Brittney Miller

UNIVERSITY CASEBOOK SERIES®

PLEADING AND PROCEDURE

CASES AND MATERIALS

ELEVENTH EDITION

by

GEOFFREY C. HAZARD, JR.

Trustee Professor of Law, University of Pennsylvania
Distinguished Professor of Law
University of California, Hastings College of the Law

WILLIAM A. FLETCHER

Richard W. Jennings Professor of Law, Emeritus
University of California, Berkeley
Circuit Judge, United States Court of Appeals for the Ninth Circuit

STEPHEN McG. BUNDY

Professor of Law, Emeritus
University of California, Berkeley

ANDREW D. BRADT

Assistant Professor of Law
University of California, Berkeley

FOUNDATION PRESS

University Casebook Series is a trademark registered in the U.S. Patent and Trademark Office.

© 1962, 1968, 1973, 1979, 1983, 1989, 1994, 1999 FOUNDATION PRESS
© 2005, 2009 By THOMSON RETUERS/FOUNDATION PRESS
© 2015 LEG, Inc. d/b/a West Academic
    444 Cedar Street, Suite 700
    St. Paul, MN 55101
    1-877-888-1330

Printed in the United States of America

ISBN: 978-1-60930-181-1

PREFACE TO THE ELEVENTH EDITION

Welcome to the most important course of the first year. Procedure is important because it sets the terms on which civil disputes are resolved and substantive legal rights enforced. For the hundreds and thousands of American lawyers and judges who work in civil litigation, procedure is central, providing the language and tools that they use and refine every day of their working lives. Our students sometimes email us from their summer jobs after their first year saying, "Now I know why Civil Procedure is so important. It is at the center of *everything*."

The first-year course in civil procedure, more than any other, exposes you to the world of practicing lawyers. In almost every case you will read in this book, you will find yourself thinking not only about legal rules, but also about a lawyer's (or judge's) strategic, tactical, or ethical choices. Those choices are often made with incomplete information and under intense pressure, and often involve high stakes. No other first-year course so consistently offers such a vivid perspective on the legal system.

Civil procedure and its effect on substantive legal regulation are at the epicenter of some of the most important and intensely debated political issues in American law today. When politicians decry "frivolous lawsuits," "greedy trial lawyers," "judicial hell holes," or "runaway juries," their underlying complaint is often with the rules of procedure studied in this course. Their immediate goal may be a change in the rules, but their ultimate goal is a change in the substantive effect of those rules. This course aims to provide you with an understanding of the real workings and underlying policy choices of the civil justice system, an understanding that will allow you to participate knowledgeably and responsibly in those important policy debates.

We like teaching and writing about civil procedure. We hope our affection and enthusiasm for the subject will be contagious. What is not to like about a subject that asks you if you can file a suit in any of several jurisdictions, obtaining in each jurisdiction a different law, a different jury, and possibly a different result? About a subject that asks you whether you can be compelled do appear in an Arkansas court because you were served with process while flying over Arkansas on a commercial airline? About a subject that teaches you how to distinguish between questions of law and questions of fact, between contentions that are creative and those that are frivolous, between jurisdiction in rem and jurisdiction in personam?

Civil procedure can sometimes be a hard subject, but this is not a hard book. Or, rather, it is no harder than the subject matter demands. Many aspects of civil procedure are, at least on their face, non-intuitive, requiring patient attention to yield up their secrets. Personal jurisdiction, subject matter jurisdiction, class actions, and preclusion are difficult subjects, even for experienced lawyers. A book that hides or glosses over difficulties does you no favors. But we have tried not to make procedure any harder than it has to be. We do not hide the ball, and we hope that our sentences are understandable on the first, rather than the second (or third), reading.

We have tried to convey a real understanding of how courts and lawyers actually work. This book contains a lot of information, some of it historical, some of it economic, sociological and psychological, and some of it practical. We have tried to take full advantage of the excellent academic literature on the operation of the civil justice system to give you a real picture of the stakes, costs, and outcomes in typical cases. Rarely will any single piece of information be critical to your understanding of a rule or case; but in the aggregate we believe that it will assist you greatly in understanding the operation of the rules and the behavior of the participants in the system.

The Federal Rules of Civil Procedure are at the center of the book, but we have also paid attention, where appropriate, to state rules of civil procedure. State rules are of course important for their own sake, but they are also important for they provide a sense of possible alternatives to the present-day federal rules. We have also paid attention to the historical development of the rules of procedure, as well as, occasionally, to procedural rules in other countries, to help you understand past and present-day alternatives to modern American rules.

This book had its origins more than fifty years ago at the University of California, Berkeley, School of Law (still known to many of us as Boalt Hall). It has changed in many ways over the years, but we like to think it is still, in spirit, the same book it was at the beginning, focusing on the hard perennial problems, and insisting on balancing both critical and practical perspectives on the material.

This edition, like earlier editions, would not have been possible without the help of many people. The current authors particularly thank Professor Stephen Bundy, who was one of the authors of the Ninth and Tenth Editions, and whose work remains an important part of the new Eleventh Edition. Professors Hazard and Fletcher welcome their new co-author, Professor Andrew Bradt, who has contributed greatly to the new edition you now have in your hands. Our academic colleagues have been indispensable sources of advice and insight. At Berkeley Law, we particularly want thank Professors Anne Joseph O'Connell, David Oppenheimer, Eleanor Swift, and Jan Vetter, each of whom has taught out of previous editions and has provided exceptionally helpful comments. At other schools, we owe particular thanks to Professors Paul McKaskle, John Oakley, Teddy Rave, Catherine Struve, and Patrick Woolley. For valuable research, editing, encouragement, and proofreading, performed variously by Jeremy Feigenbaum, Sophia Goren, Alex Hemmer, Uyen Koh, Rachel Shalev, Haley Shellito, Dylan Silva, and Heather Welles, we are very grateful.

G.C.H., Jr.

W.A.F.

A.D.B.

April 2015

SUMMARY OF CONTENTS

TABLE OF CONTENTS

TABLE OF CASES

The principal cases are in bold type.

ABBREVIATIONS AND DELETIONS

We have adopted the following short-form citations:

Calif.Civ.C.—California Civil Code

Calif.C.Civ.P.—California Code of Civil Procedure

Fed.R.Civ.P.—Federal Rules of Civil Procedure

Ill.C.Civ.P.—Illinois Code of Civil Procedure

N.Y.C.P.L.R.—New York Civil Practice Law and Rules

In editing cases and other materials, we have used asterisks (* * *) to indicate where we have deleted text from the original, and dots (. . .) to indicate where text was deleted by the author of the original. In editing cases, we have not provided any signal to indicate deletion of citations or footnotes. Where footnotes are retained, we have retained their original numbering from the case.

TABLE OF STATUTES

TABLE OF RULES

TABLE OF AUTHORITIES

UNIVERSITY CASEBOOK SERIES®

PLEADING AND PROCEDURE

CASES AND MATERIALS

ELEVENTH EDITION

CHAPTER 1

INTRODUCTION

A. THE STRUCTURE OF A LAWSUIT

NOTE ON THE STRUCTURE OF A LAWSUIT

A lawsuit is a process by which a court resolves a dispute. For example, if two drivers have a collision, there may be a dispute over who should pay for the damage caused. It is possible to imagine that the two drivers could simply walk into court, tell their story to a judge, and have her give them a decision. Such a procedure would require very few and very simple rules. Unhappily, the procedure is not that simple.

Procedural problems in lawsuits can be very complex. Because you may sometimes lose your bearings in the complexities, it may be helpful to describe in rough outline how a lawsuit is conducted, employing some of the terms frequently encountered. The following description is somewhat simplified, and we warn you that the procedures, and their names, vary from one jurisdiction to another.

Suppose that Bill Smith lives in Placerville, California, a small town in El Dorado County, in the foothills of the Sierra Nevada mountains. He buys a kerosene space heater from Sierra Appliance, a store in Placerville. Sierra Appliance is one of several stores in California and Nevada owned and operated by Sierra Appliance, Inc., a Nevada corporation with its principal place of business in Nevada. The space heater is manufactured by Heaters, Inc., a Maine corporation whose manufacturing plant and offices are located in Portland, Maine. Sierra Appliances is an authorized dealer for Heaters' space heaters.

One evening shortly after purchasing the heater, Smith leaves the heater on while he dozes in his chair. He wakes up to find his living room in flames. He escapes from the house alive, but is badly burned. The house burns to the ground. Smith subsequently learns that a neighbor had bought a Heaters, Inc., kerosene space heater that also caught fire. Smith contacts both Sierra Appliance and Heaters. He tries to obtain compensation for medical bills, lost time from work, pain and suffering, and the value of the house. He estimates that the total damages are somewhere in the neighborhood of $500,000. Neither Sierra Appliance nor Heaters is willing to offer him a satisfactory settlement. How does Smith go about bringing a lawsuit to recover for harm to himself and his property?

1. **Preliminaries.** Probably the first thing Smith does is to get a lawyer. The lawyer will give Smith her professional advice about whether a lawsuit is in Smith's best interest. If it is, and if Smith decides to go forward with it, she will handle all the steps in the litigation. For narrative convenience, we will frequently refer to the various steps as being made by Smith, but in fact they will be taken by his lawyer. The consequences of errors by the lawyer will ordinarily be borne by Smith rather than his lawyer, so Smith should choose his lawyer carefully. The lawyer is not obliged to take Smith's case, but here the injury to Smith and the harm to his property are sufficiently substantial to promise a significant legal fee. A person who

cannot or will not retain a lawyer, whether for a fee or through legal aid, is legally entitled to represent himself, but in litigation of any complexity this is almost always a bad idea.

The first thing Smith's lawyer will do is make as thorough an investigation of the facts as she can at this preliminary stage. The lawyer does this to fulfil her obligation to Smith to make the best possible case on his behalf and to fulfil her ethical obligation to the court to ensure that any claim she brings has an adequate factual and legal foundation. This investigation will likely involve an interview with Smith, an inspection of Smith's medical records, and interviews with the neighbor, with the Placerville Fire Department, and with people who deal professionally with space heaters. Fact investigation will continue as the case progresses.

The legal problem is whether Sierra Appliance or Heaters, or anyone else the lawyer can think of, has a legal responsibility to compensate Smith. To find this out, the lawyer will have to consult the law of contracts and torts. Smith bought the heater from Sierra Appliance, so there was a contract of sale between them. Was it breached because of a defect in the heater? If so, what are the legally recoverable damages caused by the breach of contract? The heater was made by Heaters. Did it breach a tort-based duty to Smith by manufacturing a defective heater? What are the legally recoverable damages in tort?

Suppose the lawyer concludes: (1) Sierra Appliance had a contractual duty to Smith to supply a heater that was free from defects, even if the defects were not due to any fault of Sierra Appliance. (2) Heaters had a tort-based duty to Smith to provide a heater free from defects. (3) If Sierra Appliance breached a duty to Smith, it owes Smith money to repay the cost of the heater, and to compensate Smith for the harm caused by the fire. (4) If Heaters breached a duty to Smith, it similarly owes money for the cost of the heater and to compensate for the harm caused. Based on a conclusion that the heater was defective and on the above legal analysis, Smith decides to file suit against both Sierra Appliance and Heaters, joining them as defendants in a single suit.

2. Which court? Territorial jurisdiction, subject matter jurisdiction, and venue. Smith is confronted at the outset with three interrelated questions about where to file suit. Smith would prefer to bring suit in California, in part because it is more convenient to his Placerville home, but also because his attorney has experience litigating in local courts

First, Smith must decide whether he can obtain *territorial jurisdiction* over the defendants in a court located in California. Territorial jurisdiction rules require a minimum level of contact between the defendant and the territorial sovereign (typically a state, sometimes the entire United States) within which the court is located. In general, any person who has sufficient "contacts" with a state is subject to the territorial jurisdiction of the courts in that state—that is, the person can be compelled to answer claims against her or else have a binding default judgment entered against her. Sometimes a federal court will have a broader territorial jurisdiction than a state court; in such a case, a plaintiff might choose to sue in federal court because it would thereby be able to assert jurisdiction over a particular defendant that would be unavailable in state court. In this case, however, the reach of the territorial jurisdiction of the federal and state courts is identical.

Territorial jurisdiction can be obtained in this case over both Sierra Appliance and Heaters. Although "presence" in a jurisdiction is a somewhat elusive concept when dealing with an artificial person such as a corporation, it is clear that Sierra Appliance is present in California for purposes of territorial jurisdiction because it has a store in California from which Smith bought the space heater. Heaters is incorporated in Maine, and has its principal place of business in Maine, and has no employees or agents in California. But the suit arises out of a purchase in California from an authorized Heaters dealer, as well as an injury in California that Smith claims is traceable to that space heater. These contacts between Heaters and the state of California are sufficient to justify the exercise of territorial jurisdiction over Heaters.

Second, Smith needs to find a court with *subject matter jurisdiction* over the suit. Subject matter jurisdiction is distinct from territorial jurisdiction: it concerns the kind of case that the court is empowered to hear. Smith must find a court that can assert both kinds of jurisdiction. There are both state and federal trial courts in California, called state Superior Courts and federal District Courts. In many suits, these courts have overlapping or "concurrent" subject matter jurisdiction, which means that a suit may be brought in either system.

California Superior Courts are courts of general subject matter jurisdiction with authority to hear all types of disputes, regardless of amount. Smith's suit clearly falls within the subject matter jurisdiction of the Superior Court.

Federal District Courts have subject matter jurisdiction over suits between citizens of different states if the amount in controversy exceeds $75,000. (There are other, additional bases for subject matter jurisdiction in federal District Courts that are unnecessary to consider here.) Jurisdiction exists because Smith, the plaintiff, is a citizen of California. Sierra Appliance, one of the defendants, is a citizen of Nevada, and Heaters, the other defendant, is a citizen of Maine. Let us assume that the amount in controversy is $500,000, well above the jurisdictional amount of $75,000.

Since both the state and federal trial courts have subject matter jurisdiction, Smith may choose either state or federal court depending on which better serves his interest.

Third, Smith can only file suit in a court with proper *venue*. (The word is derived from the French verb "venir," meaning "to come.") There are fifty-eight state Superior Courts in California, one for each county. Venue in a contract suit is proper in a county where the defendant resides, where the contract was entered into, or where the contract was to be performed. Venue in a tort suit for personal injury or property damages is proper where the defendant resides or where the injury took place. Venue is therefore proper in El Dorado County. The Superior Court for El Dorado County is in Placerville, the county seat, where Smith lives.

There are four federal judicial districts in California. The most common criteria for venue in federal District Court are the district where a defendant resides if both defendants reside in the same state, or the district where a substantial part of the events or omissions giving rise to the suit occurred. Because the purchase and the accident both took place in Placerville, venue is proper in the federal district that encompasses Placerville, which is the

Eastern District of California. The federal District Court for the Eastern District sits in Sacramento, about 45 miles from Placerville.

Smith is now in a position to choose whether to file suit in state or federal court. Smith's lawyer might think that a Sacramento jury, drawn from the city, is more likely to return a large verdict for plaintiff than a Placerville jury, drawn from a predominantly rural area. On the other hand, Smith may not want to travel 45 miles to Sacramento to file, and eventually try, his suit. Not only is the distance a problem, but Smith may also feel that he is likely to get a more sympathetic hearing from a local Placerville judge and jury. The choice between federal and state court can be influenced by other things, too. For example, the state court's calendar may be particularly crowded, with the result that Smith's case will come to trial more quickly in federal court. Or Smith's lawyer may have practiced primarily in state court, and feel nervous about the unfamiliar procedural rules and judges of the federal court. One thing that will not affect the decision is the substantive contract and tort law to be applied. The substantive law applicable in a lawsuit brought in the diversity subject matter jurisdiction of the district court is the substantive law of the state in which the federal court sits.

After some deliberation, Smith's lawyer decides to file in federal court. Had she chosen to file in state court, the case might have ended up in federal court anyway. Defendants often have the right to remove the suit from state to federal court, and indeed have that right in Smith's case.

3.   Drafting the complaint, filing, and service of process. Smith now writes a statement of his claim against the defendants. The statement will alert the defendants to the nature of Smith's claims against them, and will help guide the court as it proceeds with the case. This statement is the *complaint*—also known in some states as the petition or declaration. In his complaint, Smith will say who he is, who the defendants are, what he alleges happened to him, and what remedy he seeks. Factual assertions in the complaint are *allegations*—also known as averments.

Everything so far has been done in the lawyer's office. Smith now takes his complaint to the federal courthouse in Sacramento and *files* it with the clerk of the District Court. By this filing, the suit is officially *commenced*. (In some states, including New York, a suit is not deemed commenced until summons is served on the defendant.) After the complaint is filed, the case will be randomly assigned to one of the district judges. In the normal course, the assigned judge will handle all further proceedings in the case, up to and including any trial. In state courts of general jurisdiction, assignment to a single judge for the entire course of proceedings is uncommon. As a case progresses in state court, different judges usually decide issues relating to jurisdiction, pleading, discovery and trial.

The District Court is advised of the suit by the filing of the complaint, but the defendants are not. The device by which the defendants are advised of the suit is the *summons*. At the same time that Smith files his complaint, he hands the clerk a form of summons, containing the names of the parties and a notice to the defendants that they must come in and defend themselves. The clerk signs and puts the court's seal on the summons, thus making it official notice. Because there are two defendants, Smith obtains a summons for each.

Smith now must *serve* the summons and complaint on the defendants to notify them of the lawsuit. In federal court, Smith may use any method of service permitted by state law, as well as a variety of others. He will most likely hire a private agency to serve process. Since Sierra Appliance has stores in California, it probably has designated an agent for service of process within the state. The process server may give the summons and complaint to that person, thereby accomplishing personal service; or he may mail the summons and complaint by first class mail to Nevada, together with an acknowledgment of receipt of service, to any of several officers of the corporation specified in the California statute. Heaters almost certainly does not have an agent designated for service of process within the state. The process server will therefore mail the summons and complaint to a corporate officer in Maine in accordance with the California statute. We will assume that personal service was accomplished without incident on the agent of Sierra Appliance, and that an officer of Heaters signed the form acknowledging receipt of the summons and complaint.

    4.   Responding to the complaint. a. Preliminary objections. The defendants may think that they have some preliminary objections to the suit. For example, Heaters may think that it is a denial of due process for California to assume territorial jurisdiction over Heaters. Heaters doesn't want to litigate in California; it would prefer to compel Smith to come to Maine to make his claim. Heaters has to be careful how it presents that objection to jurisdiction. In federal court, if Heaters doesn't make that objection in its very first filing with the court, which may be a *motion to dismiss* or an *answer,* it will be held to have waived that objection and to have *consented* to the jurisdiction of the California court. In a California state court, the defendant must make that objection in a *motion to quash,* that is, to nullify, the summons, before filing any answer on the merits of the case.

    Suppose that Heaters makes a *motion to dismiss* on the ground that the court lacks territorial jurisdiction over it. A *motion* is a request for the court to take action, either by entering an order or by granting specified relief. In the heat of trial, motions may be made orally and on the spur of the moment. But pretrial motions must be made in writing and are normally made on *notice*—that is, the court and the opponent are advised in writing of the party's motion and the grounds supporting it, and are given an opportunity respond to the motion in writing. To make the motion, Heaters will file the motion with the court and serve it upon Smith. The motion will typically be accompanied by a *memorandum of law* (sometimes called a *memorandum of points and authorities*) setting forth the legal arguments supporting the request. It may be accompanied as well by evidentiary materials, frequently in the form of *affidavits*—sworn written statements of facts, given by competent witnesses. In this case, Heaters will want to present affidavits from witnesses tending to show that the company has had little relevant contact with California. Plaintiff will respond with its own memorandum of law and affidavits, and may request some discovery—compelled disclosure of evidence, about which more below—from Heaters if it thinks that such discovery is likely to uncover evidence that Heaters has more extensive contacts with California than it was willing to acknowledge in its motion. If necessary, the court will postpone the hearing on the motion to permit such discovery. On the date noticed for the motion, the court will hear argument from Heaters and Smith on the jurisdictional issue. If Heaters' motion to dismiss is granted, the effect will be the same as if Heaters had never been served at all, and Smith will have to proceed against Sierra Appliance alone. If its motion is denied, however, Heaters will be subjected to the jurisdiction of the court. We will assume that the motion is denied.

b. **Default and default judgment.** Suppose that one of the defendants, after being served with the summons and complaint, fails to do anything. This is a common response to litigation in cases involving small amounts, but relatively uncommon in cases of this magnitude. After due notice to the defendant who failed to respond, Smith would instruct the clerk of the court to note the fact that the defendant was in *default* and would then apply to the court for a *default judgment.* The judge would conduct a brief ex parte hearing (a hearing at which only Smith is present) on the question of the amount of damages Smith has sustained and would enter a judgment against the defaulting defendant, ending the action as to that defendant. The judgment can then be enforced in any state in the nation, unless the defendant who defaulted can show that the judgment was rendered without proper notice or that the rendering court lacked jurisdiction.

If a default judgment has been entered, either Sierra Appliances or Heaters may have a basis for setting it aside. Perhaps Jones, the officer of Sierra Appliance who was served with the summons and complaint, was killed the day after she was served, and failed to pass on the complaint before her death. After the default judgment has been entered, Sierra Appliance discovers the complaint. Under these circumstances, Sierra Appliances would probably succeed in a motion *to set aside the judgment.*

c. **Pleading in response to the complaint.** Many problems may arise in preparing and defending against a complaint. We shall only consider a few major points.

The first problem is whether, as against each of the defendants considered separately, the complaint describes a violation of law which, if proved, would entitle Smith to recover damages. Note that at this stage, Smith is not trying to prove anything; he is merely *alleging* what he hopes and expects can be proved at trial. If his complaint does describe a violation of law, his complaint *states a claim upon which relief can be granted* (in a California state court, *states a cause of action*).

For example, as to Heaters, the law of torts recognizes that a manufacturer of goods is liable in damages to any person whom the manufacturer could foresee would be injured by a defect in the goods. Suppose that Smith's complaint alleges that Heaters manufactured the heater, that the heater was defective, and that the defect led to a kerosene leak, which in turn was the proximate cause of the fire. Is Smith's complaint sufficient as a matter of "substantive law," in this case the applicable tort law? If negligence on Heaters' part is required under the substantive law then Smith's complaint is *not* sufficient, for he has not alleged that Heaters was negligent in the way it manufactured the heater. But if a manufacturer is liable whenever its product is defective, regardless of whether the manufacturer was negligent in making it, then Smith's complaint does state a cause of action.

Apart from the requirement that the complaint be sufficient in its substance, the rules of procedure require that the complaint comply with certain rules of form. The most important such rule is that the complaint must describe the claim in sufficient detail to give defendants fair notice of the nature of the claim being asserted against them. We will assume that Smith's complaint is sufficiently specific to meet the formal requirements for a complaint.

If Heaters believes that it is liable to Smith only if it was negligent in manufacturing the space heater, and if Smith has not alleged negligence, it will move to dismiss the complaint for *failure to state a claim upon which relief can be granted.* In California and some other states, Heaters would raise this point by means of a *general demurrer.* The effect of such a motion, in either federal or state court, is to say: "Even if what you say is true, you are not entitled to recover under the substantive law."

Assume that Sierra Appliance and Heaters move to dismiss for failure to state a claim. The judge decides, however, that the complaint is sufficient in point of substantive law. She therefore *denies* the motion.

The defendants now consider their possible defenses based on disputing Smith's factual allegations. They will expressly *admit* some of the matters alleged by Smith, such as the fact that he bought the heater. They will be *deemed to admit* allegations that they don't deny, so they will be careful to deny allegations which they wish to contest. For example, they may deny that the heater was defective, that it caused the fire, and that Smith was injured. They may suspect that Smith was injured in some degree, but they are not sure how much. To be on the safe side, they will deny that he was injured at all.

The defendants' denials will be set forth in their *answer* to Smith's complaint. The answer is the pleading by which the defendant joins issue with plaintiff on the factual matters alleged in the complaint. The factual denials constitute *negative defenses.* But defendants may also have *affirmative defenses*—contentions that there are other factual circumstances which, if proven, would exonerate them even if the facts alleged by Smith are established. For example, suppose that Heaters suspects that Smith did not use the right type of fuel in the heater and that this led to the fire. In its answer, Heaters would allege that Smith used the wrong kind of fuel, that this was a proximate contributing cause of the explosion, and hence that Smith was comparatively negligent. Heaters would thus allege in its answer that even if it was liable, there are additional facts which, under the substantive law, result in Smith's being unable to recover or which reduce the amount of his recovery.

Smith might have objections to the defendants' answers very similar to those discussed in connection with the complaint. For example, Smith might think the allegations of the affirmative defense are not sufficient in point of substantive law. If so, he could make a *motion to strike* the defense as insufficient in point of law or, in code pleading states, demur to defendants' answers.

Suppose, however, that Smith does not so move or demur. One might suppose that Smith should controvert allegations of comparative negligence. In most procedural systems, however, allegations in the answer, even if unanswered, are *deemed denied.* Hence, Smith need not file any additional pleading. At this point, therefore, the dispute is framed and the *pleadings are closed.*

5. Discovery, summary judgment, and settlement. The procedure through which each side, with the aid of the court, investigates its own claims and those of its opponent is called *discovery.* In American courts, discovery reaches all information relevant to the contested issues in the case, except information protected by an evidentiary privilege.

In federal court, the parties must exchange some basic discovery at the outset of the case, without a formal request from the other side. The information includes the names and identifying information of witnesses that the party expects to call in its own case, the identity and location of relevant documents, and, for the plaintiff, a calculation of damages. Most state courts do not have this system of initial disclosures. In addition, parties in federal court must try to agree upon and present to the court a plan for conducting discovery. Depending on the degree to which the parties are able to cooperate in the planning and conduct of discovery, the court may be called upon, or may decide on its own, to intervene in the discovery process from time to time to resolve disputes.

There are three main forms of discovery: interrogatories, requests for production or inspection, and depositions. They are often used in sequence to build a party's case.

Even after receiving defendants' initial disclosures, Smith may still have little sense of the who, what, when, and how of Heaters' design and manufacture of the space heater. To get a better sense of the facts, he may use, at least in the first instance, *interrogatories to a party*. These are *written* questions addressed to Heaters. Heaters must disclose the information demanded if it has that information. For example, Smith's interrogatories to Heaters might ask for names of personnel involved in the design and manufacture of the product, the date on which the heater was made, the information provided to customers concerning proper fuel, any studies that were done concerning the product's safety, etc. Obviously such interrogatories are more important in state courts where initial disclosures are not made.

Smith, Sierra Appliance and Heaters will probably all make use of the *request for production of documents and things and entry upon land for inspection*. Smith will request documents relevant to the design and manufacture of the heater, its safety, and warnings concerning its use. The documents requested will include emails and other data in electronic form. Sierra Appliance and Heaters may request documents supporting Smith's claims of financial loss. They may also demand production of the heater itself, or what is left of it. And they may demand the right to visit the burnt out premises to see if they can identify other causes of the heater's failure or the fire itself. The defendants may also seek a physical examination of Smith by a doctor of their choosing in order to verify and assess the extent of Smith's injuries.

After this background preparation, both parties will likely make use of a *deposition on oral examination*, or, as it normally called, simply a *deposition*. This is a device by which one party may require witnesses to appear before a court reporter and/or video camera and answer questions put to him them the lawyers for the parties. A deposition may be taken not only of a *party* to the action, such as Smith or Sierra Appliance, but also of witnesses who are not parties, such as Smith's neighbor. When the lawyer asks questions of the *deponent*, he is said to be *taking* the witness's deposition. The lawyer will try to find out the other side's version of the facts, seeking to find weaknesses and to pin down the testimony. For example, Heaters will take Smith's deposition. Normally, the lawyers for Smith and Heaters will agree on a mutually satisfactory time, Heaters will arrange to have a court reporter on hand, and the deposition will be taken at the office of Heaters' lawyer. There, Smith will be asked to identify himself, placed under oath, and questioned in detail concerning his account of buying the heater and of the fire. He will be asked about his injuries. He will be asked if there was anyone with him at the time of the fire and, if so, to give his companion's name. Probably, Heaters' lawyer will later take the deposition of the companion, if there was one. Smith will take depositions from Sierra Appliance's and Heaters' personnel, using the mandatory disclosures, answers to interrogatories, and documents to identify the key personnel and the questions to be put to them.

In a products liability case of this kind, each side is likely to have expert witnesses, retained to testify at trial. Expert witnesses do not testify about historical facts that they perceived in connection with events giving rise to the suit. Instead, they testify by way of expert opinion based upon their review of facts provided to them. For example, Smith may have retained a medical expert to testify concerning the severity of his permanent injuries and an engineer to testify to the safety of the design of the heater. Sierra Appliance and Heater are entitled to take those experts' depositions and to interrogate them intensively concerning the basis and rationale for their opinions. Smith is entitled to do the same with respect to experts retained by the defendants.

The discovery process may result in eliminating some of the issues raised by the pleadings. For example, Smith's testimony may make it quite clear that he was injured by the fire. Hence, the defendants probably will no longer wish to contest that point. On the other hand, the discovery process may open up new issues, for example, the possibility that Smith had left flammable material too close to the heater. Heaters therefore would want to amend its answer to assert this additional basis of defense.

As discovery proceeds, the parties will normally explore ways of disposing of the case without the costs and risks of trial. An important procedural device for disposing of the case without trial is *summary judgment*. It is always possible that there is some fact crucial to the lawsuit that can be established as true beyond legitimate dispute. For example, suppose that Sierra Appliance sold Smith the heater under a contract which expressly provided that Sierra Appliance would in no event be liable to the purchaser (Smith) for any amount beyond the cost of the heater itself. Assume that the contract was drafted with such care that it clearly bars Smith's claims for damages against Sierra Appliance, at least to the extent that those claims exceed the purchase price.

Smith, it will be recalled, pleaded that he was entitled to damages for personal injury and loss of property under the contract with Sierra Appliance, and Sierra Appliance denied this, so the issue is in dispute according to the pleadings. But if Sierra Appliance could produce the contract before the judge, and establish by *affidavit* that it was the contract in question, it could then urge that the contract's legal effect was to bar any liability on its part for those damages. Sierra Appliance could, therefore, move for *summary judgment*—judgment rendered on the basis of a paper record and without a trial. If Smith does not file a counter affidavit, it will be pretty clear that there is *no genuine dispute of fact* whether this was the contract under which the heater was sold. However, if Smith files an affidavit in which he denies that he signed the contract attached to Sierra Appliance's affidavit, there would be a genuine issue of fact as to whether that was the contract and summary judgment would be denied. The truth would have to be decided at the trial.

As the case approaches trial, it is likely that the parties will consider settlement. (Indeed, the parties will likely have considered settlement at earlier stages in the proceedings.) A settlement in this type of action would typically involve a payment by one or both of the defendants to the plaintiff, in exchange for plaintiff's release of his claim and agreement to dismiss his suit with prejudice. Settlement is often attractive to both parties because it saves the costs of further litigation and eliminates the risk of an extreme outcome in which either plaintiff would take nothing or defendant would pay an outsize award. Settlement is attractive to the court system as well, because it saves the high public costs of a trial. For that reason, courts often require parties to explore the potential for settlement or to participate in procedures designed to facilitate it. Settlement is by far the most common disposition in disputes that reach court. Indeed, many civil disputes settle even before a complaint is filed.

In those relatively rare cases that actually go to trial, it is helpful if, prior to trial, the parties agree on what should actually be tried. This is done at a final *pretrial conference*, a meeting, held either in the courtroom or in the judge's chambers, among the lawyers for the various parties. Sometimes, though rarely, the parties themselves will be present. At the pretrial conference, the judge will determine whether there are any required amendments to the pleadings, adding issues or eliminating them. She will also inquire about the possibilities of settlement, for the parties may now be close together in their appraisal of the case. She may take care of routine matters which would be time-consuming at the trial, such as the formal identification of documentary evidence (medical records and so on). Finally, the judge may try to ascertain whether there are any points of law that will probably come up at trial which can be decided beforehand. In short, the purpose of the pretrial conference is to put the case in final shape for trial.

6.   Trial. Only a small fraction of filed civil cases are actually tried to verdict and judgment. Assume, however, that this case is not resolved by summary judgment or settlement, and a trial date is set. On the appointed day, the lawyers and parties will convene in court and the trial will commence. A threshold question will be whether the case should be tried to a jury or not. This being an action *at law*, since it is for damages, it would be triable to a jury on demand of either party. (In contrast, a suit for an injunction is in *equity* and normally is triable to the judge sitting without a jury.) Let us assume that one of the parties has made a timely demand for jury trial (usually when the complaint or answer is filed). Failure to make a timely jury demand constitutes a waiver of the right to jury trial.

At the trial the first task is the selection of the jury. In most state courts, a jury in a civil case consists of twelve persons; in many federal districts, a six person jury is used in civil cases. A court official will have herded a group of prospective jurors into the courtroom. The lawyers will proceed to interrogate them, to find out if they are qualified and fair minded and what they are like as people. This is called the *voir dire examination*. Sometimes the primary questioning is done by the judge, but the lawyers in most states are given a chance to ask questions if they wish. A juror revealing bias or some other disqualification will be *challenged for cause*. If a juror has no such disqualification, but one party nevertheless does not want him on the jury, the party may excuse the would-be juror by using one of his limited number of *peremptory challenges*. When this process is completed, the jury is sworn by the clerk of the court. It is thereby *impaneled*.

The lawyers now make their *opening statements*. Smith, the plaintiff, goes first. His lawyer tells the jury what the case is about and what he expects to prove. The defendants may make an opening statement at this time or postpone doing so until after the plaintiff has put in his evidence. The next thing that happens is that the plaintiff puts in his *case in chief*. Plaintiff has the burden of proof of most matters alleged in his complaint. Smith himself will testify and his doctor will testify about Smith's injuries. Smith might have an expert witness testify concerning the alleged defect in the heater. When Smith, and the other witnesses put on by him, are questioned by Smith's attorney, this is *direct examination*. When the direct examination of each of Smith's witnesses is concluded, defendants' attorneys may ask him questions, seeking to bring out uncertainties, weaknesses and mistakes. This is *cross-examination*.

After plaintiff has put in his case, he *rests*. By resting, plaintiff says that he has proved enough so that, if the jury believes his evidence, a verdict may be rendered in his favor. Defendants may not think so. For example, suppose that Smith offered no evidence from which it could be concluded that the heater was defective. Heaters could raise the objection by moving for a *judgment as a matter of law* (called a *non-suit* or *directed verdict* in many state courts) requesting the judge to dismiss the plaintiff's claim without submitting it to the jury, on the ground that Smith's proof as a matter of law fails to make out the elements of a valid claim.

Suppose that the judge denies the defendant's motion. She may do so either because she disagrees with Heaters' argument that the evidence is legally insufficient, or because she prefers to see what evidence Heaters develops prior to making her ruling. Defendants would then present their *case in chief*. If defendants had not previously made their opening statements, the presentation of their case would be preceded by those statements.

In their case in chief, defendants will introduce evidence tending to disprove Smith's case. For example, defendants very likely would have their own medical testimony, tending to show that Smith wasn't as badly injured as Smith's evidence seems to indicate. Defendants would also put in evidence to support any affirmative defenses they might have, such as contributory negligence. For this purpose, they may well call plaintiff himself in their own case as an *adverse witness*. They might also call other witnesses, such as Smith's neighbor. Each witness will be directly examined by defendants and may be cross-examined by plaintiff.

At the end of the case, defendants might again move for *judgment as a matter of law*. Smith himself might move for *judgment as a matter of law*, claiming that no material evidence offered by defendants disproves his claim. Usually, if a case has gotten this far, the judge will deny the motion, preferring to let the jury render a verdict. (In the unlikely event the jury renders a verdict that is not supported by the evidence, the judge can set the verdict aside, as described below.)

The plaintiff now makes his *concluding or closing argument*. He reviews the evidence, stressing the points most favorable to him and playing down the defendants' evidence. He will urge the jury to find for Smith and, within limits, encourage the jury to see the evidence in a sympathetic light. Often the plaintiff will reserve the right to rebuttal. Then the defendants will make their closing argument, stressing the evidence favorable to them and trying to discount considerations of sympathy. When defendants are done with this argument, Smith returns with his *closing or rebuttal argument*. Finally, the judge will *instruct the jury* concerning the controlling law.

The jury then retires for *deliberation*. The jury first elects a foreperson and then proceeds to decide what they think the facts are. Usually, the jury will be asked to render a *general verdict*, which simply states the name of the prevailing party, and, if the plaintiff has prevailed, the damages he should recover. The lawyers may have requested the judge to require a *special verdict* from the jury. If the judge grants the request, the jury will be given a series of specific questions they must answer. For example, the questions might be: Did Heaters make a proper inspection of the heaters it manufactured? Did plaintiff use proper fuel?

In federal courts and in some state courts, the jury must reach unanimity in order to render a valid verdict, although the Federal Rules of Civil Procedure and some state procedural rules permit the parties to stipulate otherwise. In California and many other states, nine out of twelve must agree in favor of one party or the other. If the jury doesn't reach a decision by the necessary majority, and if the judge thinks further deliberation will be useless, she may discharge the jury and order a new trial.

If the jury does reach a verdict, it returns to the courtroom, the foreperson gives the verdict to the clerk or judge, and the judge then reads it. The parties may ask that the jury be *polled*, i.e., that each juror be individually asked whether he or she concurs in the verdict. Assuming the necessary majority does concur, the verdict will be accepted by the court and the jury will be *discharged*.

7.   Post-trial or post-judgment motions. There are two principal post-verdict or post-judgment motions. First, a party may contend that the jury's verdict should be set aside because it is insufficiently supported by the evidence. In federal court, the party would raise the point by renewing his earlier motions for *judgment as a matter of law*. In most states, the point would be raised by a motion for *judgment notwithstanding the verdict*. (The Latin term for this is judgment *non obstante veredicto*, from which is derived the commonly used name for this motion, *judgment n.o.v.*) If the motion is granted, the judge will enter judgment for the moving party.

Second, a party may seek a new trial. New trials may be sought on the basis of asserted errors that occurred in the trial itself—errors in the admission of evidence, in the conduct of attorneys, litigants, jurors or judge, and, perhaps most frequently, errors in the instructions to the jury. New trials can also be sought on the ground that the jury verdict, while perhaps not wholly without factual and legal foundation, nonetheless represented a serious miscarriage of justice. The moving party may claim that the jury's verdict on liability was against the great weight of the evidence, or that the damages awarded were grossly excessive or grossly insufficient. The district court has discretion to order a new trial on those grounds as well.

8.   Appeal. After a final judgment has been entered by the trial judge, the losing party may *appeal*.

First, in general an appeal may be taken only from a *final judgment*. As the trial progresses, a judge makes all kinds of rulings—on demurrers, motions, evidence, instructions and post-trial motions. At any point, the judge may make a mistake that will confuse or render erroneous all the subsequent stages of the proceeding. The litigants might hope that such a serious error could be corrected by immediate appeal. However, except in limited situations, no appeal may be taken until the final judgment, for better or worse, has been rendered.

This "final judgment rule" creates a good deal of difficulty. Sometimes a trial judge will make an error at the threshold of litigation that is so important that the rest of the proceedings become pointless. For example, suppose that the trial judge overruled Heaters' motion to dismiss for lack of jurisdiction. Under the "final judgment rule," this means that Heaters will have to go through the whole trial before it can appeal the ruling on the motion to dismiss. Sometimes statutes and case law provide special remedies for such situations. In the federal courts and many state courts, certain kinds of orders can be appealed before final judgment; this is called *interlocutory appeal*. Another procedure is the use of the "extraordinary writs," chiefly *mandamus* (or mandate, to use the name in California) and *prohibition*. The first writ commands the trial judge to do something; the second prohibits her from doing something.

Second, an appellate court is supposed to correct errors, not to render what it thinks is a more just result in the particular case. If the trial judge made a mistake of law and the mistake affected the outcome, then the appellate court will do something about it—usually, reverse the judgment and order a new trial. This is *reversible error* on the part of the trial court. If the trial judge made a mistake but it didn't seem to have affected the result below, the appellate court will not do anything about it. This is *harmless error* on the part of the trial court. Third, appellate courts in general do not review lower court decisions on matters of *fact*; review is ordinarily limited to questions of *law*. This general rule is subject to the important qualification that a factual determination may be reversed on appeal if the appellate court thinks there is no substantial evidence to support the factual determination in question. Obviously this leaves some latitude to the appellate courts, for "substantial" is a pretty vague criterion.

Finally, the appellate court will not ordinarily consider objections that were not first presented to the trial court. A corollary of this proposition is that, except for undisputed matters subject to *judicial notice*, the appellate court will not consider any evidence not contained in the record made in the trial court.

B. THE STRUCTURE OF THE COURT SYSTEM

NOTE ON THE STRUCTURE OF THE COURT SYSTEM

Courts in the American system are of two principal types: trial courts and appellate courts. Trial courts are those tribunals in which proceedings are initiated, the disputed issues framed, the proofs taken and the initial decision handed down. Unless timely application for appellate review is made, the disposition of the trial court is final. And even when appellate review is obtained, the function of the appellate court, speaking generally, is solely that of inquiring whether the trial court properly disposed of the case as presented to it.

1. **State courts.** State courts, as distinguished from federal courts, are the courts in which most disputes are heard.

a.   Trial courts. (1) Courts of limited jurisdiction. Most states have courts of limited jurisdiction, i.e., courts that are authorized to hear and determine cases involving a relatively small amount in controversy and (ordinarily) simple issues. The historic prototypes of the courts of limited jurisdiction are the rural justice court, presided over by a justice of the peace, and the municipal court, presided over by a magistrate. The justice court historically had authority to hear civil cases involving claims for money in a small amount, typically $20, and criminal cases involving minor offenses, typically misdemeanors. The municipal court had a similarly limited jurisdiction.

In a few states the historic pattern still prevails. In most, the court systems have been reorganized in the following directions: the justice courts have been reduced in number and professionalized (i.e., the justice is required to have legal training), and their maximum monetary jurisdiction has been increased. The municipal courts have been made uniform in their jurisdiction (so that the authority of municipal courts is the same throughout the particular state), professionalized, and have had their monetary jurisdiction increased. The names and authority of courts of limited jurisdiction vary from state to state. Most states still have courts known as justice courts, some have a court analogous to the municipal court, and many have a court of limited jurisdiction known as the "county" court. See Department of Justice, National Criminal Justice Information and Statistics Service, National Survey of Court Organization (1973). All states have what are called "small claims courts," although they are typically not a separate court. Rather, the term usually refers to a simplified form of procedure available in courts of limited jurisdiction, such as the justice or municipal court, for the trial of cases involving a relatively small amount, the precise amount varying from state to state.

(2) Courts of general jurisdiction. All states have trial courts, usually organized along county lines, for hearing cases of all types, unlimited by subject matter or amount in controversy. Such a court is referred to as a trial court of general jurisdiction. The court of general jurisdiction is known by different names in different states: in California it is the Superior Court; in New York, it is the Supreme Court; in many states it is the Circuit Court; in other states it is known as the District Court, the County Court, the Court of Common Pleas.

The hearing of cases in trial courts, whether of limited or general jurisdiction, is ordinarily conducted by a single judge. The trial bench in urban areas usually has more than one judge, and in such courts different judges may be called upon seriatim to hear various phases of a particular case. Thus, one judge may pass upon preliminary pleading questions, another on questions arising in discovery matters, and yet another preside at trial. But at any hearing only one judge ordinarily sits and decides. This is to be contrasted with the practice in continental civil procedure, where many hearings (at least in trial courts of general jurisdiction) are before a panel of three judges.

States also have specialized types of "courts," such as the "probate" court, the "domestic relations" court and others. In some states, these are separate courts staffed by separate judges. Thus, in New York there is a separate tribunal known as the Surrogate's Court which has probate jurisdiction, i.e., authority to hear matters pertaining to decedents' estates. In many states, however, the terms "probate court" or "domestic relations court" do not refer to separate courts but to specialized procedures applied in the court of general jurisdiction to these particular types of cases.

b. Appellate courts. (1) Appeals from courts of limited jurisdiction. Most states permit appeal of the determinations made by courts of limited jurisdiction. In some states, the mode of appeal is by trial de novo in the court of general jurisdiction, so that a litigant dissatisfied with the result of the disposition by the inferior court may request that the case be retried in the court of general jurisdiction. Retrial is usually limited to the issues framed in the lower court, but additional evidence as well as additional argument may be presented. In other states, the mode of appeal is strictly review. That is, the record of the proceedings in the inferior court is presented to the court of general jurisdiction for consideration of the correctness of the disposition of the case as it was presented below. In some states, the appeal to the court of general jurisdiction is the final appeal and no further review may be obtained. In others, the disposition of the court of general jurisdiction may itself be reviewed by further appeal.

(2) Appeals from courts of general jurisdiction. All states permit appellate review of the disposition of cases in courts of general jurisdiction. In a few very small states there is a single appellate court, the state supreme court, that hears appeals from the trial courts of general jurisdiction. Most states, however, have intermediate appellate courts to which appeals are taken before they may be taken to the state supreme court.

The subject matter jurisdiction of intermediate appellate courts varies from state to state. The typical pattern is that all types of appeals from the trial courts are taken to the intermediate appellate court; further appellate review in the state supreme court is obtainable only in the discretion of the supreme court or upon special request of the intermediate appellate court. The procedural device for such further review may be simply an "appeal"; more often it is known as certiorari.

The highest appellate court of a state consists of several judges, the number varying from state to state but typically being seven, as in California, Illinois and New York. The intermediate appellate courts usually consist of a number of judges who sit in panels of three. In the New York Appellate Division five judges sit on any particular appeal.

2. Federal courts. The federal court system parallels the court systems of the states, except that there are no federal courts of general jurisdiction. The authority of federal courts is limited in the kind of cases they can hear.

a. Trial courts. The principal trial court of the federal system is the District Court. Originally, the federal system had two types of trial courts, the District Courts and the Circuit Courts. As the result of a series of statutory changes since 1789, the District Court has become the only ordinary trial court in the federal system and the Circuit Court has become exclusively an appellate court.

The District Courts are organized along territorial lines called districts. Each district comprises a state or a portion of a state. Thus, the territory of the Federal District Court for the District of Oregon consists of the state of Oregon. Florida is divided into three—Northern, Middle and Southern; California and New York are divided into four. Some of these districts are divided for administrative purposes into divisions, each of which has a headquarters in a different place within the district. See 28 U.S.C. § 81 et seq.

The federal District Courts have jurisdiction over several types of cases. A principal type includes actions between citizens of different states where the amount in controversy exceeds $75,000. This is known as the "diversity" jurisdiction, and it extends, generally speaking, without regard to the subject matter of the controversy. The diversity jurisdiction of the federal courts is concurrent with that of the state courts. A second principal type includes suits "arising under" federal law, known as the "federal question" jurisdiction. District Courts have general federal question jurisdiction without regard to the amount in controversy. In some types of federal question jurisdiction, for example patent infringement suits, the jurisdiction of the federal district courts is exclusive of the states; in others, the state courts have concurrent jurisdiction. A third principal type of federal jurisdiction is actions by or against the federal government and its agencies. A fourth principal type of federal jurisdiction is admiralty, or maritime, suits. In all of these types of civil suits, the Federal Rules of Civil Procedure govern the conduct of the litigation. These rules will be considered in detail in this book.

In addition to the federal District Courts, there are a number of specialized federal courts. The study of these courts is beyond the scope of this book, but several deserve mention. Bankruptcy Courts operate as "adjuncts" to the federal District Courts. They decide a wide range of cases relating to the federal bankruptcy laws and are staffed by special bankruptcy judges. Appeal from the Bankruptcy Courts is to the federal District Court, or in some circuits to a Bankruptcy Appellate Panel, and thereafter to the federal Court of Appeals. Federal Magistrate Judges also operate as "adjuncts" to the federal District Court. They decide a wide range of procedural matters, and, with the consent of the parties, are authorized to try entire civil cases. The Claims Court is a specialized tribunal authorized to hear claims for money judgments against the United States. The Tax Court hears claims under the federal Internal Revenue Code. Neither the Claims nor the Tax Court is an "adjunct" court; rather, both are free-standing courts with separate routes of appeal.

b.   Appellate courts. Determinations made in the federal District Courts are ordinarily appealable to the Courts of Appeals, the intermediate appellate courts of the federal system. With one exception, the Courts of Appeals are organized territorially. For example, the Court of Appeals for the Second Circuit hears appeals from federal District Courts located in the states of New York, Connecticut and Vermont. There are twelve geographically organized circuits. Eleven of them have numbers (First Circuit, Second Circuit, etc.); the twelfth is the Court of Appeals for the District of Columbia. All of these circuits hear appeals from cases in particular areas of the country. There is a thirteenth circuit whose jurisdiction is based on subject matter, the Court of Appeals for the Federal Circuit. It hears appeals in cases involving specific areas of law, including patents and international trade. Each Court of Appeals consists of several judges who ordinarily sit in panels of three judges each, but who occasionally hear cases en banc, i.e., with all or, in the Ninth Circuit, a substantial fraction of the entire membership sitting. The Courts of Appeals also have important appellate jurisdiction of cases originating in the federal administrative agencies.

The highest court in the federal system is the Supreme Court of the United States. The Supreme Court has *original* jurisdiction of a very limited class of cases, chiefly actions between states. Otherwise, the Supreme Court's jurisdiction is *appellate*. The Supreme Court has appellate jurisdiction of cases originating in the lower federal courts and of certain types of cases originating in the courts of the states. Potentially, any case originating in a federal District Court may be taken to the Supreme Court. Most such cases must be appealed initially to the Courts of Appeals and may be thereafter taken to the Supreme Court only with the latter's permission. Of cases originating in the courts of the states, only those presenting determinative questions of federal law may be considered by the Supreme Court. Its consideration of such a case is limited to the federal issues involved. The Supreme Court therefore has but limited, though vitally important, appellate supervision over decisions of state courts. The state court from which an appeal to the Supreme Court may be taken is the highest state court authorized to hear the case. Ordinarily, this means that an appeal to the Supreme Court of the United States will be from the state's supreme court. If, however, the state court system is so organized that appellate review by the state's supreme court is not available in a particular case, then an appeal to the United States Supreme Court may be taken from the lower state court.

The procedure for Court of Appeals review of District Court decisions is by appeal or, in unusual cases, by extraordinary writ. The procedure for appellate review by the Supreme Court is by writ of certiorari in almost all cases. The choice of which cases to review by writ of certiorari is entirely within the discretion of the Supreme Court. In recent years, the Supreme Court has decided fewer cases, deciding only 70 cases out of more than 10,000 cases in which review was sought in the 2014 term. In practice, the Supreme Court uses its power of appellate review to decide important or unsettled questions of federal law rather than to correct errors of the lower courts.

C. AN INTRODUCTION TO THE HISTORY OF ANGLO-AMERICAN PROCEDURE

HISTORICAL NOTE ON PROCEDURE

1. Early evolution of the writ system. William's conquest of England in 1066 and the years following witnessed the superimposition of Norman feudal institutions on Anglo-Saxon royal and communal institutions and the subsequent emergence of a royal administrative and judicial system that was stronger than either of its predecessors. For present purposes, the significant Anglo-Saxon institutions at the time of the conquest were the crown and the local tribunals. The English crown, theoretically at least, had a responsibility to see that justice was done throughout the realm, i.e., had a direct legitimate interest in all legal disputes. Of English local tribunals there were two principal kinds, the hundred courts (village courts) and the shire courts (analogous to the county courts). Communal forums, these courts by the time of the conquest had assumed a territorial jurisdiction in the sense that they were recognized as the appropriate tribunals for disposition of controversies arising in the territory in which they were located. Both acted under a nominal supervision of the crown, thus representing in theory the implementation of the royal interest in justice.

The principal shortcoming of the local tribunals was that they were slow and uncertain in operation.

On top of this indigenous English institutional structure the invaders of 1066 erected a para-military governing system. The hierarchy was a pyramid of power built on land grants descending in the first instance from William to his tenants in chief, from the tenants in chief to their feudal subordinates, and from these subordinates to the petty lords of the manor. The lord's authority and responsibility included the power and duty to hold court and to render justice for his tenants. This was the Norman "feudal" court. With the invasion, the Norman court system was transplanted to England and functioned side by side with the English local courts.

As suggested above, the exercise of royal authority in a dispute between man and man could be justified under the Anglo-Saxon theory of the crown. William and his successors held that crown. But such an exercise would also constitute an intrusion into the feudal courts—an invasion of established jurisdiction in derogation of constituted authority. Hence, assertion of royal jurisdiction was impeded both by theoretical limitations imposed by feudalism and by practical objections raised by the barons. Furthermore, the process of royal intrusion, like most constitutional developments, was a series of ad hoc reactions which only in retrospect could be seen as following a pattern.

The earliest forms of royal intervention were not strictly speaking judicial but executive or administrative. The occasion for these early interventions was a wrong, typically involving a breach of the peace, committed somewhere in the realm and unredressed by the local or feudal courts. The instrument of royal intervention was the writ. The writ was nothing more than a written directive from the king to a royal official or to an individual or group of individuals, ordering the addressees to do or refrain from doing a designated act. An example of such a writ, from the reign of Stephen (1135–54), reprinted and translated in R. van Caenegem, Royal Writs in England from the Conquest to Glanvill 453–54 (Selden Soc'y 1959), is as follows:

> Stephen, king of the English to the bishop of Norwich, greeting. I order to reseise the monks of St. Edmunds of their church of Caistor as fully and justly as they were seised on the day when their abbot left for Rome. And if anything has since been taken away there, let it be justly restored. And let them keep it in peace that no injury is done to them thereof. Witness: Aubrey de Ver. At Westminster.

This method of executive intervention afforded a swift and effective remedy. But it also was easily abused. The writ issued upon the complaint of the alleged injured party: if he had misrepresented the facts, royal intervention would work not justice but injustice. The crown's desire to provide swift redress for wrong was tempered by its desire to be assured that wrong in fact had been done, an age-old dilemma in the administration of justice. In the 12th century, this dilemma was solved in two different ways, both of which, however, resulted in bringing the case before royal officials for hearing. One method directed the sheriff or some other official to advise himself of the facts before proceeding to act. At first, the writs were silent on how the sheriff was to advise himself, but reliance came to be placed on recognition by men of the vicinage, i.e., a jury. By the other method, the alleged wrongdoer was ordered to right the wrong or to appear before the king or his justices and show cause why he had not done so. At the show-cause hearing the merits of the case would be determined. This form of writ was known as a "praecipe," from the Latin word for "order" appearing first after the greeting in the writ. An example, from van Caenegem, supra at 437, is as follows:

> The king to the sheriff, greeting. Order N. to give back justly and without delay to R. a hundred marks which he owes him, so he says, and of which he complains that he deforces him unjustly. And if he does not do it, summon him by good summoners that he be before me or my justices at Westminster a fortnight after the octave of Easter to show why he has not done it. And have there with you the summoners and this writ. Witness: N. At M.

By this development, a writ that was originally an extraordinary executive interference with the normal course of feudal or local procedure became the triggering device of an ordinary judicial function of the crown.

The procedural steps by which each writ was prosecuted were not uniform but varied from writ to writ. Partly these differences were the consequence of differences in the origin of the various writs. Thus, the *praecipe* type of writ originated as an executive command made without inquiry; when judicialized, it still took the form of a command, the judicial inquiry being made when the defendant appeared in court to "show cause" why he had not obeyed the command. In contrast, the writ of novel disseisin derived from a procedure in which a judicial inquest of complaints was heard first and then executive action followed. This writ is of the *querela* (complaint) type. Other differences in the writs were the products of clerical variation in the Chancery (the royal secretariat from which the writs issued), while still others were the consequence of the age in which the writ was developed. But the point holds that each writ had its own procedure.

The earliest writs concerned controversies over land tenure and its incidents: the writ of novel disseisin was available to remedy a tenant's recent ("novel") ouster from his lands; the writ of mort d'ancestor enabled an heir to recover estates to which he was entitled on the death of a predecessor in interest who died seised in demesne and of right; the writs of debt, detinue, covenant and account, all writs developed in the 12th and 13th centuries, were used chiefly as vehicles for determining controversies over feudal dues between holders of landed estates and those claiming adversely to them. The extent to which new royal writs were fashioned was determined by the felt necessities of the time and the prevailing balance of power between the king on the one hand and the keepers of the feudal courts—the barons—on the other. The resistance of the barons to royal incursions was expressed most dramatically, but only illustratively, in Magna Carta. By the middle of the 13th century or thereabouts, the barons' resistance was strong enough to stem the flow of new common law writs. Further evolution of the writs awaited the appearance of stronger kings and stronger calls for effective justice.

In the meantime, the feudal courts, the local courts, and the borough courts (tribunals of the emergent municipalities) disposed of most of the daily grist of litigation.

See generally W. Warren, The Governance of Norman and Angevin England (1987); R. Turner, The English Judiciary in the Age of Glanvill and

Bracton (1985); H. Richardson & G. Sayles, The Governance of Medieval England from the Conquest to Magna Carta (1963); D. Stenton, English Justice Between the Norman Conquest and the Great Charter (1964); S. Milsom, Historical Foundations of the Common Law (2d ed. 1981). Compare Watkin, The Significance of "In Consimili Casu," 23 Am. J. Legal Hist. 283 (1979).

Another line of royal intervention also had great significance, both contemporaneous and modern. This was the king's direct entertainment of complaints of his subjects. Proceedings before the king and his councillors regarding the complaints—or petitions or "bills" of complaint as they came to be called—start at an early date and are directly related to the Anglo-Saxon theory of kingship as implemented by Norman monarchical vigor. They continue in the 12th and 13th centuries in the form of proceedings by petition or bill (rather than by writ) before the king's justices; they continue in the 13th, 14th and 15th centuries in the form of proceedings by bill before the King's Council or special branches of it known in the 15th and 16th centuries as the Star Chamber and the Court of Requests; they continue in the 15th and subsequent centuries in the form of proceedings by bill before the Chancellor (the pre-eminent member of the King's Council) in what came to be the Court of Chancery. Compare H. Richardson & G. Sayles, Introduction, in Select Cases of Procedure Without Writ Under Henry III (Selden Soc'y 1941); G. Sayles, Introduction, in 5 Select Cases in the Court of King's Bench Under Edward III (Selden Soc'y 1958); S. Leadam & L. Baldwin, Introduction, in Select Cases Before the King's Council 1243–1482 (Selden Soc'y 1918); C. Bayne, Introduction, in Select Cases in the Council of Henry VII (Selden Soc'y 1958).

In medieval times, invocation of royal justice by means of writ and by means of petition or bill were overlapping and at times alternative methods of procedure. In later times, procedure by writ became distinctively associated with then-evolved separate royal tribunals, referred to loosely as the common law courts and including the Court of Exchequer, the Court of Common Bench or Court of Common Pleas and the Court of King's Bench; procedure by bill became chiefly associated with the then-evolved Court of Chancery. This difference in procedure is felt even today, particularly in regard to the right to jury trial.

The formalization of procedure during this period was accompanied by the emergence of procedural specialists who understood how the system worked. These specialists were the professional ancestors of modern litigation lawyers. See Symposium, Origins of the English Legal Profession, 5 Law & Hist. Rev. 1 (1987) .

2. Early evolution of the royal courts. The medieval central government was the King's court or *curia regis*. The *curia regis* consisted of a more or less regularly constituted group of chief lords, advisers, retainers and auxiliaries who traveled with the king, giving him counsel, taking care of administrative detail and executing his orders. The chief secretary of the *curia* was the Chancellor; his administrative corps, the Chancery, was principally responsible for the preparation of documents embodying the directives of the king—diplomatic messages, grants of land or privilege, and so on, including the common law writs. So it was that the writs of the common law issued out of Chancery, a practice that continued into the 19th century. Several circumstances conspired, however, to produce specialization of functions within the *curia,* in the form of separate branches of the *curia* that came in time to be referred to as separate courts.

The first of these circumstances was the administrative necessity for orderly record keeping. When the keeping of royal records simply in chronological order became intolerably burdensome, certain types of records were collected not in the "general file" (to use a modern analogue), but in special collections dealing with particular subject matter and, in time, placed in the charge of a particular clerk. Thus, the records dealing with the king's own financial affairs were at an early date consigned to special clerical treatment in the counting house or "exchequer." This was the antecedent of what soon developed into the Court of Exchequer. But in the 12th and early 13th centuries, the chief personnel of the *curia* continued to participate in the administration of most matters concerning the crown, so that it is not possible to speak of special judges of the Court of Exchequer during this period. Separation of aspects of the king's business was manifested not by the assignment of certain tasks to particular *curiae* but by the maintenance of separate records by particular clerks in the *curia.* The notion that the judges were occupants of independent tribunals, rather than simply a particular group of functionaries in the service of the Crown, did not gain full recognition in legal doctrine until about the time of James I in the early 17th century.

The second principal circumstance that led to the differentiation of the *curia*'s functions into separate courts was the historical fact that the early Plantagenet kings had domains in France that were more important to them than England and which required their presence on the continent for long periods of time. In the king's absence, an official known as the Justiciar served in his name and stead. During the long absences of the king abroad, Englishmen became accustomed to the convenience of coming to a royal court stationary at Westminster, rather than trying to catch up with its perambulations over the countryside. This was the origin of the Court of Common Pleas, or Common Bench as it was also known. That branch of the *curia* which still traveled with the king came to be known as the King's Bench, retaining that name and gradually achieving separate organization, even though the royal household had by the 15th century become customarily stationary. The jurisdiction of Common Pleas and King's Bench was not sharply differentiated in the 13th and 14th centuries. By and large, choice between the courts was largely a matter of convenience to the litigants.

This, in radically brief form, is the evolution of the three common law courts—Exchequer, Common Pleas, and King's Bench. Before considering the evolution of the Court of Chancery, it is necessary to touch briefly on the procedure of the common law.

3. **Common law procedure.** In the medieval period, common law procedure for hearing cases was relatively simple and flexible. In proceedings by writ, the terms of the writ disclosed the general nature of the plaintiff's complaint. Upon the defendant's appearance, plaintiff stated his complaint orally and in greater detail, the statement being known as plaintiff's declaration. It was required that the claim made in the declaration come within the bounds of the writ. For example, a plaintiff who had obtained a writ of novel disseisin could not "count" (as the making of the declaration came to be known) on some other kind of claim. This requirement was conformable to the principle that the writ alone authorized the hearing

of the case, so that a departure from the writ would lead the court beyond its authority. (The requirement of conformity was later administered in a highly technical spirit and made for the procedural casuistries for which common law pleading later came to be justly notorious.)

Defendant responded, also orally, perhaps by denying one of plaintiff's factual contentions, perhaps by arguing that his conduct was not wrongful by the law of the land (i.e., the common law), perhaps by alleging that he was justified in his conduct by reason of certain circumstances which he proceeded to allege. It must be borne in mind that in the background of all medieval litigation was the hope of bringing the parties to some sort of voluntary accord. Hence, judicial responses at all stages of litigation might be more or less tentative suggestions designed to induce one party or the other to yield, rather than flat pronouncements directing a party to do so. Indeed, in the 12th and early 13th centuries, and perhaps even later, the function of the "jurors" was not so much to decide the case as to indicate what they thought to be the facts of the matter. In this early period, if these suggestions were not taken by the parties as a basis for settlement, there would have to be a trial. Only later was the jury's response taken as dispositive of the issues raised.

Jury trial in the middle ages remains a largely unexplored chapter in procedural history. Nevertheless, some points seem clear. The basic theory of medieval jury trial was that the jurors made a finding not so much on evidence presented to them as on the strength of their own knowledge of the facts—personal or by common neighborhood account. One application of this principle was that the jury was to be composed of veniremen from the place where the disputed transaction occurred; another was that special juries would be summoned where the facts of the matter were known to a peculiar group. In effect, the jury would be made up of the known witnesses to the transaction. See, e.g., G. Sayles, Introduction, in Select Cases in the Court of King's Bench Under Edward III (Selden Soc'y 1958). Nevertheless, it appears that even at an early date evidence was presented to juries. Between 1300 and 1700 the rule evolved that juries were to give their verdict solely on evidence presented in open court, though it may well be supposed that verdicts always were importantly influenced by the litigants' standing and repute in the vicinity. More importantly, jury trial came to be the distinctive method of determining facts in the common law courts. See generally Moore, The Jury: Tool of Kings, Palladium of Liberty (2d ed. 1988); Groot, The Jury of Presentment Before 1215, 26 Am. J. Legal Hist. 1 (1982).

As noted above, in early common law procedure all pleadings were oral. No doubt as a means of saving time in routine cases, written pleadings came into use. By the 15th century, written pleadings were the norm and, in time, the requirement. While written pleadings saved time they also invited technicality and delay. Beyond this, from the 14th century onward there was an intermittent but continuing effort by the common law courts to extend the scope of their writs to include types of controversies which previously were outside their bounds. These extensions were not made directly by the frank creation of new writs but indirectly by various linguistic and procedural stratagems: plaintiffs were allowed to allege certain facts that were known to be false (such as the fact that defendant used force in committing the act in question); fictitious parties were allowed to be charged with conduct that was then attributed to the defendant, etc.

By reason of its technicality and its fictions, common law pleading as it stood in the early 19th century could be mastered only by long years of diligent application. Its mysteries sheltered the bar inside a shroud of arcana that was finally pierced only by the assault of Bentham and Dickens and those who took up their demands for reform. On the state of the English courts in the early 19th century, see Christopher (Baron Bowen), Progress in the Administration of Justice During the Victorian Period, in 1 Select Essays in Anglo-American Legal History at 516 (1907).

In the sea of technicality there emerged islands of simplicity. One of these was the development, under the action of assumpsit, of the so-called "common counts." See Lucke, Slade's Case and the Origin of the Common Counts, 81 Law Q. Rev. 422, 539 (1965), 82 Law Q. Rev. 81 (1966). For example, plaintiff would simply aver that he had at defendant's special instance and request furnished defendant with goods or services at an agreed price and that defendant promised to pay therefor but despite plaintiff's demand had failed to do so, to plaintiff's damage in the stated amount. This was the "indebitatus" count. Similar counts could be made in quantum meruit for the reasonable value of services rendered where no price for them had been expressly agreed upon; in quantum valebat for the reasonable value of goods sold and delivered where no price had been agreed to; and account, which alleged that there was an account owing to plaintiff from defendant (arising out of the sale of goods or rendition of services) and that despite demand, it remained unpaid. Taken together—and they were often pleaded together—these constituted the "common counts" and represented an uncomplicated and reasonably certain method of pleading informal contractual claims. So attractive were the "common counts" in simple contract actions that they survived the general reform of common law pleading in the Field Code, considered below. Compare Fed. R. Civ. P. Appendix of Forms, Form 10.

4.   Emergence of the Court of Chancery. It will be recalled that the basis of royal justice was the complaint of subject to king, praying that justice be done. Subjects continued to appeal to the king not alone by reason of failures of justice in the local and baronial courts, but also by reason of failures of justice in the king's own courts. A principal ground was the application of a plaintiff to have the advantage of his ordinary common law rights notwithstanding the existence of some special privilege, such as a royal grant of immunity to the defendant that prevented enforcement of those rights. Another ground was the inability of plaintiff to prove his right because the transaction had occurred out of the presence of witnesses (who could give the facts to or as a part of a jury), or because the evidence of the transaction belied the truth, as where execution of a document had been induced by fraud or duress.

In the 13th, 14th and 15th centuries these petitions were addressed to and acted upon by the King's Council, the effective successor of the old *curia regis*. In the early years all petitions were passed on by the Council and into the reign of the Stuarts this was so of many petitions touching important matters. Even as late as the early 17th century, the Council *qua* Council retained in its own hands some judicial matters, usually those laden with extraordinary political implications. Apparently matters of a relatively routine, non-criminal nature were referred to the Chancellor, at first with instructions directing him how to proceed, and later simply with the view that he proceed appropriately with the matter. Again, administrative routine was the genesis of jurisdiction. Just when the Chancellor can be identified as a judicial officer is not clear. It was no earlier than 1340 and no later than 1487. In the 16th century, Chancery emerged unmistakably as a court, in the sense of a tribunal with distinct officials, procedure and jurisdiction.

In the pre-Renaissance period, Chancery administered the common law and not the mysterious and supposedly subtler body of doctrine known as "equity" that in later years was said to be its chief characteristic. Indeed, taken as a whole, Chancery proceedings involved not so much a peculiar body of doctrine as a procedure and remedy that were importantly different from the common law. The pleadings in Chancery consisted of the petition or bill, the answer and, if further statements of position were required, plaintiff's replication to the answer and defendant's rejoinder to the replication. All this was similar to bill procedure in the common law courts and, it may be added, substantially identical with procedure in the Star Chamber. See W. Jones, The Elizabethan Court of Chancery (1967). The features of Chancery procedure that distinguished it from the common law courts were the subpoena and interrogatories, by which the defendant (and the plaintiff as well) could be compelled to testify. Whereas at common law litigants could not be compelled to testify and in later years were not even permitted to do so, the Chancery inquiry permitted the plaintiff to obtain admissions of facts for which he would otherwise be at a loss for proof. This is apparently the true basis for characterizing Chancery as a "court of conscience"—not the Chancellor acting on the basis of his "conscience," but the Chancellor presiding in a court in which defendant's "conscience" was examined. And it would seem that this is the reason why Chancery seemed to be administering a body of doctrine apparently different from the common law courts: a court in which one can get proof of fraud, mistake and breach of trust would seem to be more "equitable" than courts in which, because of barriers to party testimony, evidence of such chicanery was ordinarily not available. At all events, Chancery became associated with "equitable" doctrines, a term still used to refer generally to rules originally applied and developed in that court and including generally problems of fraud, mistake and breach of fiduciary duty. By way of remedies, Chancery typically issued orders commanding restoration of the rightful situation. The common law courts, which had originally granted redress of this character, by the 14th century had come ordinarily to give only damages. The Chancellor's remedial order or injunction remains the distinctive feature of "equity."

The other distinguishing characteristic of modern "equity" is the mode of trial: the determinations of fact are made by the judge and not by a jury. How this developed has not been explored. Certainly at an early stage the Chancellor, when in doubt as to the facts, referred the matter to the common law courts. And there is reason to believe that this was often if not invariably done down through the 18th century.

At the turn of the 18th century in England there were, then, three common law courts—Exchequer, King's Bench and Common Pleas—and the Court of Chancery. A peculiar consequence of the side-by-side evolution of the common law courts and the Court of Chancery was that claims and defenses relating to the same transaction might have to be put forth in two different courts. Thus, if plaintiff purchased a quantity of goods on the basis of false representations, he could sue either in the common law courts for damages for deceit or in equity to rescind the contract and have the money he paid restored to him. But he could not assert these claims in the alternative in one proceeding. This procedural separation of legal and equitable rights and remedies added to the cumbersomeness of early 19th century litigation.

5. **Early evolution of procedure in the United States.** In the United States, after initial development of courts modeled on the more informal pattern of English local and borough courts, the procedural trappings of the common law were imported. The importation was limited, however, in two respects. First, *separate* common law courts were not created; rather, the jurisdiction of all the common law courts was vested in a single court. Cf. In re Steinway, 159 N.Y. 250, 53 N.E. 1103 (1899). This went a long way to simplifying common law procedure in this country, for the peculiar procedures of the three English courts were blended into one (at times irregular) "common law" procedure. Second, the Court of Chancery very nearly missed being transplanted. In some states, notably Pennsylvania, no court of "equity" was established before 1800; in New York, the powers of a court of equity were assumed by the Supreme Court, which in that state was (and still is) the trial court of general common law jurisdiction; in other states a separate Court of Chancery was created, perpetuating in virgin soil the bifurcation of jurisdiction that had its roots in ancient English history. See Wilson, Courts of Chancery in the American Colonies, in 2 Select Essays in Anglo-American Legal History 779 (1908); Surrency, The Courts in the American Colonies, 11 Am. J. Legal Hist. 253 (1967); Smith & Hershkowitz, Courts of Equity in the Province of New York: The Cosby Controversy, 1732–1736, 16 Am. J. Legal Hist. 1 (1972).

There survived in the England of 1800 some specialized courts. Notable among these were the Court of Admiralty, having jurisdiction of maritime controversies, and the Ecclesiastical Courts, having jurisdiction of certain matrimonial and testamentary matters. By Article III of the United States Constitution, the jurisdiction exercised in England by the Court of Admiralty was conferred on the courts of the new federal government (and remains one of the heads of federal jurisdiction). The disestablishment of religion in this country left the matter of ecclesiastical jurisdiction in limbo for a time; ultimately, jurisdiction of matrimonial causes was conferred on state trial courts of general jurisdiction, while the administration of decedents' estates was vested in state "probate" courts.

6. **Legislative reform.** By the early decades of the 19th century the English courts had become a public scandal. The common law courts were entangled in procedural subtleties from which they had seemingly little chance and certainly little inclination to extricate themselves. Chancery procedure was in almost equal degree preoccupied with niceties and was hopelessly delayed: suits took decades and more to reach finality. Parliament initiated investigations of Chancery in the 1820's, but little came of it immediately. The obtuse response of the common lawyers to the criticisms of common law pleading was a revision of common law pleading rules, known as the Hilary Rules because adopted in Hilary Term, 1834, which accentuated pleading technicality beyond even the traditional extremes. See Holdsworth, The New Rules of Pleading of the Hilary Term, 1834, 1 Cambridge L. J. 261 (1923).

The impulse to reform continued. A series of changes ensued: parties were made competent as witnesses, common law procedure was simplified and made more uniform, Chancery procedure was streamlined and the court authorized to take oral testimony. In 1873, all the old English central courts were consolidated into one Supreme Court of Judicature and a single body of procedural rules adopted for all controversies without regard to their character as "legal" or "equitable." See Sunderland, The English Struggle for Procedural Reform, 39 Harv. L. Rev. 725 (1926).

In this country the state legislatures even prior to the Revolution had shown a disposition to amend away some of the common law's technicalities, a trend that continued into the 19th century. See P. Millar, Civil Procedure of the Trial Court in Historical Perspective 39–42, 176 (1952). Cf. Brown, Frontier Justice: Wayne County 1796–1836, 16 Am. J. Legal Hist. 126 (1972); L. Wunder, Inferior Courts, Superior Justice: A History of the Justices of the Peace on the Northwest Frontier (1979). The capital event, however, was the sweeping reform embodied in the Field Code of 1848. The Code, known after its chief architect, David Dudley Field of the New York Bar, was a comprehensive reconstitution of rules of procedure, embodying the following chief features:

1.   The forms of action, i.e., the writ system, were abolished. In their stead, a single mode of procedure was made applicable alike to all kinds of civil actions, legal and equitable.

2.   The pleading stage of litigation was sharply curtailed by reducing the allowable pleadings to the complaint, the answer and (in some states) a reply.

3.   Law and equity (in some states) were "merged," in that types of claims and defenses previously cognizable only in courts of law or in courts of equity could now be asserted in the new unitary proceeding, the "one form" of action.

4.   An attempt was made to rationalize and restate the rules governing the joinder of claims and of parties.

The Field Code was enacted in New York in 1848. The California legislature of 1849 adopted a version of the Field Code substantially similar to that of New York. From New York, the Field Code was carried westward into most of the states of the Old Northwest and the Great Plains; from California, it was carried eastward into the mountain states. Within 30 years, 28 states had adopted the code, typically devising local minor variations. See Clark on Code Pleading 23 et seq. (2d ed. 1947). That Code remains, much amended, the procedural system of California and is the principal antecedent of the Federal Rules of Civil Procedure and the New York Civil Practice Act.

7.   Federal Rules of Civil Procedure. a. The Federal Rules. The most significant procedural reform of the twentieth century was the adoption of the Federal Rules of Civil Procedure. After a long period of agitation, Congress in 1934 adopted the Federal Rules Enabling Act, which conferred on the Supreme Court the power to propose rules of procedure for the federal District Courts. The Supreme Court appointed an Advisory Committee, for which Dean (later Judge) Charles E. Clark was chief draftsman. The Advisory Committee's draft, after minor changes, was adopted in 1938.

Prior to 1938 the Federal courts had two "sides"—law and equity. Different rules of procedure governed the respective sides. On the equity side, the procedure was uniform throughout the country and followed in its main contours the procedure of the English Court of Chancery. That procedure, as modified by decisional law developed over the years in the federal courts sitting in equity, was supplemented and in part superseded by rules promulgated from time to time by the United States Supreme Court, most notable of which were the relatively comprehensive Equity Rules of 1912. On the "law" side of the federal District Courts, however, the procedure was that of the state in which the federal District Court sat. But this general policy of conformity to state procedure, set forth in the Conformity Acts (part of the Judiciary Act of 1789 and subsequent amendatory provisions), was subject to exceptions laid down by statute and developed by case law. The number and uncertainty of the exceptions were substantial. The resulting confusion was an important consideration behind the drive for uniform federal rules.

The Federal Rules of Civil Procedure are adopted in a drawn-out and curious way. In a general sense, the United States Supreme Court is responsible for proposing rules to Congress, but, in practical fact, the Court usually serves as no more than a conduit to Congress for rules formulated by others. The federal rulemaking system works as follows:

The Judicial Conference of the United States appoints a Standing Committee on Rules of Practice and Procedure, as well as an Advisory Committee on the Civil Rules. The Judicial Conference is composed of the Chief Justice of the United States, the Chief Judges of the twelve Courts of Appeals and of the Court of International Trade, the Chief Judge of the Court of Appeals for the Federal Circuit, and twelve District Court Judges. The Standing Committee and the Advisory Committee are composed of federal court of appeals and district judges, law professors, and members of the practicing bar.

The Advisory Committee drafts and publishes proposed rules, and receives public comment. It redrafts the proposed rules as it sees fit in light of the comments, and forwards them to the Standing Committee. The Standing Committee has the power to accept, reject, or modify the proposed rules, but generally forwards them to the Judicial Conference unaltered. The Judicial Conference in its turn has the power to accept, reject, or modify the proposed rules, but it too generally forwards them unaltered, this time to the Supreme Court. Finally, the Supreme Court, in its turn, forwards the proposed rules to Congress by May 1 of the year in which they are to take effect. The Court has rarely refused to forward to Congress all of the rules proposed by the Judicial Conference, although it did reject some rules in the spring of 1991. If Congress does nothing with the rules forwarded by the Supreme Court, they automatically become law on December 1 of the year in which they are forwarded.

Some members of the Supreme Court have been uncomfortable with the role of the Supreme Court in this system. Justices Black and Douglas were particularly outspoken in their opposition in the 1950s and 60s. Other Justices who have expressed reservations about the rulemaking process include Justices White, Scalia and Thomas. As Chief Justice Rehnquist noted, in his letter to Congress accompanying the proposed 1993 amendments to the civil rules, "[T]his transmittal does not necessarily indicate that the Court itself would have proposed these amendments in the form submitted." 146 F.R.D. 401, 403 (1993).

Because the real drafting work is done outside Congress, any rules adopted have a restricted scope. The Rules Enabling Act provides that the Federal Rules of Civil Procedure "shall not abridge, enlarge or modify any substantive right." 28 U.S.C. § 2072(b). Although the Supreme Court has several times construed federal rules of procedure narrowly to avoid conflict with the Act, no Federal Rule of Civil Procedure has ever been invalidated on account of its "abridging, enlarging, or modifying" a substantive right. See the materials on Erie R.R. v. Tompkins, 304 U.S. 64, 58 S.Ct. 817, 82 L.Ed. 1188 (1938), in Chapter 3, infra, for exploration of the relationship among the Rules, the Rules Enabling Act, and the substantive law.

The Federal Rules of Civil Procedure have been amended a number of times since they were enacted. Amendments in 2007 rewrote the rules to make the style and terminology consistent throughout. When you read pre-2007 cases, you will sometimes encounter terminology that is no longer employed.

On the history of procedure in the federal courts, see the concise treatment in R. Fallon, J. Manning, D. Meltzer & D. Shapiro, Hart and Wechsler's The Federal Courts and the Federal System ch. 6 (6th ed. 2009). For the history of the movement leading up to the Federal Rules, see Burbank, The Rules Enabling Act of 1934, 130 U. Pa. L. Rev. 1015 (1982); Subrin, How Equity Conquered Common Law: The Federal Rules of Civil Procedure in Historical Perspective, 135 U. Pa. L. Rev. 909 (1987). Since the promulgation of the Federal Rules of Civil Procedure, a number of states have adopted their provisions substantially intact and many others have taken over substantial portions of them. See Oakley & Coon, The Federal Rules in State Courts: A Survey of State Court Systems of Civil Procedure, 61 Wash. L. Rev. 1367 (1986).

b.   Local rules. A principal aim of the Federal Rules in 1938 was to produce a uniform system of procedure in civil cases in the federal courts. On the whole, the federal rules have been successful in achieving that uniformity, but there are significant local variations. One reason for local variation is the fact that federal District Courts all have local rules that supplement the Federal Rules of Civil Procedure. 28 U.S.C. § 2071 authorizes individual federal District Courts to adopt local rules. Federal Rule 83 essentially implements § 2071:

> After giving public notice and an opportunity for comment, a district court, acting by a majority of its district judges, may adopt and amend rules governing its practice. A local rule must be consistent with—but not duplicate—federal statutes and rules adopted under 28 U.S.C. §§ 2072 and 2075, and must conform to any uniform numbering system prescribed by the Judicial Conference of the United States.

Local rules have proliferated. A 1989 study concluded that some local rules "modify or contradict the Federal Rules," despite the requirement of § 2071 and Rule 83 that they be "consistent" with the Rules. Further,

> There are nearly 5,000 local rules in the 94 federal districts, and the number is growing. There are thousands of additional standing orders. To give one example, the Central District of California, based in Los Angeles, has 31 local rules with 434 subrules, supplemented by 275 standing orders. These are published in three volumes that are hard even to lift, let alone read. At the other extreme, the Middle District of Georgia, based in Macon, has only one local rule and just 11 standing orders.

Coquillete, Squiers & Subrin, The Role of Local Rules, 75 A.B.A.J. 62 (4) (1989). See also Subrin, Federal Rules, Local Rules, and State Rules: Uniformity, Divergence, and Emerging Procedural Patterns, 137 U. Pa. L. Rev. 1999 (1989).

8.   Modern litigation. There are several notable trends in modern civil litigation. One is the sharp reduction in the proportion of filed cases that are resolved at trial. A much higher percentage of cases are disposed of through pretrial motions or settlement. One consequence of the shift away from trials is the decreasing control of appellate courts over the day-to-day, or "retail," administration of justice. Professor Yeazell summarizes this trend:

> [Previously,] trials lay at the center of litigation, and appellate courts could control the outcome of trials. Neither proposition holds true today. "Litigation," usually meaning discovery, summary judgment, settlement negotiations, alternatives to judicial process, sanctions for lawyer misbehavior, and similar pretrial matters, lies at the center of judges' and lawyers' attention. Trials are an endangered species. Appellate courts, while now more active than ever, no longer control the outcome of a high proportion of cases.

Yeazell, The Misunderstood Consequences of Modern Civil Process, 1994 Wis. L. Rev. 631, 666–67. See also Resnik, From "Cases" to "Litigation," 54 Law & Contemp. Probs. 5 (1991); Resnik, Failing Faith: Adjudicatory Procedure in Decline, 53 U. Chi. L. Rev. 494 (1986).

A second shift has been the increase in the range of cases where adjudication on the merits involves large continuing consequences for the parties to the litigation and the communities of which they are a part. In these types of cases, it is sometimes said that there has been a shift in the function of litigation from dispute resolution to regulation. These are often disputes which previously were resolved, if at all, by administrative agencies, by the legislature, or by the executive. The first and most salient example is the desegregation litigation beginning with Brown v. Board of Education, 347 U.S. 483, 74 S.Ct. 686, 98 L.Ed. 873 (1954), and continuing with comprehensive decrees concerning pupil assignment in the public schools. See O. Fiss, The Civil Rights Injunction (1978); G. Metcalf, From Little Rock to Boston: The History of School Desegregation (1983). Other examples include the cases involving "one-person one-vote" beginning with Baker v. Carr, 369 U.S. 186, 82 S.Ct. 691, 7 L.Ed.2d 663 (1962); reform of prisons and hospitals, e.g., Brown v. Plata, 570 U.S. __, 131 S.Ct. 1910 (2011), 179 L.Ed. 2d 969; Wyatt v. Stickney, 344 F. Supp. 373 (M.D. Ala. 1972), aff'd in part sub nom. Wyatt v. Aderholt, 503 F.2d 1305 (5th Cir. 1974); reform of public school finance, e.g., Serrano v. Priest, 5 Cal.3d 584, 96 Cal.Rptr. 601, 487 P.2d 1241 (1971); and a range of other regulatory and civil rights actions. These cases characteristically involve complex factual and legal issues, intense public controversy, and direct or secondary involvement of many different parties and interests. See generally Chayes, The Role of the Judge in Public Law Litigation, 89 Harv. L. Rev. 1281 (1976); Fletcher, The Discretionary Constitution: Institutional Remedies and Judicial Legitimacy, 91 Yale L.J. 635 (1982). The rise of public law litigation and the role of "activist" trial judges was praised by many political liberals and decried by conservatives.

In recent decades, much of the highly consequential regulatory litigation has been in the form of actions for money damages brought under federal and state law. Sometimes these cases are brought individually. Others are brought as class actions. Class actions under the federal antitrust and securities laws have been important sources of litigation for 40 years. State-law class actions have also been important. Sometimes state-law cases or groups of cases have involved a single product or company, as in the case of silicone gel breast implants, Agent Orange (a defoliant used during the Vietnam War) and the Ford Explorer. At other times, they have embroiled entire industries, such as asbestos and tobacco. Whether these cases proceed individually or collectively, they present situations in which private lawsuits subject to decision by a series of juries—or in the case of class actions, a single jury—have the potential to move sums in the hundreds of millions or billions of dollars into the hands of plaintiffs and their lawyers, to drive products and companies from the market place, and to generate extraordinary litigation costs. In 2005, in response to complaints by business groups that some state courts have been overly sympathetic to class action plaintiffs, Congress passed the Class Action Fairness Act ("CAFA"). CAFA makes it easier to remove diversity jurisdiction class actions, based on substantive state law, from state to federal court. See 28 U.S.C. §§ 1332(d), 1453, 1711–1715.

Because of their social significance and difficulty, these cases have placed unprecedented responsibilities and strains on the system of litigation at the trial court level. One does not have to be a political scientist to know that the "activist judges" of public law litigation and the "greedy plaintiffs' lawyers" of mass tort litigation have been the subject of partisan debate in many recent elections at both the national and state levels. Given these developments, it is hardly surprising that some believe that civil rule making, and judicial interpretation of existing rules, have come to have political overtones. Consider, for example, the following comments made at a conference celebrating the 50th Anniversary of the Federal Rules of Civil Procedure:

> [A] remarkable aspect of this conference has been the repeated references to the "political" aspects of the Federal Rules of Civil Procedure. From a variety of perspectives, many of the speakers have made comments about the political implications of various Rules. Others, seeming to accept the political content of the Rules, have warned that "we" (that is, all litigants) are safer when the facade, if not the reality, is maintained that "neutral" Rules are applied to "anonymous" (that is, not identifiable in advance) plaintiffs and defendants. I believe we cannot and should not ignore the political content and consequences of procedural rules. Over the last decade, a variety of powerful "repeat players" have sought, sometimes openly, to influence "court reform" efforts. By and large, that work has been done not by letters written to the Advisory Committee on Civil Rules, but rather by lobbying efforts directed towards legislatures and the public, by well-financed media campaigns, and by support for conferences and meetings to address and describe the "litigation crisis." However appealing might be the notion that writing the Rules of Civil Procedure (in contrast to the Rules of Criminal Procedure) is a "neutral" task with diverse consequences on anonymous and interchangeable civil plaintiffs and defendants, that description is no longer available.

Resnik, The Domain of Courts, 137 U. Pa. L. Rev. 2219 (1989). For a sophisticated argument that the federal rule making process is legitimate despite the impact of procedural rules on the operation of substantive law, and despite the high political stakes involved, see Bone, The Process of Making Process: Court Rulemaking, Democratic Legitimacy, and Procedural Efficacy, 87 Geo. L.J. 887 (1999). See also Lesnick, The Federal Rule-Making Process: A Time for Re-examination, 61 A.B.A. J. 579 (1979); Carrington, "Substance" and "Procedure" in the Rules Enabling Act, 1989 Duke L.J. 281; Burbank, Hold the Corks: A Comment on Paul Carrington's "Substance" and "Procedure" in the Rules Enabling Act, 1989 Duke L.J. 1012.

D. AMERICAN UNIQUENESS: A COMPARATIVE PERSPECTIVE

In recent decades, the growth of international trade and globalization, coupled with an increase in comparative procedural scholarship, have generated a much greater awareness of the different approaches to civil justice both between common and civil law systems, and between the American version of the common law system and virtually every other national system of civil justice. These differences have in turn led to efforts to derive principles that can command assent for the resolution of transnational disputes having links to legal systems with very different premises and procedures. The authors of one such set of rules offer a description of some of the ways in which American procedure is different.

The American Law Institute and Unidroit, ALI/Unidroit Principles of Transnational Civil Procedure 4–7 (2006)

In undertaking international harmonization of procedural law, the Reporters have come to identify both fundamental similarities and fundamental differences among procedural systems. Obviously, it is the fundamental differences that present the difficulties. However, it is important to keep in mind that all modern civil procedural systems have fundamental similarities. These similarities result from the fact that a procedural system must respond to several inherent requirements. Recognition of these requirements makes easier the task of identifying functional similarities in diverse legal systems and, at the same time, puts into sharper perspective the ways in which procedural systems differ from one another.

The fundamental similarities among procedural systems can be summarized as follows:

- Standards governing assertion of personal jurisdiction and subject-matter jurisdiction,
- Specifications for a neutral adjudicator,
- Procedure for notice to defendant,
- Rules for formulation of claims,
- Explication of applicable substantive law,
- Establishment of facts through proof,
- Provision for expert testimony,
- Rules for deliberation, decision, and appellate review,

- Rules of finality of judgments.

Of these, the rules of jurisdiction, notice, and recognition of judgments are sufficiently similar from one country to another that they have been susceptible to substantial resolution through international practice and formal conventions. Concerning jurisdiction, the United States is aberrant in that it has an expansive concept of "long-arm" jurisdiction, although this difference is one of degree rather than one of kind, and in that United States law governing authority of its constituent states perpetuates jurisdiction based on simple presence of the person ("tag" jurisdiction). Specification of a neutral adjudicator begins with realization that all legal systems have rules to assure that a judge or other adjudicator should be disinterested. Accordingly, in transnational litigation reliance generally can be placed on the local rules expressing that principle. Similarly, an adjudicative system by definition requires a principle of finality. Therefore, the concept of "final" judgment is also generally recognized, although some legal systems permit the reopening of a determination more liberally than other systems do. The corollary concept of mutual recognition of judgments is also universally accepted.

The differences in procedural systems are, along one division, differences between the common-law systems and the civil-law systems. The common-law systems all derive from England and include, Canada, Australia, New Zealand, South Africa, India, and the United States, as well as Israel, Singapore, and Bermuda. The civil-law systems originated on the European continent and include those derived from Roman law (the law of the Roman Empire codified in the Justinian Code) and canon law (the law of the Roman Catholic Church, itself substantially derived from Roman law). The civil-law systems include those of France, Germany, Italy, Spain, and virtually all other European countries and, in a borrowing or migration of legal systems, those of Latin America, Japan, and China.

The significant differences between common-law and civil-law systems are as follows:

- The judge in civil-law systems, rather than the advocates in common-law systems, has primary responsibility for development of the evidence and articulation of the legal concepts that should govern decision. However, there is great variance among civil law systems in the manner and degree to which this responsibility is exercised, and no doubt variance among the judges in any given system.

- Civil-law litigation in many systems proceeds through a series of short hearing sessions—sometimes less than an hour each—for reception of evidence, which is then consigned to the case file until an eventual final stage of analysis and decision. In contrast, common-law litigation has a preliminary or pretrial stage (sometimes more than one) and then a trial at which all the evidence is received consecutively.

- A civil-law judgment in the court of first instance is generally subject to more searching reexamination in the court of second instance than a common-law judgment.

Reexamination in the civil-law systems extends to facts as well as law.

- The judges in civil-law systems typically serve a professional lifetime as judge, whereas the judges in common-law systems generally are selected from the ranks of the bar. Thus, most civil-law judges lack the experience of having been a lawyer, whatever effects that may have.

These are important differences, but they are not irreconcilable.

The American version of the common-law system has differences from other common-law systems that are of at least equal significance. The American system is unique in the following respects:

- Jury trial is a broadly available right in the American federal and state courts. No other country routinely uses juries in civil cases.

- American rules of discovery give wide latitude for exploration of potentially relevant information and evidence, including through oral deposition.

- The American adversary system generally affords the advocates far greater latitude in presentation of a case than is customary in other common-law systems.

- The American system operates through a cost rule under which each party ordinarily pays that party's own lawyer and cannot recover that expense from a losing opponent. In almost all other countries, except Japan and China, the winning party, whether plaintiff or defendant, recovers at least a substantial portion of litigation costs.

- American judges are selected through a variety of ways in which political affiliation plays an important part. In most other common-law countries judges are selected on the basis of professional standards.

Most of the major differences between the United States and other common-law systems stem from the use of juries in American litigation. American proceedings conducted by judges without juries closely resemble their counterparts in other common-law countries.

NOTE ON THE UNIQUENESS OF AMERICAN PROCEDURE

The pronounced differences between the American procedural system and those of all other developed nations presents an increasing number of practical problems for clients and lawyers engaged in international activity. They also raise questions about the wisdom of American choices that ought to be kept in mind throughout a basic course in procedure. If American choices are wise, why have they found so little acceptance elsewhere? Are other nations simply misguided? Or is it the case that American procedure is right for us, given our system of governance, our political values, and our historical traditions, though it would not be right for other nations? If American procedure is right for American conditions, but not for others, to what extent is it fair to insist on American procedures in disputes that have connections with or are centered in other nations? Finally, is it possible that the fundamental differences between American procedures and those of other developed nations represent flaws in the American system that, whatever their origins, are now maintained less because they serve the interests of justice than because they serve the interests of powerful constituents of the civil justice system, perhaps most notably the legal profession? For reflections on these issues, consider, R. Kagan, Adversarial Legalism: The American Way of Law (2001), G. Hazard & M. Taruffo, American Civil Procedure (1993), M. Damaska, The Faces of Justice and State Authority: A Comparative Approach to the Legal Process (1986). Useful articles include, Kritzer, American Adversarialism, 38 Law & Soc'y Rev. 349 (2004), Langbein, The German Advantage in Civil Procedure, 52 U. Chi. L. Rev. 823 (1985).

E. AN INTRODUCTION TO JUDICIAL REMEDIES

NOTE ON REMEDIES

1. **The nature of judicial remedies.** The law of judicial remedies defines the nature and scope of the court-ordered relief available to a plaintiff who can demonstrate that she has a valid claim under the applicable substantive law. For example, in an action for breach of contract, the court or jury must first apply the substantive law to the evidence presented by the parties to determine whether there was a contract and whether the defendant breached that contract. Only if it finds a substantive violation will the court reach the question of what remedy should be awarded the plaintiff. The plaintiff must plead and prove her entitlement to the remedy or remedies requested under the same procedural and evidentiary standards that govern the determination of substantive claims. See Fed. R. Civ. P. 8 (a)(3) (pleading of demand for relief), Fed. R. Civ. P. 26(a)(1)(C) (mandatory disclosure of information relating to claimed damages.)

The nature and scope of the remedy awarded by the court is closely tied to the specific goals and policies of the underlying substantive law. The remedy granted is the court's best effort to vindicate the substantive right at issue in the case. The substantive impact of the law of remedies extends beyond the very small percentage of cases in which a trial is held, a substantive violation found, and a remedy awarded. The availability of judicial remedies influences plaintiffs' decisions whether to bring suit when a violation has occurred, how much the parties will invest in prosecuting and defending the case, and the parties' decisions about whether, and on what terms, to settle. In the world outside the courtroom, the threat of judicial remedies also influences many everyday decisions about compliance with the law. Because remedies are specific to particular substantive areas, there are distinct subsets of remedial law closely tailored to the goals of areas of law as diverse as contract, tort, property, environmental law, intellectual property, civil rights, and employment discrimination and that are often studied in detail in courses concerning those subjects. The subject is also covered from an overarching perspective in a Remedies course. The discussion here is intended to provide helpful background for thinking about the intersections between the law of remedies and the law of procedure.

2. **Compensatory damages. a. Tort cases.** Tort and contract disputes make up a very high percentage of the civil caseload of American courts. In those cases, the primary plenary remedy of damages. Damages are generally the only remedy for serious personal injury that has already

occurred, and are probably the most efficient form of relief in cases of economic loss that has already occurred. The chief problems in the damages remedy are how to measure it and how to collect it.

Most tort suits seek only compensatory damages, that is, damages intended to make a party whole for harm suffered. The compensable elements of harm are determined by the substantive law. Damages are awarded in a lump sum that encompasses both past harms and those anticipated to flow from the defendant's conduct in the future. Many courts and commentators believe that tort damages also serve a deterrent function because the possibility of damages must factor into a potential defendant's economic function. Thus, some argue that tort liability discourages risky behavior and encourages safety precautions. But others question the validity of the deterrence theory in light of such factors as the ability of defendants to insure, the uncertainty of liability, and the failure of potential defendants to behave rationally. For a broad overview of arguments offered by proponents and critics of the deterrence theory, see Schwartz, Reality in the Economic Analysis of Tort Law: Does Tort Law Really Deter?, 42 UCLA L. Rev. 377 (1994).

In personal injury lawsuits, the items of damage allowed include: medical expenses, economic losses attributable to the interruption of normal life on account of the injury, lost income during the period required for recovery, and economic loss attributable to any permanent injury. In addition, plaintiff can recover the monetary amount that the trier of fact assigns for "pain and suffering" endured by plaintiff, temporarily during recovery and permanently as a result of incomplete recovery. While certain types of damages—past medical expenses, for example—are relatively simple to establish, others are far more complicated. Where, for example, a plaintiff suffers a lasting injury that interferes with her long-term ability to work, the court must take into consideration such inherently uncertain factors as her long-term career path and likely age of retirement in order to determine future damages. Such problems are all the more acute when juries are asked to calculate noneconomic damages; the process of translating pain and suffering into a monetary award can be both subjective and unpredictable. For more on what is meant by "adequate compensation" in a personal injury case, see D. Dobbs, Law of Remedies ch. 8 (2d ed. 1993).

b. Contract cases. In breach of contract cases, the general measure of damages is that amount which is required to give the plaintiff the "benefit of the bargain," that is to make him as well off as he would have been if the defendant had performed instead of breaching the agreement. Often the benefit of the bargain is measured by the difference between the contract price and the market price. If the defendant promises to sell 10,000 barrels of oil to the plaintiff for $4 million, and breaches after the market price has risen to $5 million, the plaintiff's damages are the difference between the contract price and the market price: $1 million. However, as an alternative to court-awarded expectation damages, parties to a contract sometimes choose to provide in advance that a certain dollar amount of damages will be available in the event of breach—a so-called "liquidated damages clause." If the court finds that a liquidated damages clause is valid, the agreed-upon amount replaces actual damages as the measure of recovery. But if a liquidated damages clause substantially exceeds the actual amount of damages the parties anticipated at the time they entered into the agreement, courts will generally find that it is a "penalty," and hence unenforceable. (By contrast, if the liquidated damages are substantially less than actual damages, the clause is enforceable.) If a liquidated damages clause is struck down as a "penalty," plaintiff may recover actual damages in the same manner as if the liquidated damages clause had never existed. See D. Dobbs, Law of Remedies § 12.9 (2d ed. 1993).

3. Are compensatory damages fully compensatory? There are a number of features of American remedies law that bear on whether an award of compensatory damages fully compensates for harm suffered.

a. Attorneys' fees. Compensatory damages normally do not include the costs of enforcing one's right to compensation. The most important such cost is attorneys' fees, which for plaintiffs with a contingent fee arrangement typically are between 25% and 40% of the ultimate recovery. For many tort plaintiffs, this means that an award of full compensation falls significantly short of making the plaintiff whole for her losses. The rule is the same in contract cases, but parties are free to provide in their contract for an award of fees to a party who prevails in litigation relating to the agreement. Finally, in certain classes of cases, of which the most important are claims under federal and state civil rights, antitrust, and regulatory statutes, the prevailing plaintiffs are entitled to recover reasonable attorneys' fees from the opposing party.

b. Interest. Full compensation should include interest between the time harm is suffered and the time damages are paid. Interest reflects the time value of money to the plaintiff; it also reduces the defendant's incentive to delay litigation. The law draws a distinction between prejudgment interest and interest on the judgment itself. Prejudgment interest, from the date of accrual of the cause of action to the date of judgment, was traditionally allowed if the suit was brought under an agreement which provided for payment of interest on sums owed. It was also permitted in actions where the amount of damages was "certain" or "ascertainable" at the time of the harm. The requirement that the amount of damages be "ascertainable" means that prejudgment interest is ordinarily not recoverable in tort actions for injury to person or property. Some states now allow prejudgment interest in tort cases as a matter of course, while others leave it to the discretion of the court or jury. See Kotzian v. Barr, 81 N.J. 360, 408 A.2d 131 (1979) (court may decline to award prejudgment interest in "exceptional cases"). Some states follow the traditional rule, allowing it to be awarded only in contract actions or where authorized by statute or in any action in which damages can be calculated with certainty. For more, see Michael S. Knoll, A Primer on Prejudgment Interest, 75 Tex. L. Rev. 293 (1996).

Post-judgment interest accrues from the time of the judgment until it is paid or otherwise satisfied, and is allowed in all types of actions, except certain suits against the federal government. Comment, Interest on Judgments in the Federal Courts, 64 Yale L.J. 1019 (1955); Note, Interest in Judgments Against the Federal Government: The Need for Full Compensation, 91 Yale L.J. 297 (1981).

The rate of interest is generally governed by statute unless otherwise specified by contract. Because the statutory rates generally are not indexed to inflation or market rates and are not frequently adjusted, the rate often varies substantially from the prevailing rate of interest. See, e.g., Calif.C.Civ.P. § 685.010 (10 percent). If the statutory interest rate is below the prevailing rate on the open market, defendants can retain their money and accumulate interest at market rates, creating a disincentive to settle or pay claims or judgments promptly. To eliminate any post-judgment incentive to delay, the federal interest statute ties the legal rate to the market rate. 28 U.S.C. § 1961.

    c. The collateral source rule. In tort cases, the plaintiff's damages are not reduced on account of payments received by the plaintiff from sources other than the potential defendants in the action—typically insurance companies. Thus, a plaintiff may recover damages from the defendant for losses that have already been compensated by first party insurance. In support of the rule, it is argued that it is unfair to reduce plaintiff's award because she had the foresight to purchase insurance. Defenders of the collateral source rule also argue that it offsets the impact of attorneys' fees and the absence of prejudgment interest. The risk of double payment has in any event declined in recent years, because insurance contracts often provide the insurer with the right to subrogation (that is, to succeed to the insured's claim) or refund of benefits upon a tort recovery. Helfend v. Southern California Rapid Transit District, 2 Cal.3d 1, 84 Cal.Rptr. 173, 465 P.2d 61 (1970). See also D. Dobbs, Law of Remedies §§ 3.6, 8.10 (2d ed. 1993). In recent years, many states have modified the rule by permitting the defendant under certain circumstances to introduce evidence of any collateral sources available to the plaintiff. See, e.g., Cal. Civ. Code § 3333.1 (permitting such evidence to be introduced in medical malpractice cases). A few states have eliminated the rule entirely in medical malpractice actions. See, e.g., Tenn. Code Ann. § 29–26–119 (limiting damages in malpractice actions to amounts not compensated by insurance).

    d. Overcompensation, undercompensation and tort reform. In contract cases, parties are able to determine their level of compensation for breach by contracting for prejudgment interest, attorneys' fees and liquidated damages. Hence the controversy concerning compensatory damages centers on tort cases. Criticism often focuses on the potential for large unjustified awards, particularly when "pain and suffering" damages are at stake. In response to a perceived explosion in the size of awards for pain and suffering, many state legislatures have sought to place statutory caps on noneconomic damages. Courts have varied in their response to challenges to the constitutionality of such caps. Compare Best v. Taylor Mach. Works, 689 N.E.2d 1057 (1997) (striking down $500,000 cap on noneconomic damages as arbitrary and inconsistent with state constitution's "special legislation" clause), with Murphy v. Edmonds, 325 Md. 342, 601 A.2d 102 (1992) (rejecting constitutional challenges to inflation-adjusted $350,000 cap) and Fein v. Permanente Med. Group, 38 Cal.3d 137, 211 Cal.Rptr. 368, 695 P.2d 665 (1985) (sustaining $250,000 cap on noneconomic damages in medical malpractice cases). For criticism of such measures, see, e.g., Shuchman, It Isn't That the Tort Lawyers Are So Right, It's Just That the Tort Reformers Are So Wrong, 49 Rutgers L. Rev. 485 (1997) and Galanter, Real World Torts: An Antidote to Anecdote, 55 Md. L. Rev. 1093 (1996). Despite these criticisms, proposals to cap on pain and suffering awards remain a staple of tort law reform from the defense side.

    The wisdom of these caps is doubtful. The evidence suggests that it is not large claims but small ones that tend to be overcompensated, while plaintiffs who have suffered severe damages often find that judgments do not cover their losses. A 1986 Alliance of American Insurers study of product liability claims, for example, found that claimants who suffered economic losses under $100,000 received five times their loss. By contrast, claimants with losses exceeding $1 million received only 58% of their economic losses. Studies of claims in automobile accidents, airline accidents, and medical malpractice cases have found similar patterns. Galanter, Real World Torts: An Antidote to Anecdote, 55 Md. L. Rev. 1093, 1117–20 (1996). For a somewhat skeptical view of Galanter's argument and an overview of the continuing debate, see Schwartz, Empiricism and Tort Law, 2002 U. Ill. L. Rev. 1067 (2002).

4.   Punitive damages. a. Basic principles. The standard criterion of liability for actual damages in tort is that the defendant must have acted negligently. Punitive damages (sometimes referred to as "exemplary damages") are awarded in tort for worse-than-negligent behavior, such as bad faith, intentional, malicious, outrageous, or reckless acts. In many cases, awards of punitive damages may reflect the same degree of societal condemnation—and the same retributive and deterrent purposes—as do criminal penalties. See Restatement (Second) of Torts § 908, comment b. Punitive damages are awarded most frequently in intentional tort, business fraud and employment cases; awards in products liability and malpractice cases are very rare. See Vidmar & Rose, Punitive Damages by Juries in Florida: In Terrorem and in Reality, 38 Harv. J. of Legis. 487 (2001). In most states, punitive damages are generally not awarded for breach of contract, even if the breach is in bad faith, unless the plaintiff can prove that the defendant's conduct constitutes an independent tort. Many states in recent years have limited the availability of punitive damages in contract actions.

One important rationale for punitive damages views them as quasi-criminal "private fines" that express moral outrage and define norms of conduct. Other justifications are economic. In classes of cases where plaintiffs are frequently unaware that they have suffered a legal wrong or where defendants' wrongdoing is difficult to prove, awarding punitive damages in the relatively rare cases where detection and proof both occur may be necessary to provide an optimal level of deterrence. See Polinsky & Shavell, Punitive Damages: An Economic Analysis, 111 Harv. L. Rev. 869 (1998). Finally, some have argued that punitive damages serve to cover costs of litigation, such as attorneys' fees, that would otherwise go uncompensated. The Supreme Court has looked with some skepticism on the deterrence and compensation explanations, focusing instead on such damages' more purely punitive purposes. See Cooper Indus. v. Leatherman Tool Group, 532 U.S. 424, 437, 121 S.Ct. 1678, 1686, 149 L.Ed.2d 674 (2001) (noting that juries do not finely calibrate punitive damages' deterrent effect and that their compensatory purposes have decreased in importance over time).

Under common law principles, an award of punitive damages is tailored to the behavior and particular circumstances of the parties. Traditionally, whereas compensatory damages are said to focus on the harm to the plaintiff, punitive damages shift attention to the wrongfulness of defendant's conduct and defendant's financial circumstances. A wealthy defendant may be required to pay more punitive damages than a poor defendant who engaged in the same conduct, on the ground that the marginal value of a dollar is greater to a poor than to a wealthy defendant. Lunsford v. Morris, 746 S.W.2d 471, 472 (Tex. 1988) (observing that at least forty-three states allow such evidence). In order to avoid double punishment for the same conduct, a defendant may introduce evidence of punitive damage awards assessed against it in other litigation arising out of the course of conduct in question. Fischer v. Johns-Manville Corp., 103 N.J. 643, 512 A.2d 466 (1986).

The general rule is that punitive damages cannot be awarded in the absence of compensatory damages. Kerr-Selgas v. American Airlines, 69 F.3d 1205, 1214–15 (1st Cir. 1995). However, some courts have sustained relatively substantial punitive damage awards in civil rights cases where the plaintiff has received nominal, or even zero, compensatory damages. In Cush-Crawford v. Adchem Corp., 271 F.3d 352 (2d Cir. 2001), the court sustained a $100,000 punitive damage award in a sexual harassment case, even though the plaintiff had received no nominal or compensatory damages.

Despite—or perhaps because of—the many factors juries are permitted to take into consideration, there is a "vast range of discretion" in the award of punitive damages. D. Laycock, Modern American Remedies 182 (4th ed. 2012).

b. Limitations on Punitive Damages. Increasingly, state law regulates the award of punitive damages in ways that reflect their hybrid civil-criminal character. Thus, in some states, punitive damages are available only upon proof by "clear and convincing evidence." See, e.g., Calif.Civ.C. § 3294(a); Kans. Stat. Ann. § 60–3701(c). Beginning in the 1980s, a number of states, under pressure to curb a perceived "explosion" in tort claims, enacted general statutory caps on punitive damage awards. States took different approaches, some defining punitive damages in terms of multiples of compensatory damages and others in terms of the defendant's income. See, e.g., Kan. Stat. Ann § 60–3702 (limiting punitive damages to 50 percent of defendant's net worth or $5 million); N.J. Stat. Ann. § 2A:15–5.14(b) (capping punitive damages at the five times the compensatory damages or $350,000); Va. Code Ann § 8.01–38.1 (providing that no more than $350,000 in total punitive damages may be awarded against all liable defendants). Other states have enacted so-called "split recovery" statutes that provide for allocation of a portion of punitive damages awards to the state treasury. See, e.g., Ga. Code Ann. § 51–12–5.1 (mandating that 75 percent of punitive damages in product liability cases be paid to the state). Supporters of caps point to the need to protect businesses from unpredictable and potentially crippling awards; opponents argue that they are an overreaction to a handful of highly publicized cases that arbitrarily deprive deserving plaintiffs of their due. While caps on punitive damages have been subject to a variety of constitutional challenges—on equal protection, due process, and takings theories—state supreme courts, with a few exceptions, have generally found the limits constitutional. In some circumstances, state constitutional provisions may also serve as an independent limit on punitive damage amounts. Colonial Pipeline Co. v. Brown, 258 Ga. 115, 365 S.E.2d 827 (1988).

The Supreme Court has imposed limits on punitive damages in cases arising under the federal common law of admiralty. In Exxon Shipping Co. v. Baker, 554 U.S. 471, 128 S.Ct. 2605, 171 L.Ed.2d 570 (2008), the Court reduced a $2.5 billion punitive damage award arising out of the Exxon Valdez oil spill in Alaska's Prince William Sound. The jury found that Exxon was reckless in its operation of its tanker, and the court awarded compensatory damages of $507.5 million. The Supreme Court conducted an extensive review of the literature on punitive damages, concluding that "[t]he real problem . . . is the stark unpredictability of punitive awards." 544 U.S. at 499. The Court considered and rejected the possibility of a multi-factor test for setting the level of awards. Instead the Court adopted the approach of pegging punitive to compensatory damages using a ratio or maximum multiple. Pointing to large scale studies of punitive awards showing a median ratio of punitive to compensatory damages of 0.65 to 1, and in light of "the need to protect against the possibility (and the disruptive cost to the legal system of awards that are unpredictable and unnecessary)," the Court settled on a 1:1 ratio as the "fair upper limit" in admiralty cases like the one before it, in which the award of actual damages was very high. Id. at 513. We should be cautious, however, in applying *Exxon*'s 1:1 ratio in cases in which the award of actual damages was low, or in non-admiralty cases.

   c.   **Federal constitutional limits on punitive damages.** In a series of opinions over the past twenty years, the Supreme Court has read the Due Process Clause to impose constitutional limitations on punitive damage awards. According to the Court, punitive damages must not be "grossly excessive" given the wrong committed. To assess proportionality, the Court looks at three factors: the reprehensibility of the defendant's conduct, the ratio between the punitive damage award and the severity of the harm inflicted or threatened (often, but not always, measured by the compensatory damage award), and the ratio between the punitive award and legislative sanctions for similar misconduct. The Court has twice applied its new standard to invalidate state court punitive damage awards as excessive. State Farm Mut. Auto. Ins. Co. v. Campbell, 538 U.S. 408, 123 S.Ct. 1513, 155 L.Ed.2d 585 (2003) (insurance bad faith; compensatory award of $1 million; punitive award of $146 million); BMW of North America, Inc. v. Gore, 517 U.S. 559, 116 S.Ct. 1589, 134 L.Ed.2d 809 (1996) (consumer deception; compensatory award $4,000; punitive award $2 million). The Court has limited the ways in which certain types of evidence may count in determining the parameters by which a punitive award can be judged. Thus, the Court has held that in an action brought by an individual, the actual or potential harm to persons other than the plaintiff may be considered in evaluating the reprehensibility of the defendant's conduct, but not in determining the measure of actual harm against which the ratio of punitive damages to harm is calculated. Philip Morris USA v. Williams, 549 U.S. 346, 127 S.Ct. 1057, 166 L.Ed.2d 940 (2007). The Court has held that both state and federal courts must provide appellate review of the amount of punitive damages awarded, Honda Motor Co. v. Oberg, 512 U.S. 415, 432, 114 S.Ct. 2331, 129 L.Ed.2d 336 (1994), and that in reviewing awards for compliance with the Due Process Clause courts must apply a standard of de novo review. Cooper Indus., Inc. v. Leatherman Tool Group, Inc., 532 U.S. 424, 121 S.Ct. 1678, 149 L.Ed.2d 674 (2001).

   5.   Specific relief: injunctions. The remedy of damages gives the plaintiff money, or, more precisely, the right to collect money through the procedures for executing a judgment. In some circumstances, the plaintiff may obtain instead, or in addition, "specific" relief, under which a court orders the defendant to perform, or refrain from performing, a specific act. Under modern procedures, an injunction is the usual means by which specific relief is provided. This has some important consequences. First, because the injunction derives from equity, the tradition is that whether and on what terms an injunction may issue is a matter of "discretion" of the court. Second, also because the injunction derives from equity, at least in some circumstances the determination of facts relevant to issuance of the injunction is for the judge and not a jury; in most states and to an uncertain degree in the federal courts, the underlying issue of whether the defendant's conduct was wrongful is also tried to the court rather than a jury.

The link between injunction and equity is historical rather than logical. Simply put, in most situations, English common law courts awarded only the remedy of damages. A party seeking specific relief had to go to equity courts. See Historical Note on Procedure, supra. The common law awarded specific relief in a few situations, of which there are remnants in modern procedure. The most significant of these is replevin, an action to recover possession of personal property. The modern version is referred to as "claim and delivery" in some states. See Calif.C.Civ.P. § 511.010 et seq.; compare N.Y.C.P.L.R. § 7101 et seq.

An injunction is distinct from an award of damages in the manner of its enforcement: A defendant who fails to obey an injunction may be held in contempt. Contempt can result in either a fine or, in some cases, even imprisonment. A judgment for damages does not directly order the defendant to pay the money, and a failure to pay a judgment is not punishable as contempt. If a defendant fails to pay a valid judgment, the plaintiff must discover and attach defendant's assets through proceedings in execution of the judgment. These proceedings may *eventually* culminate in an order directing defendant to place his property at the disposal of the court for judicial sale. Such an order is an injunction and as such creates a "personal" obligation to obey, enforceable in contempt. See Rendleman, Compensatory Contempt: Plaintiff's Remedy When a Defendant Violates an Injunction, 1980 U. Ill. L.F. 971.

In part because an injunction is seen as imposing unusual restrictions on defendant's liberty, the tradition was, and to some extent still is, that relief by injunction rather than damages may be obtained only in "extraordinary" circumstances. The conventional formulation is that equitable remedies, such as injunctions, are available only when legal remedies, such as damages, are "inadequate."

In private litigation, "inadequacy" is found in many kinds of suits. In tort suits, injunctions are available to prevent physical injury to individuals, or to reduce the threat of such injury. Further, injunctions are frequently available to prevent physical trespass on plaintiff's real property. Injunctions are also given, though not routinely, to restrain nuisances. See, e.g., Scott v. Jordan, 99 N.M. 567, 661 P.2d 59 (1983); Christopher v. Jones, 231 Cal.App.2d 408, 41 Cal.Rptr. 828 (1964). An injunction will not issue if the threat of harm has ended. See Rondeau v. Mosinee Paper Corp., 422 U.S. 49, 95 S.Ct. 2069, 45 L.Ed.2d 12 (1975). The functional equivalent of an injunction is available in many contract suits, though the remedy is called a "specific performance decree" rather than an injunction. For example, in a suit by a purchaser of real property when the seller refuses to convey the land, the purchaser usually may obtain a specific performance decree ordering the seller to convey.

The formal doctrinal requirements for the issuance of injunctions continue to be stated in the cases, but in practice they were softened in the second half of the 20th century. Professor Laycock has argued that the traditional linked requirements that there must be an irreparable injury, and that there be no effective legal remedy, are effectively dead. Based on a survey of over fourteen hundred cases, he concludes, "The irreparable injury rule says that equitable remedies are unavailable if legal remedies will adequately repair the harm. * * * In fact, the rule does no such thing. Courts have escaped the rule by defining adequacy in such a way that damages are never an adequate substitute for plaintiff's losses. Thus, our law embodies a preference for specific relief if plaintiff wants it. The principal doctrinal expression of this preference is the rule that damages are inadequate unless they can be used to replace the specific thing that plaintiff lost. Damages can be used in this way for only one category of losses: to replace fungible goods or routine services in an orderly market." Laycock, The Death of the Irreparable Injury Rule, 103 Harv. L. Rev. 687, 689, 691 (1990).

In a wide range of public law litigation, structural injunctions have become a common form of relief. They are called "structural" because they fundamentally restructure some governmental entity or operation. Examples include injunctions ordering busing of school children to achieve racial desegregation, Swann v. Charlotte-Mecklenburg Board of Education, 402 U.S. 1, 91 S.Ct. 1267, 28 L.Ed.2d 554 (1971); ordering the redrawing of malapportioned legislative districts, Reynolds v. Sims, 377 U.S. 533, 84 S.Ct. 1362, 12 L.Ed.2d 506 (1964); ordering the improvement of conditions in prisons, Brown v. Plata, 570 U.S. __,131 S.Ct. 1910, 179 L.Ed.2d 969 (2011), Hutto v. Finney, 437 U.S. 678, 98 S.Ct. 2565, 57 L.Ed.2d 522 (1978); and ordering the improvement of conditions in mental institutions, Wyatt v. Stickney, 325 F. Supp. 781 (M.D.Ala. 1971), aff'd in part sub nom. Wyatt v. Aderholt, 503 F.2d 1305 (5th Cir. 1974). Defenders of such injunctions argue that they fit well into traditional equitable strictures on relief. Damage relief is not usually practicable. In most cases, the harm is irreparable in the normal legal sense of not being susceptible to adequate remedy by monetary payment. How, for example, does one calculate damage to a student educated in racially segregated schools, or to a voter deprived of an effective vote? Further, the defendants in many cases are state governments, which are protected from damage judgments by the principle of sovereign immunity, or state or local officials, who are substantially protected by doctrines of official immunity. In the majority of cases, courts have issued structural injunctions as a last resort, only when the administrative or political institutions that should cure the legal violations have refused to do so. The Supreme Court's statement in *Reynolds v. Sims* is representative of the general approach: "[J]udicial relief becomes appropriate only when a legislature fails to reapportion according to federal constitutional requisites in a timely fashion after having had an adequate opportunity to do so." 377 U.S. at 586. See, e.g., O. Fiss, The Civil Rights Injunction (1978); Chayes, The Role of the Judge in Public Law Litigation, 89 Harv.L.Rev. 1281 (1976); Fletcher, The Discretionary Constitution: Institutional Remedies and Judicial Legitimacy, 91 Yale L.J. 635 (1982).

6. Restitutionary remedies: constructive trusts, and rescission or cancellation. Equity courts developed a number of remedies to prevent "unjust enrichment" of the defendant. Often (and confusingly for students of the right to jury trial), these remedies involve an award of money to the plaintiff. But the principle of measurement in a restitutionary award is not the plaintiff's losses, but the defendant's gains. One important restitutionary remedy is the imposition of a "constructive trust." The trust is imposed on property to which defendant has title but which in justice belongs or ought to be restored to plaintiff. See Restatement of Restitution § 160 et seq.; Restatement of Trusts § 44 et seq. The "constructive trustee" is then ordered to convey the property to the plaintiff. Another important restitutionary remedy is rescission or cancellation of a contract. When because of mistake, fraud or other recognized ground, one party has the right to withdraw from a contract which he has made, he may obtain judicial authorization to do so by seeking rescission of the contract. The resulting decree customarily speaks in terms of "canceling" the contract and provides for restoration of payments made or other measures necessary to restore the status quo ante. See, e.g., Williams v. Marshall, 37 Cal.2d 445, 235 P.2d 372 (1951); Star Pac. Investments, Inc. v. Oro Hills Ranch, Inc., 121 Cal.App.3d 447, 176 Cal.Rptr. 546 (1981).

7. Other equitable remedies. a. Reorganization of financial affairs. Equity also affords remedies to straighten out tangled business transactions, among them accounting between parties to a complex financial arrangement. See, e.g., National Bank of Alaska v. J.B.L. & K. of Alaska, Inc., 546 P.2d 579 (Alaska 1976), and receivership for business ventures that are in financial difficulty.

b. Suits to determine title to land. The suit to quiet title originated as the remedy of a land occupant to end repeated ejectment actions (which were brought in the law courts) against him. In time, it was enlarged to provide a remedy to settle and protect interests in land that could not be determined in ejectment, such as rights in easements and rights based on equitable title. It was the precursor of the modern statutory remedy for determination of title. See Wehrman v. Conklin, 155 U.S. 314, 321–22, 15 S.Ct. 129, 39 L.Ed. 167 (1894). At the beginning of the 19th century the equity courts developed yet another remedy for clearing title to land, a bill to remove a cloud. It was a form of *quia timet* ("because he fears") relief, granted to a plaintiff whose possession was as yet undisturbed but who feared that the existence of a document purporting to vest title or interest in the land in someone else would lead to later disturbance of plaintiff's possession. Its history is described in Howard, Bills to Remove Cloud from Title, 25 W.Va. L.Q. 4 (1917). Compare Leubsdorf, Remedies for Uncertainty, 61 B.U. L. Rev. 132 (1981).

8. Declaratory relief. A declaratory judgment is a judgment that declares the legal rights of the parties, without any other relief. The classic claimant for a declaratory judgment is a party who fears a lawsuit from someone else based upon something he has done or intends to do. A declaratory judgment enables the plaintiff to obtain a judgment declaring that he or she is not liable to the defendant. All American jurisdictions have adopted some form of declaratory relief, typically by adoption of a statute patterned after the Uniform Declaratory Judgments Act, 12 U.L.A. 111 (Master ed. 1975); see, e.g., Calif.C.Civ.P. § 1060 et seq. See also the Federal Declaratory Judgment Act, 28 U.S.C. §§ 2201–2202; Fed. R. Civ. P. 57; Restatement Second of Judgments § 33.

The chief prerequisite for a declaratory judgment is a real showing that the plaintiff is at serious risk of adverse consequences unless the court declares her non-liability. Courts have historically been wary that the remedy would allow parties to apply for gratuitous judicial advice on legal problems that troubled the parties but that had not yet ripened into full-scale legal disputes. See Liberty Warehouse Co. v. Grannis, 273 U.S. 70, 47 S.Ct. 282, 71 L.Ed. 541 (1927); Willing v. Chicago Auditorium Ass'n, 277 U.S. 274, 48 S.Ct. 507, 72 L.Ed. 880 (1928) (suggesting that declaratory judgments were beyond the authority of the federal courts under the "cases and controversies" provision of U.S. Const. Art. III). The declaratory remedy is now generally available if the applicant for a declaration can show that he confronts real risk if he proceeds with the course of conduct which he seeks to follow. Compare Gilliland v. County of Los Angeles, 126 Cal.App.3d 610, 179 Cal.Rptr. 73 (1981) (dispute not ripe for adjudication), with Berkeley v. Alameda County Bd. of Supervisors, 40 Cal.App.3d 961, 115 Cal.Rptr. 540 (1974) (where plaintiff alleged a real situation of uncertainty, but defendant's position was legally valid, court should declare for defendant and not dismiss the action).

9. Provisional remedies: attachment. A provisional remedy is a judicial order, obtained at an early stage of litigation, designed to stabilize the situation pending the final disposition of the case or to provide security to a plaintiff so that if she succeeds in obtaining judgment she will be able to enforce it effectively. Traditional provisional remedies include seizure of property (called attachment), temporary and preliminary injunctions and analogous remedies. Provisional remedies are typically awarded at an early stage of the case and on the basis of a less thorough investigation than is possible prior to the issuance of a plenary remedy. Because the risk of error is higher in such proceedings, a party who seeks a provisional remedy is normally required to post a bond undertaking to make good on any losses to the defendant resulting from the wrongful issuance of the injunction.

Typical statutes permit attachment against nonresident and resident defendants in actions to recover debts, or in actions predicated on fraud, or both. In a series of cases beginning with Sniadach v. Family Fin. Corp., 395 U.S. 337, 89 S.Ct. 1820, 23 L.Ed.2d 349 (1969), the Supreme Court imposed due process restrictions on the use of attachment where, as had been usual, property of individuals was attached without a preliminary showing of the validity of the claim being enforced and of the need to prevent defendant from absconding with the property.

10. Provisional remedies: temporary restraining orders and preliminary injunctions. If a plaintiff needs to maintain the status quo *pendente lite* ("during or pending the litigation"), her first step is to seek a temporary restraining order, commonly referred to as a TRO. The TRO may be issued *ex parte* (that is, with only the plaintiff present) if immediate relief is necessary to prevent irreparable harm and the defendant's presence cannot (or in rare circumstances, should not) be secured in time for a hearing. See Calif.C.Civ.P. § 527. For discussion of the circumstances under which a TRO may be issued *ex parte,* see United Farm Workers v. Superior Court, 14 Cal.3d 902, 122 Cal.Rptr. 877, 537 P.2d 1237 (1975); Dorr & Traphagen, Federal Ex Parte Temporary Relief, 61 Denv. U. L.J. 767 (1984). A bond to indemnify the defendant against loss or expense resulting from the TRO is ordinarily required. The TRO is made "returnable" as soon as possible. See Calif.C.Civ.P. § 527 ("not later than 15 days or, if good cause appears to the court, 22 days from the date the temporary restraining order is issued.").

The defendant has an unqualified right to appear at the hearing on the "return" date to seek the dissolution of the injunction, and to oppose the granting of further injunctive relief. The plaintiff at this hearing will seek to continue the court's order by transforming the TRO into a preliminary injunction. The requirements for a preliminary injunction are variously stated, but a plaintiff will need to show essentially the following: (1) a need to maintain the status quo pending the outcome of the litigation; (2) a likelihood that she will ultimately prevail on the merits in the litigation; and (3) a difference in hardships between the plaintiff and defendant, such that plaintiff will be more hurt if the injunction is denied than defendant will be hurt if it is granted. The Supreme Court articulated the standard for a preliminary injunction in federal court in Winter v. Natural Resources Defense Council, 555 U.S. 7, 129 S.Ct. 365, 172 L.Ed.2d 249 (2008). For a good historical and analytic treatment of preliminary injunctions, see Leubsdorf, The Standard for Preliminary Injunctions, 91 Harv. L. Rev. 525 (1978).

The federal procedure for TROs and preliminary injunctions is essentially identical to state court procedures. See Fed. R. Civ. P. 65; Granny Goose Foods, Inc. v. Brotherhood of Teamsters, 415 U.S. 423, 94 S.Ct. 1113, 39 L.Ed.2d 435 (1974); 11A C. Wright, A. Miller & M. Kane, Federal Practice and Procedure §§ 2941 et seq. (1995).

CHAPTER 2

CHOOSING THE PROPER COURT

After a lawyer decides that a suit is worth pursuing, she must decide where to file it. Sometimes only one court is available, but often there is a choice between two or among several. The lawyer must not only determine where the plaintiff has a legal right to bring suit, but also, among the legally available courts, where it will be to plaintiff's greatest advantage. In many cases, the choice is easy and obvious. In others, it is complex and subtle. One of the most important considerations in the choice of court is convenience to the plaintiff. If the litigants live in different places, a plaintiff ordinarily would prefer to litigate at home, making the defendant come to him. Another consideration is the procedural rules applied. For example, state and federal courts may both be available choices; each may be (and often is) governed by a different set of procedural rules. Another is that the plaintiff may sometimes obtain a different substantive law depending on the state in which he files suit. Or, a plaintiff might wish to take advantage of prejudice against out-of-state or big-city defendants. Finally, there may be any number of other factors such as the familiarity of the lawyer with a particular court and set of rules; the quality of judges sitting on a particular court; the social and economic characteristics of jurors in a particular court; or the backlog of cases, and hence waiting time for trial.

Four requirements must be satisfied before a suit can be brought in a particular court. They are (1) territorial jurisdiction; (2) subject matter jurisdiction; (3) venue; and (4) ability to withstand a motion to dismiss for *forum non conveniens*. We will consider them in turn.

A. TERRITORIAL JURISDICTION

PRELIMINARY NOTE ON TERRITORIAL JURISDICTION

Territorial jurisdiction concerns the power of a court to engage in binding adjudication over a person or thing. Some cases are easy. For example, if a person lives in a state and has been involved in an automobile accident in that state, the courts of the state clearly have territorial jurisdiction in a suit brought against her. The conventional term for jurisdiction over her "person" is *in personam* jurisdiction. Or, for example, there may be a dispute over ownership of real property within a state. The courts of the state clearly have jurisdiction in a quiet title action designed to settle the question of ownership. The conventional terms for jurisdiction over property are *in rem* and *quasi in rem* jurisdiction. As we shall see, the domain of *in rem* and *quasi in rem* jurisdiction was dramatically reduced in the second half of the twentieth century.

Some cases are more difficult. From the beginning of our federal system, courts have had to grapple with the problem of the authority of a state to assert jurisdiction over parties and property in cases involving transactions not occurring entirely within the boundaries of a single state. For example, suppose a family in California buys a child's pajamas through a mail-order catalogue from a company located in Wisconsin. While the family is on vacation in Oregon, the pajamas catch fire from a space heater, burning the child. Can the catalogue company be sued in the Oregon courts? As will be seen, such questions often do not have simple, bright-line answers. As will also be seen, the requirements of adequate notice of the pendency of a lawsuit have historically been intertwined with the requirement that a court have territorial jurisdiction.

The Restatement (Second) of Judgments § 4, Comment a, provides the following introduction to territorial jurisdiction:

> The relevance of territorial boundaries to the exercise of jurisdiction by states within the federal union, and by courts of this country within the international community, arises from the fact that the states and nations are defined as political and legal entities in terms of their geographical boundaries. Since these entities are legally defined in terms of geographical place, the geographical location of a transaction is significant in determining whether a court of such an entity may properly exercise jurisdiction in a particular controversy. At one time, this relationship was expressed in terms of "power," referring to the authority of a state's or nation's executive officials to use direct coercion to enforce legal obligations. Under prevailing law, such executive authority could be exercised only in the state or nation in which there was physically present the person or thing to which coercion was to be applied. Accordingly, territorial jurisdiction was defined in terms of presence of the person or thing involved in the litigation, and also voluntary submission to the authority of the court. "Power" in this sense remains significant at least as a residual basis of jurisdiction.

Broadly speaking, the development of territorial jurisdiction doctrine proceeded from this early focus on physical presence in a state to the modern concept of "minimum contacts" between a party and a state. In the cases that follow, note the changing conceptions of the proper role and authority of the states within the federal system.

Beginning with the federal Judiciary Act of 1789, the territorial jurisdiction of the federal courts has been primarily tied to the rules of territorial jurisdiction of the state courts in states in which the federal courts sit. In form, the limitation is typically expressed by limiting the authority of the federal courts to serve process on potential parties. See Fed. R. Civ. P. 4. In most cases, a federal court may exercise territorial jurisdiction over a nonresident defendant only if the courts of the state in which it sits may exercise jurisdiction over that defendant. Some states have "long-arm" jurisdictional statutes that assert territorial jurisdiction to the full extent permitted by the federal Constitution. Other states have statutes that do not assert jurisdiction to the full constitutional extent. The federal courts are generally limited by the reach of jurisdiction asserted by the state, so they have more limited territorial jurisdiction in states that have more limited statutes. In some cases, however, federal courts are specifically authorized by federal statute (and, sometimes, federal procedural rule) to assert jurisdiction more broadly than the states. In cases of so-called "nationwide jurisdiction," a federal court may assert territorial jurisdiction over a defendant anywhere in the United States, irrespective of whether the defendant has had any contacts with the state in which the federal court happens to sit. , .

1. HISTORICAL FORMULAE: THE RELEVANCE OF STATE BOUNDARIES

Pennoyer v. Neff

Supreme Court of the United States, 1877.
95 U.S. (5 Otto) 714, 24 L.Ed. 565.

[On November 3, 1865, J. H. Mitchell brought suit against Marcus Neff in Oregon state trial court for Multnomah County, Oregon, for $253.14. Mitchell, a lawyer, alleged that Neff owed the money for legal services rendered in 1862 and 1863. Mitchell asserted by affidavit that Neff owned property in Multnomah County but that he could not be found within the state of Oregon. Purporting to act under an Oregon statutory procedure, the court permitted Mitchell to go forward with his suit, provided that he publish notice of the suit for six successive weeks. Mitchell put the notice in the Pacific Christian Advocate, a weekly newspaper published in the county.

Neff did not appear to defend the suit. On February 19, 1866, a default judgment for $294.98 (including court costs) was entered against him. On March 19, 1866, a patent (deed) to property in Multnomah County was issued to Neff in Washington, D.C. In July, 1866, Mitchell sought a writ of execution of his default judgment, under which Neff's property was attached and sold. The property was sold at a sheriff's sale on August 7, 1866, for $341.60 to Mitchell. Mitchell then sold the property three days later to Sylvester Pennoyer for an undisclosed amount.

Eight years later, on September 10, 1874, Neff filed suit against Pennoyer in the federal Circuit Court for the District of Oregon, seeking to recover his property, alleging that the property was worth $15,000.00. The Circuit Court held for Neff on the ground that Mitchell's affidavit in the Oregon trial court had not complied with the procedural requirements of the Oregon statute. Pennoyer sought review in the United States Supreme Court.*]

■ MR. JUSTICE FIELD delivered the opinion of the Court.

* * * The plaintiff asserts title to the premises by a patent of the United States issued to him in 1866, under the act of Congress of Sept. 27, 1850, usually known as the Donation Law of Oregon. The defendant claims to have acquired the premises under a sheriff's deed, made upon a sale of the property on execution issued upon a judgment recovered against the plaintiff in one of the circuit courts of the State. The case turns upon the validity of this judgment.

It appears from the record that the judgment was rendered in February, 1866, in favor of J.H. Mitchell, for less than $300, including costs, in an action brought by him upon a demand for services as an

---

*　Some of the material in brackets is taken from Perdue, Sin, Scandal, and Substantive Due Process: Personal Jurisdiction and *Pennoyer* Reconsidered, 62 Wash.L.Rev. 479 (1987).

attorney; that, at the time the action was commenced and the judgment rendered, the defendant therein, the plaintiff here, was a non-resident of the State; that he was not personally served with process, and did not appear therein; and that the judgment was entered upon his default in not answering the complaint, upon a constructive service of summons by publication.

The Code of Oregon provides for such service when an action is brought against a non-resident and absent defendant, who has property within the State. It also provides, where the action is for the recovery of money or damages, for the attachment of the property of the non-resident. And it also declares that no natural person is subject to the jurisdiction of a court of the State, "unless he appear in the court, or be found within the State, or be a resident thereof, or have property therein; and, in the last case, only to the extent of such property at the time the jurisdiction attached." Construing this latter provision to mean, that, in an action for money or damages where a defendant does not appear in the court, and is not found within the State, and is not a resident thereof, but has property therein, the jurisdiction of the court extends only over such property, the declaration expresses a principle of general, if not universal, law. The authority of every tribunal is necessarily restricted by the territorial limits of the State in which it is established. Any attempt to exercise authority beyond those limits would be deemed in every other forum, as has been said by this court, an illegitimate assumption of power, and be resisted as mere abuse. D'Arcy v. Ketchum et al., 11 How. 165. In the case against the plaintiff, the property here in controversy sold under the judgment rendered was not attached, nor in any way brought under the jurisdiction of the court. Its first connection with the case was caused by a levy of the execution. It was not, therefore, disposed of pursuant to any adjudication, but only in enforcement of a personal judgment, having no relation to the property, rendered against a non-resident without service of process upon him in the action, or his appearance therein. The court below did not consider that an attachment of the property was essential to its jurisdiction or to the validity of the sale, but held that the judgment was invalid from defects in the affidavit upon which the order of publication was obtained, and in the affidavit by which the publication was proved.

There is some difference of opinion among the members of this court as to the rulings upon these alleged defects. * * *

If, therefore, we were confined to the rulings of the court below upon the defects in the affidavits mentioned, we should be unable to uphold its decision. But it was also contended in that court, and is insisted upon here, that the judgment in the State court against the plaintiff was void for want of personal service of process on him, or of his appearance in the action in which it was rendered, and that the premises in controversy could not be subjected to the payment of the demand of a resident creditor except by a proceeding *in rem;* that is, by a direct proceeding against the property for that purpose. If these positions are sound, the ruling of the Circuit Court as to the invalidity of that judgment must be sustained, notwithstanding our dissent from the reasons upon which it was made. And that they are sound would seem to follow from two well-established principles of public law respecting the jurisdiction of an independent State over persons and property. The several States of the Union are not, it is true, in every respect independent, many of the rights and powers which originally belonged to them being now vested in the government created by the Constitution. But, except as restrained and limited by that instrument, they possess and exercise the authority of independent States, and the principles of public law to which we have referred are applicable to them. One of these principles is, that every State possesses exclusive jurisdiction and sovereignty over persons and property within its territory. As a consequence, every State has the power to determine for itself the civil *status* and capacities of its inhabitants; to prescribe the subjects upon which they may contract, the forms and solemnities with which their contracts shall be executed, the rights and obligations arising from them, and the mode in which their validity shall be determined and their obligations enforced; and also to regulate the manner and conditions upon which property situated within such territory, both personal and real, may be acquired, enjoyed, and transferred. The other principle of public law referred to follows from the one mentioned; that is, that no State can exercise direct jurisdiction and authority over persons or property without its territory. Story, Confl.Laws, c. 2; Wheat.Int.Law, pt. 2, c. 2. The several States are of equal dignity and authority, and the independence of one implies that exclusion of power from all others. And so it is laid down by jurists, as an elementary principle, that the laws of one State have no operation outside of its territory, except so far as is allowed by comity; and that no tribunal established by it can extend its process beyond that territory so as to subject either persons or property to its decisions. "Any exertion of authority of this sort beyond this limit," says Story, "is a mere nullity, and incapable of binding such persons or property in any other tribunals." Story, Confl.Laws, sect. 539.

But as contracts made in one State may be enforceable only in another State, and property may be held by non-residents, the exercise of the jurisdiction which every State is admitted to possess over persons and property within its own territory will often affect persons and property without it. To any influence exerted in this way by a State affecting persons resident or property situated elsewhere, no objection can be justly taken; whilst any direct exertion of authority upon them, in an attempt to give ex-territorial operation to its laws, or to enforce an ex-territorial jurisdiction by its tribunals, would be deemed an encroachment upon the independence of the State in which the persons are domiciled or the property is situated, and be resisted as usurpation.

* * *

So the State, through its tribunals, may subject property situated within its limits owned by non-residents to the payment of the demand of its own citizens against them; and the exercise of this jurisdiction in no respect infringes upon the sovereignty of the State where the owners are domiciled. Every State owes protection to its own citizens; and, when non-residents deal with them, it is a legitimate and just exercise of authority to hold and appropriate any property owned by such non-residents to satisfy the claims of its citizens. It is in virtue of the State's jurisdiction over the property of the non-resident situated within its limits that its tribunals can inquire into that non-resident's obligations to its own citizens, and the inquiry can then be carried only to the extent necessary to control the disposition of the property. If the non-resident have no property in the State, there is nothing upon which the tribunals can adjudicate.

These views are not new. They have been frequently expressed, with more or less distinctness, in opinions of eminent judges, and have been carried into adjudications in numerous cases. * * *

* * * It is the only doctrine consistent with proper protection to citizens of other States. If, without personal service, judgments *in personam,* obtained *ex parte* against non-residents and absent parties, upon mere publication of process, which, in the great majority of cases, would never be seen by the parties interested, could be upheld and enforced, they would be the constant instruments of fraud and oppression. Judgments for all sorts of claims upon contracts and for torts, real or pretended, would be thus obtained, under which property would be seized, when the evidence of the transactions upon which they were founded, if they ever had any existence, had perished.

Substituted service by publication, or in any other authorized form, may be sufficient to inform parties of the object of proceedings taken where property is once brought under the control of the court by seizure or some equivalent act. The law assumes that property is always in the possession of its owner, in person or by agent; and it proceeds upon the theory that its seizure will inform him, not only that it is taken into the custody of the court, but that he must look to any proceedings authorized by law upon such seizure for its condemnation and sale. Such service may also be sufficient in cases where the object of the action is to reach and dispose of property in the State, or of some interest therein, by enforcing a contract or a lien respecting the same, or to partition it among different owners, or, when the public is a party, to condemn and appropriate it for a public purpose. In other words, such service may answer in all actions which are substantially proceedings *in rem.* But where the entire object of the action is to determine the personal rights and obligations of the defendants, that is, where the suit is merely *in personam,* constructive service in this form upon a non-resident is ineffectual for any purpose. Process from the tribunals of one State cannot run into another State, and summon parties there domiciled to leave its territory and respond to proceedings against them. Publication of process or notice within the State where the tribunal sits cannot create any greater obligation upon the non-resident to appear. Process sent to him out of the State, and process published within it, are equally unavailing in proceedings to establish his personal liability.

The want of authority of the tribunals of a State to adjudicate upon the obligations of non-residents, where they have no property within its limits, is not denied by the court below; but the position is assumed, that, where they have property within the State, it is immaterial whether the property is in the first instance brought under the control of the court by attachment or some other equivalent act, and afterwards applied by its judgment to the satisfaction of demands against its owner; or such demands be first established in a personal action, and the property of the non-resident be afterwards seized and sold on execution. But the answer to this position has already been given in the statement, that the jurisdiction of the court to inquire into and determine his obligations at all is only incidental to its jurisdiction over the property. Its jurisdiction in that respect cannot be made to depend upon facts to be ascertained after it has tried the cause and rendered the judgment. If the judgment be previously void, it will not become valid by the subsequent discovery of property of the defendant, or by his subsequent acquisition of it. The judgment, if void when rendered, will always remain void: it cannot occupy the doubtful position of being valid if property be found, and void if there be none. * * *

The force and effect of judgments rendered against non-residents without personal service of process upon them, or their voluntary appearance, have been the subject of frequent consideration in the courts of the United States and of the several States, as attempts have been made to enforce such judgments in States other than those in which they were rendered, under the provision of the Constitution requiring that "full faith and credit shall be given in each State to the public acts, records, and judicial proceedings of every other State;" and the act of Congress providing for the mode of authenticating such acts, records, and proceedings, and declaring that, when thus authenticated, "they shall have such faith and credit given to them in every court within the United States as they have by law or usage in the courts of the State from which they are or shall be taken." In the earlier cases, it was supposed that the act gave to all judgments the same effect in other States which they had by law in the State where rendered. But this view was afterwards qualified so as to make the act applicable only when the court rendering the judgment had jurisdiction of the parties and of the subject-matter, and not to preclude an inquiry into the jurisdiction of the court in which the judgment was rendered, or the right of the State itself to exercise authority over the person or the subject-matter. * * *

* * * In several of the cases, the decision has been accompanied with the observation that a personal judgment thus recovered has no binding force without the State in which it is rendered, implying that in such State it may be valid and binding. But if the court has no jurisdiction over the person of the defendant by reason of his non-residence, and, consequently, no authority to pass upon his personal rights and obligations; if the whole proceeding, without service upon him or his appearance, is *coram non judice* and void; if to hold a defendant bound by such a judgment is contrary to the first principles of justice,—it is difficult to see how the judgment can legitimately have any force within the State. The language used can be justified only on the ground that there was no mode of directly reviewing such judgment or impeaching its validity within the State where rendered; and that, therefore, it could be called in question only when its enforcement was elsewhere attempted. In later cases, this language is repeated with less frequency than formerly, it beginning to be considered, as it always ought to have been, that a judgment which can be treated in any State of this Union as contrary to the first principles of justice, and as an absolute nullity, because rendered without any jurisdiction of the tribunal over the party, is not entitled to any respect in the State where rendered. Smith v. McCutchen, 38 Mo. 415; Darrance v. Preston, 18 Iowa 396; Hakes v. Shupe, 27 id. 465; Mitchell's Administrator v. Gray, 18 Ind. 123.

        * * *

Since the adoption of the Fourteenth Amendment to the Federal Constitution, the validity of such judgments may be directly questioned, and their enforcement in the State resisted, on the ground that proceedings in a court of justice to determine the personal rights and obligations of parties over whom that court has no jurisdiction do not constitute due process of law. Whatever difficulty may be experienced in giving to those terms a definition which will embrace every permissible exertion of power affecting private rights, and exclude such as is forbidden, there can be no doubt of their meaning when applied to judicial proceedings. They then mean a course of legal proceedings according to those rules and principles which have been established in our systems of jurisprudence for the protection and enforcement of private rights. To give such proceedings any validity, there must be a tribunal competent by its constitution—that is, by the law of its creation—to pass upon the subject-matter of the suit; and, if that involves merely a determination of the personal liability of the defendant, he must be brought within its jurisdiction by service of process within the State, or his voluntary appearance.

Except in cases affecting the personal *status* of the plaintiff, and cases in which that mode of service may be considered to have been assented to in advance, as hereinafter mentioned, the substituted service of process by publication, allowed by the law of Oregon and by similar laws in other States, where actions are brought against nonresidents, is effectual only where, in connection with process against the person for commencing the action, property in the State is brought under the control of the court, and subjected to its disposition by process adapted to that purpose, or where the judgment is sought as a means of reaching such property or affecting some interest therein; in other words, where the action is in the nature of a proceeding *in rem*. As stated by Cooley in his Treatise on Constitutional Limitations, 405, for any other purpose than to subject the property of a non-resident to valid claims against him in the State, "due process of law would require appearance or personal service before the defendant could be personally bound by any judgment rendered."

It is true that, in a strict sense, a proceeding *in rem* is one taken directly against property, and has for its object the disposition of the property, without reference to the title of individual claimants; but, in a larger and more general sense, the terms are applied to actions between parties, where the direct object is to reach and dispose of property owned by them, or of some interest therein. Such are cases commenced by attachment against the property of debtors, or instituted to partition real estate, foreclose a mortgage, or enforce a lien. So far as they affect property in the State, they are substantially proceedings *in rem* in the broader sense which we have mentioned.

      * * *

It follows from the views expressed that the personal judgment recovered in the State Court of Oregon against the plaintiff herein, then a non-resident of the State, was without any validity, and did not authorize a sale of the property in controversy.

To prevent any misapplication of the views expressed in this opinion, it is proper to observe that we do not mean to assert, by anything we have said, that a State may not authorize proceedings to determine the *status* of one of its citizens towards a non-resident, which would be binding within the State, though made without service of process or personal notice to the non-resident. The jurisdiction which every State possesses to determine the civil *status* and capacities of all its inhabitants involves authority to prescribe the conditions on which proceedings affecting them may be commenced and carried on within its territory. The State, for example, has absolute right to prescribe the conditions upon which the marriage relation between its own citizens shall be created, and the causes for which it may be dissolved. One of the parties guilty of acts for which, by the law of the State, a dissolution may be granted, may have removed to a State where no dissolution is permitted. The complaining party would, therefore, fail if a divorce were sought in the State of the defendant; and if application could not be made to the tribunals of the complainant's domicile in such case, and proceedings be there instituted without personal service of process or personal notice to the offending party, the injured citizen would be without redress. Bish.Marr. and Div., sect. 156.

Neither do we mean to assert that a State may not require a nonresident entering into a partnership or association within its limits, or making contracts enforceable there, to appoint an agent or representative in the State to receive service of process and notice in legal proceedings instituted with respect to such partnership, association, or contracts, or to designate a place where such service may be made and notice given, and provide, upon their failure, to make such appointment or to designate such place that service may be made upon a public officer designated for that purpose, or in some other prescribed way, and that judgments rendered upon such service may not be binding upon the non-residents both within and without the State. * * * The Lafayette Insurance Co. v. French et al., 18 How. 404. * * * Nor do we doubt that a State, on creating corporations or other institutions for pecuniary or charitable purposes, may provide a mode in which their conduct may be investigated, their obligations enforced, or their charters revoked, which shall require other than personal service upon their officers or members. Parties becoming members of such corporations or institutions would hold their interest subject to the conditions prescribed by law. Copin v. Adamson, Law Rep. 9 Ex. 345.

In the present case, there is no feature of this kind, and, consequently, no consideration of what would be the effect of such legislation in enforcing the contract of a non-resident can arise. The question here respects only the validity of a money judgment rendered in one State, in an action upon a simple contract against the resident of another, without service of process upon him, or his appearance therein.

Judgment affirmed.

[The dissenting opinion of Justice Hunt is omitted.]

NOTE ON *PENNOYER V. NEFF*, TYPES OF JURISDICTION, AND THE RELEVANCE OF STATE BOUNDARIES

1. **Historical background.** Professor Wendy Perdue has written a fascinating background study of *Pennoyer*. Perdue, Sin, Scandal, and Substantive Due Process: Personal Jurisdiction and *Pennoyer* Reconsidered, 62 Wash. L. Rev. 479 (1987). J. H. Mitchell's real name was John Hipple. He had been a schoolteacher in Pennsylvania, where he seduced a fifteen-year-old student whom he was then forced to marry. He gave up teaching to

become a lawyer and, after practicing in Pennsylvania for several years, left for California in 1860 with a mistress and $4,000 of his clients' money. He soon thereafter abandoned his mistress in California and moved to Portland, Oregon. He adopted the name John H. Mitchell and became a successful lawyer specializing in land litigation and railroad right-of-way cases. His success appears to have been based less on legal skill than on "exceptional political instincts" and "a friendly handshake."

Marcus Neff was an illiterate who had left Iowa by wagon train in 1848 at age 24. In 1850, he filed for land under the Oregon Land Donation Act, which provided for grants of land to settlers upon fulfillment of certain conditions. In 1856, he filed affidavits as evidence that he had fulfilled the requirements of the Act. The United States government was notoriously slow in processing land applications. Neff consulted Mitchell in 1862, possibly concerning his application. Neff paid Mitchell $6.50 for his services. Sometime before November 1865, Neff moved to California.

Sylvester Pennoyer was, like Mitchell, a successful land lawyer. He was also a politician. He bought the Neff parcel from Mitchell three days after Mitchell purchased it at the sheriff's sale. Mitchell conveyed title by quitclaim deed. (A warranty deed would have guaranteed good title to the property. A quitclaim deed conveyed only such title as Mitchell had, with no accompanying guarantee that the title was good.) Pennoyer fought Neff's suit bitterly, and, ultimately, unsuccessfully. He was elected Governor of Oregon ten years later. He complained about the result in *Pennoyer v. Neff* in his inaugural address, describing it as a usurpation of state power.

Mitchell was elected United States Senator from Oregon in 1872. He lost his seat after one term, but was reelected in 1885. During the 1885 election, the federal circuit judge who had sat at trial in *Pennoyer v. Neff* came into possession of a set of love letters Mitchell had written to his second wife's younger sister during a five-year love affair. The judge released the letters to the *Oregonian*, which promptly published them. (The *Oregonian* was, and is, the primary newspaper for the Portland area. The *Pacific Christian Advocate*, in which the notice of Mitchell's suit against Neff was published, was a small weekly newspaper largely devoted to religious news and inspirational articles.) Despite the publication of the letters, Mitchell was again elected to the Senate, where he remained until his death, in 1905, of complications resulting from a tooth extraction. At the time of his death, Mitchell was appealing a felony conviction in a massive land fraud scheme.

We know little about Neff's subsequent history. He had apparently prospered in California prior to his return to Oregon to recover his land from Pennoyer. How long he remained in Oregon after his success against Pennoyer is unclear. We do know that he, his wife, and two children were present in Multnomah County, Oregon, for the 1880 census.

2.   The constitutionalization of territorial jurisdiction. Prior to *Pennoyer*, the states recognized, under legal concepts derived from international law, that there were limitations on their authority to exercise jurisdiction in cases involving persons or property outside their boundaries. Before the Civil War, the Full Faith and Credit Clause of the federal Constitution required a state to enforce the judgment of another state, but the Constitution was otherwise silent on questions related to territorial jurisdiction. The Fourteenth Amendment to the Constitution was adopted after the Civil War. The Court in *Pennoyer* relied on old pre-war, largely state-law, decisions for its conceptual apparatus, but subsumed them under the Due Process Clause of the new amendment. The result was to convert what had theretofore been primarily a body of state-law principles into a body of federal constitutional law binding on the states under the Supremacy Clause. Previously, the Full Faith and Credit Clause had permitted a state court to treat as invalid, and to refuse to enforce, a judgment of another state's court when the judgment was rendered without territorial jurisdiction. Now, as held in *Pennoyer*, the Due Process Clause required a judgment rendered without jurisdiction to be treated as invalid not only in other states but also in the state in which it was rendered.

The Restatement (Second) of Conflict of Laws § 24, Comment e, summarizes:

> In the United States, the due process clause of the Fourteenth Amendment * * * prohibits the States from acting through their courts when they have no judicial jurisdiction * * * A judgment rendered in this country without judicial jurisdiction is void, even in the State where rendered, and is not entitled to full faith and credit in sister States. Since the extent of the judicial jurisdiction of the * * * individual States is a constitutional question, the decisions of the Supreme Court of the United States are controlling.

The history of jurisdiction since *Pennoyer* is in an important sense the evolution of principles of territorial jurisdiction in the context of the increasing economic and social integration of the states. For a review of the *Pennoyer* conceptual framework in historical perspective, and a critique of its analysis, see Hazard, A General Theory of State-Court Jurisdiction, 1965 Sup.Ct.Rev. 241. For further historical material, see Oakley, The Pitfalls of "Hint and Run" History: A Critique of Professor Borcher's "Limited View" of *Pennoyer v. Neff*, 28 U.C.Davis L.Rev. 591 (1995).

3. **Presence and physical power.** Mitchell was unable to establish *in personam* jurisdiction over the absent Neff. The Supreme Court held that Neff was beyond the reach of the Oregon courts. Why? Recall that Mitchell claimed Neff had not paid a bill for legal services that had been requested by Neff in Oregon and that had been performed by Mitchell in Oregon. Justice Holmes later wrote, "The foundation of jurisdiction is physical power." McDonald v. Mabee, 243 U.S. 90, 91, 37 S.Ct. 343, 61 L.Ed. 608 (1917). Does this statement help us understand *Pennoyer* ?

4. **Types of territorial jurisdiction.** An action *in personam* is brought, as the name suggests, against a person. An action *in rem* is brought against a thing. "Res" (or, in the accusative case, "rem") is Latin for "thing." *In personam* actions bind a defendant personally, typically providing damages or injunctive relief. Examples of *in personam* actions are suits for damages arising out of tort or breach of contract, or for an injunction against wrongful acts. "True" *in rem* actions bind property in the sense of adjudicating the rights of *all* persons who claim interest in the property. Examples of *in rem* actions are suits to settle all potential claims to a fixed sum, as in a quiet title action to settle all possible claims to land, in an admiralty "limitation of liability" proceeding where all litigants look to a particular vessel for satisfaction of their claims, and in a probate proceeding to settle all claims to a decedent's estate. *Quasi in rem* jurisdiction is distinct from true *in rem* jurisdiction in that it settles property rights only of specific

persons; it does not settle rights in property against all persons, or, as the saying goes, "against the world."

There are two types of *quasi in rem* actions. Restatement of Judgments § 32 (1942). A "type one" *quasi in rem* action resolves a dispute about the property itself. An example is a suit to quiet title to land which would not extinguish claims of persons outside the jurisdiction of the court. Another example is a suit to foreclose a mortgage on property within the jurisdiction of the court where one or more claimants are outside the court's jurisdiction.

A "type two" *quasi in rem* action establishes rights to property, but the underlying dispute is unrelated to the property. Examples are tort or contract claims for damages against an absent defendant who owns real property within the state. In a "type two" action, the property is brought within the jurisdiction of the court by "attachment," and the absent defendant is then put to the choice either of coming into the state to litigate the claim at issue or of staying outside the state and losing the litigation (and the property) through a default judgment.

Under this terminology, *Pennoyer* involved "type two" *quasi in rem* jurisdiction. In Justice Field's words, it was "in the nature of a proceeding *in rem*." This kind of jurisdiction is often called "attachment jurisdiction." See Restatement Second of Judgments § 8.

     5.   **The relevance of attachment in an *in rem* suit.** Justice Field indicates that had the Oregon court attached Neff's property at the outset of his suit, there would have been valid *quasi in rem* jurisdiction. In actual fact, the property was attached after the judgment was rendered, and sold as a means of satisfying the judgment. Why should it make a difference whether the property was attached at the beginning or at the end of the suit? Justice Field's answer (in part) appears to be that attachment at the outset will make it more likely that a diligent owner of property would be alerted to the existence of a suit against him. Attachment of property will ordinarily have the physical manifestation of posting signs on the property, and if the owner has a tenant or caretaker, or someone who checks on the property from time to time, Justice Field may be right. But even conceding that in some cases attachment of the property at the outset of the suit will be fairer to the defendant than attachment to enforce a judgment already rendered, why should we ever allow attachment of property to be a basis for asserting jurisdiction that would otherwise be unavailable?

     6.   **The relevance of service of process in an *in personam* suit.** *Pennoyer* tells us that the presence of property within a state justifies the exercise of *in rem* and *quasi in rem* jurisdiction (provided the property is attached at the beginning of the suit). Similarly, the presence of a person within a state justifies the exercise of *in personam* jurisdiction (provided the person is served with process at the beginning of the suit).

What if Smith lives in California and enters into a contract with Mitchell in California for legal services during the short time Mitchell is in that state? After rendering the services in California, Mitchell moves to Oregon and begins law practice there. Smith then visits Portland briefly on an unrelated matter. Mitchell finds out about Smith's presence in Oregon, and serves him with a copy of a complaint in a suit seeking recovery of unpaid fees for the legal services rendered in California. Should Smith be forced to litigate the suit in Oregon? Merely because he was served with process in Oregon?

In Grace v. MacArthur, 170 F. Supp. 442 (E.D.Ark.1959), a passenger was served with process in Arkansas airspace on a non-stop flight between Tennessee and Texas. Can Arkansas courts thereby obtain *in personam* jurisdiction over the passenger? The federal District Court held that service was proper under Fed. R. Civ. P. 4(f) which, as it then read, required that service be accomplished within the "territorial limits" of a state: "All process other than a subpoena may be served anywhere within the territorial limits of the state in which the district court is held * * *."

7.   A tidy framework? Near the beginning of his opinion, Justice Field says that "no State can exercise direct jurisdiction and authority over persons or property without its territory," and that "no tribunal established by it can extend its process beyond that territory so as to subject either persons or property to its decisions." But at the end of the opinion, Justice Field says that, of course, the decision is not to be understood as interfering with the right of a state court (1) to assert jurisdiction in a divorce case where one of the parties is a non-resident; and (2) to assert jurisdiction over a non-resident who enters into a business partnership or association within the state. What threat do these two exceptions pose to the otherwise tidy analytic scheme of *Pennoyer*? The business relationship between Neff and Mitchell?

8.   What is at stake? One of the things at stake in determining jurisdiction is the litigating convenience of the parties: Can Mitchell file suit in Oregon and oblige Neff to return to defend himself, or can Neff remain in California and force Mitchell to pursue him there? Is more than mere litigating convenience at stake? Possibly. For example, by litigating in his home state, a party may wish to take advantage of prejudice against outsiders. Or, for example, in some cases the courts of one state court may apply different substantive legal rules than the courts of another state.

Harris v. Balk

Supreme Court of the United States, 1905.
198 U.S. 215, 25 S.Ct. 625, 49 L.Ed. 1023.

[Balk, a North Carolina merchant, owed $344.00 to Epstein, a Maryland merchant. Harris, a North Carolina acquaintance of Balk, owed $180.00 to Balk. Harris' debt to Balk was not formalized in any written instrument. Harris travelled to Baltimore, Maryland, on business. While Harris was in Baltimore, Epstein caused a writ of attachment to be served on Harris, attaching the debt owed by Harris to Balk. Harris returned to North Carolina and through his attorney in Maryland consented to the entry of judgment against him for that amount. He paid the amount of the judgment to a North Carolina attorney employed by Epstein.

Balk brought suit in North Carolina against Harris for $180.00. Harris responded that he had already paid that amount under the judgment of the Maryland court, and that the judgment was entitled to full faith and credit. The North Carolina courts held that the Maryland judgment was rendered without jurisdiction "because Harris was but temporarily in the state, and the situs of the debt was in North Carolina." Therefore, the North Carolina courts did not have to give the judgment full faith and credit. Harris sought review in the United States Supreme Court by writ of error.]

■ MR. JUSTICE PECKHAM * * * delivered the opinion of the court:

The state court of North Carolina has refused to give any effect in this action to the Maryland judgment; and the Federal question is whether it did not thereby refuse the full faith and credit to such judgment which is required by the Federal Constitution. If the Maryland court had jurisdiction to award it, the judgment is valid and entitled to the same full faith and credit in North Carolina that it has in Maryland as a valid domestic judgment.

The defendant in error contends that the Maryland court obtained no jurisdiction to award the judgment of condemnation, because the garnishee, although at the time in the state of Maryland, and personally served with process therein, was a nonresident of that state, only casually or temporarily within its boundaries; that the situs of the debt due from Harris, the garnishee, to the defendant in error herein, was in North Carolina, and did not accompany Harris to Maryland; that, consequently, Harris, though within the state of Maryland, had not possession of any property of Balk, and the Maryland state court therefore obtained no jurisdiction over any property of Balk in the attachment proceedings, and the consent of Harris to the entry of the judgment was immaterial. The plaintiff in error, on the contrary, insists that, though the garnishee were but temporarily in Maryland, yet the laws of that state provide for an attachment of this nature if the debtor, the garnishee, is found in the state, and the court obtains jurisdiction over him by the service of process therein; that the judgment, condemning the debt from Harris to Balk, was a valid judgment, provided Balk could himself have sued Harris for the debt in Maryland. This, it is asserted, he could have done, and the judgment was therefore entitled to full faith and credit in the courts of North Carolina.

* * *

Attachment is the creature of the local law; that is, unless there is a law of the state providing for and permitting the attachment, it cannot be levied there. If there be a law of the state providing for the attachment of the debt, then, if the garnishee be found in that state, and process be personally served upon him therein, we think the court thereby acquires jurisdiction over him, and can garnish the debt due from him to the debtor of the plaintiff, and condemn it, provided the garnishee could himself be sued by his creditor in that state. * * * We do not see the materiality of the expression "situs of the debt," when used in connection with attachment proceedings. If by situs is meant the place of the creation of the debt, that fact is immaterial. If it be meant that the obligation to pay the debt can only be enforced at the situs thus fixed, we think it plainly untrue. The obligation of the debtor to pay his debt clings to and accompanies him wherever he goes. He is as much bound to pay his debt in a foreign state when therein sued upon his obligation by his creditor, as he was in the state where the debt was contracted. We speak of ordinary debts, such as the one in this case. It would be no defense to such suit for the debtor to plead that he was only in the foreign state casually or temporarily. His obligation to pay would be the same whether he was there in that way or with an intention to remain. It is nothing but the obligation to pay which is garnished or attached. This obligation can be enforced by the courts of the foreign state after personal service of process therein, just as well as by the courts of the domicil of the debtor.

If the debtor leave the foreign state without appearing, a judgment by default may be entered, upon which execution may issue, or the judgment may be sued upon in any other state where the debtor might be found.
* * *

      * * *

It seems to us, therefore, that the judgment against Harris in Maryland, condemning the $180 which he owed to Balk, was a valid judgment, because the court had jurisdiction over the garnishee by personal service of process within the state of Maryland.

It ought to be and it is the object of courts to prevent the payment of any debt twice over. Thus, if Harris, owing a debt to Balk, paid it under a valid judgment against him, to Epstein, he certainly ought not to be compelled to pay it a second time, but should have the right to plead his payment under the Maryland judgment. It is objected, however, that the payment by Harris to Epstein was not under legal compulsion. Harris in truth owed the debt to Balk, which was attached by Epstein. He had, therefore, as we have seen, no defense to set up against the attachment of the debt. Jurisdiction over him personally had been obtained by the Maryland court. As he was absolutely without defense, there was no reason why he should not consent to a judgment impounding the debt, which judgment the plaintiff was legally entitled to, and which he could not prevent. There was no merely voluntary payment within the meaning of that phrase as applicable here.

But most rights may be lost by negligence, and if the garnishee were guilty of negligence in the attachment proceeding, to the damage of Balk, he ought not to be permitted to set up the judgment as a defense. Thus it is recognized as the duty of the garnishee to give notice to his own creditor, if he would protect himself, so that the creditor may have the opportunity to defend himself against the claim of the person suing out the attachment. * * * Fair dealing requires this at the hands of the garnishee. In this case, while neither the defendant nor the garnishee appeared, the court, while condemning the credits attached, could not, by the terms of the Maryland statute, issue the writ of execution unless the plaintiff gave bond or sufficient security before the court awarding the execution, to make restitution of the money paid if the defendant should, at any time within a year and a day, appear in the action and show that the plaintiff's claim, or some part thereof, was not due to the plaintiff. The defendant in error, Balk, had notice of this attachment, certainly within a few days after the issuing thereof and the entry of judgment thereon, because he sued the plaintiff in error to recover his debt within a few days after his (Harris') return to North Carolina, in which suit the judgment in Maryland was set up by Harris as a plea in bar to Balk's claim. Balk, therefore, had an opportunity for a year and a day after the entry of the judgment to litigate the question of his liability in the Maryland court, and to show that he did not owe the debt, or some part of it, as was claimed by Epstein. He, however, took no proceedings to that end, so far as the record shows, and the reason may be supposed to be that he could not successfully defend the claim, because he admitted in this case that he did, at the time of the attachment proceeding, owe Epstein some $344.

Generally, though, the failure on the part of the garnishee to give proper notice to his creditor of the levying of the attachment would be such a neglect of duty on the part of the garnishee which he owed to his creditor as would prevent his availing himself of the judgment in the attachment suit as a bar to the suit of his creditor against himself, which might therefore result in his being called upon to pay the debt twice.

The judgment of the Supreme Court of North Carolina must be reversed, and the cause remanded for further proceedings not inconsistent with the opinion of this court.

Reversed.

■ MR. JUSTICE HARLAN and MR. JUSTICE DAY dissented.

NOTE ON *HARRIS V. BALK* AND THE EXPANSION OF IN REM JURISDICTION

1.   **Historical background.** Professor Andreas Lowenfeld provides useful background information about *Harris v. Balk*. Epstein was an importer and wholesaler of general merchandise in Baltimore. Balk was a dry goods retailer in the town of Washington, North Carolina, and a regular customer of Epstein. Between August and November of 1895, Epstein made four separate shipments to Balk, for a total of $569.00. Balk had paid $225.00 of this amount, leaving $344.00 still owing. Harris was also a dry goods retailer in Washington, North Carolina. He was in the habit of borrowing money from Balk, and had borrowed $10.00 just before going to Baltimore (in addition to $170.00 borrowed previously). At Balk's request, Harris carried the message to Epstein that Balk would come to Baltimore "soon." Harris swore that he did not tell Epstein of his debt to Balk, but obviously Epstein either knew or suspected its existence. Harris was not detained in Baltimore after the attachment of his debt to Balk, and was not required to post any bond. Harris had purchased goods while in Baltimore (possibly from Epstein) and discovered after his return that they were not being shipped. This discovery prompted him to pay the $180.00 to Epstein's lawyer in North Carolina. Lowenfeld, In Search of the Intangible: A Comment on *Shaffer v. Heitner*, 53 N.Y.U.L.Rev. 102 (1978).

Despite Professor Lowenfeld's work, the motives of the principal actors remain somewhat mysterious. As the opinion makes clear, Balk had the option of going to Maryland to defend the suit, or, within a year and a day of entry of judgment, to reopen the judgment. Why didn't Balk do so? The Court assumes (probably correctly) that Balk had no defense on the merits. Then why didn't Balk simply pay the money to Epstein in the first place? Was Balk trying to "stiff" Epstein? If so, why did Balk send a message with Harris that he would come to Baltimore soon, which suggests that he wished continued relations with Epstein? Was Balk having financial difficulties? The fact that he lent $180.00 to Harris suggests otherwise. Was Balk a "slow pay" (a familiar creature in the commercial world) with whom Epstein had lost patience? The case came before the North Carolina Supreme Court three times before it finally came before the United States Supreme Court. Why did Balk pursue Harris so vigorously? Why did Harris resist so strongly?

Even in 1890 dollars, $180.00 would not have been a large enough sum to justify such litigation. Harris' brief before the United States Supreme Court said as much: "The amount of money involved in the controversy is insignificant, but the legal question is of considerable importance to the mercantile and business world, and is fraught with much interest." Quoted in Lowenfeld, at 104. When the sum involved is small in relation to litigation expenses, the explanation is likely to be that the litigation is either a test case or a grudge match. Whether intended as a test case or not, *Harris v. Balk* turned out to be one, settling a previously undecided point about the "situs" of intangible property.

2. Tangible and intangible property, and the problem of geographical location. The Court held that the "situs" of Balk's property was Maryland so long as Harris was in that state, on the ground that a creditor's property accompanies the debtor wherever he goes. The North Carolina courts had agreed that the debt was property, but had disagreed as to its situs. Where would you say the property was located? Why? Would your answer be different if the debt were evidenced by an informal, but written, I.O.U.? By a formal legal document? By a formal legal document specifically stating that Harris would pay the debt in North Carolina? Should it matter where the formal document was kept?

The jurisdiction at issue in *Harris v. Balk* is *quasi in rem* ("type two"), as it was in *Pennoyer*, even though one is based on intangible personal property and the other on real property. How similar, in fact, are the two cases?   In this case attachment @ the onset

3. Limited and general appearances. What if Balk had wanted to defend the suit on the merits in Maryland? Would he have been allowed to defend, but to subject himself to liability only up to the value of the property that served as the basis for jurisdiction? The technical term for such a defense is a "limited appearance." Or would he have had to subject himself to liability for the full amount of the asserted debt? This is called a "general appearance."

When *quasi in rem* suits were widely employed, most states allowed limited appearances. See, e.g., Simpson v. Loehmann, 21 N.Y.2d 990, 290 N.Y.S.2d 914, 238 N.E.2d 319 (1968). A few, however, required a defendant to enter a general appearance as a condition of being permitted to defend on the merits at all. See, e.g., Shaffer v. Heitner, 433 U.S. 186, 195 n. 12, 97 S.Ct. 2569, 53 L.Ed.2d 683 (1977) (describing a Delaware statute), infra p. 143.

4. A theory-based solution to a common practical problem. The underlying practical problem posed by *Harris v. Balk* can be difficult even today. Two merchants in two different states, communicating by mail or email, agree to buy and to sell certain merchandise. A dispute arises about the merchandise or the payment. Can the dissatisfied party sue in her home state, or must she pursue the other party in the other state? How satisfactory is the solution offered by *Harris v. Balk*? Does the solution address the underlying problem directly?

5. Actual notice. Note that Balk, unlike Neff, appears to have had timely notice of the existence of the suit. The Supreme Court was careful to say that if he had not had such notice, Harris could not have asserted the prior judgment as a defense. What is the basis for that proposition?

6. Time for a reconceptualization? At various points in the development of judge-made law, the accumulated weight of legal fictions, artificial reasoning, and unjust or inefficient outcomes becomes unbearable. When this happens, courts discard the old conceptual framework and replace it with a new one. In your opinion, were we due for a reconceptualization in 1905, when *Harris v. Balk* was decided? As we will see in the next principal case, *International Shoe Co. v. Washington*, the Supreme Court finally reconceptualized the law of territorial jurisdiction in 1945. But the old conceptual framework did not entirely disappear. After the abolition of the old forms of action at common law in England, the great legal historian F. W. Maitland wrote, "The forms of action we have buried, but they still rule us from their graves." F. Maitland, Equity, and the Forms of Action at Common Law 296 (1909). As you read through the rest of the section on territorial jurisdiction, ask yourself how much *Pennoyer* and the cases it spawned still rule us from their graves.

2. TWENTIETH CENTURY SYNTHESES

a. MINIMUM CONTACTS

International Shoe Co. v. Washington

Supreme Court of the United States, 1945.
326 U.S. 310, 66 S.Ct. 154, 90 L.Ed. 95.

■ MR. CHIEF JUSTICE STONE delivered the opinion of the Court.

The questions for decision are (1) whether, within the limitations of the due process clause of the Fourteenth Amendment, appellant, a Delaware corporation, has by its activities in the State of Washington rendered itself amenable to proceedings in the courts of that state to recover unpaid contributions to the state unemployment compensation fund exacted by state statutes, Washington Unemployment Compensation Act, Washington Revised Statutes, § 9998–103a through § 9998–123a, 1941 Supp., and (2) whether the state can exact those contributions consistently with the due process clause of the Fourteenth Amendment.

The statutes in question set up a comprehensive scheme of unemployment compensation, the costs of which are defrayed by contributions required to be made by employers to a state unemployment compensation fund. The contributions are a specified percentage of the wages payable annually by each employer for his employees' services in the state. The assessment and collection of the contributions and the fund are administered by respondents. Section 14(c) of the Act, Wash.Rev.Stat.1941 Supp., § 9998–114c, authorizes respondent Commissioner to issue an order and notice of assessment of delinquent contributions upon prescribed personal service of the notice upon the employer if found within the state, or, if not so found, by mailing the notice to the employer by registered mail at his last known address. That section also authorizes the Commissioner to collect the assessment by distraint if it is not paid within ten days after service of the notice. By §§ 14(e) and 6(b) the order of assessment may be administratively reviewed by an appeal tribunal within the office of unemployment upon petition of the employer, and this determination is by § 6(i) made subject to judicial review on questions of law by the state Superior Court, with further right of appeal in the state Supreme Court as in other civil cases.

In this case notice of assessment for the years in question was personally served upon a sales solicitor employed by appellant in the State of Washington, and a copy of the notice was mailed by registered mail to appellant at its address in St. Louis, Missouri. Appellant appeared specially before the office of unemployment and moved to set aside the order and notice of assessment on the ground that the service upon appellant's salesman was not proper service upon appellant; that appellant was not a corporation of the State of Washington and was not doing business within the state; that it had no agent within the state upon whom service could be made; and that appellant is not an employer and does not furnish employment within the meaning of the statute.

The motion was heard on evidence and a stipulation of facts by the appeal tribunal which denied the motion and ruled that respondent Commissioner was entitled to recover the unpaid contributions. That action was affirmed by the Commissioner; both the Superior Court and the Supreme Court affirmed. 154 P.2d 801. Appellant in each of these courts assailed the statute as applied, as a violation of the due process clause of the Fourteenth Amendment, and as imposing a constitutionally prohibited burden on interstate commerce. * * *

The facts as found by the appeal tribunal and accepted by the state Superior Court and Supreme Court, are not in dispute. Appellant is a Delaware corporation, having its principal place of business in St. Louis, Missouri, and is engaged in the manufacture and sale of shoes and other footwear. It maintains places of business in several states, other than Washington, at which its manufacturing is carried on and from which its merchandise is distributed interstate through several sales units or branches located outside the State of Washington.

Appellant has no office in Washington and makes no contracts either for sale or purchase of merchandise there. It maintains no stock of merchandise in that state and makes no deliveries of goods in intrastate commerce. During the years from 1937 to 1940, now in question, appellant employed eleven to thirteen salesmen under direct supervision and control of sales managers located in St. Louis. These salesmen resided in Washington; their principal activities were confined to that state; and they were compensated by commissions based upon the amount of their sales. The commissions for each year totaled more than $31,000. Appellant supplies its salesmen with a line of samples, each consisting of one shoe of a pair, which they display to prospective purchasers. On occasion they rent permanent sample rooms, for exhibiting samples, in business buildings, or rent rooms in hotels or business buildings temporarily for that purpose. The cost of such rentals is reimbursed by appellant.

The authority of the salesmen is limited to exhibiting their samples and soliciting orders from prospective buyers, at prices and on terms fixed by appellant. The salesmen transmit the orders to appellant's office in St. Louis for acceptance or rejection, and when accepted the merchandise for filling the orders is shipped f.o.b. from points outside Washington to the purchasers within the state. All the merchandise shipped into Washington is invoiced at the place of shipment from which collections are made. No salesman has authority to enter into contracts or to make collections.

The Supreme Court of Washington was of opinion that the regular and systematic solicitation of orders in the state by appellant's salesmen, resulting in a continuous flow of appellant's product into the state, was sufficient to constitute doing business in the state so as to make appellant amenable to suit in its courts. But it was also of opinion that there were sufficient additional activities shown to bring the case within the rule frequently stated, that solicitation within a state by the agents of a foreign corporation plus some additional activities there are sufficient to render the corporation amenable to suit brought in the courts of the state to enforce an obligation arising out of its activities there. International Harvester Co. v. Kentucky, 234 U.S. 579, 587, 34 S.Ct. 944, 946, 58 L.Ed. 1479; People's Tobacco Co. v. American Tobacco Co., 246 U.S. 79, 87, 38 S.Ct. 233, 235, 62 L.Ed. 587, Ann.Cas.1918C, 537; Frene v. Louisville Cement Co., 77 U.S.App.D.C. 129, 134 F.2d 511, 516, 146 A.L.R. 926. The court found such additional activities in the salesmen's display of samples sometimes in permanent display rooms, and the salesmen's residence within the state, continued over a period of years, all resulting in a substantial volume of merchandise regularly shipped by appellant to purchasers within the state. The court also held that the statute as applied did not invade the constitutional power of Congress to regulate interstate commerce and did not impose a prohibited burden on such commerce.

Appellant's argument, renewed here, that the statute imposes an unconstitutional burden on interstate commerce need not detain us. For 53 Stat. 1391, 26 U.S.C. § 1606(a), 26 U.S.C.A. Int.Rev.Code, § 1606(a), provides that "No person required under a State law to make payments to an unemployment fund shall be relieved from compliance therewith on the ground that he is engaged in interstate or foreign commerce, or that the State law does not distinguish between employees engaged in interstate or foreign commerce and those engaged in intrastate commerce." It is no longer debatable that Congress, in the exercise of the commerce power, may authorize the states, in specified ways, to regulate interstate commerce or impose burdens upon it.

Appellant also insists that its activities within the state were not sufficient to manifest its "presence" there and that in its absence the state courts were without jurisdiction, [and] that consequently it was a denial of due process for the state to subject appellant to suit. It refers to those cases in which it was said that the mere solicitation of orders for the purchase of goods within a state, to be accepted without the state and filled by shipment of the purchased goods interstate, does not render the corporation seller amenable to suit within the state. See Green v. Chicago, Burlington & Quincy R. Co., 205 U.S. 530, 533, 27 S.Ct. 595, 596, 51 L.Ed. 916; International Harvester Co. v. Kentucky, supra, 234 U.S. 579, 587, 34 S.Ct. 944, 946, 58 L.Ed. 1479; Philadelphia & Reading R. Co. v. McKibbin, 243 U.S. 264, 268, 37 S.Ct. 280, 61 L.Ed. 710; People's Tobacco Co. v. American Tobacco Co., supra, 246 U.S. 79, 38 S.Ct. 233, 62 L.Ed. 587, Ann.Cas.1918C, 537. And appellant further argues that since it was not present within the state, it is a denial of due process to subject it to taxation or other money exaction. It thus denies the power of the state to lay the tax or to subject appellant to a suit for its collection.

Historically the jurisdiction of courts to render judgment in personam is grounded on their de facto power over the defendant's person. Hence his presence within the territorial jurisdiction of a court was prerequisite to its rendition of a judgment personally binding him. Pennoyer v. Neff, 95 U.S. 714, 733, 24 L.Ed. 565. But now that the capias ad respondendum has given way to personal service of summons or other form of notice, due process requires only that in order to subject a defendant to a judgment in personam, if he be not present within the territory of the forum, he have certain minimum contacts with it such that the maintenance of the suit does not offend "traditional notions of fair play and substantial justice." Milliken v. Meyer, 311 U.S. 457, 463, 61 S.Ct. 339, 343, 85 L.Ed. 278, 132 A.L.R. 1357.

Since the corporate personality is a fiction, although a fiction intended to be acted upon as though it were a fact, Klein v. Board of Tax Supervisors, 282 U.S. 19, 24, 51 S.Ct. 15, 16, 75 L.Ed. 140, 73 A.L.R. 679, it is clear that unlike an individual its "presence" without, as well as within, the state of its origin can be manifested only by activities carried on in its behalf by those who are authorized to act for it. To say that the corporation is so far "present" there as to satisfy due process requirements, for purposes of taxation or the maintenance of suits against it in the courts of the state, is to beg the question to be decided. For the terms "present" or "presence" are used merely to symbolize those activities of the corporation's agent within the state which courts will deem to be sufficient to satisfy the demands of due process. L. Hand, J., in Hutchinson v. Chase & Gilbert, 2 Cir., 45 F.2d 139, 141. Those demands may be met by such contacts of the corporation with the state of the forum as make it reasonable, in the context of our federal system of government, to require the corporation to defend the particular suit which is brought there. An "estimate of the inconveniences" which would result to the corporation from a trial away from its "home" or principal place of business is relevant in this connection. Hutchinson v. Chase & Gilbert, supra, 45 F.2d at 141.

"Presence" in the state in this sense, has never been doubted when the activities of the corporation there have not only been continuous and systematic, but also give rise to the liabilities sued on, even though no consent to be sued or authorization to an agent to accept service of process has been given. Conversely it has been generally recognized that the casual presence of the corporate agent or even his conduct of single or isolated items of activities in a state in the corporation's behalf are not enough to subject it to suit on causes of action unconnected with the activities there. To require the corporation in such circumstances to defend the suit away from its home or other jurisdiction where it carries on more substantial activities has been thought to lay too great and unreasonable a burden on the corporation to comport with due process.

While it has been held in cases on which appellant relies that continuous activity of some sorts within a state is not enough to support the demand that the corporation be amenable to suits unrelated to that activity, there have been instances in which the continuous corporate operations within a state were thought so substantial and of such a nature as to justify suit against it on causes of action arising from dealings entirely distinct from those activities.

Finally, although the commission of some single or occasional acts of the corporate agent in a state sufficient to impose an obligation or liability on the corporation has not been thought to confer upon the state authority to enforce it, Rosenberg Bros. & Co. v. Curtis Brown Co., 260 U.S. 516, 43 S.Ct. 170, 67 L.Ed. 372, other such acts, because of their nature and quality and the circumstances of their commission, may be deemed sufficient to render the corporation liable to suit. Cf. Kane v. New Jersey, 242 U.S. 160, 37 S.Ct. 30, 61 L.Ed. 222; Hess v. Pawloski, supra. True, some of the decisions holding the corporation amenable to suit have been supported by resort to the legal fiction that it has given its consent to service and suit, consent being implied from its presence in the state through the acts of its authorized agents. Lafayette Insurance Co. v. French, 18 How. 404, 407, 15 L.Ed. 451. But more realistically it may be said that those authorized acts were of such a nature as to justify the fiction. Smolik v. Philadelphia & R.C. & I. Co., D.C., 222 F. 148, 151. Henderson, The Position of Foreign Corporations in American Constitutional Law, 94, 95. *legal fiction of the Corp.*

Implication of consent

It is evident that the criteria by which we mark the boundary line between those activities which justify the subjection of a corporation to suit, and those which do not, cannot be simply mechanical or quantitative. The test is not merely, as has sometimes been suggested, whether the activity, which the corporation has seen fit to procure through its agents in another state, is a little more or a little less. St. Louis S.W.R. Co. v. Alexander, supra, 227 U.S. 218, 33 S.Ct. 245, 57 L.Ed. 486, Ann.Cas.1915B, 77; International Harvester Co. v. Kentucky, supra, 234 U.S. 579, 34 S.Ct. 944, 58 L.Ed. 1479. Whether due process is satisfied must depend rather upon the quality and nature of the activity in relation to the fair and orderly administration of the laws which it was the purpose of the due process clause to insure. That clause does not contemplate that a state may make binding a judgment in personam against an individual or corporate defendant with which the state has no contacts, ties, or relations. Cf. Pennoyer v. Neff, supra; Minnesota Commercial Men's Ass'n v. Benn, 261 U.S. 140, 43 S.Ct. 293, 67 L.Ed. 573.

But to the extent that a corporation exercises the privilege of conducting activities within a state, it enjoys the benefits and protection of the laws of that state. The exercise of that privilege may give rise to obligations; and, so far as those obligations arise out of or are connected with the activities within the state, a procedure which requires the corporation to respond to a suit brought to enforce them can, in most instances, hardly be said to be undue.

Applying these standards, the activities carried on in behalf of appellant in the State of Washington were neither irregular nor casual. They were systematic and continuous throughout the years in question. They resulted in a large volume of interstate business, in the course of which appellant received the benefits and protection of the laws of the state, including the right to resort to the courts for the enforcement of its rights. The obligation which is here sued upon arose out of those very activities. It is evident that these operations establish sufficient contacts or ties with the state of the forum to make it reasonable and just according to our traditional conception of fair play and substantial justice to permit the state to enforce the obligations which appellant has incurred there. Hence we cannot say that the maintenance of the present suit in the State of Washington involves an unreasonable or undue procedure.

We are likewise unable to conclude that the service of the process within the state upon an agent whose activities establish appellant's "presence" there was not sufficient notice of the suit, or that the suit was so unrelated to those activities as to make the agent an inappropriate vehicle for communicating the notice. It is enough that appellant has established such contacts with the state that the particular form of substituted service adopted there gives reasonable assurance that the notice will be actual; McDonald v. Mabee, supra; Milliken v. Meyer, supra. Nor can we say that the mailing of the notice of suit to appellant by registered mail at its home office was not reasonably calculated to *rule* apprise appellant of the suit. Compare Hess v. Pawloski, supra, with McDonald v. Mabee, supra, 243 U.S. 92, 37 S.Ct. 344, 61 L.Ed. 608, L.R.A.1917F, 458, and Wuchter v. Pizzutti, 276 U.S. 13, 19, 24, 48 S.Ct. 259, 260, 262, 72 L.Ed. 446, 57 A.L.R. 1230.

* * *

Appellant having rendered itself amenable to suit upon obligations arising out of the activities of its salesmen in Washington, the state may maintain the present suit in personam to collect the tax laid upon the exercise of the privilege of employing appellant's salesmen within the state. For Washington has made one of those activities, which taken together establish appellant's "presence" there for purposes of suit, the taxable event by which the state brings appellant within the reach of its taxing power. The state thus has constitutional power to lay the tax and to subject appellant to a suit to recover it. The activities which establish its "presence" subject it alike to taxation by the state and to suit to recover the tax.

Affirmed.

■ MR. JUSTICE JACKSON took no part in the consideration or decision of this case.

■ MR. JUSTICE BLACK delivered the following opinion.

* * *

Certainly appellant can not in the light of our past decisions meritoriously claim that notice by registered mail and by personal service on its sales solicitors in Washington did not meet the requirements of procedural due process. And the due process clause is not brought in issue any more by appellant's further conceptualistic contention that Washington could not levy a tax or bring suit against the corporation because it did not honor that State with its mystical "presence." For it is unthinkable that the vague due process clause was ever intended to prohibit a State from regulating or taxing a business carried on within its boundaries simply because this is done by agents of a corporation organized and having its headquarters elsewhere. To read this into the due process clause would in fact result in depriving a State's citizens of due process by taking from the State the power to protect them in their business dealings within its boundaries with representatives of a foreign corporation. Nothing could be more irrational or more designed to defeat the function of our federative system of government. Certainly a State, at the very least, has power to tax and sue those dealing with its citizens within its boundaries, as we have held before. Hoopeston Canning Co. v. Cullen, 318 U.S. 313, 63 S.Ct. 602, 87 L.Ed. 777, 145 A.L.R. 1113. Were the Court to follow this principle, it would provide a workable standard for cases where, as here, no other questions are involved. The Court has not chosen to do so, but instead has engaged in an unnecessary discussion in the course of which it has announced vague Constitutional criteria applied for the first time to the issue before us. It has thus introduced uncertain elements confusing the simple pattern and tending to curtail the exercise of State powers to an extent not justified by the Constitution.

The criteria adopted insofar as they can be identified read as follows: Due process does permit State courts to "enforce the obligations which appellant has incurred" if it be found "reasonable and just according to our traditional conception of fair play and substantial justice." And this in turn means that we will "permit" the State to act if upon "an 'estimate of the inconveniences' which would result to the corporation from a trial away from its 'home' or principal place of business," we conclude that it is "reasonable" to subject it to suit in a State where it is doing business.

It is true that this Court did use the terms "fair play" and "substantial justice" in explaining the philosophy underlying the holding that it could not be "due process of law" to render a personal judgment against a defendant without notice to and an opportunity to be heard by him. *Milliken v. Meyer*, 311 U.S. 457, 61 S.Ct. 339, 85 L.Ed. 278, 132 A.L.R. 1357. In *McDonald v. Mabee*, 243 U.S. 90, 91, 37 S.Ct. 343, 61 L.Ed. 608, L.R.A. 1917F, 458, cited in the *Milliken* case, Mr. Justice Holmes speaking for the Court warned against judicial curtailment of this opportunity to be heard and referred to such a curtailment as a denial of "fair play," which even the common law would have deemed "contrary to natural justice." And previous cases had indicated that the ancient rule against judgments without notice had stemmed from "natural justice" concepts. These cases, while giving additional reasons why notice under particular circumstances is inadequate, did not mean thereby that all legislative enactments which this Court might deem to be contrary to natural justice ought to be held invalid under the due process clause. None of the cases purport to support or could support a holding that a State can tax and sue corporations only if its action comports with this Court's notions of "natural justice." I should have thought the Tenth Amendment settled that.

I believe that the Federal Constitution leaves to each State, without any "ifs" or "buts," a power to tax and to open the doors of its courts for its citizens to sue corporations whose agents do business in those States. Believing that the Constitution gave the States that power, I think it a judicial deprivation to condition its exercise upon this Court's notion of "fair play," however appealing that term may be. Nor can I stretch the meaning of due process so far as to authorize this Court to deprive a State of the right to afford judicial protection to its citizens on the ground that it would be more "convenient" for the corporation to be sued somewhere else.

There is a strong emotional appeal in the words "fair play," "justice," and "reasonableness." But they were not chosen by those who wrote the original Constitution or the Fourteenth Amendment as a measuring rod for this Court to use in invalidating State or Federal laws passed by elected legislative representatives. No one, not even those who most feared a democratic government, ever formally proposed that courts should be given power to invalidate legislation under any such elastic standards. Express prohibitions against certain types of legislation are found in the Constitution, and under the long settled practice, courts invalidate laws found to conflict with them. This requires interpretation, and interpretation, it is true, may result in extension of the Constitution's purpose. But that is no reason for reading the due process clause so as to restrict a State's power to tax and sue those whose activities affect persons and businesses within the State, provided proper service can be had. Superimposing the natural justice concept on the Constitution's specific prohibitions could operate as a drastic abridgment of democratic safeguards they embody, such as freedom of speech, press and religion, and the right to counsel. This has already happened. Betts v. Brady, 316 U.S. 455, 62 S.Ct. 1252, 86 L.Ed. 1595. Compare Feldman v. United States, 322 U.S. 487, 494–503, 64 S.Ct. 1082, 1085–1089, 88 L.Ed. 1408, 154 A.L.R. 982. For application of this natural law concept, whether under the terms "reasonableness," "justice," or "fair play," makes judges the supreme arbiters of the country's laws and practices. This result, I believe, alters the form of government our Constitution provides. I cannot agree.

[handwritten: issues w/14th ammendment]

True, the State's power is here upheld. But the rule announced means that tomorrow's judgment may strike down a State or Federal enactment on the ground that it does not conform to this Court's idea of natural justice. I therefore find myself moved by the same fears that caused Mr. Justice Holmes to say in 1930:

"I have not yet adequately expressed the more than anxiety that I feel at the ever increasing scope given to the Fourteenth Amendment in cutting down what I believe to be the constitutional rights of the States. As the decisions now stand, I see hardly any limit but the sky to the invalidating of those rights if they happen to strike a majority of this Court as for any reason undesirable." Baldwin v. Missouri, 281 U.S. 586, 595, 50 S.Ct. 436, 439, 74 L.Ed. 1056, 72 A.L.R. 1303.

NOTES AND QUESTIONS

1. **"Minimum contacts":** *International Shoe* provided an intellectual construct for dealing with what had become obvious by the 1930s and 40s: Under a wide range of circumstances, a state should be able to assert *in personam* jurisdiction over an out-of-state defendant. In shorthand fashion, the scheme of *International Shoe* requires that the defendant have "minimum contacts" with the forum. Can you describe the scheme of *International Shoe* in a more elaborated fashion?

2. **Legislative power and adjudicative power.** The Court held that the activities of International Shoe Company in the state of Washington were such that Washington had the power to tax the company. Should it follow automatically that Washington should also have the power to enforce the payment of such taxes through its courts? *[handwritten: yes, as held by the Court in International Shoe]*

3. **Presence of natural and artificial persons.** It is usually very easy to determine whether a natural person is present in a state. She is either physically present, or she is not. But the question is not so easy for an artificial person such as a corporation. In *International Shoe*, the out-of-state defendant is a corporation rather than a natural person. What should count as "presence" for a corporation? Presence of the corporate president? Should it matter whether he or she is in the state for business, or for pleasure unrelated to business? Presence of the corporate headquarters? Presence of

the manufacturing plant? Significant sales activities? Incorporation in the state? Even for Delaware corporations? (Delaware is the preferred state of incorporation for large, publicly traded American corporations; many Delaware corporations have their corporate headquarters and manufacturing plants outside Delaware.) The *International Shoe* "minimum contacts" formula was designed with questions like these in mind. The formula does not provide a specific, bright-line answer, but it does provide a framework within which an answer can be given.

    4.   A more certain test? In *International Shoe* Justice Black objects to the formulation in the majority opinion on the ground that the criterion of "fair play" affords too much leeway to courts to deny states the right to assert judicial jurisdiction over out-of-state defendants. What test does Justice Black prefer? Does it provide any greater certainty of application? *Natural Justice*

    5.   Additional reading. For an interesting historical narrative of the litigation in *International Shoe,* see Cameron and Johnson, "Death of a Salesman? Forum Shopping and Outcome Determination under *International Shoe,*" 28 U.C.Davis L.Rev. 769 (1995).

NOTE ON GENERAL AND SPECIFIC JURISDICTION

    1.   Origin of the terminology. Twenty-one years after *International Shoe*, Professors Arthur von Mehren and Donald Trautman suggested a terminology that sought to encapsulate the Court's way of thinking. Von Mehren and Trautman, Jurisdiction to Adjudicate: A Suggested Analysis, 79 Harv. L. Rev. 1121 (1966). Under the von Mehren and Trautman analysis, there are two kinds of jurisdiction, "general" and "specific." "General jurisdiction" exists when the number and quality of a defendant's contacts with the forum state are sufficiently substantial that one may litigate any dispute in the courts of the forum, whether or not that dispute grows out of those contacts. "Specific jurisdiction" exists when the contacts with the forum are related to the dispute sought to be adjudicated. Professor Mary Twitchell has suggested that we replace the terms "general" and "specific" with "dispute-blind" and "dispute-specific." She "proposes that courts use the term 'dispute-blind' to refer to an exercise of jurisdiction made without regard to the nature of the claim presented, and the term 'dispute-specific' to refer to an exercise of jurisdiction based in any way on the nature of the controversy." Twitchell, The Myth of General Jurisdiction, 101 Harv. L. Rev. 610, 613 (1988).

    The terms general and specific jurisdiction likely would not have surprised Chief Justice Stone. What von Mehren and Trautman called general jurisdiction existed, in the language of *International Shoe*, when "the continuous corporate operations within a state were thought so substantial and of such a nature as to justify suit against it on causes of action arising from dealings entirely distinct from those activities." Specific jurisdiction existed when "the commission of some single or occasional act of the corporate agent in a state * * * because of their nature and quality and the circumstances of their commission, may be deemed sufficient to render the corporation liable to suit."

    2.   Late adoption of terminology by the Supreme Court. The Supreme Court was slow to adopt the terms general and specific jurisdiction. The Court first used the terms in Helicopteros Nacionales de Colombia, S.A.

v. Hall, 466 U.S. 408, 414 n.9, 104 S.Ct. 1868, 80 L.Ed.2d 404 (1984), almost forty years after its decision in *International Shoe*.

3. Examples of general and specific jurisdiction. How have the concepts of general and specific jurisdiction functioned in practice? Here are some early examples.

General jurisdiction. In Perkins v. Benguet Consolidated Mining Co., 342 U.S. 437, 72 S.Ct. 413, 96 L.Ed. 485 (1952), a Philippine mining corporation was sued in Ohio for dividends and for damages allegedly arising out of the failure to issue stock certificates. The plaintiff was a non-resident, and it was conceded that the suit alleged a "cause of action not arising out of the corporation's activities in the State of the forum." 342 U.S. at 446. During the Second World War, the activities of the corporation in the Philippines were completely halted because of the Japanese occupation of the islands. During that time, the president of the company (who was also the general manager and principal stockholder) returned to his home in Ohio. "[H]e carried on in Ohio a continuous and systematic supervision of the necessarily limited wartime activities of the company * * * both during the occupation of the company's properties by the Japanese and immediately thereafter." Id. at 448. The Court held that this was sufficient activity to support jurisdiction over the company in Ohio. We would today call this "general jurisdiction," although this term had not yet been proposed.

Specific jurisdiction. In McGee v. International Life Insurance Co., 355 U.S. 220, 78 S.Ct. 199, 2 L.Ed.2d 223 (1957), Lulu McGee recovered a judgment in California state court against the International Life Insurance Company as the beneficiary of a life insurance contract between the company and her son, Lowell Franklin. Franklin had purchased life insurance from a different life insurance company in 1944. In 1948, International Life agreed with that company to assume its insurance obligations. It wrote to Franklin in California, offering to continue insuring him on the same terms as his policy with the previous company. Franklin accepted the offer and paid premiums on his policy with International Life until his death in 1950. After his death, International Life refused to pay on the ground that he had committed suicide. International Life apparently never had an office or insurance agent in California. So far as the record before the Court showed, International Life had never solicited or done any business in California apart from the policy in question.

Mrs. McGee sought to enforce her California judgment against International Life in Texas, its principal place of business. The Texas courts refused to enforce the judgment on the ground that it had been rendered without jurisdiction over International Life and was therefore not entitled to full faith and credit. The Supreme Court reversed, saying, "It is sufficient for purposes of due process that the suit was based on a contract which had substantial connection with [California]. The contract was delivered in California, the premiums were mailed from there and the insured was a resident of that State when he died. It cannot be denied that California has a manifest interest in providing effective means of redress for its residents when their insurers refuse to pay claims. These residents would be at a severe disadvantage if they were forced to follow the insurance company to a distant State in order to hold it legally accountable." 355 U.S. at 223. *McGee* is an example of what we would today call specific jurisdiction.

Whenever specific jurisdiction is at issue, a court must consider the relation of the contacts to the cause of action against the defendant. What was the nature of the contacts in *McGee*? So far as the record showed, the insurance company solicited the purchase of only one life insurance policy in California—that of the plaintiff's decedent, Franklin. This one policy was enough to support jurisdiction when the suit arose out of that same policy. What do you make of the Court's reference to California's interest in providing its residents an "effective means of redress"? Is the Court considering the plaintiff's residence as an additional factor, over and above the contacts between the defendant and the forum state? What if Franklin (the decedent) had lived in Oregon at all relevant times, but his mother (the plaintiff) had lived in California? Would California have had jurisdiction? What if Franklin had lived in California and his mother in Oregon?

4. No specific jurisdiction. In Hanson v. Denckla, 357 U.S. 235, 78 S.Ct. 1228, 2 L.Ed.2d 1283 (1958), Dora Donner, then a resident of Pennsylvania, established a trust in Delaware, naming a Delaware company as trustee. Under the terms of the trust, Mrs. Donner was to have the income from securities held by the trust during her lifetime. At her death, the securities were to go to whomever she designated either by "appointment" during her lifetime, or by her will at death. Mrs. Donner moved to Florida in 1944 and died in that state in 1952. During the eight years in Florida, Mrs. Donner communicated with the Delaware trustee concerning trust business and regularly received income payments from the trust.

Mrs. Donner had three daughters. On the day of her death, she "appointed" $400,000 from the trust ($200,000 each) to the two children of one of the daughters, Elizabeth Hanson. She allowed the rest of the trust, about $1,000,000, to pass through the residuary clause of her will to her two other daughters, Katherine Denckla and Dorothy Stewart ($500,000 each). During the probate of Mrs. Donner's will in Florida state court, Mrs. Denckla and Mrs. Stewart challenged the validity of the appointment of the $400,000 to the two children of their sister, Mrs. Hanson. The Florida court found that it had jurisdiction over the Delaware trustee and possibly the trust *res* as well, and held that the appointment was invalid. The consequence of the holding was to return the $400,000 to Mrs. Donner's estate, where it would then pass through Mrs. Donner's will to Mrs. Denckla and Mrs. Stewart. Before judgment was rendered in the Florida case, Mrs. Hanson instituted a separate suit in Delaware seeking a declaratory judgment that the appointment of the $400,000 to her two children was valid. The Delaware court held, contrary to the holding by the Florida court, that the appointment was valid. The consequence of the Delaware judgment was to give the $400,000 to the two children of Mrs. Hanson rather than to Mrs. Hanson's two sisters.

The Florida case went to final judgment before the Delaware case was concluded. Mrs. Denkla and Mrs. Stewart argued in the Delaware court that the Florida judgment was binding, on the ground that the Delaware court was constitutionally required to give full faith and credit to a valid final judgment of a court of its sister state. The United States Supreme Court held that the Florida court did not have *in rem* jurisdiction over the assets of Mrs. Donner's trust (which had been established in Delaware), and did not have *in personam* jurisdiction over the Delaware trustee. The Court held that under Florida law the trustee was an indispensable party to the Florida suit.

Since there was no jurisdiction over the trustee or the trust, the Florida judgment was invalid and not entitled to full faith and credit.

The Court distinguished *McGee*, and refused to extend without limit "the trend of expanding personal jurisdiction over nonresidents." "[I]t is a mistake to assume that this trend heralds the eventual demise of all restrictions on the personal jurisdiction of state courts. Those restrictions are more than a guarantee of immunity from inconvenient or distant litigation. They are the consequence of territorial limitations on the power of the respective States * * *. The defendant trust company has no office in Florida, and transacts no business there. None of the trust assets has ever been held or administered in Florida, and the record discloses no solicitation of business in that State either in person or by mail." 357 U.S. at 250–51.

Despite what the Supreme Court wrote, it is difficult to see a clear distinction between *McGee* and *Hanson v. Denckla*. After she moved to Florida, Mrs. Donner conducted business with the Delaware trustee and regularly received payments from the trust. Further, to conclude that no trust assets were in Florida was to give a definite "situs" to intangible property (here, securities) much as the Court did in *Harris v. Balk*. At the very least, *Hanson v. Denckla* was a close case. Because it was a close case, the result may have been determined by the clear sympathy of the Court for Mrs. Hanson and its equally clear distaste for her sisters, Mrs. Denckla and Mrs. Stewart. (For example, see the following sentence from the Court's opinion: "Residuary legatees Denckla and Stewart, already the recipients of over $500,000 each, urge that the power of appointment over the $400,000 appointed to sister Elizabeth's children was not 'effectively exercised' and that the property should accordingly pass to them." Id. at 240.)

Hard cases like *Hanson v. Denckla* often make bad law but good stories. For two additional stories (one classic and one modern) of three daughters and disputes over inheritance, see W. Shakespeare, King Lear (circa 1603–06); J. Smiley, A Thousand Acres (1991).

5.   Too simplistic? Is it too simplistic to say that jurisdiction must be either "general" or "specific"? These are labels for polar positions on the jurisdictional spectrum. Is there a danger that the cases in between will be analyzed as either one or the other, losing the subtlety of the formulation actually employed by Justice Stone in *International Shoe*?

World-Wide Volkswagen Corp. v. Woodson

Supreme Court of the United States, 1980.
444 U.S. 286, 100 S.Ct. 559, 62 L.Ed.2d 490.

■ MR. JUSTICE WHITE delivered the opinion of the Court.

The issue before us is whether, consistently with the Due Process Clause of the Fourteenth Amendment, an Oklahoma court may exercise *in personam* jurisdiction over a nonresident automobile retailer and its wholesale distributor in a products-liability action, when the defendants' only connection with Oklahoma is the fact that an automobile sold in New York to New York residents became involved in an accident in Oklahoma.

I

Respondents Harry and Kay Robinson purchased a new Audi automobile from petitioner Seaway Volkswagen, Inc. (Seaway), in

Facts

Massena, N.Y., in 1976. The following year the Robinson family, who resided in New York, left that State for a new home in Arizona. As they passed through the State of Oklahoma, another car struck their Audi in the rear, causing a fire which severely burned Kay Robinson and her two children.

The Robinsons subsequently brought a products-liability action in the District Court for Creek County, Okla., claiming that their injuries resulted from defective design and placement of the Audi's gas tank and fuel system. They joined as defendants the automobile's manufacturer, Audi NSU Auto Union Aktiengesellschaft (Audi); its importer Volkswagen of America, Inc. (Volkswagen); its regional distributor, petitioner World-Wide Volkswagen Corp. (World-Wide); and its retail dealer, petitioner Seaway. Seaway and World-Wide entered special appearances,[3] claiming that Oklahoma's exercise of jurisdiction over them would offend the limitations on the State's jurisdiction imposed by the Due Process Clause of the Fourteenth Amendment.

The facts presented to the District Court showed that World-Wide is incorporated and has its business office in New York. It distributes vehicles, parts, and accessories, under contract with Volkswagen, to retail dealers in New York, New Jersey, and Connecticut. Seaway, one of these retail dealers, is incorporated and has its place of business in New York. Insofar as the record reveals, Seaway and World-Wide are fully independent corporations whose relations with each other and with Volkswagen and Audi are contractual only. Respondents adduced no evidence that either World-Wide or Seaway does any business in Oklahoma, ships or sells any products to or in that State, has an agent to receive process there, or purchases advertisements in any media calculated to reach Oklahoma. In fact, as respondents' counsel conceded at oral argument, Tr. of Oral Arg. 32, there was no showing that any automobile sold by World-Wide or Seaway has ever entered Oklahoma with the single exception of the vehicle involved in the present case.

Despite the apparent *smaller or insufficient quantities* paucity of contacts between petitioners and Oklahoma, the District Court rejected their constitutional claim and reaffirmed that ruling in denying petitioners' motion for reconsideration. Petitioners then sought a writ of prohibition in the Supreme Court of Oklahoma to restrain the District Judge, respondent Charles S. Woodson, from exercising *in personam* jurisdiction over them. * * *

* * *

II

The Due Process Clause of the Fourteenth Amendment limits the power of a state court to render a valid personal judgment against a nonresident defendant. Kulko v. California Superior Court, 436 U.S. 84, 91, 98 S.Ct. 1690, 1696, 56 L.Ed.2d 132 (1978). A judgment rendered in violation of due process is void in the rendering State and is not entitled to full faith and credit elsewhere. Pennoyer v. Neff, 95 U.S. 714, 732–733, 24 L.Ed. 565 (1878). Due process requires that the defendant be given adequate notice of the suit, Mullane v. Central Hanover Trust Co., 339

---

[3]   Volkswagen also entered a special appearance in the District Court, but unlike World-Wide and Seaway did not seek review in the Supreme Court of Oklahoma and is not a petitioner here. Both Volkswagen and Audi remain as defendants in the litigation pending before the District Court in Oklahoma.

U.S. 306, 313–314, 70 S.Ct. 652, 657, 94 L.Ed. 865 (1950), and be subject to the personal jurisdiction of the court. International Shoe Co. v. Washington, 326 U.S. 310, 66 S.Ct. 154, 90 L.Ed. 95 (1945). In the present case, it is not contended that notice was inadequate; the only question is whether these particular petitioners were subject to the jurisdiction of the Oklahoma courts.

As has long been settled, and as we reaffirm today, a state court may exercise personal jurisdiction over a nonresident defendant only so long as there exist "minimum contacts" between the defendant and the forum State. International Shoe Co. v. Washington, supra, at 316, 66 S.Ct., at 158. The concept of minimum contacts, in turn, can be seen to perform two related, but distinguishable, functions. It protects the defendant against the burdens of litigating in a distant or inconvenient forum. And it acts to ensure that the States through their courts, do not reach out beyond the limits imposed on them by their status as coequal sovereigns in a federal system.

The protection against inconvenient litigation is typically described in terms of "reasonableness" or "fairness." We have said that the defendant's contacts with the forum State must be such that maintenance of the suit "does not offend 'traditional notions of fair play and substantial justice.' " International Shoe Co. v. Washington, supra, at 316, 66 S.Ct., at 158, quoting Milliken v. Meyer, 311 U.S. 457, 463, 61 S.Ct. 339, 342, 85 L.Ed. 278 (1940). The relationship between the defendant and the forum must be such that it is "reasonable . . . to require the corporation to defend the particular suit which is brought there." 326 U.S., at 317, 66 S.Ct., at 158. Implicit in this emphasis on reasonableness is the understanding that the burden on the defendant, while always a primary concern, will in an appropriate case be considered in light of other relevant factors, including the forum State's interest in adjudicating the dispute, see McGee v. International Life Ins. Co., 355 U.S. 220, 223, 78 S.Ct. 199, 201, 2 L.Ed.2d 223 (1957); the plaintiff's interest in obtaining convenient and effective relief, see Kulko v. California Superior Court, supra, 436 U.S., at 92, 98 S.Ct., at 1697, at least when that interest is not adequately protected by the plaintiff's power to choose the forum, cf. Shaffer v. Heitner, 433 U.S. 186, 211, n. 37, 97 S.Ct. 2569, 2583, n. 37, 53 L.Ed.2d 683 (1977); the interstate judicial system's interest in obtaining the most efficient resolution of controversies; and the shared interest of the several States in furthering fundamental substantive social policies, see Kulko v. California Superior Court, supra, 436 U.S., at 93, 98, 98 S.Ct., at 1697, 1700.

The limits imposed on state jurisdiction by the Due Process Clause, in its role as a guarantor against inconvenient litigation, have been substantially relaxed over the years. As we noted in McGee v. International Life Ins. Co., supra, 355 U.S., at 222–223, 78 S.Ct., at 201, this trend is largely attributable to a fundamental transformation in the American economy:

"Today many commercial transactions touch two or more States and may involve parties separated by the full continent. With this increasing nationalization of commerce has come a great increase in the amount of business conducted by mail across state lines. At the same time modern transportation and communication have made it much less burdensome for a party sued to defend himself in a State where he engages in economic activity."

The historical developments noted in *McGee,* of course, have only accelerated in the generation since that case was decided.

Nevertheless, we have never accepted the proposition that state lines are irrelevant for jurisdictional purposes, nor could we, and remain faithful to the principles of interstate federalism embodied in the Constitution. The economic interdependence of the States was foreseen and desired by the Framers. In the Commerce Clause, they provided that the Nation was to be a common market, a "free trade unit" in which the States are debarred from acting as separable economic entities. H.P. Hood & Sons, Inc. v. Du Mond, 336 U.S. 525, 538, 69 S.Ct. 657, 665, 93 L.Ed. 865 (1949). But the Framers also intended that the States retain many essential attributes of sovereignty, including, in particular, the sovereign power to try causes in their courts. The sovereignty of each State, in turn, implied a limitation on the sovereignty of all of its sister States—a limitation express or implicit in both the original scheme of the Constitution and the Fourteenth Amendment.

Hence, even while abandoning the shibboleth that "[t]he authority of every tribunal is necessarily restricted by the territorial limits of the State in which it is established," Pennoyer v. Neff, supra, 95 U.S., at 720, we emphasized that the reasonableness of asserting jurisdiction over the defendant must be assessed "in the context of our federal system of government," International Shoe Co. v. Washington, 326 U.S., at 317, 66 S.Ct., at 158, and stressed that the Due Process Clause ensures not only fairness, but also the "orderly administration of the laws," id., at 319, 66 S.Ct., at 159. As we noted in Hanson v. Denckla, 357 U.S. 235, 250–251, 78 S.Ct. 1228, 2 L.Ed.2d 1283 (1958):

> "As technological progress has increased the flow of commerce between the States, the need for jurisdiction over nonresidents has undergone a similar increase. At the same time, progress in communications and transportation has made the defense of a suit in a foreign tribunal less burdensome. In response to these changes, the requirements for personal jurisdiction over nonresidents have evolved from the rigid rule of Pennoyer v. Neff, 95 U.S. 714, 24 L.Ed. 565, to the flexible standard of International Shoe Co. v. Washington, 326 U.S. 310, 66 S.Ct. 154, 90 L.Ed. 95. But it is a mistake to assume that this trend heralds the eventual demise of all restrictions on the personal jurisdiction of state courts. [Citation omitted.] Those restrictions are more than a guarantee of immunity from inconvenient or distant litigation. They are a consequence of territorial limitations on the power of the respective States."

Thus, the Due Process Clause "does not contemplate that a state may make binding a judgment *in personam* against an individual or corporate defendant with which the state has no contacts, ties, or relations." International Shoe Co. v. Washington, 326 U.S., at 319, 66 S.Ct., at 159. Even if the defendant would suffer minimal or no inconvenience from being forced to litigate before the tribunals of another State; even if the forum State has a strong interest in applying its law to the controversy; even if the forum State is the most convenient location for litigation, the

Due Process Clause, acting as an instrument of interstate federalism, may sometimes act to divest the State of its power to render a valid judgment. Hanson v. Denckla, supra, 357 U.S., at 251, 254, 78 S.Ct., at 1238, 1240.

III

Applying these principles to the case at hand,[10] we find in the record before us a total absence of those affiliating circumstances that are a necessary predicate to any exercise of state-court jurisdiction. Petitioners carry on no activity whatsoever in Oklahoma. They close no sales and perform no services there. They avail themselves of none of the privileges and benefits of Oklahoma law. They solicit no business there either through salespersons or through advertising reasonably calculated to reach the State. Nor does the record show that they regularly sell cars at wholesale or retail to Oklahoma customers or residents or that they indirectly, through others, serve or seek to serve the Oklahoma market. In short, respondents seek to base jurisdiction on one, isolated occurrence and whatever inferences can be drawn therefrom: the fortuitous circumstance that a single Audi automobile, sold in New York to New York residents, happened to suffer an accident while passing through Oklahoma.

It is argued, however, that because an automobile is mobile by its very design and purpose it was "foreseeable" that the Robinsons' Audi would cause injury in Oklahoma. Yet "foreseeability" alone has never been a sufficient benchmark for personal jurisdiction under the Due Process Clause. In *Hanson v. Denckla,* supra, it was no doubt foreseeable that the settlor of a Delaware trust would subsequently move to Florida and seek to exercise a power of appointment there; yet we held that Florida courts could not constitutionally exercise jurisdiction over a Delaware trustee that had no other contacts with the forum State. In Kulko v. California Superior Court, 436 U.S. 84, 98 S.Ct. 1690, 56 L.Ed.2d 132 (1978), it was surely "foreseeable" that a divorced wife would move to California from New York, the domicile of the marriage, and that a minor daughter would live with the mother. Yet we held that California could not exercise jurisdiction in a child-support action over the former husband who had remained in New York.

If foreseeability were the criterion, a local California tire retailer could be forced to defend in Pennsylvania when a blowout occurs there, see Erlanger Mills, Inc. v. Cohoes Fibre Mills, Inc., 239 F.2d 502, 507 (C.A.4 1956); a Wisconsin seller of a defective automobile jack could be haled before a district court for damage caused in New Jersey, Reilly v. Phil Tolkan Pontiac, Inc., 372 F. Supp. 1205 (D.N.J.1974); or a Florida soft-drink concessionaire could be summoned to Alaska to account for injuries happening there, see Uppgren v. Executive Aviation Services, Inc., 304 F. Supp. 165, 170–171 (D.Minn.1969). Every seller of chattels would in effect appoint the chattel his agent for service of process. His

---

[10] Respondents argue, as a threshold matter, that petitioners waived any objections to personal jurisdiction by (1) joining with their special appearances a challenge to the District Court's subject-matter jurisdiction, see n. 4, supra, and (2) taking depositions on the merits of the case in Oklahoma. The trial court, however, characterized the appearances as "special," and the Oklahoma Supreme Court, rather than finding jurisdiction waived, reached and decided the statutory and constitutional questions. Cf. Kulko v. California Superior Court, 436 U.S. 84, 91, n. 5, 98 S.Ct. 1690, 1696, n. 5, 56 L.Ed.2d 132 (1978).

amenability to suit would travel with the chattel. We recently abandoned the outworn rule of Harris v. Balk, 198 U.S. 215, 25 S.Ct. 625, 49 L.Ed. 1023 (1905), that the interest of a creditor in a debt could be extinguished or otherwise affected by any State having transitory jurisdiction over the debtor. Shaffer v. Heitner, 433 U.S. 186, 97 S.Ct. 2569, 53 L.Ed.2d 683 (1977). Having interred the mechanical rule that a creditor's amenability to a *quasi in rem* action travels with his debtor, we are unwilling to endorse an analogous principle in the present case.[11]

This is not to say, of course, that foreseeability is wholly irrelevant. But the foreseeability that is critical to due process analysis is not the mere likelihood that a product will find its way into the forum State. Rather, it is that the defendant's conduct and connection with the forum State are such that he should reasonably anticipate being haled into court there. See Kulko v. California Superior Court, supra, 436 U.S., at 97–98, 98 S.Ct., at 1699–1700; Shaffer v. Heitner, 433 U.S., at 216, 97 S.Ct., at 2586, and see id., at 217–219, 97 S.Ct., at 2586–2587 (Stevens, J., concurring in judgment). The Due Process Clause, by ensuring the "orderly administration of the laws," International Shoe Co. v. Washington, 326 U.S., at 319, 66 S.Ct., at 159, gives a degree of predictability to the legal system that allows potential defendants to structure their primary conduct with some minimum assurance as to where that conduct will and will not render them liable to suit.

When a corporation "purposefully avails itself of the privilege of conducting activities within the forum State," Hanson v. Denckla, 357 U.S., at 253, 78 S.Ct., at 1240, it has clear notice that it is subject to suit there, and can act to alleviate the risk of burdensome litigation by procuring insurance, passing the expected costs on to customers, or, if the risks are too great, severing its connection with the State. Hence if the sale of a product of a manufacturer or distributor such as Audi or Volkswagen is not simply an isolated occurrence, but arises from the efforts of the manufacturer or distributor to serve directly or indirectly, the market for its product in other States, it is not unreasonable to subject it to suit in one of those States if its allegedly defective merchandise has there been the source of injury to its owner or to others. The forum State does not exceed its powers under the Due Process Clause if it asserts personal jurisdiction over a corporation that delivers its products into the stream of commerce with the expectation that they will be purchased by consumers in the forum State. Cf. Gray v. American Radiator & Standard Sanitary Corp., 22 Ill.2d 432, 176 N.E.2d 761 (1961).

But there is no such or similar basis for Oklahoma jurisdiction over World-Wide or Seaway in this case. Seaway's sales are made in Massena,

---

[11] Respondents' counsel, at oral argument, see Tr. of Oral Arg. 19–22, 29, sought to limit the reach of the foreseeability standard by suggesting that there is something unique about automobiles. It is true that automobiles are uniquely mobile, see Tyson v. Whitaker & Son, Inc., 407 A.2d 1, 6, and n. 11 (Me.1979) (McKusick, C.J.), that they did play a crucial role in the expansion of personal jurisdiction through the fiction of implied consent, e.g., Hess v. Pawloski, 274 U.S. 352, 47 S.Ct. 632, 71 L.Ed. 1091 (1927), and that some of the cases have treated the automobile as a "dangerous instrumentality." But today, under the regime of *International Shoe,* we see no difference for jurisdictional purposes between an automobile and any other chattel. The "dangerous instrumentality" concept apparently was never used to support personal jurisdiction; and to the extent it has relevance today it bears not on jurisdiction but on the possible desirability of imposing substantive principles of tort law such as strict liability.

N.Y. World-Wide's market, although substantially larger, is limited to dealers in New York, New Jersey, and Connecticut. There is no evidence of record that any automobiles distributed by World-Wide are sold to retail customers outside this tristate area. It is foreseeable that the purchasers of automobiles sold by World-Wide and Seaway may take them to Oklahoma. But the mere "unilateral activity of those who claim some relationship with a nonresident defendant cannot satisfy the requirement of contact with the forum State." Hanson v. Denckla, supra, at 253, 78 S.Ct., at 1239–1240.

In a variant on the previous argument, it is contended that jurisdiction can be supported by the fact that petitioners earn substantial revenue from goods used in Oklahoma. The Oklahoma Supreme Court so found, 585 P.2d, at 354–355, drawing the inference that because one automobile sold by petitioners had been used in Oklahoma, others might have been used there also. While this inference seems less than compelling on the facts of the instant case, we need not question the court's factual findings in order to reject its reasoning.

This argument seems to make the point that the purchase of automobiles in New York, from which the petitioners earn substantial revenue, would not occur *but for* the fact that the automobiles are capable of use in distant States like Oklahoma. Respondents observe that the very purpose of an automobile is to travel, and that travel of automobiles sold by petitioners is facilitated by an extensive chain of Volkswagen service centers throughout the country, including some in Oklahoma. However, financial benefits accruing to the defendant from a collateral relation to the forum State will not support jurisdiction if they do not stem from a constitutionally cognizable contact with that State. See Kulko v. California Superior Court, 436 U.S., at 94–95, 98 S.Ct., at 1698–1699. In our view, whatever marginal revenues petitioners may receive by virtue of the fact that their products are capable of use in Oklahoma is far too attenuated a contact to justify that State's exercise of *in personam* jurisdiction over them.

Because we find that petitioners have no "contacts, ties, or relations" with the State of Oklahoma, *International Shoe Co. v. Washington*, supra, 326 U.S., at 319, 66 S.Ct., at 159, the judgment of the Supreme Court of Oklahoma is

Reversed.

■ MR. JUSTICE BRENNAN, dissenting.

     * * *

I

     * * * [The Court accords] too little weight to the strength of the forum State's interest in the case and fail to explore whether there would be any actual inconvenience to the defendant. The essential inquiry in locating the constitutional limits on state court jurisdiction over absent defendants is whether the particular exercise of jurisdiction offends " 'traditional notions of fair play and substantial justice.' "

     * * *

II

B

* * * [T]he interest of the forum State and its connection to the litigation is strong. The automobile accident under the litigation occurred in Oklahoma. The plaintiffs were hospitalized in Oklahoma when they brought suit. Essential witnesses and evidence were in Oklahoma. The State has a legitimate interest in enforcing its laws designed to keep its highway system safe, and the trial can proceed at least as efficiently in Oklahoma as anywhere else.

The petitioners are not unconnected with the forum. Although both sell automobiles within limited sales territories, each sold the automobile which in fact was driven to Oklahoma where it was involved in an accident. It may be true, as the Court suggests, that each sincerely intended to limit its commercial impact to the limited territory, and that each intended to accept the benefits and protection of the laws only of those States within the territory. But obviously these were unrealistic hopes that cannot be treated as an automatic constitutional shield.

An automobile simply is not a stationary item or one designed to be used in one place. An automobile is *intended* to be moved around. Someone in the business of selling large numbers of automobiles can hardly plead ignorance of their mobility or pretend that the automobiles stay put after they are sold. It is not merely that a dealer in automobiles foresees that they will move. * * * The dealer actually intends that the purchaser will use the automobile to travel to distant States where the dealer does not directly "do business." The sale of an automobile does *purposefully* inject the vehicle into the stream of interstate commerce so that it can travel to distant States. * * *

* * *

Thus, the Court errs in its conclusion * * * that "petitioners have *no* 'contacts, ties or relations' " with Oklahoma. There obviously are contacts, and, given Oklahoma's connection to the litigation, the contacts are sufficiently significant to make it fair and reasonable for the petitioners to submit to Oklahoma's jurisdiction.

III

* * *

In answering the question whether or not it is fair and reasonable to allow a particular forum to hold a trial binding on a particular defendant, the interests of the forum State and other parties loom large in today's world and surely are entitled to as much weight as are the interests of the defendant. The "orderly administration of the laws" provides a firm basis for according some protection to the interests of plaintiffs and States as well as of defendants. Certainly, I cannot see how a defendant's right to due process is violated if the defendant suffers no inconvenience. * * *

The conclusion I draw is that constitutional concepts of fairness no longer require the extreme concern for defendants that was once necessary. Rather, as I wrote in dissent in Shaffer v. Heitner, [433 U.S., at 220 (1977)] (emphasis added), minimum contacts must exist "among the *parties*, the contested transaction, and the forum state."

* * *

The plaintiffs in each of these cases brought suit in a forum in which they had significant contacts and which had significant contacts with the litigation. I am not convinced that the defendants would suffer and "heavy and disproportionate burden" in defending the suits. Accordingly, I would hold that the Constitution should not shield the defendants from appearing and defending in the plaintiffs' chosen forum.

[The dissenting opinions of Justices Marshall and Blackmun are omitted.]

NOTES AND QUESTIONS

1. **Why did the Robinsons care?** Why did the Robinsons fight so hard to keep World-Wide Volkswagen and Seaway in the case? There are four potential defendants in the case: Audi, the manufacturer; Volkswagen of America, the nation-wide importer; World-Wide Volkswagen, the regional distributor for New York, New Jersey, and Connecticut; and Seaway, the local retailer in Massena, New York. Audi did not contest jurisdiction in Oklahoma. Volkswagen of America contested jurisdiction, but lost in the state court, and did not pursue the question to the Supreme Court. Only World-Wide and Seaway sought review in the Supreme Court.

It is easy to see why World-Wide and Seaway sought to escape jurisdiction in Oklahoma. They did not want to defend there, or indeed at all. If they could successfully object to appearing in Oklahoma, the worst that could have happened is that they would have had to defend a suit closer to home, probably in New York. The best (and most likely) thing that could have happened is that the plaintiffs would have pursued only their Oklahoma suit against Audi or Volkswagen of America. It is harder to see why the Robinsons wanted to keep World-Wide and Seaway in the Oklahoma suit. Recall that this was a product liability case in which, if liability were found, Audi and Volkswagen of America would be liable to pay the full amount of damages. There was no question about the ability of Audi and Volkswagen of America to pay any judgment, and there appear to have been no difficulties about access to proof that would have been ameliorated by having World-Wide and Seaway as defendants. Why, then, did the Robinsons incur considerable expense and delay in trying to keep Seaway and World-Wide Volkswagen in the litigation?

The answer has nothing to do with personal jurisdiction, deep pockets, or access to proof. It has to do, instead, with the place within Oklahoma where the trial would take place. You need to know a little about the subject matter jurisdiction of the federal courts to understand how this worked. (Subject matter jurisdiction will be treated in detail later in this chapter.) The suit was filed in state court in Creek County, Oklahoma. The Robinsons were citizens of New York. (Until they established their new home in Arizona, they retained the citizenship of their former home state.) Audi and Volkswagen of America were foreign citizens. If the suit were filed only against Audi and Volkswagen of America, there would be "complete diversity" of citizenship between the plaintiffs and the defendants, and the defendants would be entitled to remove the suit from state to federal court. World-Wide and Seaway were both citizens of New York. If they were added as defendants, there would not be complete diversity between the plaintiffs and the defendants, and the defendants would have had to stay in state court.

Why did the plaintiffs care whether the suit was tried in state or federal court? There are differences in procedures between state and federal courts that sometimes affect a litigant's choice of forum, but that is not the explanation here. Rather, the answer lies in the geographical location of the two courts. Creek County, where the state court suit was filed, is immediately to the southwest of Tulsa. The nearest federal court is in Tulsa itself. If the suit had been removed from state to federal court, it would have been removed from the Creek County courthouse to the federal courthouse in Tulsa. The jury pools in the two locations were very different, and Creek County juries were much more favorable to plaintiffs than Tulsa juries. In the words of the Robinson's lawyer, "Creek County, Oklahoma, * * * is one of the best jurisdictions in the United States in which to try a plaintiff's lawsuit. It ranks on a par with Dade County, Florida, and Cook County, Illinois * * *." Weintraub, Due Process Limitations on the Personal Jurisdiction of State Courts: Time for Change, 63 Or. L. Rev. 485, 500 n. 98 (1984).

After the Supreme Court denied *in personam* jurisdiction over World-Wide and Seaway, the remaining defendants, as expected, removed the suit to federal court. After trial in federal court in Tulsa, a verdict for defendants was returned, most probably on the ground that the explosion of the gas tank resulted from negligent action of the driver who had hit the Robinsons' car rather than from a design defect in their Audi. The other driver had been traveling at a speed between 90 and 100 miles per hour at the time of the collision. A. Lowenfeld, Conflict of Laws 565 (1986).

2.   Is foreseeability circular? Justice White says that foreseeability of litigation affects the jurisdictional decision. In his words, the question is whether "the defendant's conduct and connection with the forum State are such that he should reasonably anticipate being haled into court there." Is this analysis circular? Doesn't the reasonable expectation of the defendant depend on what the Court says about the nature of conduct and connections necessary to create jurisdiction? Or is Justice White saying more than that? Is he referring to a defendant's intuitive expectation and sense of fairness? Such an intuition could be informed, of course, by how the United States Supreme Court has treated comparable cases. But the Court's decisions need not be the only thing that would inform the defendant's expectation and sense of fairness. Should we distinguish between sophisticated "repeat players" with strong incentives to structure their behavior in accordance with legal advice, on the one hand, and individual litigants who would not ordinarily seek legal advice, on the other? If we do differentiate between defendants in this way, how would you characterize the defendants in *World-Wide Volkswagen*?

3.   Jurisdiction over Audi and Volkswagen of America. Is it obvious that *in personam* jurisdiction existed in Oklahoma over Audi and Volkswagen of America? What factors led to a finding of jurisdiction over them? Is this "general jurisdiction"? Before you settle on an answer to this last question, ask yourself whether an Idaho-based Audi dealer who had been involved in a contract dispute with Audi in Idaho should be allowed to sue Audi in Oklahoma.

4.   Due Process and federalism. Justice White writes in *World-Wide Volkswagen*, "The concept of minimum contacts * * * can be seen to perform two related, but distinguishable, functions. It protects the defendant against the burdens of litigating in a distant or inconvenient forum. And it acts to ensure that the States, through their courts, do not reach out beyond the limits imposed on them by their status as coequal sovereigns in a federal system." Two years later, Justice White appeared to back away from that statement, writing in a footnote in Insurance Corp. of Ireland v. Compagnie des Bauxites de Guinee, 456 U.S. 694, 702 n.10, 102 S.Ct. 2099, 72 L.Ed.2d 492 (1982), "It is true that we have stated that the requirement of personal jurisdiction, as applied to state courts, reflects an element of federalism and the character of state sovereignty vis-a-vis other States * * *. The restriction on state sovereign power described in World-Wide Volkswagen Corp., however, must be seen as ultimately a function of the individual liberty interest preserved by the Due Process Clause. That Clause is the only source of the personal jurisdiction requirement and the Clause itself makes no mention of federalism concerns. Furthermore, if the federalism concept operated as an independent restriction on the sovereign power of the court, it would not be possible to waive the personal jurisdiction requirement: Individual actions cannot change the powers of sovereignty, although the individual can subject himself to powers from which he may otherwise be protected."

Justice White says that the Due Process Clause does not mention federalism. Should it have to? Justice Field, writing in *Pennoyer*, pretty clearly thought the clause limited the sovereign power of the states. Is Justice White saying that Justice Field got it wrong? Or that he himself got it wrong in *World-Wide Volkswagen*? As a matter of original intention of the adopters of the Fourteenth Amendment? As a matter of "plain meaning" of the phrase "due process"?

5.   Justice Brennan's dissent a foreshadowing of the Court's opinion in *Burger King*. Justice Brennan, in dissent in *World-Wide Volkswagen*, argues for a more flexible test that would consider not only the connection between the defendant and the forum. He would also consider the connection between the plaintiff and the forum, the interest of the forum in adjudicating the case, and the degree of burden on the defendant. Would Justice Brennan's test be less determinate or less fair than the test employed by the Court? Recall Justice Brennan's dissent when you read the Court's opinion in *Burger King Corp. v. Rudzewicz*, immediately following, and then again when you read the Court's opinion in *J. McIntyre Machinery v. Nicastro*, infra p. 99. For a suggestion that the Court adopt a test of "proportionality," whereby the degree of burden imposed on the defendant would be weighed against the number and quality of contacts with the forum state, see McMunigal, Desert, Utility, and Minimum Contacts: Toward a Mixed Theory of Personal Jurisdiction, 108 Yale L.J. 189 (1998).

b.   MINIMUM CONTACTS: SPECIFIC JURISDICTION

Burger King Corp. v. Rudzewicz

Supreme Court of the United States, 1985.
471 U.S. 462, 105 S.Ct. 2174, 85 L.Ed.2d 528.

■ JUSTICE BRENNAN delivered the opinion of the Court.

The State of Florida's long-arm statute extends jurisdiction to "[a]ny person, whether or not a citizen or resident of this state," who, inter alia, "[b]reach[es] a contract in this state by failing to perform acts required by the contract to be performed in this state," so long as the cause of action arises from the alleged contractual breach. Fla.Stat. § 48.193(1)(g) (Supp.1984). The United States District Court for the Southern District of Florida, sitting in diversity, relied on this provision in exercising personal jurisdiction over a Michigan resident who allegedly had breached a franchise agreement with a Florida corporation by failing to make required payments in Florida. The question presented is whether this exercise of long-arm jurisdiction offended "traditional conception[s] of fair play and substantial justice" embodied in the Due Process Clause of the Fourteenth Amendment. International Shoe Co. v. Washington, 326 U.S. 310, 320, 66 S.Ct. 154, 160, 90 L.Ed. 95 (1945).

I

A

Burger King Corporation is a Florida corporation whose principal offices are in Miami. It is one of the world's largest restaurant organizations, with over 3,000 outlets in the 50 States, the Commonwealth of Puerto Rico, and 8 foreign nations. Burger King conducts approximately 80% of its business through a franchise operation that the company styles the "Burger King System"—"a comprehensive restaurant format and operating system for the sale of uniform and quality food products." * * * Burger King licenses its franchisees to use its trademarks and service marks for a period of 20 years and leases standardized restaurant facilities to them for the same term. In addition, franchisees acquire a variety of proprietary information concerning the "standards, specifications, procedures and methods for operating a Burger King Restaurant." * * * They also receive market research and advertising assistance; ongoing training in restaurant management;[2] and accounting, cost-control, and inventory-control guidance. By permitting franchisees to tap into Burger King's established national reputation and to benefit from proven procedures for dispensing standardized fare, this system enables them to go into the restaurant business with significantly lowered barriers to entry.

In exchange for these benefits, franchisees pay Burger King an initial $40,000 franchise fee and commit themselves to payment of monthly royalties, advertising and sales promotion fees, and rent computed in part from monthly gross sales. Franchisees also agree to submit to the national organization's exacting regulation of virtually every conceivable aspect of their operations. Burger King imposes these standards and undertakes its rigid regulation out of conviction that "[u]niformity of service, appearance, and quality of product is essential to the preservation of the Burger King image and the benefits accruing therefrom to both Franchisee and Franchisor." * * *

Burger King oversees its franchise system through a two-tiered administrative structure. The governing contracts provide that the franchise relationship is established in Miami and governed by Florida law, and call for payment of all required fees and forwarding of all relevant notices to the Miami headquarters. The Miami headquarters sets policy and works directly with its franchisees in attempting to

---

[2]   Mandatory training seminars are conducted at Burger King University in Miami and at Whopper College Regional Training Centers around the country. * * *

resolve major problems. * * * Day-to-day monitoring of franchisees, however, is conducted through a network of 10 district offices which in turn report to the Miami headquarters.

The instant litigation grows out of Burger King's termination of one of its franchisees, and is aptly described by the franchisee as "a divorce proceeding among commercial partners." * * * The appellee John Rudzewicz, a Michigan citizen and resident, is the senior partner in a Detroit accounting firm. In 1978, he was approached by Brian MacShara, the son of a business acquaintance, who suggested that they jointly apply to Burger King for a franchise in the Detroit area. MacShara proposed to serve as the manager of the restaurant if Rudzewicz would put up the investment capital; in exchange, the two would evenly share the profits. Believing that MacShara's idea offered attractive investment and tax-deferral opportunities, Rudzewicz agreed to the venture. * * *

Rudzewicz and MacShara jointly applied for a franchise to Burger King's Birmingham, Michigan district office in the autumn of 1978. Their application was forwarded to Burger King's Miami headquarters, which entered into a preliminary agreement with them in February 1979. During the ensuing four months it was agreed that Rudzewicz and MacShara would assume operation of an existing facility in Drayton Plains, Michigan. MacShara attended the prescribed management courses in Miami during this period, see n. 2, supra, and the franchisees purchased $165,000 worth of restaurant equipment from Burger King's Davmor Industries division in Miami. Even before the final agreements were signed, however, the parties began to disagree over site-development fees, building design, computation of monthly rent, and whether the franchisees would be able to assign their liabilities to a corporation they had formed. During these disputes Rudzewicz and MacShara negotiated both with the Birmingham district office and with the Miami headquarters. With some misgivings, Rudzewicz and MacShara finally obtained limited concessions from the Miami headquarters, signed the final agreements, and commenced operations in June 1979. By signing the final agreements, Rudzewicz obligated himself personally to payments exceeding $1 million over the 20-year franchise relationship.

The Drayton Plains facility apparently enjoyed steady business during the summer of 1979, but patronage declined after a recession began later that year. Rudzewicz and MacShara soon fell far behind in their monthly payments to Miami. Headquarters sent notices of default, and an extended period of negotiations began among the franchisees, the Birmingham district office, and the Miami headquarters. After several Burger King officials in Miami had engaged in prolonged but ultimately unsuccessful negotiations with the franchisees by mail and by telephone, headquarters terminated the franchise and ordered Rudzewicz and MacShara to vacate the premises. They refused and continued to occupy and operate the facility as a Burger King restaurant.

B

Burger King commenced the instant action in the United States District Court for the Southern District of Florida in May 1981, invoking that court's diversity jurisdiction pursuant to 28 U.S.C. § 1332(a) and its original jurisdiction over federal trademark disputes pursuant to

§ 1338(a). Burger King alleged that Rudzewicz and MacShara had breached their franchise obligations "within [the jurisdiction of] this district court" by failing to make the required payments "at plaintiff's place of business in Miami, Dade County, Florida," * * * and also charged that they were tortiously infringing its trademarks and service marks through their continued, unauthorized operation as a Burger King restaurant * * *. Burger King sought damages, injunctive relief, and costs and attorney's fees.

* * *

II

A

* * *

We have noted several reasons why a forum legitimately may exercise personal jurisdiction over a nonresident who "purposefully directs" his activities toward forum residents. A State generally has a "manifest interest" in providing its residents with a convenient forum for redressing injuries inflicted by out-of-state actors. Id., at 223, 78 S.Ct., at 201; see also Keeton v. Hustler Magazine, Inc., supra, 465 U.S., at 776, 104 S.Ct., at 1479. Moreover, where individuals "purposefully derive benefit" from their interstate activities, Kulko v. California Superior Court, 436 U.S. 84, 96, 98 S.Ct. 1690, 1699, 56 L.Ed.2d 132 (1978), it may well be unfair to allow them to escape having to account in other States for consequences that arise proximately from such activities; the Due Process Clause may not readily be wielded as a territorial shield to avoid interstate obligations that have been voluntarily assumed. And because "modern transportation and communications have made it much less burdensome for a party sued to defend himself in a State where he engages in economic activity," it usually will not be unfair to subject him to the burdens of litigating in another forum for disputes relating to such activity. McGee v. International Life Insurance Co., supra, 355 U.S., at 223, 78 S.Ct., at 201.

Notwithstanding these considerations, the constitutional touchstone remains whether the defendant purposefully established "minimum contacts" in the forum State. International Shoe Co. v. Washington, supra, 326 U.S., at 316, 66 S.Ct., at 158. Although it has been argued that foreseeability of causing *injury* in another State should be sufficient to establish such contacts there when policy considerations so require,[16] the Court has consistently held that this kind of foreseeability is not a "sufficient benchmark" for exercising personal jurisdiction. World-Wide Volkswagen Corp. v. Woodson, 444 U.S., at 295, 100 S.Ct., at 566. Instead, "the foreseeability that is critical to due process analysis . . . is that the defendant's conduct and connection with the forum State are such that he should reasonably anticipate being haled into court there." Id., at 297, 100 S.Ct., at 567.

Jurisdiction * * * may not be avoided merely because the defendant did not *physically* enter the forum State. Although territorial presence frequently will enhance a potential defendant's affiliation with a State

---

[16] See, e.g., World-Wide Volkswagen Corp. v. Woodson, 444 U.S. 286, 299, 100 S.Ct. 559, 568, 62 L.Ed.2d 490 (1980) (Brennan, J., dissenting); Shaffer v. Heitner, 433 U.S. 186, 219, 97 S.Ct. 2569, 2588, 53 L.Ed.2d 683 (1977) (Brennan, J., concurring in part and dissenting in part).

and reinforce the reasonable foreseeability of suit there, it is an inescapable fact of modern commercial life that a substantial amount of business is transacted solely by mail and wire communications across state lines, thus obviating the need for physical presence within a State in which business is conducted. So long as a commercial actor's efforts are "purposefully directed" toward residents of another State, we have consistently rejected the notion that an absence of physical contacts can defeat personal jurisdiction there. Keeton v. Hustler Magazine, Inc., supra, 465 U.S., at 774–775, 104 S.Ct., at 1478; see also Calder v. Jones, 465 U.S., at 778–790, 104 S.Ct., at 1486–1487; McGee v. International Life Insurance Co., 355 U.S., at 222–223, 78 S.Ct., at 200–201. Cf. Hoopeston Canning Co. v. Cullen, 318 U.S. 313, 317, 63 S.Ct. 602, 605, 87 L.Ed. 777 (1943).

Rule

Once it has been decided that a defendant purposefully established minimum contacts within the forum State, these contacts may be considered in light of other factors to determine whether the assertion of personal jurisdiction would comport with "fair play and substantial justice." International Shoe Co. v. Washington, 326 U.S., at 320, 66 S.Ct., at 160. Thus courts in "appropriate case[s]" may evaluate "the burden on the defendant," "the forum State's interest in adjudicating the dispute," "the plaintiff's interest in obtaining convenient and effective relief," "the interstate judicial system's interest in obtaining the most efficient resolution of controversies," and the "shared interest of the several States in furthering fundamental substantive social policies." World-Wide Volkswagen Corp. v. Woodson, supra, 444 U.S., at 292, 100 S.Ct., at 564. These considerations sometimes serve to establish the reasonableness of jurisdiction upon a lesser showing of minimum contacts than would otherwise be required. See, e.g., Keeton v. Hustler Magazine, Inc., supra, 465 U.S., at 780, 104 S.Ct., at 1481; Calder v. Jones, supra, 465 U.S., at 788–789, 104 S.Ct., at 1486–1487; McGee v. International Life Insurance Co., supra, 355 U.S., at 223–224, 78 S.Ct., at 201–202. On the other hand, where a defendant who purposefully has directed his activities at forum residents seeks to defeat jurisdiction, he must present a compelling case that the presence of some other considerations would render jurisdiction unreasonable.

* * *

B

(1)

* * *

Applying these principles to the case at hand, we believe there is substantial record evidence supporting the District Court's conclusion that the assertion of personal jurisdiction over Rudzewicz in Florida for the alleged breach of his franchise agreement did not offend due process. In this case, no physical ties to Florida can be attributed to Rudzewicz other than MacShara's brief training course in Miami. Rudzewicz did not maintain offices in Florida and, for all that appears from the record, has never even visited there. Yet this franchise dispute grew directly out of "a contract which had a *substantial* connection with that State." McGee v. International Life Insurance Co., 355 U.S., at 223, 78 S.Ct., at 201 (emphasis added). Eschewing the option of operating an independent local enterprise, Rudzewicz deliberately "reach[ed] out beyond" Michigan and negotiated with a Florida corporation for the purchase of a long-term franchise and the manifold benefits that would derive from affiliation with a nationwide organization. Travelers Health Assn. v. Virginia, 339 U.S., at 647, 70 S.Ct., at 929. Upon approval, he entered into a carefully structured 20-year relationship that envisioned continuing and wide-reaching contacts with Burger King in Florida. In light of Rudzewicz's voluntary acceptance of the long-term and exacting regulation of his business from Burger King's Miami headquarters, the "quality and nature" of his relationship to the company in Florida can in no sense be viewed as "random," "fortuitous," or "attenuated." Hanson v. Denckla, 357 U.S., at 253, 78 S.Ct., at 1239; Keeton v. Hustler Magazine, Inc., 465 U.S., at 774, 104 S.Ct., at 1478; World-Wide Volkswagen Corp. v. Woodson, 444 U.S., at 299, 100 S.Ct., at 568. Rudzewicz's refusal to make the contractually required payments in Miami, and his continued use of Burger King's trademarks and confidential business information after his termination, caused foreseeable injuries to the corporation in Florida. For these reasons it was, at the very least, presumptively reasonable for Rudzewicz to be called to account there for such injuries.

* * *

[W]e believe the Court of Appeals gave insufficient weight to provisions in the various franchise documents providing that all disputes would be governed by Florida law. The franchise agreement, for example, stated:

> "This Agreement shall become valid when executed and accepted by BKC at Miami, Florida; it shall be deemed made and entered into in the State of Florida and shall be governed and construed under and in accordance with the laws of the State of Florida. The choice of law designation does not require that all suits concerning this Agreement be filed in Florida."
> * * *

The Court of Appeals reasoned that choice-of-law provisions are irrelevant to the question of personal jurisdiction, relying on Hanson v. Denckla for the proposition that "the center of gravity for choice-of-law purposes does not necessarily confer the sovereign prerogative to assert jurisdiction." 724 F.2d, at 1511–1512, n. 10, citing 357 U.S., at 254, 78 S.Ct., at 1240. This reasoning misperceives the import of the quoted proposition. The Court in *Hanson* and subsequent cases has emphasized that choice-of-law *analysis*—which focuses on all elements of a transaction, and not simply on the defendant's conduct—is distinct from minimum-contacts jurisdictional analysis—which focuses at the threshold solely on the defendant's purposeful connection to the forum.[23] Nothing in our cases, however, suggests that a choice-of-law *provision* should be ignored in considering whether a defendant has "purposefully invoked the benefits and protections of a State's laws" for jurisdictional purposes. Although such a provision standing alone would be insufficient to confer jurisdiction, we believe that, when combined with the 20-year interdependent relationship Rudzewicz established with Burger King's Miami headquarters, it reinforced his deliberate affiliation with the

---

[23] Hanson v. Denckla, 357 U.S., at 253–254, 78 S.Ct., at 1239–1240. See also Keeton v. Hustler Magazine, Inc., 465 U.S., at 778, 104 S.Ct., at 1480; Kulko v. California Superior Court, 436 U.S., at 98, 98 S.Ct., at 1700; Shaffer v. Heitner, 433 U.S., at 215, 97 S.Ct., at 2585.

forum State and the reasonable foreseeability of possible litigation there.
* * *

* * *

* * * Because Rudzewicz established a substantial and continuing relationship with Burger King's Miami headquarters, received fair notice from the contract documents and the course of dealing that he might be subject to suit in Florida, and has failed to demonstrate how jurisdiction in that forum would otherwise be fundamentally unfair, we conclude that the District Court's exercise of jurisdiction pursuant to Florida Stat. § 48.193(1)(g) (Supp.1984) did not offend due process. The judgment of the Court of Appeals is accordingly reversed, and the case is remanded for further proceedings consistent with this opinion.

It is so ordered.

[Justice Powell took no part in the consideration or decision.]

[The dissenting opinion of Justice Stevens, joined by Justice White, is omitted.]

NOTES AND QUESTIONS ON *BURGER KING* AND "MINIMUM CONTACTS"

1. **The *Burger King* formulation: "minimum contacts" and "reasonableness."** *Burger King* does not abandon the "minimum contacts" approach of *International Shoe*, but it provides a somewhat different formulation. Writing for the Court, Justice Brennan states that once minimum contacts are found, "other factors" may be considered. Those factors include the burden on the defendant; the forum state's interest in adjudicating the dispute; the plaintiff's interest in obtaining convenient and effective relief; the interest of the interstate judicial system in efficient resolution of controversies; and the shared interest of the states in furthering fundamental substantive social policies. Depending on the presence or absence of these factors, more or fewer contacts will suffice. These factors allow a court to determine whether the exercise of *in personam* jurisdiction is "reasonable." In the words of the Court, "These considerations sometimes serve to establish the reasonableness of jurisdiction upon a lesser showing of minimum contacts."

2. **Purposeful availment.** The Court holds that Rudzewicz had minimum contacts with Florida. Did he "purposely avail himself of the privilege of conducting activities within the forum State, thus invoking the benefits and protection of its laws"? Should the choice-of-law clause providing that Florida law governs be relevant to a determination of "purposeful availment"? Who do you suppose wrote the clause requiring that Florida law be applied? (Hint: It wasn't Rudzewicz.)

3. **No contractual waiver of objection to jurisdiction.** Sometimes a contract contains a clause by which one of the parties waives objection to *in personam* jurisdiction in a particular forum. There was no such clause in the contract Rudzewicz signed with Burger King. If Rudzewicz had signed a clause agreeing to suit in Florida in any dispute arising out of the franchise agreement, Burger King's ability to sue in Florida would have been beyond question. Why do you suppose Burger King did not put such a clause in the contract?

In 1984, Michigan amended its franchise statute to make illegal any "provision requiring that arbitration or litigation be conducted outside this state." Michigan Compiled Laws § 445.1527(f). How far does this provision go in protecting franchisees in the position of Rudzewicz? Could Michigan have required out-of-state franchisors to agree to bring any suit against in-state franchisees in the state of Michigan?

Asahi Metal Industry Co. v. Superior Court

Supreme Court of the United States, 1987.
480 U.S. 102, 107 S.Ct. 1026, 94 L.Ed.2d 92.

■ JUSTICE O'CONNOR announced the judgment of the Court and delivered the unanimous opinion of the Court with respect to Part I, the opinion of the Court with respect to Part II–B, in which THE CHIEF JUSTICE, JUSTICE BRENNAN, JUSTICE WHITE, JUSTICE MARSHALL, JUSTICE BLACKMUN, JUSTICE POWELL, and JUSTICE STEVENS join, and an opinion with respect to Parts II–A and III, in which THE CHIEF JUSTICE, JUSTICE POWELL, and JUSTICE SCALIA join.

This case presents the question whether the mere awareness on the part of a foreign defendant that the components it manufactured, sold, and delivered outside the United States would reach the forum state in the stream of commerce constitutes "minimum contacts" between the defendant and the forum state such that the exercise of jurisdiction "does not offend 'traditional notions of fair play and substantial justice.' " International Shoe Co. v. Washington, 326 U.S. 310, 316, 66 S.Ct. 154, 158, 90 L.Ed. 95 (1945), quoting Milliken v. Meyer, 311 U.S. 457, 463, 61 S.Ct. 339, 342, 85 L.Ed. 278 (1940).

I

On September 23, 1978, on Interstate Highway 80 in Solano County, California, Gary Zurcher lost control of his Honda motorcycle and collided with a tractor. Zurcher was severely injured, and his passenger and wife, Ruth Ann Moreno, was killed. In September 1979, Zurcher filed a product liability action in the Superior Court of the State of California in and for the County of Solano. Zurcher alleged that the 1978 accident was caused by a sudden loss of air and an explosion in the rear tire of the motorcycle, and alleged that the motorcycle tire, tube, and sealant were defective. Zurcher's complaint named, *inter alia,* Cheng Shin Rubber Industrial Co., Ltd. (Cheng Shin), the Taiwanese manufacturer of the tube. Cheng Shin in turn filed a cross-complaint seeking indemnification from its codefendants and from petitioner, Asahi Metal Industry Co., Ltd. (Asahi), the manufacturer of the tube's valve assembly. Zurcher's claims against Cheng Shin and the other defendants were eventually settled and dismissed, leaving only Cheng Shin's indemnity action against Asahi.

California's long-arm statute authorizes the exercise of jurisdiction "on any basis not inconsistent with the Constitution of this state or of the United States." Cal.Code Civ.Proc.Ann. § 410.10 (West 1973). Asahi moved to quash Cheng Shin's service of summons, arguing the State could not exert jurisdiction over it consistent with the Due Process Clause of the Fourteenth Amendment.

In relation to the motion, the following information was submitted by Asahi and Cheng Shin. Asahi is a Japanese corporation. It manufactures tire valve assemblies in Japan and sells the assemblies to Cheng Shin, and to several other tire manufacturers, for use as components in finished tire tubes. Asahi's sales to Cheng Shin took place in Taiwan. The shipments from Asahi to Cheng Shin were sent from Japan to Taiwan. Cheng Shin bought and incorporated into its tire tubes 150,000 Asahi valve assemblies in 1978; 500,000 in 1979; 500,000 in 1980; 100,000 in 1981; and 100,000 in 1982. Sales to Cheng Shin accounted for 1.24 percent of Asahi's income in 1981 and 0.44 percent in 1982. Cheng Shin alleged that approximately 20 percent of its sales in the United States are in California. Cheng Shin purchases valve assemblies from other suppliers as well, and sells finished tubes throughout the world.

In 1983 an attorney for Cheng Shin conducted an informal examination of the valve stems of the tire tubes sold in one cyclery in Solano County. The attorney declared that of the approximately 115 tire tubes in the store, 97 were purportedly manufactured in Japan or Taiwan, and of those 97, 21 valve stems were marked with the circled letter "A", apparently Asahi's trademark. Of the 21 Asahi valve stems, 12 were incorporated into Cheng Shin tire tubes. The store contained 41 other Cheng Shin tubes that incorporated the valve assemblies of other manufacturers. Declaration of Kenneth B. Shepard in Opposition to Motion to Quash Subpoena, App. to Brief for Respondent 5–6. An affidavit of a manager of Cheng Shin whose duties included the purchasing of component parts stated: " 'In discussions with Asahi regarding the purchase of valve stem assemblies the fact that my Company sells tubes throughout the world and specifically the United States has been discussed. I am informed and believe that Asahi was fully aware that valve stem assemblies sold to my Company and to others would end up throughout the United States and in California.' " 39 Cal.3d 35, 48, n. 4, 216 Cal.Rptr. 385, 392, n. 4, 702 P.2d 543, 549–550, n. 4 (1985). An affidavit of the president of Asahi, on the other hand, declared that Asahi "has never contemplated that its limited sales of tire valves to Cheng Shin in Taiwan would subject it to lawsuits in California." Ibid.
* * *

         * * *

The [Supreme Court of California] observed that "Asahi has no offices, property or agents in California. It solicits no business in California and has made no direct sales [in California]." Id., at 48, 216 Cal.Rptr., at 392, 702 P.2d, at 549. Moreover, "Asahi did not design or control the system of distribution that carried its valve assemblies into California." Id., at 49, 216 Cal.Rptr., at 392, 702 P.2d, at 549. Nevertheless, the court found the exercise of jurisdiction over Asahi to be consistent with the Due Process Clause. It concluded that Asahi knew that some of the valve assemblies sold to Cheng Shin would be incorporated into tire tubes sold in California, and that Asahi benefited indirectly from the sale in California of products incorporating its components. The court considered Asahi's intentional act of placing its components into the stream of commerce—that is, by delivering the components to Cheng Shin in Taiwan—coupled with Asahi's awareness that some of the components would eventually find their way into

California, sufficient to form the basis for state court jurisdiction under the Due Process Clause.

We granted certiorari, 475 U.S. 1044, 106 S.Ct. 1258, 89 L.Ed.2d 569 (1986), and now reverse.

II

A

The Due Process Clause of the Fourteenth Amendment limits the power of a state court to exert personal jurisdiction over a nonresident defendant. "[T]he constitutional touchstone" of the determination whether an exercise of personal jurisdiction comports with due process "remains whether the defendant purposefully established 'minimum contacts' in the forum State." Burger King Corp. v. Rudzewicz, 471 U.S. 462, 474, 105 S.Ct. 2174, 2183, 85 L.Ed.2d 528 (1985), quoting International Shoe Co. v. Washington, 326 U.S. 310, 316, 66 S.Ct. 154, 158, 90 L.Ed. 95 (1945). Most recently we have reaffirmed the oft-quoted reasoning of Hanson v. Denckla, 357 U.S. 235, 253, 78 S.Ct. 1228, 1239, 2 L.Ed.2d 1283 (1958), that minimum contacts must have a basis in "some act by which the defendant purposefully avails itself of the privilege of conducting activities within the forum State, thus invoking the benefits and protections of its laws." Burger King, 471 U.S., at 475, 105 S.Ct., at 2183. "Jurisdiction is proper . . . where the contacts proximately result from actions by the defendant himself that create a 'substantial connection' with the forum State." Ibid., quoting McGee v. International Life Insurance Co., 355 U.S. 220, 223, 78 S.Ct. 199, 201, 2 L.Ed.2d 223 (1957) (emphasis in original).

* * *

In World-Wide Volkswagen * * *, the state court sought to base jurisdiction not on any act of the defendant, but on the foreseeable unilateral actions of the consumer. Since World-Wide Volkswagen, lower courts have been confronted with cases in which the defendant acted by placing a product in the stream of commerce, and the stream eventually swept defendant's product into the forum State, but the defendant did nothing else to purposefully avail itself of the market in the forum state. Some courts have understood the Due Process Clause, as interpreted in World-Wide Volkswagen, to allow an exercise of personal jurisdiction to be based on no more than the defendant's act of placing the product in the stream of commerce. Other courts have understood the Due Process Clause and the above-quoted language in World-Wide Volkswagen to require the action of the defendant to be more purposefully directed at the forum State than the mere act of placing a product in the stream of commerce.

The reasoning of the Supreme Court of California in the present case illustrates the former interpretation of World-Wide Volkswagen. The Supreme Court of California held that, because the stream of commerce eventually brought some valves Asahi sold Cheng Shin into California, Asahi's awareness that its valves would be sold in California was sufficient to permit California to exercise jurisdiction over Asahi consistent with the requirements of the Due Process Clause. * * *

Other courts, however, have understood the Due Process Clause to require something more than that the defendant was aware of its product's entry into the forum State through the stream of commerce in order for the state to exert jurisdiction over the defendant. * * *

We now find this latter position to be consonant with the requirements of due process. The "substantial connection," *Burger King,* 471 U.S., at 475, 105 S.Ct., at 2184; *McGee,* 355 U.S., at 223, 78 S.Ct., at 201, between the defendant and the forum State necessary for a finding of minimum contacts must come about by *an action of the defendant purposefully directed toward the forum State. Burger King,* supra, 471 U.S., at 476, 105 S.Ct., at 2184; Keeton v. Hustler Magazine, Inc., 465 U.S. 770, 774, 104 S.Ct. 1473, 1478, 79 L.Ed.2d 790 (1984). The placement of a product into the stream of commerce, without more, is not an act of the defendant purposefully directed toward the forum State. Additional conduct of the defendant may indicate an intent or purpose to serve the market in the forum State, for example, designing the product for the market in the forum State, advertising in the forum State, establishing channels for providing regular advice to customers in the forum State, or marketing the product through a distributor who has agreed to serve as the sales agent in the forum State. But a defendant's awareness that the stream of commerce may or will sweep the product into the forum State does not convert the mere act of placing the product into the stream into an act purposefully directed toward the forum State.

* * * On the basis of these facts, the exertion of personal jurisdiction over Asahi by the Superior Court of California exceeds the limits of due process.

B

The strictures of the Due Process Clause forbid a state court from exercising personal jurisdiction over Asahi under circumstances that would offend "traditional notions of fair play and substantial justice." International Shoe Co. v. Washington, 326 U.S., at 316, 66 S.Ct., at 158; quoting Milliken v. Meyer, 311 U.S., at 463, 61 S.Ct., at 342.

We have previously explained that the determination of the reasonableness of the exercise of jurisdiction in each case will depend on an evaluation of several factors. A court must consider the burden on the defendant, the interests of the forum state, and the plaintiff's interest in obtaining relief. It must also weigh in its determination "the interstate judicial system's interest in obtaining the most efficient resolution of controversies; and the shared interest of the several States in furthering fundamental substantive social policies." *World-Wide Volkswagen,* 444 U.S., at 292, 100 S.Ct., at 564 (citations omitted).

A consideration of these factors in the present case clearly reveals the unreasonableness of the assertion of jurisdiction over Asahi, even apart from the question of the placement of goods in the stream of commerce.

Certainly, the burden on the defendant in this case is severe. Asahi has been commanded by the Supreme Court of California not only to traverse the distance between Asahi's headquarters in Japan and the Superior Court of California in and for the County of Solano, but also to submit its dispute with Cheng Shin to a foreign nation's judicial system. The unique burdens placed upon one who must defend oneself in a foreign legal system should have significant weight in assessing the reasonableness of stretching the long arm of personal jurisdiction over national borders.

When minimum contacts have been established, often the interests of the plaintiff and the forum in the exercise of jurisdiction will justify even the serious burdens placed on the alien defendant. In the present case, however, the interests of the plaintiff and the forum in California's assertion of jurisdiction over Asahi are slight. All that remains is a claim for indemnification asserted by Cheng Shin, a Taiwanese corporation, against Asahi. The transaction on which the indemnification claim is based took place in Taiwan; Asahi's components were shipped from Japan to Taiwan. Cheng Shin has not demonstrated that it is more convenient for it to litigate its indemnification claim against Asahi in California rather than in Taiwan or Japan.

Because the plaintiff is not a California resident, California's legitimate interests in the dispute have considerably diminished. The Supreme Court of California argued that the State had an interest in "protecting its consumers by ensuring that foreign manufacturers comply with the state's safety standards." 39 Cal.3d, at 49, 216 Cal.Rptr., at 392, 702 P.2d, at 550. The State Supreme Court's definition of California's interest, however, was overly broad. The dispute between Cheng Shin and Asahi is primarily about indemnification rather than safety standards. Moreover, it is not at all clear at this point that California law should govern the question whether a Japanese corporation should indemnify a Taiwanese corporation on the basis of a sale made in Taiwan and a shipment of goods from Japan to Taiwan. Phillips Petroleum v. Shutts, 472 U.S. 797, 821–822, 105 S.Ct. 2965, 2979, 86 L.Ed.2d 628 (1985); Allstate Insurance Co. v. Hague, 449 U.S. 302, 312–313, 101 S.Ct. 633, 639–640, 66 L.Ed.2d 521 (1981). * * *

        * * *

Considering the international context, the heavy burden on the alien defendant, and the slight interests of the plaintiff and the forum State, the exercise of personal jurisdiction by a California court over Asahi in this instance would be unreasonable and unfair.

III

Because the facts of this case do not establish minimum contacts such that the exercise of personal jurisdiction is consistent with fair play and substantial justice, the judgment of Supreme Court of California is reversed, and the case is remanded for further proceedings not inconsistent with this opinion.

It is so ordered.

■ JUSTICE BRENNAN, with whom JUSTICE WHITE, JUSTICE MARSHALL, and JUSTICE BLACKMUN join, concurring in part and in the judgment.

I do not agree with the interpretation in Part II–A of the stream-of-commerce theory, nor with the conclusion that Asahi did not "purposely avail itself of the California market." * * * I do agree, however, with the Court's conclusion in Part II–B that the exercise of personal jurisdiction over Asahi in this case would not comport with "fair play and substantial justice," International Shoe Co. v. Washington, 326 U.S. 310, 320, 66 S.Ct. 154, 160, 90 L.Ed. 95 (1945). This is one of those rare cases in which "minimum requirements inherent in the concept of 'fair play and substantial justice' . . . defeat the reasonableness of jurisdiction even [though] the defendant has purposefully engaged in forum activities." I therefore join Parts I and II–B of the Court's opinion, and write separately to explain my disagreement with Part II–A.

Part II–A states that "a defendant's awareness that the stream of commerce may or will sweep the product into the forum State does not convert the mere act of placing the product into the stream into an act purposefully directed toward the forum State." * * * Under this view, a plaintiff would be required to show "[a]dditional conduct" directed toward the forum before finding the exercise of jurisdiction over the defendant to be consistent with the Due Process Clause. * * * I see no need for such a showing, however. The stream of commerce refers not to unpredictable currents or eddies, but to the regular and anticipated flow of products from manufacture to distribution to retail sale. As long as a participant in this process is aware that the final product is being marketed in the forum State, the possibility of a lawsuit there cannot come as a surprise. Nor will the litigation present a burden for which there is no corresponding benefit. A defendant who has placed goods in the stream of commerce benefits economically from the retail sale of the final product in the forum State, and indirectly benefits from the State's laws that regulate and facilitate commercial activity. These benefits accrue regardless of whether that participant directly conducts business in the forum State, or engages in additional conduct directed toward that State. Accordingly, most courts and commentators have found that jurisdiction premised on the placement of a product into the stream of commerce is consistent with the Due Process Clause, and have not required a showing of additional conduct.

The endorsement in Part II–A of what appears to be the minority view among Federal Courts of Appeals represents a marked retreat from the analysis in World-Wide Volkswagen v. Woodson, 444 U.S. 286, 100 S.Ct. 559, 62 L.Ed.2d 490 (1980. In that case, "respondents [sought] to base jurisdiction on one, isolated occurrence and whatever inferences can be drawn therefrom: the fortuitous circumstance that a single Audi automobile, sold in New York to New York residents, happened to suffer an accident while passing through Oklahoma." Id., at 295, 100 S.Ct., at 566. The Court held that the possibility of an accident in Oklahoma, while to some extent foreseeable in light of the inherent mobility of the automobile, was not enough to establish minimum contacts between the forum State and the retailer or distributor. Id., at 295–296, 100 S.Ct., at 566. The Court then carefully explained:

> "[T]his is not to say, of course, that foreseeability is wholly irrelevant. But the foreseeability that is critical to due process analysis is not the mere likelihood that a product will find its way into the forum State. Rather, it is that the defendant's conduct and connection with the forum State are such that he should reasonably anticipate being haled into Court there." Id., at 297, 100 S.Ct. at 567.

The Court reasoned that when a corporation may reasonably anticipate litigation in a particular forum, it cannot claim that such litigation is unjust or unfair, because it "can act to alleviate the risk of burdensome litigation by procuring insurance, passing the expected costs on to consumers, or, if the risks are too great, severing its connection with the State." Ibid.

* * *

[The opinion of Justice Stevens, joined by Justices White and Blackmun, concurring in Parts I and II-B, and in the judgment, is omitted.]

NOTES AND QUESTIONS

1. **Plurality opinions.** Sort out the various opinions carefully. Part I of Justice O'Connor's opinion is joined by all the justices. Part II–B is joined by all except Justice Scalia. Part II–A is a plurality, joined only by three other justices. Justice Brennan dissents from Part II–A, joined by three justices (not including Justice Stevens). Justice Stevens dissents separately from Part II–A, joined by two of the justices who joined Justice Brennan. A plurality opinion does not state the law. It agrees with the result reached by the Court, but as to the reasoning employed, it is, in effect, a dissent. What is the law after *Asahi*? What statement or statements of law command a majority of the Court?

2. **A different rule for manufacturers of component parts?** Recall that in *World-Wide Volkswagen* no one questioned the susceptibility of Audi, the manufacturer, to suit in Oklahoma. Would Justice O'Connor subject the automobile manufacturer to suit in whatever the accident occurred, but not subject the manufacturer of a component part to suit in that forum? Why should the manufacturer of a defective part be protected, but not the automobile manufacturer who unwittingly incorporated the defective product? Are Justice O'Conner and the three justices who joined Part II–A unhappy with the implicit conclusion in *World-Wide Volkswagen* that Audi is subject to *in personam* jurisdiction in Oklahoma?

3. **Compare *Asahi* to a *forum non conveniens* case.** *In personam* jurisdiction is not the only hurdle that a plaintiff must overcome in order to bring suit in the forum of his or her choice. There must also be subject matter jurisdiction and proper venue, and the suit must be able to withstand a *forum non conveniens* objection. We will study these requirements later in this chapter, but a quick glance at *forum non conveniens* may help us understand *Asahi*. (Or perhaps it will deepen the mystery.)

The doctrine of *forum non conveniens* allows a court to dismiss a suit in which it has valid *in personam* jurisdiction but when the forum is nonetheless extremely "inconvenient." The court will weigh a variety of factors including convenience of the parties, access to proof, burden on the court system asked to decide the case, and adequacy of the remedy in the alternative forum. The plaintiff's forum choice will not be disturbed unless the balance of these factors is strongly against the plaintiff's choice. See Piper Aircraft Co. v. Reyno, 454 U.S. 235, 102 S.Ct. 252, 70 L.Ed.2d 419 (1981), and discussion infra p. 321. Look again at the formulation set forth in *Asahi* and *Burger King* for *in personam* jurisdiction. Is it replicating, under a different doctrinal heading, the *forum non conveniens* analysis?

4. **Plaintiff's contacts with the forum.** The suit in *Asahi* had originally been a suit by Zurcher against Cheng Shin. Cheng Shin then impleaded Asahi for indemnification. By the time the case came to the Supreme Court, Zurcher had settled with Cheng Shin, leaving only the

indemnification suit between Cheng Shin and Asahi. With the case in this posture, the Court dismissed the suit against Asahi for lack of *in personam* jurisdiction. Would the Court have dismissed the indemnification suit against Asahi for lack of jurisdiction if the underlying suit by Zurcher against Cheng Shin had still been pending? Would the Court have dismissed if Zurcher had sued Asahi directly? If the answer to either of these two questions is "No," isn't it clear that *Asahi* is dealing with more than Asahi's contacts with the forum state? Isn't it clear that the Court is looking at *plaintiff's* (not just defendant's) contacts with the forum?

J. McIntyre Machinery, Ltd. v. Nicastro

Supreme Court of the United States, 2011.
564 U.S. ___, 131 S.Ct. 2780, 180 L.Ed.2d 765.

■ JUSTICE KENNEDY announced the judgment of the Court and delivered an opinion in which THE CHIEF JUSTICE, JUSTICE SCALIA, and JUSTICE THOMAS join.

Whether a person or entity is subject to the jurisdiction of a state court despite not having been present in the State either at the time of suit or at the time of the alleged injury, and despite not having consented to the exercise of jurisdiction, is a question that arises with great frequency in the routine course of litigation. The rules and standards for determining when a State does or does not have jurisdiction over an absent party have been unclear because of decades-old questions left open in Asahi Metal Industry Co. v. Superior Court of Cal., Solano Cty., 480 U.S. 102 (1987).

Here, the Supreme Court of New Jersey, relying in part on *Asahi,* held that New Jersey's courts can exercise jurisdiction over a foreign manufacturer of a product so long as the manufacturer "knows or reasonably should know that its products are distributed through a nationwide distribution system that might lead to those products being sold in any of the fifty states." Applying that test, the court concluded that a British manufacturer of scrap metal machines was subject to jurisdiction in New Jersey, even though at no time had it advertised in, sent goods to, or in any relevant sense targeted the State.

That decision cannot be sustained. Although the New Jersey Supreme Court issued an extensive opinion with careful attention to this Court's cases and to its own precedent, the "stream of commerce" metaphor carried the decision far afield. Due process protects the defendant's right not to be coerced except by lawful judicial power. As a general rule, the exercise of judicial power is not lawful unless the defendant "purposefully avails itself of the privilege of conducting activities within the forum State, thus invoking the benefits and protections of its laws." There may be exceptions, say, for instance, in cases involving an intentional tort. But the general rule is applicable in this products-liability case, and the so-called "stream-of-commerce" doctrine cannot displace it.

I

This case arises from a products-liability suit filed in New Jersey state court. Robert Nicastro seriously injured his hand while using a metal-shearing machine manufactured by J. McIntyre Machinery, Ltd.

(J. McIntyre). The accident occurred in New Jersey, but the machine was manufactured in England, where J. McIntyre is incorporated and operates. The question here is whether the New Jersey courts have jurisdiction over J. McIntyre, notwithstanding the fact that the company at no time either marketed goods in the State or shipped them there. Nicastro was a plaintiff in the New Jersey trial court and is the respondent here; J. McIntyre was a defendant and is now the petitioner.

At oral argument in this Court, Nicastro's counsel stressed three primary facts in defense of New Jersey's assertion of jurisdiction over J. McIntyre.

First, an independent company agreed to sell J. McIntyre's machines in the United States. J. McIntyre itself did not sell its machines to buyers in this country beyond the U.S. distributor, and there is no allegation that the distributor was under J. McIntyre's control.

Second, J. McIntyre officials attended annual conventions for the scrap recycling industry to advertise J. McIntyre's machines alongside the distributor. The conventions took place in various States, but never in New Jersey.

Third, no more than four machines (the record suggests only one, see App. to Pet. for Cert. 130a), including the machine that caused the injuries that are the basis for this suit, ended up in New Jersey.

In addition to these facts emphasized by petitioner, the New Jersey Supreme Court noted that J. McIntyre held both United States and European patents on its recycling technology. It also noted that the U.S. distributor "structured [its] advertising and sales efforts in accordance with" J. McIntyre's "direction and guidance whenever possible," and that "at least some of the machines were sold on consignment to" the distributor.

In light of these facts, the New Jersey Supreme Court concluded that New Jersey courts could exercise jurisdiction over petitioner without contravention of the Due Process Clause. Jurisdiction was proper, in that court's view, because the injury occurred in New Jersey; because petitioner knew or reasonably should have known "that its products are distributed through a nationwide distribution system that might lead to those products being sold in any of the fifty states"; and because petitioner failed to "take some reasonable step to prevent the distribution of its products in this State."

Both the New Jersey Supreme Court's holding and its account of what it called "[t]he stream-of-commerce doctrine of jurisdiction," were incorrect, however. This Court's *Asahi* decision may be responsible in part for that court's error regarding the stream of commerce, and this case presents an opportunity to provide greater clarity.

II

The Due Process Clause protects an individual's right to be deprived of life, liberty, or property only by the exercise of lawful power. This is no less true with respect to the power of a sovereign to resolve disputes through judicial process than with respect to the power of a sovereign to prescribe rules of conduct for those within its sphere. As a general rule, neither statute nor judicial decree may bind strangers to the State.

A court may subject a defendant to judgment only when the defendant has sufficient contacts with the sovereign "such that the maintenance of the suit does not offend 'traditional notions of fair play and substantial justice.'" International Shoe Co. v. Washington, 326 U.S. 310 (1945). Freeform notions of fundamental fairness divorced from traditional practice cannot transform a judgment rendered in the absence of authority into law. As a general rule, the sovereign's exercise of power requires some act by which the defendant "purposefully avails itself of the privilege of conducting activities within the forum State, thus invoking the benefits and protections of its laws," though in some cases, as with an intentional tort, the defendant might well fall within the State's authority by reason of his attempt to obstruct its laws. In products-liability cases like this one, it is the defendant's purposeful availment that makes jurisdiction consistent with "traditional notions of fair play and substantial justice."

A person may submit to a State's authority in a number of ways. There is, of course, explicit consent. E.g., Insurance Corp. of Ireland v. Compagnie des Bauxites de Guinee, 456 U.S. 694, 703 (1982). Presence within a State at the time suit commences through service of process is another example. Citizenship or domicile—or, by analogy, incorporation or principal place of business for corporations—also indicates general submission to a State's powers. Goodyear Dunlop Tires Operations, S.A. v. Brown, [131 S.Ct. 2846 (2011)]. Each of these examples reveals circumstances, or a course of conduct, from which it is proper to infer an intention to benefit from and thus an intention to submit to the laws of the forum State. These examples support exercise of the general jurisdiction of the State's courts and allow the State to resolve both matters that originate within the State and those based on activities and events elsewhere. Helicopteros Nacionales de Colombia, S.A. v. Hall, 466 U.S. 408, 414, and n. 9 (1984). By contrast, those who live or operate primarily outside a State have a due process right not to be subjected to judgment in its courts as a general matter.

There is also a more limited form of submission to a State's authority for disputes that "arise out of or are connected with the activities within the state." Where a defendant "purposefully avails itself of the privilege of conducting activities within the forum State, thus invoking the benefits and protections of its laws," it submits to the judicial power of an otherwise foreign sovereign to the extent that power is exercised in connection with the defendant's activities touching on the State. In other words, submission through contact with and activity directed at a sovereign may justify specific jurisdiction "in a suit arising out of or related to the defendant's contacts with the forum."

The imprecision arising from *Asahi,* for the most part, results from its statement of the relation between jurisdiction and the "stream of commerce." The stream of commerce, like other metaphors, has its deficiencies as well as its utility. It refers to the movement of goods from manufacturers through distributors to consumers, yet beyond that descriptive purpose its meaning is far from exact. This Court has stated that a defendant's placing goods into the stream of commerce "with the expectation that they will be purchased by consumers within the forum State" may indicate purposeful availment. World-Wide Volkswagen Corp. v. Woodson, 444 U.S. 286, 298 (1980). But that statement does not amend the general rule of personal jurisdiction. It merely observes that a defendant may in an appropriate case be subject to jurisdiction without entering the forum—itself an unexceptional proposition—as where manufacturers or distributors "seek to serve" a given State's market. The *Issue* principal inquiry in cases of this sort is whether the defendant's activities manifest an intention to submit to the power of a sovereign. In other words, the defendant must "purposefully avai[l] itself of the privilege of conducting activities within the forum State, thus invoking the benefits and protections of its laws." Sometimes a defendant does so by sending its goods rather than its agents. The defendant's transmission of goods permits the exercise of jurisdiction only where the defendant can be said *Rule* to have targeted the forum; as a general rule, it is not enough that the defendant might have predicted that its goods will reach the forum State.

In *Asahi,* an opinion by Justice Brennan for four Justices outlined a different approach. It discarded the central concept of sovereign authority in favor of considerations of fairness and foreseeability. As that concurrence contended, "jurisdiction premised on the placement of a product into the stream of commerce [without more] is consistent with the Due Process Clause," for "[a]s long as a participant in this process is aware that the final product is being marketed in the forum State, the possibility of a lawsuit there cannot come as a surprise." It was the premise of the concurring opinion that the defendant's ability to anticipate suit renders the assertion of jurisdiction fair. In this way, the opinion made foreseeability the touchstone of jurisdiction.   *Asahi Opinion*

The standard set forth in Justice Brennan's concurrence was rejected in an opinion written by Justice O'Connor; but the relevant part of that opinion, too, commanded the assent of only four Justices, not a majority of the Court. That opinion stated: "The 'substantial connection' between the defendant and the forum State necessary for a finding of minimum contacts must come about by an action of the defendant purposefully directed toward the forum State. The placement of a product into the stream of commerce, without more, is not an act of the defendant purposefully directed toward the forum State."

Since *Asahi* was decided, the courts have sought to reconcile the competing opinions. But Justice Brennan's concurrence, advocating a rule based on general notions of fairness and foreseeability, is *Def.* inconsistent with the premises of lawful judicial power. This Court's *actions v.* precedents make clear that it is the defendant's actions, not his *expectation* expectations, that empower a State's courts to subject him to judgment.

* * *

Two principles are implicit in the foregoing. First, personal jurisdiction requires a forum-by-forum, or sovereign-by-sovereign, analysis. The question is whether a defendant has followed a course of conduct directed at the society or economy existing within the jurisdiction of a given sovereign, so that the sovereign has the power to subject the defendant to judgment concerning that conduct. Personal jurisdiction, of course, restricts "judicial power not as a matter of sovereignty, but as a matter of individual liberty," for due process protects the individual's right to be subject only to lawful power. But whether a judicial judgment is lawful depends on whether the sovereign has authority to render it.

The second principle is a corollary of the first. Because the United States is a distinct sovereign, a defendant may in principle be subject to the jurisdiction of the courts of the United States but not of any particular State. This is consistent with the premises and unique genius of our Constitution. Ours is "a legal system unprecedented in form and design, establishing two orders of government, each with its own direct relationship, its own privity, its own set of mutual rights and obligations to the people who sustain it and are governed by it." For jurisdiction, a litigant may have the requisite relationship with the United States Government but not with the government of any individual State. That would be an exceptional case, however. If the defendant is a domestic domiciliary, the courts of its home State are available and can exercise general jurisdiction. And if another State were to assert jurisdiction in an inappropriate case, it would upset the federal balance, which posits that each State has a sovereignty that is not subject to unlawful intrusion by other States. Furthermore, foreign corporations will often target or concentrate on particular States, subjecting them to specific jurisdiction in those forums.

It must be remembered, however, that although this case and *Asahi* both involve foreign manufacturers, the undesirable consequences of Justice Brennan's approach are no less significant for domestic producers. The owner of a small Florida farm might sell crops to a large nearby distributor, for example, who might then distribute them to grocers across the country. If foreseeability were the controlling criterion, the farmer could be sued in Alaska or any number of other States' courts without ever leaving town. And the issue of foreseeability may itself be contested so that significant expenses are incurred just on the preliminary issue of jurisdiction. Jurisdictional rules should avoid these costs whenever possible.

The conclusion that the authority to subject a defendant to judgment depends on purposeful availment, consistent with Justice O'Connor's opinion in *Asahi,* does not by itself resolve many difficult questions of jurisdiction that will arise in particular cases. The defendant's conduct and the economic realities of the market the defendant seeks to serve will differ across cases, and judicial exposition will, in common-law fashion, clarify the contours of that principle.

III

In this case, petitioner directed marketing and sales efforts at the United States. It may be that, assuming it were otherwise empowered to legislate on the subject, the Congress could authorize the exercise of jurisdiction in appropriate courts. That circumstance is not presented in this case, however, and it is neither necessary nor appropriate to address here any constitutional concerns that might be attendant to that exercise of power. Nor is it necessary to determine what substantive law might apply were Congress to authorize jurisdiction in a federal court in New Jersey. A sovereign's legislative authority to regulate conduct may present considerations different from those presented by its authority to subject a defendant to judgment in its courts. Here the question concerns the authority of a New Jersey state court to exercise jurisdiction, so it is petitioner's purposeful contacts with New Jersey, not with the United States, that alone are relevant.

Respondent has not established that J. McIntyre engaged in conduct purposefully directed at New Jersey. Recall that respondent's claim of jurisdiction centers on three facts: The distributor agreed to sell J. McIntyre's machines in the United States; J. McIntyre officials attended trade shows in several States but not in New Jersey; and up to four machines ended up in New Jersey. The British manufacturer had no office in New Jersey; it neither paid taxes nor owned property there; and it neither advertised in, nor sent any employees to, the State. Indeed, after discovery the trial court found that the "defendant does not have a single contact with New Jersey short of the machine in question ending up in this state." These facts may reveal an intent to serve the U.S. market, but they do not show that J. McIntyre purposefully availed itself of the New Jersey market.

It is notable that the New Jersey Supreme Court appears to agree, for it could "not find that J. McIntyre had a presence or minimum contacts in this State—in any jurisprudential sense—that would justify a New Jersey court to exercise jurisdiction in this case." The court nonetheless held that petitioner could be sued in New Jersey based on a "stream-of-commerce theory of jurisdiction." *Ibid.* As discussed, however, the stream-of-commerce metaphor cannot supersede either the mandate of the Due Process Clause or the limits on judicial authority that Clause ensures. The New Jersey Supreme Court also cited "significant policy reasons" to justify its holding, including the State's "strong interest in protecting its citizens from defective products." That interest is doubtless strong, but the Constitution commands restraint before discarding liberty in the name of expediency.

* * *

Due process protects petitioner's right to be subject only to lawful authority. At no time did petitioner engage in any activities in New Jersey that reveal an intent to invoke or benefit from the protection of its laws. New Jersey is without power to adjudge the rights and liabilities of J. McIntyre, and its exercise of jurisdiction would violate due process. The contrary judgment of the New Jersey Supreme Court is

Reversed.

■ JUSTICE BREYER, with whom JUSTICE ALITO joins, concurring in the judgment.

The Supreme Court of New Jersey adopted a broad understanding of the scope of personal jurisdiction based on its view that "[t]he increasingly fast-paced globalization of the world economy has removed national borders as barriers to trade." I do not doubt that there have been many recent changes in commerce and communication, many of which are not anticipated by our precedents. But this case does not present any of those issues. So I think it unwise to announce a rule of broad applicability without full consideration of the modern-day consequences.

In my view, the outcome of this case is determined by our precedents.

* * *

None of our precedents finds that a single isolated sale, even if accompanied by the kind of sales effort indicated here, is sufficient. * * *

Here, the relevant facts found by the New Jersey Supreme Court show no "regular . . . flow" or "regular course" of sales in New Jersey; and there is no "something more," such as special state-related design, advertising, advice, marketing, or anything else. Mr. Nicastro, who here bears the burden of proving jurisdiction, has shown no specific effort by the British Manufacturer to sell in New Jersey. He has introduced no list of potential New Jersey customers who might, for example, have regularly attended trade shows. And he has not otherwise shown that the British Manufacturer "purposefully avail[ed] itself of the privilege of conducting activities" within New Jersey, or that it delivered its goods in the stream of commerce "with the expectation that they will be purchased" by New Jersey users.

There may well have been other facts that Mr. Nicastro could have demonstrated in support of jurisdiction. And the dissent considers some of those facts. But the plaintiff bears the burden of establishing jurisdiction, and here I would take the facts precisely as the New Jersey Supreme Court stated them.

Accordingly, on the record present here, resolving this case requires no more than adhering to our precedents.

II

I would not go further. Because the incident at issue in this case does not implicate modern concerns, and because the factual record leaves many open questions, this is an unsuitable vehicle for making broad pronouncements that refashion basic jurisdictional rules.

A

The plurality seems to state strict rules that limit jurisdiction where a defendant does not "inten[d] to submit to the power of a sovereign" and cannot "be said to have targeted the forum." But what do those standards mean when a company targets the world by selling products from its Web site? And does it matter if, instead of shipping the products directly, a company consigns the products through an intermediary (say, Amazon.com) who then receives and fulfills the orders? And what if the company markets its products through popup advertisements that it knows will be viewed in a forum? Those issues have serious commercial consequences but are totally absent in this case.

[handwritten margin note: Rules of the Majority]

B

But though I do not agree with the plurality's seemingly strict no-jurisdiction rule, I am not persuaded by the absolute approach adopted by the New Jersey Supreme Court and urged by respondent and his *amici.* Under that view, a producer is subject to jurisdiction for a products-liability action so long as it "knows or reasonably should know that its products are distributed through a nationwide distribution system that *might* lead to those products being sold in any of the fifty states." In the context of this case, I cannot agree.

For one thing, to adopt this view would abandon the heretofore accepted inquiry of whether, focusing upon the relationship between "the defendant, the *forum,* and the litigation," it is fair, in light of the defendant's contacts *with that forum,* to subject the defendant to suit there. Shaffer v. Heitner, 433 U.S. 186, 204, 97 S.Ct. 2569, 53 L.Ed.2d 683 (1977) (emphasis added). * * *

* * * *[handwritten: → that case dealt w/ Quasi in Rem Jurisdiction]*

[handwritten note: (Prof. does not agree w/this analogy)]

For another, I cannot reconcile so automatic a rule with the constitutional demand for "minimum contacts" and "purposefu[l] avail[ment]," each of which rest upon a particular notion of defendant-focused fairness. * * *

* * *

It may be that a larger firm can readily "alleviate the risk of burdensome litigation by procuring insurance, passing the expected costs on to customers, or, if the risks are too great, severing its connection with the State." But manufacturers come in many shapes and sizes. It may be fundamentally unfair to require a small Egyptian shirt maker, a Brazilian manufacturing cooperative, or a Kenyan coffee farmer, selling its products through international distributors, to respond to products-liability tort suits in virtually every State in the United States, even those in respect to which the foreign firm has no connection at all but the sale of a single (allegedly defective) good. And a rule like the New Jersey Supreme Court suggests would require every product manufacturer, large or small, selling to American distributors to understand not only the tort law of every State, but also the wide variance in the way courts within different States apply that law.

C

At a minimum, I would not work such a change to the law in the way either the plurality or the New Jersey Supreme Court suggests without a better understanding of the relevant contemporary commercial circumstances.

This case presents no such occasion, and so I again reiterate that I would adhere strictly to our precedents and the limited facts found by the New Jersey Supreme Court. And on those grounds, I do not think we can find jurisdiction in this case. Accordingly, though I agree with the plurality as to the outcome of this case, I concur only in the judgment of that opinion and not its reasoning.

■ JUSTICE GINSBURG, with whom JUSTICE SOTOMAYOR and JUSTICE KAGAN join, dissenting.

A foreign industrialist seeks to develop a market in the United States for machines it manufactures. It hopes to derive substantial revenue from sales it makes to United States purchasers. Where in the United States buyers reside does not matter to this manufacturer. Its goal is simply to sell as much as it can, wherever it can. It excludes no region or State from the market it wishes to reach. But, all things considered, it prefers to avoid products liability litigation in the United States. To that end, it engages a U.S. distributor to ship its machines stateside. Has it succeeded in escaping personal jurisdiction in a State where one of its products is sold and causes injury or even death to a local user?

Under this Court's pathmarking precedent in International Shoe Co. v. Washington, 326 U.S. 310, 66 S.Ct. 154, 90 L.Ed. 95 (1945), and subsequent decisions, one would expect the answer to be unequivocally, "No." But instead, six Justices of this Court, in divergent opinions, tell us that the manufacturer has avoided the jurisdiction of our state courts, except perhaps in States where its products are sold in sizeable quantities. Inconceivable as it may have seemed yesterday, the splintered majority today "turn[s] the clock back to the days before modern long-arm statutes when a manufacturer, to avoid being haled into court where a user is injured, need only Pilate-like wash its hands of a product by having independent distributors market it." Weintraub, A Map Out of the Personal Jurisdiction Labyrinth, 28 U.C. Davis L. Rev. 531, 555 (1995).

I

On October 11, 2001, a three-ton metal shearing machine severed four fingers on Robert Nicastro's right hand. Alleging that the machine was a dangerous product defectively made, Nicastro sought compensation from the machine's manufacturer, J. McIntyre Machinery Ltd. (McIntyre UK). Established in 1872 as a United Kingdom corporation, and headquartered in Nottingham, England, McIntyre UK "designs, develops and manufactures a complete range of equipment for metal recycling." The company's product line, as advertised on McIntyre UK's Web site, includes "metal shears, balers, cable and can recycling equipment, furnaces, casting equipment and . . . the world's best aluminium dross processing and cooling system." McIntyre UK holds both United States and European patents on its technology.

The machine that injured Nicastro, a "McIntyre Model 640 Shear," sold in the United States for $24,900 in 1995, and features a "massive cutting capacity." According to McIntyre UK's product brochure, the machine is "use[d] throughout the [w]orld." McIntyre UK represented in the brochure that, by "incorporat[ing] off-the-shelf hydraulic parts from suppliers with international sales outlets," the 640 Shear's design guarantees serviceability "wherever [its customers] may be based." The instruction manual advises "owner[s] and operators of a 640 Shear [to] make themselves aware of [applicable health and safety regulations]," including "the American National Standards Institute Regulations (USA) for the use of Scrap Metal Processing Equipment."

Nicastro operated the 640 Shear in the course of his employment at Curcio Scrap Metal (CSM) in Saddle Brook, New Jersey. "New Jersey has long been a hotbed of scrap-metal businesses . . . ." See Drake, The Scrap-Heap Rollup Hits New Jersey, Business News New Jersey, June 1, 1998, p. 1. In 2008, New Jersey recycling facilities processed 2,013,730 tons of scrap iron, steel, aluminum, and other metals—more than any other State—outpacing Kentucky, its nearest competitor, by nearly 30 percent. Von Haaren, Themelis, & Goldstein, The State of Garbage in America, BioCycle, Oct. 2010, p. 19.

CSM's owner, Frank Curcio, "first heard of [McIntyre UK's] machine while attending an Institute of Scrap Metal Industries [(ISRI)] convention in Las Vegas in 1994 or 1995, where [McIntyre UK] was an exhibitor." ISRI "presents the world's largest scrap recycling industry trade show each year." The event attracts "owners [and] managers of scrap processing companies" and others "interested in seeing—and purchasing—new equipment." According to ISRI, more than 3,000 potential buyers of scrap processing and recycling equipment attend its annual conventions, "primarily because th[e] exposition provides them with the most comprehensive industry-related shopping experience concentrated in a single, convenient location." Exhibitors who are ISRI members pay $3,000 for 10' x 10' booth space.

McIntyre UK representatives attended every ISRI convention from 1990 through 2005. These annual expositions were held in diverse venues across the United States; in addition to Las Vegas, conventions were held 1990–2005 in New Orleans, Orlando, San Antonio, and San Francisco. McIntyre UK's president, Michael Pownall, regularly attended ISRI conventions. He attended ISRI's Las Vegas convention the year CSM's owner first learned of, and saw, the 640 Shear. McIntyre UK exhibited its products at ISRI trade shows, the company acknowledged, hoping to reach "anyone interested in the machine from anywhere in the United States."

Although McIntyre UK's U.S. sales figures are not in the record, it appears that for several years in the 1990's, earnings from sales of McIntyre UK products in the United States "ha[d] been good" in comparison to "the rest of the world." In response to interrogatories, McIntyre UK stated that its commissioning engineer had installed the company's equipment in several States—Illinois, Iowa, Kentucky, Virginia, and Washington.

From at least 1995 until 2001, McIntyre UK retained an Ohio-based company, McIntyre Machinery America, Ltd. (McIntyre America), "as its exclusive distributor for the entire United States." Though similarly named, the two companies were separate and independent entities with "no commonality of ownership or management." In invoices and other written communications, McIntyre America described itself as McIntyre UK's national distributor, "America's Link" to "Quality Metal Processing Equipment" from England. App.

In a November 23, 1999 letter to McIntyre America, McIntyre UK's president spoke plainly about the manufacturer's objective in authorizing the exclusive distributorship: "All we wish to do is sell our products in the [United] States—and get paid!" Notably, McIntyre America was concerned about U.S. litigation involving McIntyre UK products, in which the distributor had been named as a defendant. McIntyre UK counseled McIntyre America to respond personally to the litigation, but reassured its distributor that "the product was built and designed by McIntyre Machinery in the UK and the buck stops here—if there's something wrong with the machine." Answering jurisdictional interrogatories, McIntyre UK stated that it had been named as a defendant in lawsuits in Illinois, Kentucky, Massachusetts, and West Virginia. And in correspondence with McIntyre America, McIntyre UK noted that the manufacturer had products liability insurance coverage.

Over the years, McIntyre America distributed several McIntyre UK products to U.S. customers, including, in addition to the 640 Shear, McIntyre UK's "Niagara" and "Tardis" systems, wire strippers, and can machines. In promoting McIntyre UK's products at conventions and demonstration sites and in trade journal advertisements, McIntyre America looked to McIntyre UK for direction and guidance. To achieve McIntyre UK's objective, *i.e.,* "to sell [its] machines to customers throughout the United States," "the two companies [were acting] closely in concert with each other," McIntyre UK never instructed its distributor to avoid certain States or regions of the country; rather, as just noted, the manufacturer engaged McIntyre America to attract customers "from anywhere in the United States."

In sum, McIntyre UK's regular attendance and exhibitions at ISRI conventions was surely a purposeful step to reach customers for its products "anywhere in the United States." At least as purposeful was McIntyre UK's engagement of McIntyre America as the conduit for sales of McIntyre UK's machines to buyers "throughout the United States." Given McIntyre UK's endeavors to reach and profit from the United States market as a whole, Nicastro's suit, I would hold, has been brought in a forum entirely appropriate for the adjudication of his claim. He alleges that McIntyre UK's shear machine was defectively designed or manufactured and, as a result, caused injury to him at his workplace. The machine arrived in Nicastro's New Jersey workplace not randomly or fortuitously, but as a result of the U.S. connections and distribution system that McIntyre UK deliberately arranged. On what sensible view of the allocation of adjudicatory authority could the place of Nicastro's injury within the United States be deemed off limits for his products liability claim against a foreign manufacturer who targeted the United States (including all the States that constitute the Nation) as the territory it sought to develop?

II

A few points on which there should be no genuine debate bear statement at the outset. * * *

* * *

[T]he constitutional limits on a state court's adjudicatory authority derive from considerations of due process, not state sovereignty. As the Court clarified in Insurance Corp. of Ireland v. Compagnie des Bauxites de Guinee, 456 U.S. 694 (1982):

> "The restriction on state sovereign power described in *World-Wide Volkswagen Corp.* . . . must be seen as ultimately a function of the individual liberty interest preserved by the Due Process Clause. That Clause is the only source of the personal jurisdiction requirement and the Clause itself makes no mention of federalism concerns. Furthermore, if the federalism concept operated as an independent restriction on the sovereign power of the court, it would not be possible to waive the personal jurisdiction requirement: Individual actions cannot change the powers of sovereignty, although the individual can subject himself to powers from which he may otherwise be protected."
> *Id.*, at 703, n. 10.

See also Shaffer v. Heitner, 433 U.S. 186, 204, and n. 20 (1977) (recognizing that "the mutually exclusive sovereignty of the States [is not] the central concern of the inquiry into personal jurisdiction"). But see *ante*, at 7 (plurality opinion) (asserting that "sovereign authority," not "fairness," is the "central concept" in determining personal jurisdiction).

Finally, in *International Shoe* itself, and decisions thereafter, the Court has made plain that legal fictions, notably "presence" and "implied consent," should be discarded, for they conceal the actual bases on which jurisdiction rests. See 326 U.S., at 316, 318; Hutchinson v. Chase & Gilbert, 45 F.2d 139, 141 (C.A.2 1930) (L.Hand, J.) ("nothing is gained by [resort to words that] concea[l] what we do"). "[T]he relationship among the defendant, the forum, and the litigation" determines whether due process permits the exercise of personal jurisdiction over a defendant,

Shaffer, 433 U.S., at 204, and "fictions of implied consent" or "corporate presence" do not advance the proper inquiry, *id.,* at 202. See also Burnham v. Superior Court of Cal., County of Marin, 495 U.S. 604, 618, 110 S.Ct. 2105, 109 L.Ed.2d 631 (1990) (plurality opinion) (*International Shoe* "cast . . . aside" fictions of "consent" and "presence").

* * *

III

This case is illustrative of marketing arrangements for sales in the United States common in today's commercial world. A foreign-country manufacturer engages a U.S. company to promote and distribute the manufacturer's products, not in any particular State, but anywhere and everywhere in the United States the distributor can attract purchasers. The product proves defective and injures a user in the State where the user lives or works. Often, as here, the manufacturer will have liability insurance covering personal injuries caused by its products.

* * *

The modern approach to jurisdiction over corporations and other legal entities, ushered in by *International Shoe,* gave prime place to reason and fairness. Is it not fair and reasonable, given the mode of trading of which this case is an example, to require the international seller to defend at the place its products cause injury? Do not litigational convenience and choice-of-law considerations point in that direction? On what measure of reason and fairness can it be considered undue to require McIntyre UK to defend in New Jersey as an incident of its efforts to develop a market for its industrial machines anywhere and everywhere in the United States? Is not the burden on McIntyre UK to defend in New Jersey fair, *i.e.,* a reasonable cost of transacting business internationally, in comparison to the burden on Nicastro to go to Nottingham, England to gain recompense for an injury he sustained using McIntyre's product at his workplace in Saddle Brook, New Jersey?

McIntyre UK dealt with the United States as a single market. Like most foreign manufacturers, it was concerned not with the prospect of suit in State X as opposed to State Y, but rather with its subjection to suit anywhere in the United States. See Hay, Judicial Jurisdiction Over Foreign-Country Corporate Defendants—Comments on Recent Case Law, 63 Ore. L.Rev. 431, 433 (1984) (hereinafter Hay). As a McIntyre UK officer wrote in an e-mail to McIntyre America: "American law—who needs it?!" If McIntyre UK is answerable in the United States at all, is it not "perfectly appropriate to permit the exercise of that jurisdiction . . . at the place of injury"? See Hay 435; Degnan & Kane, The Exercise of Jurisdiction Over and Enforcement of Judgments Against Alien Defendants, 39 Hastings L.J. 799, 813–815 (1988) (noting that "[i]n the international order," the State that counts is the United States, not its component States, and that the fair place of suit within the United States is essentially a question of venue).

In sum, McIntyre UK, by engaging McIntyre America to promote and sell its machines in the United States, "purposefully availed itself " of the United States market nationwide, not a market in a single State or a discrete collection of States. McIntyre UK thereby availed itself of the market of all States in which its products were sold by its exclusive distributor. "Th[e] 'purposeful availment' requirement," this Court has explained, simply "ensures that a defendant will not be haled into a jurisdiction solely as a result of 'random,' 'fortuitous,' or 'attenuated' contacts." *Burger King,* 471 U.S., at 475. Adjudicatory authority is appropriately exercised where "actions by the defendant *himself* " give rise to the affiliation with the forum. *Ibid.* How could McIntyre UK not have intended, by its actions targeting a national market, to sell products in the fourth largest destination for imports among all States of the United States and the largest scrap metal market?

Courts, both state and federal, confronting facts similar to those here, have rightly rejected the conclusion that a manufacturer selling its products across the USA may evade jurisdiction in any and all States, including the State where its defective product is distributed and causes injury. They have held, instead, that it would undermine principles of fundamental fairness to insulate the foreign manufacturer from accountability in court at the place within the United States where the manufacturer's products caused injury. See, *e.g., Tobin v. Astra Pharmaceutical Prods., Inc.,* 993 F.2d 528, 544 (C.A.6 1993); *A. Uberti & C. v. Leonardo,* 181 Ariz. 565, 573, 892 P.2d 1354, 1362 (1995).

IV

A

While this Court has not considered in any prior case the now-prevalent pattern presented here—a foreign-country manufacturer enlisting a U.S. distributor to develop a market in the United States for the manufacturer's products—none of the Court's decisions tug against the judgment made by the New Jersey Supreme Court. McIntyre contends otherwise, citing *World-Wide Volkswagen,* and *Asahi Metal Industry Co. v. Superior Court of Cal., Solano Cty.,* 480 U.S. 102 (1987).

* * *

Notably, the foreign manufacturer of the Audi in *World-Wide Volkswagen* did not object to the jurisdiction of the Oklahoma courts and the U.S. importer abandoned its initially stated objection. And most relevant here, the Court's opinion indicates that an objection to jurisdiction by the manufacturer or national distributor would have been unavailing. To reiterate, the Court said in *World-Wide Volkswagen* that, when a manufacturer or distributor aims to sell its product to customers in several States, it is reasonable "to subject it to suit in [any] one of those States if its allegedly defective [product] has there been the source of injury."

* * * *

The [*Asahi*] decision was not a close call. The Court had before it a foreign plaintiff, the Taiwanese manufacturer, and a foreign defendant, the Japanese valve-assembly maker, and the indemnification dispute concerned a transaction between those parties that occurred abroad. All agreed on the bottom line: The Japanese valve-assembly manufacturer was not reasonably brought into the California courts to litigate a dispute with another foreign party over a transaction that took place outside the United States.

Given the confines of the controversy, the dueling opinions of Justice Brennan and Justice O'Connor were hardly necessary. * * *

* * *

In any event, Asahi, unlike McIntyre UK, did not itself seek out customers in the United States, it engaged no distributor to promote its wares here, it appeared at no tradeshows in the United States, and, of course, it had no Web site advertising its products to the world. Moreover, Asahi was a component-part manufacturer with "little control over the final destination of its products once they were delivered into the stream of commerce." It was important to the Court in *Asahi* that "those who use Asahi components in their final products, and sell those products in California, [would be] subject to the application of California tort law." To hold that *Asahi* controls this case would, to put it bluntly, be dead wrong.

* * *

For the reasons stated, I would hold McIntyre UK answerable in New Jersey for the harm Nicastro suffered at his workplace in that State using McIntyre UK's shearing machine. While I dissent from the Court's judgment, I take heart that the plurality opinion does not speak for the Court, for that opinion would take a giant step away from the "notions of fair play and substantial justice" underlying *International Shoe.* 326 U.S., at 316 (internal quotation marks omitted).

NOTES AND QUESTIONS

1. **Assessment of *Nicastro*.** *Nicastro* and *Goodyear Dunlop Tires*, our next principal case, were the first personal jurisdiction cases taken by the Supreme Court in over two decades. In his plurality opinion in *Nicastro*, Justice Kennedy notes that the jurisdictional "rules and standards" are "unclear because of decades-old questions left open in *Asahi*," and that "this case presents an opportunity to provide greater clarity." There was widespread hope that the Court would use these two cases to clarify the law of personal jurisdiction, including two issues disputed and left open in *Asahi*: the role in jurisdictional analysis of (a) state sovereignty and (b) the "stream of commerce."

As even a quick reading of the opinions in *Nicastro* reveals, the Court was unable to take advantage of the "opportunity to provide greater clarity." The academic response to *Nicastro* has been harsh. Professor Patrick Borchers characterizes the plurality opinion as "quite possibly the most poorly reasoned and obtuse decision of the entire minimum contacts era." Borchers, *J. McIntyre Machinery, Goodyear*, and the Incoherence of the Minimum Contacts Test, 44 Creighton L.Rev. 1245 (2011). Professor Wendy Perdue writes, "Personal jurisdiction * * * seems to inspire foolish remarks and poor opinions, and *Nicastro* may set a new low in that regard." Perdue, What's "Sovereignty" Got to Do With It? Due Process, Personal Jurisdiction, and the Supreme Court, 63 S.C.L.Rev. 729 (2012). Do you agree with these assessments?

2. **State sovereignty.** The role of state sovereignty in jurisdictional analysis has been a matter of continuous debate ever since *Pennoyer*. Sometimes, as in the Court's opinion in *World-Wide Volkswagen*, and in Justice O'Connor's plurality opinion for four justices in *Asahi*, the Court has treated state sovereignty as relevant to the jurisdictional analysis. At other times, as in the Court's opinion in Insurance Corp. of Ireland v. Compagnie des Bauxites de Guinee, 456 U.S. 694, 702 n.4, 102 S.Ct. 2099, 72 L.Ed.2d 492 (1982), and in Justice Brennan's dissenting opinion for four justices in

Asahi, state sovereignty has been explicitly excluded from the analysis. In Justice Kennedy's plurality opinion in *Nicastro*, state sovereignty is the centerpiece of the analysis.

So long as the "minimum contacts" analysis of *International Shoe* is the core concept, some attention to the sovereign status of states is inevitable, for we are instructed to assess minimum contacts with the particular state in which the suit is brought. This state-centered analysis works tolerably well for domestic defendants, but it can produce odd results when the defendant is a foreign corporation. McIntyre, a foreign corporation, sought to avoid not only having to defend in New Jersey; it also sought to avoid having to defend anywhere in the United States. The combined result of Justice Kennedy's plurality opinion and Justice Breyer's opinion concurring in the result enables it to do just that.

It is undisputed that McIntyre does a substantial amount of business in the United States. It sends its own employees to trade conventions, markets through an exclusive American distributor, and it sells many machines to American buyers. It is thus clear that McIntyre has purposefully targeted the United States as a whole as a profitable market. But six justices conclude in *Nicastro* that specific jurisdiction is unavailable in New Jersey because "purposeful" contacts with that state have not been shown. Under the Court's analysis, there appears to be no other state where Nicastro could have brought suit. McIntyre has purposeful contacts with Ohio, where it deals with its Ohio-based American distributor, as well as with states where its officials have attended national scrap metal conventions to advertise McIntyre's machines. These contacts may be enough to support jurisdiction over McIntyre in cases where injuries occurred in those states. That does not help Nicastro, for his claim does not arise out of or relate to these contacts. Does it make sense that a scrap metal worker injured by a McIntyre machine in Nevada or California, where conventions were held, may bring suit in those states, but a worker injured by a McIntyre machine in New Jersey, where no convention was held, may not bring suit in that state? Is there any reason to think that McIntyre expected to sell more scrap metal machines in states where the conventions were held? Isn't it likely, at least with respect to Nevada, that the convention was held there because of the attractions of Las Vegas, not because of an expectation of significant sales to Nevada purchasers? Is Nevada a more appropriate and predictable location for a lawsuit against McIntyre than New Jersey? Recall that Justice Ginsburg called New Jersey a "hotbed" of the scrap-metal industry.

Justice Kennedy writes, without apparent irony, of the "premises and unique genius of our Constitution." He suggests that "[i]t may be that, assuming it were otherwise empowered to legislate on the subject, the Congress could authorize the exercise of jurisdiction in appropriate courts." Is Justice Kennedy suggesting that plaintiffs in New Jersey and other states that have not hosted annual scrap metal conventions must lobby Congress for a federal products liability statute, and a federal statute conferring *in personam* jurisdiction, if they wish to bring suit in a court in the United States? How likely is it that Congress will pass such a statute? Why should Congress have to do so, given that all the states, including New Jersey, already have product liability statutes? Wouldn't it make more sense, in the case of a foreign corporate defendant, to evaluate "minimum contacts" with the nation a whole, and then to allow suit in the state where the injury occurred? Some version of this jurisdictional analysis, which would allow suit somewhere in the forum country, is standard in other western industrialized countries. Why is it not standard here?

Consider the following, written shortly after the Court decided *World-Wide Volkswagen*:

> In the international order, there is no such thing as Oklahoma. Oklahoma is an address, not a state. It is a fabled land in musical comedy, where the corn grows as high as an elephant's eye and wind goes sweeping across the plain. But it is just as mythical as Ruritania. It fields no army, sails no navy, prints no stamps and coins no money. Most important of all, it has no diplomatic relations and can conclude no treaties. In short, it lacks every single attribute of a "state" for international purposes.

Degnan and Kane, The Exercise of Jurisdiction Over and Enforcement of Judgments Against Alien Defendants, 39 Hast.L.J. 799, 813 (1988).

3. **"Stream of commerce."** Justice Kennedy writes in *Nicastro*, "The stream of commerce, like other metaphors, has its deficiencies as well as its utility. It refers to the movement of goods from manufacturers through distributors to consumers, yet beyond that descriptive purpose its meaning is far from exact." The stream of commerce metaphor had been used in earlier cases as a powerful argument in favor of *in personam* jurisdiction. If a manufacturer places its products in the stream of commerce with the hope and reasonable expectation that some of its products will be sold in a particular state, why is that not "purposeful" targeting of that state? A core concept in tort law is that a person can be held responsible for the "natural and probable consequences" of his or her actions. Why should not that concept be applied here, too? Justice Kennedy distinguishes between a defendant who can merely "predict" that his products will reach a forum state, and a defendant who "can be said to have targeted the forum." The second defendant is subject to *in personam* jurisdiction; the first defendant is not. How workable is Justice Kennedy's distinction? It would be an extremely unusual manufacturer who puts his products into the stream of commerce, predicting that some of them will be sold in a particular state, who does not affirmatively desire that they be sold in that state. How does Justice Kennedy expect us to distinguish between a defendant who merely desires that his products be sold in a particular state, on the one hand, and a defendant who "targets" that state, on the other?

4. **A possible practical solution for plaintiffs in product liability suits:** Recall that in *World-Wide Volkswagen*, the plaintiffs were able to assert *in personam* jurisdiction over both Audi, the manufacturer, and World-Wide Volkswagen, the nationwide importer and distributor. Why couldn't Nicastro seek redress in New Jersey from McIntyre America, the exclusive United States distributor for McIntyre UK? The answer is that McIntyre America was bankrupt and therefore judgment-proof. See Nicastro v. McIntyre Machinery America, Ltd., 987 A.2d 575, 578 n.2 (N.J. 2010) ("McIntyre America, the distributor, filed for bankruptcy in 2001 and has not participated in this lawsuit."). Even though a lawsuit in New Jersey against the nationwide distributor was not a viable remedy in *Nicastro* because of the McIntyre America's bankruptcy, a product liability suit against the distributor will usually be a viable remedy if *World-Wide Volkswagen* remains good law.

5.   Search for clarity. How easy will it be for a foreign manufacturer to know, based on the various opinions in *Nicastro*, whether it will be subject to *in personam* jurisdiction in an American state? Note the refusal of Justice Breyer (joined by Justice Alito) to state how he would decide the case on the basis of the factual narrative provided in Justice Ginsburg's dissent. Suppose you are asked by a German manufacturer of machine tools used in the American automobile industry whether it can use a single United States distributor as a means of avoiding avoid jurisdiction in personal injury suits brought by Michigan, Illinois or Tennessee plaintiffs injured while using the equipment on an automobile assembly line. Could you give a confident answer without knowing more facts about the American industry and how big ticket items like machine tools are marketed within that industry?

The Fifth Circuit recently took a narrow view of *McIntyre*. In Ainsworth v. Moffett Engineering, Ltd., 716 F.3d 174 (5th Cir. 2013), the plaintiff was the widow of a man who had been killed by an allegedly defective forklift manufactured by Moffett, an Irish corporation with its principal place of business in Ireland. Moffett had sold the forklift to Cargotec, a Delaware corporation whose principal place of business was Ohio, under an exclusive sales and distribution agreement. The American corporation then sold the forklift to Ainsworth's employer in Mississippi. The district court found "that *McIntyre*'s fractured opinion limited its applicability, and that the present case fell outside of *McIntyre*'s narrow holding." The Fifth Circuit agreed. Acknowledging that the Fifth Circuit's stream-of-commerce precedent, requiring only "mere foreseeability or awareness," is in tension with the *McIntyre* plurality, the court declined to find the plurality binding, instead looking to Justice Breyer's concurrence. It held that where over ten years Cargotec had sold 203 forklifts to Mississippi, worth nearly $4 million, and accounting for 1.55% of Moffett's United States sales, Moffett "reasonably could have expected" that its forklifts would be sold in Mississippi, and that the court therefore had personal jurisdiction over Moffett.

6.   Protecting small players. Justice Kennedy's and Justice Breyer's opinions both express concern that jurisdiction based upon the mere foreseeability of sale in a distant forum might expose small players, such as small American farmers or small Egyptian shirt makers, to product liability suits in every state where their product was distributed. If jurisdiction could be asserted over such small players, a possible (but likely somewhat impractical answer) would be that they could protect themselves by purchasing insurance against liability and the cost of defense. A possibly better answer would be to rely on a "reasonableness" factor derived from *Burger King* and *Asahi* to hold that it is unreasonable to subject small players to *in personam* jurisdiction in distant fora. The reasonableness factor might have a quite different application in cases involving large-scale players. Why should McIntyre, a relatively large-scale manufacturer and importer into the United States, be able to avoid *in personam* jurisdiction in New Jersey by hiding behind a hypothetical small Egyptian shirt maker? Stated differently, why is a large insured manufacturer like McIntyre protected from suit in the United States, when the effect is to force a crippled working-class plaintiff who was injured at his workplace in New Jersey by a McIntyre machine to bring his claim in the United Kingdom?

NOTE ON PURPOSEFUL AVAILMENT AND PURPOSEFUL DIRECTION

1. Purposeful availment and purposeful direction. The Supreme Court has often referred to a would-be defendant as having "purposefully availed" itself of the privilege of conducting activities in a forum State, and having "purposefully directed" its activities toward that State. For example, quoting from its earlier opinion in Hanson v. Denckla, 357 U.S. 235, 253, 78 S.Ct. 1228, 2 L.Ed.2d 1283 (1958), the Court in *Burger King* referred to the "purposeful availment" criterion for *in personam* jurisdiction:

> The unilateral activity of those who claim some relationship with a nonresident defendant cannot satisfy the requirement of contact with the forum State. The application of that rule will vary with the quality and nature of the defendant's activity, but it is essential in each case that there be some act by which the defendant *purposefully avails itself of the privilege of conducting activities within the forum State*, thus invoking the benefits and protections of its laws.

471 U.S. at 474–75 (emphasis added). Later in its opinion in *Burger King*, the Court spoke of "purposeful direction":

> So long as a commercial actor's efforts are "purposefully directed" toward residents of another State, we have consistently rejected the notion that an absence of physical contacts can defeat personal jurisdiction there.

Id. at 476.

2. Distinction between purposeful availment and purposeful direction. The Court in *Burger King* did not explicitly differentiate between "purposeful availment" and "purposeful direction." Indeed, some lower courts use "purposeful availment" as umbrella term to refer to both "purposeful availment" and "purposeful direction," but they may be seen as referring to two different ideas. "Purposeful availment" emphasizes the benefits a would-be defendant has obtained from its business activities conducted within the forum state, often involving contractual relations with forum residents. "Purposeful direction," on the other hand, emphasizes defendant's activities outside the forum state that have consequences inside the forum state. Consider the following rough sorting principle articulated in Schwarzenegger v. Fred Martin Motor Co., 374 F.3d 797, 802 (9th Cir. 2004): "A purposeful availment analysis is most often used in suits sounding in contract. A purposeful direction analysis, on the other hand, is most often used in suits sounding in tort."

3. Restatement formulation. The Restatement (Second) of Conflict of Laws, § 27, offers a number of grounds for asserting territorial jurisdiction. Among them are: "(a) presence"; (g) "doing business in a state"; (h) "an act done in a state"; and (i) "causing an effect in the state by an act done elsewhere." Ground (g) approximates, but is narrower than, "purposeful availment." Ground (i) approximates "purposeful direction."

4. Purposeful availment. In *International Shoe*, the shoe company sent its salesmen into the State of Washington to solicit orders. The company then entered into contracts with Washington residents under which they sent them shoes in return for the purchase price. The Supreme Court was explicit in recognizing a quid pro quo under which, in return for the privilege of doing business in Washington State, the company was obliged to defend suits in Washington arising out of that business:

> [T]o the extent that a corporation exercises the privilege of conducting activities within a state, it enjoys the benefits and protection of the laws of that state. The exercise of that privilege may give rise to obligations; and, so far as those obligations arise out of or are connected with the activities within the state, a procedure which requires the corporation to respond to a suit brought to enforce them can, in most instances, hardly be said to be undue.

326 U.S. 310, 319, 66 S.Ct. 154, 90 L.Ed. 95 (1945). In *McGee v. International Life Insurance Co.*, 355 U.S. 220, 78 S.Ct. 199, 2 L.Ed.2d 223 (1957), supra p. 73 note 3, a life insurance company based in Texas entered into a contractual relationship with an insured in California. When the insured died, the beneficiary brought suit in California. The Supreme Court upheld the exercise of *in personam* jurisdiction in California.

    5. Purposeful direction. In Calder v. Jones, 465 U.S. 783, 104 S.Ct. 1482, 79 L.Ed.2d 804 (1984), entertainer Shirley Jones and her husband sued the National Enquirer, its local distributing company, a reporter, and the magazine's president and editor in California state court, alleging that Jones had been libeled by a story reporting that she "drank so heavily as to prevent her from fulfilling her professional obligations." 465 U.S. at 788, n.9. The reporter lived and worked in Florida, which was the headquarters of the Enquirer, but traveled frequently to California on business. He conducted most of his research for the article on Jones by telephone from Florida. The trial court found that he made one trip to California in connection with the story. The president/editor " 'over[saw] just about every function of the Enquirer,' " approved the subject of the article, and edited the article in its final form. Id. at 786. The reporter and the president/editor challenged the assertion of *in personam* jurisdiction in California courts. The trial court denied jurisdiction on the ground that "First Amendment concerns weighed against an assertion of jurisdiction otherwise proper under the Due Process Clause." Id. at 785.

    The Supreme Court found jurisdiction proper. The defendants' "intentional, and allegedly tortious, actions were *expressly aimed* at California. * * * [T]hey knew that the brunt of that injury would be felt by respondent in the State in which she lives and works and in which the National Enquirer has its largest circulation. * * * An individual injured in California need not go to Florida to seek redress from persons who, though remaining in Florida, knowingly cause the injury in California." Id. at 789–90 (emphasis added). The Court denied that the First Amendment affected the jurisdictional analysis. "The infusion of [First Amendment] considerations would needlessly complicate an already imprecise inquiry. Moreover, the potential chill on protected First Amendment activity stemming from libel and defamation actions is already taken into account in the constitutional limitations on the substantive law governing such suits. To reintroduce those concerns at the jurisdictional stage would be a form of double counting." Id. at 790.

    Calder is commonly described as providing an "effects test." After the Court's decision in *Calder*, the "effects test" was increasingly cited in the lower federal courts in tort cases. The following is a typical example:

In *Calder*, the Supreme Court held that a foreign act that is both aimed at and has effect in the forum state satisfies the purposeful availment prong of the specific jurisdiction analysis. To meet *the effects test*, the defendant must have (1) committed an intentional act, which was (2) expressly aimed at the forum state, and (3) caused harm, the brunt of which is suffered and which the defendant knows is likely to be suffered in the forum state.

Effects test Rule

Bancroft & Masters, Inc. v. Augusta National, Inc., 223 F.3d 1082, 1087 (9th Cir. 2000) (emphasis added).

In Walden v. Fiore, 571 U.S. ___, 134 S.Ct. 1115, 188 L.Ed.2d 12 (2014), plaintiffs were professional gamblers traveling from Puerto Rico to Las Vegas, with a connecting flight in Atlanta, Georgia. At a security check point at the airport in Atlanta, a search of plaintiff's carry-on baggage revealed $97,000 in cash. Federal DEA agent Walden, a Georgia resident, seized the cash on suspicion that it was illicit drug money. Plaintiffs provided California identification to Walden, informed him that they were professional gamblers, and informed him that they had residences in Nevada and California. Plaintiffs sued Walden in federal district court in Nevada, alleging that his seizure of their cash violated the Fourth Amendment. They argued that *in personam* jurisdiction was proper because Walden knew that seizing the cash would have an adverse effect on them in Nevada, where they were going and where they had a residence. The Supreme Court held in a unanimous opinion that there was no jurisdiction over Walden in Nevada. The Court wrote, "It is undisputed that no part of [Walden's] course of conduct occurred in Nevada. * * * [Walden] never traveled to, conducted activities within, contacted anyone in, or sent anything or anyone to Nevada. In short, when viewed through the proper lens—whether the defendant's action connect him to the forum—[Walden] formed no jurisdictionally relevant contacts with Nevada." 134 S.Ct. at 1124. Why isn't it "jurisdictionally relevant" that Walden purposely performed an act that he knew would have an adverse effect on plaintiffs in Nevada? Is *Calder* still good law?

In Gray v. American Radiator & Standard Sanitary Corp., 22 Ill.2d 432, 176 N.E.2d 761 (1961), a water heater exploded in Illinois, injuring the plaintiff. She sued American Radiator, the manufacturer of the water heater, and Titan Valve, the manufacturer of an allegedly defective safety valve. Titan Valve manufactured its valves in Ohio and sold them to American Standard, who incorporated them into its water heaters at its manufacturing plant in Pennsylvania. The water heater in question was then sold in the ordinary course of business in Illinois. The record showed no other contacts between Titan Valve and Illinois. The Illinois Supreme Court held that Titan Valve could be required to appear in Illinois state court consistent with the due process clause. Justice O'Connor cites *American Radiator* disapprovingly in her plurality opinion in *Asahi* (Part II–A), but the majority appears to agree with its holding. Is *Gray v. American Radiator* still good law?

6. Not water-tight compartments. "Purposeful availment" and "purposeful direction," while distinct concepts, are not water-tight compartments. A defendant's conduct may involve both purposeful availment and purposeful direction. For example, the Court in *Burger King* spoke both of purposeful availment, largely involving Rudzewicz's franchising contract with Burger King, and of purposeful direction, largely involving the economic harm Rudzewicz's conduct caused Burger King in Florida.

    7.   **Extensions of *Calder*.** The *Calder* "effects test" has supported jurisdiction in a number of cases where a defendant's acts outside the forum have had foreseeable consequences in the forum. For example, *Calder* supports cases in which personal jurisdiction has been found over the operators of Internet web sites, when those sites have had predictable adverse effects in the forum. See discussion in Note on Internet-Based Jurisdiction, infra p. 136. See also Pugh v. Socialist People's Libyan Arab Jamahiriya, 290 F. Supp. 2d 54 (D.D.C. 2003), in which plaintiffs were executors of American citizens killed when a bomb planted by defendants destroyed a French airliner flying from Africa to Paris. The court held that the individual defendants could constitutionally be subjected to jurisdiction in the United States because they knew that the plane they were bombing was an international flight, because it was foreseeable that citizens of many nations, including the United States, would be on board, and because the United States has a strong interest in preventing and punishing international terrorism. Does this amount to a holding that every act of international terrorism with foreseeable consequences for an American citizen creates "minimum contacts" with the United States? Is this line of cases threatened by the Court's unanimous holding in *Walden v. Fiore*? Are website operators and international terrorists different from DEA agents for purposes of *in personam* jurisdiction?

c.   MINIMUM CONTACTS: GENERAL JURISDICTION

Goodyear Dunlop Tires Operations, S.A. v. Brown

Supreme Court of the United States, 2011.
564 U.S.___, 131 S.Ct. 2846, 180 L.Ed.2d 796.

■ JUSTICE GINSBURG delivered the opinion of the Court.

    This case concerns the jurisdiction of state courts over corporations organized and operating abroad. We address, in particular, this question: Are foreign subsidiaries of a United States parent corporation amenable to suit in state court on claims unrelated to any activity of the subsidiaries in the forum State? - Issue

    A bus accident outside Paris that took the lives of two 13-year-old boys from North Carolina gave rise to the litigation we here consider. Attributing the accident to a defective tire manufactured in Turkey at the plant of a foreign subsidiary of The Goodyear Tire and Rubber Company (Goodyear USA), the boys' parents commenced an action for damages in a North Carolina state court; they named as defendants Goodyear USA, an Ohio corporation, and three of its subsidiaries, organized and operating, respectively, in Turkey, France, and Luxembourg. Goodyear USA, which had plants in North Carolina and regularly engaged in commercial activity there, did not contest the North Carolina court's jurisdiction over it; Goodyear USA's foreign subsidiaries, however, maintained that North Carolina lacked adjudicatory authority over them.

    A state court's assertion of jurisdiction exposes defendants to the State's coercive power, and is therefore subject to review for compatibility with the Fourteenth Amendment's Due Process Clause. *International Shoe Co. v. Washington*, 326 U.S. 310 (1945) (assertion of jurisdiction over out-of-state corporation must comply with " 'traditional notions of fair play and substantial justice' "). Opinions in the wake of the pathmarking *International Shoe* decision have differentiated between general or all-purpose jurisdiction, and specific or case-linked jurisdiction. *Helicopteros Nacionales de Colombia, S.A. v. Hall*, 466 U.S. 408, 414, nn. 8, 9 (1984).

A court may assert general jurisdiction over foreign (sister-state or foreign-country) corporations to hear any and all claims against them when their affiliations with the State are so "continuous and systematic" as to render them essentially at home in the forum State. See *International Shoe*, 326 U.S., at 317, 66 S.Ct. 154. Specific jurisdiction, on the other hand, depends on an "affiliatio[n] between the forum and the underlying controversy," principally, activity or an occurrence that takes place in the forum State and is therefore subject to the State's regulation. von Mehren & Trautman, Jurisdiction to Adjudicate: A Suggested Analysis, 79 Harv. L.Rev. 1121, 1136 (1966) (hereinafter von Mehren & Trautman); see Brilmayer et al., A General Look at General Jurisdiction, 66 Texas L.Rev. 721, 782 (1988) (hereinafter Brilmayer). In contrast to general, all-purpose jurisdiction, specific jurisdiction is confined to adjudication of "issues deriving from, or connected with, the very controversy that establishes jurisdiction." von Mehren & Trautman 1136.

Because the episode-in-suit, the bus accident, occurred in France, and the tire alleged to have caused the accident was manufactured and sold abroad, North Carolina courts lacked specific jurisdiction to adjudicate the controversy. The North Carolina Court of Appeals so acknowledged. Were the foreign subsidiaries nonetheless amenable to general jurisdiction in North Carolina courts? Confusing or blending general and specific jurisdictional inquiries, the North Carolina courts answered yes. Some of the tires made abroad by Goodyear's foreign subsidiaries, the North Carolina Court of Appeals stressed, had reached North Carolina through "the stream of commerce"; that connection, the Court of Appeals believed, gave North Carolina courts the handle needed for the exercise of general jurisdiction over the foreign corporations.

A connection so limited between the forum and the foreign corporation, we hold, is an inadequate basis for the exercise of general jurisdiction. Such a connection does not establish the "continuous and systematic" affiliation necessary to empower North Carolina courts to entertain claims unrelated to the foreign corporation's contacts with the State.

On April 18, 2004, a bus destined for Charles de Gaulle Airport overturned on a road outside Paris, France. Passengers on the bus were young soccer players from North Carolina beginning their journey home. Two 13-year-olds, Julian Brown and Matthew Helms, sustained fatal injuries. The boys' parents, respondents in this Court, filed a suit for wrongful-death damages in the Superior Court of Onslow County, North Carolina, in their capacity as administrators of the boys' estates. Attributing the accident to a tire that failed when its plies separated, the parents alleged negligence in the "design, construction, testing, and inspection" of the tire.

Goodyear Luxembourg Tires, SA (Goodyear Luxembourg), Goodyear Lastikleri T.A.S. (Goodyear Turkey), and Goodyear Dunlop Tires France, SA (Goodyear France), petitioners here, were named as defendants. Incorporated in Luxembourg, Turkey, and France, respectively, petitioners are indirect subsidiaries of Goodyear USA, an Ohio corporation also named as a defendant in the suit. Petitioners manufacture tires primarily for sale in European and Asian markets. Their tires differ in size and construction from tires ordinarily sold in the United States. They are designed to carry significantly heavier loads, and to serve under road conditions and speed limits in the manufacturers' primary markets. *[handwritten: designed specifically for the market]* *[margin handwritten: tire differs from those normally sold in US]*

In contrast to the parent company, Goodyear USA, which does not contest the North Carolina courts' personal jurisdiction over it, petitioners are not registered to do business in North Carolina. They have no place of business, employees, or bank accounts in North Carolina. They do not design, manufacture, or advertise their products in North Carolina. And they do not solicit business in North Carolina or themselves sell or ship tires to North Carolina customers. Even so, a small percentage of petitioners' tires (tens of thousands out of tens of millions manufactured between 2004 and 2007) were distributed within North Carolina by other Goodyear USA affiliates. These tires were typically custom ordered to equip specialized vehicles such as cement mixers, waste haulers, and boat and horse trailers. Petitioners state, and respondents do not here deny, that the type of tire involved in the accident, a Goodyear Regional RHS tire manufactured by Goodyear Turkey, was never distributed in North Carolina. *[handwritten: specific tire never distributed in NC]*

Petitioners moved to dismiss the claims against them for want of personal jurisdiction. The trial court denied the motion, and the North Carolina Court of Appeals affirmed. Acknowledging that the claims neither "related to, nor . . . ar[o]se from, [petitioners'] contacts with North Carolina," the Court of Appeals confined its analysis to "general rather than specific jurisdiction," which the court recognized required a "higher threshold" showing: A defendant must have "continuous and systematic contacts" with the forum. That threshold was crossed, the court determined, when petitioners placed their tires ["in the stream of interstate commerce without any limitation on the extent to which those tires could be sold in North Carolina."] *[handwritten: - reasoning by appellate court]* *[margin handwritten: threshold for specific v. general jurisdiction]*

Nothing in the record, the court observed, indicated that petitioners "took any affirmative action to cause tires which they had manufactured to be shipped into North Carolina." The court found, however, that tires made by petitioners reached North Carolina as a consequence of a "highly-organized distribution process" involving other Goodyear USA subsidiaries. Petitioners, the court noted, made "no attempt to keep these tires from reaching the North Carolina market." Indeed, the very tire involved in the accident, the court observed, conformed to tire standards established by the U.S. Department of Transportation and bore markings required for sale in the United States. As further support, the court invoked North Carolina's "interest in providing a forum in which its citizens are able to seek redress for [their] injuries," and noted the hardship North Carolina plaintiffs would experience "[were they] required to litigate their claims in France," a country to which they have no ties. The North Carolina Supreme Court denied discretionary review. *[margin handwritten: tire standards consistent]* *[margin handwritten: interest in providing forum]*

We granted certiorari to decide whether the general jurisdiction the North Carolina courts asserted over petitioners is consistent with the Due Process Clause of the Fourteenth Amendment.

II

A

The Due Process Clause of the Fourteenth Amendment sets the outer boundaries of a state tribunal's authority to proceed against a defendant. The canonical opinion in this area remains *International Shoe,* in which we held that a State may authorize its courts to exercise personal jurisdiction over an out-of-state defendant if the defendant has "certain minimum contacts with [the State] such that the maintenance of the suit does not offend 'traditional notions of fair play and substantial justice.'"

Endeavoring to give specific content to the "fair play and substantial justice" concept, the Court in *International Shoe* classified cases involving out-of-state corporate defendants. First, as in *International Shoe* itself, jurisdiction unquestionably could be asserted where the corporation's in-state activity is "continuous and systematic" and that activity gave rise to the episode-in-suit. Further, the Court observed, the commission of certain "single or occasional acts" in a State may be *specific* sufficient to render a corporation answerable in that State with respect to those acts, though not with respect to matters unrelated to the forum connections. The heading courts today use to encompass these two *International Shoe* categories is "specific jurisdiction." See von Mehren & Trautman 1144–1163. Adjudicatory authority is "specific" when the suit "aris[es] out of or relate[s] to the defendant's contacts with the forum."

International Shoe distinguished from cases that fit within the "specific jurisdiction" categories, "instances in which the continuous corporate operations within a state [are] so substantial and of such a nature as to justify suit against it on causes of action arising from dealings entirely distinct from those activities." Adjudicatory authority so grounded is today called "general jurisdiction." For an individual, the paradigm forum for the exercise of general jurisdiction is the individual's domicile; for a corporation, it is an equivalent place, one in which the corporation is fairly regarded as at home. See Brilmayer 728 (identifying *general* domicile, place of incorporation, and principal place of business as "paradig[m]" bases for the exercise of general jurisdiction).

* * *

B

To justify the exercise of general jurisdiction over petitioners, the North Carolina courts relied on the petitioners' placement of their tires in the "stream of commerce." The stream-of-commerce metaphor has been invoked frequently in lower court decisions permitting "jurisdiction in products liability cases in which the product has traveled through an extensive chain of distribution before reaching the ultimate consumer." Typically, in such cases, a nonresident defendant, acting outside the forum, places in the stream of commerce a product that ultimately causes harm inside the forum.

Many States have enacted long-arm statutes authorizing courts to exercise specific jurisdiction over manufacturers when the events in suit, or some of them, occurred within the forum state. For example, the "Local Injury; Foreign Act" subsection of North Carolina's long-arm statute authorizes North Carolina courts to exercise personal jurisdiction in "any action claiming injury to person or property within this State arising out of [the defendant's] act or omission outside this State," if, "in addition[,] at or about the time of the injury," "[p]roducts . . . manufactured by the defendant were used or consumed, within this State in the ordinary course of trade." N.C. Gen.Stat. Ann. § 1–75.4(4)(b) (Lexis 2009). As the North Carolina Court of Appeals recognized, this provision of the State's long-arm statute "does not apply to this case," for both the act alleged to have caused injury (the fabrication of the allegedly defective tire) and its impact (the accident) occurred outside the forum.[4]

The North Carolina court's stream-of-commerce analysis elided the essential difference between case-specific and all-purpose (general) jurisdiction. Flow of a manufacturer's products into the forum, we have explained, may bolster an affiliation germane to specific jurisdiction. See, e.g., World-Wide Volkswagen [v. Woodson], 444 U.S. [286], 297 [(1980)] (where "the sale of a product . . . is not simply an isolated occurrence, but arises from the efforts of the manufacturer or distributor to serve . . . the market for its product in [several] States, it is not unreasonable to subject it to suit in one of those States if its allegedly defective merchandise *has there been the source of injury to its owner or to others*" (emphasis added)). But ties serving to bolster the exercise of specific jurisdiction do not warrant a determination that, based on those ties, the forum has general jurisdiction over a defendant.

A corporation's "continuous activity of some sorts within a state," *International Shoe* instructed, "is not enough to support the demand that the corporation be amenable to suits unrelated to that activity." Our 1952 decision in *Perkins v. Benguet Consol. Mining Co.*[, 342 U.S. 437 (1952),] remains "[t]he textbook case of general jurisdiction appropriately exercised over a foreign corporation that has not consented to suit in the forum."

Sued in Ohio, the defendant in *Perkins* was a Philippine mining corporation that had ceased activities in the Philippines during World War II. To the extent that the company was conducting any business during and immediately after the Japanese occupation of the Philippines, it was doing so in Ohio: the corporation's president maintained his office there, kept the company files in that office, and supervised from the Ohio office "the necessarily limited wartime activities of the company." Although the claim-in-suit did not arise in Ohio, this Court ruled that it would not violate due process for Ohio to adjudicate the controversy. *Ibid.*; see Keeton v. Hustler Magazine, Inc., 465 U.S. 770, 779–780, n. 11 (1984) (Ohio's exercise of general jurisdiction was permissible in Perkins because "Ohio was the corporation's principal, if temporary, place of business").

---

[4] The court instead relied on N.C. Gen.Stat. Ann. § 1–75.4(1)(d), which provides for jurisdiction, "whether the claim arises within or without [the] State," when the defendant "[i]s engaged in substantial activity within this State, whether such activity is wholly interstate, intrastate, or otherwise." This provision, the North Carolina Supreme Court has held, was "intended to make available to the North Carolina courts the full jurisdictional powers permissible under federal due process."

We next addressed the exercise of general jurisdiction over an out-of-state corporation over three decades later, in *Helicopteros*. In that case, survivors of United States citizens who died in a helicopter crash in Peru instituted wrongful-death actions in a Texas state court against the owner and operator of the helicopter, a Colombian corporation. The Colombian corporation had no place of business in Texas and was not licensed to do business there. "Basically, [the company's] contacts with Texas consisted of sending its chief executive officer to Houston for a contract-negotiation session; accepting into its New York bank account checks drawn on a Houston bank; purchasing helicopters, equipment, and training services from [a Texas enterprise] for substantial sums; and sending personnel to [Texas] for training." These links to Texas, we determined, did not "constitute the kind of continuous and systematic general business contacts . . . found to exist in *Perkins*," and were insufficient to support the exercise of jurisdiction over a claim that neither "ar[o]se out of . . . no[r] related to" the defendant's activities in Texas.

Helicopteros concluded that "mere purchases [made in the forum State], even if occurring at regular intervals, are not enough to warrant a State's assertion of [general] jurisdiction over a nonresident corporation in a cause of action not related to those purchase transactions." We see no reason to differentiate from the ties to Texas held insufficient in *Helicopteros*, the sales of petitioners' tires sporadically made in North Carolina through intermediaries. Under the sprawling view of general jurisdiction urged by respondents and embraced by the North Carolina Court of Appeals, any substantial manufacturer or seller of goods would be amenable to suit, on any claim for relief, wherever its products are distributed. But cf. *World-Wide Volkswagen*, 444 U.S., at 296 (every seller of chattels does not, by virtue of the sale, "appoint the chattel his agent for service of process").

Measured against *Helicopteros* and *Perkins*, North Carolina is not a forum in which it would be permissible to subject petitioners to general jurisdiction. Unlike the defendant in *Perkins*, whose sole wartime business activity was conducted in Ohio, petitioners are in no sense at home in North Carolina. Their attenuated connections to the State, fall far short of the "the continuous and systematic general business contacts" necessary to empower North Carolina to entertain suit against them on claims unrelated to anything that connects them to the State. *Helicopteros*, 466 U.S., at 416, 104 S.Ct. 1868.[5]

C

Respondents belatedly assert a "single enterprise" theory, asking us to consolidate petitioners' ties to North Carolina with those of Goodyear USA and other Goodyear entities. In effect, respondents would have us

---

[5] As earlier noted, the North Carolina Court of Appeals invoked the State's "well-recognized interest in providing a forum in which its citizens are able to seek redress for injuries that they have sustained." But "[g]eneral jurisdiction to adjudicate has in [United States] practice never been based on the plaintiff's relationship to the forum. There is nothing in [our] law comparable to . . . article 14 of the Civil Code of France (1804) under which the French nationality of the plaintiff is a sufficient ground for jurisdiction." von Mehren & Trautman 1137; see Clermont & Palmer, Exorbitant Jurisdiction, 58 Me. L.Rev. 474, 492–495 (2006) (French law permitting plaintiff-based jurisdiction is rarely invoked in the absence of other supporting factors). When a defendant's act outside the forum causes injury in the forum, by contrast, a plaintiff's residence in the forum may strengthen the case for the exercise of *specific jurisdiction*.

pierce Goodyear corporate veils, at least for jurisdictional purposes. See Brilmayer & Paisley, Personal Jurisdiction and Substantive Legal Relations: Corporations, Conspiracies, and Agency, 74 Cal. L.Rev. 1, 14, 29–30 (1986) (merging parent and subsidiary for jurisdictional purposes requires an inquiry "comparable to the corporate law question of piercing the corporate veil"). Neither below nor in their brief in opposition to the petition for certiorari did respondents urge disregard of petitioners' discrete status as subsidiaries and treatment of all Goodyear entities as a "unitary business," so that jurisdiction over the parent would draw in the subsidiaries as well. Respondents have therefore forfeited this contention, and we do not address it.

* * *

For the reasons stated, the judgment of the North Carolina Court of Appeals is *Reversed*.

NOTES AND QUESTIONS

1. **The basic concept of general jurisdiction.** The basic concept of general jurisdiction as described in *Goodyear* is clear enough. If the quantity and quality of a defendant's purposeful contacts with a state are sufficient to justify the exercise of general jurisdiction, any claim may be brought against the defendant in that state, whether or not it arises out of or relates to those contacts. The Court in *Goodyear* tells us that general jurisdiction over a corporation is appropriate when its contacts with a forum state "are 'so continuous and systematic' as to render" the corporation "essentially at home" in that state. General jurisdiction can lead to extreme results. For example, if Goodyear Turkey had been subject to general jurisdiction in North Carolina, it could have been sued there by a class of its Turkish employees seeking payment of unpaid wages.

2. **General jurisdiction over corporations**. Ever since *International Shoe* (and perhaps earlier), there has been general agreement that a corporation should be subject to general jurisdiction somewhere. Many large American corporations choose Delaware as their state of incorporation, even though their principal places of business are elsewhere. The location of a corporation's principal place of business is not always easy to determine. See, for example, Hertz Corp. v. Friend, 559 U.S. 77, 130 S.Ct. 1181, 175 L.Ed.2d 1029 (2010), infra p. 245. Goodyear USA is somewhat unusual for a large corporation. It is incorporated in Ohio and also has its principal place of business in Ohio.

Should Goodyear USA employees working at a Goodyear USA factory in California be allowed to bring suit in Ohio alleging that Goodyear has violated overtime rules prescribed by California law? If there is general jurisdiction over Goodyear USA in Ohio, there can be no jurisdictional objection to the suit. But territorial jurisdiction is not the only factor in determining where a suit may be brought. As we will see later in this chapter, venue and change-of-venue rules, as well as principles of *forum non conveniens*, are important fine-tuning devices that help determine where a suit is ultimately brought.

3. **"Essentially at home."** The Court in *Goodyear* tells us that there is general jurisdiction over a corporation where it is "essentially at home." Is it safe to assume that a corporation is "essentially at home" both in the state

where it is incorporated and in the state where it has its principal place of business?

Professors von Mehren and Trautman would have subjected a corporation to general jurisdiction at the "corporate headquarters— presumably both the place of incorporation and the principal place of business, where these differ." Von Mehren and Trautman, Jurisdiction to Adjudicate: A Suggested Analysis, 79 Harv. L. Rev. 1121, 1179 (1966). Professor Twitchell would allow general jurisdiction "wherever the corporation is headquartered." For Twitchell, this definitely means the principal place of business, although she is less certain about whether the state of incorporation should in all cases support general jurisdiction. She is still less certain about whether continuous and systematic contacts with the forum should permit general jurisdiction. Twitchell, The Myth of General Jurisdiction, 101 Harv. L. Rev. 610, 669–79 (1988).

4. Jurisdiction over *Goodyear* subsidiaries The Court holds unanimously in *Goodyear* that none of Goodyear's three foreign subsidiaries is subject to general jurisdiction in North Carolina. That is, none of them is "essentially at home" in that state. Should any of the subsidiaries be subject to specific jurisdiction? The Court notes that between 2003 and 2007 a few tens of thousands of tires manufactured by the three foreign Goodyear subsidiaries were distributed in North Carolina. The Court does not tell us whether this distribution constituted "purposeful" contact by these defendants. Whether purposeful or not, the Court appears to have concluded that these contacts were insufficiently connected to the suit brought by plaintiffs to justify specific jurisdiction. Do you agree? Recall that the imported tires were typically custom ordered and were used as equipment on special purpose vehicles. None of the tires imported into North Carolina was the same type as the tire that allegedly caused the accident in France.

5. No general jurisdiction in a more recent corporate case. In Daimler AG v. Bauman, 571 U.S. ___, 134 S.Ct. 746, 187 L.Ed.2d 624 (2014), a complaint was filed in federal District Court in the Northern District of California by twenty-two residents of Argentina who alleged that Mercedes-Benz Argentina, a wholly owned subsidiary of the German parent, Daimler AG ("Daimler"), collaborated with state security forces during Argentina's "dirty war" in detaining, torturing and killing Mercedes-Benz Argentina workers, including plaintiffs or persons closely related to them. The complaint named Daimler as a defendant, asserting general jurisdiction based on the contacts with California of Mercedes-Benz USA ("MBUSA"), another wholly owned subsidiary of Daimler. The complaint alleged violation of two federal statutes, the Alien Tort Statute and the Torture Victim Protection Act of 1991.

The Supreme Court assumed *arguendo* that the contacts of MBUSA with California were attributable to Daimler. But even employing that debatable assumption, the Court held that there was no general jurisdiction over Daimler in California:

> Here, neither Daimler nor MBUSA is incorporated in California, nor does either entity have its principal place of business there. If Daimler's California activities sufficed to allow adjudication of this Argentina-rooted case in California, the same global reach would presumably be available in every other State in which MBUSA's sales are sizable. Such exorbitant exercises of all-purpose

jurisdiction would scarcely permit out-of-state defendants "to structure their primary conduct with some minimum assurance as to where that conduct will and will not render them liable to suit." *Burger King Corp.*, 471 U.S., at 472.

34 S.Ct. at 761–62. Should it make a difference to the jurisdictional analysis that at least some of the alleged "primary conduct" of Mercedes-Benz Argentina—torture and killing—violated international law and would thus likely have been held illegal by any court in which suit would have been brought?

6. **Cases likely overruled by *Goodyear* and *Daimler*.** In a number of cases leading up to *Goodyear* and *Daimler*, lower courts had relied an expansive notion of general jurisdiction based on continuous and systematic sales in a state. See, for example, Gator.com Corp. v. L.L. Bean, Inc., 341 F.3d 1072 (9th Cir. 2003), in which the Court found general jurisdiction in California based on L.L. Bean's having made 6% of its total retail sales in California through its mail order catalogue, its toll-free telephone number, and its Internet website, even though L.L. Bean had no assets and no employees in California. The Ninth Circuit took this decision en banc, but then dismissed the appeal as moot after the parties settled. 398 F.3d 1125 (9th Cir. 2005). See also Lakin v. Prudential Securities, Inc., 348 F.3d 704 (8th Cir. 2003), indicating that if Prudential's home equity loans and lines of credit in Missouri amounted to $10,000,000 (1% of Prudential's total loan portfolio) there was general jurisdiction over Prudential in Missouri. Decisions such as these almost certainly do not survive *Goodyear* and *Daimler*.

Recall that Goodyear USA consented to jurisdiction in North Carolina. Under the prevailing precedent before *Goodyear* and *Daimler*, this was almost certainly a rational decision because Goodyear USA was likely subject to general jurisdiction in North Carolina based on its extensive business and activities in that state. Recall also *Worldwide Volkswagen*. In that case, neither Audi nor Volkswagen of America contested jurisdiction in Oklahoma when the case came to the Supreme Court. If that case were litigated today, do you think either of those two defendants could successfully challenge *in personam* jurisdiction in Oklahoma?

7. **A continuous spectrum?** It can be argued that general jurisdiction should stand at one end of a continuous spectrum of cases. Along that spectrum, the availability of territorial jurisdiction is based on a combination of factors: the quantity and quality of purposeful forum contacts, the relationship between the claims and the contacts, and other factors bearing on the fairness of the exercise of jurisdiction. In such an analysis, a weaker showing of purposeful availment might be counteracted by strong showings of relatedness, forum state interest and/or hardship to the plaintiff. Similarly, a weaker showing of relatedness could be counteracted by strong showings of purposeful availment and convenience. There is support in *International Shoe* itself for such an analysis. Do you see any support for such an analysis in *Goodyear*, in which its analysis of general jurisdiction essentially like an on-off switch in which a defendant corporation either is, or is not, "essentially at home"? Should we read *Goodyear* as barring such a balancing approach in the law of specific jurisdiction? That is, should we read *Goodyear* as casting doubt on the relatively nuanced approach of the Court in personal jurisdiction cases such as *World-Wide*

[handwritten margin note: factors re general jurisdiction]

Volkswagen, Burger King, and *Asahi*? Should we also read *Nicastro* as casting doubt on the nuanced approach of those cases?

d. LONG-ARM STATUTES

So far we have explored the outer constitutional boundaries of jurisdiction under the due process clause of the federal Constitution. But this is, from one perspective, to skip a step. A court cannot exercise *in personam* jurisdiction unless there is statutory authorization for the exercise of that jurisdiction. Jurisdictional statutes that reach across state lines are typically referred to as "long-arm" statutes: The statute asserts the state's authority to reach its "long arm" across the state boundary into another state or country, and thereby to subject a person or corporation to its jurisdiction.

Some states' long-arm statutes authorize jurisdiction to the maximum extent permitted by the federal Constitution. For example, California's statute provides, quite simply, "A court of this state may exercise jurisdiction on any basis not inconsistent with the Constitution of this state or of the United States." Calif.C.Civ.P. § 410.10. See Cornelison v. Chaney, 16 Cal.3d 143, 127 Cal.Rptr. 352, 545 P.2d 264 (1976). Rhode Island has a similar statute. R.I.Gen.L § 9–5–33(a). In such states, the only relevant jurisdictional question is what the Due Process Clause requires.

Other states have more detailed long-arm statutes, setting out particular circumstances under which state courts may exercise jurisdiction. Usually, these detailed statutes do not extend jurisdiction to the full extent permitted by the Due Process Clause. See, e.g., N.Y.C.P.L.R. § 302(a); Bensusan Restaurant Corp. v. King, 126 F.3d 25 (2d Cir. 1997); Feathers v. McLucas, 15 N.Y.2d 443, 261 N.Y.S.2d 8, 209 N.E.2d 68 (1965); Ill.C.Civ.P. § 2–209; Gray v. American Radiator & Standard Sanitary Corp., 22 Ill.2d 432, 176 N.E.2d 761 (1961); Fla. Stat. § 48.193(1)–(2); Licciardello v. Lovelady, 544 F.3d 1280 (11th Cir. 2008). In states with such statutes, a plaintiff must first satisfy the state statutory requirements for exercising jurisdiction. If the statutory requirements are met, the plaintiff must also satisfy federal due process requirements under the Fourteenth Amendment. In almost all states with such statutes, courts do not exercise territorial jurisdiction to the maximum extent permitted by the Due Process Clause. However, in at least one state with a detailed long-arm jurisdictional statute, judicial construction has resulted in the statute's being extended to the maximum permitted by the Due Process Clause. See Hall v. Helicopteros Nacionales De Colombia, S.A., 638 S.W.2d 870, 872 (Tex.1982), rev'd on other grounds, 466 U.S. 408 (1984). Sometimes, as we have seen, states go too far, interpreting their long-arm statutes to authorize jurisdiction beyond that allowed by the Due Process Clause, as in *Goodyear* and *Nicastro*.

Federal district courts usually rely on the long-arm statutes of the state in which they sit. However, there are a few federal long-arm statutes that assert nationwide *in personam* jurisdiction. See, e.g., 15 U.S.C. § 25 (anti-trust); 15 U.S.C. § 77v(a) (securities); 28 U.S.C. § 1335 (interpleader).

Omni Capital International v. Rudolf Wolff & Co.

Supreme Court of the United States, 1987.
484 U.S. 97, 108 S.Ct. 404, 98 L.Ed.2d 415.

■ JUSTICE BLACKMUN delivered the opinion of the Court.

This case presents questions concerning the prerequisites to a federal court's exercise of *in personam* jurisdiction.

I

Petitioners Omni Capital International, Ltd., and Omni Capital Corporation (collectively Omni), New York corporations, marketed an investment program involving commodity-futures trades on the London Metals Exchange. Omni employed respondent Rudolf Wolff & Co., Ltd., a British corporation with its offices in London, as a broker to handle trades on that Exchange. Respondent James Gourlay, a citizen and resident of the United Kingdom, served as Wolff's representative in soliciting this business from Omni.

The United States Internal Revenue Service disallowed income tax deductions, claimed by the participants in Omni's investment program, and did so on the ground that the program's commodities trades on the London Metals Exchange were not bona fide arm's-length transactions. A number of corporate and individual investors who participated in Omni's program then sued Omni in four separate actions in the United States District Court for the Eastern District of Louisiana. The plaintiffs in each action charged that, by misrepresenting its tax benefits and future profits, Omni fraudulently induced them to participate in the investment program. Omni, in turn, impleaded Wolff and Gourlay, contending that its liability, if any, was caused by their improper trading activities.

* * *

Wolff and Gourlay moved to dismiss the claims against them for lack of personal jurisdiction, and, as an additional ground, argued that the securities law claims failed to state causes of action. * * *

* * *

Because of a possible conflict with views of the Sixth Circuit expressed in Handley v. Indiana & Michigan Electric Co., 732 F.2d 1265, 1272 (1984), we granted certiorari to decide whether, in this federal-question litigation arising under the [Commodity Exchange Act (CEA)] the District Court may exercise personal jurisdiction over Wolff and Gourlay. — Issue?

II

Omni's primary and fundamental contention is that in a suit under the CEA, the only limits on a district court's power to exercise personal jurisdiction derive from the Due Process Clause of the Fifth Amendment. The objection of the Court of Appeals, and of Wolff and Gourlay before this Court, is that, even if an exercise of personal jurisdiction would comport with that Due Process Clause,[5] the District Court cannot

---

[5] Under Omni's theory, a federal court could exercise personal jurisdiction, consistent with the Fifth Amendment, based on an aggregation of the defendant's contacts with the Nation as a whole, rather than on its contacts with the State in which the federal court sits. As was the

exercise personal jurisdiction over Wolff and Gourlay because they are not amenable to service of summons in the absence of a statute or rule authorizing such service.

Omni attempts to meet this objection in a variety of ways. First, Omni argues that the District Court may exercise personal jurisdiction because Wolff and Gourlay have constitutionally sufficient contacts with the forum and, as well, have notice of the suits. Second, Omni contends that even if a rule authorizing service is a prerequisite to effective service and thus to the exercise of personal jurisdiction, Congress implicitly authorized nationwide service for private causes of action under the CEA. Third, Omni presses upon us the view of the Fifth Circuit dissenters that, even if authorization for service of process is required and cannot be found in a statute or rule, such authorization should be created by fashioning a remedy to fill a gap in the Federal Rules of Civil Procedure. We examine these contentions in turn.

III

A

Omni argues that the jurisdictional limits that Art. III of the Constitution places on the federal courts relate to subject-matter jurisdiction only. In this view, although Art. III, § 1, leaves it to Congress to "ordain and establish" inferior federal courts, the only limits on those courts, once established, in their exercise of personal jurisdiction, relate to due process. Thus, Omni contends, the District Court may exercise personal jurisdiction over Wolff and Gourlay if the Due Process Clause of the Fifth Amendment does not forbid it.

Omni's argument that Art. III does not itself limit a court's personal jurisdiction is correct. "The requirement that a court have personal jurisdiction flows not from Art. III, but from the Due Process Clause. . . . It represents a restriction on judicial power not as a matter of sovereignty, but as a matter of individual liberty." Insurance Corp. of Ireland v. Compagnie des Bauxites de Guinee, 456 U.S. 694, 702, 102 S.Ct. 2099, 2104, 72 L.Ed.2d 492 (1982). Omni's argument fails, however, because there are other prerequisites to a federal court's exercise of personal jurisdiction.

Before a federal court may exercise personal jurisdiction over a defendant, the procedural requirement of service of summons must be satisfied. "[S]ervice of summons is the procedure by which a court having venue and jurisdiction of the subject matter of the suit asserts jurisdiction over the person of the party served." Mississippi Publishing Corp. v. Murphree, 326 U.S. 438, 444–445, 66 S.Ct. 242, 245–246, 90 L.Ed. 185 (1946). Thus, before a court may exercise personal jurisdiction over a defendant, there must be more than notice to the defendant and a constitutionally sufficient relationship between the defendant and the forum. There also must be a basis for the defendant's amenability to service of summons. Absent consent, this means there must be authorization for service of summons on the defendant.

---

case in Asahi Metal Industry Co. v. Superior Court of Cal., 480 U.S. 102, 107 S.Ct. 1026, 94 L.Ed.2d 92 (1987), "[w]e have no occasion" to consider the constitutional issues raised by this theory. Id., at 113, n. *, 107 S.Ct., at 1032, n. *.

B

The next question, then, is whether there is authorization to serve summons in this litigation. Today, service of process in a federal action is covered generally by Rule 4 of the Federal Rules of Civil Procedure. [Editors' note: References in the opinion are to Rule 4 as it existed before amendment in 1993.] Rule 4(f) describes where process "may be served." It authorizes service in the State in which the action is brought, or anywhere else authorized by a federal statute or by the Rules.

The "most obvious reference" of this last provision is to Rule 4(e). See D. Currie, Federal Courts 373 (3d ed. 1982). The first sentence of the Rule speaks to the ability to serve summons on an out-of-state defendant when a federal statute authorizes such service. The second sentence, as an additional method, authorizes service of summons "under the circumstances" prescribed in a state statute or rule. Thus, under Rule 4(e), a federal court normally looks either to a federal statute or to the long-arm statute of the State in which it sits to determine whether a defendant is amenable to service, a prerequisite to its exercise of personal jurisdiction.

Omni argues that Wolff and Gourlay are amenable to service under Rule 4(e) because the CEA implicitly "provides for service . . . upon a party not an inhabitant of or found within the state." * * *

Neither the majority nor the dissent in the Court of Appeals found that the CEA contained an implied provision for nationwide service of process in a private cause of action. We, too, decline to draw that inference. * * *

* * *

Since the CEA does not authorize service of summons on Wolff and Gourlay, we look to the second sentence of Rule 4(e), which points to the long-arm statute of the State in which the District Court sits—here, Louisiana. * * * Before us, Omni has not contended that Wolff and Gourlay may be reached under the Louisiana long-arm statute. Indeed, Omni has conceded that they may not. See Tr. of Oral Arg. 4. Thus, neither part of Rule 4(e) authorizes the service of summons on Wolff and Gourlay.

C

The dissenters in the Court of Appeals argued that even if authorization to serve process is necessary and cannot be found in Rule 4(e), the federal courts should act to fill the "interstices in the law inadvertently left by legislative enactment" by creating their own rule authorizing service of process in this litigation. See 795 F.2d, at 431–432. We decline to embark on that adventure.

* * *

We would consider it unwise for a court to make its own rule authorizing service of summons. It seems likely that Congress has been acting on the assumption that federal courts cannot add to the scope of service of summons Congress has authorized. This Court in the past repeatedly has stated that a legislative grant of authority is necessary. See, e.g., Georgia v. Pennsylvania R. Co., 324 U.S. 439, 467–468, 65 S.Ct. 716, 731, 89 L.Ed. 1051 (1945). * * *

The strength of this longstanding assumption, and the network of statutory enactments and judicial decisions tied to it, argue strongly against devising common-law service of process provisions at this late date for at least two reasons. First, since Congress concededly has the power to limit service of process, circumspection is called for in going beyond what Congress has authorized. Second, as statutes and rules have always provided the measures for service, courts are inappropriate forums for deciding whether to extend them. Legislative rulemaking better ensures proper consideration of a service rule's ramifications within the pre-existing structure and is more likely to lead to consistent application.

legislation required in determining service

* * *

We are not blind to the consequences of the inability to serve process on Wolff and Gourlay. A narrowly tailored service of process provision, authorizing service on an alien in a federal-question case when the alien is not amenable to service under the applicable state long-arm statute, might well serve the ends of the CEA and other federal statutes. It is not for the federal courts, however, to create such a rule as a matter of common law. That responsibility, in our view, better rests with those who propose the Federal Rules of Civil Procedure and with Congress.

IV

Holding

In summary, the District Court may not exercise jurisdiction over Wolff and Gourlay without authorization to serve process. That authorization is not found in either the CEA or the Louisiana long-arm statute to which we look under Rule 4(e). We reject the suggestion that we should create a common-law rule authorizing service of process, since we would consider that action unwise, even were it within our power.

—The judgment of the Court of Appeals is affirmed.

* * *

NOTES AND QUESTIONS

1.   **Foreign defendants.** The specific question posed by *Omni Capital* was resolved in 1993 when Federal Rule of Civil Procedure 4(k)(2) was adopted. Rule 4(k)(2) allows aggregation of all contacts between the defendant and the United States as a whole as a basis for jurisdiction in a suit brought under federal law in federal district court when a defendant is not subject to jurisdiction in the court of any state.

Note that in footnote 5 of *Omni Capital* the Supreme Court left open the question whether aggregation of national contacts is permissible in assessing jurisdiction over foreign defendants. Was the Supreme Court merely being coy in leaving the question open? Has the question been squarely presented by the adoption of Rule 4(k)(2)?

A possibly more difficult question is whether such a result produced by Rule 4(k)(2) may permissibly be achieved through the Federal Rules of Civil Procedure. The Rules Enabling Act provides that the Federal Rules "shall not abridge, enlarge, or modify any substantive right." 28 U.S.C. § 2072(b). Extending *in personam* jurisdiction in this fashion may be thought to "enlarge" the scope of substantive federal law under which the defendant is being sued. The Advisory Committee on the Civil Rules, which was primarily responsible for drafting the amendment to Rule 4, was acutely aware of the problem. At the beginning of the Committee Notes, written in italics, is the following: "*SPECIAL NOTE: Mindful of the constraints of the Rules Enabling Act, the Committee calls the attention of the Supreme Court and Congress to new subdivision (k)(2). Should this limited extension of service be disapproved, the Committee nevertheless recommends adoption of the balance of the rule*[.]" 113 S.Ct. 631–3 (1993). Somewhat oddly, the Supreme Court in *Omni Capital* appears to have thought this problem unimportant. Note that if the only problem with the amended Rule 4 is that it is inconsistent with the Rules Enabling Act, Congress is perfectly free to enact the rule as a free-standing statute. For discussion of Rule 4(k)(2), see Burbank, The United States' Approach to International Civil Litigation: Recent Developments in Forum Selection, 19 U.Pa.J. of Int'l Econ.L. 1, 8–14 (1998). For a vigorous argument that Rule 4(k)(2) oversteps the boundaries of the Rules Enabling Act, see Kelleher, Amenability of Jurisdiction as a "Substantive Right": The Invalidity of Rule 4(k)(2) under the Rules Enabling Act, 75 Ind.L.J. 1191 (2000).

The lower federal courts have not been troubled by Rules Enabling Act problems. They have simply applied Rule 4(k)(2). See, e.g., Merial, Ltd. v. BASF Agro B.V., 681 F.3d 1283 (Fed.Cir. 2012); Smith v. J&B Tours, Ltd., 594 F.3d 842 (11th Cir. 2010); Porina v. Marward Shipping Co., Ltd, 521 F.3d 122, 126–27 (2d Cir. 2008); Fortis Corp. Ins. v. Viken Ship Mgmt., 450 F.3d 214, 222 (6th Cir. 2006); Mwani v. bin Laden, 417 F.3d 1, 11 (D.C.Cir. 2005).

2. Relationship between federal and state court *in personam* jurisdiction. A federal court usually asserts *in personam* jurisdiction to the same extent as a state court in which the federal court is sitting. This is true in cases both where the claim arises under federal law, and where the claim arises under state law and subject matter jurisdiction is based on diversity of citizenship. However, a federal statute sometimes explicitly provides for *in personam* jurisdiction beyond that authorized by the state. Several federal statutes provide for nationwide jurisdiction, meaning that a defendant can be summoned from anywhere in the United States to appear in any federal court in the United States. Most such statutes involve suits based on federal law, but there is also nationwide jurisdiction in federal court over a few suits based on state law. See Fed. R. Civ. P. 4(k)(1).

3. Suits based on federal law. A number of federal statutes provide for nationwide jurisdiction in cases based on federal law. See Fed. R. Civ. P. 4(k)(1)(C). They include antitrust cases, 15 U.S.C. § 25; and securities cases, 15 U.S.C. §§ 77v(a), 78aa. Bankruptcy cases can also be included in this category, although they often involve questions of state law, or of mixed federal and state law. See 11 U.S.C. Bankruptcy Rule 7004(d).

If the basis for *in personam* jurisdiction is sovereignty, it should be axiomatic that a federal court can have nationwide jurisdiction in a suit based on federal law. Just as the state can exert jurisdiction over anyone found within the geographical territory of the state, the nation should be able to exert jurisdiction over anyone found within the geographical territory of the nation. But this brings us back to the question highlighted by Justice White in *World-Wide Volkswagen* and *Insurance Corp. of Ireland*, and reprised by Justice Kennedy in *Nicastro*. To what degree is territorial jurisdiction premised on sovereignty? Should nationwide *in personam* jurisdiction in the federal courts also be limited by considerations of personal convenience and fairness?

The Supreme Court as a whole has not spoken to the constitutionality of nationwide *in personam* jurisdiction in the federal courts in extreme cases where the defendant has strong fairness grounds to object to *in personam* jurisdiction. Justice Stewart, joined by Justice Brennan, has stated that the "short answer * * * is that due process requires only certain minimum contacts between the defendant and the sovereign that has created the court. * * * The cases before us involve suits against residents of the United States in the courts of the United States. No due process problem exists." Stafford v. Briggs, 444 U.S. 527, 554, 100 S.Ct. 774, 63 L.Ed.2d 1 (1980) (Stewart, J., dissenting). The majority opinion did not reach the question answered by Justice Stewart. The lower federal courts have generally agreed with Justice Stewart. See, e.g., In re Federal Fountain, Inc. v. KR Entertainment, Inc., 165 F.3d 600, 602 (8th Cir. 1999) (en banc); Mariash v. Morrill, 496 F.2d 1138 (2d Cir. 1974). A few courts, however, disagree. See, e.g., Peay v. BellSouth Medical Assistance Plan, 205 F.3d 1206 (10th Cir. 2000). Professor Fullerton has argued extensively that due process in federal court should not be satisfied merely because a defendant can be found somewhere within the territory of the federal sovereign. Fullerton, Constitutional Limits on Nationwide Personal Jurisdiction in the Federal Courts, 79 N.W.U.L.Rev. 1 (1984).

In practice, the fairness problem is rarely presented in acute form, for federal venue statutes restrict the ability of a plaintiff to bring suit in an inconvenient federal court. 28 U.S.C. § 1391 (general venue statute); 15 U.S.C. §§ 15, 22 (antitrust venue statute); 15 U.S.C. § 77v(a) (securities venue statute). Further, change of venue from one federal court to another is available for the convenience of parties, witnesses, and will almost certainly allow transfers in cases of extreme hardship. 28 U.S.C. § 1404(a). Venue and change of venue are discussed in detail later in this chapter.

A few courts of appeals have held that if a plaintiff brings suit under a federal law that authorizes nationwide jurisdiction, "pendent personal jurisdiction" may be exercised over the defendant to decide a joined state law claim even if there are insufficient minimum contacts with the state forum to justify trying the state law claim alone. "Under this doctrine, a court may assert pendent personal jurisdiction over a defendant with respect to a claim for which there is no independent basis for personal jurisdiction so long as it arises out of a common nucleus of operative facts with a claim in the same suit over which the court does have personal jurisdiction." Action Embroidery Corp. v. Atlantic Embroidery, Inc., 368 F.3d 1174, 1180 (9th Cir. 2004). See also United States v. Botefuhr, 309 F.3d 1263, 1272–75 (10th Cir. 2002); Robinson Engineering Co. Ltd. Pension Plan Trust v. George, 223 F.3d 445, 449–50 (7th Cir. 2000); ESAB Group, Inc. v. Centricut, Inc., 126 F.3d 617, 629 (4th Cir. 1997).

4.   Suits based on state law. The cleanest example of a federal nationwide jurisdiction statute for suits based on state law is federal statutory interpleader. In 1910, an insurance company brought an interpleader proceeding in a Pennsylvania state court to determine which of two competing beneficiaries was entitled to payment under a life insurance policy. One of the claimants lived in Pennsylvania; the other lived in California. The California claimant was notified of the suit but declined to appear. The Pennsylvania court decided for the Pennsylvania claimant, and the insurance company paid him pursuant to the court's judgment. The California claimant then brought suit on the policy in federal court in

California, where the insurance company interposed the Pennsylvania judgment as a defense. The United States Supreme Court held that the Pennsylvania court had not had *in personam* jurisdiction, and affirmed a judgment in favor of the California claimant. The result was that the insurance company paid twice on the same policy. New York Life Insurance Co. v. Dunlevy, 241 U.S. 518, 36 S.Ct. 613, 60 L.Ed. 1140 (1916).

The next year, Congress passed the Federal Interpleader Act of 1917, under which nationwide *in personam* jurisdiction in federal court was made available in interpleader suits. The modern successors to that statute are 28 U.S.C. §§ 1335, 1397, and 2361. See Fed. R. Civ. P. 4(k)(1)(C). Section 2361 permits service of process on interpleader claimants wherever they "reside or may be found." A special venue provision protects claimants by permitting suit to be brought only in a judicial district in which one or more of the claimants may be found. 28 U.S.C. § 1397. It is easy to see why insurance companies went to Congress for help after the *Dunlevy* decision in 1916, before the Supreme Court's decision in *International Shoe* and before the advent of state long-arm statutes. Is a federal interpleader statute necessary today? Should a federal court be able to assert nationwide *in personam* jurisdiction in a suit based on state rather than federal law? For a more extensive treatment of interpleader, see infra p. 628.

5. Federal Rule of Civil Procedure 4. Rule 4 is directed both to the manner of service of process and to the assertion of *in personam* jurisdiction. Under the Rule as it existed when *Omni Capital* was decided, Rule 4(e) directed the federal courts to follow the state long-arm statute in the absence of a federal statute or rule authorizing broader jurisdiction ("service may * * * be made under the circumstances and in the manner prescribed in the [state] statute or rule"). The disparate and somewhat incomplete provisions of the old Rule 4, including Rule 4(e), were renumbered and fleshed out in new Rule 4(k), adopted in 1993. Stylistic changes were made to Rule 4 in 2007.

Rule 4(k)(1) provides the framework for exercising territorial jurisdiction over defendants found within the United States. Rule 4(k)(1)(A) provides that the long-arm statute of the state in which the federal district court sits governs in the absence of a contrary federal rule or statute. Rule 4(k)(1)(B) provides that, in addition to state long-arm statutes, third-party defendants impleaded under Rule 14 and additional parties needed for just adjudication under Rule 19 are subject to *in personam* jurisdiction in federal court, provided they can be served with process within 100 miles of the federal courthouse from which the summons is issued. This so-called "bulge" jurisdiction is available in federal question cases, diversity cases, and any other cases over which the federal court has subject matter jurisdiction. Finally, Rule 4(k)(1)(C) provides that, in addition to the jurisdiction available under Rule 4(k)(1)(A) and (B), a federal court may exercise whatever *in personam* jurisdiction is authorized by a federal statute.

Rule 4(k)(2) provides the framework for exercising territorial jurisdiction over defendants found outside the United States. Note how restricted Rule 4(k)(2) is. It allows nationwide aggregation of contacts for purposes of assertion of jurisdiction over a foreign defendant, but only in cases where the claim arises under federal law, and only where there is no state that can exercise jurisdiction over that defendant.

NOTE ON INTERNET-BASED JURISDICTION

1. **New wine in old bottles.** The Internet poses many new legal problems, not limited to jurisdiction. Are the jurisdictional problems posed by the Internet so out of the ordinary that courts will have to modify the minimum contacts framework?

2. **Internet websites.** Internet sites are either passive or interactive. A passive website may be visited by anyone from anywhere in the world, but the visitor can only read or look at what is on the site. An interactive website may also be visited by anyone from anywhere in the world, but the visitor may interact in various ways.

An important characteristic of both passive and interactive sites is that a visitor to the site must take the initiative by turning on her computer and seeking out the site or at least clicking on a link. Another important characteristic of Internet sites is that each has a specific domain name, or address. Such domain names are valuable to commercial enterprises. For example, the domain names of two well-known sellers of high-quality outdoor gear, L.L. Bean and Eddie Bauer, are llbean.com and eddiebauer.com.

Some passive sites are noncommercial, seeking merely to make available information of various kinds. Some interactive sites are the cyberspace equivalent of mail-order catalogues, allowing visitors to order books, clothing, etc. from an Internet retailer. Other interactive sites allow postings by Internet users seeking to buy or sell goods or services from each other, comparable to a newspaper's classified ad section. Other sites conduct internet auctions of goods offered for sale by Internet users. Still other sites allow communication by Internet users through an Internet bulletin board. Some bulletin boards are carefully screened by the site operator; others are not. Still others allow internet users to "chat" with each other in real time.

3. **An early influential formulation.** The most widely cited Internet jurisdiction case is Zippo Manufacturing Co. v. Zippo Dot Com, Inc., 952 F. Supp. 1119 (W.D.Pa. 1997). Zippo Manufacturing is a Pennsylvania corporation with its principal place of business in Pennsylvania. It manufactures a well-known brand of cigarette lighters. Zippo Dot Com, the defendant, was a California corporation with its principal place of business in California. It operated an Internet news service with 140,000 paying subscribers, of whom about 3,000 lived in Pennsylvania. Subscribers could purchase the news service on line at Zippo Dot Com's Internet site. Zippo Dot Com had the following domain names: zippo.com, zippo.net, and zipponews.com. Zippo Manufacturing sued in district court in Pennsylvania alleging various federal and state trademark-related violations. The district court upheld jurisdiction in Pennsylvania.

The district court set forth a general test for jurisdiction in Internet cases:

> [T]he likelihood that personal jurisdiction can be constitutionally exercised is directly proportionate to the nature and quality of commercial activity that an entity conducts over the Internet. This sliding scale is consistent with well developed personal jurisdictional principles. At one end of the spectrum are situations where a defendant clearly does business over the Internet. If the defendant enters into contracts with residents of a foreign

jurisdiction that involve the knowing and repeated transmission of computer files over the Internet, personal jurisdiction is proper. At the opposite end are situations where a defendant has simply posted information on an Internet Web site which is accessible to users in foreign jurisdictions. A passive Web site that does little more than make information available to those who are interested in it is not grounds for the exercise of personal jurisdiction. The middle ground is occupied by interactive Web sites where a user can exchange information with the host computer. In these cases, the exercise of jurisdiction is determined by examining the level of interactivity and commercial nature of the exchange of information that occurs on the Web site.

952 F. Supp. at 1124

The *Zippo* "sliding scale" formulation may make jurisdiction both too easy and too difficult to obtain. *Zippo* appears to say that general jurisdiction exists where a "defendant enters into contracts with residents of a foreign jurisdiction that involve the knowing and repeated transmission of computer files over the Internet." After the Court's opinion in *Goodyear*, this is clearly too broad a formulation of the criteria for general jurisdiction. At the other end of the spectrum, *Zippo* provides that a passive website "that does little more than make information available to those who are interested in it is not grounds for personal jurisdiction." What if the information is defamatory, and the web site operator intends it to harm the defamed person where she lives? Doesn't *Calder v. Jones* tell us that there is personal jurisdiction over the defamer where the defamed person lives? See description of *Calder* and the "effects test," supra p. 117, n. 5.

Lower federal courts relied heavily on *Zippo* in the first few years after the decision. In 2003, the Third Circuit wrote, "The opinion in [*Zippo*] has become a seminal authority regarding personal jurisdiction based upon the operation of an Internet web site." Toys "R" Us, Inc. v. Step Two, S.A., 318 F.3d 446, 452 (3d Cir. 2003). More recently, however, many courts of appeals have had second thoughts. In 2010, the Seventh Circuit explicitly backed away from the *Zippo* formulation, concluding that the traditional jurisdictional analyses apply to Internet as well as non-Internet cases, and that an Internet-specific formulation is not necessary. The court wrote:

> *Zippo*'s sliding scale was always just shorthand for determining whether a defendant had established sufficient minimum contacts with a forum to justify exercising personal jurisdiction over him in the forum state. But we think that the traditional due process inquiry * * * is not so difficult to apply to cases involving Internet contacts that courts need some sort of easier-to-apply categorical test.

Illinois v. Hemi Group LLC, 622 F.3d 754, 759 (7th Cir. 2010). See also Mavrix Photo, Inc. v. Brand Technologies, 647 F.3d 1218, 1227 (9th Cir. 2011) (refusing to apply the *Zippo* formulation to determine whether general jurisdiction existed).

4. **Recent cases.** A number of recent cases have recognized the limitations of the *Zippo* formulation, even when they cite it and appear to rely on it. These cases suggest, sometimes only implicitly, that personal jurisdiction problems posed by the Internet can be resolved by applying

Calder, Burger King, Asahi, and *Nicastro,* and that a special intellectual framework for Internet cases is unnecessary. Several examples:

In Panavision International L.P. v. Toeppen, 141 F.3d 1316 (9th Cir. 1998), Dennis Toeppen, an individual living in Illinois, registered as his own domain names the names of over 100 well-known companies. One of the domain names was panavision.com. Panavision International, the owner of the trademark "Panavision," sought to register panavision.com as a domain name, but discovered that Toeppen had already done so. Panavision's counsel wrote a letter to Toeppen from California, informing him that "Panavision" was a registered trademark and requesting that he cease using this domain name. Toeppen responded in a letter to California offering to cease using the name and to "settle" the matter for $13,000. Panavision refused the offer of settlement. Toeppen then registered another Panavision trademark, "Panaflex," as a domain name. Panavision responded by filing suit in federal district court in California, alleging violations of federal trademark law and California's "anti-dilution" law. The court cited *Zippo,* but did not rely on its "sliding scale" test. Relying instead on *Burger King* and *Calder,* the court upheld jurisdiction in California, noting that Toeppen knew that Panavision's principal place of business was California, and that he had registered its trademarks as his own domain names "for the purpose of extorting money from Panavision." Id. at 1322. (The "cybersquatting" problem created by people like Toeppen prompted the passage a year later of the federal Anticybersquatting Consumer Protection Act, 15 U.S.C. § 1125(d).)

In Young v. New Haven Advocate, 315 F.3d 256 (4th Cir. 2002), a Virginia state prison warden sued two Connecticut newspapers for defamation in federal district court in Virginia. The State of Connecticut had solved an overcrowding problem in its prisons by shipping about 500 prisoners to a state prison in Virginia. Reporters for the newspapers wrote articles criticizing this solution. In the course of the articles, they criticized the prison in Virginia to which the prisoners had been sent. Warden Young was mentioned unflatteringly in one of the articles. The newspapers were not circulated to Virginia, but the articles were posted on the newspapers' websites. Relying on *Calder,* the court carefully analyzed the articles, the conduct of the reporters, and the intent of the newspapers. It concluded that the articles were written to address a local controversy in Connecticut and were not "expressly aimed" at Virginia. It therefore denied personal jurisdiction in Virginia. The court did not cite *Zippo,* and did not conclude that there was no jurisdiction simply because the articles were posted on passive websites.

In Boschetto v. Hansing, 539 F.3d 1011 (9th Cir. 2008), Boschetto, a California resident, purchased a used car on eBay's Internet auction site from Hansing, a Wisconsin resident. Pursuant to the terms of purchase, Boschetto arranged for the car to be shipped to California at his own expense. Boschetto brought suit against Hansing in federal district court in California, alleging that when the car arrived he discovered that it was not as advertised. The court held that there was no personal jurisdiction over Hansing in California based on this "one-time contract for the sale of a good that involved the forum state only because that is where the purchaser happened to reside." Id. at 1019. The concurring opinion pointed out that as an eBay seller Hansing was obliged to accept the highest bid for his car irrespective of the state of residence of the bidder, and that Hansing therefore did not "purposefully direct any activity at California." Id. at 1022 (Rymer, J., concurring).

In Louis Vuitton Malletier v. Mosseri, 736 F.3d 1139 (11th Cir. 2013), Louis Vuitton brought suit in federal district court in Florida against an on-line retailer alleging federal trademark infringement. Mosseri sold "knock-off" Louis Vuitton products at extremely low prices. Louis Vuitton purchased at least one Louis Vuitton knock-off and had it shipped to Florida. After filing suit, Louis Vuitton had conducted extensive discovery, eventually learning the identity of Mosseri, the seller, who had been hiding behind various corporate names. The court upheld jurisdiction over Mosseri in Florida, noting that he "purposefully solicited business from Florida residents" on the Internet and "received orders from multiple Florida residents to ship goods into Florida," and that he therefore "purposefully availed himself of the Florida forum." Id. at 1357. The court did not rely on, or even cite, *Zippo*.

5. Availability of "geographically restrictive techniques." Professor A. Benjamin Spencer argues that problems of Internet jurisdiction can be analyzed using traditional notions of purposeful direction or purposeful availment. Spencer, Jurisdiction and the Internet: Returning to Traditional Principles to Analyze Network Mediated Contacts, 2006 U.Ill.L.Rev. 71 (2006). He contends that the increasingly availability of "geographically restrictive techniques," including mapping and screening technologies to bar users seeking to access a website from specific remote locations, "click wrap" consents to jurisdiction by remote users, and geographical disclaimers, now make it possible to limit the geographic reach of Internet websites and postings. Accordingly, he suggests that it is presumptively fair to treat any remote user's viewing of a website as a purposeful contact by the owner or operator of the website, since the owner or operator could have taken measures to block access but chose not to do so. How would such an approach affect cases like *Young v. New Haven Advocate* and *Carefirst*?

6. Additional reading. There is a great deal of very good academic writing on personal jurisdiction and the Internet, including Dunham, *Zippo*-ing the Wrong Way: How the Internet Has Misdirected the Federal Courts in Their Personal Jurisdiction Analysis, 43 U.S.F.L.Rev. 559 (2009); Floyd and Baradaran-Robison, Toward a Unified Test of Personal Jurisdiction in an Era of Widely Diffused Wrongs: The Relevance of Purpose and Effects, 81 Ind.L.J. 601 (2006); Yokoyama, You Can't Always Use the *Zippo* Code: The Fallacy of a Uniform Theory of Internet Personal Jurisdiction, 54 DePaul L.Rev. 1147 (2005); Symposium, Personal Jurisdiction in the Internet Age, 98 Nw.U.L.Rev. 411 (2004); Nguyen, A Survey of Personal Jurisdiction Based on Internet Activity: A Return to Tradition, 19 Berk.Tech.L.J. 519 (2004); Struve and Wagner, Realspace Sovereigns in Cyberspace: Problems with the Anticybersquatting Consumer Protection Act, 17 Berk.Tech.L.J. 989 (2002); Berman, The Globalization of Jurisdiction, 151 U.Pa.L.Rev. 311 (2002).

NOTE ON FOREIGN DEFENDANTS IN AMERICAN COURTS

In four of the principal cases of this chapter, the defendants were foreign companies or individuals. In *Asahi Metal Industry Co. v. Superior Court*, the defendant was a Japanese manufacturer of tire valves incorporated into tires manufactured in Taiwan. The accident from which the suit arose occurred in

California. In *J. McIntyre Machinery v. Nicastro*, the defendant was a heavy equipment manufacturer in the United Kingdom with substantial sales in the United States as a whole but limited sales in New Jersey. The accident occurred in New Jersey. In *Goodyear Dunlop Tires v. Brown*, three of the defendants were wholly owned foreign subsidiaries of Goodyear USA. The accident occurred in France. In *Omni Capital International v. Rudolf Wolff & Co., Ltd.*, the defendants were a British securities company and an individual British broker. The alleged wrongdoing largely took place in the United Kingdom. In none of these four cases did the Supreme Court come fully to grips with whether, or how, foreign defendants should be treated differently from out-of-state domestic defendants.

The jurisdictional world of *Pennoyer v. Neff* was, to a significant extent, shaped by an assumption that the individual states of the United States should be treated, for purposes of territorial jurisdiction, largely as if they were separate sovereignties analogous to foreign countries. In the century since *Pennoyer*, the states have increasingly come to be seen as parts of an integrated larger nation.

The analogy between the states and foreign countries, so strong in *Pennoyer*, has rhetorical and analytical vestiges today. The analogy may be seen in small, almost trivial matters of vocabulary. For example, it is still commonplace to refer to out-of-state domestic corporations as "foreign" corporations. More importantly, it may also be seen in the intellectual structure of Supreme Court opinions. For example, Justice Kennedy's plurality opinion in *Nicastro* emphasizes the limited reach of a sovereign state and concludes that New Jersey cannot exercise *in personam* jurisdiction over a foreign manufacturer whose allegedly defective product injured a New Jersey worker.

Even when the Court is able to recognize openly that a case requires special treatment because a defendant is foreign, it has difficulty constructing an appropriate analytic framework. In *Asahi*, the Court dismissed for lack of *in personam* jurisdiction, although the considerations that led to that conclusion would have been more easily accommodated by a *forum non conveniens* analysis. After the initial suit by the original plaintiff, Zurcher, was settled, the only parties left were the original defendant, Cheng Shin, and the third-party defendant, Asahi. The basis of the suit between them was their contractual relation which was entered into outside of the United States and would certainly be governed by non-American law. With the suit in this posture, the Court dismissed the suit, essentially on the ground that the suit had very little to do with the United States. In *Omni Capital*, the Court found that there were insufficient contacts between the state of Louisiana and the foreign defendants. The Court recognized an argument in favor of looking to the contacts between the foreign defendants and the United States as a whole, but declined to discuss it in the absence of a federal rule or statute specifically authorizing the exercise of jurisdiction on that basis.

It had been suggested in the academic literature for many years that contacts with the United States as a whole should be "aggregated" when the defendant is a foreigner. See, e.g., Green, Federal Jurisdiction in Personam of Corporations and Due Process, 14 Vand.L.Rev. 967 (1961); Lilly, Jurisdiction over Domestic and Alien Defendants, 69 Va.L.Rev. 85 (1983). But the Court has refused to aggregate contacts without explicit rule or statutory direction. As may be seen in the results in cases with foreign defendants, the Supreme Court has recognized that there is something special about such cases. But the Court has been unwilling, perhaps even unable, to articulate a satisfactory doctrinal framework for dealing with the problems that such cases entail. It would be unrealistic to expect Congress quickly and easily to provide a fully satisfactory solution to what are, in fact, a cluster of interrelated problems involving foreign litigants.

Congress can sometimes be induced to act in discrete areas, as may be seen, for example, in the Foreign Sovereign Immunities Act. The Act asserts jurisdiction over foreign countries and companies owned by such countries based on their contacts with the United States as a whole. 28 U.S.C. § 1608; Seetransport Wiking Trader v. Navimpex Centrala Navala, 989 F.2d 572, 580 (2d Cir. 1993); Texas Trading & Milling Corp. v. Federal Republic of Nigeria, 647 F.2d 300, 314 (2d Cir. 1981), cert. den. 454 U.S. 1148 (1982). It confers concurrent jurisdiction on state and federal courts, allowing jurisdiction in either court to be assessed by aggregating contacts with the nation as a whole rather than with the particular state in which the court happens to sit. For a thorough analysis of the Act, see Kane, Suing Foreign Sovereigns: A Procedural Compass, 34 Stan.L.Rev. 385 (1982). Further, Congress and the Supreme Court acted together in 1993 to adopt amended Rule 4(k)(2), providing for the nationwide aggregation of contacts between a foreign defendant and the United States in order to assert territorial jurisdiction in federal court for causes of action arising under federal law.

Rule 4(k)(2) Jurisdiction in Fed. Court arising under Fed. law

But significant gaps still remain: What about litigation in federal court under state law? What about litigation in state court under either federal or state law? Should Congress pass a statute conferring broad jurisdiction on the state courts in cases brought against foreign defendants? Is there reason to distrust the state courts when dealing with foreign defendants?

NOTE ON JURISDICTION AND JUDGMENTS IN INTERNATIONAL LITIGATION

The United States has historically had a more expansive view than most industrialized countries of the permissible bases for the exercise of territorial jurisdiction, although this may change in the wake of *Nicastro*. Consider whether the concept of "minimum contacts," as elaborated in the context of domestic litigation in the United States, is well-suited to analyzing jurisdictional questions in international cases. It is one thing to subject an American defendant to jurisdiction in California based on slight contacts with that state. It may be quite another to subject a German defendant to jurisdiction in the United States based on slight contacts with the United States as a whole, particularly if such an assertion of jurisdiction is markedly more aggressive than assertions of jurisdiction by most other countries. The Restatement (Third) of Foreign Relations Law offers "international rules and guidelines for the exercise of jurisdiction to adjudicate in cases having international implications, applicable to courts both in the United States and in other states," derived from customary international law and international agreements. (The term "state" as used by the Restatement means "country.") See § 421, Jurisdiction to Adjudicate.

In 1992, thirty-five countries began efforts to draft an international convention on jurisdiction and foreign judgments under the auspices of the Hague Conference on Private International Law. The United States helped launch these efforts in an attempt to remedy the imbalance between the broad recognition granted to foreign judgments in the United States and the more restricted recognition accorded American judgments in many foreign countries, particularly in the European Union (EU). Since 1968, many European countries have followed the Brussels Convention on Jurisdiction and the Enforcement of Judgments in Civil and Commercial Matters, which was adopted as an EU regulation in 2002. The Brussels Convention allows for broad mutual enforcement of member states' judgments provided those states adhere to a common set of somewhat restrictive jurisdictional rules. However, EU member countries may exercise jurisdiction more broadly with respect to defendants from non-member countries, and they are under no obligation to enforce judgments of non-member countries such as the United States. The United States, therefore, frequently has the worst of both worlds: American defendants can be haled into European courts fairly easily, and the resulting judgments generally will be enforced in the United States; but American judgments against EU and other foreign defendants are often denied recognition in the home countries of those defendants.

The United States has had only limited success in securing a new Hague Convention. A 1999 draft of the Hague Convention on Jurisdiction and Foreign Judgments would have made enforcement of judgments contingent on whether personal jurisdiction was proper. The jurisdictional rules of the draft were far closer to the Brussels Convention approach, which employs relatively bright-line rules based on factors such as the defendant's domicile and the place of injury, than they were to the American approach, which employs a fact-intensive inquiry into the number and nature of the contacts between the defendant and the forum. The 1999 draft prohibited several grounds of jurisdiction available in the United States, including "tag" jurisdiction allowing a defendant to be haled into court wherever he is served with process, and general jurisdiction based on a defendant's doing a certain amount of business in a particular forum. The United States was dissatisfied with the 1999 draft, and other countries objected that the draft did not adequately address new jurisdictional issues posed by the Internet and e-commerce. As a result, negotiations broke down in 2000.

A scaled down agreement, applicable to choice-of-forum agreements between commercial parties, the Hague Convention on Choice of Court Agreements, was reached in 2005. The fate of this Convention is not certain. So far, only Mexico has ratified the Convention. As of the fall of 2014, the European Union was in the final stages of ratification; when that ratification is complete, the convention will bind the 27 member states of the European Union. See generally Woodward, Saving the Hague Choice of Court Convention, 29 U.Pa.J.Int'l L. 657 (2008).

The American Law Institute, with Professors Andreas Lowenfeld and Linda Silberman acting as Reporters, has proposed a new federal statute dealing with jurisdiction and judgments in international litigation. Recognition and Enforcement of Foreign Judgments: Analysis and Proposed Federal Statute (ALI 2006). The proposed federal statute would preempt state law and would require reciprocity from countries whose judgments are recognized by American courts. For criticism of the reciprocity provision, see Miller, Playground Politics: Assessing the Wisdom of Writing a Reciprocity Requirement into U.S. International Recognition and Enforcement Law, 35 Geo.J.Int'l L. 239 (2004).

Useful additional reading includes Silberman, Some Judgements on Judgments: A View from America, 19 King's L.J. 235 (2008); Burbank,

Jurisdictional Conflict and Jurisdictional Equilibration: Paths to a Via Media?, 26 Hous.J.Int'l L. 385 (2004); Clermont, A Global Law of Jurisdiction and Judgments: Views from the United States and Japan, 37 Cornell Int'l L.J. 1 (2004); Traynor, An Introductory Framework for Analyzing the Proposed Hague Convention on Jurisdiction and Foreign Judgments in Civil and Commercial Matters: US and European Perspectives, 6 Ann.Surv.Int'l & Comp.L. 1 (2000); Degnan and Kane, The Exercise of Jurisdiction Over and Enforcement of Judgments Against Alien Defendants, 39 Hast.L.J. 799 (1988).

e. PRESENCE

INTRODUCTORY NOTE ON PRESENCE

In the world of *Pennoyer v. Neff*, physical presence within the territory of a state was sufficient for the state to exercise jurisdiction. The presence of property alone could justify *in rem* and *quasi in rem* jurisdiction. The presence of a person could justify *in personam* jurisdiction. If the test of jurisdiction is power, presence within the territory of a state is probably a sufficient justification. But what if the test of jurisdiction is fairness? In *International Shoe*, the Court declared that the due process clause requires that there be sufficient "minimum contacts" with the forum state "such that the maintenance of the suit does not offend 'traditional notions of fair play and substantial justice.' " Does this mean that in some cases mere presence in a state is not enough to satisfy due process?

1. *Property*

Shaffer v. Heitner

Supreme Court of the United States, 1977.
433 U.S. 186, 97 S.Ct. 2569, 53 L.Ed.2d 683.

■ MR. JUSTICE MARSHALL delivered the opinion of the Court.

The controversy in this case concerns the constitutionality of a Delaware statute that allows a court of that State to take jurisdiction of a lawsuit by sequestering any property of the defendant that happens to be located in Delaware. Appellants contend that the sequestration statute as applied in this case violates the Due Process Clause of the Fourteenth Amendment both because it permits the state courts to exercise jurisdiction despite the absence of sufficient contacts among the defendants, the litigation, and the State of Delaware and because it authorizes the deprivation of defendants' property without providing adequate procedural safeguards. We find it necessary to consider only the first of these contentions.

I

Appellee Heitner, a nonresident of Delaware, is the owner of one share of stock in the Greyhound Corp., a business incorporated under the laws of Delaware with its principal place of business in Phoenix, Ariz. On May 22, 1974, he filed a shareholder's derivative suit in the Court of Chancery for New Castle County, Del., in which he named as defendants

Greyhound, its wholly owned subsidiary Greyhound Lines, Inc.,[1] and 28 present or former officers or directors of one or both of the corporations. In essence, Heitner alleged that the individual defendants had violated their duties to Greyhound by causing it and its subsidiary to engage in actions that resulted in the corporations being held liable for substantial damages in a private antitrust suit[2] and a large fine in a criminal contempt action.[3] The activities which led to these penalties took place in Oregon.

Simultaneously with his complaint, Heitner filed a motion for an order of sequestration of the Delaware property of the individual defendants pursuant to Del.Code Ann., Tit. 10, § 366 (1975). This motion was accompanied by a supporting affidavit of counsel which stated that the individual defendants were nonresidents of Delaware. * * * The requested sequestration order was signed the day the motion was filed. Pursuant to that order, the sequestrator "seized" approximately 82,000 shares of Greyhound common stock belonging to 19 of the defendants, and options belonging to another two defendants. These seizures were accomplished by placing "stop transfer" orders or their equivalents on the books of the Greyhound Corporation. So far as the record shows, none of the certificates representing the seized property was physically present in Delaware. The stock was considered to be in Delaware, and so subject to seizure, by virtue of Del.Code Ann., Tit. 8, § 169 (1975), which makes Delaware the situs of ownership of all stock in Delaware corporations.

All 28 defendants were notified of the initiation of the suit by certified mail directed to their last known addresses and by publication in a New Castle County newspaper. The 21 defendants whose property was seized (hereafter referred to as appellants) responded by entering a special appearance for the purpose of moving to quash service of process and to vacate the sequestration order. They contended that the *ex parte* sequestration procedure did not accord them due process of law and that the property seized was not capable of attachment in Delaware. In addition, appellants asserted that under the rule of International Shoe Co. v. Washington, 326 U.S. 310, 66 S.Ct. 154, 90 L.Ed. 95 (1945), they did not have sufficient contacts with Delaware to sustain the jurisdiction of that State's courts.

* * *

II

The Delaware courts rejected appellants' jurisdictional challenge by noting that this suit was brought as a *quasi in rem* proceeding. Since *quasi in rem* jurisdiction is traditionally based on attachment or seizure of property present in the jurisdiction, not on contacts between the defendant and the State, the courts considered appellants' claimed lack of contacts with Delaware to be unimportant. This categorical analysis

---

[1] Greyhound Lines, Inc., is incorporated in California and has its principal place of business in Phoenix, Ariz.

[2] A judgment of $13,146,090 plus attorneys fees was entered against Greyhound in Mt. Hood Stages, Inc. v. Greyhound Corp., 1972–3 Trade Cas. ¶ 74,824, aff'd 555 F.2d 687 (C.A.9 1977). App. 10.

[3] See United States v. Greyhound Corp., 363 F. Supp. 525 (N.D.Ill.1973), 370 F. Supp. 881 (N.D.Ill.), aff'd 508 F.2d 529 (C.A.7 1974). Greyhound was fined $100,000 and Greyhound Lines $500,000.

assumes the continued soundness of the conceptual structure founded on the century-old case of Pennoyer v. Neff, 95 U.S. 714, 24 L.Ed. 565 (1877).

Pennoyer was an ejectment action brought in federal court under the diversity jurisdiction. Pennoyer, the defendant in that action, held the land under a deed purchased in a sheriff's sale conducted to realize on a judgment for attorney's fees obtained against Neff in a previous action by one Mitchell. At the time of Mitchell's suit in an Oregon State court, Neff was a nonresident of Oregon. An Oregon statute allowed service by publication on nonresidents who had property in the State, and Mitchell had used that procedure to bring Neff before the Court. The United States Circuit Court for the District of Oregon, in which Neff brought his ejectment action, refused to recognize the validity of the judgment against Neff in Mitchell's suit, and accordingly awarded the land to Neff. This Court affirmed.

* * *

From our perspective, the importance of *Pennoyer* is not its result, but the fact that its principles and corollaries derived from them became the basic elements of the constitutional doctrine governing state court jurisdiction. See, e.g., Hazard, A General Theory of State-Court Jurisdiction, 1965 Sup.Ct.Rev. 241 (hereafter Hazard). As we have noted, under *Pennoyer* state authority to adjudicate was based on the jurisdiction's power over either persons or property. This fundamental concept is embodied in the very vocabulary which we use to describe judgments. If a court's jurisdiction is based on its authority over the defendant's person, the action and judgment are denominated "in personam" and can impose a personal obligation on the defendant in favor of the plaintiff. If jurisdiction is based on the court's power over property within its territory, the action is called "in rem" or "quasi in rem." The effect of a judgment in such a case is limited to the property that supports jurisdiction and does not impose a personal liability on the property owner, since he is not before the court.[17] In *Pennoyer's* terms, the owner is affected only "indirectly" by an *in rem* judgment adverse to his interest in the property subject to the court's disposition.

By concluding that "[t]he authority of every tribunal is necessarily restricted by the territorial limits of the State in which it is established," 95 U.S., at 720, *Pennoyer* sharply limited the availability of *in personam* jurisdiction over defendants not resident in the forum State. If a nonresident defendant could not be found in a State, he could not be sued there. On the other hand, since the State in which property was located was considered to have exclusive sovereignty over that property, *in rem* actions could proceed regardless of the owner's location. Indeed, since a State's process could not reach beyond its borders, this Court held after *Pennoyer* that due process did not require any effort to give a property

---

[17] "A judgment *in rem* affects the interests of all persons in designated property. A judgment *quasi in rem* affects the interests of particular persons in designated property. The latter is of two types. In one the plaintiff is seeking to secure a pre-existing claim in the subject property and to extinguish or establish the nonexistence of similar interests of particular persons. In the other the plaintiff seeks to apply what he concedes to be the property of the defendant to the satisfaction of a claim against him. Restatement, Judgments, 5–9." Hanson v. Denckla, 357 U.S. 235, 246 n. 12, 78 S.Ct. 1228, 1235, 2 L.Ed.2d 1283 (1958).

As did the Court in *Hanson*, we will for convenience generally use the term "in rem" in place of "in rem and quasi in rem."

owner personal notice that his property was involved in an *in rem* proceeding. See, e.g., Ballard v. Hunter, 204 U.S. 241, 27 S.Ct. 261, 51 L.Ed. 461 (1907); Arndt v. Griggs, 134 U.S. 316, 10 S.Ct. 557, 33 L.Ed. 918 (1890); Huling v. Kaw Valley R. Co., 130 U.S. 559, 9 S.Ct. 603, 32 L.Ed. 1045 (1889).

The *Pennoyer* rules generally favored nonresident defendants by making them harder to sue. This advantage was reduced, however, by the ability of a resident plaintiff to satisfy a claim against a non-resident defendant by bringing into court any property of the defendant located in the plaintiff's State. * * *

Pennoyer itself recognized that its rigid categories * * * could not accommodate some necessary litigation. Accordingly, Mr. Justice Field's opinion carefully noted that cases involving the personal status of the plaintiff, such as divorce actions, could be adjudicated in the plaintiff's home State even though the defendant could not be served within that State. 95 U.S., at 733–735. Similarly, the opinion approved the practice of considering a foreign corporation doing business in a State to have consented to being sued in that State. Id., at 735–736; see Lafayette Ins. Co. v. French, 18 How. 404, 15 L.Ed. 451 (1856). This basis for *in personam* jurisdiction over foreign corporations was later supplemented by the doctrine that a corporation doing business in a State could be deemed "present" in the State, and so subject to service of process under the rule of *Pennoyer*. See, e.g., International Harvester Co. v. Kentucky, 234 U.S. 579, 34 S.Ct. 944, 58 L.Ed. 1479 (1914); Philadelphia & R.R. Co. v. McKibbin, 243 U.S. 264, 37 S.Ct. 280, 61 L.Ed. 710 (1917). See generally Note, Developments in the Law, State-Court Jurisdiction, 73 Harv.L.Rev. 909, 919–923 (1960).

The advent of automobiles, with the concomitant increase in the incidence of individuals causing injury in States where they were not subject to *in personam* actions under *Pennoyer,* required further moderation of the territorial limits on jurisdictional power. This modification, like the accommodation to the realities of interstate corporate activities, was accomplished by use of a legal fiction that left the conceptual structure established in *Pennoyer* theoretically unaltered. Cf. Olberding v. Illinois Central R. Co., 346 U.S. 338, 340–341, 74 S.Ct. 83, 85–86, 98 L.Ed. 39 (1953). The fiction used was that the out-of-state motorist, who it was assumed could be excluded altogether from the State's highways, had by using those highways appointed a designated state official as his agent to accept process. See Hess v. Pawloski, 274 U.S. 352, 47 S.Ct. 632, 71 L.Ed. 1091 (1927). Since the motorist's "agent" could be personally served within the State, the state courts could obtain *in personam* jurisdiction over the nonresident driver.

The motorists' consent theory was easy to administer since it required only a finding that the out-of-state driver had used the State's roads. By contrast, both the fictions of implied consent to service on the part of a foreign corporation and of corporate presence required a finding that the corporation was "doing business" in the forum State. Defining the criteria for making that finding and deciding whether they were met absorbed much judicial energy. See, e.g., International Shoe Co. v. Washington, 326 U.S., at 317–319, 66 S.Ct., at 158–160. While the essentially quantitative tests which emerged from these cases purported simply to identify circumstances under which presence or consent could be attributed to the corporation, it became clear that they were in fact attempting to ascertain "what dealings make it just to subject a foreign corporation to local suit". Hutchinson v. Chase & Gilbert, 45 F.2d 139, 141 (C.A.2 1930) (L. Hand, J.). In *International Shoe* we acknowledged that fact.

The question in *International Shoe* was whether the corporation was subject to the judicial and taxing jurisdiction of Washington. Mr. Chief Justice Stone's opinion for the Court began its analysis of that question by noting that the historical basis of *in personam* jurisdiction was a court's power over the defendant's person. That power, however, was no longer the central concern:

> "But now that the *capias ad respondendum* has given way to personal service of summons or other form of notice, due process requires only that in order to subject a defendant to a judgment *in personam,* if he be not present within the territory of the forum, he have certain minimum contacts with it such that the maintenance of the suit does not offend 'traditional notions of fair play and substantial justice.' Milliken v. Meyer, 311 U.S. 457, 463, 61 S.Ct. 339, 343, 85 L.Ed. 278." 326 U.S., at 316, 66 S.Ct., at 158.

Thus, the inquiry into the State's jurisdiction over a foreign corporation appropriately focused not on whether the corporation was "present" but on whether there have been

> "such contacts of the corporation with the state of the forum as make it reasonable, in the context of our federal system of government, to require the corporation to defend the particular suit which is brought there." Id., at 317, 66 S.Ct., at 158.

Mechanical or quantitative evaluations of the defendant's activities in the forum could not resolve the question of reasonableness:

> "Whether due process is satisfied must depend rather upon the quality and nature of the activity in relation to the fair and orderly administration of the laws which it was the purpose of the due process clause to insure. That clause does not contemplate that a state may make binding a judgment *in personam* against an individual or corporate defendant with which the state has no contacts, ties, or relations." Id., at 319, 66 S.Ct., at 160.

noted in class

Thus, the relationship among the defendant, the forum, and the litigation, rather than the mutually exclusive sovereignty of the States on which the rules of *Pennoyer* rest, became the central concern of the inquiry into personal jurisdiction. The immediate effect of this departure from *Pennoyer's* conceptual apparatus was to increase the ability of the state courts to obtain personal jurisdiction over nonresident defendants. See, e.g., Green, Jurisdictional Reform in California, 21 Hastings L.J. 1219, 1231–1233 (1970); Currie, The Growth of the Long Arm: Eight Years of Extended Jurisdiction in Illinois, 1963 U.Ill.L.F. 533; Developments at 1000–1008.

No equally dramatic change has occurred in the law governing jurisdiction *in rem*. There have, however, been intimations that the collapse of the *in personam* wing of *Pennoyer* has not left that decision unweakened as a foundation for *in rem* jurisdiction. Well-reasoned lower court opinions have questioned the proposition that the presence of property in a State gives that State jurisdiction to adjudicate rights to the property regardless of the relationship of the underlying dispute and the property owner to the forum. * * *

　　　* * *

　　It is clear, therefore, that the law of state-court jurisdiction no longer stands securely on the foundation established in *Pennoyer*. We think that the time is ripe to consider whether the standard of fairness and substantial justice set forth in *International Shoe* should be held to govern actions *in rem* as well as *in personam*.

III

　　The case for applying to jurisdiction *in rem* the same test of "fair play and substantial justice" as governs assertions of jurisdiction *in personam* is simple and straightforward. It is premised on recognition that "[t]he phrase, 'judicial jurisdiction over a thing', is a customary elliptical way of referring to jurisdiction over the interests of persons in a thing," Restatement (Second) of Conflict of Laws § 56, Introductory Note (1971) (hereafter Restatement).[22] This recognition leads to the conclusion that in order to justify an exercise of jurisdiction *in rem*, the basis for jurisdiction must be sufficient to justify exercising "jurisdiction over the interests of persons in a thing."[23] The standard for determining whether an exercise of jurisdiction over the interests of persons is consistent with the Due Process Clause is the minimum-contacts standard elucidated in *International Shoe*.

　　This argument, of course, does not ignore the fact that the presence of property in a State may bear on the existence of jurisdiction by providing contacts among the forum State, the defendant, and the litigation. For example, when claims to the property itself are the source of the underlying controversy between the plaintiff and the defendant,[24] it would be unusual for the State where the property is located not to have jurisdiction. In such cases, the defendant's claim to property located in the State would normally indicate that he expected to benefit from the State's protection of his interest. The State's strong interests in assuring the marketability of property within its borders and in providing a procedure for peaceful resolution of disputes about the possession of that property would also support jurisdiction, as would the likelihood that important records and witnesses will be found in the State. The presence of property may also favor jurisdiction in cases such as suits for injury suffered on the land of an absentee owner, where the defendant's

---

[22] "All proceedings, like all rights, are really against persons. Whether they are proceedings or rights *in rem* depends on the number of persons affected." Tyler v. Court of Registration, 175 Mass. 71, 76, 55 N.E. 812, 814 (Holmes, C.J.), appeal dismissed, 179 U.S. 405, 21 S.Ct. 206, 45 L.Ed. 252 (1900).

[23] It is true that the potential liability of a defendant in an *in rem* action is limited by the value of the property, but that limitation does not affect the argument. The fairness of subjecting a defendant to state-court jurisdiction does not depend on the size of the claim being litigated. Cf. Fuentes v. Shevin, 407 U.S., at 88–90, 92 S.Ct., at 1998–1999 (1972); n. 32, infra.

[24] This category includes true *in rem* actions and the first type of *quasi in rem* proceedings. See n. 17, supra.

ownership of the property is conceded but the cause of action is otherwise related to rights and duties growing out of that ownership.

It appears, therefore, that jurisdiction over many types of actions which now are or might be brought *in rem* would not be affected by a holding that any assertion of state-court jurisdiction must satisfy the *International Shoe* standard. For the type of *quasi in rem* action typified by Harris v. Balk and the present case, however, accepting the proposed analysis would result in significant change. These are cases where the property which now serves as the basis for state court jurisdiction is completely unrelated to the plaintiff's cause of action. Thus, although the presence of the defendant's property in a State might suggest the existence of other ties among the defendant, the State, and the litigation, the presence of the property alone would not support the State's jurisdiction. If those other ties did not exist, cases over which the State is now thought to have jurisdiction could not be brought in that forum.

Since acceptance of the *International Shoe* test would most affect this class of cases, we examine the arguments against adopting that standard as they relate to this category of litigation. Before doing so, however, we note that this type of case also presents the clearest illustration of the argument in favor of assessing assertions of jurisdiction by a single standard. For in cases such as *Harris [v. Balk]* and this one, the only role played by the property is to provide the basis for bringing the defendant into court. Indeed, the express purpose of the Delaware sequestration procedure is to compel the defendant to enter a personal appearance.[33] In such cases, if a direct assertion of personal jurisdiction over the defendant would violate the Constitution, it would seem that an indirect assertion of that jurisdiction should be equally impermissible.

* * *

It might * * * be suggested that allowing *in rem* jurisdiction avoids the uncertainty inherent in the *International Shoe* standard and assures a plaintiff of a forum.[37] We believe, however, that the fairness standard of *International Shoe* can be easily applied in the vast majority of cases. Moreover, when the existence of jurisdiction in a particular forum under *International Shoe* is unclear, the cost of simplifying the litigation by avoiding the jurisdictional question may be the sacrifice of "fair play and substantial justice." That cost is too high.

We are left, then, to consider the significance of the long history of jurisdiction based solely on the presence of property in a State. * * * This history must be considered as supporting the proposition that jurisdiction based solely on the presence of property satisfies the demands of due process, cf. Ownbey v. Morgan, supra, 256 U.S., at 111, 41 S.Ct., at 438 (1921), but it is not decisive. "[T]raditional notions of fair play and substantial justice" can be as readily offended by the perpetuation of ancient forms that are no longer justified as by the adoption of new procedures that are inconsistent with the basic values of

---

[33] This purpose is emphasized by Delaware's refusal to allow any defense on the merits unless the defendant enters a general appearance, thus submitting to full *in personam* liability.

[37] This case does not raise, and we therefore do not consider, the question whether the presence of a defendant's property in a State is a sufficient basis for jurisdiction when no other forum is available to the plaintiff.

our constitutional heritage. Cf. Sniadach v. Family Finance Corp., 395 U.S., at 340, 89 S.Ct., at 1822; Wolf v. Colorado, 338 U.S. 25, 27, 69 S.Ct. 1359, 1361, 93 L.Ed. 1782 (1949). The fiction that an assertion of jurisdiction over property is anything but an assertion of jurisdiction over the owner of the property supports an ancient form without substantial modern justification. Its continued acceptance would serve only to allow state court jurisdiction that is fundamentally unfair to the defendant.

We therefore conclude that all assertions of state court jurisdiction must be evaluated according to the standards set forth in *International Shoe* and its progeny.

Holding

IV

The Delaware courts based their assertion of jurisdiction in this case solely on the statutory presence of appellants' property in Delaware. Yet that property is not the subject matter of this litigation, nor is the underlying cause of action related to the property. Appellants' holdings in Greyhound do not, therefore, provide contacts with Delaware sufficient to support the jurisdiction of that State's courts over appellants. If it exists, that jurisdiction must have some other foundation.

Appellee Heitner did not allege and does not now claim that appellants have ever set foot in Delaware. Nor does he identify any act related to his cause of action as having taken place in Delaware. Nevertheless, he contends that appellants' positions as directors and officers of a corporation chartered in Delaware provide sufficient "contacts, ties, or relations", International Shoe Co. v. Washington, 326 U.S., at 319, 66 S.Ct., at 160, with that State to give its courts jurisdiction over appellants in this stockholder's derivative action. This argument is based primarily on what Heitner asserts to be the strong interest of Delaware in supervising the management of a Delaware corporation. That interest is said to derive from the role of Delaware law in establishing the corporation and defining the obligations owed to it by its officers and directors. In order to protect this interest, appellee concludes, Delaware's courts must have jurisdiction over corporate fiduciaries such as appellants.

This argument is undercut by the failure of the Delaware Legislature to assert the state interest appellee finds so compelling. Delaware law bases jurisdiction not on appellants' status as corporate fiduciaries, but rather on the presence of their property in the State. Although the sequestration procedure used here may be most frequently used in derivative suits against officers and directors, Hughes Tool Co. v. Fawcett Publications, Inc., 290 A.2d 693, 695 (Del.Ch.1972), the authorizing statute evinces no specific concern with such actions. Sequestration can be used in any suit against a nonresident, see e.g., U.S. Industries v. Gregg, supra (breach of contract); Hughes Tool Co. v. Fawcett Publications, Inc., supra (same), and reaches corporate fiduciaries only if they happen to own interests in a Delaware corporation, or other property in the State. But as Heitner's failure to secure jurisdiction over seven of the defendants named in his complaint demonstrates, there is no necessary relationship between holding a position as a corporate fiduciary and owning stock or other interests in the corporation.[43] If Delaware perceived its interest in securing

---

[43] Delaware does not require directors to own stock. 8 Del.C. § 141(b).

jurisdiction over corporate fiduciaries to be as great as Heitner suggests, we would expect it to have enacted a statute more clearly designed to protect that interest.

* * *

Appellee suggests that by accepting positions as officers or directors of a Delaware corporation, appellants performed the acts required by Hanson v. Denckla. He notes that Delaware law provides substantial benefits to corporate officers and directors, and that these benefits were at least in part the incentive for appellants to assume their positions. It is, he says, "only fair and just" to require appellants, in return for these benefits, to respond in the State of Delaware when they are accused of misusing their powers. * * *

But like Heitner's first argument, this line of reasoning establishes only that it is appropriate for Delaware law to govern the obligations of appellants to Greyhound and its stockholders. It does not demonstrate that appellants have "purposefully avail[ed themselves] of the privilege of conducting activities within the forum State," Hanson v. Denckla, supra, at 253, 78 S.Ct., at 1240, in a way that would justify bringing them before a Delaware tribunal. Appellants have simply had nothing to do with the State of Delaware. Moreover, appellants had no reason to expect to be haled before a Delaware court. Delaware, unlike some States, has not enacted a statute that treats acceptance of a directorship as consent to jurisdiction in the State. And "[i]t strains reason . . . to suggest that anyone buying securities in a corporation formed in Delaware 'impliedly consents' to subject himself to Delaware's . . . jurisdiction on any cause of action." Appellants, who were not required to acquire interests in Greyhound in order to hold their positions, did not by acquiring those interests surrender their right to be brought to judgment only in States with which they had had "minimum contacts."

[handwritten margin note: excepting and operating in Del. corp. does not put you on notice of accepting jurisdiction]

The Due Process Clause

> "does not contemplate that a state may make binding a judgment . . . against an individual or corporate defendant with which the state has no contacts, ties, or relations." International Shoe Co. v. Washington, 326 U.S., at 319, 66 S.Ct., at 160.

Delaware's assertion of jurisdiction over appellants in this case is inconsistent with that constitutional limitation on state power. The judgment of the Delaware Supreme Court must, therefore, be reversed.

It is so ordered.

■ MR. JUSTICE REHNQUIST took no part in the consideration or decision of this case.

■ MR. JUSTICE POWELL, concurring.

I agree that the principles of International Shoe Co. v. Washington, 326 U.S. 310, 66 S.Ct. 154, 90 L.Ed. 95 (1945), should be extended to govern assertions of *in rem* as well as *in personam* jurisdiction in state court. I also agree that neither the statutory presence of appellants' stock in Delaware nor their positions as directors and officers of a Delaware corporation can provide sufficient contacts to support the Delaware courts' assertion of jurisdiction in this case.

I would explicitly reserve judgment, however, on whether the ownership of some forms of property whose situs is indisputably and permanently located within a State may, without more, provide the contacts necessary to subject a defendant to jurisdiction within the State to the extent of the value of the property. In the case of real property, in particular, preservation of the common-law concept of *quasi in rem* jurisdiction arguably would avoid the uncertainty of the general *International Shoe* standard without significant cost to " 'traditional notions of fair play and substantial justice.' " Id., at 316, 66 S.Ct., at 158, quoting Milliken v. Meyer, 311 U.S. 457, 463, 61 S.Ct. 339, 343, 85 L.Ed. 278 (1940).

Subject to that reservation, I join the opinion of the Court.

■ MR. JUSTICE STEVENS, concurring in the judgment.

* * *

One who purchases shares of stock on the open market can hardly be expected to know that he has thereby become subject to suit in a forum remote from his residence and unrelated to the transaction. As a practical matter, the Delaware sequestration statute creates an unacceptable risk of judgment without notice. Unlike the 49 other States, Delaware treats the place of incorporation as the situs of the stock, even though both the owner and the custodian of the shares are elsewhere. Moreover, Delaware denies the defendant the opportunity to defend the merits of the suit unless he subjects himself to the unlimited jurisdiction of the court. Thus, it coerces a defendant either to submit to personal jurisdiction in a forum which could not otherwise obtain such jurisdiction or to lose the securities which have been attached. If its procedure were upheld, Delaware would, in effect, impose a duty of inquiry on every purchaser of securities in the national market. For unless the purchaser ascertains both the State of incorporation of the company whose shares he is buying, and also the idiosyncrasies of its law, he may be assuming an unknown risk of litigation. I therefore agree with the Court that on the record before us no adequate basis for jurisdiction exists and that the Delaware statute is unconstitutional on its face.

How the Court's opinion may be applied in other contexts is not entirely clear to me. I agree with Mr. Justice Powell that it should not be read to invalidate *in rem* jurisdiction where real estate is involved. I would also not read it as invalidating other long-accepted methods of acquiring jurisdiction over persons with adequate notice of both the particular controversy and also that their local activities might subject them to suit. My uncertainty as to the reach of the opinion, and my fear that it purports to decide a great deal more than is necessary to dispose of this case, persuade me merely to concur in the judgment.

■ MR. JUSTICE BRENNAN, concurring in part and dissenting in part.

I join Parts I–III of the Court's opinion. I fully agree that the minimum-contacts analysis developed in International Shoe Co. v. Washington, 326 U.S. 310, 66 S.Ct. 154, 90 L.Ed. 95 (1945), represents a far more sensible construct for the exercise of state-court jurisdiction than the patchwork of legal and factual fictions that has been generated from the decision in Pennoyer v. Neff, 95 U.S. 714, 24 L.Ed. 565 (1877). It is precisely because the inquiry into minimum contacts is now of such overriding importance, however, that I must respectfully dissent from Part IV of the Court's opinion.

I

The primary teaching of Parts I–III of today's decision is that a State, in seeking to assert jurisdiction over a person located outside its borders, may only do so on the basis of minimum contacts among the parties, the contested transaction, and the forum state. The Delaware Supreme Court could not have made plainer, however, that its sequestration statute, Del.Code Ann., Tit. 10, § 366 (1975), does not operate on this basis, but instead is strictly an embodiment of *quasi in rem* jurisdiction, a jurisdictional predicate no longer constitutionally viable:

> "[J]urisdiction under § 366 remains . . . *quasi in rem* founded on the presence of capital stock here, not on prior contact by defendants with this forum." 361 A.2d 225, 229 (1976).

This state-court ruling obviously comports with the understanding of the parties, for the issue of the existence of minimum contacts was never pleaded by appellee, made the subject of discovery, or ruled upon by the Delaware courts. These facts notwithstanding, the Court in Part IV reaches the minimum-contacts question and finds such contacts lacking as applied to appellants. Succinctly stated, once having properly and persuasively decided that the *quasi in rem* statute that Delaware admits to having enacted is invalid, the Court then proceeds to find that a minimum-contacts law that Delaware expressly *denies* having enacted also could not be constitutionally applied in this case.

In my view, a purer example of an advisory opinion is not to be found. True, appellants do not deny having received actual notice of the action in question. * * * Recognizing that today's decision fundamentally alters the relevant jurisdictional ground rules, I certainly would not want to rule out the possibility that Delaware's courts might decide that the legislature's overriding purpose of securing the personal appearance in state courts of defendants would best be served by reinterpreting its statute to permit state jurisdiction on the basis of constitutionally permissible contacts rather than stock ownership. Were the state courts to take this step, it would then become necessary to address the question of whether minimum contacts exist here. But in the present posture of this case, the Court's decision of this important issue is purely an abstract ruling.

     * * *

NOTES AND QUESTIONS

1. **What was the problem?** Did the Supreme Court hold that the corporate directors could not constitutionally be subjected to *in personam* jurisdiction in Delaware on the facts of this suit? Or did it merely hold that the Delaware statute was improperly drawn? Would a Delaware statute asserting *in personam* jurisdiction over directors of Delaware corporations in suits alleging violation of Delaware corporate law be constitutional?

2. **Quick fix.** The Supreme Court announced its decision in *Shaffer v. Heitner* on June 24, 1977. On July 7, 1977, the Delaware legislature passed a new jurisdictional statute under which an out-of-state resident who accepts

a position as a director of a Delaware corporation after September 1, 1977, or who serves in such capacity after June 30, 1978, is deemed to have consented to the appointment of an agent for service of process within the state. 10 Delaware Code § 3114. Did the statute need to rely on the "consent" of the director? The Supreme Court of Delaware upheld the constitutionality of the statute in Armstrong v. Pomerance, 423 A.2d 174 (Del.1980). In Pestolite, Inc. v. Cordura Corp., 449 A.2d 263, 267 (Del.Super.1982), the Delaware court construed the statute to assert jurisdiction only when the director's acts arise out of or relate to breaches of duties imposed by Delaware corporate law. It held that unrelated contract or tort actions against a director are not covered by the statute, and the assertion of jurisdiction over such suits "would violate 'traditional notions of fair play and substantial justice.' "

Why do you suppose the Delaware legislature was so anxious to preserve the possibility of jurisdiction in Delaware courts over directors of Delaware corporations? (Hint: Lawyers involved in litigation in Delaware against Delaware corporations and their officers are paid a lot of money.)

3. **Using a *quasi in rem* statute to fill a gap when due process not violated.** In Banco Ambrosiano, S.P.A. v. Artoc Bank & Trust, Ltd., 62 N.Y.2d 65, 476 N.Y.S.2d 64, 464 N.E.2d 432 (1984), assets of Artoc deposited in a bank account in New York were attached under New York's *quasi in rem* statute as the jurisdictional basis for a suit by Banco Ambrosiano against Artoc. The matter in dispute between the parties was the right to the funds that had been attached. Defendant Artoc neither was incorporated in New York nor had an office in the state. The New York *in personam* long-arm statute did not reach defendant Artoc. The New York Court of Appeals held that the case fell into a " 'gap' * * * in which the necessary minimum contacts, including the presence of defendant's property within the State, are present, but personal jurisdiction is not authorized by [the New York long-arm statute]." The court held that the New York *quasi in rem* statute could be used to fill in the gap.

Is *Banco Ambrosiano* consistent with *Shaffer v. Heitner*? Was the Delaware *quasi in rem* statute just filling a "gap" left by the state long-arm statute? Is the later Delaware statute filling the "gap" previously filled by the *quasi in rem* statute? Should we ignore the part of *Shaffer v. Heitner* that strikes down the actual assertion of jurisdiction in the case, and pay attention only to the Court's pronouncement that all assertions of jurisdiction, however denominated, will henceforth be tested under the fair play and substantial justice standard of *International Shoe*?

4. ***In rem* jurisdiction in domain name cases**. The federal Anticybersquatting Consumer Protection Act ("ACPA"), passed in 1999, deals with disputes over ownership rights in Internet domain names (like google.com, yahoo.com, berkeley.edu). See 15 U.S.C. § 1125(d). A domain name is a form of intangible property. What happens when the owner of a valuable trademark finds that another person or individual has already registered the domain name or names containing that trademark? In relevant part, the ACPA provides:

> The owner of a mark may file an in rem civil action against a domain name in the judicial district in which the domain name registrar, domain name registry, or other domain name authority that registered or assigned the domain name is located if

(i)   the domain name violates any right of the owner of a mark registered in the Patent and Trademark Office . . . ; and

(ii)   the court finds that the owner—

(I)   is not able to obtain in personam jurisdiction over a person who would have been a defendant in a civil action. . . .

15 U.S.C. § 1125(d)(2)(A). A number of recent cases have upheld jurisdiction under the ACPA over alleged cybersquatters who apparently had no contacts with the United States other than their use and claim to ownership of a contested domain name. See, e.g., Porsche Cars North America, Inc. v. Porsche.Net, 302 F.3d 248 (4th Cir. 2002); Harrods Ltd. v. Sixty Internet Domain Names, 302 F.3d 214 (4th Cir. 2002). The ACPA assumes that there is a class of cases where designating contested intangible property as located in the United States will justify the exercise of in rem jurisdiction even though principles of specific jurisdiction would not do so. Is that assumption consistent with *Shaffer*? If all assertions of *in rem* jurisdiction must meet the test of *International Shoe*, does it follow that the *in rem* jurisdictional provision of the Act is unconstitutional? Is the ownership of a trademark sufficiently like ownership of real property that a suit under the ACPA can be analogized to a quiet title action? For an argument that *in rem* jurisdiction under the ACPA violates due process, see Struve and Wagner, Realspace Sovereigns in Cyberspace: Problems with the Anticybersquatting Consumer Protection Act, 17 Berkeley Tech. L.J. 989 (2002).

5.   Jurisdiction based on presence of a person rather than property. What does *Shaffer* portend for *in personam* jurisdiction in cases where the assertion of jurisdiction is based on the transient presence of an individual defendant who is in a state only long enough for process to be served on her? Should the "fair play and substantial justice" standard of *International Shoe* apply to such cases, too? For an answer (perhaps a bad answer), see *Burnham v. Superior Court of California*, immediately following.

6.   Additional reading. There has been a great deal of excellent academic writing on *Shaffer v. Heitner*. See particularly Silberman, *Shaffer v. Heitner*: The End of an Era, 53 N.Y.U.L.Rev. 33 (1978), and Casad, *Shaffer v. Heitner*: An End to Ambivalence in Jurisdiction Theory, 26 Kan.L.Rev. 61 (1977), which came out immediately after the Court's decision. See also Maltz, Reflections on a Landmark: *Shaffer v. Heitner* Viewed from a Distance, 1986 B.Y.U.L.Rev. 1043.

2.   Person

Burnham v. Superior Court of California

Supreme Court of the United States, 1990.
495 U.S. 604, 110 S.Ct. 2105, 109 L.Ed.2d 631.

■ JUSTICE SCALIA announced the judgment of the Court and delivered an opinion in which THE CHIEF JUSTICE and JUSTICE KENNEDY join, and in which JUSTICE WHITE joins with respect to Parts I, II–A, II–B, and II–C.

The question presented is whether the Due Process Clause of the Fourteenth Amendment denies California courts jurisdiction over a nonresident, who was personally served with process while temporarily in that State, in a suit unrelated to his activities in the State.

I

Petitioner Dennis Burnham married Francie Burnham in 1976, in West Virginia. In 1977 the couple moved to New Jersey, where their two children were born. In July 1987 the Burnhams decided to separate. They agreed that Mrs. Burnham, who intended to move to California, would take custody of the children. Shortly before Mrs. Burnham departed for California that same month, she and petitioner agreed that she would file for divorce on grounds of "irreconcilable differences."

In October 1987, petitioner filed for divorce in New Jersey state court on grounds of "desertion." Petitioner did not, however, obtain an issuance of summons against his wife, and did not attempt to serve her with process. Mrs. Burnham, after unsuccessfully demanding that petitioner adhere to their prior agreement to submit to an "irreconcilable differences" divorce, brought suit for divorce in California state court in early January 1988.

In late January, petitioner visited southern California on business, after which he went north to visit his children in the San Francisco Bay area, where his wife resided. He took the older child to San Francisco for the weekend. Upon returning the child to Mrs. Burnham's home on January 24, 1988, petitioner was served with a California court summons and a copy of Mrs. Burnham's divorce petition. He then returned to New Jersey.

Later that year, petitioner made a special appearance in the California Superior Court, moving to quash the service of process on the ground that the court lacked personal jurisdiction over him because his only contacts with California were a few short visits to the State for the purposes of conducting business and visiting his children. The Superior Court denied the motion, and the California Court of Appeal denied mandamus relief, rejecting petitioner's contention that the Due Process Clause prohibited California courts from asserting jurisdiction over him because he lacked "minimum contacts" with the State. The court held it to be "a valid jurisdictional predicate for *in personam* jurisdiction" that the "defendant [was] present in the forum state and personally served with process." We granted certiorari. 493 U.S. 807, 110 S.Ct. 47, 107 L.Ed.2d 16 (1989).

[handwritten margin note: Appellate Court's holding re/jurisdiction]

II

A

The proposition that the judgment of a court lacking jurisdiction is void traces back to the English Year Books, see Bowser v. Collins, Y.B.Mich., 22 Edw. 4, f. 30, pl. 11, 145 Eng.Rep. 97 (1482), and was made settled law by Lord Coke in Case of the Marshalsea, 10 Co.Rep. 68b, 77 Eng.Rep. 1027, 1041 (K.B.1612). Traditionally that proposition was embodied in the phrase *coram non judice,* "before a person not a judge"— meaning, in effect, that the proceeding in question was not a *judicial* proceeding because lawful judicial authority was not present, and could therefore not yield a *judgment.* American courts invalidated, or denied recognition to, judgments that violated this common-law principle long before the Fourteenth Amendment was adopted. See, *e.g.,* Grumon v.

Raymond, 1 Conn. 40 (1814); Picquet v. Swan, 19 F.Cas. 609 (No. 11,134) (CC Mass.1828); Dunn v. Dunn, 4 Paige 425 (N.Y.Ch.1834); Evans v. Instine, 7 Ohio 273 (1835); Steel v. Smith, 7 Watts & Serg. 447 (Pa.1844); Boswell's Lessee v. Otis, 50 U.S. (9 How.) 336, 350, 13 L.Ed. 164 (1850). In Pennoyer v. Neff, 95 U.S. 714, 732, 24 L.Ed. 565 (1877), we announced that the judgment of a court lacking personal jurisdiction violated the Due Process Clause of the Fourteenth Amendment as well.

To determine whether the assertion of personal jurisdiction is consistent with due process, we have long relied on the principles traditionally followed by American courts in marking out the territorial limits of each State's authority. That criterion was first announced in Pennoyer v. Neff, *supra,* in which we stated that due process "mean[s] a course of legal proceedings according to those rules and principles which have been established in our systems of jurisprudence for the protection and enforcement of private rights," id., at 733, including the "well-established principles of public law respecting the jurisdiction of an independent State over persons and property," id., at 722. In what has become the classic expression of the criterion, we said in International Shoe Co. v. Washington, 326 U.S. 310, 66 S.Ct. 154, 90 L.Ed. 95 (1945), that a State court's assertion of personal jurisdiction satisfies the Due Process Clause if it does not violate " 'traditional notions of fair play and substantial justice.' " Id., at 316, 66 S.Ct., at 158, quoting Milliken v. Meyer, 311 U.S. 457, 463, 61 S.Ct. 339, 343, 85 L.Ed. 278 (1940). See also Insurance Corp. of Ireland v. Compagnie des Bauxites de Guinee, 456 U.S. 694, 703, 102 S.Ct. 2099, 2105, 72 L.Ed.2d 492 (1982). Since *International Shoe,* we have only been called upon to decide whether these "traditional notions" permit States to exercise jurisdiction over absent defendants in a manner that deviates from the rules of jurisdiction applied in the 19th century. We have held such deviations permissible, but only with respect to suits arising out of the absent defendant's contacts with the State.[1] See, *e.g.,* Helicopteros Nacionales de Colombia v. Hall, 466 U.S. 408, 414, 104 S.Ct. 1868, 1872, 80 L.Ed.2d 404 (1984). The question we must decide today is whether due process requires a similar connection between the litigation and the defendant's contacts with the State in cases where the defendant is physically present in the State at the time process is served upon him.

B

Among the most firmly established principles of personal jurisdiction in American tradition is that the courts of a State have jurisdiction over nonresidents who are physically present in the State.

---

[1] We have said that "[e]ven when the cause of action does not arise out of or relate to the foreign corporation's activities in the forum State, due process is not offended by a State's subjecting the corporation to its *in personam* jurisdiction when there are sufficient contacts between the State and the foreign corporation." Helicopteros Nacionales de Colombia v. Hall, 466 U.S., at 414, 104 S.Ct., at 1872. Our only holding supporting that statement, however, involved "regular service of summons upon [the corporation's] president while he was in [the forum State] acting in that capacity." See Perkins v. Benguet Consolidated Mining Co., 342 U.S. 437, 440, 72 S.Ct. 413, 415, 96 L.Ed. 485 (1952). It may be that whatever special rule exists permitting "continuous and systematic" contacts, id., at 438, to support jurisdiction with respect to matters unrelated to activity in the forum, applies *only* to corporations, which have never fitted comfortably in a jurisdictional regime based primarily upon "de facto power over the defendant's person." International Shoe Co. v. Washington, 326 U.S. 310, 316, 66 S.Ct. 154, 158, 90 L.Ed. 95 (1945). We express no views on these matters—and, for simplicity's sake, omit reference to this aspect of "contacts"-based jurisdiction in our discussion.

The view developed early that each State had the power to hale before its courts any individual who could be found within its borders, and that once having acquired jurisdiction over such a person by properly serving him with process, the State could retain jurisdiction to enter judgment against him, no matter how fleeting his visit. See, *e.g.*, Potter v. Allin, 2 Root 63, 67 (Conn.1793); Barrell v. Benjamin, 15 Mass. 354 (1819). That view had antecedents in English common-law practice, which sometimes allowed "transitory" actions, arising out of events outside the country, to be maintained against seemingly nonresident defendants who were present in England. See, e.g., Mostyn v. Fabrigas, 98 Eng.Rep. 1021 (K.B.1774); Cartwright v. Pettus, 22 Eng.Rep. 916 (Ch.1675). Justice Story believed the principle, which he traced to Roman origins, to be firmly grounded in English tradition: "[B]y the common law[,] personal actions, being transitory, may be brought in any place, where the party defendant may be found," for "every nation may . . . rightfully exercise jurisdiction over all persons within its domains." J. Story, Commentaries on the Conflict of Laws §§ 554, 543 (1846). See also §§ 530–538; Picquet v. Swan, supra, at 611–612 (Story, J.) ("Where a party is within a territory, he may justly be subjected to its process, and bound personally by the judgment pronounced, on such process, against him").

Recent scholarship has suggested that English tradition was not as clear as Story thought, see Hazard, A General Theory of State-Court Jurisdiction, 1965 Sup.Ct.Rev. 241, 253–260; Ehrenzweig, The Transient Rule of Personal Jurisdiction: The "Power" Myth and Forum Conveniens, 65 Yale L.J. 289 (1956). Accurate or not, however, judging by the evidence of contemporaneous or near-contemporaneous decisions one must conclude that Story's understanding was shared by American courts at the crucial time for present purposes: 1868, when the Fourteenth Amendment was adopted. The following passage in a decision of the Supreme Court of Georgia, in an action on a debt having no apparent relation to the defendant's temporary presence in the State, is representative:

> "Can a citizen of Alabama be sued in this State, as he passes through it?

> "Undoubtedly he can. The second of the axioms of *Huberus,* as translated by *Story,* is: 'that all persons who are found within the limits of a government, whether their residence is permanent or temporary, are to be deemed subjects thereof.' (*Stor. Conf.Laws, § 29, Note 3.*)

> ". . . [A] citizen of another State, who is merely passing through this, resides, as he passes, wherever he is. Let him be sued, therefore, wherever he may, he will be sued where he resides.

> "The plaintiff in error, although a citizen of Alabama, was passing through the County of Troup, in this State, and whilst doing so, he was sued in Troup. He was liable to be sued in this State, and in Troup County of this State." Murphy v. J.S. Winter & Co., 18 Ga. 690, 691–692 (1855).

See also, e.g., Peabody v. Hamilton, 106 Mass. 217, 220 (1870) (relying on Story for the same principle); Alley v. Caspari, 80 Me. 234, 236–237, 14 A. 12, 13 (1888) (same).

Decisions in the courts of many States in the 19th and early 20th centuries held that personal service upon a physically present defendant sufficed to confer jurisdiction, without regard to whether the defendant was only briefly in the State or whether the cause of action was related to his activities there. * * * Most States, moreover, had statutes or common-law rules that exempted from service of process individuals who were brought into the forum by force or fraud, see, *e.g.,* Wanzer v. Bright, 52 Ill. 35 (1869), or who were there as a party or witness in unrelated judicial proceedings, see, e.g., Burroughs v. Cocke & Willis, 56 Okla. 627, 156 P. 196 (1916); Malloy v. Brewer, 7 S.D. 587, 64 N.W. 1120 (1895). These exceptions obviously rested upon the premise that service of process conferred jurisdiction. See Anderson v. Atkins, 161 Tenn. 137, 140, 29 S.W.2d 248, 249 (1930). Particularly striking is the fact that, as far as we have been able to determine, *not one* American case from the period (or, for that matter, not one American case until 1978) held, or even suggested, that in-state personal service on an individual was insufficient to confer personal jurisdiction. Commentators were also seemingly unanimous on the rule. See, e.g., 1 A. Freeman, Law of Judgments 470–471 (1873); 1 H. Black, Law of Judgments 276–277 (1891); W. Alderson, Law of Judicial Writs and Process 225–226 (1895). See also Restatement of Conflict of Laws, §§ 77–78 (1934).

This American jurisdictional practice is, moreover, not merely old; it is continuing. It remains the practice of, not only a substantial number of the States, but as far as we are aware *all* the States and the federal government—if one disregards (as one must for this purpose) the few opinions since 1978 that have erroneously said, on grounds similar to those that petitioner presses here, that this Court's due-process decisions render the practice unconstitutional. See Nehemiah v. Athletics Congress of the U.S.A., 765 F.2d 42, 46–47 (C.A.3 1985); Schreiber v. Allis-Chalmers Corp., 448 F. Supp. 1079, 1088–1091 (D.Kan.1978), rev'd on other grounds, 611 F.2d 790 (C.A.10 1979); Harold M. Pitman Co. v. Typecraft Software, 626 F. Supp. 305, 310–314 (N.D.Ill.1986); Bershaw v. Sarbacher, 700 P.2d 347, 349 (Wash.1985); Duehring v. Vasquez, 490 So.2d 667, 671 (La.App.1986). We do not know of a single State or federal statute, or a single judicial decision resting upon State law, that has abandoned in-State service as a basis of jurisdiction. Many recent cases reaffirm it. See Hutto v. Plagens, 254 Ga. 512, 513, 330 S.E.2d 341, 342 (1985); * * *.

　　* * *

C

Despite this formidable body of precedent, petitioner contends, in reliance on our decisions applying the *International Shoe* standard, that in the absence of "continuous and systematic" contacts with the forum, see note 1, supra, a nonresident defendant can be subjected to judgment only as to matters that arise out of or relate to his contacts with the forum. This argument rests on a thorough misunderstanding of our cases.

The view of most courts in the 19th century was that a court simply could not exercise *in personam* jurisdiction over a nonresident who had not been personally served with process in the forum. See, e.g., Reber v. Wright, 68 Pa. 471, 476–477 (1871); Sturgis v. Fay, 16 Ind. 429, 431

(1861); Weil v. Lowenthal, 10 Iowa 575, 578 (1860); Freeman, Law of Judgments, at 468–470; see also D'Arcy v. Ketchum, 52 U.S. (11 How.) 165, 176, 13 L.Ed. 648 (1850); Knowles v. Logansport Gaslight & Coke Co., 86 U.S. (19 Wall.) 58, 61, 22 L.Ed. 70 (1873). Pennoyer v. Neff, while renowned for its statement of the principle that the Fourteenth Amendment prohibits such an exercise of jurisdiction, in fact set that forth only as dictum, and decided the case (which involved a judgment rendered more than two years before the Fourteenth Amendment's ratification) under "well-established principles of public law." 95 U.S., at 722. Those principles, embodied in the Due Process Clause, required (we said) that when proceedings "involv[e] merely a determination of the personal liability of the defendant, he must be brought within [the court's] jurisdiction by service of process within the State, or his voluntary appearance." Id., at 733. We invoked that rule in a series of subsequent cases, as either a matter of due process or a "fundamental principl[e] of jurisprudence," Wilson v. Seligman, 144 U.S. 41, 46, 12 S.Ct. 541, 542, 36 L.Ed. 338 (1892). See e.g., New York Life Ins. Co. v. Dunlevy, 241 U.S. 518, 522–523, 36 S.Ct. 613, 614, 60 L.Ed. 1140 (1916); Goldey v. Morning News, 156 U.S. 518, 521, 15 S.Ct. 559, 560, 39 L.Ed. 517 (1895).

Later years, however, saw the weakening of the *Pennoyer* rule. In the late 19th and early 20th centuries, changes in the technology of transportation and communication, and the tremendous growth of interstate business activity, led to an "inevitable relaxation of the strict limits on state jurisdiction" over nonresident individuals and corporations. Hanson v. Denckla, 357 U.S. 235, 260, 78 S.Ct. 1228, 1243, 2 L.Ed.2d 1283 (1958) (BLACK, J., dissenting). States required, for example, that nonresident corporations appoint an in-state agent upon whom process could be served as a condition of transacting business within their borders, see, e.g., St. Clair v. Cox, 106 U.S. 350, 1 S.Ct. 354, 27 L.Ed. 222 (1882), and provided in-state "substituted service" for nonresident motorists who caused injury in the State and left before personal service could be accomplished, see, e.g., Kane v. New Jersey, 242 U.S. 160, 37 S.Ct. 30, 61 L.Ed. 222 (1916); Hess v. Pawloski, 274 U.S. 352, 47 S.Ct. 632, 71 L.Ed. 1091 (1927). We initially upheld these laws under the Due Process Clause on grounds that they complied with *Pennoyer's* rigid requirement of either "consent," see, e.g., Hess v. Pawloski, *supra,* at 356, 47 S.Ct., at 633, or "presence," see, e.g., Philadelphia & Reading R. Co. v. McKibbin, 243 U.S. 264, 265, 37 S.Ct. 280, 280, 61 L.Ed. 710 (1917). As many observed, however, the consent and presence were purely fictional. See, e.g., 1 J. Beale, Treatise on the Conflict of Laws 360, 384 (1935); Hutchinson v. Chase & Gilbert, Inc., 45 F.2d 139, 141 (C.A.2 1930) (L. Hand, J.). Our opinion in *International Shoe* cast those fictions aside, and made explicit the underlying basis of these decisions: due process does not necessarily *require* the States to adhere to the unbending territorial limits on jurisdiction set forth in *Pennoyer.* The validity of assertion of jurisdiction over a nonconsenting defendant who is not present in the forum depends upon whether "the quality and nature of [his] activity" in relation to the forum, 326 U.S., at 319, 66 S.Ct., at 158, renders such jurisdiction consistent with "'traditional notions of fair play and substantial justice.'" Id., at 316, 66 S.Ct., at 158 (citation omitted). Subsequent cases have derived from the *International Shoe* standard the general rule that a State may dispense with in-forum personal service on nonresident defendants in suits arising out of their activities in the State. * * *

Nothing in *International Shoe* or the cases that have followed it, however, offers support for the very different proposition petitioner seeks to establish today: that a defendant's presence in the forum is not only unnecessary to validate novel, nontraditional assertions of jurisdiction, but is itself no longer sufficient to establish jurisdiction. That proposition is unfaithful to both elementary logic and the foundations of our due process jurisprudence. * * *

[handwritten: Argument of NY re jurisdiction]

The short of the matter is that jurisdiction based on physical presence alone constitutes due process because it is one of the continuing traditions of our legal system that define the due process standard of "traditional notions of fair play and substantial justice." That standard was developed by *analogy* to "physical presence," and it would be perverse to say it could now be turned against that touchstone of jurisdiction.

[handwritten: Jurisdiction based on physical presence alone = due process]

D

Petitioner's strongest argument, though we ultimately reject it, relies upon our decision in *Shaffer v. Heitner*, 433 U.S. 186, 97 S.Ct. 2569, 53 L.Ed.2d 683 (1977). In that case, a Delaware court hearing a shareholder's derivative suit against a corporation's directors secured jurisdiction *quasi in rem* by sequestering the out-of-State defendants' stock in the company, the situs of which was Delaware under Delaware law. Reasoning that Delaware's sequestration procedure was simply a mechanism to compel the absent defendants to appear in a suit to determine their personal rights and obligations, we concluded that the normal rules we had developed under *International Shoe* for jurisdiction over suits against absent defendants should apply—viz, Delaware could not hear the suit because the defendants' sole contact with the State (ownership of property there) was unrelated to the lawsuit. 433 U.S., at 213–215, 97 S.Ct., at 2584–2585. [handwritten: ↳ Rule (Shaffer v. Heitner)]

It goes too far to say, as petitioner contends, that Shaffer compels the conclusion that a State lacks jurisdiction over an individual unless the litigation arises out of his activities in the State. *Shaffer,* like *International Shoe,* involved jurisdiction over an *absent defendant,* and it stands for nothing more than the proposition that when the "minimum contact" that is a substitute for physical presence consists of property ownership it must, like other minimum contacts, be related to the litigation. Petitioner wrenches out of its context our statement in *Shaffer* that "all assertions of state-court jurisdiction must be evaluated according to the standards set forth in *International Shoe* and its progeny," 433 U.S., at 212, 97 S.Ct., at 2584. When read together with the two sentences that preceded it, the meaning of this statement becomes clear:

[handwritten: Shaffer and International Shoe w/ regards to absent Δs — min contact as a sub. for physical presence — Min contacts related to the litigation]

> "The fiction that an assertion of jurisdiction over property is anything but an assertion of jurisdiction over the owner of the property supports an ancient form without substantial modern justification. Its continued acceptance would serve only to allow state-court jurisdiction that is fundamentally unfair to the defendant.

"We *therefore conclude* that all assertions of state-court jurisdiction must be evaluated according to the standards set forth in *International Shoe* and its progeny." *Ibid.* (emphasis added).

Shaffer was saying, in other words, not that all bases for the assertion of *in personam* jurisdiction (including, presumably, in-state service) must be treated alike and subjected to the "minimum contacts" analysis of *International Shoe;* but rather that *quasi in rem* jurisdiction, that fictional "ancient form," and *in personam* jurisdiction, are really one and the same and must be treated alike—leading to the conclusion that *quasi in rem* jurisdiction, i.e., that form of *in personam* jurisdiction based upon a "property ownership" contact and by definition unaccompanied by personal, in-state service, must satisfy the litigation-relatedness requirement of *International Shoe.* The logic of *Shaffer's* holding—which places all suits against absent nonresidents on the same constitutional footing, regardless of whether a separate Latin label is attached to one particular basis of contact—does not compel the conclusion that physically present defendants must be treated identically to absent ones. As we have demonstrated at length, our tradition has treated the two classes of defendants quite differently, and it is unreasonable to read *Shaffer* as casually obliterating that distinction. *International Shoe* confined its "minimum contacts" requirement to situations in which the defendant "be not present within the territory of the forum," 326 U.S., at 316, 66 S.Ct., at 158, and nothing in *Shaffer* expands that requirement beyond that.

* * *

III

A few words in response to JUSTICE BRENNAN'S concurrence: It insists that we apply "contemporary notions of due process" to determine the constitutionality of California's assertion of jurisdiction. * * *

But the concurrence's proposed standard of "contemporary notions of due process" * * * measures state-court jurisdiction not only against traditional doctrines in this country, including current state-court practice, but against each Justice's subjective assessment of what is fair and just. Authority for that seductive standard is not to be found in any of our personal jurisdiction cases. It is, indeed, an outright break with the test of "traditional notions of fair play and substantial justice," which would have to be reformulated "*our* notions of fair play and substantial justice."

The subjectivity, and hence inadequacy, of this approach becomes apparent when the concurrence tries to explain *why* the assertion of jurisdiction in the present case meets its standard of continuing-American-tradition-*plus*-innate-fairness. JUSTICE BRENNAN lists the "benefits" Mr. Burnham derived from the State of California—the fact that, during the few days he was there, "his health and safety [were] guaranteed by the State's police, fire, and emergency medical services; he [was] free to travel on the State's roads and waterways; he likely enjoy[ed] the fruits of the State's economy." * * * Three days' worth of these benefits strike us as powerfully inadequate to establish, as an abstract matter, that it is "fair" for California to decree the ownership of all Mr. Burnham's worldly goods acquired during the ten years of his marriage, and the custody over his children. We daresay a contractual exchange swapping those benefits for that power would not survive the "unconscionability" provision of the Uniform Commercial Code. Even less persuasive are the other "fairness" factors alluded to by JUSTICE BRENNAN. It would create "an asymmetry," we are told, if Burnham were *permitted* (as he is) to appear in California courts as a plaintiff, but were not *compelled* to appear in California courts as defendant; and travel being as easy as it is nowadays, and modern procedural devices being so convenient, it is no great hardship to appear in California courts. * * *. The problem with these assertions is that they justify the exercise of jurisdiction over *everyone, whether or not* he ever comes to California. The only "fairness" elements setting Mr. Burnham apart from the rest of the world are the three-days' "benefits" referred to above—and even those, do not set him apart from many other people who have enjoyed three days in the Golden State (savoring the fruits of its economy, the availability of its roads and police services) but who were fortunate enough not to be served with process while they were there and thus are not (simply by reason of that savoring) subject to the general jurisdiction of California's courts. See, e.g., Helicopteros Nacionales de Colombia v. Hall, 466 U.S., at 414–416, 104 S.Ct., at 1872–1873. In other words, even if one agreed with JUSTICE BRENNAN'S conception of an equitable bargain, the "benefits" we have been discussing would explain why it is "fair" to assert general jurisdiction over Burnham-returned-to-New-Jersey-after-service only at the expense of proving that it is also "fair" to assert general jurisdiction over Burnham-returned-to-New-Jersey-*without*-service— which we *know* does not conform with "contemporary notions of due process."

There is, we must acknowledge, one factor mentioned by JUSTICE BRENNAN that *both* relates distinctively to the assertion of jurisdiction on the basis of personal in-state service *and* is fully persuasive—namely, the fact that a defendant voluntarily present in a particular State has a "reasonable expectatio[n]" that he is subject to suit there. * * * By formulating it as a "reasonable expectation" JUSTICE BRENNAN makes that seem like a "fairness" factor; but in reality, of course, it is just tradition, masquerading as "fairness." The only reason for charging Mr. Burnham with the reasonable expectation of being subject to suit is that the States of the Union assert adjudicatory jurisdiction over the person, and have always asserted adjudicatory jurisdiction over the person, by serving him with process during his temporary physical presence in their territory. That continuing tradition, which anyone entering California should have known about, renders it "fair" for Mr. Burnham, who voluntarily entered California, to be sued there for divorce—at least "fair" in the limited sense that he has no one but himself to blame. JUSTICE BRENNAN'S long journey is a circular one, leaving him, at the end of the day, in complete reliance upon the very factor he sought to avoid: The existence of a continuing tradition is not enough, fairness also must be considered; fairness exists here because there is a continuing tradition.

* * *

Because the Due Process Clause does not prohibit the California courts from exercising jurisdiction over petitioner based on the fact of in-state service of process, the judgment is

Affirmed.

■ JUSTICE WHITE, concurring in part and concurring in the judgment.

I join Part I and Parts II–A, II–B, and II–C of JUSTICE SCALIA'S opinion and concur in the judgment of affirmance. The rule allowing jurisdiction to be obtained over a non-resident by personal service in the forum state, without more, has been and is so widely accepted throughout this country that I could not possibly strike it down, either on its face or as applied in this case, on the ground that it denies due process of law guaranteed by the Fourteenth Amendment. Although the Court has the authority under the Amendment to examine even traditionally accepted procedures and declare them invalid, e.g., Shaffer v. Heitner, 433 U.S. 186, 97 S.Ct. 2569, 53 L.Ed.2d 683 (1977), there has been no showing here or elsewhere that as a general proposition the rule is so arbitrary and lacking in common sense in so many instances that it should be held violative of Due Process in every case. Furthermore, until such a showing is made, which would be difficult indeed, claims in individual cases that the rule would operate unfairly as applied to the particular non-resident involved need not be entertained. At least this would be the case where presence in the forum state is intentional, which would almost always be the fact. Otherwise, there would be endless, fact-specific litigation in the trial and appellate courts, including this one. Here, personal service in California, without more, is enough, and I agree that the judgment should be affirmed.

      * * *

■ JUSTICE BRENNAN, with whom JUSTICE MARSHALL, JUSTICE BLACKMUN, and JUSTICE O'CONNOR join, concurring in the judgment.

I agree with JUSTICE SCALIA that the Due Process Clause of the Fourteenth Amendment generally permits a state court to exercise jurisdiction over a defendant if he is served with process while voluntarily present in the forum State.[1] I do not perceive the need, however, to decide that a jurisdictional rule that " 'has been immemorially the actual law of the land,' " * * * quoting Hurtado v. California, 110 U.S. 516, 528, 4 S.Ct. 111, 117, 28 L.Ed. 232 (1884), automatically comports with due process simply by virtue of its "pedigree." Although I agree that history is an important factor in establishing whether a jurisdictional rule satisfies due process requirements, I cannot agree that it is the *only* factor such that all traditional rules of jurisdiction are, *ipso facto,* forever constitutional. Unlike JUSTICE SCALIA, I would undertake an "independent inquiry into the . . . fairness of the prevailing in-state service rule." * * * I therefore concur only in the judgment.

I

I believe that the approach adopted by JUSTICE SCALIA'S opinion today—reliance solely on historical pedigree—is foreclosed by our decisions in International Shoe Co. v. Washington, 326 U.S. 310, 66 S.Ct. 154, 90 L.Ed. 95 (1945), and Shaffer v. Heitner, 433 U.S. 186, 97 S.Ct. 2569, 53 L.Ed.2d 683 (1977). In *International Shoe,* we held that a state court's assertion of personal jurisdiction does not violate the Due Process

---

[1]   I use the term "transient jurisdiction" to refer to jurisdiction premised solely on the fact that a person is served with process while physically present in the forum State.

Clause if it is consistent with " 'traditional notions of fair play and substantial justice.' " 326 U.S., at 316, 66 S.Ct., at 158, quoting Milliken v. Meyer, 311 U.S. 457, 463, 61 S.Ct. 339, 342–343, 85 L.Ed. 278 (1940).[2] In Shaffer, we stated that "*all* assertions of state court jurisdiction must be evaluated according to the standards set forth in *International Shoe* and its progeny." 433 U.S. 212, 97 S.Ct., at 2584 (emphasis added). The critical insight of *Shaffer* is that all rules of jurisdiction, even ancient ones, must satisfy contemporary notions of due process. No longer were we content to limit our jurisdictional analysis to pronouncements that "[t]he foundation of jurisdiction is physical power," McDonald v. Mabee, 243 U.S. 90, 91, 37 S.Ct. 343, 343, 61 L.Ed. 608 (1917), and that "every State possesses exclusive jurisdiction and sovereignty over persons and property within its territory." Pennoyer v. Neff, 95 U.S. 714, 722, 24 L.Ed. 565 (1877). While acknowledging that "history must be considered as supporting the proposition that jurisdiction based solely on the presence of property satisfie[d] the demands of due process," we found that this factor could not be "decisive." 433 U.S., at 211–212, 97 S.Ct., at 2583. We recognized that " '[t]raditional notions of fair play and substantial justice' can be as readily offended by the perpetuation of ancient forms that are no longer justified as by the adoption of new procedures that are inconsistent with the basic values of our constitutional heritage." Id., at 212, 97 S.Ct., at 2584 (citations omitted). I agree with this approach and continue to believe that "the minimum-contacts analysis developed in *International Shoe* . . . represents a far more sensible construct for the exercise of state-court jurisdiction than the patchwork of legal and factual fictions that has been generated from the decision in *Pennoyer v. Neff*". Id., at 219, 97 S.Ct., at 2588 (citation omitted) (BRENNAN, J., concurring in part and dissenting in part).

While our *holding* in *Schaffer* may have been limited to *quasi in rem* jurisdiction, our mode of analysis was not. Indeed, that we were willing in *Schaffer* to examine anew the appropriateness of the *quasi in rem* rule—until that time dutifully accepted by American courts for at least a century—demonstrates that we did not believe that the "pedigree" of a jurisdictional practice was dispositive in deciding whether it was consistent with due process. * * * If we could discard an "ancient form without substantial modern justification" in *Shaffer,* supra, at 212, 97 S.Ct., at 2584, we can do so again. Lower courts, commentators, and the American Law Institute[6] all have interpreted *International Shoe* and

---

[2]   Our reference in *International Shoe* to " 'traditional notions of fair play and substantial justice,' " 326 U.S., at 316, 66 S.Ct., at 158, meant simply that those concepts are indeed traditional ones, not that, as JUSTICE SCALIA'S opinion suggests, * * * their specific *content* was to be determined by tradition alone. We recognized that contemporary societal norms must play a role in our analysis. See, e.g., 326 U.S., at 317, 66 S.Ct., at 158–159 (considerations of "reasonable[ness], in the context of our federal system of government").

[6]   See Restatement (Second) of Conflict of Laws § 24, Comment *b,* p. 29 (Proposed Revisions 1986) ("One basic principle underlies all rules of jurisdiction. This principle is that a state does not have jurisdiction in the absence of some reasonable basis for exercising it. With respect to judicial jurisdiction, this principle was laid down by the Supreme Court of the United States in International Shoe. . . ."); id., at 30 ("Three factors are primarily responsible for existing rules of judicial jurisdiction. Present-day notions of fair play and substantial justice constitute the first factor"); *d.,* at 41, § 28, Comment *b,* ("The Supreme Court held in Shaffer v. Heitner that the presence of a thing in a state gives that state jurisdiction to determine interests in the thing only in situations where the exercise of such jurisdiction would be reasonable. . . . It must likewise follow that considerations of reasonableness qualify the power of a state to exercise personal jurisdiction over an individual on the basis of his physical presence within its

Shaffer to mean that *every* assertion of state-court jurisdiction, even one pursuant to a "traditional" rule such as transient jurisdiction, must comport with contemporary notions of due process. Notwithstanding the nimble gymnastics of JUSTICE SCALIA'S opinion today, it is not faithful to our decision in *Schaffer*.

II

Tradition, though alone not dispositive, is of course *relevant* to the question whether the rule of transient jurisdiction is consistent with due process. Tradition is salient not in the sense that practices of the past are automatically reasonable today; indeed, under such a standard, the legitimacy of transient jurisdiction would be called into question because the rule's historical "pedigree" is a matter of intense debate. The rule was a stranger to the common law[8] and was rather weakly implanted in American jurisprudence "at the crucial time for present purposes: 1868, when the Fourteenth Amendment was adopted." * * * For much of the 19th century, American courts did not uniformly recognize the concept of transient jurisdiction, and it appears that the transient rule did not receive wide currency until well after our decision in Pennoyer v. Neff, 95 U.S. 714, 24 L.Ed. 565 (1877).

Rather, I find the historical background relevant because, however murky the jurisprudential origins of transient jurisdiction, the fact that American courts have announced the rule for perhaps a century (first in dicta, more recently in holdings) provides a defendant voluntarily present in a particular State *today* "clear notice that [he] is subject to suit" in the forum. World-Wide Volkswagen Corp. v. Woodson, 444 U.S. 286, 297, 100 S.Ct. 559, 567, 62 L.Ed.2d 490 (1980). Regardless of whether Justice Story's account of the rule's genesis is mythical, our common understanding *now,* fortified by a century of judicial practice, is that jurisdiction is often a function of geography. The transient rule is consistent with reasonable expectations and is entitled to a strong presumption that it comports with due process. "If I visit another State, . . . I knowingly assume some risk that the State will exercise its power over my property or my person while there. My contact with the State, though minimal, gives rise to predictable risks." *Shaffer,* 433 U.S., at 218, 97 S.Ct., at 2587 (STEVENS, J., concurring in judgment); see also Burger King Corp. v. Rudzewicz, 471 U.S. 462, 476, 105 S.Ct. 2174, 2184, 85 L.Ed.2d 528 (1985) ("[t]erritorial presence frequently will enhance a potential defendant's affiliation with a State and reinforce the reasonable foreseeability of suit there"); Glen, An Analysis of "Mere Presence" and Other Traditional Bases of Jurisdiction, 45 Brooklyn L.Rev. 607, 611–612 (1979). Thus, proposed revisions to the restatement (Second) of Conflict of Laws § 28, p. 39 (1986), provide that "[a] state has power to

---

territory"); Restatement (Second) of Judgments § 8, Comment *a,* p. 64 (Tent.Draft No. 5, Mar. 10, 1978) (*Shaffer* establishes " 'minimum contacts' in place of presence as the principal basis for territorial jurisdiction").

    [8]   As JUSTICE SCALIA'S opinion acknowledges, American courts in the 19th century erected the theory of transient jurisdiction largely upon JUSTICE STORY'S historical interpretation of Roman and continental sources. JUSTICE SCALIA'S opinion concedes that the rule's tradition "was not as clear as Story thought," * * * in fact, it now appears that as a historical matter Story was almost surely wrong. See Ehrenzweig, The Transient Rule of Personal Jurisdiction: The "Power" Myth and Forum Conveniens, 65 Yale L.J. 289, 293–303 (1956); Hazard, A General Theory of State-Court Jurisdiction, 1965 Sup.Ct.Rev. 241, 261 ("Story's system reflected neither decided authority nor critical analysis"). * * *

exercise judicial jurisdiction over an individual who is present within its territory unless the individual's relationship to the state is so attenuated as to make the exercise of such jurisdiction unreasonable."[11]

By visiting the forum State, a transient defendant actually "avail[s]" himself, *Burger King,* supra, at 476, 105 S.Ct., at 2184, of significant benefits provided by the State. His health and safety are guaranteed by the State's police, fire, and emergency medical services; he is free to travel on the State's roads and waterways; he likely enjoys the fruits of the State's economy as well. Moreover, the Privileges and Immunities Clause of Article IV prevents a state government from discriminating against a transient defendant by denying him the protections of its law or the right of access to its courts. See Supreme Court of New Hampshire v. Piper, 470 U.S. 274, 281 n. 10, 105 S.Ct. 1272, 1276, n. 10, 84 L.Ed.2d 205 (1985); Baldwin v. Montana Fish and Game Comm'n of Montana, 436 U.S. 371, 387, 98 S.Ct. 1852, 1862, 56 L.Ed.2d 354 (1978); see also Supreme Court of Virginia v. Friedman, 487 U.S. 59, 64–65, 108 S.Ct. 2260, 2264, 101 L.Ed.2d 56 (1988). Subject only to the doctrine of *forum non conveniens,* an out-of-state plaintiff may use state courts in all circumstances in which those courts would be available to state citizens. Without transient jurisdiction, an asymmetry would arise: a transient would have the full benefit of the power of the forum State's courts as a plaintiff while retaining immunity from their authority as a defendant. See Maltz, Sovereign Authority, Fairness, and Personal Jurisdiction: The Case for the Doctrine of Transient Jurisdiction, 66 Wash.U.L.Q. 671, 698–699 (1988).

The potential burdens on a transient defendant are slight. " [M]odern transportation and communications have made it much less burdensome for a party sued to defend himself' " in a State outside his place of residence. *Burger King,* 471 U.S., at 474, 105 S.Ct., at 2183, quoting McGee v. International Life Insurance Co., 355 U.S. 220, 223, 78 S.Ct. 199, 201, 2 L.Ed.2d 223 (1957). That the defendant has already journeyed at least once before to the forum—as evidenced by the fact that he was served with process there—is an indication that suit in the forum likely would not be prohibitively inconvenient. Finally, any burdens that do arise can be ameliorated by a variety of procedural devices.[13] For these reasons, as a rule the exercise of personal jurisdiction over a defendant based on his voluntary presence in the forum will satisfy the requirements of due process. See n. 11, supra.

---

[11] As the Restatement suggests, there may be cases in which a defendant's involuntary or unknowing presence in a State does not support the exercise of personal jurisdiction over him. The facts of the instant case do not require us to determine the outer limits of the transient jurisdiction rule.

[13] For example, in the federal system, a transient defendant can avoid protracted litigation of a spurious suit through a motion to dismiss for failure to state a claim or through a motion for summary judgment. Fed.Rules Civ.Proc. 12(b)(6) and 56. He can use relatively inexpensive methods of discovery, such as oral deposition by telephone (Rule 30(b)(7)), deposition upon written questions (Rule 31), interrogatories (Rule 33), and requests for admission (Rule 36), while enjoying protection from harassment (Rule 26(c)), and possibly obtaining costs and attorney's fees for some of the work involved (Rule 37(a)(4), (b)–(d)). Moreover, a change of venue may be possible. 28 U.S.C. § 1404. In state court, many of the same procedural protections are available, as is the doctrine of *forum non conveniens,* under which the suit may be dismissed. See generally Abrams, Power, Convenience, and the Elimination of Personal Jurisdiction in the Federal Courts, 58 Ind.L.J. 1, 23–25 (1982).

In this case, it is undisputed that petitioner was served with process while voluntarily and knowingly in the State of California. I therefore concur in the judgment.

■ JUSTICE STEVENS, concurring in the judgment.

As I explained in my separate writing, I did not join the Court's opinion in Shaffer v. Heitner, 433 U.S. 186, 97 S.Ct. 2569, 53 L.Ed.2d 683 (1977), because I was concerned by its unnecessarily broad reach. Id., at 217–219, 97 S.Ct., at 2586–2588 (opinion concurring in judgment). The same concern prevents me from joining either JUSTICE SCALIA'S or JUSTICE BRENNAN'S opinion in this case. For me, it is sufficient to note that the historical evidence and consensus identified by JUSTICE SCALIA, the considerations of fairness identified by JUSTICE BRENNAN, and the common sense displayed by JUSTICE WHITE, all combine to demonstrate that this is, indeed, a very easy case. Accordingly, I agree that the judgment should be affirmed.

NOTES AND QUESTIONS

1. **A narrow or broad construction of the intent of the adopters of the Due Process Clause.** Under the traditional scheme, service of process on a person physically present in a state sufficed for general *in personam* jurisdiction over that person, even if the person was only in the state temporarily. After *Shaffer v. Heitner*, it was widely anticipated that such "transient" or "tag" jurisdiction would be unconstitutional unless it independently satisfied the fair play and substantial justice standard of *International Shoe*. Justice Scalia, joined by three other justices, and joined in large part by Justice White, would uphold the traditional form of "transient" or "tag" jurisdiction. Are you persuaded that the intent of the adopters of the Due Process Clause of the Fourteenth Amendment is the best place to look for a resolution of the issue? Would you overrule *International Shoe* and *Shaffer v. Heitner* as inconsistent with the adopters' intent? Would you uphold *International Shoe* and *Shaffer v. Heitner* on the ground that economic conditions, methods of transportation, and means of communication have so changed that a narrowly construed intent of the adopters cannot be meaningfully and sensibly applied? Would that reasoning lead you to disagree with Justice Scalia?

2. **Airplanes and the intent of the adopters.** Recall Grace v. MacArthur, 170 F. Supp. 442 (E.D. Ark.1959), in which process was served on an airplane flying over the state of Arkansas on a nonstop flight between Tennessee and Texas. Would the assertion of personal jurisdiction based on such service comport with due process in Justice Scalia's view? If not, would it be because the airplane had not been invented when the due process clause was adopted? Recall that the district court in *MacArthur* upheld the assertion of jurisdiction.

3. **"Tag" jurisdiction and corporations.** Does "tag" jurisdiction under *Burnham* extend to a high-ranking corporate official temporarily in a state, such that *in personam* jurisdiction can thereby be established over the corporation? The answer is pretty clearly "no." In Mendoza Martinez v. AeroCaribbean, 764 F.3d 1062 (9th Cir. 2014), a corporate officer of a French airplane manufacturer, Avions de Transport Regional (ATR), was served in California with a complaint in a product liability suit arising out of a crash in the Caribbean. Relying on *Burnham*, plaintiffs contended that on the

corporate officer established general jurisdiction over ATR in California. Citing *Daimler AG v. Bauman*, the Ninth Circuit held that transient presence of a corporate officer in a state does not make the corporation "essentially at home" in that state. It wrote, "*Burnham* does not authorize tag jurisdiction over corporations, and ATR's contacts with California are insufficient to support general jurisdiction." Id. at 1071.

   4.   Presence and domicile. Natural persons have traditionally been held subject to general jurisdiction in the state of their domicile even when they are not physically present in that state. In Milliken v. Meyer, 311 U.S. 457, 61 S.Ct. 339, 85 L.Ed. 278 (1940), the plaintiff sued Meyer, a Wyoming domiciliary, in a Wyoming court concerning a dispute over profits from Colorado oil properties. Meyer was personally served in Colorado with process from the Wyoming suit. The Supreme Court upheld *in personam* jurisdiction, indicating that even some form of constructive or substituted service would suffice: "Domicile in the state is alone sufficient to bring an absent defendant within the reach of the state's jurisdiction for purposes of a personal judgment by means of [personal or] appropriate substituted service." 311 U.S. at 462.

   Milliken v. Meyer was decided in 1940, five years before *International Shoe*. Is the Court's statement in *Milliken* that domicile alone is sufficient for *in personam* jurisdiction still valid? Imagine someone who lives in California and enlists in the Army. He does not know where he will want to live when he is eventually discharged from military service, but he knows that he does not want to return to California. Under established law, such a person remains a California domiciliary until he affirmatively establishes a new domicile. Two years later, while stationed in New York, he buys a car from a fellow soldier who is about to be transferred. He makes a small down payment and promises to pay the balance within three months. The seller is transferred to California. When the buyer fails to pay, the seller sues in California to recover the balance. Are there sufficient "minimum contacts" between the defendant and California "such that the maintenance of the suit does not offend 'traditional notions of fair play and substantial justice'"? How would Justice Scalia decide this case?

   5.   Fraudulently induced presence. Even under the traditional view of transient jurisdiction, service of process on someone who has been fraudulently enticed into the state will not confer *in personam* jurisdiction. In Wyman v. Newhouse, 93 F.2d 313 (2d Cir. 1937), a man and woman had carried on for some years an illicit love affair. The affair was coming to an end, or perhaps had already ended. The woman lived in Florida, the man in New York. The woman urged the man to come visit her in Florida one last time, asserting that she was leaving the United States forever to return to her dying mother in Ireland. When the man arrived in Florida, he was met at the airport by the woman and her sister, by a deputy sheriff who served him with process, and by a photographer who attempted to take his picture. The suit alleged money lent and seduction under promise of marriage, and sought $500,000 in damages. The man returned to New York without responding to the suit, and default judgment was entered against him in Florida. When enforcement of the judgment was sought against him in New York, the federal court in New York held that *in personam* jurisdiction was not established by the service of process in Florida because he had been fraudulently enticed into the forum state.

The fraudulent enticement doctrine applies to potential defendants who come into a forum to conduct settlement negotiations concerning a dispute in which a suit has not yet been filed. If a defendant is not warned by the plaintiff that he may be served when he comes into the forum, service of process will be quashed. See, e.g., Henkel Corp. v. Degremont, S.A., 136 F.R.D. 88 (E.D.Pa.1991); Coyne v. Grupo Industrial Trieme, S.A., 105 F.R.D. 627 (D.D.C.1985).

6. Additional reading. For a series of articles on *Burnham*, see Symposium, The Future of Personal Jurisdiction: A Symposium on *Burnham v. Superior Court*, 22 Rutgers L.J. 559 (1991).

f.   NOTICE

Mullane v. Central Hanover Bank & Trust

Supreme Court of the United States, 1950.
339 U.S. 306, 70 S.Ct. 652, 94 L.Ed. 865.

■ MR. JUSTICE JACKSON delivered the opinion of the Court.

This controversy questions the constitutional sufficiency of notice to beneficiaries on judicial settlement of accounts by the trustee of a common trust fund established under the New York Banking Law, Consol.Laws, c. 2. The New York Court of Appeals considered and overruled objections that the statutory notice contravenes requirements of the Fourteenth Amendment and that by allowance of the account beneficiaries were deprived of property without due process of law. 299 N.Y. 697, 87 N.E.2d 73. The case is here on appeal under 28 U.S.C. § 1257, 28 U.S.C.A. § 1257.

Common trust fund legislation is addressed to a problem appropriate for state action. Mounting overheads have made administration of small trusts undesirable to corporate trustees. In order that donors and testators of moderately sized trusts may not be denied the service of corporate fiduciaries, the District of Columbia and some thirty states other than New York have permitted pooling small trust estates into one fund for investment administration. The income, capital gains, losses and expenses of the collective trust are shared by the constituent trusts in proportion to their contribution. By this plan, diversification of risk and economy of management can be extended to those whose capital standing alone would not obtain such advantage.

Statutory authorization for the establishment of such common trust funds is provided in the New York Banking Law, § 100–c, c. 687, L.1937, as amended by c. 602, L.1943, and c. 158, L.1944. Under this Act a trust company may, with approval of the State Banking Board, establish a common fund and, within prescribed limits, invest therein the assets of an unlimited number of estates, trusts or other funds of which it is trustee. Each participating trust shares ratably in the common fund, but exclusive management and control is in the trust company as trustee, and neither a fiduciary nor any beneficiary of a participating trust is deemed to have ownership in any particular asset or investment of this common fund. The trust company must keep fund assets separate from its own, and in its fiduciary capacity may not deal with itself or any affiliate. Provisions are made for accountings twelve to fifteen months

[handwritten: every third year]

after the establishment of a fund and triennially thereafter. The decree in each such judicial settlement of accounts is made binding and conclusive as to any matter set forth in the account upon everyone having any interest in the common fund or in any participating estate, trust or fund.

In January, 1946, Central Hanover Bank and Trust Company established a common trust fund in accordance with these provisions, and in March, 1947, it petitioned the Surrogate's Court for settlement of its first account as common trustee. During the accounting period a total of 113 trusts, approximately half *inter vivos* and half testamentary, participated in the common trust fund, the gross capital of which was nearly three million dollars. The record does not show the number or residence of the beneficiaries, but they were many and it is clear that some of them were not residents of the State of New York.

The only notice given beneficiaries of this specific application was by publication in a local newspaper in strict compliance with the minimum requirements of N.Y. Banking Law § 100–c(12): "After filing such petition [for judicial settlement of its account] the petitioner shall cause to be issued by the court in which the petition is filed and shall publish not less than once in each week for four successive weeks in a newspaper to be designated by the court a notice or citation addressed generally without naming them to all parties interested in such common trust fund and in such estates, trusts or funds mentioned in the petition, all of which may be described in the notice or citation only in the manner set forth in said petition and (without setting forth the residence of any such decedent or donor of any such estate, trust or fund)." Thus the only notice required, *[handwritten: Notice given to]* and the only one given, was by newspaper publication setting forth merely the name and address of the trust company, the name and the date of establishment of the common trust fund, and a list of all participating estates, trusts or funds.

At the time the first investment in the common fund was made on behalf of each participating estate, however, the trust company, pursuant to the requirements of § 100–c(9), had notified by mail each person of full age and sound mind whose name and address was then known to it and who was "entitled to share in the income therefrom . . . [or] . . . who would be entitled to share in the principal if the event upon which such estate, trust or fund will become distributable should have occurred at the time of sending such notice." Included in the notice was a copy of those provisions of the Act relating to the sending of the notice itself and to the judicial settlement of common trust fund accounts. *[handwritten: Prior notice mailed upon 1st Investment]*

Upon the filing of the petition for the settlement of accounts, appellant was, by order of the court pursuant to § 100–c(12), appointed special guardian and attorney for all persons known or unknown not otherwise appearing who had or might thereafter have any interests in the income of the common trust fund; and appellee Vaughan was appointed to represent those similarly interested in the principal. There were no other appearances on behalf of any one interested in either interest or principal.

Appellant appeared specially, objecting that notice and the statutory provisions for notice to beneficiaries were inadequate to afford due process under the Fourteenth Amendment, and therefore that the court was without jurisdiction to render a final and binding decree. Appellant's objections were entertained and overruled, the Surrogate holding that the notice required and given was sufficient. 75 N.Y.S.2d 397. A final decree accepting the accounts has been entered, affirmed by the Appellate Division of the Supreme Court, In re Central Hanover Bank & Trust Co., 275 App.Div. 769, 88 N.Y.S.2d 907, and by the Court of Appeals of the State of New York, 299 N.Y. 697, 87 N.E.2d 73.

The effect of this decree, as held below, is to settle "all questions respecting the management of the common fund." We understand that every right which beneficiaries would otherwise have against the trust company, either as trustee of the common fund or as trustee of any individual trust, for improper management of the common trust fund during the period covered by the accounting is sealed and wholly terminated by the decree. See Matter of Hoaglund's Estate, 194 Misc. 803, 811–812, 74 N.Y.S.2d 156, 164, affirmed 272 App.Div. 1040, 74 N.Y.S.2d 911, affirmed 297 N.Y. 920, 79 N.E.2d 746; Matter of Bank of New York, 189 Misc. 459, 470, 67 N.Y.S.2d 444, 453; Matter of Security Trust Co. of Rochester, 189 Misc. 748, 760, 70 N.Y.S.2d 260, 271; Matter of Continental Bank & Trust Co., 189 Misc. 795, 797, 67 N.Y.S.2d 806, 807–808.

We are met at the outset with a challenge to the power of the State— the right of its courts to adjudicate at all as against those beneficiaries who reside without the State of New York. It is contended that the proceeding is one *in personam* in that the decree affects neither title to nor possession of any *res,* but adjudges only personal rights of the beneficiaries to surcharge their trustee for negligence or breach of trust. Accordingly, it is said, under the strict doctrine of Pennoyer v. Neff, 95 U.S. 714, 24 L.Ed. 565, the Surrogate is without jurisdiction as to nonresidents upon whom personal service of process was not made.

Distinctions between actions *in rem* and those *in personam* are ancient and originally expressed in procedural terms what seems really to have been a distinction in the substantive law of property under a system quite unlike our own. Buckland and McNair, Roman Law and Common Law, 66; Burdick, Principles of Roman Law and Their Relation to Modern Law, 298. The legal recognition and rise in economic importance of incorporeal or intangible forms of property have upset the ancient simplicity of property law and the clarity of its distinctions, while new forms of proceedings have confused the old procedural classification. American courts have sometimes classed certain actions as *in rem* because personal service of process was not required, and at other times have held personal service of process not required because the action was *in rem.* See cases collected in Freeman on Judgments, §§ 1517 et seq. (5th ed.).

Judicial proceedings to settle fiduciary accounts have been sometimes termed *in rem,* or more indefinitely *quasi in rem,* or more vaguely still, "in the nature of a proceeding *in rem.*" It is not readily apparent how the courts of New York did or would classify the present proceeding, which has some characteristics and is wanting in some features of proceedings both *in rem* and *in personam.* But in any event we think that the requirements of the Fourteenth Amendment to the Federal Constitution do not depend upon a classification for which the standards are so elusive and confused generally and which, being primarily for state courts to define, may and do vary from state to state. Without disparaging the usefulness of distinctions between actions *in rem* and those *in personam* in many branches of law, or on other issues, or the reasoning which underlies them, we do not rest the power of the State to resort to constructive service in this proceeding upon how its courts or this Court may regard this historic antithesis. It is sufficient to observe that, whatever the technical definition of its chosen procedure, the interest of each state in providing means to close trusts that exist by the grace of its laws and are administered under the supervision of its courts is so insistent and rooted in custom as to establish beyond doubt the right of its courts to determine the interests of all claimants, resident or nonresident, provided its procedure accords full opportunity to appear and be heard.

Quite different from the question of a state's power to discharge trustees is that of the opportunity it must give beneficiaries to contest. Many controversies have raged about the cryptic and abstract words of the Due Process Clause but there can be no doubt that at a minimum they require that deprivation of life, liberty or property by adjudication be preceded by notice and opportunity for hearing appropriate to the nature of the case.

In two ways this proceeding does or may deprive beneficiaries of property. It may cut off their rights to have the trustee answer for negligent or illegal impairments of their interests. Also, their interests are presumably subject to diminution in the proceeding by allowance of fees and expenses to one who, in their names but without their knowledge, may conduct a fruitless or uncompensatory contest. Certainly the proceeding is one in which they may be deprived of property rights and hence notice and hearing must measure up to the standards of due process.

Personal service of written notice within the jurisdiction is the classic form of notice always adequate in any type of proceeding. But the vital interest of the State in bringing any issues as to its fiduciaries to a final settlement can be served only if interests or claims of individuals who are outside of the State can somehow be determined. A construction of the Due Process Clause which would place impossible or impractical obstacles in the way could not be justified.

Against this interest of the State we must balance the individual interest sought to be protected by the Fourteenth Amendment. This is defined by our holding that "The fundamental requisite of due process of law is the opportunity to be heard." Grannis v. Ordean, 234 U.S. 385, 394, 34 S.Ct. 779, 783, 58 L.Ed. 1363. This right to be heard has little reality or worth unless one is informed that the matter is pending and can choose for himself whether to appear or default, acquiesce or contest.

The Court has not committed itself to any formula achieving a balance between these interests in a particular proceeding or determining when constructive notice may be utilized or what test it must meet. Personal service has not in all circumstances been regarded as indispensable to the process due to residents, and it has more often been held unnecessary as to nonresidents. We disturb none of the established rules on these subjects. No decision constitutes a controlling or even a very illuminating precedent for the case before us. But a few general principles stand out in the books.

An elementary and fundamental requirement of due process in any proceeding which is to be accorded finality is notice reasonably calculated, under all the circumstances, to apprise interested parties of the pendency of the action and afford them an opportunity to present their objections. Milliken v. Meyer, 311 U.S. 457, 61 S.Ct. 339, 85 L.Ed. 278, 132 A.L.R. 1357; Grannis v. Ordean, 234 U.S. 385, 34 S.Ct. 779, 58 L.Ed. 1363; Priest v. Board of Trustees of Town of Las Vegas, 232 U.S. 604, 34 S.Ct. 443, 58 L.Ed. 751; Roller v. Holly, 176 U.S. 398, 20 S.Ct. 410, 44 L.Ed. 520. The notice must be of such nature as reasonably to convey the required information, Grannis v. Ordean, supra, and it must afford a reasonable time for those interested to make their appearance, Roller v. Holly, supra, and cf. Goodrich v. Ferris, 214 U.S. 71, 29 S.Ct. 580, 53 L.Ed. 914. But if with due regard for the practicalities and peculiarities of the case these conditions are reasonably met the constitutional requirements are satisfied. "The criterion is not the possibility of conceivable injury, but the just and reasonable character of the requirements, having reference to the subject with which the statute deals." American Land Co. v. Zeiss, 219 U.S. 47, 67, 31 S.Ct. 200, 207, 55 L.Ed. 82, and see Blinn v. Nelson, 222 U.S. 1, 7, 32 S.Ct. 1, 2, 56 L.Ed. 65, Ann.Cas.1913B, 555.

But when notice is a person's due, process which is a mere gesture is not due process. The means employed must be such as one desirous of actually informing the absentee might reasonably adopt to accomplish it. The reasonableness and hence the constitutional validity of any chosen method may be defended on the ground that it is in itself reasonably certain to inform those affected, compare Hess v. Pawloski, 274 U.S. 352, 47 S.Ct. 632, 71 L.Ed. 1091, with Wuchter v. Pizzutti, 276 U.S. 13, 48 S.Ct. 259, 72 L.Ed. 446, 57 A.L.R. 1230, or, where conditions do not reasonably permit such notice, that the form chosen is not substantially less likely to bring home notice than other of the feasible and customary substitutes.

It would be idle to pretend that publication alone as prescribed here, is a reliable means of acquainting interested parties of the fact that their rights are before the courts. It is not an accident that the greater number of cases reaching this Court on the question of adequacy of notice have been concerned with actions founded on process constructively served through local newspapers. Chance alone brings to the attention of even a local resident an advertisement in small type inserted in the back pages of a newspaper, and if he makes his home outside the area of the newspaper's normal circulation the odds that the information will never reach him are large indeed. The chance of actual notice is further reduced when as here the notice required does not even name those whose attention it is supposed to attract, and does not inform acquaintances who might call it to attention. In weighing its sufficiency on the basis of equivalence with actual notice we are unable to regard this as more than a feint.

Nor is publication here reinforced by steps likely to attract the parties' attention to the proceeding. It is true that publication traditionally has been acceptable as notification supplemental to other action which in itself may reasonably be expected to convey a warning.

The ways of an owner with tangible property are such that he usually arranges means to learn of any direct attack upon his possessory or proprietary rights. Hence, libel of a ship, attachment of a chattel or entry upon real estate in the name of law may reasonably be expected to come promptly to the owner's attention. When the state within which the owner has located such property seizes it for some reason, publication or posting affords an additional measure of notification. A state may indulge the assumption that one who has left tangible property in the state either has abandoned it, in which case proceedings against it deprive him of nothing, cf. Anderson National Bank v. Luckett, 321 U.S. 233, 64 S.Ct. 599, 88 L.Ed. 692, 151 A.L.R. 824; Security Savings Bank v. California, 263 U.S. 282, 44 S.Ct. 108, 68 L.Ed. 301, 31 A.L.R. 391, or that he has left some caretaker under a duty to let him know that it is being jeopardized. Ballard v. Hunter, 204 U.S. 241, 27 S.Ct. 261, 51 L.Ed. 461; Huling v. Kaw Valley Ry. & Imp. Co., 130 U.S. 559, 9 S.Ct. 603, 32 L.Ed. 1045. As phrased long ago by Chief Justice Marshall in The Mary, 9 Cranch 126, 144, 3 L.Ed. 678, "It is the part of common prudence for all those who have any interest in [a thing], to guard that interest by persons who are in a situation to protect it."

In the case before us there is, of course, no abandonment. On the other hand these beneficiaries do have a resident fiduciary as caretaker of their interest in this property. But it is their caretaker who in the accounting becomes their adversary. Their trustee is released from giving notice of jeopardy, and no one else is expected to do so. Not even the special guardian is required or apparently expected to communicate with his ward and client, and, of course, if such a duty were merely transferred from the trustee to the guardian, economy would not be served and more likely the cost be increased.

This Court has not hesitated to approve of resort to publication as a customary substitute in another class of cases where it is not reasonably possible or practicable to give more adequate warning. Thus it has been recognized that, in the case of persons missing or unknown, employment of an indirect and even a probably futile means of notification is all that the situation permits and creates no constitutional bar to a final decree foreclosing their rights. Cunnius v. Reading School District, 198 U.S. 458, 25 S.Ct. 721, 49 L.Ed. 1125, 3 Ann.Cas. 1121; Blinn v. Nelson, 222 U.S. 1, 32 S.Ct. 1, 56 L.Ed. 65, Ann.Cas.1913B, 555; and see Jacob v. Roberts, 223 U.S. 261, 32 S.Ct. 303, 56 L.Ed. 429.

Those beneficiaries represented by appellant whose interests or whereabouts could not with due diligence be ascertained come clearly within this category. As to them the statutory notice is sufficient. However great the odds that publication will never reach the eyes of such unknown parties, it is not in the typical case much more likely to fail than any of the choices open to legislators endeavoring to prescribe the best notice practicable.

Nor do we consider it unreasonable for the State to dispense with more certain notice to those beneficiaries whose interests are either conjectural or future or, although they could be discovered upon investigation, do not in due course of business come to knowledge of the common trustee. Whatever searches might be required in another situation under ordinary standards of diligence, in view of the character of the proceedings and the nature of the interests here involved we think them unnecessary. We recognize the practical difficulties and costs that would be attendant on frequent investigations into the status of great numbers of beneficiaries, many of whose interests in the common fund are so remote as to be ephemeral; and we have no doubt that such impracticable and extended searches are not required in the name of due process. The expense of keeping informed from day to day of substitutions among even current income beneficiaries and presumptive remaindermen, to say nothing of the far greater number of contingent beneficiaries, would impose a severe burden on the plan, and would likely dissipate its advantages. These are practical matters in which we should be reluctant to disturb the judgment of the state authorities.

Accordingly we overrule appellant's constitutional objections to published notice insofar as they are urged on behalf of any beneficiaries whose interests or addresses are unknown to the trustee.

As to known present beneficiaries of known place of residence, however, notice by publication stands on a different footing. Exceptions in the name of necessity do not sweep away the rule that within the limits of practicability notice must be such as is reasonably calculated to reach interested parties. Where the names and post office addresses of those affected by a proceeding are at hand, the reasons disappear for resort to means less likely than the mails to apprise them of its pendency.

The trustee has on its books the names and addresses of the income beneficiaries represented by appellant, and we find no tenable ground for dispensing with a serious effort to inform them personally of the accounting, at least by ordinary mail to the record addresses. Cf. Wuchter v. Pizzutti, supra. Certainly sending them a copy of the statute months and perhaps years in advance does not answer this purpose. The trustee periodically remits their income to them, and we think that they might reasonably expect that with or apart from their remittances word might come to them personally that steps were being taken affecting their interests.

We need not weigh contentions that a requirement of personal service of citation on even the large number of known resident or nonresident beneficiaries would, by reasons of delay if not of expense, seriously interfere with the proper administration of the fund. Of course personal service even without the jurisdiction of the issuing authority serves the end of actual and personal notice, whatever power of compulsion it might lack. However, no such service is required under the circumstances. This type of trust presupposes a large number of small interests. The individual interest does not stand alone but is identical with that of a class. The rights of each in the integrity of the fund and the fidelity of the trustee are shared by many other beneficiaries. Therefore notice reasonably certain to reach most of those interested in objecting is likely to safeguard the interests of all, since any objections sustained would inure to the benefit of all. We think that under such circumstances reasonable risks that notice might not actually reach every beneficiary are justifiable. "Now and then an extraordinary case may turn up, but constitutional law, like other mortal contrivances, has to take some chances, and in the great majority of instances, no doubt, justice will be done." Blinn v. Nelson, supra, 222 U.S. at page 7, 32 S.Ct. at page 2, 56 L.Ed. 65, Ann.Cas.1913B, 555.

The statutory notice to known beneficiaries is inadequate, not because in fact it fails to reach everyone, but because under the circumstances it is not reasonably calculated to reach those who could easily be informed by other means at hand. However it may have been in former times, the mails today are recognized as an efficient and inexpensive means of communication. Moreover, the fact that the trust company has been able to give mailed notice to known beneficiaries at the time the common trust fund was established is persuasive that postal notification at the time of accounting would not seriously burden the plan.

In some situations the law requires greater precautions in its proceedings than the business world accepts for its own purposes. In few, if any, will it be satisfied with less. Certainly it is instructive, in determining the reasonableness of the impersonal broadcast notification here used, to ask whether it would satisfy a prudent man of business, counting his pennies but finding it in his interest to convey information to many persons whose names and addresses are in his files. We are not satisfied that it would. Publication may theoretically be available for all the world to see, but it is too much in our day to suppose that each or any individual beneficiary does or could examine all that is published to see if something may be tucked away in it that affects his property interests. We have before indicated in reference to notice by publication that, "Great caution should be used not to let fiction deny the fair play that can be secured only by a pretty close adhesion to fact." McDonald v. Mabee, 243 U.S. 90, 91.

We hold the notice of judicial settlement of accounts required by the New York Banking Law § 100–c(12) is incompatible with the requirements of the Fourteenth Amendment as a basis for adjudication depriving known persons whose whereabouts are also known of substantial property rights. Accordingly the judgment is reversed and the cause remanded for further proceedings not inconsistent with this opinion.

Reversed.

■ MR. JUSTICE DOUGLAS took no part in the consideration or decision of this case.

■ MR. JUSTICE BURTON, dissenting.

These common trusts are available only when the instruments creating the participating trusts permit participation in the common fund. Whether or not further notice to beneficiaries should supplement the notice and representation here provided is properly within the discretion of the State. The Federal Constitution does not require it here.

NOTES AND QUESTIONS

1. **Practicalities of giving notice.** The great achievement of *Mullane* was to dissociate the question of the constitutionality of a method of service of process from the classification of the underlying cause of action as *in personam, quasi in rem,* or *in rem. Mullane* makes it clear that the constitutional adequacy of service of process must be judged by the practicalities of giving notice rather than by its technical classification under concepts of territorial jurisdiction. In Justice Jackson's words, the

Rule

Constitution requires "notice reasonably calculated, under all the circumstances, to apprise interested parties of the pendency of the action and afford them an opportunity to present their objections."

2. Were there minimum contacts? Assuming for the moment that notice was constitutionally adequate, are you satisfied that the litigants had sufficient "minimum contacts" with New York that they could be required to appear in a New York court, on pain of losing their right to contest the accounting?

3. Purpose of the accounting proceeding. What is the purpose of the accounting proceeding? Whose rights are being adjudicated? Who is being protected? The Court holds that notice by publication, by itself, is insufficient because interested persons are unlikely to receive actual notice of the proceedings. Yet it does not require that actual notice be provided to all persons who can be identified and who have an interest in the proceedings. Why not? See Restatement (Second) of Judgments § 2, Comment g:

> The rule in Mullane v. Central Hanover Bank & Trust Co. recognizes that persons can be bound even if they cannot be found through reasonably diligent search. Assuming that such a search has been made, the fiction is indulged that publication notifies the absentee. 339 U.S. at 317. The underlying rationale, however, is that the interests of a person so remotely situated may justly be sacrificed to those of persons having need to go forward in the practical affairs that the absentee could otherwise subsequently disrupt. It is the search for the absentee that gives expression to the concern for protection of his opportunity to be heard.

4. Due process notice decisions fact-dependent. *Mullane*'s emphasis on the practicalities of giving notice means that a due process analysis of the adequacy of notice must pay close attention the factual details of the particular case. Examples include:

a. In Jones v. Flowers, 547 U.S. 220, 126 S.Ct. 1708, 164 L.Ed.2d 415 (2006), Jones purchased a house in 1967, subject to a thirty-year mortgage. Under the terms of the mortgage, the mortgage company paid the property taxes for the duration of the mortgage. Jones separated from his wife in 1993 and moved into an apartment. His wife continued to live in the house. Jones paid off the mortgage in 1997. At that point, the mortgage company quit paying the property taxes. The taxes went unpaid, and the property was certified as delinquent. In 2000, the Arkansas State Lands Commissioner sent a certified letter to the house, addressed to Jones. The letter informed Jones that the taxes were delinquent, and that if they were not paid within the next two years the property would be sold to satisfy the unpaid taxes. A letter sent by certified mail requires that someone sign for the letter; if no one comes to the door to sign for the letter (or if the person who comes to the door refuses to sign for it), a notice of failed delivery is left at the house, stating that the letter may be picked up at the post office. No one signed for the letter. When no one came to the post office to pick up the letter within fifteen days, it was returned to the Commissioner's office marked "unclaimed." Two years later, a second certified letter was sent to the house, again addressed to Jones. This letter, like the first, was returned to the Commissioner's office marked "unclaimed." The property, which had a fair market value of $80,000, was then sold to Flowers for $21,042.15. Flowers filed an action for eviction and personally served notice of the suit on Jones's daughter, who lived at the house. Notified by his daughter of the unlawful detainer action, Jones brought suit in state court seeking to set aside the sale, contending that the notice provided by the two certified mail letters did not satisfy due process, at least when the state had knowledge that the letters had been returned unclaimed. In a 5–4 decision, the Supreme Court agreed with Jones, holding that under the circumstances more was required than sending two letters by certified mail. Writing for the Court, Chief Justice Roberts suggested that among the *additional* "reasonable steps" the Commissioner could have taken were sending a letter to Jones by regular mail, sending a letter to "occupant" by regular mail, and posting a notice on the front door of the house. In dissent, Justice Thomas argued that Jones' loss of his property was due to his "own failure to be a prudent ward of his interests. The meaning of the Constitution should not turn on the antics of tax evaders and scofflaws." Id. at 248.

Mortgage and Property tax examples

2 certified mail letters not sufficient

   b.   In Dusenbery v. United States, 534 U.S. 161, 122 S.Ct. 694, 151 L.Ed.2d 597 (2002), a federal prisoner contested the adequacy of the government's notice of its intended forfeiture of cash seized from his residence. The government established that it had sent by certified mail notice of the proposed forfeiture to the prison where he was incarcerated, and that a prison official had signed for the mail in accord with usual practice. The government established that the usual practice would then have been for the mail to be logged in, signed for by a member of the plaintiff's "Unit Team" of case workers, and distributed to the petitioner during "mail call." But the government provided no evidence that the usual practice had actually been followed in plaintiff's case. By a 5–4 margin, the Supreme Court held that the method of handling the prisoner's mail satisfied due process. All the Justices agreed that certified mail was a sufficient means for conveying notice as far as the prison mail room, but they divided on whether the procedure for the subsequent logging and distribution of mail within the prison was adequate. The dissenters pointed to changes in prison procedures that had been instituted after the events giving rise to the prisoner's suit, including requirements that the prisoner himself sign a log book to indicate receipt of certified mail, that prison officials document in writing any refusal to sign, and that official mail such as legal notices be marked as "special mail" to be "opened only in the inmate's presence." The dissenters contended that these changes were compelling evidence that the former procedures were "substantially less likely" to result in actual notice than a readily feasible alternative.

Inmate example - procedures in the mail room

   c.   In Tulsa Professional Collection Services, Inc. v. Pope, 485 U.S. 478, 108 S.Ct. 1340, 99 L.Ed.2d 565 (1988), an Oklahoma "nonclaim statute" provided that claims against the estate of a decedent are barred unless presented to the executor or executrix of the estate within two months after publication of notice advising potential claimants of the commencement of probate proceedings. Jeanne Pope, the surviving spouse and executrix, published the statutorily required notice. Tulsa Professional Collection Services, a subsidiary of the hospital in which the decedent had died, presented its claim for medical services more than two months after publication of the notice. Pope argued that the two-month period was a "self-executing statute of limitations" that did not require any notice to be effective in barring claims outside the period. (It is established law that notice is not required for a statute of limitations to be effective in barring a claim.) The Supreme Court held that the two-month period was not a "self-executing

Statute of limitations

Hospital Creditor Ex.
If known by notice by mail or other means as Certainly to ensure actual notice

statute of limitations" because it was triggered by the commencement of a judicial proceeding, and because the state was intimately involved in the filing of notice by publication. The Court remanded for a determination of whether Professional Collection Services' "identity as a creditor was known or reasonably ascertainable." If it was, "notice by mail or other means as certain to ensure actual notice" was required. 485 U.S. at 491.

d.   In Lehr v. Robertson, 463 U.S. 248, 103 S.Ct. 2985, 77 L.Ed.2d 614 (1983), a natural father sought to set aside an adoption of his child on the ground that he had not received notice of the adoption proceeding. Jessica M., the child, was born out of wedlock. The father, Jonathan Lehr, lived with Lorraine, the mother, prior to the birth and visited her in the hospital. Lehr did not live with Lorraine or Jessica after the birth, and he never provided financial support. Eight months after Jessica's birth, Lorraine married Richard Robertson. When Jessica was just over two years old, Lorraine and Richard Robertson began formal adoption proceedings for Jessica in New York state court. They did not notify Lehr of the proceedings. One month after the beginning of the adoption proceedings, Lehr began proceedings in another New York court, in which he sought a determination of paternity, an order of child support, and visitation rights. During the course of the paternity proceedings, Lehr learned of the adoption proceedings. He promptly sought a stay of the adoption proceedings, but was informed that the judge had signed the final adoption papers earlier that day.

Adoption Proceedings

The Supreme Court noted that New York required notice to a father for whom any of the following things is true: he has entered his name on a "putative father registry"; he has been adjudicated to be the father; his name is on the child's birth certificate; he lives openly with the child and mother; he has been identified as the father in a sworn statement by the mother; or he married the mother within six months of the child's birth. None of these things was true for Lehr. Under the circumstances, the Supreme Court held that Lehr had no due process right to receive notification of the adoption proceedings, even though the Robertsons knew his identity and knew that he was seeking to establish paternity, child support and visitation rights.

No notice per NY requirement

Is there a conflict between *Lehr* and *Mullane*?

e.   In Mennonite Board of Missions v. Adams, 462 U.S. 791, 103 S.Ct. 2706, 77 L.Ed.2d 180 (1983), the Mennonite Board of Missions (MBM) lent money, secured by a mortgage on real property. The owner of the property failed to pay taxes on the property. Pursuant to state statute, the county sold the property to satisfy the delinquent taxes. Notice of the tax sale was provided to the owner but not to MBM, even though MBM was identified as the mortgagee in county records. The purchaser at the tax sale eventually brought a quiet title suit to the property in order to establish that MBM's mortgage had been extinguished by the tax sale. MBM argued that the tax sale was invalid because it had not received notice of the proceeding. The Supreme Court agreed with MBM: "When the mortgagee is identified in a mortgage that is publicly recorded, constructive notice by publication must be supplemented by notice mailed to the mortgagee's last known available address, or by personal service." 462 U.S. at 798.

The Court then added in a footnote, "In this case, the mortgage on file with the County Recorder identified the mortgagee only as 'MENNONITE BOARD OF MISSIONS a corporation, of Wayne County, in the State of Ohio.' We assume that the mortgagee's address could have been ascertained by reasonably diligent efforts [citing *Mullane*]. Simply mailing a letter to 'Mennonite Board of Missions, Wayne County, Ohio,' quite likely would have provided actual notice, given 'the well-known skill of postal officials and employees in making proper delivery of letters defectively addressed.' *Grannis v. Ordean*, 234 U.S. 385, 397–398, 34 S.Ct. 779, 58 L.Ed. 1363 (1914)." Id. at 798 n. 4. What does the Court mean? That if the plaintiff could have ascertained the proper address through "reasonably diligent efforts," it should have done so? (This was in the pre-Google days.) That the plaintiff could simply have mailed the notice to MBM using the incomplete address on file with the county? Is the likely behavior of the Post Office in the 1980s something that can be established through citation of a 1914 case, as if the behavior were a matter of judicial precedent?

In the 1990s, after reading this footnote, a student at Boalt Hall (Berkeley Law) tested the " 'well-known skill of postal officials and employees' " by sending a letter to MBM addressed "Mennonite Board of Missions, Wayne County, Ohio." The Post Office returned the letter because of "insufficient address." Seeking to replicate the result of his student's experiment, Prof. Fletcher sent a letter addressed in the same way. About two weeks later he received a telephone call from Rev. Wayne Nitzsche of the Wooster Mennonite Church in Wooster, Ohio, located in Wayne County. His letter had been delivered to Rev. Nitzsche's church, which is the only Mennonite church in the county. Rev. Nitzsche graciously gave Prof. Fletcher the proper address of the Mennonite Board of Missions in Elkhart, Indiana, and offered to forward the letter. When Prof. Fletcher admitted what he was up to, Rev. Nitzsche had the good manners not to scold him for wasting his time and the church's long-distance telephone money. (This was in the pre-cell phone, pre-call-anywhere-in-the-United-States-for-the-same-price, days.)

f. In *Greene v. Lindsey*, 456 U.S. 444, 102 S.Ct. 1874, 72 L.Ed.2d 249 (1982), a Kentucky statute made specific provision for service of process in forcible entry and detainer actions. (These are eviction actions by a landlord against a tenant.) The statute required the process server to try to serve the tenant personally. After one unsuccessful try at personal service, the process server was permitted to post a copy of the notice "in a conspicuous place on the premises." Ky. Rev. Stat. § 454.030. The general practice of process servers in the housing project in question in *Greene* was to post the notice on the door of the defendant's apartment. There was evidence in the record that children in the housing project occasionally tore notices off doors. The notice in *Greene* was posted on the door; the defendants failed to respond; and a default judgment was entered against them. The defendants claimed that they had never seen the notice, and that they first learned of the suit when served with writs of possession resulting from the judgment.

The Court held that, under the circumstances, posting notice was constitutionally insufficient, and strongly suggested that mailing the notice would have sufficed. Justice O'Connor, joined by Chief Justice Burger and Justice Rehnquist, dissented. She argued for the constitutionality of posting, contending that the evidence of notices being torn off doors was "hardly compelling." 456 U.S. at 458. She noted, further, that there was no evidence that mailing was a superior method of providing notice: "[T]he Court is unable, on the present record, to evaluate the risks that notice mailed to public housing projects might fail due to loss, misdelivery, lengthy delay or theft. * * * It is no secret, after all, that unattended mailboxes are subject to plunder by thieves." Id. at 460.

Justice O'Connor's point about the difficulties with service by mail seems well taken. If you were a Kentucky legislator trying to draft a constitutional statute, what would you do? Should the statute require the process server to try more than once to make personal service, and to make such attempts at times that a resident is likely to be at home? Should the statute require, upon failure of personal service, posting *and* mailing? Does the Court's 2006 opinion in *Jones v. Flowers*, supra, suggest as much?

NOTE ON SERVICE OF PROCESS

1. **Mechanics of service of process.** As seen in *Mullane* and the cases described in the preceding note, supra, the question of what constitutes constitutionally sufficient notice occasionally arises in actual litigation. But the notice questions that arise in the day-to-day life of a practicing lawyer are typically statutory rather than constitutional.

a. **Federal district court.** The mechanics of notice in federal district court suits are regulated under federal Rule 4. The principal provisions are summarized here. Service of process to commence a lawsuit requires delivery of both a "summons" (a command to appear in court) and a copy of the complaint. Rule 4(c)(1). In most circumstances, service can be made by any non-party over 18 years of age. Rule 4(c)(2). Service by mail can be made by parties as well as non-parties. Rule 4(d).

(1) **Service on individuals.** Service on competent adults may be accomplished in a variety of ways.

(a) **Personal service.** The most reliable method of service on an individual defendant is personal delivery of the summons and complaint. Rule 4(e)(2)(A). Ordinarily, the summons and complaint are handed to the defendant personally. If a defendant attempts to evade personal service, it is sufficient that the papers be left near the person so long as it is made clear what they are. In Errion v. Connell, 236 F.2d 447, 457 (9th Cir. 1956), the sheriff testified that he saw the defendant and spoke to her, and when she ducked behind a door, he "pitched" the papers through a hole in the screen door and told her brother he was serving process. The testimony was in conflict, but the court believed the sheriff and found service properly made. However, in Weiss v. Glemp, 792 F. Supp. 215 (S.D.N.Y. 1992), service was attempted on Polish Cardinal Jozef Glemp in a libel suit brought by Rabbi Avi Weiss. The suit arose out of a protest by Rabbi Weiss at a Carmelite convent on the outskirts of the former Auschwitz concentration camp in Poland, and subsequent criticism in Poland of Rabbi Weiss by Cardinal Glemp. When Glemp was in Albany, New York, on a visit to the United States, he led an out-door procession in which service was attempted. The testimony was in conflict, but the District Court found that although a private process server thrust the papers toward Glemp, the papers never touched him, and he did not know what they were. The court quashed service, and, because *in personam* jurisdiction was premised on the service of process, dismissed for lack of jurisdiction. In comparing *Errion v. Connell* and *Weiss v. Glemp*, note that the testimony of the sheriff who served process was believed, but the testimony of the private process server was not. After 1983 amendments to Rule 4, personal service is almost always made by private process servers. Rule 4(c)(2).

(b) "Dwelling or usual place of abode." A process server may also leave the summons and complaint "at the individual's dwelling or usual place of abode with someone of suitable age and discretion who resides there." Rule 4(e)(2)(B). In National Development Co. v. Triad Holding Corp., 930 F.2d 253 (2d Cir. 1991), the court upheld service when papers were left at the New York apartment of a Saudi Arabian national who was living temporarily in New York. In Cox v. Quigley, 141 F.R.D. 222 (D.Me.1992), the court quashed service when papers were left at defendant's parents' home. Defendant had gone into the merchant marine after college; if he had any "dwelling house or usual place of abode," it was his ship.

Rabbi Weiss, who had unsuccessfully attempted personal service in New York, tried again, this time in Washington state. In Weiss v. Glemp, 127 Wash.2d 726, 903 P.2d 455 (1995), Archbishop Glemp made a three-day visit to Seattle. Rabbi Weiss filed suit in a Washington state court, and a process server, accompanied by a Polish interpreter, came to the rectory where Glemp was staying. A priest came to the door, said that Glemp was having breakfast, and asked them to return later. After waiting about two hours for Glemp to emerge, the process server went to a window through which he could see Glemp about four feet away. He yelled, "Jozef Glemp, Oficjaline dostracham [official documents]! Jozef Glemp, you have been served!" Glemp turned to look at the process server who then placed the documents on the sill outside the window. The Washington Supreme Court held that such service did not comply with Washington State's service of process rules (which parallel the relevant federal rules) for personal service, because the court held that the process server had not served Glemp "personally." Further, without deciding whether a three-day stay qualified the rectory as a "place of abode," the court held that the process server had not left the documents with "some person of suitable age and discretion." If the court had reached the question of whether the rectory was Glemp's "usual place of abode" within the meaning of the rule, what should it have decided? No

(c) Mail. Under a 1993 amendment to the Rule, plaintiff may mail two copies of the summons, together with the complaint to the defendant, and request that the defendant return a "waiver" of service. Rule 4(d). The defendant has a duty to minimize the costs of serving process. Accordingly, if the defendant "fails, without good cause, to sign and return a waiver requested by a plaintiff located within the United States," she will be liable for all costs subsequently incurred in effecting service, as well as expenses, including attorneys' fees, incurred in collecting those costs. Rule 4(d)(2). The return of a "waiver" has the same effect as an actual service of process. If the defendant returns the waiver, she has 60 days from the date the request for waiver was sent in which to answer if she is located in the United States (90 days if she is located outside the United States). Rule 4(d)(3). (This is an extension of the time ordinarily available. Rule 12(a) allows only 21 days after service of the complaint in which to answer.) The amended Rule uses the term "waiver of service" to avoid the mistaken impression some lawyers had under the previous version of the rule that all they had to do was ensure that the defendant actually received the summons and complaint. Under the rule, service is not complete (or "waived") until the defendant has returned the waiver of service.

(d) Agent appointed to accept process. Service may be made on someone appointed as an agent for acceptance of service of process. Rule 4(e)(2)(C). In National Equipment Rental, Ltd. v. Szukhent, 375 U.S. 311, 84

S.Ct. 411, 11 L.Ed.2d 354 (1964), two Michigan farmers leased incubators from National Equipment Rental. In a form lease contract signed in Michigan, the farmers agreed to appoint a person in New York as an agent for service of process. The Court upheld the appointment and service on the agent, and upheld *in personam* jurisdiction over the farmers in New York.

(e) In compliance with state law. Even if not done in accordance with the foregoing provisions, service of process is sufficient if it complies either with the law of the state in which the district court is sitting, or of the state in which the service is effected. Rule 4(e)(1).

(2) Infants and incompetents. Service on infants and incompetents must be made in accordance with the law of the state in which the service is made. Rule 4(g).

(3) Corporations and unincorporated associations. Service on corporations and unincorporated associations may be made by obtaining a waiver of service under Rule 4(d); by service in accordance with state law; or by delivery of a copy of the summons and complaint to an "officer, a managing or general agent, or to any other agent authorized by appointment or by law to receive service of process." Rule 4(h)(1).

(4) Governmental defendants. There are special provisions for service on the United States, on state and local governments, and on foreign governments. Rule 4(i) and (j).

(5) *In rem* and *quasi in rem* jurisdiction. (a) Actions relating to title to property. A district court may assert jurisdiction over, and adjudicate interests in, property in accordance with applicable federal statutes. Rule 4(n)(1). The statute contemplated by (but not mentioned in) Rule 4 is 28 U.S.C. § 1655, which governs actions to enforce or to remove liens or encumbrances, or to remove clouds on title, for property within the district. Under § 1655, an order to appear "shall be served on the absent defendant personally if practicable, wherever found, and also on the person or persons in possession of such property, if any. Where personal service is not practicable, the order shall be published as the court may direct, not less than once a week for six consecutive weeks."

(b) Other actions. In other cases where personal jurisdiction cannot be obtained over a defendant, the federal court may assert *quasi in rem* jurisdiction based on seizure of defendant's assets within the jurisdiction, in accordance with the law of the state in which the federal district court sits. Rule 4(n)(2). This provision has limited applicability, given the extensive reach of most state's long-arm statutes and the due process limitations imposed by *Shaffer v. Heitner*.

(6) Service in foreign countries. Service in foreign countries is governed by a combination of the international Convention on the Service Abroad of Judicial and Extrajudicial Documents (the "Hague Convention") and Rule 4(f). Rule 4(f)(1) specifies that service may be made in accordance with the provisions of the Hague Convention. The Convention allows service through a "Central Authority" in the foreign country. The plaintiff sends the summons and complaint, translated into the language of that county, to the Central Authority, which then serves the documents on the defendant. Rule 4(f)(2) authorizes additional methods of service, including service by registered mail (return receipt required) when sent by the clerk of the federal district court. Rule 4(f)(2)(C)(ii). In unusual cases, Rule 4(f)(3) authorizes the district court to authorize any form of service not prohibited by international agreement. For example, in Rio Properties, Inc. v. Rio International Interlink, 284 F.3d 1007, 1016 (9th Cir. 2002), the district court authorized service by email when an "elusive foreign defendant . . . structured its business such that it could be contacted only via its email address." For a detailed discussion of service on foreign defendants, see Brockmeyer v. May, 383 F.3d 798 (9th Cir. 2004).

(7) Geographical scope. The geographical scope of service of process in federal district court is the same as that in the state courts except: **(a) Foreign defendants.** Foreign defendants for whom there are insufficient contacts with any single state to establish *in personam* jurisdiction may be subjected to suit in federal court on causes of action arising under federal law if there are sufficient contacts with the United States considered as a whole. Rule 4(k)(2). **(b) Federal statutes.** Some federal statutes provide for nationwide jurisdiction in suits brought under them. Examples are federal anti-trust and securities suits, and state-law interpleader suits brought under the federal interpleader statute. Rule 4(k)(1)(C). **(c) "Bulge jurisdiction."** Third-party defendants impleaded into an existing federal suit under Rule 14, and additional parties needed for just adjudication under Rule 19, may be served and brought within the jurisdiction of the District Court, provided that the party can be served within 100 miles of the courthouse in which the action is commenced. Rule 4(k)(1)(B). This jurisdiction—often called "bulge jurisdiction"—is designed to permit efficient adjudication in cases brought in federal courts located close to state borders, such as the Southern District of New York, located in Manhattan, across the river from New Jersey.

b. State court. State service of process statutes operate much like federal Rule 4, except that there is a greater variety of rules, roughly corresponding to the greater variety of cases heard by state courts. Note that the geographical scope of a state trial court's jurisdiction is sometimes more limited than that of a federal district court.

The principal provisions of California law will be taken as an example. As in federal court, both a summons and a copy of the complaint must be served.

(1) Service on individuals. Service on individual defendants may be made:

(a) By **personal delivery** of the summons and complaint to the defendant personally. Calif.C.Civ.P. § 415.10.

(b) By **delivery at the person's "dwelling house, usual place of abode, or usual place of business or usual mailing address"** in the presence of a competent member of the household or person in charge of the office of at least 18 years of age, *and* by thereafter mailing a copy to the same place where the summons and complaint were previously delivered. Calif.C.Civ.P. § 415.20(b).

(c) By **mailing** to a defendant in California via first-class mail the summons and complaint, together with an acknowledgement with a postage-paid return envelope. If the defendant returns the acknowledgement of service, service is deemed completed on the date the acknowledgement is executed. If the defendant does not return the acknowledgement within 20 days of the date of its mailing, she is liable for reasonable expenses incurred in attempting to serve her by other means. Calif.C.Civ.P. § 415.30. An out-of-state defendant may be served by a first-class mailing of the summons and complaint, return receipt requested. Calif.C.Civ.P. § 415.40.

(d) If the court approves, by **publication** in a California newspaper that is "most likely to give actual notice" if the defendant cannot with reasonable diligence be served by another method, either in an ordinary *in personam* action, or in an action in which an interest in property is claimed by the defendant. Notice must *also* be mailed to the defendant if her address is learned before the time for publication has expired. Calif.C.Civ.P. § 415.50.

(2) Service on minors, and on wards and conservatees. Service on a minor must be made by any of the above methods on a parent, guardian, conservator, or similar fiduciary of the minor; if no such person can with reasonable diligence be found, service may be made on any person having care and control of the minor, with whom he resides, or for whom he works, or on the minor himself if he is at least 12 years old. Calif.C.Civ.P. § 416.60. Service on a non-minor for whom a guardian, conservator, or similar fiduciary has been appointed may be made on the guardian, etc. Calif.C.Civ.P. § 416.70. Note that federal Rule 4(g) defers to state law methods of service of process on "infants" and "incompetents," supra. Thus, these provisions of California law control service of process in federal district court in California.

(3) Corporations and unincorporated associations. Service may be made on any agent appointed to accept service of process, or on any of several specified officers of the corporation or association. Calif.C.Civ.P. §§ 416.10, 416.40.

(4) Governmental defendants. There are special provisions for service on the State of California and on local governing bodies. Calif.C.Civ.P. § 416.50; Calif.Gov.C. § 53051(c).

(5) Special statutes providing for service by publication. A number of special statutes provide for service by publication where rights to real property are at issue. See, e.g., Calif.C.Civ.P. § 751.54 (action to quiet title to property disturbed by earth movement (this is California after all)); § 763.010 et seq. (quiet title action); § 872.310 (partition action); § 1250.120 (condemnation action).

2. Statutes of limitations and service of process. a. In general. A statute of limitations bars suit when a certain time has elapsed after a cause of action has accrued. The statutory period varies depending on the cause of action; for example, statutes of limitations tend to be longer for contract than for tort causes of action. Further, there are special rules that toll the statute of limitations in certain cases. For example, a statute of limitations generally is tolled during the time a plaintiff is a minor, and is tolled in a medical malpractice case until the plaintiff has reason to know that the doctor might have committed malpractice.

b. Time of commencing a suit. What constitutes commencing a suit for purposes of tolling a statute of limitations? Some states hold that a suit is commenced at the time the complaint is filed with the court, even if service of process on the defendant is not accomplished until some time later. An extreme example is California, in which filing the action tolls the statute of limitations, provided service is accomplished within three years. Calif.C.Civ.P. §§ 350, 583.210. In other states, a suit is commenced and the statute of limitations tolled only when service of process is accomplished. See, e.g., Kansas Stat. Ann. § 60–306; Ragan v. Merchants Transfer & Warehouse Co., 337 U.S. 530, 69 S.Ct. 1233, 93 L.Ed. 1520 (1949) (applying the Kansas statute).

     c.   **John Doe defendants.** California has an unusual practice in the case of unknown defendants. If plaintiff knows or suspects that there is a cause of action against unknown defendants, plaintiff may state the cause of action in the complaint and name them as "Doe" defendants. Calif.C.Civ.P. § 474. Upon discovery of their true identity, plaintiff may amend the complaint to state their names, and may serve process upon them. If plaintiff serves them within three years of filing the complaint, the statute of limitations is tolled as of the time of the original filing. See, e.g., Taito v. Owens Corning, 7 Cal.App.4th 798, 9 Cal.Rptr.2d 687 (1992); Hazel v. Hewlett, 201 Cal.App.3d 1458, 247 Cal.Rptr. 723 (1988).

     d.   **Differing tolling rules in federal court depending on whether suit is brought under state or federal law.** Federal Rule 3 provides, "A civil action is commenced by filing a complaint with the court." Federal Rule 4(m) provides that an action will be dismissed if service is not made within 120 days after filing the complaint, absent "good cause" for failure to serve within that time. Neither rule specifies that it applies differently depending on whether the underlying case is based on state or federal law. A casual (or even a careful) reading of these two rules thus suggests that the statute of limitations is tolled in federal district court when the action is filed, provided service of process is accomplished within 120 days, irrespective of the law on which the underlying case is based. In Walker v. Armco Steel Corp., 446 U.S. 740, 100 S.Ct. 1978, 64 L.Ed.2d 659 (1980), the Supreme Court held that in cases based on state law, the tolling rules of the state in which the district court sits should be followed. But in West v. Conrail, 481 U.S. 35, 107 S.Ct. 1538, 95 L.Ed.2d 32 (1987), the Court held that in cases based on federal law, federal Rules 3 and 4(m) provide the tolling rule, so that if a complaint is filed and service of process is accomplished within the 120-day period prescribed by Rule 4(m), the statute of limitations is tolled as of the date of filing the complaint. The contrasting results in *Walker v. Armco Steel* and in *West v. Conrail* are tied to the Court's jurisprudence under *Erie Rr. v. Tompkins*. See discussion infra p. 375.

     e.   **Misnaming of defendant.** Both state and federal court rules deal with the (unfortunately) relatively common problem of misnaming the defendant in the complaint. When the defendant is an individual and the misnaming does not prevent the true defendant from being notified of the suit, the statute of limitations is typically tolled as of the time of the filing of the suit or of service of process, depending on which of the two times governs in the practice of the state. Litigants and courts have had more difficulty in dealing with misnaming of corporate defendants. See, e.g., Schiavone v. Fortune, 477 U.S. 21, 106 S.Ct. 2379, 91 L.Ed.2d 18 (1986), in which plaintiffs sued Fortune magazine for an alleged libel. However, Fortune is not a corporation, but rather the name of a magazine published by Time, Inc. Plaintiffs served complaints on Time's registered agent for acceptance of service of process, but the agent refused service because Time was not named as the defendant. By the time properly captioned amended complaints were served, the statute of limitations had run. The Supreme Court upheld the dismissal of the actions as time-barred. (Sorry.) Federal Rule 15(c), which permits "relation back" of an amended complaint for purposes of the statute of limitations, was subsequently amended to extend the period during which "relation back" is permitted; but the amended rule did nothing to ease the underlying problem of the harsh consequences of misnaming the corporate defendant.

3. **"Sewer service."** Private process servers are occasionally tempted to state falsely that proper service has been accomplished. (Does this partially account for the willingness of the court in *Errion v. Connell* to believe the sheriff, and the unwillingness of the court in the first *Weiss v. Glemp* case to believe the private process server? See supra n. 1.) At one time, the problem was particularly acute in New York City. In small-stakes cases—often in suits alleging defaults in consumer installment contracts—process servers simply discarded the summonses and complaints, and then falsely swore that service had been made. Predictably, the defendants never appeared, and default judgments were entered. For a discussion of the practice, see Comment, Abuse of Process: Sewer Service, 3 Colum.J.L. & Soc. Probs. 17 (1967); Turkheimer, Service of Process in New York City: A Proposed End to Unregulated Criminality, 72 Colum.L.Rev. 847 (1972). In United States v. Brand Jewelers, Inc., 318 F. Supp. 1293 (S.D.N.Y.1970), the United States was granted standing to seek an injunction against systematic "sewer service." In United States v. Wiseman, 445 F.2d 792 (2d Cir.), cert. den. 404 U.S. 967 (1971), two process servers were criminally convicted for violating the federal civil rights of those to whom the process should have been delivered. A default judgment can be set aside upon proof that there was no service, but this is an expensive and time-consuming process. The Supreme Court has held that it violates due process to require that a defendant show a defense on the merits as a condition of setting aside a default judgment. Peralta v. Heights Medical Center, Inc., 485 U.S. 80, 108 S.Ct. 896, 99 L.Ed.2d 75 (1988).

David Segal, Big Year for the Bad News Bearers; Suits Produce Deliveries Fast and Furious for Process Servers

The Washington Post, December 24, 1998, p. A1.*

Hurtling down a stretch of East Capitol Street at 55 mph, Ken Margolis is weaving his Honda through traffic and reflecting on the happiest, most frenetic 12 months of his working life.

Among the highlights: the time he met White House consultant James Carville, who graciously invited him into his Capitol Hill office to chat about sports. Then there was a visit to the home of former White House deputy chief of staff Harold M. Ickes, who came to the door wearing nothing but his underwear and a frown.

"Mr. Ickes seemed a little annoyed," Margolis recalled with a wry smile. "But he was a gentleman about it."

The Year of the Subpoena has produced few outright winners in Washington. But for process servers—the men and women who hand-deliver legal papers—1998 was nirvana. They've enjoyed record

---

paychecks and more work than they can handle, they say, as well as occasional brushes with Washington luminaries.

"It's been absolutely excellent," Margolis said, dashing toward a law firm to pick up his seventh summons of the day. "Everybody is suing everybody."

Washington is one of the world's process-serving capitals. Most litigation against the government is filed here, the town is crammed with lawyers, and the U.S. Marshals Service stopped serving legal papers years ago. Since then, dozens of private process servers have been crisscrossing the city every day, pocketing about $50 a pop.

The best in the business drive like Mario Andretti, snoop like Columbo and stalk like a repo man. A gift for subterfuge and a car trunk filled with costumes are a plus. Though most process serving is akin to routine courier work, some would-be defendants try to "duck the paper."

Then the job becomes a high-stakes game of tag—and occasionally a dangerous one. Process servers are sometimes threatened, even attacked. Contrary to lore, however, servers don't need to actually touch or hand anything to their targets. To withstand a possible court challenge, servers must merely ensure that they have the right person and that the person realizes the papers have been delivered.

"You can drop it at their feet," said Terry Merrifield of Merrifield Associates. "I've done effective service sliding the paper under a door, as long as I know the person is on the other side of that door."

Negotiating skills can come in handy, too. Merrifield, for instance, once served business magnate Herbert Haft at his Washington mansion. As Merrifield tells it, when Haft saw Merrifield coming, he bolted toward the house.

"I said, 'Don't run, Herb, I don't want to chase you,' " Merrifield recalls. "He stopped, then asked if I would mind serving the papers directly to his lawyers. I asked for his lawyers' names. He couldn't remember them. So I was like, 'Herb, you've been served.' "

Hard data in this largely unregulated business are tough to find. In most states, as well as the District, there are no licensing or registration requirements; anyone over 18 can do it. The National Association of Professional Process Servers claims 1,300 member companies, but there are far more than that, the group's president, Alan Crowe, speculates.

As for the tally of papers served, nobody has a decent guess. There were 250,000 lawsuits filed in the federal court system in 1996, and 87.5 million civil and criminal cases in state courts, Crowe said. Some cases generate 40 subpoenas, some none at all.

A few lawsuits target the process servers themselves. Most commonly, people claim they were assaulted by over-aggressive servers, were the victims of obnoxious or illegal tactics, or weren't properly served. There are, of course, financial incentives to bend the rules and leave papers even when the intended recipient is nowhere in sight. Virtually everyone in the business has been sued or been asked to testify in a trial.

"It's usually our word against theirs," Merrifield said, "You end up building a reputation with the courts."

* * *

For the hard cases, corporate and plaintiffs' lawyers call in the likes of Joel Kaplan, the owner of Action Investigative Services and a specialist in hunting the hard-to-serve.

Kaplan and his employees have donned some eye-catching get-ups over the years. There's the pizza-deliveryman outfit with its inevitable punch line, the subpoena in a pizza box—one of the oldest tricks in the book. There's the matching brown pants, shirt and baseball cap, a United Parcel Service uniform knockoff. (Most servers are careful to wear close approximations of such uniforms rather than the real thing, to avoid litigation.) Sometimes a priest's collar with a black shirt does the trick.

"You knock on someone's door at 11 a.m. on a Sunday morning and you look like Guido Sarducci," Kaplan said, referring to the Italian-priest character on the old "Saturday Night Live."

For those who won't answer their door, there's the confrontational approach. Kaplan says he has backed tow trucks into driveways, rousting nervous car owners, and has yanked out a house's electrical meter, causing an instant blackout.

"They come running out the door," Kaplan said. "They don't know what the hell happened."

Kaplan acknowledges that this is probably illegal. But it might be preferable to another of his favorite techniques.

"I'll go to the front door and say: 'Look, I saw your ugly face staring out the window. You can either come out here and get it or I'll go get the megaphone and scream at you,'" Kaplan said.

Other tactics employed by veteran servers:

They wait till the target is halfway between the car and the house. That way the person doesn't know which way to run.

They address their targets by first name. It defuses the situation.

They send women in miniskirts.

"Our female agents have done very well," said David Frizelle of U.S. Process Service. "If you need to serve a man and another company has tried to serve him with a pimply 18-year-old kid, then you're going to have an advantage by sending an attractive lady in high heels."

Kaplan of Action Investigative, who has used these and other tricks of the trade, suffers few pangs of conscience.

"Does a cop feel bad for giving you a ticket at the airport when you've been sitting in your car for four minutes?" he asked. "It's a job. Everybody has a job."

Ken Margolis would be considered a by-the-book type if the business had a book. A burly 36-year-old in black cowboy boots, he began this career soon after his family sold the gourmet food business where he'd worked for more than a decade. One afternoon, a process server showed up to slap his father with a lawsuit. Margolis, seeking a new calling, was intrigued.

"Out of the blue, I called up this guy who owned a process company and said I'd like to give this a shot." Margolis recalled. "The next week he handed me a stack of paper and said, 'Go serve.'"

That was five years ago. Margolis has since been knocking on doors, bluffing his way past security guards and sweet-talking secretaries across the Washington area. Nobody is particularly happy to see him, and he's physically threatened almost every month. Not long ago, a Capitol Heights resident threatened to shoot him.

On a recent afternoon, Margolis demonstrates his methods. First stop is Fort McNair, where he seeks out a man being sued for $7,000 in an Illinois court. Puffing after climbing three flights of stairs in an office building, Margolis pokes his head into a few rooms until he locates his quarry and quickly hands off the documents.

"Take them back," the man replies acidly after skimming the papers.

Margolis declines and rushes back to his Honda. He earns $27 for each document he delivers, and on a good day he crams in as many as 20 deliveries. The hard part is finding the "kitty cats," as he calls avoiders, and legal parking spots. He racked up so many parking tickets in his last car—$7,000 worth—that he abandoned it the day police strapped on a Denver boot.

After a speedy drive across the city, he's taking the elevator to the third floor of Superior Court Building A. There, he finds the office of a court-appointed therapist and pounds a little too hard on her door.

"You scared the liver out of me," she says, amiably accepting a subpoena.

Margolis apologizes, hops in the car and scoots to Northeast. After a failed effort to find a detective, he strikes unexpected pay dirt with a visit to the home of a Washington lawyer being dunned by a court-reporting company. The company contends the lawyer failed to pay $600 in transcription services.

"I'm not going to jump off a roof or do something stupid to avoid you," says the lawyer in a Caribbean accent, signing for the documents and grimacing.

That's a relief. In November, Margolis was trying without success to serve a man named Ivin L. Pointer. One day, he finally spotted him on, of all places, the evening news. Pointer was threatening to leap off the Woodrow Wilson Bridge, causing police to shut the bridge down and backing up traffic for five hours.

"That was the end of that case," Margolis says.

It's now 2:30, but he isn't thinking about lunch. A former gambling addict, Margolis is unabashedly hooked on the action, and once he strings together a few successes, food breaks are off the agenda. There are at least 10 subpoenas left in his back seat, and his boss tells him via cell phone that a rush job awaits him in a downtown law firm. He heads toward Southeast for a quick delivery, then points his car toward K Street NW and floors it.

"We're on a roll," he says. "If we stop, we'll cool off."

Margolis's modus operandi tends toward the straightforward, but he's not above subtle deceptions, such as carrying FedEx boxes into offices. The most memorable trick he can recall, though, was one played on him. A woman called him last year and said, "Ken, I hear you're a great process server."

"I was like, 'Really? Who referred you?' She said, 'I can't remember, but come up to Gaithersburg tomorrow morning and I'll give you some papers to serve.'"

When Margolis got there, the woman greeted him at the door—with a lawsuit. He was being sued by a teacher who claimed that Margolis embarrassed her when he showed up at school with a notice that her wages were being garnisheed. The case was eventually dropped.

"Bam," remembers Margolis, "she slapped it right on me, That case cost me 900 bucks."

g.   CONSENT TO JURISDICTION

1.   *Consent by Appearance*

NOTE ON CONSENT BY APPEARANCE

1.   **Consent by general appearance.** A defect in territorial jurisdiction is waivable. A defendant who makes a general appearance will be deemed to have consented to territorial jurisdiction in the suit in which she appears. A general appearance may be deliberate. For example, a defendant may have a plausible jurisdictional defense, but may decide that, all things considered, it is in his best interest simply to litigate the merits and to forgo contesting jurisdiction. A general appearance may also be inadvertent. All jurisdictions, state and federal, will find that a defendant has submitted to the territorial jurisdiction of a court if she fails to make a timely objection. A state example is Cuellar v. Cuellar, 406 S.W.2d 510 (Tex.Civ.App.1966), in which plaintiff brought a child support action in Texas against her former husband, who then lived in Indiana. The court held that the husband "voluntarily submitted himself to the court's jurisdiction when * * * he filed a written answer to plaintiff's motion which did not raise any jurisdictional point." 406 S.W.2d at 512. Federal practice is set forth in Federal Rule of Civil Procedure 12. Rule 12(h)(1) provides that a defense of lack of personal jurisdiction is waived if a responsive pleading, such as an answer, is filed under Rule 12(a) without simultaneously moving to dismiss for lack of personal jurisdiction under Rule 12(b)(2). A motion to dismiss for failure to state a claim under Rule 12(b)(6) that does not include a motion for dismissal for want of personal jurisdiction under Rule 12(b)(2) also results in a waiver of the defense of lack of personal jurisdiction.

2.   **Consent by filing suit.** A plaintiff is deemed to have consented to jurisdiction, at least for certain purposes, in a forum in which she has filed suit.

a.   In Adam v. Saenger, 303 U.S. 59, 58 S.Ct. 454, 82 L.Ed. 649 (1938), a Texas corporation brought suit in California against a California defendant. The California defendant filed a "cross-claim" (a Rule 13 "counterclaim" in the terminology of the federal rules) against the plaintiff. The Texas corporation (plaintiff in the primary suit, and defendant on the cross-claim) defaulted on the cross-claim. Suit was then brought in Texas to enforce the resulting California default judgment. The controlling question in the Texas suit was whether there had been *in personam* jurisdiction over the Texas corporation in California. The Supreme Court held that the Texas corporation, by filing suit, had consented to *in personam* jurisdiction on the cross-claim: "The plaintiff having, by his voluntary act in demanding justice from the defendant, submitted himself to the jurisdiction of the court, there is nothing arbitrary or unreasonable in treating him as being there for all purposes for which justice to the defendant requires his presence." 303 U.S. at 67–68. The Court did not distinguish between a compulsory and a permissive cross-claim. That is, it did not insist that the subject matter of the cross-claim be related to the subject matter of the plaintiff's original complaint.

b. In Phillips Petroleum Co. v. Shutts, 472 U.S. 797, 105 S.Ct. 2965, 86 L.Ed.2d 628 (1985), a class action seeking money damages was filed in Kansas state court. Unnamed members of the class lived in all 50 states, in the District of Columbia, and in several foreign countries. Many of these unnamed class members had no contact with Kansas other than the suit in which they were plaintiffs, and did not even know of the suit until they were informed by mail that it had been filed. Because of special protections provided by the class action device, the Court held that there was *in personam* jurisdiction for purposes of binding plaintiffs to the judgment. Among other things, plaintiffs were permitted to "opt out" of the class at the beginning of the suit; the quality of legal representation was policed by the court; and any settlement had to be approved by the court.

2. Consent by Contract

Carnival Cruise Lines, Inc. v. Shute

Supreme Court of the United States, 1991.
499 U.S. 585, 111 S.Ct. 1522, 113 L.Ed.2d 622.

■ JUSTICE BLACKMUN delivered the opinion of the Court.

In this admiralty case we primarily consider whether the United States Court of Appeals for the Ninth Circuit correctly refused to enforce a forum-selection clause contained in tickets issued by petitioner Carnival Cruise Lines, Inc., to respondents Eulala and Russel Shute.

I

The Shutes, through an Arlington, Wash., travel agent, purchased passage for a 7-day cruise on petitioner's ship, the TROPICALE. Respondents paid the fare to the agent who forwarded the payment to petitioner's headquarters in Miami, Fla. Petitioner then prepared the tickets and sent them to respondents in the State of Washington. The face of each ticket, at its left-hand lower corner, contained this admonition:

"SUBJECT TO CONDITIONS OF CONTRACT ON LAST PAGES **IMPORTANT!** PLEASE READ CONTRACT—ON LAST PAGES 1, 2, 3"

The following appeared on "contract page 1" of each ticket:

*"TERMS AND CONDITIONS OF
PASSAGE CONTRACT TICKET*

"3. (a) The acceptance of this ticket by the person or persons named hereon as passengers shall be deemed to be an acceptance and agreement by each of them of all of the terms and conditions of this Passage Contract Ticket.

"8. It is agreed by and between the passenger and the Carrier that all disputes and matters whatsoever arising under, in connection with or incident to this Contract shall be litigated, if at all, in and before a Court located in the State of Florida, U.S.A., to the exclusion of the Courts of any other state or country."

The last quoted paragraph is the forum-selection clause at issue.

II

Respondents boarded the TROPICALE in Los Angeles, Cal. The ship sailed to Puerto Vallarta, Mexico, and then returned to Los Angeles. While the ship was in international waters off the Mexican coast, respondent Eulala Shute was injured when she slipped on a deck mat during a guided tour of the ship's galley. Respondents filed suit against petitioner in the United States District Court for the Western District of Washington, claiming that Mrs. Shute's injuries had been caused by the negligence of Carnival Cruise Lines and its employees.

Petitioner moved for summary judgment, contending that the forum clause in respondents' tickets required the Shutes to bring their suit against petitioner in a court in the State of Florida. Petitioner contended, alternatively, that the District Court lacked personal jurisdiction over petitioner because petitioner's contacts with the State of Washington were insubstantial. The District Court granted the motion, holding that petitioner's contacts with Washington were constitutionally insufficient to support the exercise of personal jurisdiction.

The Court of Appeals reversed. Reasoning that "but for" petitioner's solicitation of business in Washington, respondents would not have taken the cruise and Mrs. Shute would not have been injured, the court concluded that petitioner had sufficient contacts with Washington to justify the District Court's exercise of personal jurisdiction. 897 F.2d 377, 385–386 (C.A.9 1990).** *— Appeal's holding re contacts w/ Washington)*

Turning to the forum-selection clause, the Court of Appeals acknowledged that a court concerned with the enforceability of such a clause must begin its analysis with The Bremen v. Zapata Off-Shore Co., 407 U.S. 1, 92 S.Ct. 1907, 32 L.Ed.2d 513 (1972), where this Court held that forum-selection clauses, although not "historically . . . favored," are "prima facie valid." Id., at 9–10, 92 S.Ct., at 1913. See 897 F.2d, at 388. The appellate court concluded that the forum clause should not be enforced because it "was not freely bargained for." Id., at 389. As an "independent justification" for refusing to enforce the clause, the Court of Appeals noted that there was evidence in the record to indicate that "the Shutes are physically and financially incapable of pursuing this

---

**   ** The Court of Appeals had filed an earlier opinion also reversing the District Court and ruling that the District Court had personal jurisdiction over the cruise line and that the forum-selection clause in the tickets was unreasonable and was not to be enforced. 863 F.2d 1437 (C.A.9 1988). That opinion, however, was withdrawn when the court certified to the Supreme Court of Washington the question whether the Washington long-arm statute, Wash.Rev.Code § 4.28.185 (1988), conferred personal jurisdiction over Carnival Cruise Lines for the claim asserted by the Shutes. See 872 F.2d 930 (C.A.9 1989). The Washington Supreme Court answered the certified question in the affirmative on the ground that the Shutes' claim "arose from" petitioner's advertisement in Washington and the promotion of its cruises there. 113 Wash.2d 763, 783 P.2d 78 (1989). The Court of Appeals then "refiled" its opinion "as modified herein." See 897 F.2d, at 380, n. 1.

litigation in Florida" and that the enforcement of the clause would operate to deprive them of their day in court and thereby contravene this Court's holding in *The Bremen.* 897 F.2d, at 389.

We granted certiorari to address the question whether the Court of Appeals was correct in holding that the District Court should hear respondents' tort claim against petitioner. 498 U.S. 807, 111 S.Ct. 39, 112 L.Ed.2d 16 (1990). Because we find the forum-selection clause to be dispositive of this question, we need not consider petitioner's constitutional argument as to personal jurisdiction.

[margin handwritten note: Issue = forum selection clause]

III

We begin by noting the boundaries of our inquiry. First, this is a case in admiralty, and federal law governs the enforceability of the forum-selection clause we scrutinize. Second, we do not address the question whether respondents had sufficient notice of the forum clause before entering the contract for passage. Respondents essentially have conceded that they had notice of the forum-selection provision. Brief for Respondent 26 ("The respondents do not contest the incorporation of the provisions nor [*sic*] that the forum selection clause was reasonably communicated to the respondents, as much as three pages of fine print can be communicated."). Additionally, the Court of Appeals evaluated the enforceability of the forum clause under the assumption, although "doubtful," that respondents could be deemed to have had knowledge of the clause. See 897 F.2d, at 389 and n. 11.

[margin handwritten note: sufficient notice was provided; forum selection clause was reasonably communicated]

Within this context, respondents urge that the forum clause should not be enforced because, contrary to this Court's teachings in *The Bremen,* the clause was not the product of negotiation, and enforcement effectively would deprive respondents of their day in court. Additionally, respondents contend that the clause violates the Limitation of Vessel Owner's Liability Act, 46 U.S.C.App. § 183c. We consider these arguments in turn.

[margin handwritten note: Δ's argue]

IV

A

Both petitioner and respondents argue vigorously that the Court's opinion in *The Bremen* governs this case, and each side purports to find ample support for its position in that opinion's broad-ranging language. This seeming paradox derives in large part from key factual differences between this case and *The Bremen,* differences that preclude an automatic and simple application of *The Bremen*'s general principles to the facts here.

In *The Bremen,* this Court addressed the enforceability of a forum-selection clause in a contract between two business corporations. An American corporation, Zapata, made a contract with Unterweser, a German corporation, for the towage of Zapata's ocean-going drilling rig from Louisiana to a point in the Adriatic Sea off the coast of Italy. The agreement provided that any dispute arising under the contract was to be resolved in the London Court of Justice. After a storm in the Gulf of Mexico seriously damaged the rig, Zapata ordered Unterweser's ship to tow the rig to Tampa, Fla., the nearest point of refuge. Thereafter, Zapata sued Unterweser in admiralty in federal court at Tampa. Citing the forum clause, Unterweser moved to dismiss. The District Court denied

Unterweser's motion, and the Court of Appeals for the Fifth Circuit, sitting en banc on rehearing, and by a sharply divided vote, affirmed. 446 F.2d 907 (1971).

This Court vacated and remanded, stating that, in general, "a freely negotiated private international agreement, unaffected by fraud, undue influence, or overweening bargaining power, such as that involved here, should be given full effect." 407 U.S., at 12–13, 92 S.Ct., at 1914–1915 (footnote omitted). The Court further generalized that "in the light of present-day commercial realities and expanding international trade we conclude that the forum clause should control absent a strong showing that it should be set aside." Id., at 15, 92 S.Ct., at 1916. The Court did not define precisely the circumstances that would make it unreasonable for a court to enforce a forum clause. Instead, the Court discussed a number of factors that made it reasonable to enforce the clause at issue in *The Bremen* and that, presumably, would be pertinent in any determination whether to enforce a similar clause.

In this respect, the Court noted that there was "strong evidence that the forum clause was a vital part of the agreement, and [that] it would be unrealistic to think that the parties did not conduct their negotiations, including fixing the monetary terms, with the consequences of the forum clause figuring prominently in their calculations." Id., at 14, 92 S.Ct., at 1915 (footnote omitted). Further, the Court observed that it was not "dealing with an agreement between two Americans to resolve their essentially local disputes in a remote alien forum," and that in such a case, "the serious inconvenience of the contractual forum to one or both of the parties might carry greater weight in determining the reasonableness of the forum clause." Id., at 17, 92 S.Ct., at 1917. The Court stated that even where the forum clause establishes a remote forum for resolution of conflicts, "the party claiming [unfairness] should bear a heavy burden of proof." Ibid.

In applying *The Bremen*, the Court of Appeals in the present litigation took note of the foregoing "reasonableness" factors and rather automatically decided that the forum-selection clause was unenforceable because, unlike the parties in *The Bremen*, respondents are not business persons and did not negotiate the terms of the clause with petitioner. Alternatively, the Court of Appeals ruled that the clause should not be enforced because enforcement effectively would deprive respondents of an opportunity to litigate their claim against petitioner.

The Bremen concerned a "far from routine transaction between companies of two different nations contemplating the tow of an extremely costly piece of equipment from Louisiana across the Gulf of Mexico and the Atlantic Ocean, through the Mediterranean Sea to its final destination in the Adriatic Sea." 407 U.S., at 13, 92 S.Ct., at 1915. These facts suggest that, even apart from the evidence of negotiation regarding the forum clause, it was entirely reasonable for the Court in *The Bremen* to have expected Unterweser and Zapata to have negotiated with care in selecting a forum for the resolution of disputes arising from their special towing contract.

In contrast, respondents' passage contract was purely routine and doubtless nearly identical to every commercial passage contract issued by petitioner and most other cruise lines. See, e.g., Hodes v. S.N.C.

Achille Lauro ed Altri-Gestione, 858 F.2d 905, 910 (C.A.3 1988), cert. dism'd, 490 U.S. 1001, 109 S.Ct. 1633, 104 L.Ed.2d 149 (1989). In this context, it would be entirely unreasonable for us to assume that respondents—or any other cruise passenger—would negotiate with petitioner the terms of a forum-selection clause in an ordinary commercial cruise ticket. Common sense dictates that a ticket of this kind will be a form contract the terms of which are not subject to negotiation, and that an individual purchasing the ticket will not have bargaining parity with the cruise line. But by ignoring the crucial differences in the business contexts in which the respective contracts were executed, the Court of Appeals' analysis seems to us to have distorted somewhat this Court's holding in *The Bremen*.

In evaluating the reasonableness of the forum clause at issue in this case, we must refine the analysis of *The Bremen* to account for the realities of form passage contracts. As an initial matter, we do not adopt the Court of Appeals' determination that a nonnegotiated forum-selection clause in a form ticket contract is never enforceable simply because it is not the subject of bargaining. Including a reasonable forum clause in a form contract of this kind well may be permissible for several reasons: First, a cruise line has a special interest in limiting the fora in which it potentially could be subject to suit. Because a cruise ship typically carries passengers from many locales, it is not unlikely that a mishap on a cruise could subject the cruise line to litigation in several different fora. See *The Bremen,* 407 U.S., at 13 and n. 15, 92 S.Ct., at 1915 and n. 15; *Hodes,* 858 F.2d, at 913. Additionally, a clause establishing *ex ante* the forum for dispute resolution has the salutary effect of dispelling any confusion about where suits arising from the contract must be brought and defended, sparing litigants the time and expense of pretrial motions to determine the correct forum, and conserving judicial resources that otherwise would be devoted to deciding those motions. See *Stewart Organization,* 487 U.S., at 33, 108 S.Ct., at 2249 (concurring opinion). Finally, it stands to reason that passengers who purchase tickets containing a forum clause like that at issue in this case benefit in the form of reduced fares reflecting the savings that the cruise line enjoys by limiting the fora in which it may be sued. Cf. Northwestern Nat. Ins. Co. v. Donovan, 916 F.2d 372, 378 (C.A.7 1990).

We also do not accept the Court of Appeals' "independent justification" for its conclusion that *The Bremen* dictates that the clause should not be enforced because "[t]here is evidence in the record to indicate that the Shutes are physically and financially incapable of pursuing this litigation in Florida." 897 F.2d, at 389. We do not defer to the Court of Appeals' findings of fact. In dismissing the case for lack of personal jurisdiction over petitioner, the District Court made no finding regarding the physical and financial impediments to the Shutes' pursuing their case in Florida. The Court of Appeals' conclusory reference to the record provides no basis for this Court to validate the finding of inconvenience. Furthermore, the Court of Appeals did not place in proper context this Court's statement in *The Bremen* that "the serious inconvenience of the contractual forum to one or both of the parties might carry greater weight in determining the reasonableness of the forum clause." 407 U.S., at 17, 92 S.Ct., at 1917. The Court made this statement in evaluating a hypothetical "agreement between two Americans to resolve their essentially local disputes in a remote alien forum." *Ibid.* In the present case, Florida is not a "remote alien forum," nor—given the fact that Mrs. Shute's accident occurred off the coast of Mexico—is this dispute an essentially local one inherently more suited to resolution in the State of Washington than in Florida. In light of these distinctions, and because respondents do not claim lack of notice of the forum clause, we conclude that they have not satisfied the "heavy burden of proof," ibid., required to set aside the clause on grounds of inconvenience.

It bears emphasis that forum-selection clauses contained in form passage contracts are subject to judicial scrutiny for fundamental fairness. In this case, there is no indication that petitioner set Florida as the forum in which disputes were to be resolved as a means of discouraging cruise passengers from pursuing legitimate claims. Any suggestion of such a bad-faith motive is belied by two facts: petitioner has its principal place of business in Florida, and many of its cruises depart from and return to Florida ports. Similarly, there is no evidence that petitioner obtained respondents' accession to the forum clause by fraud or overreaching. Finally, respondents have conceded that they were given notice of the forum provision and, therefore, presumably retained the option of rejecting the contract with impunity. In the case before us, therefore, we conclude that the Court of Appeals erred in refusing to enforce the forum-selection clause.

B

Respondents also contend that the forum-selection clause at issue violates 46 U.S.C.App. § 183c. That statute, enacted in 1936, see 49 Stat. 1480, provides:

> "It shall be unlawful for the . . . owner of any vessel transporting passengers between ports of the United States or between any such port and a foreign port to insert in any rule, regulation, contract, or agreement any provision or limitation (1) purporting, in the event of loss of life or bodily injury arising from the negligence or fault of such owner or his servants, to relieve such owner . . . from liability, or from liability beyond any stipulated amount, for such loss or injury, or (2) purporting in such event to lessen, weaken, or avoid the right of any claimant to a trial by court of competent jurisdiction on the question of liability for such loss or injury, or the measure of damages therefor. All such provisions or limitations contained in any such rule, regulation, contract, or agreement are declared to be against public policy and shall be null and void and of no effect."

By its plain language, the forum-selection clause before us does not take away respondents' right to "a trial by [a] court of competent jurisdiction" and thereby contravene the explicit proscription of § 183c. Instead, the clause states specifically that actions arising out of the passage contract shall be brought "if at all," in a court "located in the State of Florida," which, plainly, is a "court of competent jurisdiction" within the meaning of the statute.

Respondents appear to acknowledge this by asserting that although the forum clause does not directly prevent the determination of claims against the cruise line, it causes plaintiffs unreasonable hardship in asserting their rights and therefore violates Congress' intended goal in enacting § 183c. Significantly, however, respondents cite no authority for their contention that Congress' intent in enacting § 183c was to avoid having a plaintiff travel to a distant forum in order to litigate. The legislative history of § 183c suggests instead that this provision was enacted in response to passenger-ticket conditions purporting to limit the shipowner's liability for negligence or to remove the issue of liability from the scrutiny of any court by means of a clause providing that "the question of liability and the measure of damages shall be determined by arbitration." See S.Rep. No. 2061, 74th Cong., 2d Sess., 6 (1936); H.R.Rep. No. 2517, 74th Cong., 2d Sess., 6 (1936). See also, Safety of Life and Property at Sea: Hearings Before the Committee on Merchant Marine and Fisheries, 74th Cong., 2d Sess., pt. 4, pp. 20, 36–37, 57, 109–110, 119 (1936). There was no prohibition of a forum-selection clause. Because the clause before us allows for judicial resolution of claims against petitioner and does not purport to limit petitioner's liability for negligence, it does not violate § 183c.

V

The judgment of the Court of Appeals is **reversed**. *Order*

It is so ordered.

■ JUSTICE STEVENS, with whom JUSTICE MARSHALL joins, dissenting.

The Court prefaces its legal analysis with a factual statement that implies that a purchaser of a Carnival Cruise Lines passenger ticket is fully and fairly notified about the existence of the choice of forum clause in the fine print on the back of the ticket. Even if this implication were accurate, I would disagree with the Court's analysis. But, given the Court's preface, I begin my dissent by noting that only the most meticulous passenger is likely to become aware of the forum selection provision. I have therefore appended to this opinion a facsimile of the relevant text, using the type size that actually appears in the ticket itself. A careful reader will find the forum-selection clause in the eighth of the twenty-five numbered paragraphs.

Of course, many passengers, like the respondents in this case will not have an opportunity to read paragraph 8 until they have actually purchased their tickets. By this point, the passengers will already have accepted the condition set forth in paragraph 16(a), which provides that "[t]he Carrier shall not be liable to make any refund to passengers in respect of . . . tickets wholly or partly not used by a passenger." Not knowing whether or not that provision is legally enforceable, I assume that the average passenger would accept the risk of having to file suit in Florida in the event of an injury, rather than canceling—without a refund—a planned vacation at the last minute. The fact that the cruise line can reduce its litigation costs, and therefore its liability insurance premiums, by forcing this choice on its passengers does not, in my opinion, suffice to render the provision reasonable. Cf. Steven v. Fidelity & Casualty Co. of New York, 58 Cal.2d 862, 883, 27 Cal.Rptr. 172, 186, 377 P.2d 284, 298 (1962) (refusing to enforce limitation on liability in insurance policy because insured "must purchase the policy before he even knows its provisions").

Even if passengers received prominent notice of the forum-selection clause before they committed the cost of the cruise, I would remain persuaded that the clause was unenforceable under traditional principles of federal admiralty law and is "null and void" under the terms of Limited Liability Act, 49 Stat. 1480, as amended, 46 U.S.C.App. § 183c, which was enacted in 1936 to invalidate expressly stipulations limiting shipowners' liability for negligence.

Exculpatory clauses in passenger tickets have been around for a long time. These clauses are typically the product of disparate bargaining power between the carrier and the passenger, and they undermine the strong public interest in deterring negligent conduct. For these reasons, courts long before the turn of the century consistently held such clauses unenforceable under federal admiralty law. Thus, in a case involving a ticket provision purporting to limit the shipowner's liability for the negligent handling of baggage, this Court wrote:

"It is settled in the courts of the United States that exemptions limiting carriers from responsibility for the negligence of themselves or their servants are both unjust and unreasonable, and will be deemed as wanting in the element of voluntary assent; and, besides, that such conditions are in conflict with public policy. This doctrine was announced so long ago, and has been so frequently reiterated, that it is elementary. We content ourselves with referring to the cases of the Baltimore & Ohio & c. Railway v. Voigt, 176 U.S. 498, 505, 507 [20 S.Ct. 385, 388, 44 L.Ed. 560 (1900)], and Knott v. Botany Mills, 179 U.S. 69, 71 [21 S.Ct. 30, 30–31, 45 L.Ed. 90 (1900)], where the previously adjudged cases are referred to and the principles by them expounded are restated." The Kensington, 183 U.S. 263, 268, 22 S.Ct. 102, 104, 46 L.Ed. 190 (1902).

* * *

Forum selection clauses in passenger tickets involve the intersection of two strands of traditional contract law that qualify the general rule that courts will enforce the terms of a contract as written. Pursuant to the first strand, courts traditionally have reviewed with heightened scrutiny the terms of contracts of adhesion, form contracts offered on a take-or-leave basis by a party with stronger bargaining power to a party with weaker power. Some commentators have questioned whether contracts of adhesion can justifiably be enforced at all under traditional contract theory because the adhering party generally enters into them without manifesting knowing and voluntary consent to all their terms. See, e.g., Rakoff, Contracts of Adhesion: An Essay in Reconstruction, 96 Harv.L.Rev. 1173, 1179–1180 (1983); Slawson, Mass Contracts: Lawful Fraud in California, 48 S.Cal.L.Rev. 1, 12–13 (1974); K. Llewellyn, The Common Law Tradition 370–371 (1960).

* * *

The second doctrinal principle implicated by forum-selection clauses is the traditional rule that "contractual provisions, which seek to limit the place or court in which an action may . . . be brought, are invalid as contrary to public policy." See Dougherty, Validity of Contractual Provision Limiting Place or Court in Which Action May Be Brought, 31 A.L.R.4th 404, 409, § 3 (1984). See also Home Insurance Co. v. Morse, 20 Wall. 445, 451, 22 L.Ed. 365 (1874). Although adherence to this general rule has declined in recent years, particularly following our decision in The Bremen v. Zapata Off-Shore Co., 407 U.S. 1, 92 S.Ct. 1907, 32 L.Ed.2d 513 (1972), the prevailing rule is still that forum-selection clauses are not enforceable if they were not freely bargained for, create additional expense for one party, or deny one party a remedy. See 31 A.L.R.4th, at 409–438 (citing cases). A forum-selection clause in a standardized passenger ticket would clearly have been unenforceable under the common law before our decision in *The Bremen,* see 407 U.S. at 9, and n. 10, 92 S.Ct., at 1912–13, and n. 10, and, in my opinion, remains unenforceable under the prevailing rule today.

bargain
expense
denial of a remedy

* * *

The stipulation in the ticket that Carnival Cruise sold to respondents certainly lessens or weakens their ability to recover for the slip and fall incident that occurred off the west coast of Mexico during the cruise that originated and terminated in Los Angeles, California. It is safe to assume that the witnesses—whether other passengers or members of the crew—can be assembled with less expense and inconvenience at a west coast forum than in a Florida court several thousand miles from the scene of the accident.

Cost of witnesses - depart from LA

* * *

The Courts of Appeals, construing an analogous provision of the Carriage of Goods by Sea Act, 46 U.S.C.App. § 1300 et seq., have unanimously held invalid as limitations on liability forum-selection clauses requiring suit in foreign jurisdictions. See, e.g., Hughes Drilling Fluids v. M/V Luo Fu Shan, 852 F.2d 840 (C.A.5 1988), cert. denied, 489 U.S. 1033, 109 S.Ct. 1171, 103 L.Ed.2d 229 (1989); Union Ins. Soc. of Canton, Ltd. v. S.S. Elikon, 642 F.2d 721, 724–25 (C.A.4 1981); Indussa Corp. v. S.S. Ranborg, 377 F.2d 200, 203–204 (C.A.2 1967). Commentators have also endorsed this view. See, e.g., G. Gilmore & C. Black, The Law of Admiralty 145, and n. 23 (2nd ed. 1975); Mendelsohn, Liberalism, Choice of Forum Clauses and the Hague Rules, 2 J. of Maritime Law & Comm. 661, 663–666 (1971). The forum-selection clause here does not mandate suit in a foreign jurisdiction, and therefore arguably might have less of an impact on a plaintiff's ability to recover. See Fireman's Fund American Ins. Cos. v. Puerto Rican Forwarding Co., 492 F.2d 1294 (C.A.1 1974). However, the plaintiffs in this case are not large corporations but individuals, and the added burden on them of conducting a trial at the opposite end of the country is likely proportional to the additional cost to a large corporation of conducting a trial overseas.[6]

Under these circumstances, the general prohibition against stipulations purporting "to lessen, weaken, or avoid" the passenger's right to a trial certainly should be construed to apply to the manifestly unreasonable stipulation in these passengers' tickets. Even without the benefit of the statute, I would continue to apply the general rule that prevailed prior to our decision in *The Bremen* to forum-selection clauses in passenger tickets.

I respectfully dissent.

---

[6] The Court does not make clear whether the result in this case would also apply if the clause required Carnival passengers to sue in Panama, the country in which Carnival is incorporated.

NOTES AND QUESTIONS

1. **Criticism of *Carnival Cruise Lines*.** *Carnival Cruise Lines* has been severely criticized. See, e.g., Purcell, Geography as a Litigation Weapon: Consumers, Forum-Selection Clauses, and the Rehnquist Court, 40 U.C.L.A.L.Rev. 423, 514–15 (1992):

> Highly technical, apparently inconsequential, and rarely noticed or understood, [forum selection clauses] suddenly become—at a crucial and perhaps devastating time for the individuals and families involved—a substantial obstacle to suit and a powerful force pressing them to abandon their claims or to discount them substantially. The law should not sanction market failures that lead to such radical disproportionalities and compromise the essential integrity of the nation's system of civil justice.

See also Goldman, My Way and the Highway: The Law and Economics of Choice of Forum Clauses in Consumer Form Contracts, 86 Nw.U.L.Rev. 700 (1992), which argues that forum selection clauses in consumer contracts should be held per se invalid. Have you ever agreed to forum selection clause? Our guess is that you have agreed to many. Take a look at your apartment lease, or at the "Terms and Conditions" in your cell phone contract.

2. **Applicable law.** *Carnival Cruise Lines* was an admiralty case. Subject to an exception not relevant here, admiralty cases come within the exclusive subject matter jurisdiction of the federal courts under 28 U.S.C. § 1333. In the absence of a governing federal statute, federal courts sitting in admiralty apply a federal common law of admiralty. See *Southern Pacific Co. v. Jensen,* 244 U.S. 205, 215, 37 S.Ct. 524, 61 L.Ed. 1086 (1917). Thus, the Supreme Court in *Carnival Cruise Lines* applied judge-made federal admiralty law in determining the validity of the forum selection clause in the Shutes' ticket. In land-based (*i.e.,* non-admiralty) cases, the applicable law for determining the validity of forum selection clauses will usually be state rather than federal.

3. **Forum selection clauses in commercial admiralty contracts.** In *M/S Bremen and Unterweser Reederei v. Zapata Off-Shore Oil Co.,* 407 U.S. 1, 92 S.Ct. 1907, 32 L.Ed.2d 513 (1972), discussed in *Carnival Cruise Lines,* the Supreme Court enforced a forum selection clause in a commercial admiralty contract. The *Carnival Cruise Lines* Court said that it "must refine the analysis of *The Bremen* to account for the realities of form passage contracts." In your opinion, did the Court sufficiently "refine" the analysis? Among other things, note that the contract in *The Bremen* was between two sophisticated parties, that the forum selection clause was a negotiated term of the contract, and that parties to the contract were acting in international commerce. Note also that the contract in *The Bremen* called for adjudication in a neutral forum, whereas the *Carnival Cruise Lines* agreement called for adjudication in Carnival Cruise Lines' "home court."

4. **Economic analysis of forum selection clauses in cruise ship contracts.** The Court in *Carnival Cruise Lines* wrote, "[I]t stands to reason that passengers who purchase tickets containing a forum clause like that at issue in this case benefit in the form of reduced fares reflecting the savings that the cruise line enjoys by limiting the fora in which it may be sued." Does this really "stand to reason"? How can the Court know, or assume, that ticket prices in the cruise ship business are cost-driven rather than demand-

driven? Further, how can it know, or assume, that cruise passengers would willingly trade a forum selection clause for whatever price reduction might result from the clause? Professors Paul Carrington and Paul Haagen write, "This benefit stands to reason only if one makes assumptions that are demonstrably false. The term is not negotiated, the specific market is not competitive, the issue of forum choice is of trivial importance to an individual passenger ex ante, and the unadvised passenger cannot be expected to assign a suitable value to the clause; hence, the savings resulting from the enforcement of the clause went straight to the bottom line of Carnival Lines." Carrington and Haagen, Contract and Jurisdiction, 1996 Sup.Ct.Rev. 331, 355–56. In a post-*Carnival Cruise Lines* case involving a forum selection clause in a passenger cruise ship ticket, Judge Guido Calabresi wrote, "A preliminary analysis leads me to think that upholding forum-selection clauses like the one involved in this case makes very little economic sense. Were we writing on a clean slate, I would want to examine the issue with great care before deciding whether we should do so." Effron v. Sun Line Cruises, Inc., 67 F.3d 7 (2d Cir. 1995) (Calabresi, J., concurring).

5. **Repeated revisions of the statute.** After *Carnival Cruise Lines*, Congress revised, and then re-revised, the relevant statute. In 1992, the word "any" was added to forbid a forum selection clause in tickets on cruises transporting passengers to or from United States ports. After the 1992 revision, the statute read:

> It shall be unlawful for the manager, agent, master or owner of any vessel transporting passengers between ports of the United States or between any such port and a foreign port to insert in any . . . contract, or agreement any provision or limitation . . . purporting . . . to lessen, weaken, or avoid the right of any claimant to a trial by *any* court of competent jurisdiction on the question of liability for such loss or injury, or the measure of damages therefor.

Update to the statute- which broadens the application

Oceans Act of 1992, Pub.L. No. 102–587, § 3006, 106 Stat. 5039, 5068 (1992), 46 U.S.C. § 183c (emph. added).

The 1992 amendment was passed as a surprise "technical clarification" buried in a 68-page act passed under a motion to suspend the normal rules—without a published bill, without a public hearing, and without a Congressional report. Professor Michael Sturley wrote:

> The [cruise line] industry's only opportunity to oppose the amendment in Congress occurred during the two days between the House passage and Senate passage. To have exercised this opportunity, the industry would need to have discovered this "technical clarification" (which is the final section in Title III—the "Marine Health and Stranding Response Act") and to have appreciated its significance. The probability that this would have happened seems similar to the probability that the typical cruise line passenger would discover and appreciate the significance of a cruise line's forum selection clause.

Sturley, Forum Selection Clauses in Cruise Line Tickets: An Update on Congressional Action "Overruling" the Supreme Court, 24 J.Mar.Law and Comm. 399 n. 5 (1993).

Repeal of "any"

In the second revision a year later, the newly added word "any" was removed. Prior to the second amendment, Representative Studds of Massachusetts explained the bill as it went to the House from Senate:

> [The Senate bill's removal of "any"] clarif[ies] that the tort action cannot be brought in just any district court of the United States, but must be filed in a court located in a district in which the vessel owner is doing business, the vessel is operating, or where the passenger boarded the vessel. For this reason, the word "any" has been deleted. We do not intend by this amendment to restore the standard set by the Supreme Court in its 1991 decision Carnival Cruise Lines versus Shute.

139 Cong. Rec. H10939 (Nov. 22, 1993). After the passage of the amendment, Senator Stevens of Alaska, Senator Breaux of Louisiana, and Senator Hollings of South Carolina took issue with Representative Studd's explanation. They contended that the Senate's removal of "any" was intended precisely to restore the result in *Carnival Cruise Lines*. 140 Cong. Rec. S1847–48 (Feb. 24, 1994).

From the degree of Congressional attention, it is apparent that forum selection clauses are very important to the cruise ship industry. This is more than a fuss over a single word. A series of cases in the federal District Court for the Eastern District of Louisiana holds that the removal of "any" has restored the result in *Carnival Cruise Lines*. See, e.g., Smith v. Doe, 991 F. Supp. 781 (E.D.La.1998); Launey v. Carnival Corp., 1997 WL 426095 (E.D.La.1997); Compagno v. Commodore Cruise Line, 1994 WL 462997 (E.D.La.1994).

The current version of the statute, 46 U.S.C. § 30509(a)(1), reads:

> The owner, master, manager, or agent of a vessel transporting passengers between ports in the United States, or between a port in the United States and a port in a foreign country, may not include in a regulation or contract a provision limiting . . . the right of a claimant for personal injury or death to a trial by court of competent jurisdiction.

In Estate of Tore Myhra v. Royal Caribbean Cruises, Ltd., 695 F.3d 1233 (11th Cir. 2012), Myhra was a British cruise ship passenger who bought a ticket in the United Kingdom for a cruise that left from and returned to a port in Florida. He died after contracting legionnaire's disease on the cruise. His estate brought suit in federal district court in Florida despite a forum selection clause in the purchase documents for his ticket that required any suits to be filed in the courts of England or Wales. Those courts would have applied the Athens Convention, which limits the liability of the cruise line to $75,000. The Eleventh Circuit enforced the forum selection clause under § 30509(a), holding that the forum selection clause and the limitation of liability had been meaningfully communicated to Myhra.

6. Forum selection clause in consumer contracts governed by state law. Some state-law decisions involving forum selection clauses in consumer contracts are more consumer friendly than the admiralty law articulated by the Court in *Carnival Cruise Lines*. For example, in Aral v. EarthLink, Inc., 134 Cal.App.4th 544, 36 Cal.Rptr.3d 229 (2005), a California Court of Appeal held that a forum selection clause requiring California consumers to litigate small claims between $40 and $50 was unreasonable and unenforceable. In Dix v. ICT Group, Inc., 160 Wash.2d 826, 161 P.3d 1016 (2007), a would-be class action brought against AOL, the Washington Supreme Court invalidated as inconsistent with Washington public policy as expressed in its Consumer Protection Act, a forum selection clause requiring suits to be brought in Virginia. Courts in Virginia would not have allowed plaintiffs to bring their suit as a class action. But see America Online, Inc. v. Booker, 781 So.2d 423 (Fla. Dist. Ct. App. 2001), in which a Florida court, based on Florida law, enforced the same forum selection clause the Washington court held invalid in *Dix*.

7. **Contractual consent to jurisdiction.** In National Equipment Rental, Ltd. v. Szukhent, 375 U.S. 311, 84 S.Ct. 411, 11 L.Ed.2d 354 (1964), two Michigan chicken farmers leased incubators from National Equipment Rental, whose principal place of business was New York. The farmers signed a form contract in Michigan that, in its last paragraph, designated Mrs. Florence Weinberg, who lived in New York, as their agent for acceptance of service of process. Mrs. Weinberg was the wife of one of the officers of National Equipment Rental. When National Equipment Rental later brought suit against the farmers for nonpayment under the lease, it asserted that this clause constituted an agreement to submit to *in personam* jurisdiction in New York. Applying Federal Rule of Civil Procedure 4(d)(1), which permits service of process on "an agent authorized by appointment," the United States Supreme Court sustained jurisdiction in New York by a vote of five to four.

[handwritten margin note: chicken farmer consent to personal jurisdiction]

Note that the clause in *National Equipment Rental* was not, strictly speaking, a forum selection clause. Rather, it was a consent to *in personam* jurisdiction, permitting the exercise of personal jurisdiction in New York. If suit were brought in New York state court, the farmers could move (probably unsuccessfully) for a dismissal on grounds of *forum non conveniens*. If the suit were in federal district court in New York, the farmers could move (possibly successfully) for transfer to federal court in Michigan under 28 U.S.C. § 1404(a). By contrast, the Shutes' tickets mandated that any suit be brought only in Florida. It provided: "[A]ll disputes * * * shall be litigated, if at all, in and before a Court located in the State of Florida, U.S.A., to the exclusion of the Courts of any other state or country."

8. **Forum selection clauses and § 1404(a) motions to transfer.** What is the effect of a forum selection clause on a motion to transfer from one federal district court to another under 28 U.S.C. § 1404(a)? In Atlantic Marine Const. v. U.S. District Court, 571 U.S. ___, 134 S.Ct. 568, 581, 187 L.Ed.2d 487 (2013), the Supreme Court upheld enforcement of a forum selection clause through a § 1404(a) transfer, writing, "When the parties have agreed to a valid forum selection clause, a district court should ordinarily transfer the case to the forum specified in the clause. Only under extraordinary circumstances unrelated to the convenience of the parties should a § 1404(a) motion be denied." See also Stewart Organization, Inc. v. Ricoh Corp., 487 U.S. 22, 108 S.Ct. 2239, 101 L.Ed.2d 22 (1988). For an expanded discussion of *forum non conveniens* and § 1404(a) transfers, see infra p. 303.

9. **The Hague Convention on Choice of Court Agreements.** Drafting of the Hague Convention on Choice of Court Agreements was concluded in 2005. The Convention provides rules for the enforceability of exclusive forum choice agreements in international commercial matters, and for the subsequent recognition of judgments rendered in a court chosen

pursuant to such agreements. A dispute is "international" for purposes of the convention unless both parties reside in the same nation and the relevant aspects of their relationship and the dispute are connected solely with that nation. The Convention provides that a court designated in any exclusive forum choice agreement "shall not decline to exercise jurisdiction on the ground that the dispute should be decided by a court of another State."

The Convention does not apply to exclusive forum choice agreements entered into by "a natural person acting primarily for personal, family, or household purposes (a consumer)" or to contracts of employment. Article 2, § 1. It also excludes a variety of subject matters, including family law and probate matters, bankruptcy, the carriage of passengers and goods, intellectual property disputes (other than copyright), anti-trust matters, claims for personal injury by natural persons, tort claims not arising from a contractual relationship, and claims relating to real property. Article 2, § 2. See Note, Hague Conference Approves Uniform Rules of Enforcement for International Forum Selection Clauses, 119 Harv. L. Rev. 931 (2006).

If the United States ratifies the Convention, it will become federal law, binding in both state and federal courts. The Convention would require enforcement of agreements like that in *The Bremen*, but would leave enforcement of contracts like that in *Carnival Cruise Lines* (which fall within the Convention's exclusions for consumers, carriage of passengers, and personal injury claims) to the current regime of federal and state statutes and rules. The Convention's exclusion of consumer contracts and personal injury claims suggests that the Supreme Court may be an international outlier in its willingness to support the use of forum selection clauses in settings like *Carnival Cruise Lines*.

h.   OBJECTING TO JURISDICTION

1.   *Special Appearance*

Insurance Corp. of Ireland, Ltd. v. Compagnie des Bauxites de Guinee

Supreme Court of the United States, 1982.
456 U.S. 694, 102 S.Ct. 2099, 72 L.Ed.2d 492.

■ JUSTICE WHITE delivered the opinion of the Court.

Rule 37(b), Federal Rules of Civil Procedure, provides that a district court may impose sanctions for failure to comply with discovery orders. Included among the available sanctions is:

"An order that the matters regarding which the order was made or any other designated facts shall be taken to be established for the purposes of the action in accordance with the claim of the party obtaining the order." Rule 37(b)(2)(A).

The question presented by this case is whether this rule is applicable to facts that form the basis for personal jurisdiction over a defendant. May a district court, as a sanction for failure to comply with a discovery order directed at establishing jurisdictional facts, proceed on the basis that personal jurisdiction over the recalcitrant party has been established? Petitioners urge that such an application of the Rule would violate due process: If a court does not have jurisdiction over a party, then it may not create that jurisdiction by judicial fiat. They contend also that until a court has jurisdiction over a party, that party need not comply with orders of the court; failure to comply, therefore, cannot provide the ground for a sanction. In our view, petitioners are attempting to create a logical conundrum out of a fairly straightforward matter.

I

Respondent Compagnie des Bauxites de Guinee (CBG) is a Delaware Corporation, 49% of which is owned by the Republic of Guinea and 51% is owned by Halco (Mining) Inc. CBG's principal place of business is in the Republic of Guinea, where it operates bauxite mines and processing facilities. Halco, which operates in Pennsylvania, has contracted to perform certain administrative services for CBG. These include the procurement of insurance.

In 1973, Halco instructed an insurance broker, Marsh & McLennan, to obtain $20 million worth of business interruption insurance to cover CBG's operations in Guinea. The first half of this coverage was provided by the Insurance Company of North America (INA). The second half, or what is referred to as the "excess" insurance, was provided by a group of 21 foreign insurance companies,[2] 14 of which are petitioners in this action (the excess insurers).

* * *

Sometime after February 12, [1974] CBG allegedly experienced mechanical problems in its Guinea operation, resulting in a business interruption loss in excess of $10 million. * * *

In December 1975, CBG filed a two count suit in the Western District of Pennsylvania, asserting jurisdiction based on diversity of citizenship. The first count was against INA; the second against the excess insurers. INA did not challenge personal or subject matter jurisdiction of the District Court. The answer of the excess insurers, however, raised a number of defenses, including lack of *in personam* jurisdiction. Subsequently, this alleged lack of personal jurisdiction became the basis of a motion for summary judgment filed by the excess insurers. The issue in this case requires an account of respondent's attempt to use discovery in order to demonstrate the court's personal jurisdiction over the excess insurers.

Respondent's first discovery request—asking for "[c]opies of all business interruption insurance policies issued by defendant during the period from January 1, 1972 to December 31, 1975"—was served on each defendant in August 1976. In January 1977, the excess insurers objected, on grounds of burdensomeness, to producing such policies. Several months later, respondent filed a motion to compel petitioners to produce the requested documents. In June, 1978, the court orally overruled

---

[2]   The district court described these excess insurers as follows:

"Of the 21 Excess Insurers, 5 are English companies representing English domestic interests but insuring risks throughout the world, particularly in Pennsylvania. Seven are English companies which represent non English parents, or affiliates. The United States, Japan, and Israel are the nationalities of two each of the Excess Insurer Defendants. Switzerland and the Republic of Ireland are the nationalities of one each of the Excess Insurer Defendants. The remaining Excess Insurer Defendant is a Belgium Company which represents the United States parent." 1 App. 196a.

petitioners' objections. This was followed by a second discovery request in which respondent narrowed the files it was seeking to policies which "were delivered in . . . Pennsylvania . . . or covered a risk located in . . . Pennsylvania." Petitioners now objected that these documents were not in their custody or control; rather, they were kept by the brokers in London. The court ordered petitioners to request the information from the brokers, limiting the request to policies covering the period from 1971 to date. That was in July 1978; petitioners were given 90 days to produce the information. On November 8, petitioners were given an additional 30 days to complete discovery. On November 24, petitioners filed an affidavit offering to make their records, allegedly some 4 million files, available at their offices in London for inspection by respondent. Respondent countered with a motion to compel production of the previously requested documents. On December 21, 1978, the court, noting that no conscientious effort had yet been made to produce the requested information and that no objection had been entered to the discovery order in July, gave petitioners 60 more days to produce the requested information. He also issued the following warning:

> "[I]f you don't get it to him in 60 days, I am going to enter an order saying that because you failed to give the information as requested, that I am going to assume, under rule of Civil Procedure 37B, subsection 2(A), that there is jurisdiction."

A few moments later he restated the warning as follows: "I will assume that jurisdiction is here with this court unless you produce statistics and other information in that regard that would indicate otherwise."

On April 19, 1979, the court, after concluding that the requested material had not been produced, imposed the threatened sanction, finding that "for the purpose of this litigation the Excess Insurers are subject to the *in personam* jurisdiction of this Court because of their business contacts with Pennsylvania." * * *

II

* * *

* * * The requirement that a court have personal jurisdiction flows not from Art. III, but from the Due Process Clause. The personal jurisdiction requirement recognizes and protects an individual liberty interest. It represents a restriction on judicial power not as a matter of sovereignty, but as a matter of individual liberty.[10] [This needs to be FN

---

[10] It is true that we have stated that the requirement of personal jurisdiction, as applied to state courts, reflects an element of federalism and the character of state sovereignty vis-a-vis other states. For example, in World-Wide Volkswagen Corp. v. Woodson, 444 U.S. 286, 291–292, 100 S.Ct. 559, 564, 62 L.Ed.2d 490 (1980), we stated:

> "[A] state court may exercise personal jurisdiction over a nonresident defendant only so long as there exist 'minimum contacts' between the defendant and the forum State. The concept of minimum contacts, in turn, can be seen to perform two related, but distinguishable, functions. It protects the defendant against the burdens of litigating in a distant or inconvenient forum. And it acts to ensure that the States, through their courts, do not reach out beyond the limits imposed on them by their status as coequal sovereigns in a federal system." (Citations omitted.)

Contrary to the suggestion of Justice Powell, post, * * * our holding today does not alter the requirement that there be "minimum contacts" between the nonresident defendant and the forum state. Rather, our holding deals with how the facts needed to show those "minimum contacts" can be established when a defendant fails to comply with court-ordered discovery. The restriction on state sovereign power described in *World-Wide*

10.] Thus, the test for personal jurisdiction requires that "the maintenance of the suit . . . not offend 'traditional notions of fair play and substantial justice.' " International Shoe v. Washington, 326 U.S. 310, 316, 66 S.Ct. 154, 158, 90 L.Ed. 95 (1945), quoting Milliken v. Meyer, 311 U.S. 457, 463, 61 S.Ct. 339, 342, 85 L.Ed. 278 (1940). Because the requirement of personal jurisdiction represents first of all an individual right, it can, like other such rights, be waived. In McDonald v. Mabee, supra, the Court indicated that regardless of the power of the state to serve process, an individual may submit to the jurisdiction of the Court by appearance. A variety of legal arrangements have been taken to represent express or implied consent to the personal jurisdiction of the court.

* * * The actions of the defendant may amount to a legal submission to the jurisdiction of the court, whether voluntary or not.

The expression of legal rights is often subject to certain procedural rules: The failure to follow those rules may well result in a curtailment of the rights. Thus, the failure to enter a timely objection to personal jurisdiction constitutes, under Rule 12(h)(1), a waiver of the objection. A sanction under Rule 37(b)(2)(A) consisting of a finding of personal jurisdiction has precisely the same effect. As a general proposition, the Rule 37 sanction applied to a finding of personal jurisdiction creates no more of a due process problem than the Rule 12 waiver. Although "a court cannot conclude all persons interested by its mere assertion of its own power," Chicago Life Ins. Co. v. Cherry, supra, at 29, 37 S.Ct., at 493, not all rules that establish legal consequences to a party's own behavior are "mere assertions" of power.

Rule 37(b)(2)(A) itself embodies the standard established in Hammond Packing Co. v. Arkansas, 212 U.S. 322, 29 S.Ct. 370, 53 L.Ed. 530 (1909), for the due process limits on such rules. There the Court held that it did not violate due process for a state court to strike the answer and render a default judgment against a defendant who failed to comply with a pretrial discovery order. Such a rule was permissible as an expression of "the undoubted right of the lawmaking power to create a presumption of fact as to the bad faith and untruth of an answer begotten from the suppression or failure to produce the proof ordered. . . . [T]he preservation of due process was secured by the presumption that the refusal to produce evidence material to the administration of due process was but an admission of the want of merit in the asserted defense." Id., at 350–351, 29 S.Ct., at 380.

* * *

Petitioners argue that a sanction consisting of a finding of personal jurisdiction differs from all other instances in which a sanction is imposed, including the default judgment in *Hammond Packing,* because a party need not obey the orders of a court until it is established that the

Volkswagen Corp., however, must be seen as ultimately a function of the individual liberty interest preserved by the Due Process Clause. That clause is the only source of the personal jurisdiction requirement and the clause itself makes no mention of federalism concerns. Furthermore, if the federalism concept operated as an independent restriction on the sovereign power of the court, it would not be possible to waive the personal jurisdiction requirement: Individual actions cannot change the powers of sovereignty, although the individual can subject himself to powers from which he may otherwise be protected.

court has personal jurisdiction over that party. If there is no obligation to obey a judicial order, a sanction cannot be applied for the failure to comply. Until the court has established personal jurisdiction, moreover, any assertion of judicial power over the party violates due process.

This argument again assumes that there is something unique about the requirement of personal jurisdiction, which prevents it from being established or waived like other rights. A defendant is always free to ignore the judicial proceedings, risk a default judgment and then challenge that judgment on jurisdictional grounds in a collateral proceeding. See Baldwin v. Traveling Men's Ass'n, 283 U.S. 522, 525, 51 S.Ct. 517, 75 L.Ed. 1244 (1931). By submitting to the jurisdiction of the court for the limited purpose of challenging jurisdiction, the defendant agrees to abide by that court's determination on the issue of jurisdiction. That decision will be *res judicata* on that issue in any further proceedings. Id., at 524, 51 S.Ct., at 517. American Surety Co. v. Baldwin, 287 U.S. 156, 166, 53 S.Ct. 98, 101, 77 L.Ed. 231 (1932). As demonstrated above, the manner in which the court determines whether it has personal jurisdiction may include a variety of legal rules and presumptions, as well as straightforward fact-finding. A particular rule may offend the due process standard of *Hammond Packing,* but the mere use of procedural rules does not in itself violate the defendant's due process rights.

III

Even if Rule 37(b)(2) may be applied to support a finding of personal jurisdiction, the question remains as to whether it was properly applied under the circumstances of this case. * * *

* * * [P]etitioners had ample warning that a continued failure to comply with the discovery orders would lead to the imposition of this sanction. Furthermore, the proposed sanction made it clear that even if there was not compliance with the discovery order, this sanction would not be applied if petitioners were to "produce statistics and other information" that would indicate an absence of personal jurisdiction. In effect, the district court simply placed the burden of proof upon petitioners on the issue of personal jurisdiction.[12] Petitioners failed to comply with the discovery order; they also failed to make any attempt to meet this burden of proof. This course of behavior coupled with the ample warnings demonstrate the "justice" of the trial court's order.

* * *

■ JUSTICE POWELL, concurring in the judgment.

* * *

In my view the Court's broadly theoretical decision misapprehends the issues actually presented for decision. Federal courts are courts of limited jurisdiction. Their personal jurisdiction, no less than their subject matter jurisdiction, is subject both to constitutional and to statutory definition. When the applicable limitations on federal jurisdiction are identified, it becomes apparent that the Court's theory could require a sweeping but largely unexplicated revision of jurisdictional doctrine. This revision could encompass not only the personal jurisdiction of federal courts but "sovereign" limitations on state jurisdiction as

---

[12] Counsel for petitioners agreed to this characterization of the sanction at oral argument. Trans. of Oral Arg. 47–48.

identified in World-Wide Volkswagen Corp. v. Woodson, 444 U.S. 286, 291–293, 100 S.Ct. 559, 564–565, 62 L.Ed.2d 490 (1980). * * *

I

This lawsuit began when the respondent Compagnie des Bauxites brought a contract action against the petitioner insurance companies in the United States District Court for the Western District of Pennsylvania. Alleging diversity jurisdiction, respondent averred that the District Court had personal jurisdiction of the petitioners, all foreign corporations, under the long-arm statute of the State of Pennsylvania. See Compagnie des Bauxites de Guinea v. Insurance Co. of North America, 651 F.2d 877, 880, 881 (C.A.3 1981). Petitioners, however, denied that they were subject to the court's personal jurisdiction under that or any other statute. Viewing the question largely as one of fact, the court ordered discovery to resolve the dispute.

* * *

Rule 37(b) is not, however, a jurisdictional provision. As recognized by the Court of Appeals, the governing jurisdictional statute remains the long-arm statute of the State of Pennsylvania. See 651 F.2d, at 881. In my view the Court fails to make clear the implications of this central fact: that the District Court in this case relied on state law to obtain personal jurisdiction.

* * *

As a result of the District Court's dependence on the law of Pennsylvania to establish personal jurisdiction—a dependence mandated by Congress under 28 U.S.C. § 1652—its jurisdiction in this case normally would be subject to the same due process limitations as a state court. See, e.g., Forsythe v. Overmyer, supra, at 782; Washington v. Norton Mfg., Inc., 588 F.2d 441, 445 (C.A.5 1979); Fisons Ltd. v. United States, 458 F.2d 1241, 1250 (C.A.7 1972). * * *

* * *

A

Under traditional principles, the due process question in this case is whether "minimum contacts" exist between petitioners and the forum State that would justify the State in exercising personal jurisdiction. See, e.g., World-Wide Volkswagen Corp. v. Woodson, supra, 444 U.S., at 291–293, 100 S.Ct., at 564–565; Shaffer v. Heitner, 433 U.S. 186, 216, 97 S.Ct. 2569, 2586, 53 L.Ed.2d 683 (1977); Hanson v. Denckla, supra, 357 U.S., at 251, 78 S.Ct., at 1238. By finding that the establishment of minimum contacts is not a prerequisite to the exercise of jurisdiction to impose sanctions under Fed.Rule Civ.Proc. 37, the Court may be understood as finding that "minimum contacts" no longer is a constitutional requirement for the exercise by a state court of personal jurisdiction over an unconsenting defendant.[5] Whenever the Court's notions of fairness are not offended, jurisdiction apparently may be upheld.

---

[5] The Court refers to the respondent's prima facie showing of "minimum contacts" only as one factor indicating that the District Court did not abuse its discretion in entering a finding of personal jurisdiction as a sanction under Rule 37(b). * * * Generally it views the requirement of personal jurisdiction as a right that may be "established or waived like other rights." * * *

Before today, of course, our cases had linked minimum contacts and fair play as *jointly* defining the "sovereign" limits on state assertions of personal jurisdiction over unconsenting defendants. See World-Wide Volkswagen Corp. v. Woodson, supra, 444 U.S., at 292–293, 100 S.Ct., at 564–565; see Hanson v. Denckla, supra, 357 U.S., at 251, 78 S.Ct., at 1238. The Court appears to abandon the rationale of these cases in a footnote. See ante, * * * n. 10. But it does not address the implications of its action. By eschewing reliance on the concept of minimum contacts as a "sovereign" limitation on the power of States—for, again, it is the State's long-arm statute that is invoked to obtain personal jurisdiction in the District Court—the Court today effects a potentially substantial change of law. For the first time it defines personal jurisdiction solely by reference to abstract notions of fair play. And, astonishingly to me, it does so in a case in which this rationale for decision was neither argued nor briefed by the parties.

B

Alternatively, it is possible to read the Court opinion, not as affecting state jurisdiction, but simply as asserting that Rule 37 of the Federal Rules of Civil Procedure represents a congressionally approved basis for the exercise of personal jurisdiction by a federal district court. On this view Rule 37 vests the federal district courts with authority to take jurisdiction over persons not in compliance with discovery orders. * * *

* * * A plaintiff is not entitled to discovery to establish essentially speculative allegations necessary to personal jurisdiction. Nor would the use of Rule 37 sanctions to enforce discovery orders constitute a mere abuse of discretion in such a case. For me at least, such a use of discovery would raise serious questions as to the constitutional as well as the statutory authority of a federal court—in a diversity case—to exercise personal jurisdiction absent some showing of minimum contacts between the unconsenting defendant and the forum State.

II

In this case the facts alone—unaided by broad jurisdictional theories—more than amply demonstrate that the District Court possessed personal jurisdiction to impose sanctions under Rule 37 and otherwise to adjudicate this case. I would decide the case on this narrow basis.

As recognized both by the District Court and the Court of Appeals, the respondent adduced substantial support for its jurisdictional assertions. By affidavit and other evidence, it made a prima facie showing of "minimum contacts." See 651 F.2d, at 881–882, 886 and n. 9. In the view of the District Court, the evidence adduced actually was sufficient to sustain a finding of personal jurisdiction independently of the Rule 37 sanction.

Where the plaintiff has made a prima facie showing of minimum contacts, I have little difficulty in holding that its showing was sufficient to warrant the District Court's entry of discovery orders. And where a defendant then fails to comply with those orders, I agree that the prima facie showing may be held adequate to sustain the court's finding that minimum contacts exist, either under Rule 37 or under a theory of "presumption" or "waiver." * * *

NOTE ON *INSURANCE CORP. OF IRELAND* AND SPECIAL APPEARANCE

1. **Consent to decide jurisdiction.** By appearing to contest jurisdiction, didn't the excess insurers consent to the exercise of jurisdiction at least for the purpose of determining whether *in personam* jurisdiction existed? Once having consented to the exercise of jurisdiction for that purpose, could the excess insurers reasonably refuse to provide information relevant to the determination of that issue? Was the district court's finding of jurisdiction a reasonable sanction for the refusal to provide relevant information? (If you are tempted to think that the sanction was unreasonable, ask yourself why the excess insurers were unwilling to provide the information.)

2. **Special appearance.** All American court systems, state and federal, provide for special appearances for the sole purpose of contesting territorial jurisdiction. Restatement (Second) of Conflict of Laws, § 81, provides:

> A state will not exercise judicial jurisdiction over an individual who appears in the action for the sole purpose of objecting that there is no jurisdiction over him.

For examples of special appearances in state courts, see Tigges v. City of Ames, 356 N.W.2d 503 (Iowa 1984); Islamic Republic of Iran v. Pahlavi, 160 Cal.App.3d 620, 206 Cal.Rptr. 752 (1984); Mladinich v. Kohn, 250 Miss. 138, 164 So.2d 785 (1964). A defendant must be careful that she does not inadvertently make a general appearance. For example, California state courts will find that a defendant has appeared generally if she answers on the merits, even if at the same time she states that she is not submitting to the jurisdiction of the court. Neihaus v. Superior Court In and For Sacramento County, 69 Cal.App.3d 340, 137 Cal.Rptr. 905 (1977); Calif.C.Civ.P. § 1014. See 2 B. Witkin, California Procedure, Jurisdiction, § 149 et seq. (1985); Note, Special Appearances in California, 10 Stan.L.Rev. 711 (1958) (warning that Calif.C.Civ.P. § 1014 does not fully describe California special appearance practice). Similarly, in Texas a defendant will be found to have made a general appearance if she answers at the same time she objects to jurisdiction. Cuellar v. Cuellar, 406 S.W.2d 510 (Tex.Civ.App.1966) Tex.R.Civ.P. 120a. See Newton and Wicker, Personal Jurisdiction and the Appearance to Challenge Jurisdiction in Texas, 38 Baylor L.Rev. 491 (1986); Thode, In Personam Jurisdiction; Article 2031B, the Texas "Long Arm" Jurisdiction Statute; and the Appearance to Challenge Jurisdiction in Texas and Elsewhere, 42 Tex.L.Rev. 279 (1964).

Special appearances are permitted in federal district court under Rule 12, although the phrase "special appearance" is not used. A defendant may move for dismissal under Rule 12(b)(2) for "lack of personal jurisdiction." A motion under Rule 12(b)(2) may be joined with other motions permitted under Rule 12(b), or with a "responsive pleading," such as an answer to the complaint. (Note that defendants in *Insurance Corp. of Ireland* answered and objected to *in personam* jurisdiction simultaneously, as is permitted under Rule 12.) An objection to personal jurisdiction is waived if it is not asserted in a responsive pleading (ordinarily, the answer) or in a motion under federal Rule 12(b)(2) to dismiss for want of personal jurisdiction. See Fed. R. Civ. P. 12(h). But a timely objection is not all that is needed. An objection may be forfeited if not pursued in a timely fashion. In Hamilton v. Atlas Turner, 197

F.3d 58 (2d Cir. 1999), the defendant objected to jurisdiction in its answer. It then waited four years before moving to dismiss. The Second Circuit held that the defendant had forfeited its right to a jurisdictional dismissal through delay, and that the district court had abused its discretion in sustaining defendant's objection. See also Peterson v. Highland Music, Inc., 140 F.3d 1313, 1318 (9th Cir. 1998) ("Rule 12(h)(1) specifies the minimum steps that a party must take in order to preserve a defense.").

3. A defendant's choices, and their consequences. If a defendant is quite confident that territorial jurisdiction does not exist in the state where suit is brought, she may be tempted to stay away from the litigation altogether. If she does that, a default judgment will most likely be entered against her. The plaintiff will then bring that judgment to the state in which the defendant is found, and seek to enforce it in the courts of that state, relying on the Full Faith and Credit Clause of the United States Constitution. The defendant may resist enforcement on the ground that the judgment was rendered without territorial jurisdiction. The court of the state in which enforcement is sought will then decide whether territorial jurisdiction existed in the court that rendered the judgment. If it existed, the judgment will be enforced. If not, it will not be. This strategy is often called "collaterally attacking" the original default judgment.

All this is very tidy, but very risky. The only question open to consideration in the court in which enforcement is sought is the jurisdictional question. Thus, if the defendant loses the argument about territorial jurisdiction in her home state, she is foreclosed from making any defense on the merits of the suit. See Restatement (Second) of Conflict of Laws § 104; Restatement (Second) of Judgments § 81 (particularly Comment b). If the jurisdictional question is somewhat close (and most are), and if the defendant has a plausible defense on the merits (and most do), risking the entire outcome of the lawsuit on the jurisdictional question may be foolish. In litigation within the United States, where the alternative forums are courts of different states, it is rare for a defendant to risk her entire suit on the outcome of the enforcement proceeding.

It is more common in international litigation for a defendant to decline to appear to litigate the existence of jurisdiction, for the risks of this strategy in such cases are often lower, and the returns higher, than in domestic cases. Although there will frequently be treaty-based obligations to enforce valid judgments of foreign countries, these typically do not have the strength of the Full Faith and Credit Clause among the states. Further, the disadvantage of litigating against a national of another country in his own courts is often much greater than the disadvantage of litigating in the courts of another state. See Degnan and Kane, The Exercise of Jurisdiction Over and Enforcement of Judgments Against Alien Defendants, 39 Hast.L.J. 799 (1988).

But even in international litigation, the stakes are sufficiently high and the risk of staying away sufficiently great that foreign and multi-national corporations generally choose to make special appearances in American courts. Professors Ugo Mattei and Jeffrey Lena have analyzed the tendency of foreign and multi-national corporations to appear and defend actions brought in the United States based on allegedly illegal foreign conduct, particularly human rights violations. They note that the principles of jurisdiction, discovery and punitive damages applied in the United States are often inconsistent with international standards (to the advantage of plaintiffs), and that enforcement of a United States judgment could therefore be successfully resisted in the corporation's home country. But these companies often do business and have assets in the United States against which enforcement may be sought in an American court, making irrelevant the unenforceability of the judgment abroad. Mattei & Lena, U.S. Jurisdiction over Conflicts Arising Outside of the United States: Some Hegemonic Implications, 24 Hastings Int'l & Comp.L.Rev. 381, 400 (2001).

4. **Special appearance subjects the defendant to the decision of the court in which the appearance is made.** A defendant who makes a special appearance for the purpose of contesting territorial jurisdiction, and loses, can only challenge the correctness of the jurisdiction decision by appealing within the court system that has asserted jurisdiction. In Baldwin v. Iowa State Traveling Men's Ass'n, 283 U.S. 522, 51 S.Ct. 517, 75 L.Ed. 1244 (1931), defendant appeared specially in federal district court in Missouri to contest *in personam* jurisdiction. The district court found that it had jurisdiction. The defendant did not participate further in the suit, and default judgment was entered against him. Plaintiff sought enforcement of the judgment against the defendant in a proceeding in federal district court in Iowa. The Supreme Court refused to allow the question to be considered by the second court:

> [T]he respondent entered the Missouri court for the very purpose of litigating the question of jurisdiction over its person. It had the election not to appear at all. If, in the absence of appearance, the court had proceeded to judgment, and the present suit had been brought thereon, respondent could have raised and tried out the issue in the present action, because it would never have had its day in court with respect to jurisdiction. It had also the right to appeal from the decision of the Missouri District Court * * *. It elected to follow neither of those courses, but, after having been defeated upon full hearing in its contention as to jurisdiction, it took no further steps, and the judgment in question resulted.

> Public policy dictates that there be an end of litigation; that those who have contested an issue shall be bound by the result of the contest; and that matters once tried shall be considered forever settled as between the parties. We see no reason why this doctrine should not apply in every case where one voluntarily appears, presents his case and is fully heard, and why he should not, in the absence of fraud, be thereafter concluded by the judgment of the tribunal to which he has submitted his cause.

283 U.S. at 525–26.

The *Baldwin* rule applies to jurisdictional decisions reached after special appearance in state courts as well. Davis v. Davis, 305 U.S. 32, 59 S.Ct. 3, 83 L.Ed. 26 (1938). See also Somportex Ltd. v. Philadelphia Chewing Gum Corp., 453 F.2d 435 (3d Cir. 1971) (enforcing an English default judgment entered when defendant refused to proceed further after having made an unsuccessful jurisdictional challenge), cert. den. 405 U.S. 1017 (1972).

2. Limited Appearance

NOTE ON LIMITED APPEARANCE

Prior to *Shaffer v. Heitner*, it happened with some frequency that a defendant was sued *quasi in rem* in a state with which he had few if any contacts beyond the property in question. The solution offered by some states in such circumstances was to allow the defendant to appear to defend the merits of the lawsuit, but to limit the potential liability in the suit to the value of the property that formed the basis for the jurisdiction. See, e.g., Cheshire National Bank v. Jaynes, 224 Mass. 14, 112 N.E. 500 (1916). Other states, including Delaware, declined to allow limited appearances in *quasi in rem* suits, and required that as a condition of defending on the merits a defendant submit himself to the jurisdiction of the court for the full amount in controversy, even if it exceeded the value of the property.

After *Shaffer*, the issue has lost much of its urgency, for *quasi in rem* jurisdiction is now rarely employed. Either there are insufficient "minimum contacts," in which case there is no jurisdiction over the defendant; or there are sufficient "minimum contacts," in which case the defendant may be submitted to the *in personam* jurisdiction of the court. In a few circumstances, however, *quasi in rem* jurisdiction continues to exist. See, e.g., Banco Ambrosiano, S.p.A. v. Artoc Bank & Trust Ltd., 62 N.Y.2d 65, 476 N.Y.S.2d 64, 464 N.E.2d 432 (1984), in which *quasi in rem* jurisdiction was used to fill a gap left between the extent of New York's long-arm statute and the constitutionally permissible reach of its jurisdiction under *International Shoe*.

For discussion of limited appearances, see Carrington, The Modern Utility of Quasi In Rem Jurisdiction, 76 Harv.L.Rev. 303, 313–16 (1976); Note, The "Right" to Defend Federal Quasi In Rem Actions Without Submitting to the Personal Jurisdiction of the Court, 48 Iowa L.Rev. 441 (1963).

i.   RELATION OF TERRITORIAL JURISDICTION TO CHOICE OF LAW

More is at stake in the choice of forum than litigating convenience and the possibility of undue sympathy for a home-town litigant. It may surprise you to learn that the substantive law applied to a case may be different depending on the forum in which the case is brought. In theory and largely in practice, federal law is uniformly applied across the country, in both federal and state courts. But state laws are not uniformly applied across the country. For example, if suit is brought in State A, the courts of that state may well apply the law of State A; but if the same suit is brought in State B, the courts of that state may well apply the law of State B. Or the courts of State A may apply the law of State A, while the courts of State B may apply the law State C, where some of the underlying events in the suit took place.

There are only modest federal constitutional constraints on the ability of a state to apply its own state law. More important constraints are imposed by the state-law choice-of-law rules followed by individual states. The Notes that follow consider the two types of constraints.

NOTE ON FEDERAL CONSTITUTIONAL CONSTRAINTS ON CHOICE OF STATE LAW

There are relatively few Supreme Court cases dealing with federal constitutional constraints on choice of state law. Three following are three of the most important cases.

In Home Insurance Co. v. Dick, 281 U.S. 397, 57 S.Ct. 129, 81 L.Ed.2d 926 (1930), Dick was an American citizen living in Mexico but with permanent residence in Texas. He brought suit in Texas state court to recover on an insurance policy for the total loss of a tugboat. The policy was issued in Mexico by a Mexican insurance company, and it covered the tugboat only in Mexican waters. The policy premium was paid in Mexico, and any payment for loss was to be made in Mexico. The policy required that any suit to recover under the policy be brought within one year of the loss. Dick brought suit in Texas state court against two New York insurance companies that had contracted to act as reinsurers under the policy. The suit was filed more than one year after the loss. It was undisputed that if suit had been brought in Mexico, the one-year limitation period would have been applied. The Texas Supreme Court applied Texas's two-year statute of limitations and held against the two reinsurers on the merits. The United States Supreme Court reversed. *In personam* jurisdiction over the defendant companies was not at issue, for each defendant had appointed an agent for service of process in Texas. The Court held that application of Texas law violated due process. The Court wrote:

> All acts relating to the making of the policy were done in Mexico. All in relation to the making of the contracts of re-insurance were done there or in New York. And, likewise, all things in regard to performance were to be done outside Texas. Neither the Texas laws nor the Texas courts were involved for any purpose, except by Dick in the bringing of this suit. The fact that Dick's permanent residence was in Texas is without significance. At all times here material, he was physically present and acting in Mexico. Texas was, therefore, without power to affect the terms of contracts so made.

281 U.S. at 408.

In Allstate Insurance Co. v. Hague, 449 U.S. 302, 101 S.Ct. 633, 66 L.Ed.2d 521 (1981), Ralph Hague was killed in Wisconsin when the motorcycle on which he was a passenger was struck by a car. Neither of the two vehicle operators carried insurance. Hague carried uninsured motorists' coverage on three vehicles he owned, with a maximum benefit of $15,000 in coverage on each. The insurance laws of Wisconsin and Minnesota differed: Wisconsin law prohibited "stacking" of the policies, making only $15,000 available for compensation of Hague's survivors. Minnesota law permitted "stacking," making $45,000 available. Hague and the two operators of the vehicles were all residents of Wisconsin, although Hague worked in Minnesota. After Hague's death, his widow moved to Minnesota. The widow brought suit in Minnesota against Hague's insurance company, and argued that the Minnesota law permitting "stacking" should be applied to the case. If the widow had brought suit in Wisconsin, Wisconsin courts would have applied Wisconsin law. But the Minnesota court applied Minnesota law, and the Supreme Court affirmed.

Justice Brennan's plurality opinion stated the test for constitutionally permissible application of state law: "[F]or a State's substantive law to be selected in a constitutionally permissible manner, that State must have a significant contact or significant aggregation of contacts, creating state interests, such that choice of its law is neither arbitrary nor fundamentally unfair." 449 U.S. at 312–13. Justice Brennan relied on three factors to justify the application of Minnesota law under this test: (1) Hague was a member of the Minnesota workforce at the time of this death; (2) the insurer, Allstate Insurance, was present and doing business in Minnesota; and (3) Hague's widow had become a resident of Minnesota prior to, and for reasons unrelated to, the litigation. Justice Stevens concurred in the result.

In Phillips Petroleum Co. v. Shutts, 472 U.S. 797, 105 S.Ct. 2965, 86 L.Ed.2d 628 (1985), a class action was brought in Kansas state court by landowners in eleven states who had leased natural gas rights to Phillips. As finally certified, the class had 28,100 lessors, of whom fewer than 1,000 lived in Kansas. About one quarter of one percent of the leases were on land in Kansas. The Court held that the class had been properly certified, even though the great bulk of the plaintiff class members neither lived in Kansas nor owned land in Kansas. *In personam* jurisdiction over Phillips was not contested. The choice-of-law issue in the case was whether (and in what amount) Phillips owed interest on royalty payments that had been suspended while requested increases in gas prices were pending with the Federal Power Commission. While the requests were pending, Phillips had charged the higher price that it had requested. The requested increases were granted with retroactive effect, so Phillips was able to keep the money it had been charging. Phillips refused to pay interest on the marginal increase in royalties it owed based on the higher prices it had already charged and received. The plaintiffs chose to sue in Kansas rather than Texas or Oklahoma, where the great bulk of the leases were located, because statutory interest rates under Kansas law were significantly higher than under either Texas or Oklahoma law. The Kansas Supreme Court applied Kansas law, including the Kansas statutory rate of interest, to all of the leases in the class.

The United States Supreme Court reversed and remanded. Applying both the Full Faith and Credit Clause and the Due Process Clause, the Court quoted the test articulated in the plurality opinion in *Hague*. 472 U.S. at 821–22. It held that while Kansas law could be permissibly applied to at least some of the leases, Kansas law could not be applied to all of them. The Court wrote, "Given Kansas' lack of 'interest' in claims unrelated to that State, and the substantive conflict with jurisdictions such as Texas, we conclude that application of Kansas law to every claim in the case is sufficiently arbitrary and unfair as to exceed constitutional limits." Id. at 822. The Court remanded to the Kansas court so permit it to apply the *Hague* test in the first instance to determine "which law must apply to the various transactions involved in this lawsuit." Id. at 823. On remand, the Kansas Supreme Court wrote an opinion reinstating its prior judgment, applying Kansas law to all of the leases. Shutts v. Phillips Petroleum Co., 240 Kan. 764, 732 P.2d 1286 (1987). Perhaps surprisingly, the United States Supreme Court denied certiorari. 487 U.S. 1223, 108 S.Ct. 2883, 101 L.Ed.2d 918 (1988).

A plaintiff's choice of forum is sometimes influenced by considerations beyond convenience and possible bias of the forum. As may be seen in these cases, a plaintiff will sometimes choose a forum because it will apply a particularly favorable law unavailable in other forums. As may also be seen, state courts have a tendency to apply their own substantive law.

When applied to final judgments of a court of another state, the Full Faith and Credit Clause has great force: A judgment of the court of one state must be enforced in the court of another state unless there was no jurisdiction in the rendering court. But when applied to a choice of law question in a case under adjudication, the Court employs both the Full Faith and Credit Clause and the Due Process Clause. As seen in *Phillips Petroleum*, in that circumstance the Full Faith and Credit Clause has only the same force as the Due Process Clause. In this context, the Full Faith and Credit Clause (and the Due Process Clause) have limited force.

The constitutional test for *in personam* jurisdiction is whether there are "minimum contacts * * * such that the maintenance of the suit does not offend 'traditional notions of fair play and substantial justice.'" *International Shoe*, supra p. 64. The constitutional test for choice of law is whether there is "a significant contact, or significant aggregation of contacts, creating state interests, such that choice of its law is neither arbitrary nor fundamentally unfair." *Hague*, 449 U.S. 312–13; *Shutts*, 472 U.S. at 821–22. The two tests overlap, but they are not identical. There can be insufficient contacts for *in personam* jurisdiction, yet sufficient contacts to justify applying the substantive law of the state. For example, the Court in *Shaffer v. Heitner* held that there was no *in personam* jurisdiction over the defendants, but had little doubt that Delaware law could be applied to the dispute. 433 U.S. at 215. Conversely, there can be sufficient contacts for *in personam* jurisdiction but insufficient contacts to justify applying the law of the forum. For example, in *Shutts* the Court upheld *in personam* jurisdiction but held that Kansas law could not be applied to all of the transactions at issue in the suit.

The consequence of *Hague*, and many lower court cases like it, is that one law will be applied if suit is brought in one state, and another law if the same suit is brought in another state. Is this a sensible way for our federal system to operate? Should the Constitution be read to prevent the system from operating in this way?

NOTE ON NON-CONSTITUTIONAL CHOICE OF LAW RULES

As we have just seen, the Supreme Court has read the Constitution to impose relatively few constraints on the states' ability to apply their own law to suits brought in their courts. Within very broad limits, a state is free to employ its own choice-of-law rules to determine when it will follow its own substantive law or the substantive law of another state. It is beyond the scope of a Civil Procedure course to study in detail the range of choice-of-law systems employed by the states. This is the subject of a separate course on Conflict of Laws. But a short review here will give some sense of the problems that choice of law addresses and of the range of solutions adopted by the states. We consider here only cases where the choice is between the laws of different states. (Cases where the choice is between federal and state law involve different considerations. Some of those will be covered during the discussion of *Erie Railroad Co. v. Tompkins* and related cases, infra p. 335).

Choice-of-law questions arise when cases involve actions in, or relationships with, more than one state. Several examples suggest the range of such cases:

(a) A state has a "guest statute" providing that a "guest" in a motor vehicle (i.e., a non-paying passenger) who is injured in an accident may recover from the driver only upon a showing of gross negligence. An adjoining state may have no guest statute, and permit recovery against the driver on a showing of ordinary negligence. Residents of the guest-statute state drive into the adjoining state, where they are involved in an accident caused by the driver's negligence. Which state's law should be applied? Modern cases typically apply the statute of the state in which the parties reside rather than of the state in which the accident occurs. See, e.g., Mellk v. Sarahson, 49 N.J. 226, 229 A.2d 625 (1967); Babcock v. Jackson, 12 N.Y.2d 473, 240 N.Y.S.2d 743, 191 N.E.2d 279 (1963). But the situation becomes much more complex when the facts are varied. For example, one party may reside in one state and the other party in another; the parties may be citizens of one state but actually live in another; the parties may both be residents of one state, but the trip may begin and end in another; etc. Modern cases are not uniform in their decisions of these variant cases.

(b) A state forbids suits to enforce payment of amounts due under a construction contract if the plaintiff is not a licensed contractor. An adjoining state permits such suits. An unlicensed contractor signs a contract in the state permitting suit, agreeing to build a house in the state denying the right to sue. The contractor later sues to enforce payment. Which state's law should be applied? In Wood Bros. Homes, Inc. v. Walker Adjustment Bureau, 198 Colo. 444, 601 P.2d 1369 (1979), the court applied the law of the state in which the contract was to be performed, denying the right to recover payment.

(c) A state has a "dram shop act," under which a person who serves alcohol to an obviously intoxicated person is liable for injuries subsequently caused by that person. A neighboring state has no such act. An obviously intoxicated person is served alcohol in the dram-shop-act state, and that person then drives into the neighboring state and causes an accident. The person injured sues the person who served alcohol in violation of the dram shop act. Which state's law should be applied? In Schmidt v. Driscoll Hotel, 249 Minn. 376, 82 N.W.2d 365 (1957), the court applied the law of the state in which the alcohol was served. In an interesting variation, an obviously intoxicated California citizen was served alcohol in a Nevada casino. The California citizen then tried to drive home and caused an accident in California. California had a dram shop act; Nevada did not. The California Supreme Court applied the California dram shop act to the Nevada casino, emphasizing the casino's advertising in California and its knowledge that many of its customers were Californians. Bernhard v. Harrah's Club, 16 Cal.3d 313, 128 Cal.Rptr. 215, 546 P.2d 719 (1976), cert. den. 429 U.S. 859 (1976).

In the nineteenth century, choice of law questions were generally resolved by a system of "comity" under which the forum state applied the law of another state, according to generally accepted principles, as a matter of good will and harmonious interstate relations. For example, the law of the state in which a tort occurred would be followed, even if suit was brought in a different state. Further, the law of the state in which a contract was entered into would govern the validity of the contract; and the law of the state in which a contract was to be performed would govern the duties prescribed under the contract. The most important single source of nineteenth century choice of law rules was a treatise by Supreme Court Justice Joseph Story. J. Story, Commentaries on the Conflict of Laws (1834).

In the twentieth century, the comity-based system of Story was refined (many would say distorted) and incorporated into the first Restatement of the Law of Conflict of Laws (1934), for which the Reporter was Professor Joseph Beale. What had been a somewhat flexible and ultimately voluntary system under Story became, under the First Restatement, a rigid system based on a theory of obligation of the states to enforce the "vested rights" of parties under the Restatement's choice of law rules. In part because of the rigidity of Beale's system, in part because of the growing twentieth-century insistence on realistic assessments of policy considerations underlying doctrinal rules, and in part because of an enormous increase in the number and complexity of interstate transactions, the First Restatement came under heavy attack.

The most important attacker was Professor Brainerd Currie, who developed a complete system of "interest analysis," under which he sought to analyze the interests of the various states in the application of their law to the transaction in dispute. B. Currie, Selected Essays on the Conflict of Laws (1963). For example, Currie argued that in some cases only one state had a strong interest in the application of its rules. Such a case would be presented if two residents of a non-guest statute state drove into a guest-statute state and had an accident there. Currie argued that the state in which the accident occurred had little interest in the application of its guest statute, and that the state in which the parties lived had a strong interest in the application of their law. Currie characterized such a case as involving a "false conflict," and refused to follow the traditional rule that would have applied the law of the state in which the accident occurred.

Prompted by the many criticisms of the First Restatement, the American Law Institute published Restatement (Second) Conflict of Laws in 1971, after almost twenty years of discussion and debate. The Second Restatement is unabashedly policy-based and rule-eschewing, so much so that its formulations often make it difficult to predict how a court applying the Second Restatement will decide any particular case. Many academics have criticized the Second Restatement, on almost as many grounds as there are critics. Probably the most vigorous critic was Professor Albert Ehrenzweig. A. Ehrenzweig, A Treatise on the Conflict of Laws (1962). When Professor Ehrenzweig published his treatise, the Second Restatement was in draft, still nine years from ultimate publication. Numerous other academics have proposed their own systems that deviate in significant respects from the approach of the Second Restatement. See, e.g., Professor Robert Leflar's "choice-influencing considerations"; R. Leflar, American Conflicts Law (1968). (The Minnesota court in *Allstate Insurance Co. v. Hague* purported to follow Professor Leflar when it applied Minnesota law.)

The result in the courts has been something close to chaos. Professor Herma Hill Kay surveyed the fifty states and the District of Columbia in 1983 and found that twenty-two followed a traditional, First Restatement-type approach; fourteen followed the Second Restatement; six followed some kind of a combined approach; three followed Professor Leflar's choice-influencing considerations; two followed Professor Currie's interest analysis; and two other groups (of two states each) followed still other approaches. Kay, Theory into Practice: Choice of Law in the Courts, 34 Mercer L.Rev. 521, 591–592 (1983). Moreover, merely to list the groups of states that follow different approaches is to understate the problem, for many of the approaches are highly indeterminate in their application and yield a wide range of results in comparable cases. In 2014, the American Law Institute announced plans to draft a Restatement (Third) of Conflict of Laws.

Further elaboration of choice of law rules in the various states will take us too far afield from Civil Procedure and into the province of Conflict of Laws. But it is apparent that a creative lawyer, with a good knowledge of the various choice-of-law approaches followed in the relevant states, will sometimes have an opportunity through an astute choice of forum to obtain a substantive rule of law that will make a material difference to the outcome of her case.

B. SUBJECT MATTER JURISDICTION

PRELIMINARY NOTE ON SUBJECT MATTER JURISDICTION

A court must have both territorial jurisdiction and subject matter jurisdiction before it can adjudicate a case. Although they share the word "jurisdiction," territorial and subject matter jurisdiction are fundamentally distinct concepts.

Territorial jurisdiction is the geographically based authority of a court to require a person, corporation or other association, or thing to submit to binding adjudication. As seen in the previous section, the United States Constitution imposes due process limitations on the power of state and federal courts to assert territorial jurisdiction. In addition, state and federal statutes often impose further restrictions, preventing the court from asserting the full extent of territorial jurisdiction that would be available if the statute were drafted more broadly. Want of territorial jurisdiction is a waivable defect. A defendant may deliberately (or inadvertently) fail to make a timely objection to want of territorial jurisdiction, and thereby subject herself to the adjudicatory authority of the court. A defendant may also consent to territorial jurisdiction, with the same consequence as a failure to make a timely objection.

Subject matter jurisdiction is the authority of a court to adjudicate a particular type of suit. Questions of subject matter jurisdiction arise in both state and federal courts. All states have a court of general jurisdiction, often called the Superior Court, which is capable of hearing any dispute brought before it, limited only by specifically described exceptions. In addition, many states have courts of limited jurisdiction which only hear cases concerning particular subject matters, such as divorce and child custody disputes, probate matters, or disputes where the claim is below a certain amount. The nature of these courts varies significantly from state to state. Federal courts, by contrast to the state courts of general jurisdiction, are all courts of limited jurisdiction, capable of hearing only those disputes for which jurisdiction is specifically conferred by both the Constitution and federal statute. Federal courts have subject matter jurisdiction either because of the nature of the law involved, or because of the identity of the parties. An example of the first is "federal question" jurisdiction under 28 U.S.C. § 1331, in which plaintiff asserts a claim arising under federal law. An example of the second is "diversity" jurisdiction under 28 U.S.C. § 1332, in which plaintiff and defendant are citizens of diverse states, say California and New York. Unlike a want of territorial jurisdiction, a want of subject matter jurisdiction cannot be cured by waiver or consent of the parties. Even if both plaintiff and defendant agree that they wish a state probate court to hear an ordinary contract dispute, or a federal court to hear a dispute based on state law between two citizens of the same state, the state and federal courts do not have subject matter jurisdiction and hence cannot hear the dispute.

1. State trial courts. Although there is variation from state to state, a description of the subject matter jurisdiction of the courts of California usefully conveys the nature of subject matter jurisdiction in state courts. The trial court of general jurisdiction in California is the Superior Court. Its jurisdiction is unlimited except where jurisdiction is specifically granted to other state tribunals. Unlike some state courts, the California Superior Court has jurisdiction over divorce and child custody disputes and probate matters. Calif.Civ.C. §§ 4351, 7007; Calif.C.Civ.P. § 1740 (domestic relations); Calif.Prob.C. §§ 301, 2200 (probate). There are "departments" within the Superior Court for specialized subject matters, including not only domestic relations and probate, but also delinquent and neglected minors, adoptions, and protection of incompetent persons.

State administrative agencies have subject matter jurisdiction over certain matters. Their trial jurisdiction is exclusive of the state courts, although there is generally appellate jurisdiction in the state court over decisions by an administrative agency.

2. Federal trial courts. The basic trial court in the federal system is the district court. Its jurisdiction is limited rather than general, and is dependent on both constitutional and statutory authorization.

Article III of the Constitution, the "judicial" article, sets out a series of heads of subject matter jurisdiction for the federal courts, including "federal question," admiralty, diversity of citizenship, United-States-as-a-party, and other less important heads. Article III is constructed on a principle comparable to Article I, the legislative article. Article I does not grant Congress a general legislative power. Rather, it grants Congress (and thereby the federal government) a number of specific legislative powers, such as the power to regulate interstate commerce, the power to tax, and the power to coin money. Legislation by the federal government is constitutional only if it is based on one of these enumerated heads of Article I power. Similarly, Article III does not grant general jurisdiction. Rather, it grants only the specified heads of jurisdiction, and the federal courts can only exercise the jurisdiction specified. Over the course of two centuries, the enumerated powers of the legislature under Article I have been construed fairly expansively, particularly the commerce power. See, e.g., Heart of Atlanta Motel v. United States, 379 U.S. 241, 85 S.Ct. 348, 13 L.Ed.2d 258 (1964) (Civil Rights Act of 1964, forbidding racial discrimination in public accommodations, is a valid exercise of the commerce power); but compare National Federation of Independent Business v. Sebelius, 567 U.S. ___, 132 S.Ct. 2566, 183 L.Ed.2d 450 (2012) (Patient Protection and Affordable Care Act of 2010, requiring individuals to purchase health care insurance, is not a valid exercise of the commerce power, but monetary assessment for failure to purchase such insurance is a valid exercise of the taxing power); United States v. Lopez, 514 U.S. 549, 115 S.Ct. 1624, 131 L.Ed.2d 626 (1995) (Gun-Free School Zones Act of 1990, forbidding the knowing possession of a firearm in a school zone, is not a valid exercise of the commerce power, at least in the absence of a requirement that the firearm have previously traveled in interstate commerce). By contrast, most of the heads of the jurisdiction under Article III have been construed fairly strictly.

In addition to constitutional authorization for the exercise of federal court jurisdiction, there must also be statutory implementation of that authorization. When the Constitution was drafted, those who were suspicious of an expanded federal government viewed with alarm the prospect of a large federal judiciary. Under a compromise suggested by James Madison, actual implementation of jurisdiction for the lower federal courts was left to Congress. In this fashion, control over the structure and jurisdiction of the federal courts was subject to the political control of the states' representatives in Congress, which made Article III much less objectionable to states' rights advocates during the constitutional ratifying debates. Congressional authority to constitute the federal courts and to define their jurisdiction was exercised by the First Congress in the Judiciary Act of 1789.

A number of statutory grants implement Article III. For example, "federal question" jurisdiction is implemented by 28 U.S.C. § 1331, "diversity" jurisdiction by 28 U.S.C. § 1332, and admiralty jurisdiction by 28 U.S.C. § 1333. In almost all instances, the statutory grant of jurisdiction does not go to the full extent of the jurisdiction authorized by the Constitution. Given that both constitutional authorization and statutory implementation are required before the district court has jurisdiction, the narrower scope of the statutory grant controls. There is an interesting historical debate about the extent of Congress' obligation to confer jurisdiction on the federal courts. Three pertinent articles are Amar, A Neo-Federalist View of Article III: Separating the Two Tiers of Federal Jurisdiction, 65 B.U.L.Rev. 205 (1985); Meltzer, The History and Structure of Article III, 138 U.Pa.L.Rev. 1569 (1990); Fletcher, Congressional Power over the Jurisdiction of Federal Courts: The Meaning of the Word "All" in Article III, 59 Duke L.J. 929 (2010).

Federal magistrate courts assist and supplement the district courts in cases over which the district court already has jurisdiction. 28 U.S.C. § 636. A magistrate judge may act as a special master in certain cases, and may hear many pretrial motions (including for discovery), without the consent of the parties. If the parties consent, a magistrate judge may hear all pretrial motions and may try both jury and non-jury civil cases. The constitutionality of the exercise of authority by magistrate judges is not clear in all instances. See C. Seron, The Roles of Magistrates in Federal District Courts (1983) (describing the roles of magistrates); Note, Article III Limits on Article I Courts: The Constitutionality of the Bankruptcy Court and the 1979 Magistrate Act, 80 Colum.L.Rev. 560 (1980) (arguing that the Magistrate Act is unconstitutional); E. Chemerinsky, Federal Jurisdiction § 4.5.2 (5th ed.2007) (describing the constitutional debate).

3.   Concurrent and exclusive jurisdiction. State and federal trial courts have concurrent subject matter jurisdiction in a large number of cases. In such cases, because both courts have subject matter jurisdiction, the litigants have some choice about where to adjudicate their dispute. The plaintiff gets to choose where to file the suit and often has the final say about where the suit is to be tried, but in some circumstances the defendant may remove to federal court a case originally filed in state court. 28 U.S.C. § 1441.

State trial courts have concurrent jurisdiction with the federal courts over most cases involving federal law. The general rule is that state courts have concurrent jurisdiction over all cases based on federal law, unless Congress has explicitly provided for exclusive jurisdiction. Claflin v. Houseman, 93 U.S. (3 Otto) 130, 23 L.Ed. 833 (1876). The only exception is federal anti-trust suits, for which there is exclusive jurisdiction even though the statute is silent. See 15 U.S.C. §§ 15, 26; Freeman v. Bee Machine Co., 319 U.S. 448, 63 S.Ct. 1146, 87 L.Ed. 1509 (1943). In all other cases of exclusive jurisdiction, an explicit federal statute so provides. See, e.g., admiralty cases (28 U.S.C. § 1333); bankruptcy proceedings (28 U.S.C. § 1334); patent and copyright cases (28 U.S.C. § 1338); and some cases under the Securities Exchange Act of 1934 (15 U.S.C. § 78aa). Except for claims that are within the exclusive jurisdiction of the federal courts, a state court has a constitutional obligation to adjudicate federal claims and defenses otherwise within their jurisdiction. See Testa v. Katt, 330 U.S. 386, 67 S.Ct. 810, 91 L.Ed. 967 (1947).

Similarly, federal district courts have concurrent jurisdiction with the state courts over many cases involving state law. So long as there is a basis for federal subject matter jurisdiction, a federal court may hear the case, even if it involves state law. Usually, jurisdiction in such a case is based on diversity of citizenship, but sometimes a federal question case involves a claim or defense based on state law. Although it is normally not phrased in this way, state courts have exclusive jurisdiction in cases where there is no federal grant of subject matter jurisdiction to the federal courts. Such cases are typically those based solely on state law in which there is no diversity of citizenship between the parties.

Problems of subject matter jurisdiction in the state courts are usually easy to deal with. They rarely cause serious difficulty to judges or practitioners trying to decide which state court or courts can hear a particular dispute. By contrast, problems of subject matter jurisdiction in the federal courts can be difficult, sometimes fiendishly so. Problems of federal court subject matter jurisdiction are explored in the materials that follow.

1. FEDERAL QUESTION JURISDICTION

Louisville & Nashville RR. Co. v. Mottley

Supreme Court of the United States, 1908.
211 U.S. 149, 29 S.Ct. 42, 53 L.Ed. 126.

* * *

The appellees (husband and wife), being residents and citizens of Kentucky, brought this suit in equity in the circuit court of the United States for the western district of Kentucky against the appellant, a railroad company and a citizen of the same state. The object of the suit was to compel the specific performance of [a] contract.

* * *

The bill alleged that in September, 1871, plaintiffs, while passengers upon the defendant railroad, were injured by the defendant's negligence, and released their respective claims for damages in consideration of the agreement for transportation during their lives, expressed in the contract. It is alleged that the contract was performed by the defendant up to January 1, 1907, when the defendant declined to renew the passes. The bill then alleges that the refusal to comply with the contract was based solely upon that part of the act of Congress of June 29, 1906 (34 Stat. at L. 584, chap. 3591, U.S.Comp.Stat.Supp.1907, p. 892), which forbids the giving of free passes or free transportation. The bill further alleges: First, that the act of Congress referred to does not prohibit the giving of passes under the circumstances of this case; and, second, that, if the law is to be construed as prohibiting such passes, it is in conflict with the 5th Amendment of the Constitution, because it deprives the plaintiffs of their property without due process of law. The defendant demurred to the bill. The judge of the circuit court overruled the demurrer, entered a decree for the relief prayed for, and the defendant appealed directly to this court.

* * *

■ MR. JUSTICE MOODY, after making the foregoing statement, delivered the opinion of the court:

Two questions of law were raised by the demurrer to the bill, were brought here by appeal, and have been argued before us. They are, first, whether that part of the act of Congress of June 29, 1906 * * * which forbids the giving of free passes or the collection of any different compensation for transportation of passengers than that specified in the tariff filed, makes it unlawful to perform a contract for transportation of persons who, in good faith, before the passage of the act, had accepted such contract in satisfaction of a valid cause of action against the railroad; and, second, whether the statute, if it should be construed to render such a contract unlawful, is in violation of the 5th Amendment of the Constitution of the United States. We do not deem it necessary, however, to consider either of these questions, because, in our opinion, the court below was without jurisdiction of the cause. Neither party has questioned that jurisdiction, but it is the duty of this court to see to it that the jurisdiction of the circuit court, which is defined and limited by statute, is not exceeded. This duty we have frequently performed of our own motion. Mansfield, C. & L.M.R. Co. v. Swan, 111 U.S. 379, 382, 28 L.Ed. 462, 463, 4 Sup.Ct.Rep. 510.

There was no diversity of citizenship, and it is not and cannot be suggested that there was any ground of jurisdiction, except that the case was a "suit . . . arising under the Constitution or laws of the United States." 25 Stat. at L. 434, chap. 866, U.S.Comp.Stat.1901, p. 509. It is the settled interpretation of these words, as used in this statute, conferring jurisdiction, that a suit arises under the Constitution and laws of the United States only when the plaintiff's statement of his own cause of action shows that it is based upon those laws or that Constitution. It is not enough that the plaintiff alleges some anticipated defense to his cause of action, and asserts that the defense is invalidated by some provision of the Constitution of the United States. Although such allegations show that very likely, in the course of the litigation, a question under the Constitution would arise, they do not show that the suit, that is, the plaintiff's original cause of action, arises under the Constitution. In Tennessee v. Union & Planters' Bank, 152 U.S. 454, 38 L.Ed. 511, 14 Sup.Ct.Rep. 654, the plaintiff, the state of Tennessee, brought suit in the circuit court of the United States to recover from the defendant certain taxes alleged to be due under the laws of the state. The plaintiff alleged that the defendant claimed an immunity from the taxation by virtue of its charter, and that therefore the tax was void, because in violation of the provision of the Constitution of the United States, which forbids any state from passing a law impairing the obligation of contracts. The cause was held to be beyond the jurisdiction of the circuit court, the court saying, by Mr. Justice Gray (p. 464): "A suggestion of one party, that the other will or may set up a claim under the Constitution or laws of the United States, does not make the suit one arising under that Constitution or those laws." * * * *precedent*

* * *

.The interpretation of the act which we have stated was first announced [in 1888] in Metcalf v. Watertown, 128 U.S. 586, 32 L.Ed. 543, 9 Sup.Ct.Rep. 173, and has since been repeated and applied in Colorado Cent. Consol. Min. Co. v. Turck, 150 U.S. 138, 142, 37 L.Ed. 1030, 1031, 14 Sup.Ct.Rep. 35; Tennessee v. Union & Planters' Bank, 152 U.S. 454, 459, 38 L.Ed. 511, 513, 14 Sup.Ct.Rep. 654; Chappell v. Waterworth, 155 U.S. 102, 107, 39 L.Ed. 85, 87, 15 Sup.Ct.Rep. 34; Postal Teleg. Cable Co. v. United States (Postal Teleg. Cable Co. v. Alabama), 155 U.S. 482, 487, 39 L.Ed. 231, 232, 15 Sup.Ct.Rep. 192; Oregon Short Line & U.N.R. Co. v. Skottowe, 162 U.S. 490, 494, 40 L.Ed. 1048, 1049, 16 Sup.Ct.Rep. 869; Walker v. Collins, 167 U.S. 57, 59, 42 L.Ed. 76, 77, 17 Sup.Ct.Rep. 738; Muse v. Arlington Hotel Co., 168 U.S. 430, 436, 42 L.Ed. 531, 533, 18 Sup.Ct.Rep. 109; Galveston, H. & S.A.R. Co. v. Texas, 170 U.S. 226, 236, 42 L.Ed. 1017, 1020, 18 Sup.Ct.Rep. 603; Third Street & Suburban R. Co. v. Lewis, 173 U.S. 457, 460, 43 L.Ed. 766, 767, 19 Sup.Ct.Rep. 451; Florida C. & P.R. Co. v. Bell, 176 U.S. 321, 327, 44 L.Ed. 486, 489, 20 Sup.Ct.Rep. 399; Houston & T.C.R. Co. v. Texas, 177 U.S. 66, 78, 44 L.Ed. 673, 680, 20 Sup.Ct.Rep. 545; Arkansas v. Kansas & T. Coal Co., 183 U.S. 185, 188, 46 L.Ed. 144, 146, 22 Sup.Ct.Rep. 47; Vicksburg Waterworks Co. v. Vicksburg, 185 U.S. 65, 68, 46 L.Ed. 808, 809, 22 Sup.Ct.Rep. 585; Boston & M. Consol. Copper & S. Min. Co. v. Montana Ore Purchasing Co., 188 U.S. 632, 639, 47 L.Ed. 626, 631, 23 Sup.Ct.Rep. 434; Minnesota v. Northern Securities Co., 194 U.S. 48, 63, 48 L.Ed. 870, 877, 24 Sup.Ct.Rep. 598; Joy v. St. Louis, 201 U.S. 332, 340, 50 L.Ed. 776, 780, 26 Sup.Ct.Rep. 478; Devine v. Los Angeles, 202 U.S. 313, 334, 50 L.Ed. 1046, 1053, 26 Sup.Ct.Rep. 652. The application of this rule to the case at bar is decisive against the jurisdiction of the circuit court.

It is ordered that the judgment be reversed and the case remitted to the circuit court with instructions to dismiss the suit for want of jurisdiction.

NOTE ON THE CONSTITUTIONAL SCOPE OF FEDERAL QUESTION JURISDICTION AND THE WELL-PLEADED COMPLAINT RULE

Article III of the Constitution confers jurisdiction on the federal courts in "all Cases, in Law and Equity, arising under this Constitution, the Laws of the United States, and Treaties made, or which shall be made, under their authority." U.S.Const., Art.III, Sec.2, para.1. The first Judiciary Act, adopted by the first Congress in 1789, authorized jurisdiction under several of the heads of jurisdiction of Article III, but failed to authorize general federal question jurisdiction. A general federal question jurisdiction statute was passed in 1801 by the outgoing Federalists in the waning days of the first Adams administration, but the incoming Jeffersonians repealed the statute in 1802. It was not until after the Civil War, in 1875, that a general federal question jurisdiction statute was again enacted. The present form of the statute is 28 U.S.C. § 1331, little changed from the form in which it was enacted in 1875. The present statute provides, in words that echo the constitutional authorization, "The district courts shall have original jurisdiction of all civil actions arising under the Constitution, laws, or treaties of the United States." Although the "arising under" words of the constitutional and statutory provisions are identical, they mean quite different things.

1.   **Constitutional scope of federal question jurisdiction.** The constitutional scope of federal question jurisdiction is exceedingly broad. In *Osborn v. Bank of the United States*, 22 U.S. (9 Wheat.) 738, 6 L.Ed. 204 (1824), the Bank of the United States was authorized by statute to sue and be sued in federal court, even in cases where the cause of action did not depend on federal law, and indeed where no question of federal law was actually at issue in the dispute. Chief Justice John Marshall wrote for the Court that it was enough that the Bank was created under a federal charter and that a question of federal law *might* arise in a suit brought by or against the Bank. *Osborn* has been criticized as going to, or perhaps beyond, the outer boundaries of federal question jurisdiction. See, e.g., Textile Workers Union v. Lincoln Mills, 353 U.S. 448, 481, 77 S.Ct. 912, 1 L.Ed.2d 972 (1957) (Frankfurter, J., dissenting) ("*Osborn* * * * appears to have been based on premises that today * * * are subject to criticism"). But the Supreme Court reaffirmed *Osborn* in American National Red Cross v. S.G. and A.E., 505 U.S. 247, 112 S.Ct. 2465, 120 L.Ed.2d 201 (1992). The American Red Cross, like the Bank of the United States in *Osborn*, is a federally chartered corporation authorized by statute to sue and be sued in federal court, even in cases where no question of federal law is at issue. The Court in *American Red Cross* cited the "long standing and settled rule" of *Osborn*, 505 U.S. at 265, and held that the mere fact of federal incorporation was a sufficient constitutional basis for federal question jurisdiction. Note that in neither *Osborn* nor *American Red Cross* was jurisdiction based on the general federal question jurisdiction statute, 28 U.S.C. § 1331. In each case, special statutes conferred jurisdiction over suits to which the Bank and the Red Cross were parties.

Another example of a far-reaching federal question jurisdiction is bankruptcy proceedings. Under the federal bankruptcy act, a trustee in bankruptcy may sue in federal court—either bankruptcy court or district court—to marshal the assets of the bankrupt, as a prelude to eventual distribution of those assets among the bankrupt's creditors. (The division of responsibility between the bankruptcy court and the district court is a complicated subject, with significant constitutional difficulties of its own, but that question is beyond the scope of this note.) Such a claim often involves a tort or a contract between the bankrupt estate and another party, in which no question of federal law is involved. Yet it is clearly established that such cases fall within the boundaries of constitutionally permissible federal question jurisdiction. For example, in Northern Pipeline Construction Co. v. Marathon Pipe Line Co., 458 U.S. 50, 102 S.Ct. 2858, 73 L.Ed.2d 598 (1982), the Court assumed without discussion that federal district courts can have jurisdiction over state-law contract suits between non-diverse parties brought as part of bankruptcy proceedings.

Rationales for these expansive interpretations of federal question jurisdiction are somewhat elusive. The most obvious rationale to sustain

Osborn and, to a lesser extent, *American National Red Cross* is that both the Bank and the Red Cross were federally chartered corporations that served federal purposes and that deserved the protection of adjudication in sympathetic federal courts. For many years, some academics have argued for a broader theory of "protective jurisdiction" that would go beyond federally chartered corporations. Professor Herbert Wechsler argued that federal courts should be able to exercise "protective jurisdiction" over all cases in which Congress has constitutional authority to enact a substantive rule to govern disposition of the controversy, even if Congress has not in fact enacted such a rule. This would allow Congress to pass a jurisdictional statute asserting federal jurisdiction over many litigants and areas of the law in which the federal government has a political interest, but without requiring Congress to replace the existing substantive state law with federal law. Wechsler, Federal Jurisdiction and the Revision of the Judicial Code, 13 Law & Contemp. Probs. 216 (1948). Professor Paul Mishkin suggested a limited version of Professor Wechsler's position, arguing for "protective jurisdiction" over cases based on substantive state law only when there is already "an articulated and active federal policy regulating a field." Mishkin, The Federal "Question" in the District Courts, 53 Colum.L.Rev. 157, 192 (1953). The Supreme Court, however, has steadfastly refused to decide whether "protective jurisdiction" can serve as a basis for federal question jurisdiction. See, e.g., Verlinden B.V. v. Central Bank of Nigeria, 461 U.S. 480, 491 n. 17, 103 S.Ct. 1962, 76 L.Ed.2d 81 (1983) ("[W]e need not consider [whether] the Act is constitutional as an aspect of so-called 'protective jurisdiction.' ").

2.   Original federal question jurisdiction and the "well pleaded complaint" rule. As seen in *Mottley*, the general federal question jurisdiction statute, 28 U.S.C. § 1331, is construed far more narrowly than the constitutional provision from which it derives. Plaintiff may not anticipate a federal defense by the defendant in her complaint and use that defense as a basis for federal jurisdiction. To the uninitiated, the well-pleaded complaint rule could be seen as a product of the words of 28 U.S.C. § 1331: The case must "arise under" federal law, meaning that the plaintiff's cause of action depends on—"arises under"—federal law. But this is too simple a reading of these words, for it is clear from cases like *Osborn* that the same words mean something much broader in Article III.

The general contours of the problem are obvious enough. Section 1331 sorts cases between federal and state courts for adjudication at trial, and is based on a rough principle that questions of federal law should be decided in a federal district court if one of the parties invokes the court's jurisdiction. But federal and state substantive law overlap and intertwine in many areas, and many disputes involve questions of both federal and state law. Therefore, a principle of federal right/federal forum is impossible to implement fully without drawing huge numbers of cases into district court, many of which will substantially depend for their resolution on questions of state law.

The problem thus is to devise a rule that will divide the cases of mixed state and federal law in a reasonable manner between the federal and state courts. The characteristics of an ideal rule would be: (1) It should send cases in which federal law predominates to federal court, and cases in which state law predominates to state court. (2) It should operate smoothly and predictably, so that parties do not spend time and energy litigating the jurisdictional question, and do not bring the case in the wrong forum only to learn, after the statute of limitations has run, that they are in the wrong place. (3) It should operate early in the litigation, so that parties can prepare their cases knowing where they will litigate.

How well does the well-pleaded complaint rule satisfy these criteria? In cases in which plaintiff relies on federal law as the basis for her cause of action, it works fairly well. In such a case, criterion (1), above, is usually satisfied because federal law is likely to form an important part of the case. Criterion (2) is satisfied because of the obvious presence of federal law as the basis for the cause of action. Criterion (3) is satisfied because the parties know as soon as the complaint is filed that federal jurisdiction is present. But what about cases in which the well-pleaded complaint rule works badly? For example, what about a case in which a defendant pleads a federal defense that proves dispositive? In other words, what about *Mottley*?

After the Mottleys were dismissed by the United States Supreme Court on jurisdictional grounds, they filed suit again, this time in Kentucky state court. The Kentucky courts sustained the Mottleys' claim against the railroad's federal defense. The railroad then appealed to the United States Supreme Court, which reversed. Louisville and Nashville RR. Co. v. Mottley, 219 U.S. 467, 31 S.Ct. 265, 55 L.Ed. 297 (1911). The Mottleys thus lost twice in the Supreme Court, the first time on jurisdiction and the second time on the merits.

What or whom should the Mottleys blame? The well-pleaded complaint rule? Perhaps the rule is not ideal from the standpoint of a defendant seeking to assert a federal defense, but the Mottleys were plaintiffs. Recall that they won in the Kentucky state courts when they refiled, so it is clear, at least in retrospect, that they had nothing to fear from state-court adjudication. Their lawyer? At the time their first case was filed in federal court, the well-pleaded complaint rule was firmly established, and dismissal by the Supreme Court was easily predictable. Recall the extraordinarily long string citation at the end of the Court's opinion.

3. Counterclaims and the "well-pleaded complaint" rule. A counterclaim that states a claim under federal law does not "arise" under federal law for purposes of federal trial court jurisdiction. In Holmes Group, Inc. v. Vornado Air Circulation Systems, 535 U.S. 826, 122 S.Ct. 1889, 153 L.Ed.2d 13 (2002), the Supreme Court considered the well-pleaded complaint rule under 28 U.S.C. § 1338, the federal question jurisdictional statute for patent cases. Applying the well-pleaded complaint rule, the Court held that the patent law counterclaim by the defendant did not "arise under" federal patent law within the meaning of § 1338. The Court acknowledged that in its prior cases it had addressed only the question of whether a federal defense, rather than a federal compulsory counterclaim, could establish "arising under" jurisdiction. But it found the well-pleaded complaint rule controlled. Since a counterclaim appears as "as part of the defendant's answer, not as part of the plaintiff's complaint," it cannot serve as the basis for "arising under" jurisdiction. Id. at 831. There is no reason to think that the Court will read § 1331, the general federal question jurisdiction statute, any differently from § 1338.

4. Original and appellate jurisdiction. The well-pleaded complaint rule applies to the original jurisdiction of the district court, but not to the appellate jurisdiction of the United States Supreme Court. The Supreme Court's appellate jurisdiction over cases coming up from the state courts is governed by 28 U.S.C. § 1257, which confers jurisdiction whenever a question of federal law may be dispositive of the case, regardless of which party asserted the right. This is why the Supreme Court took jurisdiction of the Mottleys' case the second time, after it had been decided by the Kentucky state court. Can you see why the appellate jurisdiction statute is written differently from the original jurisdiction statute?

Merrell Dow Pharmaceuticals Inc. v. Thompson

Supreme Court of the United States, 1986.
478 U.S. 804, 106 S.Ct. 3229, 92 L.Ed.2d 650.

■ JUSTICE STEVENS delivered the opinion of the Court.

The question presented is whether the incorporation of a federal standard in a state-law private action, when Congress has intended that there not be a federal private action for violations of that federal standard, makes the action one "arising under the Constitution, laws, or treaties of the United States," 28 U.S.C. § 1331.

I

The Thompson respondents are residents of Canada and the MacTavishes reside in Scotland. They filed virtually identical complaints against petitioner, a corporation, that manufactures and distributes the drug Bendectin. The complaints were filed in the Court of Common Pleas in Hamilton County, Ohio. Each complaint alleged that a child was born with multiple deformities as a result of the mother's ingestion of Bendectin during pregnancy. In five of the six counts, the recovery of substantial damages was requested on common-law theories of negligence, breach of warranty, strict liability, fraud, and gross negligence. In Count IV, respondents alleged that the drug Bendectin was "misbranded" in violation of the Federal Food, Drug, and Cosmetic Act (FDCA) because its labeling did not provide adequate warning that its use was potentially dangerous. Paragraph 26 alleged that the violation of the FDCA "in the promotion" of Bendectin "constitutes a rebuttable presumption of negligence." Paragraph 27 alleged that the "violation of said federal statutes directly and proximately caused the injuries suffered" by the two infants.

Petitioner filed a timely petition for removal from the state court to the Federal District Court alleging that the action was "founded, in part, on an alleged claim arising under the laws of the United States." After removal, the two cases were consolidated. Respondents filed a motion to remand to the state forum on the ground that the federal court lacked subject-matter jurisdiction. Relying on our decision in Smith v. Kansas City Title & Trust Co., 255 U.S. 180, 41 S.Ct. 243, 65 L.Ed. 577 (1921), the District Court held that Count IV of the complaint alleged a cause of action arising under federal law and denied the motion to remand. It then granted petitioner's motion to dismiss on *forum non conveniens* grounds.

The Court of Appeals for the Sixth Circuit reversed. After quoting one sentence from the concluding paragraph in our recent opinion in Franchise Tax Board v. Construction Laborers Vacation Trust, 463 U.S. 1, 103 S.Ct. 2841, 77 L.Ed.2d 420 (1983), and noting "that the FDCA does not create or imply a private right of action for individuals injured as a result of violations of the Act," it explained:

"Federal question jurisdiction would, thus, exist only if plaintiffs' right to relief depended necessarily on a substantial question of federal law. Plaintiffs' causes of action referred to the FDCA merely as one available criterion for determining whether Merrell Dow was negligent. Because the jury could find negligence on the part of Merrell Dow without finding a violation of the FDCA, the plaintiffs' causes of action did not depend necessarily upon a question of federal law. Consequently, the causes of action did not arise under federal law and, therefore, were improperly removed to federal court." 766 F.2d, at 1006.

We granted certiorari, and we now affirm.

II

Article III of the Constitution gives the federal courts power to hear cases "arising under" federal statutes. That grant of power, however, is not self-executing, and it was not until the Judiciary Act of 1875 that Congress gave the federal courts general federal-question jurisdiction. Although the constitutional meaning of "arising under" may extend to all cases in which a federal question is "an ingredient" of the action, Osborn v. Bank of the United States, 9 Wheat. 738, 823, 6 L.Ed. 204 (1824), we have long construed the statutory grant of federal-question jurisdiction as conferring a more limited power.

Under our longstanding interpretation of the current statutory scheme, the question whether a claim "arises under" federal law must be determined by reference to the "well-pleaded complaint." Franchise Tax Board, 463 U.S., at 9–10, 103 S.Ct., at 2846–2847. A defense that raises a federal question is inadequate to confer federal jurisdiction. Louisville & Nashville R. Co. v. Mottley, 211 U.S. 149, 29 S.Ct. 42, 53 L.Ed. 126 (1908). Since a defendant may remove a case only if the claim could have been brought in federal court, 28 U.S.C. § 1441(b), moreover, the question for removal jurisdiction must also be determined by reference to the "well-pleaded complaint."

[T]he propriety of the removal in this case thus turns on whether the case falls within the original "federal question" jurisdiction of the federal courts. There is no "single, precise definition" of that concept; rather, "the phrase 'arising under' masks a welter of issues regarding the interrelation of federal and state authority and the proper management of the federal judicial system." Id., 463 U.S., at 8, 103 S.Ct., at 2846.

This much, however, is clear. The "vast majority" of cases that come within this grant of jurisdiction are covered by Justice Holmes' statement that a " 'suit arises under the law that creates the cause of action.' " Id., at 8–9, 103 S.Ct., at 2846, quoting American Well Works Co. v. Layne & Bowler Co., 241 U.S. 257, 260, 36 S.Ct. 585, 586, 60 L.Ed. 987 (1916). Thus, the vast majority of cases brought under the general federal-question jurisdiction of the federal courts are those in which federal law creates the cause of action.

We have, however, also noted that a case may arise under federal law "where the vindication of a right under state law necessarily turned on some construction of federal law." Franchise Tax Board, 463 U.S., at

9, 103 S.Ct., at 2846.[5] Our actual holding in *Franchise Tax Board* demonstrates that this statement must be read with caution: the central issue presented in that case turned on the meaning of the Employee Retirement Income Security Act of 1974 (1982 ed. and Supp. III), but we nevertheless concluded that federal jurisdiction was lacking.

This case does not pose a federal question of the first kind; respondents do not allege that federal law creates any of the causes of action that they have asserted. This case thus poses what Justice Frankfurter called the "litigation-provoking problem," Textile Workers v. Lincoln Mills, 353 U.S. 448, 470, 77 S.Ct. 912, 928, 1 L.Ed.2d 972 (1957) (dissenting opinion)—the presence of a federal issue in a state-created cause of action.

* * *

In this case, both parties agree with the Court of Appeals' conclusion that there is no federal cause of action for FDCA violations. For purposes of our decision, we assume that this is a correct interpretation of the FDCA. Thus, as the case comes to us, it is appropriate to assume that, under the settled framework for evaluating whether a federal cause of action lies, some combination of the following factors is present: (1) the plaintiffs are not part of the class for whose special benefit the statute was passed; (2) the indicia of legislative intent reveal no congressional purpose to provide a private cause of action; (3) a federal cause of action would not further the underlying purposes of the legislative scheme; and (4) the respondents' cause of action is a subject traditionally relegated to state law.[7] In short, Congress did not intend a private federal remedy for violations of the statute that it enacted.

This is the first case in which we have reviewed this type of jurisdictional claim in light of these factors. That this is so is not surprising. The development of our framework for determining whether a private cause of action exists has proceeded only in the last 11 years, and its inception represented a significant change in our approach to congressional silence on the provision of federal remedies.

---

[5] The case most frequently cited for that proposition is Smith v. Kansas City Title Trust Co., 255 U.S. 180, 41 S.Ct. 243, 65 L.Ed. 577 (1921). In that case the Court upheld federal jurisdiction of a shareholder's bill to enjoin the corporation from purchasing bonds issued by the federal land banks under the authority of the Federal Farm Loan Act on the ground that the federal statute that authorized the issuance of the bonds was unconstitutional. The Court stated:

"The general rule is that where it appears from the bill or statement of the plaintiff that the right to relief depends upon the construction or application of the Constitution or laws of the United States, and that such federal claim is not merely colorable, and rests upon a reasonable foundation, the District Court has jurisdiction under this provision." Id., at 199, 41 S.Ct., at 245.

The effect of this view, expressed over Justice Holmes' vigorous dissent, on his *American Well Works* formulation has been often noted. See, e.g., Franchise Tax Board, 463 U.S., at 9, 103 S.Ct., at 2846 ("[I]t is well settled that Justice Holmes' test is more useful for describing the vast majority of cases that come within the district courts' original jurisdiction than it is for describing which cases are beyond district court jurisdiction"); T.B. Harms Co. v. Eliscu, 339 F.2d 823, 827 (C.A.2 1964) (Friendly, J.) ("It has come to be realized that Mr. Justice Holmes' formula is more useful for inclusion than for the exclusion for which it was intended").

[7] See California v. Sierra Club, 451 U.S. 287, 293, 101 S.Ct. 1775, 1778, 68 L.Ed.2d 101 (1981); Cannon v. University of Chicago, 441 U.S. 677, 689–709, 99 S.Ct. 1946, 1953–1964, 60 L.Ed.2d 560 (1979); Cort v. Ash, 422 U.S. 66, 78, 95 S.Ct. 2080, 2087, 45 L.Ed.2d 26 (1975).

* * *

III

Petitioner advances three arguments to support its position that, even in the face of this congressional preclusion of a federal cause of action for a violation of the federal statute, federal-question jurisdiction may lie for the violation of the federal statute as an element of a state cause of action.

First, petitioner contends that the case represents a straightforward application of the statement in *Franchise Tax Board* that federal-question jurisdiction is appropriate when "it appears that some substantial, disputed question of federal law is a necessary element of one of the well-pleaded state claims." 463 U.S., at 13, 103 S.Ct., at 2848. *Franchise Tax Board,* however, did not purport to disturb the long-settled understanding that the mere presence of a federal issue in a state cause of action does not automatically confer federal-question jurisdiction. * * *

Far from creating some kind of automatic test, *Franchise Tax Board* thus candidly recognized the need for careful judgments about the exercise of federal judicial power in an area of uncertain jurisdiction. Given the significance of the assumed congressional determination to preclude federal private remedies, the presence of the federal issue as an element of the state tort is not the kind of adjudication for which jurisdiction would serve congressional purposes and the federal system. * * *

Second, petitioner contends that there is a powerful federal interest in seeing that the federal statute is given uniform interpretations, and that federal review is the best way of insuring such uniformity. In addition to the significance of the congressional decision to preclude a federal remedy, we do not agree with petitioner's characterization of the federal interest and its implications for federal-question jurisdiction. To the extent that petitioner is arguing that state use and interpretation of the FDCA pose a threat to the order and stability of the FDCA regime, petitioner should be arguing, not that federal courts should be able to review and enforce state FDCA-based causes of action as an aspect of federal-question jurisdiction, but that the FDCA pre-empts state-court jurisdiction over the issue in dispute. Petitioner's concern about the uniformity of interpretation, moreover, is considerably mitigated by the fact that, even if there is no original district court jurisdiction for these kinds of action, this Court retains power to review the decision of a federal issue in a state cause of action.

Finally, petitioner argues that, whatever the general rule, there are special circumstances that justify federal-question jurisdiction in this case. Petitioner emphasizes that it is unclear whether the FDCA applies to sales in Canada and Scotland; there is, therefore, a special reason for having a federal court answer the novel federal question relating to the extraterritorial meaning of the Act. We reject this argument. We do not believe the question whether a particular claim arises under federal law depends on the novelty of the federal issue. * * *

IV

We conclude that a complaint alleging a violation of a federal statute as an element of a state cause of action, when Congress has determined that there should be no private, federal cause of action for the violation, does not state a claim "arising under the Constitution, laws, or treaties of the United States." 28 U.S.C. § 1331.

The judgment of the Court of Appeals is affirmed.

* * *

■ JUSTICE BRENNAN, with whom JUSTICE WHITE, JUSTICE MARSHALL, and JUSTICE BLACKMUN join, dissenting.

* * *

* * * I believe that the limitation on federal jurisdiction recognized by the Court today is inconsistent with the purposes of § 1331. Therefore, I respectfully dissent.

I

While the majority of cases covered by § 1331 may well be described by Justice Holmes' adage that "[a] suit arises under the law that creates the cause of action," American Well Works Co. v. Layne & Bowler Co., 241 U.S. 257, 260, 36 S.Ct. 585, 586, 60 L.Ed. 987 (1916), it is firmly settled that there may be federal-question jurisdiction even though both the right asserted and the remedy sought by the plaintiff are state created. The rule as to such cases was stated in what Judge Friendly described as "[t]he path-breaking opinion" in Smith v. Kansas City Title & Trust Co., 255 U.S. 180, 41 S.Ct. 243, 65 L.Ed. 577 (1921). T.B. Harms Co. v. Eliscu, 339 F.2d 823, 827 (C.A.2 1964). * * * Although the cause of action was wholly state created, the Court held that there was original federal jurisdiction over the case:

> "The general rule is that where it appears from the bill or statement of the plaintiff that the right to relief depends upon the construction or application of the Constitution or laws of the United States, and that such federal claim is not merely colorable, and rests upon a reasonable foundation, the District Court has jurisdiction under [the statute granting federal question jurisdiction]." 255 U.S., at 199, 41 S.Ct., at 245.

The continuing vitality of *Smith* is beyond challenge. We have cited it approvingly on numerous occasions, and reaffirmed its holding several times—most recently just three Terms ago by a unanimous Court in Franchise Tax Board v. Construction Laborers Vacation Trust, supra, 463 U.S., at 9, 103 S.Ct., at 2846. * * * Moreover, in addition to Judge Friendly's authoritative opinion in T.B. Harms Co. v. Eliscu, supra, at 827, Smith has been widely cited and followed in the lower federal courts. Furthermore, the principle of the Smith case has been recognized and endorsed by most commentators as well.

There is, to my mind, no question that there is federal jurisdiction over the respondents' fourth cause of action under the rule set forth in *Smith* and reaffirmed in *Franchise Tax Board*. Respondents pleaded that petitioner's labeling of the drug Bendectin constituted "misbranding" in violation of §§ 201 and 502(f)(2) and (j) of the Federal Food, Drug, and Cosmetic Act (FDCA), and that this violation "directly and proximately caused" their injuries. Respondents asserted in the complaint that this violation established petitioner's negligence per se and entitled them to recover damages without more. * * * As pleaded, then, respondents' "right to relief depend[ed] upon the construction or application of the

Constitution or laws of the United States." * * * Thus, the statutory question is one which "discloses a need for determining the meaning or application of [the FDCA]," T.B. Harms Co. v. Eliscu, 339 F.2d, at 827, and the claim raised by the fourth cause of action is one "arising under" federal law within the meaning of § 1331.

II

The Court apparently does not disagree with any of this—except, of course, for the conclusion. According to the Court, if we assume that Congress did not intend that there be a private federal cause of action under a particular federal law (and, presumably, *a fortiori* if Congress' decision not to create a private remedy is express), we must also assume that Congress did not intend that there be federal jurisdiction over a state cause of action that is determined by that federal law. Therefore, assuming—only because the parties have made a similar assumption— that there is no private cause of action under the FDCA,[4] the Court holds that there is no federal jurisdiction over the plaintiffs' claim.

* * *

The Court nowhere explains the basis for this conclusion. Yet it is hardly self-evident. Why should the fact that Congress chose not to create a private federal *remedy* mean that Congress would not want there to be federal *jurisdiction* to adjudicate a state claim that imposes liability for violating the federal law? Clearly, the decision not to provide a private federal remedy should not affect federal jurisdiction unless the reasons Congress withholds a federal remedy are also reasons for withholding federal jurisdiction. Thus, it is necessary to examine the reasons for Congress' decisions to grant or withhold both federal jurisdiction and private remedies, something the Court has not done.

A

In the early days of our Republic, Congress was content to leave the task of interpreting and applying federal laws in the first instance to the state courts; with one short-lived exception,[5] Congress did not grant the inferior federal courts original jurisdiction over cases arising under federal law until 1875. The reasons Congress found it necessary to add this jurisdiction to the district courts are well known. First, Congress recognized "the importance, and even necessity of *uniformity* of decisions throughout the whole United States, upon all subjects within the purview of the constitution." * * * [W]hile perfect uniformity may not have been achieved, experience indicates that the availability of a federal forum in federal-question cases has done much to advance that goal. * * *

In addition, § 1331 has provided for adjudication in a forum that specializes in federal law and that is therefore more likely to apply that law correctly. * * *

These reasons for having original federal-question jurisdiction explain why cases like this one and *Smith*—i.e., cases where the cause of

---

4   It bears emphasizing that the Court does not hold that there is no private cause of action under the FDCA. Rather, it expressly states that "[f]or purposes of our decision, we assume that this is a correct interpretation of the FDCA." * * *

5   Congress granted original federal-question jurisdiction briefly in the Midnight Judges Act, ch. 4, § 11, 2 Stat. 92 (1801), which was repealed in 1802, Act of Mar. 8, 1802, ch. 8, § 1, 2 Stat. 132.

action is a creature of state law, but an essential element of the claim is federal—"arise under" federal law within the meaning of § 1331. Congress passes laws in order to shape behavior; a federal law expresses Congress' determination that there is a federal interest in having individuals or other entities conform their actions to a particular norm established by that law. * * * Congress determined that the availability of a federal forum to adjudicate cases involving federal questions would make it more likely that federal laws would shape behavior in the way that Congress intended.

By making federal law an essential element of a state-law claim, the State places the federal law into a context where it will operate to shape behavior: the threat of liability will force individuals to conform their conduct to interpretations of the federal law made by courts adjudicating the state-law claim. * * * It therefore follows that there is federal jurisdiction under § 1331.

B

The only remaining question is whether the assumption that Congress decided not to create a private cause of action alters this analysis in a way that makes it inappropriate to exercise original federal jurisdiction. According to the Court, "the very reasons for the development of the modern implied remedy doctrine" support the conclusion that, where the legislative history of a particular law shows (whether expressly or by inference) that Congress intended that there be no private federal remedy, it must also mean that Congress would not want federal courts to exercise jurisdiction over a state-law claim making violations of that federal law actionable. These reasons are " 'the increased complexity of federal legislation,' " " 'the increased volume of federal litigation,' " and " 'the desirability of a more careful scrutiny of legislative intent.' "

These reasons simply do not justify the Court's holding. Given the relative expertise of the federal courts in interpreting federal law, * * *, the increased complexity of federal legislation argues rather strongly in favor of recognizing federal jurisdiction. * * *

     * * *

It may be that a decision by Congress not to create a private remedy is intended to preclude all private enforcement. If that is so, then a state cause of action that makes relief available to private individuals for violations of the FDCA is pre-empted. But if Congress' decision not to provide a private federal remedy does *not* pre-empt such a state remedy, then, in light of the FDCA's clear policy of relying on the federal courts for enforcement, it also should not foreclose federal jurisdiction over that state remedy. Both § 1331 and the enforcement provisions of the FDCA reflect Congress' strong desire to utilize the federal courts to interpret and enforce the FDCA, and it is therefore at odds with both these statutes to recognize a private state-law remedy for violating the FDCA but to hold that this remedy cannot be adjudicated in the federal courts.

The Court's contrary conclusion requires inferring from Congress' decision not to create a private federal remedy that, while some private enforcement is permissible in state courts, it is "bad" if that enforcement comes from the *federal* courts. But that is simply illogical. * * *

FURTHER NOTE ON 28 U.S.C. § 1331

The well-pleaded complaint rule works moderately well, both as a means of sorting cases that should go into federal and state courts and as a means of predicting how courts will construe 28 U.S.C. § 1331. As seen in *Merrell Dow* and *Mottley*, however, the rule does not work perfectly. No one disputed that the *Merrell Dow* plaintiffs' federal question was properly pleaded in their complaint, but the Supreme Court denied jurisdiction anyway. The Court had noted earlier, in Franchise Tax Board of California v. Construction Laborers Vacation Trust, 463 U.S. 1, 9, 11, 12, 103 S.Ct. 2841, 77 L.Ed.2d 420 (1983), that while it is a "powerful doctrine" and a "quick rule of thumb," the well-pleaded complaint rule can "produce awkward results." The Court in *Franchise Tax Board* had in mind the inability of a defendant to rely on a federal defense, but its words might also apply to *Merrell Dow*, where the well-pleaded complaint rule was satisfied but the Court nevertheless declined to find jurisdiction. Professor William Cohen argued that no single rule was ever likely to suffice for interpreting the general federal question statute. Cohen, The Broken Compass: The Requirement that a Case Arise "Directly" Under Federal Law, 115 U.Pa.L.Rev. 890 (1967). Nothing has happened in the more than half-century since the publication of Professor Cohen's article to prove him wrong.

1. Justice Holmes, the cause of action test, and the incorporation of federal law into a state cause of action. In American Well Works Co. v. Layne & Bowler Co., 241 U.S. 257, 260, 36 S.Ct. 585, 60 L.Ed. 987 (1916), Justice Holmes suggested that federal question jurisdiction should exist under § 1331 only when federal law creates the cause of action: "A suit arises under the law that creates the cause of action." But this test is somewhat restrictive. If a case satisfies the test, there is clearly federal question jurisdiction under § 1331. Later Supreme Court cases have made clear that some cases that do not satisfy the *American Well Works* cause-of-action test are nevertheless properly heard by the district court. In the words of the *Franchise Tax Board* Court, Justice Holmes' cause-of-action test "is more useful for describing the vast majority of cases that come within the district courts' original jurisdiction than it is for describing which cases are beyond district court jurisdiction." 463 U.S. at 9.

For example, in Smith v. Kansas City Title & Trust Co., 255 U.S. 180, 41 S.Ct. 243, 65 L.Ed. 577 (1921), plaintiff was a shareholder in a corporation that sought to purchase bonds issued by Federal and Joint Stock Land Banks established under the Federal Farm Loan Act. Plaintiff asserted a state law cause of action under which a shareholder could bring a derivative suit to prevent the corporation from purchasing invalid bonds. Plaintiff argued that the bonds were invalid under federal law on the ground that the federal statute under which they were issued was unconstitutional. The validity of the bonds was the central, indeed the only, issue in the case. Thus, the cause of action was created under state law, but the only question actually presented was federal. The Court held that there was jurisdiction under § 1331. Justice Holmes' cause-of-action test was of course not satisfied; indeed, Justice Holmes dissented, but he was alone in so doing.

How can *Merrell Dow* and *Kansas City Title & Trust* be reconciled? By comparing the importance of the federal question in the two cases? If this is the answer (as it seems to be), is there jurisdiction under § 1331 if the federal question appears in a well-pleaded complaint (even if embedded in a state-law cause of action) *and* it is of sufficient importance to pass a threshold established in *Merrell Dow*? What, exactly, is the threshold established in *Merrell Dow*?

2. **Reading *Merrell Dow* narrowly.** It is possible to read some of the language in *Merrell Dow* as overruling *Kansas City Title & Trust* and embracing Justice Holmes's opinion in *American Well Works*. The Court's concluding statement in *Merrell Dow* would certainly support such a reading. The Court wrote, "We conclude that a complaint alleging a violation of a federal statute as an element of a state cause of action, when Congress has determined that there should be no private, federal cause of action for the violation, does not state a claim 'arising under [federal law].'" Yet, as Justice Brennan is at pains to point out, *Merrell Dow* cited and did not overrule *Kansas City Title & Trust*. Cases decided after *Merrell Dow* make clear that *Kansas City Title & Trust* is alive and well.

3. ***Grable & Sons Metal Products.*** In Grable & Sons Metal Products, Inc. v. Darue Engineering and Manufacturing, 545 U.S. 308, 125 S.Ct. 2363, 162 L.Ed.2d 257 (2005), Grable brought a state-law quiet title action in state court to contest the validity of the title to real property bought at a federal tax sale by Darue. Darue removed the suit to federal district court under 28 U.S.C. § 1441, contending that Grable's suit arose under federal law within the meaning of § 1331. Grable had owned the real property but had fallen behind in paying federal taxes. The IRS seized the property and notified Grable by certified mail that it would sell the property at a tax sale if Grable failed to redeem the property by a certain date. Grable received the notice but did nothing. The property was then sold to Darue at the tax sale. Grable's quiet title action acknowledged actual receipt of the notice but alleged that the sale was invalid because the form of notice was improper under federal law. Grable's cause of action was based on state law, and the federal notice law upon which it relied did not provide a private cause of action. The Court nevertheless upheld federal question jurisdiction.

The Court formulated the general test as follows: "[D]oes a state-law claim necessarily raise a stated federal issue, actually disputed and substantial, which a federal forum may entertain without disturbing any congressionally approved balance of federal and state judicial responsibilities." Id. at 314. Applying the test, the Court wrote:

> Whether Grable was given notice within the meaning of the federal statute is * * * an essential element of its quiet title claim, and the meaning of the federal statute is actually in dispute; it appears to the only legal or factual issue contested in the case. The meaning of the federal tax provision is an important issue of federal law that sensibly belongs in federal court. The Government has a strong interest in the "prompt and certain collection of delinquent taxes," and the ability of the IRS to satisfy its claims from the property of delinquents requires clear terms of notice to allow buyers like Darue to satisfy themselves that the Service has touched the bases necessary for good title. The Government thus has a direct interest in the availability of a federal forum to vindicate its own administrative actions, and buyers (as well as tax delinquents) may find it valuable to come before judges used to federal tax matters. Finally, because it will be the rare state title case that raises a contested matter of federal law, federal jurisdiction to resolve

genuine disagreements over federal tax provisions will portend only a microscopic effect on the federal-state division of labor.

Id. at 315. The Court explicitly narrowed *Merrell Dow*, adding: "*Merrell Dow* should be read in its entirety as treating the absence of a federal private right of action as evidence relevant to, but not dispositive of, the 'sensitive judgments about congressional intent' that § 1331 requires. * * * The Court [in *Merrell Dow*] saw the missing cause of action not as a missing federal door key, always required, but as a missing welcome mat, required in the circumstances, when exercising federal jurisdiction over a state misbranding action that would have attracted a horde of original filings and removal cases raising other state claims with embedded federal issues." Id. at 318.

Justice Thomas concurred separately, strongly suggesting that he would be willing to abandon *Kansas City Title & Trust* and adopt Justice Holmes's position in *American Well Works*. He wrote, "Jurisdictional rules should be clear. Whatever the virtues of the [*Kansas City Title & Trust*] standard, it is anything but clear. * * * Whatever the vices of the *American Well Works* rule, it is clear. Moreover, it accounts for the 'vast majority' of cases that come within § 1331 under our current case law—further indication that trying to sort out which cases fall within the smaller [*Kansas City Title & Trust*] category may not be worth the uncertainty it entails." Id. at 321 (Thomas, J., concurring).

For a thorough analysis of *Grable* and lower court cases interpreting it, see Bradt, Grable on the Ground: Mitigating Unchecked Jurisdictional Discretion, 44 U.C. Davis L.Rev. 1153 (2011).

4. ***Empire Healthchoice.*** In Empire Healthchoice Assurance, Inc. v. McVeigh, 547 U.S. 677, 126 S.Ct. 211, 165 L.Ed.2d 131 (2006), McVeigh was a federal employee covered under a health care policy issued under the Federal Employees Health Benefits Act (FEHBA). The contract between the federal government and McVeigh's insurer pursuant to the FEHBA required the insurer to recoup damage recoveries obtained by the insured from a tortfeasor third party as reimbursement for health care expenditures made by the insurer. McVeigh was injured in an accident and eventually died from his injuries. The insurer paid $157,309 in health care expenses in caring for McVeigh after the accident. McVeigh's estate recovered a settlement of a little over $3,000,000 from the tortfeasor, and the insurer brought suit to recover the $157,309. The right of the insurer to recover this amount arose out of the contract between the federal government and the insurer, and the contract implemented the FEHBA. The Court nevertheless held that there was no jurisdiction under § 1331. The insurer's "contract-derived claim for reimbursement is not a 'creature of federal law.'" Id. at 696. Justice Breyer dissented, joined by three other Justices. He would have held that the contract was governed by federal common law, and that any claim for reimbursement under the contract therefore arose under federal law. Federal common law is judge-made law that is both jurisdiction-conferring under § 1331 and supreme under the Supremacy Clause. Federal common law is covered, infra p. 427.

5. ***Gunn v. Minton.*** In Gunn v. Minton, 568 U.S. ___, 133 S.Ct. 1059, 185 L.Ed.2d 72 (2013), Minton had been represented in federal court by attorney Gunn in a patent dispute. Minton's suit failed. Minton then sued Gunn in Texas state court for malpractice. An essential ingredient of his state-law malpractice claim was his contention that Gunn has failed to make what would have been a winning argument under federal patent law. The Texas Supreme Court held that there was federal question jurisdiction under 28 U.S.C. § 1338. Section 1338 confers exclusive jurisdiction on the federal courts in patent cases. The Texas Supreme Court dismissed Minton's suit based on its conclusion that it arose under federal patent law and therefore came within the exclusive jurisdiction of the federal courts. The United States Supreme Court reversed. It acknowledged that the boundaries of federal question "arising under" jurisdiction when the federal issue is embedded in a state-law cause of action are not entirely clear. It wrote, "In outlining the contours of this 'slim category' [of federal question cases], we do not paint on a blank canvas. Unfortunately, the canvas looks like one that Jackson Pollock got to first." 133 S.Ct. at 1065.

The Court first noted that the "arising under" test is identical under the general federal question jurisdictional statute, § 1331, and the patent federal question jurisdiction statute, § 1338. Id. at 1064. It then derived the following test from *Grable*:

> [F]ederal jurisdiction over a state law claim will lie if a federal issue is: (1) necessarily raised, (2) actually disputed, (3) substantial, and (4) capable of resolution in federal court without disrupting the federal-state balance approved by Congress.

Id. at 1065. "The substantiality inquiry under *Grable* looks * * * to the importance of the issue to the federal system as a whole." Id. at 1066. The Court noted that the underlying patent question in the malpractice suit was hypothetical: What would the federal court have held in the patent case if Gunn had made the argument Minton now says he should have made? The Court concluded that the answer to this hypothetical question, in the context of a state-law malpractice suit, would have extremely limited effect on patent law in general, and that the question was not "substantial" in the sense intended by *Grable*.

6. Is the cost of clarity too high? The Court itself has conceded that the picture of federal question jurisdiction in cases in which the federal question is embedded in a state-law cause of action looks like a canvas "that Jackson Pollock got to first." Eliminating the uncertainty entailed in determining whether there is federal question jurisdiction in such cases is obviously desirable. Is Justice Thomas right to prefer the clarity of Justice Holmes's *American Well Works* cause-of-action test? The cost of adopting Justice Holmes's test would be the exclusion from federal district court of cases in which "substantial" questions of federal law are embedded in state-law causes of action. Would that cost be too high?

7. Declaratory judgments and the well-pleaded complaint rule. In 1934, Congress adopted the Federal Declaratory Judgment Act, 28 U.S.C. § 2201, under which a plaintiff may request from a federal district court a declaration of rights "in a case of actual controversy within its jurisdiction." A declaratory judgment suit is used to obtain an early judicial determination of rights. It is an extremely useful device where a party would otherwise have to act based only on a guess about her rights, and would be subjected to (and would lose) a suit for damages or injunction if she guessed incorrectly. A plaintiff in a declaratory judgment suit is thus often someone who would have been a defendant had she simply gone ahead with her contemplated acts. This means that a plaintiff's well-pleaded declaratory judgment complaint will often assert rights based on federal law, whereas that same assertion of federal rights would have appeared as federal defenses in the answer had plaintiff waited to be made a defendant in a "coercive suit" for damages or an injunction. How does the well-pleaded complaint rule apply to declaratory judgment suits?

In Skelly Oil Co. v. Phillips Petroleum Co., 339 U.S. 667, 671, 70 S.Ct. 876, 94 L.Ed. 1194 (1950), the Court held, in an opinion by Justice Frankfurter, that in passing the Federal Declaratory Judgment Act, "Congress enlarged the range of remedies available in the federal courts but did not extend their jurisdiction." According to *Skelly Oil*, Congress did not intend to expand the practical reach of federal question subject matter jurisdiction by allowing declaratory judgment plaintiffs to rely on federal rights that before the passage of the Act could only have been asserted as defenses in a "coercive suit" for damages or an injunction. According to *Skelly Oil*, federal question jurisdiction cannot be determined by reading the actual complaint filed in the case. Rather, jurisdiction is determined by *hypothesizing* what a complaint would have looked like in the "coercive suit" that would have been filed if plaintiff had simply acted, and had thus been a defendant instead of a plaintiff. If a question of federal law is presented in this well-pleaded, but hypothetical, complaint, then there is federal question jurisdiction in the district court. Justice Frankfurter's explanation for the result in *Skelly Oil* was that if the plaintiff's actual complaint were consulted, "It would turn into the federal courts a vast current of litigation indubitably arising under State law. * * * [This would] disregard the effective functioning of the federal judicial system and distort the limited procedural purpose of the Declaratory Judgment Act." 339 U.S. at 673–74.

In Franchise Tax Board of California v. Construction Laborers Vacation Trust, 463 U.S. 1, 103 S.Ct. 2841, 77 L.Ed.2d 420 (1983), plaintiff brought a declaratory judgment action in state court under the state declaratory judgment act, asserting a federal right to be free of state taxation. Defendant sought to remove to federal district court, arguing that *Skelly Oil* was based on a construction of the Federal Declaratory Judgment Act and should not apply to limit removal of suits brought under a state act. The Court reaffirmed and extended *Skelly Oil*, writing, "At this point, any adjustment in the system that has evolved under the *Skelly Oil* rule must come from Congress." The Court noted that *Skelly Oil* did not directly govern a case brought in state court under a state declaratory judgment act, but noted that it would become a "dead letter" if a state law declaratory judgment case could be removed to federal court based on the federal right asserted in the state court complaint. 463 U.S. at 18 and n. 17.

The Supreme Court's application of the well-pleaded complaint rule to declaratory judgments has been criticized vigorously and repeatedly. See, e.g., American Law Institute, Study of the Division of Jurisdiction Between State and Federal Courts § 1311, at 170–71 (1969) (criticizing *Skelly Oil*); Doernberg, There's No Reason for It; It's Just Our Policy: Why the Well-Pleaded Complaint Rule Sabotages the Purposes of Federal Question Jurisdiction, 38 Hastings L.J. 597, 640–46 (1987) (criticizing both *Skelly Oil* and *Franchise Tax Board*). The Court has made it clear that it considers any change to be a matter for Congress. Congress, meanwhile, has shown no interest in the topic.

2. DIVERSITY JURISDICTION

Mas v. Perry

United States Court of Appeals for the Fifth Circuit, 1974.
489 F.2d 1396.

■ AINSWORTH, CIRCUIT JUDGE:

* * *

Appellees Jean Paul Mas, a citizen of France, and Judy Mas were married at her home in Jackson, Mississippi. Prior to their marriage, Mr. and Mrs. Mas were graduate assistants, pursuing coursework as well as performing teaching duties, for approximately nine months and one year, respectively, at Louisiana State University in Baton Rouge, Louisiana. Shortly after their marriage, they returned to Baton Rouge to resume their duties as graduate assistants at LSU. They remained in Baton Rouge for approximately two more years, after which they moved to Park Ridge, Illinois. At the time of the trial in this case, it was their intention to return to Baton Rouge while Mr. Mas finished his studies for the degree of Doctor of Philosophy. Mr. and Mrs. Mas were undecided as to where they would reside after that.

Upon their return to Baton Rouge after their marriage, appellees rented an apartment from appellant Oliver H. Perry, a citizen of Louisiana. This appeal arises from a final judgment entered on a jury verdict awarding $5,000 to Mr. Mas and $15,000 to Mrs. Mas for damages incurred by them as a result of the discovery that their bedroom and bathroom contained "two-way" mirrors and that they had been watched through them by the appellant during three of the first four months of their marriage.

At the close of the appellees' case at trial, appellant made an oral motion to dismiss for lack of jurisdiction. The motion was denied by the district court. Before this Court, appellant challenges the final judgment below solely on jurisdictional grounds, contending that appellees failed to prove diversity of citizenship among the parties and that the requisite jurisdictional amount is lacking with respect to Mr. Mas. Finding no merit to these contentions, we affirm. Under section 1332(a)(2), the federal judicial power extends to the claim of Mr. Mas, a citizen of France, against the appellant, a citizen of Louisiana. Since we conclude that Mrs. Mas is a citizen of Mississippi for diversity purposes, the district court also properly had jurisdiction under section 1332(a)(1) of her claim.

It has long been the general rule that complete diversity of parties is required in order that diversity jurisdiction obtain; that is, no party on one side may be a citizen of the same State as any party on the other side. Strawbridge v. Curtiss, 7 U.S. (3 Cranch) 267, 2 L.Ed. 435 (1806). This determination of one's State citizenship for diversity purposes is controlled by federal law, not by the law of any State. As is the case in other areas of federal jurisdiction, the diverse citizenship among adverse parties must be present at the time the complaint is filed. Mollan v. Torrance, 22 U.S. (9 Wheat.) 537, 539, 6 L.Ed. 154, 155 (1824). Jurisdiction is unaffected by subsequent changes in the citizenship of the parties. Morgan's Heirs v. Morgan, 15 U.S. (2 Wheat.) 290, 297, 4 L.Ed. 242, 244 (1817). The burden of pleading the diverse citizenship is upon the party invoking federal jurisdiction, see Cameron v. Hodges, 127 U.S. 322, 8 S.Ct. 1154, 32 L.Ed. 132 (1888); and if the diversity jurisdiction is properly challenged, that party also bears the burden of proof, McNutt v. General Motors Acceptance Corp., 298 U.S. 178, 56 S.Ct. 780, 80 L.Ed. 1135 (1936).

To be a citizen of a State within the meaning of section 1332, a natural person must be both a citizen of the United States, and a domiciliary of that State. For diversity purposes, citizenship means domicile; mere residence in the State is not sufficient.

A person's domicile is the place of "his true, fixed, and permanent home and principal establishment, and to which he has the intention of returning whenever he is absent therefrom. . . ." A change of domicile may be effected only by a combination of two elements: (a) taking up residence in a different domicile with (b) the intention to remain there.

It is clear that at the time of her marriage, Mrs. Mas was a domiciliary of the State of Mississippi. While it is generally the case that the domicile of the wife—and, consequently, her State citizenship for purposes of diversity jurisdiction—is deemed to be that of her husband, we find no precedent for extending this concept to the situation here, in which the husband is a citizen of a foreign state but resides in the United States. Indeed, such a fiction would work absurd results on the facts before us. If Mr. Mas were considered a domiciliary of France—as he would be since he had lived in Louisiana as a student-teaching assistant prior to filing this suit, then Mrs. Mas would also be deemed a domiciliary, and thus, fictionally at least, a citizen of France. She would not be a citizen of any State and could not sue in a federal court on that basis; nor could she invoke the alienage jurisdiction to bring her claim in federal court, since she is not an alien. On the other hand, if Mrs. Mas's domicile were Louisiana, she would become a Louisiana citizen for diversity purposes and could not bring suit with her husband against appellant, also a Louisiana citizen, on the basis of diversity jurisdiction. These are curious results under a rule arising from the theoretical identity of person and interest of the married couple.

An American woman is not deemed to have lost her United States citizenship solely by reason of her marriage to an alien. 8 U.S.C. § 1489. Similarly, we conclude that for diversity purposes a woman does not have her domicile or State citizenship changed solely by reason of her marriage to an alien.

Mrs. Mas's Mississippi domicile was disturbed neither by her year in Louisiana prior to her marriage nor as a result of the time she and her husband spent at LSU after their marriage, since for both periods she was a graduate assistant at LSU. Though she testified that after her marriage she had no intention of returning to her parents' home in Mississippi, Mrs. Mas did not effect a change of domicile since she and Mr. Mas were in Louisiana only as students and lacked the requisite intention to remain there. Until she acquires a new domicile, she remains a domiciliary, and thus a citizen, of Mississippi.

Appellant also contends that Mr. Mas's claim should have been dismissed for failure to establish the requisite jurisdictional amount for diversity cases of more than $10,000. In their complaint Mr. and Mrs.

Mas alleged that they had each been damaged in the amount of $100,000. As we have noted, Mr. Mas ultimately recovered $5,000.

It is well settled that the amount in controversy is determined by the amount claimed by the plaintiff in good faith. Federal jurisdiction is not lost because a judgment of less than the jurisdictional amount is awarded. That Mr. Mas recovered only $5,000 is, therefore, not compelling. As the Supreme Court stated in St. Paul Mercury Indemnity Co. v. Red Cab Co., 303 U.S. 283, 288–290, 58 S.Ct. 586, 590–591, 82 L.Ed. 845:

> [T]he sum claimed by the plaintiff controls if the claim is apparently made in good faith.
>
> It must appear to a legal certainty that the claim is really for less than the jurisdictional amount to justify dismissal. The inability of the plaintiff to recover an amount adequate to give the court jurisdiction does not show his bad faith or oust the jurisdiction. . . .
>
> . . . His good faith in choosing the federal forum is open to challenge not only by resort to the face of his complaint, but by the facts disclosed at trial, and if from either source it is clear that his claim never could have amounted to the sum necessary to give jurisdiction there is no injustice in dismissing the suit.

Having heard the evidence presented at the trial, the district court concluded that the appellees properly met the requirements of section 1332 with respect to jurisdictional amount. Upon examination of the record in this case, we are also satisfied that the requisite amount was in controversy.

Thus the power of the federal district court to entertain the claims of appellees in this case stands on two separate legs of diversity jurisdiction: a claim by an alien against a State citizen; and an action between citizens of different States. We also note, however, the propriety of having the federal district court entertain a spouse's action against a defendant, where the district court already has jurisdiction over a claim, arising from the same transaction, by the other spouse against the same defendant. In the case before us, such a result is particularly desirable. The claims of Mr. and Mrs. Mas arise from the same operative facts, and there was almost complete interdependence between their claims with respect to the proof required and the issues raised at trial. Thus, since the district court had jurisdiction of Mr. Mas's action, sound judicial administration militates strongly in favor of federal jurisdiction of Mrs. Mas's claim.

Affirmed.

Hertz Corp. v. Friend

Supreme Court of the United States, 2010.
559 U.S. 77, 130 S.Ct. 1181, 175 L.Ed.2d 1029.

■ JUSTICE BREYER delivered the opinion of the Court.

The federal diversity jurisdiction statute provides that "a corporation shall be deemed to be a citizen of any State by which it has been incorporated *and of the State where it has its principal place of* business." 28 U.S.C. § 1332(c)(1) (emphasis added). We seek here to resolve different interpretations that the Circuits have given this phrase. In doing so, we place primary weight upon the need for judicial administration of a jurisdictional statute to remain as simple as possible. And we conclude that the phrase "principal place of business" refers to the place where the corporation's high level officers direct, control, and coordinate the corporation's activities. Lower federal courts have often metaphorically called that place the corporation's "nerve center." We believe that the "nerve center" will typically be found at a corporation's headquarters.

I

In September 2007, respondents Melinda Friend and John Nhieu, two California citizens, sued petitioner, the Hertz Corporation, in a California state court. They sought damages for what they claimed were violations of California's wage and hour laws. And they requested relief on behalf of a potential class composed of California citizens who had allegedly suffered similar harms.

Hertz filed a notice seeking removal to a federal court. Hertz claimed that the plaintiffs and the defendant were citizens of different States. Hence, the federal court possessed diversity-of-citizenship jurisdiction. Friend and Nhieu, however, claimed that the Hertz Corporation was a California citizen, like themselves, and that, hence, diversity jurisdiction was lacking.

To support its position, Hertz submitted a declaration by an employee relations manager that sought to show that Hertz's "principal place of business" was in New Jersey, not in California. The declaration stated, among other things, that Hertz operated facilities in 44 States; and that California-which had about 12% of the Nation's population, accounted for 273 of Hertz's 1,606 car rental locations; about 2,300 of its 11,230 full-time employees; about $811 million of its $4.371 billion in annual revenue; and about 3.8 million of its approximately 21 million annual transactions, *i.e.,* rentals. The declaration also stated that the "leadership of Hertz and its domestic subsidiaries" is located at Hertz's "corporate headquarters" in Park Ridge, New Jersey; that its "core executive and administrative functions * * * are carried out" there and "to a lesser extent" in Oklahoma City, Oklahoma; and that its "major administrative operations * * * are found" at those two locations.

The District Court of the Northern District of California accepted Hertz's statement of the facts as undisputed. But it concluded that, given those facts, Hertz was a citizen of California. In reaching this conclusion, the court applied Ninth Circuit precedent, which instructs courts to identify a corporation's "principal place of business" by first determining the amount of a corporation's business activity State by State. If the amount of activity is "significantly larger" or "substantially predominates" in one State, then that State is the corporation's "principal place of business." If there is no such State, then the "principal place of business" is the corporation's "nerve center," *i.e.,* the place where " 'the majority of its executive and administrative functions are performed.' "

Applying this test, the District Court found that the "plurality of each of the relevant business activities" was in California, and that "the differential between the amount of those activities" in California and the amount in "the next closest state" was "significant." Hence, Hertz's "principal place of business" was California, and diversity jurisdiction was thus lacking. The District Court consequently remanded the case to the state courts.

Hertz appealed the District Court's remand order. The Ninth Circuit affirmed in a brief memorandum opinion. Hertz filed a petition for certiorari. And, in light of differences among the Circuits in the application of the test for corporate citizenship, we granted the writ.

* * *

III

We begin our "principal place of business" discussion with a brief review of relevant history. The Constitution provides that the "judicial Power shall extend" to "Controversies * * * between Citizens of different States." Art. III, § 2. This language, however, does not automatically confer diversity jurisdiction upon the federal courts. Rather, it authorizes Congress to do so and, in doing so, to determine the scope of the federal courts' jurisdiction within constitutional limits.

Congress first authorized federal courts to exercise diversity jurisdiction in 1789 when, in the First Judiciary Act, Congress granted federal courts authority to hear suits "between a citizen of the State where the suit is brought, and a citizen of another State." § 11, 1 Stat. 78. The statute said nothing about corporations. In 1809, Chief Justice Marshall, writing for a unanimous Court, described a corporation as an "invisible, intangible, and artificial being" which was "certainly not a citizen." *Bank of United States v. Deveaux,* 5 Cranch 61, 86, 3 L.Ed. 38 (1809). But the Court held that a corporation could invoke the federal courts' diversity jurisdiction based on a pleading that the corporation's shareholders were all citizens of a different State from the defendants, as "the term citizen ought to be understood as it is used in the constitution, and as it is used in other laws. That is, to describe the real persons who come into court, in this case, under their corporate name." *Id.,* at 91–92.

In *Louisville, C. & C.R. Co. v. Letson,* 2 How. 497, 11 L.Ed. 353 (1844), the Court modified this initial approach. It held that a corporation was to be deemed an artificial person of the State by which it had been created, and its citizenship for jurisdictional purposes determined accordingly. *Id.,* at 558–559. Ten years later, the Court in *Marshall v. Baltimore & Ohio R. Co.,* 16 How. 314, 14 L.Ed. 953 (1854), held that the reason a corporation was a citizen of its State of incorporation was that, for the limited purpose of determining corporate citizenship, courts could conclusively (and artificially) presume that a corporation's *shareholders* were citizens of the State of incorporation. *Id.,* at 327–328. And it reaffirmed *Letson.* 16 How., at 325–326, 14 L.Ed. 953. Whatever the rationale, the practical upshot was that, for diversity purposes, the federal courts considered a corporation to be a citizen of the State of its incorporation. 13F C. Wright, A. Miller, & E. Cooper, Federal Practice and Procedure § 3623, pp. 1–7 (3d ed. 2009) (hereinafter Wright & Miller).

In 1928 this Court made clear that the "state of incorporation" rule was virtually absolute. It held that a corporation closely identified with State A could proceed in a federal court located in that State as long as the corporation had filed its incorporation papers in State B, perhaps a State where the corporation did no business at all. Subsequently, many in Congress and those who testified before it pointed out that this interpretation was at odds with diversity jurisdiction's basic rationale, namely, opening the federal courts' doors to those who might otherwise suffer from local prejudice against out-of-state parties. Through its choice of the State of incorporation, a corporation could manipulate federal-court jurisdiction, for example, opening the federal courts' doors in a State where it conducted nearly all its business by filing incorporation papers elsewhere. Although various legislative proposals to curtail the corporate use of diversity jurisdiction were made, none of these proposals were enacted into law.

At the same time as federal dockets increased in size, many judges began to believe those dockets contained too many diversity cases. A committee of the Judicial Conference of the United States studied the matter. And on March 12, 1951, that committee, the Committee on Jurisdiction and Venue, issued a report.

Among its observations, the committee found a general need "to prevent frauds and abuses" with respect to jurisdiction. The committee recommended against eliminating diversity cases altogether. Instead it recommended, along with other proposals, a statutory amendment that would make a corporation a citizen both of the State of its incorporation and any State from which it received more than half of its gross income. If, for example, a citizen of California sued (under state law in state court) a corporation that received half or more of its gross income from California, that corporation would not be able to remove the case to federal court, even if Delaware was its State of incorporation.

During the spring and summer of 1951 committee members circulated their report and attended circuit conferences at which federal judges discussed the report's recommendations. Reflecting those criticisms, the committee filed a new report in September, in which it revised its corporate citizenship recommendation. It now proposed that " 'a corporation shall be deemed a citizen of the state of its original creation . . . [and] shall also be deemed a citizen of a state where it has its principal place of business.' " The committee wrote that this new language would provide a "simpler and more practical formula" than the "gross income" test. * * *

   * * *

  * * * Subsequently, in 1958, Congress both codified the courts' traditional place of incorporation test and also enacted into law a slightly modified version of the Conference Committee's proposed "principal place of business" language. A corporation was to "be deemed a citizen of any State by which it has been incorporated and of the State where it has its principal place of business." § 2, 72 Stat. 415.

IV

   * * *

[S]uppose those corporate headquarters, including executive offices, are in one State, while the corporation's plants or other centers of business activity are located in other States. In 1959 a distinguished federal district judge, Edward Weinfeld, [wrote]:

"Where a corporation is engaged in far-flung and varied activities which are carried on in different states, its principal place of business is the nerve center from which it radiates out to its constituent parts and from which its officers direct, control and coordinate all activities without regard to locale, in the furtherance of the corporate objective. The test applied by our Court of Appeals, is that place where the corporation has an 'office from which its business was directed and controlled'-the place where 'all of its business was under the supreme direction and control of its officers.' " *Scot Typewriter Co.*, 170 F. Supp., at 865.

Numerous Circuits have since followed this rule, applying the "nerve center" test for corporations with "far-flung" business activities.

Scot's analysis, however, did not go far enough. For it did not answer what courts should do when the operations of the corporation are not "far-flung" but rather limited to only a few States. When faced with this question, various courts have focused more heavily on where a corporation's actual business activities are located.

Perhaps because corporations come in many different forms, involve many different kinds of business activities, and locate offices and plants for different reasons in different ways in different regions, a general "business activities" approach has proved unusually difficult to apply. Courts must decide which factors are more important than others: for example, plant location, sales or servicing centers; transactions, payrolls, or revenue generation.

* * *

V

A

In an effort to find a single, more uniform interpretation of the statutory phrase, we have reviewed the Courts of Appeals' divergent and increasingly complex interpretations. Having done so, we now return to, and expand, Judge Weinfeld's approach, as applied in the Seventh Circuit. We conclude that "principal place of business" is best read as referring to the place where a corporation's officers direct, control, and coordinate the corporation's activities. It is the place that Courts of Appeals have called the corporation's "nerve center." And in practice it should normally be the place where the corporation maintains its headquarters-provided that the headquarters is the actual center of direction, control, and coordination, *i.e.,* the "nerve center," and not simply an office where the corporation holds its board meetings (for example, attended by directors and officers who have traveled there for the occasion).

Three sets of considerations, taken together, convince us that this approach, while imperfect, is superior to other possibilities. First, the statute's language supports the approach. The statute's text deems a corporation a citizen of the "State where it has its principal place of business." 28 U.S.C. § 1332(c)(1). The word "place" is in the singular, not the plural. The word "principal" requires us to pick out the "main, prominent" or "leading" place. 12 Oxford English Dictionary 495 (2d ed. 1989) (def. (A)(I)(2)). Cf. *Commissioner v. Soliman,* 506 U.S. 168, 174, 113

S.Ct. 701, 121 L.Ed.2d 634 (1993) (interpreting "principal place of business" for tax purposes to require an assessment of "whether any one business location is the 'most important, consequential, or influential' one"). And the fact that the word "place" follows the words "State where" means that the "place" is a place *within* a State. It is not the State itself.

* * *

Second, administrative simplicity is a major virtue in a jurisdictional statute. Complex jurisdictional tests complicate a case, eating up time and money as the parties litigate, not the merits of their claims, but which court is the right court to decide those claims. Complex tests produce appeals and reversals, encourage gamesmanship, and, again, diminish the likelihood that results and settlements will reflect a claim's legal and factual merits. Judicial resources too are at stake. Courts have an independent obligation to determine whether subject-matter jurisdiction exists, even when no party challenges it. So courts benefit from straightforward rules under which they can readily assure themselves of their power to hear a case.

Simple jurisdictional rules also promote greater predictability. Predictability is valuable to corporations making business and investment decisions. Predictability also benefits plaintiffs deciding whether to file suit in a state or federal court.

A "nerve center" approach, which ordinarily equates that "center" with a corporation's headquarters, is simple to apply *comparatively speaking*. The metaphor of a corporate "brain," while not precise, suggests a single location. By contrast, a corporation's general business activities more often lack a single principal place where they take place. That is to say, the corporation may have several plants, many sales locations, and employees located in many different places. If so, it will not be as easy to determine which of these different business locales is the "principal" or most important "place."

Third, the statute's legislative history, for those who accept it, offers a simplicity-related interpretive benchmark. The Judicial Conference provided an initial version of its proposal that suggested a numerical test. A corporation would be deemed a citizen of the State that accounted for more than half of its gross income. The Conference changed its mind in light of criticism that such a test would prove too complex and impractical to apply. That history suggests that the words "principal place of business" should be interpreted to be no more complex than the initial "half of gross income" test. A "nerve center" test offers such a possibility. A general business activities test does not.

B

We recognize that there may be no perfect test that satisfies all administrative and purposive criteria. We recognize as well that, under the "nerve center" test we adopt today, there will be hard cases. For example, in this era of telecommuting, some corporations may divide their command and coordinating functions among officers who work at several different locations, perhaps communicating over the Internet. That said, our test nonetheless points courts in a single direction, towards the center of overall direction, control, and coordination. Courts do not have to try to weigh corporate functions, assets, or revenues different in kind, one from the other. Our approach provides a sensible test that is relatively easier to apply, not a test that will, in all instances, automatically generate a result.

We also recognize that the use of a "nerve center" test may in some cases produce results that seem to cut against the basic rationale for 28 U.S.C. § 1332. For example, if the bulk of a company's business activities visible to the public take place in New Jersey, while its top officers direct those activities just across the river in New York, the "principal place of business" is New York. One could argue that members of the public in New Jersey would be *less* likely to be prejudiced against the corporation than persons in New York-yet the corporation will still be entitled to remove a New Jersey state case to federal court. And note too that the same corporation would be unable to remove a New York state case to federal court, despite the New York public's presumed prejudice against the corporation.

We understand that such seeming anomalies will arise. However, in view of the necessity of having a clearer rule, we must accept them. Accepting occasionally counterintuitive results is the price the legal system must pay to avoid overly complex jurisdictional administration while producing the benefits that accompany a more uniform legal system.

* * *

NOTE ON ASSORTED PROBLEMS OF DIVERSITY JURISDICTION

1.   Citizenship. a. Natural persons. A natural person is a citizen of a state in which he or she is domiciled. Domicile is distinct from residence. (Venue under 28 U.S.C. § 1391 and related statutes relies on residence rather than domicile. See infra p. 300). Note the oddity of the statute as it applies to *Mas v. Perry*. An American citizen domiciled abroad may not use § 1332 as the basis for jurisdiction because the statute requires citizenship "of a state."

Under the current version of § 1332, there are two ways a diversity suit can be based on alienage or include an alien. First, under § 1332(a)(2) there is jurisdiction over suits between citizens of a state and "citizens or subjects of a foreign state." (The French are "citizens"; the British are, or at least used to be, "subjects.") Note, however, that an alien lawfully admitted for permanent residence in the United States (i.e., a holder of a "green card") is "deemed" a citizen of the state in which he or she is domiciled. Aliens lawfully in the country on work or student visas do not qualify as lawfully admitted permanent residents. Second, under § 1332(a)(3), a citizen or subject of a foreign state can join as an "additional party" a diversity suit between citizens of different states.

The odd distinction between aliens and Americans domiciled abroad was applied in Twentieth Century-Fox Film Corp. v. Taylor, 239 F. Supp. 913 (S.D.N.Y.1965). Richard Burton and Elizabeth Taylor disagreed with Twentieth Century-Fox during the filming of "Cleopatra." In the ensuing litigation, there was diversity between Burton, a British "subject," and Twentieth Century-Fox, an American corporation. But there was no diversity between Taylor and Twentieth Century-Fox because, although she was an American citizen, she was not then domiciled in the United States. For a discussion of diversity jurisdiction based on alienage, see Johnson, Why Alienage Jurisdiction? Historical Foundations and Modern Justifications for

Federal Jurisdiction over Disputes Involving Noncitizens, 21 Yale J.Int'l L. 1 (1996).

b.   Artificial persons. For purposes of federal diversity jurisdiction, a corporation is treated as a citizen of both its state of incorporation and its principal place of business. The place of incorporation is easy to determine, but note that a few corporations are incorporated in more than one state. The principal place of business is sometimes more difficult to determine. Before the Court's decision in *Hertz*, there were two separate lines of authority. Under one line of cases, the principal place of business was where the corporation carries on its primary production or service activities. See, e.g., Kelly v. United States Steel Corp., 284 F.2d 850 (3d Cir. 1960). Under the other, the principal place of business was where the corporation's administrative office, or "nerve center," was located. See, e.g., Scot Typewriter Co. v. Underwood Corp., 170 F. Supp. 862 (S.D.N.Y.1959). The Court in *Hertz* resolved this split in favor of the "nerve center."

Under the general diversity jurisdiction statute, 28 U.S.C. § 1332(c), an unincorporated association is a citizen of all the states in which the members of the association are citizens. This rule has most frequent application to business partnerships and labor unions. See Carden v. Arkoma Associates, 494 U.S. 185, 110 S.Ct. 1015, 108 L.Ed.2d 157 (1990) (business partnership); United Steelworkers of America v. R.H. Bouligny, Inc., 382 U.S. 145, 86 S.Ct. 272, 15 L.Ed.2d 217 (1965) (labor union). A suit on behalf of a trust, including a business trust, may be brought solely in the name of the trustee. The citizenship of the trustee, and not that of the trust beneficiaries, will be considered for purposes of diversity. Navarro Savings Ass'n v. Lee, 446 U.S. 458, 100 S.Ct. 1779, 64 L.Ed.2d 425 (1980). Under the Class Action Fairness Act of 2005 (CAFA), however, an unincorporated association is treated like a corporation. CAFA specifies that for purposes of class actions that qualify for CAFA treatment, an unincorporated association is a citizen of the state where it has its principal place of business and of the state under whose laws it is organized. 28 U.S.C. § 1332(d)(10).

2.   Complete diversity. In Strawbridge v. Curtiss, 7 U.S. (3 Cranch) 267, 2 L.Ed. 435 (1806), Chief Justice John Marshall held that "complete diversity" is required under the statute that later became § 1332. "Complete diversity" means that all the plaintiffs must be of a different citizenship from all the defendants. Thus, if all the plaintiffs are citizens of California and all the defendants are citizens of New York or Illinois, there is complete diversity. But if a citizen of California is joined as a defendant, in addition to the New York and Illinois citizens, complete diversity is destroyed and jurisdiction under § 1332 is defeated. Complete diversity is a statutory requirement under § 1332. It is not a constitutional requirement. One example of a statute that does not require complete diversity is the federal interpleader statute, 28 U.S.C. § 1335, which requires only minimal diversity. That is, it is enough if any defendant has a different citizenship from any plaintiff. State Farm Fire & Casualty Co. v. Tashire, 386 U.S. 523, 87 S.Ct. 1199, 18 L.Ed.2d 270 (1967). Another example is CAFA, which is applicable to class actions in which the aggregate amount in controversy exceeds $5,000,000. CAFA class actions require only minimal diversity. 28 U.S.C. § 1332(d)(2).

The Multiparty, Multiforum Trial Jurisdiction Act of 2002 gives federal district courts original jurisdiction over civil suits arising from a single accident in which at least 75 people have died, provided certain multi-state elements are present. See 28 U.S.C. §§ 1369 and 1441(e). Only minimal diversity is required under the Act. However, the statute instructs a district court to "abstain from hearing" the suit if "the substantial majority of all plaintiffs are citizens of a single State of which the primary defendants are also citizens; and the claims asserted will be governed primarily by the laws of that state." 28 U.S.C. § 1369(b)(1) and (2). The Act contains an unusual provision allowing remand of removed actions. Once the federal district court has determined liability, it must remand to the state court for determination of the amount of damages "unless the [district] court finds that, for the convenience of parties and witnesses and in the interest of justice, the action should be retained" in the district court. 28 U.S.C. § 1441(e)(2). See Wallace v. Louisiana Citizens Property Ins. Corp., 444 F.3d 697 (5th Cir. 2006) (suit arising out of Hurricane Katrina); Passa v. Derderian, 308 F. Supp. 2d 43 (D.R.I. 2004) (suit arising out of night club fire in Rhode Island); Effron, Disaster-Specific Mechanisms for Consolidation, 82 Tul.L.Rev. 2423 (2008).

In a suit originally filed in federal court against several defendants, one of whom would defeat complete diversity, or in a suit removed from state court in which such a defendant is added after removal, the district court may dismiss the defendant under federal Rule 21 in order to preserve its jurisdiction. The dismissal is in the sound discretion of the district judge. However, the district court should not dismiss if dismissal is improper under the criteria provided in Rule 19(b). See, e.g., Filippini v. Ford Motor Co., 110 F.R.D. 131 (N.D.Ill.1986). A court of appeals also has the power to dismiss such a defendant; a remand to the district court for a dismissal under Rule 21 is unnecessary. Newman-Green, Inc. v. Alfonzo-Larrain, 490 U.S. 826, 109 S.Ct. 2218, 104 L.Ed.2d 893 (1989). Compare the higher standard where plaintiff has joined a non-diverse defendant in a suit originally filed in state court, and where defendant seeks to remove. A diverse defendant seeking to dismiss a non-diverse defendant in order to permit removal must show that plaintiff joined the non-diverse defendant "fraudulently" as a means to defeat removal. Batoff v. State Farm Insurance Co., 977 F.2d 848 (3d Cir. 1992). See discussion of removal, infra p. 286.

3. **Amount in controversy.** The diversity jurisdiction statute has always required that the amount in controversy exceed a certain minimum. Under the Judiciary Act of 1789, the amount was $500. It is now $75,000, increased in 1997 from $50,000. (The general federal question jurisdiction statute, 28 U.S.C. § 1331, had a $10,000 amount in controversy requirement for many years, but the requirement was removed entirely in 1980.) Two functions are served, at least to some degree, by the amount in controversy requirement. First, the requirement preserves federal judicial resources by keeping small diversity cases out of the federal courts. Second, it protects plaintiffs in small diversity cases filed in rural state courts from being removed to federal courts located in urban centers.

a. **Legal certainty test.** The "legal certainty" test of St. Paul Mercury Indemnity Co. v. Red Cab Co., 303 U.S. 283, 58 S.Ct. 586, 82 L.Ed. 845 (1938), requires a defendant opposing jurisdiction to prove to a "legal certainty" that plaintiff cannot recover damages in excess of $75,000. The test is obviously designed to favor plaintiffs, but it is not an "open sesame" for all claims, even when plaintiff has suffered substantial harm. For example, in Kahn v. Hotel Ramada of Nevada, 799 F.2d 199 (5th Cir. 1986), plaintiff entrusted his luggage and a briefcase containing valuable jewelry to a hotel bellman at a Las Vegas hotel. When he returned an hour later, it had been stolen. Plaintiff sued in federal district court for the alleged value of the property, an amount substantially in excess of the jurisdictional amount. The hotel moved to dismiss on the ground that a Nevada hotelkeepers statute limited its liability to $750. The court found that the statute governed, and sustained a dismissal by the district court for lack of jurisdiction. (Question: If plaintiff Kahn now files suit in state court, what will be the effect of the federal court's dismissal for want of jurisdiction? Will the state court be required to follow the federal court's decision on the meaning of the statute? The federal court clearly found as a matter of law that the statute governed, but did it do so "on the merits"? See materials on issue preclusion, infra p. 1072.) Claims for punitive damages are part of the jurisdictional amount, but "a claim for punitive damages is to be given closer scrutiny, and the trial judge accorded greater discretion than a claim for actual damages." Zahn v. International Paper Co., 469 F.2d 1033 n. 1 (2d Cir. 1972), aff'd on other grounds 414 U.S. 291 (1973).

b. Injunctions, and plaintiff's or defendant's viewpoint. Injunctions present special problems of valuation. Not only may the dollar amount at stake be hard to calculate, but, in addition, the value to the plaintiff and the cost to the defendant may be different. For example, in Glenwood Light & Water Co. v. Mutual Light, Heat & Power Co., 239 U.S. 121, 36 S.Ct. 30, 60 L.Ed. 174 (1915), plaintiff sought an injunction that would have forced defendant to move certain electrical poles and wires. The value to the plaintiff was more than the jurisdictional amount, but the cost to the defendant was less. The Supreme Court upheld jurisdiction, viewing the jurisdictional amount from the plaintiff's perspective. Although the cases are not uniform, the general tendency is to find jurisdiction if the amount in controversy is satisfied when viewed from *either* the plaintiff's or the defendant's perspective. 14B C. Wright, A. Miller, and E. Cooper, Federal Practice and Procedure § 3703 (2009).

c. Aggregation of claims. The general rule is that a single plaintiff can aggregate all claims brought in a single complaint—even if the causes of action are unrelated to one another—to satisfy the jurisdictional amount. Multiple plaintiffs, however, cannot aggregate their claims to satisfy the jurisdictional amount. Snyder v. Harris, 394 U.S. 332, 89 S.Ct. 1053, 22 L.Ed.2d 319 (1969). However, if the claim of one plaintiff satisfies the jurisdictional amount, often plaintiffs whose claims do not satisfy the jurisdictional amount may join the suit under either Rule 20 (joinder) or Rule 23 (class action). See Exxon Mobil v. Allapattah Services, Inc., 545 U.S. 546, 125 S.Ct. 2611, 162 L.Ed.2d 502 (2005), infra p. 276. If individual or class plaintiffs have an undivided interest in the claim, the value of the entire interest may be considered. For example, in Eagle v. American Telephone and Telegraph Co., 769 F.2d 541 (9th Cir. 1985), cert. den. 475 U.S. 1084 (1986), plaintiffs were a class of minority shareholders alleging wrongful depletion of corporate assets resulting from a merger. The court held that the interests of shareholders under California law in such a case were "common and undivided," and upheld jurisdiction based on the dollar amount of injury to the entire class of shareholders. 769 F.2d at 546–47. For a useful description of the rules governing aggregation and a proposed statute see Rensberger, The Amount in Controversy: Understanding the Rules of Aggregation, 26 Ariz.St.L.J. 925 (1994).

d. Counterclaims. Amounts sought in permissive counterclaims under federal Rule 13(b) are not considered part of the amount in controversy. The same is generally true of amounts sought in compulsory counterclaims under Rule 13(a), at least for suits filed directly in federal district court. (The only exception is a case that appears to be a "sport." Horton v. Liberty Mutual Insurance Co., 367 U.S. 348, 81 S.Ct. 1570, 6 L.Ed.2d 890 (1961).) However, when the defendant seeks an amount over $75,000 in a compulsory counterclaim in state court, and then removes the case to federal court based on that amount in controversy, the cases are split. Some allow removal; some do not. For extended discussion, see 14B C. Wright, A. Miller, and E. Cooper, Federal Practice and Procedure § 3706 (2009).

4. Improper or collusive assignment or joinder to create diversity. 28 U.S.C. § 1359 provides that assignment or joinder of parties may not be done "improperly or collusively" in order to invoke jurisdiction. In Kramer v. Caribbean Mills, Inc., 394 U.S. 823, 89 S.Ct. 1487, 23 L.Ed.2d 9 (1969), a Haitian and a Panamanian corporation became embroiled in a contract dispute. The Panamanian corporation assigned its entire claim of $165,000 under the contract to its lawyer, Kramer, a Texas citizen, for $1. In a separate agreement, signed on the same day as the assignment, Kramer agreed to pay 95% of any recovery on the assigned cause of action to the corporation, "solely as a bonus." The net effect of the assignment and the separate agreement was to give Kramer a contingency fee of 5% of any recovery in the suit. Kramer then filed suit in his own name in diversity in federal district court in Texas. The jury returned a verdict for $165,000, but the Supreme Court sustained a dismissal for want of jurisdiction. The Court reasoned:

> If federal jurisdiction could be created by assignments of this kind, which are easy to arrange and involve few disadvantages for the assignor, then a vast quantity of ordinary contract and tort litigation could be channeled into the federal courts at the will of one of the parties.

394 U.S. at 828–29.

5. Probate and domestic relations. Although no explicit exception is made in 28 U.S.C. § 1332, under long-established case law diversity jurisdiction does not include probate proceedings, or domestic relations suits seeking divorce, alimony, or child custody. The Supreme Court reaffirmed the domestic relations exception in Ankenbrandt v. Richards, 504 U.S. 689, 112 S.Ct. 2206, 119 L.Ed.2d 468 (1992). Plaintiff brought a damages suit on behalf of her two daughters against her former husband (the girls' father) and his female companion, alleging physical and sexual abuse. The Court sustained jurisdiction, noting the existence of the domestic relations exception but holding that this tort suit fell outside it.

You may wish to consider the following views on the domestic relations exception:

> [R]ecognizing the increasing federalization of family law as well as past discrimination against these issues, federal courts should treat family law cases like any other diversity cases. * * * Domestic relations issues are of paramount importance to the litigants who bring these cases; these litigants deserve as much respect as litigants in any other diversity case.

Cahn, Family Law, Federalism, and the Federal Courts, 79 Iowa L.Rev. 1073, 1126 (1994).

> Women and the families they sometimes inhabit are not only assumed to be outside the federal courts, they are also assumed not to be related to the "national issues" to which the federal judiciary is to devote its interests. Jurisdictional lines have not been drawn according to the laws of nature but by men, who today are seeking to confirm their prestige as members of the most important judiciary in the country. * * * Dealing with women—in and out of families, arguing about federal statutory rights of relatively small value—is not how they want to frame their job.

Resnik, "Naturally" without Gender: Women, Jurisdiction, and the Federal Courts, 66 N.Y.U.L.Rev. 1682, 1749 (1991). For an argument in favor of a special category of "*Akenbrandt* abstention," under which federal courts would have jurisdiction but would abstain from deciding "core" domestic relations cases and, in addition, cases raising difficult questions of unresolved state law, see Stein, The Domestic Relations Exception to Federal Jurisdiction: Rethinking an Unsettled Federal Courts Doctrine, 36 Boston Coll.L.Rev. 669 (1995).

NOTE ON THE ORIGIN AND PURPOSES OF DIVERSITY JURISDICTION

Article III of the Constitution confers jurisdiction on the federal courts over "Controversies * * * between Citizens of different States; * * * and between a State, or the Citizens thereof, and foreign States, Citizens or Subjects." U.S.Const., Art.III, Sec.2, para.1. The Judiciary Act of 1789 implemented the constitutional grant of diversity jurisdiction, and the federal trial courts have exercised diversity jurisdiction ever since. Compare the early statutory grant of diversity jurisdiction (1789) to the late permanent grant of general federal question jurisdiction (1875). Why do you suppose the one was so early and the other so late? The 1789 statute provided that "the circuit courts shall have original cognizance, concurrent with the courts of the several States, of all suits of a civil nature at common law or in equity, where the matter in dispute exceeds, exclusive of costs, the sum or value of five hundred dollars, and * * * an alien is a party, or the suit is between a citizen of the State where the suit is brought, and a citizen of another State." 1 Stat. 73, 78, § 11 (Sept. 24, 1789). Except for the fact that district courts have now replaced circuit courts as the primary federal trial courts, the modern diversity statute, 28 U.S.C. § 1332, is remarkably similar to the 1789 version.

The most obvious purpose of diversity jurisdiction was to protect out-of-state litigants against local prejudice. As Alexander Hamilton wrote in *The Federalist* No. 80: "The reasonableness of the agency of the national courts in cases in which the State tribunals cannot be supposed to be impartial speaks for itself. * * * This principle has no inconsiderable weight in designating the federal courts as the proper tribunals for the determination of controversies between different States and their citizens." Chief Justice John Marshall wrote to the same effect in Bank of the United States v. Deveaux, 9 U.S. (5 Cranch) 61, 87, 3 L.Ed. 38 (1809): "However true the fact may be, that the tribunals of the states will administer justice as impartially as those of the nation, to parties of every description, it is not less true that the constitution itself either entertains apprehensions on this subject, or views with such indulgence the possible fears and apprehensions of suitors, that it has established national tribunals for the decision of controversies between aliens and a citizen, or between citizens of different states."

Yet diversity jurisdiction was not universally accepted, and prejudice against out-of-staters not universally conceded. Consider the following exchange during the Virginia debates over the ratification of the Constitution. It anticipates modern debates over diversity both in the vigor of the attack and in the somewhat tepid defense. George Mason, a venerated Virginia lawyer, argued, "[The federal courts'] *jurisdiction* extends to controversies between citizens of different states. Can we not trust our state courts with the decision of these? If I have a controversy with a man in Maryland,—if a man in Maryland has my bond for a hundred pounds,—are not the state courts competent to try it? Is it suspected that they would enforce the payment if unjust, or refuse to enforce it if just? The very idea is ridiculous." James Madison, one of the authors of *The Federalist* and probably more responsible than any other single person for the structure of the federal judiciary, responded, "As to its cognizance of disputes between citizens of different states, I will not say it is a matter of much importance. Perhaps it might be left to the state courts. But I sincerely believe this provision will be rather salutary than otherwise." 3 J. Elliot, Debates in the Several State Conventions on the Adoption of the Federal Constitution 526, 533 (1881). For early scholarly argument on the role of prejudice against out-of-staters, compare Friendly, The Historic Basis of Diversity Jurisdiction, 41 Harv.L.Rev. 483 (1928) (prejudice against out-of-staters was speculative in 1789), and Frankfurter, Distribution of Judicial Power Between United States and State Courts, 13 Cornell L.Q. 499 (1928) (same, relying on Friendly), with Yntema and Jaffin, Preliminary Analysis of Concurrent Jurisdiction, 79 U.Pa.L.Rev. 869 (1931) (protection against prejudice was a likely purpose).

Another purpose, or at least function, of diversity jurisdiction was to provide a nationwide system of courts in which important commercial disputes could be adjudicated and a uniform system of law applied. At that time, commercial law was almost entirely judge-made common law which could vary from state to state. State courts had no obligation to adopt the commercial law of their neighboring states and had no ready mechanism to coordinate their common law decisions with those of neighboring states even when they wanted to do so. The federal courts, by contrast, were governed by a single appellate court—the Supreme Court—and applied uniform rules of general common law in commercial cases throughout the country. See Swift v. Tyson, 41 U.S. (16 Pet.) 1, 10 L.Ed. 865 (1842). By and large, particularly in the years before the Civil War, state courts appreciated the stability and uniformity of the federal courts' decisions in commercial cases and voluntarily conformed their decisions to those of the federal courts as a way of creating and maintaining a nationally uniform general common law in commercial cases. See, e.g., Fletcher, The General Common Law and Section 34 of the Judiciary Act of 1789: The Example of Marine Insurance, 97 Harv.L.Rev. 1513 (1984); Frank, Historical Bases of the Federal Judicial System, 13 Law & Contemp. Probs. 3, 28 (1948).

What are the purposes served by diversity jurisdiction today? The general common law of *Swift v. Tyson* was abandoned by the Supreme Court in Erie Railroad Co. v. Tompkins, 304 U.S. 64, 58 S.Ct. 817, 82 L.Ed. 1188

(1938), and federal courts now follow the laws of the states in which they sit. Thus, whatever advantage diversity jurisdiction and the general common law might once have provided in achieving uniformity of law is now gone. Indeed, this advantage had disappeared or was at least outweighed by problems associated with the general common law before the end of the nineteenth century. For further exploration of *Swift v. Tyson*, *Erie Railroad v. Tompkins*, and the role of the general common law, see infra p. 348.

Therefore, of the original purposes of diversity, only protection of out-of-staters remains. Is such prejudice a problem today? Are there other purposes that modern diversity jurisdiction serves? For most of the twentieth century, many scholars and judges, and some members of the practicing bar, recommended abolishing or curtailing diversity jurisdiction. The great majority of practicing lawyers, however, have favored its retention. For discussion, see, e.g., Report of the Federal Courts Study Committee 38 (1990) (urging severe curtailment); Rowe, Abolishing Diversity Jurisdiction: Positive Side Effects and Potential for Further Reform, 92 Harv.L.Rev. 963 (1979) (urging abolition); Kramer, Diversity Jurisdiction, 1990 B.Y.U.L.Rev. 97 (urging practical abolition or severe curtailment); American Law Institute, Study of the Division of Jurisdiction Between State and Federal Courts 99 (1969) (urging retention); Shapiro, Federal Diversity Jurisdiction: A Survey and a Proposal, 91 Harv.L.Rev. 317 (1977) (urging retention or abolition depending on local needs).

Prejudice against out-of-staters. Anecdotal evidence suggests that diversity jurisdiction is still a useful protection for out-of-staters. Consider the following two cases:

In *Pappas v. Middle Earth Condominium Ass'n*, 963 F.2d 534 (2d Cir. 1992), a New Jersey citizen brought a diversity suit in federal district court in Vermont against a Vermont citizen, based on a severe injury suffered when he slipped on ice outside defendant's condominium. Defendant's lawyer argued to the jury: "But isn't what they're really asking is that they can come up * * * here from New Jersey to Vermont to enjoy what we experience every year, for those of us who are here originally for most of our lives * * * and without a care in the world for their own safety when they encounter what we, ourselves do not take for granted, and then can injure themselves, and they can sit back and say, * * * 'I'd like you to retire me.' " 963 F.2d at 536–37. The court of appeals reversed a jury verdict for the defendant and remanded for a new trial, based on the regional bias in the defendant's argument.

In *TXO Production Corp. v. Alliance Resources Corp.*, 509 U.S. 443, 113 S.Ct. 2711, 125 L.Ed.2d 366 (1993), a state court jury in West Virginia returned a $10,000,000 punitive damages verdict against TXO, a large Texas corporation. The attorney for Allied Resources had begun his rebuttal argument, "Ladies and gentlemen of the jury, this greedy bunch from down in Texas doesn't understand this case." He called them "Texas high rollers, wildcatters," and compared TXO to a wealthy out-of-town visitor who "stays here all day" but refuses to put a quarter in the parking meter to pay for local fire and police departments. 509 U.S. at 493–94 (O'Connor, J., dissenting). The Supreme Court sustained the punitive damages award. Justice O'Connor argued in dissent that the award of punitive damages was excessive, using the regional bias to support her argument. No one, including Justice O'Connor, argued that the evident regional bias in the attorney's argument was itself sufficient to warrant setting aside the verdict. What would the Court's response have been if the case had been tried in federal court under diversity jurisdiction rather than in state court?

A 1992 survey of cases removed from state to federal court provides further evidence. Lawyers for the defendants in 56.3% of the diversity cases removed to federal court reported that bias against out-of-staters in the state court was an important consideration in seeking removal. More experienced lawyers reported bias more frequently than less experienced lawyers. Bias against out-of-staters was reported at relatively higher levels in the South and the non-industrialized Midwest, and at relatively lower levels in the Northeast, the industrialized Midwest, and the Far West. Miller, An Empirical Study of Forum Choices in Removal Cases Under Diversity and Federal Question Jurisdiction, 41 Am.U.L.Rev. 369, 409–10 (1992).

Other purposes. There may be other purposes for, or at least consequences of, diversity jurisdiction.

Protection from rural prejudice is related to but distinct from protection from prejudice against out-of-staters. State courts are located all over a state. Usually there is at least one trial court of general jurisdiction in every county. Federal courts, by contrast, are located only in the major cities. Therefore, removal from a state court in a rural county to the nearest federal court will necessarily mean that the trial will be held in an urban area, and the jury will be drawn from an urban rather than a rural population. In Gentle v. Lamb-Weston, Inc., 302 F. Supp. 161 (D.Me.1969), eleven Maine potato farmers sued an Oregon food processing corporation in state court in rural Aroostook County. Each farmer assigned 1/100th of his claim to a law school classmate of their attorney; the classmate was an Oregon citizen, who became the twelfth plaintiff by virtue of the assignments. The presence of the Oregon citizen as a plaintiff defeated removal to the federal district court in Portland because it destroyed complete diversity. The district judge wrote, "Through this cynical device, plaintiffs seek to benefit from whatever local prejudice a trial against a foreign corporation before an Aroostook County jury might afford them." 302 F. Supp. at 163. The judge allowed removal despite the assignment.

It is also argued, and sometimes stated as if beyond argument, that federal judges and procedures are better than those of the states. A representative statement is, "Without disparagement of the quality of justice in many state courts throughout the country, it may be granted that often the federal courts do have better judges, better juries, and better procedures. Life tenure gives a degree of independence to a federal judge that a state judge facing re-election may find it hard to maintain, and in some types of cases this difference might be very significant." American Law Institute, Study of the Division of Jurisdiction Between State and Federal Courts 100 (1969).

Cross-fertilization between the court systems, and broadening of federal judges through continued exposure to state law, are also asserted as advantages stemming from diversity jurisdiction. The evidence on these factors is genuine but somewhat equivocal. For a thoughtful exploration, see Shapiro, Federal Diversity Jurisdiction: A Survey and a Proposal, 91 Harv.L.Rev. 317, 321–29 (1977).

Arguments against diversity. With all of that, what are the arguments against diversity jurisdiction? Former Dean Larry Kramer gives six: First, diversity cases consume federal judicial resources, and "perhaps no other major class of cases has a weaker claim on federal judicial resources." The federal courts' most important business is to decide cases involving questions of federal law. Second, federal courts bring no "special expertise" to questions of state law. Third, "diversity jurisdiction is frequently a source of friction between state and federal courts." This results not only from disagreements between federal and state courts about the meaning of state law, but also from the awkwardness produced when parties file (as they sometimes do) simultaneous parallel suits in federal and state court. Fourth, minimizing frictions between the two court systems is expensive and time-consuming. Fifth, "diversity jurisdiction reduces pressure to improve state judicial systems." Sixth, "while it would be an overstatement to say that there are no benefits from diversity jurisdiction, most of its original justifications no longer exist." Kramer, Diversity Jurisdiction, 1990 B.Y.U.L.Rev. 97, 102–107.

3. SUPPLEMENTAL JURISDICTION

United Mine Workers of America v. Gibbs

Supreme Court of the United States, 1966.
383 U.S. 715, 86 S.Ct. 1130, 16 L.Ed.2d 218.

■ MR. JUSTICE BRENNAN delivered the opinion of the Court.

Respondent Paul Gibbs was awarded compensatory and punitive damages in this action against petitioner United Mine Workers of America (UMW) for alleged violations of § 303 of the Labor Management Relations Act, 1947, and of the common law of Tennessee. The case grew out of the rivalry between the United Mine Workers and the Southern Labor Union over representation of workers in the southern Appalachian coal fields. Tennessee Consolidated Coal Company, not a party here, laid off 100 miners of the UMW's Local 5881 when it closed one of its mines in southern Tennessee during the spring of 1960. Late that summer, Grundy Company, a wholly owned subsidiary of Consolidated, hired respondent as mine superintendent to attempt to open a new mine on Consolidated's property at nearby Gray's Creek through use of members of the Southern Labor Union. As part of the arrangement, Grundy also gave respondent a contract to haul the mine's coal to the nearest railroad loading point.

On August 15 and 16, 1960, armed members of Local 5881 forcibly prevented the opening of the mine, threatening respondent and beating an organizer for the rival union. The members of the local believed Consolidated had promised them the jobs at the new mine; they insisted that if anyone would do the work, they would. At this time, no representative of the UMW, their international union, was present. George Gilbert, the UMW's field representative for the area including Local 5881, was away at Middlesboro, Kentucky, attending an Executive Board meeting when the members of the local discovered Grundy's plan; he did not return to the area until late in the day of August 16. There was uncontradicted testimony that he first learned of the violence while at the meeting, and returned with explicit instructions from his international union superiors to establish a limited picket line, to prevent any further violence, and to see to it that the strike did not spread to neighboring mines. There was no further violence at the mine site; a picket line was maintained there for nine months; and no further attempts were made to open the mine during that period.

Respondent lost his job as superintendent, and never entered into performance of his haulage contract. He testified that he soon began to lose other trucking contracts and mine leases he held in nearby areas. Claiming these effects to be the result of a concerted union plan against him, he sought recovery not against Local 5881 or its members, but only against petitioner, the international union. The suit was brought in the United States District Court for the Eastern District of Tennessee, and jurisdiction was premised on allegations of secondary boycotts under § 303. The state law claim, for which jurisdiction was based upon the doctrine of pendent jurisdiction, asserted "an unlawful conspiracy and an unlawful boycott aimed at him and [Grundy] to maliciously, wantonly and willfully interfere with his contract of employment and with his contract of haulage."

* * * The jury's verdict was that the UMW had violated both § 303 and state law. Gibbs was awarded $60,000 as damages under the employment contract and $14,500 under the haulage contract; he was also awarded $100,000 punitive damages. On motion, the trial court set aside the award of damages with respect to the haulage contract on the ground that damage was unproved. It also held that union pressure on Grundy to discharge respondent as supervisor would constitute only a primary dispute with Grundy, as respondent's employer, and hence was not cognizable as a claim under § 303. Interference with the employment relationship was cognizable as a state claim, however, and a remitted award was sustained on the state law claim. We granted certiorari. We reverse.

I.

A threshold question is whether the District Court properly entertained jurisdiction of the claim based on Tennessee law. * * *

* * *

* * * The Court held in Hurn v. Oursler, 289 U.S. 238, 53 S.Ct. 586, 77 L.Ed. 1148, that state law claims are appropriate for federal court determination if they form a separate but parallel ground for relief also sought in a substantial claim based on federal law. * * *

Hurn was decided in 1933, before the unification of law and equity by the Federal Rules of Civil Procedure. At the time, the meaning of "cause of action" was a subject of serious dispute; the phrase might "mean one thing for one purpose and something different for another."

* * *

With the adoption of the Federal Rules of Civil Procedure and the unified form of action, Fed.Rule Civ.Proc. 2, much of the controversy over "cause of action" abated. The phrase remained as the keystone of the *Hurn* test, however, and, as commentators have noted, has been the source of considerable confusion. Under the Rules, the impulse is toward entertaining the broadest possible scope of action consistent with fairness to the parties; joinder of claims, parties and remedies is strongly encouraged. Yet because the *Hurn* question involves issues of jurisdiction as well as convenience, there has been some tendency to limit its application to cases in which the state and federal claims are, as in *Hurn,* "little more than the equivalent of different epithets to characterize the same group of circumstances." 289 U.S., at 246, 53 S.Ct., at 590.

This limited approach is unnecessarily grudging. Pendent jurisdiction, in the sense of judicial *power,* exists whenever there is a claim "arising under [the] Constitution, the Laws of the United States, and Treaties made, or which shall be made, under their Authority * * *," U.S. Const., Art. III, § 2, and the relationship between that claim and the state claim permits the conclusion that the entire action before the court comprises but one constitutional "case." The federal claim must have substance sufficient to confer subject matter jurisdiction on the court. Levering & Garrigues Co. v. Morrin, 289 U.S. 103, 53 S.Ct. 549, 77 L.Ed. 1062. The state and federal claims must derive from a common nucleus of operative fact. But if, considered without regard to their federal or state character, a plaintiff's claims are such that he would ordinarily be expected to try them all in one judicial proceeding, then, assuming substantiality of the federal issues, there is *power* in federal courts to hear the whole.

That power need not be exercised in every case in which it is found to exist. It has consistently been recognized that pendent jurisdiction is a doctrine of discretion, not of plaintiff's right. Its justification lies in considerations of judicial economy, convenience and fairness to litigants; if these are not present a federal court should hesitate to exercise jurisdiction over state claims, even though bound to apply state law to them, Erie R. Co. v. Tompkins, 304 U.S. 64, 58 S.Ct. 817, 82 L.Ed. 1188. Needless decisions of state law should be avoided both as a matter of comity and to promote justice between the parties, by procuring for them a surer-footed reading of applicable law. Certainly, if the federal claims are dismissed before trial, even though not insubstantial in a jurisdictional sense, the state claims should be dismissed as well. Similarly, if it appears that the state issues substantially predominate, whether in terms of proof, of the scope of the issues raised, or of the comprehensiveness of the remedy sought, the state claims may be dismissed without prejudice and left for resolution to state tribunals. There may, on the other hand, be situations in which the state claim is so closely tied to questions of federal policy that the argument for exercise of pendent jurisdiction is particularly strong. In the present case, for example, the allowable scope of the state claim implicates the federal doctrine of pre-emption; while this interrelationship does not create statutory federal question jurisdiction, Louisville & N.R. Co. v. Mottley, 211 U.S. 149, 29 S.Ct. 42, 53 L.Ed. 126, its existence is relevant to the exercise of discretion. Finally, there may be reasons independent of jurisdictional considerations, such as the likelihood of jury confusion in treating divergent legal theories of relief, that would justify separating state and federal claims for trial, Fed.Rule Civ.Proc. 42(b). If so, jurisdiction should ordinarily be refused.

The question of power will ordinarily be resolved on the pleadings. But the issue whether pendent jurisdiction has been properly assumed is one which remains open throughout the litigation. Pretrial procedures or even the trial itself may reveal a substantial hegemony of state law claims, or likelihood of jury confusion, which could not have been anticipated at the pleading stage. Although it will of course be appropriate to take account in this circumstance of the already completed course of the litigation, dismissal of the state claim might even then be merited. For example, it may appear that the plaintiff was well aware of the nature of his proofs and the relative importance of his claims; recognition of a federal court's wide latitude to decide ancillary questions of state law does not imply that it must tolerate a litigant's effort to impose upon it what is in effect only a state law case. Once it appears that a state claim constitutes the real body of a case, to which the federal claim is only an appendage, the state claim may fairly be dismissed.

We are not prepared to say that in the present case the District Court exceeded its discretion in proceeding to judgment on the state claim. We may assume for purposes of decision that the District Court was correct in its holding that the claim of pressure on Grundy to terminate the employment contract was outside the purview of § 303. Even so, the § 303 claims based on secondary pressures on Grundy relative to the haulage contract and on other coal operators generally were substantial. Although § 303 limited recovery to compensatory damages based on secondary pressures, Local 20, Teamsters, Chauffeurs and Helpers Union v. Morton, supra, and state law allowed both compensatory and punitive damages, and allowed such damages as to both secondary and primary activity, the state and federal claims arose from the same nucleus of operative fact and reflected alternative remedies. Indeed, the verdict sheet sent in to the jury authorized only one award of damages, so that recovery could not be given separately on the federal and state claims.

It is true that the § 303 claims ultimately failed and that the only recovery allowed respondent was on the state claim. We cannot confidently say, however, that the federal issues were so remote or played such a minor role at the trial that in effect the state claim only was tried. * * *

* * * Moreover, the question whether the permissible scope of the state claim was limited by the doctrine of pre-emption afforded a special reason for the exercise of pendent jurisdiction; the federal courts are particularly appropriate bodies for the application of pre-emption principles. We thus conclude that although it may be that the District Court might, in its sound discretion, have dismissed the state claim, the circumstances show no error in refusing to do so.

II.

[The Supreme Court then reversed the judgment on the merits.]

Reversed.

■ THE CHIEF JUSTICE took no part in the decision of this case.

[A concurring opinion by JUSTICE HARLAN joined by JUSTICE CLARK, is omitted.]

NOTES AND QUESTIONS

1. **Why no diversity jurisdiction?** Why was there no diversity between plaintiff Gibbs and defendant United Mine Workers of America? (Hint: United Mine Workers of America is not a corporation.)

2. **Additional claim against the same defendant.** *UMW v. Gibbs* was a fairly easy case in which to find subject matter jurisdiction. Plaintiff

was already in federal district court on a federal question claim, and sought merely to add an additional state-law claim, arising out of the same set of facts, against the same defendant. Should there have been jurisdiction if plaintiff had sought to add a claim against an additional party?

3. Additional claim against an additional party. In Aldinger v. Howard, 427 U.S. 1, 96 S.Ct. 2413, 49 L.Ed.2d 276 (1976), plaintiff brought a federal civil rights claim against several individual defendants under 28 U.S.C. § 1343 and 42 U.S.C. § 1983, and a state-law claim arising out of the same set of facts against Spokane County. The Supreme Court denied jurisdiction over the state-law claim against the additional party, Spokane County. In *Aldinger*, plaintiff could have sued all the defendants, including the county, in state court. The Court noted that a different case would be presented if one of the defendants could be sued only in federal court:

> Other statutory grants [than §§ 1343 and 1983] and other alignments of parties and claims might call for a different result. When the grant of jurisdiction to a federal court is exclusive, for example, as in the prosecution of tort claims against the United States under 28 U.S.C. § 1346, the argument of judicial economy and convenience can be coupled with the additional argument that *only* in a federal court may all of the claims be tried together.

427 U.S. at 18 (emphasis in original).

4. Further discussion. For further discussion of *UMW v. Gibbs*, see Note on Supplemental Jurisdiction following the next case.

Owen Equipment & Erection Co. v. Kroger

Supreme Court of the United States, 1978.
437 U.S. 365, 98 S.Ct. 2396, 57 L.Ed.2d 274.

■ MR. JUSTICE STEWART delivered the opinion of the Court.

In an action in which federal jurisdiction is based on diversity of citizenship, may the plaintiff assert a claim against a third-party defendant when there is no independent basis for federal jurisdiction over that claim? * * *

I

On January 18, 1972, James Kroger was electrocuted when the boom of a steel crane next to which he was walking came too close to a high-tension electric power line. The respondent (his widow, who is the administratrix of his estate) filed a wrongful-death action in the United States District Court for the District of Nebraska against the Omaha Public Power District (OPPD). Her complaint alleged that OPPD's negligent construction, maintenance, and operation of the power line had caused Kroger's death. Federal jurisdiction was based on diversity of citizenship, since the respondent was a citizen of Iowa and OPPD was a Nebraska corporation.

OPPD then filed a third-party complaint pursuant to Fed.Rule Civ.Proc. 14(a)[2] against the petitioner, Owen Equipment and Erection

---

[2]   Rule 14(a) provides in relevant part:

"At any time after commencement of the action a defending party, as a third-party plaintiff, may cause a summons and complaint to be served upon a person not a party

Co. (Owen), alleging that the crane was owned and operated by Owen, and that Owen's negligence had been the proximate cause of Kroger's death. OPPD later moved for summary judgment on the respondent's complaint against it. While this motion was pending, the respondent was granted leave to file an amended complaint naming Owen as an additional defendant. Thereafter, the District Court granted OPPD's motion for summary judgment in an unreported opinion. The case thus went to trial between the respondent and the petitioner alone.

The respondent's amended complaint alleged that Owen was "a Nebraska corporation with its principal place of business in Nebraska." Owen's answer admitted that it was "a corporation organized and existing under the laws of the State of Nebraska," and denied every other allegation of the complaint. On the third day of trial, however, it was disclosed that the petitioner's principal place of business was in Iowa, not Nebraska,[5] and that the petitioner and the respondent were thus both citizens of Iowa. The petitioner then moved to dismiss the complaint for lack of jurisdiction. The District Court reserved decision on the motion, and the jury thereafter returned a verdict in favor of the respondent. In an unreported opinion issued after the trial, the District Court denied the petitioner's motion to dismiss the complaint.

The judgment was affirmed on appeal. 558 F.2d 417. The Court of Appeals held that under this Court's decision in Mine Workers v. Gibbs, 383 U.S. 715, 86 S.Ct. 1130, 16 L.Ed.2d 218, the District Court had jurisdictional power, in its discretion, to adjudicate the respondent's claim against the petitioner because that claim arose from the "core of 'operative facts' giving rise to both [respondent's] claim against OPPD and OPPD's claim against Owen." 558 F.2d at 424. It further held that the District Court had properly exercised its discretion in proceeding to decide the case even after summary judgment had been granted to OPPD, because the petitioner had concealed its Iowa citizenship from the respondent. Rehearing en banc was denied by an equally divided court. 558 F.2d 417.

II

It is undisputed that there was no independent basis of federal jurisdiction over the respondent's state-law tort action against the petitioner, since both are citizens of Iowa. And although Fed.Rule

---

to the action who is or may be liable to him for all or part of the plaintiff's claim against him. * * * The person served with the summons and third-party complaint, hereinafter called the third-party defendant, shall make his defenses to the third-party plaintiff's claim as provided in Rule 12 and his counterclaims against the third-party plaintiff and cross-claims against other third-party defendants as provided in Rule 13. The third-party defendant may assert against the plaintiff any defenses which the third-party plaintiff has to the plaintiff's claim. The third-party defendant may also assert any claim against the plaintiff arising out of the transaction or occurrence that is the subject matter of the plaintiff's claim against the third-party plaintiff. The plaintiff may assert any claim against the third-party defendant arising out of the transaction or occurrence that is the subject matter of the plaintiff's claim against the third-party plaintiff, and the third-party defendant thereupon shall assert his defenses as provided in Rule 12 and his counter-claims and cross-claims as provided in Rule 13."

[5]   The problem apparently was one of geography. Although the Missouri River generally marks the boundary between Iowa and Nebraska, Carter Lake, Iowa, where the accident occurred and where Owen had its main office, lies west of the river, adjacent to Omaha, Neb. Apparently the river once avulsed at one of its bends, cutting Carter Lake off from the rest of Iowa.

Civ.Proc. 14(a) permits a plaintiff to assert a claim against a third-party defendant, it does not purport to say whether or not such a claim requires an independent basis of federal jurisdiction. Indeed, it could not determine that question, since it is axiomatic that the Federal Rules of Civil Procedure do not create or withdraw federal jurisdiction.[7]

In affirming the District Court's judgment, the Court of Appeals relied upon the doctrine of ancillary jurisdiction, whose contours it believed were defined by this Court's holding in *Mine Workers v. Gibbs, supra.* The *Gibbs* case differed from this one in that it involved pendent jurisdiction, which concerns the resolution of a plaintiff's federal-and state-law claims against a single defendant in one action. By contrast, in this case there was no claim based upon substantive federal law, but rather state-law tort claims against two different defendants. Nonetheless, the Court of Appeals was correct in perceiving that *Gibbs* and this case are two species of the same generic problem: Under what circumstances may a federal court hear and decide a state-law claim arising between citizens of the same State?[8] But we believe that the Court of Appeals failed to understand the scope of the doctrine of the *Gibbs* case.

* * *

It is apparent that *Gibbs* delineated the constitutional limits of federal judicial power. But even if it be assumed that the District Court in the present case had constitutional power to decide the respondent's lawsuit against the petitioner,[10] it does not follow that the decision of the Court of Appeals was correct. Constitutional power is merely the first hurdle that must be overcome in determining that a federal court has jurisdiction over a particular controversy. For the jurisdiction of the federal courts is limited not only by the provisions of Art. III of the Constitution, but also by Acts of Congress. * * *

III

The relevant statute in this case, 28 U.S.C. § 1332(a)(1), confers upon federal courts jurisdiction over "civil actions where the matter in controversy exceeds the sum or value of $10,000 * * * and is between * * * citizens of different States." This statute and its predecessors have consistently been held to require complete diversity of citizenship.[13] That is, diversity jurisdiction does not exist unless each defendant is a citizen of a different State from each plaintiff. Over the years Congress has

---

[7]   Fed.Rule Civ.Proc. 82; see Snyder v. Harris, 394 U.S. 332, 89 S.Ct. 1053, 22 L.Ed.2d 319; Sibbach v. Wilson & Co., 312 U.S. 1, 10, 61 S.Ct. 422, 424, 85 L.Ed. 479.

[8]   No more than in Aldinger v. Howard, 427 U.S. 1, 96 S.Ct. 2413, 49 L.Ed.2d 276, is it necessary to determine here "whether there are any 'principled' differences between pendent and ancillary jurisdiction; or, if there are, what effect *Gibbs* had on such differences." Id., at 13, 96 S.Ct., at 2420.

[10]   Federal jurisdiction in *Gibbs* was based upon the existence of a question of federal law. The Court of Appeals in the present case believed that the "common nucleus of operative fact" test also determines the outer boundaries of constitutionally permissible federal jurisdiction when that jurisdiction is based upon diversity of citizenship. We may assume without deciding that the Court of Appeals was correct in this regard. See also n. 13, infra.

[13]   E.g., Strawbridge v. Curtiss, 3 Cranch 267, 2 L.Ed. 435; Coal Co. v. Blatchford, 11 Wall. 172, 20 L.Ed. 179; Indianapolis v. Chase Nat. Bank, 314 U.S. 63, 69, 62 S.Ct. 15, 16, 86 L.Ed. 47; American Fire & Cas. Co. v. Finn, 341 U.S. 6, 17, 71 S.Ct. 534, 541, 95 L.Ed. 702. It is settled that complete diversity is not a constitutional requirement. State Farm Fire & Cas. Co. v. Tashire, 386 U.S. 523, 530–531, 87 S.Ct. 1199, 1203–1204, 18 L.Ed.2d 270.

repeatedly re-enacted or amended the statute conferring diversity jurisdiction, leaving intact this rule of complete diversity. Whatever may have been the original purposes of diversity-of-citizenship jurisdiction, this subsequent history clearly demonstrates a congressional mandate that diversity jurisdiction is not to be available when any plaintiff is a citizen of the same State as any defendant.

Thus it is clear that the respondent could not originally have brought suit in federal court naming Owen and OPPD as codefendants, since citizens of Iowa would have been on both sides of the litigation. Yet the identical lawsuit resulted when she amended her complaint. Complete diversity was destroyed just as surely as if she had sued Owen initially. In either situation, in the plain language of the statute, the "matter in controversy" could not be "between * * * citizens of different States."

It is a fundamental precept that federal courts are courts of limited jurisdiction. The limits upon federal jurisdiction, whether imposed by the Constitution or by Congress, must be neither disregarded nor evaded. Yet under the reasoning of the Court of Appeals in this case, a plaintiff could defeat the statutory requirement of complete diversity by the simple expedient of suing only those defendants who were of diverse citizenship and waiting for them to implead nondiverse defendants.[17] If, as the Court of Appeals thought, a "common nucleus of operative fact" were the only requirement for ancillary jurisdiction in a diversity case, there would be no principled reason why the respondent in this case could not have joined her cause of action against Owen in her original complaint as ancillary to her claim against OPPD. Congress' requirement of complete diversity would thus have been evaded completely.

It is true, as the Court of Appeals noted, that the exercise of ancillary jurisdiction over nonfederal claims has often been upheld in situations involving impleader, cross-claims or counterclaims. But in determining whether jurisdiction over a nonfederal claim exists, the context in which the nonfederal claim is asserted is crucial. And the claim here arises in a setting quite different from the kinds of nonfederal claims that have been viewed in other cases as falling within the ancillary jurisdiction of the federal courts.

First, the nonfederal claim in this case was simply not ancillary to the federal one in the same sense that, for example, the impleader by a defendant of a third-party defendant always is. A third-party complaint depends at least in part upon the resolution of the primary lawsuit. Its relation to the original complaint is thus not mere factual similarity but logical dependence. The respondent's claim against the petitioner, however, was entirely separate from her original claim against OPPD, since the petitioner's liability to her depended not at all upon whether or

---

[17] This is not an unlikely hypothesis, since a defendant in a tort suit such as this one would surely try to limit his liability by impleading any joint tortfeasors for indemnity or contribution. Some commentators have suggested that the possible abuse of third-party practice could be dealt with under 28 U.S.C. § 1359, which forbids collusive attempts to create federal jurisdiction. See, e.g., 3 J. Moore, Federal Practice 14.27[1], p. 14–571 (2d ed. 1974); 6 C. Wright & A. Miller, Federal Practice and Procedure § 1444, pp. 231–232 (1971); Note, Rule 14 Claims and Ancillary Jurisdiction, 57 Va.L.Rev. 265, 274–275 (1971). The dissenting opinion today also expresses this view. Post, at 2407. But there is nothing necessarily collusive about a plaintiff's selectively suing only those tortfeasors of diverse citizenship, or about the named defendants' desire to implead joint tortfeasors. Nonetheless, the requirement of complete diversity would be eviscerated by such a course of events.

not OPPD was also liable. Far from being an ancillary and dependent claim, it was a new and independent one.

Second, the nonfederal claim here was asserted by the plaintiff, who voluntarily chose to bring suit upon a state-law claim in a federal court. By contrast, ancillary jurisdiction typically involves claims by a defending party haled into court against his will, or by another person whose rights might be irretrievably lost unless he could assert them in an ongoing action in a federal court. A plaintiff cannot complain if ancillary jurisdiction does not encompass all of his possible claims in a case such as this one, since it is he who has chosen the federal rather than the state forum and must thus accept its limitations. "[T]he efficiency plaintiff seeks so avidly is available without question in the state courts." Kenrose Mfg. Co. v. Fred Whitaker Co., 512 F.2d 890, 894 (CA4).[20]

It is not unreasonable to assume that, in generally requiring complete diversity, Congress did not intend to confine the jurisdiction of federal courts so inflexibly that they are unable to protect legal rights or effectively to resolve an entire, logically entwined lawsuit. Those practical needs are the basis of the doctrine of ancillary jurisdiction. But neither the convenience of litigants nor considerations of judicial economy can suffice to justify extension of the doctrine of ancillary jurisdiction to a plaintiff's cause of action against a citizen of the same State in a diversity case. Congress has established the basic rule that diversity jurisdiction exists under 28 U.S.C. § 1332 only when there is complete diversity of citizenship. "The policy of the statute calls for its strict construction." To allow the requirement of complete diversity to be circumvented as it was in this case would simply flout the congressional command.[21]

Accordingly, the judgment of the Court of Appeals is reversed.

■ MR. JUSTICE WHITE, with whom MR. JUSTICE BRENNAN joins, dissenting.

The Court today states that "[i]t is not unreasonable to assume that, in generally requiring complete diversity, Congress did not intend to confine the jurisdiction of federal courts so inflexibly that they are unable * * * effectively to resolve an entire, logically entwined lawsuit." In spite of this recognition, the majority goes on to hold that in diversity suits federal courts do not have the jurisdictional power to entertain a claim asserted by a plaintiff against a third-party defendant, no matter how entwined it is with the matter already before the court, unless there is an independent basis for jurisdiction over that claim. Because I find no support for such a requirement in either Art. III of the Constitution or in

Holding by Majority

---

[20] Whether Iowa's statute of limitations would now bar an action by the respondent in an Iowa court is, of course, entirely a matter of state law. See Iowa Code § 614.10 (1977). Compare 558 F.2d at 420, with id., at 432 n. 42 (Bright, J., dissenting; cf. Burnett v. New York Central R. Co., 380 U.S. 424, 431–432, and n. 9, 85 S.Ct. 1050, 1056–1057, 13 L.Ed.2d 941.

[21] Our holding is that the District Court lacked power to entertain the respondent's lawsuit against the petitioner. Thus, the asserted inequity in the [petitioner's] alleged concealment of its citizenship is irrelevant. Federal judicial power does not depend upon "prior action or consent of the parties."American Fire & Cas. Co. v. Finn, 341 U.S., at 17–18, 71 S.Ct., at 542.

any statutory law, I dissent from the Court's "unnecessarily grudging"[1] approach.

* * *

In the present case, the only indication of congressional intent that the Court can find is that contained in the diversity jurisdictional statute, 28 U.S.C. § 1332(a), which states that "district courts shall have original jurisdiction of all civil actions where the matter in controversy exceeds the sum or value of $10,000 * * * and is between * * * citizens of different States * * * " Because this statute has been interpreted as requiring complete diversity of citizenship between each plaintiff and each defendant, Strawbridge v. Curtiss, 7 U.S. (3 Cranch) 267, 2 L.Ed. 435 (1806), the Court holds that the District Court did not have ancillary jurisdiction over Mrs. Kroger's claim against Owen. In so holding, the Court unnecessarily expands the scope of the complete-diversity requirement while substantially limiting the doctrine of ancillary jurisdiction.

* * *

Because in the instant case Mrs. Kroger merely sought to assert a claim against someone already a party to the suit, considerations of judicial economy, convenience, and fairness to the litigants—the factors relied upon in *Gibbs*—support the recognition of ancillary jurisdiction here. Already before the court was the whole question of the cause of Mr. Kroger's death. Mrs. Kroger initially contended that OPPD was responsible; OPPD in turn contended that Owen's negligence had been the proximate cause of Mr. Kroger's death. In spite of the fact that the question of Owen's negligence was already before the District Court, the majority requires Mrs. Kroger to bring a separate action in state court in order to assert that very claim. Even if the Iowa statute of limitations will still permit such a suit, see ante n. 20, considerations of judicial economy are certainly not served by requiring such duplicative litigation.[4]

The majority, however, brushes aside such considerations of convenience, judicial economy, and fairness because it concludes that recognizing ancillary jurisdiction over a plaintiff's claim against a third-party defendant would permit the plaintiff to circumvent the complete-diversity requirement and thereby "flout the congressional command." Since the plaintiff in such a case does not bring the third-party defendant into the suit, however, there is no occasion for deliberate circumvention of the diversity requirement, absent collusion with the defendant. In the

---

[1] See Mine Workers v. Gibbs, 383 U.S. 715, 725, 86 S.Ct. 1130, 1138, 16 L.Ed.2d 218 (1966).

[4] It is true that prior to trial OPPD was dismissed as a party to the suit and that, as we indicated in *Gibbs,* the dismissal prior to trial of the federal claim will generally require the dismissal of the nonfederal claim as well. See 383 U.S., at 726, 86 S.Ct., at 1139. Given the unusual facts of the present case, however—in particular, the fact that the actual location of Owen's principal place of business was not revealed until the third day of trial—fairness to the parties would lead me to conclude that the District Court did not abuse its discretion in retaining jurisdiction over Mrs. Kroger's claim against Owen. Under the Court's disposition, of course, it would not matter whether or not the federal claim is tried, for in either situation the court would have no jurisdiction over the plaintiff's nonfederal claim against the third-party defendant.

case of such collusion, of which there is absolutely no indication here,[5] the court can dismiss the action under the authority of 28 U.S.C. § 1359.[6] In the absence of such collusion, there is no reason to adopt an absolute rule prohibiting the plaintiff from asserting those claims that he may properly assert against the third-party defendant pursuant to Fed.Rule Civ.Proc. 14(a). The plaintiff in such a situation brings suit against the defendant only with absolutely no assurance that the defendant will decide or be able to implead a particular third-party defendant. Since the plaintiff has no control over the defendant's decision to implead a third party, the fact that he could not have originally sued that party in federal court should be irrelevant. Moreover, the fact that a plaintiff in some cases may be able to foresee the subsequent chain of events leading to the impleader does not seem to me to be a sufficient reason to declare that a district court does not have the *power* to exercise ancillary jurisdiction over the plaintiff's claims against the third-party defendant.

* * *

NOTE ON SUPPLEMENTAL JURISDICTION

In 1990, Congress enacted 28 U.S.C. § 1367, conferring "supplemental jurisdiction" on the federal courts. "Supplemental jurisdiction" was a new term, subsuming the old categories of "pendent jurisdiction," "ancillary jurisdiction," and "pendent party jurisdiction." As explained in this note, the supplemental jurisdiction statute preserves the results reached by the Supreme Court in both *UMW v. Gibbs* and *Owen Equipment*.

1.   The problem. The limitations on subject matter jurisdiction of the federal courts can make efficient resolution of some disputes impossible in federal court. Sometimes a dispute will involve several different claims: If those claims are considered independently, there may be subject matter jurisdiction over some of the claims, but not over others. Or a dispute may involve several parties: If the claims among those parties are considered independently, there may be subject matter jurisdiction over claims among some of the parties, but not over claims among the others.

The modern notion of judicial efficiency, reflected in the Federal Rules of Civil Procedure, is that a court should resolve as much as reasonably possible in a single proceeding. The rules governing joinder of claims and parties are considered in detail later. See infra Chapter 4. For now, a summary list will convey the idea: Federal Rule 18 allows a party to join as many claims as he has against the opposing party, whether or not those claims are related to one another. Rule 20 allows all persons to join as co-parties who assert a right to relief arising out of the same transaction, so long as their claims share a common question of law or fact. Rules 13(a) and (b) require a defendant to assert "compulsory" counterclaims against a plaintiff, and permit a defendant to assert "permissive" counterclaims, depending on the relationship between the counterclaim and the plaintiff's claim. Rule 13(g) permits co-parties to cross-claim against one another. Rule

---

[5]   When Mrs. Kroger brought suit, it was believed that Owen was a citizen of Nebraska, not Iowa. Therefore, had she desired at that time to make Owen a party to the suit, she would have done so directly by naming Owen as a defendant.

[6]   Section 1359 states: "A district court shall not have jurisdiction of a civil action in which any party, by assignment or otherwise, has been improperly or collusively made or joined to invoke the jurisdiction of such court."

14(a) allows a defendant to bring in as a third-party defendant a person who is or may be liable to the defendant for the claim asserted against the defendant by the plaintiff. Rule 24(a) and (b) allow parties to intervene in existing suits either "as or right" or "permissively," depending on the strength of their interest in the litigation into which they seek to intervene.

But efficient resolution of disputes, as envisioned by the federal rules, is not always possible. Rule 82 makes explicit what would almost certainly be true even if it were not explicitly stated: The "rules do not extend or limit the jurisdiction of the district courts." That is, if the federal rules would permit a claim or party to be joined but the jurisdictional statutes do not permit it, the federal rules must give way. The controlling limitation, which must always be addressed, is federal subject matter jurisdiction.

2. Definitions. "Supplemental jurisdiction" is jurisdiction over claims brought between existing parties, or between existing and new parties, for which there is no federal subject matter jurisdiction if those claims are considered independently. To take a simple example based on *UMW v. Gibbs*, a plaintiff who is a co-citizen with the defendant may have two claims against the defendant, one based on federal law and one based on state law. There is federal question jurisdiction under 28 U.S.C. § 1331 over the federal-law claim, but there is no subject matter jurisdiction over the state-law claim if that claim is considered independently of the federal-law claim. If federal subject matter jurisdiction over the state-law claim exists, it will be by virtue of "supplemental jurisdiction."

Prior to enactment of the new supplemental jurisdiction statute, several different terms were used. Precise definitions were never provided by the courts, but practical definitions could be inferred from usage. "Pendent jurisdiction," at issue in *UMW v. Gibbs*, was jurisdiction over additional claims brought by the same plaintiff against the same defendant. "Ancillary jurisdiction," at issue in *Owen Equipment*, was jurisdiction over additional claims brought by existing parties other than the plaintiff (usually the defendant), or over claims brought by or against additional parties. "Pendent party jurisdiction," a subcategory of "ancillary jurisdiction," was jurisdiction over claims brought against additional parties, as in *Owen Equipment*.

3. Historical background of the supplemental jurisdiction statute. Intermittent calls for reform of pendent and ancillary jurisdiction doctrines went unheeded until the Supreme Court decided *Finley v. United States*, 490 U.S. 545, 109 S.Ct. 2003, 104 L.Ed.2d 593 (1989). In *Finley*, a private plaintiff sued the United States under the Federal Tort Claims Act, 28 U.S.C. § 1346(b), after an airplane crash in which the plane became entangled in power lines near the San Diego municipal airport. Plaintiff sought to join to its claim against the United States a state-law claim against the city of San Diego and against the power company. Neither of these additional parties was of diverse citizenship from the plaintiff. Since there was no independent basis for jurisdiction, plaintiff relied on ancillary jurisdiction.

Ordinarily, plaintiffs in pendent and ancillary jurisdiction cases have a choice of either federal or state court. If the federal court cannot, or will not, hear the pendent or ancillary state-law claims, plaintiff can choose to have the entire dispute heard in state court. Judicial efficiency is still served; it is just served in state rather than federal court. But suits brought against the United States under the Federal Torts Claim Act (FTCA) are within the exclusive jurisdiction of the federal courts. Plaintiff's argument for ancillary jurisdiction in *Finley* was therefore particularly strong, since there was no forum capable of resolving all plaintiff's claims if the federal forum were unavailable for the state-law claims. Previously, in dictum, the Supreme Court had explicitly indicated that ancillary jurisdiction over additional defendants might be available in an FTCA suit: "When the grant of jurisdiction to a federal court is exclusive, for example, as in the prosecution of tort claims against the United States under 28 U.S.C. § 1346, the argument of judicial economy and convenience can be coupled with the additional argument that *only* in a federal court may all of the claims be tried together." Aldinger v. Howard, 427 U.S. 1, 18, 96 S.Ct. 2413, 49 L.Ed.2d 276 (1976). Nevertheless, the Court held in *Finley* that there was no ancillary jurisdiction over plaintiff's claims against the two additional parties.

Prompted by *Finley*, a Federal Courts Study Committee recommended a new "supplemental jurisdiction" statute. Report of the Federal Courts Study Committee 47–48 (1990) (recommendation); I Federal Courts Study Committee Working Papers and Subcommittee Reports 546–68 (1990) (report). A variation of the proposed statute was passed in late 1990 and was codified at 28 U.S.C. § 1367.

4.   **Structure of the supplemental jurisdiction statute.** The structure of the statute is fairly straightforward. The old terms are replaced by the single term "supplemental jurisdiction." Section 1367(a) confers supplemental jurisdiction on the federal courts to the extent permitted by Article III of the Constitution over claims and parties for which there is no independent basis for jurisdiction, subject to the exceptions set out in subsections (b) and (c). Subsection 1367(b) excepts from supplemental jurisdiction certain claims and parties where jurisdiction is based on diversity of citizenship. The combined effect of subsections (a) and (b) is to authorize broad supplemental jurisdiction over claims combined with claims brought under federal question jurisdiction, and to authorize a somewhat narrower supplemental jurisdiction over claims combined with state-law claims brought under diversity jurisdiction. Section 1367(c) specifies circumstances under which a district court may decline to exercise supplemental jurisdiction.

a.   **Federal question cases.** Supplemental jurisdiction under § 1367(a) is as broad as Article III will permit for the exercise of original jurisdiction. Given the limitation in subsection (b) on diversity cases, this broad grant of supplemental jurisdiction applies fully only to cases in which the original claim is based on federal law. This is a significant broadening of the case law, going beyond a mere overruling of *Finley*. Also overruled are cases in which plaintiff brought suit against one defendant under federal law and then sought to add additional defendants based on state-law claims, but in which, unlike in *Finley*, there was concurrent jurisdiction in state court over the federal claim. *Aldinger v. Howard*, supra, was such a case.

b.   **Diversity cases.** The exceptions in § 1367(b) from the broad grant in subsection (a) make supplemental jurisdiction more narrowly available in diversity than in federal question cases. The rationale for distinguishing between federal question and diversity cases is fairly obvious. In federal question cases, broad supplemental jurisdiction facilitates the core business of the federal courts of adjudicating cases involving questions of federal law in an effective and efficient way. In diversity cases, by contrast, supplemental jurisdiction is restricted as a way of conserving the resources of the federal courts, and of encouraging litigants to take such disputes to state courts. The drafting of § 1367(b) is awkward, but its clear purpose is largely to preserve the prior law of pendent and ancillary jurisdiction in diversity cases. For example, the denial of ancillary (now supplemental) jurisdiction in *Owen Equipment* is preserved, since jurisdiction over plaintiff Kroger's original claim was based on diversity of citizenship.

   c.   **When jurisdiction may be declined.** Even when supplemental jurisdiction exists, there are circumstances under which a district court may decline to exercise that jurisdiction. *UMW v. Gibbs* had described some of those circumstances, and § 1367(c) codifies a list derived from (but not identical to) those described in the case. When the criteria governing remand given in § 1367(c) are inconsistent with those given in *UMW v. Gibbs,* the criteria of § 1367(c) control. Executive Software North America, Inc. v. United States District Court, 24 F.3d 1545 (9th Cir. 1994). If neither party requests remand of state-law claims to state court under § 1367(c), the district court is not required to remand sua sponte. Acri v. Varian Assoc., Inc., 114 F.3d 999 (9th Cir. 1997); Myers v. County of Lake, 30 F.3d 847 (7th Cir. 1994). If a case is removed from state to federal court, and the district court decides not to exercise supplemental jurisdiction over certain claims, those claims should be remanded to state court rather than dismissed for want of jurisdiction. Carnegie-Mellon University v. Cohill, 484 U.S. 343, 108 S.Ct. 614, 98 L.Ed.2d 720 (1988).

   d.   **Tolling of the state statute of limitations.** Section 1367(d) provides that statutes of limitations for claims over which the district court has supplemental jurisdiction, including state-law claims, are tolled during the period the claims are pending in federal court. This protection is necessary for claims in cases that were filed originally in federal court, for those claims will be dismissed and must be refiled. However, the protection is unnecessary in removed cases, for the claims will not be dismissed. Rather, they will simply be remanded to state court. The Supreme Court sustained the constitutionality of the tolling provision as applied to state causes of action and state statutes of limitation in Jinks v. Richland County, 538 U.S. 456, 123 S.Ct. 1667, 155 L.Ed.2d 631 (2003) (reversing decision of the Supreme Court of South Carolina). If § 1367(d) had been in effect during the litigation in *Owen Equipment*, would Mrs. Kroger and Owen Equipment have fought about the denial of subject matter jurisdiction all the way to the United States Supreme Court?

   5.   **The scope of a constitutional "case."** The constitutional test in *UMW v. Gibbs* of what constitutes a "case" for purposes of pendent jurisdiction is that the claims "must derive from a common nucleus of operative fact," and must be such that plaintiff "would ordinarily be expected to try them all in one judicial proceeding." Note that Rule 18, which allows a plaintiff to join all claims she has against a defendant in a single complaint whether or not the claims are related, permits a plaintiff to assert claims that satisfy the second but not the first part of the test. Why did *UMW v. Gibbs* write the test more narrowly than Rule 18? The Court based its test on its own definition of a "constitutional 'case.'" Although the term "case" is used in the Constitution, it is nowhere defined in that document; nor does the Court in *UMW v. Gibbs* give any historical basis for its reading of the term. Obviously, Rule 18 has a different definition of "case" in mind from that employed in *UMW v. Gibbs* when it permits a plaintiff to join unrelated claims in the same complaint.

Several of the federal rules governing joinder have requirements of relatedness. See, e.g., Rule 13(a)(1)(A) (compulsory counterclaim) ("arises out of the transaction or occurrence that is the subject matter of the opposing party's claim"); Rule 13(g) (cross-claim) ("arises out of the transaction or occurrence that is the subject matter of the original action or of a counterclaim"); Rule 14(a) (impleader) (claim against a third-party "who is or may be liable * * * for all or part of the claim against it"); Rule 24(a) (intervention of right) ("an interest relating to the property or transaction that is the subject of the action"). Other rules have little or no requirement of relatedness. See, e.g., Rule 13(b)(1)(B) (permissive counterclaim) ("any claim that is not compulsory"); Rule 24(b) (permissive intervention) ("a claim or defense that shares with the main action a common question of law of fact"). If the relatedness requirements of the first set of rules are satisfied, the constitutional test of *UMW v. Gibbs* is likely satisfied. What about the rules in which there is little or no relatedness test?

UMW v. Gibbs states a constitutional test for a "case" under pendent jurisdiction. Did *UMW v. Gibbs* also intend to state the constitutional test for ancillary jurisdiction? Note that if claims are permitted under any of the above rules they would qualify under what used to be called ancillary jurisdiction. The Supreme Court was never willing to define pendent and ancillary jurisdiction carefully, and was hesitant to extend *UMW v. Gibbs* beyond the federal question and pendent jurisdiction context in which it arose. The Court wrote in footnotes to *Owen Equipment*, "[It is unnecessary] to determine here 'whether there are any "principled" ' differences between pendent and ancillary jurisdiction; or, if there are, what effect *Gibbs* had on such differences." It noted that *UMW v. Gibbs* was a federal question case, but only "assume[d] without deciding" that the " 'common nucleus of operative fact' " test also determines the outer boundaries of constitutionally permissible federal jurisdiction when that jurisdiction is based on diversity of citizenship. 437 U.S., at 370 n.8, 371 n.10. The supplemental jurisdiction statute extends jurisdiction to "all other claims that are so related to claims in the action within such original jurisdiction that they form part of the same case or controversy under Article III of the United States Constitution." *UMW v. Gibbs* and its "common nucleus of operative fact" test are nowhere mentioned.

The question is most clearly posed in cases of set-off, where a plaintiff sues for, say, $100,000, and defendant wishes to set off against any possible recovery an unrelated debt of $20,000 owed to him by plaintiff. Obviously, defendant would prefer to pay a net amount of $80,000 than to pay $100,000 and hope to recover $20,000 in a separate proceeding. The fairness and efficiency of allowing set-off in such a circumstance was recognized as early as Roman law, and set-off for unrelated claims was well-established in English courts before the adoption of the Constitution. Is it constitutionally permissible for a defendant in federal court to counterclaim for a set-off based on a debt owed by plaintiff to defendant, but arising out an unrelated transaction? Such a counterclaim for set-off is available under Rule 13(b) (permissive counterclaim). But it would pretty clearly not be permitted if *UMW v. Gibbs* provides the correct definition of a constitutional case, for the set-off claim does not "derive from a common nucleus of operative fact." But it is also pretty silly to force a defendant to pay a judgment to plaintiff without allowing her to subtract an amount that plaintiff owes her, as English courts long ago recognized in allowing such a set-off. Is that historical fact significant in defining the scope of a "case" with the meaning of Article III? The Supreme Court has never addressed the issue. For many years, lower courts have held that a counterclaim for an unrelated set-off is permitted. See, e.g., Curtis v. J.E. Caldwell & Co., 86 F.R.D. 454 (E.D.Pa.1980); Marks v. Spitz, 4 F.R.D. 348 (D.Mass.1945). For argument that "common nucleus of operative fact" does not define the outer boundary of the term "case" in Article III, see Fletcher, "Common Nucleus of Operative Fact" and Defensive Set-off: Beyond the *Gibbs* Test, 74 Ind.L.J. 171 (1998).

Two recent cases have held that the "common nucleus of operative fact" test does not describe the outer boundary of a "case." Global Naps, Inc. v. Verizon of New England, Inc., 603 F.3d 71 (1st Cir. 2010) (supplemental jurisdiction exists over a permissive counterclaim); Jones v. Ford Motor Credit Co., 358 F.3d 205 (2d Cir. 2004) (same). Compare Channell v. Citicorp National Services, Inc., 89 F.3d 379, 385 (7th Cir. 1996) (no supplemental jurisdiction over permissive counterclaim for set-off); Ambromovage v. United Mine Workers, 726 F.2d 972, 998, 990 (3d Cir. 1984) (same).

6. American Law Institute analysis of § 1367. Under the direction of Reporter (and Professor) John Oakley, the American Law Institute conducted a comprehensive study of the federal subject matter jurisdiction, removal, and venue. Federal Judicial Code Revision Project (2004). The study makes clear what is only implicit in § 1367. Under § 1367 as it is written, subsection (a) confers supplemental jurisdiction over claims related to "any civil action of which the district courts have original jurisdiction." However, for § 1367(a) to make sense, the "*civil action* of which the district court[ ] ha[s] original jurisdiction" must be understood to refer not to the civil action as a whole but to *claims in that civil action*. That is, a court must determine whether it has subject matter jurisdiction over one or more claims in the complaint. If it does have jurisdiction over one or more claims, the court must then examine other claims in the complaint over which it would not have jurisdiction if those claims were considered on their own. If those other claims satisfy the criteria of § 1367, there is supplemental jurisdiction over them. To make this analytically clear, the Project proposes a revision of § 1367 that would divide claims into two categories: "freestanding" claims and "supplemental" claims. For additional discussion of the ALI Project see Hartnett, Would the *Kroger* Rule Survive the ALI's Proposed Revision of § 1367?, 51 Duke L.J. 647 (2001); Oakley, *Kroger* Redux, 51 Duke L.J. 663 (2001).

7. Academic assessments. For useful treatments of the supplemental jurisdiction statute, see Floyd, Three Faces of Supplemental Jurisdiction after the Demise of *United Mine Workers v. Gibbs*, 60 Fla. L.Rev. 277 (2008); Steinman, Claims, Civil Actions, Congress & the Court: Limiting the Reasoning of Cases Construing Poorly Drawn Statutes, 65 Wash. & Lee L.Rev. 1593 (2008); Pfander, Supplemental Jurisdiction and Section 1367: The Case for a Sympathetic Textualism, 148 U. Pa. L.Rev. 109 (1999); Symposium, A Reappraisal of the Supplemental Jurisdiction Statute: Title 28 U.S.C. § 1367, 74 Ind. L.J. 1 (1998); McLaughlin, The Federal Supplemental Jurisdiction Statute—A Constitutional and Statutory Analysis, 24 Ariz.St. L.J. 849 (1992).

When the statute was first passed, there was a debate about the quality of its drafting, the tone of which is suggested by the titles of the articles. Freer, Compounding Confusion and Hampering Diversity: Life After *Finley* and the Supplemental Jurisdiction Statute, 40 Emory L.J. 445 (1991); Rowe, Burbank, and Mengler, Compounding or Creating Confusion about

Supplemental Jurisdiction? A Reply to Professor Freer, id. 943; Arthur and Freer, Grasping at Burnt Straws: The Disaster of the Supplemental Jurisdiction Statute, id. 963; Rowe, Burbank, and Mengler, A Coda on Supplemental Jurisdiction, id. 993; Arthur and Freer, Close Enough for Government Work: What Happens When Congress Doesn't Do Its Job, id. 1007.

Exxon Mobil Corp. v. Allapattah Services, Inc.

Supreme Court of the United States, 2005.
545 U.S. 546, 125 S.Ct. 2611, 162 L.Ed.2d 502.

■ JUSTICE KENNEDY delivered the opinion of the Court.

These consolidated cases present the question whether a federal court in a diversity action may exercise supplemental jurisdiction over additional plaintiffs whose claims do not satisfy the minimum amount-in-controversy requirement, provided the claims are part of the same case or controversy as the claims of plaintiffs who do allege a sufficient amount in controversy. Our decision turns on the correct interpretation of 28 U.S.C. § 1367. The question has divided the Courts of Appeals, and we granted certiorari to resolve the conflict.

We hold that, where the other elements of jurisdiction are present and at least one named plaintiff in the action satisfies the amount-in-controversy requirement, § 1367 does authorize supplemental jurisdiction over the claims of other plaintiffs in the same Article III case or controversy, even if those claims are for less than the jurisdictional amount specified in the statute setting forth the requirements for diversity jurisdiction. We affirm the judgment of the Court of Appeals for the Eleventh Circuit in No. 04–70, and we reverse the judgment of the Court of Appeals for the First Circuit in No. 04–79.

I

In 1991, about 10,000 Exxon dealers filed a class-action suit against the Exxon Corporation in the United States District Court for the Northern District of Florida. The dealers alleged an intentional and systematic scheme by Exxon under which they were overcharged for fuel purchased from Exxon. The plaintiffs invoked the District Court's § 1332(a) diversity jurisdiction. After a unanimous jury verdict in favor of the plaintiffs, the District Court certified the case for interlocutory review, asking whether it had properly exercised § 1367 supplemental jurisdiction over the claims of class members who did not meet the jurisdictional minimum amount in controversy.

The Court of Appeals for the Eleventh Circuit upheld the District Court's extension of supplemental jurisdiction to these class members. Allapattah Services, Inc. v. Exxon Corp., 333 F.3d 1248 (2003). "[W]e find," the court held, "that § 1367 clearly and unambiguously provides district courts with the authority in diversity class actions to exercise supplemental jurisdiction over the claims of class members who do not meet the minimum amount in controversy as long as the district court has original jurisdiction over the claims of at least one of the class representatives." Id., at 1256. This decision accords with the views of the Courts of Appeals for the Fourth, Sixth, and Seventh Circuits. The Courts of Appeals for the Fifth and Ninth Circuits, adopting a similar analysis of the statute, have held that in a diversity class action the unnamed class members need not meet the amount-in-controversy requirement, provided the named class members do. These decisions, however, are unclear on whether all the named plaintiffs must satisfy this requirement.

In the other case now before us the Court of Appeals for the First Circuit took a different position on the meaning of § 1367(a). 370 F.3d 124 (2004). In that case, a 9-year-old girl sued Star-Kist in a diversity action in the United States District Court for the District of Puerto Rico, seeking damages for unusually severe injuries she received when she sliced her finger on a tuna can. Her family joined in the suit, seeking damages for emotional distress and certain medical expenses. The District Court granted summary judgment to Star-Kist, finding that none of the plaintiffs met the minimum amount-in-controversy requirement. The Court of Appeals for the First Circuit, however, ruled that the injured girl, but not her family members, had made allegations of damages in the requisite amount.

The Court of Appeals then addressed whether, in light of the fact that one plaintiff met the requirements for original jurisdiction, supplemental jurisdiction over the remaining plaintiffs' claims was proper under § 1367. The court held that § 1367 authorizes supplemental jurisdiction only when the district court has original jurisdiction over the action, and that in a diversity case original jurisdiction is lacking if one plaintiff fails to satisfy the amount-in-controversy requirement. Although the Court of Appeals claimed to "express no view" on whether the result would be the same in a class action, id., at 143, n. 19, its analysis is inconsistent with that of the Court of Appeals for the Eleventh Circuit. The Court of Appeals for the First Circuit's view of § 1367 is, however, shared by the Courts of Appeal for the Third, Eighth, and Tenth Circuits, and the latter two Courts of Appeals have expressly applied this rule to class actions.

II

A

The district courts of the United States, as we have said many times, are "courts of limited jurisdiction. They possess only that power authorized by Constitution and statute," Kokkonen v. Guardian Life Ins. Co. of America, 511 U.S. 375, 377, 114 S.Ct. 1673, 128 L.Ed.2d 391 (1994). In order to provide a federal forum for plaintiffs who seek to vindicate federal rights, Congress has conferred on the district courts original jurisdiction in federal-question cases—civil actions that arise under the Constitution, laws, or treaties of the United States. 28 U.S.C. § 1331. In order to provide a neutral forum for what have come to be known as diversity cases, Congress also has granted district courts original jurisdiction in civil actions between citizens of different States, between U.S. citizens and foreign citizens, or by foreign states against U.S. citizens. § 1332. To ensure that diversity jurisdiction does not flood the federal courts with minor disputes, § 1332(a) requires that the matter in controversy in a diversity case exceed a specified amount, currently $75,000. § 1332(a).

Although the district courts may not exercise jurisdiction absent a statutory basis, it is well established—in certain classes of cases—that, once a court has original jurisdiction over some claims in the action, it may exercise supplemental jurisdiction over additional claims that are part of the same case or controversy. The leading modern case for this principle is Mine Workers v. Gibbs, 383 U.S. 715, 86 S.Ct. 1130, 16 L.Ed.2d 218 (1966). * * *

* * *

We have not, however, applied Gibbs' expansive interpretive approach to other aspects of the jurisdictional statutes. For instance, we have consistently interpreted § 1332 as requiring complete diversity: In a case with multiple plaintiffs and multiple defendants, the presence in the action of a single plaintiff from the same State as a single defendant deprives the district court of original diversity jurisdiction over the entire action. Strawbridge v. Curtiss, 3 Cranch 267 (1806); Owen Equipment & Erection Co. v. Kroger, 437 U.S. 365, 375 (1978). The complete diversity requirement is not mandated by the Constitution, State Farm Fire & Casualty Co. v. Tashire, 386 U.S. 523, 530–531 (1967), or by the plain text of § 1332(a). The Court, nonetheless, has adhered to the complete diversity rule in light of the purpose of the diversity requirement, which is to provide a federal forum for important disputes where state courts might favor, or be perceived as favoring, home-state litigants. The presence of parties from the same State on both sides of a case dispels this concern, eliminating a principal reason for conferring § 1332 jurisdiction over any of the claims in the action. The specific purpose of the complete diversity rule explains both why we have not adopted Gibbs' expansive interpretive approach to this aspect of the jurisdictional statute and why Gibbs does not undermine the complete diversity rule. In order for a federal court to invoke supplemental jurisdiction under Gibbs, it must first have original jurisdiction over at least one claim in the action. Incomplete diversity destroys original jurisdiction with respect to all claims, so there is nothing to which supplemental jurisdiction can adhere.

In contrast to the diversity requirement, most of the other statutory prerequisites for federal jurisdiction, including the federal-question and amount-in-controversy requirements, can be analyzed claim by claim. True, it does not follow by necessity from this that a district court has authority to exercise supplemental jurisdiction over all claims provided there is original jurisdiction over just one. Before the enactment of § 1367, the Court declined in contexts other than the pendent-claim instance to follow Gibbs' expansive approach to interpretation of the jurisdictional statutes. The Court took a more restrictive view of the proper interpretation of these statutes in so-called pendent-party cases involving supplemental jurisdiction over claims involving additional parties—plaintiffs or defendants—where the district courts would lack original jurisdiction over claims by each of the parties standing alone.

Thus, with respect to plaintiff-specific jurisdictional requirements, the Court held in Clark v. Paul Gray, Inc., 306 U.S. 583, 59 S.Ct. 744, 83 L.Ed. 1001 (1939), that every plaintiff must separately satisfy the amount-in-controversy requirement. Though Clark was a federal-question case, at that time federal-question jurisdiction had an amount-in-controversy requirement analogous to the amount-in-controversy requirement for diversity cases. "Proper practice," Clark held, "requires that where each of several plaintiffs is bound to establish the jurisdictional amount with respect to his own claim, the suit should be dismissed as to those who fail to show that the requisite amount is involved." Id., at 590, 59 S.Ct. 744. The Court reaffirmed this rule, in the context of a class action brought invoking § 1332(a) diversity jurisdiction, in Zahn v. International Paper Co., 414 U.S. 291, 94 S.Ct. 505, 38 L.Ed.2d 511 (1973). It follows "inescapably" from Clark, the Court held in Zahn, that "any plaintiff without the jurisdictional amount must be dismissed from the case, even though others allege jurisdictionally sufficient claims." 414 U.S., at 300, 94 S.Ct. 505.

* * *

B

In Finley [v. United States, 490 U.S. 545 (1989) (holding no supplemental jurisdiction over claim against an additional party in a suit brought under the Federal Tort Claims Act),] we emphasized that "[w]hatever we say regarding the scope of jurisdiction conferred by a particular statute can of course be changed by Congress." 490 U.S., at 556, 109 S.Ct. 2003. In 1990, Congress accepted the invitation. It passed the Judicial Improvements Act, 104 Stat. 5089, which enacted § 1367, the provision which controls these cases.

Section 1367 provides, in relevant part:

(a)   Except as provided in subsections (b) and (c) or as expressly provided otherwise by Federal statute, in any civil action of which the district courts have original jurisdiction, the district courts shall have supplemental jurisdiction over all other claims that are so related to claims in the action within such original jurisdiction that they form part of the same case or controversy under Article III of the United States Constitution. Such supplemental jurisdiction shall include claims that involve the joinder or intervention of additional parties.

(b)   In any civil action of which the district courts have original jurisdiction founded solely on section 1332 of this title, the district courts shall not have supplemental jurisdiction under subsection (a) over claims by plaintiffs against persons made parties under Rule 14, 19, 20, or 24 of the Federal Rules of Civil Procedure, or over claims by persons proposed to be joined as plaintiffs under Rule 19 of such rules, or seeking to intervene as plaintiffs under Rule 24 of such rules, when exercising supplemental jurisdiction over such claims would be inconsistent with the jurisdictional requirements of section 1332.

All parties to this litigation and all courts to consider the question agree that § 1367 overturned the result in Finley. There is no warrant, however, for assuming that § 1367 did no more than to overrule Finley and otherwise to codify the existing state of the law of supplemental jurisdiction. We must not give jurisdictional statutes a more expansive interpretation than their text warrants; but it is just as important not to adopt an artificial construction that is narrower than what the text provides. * * *

Section 1367(a) is a broad grant of supplemental jurisdiction over other claims within the same case or controversy, as long as the action is one in which the district courts would have original jurisdiction. The last sentence of § 1367(a) makes it clear that the grant of supplemental jurisdiction extends to claims involving joinder or intervention of additional parties. The single question before us, therefore, is whether a diversity case in which the claims of some plaintiffs satisfy the amount-in-controversy requirement, but the claims of others plaintiffs do not, presents a "civil action of which the district courts have original jurisdiction." If the answer is yes, § 1367(a) confers supplemental jurisdiction over all claims, including those that do not independently satisfy the amount-in-controversy requirement, if the claims are part of the same Article III case or controversy. If the answer is no, § 1367(a) is inapplicable and, in light of our holdings in Clark and Zahn, the district court has no statutory basis for exercising supplemental jurisdiction over the additional claims.

We now conclude the answer must be yes. When the well-pleaded complaint contains at least one claim that satisfies the amount-in-controversy requirement, and there are no other relevant jurisdictional defects, the district court, beyond all question, has original jurisdiction over that claim. The presence of other claims in the complaint, over which the district court may lack original jurisdiction, is of no moment. If the court has original jurisdiction over a single claim in the complaint, it has original jurisdiction over a "civil action" within the meaning of § 1367(a), even if the civil action over which it has jurisdiction comprises fewer claims than were included in the complaint. Once the court determines it has original jurisdiction over the civil action, it can turn to the question whether it has a constitutional and statutory basis for exercising supplemental jurisdiction over the other claims in the action.

Section 1367(a) commences with the direction that §§ 1367(b) and (c), or other relevant statutes, may provide specific exceptions, but otherwise § 1367(a) is a broad jurisdictional grant, with no distinction drawn between pendent-claim and pendent-party cases. In fact, the last sentence of § 1367(a) makes clear that the provision grants supplemental jurisdiction over claims involving joinder or intervention of additional parties. The terms of § 1367 do not acknowledge any distinction between pendent jurisdiction and the doctrine of so-called ancillary jurisdiction. Though the doctrines of pendent and ancillary jurisdiction developed separately as a historical matter, the Court has recognized that the doctrines are "two species of the same generic problem," Kroger, 437 U.S., at 370, 98 S.Ct. 2396. Nothing in § 1367 indicates a congressional intent to recognize, preserve, or create some meaningful, substantive distinction between the jurisdictional categories we have historically labeled pendent and ancillary.

If § 1367(a) were the sum total of the relevant statutory language, our holding would rest on that language alone. The statute, of course, instructs us to examine § 1367(b) to determine if any of its exceptions apply, so we proceed to that section. While § 1367(b) qualifies the broad rule of § 1367(a), it does not withdraw supplemental jurisdiction over the claims of the additional parties at issue here. The specific exceptions to § 1367(a) contained in § 1367(b), moreover, provide additional support for our conclusion that § 1367(a) confers supplemental jurisdiction over these claims. Section 1367(b), which applies only to diversity cases, withholds supplemental jurisdiction over the claims of plaintiffs proposed to be joined as indispensable parties under Federal Rule of Civil Procedure 19, or who seek to intervene pursuant to Rule 24. Nothing in the text of § 1367(b), however, withholds supplemental jurisdiction over the claims of plaintiffs permissively joined under Rule 20 (like the additional plaintiffs in No. 04–79) or certified as class-action members pursuant to Rule 23 (like the additional plaintiffs in No. 04–70). The natural, indeed the necessary, inference is that § 1367 confers supplemental jurisdiction over claims by Rule 20 and Rule 23 plaintiffs. This inference, at least with respect to Rule 20 plaintiffs, is strengthened by the fact that § 1367(b) explicitly excludes supplemental jurisdiction over claims against defendants joined under Rule 20.

We cannot accept the view, urged by some of the parties, commentators, and Courts of Appeals, that a district court lacks original jurisdiction over a civil action unless the court has original jurisdiction over every claim in the complaint. As we understand this position, it requires assuming either that all claims in the complaint must stand or fall as a single, indivisible "civil action" as a matter of definitional necessity—what we will refer to as the "indivisibility theory"—or else that the inclusion of a claim or party falling outside the district court's original jurisdiction somehow contaminates every other claim in the complaint, depriving the court of original jurisdiction over any of these claims—what we will refer to as the "contamination theory."

The indivisibility theory is easily dismissed, as it is inconsistent with the whole notion of supplemental jurisdiction. If a district court must have original jurisdiction over every claim in the complaint in order to have "original jurisdiction" over a "civil action," then in Gibbs there was no civil action of which the district court could assume original jurisdiction under § 1331, and so no basis for exercising supplemental jurisdiction over any of the claims. The indivisibility theory is further belied by our practice—in both federal-question and diversity cases—of allowing federal courts to cure jurisdictional defects by dismissing the offending parties rather than dismissing the entire action. Clark, for example, makes clear that claims that are jurisdictionally defective as to amount in controversy do not destroy original jurisdiction over other claims. 306 U.S., at 590, 59 S.Ct. 744 (dismissing parties who failed to meet the amount-in-controversy requirement but retaining jurisdiction over the remaining party). If the presence of jurisdictionally problematic claims in the complaint meant the district court was without original jurisdiction over the single, indivisible civil action before it, then the district court would have to dismiss the whole action rather than particular parties.

We also find it unconvincing to say that the definitional indivisibility theory applies in the context of diversity cases but not in the context of federal-question cases. The broad and general language of the statute does not permit this result. The contention is premised on the notion that the phrase "original jurisdiction of all civil actions" means different things in § 1331 and § 1332. It is implausible, however, to say that the identical phrase means one thing (original jurisdiction in all actions where at least one claim in the complaint meets the following requirements) in § 1331 and something else (original jurisdiction in all actions where every claim in the complaint meets the following requirements) in § 1332.

The contamination theory, as we have noted, can make some sense in the special context of the complete diversity requirement because the presence of nondiverse parties on both sides of a lawsuit eliminates the justification for providing a federal forum. The theory, however, makes little sense with respect to the amount-in-controversy requirement, which is meant to ensure that a dispute is sufficiently important to warrant federal-court attention. The presence of a single nondiverse party may eliminate the fear of bias with respect to all claims, but the presence of a claim that falls short of the minimum amount in controversy does nothing to reduce the importance of the claims that do meet this requirement.

It is fallacious to suppose, simply from the proposition that § 1332 imposes both the diversity requirement and the amount-in-controversy requirement, that the contamination theory germane to the former is also relevant to the latter. There is no inherent logical connection between the amount-in-controversy requirement and § 1332 diversity jurisdiction. After all, federal-question jurisdiction once had an amount-in-controversy requirement as well. If such a requirement were revived under § 1331, it is clear beyond peradventure that § 1367(a) provides supplemental jurisdiction over federal-question cases where some, but not all, of the federal-law claims involve a sufficient amount in controversy. In other words, § 1367(a) unambiguously overrules the holding and the result in Clark. If that is so, however, it would be quite extraordinary to say that § 1367 did not also overrule Zahn, a case that was premised in substantial part on the holding in Clark.

* * *

* * * When the well-pleaded complaint in district court includes multiple claims, all part of the same case or controversy, and some, but not all, of the claims are within the court's original jurisdiction, does the court have before it "any civil action of which the district courts have original jurisdiction"? It does. Under § 1367, the court has original jurisdiction over the civil action comprising the claims for which there is no jurisdictional defect. No other reading of § 1367 is plausible in light of the text and structure of the jurisdictional statute. Though the special nature and purpose of the diversity requirement mean that a single nondiverse party can contaminate every other claim in the lawsuit, the contamination does not occur with respect to jurisdictional defects that go only to the substantive importance of individual claims.

It follows from this conclusion that the threshold requirement of § 1367(a) is satisfied in cases, like those now before us, where some, but not all, of the plaintiffs in a diversity action allege a sufficient amount in controversy. We hold that § 1367 by its plain text overruled Clark and Zahn and authorized supplemental jurisdiction over all claims by diverse parties arising out of the same Article III case or controversy, subject only to enumerated exceptions not applicable in the cases now before us.

C

The proponents of the alternative view of § 1367 insist that the statute is at least ambiguous and that we should look to other interpretive tools, including the legislative history of § 1367, which supposedly demonstrate Congress did not intend § 1367 to overrule Zahn. We can reject this argument at the very outset simply because § 1367 is not ambiguous. For the reasons elaborated above, interpreting § 1367 to foreclose supplemental jurisdiction over plaintiffs in diversity cases who do not meet the minimum amount in controversy is inconsistent with the text, read in light of other statutory provisions and our established jurisprudence. Even if we were to stipulate, however, that the reading these proponents urge upon us is textually plausible, the legislative history cited to support it would not alter our view as to the best interpretation of § 1367.

[Discussion of legislative history omitted.]

D

Finally, we note that the Class Action Fairness Act (CAFA), Pub.L. 109–2, 119 Stat. 4, enacted this year, has no bearing on our analysis of these cases. Subject to certain limitations, the CAFA confers federal diversity jurisdiction over class actions where the aggregate amount in controversy exceeds $5 million. It abrogates the rule against aggregating claims, a rule this Court recognized in Ben-Hur and reaffirmed in Zahn. The CAFA, however, is not retroactive, and the views of the 2005 Congress are not relevant to our interpretation of a text enacted by Congress in 1990. The CAFA, moreover, does not moot the significance of our interpretation of § 1367, as many proposed exercises of supplemental jurisdiction, even in the class-action context, might not fall within the CAFA's ambit. The CAFA, then, has no impact, one way or the other, on our interpretation of § 1367.

The judgment of the Court of Appeals for the Eleventh Circuit is affirmed. The judgment of the Court of Appeals for the First Circuit is reversed, and the case is remanded for proceedings consistent with this opinion.

■ JUSTICE STEVENS' dissenting opinion, joined by JUSTICE BREYER, is omitted. JUSTICE GINSBURG'S dissenting opinion, joined by JUSTICES STEVENS, O'CONNOR, and BREYER, is omitted.

NOTES AND QUESTIONS

1. **Two questions.** The Supreme Court answered two questions in *Exxon Mobil*. The first, in the Eleventh Circuit case, was whether, in a diversity class action brought under Federal Rule of Civil Procedure 23, more than one plaintiff must satisfy the amount in controversy requirement of 28 U.S.C. § 1332(a) (amount in controversy must exceed $75,000). The second, in the First Circuit case, was whether, in a diversity action with multiple plaintiffs permissively joined under Federal Rule of Civil Procedure 20, more than one plaintiff must satisfy the amount in controversy requirement. The Court answered both questions the same way: in both class actions brought under Rule 23 and multiple plaintiff suits brought under Rule 20, only one plaintiff needs to satisfy the amount in controversy requirement. Other plaintiffs' claims that do not satisfy the amount in controversy requirement may be heard under the supplemental jurisdiction granted by § 1367(a).

2. **A long-awaited decision.** The two questions answered by the Court were apparent almost from the moment § 1367 was passed in 1990. Although the Court concluded in *Exxon Mobil* that the statutory text was clear, this result was not a foregone conclusion. At least as to Rule 23, the wording might have been due to an oversight in drafting. The three law

professors primarily responsible for drafting § 1367 published an article almost immediately after its enactment suggesting that the statute should be read to preserve the rule of Zahn v. International Paper Co., 414 U.S. 291, 94 S.Ct. 505, 38 L.Ed.2d 511 (1973), in class action cases, even though its text did not appear to say so. See T. Mengler, S. Burbank, and T. Rowe, Congress Accepts Supreme Court's Invitation to Codify Supplemental Jurisdiction, 74 Judicature 213 (1991). The Court granted certiorari in a case presenting the Rule 23 (but not the Rule 20) question, but the Court divided four to four, affirming without opinion by an equally divided Court. Free v. Abbott Laboratories, Inc., 529 U.S. 333, 120 S.Ct. 1578, 146 L.Ed.2d 306 (2000). As indicated at the beginning of the Court's opinion in *Exxon Mobil*, the courts of appeals were divided on both questions. Fifteen years after the adoption of § 1367, we finally got the answers.

The Court presents its decision as an exercise in applying the language of the statute to the exclusion of its legislative history. Are you persuaded that the Court's "claim by claim" theory is consistent with the statutory language? (Recall that the ALI Project, described in the supplemental jurisdiction note following *Kroger*, suggested a revision of the text to make clear that 1367 intended a claim by claim analysis.) In particular, are you persuaded by the distinction that the Court draws between failures by some plaintiffs to meet the jurisdictional minimum amount (which the Court holds are cured by the statute when at least one plaintiff is diverse from all defendants and has a claim satisfying the minimum) and failures to satisfy complete diversity (which the Court states in dictum are not cured, even when at least one plaintiff is diverse from all defendants and satisfies the minimum)? Where is that distinction reflected in the language of the statute? If the distinction drawn is not supported by the language of the statute, is it nonetheless wise as a matter of policy?

3.   **What was at stake in the Rule 23 case?** Prior to the adoption of § 1367, the established rule under *Zahn v. International Paper* was that all plaintiffs in a diversity class action under Rule 23 had to satisfy the amount in controversy requirement of § 1332(a). The conventional view was that the rule in *Zahn* was harmful to plaintiffs' interests, and that overruling *Zahn* would help plaintiffs by increasing their options, allowing them to choose between a state and a federal forum. That view is now dated. It has become increasingly clear that there are sharp differences between the federal courts and some state courts on issues bearing on class action practice, including standards for certification, awards of punitive damages, and review of settlements, and that these differences present strategic opportunities for both plaintiffs and defendants. For example, plaintiffs may (and often do) choose a plaintiff-favorable state court, creating tremendous litigation exposure for the defendant. In cases leading up to *Exxon Mobil*, it was usually corporate defendants who argued that § 1367 overrules *Zahn* because they wished to remove the class action to what they thought would be the more defendant-favorable federal forum. For a vivid example see McCauley v. Ford Motor Co., 264 F.3d 952 (9th Cir. 2001), cert. dismissed, 537 U.S. 1, 123 S.Ct. 584, 154 L.Ed.2d 1 (2002).

4.   **Overtaken by events?** Responding to pressure from corporate class action defendants (and corporations who feared that they would become such defendants in the future), Congress enacted the Class Action Fairness Act of 2005 (CAFA), greatly expanding diversity jurisdiction over class actions. See 28 U.S.C. §§ 1332(d) (original jurisdiction) and 1453 (removal).

CAFA authorizes subject matter jurisdiction in federal district court in class actions in which there is more than $5,000,000 in controversy for the entire class. Only minimal diversity is required. § 1332(d)(2). Removal to federal court is much easier than removal in general diversity cases. See discussion of removal, infra p. 286. Federal district court jurisdiction is not authorized in class actions with a particularly strong connection to a single state, but the overall effect of the Act is to allow defendants to remove most diversity class actions to federal court.

CAFA greatly diminishes the practical importance of supplemental jurisdiction in diversity class actions. The only diversity class actions in which supplemental jurisdiction now makes a difference are those in which the aggregate amount in controversy for the entire class is $5,000,000 or less, or in which the connection to a single state is particularly strong. The Court in *Exxon Mobil* writes that "the Class Action Fairness Act * * * has no bearing on our analysis of these cases." The Court is correct in saying that the Act has no bearing on its analysis of the text of § 1367. But CAFA does have a substantial impact on the practical importance of that analysis.

5.   What was at stake in the Rule 20 case? The stakes in a Rule 20 case replicate, to a lesser degree and on a much smaller scale, the stakes in a Rule 23 class action case. Generally speaking, corporate defendants in diversity cases prefer litigating in federal rather than state court. The Court's answer in the Rule 20 case makes it somewhat easier for defendants to remove multiple-plaintiff diversity cases to federal court, for so long as all of the plaintiffs are of diverse citizenship from all of the defendants, only one of the plaintiffs need satisfy the amount in controversy requirement of § 1332(a). But it is fair to say that there had been no organized effort, comparable to the effort in class action cases, to allow broader removal in Rule 20 permissive joinder diversity cases.

6.   Supplemental jurisdiction based on something other than § 1367. Is § 1367 the only basis on which federal courts can assert supplemental (or ancillary or pendent) jurisdiction? The answer is almost certainly no. In Kokkonen v. Guardian Life Insurance Co. of America, 511 U.S. 375, 114 S.Ct. 1673, 128 L.Ed.2d 391 (1994), the district court had entered an unconditional order dismissing plaintiff's claim pursuant to a settlement agreement. When defendant failed to live up to the agreement, plaintiff returned to the federal court seeking an enforcement order. The Supreme Court held that there had to be an independent basis for subject matter jurisdiction to support plaintiff's suit to enforce the agreement, and that no such basis existed here. But the Court noted explicitly that if the parties had incorporated into the order of dismissal a condition that the defendant comply with the settlement, the district court would have had ancillary jurisdiction: "In that event, a breach of the agreement would be a violation of the order, and ancillary jurisdiction to enforce the agreement would therefore exist." Id. at 381. The Court nowhere mentioned § 1367 in its opinion. For an analysis of Kokkonen, see Green, Justice Scalia and Ancillary Jurisdiction: Teaching a Lame Duck New Tricks in *Kokkonen v. Guardian Life Insurance Company of America*, 81 Va.L.Rev. 1631 (1995).

4. REMOVAL

Caterpillar Inc. v. Williams

Supreme Court of the United States, 1987.
482 U.S. 386, 107 S.Ct. 2425, 96 L.Ed.2d 318.

■ JUSTICE BRENNAN delivered the opinion of the Court.

The question for decision is whether respondents' state-law complaint for breach of individual employment contracts is completely pre-empted by § 301 of the Labor Management Relations Act, 1947 (LMRA), and therefore removable to Federal District Court.

I

At various times between 1956 and 1968, Caterpillar Tractor Company (Caterpillar) hired respondents to work at its San Leandro, California, facility. Initially, each respondent filled a position covered by the collective-bargaining agreement between Caterpillar and Local Lodge No. 284, International Association of Machinists (Union). Each eventually became either a managerial or a weekly salaried employee, positions outside the coverage of the collective-bargaining agreement. Respondents held the latter positions for periods ranging from 3 to 15 years; all but two respondents served 8 years or more.

Respondents allege that, "[d]uring the course of [their] employment, as management or weekly salaried employees," Caterpillar made oral and written representations that "they could look forward to indefinite and lasting employment with the corporation and that they could count on the corporation to take care of them." More specifically, respondents claim that, "while serving Caterpillar as managers or weekly salaried employees, [they] were assured that if the San Leandro facility of Caterpillar ever closed, Caterpillar would provide employment opportunities for [them] at other facilities of Caterpillar, its subsidiaries, divisions, or related companies." Respondents maintain that these "promises were continually and repeatedly made," and that they created "a total employment agreement wholly independent of the collective-bargaining agreement pertaining to hourly employees." In reliance on these promises, respondents assert, they "continued to remain in Caterpillar's employ rather than seeking other employment."

Between May 1980 and January 1984, Caterpillar downgraded respondents from managerial and weekly salaried positions to hourly positions covered by the collective-bargaining agreement. Respondents allege that, at the time they were downgraded to unionized positions, Caterpillar supervisors orally assured them that the downgrades were temporary. On December 15, 1983, Caterpillar notified respondents that its San Leandro plant would close and that they would be laid off.

On December 17, 1984, respondents filed an action based solely on state law in California state court, contending that Caterpillar "breached [its] employment agreement by notifying [respondents] that the San Leandro plant would be closed and subsequently advising [respondents] that they would be terminated" without regard to the individual employment contracts. Caterpillar then removed the action to federal court, arguing that removal was proper because any individual employment contracts made with respondents "were, as a matter of federal substantive labor law, merged into and superseded by the . . . collective bargaining agreements." Respondents denied that they alleged any federal claim and immediately sought remand of the action to the state court. In an oral opinion, the District Court held that removal to federal court was proper, and dismissed the case when respondents refused to amend their complaint to attempt to state a claim under § 301 of the LMRA.

The Court of Appeals for the Ninth Circuit reversed, holding that the case was improperly removed. * * *

We granted certiorari, and now affirm.

II

A

* * *

Only state-court actions that originally could have been filed in federal court may be removed to federal court by the defendant. Absent diversity of citizenship, federal-question jurisdiction is required. The presence or absence of federal-question jurisdiction is governed by the "well-pleaded complaint rule," which provides that federal jurisdiction exists only when a federal question is presented on the face of the plaintiff's properly pleaded complaint. See Gully v. First National Bank, 299 U.S. 109, 112–113, 57 S.Ct. 96, 97–98, 81 L.Ed. 70 (1936). The rule makes the plaintiff the master of the claim; he or she may avoid federal jurisdiction by exclusive reliance on state law.

Ordinarily federal pre-emption is raised as a defense to the allegations in a plaintiff's complaint. Before 1887, a federal defense such as pre-emption could provide a basis for removal, but, in that year, Congress amended the removal statute. We interpret that amendment to authorize removal only where original federal jurisdiction exists. See Act of Mar. 3, 1887. Thus, it is now settled law that a case may *not* be removed to federal court on the basis of a federal defense, including the defense of pre-emption, even if the defense is anticipated in the plaintiff's complaint, and even if both parties concede that the federal defense is the only question truly at issue.

There does exist, however, an "independent corollary" to the well-pleaded complaint rule, known as the "complete pre-emption" doctrine. On occasion, the Court has concluded that the pre-emptive force of a statute is so "extraordinary" that it "converts an ordinary state common-law complaint into one stating a federal claim for purposes of the well-pleaded complaint rule." * * *

The complete pre-emption corollary to the well-pleaded complaint rule is applied primarily in cases raising claims pre-empted by § 301 of the LMRA. Section 301 provides:

> "Suits for violation of contracts between an employer and a labor organization representing employees in an industry affecting commerce as defined in this chapter, or between any such labor organizations, may be brought in any district court of the United States having jurisdiction of the parties, without respect of the amount in controversy or without regard to the citizenship of the parties." 29 U.S.C. § 185(a).

In Avco Corp. v. Machinists, the Court of Appeals decided that "[s]tate law does not exist as an independent source of private rights to enforce collective bargaining contracts." 376 F.2d 337, 340 (C.A.6 1967), aff'd, 390 U.S. 557, 88 S.Ct. 1235, 20 L.Ed.2d 126 (1968). In affirming, we held that, when "[t]he heart of the [state-law] complaint [is] a . . . clause in the collective bargaining agreement," id., at 558, 88 S.Ct., at 1236, that complaint arises under federal law:

> "[T]he pre-emptive force of § 301 is so powerful as to displace entirely any state cause of action 'for violation of contracts between an employer and a labor organization.' Any such suit is purely a creature of federal law, notwithstanding the fact that state law would provide a cause of action in the absence of § 301." Franchise Tax Board, supra, 463 U.S., at 23, 103 S.Ct., at 2853–2854.

B

Caterpillar asserts that respondents' state-law contract claims are in reality completely pre-empted § 301 claims, which therefore arise under federal law. We disagree. Section 301 governs claims founded directly on rights created by collective-bargaining agreements, and also claims "substantially dependent on analysis of a collective-bargaining agreement." Respondents allege that Caterpillar had entered into and breached individual employment contracts with them. Section 301 says nothing about the content or validity of individual employment contracts. It is true that respondents, bargaining unit members at the time of the plant closing, possessed substantial rights under the collective agreement, and could have brought suit under § 301. As masters of the complaint, however, they chose not to do so.

* * *

Caterpillar next relies on this Court's decision in *J.I. Case Co. v. NLRB,* 321 U.S. 332, 64 S.Ct. 576, 88 L.Ed. 762 (1944), arguing that when respondents returned to the collective-bargaining unit, their individual employment agreements were subsumed into, or eliminated by, the collective-bargaining agreement. Thus, Caterpillar contends, respondents' claims under their individual contracts actually are claims under the collective agreement and pre-empted by § 301.

Caterpillar is mistaken. * * *

* * *

* * * Caterpillar's basic error is its failure to recognize that a plaintiff covered by a collective-bargaining agreement is permitted to assert legal rights independent of that agreement, including state-law contract rights, so long as the contract relied upon is not a collective-bargaining agreement. Caterpillar impermissibly attempts to create the prerequisites to removal by ignoring the set of facts (i.e., the individual employment contracts) presented by respondents, along with their legal characterization of those facts, and arguing that there are different facts respondents might have alleged that would have constituted a federal claim. In sum, Caterpillar does not seek to point out that the contract relied upon by respondents is in fact a collective agreement; rather it attempts to justify removal on the basis of facts not alleged in the complaint. The "artful pleading" doctrine cannot be invoked in such circumstances.

[I]f an employer wishes to dispute the continued legality or viability of a pre-existing individual employment contract because an employee has taken a position covered by a collective agreement, it may raise this question in state court. The employer may argue that the individual employment contract has been pre-empted due to the principle of exclusive representation in § 9(a) of the National Labor Relations Act (NLRA), 29 U.S.C. § 159(a). Or the employer may contend that enforcement of the individual employment contract arguably would constitute an unfair labor practice under the NLRA, and is therefore pre-empted. The fact that a defendant might ultimately prove that a plaintiff's claims are pre-empted under the NLRA does not establish that they are removable to federal court.

Finally, Caterpillar argues that § 301 pre-empts a state-law claim even when the employer raises only a defense that requires a court to interpret or apply a collective-bargaining agreement. Caterpillar asserts such a defense claiming that, in its collective-bargaining agreement, its unionized employees waived any pre-existing individual employment contract rights.[13]

It is true that when a defense to a state claim is based on the terms of a collective-bargaining agreement, the state court will have to interpret that agreement to decide whether the state claim survives. But the presence of a federal question, even a § 301 question, in a defensive argument does not overcome the paramount policies embodied in the well-pleaded complaint rule—that the plaintiff is the master of the complaint, that a federal question must appear on the face of the complaint, and that the plaintiff may, by eschewing claims based on federal law, choose to have the cause heard in state court. When a plaintiff invokes a right created by a collective-bargaining agreement, the plaintiff has *chosen* to plead what we have held must be regarded as a federal claim, and removal is at the defendant's option. But a *defendant* cannot, merely by injecting a federal question into an action that asserts what is plainly a state-law claim, transform the action into one arising under federal law, thereby selecting the forum in which the claim shall be litigated. If a defendant could do so, the plaintiff would be master of nothing. Congress has long since decided that federal defenses do not provide a basis for removal.

III

Respondents' claims do not arise under federal law and therefore may not be removed to federal court. The judgment of the Court of Appeals is

Affirmed.

NOTE ON REMOVAL

1.   Federal question removal. *Caterpillar* illustrates two important general principles applicable to federal question removal cases under 28

---

[13] We intimate no view on the merits of this or any of the pre-emption arguments discussed above. These are questions that must be addressed in the first instance by the state court in which respondents filed their claims.

U.S.C. § 1441: (a) plaintiff is "master" of his or her complaint, and (b) federal defenses may not be used as a basis for removal.

      a.   Plaintiff as master of the complaint. It sometimes happens that plaintiff has available both federal- and state-law causes of action. If plaintiff is willing to forgo her federal-law cause of action, she may prevent removal from state to federal court by confining her complaint to her state-law cause of action. See The Fair v. Kohler Die and Specialty Co., 228 U.S. 22, 25, 33 S.Ct. 410, 57 L.Ed. 716 (1913) ("Of course the party who brings a suit is master to decide what law he will rely upon."); Garibaldi v. Lucky Food Stores, Inc., 726 F.2d 1367, 1370 (9th Cir. 1984) ("[P]laintiff is the master of his or her own complaint and is free to ignore the federal cause of action and rest the claim solely on a state cause of action."). In *Caterpillar*, plaintiffs chose to rely only on state-law claims under individual contracts between themselves and the company, forgoing possible federal-law claims under the collective bargaining contract between their union and the company.

      b.   Federal defenses not available as a basis for removal. 28 U.S.C. § 1441(a) permits a defendant to remove from state to federal court "any civil action * * * of which the district courts of the United States have original jurisdiction." The statute has been construed to mean that removal is proper only if the plaintiff could have filed the suit in federal court in the first place. In other words, the well-pleaded complaint rule applies to removal by the defendant as well as to initial filing by the plaintiff.

      Is this sensible? An important justification for the well-pleaded complaint rule is that it can be applied at an early stage in litigation, on the basis of pleadings actually in front of the court. Plaintiff cannot rely on an anticipated federal defense as a basis for subject matter jurisdiction when she files the case, in part because defendant might not in fact assert that defense. Removal is generally sought early in the case. And if a federal defense is pleaded as a basis for removal, it is no longer a hypothetical matter whether the federal defense will be pleaded. Further, if we think that parties relying on federal law should have a federal forum to determine their federal rights, the well-pleaded complaint is proper as applied to plaintiffs, but perverse as applied to defendants. As the rule now stands, defendants can remove only when plaintiffs assert federal rights.

      Reformulation of § 1441(a) to allow removal based on the assertion of a federal defense is not a new idea. Professor Herbert Wechsler suggested it in 1948. Wechsler, Federal Jurisdiction and the Revision of the Judicial Code, 13 Law & Contemp. Probs. 216, 233–34 (1948). The American Law Institute recommended it again in 1969. ALI, Study of the Division of Jurisdiction Between State and Federal Courts 188–194 (1969). But Congress has refused to act, and the Court has refused to reread the statute as it stands. Franchise Tax Board of California v. Construction Laborers Vacation Trust, 463 U.S. 1, 10 n. 9, 103 S.Ct. 2841, 77 L.Ed.2d 420 (1983) ("Commentators have repeatedly proposed that some mechanism be established to permit removal of cases in which a federal defense may be dispositive. * * * But those proposals have not been adopted."). The general rule is that only defendants have the right to remove. Under this rule, a plaintiff may not remove based on a defendant's counterclaim asserting a right under federal law. Shamrock Oil & Gas Corp. v. Sheets, 313 U.S. 100, 61 S.Ct. 868, 85 L.Ed. 1214 (1941). However, under a narrow 2011 amendment to the removal statute, a plaintiff may remove based on a counterclaim or third-party claim arising under federal patent, plant variety protection, or copyright laws. 28 U.S.C. § 1454.

2. Complete preemption removal. The result in *Caterpillar* was not as obvious as it might appear from the preceding principles. The Supreme Court has developed an odd and somewhat unruly exception that permits removal where the plaintiff has tried to plead a state-law cause of action that is completely preempted by federal law. Thus, in Avco Corp. v. Aero Lodge No. 735, International Association of Machinists and Aerospace Workers, 390 U.S. 557, 88 S.Ct. 1235, 20 L.Ed.2d 126 (1968), plaintiff-employer sued under state law in state court to enjoin a strike, relying on a no-strike clause in its collective bargaining agreement with the union. The Supreme Court upheld removal to federal district court on the ground that a claim under a collective bargaining agreement was entirely preempted by federal labor law. In Metropolitan Life Insurance Co. v. Taylor, 481 U.S. 58, 107 S.Ct. 1542, 95 L.Ed.2d 55 (1987), an employee sued his employer in state court, seeking recovery under state law from the employer's plan for ill and disabled workers. The Court upheld removal to federal district court on the ground that any state-law claim against the plan was entirely preempted by the federal Employee Retirement Income Security Act (ERISA).

It is somewhat unclear why defenses based on assertions of complete federal preemption are entitled to special treatment in removal, for preemption defenses are not necessarily more difficult for a state court to address than other federal defenses. The Court's decisions in *Avco* and *Taylor* may have been motivated by a particular distrust of the state courts' ability to deal with federal labor law and with ERISA. There is a history of conflict between the federal government and the states over their respective spheres of authority in labor law, and both federal labor law and ERISA are notoriously complicated. Even if the complete preemption doctrine is confined to these two areas, removal on this basis is not simple, for there is complication and ambiguity as to the meaning and preemptive scope of the substantive law, as is evident from the Court's opinion in *Caterpillar*.

The Supreme Court has repeated the mantra that only "complete" (not merely partial) preemption is required, noting that "artful pleading" of a preempted state claim will not be permitted to disguise the preempted claim's inescapably federal nature. See Rivet v. Regions Bank of Louisiana, 522 U.S. 470, 118 S.Ct. 921, 139 L.Ed.2d 912, 925 (1998) (citations omitted):

> The artful pleading doctrine allows removal where federal law completely preempts a plaintiff's state-law claim. Although federal preemption is ordinarily a defense, "[o]nce an area of state law has been completely pre-empted, any claim purportedly based on that pre-empted state-law claim is considered, from its inception, a federal claim, and therefore arises under federal law."

However, neither the justification for the doctrine, nor the scope of its application, is readily apparent. The Court's latest foray is Beneficial National Bank v. Anderson, 539 U.S. 1, 123 S.Ct. 2058, 156 L.Ed.2d 1 (2003). The Court held that federal regulation of interest rates chargeable by nationally chartered banks completely preempt state usury laws, allowing removal of a state-law usury suit brought against a national bank. Justice Scalia dissented vigorously. He criticized the Court's earlier decisions in *Avco* and *Taylor* as without sufficient theoretical foundation, and objected to the expansion of those decisions in *Anderson*: "[A]s between an inexplicable narrow holding [in *Avco* and *Taylor*] and an inexplicable broad one [in this case], the former is the lesser evil[.]" Id. at 21.

For analysis and criticism, see Tarkington, Rejecting the Touchstone: Complete Preemption and Congressional Intent after *Beneficial National Bank v. Anderson*, 59 S. Car. L.Rev.225 (2008); Pursley, Rationalizing Complete Preemption after *Beneficial National Bank v. Anderson*: A New Rule, a New Justification, 54 Drake L.Rev. 371 (2006); Ragazzo, Reconsidering the Artful Pleading Doctrine, 44 Hast. L.J. 273 (1993). See also Miller, Artful Pleading: A Doctrine in Search of a Definition, 76 Tex.L.Rev. 1781 (1998); Twitchell, Characterizing Federal Claims: Preemption, Removal, and the Arising-Under Jurisdiction of the Federal Courts, 54 Geo.Wash.L.Rev. 812 (1986).

3.   Diversity removal. a. Narrower scope of removal. Removal in a diversity case, unlike that in a federal question case, is narrower than original jurisdiction in federal district court. Original jurisdiction in diversity under 28 U.S.C § 1332 requires only that plaintiff and defendant be citizens of different states. It does not matter if plaintiff—the party seeking the presumptively unbiased federal forum—is a citizen of the state in which the district court sits. By contrast, removal is unavailable in diversity if any defendant named and served is a citizen of the state in which the suit is brought, on the ground that a defendant need not fear bias in his or her own state court. 28 U.S.C. § 1441(b). The American Law Institute has recommended that treatment between in-state plaintiffs and in-state defendants be equalized by eliminating the right of an in-state plaintiff to invoke original diversity jurisdiction. ALI, Study of the Division of Jurisdiction between State and Federal Courts 124 (1969) ("The right of an in-state plaintiff to institute a diversity action against an out-of-state defendant * * * is not responsive to any acceptable justification for diversity jurisdiction. The in-stater can hardly be heard to ask the federal government to spare him from litigation in the courts of his own state.").

b.   Devices to defeat diversity removal. A plaintiff may defeat removal in a diversity suit by choosing to forego a damage recovery in excess of $75,000. Plaintiff must make it plain before removal that she seeks $75,000 or less; she may not obtain a remand to state court by reducing her damage claim after removal. St. Paul Mercury Indemnity Co. v. Red Cab Co., 303 U.S. 283, 292, 58 S.Ct. 586, 82 L.Ed. 845 (1938). See also Rogers v. Wal-Mart Stores, Inc., 230 F.3d 868 (6th Cir. 2000); In re Shell Oil Co., 970 F.2d 355 (7th Cir. 1992). Some states do not require a plaintiff to state in the complaint how much she is claiming; other states forbid a plaintiff from doing so. To deal with complaints filed in these states (as well as cases in which non-monetary relief is sought), Congress amended the removal statute in 2011. The defendant needs only to allege plausibly in the notice of removal an amount in controversy that satisfies the jurisdictional amount. 28 U.S.C. § 1446. If plaintiff contests defendant's allegation, defendant must show, by a preponderance of the evidence, that the alleged amount is true. See Dart Cherokee Basin Operating Co., LLC v. Owens, 574 U.S. ___, 135 S.Ct. 547, 190 L.Ed.2d 495 (2014).

The Class Action Fairness Act of 2005 (CAFA) takes a different approach to stipulated amounts in controversy. In Standard Fire Ins. v. Knowles, 568 U.S. ___, 133 S.Ct. 1345, 185 L.Ed.2d 439 (2013), the Supreme Court held that a stipulation attached to the complaint that damages in excess of $5,000,000 (i.e., damages satisfying the CAFA jurisdictional amount) will not be sought cannot defeat removal. Removal in a CAFA case typically takes place before a class is certified, The Court reasoned that a binding stipulation is not possible because a named plaintiff in an uncertified class action has no authority to bind members of the would-be class.

Recall that 28 U.S.C. § 1359 does not permit improper or collusive assignments or joinder to invoke diversity. See, supra p. 255. The conventional view is that § 1359 speaks only to attempts to invoke jurisdiction, leaving the parties to their own ingenious devices to defeat jurisdiction. In Mecom v. Fitzsimmons Drilling Co., 284 U.S. 183, 52 S.Ct. 84, 76 L.Ed. 233 (1931), an Oklahoma citizen three times filed separate wrongful death suits in state court as administratrix of the estate of her deceased husband. Each time defendant, a Louisiana citizen, removed to federal court based on diversity of citizenship. After each removal, plaintiff took voluntary dismissals and refiled the suit. After the first two dismissals, she refiled in state court as administratrix. After the third dismissal, she resigned as administratrix, and had a Louisiana citizen appointed in her place. The Louisiana citizen then filed suit in state court and successfully resisted removal on the ground that diversity of citizenship no longer existed.

The specific problem posed in *Mecom* is now handled by statute. In 1988, 28 U.S.C. § 1332(c)(2) was added, providing that the legal representative of an estate is deemed to be a citizen of the same state as the decedent. But the general problem remains: Can a litigant assign her interest to a non-diverse party in order to defeat diversity? In Provident Savings Life Assurance Society v. Ford, 114 U.S. 635, 5 S.Ct. 1104, 29 L.Ed. 261 (1885), the Supreme Court upheld an assignment to defeat diversity, and the case has not been overruled in the more than one hundred years since the decision. But the lower federal courts have begun to move away from *Provident*. For example, in Grassi v. Ciba-Geigy, Ltd., 894 F.2d 181 (5th Cir. 1990), the court disregarded an assignment made for the purpose of remaining in state court. See also Gentle v. Lamb-Weston, Inc., 302 F. Supp. 161 (D. Me. 1969), supra p. 259.

Plaintiff may also prevent removal by joining defendants who would destroy complete diversity. If joinder of a defendant is "fraudulent" in the sense that there is no colorable ground supporting the claim, or if plaintiff has no real intention of prosecuting the claim against the defendant, the case may be removed and the defendant dismissed. But fraudulent joinder is not always easy to show. See, e.g., Batoff v. State Farm Insurance Co., 977 F.2d 848, 851–54 (3d Cir. 1992) (denying removal because defendant did not meet "heavy burden of persuasion" to show that joinder was fraudulent). Further, a diversity case must be removed within one year of its filing in state court. 28 U.S.C. § 1446(b). For many years, the one-year limitation would not be extended even if the defendant seeking to remove could not discover within that time that the joinder was fraudulent. Congress changed the rule in 2011. Under 28 U.S.C. § 1441(c)(1), a district court now has discretion to extend the period for removal if it finds that the plaintiff "acted in bad faith in order to prevent the defendant from removing the action."

4. Removal under the Class Action Fairness Act of 2005. Corporate defendants in class actions have long preferred federal courts. The Class Action Fairness Act of 2005 was enacted to benefit corporations by expanding federal court subject matter jurisdiction in diversity class actions. Subject to exceptions for actions with a particularly strong connection to a single state, federal courts now have concurrent subject matter jurisdiction over all diversity class actions in which the aggregate amount in controversy exceeds $5,000,000, and in which there is minimal diversity of citizenship.

28 U.S.C. § 1332(d). If the action is filed in state court, removal is governed by the newly enacted 28 U.S.C. § 1453. By comparison to removal under §§ 1441 and 1446, removal under § 1453 is very easy. First, a defendant may remove even if it is a citizen of the state in which the action is brought. § 1453(b). Compare § 1441(b) (no removal in diversity cases if any of the defendants is a citizen of the state in which the suit is brought). Second, one defendant may remove the entire action to federal court, even if other defendants do not want to remove. § 1453(b). Compare § 1446(a) (all defendants must agree to remove). Third, there is no time limit on removal. § 1435(b). Compare § 1446(b) (one-year time limit on removal). Fourth, a district court's order remanding to state court is reviewable on appeal. § 1453(c)(1). Compare § 1447(d) (remand order not reviewable on appeal or otherwise; but see discussion of the *Hermansdorfer* case, infra note 6). For a history of the passage of CAFA, see Burbank, The Class Action Fairness Act of 2005 in Historical Context, 156 U. Pa. L. Rev. 1439 (2008); Marcus, Erie, the Class Action Fairness Act, and Some Federalism Implications of Diversity Jurisdiction, 48 Wm. & Mary L. Rev. 1247 (2007).

    5.   Non-removable claims. Some claims are specifically made non-removable. For example, claims under the Federal Employers Liability Act (FELA) are made non-removable by 28 U.S.C. § 1445(a). FELA is a statute under which workers on interstate railroads can recover for injuries negligently caused during the course of their employment. When FELA was enacted in 1908, it was an innovative, pro-worker statute that, among other things, introduced the concept of comparative negligence to land-based tort law. (Previously, comparative negligence had been used only in maritime torts.) In 1910, Congress made FELA cases filed in state court non-removable to federal court. 36 Stat. 291 (April 5, 1910). Senator Dixon of Montana supported the amendment because, in his words, "It has been my experience that in suits of this kind in the West * * * whenever a personal-injury suit was brought against a railroad the invariable custom was to transfer the case to the federal courts; in my own State taking the plaintiff a distance in many cases of 400 miles to the federal court, involving a tremendous expense of witnesses and in many cases amounting actually to a denial of justice." 46 Congressional Record 4092 (61st Cong., 2d Sess., Sen., April 1, 1910).

    Later in the book, you will encounter a choice-of-law question—a so-called "reverse *Erie*" question—in a FELA case, Dice v. Akron, Canton & Youngstown RR. Co., 342 U.S. 359, 72 S.Ct. 312, 96 L.Ed. 398 (1952). See infra p. 410. As you study *Dice*, you may wish to consider this rationale for non-removability of FELA cases.

    6.   Non-appealability of remand orders. Section 1447(d) provides that remands to state court of cases removed under § 1441 are "not reviewable on appeal or otherwise." But see Thermtron Products, Inc. v. Hermansdorfer, 423 U.S. 336, 96 S.Ct. 584, 46 L.Ed.2d 542 (1976). District Judge Hermansdorfer relied on the non-reviewability of remand orders and acted out the hostility felt by many district judges toward diversity cases. During 1973, fourteen diversity cases were removed from Kentucky state courts to Judge Hermansdorfer's court. In each case Judge Hermansdorfer issued an order to show cause why it should not be remanded, and entered orders of remand in twelve of the fourteen cases. *Thermtron Products*, one of these twelve cases, was an ordinary diversity case arising out of an automobile accident. On the record, Judge Hermansdorfer noted his crowded docket, complained that the case interfered with cases of higher priority, stated that defendant had failed to show how he would be prejudiced in state court, and remanded. The Supreme Court granted mandamus, reversing his order. It held that only remands based on lack of subject matter jurisdiction are non-reviewable, and Judge Hermansdorfer had made it painfully clear that he was remanding for other reasons. After *Thermtron Products*, a remand is still non-reviewable when based on a finding that subject matter jurisdiction is lacking, even if that finding is clearly mistaken. See, e.g., Tillman v. CSX Transportation, Inc., 929 F.2d 1023 (5th Cir.), cert. den. 502 U.S. 859 (1991). To get a sense of the strength of the non-reviewability principle, see Liberty Mutual Insurance Co. v. Ward Trucking Corp., 48 F.3d 742 (3d Cir. 1995), in which defendant removed a diversity case to federal court. The district court remanded on the ground of insufficient amount in controversy. During discovery, defendant learned that plaintiff had incurred damages of over $150,000, and again removed. The district court remanded to state court without allowing defendant an opportunity to respond to plaintiff's motion to remand. The court of appeals held the remand order non-reviewable.

The Supreme Court has since reaffirmed the narrow scope of the *Thermtron Products* exception to the non-reviewability of remand orders. In Kircher v. Putnam Funds Trust, 547 U.S. 633, 126 S.Ct. 2145, 165 L.Ed.2d 92 (2006), the district court remanded to state court based upon its conclusion that the suit did not satisfy the requirements of the special removal provision of the Securities Litigation Uniform Standards Act of 1998. The district court's reading of the removal provision was logically dependent on its reading of a substantive provision of the same Act. The Supreme Court, in another case, had just held that the district court's reading of the substantive provision of the Act was wrong, which meant that its decision to remand was necessarily wrong. Nonetheless, the Court held that the district court's order remanding the case to state court was not reviewable on appeal. The Court wrote:

> The District Court said that it was remanding for lack of jurisdiction, an unreviewable ground[.] * * * [O]n the District Court's understanding [of the substantive provision], the court had no subject matter jurisdiction. * * * And "[w]here the order is based on one of the [grounds enumerated in 28 U.S.C. § 1447(c)], review is unavailable no matter how plain the legal error in ordering the remand."

547 U.S. at 641–42 (citation omitted).

In contrast to remand orders based on lack of subject matter jurisdiction under 28 U.S.C. § 1331 and comparable statutes, remand orders under the supplemental jurisdiction statute, § 1367(c), are not based on a lack of subject matter jurisdiction. The district court has the authority under § 1367(c) to retain the claim over which there is supplemental jurisdiction after the federal question or diversity-based claim has been dismissed, but it need not do so. A district court's decision to remand a claim under § 1367(c) is based on discretionary or judgment-based criteria such as whether the remanded claim "raises a novel or complex issue of State law." § 1367(c)(1). Remands under § 1367(c) are reviewable by appeal rather than mandamus.

   7.   Procedure. To seek removal, defendant or defendants file a notice of removal in the state court. Ordinarily, all defendants must join in the notice. A defendant has thirty days from service of the complaint to file a timely notice of removal, if the facts alleged in the complaint show the case is removable; if not, the defendant has 30 days from receipt of some other document showing the case is removable. 28 U.S.C. § 1446(b). If the defendant has independent knowledge of facts making a case removable, it may remove based on those facts. Roth v. CHA Hollywood Medical Ctr., 720 F.3d 1121 (9th Cir. 2013). Before 2011, the operation of the 30-day rule was confusing in a case with multiple defendants served at different times. The statute now provides that each defendant has 30 days to file a notice of removal after service on that defendant. 28 U.S.C. § 1446(b)(1). Earlier-served defendants may then satisfy the requirement of unanimity by consenting to the later-served defendant's removal notice. § 1446(b)(2)(C). A motion to remand must be made within 30 days of removal for anything other than a defect in subject matter jurisdiction. § 1447(c).

8.   **Post-removal cure of improper removal.** The general rule is that if the removal is improper because of lack of subject matter jurisdiction, a motion to remand may (indeed, must) be entertained at any time. However, in Caterpillar Inc. v. Lewis, 519 U.S. 61, 117 S.Ct. 467, 136 L.Ed.2d 437 (1996), a diversity suit was improperly removed to federal court, and the federal district court wrongly denied a timely motion to remand. (At the time of removal, there was incomplete diversity because one of the defendants had the same citizenship as the plaintiff.) The non-diverse defendant then settled out of the suit. Because the non-diverse defendant was now gone, the federal district court now had subject matter jurisdiction, even though it had not had jurisdiction at the time of removal. The wrongly removed plaintiff went to trial and lost on the merits. He then renewed his objection to removal. The Supreme Court conceded that removal had been improper and that the district court had wrongly denied the motion to remand. But "no jurisdictional defect lingered through judgment in the district court. To wipe out the adjudication post-judgment, and return to the state court a case now satisfying all federal jurisdictional requirements, would impose an exorbitant cost on our dual court system, a cost incompatible with the fair and unprotracted administration of justice." 519 U.S. at 477. But compare Grupo Dataflux v. Atlas Global Group, L.P., 541 U.S. 567, 124 S.Ct. 1920, 158 L.Ed.2d 866 (2004), in which plaintiff Atlas was a limited partnership and defendant a Mexican corporation. Plaintiff filed a state-law claim in federal court. At the time of filing, two of the partners in Atlas were Mexican citizens. Hence, under the rule that a partnership is a citizen of each state or foreign country of which any of its partners is a citizen, there was a lack of complete diversity. Before trial, however, the two Mexican partners were bought out, so that at the time of trial there were no non-diverse partners in Atlas and diversity was complete. After losing at trial, defendant moved to dismiss for lack of subject matter jurisdiction because of the lack of diversity at the time of filing. The Court held that the suit should have been dismissed. It distinguished *Caterpillar* on the ground that the correction of the defect in that case had been accomplished by dismissing a non-diverse party, while the correction in *Grupo Dataflux* had been accomplished by changing the citizenship of a continuing party. Has the Supreme Court lost its way?

9.   **Other removal statutes.** In addition to the general removal statute and the newly enacted CAFA removal statute, several other statutes permit removal in specific types of cases. For example, removal is permitted in civil or criminal suits brought against individual federal officers so long as a federal defense is asserted. 28 U.S.C. § 1442; Mesa v. California, 489

U.S. 121, 109 S.Ct. 959, 103 L.Ed.2d 99 (1989). Further, removal is permitted in suits brought against private individuals where the defendant is denied or cannot enforce "equal civil rights." 28 U.S.C. § 1443(1). This statute has been narrowly construed, however, and is rarely employed. Georgia v. Rachel, 384 U.S. 780, 86 S.Ct. 1783, 16 L.Ed.2d 925 (1966) ("equal civil rights" refers only to racial equality); City of Greenwood v. Peacock, 384 U.S. 808, 86 S.Ct. 1800, 16 L.Ed.2d 944 (1966) ("pervasive and explicit" state law denying equality is required; mere allegation of unequal treatment is not sufficient)

10. Additional reading. For recent thoughtful articles on removal, see Field, Removal Reform: A Solution for Federal Question Jurisdiction, Forum Shopping, and Duplicative Federal Litigation, 88 Ind. L.J. 611 (2013); Bassett and Perschbacher, The Roots of Removal, 77 Brook. L.Rev. 1 (2011).

5. CHALLENGING FEDERAL SUBJECT MATTER JURISDICTION

NOTE ON DIRECT CHALLENGE TO FEDERAL SUBJECT MATTER JURISDICTION

A defect of federal subject matter jurisdiction is not waivable in district court or on appeal. It may be challenged directly until a judgment has become final and appeals are no longer possible. It may be raised in the district court at any time before judgment. Rule 12(b)(1), (h)(3). It may also be raised on appeal, even if not previously raised in the trial court. It may be raised by any party. It may even be—indeed, must be—raised by the federal court *sua sponte* if it comes to the court's attention. See Mansfield, Coldwater & Lake Michigan Ry. v. Swan, 111 U.S. 379, 4 S.Ct. 510, 28 L.Ed. 462 (1884). A federal court must find that it has subject matter jurisdiction before it can decide any question on the merits. The Supreme Court has disapproved a "doctrine of hypothetical jurisdiction" under which a court could assume that it had subject matter jurisdiction in order to dismiss a case on the merits when the merits question was easier than the jurisdiction question, and when the result would be the same as if jurisdiction were denied. Steel Company v. Citizens for a Better Environment, 523 U.S. 83, 118 S.Ct. 1003, 140 L.Ed.2d 210 (1998). However, a collateral attack on subject matter jurisdiction (i.e., an attack in a separate proceeding) is treated differently from a direct challenge and is usually unavailing.

The consequences of a successful, late-raised objection to subject matter jurisdiction are apparent in both *Louisville & Nashville Rr. v. Mottley* and *Owen Equipment & Erection Co. v. Kroger*, supra pp. 225, 264. At best, the consequence is a significant expenditure of time and money, as in *Mottley*. At worst, the consequence is the potential loss of a cause of action because of the running of the statute of limitations, as in *Owen Equipment*. (This is probably why the parties fought the jurisdictional question all the way to the Supreme Court in *Owen Equipment*. By the time the district court dismissed Mrs. Kroger's suit, it may have been too late to refile in state court because the statute of limitations had run.)

The most extreme case may be American Fire & Casualty Co. v. Finn, 341 U.S. 6, 71 S.Ct. 534, 95 L.Ed. 702 (1951). Plaintiff Finn suffered a loss due to fire and brought suit in state court against three defendants, including

American Fire and Casualty Company. Defendants removed the suit to federal court. After unsuccessfully seeking a remand to state court, Finn tried his case on the merits in federal district court and won a judgment against American Fire. American Fire then moved to vacate the judgment and to remand to the state court on the ground that there was no subject matter jurisdiction in the federal court, and that the case had therefore been improperly removed. This was, of course, precisely the remand plaintiff Finn had sought, and American Fire had resisted, before trial. But now, after having lost on the merits, American Fire sought to avoid the judgment of the court to which it had sought removal, on the ground that the removal was improper. The Supreme Court held that there was no subject matter jurisdiction in the district court and vacated the judgment.

Recall that a defect in *in personam* jurisdiction is waivable. Indeed, it is so easily waived that a defendant sometimes waives it inadvertently. But a defect in federal subject matter jurisdiction is not waivable, even in the most extreme circumstances. Why are the two kinds of jurisdiction treated so differently? The standard answer is that an *in personam* jurisdictional objection is a personal right, designed to protect an individual defendant from undue inconvenience and expense. If the individual decides to forgo the objection, she should be able to do so. By contrast, a subject matter jurisdictional objection is not based on a personal right but rather a structural principle. It is designed to protect the dignity and respective jurisdictions of the federal and state court systems. Private individuals should not be able for their own purposes to deprive the state court system of a case that should rightfully be tried in that system. How do you think Mrs. Kroger or Mr. Finn would respond to this principled explanation?

There may be a small crack in the dike. In Ruhrgas, AG v. Marathon Oil Co., 526 U.S. 574, 119 S.Ct. 1563, 143 L.Ed.2d 760 (1999), the Supreme Court held that an objection to personal jurisdiction may be decided before deciding an objection to subject matter jurisdiction if the personal jurisdiction issue is easier and will allow dismissal of the case. For discussion, see Friedenthal, The Crack in the Steel Case, 68 Geo. Wash.L.Rev. 258 (2000). For sharp criticism of *Ruhrgas*, see Idleman, The Emergence of Jurisdictional Resequencing in the Federal Courts, 87 Cornell L.Rev. 1 (2001). Does *Ruhrgas* undermine cases like *Finn*? That is, if a federal court may avoid deciding whether it has subject matter jurisdiction (and thereby run the risk that it is acting in a case over which it has no subject matter jurisdiction) for reasons of administrative convenience, shouldn't the court also be able act in order to avoid serious unfairness caused by the disingenuous conduct of one of the parties, in a case such as *Finn*?

The academic community has severely criticized this so-called "first principle" of federal jurisdiction. The American Law Institute, echoing Professor J. William Moore, has written, "[T]his fetish of federal jurisdiction is wholly inconsistent with sound judicial administration and can only serve to diminish respect for a system that tolerates it." ALI, Study of the Division of Jurisdiction Between State and Federal Courts 366 (1969).

C. VENUE

Even if a court has *in personam* jurisdiction over the defendants and subject matter jurisdiction over the dispute, it must also have proper venue. "Venue" is the past participle of the French infinitive "venir," meaning "to come." Venue is a separate, largely statutory requirement designed to fine-tune the decision about the proper place to bring an action. The primary purpose of venue is to protect the defendant, since the plaintiff, who has the initial choice of forum, will have taken her own interests into account in making her initial forum choice. "In most instances, the purpose of statutorily specified venue is to protect the *defendant* against the risk that a plaintiff will select an unfair or inconvenient place of trial." Leroy v. Great Western United Corp., 443 U.S. 173, 183–84, 99 S.Ct. 2710, 61 L.Ed.2d 464 (1979) (emphasis in original). Both the state and federal court systems have venue requirements.

1. STATE COURTS

NOTE ON VENUE IN STATE COURTS

State court venue systems restrict a litigant's choice of forum within the state, generally requiring that a suit be brought in a particular county. *In personam* jurisdiction within the state as a whole is assumed. Venue requirements, like *in personam* jurisdiction requirements, are generally waivable by the affected party or parties. A very few venue requirements are like subject matter jurisdiction requirements, and are not waivable. Although the factors involved in state court venue decisions vary from state to state, most states resemble one another fairly closely. "Local actions"— actions involving title to real estate or other intensely local actions—must be tried in the county where the real estate is located. "Transitory actions"—all other actions—are usually triable in more than one county. Venue in transitory actions depends on the place where the cause of action arose, on the subject matter of the suit, and on the residence and character of the parties. In transitory actions, venue is generally available where the events giving rise to the cause of action took place, or where the defendant resides or is doing business. Definitions of residence differ depending on whether the defendant is a private individual, a corporation, or an unincorporated association. Special venue provisions govern suits against the State and its officials. Stevens, Venue Statutes: Diagnosis and Proposed Cure, 49 Mich.L.Rev. 307 (1951), is still the best general treatment of venue in state courts. For venue in specific states, see, e.g., Note, Forum Shopping and Venue Transfers in Alabama, 48 Ala.L.Rev. 671 (1997); Clark, Venue in Civil Actions, 36 Okla.L.Rev. 643 (1983) (Oklahoma).

California venue provisions are fairly typical. The following is a brief overview. "Local actions" in California include numerous actions related to real estate, such as condemnation, quiet title, specific performance of a land sale contract, unlawful detainer, ejectment, trespass, slander of title, partition of land, or foreclosure of a mortgage on land. Calif.C.Civ.P. §§ 392(1), 110(b)(1). In all such actions, suit must be filed in the county where the land is located. "Local actions" also include marriage dissolutions (suit must be filed in the county where the petitioner-spouse resides), child support proceedings (where the child resides), and adoptions (where the adopting parent resides). Calif.C.Civ.P. §§ 395(a), 226. Defective venue in a local action suit may be waived, unless the suit is for condemnation of land. Calif.C.Civ.P. § 1250.020.

"Transitory actions" are all other actions, typically described as actions in which the claim might have arisen anywhere. Transitory actions include actions for personal injury or death, for injury to personal property, or for breach of contract. The general rule for transitory actions against individual defendants is that they must be filed in a county where one of the defendants resides, although this general rule is supplemented by a number of specific provisions. Calif.C.Civ.P. § 395(a). Residence, for purposes of California state venue, is synonymous with domicile. (Compare federal venue, where residence is not synonymous with domicile.) Actions for personal injury or death, or for injury to personal property, may be tried in the county where the injury occurred or where a defendant resides. Calif.C.Civ.P. § 395(a). Actions for breach of non-consumer contracts may be tried in the county where the defendant resides, where the contract was entered into, or where the contract was to be performed. Calif.C.Civ.P. § 395(a). Actions for breach of consumer contracts, and of contracts resulting from unsolicited telephone calls from the seller, may be tried where the contract was signed, where the purchaser resided when the contract was entered into, or where the purchaser resides at the commencement of the action. Calif.C.Civ.P. § 395(b). Venue is available more broadly against a corporate defendant than an individual defendant. Venue is proper in the county where the corporation resides (its principal office), where a contract was made or to be performed, or where a tort obligation arose or injury occurred. Calif.C.Civ.P. § 395.5. In "mixed" cases, where causes of action governed by different venue provisions are joined, venue is available only where it is proper as to all causes of action.

Venue may be changed in both local and transitory actions. If venue is improper because laid in the wrong county, it may be changed. Calif.C.Civ.P. § 397(1). Even if venue is proper, it may be changed "when the convenience of witnesses and the ends of justice would be promoted by the change." Calif.C.Civ.P. § 397(3). An initial choice of venue and a subsequent change of venue within California will not result in a change of the substantive law being applied.

2.   FEDERAL COURTS

a.   VENUE

NOTE ON VENUE IN FEDERAL COURTS

The judicial district is the organizing unit in the federal venue scheme, comparable to the county in state venue schemes. Small or sparsely populated states have a single federal judicial district for the entire state. For example, Massachusetts, Rhode Island, New Jersey, Kansas, Colorado, Montana, Nevada, and Alaska each have a single federal judicial district. Large, populous states have two, or sometimes several, districts. Pennsylvania has Eastern and Western Districts. New York has Eastern, Northern, Southern, and Western Districts. California has Central, Eastern, Northern, and Southern Districts. The district court for a judicial district ordinarily sits in the largest city in the district, although in some districts there are divisions of the district court that also sit in smaller cities in the district. The names of the districts can occasionally mislead. Contrary to what one might think, the District Court for the Central District of California sits in Los Angeles.

The Federal Courts Jurisdiction and Clarification Act of 2011 has substantially reworked elements of federal venue law.

1.   Venue defined. The new statute defines venue as "the geographic specification of the proper court or courts for the litigation of a civil action that is within the subject matter jurisdiction of the district courts in general." 28 U.S.C. § 1390(a).

2.   "Local" and "transitory" actions. Until 2011, federal venue distinguished between "local" and "transitory" actions. Previously, federal courts had applied the local action venue rules of the particular state in which the federal court was located. The most famous local action venue case is Livingston v. Jefferson, 15 F.Cas. 660 (C.C.D.Va.1811). The suit arose out of a long-running dispute over a valuable sandbank (or "batture") bordering the Mississippi River at New Orleans, in Louisiana. Edward Livingston claimed ownership of the land, but a United States marshal, acting at the direction of President Jefferson, evicted Livingston and his employees from the property. After Jefferson had returned to private life in Virginia, Livingston brought suit for trespass in federal circuit court in Virginia. (The circuit courts were the primary federal trial courts in those days.) Chief Justice John Marshall, Jefferson's bitter enemy, presided over the court as Circuit Justice. Livingston brought suit in Virginia because under early 19th-century principles of *in personam* jurisdiction, Jefferson was not susceptible to suit in Louisiana. If the local action venue rule applied, venue could be laid only in Louisiana because the suit was for trespass to land. To Jefferson's surprise, Marshall applied the local action rule and dismissed. The result was that the suit could not be brought in Virginia, or, for that matter, anywhere. For discussion, see Degnan, *Livingston v. Jefferson*—A Freestanding Footnote, 75 Calif.L.Rev. 115 (1987).

The new statute has abolished the distinction between local and transitory actions for venue purposes. 28 U.S.C. § 1391(a)(2). All civil actions (except admiralty cases) are now governed by the same general venue statute.

3.   The general venue statute, 28 U.S.C. § 1391. The general venue statute is 28 U.S.C. § 1391. Before 2011, the first two subsections of the statute provided separately for venue in diversity and federal question cases. The wording of the subsections was substantially identical, and the minor differences were traceable to decades-old drafting errors. This led many to ask why Congress did not consolidate the subsection into a single section applicable to both kinds of cases. The 2011 statute finally accomplished this step.

a.   § 1391(b)(1): venue based on defendant's residence. Under § 1391(b)(1), venue is available in any judicial district where a defendant resides, so long as all the defendants reside in the state in which that district is located. If there are two defendants, one residing in New York and one in New Jersey, venue is not available under this subsection. Natural persons, including aliens lawfully admitted for permanent residence, are deemed to reside in the district where they are domiciled. § 1391(c)(1). Corporations and unincorporated associations are deemed to reside in any district in which they are subject to personal jurisdiction in the action in question. § 1391(c)(2). (Compare citizenship of a corporation for purposes of diversity jurisdiction, § 1332(a) (corporation is a citizen of the state in which it is incorporated and in which it has its principal place of business); and of an unincorporated association for purposes of diversity jurisdiction, § 1332(c) (unincorporated association is a citizen of every state in which a member of the association is domiciled).)

If a defendant is subject to personal jurisdiction in a state with more than one judicial district, that defendant will be deemed to reside in each district where its contacts would be sufficient support personal jurisdiction if the district were a separate state, or, if there is no such district, in the district with which it has the most significant contacts. § 1391(d).

b.   § 1391(b)(2): venue based on events or property. Under § 1391(b)(2), venue is available in a judicial district "in which a substantial part of the events or omissions giving rise to the claim occurred," or "a substantial part of property that is the subject of the action is situated." Under an earlier, stricter version of this subsection, venue was available only in the district "in which the claim arose." In Leroy v. Great Western United Corp., 443 U.S. 173, 99 S.Ct. 2710, 61 L.Ed.2d 464 (1979), decided under the earlier standard, the Court held that it was conceivable, but unlikely, that a claim could arise, and venue be available, in more than one district. Under the more liberal standard now in effect, venue can often be available in more than one district under this provision.

c.   § 1391(b)(3). Subsections 1391(b)(3) is a fallback provision, available only when venue is available under neither § 1391(b)(1) nor (b)(2). Under the fallback provision, venue is available in any district in which any defendant is subject to personal jurisdiction in the action in question.

4.   Venue in suits against defendants residing outside the United States. A defendant (whether an alien or U.S. citizen) who resides outside the United States may be sued in any district. Joinder of such a defendant is disregarded for purposes of determining whether a suit may be brought with respect to other defendants. 28 U.S.C. § 1391(c)(3).

5.   Venue in suits against officers, employees, and administrative agencies of the United States, or against the United States itself. Section 1391(e) provides that venue in suits against officers or employees of the United States, or against its administrative agencies, is available (1)(A) where the defendant resides, §1391(e)(1)(A); where a substantial part of the event or omissions giving rise to the claim occurred, or a substantial part of the property that is the subject of the action is situated, § 1391(e)(1)(B); or where the plaintiff resides if no real property is involved in the action, § 1391(e)(1)(C). The first two subsections replicate the general venue statute. The third subsection was added in 1962 in order to allow litigation involving the federal government to be decided, at plaintiff's option, where it is likely to be most convenient for plaintiff. Suits brought under this subsection will usually be decided outside of the "Beltway" of Washington, D.C., in a court that has some understanding of the local matter in dispute and, perhaps, some sympathy for the local plaintiff. Note that subsection (e)(1)(C) is not a fallback provision. A plaintiff may bring suit in the district where she resides without having to show that venue is unavailable under the two preceding subsections. Proposals were made in the early 1980s for venue statutes that would have *required* administrative law cases of particular local interest to be brought outside of Washington, D.C. These proposals were not adopted. For discussion, see Sunstein, Participation, Public Law, and Venue Reform, 49 U.Chi.L.Rev. 976 (1982). Venue in suits against the United States itself (rather than against its officers, employees, or agencies) is determined under 28 U.S.C. § 1402 rather than § 1391(e). The text of § 1391(e)(1) appears to authorize venue in suits brought directly against the United States, but those words have been ignored. See, e.g., Misko v. United States, 77 F.R.D. 425, 429 n. 7 (D.D.C.1978).

6. Special venue statutes. There are several special venue statutes governing particular kinds of suits. Some are supplemental, allowing venue under either the general venue statute or under the special statute. Examples are federal antitrust suits, 15 U.S.C. §§ 15, 22, and suits for the collection of internal revenue, 28 U.S.C. § 1396. The Supreme Court has recently held that the special venue provision of the Federal Arbitration Act, 9 U.S.C. § 9, is supplemental. See Cortez Byrd Chips, Inc. v. Bill Harbert Construction Co., 529 U.S. 193, 120 S.Ct. 1331, 146 L.Ed.2d 171 (2000). Other special venue statutes are exclusive, allowing venue only under the provisions of the special statute. Examples are patent infringement suits, 28 U.S.C. § 1400(b), employment discrimination suits, 42 U.S.C. § 2000e–5, and suits under the federal Interpleader Act, 28 U.S.C. § 1397. If a suit contains multiple claims, and if the claims are subject to different (and incompatible) exclusive special venue provisions, what happens? Do the claims have to be split up and tried in separate suits in separate courts? Some courts have held, by analogy to pendent subject matter jurisdiction, that the claims may be heard together, even though venue is lacking for one or more of the claims. For a useful discussion, see Corn, Pendent Venue: A Doctrine in Search of a Theory, 68 U.Chi.L.Rev. 931 (2001).

7. Removed cases. The 2011 Act makes explicit what had long been assumed: Federal venue requirements do not apply to cases removed from state court. 28 U.S.C. § 1390(c). The general removal statute, 28 U.S.C. § 1441(a), requires only that a suit be removed to the federal district court of the district embracing the place where the state court sits, even if venue would not have been available if the suit had been filed in the district court in the first instance. Polizzi v. Cowles Magazines, Inc., 345 U.S. 663, 73 S.Ct. 900, 97 L.Ed. 1331 (1953).

b.   CHANGE OF VENUE AND RELATED TOPICS

Ferens v. John Deere Co.
Supreme Court of the United States, 1990.
494 U.S. 516, 110 S.Ct. 1274, 108 L.Ed.2d 443.

■ JUSTICE KENNEDY delivered the opinion of the Court.

Section 1404(a) of Title 28 states: "For the convenience of parties and witnesses, in the interest of justice, a district court may transfer any civil action to any other district or division where it might have been brought." 28 U.S.C. § 1404(a) (1982 ed.). In Van Dusen v. Barrack, 376 U.S. 612, 84 S.Ct. 805, 11 L.Ed.2d 945 (1964), we held that, following a transfer under § 1404(a) initiated by a defendant, the transferee court must follow the choice of law rules that prevailed in the transferor court. We now decide that, when a plaintiff moves for the transfer, the same rule applies.

I

Albert Ferens lost his right hand when, the allegation is, it became caught in his combine harvester, manufactured by Deere & Company. The accident occurred while Ferens was working with the combine on his farm in Pennsylvania. For reasons not explained in the record, Ferens delayed filing a tort suit and Pennsylvania's 2-year limitations period expired. In the third year, he and his wife sued Deere in the United States District Court for the Western District of Pennsylvania, raising contract and warranty claims as to which the Pennsylvania limitations period had not yet run. The District Court had diversity jurisdiction, as Ferens and his wife are Pennsylvania residents, and Deere is incorporated in Delaware with its principal place of business in Illinois.

Not to be deprived of a tort action, the Ferenses in the same year filed a second diversity suit against Deere in the United States District Court for the Southern District of Mississippi, alleging negligence and products liability. Diversity jurisdiction and venue were proper. The Ferenses sued Deere in the District Court in Mississippi because they knew that, under Klaxon Co. v. Stentor Electric Mfg. Co., 313 U.S. 487, 496, 61 S.Ct. 1020, 1021, 85 L.Ed. 1477 (1941), the federal court in the exercise of diversity jurisdiction must apply the same choice of law rules that Mississippi state courts would apply if they were deciding the case. A Mississippi court would rule that Pennsylvania substantive law controls the personal injury claim but that Mississippi's own law governs the limitation period.

Although Mississippi has a borrowing statute which, on its face, would seem to enable its courts to apply statutes of limitations from other jurisdictions, see Miss.Code Ann. § 15–1–65 (1972), the State Supreme Court has said that the borrowing statute "only applies where a nonresident [defendant] in whose favor the statute has accrued afterwards moves into this state." Louisiana & Mississippi R. Transfer Co. v. Long, 159 Miss. 654, 667, 131 So. 84, 88 (1930). The borrowing statute would not apply to the Ferenses' action because, as the parties agree, Deere was a corporate resident of Mississippi before the cause of action accrued. The Mississippi courts, as a result, would apply Mississippi's 6-year statute of limitations to the tort claim arising under Pennsylvania law and the tort action would not be time-barred under the Mississippi statute. See Miss.Code Ann. § 15–1–49 (1972).

The issue now before us arose when the Ferenses took their forum shopping a step further: having chosen the federal court in Mississippi to take advantage of the State's limitations period, they next moved, under § 1404(a), to transfer the action to the federal court in Pennsylvania on the ground that Pennsylvania was a more convenient forum. The Ferenses acted on the assumption that, after the transfer, the choice of law rules in the Mississippi forum, including a rule requiring application of the Mississippi statute of limitations, would continue to govern the suit.

Deere put up no opposition, and the District Court in Mississippi granted the § 1404(a) motion. The Court accepted the Ferenses' arguments that they resided in Pennsylvania; that the accident occurred there; that the claim had no connection to Mississippi; that a substantial number of witnesses resided in the Western District of Pennsylvania but none resided in Mississippi; that most of documentary evidence was located in the Western District of Pennsylvania but none was located in Mississippi; and that the warranty action pending in the Western District of Pennsylvania presented common questions of law and fact.

The District Court in Pennsylvania consolidated the transferred tort action with the Ferenses' pending warranty action but declined to honor the Mississippi statute of limitations as the District Court in Mississippi would have done. It ruled instead that, because the Ferenses had moved for transfer as plaintiffs, the rule in *Van Dusen* did not apply. Invoking the 2-year limitations period set by Pennsylvania law, the District Court dismissed their tort action. Ferens v. Deere & Co., 639 F. Supp. 1484 (W.D.Pa.1986).

The Court of Appeals for the Third Circuit affirmed, but not, at first, on grounds that the Ferenses had lost their entitlement to Mississippi choice of law rules by their invoking § 1404(a). The Court of Appeals relied at the outset on the separate theory that applying Mississippi's statute of limitations would violate due process because Mississippi had no legitimate interest in the case. Ferens v. Deere & Co., 819 F.2d 423 (1987). We vacated this decision and remanded in light of Sun Oil Co. v. Wortman, 486 U.S. 717, 108 S.Ct. 2117, 100 L.Ed.2d 743 (1988), in which we held that a State may choose to apply its own statute of limitations to claims governed by the substantive laws of another State without violating either the Full Faith and Credit Clause or the Due Process Clause. Ferens v. Deere & Co., 487 U.S. 1212, 108 S.Ct. 2862, 101 L.Ed.2d 898 (1988). On remand, the Court of Appeals again affirmed, this time confronting the *Van Dusen* question and ruling that a transferor court's choice of law rules do not apply after a transfer under § 1404(a) on a motion by a plaintiff. 862 F.2d 31 (C.A.3 1988).

II

Section 1404(a) states only that a district court may transfer venue for the convenience of the parties and witnesses when in the interest of justice. It says nothing about choice of law, and nothing about affording plaintiffs different treatment from defendants. We touched upon these issues in *Van Dusen,* but left open the question presented in this case. See 376 U.S., at 640, 84 S.Ct., at 821. In *Van Dusen,* an airplane flying from Boston to Philadelphia crashed into Boston Harbor soon after take-off. The personal representatives of the accident victims brought more than 100 actions in the District Court for the District of Massachusetts and more than 40 actions in the District Court for the Eastern District of Pennsylvania. When the defendants moved to transfer the actions brought in Pennsylvania to the federal court in Massachusetts, a number of the Pennsylvania plaintiffs objected because they lacked capacity under Massachusetts law to sue as representatives of the decedents. The plaintiffs also averred that the transfer would deprive them of the benefits of Pennsylvania's choice of law rules because the transferee forum would apply to their wrongful death claims a different substantive rule. The plaintiffs obtained from the Court of Appeals a writ of mandamus ordering the District Court to vacate the transfer. See id., at 613–615, 84 S.Ct., at 807–08.

We reversed. After considering issues not related to the present dispute, we held that the Court of Appeals erred in its assumption that

Massachusetts law would govern the action following transfer. The legislative history of § 1404(a) showed that Congress had enacted the statute because broad venue provisions in federal acts often resulted in inconvenient forums and that Congress had decided to respond to this problem by permitting transfer to a convenient federal court under § 1404(a). 376 U.S., at 634–636, 84 S.Ct., at 818–19. We said:

> "This legislative background supports the view that § 1404(a) was not designed to narrow the plaintiff's venue privilege or to defeat the state-law advantages that might accrue from the exercise of this venue privilege but rather the provision was simply to counteract the inconveniences that flowed from the venue statutes by permitting transfer to a convenient federal court. The legislative history of § 1404(a) certainly does not justify the rather startling conclusion that one might 'get a change of a law as a bonus for a change of venue.' Indeed, an interpretation accepting such a rule would go far to frustrate the remedial purposes of § 1404(a). If a change in the law were in the offing, the parties might well regard the section primarily as a forum-shopping instrument. And, more importantly, courts would at least be reluctant to grant transfers, despite considerations of convenience, if to do so might conceivably prejudice the claim of a plaintiff who initially selected a permissible forum. We believe, therefore, that both the history and purposes of § 1404(a) indicate that it should be regarded as a federal judicial housekeeping measure, dealing with the placement of litigation in the federal courts and generally intended, on the basis of convenience and fairness, simply to authorize a change of courtrooms." Id., at 635–637, 84 S.Ct., at 818–19 (footnotes omitted).

We thus held that the law applicable to a diversity case does not change upon a transfer initiated by a defendant.

III

The quoted part of *Van Dusen* reveals three independent reasons for our decision. First, § 1404(a) should not deprive parties of state law advantages that exist absent diversity jurisdiction. Second, § 1404(a) should not create or multiply opportunities for forum shopping. Third, the decision to transfer venue under § 1404(a) should turn on considerations of convenience and the interest of justice rather than on the possible prejudice resulting from a change of law. Although commentators have questioned whether the scant legislative history of § 1404(a) compels reliance on these three policies, see Note, Choice of Law after Transfer of Venue, 75 Yale L.J. 90, 123 (1965), we find it prudent to consider them in deciding whether the rule in *Van Dusen* applies to transfers initiated by plaintiffs. We decide that, in addition to other considerations, these policies require a transferee forum to apply the law of the transferor court, regardless of who initiates the transfer. A transfer under § 1404(a), in other words, does not change the law applicable to a diversity case.

A

The policy that § 1404(a) should not deprive parties of state law advantages, although perhaps discernible in the legislative history, has its real foundation in Erie R. Co. v. Tompkins, 304 U.S. 64, 58 S.Ct. 817, 82 L.Ed. 1188 (1938). See *Van Dusen,* 376 U.S., at 637, 84 S.Ct., at 819. The *Erie* rule remains a vital expression of the federal system and the concomitant integrity of the separate States. We explained *Erie* in Guaranty Trust Co. v. York, 326 U.S. 99, 109, 65 S.Ct. 1464, 1470, 89 L.Ed. 2079 (1945), as follows:

> "In essence, the intent of [the *Erie*] decision was to insure that, in all cases where a federal court is exercising jurisdiction solely because of the diversity of citizenship of the parties, the outcome of the litigation in the federal court should be substantially the same, so far as legal rules determine the outcome of a litigation, as it would be if tried in a State court. The nub of the policy that underlies Erie R. Co. v. Tompkins is that for the same transaction the accident of a suit by a non-resident litigant in a federal court instead of in a State court a block away should not lead to a substantially different result."

In Hanna v. Plumer, 380 U.S. 460, 473, 85 S.Ct. 1136, 1145, 14 L.Ed.2d 8 (1965), we held that Congress has the power to prescribe procedural rules that differ from state law rules even at the expense of altering the outcome of litigation. This case does not involve a conflict. As in *Van Dusen,* our interpretation of § 1404(a) is in full accord with the *Erie* rule.

The *Erie* policy had a clear implication for *Van Dusen.* The existence of diversity jurisdiction gave the defendants the opportunity to make a motion to transfer venue under § 1404(a), and if the applicable law were to change after transfer, the plaintiff's venue privilege and resulting state-law advantages could be defeated at the defendant's option. 376 U.S., at 638, 84 S.Ct., at 820. To allow the transfer and at the same time preserve the plaintiff's state-law advantages, we held that the choice of law rules should not change following a transfer initiated by a defendant. Id., at 639, 84 S.Ct., at 821.

Transfers initiated by a plaintiff involve some different considerations, but lead to the same result. Applying the transferor law, of course, will not deprive the plaintiff of any state law advantages. A defendant, in one sense, also will lose no legal advantage if the transferor law controls after a transfer initiated by the plaintiff; the same law, after all, would have applied if the plaintiff had not made the motion. In another sense, however, a defendant may lose a nonlegal advantage. Deere, for example, would lose whatever advantage inheres in not having to litigate in Pennsylvania, or, put another way, in forcing the Ferenses to litigate in Mississippi or not at all.

We, nonetheless, find the advantage that the defendant loses slight. A plaintiff always can sue in the favorable state court or sue in diversity and not seek a transfer. By asking for application of the Mississippi statute of limitations following a transfer to Pennsylvania on grounds of convenience, the Ferenses are seeking to deprive Deere only of the advantage of using against them the inconvenience of litigating in Mississippi. The text of § 1404(a) may not say anything about choice of law, but we think it not the purpose of the section to protect a party's ability to use inconvenience as a shield to discourage or hinder litigation otherwise proper. The section exists to eliminate inconvenience without altering permissible choices under the venue statutes. See *Van Dusen,* supra, at 634–635, 84 S.Ct. at 818–19. This interpretation should come as little surprise. As in our previous cases, we think that "[t]o construe § 1404(a) this way merely carries out its design to protect litigants, witnesses and the public against unnecessary inconvenience and expense, not to provide a shelter for . . . proceedings in costly and inconvenient forums." Continental Grain Co. v. Barge FBL–585, 364 U.S. 19, 27, 80 S.Ct. 1470, 1475, 4 L.Ed.2d 1540 (1960). By creating an opportunity to have venue transferred between courts in different States on the basis of convenience, an option that does not exist absent federal jurisdiction, Congress, with respect to diversity, retained the *Erie* policy while diminishing the incidents of inconvenience.

Applying the transferee law, by contrast, would undermine the *Erie* rule in a serious way. It would mean that initiating a transfer under § 1404(a) changes the state law applicable to a diversity case. We have held, in an isolated circumstance, that § 1404(a) may pre-empt state law. See Stewart Organization, Inc. v. Ricoh Corp., 487 U.S. 22, 108 S.Ct. 2239, 101 L.Ed.2d 22 (1988) (holding that federal law determines the validity of a forum selection clause). In general, however, we have seen § 1404(a) as a housekeeping measure that should not alter the state law governing a case under *Erie*. See *Van Dusen,* supra, 376 U.S., at 636–637, 84 S.Ct., at 819–20; see also *Stewart Organization,* supra, 487 U.S., at 37, 108 S.Ct., at 2247 (SCALIA, J., dissenting) (finding the language of § 1404(a) "plainly insufficient" to work a change in the applicable state law through pre-emption). The Mississippi statute of limitations, which everyone agrees would have applied if the Ferenses had not moved for a transfer, should continue to apply in this case.

In any event, defendants in the position of Deere would not fare much better if we required application of the transferee law instead of the transferor law. True, if the transferee law were to apply, some plaintiffs would not sue these defendants for fear that they would have no choice but to litigate in an inconvenient forum. But applying the transferee law would not discourage all plaintiffs from suing. Some plaintiffs would prefer to litigate in an inconvenient forum with favorable law than to litigate in a convenient forum with unfavorable law or not to litigate at all. The Ferenses, no doubt, would have abided by their initial choice of the District Court in Mississippi had they known that the District Court in Pennsylvania would dismiss their action. If we were to rule for Deere in this case we would accomplish little more than discouraging the occasional motions by plaintiffs to transfer inconvenient cases. Other plaintiffs would sue in an inconvenient forum with the expectation that the defendants themselves would seek transfer to a convenient forum, resulting in application of the transferor law under *Van Dusen.* See Note, Choice of Law in Federal Court After Transfer of Venue, 63 Cornell L.Rev. 149, 156 (1977). In this case, for example, Deere might have moved for a transfer if the Ferenses had not.

B

Van Dusen also sought to fashion a rule that would not create opportunities for forum shopping. Some commentators have seen this policy as the most important rationale of *Van Dusen,* see, e.g., 19 C. Wright, A. Miller, & E. Cooper, Federal Practice and Procedure § 4506, p. 79 (1982), but few attempt to explain the harm of forum shopping when the plaintiff initiates a transfer. An opportunity for forum shopping exists whenever a party has a choice of forums that will apply different laws. The *Van Dusen* policy against forum shopping simply requires us to interpret § 1404(a) in a way that does not create an opportunity for obtaining a more favorable law by selecting a forum through a transfer of venue. In the *Van Dusen* case itself, this meant that we could not allow defendants to use a transfer to change the law. 376 U.S., at 636, 84 S.Ct., at 819.

No interpretation of § 1404(a), however, will create comparable opportunities for forum shopping by a plaintiff because, even without § 1404(a), a plaintiff already has the option of shopping for a forum with the most favorable law. The Ferenses, for example, had an opportunity for forum shopping in the state courts because both the Mississippi and Pennsylvania courts had jurisdiction and because they each would have applied a different statute of limitations. Diversity jurisdiction did not eliminate these forum shopping opportunities; instead, under *Erie,* the federal courts had to replicate them. See Klaxon Co. v. Stentor Electric Mfg. Co., Inc., 313 U.S., at 496, 61 S.Ct., at 1021 ("Whatever lack of uniformity [*Erie*] may produce between federal courts in different states is attributable to our federal system, which leaves to a state, within the limits permitted by the Constitution, the right to pursue local policies diverging from those of its neighbors"). Applying the transferor law would not give a plaintiff an opportunity to use a transfer to obtain a law that he could not obtain through his initial forum selection. If it does make selection of the most favorable law more convenient, it does no more than recognize a forum shopping choice that already exists. This fact does not require us to apply the transferee law. Section 1404(a), to reiterate, exists to make venue convenient and should not allow the defendant to use inconvenience to discourage plaintiffs from exercising the opportunities that they already have.

Applying the transferee law, by contrast, might create opportunities for forum shopping in an indirect way. The advantage to Mississippi's personal injury lawyers that resulted from the State's then applicable 6-year statute of limitations has not escaped us; Mississippi's long limitation period no doubt drew plaintiffs to the State. Although *Sun Oil* held that the federal courts have little interest in a State's decision to create a long statute of limitations or to apply its statute of limitations to claims governed by foreign law, we should recognize the consequences of our interpretation of § 1404(a). Applying the transferee law, to the extent that it discourages plaintiff-initiated transfers, might give States incentives to enact similar laws to bring in out-of-state business that would not be moved at the instance of the plaintiff.

C

Van Dusen also made clear that the decision to transfer venue under § 1404(a) should turn on considerations of convenience rather than on the possibility of prejudice resulting from a change in the applicable law. See 376 U.S., at 636, 84 S.Ct., at 819; Piper Aircraft Co. v. Reyno, 454 U.S. 235, 253–254, and n. 20, 102 S.Ct. 252, 264–65, and n. 20, 70 L.Ed.2d 419 (1981). We reasoned in *Van Dusen* that, if the law changed following a transfer initiated by the defendant, a district court "would at least be reluctant to grant transfers, despite considerations of convenience, if to do so might conceivably prejudice the claim of a plaintiff." 376 U.S., at 636, 84 S.Ct., at 819. The court, to determine the prejudice, might have to make an elaborate survey of the law, including statutes of limitations, burdens of proof, presumptions, and the like. This would turn what is supposed to be a statute for convenience of the courts into one expending extensive judicial time and resources. Because this difficult task is contrary to the purpose of the statute, in *Van Dusen* we made it unnecessary by ruling that a transfer of venue by the defendant does not result in a change of law. This same policy requires application of the transferor law when a plaintiff initiates a transfer.

If the law were to change following a transfer initiated by a plaintiff, a district court in a similar fashion would be at least reluctant to grant a transfer that would prejudice the defendant. Hardship might occur because plaintiffs may find as many opportunities to exploit application of the transferee law as they would find opportunities for exploiting application of the transferor law. See Note, 63 Cornell L.Rev., at 156. If the transferee law were to apply, moreover, the plaintiff simply would not move to transfer unless the benefits of convenience outweighed the loss of favorable law.

Some might think that a plaintiff should pay the price for choosing an inconvenient forum by being put to a choice of law versus forum. But this assumes that § 1404(a) is for the benefit only of the moving party. By the statute's own terms, it is not. Section 1404(a) also exists for the benefit of the witnesses and the interest of justice, which must include the convenience of the court. Litigation in an inconvenient forum does not harm the plaintiff alone. As Justice Jackson said:

> "Administrative difficulties follow for courts when litigation is piled up in congested centers instead of being handled at its origin. Jury duty is a burden that ought not to be imposed upon the people of a community which has no relation to the litigation. In cases which touch the affairs of many persons, there is reason for holding the trial in their view and reach rather than in remote parts of the country where they can learn of it by report only. There is a local interest in having localized controversies decided at home. There is an appropriateness too, in having the trial of a diversity case in a forum that is at home with the state law that must govern the case, rather than having a court in some other forum untangle problems in conflicts of laws, and in law foreign to itself." Gulf Oil Corp. v. Gilbert, 330 U.S. 501, 508–509, 67 S.Ct. 839, 843, 91 L.Ed. 1055 (1947).

The desire to take a punitive view of the plaintiff's actions should not obscure the systemic costs of litigating in an inconvenient place.

D

This case involves some considerations to which we perhaps did not give sufficient attention in *Van Dusen*. Foresight and judicial economy now seem to favor the simple rule that the law does not change following a transfer of venue under § 1404(a). Affording transfers initiated by plaintiffs different treatment from transfers initiated by defendants may seem quite workable in this case, but the simplicity is an illusion. If we were to hold that the transferee law applies following a § 1404(a) motion by a plaintiff, cases such as this would not arise in the future. Although applying the transferee law, no doubt, would catch the Fereses by surprise, in the future no plaintiffs in their position would move for a change of venue.

Other cases, however, would produce undesirable complications. The rule would leave unclear which law should apply when both a defendant and a plaintiff move for a transfer of venue or when the court transfers venue on its own motion. See Note, 63 Cornell L.Rev., at 158. The rule also might require variation in certain situations, such as when the plaintiff moves for a transfer following a removal from state court by the defendant, or when only one of several plaintiffs requests the transfer, or when circumstances change through no fault of the plaintiff making a once convenient forum inconvenient. True, we could reserve any consideration of these questions for a later day. But we have a duty, in deciding this case, to consider whether our decision will create litigation and uncertainty. On the basis of these considerations, we again conclude that the transferor law should apply regardless who makes the § 1404(a) motion.

IV

Some may object that a district court in Pennsylvania should not have to apply a Mississippi statute of limitations to a Pennsylvania cause of action. This point, although understandable, should have little to do with the outcome of this case. Congress gave the Ferenses the power to seek a transfer in § 1404(a) and our decision in *Van Dusen* already could require a district court in Pennsylvania to apply the Mississippi statute of limitations to Pennsylvania claims. Our rule may seem too generous because it allows the Ferenses to have both their choice of law and their choice of forum, or even to reward the Ferenses for conduct that seems manipulative. We nonetheless see no alternative rule that would produce a more acceptable result. Deciding that the transferee law should apply, in effect, would tell the Ferenses that they should have continued to litigate their warranty action in Pennsylvania and their tort action in Mississippi. Some might find this preferable, but we do not. We have made quite clear that "[t]o permit a situation in which two cases involving precisely the same issues are simultaneously pending in different District Courts leads to the wastefulness of time, energy and money that § 1404(a) was designed to prevent." *Continental Grain*, 364 U.S., at 26, 80 S.Ct., at 1474.

From a substantive standpoint, two further objections give us pause but do not persuade us to change our rule. First, one might ask why we require the Ferenses to file in the District Court in Mississippi at all. Efficiency might seem to dictate a rule allowing plaintiffs in the Ferenses' position not to file in an inconvenient forum and then to return to a convenient forum through a transfer of venue, but instead simply to file in the convenient forum and ask for the law of the inconvenient forum to apply. Although our rule may invoke certain formality, one must remember that § 1404(a) does not provide for an automatic transfer of venue. The section, instead, permits a transfer only when convenient and "in the interest of justice." Plaintiffs in the position of the Ferenses must go to the distant forum because they have no guarantee, until the court there examines the facts, that they may obtain a transfer. No one has contested the justice of transferring this particular case, but the option remains open to defendants in future cases. Although a court cannot ignore the systemic costs of inconvenience, it may consider the course that the litigation already has taken in determining the interest of justice.

Second, one might contend that, because no *per se* rule requiring a court to apply either the transferor law or the transferee law will seem appropriate in all circumstances, we should develop more sophisticated federal choice of law rules for diversity actions involving transfers. See Note, 75 Yale L.J., at 130–35. To a large extent, however, state conflicts of law rules already ensure that appropriate laws will apply to diversity cases. Federal law, as a general matter, does not interfere with these rules. See *Sun Oil,* 486 U.S., at 727–729. In addition, even if more elaborate federal choice of law rules would not run afoul of *Klaxon* and *Erie,* we believe that applying the law of the transferor forum effects the appropriate balance between fairness and simplicity. Cf. R. Leflar, American Conflicts Law § 143, p. 293 (3d ed. 1977) (arguing against a federal common law of conflicts).

For the foregoing reasons, we conclude that Mississippi's statute of limitations should govern the Ferenses' action. We reverse and remand for proceedings consistent with this opinion.

It is so ordered.

■ JUSTICE SCALIA, with whom JUSTICE BRENNAN, JUSTICE MARSHALL, and JUSTICE BLACKMUN join, dissenting.

     * * *

The Court suggests that applying the choice-of-law rules of the forum court to a transferred case ignores the interest of the federal courts themselves in avoiding the "systemic costs of litigating in an inconvenient place," quoting Justice Jackson's eloquent remarks on that subject in Gulf Oil Corp. v. Gilbert, 330 U.S. 501, 509, 67 S.Ct. 839, 843, 91 L.Ed. 1055 (1947). * * * The point, apparently, is that these systemic costs will increase because the change in law attendant to transfer will not only deter the plaintiff from moving to transfer but will also deter the court from ordering *sua sponte* a transfer that will harm the plaintiff's case. Justice Jackson's remarks were addressed, however, not to the operation of § 1404(a), but to "those rather rare cases where the doctrine [of *forum non conveniens*] should be applied." 330 U.S., at 509, 67 S.Ct., at 843. Where the systemic costs are that severe, transfer ordinarily will occur whether the plaintiff moves for it or not; the district judge can be expected to order it *sua sponte.* I do not think that the prospect of depriving the plaintiff of favorable law will any more deter a district judge from transferring[1] than it would have deterred a district judge, under the prior regime, from ordering a dismissal *sua sponte* pursuant to the doctrine of *forum non conveniens.* In fact the deterrence to *sua sponte* transfer will be considerably less, since transfer involves no risk of statute-of-limitations bars to refiling.

---

[1]   The prospective transferor court would not be deterred at all, of course, if we simply extended the *Van Dusen* rule to court-initiated transfers. In my view that would be inappropriate, however, since court-initiated transfer, like plaintiff-initiated transfer, does not confer upon the defendant the advantage of forum-shopping for law, Van Dusen v. Barrack, 376 U.S. 612, 636, 84 S.Ct. 805, 819, 11 L.Ed.2d 945 (1964), and does not enable the defendant "to utilize a transfer to achieve a result in federal court which could not have been achieved in the courts of the State where the action was filed," id., at 638, 84 S.Ct., at 820.

Thus, it seems to me that a proper calculation of systemic costs would go as follows: Saved by the Court's rule will be the incremental cost of trying in forums that are inconvenient (but not so inconvenient as to prompt the court's *sua sponte* transfer) those suits that are now filed in such forums for choice-of-law purposes. But incurred by the Court's rule will be the costs of considering and effecting transfer, not only in those suits but in the indeterminate number of additional suits that will be filed in inconvenient forums now that filing-and-transfer is an approved form of shopping for law; plus the costs attending the necessity for transferee courts to figure out the choice-of-law rules (and probably the substantive law) of distant States much more often than our *Van Dusen* decision would require. It should be noted that the file-and-transfer ploy sanctioned by the Court today will be available not merely to achieve the relatively rare (and generally unneeded) benefit of a longer statute of limitations, but also to bring home to the desired state of litigation all sorts of favorable choice-of-law rules regarding substantive liability—in an era when the diversity among the States in choice-of-law principles has become kaleidoscopic.[2]

The Court points out, apparently to deprecate the prospect that filing-and-transfer will become a regular litigation strategy, that there is "no guarantee" that a plaintiff will be accorded a transfer; that while "[n]o one has contested the justice of transferring this particular case," that option "remains open to defendants in future cases"; and that "[a]lthough a court cannot ignore the systemic costs of inconvenience, it may consider the course that the litigation already has taken in determining the interest of justice." * * * I am not sure what this means—except that it plainly does not mean what it must mean to foreclose the filing-and-transfer option, namely, that transfer can be denied because the plaintiff was law-shopping. The whole theory of the Court's opinion is that it is not in accord with the policy of § 1404(a) to deprive the plaintiff of the "state-law advantages" to which his "venue privilege" entitles him. * * * The Court explicitly repudiates "[t]he desire to take a punitive view of the plaintiff's actions," * * *, and to make him "pay the price for choosing an inconvenient forum by being put to a choice of law versus forum," * * *. Thus, all the Court is saying by its "no guarantee" language is that the plaintiff must be careful to choose a *really inconvenient* forum if he wants to be sure about getting a transfer. That will often not be difficult. In sum, it seems to me quite likely that today's decision will cost the federal courts more time than it will save them.

* * *

For the foregoing reasons, I respectfully dissent.

---

[2]   The current edition of Professor Leflar's treatise on American Conflicts Law lists 10 separate theories of choice of law that are applied, individually or in various combinations, by the 50 States. See R. Leflar, L. McDougall III, & R. Felix, American Conflicts Law §§ 86–91, 93–96 (4th ed. 1986). See also Kay, Theory into Practice: Choice of Law in the Courts, 34 Mercer L.Rev. 521, 525–584, 591–592 (1983).

NOTE ON *FERENS V. JOHN DEERE*, CHANGE OF VENUE UNDER § 1404(a), DISMISSAL OR TRANSFER FOR LACK OF VENUE UNDER § 1406(a), AND OTHER TRANSFERS

1.   **Prelude.** In Baltimore & Ohio R.R. Co. v. Kepner, 314 U.S. 44, 62 S.Ct. 6, 86 L.Ed. 28 (1941), plaintiff Kepner had brought suit against the railroad in federal district court in New York under the Federal Employers Liability Act (FELA) for injuries suffered in a railroad accident. *In personam* jurisdiction and venue were proper. Kepner was an Ohio resident; the accident took place in Ohio; and about twenty-five witnesses from Ohio would be required at the trial in New York. The railroad brought suit in state court in Ohio seeking an injunction against Kepner's continued prosecution of his suit in district court in New York. The Ohio Supreme Court denied the injunction, and the United States Supreme Court affirmed. *Kepner* was typical of a large number of cases in which FELA plaintiffs brought suit in distant forums in order to secure litigating advantages not available at home. During the mid-1940s the railroads pressed hard for some kind of legislative solution that would restrict the ability of FELA plaintiffs to shop freely among the federal district courts for the most advantageous forum. See E. Purcell, Litigation and Inequality 230–37 (1992).

Six years after *Kepner*, in Gulf Oil Corp. v. Gilbert, 330 U.S. 501, 67 S.Ct. 839, 91 L.Ed. 1055 (1947), plaintiff Gilbert brought a diversity suit in federal district court in New York for damages arising out of a fire that destroyed his warehouse in Lynchburg, Virginia. As in *Kepner*, *in personam* jurisdiction and venue were proper in New York because the corporation had a substantial presence in the state. The Supreme Court upheld a *forum non conveniens* dismissal, for the first time squarely endorsing the use of the doctrine by the federal courts. The Court was careful to say that *forum non conveniens* was not available in FELA cases because of the special character of that statute, and the Court emphasized that the doctrine should be employed rarely even in non-FELA cases. But in this case numerous factors weighed against the New York federal district court. The plaintiff and his warehouse were in Virginia; the fire and any negligent acts took place there; all the witnesses (with the possible exception of experts) lived there; and the district court in Virginia was familiar with Virginia law.

In both *Kepner* and *Gilbert*, plaintiffs brought suit in the distant New York forum in hopes of obtaining a larger recovery than they would have obtained at home. In FELA cases such as *Kepner*, there was no judicial mechanism to restrict forum shopping by plaintiffs, even after *Gulf Oil*. And even in non-FELA cases, a *forum non conveniens* dismissal was not the optimal solution for an inappropriate forum choice in federal court. As the Supreme Court had articulated the doctrine in *Gulf Oil*, it was available only in extreme cases. Further, *forum non conveniens* had developed in the state courts with limited means of coordinating their activities across state lines, and a successful invocation of the doctrine resulted in an outright dismissal of the case. In 1948, prompted by *Kepner* and other FELA cases, and possibly encouraged by *Gulf Oil*, Congress enacted 28 U.S.C. § 1404(a), permitting a transfer from one federal district court to another "for the convenience of parties and witnesses, in the interest of justice."

2.   **Transfer under § 1404(a).** A transfer under § 1404(a) resembles a *forum non conveniens* dismissal in that both are premised on a finding that the initial forum choice is inappropriate, but transfer under § 1404(a) is

available on a significantly lesser showing of inconvenience than dismissal for *forum non conveniens*. Norwood v. Kirkpatrick, 349 U.S. 29, 75 S.Ct. 544, 99 L.Ed. 789 (1955). Further, § 1404(a) permits transfer rather than dismissal, and it permits transfer of cases brought under both state and federal law, including FELA cases.

The central function of § 1404(a) is to allow a defendant to escape a seriously inconvenient forum choice by plaintiff. However, as *Ferens* makes clear, either party may seek a transfer. The decision to transfer lies in the discretion of the district court. Ross v. Buckeye Cellulose Corp., 980 F.2d 648 (11th Cir. 1993). Factors that a district court should consider include "the place where the operative facts occurred; the convenience of the parties; the convenience of the witnesses; the relative ease of access to the sources of proof and the availability of process to compel attendance of unwilling witnesses; the plaintiff's choice of forum; a forum's familiarity with the governing law; trial efficiency; and the interests of justice." Don King Productions, Inc. v. Douglas, 735 F. Supp. 522, 533 (S.D.N.Y.1990). For a thorough discussion and application of § 1404(a), see McDevitt & Street Co. v. Fidelity and Deposit Co. of Maryland, 737 F. Supp. 351 (W.D.N.C.1990).

What is the effect of a forum selection clause when one federal forum is specified in the clause but plaintiff files in a different federal forum? In Atlantic Marine Const. v. U.S. District Court, 571 U.S. ___, 134 S.Ct. 568, 581, 187 L.Ed.2d 487 (2013), the Court wrote: "When the parties have agreed to a valid forum selection clause, a district court should ordinarily transfer the case to the forum specified in the clause. Only under extraordinary circumstances unrelated to the convenience of the parties should a § 1404(a) motion be denied." See also Stewart Organization, Inc. v. Ricoh Corp., 487 U.S. 22, 108 S.Ct. 2239, 101 L.Ed.2d 22 (1988). The Court held in *Atlantic Marine* that § 1404(a) rather than § 1406(a) is the proper mechanism for enforcing a forum selection clause. The Court was at pains to emphasize three things. First, a plaintiff's choice of forum "merits no weight" in the determination whether to transfer to the forum specified in the clause. Id. Second, the parties' private interests are irrelevant to the determination whether to transfer. Third, unlike ordinary transfers under § 1404(a), a transfer to enforce a forum selection clause does not result in application of the law of the transferor forum; rather the law of the specified transferee forum applies.

3.   **Practical impact of change of venue under § 1404(a).** Does change of venue under § 1404(a) have much practical impact? A study covering all ninety-four federal districts from 1979 to 1991 and including 2,804,640 cases that terminated in judgments, suggests that it does. Clermont and Eisenberg, Exorcising the Evil of Forum-Shopping, 80 Cornell L.Rev. 1507 (1995). Professors Kevin Clermont and Theodore Eisenberg conclude that plaintiffs' "win rate" in cases that remained in the forum in which they were filed was 58%. In cases transferred to another forum under § 1404(a), plaintiffs' win rate dropped to 29%. Reasons other than favorable or unfavorable forums might account for the difference in win rates. For example, the set of transferred cases may be, on the merits, weaker cases than the set of non-transferred cases. The authors conclude that this explanation "contributes to," but "probably does not fully explain the effect" of transfer. "Our empirical investigation suggests that transfer offers the considerable advantage of countering the very real detriments of forum-shopping, and that it does so without undue burden. The new empirical

evidence is not definitive, but the transfer critics can find no support in it. Good policy calls, at the least, for preserving the transfer mechanism." Id. at 1517, 1530. For an argument that Professors Clermont and Eisenberg have overstated the effect of transfer on the outcomes of cases, see Steinberg, Simplifying the Choice of Forum: A Response to Professor Clermont and Professor Eisenberg, 75 Wash.U.L.Q. 1479 (1997); for a response, see Clermont and Eisenberg, Simplifying the Choice of Forum: A Reply, 75 Wash.U.L.Q. 1551 (1997).

In Smith v. Colonial Penn Ins. Co., 943 F. Supp. 782 (S.D.Tex.1996), the defendant was an insurance company headquartered in the northeastern United States. The suit was brought in the Galveston division of the Southern District of Texas. Defendant moved for a change of venue to the Houston division of the Southern District. (Intra-district changes of venue are governed by the same criteria as inter-district changes.) The district court did not take kindly to the motion:

> Defendant's request for a transfer of venue is centered around the fact that Galveston does not have a commercial airport into which Defendant's employees and corporate representatives may fly and out of which they may be expediently whisked to the federal courthouse in Galveston. Rather, Defendant contends that it will be faced with the huge "inconvenience" of flying into Houston and driving less than forty miles to the Galveston courthouse, an act that will "encumber" it with "unnecessary driving time and expenses." * * * The Court being somewhat familiar with the Northeast, notes that perceptions about travel are different in that part of the country than they are in Texas. A litigant in that part of the country might be shocked at having to travel fifty miles to try a case, but in this vast state of Texas, such a travel distance would not be viewed with any surprise or consternation. Defendant should be assured that it is not embarking on a three-week-long trip via covered wagons when it travels to Galveston. Rather, Defendant will be pleased to discover that the highway is paved and lighted all the way to Galveston, and thanks to the efforts of this Court's predecessor, Judge Roy Bean, the trip should be free from rustlers, hooligans, or vicious varmints of unsavory kind * * *. Defendant will * * * be pleased to know that regular limousine service is available from Hobby Airport, even to the steps of this humble courthouse, which has got lights, indoor plummin', 'lectric doors, and all sorts of new stuff, almost like them big courthouses back East.'

Id. at 783–84 and n.2.

All lawyers dread being "home-towned." Did the defendant really want (but have no grounds for seeking) a transfer out of Texas altogether? Does the tone of the opinion give some reason to believe that defendant wanted out of the courtroom of this particular judge?

4.　Transfer to a district "where it might have been brought." For many years, § 1404(a) simply provided that an action could be transferred only to a district "where it might have been brought." In Hoffman v. Blaski, 363 U.S. 335, 80 S.Ct. 1084, 4 L.Ed.2d 1254 (1960), the Supreme Court held that a transfer under § 1404(a) can only be to a district court in which venue is proper, independent of any waiver by defendant. The defendant in *Hoffman* was willing to waive the lack of venue in the transferee forum (as it clearly would have been entitled to do if it had been sued there in the first instance), but the Court held that such a waiver did not mean that the suit "might have been brought" in the transferee forum. *Hoffman* was heavily criticized, and has now been partially overruled. After a 2011 amendment, § 1404(a) now provides that an action may be transferred to "any other district or division where it might have been brought or to any district or division to which all parties have consented." The requirement of unanimous party consent means that the plaintiff has to agree to the transfer to a district where the suit could not have been brought originally. It is not enough that the defendant wishes to, and would consent to, transfer to that district.

5.   Change of courtrooms, not a change of law. As is evident from the Court's opinion, the foundation case for *Ferens* is Van Dusen v. Barrack, 376 U.S. 612, 84 S.Ct. 805, 11 L.Ed.2d 945 (1964). *Van Dusen* arose out of a commercial airplane crash in Boston harbor, just after take-off for Philadelphia. More than 100 suits were filed in the district court in Massachusetts, and more than 45 were filed in the district court in Pennsylvania. Defendants in the Pennsylvania suits successfully moved for transfer to the district court in Massachusetts under § 1404(a). Pennsylvania law allowed a much more generous damage recovery in wrongful death cases than did Massachusetts law. The plaintiffs in *Van Dusen* hoped that the district court in Pennsylvania would apply the generous Pennsylvania law to their cases, and they feared that the district court in Massachusetts would apply the ungenerous Massachusetts law. The Supreme Court held that the transferred plaintiffs should not be deprived of favorable law because of the transfer: "A change of venue under § 1404(a) generally should be, with respect to state law, but a change of courtrooms." 376 U.S. at 639.

A federal district court is required to apply the state law of the state in which it sits. See Erie RR. v. Tompkins, 304 U.S. 64, 58 S.Ct. 817, 82 L.Ed. 1188 (1938), infra p. 335. The applicable state law is not necessarily the substantive law of that state, for in some cases the courts of the state will apply the law of another state. For example, under conventional choice-of-law rules a court will follow the substantive tort law of the state in which an accident occurred rather than of the state in which the case is tried. A federal district court will follow the choice-of-law rules of the state in which is sits, and then apply the law to which it is directed by those choice-of-law rules. Klaxon Co. v. Stentor Electric Mfg. Co., 313 U.S. 487, 61 S.Ct. 1020, 85 L.Ed. 1477 (1941). However, not all states follow the same choice-of-law rules, and different states might apply different law to identical cases brought in their respective jurisdictions. Among other things, states tend to find that their choice-of-law rules direct them to apply their own substantive law. See discussion of choice of law, supra p. 219. The net effect of the Supreme Court's holding in *Van Dusen* was that the District Court in Massachusetts, in the cases transferred from the district court in Pennsylvania, would apply the choice-of-law rules that the Pennsylvania state courts would have applied. In the cases originally filed in the district court in Massachusetts, the court would follow the Massachusetts choice-of-law rules.

The Court in *Van Dusen* left two questions open: "We do not attempt to determine whether * * * the same considerations would govern if a plaintiff sought transfer under § 1404(a), or if it was contended that the transferor

State would simply have dismissed the action on the ground of *forum non conveniens*." 376 U.S. at 640. The Court in *Ferens* has now answered the first of those two questions. Did it answer correctly, in your view? If you are uncomfortable with the result in *Ferens*, is it because of the incentives it provides for forum shopping? *Ferens* allows a plaintiff to seek out an inconvenient forum that has favorable law, and then to transfer to a convenient forum with the favorable law now applicable to that case. As the discussion in *Ferens* makes clear, plaintiff could not have obtained the favorable law simply by filing suit directly in the Pennsylvania forum to which the suit was eventually transferred. Do you disapprove of the Mississippi court's applying the longer Mississippi statute of limitations to a cause of action arising out of an accident in Pennsylvania, brought by a Pennsylvania plaintiff whose sole reason for suing in Mississippi was to obtain the favorable Mississippi statute of limitations?

The Mississippi court's willingness in *Ferens* to apply its own statute of limitations to a cause of action arising in another state is common in state courts. The Supreme Court has held that application of the forum state's statute of limitations in such circumstances does not violate the Full Faith and Credit Clause of the federal Constitution. Sun Oil Co. v. Wortman, 486 U.S. 717, 108 S.Ct. 2117, 100 L.Ed.2d 743 (1988). In Frazier v. Commercial Credit Equipment Corp., 755 F. Supp. 163 (S.D.Miss.1991), a District Court in Mississippi declined to transfer a case to a district court in West Virginia under § 1404(a). The case arose out of an accident in West Virginia. Suit was time-barred if the West Virginia statute of limitations were applied. Plaintiffs filed suit in Mississippi to take advantage of its long statute of limitations, as plaintiffs had done in *Ferens*. The district court noted that the "justice" of the particular transfer in *Ferens* had not been contested, and it held that transfer in this case was not "in the interest of justice." 755 F. Supp. at 166. Did the district court in *Frazier* effectively negate the Supreme Court's holding in *Ferens*?

6. ***Van Dusen*'s unanswered question.** How should the Court rule when the forum choice in the initial forum is so inappropriate that the case would have been dismissed for *forum non conveniens* if § 1404(a) had not permitted transfer? (Recall that § 1404(a) transfers are available on a lesser showing of inconvenience than *forum non conveniens* dismissals.) The following may help answer the question: Whenever state law is at issue, the federal district court will try to apply the state law that would have been applied if the suit had been filed in state rather than federal court. If a suit is filed in state court and a motion for *forum non conveniens* is defeated, the state court will follow its own choice-of-law rules and whatever substantive law those rules select. But if a *forum non conveniens* motion is granted by the state court, plaintiff will have to refile her suit in the court of another state. The court in the second state will follow its own choice-of-law rules, rather than those of the court in the first state that dismissed the case, and the rules followed by the court in the second state may direct it to a different substantive law.

7. **Different federal law.** Notice that the Court in *Van Dusen* stated that a change of venue under § 1404(a) was a nothing more than a change of courtrooms "with respect to state law." But the *Van Dusen* problem is not confined to state law. Federal law is not uniform throughout the country. It sometimes happens, particularly in new or rapidly developing areas of law, that the federal courts of appeals will follow one interpretation of a federal

statute in some circuits and another interpretation in other circuits. Such conflicts among the circuits are resolved eventually, usually by Supreme Court decisions, but meanwhile a different interpretation of federal law is followed in different circuits. What if a suit is transferred under § 1404(a) between two conflicting circuits? Should the transferee federal district court follow the rule of the transferor or the transferee circuit? In a case transferred under a somewhat analogous statute, 28 U.S.C. § 1407, the Court of Appeals for the District of Columbia followed what it thought to be the correct interpretation of federal law, irrespective of the interpretation followed in the transferor circuit. In re Korean Air Lines Disaster of September 1, 1983, 829 F.2d 1171 (D.C. Cir. 1987) (R.B. Ginsburg, J.), aff'd, 490 U.S. 122 (1989). Later court of appeals decisions dealing with transfers under § 1404(a) have followed *Korean Air Lines*, holding that where there is a conflict between the circuits on a question of federal law the transferee court should follow the interpretation of its own circuit. See, e.g., Lanfear v. Home Depot, Inc., 536 F.3d 1217, 1223 (11th Cir. 2008); McMasters v. United States, 260 F.3d 814, 819–20 (7th Cir. 2001); Murphy v. F.D.I.C., 208 F.3d 959, 966 (11th Cir. 2000); Bradley v. United States, 161 F.3d 777, 782 n.4 (4th Cir. 1998). In an interesting variation, a court of appeals has held that the transferee court should follow its own interpretation of federal law but the transferor court's interpretation of state law embedded in question of the federal law. See Hooper v. Lockheed Martin Corp., 688 F.3d 1037 (9th Cir. 2012).

Why should federal law be treated differently from state law after a transfer between federal district courts? For thoughtful discussions, see Marcus, Conflict Among Circuits and Transfers Within the Federal Judicial System, 93 Yale L.J. 677 (1984) (advocating the result later reached in *Korean Air Lines*), and Ragazzo, Transfer and Choice of Federal Law: The Appellate Model, 93 Mich.L.Rev. 703 (1995). Professor Ragazzo argues that cases should be treated differently depending on whether they are transferred under 28 U.S.C. § 1407 or under §§ 1404 and 1406. Section 1407 allows transfer of mass tort or complex litigation cases to a single federal court for coordinated or consolidated pretrial treatment. See n. 10, infra. It contemplates that cases will be transferred back to their original district for trial (although many cases are decided on pretrial motions or are settled, and are therefore never sent back to the transferor forum). Sections 1404 and 1406 provide for permanent transfers. Professor Ragazzo argues that in § 1407 cases the federal law of the transferor forum should apply, but that in §§ 1404 and 1406 cases the federal law of the transferee forum should apply. (Recall that *Korean Air Lines*, holding that the federal law of the transferee forum should apply, was a § 1407 case.)

8. **Transfer or dismissal under 28 U.S.C. § 1406(a).** Section 1406(a) provides that the "district court of a district in which is filed a case laying venue in the wrong division or district shall dismiss, or if it be in the interest of justice, transfer such case to any district or division in which it could have been brought." The purpose of § 1406(a) is to permit transfer rather than dismissal, thereby protecting a plaintiff from a statute of limitations defense that might be available if plaintiff were forced to refile the suit in a proper court. The Supreme Court has applied the statute expansively, allowing transfer when there is no *in personam* jurisdiction over the defendant, as well as when there is a defect in venue in the transferor forum. Goldlawr, Inc. v. Heiman, 369 U.S. 463, 82 S.Ct. 913, 8 L.Ed.2d 39 (1962). In *Goldlawr*, both *in personam* jurisdiction and venue were lacking,

and the Court's decision was consistent with § 1406(a) in the sense that the statutory premise of "venue in the wrong division or district" was satisfied. Most of the courts to address the question have gone beyond *Goldlawr* to permit transfers even when venue is good, but there is no *in personam* jurisdiction. See, e.g., Saudi v. Northrup Grumman Corp., 427 F.3d 271, 277 (4th Cir. 2005); Corke v. Samejet M.S. Song of Norway, 572 F.3d 77, 80 (2d Cir. 1978); Dubin v. United States, 380 F.2d 813 (5th Cir. 1967). A few courts have not permitted transfers in this circumstance. See, e.g., Ellis v. Great Southwestern Corp., 646 F.2d 1099 (5th Cir. 1981).

The law of the transferor court does not apply after a transfer under § 1406(a) because the transferor court was never a proper forum. Nelson v. International Paint Co., 716 F.2d 640 (9th Cir. 1983). Recall that the Court held in *Atlantic Marine*, supra, that transfers under § 1404(a) pursuant to a forum selection clause designating the transferee court as the proper forum are treated, for choice-of-law purposes, like transfers under § 1406(a).

9.   **Transfer under 28 U.S.C. § 1631.** Section 1631, enacted in 1982 as part of a statute creating the new Court of Appeals for the Federal Circuit in Washington, D.C., provides that certain federal courts in which there is a "want of jurisdiction" may transfer the case to certain other federal courts in which there is jurisdiction. The legislative history makes clear that Congress had in mind defects of subject matter jurisdiction in administrative law cases where allocations of jurisdiction among the federal courts often pose difficult questions. See 1982 U.S.Code and Admin.News, Federal Courts Improvement Act of 1982 11, 21 (1982) (Senate Report). The legislative history nowhere mentions defects in *in personam* jurisdiction. The overwhelming majority of cases allowing transfer under § 1631 have involved defects in subject matter jurisdiction. But a few courts have held that § 1631 allows transfer to cure defects in *in personam* jurisdiction as well as subject matter jurisdiction. See, e.g., Roman v. Ashcroft, 340 F.3d 314, 328–29 (6th Cir. 2003); Ross v. Colorado Outward Bound School, Inc., 822 F.2d 1524 (10th Cir. 1987). Compare SongByrd, Inc. v. Estate of Grossman, 206 F.3d 172, 179 n.2 (2d Cir. 2000) ("the legislative history of section 1631 provides some reason to believe that this section authorizes transfers only to cure lack of subject matter jurisdiction"). If § 1631 applies to *in personam* jurisdiction, it obviously supplements (and possibly supplants) § 1406(a) transfers for want of jurisdiction.

10.   **Transfer under 28 U.S.C. § 1407.** Section 1407 provides, "When civil actions involving one or more common questions of fact are pending in different districts, such actions may be transferred to any district for coordinated or consolidated pretrial proceedings." This section is typically employed in mass tort cases or other complex litigation in which numerous cases arising out of the same occurrence or transaction are filed in different federal district courts around the country. The decision whether to transfer cases is made by the Judicial Panel on Multidistrict Litigation, composed of seven specially assigned federal district and circuit judges. Consolidation for pretrial proceedings allows efficiencies in litigation, particularly in conducting discovery and in avoiding inconsistent rulings among district courts on pretrial motions. Section 1407 contemplates that after pretrial proceedings are complete, a case will be transferred back to the original transferor court for trial if it has not been settled or otherwise disposed of during pretrial proceedings. For many years, transferee courts under § 1407 kept some transferred cases for trial despite the clear language of § 1407(a)

providing, "Each action so transferred shall be remanded * * * at or before the conclusion of such pretrial proceedings to the district from which it was transferred unless it shall have been previously terminated." The Supreme Court eventually prohibited such "self-assignments": "[Defendant] may or may not be correct that permitting transferee courts to make self-assignments would be more desirable than [what the § 1407 requires], but the proper venue for resolving that issue remains the floor of Congress." Lexecon Inc. v. Milberg Weiss Bershad Hynes & Lerach, 523 U.S. 26, 40, 118 S.Ct. 956, 140 L.Ed.2d 62 (1998).

For an good early description of the workings of § 1407, written by a long-time member of the Judicial Panel, see Weigel, The Judicial Panel on Multidistrict Litigation, Transferor Courts and Transferee Courts, 78 F.R.D. 575 (1978). For a good recent description, see Bradt, The Shortest Distance: Direct Filing and Choice of Law in Multidistrict Litigation, 88 Notre Dame L.Rev. 759, 785–791 (2012). Multidistrict litigation (MDL) cases occupy a surprisingly large percentage of the federal courts' civil docket. Professor Bradt writes:

> Recent empirical work by the Federal Judicial Center reveals that one third of all civil cases in the federal courts right now are part of a pending MDL. * * * [N]inety percent of these cases are products-liability cases. And many of these MDLs are massive, comprising thousands of cases.

Id. at 784. See also Steinman, Law of the Case: A Judicial Puzzle in Consolidated Cases and in Multidistrict Litigation, 135 U.Pa.L.Rev. 595 (1987).

D. FORUM NON CONVENIENS

Piper Aircraft Co. v. Reyno

Supreme Court of the United States, 1981.
454 U.S. 235, 102 S.Ct. 252, 70 L.Ed.2d 419.

■ JUSTICE MARSHALL delivered the opinion of the Court.

These cases arise out of an air crash that took place in Scotland. Respondent, acting as representative of the estates of several Scottish citizens killed in the accident, brought wrongful death actions against petitioners in the United States District Court for the Middle District of Pennsylvania. Petitioners moved to dismiss on the ground of *forum non conveniens*. After noting that an alternative forum existed in Scotland, the District Court granted their motions. 479 F. Supp. 727 (1979). The United States Court of Appeals for the Third Circuit reversed. 630 F.2d 149 (1980). The Court of Appeals based its decision, at least in part, on the ground that dismissal is automatically barred where the law of the alternative forum is less favorable to the plaintiff than the law of the forum chosen by the plaintiff. Because we conclude that the possibility of an unfavorable change in law should not, by itself, bar dismissal, and because we conclude that the District Court did not otherwise abuse its discretion, we reverse.

I

A

In July 1976, a small commercial aircraft crashed in the Scottish highlands during the course of a charter flight from Blackpool to Perth. The pilot and five passengers were killed instantly. The decedents were all Scottish subjects and residents, as are their heirs and next of kin. There were no eyewitnesses to the accident. At the time of the crash the plane was subject to Scottish air traffic control.

The aircraft, a twin engine Piper Aztec, was manufactured in Pennsylvania by petitioner Piper Aircraft Company (Piper). The propellers were manufactured in Ohio by petitioner Hartzell Propeller, Inc. (Hartzell). At the time of the crash the aircraft was registered in Great Britain and was owned and maintained by Air Navigation and Trading Co., Ltd. (Air Navigation). It was operated by McDonald Aviation, Ltd. (McDonald), a Scottish air taxi service. Both Air Navigation and McDonald were organized in the United Kingdom. The wreckage of the plane is now in a hangar in Farnsborough, England.

The British Department of Trade investigated the accident several months after it occurred. A preliminary report found that the plane crashed after developing a spin, and suggested that mechanical failure in the plane or the propeller was responsible. At Hartzell's request, this report was reviewed by a three-member Review Board, which held a nine-day adversary hearing attended by all interested parties. The Review Board found no evidence of defective equipment and indicated that pilot error may have contributed to the accident. The pilot, who had obtained his commercial pilot's license only three months earlier, was flying over high ground at an altitude considerably lower than the minimum height required by his company's operations manual.

In July 1977, a California probate court appointed respondent Gaynell Reyno administratrix of the estates of the five passengers. Reyno is not related to and does not know any of the decedents or their survivors; she was a legal secretary to the attorney who filed this lawsuit. Several days after her appointment, Reyno commenced separate wrongful death actions against Piper and Hartzell in the Superior Court of California, claiming negligence and strict liability. Air Navigation, McDonald, and the estate of the pilot are not parties to this litigation. The survivors of the five passengers whose estates are represented by Reyno filed a separate action in the United Kingdom against Air Navigation, McDonald, and the pilot's estate. Reyno candidly admits that the action against Piper and Hartzell was filed in the United States because its laws regarding liability, capacity to sue, and damages are more favorable to her position than are those of Scotland. Scottish law does not recognize strict liability in tort. Moreover, it permits wrongful death actions only when brought by a decedent's relatives. The relatives may sue only for "loss of support and society."

On petitioners' motion, the suit was removed to the United States District Court for the Central District of California. Piper then moved for transfer to the United States District Court for the Middle District of Pennsylvania, pursuant to 28 U.S.C. § 1404(a). Hartzell moved to dismiss for lack of personal jurisdiction, or in the alternative, to transfer.[5] In December 1977, the District Court quashed service on Hartzell and transferred the case to the Middle District of Pennsylvania. Respondent then properly served process on Hartzell.

B

In May 1978, after the suit had been transferred, both Hartzell and Piper moved to dismiss the action on the ground of *forum non conveniens.* The District Court granted these motions in October 1979. It relied on the balancing test set forth by this Court in Gulf Oil Corp. v. Gilbert, 330 U.S. 501, 67 S.Ct. 839, 91 L.Ed. 1055 (1947), and its companion case, Koster v. Lumbermens Mut. Cas. Co., 330 U.S. 518, 67 S.Ct. 828, 91 L.Ed. 1067 (1947). In those decisions, the Court stated that a plaintiff's choice of forum should rarely be disturbed. However, when an alternative forum has jurisdiction to hear the case, and when trial in the chosen forum would "establish . . . oppressiveness and vexation to a defendant out of all proportion to plaintiff's convenience," or when the "chosen forum [is] inappropriate because of considerations affecting the court's own administrative and legal problems," the court may, in the exercise of its sound discretion, dismiss the case. *Koster,* supra, at 524, 67 S.Ct., at 831–32. To guide trial court discretion, the Court provided a list of "private interest factors" affecting the convenience of the litigants, and a list of "public interest factors" affecting the convenience of the forum. *Gilbert,* supra, 330 U.S. at 508–509, 67 S.Ct., at 843.[6]

After describing our decisions in *Gilbert* and *Koster,* the District Court analyzed the facts of this case. It began by observing that an alternative forum existed in Scotland; Piper and Hartzell had agreed to submit to the jurisdiction of the Scottish courts and to waive any statute of limitations defense that might be available. It then stated that plaintiff's choice of forum was entitled to little weight. The court recognized that a plaintiff's choice ordinarily deserves substantial deference. It noted, however, that Reyno "is a representative of foreign citizens and residents seeking a forum in the United States because of the more liberal rules concerning products liability law," and that "the courts have been less solicitous when the plaintiff is not an American citizen or resident, and particularly, when the foreign citizens seek to benefit from the more liberal tort rules provided for the protection of citizens and residents of the United States." 479 F. Supp. at 731.

The District Court next examined several factors relating to the private interests of the litigants, and determined that these factors

---

[5]   The District Court concluded that it could not assert personal jurisdiction over Hartzell consistent with due process. However, it decided not to dismiss Hartzell because the corporation would be amenable to process in Pennsylvania.

[6]   The factors pertaining to the private interests of the litigants included the "relative ease of access to sources of proof; availability of compulsory process for attendance of unwilling, and the cost of obtaining attendance of willing, witnesses; possibility of view of premises, if view would be appropriate to the action; and all other practical problems that make trial of a case easy, expeditious, and inexpensive." *Gilbert,* 330 U.S. at 508, 67 S.Ct., at 843. The public factors bearing on the question included the administrative difficulties flowing from court congestion; the "local interest in having localized controversies decided at home"; the interest in having the trial of a diversity case in a forum that is at home with the law that must govern the action; the avoidance of unnecessary problems in conflicts of law, or in the application of foreign law; and the unfairness of burdening citizens in an unrelated forum with jury duty. Id., at 509, 67 S.Ct., at 843.

strongly pointed towards Scotland as the appropriate forum. Although evidence concerning the design, manufacture, and testing of the plane and propeller is located in the United States, the connections with Scotland are otherwise "overwhelming." Id., at 732. The real parties in interest are citizens of Scotland, as were all the decedents. Witnesses who could testify regarding the maintenance of the aircraft, the training of the pilot, and the investigation of the accident—all essential to the defense—are in Great Britain. Moreover, all witnesses to damages are located in Scotland. Trial would be aided by familiarity with Scottish topography, and by easy access to the wreckage.

The District Court reasoned that because crucial witnesses and evidence were beyond the reach of compulsory process, and because the defendants would not be able to implead potential Scottish third-party defendants, it would be "unfair to make Piper and Hartzell proceed to trial in this forum." Id., at 733. The survivors had brought separate actions in Scotland against the pilot, McDonald, and Air Navigation. "[I]t would be fairer to all parties and less costly if the entire case was presented to one jury with available testimony from all relevant witnesses." Ibid. Although the court recognized that if trial were held in the United States, Piper and Hartzell could file indemnity or contribution actions against the Scottish defendants, it believed that there was a significant risk of inconsistent verdicts.[7]

The District Court concluded that the relevant public interests also pointed strongly towards dismissal. The court determined that Pennsylvania law would apply to Piper and Scottish law to Hartzell if the case were tried in the Middle District of Pennsylvania.[8] As a result, "trial in this forum would be hopelessly complex and confusing for a jury." Id., at 734. In addition, the court noted that it was unfamiliar with Scottish law and thus would have to rely upon experts from that country. The court also found that the trial would be enormously costly and time-consuming; that it would be unfair to burden citizens with jury duty when the Middle District of Pennsylvania has little connection with the controversy; and that Scotland has a substantial interest in the outcome of the litigation.

In opposing the motions to dismiss, respondent contended that dismissal would be unfair because Scottish law was less favorable. The District Court explicitly rejected this claim. It reasoned that the possibility that dismissal might lead to an unfavorable change in the law

---

[7]   The District Court explained that inconsistent verdicts might result if petitioners were held liable on the basis of strict liability here, and then required to prove negligence in an indemnity action in Scotland. Moreover, even if the same standard of liability applied, there was a danger that different juries would find different facts and produce inconsistent results.

[8]   Under Klaxon v. Stentor Electric Manufacturing Co., 313 U.S. 487, 61 S.Ct. 1020, 85 L.Ed. 1477 (1941), a court ordinarily must apply the choice-of-law rules of the state in which it sits. However, where a case is transferred pursuant to 28 U.S.C. § 1404(a), it must apply the choice-of-law rules of the state from which the case was transferred. Van Dusen v. Barrack, 376 U.S. 612, 84 S.Ct. 805, 11 L.Ed.2d 945 (1964). Relying on these two cases, the District Court concluded that California choice-of-law rules would apply to Piper, and Pennsylvania choice-of-law rules would apply to Hartzell. It further concluded that California applied a "governmental interests" analysis in resolving choice-of-law problems, and that Pennsylvania employed a "significant contacts" analysis. The court used the "governmental interests" analysis to determine that Pennsylvania liability rules would apply to Piper, and the "significant contacts" analysis to determine that Scottish liability rules would apply to Hartzell.

did not deserve significant weight; any deficiency in the foreign law was a "matter to be dealt with in the foreign forum." Id., at 738.

On appeal, the United States Court of Appeals for the Third Circuit reversed and remanded for trial. The decision to reverse appears to be based on two alternative grounds. First, the Court held that the District Court abused its discretion in conducting the *Gilbert* analysis. Second, the Court held that dismissal is never appropriate where the law of the alternative forum is less favorable to the plaintiff.

* * *

II

The Court of Appeals erred in holding that plaintiffs may defeat a motion to dismiss on the ground of *forum non conveniens* merely by showing that the substantive law that would be applied in the alternative forum is less favorable to the plaintiffs than that of the present forum. The possibility of a change in substantive law should ordinarily not be given conclusive or even substantial weight in the *forum non conveniens* inquiry.

We expressly rejected the position adopted by the Court of Appeals in our decision in Canada Malting Co. v. Paterson Steamships, Ltd., 285 U.S. 413, 52 S.Ct. 413, 76 L.Ed. 837 (1932). That case arose out of a collision between two vessels in American waters. The Canadian owners of cargo lost in the accident sued the Canadian owners of one of the vessels in Federal District Court. The cargo owners chose an American court in large part because the relevant American liability rules were more favorable than the Canadian rules. The District Court dismissed on grounds of *forum non conveniens*. The plaintiffs argued that dismissal was inappropriate because Canadian laws were less favorable to them. This Court nonetheless affirmed:

> "We have no occasion to enquire by what law the rights of the parties are governed, as we are of the opinion that, under any view of that question, it lay within the discretion of the District Court to decline jurisdiction over the controversy. . . . '[T]he court will not take cognizance of the case if justice would be as well done by remitting the parties to their home forum.'" Id., at 419–420, 52 S.Ct., at 414, quoting Charter Shipping Co. v. Bowring, Jones & Tidy, 281 U.S. 515, 517, 50 S.Ct. 400, 414, 74 L.Ed. 1008 (1930).

The Court further stated that "there was no basis for the contention that the District Court abused its discretion." 285 U.S., at 423, 52 S.Ct., at 415–16.

It is true that *Canada Malting* was decided before *Gilbert,* and that the doctrine of *forum non conveniens* was not fully crystallized until our decision in that case.[13] * * *

---

[13] The doctrine of *forum non conveniens* has a long history. It originated in Scotland, see Braucher, The Inconvenient Federal Forum, 60 Harv.L.Rev. 908, 909–911 (1947), and became part of the common law of many states, see id., at 911–912; Blair, The Doctrine of Forum Non Conveniens in Anglo-American Law, 29 Colum.L.Rev. 1 (1929). The doctrine was also frequently applied in federal admiralty actions. See, e.g., Canada Malting Co. v. Paterson Steamships, Ltd., 285 U.S. 413, 52 S.Ct. 413, 76 L.Ed. 837 (1932); see also Bickel, The Doctrine of Forum Non Conveniens As Applied in the Federal Courts in Matters of Admiralty, 35 Cornell L.Q. 12 (1949). In Williams v. Green Bay & Western R., 326 U.S. 549, 66 S.Ct. 284, 90 L.Ed. 311 (1946), the

* * *

[I]f conclusive or substantial weight were given to the possibility of a change in law, the *forum non conveniens* doctrine would become virtually useless. Jurisdiction and venue requirements are often easily satisfied. As a result, many plaintiffs are able to choose from among several forums. Ordinarily, these plaintiffs will select that forum whose choice of law rules are most advantageous. Thus, if the possibility of an unfavorable change in substantive law is given substantial weight in the *forum non conveniens* inquiry, dismissal would rarely be proper.

* * *

* * * The flow of litigation into the United States would increase and further congest already crowded courts.

The Court of Appeals based its decision, at least in part, on an analogy between dismissals on grounds of *forum non conveniens* and transfers between federal courts pursuant to § 1404(a). In Van Dusen v. Barrack, 376 U.S. 612, 84 S.Ct. 805, 11 L.Ed.2d 945 (1964), this Court ruled that a § 1404(a) transfer should not result in a change in the applicable law. * * *

* * *

The reasoning employed in Van Dusen v. Barrack is simply inapplicable to dismissals on grounds of *forum non conveniens*. That case did not discuss the common-law doctrine. Rather, it focused on "the construction and application" of § 1404(a). 376 U.S., at 613, 84 S.Ct., at 807–08. Emphasizing the remedial purpose of the statute, *Barrack* concluded that Congress could not have intended a transfer to be accompanied by a change in law. Id., at 622, 84 S.Ct., at 812. The statute was designed as a "federal housekeeping measure," allowing easy change of venue within a unified federal system. Id., at 613, 84 S.Ct., at 807–08. The Court feared that if a change in venue were accompanied by a change in law, forum-shopping parties would take unfair advantage of the relaxed standards for transfer. The rule was necessary to ensure the just and efficient operation of the statute.

We do not hold that the possibility of an unfavorable change in law should *never* be a relevant consideration in a *forum non conveniens* inquiry. Of course, if the remedy provided by the alternative forum is so clearly inadequate or unsatisfactory that it is no remedy at all, the unfavorable change in law may be given substantial weight; the district court may conclude that dismissal would not be in the interests of justice. In this case, however, the remedies that would be provided by the

---

Court first indicated that motions to dismiss on grounds of *forum non conveniens* could be made in federal diversity actions. The doctrine became firmly established when *Gilbert* and *Koster* were decided one year later.

In previous *forum non conveniens* decisions, the Court has left unresolved the question whether under Erie R. v. Tompkins, 304 U.S. 64, 58 S.Ct. 817, 82 L.Ed. 1188 (1938), state or federal law of *forum non conveniens* applies in a diversity case. *Gilbert,* supra, 330 U.S. at 509, 67 S.Ct., at 843; *Koster,* supra, 330 U.S. at 529, 67 S.Ct., at 834; Williams v. Green Bay & Western R., supra, 326 U.S. at 551, 558–559, 66 S.Ct., at 288–89 (1946). The Court did not decide this issue because the same result would have been reached in each case under federal or state law. The lower courts in this case reached the same conclusion: Pennsylvania and California law on *forum non conveniens* dismissals are virtually identical to federal law. See Reyno v. Piper Aircraft Co., 630 F.2d 149, 158 (C.A.3 1980). Thus, here, also, we need not resolve the *Erie* question.

Scottish courts do not fall within this category. Although the relatives of the decedents may not be able to rely on a strict liability theory, and although their potential damage award may be smaller, there is no danger that they will be deprived of any remedy or treated unfairly.

III

* * * Furthermore, we do not believe that the District Court abused its discretion in weighing the private and public interests.

A

The District Court acknowledged that there is ordinarily a strong presumption in favor of the plaintiff's choice of forum, which may be overcome only when the private and public interest factors clearly point towards trial in the alternative forum. It held, however, that the presumption applies with less force when the plaintiff or real parties in interest are foreign.

The District Court's distinction between resident or citizen plaintiffs and foreign plaintiffs is fully justified. In *Koster,* the Court indicated that a plaintiff's choice of forum is entitled to greater deference when the plaintiff has chosen the home forum. *Koster,* supra, 330 U.S., at 524, 67 S.Ct., at 831–32. When the home forum has been chosen, it is reasonable to assume that this choice is convenient. When the plaintiff is foreign, however, this assumption is much less reasonable. Because the central purpose of any *forum non conveniens* inquiry is to ensure that the trial is convenient, a foreign plaintiff's choice deserves less deference.

B

The *forum non conveniens* determination is committed to the sound discretion of the trial court. It may be reversed only when there has been a clear abuse of discretion; where the court has considered all relevant public and private interest factors, and where its balancing of these factors is reasonable, its decision deserves substantial deference. * * * In examining the District Court's analysis of the public and private interests, however, the Court of Appeals seems to have lost sight of this rule, and substituted its own judgment for that of the District Court.

* * *

Reversed.

■ [The separate opinions of JUSTICE WHITE, concurring and dissenting in part, and of JUSTICE STEVENS, dissenting, are omitted.]

NOTE ON *FORUM NON CONVENIENS*

1. Scope of *forum non conveniens* in the federal courts. A motion to dismiss on grounds of *forum non conveniens* in federal district court is proper only when the alternative forum is in a foreign country, as it was in *Piper.* If the alternative forum is in the United States, the proper motion is for transfer to another federal district court under 28 U.S.C. § 1404(a).

Is an essential purpose of *forum non conveniens* as applied by the Supreme Court in *Piper* to protect American corporations from suits in the United States arising out of injuries to foreigners in foreign countries? What if one of the decedents in the accident in *Piper* had been an American citizen residing permanently in Great Britain? An American citizen residing in the United States but on vacation in Great Britain?

2.   Conditions on dismissal. It is common for a court to condition a *forum non conveniens* dismissal on an agreement by the defendant to waive the statute of limitations, an *in personam* jurisdiction objection, or other defenses in the alternative forum. State courts do not have the power directly to transfer cases to courts outside the state, but the power to impose conditions on dismissal such as waiver of defenses in the alternative forum has much the same practical effect. An example is Stangvik v. Shiley Inc., 54 Cal.3d 744, 1 Cal.Rptr.2d 556, 819 P.2d 14 (1991), in which two men, one Swedish and the other Norwegian, in separate operations in their own countries, received artificial heart valves manufactured in California. The valves failed causing the deaths of the two men, and suits were brought against the manufacturer in California state court. The trial court granted a *forum non conveniens* dismissal, subject to the defendant's complying with the following conditions:

> (1) submission to jurisdiction in Sweden and Norway; (2) compliance with discovery orders of the Scandinavian courts; (3) agreement to make past and present employees reasonably available to testify in Sweden and Norway at defendants' cost if so ordered within the discretion of Scandinavian courts; (4) tolling of the statute of limitations during the pendency of the actions in California; (5) agreement to make documents in their possession in the United States available for inspection in Sweden and Norway, as required by Scandinavian law, at defendants' expense; (6) agreement that depositions in the United States might proceed under section 2029 [of the California Civil Code]; and (7) agreement to pay any final judgments rendered in the Scandinavian actions.

54 Cal.3d at 750 n. 2. The California Supreme Court affirmed the dismissal, partially relying on the conditions to which the defendant agreed.

The power to impose conditions is not unlimited, however. In re Union Carbide Corp. Gas Plant Disaster at Bhopal, 809 F.2d 195 (2d Cir.), cert. den. 484 U.S. 871 (1987), arose out of a catastrophic gas leak at a Union Carbide plant in India, in which over 2,000 people were killed and another 200,000 seriously injured. Some 145 would-be class actions were filed in the United States. They were consolidated and transferred to federal District Court in the Southern District of New York by the Judicial Panel on Multidistrict Litigation under 28 U.S.C. § 1407. After consolidation, Union Carbide moved for a *forum non conveniens* dismissal. The district court dismissed on the condition that Union Carbide submit to discovery in Indian courts in accordance with the standards of the Federal Rules of Civil Procedure. (Indian discovery is patterned after the relatively restrictive British discovery rules.) The court of appeals reversed, holding that such a condition could not be imposed as a condition of dismissal under *forum non conveniens*.

3.   Adequacy of the remedy in the alternate forum. There are no bright-line answers to the question whether the remedy in the alternative forum is adequate. Compare the following two cases. In Gonzalez v. Chrysler Corporation, 301 F.3d 377 (5th Cir. 2002), the plaintiff's child was killed by the passenger-side airbag in a car manufactured by Chrysler. Mexico has a $2,500 cap on damages in a wrongful death suit. The plaintiff had shopped for the car in Houston, but had bought it in Mexico. The accident took place in Mexico. Both drivers and all witnesses were Mexican. Among other things, plaintiff argued that the recovery was so small that, as a practical matter, no suit would be filed in Mexico. The Fifth Circuit affirmed the trial court's dismissal based on *forum non conveniens*. The $2,500 limit reflected Mexico's "deliberate choice * * * as a sovereign nation * * * to limit tort damages with respect to a child's death" which a United States court was obliged to respect as a matter of comity. Id. at 381–82.

In Nemariam v. Federal Democratic Republic of Ethiopia, 315 F.3d 390 (D.C. Cir. 2003), the plaintiff, an Eritrean national, claimed that the Ethiopian government had expropriated her property during the Eritrean–Ethiopian border war, in violation of international law. The district court dismissed based on *forum non conveniens*, holding that the Ethiopia/Eritrea Claims Commission, created by the Peace Treaty that concluded the war, was a more appropriate forum. The court of appeals reversed, holding that the remedy provided by the Claims Commission was inadequate. Individuals could not bring their own claims before the Commission, but instead had to rely on the Eritrean government to do so on their behalf. Further, the Eritrean government had the right to compromise individual damage claims as part of an overall settlement of claims between the two nations.

The court in *Nemarian* distinguished *Gonzalez v. Chrysler* on the ground that Mexican law at least guaranteed some remedy, "whereas Ethiopia cannot assure Nemariam of recovering any award at all, even if the Commission upholds her claim in full." Id. at 394–95. Is *Nemariam* consistent with *Gonzalez*? Are you persuaded by the court's distinction between a suit that is not economically viable and a suit that, while viable, may be controlled or compromised by the state of which the plaintiff is a citizen? Does the *Nemariam* court adequately deal with the issue of respect for Eritrean sovereignty?

4. Examples. In Ravelo Monegro v. Rosa, 211 F.3d 509 (9th Cir. 2000), plaintiffs were thirteen aspiring professional baseball players in the Dominican Republic who were induced to sign minor league baseball contracts with the San Francisco Giants by Rosa, the Giants' Latin America scout. Plaintiffs sued Rosa and the Giants in federal District Court for the Northern District of California (i.e., in San Francisco), alleging that Rosa conditioned their continued employment on submitting to his sexual advances, and that he misappropriated their signing bonuses to his own use. A parallel combined criminal and civil proceeding was instituted in the Dominican Republic. In denying a motion for a dismissal under *forum non conveniens*, the court of appeals distinguished *Piper*:

> This case is unlike *Piper* in a number of respects. First, unlike *Piper*, plaintiffs' chosen forum is more than merely the American defendants' home forum. It is also a forum with a substantial relation to the action. * * * Second, unlike *Piper*, there are no possible co-defendants or third-party defendants who could not be made to appear in the American forum. Indeed, quite the opposite problem exists in this case: If this suit were dismissed in favor of a suit in the Dominican Republic, it is not clear that defendant Rosa would appear, or could be compelled to appear, in that forum. * * * Third, unlike *Piper*, there is no showing that access to proof—even aside from Rosa's testimony—would be easier in the Dominican Republic.

Id. at 514–15.

In Creative Technology, Ltd. v. Aztech System Pte., Ltd., 61 F.3d 696 (9th Cir. 1995), one Singapore company sued another for alleged violations of American copyright law arising out of distribution of competing computer "sound cards" in the United States. The court of appeals sustained a *forum non conveniens* dismissal by the district court, writing, "This is essentially a dispute between two Singapore corporations as to which of them was the original developer of the disputed sound card technology. This is not a case involving the piracy of American made products or substantively involving American companies." Id. at 704. In Bhatnagar v. Surrendra Overseas Ltd., 52 F.3d 1220 (3d Cir. 1995), plaintiff, a six-year-old girl, was injured aboard an Indian merchant ship in international waters. She was an Indian citizen residing in India, but she had boarded the ship in the United States and had been flown to the United States for emergency medical treatment. The district court found that "the Indian legal system has a tremendous backlog of cases—so great that it could take up to a quarter of a century to resolve this litigation if it were filed in India." The court of appeals upheld the refusal of the district court to dismiss on ground of *forum non conveniens*: "[T]he district court did not commit legal error in concluding that delay can render a putative alternative forum clearly inadequate." Id. at 1227, 1230. Note that in both *Creative Technology* and *Bhatnagar* the court of appeals sustained the decision of the district court, in the one case to dismiss and in the other to deny dismissal, illustrating that *forum non conveniens* accords considerable discretion to the trial court.

5.   *Forum non conveniens* in state courts. There is significant variation among the states in the ease or difficulty with which a *forum non conveniens* dismissal may be obtained. The Court in *Reyno* wrote that the federal law of *forum non conveniens* was essentially identical to that of California and Pennsylvania. When the Court wrote this, it was almost certainly wrong; California law was much more favorable to plaintiffs than the Court's holding in *Reyno*. See Holmes v. Syntex Laboratories, 156 Cal.App.3d 372, 202 Cal.Rptr. 773 (1984). However, California law has come substantially into line with *Reyno* since then. Stangvik v. Shiley Inc., 54 Cal.3d 744, 1 Cal.Rptr.2d 556, 819 P.2d 14 (1991). Other state courts are much more favorable to plaintiffs than *Reyno*. For a time, Texas abolished *forum non conveniens* by statute. See Dow Chemical Co. v. Alfaro, 786 S.W.2d 674 (Tex.1990), cert. den. 498 U.S. 1024 (1991); Guardian Royal Exchange Assurance, Ltd. v. English China Clays, P.L.C., 815 S.W.2d 223 (Tex.1991). Texas reinstated a limited form of *forum non conveniens* in August 1993. See Tex.Civ.Pract. & Rem.C. § 71.051.

Forum non conveniens issues can arise in the state courts in various ways. In Myers v. Boeing Co., 115 Wash.2d 123, 794 P.2d 1272 (1990), the dismissal was for only part of the suit. Seventy-one Japanese nationals sued Boeing in Washington state courts arising out of the crash of a Boeing 747 in Japan. The state court found that Boeing was liable to the plaintiffs, but entered a *forum non conveniens* dismissal on condition that "Boeing submit to jurisdiction in Japan, waive any statute of limitations defenses, admit liability for compensatory damages, and not oppose recognition in Japan of the judgment of liability entered" by the Washington court. In MacLeod v. MacLeod, 383 A.2d 39 (Me.1978), plaintiff, who lived in Virginia, brought a damages suit in a Maine court against her former husband for failure to make payments under a French divorce decree. The former husband, a CIA employee, lived in Thailand. He was an American citizen, but his "sole contact with the United States [was] his Virginia driver's license." Plaintiff sued defendant in Maine "because it was the sole place within American territory where she could catch Mr. MacLeod for service of process." The Maine Supreme Court stayed the Maine action on the condition that Mr. MacLeod submit to suit for damages in Virginia.

6.   Relationship between *forum non conveniens* dismissals and *in personam* jurisdiction dismissals. Professor Alex Albright has argued persuasively that after the statutory abolition of *forum non conveniens* Texas courts used *in personam* jurisdiction rulings to produce dismissals that previously would have been available under *forum non conveniens*. Albright, *In Personam* Jurisdiction: A Confused and Inappropriate Substitute for *Forum Non Conveniens*, 71 Tex.L.Rev. 351 (1992). Recall the Supreme Court's dismissal for want of *in personam* jurisdiction in Asahi Metal Industry Co. v. Superior Court, 480 U.S. 102, 107 S.Ct. 1026, 94 L.Ed.2d 92 (1987), supra p. 92. So long as *forum non conveniens* is not federal law that is binding on the state courts, the United States Supreme Court cannot require a state court to dismiss on *forum non conveniens* grounds, for its authority in cases coming up on appeal from state courts is limited to questions of federal law. Was the U.S. Supreme Court doing the same thing in *Asahi* as the Texas courts? That is, was the Court using its authority under the federal Due Process Clause to dismiss for want of *in personam* jurisdiction, in order to achieve a result that it was powerless to achieve under *forum non conveniens*?

7.   State or federal law? Why didn't the Supreme Court in *Piper* admit what was obvious to any competent California lawyer at the time— that the California law of *forum non conveniens* was almost certainly more generous to plaintiffs than the law applied by the Court in *Piper*? The answer is that the Supreme Court was unwilling to face up to the issue of the federal or state character of *forum non conveniens* law. By pretending that the California and federal laws of *forum non conveniens* were identical, the Court did not have to choose between them. If the Court had recognized that California law was different, it would have had to answer the question posed under *Erie RR. v. Tompkins*: Should federal courts follow the law of *forum non conveniens* of the states in which they sit, or should they follow their own independent federal law of *forum non conveniens*?

The lower federal courts have answered the question avoided by the Supreme Court in *Piper*. The now-standard answer in the lower federal courts is that federal *forum non conveniens* law is applicable irrespective of any differences from the *forum non conveniens* law of the state in which the federal court sits. See, e.g., Esfeld v. Costa Crociere, S.P.A., 289 F.3d 1300, 1315 (11th Cir. 2002); Ravelo Monegro v. Rosa, 211 F.3d 509, 511–12 (9th Cir. 2000); Rivendell Forest Prods. Ltd. v. Canadian Pac. Ltd., 2 F.3d 990, 992 (10th Cir. 1993); Royal Bed & Spring Co. v. Famossul Industria e Comercio de Moveis, Ltda., 906 F.2d 45, 50 (1st Cir. 1990). For an argument that state law should be followed in some circumstances, see Stein, *Erie* and Court Access, 100 Yale L.J. 1935 (1991).

Perhaps the question should be pushed further. In cases where the alternative forum is in a foreign country—in other words, in the cases where federal courts apply the doctrine of *forum non conveniens*—isn't there a good argument for a uniform federal rule that binds both state and federal courts? Foreign relations and foreign commerce have been the traditional and particular concern of the national government, and have been an area where uniform federal rules are most frequently applied. For an excellent article arguing for a uniform federal standard binding both federal and state courts in such cases, see Greenberg, The Appropriate Source of Law for Forum Non Conveniens Decisions in International Cases: A Proposal for the Development of Federal Common Law, 4 Int'l Tax and Bus.Law 155 (1986). For a contrary argument, see Comment, Forum Non Conveniens and State Control of Foreign Plaintiff Access to U.S. Courts in International Tort Actions, 58 U.Chi.L.Rev. 1369 (1991).

The Supreme Court has provided cryptic, and somewhat contradictory, guidance on this question. In Chick Kam Choo v. Exxon Corp., 486 U.S. 140, 148, 108 S.Ct. 1684, 100 L.Ed.2d 127 (1988), the Court refused to enjoin a Texas state court from proceeding in an admiralty suit involving a foreign plaintiff and foreign substantive law that had previously been dismissed from federal court on ground of *forum non conveniens*: "Federal *forum non conveniens* principles simply cannot determine whether Texas courts, which operate under a broad 'open courts' mandate, would consider themselves an appropriate forum for petitioner's lawsuit." Six years later, in American Dredging Co. v. Miller, 510 U.S. 443, 457, 114 S.Ct. 981, 127 L.Ed.2d 285 (1994), the Court held that in an admiralty suit filed in state court between domestic parties, federal *forum non conveniens* law does not pre-empt Louisiana law. But it was careful to indicate that it did not decide whether there should be a uniform federal law of *forum non conveniens* in cases involving foreign parties: "[T]he Solicitor General has urged that we limit our holding, that *forum non conveniens* is not part of the uniform law of admiralty, to cases involving domestic entities. We think it unnecessary to do that. Since the parties to this suit are domestic entities it is quite impossible for our holding to be any broader."

8.   Injunctions to control improper forum choice. Defendants sued in an inconvenient forum can, and often do, move in that forum for a dismissal on grounds of *forum non conveniens*. Another strategy is to seek from the more convenient forum (which is frequently the forum where the plaintiff resides) an injunction forbidding the plaintiff to pursue the suit in the inconvenient forum. This was the strategy pursued (unsuccessfully) by the railroad in Baltimore & Ohio Rr. Co. v. Kepner, 314 U.S. 44, 62 S.Ct. 6, 86 L.Ed. 28 (1941), discussed supra p. 314, note 1.

In domestic litigation, such injunctions are almost never available. The Supreme Court has flatly prohibited state court injunctions against federal court *in personam* litigation. General Atomic Co. v. Felter, 434 U.S. 12, 12, 98 S.Ct. 76, 54 L.Ed.2d 199 (1977) ("it is not within the power of state courts to bar litigants from filing and prosecuting *in personam* actions in the federal courts"); Donovan v. City of Dallas, 377 U.S. 408, 84 S.Ct. 1579, 12 L.Ed.2d 409 (1964). Conversely, the power of federal courts to enjoin state court litigation is narrowly circumscribed by the Anti-Injunction Act, 28 U.S.C. § 2283. In practical fact, the Act prevents federal injunctions against state court proceedings when the only argument is that the state forum is inconvenient. State courts do have the power to enjoin parties before them from engaging in litigation in other state courts, but it is rarely employed. The general rule is that a suit in another state will be enjoined only "when the injunction will prevent a multiplicity of suits or will protect a party from vexatious or harassing litigation." Christensen v. Integrity Insurance Co., 719 S.W.2d 161, 163 (Tex.1986).

In international litigation, an injunction is sometimes issued by the courts of one country against litigation in another country. See, e.g., Laker Airways Ltd. v. Sabena, Belgian World Airlines, 731 F.2d 909 (D.C. Cir. 1984), in which a British court had enjoined Laker Airways from continuing an antitrust suit it had filed in federal court in the United States. The federal court in turn enjoined KLM and Sabena (the plaintiffs in the British injunction proceeding and the defendants in the United States antitrust suit) from continuing to take part in the British proceeding. The impasse finally ended when the House of Lords vacated the British injunction. British Airways Bd. v. Laker Airways, 1985 App.Cas. 58, 96. For discussion of injunctions in international cases, see Bermann, The Use of Anti-Suit Injunctions in International Litigation, 28 Colum.J.Transnat'l L. 589 (1990).

9. *Forum non conveniens* **dismissal as an alternative to dismissal on jurisdictional grounds.** In Sinochem International Co. v. Malaysia International Shipping Corp., 549 U.S. 422, 127 S.Ct. 1184, 167 L.Ed.2d 15 (2007), the district court dismissed a case on *forum non conveniens* grounds without resolving whether it had personal jurisdiction over the defendant. The Supreme Court upheld the dismissal: "A district court * * * may dispose of an action by a *forum non conveniens* dismissal, bypassing questions of subject matter and personal jurisdiction, when considerations of convenience, fairness and judicial economy so warrant." 549 U.S. at 432. The Court wrote that *forum non conveniens* was not a determination on the merits, but rather "a determination that the merits should be adjudicated elsewhere." Id.

CHAPTER 3

THE *ERIE* PROBLEM

A. THE LAW APPLIED IN FEDERAL COURT: THE PROBLEM OF *ERIE RAILROAD V. TOMPKINS*

INTRODUCTORY NOTE ON THE LAW APPLIED IN FEDERAL COURTS

Determining that a federal district court has jurisdiction to hear a case does not determine what law it should use in deciding that case. When the choice is between federal and state law, the problem is conventionally referred to as the *Erie* problem, after Erie Railroad Co. v. Tompkins, 304 U.S. 64, 58 S.Ct. 817, 82 L.Ed. 1188 (1938).

1. Relationship between federal and state law. The starting point in considering whether federal or state law applies to a legal controversy is the organization of the federal system. Professor Henry Hart wrote:

> The law which governs daily living in the United States is a single system of law: it speaks in relation to any particular question with only one ultimately authoritative voice, however difficult it may be on occasion to discern in advance which of two or more conflicting voices really carries authority. In the long run and in the large, this must be so. People repeatedly subjected, like Pavlov's dogs, to two or more inconsistent sets of directions, without means of resolving the inconsistencies, could not fail in the end to react as the dogs did. The society, collectively, would suffer a nervous breakdown.

> Yet the sources of the laws which say what Americans can, may or must do or not do and what happens if they act differently, or which seek to influence by official action what they are able to choose to do on their own account in the infinity of situations in which they have to decide whether to do or not do something, are exceedingly diverse. The problems of developing the necessary mechanisms for evoking or enforcing harmony are correspondingly complex.

> * * *

> In any system of government, responsibility for doing these things is divided among the government's various branches. In a federal system, it is further divided between the federal government and the governments of the states and their political subdivisions.

Hart, The Relation Between State and Federal Law, 54 Colum.L.Rev. 489, 489–90 (1954).

The relationship between federal and state law was further described by Professors Hart and Herbert Wechsler:

> Federal law is generally interstitial in its nature. It rarely occupies a legal field completely, totally excluding all participation by the legal systems of the states. This was plainly true in the beginning when the federal legislative product (including the Constitution) was extremely small. It is significantly true today, despite the volume of Congressional enactments, and even within areas where Congress has been very active. Federal legislation, on the whole, has been conceived and drafted on an *ad hoc* basis to accomplish limited objectives. It builds upon legal relationships established by the states, altering or supplanting them only so far as necessary for the special purpose. Congress acts, in short, against the background of the total *corpus juris* of the states in much the way that a state legislature acts against the background of the common law, assumed to govern unless changed by legislation.

R. Fallon, J. Manning, D. Meltzer, and D. Shapiro, Hart and Wechsler's The Federal Courts and the Federal System 459 (6th ed. 2009). This passage was originally written in 1953, but it remains largely true today.

2.   Law applied in the federal and state courts, substantive and procedural. The federal courts hear cases involving many kinds of law— federal, state, local, foreign, and international. The state courts hear cases involving the same variety. For ease of discussion, we usually speak of the courts as deciding questions of federal and state law, but this is a simplifying shorthand.

In a well-designed domestic legal system, the same law should apply to a case irrespective of the court in which it is tried. By that criterion, the American system is imperfect, for the law applied to the same set of facts can differ depending on which state court hears the case. (Recall from the previous chapter the choice-of-forum maneuvering to obtain favorable law through the choice of a particular state court. See also Note on Non-constitutional Choice of Law Rules, supra p. 219.)

When the comparison is between the state courts and the federal courts sitting in that state, rather than between the state courts of two different states, the situation is improved but not problem-free. The state and federal courts in the same state always apply the same substantive law, but sometimes apply different procedural law. Because there is not always a clear line between substantive and procedural law, and because even clearly procedural law affects the application of substantive law, the choice between federal and state courts can have important consequences. The interplay between the substantive and procedural law in the federal and state courts forms the basis for the modern "*Erie*" problem.

3.   *Swift v. Tyson.* Although the *Erie* problem is modern, its origins lie in the eighteenth and nineteenth centuries. The centerpiece of the story is the most misunderstood and reviled choice-of-law case in our history, Swift v. Tyson, 41 U.S. (16 Pet.) 1, 10 L.Ed. 865 (1842). *Swift v. Tyson* involved a common problem of negotiable instruments law. A bill of exchange is a negotiable instrument, somewhat like a modern check except that the promise to pay is made by a private party rather than by a bank. Plaintiff

Swift owned a bill of exchange (i.e., a written promise to pay) that had originally been made by Tyson to two other men. Those two men had endorsed it over to Swift. When Swift sued Tyson in federal court for payment, Tyson responded that the two men had not performed the contract in return for which he had given the bill of exchange. The issue in the case was whether a "remote endorsee" (i.e., Swift) took the bill of exchange free of an underlying defense against the two original payees. Under the "local law" of New York, followed by the New York state courts, the defense against the two original payees was also good against Swift. Under the "general law" of the United States, followed by the federal courts, the defense was not available against Swift. Thus, the result in the case depended on whether the "local law" or the "general law" was followed.

To the extent that a statute governed the result in *Swift v. Tyson*, it was the predecessor to the modern Rules of Decision Act, 28 U.S.C. § 1652, Section 34 of the Judiciary Act of 1789:

> *And be it further enacted* That the laws of the several states, except where the constitution, treaties or statutes of the United States shall otherwise require or provide, shall be regarded as rules of decision in trials at common law in the courts of the United States in cases where they apply.

Jud. Act of 1789, § 34, 1 Stat. 73, 92. In a general sense, the statute was clear enough. It required the federal courts to follow the "laws of the several states * * * in cases where they apply." But what were the "laws of the several states"?

At the time of *Swift v. Tyson*, there were three kinds of law relevant to the question:

a. Federal law: Federal law was the law of the national government, based on the Constitution, treaties, or statutes. At the time of *Swift v. Tyson*, there was no "federal common law"; that is, there was no judge-made federal law. The Supreme Court had made this clear in Wheaton v. Peters, 33 U.S. (8 Pet.) 591, 8 L.Ed. 1055 (1834), when it declined to find a federal common law of copyright: "It is clear, there can be no common law of the United States. * * * The common law could be made a part of our federal system, only by legislative adoption." (As we shall see, infra p. 427, there is federal common law today.)

Federal law was both jurisdiction-conferring and supreme. Federal law could serve as the basis for jurisdiction in the federal courts under the "federal question" jurisdiction authorized under Article III of the Constitution. At the time of *Swift v. Tyson*, original federal question jurisdiction existed in a few specific instances, such as suits by or against the Bank of the United States. See Osborn v. Bank of the United States, 22 U.S. (9 Wheat.) 738, 6 L.Ed. 204 (1824). Appellate federal question jurisdiction existed under Section 25 of the Judiciary Act of 1789, permitting Supreme Court review of state court decisions on questions of federal law. See Martin v. Hunter's Lessee, 14 U.S. (1 Wheat.) 304, 4 L.Ed. 97 (1816). Federal law was also supreme law under the Supremacy Clause of the Constitution. This meant that state courts had to follow federal law whenever it applied, and that inconsistent general or state law had to give way.

b. General law. General law was a general common law, applied more or less uniformly by all civil courts, federal and state, in the United States. There is no precise modern equivalent. Perhaps the closest modern domestic analogy is the general law summarized in the Restatements of the American Law Institute. For example, the Restatement (Second) of Contracts describes the law of contracts as generally applied in American courts. The law of the Restatement is not that of any single jurisdiction, but serves as a source of law for courts seeking to conform to a general national standard. The closest international analogy is probably customary international law. By custom and practice, certain international norms have become established. No single country is the source of these norms; rather, they have been developed through longstanding and relatively uniform practices in the international community. In the absence of a country's clear indication of intent to deviate from these norms, they govern a dispute to which they apply.

The general law in the United States at the time of *Swift v. Tyson* covered commercial subjects like contracts, insurance, and negotiable instruments. Because there was no supreme federal commercial law, American merchants and their lawyers used the general law to establish relatively uniform rules governing commercial dealings in the various states. General law was neither jurisdiction-conferring nor supreme. It was not federal law in the sense of serving as the basis for federal court jurisdiction under the "federal question" provision of Article III. To the extent that the federal courts heard cases involving questions of general law, their jurisdiction was based on diversity of citizenship or admiralty. Nor was the general law supreme federal law in the sense of obliging the state courts to follow it under the Supremacy Clause. If a state court decided that the state law of negotiable instruments on a particular point required one thing, whereas the general law of negotiable instruments on the same point required another, the state court was free to depart from the general law.

c. **State (or "local") law.** State law at the time of *Swift v. Tyson* was non-federal, non-general law. In the terminology of the period, it was often called "local" law. State, or local, law covered particular subject areas to which the general law did not extend, such as marriage, inheritance, and real property. Federal courts routinely followed the state, or local, law of the states in which they sat in all of these subject areas, with the result that the rules applied in such cases were the same in federal and state courts.

State, or local, law also included particular rules of commercial law where the state had clearly departed from the uniform rule of the general law. On the specific rule at issue in *Swift v. Tyson*, the New York courts had established a "local" law different from the "general" law of negotiable instruments. The question before the Supreme Court was whether the federal courts had to follow this rule of "local" state law when there was a rule of a "general" law that was also capable of serving as the rule of decision. In the 53 years since the adoption of the Judiciary Act, *Swift v. Tyson* was the first case to come before the Supreme Court in which, on the issue in dispute, a local state rule clearly departed from a general rule of commercial law. The Court held that the federal court was not obliged to follow the "local" law of New York, and that it should, instead, follow the "general" law.

4. **Justice Story's opinion.** Justice Joseph Story, possibly the foremost expert on commercial law in the United States, wrote for the Court:

> But, admitting the doctrine to be fully settled in New York, it remains to be considered, whether it is obligatory upon this court, if it differs from the principles established in the general

commercial law. It is observable that the courts of New York do not found their decision upon this point upon any local statute, or positive, fixed, or ancient local usage; but they deduce the doctrine from the general principles of commercial law. It is, however, contended, that the [Rules of Decision Act] furnishes a rule obligatory upon this Court to follow the decisions of the state tribunals in all cases to which they apply. * * * In order to maintain the argument, it is essential, therefore, to hold, that the word "laws," in this section, includes within the scope of its meaning the decisions of the local tribunals. In the ordinary use of language it will be hardly contended that the decisions of courts constitute laws. They are, at most, only evidence of what the laws are, and are not of themselves laws. * * * The laws of a state are more usually understood to mean the rules and enactments promulgated by the legislative authority thereof, or long-established local customs having the force of laws. In all the various cases which have hitherto come before us for decision, this Court have uniformly supposed, that the true interpretation of [the Act] limited its application to State laws strictly local, that is to say, to the positive statutes of the State, and the construction thereof adopted by the local tribunals, and to rights and titles to things having a permanent locality, such as the rights and titles to real estate, and other matters immovable and intraterritorial in their nature and character. It never has been supposed by us, that the section did apply, or was designed to apply, to questions of a more general nature, not at all dependent upon local statutes or local usages of a fixed and permanent operation, as, for example, to the construction of ordinary contracts or other written instruments, and especially to questions of general commercial law, where the State tribunals are called upon to perform the like functions as ourselves, that is, to ascertain upon general reasoning and legal analogies, what is the true exposition of the contract or instrument, or what is the just rule furnished by the principles of commercial law to govern the case.

41 U.S. (16 Pet.) at 18–19. The Court was unanimous in holding that the federal courts should follow the general law rather than a state's local law in cases where the state law deviated from the general law. Justice Catron dissented, but only on the substantive point of what the general rule of law actually was.

By the end of the nineteenth century, *Swift v. Tyson* had come to be seen as a case of enormous importance. But when it was decided, it was seen as both correctly decided and relatively unimportant. The obvious correctness of *Swift v. Tyson* to the lawyers of the period can perhaps be best seen by consulting the two-volume biography of Story written by his admiring son, William Wetmore Story. William recounted at great length his father's important achievements and opinions, but he nowhere mentioned *Swift v. Tyson*. W. Story, Life and Letters of Joseph Story (1851).

5.   General law under *Swift v. Tyson* before the Civil War. From 1789 to the Civil War, by far the largest part of the federal courts' docket was commercial cases brought in their diversity jurisdiction. (With one short-lived exception, there was no general original federal question jurisdiction statute until 1875.) During this period, the federal courts, and in particular the Supreme Court, provided a valuable service in assisting the state courts to develop and maintain a uniform body of general law. At a time when the reporting systems of many state courts were rudimentary or nonexistent, and when commercial law was developing rapidly, the Supreme Court's opinions were well-respected and, perhaps just as important, widely and accurately reported. Chief Justice Marshall, in arguing to Congress that it should pay the reporter of the Supreme Court's decisions, described the role of the Court in the federal system as it then existed:

> It is a minor consideration, but not perhaps to be entirely overlooked, that, even in cases where the decisions of the Supreme Court are not to be considered as authority except in the courts of the United States, some advantage may be derived from their being known. It is certainly to be wished that independent tribunals having concurrent jurisdiction over the same subject should concur in the principles on which they determine the causes coming before them. This concurrence can be obtained only by communicating to each the judgments of the other, and by that mutual respect which will probably be inspired by a knowledge of the grounds on which their judgments respectively stand. On great commercial questions, especially, it is desirable that the judicial opinions of all parts of the Union should be the same.

Letter to Congress Feb. 7, 1817, *reprinted in* 2 W. Crosskey, Politics and the Constitution in the History of the United States 1246 (1953). Further, lower federal courts were obliged to follow the decisions of the Supreme Court on questions of general law, even though the state courts were not. This meant that if the state courts deviated from the general law as construed by the Supreme Court, they would have a federal trial court within their state following a different rule from that followed by the state courts. The awkwardness that would result from such a disagreement provided further incentive to the state courts to follow the decisions of the federal courts.

For the entire pre-Civil War period, the state and federal courts lived in relative harmony, with the state courts deferring—usually gratefully—to the decisions of the United States Supreme Court on questions of general law. Justice William Tilghman of the Pennsylvania Supreme Court expressed the usual view of the state courts during this period:

> The decisions of the Supreme Court of the *United States* have no obligatory authority over this court, except in cases growing out of the constitution, of which this is not one. Yet so great is the importance of preserving uniformy [sic] of commercial law, throughout the *United States*; and so great the respect which I feel for the highest tribunal in the union, that I shall always be inclined to adopt its opinions, rather than those of any foreign court, unless I am well satisfied, it is in the wrong. That is more than I can say on the present occasion.

Waln v. Thompson, 9 Serg. & Rawle 115, 122 (Pa.1822).

6.   Growing unpopularity of *Swift v. Tyson* after the Civil War. After the Civil War, the economic interests of the states began increasingly to diverge, as the eastern seaboard states became disproportionately the home of financiers, factory owners, and creditors, and the other states the home of farmers, workers, and debtors. In this new post-war setting, the federal courts did two things to destroy the harmony of the earlier system. First, the Supreme Court expanded the scope of the general law, so that it included for the first time a general law of tort. This meant that industrial accidents were governed in the federal courts by the general law rather than by the law of the state in which the federal court sat. Second, the Supreme Court and lower federal courts constructed a general law that increasingly favored the creditors and employers. Many state courts refused to follow the lead of the federal courts and instead developed state laws sympathetic to the debtors and workers.

By the end of the century, the battle lines were clearly drawn. For those who favored the results achieved in the state courts, *Swift v. Tyson* was no longer the natural outgrowth of a harmonious system. It was now the essential tool of the enemy. *Swift v. Tyson* and its author were attacked unmercifully. Professor John Chipman Gray of the Harvard Law School, now remembered primarily for his formulation of the Rule against Perpetuities, wrote:

> Among the causes which led to the decision in *Swift v. Tyson*, the chief seems to have been the character and position of Judge Story. He was then by far the oldest judge in commission on the bench; he was a man of great learning, and of reputation for learning greater even than the learning itself; he was occupied at the time in writing a book on bills of exchange, which would, of itself, lead him to dogmatize on the subject; he had had great success in extending the jurisdiction of the Admiralty; he was fond of glittering generalities; and he was possessed by a restless vanity. All these things conspired to produce the result.

J. Gray, The Nature and Sources of the Law 238–39 (1909).

7. Additional reading. After a long period of neglect and distortion, several modern studies of *Swift v. Tyson* and its jurisprudential underpinnings have appeared. R. Bridwell & R. Whitten, The Constitution and the Common Law (1977); T. Freyer, Forums of Order: The Federal Courts and Business in American History (1977); Harmony and Dissonance: The *Swift* and *Erie* Cases in American Federalism (1981); Fletcher, The General Common Law and Section 34 of the Judiciary Act of 1789: The Example of Marine Insurance, 97 Harv.L.Rev. 1513 (1984); Jay, Origins of Federal Common Law: Part One and Part Two, 133 U.Pa.L.Rev. 1003, 1231 (1985). There is no comprehensive legal history of *Swift* during the post-Civil War period. Two excellent histories covering some of this ground are C. Fairman, Reconstruction and Reunion, 1864–88, Part One 918–1116 (1971); E. Purcell, Litigation and Inequality (1992). See also E. Purcell, Brandeis and the Progressive Constitution: *Erie*, the Judicial Power, and the Politics of the Federal Courts in Twentieth-Century America (2000).

Erie Railroad Co. v. Tompkins

Supreme Court of the United States, 1938.
304 U.S. 64, 58 S.Ct. 817, 82 L.Ed. 1188.

■ MR. JUSTICE BRANDEIS delivered the opinion of the Court.

The question for decision is whether the oft-challenged doctrine of Swift v. Tyson shall now be disapproved.

Tompkins, a citizen of Pennsylvania, was injured on a dark night by a passing freight train of the Erie Railroad Company while walking along its right of way at Hughestown in that state. He claimed that the accident occurred through negligence in the operation, or maintenance, of the train; that he was rightfully on the premises as licensee because on a commonly used beaten footpath which ran for a short distance alongside the tracks; and that he was struck by something which looked like a door projecting from one of the moving cars. To enforce that claim he brought an action in the federal court for Southern New York, which had jurisdiction because the company is a corporation of that state. It denied liability; and the case was tried by a jury.

The Erie insisted that its duty to Tompkins was no greater than that owed to a trespasser. It contended, among other things, that its duty to Tompkins, and hence its liability, should be determined in accordance with Pennsylvania law; that under the law of Pennsylvania, as declared by its highest court, persons who use pathways along the railroad right of way—that is, a longitudinal pathway as distinguished from a crossing—are to be deemed trespassers; and that the railroad is not liable for injuries to undiscovered trespassers resulting from its negligence unless it be wanton or willful. Tompkins denied that any such rule had been established by the decisions of the Pennsylvania courts; and contended that, since there was no statute of the state on the subject, the railroad's duty and liability is to be determined in federal courts as a matter of general law.

The trial judge refused to rule that the applicable law precluded recovery. The jury brought in a verdict of $30,000; and the judgment entered thereon was affirmed by the Circuit Court of Appeals, which held (2 Cir., 90 F.2d 603, 604), that it was unnecessary to consider whether the law of Pennsylvania was as contended, because the question was one not of local, but of general, law, and that "upon questions of general law the federal courts are free, in absence of a local statute, to exercise their independent judgment as to what the law is; and it is well settled that the question of the responsibility of a railroad for injuries caused by its servants is one of general law. . . . Where the public has made open and notorious use of a railroad right of way for a long period of time and without objection, the company owes to persons on such permissive pathway a duty of care in the operation of its trains. . . . It is likewise generally recognized law that a jury may find that negligence exists toward a pedestrian using a permissive path on the railroad right of way if he is hit by some object projecting from the side of the train."

The Erie had contended that application of the Pennsylvania rule was required, among other things, by section 34 of the Federal Judiciary Act of September 24, 1789, c. 20, 28 U.S.C. § 725, 28 U.S.C.A. § 725, which provides: "The laws of the several States, except where the Constitution, treaties, or statutes of the United States otherwise require or provide, shall be regarded as rules of decision in trials at common law, in the courts of the United States, in cases where they apply."*

Because of the importance of the question whether the federal court was free to disregard the alleged rule of the Pennsylvania common law, we granted certiorari. 302 U.S. 671, 58 S.Ct. 50, 82 L.Ed. 518.

First. Swift v. Tyson, 16 Pet. 1, 18, 10 L.Ed. 865, held that federal courts exercising jurisdiction on the ground of diversity of citizenship need not, in matters of general jurisprudence, apply the unwritten law of the state as declared by its highest court; that they are free to exercise an independent judgment as to what the common law of the state is—or should be; and that, as there stated by Mr. Justice Story, "the true interpretation of the 34th section limited its application to state laws, strictly local, that is to say, to the positive statutes of the state, and the construction thereof adopted by the local tribunals, and to rights and titles to things having a permanent locality such as the rights and titles to real estate, and other matters immovable and intra-territorial in their nature and character. It never has been supposed by us, that the section did apply, or was designed to apply, to questions of a more general nature, not at all dependent upon local statutes or local usages of a fixed and permanent operation, as, for example, to the construction of ordinary contracts or other written instruments, and especially to questions of general commercial law, where the state tribunals are called upon to perform the like functions as ourselves, that is, to ascertain, upon general reasoning and legal analogies, what is the true exposition of the contract or instrument, or what is the just rule furnished by the principles of commercial law to govern the case."

The Court in applying the rule of section 34 to equity cases, in Mason v. United States, 260 U.S. 545, 559, 43 S.Ct. 200, 204, 67 L.Ed. 396, said: "The statute, however, is merely declarative of the rule which would exist in the absence of the statute." The federal courts assumed, in the broad field of "general law," the power to declare rules of decision which Congress was confessedly without power to enact as statutes. Doubt was repeatedly expressed as to the correctness of the construction given section 34, and as to the soundness of the rule which it introduced. But it was the more recent research of a competent scholar, who examined the original document, which established that the construction given to it by the Court was erroneous; and that the purpose of the section was merely to make certain that, in all matters except those in which some federal law is controlling, the federal courts exercising jurisdiction in diversity of citizenship cases would apply as their rules of decision the law of the state, unwritten as well as written.[5]

Criticism of the doctrine became widespread after the decision of Black & White Taxicab & Transfer Co. v. Brown & Yellow Taxicab & Transfer Co., 276 U.S. 518, 48 S.Ct. 404, 72 L.Ed. 681, 57 A.L.R. 426. There, Brown & Yellow, a Kentucky corporation owned by Kentuckians, and the Louisville & Nashville Railroad, also a Kentucky corporation,

---

* [Now 28 U.S.C.A. § 1652, applying to "civil actions" rather than merely to "trials at common law" by reason of the 1948 revision of the Judicial Code.]

[5] Charles Warren, New Light on the History of the Federal Judiciary Act of 1789 (1923) 37 Harv.L.Rev. 49, 51–52, 81–88, 108.

wished that the former should have the exclusive privilege of soliciting passenger and baggage transportation at the Bowling Green, Ky., railroad station; and that the Black & White, a competing Kentucky corporation, should be prevented from interfering with that privilege. Knowing that such a contract would be void under the common law of Kentucky, it was arranged that the Brown & Yellow reincorporate under the law of Tennessee, and that the contract with the railroad should be executed there. The suit was then brought by the Tennessee corporation in the federal court for Western Kentucky to enjoin competition by the Black & White; an injunction issued by the District Court was sustained by the Court of Appeals; and this Court, citing many decisions in which the doctrine of Swift v. Tyson had been applied, affirmed the decree.

Second. Experience in applying the doctrine of Swift v. Tyson, had revealed its defects, political and social; and the benefits expected to flow from the rule did not accrue. Persistence of state courts in their own opinions on questions of common law prevented uniformity; and the impossibility of discovering a satisfactory line of demarcation between the province of general law and that of local law developed a new well of uncertainties.

On the other hand, the mischievous results of the doctrine had become apparent. Diversity of citizenship jurisdiction was conferred in order to prevent apprehended discrimination in state courts against those not citizens of the state. Swift v. Tyson introduced grave discrimination by noncitizens against citizens. It made rights enjoyed under the unwritten "general law" vary according to whether enforcement was sought in the state or in the federal court; and the privilege of selecting the court in which the right should be determined was conferred upon the noncitizen. Thus, the doctrine rendered impossible equal protection of the law. In attempting to promote uniformity of law throughout the United States, the doctrine had prevented uniformity in the administration of the law of the state.

The discrimination resulting became in practice far-reaching. This resulted in part from the broad province accorded to the so-called "general law" as to which federal courts exercised an independent judgment. In addition to questions of purely commercial law, "general law" was held to include the obligations under contracts entered into and to be performed within the state; the extent to which a carrier operating within a state may stipulate for exemption from liability for his own negligence or that of his employee; the liability for torts committed within the state upon persons resident or property located there, even where the question of liability depended upon the scope of a property right conferred by the state; and the right to exemplary or punitive damages. Furthermore, state decisions construing local deeds, mineral conveyances, and even devises of real estate, were disregarded.

In part the discrimination resulted from the wide range of persons held entitled to avail themselves of the federal rule by resort to the diversity of citizenship jurisdiction. Through this jurisdiction individual citizens willing to remove from their own state and become citizens of another might avail themselves of the federal rule. And, without even change of residence, a corporate citizen of the state could avail itself of the federal rule by reincorporating under the laws of another state, as was done in the Taxicab Case.

The injustice and confusion incident to the doctrine of Swift v. Tyson have been repeatedly urged as reasons for abolishing or limiting diversity of citizenship jurisdiction. Other legislative relief has been proposed.[21] If only a question of statutory construction were involved, we should not be prepared to abandon a doctrine so widely applied throughout nearly a century.[22] But the unconstitutionality of the course pursued has now been made clear, and compels us to do so.

Third. Except in matters governed by the Federal Constitution or by acts of Congress, the law to be applied in any case is the law of the state. And whether the law of the state shall be declared by its Legislature in a statute or by its highest court in a decision is not a matter of federal concern. There is no federal general common law. Congress has no power to declare substantive rules of common law applicable in a state whether they be local in their nature or "general," be they commercial law or a part of the law of torts. And no clause in the Constitution purports to confer such a power upon the federal courts. As stated by Mr. Justice Field when protesting in Baltimore & Ohio R.R. Co. v. Baugh, 149 U.S. 368, 401, 13 S.Ct. 914, 927, 37 L.Ed. 772, against ignoring the Ohio common law of fellow-servant liability: "I am aware that what has been termed the general law of the country—which is often little less than what the judge advancing the doctrine thinks at the time should be the general law on a particular subject—has been often advanced in judicial opinions of this court to control a conflicting law of a state. I admit that learned judges have fallen into the habit of repeating this doctrine as a convenient mode of brushing aside the law of a state in conflict with their views. And I confess, that, moved and governed by the authority of the great names of those judges, I have, myself, in many instances, unhesitatingly and confidently, but I think now erroneously, repeated the same doctrine. But, notwithstanding the great names which may be cited in favor of the doctrine, and notwithstanding the frequency with which the doctrine has been reiterated, there stands, as a perpetual protest against its repetition, the constitution of the United States, which recognizes and preserves the autonomy and independence of the states,— independence in their legislative and independence in their judicial departments. Supervision over either the legislative or the judicial action of the states is in no case permissible except as to matters by the constitution specifically authorized or delegated to the United States. Any interference with either, except as thus permitted, is an invasion of

---

[21] Thus, bills which would abrogate the doctrine of Swift v. Tyson have been introduced. S. 4333, 70th Cong., 1st Sess.; S. 96, 71st Cong., 1st Sess.; H.R. 8094, 72d Cong., 1st Sess. See, also, Mills, supra, note 4 at 68, 69; Dobie, supra, note 6, at 241; Frankfurter, supra, note 6, at 530; Campbell, supra, note 6, at 811. State statutes on conflicting questions of "general law" have also been suggested. See Heiskell, supra, note 4, at 760; Dawson, supra, note 6; Dobie, supra, note 6, at 241.

[22] The doctrine has not been without defenders. See Eliot, The Common Law of the Federal Courts (1902) 36 Am.L.Rev. 498, 523–525; A.B. Parker, The Common Law Jurisdiction of the United States Courts (1907) 17 Yale L.J. 1; Schofield, Swift v. Tyson: Uniformity of Judge-Made State Law in State and Federal Courts (1910) 4 Ill.L.Rev. 533; Brown, The Jurisdiction of the Federal Courts Based on Diversity of Citizenship (1929) 78 U. of Pa.L.Rev. 179, 189–191; J.J. Parker, The Federal Jurisdiction and Recent Attacks Upon It (1932) 18 A.B.A.J. 433, 438; Yntema, The Jurisdiction of the Federal Courts in Controversies Between Citizens of Different States (1933) 19 A.B.A.J. 71, 74, 75; Beutel, Common Law Judicial Technique and the Law of Negotiable Instruments—Two Unfortunate Decisions (1934) 9 Tulane L.Rev. 64.

the authority of the state, and, to that extent, a denial of its independence."

The fallacy underlying the rule declared in Swift v. Tyson is made clear by Mr. Justice Holmes.[23] The doctrine rests upon the assumption that there is "a transcendental body of law outside of any particular State but obligatory within it unless and until changed by statute," that federal courts have the power to use their judgment as to what the rules of common law are; and that in the federal courts "the parties are entitled to an independent judgment on matters of general law":

"But the law in the sense in which courts speak of it today does not exist without some definite authority behind it. The common law so far as it is enforced in a State, whether called common law or not, is not the common law generally but the law of that State existing by the authority of that State without regard to what it may have been in England or anywhere else. . . .

"The authority and only authority is the State, and if that be so, the voice adopted by the State as its own [whether it be of its Legislature or of its Supreme Court] should utter the last word."

Thus the doctrine of Swift v. Tyson is, as Mr. Justice Holmes said, "an unconstitutional assumption of powers by the Courts of the United States which no lapse of time or respectable array of opinion should make us hesitate to correct." In disapproving that doctrine we do not hold unconstitutional section 34 of the Federal Judiciary Act of 1789 or any other act of Congress. We merely declare that in applying the doctrine this Court and the lower courts have invaded rights which in our opinion are reserved by the Constitution to the several states.

Fourth. The defendant contended that by the common law of Pennsylvania as declared by its highest court in Falchetti v. Pennsylvania R. Co., 307 Pa. 203, 160 A. 859, the only duty owed to the plaintiff was to refrain from willful or wanton injury. The plaintiff denied that such is the Pennsylvania law. In support of their respective contentions the parties discussed and cited many decisions of the Supreme Court of the state. The Circuit Court of Appeals ruled that the question of liability is one of general law; and on that ground declined to decide the issue of state law. As we hold this was error, the judgment is reversed and the case remanded to it for further proceedings in conformity with our opinion.

Reversed.*

■ MR. JUSTICE CARDOZO took no part in the consideration or decision of this case.

■ MR. JUSTICE REED (concurring in part).

I concur in the conclusion reached in this case, in the disapproval of the doctrine of Swift v. Tyson, and in the reasoning of the majority opinion, except in so far as it relies upon the unconstitutionality of the "course pursued" by the federal courts.

---

[23] Kuhn v. Fairmont Coal Co., 215 U.S. 349, 370–372, 30 S.Ct. 140, 54 L.Ed. 228; Black & White Taxicab, etc., Co. v. Brown & Yellow Taxicab, etc., Co., 276 U.S. 518, 532–536, 48 S.Ct. 404, 408, 409, 72 L.Ed. 681, 57 A.L.R. 426.

* The dissenting opinion of Butler, J., joined by McReynolds, J., is omitted.

The "doctrine of Swift v. Tyson," as I understand it, is that the words "the laws," as used in section 34, line 1, of the Federal Judiciary Act of September 24, 1789, 28 U.S.C.A. § 725, do not include in their meaning "the decisions of the local tribunals." Mr. Justice Story, in deciding that point, said, 16 Pet. 1, 19, 10 L.Ed. 865: "Undoubtedly, the decisions of the local tribunals upon such subjects are entitled to, and will receive, the most deliberate attention and respect of this court; but they cannot furnish positive rules, or conclusive authority, by which our own judgments are to be bound up and governed."

To decide the case now before us and to "disapprove" the doctrine of Swift v. Tyson requires only that we say that the words "the laws" include in their meaning the decisions of the local tribunals. As the majority opinion shows, by its reference to Mr. Warren's researches and the first quotation from Mr. Justice Holmes, that this Court is now of the view that "laws" includes "decisions," it is unnecessary to go further and declare that the "course pursued" was "unconstitutional," instead of merely erroneous.

The "unconstitutional" course referred to in the majority opinion is apparently the ruling in Swift v. Tyson that the supposed omission of Congress to legislate as to the effect of decisions leaves federal courts free to interpret general law for themselves. I am not at all sure whether, in the absence of federal statutory direction, federal courts would be compelled to follow state decisions. There was sufficient doubt about the matter in 1789 to induce the first Congress to legislate. No former opinions of this Court have passed upon it. Mr. Justice Holmes evidently saw nothing "unconstitutional" which required the overruling of Swift v. Tyson, for he said in the very opinion quoted by the majority, "I should leave Swift v. Tyson undisturbed, as I indicated in Kuhn v. Fairmont Coal Co., but I would not allow it to spread the assumed dominion into new fields." Black & White Taxicab Co. v. Brown & Yellow Taxicab Co., 276 U.S. 518, 535, 48 S.Ct. 404, 409, 72 L.Ed. 681, 57 A.L.R. 426. If the opinion commits this Court to the position that the Congress is without power to declare what rules of substantive law shall govern the federal courts, that conclusion also seems questionable. The line between procedural and substantive law is hazy, but no one doubts federal power over procedure. Wayman v. Southard, 10 Wheat. 1, 6 L.Ed. 253. The Judiciary Article, 3, and the "necessary and proper" clause of article 1, § 8, may fully authorize legislation, such as this section of the Judiciary Act.

In this Court, stare decisis, in statutory construction, is a useful rule, not an inexorable command. Burnet v. Coronado Oil & Gas Co., 285 U.S. 393, dissent, page 406, note 1, 52 S.Ct. 443, 446, 76 L.Ed. 815. Compare Read v. Bishop of Lincoln, [1892] A.C. 644, 655; London Street Tramways v. London County Council, [1898] A.C. 375, 379. It seems preferable to overturn an established construction of an act of Congress, rather than, in the circumstances of this case, to interpret the Constitution. Cf. United States v. Delaware & Hudson Co., 213 U.S. 366, 29 S.Ct. 527, 53 L.Ed. 836.

There is no occasion to discuss further the range or soundness of these few phrases of the opinion. It is sufficient now to call attention to them and express my own nonacquiescence.

■ Dissenting opinion of MR. JUSTICE BUTLER, joined by MR. JUSTICE MCREYNOLDS, is omitted.]

NOTE ON *ERIE*

1.   *Erie* as a surprise. The litigants in *Erie* were somewhat surprised by the Court's holding. Although Justice Brandeis' opinion begins, "The question for decision is whether the oft-challenged doctrine of Swift v. Tyson shall now be disapproved," that question had not been addressed by the parties at any stage of the proceedings. Review had been granted to determine, and argument before the Supreme Court had been limited to, the question of whether the responsibility of the railroad to Mr. Tompkins was governed by local or general law. But the "question for decision" had been in the minds of the Justices, and the profession at large, for more than a generation, and it is unlikely that the parties could have written or said anything to change the minds of any of the Justices. Note the alignment of the parties in *Erie*. The railroad argued that the local (i.e., Pennsylvania) law governed the dispute, and Tompkins argued that the general law governed. That the parties should have been so aligned was unusual, for big business had been the prime beneficiary of the regime of *Swift v. Tyson* and the general law.

2.   Grounds for the decision in *Erie*. Justice Brandeis gave essentially three grounds for the Court's decision in *Erie*. The first was almost certainly wrong; the second valid and important; and the third valid only in a very limited sense.

a.   *Swift v. Tyson* misinterpreted the Rules of Decision Act. Justice Brandeis concludes that *Swift v. Tyson* misinterpreted Section 34 of the Judiciary Act of 1789, now known as the Rules of Decision Act. In support of this conclusion, he cites the work of a noted historian, Charles Warren, who had found an original draft of the Judiciary Act of 1789. The draft showed that in an amendment to Section 34 of the Act, the phrase "*statute law* of the several States" had been struck and then replaced by the word "*laws* of the several States." Warren concluded from the change—almost certainly correctly—that the Judiciary Act's adopters intended to include not only statutory law but also judge-made common law. But Warren missed the distinction between "local" law and "general" law, and therefore concluded— almost certainly incorrectly—that federal courts were required by the statute to follow *all* rules of judge-made law established by the state courts, both local and general. Thus, according to Warren, the state law that federal courts were obliged to follow necessarily included rules of "local" law in areas where rules of "general" law were also available. Warren's ultimate conclusion was that Story and the *Swift v. Tyson* Court had plainly misconstrued Section 34: "Had Judge Story seen this original draft of the amendment, it is almost certain that his decision would have been the reverse of what it was." Warren, New Light on the History of the Federal Judiciary Act of 1789, 37 Harv.L.Rev. 49, 52 (1923).

b.   The experience under *Swift v. Tyson* revealed its practical defects. Justice Brandeis points to the injustice and confusion that resulted from *Swift v. Tyson*. The accident of diversity of citizenship could result in the availability of a federal forum with a different and more advantageous rule of law. Indeed, in the famous *Black & White Taxicab* case, discussed in Brandeis' opinion, a company reincorporated in another state for no other reason than to create diversity of citizenship and to seek the advantageous federal rule. Moreover, as Justice Brandeis points out, the benefits of uniformity "expected to flow from the rule" of *Swift v. Tyson* had largely disappeared in the late nineteenth and early twentieth centuries. For discussion, see Gilmore, Legal Realism: Its Cause and Cure, 70 Yale L.J. 1037 (1961) (arguing that other mechanisms, such as ALI Restatements, better served *Swift*'s function of encouraging uniformity). Observe, however, that Brandeis refers to "unequal protection of the law" concerning "rights," suggesting that he views the matter as involving more than merely practical problems.

     c.   ***Swift v. Tyson* went beyond the powers granted to the federal government.** Justice Brandeis writes that the federal government unconstitutionally usurped the powers belonging to the states, saying that the federal government as a whole is disabled from legislating rules of tort or contract law in the areas covered by the general common law. This statement was close-to-untrue when made, and became clearly untrue soon thereafter, for the Supreme Court was at that very moment embarking on an expanded interpretation of the powers of the federal government under the Commerce Clause of the Constitution. See, e.g., NLRB v. Jones & Laughlin Steel Corp., 301 U.S. 1, 57 S.Ct. 615, 81 L.Ed. 893 (1937); United States v. Darby, 312 U.S. 100, 61 S.Ct. 451, 85 L.Ed. 609 (1941). Justice Brandeis appears also to argue that the federal judiciary, as distinct from the federal government as a whole, is not constitutionally empowered to create rules in these areas, especially when those rules are available only to litigants who can invoke the diversity jurisdiction. This is an important argument, based partly on separation of powers and partly on fairness. It is not clear, however, that the argument sustains a conclusion of unconstitutionality of judicial action. Further, the argument in no way disables the federal government from enacting generally applicable federal statutory law in these areas.

     3.   ***Swift v. Tyson*, *Erie*, and the changing meaning of the Rules of Decision Act.** Both *Swift v. Tyson* and *Erie* interpreted the Rules of Decision Act, construing it to fit the conceptual frameworks and practical needs of their respective centuries. The present Rules of Decision Act provides:

> The laws of the several states, except where the Constitution or treaties of the United States or Acts of Congress otherwise require or provide, shall be regarded as rules of decision in civil actions in the courts of the United States, in cases where they apply.

28 U.S.C. § 1652. The words of the statute, "the laws of the several states," remain unchanged from the original Section 34 of the 1789 Judiciary Act. But their meaning has changed. Under *Swift v. Tyson*, there were three categories of domestic law—federal, general, and state. Erie abolished the category of general law. Now, after *Erie*, there are only two categories—federal and state. If a domestic law is not federal, it is necessarily state, for now, in the words of Justice Brandeis in *Erie*, "There is no federal general common law."

     4.   ***Erie* and "positive" law.** The Justices who decided *Swift v. Tyson* relied on the concept of a general law shared among states but not belonging to any single state. Peter DuPonceau, an early nineteenth century lawyer, described this general or common law as

a general system of jurisprudence, constantly hovering over the local legislation and filling up its interstices. It was ready to pour in at every opening that it could find. Like the sun under a cloud, it was overshadowed, not extinguished by the local laws * * *. It burst in at the moment of the adoption of the Constitution of the United States, and filled up every space which the State laws ceased to occupy.

P. DuPonceau, A Dissertation on the Nature and Extent of the Jurisdiction of the Courts of the United States 88 (1824). A reviewer of DuPonceau's book enthusiastically endorsed his metaphor, referring to the general law as a law "floating in the atmosphere." 21 North American Review 104, 139 (1825).

Justice Holmes, almost one hundred years later, disagreed as to the nature of law. Possibly taking deliberate aim at DuPonceau and his reviewer, he wrote: "The common law is not some brooding omnipresence in the sky, but the articulate voice of some sovereign or quasi-sovereign that can be identified." Southern Pacific Co. v. Jensen, 244 U.S. 205, 222, 37 S.Ct. 524, 61 L.Ed. 1086 (1917). In the almost-century between DuPonceau and Holmes, the concept of a general law shared among sovereigns had largely disappeared, replaced by the concept of a "positive" law created and sustained by a single sovereign (or quasi-sovereign) government.

5.   **Related developments in constitutional law.** It would take us too far afield from Civil Procedure to explore the topic thoroughly, but contemporaneous developments in constitutional law cast an interesting cross-light on *Erie*. One year before *Erie*, in West Coast Hotel Co. v. Parrish, 300 U.S. 379, 57 S.Ct. 578, 81 L.Ed. 703 (1937), the Court had upheld, by a five to four vote, a state minimum wage statute against a federal constitutional challenge. This case, and several others decided in the next few years, were the culmination of a bitter fight between President Franklin Roosevelt and the conservative Justices of the Supreme Court. During the early years of the twentieth century, the Court had repeatedly struck down as unconstitutional economic legislation enacted by the states and, during the 1930s, by the U.S. Congress. Roughly speaking, such legislation, both state and federal, sought to control business enterprises and to protect workers and consumers. In early 1937, Roosevelt sought legislation that would have expanded the membership of the Supreme Court. Roosevelt planned to fill the new positions with Justices sympathetic to the New Deal, so that, with a newly created liberal majority, the enlarged Court would sustain rather than strike down such economic legislation. In *West Coast Hotel*, Justice Roberts abandoned his generally conservative position to vote with the liberal majority and to sustain the challenged state minimum wage statute. When it became apparent that the Court would sustain this and comparable legislation in the future, Congress' support for Roosevelt's Court-packing plan dissipated, and the membership of the Court remained at nine. (Roberts' change of position came to be known as the "switch in time that saved nine.") Then, within a year of *West Coast Hotel*, Justices of the old conservative majority began resigning, giving Roosevelt the appointments he had unsuccessfully sought through his plan. See Leuchtenburg, The Origins of Franklin D. Roosevelt's "Court-Packing" Plan, 1966 Sup.Ct.Rev. 347.

The decision in *West Coast Hotel* was of a piece with *Erie*. The Justices who had previously struck down the state and federal economic legislation were largely those who had previously voted to uphold *Swift v. Tyson* and its general law. This is not surprising, for the social and economic considerations that led to a distaste for Progressive and Democratic economic legislation also led to an affection for *Swift v. Tyson*. The kinship of *West Coast Hotel* and *Erie* may been seen in the alignment of the Justices. In *West Coast Hotel*, the majority consisted of Chief Justice Hughes, joined by Justices Brandeis, Cardozo, Roberts and Stone. The four dissenters were Justices Butler, McReynolds, Sutherland, and VanDevanter. In the Court's last major pre-*Erie* encounter with *Swift*, the four *West Coast Hotel* dissenters were in the majority, and they supported an expansive interpretation of *Swift v. Tyson* and the general law. Black and White Taxicab & Transfer Co. v. Brown and Yellow Taxicab & Transfer Co., 276 U.S. 518, 48 S.Ct. 404, 72 L.Ed.2d 681 (1928). (Justice Roberts was not in either group, for he was not appointed to the Court until 1930, two years later.) In *Erie* itself, the majority consisted of Justice Brandeis, joined by Chief Justice Hughes and Justices Black, Reed, Roberts, and Stone. (Justice Cardozo did not participate due to illness.) Black and Reed were two new Roosevelt appointees, replacing Sutherland and VanDevanter. Justice Butler, joined by McReynolds, wrote separately to object to the sudden overruling of *Swift v. Tyson*.

6. Additional reading. There is an enormous literature on *Erie*. A sampling includes Shulman, The Demise of *Swift v. Tyson*, 47 Yale L.J. 1336 (1938); Clark, State Law in the Federal Courts: The Brooding Omnipresence of *Erie v. Tompkins*, 55 Yale L.J. 267 (1946); Kurland, Mr. Justice Frankfurter, the Supreme Court and the *Erie* Doctrine in Diversity Cases, 67 Yale L.J. 187 (1957); Friendly, In Praise of *Erie*—and of the New Federal Common Law, 39 N.Y.U. L. Rev. 383 (1964); Ely, The Irrepressible Myth of *Erie*, 87 Harv. L. Rev. 693 (1974); Younger, What Happened in *Erie*, 56 Tex. L.Rev. 1011 (1978) (includes picture); Westen and Lehman, Is There Life for *Erie* after the Death of Diversity?, 78 Mich. L. Rev. 311 (1981), Redish, Continuing the *Erie* Debate: A Response to Westen and Lehman, 78 Mich. L. Rev. 959 (1982); Westen, After "Life for *Erie*"—A Reply, 78 Mich. L. Rev. 971 (1982); Ides, The Supreme Court and the Law to Be Applied in Diversity Cases: A Critical Guide to the Development and Application of the *Erie* Doctrine and Related Problems, 163 F.R.D. 21 (1995); Bauer, The *Erie* Doctrine Revisited: How a Conflicts Perspective Can Aid the Analysis, 74 Notre Dame L. Rev. 1235 (1999).

NOTE ON *ERIE* AND THE SUBSTANCE/PROCEDURE DISTINCTION

1. The substance/procedure distinction. The effect of *Erie* on substantive law is plain. Two previous categories of substantive law—general and local—were collapsed into one, and became, for purposes of the Rules of Decision Act, state law that the federal courts were obliged to follow. But what about procedural law? Did *Erie* and the Rules of Decision Act apply to matters of procedure? Most of the cases in the remainder of the chapter will deal with this question.

2. The Rules Enabling Act and the Federal Rules of Civil Procedure. For 150 years, the federal courts mostly followed the procedural rules of the states in which they sat. The most recent regulation of the matter prior to the Rules Enabling Act of 1934 was the Conformity Act of 1872, which provided:

> The practice, pleadings, and forms and modes of proceeding, in other than equity and admiralty cases * * * shall conform, as near as may be, to the practice, pleadings and forms and modes of proceedings existing at the time in like causes in the courts of record of the State within which such * * * District Courts are held * * *.

17 Stat. 196, 197 (June 1, 1872). Under the Conformity Act, the federal courts in New York and Massachusetts, in cases at law (that is, non-equity and non-admiralty cases), followed different procedural rules, more or less to the extent that the state courts of New York and Massachusetts themselves followed different rules. As a corollary, within the same state the federal and state courts in cases at law followed "as near as may be" the same procedural rules. Had the Conformity Act remained in effect, the substance/procedure question under *Erie* thus would have arisen infrequently in cases at law, for the federal courts would have been required by the Act to adhere fairly closely to state procedures. The question would rarely have arisen in admiralty, for the state courts had (and have) no admiralty jurisdiction.

In equity, however, the federal and state courts followed different rules. Some, though not all, states declined to create equity courts at all after the Revolution. In those states it obviously would have been impossible for the federal courts to follow local or state equity procedures. But even in the states that had equity courts, the federal courts went their own way, with the consequence that the federal courts developed, independently of the states, a full system of procedural rules governing suits brought in equity. See generally Subrin, How Equity Conquered Common Law: The Federal Rules of Civil Procedure in Historical Perspective, 135 U.Pa.L.Rev. 909 (1987).

At the same time the Supreme Court moved in *Erie* to require the federal courts to conform their decisions to those of the states on matters of substantive law, Congress moved in precisely the opposite direction on matters of procedural law. In 1934, four years before the Court's decision in *Erie*, Congress enacted the Rules Enabling Act, authorizing the adoption of a uniform system of procedural rules for civil cases in the federal courts. The Act provided:

> [T]he Supreme Court * * * shall have the power to prescribe by general rules, for the District Courts * * * the forms of process, writs, pleadings, and motions, and the practice and procedure in civil actions at law. Said rules shall neither abridge, enlarge or modify the substantive rights of any litigant. * * * The court may at any time unite the general rules prescribed by it for cases in equity with those in actions at law so as to secure one form of civil action and procedure for both.

Reprinted in Burbank, The Rules Enabling Act of 1934, 130 U.Pa.L.Rev. 1015, 1097–98 (1982). (The present form of the Act is at 28 U.S.C. § 2072.) Then in 1938, the same year *Erie* was decided, the Federal Rules of Civil Procedure were adopted. In their current form, "These rules govern the procedure in all civil actions and proceedings in the United States district courts, except as stated in Rule 81." Fed. R. Civ. P. 1. For an excellent history of the Act, see Burbank, supra.

Guaranty Trust Co. v. York

Supreme Court of the United States, 1945.
326 U.S. 99, 65 S.Ct. 1464, 89 L.Ed. 2079.

[In 1942 plaintiff York filed in New York federal District Court a diversity suit in equity for fraud in connection with certain transactions in which defendant participated in 1931. Defendant pleaded the statute of limitations, invoking the New York rule that the statute of limitations period applied alike to actions at law and in equity. Plaintiff contended that the more flexible doctrine of laches, traditionally followed by the federal courts in equity suits, should be followed. The Court of Appeals held that the federal trial court should have applied, not the New York "strict" time rule, but the more elastic federal laches doctrine, and accordingly reversed a summary judgment which had been entered for defendant. Defendant sought certiorari.]

■ MR. JUSTICE FRANKFURTER delivered the opinion of the Court.

* * *

[T]his case reduces itself to the narrow question whether, when no recovery could be had in a State court because the action is barred by the statute of limitations, a federal court in equity can take cognizance of the suit because there is diversity of citizenship between the parties. Is the outlawry, according to State law, of a claim created by the States a matter of "substantive rights" to be respected by a federal court of equity when that court's jurisdiction is dependent on the fact that there is a State-created right, or is such statute of "a mere remedial character," Henrietta Mills v. Rutherford Co., supra, 281 U.S. at page 128, 50 S.Ct. at page 272, 74 L.Ed. 737, which a federal court may disregard?

Matters of "substance" and matters of "procedure" are much talked about in the books as though they defined a great divide cutting across the whole domain of law. But, of course, "substance" and "procedure" are the same key-words to very different problems. Neither "substance" nor "procedure" represents the same invariants. Each implies different variables depending upon the particular problem for which it is used. See Home Ins. Co. v. Dick, 281 U.S. 397, 409, 50 S.Ct. 338, 341, 74 L.Ed. 926, 74 A.L.R. 701. And the different problems are only distantly related at best, for the terms are in common use in connection with situations turning on such different considerations as those that are relevant to questions pertaining to ex post facto legislation, the impairment of the obligations of contract, the enforcement of federal rights in the State courts and the multitudinous phases of the conflict of laws.

Here we are dealing with a right to recover derived not from the United States but from one of the States. When, because the plaintiff happens to be a non-resident, such a right is enforceable in a federal as well as in a State court, the forms and mode of enforcing the right may at times, naturally enough, vary because the two judicial systems are not identic. But since a federal court adjudicating a state-created right solely because of the diversity of citizenship of the parties is for that purpose, in effect, only another court of the State, it cannot afford recovery if the right to recover is made unavailable by the State nor can it substantially affect the enforcement of the right as given by the State.

And so the question is not whether a statute of limitations is deemed a matter of "procedure" in some sense. The question is whether such a statute concerns merely the manner and the means by which a right to recover, as recognized by the State, is enforced, or whether such statutory limitation is a matter of substance in the aspect that alone is relevant to our problem, namely, does it significantly affect the result of a litigation for a federal court to disregard a law of a State that would be controlling in an action upon the same claim by the same parties in a State court?

It is therefore immaterial whether statutes of limitation are characterized either as "substantive" or "procedural" in State court opinions in any use of those terms unrelated to the specific issue before us. Erie R. Co. v. Tompkins was not an endeavor to formulate scientific legal terminology. It expressed a policy that touches vitally the proper distribution of judicial power between State and federal courts. In essence, the intent of that decision was to insure that, in all cases where a federal court is exercising jurisdiction solely because of the diversity of citizenship of the parties, the outcome of the litigation in the federal court should be substantially the same, so far as legal rules determine the outcome of a litigation, as it would be if tried in a State court. The nub of the policy that underlies Erie R. Co. v. Tompkins is that for the same transaction the accident of a suit by a non-resident litigant in a federal court instead of in a State court a block away, should not lead to a substantially different result. And so, putting to one side abstractions regarding "substance" and "procedure", we have held that in diversity cases the federal courts must follow the law of the State as to burden of proof, Cities Service Oil Co. v. Dunlap, 308 U.S. 208, 60 S.Ct. 201, 84 L.Ed. 196, as to conflict of laws, Klaxon Co. v. Stentor Co., 313 U.S. 487, 61 S.Ct. 1020, 85 L.Ed. 1477, as to contributory negligence, Palmer v. Hoffman, 318 U.S. 109, 117, 63 S.Ct. 477, 482, 87 L.Ed. 645, 144 A.L.R. 719. Erie R. Co. v. Tompkins has been applied with an eye alert to essentials in avoiding disregard of State law in diversity cases in the federal courts. A policy so important to our federalism must be kept free from entanglements with analytical or terminological niceties.

Plainly enough, a statute that would completely bar recovery in a suit if brought in a State court bears on a State-created right vitally and not merely formally or negligibly. As to consequences that so intimately affect recovery or nonrecovery a federal court in a diversity case should follow State law. The fact that under New York law a statute of limitations might be lengthened or shortened, that a security may be foreclosed though the debt be barred, that a barred debt may be used as a set-off, are all matters of local law properly to be respected by federal courts sitting in New York when their incidence comes into play there. Such particular rules of local law, however, do not in the slightest change the crucial consideration that if a plea of the statute of limitations would bar recovery in a State court, a federal court ought not to afford recovery.

* * *

To make an exception to Erie R. Co. v. Tompkins on the equity side of a federal court is to reject the considerations of policy which, after long travail, led to that decision. Judge Augustus N. Hand thus summarized below the fatal objection to such inroad upon Erie R. Co. v. Tompkins: "In my opinion it would be a mischievous practice to disregard state statutes of limitations whenever federal courts think that the result of adopting them may be inequitable. Such procedure would promote the choice of United States rather than of state courts in order to gain the advantage of different laws. The main foundation for the criticism of Swift v. Tyson was that a litigant in cases where federal jurisdiction is based only on diverse citizenship may obtain a more favorable decision by suing in the United States courts." 2 Cir., 143 F.2d 503, 529, 531.

Diversity jurisdiction is founded on assurance to non-resident litigants of courts free from susceptibility to potential local bias. The Framers of the Constitution, according to Marshall, entertained "apprehensions" lest distant suitors be subjected to local bias in State courts, or, at least, viewed with "indulgence the possible fears and apprehensions" of such suitors. Bank of the United States v. Deveaux, 5 Cranch 61, 87, 3 L.Ed. 38. And so Congress afforded out-of-State litigants another tribunal, not another body of law. The operation of a double system of conflicting laws in the same State is plainly hostile to the reign of law. Certainly, the fortuitous circumstance of residence out of a State of one of the parties to a litigation ought not to give rise to a discrimination against others equally concerned but locally resident. The source of substantive rights enforced by a federal court under diversity jurisdiction, it cannot be said too often, is the law of the States. Whenever that law is authoritatively declared by a State, whether its voice be the legislature or its highest court, such law ought to govern in litigation founded on that law, whether the forum of application is a State or a federal court and whether the remedies be sought at law or may be had in equity.

Dicta may be cited characterizing equity as an independent body of law. To the extent that we have indicated, it is. But insofar as these general observations go beyond that, they merely reflect notions that have been replaced by a sharper analysis of what federal courts do when they enforce rights that have no federal origin. And so, before the true source of law that is applied by the federal courts under diversity jurisdiction was fully explored, some things were said that would not now be said. But nothing that was decided, unless it be the Kirby case, needs to be rejected.

The judgment is reversed and the case is remanded for proceedings not inconsistent with this opinion.

■ MR. JUSTICE ROBERTS and MR. JUSTICE DOUGLAS took no part in the consideration or decision of this case.

■ MR. JUSTICE RUTLEDGE.

I dissent. * * *

The words "substantive" and "procedural" or "remedial" are not talismanic. Merely calling a legal question by one or the other does not resolve it otherwise than as a purely authoritarian performance. But they have come to designate in a broad way large and distinctive legal domains within the greater one of the law and to mark, though often indistinctly or with overlapping limits, many divides between such regions.

One of these historically has been the divide between the substantive law and the procedural or remedial law to be applied by the federal courts in diversity cases, a division sharpened but not wiped out by Erie R. Co.

v. Tompkins and subsequent decisions extending the scope of its ruling. The large division between adjective law and substantive law still remains, to divide the power of Congress from that of the states and consequently to determine the power of the federal courts to apply federal law or state law in diversity matters.

This division, like others drawn by the broad allocation of adjective or remedial and substantive, has areas of admixture of these two aspects of the law. In these areas whether a particular situation or issue presents one aspect or the other depends upon how one looks at the matter. As form cannot always be separated from substance in a work of art, so adjective or remedial aspects cannot be parted entirely from substantive ones in these borderland regions.

* * *

Applicable statutes of limitations in state tribunals are not always the ones which would apply if suit were instituted in the courts of the state which creates the substantive rights for which enforcement is sought. The state of the forum is free to apply its own period of limitations, regardless of whether the state originating the right has barred suit upon it. Whether or not the action will be held to be barred depends therefore not upon the law of the state which creates the substantive right, but upon the law of the state where suit may be brought. This in turn will depend upon where it may be possible to secure service of process, and thus jurisdiction of the person of the defendant. It may be therefore that because of the plaintiff's inability to find the defendant in the jurisdiction which creates his substantive right, he will be foreclosed of remedy by the sheer necessity of going to the haven of refuge within which the defendant confines its "presence" for jurisdictional purposes. The law of the latter may bar the suit even though suit still would be allowed under the law of the state creating the substantive right.

* * *

■ MR. JUSTICE MURPHY joins in this opinion.

NOTES AND QUESTIONS

1.   **The "outcome determinative" test.** *York* is often described as using an "outcome determinative" test. Justice Frankfurter framed the question as follows: "[D]oes it significantly affect the result of the litigation for a federal court to disregard a law of a State that would be controlling in an action upon the same claim by the same parties in a State court?" What does that mean? If the state statute of limitations applied in *York*, plaintiff lost, whereas if the federal laches period applied, plaintiff could pursue the suit. But aren't many procedural rules outcome determinative if they are disobeyed? For example, what about a state rule that requires a defendant to answer a complaint within 30 days, compared with federal Rule 12(a), which requires an answer with 21 days? The *York* Court cannot possibly mean that a federal court would have to allow 30 days for an answer in such a case.

2.   **Pre-*York* cases.** In one case before *York*, the Court upheld a Federal Rule of Civil Procedure against a challenge under Rules Enabling

Act and then followed the federal Rule. In several others, where there was no applicable federal Rule, the Court followed the state rule.

a.   Challenge under the Rules Enabling Act. In Sibbach v. Wilson & Co., 312 U.S. 1, 61 S.Ct. 422, 85 L.Ed. 479 (1941), plaintiff brought a diversity action for personal injuries in federal district court in Illinois. The district court ordered plaintiff to submit to a physical examination by a doctor under federal Rule 35(a). Compulsory physical examination of a party was not authorized in Illinois state courts. When plaintiff refused to submit to the examination, she was held in contempt under Rule 37. Plaintiff contended that these rules violated the restriction of the Rules Enabling Act that the "rules shall neither abridge, enlarge, nor modify the substantive rights of any litigant." The Supreme Court disagreed:

> * * * [P]etitioner admits, and we think, correctly, that Rules 35 and 37 are rules of procedure. She insists, nevertheless, that by the prohibition against abridging substantive rights, Congress has banned the rules here challenged. In order to reach this result she translates "substantive" into "important" or "substantial" rights. And she urges that if a rule affects such a right, albeit the rule is one of procedure merely, its prescription is not within the statutory grant of power embodied in the Act of June 19, 1934.
>
> * * *
>
> * * * If we were to adopt the suggested criterion of the importance of the alleged right we should invite endless litigation and confusion worse confounded. The test must be whether a rule really regulates procedure,—the judicial process for enforcing rights and duties recognized by substantive law and for justly administering remedy and redress for disregard or infraction of them. That the rules in question are such is admitted.

312 U.S. at 11, 14. Justice Frankfurter, joined by three other Justices, dissented. He would have held that Rule 35(a), authorizing a compelled physical examination, violated the Rules Enabling Act:

> [A] drastic change in public policy in a matter deeply touching the sensibilities of people or even their prejudices as to privacy, ought not to be inferred from a general authorization to formulate rules for the more uniform and effective dispatch of business on the civil side of the federal courts. I deem a requirement as to the invasion of the person to stand on a very different footing from questions pertaining to the discovery of documents, pre-trial procedure and other devices for the expeditious, economic and fair conduct of litigation. * * * I conclude that to make the drastic change that Rule 35 sought to introduce would require explicit legislation.

Id. at 18.

b.   No applicable federal Rule. There was (and is) no applicable Federal Rule of Civil Procedure governing burden of proof and choice of law.

(1)   Burden of proof. In Cities Service Oil Co. v. Dunlap, 308 U.S. 208, 60 S.Ct. 201, 84 L.Ed. 196 (1939), plaintiff filed a quiet title suit in federal district court in Texas. Under Texas law, the burden of proof of was on the defendant. There was no applicable Federal Rule of Civil Procedure. The Supreme Court followed the Texas rule: "We cannot accept the view that the question presented was only one of practice in courts of equity. Rather we think it relates to a substantial right upon which the holder of recorded legal title to Texas land may confidently rely." Id. at 212.

In Palmer v. Hoffman, 318 U.S. 109, 63 S.Ct. 477, 87 L.Ed. 645 (1943), plaintiff sued in federal district court in New York for personal injuries. The district judge instructed the jury that defendant had the burden of proving the defense of contributory negligence. Relying on *Cities Service*, the Supreme Court disagreed:

> [Plaintiff] contends in the first place that the charge was correct because of the fact that Rule 8(c) of the Rules of Civil Procedure makes contributory negligence an affirmative defense. * * * Rule 8(c) covers only the manner of pleading. The question of the burden of establishing contributory negligence is a question of local law which federal courts in diversity of citizenship cases * * * must apply.

Id. at 117.

(2) Choice of law. In Klaxon Co. v. Stentor Elec. Mfg. Co., 313 U.S. 487, 61 S.Ct. 1020, 85 L.Ed. 1477 (1941), plaintiff brought a breach of contract suit in federal district court in Delaware. The parties disagreed about whether New York law applied to one aspect of the suit. The Court held that the federal district court was required by *Erie* to follow the conflict of laws rules of the state in which it sat (in this case, Delaware):

> The conflict of laws rules to be applied by the federal court in Delaware must conform to those prevailing in Delaware's state courts. Otherwise the accident of diversity of citizenship would constantly disturb equal administration of justice in coordinate state and federal courts sitting side by side.

Id. at 496.

c. Post-*York* cases. Several cases after *York* are fairly straightforward applications of the *York* "outcome determinative" test, in which there was no applicable federal rule. But there is one puzzling case.

(1) Applications of *York*—no applicable federal Rule. In Angel v. Bullington, 330 U.S. 183, 67 S.Ct. 657, 91 L.Ed. 832 (1947), plaintiff sued, and lost, in North Carolina state court. He then brought suit in federal district court in North Carolina. The Supreme Court held that the federal court should give the same res judicata effect to the North Carolina state court judgment as the courts of that state would give it. (Today, this case would be resolved by relying on the full faith and credit statute, 28 U.S.C. § 1738. See discussion, infra p. 1121. But the answer is the same.)

In Cohen v. Beneficial Industrial Loan Corp., 337 U.S. 541, 69 S.Ct. 1221, 93 L.Ed. 1528 (1949), plaintiff brought a shareholder derivative suit in federal district court in New Jersey. The Supreme Court applied a New Jersey rule requiring that losing plaintiffs in shareholder derivative suits pay the other side's attorneys' fees, and that a plaintiffs post a bond for such fees as a precondition to filing suit.

> If all the Act did was to create this [new] liability [for attorneys' fees], it would clearly be substantive. But this new liability would

be without meaning and value in many cases if it resulted in nothing but a judgment for expenses at or after the end of the case. Therefore, a procedure is prescribed by which the liability is insured by entitling the corporate defendant to a bond of indemnity before the outlay is incurred. We do not think a statute which so conditions the stockholder's action can be disregarded by the federal court as a mere procedural device.

Id. at 555–56.

In Woods v. Interstate Realty Co., 337 U.S. 535, 69 S.Ct. 1235, 93 L.Ed. 1524 (1949), a Tennessee corporation sued in federal district court in Mississippi to collect a commission earned on the sale of Mississippi land. The Supreme Court refused to allow the suit, relying on a Mississippi statute denying access to Mississippi courts to out-of-state corporations that had not qualified to do business in Mississippi.

Finally, in Bernhardt v. Polygraphic Co. of America, 350 U.S. 198, 76 S.Ct. 273, 100 L.Ed. 199 (1956), plaintiff sued for breach of an employment contract that contained an arbitration clause. The Supreme Court required the district court to follow Vermont law on the enforceability of the arbitration clause:

If the federal court allows arbitration where the state court would disallow it, the outcome of litigation might depend on the courthouse where suit is brought. For the remedy by arbitration, whatever its merits or shortcomings, substantially affects the cause of action created by the State. The nature of the tribunal where suits are tried is an important part of the parcel of rights behind a cause of action. The change from a court of law to an arbitration panel may make a radical difference in ultimate result.

Id. at 203.

(2) **The puzzling case—a potentially applicable federal Rule**. In Ragan v. Merchants Transfer & Warehouse Co., 337 U.S. 530, 69 S.Ct. 1233, 93 L.Ed. 1520 (1949), plaintiff sued in diversity for personal injuries. He filed his complaint within the applicable state statute of limitations period, but served process only after the expiration of that period. Federal Rule 3 provides, "A civil action is commenced by filing a complaint with the court." Relying on Rule 3, plaintiff contended that his suit satisfied the statute of limitations. The state rule, applicable in state courts, provided that "an action shall be deemed commenced, within the meaning of this article, as to each defendant, at the date of the summons which is served on him." Relying on the state rule, defendant contended that plaintiff's suit was time-barred. The Supreme Court followed the state rule:

[L]ocal law undertook to determine the life of the cause of action. We cannot give it longer life in the federal court than it would have had in the state court without adding something to the cause of action. We may not do that consistently with *Erie R. Co. v. Tompkins*.

Id. at 533–34. The Court's opinion did not make clear whether federal Rule 3, stating when a "civil action is commenced" in federal court, applied but was overridden by conflicting state law, or whether Rule 3 simply did not apply. Does the choice between these two alternatives make a difference?

You may wish to come back to this question after you have read *Hanna v. Plumer* and the notes following.

Byrd v. Blue Ridge Rural Electric Cooperative

Supreme Court of the United States, 1958.
356 U.S. 525, 78 S.Ct. 893, 2 L.Ed.2d 953.

■ MR. JUSTICE BRENNAN delivered the opinion of the Court.

This case was brought in the District Court for the Western District of South Carolina. Jurisdiction was based on diversity of citizenship. 28 U.S.C. § 1332. The petitioner, a resident of North Carolina, sued respondent, a South Carolina corporation, for damages for injuries allegedly caused by the respondent's negligence. He had judgment on a jury verdict. The Court of Appeals for the Fourth Circuit reversed and directed the entry of judgment for the respondent. 238 F.2d 346. We granted certiorari, 352 U.S. 999, 77 S.Ct. 557, 1 L.Ed.2d 544, and subsequently ordered reargument, 355 U.S. 950, 78 S.Ct. 530, 2 L.Ed.2d 527.

The respondent is in the business of selling electric power to subscribers in rural sections of South Carolina. The petitioner was employed as a lineman in the construction crew of a construction contractor. The contractor, R.H. Bouligny, Inc., held a contract with the respondent in the amount of $334,300 for the building of some 24 miles of new power lines, the reconversion to higher capacities of about 88 miles of existing lines, and the construction of 2 new substations and a breaker station. The petitioner was injured while connecting power lines to one of the new substations.

One of respondent's affirmative defenses was that under the South Carolina Workmen's Compensation Act the petitioner—because the work contracted to be done by his employer was work of the kind also done by the respondent's own construction and maintenance crews—had the status of a statutory employee of the respondent and was therefore barred from suing the respondent at law because obliged to accept statutory compensation benefits as the exclusive remedy for his injuries. Two questions concerning this defense are before us: (1) whether the Court of Appeals erred in directing judgment for respondent without a remand to give petitioner an opportunity to introduce further evidence; and (2) whether petitioner, state practice notwithstanding, is entitled to a jury determination of the factual issues raised by this defense.

* * *†

A question is also presented as to whether on remand the factual issue is to be decided by the judge or by the jury. The respondent argues on the basis of the decision of the Supreme Court of South Carolina in Adams v. Davison-Paxon Co., 230 S.C. 532, 96 S.E.2d 566, that the issue of immunity should be decided by the judge and not by the jury. That was a negligence action brought in the state trial court against a store owner by an employee of an independent contractor who operated the store's

---

†   [The Court held that since the Court of Appeals differed from the trial court in the proper interpretation to be given the South Carolina statute, it should have remanded the case for new trial to allow plaintiff the opportunity to establish his case in the light of that interpretation.]

millinery department. The trial judge denied the store owner's motion for a directed verdict made upon the ground that [South Carolina statute] § 72–111 barred the plaintiff's action. The jury returned a verdict for the plaintiff. The South Carolina Supreme Court reversed, holding that it was for the judge and not the jury to decide on the evidence whether the owner was a statutory employer, and that the store owner had sustained his defense. The court rested its holding on decisions * * * involving judicial review of the Industrial Commission and said:

> "Thus the trial court should have in this case resolved the conflicts in the evidence and determined the fact of whether [the independent contractor] was performing a part of the 'trade, business or occupation' of the department store-appellant and, therefore, whether [the employee's] remedy is exclusively under the Workmen's Compensation Law." 230 S.C. at page 543, 96 S.E.2d at page 572.

The respondent argues that this state-court decision governs the present diversity case and "divests the jury of its normal function" to decide the disputed fact question of the respondent's immunity under § 72–111. This is to contend that the federal court is bound under Erie R. Co. v. Tompkins, 304 U.S. 64, 58 S.Ct. 817, 82 L.Ed. 1188, to follow the state court's holding to secure uniform enforcement of the immunity created by the State.

First. It was decided in Erie R. Co. v. Tompkins that the federal courts in diversity cases must respect the definition of state-created rights and obligations by the state courts. We must, therefore, first examine the rule in Adams v. Davison-Paxon Co. to determine whether it is bound up with these rights and obligations in such a way that its application in the federal court is required.

The Workmen's Compensation Act is administered in South Carolina by its Industrial Commission. The South Carolina courts hold that, on judicial review of actions of the Commission under § 72–111, the question whether the claim of an injured workman is within the Commission's jurisdiction is a matter of law for decision by the court, which makes its own findings of fact relating to that jurisdiction. The South Carolina Supreme Court states no reasons in Adams v. Davison-Paxon Co. why, although the jury decides all other factual issues raised by the cause of action and defenses, the jury is displaced as to the factual issue raised by the affirmative defense under § 72–111. The decisions cited to support the holding * * * are concerned solely with defining the scope and method of judicial review of the Industrial Commission. A State may, of course, distribute the functions of its judicial machinery as it sees fit. The decisions relied upon, however, furnish no reason for selecting the judge rather than the jury to decide this single affirmative defense in the negligence action. They simply reflect a policy, that administrative determination of "jurisdictional facts" should not be final but subject to judicial review. The conclusion is inescapable that the Adams holding is grounded in the practical consideration that the question had theretofore come before the South Carolina courts from the Industrial Commission and the courts had become accustomed to deciding the factual issue of immunity without the aid of juries. We find nothing to suggest that this rule was announced as an integral part of the special relationship created by the statute. Thus the requirement appears to be merely a form and mode of enforcing the immunity, Guaranty Trust Co. of New York v. York, 326 U.S. 99, 108, 65 S.Ct. 1464, 1469, 89 L.Ed. 2079, and not a rule intended to be bound up with the definition of the rights and obligations of the parties. The situation is therefore not analogous to that in Dice v. Akron, C. & Y.R. Co., 342 U.S. 359, 72 S.Ct. 312, 96 L.Ed. 398, where this Court held that the right to trial by jury is so substantial a part of the cause of action created by the Federal Employers' Liability Act, 45 U.S.C.A. § 51 et seq., that the Ohio courts could not apply, in an action under that statute, the Ohio rule that the question of fraudulent release was for determination by a judge rather than by a jury.

Second. But cases following Erie have evinced a broader policy to the effect that the federal courts should conform as near as may be—in the absence of other considerations—to state rules even of form and mode where the state rules may bear substantially on the question whether the litigation would come out one way in the federal court and another way in the state court if the federal court failed to apply a particular local rule. Concededly the nature of the tribunal which tries issues may be important in the enforcement of the parcel of rights making up a cause of action or defense, and bear significantly upon achievement of uniform enforcement of the right. It may well be that in the instant personal-injury case the outcome would be substantially affected by whether the issue of immunity is decided by a judge or a jury. Therefore, were "outcome" the only consideration, a strong case might appear for saying that the federal court should follow the state practice.

But there are affirmative countervailing considerations at work here. The federal system is an independent system for administering justice to litigants who properly invoke its jurisdiction. An essential characteristic of that system is the manner in which, in civil common-law actions, it distributes trial functions between judge and jury and, under the influence—if not the command[10]—of the Seventh Amendment, assigns the decisions of disputed questions of fact to the jury. Jacob v. City of New York, 315 U.S. 752, 62 S.Ct. 854, 86 L.Ed. 1166.[11] The policy of uniform enforcement of state-created rights and obligations, see e.g., Guaranty Trust Co. of New York v. York, supra, cannot in every case exact compliance with a state rule[12]—not bound up with rights and obligations—which disrupts the federal system of allocating functions between judge and jury. Herron v. Southern Pacific Co., 283 U.S. 91, 51

---

[10] Our conclusion makes unnecessary the consideration of—and we intimate no view upon—the constitutional question whether the right of jury trial protected in federal courts by the Seventh Amendment embraces the factual issue of statutory immunity when asserted, as here, as an affirmative defense in a common-law negligence action.

[11] The Courts of Appeals have expressed varying views about the effect of Erie R. Co. v. Tompkins on judge-jury problems in diversity cases. Federal practice was followed in Gorham v. Mutual Benefit Health & Accident Ass'n, 4 Cir.1940, 114 F.2d 97; Diederich v. American News Co., 10 Cir., 1942, 128 F.2d 144; McSweeney v. Prudential Ins. Co., 4 Cir., 1942, 128 F.2d 660; Ettelson v. Metropolitan Life Ins. Co., 3 Cir., 1943, 137 F.2d 62; Order of United Commercial Travelers of America v. Duncan, 6 Cir., 1955, 221 F.2d 703. State practice was followed in Cooper v. Brown, 3 Cir., 1942, 126 F.2d 874; Gutierrez v. Public Service Interstate Transportation Co., 2 Cir., 1948, 168 F.2d 678; Prudential Ins. Co. of America v. Glasgow, 2 Cir., 1953, 208 F.2d 908; Pierce Consulting Engineering Co. v. City of Burlington, 2 Cir., 1955, 221 F.2d 607; Rowe v. Pennsylvania Greyhound Lines, 2 Cir., 1956, 231 F.2d 922.

[12] This Court held in Sibbach v. Wilson & Co., 312 U.S. 1, 655, 61 S.Ct. 422, 85 L.Ed. 479, that Federal Rules of Civil Procedure 35 should prevail over a contrary state rule.

S.Ct. 383, 75 L.Ed. 857. Thus the inquiry here is whether the federal policy favoring jury decisions of disputed fact questions should yield to the state rule in the interest of furthering the objective that the litigation should not come out one way in the federal court and another way in the state court.

We think that in the circumstances of this case the federal court should not follow the state rule. It cannot be gainsaid that there is a strong federal policy against allowing state rules to disrupt the judge-jury relationship in the federal courts. In Herron v. Southern Pacific Co., supra, the trial judge in a personal-injury negligence action brought in the District Court for Arizona on diversity grounds directed a verdict for the defendant when it appeared as a matter of law that the plaintiff was guilty of contributory negligence. The federal judge refused to be bound by a provision of the Arizona Constitution which made the jury the sole arbiter of the question of contributory negligence.[13] This Court sustained the action of the trial judge, holding that "state laws cannot alter the essential character or function of a federal court" because that function "is not in any sense a local matter, and state statutes which would interfere with the appropriate performance of that function are not binding upon the federal court under either the Conformity Act or the 'Rules of Decision Act." Perhaps even more clearly in light of the influence of the Seventh Amendment, the function assigned to the jury 'is an essential factor in the process for which the Federal Constitution provides.' " Concededly the Herron case was decided before Erie R. Co. v. Tompkins, but even when Swift v. Tyson, 16 Pet. 1, 10 L.Ed. 865, was governing law and allowed federal courts sitting in diversity cases to disregard state decisional law, it was never thought that state statutes or constitutions were similarly to be disregarded.

Third. We have discussed the problem upon the assumption that the outcome of the litigation may be substantially affected by whether the issue of immunity is decided by a judge or a jury. But clearly there is not present here the certainty that a different result would follow, cf. Guaranty Trust Co. of New York v. York, supra, or even the strong possibility that this would be the case, cf. Bernhardt v. Polygraphic Co., supra. There are factors present here which might reduce that possibility. The trial judge in the federal system has powers denied the judges of many States to comment on the weight of evidence and credibility of witnesses, and discretion to grant a new trial if the verdict appears to him to be against the weight of the evidence. We do not think the likelihood of a different result is so strong as to require the federal practice of jury determination of disputed factual issues to yield to the state rule in the interest of uniformity of outcome.

The Court of Appeals did not consider other grounds of appeal raised by the respondent because the ground taken disposed of the case. We accordingly remand the case to the Court of Appeals for the decision of the other questions, with instructions that, if not made unnecessary by the decision of such questions, the Court of Appeals shall remand the case to the District Court for a new trial of such issues as the Court of Appeals may direct.

---

[13] "The defense of contributory negligence or of assumption of risk shall, in all cases whatsoever, be a question of fact and shall, at all times, be left to the jury." § 5, Art. 18, A.R.S.

Reversed and remanded.*

NOTES AND QUESTIONS

1.   *Byrd's* **analysis.** *Byrd's* analysis is in three parts. **a. "Integral part" of the state statute.** In *Adams v. Davison-Paxon Co.*, discussed in *Byrd*, the Supreme Court of South Carolina held that a judge rather than a jury should decide factual issues on which the jurisdiction of the state's Industrial Commission depends. But the U.S. Supreme Court discounted *Adams* as not reflecting a considered judgment that this judge/jury division was an integral part of the state workers' compensation statute. How reliable is the U.S. Supreme Court as an interpreter of a state supreme court decision on the meaning of a state statute? Remember this aspect of *Byrd* when you read *Dice v. Akron, Canton & Youngstown Rr. Co.*, infra p. 410. **b. Importance of the federal interest.** Note the curious formulation of the federal interest in Justice Brennan's opinion: "under the influence—if not the command—of the Seventh Amendment." The Seventh Amendment may or may not command that the issue be decided by a jury; the Court refuses to decide that question. But under the "influence" of the amendment, the Court finds that the strong federal interest in providing a jury trial outweighs the interest in achieving uniformity between the state and federal courts. For the contours of the Seventh Amendment jury trial guarantee, see infra p. 898. **c. Outcome determinativeness.** At the end of its opinion, the Court backs away from its earlier concession that the judge/jury choice "may well" substantially affect the outcome. Which part of the opinion do you believe?

2.   *Byrd's* **"balancing" test.** *York* is known, in shorthand fashion, for providing an "outcome determinative" test. *Byrd* is known for its "balancing" test, under which the relative strengths of the state and federal interests are weighed. How much guidance does the Court give us in applying the balancing test?

3.   *Forum non conveniens.* To test your understanding of *York* and *Byrd*, ask yourself the question the Supreme Court avoided in *Piper Aircraft Co. v. Reyno*, supra p. 321. The issue in *Piper* was whether a suit arising out a crash of a small airplane in Scotland should be dismissed by a federal district court in Pennsylvania. The Supreme Court found that the *forum non conveniens* law of California (where the suit had been originally filed), of Pennsylvania (where the suit had been transferred), and of the federal courts was the same. Therefore, the Court did not have to choose between a state and a federal law of *forum non conveniens*. See supra, p. 325, n.13. Imagine a case in which the federal law of *forum non conveniens* would result in dismissal, but the state law would not. If the case is filed in federal court, should the state or federal law of *forum non conveniens* apply? Is *forum non conveniens* outcome determinative within the meaning of *York*? What is the balance of federal and state interests under *Byrd*? Note that the alternative forum is necessarily in a foreign country, since that is the only situation in which the federal courts' law of *forum non conveniens* applies. (If the alternative forum is domestic, a federal district court transfers to another federal district court under 28 U.S.C. § 1404(a).)

---

*   The opinions of Justice Whittaker, concurring and dissenting, and Justice Frankfurter, with whom Justice Harlan joined in dissenting, are omitted.

Hanna v. Plumer

Supreme Court of the United States, 1965.
380 U.S. 460, 85 S.Ct. 1136, 14 L.Ed.2d 8.

■ MR. CHIEF JUSTICE WARREN delivered the opinion of the Court.

The question to be decided is whether, in a civil action where the jurisdiction of the United States district court is based upon diversity of citizenship between the parties, service of process shall be made in the manner prescribed by state law or that set forth in Rule 4(d)(1) of the Federal Rules of Civil Procedure.

On February 6, 1963, petitioner, a citizen of Ohio, filed her complaint in the District Court for the District of Massachusetts, claiming damages in excess of $10,000 for personal injuries resulting from an automobile accident in South Carolina, allegedly caused by the negligence of one Louise Plumer Osgood, a Massachusetts citizen deceased at the time of the filing of the complaint. Respondent, Mrs. Osgood's executor and also a Massachusetts citizen, was named as defendant. On February 8, service was made by leaving copies of the summons and the complaint with respondent's wife at his residence, concededly in compliance with Rule 4(d)(1), which provides:

> "The summons and complaint shall be served together. The plaintiff shall furnish the person making service with such copies as are necessary. Service shall be made as follows:
>
> > "(1) Upon an individual other than an infant or an incompetent person, by delivering a copy of the summons and of the complaint to him personally or by leaving copies thereof at his dwelling house or usual place of abode with some person of suitable age and discretion then residing therein. . . ."

[handwritten margin note: Fed. rule service of process]

Respondent filed his answer on February 26, alleging, *inter alia,* that the action could not be maintained because it had been brought "contrary to and in violation of the provisions of Massachusetts General Laws (Ter.Ed.) Chapter 197, Section 9." That section provides:

> "Except as provided in this chapter, an executor or administrator shall not be held to answer to an action by a creditor of the deceased which is not commenced within one year from the time of his giving bond for the performance of his trust, or to such an action which is commenced within said year unless before the expiration thereof the writ in such action has been served by delivery in hand upon such executor or administrator or service thereof accepted by him or a notice stating the name of the estate, the name and address of the creditor, the amount of the claim and the court in which the action has been brought has been filed in the proper registry of probate. . . ." Mass.Gen.Laws Ann., c. 197, § 9 (1958).

[handwritten margin note: state rule]

On October 17, 1963, the District Court granted respondent's motion for summary judgment, citing Ragan v. Merchants Transfer & Warehouse Co., 337 U.S. 530, 69 S.Ct. 1233, and Guaranty Trust Co. v. York, 326 U.S. 99, 65 S.Ct. 1464, in support of its conclusion that the adequacy of the service was to be measured by § 9, with which, the court held, petitioner had not complied. On appeal, petitioner admitted noncompliance with § 9, but argued that Rule 4(d)(1) defines the method by which service of process is to be effected in diversity actions. The Court of Appeals for the First Circuit, finding that "[r]elatively recent amendments [to § 9] evince a clear legislative purpose to require personal notification within the year,"[1] concluded that the conflict of state and federal rules was over "a substantive rather than a procedural matter," and unanimously affirmed. 331 F.2d 157. Because of the threat to the goal of uniformity of federal procedure posed by the decision below,[2] we granted certiorari, 379 U.S. 813, 85 S.Ct. 52.

We conclude that the adoption of Rule 4(d)(1), designed to control service of process in diversity actions, neither exceeded the congressional mandate embodied in the Rules Enabling Act nor transgressed constitutional bounds, and that the Rule is therefore the standard against which the District Court should have measured the adequacy of the service. Accordingly, we reverse the decision of the Court of Appeals.

The Rules Enabling Act, 28 U.S.C.A. § 2072 provides, in pertinent part:

> "The Supreme Court shall have the power to prescribe, by general rules, the forms of process, writs, pleadings, and motions, and the practice and procedure of the district courts of the United States in civil actions.

> "Such rules shall not abridge, enlarge or modify any substantive right and shall preserve the right of trial by jury. . . ."

Under the cases construing the scope of the Enabling Act, Rule 4(d)(1) clearly passes muster. Prescribing the manner in which a defendant is to be notified that a suit has been instituted against him, it relates to the "practice and procedure of the district courts."

> "The test must be whether a rule really regulates procedure,—the judicial process for enforcing rights and duties recognized by substantive law and for justly administering remedy and redress for disregard or infraction of them." Sibbach v. Wilson & Co., 312 U.S. 1, 14, 61 S.Ct. 422, 426.

In Mississippi Pub. Corp. v. Murphree, 326 U.S. 438, 66 S.Ct. 242, this Court upheld Rule 4(f), which permits service of a summons anywhere within the State (and not merely the district) in which a district court sits:

> "We think that Rule 4(f) is in harmony with the Enabling Act. . . . Undoubtedly most alterations of the rules of practice and procedure may and often do affect the rights of litigants.

---

[1] Section 9 is in part a statute of limitations, providing that an executor need not "answer to an action . . . which is not commenced within one year from the time of his giving bond. . . ." This part of the statute, the purpose of which is to speed the settlement of estates, is not involved in this case, since the action clearly was timely commenced. * * *

Section 9 also provides for the manner of service. * * *

[2] There are a number of state service requirements which would not necessarily be satisfied by compliance with Rule 4(d)(1). See, e.g., Cal.Civ.Proc.Code § 411(8); Idaho Code Ann. § 5–507(7) (1948); Ill.Rev.Stat., c. 110, § 13.2 (1963); Ky.Rev.Stat., Rules Civ.Proc., Rule 4.04 (1962); Md.Ann.Code, Rules Proc., Rule 104b (1963); Mich.Rev.Jud.Act § 600.1912 (1961); N.C.Gen.Stat. § 1–94 (1953); S.D.Code § 33.0807(8) (Supp.1960); Tenn.Code Ann. § 20–214 (1955).

Congress' prohibition of any alteration of substantive rights of litigants was obviously not addressed to such incidental effects as necessarily attend the adoption of the prescribed new rules of procedure upon the rights of litigants who, agreeably to rules of practice and procedure, have been brought before a court authorized to determine their rights. Sibbach v. Wilson & Co., 312 U.S. 1, 11–14, 61 S.Ct. 422, 425–427. The fact that the application of Rule 4(f) will operate to subject petitioner's rights to adjudication by the district court for northern Mississippi will undoubtedly affect those rights. But it does not operate to abridge, enlarge or modify the rules of decision by which that court will adjudicate its rights." Id., at 445–446, 66 S.Ct. at 246.

Thus were there no conflicting state procedure, Rule 4(d)(1) would clearly control. National Rental v. Szukhent, 375 U.S. 311, 316, 84 S.Ct. 411, 414. However, respondent, focusing on the contrary Massachusetts rule, calls to the Court's attention another line of cases, a line which—like the Federal Rules—had its birth in 1938. Erie R. Co. v. Tompkins, 304 U.S. 64, 58 S.Ct. 817, overruling Swift v. Tyson, 16 Pet. 1, held that federal courts sitting in diversity cases when deciding questions of "substantive" law, are bound by state court decisions as well as state statutes. The broad command of *Erie* was therefore identical to that of the Enabling Act: federal courts are to apply state substantive law and federal procedural law. However, as subsequent cases sharpened the distinction between substance and procedure, the line of cases following *Erie* diverged markedly from the line construing the Enabling Act. Guaranty Trust Co. v. York, 326 U.S. 99, 65 S.Ct. 1464, made it clear that *Erie*-type problems were not to be solved by reference to any traditional or common-sense substance-procedure distinction:

> "And so the question is not whether a statute of limitations is deemed a matter of 'procedure' in some sense. The question is . . . does it significantly affect the result of a litigation for a federal court to disregard a law of a State that would be controlling in an action upon the same claim by the same parties in a State court?" 326 U.S., at 109, 65 S.Ct., at 1470.[5]

Respondent, by placing primary reliance on *York* and *Ragan,* suggests that the *Erie* doctrine acts as a check on the Federal Rules of Civil Procedure, that despite the clear command of Rule 4(d)(1), *Erie* and its progeny demand the application of the Massachusetts rule. Reduced to essentials, the argument is: (1) *Erie,* as refined in *York,* demands that federal courts apply state law whenever application of federal law in its stead will alter the outcome of the case. (2) In this case, a determination that the Massachusetts service requirements obtain will result in immediate victory for respondent. If, on the other hand, it should be held that Rule 4(d)(1) is applicable, the litigation will continue, with possible victory for petitioner. (3) Therefore, *Erie* demands application of the Massachusetts rule. The syllogism possesses an appealing simplicity, but is for several reasons invalid.

---

[5]   See also Ragan v. Merchants Transfer Co., supra; Woods v. Interstate Realty Co., 337 U.S. 535, 69 S.Ct. 1235; Bernhardt v. Polygraphic Co., 350 U.S. 198, 203–204, 207–208, 76 S.Ct. 273, 276–279; cf. Byrd v. Blue Ridge Cooperative, 356 U.S. 525, 78 S.Ct. 893.

In the first place, it is doubtful that, even if there were no Federal Rule making it clear that in-hand service is not required in diversity actions, the *Erie* rule would have obligated the District Court to follow the Massachusetts procedure. "Outcome-determination" analysis was never intended to serve as a talisman. Byrd v. Blue Ridge Rural Cooperative, 356 U.S. 525, 537, 78 S.Ct. 893, 900. Indeed, the message of *York* itself is that choices between state and federal law are to be made not by application of any automatic, "litmus paper" criterion, but rather by reference to the policies underlying the *Erie* rule.

The *Erie* rule is rooted in part in a realization that it would be unfair for the character or result of a litigation materially to differ because the suit had been brought in a federal court.

> "Diversity of citizenship jurisdiction was conferred in order to prevent apprehended discrimination in state courts against those not citizens of the State. Swift v. Tyson introduced grave discrimination by non-citizens against citizens. It made rights enjoyed under the unwritten 'general law' vary according to whether enforcement was sought in the state or in the federal court; and the privilege of selecting the court in which the right should be determined was conferred upon the non-citizen. Thus, the doctrine rendered impossible equal protection of the law." Erie R. Co. v. Tompkins, supra, 304 U.S. at 74–75, 58 S.Ct. at 820–821.

The decision was also in part a reaction to the practice of "forum-shopping" which had grown up in response to the rule of Swift v. Tyson. That the *York* test was an attempt to effectuate these policies is demonstrated by the fact that the opinion framed the inquiry in terms of "substantial" variations between state and federal litigation. 326 U.S., at 109. Not only are nonsubstantial or trivial variations not likely to raise the sort of equal protection problems which troubled the Court in *Erie;* they are also unlikely to influence the choice of a forum. The "outcome-determination" test therefore cannot be read without reference to the twin aims of the *Erie* rule: discouragement of forum-shopping and avoidance of inequitable administration of the laws.

The difference between the conclusion that the Massachusetts rule is applicable, and the conclusion that it is not, is of course at this point "outcome-determinative" in the sense that if we hold the state rule to apply, respondent prevails, whereas if we hold that Rule 4(d)(1) governs, the litigation will continue. But in this sense *every* procedural variation is "outcome-determinative." For example, having brought suit in a federal court, a plaintiff cannot then insist on the right to file subsequent pleadings in accord with the time limits applicable in the state courts, even though enforcement of the federal timetable will, if he continues to insist that he must meet only the state time limit, result in determination of the controversy against him. So it is here. Though choice of the federal or state rule will at this point have a marked effect upon the outcome of the litigation, the difference between the two rules would be of scant, if any, relevance to the choice of a forum. Petitioner, in choosing her forum, was not presented with a situation where application of the state rule would wholly bar recovery;[10] rather, adherence to the state rule would have resulted only in altering the way in which process was served.[11] Moreover, it is difficult to argue that permitting service of defendant's wife to take the place of in-hand service of defendant himself alters the mode of enforcement of state-created rights in a fashion sufficiently "substantial" to raise the sort of equal protection problems to which the *Erie* opinion alluded.

There is, however, a more fundamental flaw in respondent's syllogism: the incorrect assumption that the rule of Erie R. Co. v. Tompkins constitutes the appropriate test of the validity and therefore the applicability of a Federal Rule of Civil Procedure. The *Erie* rule has never been invoked to void a Federal Rule. It is true that there have been cases where this Court has held applicable a state rule in the face of an argument that the situation was governed by one of the Federal Rules. But the holding of each such case was not that *Erie* commanded displacement of a Federal Rule by an inconsistent state rule, but rather that the scope of the Federal Rule was not as broad as the losing party urged, and therefore, there being no Federal Rule which covered the point in dispute, *Erie* commanded the enforcement of state law.

> "Respondent contends, in the first place, that the charge was correct because of the fact that Rule 8(c) of the Rules of Civil Procedure makes contributory negligence an affirmative defense. We do not agree. Rule 8(c) covers only the manner of pleading. The question of the burden of establishing contributory negligence is a question of local law which federal courts in diversity of citizenship cases (Erie R. Co. v. Tompkins, 304 U.S. 64, 58 S.Ct. 817) must apply." Palmer v. Hoffman, 318 U.S. 109, 117, 63 S.Ct. 477, 482.[12]

(Here, of course, the clash is unavoidable; Rule 4(d)(1) says—implicitly, but with unmistakable clarity—that in-hand service is not required in federal courts.) At the same time, in cases adjudicating the validity of Federal Rules, we have not applied the *York* rule or other refinements of *Erie,* but have to this day continued to decide questions concerning the scope of the Enabling Act and the constitutionality of specific Federal Rules in light of the distinction set forth in *Sibbach*. E.g., Schlagenhauf v. Holder, 379 U.S. 104, 85 S.Ct. 234.

---

[10] See Guaranty Trust Co. v. York, supra, at 326 U.S. 108–109, 65 S.Ct. at 1469; Ragan v. Merchants Transfer Co., supra, 337 U.S. at 532, 69 S.Ct. at 1234; Woods v. Interstate Realty Co., supra, note 5, 337 U.S. at 538, 69 S.Ct. at 1237.

Similarly, a federal court's refusal to enforce the New Jersey rule involved in Cohen v. Beneficial Loan Corp., 337 U.S. 541, 69 S.Ct. 1221, requiring the posting of security by plaintiffs in stockholders' derivative actions, might well impel a stockholder to choose to bring suit in the federal, rather than the state, court.

[11] Cf. Monarch Insurance Co. of Ohio v. Spach, 281 F.2d 401, 412 (C.A.5th Cir.1960). We cannot seriously entertain the thought that one suing an estate would be led to choose the federal court because of a belief that adherence to Rule 4(d)(1) is less likely to give the executor actual notice than § 9, and therefore more likely to produce a default judgment. Rule 4(d)(1) is well designed to give actual notice, as it did in this case. See note 1, supra.

[12] To the same effect, see Ragan v. Merchants Transfer Co., supra; Cohen v. Beneficial Loan Corp., supra, note 10, 337 U.S. at 556, 69 S.Ct. at 1230; Id., at 557, 69 S.Ct. at 1230 (Douglas, J., dissenting); cf. Bernhardt v. Polygraphic Co., supra, note 5, 350 U.S. at 201–202, 76 S.Ct. at 275; see generally Iovino v. Waterson, supra, note 6, at 47–48.

Nor has the development of two separate lines of cases been inadvertent. The line between "substance" and "procedure" shifts as the legal context changes. "Each implies different variables depending upon the particular problem for which it is used." Guaranty Trust Co. v. York, supra, 326 U.S. at 108, 65 S.Ct. at 1469; Cook, The Logical and Legal Bases of the Conflict of Laws, pp. 154–183 (1942). It is true that both the Enabling Act and the *Erie* rule say, roughly, that federal courts are to apply state "substantive" law and federal "procedural" law, but from that it need not follow that the tests are identical. For they were designed to control very different sorts of decisions. When a situation is covered by one of the Federal Rules, the question facing the court is a far cry from the typical, relatively unguided *Erie* choice: the court has been instructed to apply the Federal Rule, and can refuse to do so only if the Advisory Committee, this Court, and Congress erred in their prima facie judgment that the Rule in question transgresses neither the terms of the Enabling Act nor constitutional restrictions.

We are reminded by the *Erie* opinion that neither Congress nor the federal courts can, under the guise of formulating rules of decision for federal courts, fashion rules which are not supported by a grant of federal authority contained in Article I or some other section of the Constitution; in such areas state law must govern because there can be no other law. But the opinion in *Erie,* which involved no Federal Rule and dealt with a question which was "substantive" in every traditional sense (whether the railroad owed a duty of care to Tompkins as a trespasser or a licensee), surely neither said nor implied that measures like Rule 4(d)(1) are unconstitutional. For the constitutional provision for a federal court system (augmented by the Necessary and Proper Clause) carries with it congressional power to make rules governing the practice and pleading in those courts, which in turn includes a power to regulate matters which, though falling within the uncertain area between substance and procedure, are rationally capable of classification as either. Cf. M'Culloch v. Maryland, 4 Wheat. 316, 421. Neither *York* nor the cases following it ever suggested that the rule there laid down for coping with situations where no Federal Rule applies is coextensive with the limitation on Congress to which *Erie* had adverted. * * *

Erie and its offspring cast no doubt on the long-recognized power of Congress to prescribe housekeeping rules for federal courts even though some of those rules will inevitably differ from comparable state rules. Cf. Herron v. Southern Pacific Co., 283 U.S. 91, 51 S.Ct. 383. "When, because the plaintiff happens to be a non-resident, such a right is enforceable in a federal as well as in a State court, the forms and mode of enforcing the right may at times, naturally enough, vary because the two judicial systems are not identic." Guaranty Trust Co. v. York, supra, 326 U.S. at 108, 65 S.Ct. at 1469; Cohen v. Beneficial Indus. Loan Corp., 337 U.S. 541, 555, 69 S.Ct. 1221, 1229. Thus, though a court, in measuring a Federal Rule against the standards contained in the Enabling Act and the Constitution, need not wholly blind itself to the degree to which the Rule makes the character and result of the federal litigation stray from the course it would follow in state courts, Sibbach v. Wilson & Co., supra, 312 U.S. at 13–14, 61 S.Ct. at 426–427, it cannot be forgotten that the *Erie* rule, and the guidelines suggested in *York,* were created to serve another purpose altogether. To hold that a Federal Rule of Civil Procedure must cease to function whenever it alters the mode of enforcing state-created rights would be to disembowel either the Constitution's grant of power over federal procedure or Congress' attempt to exercise that power in the Enabling Act. Rule 4(d)(1) is valid and controls the instant case.

Holding ✓

Reversed.

■ MR. JUSTICE BLACK concurs in the result.

■ MR. JUSTICE HARLAN, concurring.

It is unquestionably true that up to now *Erie* and the cases following it have not succeeded in articulating a workable doctrine governing choice of law in diversity actions. I respect the Court's effort to clarify the situation in today's opinion. However, in doing so I think it has misconceived the constitutional premises of *Erie* and has failed to deal adequately with those past decisions upon which the courts below relied.

Erie was something more than an opinion which worried about "forum-shopping and avoidance of inequitable administration of the laws," * * * although to be sure these were important elements of the decision. I have always regarded that decision as one of the modern cornerstones of our federalism, expressing policies that profoundly touch the allocation of judicial power between the state and federal systems. *Erie* recognized that there should not be two conflicting systems of law controlling the primary activity of citizens, for such alternative governing authority must necessarily give rise to a debilitating uncertainty in the planning of everyday affairs. And it recognized that the scheme of our Constitution envisions an allocation of law-making functions between state and federal legislative processes which is undercut if the federal judiciary can make substantive law affecting state affairs beyond the bounds of congressional legislative powers in this regard. Thus, in diversity cases *Erie* commands that it be the state law governing primary private activity which prevails.

The shorthand formulations which have appeared in some past decisions are prone to carry untoward results that frequently arise from oversimplification. The Court is quite right in stating that the "outcome-determinative" test of Guaranty Trust Co. v. York, 326 U.S. 99, 65 S.Ct. 1464, if taken literally, proves too much, for any rule, no matter how clearly "procedural," can affect the outcome of litigation if it is not obeyed. In turning from the "outcome" test of *York* back to the unadorned forum-shopping rationale of *Erie,* however, the Court falls prey to like oversimplification, for a simple forum-shopping rule also proves too much; litigants often choose a federal forum merely to obtain what they consider the advantages of the Federal Rules of Civil Procedure or to try their cases before a supposedly more favorable judge. To my mind the proper line of approach in determining whether to apply a state or a federal rule, whether "substantive" or "procedural," is to stay close to basic principles by inquiring if the choice of rule would substantially affect those primary decisions respecting human conduct which our constitutional system leaves to state regulation. If so, *Erie* and the Constitution require that the state rule prevail, even in the face of a conflicting federal rule.

The Court weakens, if indeed it does not submerge, this basic principle by finding, in effect, a grant of substantive legislative power in the constitutional provision for a federal court system (compare Swift v.

Tyson, 16 Pet. 1), and through it, setting up the Federal Rules as a body of law inviolate.

> "[T]he constitutional provision for a federal court system . . . carries with it congressional power . . . to regulate matters which, though falling within the uncertain area between substance and procedure, *are rationally capable of classification as either.*" * * * (Emphasis supplied.)

So long as a reasonable man could characterize any duly adopted federal rule as "procedural," the Court, unless I misapprehend what is said, would have it apply no matter how seriously it frustrated a State's substantive regulation of the primary conduct and affairs of its citizens. Since the members of the Advisory Committee, the Judicial Conference, and this Court who formulated the Federal Rules are presumably reasonable men, it follows that the integrity of the Federal Rules is absolute. Whereas the unadulterated outcome and forum-shopping tests may err too far toward honoring state rules, I submit that the Court's "arguably procedural, *ergo* constitutional" test moves too fast and far in the other direction.

The courts below relied upon this Court's decisions in Ragan v. Merchants Transfer & Warehouse Co., 337 U.S. 530, 69 S.Ct. 1233, and Cohen v. Beneficial Indus. Loan Corp., 337 U.S. 541, 69 S.Ct. 1221. Those cases deserve more attention than this Court has given them, particularly *Ragan* which, if still good law, would in my opinion call for affirmance of the result reached by the Court of Appeals. Further, a discussion of these two cases will serve to illuminate the "diversity" thesis I am advocating.

In *Ragan* a Kansas statute of limitations provided that an action was deemed commenced when service was made on the defendant. Despite Federal Rule 3 which provides that an action commences with the filing of the complaint, the Court held that for the purposes of the Kansas statute of limitations a diversity tort action commenced only when service was made upon the defendant. The effect of this holding was that although the plaintiff had filed his federal complaint within the state period of limitations, his action was barred because the federal marshal did not serve a summons on the defendant until after the limitations period had run. I think that the decision was wrong. At most, application of the Federal Rule would have meant that potential Kansas tort defendants would have to defer for a few days the satisfaction of knowing that they had not been sued within the limitations period. The choice of the Federal Rule would have had no effect on the primary stages of private activity from which torts arise, and only the most minimal effect on behavior following the commission of the tort. In such circumstances the interest of the federal system in proceeding under its own rules should have prevailed.

Cohen v. Beneficial Indus. Loan Corp. held that a federal diversity court must apply a state statute requiring a small stockholder in a stockholder derivative suit to post a bond securing payment of defense costs as a condition to prosecuting an action. Such a statute is not "outcome determinative"; the plaintiff can win with or without it. The Court now rationalizes the case on the ground that the statute might affect the plaintiff's choice of forum * * *, but as has been pointed out, a simple forum-shopping test proves too much. The proper view of *Cohen* is, in my opinion, that the statute was meant to inhibit small stockholders from instituting "strike suits," and thus it was designed and could be expected to have a substantial impact on private primary activity. Anyone who was at the trial bar during the period when *Cohen* arose can appreciate the strong state policy reflected in the statute. I think it wholly legitimate to view Federal Rule 23 as not purporting to deal with the problem. But even had the Federal Rules purported to do so, and in so doing provided a substantially less effective deterrent to strike suits, I think the state rule should still have prevailed. That is where I believe the Court's view differs from mine; for the Court attributes such overriding force to the Federal Rules that it is hard to think of a case where a conflicting state rule would be allowed to operate, even though the state rule reflected policy considerations which, under *Erie,* would lie within the realm of state legislative authority.

It remains to apply what has been said to the present case. The Massachusetts rule provides that an executor need not answer suits unless in-hand service was made upon him or notice of the action was filed in the proper registry of probate within one year of his giving bond. The evident intent of this statute is to permit an executor to distribute the estate which he is administering without fear that further liabilities may be outstanding for which he could be held personally liable. If the Federal District Court in Massachusetts applies Rule 4(d)(1) of the Federal Rules of Civil Procedure instead of the Massachusetts service rule, what effect would that have on the speed and assurance with which estates are distributed? As I see it, the effect would not be substantial. It would mean simply that an executor would have to check at his own house or the federal courthouse as well as the registry of probate before he could distribute the estate with impunity. As this does not seem enough to give rise to any real impingement on the vitality of the state policy which the Massachusetts rule is intended to serve, I concur in the judgment of the Court.

NOTE ON *ERIE, HANNA V. PLUMER,* AND THE FEDERAL RULES OF CIVIL PROCEDURE

Does the Supreme Court in *Hanna* have an appropriate understanding of *Erie* and the roles of substance and procedure in federal court? A careful reading of *Hanna*, and of Ely, The Irrepressible Myth of *Erie*, 87 Harv. L. Rev. 693 (1974), suggests the following analysis:

1. **Valid Federal Rules of Civil Procedure control over inconsistent state rules.** Valid Federal Rules of Civil Procedure, applicable in federal district courts, control matters within their scope, even when state procedural rules would, if applicable, require something different. That the federal Rules control over inconsistent state law flows from the principle of supremacy of federal law, and from the Rules of Decision Act, 28 U.S.C. § 1652, which provides, in pertinent part, "The laws of the several States, *except where* the Constitution or treaties of the United States or *Acts of Congress otherwise require or provide*, shall be regarded as rules of decision * * *. (emphasis added). The federal Rules, promulgated under the Rules Enabling Act, 28 U.S.C. § 2072, are Acts of Congress for purposes of the Rules of Decision Act.

2. Valid Federal Rules of Appellate Procedure also control over inconsistent state rules. Valid Federal Rules of Appellate Procedure, applicable in federal courts of appeal, also control matters within their scope and prevail over inconsistent state procedural rules. See Burlington Northern Railroad Co. v. Woods, 480 U.S. 1, 107 S.Ct. 967, 94 L.Ed.2d 1 (1987).

3. Federal Rules of Civil and Appellate Procedure must be valid and applicable. a. Rule must be valid. The Federal Rules of Civil Procedure (and the Federal Rules of Appellate Procedure) are promulgated under the authority of the Rules Enabling Act, 28 U.S.C. § 2072. In its present form, the Act provides, in pertinent part, "The Supreme Court shall have the power to prescribe general rules of practice and procedure and rules of evidence for cases in the United States District Courts * * *. Such rules shall not abridge, enlarge or modify any substantive right." The original reason for the restriction in the second quoted sentence was unrelated to *Erie*; but the restriction has, today, become intimately related to the *Erie* analysis.

The Rules Enabling Act was originally passed in 1934, four years before *Erie*. Because *Swift v. Tyson* was then still the law, there was little concern that a new system of federal rules would unduly interfere with the enforcement of state law in the federal courts. Rather, the concern was that the rulemakers would exceed the permissible boundaries of their delegated authority from Congress. The manner of adopting the Federal Rules of Civil Procedure is described in detail in Chapter One. It is sufficient to note here the basic mechanism: The Supreme Court, assisted significantly by various advisory groups, proposes rules to Congress. If Congress does nothing to the proposed rules within a prescribed period, the rules automatically become law. When the Act was passed in 1934, there was real concern about the constitutionality of excessive delegation of congressional legislative power, as well as about the wisdom of such delegation, under the Act. The restriction in the Act was designed to ensure that any federal rules thus adopted would not be an unconstitutional product of unrestricted delegated power. See Burbank, The Rules Enabling Act of 1934, 130 U. Pa. L. Rev. 1015 (1982).

After the Court's decision in *Erie*, the temptation to read the Rules Enabling Act in light of that decision proved irresistible. To the extent that the Act was thought relevant to an understanding of the permissible scope of the rules, its restriction was understood after 1938 to protect state substantive law from undue distortion by the application of federal procedural rules. Thus, a statutory restriction with a rationale originally based on separation of powers came, after 1938, to have a further and continuing rationale based on federalism. Based on this federalism rationale, Justice Harlan argues in his concurrence for greater deference to the principles embodied in state law than the majority opinion in *Hanna v. Plumer* is willing to grant.

The Supreme Court has never struck down a Federal Rule of Civil Procedure as invalid because it exceeds the restriction of the Rules Enabling Act. But the restriction has occasionally had real consequence on the drafting of the rules proposed by the Supreme Court under the Act, and on the interpretation of the rules adopted.

b. Federal Rule must be applicable. A federal Rule must not only be valid; it must also be applicable to the issue at hand. Ordinarily, the meaning and scope of a federal rule is fairly obvious. From time to time, however, the Supreme Court has not seen it that way. See, e.g., Rule 3, *Walker v. Armco Steel Corp.*, and *West v. Conrail*, discussed in note 6, infra.

4. No applicable federal procedural Rule. An arguably procedural issue not governed by the federal rules occasionally arises, in which the federal courts follow one practice and the state courts another, and in which no Federal Rule of Civil Procedure requires the federal practice. In that event, either the "outcome determinative" test of *York* or the "balancing" test of *Byrd* applies (or perhaps some combination of the two).

5. Does *Erie* apply only in diversity cases? It is customary to speak of *Erie* as applying to diversity cases. This is an understandable shorthand, for the federal courts are usually sitting in diversity when they decide issues of state law. But even if we confine the universe of "*Erie* questions" to procedure/substance questions that arise in the course of deciding issues of state law, this shorthand is not fully accurate. Issues of state law arise not only in diversity cases, but also in cases brought under other heads of jurisdiction, including federal question and supplemental jurisdiction, 28 U.S.C. §§ 1331, 1367. The Rules of Decision Act does not distinguish between diversity and other bases for the federal court jurisdiction. It provides simply that the laws of the states "shall be regarded as rules of decision in civil actions in the courts of the United States." Thus, *Erie* applies to all cases in federal courts, regardless of the basis for subject matter jurisdiction. See, e.g., Vess v. Ciba-Geigy Corp. USA, 317 F.3d 1097, 1102 (9th Cir. 2003); Maternally Yours v. Your Maternity Shop, Inc., 234 F.2d 538 (2d Cir. 1956).

6. Do the federal Rules apply equally to cases based on state and on federal law? The analysis in *Hanna* strongly suggests that so long as a Federal Rule of Civil Procedure is valid and applicable, it is equally applicable to cases based on state and on federal law. For the most part, this is true. In the great majority of cases, federal district courts simply apply the federal Rules to cases pending before them, without regard to whether the case (or a particular claim within the case) is based on state or federal law. For at least one rule, however, this is not true.

Federal Rule 3 provides, in its entirety, "A civil action is commenced by filing a complaint with the court." In Walker v. Armco Steel Corp., 446 U.S. 740, 100 S.Ct. 1978, 64 L.Ed.2d 659 (1980), a suit based on state substantive law, the Supreme Court held that the suit was not "commenced" for purposes of tolling the state statute of limitations by "filing a complaint." Rather, following Ragan v. Merchants Transfer & Warehouse, Inc., 337 U.S. 530, 69 S.Ct. 1233, 93 L.Ed. 1520 (1949), the Court held that the state tolling rule applied. The state rule was that the statute was not tolled until the complaint was served. In footnote 11 of its opinion, the *Walker* Court left open the question whether Rule 3 would provide the tolling rule in a case based on federal rather than state law. The Court answered the question left open in *Walker* in West v. Conrail, 481 U.S. 35, 107 S.Ct. 1538, 95 L.Ed.2d 32 (1987), holding that a suit based on federal law is "commenced" and the statute of limitations tolled when a complaint is filed. Rule 3 is now routinely regarded as providing the tolling rule for federal causes of action. See, e.g., Lewis v. Richmond City Police Dept., 947 F.2d 733 (4th Cir. 1991). Professor Stephen Burbank has vigorously criticized both footnote 11 of *Walker* and the Court's decision in *West v. Conrail*. Burbank, Of Rules and Discretion:

The Supreme Court, Federal Rules and Common Law, 63 Notre Dame L.Rev. 693, 698–719 (1988).

Rule 3 is thus construed differently depending on whether it is applied to a federal or state cause of action. Is this because a tolling rule for a statute of limitations is substantive, and because the Rules Enabling Act requires Rule 3 to give way when there is a contrary state rule? Has the Court forgotten the reason for the restriction written into the Rules Enabling Act? See discussion supra note 3a. Should other federal Rules, in addition to Rule 3, be construed differently depending on whether they are applied to a federal or state cause of action?

Gasperini v. Center for Humanities, Inc.

Supreme Court of the United States, 1996.
518 U.S. 415, 116 S.Ct. 2211, 135 L.Ed.2d 659.

■ JUSTICE GINSBURG delivered the opinion of the Court.

Under the law of New York, appellate courts are empowered to review the size of jury verdicts and to order new trials when the jury's award "deviates materially from what would be reasonable compensation." N.Y. Civ. Prac. Law and Rules (CPLR) § 5501(c) (McKinney 1995). Under the Seventh Amendment, which governs proceedings in federal court, but not in state court, "the right of trial by jury shall be preserved, and no fact tried by a jury, shall be otherwise re-examined in any Court of the United States, than according to the rules of the common law." U.S. Const., Amdt. 7. The compatibility of these provisions, in an action based on New York law but tried in federal court by reason of the parties' diverse citizenship, is the issue we confront in this case. We hold that New York's law controlling compensation awards for excessiveness or inadequacy can be given effect, without detriment to the Seventh Amendment, if the review standard set out in CPLR § 5501(c) is applied by the federal trial court judge, with appellate control of the trial court's ruling limited to review for "abuse of discretion."

Holding

I

Petitioner William Gasperini, a journalist for CBS News and the Christian Science Monitor, began reporting on events in Central America in 1984. He earned his living primarily in radio and print media and only occasionally sold his photographic work. During the course of his seven-year stint in Central America, Gasperini took over 5,000 slide transparencies, depicting active war zones, political leaders, and scenes from daily life. In 1990, Gasperini agreed to supply his original color transparencies to The Center for Humanities, Inc. (Center) for use in an educational videotape, *Conflict in Central America*. Gasperini selected 300 of his slides for the Center; its videotape included 110 of them. The Center agreed to return the original transparencies, but upon the completion of the project, it could not find them.

Gasperini commenced suit in the United States District Court for the Southern District of New York, invoking the court's diversity jurisdiction pursuant to 28 U.S.C. § 1332. He alleged several state-law claims for relief, including breach of contract, conversion, and negligence. The Center conceded liability for the lost transparencies and the issue of damages was tried before a jury.

At trial, Gasperini's expert witness testified that the "industry standard" within the photographic publishing community valued a lost transparency at $1,500. This industry standard, the expert explained, represented the average license fee a commercial photograph could earn over the full course of the photographer's copyright, *i.e.,* in Gasperini's case, his lifetime plus 50 years. Gasperini estimated that his earnings from photography totaled just over $10,000 for the period from 1984 through 1993. He also testified that he intended to produce a book containing his best photographs from Central America.

After a three-day trial, the jury awarded Gasperini $450,000 in compensatory damages. This sum, the jury foreperson announced, "is [$]1500 each, for 300 slides." Moving for a new trial under Federal Rule *FRCP 59* of Civil Procedure 59, the Center attacked the verdict on various grounds, including excessiveness. Without comment, the District Court denied the motion.

The Court of Appeals for the Second Circuit vacated the judgment entered on the jury's verdict. 66 F.3d 427 (1995). Mindful that New York law governed the controversy, the Court of Appeals endeavored to apply CPLR § 5501(c), which instructs that, when a jury returns an itemized verdict, as the jury did in this case, the New York Appellate Division "shall determine that an award is excessive or inadequate if it deviates materially from what would be reasonable compensation." The Second Circuit's application of § 5501(c) as a check on the size of the jury's verdict followed Circuit precedent elaborated two weeks earlier in *Consorti v. Armstrong World Industries, Inc.,* 64 F.3d 781, superseded, 72 F.3d 1003 (1995). Surveying Appellate Division decisions that reviewed damage awards for lost transparencies, the Second Circuit concluded that testimony on industry standard alone was insufficient to justify a verdict; prime among other factors warranting consideration were the uniqueness of the slides' subject matter and the photographer's earning level.

Guided by Appellate Division rulings, the Second Circuit held that the $450,000 verdict "materially deviates from what is reasonable compensation." 66 F.3d, at 431. Some of Gasperini's transparencies, the Second Circuit recognized, were unique, notably those capturing combat situations in which Gasperini was the only photographer present. *Id.,* at 429. But others "depicted either generic scenes or events at which other professional photojournalists were present." *Id.,* at 431. No more than 50 slides merited a $1,500 award, the court concluded, after "[g]iving Gasperini every benefit of the doubt." *Ibid.* Absent evidence showing significant earnings from photographic endeavors or concrete plans to publish a book, the court further determined, any damage award above $100 each for the remaining slides would be excessive. Remittiturs "presen[t] difficult problems for appellate courts," the Second Circuit acknowledged, for court of appeals judges review the evidence from "a cold paper record." *Ibid.* Nevertheless, the Second Circuit set aside the $450,000 verdict and ordered a new trial, unless Gasperini agreed to an award of $100,000.

This case presents an important question regarding the standard a federal court uses to measure the alleged excessiveness of a jury's verdict in an action for damages based on state law. * * *

II

Before 1986, state and federal courts in New York generally invoked the same judge-made formulation in responding to excessiveness attacks on jury verdicts: courts would not disturb an award unless the amount was so exorbitant that it "shocked the conscience of the court." See *Consorti*, 72 F.3d, at 1012–1013 (collecting cases). As described by the Second Circuit:

> "The standard for determining excessiveness and the appropriateness of remittitur in New York is somewhat ambiguous. Prior to 1986, New York law employed the same standard as the federal courts, *see Matthews v. CTI Container Transport Int'l Inc.*, 871 F.2d 270, 278 (2d Cir.1989), which authorized remittitur only if the jury's verdict was so excessive that it 'shocked the conscience of the court.' " *Id.*, at 1012.

* * *

In both state and federal courts, trial judges made the excessiveness assessment in the first instance, and appellate judges ordinarily deferred to the trial court's judgment. See, *e.g.*, *McAllister v. Adam Packing Corp.*, 66 App.Div.2d 975, 976, 412 N.Y.S.2d 50, 52 (3d Dept.1978) ("The trial court's determination as to the adequacy of the jury verdict will only be disturbed by an appellate court where it can be said that the trial court's exercise of discretion was not reasonably grounded."); *Martell v. Boardwalk Enterprises, Inc.*, 748 F.2d 740, 750 (C.A.2 1984) ("The trial court's refusal to set aside or reduce a jury award will be overturned only for abuse of discretion.").

In 1986, as part of a series of tort reform measures,[3] New York codified a standard for judicial review of the size of jury awards. Placed in CPLR § 5501(c), the prescription reads:

> "In reviewing a money judgment . . . in which it is contended that the award is excessive or inadequate and that a new trial should have been granted unless a stipulation is entered to a different award, the appellate division shall determine that an award is excessive or inadequate if it deviates materially from what would be reasonable compensation."

* * *

New York state-court opinions confirm that § 5501(c)'s "deviates materially" standard calls for closer surveillance than "shock the conscience" oversight. See, *e.g.*, *O'Connor v. Graziosi*, 131 App.Div.2d 553, 554, 516 N.Y.S.2d 276, 277 (2d Dept.1987) ("apparent intent" of 1986 legislation was "to facilitate appellate changes in verdicts")[.] * * *

Although phrased as a direction to New York's intermediate appellate courts, § 5501(c)'s "deviates materially" standard, as construed by New York's courts, instructs state trial judges as well. * * * Application of § 5501(c) at the trial level is key to this case.

To determine whether an award "deviates materially from what would be reasonable compensation," New York state courts look to

---

[3] The legislature sought, particularly, to curtail medical and dental malpractice, and to contain "already high malpractice premiums." Legislative Findings and Declaration, Ch. 266, 1986 N.Y. Laws 470 (McKinney).

awards approved in similar cases. * * * The "deviates materially" standard, however, in design and operation, influences outcomes by tightening the range of tolerable awards. See, *e.g., Consorti,* 72 F.3d, at 1013, and n. 10, 1014–1015, and n. 14.

III

In cases like Gasperini's, in which New York law governs the claims for relief, does New York law also supply the test for federal court review of the size of the verdict? The Center answers yes. The "deviates materially" standard, it argues, is a substantive standard that must be applied by federal appellate courts in diversity cases. The Second Circuit agreed. See 66 F.3d, at 430; see also *Consorti,* 72 F.3d, at 1011 ("[CPLR § 5501(c)] is the substantive rule provided by New York law."). Gasperini, emphasizing that § 5501(c) trains on the New York Appellate Division, characterizes the provision as procedural, an allocation of decisionmaking authority regarding damages, not a hard cap on the amount recoverable. Correctly comprehended, Gasperini urges, § 5501(c)'s direction to the Appellate Division cannot be given effect by federal appellate courts without violating the Seventh Amendment's re-examination clause.

As the parties' arguments suggest, CPLR § 5501(c), appraised under *Erie R. Co. v. Tompkins,* 304 U.S. 64, 58 S.Ct. 817, 82 L.Ed. 1188 (1938), and decisions in *Erie*'s path, is both "substantive" and "procedural": "substantive" in that § 5501(c)'s "deviates materially" standard controls how much a plaintiff can be awarded; "procedural" in that § 5501(c) assigns decisionmaking authority to New York's Appellate Division. Parallel application of § 5501(c) at the federal appellate level would be out of sync with the federal system's division of trial and appellate court functions, an allocation weighted by the Seventh Amendment. The dispositive question, therefore, is whether federal courts can give effect to the substantive thrust of § 5501(c) without untoward alteration of the federal scheme for the trial and decision of civil cases.

A

Federal diversity jurisdiction provides an alternative forum for the adjudication of state-created rights, but it does not carry with it generation of rules of substantive law. As *Erie* read the Rules of Decision Act: "Except in matters governed by the Federal Constitution or by Acts of Congress, the law to be applied in any case is the law of the State." 304 U.S., at 78, 58 S.Ct., at 822. Under the *Erie* doctrine, federal courts sitting in diversity apply state substantive law and federal procedural law.

Classification of a law as "substantive" or "procedural" for *Erie* purposes is sometimes a challenging endeavor. *Guaranty Trust Co. v. York,* 326 U.S. 99, 65 S.Ct. 1464, 89 L.Ed. 2079 (1945), an early interpretation of *Erie,* propounded an "outcome-determination" test: "[D]oes it significantly affect the result of a litigation for a federal court to disregard a law of a State that would be controlling in an action upon the same claim by the same parties in a State court?" 326 U.S., at 109, 65 S.Ct., at 1470. Ordering application of a state statute of limitations to an equity proceeding in federal court, the Court said in *Guaranty Trust:* "[W]here a federal court is exercising jurisdiction solely because of the diversity of citizenship of the parties, the outcome of the litigation in the federal court should be substantially the same, so far as legal rules determine the outcome of a litigation, as it would be if tried in a State court." *Ibid;* see also *Ragan v. Merchants Transfer & Warehouse Co.,* 337 U.S. 530, 533, 69 S.Ct. 1233, 1235, 93 L.Ed. 1520 (1949) (when local law that creates the cause of action qualifies it, "federal court must follow suit," for "a different measure of the cause of action in one court than in the other [would transgress] the principle of *Erie*"). A later pathmarking case, qualifying *Guaranty Trust,* explained that the "outcome-determination" test must not be applied mechanically to sweep in all manner of variations; instead, its application must be guided by "the twin aims of the *Erie* rule: discouragement of forum-shopping and avoidance of inequitable administration of the laws." *[Hanna v. Plumer,]* 380 U.S. 460, 468, 85 S.Ct. 1136, 1142, 14 L.Ed.2d 8 (1965).

Informed by these decisions, we address the question whether New York's "deviates materially" standard, codified in CPLR § 5501(c), is outcome-affective in this sense: Would "application of the [standard] . . . have so important an effect upon the fortunes of one or both of the litigants that failure to [apply] it would [unfairly discriminate against citizens of the forum State, or] be likely to cause a plaintiff to choose the federal court"? *Id.,* at 468, n. 9, 85 S.Ct., at 1142, n. 9.

We start from a point the parties do not debate. Gasperini acknowledges that a statutory cap on damages would supply substantive law for *Erie* purposes.* * * Although CPLR § 5501(c) is less readily classified, it was designed to provide an analogous control.

New York's Legislature codified in § 5501(c) a new standard, one that requires closer court review than the common law "shock the conscience" test. More rigorous comparative evaluations attend application of § 5501(c)'s "deviates materially" standard. To foster predictability, the legislature required the reviewing court, when overturning a verdict under § 5501(c), to state its reasons, including the factors it considered relevant. See CPLR § 5522(b). We think it a fair conclusion that CPLR § 5501(c) differs from a statutory cap principally "in that the maximum amount recoverable is not set by statute, but rather is determined by case law." * * * In sum, § 5501(c) contains a procedural instruction, but the State's objective is manifestly substantive. Cf. *S.A. Healy Co. v. Milwaukee Metropolitan Sewerage Dist.,* 60 F.3d 305, 310 (C.A.7 1995).

It thus appears that if federal courts ignore the change in the New York standard and persist in applying the "shock the conscience" test to damage awards on claims governed by New York law, " 'substantial' variations between state and federal [money judgments]" may be expected. See *Hanna,* 380 U.S., at 467–468, 85 S.Ct., at 1142. * * * Just as the *Erie* principle precludes a federal court from giving a state-created claim "longer life . . . than [the claim] would have had in the state court," *Ragan,* 337 U.S., at 533–534, 69 S.Ct., at 1235, so *Erie* precludes a recovery in federal court significantly larger than the recovery that would have been tolerated in state court.

B

CPLR § 5501(c), as earlier noted, is phrased as a direction to the New York Appellate Division. Acting essentially as a surrogate for a New York appellate forum, the Court of Appeals reviewed Gasperini's award to determine if it "deviate[d] materially" from damage awards the Appellate Division permitted in similar circumstances. The Court of Appeals performed this task without benefit of an opinion from the District Court, which had denied "without comment" the Center's Rule 59 motion. 66 F.3d, at 428. Concentrating on the authority § 5501(c) gives to the Appellate Division, Gasperini urges that the provision shifts fact-finding responsibility from the jury and the trial judge to the appellate court. Assigning such responsibility to an appellate court, he maintains, is incompatible with the Seventh Amendment's re-examination clause, and therefore, Gasperini concludes, § 5501(c) cannot be given effect in federal court. Although we reach a different conclusion than Gasperini, we agree that the Second Circuit did not attend to "[a]n essential characteristic of [the federal-court] system," *Byrd v. Blue Ridge Rural Elec. Cooperative, Inc.*, 356 U.S. 525, 537, 78 S.Ct. 893, 901, 2 L.Ed.2d 953 (1958), when it used § 5501(c) as "the standard for [federal] appellate review," *Consorti*, 72 F.3d, at 1013; see also 66 F.3d, at 430.

That "essential characteristic" was described in *Byrd*, a diversity suit for negligence in which a pivotal issue of fact would have been tried by a judge were the case in state court. The *Byrd* Court held that, despite the state practice, the plaintiff was entitled to a jury trial in federal court. In so ruling, the Court said that the *Guaranty Trust* "outcome-determination" test was an insufficient guide in cases presenting countervailing federal interests. See *Byrd*, 356 U.S., at 537, 78 S.Ct., at 901. The Court described the countervailing federal interests present in *Byrd* this way:

> "The federal system is an independent system for administering justice to litigants who properly invoke its jurisdiction. An essential characteristic of that system is the manner in which, in civil common-law actions, it distributes trial functions between judge and jury and, under the influence—if not the command—of the Seventh Amendment, assigns the decisions of disputed questions of fact to the jury." *Ibid.* (footnote omitted).

The Seventh Amendment, which governs proceedings in federal court, but not in state court, bears not only on the allocation of trial functions between judge and jury, the issue in *Byrd;* it also controls the allocation of authority to review verdicts, the issue of concern here. The Amendment reads:

> "In Suits at common law, where the value in controversy shall exceed twenty dollars, the right of trial by jury shall be preserved, and no fact tried by a jury, shall be otherwise re-examined in any Court of the United States, than according to the rules of the common law." U.S. Const., Amdt. 7.

Byrd involved the first clause of the Amendment, the "trial by jury" clause. This case involves the second, the "re-examination" clause. In keeping with the historic understanding, the re-examination clause does not inhibit the authority of trial judges to grant new trials "for any of the reasons for which new trials have heretofore been granted in actions at law in the courts of the United States." Fed. Rule Civ. Proc. 59(a). That authority is large. * * * "The trial judge in the federal system," we have reaffirmed, "has . . . discretion to grant a new trial if the verdict appears to [the judge] to be against the weight of the evidence." *Byrd,* 356 U.S., at 540, 78 S.Ct., at 902. This discretion includes overturning verdicts for excessiveness and ordering a new trial without qualification, or conditioned on the verdict winner's refusal to agree to a reduction (remittitur). See *Dimick v. Schiedt,* 293 U.S. 474, 486–487, 55 S.Ct. 296, 301, 79 L.Ed. 603 (1935) (recognizing that remittitur withstands Seventh Amendment attack, but rejecting additur as unconstitutional).

In contrast, appellate review of a federal trial court's denial of a motion to set aside a jury's verdict as excessive is a relatively late, and less secure, development. Such review was once deemed inconsonant with the Seventh Amendment's re-examination clause. See, *e.g., Lincoln v. Power,* 151 U.S. 436, 437–438, 14 S.Ct. 387, 388, 38 L.Ed. 224 (1894); *Williamson v. Osenton,* 220 F. 653, 655 (C.A.4 1915); see also 6A Moore's Federal Practice ¶ 59.08[6], at 59–167 (collecting cases). We subsequently recognized that, even in cases in which the *Erie* doctrine was not in play—cases arising wholly under federal law—the question was not settled; we twice granted certiorari to decide the unsettled issue, but ultimately resolved the cases on other grounds. See *Grunenthal v. Long Island R. Co.,* 393 U.S. 156, 158, 89 S.Ct. 331, 333, 21 L.Ed.2d 309 (1968); *Neese v. Southern R. Co.,* 350 U.S. 77, 77, 76 S.Ct. 131, 131–132, 100 L.Ed. 60 (1955).

Before today, we have not "expressly [held] that the Seventh Amendment allows appellate review of a district court's denial of a motion to set aside an award as excessive." *Browning-Ferris Industries of Vt., Inc. v. Kelco Disposal, Inc.,* 492 U.S. 257, 279, n. 25, 109 S.Ct. 2909, 2922, n. 25, 106 L.Ed.2d 219 (1989). But in successive reminders that the question was worthy of this Court's attention, we noted, without disapproval, that courts of appeals engage in review of district court excessiveness determinations, applying "abuse of discretion" as their standard. See *Grunenthal,* 393 U.S., at 159, 89 S.Ct., at 333. We noted the Circuit decisions in point, *id.,* at 157, n. 3, 89 S.Ct., at 332, n. 3, and, in *Browning-Ferris,* we again referred to appellate court abuse-of-discretion review:

> "[T]he role of the district court is to determine whether the jury's verdict is within the confines set by state law, and to determine, by reference to federal standards developed under Rule 59, whether a new trial or remittitur should be ordered. The court of appeals should then review the district court's determination under an abuse-of-discretion standard." 492 U.S., at 279, 109 S.Ct., at 2922.[18]

As the Second Circuit explained, appellate review for abuse of discretion is reconcilable with the Seventh Amendment as a control necessary and proper to the fair administration of justice: "We must give the benefit of every doubt to the judgment of the trial judge; but surely there must be an upper limit, and whether that has been surpassed is not a question of fact with respect to which reasonable men may differ, but a question of law." *Dagnello v. Long Island R. Co.,* 289 F.2d 797, 806

---

[18] *Browning-Ferris* concerned punitive damages. We agree with the Second Circuit, however, that "[f]or purposes of deciding whether state or federal law is applicable, the question whether an award of *compensatory* damages exceeds what is permitted by law is not materially different from the question whether an award of *punitive* damages exceeds what is permitted by law." *Consorti,* 72 F.3d, at 1012.

(C.A.2 1961) (quoted in *Grunenthal,* 393 U.S., at 159, 89 S.Ct., at 333). All other Circuits agree. * * * We now approve this line of decisions, and thus make explicit what Justice Stewart thought implicit in our *Grunenthal* disposition: "[N]othing in the Seventh Amendment . . . precludes appellate review of the trial judge's denial of a motion to set aside [a jury verdict] as excessive." 393 U.S., at 164, 89 S.Ct., at 336 (Stewart, J., dissenting) (internal quotation marks and footnote omitted).

C

In *Byrd,* the Court faced a one-or-the-other choice: trial by judge as in state court, or trial by jury according to the federal practice. In the case before us, a choice of that order is not required, for the principal state and federal interests can be accommodated. The Second Circuit correctly recognized that when New York substantive law governs a claim for relief, New York law and decisions guide the allowable damages. See 66 F.3d, at 430; see also *Consorti,* 72 F.3d, at 1011. But that court did not take into account the characteristic of the federal-court system that caused us to reaffirm: "The proper role of the trial and appellate courts in the federal system in reviewing the size of jury verdicts is . . . a matter of federal law." *Donovan v. Penn Shipping Co.,* 429 U.S. 648, 649, 97 S.Ct. 835, 837, 51 L.Ed.2d 112 (1977) *(per curiam);* see also *Browning-Ferris,* 492 U.S., at 279, 109 S.Ct., at 2922 ("[T]he role of the district court is to determine whether the jury's verdict is within the confines set by state law. . . . The court of appeals should then review the district court's determination under an abuse-of-discretion standard.").

New York's dominant interest can be respected, without disrupting the federal system, once it is recognized that the federal district court is capable of performing the checking function, *i.e.,* that court can apply the State's "deviates materially" standard in line with New York case law evolving under CPLR § 5501(c).[22] We recall, in this regard, that the "deviates materially" standard serves as the guide to be applied in trial as well as appellate courts in New York. * * *

New York's dominant interest can be respected, without disrupting the federal system, once it is recognized that the federal district court is capable of performing the checking function, *i.e.,* that court can apply the State's "deviates materially" standard in line with New York case law

---

[22] JUSTICE SCALIA finds in Federal Rule of Civil Procedure 59 a "federal standard" for new trial motions in " 'direct collision' " with, and " 'leaving no room for the operation of,' " a state law like CPLR § 5501(c). *Post,* at 2239–40 (quoting *Burlington Northern R. Co.,* 480 U.S., at 4–5, 107 S.Ct., at 969). The relevant prescription, Rule 59(a), has remained unchanged since the adoption of the Federal Rules by this Court in 1937. 302 U.S. 783. Rule 59(a) is as encompassing as it is uncontroversial. It is indeed "Hornbook" law that a most usual ground for a Rule 59 motion is that "the damages are excessive." See C. Wright, Law of Federal Courts 676–677 (5th ed.1994). Whether damages are excessive for the claim-in-suit must be governed by *some law.* And there is no candidate for that governance other than the law that gives rise to the claim for relief—here, the law of New York. See 28 U.S.C. § 2072(a) and (b) ("Supreme Court shall have the power to prescribe general rules of . . . procedure"; "[s]uch rules shall not abridge, enlarge or modify any substantive right"); *Browning-Ferris,* 492 U.S., at 279, 109 S.Ct., at 2922 ("standard of excessiveness" is a "matte[r] of state, and not federal, common law"); see also R. Fallon, D. Meltzer, & D. Shapiro, Hart and Wechsler's The Federal Courts and the Federal System 729–730 (4th ed.1996) (observing that Court "has continued since [*Hanna v. Plumer,* 380 U.S. 460, 85 S.Ct. 1136, 14 L.Ed.2d 8 (1965)] to interpret the federal rules to avoid conflict with important state regulatory policies," citing *Walker v. Armco Steel Corp.,* 446 U.S. 740, 100 S.Ct. 1978, 64 L.Ed.2d 659 (1980)).

evolving under CPLR § 5501(c). We recall, in this regard, that the "deviates materially" standard serves as the guide to be applied in trial as well as appellate courts in New York. * * *

Within the federal system, practical reasons combine with Seventh Amendment constraints to lodge in the district court, not the court of appeals, primary responsibility for application of § 5501(c)'s "deviates materially" check. Trial judges have the "unique opportunity to consider the evidence in the living courtroom context," *Taylor v. Washington Terminal Co.*, 409 F.2d 145, 148 (C.A.D.C.1969), while appellate judges see only the "cold paper record," 66 F.3d, at 431.

District court applications of the "deviates materially" standard would be subject to appellate review under the standard the Circuits now employ when inadequacy or excessiveness is asserted on appeal: abuse of discretion. * * * In light of *Erie*'s doctrine, the federal appeals court must be guided by the damage-control standard state law supplies, but as the Second Circuit itself has said: "If we reverse, it must be because of an abuse of discretion. . . . The very nature of the problem counsels restraint. . . . We must give the benefit of every doubt to the judgment of the trial judge." *Dagnello*, 289 F.2d, at 806.

IV

It does not appear that the District Court checked the jury's verdict against the relevant New York decisions demanding more than "industry standard" testimony to support an award of the size the jury returned in this case. As the Court of Appeals recognized, see 66 F.3d, at 429, the uniqueness of the photographs and the plaintiff's earnings as photographer—past and reasonably projected—are factors relevant to appraisal of the award. See, *e.g., Blackman v. Michael Friedman Publishing Group, Inc.*, 201 App.Div.2d 328, 328, 607 N.Y.S.2d 43, 44 (1st Dept.1994); *Nierenberg v. Wursteria, Inc.*, 189 App.Div.2d 571, 571–572, 592 N.Y.S.2d 27, 27–28 (1st Dept.1993). Accordingly, we vacate the judgment of the Court of Appeals and instruct that court to remand the case to the District Court so that the trial judge, revisiting his ruling on the new trial motion, may test the jury's verdict against CPLR § 5501(c)'s "deviates materially" standard.

It is so ordered.

■ JUSTICE STEVENS, dissenting.

While I agree with most of the reasoning in the Court's opinion, I disagree with its disposition of the case. I would affirm the judgment of the Court of Appeals. I would also reject the suggestion that the Seventh Amendment limits the power of a federal appellate court sitting in diversity to decide whether a jury's award of damages exceeds a limit established by state law.

* * *

■ JUSTICE SCALIA, with whom the CHIEF JUSTICE and JUSTICE THOMAS join, dissenting.

Today the Court overrules a longstanding and well-reasoned line of precedent that has for years prohibited federal appellate courts from reviewing refusals by district courts to set aside civil jury awards as contrary to the weight of the evidence. * * * It is not for us, much less for the courts of appeals, to decide that the Seventh Amendment's restriction on federal-court review of jury findings has outlived its usefulness.

The Court also holds today that a state practice that relates to the division of duties between state judges and juries must be followed by federal courts in diversity cases. On this issue, too, our prior cases are directly to the contrary.

As I would reverse the judgment of the Court of Appeals, I respectfully dissent.

I

Because the Court and I disagree as to the character of the review that is before us, I recount briefly the nature of the New York practice rule at issue. Section 5501(c) of the N.Y. Civ. Prac. Law and Rules (CPLR) (McKinney 1995) directs New York intermediate appellate courts faced with a claim "that the award is excessive or inadequate and that a new trial should have been granted" to determine whether the jury's award "deviates materially from what would be reasonable compensation." In granting respondent a new trial under this standard, the Court of Appeals necessarily engaged in a two-step process. As it has explained the application of § 5501(c), that provision "requires the reviewing court to determine the range it regards as reasonable, and to determine whether the particular jury award deviates materially from that range." *Consorti v. Armstrong World Industries, Inc.,* 72 F.3d 1003, 1013 (1995) (amended). The first of these two steps—the determination as to "reasonable" damages—plainly requires the reviewing court to reexamine a factual matter tried by the jury: the appropriate measure of damages, on the evidence presented, under New York law. The second step—the determination as to the degree of difference between "reasonable" damages and the damages found by the jury (whether the latter "deviates materially" from the former)—establishes the degree of judicial tolerance for awards found not to be reasonable, whether at the trial-level or by the appellate court. No part of this exercise is appropriate for a federal court of appeals, whether or not it is sitting in a diversity case.

A

Granting appellate courts authority to decide whether an award is "excessive or inadequate" in the manner of CPLR § 5501(c) may reflect a sound understanding of the capacities of modern juries and trial judges. That is to say, the people of the State of New York may well be correct that such a rule contributes to a more just legal system. But the practice of *federal* appellate reexamination of facts found by a jury is precisely what the People of the several States considered *not* to be good legal policy in 1791. Indeed, so fearful were they of such a practice that they constitutionally prohibited it by means of the Seventh Amendment.

* * *

The second clause of the Amendment responded to that concern by providing that "[i]n [s]uits at common law . . . no fact tried by a jury, shall be otherwise re-examined in any Court of the United States, than according to the rules of the common law." U.S. Const., Amdt. 7. The Reexamination Clause put to rest "apprehensions" of "new trials by the appellate courts," *Wonson,* 28 F.Cas., at 750, by adopting, in broad fashion, "the rules of the common law" to govern federal-court interference with jury determinations. The content of that law was familiar and fixed. * * * It quite plainly barred reviewing courts from entertaining claims that the jury's verdict was contrary to the evidence.

* * *

Nor was the common law proscription on reexamination limited to review of the correctness of the jury's determination of liability on the facts. No less than the existence of liability, the proper measure of damages "involves only a question of fact," *St. Louis, I.M. & S.R. Co. v. Craft,* 237 U.S. 648, 661, 35 S.Ct. 704, 707, 59 L.Ed. 1160 (1915), as does a "motio[n] for a new trial based on the ground that the damages . . . are excessive," *Metropolitan R. Co. v. Moore,* 121 U.S. 558, 574, 7 S.Ct. 1334, 1342, 30 L.Ed. 1022 (1887). As appeals from denial of such motions necessarily pose a factual question, courts of the United States are constitutionally forbidden to entertain them. * * * This view was for long years not only unquestioned in our cases, but repeatedly affirmed.

* * *

C

The Court, as is its wont of late, all but ignores the relevant history. * * *

II

The Court's holding that federal courts of appeals may review district court denials of motions for new trials for error of fact is not the only novel aspect of today's decision. The Court also directs that the case be remanded to the District Court, so that it may "test the jury's verdict against CPLR § 5501(c)'s 'deviates materially' standard." This disposition contradicts the principle that "[t]he proper role of the trial and appellate courts in the federal system in reviewing the size of jury verdicts is . . . a matter of federal law." *Donovan v. Penn Shipping Co.,* 429 U.S. 648, 649, 97 S.Ct. 835, 837, 51 L.Ed.2d 112 (1977) *(per curiam).*

The Court acknowledges that state procedural rules cannot, as a general matter, be permitted to interfere with the allocation of functions in the federal court system. Indeed, it is at least partly for this reason that the Court rejects direct application of § 5501(c) at the appellate level as inconsistent with an " 'essential characteristic' " of the federal court system—by which the Court presumably means abuse-of-discretion review of denials of motions for new trials. But the scope of the Court's concern is oddly circumscribed. The "essential characteristic" of the federal jury, and, more specifically, the role of the federal trial court in reviewing jury judgments, apparently counts for little. The Court approves the "accommodat[ion]" achieved by having district courts review jury verdicts under the "deviates materially" standard, because it regards that as a means of giving effect to the State's purposes "without disrupting the federal system." But changing the standard by which trial judges review jury verdicts *does* disrupt the federal system, and is plainly inconsistent with "the strong federal policy against allowing state rules to disrupt the judge-jury relationship in federal court." *Byrd v. Blue Ridge Rural Elec. Cooperative, Inc.,* 356 U.S. 525, 538, 78 S.Ct. 893, 901, 2 L.Ed.2d 953 (1958). The Court's opinion does not even acknowledge, let alone address, this dislocation.

We discussed precisely the point at issue here in *Browning-Ferris Industries of Vt., Inc. v. Kelco Disposal, Inc.,* 492 U.S. 257, 109 S.Ct. 2909, 106 L.Ed.2d 219 (1989), and gave an answer altogether contrary to the one provided today. *Browning-Ferris* rejected a request to fashion a federal common-law rule limiting the size of punitive-damages awards in federal courts, reaffirming the principle of *Erie R. Co. v. Tompkins,* 304 U.S. 64, 58 S.Ct. 817, 82 L.Ed. 1188 (1938), that "[i]n a diversity action, or in any other lawsuit where state law provides the basis of decision, the propriety of an award of punitive damages . . . and the factors the jury may consider in determining their amount, are questions of state law." 492 U.S., at 278, 109 S.Ct., at 2921–2922. But the opinion expressly stated that "[f]ederal law . . . will control on those issues involving the proper review of the jury award by a federal district court and court of appeals." *Id.,* at 278–279, 109 S.Ct., at 2922. * * * The same distinction necessarily applies where the judgment under review is for compensatory damages: State substantive law controls what injuries are compensable and in what amount; but federal standards determine whether the award exceeds what is lawful to such degree that it may be set aside by order for new trial or remittitur.

The Court does not disavow those statements in *Browning-Ferris* (indeed, it does not even discuss them), but it presumably overrules them, at least where the state rule that governs "whether a new trial or remittitur should be ordered" is characterized as "substantive" in nature. That, at any rate, is the reason the Court asserts for giving § 5501(c) dispositive effect. The objective of that provision, the Court states, "is manifestly substantive", since it operates to "contro[l] how much a plaintiff can be awarded" by "tightening the range of tolerable awards." Although "less readily classified" as substantive than "a statutory cap on damages," it nonetheless "was designed to provide an analogous control", by making a new trial mandatory when the award "deviat[es] materially" from what is reasonable.

I do not see how this can be so. It seems to me quite wrong to regard this provision as a "substantive" rule for *Erie* purposes. The "analog[y]" to "a statutory cap on damages" fails utterly. There is an absolutely fundamental distinction between a *rule of law* such as that, which would ordinarily be imposed upon the jury in the trial court's instructions, and a *rule of review,* which simply determines how closely the jury verdict will be scrutinized for compliance with the instructions. A tighter standard for reviewing jury determinations can no more plausibly be called a "substantive" disposition than can a tighter appellate standard for reviewing trial-court determinations. The one, like the other, provides additional assurance *that the law has been complied with;* but the other, like the one, *leaves the law unchanged.*

The Court commits the classic *Erie* mistake of regarding whatever changes the outcome as substantive, see *ante,* at 2220–21. That is not the only factor to be considered. See *Byrd,* 356 U.S., at 537, 78 S.Ct., at 900 ("[W]ere 'outcome' the only consideration, a strong case might appear for saying that the federal court should follow the state practice. But there are affirmative countervailing considerations at work here"). Outcome-determination "was never intended to serve as a talisman," *Hanna v. Plumer,* 380 U.S. 460, 466–467, 85 S.Ct. 1136, 1141, 14 L.Ed.2d 8 (1965), and does not have the power to convert the most classic elements of the *process* of assuring that the law is observed into the substantive law itself. * * *

In any event, the Court exaggerates the difference that the state standard will make. It concludes that different outcomes are likely to ensue depending on whether the law being applied is the state "deviates materially" standard of § 5501(c) or the "shocks the conscience" standard. Of course it is not the federal *appellate* standard but the federal *district-court* standard for granting new trials that must be compared with the New York standard to determine whether substantially different results will obtain—and it is far from clear that the district-court standard *ought* to be "shocks the conscience." Indeed, it is not even clear (as the Court asserts) that "shocks the conscience" *is* the standard (erroneous or not) actually applied by the district courts of the Second Circuit. The Second Circuit's test for reversing a grant of a new trial for an excessive verdict is whether the award was "*clearly* within the maximum limit of a reasonable range." *Ismail v. Cohen,* 899 F.2d 183, 186 (C.A.2 1990) (internal quotation marks omitted), so any district court that uses that standard will be affirmed. And while many district-court decisions express the "shocks the conscience" criterion, see, *e.g., Koerner v. Club Mediterranee, S.A.,* 833 F. Supp. 327, 333 (S.D.N.Y.1993), some have used a standard of "indisputably egregious," *Banff v. Express, Inc.,* 921 F. Supp. 1065, 1069 (S.D.N.Y.1995), or have adopted the inverse of the Second Circuit's test for reversing a grant of new trial, namely, "*clearly* outside the maximum limit of a reasonable range," *Paper Corp. v. Schoeller Technical Papers, Inc.,* 807 F. Supp. 337, 350–351 (S.D.N.Y.1992). * * * In sum, it is at least highly questionable whether the consistent outcome differential claimed by the Court even exists. What seems to me far more likely to produce forum-shopping is the consistent difference between the state and federal *appellate* standards, which the Court leaves untouched. Under the Court's disposition, the Second Circuit reviews only for abuse of discretion, whereas New York's appellate courts engage in a *de novo* review for material deviation, giving the defendant a double shot at getting the damages award set aside. The only result that would produce the conformity the Court erroneously believes *Erie* requires is the one adopted by the Second Circuit and rejected by the Court: *de novo* federal appellate review under the § 5501(c) standard.

To say that application of § 5501(c) in place of the federal standard will not consistently produce disparate results is not to suggest that the decision the Court has made today is not a momentous one. The *principle* that the state standard governs is of great importance, since it bears the potential to destroy the uniformity of federal practice and the integrity of the federal court system. Under the Court's view, a state rule that directed courts "to determine that an award is excessive or inadequate if it deviates *in any degree* from *the proper measure of compensation*" would have to be applied in federal courts, effectively requiring federal judges to determine the amount of damages *de novo,* and effectively taking the matter away from the jury entirely. Cf. *Byrd,* 356 U.S., at 537–538, 78 S.Ct., at 901. * * *

The foregoing describes why I think the Court's *Erie* analysis is flawed. But in my view, one does not even reach the *Erie* question in this case. The standard to be applied by a district court in ruling on a motion for a new trial is set forth in Rule 59 of the Federal Rules of Civil Procedure, which provides that "[a] new trial may be granted . . . for any of the reasons for which new trials have heretofore been granted in actions at law *in the courts of the United States*" (emphasis added). That is undeniably a federal standard. Federal district courts in the Second Circuit have interpreted that standard to permit the granting of new trials where " 'it is quite clear that the jury has reached a seriously erroneous result' " and letting the verdict stand would result in a " 'miscarriage of justice.' " Koerner v. Club Mediterranee, S. A., 833 F. Supp. 327 (S.D.N.Y.1993) (quoting Bevevino v. *Saydjari*, 574 F.2d 676, 684 (C.A.2 1978)). Assuming (as we have no reason to question) that this is a correct interpretation of what Rule 59 requires, it is undeniable that the federal rule is " 'sufficiently broad' to cause a 'direct collision' with the state law or, implicitly, to 'control the issue' before the court, thereby leaving no room for the operation of that law." *Burlington Northern R. Co. v. Woods*, 480 U.S. 1, 4–5, 107 S.Ct. 967, 969, 94 L.Ed.2d 1 (1987). It is simply not possible to give controlling effect both to the federal standard and the state standard in reviewing the jury's award. That being so, the court has no choice but to apply the Federal Rule, which is an exercise of what we have called Congress's "power to regulate matters which, though falling within the uncertain area between substance and procedure, are rationally capable of classification as either." *Hanna*, 380 U.S., at 472, 85 S.Ct., at 1144.

* * *

There is no small irony in the Court's declaration today that appellate review of refusals to grant new trials for error of fact is "a control necessary and proper to the fair administration of justice." It is objection to *precisely* that sort of "control" by federal appellate judges that gave birth to the Reexamination Clause of the Seventh Amendment. Alas, those who drew the Amendment, and the citizens who approved it, did not envision an age in which the Constitution means whatever this Court thinks it ought to mean—or indeed, whatever the courts of appeals have recently thought it ought to mean.

When there is added to the revision of the Seventh Amendment the Court's precedent-setting disregard of Congress's instructions in Rule 59, one must conclude that this is a bad day for the Constitution's distinctive Article III courts in general, and for the role of the jury in those courts in particular. I respectfully dissent.

NOTES AND QUESTIONS

1. *York* and *Byrd* revisited. *Gasperini* is the first Supreme Court case after *Byrd* itself to apply a *Byrd* analysis to an *Erie* problem, and is necessarily also the first case to apply a combined *York* and *Byrd* analysis.

2. Two *Erie* questions. The majority opinion is somewhat opaque, but with a little work you can see that the Court is deciding not one, but two, *Erie* questions. The first is a question about procedure in the district court: What standard should the district court use in determining whether to grant a new trial? The second is a question about procedure in the court of appeals: What standard should the court of appeals use to determine whether the district court properly denied the motion for a new trial?

3. **The *Erie* question in the district court. a. Does federal Rule)(a) provide a federal standard governing whether the district urt should have granted a new trial?** At the time of the Court's cision in *Gasperini*, Rule 59(a) provided, "A new trial may be granted * * * an action in which there has been a trial by jury, for any of the reasons for which new trials have heretofore been granted in actions at law in the courts of the United States." (The wording of the rule is now slightly different but to the same effect.) The Court in *Gasperini* holds that Rule 59(a) does not provide a federal standard governing whether the district court should grant a new trial because of an excessive jury verdict. The Court writes, "Whether damages are excessive for the claim-in-suit must be governed by some law. And there is no candidate for that governance other than the law that gives rise to the claim for relief—here the law of New York." See footnote 22 in the Court's opinion. Can the Court really mean that there is "no candidate"? Rule 59(a) specifically stated that a new trial "may be granted for * * * any of the reasons for which new trials have heretofore been granted in actions at law in the courts of the United States."

Why doesn't the language of Rule 59(a) instruct the federal district court to apply the "shock-the-conscience" standard that district courts have heretofore applied in reviewing jury verdicts for excessiveness under Rule 59(a)? The Court's answer appears to be that if Rule 59(a) were read in this case to contain a federal standard of review for excessiveness, the Rule would violate the limitation provided in the Rules Enabling Act. That is, the Rules Enabling Act provides that the federal Rules "shall not abridge, enlarge or modify any substantive right." 28 U.S.C. § 2072. The citations contained in its footnote 22 suggest that this is the Court's answer. In *Gasperini*, the Court is dealing with an action brought under the substantive law of New York. But if the "shock-the conscience" standard is not applied in *Gasperini* because of the limitation of the Rules Enabling Act, can the "shock-the-conscience" standard ever be applied under Rule 59(a)? The Rules Enabling Act does not distinguish between substantive rights based on state law and those based on federal law. Recall that Rule 3 means something different depending on whether the action is based on state or federal law. See the discussion following *Hanna v. Plumer*, supra p. 375 note 6. Has Rule 59(a) now joined the anomalous Rule 3?

Justice Scalia, in dissent, contends that Rule 59(a) prescribes a federal standard of review for excessiveness, which the district court must use in deciding whether to grant a new trial. If Rule 59(a) does prescribe a federal standard for granting a new trial, the *Erie* question in this case is relatively easy. Under *Hanna v. Plumer*, the Court would decide if Rule 59(a) is valid under the Rules Enabling Act; if Rule 59(a) is valid, the federal standard prescribed by the Rule must be applied by the district court.

What is the support for Justice Scalia's contention that Rule 59(a) prescribes a federal standard of review for excessiveness? Recall that Rule 59(a) provides that a new trial may be granted "for any of the reasons for which new trials have heretofore been granted in actions at law in the courts of the United States." Justice Scalia quotes Rule 59(a), italicizing the words "in the courts of the United States." He then asserts, as if it follows from the italicized words, "That is undeniably a federal standard." Can Justice Scalia really mean that merely because a standard has "heretofore" been applied "in the courts of the United States," it is necessarily a federal standard? Is he forgetting that federal courts routinely apply state law? Further and more specifically, as the Court points out in footnote 22, the text of Rule 59(a) had remained unchanged since its original approval by the Court in 1937, and its tacit approval by Congress in 1938. Until the adoption of Rule 59(a), the federal Conformity Act required federal district courts "in actions at law" to follow the procedural rules of the state in which they sat. Thus, at the time of the adoption of Rule 59(a), the standard of review of jury verdicts that had "heretofore" been applied "in the courts of the United States" had been supplied by state law. In the first half of his dissent, Justice Scalia insists on adherence to the original meaning of the Seventh Amendment. Why does he not similarly insist on adherence to the original meaning of Rule 59(a)?

b. In the absence of an applicable Federal Rule of Civil Procedure. Because Rule 59(a) does not (probably because it cannot) provide a federal standard, there is no applicable federal Rule. Because there is no applicable federal Rule, and because the New York standard is "manifestly objective," does it follow that New York law must be applied?

4. The *Erie* question in the court of appeals. a. Does the Seventh Amendment provide the governing rule? Until *Gasperini*, it was an open question whether the Seventh Amendment permits a federal court of appeals to reduce a jury verdict. The Court in *Gasperini* resolves the question, holding that a court of appeals may do so. If the Seventh Amendment had provided the controlling standard and had forbidden a federal court to reduce the amount of a jury's damage award, an *Erie* analysis would have been unnecessary, for the Seventh Amendment would simply have prevailed over inconsistent state law by virtue of the supremacy of federal law. But because the Seventh Amendment does not provide the controlling standard, the Court in *Gasperini*, like the Court in *Byrd*, is dealing with a federal court practice that is not constitutionally required.

b. In the absence of a controlling Federal Rule of Appellate Procedure. Not only is there no controlling constitutional provision in *Gasperini*. There is also no applicable statute or Federal Rule of Appellate Procedure. The "abuse of discretion" standard that the federal courts of appeal normally apply in reviewing a district court decision whether, and by how much, to reduce a jury verdict is not contained in a rule, but is, rather, a practice based on judge-made law. Therefore, the Court must make the "relatively unguided *Erie* choice" that is required in the absence of an applicable federal Rule. That is, the Court must engage in a *York/Byrd* analysis to determine whether to follow the federal appellate practice of reviewing the district court decision for "abuse of discretion."

The competing New York state appellate standard of review is "deviates materially from what would be reasonable compensation." This standard is applied by the state appellate court in reviewing the decision of the trial court, as well as by the state trial court in evaluating the jury verdict in the first instance. The Supreme Court does not bother with an explicit *York* outcome-determinative analysis, perhaps because it is clear that the choice between the two is not "outcome-determinative." But the Court does engage in a *Byrd* interest-balancing analysis. The Court concludes that the interest of the state in "checking" excessive jury verdicts, expressed in its "deviates materially" standard, is sufficiently protected by the federal *district court's* application of the "deviates materially" standard. Therefore, the federal court of appeals can continue to use its customary "abuse of discretion" standard in its appellate review of the district court's decision. Do you agree with the Court that the standard of review by the court of appeals of the district court's action, unlike the standard of review by the district court of the size of the jury damage verdict, should be governed by the federal rather than the state standard?

5. Additional reading. For insightful academic writing on *Gasperini*, see Floyd, Erie Awry: A Comment on *Gasperini v. Center for Humanities, Inc.*, 1997 B.Y.U. L. Rev. 267; Freer, Some Thoughts on the State of *Erie* After *Gasperini*, 76 Tex. L. Rev. 1637, 1663 (1998); Rowe, Not Bad for Government Work: Does Anyone Else Think the Supreme Court is Doing a Halfway Decent Job in Its *Erie-Hanna* Jurisprudence? 73 Notre Dame L. Rev. 963, 966 (1998).

Shady Grove Orthopedic Assocs., P.A. v. Allstate Ins. Co.

Supreme Court of the United States, 2010.
559 U.S. 393, 130 S.Ct. 1431, 176 L.Ed.2d 311.

■ JUSTICE SCALIA announced the judgment of the Court and delivered the opinion of the Court with respect to Parts I and II–A, an opinion with respect to Parts II–B and II–D, in which THE CHIEF JUSTICE, JUSTICE THOMAS, and JUSTICE SOTOMAYOR join, and an opinion with respect to Part II–C, in which THE CHIEF JUSTICE and JUSTICE THOMAS join.

New York law prohibits class actions in suits seeking penalties or statutory minimum damages.[1] We consider whether this precludes a federal district court sitting in diversity from entertaining a class action under Federal Rule of Civil Procedure 23.

I

The petitioner's complaint alleged the following: Shady Grove Orthopedic Associates, P. A., provided medical care to Sonia E. Galvez for injuries she suffered in an automobile accident. As partial payment for that care, Galvez assigned to Shady Grove her rights to insurance benefits under a policy issued in New York by Allstate Insurance Co. Shady Grove tendered a claim for the assigned benefits to Allstate, which under New York law had 30 days to pay the claim or deny it. * * * Allstate apparently paid, but not on time, and it refused to pay the statutory

---

[1]   New York Civ. Prac. Law Ann. § 901 (West 2006) provides:

"(a) One or more members of a class may sue or be sued as representative parties on behalf of all if:

"1. the class is so numerous that joinder of all members, whether otherwise required or permitted, is impracticable;

"2. there are questions of law or fact common to the class which predominate over any questions affecting only individual members;

"3. the claims or defenses of the representative parties are typical of the claims or defenses of the class;

"4. the representative parties will fairly and adequately protect the interests of the class; and

"5. a class action is superior to other available methods for the fair and efficient adjudication of the controversy.

"(b) Unless a statute creating or imposing a penalty, or a minimum measure of recovery specifically authorizes the recovery thereof in a class action, an action to recover a penalty, or minimum measure of recovery created or imposed by statute may not be maintained as a class action."

interest that accrued on the overdue benefits (at two percent per month)[.]

Shady Grove filed this diversity suit in the Eastern District of New York to recover the unpaid statutory interest. Alleging that Allstate routinely refuses to pay interest on overdue benefits, Shady Grove sought relief on behalf of itself and a class of all others to whom Allstate owes interest. The District Court dismissed the suit for lack of jurisdiction. * * * It reasoned that N.Y. Civ. Prac. Law Ann. § 901(b), which precludes a suit to recover a "penalty" from proceeding as a class action, applies in diversity suits in federal court, despite Federal Rule of Civil Procedure 23. Concluding that statutory interest is a "penalty" under New York law, it held that § 901(b) prohibited the proposed class action. And, since Shady Grove conceded that its individual claim (worth roughly $500) fell far short of the amount-in-controversy requirement for individual suits under 28 U.S.C. § 1332(a), the suit did not belong in federal court.[3]

The Second Circuit affirmed. * * *

II

The framework for our decision is familiar. We must first determine whether Rule 23 answers the question in dispute. *Burlington Northern R. Co.* v. *Woods*, 480 U.S. 1, 4–5, 107 S.Ct. 967, 94 L.Ed.2d 1 (1987). If it does, it governs—New York's law notwithstanding—unless it exceeds statutory authorization or Congress's rulemaking power. *Id.*, at 5, 107 S.Ct. 967, 94 L.Ed.2d 1; see *Hanna* v. *Plumer*, 380 U.S. 460, 463–464, 85 S.Ct. 1136, 14 L.Ed.2d 8 (1965). We do not wade into *Erie*'s murky waters unless the federal rule is inapplicable or invalid. See 380 U.S., at 469–471, 85 S.Ct. 1136, 14 L.Ed.2d 8.

A

The question in dispute is whether Shady Grove's suit may proceed as a class action. Rule 23 provides an answer. It states that "[a] class action may be maintained" if two conditions are met: The suit must satisfy the criteria set forth in subdivision (a) (*i.e.*, numerosity, commonality, typicality, and adequacy of representation), and it also must fit into one of the three categories described in subdivision (b). Fed. Rule Civ. Proc. 23(b). By its terms this creates a categorical rule entitling a plaintiff whose suit meets the specified criteria to pursue his claim as a class action. * * * Thus, Rule 23 provides a one-size-fits-all formula for deciding the class-action question. Because § 901(b) attempts to answer the same question—*i.e.*, it states that Shady Grove's suit "may *not* be maintained as a class action" (emphasis added) because of the relief it seeks—it cannot apply in diversity suits unless Rule 23 is ultra vires.

The Second Circuit believed that § 901(b) and Rule 23 do not conflict because they address different issues. Rule 23, it said, concerns only the criteria for determining whether a given class can and should be certified; § 901(b), on the other hand, addresses an antecedent question: whether the particular type of claim is eligible for class treatment in the first place—a question on which Rule 23 is silent." * *

---

[3] Shady Grove had asserted jurisdiction under 28 U.S.C. § 1332(d)(2), which relaxes, for class actions seeking at least $5 million, the rule against aggregating separate claims for calculation of the amount in controversy. See *Exxon Mobil Corp.* v. *Allapattah Services, Inc.*, 545 U.S. 546, 571, 125 S.Ct. 2611, 162 L.Ed.2d 502 (2005).

We disagree. To begin with, the line between eligibility and certifiability is entirely artificial. Both are preconditions for maintaining a class action. * * *

There is no reason * * * to read Rule 23 as addressing only whether claims made eligible for class treatment by some *other* law should be certified as class actions. Allstate asserts that Rule 23 neither explicitly nor implicitly empowers a federal court "to certify a class in each and every case" where the Rule's criteria are met. * * * But that is *exactly* what Rule 23 does: It says that if the prescribed preconditions are satisfied "[a] class action *may be maintained*" (emphasis added)—not "*a class action may be permitted*." Courts do not maintain actions; litigants do. The discretion suggested by Rule 23's "may" is discretion residing in the plaintiff: He may bring his claim in a class action if he wishes. And like the rest of the Federal Rules of Civil Procedure, Rule 23 *automatically* applies "in all civil actions and proceedings in the United States district courts," Fed. Rule Civ. Proc. 1. * * *

Allstate points out that Congress has carved out some federal claims from Rule 23's reach, see, *e.g.*, 8 U.S.C. § 1252(e)(1)(B)—which shows, Allstate contends, that Rule 23 does not authorize class actions for all claims, but rather leaves room for laws like § 901(b). But Congress, unlike New York, has ultimate authority over the Federal Rules of Civil Procedure; it can create exceptions to an individual rule as it sees fit—either by directly amending the rule or by enacting a separate statute overriding it in certain instances. * * * The fact that Congress has created specific exceptions to Rule 23 hardly proves that the Rule does not apply generally. In fact, it proves the opposite. If Rule 23 did *not* authorize class actions across the board, the statutory exceptions would be unnecessary.

Allstate next suggests that the structure of § 901 shows that Rule 23 addresses only certifiability. Section 901(*a*), it notes, establishes class-certification criteria roughly analogous to those in Rule 23 (wherefore it agrees *that* subsection is pre-empted). But § 901(b)'s rule barring class actions for certain claims is set off as its own subsection, and where it applies, § 901(a) does not. This shows, according to Allstate, that § 901(b) concerns a separate subject. Perhaps it does concern a subject separate from the subject of § 901(a). But the question before us is whether it concerns a subject separate from the subject of *Rule 23*—and for purposes of answering *that* question the way New York has structured its statute is immaterial. Rule 23 permits all class actions that meet its requirements, and a State cannot limit that permission by structuring one part of its statute to track Rule 23 and enacting another part that imposes additional requirements. Both of § 901's subsections undeniably answer the same question as Rule 23: whether a class action may proceed for a given suit. * * *

The dissent argues that § 901(b) has nothing to do with whether Shady Grove may maintain its suit as a class action, but affects only the *remedy* it may obtain if it wins. * * * Whereas "Rule 23 governs procedural aspects of class litigation" by "prescrib[ing] the considerations relevant to class certification and postcertification proceedings," § 901(b) addresses only "the size of a monetary award a class plaintiff may pursue." * * * Accordingly, the dissent says, Rule 23 and New York's law may coexist in peace.

We need not decide whether a state law that limits the remedies available in an existing class action would conflict with Rule 23; that is not what § 901(b) does. By its terms, the provision precludes a plaintiff from "maintain[ing]" a class action seeking statutory penalties. Unlike a law that sets a ceiling on damages (or puts other remedies out of reach) in properly filed class actions, § 901(b) says nothing about what remedies a court may award; it prevents the class actions it covers from coming into existence at all. * * *

* * *

The dissent all but admits that the literal terms of § 901(b) address the same subject as Rule 23—*i.e.*, whether a class action may be maintained—but insists the provision's *purpose* is to restrict only remedies. * * * Unlike Rule 23, designed to further procedural fairness and efficiency, § 901(b) (we are told) "responds to an entirely different concern": the fear that allowing statutory damages to be awarded on a class wide basis would "produce overkill." * * * The dissent reaches this conclusion on the basis of (1) constituent concern recorded in the law's bill jacket; (2) a commentary suggesting that the Legislature "apparently fear[ed]" that combining class actions and statutory penalties "could result in annihilating punishment of the defendant," * * * (3) a remark by the Governor in his signing statement that § 901(b) " 'provides a controlled remedy,' " * * * and (4) a state court's statement that the final text of § 901(b) " 'was the result of a compromise among competing interests[.]' " * * *

This evidence of the New York Legislature's purpose is pretty sparse. But even accepting the dissent's account of the legislature's objective at face value, it cannot override the statute's clear text. Even if its aim is to restrict the remedy a plaintiff can obtain, § 901(b) achieves that end by limiting a plaintiff's power to maintain a class action. * * *

The dissent's approach of determining whether state and federal rules conflict based on the subjective intentions of the state legislature is an enterprise destined to produce "confusion worse confounded," *Sibbach v. Wilson & Co.*, 312 U.S. 1, 14, 61 S.Ct. 422, 85 L. Ed. 479 (1941). It would mean, to begin with, that one State's statute could survive preemption (and accordingly affect the procedures in federal court) while another State's identical law would not, merely because its authors had different aspirations. It would also mean that district courts would have to discern, in every diversity case, the purpose behind any putatively preempted state procedural rule, even if its text squarely conflicts with federal law. That task will often prove arduous. Many laws further more than one aim, and the aim of others may be impossible to discern. Moreover, to the extent the dissent's purpose-driven approach depends on its characterization of § 901(b)'s aims as substantive, it would apply to many state rules ostensibly addressed to procedure. * * *

But while the dissent does indeed artificially narrow the scope of § 901(b) by finding that it pursues only substantive policies, that is not the central difficulty of the dissent's position. The central difficulty is that even artificial narrowing cannot render § 901(b) compatible with Rule 23. * * * Rule 23 unambiguously authorizes *any* plaintiff, in *any* federal civil proceeding, to maintain a class action if the Rule's prerequisites are met. We cannot contort its text, even to avert a collision with state law that might render it invalid. See *Walker* v. *Armco Steel Corp.*, 446 U.S. 740, 750, n. 9, 100 S.Ct. 1978, 64 L.Ed.2d 659 (1980). What the dissent's approach achieves is not the avoiding of a "conflict between Rule 23 and § 901(b)," * * *, but rather the invalidation of Rule 23 (pursuant to § 2072(b) of the Rules Enabling Act) to the extent that it conflicts with the substantive policies of § 901. There is no other way to reach the dissent's destination. We must therefore confront head-on whether Rule 23 falls within the statutory authorization.

B

In the Rules Enabling Act, Congress authorized this Court to promulgate rules of procedure subject to its review, 28 U.S.C. § 2072(a), but with the limitation that those rules "shall not abridge, enlarge or modify any substantive right," § 2072(b).

We have long held that this limitation means that the Rule must "really regulat[e] procedure,—the judicial process for enforcing rights and duties recognized by substantive law and for justly administering remedy and redress for disregard or infraction of them," *Sibbach*, 312 U.S., at 14, 61 S.Ct. 422, 85 L. Ed. 479; see *Hanna, supra*, at 464, 85 S.Ct. 1136, 14 L.Ed.2d 8; *Burlington*, 480 U.S., at 8, 107 S.Ct. 967, 94 L.Ed.2d 1. The test is not whether the rule affects a litigant's substantive rights; most procedural rules do. *Mississippi Publishing Corp. v. Murphree*, 326 U.S. 438, 445, 66 S.Ct. 242, 90 L. Ed. 185 (1946). What matters is what the rule itself *regulates:* If it governs only "the manner and the means" by which the litigants' rights are "enforced," it is valid; if it alters "the rules of decision by which [the] court will adjudicate [those] rights," it is not. *Id.*, at 446, 66 S.Ct. 242, 90 L. Ed. 185 (internal quotation marks omitted).

Applying that test, we have rejected every statutory challenge to a Federal Rule that has come before us. We have found to be in compliance with § 2072(b) rules prescribing methods for serving process, see *id.*, at 445–446, 66 S.Ct. 242, 90 L. Ed. 185 (Fed. Rule Civ. Proc. 4(f)); *Hanna, supra*, at 463–465, 85 S.Ct. 1136, 14 L.Ed.2d 8 (Fed. Rule Civ. Proc. 4(d)(1)), and requiring litigants whose mental or physical condition is in dispute to submit to examinations, see *Sibbach, supra*, at 14–16, 61 S.Ct. 422, 85 L. Ed. 479 (Fed. Rule Civ. Proc. 35); *Schlagenhauf* v. *Holder*, 379 U.S. 104, 113–114, 85 S.Ct. 234, 13 L.Ed.2d 152 (1964) (same). Likewise, we have upheld rules authorizing imposition of sanctions upon those who file frivolous appeals, see *Burlington, supra*, at 8, 107 S.Ct. 967, 94 L.Ed.2d 1 (Fed. Rule App. Proc. 38), or who sign court papers without a reasonable inquiry into the facts asserted, see *Business Guides, Inc.* v. *Chromatic Communications Enterprises, Inc.*, 498 U.S. 533, 551–554, 111 S.Ct. 922, 112 L.Ed.2d 1140 (1991) (Fed. Rule Civ. Proc. 11). Each of these rules had some practical effect on the parties' rights, but each undeniably regulated only the process for enforcing those rights; none altered the rights themselves, the available remedies, or the rules of decision by which the court adjudicated either.

Applying that criterion, we think it obvious that rules allowing multiple claims (and claims by or against multiple parties) to be litigated together are also valid. See, *e.g.*, Fed. Rules Civ. Proc. 18 (joinder of claims), 20 (joinder of parties), 42(a) (consolidation of actions). Such rules neither change plaintiffs' separate entitlements to relief nor abridge defendants' rights; they alter only how the claims are processed. For the same reason, Rule 23—at least insofar as it allows willing plaintiffs to join their separate claims against the same defendants in a class action—falls within § 2072(b)'s authorization. A class action, no less than traditional joinder (of which it is a species), merely enables a federal court to adjudicate claims of multiple parties at once, instead of in separate suits. And like traditional joinder, it leaves the parties' legal rights and duties intact and the rules of decision unchanged.

Allstate contends that the authorization of class actions is not substantively neutral: Allowing Shady Grove to sue on behalf of a class "transform[s] [the] dispute over a five *hundred* dollar penalty into a dispute over a five *million* dollar penalty." * * * Allstate's aggregate liability, however, does not depend on whether the suit proceeds as a class action. Each of the 1,000-plus members of the putative class could (as Allstate acknowledges) bring a freestanding suit asserting his individual claim. It is undoubtedly true that some plaintiffs who would not bring individual suits for the relatively small sums involved will choose to join a class action. That has no bearing, however, on Allstate's or the plaintiffs' legal rights. The likelihood that some (even many) plaintiffs will be induced to sue by the availability of a class action is just the sort of "incidental effec[t]" we have long held does not violate § 2072(b), *Mississippi Publishing*, *supra*, at 445, 66 S.Ct. 242, 90 L. Ed. 185.

Allstate argues that Rule 23 violates [the Rules Enabling Act], § 2072(b), because the state law it displaces, § 901(b), creates a right that the Federal Rule abridges—namely, a "substantive right . . . not to be subjected to aggregated class-action liability" in a single suit. * * * To begin with, we doubt that that is so. Nothing in the text of § 901(b) (which is to be found in New York's procedural code) confines it to claims under New York law; and of course New York has no power to alter substantive rights and duties created by other sovereigns. As we have said, the *consequence* of excluding certain class actions may be to cap the damages a defendant can face in a single suit, but the law itself alters only procedure. In that respect, § 901(b) is no different from a state law forbidding simple joinder. As a fallback argument, Allstate argues that even if § 901(b) is a procedural provision, it was enacted "for *substantive reasons*[.]" * * * Its end was not to improve "the conduct of the litigation process itself" but to alter "the outcome of that process." * * *

The fundamental difficulty with both these arguments is that the substantive nature of New York's law, or its substantive purpose, *makes no difference*. A Federal Rule of Procedure is not valid in some jurisdictions and invalid in others—or valid in some cases and invalid in others—depending upon whether its effect is to frustrate a state substantive law (or a state procedural law enacted for substantive purposes). * * *

   * * *

In sum, it is not the substantive or procedural nature or purpose of the affected state law that matters, but the substantive or procedural nature of the Federal Rule. We have held since *Sibbach*, and reaffirmed repeatedly, that the validity of a Federal Rule depends entirely upon whether it regulates procedure. See *Sibbach*, *supra*, at 14, 61 S.Ct. 422,

85 L. Ed. 479; *Hanna, supra,* at 464, 85 S.Ct. 1136, 14 L.Ed.2d 8; *Burlington,* 480 U.S., at 8, 107 S.Ct. 967, 94 L.Ed.2d 1. If it does, it is authorized by § 2072 and is valid in all jurisdictions, with respect to all claims, regardless of its incidental effect upon state-created rights.

C

A few words in response to the concurrence. We understand it to accept the framework we apply—which requires first, determining whether the federal and state rules can be reconciled (because they answer different questions), and second, if they cannot, determining whether the Federal Rule runs afoul of § 2072(b). * * * The concurrence agrees with us that Rule 23 and § 901(b) conflict,* * * and departs from us only with respect to the second part of the test, *i.e.,* whether application of the Federal Rule violates § 2072(b)[.] * * * Like us, it answers no, but for a reason different from ours. * * *

The concurrence would decide this case on the basis, not that Rule 23 is procedural, but that the state law it displaces is procedural, in the sense that it does not "function as a part of the State's definition of substantive rights and remedies." * * *

* * * Recognizing the impracticability of a test that turns on the idiosyncrasies of state law, *Sibbach* adopted and applied a rule with a single criterion: whether the Federal Rule "really regulates procedure." 312 U.S., at 14, 61 S.Ct. 422, 85 L. Ed. 479. * * *

In reality, the concurrence seeks not to apply *Sibbach*, but to overrule it (or, what is the same, to rewrite it). Its approach, the concurrence insists, gives short shrift to the statutory text forbidding the Federal Rules from "abridg[ing], enlarg[ing], or modify[ing] any substantive right," § 2072(b). * * * There is something to that. It is possible to understand how it can be determined whether a Federal Rule "enlarges" substantive rights without consulting State law: If the Rule creates a substantive right, even one that duplicates some state-created rights, it establishes a new *federal* right. But it is hard to understand how it can be determined whether a Federal Rule "abridges" or "modifies" substantive rights without knowing what state-created rights would obtain if the Federal Rule did not exist. *Sibbach*'s exclusive focus on the challenged Federal Rule—driven by the very real concern that Federal Rules which vary from State to State would be chaos, see 312 U.S., at 13–14, 61 S.Ct. 422, 85 L. Ed. 479—is hard to square with § 2072(b)'s terms.

Sibbach has been settled law, however, for nearly seven decades. Setting aside any precedent requires a "special justification" beyond a bare belief that it was wrong. *Patterson* v. *McLean Credit Union*, 491 U.S. 164, 172, 109 S.Ct. 2363, 105 L.Ed.2d 132 (1989) (internal quotation marks omitted). And a party seeking to overturn a *statutory* precedent bears an even greater burden, since Congress remains free to correct us, *ibid.*, and adhering to our precedent enables it do so, see, *e.g., Finley* v. *United States*, 490 U.S. 545, 556, 109 S.Ct. 2003, 104 L.Ed.2d 593 (1989); 28 U.S.C. § 1367; *Exxon Mobil Corp.* v. *Allapattah Services, Inc.*, 545 U.S. 546, 558, 125 S.Ct. 2611, 162 L.Ed.2d 502 (2005). We do Congress no service by presenting it a moving target. * * *

* * *

* * * At the end of the day, one must come face to face with the decision whether or not the state policy (with which a putatively procedural state rule may be "bound up") pertains to a "substantive right or remedy"—that is, whether it is substance or procedure. The more one explores the alternatives to *Sibbach*'s rule, the more its wisdom becomes apparent.

D

We must acknowledge the reality that keeping the federal-court door open to class actions that cannot proceed in state court will produce forum shopping. That is unacceptable when it comes as the consequence of judge-made rules created to fill supposed "gaps" in positive federal law. But divergence from state law, with the attendant consequence of forum shopping, is the inevitable (indeed, one might say the intended) result of a uniform system of federal procedure. Congress itself has created the possibility that the same case may follow a different course if filed in federal instead of state court. Cf. *Hanna*, 380 U.S., at 472–473, 85 S.Ct. 1136, 14 L.Ed.2d 8. The short of the matter is that a Federal Rule governing procedure is valid whether or not it alters the outcome of the case in a way that induces forum shopping. To hold otherwise would be to "disembowel either the Constitution's grant of power over federal procedure" or Congress's exercise of it. *Id.*, at 473–474, 85 S.Ct. 1136, 14 L.Ed.2d 8.

The judgment of the Court of Appeals is reversed, and the case is remanded for further proceedings.

■ JUSTICE STEVENS, concurring in part and concurring in the judgment.

The New York law at issue is a procedural rule that is not part of New York's substantive law. Accordingly, I agree with JUSTICE SCALIA that Federal Rule of Civil Procedure 23 must apply in this case and join Parts I and II–A of the Court's opinion. But I also agree with JUSTICE GINSBURG that there are some state procedural rules that federal courts must apply in diversity cases because they function as a part of the State's definition of substantive rights and remedies.

I

It is a long-recognized principle that federal courts sitting in diversity "apply state substantive law and federal procedural law." *Hanna v. Plumer*, 380 U.S. 460, 465, 85 S.Ct. 1136, 14 L.Ed.2d 8 (1965). This principle is governed by a statutory framework, and the way that it is administered varies depending upon whether there is a federal rule addressed to the matter. See *id.*, at 469–472, 85 S.Ct. 1136, 14 L.Ed.2d 8. If no federal rule applies, a federal court must follow the Rules of Decision Act, 28 U.S.C. § 1652, and make the "relatively unguided *Erie* choice," *Hanna*, 380 U.S., at 471, 85 S.Ct. 1136, 14 L.Ed.2d 8, to determine whether the state law is the "rule of decision." But when a situation is covered by a federal rule, the Rules of Decision Act inquiry by its own terms does not apply. See § 1652; *Hanna*, 380 U.S., at 471, 85 S.Ct. 1136, 14 L.Ed.2d 8. Instead, the Rules Enabling Act (Enabling Act) controls. See 28 U.S.C. § 2072.

That does not mean, however, that the federal rule always governs. * * *

* * *

II

When both a federal rule and a state law appear to govern a question before a federal court sitting in diversity, our precedents have set out a two-step framework for federal courts to negotiate this thorny area. At both steps of the inquiry, there is a critical question about what the state law and the federal rule mean.

The court must first determine whether the scope of the federal rule is " 'sufficiently broad' " to " 'control the issue' " before the court, "thereby leaving no room for the operation" of seemingly conflicting state law. See *Burlington Northern R. Co.* v. *Woods*, 480 U.S. 1, 4–5, 107 S.Ct. 967, 94 L.Ed.2d 1 (1987); *Walker* v. *Armco Steel Corp.*, 446 U.S. 740, 749–750, and n. 9, 100 S.Ct. 1978, 64 L.Ed.2d 659 (1980). If the federal rule does not apply or can operate alongside the state rule, then there is no "Ac[t] of Congress" governing that particular question, 28 U.S.C. § 1652, and the court must engage in the traditional Rules of Decision Act inquiry under *Erie* and its progeny. In some instances, the "plain meaning" of a federal rule will not come into " 'direct collision' " with the state law, and both can operate. *Walker*, 446 U.S., at 750, n. 9, 749, 100 S.Ct. 1978, 64 L.Ed.2d 659. In other instances, the rule "when fairly construed," *Burlington Northern R. Co.*, 480 U.S., at 4, 107 S.Ct. 967, 94 L.Ed.2d 1, with "sensitivity to important state interests and regulatory policies," *Gasperini*, 518 U.S., at 427, n. 7, 116 S.Ct. 2211, 135 L.Ed.2d 659, will not collide with the state law.

If, on the other hand, the federal rule is "sufficiently broad to control the issue before the Court," such that there is a "direct collision," *Walker*, 446 U.S., at 749–750, 100 S.Ct. 1978, 64 L.Ed.2d 659, the court must decide whether application of the federal rule "represents a valid exercise" of the "rulemaking authority . . . bestowed on this Court by the Rules Enabling Act." *Burlington Northern R. Co.*, 480 U.S., at 5, 107 S.Ct. 967, 94 L.Ed.2d 1; see also *Gasperini*, 518 U.S., at 427, n. 7, 116 S.Ct. 2211, 135 L.Ed.2d 659; *Hanna*, 380 U.S., at 471–474, 85 S.Ct. 1136, 14 L.Ed.2d 8. The Enabling Act requires, *inter alia*, that federal rules "not abridge, enlarge or modify *any* substantive right." 28 U.S.C. § 2072(b) (emphasis added). Unlike Justice Scalia, I believe that an application of a federal rule that effectively abridges, enlarges, or modifies a state-created right or remedy violates this command. Congress may have the constitutional power "to supplant state law" with rules that are "rationally capable of classification as procedure," * * * but we should generally presume that it has not done so. Cf. *Wyeth* v. *Levine*, 555 U.S. 555, 565, 129 S.Ct. 1187, 1195, 173 L.Ed.2d 51 (2009)) (observing that "we start with the assumption" that a federal statute does not displace a State's law "unless that was the clear and manifest purpose of Congress" (internal quotation marks omitted)). Indeed, the mandate that federal rules "shall not abridge, enlarge or modify any substantive right" evinces the opposite intent, as does Congress' decision to delegate the creation of rules to this Court rather than to a political branch, see 19 C. Wright, A. Miller, & E. Cooper, Federal Practice and Procedure § 4509, p. 265 (2d ed. 1996) (hereinafter Wright).

* * *

JUSTICE SCALIA believes that the sole Enabling Act question is whether the federal rule "really regulates procedure," * * * which means, apparently, whether it regulates "the manner and the means by which the litigants' rights are enforced[.]" * * * I respectfully disagree. This interpretation of the Enabling Act is consonant with the Act's first limitation to "general rules of practice and procedure," § 2072(a). But it ignores the second limitation that such rules also "not abridge, enlarge or modify *any* substantive right," § 2072(b) (emphasis added), and in so doing ignores the balance that Congress struck between uniform rules of federal procedure and respect for a State's construction of its own rights and remedies. It also ignores the separation-of-powers presumption, see Wright § 4509, at 265, and federalism presumption * * *, that counsel against judicially created rules displacing state substantive law.

Although the plurality appears to agree with much of my interpretation of § 2072, * * * it nonetheless rejects that approach for two reasons, both of which are mistaken. First, JUSTICE SCALIA worries that if federal courts inquire into the effect of federal rules on state law, it will enmesh federal courts in difficult determinations about whether application of a given rule would displace a state determination about substantive rights. * * * I do not see why an Enabling Act inquiry that looks to state law necessarily is more taxing than JUSTICE SCALIA's. But in any event, that inquiry is what the Enabling Act requires: While it may not be easy to decide what is actually a "substantive right," "the designations substantive and procedural become important, for the Enabling Act has made them so." * * *

Second, the plurality argues that its interpretation of the Enabling Act is dictated by this Court's decision in *Sibbach*, which applied a Federal Rule about when parties must submit to medical examinations. But the plurality misreads that opinion. * * *

    * * *

III

JUSTICE GINSBURG views the basic issue in this case as whether and how to apply a federal rule that dictates an answer to a traditionally procedural question (whether to join plaintiffs together as a class), when a state law that "defines the dimensions" of a state-created claim dictates the opposite answer. * * * As explained above, I readily acknowledge that if a federal rule displaces a state rule that is " 'procedural' in the ordinary sense of the term," * * * but sufficiently interwoven with the scope of a substantive right or remedy, there would be an Enabling Act problem, and the federal rule would have to give way. In my view, however, this is not such a case.

    * * *

Because Rule 23 governs class certification, the only decision is whether certifying a class in this diversity case would "abridge, enlarge or modify" New York's substantive rights or remedies. § 2072(b). Although one can argue that class certification would enlarge New York's "limited" damages remedy, * * * such arguments rest on extensive speculation about what the New York Legislature had in mind when it created § 901(b). But given that there are two plausible competing narratives, it seems obvious to me that we should respect the plain textual reading of § 901(b), a rule in New York's procedural code about when to certify class actions brought under any source of law, and respect Congress' decision that Rule 23 governs class certification in federal courts. In order to displace a federal rule, there must be more than just a possibility that the state rule is different than it appears.

Accordingly, I concur in part and concur in the judgment.

■ JUSTICE GINSBURG, with whom JUSTICE KENNEDY, JUSTICE BREYER, and JUSTICE ALITO join, dissenting.

The Court today approves Shady Grove's attempt to transform a $500 case into a $5,000,000 award, although the State creating the right to recover has proscribed this alchemy. If Shady Grove had filed suit in New York state court, the 2% interest payment authorized by New York Ins. Law Ann. § 5106(a) as a penalty for overdue benefits would, by Shady Grove's own measure, amount to no more than $500. By instead filing in federal court based on the parties' diverse citizenship and requesting class certification, Shady Grove hopes to recover, for the class, statutory damages of more than $5,000,000. The New York Legislature has barred this remedy, instructing that, unless specifically permitted, "an action to recover a penalty, or minimum measure of recovery created or imposed by statute may not be maintained as a class action." N.Y. Civ. Prac. Law Ann. (CPLR) § 901(b). The Court nevertheless holds that Federal Rule of Civil Procedure 23, which prescribes procedures for the conduct of class actions in federal courts, preempts the application of § 901(b) in diversity suits.

The Court reads Rule 23 relentlessly to override New York's restriction on the availability of statutory damages. Our decisions, however, caution us to ask, before undermining state legislation: Is this conflict really necessary? Cf. Traynor, Is This Conflict Really Necessary? 37 Tex. L. Rev. 657 (1959). Had the Court engaged in that inquiry, it would not have read Rule 23 to collide with New York's legitimate interest in keeping certain monetary awards reasonably bounded. I would continue to interpret Federal Rules with awareness of, and sensitivity to, important state regulatory policies. Because today's judgment radically departs from that course, I dissent.

I

A

"Under the *Erie* doctrine," it is long settled, "federal courts sitting in diversity apply state substantive law and federal procedural law." *Gasperini* v. *Center for Humanities, Inc.,* 518 U.S. 415, 427, 116 S.Ct. 2211, 135 L.Ed.2d 659 (1996); see *Erie R. Co.* v. *Tompkins,* 304 U.S. 64, 58 S.Ct. 817, 82 L. Ed. 1188 (1938). Justice Harlan aptly conveyed the importance of the doctrine; he described *Erie* as "one of the modern cornerstones of our federalism, expressing policies that profoundly touch the allocation of judicial power between the state and federal systems." *Hanna* v. *Plumer,* 380 U.S. 460, 474, 85 S.Ct. 1136, 14 L.Ed.2d 8 (1965) (concurring opinion). Although we have found *Erie*'s application "sometimes [to be] a challenging endeavor," *Gasperini,* 518 U.S., at 427, 116 S.Ct. 2211, 135 L.Ed.2d 659, two federal statutes mark our way.

The first, the Rules of Decision Act, prohibits federal courts from generating substantive law in diversity actions. See *Erie,* 304 U.S., at 78, 58 S.Ct. 817, 82 L. Ed. 1188. Originally enacted as part of the Judiciary Act of 1789, this restraint serves a policy of prime importance to our federal system. We have therefore applied the Act "with an eye alert to

. . . avoiding disregard of State law." *Guaranty Trust Co.* v. *York*, 326 U.S. 99, 110, 65 S.Ct. 1464, 89 L. Ed. 2079 (1945).

The second, the Rules Enabling Act, enacted in 1934, authorizes us to "prescribe general rules of practice and procedure" for the federal courts, but with a crucial restriction: "Such rules shall not abridge, enlarge or modify any substantive right." 28 U.S.C. § 2072. Pursuant to this statute, we have adopted the Federal Rules of Civil Procedure. In interpreting the scope of the Rules, including, in particular, Rule 23, we have been mindful of the limits on our authority. See, *e.g., Ortiz* v. *Fibreboard Corp.*, 527 U.S. 815, 845, 119 S.Ct. 2295, 144 L.Ed.2d 715 (1999) (The Rules Enabling Act counsels against "adventurous application" of Rule 23; any tension with the Act "is best kept within tolerable limits.")[.] * * *

If a Federal Rule controls an issue and directly conflicts with state law, the Rule, so long as it is consonant with the Rules Enabling Act, applies in diversity suits. See *Hanna*, 380 U.S., at 469–474, 85 S.Ct. 1136, 14 L.Ed.2d 8. If, however, no Federal Rule or statute governs the issue, the Rules of Decision Act, as interpreted in *Erie*, controls. That Act directs federal courts, in diversity cases, to apply state law when failure to do so would invite forum-shopping and yield markedly disparate litigation outcomes. See *Gasperini*, 518 U.S., at 428, 116 S.Ct. 2211, 135 L.Ed.2d 659; *Hanna*, 380 U.S., at 468, 85 S.Ct. 1136, 14 L.Ed.2d 8. Recognizing that the Rules of Decision Act and the Rules Enabling Act simultaneously frame and inform the *Erie* analysis, we have endeavored in diversity suits to remain safely within the bounds of both congressional directives.

B

In our prior decisions in point, many of them not mentioned in the Court's opinion, we have avoided immoderate interpretations of the Federal Rules that would trench on state prerogatives without serving any countervailing federal interest. "Application of the *Hanna* analysis," we have said, "is premised on a 'direct collision' between the Federal Rule and the state law." *Walker* v. *Armco Steel Corp.*, 446 U.S. 740, 749–750, 100 S.Ct. 1978, 64 L.Ed.2d 659 (1980) (quoting *Hanna*, 380 U.S., at 472, 85 S.Ct. 1136, 14 L.Ed.2d 8). To displace state law, a Federal Rule, "when fairly construed," must be " 'sufficiently broad' " so as "to 'control the issue' before the court, thereby leaving *no room* for the operation of that law." *Burlington Northern R. Co.* v. *Woods*, 480 U.S. 1, 4–5, 107 S.Ct. 967, 94 L.Ed.2d 1 (1987) (quoting *Walker*, 446 U.S., at 749–750, and n. 9, 100 S.Ct. 1978, 64 L.Ed.2d 659; emphasis added); cf. *Stewart Organization, Inc.* v. *Ricoh Corp.*, 487 U.S. 22, 37–38, 108 S.Ct. 2239, 101 L.Ed.2d 22 (1988) (Scalia, J., dissenting) ("[I]n deciding whether a federal . . . Rule of Procedure encompasses a particular issue, a broad reading that would create significant disuniformity between state and federal courts should be avoided if the text permits.").

In pre-*Hanna* decisions, the Court vigilantly read the Federal Rules to avoid conflict with state laws. * * *

* * *

We were similarly attentive to a State's regulatory policy in *Gasperini*. * * *

* * *

In sum, both before and after *Hanna*, the above-described decisions show, federal courts have been cautioned by this Court to "interpre[t] the Federal Rules . . . with sensitivity to important state interests," *Gasperini*, 518 U.S., at 427, n. 7, 116 S.Ct. 2211, 135 L.Ed.2d 659, and a will "to avoid conflict with important state regulatory policies," *id.*, at 438, n. 22, 116 S.Ct. 2211, 135 L.Ed.2d 659 (internal quotation marks omitted).[2] The Court veers away from that approach—and conspicuously, its most recent reiteration in *Gasperini*, * * *—in favor of a mechanical reading of Federal Rules, insensitive to state interests and productive of discord.

C

Our decisions instruct over and over again that, in the adjudication of diversity cases, state interests—whether advanced in a statute, * * *, or a procedural rule, *e.g.*, *Gasperini*—warrant our respectful consideration. Yet today, the Court gives no quarter to New York's limitation on statutory damages and requires the lower courts to thwart the regulatory policy at stake: To prevent excessive damages, New York's law controls the penalty to which a defendant may be exposed in a single suit. * * *

* * *

"[T]he final bill . . . was the result of a compromise among competing interests." * * * Section 901(a) allows courts leeway in deciding whether to certify a class, but § 901(b) rejects the use of the class mechanism to pursue the particular remedy of statutory damages. The limitation was not designed with the fair conduct or efficiency of litigation in mind. Indeed, suits seeking statutory damages are arguably *best* suited to the class device because individual proof of actual damages is unnecessary. New York's decision instead to block class-action proceedings for statutory damages therefore makes scant sense, except as a means to a manifestly substantive end: Limiting a defendant's liability in a single lawsuit in order to prevent the exorbitant inflation of penalties— remedies the New York Legislature created with individual suits in mind.

D

Shady Grove contends—and the Court today agrees—that Rule 23 unavoidably preempts New York's prohibition on the recovery of statutory damages in class actions. * * *

The Court, I am convinced, finds conflict where none is necessary. * * * Sensibly read, Rule 23 governs procedural aspects of class litigation, but allows state law to control the size of a monetary award a class plaintiff may pursue.

---

[2]   JUSTICE STEVENS stakes out common ground on this point[.] * * * Nevertheless, JUSTICE STEVENS sees no reason to read Rule 23 with restraint in this particular case; the Federal Rule preempts New York's damages limitation, in his view, because § 901(b) is "a procedural rule that is not part of New York's substantive law." * * * This characterization of § 901(b) does not mirror reality, as I later explain. * * * But a majority of this Court, it bears emphasis, agrees that Federal Rules should be read with moderation in diversity suits to accommodate important state concerns.

In other words, Rule 23 describes a method of enforcing a claim for relief, while § 901(b) defines the dimensions of the claim itself. In this regard, it is immaterial that § 901(b) bars statutory penalties in wholesale, rather than retail, fashion. The New York Legislature could have embedded the limitation in every provision creating a cause of action for which a penalty is authorized; § 901(b) operates as shorthand to the same effect. It is as much a part of the delineation of the claim for relief as it would be were it included claim by claim in the New York Code.

* * *

The absence of an inevitable collision between Rule 23 and § 901(b) becomes evident once it is comprehended that a federal court sitting in diversity can accord due respect to both state and federal prescriptions. Plaintiffs seeking to vindicate claims for which the State has provided a statutory penalty may pursue relief through a class action if they forgo statutory damages and instead seek actual damages or injunctive or declaratory relief; any putative class member who objects can opt out and pursue actual damages, if available, and the statutory penalty in an individual action. * * * In sum, while phrased as responsive to the question whether certain class actions may begin, § 901(b) is unmistakably aimed at controlling how those actions must end. On that remedial issue, Rule 23 is silent.

Any doubt whether Rule 23 leaves § 901(b) in control of the remedial issue at the core of this case should be dispelled by our *Erie* jurisprudence, including *Hanna*, which counsels us to read Federal Rules moderately and cautions against stretching a rule to cover every situation it could conceivably reach. * * *

* * *

By finding a conflict without considering whether Rule 23 rationally should be read to avoid any collision, the Court unwisely and unnecessarily retreats from the federalism principles undergirding *Erie*. Had the Court reflected on the respect for state regulatory interests endorsed in our decisions, it would have found no cause to interpret Rule 23 so woodenly—and every reason not to do so. * * *

II

Because I perceive no unavoidable conflict between Rule 23 and § 901(b), I would decide this case by inquiring "whether application of the [state] rule would have so important an effect upon the fortunes of one or both of the litigants that failure to [apply] it would be likely to cause a plaintiff to choose the federal court." *Hanna*, 380 U.S., at 468, n. 9, 85 S.Ct. 1136, 14 L.Ed.2d 8. See *Gasperini*, 518 U.S., at 428, 116 S.Ct. 2211, 135 L.Ed.2d 659.

Seeking to pretermit that inquiry, Shady Grove urges that the class-action bar in § 901(b) must be regarded as "procedural" because it is contained in [New York's Civil Practice Law and Rules], which "govern[s] the *procedure* in civil judicial proceedings *in all courts of the state*." * * *

Shady Grove also ranks § 901(b) as "procedural" because "nothing in [the statute] suggests that it is limited to rights of action based on New York state law, as opposed to federal law or the law of other states"; instead it "applies to actions seeking penalties under *any* statute." * * *

It is true that § 901(b) is not specifically *limited* to claims arising under New York law. But neither is it expressly *extended* to claims arising under foreign law. The rule prescribes, without elaboration either way, that "an action to recover a penalty . . . may not be maintained as a class action." * * *

* * * Shady Grove overlooks the most likely explanation for the absence of limiting language: New York legislators make law with New York plaintiffs and defendants in mind, *i.e.*, as if New York were the universe. * * *

The point was well put by Brainerd Currie in his seminal article on governmental interest analysis in conflict-of-laws cases. The article centers on a now-archaic Massachusetts law that prevented married women from binding themselves by contract as sureties for their husbands. Discussing whether the Massachusetts prescription applied to transactions involving foreign factors (a foreign forum, foreign place of contracting, or foreign parties), Currie observed:

> "When the Massachusetts legislature addresses itself to the problem of married women as sureties, the undeveloped image in its mind is that of *Massachusetts* married women, husbands, creditors, transactions, courts, and judgments. In the history of Anglo-American law the domestic case has been normal, the conflict-of-laws case marginal." Married Women's Contracts: A Study in Conflict-of-Laws Method, 25 U. Chi. L. Rev. 227, 231 (1958) (emphasis added).

Shady Grove's suggestion that States must specifically limit their laws to domestic rights of action if they wish their enactments to apply in federal diversity litigation misses the obvious point: State legislators generally do not focus on an interstate setting when drafting statutes.

* * *

In short, Shady Grove's effort to characterize § 901(b) as simply "procedural" cannot successfully elide this fundamental norm: When no federal law or rule is dispositive of an issue, and a state statute is outcome affective in the sense our cases on *Erie* (pre- and post-*Hanna*) develop, the Rules of Decision Act commands application of the State's law in diversity suits. *Gasperini*, 518 U.S., at 428, 116 S.Ct. 2211, 135 L.Ed.2d 659; *Hanna*, 380 U.S., at 468, n. 9, 85 S.Ct. 1136, 14 L.Ed.2d 8; *York*, 326 U.S., at 109, 65 S.Ct. 1464, 89 L. Ed. 2079. As this case starkly demonstrates, if federal courts exercising diversity jurisdiction are compelled by Rule 23 to award statutory penalties in class actions while New York courts are bound by § 901(b)'s proscription, "substantial variations between state and federal [money judgments] may be expected." *Gasperini*, 518 U.S., at 430, 116 S.Ct. 2211, 135 L.Ed.2d 659 (quoting *Hanna*, 380 U.S., at 467–468, 85 S.Ct. 1136, 14 L.Ed.2d 8 (internal quotation marks omitted)). The "variation" here is indeed "substantial." Shady Grove seeks class relief that is *ten thousand times* greater than the individual remedy available to it in state court. As the plurality acknowledges, * * * forum shopping will undoubtedly result if a plaintiff need only file in federal instead of state court to seek a massive monetary award explicitly barred by state law. See *Gasperini*, 518 U.S., at 431, 116 S.Ct. 2211, 135 L.Ed.2d 659 ("*Erie* precludes a recovery in federal court significantly larger than the recovery that would have been tolerated in state court."). * * *

* * *

Gasperini's observations apply with full force in this case. By barring the recovery of statutory damages in a class action, § 901(b) controls a defendant's maximum liability in a suit seeking such a remedy. * * *

* * * In sum, because "New York substantive law governs [this] claim for relief, New York law . . . guide[s] the allowable damages." *Gasperini*, 518 U.S., at 437, 116 S.Ct. 2211, 135 L.Ed.2d 659.

III

The Court's erosion of *Erie's* federalism grounding impels me to point out the large irony in today's judgment. Shady Grove is able to pursue its claim in federal court only by virtue of the recent enactment of the Class Action Fairness Act of 2005 (CAFA), 28 U.S.C. § 1332(d). In CAFA, Congress opened federal-court doors to state-law-based class actions so long as there is minimal diversity, at least 100 class members, and at least $5,000,000 in controversy. *Ibid.* By providing a federal forum, Congress sought to check what it considered to be the overreadiness of some state courts to certify class actions. See, *e.g.*, S. Rep. No. 109–14, p. 4 (2005) (CAFA prevents lawyers from "gam[ing] the procedural rules [to] keep nationwide or multi-state class actions in state courts whose judges have reputations for readily certifying classes." (internal quotation marks omitted)); *id.*, at 22 (disapproving "the 'I never met a class action I didn't like' approach to class certification" that "is prevalent in state courts in some localities"). In other words, Congress envisioned fewer—not more—class actions overall. Congress surely never anticipated that CAFA would make federal courts a mecca for suits of the kind Shady Grove has launched: class actions seeking state-created penalties for claims arising under state law—claims that would be barred from class treatment in the State's own courts. Cf. *Woods*, 337 U.S., at 537, 69 S.Ct. 1235, 93 L. Ed. 1524 ("[T]he policy of *Erie* . . . preclude[s] maintenance in . . . federal court . . . of suits to which the State ha[s] closed its courts.").

I would continue to approach *Erie* questions in a manner mindful of the purposes underlying the Rules of Decision Act and the Rules Enabling Act, faithful to precedent, and respectful of important state interests. I would therefore hold that the New York Legislature's limitation on the recovery of statutory damages applies in this case, and would affirm the Second Circuit's judgment.

NOTES AND QUESTIONS

1. **Controlling opinion?** Is there a controlling opinion on the question of *Erie* methodology?

Justice Scalia wrote for himself and three others. His opinion looks only to the text and operation of Rule 23, independent of the nature and strength of the state policy embodied in New York's Civil Practice Law § 901(b) and the effect of Rule 23 on that policy. In his words (italics his), "[T]he substantive nature of New York's law, or its substantive purpose, *makes no difference.*" Justice Scalia's approach would ensure that a valid federal Rule, whether Rule 23 or some other Rule, will have the same meaning in all states, irrespective of the differences in individual state substantive statutes and the nature and strength of the state policies they embody.

Justice Ginsburg wrote for herself and three others. Her opinion looks at the text, and the policy behind, § 901(b). She concludes that New York has a strong substantive policy, expressed in § 901(b), against allowing class actions to enforce statutory damage provisions of New York laws. Statutory damages are defined in § 901(a) as a "penalty, or a minimum measure of recovery." Even though the text of § 901(a) did not confine itself to New York laws authorizing statutory damage remedies, Justice Ginsburg understood § 901(a) as a substantive law whose purpose was only to limit the manner in which statutory damages under New York law may be recovered, rather than a procedural law whose purpose was generally to limit access to class actions to recover statutory damages under any law, state or federal. In her view, given the nature and strength of the state substantive policy embodied in § 901(b), Rule 23 should be read as not addressing the question whether damage remedies may be limited by a state law that forbids class actions that would otherwise be available under Rule 23. How convincing do you find Justice Ginsburg's understanding of the purpose of § 901(a) and her reading of Rule 23?

Justice Stevens wrote for himself alone. He agrees with Justice Scalia that Rule 23 directly conflicts with § 901(a). And he agrees with Justice Ginsburg that the nature and strength of a state policy should be considered in conducting an *Erie* analysis. But for Justice Stevens, the analysis does not result in a construction of Rule 23 that avoids a conflict with § 901(a); in his view, the text of Rule 23 is sufficiently clear and comprehensive that a conflict between the Rule and § 901(a) is inescapable. So for him, the question is whether the effect of Rule 23 on the policy embodied in § 901(a) violates the Rules Enabling Act. That is, Justice Stevens considers the nature and strength of the state policy expressed in § 901(a). But unlike Justice Ginsburg, he does not consider them as a means of construing Rule 23(a). Rather, he considers them as a means of determining whether the Rule is invalid as "enlarg[ing], abridg[ing], or modify[ing] any substantive right." 28 U.S.C. § 2072(b).

Can we at least say that a majority of the Court rejects Justice Scalia's statement that, for purposes of *Erie* "the substantive nature of New York's law, or its substantive purpose, *makes no difference*"?

2. *Gasperini* **redux?** Their respective opinions in *Shady Grove* suggest that Justices Scalia and Ginsburg are refighting the battle they fought (and Justice Ginsburg won) in *Gasperini*. In *Gasperini*, Justice Ginsburg, writing for the Court, construed Rule 59(a) as not providing a controlling federal standard for granting a new trial based on excessiveness of the jury verdict. In *Shady Grove*, Justice Ginsburg, writing in dissent, construed Rule 23 as not providing a federal standard under which a class action should be certified regardless of the damages sought. In both cases, Justice Ginsburg construed federal Rules narrowly so as to avoid conflict with state policies. In *Gasperini*, Justice Scalia read Rule 59(a) as providing a federal standard for reviewing a jury verdict for excessiveness. In *Shady Grove*, Justice Scalia construed Rule 23 as providing a broad rule for class certification, applicable in suits seeking statutory damages, despite New York's clear language in § 901(b) precluding class action treatment in such cases. In both cases, Justice Scalia construed federal Rules broadly despite the conflict, or potential conflict, with state policies.

The different federal-state balances preferred by Justices Ginsburg and Scalia are pretty obvious. Justice Ginsburg agrees with the preference expressed by Justice Harlan in his concurrence in *Hanna v. Plumer*. Justice Scalia, on the other hand, agrees with a strong version of the majority opinion in *Hanna v. Plumer*. Would you agree that Justice Scalia has a weak argument in support of his reading of Rule 59(a) in *Gasperini*, and that the same can be said of Justice Ginsburg's argument in support of her reading of Rule 23 in *Shady Grove*? Are the justices' policy preferences exerting an unduly strong influence on their legal analyses?

3.   Dissent's reference to the "Court's opinion." Did you notice that at the beginning of Part I.B of her dissent Justice Ginsburg referred to the "Court's opinion"? Because Justice Scalia's opinion got only four votes (counting his own), his is not an opinion of the Court; rather, it is only a plurality opinion. So Justice Ginsburg is mistaken in referring to the "Court's opinion." This mistake suggests (but no more than suggests) that Justice Scalia originally had five votes for his opinion, and that Justice Ginsburg was originally dissenting from the "Court's opinion." If this is right, someone (probably Justice Stevens) deserted Justice Scalia's draft opinion, leaving him with only a plurality; then, in editing the final version of her dissent, Justice Ginsburg failed to change the reference from the "Court's opinion" to the "plurality opinion."

4.   Not ideological or political in the usual sense. It is refreshing to note that the differences of opinion among the justices in *Gasperini* and *Shady Grove* are not ideological or political in the usual sense. The division among the justices in *Gasperini* is as follows: Majority opinion: Justice Ginsburg, joined by Justices O'Connor, Kennedy, Souter, and Breyer. Concurring opinion: Justice Stevens. Dissent: Justice Scalia, joined by Chief Justice Rehnquist and Thomas. The division in *Shady Grove* is as follows: Plurality opinion: Justice Scalia, joined by Chief Justice Roberts and Justices Thomas and Sotomayor. Concurring opinion: Justice Stevens. Dissent: Justice Ginsburg, joined by Justices Kennedy, Breyer, and Alito.

5.   Are uniformity and simplicity preferable? Justice Scalia argues in favor of his reading of Rule 23(a), and of the federal Rules generally, on the ground that uniformity and simplicity are preferable to variation and complexity. In his view, it is better to have a uniform reading of the federal Rules that does not have to take into account, on a state-by-state and case-by-case basis, the different strengths of state policies. A disadvantage of the approach of Justice Ginsburg, as well as that of Justice Stevens, is that there may be different readings of the federal Rules depending on the policies of the different states in which the district courts sit. Do you agree with Justice Scalia?

As you think about this question, recall the original reason for the limitation on the Rules contained in the Rules Enabling Act. As discussed by Professor Burbank, Congress was concerned that unless there was some limitation on the reach of the Rules they would be held unconstitutional as an undue delegation of the legislative power. Burbank, The Rules Enabling Act of 1934, 130 U.Pa.L.Rev. 1015 (1982). As originally conceived, the limitation in the Rules Enabling Act had nothing to do with preserving or achieving a proper federal-state balance. See also Burbank & Wolff, Redeeming the Missed Opportunities of *Shady Grove*, 159 U.Pa.L.Rev. 17 (2010).

B. "REVERSE *ERIE*": FEDERAL LAW IN STATE COURTS

Dice v. Akron, Canton & Youngstown Railroad Co.

Supreme Court of the United States, 1952.
342 U.S. 359, 72 S.Ct. 312, 96 L.Ed. 398.

■ Opinion of the Court by MR. JUSTICE BLACK, announced by MR. JUSTICE DOUGLAS.

Petitioner, a railroad fireman, was seriously injured when an engine in which he was riding jumped the track. Alleging that his injuries were due to respondent's negligence, he brought this action for damages under the Federal Employers' Liability Act, 35 Stat. 65, 45 U.S.C. § 51 et seq., 45 U.S.C.A. § 51 et seq., in an Ohio court of common pleas. Respondent's defenses were (1) a denial of negligence and (2) a written document signed by petitioner purporting to release respondent in full for $924.63. Petitioner admitted that he had signed several receipts for payments made him in connection with his injuries but denied that he had made a full and complete settlement of all his claims. He alleged that the purported release was void because he had signed it relying on respondent's deliberately false statement that the document was nothing more than a mere receipt for back wages.

After both parties had introduced considerable evidence the jury found in favor of petitioner and awarded him a $25,000 verdict. The trial judge later entered judgment notwithstanding the verdict. In doing so he reappraised the evidence as to fraud, found that petitioner had been "guilty of supine negligence" in failing to read the release, and accordingly held that the facts did not "sustain either in law or equity the allegations of fraud by clear, unequivocal and convincing evidence." This judgment notwithstanding the verdict was reversed by the Court of Appeals of Summit County, Ohio, on the ground that under federal law, which controlled, the jury's verdict must stand because there was ample evidence to support its finding of fraud. The Ohio Supreme Court, one judge dissenting, reversed the Court of Appeals' judgment and sustained the trial court's action, holding that: (1) Ohio, not federal, law governed; (2) under that law petitioner, a man of ordinary intelligence who could read, was bound by the release even though he had been induced to sign it by the deliberately false statement that it was only a receipt for back wages; and (3) under controlling Ohio law factual issues as to fraud in the execution of this release were properly decided by the judge rather than by the jury. 155 Ohio St. 185, 98 N.E.2d 301. We granted certiorari because the decision of the Supreme Court of Ohio appeared to deviate from previous decisions of this Court that federal law governs cases arising under the Federal Employers' Liability Act. 342 U.S. 811, 72 S.Ct. 59.

First. We agree with the Court of Appeals of Summit County, Ohio, and the dissenting judge in the Ohio Supreme Court and hold that validity of releases under the Federal Employers' Liability Act raises a federal question to be determined by federal rather than state law. Congress in § 1 of the Act granted petitioner a right to recover against his employer for damages negligently inflicted. State laws are not controlling in determining what the incidents of this federal right shall be. Manifestly the federal rights affording relief to injured railroad employees under a federally declared standard could be defeated if states were permitted to have the final say as to what defenses could and could not be properly interposed to suits under the Act. Moreover, only if federal law controls can the federal Act be given that uniform application throughout the country essential to effectuate its purposes. Releases and other devices designed to liquidate or defeat injured employees' claims play an important part in the federal Act's administration. Their validity is but one of the many interrelated questions that must constantly be determined in these cases according to a uniform federal law.

Second. In effect the Supreme Court of Ohio held that an employee trusts his employer at his peril, and that the negligence of an innocent worker is sufficient to enable his employer to benefit by its deliberate fraud. Application of so harsh a rule to defeat a railroad employee's claim is wholly incongruous with the general policy of the Act to give railroad employees a right to recover just compensation for injuries negligently inflicted by their employers. And this Ohio rule is out of harmony with modern judicial and legislative practice to relieve injured persons from the effect of releases fraudulently obtained. We hold that the correct federal rule is that announced by the Court of Appeals of Summit County, Ohio, and the dissenting judge in the Ohio Supreme Court—a release of rights under the Act is void when the employee is induced to sign it by the deliberately false and material statements of the railroad's authorized representatives made to deceive the employee as to the contents of the release. The trial court's charge to the jury correctly stated this rule of law.

Third. Ohio provides and has here accorded petitioner the usual jury trial of factual issues relating to negligence. But Ohio treats factual questions of fraudulent releases differently. It permits the judge trying a negligence case to resolve all factual questions of fraud "other than fraud in the factum." The factual issue of fraud is thus split into fragments, some to be determined by the judge, others by the jury.

It is contended that since a state may consistently with the Federal Constitution provide for trial of cases under the Act by a non-unanimous verdict, Minneapolis & St. Louis R. Co. v. Bombolis, 241 U.S. 211, 36 S.Ct. 595, 60 L.Ed. 961, Ohio may lawfully eliminate trial by jury as to one phase of fraud while allowing jury trial as to all other issues raised. The Bombolis case might be more in point had Ohio abolished trial by jury in all negligence cases including those arising under the federal Act. But Ohio has not done this. It has provided jury trials for cases arising under the federal Act but seeks to single out one phase of the question of fraudulent releases for determination by a judge rather than by a jury. Compare Testa v. Katt, 330 U.S. 386, 67 S.Ct. 810, 91 L.Ed. 967.

We have previously held that "The right to trial by jury is 'a basic and fundamental feature of our system of federal jurisprudence' " and that it is "part and parcel of the remedy afforded railroad workers under the Employers' Liability Act." Bailey v. Central Vermont R. Co., 319 U.S. 350, 354, 63 S.Ct. 1062, 1064, 87 L.Ed. 1444. We also recognized in that case that to deprive railroad workers of the benefit of a jury trial where there is evidence to support negligence "is to take away a goodly portion of the relief which Congress has afforded them." It follows that the right to trial by jury is too substantial a part of the rights accorded by the Act to permit it to be classified as a mere "local rule of procedure" for denial in the manner that Ohio has here used. Brown v. Western R. Co., 338 U.S. 294, 70 S.Ct. 105, 94 L.Ed. 100.

The trial judge and the Ohio Supreme Court erred in holding that petitioner's rights were to be determined by Ohio law and in taking away petitioner's verdict when the issues of fraud had been submitted to the jury on conflicting evidence and determined in petitioner's favor. The judgment of the Court of Appeals of Summit County, Ohio, was correct and should not have been reversed by the Supreme Court of Ohio. The cause is reversed and remanded to the Supreme Court of Ohio for further action not inconsistent with this opinion.

It is so ordered.

Reversed and remanded with directions.

■ MR. JUSTICE FRANKFURTER, whom MR. JUSTICE REED, MR. JUSTICE JACKSON and MR. JUSTICE BURTON join, concurring for reversal but dissenting from the Court's opinion.

Ohio, as do many other States, maintains the old division between law and equity as to the mode of trying issues, even though the same judge administers both. The Ohio Supreme Court has told us what, on one issue, is the division of functions in all negligence actions brought in the Ohio courts: "Where it is claimed that a release was induced by fraud (other than fraud in the factum) or by mistake, it is . . . necessary, before seeking to enforce a cause of action which such release purports to bar, that equitable relief from the release be secured." 155 Ohio St. 185, 186, 98 N.E.2d 301, 304. Thus, in all cases in Ohio, the judge is the trier of fact on this issue of fraud, rather than the jury. It is contended that the Federal Employers' Liability Act requires that Ohio courts send the fraud issue to a jury in the cases founded on that Act. To require Ohio to try a particular issue before a different fact-finder in negligence actions brought under the Employers' Liability Act from the fact-finder on the identical issue in every other negligence case disregards the settled distribution of judicial power between Federal and State courts where Congress authorizes concurrent enforcement of federally-created rights.

It has been settled ever since the Second Employers' Liability Cases (Mondou v. New York, N.H. & H.R. Co.) 223 U.S. 1, 32 S.Ct. 169, 56 L.Ed. 327, that no State which gives its courts jurisdiction over common law actions for negligence may deny access to its courts for a negligence action founded on the Federal Employers' Liability Act. Nor may a State discriminate disadvantageously against actions for negligence under the Federal Act as compared with local causes of action in negligence. McKnett v. St. Louis & S.F.R. Co., 292 U.S. 230, 234, 54 S.Ct. 690, 692, 78 L.Ed. 1227; Missouri ex rel. Southern R. Co. v. Mayfield, 340 U.S. 1, 4, 71 S.Ct. 1, 3, 95 L.Ed. 3. Conversely, however, simply because there is concurrent jurisdiction in Federal and State courts over actions under the Employers' Liability Act, a State is under no duty to treat actions arising under that Act differently from the way it adjudicates local actions for negligence, so far as the mechanics of litigation, the forms in which law is administered, are concerned. This surely covers the distribution of functions as between judge and jury in the determination of the issues in a negligence case.

[Justice Frankfurter concurred with the majority's holding that federal law governed the standard for what constituted a valid release from liability.]

NOTE ON FEDERAL LAW IN STATE COURTS

1. State courts required to hear federal causes of action. A state court of general jurisdiction is required to hear civil suits based on federal causes of action. In Testa v. Katt, 330 U.S. 386, 67 S.Ct. 810, 91 L.Ed. 967 (1947), a Rhode Island state court refused to hear a civil suit for treble damages arising out of a violation of federal law, even though Rhode Island courts adjudicated this type of case arising under state law. The Supreme Court held that a state court with "jurisdiction adequate and appropriate under established local law to adjudicate this action" could not decline to hear a case based on federal law.

But *Testa v. Katt* does not end the inquiry. Granted that the state court must hear the case, what procedures may the state court employ?

2. "Reverse-*Erie*." *Dice* is often referred to as a "reverse-*Erie*" case. Why?

3. Having it both ways? Can both *Dice* and *Byrd v. Blue Ridge* be right? Justice Black's justification for requiring the state to follow the federal practice in *Dice* was that the right to a jury decision was "part and parcel" of the Federal Employers' Liability Act (FELA). Justice Brennan's justification for not following the state practice in *Byrd* was that the state assignment of responsibility to judge and jury was not an "integral part" of the South Carolina workers' compensation statute. Did the Supreme Court read the two statutes correctly?

Think for a moment about the jurisdictional structure of the federal and state courts. The U.S. Supreme Court had the last word on the meaning of FELA in *Dice*, overruling the decision of the Ohio Supreme Court. The U.S. Supreme Court also had the last word on the meaning of the state workers' compensation statute in *Byrd*, in a case that came up through the federal courts without ever going to the state courts. Is there something wrong with a system that gives the federal courts such power over questions of state law? Was the U.S. Supreme Court unduly sympathetic to federal interests and insufficiently sympathetic to state interests in these two cases?

4. Must federal law "take the state courts as it finds them"? In a famous article, Professor Henry Hart argued that Congress should be free to require the state courts to hear cases based on federal law, but that the state courts, on their side, should be free to follow their own procedures. In Hart's words, "The general rule, bottomed deeply in belief in the importance of state control of state judicial procedure, is that federal law takes the state courts as it finds them." Hart, The Relations Between State and Federal Law, 54 Colum.L.Rev. 489, 508 (1954). How far should this "general rule" go?

5. *Dice* and FELA. Putting to one side the correctness of *Byrd*, how defensible is the Court's decision in *Dice* ?

FELA is an avowedly pro-plaintiff statute, designed to provide an effective remedy to injured railroad workers. Under FELA, the plaintiff may file suit in either state or federal court. If he files in state court, the defendant railroad may not remove to federal court. 28 U.S.C. § 1445(a). One of the reasons for nonremovability is that removal can impose severe hardship on plaintiffs, particularly in large Western states. In such states, the nearest federal court is often hundreds of miles from the state court nearest the home of the plaintiff. Under the Court's decision in *Dice*, a plaintiff could litigate close to home, in state court, without sacrificing his federal procedural rights. Was Congress justified in FELA cases in deviating from the "general rule" of taking the state courts as it finds them? Or, to put the matter somewhat differently, was the Court justified in concluding that Congress intended this result in FELA cases?

In another FELA case, Brown v. Western Ry. of Alabama, 338 U.S. 294, 70 S.Ct. 105, 94 L.Ed. 100 (1949), the Georgia Court of Appeals upheld a demurrer to plaintiff's complaint because he failed to plead facts with sufficient particularity to satisfy strict Georgia pleading rules. The U.S. Supreme Court required the Georgia courts to abandon their usual pleading requirements, and to adopt instead a relaxed pleading standard similar to that of the federal rules in FELA cases. Justice Black wrote for the Court:

> Strict local rules of pleading cannot be used to impose unnecessary burdens upon rights of recovery authorized by federal laws. "Whatever springes the State may set for those who are endeavoring to assert rights that the State confers, the assertion of federal rights, when plainly and reasonably made, is not to be defeated under the name of local practice." * * * Should this Court fail to protect federally protected rights from dismissal because of over-exacting local requirements for meticulous pleadings, desirable uniformity in adjudication of federally created rights could not be achieved.

338 U.S. at 298–99.

Justice Frankfurter dissented, pointing out that Georgia allowed amendment of a complaint to supply greater particularity and that plaintiff had declined to amend. He wrote:

> Congress has authorized State courts to enforce Federal rights, and Federal courts State-created rights. Neither system of courts can impair these respective rights, but both may have their own requirements for stating claims (pleading) and conducting litigation (practice).
>
> In the light of these controlling considerations, I cannot find that the Court of Appeals of Georgia has either sought to evade the law of the United States or did so unwittingly. * * * [The Georgia court] has not contracted rights under the Federal Act nor hobbled the plaintiff in getting a judgment to which he may be entitled.

338 U.S. at 301–03.

How much interference with the enforcement of federal rights is necessary before a state court should be required to adopt federal procedures in a FELA case? Did the Court go too far in *Brown*?

6. Non-FELA cases. In Felder v. Casey, 487 U.S. 131, 108 S.Ct. 2302, 101 L.Ed.2d 123 (1988), plaintiff brought a federal civil rights claim in Wisconsin state court under 42 U.S.C. § 1983 against the City of Milwaukee and several of its police officers. In suits against municipalities, Wisconsin courts apply a notice-of-claim requirement, under which a plaintiff is required within 120 days of an incident to notify the city of a claim, and of his or her intent to hold the city liable. If the city has not been so notified, no claim may be brought thereafter. The practical consequence of the notice-of-claim requirement is to impose a *de facto* 120-day statute of limitations. The actual statute of limitations for § 1983 claims is the most closely analogous state statute of limitations, which, in Wisconsin, is two years.

The Supreme Court held that the Wisconsin notice-of-claim requirement unduly interfered with the operation of 42 U.S.C. § 1983:

> Federal law takes state courts as it finds them only insofar as those courts employ rules that do not "impose unnecessary burdens upon rights of recovery authorized by federal laws." [citing *Brown*] * * * [E]nforcement of the notice-of-claim statute in § 1983 actions brought in state court so interferes with and frustrates the substantive right Congress created that, under the Supremacy Clause, it must yield to the federal interest.

487 U.S. at 150–51.

In Johnson v. Fankell, 520 U.S. 911, 117 S.Ct. 1800, 138 L.Ed.2d 108 (1997), plaintiff brought a federal civil rights suit in Idaho state court under 42 U.S.C. § 1983 against state officials who asserted a federal defense of "qualified immunity." The trial court rejected the defense and denied their motion to dismiss. Defendants then tried to take an interlocutory appeal, but the Idaho Supreme Court refused to hear it because the ruling did not constitute a "final judgment" under Idaho law. In suits in federal court, defendants are entitled to take interlocutory appeals on qualified immunity rulings in § 1983 cases. The United States Supreme Court held that Idaho state courts were not required to grant an interlocutory appeal. It distinguished *Felder v. Casey* on the ground that, unlike the 120-day notice-of-claim requirement in *Felder*, the availability of an interlocutory appeal was not "outcome determinative." Id. at 920–21. "When pre-emption of state law is at issue, we must respect the 'principles [that] are fundamental to a system of federalism in which the state courts share responsibility for the application and enforcement of federal law.' . . . This respect is at its apex when we confront a claim that federal law requires a State to undertake something as fundamental as the restructuring as the operations of its courts." Id. at 922.

7. Additional reading. For additional discussion, see Hill, Substance and Procedure in State FELA Actions—the Converse of the *Erie* Problem?, 17 Ohio St.L.J. 384 (1956); Meltzer, State Court Forfeitures of Federal Rights, 99 Harv.L.Rev. 1128 (1986); Neuborne, Toward Procedural Parity in Constitutional Litigation, 22 Wm. & Mary L.Rev. 725 (1981).

C. ASCERTAINING STATE LAW

DeWeerth v. Baldinger

United States Court of Appeals for the Second Circuit, 1987.
836 F.2d 103.

■ JON O. NEWMAN, CIRCUIT JUDGE:

This appeal concerns a dispute over ownership of a painting by Claude Monet that disappeared from Germany at the end of World War

II and has been in the possession of a good-faith purchaser for the last 30 years. The appeal presents primarily the issue whether New York law, which governs this dispute, requires an individual claiming ownership of stolen personal property to use due diligence in trying to locate the property in order to postpone the running of the statute of limitations in a suit against a good-faith purchaser. The issue arises on an appeal from a judgment of the District Court for the Southern District of New York (Vincent L. Broderick, Judge) ruling that plaintiff-appellee Gerda Dorothea DeWeerth, a citizen of West Germany who owned the Monet from 1922 until 1943, was entitled to recover it from defendant-appellant Edith Marks Baldinger, an American citizen who purchased the painting in New York in 1957 and who has possessed it ever since. We conclude that New York law imposes a due diligence requirement, that the undisputed facts show that DeWeerth failed to exercise reasonable diligence in locating the painting after its disappearance, and that her action for recovery is untimely. We therefore reverse the judgment of the District Court.

Background

* * *

The painting in the pending case, Monet's "Champs de Blé à Vétheuil," is one of a series of similar impressionistic landscapes painted by the artist near the town of Vétheuil, located on the Seine in Northern France. The oil painting, measuring 65 by 81 centimeters, shows a wheat field, a village, and trees. It is signed and dated "Claude Monet '79." The painting is estimated to be worth in excess of $500,000.

Plaintiff Gerda Dorothea DeWeerth is a citizen of West Germany. Her father, Karl von der Heydt, the owner of a substantial art collection, purchased the Monet in 1908. DeWeerth inherited the painting in 1922 along with other works of art from her father's estate. She kept the painting in her home in Wuppertal-Elberfeld, Germany, from 1922 until 1943, except for the two-year period 1927–1929 when the Monet was in the possession of her mother. A photograph taken in 1943 shows the Monet hanging on a wall in DeWeerth's residence.

In August 1943, DeWeerth sent the Monet and other valuables to the home of her sister, Gisela von Palm, for safekeeping during World War II. Von Palm lived in a castle in Oberbalzheim, Southern Germany. Von Palm received the shipment, including the Monet, which she hung in the castle. In 1945, at the end of the war, American soldiers were quartered in von Palm's residence. Following the soldiers' departure, von Palm noticed that the Monet was missing. She informed her sister of the painting's disappearance in the fall of 1945.

DeWeerth contacted several authorities concerning the lost Monet. In 1946, she filed a report with the military government administering the Bonn-Cologne area after the war. The report is no longer extant, but DeWeerth testified that it was a standard government form in which she briefly described items she had lost during the war. In 1948, in a letter to her lawyer, Dr. Heinz Frowein, regarding insurance claims on property she had lost, DeWeerth expressed regret about the missing Monet and inquired whether it was "possible to do anything about it." Frowein wrote back that the Monet would not be covered by insurance; he did not initiate an investigation. In 1955, DeWeerth sent the 1943 photograph of the Monet to Dr. Alfred Stange, a former professor of art and an expert in medieval painting, and asked him to investigate the painting's whereabouts. Stange responded that the photo was insufficient evidence with which to begin a search, and DeWeerth did not pursue the matter with him further. Finally, in 1957 DeWeerth sent a list of art works she had lost during the war to the *Bundeskriminalamt,* the West German federal bureau of investigation. None of DeWeerth's efforts during the period 1945–1957 to locate the Monet was fruitful. DeWeerth made no further attempts to recover the painting after 1957.

In the meantime, the Monet had reappeared in the international art market by 1956. In December of that year, third-party defendant-appellant Wildenstein & Co., Inc., an art gallery in New York City, acquired the Monet on consignment from Francois Reichenbach, an art dealer in Geneva, Switzerland. From December 1956 until June 1957, the painting was in the possession of Wildenstein in New York, where it was shown to several prospective buyers. Defendant Edith Marks Baldinger eventually purchased the painting in June 1957 for $30,900. The parties have stipulated that Baldinger purchased for value, in good faith, and without knowledge of any adverse claim.

Since 1957, Baldinger has kept the Monet in her New York City apartment, except for two occasions when it was displayed at public exhibitions. From October 29 to November 1, 1957, it was shown at a benefit at the Waldorf-Astoria Hotel, and in 1970 it was loaned to Wildenstein for an exhibition in its New York gallery for approximately one month.

DeWeerth learned of Baldinger's possession of the Monet through the efforts of her nephew, Peter von der Heydt. In 1981, von der Heydt was told by a cousin that DeWeerth had owned a Monet that had disappeared during the war. Shortly thereafter, von der Heydt identified the painting in a published volume of Monet's works, Claude Monet: Bibliographie et Catalogue Raisonné, Vol. I 1840–1881 (intro. by Daniel Wildenstein, La Bibliothèque des Arts, Lausanne and Paris, 1974), which he found at the Wallraf-Richartz Museum in Cologne, less than 20 miles from where DeWeerth has been living since 1957. The Catalogue Raisonné indicated that the painting had been sold by Wildenstein in 1957 and that Wildenstein had exhibited it in 1970. In 1982, DeWeerth retained counsel in New York and requested Wildenstein to identify the current owner. When Wildenstein refused, DeWeerth brought an action in New York Supreme Court under N.Y.Civ.Prac.L. & R. § 3102(c) (McKinney 1970) for "disclosure to aid in bringing an action." In December 1982, the court ruled in favor of DeWeerth, and Wildenstein was compelled to identify Baldinger. By letter dated December 27, 1982, DeWeerth demanded return of the Monet from Baldinger. By letter dated February 1, 1983, Baldinger rejected the demand.

DeWeerth instituted the present action to recover the Monet on February 16, 1983.[2] At the conclusion of discovery, the parties submitted the case to Judge Broderick for decision on the record. The District Court adjudged DeWeerth the owner of the painting and ordered Baldinger to return it. The District Judge found that DeWeerth had superior title and

---

[2] Baldinger brought a third-party action against Wildenstein. That action has been severed pursuant to Fed.R.Civ.P. 42(b).

that the action was timely as she had exercised reasonable diligence in finding the painting. DeWeerth v. Baldinger, 658 F.Supp. 688 (S.D.N.Y.1987).

Discussion

* * *

The New York statute of limitations governing actions for recovery of stolen property requires that suit be brought within three years of the time the action accrued. N.Y.Civ.Prac.L. & R. § 214(3) (McKinney 1972). The date of accrual depends upon the identity of the party from whom recovery is sought. Where an owner pursues the party who took his property, the three-year period begins to run when the property was taken. See Sporn v. M.C.A. Records, Inc., 58 N.Y.2d 482, 487–88, 462 N.Y.S.2d 413, 415–16, 448 N.E.2d 1324, 1326–27 (1983). This is so even where the property owner was unaware of the unlawful taking at the time it occurred. See Varga v. Credit-Suisse, 5 A.D.2d 289, 291–92, 171 N.Y.S.2d 674, 677–78 (1st Dep't), aff'd, 5 N.Y.2d 865, 182 N.Y.S.2d 17, 155 N.E.2d 865 (1958); Two Clinton Square Corp. v. Friedler, 91 A.D.2d 1193, 1194, 459 N.Y.S.2d 179, 181 (4th Dep't 1983). In contrast, where the owner proceeds against one who innocently purchases the property in good faith, the limitations period begins to run only when the owner demands return of the property and the purchaser refuses. Menzel v. List, 22 A.D.2d 647, 253 N.Y.S.2d 43, 44 (1st Dep't 1964), on remand, 49 Misc.2d 300, 267 N.Y.S.2d 804 (Sup.Ct.1966), modified on other grounds, 28 A.D.2d 516, 279 N.Y.S.2d 608 (1st Dep't 1967), modification rev'd, 24 N.Y.2d 91, 298 N.Y.S.2d 979, 246 N.E.2d 742 (1969); Duryea v. Andrews, 12 N.Y.S. 42 (2d Dep't 1890); accord Kunstsammlungen Zu Weimar v. Elicofon, 536 F. Supp. 829, 848–49 (E.D.N.Y.1981) (applying New York law), aff'd, 678 F.2d 1150, 1161 (2d Cir.1982). Until demand and refusal, the purchaser in good faith is not considered a wrongdoer, Gillet v. Roberts, 57 N.Y. 28 (1874), even though this rule somewhat anomalously affords the owner more time to sue a good-faith purchaser than a thief.

In the present case, it is undisputed that DeWeerth initiated her suit within three years of the date her demand for return of the Monet was refused. However, the fact that her action was brought soon after refusal does not end the inquiry. Under New York law, even though the three-year limitations period begins to run only once a demand for return of the property is refused, a plaintiff may not delay the action simply by postponing his demand. Where demand and refusal are necessary to start a limitations period, the demand may not be unreasonably delayed. See Heide v. Glidden Buick Corp., 188 Misc. 198, 67 N.Y.S.2d 905 (1st Dep't 1947) (contract action); Austin v. Board of Higher Education, 5 N.Y.2d 430, 442–43, 186 N.Y.S.2d 1, 10–11, 158 N.E.2d 681, 687–88 (1959) (mandamus proceeding); Reid v. Board of Supervisors, 128 N.Y. 364, 373, 28 N.E. 367, 369 (1891) (reimbursement for price of real estate purchased at tax sale); Kunstsammlungen Zu Weimar v. Elicofon, supra, 536 F. Supp. at 849 (recovery of stolen art). While this proscription against unreasonable delay has been referred to as "laches," the New York courts have explained that the doctrine refers solely to an unexcused lapse of time and not to the equitable principle of laches, which requires prejudice to the defendant as well as delay. See Devens v. Gokey, 12 A.D.2d 135, 137, 209 N.Y.S.2d 94, 97 (4th Dep't), aff'd, 10 N.Y.2d 898, 223 N.Y.S.2d

515, 179 N.E.2d 516 (1961); Curtis v. Board of Education, 107 A.D.2d 445, 448, 487 N.Y.S.2d 439, 441 (4th Dep't 1985).

Baldinger asserts that DeWeerth's action is untimely because the delay between the painting's disappearance in Europe in 1945 and DeWeerth's demand for its return in 1982 was unreasonable. DeWeerth responds that she cannot be charged with unreasonable delay before learning the identity of Baldinger in 1982 because she could not have known before that time to whom to make the demand. These contentions frame the precise issue presented by this appeal: Whether New York law imposes upon a person who claims ownership of stolen personal property an obligation to use due diligence in attempting to locate the property. DeWeerth points out that no New York court has ever held that the unreasonable delay rule applies *before* the plaintiff has learned the identity of the person to whom demand must be made. In *Glidden Buick, Reid,* and *Austin,* plaintiffs were barred for unreasonably delaying demands to known defendants. DeWeerth suggests that in the absence of New York authority directly on point, her actions before she discovered that Baldinger possessed the Monet cannot be subject to the unreasonable delay rule. Baldinger responds that New York courts, confronting the issue, would impose an obligation of due diligence to attempt to locate the person in possession of another's property. The District Court did not decide the issue, concluding that plaintiff had exercised due diligence in any event. 658 F.Supp. at 694.

This Court's role in exercising its diversity jurisdiction is to sit as another court of the state. Guaranty Trust Co. v. York, 326 U.S. 99, 108, 65 S.Ct. 1464, 1469, 89 L.Ed. 2079 (1945). When presented with an absence of controlling state authority, we must "make an estimate of what the state's highest court would rule to be its law." In making that determination, this Court may consider all of the resources that the New York Court of Appeals could use, including New York's stated policies and the law of other jurisdictions. We determine that in an action for the recovery of stolen personal property, the New York Court of Appeals would not make an exception to the unreasonable delay rule for plaintiff's actions prior to learning the identity of the current possessor. Rather, we believe that the New York courts would impose a duty of reasonable diligence in attempting to locate stolen property, in addition to the undisputed duty to make a demand for return within a reasonable time after the current possessor is identified.[5]

An obligation to attempt to locate stolen property is consistent with New York's treatment of the good-faith purchaser. The purpose of the rule whereby demand and refusal are substantive elements of a conversion action against a good-faith purchaser is to protect the innocent party by assuring him notice before he is held liable in tort:

---

[5]   We have elected not to submit the unresolved state law issue in this appeal to the New York Court of Appeals pursuant to the recently authorized procedure permitting that Court to answer questions certified to it by the United States Supreme Court, a United States Court of Appeals, or a court of last resort of any state. See N.Y.Rules of Court § 500.17 (N.Y.Ct.App.) (McKinney 1987). That valuable procedure should be confined to issues likely to recur with some frequency. See Kidney v. Kolmar Laboratories, Inc., 808 F.2d 955, 957 (2d Cir.1987). Though the issue presented by this appeal is interesting, we do not think it will recur with sufficient frequency to warrant use of the certification procedure.

> The rule is a reasonable and just one, that an innocent purchaser of personal property from a wrong-doer shall first be informed of the defect in his title and have an opportunity to deliver the property to the true owner, before he shall be made liable as a tort-feasor for a wrongful conversion.

Gillet v. Roberts, supra, 57 N.Y. at 34; accord Kunstsammlungen Zu Weimar v. Elicofon, supra, 536 F.Supp. at 848. The rule may disadvantage the good-faith purchaser, however, if demand can be indefinitely postponed. For if demand is delayed, then so is accrual of the cause of action, and the good-faith purchaser will remain exposed to suit long after an action against a thief or even other innocent parties would be time-barred. See, e.g., Varga v. Credit-Suisse, supra, 5 A.D.2d at 291, 171 N.Y.S.2d at 677–78 (action against converter accrues when property is taken); Federal Insurance Co. v. Fries, 78 Misc.2d 805, 810, 355 N.Y.S.2d 741, 747 (Civ.Ct.1974) (action against recipient of mistaken delivery accrues at time of delivery). As the court in Elicofon observed, the unreasonable delay rule serves to mitigate the inequity of favoring a thief over a good-faith purchaser. 536 F.Supp. at 849. In this case, plaintiff's proposed exception to the rule would rob it of all of its salutary effect: The thief would be immune from suit after three years, while the good-faith purchaser would remain exposed as long as his identity did not fortuitously come to the property owner's attention. A construction of the rule requiring due diligence in making a demand to include an obligation to make a reasonable effort to locate the property will prevent unnecessary hardship to the good-faith purchaser, the party intended to be protected.

* * *

A rule requiring reasonable diligence in attempting to locate stolen property is especially appropriate with respect to stolen art. Much art is kept in private collections, unadvertised and unavailable to the public. An owner seeking to recover such property will almost never learn of its whereabouts by chance. Yet the location of stolen art may frequently be discovered through investigation. *See* F. Feldman & B. Burnham, *An Art Archive: Principles and Realization,* 10 Conn.L.Rev. 702, 724 (1978) (French and Italian authorities credit stolen art registries and investigation efforts for recovery rates as high as 75%). Unlike many other items of stolen personal property, such as jewelry or automobiles, art loses its value if it is altered or disguised. Moreover, valuable works of art, unlike fungible items like stereo components, tend to be easily remembered by those who have seen them. Thus, the owner of stolen art has a better chance than most owners of stolen property in tracking down the item he has lost.

Other jurisdictions have adopted limitations rules that encourage property owners to search for their missing goods. In virtually every state except New York, an action for conversion accrues when a good-faith purchaser acquires stolen property; demand and refusal are unnecessary. *See Restatement (Second) of Torts* § 229 & comment h (1965); Prosser, *Law of Torts* 93–94 (5th ed. 1984); 51 Am.Jur.2d *Limitation of Actions* § 125; *Federal Insurance Co. v. Fries, supra,* 78 Misc.2d at 807, 355 N.Y.S.2d at 744. In these states, the owner must find the current possessor within the statutory period or his action is barred. Obviously, this creates an incentive to find one's stolen property. It is true that New York has chosen to depart from the majority view. Nevertheless, the fact that plaintiff's interpretation of New York law would exaggerate its inconsistency with the law of other jurisdictions weighs against adopting such a view. At least one other state has recently confronted the limitations problem in the context of stolen art and has imposed a duty of reasonable investigation. *See O'Keeffe v. Snyder,* 83 N.J. 478, 416 A.2d 862 (1980); *See also* Comment, *The Recovery of Stolen Art: Of Paintings, Statues and Statutes of Limitations,* 27 U.C.L.A.L.Rev. 1122 (1980).

In light of New York's policy of favoring the good faith purchaser and discouraging stale claims and the approach to actions to recover property in other jurisdictions, we hold that under New York law an owner's obligation to make a demand without unreasonable delay includes an obligation to use due diligence to locate stolen property.

* * *

The question of what constitutes unreasonable delay in making a demand that starts the statute of limitations depends upon the circumstances of the case. * * *

* * * DeWeerth's investigation was minimal. * * *

* * *

This case illustrates the problems associated with the prosecution of stale claims. Gisela von Palm, the only witness who could verify what happened to the Monet in 1945 is dead. Key documents, including DeWeerth's father's will and reports to the military authorities, are missing. DeWeerth's claim of superior title is supported largely by hearsay testimony of questionable value. Memories have faded. To require a good-faith purchaser who has owned a painting for 30 years to defend under these circumstances would be unjust. New York law avoids this injustice by requiring a property owner to use reasonable diligence in locating his property. In this case, DeWeerth failed to meet that burden. Accordingly, the judgment of the District Court is reversed.

Solomon R. Guggenheim Foundation v. Lubell

Court of Appeals of New York, 1991.

77 N.Y.2d 311, 567 N.Y.S.2d 623, 569 N.E.2d 426.

■ WACHTLER, CHIEF JUDGE.

The backdrop for this replevin action is the New York City art market, where masterpieces command extraordinary prices at auction and illicit dealing in stolen merchandise is an industry all its own. The Solomon R. Guggenheim Foundation, which operates the Guggenheim Museum in New York City, is seeking to recover a Chagall gouache worth an estimated $200,000. The Guggenheim believes that the gouache was stolen from its premises by a mailroom employee sometime in the late 1960s. The appellant Rachel Lubell and her husband, now deceased, bought the painting from a well-known Madison Avenue gallery in 1967 and have displayed it in their home for more than 20 years. Mrs. Lubell claims that before the Guggenheim's demand for its return in 1986, she had no reason to believe that the painting had been stolen.

* * *

* * * The trial court granted [Mrs. Lubell's] cross motion for summary judgment, relying on DeWeerth v. Baldinger, 836 F.2d 103, an opinion from the United States Court of Appeals for the Second Circuit. * * *

* * *

In *DeWeerth v. Baldinger* * * *, the Second Circuit took note of the fact that New York case law treats thieves and good-faith purchasers differently and looked to that difference as a basis for imposing a reasonable diligence requirement on the owners of stolen art. Although the court acknowledged that the question posed by the case was an open one, it declined to certify it to this Court (see, 22 NYCRR 500.17), stating that it did not think that it "[would] recur with sufficient frequency to warrant use of the certification procedure" (836 F.2d, at 108, n. 5). Actually, the issue has recurred several times in the three years since DeWeerth was decided (see, e.g., Republic of Turkey v. Metropolitan Museum of Art, No. 87 Civ. 3750 [VLB], slip opn. [S.D.N.Y. July 16, 1990]), including the case now before us. We have reexamined the relevant New York case law and we conclude that the Second Circuit should not have imposed a duty of reasonable diligence on the owners of stolen art work for purposes of the Statute of Limitations.

While the demand and refusal rule is not the only possible method of measuring the accrual of replevin claims, it does appear to be the rule that affords the most protection to the true owners of stolen property. [Lengthy discussion of New York law omitted.]

* * * New York enjoys a worldwide reputation as a preeminent cultural center. To place the burden of locating stolen artwork on the true owner and to foreclose the rights of that owner to recover its property if the burden is not met would, we believe, encourage illicit trafficking in stolen art. Three years after the theft, any purchaser, good faith or not, would be able to hold onto stolen art work unless the true owner was able to establish that it had undertaken a reasonable search for the missing art. This shifting of the burden onto the wronged owner is inappropriate. In our opinion, the better rule gives the owner relatively greater protection and places the burden of investigating the provenance of a work of art on the potential purchaser.

Despite our conclusion that the imposition of a reasonable diligence requirement on the museum would be inappropriate for purposes of the Statute of Limitations, our holding today should not be seen as either sanctioning the museum's conduct or suggesting that the museum's conduct is no longer an issue in this case. [Mrs. Lubell's] contention that the museum did not exercise reasonable diligence in locating the painting will be considered by the Trial Judge in the context of her laches defense. The conduct of both the appellant and the museum will be relevant to any consideration of this defense at the trial level, and as the Appellate Division noted, prejudice will also need to be shown * * *.

* * *

DeWeerth v. Baldinger

United States District Court for the Southern District of New York, 1992.
804 F.Supp. 539.

■ VINCENT L. BRODERICK, DISTRICT JUDGE.

* * *

This action concerns plaintiff's claim to the ownership of a painting by Claude Monet entitled "Champs de Blé à Vétheuil" (the "Monet"), which was stolen from plaintiff in 1945 and purchased in good faith by the defendant in 1957 from third-party defendant Wildenstein & Co. On April 20, 1987, after a bench trial, I issued a decision including findings of fact and conclusions of law in this matter and ordered that judgment be rendered for the plaintiff requiring that the painting be returned to the plaintiff. [T]hat decision was subsequently reversed by the Court of Appeals. The Court of Appeals found that in this diversity case I had misapplied New York law.

Plaintiff has now moved for relief under [Fed. R. Civ. P. 60(b)(6), a catch-all provision that, in the wording used at the time of the court's decision, allowed relief from a final judgment for "any other reason justifying relief from the operation of the judgment."]

* * * I conclude that the Rule 60 motion must be granted. In summary, the highest court of New York State has now ruled in Guggenheim v. Lubell, 77 N.Y.2d 311, 567 N.Y.S.2d 623, 569 N.E.2d 426 (1991), subsequent to the 1987 Second Circuit decision, that state law requires—and, according to the state court ruling, would previously have also required—a result which is consonant with my original determination. Because of the primacy of the state courts in determining interpretation of state law under principles of federalism, * * * the *Guggenheim* decision, albeit stating that it also reflects prior law, is a new development justifying Rule 60 relief.

[Lengthy discussion omitted.]

NOTE ON ASCERTAINING STATE LAW

1.   **Coda.** In DeWeerth v. Baldinger, 38 F.3d 1266 (2d Cir. 1994), the court of appeals reversed the decision of the district court granting relief under federal Rule 60(b)(6), thereby reinstating the court of appeals' incorrect interpretation of New York law. The court of appeals wrote:

> It turned out that the *DeWeerth* panel prediction was wrong. However, by bringing this suit, DeWeerth exposed herself to the possibility that her adversaries would argue for a change in the applicable rules of law. By filing her state law claim in a federal forum, she knew that any open question of state law would be decided by a federal court as opposed to a New York state court. The subsequent outcome of the *Guggenheim* decision does not impugn the integrity of the *DeWeerth* decision or the fairness of the process that was accorded DeWeerth. The result in this case would be no different if DeWeerth had filed her claim in state court and Baldinger had removed the action to federal court. The very nature of diversity jurisdiction leaves open the possibility that a state court will subsequently disagree with a federal court's

interpretation of state law. However, this aspect of our dual justice system does not mean that all diversity judgments are subject to revision once a state court later addresses the litigated issues. Such a rule would be tantamount to holding that the doctrine of finality does not apply to diversity judgments, a theory that has no basis in *Erie* or its progeny.

Id. at 1273–4. Are you convinced? In Batts v. Tow-Motor Forklift Co., 66 F.3d 743 (5th Cir. 1995), the Court of Appeals for the Fifth Circuit refused to reopen a judgment under Rule 60(b)(6) under circumstances similar to those in *DeWeerth*, relying on the Second Circuit's "well-reasoned opinion."

2. Compare practice in cases on direct appellate review. In Thomas v. American Home Products, Inc., 519 U.S. 913, 117 S.Ct. 282, 136 L.Ed.2d 201 (1996), the Eleventh Circuit decided a case based on Georgia state law. After the court of appeals' decision but before a petition for certiorari was filed in the Supreme Court, a decision of the Georgia Supreme Court made it clear that the court of appeals' interpretation of Georgia law was incorrect. The U.S. Supreme Court granted the petition for certiorari, vacated the judgment of the court of appeals, and remanded the case for reconsideration in light of the later decision of the Georgia Supreme Court. See also Lords Landing Village Condominium Council of Unit Owners v. Continental Insurance Co., 520 U.S. 893, 117 S.Ct. 1731, 138 L.Ed.2d 91 (1997) (same). Note that in *DeWeerth*, unlike in *Thomas* and *Lords Landing*, the losing party sought to reopen a judgment after the time for direct appellate review had expired.

3. Federal court "in effect, sitting as a state court." When deciding a question of state law, a federal court should put itself in the position of a state court of the state in which it sits. In the years immediately following *Erie*, the federal courts thought themselves required to follow mechanically lower state court decisions of doubtful authority. In the words of Judge Jerome Frank, they were sometimes reduced to playing "the role of ventriloquist's dummy" to the lower courts of the state. Richardson v. Commissioner, 126 F.2d 562, 567 (2d Cir. 1942). The Supreme Court eventually described the federal courts' task more realistically:

> [When] the underlying substantive rule involved is based on state law, * * * the State's highest court is the best authority on its own law. If there be no decision by that court then federal authorities must apply what they find to be the state law after giving 'proper regard' to relevant rulings of other courts of the State. In this respect, it may be said to be, in effect, sitting as a state court.

Commissioner v. Estate of Bosch, 387 U.S. 456, 465, 87 S.Ct. 1776, 18 L.Ed.2d 886 (1967). *Estate of Bosch* does not make the task easy, for deciding unsettled questions of law is inherently a complex matter. But at least the federal courts, which are "in effect, sitting as a state court," now have the same freedom as the state courts to consider a range of sources and policy considerations in arriving at their determination of state law.

4. Federal courts apply state court choice of law rules. A federal court is required to apply the choice of law principles of the state in which it is sitting. Klaxon Co. v. Stentor Electric Mfg. Co., 313 U.S. 487, 61 S.Ct. 1020, 85 L.Ed. 1477 (1941). This ordinarily leads to application of the substantive law of that state. But it leads to the substantive law of another state when the courts of the state in which the federal court is sitting would apply that law. Judge Henry Friendly once began an opinion in such a case: "Our principal task, in this diversity of citizenship case, it to determine what the New York courts would think the California courts would think on an issue about which neither has thought." Nolan v. Transocean Air Lines, 276 F.2d 280, 281 (2d Cir. 1960).

5. **No deference to decisions of the district court on questions of state law.** A decision by the federal district court on a question of state law is entitled to no special deference from the court of appeals. It is reviewed in the same manner as any other decision on a question of law. Salve Regina College v. Russell, 499 U.S. 225, 111 S.Ct. 1217, 113 L.Ed.2d 190 (1991). Prior to the Court's decision in *Salve Regina*, most federal courts of appeals treated district court decisions on questions of state law almost as if they were findings of fact, subject to reversal only if clearly erroneous.

6. **Special difficulties inherent in the federal system.** As *DeWeerth* shows, it is sometimes difficult for a federal court to determine the law of a state. This is not surprising, for the law—whether state or federal—is sometimes unclear. But the difficulties take on a special character because of the jurisdictional structure of the federal system.

a. **Federal law in state court.** If a state trial or appellate court makes a mistake of federal law, the U.S. Supreme Court is potentially available to correct it. In fact, however, the appellate jurisdiction of the U.S. Supreme Court is discretionary, and the Court takes very few of the cases in which review is sought. But the Court always has the option of correcting a mistake of federal law by a state court if the parties seek review and if the Court deems the case sufficiently important.

b. **State law in federal court.** By contrast, if a federal court makes a mistake of state law, the only possible appeal is within the federal court system. There is no appeal to a state court from a federal court decision on a question of state law.

7. **Devices to obtain authoritative determinations of state law by state courts.** There are special devices by which the federal courts can seek determination by the state courts of particularly difficult questions of state law.

a. **Certification.** All states courts except those of North Carolina and Missouri are willing to answer questions of state law "certified" from a federal court, although the procedures for certifying a question vary somewhat from state to state. See Klotz, Comment, Avoiding Inconsistent Interpretations: *United States v. Kelly*, the Fourth Circuit, and the Need for a Certification Procedure in North Carolina, 49 Wake Forest L.Rev. 1173 (2014). A certified question in *DeWeerth* would have read something like: "Does the law of New York impose upon the person claiming ownership of stolen personal property an obligation to use due diligence in attempting to locate the property?" If a certified question procedure had been employed, the federal court would have sent the question to the New York Court of Appeals (the highest court in the state). If New York Court of Appeals had answered the question, the federal court would then have relied on the answer. The federal court of appeals in *DeWeerth* declined to use the certification procedure because, in its judgment, the question was not likely to arise frequently. (Did you note the response of the New York Court of Appeals to this assertion by the federal court?)

b.   Abstention. Under certain circumstances, a federal district court will "abstain" from deciding a case. While the federal court abstains, the parties file a separate suit to bring the state-law question before a state court. There are several kinds of abstention, named after the leading Supreme Court cases for each of them. They are *Pullman* abstention, after Railroad Commission of Texas v. Pullman Co., 312 U.S. 496, 61 S.Ct. 643, 85 L.Ed. 971 (1941) (abstention proper when state law is uncertain, and a decision on state law grounds may permit the federal court to avoid deciding a federal constitutional question); *Burford* abstention, after Burford v. Sun Oil Co., 319 U.S. 315, 63 S.Ct. 1098, 87 L.Ed. 1424 (1943) (abstention proper when erroneous decision of state law would disrupt an important complex state regulatory scheme, such as regulation of oil drilling in Texas); *Thibodaux* abstention, after Louisiana Power and Light Co. v. City of Thibodaux, 360 U.S. 25, 79 S.Ct. 1070, 3 L.Ed.2d 1058 (1959) (abstention proper where state law is unsettled in an area of particular local concern, such as eminent domain proceedings for condemnation of real property); *Colorado River* abstention, after Colorado River Water Conservation District v. United States, 424 U.S. 800, 96 S.Ct. 1236, 47 L.Ed.2d 483 (1976) (abstention proper in certain water rights cases). Another kind of abstention, not strictly relevant here, is *Younger* abstention, after Younger v. Harris, 401 U.S. 37, 91 S.Ct. 746, 27 L.Ed.2d 669 (1971) (federal court will not enjoin a pending state criminal prosecution).

c.   Certified question device now more commonly used than abstention. The certified question device has now become the more commonly used method of obtaining answers to state-law questions. The majority of state courts accept most certified questions and answer fairly quickly. Between 1990 and 1994, state courts answered 119 certified questions from federal courts of appeal and 165 certified questions from federal district courts. During that period, they declined to answer only seven questions. J. Goldschmidt, Certification of Questions of Law: Federalism in Practice 34–35 (1995). California did not have a certified question procedure until 1998. Under the California procedure, only sister state courts and the federal court of appeals may certify questions. Between 1998 and 2005, the California Supreme Court declined to accept certified questions on seven occasions. Shatz & Martin, You've Got to Know How to Ask: A Look at Eight Years of "Certified" Questions to the California Supreme Court, 27 CEB Civil Litigation Reporter 132 (Aug. 2005).

In Arizonans for Official English v. Arizona, 520 U.S. 43, 75–80, 117 S.Ct. 1055, 137 L.Ed.2d 170 (1997), the Supreme Court sharply rebuked the Ninth Circuit for failing to certify to the Arizona Supreme Court a question about the construction of a state statute that had been challenged on federal constitutional grounds. Perhaps responding to the Court's rebuke in *Arizonans for Official English*, the Ninth Circuit twice during the course of an extended appellate process certified questions to the California Supreme Court about the meaning of the No Aid and No Preference Clauses in the California Constitution. San Diego's leasing of city park land to the Boy Scouts, who discriminated on grounds of religion and sexual orientation, had been challenged on state and federal constitutional grounds. If the leases had been struck down on state-law grounds, the court of appeals would not have had to reach the federal constitutional questions. The California Supreme Court both times declined to answer the certified questions. Barnes-Wallace v. City of San Diego, 704 F.3d 1067, 1075 (9th Cir. 2012).

D. FEDERAL COMMON LAW

Clearfield Trust Co. v. United States

Supreme Court of the United States, 1943.
318 U.S. 363, 63 S.Ct. 573, 87 L.Ed. 838.

■ MR. JUSTICE DOUGLAS delivered the opinion of the Court.

On April 28, 1936, a check was drawn on the Treasurer of the United States through the Federal Reserve Bank of Philadelphia to the order of Clair A. Barner in the amount of $24.20. It was dated at Harrisburg, Pennsylvania and was drawn for services rendered by Barner to the Works Progress Administration. The check was placed in the mail addressed to Barner at his address in Mackeyville, Pa. Barner never received the check. Some unknown person obtained it in a mysterious manner and presented it to the J.C. Penney Co. store in Clearfield, Pa., representing that he was the payee and identifying himself to the satisfaction of the employees of J.C. Penney Co. He endorsed the check in the name of Barner and transferred it to J.C. Penney Co. in exchange for cash and merchandise. Barner never authorized the endorsement nor participated in the proceeds of the check. J.C. Penney Co. endorsed the check over to the Clearfield Trust Co. which accepted it as agent for the purpose of collection and endorsed it as follows: "Pay to the order of Federal Reserve Bank of Philadelphia, Prior Endorsements Guaranteed." Clearfield Trust Co. collected the check from the United States through the Federal Reserve Bank of Philadelphia and paid the full amount thereof to J.C. Penney Co. Neither the Clearfield Trust Co. nor J.C. Penney Co. had any knowledge or suspicion of the forgery. Each acted in good faith. On or before May 10, 1936, Barner advised the timekeeper and the foreman of the W.P.A. project on which he was employed that he had not received the check in question. This information was duly communicated to other agents of the United States and on November 30, 1936, Barner executed an affidavit alleging that the endorsement of his name on the check was a forgery. No notice was given the Clearfield Trust Co. or J.C. Penney Co. of the forgery until January 12, 1937, at which time the Clearfield Trust Co. was notified. The first notice received by Clearfield Trust Co. that the United States was asking reimbursement was on August 31, 1937.

This suit was instituted in 1939 by the United States against the Clearfield Trust * * *. The cause of action was based on the express guaranty of prior endorsements made by the Clearfield Trust Co. J.C. Penney Co. intervened as a defendant. The case was heard on complaint, answer and stipulation of facts. The District Court held that the rights of the parties were to be determined by the law of Pennsylvania and that since the United States unreasonably delayed in giving notice of the forgery to the Clearfield Trust Co., it was barred from recovery under the rule of Market Street Title & Trust Co. v. Chelten T. Co., 296 Pa. 230, 145 A. 848. It accordingly dismissed the complaint. On appeal the Circuit Court of Appeals reversed. * * *

We agree with the Circuit Court of Appeals that the rule of Erie R. Co. v. Tompkins, 304 U.S. 64, 58 S.Ct. 817, 82 L.Ed. 1188, 114 A.L.R. 1487, does not apply to this action. The rights and duties of the United

States on commercial paper which it issues are governed by federal rather than local law. When the United States disburses its funds or pays its debts, it is exercising a constitutional function or power. This check was issued for services performed under the Federal Emergency Relief Act of 1935. The authority to issue the check had its origin in the Constitution and the statutes of the United States and was in no way dependent on the laws of Pennsylvania or of any other state. The duties imposed upon the United States and the rights acquired by it as a result of the issuance find their roots in the same federal sources. In absence of an applicable Act of Congress it is for the federal courts to fashion the governing rule of law according to their own standards. * * *

In our choice of the applicable federal rule we have occasionally selected state law. But reasons which may make state law at times the appropriate federal rule are singularly inappropriate here. The issuance of commercial paper by the United States is on a vast scale and transactions in that paper from issuance to payment will commonly occur in several states. The application of state law, even without the conflict of laws rules of the forum, would subject the rights and duties of the United States to exceptional uncertainty. It would lead to great diversity in results by making identical transactions subject to the vagaries of the laws of the several states. The desirability of a uniform rule is plain. And while the federal law merchant developed for about a century under the regime of Swift v. Tyson, 16 Pet. 1, 10 L.Ed. 865, represented general commercial law rather than a choice of a federal rule designed to protect a federal right, it nevertheless stands as a convenient source of reference for fashioning federal rules applicable to these federal questions.

United States v. National Exchange Bank, 214 U.S. 302, 29 S.Ct. 665, 53 L.Ed. 1006, falls in that category. The Court held that the United States could recover as drawee from one who presented for payment a pension check on which the name of the payee had been forged, in spite of a protracted delay on the part of the United States in giving notice of the forgery. * * *

* * *

The National Exchange Bank case went no further than to hold that prompt notice of the discovery of the forgery was not a condition precedent to suit. It did not reach the question whether lack of prompt notice might be a defense. We think it may. If it is shown that the drawee on learning of the forgery did not give prompt notice of it and that damage resulted, recovery by the drawee is barred. The fact that the drawee is the United States and the laches those of its employees are not material. The United States as drawee of commercial paper stands in no different light than any other drawee. As stated in United States v. National Exchange Bank, 270 U.S. 527, 534, 46 S.Ct. 388, 389, 70 L.Ed. 717, "The United States does business on business terms." It is not excepted from the general rules governing the rights and duties of drawees "by the largeness of its dealings and its having to employ agents to do what if done by a principal in person would leave no room for doubt." But the damage occasioned by the delay must be established and not left to conjecture. * * * But we do not think that he who accepts a forged signature of a payee deserves that preferred treatment. It is his neglect or error in accepting the forger's signature which occasions the loss. See Bank of Commerce v. Union Bank, 3 N.Y. 230, 236. He should be allowed to shift that loss to the drawee only on a clear showing that the drawee's delay in notifying him of the forgery caused him damage. See Woodward, Quasi Contracts (1913) § 25. No such damage has been shown by Clearfield Trust Co. who so far as appears can still recover from J.C. Penney Co. The only showing on the part of the latter is contained in the stipulation to the effect that if a check cashed for a customer is returned unpaid or for reclamation a short time after the date on which it is cashed, the employees can often locate the person who cashed it. It is further stipulated that when J.C. Penney Co. was notified of the forgery in the present case none of its employees was able to remember anything about the transaction or check in question. The inference is that the more prompt the notice the more likely the detection of the forger. But that falls short of a showing that the delay caused a manifest loss. Third Nat. Bank v. Merchants' Nat. Bank, 76 Hun. 475, 27 N.Y.S. 1070. It is but another way of saying that mere delay is enough.

Affirmed.

■ MR. JUSTICE MURPHY and MR. JUSTICE RUTLEDGE did not participate in the consideration or decision of this case.

NOTES AND QUESTIONS

1. **The nature of federal common law.** Federal common law is judge-made federal law. It is both jurisdiction-conferring under the federal courts' federal question jurisdiction and supreme under the Supremacy Clause of the Constitution. Federal common law is fundamentally distinct from the general common law of *Swift v. Tyson*. The general common law was neither jurisdiction-conferring nor supreme federal law. See discussion supra p. 335, Introductory Note on the Law Applied in Federal Courts.

The Court that overruled *Swift v. Tyson* in *Erie* clearly understood the distinction between the federal common law and general common law. On the same day the Court decided *Erie*, it also decided Hinderlider v. La Plata River & Cherry Creek Ditch Co., 304 U.S. 92, 58 S.Ct. 803, 82 L.Ed. 1202 (1938), applying the long-standing federal common law rule of equitable apportionment of water from interstate streams. See also D'Oench, Duhme & Co. v. FDIC, 315 U.S. 447, 469, 62 S.Ct. 676, 86 L.Ed. 956 (1942) (distinguishing federal common law from general common law). Judge Henry Friendly praised *Erie*, in part because the abandonment of the general common law of *Swift v. Tyson* cleared the way for further development of a true federal common law:

> My view is that, by banishing the spurious uniformity of *Swift v. Tyson* * * * and by leaving to the states what ought to be left to them, *Erie* led to the emergence of a federal decisional law in areas of national concern that is truly uniform because, under the supremacy clause, it is binding in every forum, and therefore it is predictable and useful as its predecessor, more general in its subject matter but limited to the federal courts, was not. The clarion yet careful pronouncement of *Erie*, "There is no federal general common law," opened the way to what, for want of a better term, we may call specialized federal common law.

Friendly, In Praise of *Erie*—and of the New Federal Common Law, 39 N.Y.U.L.Rev. 382, 405 (1964).

2. Early history. At the beginning of the federal system, there was no federal common law. After an early period of uncertainty, the Supreme Court specifically renounced it in 1834. Wheaton v. Peters, 33 U.S. (8 Pet.) 591, 8 L.Ed. 1055 (1834) (refusing to find a federal common law of copyright). Further, the original Rules of Decision Act did not mention federal common law. It provided

> That the laws of the several states, except where *the constitution, treaties or statutes of the United States* shall otherwise require or provide shall be regarded as the rules of decision * * *.

Jud. Act of 1789, § 34, 1 Stat. 73, 92 (emphasis added). The modern Rules of Decision Act is essentially unchanged, providing, "except where the Constitution or treaties of the United States or Acts of Congress otherwise require or provide." 28 U.S.C. § 1652. By the second half of the nineteenth century, however, a federal common law had begun to emerge, primarily in interstate litigation. As seen in *Clearfield Trust* and in the excerpt from Judge Friendly, federal common law is now an important and accepted part of federal law, notwithstanding its omission from the Rules of Decision Act.

For a lively exchange on the significance of the failure to mention federal common law in the Rules of Decision Act, see Redish, Continuing the *Erie* Debate: A Response to Westen and Lehman, 78 Mich.L.Rev. 959 (1982); Westen, After "Life for *Erie*"—A Reply, 78 Mich.L.Rev. 971 (1982).

3. Compare *United States v. Yazell*. Compare *Clearfield Trust* with United States v. Yazell, 382 U.S. 341, 86 S.Ct. 500, 15 L.Ed.2d 404 (1966). Mr. and Mrs. Yazell received a loan from the federal Small Business Administration to help their small business recover from a natural disaster. After the Yazells defaulted on the loan, the United States sought recovery from both of them, including from the separate property of Mrs. Yazell. Under Texas law of coverture, Mrs. Yazell's separate property was not available to satisfy the loan. The United States argued for a uniform rule of federal common law, applicable to all federal loans, that would disregard state-law defenses such as coverture. The Supreme Court refused to adopt a federal common law rule. It wrote:

> We do not here consider the question of the constitutional power of Congress to override state law in these circumstances by direct legislation * * *. We decide only that this Court, in the absence of specific congressional action, should not decree in this situation that implementation of federal interests requires overriding the particular state rule involved here. Both theory and the precedents of this Court teach us solicitude for state interests, particularly in the field of family and family-property arrangements. They should be overridden by the federal courts only where clear and substantial interests of the National Government, which cannot be served consistently with respect for such interests, will suffer major damage if the state law is applied.

382 U.S. at 352. Are *Clearfield Trust* and *Yazell* both properly decided?

4. Federal common law inferred solely from strength of federal interests. The Supreme Court has formulated federal common law in a number of areas without relying on specific federal constitutional, treaty, or statutory provisions. These areas include: **a. Cases in which the United States is a party.** See, e.g., *Clearfield Trust*. The fact that the

United States is a party is not enough, by itself, to support a federal common law rule. There must be, in addition, a strong federal interest in the formulation and application of a uniform federal rule. See, e.g., *Yazell*, supra. **b. Cases involving foreign relations.** See, e.g., Sosa v. Alvarez-Machain, 542 U.S. 692, 124 S.Ct. 2739, 159 L.Ed.2d 718 (2004) (some aspects of customary international law); Banco Nacional de Cuba v. Sabbatino, 376 U.S. 398, 84 S.Ct. 923, 11 L.Ed.2d 804 (1964) ("act of state" doctrine of international law). **c. Interstate disputes.** See, e.g., *Hinderlider*, supra (interstate allocation of water); Illinois v. City of Milwaukee, 406 U.S. 91, 92 S.Ct. 1385, 31 L.Ed.2d 712 (1972) (interstate pollution). **d. Admiralty.** See, e.g., Exxon Shipping Co. v. Baker, 554 U.S. 471, 128 S.Ct. 2605, 171 L.Ed.2d570 (2008) (standard for awarding punitive damages); Pope & Talbot, Inc. v. Hawn, 346 U.S. 406, 74 S.Ct. 202, 98 L.Ed. 143 (1953) (comparative negligence in maritime accidents). **e. Cases involving Indian tribes.** See, e.g., Michigan v. Bay Mills Indian Community, 572 U.S. ___, 134 S.Ct. 2024, 188 L.Ed.2d 1071 (2014) (scope of tribal sovereign immunity).

5. Federal common law inferred from statutory or constitutional provisions. Federal common law is sometimes inferred from federal statutory or constitutional provisions. This is not free-standing common law, for it is tied—however loosely—to these provisions. But it is common law in the sense that judge-made law is inferred from very general text or fills important gaps. Professor Paul Mishkin describes law inferred from statutory provisions as based on the "power in the federal courts to declare, as a matter of common law, or 'judicial legislation,' rules which may be necessary to fill in interstitially or otherwise effectuate the statutory patterns enacted in the large by Congress." Mishkin, The Variousness of "Federal Law": Competence and Discretion in the Choice of National and State Rules for Decision, 105 U.Pa.L.Rev. 797, 800 (1957).

Examples of common law inferred from statutes include Textile Workers Union v. Lincoln Mills, 353 U.S. 448, 77 S.Ct. 912, 1 L.Ed.2d 972 (1957) (common law of collective bargaining agreements inferred from grant of jurisdiction to the federal courts over suits based on breach of such agreements); Cannon v. University of Chicago, 441 U.S. 677, 99 S.Ct. 1946, 60 L.Ed.2d 560 (1979) (private cause of action inferred from federal statute prohibiting sex-based discrimination by educational institutions); Feres v. United States, 340 U.S. 135, 71 S.Ct. 153, 95 L.Ed. 152 (1950) (exemption from coverage under the Federal Tort Claims Act inferred for active duty members of the military); DelCostello v. International Brotherhood of Teamsters, 462 U.S. 151, 103 S.Ct. 2281, 76 L.Ed.2d 476 (1983) (federal statute of limitations inferred for breach of collective bargaining agreement).

Examples of common law inferred from constitutional provisions include Bivens v. Six Unknown Federal Narcotics Agents, 403 U.S. 388, 91 S.Ct. 1999, 29 L.Ed.2d 619 (1971) (private cause of action for damages for illegal search and seizure by federal agents inferred from the Fourth Amendment); Davis v. Passman, 442 U.S. 228, 99 S.Ct. 2264, 60 L.Ed.2d 846 (1979) (private cause of action for damages for sex-based employment discrimination by Member of Congress inferred from Due Process Clause of the Fifth Amendment).

6. Recent reluctance to formulate rules of federal common law. In recent years, the Supreme Court has shown a marked reluctance to formulate or rely on rules of federal common law. In American Electric Power Co., Inc. v. Connecticut, 564 U.S. ___, 131 S.Ct. 2527, 180 L.Ed.2d 435 (2011), the Court held that the federal Clean Air Act displaced the previously applicable federal common law of public nuisance applicable to power plant emissions, even in the absence of promulgated regulations under the Act. The Court wrote, "Recognition that a subject is meet for federal law governance * * * does not mean that federal courts should create the controlling law." Id. at 2536. In O'Melveny & Myers v. Federal Deposit Insurance Corp., 512 U.S. 79, 114 S.Ct. 2048, 129 L.Ed.2d 67 (1994), the Court declined to fashion a federal common law rule governing tort liability of attorneys who provide legal services to savings and loans. It wrote, "[T]his is not one of those extraordinary cases in which the judicial creation of a federal rule of decision is warranted." Id. at 89. See also Atherton v. Federal Deposit Insurance Corp., 519 U.S. 213, 117 S.Ct. 666, 136 L.Ed.2d 656 (1997) (quoting *O'Melveny & Myers* and refusing to create a federal common law rule governing liability of officers and directors of federally insured savings institutions). For a useful analysis, see Lund, The Decline of Federal Common Law, 76 B.U.L.Rev. 895 (1996).

7. Additional reading. For additional reading, see Dellinger, Of Rights and Remedies: The Constitution as a Sword, 85 Harv.L.Rev. 1532 (1972); Field, Sources of Law: The Scope of Federal Common Law, 99 Harv.L.Rev. 881 (1986); Meltzer, State Court Forfeitures of Federal Rights, 99 Harv.L.Rev. 1128 (1986); Merrill, The Common Law Powers of Federal Courts, 52 U.Chi.L.Rev. 1 (1985); Monaghan, The Supreme Court 1974 Term—Foreword: Constitutional Common Law, 89 Harv.L.Rev. 1 (1975).

CHAPTER 4

PLEADINGS

A. INTRODUCTION

A modern lawsuit is commenced by the parties' filing statements of their claims and defenses, in writing, with a trial court. These written statements are called "pleadings." Federal Rule 7(a) lists the types of pleadings in federal litigation. The plaintiff's statement of claim is called a "complaint," and the defendant's response to the plaintiff's claim is called an "answer." If the defendant wishes to assert a claim against the plaintiff, she files a "counterclaim." If the defendant wishes to assert a claim against a co-defendant, she files a "cross-claim." In certain defined circumstances, the defendant may also file a complaint against a person who is not already a party to the action. In federal practice, this is called a "third-party complaint." A plaintiff, a co-defendant, or a third-party defendant responding to the defendant files a "reply" to a counterclaim and an answer to a cross-claim or third-party complaint. The court may order that a reply be filed to an answer but does not usually do so. Fed. R. Civ. P. 7(a)(7). Broadly speaking, the pleadings set the "agenda" for the case by describing the nature of the dispute between the parties. Although there is significant debate over how specific the pleadings must be, in essence there is a consensus that the pleadings serve to notify the parties of their claims and defenses against one another and to clarify the issues that are joined and which must eventually be resolved by a judge or jury, if the parties do not settle.

There are two systems of pleading in modern American civil litigation: "notice" and "code" pleading. They are principally distinguished by the extent to which they require the pleader to provide specific details. Notice pleading is used in federal district court and in most state trial courts. Code pleading is used in a minority of state courts, but a minority that includes large and influential jurisdictions like California, Illinois, and New York. Notice pleading has historically been thought to require very little of the pleader. To assert a substantive claim in federal district court in an ordinary case, a complaint need only provide "a short and plain statement of the claim showing that the pleader is entitled to relief." Fed. R. Civ. P. 8(a)(2). Code pleading, sometimes called "fact pleading," requires somewhat (but not a great deal) more. For example, a complaint in California state court must provide "[a] statement of the facts constituting the cause of action, in ordinary and concise language." Calif.C.Civ.P. § 425.10(a)(1).

Both the notice and code pleading systems are relatively recent innovations and are considerable improvements upon the highly technical system that they replaced. Until the mid-nineteenth century, both the English and American court systems had the ambitious aims of using an extended series of pleadings to identify the precise legal and factual issues in dispute and, when the disputes proved to be solely legal, to permit early disposition by the court without convening a jury. In theory, this lengthy back-and-forth of competing pleadings would narrow the factual issues in dispute, and a jury would be convened for the sole purpose of resolving those disputes.

In the view of contemporary critics, the resulting system often failed to achieve its stated goals and was technical, expensive, and prone to unfair manipulation. In the United States, code pleading was the reformist response, first introduced in the Field Code in New York in 1848. ("Code" pleading is so named because its requirements were laid out in a legislated code.) The Field Code provided the model for the adoption of code pleading a year later in Missouri, and two years later in California. Hepburn, The Development of Code Pleading 92–94 (1897). By 1875, twenty-four states had adopted some form of code pleading, and by the 1930s most American states had followed suit. Clark, Code Pleading 24 (2d ed. 1947).

Notice pleading was first adopted in 1938 in the federal courts as part of the new Federal Rules of Civil Procedure. Most states have now adopted the federal rules and notice pleading for use in their own courts, although a minority of states have retained modernized versions of code pleading. See Oakley, A Fresh Look at the Federal Rules in State Courts, 3 Nev. L.J. 354 (2003).

In both notice and code pleading systems, relatively little time and energy are spent on pleading compared to the old common law system. Instead, the center of gravity in contested civil litigation is discovery. In the old common law system, there was very little discovery at all. In both notice and code pleading, it is often said that the function of the pleadings is simply to provide notice to the other party of the pendency of the action and the nature of the pleader's contentions, so as to facilitate informed preparation for discovery or settlement. In fact, however, we expect written pleadings to do more than that, even in a pure notice pleading system. In some cases, the pleadings provide the basis for a prompt and inexpensive resolution of the case at the outset on the ground of legal insufficiency of a claim or defense. Often, the exchange of pleadings discloses that some matters of fact are not in dispute, so that the parties and the court can focus their time and financial resources on the disputed contentions. After the close of the case, the pleadings provide a record of what was disputed and decided.

Although there is consensus that notice pleading is a considerable improvement over the old common law pleading system, it has become increasingly controversial as cases involving substantial discovery have become more frequent and discovery has become more expensive and time consuming. Many believe that notice pleading makes it too easy for plaintiffs to advance non-meritorious claims at the outset of the case, forcing the defendant to an unfair choice between coerced settlement and paying the costs of defending itself. For several decades, efforts have been made to change the rules and pass statutes that require more detailed pleadings for claims judged to be less socially desirable or likely to be without merit, and to sanction attorneys whose pleadings prove to have been frivolous. Recently, as we shall see, the Supreme Court has acknowledged these concerns and has raised the burdens on parties filing pleadings in all cases in federal court. See Miller, From Conley to Twombly to Iqbal: A Double Play on the Federal Rules of Civil Procedure, 60 Duke L.J. 1 (2010).

This fight over pleading doctrine has long been hard fought, especially over the last forty years. As you consider the developments in the modern law of pleading over that span of time, ask yourself why the fight has been so loud and intense. Why are judges, lawyers, and law professors so worked up over pleading? What should the burden on parties be in pleading their claims and defenses? And who should set that burden—legislatures, judges, or rulemakers?

B. DETERMINING THE SUBSTANTIVE SUFFICIENCY OF THE COMPLAINT

UNITED STATES DISTRICT COURT

FOR THE SOUTHERN DISTRICT OF FLORIDA

CASE NO. 02–21734

CIV-SEITZ

ACCESS NOW, INC., a Florida non-profit corporation, and ROBERT GUMSON, Plaintiffs,

v.

SOUTHWEST AIRLINES CO., a Texas corporation, Defendant.

COMPLAINT

Plaintiffs, ACCESS NOW, INC. ("ACCESS NOW"), and ROBERT GUMSON ("GUMSON"), by their undersigned counsel, sue the Defendant, SOUTHWEST AIRLINES, CO., a Texas corporation, ("SOUTHWEST") and states:

SUMMARY OF THE CASE

1. ACCESS NOW, a non-profit, access advocacy organization for disabled individuals, and GUMSON, who is a blind individual, bring this action for injunctive and declaratory relief to require SOUTHWEST to bring the internet website SOUTHWEST.COM (the "SOUTHWEST.COM website") into compliance with the Americans with Disabilities Act ("ADA"), 42 U.S.C. §§ 12101, GUMSON, as well as certain other members of ACCESS NOW are blind and therefore, can only navigate the internet by employing a screen access software program ("screen reader") that converts website content into synthesized speech. The SOUTHWEST.COM website is incompatible with screen readers, denying plaintiffs of their access to services offered through SOUTHWEST.COM.[1] Despite being the first airline to establish a home page on the internet, SOUTHWEST has failed to remove

---

[1] Southwest, Through its Website, represents that it is a publicly traded company on the New York Stock exchange under symbol "LUV" with a total operating revenue in the year 2001 of 5.6 billion dollars. Southwest employs more than 34,000 employees, flies to 58 cities in approximately 30 states. Moreover, Southwest represents that it was the most admired airline in the world for the years 1997 through 2000; one of the most admired companies in the world; and has been named one of the top 100 E-businesses in the United States.

communications barriers inherent in the SOUTHWEST.COM website, thus denying the blind, independent access to purchase products,[2] in violation of Title III of the ADA, 42 U.S.C. §§ 12181, *et seq.*

JURISDICTION AND PARTIES

2. This is an action for declaratory and injunctive relief pursuant to Title III of the Americans With Disabilities Act, 42 U.S.C. §§ 12181, *et seq.* (hereinafter the "ADA") and 28 U.S.C. §§ 2201–02. This Court has jurisdiction pursuant to 28 U.S.C. § 1331. Venue is proper in this district (Miami division), pursuant to 28 U.S.C. §§ 1391(b) and (c) in that a substantial part of the events giving rise to the action occurred and continue to occur in this district and/or the Defendant conducts substantial and regular business within this district. Defendant operates for profit, 24 hours a day, 7 days a week, an inter-active website(s) to solicit and sell their services to the public living within the district.

3. Plaintiff, ACCESS NOW, is a Florida not-for-profit corporation, with over 600 nationwide members, many of whom are disabled. One of the purposes of Access Now is to assure that public spaces, public accommodations and commercial premises are accessible to and useable by its members; to assure its members are not excluded from the enjoyment and use of the benefits and services, programs and activities of public accommodations; and to assure that its members are not discriminated against because of their disabilities. ACCESS NOW and its blind members, including GUMSON, have suffered as a result of SOUTHWEST'S actions and/or inactions as stated herein.

4. Plaintiff, GUMSON is an individual, *sui juris* with a disability defined by the ADA, 42 U.S.C. § 12102(2). GUMSON has a computer on which he installed a screen reader and on which he uses the internet and has e-mail capabilities. He has attempted, prior to the filing of this lawsuit, to use the SOUTHWEST.COM website to purchase airline tickets [and] other products, however, he was/is unable to gain access to the goods and services offered by SOUTHWEST.COM as they are inaccessible to a blind person using a screen reader. SOUTHWEST.COM offers the sighted customer the promise of independence of on-line airline/hotel booking in the comfort and safety of their home. Yet, even if a blind person like GUMSON has a screen reader with a voice synthesizer on their computer, they are prevented from using the SOUTHWEST.COM website because of its failure to allow access.

5. To help its sighted customers tailor their searches, SOUTHWEST.COM provides tabs marked "Reservations, Schedules and Fares" and a "click and save program", "travel center" and "rapid rewards" program, thereby offering its sighted customers a customized and money saving booking experience.

6. In fact, SOUTHWEST.COM states on its website that more [than] 3.5 million people subscribe to SOUTHWEST'S weekly click and save e-mails. Moreover, SOUTHWEST touts itself as exemplary of the highest level of design effectiveness and innovative technology achievable on the web today. Unfortunately, this "innovative technology"

---

[2] Southwest represents on its Website that internet users search for Southwest more than any other airline on the web.

excludes plaintiffs as SOUTHWEST. COM fails to accommodate the disability, despite the relative ease to accommodate.

FACTUAL BACKGROUND

7.   In 1990, Congress enacted the ADA (42 U.S.C. § 12101) wherein commercial enterprises were provided one and a half years from the enactment of the statute to implement its requirements. The effective date of Title III of the ADA was January 26, 1993. 42 U.S.C. § 12181; 28 C.F.R. § 36.508(a).

8.   The stated purpose of the ADA can best be surmised by Justice Kennedy's concurring opinion in the recent United States Supreme Court's opinion, Board of Trustees of Univ. of Alabama v. Patricia Garrett, 531 U.S. 356, 121 S.Ct. 955, 148 L.Ed.2d 866 (2001) (Kennedy, J., O'Connor, J., concurring).

> Prejudice we are beginning to understand, rises not from malice or hostile animus alone. It may result as well from insensitivity caused by simple want of careful, rational reflection or from some instinctive mechanism to guard against people who appear to be different in some respects from ourselves. . . . [K]nowledge of our own human instincts teaches that persons who find it difficult to perform routine functions by reason of some mental or physical impairment might at first seem unsettling to us, unless we are guided by the better angels of our nature. There can be little doubt, then, that persons with mental or physical impairments are confronted with prejudice which can stem from indifference or insecurity as well as from malicious ill will.

> One of the undoubted achievements of statutes designed to assist those with impairments is that citizens have an incentive, flowing from a legal duty, to develop a better understanding, a more decent perspective, for accepting persons with impairments or disabilities into the larger society. The law works this way because the law can be a teacher. . . . [T]he Americans with Disabilities Act of 1990 will be a milestone on the path to a more decent, tolerant, progressive society.

Id.

9.   The SOUTHWEST. COM website is a public accommodation as defined by Title III of the ADA, 42 U.S.C. § 12181(7), in that it is a place of exhibition, display and a sales establishment. SOUTHWEST has discriminated and continues to discriminate against Plaintiffs, and others who are similarly situated, by denying access to, and full and equal enjoyment of the goods, services, facilities, privileges, advantages and/or accommodations of their website (SOUTHWEST.COM) in derogation of the ADA.

10. Specifically, blind members of ACCESS NOW, including GUMSON do not have use of a monitor, nor a computer mouse due to their disability. Instead of reading web pages or viewing the images, they listen to the web through a software program known as a screen reader. A screen reader converts text into speech using an integrated voice synthesizer, and the computer's sound card to output the content of a website to the computer's speakers.

11. Blind members of ACCESS NOW and GUMSON, in employing their screen readers, have been denied access to the SOUTHWEST.COM website based solely on their disability, prior to the filing of this lawsuit. Specifically, the SOUTHWEST.COM website fails to provide "alternative text" which would provide a "screen reader" program the ability to communicate via synthesized speech what is visually displayed on the website.

12. Additionally, the SOUTHWEST.COM web site also fails to provide online forms which can be readily filled out by ACCESS NOW and GUMSON and fails to provide a "skip navigation link" which facilitates access for these blind consumers by permitting them to bypass the navigation bars on a website and proceed to the main content.

13. SOUTHWEST.COM accessibility barriers include, without limitation, the following:

(a) Approximately 45 instances of failure to provide alternative text for all images on the home page alone ("unlabeled graphics");

(b) Data tables are not adequately labeled with headers for the table rows and columns;

(c) Online forms which cannot be completed by a blind consumer; and

(d) Absence of "skip navigation link".

14. Accordingly, the SOUTHWEST. COM website does not allow screen readers to effectively monitor the computer screen and to fully convert the information into synthesized speech. SOUTHWEST. COM's use of (a) unlabeled graphics, (b) inadequately labeled data tables, (c) online forms not accessible to the blind and its lack of a (d)"skip navigation link" deny plaintiffs access to on-line bookings and other items offered through SOUTHWEST.COM. In fact, what often appears to be text—such as the tabs for reservations and schedules—are in fact unlabeled graphics. For example:

(a) **Navigating**: Although SOUTHWEST.COM'S home screen contains some text (i.e., "Reservations, Schedules and Fares"), in actuality, the "text" is a graphic that while capable of being read by a screen reader does not allow proper navigation. Due to the lack of any alternative, plaintiffs were/are forced to listen to a never ending recitation of text that cannot even be reduced to recognizable terms when they should hear a simple term such as "Reservations."

Specifically, while a sighted consumer sees a link labeled as "Fares", plaintiffs hear "CGI-bin/request Fares." Moreover, while a sighted customer sees "GO", plaintiffs hear "images/sidego.gif." Also, a sighted customer sees "contact SWA", while plaintiffs hear "travel-center/luvbook.html." Lastly, while a sighted user can focus in immediately to the main content of a page, the plaintiffs must listen to hundreds of items before arriving at the main content. Compounding the many navigational challenges facing plaintiffs when they visit SOUTHWEST.COM is the lack of a "skip navigation link." Once plaintiffs select a link to follow, the navigation bars from the

home page are repeated. Accordingly, plaintiffs are forced to
listen to the recitation of non-alternative text before hearing the
main content of that particular webpage, i.e. the home page
and/or ordering page.

(b) **Purchasing**: Although technically possible, plaintiffs
found purchasing a ticket to be extremely difficult and thereby
they have been denied equal access. For example, a sighted
customer goes to the visual prompt indicating "Reservations,"
however, plaintiffs hear "CGI-bin/billeditenarary." This sighted
customer would then proceed to the visual prompt "Hotel,"
however, plaintiffs hear "CGI-bin/hoteltab."

Then the sighted customer would see the visual prompt
"stay near downtown," however, a screen reader would prompt
plaintiff, another blind customer, to press the tab key which
automatically checks the "other city" radio button. While a
sighted customer could proceed to the "negotiated corporate rate
code," plaintiffs hear "edit box." Further, a sighted customer
could proceed to a visual prompt "air," while plaintiffs hear
"ss=0 & disc=3:1020187129.580657:49368@22de40b7c17e5db
60052564bf9c7071c65e291eb." Therefore, blind users are denied
the independent ability to purchase airline tickets or any other
item from SOUTHWEST.COM.

15. Without injunctive relief, GUMSON and other blind members
of ACCESS NOW will continue to be discriminated against and unable
to independently access and use Defendant's, SOUTHWEST.COM,
website in violation of their rights under the ADA. Providing accessibility
would neither fundamentally, alter the nature of Defendant's website nor
unduly burden Defendant. It is readily achievable.

16. Plaintiffs have no adequate remedy at law.

CLAIMS FOR RELIEF

COUNT I–VIOLATION OF THE ADA'S
COMMUNICATION BARRIERS REMOVAL MANDATE

17. Plaintiffs reallege paragraphs 1 through 16 as if fully set forth
herein.

18. Defendant, SOUTHWEST'S website denies access to Plaintiffs
through the use of a screen reader and therefore violates the
communication barriers removal provision of the ADA, 42 U.S.C.
§ 12182(b)(2)(A)(iv), because it constitutes a failure to remove existing
communication barriers from the website.

19. Redesigning the SOUTHWEST.COM website to permit the
blind to use it through a screen reader is readily achievable and the
requested modification is reasonable.

20. These remedial measures (SOUTHWEST redesigning the
portions of the website to enable access through a screen reader) are
effective, practical and financially manageable.

COUNT II–VIOLATION OF THE ADA'S
AUXILIARY AIDS SERVICES MANDATE

21. Plaintiffs reallege paragraphs 1 through 16, as if fully set forth
herein.

22. Defendant's website violates the auxiliary aids and services provision of the ADA, 42 U.S.C. § 12182(b)(2)(A)(iii), because it constitutes a failure to take steps to ensure that individuals who are blind are not denied access to the website, and does not provide an effective method of making this "visually delivered material available to individuals with visual impairments." 42 U.S.C. § 12102(1)(b).

23. Providing auxiliary aids and services that would make Defendant's SOUTHWEST.COM website accessible to and independently usable by persons who are blind.

COUNT III–VIOLATION OF ADA'S
REASONABLE MODIFICATION MANDATE

24. Plaintiffs reallege paragraphs 1 through 16, as if fully set forth herein.

25. Defendant's website denying access to the Plaintiffs to use it through a screen reader violates the reasonable modifications provisions of the ADA, 42 U.S.C. § 12182(b)(2)(A)(ii), in that it constitutes a failure to make reasonable modifications to policies, practices and procedures necessary to afford access to the website to persons who are blind. Modifying its policies, practices and procedures to afford access to SOUTHWEST.COM by redesigning the web site, would not fundamentally alter the nature of SOUTHWEST.COM'S website.

COUNT IV–VIOLATION OF THE ADA'S
FULL AND EQUAL ENJOYMENT MANDATE

26. Plaintiffs reallege paragraphs 1 through 16, as if fully set forth herein.

27. Defendant's internet website violates the full and equal enjoyment and participation provisions of the ADA pertaining to access to goods and services and advantages offered by SOUTHWEST.COM (42 U.S.C. §§ 12182(a), 12182(b)(1)(A)(i), and 12182(b)(1)(A)(ii)), in that it constitutes a failure to make the website fully accessible and independently usable by individuals who are blind.

RELIEF

WHEREFORE, Plaintiffs, ACCESS NOW, INC. and ROBERT GUMSON, request this court grant the following relief:

(a) Declare that Defendant's, SOUTHWEST AIRLINES CO., actions and inactions with respect to its SOUTHWEST.COM internet website violate Title III of the ADA, 42 U.S.C. § 12182 as alleged in Counts 1–4;

(b) Enjoin Defendant, SOUTHWEST AIRLINES CO. from continuing to violate the ADA and order Defendant to make its SOUTHWEST.COM website accessible and to take such other and further steps as are necessary to allow independent access through screen access programs by persons who are blind; and

(c) Grant Plaintiffs, ACCESS NOW, INC. and ROBERT GUMSON. such other relief as the Court deems just, equitable, and appropriate, including without limitation, an award of reasonable attorneys' fees, litigation expenses and costs under 42 U.S.C. § 12205.

TRIAL BY JURY IS DEMANDED ON ALL CLAIMS SO TRIABLE.

DATED this 10th day of June, 2002.

RASCO REININGER PEREZ & ESQUENAZI,
PL

Attorneys for Plaintiffs
283 Catalonia Avenue, Second Floor
Coral Gables, Florida 33134
Telephone: (305) 476–7100
Facsimile: (305) 476–7102

By: HOWARD R. BEHAR
Florida Bar No. 054471

By: STEVEN R. REININGER
Florida Bar No. 202002

NOTE ON THE ELEMENTS OF A COMPLAINT

1. Caption and form. The complaint is the formal opening salvo of the litigation. Although the parties may have corresponded before the complaint is filed, the complaint represents the formal commencement of the case. See Fed. R. Civ. P. 3. The required format of pleadings and other papers is prescribed in part by statute, in part by rule, and in part by custom. See, e.g., Fed. R. Civ. P. 10. In general, pleadings and other papers have a caption containing the name of the court, the title of the action, the name, address, and telephone number of the attorney presenting the pleading, and a brief designation of the nature of the paper (e.g., "complaint"). Papers ordinarily must be typed and double spaced, with proper margins.

2. Body. In the body of pleadings, it is mandatory (or sometimes merely customary) to set forth allegations in separately numbered paragraphs. See, e.g., Fed. R. Civ. P. 10(b). The organization of the paragraphs is largely up to the drafter, subject to three principal considerations. First, separate claims or causes of action must be stated separately. Second, each paragraph should deal with a limited subject. Third, allegations unlikely to be contested (e.g., ownership of a car) should be stated in separate paragraphs from allegations likely to be contested (e.g., negligence of the driver). This organization permits a person responding to the pleading to admit or deny allegations efficiently and precisely.

3. The required content of the complaint. In federal court, a complaint or other claim for relief must contain three required elements: (1) "a short and plain statement of the grounds of the court's jurisdiction"; (2) "a short and plain statement of the claim showing that the pleader is entitled to relief;" and (3) "a demand for the relief sought." See Fed. R. Civ. P. 8(a). Can you identify the portions of the complaint where the plaintiffs attempt to supply each of those elements? Where do you suppose that Paragraph 8 of the Complaint fits in the scheme of required elements?

4. Pleading subject matter jurisdiction in federal court. The requirement that the complaint in a federal court plead the basis of the court's jurisdiction reflects the fact that federal courts' subject matter jurisdiction is limited by the Constitution and by statute. For example, the outer boundaries of federal question jurisdiction are set by Article III: "The judicial Power shall extend to all Cases, in Law and Equity, arising under this Constitution, the Laws of the United States, and Treaties made, or which shall be made, under their Authority." U.S. Const. art. III, § 2, cl. 1.

But Article III is not enough by itself to confer jurisdiction. A statute conferring all or part of the constitutionally authorized jurisdiction is also required. The most important statute conferring federal question jurisdiction is 28 U.S.C. § 1331: "The district courts shall have original jurisdiction of all civil actions arising under the Constitution, laws, or treaties of the United States." Comparable provisions for diversity jurisdiction are U.S. Const. art. III, § 2, cl. 1 and 28 U.S.C. § 1332(a). What is the claimed basis for the court's jurisdiction in *Access Now?*

State trial courts are typically courts of general rather than limited jurisdiction and usually do not require allegations of jurisdiction in the complaint.

5. **The "claims for relief."** By convention, most complaints include "claims for relief," or "counts" describing the plaintiff's legal theories. *Access Now* is typical in this regard. But this section of the complaint is not formally required. All federal Rule 8 requires, for instance, is a "short and plain statement of the claim showing that the pleader is entitled to relief." The Supreme Court has on several occasions explained that "a complaint need not pin plaintiff's claim to a precise legal theory." Skinner v. Switzer, 562 U.S. 521, 131 S.Ct. 1289, 179 L.Ed.2d 233 (2011); see also Johnson v. City of Shelby, Miss., 574 U.S. ___, 135 S.Ct. 346, 190 L.Ed.2d 309 (2014) (per curiam) (holding that the rules "do not countenance dismissal of a complaint for imperfect statement of the legal theory supporting the claim asserted"). Why do you suppose the drafters of Rule 8 did not require plaintiffs to plead their legal theories? And why do you suppose most plaintiffs do so anyway?

6. **Prayer for relief.** At the conclusion of the complaint, plaintiff "prays" or makes a "demand" for the relief, or remedies, she seeks. See, e.g., Fed. R. Civ. P. 8(a)(3). A foundation for the prayer must be laid by appropriate allegations in the body of the complaint describing the nature and extent of the harm suffered. If the suit is contested by the defendant, the relief awarded is not limited by the amount or kind of relief sought in the prayer. But if the defendant fails to answer and a default judgment is entered, the relief will be limited to that sought in the prayer. See Fed. R. Civ. P. 54(c). What is the relief that the plaintiffs are seeking in *Access Now* and how does the complaint lay the foundation for the requested relief? For background see Chapter 1.E., An Introduction to Judicial Remedies.

7. **Designation of parties.** When a party is a person other than a natural person suing in his own right, the party's capacity is specifically designated. When a corporation is named, its state of incorporation is given. (In suits in federal district court in which jurisdiction is based on diversity, both the state of incorporation and the state in which the corporation has its principal place of business are given, for the corporation is a citizen of both states for purposes of the diversity statute, 28 U.S.C. § 1332.) A natural person suing or being sued in a special capacity, such as an executor, trustee, receiver, or public officer, is named in that capacity. Under older doctrine, a failure to specify the capacity of a person suing or being sued in a special capacity was a fatal error, but such a mistake is today regarded as harmless or correctable by amendment.

8. **Signing and verification.** Statutes or rules require that all pleadings be signed by the party or her attorney. See, e.g., Fed. R. Civ. P. 11(a). By statute or rule in some states, and by custom in others, all papers other than pleadings are signed by the attorney (or by the party if she is

unrepresented). Some jurisdictions require that all complaints be verified; that is, accompanied by an affidavit stating that the person knows, or states on information and belief, that the matters contained in the pleading are true. In other states, verification is required only for certain kinds of claims or is optional.

Access Now, Inc. v. Southwest Airlines Co.

United States District Court, Southern District of Florida, 2002.
227 F. Supp. 2d 1312.

■ SEITZ, DISTRICT JUDGE.

This matter is before the Court on Defendant Southwest Airlines, Co.'s ("Southwest") Motion to Dismiss Plaintiffs' Complaint. Plaintiffs, Access Now, Inc. ("Access Now"), a non-profit, access advocacy organization for disabled individuals, and Robert Gumson ("Gumson"), a blind individual, filed this four-count Complaint for injunctive and declaratory relief under the Americans with Disabilities Act ("ADA"), 42 U.S.C. §§ 12101 et seq. Plaintiffs contend that Southwest's Internet website, southwest.com, excludes Plaintiffs in violation of the ADA, as the goods and services Southwest offers at its "virtual ticket counters" are inaccessible to blind persons. Southwest has moved to dismiss Plaintiffs' Complaint on the grounds that southwest.com is not a "place of public accommodation" and, therefore, does not fall within the scope of Title III of the ADA. The Court has considered the parties' thorough papers, the extremely informative argument of counsel, and the exhibits presented during oral argument. For the reasons stated below, The Court will grant Southwest's motion to dismiss.

Background

Having found that nearly forty-three million Americans have one or more mental or physical disabilities, that such individuals continually encounter various forms of discrimination, and that "the continuing existence of unfair and unnecessary discrimination and prejudice denies people with disabilities the opportunity to compete on an equal basis and to pursue those opportunities for which our free society is justifiably famous," Congress enacted the ADA in 1990. Congress' stated purposes in enacting the ADA were, among other things, to provide "a clear and comprehensive national mandate for the elimination of discrimination against individuals with disabilities," and "clear, strong, consistent, enforceable standards addressing discrimination against individuals with disabilities." Among the statutorily created rights embodied within the ADA, is Title III's prohibition against discrimination in places of public accommodation. 42 U.S.C. § 12182(a).

Since President George Bush signed the ADA into law on July 26, 1990, this Nation, as well the rest of the world, has experienced an era of rapidly changing technology and explosive growth in the use of the Internet. Today, millions of people across the globe utilize the Internet on a regular basis for communication, news gathering, and commerce. Although this increasingly widespread and swiftly developing technology provides great benefits for the vast majority of Internet users, individuals who suffer from various physical disabilities may be unable to access the goods and services offered on many Internet websites. According to

Plaintiffs, of the nearly ten million visually impaired persons in the United States, approximately 1.5 million of these individuals use the Internet.

In an effort to accommodate the needs of the visually impaired, a number of companies within the computer software industry have developed assistive technologies, such as voice-dictation software, voice-navigation software, and magnification software to assist visually impaired persons in navigating through varying degrees of text and graphics found on different websites. However, not only do each of the different assistive software programs vary in their abilities to successfully interpret text and graphics, but various websites also differ in their abilities to allow different assistive technologies to effectively convert text and graphics into meaningful audio signals for visually impaired users. This lack of coordination between programmers and assistive technology manufacturers has created a situation where the ability of a visually impaired individual to access a website depends upon the particular assistive software program being used and the particular website being visited.

In light of this rapidly developing technology, and the accessibility problems faced by numerous visually impaired Internet users, the question remains whether Title III of the ADA mandates that Internet website operators modify their sites so as to provide complete access to visually impaired individuals.[3] Because no court within this Circuit has squarely addressed this issue, the Court is faced with a question of first impression, namely, whether Southwest's Internet website, southwest.com, is a place of public accommodation as defined by the ADA, and if so, whether Title III of the ADA requires Southwest to make the goods and services available at its "virtual ticket counters" accessible to visually impaired persons.

Southwest, the fourth largest U.S. airline (in terms of domestic customers carried), was the first airline to establish a home page on the Internet. See Southwest Airlines Fact Sheet, at http://www.southwest.com/about_swa/press/factsheet.html (Last visited Oct. 16, 2002). Southwest's Internet website, southwest.com, provides consumers with the means to, among other things, check airline fares and schedules, book airline, hotel, and car reservations, and stay informed of Southwest's sales and promotions. Employing more than 35,000 employees, and conducting approximately 2,800 flights per day, Southwest reports that "approximately 46 percent, or over $500 million, of its passenger revenue for first quarter 2002 was generated by online bookings via southwest.com." Id. According to Southwest, "more than 3.5 million people subscribe to Southwest's weekly Click 'N Save e-mails,' " Id. Southwest prides itself on operating an Internet website that provides

---

[3]   Some commentators, while recognizing the paucity of case law in this area, have suggested that Internet websites fall within the scope of the ADA. See, e.g. Jeffrey Scott Raneu, Note, Was Blind But Now I See: The Argument for ADA Applicability to the Internet, 22 B.C. Third World L.J. 389 (2002); Adam M. Schloss, Web-Sight for Visually-Disabled People; Does Title III of the Americans with Disabilities Act Apply to Internet Websites?, 35 Colum. J.L. & Soc. Probs. 35 (2001); Matthew A. Stowe, Note, Interpreting "Place of Public Accommodation" Under Title III of the ADA: A Technical Determination with Potentially Broad Civil Rights Implications, 50 Duke L.J. 297 (2000); Jonathan Bick, Americans with Disabilities Act and the Internet, 10 Alb. L.J. Sci. & Tech. 205 (2000).

"the highest level of business value, design effectiveness, and innovative technology use achievable on the Web today." Id.

Despite the apparent success of Southwest's website, Plaintiffs contend that Southwest's technology violates the ADA, as the goods and services offered on southwest.com are inaccessible to blind persons using a screen reader.[4] (Compl. ¶ 4). Plaintiffs allege that although "southwest.com offers the sighted customer the promise of independence of on-line airline/hotel booking in the comfort and safety of their home . . . even if a blind person like [Plaintiff] Gumson has a screen reader with a voice synthesizer on their computer, they are prevented from using the southwest.com website because of its failure to allow access" (Compl. ¶ 4). Specifically, Plaintiffs maintain that "the southwest.com website fails to provide 'alternative text' which would provide a 'screen reader' program the ability to communicate via synthesized speech what is visually displayed on the website." (Compl. ¶ 11). Additionally, Plaintiffs assert that the southwest.com website "fails to provide online forms which can be readily filled out by [Plaintiffs] and fails to provide a 'skip navigation link' which facilitates access for these blind consumers by permitting them to bypass the navigation bars on a website and proceed to the main content." (Compl. ¶ 12).

Plaintiffs' four-count Complaint seeks a declaratory judgment that Southwest's website violates the communication barriers removal provision of the ADA (Count I), violates the auxiliary aids and services provision of the ADA (Count II), violates the reasonable modifications provisions of the ADA (Count III), and violates the full and equal enjoyment and participation provisions of the ADA (Count IV).[5] Plaintiffs ask this Court to enjoin Southwest from continuing to violate the ADA, to order Southwest to make its website accessible to persons who are blind, and to award Plaintiffs attorneys' fees and costs. Southwest has moved to dismiss Plaintiffs' Complaint pursuant to Fed. R. Civ. P. 12(b)(6). The Court has federal question jurisdiction over this matter pursuant to 28 U.S.C. § 1331.

Discussion

A. Standard of Review

Federal Rule of Civil Procedure 12(b)(6) provides that dismissal of a claim is appropriate when "it is clear that no relief could be granted under any set of facts that could be proved consistent with the allegations." Blackston v. Alabama, 30 F.3d 117, 120 (11th Cir. 1994) (quoting Hishon v. King & Spalding, 467 U.S. 69, 73, 104 S.Ct. 2229, 81 L.Ed.2d 59 (1984)). At this stage of the case, the Court must accept Plaintiffs' allegations in the Complaint as true and view those allegations in a light most favorable to Plaintiffs to determine whether the Complaint fails to

---

[4] Plaintiffs claim that although purchasing tickets at southwest.com is "technically possible, plaintiffs found purchasing a ticket to be extremely difficult . . ." (Compl. at 7). Plaintiffs do not argue that they are unable to access such goods and services via alternative means such as telephone or by visiting a particular airline ticket counter or travel agency.

[5] Plaintiffs' Counsel informed the Court that Plaintiffs made no effort to resolve this dispute prior to filing their Complaint. Although the law does not require Plaintiffs to confer with Southwest prior to filing this action, in light of Plaintiffs' Counsel's discussion of the proactive measures that other companies, such as Amazon.com, have taken to modify their websites to make them more accessible to visually impaired persons, it is unfortunate that Plaintiffs made no attempt to resolve this matter before resorting to litigation.

state a claim for relief. S & Davis Int'l, Inc. v. Republic of Yemen, 218 F.3d 1292, 1298 (11th Cir. 2000).

B. Plaintiffs Have Failed to State a Claim Upon Which Relief Can be Granted

The threshold issue of whether an Internet website, such as southwest.com, is a "place of public accommodation" as defined by the ADA, presents a question of statutory construction. As in all such disputes, the Court must begin its analysis with the plain language of the statute in question. Rendon v. Valleycrest Prods., Ltd., 294 F.3d 1279, 1283 n. 6 (11th Cir. 2002) (citing Kmart v. Cartier, Inc., 486 U.S. 281, 291, 108 S.Ct. 1811, 100 L.Ed.2d 313 (1988)). The "first step in interpreting a statute is to determine whether the language at issue has a plain and unambiguous meaning with regard to the particular dispute in the case." Rendon, 294 F.3d at 1283 n. 6. (quoting Robinson v. Shell Oil Co., 519 U.S. 337, 340, 117 S.Ct. 843, 136 L.Ed.2d 808 (1997)). A court need look no further where the statute in question provides a plain and unambiguous meaning. Rendon, 294 F.3d at 1283 n.6.

1. Southwest.com is Not a "Place of Public Accommodation" as Defined by the Plain and Unambiguous Language of the ADA

Title III of the ADA sets forth the following general rule against discrimination in places of public accommodation:

> No individual shall be discriminated against on the basis of disability in the full and equal enjoyment of the goods, services, facilities, privileges, advantages, or accommodations of any *place of public accommodation* by any person who owns, leases (or leases to), or operates a *place of public accommodation*.

42 U.S.C. § 12182 (a) (emphasis added).

The statute specifically identifies twelve (12) particularized categories of "places of public accommodation." 42 U.S.C. § 12181(7). "Public accommodations" include:

> (A) an inn, hotel, motel, or other place of lodging, except for an establishment located within a building that contains not more than five rooms for rent or hire and that is actually occupied by the proprietor of such establishment as the residence of such proprietor;
>
> (B) a restaurant, bar, or other establishment serving food or drink;
>
> (C) a motion picture house, theater, concert hall, stadium, or other place of exhibition or entertainment;
>
> (D) an auditorium, convention center, lecture hall, or other place of public gathering;
>
> (E) a bakery, grocery store, clothing store, hardware store, shopping center, or other sales or rental establishment;
>
> (F) a laundromat dry-cleaner, bank, barber shop, beauty shop, travel service, shoe repair service, funeral parlor, gas station, office of an accountant or lawyer, pharmacy, insurance

office, professional office of a health care provider, hospital, or other service establishment;,

(G) a terminal, depot, or other station used for specified public transportation;

(H) a museum, library, gallery, or other place of public display or collection;

(I) a park, zoo, amusement park, or other place of recreation;

(J) a nursery, elementary, secondary, undergraduate, or postgraduate private school, or other place of education;

(K) a day care center, senior citizen center, homeless shelter, food bank, adoption agency, or other social service center establishment; and

(L) a gymnasium, health spa, bowling alley, golf course, or other place of exercise or recreation.

42 U.S.C. § 12181(7).

Furthermore, pursuant to Congress' grant of authority to the Attorney General to issue regulations to carry out the ADA, the applicable federal regulations also define a "place of public accommodation" as "a facility, operated by a private entity, whose operations affect commerce and fall within at least one of the [twelve (12) enumerated categories set forth in 42 U.S.C. § 12181(7).]" 28 C.F.R. § 36.101.[6] Section 36.104 defines "facility" as "all or any portion of buildings, structures, sites, complexes, equipment, rolling stock or other conveyances, roads, walks, passageways, parking lots, or other real or personal property, including the site where the building, property, structure, or equipment is located." 28 C.F.R. § 36.104. In interpreting the plain and unambiguous language of the ADA, and its applicable federal regulations, the Eleventh Circuit has recognized Congress' clear intent that Title III of the ADA governs solely access to physical, concrete places of public accommodation. Rendon, 294 F.3d at 1283–84; Stevens v. Premier Cruises, Inc., 215 F.3d 1237, 1241 (11th Cir. 2000) (noting that "because Congress has provided such a comprehensive definition of 'public accommodation,' we think that the intent of Congress is clear enough"). Where Congress has created specifically enumerated rights and expressed the intent of setting forth "clear, strong, consistent, enforceable standards," courts must follow the law as written and wait for Congress to adopt or revise legislatively-defined standards that apply to those rights. Here, to fall within the scope of the ADA as presently drafted, a public accommodation must be a physical, concrete structure. To expand the ADA to cover "virtual" spaces would be to create new rights without well-defined standards.

Notwithstanding the fact that the plain and unambiguous language of the statute and relevant regulations does not include Internet websites among the definitions of "places of public accommodation," Plaintiffs allege that the southwest.com website falls within the scope of Title III,

---

[6]   The Court may consider the C.F.R. definitions, as Congress specifically directed the Attorney General to "issue regulations in an accessible format to carry out the provisions of [the ADA] . . . that include standards applicable to facilities and vehicles covered under section 12182 of [the ADA.]" 42 U.S.C. § 12186(b).

in that it is a place of "exhibition, display and a sales establishment." (Compl. ¶ 9). Plaintiffs' argument rests on a definition they have created by selecting language from three separate statutory subsections of 42 U.S.C. § 12181(7). See § 42 U.S.C. §§ 12181(7)(C), (H) & (E).[7] While Plaintiffs can, as advocates, combine general terms from three separate statutory subsections, and apply them to an unenumerated specific term, namely Internet websites, the Court must view these general terms in the specific context in which Congress placed each of them.

Under the rule of ejusdem generis, where general words follow a specific enumeration of persons or things, the general words should be limited to persons or things similar to those specifically enumerated." Allen v. A.G. Thomas, 161 F.3d 667, 671 (11th Cir. 1998) (quoting United States v. Turkette, 452 U.S. 576, 581–82, 101 S.Ct. 2524, 69 L.Ed.2d 246 (1981)). Here, the general terms, "exhibition," "display," and "sales establishment," are limited to their corresponding specifically enumerated terms, all of which are physical, concrete structures, namely: "motion picture house, theater, concert hall, stadium"; and "museum, library, gallery"; and "bakery, grocery store, clothing store, hardware store, shopping center," respectively. 42 U.S.C. §§ 12181(7)(C), (H) & (E). Thus, this Court cannot properly construe "a place of public accommodation" to include Southwest's Internet website, SOUTHWEST.COM.

2. Plaintiffs Have Not Established a Nexus Between Southwest.com and a Physical, Concrete Place of Public Accommodation

Although Internet websites do not fall within the scope of the ADA's plain and unambiguous language, Plaintiffs contend that the Court is not bound by the statute's plain language, and should expand the ADA's application into cyberspace.[8] As part of their argument, Plaintiffs encourage the Court to follow Carparts Distribution Ctr., Inc. v. Automotive Wholesaler's Assoc. of New England, in which the First Circuit broadly held that the ADA's definition of "public accommodation" is not limited to actual physical structures, but includes, *inter alia*, health-benefit plans. *Carparts*, 37 F.3d 12, 19 (1st Cir. 1994).[9] While

---

[7]   Plaintiffs created definition from the following italicized language in three subsection of 42 U.S.C. § 12181(7);

"a motion picture house, theater, concert hall, stadium, or other *place of exhibition* or entertainment," 42 U.S.C. § 12181(7)(C);

"a museum, library, gallery, or other place of public *display* or collection," 42 U.S.C. § 12181(7)(H);

and "a bakery, grocery store, clothing store, hardware store, shopping center, or other *sales* or rental *establishment*," 42 U.S.C. § 12181(7)(E).

[8]   Plaintiffs concede that neither the legislative history of the ADA nor the plain language of the statute and applicable federal regulations, contain any specific reference to the Internet or cyberspace.

[9]   Although *Carparts* does not explicitly address the issue of whether an Internet website falls within the definition of "public accommodation," Plaintiffs focus on the First Circuit's dicta discussing the public policy reasons for why the ADA's definition of "public accommodations" should be read broadly:

By including "travel service" among the list of services considered "public accommodations," Congress clearly contemplated that "service establishment" include providers of services which do not require a person no physically enter an actual physical structure. Many travel services conduct by telephone or correspondence

application of the broad holding and dicta in *Carparts* to the facts in this case might arguably require this Court to include Internet websites within the ADA's definition of "public accommodations," the Eleventh Circuit has not read Title III of the ADA nearly as broadly as the First Circuit.[10] See *Rendon*, 294 F.3d 1279.

In *Rendon*, a recent Eleventh Circuit case addressing the scope of Title III, a group of individuals with hearing and upper-body mobility impairments sued the producers of the television game show, "Who Wants To Be A Millionaire," alleging that the use of an automated fast finger telephone selection process violated the ADA because it excluded disabled individuals from participating. The district court dismissed the complaint on grounds that the automated telephone selection process was not conducted at a physical location, and therefore, was not a "place of public accommodation" as defined by the ADA. The Eleventh Circuit reversed, holding that the telephone selection process was "a discriminatory screening mechanism . . . which deprives [the plaintiffs] of the opportunity to compete for the privilege of being a contestant on the [game show]." *Rendon*, 294 F.3d at 1286. The Eleventh Circuit

---

without requiring their customers to enter an office in order to obtain their services. Likewise, one can easily imagine the existence of other service establishments conducting business by mail and without providing facilities for their customers to enter in order to utilize their services. It would be irrational to conclude that persons who enter an office to purchase service are protected by the ADA, but persons who purchase the same services over the telephone or by mail are not. Congress could not have intended such an absurd result.

Carparts, 37 F.3d at 19.

[10] In addition to *Carparts*, Plaintiffs encourage this Court to follow Doe v. Mutual of Omaha Ins. Co., 179 F.3d 557 (7th Cir. 1999), in which Chief Judge Posner approvingly cited to *Carparts* and stated in dicta that;

The core meaning of [42 U.S.C. § 12182(a)], plainly enough, is that the owner or operator of a store, hotel, restaurant, dentist's office, travel agency, theater, Website, or other facility (whether in physical space or in electronic space, [*Carparts*]), that is open to the public cannot exclude disabled persons from entering the facility and, once in, from using the facility in the same way that the nondisabled do.

Plaintiffs also cite to a September 9, 1996 letter from Deval L. Patrick, Assistant Attorney General, Civil Rights Division, United States Department of Justices, to U.S. Senator Tom Harkin, advising the Senator that "covered entities that use the Internet for communications regarding their programs, goods, or services must be prepared to offer those communications through accessible means as well." Finally Plaintiffs cite the recent unpublished opinion in Vincent Martin et al. v. Metro Atlanta Rapid Transit Authority, 225 F. Supp. 2d 1362, 2002 (N.D. Ga. 2002), in which U.S. District Judge Thomas W. Thrash, Jr. held that until the Metropolitan Atlanta Rapid Transit Authority ("MARTA") reformats its Internet website in such a way that it can be read by visually impaired persons using screen readers, MARTA is "violating the ADA mandate of making adequate communications capacity available, through accessible formats and technology, to enable users to obtain information and schedule service." Vincent Martin et. al. v. Metro. Atlanta Rapid Transit Authority, 225 F. Supp. 2d 1362, 1374 (N.D. Ga. Oct. 7, 2002) (quoting 49 C.F.R. § 37.167(f)). That case, however, is distinguishable in one critical respect: Plaintiffs in *Vincent Martin* filed suit under both the Rehabilitation Act of 1973, as amended, 29 U.S.C. § 794 et seq., and Title II of the ADA, 42 U.S.C. 12132, not Title III as in the present case. Title II prohibits qualified individuals from being "excluded from participation in or [being] denied the benefits of the services, programs, activities of a public entity, or [being] subjected to discrimination by any such entity." 42 U.S.C. § 12132. Title II of the ADA defines "public entity" as "(A) any State or local government; (B) any department, agency, special purpose district, or other instrumentality of a State or States or local government; and (C) the National Railroad Passenger Corporation, and any commuter authority. . . ." 42 U.S.C. § 12131. Because the present case deals with Title III, not Title II of the ADA, and Plaintiffs could not allege any facts that would place Southwest within the definition of a "public entity" under Title II, *Vincent Martin* is inapplicable.

observed that "there is nothing in the text of the statute to suggest that discrimination via an imposition of screening or eligibility requirements must occur on site to offend the ADA." Id. at 1283–84. Most significantly, the Eleventh Circuit noted that the plaintiffs stated a claim under Title III because they demonstrated "a nexus between the challenged service and the premises of the public accommodation," namely the concrete television studio. Id. at 1284 n. 8.

Plaintiffs contend that the Eleventh Circuit in *Rendon* aligned itself with the First Circuit in Carparts, and that *Rendon* requires a broad reading of the ADA to include Internet websites within the "public accommodations" definition. However, these arguments, while emotionally attractive, are not legally viable for at least two reasons. First, contrary to Plaintiffs' assertion that the Eleventh Circuit aligned itself with *Carparts*, the Eleventh Circuit in *Rendon* not only did not approve of *Carparts*, it failed even to cite it.

Second, whereas the defendants in *Rendon* conceded, and the Eleventh Circuit agreed, that the game show at issue took place at a physical, public accommodation (a concrete television studio), and that the fast finger telephone selection process used to select contestants tended to screen out disabled individuals, the Internet website at issue here is neither a physical, public accommodation itself as defined by the ADA, nor a means to accessing a concrete space such as the specific television studio in *Rendon*.[11] 294 F.3d at 1284. Although Plaintiffs contend that this "is a case seeking equal access to Southwest's virtual 'ticket counters' as they exist on-line," the Supreme Court and the Eleventh Circuit have both recognized that the Internet is "a unique medium—known to its users as 'cyberspace'—*located in no particular geographical location* but available to anyone, anywhere in the world, with access to the Internet." Voyeur Dorm, L.C. v. City of Tampa, 265 F.3d 1232, 1237 n.3 (11th Cir. 2001) (quoting Reno v. ACLU, 521 U.S. 844, 851, 117 S.Ct. 2329, 138 L.Ed.2d 874 (1997)). Thus, because the Internet website, southwest.com, does not exist in any particular geographical location, Plaintiffs are unable to demonstrate that Southwest's website impedes their access to a specific, physical, concrete space such as a particular airline ticket counter or travel agency.[12] Having failed to establish a nexus between southwest.com and a physical, concrete place of public accommodation, Plaintiffs have failed to state a claim upon which relief can be granted under Title III of the ADA.[13]

---

[11] In recognizing the requirement that a plaintiff establish "a nexus between the challenged service and the premises of the public accommodation," the Eleventh Circuit noted that the plaintiffs in *Rendon* stated a claim under Title III of the ADA because they sought "the privilege of competing in a contest held in a *concrete space* . . ." *Rendon*, 294 F.3d at 1284 (emphasis added).

[12] It is important to note that aircrafts are explicitly exempt from Title III of the ADA. 42 U.S.C. § 12181(10). Plaintiffs do not argue that Southwest's website impedes their access to aircrafts.

[13] Given the number of visually impaired persons who utilize the Internet for commerce, and the significant amount of business that Southwest obtains through its Internet website, it is unfortunate that the parties have not cooperated to develop a creative solution that benefits both parties and which avoids the costs and polarizing effects of litigation. It is especially surprising that Southwest, a company which prides itself on its consumer relations, has not voluntarily seized the opportunity to employ all available technologies to expand accessibility to its website for visually impaired customers who would be an added source of revenue. That

Conclusion

Accordingly, based upon the foregoing reasons, it is hereby

ORDERED that Defendant Southwest's Motion to Dismiss Plaintiffs' Complaint is GRANTED, and this action is DISMISSED WITH PREJUDICE. All pending motions not otherwise ruled upon are denied as moot, and this case is CLOSED.

NOTE ON DEVICES FOR CHALLENGING THE SUBSTANTIVE SUFFICIENCY OF A COMPLAINT

1. The procedural requirements for a sufficient complaint. As noted above, Rule 8(a) specifies the required components of a pleading in federal court. What component of the plaintiff's complaint in *Access Now* does the defendant contend is defective?

2. Devices for testing legal sufficiency: the motion to dismiss for failure to state a claim under Fed. R. Civ. P. 12(b)(6). In federal court, and in state courts following the federal Rules, the legal sufficiency of a complaint's allegations is tested by a motion under Rule 12(b)(6) to dismiss for failure to state a claim upon which relief can be granted. Indeed, the "12(b)(6) motion" is common parlance for litigators. A motion to dismiss under Rule 12(b)(6) admits the truth of the allegations of the complaint, for purposes of the motion only, and in ruling on the motion the court must treat them as true. Moreover, where the complaint is ambiguous or permits different readings, the court ruling on the motion is required to construe it in favor of the pleader. If the motion is denied and the suit proceeds, the defendant may later challenge the factual allegations of the complaint as unsupported by the evidence. Did the court properly apply these standards in judging the substantive sufficiency of the complaint in *Access Now?*

In code pleading states, the function served by the Rule 12(b)(6) motion is filled by the demurrer. A demurrer is in essence a motion directed to the face of the complaint. The so-called general demurrer is a motion asserting that the "pleading does not state facts sufficient to constitute a cause of action." Calif.C.Civ.P. § 430.10(e). A general demurrer is described in Raneri v. DePolo, 441 A.2d 1373, 1375, 65 Pa. Cmwlth. 183 (1982):

> A demurrer, which tests a complaint's legal sufficiency, is an assertion that the pleading does not set forth a cause of action upon which relief can be granted . . . and admits every well-pleaded material fact plus all reasonable inferences therefrom. . . . [Plaintiff] is not required here to prove his cause of action; the only issue now before us is whether or not the allegations, if proved, are sufficient to entitle the plaintiff to relief.

In modern federal and code pleading practice, the defendant retains the right to challenge the factual sufficiency of the evidence supporting the complaint if the challenge to legal sufficiency fails. It was not always so. The

being said, in light of the rapidly developing technology at issue, and the lack of well-defined standards for bringing a virtually infinite number of Internet websites into compliance with the ADA, a precondition for taking the ADA into "virtual" space is a meaningful input from all interested parties via the legislative process. As Congress has created the statutory defined rights under the ADA, it is the role of Congress, and not this Court, to specifically expand the ADA's definition of "public accommodation" beyond physical, concrete places of public accommodation, to include "virtual" places of public accommodation.

early common law demurrer required defendant to elect between the two options. In order to demur generally (that is, to challenge the legal sufficiency of the complaint), a defendant was required to admit *conclusively* the factual allegations of the plaintiff. If the defendant prevailed on the demurrer, judgment could be entered in his favor. But if he lost on the issue of law, then judgment would be entered against him, because he would be deemed to have admitted the truth of plaintiff's claim. Why do you suppose the requirement that defendant elect between challenging legal and factual sufficiency was eliminated?

3.   The measure of substantive sufficiency. The substantive "elements" of a sufficient complaint are well established for most commonly recurring claims. When the claim is based on judge-made common law, in most jurisdictions there are cases that recite the elements of a particular type of claim. See Hazard, Leubsdorf & Bassett, Civil Procedure § 4.8 (6th ed. 2011).

When the substantive law governing the claim is statutory, the method for deriving the elements begins with the statutory language. How does the court derive the required elements of a claim from the statutory language in *Access Now*? What element or elements of the claim does the defendant contend has not been pleaded? What other sources of law does the court consider in addition to the language itself in deciding whether that element has been pleaded? If you had to characterize the issue decided in *Access Now* as one of fact or law, which characterization would you think was more nearly correct?

4.   The substantive law. Did the *Access Now* court get the substantive law right? The substantive question resolved in *Access Now* has now been considered by another federal district court, which sustained the plaintiff's complaint against a motion to dismiss. National Federation of the Blind v. Target Corp., 452 F. Supp. 2d 946 (N.D. Cal. 2006). The pertinent part of the court's decision reads as follows:

> Defendant contends that Target.com is not a place of public accommodation within the meaning of the ADA, and therefore plaintiffs cannot state a claim under the ADA. Specifically, defendant claims that the complaint is deficient because it does not allege that "individuals with vision impairments are denied access to one of Target's brick and mortar stores or the goods they contain." However, the complaint states that "due to Target's failure and refusal to remove access barriers to Target.com, blind individuals have been and are being denied equal access to Target stores, as well as to the numerous goods, services and benefits offered to the public through Target.com." Complaint P 24. Plaintiffs' legal theory is that unequal access to Target.com denies the blind the full enjoyment of the goods and services offered at Target stores, which are places of public accommodation.

> Defendant contends that even if Target.com is the alleged service of Target stores, plaintiffs still do not state a claim because they fail to assert that they are denied physical access to Target stores. * * * *

> The case law does not support defendant's attempt to draw a false dichotomy between those services which impede physical

access to a public accommodation and those merely offered by the
facility. Such an interpretation would effectively limit the scope of
Title III to the provision of ramps, elevators and other aids that
operate to remove physical barriers to entry. Although the Ninth
Circuit has determined that a place of public accommodation is a
physical space, the court finds unconvincing defendant's attempt to
bootstrap the definition of accessibility to this determination,
effectively reading out of the ADA the broader provisions enacted
by Congress. In *Rendon* [*v. Valleycrest Prods, Inc.*], even though the
disabled individual did not contest the actual physical barriers of
the facility in question, the Eleventh Circuit found that Title III
was implicated because a "discriminatory procedure that deprived
[the individual] of the opportunity to compete to be a contestant
* * * *at* a place of public accommodation" was utilized. *Rendon*, 294
F.3d at 1281 (emphasis added). Similarly, in the present action,
plaintiffs have alleged that the inaccessibility of Target.com denies
the blind the ability to enjoy the services of Target stores. The
Ninth Circuit has stated that the "ordinary meaning" of the ADA's
prohibition against "discrimination in the enjoyment of goods,
services, facilities or privileges, is 'that *whatever* goods or services
the place provides, it cannot discriminate on the basis of disability
in providing enjoyment of those goods and services.'" Defendant's
argument is unpersuasive and the court declines to dismiss the
action for failure to allege a denial of physical access to the Target
stores.

452 F. Supp. 2d 946, 951–52, 955. Does the difference in outcomes between
Access Now and *National Federation of the Blind* reflect a difference in what
was pleaded in the two cases or a different view of the applicable substantive
law?

District courts continue to remain divided over whether a website itself
may be a place of public accommodation even if there is no plausible nexus
to a physical location. In National Association of the Deaf v. Netflix, Inc., 869
F. Supp. 2d 196 (D. Mass. 2012), deaf and hearing-impaired plaintiffs sued
Netflix under the ADA for discrimination on the ground that only a small
portion of its content provided closed captioning. The district court rejected
the defendant's 12(b)(6) motion, which was premised on the argument that
Netflix's in-home video-streaming service was not a place of public
accommodation:

Plaintiffs convincingly argue that the Watch Instantly web site
falls within at least one, if not more, of the enumerated ADA
categories. The web site may qualify as: a "service establishment"
in that it provides customers with the ability to stream video
programming through the internet; a "place of exhibition or
entertainment" in that it displays movies, television programming,
and other content; and a "rental establishment" in that it engages
customers to pay for the rental of video programming.

Id. at. 200.

Conversely, in dealing with a virtually identical lawsuit against Netflix,
a California district court dismissed the plaintiff's ADA claim under Rule
12(b)(6) on the ground that "websites are not places of public

accommodations under the ADA because they are not actual physical places." Cullen v. Netflix, 880 F. Supp. 2d 1017 (N.D. Cal. 2012). See also Young v. Facebook, Inc., 790 F. Supp. 2d 1110 (N.D. Cal. 2011) (dismissing ADA claim against Facebook because it "operates only in cyberspace and is thus not 'a place of public accommodation' ").

5.   Leave to amend. If the court grants a motion to dismiss under Rule 12(b)(6), the plaintiff is routinely given leave to amend the complaint. The rationale behind granting leave to amend is to ensure that the failure to plead the missing element or elements reflects a real lack of proof available to the plaintiff, rather than remediable error or inadvertence. Under such circumstances, a plaintiff should not lose the opportunity to litigate a meritorious claim due to a curable deficiency in the complaint. Failure to grant leave to amend at least once is almost invariably held an abuse of discretion, unless it is certain that any amendment would be futile. The measure of indulgence varies from jurisdiction to jurisdiction, but on the whole it is quite generous. Federal courts are likely to grant leave to amend even when the proposed amendments are inconsistent with the original allegations in the complaint. See West Run Student Housing Associates v. Huntington National Bank, 712 F.3d 165 (3d Cir. 2013).

For a description of federal practice under Rule 12(b)(6), see, e.g., Bausch v. Stryker Corp., 630 F.3d 546 (7th Cir. 2010) (denial of motions for leave to amend are disfavored). According to the subsequent opinion in the court of appeals, Access Now, Inc. v. Southwest Airlines Co., 385 F.3d 1324, 1331 n.3 (11th Cir. 2004), the plaintiffs did not seek leave to amend their complaint. Had they done so, it would presumably have been an abuse of discretion for the district court to deny at least one such opportunity.

6.   What next for the plaintiff? When, as in *Access Now*, the dismissal of the complaint for failure to state a claim leaves plaintiff with no remaining viable theory on which relief can be sought, plaintiff is entitled to appeal from the court's final judgment dismissing the action. Because the question is one of law, the reviewing court will apply a de novo standard of review. In *Access Now*, the court of appeals dismissed the plaintiff's appeal. 385 F.3d 1324 (11th Cir. 2004). The plaintiff's principal argument on appeal was that its complaint should have been sustained because it had pleaded that Southwest.com was a "nexus" to Southwest Airlines, which was itself a "travel service" within the meaning of 42 U.S.C. § 12181(7)(F). The court of appeals responded to this argument by refusing to consider the merits: "[T]he claim presented to the district court—that Southwest.com is itself a place of public accommodation—appears to us to have been abandoned on appeal, and a new (and fact-specific) theory—that Southwest.com has a 'nexus' to Southwest Airlines' 'travel service'—has been raised for the first time on appeal." 385 F.3d at 1329. The court refused to consider either theory, on the ground that the first had been abandoned, while the second had not been pleaded or argued in the lower court. Rereading the complaint in the light most favorable to the plaintiff, and considering the district court's discussion of *Rendon*, do you agree with the court of appeals that the plaintiff's "nexus" theory was not adequately pleaded or argued in the district court? Was the failure of plaintiff's counsel to seek leave to amend in the district court a serious error in judgment?

C. ALLOCATING THE BURDEN OF PLEADING

Gomez v. Toledo

Supreme Court of the United States, 1980.
446 U.S. 635, 100 S.Ct. 1920, 64 L.Ed.2d 572.

■ MR. JUSTICE MARSHALL delivered the opinion of the Court.

The question presented is whether, in an action brought under 42 U.S.C. § 1983 against a public official whose position might entitle him to qualified immunity, a plaintiff must allege that the official has acted in bad faith in order to state a claim for relief or, alternatively, whether the defendant must plead good faith as an affirmative defense.

      - Issue

I

Petitioner Carlos Rivera Gomez brought this action against respondent, the Superintendent of the Police of the Commonwealth of Puerto Rico, contending that respondent had violated his right to procedural due process by discharging him from employment with the Police Department's Bureau of Criminal Investigation. Basing jurisdiction on 28 U.S.C. § 1343(3),[2] petitioner alleged the following facts in his complaint.[3] Petitioner had been employed as an agent with the Puerto Rican police since 1968. In April 1975, he submitted a sworn statement to his supervisor in which he asserted that two other agents had offered false evidence for use in a criminal case under their investigation. As a result of this statement, petitioner was immediately transferred from the Criminal Investigation Corps for the Southern Area to Police Headquarters in San Juan, and a few weeks later to the Police Academy in Gurabo, where he was given no investigative authority. In the meantime respondent ordered an investigation of petitioner's claims, and the Legal Division of the Police Department concluded that all of petitioner's factual allegations were true.

In April 1976, while still stationed at the Police Academy, petitioner was subpoenaed to give testimony in a criminal case arising out of the evidence that petitioner had alleged to be false. At the trial petitioner, appearing as a defense witness, testified that the evidence was in fact false. As a result of this testimony, criminal charges, filed on the basis of information furnished by respondent, were brought against petitioner for the allegedly unlawful wiretapping of the agents' telephones. Respondent suspended petitioner in May 1976 and discharged him without a hearing in July. In October, the District Court of Puerto Rico found no probable cause to believe that petitioner was guilty of the allegedly unlawful wiretapping and, upon appeal by the prosecution, the Superior Court affirmed. Petitioner in turn sought review of his discharge before the Investigation, Prosecution, and Appeals Commission of Puerto Rico,

---

[2] That section grants the federal district courts jurisdiction "[t]o redress the deprivation, under color of any State law, statute, ordinance, regulation, custom or usage, of any right, privilege or immunity secured by the Constitution of the United States or by any Act of Congress providing for equal rights of citizens or of all persons within the jurisdiction of the United States."

[3] At this stage of the proceedings, of course, all allegations of the complaint must be accepted as true.

which, after a hearing, revoked the discharge order rendered by respondent and ordered that petitioner be reinstated with back pay.

Based on the foregoing factual allegations, petitioner brought this suit for damages, contending that his discharge violated his right to procedural due process, and that it had caused him anxiety, embarrassment, and injury to his reputation in the community. In his answer, respondent denied a number of petitioner's allegations of fact and asserted several affirmative defenses. Respondent then moved to dismiss the complaint for failure to state a cause of action, see Fed. Rule Civ. Proc. 12(b)(6), and the District Court granted the motion. Observing that respondent was entitled to qualified immunity for acts done in good faith within the scope of his official duties, it concluded that petitioner was required to plead as part of his claim for relief that, in committing the actions alleged, respondent was motivated by bad faith. The absence of any such allegation, it held, required dismissal of the complaint. The United States Court of Appeals for the First Circuit affirmed. 602 F.2d 1018 (1979).

* * *

II

Section 1983 provides a cause of action for "the deprivation of any rights, privileges, or immunities secured by the Constitution and laws" by any person acting "under color of any statute, ordinance, regulation, custom, or usage, or any State or Territory." 42 U.S.C. § 1983.[6] This statute, enacted to aid in " 'the preservation of human liberty and human rights,' " Owen v. City of Independence, 445 U.S. 622, 636 (1980), quoting Cong.Globe, 42d Cong., 1st Sess., App. 68 (1871) (Rep. Shellabarger), reflects a congressional judgment that a "damages remedy against the offending party is a vital component of any scheme for vindicating cherished constitutional guarantees," 445 U.S., at 651, 100 S.Ct., at 1415. As remedial legislation, § 1983 is to be construed generously to further its primary purpose. See 445 U.S., at 636.

In certain limited situations, we have held that public officers are entitled to a qualified immunity from damages liability under § 1983. This conclusion has been based on an unwillingness to infer from legislative silence a congressional intention to abrogate immunities that were both "well-established at common law" and "compatible with the purposes of the Civil Rights Act." 445 U.S., at 638. Findings of immunity have thus been "predicated upon a considered inquiry into the immunity historically accorded the relevant official at common law and the intentions behind it." Imbler v. Pachtman, 424 U.S. 409, 421 (1976). In Pierson v. Ray, 386 U.S. 547, 555 (1967), for example, we concluded that a police officer would be "excus[ed] from liability for acting under a statute that he reasonably believed to be valid but that was later held unconstitutional, on its face or as applied." And in other contexts we have held, on the basis of "[c]ommon-law tradition . . . and strong public-policy reasons," Wood v. Strickland, 420 U.S. 308, 318 (1975), that certain

---

    6   Section 1983 provides in full: "Every person who, under color of any statute, ordinance, regulation, custom, or usage, of any State or Territory, subjects, or causes to be subjected, any citizen of the United States or other person within the jurisdiction thereof to the deprivation of any rights, privileges, or immunities secured by the Constitution and laws, shall be liable to the person injured in an action at law, suit in equity, or other proper proceeding for redress."

categories of executive officers should be allowed qualified immunity from liability for acts done on the basis of an objectively reasonable belief that those acts were lawful. * * *

Nothing in the language or legislative history of § 1983, however, suggests that in an action brought against a public official whose position might entitle him to immunity if he acted in good faith, a plaintiff must allege bad faith in order to state a claim for relief. By the plain terms of § 1983, two—and only two—allegations are required in order to state a cause of action under that statute. First, the plaintiff must allege that some person has deprived him of a federal right. Second, he must allege that the person who has deprived him of that right acted under color of state or territorial law. See Monroe v. Pape, 365 U.S. 167 (1961). Petitioner has made both of the required allegations. He alleged that his discharge by respondent violated his right to procedural due process, see Board of Regents v. Roth, 408 U.S. 564 (1972), and that respondent acted under color of Puerto Rican law. See Monroe v. Pape, supra, at 172–187.

[handwritten margin note: 1. deprived right 2. that person has acted under the color of state or territorial law]

Moreover, this Court has never indicated that qualified immunity is relevant to the existence of the plaintiff's cause of action; instead we have described it as a defense available to the official in question. See Procunier v. Navarette, 434 U.S. 555, at 562 (1978); Pierson v. Ray, supra, 386 U.S. 547, at 556, 557 (1967); Butz v. Economou, 438 U.S. 478, 508 (1978). Since qualified immunity is a defense, the burden of pleading it rests with the defendant. See Fed. Rule Civ.Proc. 8(c) (defendant must plead any "matter constituting an avoidance or affirmative defense"); 5 C. Wright & A. Miller, Federal Practice and Procedure § 1271 (1969). It is for the official to claim that his conduct was justified by an objectively reasonable belief that it was lawful. We see no basis for imposing on the plaintiff an obligation to anticipate such a defense by stating in his complaint that the defendant acted in bad faith.

Our conclusion as to the allocation of the burden of pleading is supported by the nature of the qualified immunity defense. As our decisions make clear, whether such immunity has been established depends on facts peculiarly within the knowledge and control of the defendant. Thus we have stated that "[i]t is the existence of reasonable grounds for the belief formed at the time and in light of all the circumstances, coupled with good-faith belief, that affords a basis for qualified immunity of executive officers for acts performed in the course of official conduct." Scheuer v. Rhodes, [416 U.S. 232] at 247–248 (1974). The applicable test focuses not only on whether the official has an objectively reasonable basis for that belief, but also on whether "[t]he official himself [is] acting sincerely and with a belief that he is doing right," Wood v. Strickland, supra, 420 U.S. 308, at 321(1975). There may be no way for a plaintiff to know in advance whether the official has such a belief or, indeed, whether he will even claim that he does. The existence of a subjective belief will frequently turn on factors which a plaintiff cannot reasonably be expected to know. For example, the official's belief may be based on state or local law, advice of counsel, administrative practice, or some other factor of which the official alone is aware. To impose the pleading burden on the plaintiff would ignore this elementary

[handwritten margin note: D's belief which P wouldn't know]

fact and be contrary to the established practice in analogous areas of the law.[7]

The decision of the Court of Appeals is reversed, and the case is remanded to that court for further proceedings consistent with this opinion.

It is so ordered.

■ MR. JUSTICE REHNQUIST joins the opinion of the Court, reading it as he does to leave open the issue of the burden of persuasion, as opposed to the burden of pleading, with respect to a defense of qualified immunity.

NOTE ON ALLOCATING THE BURDEN OF PLEADING

1.   The elements of a sufficient complaint. If a plaintiff's claim fails to include allegations of all of the elements of a claim, it is legally insufficient. In most cases, the required elements of a legal claim are clearly defined, either by the relevant common law or the statute creating the claim. In *Gomez*, for instance, Justice Marshall explains that there are only two elements of a claim under 28 U.S.C. § 1983 that must be included in the complaint: (1) that "some person has deprived him of a federal right," and (2) that "the person who has deprived him of that right acted under color of state or territorial law." Although the complaint need not specifically reference § 1983, the factual allegations in the complaint must satisfy each of the elements. As the Supreme Court recently explained in Johnson v. City of Shelby, Miss., 574 U.S. ___, 135 S.Ct. 346, 190 L.Ed.2d 309 (2014) (per curiam), "no heightened pleading rule requires plaintiffs seeking damages for violations of constitutional rights to invoke § 1983 expressly in order to state a claim. * * * A plaintiff * * * must plead facts to show that her claim has substantive plausibility."

2.   Affirmative defenses. Rule 8(c) lists nineteen "affirmative defenses" that must be pleaded by a defendant (or, more broadly, by a party responding to a "pleading"). This list, which is not exclusive, includes such defenses as "contributory negligence," "statute of limitations," and "res judicata." An affirmative defense (as opposed to a denial of plaintiff's allegations, which is a "negative defense") alleges facts not included in the plaintiff's complaint that will defeat the plaintiff's claim. Consider *Gomez* and the defense of qualified immunity. Qualified immunity is an affirmative defense because it rests on an allegation not included in the complaint (that the defendant's actions were based on a reasonable belief that they were lawful), and it provides a defense to the plaintiff's claim without which that claim would be valid.

3.   Allocating the burden of pleading. *Gomez* holds that the plaintiff need not plead that the defendant acted in bad faith because

---

[7]   As then-Dean Charles Clark stated over forty years ago: "It seems to be considered only fair that certain types of things which in common law pleading were matters in confession and avoidance—i.e., matters which seemed more or less to admit the general complaint and yet to suggest some other reason why there was no right—must be specifically pleaded in the answer, and that has been a general rule." ABA Proceedings, Institute at Washington and Symposium at New York City on the Federal Rules of Civil Procedure 49 (1939). See also 5 C. Wright & A. Miller, Federal Practice and Procedure §§ 1270–1271 (1969). Cf. FTC v. A.E. Staley Mfg. Co., 324 U.S. 746, 759 (1945) (good-faith defense under Robinson-Patman Act); Barcellona v. Tiffany English Pub, Inc., 597 F.2d 464, 468 (C.A.5 1979); Cohen v. Ayers, 596 F.2d 733, 739–740 (C.A.7 1979); United States v. Kroll, 547 F.2d 393 (C.A.7 1977).

qualified immunity is an affirmative defense. The lack of bad faith on the part of the defendant is not an element of the claim that must be pleaded in the complaint. Indeed, courts often repeat that a plaintiff "is not required to negate an affirmative defense in his complaint." Tregenza v. Great American Communications Co., 12 F.3d 717 (7th Cir. 1993). See also Jones v. Bock, 549 U.S. 199, 127 S.Ct. 910, 166 L.Ed.2d 798 (2007) (holding that a plaintiff need not plead that it exhausted administrative remedies because such exhaustion is an affirmative defense).

But what determines which allegations are elements of a claim, and which are affirmative defenses? That is, how are we to know what a plaintiff must include in her complaint, and what she can save for later in response to a defense asserted by the defendant in the answer? As Professors Hazard, Leubsdorf, and Bassett summarize, "there is often room to dispute which party should be required to plead and prove a given circumstance. Allocation to either plaintiff or defendant is coherent as a matter of substantive law and procedural logic." Hazard, Leubsdorf & Bassett, Civil Procedure § 4.9 (6th ed. 2011). So how should the allocation be done?

In an influential article, Professor Cleary suggested three benchmarks courts might follow when allocating burdens between the plaintiff and defendant. One such benchmark is policy, which "extend[s] into the stage of allocating those elements by way of favoring one or the other party to a particular kind of litigation." Allocating burdens to the plaintiff makes pleading in the complaint a more difficult enterprise, and vice versa, so the allocation of pleading burdens is inescapably a policy decision about how difficult pleading a particular claim ought to be. The second benchmark is fairness: "The nature of a particular element may indicate that evidence relating to it lies more within the control of one party, which suggests the fairness of allocating that element to him. Examples are payment, discharge in bankruptcy, and license, all of which are commonly treated as affirmative defenses." The third benchmark Cleary offers is probability: "a judicial, i.e., wholly nonstatistical, estimate of the probabilities of the situation, with the burden being put on the party who will be benefited by a departure from the supposed norm." Cleary, Presuming and Pleading: An Essay on Juristic Immaturity, 12 Stan. L. Rev. 5 (1959).

> Commenting on Professor Cleary's article, Professor Hazard explains:
>
> I understand him to say that the definition of a prima facie case of legal wrong is a construct based on experience of two kinds. One is experience with everyday events that give rise to disputes over claims of right. That experience is the origin of our expectations about people's capacities, limitations, and propensities, and hence the points on which the outcome is likely to depend. The other body of experience is with legal controversy itself, particularly litigation. It is from that experience that we learn what points are likely to be difficult to resolve in disputes of various kinds, and hence the points on which outcome is likely to depend.

Hazard, Introduction to Cleary's Presuming and Pleading: An Essay on Juristic Immaturity, 1979 Ariz. St. L.J. 111 (1979).

How do Professor Cleary's standards apply to the issue of official immunity that was contested in *Gomez v. Toledo*? Is Justice Marshall correct that the relevant statutory language suggests that immunity is a defense? Assuming that the statute provides limited guidance, what is the proper allocation of the pleading burden in light of the considerations of fairness, probability, and policy that Professor Cleary suggests should control? Which factor does Justice Marshall think is decisive?

4. Does it matter who bears the burden of pleading? The Supreme Court in *Gomez* holds that plaintiff is not required to allege in the complaint that defendant acted in bad faith. Instead the defendant must allege good faith as an affirmative defense in the answer. Most lawyers would probably say that, standing alone, the question of who bears the burden of pleading an element of the claim is not very important. A lawyer may properly plead bad or good faith if she has evidentiary support for the claim or reasonably believes she will do so after discovery. See Fed. R. Civ. P. 11(b). In practice, this standard will seldom bar an averment of bad faith by the plaintiff or an averment of good faith by the defendant.

5. Burden of pleading and burdens of production and persuasion. The more important issues are not the "burden of pleading," but rather the "burden of production" and the "burden of persuasion." What is the difference? The burden of pleading an element determines who must *allege* that element in the pleadings. The burdens of production and persuasion, however, go to the method and adequacy of the proof of a claim before the finder of fact. Though these two terms are often lumped together by laypersons (and casual lawyers) under the heading "burden of proof," they in fact have distinct meanings and practical significance. The classic article explaining the difference is James, Burdens of Proof, 47 Va. L. Rev. 51 (1961).

A party having the "burden of production" has the burden of placing sufficient evidence in the record supporting all essential elements of her claim to allow the finder of fact—judge or jury—to find in her favor. If the party with the burden of production presents no evidence, or evidence that the judge decides does not meet the sufficiency standard, then the judge has the power to declare her the loser without any consideration of her case by the jury. See discussion of judgment as a matter of law and Fed. R. Civ. P. 50, infra at pp. 993–1001. Note that "burden of pleading," as used in *Gomez*, is not the same thing as burden of production. "Pleading" refers to making allegations; "production" refers to producing evidence supporting those allegations. Thus, when the Court in *Gomez* holds that defendant has the burden of pleading good faith, this burden requires only that defendant assert good faith as a defense in his pleadings. Defendant may also have at least the initial burden of producing evidence on the issue of his good faith, but that is an analytically distinct issue from whether he has the burden of pleading.

The "burden of persuasion," in contrast, describes the standard that the finder of fact is required to apply in determining whether it believes that a factual claim is true. Depending on the issue and on the type of case, the party with the burden of persuasion must meet different standards of persuasiveness. In ordinary civil cases, the burden of persuasion is that plaintiff must prove her case by a "preponderance of the evidence." On certain issues in a civil case, such as fraud, the burden of proof can be higher, requiring proof by "clear and convincing evidence." In a criminal case, the burden of proof requires that the prosecutor prove a defendant's guilt "beyond a reasonable doubt."

A party is said to bear the "burden of persuasion" or "the risk of nonpersuasion" on an issue when the finder of fact must hold against that party if the evidence fails to meet the specified degree of persuasiveness. For example, if the plaintiff has presented sufficient evidence to permit a decision in her favor (that is, if the plaintiff has satisfied her burden of production), the full case is then submitted to the finder of fact, judge or jury. The jury or judge may still find, after considering both the plaintiff's and the defendant's evidence, that the plaintiff has not proved her case, meaning that the plaintiff has failed to satisfy her burden of persuasion. An example of this usage is the federal Administrative Procedure Act, which provides that a "proponent of a rule or order has the burden of proof." 5 U.S.C. § 556(d). The Supreme Court explained that burden of proof, as used in the Act, means burden of persuasion: "Burden of proof was frequently used [in the past] to refer to what we now call the burden of persuasion—the notion that if the evidence is evenly balanced, the party that bears the burden of persuasion must lose." Director, Office of Workers' Comp. Programs v. Greenwich Collieries, 512 U.S. 267, 272, 114 S.Ct. 2251, 129 L.Ed.2d 221 (1994).

6. **Burden of persuasion of defendant's good faith under 42 U.S.C. § 1983.** The normal rule of thumb is, "He who pleads must prove," meaning that the party with the burden of pleading also has the burdens of production and persuasion. Justice Rehnquist in *Gomez* points out that the Court decides only who has the burden of pleading, explicitly leaving the burden of persuasion (and implicitly, the burden of production) for another day. Assuming that the *Gomez* Court's holding on the burden of pleading is correct, does Professor Cleary's analysis suggest any reason to depart from the normal rule that the pleader bears the burden of production and persuasion when the issue is the good faith of an official sued under 42 U.S.C. § 1983?

7. **Immunity for an official's good faith actions becomes an objective standard.** Justice Marshall, writing for the Court in *Gomez*, assumed that an official's good faith immunity was a subjective question, depending on what was actually in the defendant's mind. But in a series of later decisions beginning with Harlow v. Fitzgerald, 457 U.S. 800, 818–19, 102 S.Ct. 2727, 73 L.Ed.2d 396 (1982), the Court reached a different conclusion, ultimately holding that the officer's subjective belief was entirely irrelevant. The Court later explained "The relevant question * * * is the objective (albeit fact-specific) question whether a reasonable officer could have believed [the search] to be lawful, in light of clearly established law and the information the searching officers possessed. [The officer's] subjective beliefs about the search are irrelevant." Anderson v. Creighton, 483 U.S. 635, 641, 107 S.Ct. 3034, 97 L.Ed.2d 523 (1987). Note that one of the grounds given by Justice Marshall for allocating the burden of pleading (and burdens of production and of persuasion, too?)—that the defendant knows his own state of mind—is inapplicable now that the standard for the official's good faith is entirely objective.

8. **The Supreme Court revisits pleading and proof of official immunity.** In Crawford-El v. Britton, 523 U.S. 574, 118 S.Ct. 1584, 140 L.Ed.2d 759 (1998), while citing with apparent approval its holding in *Gomez*, the Supreme Court offered the following dictum on the handling of cases involving the qualified immunity defense:

> When a plaintiff files a complaint against a public official alleging a claim that requires proof of wrongful motive, the trial court must exercise its discretion in a way that protects the substance of the

qualified immunity defense. * * * The district judge has two primary options prior to permitting any discovery at all. First, the court may order a reply to the defendant's or a third party's answer under Federal Rule of Civil Procedure 7(a), or grant the defendant's motion for a more definite statement under Rule 12(e). Thus, the court may insist that the plaintiff "put forward specific, nonconclusory factual allegations" that establish improper motive causing cognizable injury in order to survive a prediscovery motion for dismissal or summary judgment. This option exists even if the official chooses not to plead the affirmative defense of qualified immunity. Second, if the defendant does plead the immunity defense, the district court should resolve that threshold question before permitting discovery.

Id. at 597–98.

What is the source of legal authority for the Court's statement in *Crawford-El* that the district court is required to order a reply or more definite statement and to resolve the immunity issue before allowing discovery? Is it the doctrine of qualified immunity itself? In the wake of *Crawford-El* most courts of appeal that have considered the issue have concluded, based on the Court's continued citation of *Gomez*, that it is not proper to require the plaintiff to plead specifically the absence of official immunity in the complaint. See Goad v. Mitchell, 297 F.3d 497 (6th Cir. 2002) (citing cases). Given the Court's statement in *Crawford-El*, does this outcome preserve the shell of *Gomez* while gutting its substance? If so, what factor or combination of factors best explains the shift in the Court's position?

D. THE FORMAL SUFFICIENCY OF THE COMPLAINT: HOW SPECIFIC MUST A PLEADING BE?

1. THE STANDARD REQUIREMENT FOR PLEADING UNDER FEDERAL RULE 8

NOTE ON THE PHILOSOPHY OF MODERN PLEADING

1. **From common law to code pleading.** The law of pleading has been an intermittent sore spot in Anglo-American law. The system of common law pleading aimed at narrowing sharply the issues in dispute on the basis of an extended exchange of written pleadings. The resulting system was heavily criticized for its cost and complexity. As Professor Burbank describes it, "Perhaps the single most salient feature of common law procedure was its unremitting search, pursued in pleading practice that sometimes resembled a ping pong match, for a single issue (of law or fact) that would enable decision of the case. The quest, in other words, was to avoid complexity at all costs, and the most important cost of common law procedure was that so many cases were decided on pleading points rather than the merits." Burbank, The Complexity of Modern American Civil Litigation: Curse or Cure, 91 Judicature 163 (2008). The successor to common law pleading in England, the notorious Hilary Term Rules of 1834, was regarded as even worse.

Code pleading, which replaced common law pleading in most American jurisdictions, avoided much of the technicality of its predecessor. But its

SECTION D

THE FORMAL SUFFICIENCY OF THE COMPLAINT:
HOW SPECIFIC MUST A PLEADING BE?

463

requirement that the complaint state "facts constituting a cause of action" came, over time, to engender significant complications centering on the definition of a "fact." "Facts," the courts held, were more specific than, and distinguishable from, "legal conclusions." A complaint that pleaded "facts" would survive a motion to dismiss; one that pleaded legal conclusions might be held insufficient, as if the element pleaded in conclusory terms had not been pleaded at all. In the words of a leading nineteenth century scholar, "the allegations must be of dry, naked, actual facts." Pomeroy, Remedies and Remedial Rights § 529, at 566.

In the words of one modern critique:

> Many judges and some legal scholars did not clearly recognize that only a matter of degree differentiates "facts" from "mere conclusions," in one direction of specificity, and differentiates them from "evidence" in the opposite direction of specificity. For example, many courts held that an allegation that a defendant acted "negligently" was a "mere conclusion," while others held that such a description was sufficient in a story about handling a horse or operating a car. There was considerable naivete, and not a little manipulation and cynicism, centering on what, exactly, were "facts." A mass of conflicting decisional law accrued on these and other particulars.

Hazard, Leubsdorf & Bassett, Civil Procedure § 4.12 (6th ed. 2011).

2. The philosophy of notice pleading under the federal Rules. The next major stage of modernization in American pleading was the Federal Rules of Civil Procedure. On the one hand, the federal Rules sought to abandon altogether the technical terminology of code pleading and its accompanying case law. The adequacy of a claim for relief under Rule 8(a) was not to turn on whether it pleaded "facts" or "legal conclusions," but rather on whether it provided fair notice of the plaintiff's claim. Instead of serving the purpose of ultimately narrowing the factual issues for trial, the drafters of the original federal Rules meant for pleading to provide the parties with fair notice of the claims and defenses alleged. Assuming the plaintiff's complaint stated a claim upon which relief could be granted, it would then open the door to discovery: the required exchange of information by the parties, based on which they could later prove their claims and defenses.

Underlying this theoretical shift are three basic insights. First, the judgment as to how much specificity to require should be based on pragmatic considerations of cost, accuracy, and fairness, not on conclusory labels. Second, resolving a dispute at the pleading stage of the litigation is the ultimate "summary" process, decided wholly on the basis of an exchange of written claims about the facts, but without any opportunity to test those claims with evidence, cross-examination or discovery. Accordingly, such resolutions should be limited to cases where it is apparent that a deeper factual inquiry is unlikely to yield improved accuracy in proportion to its cost. Otherwise, using pleading in its pure summary form to try to resolve or even significantly narrow factual disputes on the merits would result in too many cases being decided inaccurately or unfairly. Third, if the pleading process is extended, for example by permitting or requiring multiple rounds of pleading, it may itself become a significant source of cost and delay, which would be particularly unfair in cases involving modest stakes. For a concise history of these developments, see Langbein, The Disappearance of Civil Trial in the United States, 122 Yale L.J. 522 (2012).

3.   *Conley v. Gibson.* Until 2007, the leading case interpreting federal Rule 8's requirement of "a short and plain statement of the claim showing the pleader is entitled to relief" was Conley v. Gibson, 355 U.S. 41, 78 S.Ct. 99, 2 L.Ed.2d 80 (1957). In *Conley*, a group of African-American railroad employees brought suit, alleging that their union had violated the federal Railway Labor Act by failing to represent them fairly in collective bargaining with the employer. Defendant sought to dismiss on several grounds, including for failure to state a claim under Rule 12(b)(6). In an opinion by Justice Black, the Supreme Court wrote:

> In summary, the complaint made the following allegations relevant to our decision: Petitioners were employees of the Texas and New Orleans Railroad at its Houston Freight House. Local 28 of the Brotherhood was the designated bargaining agent under the Railway Labor Act for the bargaining unit to which petitioners belonged. A contract existed between the Union and the Railroad which gave the employees in the bargaining unit certain protection from discharge and loss of seniority. In May 1954, the Railroad purported to abolish 45 jobs held by petitioners or other Negroes all of whom were either discharged or demoted. In truth the 45 jobs were not abolished at all but instead filled by whites as the Negroes were ousted, except for a few instances where Negroes were rehired to fill their old jobs but with loss of seniority. Despite repeated pleas by petitioners, the Union, acting according to plan, did nothing to protect them against these discriminatory discharges and refused to give them protection comparable to that given white employees. The complaint then went on to allege that the Union had failed in general to represent Negro employees equally and in good faith. It charged that such discrimination constituted a violation of petitioners' right under the Railway Labor Act to fair representation from their bargaining agent.

> * * *

> In appraising the sufficiency of the complaint we follow, of course, the accepted rule that a complaint should not be dismissed for failure to state a claim *unless it appears beyond doubt that the plaintiff can prove no set of facts in support of his claim which would entitle him to relief.*

355 U.S. at 42–43, 45–46 (emphasis added).

The Court had no difficulty in holding that under the Railway Labor Act the union had an obligation to represent its members fairly, and that systematic discrimination against African-American members, if proven, would violate that obligation. It then rejected the argument that the complaint had not described the claim with sufficient specificity:

> The decisive answer to this is that the Federal Rules of Civil Procedure do not require a claimant to set out in detail the facts upon which he bases his claim. To the contrary, all the Rules require is a "short and plain statement of the claim" that will give the defendant fair notice of what the plaintiff's claim is and the

SECTION D

THE FORMAL SUFFICIENCY OF THE COMPLAINT:
HOW SPECIFIC MUST A PLEADING BE?

465

grounds upon which it rests. * * * Such simplified "notice pleading" is made possible by the liberal opportunity for discovery and the other pretrial procedures established by the Rules to disclose more precisely the basis of both claim and defense and to define more narrowly the disputed facts and issues. Following the simple guide of Rule 8(f) that "all pleadings shall be so construed as to do substantial justice," we have no doubt that petitioners' complaint adequately set forth a claim and gave the respondents fair notice of its basis. The Federal Rules reject the approach that pleading is a game of skill in which one misstep by counsel may be decisive to the outcome and accept the principle that the purpose of pleading is to facilitate a proper decision on the merits.

Id. at 47–48. The case that follows is a representative example of how the Supreme Court applied *Conley* for fifty years.

Swierkiewicz v. Sorema, N.A.

Supreme Court of the United States, 2002.
534 U.S. 506, 122 S.Ct. 992, 152 L.Ed.2d 1.

■ JUSTICE THOMAS delivered the opinion of the Court.

This case presents the question whether a complaint in an employment discrimination lawsuit must contain specific facts establishing a prima facie case of discrimination under the framework set forth by this Court in McDonnell Douglas Corp. v. Green, 411 U.S. 792, 36 L.Ed.2d 668, 93 S.Ct. 1817 (1973). We hold that an employment discrimination complaint need not include such facts and instead must contain only "a short and plain statement of the claim showing that the pleader is entitled to relief." Fed. Rule Civ. Proc. 8(a)(2).

I

Petitioner Akos Swierkiewicz is a native of Hungary, who at the time of his complaint was 53 years old. In April 1989, petitioner began working for respondent Sorema N. A., a reinsurance company headquartered in New York and principally owned and controlled by a French parent corporation. Petitioner was initially employed in the position of senior vice president and chief underwriting officer (CUO). Nearly six years later, Francois M. Chavel, respondent's Chief Executive Officer, demoted petitioner to a marketing and services position and transferred the bulk of his underwriting responsibilities to Nicholas Papadopoulo, a 32-year-old who, like Mr. Chavel, is a French national. About a year later, Mr. Chavel stated that he wanted to "energize" the underwriting department and appointed Mr. Papadopoulo as CUO. Petitioner claims that Mr. Papadopoulo had only one year of underwriting experience at the time he was promoted, and therefore was less experienced and less qualified to be CUO than he, since at that point he had 26 years of experience in the insurance industry.

Following his demotion, petitioner contends that he "was isolated by Mr. Chavel . . . excluded from business decisions and meetings and denied the opportunity to reach his true potential at SOREMA." Petitioner unsuccessfully attempted to meet with Mr. Chavel to discuss his discontent. Finally, in April 1997, petitioner sent a memo to Mr. Chavel outlining his grievances and requesting a severance package. Two weeks later, respondent's general counsel presented petitioner with two options: He could either resign without a severance package or be dismissed. Mr. Chavel fired petitioner after he refused to resign.

Petitioner filed a lawsuit alleging that he had been terminated on account of his national origin in violation of Title VII of the Civil Rights Act of 1964, 42 U.S.C. § 2000e *et seq.*, and on account of his age in violation of the Age Discrimination in Employment Act of 1967 (ADEA), 29 U.S.C. § 621 *et seq.* The United States District Court for the Southern District of New York dismissed petitioner's complaint because it found that he "had not adequately alleged a prima facie case, in that he had not adequately alleged circumstances that support an inference of discrimination." The United States Court of Appeals for the Second Circuit affirmed the dismissal, relying on its settled precedent, which requires a plaintiff in an employment discrimination complaint to allege facts constituting a prima facie case of discrimination under the framework set forth by this Court in *McDonnell Douglas, supra,* at 802. The Court of Appeals held that petitioner had failed to meet his burden because his allegations were "insufficient as a matter of law to raise an inference of discrimination." We granted certiorari to resolve a split among the Courts of Appeals concerning the proper pleading standard for employment discrimination cases, and now reverse.

II

Applying Circuit precedent, the Court of Appeals required petitioner to plead a prima facie case of discrimination in order to survive respondent's motion to dismiss. In the Court of Appeals' view, petitioner was thus required to allege in his complaint: (1) membership in a protected group; (2) qualification for the job in question; (3) an adverse employment action; and (4) circumstances that support an inference of discrimination. *Ibid.*; cf. *McDonnell Douglas,* 411 U.S. at 802; Texas Dept. of Community Affairs v. Burdine, 450 U.S. 248, 253–254, n. 6, 67 L.Ed.2d 207, 101 S.Ct. 1089 (1981).

The prima facie case under *McDonnell Douglas*, however, is an evidentiary standard, not a pleading requirement. In *McDonnell Douglas*, this Court made clear that "the critical issue before us concerned the order and allocation *of proof* in a private, non-class action challenging employment discrimination." 411 U.S. at 800 (emphasis added). In subsequent cases, this Court has reiterated that the prima facie case relates to the employee's burden of presenting evidence that raises an inference of discrimination. See *Burdine,* 450 U.S. at 252–253.

This Court has never indicated that the requirements for establishing a prima facie case under *McDonnell Douglas* also apply to the pleading standard that plaintiffs must satisfy in order to survive a motion to dismiss. For instance, we have rejected the argument that a Title VII complaint requires greater "particularity," because this would "too narrowly constrict the role of the pleadings." McDonald v. Santa Fe Trail Transp. Co., 427 U.S. 273, 283, n. 11, 49 L.Ed.2d 493, 96 S.Ct. 2574 (1976). Consequently, the ordinary rules for assessing the sufficiency of a complaint apply. See, e.g., Scheuer v. Rhodes, 416 U.S. 232, 236, 40 L.Ed.2d 90, 94 S.Ct. 1683 (1974) ("When a federal court reviews the sufficiency of a complaint, before the reception of any evidence either by

SECTION D

THE FORMAL SUFFICIENCY OF THE COMPLAINT:
HOW SPECIFIC MUST A PLEADING BE?

467

affidavit or admissions, its task is necessarily a limited one. The issue is not whether a plaintiff will ultimately prevail but whether the claimant is entitled to offer evidence to support the claims").

In addition, under a notice pleading system, it is not appropriate to require a plaintiff to plead facts establishing a prima facie case because the *McDonnell Douglas* framework does not apply in every employment discrimination case. For instance, if a plaintiff is able to produce direct evidence of discrimination, he may prevail without proving all the elements of a prima facie case. See Trans World Airlines, Inc. v. Thurston, 469 U.S. 111, 121, 83 L.Ed.2d 523, 105 S.Ct. 613 (1985) ("The *McDonnell Douglas* test is inapplicable where the plaintiff presents direct evidence of discrimination"). Under the Second Circuit's heightened pleading standard, a plaintiff without direct evidence of discrimination at the time of his complaint must plead a prima facie case of discrimination, even though discovery might uncover such direct evidence. It thus seems incongruous to require a plaintiff, in order to survive a motion to dismiss, to plead more facts than he may ultimately need to prove to succeed on the merits if direct evidence of discrimination is discovered.

Moreover, the precise requirements of a prima facie case can vary depending on the context and were "never intended to be rigid, mechanized, or ritualistic." Furnco Constr. Corp. v. Waters, 438 U.S. 567, 577, 57 L.Ed.2d 957, 98 S.Ct. 2943 (1978);. Before discovery has unearthed relevant facts and evidence, it may be difficult to define the precise formulation of the required prima facie case in a particular case. Given that the prima facie case operates as a flexible evidentiary standard, it should not be transposed into a rigid pleading standard for discrimination cases.

Furthermore, imposing the Court of Appeals' heightened pleading standard in employment discrimination cases conflicts with Federal Rule of Civil Procedure 8(a)(2), which provides that a complaint must include only "a short and plain statement of the claim showing that the pleader is entitled to relief." Such a statement must simply "give the defendant fair notice of what the plaintiff's claim is and the grounds upon which it rests." Conley v. Gibson, 355 U.S. 41, 47, 2 L.Ed.2d 80, 78 S.Ct. 99 (1957). This simplified notice pleading standard relies on liberal discovery rules and summary judgment motions to define disputed facts and issues and to dispose of unmeritorious claims. See *id.* at 47–48, Leatherman v. Tarrant County Narcotics Intelligence and Coordination Unit, 507 U.S. 163, 168–169, 122 L.Ed.2d 517, 113 S.Ct. 1160 (1993). "The provisions for discovery are so flexible and the provisions for pretrial procedure and summary judgment so effective, that attempted surprise in federal practice is aborted very easily, synthetic issues detected, and the gravamen of the dispute brought frankly into the open for the inspection of the court." 5 C. Wright & A. Miller, Federal Practice and Procedure § 1202, p. 76 (2d ed. 1990).

Rule 8(a)'s simplified pleading standard applies to all civil actions, with limited exceptions. Rule 9(b), for example, provides for greater particularity in all averments of fraud or mistake. This Court, however, has declined to extend such exceptions to other contexts. In *Leatherman* we stated: "The Federal Rules do address in Rule 9(b) the question of the need for greater particularity in pleading certain actions, but do not include among the enumerated actions any reference to complaints alleging municipal liability under § 1983. *Expressio unius est exclusio alterius.*" 507 U.S. at 168. Just as Rule 9(b) makes no mention of municipal liability under Rev. Stat. § 1979, 42 U.S.C. § 1983, neither does it refer to employment discrimination. Thus, complaints in these cases, as in most others, must satisfy only the simple requirements of Rule 8(a).

Other provisions of the Federal Rules of Civil Procedure are inextricably linked to Rule 8(a)'s simplified notice pleading standard. Rule 8(e)(1) states that "no technical forms of pleading or motions are required," and Rule 8(f) provides that "all pleadings shall be so construed as to do substantial justice." Given the Federal Rules' simplified standard for pleading, "[a] court may dismiss a complaint only if it is clear that no relief could be granted under any set of facts that could be proved consistent with the allegations." Hishon v. King & Spalding, 467 U.S. 69, 73, 81 L.Ed.2d 59, 104 S.Ct. 2229 (1984). If a pleading fails to specify the allegations in a manner that provides sufficient notice, a defendant can move for a more definite statement under Rule 12(e) before responding. Moreover, claims lacking merit may be dealt with through summary judgment under Rule 56. The liberal notice pleading of Rule 8(a) is the starting point of a simplified pleading system, which was adopted to focus litigation on the merits of a claim. See *Conley, supra,* at 48 ("The Federal Rules reject the approach that pleading is a game of skill in which one misstep by counsel may be decisive to the outcome and accept the principle that the purpose of pleading is to facilitate a proper decision on the merits").

Applying the relevant standard, petitioner's complaint easily satisfies the requirements of Rule 8(a) because it gives respondent fair notice of the basis for petitioner's claims. Petitioner alleged that he had been terminated on account of his national origin in violation of Title VII and on account of his age in violation of the ADEA. His complaint detailed the events leading to his termination, provided relevant dates, and included the ages and nationalities of at least some of the relevant persons involved with his termination. These allegations give respondent fair notice of what petitioner's claims are and the grounds upon which they rest. See *Conley, supra,* at 47. In addition, they state claims upon which relief could be granted under Title VII and the ADEA.

Respondent argues that allowing lawsuits based on conclusory allegations of discrimination to go forward will burden the courts and encourage disgruntled employees to bring unsubstantiated suits. Whatever the practical merits of this argument, the Federal Rules do not contain a heightened pleading standard for employment discrimination suits. A requirement of greater specificity for particular claims is a result that "must be obtained by the process of amending the Federal Rules, and not by judicial interpretation." *Leatherman, supra,* at 168. Furthermore, Rule 8(a) establishes a pleading standard without regard to whether a claim will succeed on the merits. "Indeed it may appear on the face of the pleadings that a recovery is very remote and unlikely but that is not the test." *Scheuer,* 416 U.S. at 236.

holding

For the foregoing reasons, we hold that an employment discrimination plaintiff need not plead a prima facie case of discrimination and that petitioner's complaint is sufficient to survive respondent's motion to dismiss. Accordingly, the judgment of the Court of Appeals is reversed, and the case is remanded for further proceedings consistent with this opinion.

It is so ordered.

NOTES AND QUESTIONS

1. **Background.** The claim in *Swierkiewicz* arises under federal employment discrimination law. The pleading issue turns in part on ways of proving discrimination through direct or circumstantial evidence. An example of direct evidence of discrimination would be a statement by an employer that expressly attributed an employment action to an individual's race, gender, or age. Because few employers will admit to discriminatory motives or attitudes, such evidence can be hard to come by. Accordingly, the courts have developed doctrines allowing circumstantial proof of discrimination. In McDonnell Douglas Corp. v. Green, 411 U.S. 792, 93 S.Ct. 1817, 36 L.Ed.2d 668 (1973), the Supreme Court set out a four-part test for proving a *prima facie* case of discrimination—that is, a case, based on circumstantial evidence that, unless rebutted, would permit the jury to infer discrimination even in the absence of direct evidence. The four elements of proof were: (1) membership in a protected group; (2) qualification for the job in question; (3) an adverse employment action; and (4) circumstances that support an inference of discrimination. 411 U.S. at 802.

2. **The holding.** It seems clear that the *prima facie* case created in *McDonnell Douglas* was intended to smooth the way for plaintiffs. What then was wrong with requiring the plaintiff to allege a *prima facie* case in the complaint? Is the problem that plaintiff cannot be expected to know the facts which would allow him to plead a *prima facie* case? Or is the problem that making the plaintiff plead such a case might undermine his ability to prove his case through direct evidence, if it were to surface? Or is the problem that making the plaintiff plead a *prima facie* case doesn't greatly increase our confidence in the merits of his claim and invites extra litigation about the details of the complaint?

3. **"Notice pleading."** The Court in *Conley* refers to pleading under Rule 8(a) as "simplified 'notice pleading.' " Judge Charles Clark, the great scholar of procedure who was the principal draftsman of the Federal Rules of Civil Procedure, disliked the label "notice pleading." He objected, "It is too often overlooked that federal pleading is still issue pleading, presenting a definite issue for adjudication; the use of the term 'notice pleading'—which was rejected by the rule-makers and never employed by them—is prejudicial to a proper operation of the federal system, since it suggests the absence of all pleadings and the necessity of some substitute by way of pre-pre-trial." Padovani v. Bruchhausen, 293 F.2d 546, 550–51 (2d Cir. 1961). Despite these pleas, it has become common to call pleading under the federal Rules "notice pleading."

What are the limits of notice pleading? One possibility is that a claim may be so vague that it simply does not tell the defendant the "who, what, where, and why" of the dispute so that it can investigate and prepare a response. Was that a problem in *Swierkiewicz*? Another possibility is that the complaint itself discloses sufficient specific facts to indicate that, no matter what other evidence plaintiff adduces, the claim is doomed to fail because a critical element of proof cannot be supplied—or as *Conley* puts it, that there is no set of facts that plaintiff could prove in support of his claim that would entitle him to relief. Was there any fatal defect like that in the *Swierkiewicz* complaint?

4. Who should decide what Rule 8 means? In *Swierkiewicz*, the defendant argued that "allowing lawsuits based on conclusory allegations of discrimination to go forward will burden the courts and encourage disgruntled employees to bring unsubstantiated suits." The Court rejected that argument, stating that imposition of any such "heightened pleading" standard for employment discrimination cases could be created only through amendment of the federal Rules. In a subsequent case, citing *Swierkiewicz*, the Court stated that "courts should generally not depart from the usual practice under the Federal Rules on the basis of perceived policy concerns," and any such policy changes "must be obtained by the process of amending the Federal Rules, and not by judicial interpretation." Jones v. Bock, 549 U.S. 199, 127 S.Ct. 910, 166 L.Ed.2d 798 (2007). Recall the discussion in Chapter 1 of the process for making and amending Federal Rules of Civil Procedure, supra at 27. Why would the Court state that a change to the interpretation of the Rules must be accomplished through that process? Is such an argument convincing?

5. Motion for more definite statement. The classic remedy for a vague complaint is not a motion to dismiss, but rather a motion for more definite statement under Rule 12(e). In fact, however, such motions are rarely made and even more rarely granted. Rule 12(e) is in obvious tension with the notice pleading policy articulated in Rule 8(a), which requires only "a short and plain statement" of plaintiff's claim. Not surprisingly, district courts are reluctant to grant Rule 12(e) motions, for if a pleading satisfies Rule 8(a) it almost certainly satisfies Rule 12(e). As a result, it is often stated that Rule 12(e) motions are "disfavored." See, e.g., Premier Payments Online, Inc. v. Payment Systems Worldwide, 848 F. Supp. 2d 514 (E.D. Pa. 2013); E.E.O.C. v. Alia Corp., 842 F. Supp. 2d 1243 (E.D. Cal. 2012).

6. When should a lawyer provide more than the minimum required by Rule 8(a)? It is clearly possible to provide more detail than the minimum that Rule 8 requires, and most lawyers will do so in cases of any complexity. Notice how much we know about plaintiff's case from the complaint in *Conley v. Gibson*, as summarized in Justice Black's opinion. Was all that information required by Rule 8(a)? A lawyer should always think about the function of the complaint in the particular case she is filing. Providing more detail can educate the defendant and the court to the compelling nature of the case or to the strength of the proof, it can help to strengthen the court's resolve in addressing the issues of law raised by the complaint, and it may help in mobilizing public opinion or other constituencies. *Access Now* may have been such a case. For another example, see Pelman v. McDonald's Corp., 2003 WL 22052778 (S.D.N.Y. 2003), rev'd, 396 F.3d 508 (2d Cir. 2005) (complaint charging that defendant was responsible for contributing to plaintiff's obesity). On the other hand, a lawyer who provides more information than strictly necessary may end up pleading the plaintiff out of court without any discovery. Did the lawyers in *Access Now* provide more information than they had to?

If, based on what she now knows, the plaintiff has a weak case, what should she do? If the currently known facts are unfavorable or inconclusive, should she draft a generally worded complaint and hope to learn better facts through discovery? If the legal arguments are weak, should she disguise the weakness by drafting a vague complaint, hoping to postpone the court's

SECTION D

THE FORMAL SUFFICIENCY OF THE COMPLAINT:
HOW SPECIFIC MUST A PLEADING BE?

471

decision on the law? Should plaintiff be allowed to pursue a case she knows is weak? Frivolous? See discussion of Fed. R. Civ. P. 11, infra p. 519.

7. The complaint as a literary work? For a fascinating though somewhat dreamy view of what a complaint could be, consider the following:

> I once had a client named Hattie Kendrick. She was a woman and an African-American, a school teacher and a civil rights warrior, spit upon, arrested, and tossed out of restaurants and clothing stores that did not "cater to the colored trade." She marched and spoke out for integration and against oppression. Her school fired her, but not before she had taught generations of black children in Cairo, Illinois, that participation in American democracy was their right and duty. In the 1940's, she sued to win equal pay for black teachers, with Thurgood Marshall as her lawyer. And in the 1970's, she was a named plaintiff in a class action asserting the voting rights of black citizens in Cairo against a city electoral system rigged to reduce the value of their votes to nothingness. All she wanted was to cast a meaningful vote in a democratic election before she died—she was in her nineties, growing blind and weak. Such a woman. Such a story. And such a voice. Listen to how she discerns the problems of her town: "Too long have the two races stood grinning in each other's faces, while they carry the fires of resentment and hate in their hearts, and with their hands hid behind their backs they carry the unsheathed sword." Yet here is how the complaint filed in federal court identifies the named plaintiffs, including Hattie Kendrick: "All plaintiffs are Blacks, citizens of the United States and of the State of Illinois, and residents of Cairo, Illinois registered to vote in Municipal Elections conducted in Cairo."

Eastman, Speaking Truth to Power: The Language of Civil Rights Litigators, 104 Yale L.J. 763, 765–66 (1995). Professor Eastman reproduces the full complaint actually filed in the case, and a complaint that, in retrospect, he would like to have filed. See id. at 836–49, 865–79.

Bell Atlantic Corp. v. Twombly

Supreme Court of the United States, 2007.
550 U.S. 544, 127 S.Ct. 1955, 167 L.Ed.2d 929.

■ JUSTICE SOUTER delivered the opinion of the Court.

Liability under § 1 of the Sherman Act, 15 U.S.C. § 1, requires a "contract, combination . . . , or conspiracy, in restraint of trade or commerce." The question in this putative class action is whether a § 1 complaint can survive a motion to dismiss when it alleges that major telecommunications providers engaged in certain parallel conduct unfavorable to competition, absent some factual context suggesting agreement, as distinct from identical, independent action. We hold that such a complaint should be dismissed.

I

The upshot of the 1984 divestiture of the American Telephone & Telegraph Company's (AT & T) local telephone business was a system of regional service monopolies (variously called "Regional Bell Operating

Companies," "Baby Bells," or "Incumbent Local Exchange Carriers" (ILECs)), and a separate, competitive market for long-distance service from which the ILECs were excluded. More than a decade later, Congress withdrew approval of the ILECs' monopolies by enacting the Telecommunications Act of 1996 (1996 Act), which "fundamentally restructured local telephone markets" and "subjected [ILECs] to a host of duties intended to facilitate market entry." In recompense, the 1996 Act set conditions for authorizing ILECs to enter the long-distance market.

"Central to the [new] scheme [was each ILEC's] obligation . . . to share its network with competitors," which came to be known as "competitive local exchange carriers" (CLECs). A CLEC could make use of an ILEC's network in any of three ways: by (1) "purchasing local telephone services at wholesale rates for resale to end users," (2) "leasing elements of the [ILEC's] network 'on an unbundled basis,'" or (3) "interconnecting its own facilities with the [ILEC's] network." Owing to the "considerable expense and effort" required to make unbundled network elements available to rivals at wholesale prices, the ILECs vigorously litigated the scope of the sharing obligation imposed by the 1996 Act, with the result that the Federal Communications Commission (FCC) three times revised its regulations to narrow the range of network elements to be shared with the CLECs.

Respondents William Twombly and Lawrence Marcus (hereinafter plaintiffs) represent a putative class consisting of all "subscribers of local telephone and/or high speed internet services . . . from February 8, 1996 to present." In this action against petitioners, a group of ILECs,[1] plaintiffs seek treble damages and declaratory and injunctive relief for claimed violations of § 1 of the Sherman Act, 15 U.S.C. § 1, which prohibits "every contract, combination in the form of trust or otherwise, or conspiracy, in restraint of trade or commerce among the several States, or with foreign nations."

The complaint alleges that the ILECs conspired to restrain trade in two ways, each supposedly inflating charges for local telephone and high-speed Internet services. Plaintiffs say, first, that the ILECs "engaged in parallel conduct" in their respective service areas to inhibit the growth of upstart CLECs. * * * *

Second, the complaint charges agreements by the ILECs to refrain from competing against one another. These are to be inferred from the ILECs' common failure "meaningfully [to] pursue" "attractive business opportunities" in contiguous markets where they possessed "substantial competitive advantages," id., ¶¶ 40–41, and from a statement of Richard Notebaert, chief executive officer (CEO) of the ILEC Qwest, that competing in the territory of another ILEC " 'might be a good way to turn a quick dollar but that doesn't make it right,' " id., ¶ 42.

---

[1]   The 1984 divestiture of AT & T's local telephone service created seven Regional Bell Operating Companies. Through a series of mergers and acquisitions, those seven companies were consolidated into the four ILECs named in this suit: BellSouth Corporation, Qwest Communications International, Inc., SBC Communications, Inc., and Verizon Communications, Inc. (successor-in-interest to Bell Atlantic Corporation). Complaint ¶ 21. Together, these ILECs allegedly control 90 percent or more of the market for local telephone service in the 48 contiguous States. Id., ¶ 48.

SECTION D

THE FORMAL SUFFICIENCY OF THE COMPLAINT:
HOW SPECIFIC MUST A PLEADING BE?

473

The complaint couches its ultimate allegations this way:

"In the absence of any meaningful competition between the [ILECs] in one another's markets, and in light of the parallel course of conduct that each engaged in to prevent competition from CLECs within their respective local telephone and/or high speed internet services markets and the other facts and market circumstances alleged above, Plaintiffs allege upon information and belief that [the ILECs] have entered into a contract, combination or conspiracy to prevent competitive entry in their respective local telephone and/or high speed internet services markets and have agreed not to compete with one another and otherwise allocated customers and markets to one another." Id., ¶ 51.[2]

The United States District Court for the Southern District of New York dismissed the complaint for failure to state a claim upon which relief can be granted. * * * *

The Court of Appeals for the Second Circuit reversed. * * * *

We granted certiorari to address the proper standard for pleading an antitrust conspiracy through allegations of parallel conduct, and now reverse.

II

A

Because § 1 of the Sherman Act "does not prohibit [all] unreasonable restraints of trade . . . but only restraints effected by a contract, combination, or conspiracy," "the crucial question" is whether the challenged anticompetitive conduct "stems from independent decision or from an agreement, tacit or express." While a showing of parallel "business behavior is admissible circumstantial evidence from which the fact finder may infer agreement," it falls short of "conclusively establishing agreement or . . . itself constituting a Sherman Act offense." Even "conscious parallelism," a common reaction of "firms in a concentrated market [that] recognize their shared economic interests and their interdependence with respect to price and output decisions" is "not in itself unlawful."

The inadequacy of showing parallel conduct or interdependence, without more, mirrors the ambiguity of the behavior: consistent with conspiracy, but just as much in line with a wide swath of rational and competitive business strategy unilaterally prompted by common perceptions of the market. * * * *

---

[2] In setting forth the grounds for § 1 relief, the complaint repeats these allegations in substantially similar language:

"Beginning at least as early as February 6, 1996, and continuing to the present, the exact dates being unknown to Plaintiffs, Defendants and their co-conspirators engaged in a contract, combination or conspiracy to prevent competitive entry in their respective local telephone and/or high speed internet services markets by, among other things, agreeing not to compete with one another and to stifle attempts by others to compete with them and otherwise allocating customers and markets to one another in violation of Section 1 of the Sherman Act." Id., ¶ 64.

B

This case presents the antecedent question of what a plaintiff must plead in order to state a claim under § 1 of the Sherman Act. Federal Rule of Civil Procedure 8(a)(2) requires only "a short and plain statement of the claim showing that the pleader is entitled to relief," in order to "give the defendant fair notice of what the . . . claim is and the grounds upon which it rests," Conley v. Gibson, 355 U.S. 41, 47, 78 S.Ct. 99, 2 L.Ed.2d 80 (1957). While a complaint attacked by a Rule 12(b)(6) motion to dismiss does not need detailed factual allegations, a plaintiff's obligation to provide the "grounds" of his "entitlement to relief" requires more than labels and conclusions, and a formulaic recitation of the elements of a cause of action will not do. Factual allegations must be enough to raise a right to relief above the speculative level, * * * on the assumption that all the allegations in the complaint are true (even if doubtful in fact), see, e.g., Swierkiewicz v. Sorema N. A., 534 U.S. 506, 508, n. 1, 122 S.Ct. 992, 152 L.Ed.2d 1 (2002).

In applying these general standards to a § 1 claim, we hold that stating such a claim requires a complaint with enough factual matter (taken as true) to suggest that an agreement was made. Asking for plausible grounds to infer an agreement does not impose a probability requirement at the pleading stage; it simply calls for enough fact to raise a reasonable expectation that discovery will reveal evidence of illegal agreement. And, of course, a well-pleaded complaint may proceed even if it strikes a savvy judge that actual proof of those facts is improbable, and "that a recovery is very remote and unlikely." In identifying facts that are suggestive enough to render a § 1 conspiracy plausible, we have the benefit of the prior rulings and considered views of leading commentators * * * that lawful parallel conduct fails to bespeak unlawful agreement. It makes sense to say, therefore, that an allegation of parallel conduct and a bare assertion of conspiracy will not suffice. Without more, parallel conduct does not suggest conspiracy, and a conclusory allegation of agreement at some unidentified point does not supply facts adequate to show illegality. Hence, when allegations of parallel conduct are set out in order to make a § 1 claim, they must be placed in a context that raises a suggestion of a preceding agreement, not merely parallel conduct that could just as well be independent action.

The need at the pleading stage for allegations plausibly suggesting (not merely consistent with) agreement reflects the threshold requirement of Rule 8(a)(2) that the "plain statement" possess enough heft to "show that the pleader is entitled to relief." A statement of parallel conduct, even conduct consciously undertaken, needs some setting suggesting the agreement necessary to make out a § 1 claim; without that further circumstance pointing toward a meeting of the minds, an account of a defendant's commercial efforts stays in neutral territory. An allegation of parallel conduct is thus much like a naked assertion of conspiracy in a § 1 complaint: it gets the complaint close to stating a claim, but without some further factual enhancement it stops short of the line between possibility and plausibility of "entitlement to relief."

* * *

Thus, it is one thing to be cautious before dismissing an antitrust complaint in advance of discovery, but quite another to forget that proceeding to antitrust discovery can be expensive. * * * * That potential expense is obvious enough in the present case: plaintiffs represent a putative class of at least 90 percent of all subscribers to local telephone or high-speed Internet service in the continental United States, in an action against America's largest telecommunications firms (with many thousands of employees generating reams and gigabytes of business records) for unspecified (if any) instances of antitrust violations that allegedly occurred over a period of seven years.

It is no answer to say that a claim just shy of a plausible entitlement to relief can, if groundless, be weeded out early in the discovery process through "careful case management," given the common lament that the success of judicial supervision in checking discovery abuse has been on the modest side. And it is self-evident that the problem of discovery abuse cannot be solved by "careful scrutiny of evidence at the summary judgment stage," much less "lucid instructions to juries;" the threat of discovery expense will push cost-conscious defendants to settle even anemic cases before reaching those proceedings. Probably, then, it is only by taking care to require allegations that reach the level suggesting conspiracy that we can hope to avoid the potentially enormous expense of discovery in cases with no " 'reasonably founded hope that the [discovery] process will reveal relevant evidence' " to support a § 1 claim. *Dura*, 544 U.S., at 347, 125 S.Ct. 1627, 161 L.Ed.2d 577.

[Plaintiffs'] * * * main argument against the plausibility standard at the pleading stage is its ostensible conflict with an early statement of ours construing Rule 8. Justice Black's opinion for the Court in *Conley v. Gibson* spoke not only of the need for fair notice of the grounds for entitlement to relief but of "the accepted rule that a complaint should not be dismissed for failure to state a claim unless it appears beyond doubt that the plaintiff can prove no set of facts in support of his claim which would entitle him to relief." This "no set of facts" language can be read in isolation as saying that any statement revealing the theory of the claim will suffice unless its factual impossibility may be shown from the face of the pleadings; and the Court of Appeals appears to have read *Conley* in some such way* * *.

On such a focused and literal reading of *Conley's* "no set of facts," a wholly conclusory statement of claim would survive a motion to dismiss whenever the pleadings left open the possibility that a plaintiff might later establish some "set of [undisclosed] facts" to support recovery. So here, the Court of Appeals specifically found the prospect of unearthing direct evidence of conspiracy sufficient to preclude dismissal, even though the complaint does not set forth a single fact in a context that suggests an agreement. It seems fair to say that this approach to pleading would dispense with any showing of a " 'reasonably founded hope' " that a plaintiff would be able to make a case, see *Dura*, 544 U.S., at 347, 125 S.Ct. 1627, 161 L.Ed.2d 577; Mr. Micawber's optimism would be enough.

Seeing this, a good many judges and commentators have balked at taking the literal terms of the *Conley* passage as a pleading standard. * * *

* * * *Conley's* "no set of facts" language has been questioned, criticized, and explained away long enough. To be fair to the *Conley* Court, the passage should be understood in light of the opinion's

preceding summary of the complaint's concrete allegations, which the Court quite reasonably understood as amply stating a claim for relief. But the passage so often quoted fails to mention this understanding on the part of the Court, and after puzzling the profession for 50 years, this famous observation has earned its retirement. The phrase is best forgotten as an incomplete, negative gloss on an accepted pleading standard: once a claim has been stated adequately, it may be supported by showing any set of facts consistent with the allegations in the complaint. *Conley*, then, described the breadth of opportunity to prove what an adequate complaint claims, not the minimum standard of adequate pleading to govern a complaint's survival.

III

When we look for plausibility in this complaint, we agree with the District Court that plaintiffs' claim of conspiracy in restraint of trade comes up short. To begin with, the complaint leaves no doubt that plaintiffs rest their § 1 claim on descriptions of parallel conduct and not on any independent allegation of actual agreement among the ILECs. Although in form a few stray statements speak directly of agreement,[9] on fair reading these are merely legal conclusions resting on the prior allegations. Thus, the complaint first takes account of the alleged "absence of any meaningful competition between [the ILECs] in one another's markets," "the parallel course of conduct that each [ILEC] engaged in to prevent competition from CLECs," "and the other facts and market circumstances alleged [earlier]"; "in light of" these, the complaint concludes "that [the ILECs] have entered into a contract, combination or conspiracy to prevent competitive entry into their . . . markets and have agreed not to compete with one another." Complaint ¶ 51.[10] The nub of the complaint, then, is the ILECs' parallel behavior, consisting of steps to keep the CLECs out and manifest disinterest in becoming CLECs themselves, and its sufficiency turns on the suggestions raised by this conduct when viewed in light of common economic experience.

We think that nothing contained in the complaint invests either the action or inaction alleged with a plausible suggestion of conspiracy. As to the ILECs' supposed agreement to disobey the 1996 Act and thwart the CLECs' attempts to compete, we agree with the District Court that nothing in the complaint intimates that the resistance to the upstarts

---

[9]   See Complaint ¶¶ 51, 64 (alleging that ILECs engaged in a "contract, combination or conspiracy" and agreed not to compete with one another).

[10]   If the complaint had not explained that the claim of agreement rested on the parallel conduct described, we doubt that the complaint's references to an agreement among the ILECs would have given the notice required by Rule 8. Apart from identifying a seven-year span in which the § 1 violations were supposed to have occurred (*i.e.*, "beginning at least as early as February 6, 1996, and continuing to the present," *id.*, ¶ 64), the pleadings mentioned no specific time, place, or person involved in the alleged conspiracies. This lack of notice contrasts sharply with the model form for pleading negligence, Form 9 [eds. note: now Form 11], which the dissent says exemplifies the kind of "bare allegation" that survives a motion to dismiss. Whereas the model form alleges that the defendant struck the plaintiff with his car while plaintiff was crossing a particular highway at a specified date and time, the complaint here furnishes no clue as to which of the four ILECs (much less which of their employees) supposedly agreed, or when and where the illicit agreement took place. A defendant wishing to prepare an answer in the simple fact pattern laid out in Form 9 would know what to answer; a defendant seeking to respond to plaintiffs' conclusory allegations in the § 1 context would have little idea where to begin.

SECTION D

THE FORMAL SUFFICIENCY OF THE COMPLAINT:
HOW SPECIFIC MUST A PLEADING BE?

477

was anything more than the natural, unilateral reaction of each ILEC intent on keeping its regional dominance. * * *

Plaintiffs' second conspiracy theory rests on the competitive reticence among the ILECs themselves in the wake of the 1996 Act, which was supposedly passed in the " 'hope that the large incumbent local monopoly companies . . . might attack their neighbors' service areas, as they are the best situated to do so.' " Complaint ¶ 38. Contrary to hope, the ILECs declined " 'to enter each other's service territories in any significant way,' " *id.*, and the local telephone and high speed Internet market remains highly compartmentalized geographically, with minimal competition. Based on this state of affairs, and perceiving the ILECs to be blessed with "especially attractive business opportunities" in surrounding markets dominated by other ILECs, the plaintiffs assert that the ILECs' parallel conduct was "strongly suggestive of conspiracy." Id., ¶ 40.

But it was not suggestive of conspiracy, not if history teaches anything. In a traditionally unregulated industry with low barriers to entry, sparse competition among large firms dominating separate geographical segments of the market could very well signify illegal agreement, but here we have an obvious alternative explanation. In the decade preceding the 1996 Act and well before that, monopoly was the norm in telecommunications, not the exception. The ILECs were born in that world, doubtless liked the world the way it was, and surely knew the adage about him who lives by the sword. Hence, a natural explanation for the noncompetition alleged is that the former Government-sanctioned monopolists were sitting tight, expecting their neighbors to do the same thing.

* * * We agree with the District Court's assessment that antitrust conspiracy was not suggested by the facts adduced under either theory of the complaint, which thus fails to state a valid § 1 claim.[14]

Plaintiffs say that our analysis runs counter to Swierkiewicz v. Sorema N. A., 534 U.S. 506, 508, 122 S.Ct. 992, 152 L.Ed.2d 1 (2002), [in] which [the Court held] that the Court of Appeals had impermissibly applied what amounted to a heightened pleading requirement by insisting that Swierkiewicz allege "specific facts" beyond those necessary to state his claim and the grounds showing entitlement to relief. Id.

Here, in contrast, we do not require heightened fact pleading of specifics, but only enough facts to state a claim to relief that is plausible on its face. Because the plaintiffs here have not nudged their claims across the line from conceivable to plausible, their complaint must be dismissed.

---

[14] In reaching this conclusion, we do not apply any "heightened" pleading standard, nor do we seek to broaden the scope of Federal Rule of Civil Procedure 9, which can only be accomplished " 'by the process of amending the Federal Rules, and not by judicial interpretation.' " Swierkiewicz v. Sorema N. A., 534 U.S. 506, 515, 122 S.Ct. 992, 152 L.Ed.2d 1 (2002) (quoting Leatherman v. Tarrant County Narcotics Intelligence and Coordination Unit, 507 U.S. 163, 168, 113 S.Ct. 1160, 122 L.Ed.2d 517 (1993)). On certain subjects understood to raise a high risk of abusive litigation, a plaintiff must state factual allegations with greater particularity than Rule 8 requires. Fed. Rules Civ. Proc. 9(b)–(c). Here, our concern is not that the allegations in the complaint were insufficiently "particularized", ibid.; rather, the complaint warranted dismissal because it failed in toto to render plaintiffs' entitlement to relief plausible.

* * *

The judgment of the Court of Appeals for the Second Circuit is reversed, and the cause is remanded for further proceedings consistent with this opinion.

It is so ordered.

■ JUSTICE STEVENS, with whom JUSTICE GINSBURG joins except as to Part IV, dissenting.

* * *

[T]his is a case in which there is no dispute about the substantive law. If the defendants acted independently, their conduct was perfectly lawful. If, however, that conduct is the product of a horizontal agreement among potential competitors, it was unlawful. Plaintiffs have alleged such an agreement and, because the complaint was dismissed in advance of answer, the allegation has not even been denied. Why, then, does the case not proceed? Does a judicial opinion that the charge is not "plausible" provide a legally acceptable reason for dismissing the complaint? I think not.

* * * *

I

Rule 8(a)(2) of the Federal Rules requires that a complaint contain "a short and plain statement of the claim showing that the pleader is entitled to relief." The rule did not come about by happenstance and its language is not inadvertent. The English experience with Byzantine special pleading rules—illustrated by the hypertechnical Hilary rules of 1834—made obvious the appeal of a pleading standard that was easy for the common litigant to understand and sufficed to put the defendant on notice as to the nature of the claim against him and the relief sought. Stateside, David Dudley Field developed the highly influential New York Code of 1848, which required "[a] statement of the facts constituting the cause of action, in ordinary and concise language, without repetition, and in such a manner as to enable a person of common understanding to know what is intended." Substantially similar language appeared in the Federal Equity Rules adopted in 1912.

A difficulty arose, however, in that the Field Code and its progeny required a plaintiff to plead "facts" rather than "conclusions," a distinction that proved far easier to say than to apply. As commentators have noted,

> "it is virtually impossible logically to distinguish among 'ultimate facts,' 'evidence,' and 'conclusions.' Essentially any allegation in a pleading must be an assertion that certain occurrences took place. The pleading spectrum, passing from evidence through ultimate facts to conclusions, is largely a continuum varying only in the degree of particularity with which the occurrences are described." Weinstein & Distler, Comments on Procedural Reform: Drafting Pleading Rules, 57 Colum. L. Rev. 518, 520–521 (1957).

Rule 8 was directly responsive to this difficulty. Its drafters intentionally avoided any reference to "facts" or "evidence" or "conclusions."

SECTION D

THE FORMAL SUFFICIENCY OF THE COMPLAINT:
HOW SPECIFIC MUST A PLEADING BE?

479

Under the relaxed pleading standards of the Federal Rules, the idea was not to keep litigants out of court but rather to keep them in. The merits of a claim would be sorted out during a flexible pretrial process and, as appropriate, through the crucible of trial. See *Swierkiewicz*, 534 U.S., at 514, 122 S.Ct. 992, 152 L.Ed.2d 1 ("The liberal notice pleading of Rule 8(a) is the starting point of a system, which was adopted to focus litigation on the merits of a claim"). * * * *

II

It is in the context of this history that Conley v. Gibson, 355 U.S. 41, 78 S.Ct. 99, 2 L.Ed.2d 80 (1957), must be understood. The *Conley* plaintiffs were black railroad workers who alleged that their union local had refused to protect them against discriminatory discharges, in violation of the National Railway Labor Act. The union sought to dismiss the complaint on the ground that its general allegations of discriminatory treatment by the defendants lacked sufficient specificity. Writing for a unanimous Court, Justice Black rejected the union's claim as foreclosed by the language of Rule 8. In the course of doing so, he articulated the formulation the Court rejects today: "In appraising the sufficiency of the complaint we follow, of course, the accepted rule that a complaint should not be dismissed for failure to state a claim unless it appears beyond doubt that the plaintiff can prove no set of facts in support of his claim which would entitle him to relief."

Consistent with the design of the Federal Rules, *Conley's* "no set of facts" formulation permits outright dismissal only when proceeding to discovery or beyond would be futile. Once it is clear that a plaintiff has stated a claim that, if true, would entitle him to relief, matters of proof are appropriately relegated to other stages of the trial process. Today, however, in its explanation of a decision to dismiss a complaint that it regards as a fishing expedition, the Court scraps *Conley's* "no set of facts" language. Concluding that the phrase has been "questioned, criticized, and explained away long enough," the Court dismisses it as careless composition.

If *Conley's* "no set of facts" language is to be interred, let it not be without a eulogy. That exact language, which the majority says has "puzzled the profession for 50 years," has been cited as authority in a dozen opinions of this Court and four separate writings. In not one of those 16 opinions was the language "questioned," "criticized," or "explained away." Indeed, today's opinion is the first by any Member of this Court to express any doubt as to the adequacy of the *Conley* formulation. Taking their cues from the federal courts, 26 States and the District of Columbia utilize as their standard for dismissal of a complaint the very language the majority repudiates: whether it appears "beyond doubt" that "no set of facts" in support of the claim would entitle the plaintiff to relief.

1st time the concern has been raised

* * * *

* * * * *Conley's* statement that a complaint is not to be dismissed unless "no set of facts" in support thereof would entitle the plaintiff to relief is hardly "puzzling." It reflects a philosophy that, unlike in the days of code pleading, separating the wheat from the chaff is a task assigned to the pretrial and trial process. *Conley's* language, in short, captures the

policy choice embodied in the Federal Rules and binding on the federal courts.

We have consistently reaffirmed that basic understanding of the Federal Rules in the half century since *Conley*. * * * *

As in the discrimination context, we have developed an evidentiary framework for evaluating claims under § 1 of the Sherman Act when those claims rest on entirely circumstantial evidence of conspiracy. See Matsushita Elec. Industrial Co. v. Zenith Radio Corp., 475 U.S. 574, 106 S.Ct. 1348, 89 L.Ed.2d 538 (1986). Under *Matsushita*, a plaintiff's allegations of an illegal conspiracy may not, at the summary judgment stage, rest solely on the inferences that may be drawn from the parallel conduct of the defendants. In order to survive a Rule 56 motion, a § 1 plaintiff "must present evidence 'that tends to exclude the possibility' that the alleged conspirators acted independently.'" That is, the plaintiff "must show that the inference of conspiracy is reasonable in light of the competing inferences of independent action or collusive action."

Everything today's majority says would therefore make perfect sense if it were ruling on a Rule 56 motion for summary judgment and the evidence included nothing more than the Court has described. * * * *

This case is a poor vehicle for the Court's new pleading rule, for we have observed that "in antitrust cases, where 'the proof is largely in the hands of the alleged conspirators,' . . . dismissals prior to giving the plaintiff ample opportunity for discovery should be granted very sparingly." Moreover, the fact that the Sherman Act authorizes the recovery of treble damages and attorney's fees for successful plaintiffs indicates that Congress intended to encourage, rather than discourage, private enforcement of the law. It is therefore more, not less, important in antitrust cases to resist the urge to engage in armchair economics at the pleading stage.

* * * *

III

* * * [T]he theory on which the Court permits dismissal is that, so far as the Federal Rules are concerned, no agreement has been alleged at all. This is a mind-boggling conclusion.

* * * [T]he plaintiffs allege in three places in their complaint, ¶¶ 4, 51, 64, that the ILECs did in fact agree both to prevent competitors from entering into their local markets and to forgo competition with each other. And as the Court recognizes, at the motion to dismiss stage, a judge assumes "that all the allegations in the complaint are true (even if doubtful in fact)."

The majority circumvents this obvious obstacle to dismissal by pretending that it does not exist. The Court admits that "in form a few stray statements in the complaint speak directly of agreement," but disregards those allegations by saying that "on fair reading these are merely legal conclusions resting on the prior allegations" of parallel conduct. The Court's dichotomy between factual allegations and "legal conclusions" is the stuff of a bygone era. That distinction was a defining feature of code pleading, but was conspicuously abolished when the Federal Rules were enacted in 1938. * * *

SECTION D

THE FORMAL SUFFICIENCY OF THE COMPLAINT:
HOW SPECIFIC MUST A PLEADING BE?

481

Even if I were inclined to accept the Court's anachronistic dichotomy and ignore the complaint's actual allegations, I would dispute the Court's suggestion that any inference of agreement from petitioners' parallel conduct is "implausible." Many years ago a truly great economist perceptively observed that "people of the same trade seldom meet together, even for merriment and diversion, but the conversation ends in a conspiracy against the public, or in some contrivance to raise prices." A. Smith, An Inquiry Into the Nature and Causes of the Wealth of Nations, in 39 Great Books of the Western World 55 (R. Hutchins & M. Adler eds. 1952). I am not so cynical as to accept that sentiment at face value, but I need not do so here. Respondents' complaint points not only to petitioners' numerous opportunities to meet with each other, but also to Notebaert's curious statement that encroaching on a fellow incumbent's territory "might be a good way to turn a quick dollar but that doesn't make it right," id., ¶ 42. What did he mean by that? One possible (indeed plausible) inference is that he meant that while it would be in his company's economic self-interest to compete with its brethren, he had agreed with his competitors not to do so. * * *

* * * * [T]he District Court was required at this stage of the proceedings to construe Notebaert's ambiguous statement in the plaintiffs' favor. The inference the statement supports—that simultaneous decisions by ILECs not even to attempt to poach customers from one another once the law authorized them to do so were the product of an agreement—sits comfortably within the realm of possibility. That is all the Rules require.

NOTES AND QUESTIONS

1. **The Court's holding.** The majority states its holding as follows:

In applying these general standards [derived from Rule 8 (a)(2)] to a [claim of conspiracy under Section 1 of the Sherman Act], we hold that stating such a claim requires a complaint with enough factual matter (taken as true) to suggest that an agreement was made. Asking for plausible grounds to infer an agreement does not impose a probability requirement at the pleading stage; it simply calls for enough fact to raise a reasonable expectation that discovery will reveal evidence of illegal agreement.

Does this holding necessarily imply a change in traditional standards of notice pleading? Consider the following questions.

2. **Revival of the code pleading prohibition on legal conclusions?** The plaintiff's complaint pleads, in so many words, that the defendants "have entered into a contract, combination or conspiracy" in restraint of trade. Why isn't that allegation sufficient, in the Court's view, to satisfy the requirements of Rule 8(a)(2)? Would the complaint in *Swierkiewicz v. Sorema* survive under the standard applied in *Twombly*?

3. **Meanings of *Conley v. Gibson*.** The most plaintiff-favoring view of the rule of *Conley v. Gibson* was that if plaintiff pleaded an element of a claim, even in conclusory form, then the complaint could not be dismissed unless the defendant had pleaded other specific facts which indisputably demonstrated that the "conclusion" would never be provable at trial. *Access Now v. Southwest Airlines Co.* is arguably an example of a case where the

specific facts pleaded demonstrated the untenable nature of a conclusory claim. In *Twombly*, are plaintiff's allegations of parallel conduct wholly inconsistent with the existence of the agreement among the defendants that the plaintiff has described, or do they merely fail to affirmatively suggest the existence of an agreement? If the latter is the case, then hasn't the strong plaintiff-favoring version of *Conley* been rejected?

Another less dramatic reading of *Conley* is that in determining whether an element has been pleaded, the court must take what has been pleaded as true and read the allegations of the complaint in the light most favorable to the plaintiff. Did the Court read every allegation of Twombly's complaint in the light most favorable to the plaintiff?

4. Determining plausibility for other kinds of claims. In assessing whether the *Twombly* complaint pleads a "plausible" claim of combination or conspiracy, the Court offers a variety of potential non-conspiratorial explanations for defendants' alleged conduct. Does this imply that in construing complaints the court should similarly theorize about the potential non-discriminatory motivations for defendants' alleged conduct in discrimination cases? About the non-negligent explanations for defendants' alleged conduct in negligence cases? What problems do you see with such theorizing?

The Court also appears to give great weight in its formulation of the "plausibility" principle to the goal of preventing costly and unproductive discovery in complex cases and to the presumed inability of judicial management or summary judgment to do so. As the Court points out, those problems are especially severe in antitrust class actions. But across the federal docket, the number of cases involving massive discovery is small as a percentage of all cases filed. Does this imply that in deciding how much "plausibility" to demand in particular kinds of complaints lower courts should analyze the risks of wasteful discovery on a claim-by-claim or subject-area-by-subject-area basis? If not, hasn't the Court allowed an unusual kind of "big case" litigation to skew the pleading standards that will apply to many routine cases which don't present the risk of extraordinary discovery costs?

For a brief period following the *Twombly* decision, some believed that its holding would be limited to the antitrust area—or at least to other kinds of cases thought to generate high discovery costs. The Supreme Court ended that speculation in the following case, decided in 2009.

Ashcroft v. Iqbal

Supreme Court of the United States, 2009.
556 U.S. 662, 129 S.Ct. 1937, 173 L.Ed.2d 868.

■ JUSTICE KENNEDY delivered the opinion of the Court.

Respondent Javaid Iqbal is a citizen of Pakistan and a Muslim. In the wake of the September 11, 2001, terrorist attacks he was arrested in the United States on criminal charges and detained by federal officials. Respondent claims he was deprived of various constitutional protections while in federal custody. To redress the alleged deprivations, respondent filed a complaint against numerous federal officials, including John Ashcroft, the former Attorney General of the United States, and Robert Mueller, the Director of the Federal Bureau of Investigation (FBI). Ashcroft and Mueller are the petitioners in the case now before us. As to these two petitioners, the complaint alleges that they adopted an unconstitutional policy that subjected respondent to harsh conditions of confinement on account of his race, religion, or national origin.

In the District Court petitioners raised the defense of qualified immunity and moved to dismiss the suit, contending the complaint was not sufficient to state a claim against them. The District Court denied the motion to dismiss, concluding the complaint was sufficient to state a claim despite petitioners' official status at the times in question. Petitioners brought an interlocutory appeal in the Court of Appeals for the Second Circuit. The court, without discussion, assumed it had jurisdiction over the order denying the motion to dismiss; and it affirmed the District Court's decision.

Respondent's account of his prison ordeal could, if proved, demonstrate unconstitutional misconduct by some governmental actors. But the allegations and pleadings with respect to these actors are not before us here. This case instead turns on a narrower question: Did respondent, as the plaintiff in the District Court, plead factual matter that, if taken as true, states a claim that petitioners deprived him of his clearly established constitutional rights. We hold respondent's pleadings are insufficient.

I

Following the 2001 attacks, the FBI and other entities within the Department of Justice began an investigation of vast reach to identify the assailants and prevent them from attacking anew. The FBI dedicated more than 4,000 special agents and 3,000 support personnel to the endeavor. By September 18 "the FBI had received more than 96,000 tips or potential leads from the public."

In the ensuing months the FBI questioned more than 1,000 people with suspected links to the attacks in particular or to terrorism in general. Of those individuals, some 762 were held on immigration charges; and a 184-member subset of that group was deemed to be "of 'high interest' " to the investigation. The high-interest detainees were held under restrictive conditions designed to prevent them from communicating with the general prison population or the outside world.

Respondent was one of the detainees. According to his complaint, in November 2001 agents of the FBI and Immigration and Naturalization Service arrested him on charges of fraud in relation to identification documents and conspiracy to defraud the United States. Pending trial for those crimes, respondent was housed at the Metropolitan Detention Center (MDC) in Brooklyn, New York. Respondent was designated a person "of high interest" to the September 11 investigation and in January 2002 was placed in a section of the MDC known as the Administrative Maximum Special Housing Unit (ADMAX SHU). As the facility's name indicates, the ADMAX SHU incorporates the maximum security conditions allowable under Federal Bureau of Prison regulations. ADMAX SHU detainees were kept in lockdown 23 hours a day, spending the remaining hour outside their cells in handcuffs and leg irons accompanied by a four-officer escort.

Respondent pleaded guilty to the criminal charges, served a term of imprisonment, and was removed to his native Pakistan. He then filed a *Bivens* action in the United States District Court for the Eastern District of New York against 34 current and former federal officials and 19 "John Doe" federal corrections officers. The defendants range from the correctional officers who had day-to-day contact with respondent during the term of his confinement, to the wardens of the MDC facility, all the way to petitioners-officials who were at the highest level of the federal law enforcement hierarchy.

The 21-cause-of-action complaint does not challenge respondent's arrest or his confinement in the MDC's general prison population. Rather, it concentrates on his treatment while confined to the ADMAX SHU. The complaint sets forth various claims against defendants who are not before us. For instance, the complaint alleges that respondent's jailors "kicked him in the stomach, punched him in the face, and dragged him across" his cell without justification, subjected him to serial strip and body-cavity searches when he posed no safety risk to himself or others, and refused to let him and other Muslims pray because there would be "[n]o prayers for terrorists."

The allegations against petitioners are the only ones relevant here. The complaint contends that petitioners designated respondent a person of high interest on account of his race, religion, or national origin, in contravention of the First and Fifth Amendments to the Constitution. The complaint alleges that "the [FBI], under the direction of Defendant MUELLER, arrested and detained thousands of Arab Muslim men . . . as part of its investigation of the events of September 11." It further alleges that "[t]he policy of holding post-September-11th detainees in highly restrictive conditions of confinement until they were 'cleared' by the FBI was approved by Defendants ASHCROFT and MUELLER in discussions in the weeks after September 11, 2001." Lastly, the complaint posits that petitioners "each knew of, condoned, and willfully and maliciously agreed to subject" respondent to harsh conditions of confinement "as a matter of policy, solely on account of [his] religion, race, and/or national origin and for no legitimate penological interest." The pleading names Ashcroft as the "principal architect" of the policy, and identifies Mueller as "instrumental in [its] adoption, promulgation, and implementation."

Petitioners moved to dismiss the complaint for failure to state sufficient allegations to show their own involvement in clearly established unconstitutional conduct. The District Court denied their motion. Accepting all of the allegations in respondent's complaint as true, the court held that "it cannot be said that there [is] no set of facts on which [respondent] would be entitled to relief as against" petitioners. *Id.*, at 136a–137a (relying on Conley v. Gibson, 355 U.S. 41, 78 S.Ct. 99, 2 L.Ed.2d 80 (1957)). Invoking the collateral-order doctrine petitioners filed an interlocutory appeal in the United States Court of Appeals for the Second Circuit. While that appeal was pending, this Court decided Bell Atlantic Corp. v. Twombly, 550 U.S. 544, 127 S.Ct. 1955, 167 L.Ed.2d 929 (2007), which discussed the standard for evaluating whether a complaint is sufficient to survive a motion to dismiss.

The Court of Appeals * * * concluded that *Twombly* called for a "flexible 'plausibility standard,' which obliges a pleader to amplify a claim with some factual allegations in those contexts where such amplification is needed to render the claim *plausible*." The court found that petitioners' appeal did not present one of "those contexts" requiring amplification. * * *

* * * We granted certiorari and now reverse.

III

In *Twombly* the Court found it necessary first to discuss the antitrust principles implicated by the complaint. Here too we begin by taking note of the elements a plaintiff must plead to state a claim of unconstitutional discrimination against officials entitled to assert the defense of qualified immunity.

* * * *

* * * Based on the rules our precedents establish, respondent correctly concedes that Government officials may not be held liable for the unconstitutional conduct of their subordinates under a theory of *respondeat superior*. Because vicarious liability is inapplicable to *Bivens* and § 1983 suits, a plaintiff must plead that each Government-official defendant, through the official's own individual actions, has violated the Constitution.

* * * Where the claim is invidious discrimination in contravention of the First and Fifth Amendments, our decisions make clear that the plaintiff must plead and prove that the defendant acted with discriminatory purpose. Under extant precedent purposeful discrimination requires more than "intent as volition or intent as awareness of consequences." *Personnel Administrator of Mass. v. Feeney,* 442 U.S. 256, 279, 99 S.Ct. 2282, 60 L.Ed.2d 870 (1979). It instead involves a decisionmaker's undertaking a course of action " 'because of,' not merely 'in spite of,' [the action's] adverse effects upon an identifiable group." *Ibid.* It follows that, to state a claim based on a violation of a clearly established right, respondent must plead sufficient factual matter to show that petitioners adopted and implemented the detention policies at issue not for a neutral, investigative reason but for the purpose of discriminating on account of race, religion, or national origin.

* * * In a § 1983 suit or a *Bivens* action-where masters do not answer for the torts of their servants-the term "supervisory liability" is a misnomer. Absent vicarious liability, each Government official, his or her title notwithstanding, is only liable for his or her own misconduct. * * *

IV

A

We turn to respondent's complaint. Under Federal Rule of Civil Procedure 8(a)(2), a pleading must contain a "short and plain statement of the claim showing that the pleader is entitled to relief." As the Court held in *Twombly,* the pleading standard Rule 8 announces does not require "detailed factual allegations," but it demands more than an unadorned, the-defendant-unlawfully-harmed-me accusation. A pleading that offers "labels and conclusions" or "a formulaic recitation of the elements of a cause of action will not do." Nor does a complaint suffice if it tenders "naked assertion[s]" devoid of "further factual enhancement."

To survive a motion to dismiss, a complaint must contain sufficient factual matter, accepted as true, to "state a claim to relief that is plausible on its face." A claim has facial plausibility when the plaintiff pleads factual content that allows the court to draw the reasonable inference that the defendant is liable for the misconduct alleged. The plausibility standard is not akin to a "probability requirement," but it asks for more than a sheer possibility that a defendant has acted unlawfully. Where a complaint pleads facts that are "merely consistent with" a defendant's liability, it "stops short of the line between possibility and plausibility of 'entitlement to relief.' "

Two working principles underlie our decision in *Twombly*. First, the tenet that a court must accept as true all of the allegations contained in a complaint is inapplicable to legal conclusions. Threadbare recitals of the elements of a cause of action, supported by mere conclusory statements, do not suffice. *Id.,* at 555, 127 S.Ct. 1955 (Although for the purposes of a motion to dismiss we must take all of the factual allegations in the complaint as true, we "are not bound to accept as true a legal conclusion couched as a factual allegation" (internal quotation marks omitted)). Rule 8 marks a notable and generous departure from the hyper-technical, code-pleading regime of a prior era, but it does not unlock the doors of discovery for a plaintiff armed with nothing more than conclusions. Second, only a complaint that states a plausible claim for relief survives a motion to dismiss. Determining whether a complaint states a plausible claim for relief will, as the Court of Appeals observed, be a context-specific task that requires the reviewing court to draw on its judicial experience and common sense. But where the well-pleaded facts do not permit the court to infer more than the mere possibility of misconduct, the complaint has alleged-but it has not "show[n]"—"that the pleader is entitled to relief." Fed. Rule Civ. Proc. 8(a)(2).

In keeping with these principles a court considering a motion to dismiss can choose to begin by identifying pleadings that, because they are no more than conclusions, are not entitled to the assumption of truth. While legal conclusions can provide the framework of a complaint, they must be supported by factual allegations. When there are well-pleaded factual allegations, a court should assume their veracity and then determine whether they plausibly give rise to an entitlement to relief. * * * *

B

Under *Twombly's* construction of Rule 8, we conclude that respondent's complaint has not "nudged [his] claims" of invidious discrimination "across the line from conceivable to plausible."

We begin our analysis by identifying the allegations in the complaint that are not entitled to the assumption of truth. Respondent pleads that petitioners "knew of, condoned, and willfully and maliciously agreed to subject [him]" to harsh conditions of confinement "as a matter of policy, solely on account of [his] religion, race, and/or national origin and for no legitimate penological interest." The complaint alleges that Ashcroft was the "principal architect" of this invidious policy, and that Mueller was "instrumental" in adopting and executing it. These bare assertions, much like the pleading of conspiracy in *Twombly,* amount to nothing more than a "formulaic recitation of the elements" of a constitutional discrimination claim, namely, that petitioners adopted a policy " 'because of,' not merely 'in spite of,' its adverse effects upon an identifiable group." As such, the allegations are conclusory and not entitled to be assumed true. To be clear, we do not reject these bald allegations on the ground that they are unrealistic or nonsensical. We do not so characterize them any more than the Court in *Twombly* rejected the plaintiffs' express allegation of a

SECTION D

THE FORMAL SUFFICIENCY OF THE COMPLAINT:
HOW SPECIFIC MUST A PLEADING BE?

487

" 'contract, combination or conspiracy to prevent competitive entry,' "because it thought that claim too chimerical to be maintained. It is the conclusory nature of respondent's allegations, rather than their extravagantly fanciful nature, that disentitles them to the presumption of truth.

We next consider the factual allegations in respondent's complaint to determine if they plausibly suggest an entitlement to relief. The complaint alleges that "the [FBI], under the direction of Defendant MUELLER, arrested and detained thousands of Arab Muslim men . . . as part of its investigation of the events of September 11." It further claims that "[t]he policy of holding post-September-11th detainees in highly restrictive conditions of confinement until they were 'cleared' by the FBI was approved by Defendants ASHCROFT and MUELLER in discussions in the weeks after September 11, 2001." Taken as true, these allegations are consistent with petitioners' purposefully designating detainees "of high interest" because of their race, religion, or national origin. But given more likely explanations, they do not plausibly establish this purpose.

The September 11 attacks were perpetrated by 19 Arab Muslim hijackers who counted themselves members in good standing of al Qaeda, an Islamic fundamentalist group. Al Qaeda was headed by another Arab Muslim-Osama bin Laden-and composed in large part of his Arab Muslim disciples. It should come as no surprise that a legitimate policy directing law enforcement to arrest and detain individuals because of their suspected link to the attacks would produce a disparate, incidental impact on Arab Muslims, even though the purpose of the policy was to target neither Arabs nor Muslims. On the facts respondent alleges the arrests Mueller oversaw were likely lawful and justified by his nondiscriminatory intent to detain aliens who were illegally present in the United States and who had potential connections to those who committed terrorist acts. As between that "obvious alternative explanation" for the arrests and the purposeful, invidious discrimination respondent asks us to infer, discrimination is not a plausible conclusion.

But even if the complaint's well-pleaded facts give rise to a plausible inference that respondent's arrest was the result of unconstitutional discrimination, that inference alone would not entitle respondent to relief. It is important to recall that respondent's complaint challenges neither the constitutionality of his arrest nor his initial detention in the MDC. Respondent's constitutional claims against petitioners rest solely on their ostensible "policy of holding post-September-11th detainees" in the ADMAX SHU once they were categorized as "of high interest." To prevail on that theory, the complaint must contain facts plausibly showing that petitioners purposefully adopted a policy of classifying post-September-11 detainees as "of high interest" because of their race, religion, or national origin.

This the complaint fails to do. Though respondent alleges that various other defendants, who are not before us, may have labeled him a person of "of high interest" for impermissible reasons, his only factual allegation against petitioners accuses them of adopting a policy approving "restrictive conditions of confinement" for post-September-11 detainees until they were " 'cleared' by the FBI." *Ibid.* Accepting the truth of that allegation, the complaint does not show, or even intimate, that petitioners purposefully housed detainees in the ADMAX SHU due to their race, religion, or national origin. All it plausibly suggests is that the Nation's top law enforcement officers, in the aftermath of a devastating terrorist attack, sought to keep suspected terrorists in the most secure conditions available until the suspects could be cleared of terrorist activity. Respondent does not argue, nor can he, that such a motive would violate petitioners' constitutional obligations. He would need to allege more by way of factual content to "nudg[e]" his claim of purposeful discrimination "across the line from conceivable to plausible." *Twombly,* 550 U.S., at 570, 127 S.Ct. 1955.

* * * *

It is important to note, however, that we express no opinion concerning the sufficiency of respondent's complaint against the defendants who are not before us. Respondent's account of his prison ordeal alleges serious official misconduct that we need not address here. Our decision is limited to the determination that respondent's complaint does not entitle him to relief from petitioners.

C

* * *

1

Respondent first says that our decision in *Twombly* should be limited to pleadings made in the context of an antitrust dispute. This argument is not supported by *Twombly* and is incompatible with the Federal Rules of Civil Procedure. Though *Twombly* determined the sufficiency of a complaint sounding in antitrust, the decision was based on our interpretation and application of Rule 8. That Rule in turn governs the pleading standard "in all civil actions and proceedings in the United States district courts." Fed. Rule Civ. Proc. 1. Our decision in *Twombly* expounded the pleading standard for "all civil actions," and it applies to antitrust and discrimination suits alike.

2

Respondent next implies that our construction of Rule 8 should be tempered where, as here, the Court of Appeals has "instructed the district court to cabin discovery[.]" * * * We have held, however, that the question presented by a motion to dismiss a complaint for insufficient pleadings does not turn on the controls placed upon the discovery process. *Twombly, supra,* at 559 ("It is no answer to say that a claim just shy of a plausible entitlement to relief can, if groundless, be weeded out early in the discovery process through careful case management given the common lament that the success of judicial supervision in checking discovery abuse has been on the modest side" (internal quotation marks and citation omitted)).

* * * *

The judgment of the Court of Appeals is reversed, and the case is remanded for further proceedings consistent with this opinion.

It is so ordered.

SECTION D

THE FORMAL SUFFICIENCY OF THE COMPLAINT:
HOW SPECIFIC MUST A PLEADING BE?

489

■ JUSTICE SOUTER, with whom JUSTICE STEVENS, JUSTICE GINSBURG, and JUSTICE BREYER join, dissenting.

* * * I respectfully dissent from both the rejection of supervisory liability as a cognizable claim in the face of petitioners' concession, and from the holding that the complaint fails to satisfy Rule 8(a)(2) of the Federal Rules of Civil Procedure.

I

A

Respondent Iqbal was arrested in November 2001 on charges of conspiracy to defraud the United States and fraud in relation to identification documents, and was placed in pretrial detention at the Metropolitan Detention Center in Brooklyn, New York. He alleges that FBI officials carried out a discriminatory policy by designating him as a person " 'of high interest' " in the investigation of the September 11 attacks solely because of his race, religion, or national origin. Owing to this designation he was placed in the detention center's Administrative Maximum Special Housing Unit for over six months while awaiting the fraud trial. As I will mention more fully below, Iqbal contends that Ashcroft and Mueller were at the very least aware of the discriminatory detention policy and condoned it (and perhaps even took part in devising it), thereby violating his First and Fifth Amendment rights.

Iqbal claims that on the day he was transferred to the special unit, prison guards, without provocation, "picked him up and threw him against the wall, kicked him in the stomach, punched him in the face, and dragged him across the room." He says that after being attacked a second time he sought medical attention but was denied care for two weeks. According to Iqbal's complaint, prison staff in the special unit subjected him to unjustified strip and body cavity searches, verbally berated him as a " 'terrorist' " and " 'Muslim killer,' " refused to give him adequate food, and intentionally turned on air conditioning during the winter and heating during the summer. He claims that prison staff interfered with his attempts to pray and engage in religious study and with his access to counsel.

* * *

* * * Ashcroft and Mueller * * * conceded in their petition for certiorari [and in their brief on the merits] that they would be liable if they had "actual knowledge" of discrimination by their subordinates and exhibited " 'deliberate indifference' " to that discrimination. * * * *

II

Given petitioners' concession, the complaint satisfies Rule 8(a)(2). Ashcroft and Mueller admit they are liable for their subordinates' conduct if they "had actual knowledge of the assertedly discriminatory nature of the classification of suspects as being 'of high interest' and they were deliberately indifferent to that discrimination." Iqbal alleges that after the September 11 attacks the Federal Bureau of Investigation (FBI) "arrested and detained thousands of Arab Muslim men," that many of these men were designated by high-ranking FBI officials as being " 'of high interest,' " and that in many cases, including Iqbal's, this designation was made "because of the race, religion, and national origin of the detainees, and not because of any evidence of the detainees' involvement in supporting terrorist activity." The complaint further alleges that Ashcroft was the "principal architect of the policies and practices challenged," and that Mueller "was instrumental in the adoption, promulgation, and implementation of the policies and practices challenged." According to the complaint, Ashcroft and Mueller "knew of, condoned, and willfully and maliciously agreed to subject [Iqbal] to these conditions of confinement as a matter of policy, solely on account of [his] religion, race, and/or national origin and for no legitimate penological interest." The complaint thus alleges, at a bare minimum, that Ashcroft and Mueller knew of and condoned the discriminatory policy their subordinates carried out. Actually, the complaint goes further in alleging that Ashcroft and Muller affirmatively acted to create the discriminatory detention policy. If these factual allegations are true, Ashcroft and Mueller were, at the very least, aware of the discriminatory policy being implemented and deliberately indifferent to it.

Ashcroft and Mueller argue that these allegations fail to satisfy the "plausibility standard" of *Twombly*. They contend that Iqbal's claims are implausible because such high-ranking officials "tend not to be personally involved in the specific actions of lower-level officers down the bureaucratic chain of command." But this response bespeaks a fundamental misunderstanding of the enquiry that *Twombly* demands. *Twombly* does not require a court at the motion-to-dismiss stage to consider whether the factual allegations are probably true. We made it clear, on the contrary, that a court must take the allegations as true, no matter how skeptical the court may be. See *Twombly,* 550 U.S., at 555 (a court must proceed "on the assumption that all the allegations in the complaint are true (even if doubtful in fact). The sole exception to this rule lies with allegations that are sufficiently fantastic to defy reality as we know it: claims about little green men, or the plaintiff's recent trip to Pluto, or experiences in time travel. That is not what we have here.

[Unlike in *Twombly,*] the allegations in the complaint are neither confined to naked legal conclusions nor consistent with legal conduct. The complaint alleges that FBI officials discriminated against Iqbal solely on account of his race, religion, and national origin, and it alleges the knowledge and deliberate indifference that, by Ashcroft and Mueller's own admission, are sufficient to make them liable for the illegal action. Iqbal's complaint therefore contains "enough facts to state a claim to relief that is plausible on its face."

I do not understand the majority to disagree with this understanding of "plausibility" under *Twombly*. Rather, the majority discards the allegations discussed above with regard to Ashcroft and Mueller as conclusory, and is left considering only two statements in the complaint: that "the [FBI], under the direction of Defendant MUELLER, arrested and detained thousands of Arab Muslim men . . . as part of its investigation of the events of September 11," and that "[t]he policy of holding post-September-11th detainees in highly restrictive conditions of confinement until they were 'cleared' by the FBI was approved by Defendants ASHCROFT and MUELLER in discussions in the weeks after September 11, 2001." I think the majority is right in saying that these allegations suggest only that Ashcroft and Mueller "sought to keep suspected terrorists in the most secure conditions available until the suspects could be cleared of terrorist activity," and that this produced "a

SECTION D

THE FORMAL SUFFICIENCY OF THE COMPLAINT:
HOW SPECIFIC MUST A PLEADING BE?

491

disparate, incidental impact on Arab Muslims." And I agree that the two allegations selected by the majority, standing alone, do not state a plausible entitlement to relief for unconstitutional discrimination.

But these allegations do not stand alone as the only significant, nonconclusory statements in the complaint, for the complaint contains many allegations linking Ashcroft and Mueller to the discriminatory practices of their subordinates. See Complaint ¶ 10 (Ashcroft was the "principal architect" of the discriminatory policy); *id.,* ¶ 11 (Mueller was "instrumental" in adopting and executing the discriminatory policy); *id.,* ¶ 96 (Ashcroft and Mueller "knew of, condoned, and willfully and maliciously agreed to subject" Iqbal to harsh conditions "as a matter of policy, solely on account of [his] religion, race, and/or national origin and for no legitimate penological interest").

The majority says that these are "bare assertions" that, "much like the pleading of conspiracy in *Twombly,* amount to nothing more than a 'formulaic recitation of the elements' of a constitutional discrimination claim" and therefore are "not entitled to be assumed true." The fallacy of the majority's position, however, lies in looking at the relevant assertions in isolation. The complaint contains specific allegations that, in the aftermath of the September 11 attacks, the Chief of the FBI's International Terrorism Operations Section and the Assistant Special Agent in Charge for the FBI's New York Field Office implemented a policy that discriminated against Arab Muslim men, including Iqbal, solely on account of their race, religion, or national origin. Viewed in light of these subsidiary allegations, the allegations singled out by the majority as "conclusory" are no such thing. Iqbal's claim is not that Ashcroft and Mueller "knew of, condoned, and willfully and maliciously agreed to subject" him to a discriminatory practice that is left undefined; his allegation is that "they knew of, condoned, and willfully and maliciously agreed to subject" him to a particular, discrete, discriminatory policy detailed in the complaint. Iqbal does not say merely that Ashcroft was the architect of some amorphous discrimination, or that Mueller was instrumental in an ill-defined constitutional violation; he alleges that they helped to create the discriminatory policy he has described. Taking the complaint as a whole, it gives Ashcroft and Mueller " 'fair notice of what the . . . claim is and the grounds upon which it rests.' " * * *

That aside, the majority's holding that the statements it selects are conclusory cannot be squared with its treatment of certain other allegations in the complaint as nonconclusory. For example, the majority takes as true the statement that "[t]he policy of holding post-September-11th detainees in highly restrictive conditions of confinement until they were 'cleared' by the FBI was approved by Defendants ASHCROFT and MUELLER in discussions in the weeks after September 11, 2001." This statement makes two points: (1) after September 11, the FBI held certain detainees in highly restrictive conditions, and (2) Ashcroft and Mueller discussed and approved these conditions. If, as the majority says, these allegations are not conclusory, then I cannot see why the majority deems it merely conclusory when Iqbal alleges that (1) after September 11, the FBI designated Arab Muslim detainees as being of " 'high interest' " "because of the race, religion, and national origin of the detainees, and not because of any evidence of the detainees' involvement in supporting terrorist activity," Complaint ¶¶ 48–50, and (2) Ashcroft and Mueller "knew of, condoned, and willfully and maliciously agreed" to that discrimination, *id.,* ¶ 96. By my lights, there is no principled basis for the majority's disregard of the allegations linking Ashcroft and Mueller to their subordinates' discrimination.

I respectfully dissent.

Notes and Questions

1. **The legal theory of *Iqbal*'s complaint.** The majority says that the only legally available claim against Ashcroft and Mueller is for their own intentional discrimination—that is, for decisions that they themselves made or actions that they took "because of" the race, religion or national origin of the plaintiffs. Accordingly, the majority holds that the plaintiff was required to adequately plead that Ashcroft and Mueller "purposefully adopted a policy of classifying post-September-11 detainees as 'of high interest' because of their race, religion, or national origin." The dissent, relying on an explicit concession by Ashcroft and Mueller, assumes without deciding that liability is also permitted on the basis that defendants, as supervisors, "had actual knowledge of the assertedly discriminatory nature of the classification of suspects as being 'of high interest' and they were deliberately indifferent to that discrimination." Does this difference in applicable legal theory explain the disagreement between the majority and the dissent concerning the adequacy of the complaint?

2. **Does the complaint fail to provide fair notice?** If you were a lawyer for Ashcroft or Mueller, could you figure out what events the plaintiffs are complaining about and what Ashcroft and Mueller's roles in those events allegedly were? Is there any doubt about what policy is being challenged? Is there any doubt about the time period in which it was adopted? Does the complaint describe any instances of how the policy was administered? Do the allegations describe the alleged illegal conduct of Ashcroft and Mueller in sufficient detail to allow them to prepare their defense? How do the allegations compare, in terms of specificity, with those approved in *Swierkiewicz* and those disapproved in *Twombly*?

3. **When is an allegation conclusory?** A key difference between the majority and dissent is how they handle the allegations (a) that defendants "knew of, condoned, and willfully and maliciously agreed to subject [him]" to harsh conditions of confinement "as a matter of policy, solely on account of [his] religion, race, and/or national origin and for no legitimate penological interest," (b) that Ashcroft was the "principal architect of the policies and practices challenged," and (c) that Mueller "was instrumental in the adoption, promulgation, and implementation of the policies and practices challenged."

As noted, supra p. 462, the drafters of the federal Rules sought to abolish the distinction in code pleading between properly pleaded facts and improperly pleaded legal conclusions. The drafters reasoned that there was no clear dividing line conceptually between facts and legal conclusions, so the emphasis on that distinction provoked litigation and resulted in inconsistent and often erroneous results. If the complaint provided adequate notice, there would be no reason to treat legal conclusions as inadequate—discovery would expose their flaws. Was the majority's dismissal of the above allegations as "conclusory" based on any concern that those allegations did not, in context, provide sufficient notice of the claim?

Another possible reason for disregarding "conclusions" is that they add nothing to what is pleaded elsewhere in the complaint. But don't the allegations that Ashcroft was "principal architect" and that Mueller was "instrumental in the adoption, promulgation, and implementation" of the policy go beyond the simple statement of the elements of the claim and convey additional information?

Twombly seems to have added an additional concern: if a legal conclusion were sufficient, standing alone, to satisfy the requirements of Rule 8(a), then too many baseless suits might reach discovery. If the concern that justifies ignoring "conclusory" language is that more detail is required in order to determine whether the allegations are worth crediting, then isn't the majority disingenuous in suggesting that it is not in fact dismissing those allegations because they are unworthy of being credited? How fair is it to require greater detail from a plaintiff in Iqbal's position who has not had any discovery?

After *Iqbal* how would you distinguish language that is impermissibly conclusory (whether or not it parrots a legal rule) from language that is sufficiently factual? Does the majority explain the distinction between the two in a way that trial judges in other cases can discern and apply?

4. Testing plausibility. The majority and dissent appear to agree that if the allegations that the majority classifies as "conclusory" are ignored then the remaining "factual" allegations pleaded in the complaint do not state a plausible claim for relief. Do you agree? Is the dissent correct that the allegations of the complaint, if read to include the portions the majority dismisses as "conclusory," do state a plausible claim?

The majority says that "determining whether a complaint states a plausible claim for relief will * * * be a context-specific task that requires the reviewing court to draw on its judicial experience and common sense." Does context-specificity mean that the lower courts will have to develop "plausibility" standards for each area of substantive law? How reliable are "judicial experience and common sense" as a guide to the likelihood that plaintiff, if allowed discovery, will find sufficient information supporting her claim to prevail at trial? Consider a judge in his first day on the job. Does the majority provide a sufficient analysis of plausibility to allow lower court judges to make such determinations consistently and reliably?

5. The benefits and costs of screening. *Twombly* and *Iqbal* together create the potential for dismissal at the pleading stage of many claims that cannot be pleaded in terms that are both non-conclusory and plausible. Some of those claims will be ones that would ultimately fail after discovery, either at summary judgment or at a trial. But what is the potential for this stronger screening rule to burden claims that would be winners after discovery, either by barring them altogether or by increasing litigation costs? Did the *Twombly* or *Iqbal* courts give sufficient consideration to those potential costs? Recall the statement in *Swierkiewicz* that "a requirement of greater specificity" for particular claims "must be obtained" by formal amendment, rather than judicial interpretation, of the federal Rules. Would the formal rulemaking process have been a better way to judge the benefits and costs of the Court's procedural innovation?

6. The role of the Supreme Court in interpreting federal Rules. As a matter of separation of powers, was it appropriate for the Court to change the interpretation of Rule 8 in such a significant way? Professors Burbank and Farhang suggest not: "The Court's recent pleading decisions were certainly bold. . . . *Twombly*, and *Iqbal* are a few recent examples of the Court using its Article III judicial power to achieve results that would have been very difficult or impossible to achieve through the exercise of delegated legislative lawmaking power under the Enabling Act." Burbank & Farhang, Litigation Reform: An Institutional Approach, 162 U. Pa. L. Rev. 1543 (2014); see also Marcus, Institutions and an Interpretive Methodology for the Federal Rules of Civil Procedure, 2011 Utah L. Rev. 927.

Professor Redish disagrees. He argues that,

> [T]he language of Rule 8(a) is no way inconsistent with a plausibility standard. . . . Although the drafters of the Federal Rules in most cases sought to break away from the unduly high barriers to suit set by the code pleading standard for required factual detail, it is difficult to believe that they intended to allow the pleading of vague and conclusory allegations to enable the plaintiff to invoke the costly and burdensome discovery process absent some showing that the case was more than fanciful.

Redish, Pleading, Discovery, and the Federal Rules: Exploring the Foundations of Modern Procedure, 64 Fla. L. Rev. 845 (2012). Do you think the Court acted appropriately in reinterpreting the meaning of Rule 8(a) in *Twombly* and *Iqbal*?

7. *Iqbal* and the use of trans-substantive rules. One of the significant developments of modern procedural reform has been the advent of so-called "trans-substantive" procedural rules, that is, procedural rules that apply to nearly all civil cases, regardless of the substantive law to be applied. With limited exceptions, such as Rule 9(b)'s requirement of pleading with particularity in cases of fraud or mistake, the federal Rules apply to all cases in federal court. Trans-substantivity was a central component of reformers' goal of simplifying procedure and shedding the technicality of common law pleading. Hence the requirement of only a "short and plain statement" in federal Rule 8(a). Unless the rulemakers or the Congress legislated otherwise, this standard was to apply in all civil cases in federal court. Recall the Court's statement in *Swierkiewicz* that, "A requirement of greater specificity for particular claims is a result that 'must be obtained by the process of amending the Federal Rules, and not by judicial interpretation." Supra, p. 468.

After *Twombly*, it was thought that the Supreme Court might be venturing down the path of creating heightened pleading burdens for different kinds of cases, particularly cases in which the costs of discovery were thought to be high, as in antitrust cases. *Iqbal* made clear that this was not the case. As Justice Kennedy explains, "Our decision in *Twombly* expounded the pleading standard for 'all civil actions,' and it applies to antitrust and discrimination suits alike."

Is the Court's commitment to trans-substantivity misplaced? Should we more commonly have different pleading standards for different types of cases? If so, in what kinds of claims should pleading standards be heightened? For discussion of this issue, see Bone, *Twombly*, Pleading Rules, and the Regulation of Court Access, 94 Iowa L. Rev. 873 (2009); Effron, The

SECTION D

THE FORMAL SUFFICIENCY OF THE COMPLAINT:
HOW SPECIFIC MUST A PLEADING BE?

495

Plaintiff Neutrality Principle: Pleading Complex Litigation in the Era of *Twombly* and *Iqbal*, 51 Wm. & Mary L. Rev. 1997 (2010).

And, despite the Court's statement that *Iqbal* provides the pleading standard for all civil cases in federal court, does its instruction that judges draw on their "judicial experience and common sense" invite individual judges to apply different standards to different kinds of cases? See Spencer, Pleading and Access to Civil Justice: A Response to *Twiqbal* Apologists, 60 U.C.L.A. L. Rev. 1710 (2013); Burbank, Pleading and the Dilemma of "General Rules," 2009 Wisc. L. Rev. 535.

8. Does *Iqbal* go further than *Twombly*? In *Iqbal*, Justice Kennedy explains that the decision extends the *Twombly* plausibility standard to all federal civil cases. But does *Iqbal* raise pleading standards even higher than *Twombly*? Consider *Iqbal*'s treatment of "legal conclusions." Is it consistent with Justice Souter's majority opinion in *Twombly*? Note that Justice Souter sides with the dissenters in *Iqbal*. Are you persuaded by his explanation why?

9. Reactions to *Twombly* and *Iqbal*. In the aftermath of *Iqbal* legislation was introduced in both houses of Congress seeking to overturn the result in *Twombly* and *Iqbal* and restore a full notice pleading regime. For example, House Bill 4115, the Open Access to Courts Act of 2009, would have prohibited dismissal of a complaint "unless it appears beyond doubt that the plaintiff can prove no set of facts in support of the claim which would entitle the plaintiff to relief." The bill further provided that "[a] court shall not dismiss a complaint * * * on the basis of a determination by the judge that the factual contents of the complaint do not show the plaintiff's claim to be plausible or are insufficient to warrant a reasonable inference that the defendant is liable for the misconduct alleged." Hearings were held on the bill, but it never made it out of Committee.

10. The impact of *Twombly* and *Iqbal*. Since the *Twombly* and *Iqbal* decisions, professional researchers and scholars have spent much energy on assessing their impact. Typical of the reaction among scholars is the statement by Professors Clermont and Yeazell that "[b]y inventing a new and foggy test for the threshold stage of every lawsuit, [the Supreme Court has] destabilized the entire system of civil litigation." Clermont & Yeazell, Inventing Tests, Destabilizing Systems, 95 Iowa L. Rev. 821 (2010). Their observation is undoubtedly correct, but the question observers have hoped to answer since *Twombly* and *Iqbal* is whether the decisions have made a real difference in federal civil litigation.

Researchers at the Federal Judicial Center (FJC) in the Administrative Office of the U.S. Courts have amassed an enormous amount of data and continue to examine the effects of *Iqbal*. Their initial study concluded that "there was no increase from 2006 to 2010 in the rate at which a grant of a motion to dismiss terminated the case." Joe Cecil et al., Federal Judicial Center, Motions to Dismiss for Failure to State a Claim After *Iqbal* (2011). Although the study found that the rate of filing of motions to dismiss increased, the rate at which those motions were granted had not significantly increased (aside from an increase in cases challenging financial instruments, which had increased significantly in the wake of the mortgage crisis in the mid-2000s). Id. at 23. The FJC study acknowledged its limitations and was an admittedly early attempt to study the problem, but it came in for significant scholarly criticism of both its methods and conclusions. See

Hoffman, *Twombly* and *Iqbal*'s Measure: An Assessment of the Federal Judicial Center's Study of Motions to Dismiss, 6 Fed. Cts. L. Rev. 1 (2011).

Professor Gelbach has provided one of the most trenchant critiques. Gelbach argues that it is misleading to assess the impact of *Twombly* and *Iqbal* by looking exclusively at whether the rate at which motions to dismiss are granted has gone up. Such an analysis ignores potential effects of *Twombly* and *Iqbal* that are not reflected in the grant rate. For instance, raised pleading standards may (1) reduce the number of cases actually brought by plaintiffs, (2) increase the likelihood that defendants will file a motion to dismiss, which may at best be successful and at least very costly to respond to, and (3) may reduce the likelihood that defendants will settle. As a result, Professor Gelbach concludes that the FJC Study seriously understates the number of cases that are "negatively affected" by *Twombly* and *Iqbal*. Using a sophisticated statistical analysis, he concludes that, "For employment discrimination and civil rights cases, switching from *Conley* to *Twombly/Iqbal* negatively affected plaintiffs in at least 15.4% and at least 18.4%, respectively, of the cases that faced [motions to dismiss] in the *Iqbal* period." Gelbach, Locking the Doors to Discovery? Assessing the Effects of *Twombly* and *Iqbal* on Access to Discovery, 121 Yale L.J. 2270 (2012).

In another illuminating study, Professor Dodson has examined the reasoning courts have given for granting motions to dismiss before and after *Twombly*. He reports:

> These data show that courts are using factual insufficiency more often as a justification for dismissals than before *Twombly*. The increases in the proportion of factual-insufficiency dismissals is fairly stark, highly significant, and in double digits for most categories [of cases]. The fairly uncontroversial conclusion is that courts are taking *Twombly* and *Iqbal* to heart.

Dodson, New Pleading in the 21st Century 97 (2013).

Massive resources continue to be devoted to the empirical puzzle of the impact of *Twombly* and *Iqbal*. It remains to be seen whether this analysis will reveal a definitive answer. A useful and penetrating analysis of empirical pleading scholarship, and empirical scholarship in civil procedure generally, can be found in Engstrom, The *Twiqbal* Puzzle and Empirical Study of Civil Procedure, 65 Stan. L. Rev. 1203 (2013).

11. Further reading. *Twombly* and *Iqbal* have prompted a deluge of scholarship. In addition to the articles noted above, other illuminating pieces include: Miller, Simplified Pleading, Meaningful Days in Court, and Trials on the Merits: Reflections on the Deformation of Federal Procedure, 88 N.Y.U. L. Rev. 439 (2012); Hartnett, Taming *Twombly*, Even After *Iqbal*, 158 U. Pa. L. Rev. 473 (2010); Spencer, Understanding Pleading Doctrine, 108 Mich. L. Rev. 1 (2009); Steinman, The Pleading Problem, 62 Stan. L. Rev. 1293 (2010).

SECTION D

THE FORMAL SUFFICIENCY OF THE COMPLAINT:
HOW SPECIFIC MUST A PLEADING BE?

497

2. HEIGHTENED PLEADING REQUIREMENTS AND DISFAVORED CLAIMS

INTRODUCTORY NOTE ON HEIGHTENED PLEADING REQUIREMENTS

1. Rule 8(a) is the usual pleading standard. In general, the pleading standard in the federal courts is provided by Rule 8(a), unless another federal Rule or statute provides otherwise. In Leatherman v. Tarrant County Narcotics Intelligence and Coordination Unit, 507 U.S. 163, 113 S.Ct. 1160, 122 L.Ed.2d 517 (1993), the Supreme Court reviewed a lower court opinion that had imposed a "heightened" pleading standard for federal civil rights actions alleging municipal liability under 42 U.S.C. § 1983. The Supreme Court reversed. The Court held that there is no "heightened pleading standard" for a complaint in a § 1983 civil rights case brought against a municipality. The Court based its holding on Rule 8(a), which requires only a "short and plain statement of the claim." It compared Rule 8(a) to Rule 9(b), which requires particularized pleading when "fraud" or "mistake" are alleged. The Court reasoned that the fact that the only express exceptions to the notice pleading rules spelled out in the rules were the particularity requirements for fraud and mistake in Rule 9 indicated that no other exceptions were contemplated or permitted. The Court stated:

> Perhaps if Rules 8 and 9 were rewritten today, claims against municipalities under § 1983 might be subjected to the added specificity requirement of Rule 9(b). But that is a result which must be obtained by the process of amending the Federal Rules, and not by judicial interpretation. In the absence of such an amendment, federal courts and litigants must rely on summary judgment and control of discovery to weed out unmeritorious claims sooner rather than later.

507 U.S. at 168–69. The Court unanimously reaffirmed this holding in *Swierkiewicz v. Sorema, N.A.*, discussed supra at p. 465.

2. Pleading fraud and mistake. The federal Rules originally contemplated requiring more specific pleading in two limited classes of cases: those involving averments of fraud or mistake. Fed. R. Civ. P. 9(b). The requirement of specificity in pleading fraud is a carry-over from the common law and code systems of pleading. Allegations of fraud appear to have been disfavored, because of their potential for damage to reputation and their consequent tendency to increase the contentiousness of any suit in which they were made. The aim of the rule is "prevent plaintiffs from stating a claim just by adding the word 'fraudulently' to a description of a financial transaction." James, Hazard & Leubsdorf, Civil Procedure § 2.19, at 222 (5th ed. 2001). To avoid that result, plaintiff is required to plead the content of the statement claimed to be false, either verbatim or in substance, and the falsity of the statement. In addition, the complaint must plead the circumstances in sufficient detail to make clear that the statement was one of material fact "rather than the kind of opinion or prophecy on which people are not entitled to rely." Id. at 222–23. See Richman et al., The Pleading of Fraud: Rhymes Without Reason, 60 S. Cal. L. Rev. 959 (1987).

3. Other claims requiring more specific pleading. Several other Rules also require particularized pleading. Under Rule 9(g), claims for "special damage" must be "specifically stated." Under Rule 23.1, a plaintiff in a shareholder derivative suit must "state with particularity: (A) any effort by the plaintiff to obtain the desired action from the directors or comparable authority and, if necessary, from the shareholders or members; and (B) the reasons for not obtaining the action or not making the effort."

4.   The effect of a failure to plead with particularity. The requirement of particularity under Rule 9(b) applies to all allegations of fraud. In cases where fraud is an essential element of the claim, failure to plead fraud with specificity is equivalent to not having pleaded the element of fraud at all. In effect, the motion to dismiss a claim "grounded in fraud under Rule 9(b) for failure to plead with particularity is the functional equivalent of a motion to dismiss under Rule 12(b)(6) for failure to state a claim." Vess v. Ciba-Geigy Corp., 317 F.3d 1097, 1107 (9th Cir. 2003). In other cases, however, the plaintiff may choose to "dress up" a claim that does not require proof of fraud by adding averments of fraudulent conduct. Because such averments, though inessential to the claim, nonetheless give rise to the possibility of reputational damage to the defendant, they are still required to be pleaded with particularity. But the failure to plead them is not necessarily fatal to the claim: instead, the insufficiently particular allegations of fraud are stripped from the claim, which is then evaluated for sufficiency without those allegations. Id.

5.   Policies favoring greater specificity. A requirement that an element of a claim or defense be pleaded with greater specificity or particularity increases the burden of pleading with respect to that element. In principle, then, an increase in specificity or particularity should be justified on the basis of the same considerations that underlay the assignment of the burden to the pleader in the first instance. Recall the discussion in the Note on Allocating the Burden of Pleading, supra p. 458. In Professor Cleary's formulation, those considerations were fairness (or access to evidence), probability, and policy. In recent years, courts and legislatures have sought to impose additional requirements of specificity for several different types of claims. As you read the following materials, ask yourself how well these additional pleading burdens are justified by the considerations that Professor Cleary identifies as central.

Tellabs, Inc. v. Makor Issues & Rights, Ltd.

Supreme Court of the United States, 2007.
551 U.S. 308, 127 S.Ct. 2499, 168 L.Ed.2d 179.

■ JUSTICE GINSBURG delivered the opinion of the Court.

This Court has long recognized that meritorious private actions to enforce federal antifraud securities laws are an essential supplement to criminal prosecutions and civil enforcement actions brought, respectively, by the Department of Justice and the Securities and Exchange Commission (SEC). Private securities fraud actions, however, if not adequately contained, can be employed abusively to impose substantial costs on companies and individuals whose conduct conforms to the law. As a check against abusive litigation by private parties, Congress enacted the Private Securities Litigation Reform Act of 1995 (PSLRA), 109 Stat. 737.

SECTION D

THE FORMAL SUFFICIENCY OF THE COMPLAINT:
HOW SPECIFIC MUST A PLEADING BE?

499

Exacting pleading requirements are among the control measures Congress included in the PSLRA. The Act requires plaintiffs to state with particularity both the facts constituting the alleged violation, and the facts evidencing scienter, *i.e.*, the defendant's intention "to deceive, manipulate, or defraud." This case concerns the latter requirement. As set out in § 21D(b)(2) of the PSLRA, plaintiffs must "state with particularity facts giving rise to a strong inference that the defendant acted with the required state of mind." 15 U.S.C. § 78u–4(b)(2).

Congress left the key term "strong inference" undefined, and Courts of Appeals have divided on its meaning. In the case before us, the Court of Appeals for the Seventh Circuit held that the "strong inference" standard would be met if the complaint "allege[d] facts from which, if true, a reasonable person could infer that the defendant acted with the required intent." That formulation, we conclude, does not capture the stricter demand Congress sought to convey in § 21D(b)(2). It does not suffice that a reasonable factfinder plausibly could infer from the complaint's allegations the requisite state of mind. Rather, to determine whether a complaint's scienter allegations can survive threshold inspection for sufficiency, a court governed by § 21D(b)(2) must engage in a comparative evaluation; it must consider, not only inferences urged by the plaintiff, as the Seventh Circuit did, but also competing inferences rationally drawn from the facts alleged. An inference of fraudulent intent may be plausible, yet less cogent than other, nonculpable explanations for the defendant's conduct. To qualify as "strong" within the intendment of § 21D(b)(2), we hold, an inference of scienter must be more than merely plausible or reasonable-it must be cogent and at least as compelling as any opposing inference of nonfraudulent intent.

I

Petitioner Tellabs, Inc., manufactures specialized equipment used in fiber optic networks. During the time period relevant to this case, petitioner Richard Notebaert was Tellabs' chief executive officer and president. Respondents (Shareholders) are persons who purchased Tellabs stock between December 11, 2000, and June 19, 2001. They accuse Tellabs and Notebaert (as well as several other Tellabs executives) of engaging in a scheme to deceive the investing public about the true value of Tellabs' stock.

Beginning on December 11, 2000, the Shareholders allege, Notebaert (and by imputation Tellabs) "falsely reassured public investors, in a series of statements . . . that Tellabs was continuing to enjoy strong demand for its products and earning record revenues," when, in fact, Notebaert knew the opposite was true. From December 2000 until the spring of 2001, the Shareholders claim, Notebaert knowingly misled the public in four ways. First, he made statements indicating that demand for Tellabs' flagship networking device, the TITAN 5500, was continuing to grow, when in fact demand for that product was waning. Second, Notebaert made statements indicating that the TITAN 6500, Tellabs' next-generation networking device, was available for delivery, and that demand for that product was strong and growing, when in truth the product was not ready for delivery and demand was weak. Third, he falsely represented Tellabs' financial results for the fourth quarter of 2000 (and, in connection with those results, condoned the practice of "channel stuffing," under which Tellabs flooded its customers with unwanted products). Fourth, Notebaert made a series of overstated revenue projections, when demand for the TITAN 5500 was drying up and production of the TITAN 6500 was behind schedule. Based on Notebaert's sunny assessments, the Shareholders contend, market analysts recommended that investors buy Tellabs' stock.

The first public glimmer that business was not so healthy came in March 2001 when Tellabs modestly reduced its first quarter sales projections. In the next months, Tellabs made progressively more cautious statements about its projected sales. On June 19, 2001, the last day of the class period, Tellabs disclosed that demand for the TITAN 5500 had significantly dropped. Simultaneously, the company substantially lowered its revenue projections for the second quarter of 2001. The next day, the price of Tellabs stock, which had reached a high of $67 during the period, plunged to a low of $15.87.

On December 3, 2002, the Shareholders filed a class action in the District Court for the Northern District of Illinois. Their complaint stated, *inter alia,* that Tellabs and Notebaert had engaged in securities fraud in violation of § 10(b) of the Securities Exchange Act of 1934, 15 U.S.C. § 78j(b), and SEC Rule 10b–5, 17 CFR § 240.10b–5 (2006), also that Notebaert was a "controlling person" under § 20(a) of the 1934 Act, 15 U.S.C. § 78t(a), and therefore derivatively liable for the company's fraudulent acts. Tellabs moved to dismiss the complaint on the ground that the Shareholders had failed to plead their case with the particularity the PSLRA requires. The District Court agreed, and therefore dismissed the complaint without prejudice.

The Shareholders then amended their complaint, adding references to 27 confidential sources and making further, more specific, allegations concerning Notebaert's mental state. The District Court again dismissed, this time with prejudice. The Shareholders had sufficiently pleaded that Notebaert's statements were misleading, the court determined, but they had insufficiently alleged that he acted with scienter.

The Court of Appeals for the Seventh Circuit reversed in relevant part. * * *

We granted certiorari to resolve the disagreement among the Circuits on whether, and to what extent, a court must consider competing inferences in determining whether a securities fraud complaint gives rise to a "strong inference" of scienter.

II

Section 10(b) of the Securities Exchange Act of 1934 forbids the "use or employ, in connection with the purchase or sale of any security . . . , [of] any manipulative or deceptive device or contrivance in contravention of such rules and regulations as the [SEC] may prescribe as necessary or appropriate in the public interest or for the protection of investors." 15 U.S.C. § 78j(b). SEC Rule 10b–5 implements § 10(b) by declaring it unlawful:

"(a) To employ any device, scheme, or artifice to defraud,

"(b) To make any untrue statement of a material fact or to omit to state a material fact necessary in order to make the statements made . . . not misleading, or

SECTION D

THE FORMAL SUFFICIENCY OF THE COMPLAINT:
HOW SPECIFIC MUST A PLEADING BE?

501

"(c) To engage in any act, practice, or course of business which operates or would operate as a fraud or deceit upon any person, in connection with the purchase or sale of any security." 17 CFR § 240.10b–5.

Section 10(b), this Court has implied from the statute's text and purpose, affords a right of action to purchasers or sellers of securities injured by its violation. To establish liability under § 10(b) and Rule 10b–5, a private plaintiff must prove that the defendant acted with scienter, "a mental state embracing intent to deceive, manipulate, or defraud."

In an ordinary civil action, the Federal Rules of Civil Procedure require only "a short and plain statement of the claim showing that the pleader is entitled to relief." Fed. Rule Civ. Proc. 8(a)(2). Although the rule encourages brevity, the complaint must say enough to give the defendant "fair notice of what the plaintiff's claim is and the grounds upon which it rests." Prior to the enactment of the PSLRA, the sufficiency of a complaint for securities fraud was governed not by Rule 8, but by the heightened pleading standard set forth in Rule 9(b). Rule 9(b) applies to "all averments of fraud or mistake"; it requires that "the circumstances constituting fraud . . . be stated with particularity" but provides that "[m]alice, intent, knowledge, and other condition of mind of a person, may be averred generally."

Courts of Appeals diverged on the character of the Rule 9(b) inquiry in § 10(b) cases: Could securities fraud plaintiffs allege the requisite mental state "simply by stating that scienter existed," or were they required to allege with particularity facts giving rise to an inference of scienter? Circuits requiring plaintiffs to allege specific facts indicating scienter expressed that requirement variously. The Second Circuit's formulation was the most stringent. Securities fraud plaintiffs in that Circuit were required to "specifically plead those [facts] which they assert give rise to a *strong inference* that the defendants had" the requisite state of mind. The "strong inference" formulation was appropriate, the Second Circuit said, to ward off allegations of "fraud by hindsight."

Setting a uniform pleading standard for § 10(b) actions was among Congress' objectives when it enacted the PSLRA. Designed to curb perceived abuses of the § 10(b) private action—"nuisance filings, targeting of deep-pocket defendants, vexatious discovery requests and manipulation by class action lawyers," [Merrill Lynch Pierce, Fenner & Smith] v. Dabit, 547 U.S. [71], at 81, 126 S.Ct. 1503 (quoting H.R. Conf. Rep. No. 104–369, p. 31 (1995), U.S.Code Cong. & Admin.News 1995, p. 730 (hereinafter H.R. Conf. Rep.))—the PSLRA installed both substantive and procedural controls. * * * [I]n § 21D(b) of the PSLRA, Congress "impose[d] heightened pleading requirements in actions brought pursuant to § 10(b) and Rule 10b–5."

Under the PSLRA's heightened pleading instructions, any private securities complaint alleging that the defendant made a false or misleading statement must: (1) "specify each statement alleged to have been misleading [and] the reason or reasons why the statement is misleading," 15 U.S.C. § 78u–4(b)(1); and (2) "state with particularity facts giving rise to a strong inference that the defendant acted with the required state of mind," § 78u–4(b)(2). In the instant case, as earlier stated, the District Court and the Seventh Circuit agreed that the

Shareholders met the first of the two requirements: The complaint sufficiently specified Notebaert's alleged misleading statements and the reasons why the statements were misleading. But those courts disagreed on whether the Shareholders, as required by § 21D(b)(2), "state[d] with particularity facts giving rise to a strong inference that [Notebaert] acted with [scienter]," § 78u–4(b)(2).

The "strong inference" standard "unequivocally raise[d] the bar for pleading scienter," and signaled Congress' purpose to promote greater uniformity among the Circuits, see H.R. Conf. Rep., p. 41. But "Congress did not . . . throw much light on what facts . . . suffice to create [a strong] inference," or on what "degree of imagination courts can use in divining whether" the requisite inference exists. While adopting the Second Circuit's "strong inference" standard, Congress did not codify that Circuit's case law interpreting the standard. See § 78u–4(b)(2). With no clear guide from Congress other than its "inten[tion] to strengthen existing pleading requirements," H.R. Conf. Rep., p. 41, Courts of Appeals have diverged again, this time in construing the term "strong inference." Among the uncertainties, should courts consider competing inferences in determining whether an inference of scienter is "strong"? Our task is to prescribe a workable construction of the "strong inference" standard, a reading geared to the PSLRA's twin goals: to curb frivolous, lawyer-driven litigation, while preserving investors' ability to recover on meritorious claims.

III

A

We establish the following prescriptions: *First,* faced with a Rule 12(b)(6) motion to dismiss a § 10(b) action, courts must, as with any motion to dismiss for failure to plead a claim on which relief can be granted, accept all factual allegations in the complaint as true. See Leatherman v. Tarrant County Narcotics Intelligence and Coordination Unit, 507 U.S. 163, 164, 113 S.Ct. 1160, 122 L.Ed.2d 517 (1993). On this point, the parties agree.

Second, courts must consider the complaint in its entirety, as well as other sources courts ordinarily examine when ruling on Rule 12(b)(6) motions to dismiss, in particular, documents incorporated into the complaint by reference, and matters of which a court may take judicial notice. The inquiry, as several Courts of Appeals have recognized, is whether *all* of the facts alleged, taken collectively, give rise to a strong inference of scienter, not whether any individual allegation, scrutinized in isolation, meets that standard.

Third, in determining whether the pleaded facts give rise to a "strong" inference of scienter, the court must take into account plausible opposing inferences. The Seventh Circuit expressly declined to engage in such a comparative inquiry. A complaint could survive, that court said, as long as it "alleges facts from which, if true, a reasonable person could infer that the defendant acted with the required intent"; in other words, only "[i]f a reasonable person could not draw such an inference from the alleged facts" would the defendant prevail on a motion to dismiss. But in § 21D(b)(2), Congress did not merely require plaintiffs to "provide a factual basis for [their] scienter allegations," *i.e.,* to allege facts from which an inference of scienter rationally *could* be drawn. Instead,

SECTION D

THE FORMAL SUFFICIENCY OF THE COMPLAINT:
HOW SPECIFIC MUST A PLEADING BE?

503

Congress required plaintiffs to plead with particularity facts that give rise to a "strong"-*i.e.,* a powerful or cogent-inference. See American Heritage Dictionary 1717 (4th ed. 2000) (defining "strong" as "[p]ersuasive, effective, and cogent"); 16 Oxford English Dictionary 949 (2d ed.1989) (defining "strong" as "[p]owerful to demonstrate or convince" (definition 16b)); cf. 7 *id.,* at 924 (defining "inference" as "a conclusion [drawn] from known or assumed facts or statements"; "reasoning from something known or assumed to something else which follows from it").

The strength of an inference cannot be decided in a vacuum. The inquiry is inherently comparative: How likely is it that one conclusion, as compared to others, follows from the underlying facts? To determine whether the plaintiff has alleged facts that give rise to the requisite "strong inference" of scienter, a court must consider plausible nonculpable explanations for the defendant's conduct, as well as inferences favoring the plaintiff. The inference that the defendant acted with scienter need not be irrefutable, *i.e.,* of the "smoking-gun" genre, or even the "most plausible of competing inferences." Recall in this regard that § 21D(b)'s pleading requirements are but one constraint among many the PSLRA installed to screen out frivolous suits, while allowing meritorious actions to move forward. Yet the inference of scienter must be more than merely "reasonable" or "permissible"—it must be cogent and compelling, thus strong in light of other explanations. A complaint will survive, we hold, only if a reasonable person would deem the inference of scienter cogent and at least as compelling as any opposing inference one could draw from the facts alleged.

B

Tellabs contends that when competing inferences are considered, Notebaert's evident lack of pecuniary motive will be dispositive. The Shareholders, Tellabs stresses, did not allege that Notebaert sold any shares during the class period. While it is true that motive can be a relevant consideration, and personal financial gain may weigh heavily in favor of a scienter inference, we agree with the Seventh Circuit that the absence of a motive allegation is not fatal. As earlier stated, allegations must be considered collectively; the significance that can be ascribed to an allegation of motive, or lack thereof, depends on the entirety of the complaint.

Tellabs also maintains that several of the Shareholders' allegations are too vague or ambiguous to contribute to a strong inference of scienter. For example, the Shareholders alleged that Tellabs flooded its customers with unwanted products, a practice known as "channel stuffing." But they failed, Tellabs argues, to specify whether the channel stuffing allegedly known to Notebaert was the illegitimate kind (*e.g.,* writing orders for products customers had not requested) or the legitimate kind (*e.g.,* offering customers discounts as an incentive to buy). We agree that omissions and ambiguities count against inferring scienter, for plaintiffs must "state with particularity facts giving rise to a strong inference that the defendant acted with the required state of mind."§ 78u–4(b)(2). We reiterate, however, that the court's job is not to scrutinize each allegation in isolation but to assess all the allegations holistically. In sum, the reviewing court must ask: When the allegations are accepted as true and taken collectively, would a reasonable person deem the inference of scienter at least as strong as any opposing inference?

IV

* * * In the instant case, provided that the Shareholders have satisfied the congressionally "prescribe[d] . . . means of making an issue," the case will fall within the jury's authority to assess the credibility of witnesses, resolve any genuine issues of fact, and make the ultimate determination whether Notebaert and, by imputation, Tellabs acted with scienter. We emphasize, as well, that under our construction of the "strong inference" standard, a plaintiff is not forced to plead more than she would be required to prove at trial. A plaintiff alleging fraud in a § 10(b) action, we hold today, must plead facts rendering an inference of scienter *at least as likely as* any plausible opposing inference. At trial, she must then prove her case by a "preponderance of the evidence." Stated otherwise, she must demonstrate that it is *more likely* than not that the defendant acted with scienter.

* * *

While we reject the Seventh Circuit's approach to § 21D(b)(2), we do not decide whether, under the standard we have described, the Shareholders' allegations warrant "a strong inference that [Notebaert and Tellabs] acted with the required state of mind," 15 U.S.C. § 78u–4(b)(2). Neither the District Court nor the Court of Appeals had the opportunity to consider the matter in light of the prescriptions we announce today. We therefore vacate the Seventh Circuit's judgment so that the case may be reexamined in accord with our construction of § 21D(b)(2).

The judgment of the Court of Appeals is vacated, and the case is remanded for further proceedings consistent with this opinion.

■ JUSTICE SCALIA, concurring in the judgment.

I fail to see how an inference that is merely "at least as compelling as any opposing inference," can conceivably be called what the statute here at issue requires: a "strong inference," 15 U.S.C. § 78u–4(b)(2). If a jade falcon were stolen from a room to which only A and B had access, could it *possibly* be said there was a "strong inference" that B was the thief? I think not, and I therefore think that the Court's test must fail. In my view, the test should be whether the inference of scienter (if any) is *more plausible* than the inference of innocence.

* * * *

■ JUSTICE ALITO, concurring in the judgment.

I agree with the Court that the Seventh Circuit used an erroneously low standard for determining whether the plaintiffs in this case satisfied their burden of pleading "with particularity facts giving rise to a strong inference that the defendant acted with the required state of mind." 15 U.S.C. § 78u–4(b)(2). I further agree that the case should be remanded to allow the lower courts to decide in the first instance whether the allegations survive under the correct standard. In two respects, however, I disagree with the opinion of the Court. First, the best interpretation of the statute is that only those facts that are alleged "with particularity" may properly be considered in determining whether the allegations of scienter are sufficient. Second, I agree with Justice SCALIA that a "strong inference" of scienter, in the present context, means an inference that is more likely than not correct.

SECTION D

THE FORMAL SUFFICIENCY OF THE COMPLAINT:
HOW SPECIFIC MUST A PLEADING BE?

505

■ JUSTICE STEVENS, dissenting.

As the Court explains, when Congress enacted a heightened pleading requirement for private actions to enforce the federal securities laws, it "left the key term 'strong inference' undefined." It thus implicitly delegated significant lawmaking authority to the Judiciary in determining how that standard should operate in practice. Today the majority crafts a perfectly workable definition of the term, but I am persuaded that a different interpretation would be both easier to apply and more consistent with the statute.

The basic purpose of the heightened pleading requirement in the context of securities fraud litigation is to protect defendants from the costs of discovery and trial in unmeritorious cases. Because of its intrusive nature, discovery may also invade the privacy interests of the defendants and their executives. Like citizens suspected of having engaged in criminal activity, those defendants should not be required to produce their private effects unless there is probable cause to believe them guilty of misconduct. Admittedly, the probable-cause standard is not capable of precise measurement, but it is a concept that is familiar to judges. As a matter of normal English usage, its meaning is roughly the same as "strong inference." Moreover, it is most unlikely that Congress intended us to adopt a standard that makes it more difficult to commence a civil case than a criminal case.

In addition to the benefit of its grounding in an already familiar legal concept, using a probable-cause standard would avoid the unnecessary conclusion that "in determining whether the pleaded facts give rise to a 'strong' inference of scienter, the court *must* take into account plausible opposing inferences." There are times when an inference can easily be deemed strong without any need to weigh competing inferences. For example, if a known drug dealer exits a building immediately after a confirmed drug transaction, carrying a suspicious looking package, a judge could draw a strong inference that the individual was involved in the aforementioned drug transaction without debating whether the suspect might have been leaving the building at that exact time for another unrelated reason.

If, using that same methodology, we assume (as we must) the truth of the detailed factual allegations attributed to 27 different confidential informants described in the complaint, and view those allegations collectively, I think it clear that they establish probable cause to believe that Tellabs' chief executive officer "acted with the required intent," as the Seventh Circuit held.[2]

---

[2] The "channel stuffing" allegations in ¶¶ 62–72 of the amended complaint are particularly persuasive. Contrary to petitioners' arguments that respondents' allegations of channel stuffing "are too vague or ambiguous to contribute to a strong inference of scienter," this portion of the complaint clearly alleges that Notebaert himself had specific knowledge of illegitimate channel stuffing during the relevant time period. ("Defendant Notebaert worked directly with Tellabs' sales personnel to channel stuff SBC"); (alleging, in describing such channel stuffing, that Tellabs took "extraordinary" steps that amounted to "an abnormal practice in the industry"; that "distributors were upset and later returned the inventory" (and, in the case of Verizon's Chairman, called Tellabs to complain); that customers "did not want" products that Tellabs sent and that Tellabs employees wrote purchase orders for; that "returns were so heavy during January and February 2001 that Tellabs had to lease extra storage space to accommodate all the returns"; and that Tellabs "backdat[ed] sales" that actually took place in 2001 to appear as having occurred in 2000). If these allegations are actually taken as true

NOTE ON LEGISLATIVE APPROACHES TO SPECIFICITY

1.   Congressional control of pleading: The Private Securities Litigation Reform Act of 1995. In general, the Supreme Court has held that the pleading standard of Rule 8(a) applies to all cases, unless there is a specific rule or statute mandating otherwise. See Leatherman v. Tarrant County Narcotics Intelligence and Coordination Unit, 507 U.S. 163, 113 S.Ct. 1160, 122 L.Ed.2d 517 (1993). Sometimes substantive legislation clearly and expressly overrides the normal pleading requirements of the federal Rules. Concerned over the amount and type of securities fraud litigation brought against publicly traded corporations, Congress passed, over President Clinton's veto, the Private Securities Litigation Reform Act of 1995. According to the Conference Committee Report:

> Congress has been prompted by significant evidence of abuse in private securities lawsuits to enact reforms to protect investors and maintain confidence in our capital markets. The House and Senate Committees heard evidence that abusive practices committed in private securities litigation include: (1) the routine filing of lawsuits against issuers of securities and others whenever there is a significant change in an issuer's stock price, without regard to any underlying culpability of the issuer, and with only faint hope that the discovery process might lead eventually to some plausible cause of action; (2) the targeting of deep pocket defendants * * *; (3) the abuse of the discovery process to impose costs so burdensome that it is often economical for the victimized party to settle; and (4) the manipulation by class action lawyers of the clients whom they purportedly represent.

H. R. Conf. Rep. No. 104–369, at 31 (1995); 1995 U.S. C.C.A.N. 730.

2.   Pleading under the Act. Among other things, the Act requires more specific pleading by the plaintiff in claims brought under the federal securities laws. A plaintiff alleging misleading statements "shall specify each statement alleged to have been misleading, * * * and, if an allegation * * * is made on information and belief, the complaint shall state with particularity all facts on which that belief is formed." 15 U.S.C. § 78u–4(b)(1). An allegation of fraudulent intent "shall * * * state with particularity facts giving rise to a strong inference that the defendant acted with the required state of mind." 15 U.S.C. § 78u–4(b)(2). The origins and controversy over the meaning of the "strong inference" standard are well described in *Tellabs*.

3.   Discovery under the Act. The Act provides that discovery shall be stayed during the pendency of any motion to dismiss for failure to meet the pleading requirements. 15 U.S.C. § 78u–4(b)(3). The Conference Committee Report explained its desire to eliminate "fishing expeditions": "The cost of discovery often forces innocent parties to settle frivolous securities class actions. According to the general counsel of an investment bank, 'discovery costs account for roughly 80% of total litigation costs in securities fraud cases.'" 1995 U.S.C.C.A.N. at 736.

4.   Interpreting and applying the standard set in *Tellabs*. How does the "strong inference" standard of *Tellabs* compare with the

---

and viewed in the collective, it is hard to imagine what competing inference could effectively counteract the inference that Notebaert and Tellabs " 'acted with the required state of mind.' "

SECTION D

THE FORMAL SUFFICIENCY OF THE COMPLAINT:
HOW SPECIFIC MUST A PLEADING BE?

507

"plausibility" standard of *Twombly* and *Iqbal*? How should the standard set out in *Tellabs* be applied? On remand, the court of appeals described the allegations of the complaint in more detail:

The complaint alleges the following: The corporate defendant, Tellabs, manufactures equipment used in fiber optic cable networks; its principal customers are telephone companies. In December 2000, the beginning of the period of alleged violations of Rule 10b–5, Tellabs's principal product, accounting for more than half its sales, was a switching system called TITAN 5500. The product was almost 10 years old when on December 11 Tellabs announced that the 5500's successor product, TITAN 6500, was "available now" and that Sprint had signed a multiyear, $100 million contract to buy the 6500, though in fact no sales pursuant to the contract closed until after the period covered by the complaint. The same announcement added that despite the advent of the 6500, sales of the 5500 would continue to grow. (Most of these and other announcements quoted in the complaint were made by Richard Notebaert, who was Tellabs's chief executive officer and, along with Tellabs, is the principal defendant.)

The following month, Tellabs announced that "customers are buying more and more Tellabs equipment" and that Tellabs had "set the stage for sustained growth" with the successful launch of several products. In February, the company told its stockholders that its growth was "robust" and that "customers are embracing" the 6500. In response to a question frequently asked by investors— whether sales of the 5500 had peaked—the company declared that "although we introduced this product nearly 10 years ago, it's still going strong." In March the company reduced its sales estimates slightly but said it was doing so because of lower than expected growth in a part of its business unrelated to the 5500 and 6500 systems, and that "interest in and demand for the 6500 continues to grow" and "we are satisfying very strong demand and growing customer demand [for the 6500, and] we are as confident as ever— that may be an understatement—about the 6500." And in response to a securities analyst's question whether Tellabs was experiencing "any weakness at all" in demand for the 5500, Notebaert responded: "No, we're not. . . . We're still seeing that product continue to maintain its growth rate; it's still experiencing strong acceptance." Yet from the outset of the period covered by the complaint Tellabs had been flooding its customers with tens of millions of dollars worth of 5500s that the customers had not requested, in order to create an illusion of demand. The company had to lease extra storage space in January and February to accommodate the large number of returns.

Just weeks after these statements Tellabs reduced its sales projections significantly because its customers were "exercising a high degree of prudence over every dollar spent." But it reiterated that the demand for the 6500 was "very strong." In April it said "we should hit our full manufacturing capacity [for the 6500] in May or June to accommodate the demand we are seeing. Everything we can build, we are building and shipping. The demand is very strong."

In June, however, at the end of the period covered by the complaint, Tellabs announced a major drop in revenues, and its share price, which at its peak during the period had been $67 and in the middle of the period had varied between $30 and $38, fell to just under $16. (It currently is below $7.00.) But the deterioration had been well under way by December as a result of the bursting of the fiber-optics bubble in the middle of the year. The market for the 5500 was evaporating; the next month (January 2001), Tellabs's largest customer, Verizon, reduced its orders for the 5500 by 50 percent—having already, the previous June, reduced them by 25 percent. And not a single 6500 system was shipped during the complaint period.

Tellabs's revenues in 2001 were 35 percent lower than the year before and its profits 125 percent lower. The drop in the second quarter (most of which was within the period covered by the complaint) over the year before was even steeper; revenues dropped 43 percent and profits 211 percent.

Makor Issues & Rights, Ltd. v. Tellabs, Inc., 513 F.3d 702, 706–07 (7th Cir. 2008). The court held that these allegations supported a sufficiently strong inference of scienter to meet the standard set by the Supreme Court. Was it right to do so?

5.   Confidential sources. Since the Court decided *Tellabs*, one issue that has split the lower courts is the effect of allegations of information from confidential sources in determining scienter. The Fifth Circuit has held that, "[f]ollowing *Tellabs*, courts must discount allegations from confidential sources." Indiana Electrical Pension Workers Trust Fund v. Shaw Group, Inc., 537 F.3d 527 (5th Cir. 2008); see also Higginbotham v. Baxter, Int'l, 495 F.3d 753 (7th Cir. 2007). Most other courts, however, have preferred a case-by-case approach, assessing in context the weight to give claims from confidential informants. See New Jersey Carpenters Pension & Annuity Funds, 537 F.3d 35 (1st Cir. 2008). Given *Tellabs'* mandate to consider plausible opposing inferences, what is the proper weight to be given allegations from confidential informants in deciding a motion to dismiss?

6.   Effects of the Act. The Act's insistence on more specific pleadings in securities class actions, its stay of discovery, and its other provisions would appear to increase costs of suit for plaintiffs' attorneys. In addition, the Act would appear to make it more difficult, or at least riskier, to file a fraud claim in the absence of "hard" public evidence that a company has engaged in fraud, such as a government investigation or a public restatement of the company's accounting results. Cases in which the details of the fraud had not drawn the government's attention or been highlighted by a corporate admission would be harder to bring, since they will depend increasingly on the cooperation of whistleblowing insiders. These effects will be beneficial if they generally tend to deter meritless lawsuits, but more disturbing if they also prevent the filing of a significant number of lawsuits that are potentially meritorious.

The empirical evidence suggests that the Act has had mixed effects. There is evidence suggesting that the Act has caused plaintiffs' lawyers to focus more directly on cases where the company has made a public admission of problems in its accounting, and those reporting such evidence argue that it reflects a desirable shift in emphasis toward cases where the likelihood of fraud is high. Marilyn F. Johnson, Karen K. Nelson, and A. C. Pritchard, Do the Merits Matter More: Class Actions Under the Private Securities Litigation Reform Act, 23 Journal of Law, Economics and Organization 627 (2007).

Other research suggests, however, that the Act is also deterring significant amounts of meritorious litigation. It appears that higher costs of litigation under the Act have shifted plaintiffs' attorneys toward suits against larger firms and have sharply reduced the incidence of class actions against smaller companies (where smaller financial losses are involved), apparently without regard to the merit or lack of merit of the claims against those companies. Choi, Do the Merits Matter Less After the Private Securities Litigation Reform Act?, 23 J.L.Econ. & Org. 598, 622 (1998). Professor Choi also finds that the Act has deterred the prosecution of a significant fraction of non-frivolous "soft evidence" claims, that is, of non-frivolous claims based on fraud whose details are not yet publicly known. These of course are the cases whose prosecution is most severely complicated by the Act's pleading requirements and restrictions on discovery.

7. Further reading. *Tellabs* has spawned an extensive literature from both scholars of civil procedure and securities law. See Miller, A Modest Proposal for Securities Law Pleadings After *Tellabs*, 75 Law & Contemp. Probs. 93 (2012); Steinberg & Gomez-Cornejo, Blurring the Lines Between Pleading Doctrines, 30 Rev. Litig. 1 (2010); Cox, Thomas & Bai, Do Differences in Pleading Standards Cause Forum Shopping in Securities Class Actions?: Doctrinal and Empirical Analyses, 2009 Wis. L. Rev. 421; Miller, Pleading After *Tellabs*, 2009 Wis. L. Rev. 507.

E. ETHICAL CONSTRAINTS ON PLEADING

1. INCONSISTENT THEORIES AND THE PROFESSIONAL OBLIGATION TO PLEAD A DOUBTFUL CASE

McCormick v. Kopmann

Illinois Court of Appeals, Third District, 1959.
23 Ill.App.2d 189, 161 N.E.2d 720.

■ PRESIDING JUSTICE REYNOLDS delivered the opinion of the court.

On the evening of November 21, 1956, Lewis McCormick was killed on Main Street in Gifford, Illinois, when a truck being operated by defendant Lorence Kopmann collided with the automobile which McCormick was driving.

This action was brought by McCormick's widow in the Circuit Court of Champaign County against Kopmann and Anna, John and Mary Huls. The complaint contains four counts; the issues raised on this appeal concern only the first and fourth counts.

Count I is brought by plaintiff as Administratrix of McCormick's Estate, against Kopmann, under the Illinois Wrongful Death Act. Plaintiff sues for the benefit of herself and her eight children, to recover for the pecuniary injury suffered by them as a result of McCormick's death. It is charged that Kopmann negligently drove his truck across the center line of Main Street and collided with McCormick's automobile. In paragraph 3 of Count I, plaintiff alleges

> "That at the time of the occurrence herein described, and for a reasonable period of time preceding it, the said decedent was in the exercise of ordinary care for his own safety and that of his property."

Count IV is brought by plaintiff as Administratrix of McCormick's Estate, against the Huls, under the Illinois Dram Shop Act. Plaintiff avers that Count IV is brought "in the alternative to Count I." She sues for the benefit of herself and her four minor children, to recover for the injury to their means of support suffered as a result of McCormick's death. It is alleged that Anna Huls operated a dramshop in Penfield, Illinois; that John and Mary Huls operated a dramshop in Gifford; that on November 21, 1956, the Huls sold alcoholic beverages to McCormick which he consumed and which rendered him intoxicated; and that "as a result of such intoxication" McCormick drove his automobile "in such a manner as to cause a collision with a truck" being driven by Kopmann on Main Street in Gifford.

Kopmann, defendant under Count I, moved to dismiss the complaint on the theory that the allegations of that Count I and Count IV were fatally repugnant and could not stand together, because McCormick could not be free from contributory negligence as alleged in Count I, if his intoxication caused the accident as alleged in Count IV. Kopmann also urged that the allegation in Count IV that McCormick's intoxication was the proximate cause of his death, is a binding judicial admission which precludes an action under the Wrongful Death Act. Kopmann's motion was denied. He raised the same defenses in his answer.

The Huls, defendants under Count IV, answered. They did not file a motion directed against Count IV.

Neither defendant sought a severance and both counts came on for trial at the same time.

Plaintiff introduced proof that at the time of the collision, McCormick was proceeding North in the northbound traffic lane, and that Kopmann's truck, traveling South, crossed the center line and struck McCormick's car. Plaintiff also introduced testimony that prior to the accident McCormick drank a bottle of beer in Anna Huls' tavern in Penfield and one or two bottles of beer in John and Mary Huls' tavern in Gifford. Plaintiff's witness Roy Lowe, who was with McCormick during the afternoon and evening of November 21, and who was seated in the front seat of McCormick's car when the collision occurred, testified on cross examination that in his opinion McCormick was sober at the time of the accident.

At the close of plaintiff's evidence, all defendants moved for directed verdicts. The motions were denied.

Kopmann, the defendant under the Wrongful Death count, introduced testimony that at the time of the collision, his truck was in the proper lane; that McCormick's automobile was backed across the center line of Main Street, thus encroaching on the southbound lane, and blocking it; that the parking lights on McCormick's automobile were turned on, but not the headlights; that Kopmann tried to swerve to avoid hitting McCormick's car; and that there was an odor of alcohol on McCormick's breath immediately after the accident. Over plaintiff's objection, the trial court permitted Kopmann's counsel to read to the jury the allegations of Count IV relating to McCormick's intoxication, as an admission.

The Huls, defendants under the Dram Shop count, introduced opinion testimony of a number of witnesses that McCormick was not intoxicated at the time of the accident. Anna Huls testified that McCormick drank one bottle of beer in her tavern. Several witnesses testified that McCormick had no alcoholic beverages in John and Mary Huls' tavern.

All defendants moved for directed verdicts at the close of all the proof. The motions were denied. The jury was instructed that Count IV was an alternative to Count I; that Illinois law permits a party who is uncertain as to which state of facts is true to plead in the alternative, and that it is for the jury to determine the facts. At Kopmann's request, the court instructed the jury on the law of contributory negligence, and further:

> ". . . if you find from all of the evidence in the case that (McCormick) was operating his automobile while intoxicated and that such intoxication, if any, contributed proximately to cause the collision in question, then in that case . . . you should find the defendant, Lorence Kopmann, not guilty."

The jury returned a verdict against Kopmann for $15,500 under Count I. The jury found the Huls not guilty under Count IV. Kopmann's motions for judgment notwithstanding the verdict, and in the alternative for a new trial, were denied.

Kopmann has appealed. His first contention is that the trial court erred in denying his pre-trial motion to dismiss the complaint. Kopmann is correct in asserting that the complaint contains inconsistent allegations. The allegation of Count I that McCormick was free from contributory negligence, cannot be reconciled with the allegation of Count IV that McCormick's intoxication was the proximate cause of his death. Freedom from contributory negligence is a prerequisite to recovery under the Wrongful Death Act. If the jury had found that McCormick was intoxicated and that his intoxication caused the accident, it could not at the same time have found that McCormick was not contributorily negligent. The Illinois Supreme Court has held that "voluntary intoxication will not excuse a person from exercising such care as may reasonably be expected from one who is sober." Keeshan v. Elgin, A. & S. Traction Co., 229 Ill. 533, 537.

In addition to this factual inconsistency, it has been held that compensation awarded under the Wrongful Death Act includes reparation for the loss of support compensable under the Dram Shop Act.

Counts I and IV, therefore, are mutually exclusive; plaintiff may not recover upon both counts. It does not follow, however, that these counts may not be pleaded together. Section 24(1) of the Illinois Civil Practice Act (Ill. Rev. Stat. Ch. 110, Sec. 24) authorizes joinder of defendants against whom a liability is asserted in the alternative arising out of the same transaction. Section 24(3) of the Act provides:

> "If the plaintiff is in doubt as to the person from whom he is entitled to redress, he may join two or more defendants, and state his claim against them in the alternative in the same count or plead separate counts in the alternative against different defendants, to the intent that the question which, if any, of the defendants is liable, and to what extent, may be determined as between the parties."

Section 34 of the Act states in part that "Relief, whether based on one or more counts, may be asked in the alternative."

Section 43(2) of the Act provides:

> "When a party is in doubt as to which of two or more statements of fact is true, he may, regardless of consistency, state them in the alternative or hypothetically in the same or different counts or defenses, whether legal or equitable. A bad alternative does not affect a good one."

Thus, the Civil Practice Act expressly permits a plaintiff to plead inconsistent counts in the alternative, where he is genuinely in doubt as to what the facts are and what the evidence will show. The legal sufficiency of each count presents a separate question. It is not ground for dismissal that allegations in one count contradict those in an alternative count. These principles have been applied recently in cases similar to that at bar.* * *

* * *

The 1955 revision of Section 43(2) of the Civil Practice Act * * * was modeled after Rule 8(e)(2) of the Federal Rules of Civil Procedure. * * * *

Sound policy weighs in favor of alternative pleading, so that controversies may be settled and complete justice accomplished in a single action. If the right is abused, as where the pleader has knowledge of the true facts (viz, he knows that the facts belie the alternative) pleading in the alternative is not justified.

* * * *

There is nothing in the record before us to indicate that plaintiff knew in advance of the trial, that the averments of Count I, and not Count IV, were true. In fact, at the trial, Kopmann attempted to establish the truth of the allegations of Count IV that McCormick was intoxicated at the time of the collision and that his intoxication caused his death. He can hardly be heard now to say that before the trial, plaintiff should have known that these were not the facts. Where * * * the injured party is still living and able to recollect the events surrounding the accident, pleading in the alternative may not be justified, but where, as in the case at bar, the key witness is deceased, pleading alternative sets of facts is often the only feasible way to proceed. * * *

We hold that, in the absence of a severance, plaintiff had the right to go to trial on both Counts I and IV, and to adduce all the proof she had under both Count I and Count IV.

Kopmann's next argument is that the allegations of Count IV regarding McCormick's intoxication constitute binding judicial admissions. He contends that plaintiff's action against him should have been dismissed on the basis of the allegations in Count IV regarding McCormick's intoxication.

* * * *

Alternative fact allegations made in good faith and based on genuine doubt are not admissions against interest so as to be admissible in evidence against the pleader. The pleader states the facts in the alternative because he is uncertain as to the true facts. Therefore, he is not "admitting" anything other than his uncertainty. An essential objective of alternative pleading is to relieve the pleader of the necessity and therefore the risk of making a binding choice, which is no more than to say that he is relieved of making an admission.

[handwritten marginalia: Rule]

[handwritten marginalia: Purpose of alternative pleading]

Kopmann next contends that the trial judge erred in denying his motion for directed verdict at the close of plaintiff's proof. Kopmann's theory is that if, as the trial judge ruled, plaintiff made out a *prima facie* case under Count IV, she necessarily negatived Kopmann's liability under Count I by proving McCormick was guilty of contributory negligence. He also urges that plaintiff is entitled to have but one of the two counts submitted to the jury, and that the trial judge should have required plaintiff to elect between Counts I and IV at the close of the evidence, and before the case was submitted to the jury.

There are several reasons why we believe Kopmann's position is unsound. First, we are of the opinion that plaintiff's evidence did not contradict the position she took in Count I, viz., that McCormick exercised due care for his own safety. Plaintiff proved only that McCormick drank two or three bottles of beer prior to the accident. Yet Lowe, who was with McCormick during the entire time from late afternoon until his death, testified during plaintiff's case in chief that McCormick was sober at the time of the accident. * * *

Moreover, even if plaintiff made out a prima facie case of McCormick's intoxication for purposes of the Dram Shop Act, she made no showing of a causal connection between the intoxication and the accident. This is a necessary element of plaintiff's case under Count IV. All of the witnesses for plaintiff who testified on the question agreed that at the time of the collision McCormick's car was facing North in the northbound traffic lane, and that Kopmann's truck swerved over the center line and struck McCormick's car. Hence, whether or not McCormick was intoxicated at the time of the collision is immaterial, because there was a complete absence of proof that the fatal collision happened "in consequence of (McCormick's) intoxication" as required by the Dram Shop Act.

The trial judge should have directed a verdict for the Huls, as to Count IV because there was no evidence of causal connection between the intoxication, if any, and death, but the error is moot on this appeal by Kopmann, the defendant under Count I, since there was a verdict of not guilty as to Count IV.

Our second reason for rejecting Kopmann's contention is more basic. Plaintiff pleaded alternative counts because she was uncertain as to what the true facts were. Even assuming she introduced proof to support all essential allegations of both Count I and Count IV, she was entitled to have all the evidence submitted to the trier of fact, and to have the jury decide where the truth lay. She was not foreclosed *ipso facto* from going to the jury under Count I, merely because she submitted proof, under Count IV, tending to prove that McCormick's intoxication proximately caused his death. If this were the rule, one who in good faith tried his case on alternative theories, pursuant to the authorization, if not the encouragement of Section 43, would run the risk of having his entire case dismissed. The provisions of the Civil Practice Act authorizing alternative pleading, necessarily contemplate that the pleader adduce proof in support of both sets of allegations or legal theories, leaving to the jury the determination of the facts.

Furthermore, in testing the sufficiency of the proof as against a motion for directed verdict, the sufficiency of the proof to support each count is to be judged separately as to each count, just as the legal sufficiency of each count is separately judged at the pleading stage. As to each count, the court will look only to the proof and inferences therefrom favorable to the plaintiff; the court cannot weigh conflicting evidence. Proof unfavorable to the plaintiff, even though the plaintiff herself introduced that proof, cannot be considered. The determination to be made is whether there is any evidence (all unfavorable evidence excluded) upon which the jury could base a verdict for the plaintiff under the count in question, and if there is, the motion as to that count must be denied and the issues submitted to the jury. Judged by these well-settled tests, it is clear that plaintiff's proof under Count I was sufficient to require the case to be submitted to the jury.

What we have said is not to say that a plaintiff assumes no risks in adducing proof to support inconsistent counts. The proof in support of one inconsistent count necessarily tends to negate the proof under the other count and to have its effect upon the jury. While the fact alone of inconsistent evidence will not bar submission of the case to the jury, it may very well affect the matter of the weight of the evidence and warrant the granting of a new trial, even though, as we have held, it does not warrant *ipso facto* a directed verdict or judgment notwithstanding the verdict.

Kopmann argues that plaintiff should have been required to elect between her alternative counts before going to the jury. The doctrine known as "election of remedies" has no application to the case at bar. Here, either of two defendants may be liable to plaintiff, depending upon what the jury finds the facts to be. It has been aptly said that "truth cannot be stated until known, and, for purposes of judicial administration, cannot be known until the trier of facts decides the fact issues." McCaskill, Illinois Civil Practice Act Annotated (1933), p. 103. Plaintiff need not choose between the alternative counts. Such a requirement would, to a large extent, nullify the salutary purposes of alternative pleading. Since she could bring actions against the defendants seriatim, or at the same time in separate suits, she is entitled to join them in a single action, introduce all her proof, and submit the entire case to the jury under appropriate instructions.

* * *

We conclude that the verdict and judgment below are correct and the judgment is affirmed.

NOTE ON PLEADING INCONSISTENT THEORIES, THE NATURE OF AN AVERMENT OR ALLEGATION, AND THE PROFESSIONAL OBLIGATION TO PLEAD A DOUBTFUL CLAIM

1. **The common law approach.** The common law pleading rules required that a pleader's allegations be consistent. Consistency was required even where the allegations referred to an out-of-court event which under the substantive law was difficult to classify, or where the pleader knew too little about the facts, at the time of pleading, to settle conclusively on a single consistent narrative.

A case illustrating the early approach is Wigton v. McKinley, 122 Colo. 14, 221 P.2d 383 (1950), a quiet-title suit in which plaintiff claimed title to real estate, first, as owner under an unrecorded deed from his wife delivered to him prior to her death and, second, as devisee under his wife's will. The court pointed out that if the deed was valid and delivered, the wife would have had nothing to devise, while the devise was valid only if the deed was not. The court held, "A party to an action may not base his cause upon inconsistent and self-destructive grounds." 221 P.2d at 385.

The common law requirement of consistency put a plaintiff in a very difficult situation. As Professor, later-Judge, Charles E. Clark explained:

> Now the difficulty is that the pleader often cannot know, and cannot reasonably be expected to know, which of two or more alternatives is the correct one. This is particularly true as to the details of the injury or breach, which often are known only to the defendant in advance of trial. * * * To enforce the rule [requiring consistency] as harshly as at common law is unfairly to trap the pleader beyond any requirement of fair notice to the defendant.

Clark, Code Pleading § 42 (2d ed. 1947). For example, if the plaintiff's pre-filing investigation and legal research disclosed two plausible alternative scenarios, and plaintiff elected scenario A, defendant could defend on the ground that the truth was actually scenario B. If plaintiff elected scenario B, defendant could rely on scenario A.

A possible solution under common law pleading was for plaintiff to sue first under scenario A, and if unsuccessful to sue again under scenario B. But this solution raised a number of difficulties, including the possibility that defendant would succeed on the basis of inconsistent defenses in the two proceedings; the certainty that plaintiff would incur additional costs in a second proceeding; and the possibility that the doctrine of res judicata would preclude plaintiff from bringing a second proceeding at all.

To eliminate the dilemma posed by the common law requirement of consistency, modern procedural regimes generally permit pleading of inconsistent or alternative allegations, so long as the pleading satisfies the basic ethical requirements of federal Rule 11 or comparable state rules. See Fed. R. Civ. P. 8(d)(2), (3). The principle is applied to cases of both factual and legal inconsistency. *McCormick v. Kopmann* is a classic application of the doctrine.

2. **Alternative pleading, party knowledge, and alternative proof.** The *McCormick* court holds explicitly that allegations in a complaint are not only not *conclusive* admissions of the matters pleaded, they are not admissions at all. If this is correct, what is the status of an allegation in a complaint? Does it do anything more than state a hypothesis concerning

what the tribunal *may* later conclude to be proven under the applicable burden of persuasion? Does the pleading say anything more than that the hypothesis can't responsibly be ruled out on the basis of pre-filing investigation?

The court in *McCormick* stresses the importance of the fact that plaintiff, the administratrix of the deceased's estate, was not present and hence not certain which version of the accident occurred. What if Mr. McCormick had survived the accident but had vehemently denied being intoxicated at the time of the accident? In Chirelstein v. Chirelstein, 8 N.J.Super. 504, 73 A.2d 628 (1950), aff'd, 79 A.2d 884 (N.J. Super. Ct. App. Div. 1951), plaintiff had earlier sued defendant for divorce in a Florida court, where a divorce decree had been entered. In the present suit, plaintiff alleged, first, that the Florida decree was valid and that pursuant to the decree she was therefore entitled to alimony as a divorcee; and, second, that the Florida decree was invalid because it had been procured through a fraud (in which she necessarily would have participated), and that she was entitled to a divorce and alimony in the present proceeding. The court held that plaintiff could take these inconsistent positions:

> I see no basis for requiring an election. Where the interplay of the facts and the law is such that the legal soundness of the respective legal positions is debatable, alternative or hypothetical claims should be permitted. I can perceive no reason for requiring a litigant in these circumstances to make a conclusive anticipation of the views of the court. * * * Where the judicial treatment of the facts is in doubt, justice demands that the litigant be permitted to assert alternative positions which depend upon the successive determinations of the issues raised by the facts.

73 A.2d at 632. See also Rader Co. v. Stone, 178 Cal.App.3d 10, 223 Cal. Rptr. 806 (1986). Does *Chirelstein v. Chirelstein* suggest that had Mr. McCormick survived the accident, he could have filed the same pleading as his wife, even if he was sure what he thought had happened, so long as his lawyer was unsure of whether the jury would view his conduct as negligent?

3. The professional obligation to assert a doubtful claim. Did the lawyer for Ms. McCormick have a professional obligation to advise the filing of the claims against both Kopmann and the Huls, assuming that both claims were non-frivolous? The issue is one of professional competence. The disciplinary ethical rules of the profession require a lawyer to "provide competent representation to a client." ABA, Model Rules of Professional Conduct, 1.1 (2007). Competence is typically defined to include reasonable inquiry into the underlying facts and law and adequate preparation. In practice, the obligation of competence is enforced through the process of professional discipline only in rare and egregious cases. Far more important to most lawyers are their own pride, the good opinion of their clients, and the threat of civil liability for professional malpractice.

To establish a claim for malpractice, a client or former client must show that he was injured by his lawyer's failure to exercise due care, defined as "the competence and diligence normally exercised by lawyers in similar circumstances." Restatement (Third) of the Law Governing Lawyers § 52 (2000). Because the judgments made by lawyers usually involve "situations and requirements of legal practice unknown to most jurors and often not familiar in detail to most judges * * * a plaintiff ordinarily must introduce expert testimony concerning the care reasonably required in the circumstances of the case and the lawyer's failure to exercise such care." Id., comment g. In Aloy v. Mash, 38 Cal.3d 413, 212 Cal.Rptr. 162, 696 P.2d 656 (1985), the plaintiff claimed that defendant had "negligently failed to assert her community property interest in [her ex-husband's] military retirement pension, which failure prevented her from receiving any share of his gross military retirement pension benefits." 38 Cal.3d at 416. Though the defendant argued that he had relied upon an older case holding that the plaintiff had no right to a share of her husband's pension, the plaintiff responded with expert testimony to the effect that (1) reasonable research would have showed that the question was unsettled and (2) family lawyers at the relevant time and place routinely claimed such benefits. The court held that plaintiff was entitled to a trial on the issue of negligence. Id. at 415–22. In a jurisdiction that followed the rule of Aloy, would you feel confident that a lawyer's decision, at the outset of the action, to decline to assert claims similar to those asserted against Kopmann and Huls would meet the applicable standard of care?

    4. Do *Twombly* and *Iqbal* affect alternative pleading? In the wake of the Supreme Court's recent decisions in *Twombly* and *Iqbal*, supra p. 471–496, one open question is whether the new rule of "plausibility pleading" affects the ability to plead in the alternative. Recall that *Twombly* instructs judges to consider an "obvious alternative explanation" for a defendant's conduct. If the plaintiff presents multiple theories against different defendants, does each theory potentially serve as a defense for one defendant against the other, as it might have in the days of common law pleading? In *McCormick*, does the plaintiff's theory of liability against Kopmann undermine the theory of liability against Huls? In the years following the *Twombly* and *Iqbal* decisions, the few courts to consider the question have held that plaintiffs may plead alternative theories so long as each is "plausible." See, e.g., Koch v. I-Flow Corp., 715 F. Supp. 2d 297 (D.R.I. 2010). Is the court's analysis in *McCormick* outdated in a world of plausibility pleading?

    5. What about the Huls? Kopmann's appeal is disadvantaged by the fact that the jury found against him. The Huls, who won at trial, did not appeal. But according to the opinion of the court, they should have had a directed verdict—that is, their case should never have reached the jury—because the record disclosed no evidence of any causal connection between their alcohol and Mr. McCormick's death. Does this wholesale failure of proof against them mean that the lawyer for Mrs. McCormick acted improperly in pleading a claim against them and taking it to trial?

2. FRIVOLOUS CLAIMS AND CONTENTIONS

NOTE ON ENSURING THE SUBSTANTIALITY OF CLAIMS AND DEFENSES

    Lawyers sometimes file pleadings that have little basis in fact or law. The lawyer may be pressed for time and unable to investigate properly, or the lawyer may be careless. The client may not have been sufficiently forthcoming about the facts as the complaint was being drawn up. The client and the lawyer may be seeking unfair strategic advantage (and settlement leverage) by filing a largely unfounded lawsuit that will cost the defendant a disproportionate amount of time and money to defend.

Verification of pleadings is a traditional device designed to preclude or discourage erroneous factual allegations. Many jurisdictions permit, and in some circumstances require, verified pleadings. Normally, a party verifies a pleading by attaching an affidavit stating under oath or under "penalty of perjury" that the allegations in the complaint are true, or that he believes them to be true. In certain circumstances, the attorney or a non-party may verify a pleading. If the plaintiff verifies his complaint, the defendant must verify his answer. Calif. C. Civ. P. § 446(a). A further, and generally more important, practical consequence of verification is that a defendant may answer an unverified complaint by general denial, but must answer a verified complaint specifically, "positively or according to the information and belief of the defendant." § 431.30(d).

The verification requirement has generally had little effect on truthfulness in pleadings, although from time to time a litigant has been seriously embarrassed on the witness stand by a discrepancy between his testimony and the allegations in his complaint. Further, courts tend to be somewhat more stringent about inconsistency between allegations in a verified complaint, or between allegations in successive verified complaints. See, e.g., Payne v. Bennion, 178 Cal.App.2d 595, 3 Cal.Rptr. 14 (1960) (verified complaint contained factually inconsistent allegations; court refused to allow amendment to cure the inconsistency without "proper explanation" by the pleader); but see Premier Elec. Constr. Co. v. La Salle Nat'l Bank, 132 Ill.App.3d 485, 87 Ill.Dec. 721, 477 N.E.2d 1249 (1984) (verified complaint alleged "legal conclusions" rather than facts and was therefore not binding on plaintiff). A verified pleading is very difficult to challenge on the ground that the verifying party had no basis for knowing the truth or falsehood of the factual allegations contained in her pleading. See, e.g., Surowitz v. Hilton Hotels Corp., 383 U.S. 363, 370–71, 86 S.Ct. 845, 15 L.Ed.2d 807 (1966) (allowing a verified complaint by an unsophisticated plaintiff with a limited knowledge of English in a shareholder derivative suit under Fed. R. Civ. P. 23.1: "Mrs. Surowitz verified the complaint, not on the basis of her own knowledge and understanding, but in the faith that her son-in-law had correctly advised her either that the statements in the complaint were true or to the best of his knowledge he believed them to be true.").

The common law also provided remedies for meritless or abusive litigation in the form of the civil torts of malicious prosecution and abuse of process. Both types of claims are difficult to win. To win a malicious prosecution claim, the plaintiff must establish (1) that the defendant instituted a proceeding against the plaintiff; (2) that the proceeding was terminated in favor of the plaintiff (by an outright win for the plaintiff); (3) that the claim was brought without probable cause; (4) that the defendant acted with malice or improper purpose; and, in a minority of jurisdictions, (5) that the plaintiff suffered "special damage" of the type required. Hazard et al., The Law and Ethics of Lawyering 690 (4th ed. 2005). The definition of probable cause varies from jurisdiction to jurisdiction. A standard formulation states that probable cause exists when, on the basis of facts which the lawyer reasonably believes to be true, the client's claim is "objectively tenable" or "may have merit." Compare Sheldon Appel Co. v. Albert & Oliker, 47 Cal.3d 863, 254 Cal.Rptr. 336, 765 P.2d 498, 499 (1989) ("objectively tenable") with Friedman v. Dozorc, 412 Mich. 1, 312 N.W.2d

585, 606 (1981) ("claim *may* be valid under the applicable law") (emphasis in original).

Abuse of process claims aim at actions taken in litigation that are technically justified under the applicable law, but undertaken with an improper motivation. The plaintiff must ordinarily show that the litigation (or procedural step within the litigation) that is complained of was undertaken primarily with a purpose for which it was not designed or, as some courts have put it, "outside the normal contemplation of private litigation." Mozzochi v. Beck, 204 Conn. 490, 529 A.2d 171, 174 (1987). If the infliction of delay, cost, or emotional distress, however deliberate, is simply the natural consequence of the "normal contemplation of private litigation," it is not actionable. Id. See Hazard et al., The Law and Ethics of Lawyering 690 (4th ed. 2005).

There are several modern devices to encourage attorneys and their clients to make only claims with a substantial basis in fact and law: Rule 11 in the federal system (and comparable rules in state systems); 28 U.S.C. § 1927, forbidding unreasonable and vexatious multiplication of proceedings; and the "inherent power" of the courts to prevent abusive litigation tactics. Unlike the traditional verification requirement, which addresses only the truthfulness of factual allegations, these devices require substantiality both in factual allegations and legal contentions.

Zuk v. Eastern Pennsylvania Psychiatric Institute of the Medical College of Pennsylvania

United States Court of Appeals, Third Circuit, 1996.
103 F.3d 294.

■ ROSENN, CIRCUIT JUDGE.

This appeal brings into focus difficult questions relating to the evolving uses and purposes of Federal Rules of Civil Procedure (Fed. R. Civ. P.) Rule 11 sanctions, the more narrow statutory function of sanctions permitted under 28 U.S.C. § 1927, and differences between the two. The sanctions here stem from a suit filed in the United States District Court for the Eastern District of Pennsylvania by Benjamin Lipman, the appellant, in behalf of Dr. Gerald Zuk for copyright infringement against the Eastern Pennsylvania Psychiatric Institute (EPPI). The district court dismissed the action on a Rule 12(b)(6) motion filed by the defendant, and appellant and his client thereafter were subjected to joint and several liability in the sum of $15,000 for sanctions and defendant's counsel fees. Dr. Zuk settled his liability and Lipman appealed. We affirm in part and vacate in part.

I.

Dr. Zuk, a psychologist on the faculty of EPPI, early in the 1970s had an EPPI technician film two of Dr. Zuk's family therapy sessions. As academic demand for the films developed, Zuk had EPPI duplicate the films and make them available for rental through their library. Zuk subsequently wrote a book which, among other things, contained transcripts of the therapy sessions. He registered the book in 1975 with the United States Copyright Office.

In 1980, upon a change in its ownership, EPPI furloughed Zuk. He thereupon requested that all copies of the films be returned to him; EPPI ignored the request. It would appear that EPPI continued to rent out the films for at least some time thereafter. For reasons which have not been made clear, after a long hiatus, Zuk renewed his attempts to recover the films in 1994. In 1995, appellant filed the suit in Zuk's behalf, alleging that EPPI was renting out the films and thereby infringed his copyright.

On June 19, 1995, EPPI moved for dismissal under Rule 12(b), and appellant filed a memorandum in opposition. While the motion was pending, EPPI mailed to Lipman a notice of its intention to move for sanctions under Rule 11(c)(1)(A) on the grounds essentially that appellant had failed to conduct an inquiry into the facts reasonable under the circumstances and into the law. The district court entered an order granting the motion to dismiss. The court found that the copyright of the book afforded no protection to the films, that EPPI owned the copies of the films in its possession and that their use was not an infringement, and that in any event, Zuk's claims were barred by the statute of limitations.

On August 16, EPPI filed a motion for attorney's fees pursuant to 17 U.S.C. § 505 which appellant opposed by a memorandum in opposition on August 31. On September 15, EPPI also filed a Rule 11 motion for sanctions, and appellant filed a memorandum in opposition. On November 1, the court entered an order to "show cause why Rule 11 sanctions should not be imposed for (a) filing the complaint, and failing to withdraw it; and (b) signing and filing each and every document presented." Appellant responded on December 1 with a declaration reiterating the facts of the case as he viewed them.

On February 1, 1996, the court, upon consideration of defendant's motion for attorney's fees and sanctions, ordered: "That plaintiff, Gerald Zuk, Ph.D., and plaintiff's counsel, Benjamin G. Lipman, Esq. are jointly and severally liable to the defendant for counsel fees in the sum of $15,000." We must ascertain the underpinnings for the Order. It appears that Dr. Zuk subsequently settled his liability with EPPI in the amount of $6,250, leaving appellant liable for $8,750. Appellant timely appealed.

II.

We turn first to the Copyright Act which provides in relevant part: "In any civil action under this title [Copyrights], the court in its discretion may allow the recovery of full costs by or against any party. . . . The court may also award a reasonable attorney's fee to the prevailing party as part of the costs." 17 U.S.C. § 505.

Under this Act, a reasonable attorney's fees may be awarded in the court's discretion to the prevailing party against the other party as costs. This court has in the past recognized that the statutory authorization is broad, does not require bad faith on the part of the adversaries, and reveals an intent to rely on the sound judgment of the district court. Lieb v. Topstone Industries, Inc. 788 F.2d 151, 155 (3rd Cir. 1986). In the instant case, the trial judge aptly recognized that fees were not automatically awarded to the prevailing party, but believed that this was the kind of case in which an award was clearly justified. He therefore concluded that reasonable compensation for all the time spent in this litigation, including the fees and sanctions issues, was to enter a total award of $15,000. Therefore the district court committed no error in making an award under this Act. However, under the statutory directive, the attorney's fee is considered an element of costs and therefore liability attached only to Dr. Zuk and not his attorney, Benjamin G. Lipman. Dr. Zuk has settled his liability, and the appellant's liability under the Copyright Act should not detain us. There is none. We therefore turn to the other statute that figures in this appeal, 28 U.S.C. § 1927.

A.

The short memorandum of the district court accompanying its Order of February 1, 1996 also shows that the district court concluded that "joint and several liability should be imposed under both Fed. R. Civ. P. 11 and 28 U.S.C. § 1927 upon plaintiff's counsel, as well as plaintiff, for the $15,000 counsel fee award." D.C. Memo at 2.

We turn first to the propriety of the district court's imposition of sanctions under 28 U.S.C. § 1927. We review a district court's decision to impose sanctions for abuse of discretion. Cooter & Gell v. Hartmarx Corp., 496 U.S. 384, 385, 110 L.Ed.2d 359, 110 S.Ct. 2447 (1990); Jones v. Pittsburgh Nat'l Corp., 899 F.2d 1350, 1357 (3rd Cir. 1990).

Section 1927 provides in pertinent part: "Any attorney or person admitted to conduct cases who so multiplies the proceeding in any case unreasonably and vexatiously may be required by the court to satisfy personally the excess costs, expenses and attorney's fees reasonably incurred because of such conduct." Although a trial court has broad discretion in managing litigation before it, the principal purpose of imposing sanctions under 28 U.S.C. § 1927 is "the deterrence of intentional and unnecessary delay in the proceedings." Beatrice Foods v. New England Printing, 899 F.2d 1171, 1177 (Fed. Cir. 1990). In this case, the trial court imposed sanctions on plaintiff and his counsel, not because of any multiplicity of the proceedings or delaying tactics, but for failure to make a reasonably adequate inquiry into the facts and law before filing the lawsuit. Thus, the statute does not apply to the set of facts before us. Furthermore, the statute is designed to discipline counsel only and does not authorize imposition of sanctions on the attorney's client.

Finally, this court has stated that "before a court can order the imposition of attorneys' fees under § 1927, it must find wilful bad faith on the part of the offending attorney." Williams v. Giant Eagle Markets, Inc., 883 F.2d 1184, 1191 (3d Cir. 1989). Although the court need not "make an express finding of bad faith in so many words," Baker Industries, Inc. v. Cerberus Ltd., 764 F.2d 204, 209 (3d Cir. 1985), there must at least be statements on the record which this court can construe as an implicit finding of bad faith. Id.

At oral argument before us, counsel for EPPI conceded that the district court had made no express finding of bad faith. Our review of the record, which in relevant part consists only of a two-page Memorandum and Order, reveals no statements which we can interpret as an implicit finding of wilful bad faith. At most, the court's statements might be interpreted to indicate a finding of negligence on appellant's part.[2]

---

[2]   For example, the court stated: "I find it impossible to avoid the conclusion that plaintiff's counsel failed to conduct an adequate investigation . . ." and "If a tolerably adequate inquiry had preceded the filing of the [sic] this lawsuit, no lawsuit would have been filed."

We have also interpreted § 1927 as requiring specific notice and the opportunity to be heard before sanctions are imposed. In Jones v. Pittsburgh Nat'l Corp., we confronted a situation very much like the current one; the appellant had been sanctioned under both Rule 11 and § 1927, but had received notice only in regard to Rule 11. In vacating the order imposing sanctions, we noted that "particularized notice is required to comport with due process," and that "the mere existence of . . . § 1927 does not constitute sufficient notice in our view." 899 F.2d 1350 at 1357.

We therefore hold that because the court had made no finding of wilful bad faith, and because it failed to give appellant notice and an opportunity to defend, it was an abuse of discretion to award sanctions against plaintiff's counsel under 28 U.S.C. § 1927.

III.

In imposing joint and several liability upon appellant, the district court stated only that it was acting pursuant to Fed. R. Civ. P. 11 and 28 U.S.C. § 1927. It did not set forth the portion of the sanctions imposed as a result of the perceived § 1927 violation, as opposed to the portion to be allocated pursuant to Rule 11. Thus, we are denied meaningful review.

This court confronted a similar situation in *Jones*, supra. In that case, we concluded that "the court did not identify and relate the violations to each source of authority in a way that would permit meaningful appellate review. . . . In consequence, the entire order imposing sanctions on appellant must be vacated." 899 F.2d 1350 at 1358. We believe that we are constrained to apply the same rationale in this case as well. We therefore will vacate the Order imposing sanctions and remand for further appropriate proceedings in accordance with this opinion.

IV.

Because the order imposing sanctions on appellant must be vacated and the matter remanded, we conclude that certain issues will probably arise on the remand and should, in the interest of justice, be addressed. We refer here specifically to the question of the proper type and amount of sanctions to be imposed pursuant to Rule 11 under the particular circumstances of this case.

A.

We note at the outset that we find no error in the district court's decision to impose sanctions pursuant to Fed. R. Civ. P. 11.[3] As noted above, we review a district court's decision to impose sanctions for abuse of discretion. Cooter & Gell, 496 U.S. at 385. An abuse of discretion in this context would occur if the court "based its ruling on an erroneous

---

[3]   Appellant contended that he was not given the benefit of Rule 11's 21-day safe harbor, because the court dismissed the action before he had had the full opportunity to withdraw it. He thus claimed that sanctions were improper under Rule 11(c)(1)(A) (upon motion by other party). EPPI maintained that the sanctions actually were imposed under Rule 11(c)(1)(B) (on the court's initiative), which has no safe harbor provision. The court issued an order to show cause, which is required only under 11(c)(1)(B), but stated that it was "in consideration of defendant's motion for sanctions." In its accompanying memorandum, the district court did not address this apparent inconsistency. At oral argument before this court, appellant acknowledged that he would not have withdrawn the complaint even if he had been given the full 21-day safe harbor. Thus, we need not address this contention.

view of the law or a clearly erroneous assessment of the evidence." Rogal v. American Broadcasting Companies, Inc., 74 F.3d 40, 44 (3d Cir. 1996).

Prior to a significant amendment in 1983, Rule 11 stated that an attorney might be subjected to disciplinary action only for a "wilful" violation of the rule. The Advisory Committee Notes to the 1983 amendment make clear that the wilfulness prerequisite has been deleted. Rather, the amended rule imposes a duty on counsel to make an inquiry into both the facts and the law which is "reasonable under the circumstances." This is a more stringent standard than the original good-faith formula, and it was expected that a greater range of circumstances would trigger its violation. The district court did not abuse its discretion in determining that appellant had not sufficiently investigated the facts of the case nor had he educated himself well enough as to copyright law. We therefore see no error in the court's decision to impose sanctions.

1. The Inquiry into The Facts

In dismissing the complaint, the court found that "it . . . seems highly probable that plaintiff's claims are barred by the three-year statute of limitations." Later, in the Memorandum and Order imposing sanctions, the court noted that the "obvious" statute of limitations issue would have been resolved and no lawsuit filed, had appellant conducted an adequate investigation. D.C. Memo at 2.

Dr. Zuk left EPPI in 1980, and it is undisputed that EPPI continued to rent out the films in question for some time thereafter. Appellant, however, had no evidence whatsoever, other than conjecture, to prove that the films were being rented in the three years preceding the commencement of this action. The Advisory Committee Notes to the 1993 amendments to Rule 11 explain:

> Tolerance of factual contentions in initial pleadings . . . when specifically identified as made on information and belief does not relieve litigants from the obligation to conduct an appropriate investigation into the facts that is reasonable under the circumstances; it is not a license to . . . make claims . . . without any factual basis or justification."

Appellant's assertions in ¶¶ 36 and 37 of the complaint (in regard to EPPI's ongoing use of the films) are based purely upon Dr. Zuk's beliefs.[4] What little investigation appellant actually conducted did not reveal any information that the films were being rented out during the relevant period. Indeed, certain pre-filing correspondence with EPPI indicated that, pursuant to Dr. Zuk's earlier instructions, the library staff was cautioned not to rent any of Dr. Zuk's films. Nor are we persuaded by appellant's contention that further information would have been obtained during discovery. The Note cited above observes that discovery is not intended as a fishing expedition permitting the speculative pleading of a case first and then pursuing discovery to support it; the plaintiff must have some basis in fact for the action. The need for a reasonable investigation with respect to distribution of the film during

---

[4] EPPI emphasizes that while ¶¶ 36 and 37 should have been pleaded on information and belief, they were instead phrased as "Dr. Zuk believes, and therefore avers,. . . ." In light of liberal federal pleading practice, we do not find this to be an important distinction.

the three-year period prior to the filing of the lawsuit is evident because of the long period allegedly spanned by the distribution.

2.   The Inquiry into The Law

Rule 11(b)(2) requires that all "claims, defenses, and other legal contentions [be] warranted by existing law or by a nonfrivolous argument for the extension, modification, or reversal of existing law or the establishment of new law." Appellant does not contend that any of the latter justifications apply, and so we must ascertain whether his legal arguments are "warranted by existing law." For reasons that follow, we conclude that they are not, and that sanctions therefore were within the sound discretion of the district court.

Appellant's legal research was faulty primarily in two particular areas: copyright law (pertaining to what the parties call the "registration issue") and the law of personal property (the "ownership issue"). Turning to the registration issue, appellant states that this was the first copyright case which he had handled, and points out that a practitioner has to begin somewhere. While we are sympathetic to this argument, its thrust is more toward the nature of the sanctions to be imposed rather than to the initial decision whether sanctions should be imposed. Regrettably, the reality of appellant's weak grasp of copyright law is that it caused him to pursue a course of conduct which was not warranted by existing law and compelled the defendant to expend time and money in needless litigation.

Appellant's primary contention is that by registering a copyright in his book, Dr. Zuk had somehow also protected the films reproduced in them. The logical progression is that because the book contained transcripts of the films, the words spoken in the films were protected, and thus so were the films. Although perhaps logical, this argument runs contrary to copyright law. "The copyright in [a derivative] work . . . does not affect or enlarge the scope, duration, ownership, or subsistence of, any copyright protection in the preexisting material." 17 U.S.C. § 103(b).

In all fairness to appellant, we should note that the cases and commentary interpreting this provision focus on derivative works which incorporate the preexisting work of a different author. Had appellant presented his argument as a matter of first impression, and argued for a new interpretation of the statute where the same individual authored both works, he might have stood upon a more solid footing. Instead, appellant's brief evidences what strikes us as a cursory reading of the copyright laws, and a strained analysis of what appears to be an inapposite case (Gamma Audio & Video, Inc. v. Ean-Chea, 11 F.3d 1106, 1257 (1st Cir. 1993)).

We now focus on the ownership issue. The parties agree that if EPPI owns the copies of the film in its possession, then 17 U.S.C. § 109[5] permits EPPI to rent out the films. Appellant maintains, however, that EPPI does not own the copies, because they were made specifically for Dr. Zuk at his behest, and as a perquisite of his faculty position at EPPI. This question raises reasonable issues as to the rights of an employer in the

---

[5]   This section states in pertinent part that a nonprofit library (such as that operated by EPPI) is free to rent, lease, or lend copywritten material without authority of the copyright owner, so long as the library owns a lawfully made copy of such material.

work product of an employee, and its resolution is not so clear as to itself warrant the sanctioning of appellant for advancing this claim.

EPPI contends, however, that it is too late in the day to raise this argument. The Pennsylvania statute of limitations on replevin is two years. Dr. Zuk demanded the return of the copies in 1980, and EPPI refused to comply, based upon a claim of ownership. EPPI's possession thereafter was open, notorious, and under claim of right, and yet Dr. Zuk did not institute an action to replevy. It would therefore appear that EPPI now holds superior title, see, e.g., Priester v. Milleman, 161 Pa. Super. 507, 55 A.2d 540 (Pa. Super. 1947), and that an inquiry into Pennsylvania personal property law would have revealed that appellant's claim was far too stale. However, EPPI raises its argument too late in this proceeding. It did not rely upon, or even mention, the adverse possession theory before the district court. Because the court could not have relied upon this aspect of the ownership issue in imposing sanctions, it is inappropriate for us to consider it at this time.

B.

Having concluded that there is no error in the district court's decision to impose sanctions upon appellant under Rule 11, we turn now to the type and amount of sanctions imposed. We review the appropriateness of the sanctions imposed for abuse of discretion. Snow Machines, Inc. v. Hedco, Inc., 838 F.2d 718, 724 (3d Cir. 1988). As the courts have undergone experience with the application of Rule 11 sanctions, its scope has broadened and the emphasis of the Rule has changed.

According to Wright & Miller:

> The 1993 revision . . . makes clear that the main purpose of Rule 11 is to deter, not to compensate. Accordingly, it changes the emphasis in the types of sanctions to be ordered. It envisions as the norm public interest remedies such as fines and reprimands, as opposed to the prior emphasis on private interest remedies. Thus, the Advisory Committee Notes state that any monetary penalty "should ordinarily be paid into the court" except "under unusual circumstances" when they should be given to the opposing party. Any sanction imposed should be calibrated to the least severe level necessary to serve the deterrent purpose of the Rule. In addition, the new Rule 11 contemplates greater use of nonmonetary sanctions, including reprimands, orders to undergo continuing education, and referrals to disciplinary authorities.

5A Charles Alan Wright & Arthur R. Miller, Federal Practice & Procedure § 1336 (2d ed. Supp. 1996).

This court has instructed the district courts that "fee-shifting is but one of several methods of achieving the various goals of Rule 11," that they should "consider a wide range of alternative possible sanctions for violation of the rule," and that the "district court's choice of deterrent is appropriate when it is the minimum that will serve to adequately deter the undesirable behavior." Doering v. Union County Bd. of Chosen Freeholders, 857 F.2d 191, 194 (3d Cir. 1988).

Thus, the district courts have been encouraged to consider mitigating factors in fashioning sanctions, most particularly the sanctioned party's ability to pay. Id. at 195. Courts were also given examples of other factors they might consider, including whether the attorney has a history of this sort of behavior, the defendant's need for compensation, the degree of frivolousness, and the "willfulness" of the violation. Id. at 197 n.6.

In *Doering*, a $25,000 sanction was imposed on a sole practitioner with less than $40,000 gross income per annum. We affirmed the district court's decision to impose sanctions, but vacated and remanded as to the amount. We noted that "in order for the district court to exercise properly its discretion in setting the amount of fees to be assessed against counsel, further evidence must be developed upon the issue of his ability to pay." Id. at 196.

Although money sanctions are not encouraged under Rule 11, they are not forbidden. Under the circumstances of this case, we see no error in the district court's imposition of fee sanctions upon the appellant, although the amount may be contrary to the current spirit of Rule 11. The present case differs from *Doering* in that appellant did not request that the district court mitigate the sanctions. Appellant also faces a lesser financial burden in that he is liable for only $8,750, his client having paid the difference. Nonetheless, when we look to the list of mitigating factors, and consider the non-punitive purpose of Rule 11, we conclude that it was error to invoke without comment a very severe penalty. On remand, the district court should apply the principles announced by this court in *Doering*.

V.

To summarize, to the extent the Order of the district court dated February 1, 1996 imposed sanctions upon appellant pursuant to Fed. R. Civ. P. 11, it will be affirmed only as to the actual imposition of such sanctions. The Order will be vacated as to the type and amount of sanctions imposed under Rule 11 and as to any sanctions imposed under 28 U.S.C. § 1927. The case will be remanded for further proceedings consistent with this opinion.

Each side to bear its own costs.

NOTE ON FEDERAL RULE 11 AND OTHER DEVICES DESIGNED TO DETER FRIVOLOUS OR ABUSIVE LITIGATION

1. **What constitutes a frivolous claim under Rule 11?** Rule 11 has four elements: (a) a requirement that every pleading, motion or other paper be signed; (b) a declaration that the signature shall be treated as a certification that the document has certain attributes; (c) a description of the required attributes—that the document has been prepared after reasonable investigation and that to the best of the signer's knowledge, information, and belief the document meets minimum standards of factual merit, legal merit, and lack of improper purpose; and (d) a description of the standards and process for the award of sanctions when a certification is found to violate the rule.

a. **Reasonable investigation and evidentiary support.** In signing a complaint or other pleading, the lawyer or unrepresented party certifies that she has made a reasonable investigation. What does a reasonable investigation consist of when your opponent controls the evidence? The court in *Zuk* writes that "pre-filing correspondence with EPPI indicated that, pursuant to Dr. Zuk's earlier instructions, the library staff was cautioned not to rent any of Dr. Zuk's films." Was Dr. Zuk required to take the statements in the correspondence at face value? If not, would it have been ethically proper for Dr. Zuk to run a sting directed to the lending counter at the library? Could Dr. Zuk's lawyer have complied with Rule 11 without conducting such a sting?

The requirement that factual claims have "evidentiary support" or, if so identified, "will likely have evidentiary support after a reasonable opportunity for further investigation or discovery" clearly permits the pleader to advance a contention without sufficient evidence in hand to permit a finding in her favor at trial, provided that there is a reasonable likelihood of such information emerging in discovery. The problem arises when, after discovery, there is a failure of proof and the party's claim or defense is dismissed. How does a court go about determining, after the fact, whether at the time of filing there was a "reasonable likelihood" that such evidence would emerge? Consider, for example, the situation of a lawyer for the plaintiff in a case alleging intentional racial discrimination in employment under Title VII of the Civil Rights Act of 1964. Suppose that the lawyer, after pre-filing investigation, has only his client's strong belief that he was discriminated against and the company's written denial that discrimination occurred. Isn't the lawyer in such a case in many ways like the lawyer in *McCormick v. Kopmann*? How does the lawyer decide whether a court will later agree that it was "reasonably likely" that such evidence would emerge from discovery if in fact such proof fails to emerge? Put another way, what is the status under Rule 11 of a claim that is not indisputably without factual merit but that is nonetheless a long shot? Is there some risk that judges will differ in their assessment of the probability of discrimination emerging after full discovery, perhaps even along political, racial or gender lines? See Uy v. Bronx Municipal Hosp. Ctr., 182 F.3d 152 (2d Cir. 1999) (Rule 11 sanctions denied because prior to discovery plaintiff's lawyer could not have known that all adverse witnesses would contradict his client's story); Yablon, The Good, the Bad, and the Frivolous Case: An Essay on Probability and Rule 11, 44 U.C.L.A. L. Rev. 65 (1996).

The statute of limitations is an affirmative defense. Fed. R. Civ. P. 8(c)(1). For that reason, Dr. Zuk did not have to plead compliance with the statute in order to survive a motion to dismiss for failure to state a claim. It was enough for him to plead the elements of a claim under the copyright laws, and it was then the defendant's option to plead or waive the affirmative defense of the statute of limitations. That does not mean that Dr. Zuk's lawyer was entitled to proceed in ignorance of the statute of limitations issue. His obligation to represent Dr. Zuk competently almost certainly required him to assess both the strength of the limitations defense and the likelihood that it would be asserted. But is it consistent with Rule 11, which governs the making of contentions, to sanction a lawyer for contending something that his complaint was not required to and did not explicitly contend? Is it consistent with the assumptions of an adversary system?

A litigant has a continuing duty to ensure that his representations to the court meet the standards of the rule. For example, if a factual allegation in the complaint is made after reasonable investigation (thus complying with the rule at the time it is made), but is later learned to be without foundation, a litigant may not continue to "present" it to court by "later advocating" it. Prohibited "presentations" to the court include oral advocacy based on written material that violates the rule. Fed. R. Civ. P. 11(b).

b.   Warranted by existing law or a non-frivolous argument for the extension, modification, or reversal of existing law, or the creation of new law. There are obviously a number of objective indicia of whether a legal argument is frivolous: the text of any relevant statute, rule, or regulation; the prominence, number, and date of decisions in the controlling jurisdiction accepting or rejecting the argument; the level of support for the argument in decisions rejecting it (for example, dissenting opinions); the treatment of the argument in cases from other jurisdictions; the power of analogous arguments drawn from the controlling jurisdiction or others; the content of academic commentary, etc. Often these sources will clearly establish the respectability of an argument. But only rarely will they conclusively establish its complete lack of merit.

Important issues of indeterminacy arise in determining when a legal argument is so clearly improper that a lawyer should be sanctioned for filing it. Although judges are fond of saying that arguments are obviously wrong or even wacky, legal frivolity turns out to be like obscenity: judges "know it when they see it." There are a significant number of cases in which arguments sanctioned as frivolous in the district court have been held to be winning arguments in the court of appeals. Meyer, When Reasonable Minds Differ, 71 N.Y.U. L. Rev. 1467, 1484 & n. 47 (1996) (cataloguing cases). There are also cases in which arguments that were accepted as winners in the district court have been held frivolous and sanctionable in the court of appeals. Professor Levinson describes one such case:

> A Texas case in which an oil company argued that a statutory requirement of a bid for an oil lease was that the royalty offer be written as a percentage. The company therefore argued that its competitor, who had offered a royalty of .82165 had not complied with the statute, which purportedly required an offer of 82.165 percent. The Fifth Circuit pronounced this argument "quite incredible," and its opinion quoted from some children's arithmetic books on how to convert decimals into percentages and vice versa. But the most notable point is that the district judge below had apparently accepted this argument, and the Fifth Circuit had to reverse him.

Levinson, Frivolous Cases: Do Lawyers Really Know Anything at All?, 24 Osgoode Hall L.J. 353, 370–71 (1986) (footnotes omitted) (citing Oil & Gas Futures, Inc. v. Andrus, 610 F.2d 287, 288 (5th Cir. 1980)). For a vivid list of apparently "odd-ball" claims that succeeded on the merits, see Rhode, Access to Justice 24–25 (2004).

Perhaps because of courts' discomfort with the lack of standards for determining legal frivolousness, many decisions sanctioning legal arguments are written in terms that avoid the force of the argument itself and instead attack the lawyer's research or the failure to identify the legal argument as novel in the papers filed with the court. Did the court in *Zuk* pursue such a strategy here? Recall Judge Rosenn's suggestion: "Had appellant presented his argument as a matter of first impression, and argued for a new interpretation of the statute where the same individual authored both works, he might have stood upon a more solid footing. Instead, appellant's brief evidences what strikes us as a cursory reading of the copyright laws, and a strained analysis of what appears to be an inapposite case." Is the court saying that a district court can sometimes decide whether an argument is frivolous based upon whether the lawyer admits its weaknesses? The Advisory Committee Notes state that although "arguments for a change of law are not required to be specifically so identified, a contention that is so identified should be viewed with greater tolerance under the rule." Is that approach consistent with encouraging vigorous advocacy for legal change? Cf. Golden Eagle Distrib. Corp. v. Burroughs Corp., 801 F.2d 1531 (9th Cir. 1986) (arguing against requiring lawyers to explicitly identify novel arguments).

c. **Not being presented for an improper purpose.** Most reported cases imposing sanctions under Rule 11 do so on the ground of lack of merit of the substantive claim or failure to perform a proper investigation. Sanctions for improper purpose are much less frequent. The courts have had difficulty with cases where the claim is not frivolous on the merits, but the party or lawyer's underlying purpose goes beyond simply winning on the merits, whether by getting revenge, dramatizing a political cause, or causing embarrassment to an opponent. The literal text of the rule indicates that presenting a minimally meritorious contention with an improper purpose constitutes a violation, but the courts have often hesitated to impose sanctions in such cases for fear of deterring meritorious claims.

Some courts hold that when a pleading or contention is neither legally nor factually frivolous, sanctions are unavailable regardless of the underlying purpose. Sussman v. Bank of Israel, 56 F.3d 450 (2d Cir. 1995) (no violation of Rule 11 when a complaint adequately grounded in law and fact is filed "with a view to exerting pressure on defendants through the generation of adverse and economically disadvantageous publicity."). Others argue that the inquiry should be whether the illicit purpose dominates over a legitimate purpose "to vindicate rights in court," In re Kunstler, 914 F.2d 505 (4th Cir. 1990), or whether the case is an "exceptional" one "where the improper purpose is objectively ascertainable." Whitehead v. Food Max of Miss., Inc., 332 F.3d 796, 805 (5th Cir. 2003). In *Whitehead*, the court affirmed an award of sanctions against a lawyer who had won a $3.2 million judgment against Kmart. The plaintiffs were a mother and child who had been kidnapped from a Kmart parking lot. The mother was then raped while the daughter was held at knife point. Three days after judgment, the lawyer for the plaintiffs obtained a writ of execution and accompanied two U.S. Marshals to the Kmart store where the kidnapping had occurred. He invited three TV stations to cover the event. At the store, the lawyer initially attempted to seize currency in the cash registers and vault, though ultimately no money was seized. The lawyer also gave interviews to the TV reporters, which were widely broadcast. The lawyer "asserted Kmart 'wo[uld no]t pay' the judgment; claimed Kmart had been 'warned' before the abduction that 'an event like [that] was going to happen' but 'didn't care'; charged his clients had been twice 'victimized' by Kmart, once by being abducted there and once by Kmart's 'not paying . . . a just debt'; and proclaimed he was there to ensure Kmart did what it was supposed to do." 332 F.2d at 800. The court of appeals, sitting en banc, affirmed the imposition of sanctions. The court found it unnecessary to decide whether the service of the writ was adequately supported in fact or law. Ordinarily, the court suggested, the district court should not "read an ulterior motive" into a document "well grounded in fact and law," but this case demonstrated "exceptional circumstances." 332 F.3d at 805. There was little evidence of a legitimate purpose, since the lawyer had no reason to think that Kmart would not pay the judgment and no hope of finding anything close to $3.2 million on the premises of a single store. The district court therefore did not abuse its discretion in finding that the lawyer had acted with two improper purposes: to embarrass Kmart and to promote himself. For a discussion of the improper purpose issue and an argument that some politically motivated suits ought to be entitled to First Amendment protection see Andrews, *Jones v. Clinton*: A Study in Politically Motivated Suits, Rule 11, and the First Amendment, 2001 B.Y.U. L. Rev. 1 (2001).

2.   **Previous versions of Rule 11.** Federal Rule 11 is now in its third principal incarnation. The original version of Rule 11 permitted sanctions only for pleadings filed in bad faith. In consequence, sanctions were rarely awarded. In 1983 the rule was amended in two critical respects. First, the standard for liability under the amended rule was changed from subjective to objective. Second, the trial court was obliged to impose sanctions whenever it found that the rule had been violated.

The 1983 amendments produced a radical change in practice under the Rule. While litigation during the first 45 years of the rule's existence had produced nine reported judicial opinions, in the 10 years following the adoption of the amended Rule 11 there were thousands of reported opinions under the rule and many more unreported opinions.

Rule 11 was substantially amended in 1993. The amendment was the product of dissatisfaction among a number of people, including some plaintiffs' groups and many members of the bar. A study of the operation of the 1983 version of the Rule in the Fifth, Seventh, and Ninth Circuits found that civil rights cases made up 11.4 percent of federal cases filed, but 22.7 percent of the cases in which Rule 11 sanctions were applied. Among civil rights plaintiffs' lawyers, 31 percent reported not pursuing a claim or defense they thought had potential merit because of Rule 11; only 17.9 percent of civil rights defendants' lawyers reported being similarly deterred. Marshall et al., The Use and Impact of Rule 11, 86 Nw. U. L. Rev. 943 (1992).

3.   **The 1993 changes in sanctioning policy and the current rule.** The concerns outlined by the Advisory Committee led to several major changes in the operation of the sanctions provisions of the rule:

a.   **"Safe harbor."** A litigant can escape sanctions by withdrawing an offending pleading or representation within 21 days of being served with a motion by an opposing party. Fed. R. Civ. P. 11(c)(2). The motion may not be filed with the court until the 21-day clock has run, and if the court takes action on the challenged pleading before the expiration of the 21-day period, no sanctions may be awarded in response to the motion. Ridder v. City of Springfield, 109 F.3d 288 (6th Cir. 1997). The safe harbor rule was designed to reduce the volume of litigation under Rule 11 and to reduce its potential chilling effect on the assertion of doubtful factual and innovative legal claims. Doesn't it also reduce the Rule's deterrent effect?

A district court may impose Rule 11 sanctions on its own motion without having to observe the 21-day safe-harbor period. Fed. R. Civ. P. 11(c)(3). According to the Advisory Committee Notes, the rule contemplates that court-initiated sanctions will be issued in a narrower range of circumstances than party-initiated sanctions. Such sanctions will " 'ordinarily be issued only in situations that are akin to a contempt of court.' " Barber v. Miller, 146 F.3d 707, 711 (9th Cir. 1998).

b.   Standards for the award of sanctions. While the award of sanctions under the former rule was mandatory upon a finding that the rule had been violated, under the current Rule the district judge may choose not to impose sanctions. Fed. R. Civ. P. 11(c). Moreover, while under the former Rule an award of costs, including attorney's fees, to the other side was the standard sanction, the current Rule cautions that sanctions under the Rule "must be limited to what suffices to deter repetition of the conduct or comparable conduct by others similarly situated." Fed. R. Civ. P. 11(c)(4). Available sanctions include "nonmonetary directives"; an order to pay money to the court; and an order to pay the expenses, including attorney's fees, to the other side but only "if imposed on motion and warranted for effective deterrence." Id.

c.   Persons liable for sanctions. The current Rule 11 also provides that if a court determines that the duty set forth in subdivision (b) is violated, it may "impose an appropriate sanction on any attorney, law firm, or party that violated the rule or is responsible for the violation." Fed. R. Civ. P. 11(c)(1). Fed. R. Civ. P. 11(c)(5)(A) provides an exception to this general rule, stating that monetary sanctions cannot be awarded against a represented party for violation of the requirement of legal merit.

The Advisory Committee Notes state that "[t]he revision permits the court to consider whether other attorneys in the firm, co-counsel, other law firms, or the party itself should be held accountable for their part in causing a violation." In the context of this sentence, "the party itself" appears to mean a represented party. If this is so, then a represented party may be "responsible" for a violation by his attorney, and, subject to Rule 11(c)(1), therefore liable for sanctions for that violation.

But under the current rule only "an attorney or unrepresented party" is instructed to sign and certify submissions to the court, and thus, under a strict reading of the language, only an attorney or unrepresented party can violate the rule. Sanctions may be imposed on a represented party only for a violation by his attorney, and only if the party is "responsible" for his attorney's violation. Assume that the party is a convincing liar. The attorney discharges her duty of making "an inquiry reasonable under the circumstances," but since the client is such a good liar, the attorney believes the story and files a complaint. Since this is not a violation of the lawyer's duty, may the client avoid sanction, even though a flagrantly unfounded complaint has been filed based on lies propounded by the client?

The few lower federal courts that have addressed sanctions for represented parties have not spent much time agonizing. See, e.g., Union Planters Bank v. L & J Dev. Co., Inc., 115 F.3d 378, 384 (6th Cir. 1997) (upholding sanctions against represented defendants "for misrepresenting key facts during both depositions and trial testimony, and knowingly bringing and pursuing claims devoid of evidentiary support"); Binghamton Masonic Temple, Inc. v. Bares, 168 F.R.D. 121 (N.D.N.Y. 1996) (sanctioning a represented party for bringing a claim with an improper purpose and for misleading both its own attorney and the opposing party). Perhaps these results may be defended, even if not covered by the literal language of Rule 11, on the ground that the court has inherent power to sanction bad faith client conduct.

4.   Other power to sanction. Rule 11 is not the only source of a federal district court's power to sanction frivolous litigation or abusive tactics.

a.   28 U.S.C. § 1927. Under 28 U.S.C. § 1927, discussed in *Zuk*, a federal district court may award costs, including attorneys' fees, against an attorney (though not a party) who "multiplies the proceedings in any case unreasonably and vexatiously." Prior to 1980, § 1927 allowed only an award of costs, and as a consequence was rarely invoked. Roadway Express, Inc. v. Piper, 447 U.S. 752, 100 S.Ct. 2455, 65 L.Ed.2d 488 (1980). After § 1927 was amended in 1980 to include attorneys' fees, § 1927 was invoked more frequently. The Supreme Court has never articulated the standard for sanctions under § 1927, and the courts of appeals disagree. Some, like the Third Circuit in *Zuk*, require subjective bad faith. See Avirgan v. Hull, 932 F.2d 1572 (11th Cir. 1991); United States v. Int'l Bhd. of Teamsters, 948 F.2d 1338 (2d Cir. 1991). Other Circuits require only an objective standard. See Miera v. Dairyland Ins. Co., 143 F.3d 1337 (10th Cir. 1998). Before imposing sanctions under § 1927, a district court must give the party notice and opportunity to defend against the threatened sanctions. Ted Lapidus, S.A. v. Vann, 112 F.3d 91 (2d Cir. 1997).

b.   Inherent power. Federal district courts also have "inherent power" to award sanctions. In Chambers v. NASCO, Inc., 501 U.S. 32, 111 S.Ct. 2123, 115 L.Ed.2d 27 (1991), the Supreme Court upheld an award of attorneys' fees and expenses totaling almost $1 million against a party for a sustained pattern of bad-faith litigating tactics. Sanctions were not available under 28 U.S.C. § 1927, which is limited to awards against attorneys, and only a portion of the conduct was covered under Rule 11. The Supreme Court sustained the entire award based on the district court's "inherent power" to sanction bad-faith litigation tactics. The Court wrote, "[Plaintiff Chambers'] entire course of conduct throughout the lawsuit evidenced bad faith and an attempt to perpetrate a fraud on the court, and the conduct sanctionable under the Rules was intertwined within conduct that only the inherent power could address. In circumstances such as these in which all of a litigant's conduct is deemed sanctionable, requiring a court first to apply Rules and statutes containing sanctioning provisions to discrete occurrences before invoking inherent power to address remaining instances of sanctionable conduct would serve only to foster extensive and needless satellite litigation, which is contrary to the aim of the Rules themselves." 501 U.S. at 51.

5.   State law counterparts. Although relatively few states have adopted Fed. R. Civ. P. 11 precisely, many states have counterparts. California has oscillated between different statutory solutions. At some times, the statute has embodied a bad faith standard. The current version of the statute, Calif. C. Civ. P. § 128.7, is virtually identical to Fed. R. Civ. P. 11.

6.   Additional reading. There is a vast literature on Rule 11. For a small sample, see Guthrie, Framing Frivolous Litigation: A Psychological Theory, 67 U. Chi. L. Rev. 163 (2000); Bone, Modeling Frivolous Suits, 145 U. Pa. L. Rev. 519 (1997); Schwarzer, Rule 11: Entering a New Era, 28 Loy. L.A. L. Rev. 7 (1994); Tobias, The 1993 Revision of Federal Rule 11, 70 Ind. L.J. 171 (1994).

F. RESPONDING TO THE COMPLAINT

1. MOTIONS AND DEFENSES UNDER RULE 12

NOTE ON MOTIONS RESPONDING TO THE COMPLAINT AND ON THE PRESENTATION AND PRESERVATION OF DEFENSES

1. **Rule 12 motions to dismiss.** The responsive pleading to a complaint is the "answer." In the answer, the defendant is required to "state in short and plain terms its defenses to each claim asserted," "admit or deny the allegations asserted against it by an opposing party," and "affirmatively state any avoidance or affirmative defense." Fed. R. Civ. P. 8(b)(1), (c). The answer must also typically state any available counterclaims the defendant intends to assert against the plaintiff. Fed. R. Civ. P. 13. As a result, preparing an answer is a rather complicated enterprise requiring a significant investment of time and resources. What if a defendant thinks that the plaintiff's case is fundamentally flawed for some reason, perhaps because it was filed in the wrong forum, or because it fails to state a legal claim? Must the defendant go to the trouble of preparing an answer if it believes that plaintiff's case should be cut off at the knees?

The answer is often, "no." Federal Rule 12 authorizes a number of *pre-answer* motions to dismiss that the defendant can make in lieu of an answer to the complaint. We have already examined two such motions: the motion to dismiss for failure to state a claim under Rule 12(b)(6) and the motion for more definite statement under Rule 12(e). In addition, Rule 12 authorizes the defendant to raise by motion several other defenses, listed in subsections (1)–(5) and (7) of Rule 12(b). These defenses are generally directed at where and how the plaintiff has asserted her claim, as opposed to the substantive merits of the claim. For instance, a Rule 12 motion may contend that the plaintiff has filed her case in a court without jurisdiction or in an improper venue. These defenses do not go to the merits of the litigation, but instead posit that the case must be dismissed and filed again in a proper forum. If a defendant believes that he can make a successful motion to dismiss on one of the grounds enumerated in Rule 12, then he may make that motion and delay filing an answer until the court has ruled. Fed. R. Civ. P. 12(a)(4).

2. **Preserving defenses under Rule 12.** Rule 12 is a minefield. That is because some Rule 12 defenses are waivable and a lawyer must be careful to assert them properly. If a lawyer fails to assert Rule 12 defenses in accordance with the rule, he may find himself, ahem, waving goodbye forever to those defenses. Read Rule 12 carefully, with special attention to Rule 12(g) and Rule 12(h). Why do you think the Rule requires that many of these defenses be raised either by pre-answer motion or in the answer?

To understand how Rule 12 works, the first thing to note is that a defendant may always elect to forgo filing a Rule 12 motion and simply file an answer including any of the Rule 12(b) defenses. If the defendant decides to take this route, she must include in the answer any of the defenses listed in Rule 12(b)(2)–(5), or she has waived them (unless she amends the answer to add such a defense pursuant to Rule 15(a)(1)). The defendant may wait to assert a defense under Rule 12(b)(6) or 12(b)(7) in a motion for judgment on the pleadings or at trial. The defendant may assert the defense of lack of subject matter jurisdiction under Rule 12(b)(1) at any point in the litigation, even for the first time after trial or on appeal.

In essence, the relative waivability of these defenses is correlated to their relative importance. The defenses listed in Rule 12(b)(2)–(5) involve personal jurisdiction, venue, and service of process. While these defenses protect important interests, each may be waived and none goes to the merits of the plaintiff's claims. The defenses in Rule 12(b)(6) and (7) (failure to state a claim, and failure to join an indispensable party) are more central to the litigation because they go to the underlying merits of the case and the court's ability to effectively resolve the controversy. As a result, these defenses are available even after the pleadings are closed. Finally, the defense of lack of subject matter jurisdiction is deemed of paramount importance because it goes to the power available to the federal courts under the Constitution and federal statutes. As a result, that defense is *never* waivable and can be raised at any time. In fact, a court has a responsibility to raise a defect in subject matter jurisdiction on its own motion.

Once you have this scheme down, we can complicate matters by considering the impact of a pre-answer motion to dismiss. *If* a defendant chooses to make a pre-answer motion to dismiss, she must raise any defenses she has among those listed in 12(b)(2)–(5), or she has waived them. Fed. R. Civ. P. 12(g). The reason for this requirement is readily apparent: it prevents the defendant from unduly delaying the litigation by making a series of motions under Rule 12 one after the other. Even if a defendant has made a pre-answer motion to dismiss, she may later raise a defense under Rule 12(b)(6) and 12(b)(7) in the answer, a motion for judgment on the pleadings, or at trial. Fed. R. Civ. P. 12(h)(2). And, again, a defendant may raise a motion to dismiss for lack of subject matter jurisdiction at any time. Fed. R. Civ. P. 12(h)(3).

Although the Rules seem irritatingly technical at first, with some practice you will get the hang of them. To test your understanding, try answering the following questions:

a.   Plaintiff files a complaint. Defendant files a motion under Rule 12(b)(6) to dismiss the complaint for failure to state a claim. The motion is denied. Defendant now files motions under Rule 12(b)(2) to dismiss for lack of jurisdiction over the person and under Rule 12(e) for a more definite statement. Plaintiff responds that the issues of lack of personal jurisdiction and indefiniteness have been waived. How should the court rule on the second set of motions and why? Rule for P   12h1

b.   Plaintiff files a complaint. Defendant files a motion under Rules 12(b)(2) and (b)(5) to dismiss for lack of jurisdiction over the person and insufficiency of service of process. The motions are denied. Defendant then files an answer asserting the defense of improper venue. Plaintiff moves to strike the defense of improper venue from Defendant's answer. How should the court rule on the motion and why? Rule for P 12h1

c.   Plaintiff files a complaint. Defendant files a motion under Rule 12(b)(2) to dismiss for lack of jurisdiction over the person. The court denies the motion. Defendant then files an answer raising the defense that the complaint failed to state a claim. Plaintiff moves to strike the defense of failure to state a claim from Defendant's answer. How should the court rule? Rule for D 12h(2)

d.   Plaintiff files a complaint. Defendant files an answer denying the principal allegations of the complaint. Later in the action, Defendant moves to amend the answer to assert the defenses of lack of personal jurisdiction, failure to state a claim, and failure to join an indispensable party under Rule 19. Plaintiff objects that those defenses have been waived. How should the court rule on the motion to amend?

e.   Plaintiff files a complaint. Defendant moves to dismiss under Rule 12(b)(6) for failure to state a claim. The court denies the motion. Defendant now files an answer asserting the defense of lack of subject matter jurisdiction, and, following the filing of the answer, moves to dismiss the action on that ground. If Plaintiff contends that the defense of subject matter jurisdiction is waived, how should the court rule and why? What if, instead of filing an answer and then moving to dismiss on grounds of lack of subject matter jurisdiction, Defendant had simply "suggested" that subject matter jurisdiction was lacking?

3.   Motion for judgment on the pleadings. Federal Rule 12(c) provides that a party may move for judgment on the pleadings "[a]fter the pleadings have closed—but early enough not to delay trial." The Rule 12(c) motion creates an opportunity to resolve a case early on in the litigation process if it can be decided based on the pleadings alone. This can be the case if the parties agree on the relevant facts and the case can be resolved through simply applying the law to those facts. For instance, if the case turns on the interpretation of a relevant statute, or the pleadings disclose that a case falls outside the applicable statute of limitations, the court may resolve the case based on the pleadings alone. As noted above, a defendant may also raise a defense under Rule 12(b)(1), 12(b)(6), or 12(b)(7) in a motion for judgment on the pleadings. See Wright, Miller & Kane, Federal Practice & Procedure § 1367 (3d ed. 2005).

4.   Presenting matters outside the pleadings. In theory, a court ought to be able to decide a motion under Rule 12(b)(6) or 12(c) by looking exclusively at the pleadings. Indeed, the whole point of offering such a motion is to provide an early opportunity to resolve litigation on the merits so the parties do not waste significant expense on discovery in a case whose result is foreordained. But sometimes such a motion demands assessment of material beyond the four corners of the pleadings and examination of factual material, such as affidavits or other documentary materials. If the court decides that proper resolution of the motion requires consideration of such materials, Rule 12(d) requires the court to convert the motion into one for summary judgment under Rule 56, which is discussed infra, Chapter 7.B. See, e.g., Perlman v. Fidelity Services, 932 F. Supp. 2d 397 (E.D.N.Y. 2013) (converting a motion for judgment on the pleadings into one for summary judgment when "the Court has relied, at least in part, on deposition excerpts and other exhibits submitted by the parties in conjunction with their moving papers").

2. THE ANSWER

Zielinski v. Philadelphia Piers, Inc.

United States District Court, Eastern District of Pennsylvania, 1956.
139 F. Supp. 408.

■ VAN DUSEN, DISTRICT JUDGE.

Plaintiff requests a ruling that, for the purposes of this case, the motordriven fork lift operated by Sandy Johnson on February 9, 1953, was owned by defendant and that Sandy Johnson was its agent acting in the course of his employment on that date. The following facts are established by the pleadings, interrogatories, depositions and uncontradicted portions of affidavits:

1.   Plaintiff filed his complaint on April 28, 1953, for personal injuries received on February 9, 1953, while working on Pier 96, Philadelphia, for J. A. McCarthy, as a result of a collision of two motor-driven fork lifts.

2.   Paragraph 5 of this complaint stated that 'a motor-driven vehicle known as a fork lift or chisel, owned, operated and controlled by the defendant, its agents, servants and employees, was so negligently and carelessly managed * * * that the same * * * did come into contact with the plaintiff causing him to sustain the injuries more fully hereinafter set forth.'

3.   The 'First Defense' of the Answer stated 'Defendant * * * (c) denies the averments of paragraph 5 * * *.'

4.   The motor-driven vehicle known as a fork lift or chisel, which collided with the McCarthy fork lift on which plaintiff was riding, had on it the initials 'P.P.I.'

5.   On February 10, 1953, Carload Contractors, Inc. made a report of this accident to its insurance company, whose policy No. CL 3964 insured Carload Contractors, Inc. against potential liability for the negligence of its employees contributing to a collision of the type described in paragraph 2 above.

6.   By letter of April 29, 1953, the complaint served on defendant was forwarded to the above-mentioned insurance company. This letter read as follows:

'Gentlemen:

'As per telephone conversation today with your office, we attach hereto 'Complaint in Trespass' as brought against Philadelphia Piers, Inc. by one Frank Zielinski for supposed injuries sustained by him on February 9, 1953.

'We find that a fork lift truck operated by an employee of Carload Contractors, Inc. also insured by yourselves was involved in an accident with another chisel truck, which, was alleged, did cause injury to Frank Zielinski, and same was reported to you by Carload Contractors, Inc. at the time, and you assigned Claim Number OL 0153–94 to this claim.

'Should not this Complaint in Trespass be issued against Carload Contractors, Inc. and not Philadelphia Piers, Inc.?

'We forward for your handling.'

7.   Interrogatories 1 to 5 and the answers thereto,[1] which were sworn to by defendant's General Manager on June 12, 1953, and filed on June 22, 1953, read as follows:

'1.   State whether you have received any information of an injury sustained by the plaintiff on February 9, 1953, South Wharves. If so, state when and from whom you first received notice of such injury. A. We were first notified of this accident on or about February 9, 1953 by Thomas Wilson.

'2.   State whether you caused an investigation to be made of the circumstances of said injury and if so, state who made such investigation and when it was made. A. We made a very brief investigation on February 9, 1953 and turned the matter over to (our insurance company) for further investigation.

'3.   Give the names and addresses of all persons disclosed by such investigation to have been witnesses to the aforesaid occurrence. A. The witnesses whose names we have obtained so far are:

'Victor Marzo, 2005 E. Hart Lane, Philadelphia

'Thomas Wilson, 6115 Reinhardt St., Philadelphia

'Sandy Johnson, 1236 S. 16th Street, Philadelphia

'4.   State whether you have obtained any written statements from such witnesses and if so, identify such statements and state when and by whom they were taken. If in writing, attach copies of same hereto. A. We have obtained written statements from Victor Marzo, Thomas Wilson and Sandy Johnson and these statements are in the possession of our counsel * * *, who advises that copies need not be attached unless we are ordered by the court to do so.

'5.   Set forth the facts disclosed by such statements and investigation concerning the manner in which the accident happened. A. Sandy Johnson was moving boxes on Pier 96 and had stopped his towmotor when a towmotor operated by an employee of McCarthy Stevedoring Company with a person on the back, apparently the plaintiff, backed into the standing towmotor, injuring the plaintiff.'

8.   At a deposition taken August 18, 1953, Sandy Johnson testified that he was the employee of defendant on February 9, 1953, and had been their employee for approximately fifteen years.

---

[1]   Plaintiff's argument that the answers to other interrogatories are misleading does not seem significant in view of the fact that plaintiff had the opportunity to frame these interrogatories (and could have filed requests for admissions) in a form that would have secured clearer answers and in view of the answer to Interrogatory 15. This order is being based on the inadequacy of the answer; and the inaccuracy of statements in the answers in the interrogatories, in view of the misleading effect of such inadequate answer and inaccurate statements under all the circumstances, including the inaccurate testimony of Sandy Johnson as described below.

9.   At a pre-trial conference held on September 27, 1955,[3] plaintiff first learned that over a year before February 9, 1953, the business of moving freight on piers in Philadelphia, formerly conducted by defendant, had been sold by it to Carload Contractors, Inc. and Sandy Johnson had been transferred to the payroll of this corporation without apparently realizing it, since the nature or location of his work had not changed.

10. As a result of the following answers to Supplementary Interrogatories 16 to 19, filed October 21, 1955, plaintiff learned the facts stated in paragraphs 5 and 6 above in the fall of 1955:

'16. With reference to your answer to Interrogatory #1, state the name and address of the person employed by you who first received notice of this accident on or about February 9, 1953. A. Joseph Nolan, Office Manager.

'17. With reference to your answer to Interrogatory #2, give the name and address of the person who conducted the investigation on February 9, 1953. A. Joseph Nolan, Office Manager.

'18. With reference to your answer to Interrogatory #2, state the name and address of the person who turned the matter over to (your insurance company) and state whether the matter was turned over by telephone or by letter. If by letter, attach copy of same hereto. A. Joseph Nolan gave the information to James L. Maher, Office Manager, of Carload Contractors, Inc., as a result of which the attached accident report signed by Jonathan Wainwright, Treasurer of Carload Contractors, Inc. was forwarded to (the insurance company) on February 10, 1953.

'19. State whether or not any person on your behalf submitted a written report of the accident to (your insurance company). If so, give the name and address of such person, the date of said written report and attach copy of same hereto. A. Yes, the attached report[4] dated April 29, 1953, was submitted to the insurance company after suit was started.'

11. Defendant now admits that on February 9, 1953, it owned the fork lift in the custody of Sandy Johnson and that this fork lift was leased to Carload Contractors, Inc. It is also admitted that the pier on which the accident occurred was leased by defendant.

12. There is no indication of action by either party in bad faith and there is no proof of inaccurate statements being made with intent to deceive. Because defendant made a prompt investigation of the accident (see answers to Interrogatories 1, 2, 16 and 17), its insurance company has been representing the defendant since suit was brought, and this company insures Carload Contractors, Inc. also, requiring defendant to defend this suit, will not prejudice it.

Under these circumstances, and for the purposes of this action, it is ordered that the following shall be stated to the jury at the trial:

---

[3]   The applicable statute of limitations prevented any suit against Carload Contractors, Inc. after February 9, 1955, 12 P.S. § 34.

[4]   This is the letter quoted in paragraph 6 above.

'It is admitted that, on February 9, 1953, the towmotor or fork lift bearing the initials 'P.P.I.' was owned by defendant and that Sandy Johnson was a servant in the employ of defendant and doing its work on that date.'

This ruling is based on the following principles:

1.   Under the circumstances of this case, the answer contains an ineffective denial of that part of paragraph 5 of the complaint which alleges that 'a motor driven vehicle known as a fork lift or chisel (was) owned, operated and controlled by the defendant, its agents, servants and employees.'

F.R.Civ.P. 8(b), 28 U.S.C. provides:

'A party shall state in short and plain terms his defenses to each claim asserted and shall admit or deny the averments upon which the adverse party relies. * * * Denials shall fairly meet the substance of the averments denied. When a pleader intends in good faith to deny only a part or a qualification of an averment, he shall specify so much of it as is true and material and shall deny only the remainder.'

For example, it is quite clear that defendant does not deny the averment in paragraph 5 that the fork lift came into contact with plaintiff, since it admits, in the answers to interrogatories, that an investigation of an occurrence of the accident had been made and that a report dated February 10, 1953, was sent to its insurance company stating 'While Frank Zielinski was riding on bumper of chisel and holding rope to secure cargo, the chisel truck collided with another chisel truck operated by Sandy Johnson causing injuries to Frank Zielinski's legs and hurt head of Sandy Johnson.' Compliance with the above-mentioned rule required that defendant file a more specific answer than a general denial. A specific denial of parts of this paragraph and specific admission of other parts would have warned plaintiff that he had sued the wrong defendant.

Paragraph 8.23 of Moore's Federal Practice (2nd Edition) Vol. II, p. 1680, says: 'In such a case, the defendant should make clear just what he is denying and what he is admitting.' This answer to paragraph 5 does not make clear to plaintiff the defenses he must be prepared to meet.

    * * *

2.   Under the circumstances of this case, principles of equity require that defendant be estopped from denying agency because, otherwise, its inaccurate statements and statements in the record, which it knew (or had the means of knowing within its control) were inaccurate, will have deprived plaintiff of his right of action.

If Interrogatory 2 had been answered accurately by saying that employees of Carload Contractors, Inc. had turned the matter over to the insurance company, it seems clear that plaintiff would have realized his mistake. The fact that if Sandy Johnson had testified accurately, the plaintiff could have brought its action against the proper party defendant within the statutory period of limitations is also a factor to be considered, since defendant was represented at the deposition and received knowledge of the inaccurate testimony.

At least one appellate court has stated that the doctrine of equitable estoppel will be applied to prevent a party from taking advantage of the statute of limitations where the plaintiff has been misled by conduct of such party. See, Peters v. Public Service Corporation, 132 N.J.Eq. 500, 29 A.2d 189, 195 (1942).[12] In that case, the court said, 29 A.2d at page 196:

> 'Of course, defendants were under no duty to advise complainants' attorney of his error, other than by appropriate pleadings, but neither did defendants have a right, knowing of the mistake, to foster it by its acts of omission.'

This doctrine has been held to estop a party from taking advantage of a document of record where the misleading conduct occurred after the recording, so that application of this doctrine would not necessarily be precluded in a case such as this where the misleading answers to interrogatories and depositions were subsequent to the filing of the answer, even if the denial in the answer had been sufficient. See, J. H. Gerlach Co., Inc. v. Noyes, 1925, 251 Mass. 558, 147 N.E. 24, 26–27, 45 A.L.R. 961; East Central Fruit Growers, etc. v. Zuritsky, 1943, 346 Pa. 335, 338, 30 A.2d 133.

Closely related to this doctrine is the principle that a party may be estopped to deny agency or ratification. See Section 103 of Restatement of Agency and Hannon v. Siegel-Cooper Co., 1901, 167 N.Y. 244, 60 N.E. 597, 52 L.R.A. 429.

Since this is a pre-trial order, it may be modified at the trial if the trial judge determines from the facts which then appear that justice so requires. See, Smith Contracting Corp. v. Trojan Const. Co., Inc., 10 Cir., 1951, 192 F.2d 234, 236, and cases there cited; cf. Fernandez v. United Fruit Co., 2 Cir., 1952, 200 F.2d 414.

NOTE ON THE ANSWER

1. **Denial or admission.** The defendant's answer must respond to the plaintiff's allegations. Conventionally it tracks the complaint paragraph by paragraph. The response to an allegation can be a denial, an admission, or silence. A *denial* puts the allegation in issue and thereby creates an issue of fact as to the allegation. An *admission* establishes the allegation as true for purposes of the case. A *failure to deny* has the same effect as an admission. See, e.g., Fed. R. Civ. P. 8(b)(6).

To understand *Zielinski*, try to articulate why the plaintiff was so confused, and why was the impact of that confusion potentially disastrous for the plaintiff's case.

2. **The legal effect of an admission.** One of the functions of pleadings is to limit the issues in dispute. If facts alleged in the complaint are admitted, they are not in dispute, and for purposes of the case, no further evidence is required to prove their existence. An admission does more than render evidence tending to prove the admitted issue unnecessary—it renders it inadmissible. Consider Fuentes v. Tucker, 31 Cal.2d 1, 187 P.2d 752

---

[12] When inaccurate statements are made under circumstances where there is foreseeable danger that another will rely on them to his prejudice, and he does in fact rely thereon, such statements are sufficient to invoke this doctrine even though fraud is not present. Chemical Nat. Bank of New York v. Kellogg, 1905, 183 N.Y. 92, 75 N.E. 1103, 2 L.R.A.,N.S., 299; Church of Christ v. McDonald, 1943, 180 Tenn. 86, 171 S.W.2d 817, 821, 146 A.L.R. 1173; cf. Reifsnyder v. Dougherty, 1930, 301 Pa. 328, 334–335, 152 A. 98.

(1947): Plaintiffs sued defendant for the wrongful death of their minor children in an automobile accident. The defendant admitted liability but contested the amount of damages. At trial, the plaintiffs offered proof of the force of the impact and of the fact that the defendant was drunk. The court held that the evidence should have been excluded:

> It follows, therefore, if an issue has been removed from a case by an admission in the answer, that it is error to receive evidence which is material solely to the excluded matter. This, of course, does not mean that an admission of liability precludes a plaintiff from showing how an accident happened if such evidence is material to the issue of damages. In an action for personal injuries, where liability is admitted and the only issue to be tried is the amount of damage, the force of the impact and the surrounding circumstances may be relevant and material to indicate the extent of plaintiff's injuries. * * *

> The defendant here by an unqualified statement in his answer admitted liability for the deaths of the children, and the sole remaining question in issue was the amount of damages suffered by the parents. In an action for wrongful death of a minor child the damages consist of the pecuniary loss to the parents in being deprived of the services, earnings, society, comfort and protection of the child. The manner in which the accident occurred, the force of the impact, or defendant's intoxication could have no bearing on these elements of damage. The evidence, therefore, was not material to any issue before the jury, and its admission was error.

187 P.2d at 755.

Think for a moment about the parties' trial strategy in *Fuentes*. On one hand, plaintiffs may be relieved that they do not have to litigate the question of liability, for it removes uncertainty on that issue and it saves the expense of investigation and trial. On the other hand, plaintiffs want to introduce evidence of defendant's drunkenness, for such evidence is likely to create antipathy toward the defendant and sympathy for themselves. Such emotions are not logically relevant to the amount of compensatory damages plaintiffs have suffered, but they can have a profound effect on the amount of damages a jury is willing to award. The defendant, of course, looks at the issue from precisely the opposite point of view. On the one hand, he may regret having to admit liability. But on the other, the admission operates to keep evidence of his drunkenness from the jury. The defendant is in the controlling position, for he may frame his answer to admit or deny liability, and thereby to exclude or allow the evidence. Could the plaintiff in *Fuentes* have avoided the tactical disadvantage created by defendant's willingness to concede negligence by adding allegations of recklessness to the complaint and demanding punitive damages?

     3. The legal consequences of a denial. Generally speaking, a denial has two consequences. First, it imposes on the plaintiff the burden of proving the allegation denied. Second, it ordinarily permits the defendant to introduce evidence that would tend to disprove the allegation. See Clark, Code Pleading 606–610 (2d ed. 1947); Hazard, Leubsdorf & Bassett, Civil Procedure, § 5.4 (6th ed. 2011).

4.   Denial for lack of information and belief. The pleading rules contemplate that the denial of an allegation in a pleading should be made based on the knowledge of the person making the denial. However, it is recognized that a defendant, at least at the time when required to answer, may not know whether a particular allegation is true or not. Accordingly, the rules permit the defendant to aver that he has no information or belief sufficient to answer and on that basis to deny the allegation. See Fed. R. Civ. P. 8(b)(5).

5.   When does a denial fail to provide fair notice? A denial may fail to provide fair notice in two ways. It may suggest that the defendant intends to contest—and has an ethical basis for contesting—matters that he in fact has no fair basis to contest, leading the plaintiff to waste time and money on proving matters that are not really in dispute. Denials having this vice ought ordinarily to run afoul of Fed. R. Civ. P. 11(b)(4), which states that the person signing the answer certifies that "after an inquiry reasonable under the circumstances * * * the denials of factual contentions are warranted on the evidence, or, if specifically so identified, are reasonably based on belief or a lack of information." Had the current version of Rule 11(b)(4) been extant at the time of the *Zielinski* decision, would any portion of the defendant's denial of Paragraph 5 of the plaintiff's complaint have violated Rule 11(b)(4)? yes

An answer may also fail to disclose the issues which defendant in fact intends to contest, suggesting to the plaintiff that there is no issue to be investigated when in fact there is such an issue. The requirement of fair notice is enforced in part by the requirements in Rule 8(b)(4) that "[a] denial must fairly respond to the substance of the allegation" and that "[a] party that intends in good faith to deny only part of an allegation must admit the part that is true and deny the rest." How did the defendant in *Zielinski* violate that rule? Was the sanction that the court imposed an appropriate remedy for those violations?

Ordinarily a denial is a sufficient basis for defendant later to introduce evidence at trial tending to disprove plaintiff's allegation by proving an inconsistency. Some courts have held in the past that proof of such an inconsistency is permitted only if, in addition to denying plaintiff's allegation, defendant alleges the inconsistent proposition. Consider, for example, Jetty v. Craco, 123 Cal.App.2d 876, 267 P.2d 1055 (1954): Plaintiff sued defendant to recover $4,000 which she alleged she had loaned to defendant to buy merchandise. Defendant denied this allegation. At trial, defendant sought to show that he and plaintiff had formed a partnership and that the money was risk capital advanced to the enterprise rather than a loan. This evidence was held properly excluded:

> In order to prove her case plaintiff was not required to prove more than the making of the loan. Defendant under his denials could prove that he did not borrow the money. But the pleadings did not create an issue whether there was some special contract or relationship between the parties that would have constituted a defense to the action. The claim of a partnership and the receipt of the money as a contribution to the partnership was new matter, which, not having been pleaded was not available as a defense to the action. If this were not true a defendant, under mere denials in

an action for money loaned, could come up with all manner of claims of special agreements to defeat the action.

267 P.2d at 1057. In effect, a rule like that in *Jetty* transforms some ways of proving that there was no loan into affirmative defenses, at least at the pleading stage. Should the availability of broad discovery devices affect the application of the pleading rules regarding defenses? If plaintiff in *Jetty* had the opportunity to take defendant's deposition and thereby obtain the defendant's complete version of the transaction, does it make sense to exclude evidence that supports defendant's story? By the same token, is it a critical argument in support of the result in *Zielinski* that the defendant cheated not only at the pleading stage but also in discovery?

6. Affirmative defenses. Some defenses must be affirmatively pleaded. In most instances, such defenses go beyond affirmative denials of plaintiff's allegations and constitute introduction of new matter. For a non-exhaustive catalogue of affirmative defenses under the federal Rules, see Rule 8(c): "In responding to a pleading, a party must affirmatively state any avoidance or affirmative defense, including:

- accord and satisfaction;
- arbitration and award;
- assumption of risk;
- contributory negligence;
- discharge in bankruptcy;
- duress;
- estoppel;
- failure of consideration;
- fraud;
- illegality;
- injury by fellow servant;
- laches;
- license;
- payment;
- release;
- res judicata;
- statute of frauds;
- statute of limitations; and
- waiver."

[handwritten annotation: examples / list not intended / to be exhaustive]

Like the claims in a complaint, the affirmative defenses in the answer need only be "simple, concise, and direct. No technical form is required." Fed. R. Civ. P. 8(d)(1). And, as in a complaint, the defendant may plead as many affirmative defenses as he has, regardless of their consistency. Fed. R. Civ. P. 8(d)(2). See also Montgomery v. Wyeth, 580 F.3d 455 (6th Cir. 2009).

After the Supreme Court's decisions in *Twombly* and *Iqbal*, it is an open question whether affirmative defenses must meet the standard of "plausibility" promulgated by those cases. Courts are split on the question. Compare Tyco Fire Products LP v. Victaulic Co., 777 F. Supp. 2d 893 (E.D.

Pa. 2011) ("An affirmative defense need not be plausible to survive; it must merely provide fair notice of the issue involved."), with Deneice Design, LLC v. Braun, 993 F. Supp. 2d 765 (S.D. Tex. 2013) (concluding that *Twombly* and *Iqbal* apply equally to complaints and affirmative defenses). What arguments would you make in favor or, or opposing, the extension of the plausibility standard to pleading affirmative defenses? See Mayer, An Implausible Standard for Affirmative Defenses, 112 Mich. L. Rev. 275 (2013).

7.   Counterclaims. A defendant may choose not only to answer plaintiff's complaint, but also to advance a claim (or claims) of her own against the plaintiff. A counterclaim is typically filed at the same time as the answer, but it is, in effect, a complaint by the defendant. See Fed. R. Civ. P. 13, and discussion, infra p. 562.

8.   Reply. The original Field Code provided for a reply by the plaintiff to any "new matter" raised in defendant's answer. The provision for a reply is found in many of the versions of the Field Code patterned after that adopted in New York. The federal Rules allow a reply only to a counterclaim, or when the court directs the plaintiff to reply to new matter in an answer. Fed. R. Civ. P. 7(a).

G. AMENDED PLEADINGS

NOTE ON AMENDING PLEADINGS

1.   Liberal pretrial amendment policy. The purpose of the pleadings is to set out the basic framework of a dispute so that claims and defenses may be presented and discovery commenced. Amendment of the pleadings is allowed liberally to allow pleaders to correct mistakes or to reflect facts revealed through discovery. See Fed. R. Civ. P. 15(a). Rule 15(a)(1) allows a party to revise a pleading "as a matter of course" (i.e., without having to seek permission) within 21 days after serving it, or, if the pleading is one to which a responsive pleading is required, within 21 days of service of the responsive pleading or a motion under Rule 12(b), (e), or (f). This provision allows a pleader to correct mistakes if she acts quickly. As discovery goes forward, the parties may learn things that cause them to revise their view of the case and perhaps to want to revise their pleadings. Once past the point where amendment is permitted as a matter of course, the parties may amend their earlier pleadings only by written consent of the other party or by leave of court. Rule 15(a)(2) specifically instructs that leave to amend "should freely be given when justice so requires."

The liberal policy favoring amendment does not mean that all amendments will be allowed. As discovery comes to an end and the date set for trial approaches, courts become increasingly hostile to amendments that involve a major shift in the theory of the case. A party proposing such an amendment will need a good explanation why he failed to seek amendment earlier (the best explanation being that the amendment is itself a response to what was recently learned in discovery). A party opposing such an amendment is more likely to prevail if the new theory was not fully covered in prior discovery, so that its investigation would significantly delay the trial. See, e.g., Boulevard Invest, LLC, 663 F. Supp. 2d 973 (D. Nev. 2009) (denying motion to amend after discovery was complete when "the new issues raised would require extra discovery, would delay trial, and likely would increase defense costs").

2. Amendments to conform to the evidence under Fed. R. Civ. P. 15(b). The common law and traditional code pleading rule was that an objection on the ground of substantive insufficiency could be leveled at any time on either of two grounds: first, that the claim was not supported by *evidence* at trial; or second, notwithstanding the evidence, that the *pleading* did not raise a substantive issue. Thus, even if a litigant had established by evidence the elements required under the substantive law, he was vulnerable to attack on the second ground if he had not properly alleged those elements in his pleading. The theory was that a judgment could not be entered unless a "foundation" for it had been laid in the pleadings. See generally Morgan, The Variance Problem, 32 Neb. L. Rev. 357 (1953).

Under the federal Rules, amendments to pleadings made in response to evidence introduced at trial are covered by Rule 15(b). Rule 15(b) covers two situations in which such amendments may be made. First, if "an issue not raised by the pleadings is tried by the parties' express or implied consent," Rule 15(b)(2) directs that it be treated as if it had been raised in the pleadings and that amendment of the pleadings be allowed to conform to the evidence presented. Second, if a party objects to the introduction of evidence at trial because it is not within the framework established by the pleadings, Rule 15(b)(1) directs the district court to "freely permit an amendment when doing so will aid in presenting the merits and the objecting party fails to satisfy the court that the evidence would prejudice that party's action or defense on the merits."

In federal practice, the normal time to put a case in final form for trial is the final pretrial conference described in Rule 16(e), discussed infra, at p. 897. This conference should bring to the surface any important variance between the pleadings and the evidence. The conference often results in a written pretrial order that specifies the issues to be tried, describes in general terms the nature of the evidence to be offered, and names the witnesses to be called. Fed. R. Civ. P. 16(c)(2), (e). An amendment to the pleadings may (and should) be made at the conference, either by including the amendment in the court's pretrial order itself or by ordering that an amended pleading be prepared and filed. Rule 16(d) provides that the pretrial order "controls the course of the action unless the court modifies it."

The liberality of amendment to conform to the evidence contemplated under Rule 15(b) is in some tension with Rule 16(e): Rule 15(b) says that introduction of evidence and amendment to the pleading should be allowed unless there would be "prejudice" to the party objecting to the amendment, whereas Rule 16(e) says that change to the pretrial order should not be allowed unless there would be "manifest injustice," presumably to the party seeking the change. For the most part, courts follow the liberal policy of Rule 15(b) rather than the more stringent policy of Rule 16(e) and allow amendment to conform to the evidence. 6A Wright, Miller & Kane, Federal Practice and Procedure § 1491 (3d ed. 2005). "This approach is consistent with the mandate of Rule 1 that the rules shall be construed to secure the 'just' determination of every action and recognizes the very explicit policy of Rule 15(b) in favor of allowing amendments." Id. A lawyer should not, however, put herself in the position of having to persuade an impatient district judge that the pretrial order should be changed to allow the introduction of evidence not within the scope of the order. See, e.g., Rigby v. Beech Aircraft Co., 548 F.2d 288 (10th Cir. 1977) (refusing to allow introduction of evidence outside the scope of the pretrial order).

3. Effect of amended pleading on prior pleadings. For most purposes, an amended pleading supersedes the prior pleading. As the First Circuit recently noted regarding the amendment of a complaint, "the earlier complaint is a dead letter and no longer performs any function in the case." *Connectu, Inc. v. Zuckerberg*, 522 F.3d 82 (1st Cir. 2008). An amended complaint must be served on opposing parties before the case may progress to further stages of the litigation such as, for example, entry of default judgment against defendant. Fed. R. Civ. P. 5(a).

Worthington v. Wilson

United States District Court for the Central District of Illinois, 1992.
790 F. Supp. 829.

■ MIHM, CHIEF JUDGE.

* * *

BACKGROUND

According to the amended complaint, the Plaintiff Richard Worthington ("Worthington") was arrested on February 25, 1989 by two police officers in the Peoria Heights Police Department. At the time of his arrest, Worthington was nursing an injured left hand and so advised the arresting officer. The officer responded by grabbing and twisting Worthington's injured hand and wrist, which prompted Worthington to shove the officer away and tell him to "take it easy." A second officer arrived on the scene and the two officers wrestled Worthington to the ground and handcuffed him. The officers then hoisted Worthington from the ground by the handcuffs, which caused him to suffer broken bones in his left hand. These allegations are taken as true by this court for purposes of the pending motions.

Exactly two years later, on February 25, 1991, Worthington, by his attorney Gary Morris, filed a complaint in the Circuit Court of Peoria County against the Village of Peoria Heights and "three unknown named police officers." This complaint recited the facts above and claimed that the officers' actions deprived Worthington of his constitutional rights in violation of the Civil Rights Act of 1964, 42 U.S.C. § 1983. * * * The Village removed the action to this court[.]

* * *

On June 17, 1991, Worthington filed an amended complaint which named as Defendants Dave Wilson and Jeff Wall ("the Defendants"), the two officers who arrested Worthington on February 25, 1989. This amended complaint contains no claim against the Village of Peoria Heights. These Defendants, represented by Jeanne Wysocki (the same attorney who represented the Village), moved to dismiss the amended complaint on the grounds that the statute of limitations had run and that the complaint failed to state a proper claim under § 1983. * * *

DISCUSSION

I. *Statute of Limitations / Relation Back*

In their motion to dismiss, the Defendants first argue that the amended complaint against them must be dismissed because the statute of limitations has run. The Defendants note that the statute of limitations for § 1983 cases in Illinois is two years, and that the amended complaint was not filed until about four months after this period had expired. Moreover, the Defendants argue that the amended complaint cannot be deemed to relate back to the filing date of the original complaint because the prerequisites of relation back under Federal Rule of Civil Procedure 15(c) have not all been met. Specifically, the Defendants argue that they did not have notice of the action before the statute of limitations period had run as required by <u>Schiavone v. Fortune,</u> 477 U.S. 21, 106 S.Ct. 2379, 91 L.Ed.2d 18 (1986), and that the renaming of fictitious parties does not constitute a "mistake" under Rule 15(c).

* * *

A. *Schiavone Notice Requirements*

As an initial matter, there is no doubt that the statute of limitations for a § 1983 action in Illinois is two years. Therefore, as noted by the Magistrate, Worthington's action against the Defendants must have been filed by February 25, 1991. Since the amended complaint was not filed until June 17, 1991, the only way the amended complaint can be found to be timely filed is if it relates back to the filing of the original complaint. Relation back of amendments under federal rules is covered by Rule 15(c).

The Defendants' first argument is that Rule 15(c), as interpreted by *Schiavone,* requires that the party to be brought in by amendment receives notice of the action before the expiration of the statute of limitations period. The Defendants argue that because they did not receive notice of this action within this time, the amended complaint does not relate back and is therefore untimely. Because this court finds that *Schiavone* no longer controls, it rejects the Defendants' first argument.

Until December 1, 1991, Rule 15(c) provided, in relevant part:

> Whenever the claim or defense asserted in the amended pleading arose out of the conduct, transaction, or occurrence set forth or attempted to be set forth in the original pleading, the amendment relates back to the date of the original pleading. An amendment changing the party against whom a claim is asserted relates back if the foregoing provision is satisfied and, within the period provided by law for commencing the action against the party to be brought in by amendment that party (1) has received such notice of the institution of the action that the party will not be prejudiced in maintaining his defense on the merits, and (2) knew or should have known that, but for a mistake concerning the identity of the proper party, the action would have been brought against the party.

In *Schiavone,* the Supreme Court interpreted this provision to require that, in addition to the amended complaint arising out of the same conduct set forth in the original complaint, the new party must have received actual notice of the action (and that it was the proper party) before the statute of limitations period expired. As noted by the Magistrate and counsel for the Defendants, it appears that the Defendants did not receive notice of this action against them by February 25, 1991. Thus, under the old version of Rule 15(c) and *Schiavone,* the amended complaint against the officers would not relate back and would thus be untimely filed.

However, as of December 1, 1991, Rule 15(c) reads differently. As will be seen momentarily, the amendment was designed to change the requirement of *Schiavone* that the new party receives notice of the action before the expiration of the limitations period. As amended on December 1, 1991, Rule 15(c) reads, in relevant part:

> An amendment of a pleading relates back to the date of the original pleading when:
>
> * * *
>
> (2) The claim or defense asserted in the amended pleading arose out of the conduct, transaction, or occurrence set forth or attempted to be set forth in the original pleading, or
>
> (3) the amendment changes the party or the naming of the party against whom a claim is asserted if the foregoing provision (2) is satisfied and, within the period provided by Rule 4[m] for service of the summons and complaint, the party to be brought in by amendment (A) has received such notice of the institution of the action that the party will not be prejudiced in maintaining a defense on the merits, and (B) knew or should have known that, but for a mistake concerning the identity of the proper party, the action would have been brought against the party.

As noted by the Advisory Committee on the Federal Rules, this amendment was designed to change the result dictated by *Schiavone.*

> Paragraph (c) (3). This paragraph has been revised to change the result in *Schiavone v. Fortune, supra,* with respect to the problem of a misnamed defendant. An intended defendant who is notified of an action within the period allowed by Rule 4[m] for service of a summons and complaint may not under the revised rule defeat the action on account of a defect in the pleading with respect to the defendants named, provided that the requirements of clauses (A) and (B) have been met. If the notice requirement is met within the Rule 4[m] period, a complaint may be amended at any time to correct a formal defect such as misnomer or misidentification. On the basis of the text of the former rule, the Court reached a result in *Schiavone v. Fortune* that was inconsistent with the liberal pleading practices secured by Rule 8.
>
> In allowing a name-correcting amendment within the time allowed by Rule 4(m), this rule allows not only the 120 days specified in that rule, but also any additional time resulting from any extension ordered by the court pursuant to that rule, as may be granted, for example, if the defendant is a fugitive from service of the summons.

(Citations omitted). Thus, relation-back is now governed by a modified standard. An amended complaint which changes the name of the defendant will relate back to the filing of the original complaint if it arises out of the same conduct contained in the original complaint and the new party was aware of the action within 120 days of the filing of the original complaint.

Thus, under the amended version of Rule 15(c), Worthington's amended complaint, which arises out of the very same conduct in its original complaint, would relate back to February 25, 1991 if the Defendants were aware, before June 25, 1991, that they were the officers referred to as "unknown named police officers" in the original complaint. At oral argument on March 12, 1992, counsel for the Defendants conceded that they were aware of the pendency of the action within this period; thus, under the new version of Rule 15(c), the amended complaint would be timely because the Defendants received notice of the action within 120 days of the original filing. Given that the two versions of Rule 15(c) dictate opposite results on this issue in this case, the question becomes which version governs here. The answer is that the new version applies.

* * *

Accordingly, this court rejects the Defendants' argument and the Magistrate's recommendation that *Schiavone* prohibits relation back of this amended complaint. Rule 15(c) no longer requires that the party to be brought in by amendment receive notice of the action prior to the expiration of the statute of limitations period.

B.   *"Mistake"*

The Defendants also argue that relation back is not permitted here under Rule 15(c) because there was no "mistake" concerning the identity of the proper party. In this regard, Rule 15(c) states that an amendment changing the naming of a party will relate back if, among other things, the party brought in by the amendment "knew or should have known that, but for a *mistake* concerning the identity of the proper party, the action would have been brought against the party." (Emphasis added). Both the old version and the new version of Rule 15(c) contain this identical language.

The Defendants argue that the failure of the original complaint to name Wilson and Wall was not due to a "mistake" but rather was due to a lack of knowledge over the proper defendant. The Defendants argue that while Rule 15(c) permits amendments which change a mistaken name in the original complaint, it does not permit a plaintiff to replace "unknown" parties with actual parties. In support of this argument, the Defendants cite Wood v. Worachek, 618 F.2d 1225, 1230 (7th Cir. 1980) and Rylewicz v. Beaton Services, Ltd., 888 F.2d 1175, 1181 (7th Cir. 1989). These cases reflect the Seventh Circuit's view that an amended complaint which replaces fictitious names with actual names due to an initial lack of knowledge concerning the proper defendant does not involve a "mistake" and is therefore not entitled to relation back under Rule 15(c). See also Norton v. International Harvester Co., 627 F.2d 18, 22 (7th Cir. 1980). But see Sassi v. Breier, 584 F.2d 234, 235 (7th Cir. 1978). These holdings would seem to control in this case, since Worthington concedes that he designated the Defendants as "unknown named police officers" in the original complaint because he was unaware of their identities at that time. Moreover, the recent amendment of Rule 15(c) would not seem to undercut the applicability of these holdings, since the language concerning mistake is identical in both versions. Accordingly, the court finds that, pursuant to the Seventh Circuit authority noted above, Worthington's amended complaint is not entitled to relation back.

However, this court will take this opportunity to respectfully express its disagreement with the above-noted Seventh Circuit decisions. First of all, this court is of the opinion that the "mistake" language in Rule 15(c) does not create a new, separate prerequisite for relation back, but rather merely refers back to the first portion of Rule 15(c)(3). The word "mistake" appears to this court to be a way of referencing, in one word, the phrase "change the party or the naming of the party" at the beginning of the subsection.

* * *

Read this way, the word mistake would not create an additional prerequisite for relation-back. The requirements for relation-back would only be three:

   (1) the amendment changes the party or the naming of the party;

   (2) the defendant received notice of the action within the service of process period; and

   (3) the defendant knew that it was the party being sued.

The above is an explanation of *how* Rule 15(c)(3) can be rationally interpreted, under its existing language, as not having a separate "mistake" requirement. The more interesting question to be addressed now is *why* such a "mistake" requirement should not be included. It must be questioned whether a fourth requirement of "mistake" logically fits in with the other three requirements listed above. Those first three requirements in essence demand that the party being brought in had *notice*—that he knew about the action and knew that he was the one intended to be sued. The focus is on the awareness of the party to be brought in, out of concern for due process. A separate "mistake" requirement improperly shifts the focus to the state of mind of the plaintiff bringing the action—whether the plaintiff named the wrong defendant out of a mistake or because he did not have enough information to identify the proper defendant at all. Such an analysis is irrelevant in this court's view. The heart of Rule 15(c) is notice to the defendant. See generally 6A Wright & Miller, Federal Practice and Procedure, § 1498. The mistake requirement does nothing to further this controlling interest.

Indeed, it can plausibly be argued that a mistake requirement would actually hinder the important interest of notice to the Defendant. As is true in this case, a complaint which does not attempt to specifically identify the proper defendants leaves open the possibility that the eventual defendants are the ones being sued. If the original complaint comes to the attention of those defendants (as it did here) and the complaint uses "John Doe" or "unknown," the defendants will be on notice that they are being sued if the content of that complaint implicates them. Contrast that with the situation where the complaint actually names defendants, but names the wrong ones. Had Worthington simply randomly chosen the names of two officers in the department, the Defendants Wilson and Wall might have been lulled into the belief that they were not being sued. As a result, a separate "mistake" requirement could be detrimental to the true purpose of Rule 15(c) and should not be included in the analysis. Having said all of this, this court recognizes that it is duty bound to follow Seventh Circuit precedent on point, and accordingly reaches the result dictated by *Wood*.

Accordingly, this court finds that Worthington's amended complaint does not relate back under Rule 15(c) because the amendment did not correct a "mistake," but rather corrected a lack of knowledge at the time of the original complaint.

* * *

CONCLUSION

For the reasons set forth above, the Defendants' motion to dismiss is GRANTED, * * *.

NOTE ON FEDERAL RULE 15(c) AND RELATION BACK

1. Relation back. Under some circumstances, Rule 15(c) allows an amended pleading to "relate back" to the date of the original pleading. Shorn of the jargon, this means simply that the court will treat the amended pleading as having been filed on the date the original pleading was filed. The purpose of the rule is to permit an amended claim to avoid the effect of the statute of limitations. So long as the original pleading is filed within the statutory limitations period, an amended pleading meeting the requirements of Rule 15(c) will be treated as having been filed within the limitations period, even if the amendment actually occurred after the statute of limitations had run.

2. Properly named defendants. When defendants are properly named, Rule 15(c)(1)(B) permits relation back of new claims against that defendant if the "amendment asserts a claim or defense that arose out of the conduct, transaction, or occurrence set out—or attempted to be set out—in the original pleading." This is an explicit departure from the old common law pleading rules that did not allow relation back of amendments asserting new causes of action. The leading case construing Rule 15(c)(1)(B) is *Tiller v. Atlantic Coast Line R.R. Co.*, 323 U.S. 574, 65 S.Ct. 421, 89 L.Ed. 465 (1945). Plaintiff initially sued under the Federal Employers' Liability Act for recovery of damages for the accidental death of her husband. Later, after the statute of limitations had run, she amended her complaint to add a cause of action under the Federal Boiler Inspection Act. The Supreme Court allowed relation back for the added statutory claim:

> The original complaint in this case alleged a failure to provide a proper lookout for deceased, to give him proper warning of the approach of the train, to keep the head car properly lighted, to warn the deceased of an unprecedented and unexpected change in the manner of shifting cars. The amended complaint charged the failure to have the locomotive properly lighted. Both of them related to the same general conduct, transaction and occurrence which involved the death of the deceased.

323 U.S. at 581.

The Ninth Circuit recently held that an amended complaint can relate back even if it includes allegations that were expressly disclaimed in the original pleading. In *ASARCO, LLC v. Union Pacific Railroad Co.*, 765 F.3d 999 (9th Cir. 2014), ASARCO sued Union Pacific for recovery of a share of the environmental cleanup costs associated with damage to the Coeur d'Alene basin, where both companies had engaged in mining operations. In the original complaint, ASARCO expressly excluded a part of the basin from its claims. It then amended the complaint—after the statute of limitations had run—to include the parts of the basin it had explicitly excluded from the original complaint. The Ninth Circuit held that the amended complaint related back because both pleadings sought contribution based on the same conduct—the pollution of the basin—and the original complaint sufficiently put the defendant on notice that the claims in the amended complaint might arise. Do you agree with the Ninth Circuit's conclusion that the defendant is not entitled to the protection of the statute of limitations in this case?

3.   Improperly named and unnamed defendants. The relatively generous treatment accorded plaintiffs who sue properly named defendants contrasts with the erratic and often ungenerous treatment accorded plaintiffs who name improperly, or fail to, name the true defendant. Plaintiffs' lawyers can get their clients (and sometimes themselves) into serious trouble by failing to name a defendant properly. Rule 15(c) is designed to protect plaintiffs who have failed to name the proper defendant, but, as seen in *Worthington,* its protections are limited.

a.   Improperly named defendants. If a defendant is named improperly because of a "mistake," an amended complaint properly naming that defendant will be allowed to relate back to the date of the original complaint if Rule 15(c)(1)(C) is satisfied. First, Rule 15(c)(1)(C) incorporates the requirement of (c)(1)(B) that the claim against the now-properly named defendant arise out of the conduct, transaction, or occurrence set forth in the original complaint. Second, Rule 15(c)(1)(C) requires that "within the period provided by Rule 4(m) for serving the summons and complaint" (i.e., within 120 days of filing), the true defendant "(i) received such notice of the action that it will not be prejudiced in defending on the merits; and (ii) knew or should have known that the action would have been brought against it, but for a mistake concerning the proper party's identity."

Note that under Rule 15(c)(1)(C)(i) and (ii), notice to the defendant may be by any means, including but not limited to notice provided by the new complaint. That is, the *original,* though mistaken, complaint (or word-of-mouth concerning it) might have provided sufficient notice to comply with the "received such notice" and "knew or should have known" conditions, even though the defendant was not properly named in that complaint. Note, further, that so long as the notice required by Rule 15(c)(1)(C) is received within 120 days, the complaint may be amended at any time, even years later.

What constitutes sufficient notice to comply with Rule 15(c)(1)(C)(i) and (ii)? Some cases are easy, such as when the defendant actually knows about the complaint and that the plaintiff has sued the wrong party. See, for example, Joseph v. Elan Motorsports Technologies Racing Corp., 638 F.3d 555 (7th Cir. 2011), which allowed relation back when the plaintiff sued Elan Corp. instead of its affiliate Elan, Inc., and defendant Elan Corp. was aware of the error.

Other cases are more difficult. See, for example, Martz v. Miller Bros. Co., 244 F.Supp. 246 (D. Del. 1965), in which plaintiff was injured on the sidewalk in front of Miller Brothers' furniture store in Newark, Delaware. Plaintiff named "Miller Brothers Company," a Delaware corporation, and served the corporate secretary, its agent for acceptance of service of process.

Unfortunately, the store in question was owned by "Miller Brothers Company of Newark," a separate Delaware corporation. The court held that an amended complaint naming the proper corporation did not relate back because no notice had been given the true defendant.

What constitutes a "mistake concerning the proper party's identity" under Rule 15(c)(1)(c)(ii)? In Krupski v. Costa Crociere S.p.A., 560 U.S. 538, 130 S.Ct. 2485, 177 L.Ed.2d 148 (2010), Krupski was injured on a cruise when she fell and broke her leg. Her ticket identified Costa Crociere S.p.A., an Italian corporation, as the carrier, and Costa Cruise Lines N.V., as the sales and marketing agent for the carrier. Plaintiff made her initial approach to Costa Cruise Lines. When settlement negotiations broke down, plaintiff filed a complaint against Costa Cruise Lines prior to the running of the statute. After the statute had run, Costa Cruise Lines filed an answer denying that it was the proper defendant and identifying Costa Crociere as the actual carrier and vessel operator. Several months later Costa Cruise Lines moved for summary judgment on the same ground. At that point, the plaintiff sought to file an amended complaint naming Costa Crociere as the defendant. The district court held, and the Eleventh Circuit affirmed on the ground, that because the ticket clearly identified both Costa Crociere and Costa Cruise Lines and because Krupski and her lawyer had access to the ticket before the running of the statute, Krupski knew or should have known that Costa Crociere was a potential defendant. Krupski had therefore not made a "mistake," but rather had made a deliberate choice to sue one party instead of another.

The Supreme Court reversed. The relevant inquiry, the Court said, was not what the plaintiff or her lawyer knew, but whether "the *defendant* knew or should have known during the Rule 4(m) period" that "it would have been named as a defendant but for an error." 130 S.Ct. at 2493 (emphasis in original). Citing Black's Law Dictionary, the Court defined "mistake" as "[a]n error, misconception, or misunderstanding; an erroneous belief." Id. at 2494. The Court acknowledged that a plaintiff's "deliberate choice to sue one party instead of another while fully understanding the factual and legal differences between the two parties is the antithesis of making a mistake." Id. But the plaintiff's knowledge of the contents of the ticket was not sufficient, standing alone, to foreclose the possibility that she nevertheless misunderstood crucial facts concerning the companies' identities. Id. at 2497.

b.   Unnamed defendants. The defendants in *Worthington* concede that they received actual notice of the suit and that they were not prejudiced by the failure to name them in the original complaint. The only problem was that Worthington had not made a "mistake" in naming them, and thus did not qualify for relation back under Rule 15(c)(1)(C). How clear a meaning does the term "mistake" have in Rule 15(c)(1)(C)(ii)? What if Worthington heard the officers call each other by their first names, Tom, Dick, and Harry? Would it suffice to sue Tom Doe, Dick Moe, and Harry Roe? What if Worthington knew what the defendants looked like but did not know their names? Would it suffice to sue the first three names in the telephone book, Paul Aaberg, Alan Aaboe, and David Aagaard?

The district judge in *Worthington* made plain his disagreement with the Seventh Circuit, but his decision was controlled by Wood v. Worachek, 618 F.2d 1225, 1230 (7th Cir. 1980) ("Rule 15(c)[(1)(C)] permits an amendment to relate back only where there has been an error made concerning the identity of the proper party and where that party is chargeable with knowledge of the mistake, but it does not permit relation back where, as here, there is a lack of knowledge of the proper party."). Consider the problem facing the plaintiff in *Worthington.* He knows he has been hurt by members of the Peoria Police Department, but he does not know who they are. Perhaps the only way he can learn their identity is to file suit and conduct discovery. If he files suit the day after the incident, there is enough time to discover the identity of the officers and still to file an amended complaint before a two-year statute of limitations elapses. But ordinary human beings often do not act that way. Many people will not see a lawyer until the statute has almost run, and too many lawyers wait until the last minute to file suit. To add to the difficulty, many statutes are much shorter than two years. If you were Worthington's attorney, and he came to you for advice on the last day before the statute of limitations ran out, what advice would you given him if he did not know the names of the officers who arrested him?

By naming a "John Doe" defendant, plaintiff indicates (correctly) that she does not know the name of the person who injured her. Is it normal English usage to say that plaintiff has made a "mistake concerning the proper party's identity" in such a case? Must the normal usage be followed if, in the view of the court, it produces injustice? Must it be followed if, in the view of the court, the drafters of Rule 15 were not thinking of the problem of a defendant whose name was unknown? If the drafters were not thinking about the problem, how can the court know what the drafters would have written if they had thought about it?

The Seventh Circuit's view of "mistake" under Rule 15(c)(1)(C) was reaffirmed on appeal. Worthington v. Wilson, 8 F.3d 1253 (7th Cir. 1993). Of the seven other circuits to consider the issue, only the Third Circuit takes a different view. See Singletary v. Pennsylvania Department of Corrections, 266 F.3d 186 (3d Cir. 2001), Varlack v. SWC Caribbean, Inc., 550 F.2d 171 (3d Cir. 1977). Does the definition of "mistake" in *Krupski*, noted above, change the result in *Worthington v. Willingham*?

c.   Misconduct by defendant. If defendant misleads the plaintiff into naming the wrong defendant, or prevents the plaintiff from discovering the identity of the true defendant, the true defendant can sometimes be estopped from asserting a statute of limitations defense to an amended complaint, depending on applicable state law governing tolling of statutes of limitations. Bechtel v. Robinson, 886 F.2d 644 (3d Cir. 1989) (applying Delaware law to find estoppel to assert the statute of limitations based on defendant's conduct).

4.   *Schiavone v. Fortune* and the period allowed for providing sufficient notice to the true defendant. The 1991 amendment to Rule 15(c)(1)(C), discussed in *Worthington,* added 120 days to the period during which plaintiff is allowed to provide notice to the true defendant. The amendment was prompted by Schiavone v. Fortune, 477 U.S. 21, 106 S.Ct. 2379, 91 L.Ed.2d 18 (1986), in which plaintiffs sued for libel arising out of an article published in *Fortune* magazine. The complaints named *Fortune* magazine as defendant and were filed within the statute of limitations, but *Fortune* was an internal division of Time, Inc., rather than a separate corporation. Service was attempted outside the statutory period but within the grace period for service allowed under New Jersey law. The Supreme Court refused to allow relation back of a later complaint that properly named Time. Although the attempted service of the first complaints would have provided sufficient actual notice to Time under Rule 15(c), the notice was simply too late. At the time the Court decided *Schiavone,* Rule 15(c)(1)(C) allowed relation back if the true defendant received notice "within the period provided by law for commencing the action." The Court held that this meant the period of the statute of limitations rather than the statute of limitations plus the period allowed for service of process.

Amended Rule 15(c)(1)(C) now provides that relation back is permitted if notice is provided to the true defendant "within the period covered by Rule 4(m) for serving the summons and complaint" (i.e., 120 days). The notes of the Advisory Committee on Civil Rules state that the revised Rule 15(c)(1)(C) is designed "to change the result in *Schiavone v. Fortune.*" How, exactly, was it changed? The amendment indicates that 120 days are to be added as a grace period. But added to what? The district court in *Worthington* assumes without discussion that the 120-day period is to be added to the date of the filing of the original complaint, and the courts of appeals that have addressed the question have agreed. See Jacobsen v. Osborne, 133 F.3d 315, 319–20 (5th Cir. 1998) (" '[R]elation back is allowed [under the amended Rule] as long as the added party had notice within 120 days following the filing of the complaint * * *.' "); Arendt v. Vetta Sports, Inc., 99 F.3d 231 (7th Cir. 1996) (same).

In *Worthington,* the attorney for the police officers conceded at oral argument before the district court that the officers had received timely notice under Rule 15(c)(1)(C) of the pendency of the suit (most likely as a result of the service of the original complaint on the defendant Village of Peoria Heights). If the failure to name the officers had been a "mistake" within the meaning of Rule 15(c)(1)(C), relation back would have been allowed.

    5.   **Additional reading.** For additional reading, see Note, Relation Back of Amendments Naming Previously Unnamed Defendants Under Federal Rule 15(c), 89 Cal. L. Rev. 1549 (2001); Rice, Meet John Doe: It Is Time for Federal Civil Procedure to Recognize John Doe Parties, 57 U. Pitt. L. Rev. 883 (1996); Lewis, The Excessive History of Federal Rule 15(c) and Its Lessons for Civil Rules Revision, 85 Mich. L. Rev. 1507 (1987) (general discussion of Rule 15(c)); Bauer, *Schiavone:* An Un-*Fortune*-ate Illustration of the Supreme Court's Role as Interpreter of the Federal Rules of Civil Procedure, 63 Notre Dame L. Rev. 720 (1988) (criticism of *Schiavone*).

CHAPTER 5

JOINDER AND CLASS ACTIONS

A. JOINDER OF CLAIMS

INTRODUCTORY NOTE ON THE SIZE OF THE LITIGATION

Litigation may arise out of a simple event involving few parties—for example, a slip-and-fall accident in the aisle of a supermarket. Or it may arise out of a complex event involving many parties—for example, a financial fraud perpetrated against thousands of investors by a group of people working in a large corporation, or physical injuries suffered by thousands of consumers as a result of an allegedly defective product designed, manufactured, and sold by a series of different corporations.

Our legal system tries to handle cases at both ends of the spectrum. The simple cases are relatively easy. In such cases, the primary impediment to litigation is not complexity but cost, for the plaintiff's injury may not be sufficiently severe to warrant the cost of full-scale litigation. By contrast, the complex cases are not only costly, but also logistically and intellectually difficult, both for the parties and the court.

A plaintiff makes the initial determination about the size of the litigation, deciding what claims to bring and how many defendants to sue. If there are several potential plaintiffs, they decide among themselves whether to sue individually or to join in the same suit. If there is a large number of potential plaintiffs, one or more individuals may seek to bring a class action, in which the named plaintiff or plaintiffs litigate on behalf of a large number of unnamed class members.

A defendant also has some say in the size and shape of the litigation. A defendant may decide not only to defend against the claims brought by the plaintiff, but also to assert its own claims against the plaintiff. A defendant may bring claims against a co-defendant already sued by the plaintiff. A defendant may also seek to bring in other parties—as additional plaintiffs, as additional defendants to the plaintiff's action, or as so-called third-party defendants whom the plaintiff has not sued but against whom the defendant wishes to assert its own claims.

Finally, an outsider to the initial litigation has some say as well. Someone concerned that a case may affect her interests may try to intervene in the case in order to protect those interests.

Modern procedural rules try to take all these possibilities into account. The basic philosophy of modern rules—both state and federal—is to allow liberal joinder of claims and parties. Sometimes, however, the federal rules allow more liberal joinder of claims and parties than the subject matter jurisdiction of the federal courts will permit. In such cases, the limitations on the federal courts' subject matter jurisdiction control, no matter what the rules appear to permit. Sometimes the rules allow joinder of claims and parties that result in a case that is unmanageable, or is potentially unfair to one or more parties. In such cases, the trial judge has discretion to refuse to hear certain claims or join additional parties.

Choices about the size of litigation have important consequences beyond the four corners of the litigation itself. Because of preclusion law, claims and issues actually decided in one case may bind the parties in a later case. In addition, claims that could have been brought in the current case, but were not, may be foreclosed in a later case. See discussion of preclusion in Chapter 9, infra. Preclusion consequences are generally predictable—and controllable—when a case is being framed and litigated. Parties should think carefully about those consequences as they make choices about the size and conduct of litigation.

Because of stare decisis, legal rules and principles established in one case generally become binding precedent in later cases. Potential stare decisis consequences sometimes induce non-parties to intervene in cases in which they would otherwise have no interest. Usually, however, stare decisis consequences of an earlier case are felt by later litigants who had no knowledge of, and no opportunity to intervene in, the earlier case.

NOTE ON HISTORICAL ATTITUDES TOWARD JOINDER

1. **Common law.** At common law—that is, in the "law" courts as distinct from the "equity" courts—there were no generalized joinder rules. Each kind of suit had a different writ, and each writ had its own characteristics. Joinder of claims depended on the particular writ under which a suit was brought. For example, the writ for trespass allowed multiple claims of trespass, whether those claims were factually related or not. However, multiple contract claims could not be asserted in the same writ even if the claims arose out of a single transaction. See generally Williams, Pleading Reform in Nineteenth Century America: The Joinder of Actions at Common Law and Under the Codes, 6 J.Legal Hist. 299 (1985).

Joinder of parties also depended on the nature of the particular writ. In tort actions, joint owners of property were required to join as plaintiffs when suing for injury to the property. See B. Shipman, Common Law Pleading 397 (3d ed. 1923). Where defendants had acted in concert, joinder of defendants was permitted though not required. See Prosser, Joint Torts and Several Liability, 25 Calif. L. Rev. 413, 414–15 (1937). In contract actions, "joint" obligees were required to join as plaintiffs and joint obligors were required to be joined as defendants. See Reed, Compulsory Joinder of Parties in Civil Actions, 55 Mich. L. Rev. 327, 356–74 (1957).

2. **Equity.** In equity—that is, in the "equity" courts—joinder of claims and parties was typically not regulated by rule. In part, this was because cases in the equity courts were often amorphous and complex; in part, it was because of the equity tradition of deciding each case on its own peculiar facts without regard to strict legal right or rule. In theory, equity courts could take any case that could not be handled fairly in the law courts because of the limitations of the common law joinder rules, but joinder in the equity courts became increasingly limited from about 1700 to 1850.

3. **The Field Code.** The modernizing Field Code of procedure was adopted in New York in 1848, and by many other states soon afterwards. The Field Code generally followed the common law writ practice for joinder of claims but adopted much of the equity practice for joinder of parties. Most states have now adopted some version of the federal rules, but some large states—such as California and New York—are still nominally "code states."

However, the modern joinder rules in the code states are functionally similar to the modern joinder rules in the federal rules.

4. Modern approaches to joinder. The general philosophy of modern procedural rules in both the federal and state systems is to allow liberal joinder of claims and parties. See generally G. Hazard, J. Leubsdorf & D. Bassett, Civil Procedure, chs. 9 and 10 (6th ed. 2011); Kaplan, Continuing Work of the Civil Committee: 1966 Amendments to the Federal Rules of Civil Procedure (II), 81 Harv. L. Rev. 591 (1968). The materials that follow explore the modern joinder and class action rules.

NOTE ON SUBJECT MATTER JURISDICTION AND JOINDER

Federal courts have limited subject matter jurisdiction, as discussed in detail in Chapter 2, supra. For students who have not read Chapter 2, the following is a brief overview of subject matter jurisdiction in the federal courts.

The term "subject matter jurisdiction" refers to the kinds of suit a court may hear. (It is different from "personal jurisdiction," which refers to the ability of a court to compel particular persons to appear before them.) Subject matter jurisdiction in the federal courts is both a constitutional and a statutory matter. Article III of the United States Constitution authorizes the federal courts to hear only certain kinds of suits. Federal statutes then authorize the federal courts to hear a subset of the suits authorized in Article III. For subject matter jurisdiction to exist there must be both constitutional and statutory authorization.

The two most common statutory bases for federal court subject matter jurisdiction are "federal question" and "diversity of citizenship," set forth in 28 U.S.C. §§ 1331 and 1332. If a plaintiff's claim arises under federal law, there is "federal question" jurisdiction under § 1331. If a plaintiff and defendant are citizens of different states and the amount in controversy in plaintiff's claim is over $75,000, there is "diversity jurisdiction" under § 1332. If a plaintiff's claim does not arise under federal law, if there is no diversity of citizenship between the parties, and if there is no other basis for jurisdiction, there is no subject matter jurisdiction in the federal courts. If the plaintiff and defendant are citizens of different states but the amount in controversy is $75,000 or less, and if the suit is not based on federal law, there is also no subject matter jurisdiction.

If there is no subject matter jurisdiction over a claim under either §§ 1331 or 1332 when that claim is considered alone, there is sometimes "supplemental" subject matter jurisdiction under 28 U.S.C. § 1367 when that claim is joined with another claim over which there is jurisdiction. For example, in a pure "federal question" suit brought under § 1331, there is supplemental jurisdiction over an additional claim arising under state law so long as the additional claim "form[s] part of the same case or controversy" with the federal claim. See § 1367(a). In a "diversity" suit brought under § 1332, in which the plaintiff has brought one state-law claim in which the amount in controversy is over $75,000, there is supplemental jurisdiction over an additional state-law claim brought by the plaintiff in which the amount in controversy is $75,000 or less, so long as that additional claim is part of the "same case or controversy."

In combination, §§ 1331, 1332, and 1367 operate to confer subject matter jurisdiction over many original and joined claims. But even with the help of supplemental jurisdiction under § 1367, there is no subject matter jurisdiction over some joined claims. To take one example, there is often no supplemental jurisdiction over a "permissive" counterclaim against the plaintiff under federal Rule 13(b). (You will learn about compulsory and permissive counterclaims under Rule 13, and their relation to supplemental jurisdiction, in *Jones v. Ford Motor Credit Co.*, infra p. 562.) So far as Rule 13(b) is concerned, the permissive counterclaim may be brought. But a federal procedural rule, such as Rule 13(b), cannot confer subject matter jurisdiction.

The federal joinder rules thus purport to allow joinder in circumstances where, because of the limitations on the federal courts' subject matter jurisdiction, joinder is impossible. The federal joinder rules must always be read in light of the limitations on the federal courts' subject matter jurisdiction. Do not be tricked by the federal Rules. They sometimes promise more than they can deliver.

1. MULTIPLE CLAIMS IN THE SAME PLEADING: RULE 18(a)

Federal Rule 18(a) provides that a party asserting a claim for relief—whether as an original claim by plaintiff, as a counterclaim by defendant, as a cross-claim against a co-party, or as a claim against a third party—may join any other claim to that claim. There is no requirement in the rule that the joined claims be related to one another beyond the requirement that they be asserted by the same party in the same pleading. Unlike other joinder rules, Rule 18(a) does not require that a joined claim arise out of the same or related transaction or occurrence. Compare, for example, federal Rule 20(a) which allows joinder of *parties* (as distinct from joinder of *claims* in Rule 18(a)) only when the claims by or against the newly joined parties "aris[e] out of the same transaction, occurrence, or series of transactions or occurrences" as the claims by or against the existing parties.

The effect of Rule 18(a) is to allow a party who brings a claim against another party to bring all of her claims against that party at the same time, whether those claims are related or not. The obvious rationale is efficiency: If one claim is already being brought against a party in an existing suit, why force the claimant to file another suit in order to bring another claim against that same party?

Note that Rule 18(a), if considered alone, would allow claims to be joined that are not within the subject matter jurisdiction of the federal courts. For example, if a plaintiff in a suit where there is no diversity of citizenship brings a claim based on federal law, there is subject matter jurisdiction under 28 U.S.C. § 1331. But if the plaintiff seeks to join a new and unrelated claim based on state law, there is no independent basis for subject matter jurisdiction over that new claim (because there is neither a federal question or diversity of citizenship). Further, there is no supplemental jurisdiction over that new claim under § 1367 because the claim is not part of the "same case or controversy" as the federal claim. Therefore, while Rule 18(a) appears to allow the new claim to be joined, the limitations on the federal courts' subject matter jurisdiction prevent joinder.

2. SEVERANCE AND CONSOLIDATION

NOTE ON SEVERANCE AND CONSOLIDATION

A case can be severed into two or more parts for separate disposition. Under federal Rule 42(b), a district court may sever "[f]or convenience, to avoid prejudice, or to expedite and economize." Severance sometimes means that the district court conducts entirely separate trials; it sometimes means that the court conducts separate trials only as to certain issues or claims. Conversely, under Rule 42(a) a district court may consolidate separately filed cases. Consolidation sometimes means that separate cases are combined for all purposes; it sometimes means that they are consolidated for only some purposes—for example, for pre-trial motions, or for trial on liability but not damages.

Use of severance and consolidation has increased under the modern rules—severance because joinder sometimes results in cases that are too large to handle in a single proceeding, and consolidation because many courts, now accustomed to handling large cases, are willing to consolidate what, in earlier times, would have been separate cases. When separate cases involving important issues in common are pending in the same district court, it is now routine to consolidate them for at least some purposes. Cases may be consolidated for pretrial purposes, especially if they involve extensive discovery. The Supreme Court wrote many years ago that "consolidation * * * does not merge the suits into a single cause, or change the rights of the parties, or make those who are parties in one suit parties in another," Johnson v. Manhattan Ry. Co., 289 U.S. 479, 496–97, 53 S.Ct. 721, 728, 77 L.Ed. 1331 (1933), but it is hard to see how the Court's statement can be entirely true. See also State Mut. Life Assur. Co. v. Deer Creek Park, 612 F.2d 259, 267 (6th Cir. 1979).

The decision to sever or consolidate is generally left to the discretion of the district judge. District judges sometimes have very different approaches. See, e.g., Arroyo v. Chardon, 90 F.R.D. 603 (D.P.R. 1981) (refusing to consolidate nine actions by public employees who had been demoted for their "association" with a political party). The trial judge's choice to sever or consolidate is ordinarily not reviewable until there has been a final judgment in the trial court. The appellate court then has to decide not merely whether the trial judge made a bad choice, but whether the choice was so bad as to justify retrial. See, e.g., Shump v. Balka, 574 F.2d 1341 (10th Cir. 1978). For a list of factors relevant to severance, see Arnold v. Eastern Air Lines, 681 F.2d 186 (4th Cir. 1982). See also Fed. R. Civ. P. 20(b) (separate trial provision in rule on permissive joinder of parties) and Fed. R. Civ. P. 21 (severance provision in rule on misjoinder and non-joinder of parties). For consolidation of cases filed in different federal districts for pretrial purposes, see 28 U.S.C. § 1407 (consolidation in a single district court for pretrial proceedings in multidistrict litigation); Lexecon, Inc. v. Milberg Weiss Bershad Hynes & Lerach, 523 U.S. 26, 118 S.Ct. 956, 140 L.Ed.2d 62 (1998).

3.   COUNTERCLAIMS: FEDERAL RULE 13(a) AND (b)

Jones v. Ford Motor Credit Company

United States Court of Appeals for the Second Circuit, 2004.
358 F.3d 205.

■ NEWMAN, CIRCUIT JUDGE.

This appeal concerns the availability of subject matter jurisdiction for permissive counterclaims. It also demonstrates the normal utility of early decision of a motion for class certification. Defendant-Appellant Ford Motor Credit Company ("Ford Credit") appeals from the [judgment of the District Court] dismissing for lack of jurisdiction its permissive counterclaims against three of the four Plaintiffs-Appellees and its conditional counterclaims against members of the putative class that the Plaintiffs-Appellees seek to certify. * * * We conclude that supplemental jurisdiction authorized by 28 U.S.C. § 1367 may be available for the permissive counterclaims, but that the District Court's discretion under subsection 1367(c) should not be exercised in this case until a ruling on the Plaintiffs' motion for class certification. We therefore vacate and remand.

Background

Plaintiffs-Appellees Joyce Jones, Martha L. Edwards, Lou Cooper, and Vincent E. Jackson ("Plaintiffs"), individually and as class representatives, sued Ford Credit alleging racial discrimination under the Equal Credit Opportunity Act ("ECOA"), 15 U.S.C. § 1691 et seq. (2003). They had purchased Ford vehicles under Ford Credit's financing plan. They alleged that the financing plan discriminated against African-Americans. Although the financing rate was primarily based on objective criteria, Ford Credit permitted its dealers to mark up the rate, using subjective criteria to assess non-risk charges. The Plaintiffs alleged that the mark-up policy penalized African-American customers with higher rates than those imposed on similarly situated Caucasian customers.

In its Answer, Ford Credit denied the charges of racial discrimination and also asserted state-law counterclaims against Jones, Edwards, and Cooper for the amounts of their unpaid car loans. Ford Credit alleged that Jones was in default on her obligations under her contract for the purchase of a 1995 Ford Windstar, and that Edwards and Cooper were in default on payments for their joint purchase of a 1995 Mercury Cougar. Additionally, in the event that a class was certified, Ford Credit asserted conditional counterclaims against any member of that class who was in default on a car loan from Ford Credit. The Plaintiffs moved to dismiss Ford Credit's counterclaims for lack of subject matter jurisdiction, Fed. R. Civ. P. 12(b)(1), lack of personal jurisdiction, Fed. R. Civ. P. 12(b)(2), improper venue, Fed. R. Civ. P. 12(b)(3), and failure to state a claim upon which relief could be granted, Fed. R. Civ. P. 12(b)(6).

The District Court granted the Plaintiffs' motion and dismissed Ford Credit's counterclaims, summarizing its reasons for doing so as follows: "Defendant's counterclaims do not meet the standard for compulsory counterclaims[, and] . . . pursuant to § 1367(c)(4), . . . there are compelling reasons to decline to exercise jurisdiction over the counterclaims." * * *

In reaching these conclusions, [District] Judge McKenna acknowledged some uncertainty. After determining that the counterclaims were permissive, he expressed doubt as to the jurisdictional consequence of that determination. On the one hand, he believed, as the Plaintiffs maintain, that permissive counterclaims must be dismissed if they lack an independent basis of federal jurisdiction. On the other hand, he acknowledged * * * that "there [was] some authority to suggest that . . . the court should determine, based on the particular circumstances of the case, whether it had authority to exercise supplemental jurisdiction under § 1367(a)" over a counterclaim, regardless of whether it was compulsory or permissive. * * *

To resolve his uncertainty, Judge McKenna initially ruled that the counterclaims, being permissive, "must be dismissed for lack of an independent basis of federal jurisdiction." He then ruled that, if he was wrong and if supplemental jurisdiction under section 1367 was available, he would still dismiss the counterclaims in the exercise of the discretion subsection 1367(c) gives district courts. Without explicitly stating on which of the four subdivisions of subsection 1367(c) he relied, Judge McKenna gave the following reasons for declining to exercise supplemental jurisdiction:

> The claims and counterclaims arise out of the same occurrence only in the loosest terms. . . . There does not exist a logical relationship between the essential facts [to be proven] in the claim and those of the counterclaims.

> Allowing defendant's counterclaims to proceed in this forum might undermine the ECOA enforcement scheme by discouraging plaintiffs from bringing ECOA claims due to the fear of counterclaims.

> The interests of judicial economy will not be served by joining the claim and counterclaims in one suit [because of] what would most likely be a tremendous number of separate collection actions, each based on facts specific to the individual plaintiffs involved.

* * * Judge McKenna stated his belief that it would be "unfair and inexpedient" to require absent class members who resided outside of New York to litigate their debt collection actions in the Southern District of New York and that there was no good reason to litigate the debt collection actions in a federal court. * * *

[handwritten margin note: unfair to include out of state collection actions]

On March 27, 2003, the District Court entered judgment pursuant to Fed. R. Civ. P. 54(b) in favor of the Plaintiffs, dismissing Ford Credit's counterclaims without prejudice. Ford Credit appeals from this decision.

Discussion

I.   Are Ford Credit's Counterclaims Permissive?

Fed. R. Civ. P. 13(a) defines a compulsory counterclaim as any claim which at the time of serving the pleading the pleader has against any opposing party, if it arises out of the transaction or occurrence that is the subject matter of the opposing party's claim and does not require for its adjudication the presence of third parties of whom the court cannot obtain jurisdiction.

Such counterclaims are compulsory in the sense that if they are not raised, they are forfeited. See Critical-Vac Filtration Corp. v. Minuteman International, Inc., 233 F.3d 697, 699 (2d Cir. 2000). Fed. R. Civ. P. 13(b) defines a permissive counterclaim as "any claim against an opposing party not arising out of the transaction or occurrence that is the subject matter of the opposing party's claim."

Whether a counterclaim is compulsory or permissive turns on whether the counterclaim "arises out of the transaction or occurrence that is the subject matter of the opposing party's claim," and this Circuit has long considered this standard met when there is a "logical relationship" between the counterclaim and the main claim. See United States v. Aquavella, 615 F.2d 12, 22 (2d Cir. 1979).[1] Although the "logical relationship" test does not require "an absolute identity of factual backgrounds," id. (internal citation omitted), the " 'essential facts of the claims [must be] so logically connected that considerations of judicial economy and fairness dictate that all the issues be resolved in one lawsuit.' " Critical-Vac, 233 F.3d at 699 (emphasis omitted) (quoting Adam v. Jacobs, 950 F.2d 89, 92 (2d Cir. 1991)); see also Harris v. Steinem, 571 F.2d 119, 123 (2d Cir. 1978); United Artists Corp. v. Masterpiece Productions, Inc., 221 F.2d 213, 216 (2d Cir. 1955).

We agree with the District Court that the debt collection counterclaims were permissive rather than compulsory. The Plaintiffs' ECOA claim centers on Ford Credit's mark-up policy, based on subjective factors, which allegedly resulted in higher finance charges on their purchase contracts than on those of similarly situated White customers. Ford Credit's debt collection counterclaims are related to those purchase contracts, but not to any particular clause or rate. Rather, the debt collection counterclaims concern the individual Plaintiffs' non-payment after the contract price was set. Thus, the relationship between the counterclaims and the ECOA claim is "logical" only in the sense that the sale, allegedly on discriminatory credit terms, was the "but for" cause of the non-payment. That is not the sort of relationship contemplated by our case law on compulsory counterclaims. The essential facts for proving the counterclaims and the ECOA claim are not so closely related that resolving both sets of issues in one lawsuit would yield judicial efficiency. Indeed, Ford Credit does not even challenge the ruling that its counterclaims are permissive.

II.   Is There Jurisdiction over the Permissive Counterclaims?

For several decades federal courts have asserted that permissive counterclaims require an independent basis of jurisdiction, i.e., that the counterclaim must be maintainable in a federal district court on some jurisdictional basis that would have sufficed had it been brought in a separate action. The origin of this proposition, the questioning of it before the statutory authorization of supplemental jurisdiction in section 1367,

---

[1]   The phrase "logical relationship," in the context of counterclaims, was first used by the Supreme Court in Moore v. New York Cotton Exchange, 270 U.S. 593, 610, 70 L. Ed. 750, 46 S.Ct. 367 (1926). Referring to a counterclaim "arising out of the transaction which is the subject matter of the suit," as stated in former Equity Rule 30, the Court explained:

> "Transaction" is a word of flexible meaning. It may comprehend a series of many occurrences, depending not so much upon the immediateness of their connection as upon their logical relationship.

Id.

and the impact of that provision upon the proposition all merit careful consideration.

(A) Origin of the independent basis doctrine

The first suggestion of the requirement of an independent basis for permissive counterclaims is believed to have appeared in Marconi Wireless Telegraph Co. of America v. National Electric Signaling Co., 206 Fed. 295 (E.D.N.Y. 1913), a case involving former Equity Rule 30. See Thomas F. Green, Jr., Federal Jurisdiction over Counterclaims, 48 Nw. U. L. Rev. 271, 283 (1953). That rule distinguished in its two parts between what we would now call compulsory counterclaims "arising out of the transaction which is the subject matter of the suit" and what we would now call permissive counterclaims "which might be the subject of an independent suit in equity." Equity Rule 30, quoted in Moore v. New York Cotton Exchange, 270 U.S. 593, 609, 70 L. Ed. 750, 46 S.Ct. 367 (1926). In Moore, the Supreme Court ruled that the counterclaim in that case bore a sufficient relation to the underlying transaction under the first part of the equity rule to be properly within federal jurisdiction and explicitly declined to "consider the point that, under the second branch [of the rule], federal jurisdiction independent of the original bill must appear." Id.

* * *

Our first holding that independent jurisdiction was required for a permissive counterclaim occurred in 1968. See O'Connell v. Erie Lackawanna R.R., 391 F.2d 156, 163 (2d Cir. 1968). Six years later, the Supreme Court stated, "If a counterclaim is compulsory, the federal court will have ancillary jurisdiction over it even though ordinarily it would be a matter for a state court," Baker v. Gold Seal Liquors, Inc., 417 U.S. 467, 469 n. 1, 41 L.Ed.2d 243, 94 S.Ct. 2504 (1974) (emphasis added), apparently implying that ancillary jurisdiction is not available for a permissive counterclaim.

Notably absent from this evolution of the case law is a reasoned explanation of why independent jurisdiction should be needed for permissive counterclaims. * * *

(B) Questioning the doctrine prior to section 1367

The first challenge to the independent jurisdiction requirement appeared in Professor Green's article in 1953. See Thomas F. Green, Jr., Federal Jurisdiction over Counterclaims, 48 Nw. U. L. Rev. 271, 283 (1953). He mounted a powerful argument against the doctrine, demonstrating how it emerged from unreasoned dicta into unexplained holdings and why it was an unwarranted deviation from the general principle that "two court actions should not be encouraged where one will do." Id. at 271 (footnote omitted). He particularly noted the incursion on the doctrine, well established even in 1953 when he wrote, that permitted some set-offs to be interposed against a plaintiff's claim in the absence of independent jurisdiction. Professor Green questioned why a defendant who can present evidence of a set-off that reduces a plaintiff's judgment to zero should not be able to obtain a counterclaim judgment to which his evidence would entitle him in a separate action. Id. at 287–88.

In 1970, Judge Friendly, the acknowledged jurisdictional scholar of our Court, changed his mind about the independent jurisdiction doctrine and "rejected the conventional learning, which [he] followed too readily in O'Connell." United States v. Heyward-Robinson Co., 430 F.2d 1077, 1088 (2d Cir. 1970) (Friendly, J., concurring). Judge Friendly noted Professor Green's persuasiveness: "The reasons why the conventional view is wrong are set out in detail in [Professor Green's article], and nothing would be gained by repetition." Id.

In 1984, the Third Circuit, in a thoughtful opinion by Judge Becker, rejected the view that independent jurisdiction is required for all permissive counterclaims. See Ambromovage v. United Mine Workers, 726 F.2d 972 (3d Cir. 1984). Considering whether jurisdiction was available for a set-off, Judge Becker declined to uphold jurisdiction based on the previously recognized set-off exception to the independent jurisdiction requirement,[3] and instead argued broadly for ancillary jurisdiction, with some exceptions, over set-offs and permissive counterclaims that satisfy the test of sharing a "common nucleus of operative fact," United Mine Workers v. Gibbs, 383 U.S. 715, 725, 16 L.Ed. 2d 218, 86 S.Ct. 1130 (1966), with the plaintiff's underlying claim. Ambromovage, 736 F.2d at 988–89. "We conclude that the determination that a counterclaim is permissive within the meaning of Rule 13 is not dispositive of the constitutional question whether there is federal jurisdiction over the counterclaim." Id. at 990.

(C)   The impact of section 1367

The judge-made doctrine of ancillary jurisdiction, which had been invoked to provide a jurisdictional basis for compulsory counterclaims, was given statutory undergirding when Congress added section 1367 to Title 28 in 1990. . . . The newly labeled "supplemental" jurisdiction explicitly extended federal courts' authority to "all other claims" in a civil action "so related to claims in the action within [the district court's] original jurisdiction that they form part of the same case or controversy under Article III of the United States Constitution." 28 U.S.C. § 1367(a) (2000).

The explicit extension to the limit of Article III of a federal court's jurisdiction over "all other claims" sought to be litigated with an underlying claim within federal jurisdiction recast the jurisdictional basis of permissive counterclaims into constitutional terms.[5] After

---

[3]   The set-off exception provides that "where the permissive counterclaim is in the nature of a set-off interposed merely to defeat or reduce the opposing party's claim and does not seek affirmative relief, no independent jurisdictional grounds are required." Heyward-Robinson, 430 F.2d at 1081 n. 1. As the court noted in Ambromovage, the "defensive set-off exception does not fit squarely within the analytic framework set forth" in United Mine Workers v. Gibbs, 383 U.S. 715, 16 L.Ed.2d 218, 86 S.Ct. 1130 (1966), because "under the exception, all defensive set-offs, whether or not they satisfy the Gibbs test, are within the ancillary jurisdiction of the court." Ambromovage, 726 F.2d at 990–92 & n. 56.

[5]   There is some doubt as to whether section 1367's expansion of supplemental jurisdiction to its constitutional limits renders the provision's scope broader than was contemplated in Gibbs. The text of subsection 1367(a) unambiguously extends jurisdiction to the limits of Article III, and the provision's legislative history indicates that Congress viewed the Gibbs "common nucleus" test as delineating those constitutional limits. See H.R. Rep. No. 101–734, reprinted in 1990 U.S.C.C.A.N. 6360, 6374–75 (stating that "subsection (a) codifies the scope of supplemental jurisdiction first articulated by the Supreme Court in United Mine Workers v. Gibbs, 383 U.S. 715, 16 L.Ed.2d 218, 86 S.Ct. 1130 (1966)"). Several commentators have suggested, however, that the extent of constitutional jurisdiction is broader than the Gibbs test, as Article III may not require a particular factual relationship between joined claims or counterclaims and federal claims that provide the basis for jurisdiction.

section 1367, it is no longer sufficient for courts to assert, without any reason other than dicta or even holdings from the era of judge-created ancillary jurisdiction, that permissive counterclaims require independent jurisdiction. Rising to the challenge, after enactment of section 1367, in a case strikingly similar to our pending case, the Seventh Circuit vacated the dismissal of a permissive counterclaim and remanded for exercise of the discretion contemplated by section 1367. Channell v. Citicorp Nat'l Servs., 89 F.3d 379 (7th Cir. 1996). Channell involved a creditor's counterclaims to collect debts in a class action alleging violations of the Consumer Leasing Act, 15 U.S.C. §§ 1667–1667e (2000). As Judge Easterbrook stated, "Now that Congress has codified the supplemental jurisdiction in § 1367(a), courts should use the language of the statute to define the extent of their powers." Id. at 385. He viewed section 1367's reach to the constitutional limits of Article III as requiring only "[a] loose factual connection between the claims," id. (internal quotation marks omitted), a standard that appears to be broader than the Gibbs test of "a common nucleus of operative facts," appropriate for permitting joinder of a plaintiff's non-federal claim. In Channell, he readily found the requisite "loose connection" to exist between the Consumer Leasing Act claim and the debt collection counterclaim. Id. at 385–86.

We share the view that section 1367 has displaced, rather than codified, whatever validity inhered in the earlier view that a permissive counterclaim requires independent jurisdiction (in the sense of federal question or diversity jurisdiction). The issue in this case therefore becomes whether supplemental jurisdiction is available for Ford Credit's counterclaims.

L/ Issue

In 1983, Professor Matasar, anticipating section 1367's authorization of supplemental jurisdiction for all claims within an Article III "case or controversy," advocated permitting joinder of all claims, whether those of the plaintiff or the defendant, to the full extent of "the system of rules lawfully adopted to govern procedure in the federal courts." See Richard A. Matasar, Rediscovering "One Constitutional Case": Procedural Rules and the Rejection of the Gibbs Test for Supplemental Jurisdiction, 71 Cal. L. Rev. 1399, 1478–79 (1983). He drew support from Chief Justice Marshall's statement that " '[the judicial] power is capable of acting only when the subject is submitted to [the judicial department], by a party who asserts his rights in the form prescribed by law.' " Id. at 1479 (quoting Osborn v. President, Directors & Co. of Bank, 22 U.S. (9 Wheat.) 738, 819, 6 L. Ed. 204 (1824) (Little, Brown 1864)). Professor Matasar would permit jurisdiction over any counterclaim authorized by federal rules, without requiring any factual relationship to the underlying claim.

More recently, Professor Fletcher (now Judge Fletcher) also advocated a broad view of the claims that could be joined in a "case or controversy" under section 1367. See William A. Fletcher, "Common Nucleus of Operative Fact" and Defensive Set-Off Beyond the Gibbs Test, 74 Ind. L. J. 171 (1998). Like Professor Matasar, Professor Fletcher urged that the constitutional test of a "case" did not require a factual connection between joined claims, but would be satisfied under either the joinder standards applicable when the Constitution was adopted or modern joinder rules. Id. at 178.

Congress's understanding of the extent of Article III is of course not binding as constitutional interpretation, and section 1367's legislative history cannot be read as an independent limit on subsection 1367(a)'s clear extension of jurisdiction to the limits of Article III. Thus, the correct reading of subsection 1367(a)'s reference to "the same case or controversy under Article III" remains unsettled.

III. Application of Section 1367's Standards for Supplemental Jurisdiction

Whether or not the Gibbs "common nucleus" standard provides the outer limit of an Article III "case,"[6] and is therefore a requirement for entertaining a permissive counterclaim that otherwise lacks a jurisdictional basis, the facts of Ford Credit's counterclaims and those of the Plaintiffs' ECOA claims satisfy that standard, even though the relationship is not such as would make the counterclaims compulsory. See Channell, 89 F.3d at 385–86.[7] The counterclaims and the underlying claim bear a sufficient factual relationship (if one is necessary) to constitute the same "case" within the meaning of Article III and hence of section 1367. Both the ECOA claim and the debt collection claims originate from the Plaintiffs' decisions to purchase Ford cars.

Satisfying the constitutional "case" standard of subsection 1367(a), however, does not end the inquiry a district court is obliged to make with respect to permissive counterclaims. A trial court must consider whether any of the four grounds set out in subsection 1367(c) are present to an extent that would warrant the exercise of discretion to decline assertion of supplemental jurisdiction. Subsection 1367(c) provides:

> The district courts may decline to exercise supplemental jurisdiction over a claim under subsection (a) if—
>
> (1) the claim raises a novel or complex issue of State law,
>
> (2) the claim substantially predominates over the claim or claims over which the district court has original jurisdiction,
>
> (3) the district court has dismissed all claims over which it has original jurisdiction, or
>
> (4) in exceptional circumstances, there are other compelling reasons for declining jurisdiction.

We have indicated that, where at least one of the subsection 1367(c) factors is applicable, a district court should not decline to exercise supplemental jurisdiction unless it also determines that doing so would not promote the values articulated in Gibbs, 383 U.S. at 726: economy, convenience, fairness, and comity. See Itar-Tass Russian News Agency v. Russian Kurier, Inc., 140 F.3d 442, 445–47 (2d Cir. 1998) (rejecting approach of 1st, 3rd, 7th, and D.C. Circuits in favor of approach adhered to by 8th, 9th, and 11th Circuits).

Clearly the exception set forth in subsection 1367(c)(1) does not apply since Ford Credit's counterclaims do not raise a novel or complex issue of state law, but merely a standard contract question. Nor does

---

[6] If the Gibbs standard marks the outer limit of an Article III "case," congressional authorization to join counterclaims with a more tenuous connection to the underlying claim would be unconstitutional unless Congress has some authority to expand the constitutional scope of "case."

[7] We note that the "common nucleus" test of Gibbs, expanding the prior test of Hurn v. Oursler, 289 U.S. 238, 245–47, 77 L. Ed. 1148, 53 S.Ct. 586 (1933), was developed to provide some limit upon the state law claims that a plaintiff could join with its federal law claims. That rationale does not necessarily apply to a defendant's counterclaims. A plaintiff might be tempted to file an insubstantial federal law claim as an excuse to tie to it one or more state law claims that do not belong in a federal court. There is no corresponding risk that a defendant will decline to file in state court an available state law claim, hoping to be lucky enough to be sued by his adversary on a federal claim so that he can assert a state law counterclaim.

subsection 1367(c)(3) apply since the District Court has not dismissed all claims over which it has original jurisdiction. That leaves subsections 1367(c)(2), permitting declination of supplemental jurisdiction where "the counterclaim substantially predominates over the claim or claims over which the district court has original jurisdiction," and 1367(c)(4), permitting declination "in exceptional circumstances, [where] there are other compelling reasons for declining jurisdiction." The District Court apparently based its decision on subsection 1367(c)(4), since it cited only that subsection in its opinion, but some of the concerns it discussed implicate the substantial predomination analysis of subsection 1367(c)(2) as well.

> * * *

Whether Ford Credit's counterclaims "predominate[ ]" over the Plaintiffs' claims and whether there are "exceptional circumstances" for declining jurisdiction cannot properly be determined until a decision has been made on the Plaintiffs' motion for class certification. Both the applicability of subsections 1367(c)(2) and (4), and the exercise of a district court's discretion in the event either or both are ruled applicable will be significantly influenced by the existence of a large class as sought by the Plaintiffs. The District Court's conclusions that it would be "unfair and inexpedient" to require out-of-state class members to litigate Ford's state law debt claims in New York, and that allowing the counterclaims might dissuade potential plaintiffs from joining the class, were therefore premature.

Class certification is to be decided "at an early practicable time" after the commencement of a suit. Fed. R. Civ. P. 23(c)(1) (amended Dec. 1, 2003). See 5 James Wm. Moore et al., Moore's Federal Practice-Civil § 23.61 (3d ed. 2003); cf. Cottone v. Blum, 571 F. Supp. 437, 440–41 (W.D.N.Y. 1983) (dismissing class action for, among other things, failure to move for class certification within 60 days of filing of complaint, as required by local rule). That course is especially important in this case. Accordingly, we remand this case with directions to rule on the class certification motion, and then, in light of that ruling, to proceed to determine whether to exercise or decline supplemental jurisdiction.

On remand, the District Court should exercise its discretion pursuant to subsection 1367(c) in light of our decision in Itar-Tass, particularly the caution there expressed concerning use of subsection 1367(c)(4), 140 F.3d at 448. In order to decline jurisdiction on this basis, the District Court should identify truly compelling circumstances that militate against exercising jurisdiction. Id. Moreover, if the Court certifies the class action, its substantial predomination analysis under subsection 1367(c)(2) should take into account the methods by which the class action might be managed in order to prevent the state law counterclaims from predominating. By bifurcating the litigation, certifying a limited class (perhaps only in-state plaintiffs), or utilizing other management tools, the District Court might be able to structure the litigation in such a way as to prevent the state law claims from predominating over the federal basis of the action, while maintaining the advantages inherent in providing a forum in which all of the litigants' claims can be litigated.

Conclusion

The judgment dismissing Ford Credit's counterclaims is vacated, and the case is remanded for further proceedings consistent with this opinion. No costs.

NOTE ON COMPULSORY AND PERMISSIVE COUNTERCLAIMS

1. Counterclaims under Rule 13. A defendant is not limited to defending against plaintiff's claims. She may assert claims of her own, called "counterclaims," against the plaintiff. A counterclaim is any claim asserted by a party against an opposing party who has already asserted a claim. A counterclaim is usually a claim asserted by a defendant against a plaintiff, but it need not be. It could also be, for example, a new claim by a plaintiff against a counterclaiming defendant. A counterclaim under Rule 13 is either compulsory under Rule 13(a) or permissive under Rule 13(b).

A counterclaim is compulsory under Rule 13(a) if it "arises out of the transaction or occurrence that is the subject matter of the opposing party's claim." As indicated by the word "compulsory," a compulsory counterclaim must be asserted in the current suit. The consequence of not asserting a compulsory counterclaim is that the defendant may not assert that claim in any subsequent suit. The compulsory counterclaim rule is subject to two important exceptions: First, a counterclaim need not be filed in the current proceeding if it is already pending as a claim in another proceeding. See Rule 13(a)(2)(A). Second, the counterclaim need not be filed if the opposing party has not obtained *in personam* jurisdiction over the party who has a potential counterclaim. See Rule 13(a)(2)(B). The compulsory counterclaim rule under Rule 13(a) is, in effect, a rule of preclusion. For further discussion of preclusion, see Preclusion Between the Same Parties, Chapter 9, infra p. 1050.

A counterclaim is permissive under Rule 13(b) if it does not arise out of the same transaction or occurrence as the plaintiff's claim. The only Rule 13(b) requirement is that a permissive counterclaim be a claim asserted by the defendant against the plaintiff (or, more precisely, by a party against an opposing party that has already asserted a claim). A failure to assert a permissive counterclaim has no preclusive consequence in later litigation.

2. Supplemental jurisdiction. The federal supplemental jurisdiction statute, 28 U.S.C. § 1367, is explained in detail in Chapter 2, supra. For students who have not read Chapter 2, the following is a brief and, for present purposes, sufficient summary. Section 1367 was enacted in 1990, codifying most but not all of the rules that had previously been established in judge-made law. Under the pre-§ 1367 judge-made law, the terms "ancillary" and "pendent jurisdiction" had been used to refer to jurisdiction over claims that were joined to claims for which there was already subject matter jurisdiction. Section 1367 invented a new term, "supplemental jurisdiction," that includes both "ancillary" and "pendent jurisdiction." (This bit of terminological history should help you read the court's opinion in *Jones*.)

The scheme of § 1367 is as follows. Section 1367(a) grants supplemental subject matter jurisdiction broadly. Under § 1367(a), there is supplemental jurisdiction over all claims that are joined with claims for which there is already subject matter jurisdiction, even if there would be no jurisdiction over the joined claims if those claims were standing alone. The only limitation in § 1367(a) is the requirement that the pre-existing and joined claims must be part of the "same case or controversy," as those terms are used in Article III of the Constitution. Section 1367(b) excepts from the broad grant of supplemental jurisdiction in § 1367(a) certain claims in cases where the sole basis for jurisdiction is diversity of citizenship. Those exceptions are defined in terms of claims made under certain federal Rules—Rules 14, 19, 20, and 24. There is no exception for claims made under Rule 13. Thus, the broad grant of supplemental jurisdiction in § 1367(b) applies in both federal question and diversity cases to all counterclaims under Rule 13, both compulsory and permissive.

A federal district court is not required to hear all claims for which there is only "supplemental" jurisdiction. Section 1367(c), quoted in *Jones*, specifies several circumstances in which the district court, in its discretion, may decline to exercise supplemental jurisdiction. The consequence of a district court's refusal to hear a claim based on the criteria of § 1367(c) is that the claim will be brought, if the party wishes to pursue it, in state court. One may understand § 1367(c) as a kind of statutory severance rule, somewhat analogous to federal Rule 42(b).

[handwritten margin note: 1367(c) discretion of courts the]

3. Effect of *Jones*. Prior to the court's decision in *Jones*, the rule in the Second Circuit was (and in some other circuits still is) that there is supplemental jurisdiction over compulsory counterclaims under Rule 13(a), but not over permissive counterclaims under Rule 13(b). *See United States v. Heyward-Robinson Co.*, 430 F.2d 1077 (2d Cir. 1970), discussed in *Jones*. *Jones* abandons *Heyward-Robinson* and holds that the same "transaction or occurrence" test of Rule 13(a) is narrower than the same "case of controversy" test of § 1367 and Article III of the Constitution. What will be the practical effect of abandoning *Heyward-Robinson*?

In *Heyward-Robinson*, the court held, over Judge Friendly's dissent, that the counterclaim in that case was compulsory under Rule 13(a). The short-term consequence of the court's holding was to allow the district court to hear the counterclaim under its "ancillary" subject matter jurisdiction (as it was then called). There was some justice, as well as efficiency, in the court's decision. The defendant's claim was likely time-barred if it had to be refiled; further, the claim had already been litigated to judgment in the district court, and the subject matter jurisdiction question had been raised for the first time on appeal. But the long-term consequence was more ambiguous. In reaching its holding, the *Heyward-Robinson* court expanded the same "transaction or occurrence" test of Rule 13(a), thereby making more counterclaims compulsory. The court's expanded reading of Rule 13(a) not only made the compulsory counterclaim rule broader, but also made its reach more uncertain. After *Heyward-Robinson*, a risk-averse defendant was well advised to assert many tangentially related claims as counterclaims even if he would have preferred to litigate them separately. (Can you see why she would have been well advised to do so?) Now, after *Jones*, the compulsory counterclaim rule (at least in the Second Circuit) is somewhat narrower, as well as somewhat clearer, giving defendants more freedom to assert, or not assert, counterclaims that are only tangentially related to the plaintiff's claim or claims.

4. Definition of part of the "same case or controversy" under Article III. When Congress enacted § 1367, it believed (or at least the three law professors who drafted § 1367 believed) that the definition of the "same case or controversy" was contained in *United Mine Workers v. Gibbs*, 383

U.S. 715, 86 S.Ct. 1130, 16 L.Ed.2d 218 (1966). See Chapter 2, supra, p. 273 n.5. In *Gibbs*, the Supreme Court held that a federal district court had "pendent" subject matter jurisdiction over a joined claim that "derived" from a "common nucleus of operative fact" as the claim over which it had federal question jurisdiction. But the "common nucleus of operative fact" test may not state the outer limits of the "same case or controversy" under § 1367 and Article III. The *Jones* court clearly thinks that it does not. In the view of the *Jones* court, what is the test for whether a claim forms part of the "same case or controversy" with another claim?

5. **Counterclaims for monetary relief, set-offs, and insurance.** Counterclaims for affirmative monetary relief or for set-off facilitate fair and efficient resolution of disputes in which there are offsetting monetary recoveries. Counterclaims for affirmative monetary relief encompass all monetary claims. A counterclaim for set-off is a subset of those counterclaims. A set-off is an amount that is or can be "liquidated" arising out of a contract or a judgment that is owed by the plaintiff to the defendant. The amount owed can be deducted, or "set off," against any amount recovered by the plaintiff.

In a jurisdiction with comparative negligence, imagine that P sues D for personal injuries and that D counterclaims for her own injuries. The jury finds that P's injuries are worth $10,000 and that P is 20% negligent. The jury finds that D's injuries are worth $100,000 and that D is 80% negligent. P is due 80% of $10,000 (i.e., $8,000) while D is due 20% of $100,000 (i.e., $20,000). If you were P, would you want to pay D $20,000 and receive $8,000 from D, or would you prefer to net it out and simply pay D $12,000? In the absence of insurance, the standard resolution is to require payment only by the party who, after combining the two offsetting recoveries, owes a net amount. Can you see why that is the fairest and most efficient way to handle the problem?

6. **Counterclaims and multiple capacities of defendant.** A defendant sued in one capacity cannot assert a counterclaim in another capacity. See, e.g., Banco Nacional de Cuba v. Chase Manhattan Bank, 658 F.2d 875 (2d Cir. 1981), in which Chase Manhattan Bank was sued as a corporate defendant, and Chase counterclaimed as a trustee of property that had been seized by the plaintiff. The court disallowed the counterclaim on the ground that it was asserted in a different capacity than the capacity in which the Bank was sued. Accord, Durham v. Bunn, 85 F.Supp. 530 (E.D.Pa.1949).

7. **State counterclaim rules.** All states have counterclaim rules comparable to Rule 13. Under California terminology, a "cross-complaint" refers to three kinds of claims, all of which have separate names under the federal rules—a counterclaim under Rule 13(a) and (b), a cross-claim under Rule 13(g), and a third-party complaint under Rule 14(a). Calif.C.Civ.P. §§ 426.10, 426.30, 428.10. For historical background of the California cross-complaint, see Friedenthal, Joinder of Claims, Counterclaims, and Cross-Complaints: Suggested Revision of the California Provisions, 23 Stan. L. Rev. 1 (1970). For comparable provisions in other states, see, e.g., N.Y.C.P.L.R. § 3019; Ill.C.C.P. § 2–608.

4. CROSS-CLAIMS: FEDERAL RULE 13(g)

Fairview Park Excavating Co. v. Al Monzo Construction Co.

United States Court of Appeals, Third Circuit, 1977.
560 F.2d 1122.

■ GARTH, CIRCUIT JUDGE.

This appeal initially presented a jurisdictional question arising out of an action brought by the plaintiff subcontractor (Fairview) against its general contractor (Monzo) and a Pennsylvania municipal authority (Robinson Township) for which the construction work in issue was being performed. After Fairview's claim against the Township had been dismissed on state law grounds, the district court then dismissed Monzo's cross-claim against the Township for lack of an independent (diversity) basis for federal subject matter jurisdiction. Monzo contends in this appeal that the dismissal of its cross-claim against the Township was erroneous. We agree. * * *

I

Fairview Park Excavating Co., Inc., the plaintiff/appellee, is an Ohio corporation which as a subcontractor provided labor and materials under certain construction contracts for Robinson Township. Al Monzo Construction Company, Inc., a defendant and the appellant in this Court, is a Pennsylvania corporation, which acted as general contractor to Robinson Township. Robinson Township Municipal Authority, the defendant/appellee, is a "citizen" of Pennsylvania. Maryland Casualty Co., a defendant/appellant, is a Maryland corporation which became a surety on Monzo's bond guaranteeing payment to subcontractors, laborers and materialmen.

Fairview completed its work as subcontractor but did not receive payment. Fairview then filed a diversity action in the United States District Court for the Western District of Pennsylvania—joining Monzo, Maryland Casualty and the Township as defendants.

The Township denied any liability to Fairview, claiming that Fairview was not in contractual privity with it. The Township asserted that it had contracted only with Monzo as its contractor, and that any monies still owing to Monzo were being withheld by the Township only until Monzo completed certain restoration work.

Monzo and Maryland Casualty, replying together, denied liability, counterclaimed against Fairview, and cross-claimed against the Township. The Township counterclaimed against Monzo for damages caused by defective work. Trial without a jury was set for March 16, 1976.

On the first day of trial, however, the district court granted the Township's motion that Fairview's complaint against it be dismissed. The district court subsequently explained the basis for its dismissal of the Township as a defendant as follows:

> * * * [U]nder the law of Pennsylvania a municipal corporation is liable to a contractor but not to a subcontractor, materialman or laborer. * * *

With the Township no longer a "defendant" in Fairview's suit, its only remaining connection to the case was provided by Monzo's cross-claim. However, even this connection was short-lived. On the same date, March 16, 1976, the district court dismissed Monzo's cross-claim because of an absence of diversity between the two parties. In its Memorandum Opinion of June 1, 1976, the district court stated: "The various disputes between Monzo and Robinson were not properly before us and are, in fact, matters for state court jurisdiction, there being no diversity of citizenship between these parties."

At this juncture, only Fairview's claim against Monzo was left. After trial, judgment was entered for Fairview. * * *

II

The primary complaint voiced by Monzo on this appeal is that the district court erred in dismissing its cross-claim against the Township on jurisdictional grounds. Monzo contends that, having once acquired jurisdiction over the Township as a defendant to its cross-claim, it could not be divested of jurisdiction by the Township's dismissal as a primary defendant to the plaintiff Fairview's claim if that dismissal was predicated (as it was) on nonjurisdictional grounds.

The Township's argument, in our view, is not to the contrary. In its brief, the Township quotes Professor Moore as follows:

If the original bill or claim in connection with which the cross-claim arises is dismissed *for lack of jurisdiction,* it would seem, on analogy to cases concerning counterclaims, that the dismissal carries with it the cross-claim unless the latter is supported by independent jurisdictional grounds.

However, reliance on that proposition affords little comfort to the Township, for here the original claim was dismissed on nonjurisdictional rather than jurisdictional grounds. As indicated earlier, the district court judge properly held that under Pennsylvania law an absence of contractual privity between the plaintiff and the Township was fatal to Fairview's cause of action. City of Philadelphia v. National Surety Corp., 140 F.2d 805, 807 (3d Cir.1944).

The basis for the distinction between jurisdictional and nonjurisdictional dismissals is readily apparent. If a federal court dismisses a plaintiff's claim for lack of subject matter jurisdiction, any cross-claims dependent upon ancillary jurisdiction must necessarily fall as well, because it is the plaintiff's claim—to which the cross-claim is ancillary—that provides the derivative source of jurisdiction for the cross-claim. Deviation from this rule would work an impermissible expansion of federal subject matter jurisdiction. Yet by the same token, once a district court judge has properly permitted a cross-claim under F.R.Civ.P. 13(g), as was the case here, the ancillary jurisdiction that results should not be defeated by a decision on the merits adverse to the plaintiff on the plaintiff's primary claim. As Judge Aldrich has stated:

[i]f [a defendant] had a proper cross-claim against its codefendants this gave the court ancillary jurisdiction even though all the parties to the cross-claim were citizens of the same state. The termination of the original claim would not affect this. This is but one illustration of the elementary

> principle that jurisdiction which has once attached is not lost by subsequent events.

Atlantic Corp. v. United States, 311 F.2d 907, 910 (1st Cir.1962) (citations omitted); see *Parris v. St. Johnsbury Trucking Co.*, 395 F.2d 543, 544 (2d Cir.1968) (reviewing decision on cross-claim between co-citizen defendants although plaintiff's diversity claim had been settled during trial); *Barker v. Louisiana & Arkansas Ry. Co.*, 57 F.R.D. 489, 491 (W.D.La.1972). The contrary rule, which the Township urges here, would operate to make subject matter jurisdiction over every ancillary cross-claim dependent upon that claim's being resolved *prior* to the plaintiff's primary action. (Otherwise a judgment on the merits adverse to the plaintiff would drain the cross-claim of jurisdiction in every instance, a completely indefensible result.) Given that cross-claims necessarily involve co-defendants, *Danner v. Anskis*, 256 F.2d 123, 124 (3d Cir.1958), a rule which would restrict the duration of federal court jurisdiction over cross-claims to the pendency of plaintiff's primary claim would be untenable: in many cases, cross-claims need not be heard until plaintiff has obtained a judgment on the merits. To permit the raising of a threat of a dismissal for want of jurisdiction at that point would destroy cross-claims otherwise properly maintainable by virtue of ancillary jurisdiction.

    * * *

NOTE ON CROSS-CLAIMS AGAINST CO-PARTIES

    1. Cross-claims under Rule 13(g). A cross-claim under Rule 13(g) may be asserted only between co-parties, typically between co-defendants. A cross-claim is always permissive. That is, a party with a possible cross-claim is under no compulsion to assert it in the current litigation. Note, however, that a cross-claim under Rule 13(g) is like a compulsory counterclaim under Rule 13(a) in the sense that both types of claims must be related to claims that have already been asserted. Rule 13(g) provides that a cross-claim is permitted "if the claim arises out of the transaction or occurrence that is the subject matter either of the original action or of a counterclaim, or if the claim relates to any property that is the subject matter of the original action."

    Why do you suppose a cross-claim must be related to a claim that has already been asserted, unlike a permissive counterclaim under Rule 13(b), for which there is no relatedness requirement? Here is one possibility: Think about the parties by whom and against whom a cross-claim and counterclaim are likely to be asserted. A cross-claim is usually asserted by a defendant against a co-defendant. Neither defendant is in court voluntarily, and neither defendant is likely to have chosen the particular court in which the suit is going forward. By contrast, a counterclaim is usually asserted by a defendant against a plaintiff who has chosen to come to court, and who has probably chosen the particular court in which the suit is going forward. In these circumstances, is there less reason to be protective of a plaintiff than of a co-defendant?

    Here is another possibility. Think about the type of suit in which cross-claims are likely to be asserted. They are, by definition, multi-party suits, and they are frequently quite complicated. The principal case, *Fairview Park*, is fairly typical. Is it inviting needless and perhaps unmanageable complication to allow a co-defendant to assert an unrelated cross-claim in a case that is likely already to be complicated?

Once a party has asserted a cross-claim against a co-party, the co-party is, as to that cross-claim, a defendant. Any claim by the co-party back against the cross-claiming party is a counterclaim as to that cross-claim. Because the claim by the co-party is a counterclaim, Rules 13(a) and (b) apply. Therefore, even though the cross-claim was not compulsory, a counterclaim in response to that cross-claim that satisfies the relatedness criterion of Rule 13(a) is a compulsory counterclaim as to that cross-claim. See Earle M. Joregenson Co. v. T.I. United States, Ltd., 133 F.R.D. 472, 475 (E.D. Pa. 1991).

2. Contribution and indemnification. Cross-claims are frequently claims for contribution between or among joint tortfeasors, or for indemnification from an insurer or bonding agent or from a co-party who may be liable only secondarily. For discussion, see Davis, Comparative Negligence, Comparative Contribution, and Equal Protection in the Trial and Settlement of Multiple Defendant Product Cases, 10 Ind. L. Rev. 831 (1977).

3. Rule 13(g) and supplemental jurisdiction. Because a cross-claim under Rule 13(g) must satisfy a fairly strict relatedness requirement, it necessarily satisfies whatever relatedness requirement inheres in the "same case or controversy" requirement of § 1367 and Article III. The court in *Fairview Park* had no trouble holding that there was "ancillary jurisdiction" (now "supplemental jurisdiction") over the cross-claim at the time it was asserted. Do you think the court was correct in holding that ancillary jurisdiction continued to exist even after the claims to which the cross-claim had been related were dismissed on the merits? Why should it have made a difference if those claims had been dismissed for lack of subject matter jurisdiction?

4. Rule 13(g) and Rule 18(a). Once a Rule 13(g) cross-claim is properly made, the cross-claiming party can add unrelated claims against the cross-claim defendant under Rule 18(a). Rule 18(a) provides, "A party asserting a claim to relief as an original claim, counterclaim, *cross-claim*, or third-party claim, may join . . . as many claims . . . as the party has against the opposing party." (Emphasis added.) See, e.g., First National Bank of Cincinnati v. Pepper, 454 F.2d 626, 635 (2d Cir. 1972).

5. State procedure. All modern procedural regimes allow cross-claims based on roughly the same criteria as federal Rule 13(g). California terminology is somewhat confusing for someone accustomed to federal terminology. Calif.C.Civ.P. § 428.10 does not differentiate in its vocabulary between what the federal rules call cross-claims, third-party claims, and counterclaims. California calls them all cross-complaints. See note 7 following the *Jones* case, supra, p. 572.

B. JOINDER OF PARTIES

INTRODUCTORY NOTE ON PARTIES AND STANDING

The term "party" is neither simple nor self-defining. A party may be a number of things—for example, a plaintiff, a defendant, a third-party plaintiff or defendant, a named or unnamed member of a plaintiff or defendant class, an intervenor, an interpleading stakeholder or an interpleaded claimant, or a party who should be joined if feasible. These terms will become familiar as you read through this section. What kind of interest must a would-be party have in order to seek affirmative relief or to participate in litigation?

1. **Interest of a plaintiff or other party seeking affirmative relief.** To sue in federal court, a plaintiff (or a defendant asserting a counterclaim or filing a third-party complaint) must be able to withstand a motion to dismiss under Rule 12(b)(6) for "failure to state a claim upon which relief can be granted." The equivalent motion in some state courts is a demurrer. Familiar ways to express this idea are to say that a plaintiff must "state a claim" or "have a cause of action." Whether plaintiff has stated a claim depends on the relevant provisions of substantive law. A Rule 12(b)(6) motion to dismiss (in federal practice) or demurrer (in the practice of some states) tests whether plaintiff's alleged facts, if true, satisfy the substantive requirements for a cause of action for negligence, for breach of contract, for violation of a statute, or for some other breach of legal obligation owed to plaintiff by the defendant.

Federal = 12b6
State = demurrer

Beginning in the 1930s, the federal courts in a few cases began to refer to the requirement that plaintiff state a claim as a "standing" requirement, as in the sentence, "Plaintiff must have standing to assert this claim against this defendant." One way to think about the standing requirement (and about the requirement that plaintiff have stated a claim) is to separate the question of defendant's duty from the question of plaintiff's right to enforce that duty. Defendant may have a duty—for example, a duty not to breach a contract. But to whom does the defendant owe that duty? She clearly owes it to the party with whom she has contracted. Does she also owe it to a non-contracting party who might be benefitted by her performance or harmed by her non-performance? The substantive law of contract divides the world of non-contracting parties into "intended beneficiaries," who may sue to enforce the contract, and "incidental beneficiaries," who may not. Restatement (Second) of Contracts §§ 302–315 (1979). Translated into the vocabulary of standing, one might say (though one ordinarily does not) that the contracting party and the "intended beneficiary" have standing to enforce the contract, but that the "incidental beneficiary" does not have standing.

As elaborated in the last half-century or so, standing law has become a complicated specialty of federal jurisdiction. The vocabulary of standing is most often employed when the defendant is either the government, or a private party whose behavior is regulated by the government (as, for example, under an anti-pollution statute). The United States Supreme Court has stated that to have standing a plaintiff must have "suffered injury in fact" or "distinct and palpable injury"; must show that the injury has resulted from the defendant's action; and must show that the injury is "fairly redressable" by the judicial remedy sought. See Friends of the Earth, Inc. v. Laidlaw Envtl. Svs. (TOC), Inc., 528 U.S. 167, 180–81 (2000); Association of Data Processing Service Orgs v. Camp, 397 U.S. 150, 152, 90 S.Ct. 827, 25 L.Ed.2d 184 (1970); Allen v. Wright, 468 U.S. 737, 751, 104 S.Ct. 3315, 82 L.Ed.2d 556 (1984). The Court has held that these requirements stem from the so-called "case or controversy" requirement of Article III of the Constitution. If a plaintiff cannot satisfy these requirements, Congress is without power to create a cause of action that plaintiff may enforce in federal court. See, for example, Lujan v. Defenders of Wildlife, 504 U.S. 555, 112 S.Ct. 2130, 119 L.Ed.2d 351 (1992) (holding unconstitutional Congress' attempt to confer standing to enforce an environmental statute against an agency of the federal government because the plaintiffs lacked "injury in fact").

The Supreme Court's standing jurisprudence has been, to some critics, erratic and unprincipled. Professor Kenneth Culp Davis has described standing law as "permeated with sophistry." 4 K. Davis, Administrative Law Treatise § 24:53 (2d ed. 1983). Justice Harlan once complained that standing law was a "word game played by secret rules." Flast v. Cohen, 392 U.S. 83, 129, 88 S.Ct. 1942, 20 L.Ed.2d 947 (1968) (Harlan, J., dissenting). For a sampling of the enormous academic writing on standing, see Albert, Standing to Challenge Administrative Action: An Inadequate Surrogate for Claims for Relief, 83 Yale L.J. 425 (1973); Fletcher, The Structure of Standing, 98 Yale L.J. 425 (1988); Sunstein, Standing and the Privatization of Public Law, 88 Colum. L. Rev. 1432 (1988).

State courts have been, for the most part, mercifully free of the standing vocabulary and analytic apparatus developed by the United States Supreme Court. One reason for the difference is that state courts are not created by Article III of the federal Constitution, and their jurisdiction is thus not restricted to "cases or controversies." Another reason is that much of the business of the state courts consists in deciding common law questions—such as whether a non-party to a contract may sue to enforce that contract—that have retained the vocabulary of the common law rather than adopted the vocabulary of standing. Finally, state courts have been less concerned about separation of powers concerns than the federal courts, and have therefore generally been willing to recognize as enforceable causes of action whatever the state legislatures have chosen to create.

2.   Interest of someone who seeks to participate in ongoing litigation. Under both federal and state procedural regimes, non-parties with an interest in ongoing litigation may join that litigation as "intervenors." See, e.g., Fed. R. Civ. P. 24. The federal courts of appeals have given different answers to the question whether an intervenor under Rule 24 must have sufficient interest in the suit to satisfy the constitutional standing requirement of Article III. Compare, e.g., Mausolf v. Babbitt, 85 F.3d 1295 (8th Cir. 1996) (Article III standing required), with United States Postal Service v. Brennan, 579 F.2d 188 (2d Cir. 1978) (contra). The Supreme Court has noted the question but has declined to answer it. Diamond v. Charles, 476 U.S. 54, 68–9 n. 5, 106 S.Ct. 1697, 90 L.Ed.2d 48 (1986). State courts have been untroubled by any comparable standing requirement for would-be intervenors in ongoing litigation.

NOTE ON THE REAL PARTY IN INTEREST RULE

1.   The real party in interest rule. Related to the doctrine of standing is the so-called real party in interest rule. In federal practice, Rule 17(a) provides, "An action must be prosecuted in the name of the real party in interest." The effect of the rule is to ensure that the person asserting a claim for relief is also the person "who, according to the governing substantive law is entitled to enforce the right." C. Wright, A. Miller & M. Kane, 6A Federal Practice and Procedure § 1543 at 475 (2010). In situations where there could be confusion about who has the right to enforce the claim, the rule is supposed to reduce the risk that the defendant may later have to respond to a second suit brought by the "real party in interest," that is, by the person who actually had the legal right to enforce the claim. When the real party in interest is not named as the plaintiff, the person who is suing is said to be a "nominal party," or party in name only.

    2.   Assignments. A claim that originally belonged to one party may have been transferred to another, by formal assignment or by operation of law. If the assignment is complete, so that the original owner has no remaining interest, then the assignee is the real party in interest. A common problem is as follows: an insurer that pays a casualty loss is subrogated to the rights of the insured against the person who caused the loss. Once the insurance company pays the loss, it becomes the owner (in effect, the assignee) of the claim by virtue of subrogation and would ordinarily be the proper party to sue for the loss. But a suit by an insurance company against some "ordinary" person (who is, herself, usually also insured) looks bad to a jury. Insurance companies sometimes respond to this problem by paying most, but not all of the claim. Where the insured retains some interest (the case of partial subrogation) the cases are divided. Some hold that both the insuror and the insured are real parties in interest and that either may sue to enforce the claim. Virginia Electric & Power Co. v. Westinghouse Electric Corp., 485 F.2d 78 (4th Cir. 1973) (applying Virginia law). Others require that the insurer participate as a named party. Bank of the Orient v. Superior Court, 67 Cal.App.3d 588, 136 Cal.Rptr. 741 (1977) (insurer, partial subrogee by virtue of partial payment of plaintiff's loss, required to be joined as real party in interest). In other cases, insurance companies use the device of "lending" the money due under the policy to the insured, pursuant to an arrangement under which the insured permits suit to be brought in her name and agrees to repay her "loan" only if the suit is successful. If plaintiff loses the suit, or if the suit recovers less than the subrogated amount, the "loan" is forgiven to that extent. The plaintiff insurer thus is disguised by its insured, just as the defendant insurer is disguised by its insured. Is that fair enough? See generally Comment, The Loan Receipt and Insurers' Subrogation, 50 Tul. L. Rev. 115 (1975).

    Another way of handling the problem is through an evidentiary rule making evidence of insurance inadmissible when not legally relevant to questions at issue in the case—such as questions about defendant's liability or the amount of plaintiff's damages. See, e.g., Calif. Evid. Code § 1155 (prohibiting admission of evidence of insurance "to prove negligence or other wrongdoing"); Continental Airlines, Inc. v. McDonnell Douglas Corp., 264 Cal.Rptr. 779, 789 (1990) ("Douglas wanted to show the jury that Continental's insurance company, not Continental, is the real party in interest in this lawsuit * * *. The trial court correctly perceived that bringing that information before the jurors would be highly prejudicial and misleading."); Morton v. Maryland Cas. Co., 1 A.D.2d 116, 123 (N.Y.1955) ("evidence that a defendant is insured, or an intimation to that effect, is ordinarily inadmissible and improper in an action for damages or negligence").

    Parties may use assignment or partial assignment to game the rules requiring complete diversity of citizenship by assigning a claim to a plaintiff who is diverse (or non-diverse) depending on whether the assignor wishes to create or defeat diversity jurisdiction. The use of assignments to create diversity jurisdiction is regulated by 28 U.S.C. § 1359, which bars jurisdiction "in which any party, by assignment or otherwise, has been improperly made or joined to invoke the jurisdiction of [the] court." The use of assignments to defeat diversity jurisdiction is not the subject of statutory regulation, but some courts have been willing to disregard assignments made to defeat jurisdiction. See Chapter 2, supra, for further discussion.

3. **Other legal relationships.** In a variety of situations, the person who legally controls the claim is not the same as the person who benefits from the prosecution of the lawsuit. The second sentence of Rule 17(a) recites some of the common situations in which this occurs, and expressly authorizes those persons to sue in their own name without joining the person who will benefit from the outcome of the suit. These relationships can also be manipulated to create or defeat diversity jurisdiction.

4. **Suits "for the use of."** In some situations, the government may sue as the nominal plaintiff "for the use of," or ex relatione (ex rel.), a private person. Suit is brought in the name of the government but on the information and at the instigation of an individual who has a private interest in the matter. See 6A C. Wright, A. Miller, and M. Kane, Federal Practice and Procedure § 1551 (2010); Fed.R.Civ.P. 17(a)(2) ("When a federal statute so provides, an action for another's use or benefit must be brought in the name of the United States.").

5. **Abolition of the real party in interest rule**. It seems doubtful that the real party in interest rule is necessary to protect defendants against the risk of multiple suits. A defendant who wants to ensure joinder of the real party in interest can often accomplish that result using the joinder rules, for example, by adding the real party under Rule 13(h) as an additional defendant, or by moving for compulsory joinder under Rule 19. Moreover, under modern doctrines of privity, the real party will sometimes be bound by actions taken by the nominal party, sometimes because the real party controlled the action (which is common, for example, when the real party is an insurer), and sometimes because the nominal party was its representative. See Restatement (Second) of Judgments § 37. A number of states have no real party in interest rule and do not appear to miss it. See, e.g., Ill.C.C.P 2–403.

1. BASIC CONCEPTS OF PARTY JOINDER

a. PERMISSIVE JOINDER: FEDERAL RULE 20(a)

Kedra v. City of Philadelphia

United States District Court for the Eastern District of Pennsylvania, 1978.
454 F. Supp. 652.

■ LUONGO, DISTRICT JUDGE.

This civil rights action arises out of an alleged series of brutal acts committed by Philadelphia policemen against the plaintiffs. The events set forth in the complaint span one and one-half years, from December 1975 to February or March 1977. The defendants have moved to dismiss. See Fed.R.Civ.P. 12(b).

I.   The Factual Allegations

Plaintiffs are Dolores M. Kedra; her children, Elizabeth, Patricia, Teresa, Kenneth, Joseph, Michael, Robert, and James; and Elizabeth's husband, Richard J. Rozanski. Michael, Robert, and James Kedra are minors, and their mother sues on their behalf as parent and natural guardian.

Defendants are the City of Philadelphia; Police Commissioner Joseph J. O'Neill; officials of the Police Department's Homicide Division Division Chief Donald Patterson, Chief Inspector Joseph Golden, Lieutenant Leslie Simmins, and Sergeant John Tiers; Homicide Detectives Richard Strohm, James Richardson, George Cassidy, and Michael Gannon; Police Lieutenant Augustus C. Miller; Police Officers James Brady, Robert Pitney, Jessie Vassor, and John J. D'Amico; an officer surnamed Tuffo; and other unidentified members of the Police Department. It is alleged that "at all times material to plaintiffs' cause of action (the City of Philadelphia) employed all of the individual defendants." It is further alleged that each of the individual defendants, "separately and in concert," acted under color of Pennsylvania law and, "pursuant to their authority as agents, servants, and employees of defendant City of Philadelphia, intentionally and deliberately engaged in the unlawful conduct described. . . ." They are sued "individually and in their official capacity" and "jointly and severally."

The series of events set forth in the complaint dates from December 22, 1975. On that evening, Richard Rozanski and Joseph and Michael Kedra were arrested at gun point without probable cause by defendants Vassor and D'Amico and taken to Philadelphia Police Headquarters (the Roundhouse). At the Roundhouse, they were separated and questioned for seventeen hours by defendants Strohm, Richardson, Cassidy, and Gannon. They were not informed of their constitutional rights and were refused requests for counsel. The complaint states:

> During the course of the interrogation, plaintiffs Richard Rozanski, Michael Kedra and Joseph Kedra were handcuffed, struck about the head, face, stomach, abdomen, arms and legs with fists and physical objects, were harassed and threatened with further physical violence by defendants Strohm, Richardson, Cassidy and Gannon; during the course of this interrogation, plaintiff Richard Rozanski's legs were held apart by two of the defendant detectives while he was kicked in the testicles, groin, buttocks and legs by defendant Strohm.

Rozanski, and Michael and Joseph Kedra each sustained serious injuries as a result of the beatings.

Meanwhile, defendant Richardson forcibly took Elizabeth Rozanski from her mother's house to the Roundhouse, where she was detained and questioned for seventeen hours by defendants Strohm, Gannon, Richardson, and Simmins. She was not advised of her rights. She was shown her husband, who had been beaten badly, and "was threatened with arrest in an attempt to coerce a false statement from her." A warrantless search of her bedroom was conducted by defendant Strohm "and others" without her consent and without probable cause.

On that same evening, Dolores Kedra voluntarily went to the Roundhouse "where she was illegally interrogated, coerced into signing a release authorizing the search of her house and forcibly detained" for nine hours by Strohm, Richardson, Cassidy, Gannon, "and other unidentified defendants."

Seven days later, on the morning of December 29, 1975, defendants Brady and Pitney went to the Kedra home, demanding to see Richard Rozanski and "falsely stating that they had papers for his appearance in Court on the following day." All of the plaintiffs except Dolores Kedra, the mother, were at home at the time. The policemen "attempted to drag (Rozanski) out of the house," but Rozanski and Kenneth Kedra shut and locked the door. Rozanski asked to see a warrant, but Brady and Pitney did not have one. Brady and Pitney then secured the aid of other policemen who, without a warrant or probable cause and "through the use of excessive force," "broke open the door with the butt end of a shotgun and forced their way into the house with shotguns, handguns, blackjacks, and nightsticks in hand." Defendants Brady, Pitney, Miller, Tiers, "and ten to fifteen other defendant members of the Philadelphia Police Department" conducted a thorough search of the house and, while doing so, physically assaulted Patricia, Joseph, Michael, and Kenneth Kedra, inflicting serious injuries. They also attempted to confiscate a camera and note pad being used by Joseph Kedra. It is alleged further that

> "(T)he defendants unlawfully detained plaintiffs within the house by blocking off both the front and rear doors, holding plaintiffs in fear of life and limb by visibly displaying shotguns, handguns and nightsticks, and through threats of violence, coercion and abusive language."

Rozanski and Joseph, Michael, and Kenneth Kedra were taken to the Roundhouse in a police van, and Kenneth was beaten while being led to the van. At the Roundhouse, Michael and Kenneth were "unlawfully detained" for twenty-four hours, and Rozanski "was struck in the face by defendant Strohm" and was denied repeated requests for counsel. "(W)ithout just or probable cause," Rozanski was charged with murder, burglary, and receiving stolen goods, and Kenneth and Joseph were charged with assault and battery, harboring a fugitive, and resisting arrest. In defending these charges, they incurred attorney's fees. All three later were acquitted on all counts.

With respect to the December 1975 events, the complaint sets forth the following general allegations:

> 17. At all times material to plaintiffs' cause of action, plaintiff Richard Rozanski, through his attorney, offered to voluntarily surrender to the Philadelphia Police; the defendants chose, however, to engage in the course of conduct described in detail above, the purpose and effect of which was to knowingly, intentionally and deliberately deprive plaintiffs of rights secured by the Constitution of the United States.

> 18. All of the aforementioned acts were committed by defendants intentionally, deliberately and maliciously, pursuant to their authority as agents, servants and employees of the Police Department of the City of Philadelphia.

> 19. The aforementioned acts were committed with the consent and knowledge and at the direction of defendants Joseph F. O'Neill in his capacity as Police Commissioner of the City of Philadelphia.

20. The aforementioned acts were committed with the knowledge and consent and at the direction of defendant Joseph Golden in his official capacity as Chief Inspector of the Homicide Division of the Police Department of the City of Philadelphia.

21. The aforementioned acts were committed with the knowledge and consent and at the direction of Captain Donald Patterson, Chief of the Homicide Division of the Philadelphia Police Department, Lieutenant Lesley Simmins and Sergeant John Tiers, in their official capacities as supervisory officials of the Philadelphia Police Department.

22. The defendants named in Paragraphs 18, 19, 20 and 21 are and were at all times material to plaintiffs' cause of action in a position to exercise direct supervision of the defendant officers and detectives and did in fact exercise such control and supervision at all times material to plaintiffs' cause of action.

23. All of the aforementioned acts were committed without just or probable cause with regard to each of the plaintiffs.

The complaint alleges further that "defendants have engaged and continue to engage in a systematic pattern of harassment, threats and coercion with the intention of, and having the effect of depriving plaintiffs of . . . rights and privileges. . . ." As part of this "pattern," Michael Kedra was arrested in June 1976 and was beaten by defendant Strohm, "who handcuffed plaintiff's hands behind his back, and struck him in the chest and stomach with a nightstick and fist." James Kedra has been "harassed and threatened without cause" by defendants D'Amico, Brady and Pitney, and in February or March 1977 "was grabbed by the shirt" by Tuffo and Pitney "and threatened with physical violence."

The complaint asserts that "as a result of the aforementioned actions, plaintiffs have suffered and continue to suffer severe emotional distress."

II. The Suit and the Motion

Plaintiffs' complaint was filed on November 23, 1977. The action is brought under the Constitution and the Civil Rights Act of 1871, 42 U.S.C. §§ 1983, 1985, 1986. Jurisdiction is based on 28 U.S.C. §§ 1331 and 1343. As a basis for their civil rights claims, the plaintiffs assert that defendants' actions deprived them of the following federal "rights, privileges and immunities":

(a) The right of free speech and the right to peacably (Sic) assemble under the First and Fourteenth Amendments.

(b) The right to be secure in their persons, houses, papers, and effects against unreasonable searches and seizures under the Fourth and Fourteenth Amendments.

(c) The prohibition against compulsory self-incrimination under the Fifth and Fourteenth Amendments.

(d) The right to be free from deprivation of life, liberty or property without due process of law under the Fifth and Fourteenth Amendments.

(e) The prohibition against cruel and unusual punishment under the Eighth and Fourteenth Amendments.

Without explanation, the complaint also cites the Equal Protection Clause of the Fourteenth Amendment and Article 1, §§ 1, 8, and 9 of the Pennsylvania Constitution. Plaintiffs also invoke the pendent jurisdiction doctrine to assert additional claims under Pennsylvania law "for false arrest, false imprisonment, malicious prosecution, assault and battery, trespass to real and personal property and negligent and intentional infliction of emotional distress." Plaintiffs seek compensatory and punitive damages in excess of $10,000 and attorneys' fees and costs.

All of the named defendants have filed the motion to dismiss. It is based on several grounds and raises questions of procedure as well as jurisdictional and substantive issues under the civil rights laws. In addition, the pendent state claims raise jurisdictional issues not discussed in the motion which should be examined in this opinion.

III. Procedural Questions

Defendants' motion raises two matters that essentially are procedural. First, they contest Dolores Kedra's prosecution of the case on behalf of her minor sons, Michael, Robert, and James. Second, they contend that there has been an improper joinder of parties.

A.   Suit on behalf of the minor children

In the list of plaintiffs in the caption of the complaint, Michael, Robert, and James Kedra are each listed as "a minor, by his parent and natural guardian, DOLORES M. KEDRA." Defendants contend that Dolores Kedra is seeking to assert her children's rights and that she lacks standing to do so. They also argue that, because she asserts no rights of her own with respect to these children's claims, the Court lacks jurisdiction over the claims.

Defendants' contentions on this matter are frivolous. The complaint makes abundantly clear that Michael, Robert, and James are plaintiffs in their own right and that their mother merely is acting as their representative since, as minors, they lack capacity to sue.[4] In light of the allegations of injury to Michael, Robert, and James, defendants do not, and could not, contend that these minors lack standing. There are no jurisdictional problems presented by their claims. The only real question, therefore, is whether suit by these children through a representative is procedurally proper. Federal Rule of Civil Procedure 17(c), which specifically contemplates such a procedure,[5] answers that question affirmatively.

---

[4]   Under Federal Rule of Civil Procedure 17(b), the capacity of these plaintiffs to sue is determined by the law of Pennsylvania. Under Pennsylvania law, a plaintiff who is a minor (defined as a person under the age of eighteen years) must be represented by a guardian who supervises and controls the action on his behalf. Pa.R.Civ.P. 2027; See Pa.R.Civ.P. 76 (definitions of "minor" and "majority"). Defendants do not contend that Michael, Robert, and James are not minors.

[5]   The rule provides:

Whenever an infant or incompetent person has a representative, such as a general guardian, committee, conservator, or other like fiduciary, the representative may sue or defend on behalf of the infant or incompetent person. If an infant or incompetent person does not have a duly appointed representative he may sue by his next friend or by a guardian ad litem. The court shall appoint a guardian ad litem for an infant or incompetent person not otherwise represented in an action or shall make such other order as it deems proper for the protection of the infant or incompetent person.

B.   Joinder

Defendants contend that there has been an improper joinder of parties under Federal Rule of Civil Procedure 20(a), which provides:

> All persons may join in one action as plaintiffs if they assert any right to relief jointly, severally, or in the alternative in respect of or arising out of the same transaction, occurrence, or series of transactions or occurrences and if any question of law or fact common to all these persons will arise in the action. All persons . . . may be joined in one action as defendants if there is asserted against them jointly, severally, or in the alternative, any right to relief in respect of or arising out of the same transaction, occurrence, or series of transactions or occurrences and if any question of law or fact common to all defendants will arise in the action. A plaintiff or defendant need not be interested in obtaining or defending against all the relief demanded. Judgment may be given for one or more of the plaintiffs according to their respective rights to relief, and against one or more defendants according to their respective liabilities.

Defendants argue that plaintiffs' claims against them do not "aris(e) out of the same transaction, occurrence, or series of transactions or occurrences" because they stem from events spanning a fourteen or fifteen month period.[6]

The joinder provisions of the Federal Rules are very liberal. As the Supreme Court noted in United Mine Workers v. Gibbs, 383 U.S. 715, 86 S.Ct. 1130, 16 L.Ed.2d 218 (1966),

> "Under the Rules, the impulse is toward entertaining the broadest possible scope of action consistent with fairness to the parties; joinder of claims, parties and remedies is strongly encouraged."

383 U.S. at 724, 86 S.Ct. at 1138 (footnote omitted).

The reason for the liberality is that unification of claims in a single action is more convenient and less expensive and time-consuming for the parties and the court. Mosley v. General Motors Corp., 497 F.2d 1330, 1332 (8th Cir. 1974). In recognition of this attitude, the "transaction or occurrence" language of Rule 20 has been interpreted to "permit all reasonably related claims for relief by or against different parties to be tried in a single proceeding. Absolute identity of all events is unnecessary." Id. at 1333.

Although the events giving rise to plaintiffs' claims in this case occurred over a lengthy time period, they all are "reasonably related." The complaint sets forth a series of alleged unlawful detentions,

---

[6]   The Federal Rules permit unlimited joinder of claims against an opposing party (Fed.R.Civ.P. 18(a)), but in multiparty cases joinder is limited by the requirement of Rule 20(a) that plaintiffs or defendants may not be joined in the same case unless some of the claims by or against each party arise out of common events and contain common factual or legal questions. Defendants have not argued that common factual and legal questions are not present in this case; the similarity of the claims against each defendant makes it abundantly clear that there are common issues. Once parties are joined under Rule 20(a), Rule 18(a)'s allowance of unlimited joinder of claims against those parties is fully applicable. See Advisory Committee on Rules, Note to 1966 Amendment to Rule 18.

searches, beatings and similar occurrences and charges defendants with "engag(ing) in a systematic pattern of harassment, threats and coercion with the intention of . . . depriving plaintiffs of (their) rights"; each of the incidents set forth is encompassed within the "systematic pattern." There is no logical reason why the systematic conduct alleged could not extend over a lengthy time period and, on the face of these allegations, there is nothing about the extended time span that attenuates the factual relationship among all of these events. The claims against the defendants "aris(e) out of the same transaction, occurrence, or series of transactions or occurrences" for purposes of Rule 20(a), and therefore joinder of defendants in this case is proper.

Apart from the procedural propriety of the joinder under Rule 20(a), however, there is a question whether a single trial of all claims against all defendants will prejudice some of the defendants. Some of the defendants were involved in only one of the several incidents alleged, and lumping them together with other defendants who were involved in more than one incident may be unfair. This problem is of particular concern with respect to the December 29, 1975 incident, which, apart from the allegations of direction, supervision, and control, appears to involve different actors than the other incidents alleged. Federal Rule 20(b) provides the court with power to remedy this situation:

> "The court may make such orders as will prevent a party from being embarrassed, delayed, or put to expense by the inclusion of a party against whom he asserts no claim and who asserts no claim against him, and may order separate trials or make other orders to prevent delay or prejudice."

At oral argument, counsel for both sides recognized the potential prejudicial effect of the joinder in this case and suggested formulation of a stipulation which would attempt to remedy the problem. It appears, however, that it will be better to deal with the problem after discovery has been completed and the case is ready for trial. At that time, the degree of involvement of each of the defendants will be more clear and potential prejudice will be easier to assess. I therefore shall defer decision of this aspect of the case. I shall retain flexibility to sever portions of it or to take other remedial actions, if necessary, once the prejudice issue is more clearly focused.

[The court then decided the following: (1) Plaintiffs sufficiently alleged in their complaint that the individual defendants acted "under color of law" to state claims under the federal civil rights laws. (2) Plaintiffs' claim against one of the individual defendants, Jessie Vassor, was barred by the statute of limitations. No other claims were time-barred. (3) Plaintiffs sufficiently alleged in their complaint that the supervisory defendants were directly involved in the wrongful acts to state claims under the federal civil rights laws. (4) Plaintiffs failed to state a claim against the City of Philadelphia under the federal civil rights laws. (5) The court had "pendent" jurisdiction over state law claims against all of the defendants, including the City of Philadelphia. The court declined to exercise pendent jurisdiction over the state-law claims against the City of Philadelphia, but retained the state-law claims over all of the other defendants.]

NOTES ON PERMISSIVE JOINDER OF PLAINTIFFS AND DEFENDANTS

1. **Federal Rule 20(a).** Federal Rule 20(a) authorizes "permissive joinder" of multiple parties, so long as two requirements are satisfied: (1) all joined plaintiffs must assert, and all joined defendants must have asserted against them, claims "arising out of the same transaction, occurrence, or series of transactions or occurrences," and (2) there must be a question of law or fact common to all of the joined parties. Rule 20(a) does not require joinder. Rather, it *permits* joinder when its two criteria are satisfied. (Compare Rule 19, which *requires* joinder of parties under certain circumstances. See discussion, infra, p. 588).

2. **Comparison with Rule 18(a).** Rule 20(a) deals with joinder of parties. Rule 18(a) deals with joinder of claims. There is no relatedness requirement in Rule 18(a). That is, insofar as Rule 18(a) is concerned, joined claims can be entirely unrelated. If there is a single plaintiff and a single defendant in a case, Rule 18(a) is the only rule that must be satisfied. But if there is potentially more than one plaintiff or more than one defendant, we are dealing with joinder of parties as well as joinder of claims. As soon as there is joinder of parties, the relatedness requirements of Rule 20(a) must be satisfied.

3. **Comparison with class actions under Rule 23.** Damage suits were very difficult to bring as class actions before 1966. As a result, Rule 20(a) was sometimes pressed into service in suits that today would likely be brought as class actions. However, Rule 23 was amended in 1966 to allow class actions in cases where "questions of law or fact common to class members predominate over any questions affecting only individual members [of the class]." See Rule 23(b)(3). Under the amended rule, class actions seeking damages are now routinely brought for large classes of plaintiffs. See discussion of class actions, infra p. 638.

4. **Application of Rule 20(a) in this case.** Was it a close question in *Kedra* whether the two criteria of Rule 20(a) were satisfied? First, was the series of events of which the plaintiffs complained—spread out over fourteen or fifteen months—"the same transaction, occurrence, or series of transactions or occurrences"? The events may have been "occurrences," but they were not the same "occurrences." The various "occurrences" took place in a "series." How related must "occurrences" in the "series" be to comply with the rule? The rule does not say. For the rule to make sense the occurrences must be related in some way. Should it be enough that the alleged police harassment and brutality was intermittent but more or less continuous over the fourteen to fifteen month period, and that the actors were all members of the same police force? Second, was there a question of law or fact in common among all the parties? Does the court tell us what the question was? Should it have done so, and if so, what would it have said? Is it enough that all the joined claims are civil rights claims? If a stronger showing of commonality was required, do you think that the plaintiffs made it?

Were the defendants objecting to the joinder of plaintiffs or of defendants? Both? Why do you suppose the defendants wanted to disaggregate the plaintiffs' suit?

5. **Supplemental jurisdiction. a. Federal question cases.** Under 28 U.S.C. § 1367(a), joinder of parties for whose claims there is no

independent basis for jurisdiction is permitted in federal question cases so long as the claims are part of the "same case or controversy" under Article III. Because of the relatedness requirement of Rule 20(a), the "same case or controversy" requirement is necessarily satisfied in all circumstances where the rule permits joinder.

b.   Diversity cases. The situation is more complicated in diversity cases. Section 1367(a) of the supplemental jurisdiction statute provides for supplemental jurisdiction as broadly as Article III permits, except as limited in diversity cases by § 1367(b). Section 1367(b) provides that in diversity cases "the district courts shall not have supplemental jurisdiction * * * over claims by plaintiffs against persons made parties under Rule * * * 20[.]" This text makes clear that there is no supplemental jurisdiction over state-law claims against *non-diverse defendants who have been joined* under Rule 20. But what about state-law claims *by non-diverse plaintiffs who have been joined*, or state-law claims *by diverse plaintiffs alleging $75,000 or less who have been joined*? In enumerating the exceptions to the supplemental jurisdiction granted by § 1367(a), § 1367(b) does not mention claims *by plaintiffs who have been joined*. Under the scheme of the statute, the failure to mention a claim in § 1367(b) means that supplemental jurisdiction exists. But this literal reading of § 1367 conflicts with deeply rooted principles of diversity jurisdiction that prevailed before the enactment of § 1367.

The Supreme Court held in Exxon Mobil Corp. v. Allapattah Services, Inc., 545 U.S. 546, 125 S.Ct. 2611, 162 L.Ed.2d 502 (2005), that there is supplemental jurisdiction in diversity cases over Rule 20 claims brought by plaintiffs. See supra, Chapter 2, p. 276. That is, the Court read the words of § 1367(b) literally. The Court wrote, "The omission of Rule 20 plaintiffs from the list of exceptions in § 1367(b) may have been an 'unintentional drafting gap.' If that is the case, it is up to Congress rather than the courts to fix it." Id. at 565.

b.   COMPULSORY JOINDER: FEDERAL RULE 19

Temple v. Synthes Corp.

Supreme Court of the United States, 1990.
498 U.S. 5, 111 S.Ct. 315, 112 L.Ed.2d 263.

■ PER CURIAM.

Petitioner Temple, a Mississippi resident, underwent surgery in October 1986 in which a "plate and screw device" was implanted in his lower spine. The device was manufactured by respondent Synthes Corp., Ltd. (U.S.A.) (Synthes), a Pennsylvania corporation. Dr. S. Henry LaRocca performed the surgery at St. Charles General Hospital in New Orleans, Louisiana. Following surgery, the device's screws broke off inside Temple's back.

Temple filed suit against Synthes in the United States District Court for the Eastern District of Louisiana. The suit, which rested on diversity jurisdiction, alleged defective design and manufacture of the device. At the same time, Temple filed a state administrative proceeding against Dr. LaRocca and the hospital for malpractice and negligence. At the conclusion of the administrative proceeding, Temple filed suit against the doctor and the hospital in Louisiana state court.

Synthes did not attempt to bring the doctor and the hospital into the federal action by means of a third-party complaint, as provided in Federal Rule of Civil Procedure 14(a). Instead, Synthes filed a motion to dismiss Temple's federal suit for failure to join necessary parties pursuant to Federal Rule of Civil Procedure 19. Following a hearing, the District Court ordered Temple to join the doctor and the hospital as defendants within 20 days or risk dismissal of the lawsuit. According to the court, the most significant reason for requiring joinder was the interest of judicial economy. The court relied on this Court's decision in Provident Tradesmens Bank & Trust Co. v. Patterson, 390 U.S. 102, 88 S.Ct. 733, 19 L.Ed.2d 936 (1968), wherein we recognized that one focus of Rule 19 is "the interest of the courts and the public in complete, consistent, and efficient settlement of controversies." Id., at 111, 88 S.Ct., at 739. When Temple failed to join the doctor and the hospital, the court dismissed the suit with prejudice.

dismissal

Temple appealed, and the United States Court of Appeals for the Fifth Circuit affirmed. The court deemed it "obviously prejudicial to the defendants to have the separate litigations being carried on," because Synthes' defense might be that the plate was not defective but that the doctor and the hospital were negligent, while the doctor and the hospital, on the other hand, might claim that they were not negligent but that the plate was defective. The Court of Appeals found that the claims overlapped and that the District Court therefore had not abused its discretion in ordering joinder under Rule 19. * * *

appeal

overlapping claims

Temple contends that it was error to label joint tortfeasors as indispensable parties under Rule 19(b) and to dismiss the lawsuit with prejudice for failure to join those parties. We agree. Synthes does not deny that it, the doctor, and the hospital are potential joint tortfeasors. It has long been the rule that it is not necessary for all joint tortfeasors to be named as defendants in a single lawsuit. See Lawlor v. National Screen Service Corp., 349 U.S. 322, 329–330, 75 S.Ct. 865, 869, 99 L.Ed. 1122 (1955); Bigelow v. Old Dominion Copper Mining & Smelting Co., 225 U.S. 111, 132, 32 S.Ct. 641, 644, 56 L.Ed. 1009 (1912). See also Nottingham v. General American Communications Corp., 811 F.2d 873, 880 (CA5) (per curiam), cert. denied, 484 U.S. 854, 108 S.Ct. 158, 98 L.Ed.2d 113 (1987). Nothing in the 1966 revision of Rule 19 changed that principle. See Provident Bank, supra, 390 U.S., at 116–117, n. 12, 88 S.Ct., at 741–742, n. 12. The Advisory Committee Notes to Rule 19(a) explicitly state that "a tortfeasor with the usual 'joint-and-several' liability is merely a permissive party to an action against another with like liability." 28 U.S.C.App., p. 595. There is nothing in Louisiana tort law to the contrary. See Mullin v. Skains, 252 La. 1009, 1014, 215 So.2d 643, 645 (1968); La.Civ.Code Ann., Arts. 1794, 1795 (West 1987).

* * *

Here, no inquiry under Rule 19(b) is necessary, because the threshold requirements of Rule 19(a) have not been satisfied. As potential joint tortfeasors with Synthes, Dr. LaRocca and the hospital were merely permissive parties. The Court of Appeals erred by failing to hold that the District Court abused its discretion in ordering them joined as defendants and in dismissing the action when Temple failed to comply with the court's order. For these reasons, we grant the petition for certiorari, reverse the judgment of the Court of Appeals for the Fifth Circuit, and remand for further proceedings consistent with this opinion.

It is so ordered.

Helzberg's Diamond Shops v. Valley West Des Moines Shopping Center

United States Court of Appeals for the Eighth Circuit, 1977.
564 F.2d 816.

■ ALSOP, DISTRICT JUDGE[*]

On February 3, 1975, Helzberg's Diamond Shops, Inc. (Helzberg), a Missouri corporation, and Valley West Des Moines Shopping Center, Inc. (Valley West), an Iowa corporation, executed a written Lease Agreement. The Lease Agreement granted Helzberg the right to operate a full line jewelry store at space 254 in the Valley West Mall in West Des Moines, Iowa. Section 6 of Article V of the Lease Agreement provides:

> (Valley West) agrees it will not lease premises in the shopping center for use as a catalog jewelry store nor lease premises for more than two full line jewelry stores in the shopping center in addition to the leased premises. This clause shall not prohibit other stores such as department stores from selling jewelry from catalogs or in any way restrict the shopping center department stores.

Subsequently, Helzberg commenced operation of a full line jewelry store in the Valley West Mall.

Between February 3, 1975 and November 2, 1976 Valley West and two other corporations entered into leases for spaces in the Valley West Mall for use as full line jewelry stores. Pursuant to those leases the two corporations also initiated actual operation of full line jewelry stores.

On November 2, 1976, Valley West and Kirk's Incorporated, Jewelers, an Iowa corporation, doing business as Lord's Jewelers (Lord's), entered into a written Lease Agreement. The Lease Agreement granted Lord's the right to occupy space 261 in the Valley West Mall. Section 1 of Article V of the Lease Agreement provides that Lord's will use space 261

> . . . only as a retail specialty jewelry store (and not as a catalogue or full line jewelry store) featuring watches, jewelry (and the repair of same) and incidental better gift items.

However, Lord's intended to open and operate what constituted a full line jewelry store at space 261.

In an attempt to avoid the opening of a fourth full line jewelry store in the Valley West Mall and the resulting breach of the Helzberg-Valley West Lease Agreement, Helzberg instituted suit seeking preliminary and permanent injunctive relief restraining Valley West's breach of the Lease Agreement. The suit was filed in the United States District Court for the Western District of Missouri. Subject matter jurisdiction was invoked pursuant to 28 U.S.C. § 1332 based upon diversity of citizenship between

---

[*] [District judge sitting by designation on the court of appeals—Ed.]

the parties and an amount in controversy which exceeded $10,000. Personal jurisdiction was established by service of process on Valley West pursuant to the Missouri "long arm" statute, Rev.Stat.Mo. § 506.500 et seq. (1977). Rule 4(e), Fed.R.Civ.P.

Valley West moved to dismiss pursuant to Rule 19 because Helzberg had failed to join Lord's as a party defendant.[1] That motion was denied. The District Court went on to order that pending the determination of (the) action on the merits, that (Valley West) be, and it is hereby, enjoined and restrained from allowing, and shall take all necessary steps to prevent, any other tenant in its Valley West Mall (including but not limited to Kirk's Incorporated, Jewelers, d/b/a Lord's Jewelers) to open and operate on March 30, 1977, or at any other time, or to be operated during the term of (Helzberg's) present leasehold, a fourth full line jewelry store * * *.

From this order Valley West appeals.

It is clear that Valley West is entitled to appeal from the order granting preliminary injunctive relief. 28 U.S.C. § 1292(a)(1). However, Valley West does not attack the propriety of the issuance of a preliminary injunction directly; instead, it challenges the District Court's denial of its motion to dismiss for failure to join an indispensable party * * *.

Ordinarily, the denial of a motion to dismiss is not reviewable. Cohen v. Beneficial Indus. Loan Corp., 337 U.S. 541, 69 S.Ct. 1221, 93 L.Ed. 1528 (1949); Catlin v. United States, 324 U.S. 229, 65 S.Ct. 631, 89 L.Ed. 911 (1945); United States v. Barket, 530 F.2d 181 (8th Cir. 1975), cert. denied, 429 U.S. 917, 97 S.Ct. 308, 50 L.Ed.2d 282 (1976). However, because the denial of Valley West's motion to dismiss enters into and becomes a part of the District Court's order granting preliminary injunctive relief and because the granting of preliminary injunctive relief is itself appealable, we can and will review the order denying Valley West's motion to dismiss. See United States v. Fort Sill Apache Tribe, 507 F.2d 861, 205 Ct.Cl. 805 (1974).

Rule 19, Fed.R.Civ.P., provides in pertinent part:

(a) [**Persons to be Joined if Feasible.**] A person who is subject to service of process and whose joinder will not deprive the court of jurisdiction over the subject matter of the action shall be joined as a party in the action if (1) in his absence complete relief cannot be accorded among those already parties, or (2) he claims an interest relating to the subject of the action and is so situated that the disposition of the action in his absence may (i) as a practical matter impair or impede his ability to protect that interest or (ii) leave any of the persons already parties subject to a substantial risk of incurring double, multiple, or otherwise inconsistent obligations by reason of his claimed interest. . . .

(b) [**Determination by Court Whenever Joinder not Feasible.**] If a person as described in subdivision (a)(1)–(2) hereof cannot be made a party, the court shall determine whether in equity and good conscience the action should proceed among the parties before it, or should be dismissed, the absent

---

[1]   Lord's was not subject to the personal jurisdiction of the District Court.

person being thus regarded as indispensable. The factors to be considered by the court include: first, to what extent a judgment rendered in the person's absence might be prejudicial to him or those already parties; second, the extent to which, by protective provisions in the judgment, by the shaping of relief, or other measures, the prejudice can be lessened or avoided; third, whether a judgment rendered in the person's absence will be adequate; fourth, whether the plaintiff will have an adequate remedy if the action is dismissed for nonjoinder.

Because Helzberg was seeking and the District Court ordered injunctive relief which may prevent Lord's from operating its jewelry store in the Valley West Mall in the manner in which Lord's originally intended, the District Court correctly concluded that Lord's was a party to be joined if feasible. See Rule 19(a)(2)(i), Fed.R.Civ.P. Therefore, because Lord's was not and is not subject to personal jurisdiction in the Western District of Missouri, the District Court was required to determine whether or not Lord's should be regarded as indispensable. After considering the factors which Rule 19(b) mandates be considered, the District Court concluded that Lord's was not to be regarded as indispensable. We agree.

The determination of whether or not a person is an indispensable party is one which must be made on a case-by-case basis and is dependent upon the facts and circumstances of each case. Provident Tradesmens Bank & Trust Co. v. Patterson, 390 U.S. 102, 88 S.Ct. 733, 19 L.Ed.2d 936 (1968); 7 C. Wright & A. Miller, Federal Practice & Procedure § 1607 (1972); 3A J. Moore, Federal Practice ¶ 19.07–2(0) (1976). An analysis of the facts and circumstances of the case before us lead us to conclude that Lord's was not an indispensable party and that, therefore, the District Court did not err in denying Valley West's motion to dismiss.

Rule 19(b) requires the court to look first to the extent to which a judgment rendered in Lord's absence might be prejudicial to Lord's or to Valley West. Valley West argues that the District Court's order granting preliminary injunctive relief does prejudice Lord's and may prejudice Valley West. We do not agree.

It seems axiomatic that none of Lord's rights or obligations will be ultimately determined in a suit to which it is not a party. See Mallow v. Hinde, 25 U.S. (12 Wheat.) 193, 6 L.Ed. 599 (1827); E. B. Elliott Adv. Co. v. Metropolitan Dade County, 425 F.2d 1141 (5th Cir.), cert. denied, 400 U.S. 805, 91 S.Ct. 12, 27 L.Ed.2d 35 (1970); 7 C. Wright & A. Miller, Federal Practice & Procedure § 1611, at 112 (1972). Even if, as a result of the District Court's granting of the preliminary injunction, Valley West should attempt to terminate Lord's leasehold interest in space 261 in the Valley West Mall, Lord's will retain all of its rights under its Lease Agreement with Valley West. None of its rights or obligations will have been adjudicated as a result of the present proceedings, proceedings to which it is not a party. Therefore, we conclude that Lord's will not be prejudiced in a way contemplated by Rule 19(b) as a result of this action.

Likewise, we think that Lord's absence will not prejudice Valley West in a way contemplated by Rule 19(b). Valley West contends that it may be subjected to inconsistent obligations as a result of a determination in this action and a determination in another forum that

Valley West should proceed in a fashion contrary to what has been ordered in these proceedings.

It is true that the obligations of Valley West to Helzberg, as determined in these proceedings, may be inconsistent with Valley West's obligations to Lord's. However, we are of the opinion that any inconsistency in those obligations will result from Valley West's voluntary execution of two Lease Agreements which impose inconsistent obligations rather than from Lord's absence from the present proceedings.

Helzberg seeks only to restrain Valley West's breach of the Lease Agreement to which Helzberg and Valley West were the sole parties. Certainly, all of the rights and obligations arising under a lease can be adjudicated where all of the parties to the lease are before the court. See Lomayaktewa v. Hathaway, 520 F.2d 1324 (9th Cir. 1975), cert. denied, 425 U.S. 903, 96 S.Ct. 1492, 47 L.Ed.2d 752 (1976). Thus, in the context of these proceedings the District Court can determine all of the rights and obligations of both Helzberg and Valley West based upon the Lease Agreement between them, even though Lord's is not a party to the proceedings.

Valley West's contention that it may be subjected to inconsistent judgments if Lord's should choose to file suit elsewhere and be awarded judgment is speculative at best. In the first place, Lord's has not filed such a suit. Secondly, there is no showing that another court is likely to interpret the language of the two Lease Agreements differently from the way in which the District Court would. Therefore, we also conclude that Valley West will suffer no prejudice as a result of the District Court's proceeding in Lord's absence. Any prejudice which Valley West may suffer by way of inconsistent judgments would be the result of Valley West's execution of Lease Agreements which impose inconsistent obligations and not the result of the proceedings in the District Court.

Rule 19(b) also requires the court to consider ways in which prejudice to the absent party can be lessened or avoided. The District Court afforded Lord's an opportunity to intervene in order to protect any interest it might have in the outcome of this litigation. Lord's chose not to do so. In light of Lord's decision not to intervene we conclude that the District Court acted in such a way as to sufficiently protect Lord's interests. Cf. 7 C. Wright & A. Miller, Federal Practice & Procedures 1610, at 103 (1972).

* * *

In sum, it is generally recognized that a person does not become indispensable to an action to determine rights under a contract simply because that person's rights or obligations under an entirely separate contract will be affected by the result of the action. 3A J. Moore, Federal Practice P 19.10, at 2349–50 (1976); see also Division 525, Railway Conductors v. Gorman, 133 F.2d 273 (8th Cir. 1943); 7 C. Wright & A. Miller, Federal Practice & Procedure s 1613, at 135 (1972). This principle applies to an action against a lessor who has entered into other leases which also may be affected by the result in the action in which the other lessees are argued to be indispensable parties. See Cherokee Nation v. Hitchcock, 187 U.S. 294, 23 S.Ct. 115, 47 L.Ed. 183 (1902). We conclude that the District Court properly denied the motion to dismiss for failure to join an indispensable party.

* * *

Affirmed.

NOTE ON COMPULSORY JOINDER OF PARTIES UNDER RULE 19

1. **Origin of the compulsory joinder rule.** A predecessor to federal Rule 19 may be found the English equity courts, which required that all persons "interested" in multi-faceted controversies be made parties. As stated in Mitford, Pleadings in the Court of Chancery 163*–164* (4th ed. Jeremy 1833):

> It is the constant aim of a court of equity to do complete justice by deciding upon and settling the rights of all persons interested in the subject of the suit, to make the performance of the order of the court perfectly safe to those who are compelled to obey it, and to prevent future litigation. For this purpose all persons materially interested in the subject ought generally to be parties to the suit, plaintiffs or defendants, however numerous they may be * * *.

The content of the term "interest" was vague, but the central objectives of the rule were simple enough: from the viewpoint of the court, to resolve the entire controversy in one proceeding; from the viewpoint of those already parties, to protect them against the consequences of subsequent litigation reaching inconsistent results; from the viewpoint of those not already made parties, to assure that they will not be adversely affected, as a practical matter, by a judgment entered in their absence.

2. **Pre-1966 version of Rule 19.** Under federal Rule 19 as it existed prior to amendment in 1966, the criteria for judging whether an absent party should be joined were not spelled out. Further, some courts appeared to be under the misapprehension that they were without jurisdiction to proceed in absence of a party who was deemed by the rule to be "indispensable," instead of merely being forbidden to do so by a Federal Rule of Civil Procedure. Two articles were particularly forceful in their criticism of the operation of the pre-1966 rule. Reed, Compulsory Joinder of Parties in Civil Actions, 55 Mich. L. Rev. 327 (1957), and Hazard, Indispensable Party: The Historical Origin of a Procedural Phantom, 61 Colum. L. Rev. 1254 (1961). Prodded by these articles and by the courts' continuing difficulty in articulating stable criteria under the rule, the Advisory Committee recommended something close to the present rule.

3. **Changing terminology of Rule 19.** The terminology used in Rule 19 has changed over the years. The changes in terminology have not appreciably changed the operation of Rule 19, but you need to understand the earlier terminology to understand earlier Rule 19 cases. In particular, you need to understand two terms that were once in the text of the rule but that have now disappeared—"necessary" party and "indispensable" party. Neither term appears in the current version of Rule 19. "Necessary" was used in the original version of Rule 19, but was eliminated in the 1966 revision. "Indispensable" was used in the post-1966 version of the rule, but was eliminated in the 2007 stylistic revision. What do (or did) those terms mean?

"Necessary" party: In the terminology of the current version of Rule 19, "person to be joined if feasible" under Rule 19(a) is the replacement term for "necessary party." If a person meets the criteria of Rule 19(a)(1) or (a)(2), she must be joined if it "feasible" to do so. Under the pre-1996 version of the rule, that person was deemed "necessary." But she was "necessary" only in the sense that she had to be joined if joinder was "feasible." Such a person was not "necessary" in the sense that a failure to join her required dismissal of the suit between the existing parties. As may be seen in *Temple*, the "necessary" party terminology was still being used by the Supreme Court twenty-four years after it had disappeared from the text of the rule. (*See, e.g.*, "Synthes filed a motion to dismiss Temple's federal suit for failure to join necessary parties pursuant to Federal Rule of Procedure 19.")

"Indispensable" party: In the terminology of the pre-2008 version of Rule 19, an "indispensable" person was a person whose absence meant that the suit between the existing parties had to be dismissed. See the version of Rule 19(b) quoted in *Helzberg's Diamond Shops*. The current version of the rule has dropped the term "indispensable." Now, the rule simply provides that if a "person required to be joined if feasible" cannot be joined, the court should consider considering the factors outlined in Rule 19(b)(1)–(4) and decide whether "in equity and good conscience" the suit should be dismissed.

4. **Application of Rule 19 depends on factual context.** The Supreme Court construed the then-newly amended Rule 19 in Provident Tradesmens Bank & Trust v. Patterson, 390 U.S. 102, 88 S.Ct. 733, 19 L.Ed.2d 936 (1968). The Court described the operation of the Rule as follows:

> Whether a person is "indispensable," that is, whether a particular lawsuit must be dismissed in the absence of that person, can only be determined in the context of a particular litigation. * * * Assuming the existence of a person who should be joined if feasible, the only further question arises when the joinder is not possible and the court must decide whether to dismiss or to proceed without him. To use the familiar but confusing terminology, the decision to proceed is a decision that the absent person is merely "necessary," while the decision to dismiss is a decision that he is "indispensable." The decision whether to dismiss (i.e., the decision whether the person missing is "indispensable") must be based on factors varying with the different cases[.] * * * To say that a court "must" dismiss in the absence of an indispensable party and that it "cannot proceed" without him puts the matter the wrong way around: a court does not know whether a particular person is indispensable until it has examined the situation to determine whether it can proceed without him.

Id. at 118–119.

5. **Person "to be joined if feasible."** Rule 19(a)(1) contains three criteria. If any one of them is satisfied, the absent person is "to be joined if feasible."

a. **Complete relief.** Under Rule 19(a)(1)(A), a person shall be joined if "in that person's absence, the court cannot accord complete relief among existing parties." This criterion sounds straightforward, but can be quite difficult to apply. This may be seen in Disabled Rights Action Committee v. Las Vegas Events, 375 F.3d 861 (9th Cir. 2004). Plaintiff Disabled Rights sued Las Vegas Events (Events) and the Professional Rodeo Cowboys Association (Cowboys) under Title III of the Americans with Disabilities Act

(ADA). Disabled Rights sought an injunction that would require the defendants to make the Rodeo accessible to people in wheelchairs. The Rodeo took place in the "Thomas & Mack Center" (Center) in Las Vegas. Defendants Events and Cowboys sought dismissal under Rule 19, contending that the owner of the Center was a "person to be joined if feasible," and was an "indispensable" person in whose absence dismissal was required. Defendants contended that complete relief could not be accorded in the absence of the owner because they had limited ability to make changes to the Center. The court of appeals held that the owner was not even a party "to be joined if feasible," let alone a party whose absence would require dismissal of the suit. The court wrote:

> Meaningful relief could * * * be granted by enjoining Events and Cowboys from making certain kinds of operational decisions regarding conditions over which they have control—e.g., enjoining them from removing accessible floor seating, or requiring the erection of temporary ramps or lifts. Meaningful relief could also be granted by requiring Events and Cowboys to hold the Rodeo at an accessible venue either immediately, or in the future, after the current provisions of its licensing agreement expire.

375 F.3d at 880. Note the court's use of the term "meaningful relief," even though Rule 19(a)(1)(A) speaks of "complete relief." Did the court misapply the Rule?

b.   Impair or impede an interest as a practical matter. Under Rule 19(a)(1)(B)(i), a person claiming an interest in the litigation must be joined if feasible if, in his absence, the litigation may "as a practical matter impair or impede the person's ability to protect the interest." "Interest" is a broader term than "right," as may be seen in American Greyhound Racing, Inc. v. Hull, 305 F.3d 1015 (9th Cir. 2002). Plaintiff Greyhound Racing was in competition with Indian-run casinos for gambling dollars in Arizona. Greyhound Racing sued the Governor of Arizona contending that compacts between the State and the Indian tribes, under which tribes operated their casinos, were illegal under federal law. At the time the suit was brought, the ten-year term of the current compacts with the tribes was about to expire. However, the compacts would be automatically extended for another five years unless either the Governor or a tribe served notice of an intent not to extend. No justification was required for a refusal to extend. The Governor moved to dismiss because no Indian tribe was joined as a defendant. The court held that the criterion of Rule 19(a)(1)(B)(i) was satisfied. Even though the tribes had no legally enforceable right to extension of the compacts, the outcome of the litigation might affect the ability of the Governor to extend the compact. The tribes therefore had an "interest" that was threatened by the litigation.

c.   Double, multiple, or otherwise inconsistent obligations. Under Rule 19(a)(1)(B)(ii), a person claiming an interest in the litigation must be joined if feasible if, in his absence, an existing party may be left "subject to a substantial risk of incurring double, multiple, or otherwise inconsistent obligations because of the interest." In Haas v. Jefferson National Bank of Miami Beach, 442 F.2d 394 (5th Cir. 1971), plaintiff Haas sued the Jefferson National Bank seeking an order that would require the bank to deliver certain shares of stock held (but not owned) by the bank, which Haas claimed to own. The bank sought a dismissal under Rule 19, contending that an absent party, Glueck, also claimed an ownership interest in the same shares of stock. If Glueck were not joined in the current suit, and if the bank were ordered to deliver the shares to Haas, Glueck might sue the bank in a later suit for delivery of the same shares. If Glueck were not a party to the first suit, he would not be bound by a holding in that suit that Haas owned the shares, and the bank could potentially be required in a later suit to pay Glueck the value of the stock it had previously delivered to Haas. The court held that Glueck was a party "to be joined if feasible" under the criterion of Rule 19(a)(1)(B)(ii).

6. **Dismissal in the absence of a person to be joined if feasible.** The criteria requiring dismissal under Rule 19(b) overlap with the criteria for a person to be joined if feasible under Rule 19(a). The overarching criterion of Rule 19(b) is whether "in equity and good conscience" the action should proceed without the absent person "to be joined if feasible." See Shields v. Barrow, 58 U.S. 130, 139 (1854) (indispensable parties are those without whom a final judgment "may be wholly inconsistent with equity and good conscience."). Rule 19(b) then goes on to give a non-exhaustive list of specific criteria for determining whether the overarching criterion has been satisfied. The absence of the Indian tribes in *Greyhound Racing* and of Glueck in *Haas v. Jefferson Bank*, supra, was held to require dismissal under these criteria.

7. **Personal jurisdiction over Lord's Jewelers.** West Valley Mall, where plaintiff Helzberg had the jewelry shop in question, was located in Iowa. Defendant Valley West was an Iowa corporation. However, Helzberg filed suit in the federal district court in Missouri, its own state of incorporation. Valley West appears not to have contested personal jurisdiction in Missouri. However, there was no personal jurisdiction in Missouri over Lord's Jewelers. (See n.1 of the court's opinion, supra p. 591.) The relevant portions of the Missouri long-arm statute in effect when *Helzberg's Diamond Shops* was decided authorized the exercise of personal jurisdiction over a corporation based either on "[t]he transaction of business within this state," or on "[t]he making of any contract within this state." Rev. Stat. Mo. § 506.500. We are not told any of the underlying facts relevant to jurisdiction, but we may infer that Lord's was not a Missouri corporation; that Lord's did no business in Missouri; and that the lease between Valley West and Lord's was not signed in Missouri. If the court had held that dismissal was required under Rule 19(b) in the absence of Lord's, Helzberg could easily have sued Valley West and Lord's in federal district court in Iowa (assuming the statute of limitations had not run). Why do you suppose Helzberg was willing to go all the way to the Eighth Circuit in order to maintain a suit in district court in Missouri rather than Iowa? To put the question the other way around, why do you suppose Valley West was willing to go to the Eighth Circuit to try to get the suit dismissed?

8. **Rule 19 and supplemental jurisdiction.** Supplemental jurisdiction is not available in a diversity case under 28 U.S.C. § 1332 when a person is sought to be joined under Rule 19. See 28 U.S.C. § 1367(b) (excluding from supplemental jurisdiction in diversity cases claims "by plaintiffs against persons made parties under Rule * * * 19," and claims "by persons proposed to be joined as plaintiffs under Rule 19"). However, supplemental jurisdiction is available, irrespective of the absent party's citizenship, if subject matter jurisdiction is based on the presence of a federal question under 28 U.S.C. § 1331. See § 1367(a).

9. Reasons for inability to join a person "to be joined if feasible." It may be infeasible to join a person for a number of reasons. (a) Sometimes (though rarely) there are so many absent persons that joinder of all of them is impracticable. See, e.g., Eldredge v. Carpenters 46 Northern California Counties Joint Apprenticeship and Training Committee, 662 F.2d 534 (9th Cir. 1981) (4,500 employers). (b) Sometimes, as in *Helzberg's Diamond Shops*, the absent party is not subject to personal jurisdiction in the forum. This has become increasingly rare as state long-arm statutes have grown longer and longer arms. (c) Sometimes the absent defendant is immune from suit. This difficulty exists in suits in which the absent defendant is an Indian tribe because tribes have sovereign immunity. A tribe may consent to be sued, but, absent consent, is immune. See, e.g., Greyhound Racing, supra; Clinton v. Babbitt, 180 F.3d 1081 (9th Cir. 1999); Kescoli v. Babbitt, 101 F.3d 1304 (9th Cir. 1996). (d) Finally, sometimes the joinder of the absent person would add a defendant of the same citizenship as the plaintiff, and thereby defeat diversity jurisdiction under 28 U.S.C. § 1332. See, e.g., *Haas v. Jefferson Bank*, supra. This final reason is the most common in the reported cases.

10. Relationship to Rules 20(a) and 14(a). a. Alternatives under the rules. The Supreme Court held in *Temple* that a joint tort-feasor is not a person "to be joined if feasible" under Rule 19(a). Therefore, plaintiff Temple was not required by Rule 19(a) to join the doctor and the hospital as co-defendants. However, Temple clearly could have joined them as co-defendants under Rule 20(a). Permissive joinder would have been available under Rule 20(a) because the actions of Synthes, the doctor, and the hospital arose "out of the same transaction, occurrence, or series of transactions or occurrences," and there was at least one common question of law or fact.

Further, as the Court pointed out, defendant Synthes may have been able to "implead" the doctor and hospital as third-party defendants under Rule 14(a). (You will encounter Rule 14(a) in the next section of this chapter.) If the doctor and hospital had been impleaded under Rule 14, they would have been required to defend against a claim by Synthes contending that they were responsible, in whole or in part, for Temple's injury. If Synthes' claim against them were successful, they would be required to reimburse Synthes, in whole or in part, for any damages awarded against Synthes.

b. Tactical considerations. Why didn't Temple join the doctor and hospital as co-defendants under Rule 20(a)? Because their presence as co-defendants would have defeated diversity jurisdiction in federal court under 28 U.S.C. § 1332? Why didn't Temple sue everyone in a single suit in state court where subject matter jurisdiction would not have been a problem?

Why didn't Synthes seek to implead the doctor and hospital under Rule 14(a)? Because Synthes preferred a dismissal of Temple's federal court suit? But if Synthes obtained a dismissal of Temple's federal court suit, couldn't Temple have sued Synthes in state court, along with the doctor and hospital? Is it possible that by the time Synthes filed its Rule 19 motion to dismiss, the statute of limitations had run, thereby preventing Temple from filing a viable state court suit against it?

11. Foreign state sovereign immunity. In Republic of the Philippines v. Pimentel, 553 U.S. 851, 128 S.Ct. 2180, 171 L.Ed.2d 131 (2008), a class of plaintiffs represented by Pimentel had obtained a judgment of nearly $2 billion against the estate of Ferdinand Marcos, the former

President of the Republic of the Philippines, for human rights abuses. The Pimentel class sought to execute part of the judgment by attaching $35 million owned by a Panamanian company established by Marcos. The funds were held in a Merrill Lynch account. Other private creditors of Marcos also asserted a right to the funds. Finally, two Philippine government entities, the Republic of the Philippines (Republic) and the Philippine Presidential Commission on Good Governance (Commission), asserted a right to the funds.

Merrill Lynch brought an interpleader action to determine ownership of the funds. (You will learn about interpleader in a later section of this chapter.) Briefly stated, an interpleader action allows a custodian of property subject to competing claims to seek a judicial determination of rights to the property. The Republic and the Commission were immune from suit under the doctrine of sovereign immunity, and they refused to waive their immunity. Instead, they sought dismissal of the interpleader under Rule 19(b). The Supreme Court held that the action should be dismissed.

12. Comparable state rules. All states have procedural rules that serve the same function as Rule 19. See, e.g., Calif.C.Civ.P. § 389(a)–(b); Atlantic Richfield Co. v. Superior Court, 51 Cal.App.3d 168, 124 Cal.Rptr. 63 (1975) (dismissing suit).

2. IMPLEADER

Banks v. City of Emeryville

United States District Court for the Northern District of California, 1985.
109 F.R.D. 535.

■ WILLIAMS, J.

On October 31, 1982, plaintiffs' decedent, Mercedes Banks, was arrested by the Emeryville City Police for public drunkenness. Ms. Banks was placed in a cell at the Emeryville Police Department Temporary Detention Facility. During the course of her detention, a fire broke out in her cell. After the fire was extinguished, the decedent was found, charred nearly beyond recognition, on a mattress which had disintegrated into burnt shreds.

In August of 1983, plaintiffs brought suit, under 42 U.S.C. § 1983, against City of Emeryville and John B. LaCoste, the latter sued as an individual and in his capacity as Chief of Police for the City of Emeryville. In particular, plaintiffs claim that the civil rights violations occurred as a direct consequence of inadequate supervision of individuals detained in Emeryville City Jail, inadequate fire safety procedures and equipment in the jail, having furnished the cell with a dangerous and defective mattress, the dangerous and defective design of the jail, and for unlawful procedures in violation of California Penal Code § 647(f). Plaintiffs have not alleged any additional causes of action beyond 42 U.S.C. § 1983, nor do they name any additional parties beyond the City of Emeryville and John B. LaCoste.

The defendants contend that the fire was a suicide in which Ms. Banks lit herself and her cell mattress on fire. The defendants deny all allegations of negligence or racially motivated misconduct which may have contributed to Ms. Banks' death.

On March 8, 1985, the defendants, City of Emeryville and John B. LaCoste, filed a third party complaint against Pacific Hospital Equipment and Supply Company, Western Medical Enterprises, Inc., ARA, Inc., ARA Services, Inc., California Mattress Company, Allen D. Fisher, Lawrence Nolan, F.L. Herbeth, Ryland P. Davis, Edward Kuntz, John R. Ranelli, Gilen French, David D. Dayton, Bedline and Vogue Bedding Company. All of the third party defendants were involved in the manufacture, distribution, or sale of the mattress which was ultimately placed in the decedent's jail cell. The defendants allege that as a direct result of the presence of this dangerous and defective mattress, the fire spread too quickly to allow the police to rescue Ms. Banks. In the third party complaint, the defendants seek indemnification or contribution based on eight separate causes of action: "general" indemnification, strict products liability, breach of warranty, breach of implied warranty of merchantibility, breach of implied warranty of fitness for particular purposes, negligence, misrepresentation and breach of contract. The third party defendants have moved for judgment on the pleadings for all eight causes of action.

DISMISSAL ON THE GROUNDS OF LATE IMPLEADER

According to the Federal Rules of Civil Procedure, Rule 14(a) leave of the court need not be obtained if a third party complaint is filed not later than ten days after the defendants serve their answer to the original complaint. In this case, the defendants' answer was filed on September 16, 1983, and the third party complaint was filed on March 8, 1985, a period exceeding ten days. The third party defendants urge the court to dismiss the third party complaint due to this late filing.

The Ninth Circuit has determined that it is within the discretionary power of the court to allow or disallow a third party to be impleaded where the third party complaint is filed beyond the ten day period following the filing of the defendant's answer. United States v. One 1977 Mercedes Benz, 708 F.2d 444, 452 (9th Cir.1983), cert. denied 464 U.S. 1071, 104 S.Ct. 981, 79 L.Ed.2d 217 (1983). * * * [T]he court has already determined that adding the third parties was appropriate. The court remains of the opinion that the third party complaint does not unnecessarily complicate the case, or prejudice any of the parties. It is clearly based on the same set of operative facts. United States v. Joe Grasso & Son, Inc., 380 F.2d 749, 751 (5th Cir.1967). Hence, late filing is not an adequate ground for dismissal.

FEDERAL JURISDICTION OVER THE THIRD PARTY COMPLAINT

Although none of the parties addressed this issue in their briefs or at oral argument, there is some question about the willingness of the Ninth Circuit to entertain state law claims against parties where no independent basis for federal jurisdiction exists as to those parties. As will be discussed more fully below, the third party defendants in this case are properly impleaded only under several state law causes of action. Thus it is necessary to determine whether an independent basis for federal subject matter jurisdiction is required as to the third party defendants.

Generally, the Ninth Circuit has been extremely hostile to the introduction of pendent state claims by plaintiffs against parties for whom no independent basis for jurisdiction exists. Safeco Ins. Co. of America v. Guyton, 692 F.2d 551, 555 (9th Cir.1982). However, the Ninth Circuit has approved the joining of a party within the ancillary jurisdiction of the court where that party is brought into the case by a party other then the plaintiff. Burke v. Ernest W. Hahn, Inc., 592 F.2d 542, 546 (9th Cir.1979). In Burke, the defendant sought to join a third party who may have been liable for some portion of the defendant's liability to the plaintiff. The court allowed the defendant to join the third party on the theory that the claims arose out of the same set of operative facts, and therefore that the claim fell within the court's ancillary jurisdiction. The situation in Burke is highly analogous to this case, because here the defendants seek to join third parties who may be liable for some portion of the defendants' liability to the plaintiffs. In this situation, the third party complaint need not have an independent basis for federal jurisdiction if the original complaint has satisfied the federal requirements for jurisdiction. United States v. United Pacific Insurance Co., 472 F.2d 792, 794 (9th Cir.1973), cert. denied 411 U.S. 982, 93 S.Ct. 2273, 36 L.Ed.2d 958 (1973); Fong v. United States, 21 F.R.D. 385, 387 (N.D.Cal.1975). Therefore, the court may exercise its ancillary jurisdiction over the state law claims in the third party complaint.

PROPRIETY OF IMPLEADING THE THIRD PARTIES UNDER RULE 14(a)

Section 1983

The central issue in this motion is whether the third party defendants may be impleaded under Federal Rules of Civil Procedure, Rule 14(a). In relevant part, Rule 14(a) provides,

"At any time after commencement of the action a defending party as a third party plaintiff, may cause a summons and complaint to be served upon a person not a party to the action who is or may be liable to him for all or part of the plaintiff's claim against him. . . ." (emphasis added)

The third party defendants assert that the defendants are trying to pass on liability for a § 1983 claim, which they claim is improper because they cannot be held liable for violating decedent's civil rights under § 1983. Third party defendants also argue that § 1983 does not provide for indemnification.

To the extent that defendants may be trying to seek indemnity by way of the third party complaint based directly on § 1983, the third party defendants are correct in asserting that impleader is improper. First, it is well settled that a private party may only incur § 1983 liability if his actions are carried out "under color of state law". Monroe v. Pape, 365 U.S. 167, 184, 81 S.Ct. 473, 482, 5 L.Ed.2d 492 (1961). In this case, there are no allegations that the third party defendants acted "under color of state law". Rather, they merely sold an allegedly defective mattress to a governmental body. This, without more, is not an action taken "under color of state law". Therefore, based on the record in this case, the third party defendants cannot be found to have violated § 1983.

Moreover, even if there were allegations that the third party defendants acted "under color of state law", defendants have not persuaded the court that § 1983 provides for indemnification. In Valdez v. City of Farmington, 580 F.Supp. 19, 21 (D.N.M.1984), the court noted that "there exists no clear authority on the question of whether a § 1983 defendant may seek indemnity from his co-defendant." In Northwest Airlines, Inc. v. Transport Workers Union of America, AFL–CIO, 451 U.S. 77, 101 S.Ct. 1571, 67 L.Ed.2d 750 (1981), a case cited in Valdez, the Supreme Court made it clear that courts are not free to read a cause of action for indemnity into statutes where no statutory basis exists for such a claim. There, the Court determined that no right to contribution exists among co-defendants under the Equal Pay Act or Title VII. Defendants have pointed to no provision of § 1983, nor any legislative history, to support their assertion that § 1983 provides for a right of contribution or indemnity. Therefore, any claims for indemnification against the third party defendants based directly upon § 1983 are impermissible.

STATE LAW THEORIES

Rather than premising liability upon a § 1983 claim, the last seven claims seeking indemnification or contribution in the third party complaint are based on several state theories of liability. Valdez and Northwest Airlines, cited by the third party defendants as grounds for dismissing the defendants' state law claims, are simply inapplicable to a situation where indemnification is based on state law claims. In both Valdez and Northwest Airlines the defendant sought contribution based upon federal statutes that did not provide for contribution. Here, in claims two through eight, the defendants seek indemnification based on state law claims, rather then on § 1983 directly. Hence, to the extent that the defendants seek indemnification or contribution based on state law theories, the claims are permissible provided that the claims satisfy the requirements of Rule 14(a) and the substantive requirements of state law.

As an initial matter, the claims for indemnity do appear to be authorized under state law. In American Motorcycle Association v. Superior Court of Los Angeles County, 20 Cal.3d 578, 146 Cal.Rptr. 182, 578 P.2d 899 (1978), the court held that a defendant may implead a third party on the grounds of comparative fault and recognized that such a finding would allow for indemnification or contribution. Subsequent cases have permitted indemnification and contribution based on comparative negligence, even in the face of wilful misconduct by the original defendant. Southern Pacific Transportation Co. v. State of California, 115 Cal.App.3d 116, 171 Cal.Rptr. 187 (1981). Therefore, claims for indemnification and contribution are cognizable under California law.

The question under Rule 14(a) is whether the defendants can potentially hold the third party defendants liable for some or all of the defendants' primary liability to the plaintiffs. The third party defendants initially argue that they can only be held liable to the defendants if they could be found to be directly liable to the plaintiffs. This assertion is directly contrary to settled law. "As a matter of procedure, Rule 14 does not require that the third party defendant be liable to the original plaintiff in order for the original defendant to proceed with his claim against a third party defendant and recover judgment thereon." Huggins v. Graves, 337 F.2d 486, 489 (6th Cir.1964). See also, Barnett v. Sears Roebuck and Co., 80 F.R.D. 662, 665 (W.D.Okla.1978). Hence, it is permissible to implead third party defendants even if there is no basis for the third party defendants to be directly liable to the plaintiffs.

Given the above, the third party defendants' argument is essentially reduced to the contention that indemnity liability cannot be transferred through dissimiliar causes of action. However, the claims upon which indemnity is based need not be similiar to the claims asserted in the original complaint. In Givoh Associates v. American Druggists Ins. Co., 562 F.Supp. 1346, 1350 (E.D.N.Y.1983), the court noted that, ". . . Rule 14 actions are normally interpreted to allow claims even though they do not allege the same cause of action or the same theory of liability as the original complaint." Indeed, impleader should be allowed if the third party complaint arises out of the same set of operative facts, and "if under some construction of facts which might be adduced at trial, recovery might be possible." Tiesler v. Martin Paint Stores, Inc., 76 F.R.D. 640, 643 (E.D.Pa.1977). "Dismissal is not favored unless it appears that in no event would the pleader be able to prove an actionable claim." Parr v. Great Lake's Express Co., 484 F.2d 767, 770 (7th Cir.1973). It is of no import that the defendants' liability is premised upon a federal statute, and the liability of the third party defendants is derived from state law. See, Kennedy v. Pennsylvania Railroad Co., 282 F.2d 705 (3rd Cir.1960) (original complaint based on Federal Employers' Liability Act and third party complaint based on various state law claims). Hence, if there is any possible scenario under which the third party defendants may be liable for all or part of the defendants' liability to the plaintiffs, the third party complaint should be allowed to stand.

Under Rule 14(a), a third party may be impleaded only if the third party "is or may be liable to him [the original defendant] for all or part of the plaintiff's claim against him." In this case, the defendants may be liable to the plaintiffs for the death of the decedent, Mercedes Banks, because of the defendants' alleged inadequate supervision, procedures, equipment and improper jail design. The defendants allege that Ms. Banks' death was due, at least in part, to the presence of highly dangerous polyurethane filling in the mattress which was sold, distributed and manufactured by the third party defendants. Due to the presence of this dangerous filling, defendants assert that the fire spread too quickly to allow the decedent to be rescued. One determination that a jury might make is that the tortious actions of the third party defendants are, in whole or in part, responsible for the decedent's death, and that the defendants should therefore be relieved of liability to the plaintiffs to that extent. Therefore, since it is possible that the third party defendants may be all or partially liable to the defendants for the plaintiffs' claim against the defendants, impleader is appropriate under Rule 14.

* * *

CONCLUSION

In the third party complaint, the defendants seek indemnification or contribution based on various state law causes of action, and, apparently, one federal claim. Although the defendants may not seek indemnification based directly on § 1983, the defendants may seek indemnification based on their state law causes of action—i.e., claims two through eight. Because California state law permits both indemnification and contribution, and the requirements of Rule 14(a) have been satisfied, defendants have stated viable claims. The question of whether indemnification or contribution would be more appropriate in this case, and the precise form that either might take, need not be decided at this time. These issues were not briefed by the parties and were not discussed at oral argument.

For the foregoing reasons, IT IS HEREBY ORDERED THAT the third party defendants' motion for judgment on the pleadings is DENIED, except as to the defendants' first claim for relief which is hereby DISMISSED.

Owen Equipment & Erection Co. v. Kroger

Supreme Court of the United States, 1978.
437 U.S. 365, 98 S.Ct. 2396, 57 L.Ed.2d 274.

[For a longer version of the Supreme Court's opinion in *Owen Equipment & Erection Co. v. Kroger*, see Chapter 2, supra.]

■ MR. JUSTICE STEWART delivered the opinion of the Court.

In an action in which federal jurisdiction is based on diversity of citizenship, may the plaintiff assert a claim against a third-party defendant when there is no independent basis for federal jurisdiction over that claim? * * *

I

On January 18, 1972, James Kroger was electrocuted when the boom of a steel crane next to which he was walking came too close to a high-tension electric power line. The respondent (his widow, who is the administratrix of his estate) filed a wrongful-death action in the United States District Court for the District of Nebraska against the Omaha Public Power District (OPPD). Her complaint alleged that OPPD's negligent construction, maintenance, and operation of the power line had caused Kroger's death. Federal jurisdiction was based on diversity of citizenship, since the respondent was a citizen of Iowa and OPPD was a Nebraska corporation.

OPPD then filed a third-party complaint pursuant to Fed.Rule Civ.Proc. 14(a) against the petitioner, Owen Equipment and Erection Co. (Owen), alleging that the crane was owned and operated by Owen, and that Owen's negligence had been the proximate cause of Kroger's death.[3] OPPD later moved for summary judgment on the respondent's complaint against it. While this motion was pending, the respondent was granted leave to file an amended complaint naming Owen as an additional defendant. Thereafter, the District Court granted OPPD's motion for summary judgment in an unreported opinion. The case thus went to trial between the respondent and the petitioner alone.

The respondent's amended complaint alleged that Owen was "a Nebraska corporation with its principal place of business in Nebraska." Owen's answer admitted that it was "a corporation organized and existing under the laws of the State of Nebraska," and denied every other

---

[3] Under Rule 14(a), a third-party defendant may not be impleaded merely because he may be liable to the *plaintiff*. * * * While the third-party complaint in this case alleged merely that Owen's negligence caused Kroger's death, and the basis of Owen's alleged liability *to OPPD* is nowhere spelled out, OPPD evidently relied upon the state common-law right of contribution among joint tort-feasors. See *Dairyland Ins. Co. v. Mumert*, 212 N.W.2d 436, 438 (Iowa); *Best v. Yerkes*, 247 Iowa 800, 77 N.W.2d 23. * * *

allegation of the complaint. On the third day of trial, however, it was disclosed that the petitioner's principal place of business was in Iowa, not Nebraska,[5] and that the petitioner and the respondent were thus both citizens of Iowa. The petitioner then moved to dismiss the complaint for lack of jurisdiction. The District Court reserved decision on the motion, and the jury thereafter returned a verdict in favor of the respondent. In an unreported opinion issued after the trial, the District Court denied the petitioner's motion to dismiss the complaint.

The judgment was affirmed on appeal. * * *

II

It is undisputed that there was no independent basis of federal jurisdiction over the respondent's state-law tort action against the petitioner, since both are citizens of Iowa. And although Fed.Rule Civ.Proc. 14(a) permits a plaintiff to assert a claim against a third-party defendant, it does not purport to say whether or not such a claim requires an independent basis of federal jurisdiction. Indeed, it could not determine that question, since it is axiomatic that the Federal Rules of Civil Procedure do not create or withdraw federal jurisdiction.[7]

* * *

III

The relevant statute in this case, 28 U.S.C. § 1332(a)(1), confers upon federal courts jurisdiction over "civil actions where the matter in controversy exceeds the sum or value of $10,000 * * * and is between * * * citizens of different States." This statute and its predecessors have consistently been held to require complete diversity of citizenship.[13] That is, diversity jurisdiction does not exist unless each defendant is a citizen of a different State from each plaintiff. Over the years Congress has repeatedly re-enacted or amended the statute conferring diversity jurisdiction, leaving intact this rule of complete diversity. Whatever may have been the original purposes of diversity-of-citizenship jurisdiction, this subsequent history clearly demonstrates a congressional mandate that diversity jurisdiction is not to be available when any plaintiff is a citizen of the same State as any defendant.

Thus it is clear that the respondent could not originally have brought suit in federal court naming Owen and OPPD as codefendants, since citizens of Iowa would have been on both sides of the litigation. Yet the identical lawsuit resulted when she amended her complaint. Complete diversity was destroyed just as surely as if she had sued Owen initially. In either situation, in the plain language of the statute, the "matter in controversy" could not be "between * * * citizens of different States."

---

[5] The problem apparently was one of geography. Although the Missouri River generally marks the boundary between Iowa and Nebraska, Carter Lake, Iowa, where the accident occurred and where Owen had its main office, lies west of the river, adjacent to Omaha, Neb. Apparently the river once avulsed at one of its bends, cutting Carter Lake off from the rest of Iowa.

[7] Fed.Rule Civ.Proc. 82[.] * * *

[13] E.g., Strawbridge v. Curtiss, 3 Cranch 267, 2 L.Ed. 435; Coal Co. v. Blatchford, 11 Wall. 172, 20 L.Ed. 179; Indianapolis v. Chase Nat. Bank, 314 U.S. 63, 69, 62 S.Ct. 15, 16, 86 L.Ed. 47; American Fire & Cas. Co. v. Finn, 341 U.S. 6, 17, 71 S.Ct. 534, 541, 95 L.Ed. 702. It is settled that complete diversity is not a constitutional requirement. State Farm Fire & Cas. Co. v. Tashire, 386 U.S. 523, 530–531, 87 S.Ct. 1199, 1203–1204, 18 L.Ed.2d 270.

* * *

Accordingly, the judgment of the Court of Appeals is reversed.

[A dissenting opinion by Justice White, joined by Justice Brennan, is omitted.]

NOTE ON IMPLEADER

1.   Nomenclature. A third-party complaint under Rule 14(a) is a complaint by the defendant against the impleaded third-party defendant. As to the third-party defendant, the defendant is a third-party plaintiff. A third-party complaint may be challenged by the third-party defendant in the same manner a defendant may challenge a complaint filed by a plaintiff.

2.   Derivative liability. The liability of a third-party defendant impleaded under Rule 14(a) is "derivative." In the words of the rule, a third-party plaintiff may serve a complaint under Rule 14(a)(1) on a person "who is or may be liable to it for all or part of the plaintiff's claim against it." Before there can be recovery on a Rule 14(a) impleader claim, there must be a recovery against the defendant/third-party plaintiff, and the third-party defendant must be liable to the defendant/third-party plaintiff for all or part of that recovery. Note the difference between the "who is or may be liable" language of Rule 14(a) describing the third-party complaint, on the one hand, and the "transaction" or "occurrence" language of Rules 13(a) (compulsory counterclaim), 13(g) (cross-claim), and 20(a) (permissive joinder of parties), on the other.

As seen in *Banks*, the theories of recovery need not be the same in the complaint and the third-party complaint. In *Banks*, the plaintiffs brought a federal civil rights claim under 42 U.S.C. § 1983, but the City of Emeryville and Police Chief LaCoste impleaded the third-party defendants based on product liability claims under state law. Further, at the time the third-party complaint is served, there is no necessity that the defendant's liability to plaintiff have already been determined. The language of Rule 14(a) specifies that the third-party defendant is a person "who is *or may be* liable" (emphasis added).

3.   Defenses and additional claims by the third-party defendant; additional claims against the third-party defendant. Once a third-party defendant is brought into the case under Rule 14(a), she must or may do a number of things. She "must" (a) answer the third-party complaint; and (b) assert any defenses that the impleading defendant/third-party plaintiff has against the original plaintiff. She "may" (a) counterclaim against the third-party plaintiff; and (b) cross-claim against any co-third-party defendants. Fed. R. Civ. P. 14(a)(2). Further, as seen in *Owen Equipment*, the original plaintiff may make a claim directly against the third-party defendant, in effect making the third-party defendant a co-defendant with the defendant/third-party plaintiff. The claim by the plaintiff against the third-party defendant must arise out of the "transaction or occurrence that is the subject matter of the plaintiff's claim against the third-party plaintiff." Fed. R. Civ. Pro. 14(a)(3). In other words, the plaintiff's claim against the third-party defendant is subject to the same relatedness restriction as a plaintiff's claim against an additional party joined under Rule 20(a). If the plaintiff asserts a claim against the third-party defendant or defendants, the third-party defendant may, in turn, counterclaim against the plaintiff and cross-claim against any co-third-party defendants.

4. **Plaintiff can implead under Rule 14(b).** Under Rule 14(b), a plaintiff against whom a claim has been asserted (most likely as a counterclaim), may claim against a third party in the same manner as a defendant may implead under Rule 14(a).

5. **Rule 14(a) and Rule 18(a).** Once a Rule 14(a) third-party impleader claim is properly made, the third-party plaintiff can add unrelated claims against the third-party defendant under Rule 18(a). Rule 18(a) provides, "A party asserting a claim, counterclaim, crossclaim, or *third-party claim* may join, as independent or alternative claims, as many claims as it has against an opposing party." (Emphasis added.) See, e.g., United States v. City of Twin Falls, 806 F.2d 862, 867–68 (9th Cir. 1986); Price v. CTB, Inc., 168 F.Supp.2d 1299, 1302 (M.D. Ala. 2001).

6. **Timing.** Under Rule 14(a)(1), if a third-party complaint is filed no later than fourteen days after service of defendant's answer, no leave of court is required. However, if more than fourteen days have elapsed, the would-be third-party plaintiff must obtain leave of the district court. (When *Banks* was decided, Rule 14(a)(1) specified ten days.) The court in *Banks* was willing to grant leave, but leave is not always given. For example, in Hicks v. Long Island Railroad, 165 F.R.D. 377 (E.D.N.Y. 1996), the plaintiff sued his employer, the Railroad, for injuries suffered when a chair broke, inflicting a severe back injury. The accident took place in May 1994, and suit was filed soon thereafter. In February 1996, after discovery was complete and the case was about to go to trial, the defendant Railroad sought leave to serve a third-party complaint on the chair manufacturer. The Railroad's attorney said that he had waited so long because he had been "too busy." The district court denied leave, stating that "the third-party action will cause undue delay which will substantially prejudice [plaintiff] Hicks, and that [the Railroad] has not shown a meritorious excuse for its delay." *Id.* at 380.

7. **Availability of impleader depends on substantive law.** As seen in both *Banks* and *Owen Equipment*, the availability of impleader under Rule 14(a) depends on the substantive law upon which the third-party plaintiff relies. See *Banks*' analysis of California state law in the "State Law Theories" section of its opinion, and *Owen Equipment*'s analysis of Iowa law in its footnote 3.

8. **Rule 14(a) and supplemental jurisdiction.** Both *Banks* and *Owen Equipment* were decided before the passage of the supplemental jurisdiction statute in 1990. See 28 U.S.C. § 1367. The court in *Banks* held that there was "ancillary" subject matter jurisdiction over the defendants' third-party claim against the various third-party defendants. ("Ancillary" jurisdiction is a pre-§ 1367 term for one aspect of what we now call supplemental jurisdiction.) The Supreme Court in *Owen Equipment* held that there was *not* "ancillary" jurisdiction over the original plaintiff's claim against the third-party defendant, Owen Equipment. The problem in *Owen Equipment* was not that Rule 14(a) forbade plaintiff to claim directly against the third-party defendant. On the contrary, such a claim is explicitly authorized by Rule 14(a)(3). The problem was, rather, that plaintiff's claim against Owen Equipment would transform the third-party defendant into a defendant. The "complete diversity" rule of 28 U.S.C. § 1332, explained in the Court's opinion, forbade the addition of a defendant with the same citizenship as the plaintiff.

Section 1367 codifies the results in *Banks* and *Owen Equipment*. Under § 1367, in both federal question and diversity cases, there is supplemental jurisdiction over claims by a defendant/third-party plaintiff against a third-party defendant under Rule 14(a). *Banks* is a federal question case because the original plaintiffs' claim is based on the federal civil rights statute, 42 U.S.C. § 1983; but the same result obtains in a diversity case for a claim by a defendant/third-party plaintiff against a third-party defendant. By contrast, in a diversity case, there is no supplemental jurisdiction under § 1367 over a claim by the plaintiff against the impleaded third-party defendant. See § 1367(b) (not authorizing supplemental jurisdiction "over claims by plaintiffs against persons made parties under Rule 14"). In a federal question case, there is supplemental jurisdiction over a claim by the plaintiff against the third-party defendant. See § 1367(a). However, *Owen Equipment* was a diversity case, so there was (and is) no supplemental jurisdiction over plaintiff's claim against the third-party defendant.

3. INTERVENTION

HISTORICAL NOTE ON INTERVENTION

Intervention under modern rules derives from two sources. The first is the equity motion or petition *pro interesse suo*, an application by a nonparty with a superior claim or interest to obtain property or the profits of property held by a sequestrator or receiver. Thus, where sequestration had been ordered in Chancery and the property was subject to a prior claim such as that of a mortgagee or landlord entitled to the rents and profits of real property, the mortgagee or landlord was allowed to appear "for his own interest" to claim those profits in priority over the claim being enforced by sequestration. See Fawcett v. Fothergill, Dick. 19, 21 E.R. 173 (Ch. 1703) (mortgagee); Dixon v. Smith, 1 Swans. 457, 36 E.R. 464 (Ch. 1818) (landlord). See generally 2 Daniel, Pleading and Practice in Chancery 1268–73 (Perkins Am. ed. 1846).

The doctrine was adapted by the federal courts as a solution to the problem of doing tolerably complete justice in a multiparty dispute where complete diversity of citizenship was lacking. See Freeman v. Howe, 65 U.S. (24 How.) 450, 16 L.Ed. 749 (1861), relying on a *pro interesse suo* type of case, Pennock v. Coe, 64 U.S. (23 How.) 117, 16 L.Ed. 436 (1860), to establish the jurisdiction of a federal court to determine adverse claims to property seized by a federal marshal pursuant to a writ of attachment. From that point the concept was expanded by degrees until it today supports a welter of instances. As said in Note, Intervention in Federal Equity Cases, 31 Colum. L. Rev. 1312 (1931), "The practice has been justified by * * * injustice."

The second source of the modern rules is the Field Code. The New York provision under the Code was that "when, in an action for the recovery of real or personal property, a person not a party to the action, but having an interest in the subject thereof, makes application to the court to be made a party, it may order him to be brought in by the proper amendment." N.Y.Laws 1851, c. 479, § 122. This provision was narrowly construed and little used, and was later replaced by a provision paralleling Federal Rule 24. See N.Y.Temp.Comm'n, First Prelim.Rep. 46–47 (1957). The broader intervention provision was framed in terms of the intervenor's "interest" in the controversy. It was drawn from the civil law rule in Louisiana, see Horn

v. Volcano Water Co., 13 Cal. 62 (1859), Millar, Civil Procedure of the Trial Court in Historical Perspective 146–48 (1952).

Atlantis Development Corp. v. United States

United States Court of Appeals, Fifth Circuit, 1967.
379 F.2d 818.

■ JOHN R. BROWN, CIRCUIT JUDGE.

* * * The District Court declined to permit mandatory intervention as a matter of right or to allow intervention as permissive. As is so often true, a ruling made to avoid delay, complications, or expense turns out to have generated more of its own. With the main case being stayed by the District Court pending this appeal, it is pretty safe to assume that the case would long have been decided on its merits (or lack of them) had intervention of either kind been allowed. And this seems especially unfortunate since it is difficult to believe that the presence of the attempted intervenor would have added much to the litigation. All of this becomes the more ironic, if not unfortunate, since the intervenor[1] and the Government sparring over why intervention ought or ought not to have been allowed, each try to persuade us the one was bound to win, the other lose on the merits which each proceeds to argue as though the parties were before or in the court. Adding to the problem, or perhaps more accurately, aiding in the solution of it, are the mid-1966 amendments to the Federal Rules of Civil Procedure including specifically those relating to intervention. We reverse.

What the jousting[2] is all about is the ownership in, or right to control the use, development of and building on a number of coral reefs or islands comprising Pacific Reef, Ajax Reef, Long Reef, an unnamed reef and Triumph Reef which the intervenor has called the "Atlantis Group" because of the name given them by Anderson, its predecessor in interest and the supposed discoverer. Discovery in the usual sense of finding a land area, continent or island heretofore unknown could hardly fit this case. For these reefs are, and have been for years, shown on Coast and Geodetic Charts[3] and, more important, they are scarcely 4½ miles off Elliott Key and 10 miles off the Coast off the Florida Mainland. Although the depth of water washing over them at mean low water is likely one of the factual controversies having some possible significance, it seems undisputed that frequently and periodically the bodies of these reefs become very apparent especially in rough seas when the rock or the top surface of the rock becomes plainly visible in the troughs of the seas.

[During the early 1960s, Atlantis tried to get permission from the State of Florida or from the United States to build on the reefs. Both governments responded that the reefs lay outside their territorial jurisdiction.] Subsequently, Atlantis spent approximately $50,000 for surveys and the construction of four prefabricated buildings, three of

---

[1] Atlantis Development Corporation, Ltd., a Bahamian corporation, will be referred to interchangeably as either Atlantis or Intervenor.

[2] The "facts" are as yet unknown since no trial of either the main or the intervention case has been had. * * *

[3] They first appeared on U.S. Coast & Geodetic Survey Chart No. 166, issued in 1878. More recently, see Coast & Geodetic Survey Chart No. 1249, as corrected through June 1, 1963.

which were destroyed by a hurricane in September 1963. Thereafter upon learning that the United States Corps of Engineers was asserting that permission was needed to erect certain structures on two of the reefs, Triumph and Long Reef, Atlantis commenced its long, but unrewarding, efforts either to convince the Corps of Engineers, the United States Attorney General, or both, that the island reefs were beyond the jurisdiction of United States control or to initiate litigation which would allow a judicial, peaceful resolution. The Engineers ultimately reaffirmed the earlier decision to require permits. In December 1964 on learning that the defendants in the main case had formally sought a permit from the Engineers, Atlantis notified the Government of its claim to ownership of the islands and the threatened unauthorized actions by the defendants. This precipitated further communications with the Department of Justice with Atlantis importuning, apparently successfully, the Government to initiate the present action.

It was against this background that the litigation commenced. The suit is brought by the United States against the main defendants.[5] The complaint was in two counts seeking injunctive relief. In the first the Government asserted that Triumph and Long Reefs are part of the bed of the Atlantic Ocean included in the Outer Continental Shelf subject to the jurisdiction, control and power of disposition of the United States. The action of the defendants (note 5, supra) in the erection of caissons on the reefs, the dredging of material from the sea bed, and the depositing of the dredged material within the caissons without authorization was charged as constituting a trespass on government property. In the second count the Government alleged that the defendants were engaged in the erection of an artificial island or fixed structure on the Outer Continental Shelf in the vicinity of the reefs without a permit from the Secretary of the Army in violation of the Outer Continental Shelf Lands Act, 43 U.S.C.A. § 1333(f) and 33 U.S.C.A. § 403. Denying that the complaint stated a claim, F.R.Civ.P. 12(b), the defendants besides interposing general denial asserted that the Secretary of the Army lacks jurisdiction to require a permit for construction on the Outer Continental Shelf and that the District Court lacks jurisdiction since the reefs and the defendants' actions thereon are outside the territorial limits of the United States. As thus framed, the issues in the main case are whether (1) the District Court has jurisdiction of subject matter, (2) the defendants are engaged in acts which constitute a trespass against government property, and (3) the defendants' construction activities without a permit violate 43 U.S.C.A. § 1333(f) and 33 U.S.C.A. § 403.

Atlantis seeking intervention by proposed answer and cross-claim against the defendants admitted the jurisdiction of the District Court. It asserted that the United States has no territorial jurisdiction, dominion or ownership in or over the reefs and cannot therefore maintain the action for an injunction, and that conversely Atlantis has title to the property by discovery and occupation. In the cross-claim, Atlantis charged the defendants as trespassers against it. Appropriate relief was sought by the prayer.[7]

---

[5] Acme General Contractors, Inc., and J.H. Coppedge Company, each Florida corporations, and Louis M. Ray, a resident of Dade County, Florida.

[7] It sought judgment adjudicating and determining (a) the rights of the parties to this action and those of the intervenor; (b) that the Government has no territorial jurisdiction over

The District Court without opinion declared in the order that intervenor "does not have such an interest in this cause as will justify its intervention, either as a matter of right or permissively." Leave was granted to appear amicus curiae.

We think without a doubt that under former F.R.Civ.P. 24(a), intervention as a matter of right was not compelled under (a)(2).[8] The situation did not present one in which the intervenor "is or may be bound" by a decree rendered in his absence in the sense articulated most recently in *Sam Fox*[9] in terms of res judicata. Although not quite so clear, we also think it did not measure up to the notions loosely reflected in a case-by-case development under which, although res judicata was technically lacking, the decree is considered "binding" since in a very practical sense it would have an immediate operative effect upon the intervenor. In none of these cases was it suggested that if the only effect of the decree in intervenor's absence would be to raise the hurdle of stare decisis, this would amount to the absentee being bound as a practical matter.

This brings us squarely to the effect of the 1966 Amendments and the new F.R.Civ.P. 24(a).[12]

* * *

In assaying the new Rule, several things stand out. The first, as the Government acknowledges, is that this amounts to a legislative repeal of the rigid *Sam Fox* (note 9, supra)[15] res judicata rule. But more important,

---

or ownership in Triumph Reef; (c) that the Secretary of Defense has no power to require application and permit for construction on the reefs; (d) that Atlantis has the paramount right, title and interest in the reefs; and that (e) the defendants have none.

8   Fed.R.Civ.P. 24. Intervention

(a)   Intervention of Right. Upon timely application anyone shall be permitted to intervene in an action: (1) when a statute of the United States confers an unconditional right to intervene; or (2) when the representation of the applicant's interest by existing parties is or may be inadequate and the applicant is or may be bound by a judgment in the action; or (3) when the applicant is so situated as to be adversely affected by a distribution or other disposition of property which is in the custody or subject to the control or disposition of the court or an officer thereof.

"(b) Permissive Intervention. Upon timely application anyone may be permitted to intervene in an action: (1) when a statute of the United States confers a conditional right to intervene; or (2) when an applicant's claim or defense and the main action have a question of law or fact in common. . . . In exercising its discretion the court shall consider whether the intervention will unduly delay or prejudice the adjudication of the rights of the original parties."

9   Sam Fox Publishing Co. v. United States, 1961, 366 U.S. 683, 81 S.Ct. 1309, 6 L.Ed.2d 604.

12   "(a) *Intervention of Right*. Upon timely application anyone shall be permitted to intervene in any action: (1) when a statute of the United States confers an unconditional right to intervene; or (2) when the applicant claims an *interest relating to the property or transaction which is the subject of the action* and he is so situated that the *disposition of the action may as a practical matter impair or impede his ability to protect that interest*, unless the applicant's interest is adequately represented by existing parties." [Emphasis added.]

Rule 24(a), F.R.Civ.P., as amended July 1, 1966 (U.S.Code Cong. & Adm.News, 89th Cong., 2d Sess., No. 3, Apr. 5, 1966, 799). See also 39 F.R.D. 69, 109–111; Cohn, The New Federal Rules of Civil Procedure, Essays reprinted from Geo.L.J. 7, 32–35 (1966).

15   39 F.R.D. 69, 110: Advisory Committee Notes.

"Original Rule 24(a)(2), however, made it a condition of intervention that 'the applicant is or may be bound by a judgment in the action,' and this created difficulties with intervention in class actions. . . . See Sam Fox Publishing Co. v. United States, 366 U.S. 683 [81 S.Ct. 1309, 6 L.Ed.2d 604] (1961). . . . This reasoning might be linguistically justified by original Rule 24(a)(2); but it could lead to poor results. Compare the discussion in International M. & I. Corp. v. Von

the revision was a coordinated one to tie more closely together the related situations of joinder, F.R.Civ.P. 19,[16] and class actions, F.R.Civ.P. 23.

As the Advisory Committee's notes reflect, there are competing interests at work in this area. On the one hand, there is the private suitor's interests in having his own lawsuit subject to no one else's direction or meddling. On the other hand, however, is the great public interest, especially in these explosive days of ever-increasing dockets, of having a disposition at a single time of as much of the controversy to as many of the parties as is fairly possible consistent with due process.[18]

In these three Rules the Advisory Committee, unsatisfied with the former Rules which too frequently defined application in terms of rigid legal concepts such as joint, common ownership, res judicata, or the like, as well as court efforts in applying them, deliberately set out on a more pragmatic course. For the purposes of our problem, this course is reflected in the almost, if not quite, uniform language concerning a party

[handwritten margin note: Suitor's interest / Interest of the / Public in reduced / amounts of / Litigation]

Clemm, 301 F.2d 857 (2d Cir.1962); Atlantic Refining Co. v. Standard Oil Co., 113 U.S.App.D.C. 20, 304 F.2d 387 (D.C.Cir.1962). [See note 10, supra]. . . .

"The amendment provides that an applicant is entitled to intervene in an action when his position is comparable to that of a person under Rule 19(a)(2)(i), as amended, unless his interest is already adequately represented in the action by existing parties. The Rule 19(a)(2)(i) criterion imports practical considerations, and the deletion of the 'bound' language similarly frees the rule from undue preoccupation with strict consideration of *res judicata*."

See also Stewart, J., dissenting, *El Paso II*, supra, note 14: "The purpose of the revision was to remedy certain logical shortcomings in the construction of the former 24(a)(2), see Sam Fox Publishing Co. v. United States, ..." 386 U.S. at 153, 87 S.Ct. at 946, 17 L.Ed.2d at 829.

[16]   F.R.Civ.P. 19 was completely rewritten:

"Joinder of Persons Needed for Just Adjudication

"(a) Persons to be Joined if Feasible. A person who is subject to service of process and whose joinder will not deprive the court of jurisdiction over the subject matter of the action shall be joined as a party in the action if (1) in his absence complete relief cannot be accorded among those already parties, or (2) *he claims an interest relating to the subject of the action* and is so situated that the *disposition of the action in his absence may (i) as a practical matter impair or impede his ability to protect that interest* or (ii) leave any of the persons already parties subject to a substantial risk of incurring double, multiple, or otherwise inconsistent obligations by reason of his claimed interest. If he has not been so joined, the court shall order that he be made a party. If he should join as a plaintiff but refuses to do so, he may be made a defendant, or, in a proper case, an involuntary plaintiff. If the joined party objects to venue and his joinder would render the venue of the action improper, he shall be dismissed from the action.

"(b) Determination by Court Whenever Joinder not Feasible. * * *

"(c) Pleading Reasons for Nonjoinder. A pleading asserting a claim for relief shall state the names, if known to the pleader, of any persons as described in subdivision (a)(1)–(2) hereof who are not joined, and the reasons why they are not joined.

"(d) Exception of Class Actions. This rule is subject to the provisions of Rule 23." [Emphasis added.]

39 F.R.D. 69, 88–89. See discussion by Cohn, supra, note 12, at pp. 7–14.

[18]   See, e.g., notes to F.R.Civ.P. 19. "New *subdivision (a)* defines the persons whose joinder in the action is desirable. . . . The interests that are being furthered here are not only those of the parties, but also that of the public in avoiding repeated lawsuits on the same essential subject matter. . . ." 39 F.R.D. 69, 91.

This Court has recently voiced the same objectives:

"The Rules allow joinder in such a case as the present; indeed in order to prevent costly, slow, multiplicitous litigation (with the danger of inconsistent results), they demand it. The Supreme Court has recently held that 'Under the Rules, the impulse is toward entertaining the broadest possible scope of action consistent with fairness to the parties; joinder of claims, parties and remedies is strongly encouraged.' United Mine Workers of America v. Gibbs, 1966, 383 U.S. 715, 724, 86 S.Ct. 1130, 1138, 16 L.Ed.2d 218, 227."

Har-Pen Truck Lines, Inc. v. Mills, 5 Cir., 1967, 378 F.2d 705, 709.

who claims an interest relating to the subject of the action and is so situated that the disposition of the action may as a practical matter impair or impede his ability to protect that interest (see the italicized portions of Rules 19(a)(2)(i), [and] 24 * * * , notes 16 [and] 12 * * * , supra.

Although this is question-begging and is therefore not a real test, this approach shows that the question of whether an intervention as a matter of right exists often turns on the unstated question of whether joinder of the intervenor was called for under new Rule 19. Were this the controlling inquiry, we find ample basis here to answer it in the affirmative. Atlantis—having formally informed the Government in detail of its claim of ownership to the very reefs in suit, that the defendants were trespassing against it, and having successfully urged the Government to institute suit against the defendants—seems clearly to occupy the position of a party who ought to have been joined as a defendant under new Rule 19(a)(2)(i) [see the italicized portion of note 16, supra].

* * *

When approached in this light, we think that both from the terms of new Rule 24(a) and its adoption of 19(a)(2)(i) intervention of right is called for here. Of course F.R.Civ.P. 24(a)(2) requires both the existence of an interest which may be impaired as a practical matter and an absence of adequate representation of the intervenor's interest by existing parties. There can be no difficulty here about the lack of representation. On the basis of the pleadings, see Kozak v. Wells, 8 Cir., 1960, 278 F.2d 104, 109, 84 A.L.R.2d 1400; cf. Stadin v. Union Electric Co., 8 Cir., 1962, 309 F.2d 912, 917, cert. denied, 1963, 373 U.S. 915, 83 S.Ct. 1298, 10 L.Ed.2d 415, Atlantis is without a friend in this litigation. The Government turns on the defendants and takes the same view both administratively and in its brief here toward Atlantis. The defendants, on the other hand, are claiming ownership in and the right to develop the very islands claimed by Atlantis.

Nor can there be any doubt that Atlantis "claims an interest relating to the property or transaction which is the subject of the action." The object of the suit is to assert the sovereign's exclusive dominion and control over two out of a group of islands publicly claimed by Atlantis. This identity with the very property at stake in the main case and with the particular transaction therein involved (the right to build structures with or without permission of the Corps of Engineers) is of exceptional importance. For 24(a)(2) is in the conjunctive requiring both an interest relating to the property or transaction and the practical harm if the party is absent. This sharply reduces the area in which stare decisis may, as we later discuss, supply the element of practical harm.

This brings us then to the question whether these papers reflect that in the absence of Atlantis, a disposition of the main suit may as a practical matter impair or impede its ability to protect that interest—its claim to ownership and the right to control, use and develop without hindrance from the Government, the Department of Defense or other agencies. Certain things are clear. Foremost, of course, is the plain proposition that the judgment itself as between Government and defendants cannot have any direct, immediate effect upon the rights of Atlantis, not a party to it.

But in a very real and practical sense is not the trial of this lawsuit the trial of Atlantis' suit as well? Quite apart from the contest of Atlantis' claim of sovereignty vis-a-vis the Government resulting from its "discovery" and occupation of the reefs, there are at least two basic substantial legal questions directly at issue, but not yet resolved in any Court at any time between the Government and the defendants which are inescapably present in the claim of Atlantis against the Government. One is whether these coral reefs built up by accretion of marine biology are "submerged lands" under the Outer Continental Shelf Lands Act, 43 U.S.C.A. § 1331 et seq. The second basic question is whether, assuming both from the standpoint of geographical location and their nature they constitute "lands," does the sovereignty of the United States extend to them with respect to any purposes not included in or done for the protection of the "exploring for, developing, removing, and transporting . . ." natural resources therefrom, 43 U.S.C.A. § 1333(a)(1). Another, closely related, is whether the authority of the Secretary of the Army to prevent obstruction of navigation extended by § 1333(f) to "artificial islands and fixed structures," includes structures other than those "erected thereon for the purpose of exploring for, developing, removing, and transporting" mineral resources therefrom (§ 1333(a)(1) * * *).

The Government would avoid all of these problems by urging us to rule as a matter of law on the face of the moving papers that the intervenors could not possibly win on the trial of the intervention and consequently intervention should be denied. In support it asserts that the claim that the reefs are beyond the jurisdiction of the United States is self-defeating, and under the plain meaning of the Outer Continental Shelf Lands Act and the facts revealed from the Coast and Geodetic Chart[25] of which we must take judicial knowledge as proof of all facts shown.

The first is at least contingently answered by § 1333(b) which invests jurisdiction in the United States District Court of the nearest adjacent state. As to the others, it is, of course, conceivable that there will be some instances in which the total lack of merit is so evident from the face of the moving papers that denial of the right of intervention rests upon a complete lack of a substantial claim. But it hardly comports with good administration, if not due process, to determine the merits of a claim asserted in a pleading seeking an adjudication through an adversary hearing by denying access to the court at all. This seems especially important when dealing with interests in the Outer Continental Shelf in view of the legislative history which reflected domestically the purpose of asserting a limited "horizontal jurisdiction" extending only to the seabed and subsoil, the limited nature of which was formally recognized by the International Convention of the Continental Shelf. See United States v. States of Louisiana, Texas, Mississippi, Alabama and Florida, 1960, 363 U.S. 1, 30–31, 80 S.Ct. 961, 979, 4 L.Ed.2d 1025, 1046.

If in its claim against the defendants in the main suit these questions are answered favorably to the Government's position, the claim of Atlantis for all practical purposes is worthless. That statement assumes, of course, that such holding is either approved or made by this Court after

---

[25] The Geodetic Chart shows the 100-fathom (600-foot) line—the seaward limit to the Outer Continental Shelf—is about three miles seaward of these reefs.

an appeal to it and thereafter it is either affirmed, or not taken for review, on certiorari. It also assumes that in the subsequent separate trial of the claim of Atlantis against the Government the prior decision would be followed as a matter of stare decisis. Do these assumptions have a realistic basis? Anyone familiar with the history of the Fifth Circuit could have but a single answer to that query. This Court, unlike some of our sister Circuit Courts who occasionally follow a different course, has long tried earnestly to follow the practice in which a decision announced by one panel of the Court is followed by all others until such time as it is reversed, either outright or by intervening decisions of the Supreme Court, or by the Court itself en banc. That means that if the defendants in the main action do not prevail upon these basic contentions which are part and parcel of the claim of Atlantis, the only way by which Atlantis can win is to secure a rehearing en banc with a successful overruling of the prior decision or, failing in either one or both of those efforts, a reversal of the earlier decision by the Supreme Court on certiorari. With the necessarily limited number of en banc hearings in this Circuit and with the small percentage of cases meriting certiorari, it is an understatement to characterize these prospects as formidable.

That is but a way of saying in a very graphic way that the failure to allow Atlantis an opportunity to advance its own theories both of law and fact in the trial (and appeal) of the pending case will if the disposition is favorable to the Government "as a practical matter impair or impede [its] ability to protect [its] interest." That is, to be sure, a determination by us that in the new language of 24(a)(2) stare decisis may now—unlike the former days under 24(a)(2)—supply that practical disadvantage which warrants intervention of right. It bears repeating, however, that this holding does not presage one requiring intervention of right in every conceivable circumstance where under the operation of the Circuit's stare decisis practice, the formidable nature of an en banc rehearing or the successful grant of a writ of certiorari, an earlier decision might afford a substantial obstacle. We are dealing here with a conjunction of a claim to and interest in the very property and the very transaction which is the subject of the main action. When those coincide, the Court before whom the potential parties in the second suit must come must itself take the intellectually straight forward, realistic view that the first decision will in all likelihood be the second and the third and the last one. Even the possibility that the decision might be overturned by en banc ruling or reversal on certiorari does not overcome its practical effect, not just as an obstacle, but as the forerunner of the actual outcome. In the face of that, it is "as a practical matter" a certainty that an absent party seeking a right to enter the fray to advance his interest against all or some of the parties as to matters upon which he is for all practical purposes shortly to be foreclosed knows the disposition in his absence will "impair or impede his ability to protect that interest, . . ." F.R.Civ.P. 24(a)(2).

Reversed.

FURTHER NOTE ON INTERVENTION

1. **Atlantis' dilemma.** Atlantis had been stymied in its effort to litigate with the federal government the question of domain over the offshore reefs. The government refused to sue Atlantis, and Atlantis apparently was unwilling to provoke a suit by making a major development investment in

616 JOINDER AND CLASS ACTIONS CHAPTER 5

the face of uncertainty as to its right to do so. Because of the doctrine of sovereign immunity, Atlantis could not sue the government without its consent. (Today, Atlantis presumably could sue the Government by virtue of 28 U.S.C. § 2409a, enacted in 1972, which limits the Government's immunity in suits over title to land.) A competitor of Atlantis finally stimulated the United States to bring suit against it; once that suit had been brought, Atlantis sought to intervene.

2. **Interest sufficient to support intervention under Rule 24(a)(2).** As described in the court's opinion, the 1966 amendment to Rule 24(a)(2) greatly expanded the nature of the interest that justifies intervention as of right. After 1966, it was clear that an enforceable legal right was no longer necessary. Instead, all that is required is an "interest relating to the property or transaction" at issue, such that the disposition of the suit "may as a practical matter impair or impede the * * * ability [of the would-be intervenor] to protect that interest." How far does Rule 24(a) go? In Cascade Natural Gas Corp. v. El Paso Natural Gas Co., 386 U.S. 129, 84 S.Ct. 1044, 12 L.Ed.2d. 12 (1967), the underlying antitrust dispute was over divestiture by El Paso Natural Gas of a pipeline company serving the Pacific Northwest. Depending on the structure of the new company created by the divestiture, Cascade Natural Gas would have access to greater or lesser amounts of natural gas. Even though Cascade did not have a legal right to a particular amount of natural gas, it was permitted to intervene in the divestiture proceeding under the new version of Rule 24(a) in order to protect its interest in avoiding a "grossly unfair division" of the gas reserves. Id. at 133.

3. **The California same-sex marriage case.** In the fall of 2008, California voters passed Proposition 8, a voter-initiated proposition defining marriage under California law as exclusively a union between a man and a woman. Two same-sex couples brought suit in federal district court challenging Proposition 8 as unconstitutional, naming the Governor and other state officials as defendants. None of the named defendants was willing to defend the constitutionality of the proposition. The official proponents of Proposition 8 were voters who had put the proposition on the ballot by following specified procedures under state law. As official proponents of the proposition, they were authorized under state law to defend the proposition's constitutionality. They intervened as of right under Rule 24(a) as defendants in the district court. Perry v. Schwarzenegger, 704 F.Supp.2d 921, 928 (N.D. Cal. 2010). The district court held Proposition 8 unconstitutional, and the state officials named as defendants refused to appeal the judgment. When the state officials refused to appeal, the official proponents did so. The Ninth Circuit certified to the California Supreme Court the question whether under state law the official proponents had the authority to appeal. Perry v. Schwarzenegger, 628 F.3d 1191 (9th Cir. 2011). The California Supreme Court responded that in this circumstance the official proponents were authorized by state law to appeal the decision of the district court as representatives of the state. Perry v. Brown, 52 Cal.4th 1116, 134 Cal.Rptr.3d 499, 265 P.3d 1002 (2011). The Ninth Circuit then heard the appeal and affirmed on the merits the district court's decision holding Proposition 8 unconstitutional. Perry v. Brown, 671 F.3d 1052 (9th Cir. 2012). On certiorari, the Supreme Court held that the official proponents did not have Article III standing to bring the appeal, despite the fact that they had been permitted to intervene as of right in the district court under Rule 24(a), and despite the fact that the California Supreme Court had held that they had the authority under state law to bring the appeal. Hollingsworth v. Perry, 570 U.S. ___, 133 S.Ct. 2652, 186 L.Ed.2d 768 (2013). In the words of the Court, the official proponents did not have a "concrete and particularized injury," and therefore any dispute they had with the plaintiffs who challenged Proposition 8 was not a "case or controversy" within the judicial power of the federal courts to decide.

It is possible, perhaps even likely, that we should not take seriously the Supreme Court's analysis and standing decision in *Hollingsworth*. The Court was clearly anxious to avoid or at least delay deciding the constitutional question presented, and the standing decision was a way to accomplish that goal. Using jurisdictional grounds to duck cases is a time-honored way for the Supreme Court to avoid politically awkward decisions. See A. Bickel, The Least Dangerous Branch: The Supreme Court at the Bar of Politics (1962). But if we do take the analysis of *Hollingsworth* seriously, are we forced to re-evaluate the liberality with which "interest" in Rule 24(a) has been defined? Can the "case or controversy" analysis of *Hollingsworth* be distinguished on the ground that the official proponents were the only parties seeking to appeal? That is, would the appeal, and the presence in the suit of the official proponents, have been treated differently if one of the named state defendants had appealed and the official proponents had sought to intervene in the existing appeal?

4.　Permissive intervention under Rule 24(b). The requirements for permissive intervention under Rule 24(b) are less demanding than for intervention as of right under Rule 24(a). Rule 24(b)(1)(B) requires only that a would-be intervenor make a "timely motion" and have "a claim or defense that shares with the main action a common question of law or fact." Rule 24(b) was a more important basis for invention before the amendment to Rule 24(a) in 1966 which expanded the bases for intervention as of right.

5.　"As a practical matter impair or impede." Observe that the "practical" impairment of Atlantis' interest was based on what was going to be the precedential, or stare decisis, effect of the court's decision. Interpreted broadly, the court's holding that Atlantis had a right to intervene under Rule 24(a) would mean that anyone concerned about the possible precedential effect of a case would qualify under Rule 24(a). The court tries to narrow its holding by suggesting that it applies only in extraordinary circumstances. Compare Alaska Excursion Cruises, Inc. v. United States, 603 F.Supp. 541 (D.D.C. 1984). See also Comment, Intervention, Joinder, and Issue Preclusion, 6 Wm. Mitchell L. Rev. 361 (1980).

6.　Timeliness. The opportunity to intervene may be lost if the would-be intervenor unduly delays in moving to intervene. See United Airlines, Inc. v. McDonald, 432 U.S. 385, 97 S.Ct. 2464, 53 L.Ed.2d 423 (1977); cf. Walker v. Jim Dandy Co., 747 F.2d 1360 (11th Cir. 1984); Note, The Timeliness Threat to Intervention of Right, 89 Yale L.J. 586 (1980); Note, Timeliness of a Motion to Intervene, 1984 B.Y.U. L. Rev. 219 (1984). Restatement (Second) of Judgments § 62 states that under certain conditions, "A person not a party to an action who has a claim arising out of the transaction that was the subject of the action, and who knew about the action prior to the rendition of judgment therein, may not thereafter maintain an action on his claim * * *."

7.　Interlocutory appeals. Denial by the district court of a motion to intervene as of right under Rule 24(a) is immediately appealable. See Rhode Island v. EPA, 378 F.3d 19, 26 (1st Cir. 2004). By contrast, denial of a motion to intervene permissively under Rule 24(b) is not immediately appealable. See United States v. Jefferson County, 720 F.2d 1511 (11th Cir. 1983).

Stuart v. Huff

United States Court of Appeals for the Fourth Circuit, 2013.
706 F.3d 345.

■ WILKINSON, CIRCUIT JUDGE.

In late 2011, plaintiffs challenged the constitutionality of the North Carolina "Woman's Right to Know Act," ("the Act"), a statute that requires certain informed consent procedures prior to the performance of an abortion, N.C. Gen.Stat. §§ 90–21.80 to –21.92. Although the North Carolina Attorney General actively sought to defend the statute, appellants—a group of pro-life medical professionals, women who have previously undergone abortions, and pregnancy counseling centers—filed a motion to intervene as defendants in the suit. The district court denied their motion. Because the court did not abuse its discretion in doing so, we affirm.

I.

The North Carolina General Assembly enacted the Woman's Right to Know Act in July 2011. The Act requires that a "physician who is to perform [an] abortion, or [a] qualified technician" must provide the pregnant woman with a real-time ultrasound display of the fetus and a "simultaneous explanation of what the display is depicting." * * * In addition to these real-time display and explanation requirements, the Act contains certain other informed consent provisions and authorizes civil remedies against persons who violate the law. * * *

Plaintiffs are a group of physicians and medical centers that provide abortion services. On September 29, 2011, they filed a complaint in the United States District Court for the Middle District of North Carolina seeking a declaration that the Act violates the First and Fourteenth Amendment rights of physicians and their patients, along with an injunction preventing enforcement of the Act. Plaintiffs also filed a motion for a temporary restraining order and preliminary injunction. The merits of plaintiffs' claims are not at issue in this appeal * * * .

On October 12, the defendants in the underlying suit—a number of state officials represented by the North Carolina Attorney General—filed their opposition to the motion for a preliminary injunction. The district court held a hearing on the motion five days later, which lasted nearly three hours. During that hearing, the Attorney General (through a special deputy) pressed numerous arguments for upholding the Act under *Planned Parenthood of Southeastern Pennsylvania v. Casey*, 505 U.S. 833, 112 S.Ct. 2791, 120 L.Ed.2d 674 (1992), which upheld an abortion informed consent statute against a similar challenge. In particular, the Attorney General argued that the Act should be upheld because *Casey* recognizes the state's "profound interest in potential life"; its "permissible purpose" of informing women considering an abortion of the procedure's "potential consequences" for their "future psychological and emotional health"; and its ability to require the communication of "truthful and non-misleading" information to patients. The Attorney

General did not introduce factual evidence in support of the Act, choosing instead to rely on the above legal arguments from *Casey*.

The district court ruled on the motion on October 25, issuing a preliminary injunction against the Act's real-time display and explanation requirements, but denying the motion with respect to the remainder of the Act. *Stuart v. Huff*, 834 F.Supp.2d 424, 437 (M.D.N.C.2011). Those unaffected portions of the Act went into effect the next day. Deciding to litigate the case to final judgment rather than appeal the preliminary injunction, the Attorney General filed an answer and moved to dismiss the complaint two weeks later.

Appellants in this matter are a group of pro-life doctors, former abortion patients, and pregnancy counseling centers. On November 8, they filed a motion to intervene as defendants in the case, the subject of this appeal. Appellants sought to intervene as a matter of right pursuant to Federal Rule of Civil Procedure 24(a), and, alternatively, as a permissive matter pursuant to Rule 24(b).

The district court denied the motion on both grounds. * * *
* * *

The would-be intervenors now appeal the district court's decision.

II.

The Federal Rules of Civil Procedure provide two avenues for intervention relevant to this appeal. Under Rule 24(a)(2), a district court must permit intervention as a matter of right if the movant can demonstrate "(1) an interest in the subject matter of the action; (2) that the protection of this interest would be impaired because of the action; and (3) that the applicant's interest is not adequately represented by existing parties to the litigation." *Teague v. Bakker*, 931 F.2d 259, 260–61 (4th Cir.1991). If intervention of right is not warranted, a court may still allow an applicant to intervene permissively under Rule 24(b), although in that case the court must consider "whether the intervention will unduly delay or prejudice the adjudication of the original parties' rights." Fed.R.Civ.P. 24(b)(3).

It is well settled that district court rulings on both types of intervention motions are to be reviewed for abuse of discretion. *In re Sierra Club*, 945 F.2d 776, 779 (4th Cir.1991). Deferential appellate review is proper here for many reasons, the first of which is that Rule 24's requirements are based on dynamics that develop in the trial court and that the court is accordingly in the best position to evaluate. * * * [I]n the intervention context, it is the trial judge who is best able to determine whether, for example, a proposed intervenor's interests are being adequately represented by an existing party pursuant to Rule 24(a)(2). Indeed, the trial court's superior vantage point was evident in this very case when the judge noted the Attorney General's "detailed, thorough, and substantial brief" and "zealous" oral argument in opposition to the preliminary injunction.

Appellate review is necessarily limited in this setting for another reason: "Questions of trial management are quintessentially the province of the district courts." *United States v. Smith*, 452 F.3d 323, 332 (4th Cir.2006); *see also, e.g., Arnold v. E. Air Lines, Inc.*, 681 F.2d 186, 194 (4th Cir.1982) (noting that "many details of trial management" are "necessarily committed to broad trial court discretion"). It is incontrovertible that motions to intervene can have profound implications for district courts' trial management functions. Additional parties can complicate routine scheduling orders, prolong and increase the burdens of discovery and motion practice, thwart settlement, and delay trial. This is particularly so where, as here, the proposed intervenors are themselves differently situated entities. The district court thus rightly expressed its concern that "[a]dding three groups of intervenors would necessarily complicate the discovery process and consume additional resources of the court and the parties."

With these boundaries of our reviewing role in mind, we examine the appellants' arguments for intervention.

III.

The district court denied the appellants' motion to intervene as of right based on its finding that the Attorney General was adequately representing their interests. The court's conclusion rested on two presumptions. First, the court reasoned that where a proposed intervenor's ultimate objective is the same as that of an existing party, the party's representation is presumptively adequate, rebuttable only by a showing of adverse interests, collusion, or nonfeasance. Second, the court explained that where the party who shares the intervenor's objective is a government agency, the intervenor has the burden of making a strong showing of inadequacy.

Appellants contend that the court's ruling was an abuse of discretion in two regards. To begin, although they concede that the court was correct to apply the first presumption, they dispute the second. That is, appellants claim that the district court was wrong to demand a strong showing of inadequacy due to the fact that the Attorney General is a government official. * * * Appellants then argue that they satisfied this minimal burden by demonstrating adversity of interest with and, alternatively, nonfeasance by the Attorney General. We consider these arguments in turn.

A.

We begin with appellants' contention that, regardless of the fact that the existing defendants are represented by a government agency, the burden of "showing inadequacy of representation" ought to be "minimal," in contrast to the "very strong showing" required by the district court.

We disagree. Although our circuit has yet to address the question of whether a more exacting showing of inadequacy should be required where the proposed intervenor shares the same objective as a government party, every circuit to rule on the matter has held in the affirmative. *See, e.g., Arakaki v. Cayetano*, 324 F.3d 1078, 1086 (9th Cir.2003); *Daggett v. Comm'n on Governmental Ethics & Election Practices*, 172 F.3d 104, 111 (1st Cir.1999); *Wade v. Goldschmidt*, 673 F.2d 182, 186 n. 7 (7th Cir.1982). We find this position persuasive for several reasons.

To start, it is among the most elementary functions of a government to serve in a representative capacity on behalf of its people. In matters of public law litigation that may affect great numbers of citizens, it is the government's basic duty to represent the public interest. And the need for government to exercise its representative function is perhaps at its apex where, as here, a duly enacted statute faces a constitutional challenge. In such cases, the government is simply the most natural party to shoulder the responsibility of defending the fruits of the democratic process. As the Supreme Court stated in the related standing context in *Diamond v. Charles*, "[b]ecause the State alone is entitled to create a legal code, only the State has the kind of direct stake" needed to defend "the standards embodied in that code" against a constitutional attack. 476 U.S. 54, 65, 106 S.Ct. 1697, 90 L.Ed.2d 48 (1986) (internal quotation marks omitted).

Moreover, when a statute comes under attack, it is difficult to conceive of an entity better situated to defend it than the government. It is after all the government that, through the democratic process, gains familiarity with the matters of public concern that lead to the statute's passage in the first place. Thus in this case, while defending the Act in district court, the Attorney General vigorously pressed the state's important interests in "protecting the woman's future psychological health," "promoting the potential life of the unborn child," and ensuring that each woman has the "opportunity to fully appreciate the consequences [of an abortion] to herself and to her unborn child."

Finally, to permit private persons and entities to intervene in the government's defense of a statute upon only a nominal showing would greatly complicate the government's job. Faced with the prospect of a deluge of potential intervenors, the government could be compelled to modify its litigation strategy to suit the self-interested motivations of those who seek party status, or else suffer the consequences of a geometrically protracted, costly, and complicated litigation. In short, "the business of the government could hardly be conducted if, in matters of litigation, individual citizens could usually or always intervene and assert individual points of view." 6 *Moore's Federal Practice* § 24.03[4][a][iv][A] (3d ed.2011).

Appellants respond that the requirement of a "very strong showing" of inadequacy by a government party is inconsistent with Supreme Court precedent and the law of this circuit. Specifically, they point to the Supreme Court's decision in *Trbovich v. United Mine Workers*, which held that Rule 24(a) is "satisfied if the applicant shows that representation of his interest may be inadequate; and the burden of making that showing should be treated as minimal." 404 U.S. 528, 538 n. 10, 92 S.Ct. 630, 30 L.Ed.2d 686 (1972) (emphasis added) (internal quotation marks omitted); *see also United Guar. Residential Ins. Co. of Iowa v. Phila. Sav. Fund Soc'y*, 819 F.2d 473, 475 (4th Cir.1987).

Appellants' argument misses the mark. For in *Trbovich* and *United Guaranty* the proposed intervenors did not even share the same ultimate objective as an existing party. Thus, in *Trbovich*, the Supreme Court expressly noted that the Secretary of Labor was compelled by statute to "serve two distinct interests," such that the Secretary's ultimate objective was not the same as that of the proposed intervenor to begin with. 404 U.S. at 538, 92 S.Ct. 630. Likewise, in *United Guaranty*, we observed that the existing defendant's objectives were apparently 'at cross purposes" with the proposed intervenor. 819 F.2d at 476.

Contrary to the appellants' claim, then, *Trbovich* and *United Guaranty* stand for the conventional proposition that where the existing party and proposed intervenor seek divergent objectives, there is less reason to presume that the party (government agency or otherwise) will adequately represent the intervenor. In such circumstances, it is perfectly sensible to require a more modest showing of inadequacy before granting intervention of right since an existing party is not likely to adequately represent the interests of another with whom it is at cross purposes in the first instance.

* * *

B.

Appellants next argue that they have sufficiently demonstrated adversity of interest with and, alternatively, nonfeasance by the Attorney General, thereby rebutting the presumption of adequacy that arises because they share the same objective. * * *

First as to adversity of interest. Appellants begin by pointing to their desire to ensure that "a pregnant woman understands the potential risk and harms to the child so that she can make the decision for the child." * * * Appellants assert that, as women who have experienced the effects of the procedure first-hand and doctors and medical centers who provide care to pregnant women, their interests are "separate and distinct from the State's." Far from showing adversity with the Attorney General, however, this argument actually underscores how the appellants and Attorney General are motivated by the same underlying concerns. Indeed, the Attorney General pressed this exact argument during the preliminary injunction hearing, noting that the state possessed an "interest in ensuring that the woman not undergo an abortion without at least having an opportunity to fully appreciate the consequences . . . to her unborn child."

* * *

At bottom, appellants' argument is that as the "class of beneficiaries protected by the Act," their interests in defending the Act are "stronger" and more "specific" than the state's general interest. But stronger, more specific interests do not adverse interests make-and they surely cannot be enough to establish inadequacy of representation since would-be intervenors will nearly always have intense desires that are more particular than the state's (or else why seek party status at all). Allowing such interests to rebut the presumption of adequacy would simply open the door to a complicating host of intervening parties with hardly a corresponding benefit.

In the absence of any identifiable adverse interests, appellants assert that the district court should have inferred adversity because, in defending the Act, the Attorney General made certain strategic decisions with which appellants disagree. In particular, appellants contend that the Attorney General relied on legal arguments at the preliminary injunction stage and chose to litigate the case to final judgment, whereas they would have presented factual evidence and immediately appealed the preliminary injunction. Appellants suggest that these "divergent approaches to the conduct of the litigation" warrant a finding of adversity because, in their view, the governing test from *United Guaranty* is whether the existing party and the intervenor's interests "may 'always dictate precisely the same approach to the conduct of the litigation.' " 819 F.2d at 475 (quoting *Trbovich*, 404 U.S. at 539, 92 S.Ct. 630).

But again, *United Guaranty* and *Trbovich* are inapposite because unlike in those cases, the appellants here concede that they share the same objective as the existing government defendants: upholding the constitutionality of the Act. In this context, the relevant and settled rule is that disagreement over how to approach the conduct of the litigation is not enough to rebut the presumption of adequacy. * * *

Nor could it be any other way. There will often be differences of opinion among lawyers over the best way to approach a case. It is not unusual for those who agree in principle to dispute the particulars. To have such unremarkable divergences of view sow the seeds for intervention as of right risks generating endless squabbles at every juncture over how best to proceed. There is much to be said, frankly, for simplifying rather than complicating the litigation process. We thus hold that the district court did not err in concluding that the appellants failed to establish adversity of interest with the Attorney General.

2.

Appellants next attempt to rebut the presumption of adequacy by repackaging their disagreements with the Attorney General's litigation decisions as "evidence of nonfeasance." According to appellants, the district court abused its discretion when it rejected this argument, concluding instead that the Attorney General's choice to rely on legal arguments under *Planned Parenthood of Southeastern Pennsylvania v. Casey*, 505 U.S. 833, 112 S.Ct. 2791, 120 L.Ed.2d 674 (1992), was a reasonable "tactical decision."

Again we find the appellants' position unavailing. The Attorney General's decision to concentrate his argument on *Casey* was hardly nonfeasance given that *Casey* upheld a Pennsylvania informed consent law that bears many similarities to the statute at bar. *See* 505 U.S. at 881–87, 112 S.Ct. 2791. * * * The reasonableness of the Attorney General's choice is particularly manifest given that it was largely successful: the district court upheld every provision of the Act except for its real-time display and explanation requirements. Moreover, the Fifth Circuit recently upheld a nearly identical real-time fetal display and explanation statute against a motion for a preliminary injunction using reasoning under *Casey* that closely tracks the arguments made by the Attorney General in this case. *See* Tex. *Med. Providers Performing Abortion Servs. v. Lakey*, 667 F.3d 570, 574–80 (5th Cir. 2012).

Nor was it nonfeasance for the Attorney General to choose to litigate the merits of the Act through to final judgment rather than appeal the preliminary injunction. It was eminently reasonable for the Attorney General to believe that the interests of North Carolina's citizens would best be served by an expeditious final ruling on the constitutionality of the Act, as opposed to prolonged intermediate litigation over the preliminary injunction. Federal case law is in accord. * * *

In sum, appellants have done little more than identify reasonable litigation decisions made by the Attorney General with which they disagree. Such differences of opinion cannot be sufficient to warrant intervention as of right, for, as already discussed, the harms that the contrary rule would inflict upon the efficiency of the judicial system and the government's representative function are all-too-obvious. The damage wrought by such a ruling would be especially senseless in a case such as this one, whereas the district court found, the existing defendants are "zealously" and "vigorously" defending the Act. We therefore hold that the district court did not abuse its discretion in rejecting appellants' claim of nonfeasance.

C.

Appellants next challenge the district court's denial of their request for permissive intervention under Rule 24(b)(1)(B), which provides that a district court "may permit" intervention if the applicant has "a claim or defense that shares with the main action a common question of law or fact." Critically, the rule also states that "[i]n exercising its discretion" to permit intervention, a district court "must consider whether the intervention will (unduly delay) . . . the adjudication." Fed.R.Civ.P. 24(b)(3).

In this case, the district court noted that "[a]dding three groups of intervenors would necessarily complicate the discovery process and consume additional resources of the court and the parties." The court further reasoned that permitting intervention would likely "result in undue delay in adjudication of the merits, without a corresponding benefit to existing litigants, the courts, or the process" because "the existing [d]efendants are zealously pursuing the same ultimate objectives" as the appellants. The court denied permissive intervention for that reason, and we find no error in its ruling.

IV.

Our decision today does not leave appellants without recourse. Appellants retain the ability to present their views in support of the Act by seeking leave to file amicus briefs both in the district court and in this court. *See Francis v. Chamber of Commerce*, 481 F.2d 192, 194–96 (4th Cir.1973) (affirming district court's decision to deny a motion to intervene and instead permit the would-be intervenor to file an amicus brief); Fed. R.App. P. 29 (describing the procedure for filing amicus briefs in the courts of appeal). Indeed, when asked at oral argument whether amicus participation would be a viable alternative to intervenor status, appellants' counsel noted that he files amicus briefs in cases like this "all the time." While a would-be intervenor may prefer party status to that of friend-of-court, the fact remains that amici often make useful contributions to litigation. The availability of such alternative avenues of expression reinforces our disinclination to drive district courts into multi-cornered lawsuits by indiscriminately granting would-be intervenors party status and all the privileges pertaining thereto.

* * *

AFFIRMED.

NOTES AND QUESTIONS

1. **Intervention as full parties.** The group of "pro-life doctors, former abortion patients, and pregnancy counseling centers" sought to intervene as additional defendants under Rule 24(a). If they had been allowed to intervene on the terms they sought, they would have had full rights as defendants in the suit. Can you see why the district court was

unwilling to allow them to intervene, and why the court of appeals declined to reverse? In some circumstances, courts have allowed and even encouraged intervention under Rule 24(a) for limited purposes. See, e.g., United States v. City of Detroit, 712 F.3d 925, 931–33 (6th Cir. 2013).

2.   **Result on the merits.** After the court of appeals affirmed the denial of intervention, the district court proceeded to a final adjudication on the merits of the case. The court of appeals then decided an appeal on the merits, holding that the "real-time and explanation requirements" of the North Carolina statute were unconstitutional as a violation of the plaintiff doctors' First Amendment rights. See Stuart v. Camnitz, 774 F.3d 238 (4th Cir. 2014). The district court had upheld the remainder of the statute; that part of the district court's decision was not appealed. The would-be intervenors had sought to become additional defendants arguing in favor of the statute's constitutionality. Do you think their participation in the suit, if they had become additional defendants, would have made any difference to the outcome on the First Amendment issue on which the state failed to prevail?

3.   **Compare to *Atlantis*.** The would-be intervenor in *Atlantis* was, in the words of the court, "without a friend in this litigation." That is, there was no existing party that was going to represent Atlantis' interests. Atlantis was adverse not only to the plaintiff, the United States, but also to the principal defendants, who were rival claimant to the reefs. While the State of North Carolina was not exactly a "friend" of the would-be intervenors, it sought essentially the same goal—a judicial holding that North Carolina's Woman's Right to Know Act is constitutional. The court held, under Rule 24(a), that although the would-be intervenors "claim[ed] an interest relating to the * * * transaction that is the subject of the action," the state party "adequately represented that interest."

4.   **Representation of would-be intervenor's interests.** What counts as an "interest" for which the existing party must be an "adequate representative"? In *Stuart v. Huff*, both the state and the would-be intervenors had an interest in obtaining a judgment upholding the constitutionality of the challenged statute. Do you think this was the would-be intervenors' sole motivation for seeking to intervene? Could additional motivations have included a felt moral obligation to do everything possible, including intervention in the suit, to bear witness to their opposition to abortion? A desire to use their intervention in the suit as a means to seek publicity for, and financial contributions to, organizations to which they belonged, as part of their effort to limit access to abortion? Are motivations such as these properly ignored by a court in deciding whether an existing party adequately represents the "interest" of a would-be intervenor under Rule 24(a)? Under existing case law, the answer is almost certainly "yes." See, e.g., Keith v. Daley, 764 F.2d 1265 (7th Cir. 1985) (upholding district court's denial of motion by a pro-life group to intervene as a defendant in an action challenging a statute restricting abortion; the group does not have "a right to intervene in every lawsuit involving abortion rights, or to forever defend statutes it helped to enact.")

5.   **"Minimal" burden of showing inadequacy of representation by an existing party.** In Trbovich v. United Mine Workers, 404 U.S. 528, n.10, 92 S.Ct. 630, 30 L.Ed.2d 686 (1972), the Supreme Court described as "minimal" the burden that must be borne by a would-be intervenor under Rule 24(a): "The requirement of the Rule is satisfied if the applicant shows

that representation of his interest 'May be' inadequate; and the burden of making that showing should be treated as minimal."

6.   Should the burden of showing inadequate representation be different when the existing party is the government? While recognizing the controlling authority of *Trbovich*, the court in *Stuart v. Huff* treats differently a case in which the "ultimate objective" of the would-be intervenor is the same as that of the existing party. The court starts out with a rebuttable assumption that if the "ultimate objective" of an existing party is that same as that of a would-be intervenor, the existing party's representation of that interest is "adequate." The court then strengthens that assumption when that existing party is the government. The court tells us that in such a case a "strong showing" or "very strong showing" is necessary to overcome the presumption of adequate representation by the government. Citing three decisions by other courts of appeals, the court writes that every other circuit to rule on the question agrees that such a "strong" or "very strong" showing of inadequate representation is required when the government is a party.

Despite what the court in *Stuart v. Huff* says, there are many cases in which intervention on the side of the government under Rule 24(a) has been readily allowed. For example, in Wildearth Guardians v. United States Forest Service, 573 F.3d 992 (10th Cir. 2009), an environmental group challenged the Forest Service's approval of a mine operator's plan for venting methane gas from its mine. The mine operator sought to intervene on the side of the Forest Service. The environmental group opposed intervention, contending that the mine operator had not shown inadequacy of representation by the government. The Tenth Circuit upheld intervention, writing that the intervenors' "showing is easily made." Id. at 996. It explained, "[T]he government's representation of the public interest generally cannot be assumed to be identical to the individual parochial interest of a particular member of the public merely because both entities occupy the same posture in the litigation. In litigating on behalf of the general public, the government is obligated to consider a broad spectrum of views, many of which may conflict with the particular interest of the would-be intervenor." Id. The Ninth Circuit, whose opinion is cited by the court in *Stuart v. Huff*, readily allows intervention on the side of the government when the "intervenors' interests are narrower than that of the government and therefore may not be adequately represented." Arakani v. Cayetano, 126 F.3d 1078, 1087 (9th Cir. 2003) (citing cases). For a useful discussion, see Black, Trashing the Presumption: Intervention on the Side of the Government, 39 Envntl.L. 481 (2009).

NOTE ON INTERVENTION IN "PUBLIC LAW LITIGATION"

There is no precise definition of "public law litigation," but we may say generally that such litigation typically involves broad questions of considerable importance not only to the plaintiffs and defendants, but also to the general public at large. In his classic article describing and analyzing public law litigation, Professor Chayes wrote:

> The party structure is sprawling and amorphous, subject to change over the course of the litigation. The traditional adversary relationship is suffused and intermixed with negotiating and mediating processes at every point. The judge is the dominant

figure in organizing and guiding the case, and he draws for support not only on the parties and their counsel, but on a wide range of outsiders—masters, experts, and oversight personnel. Most important, the trial judge has increasingly become the creator and manager of complex forms of ongoing relief, which have widespread effects on persons not before the court and require the judge's continuing involvement in administration and implementation. School desegregation, employment discrimination, and prisoners' or inmates' rights cases come readily to mind. * * * Antitrust, securities fraud and other aspects of the conduct of corporate business, bankruptcy and reorganizations, union governance, consumer fraud, housing discrimination, electoral reapportionment, environmental management—cases in all these fields display in varying degrees the features of public law litigation.

Chayes, The Role of the Judge in Public Law Litigation, 89 Harv.L.Rev. 1281 (1976).

Then-professor Fletcher commented on the judge's need for information about the possible effects of remedial decrees in public law litigation. He wrote:

The obvious way [for the district court] to obtain the information is to permit the people affected to participate in the suit. The most structured form of such participation is that provided by the Federal Rules of Civil Procedure, which allow intervention as of right under Rule 24(a), or permissively under Rule 24(b). But Rule 24 by no means exhausts the mechanisms for participation by non-parties. Another method is a special form of intervention—participation by the United States either as an outright intervenor or as an amicus. A certain amount of additional information may also be provided by witnesses who are neither parties nor intervenors, but who are potentially affected by the suit. A special form of such participation occurs when an expert witness testifies before the court to a consensus among the members of his or her particular profession, which in turn may represent a consensus or compromise among the various constituencies served by the profession. Finally, court-appointed masters or special administrators may also bring valuable information before the court.

Fletcher, The Discretionary Constitution: Institutional Remedies and Judicial Legitimacy, 91 Yale L.J. 635, 657 (1982).

There has been considerable pressure in public law litigation to use intervention under Rule 24 as a means of providing information to the district court, and a widespread willingness by district judges to interpret Rule 24 broadly to that end. An interesting example is intervention by the California prison guard union in Coleman v. Schwarzenegger, 922 F.Supp.2d 882 (N.D. Cal. 2009), in which California state prisoners contended that, partly as a result of prison overcrowding, mental and physical health care for prisoners fell below the standard mandated by the Eighth Amendment. The prison guard union intervened as a plaintiff in the district court, on the side of the prisoners. Id. at 912. The district court ordered release of prisoners in order to reduce overcrowding and to bring California prisons into compliance with the Eighth Amendment. The Supreme Court affirmed. Brown v. Plata, 563 U.S. ___, 131 S.Ct. 1910, 179 L.Ed.2d 969 (2011).

Useful articles include Hall, Standing of Intervenor-Defendants in Public Law Litigation, 80 Fordham L.Rev. 1539 (2012); Appel, Intervention in Public Law Litigation, 78 Wash.U.L.Q. 215 (2000); Symposium, Problems of Intervention in Public Law Litigation, 13 U.C.D. L. Rev. 211 (1980); Yeazell, Intervention and the Idea of Litigation: A Commentary on the Los Angeles School Case, 25 UCLA L. Rev. 244 (1977); Kennedy, Let's All Join In: Intervention Under Federal Rule 24, 57 Ky.L.J. 329 (1969); Shapiro, Some Thoughts on Intervention Before Courts, Agencies, and Arbitrators, 81 Harv. L. Rev. 721 (1968).

4. INTERPLEADER

State Farm Fire & Casualty Co. v. Tashire

Supreme Court of the United States, 1967.
386 U.S. 523, 87 S.Ct. 1199, 18 L.Ed.2d 270.

■ MR. JUSTICE FORTAS delivered the opinion of the Court.

Early one September morning in 1964, a Greyhound bus proceeding northward through Shasta County, California, collided with a southbound pickup truck. Two of the passengers aboard the bus were killed. Thirty-three others were injured, as were the bus driver, the driver of the truck and its lone passenger. One of the dead and 10 of the injured passengers were Canadians; the rest of the individuals involved were citizens of five American States. The ensuing litigation led to the present case, which raises important questions concerning administration of the interpleader remedy in the federal courts.

The litigation began when four of the injured passengers filed suit in California state courts, seeking damages in excess of $1,000,000. Named as defendants were Greyhound Lines, Inc., a California corporation; Thereon Nauta, the bus driver; Ellis Clark, who drove the truck; and Kenneth Glasgow, the passenger in the truck who was apparently its owner as well. Each of the individual defendants was a citizen and resident of Oregon. Before these cases could come to trial and before other suits were filed in California or elsewhere, petitioner, State Farm Fire & Casualty Company, an Illinois corporation, brought this action in the nature of interpleader in the United States District Court for the District of Oregon.

In its complaint State Farm asserted that at the time of the Shasta County collision it had in force an insurance policy with respect to Ellis Clark, driver of the truck, providing for bodily injury liability up to $10,000 per person and $20,000 per occurrence and for legal representation of Clark in actions covered by the policy. It asserted that actions already filed in California and others which it anticipated would be filed far exceeded in aggregate damages sought the amount of its maximum liability under the policy. Accordingly, it paid into court the sum of $20,000 and asked the court (1) to require all claimants to establish their claims against Clark and his insurer in this single proceeding and in no other, and (2) to discharge State Farm from all further obligations under its policy—including its duty to defend Clark in lawsuits arising from the accident. Alternatively, State Farm expressed its conviction that the policy issued to Clark excluded from coverage accidents resulting from his operation of a truck which belonged to another and was being used in the business of another. The complaint, therefore, requested that the court decree that the insurer owed no duty to Clark and was not liable on the policy, and it asked the court to refund the $20,000 deposit. *complaint*

Joined as defendants were Clark, Glasgow, Nauta, Greyhound Lines, and each of the prospective claimants. Jurisdiction was predicated upon 28 U.S.C.A. § 1335, the federal interpleader statute,[1] and upon general diversity of citizenship, there being diversity between two or more of the claimants to the fund and between State Farm and all of the named defendants.

An order issued, requiring each of the defendants to show cause why it should not be restrained from filing or prosecuting "any proceeding in any state or United States Court affecting the property or obligation involved in this interpleader action, and specifically against the plaintiff and the defendant Ellis D. Clark." Personal service was effected on each of the American defendants, and registered mail was employed to reach the 11 Canadian claimants. Defendants Nauta, Greyhound, and several of the injured passengers responded, contending that the policy did cover this accident and advancing various arguments for the position that interpleader was either impermissible or inappropriate in the present circumstances. Greyhound, however, soon switched sides and moved that the court broaden any injunction to include Nauta and Greyhound among those who could not be sued except within the confines of the interpleader proceeding.

When a temporary injunction along the lines sought by State Farm was issued by the United States District Court for the District of Oregon, the present respondents moved to dismiss the action and, in the alternative, for a change of venue—to the Northern District of California, in which district the collision had occurred. After a hearing, the court declined to dissolve the temporary injunction, but continued the motion for a change of venue. The injunction was later broadened to include the protection sought by Greyhound, but modified to permit the filing— although not the prosecution—of suits. The injunction, therefore, provided that all suits against Clark, State Farm, Greyhound, and Nauta be prosecuted in the interpleader proceeding.

On interlocutory appeal,[2] the Court of Appeals for the Ninth Circuit reversed. 363 F.2d 7. The court found it unnecessary to reach

---

[1] 28 U.S.C.A. § 1335(a) provides: "The district courts shall have original jurisdiction of any civil action of interpleader or in the nature of interpleader filed by any person, firm, or corporation, association, or society having in his or its custody or possession money or property of the value of $500 or more, or having issued a . . . policy of insurance . . . of value or amount of $500 or more . . . if

"(1) Two or more adverse claimants, of diverse citizenship as defined in section 1332 of this title, are claiming or may claim to be entitled to such money or property, or to any one or more of the benefits arising by virtue of any . . . policy . . . ; and if (2) the plaintiff has . . . paid . . . the amount due under such obligation into the registry of the court, there to abide the judgment of the court. . . ."

[See also 28 U.S.C.A. §§ 1397, 2361.—Ed.]

[2] 28 U.S.C.A. § 1292(A)(1).

respondents' contentions relating to service of process and the scope of the injunction, for it concluded that interpleader was not available in the circumstances of this case. It held that in States like Oregon which do not permit "direct action" suits against the insurance company until judgments are obtained against the insured, the insurance company may not invoke federal interpleader until the claims against the insured, the alleged tortfeasor, have been reduced to judgment. Until that is done, said the court, claimants with unliquidated tort claims are not "claimants" within the meaning of § 1335, nor are they "[p]ersons having claims against the plaintiff" within the meaning of Rule 22 of the Federal Rules of Civil Procedure.[3] Id., at 10. In accord with that view, it directed dissolution of the temporary injunction and dismissal of the action. Because the Court of Appeals' decision on this point conflicts with those of other federal courts, and concerns a matter of significance to the administration of federal interpleader, we granted certiorari. 385 U.S. 811, 87 S.Ct. 90, 17 L.Ed.2d 52 (1966). Although we reverse the decision of the Court of Appeals upon the jurisdictional question, we direct a substantial modification of the District Court's injunction for reasons which shall appear.

I

Before considering the issues presented by the petition for certiorari, we find it necessary to dispose of a question neither raised by the parties nor passed upon by the courts below. Since the matter concerns our jurisdiction, we raise it on our own motion. Treinies v. Sunshine Mining Co., 308 U.S. 66, 70, 60 S.Ct. 44, 47, 84 L.Ed. 85 (1939). The interpleader statute, 28 U.S.C.A. § 1335, applies where there are "Two or more adverse claimants, of diverse citizenship. . . ." This provision has been uniformly construed to require only "minimal diversity," that is, diversity of citizenship between two or more claimants, without regard to the circumstance that other rival claimants may be co-citizens. The language of the statute, the legislative purpose broadly to remedy the problems posed by multiple claimants to a single fund, and the consistent judicial interpretation tacitly accepted by Congress, persuade us that the statute requires no more. There remains, however, the question whether such a statutory construction is consistent with Article III of our Constitution, which extends the federal judicial power to "Controversies . . . between citizens of different States . . . and between a State, or the Citizens thereof, and foreign States, Citizens or Subjects." In Strawbridge v. Curtiss, 3 Cranch 267, 2 L.Ed. 435 (1806), this Court held that the diversity of citizenship statute required "complete diversity": where co-citizens appeared on both sides of a dispute, jurisdiction was lost. But

---

[3] We need not pass upon the Court of Appeals' conclusions with respect to the interpretation of interpleader under Rule 22, which provides that "(1) Persons having claims against the plaintiff may be joined as defendants and required to interplead when their claims are such that the plaintiff is or may be exposed to double or multiple liability. . . ." First, as we indicate today, this action was properly brought under § 1335. Second, State Farm did not purport to invoke Rule 22. Third, State Farm could not have invoked it in light of venue and service of process limitations. Whereas statutory interpleader may be brought in the district where any claimant resides (28 U.S.C. § 1397), Rule interpleader based upon diversity of citizenship may be brought only in the district where all plaintiffs or all defendants reside (28 U.S.C. § 1391(A)). And whereas statutory interpleader enables a plaintiff to employ nationwide service of process (28 U.S.C. § 2361), service of process under Rule 22 is confined to that provided in Rule 4. See generally, 3 Moore, Fed.Prac. ¶ 22.04.

* * *

Chief Justice Marshall there purported to construe only "The words of the act of Congress," not the Constitution itself. And in a variety of contexts this Court and the lower courts have concluded that Article III poses no obstacle to the legislative extension of federal jurisdiction, founded on diversity, so long as any two adverse parties are not co-citizens. Accordingly, we conclude that the present case is properly in the federal courts.

II

We do not agree with the Court of Appeals that, in the absence of a state law or contractual provision for "direct action" suits against the insurance company, the company must wait until persons asserting claims against its insured have reduced those claims to judgment before seeking to invoke the benefits of federal interpleader. That may have been a tenable position under the 1926 and 1936 interpleader statutes. These statutes did not carry forward the language in the 1917 Act authorizing interpleader where adverse claimants "may claim" benefits as well as where they "are claiming" them. In 1948, however, in the revision of the Judicial Code, the "may claim" language was restored. Until the decision below, every court confronted by the question has concluded that the 1948 revision removed whatever requirement there might previously have been that the insurance company wait until at least two claimants reduced their claims to judgments. The commentators are in accord.

Considerations of judicial administration demonstrate the soundness of this view which, in any event, seems compelled by the language of the present statute, which is remedial and to be liberally construed. Were an insurance company required to await reduction of claims to judgment, the first claimants to obtain such a judgment or to negotiate a settlement might appropriate all or a disproportionate slice of the fund before his fellow claimants were able to establish their claims. The difficulties such a race to judgment pose for the insurer, and the unfairness which may result to some claimants, were among the principal evils the interpleader device was intended to remedy.[15]

III

The fact that State Farm had properly invoked the interpleader jurisdiction under § 1335 did not, however, entitle it to an order both enjoining prosecution of suits against it outside the confines of the interpleader proceeding and also extending such protection to its insured, the alleged tortfeasor. Still less was Greyhound Lines entitled to have that order expanded so as to protect itself and its driver, also alleged to be tortfeasors, from suits brought by its passengers in various state or federal courts. Here, the scope of the litigation, in terms of parties and claims, was vastly more extensive than the confines of the "fund," the deposited proceeds of the insurance policy. In these circumstances, the mere existence of such a fund cannot, by use of interpleader, be employed

---

[15] The insurance problem envisioned at the time was that of an insurer faced with conflicting but mutually exclusive claims to a policy, rather than an insurer confronted with the problem of allocating a fund among various claimants whose independent claims may exceed the amount of the fund. S.Rep. No. 558, 74th Cong., 1st Sess., 2–3, 7, 8 (1935); Chafee, Modernizing Interpleader, 30 Yale L.J. 814, 818–819 (1921).

to accomplish purposes that exceed the needs of orderly contest with respect to the fund.

There are situations, of a type not present here, where the effect of interpleader is to confine the total litigation to a single forum and proceeding. One such case is where a stakeholder, faced with rival claims to the fund itself, acknowledges—or denies—his liability to one or the other of the claimants.[16] In this situation, the fund itself is the target of the claimants. It marks the outer limits of the controversy. It is, therefore, reasonable and sensible that interpleader, in discharge of its office to protect the fund, should also protect the stakeholder from vexatious and multiple litigation. In this context, the suits sought to be enjoined are squarely within the language of 28 U.S.C.A. § 2361, which provides in part:

> "In any civil action of interpleader or in the nature of interpleader under section 1335 of this title, a district court may issue its process for all claimants and enter its order restraining them from instituting or prosecuting *any proceeding* in any State or United States court *affecting the property, instrument or obligation involved in the interpleader action. . . .*" (Emphasis added.)

But the present case is another matter. Here, an accident has happened. Thirty-five passengers or their representatives have claims which they wish to press against a variety of defendants: the bus company, its driver, the owner of the truck, and the truck driver. The circumstance that one of the prospective defendants happens to have an insurance policy is a fortuitous event which should not of itself shape the nature of the ensuing litigation. For example, a resident of California, injured in California aboard a bus owned by a California corporation should not be forced to sue that corporation anywhere but in California simply because another prospective defendant carried an insurance policy. And an insurance company whose maximum interest in the case cannot exceed $20,000 and who in fact asserts that it has no interest at all, should not be allowed to determine that dozens of tort plaintiffs must be compelled to press their claims—even those claims which are not against the insured and which in no event could be satisfied out of the meager insurance fund—in a single forum of the insurance company's choosing. There is nothing in the statutory scheme, and very little in the judicial and academic commentary upon that scheme, which requires that the tail be allowed to wag the dog in this fashion.

State Farm's interest in this case, which is the fulcrum of the interpleader procedure, is confined to its $20,000 fund. That interest receives full vindication when the court restrains claimants from seeking to enforce against the insurance company any judgment obtained against its insured, except in the interpleader proceeding itself. To the extent that the District Court sought to control claimants' lawsuits against the insured and other alleged tortfeasors, it exceeded the powers granted to it by the statutory scheme.

We recognize, of course, that our view of interpleader means that it cannot be used to solve all the vexing problems of multiparty litigation

---

[16] This was the classic situation envisioned by the sponsors of interpleader. See n. 15, supra.

arising out of a mass tort. But interpleader was never (intended) to perform such a function, to be an all-purpose "bill of peace." Had it been so intended, careful provision would necessarily have been made to insure that a party with little or no interest in the outcome of a complex controversy should not strip truly interested parties of substantial rights—such as the right to choose the forum in which to establish their claims, subject to generally applicable rules of jurisdiction, venue, service of process, removal, and change of venue. None of the legislative and academic sponsors of a modern federal interpleader device viewed their accomplishment as a "bill of peace," capable of sweeping dozens of lawsuits out of the various state and federal courts in which they were brought and into a single interpleader proceeding. And only in two reported instances has a federal interpleader court sought to control the underlying litigation against alleged tortfeasors as opposed to the allocation of a fund among successful tort plaintiffs. See Commercial Union Ins. Co. of New York v. Adams, 231 F.Supp. 860 (D.C.S.D.Ind.1964) (where there was virtually no objection and where all of the basic tort suits would in any event have been prosecuted in the forum state), and Pan American Fire & Cas. Co. v. Revere, 188 F.Supp. 474 (D.C.E.D.La.1960). Another district court, on the other hand, has recently held that it lacked statutory authority to enjoin suits against the alleged tortfeasor as opposed to proceedings against the fund itself. Travelers Indem. Co. v. Greyhound Lines, Inc., 260 F.Supp. 530 (D.C.W.D.La.1966).

In light of the evidence that federal interpleader was not intended to serve the function of a "bill of peace" in the context of multiparty litigation arising out of a mass tort, of the anomalous power which such a construction of the statute would give the stakeholder, and of the thrust of the statute and the purpose it was intended to serve, we hold that the interpleader statute did not authorize the injunction entered in the present case. Upon remand, the injunction is to be modified consistently with this opinion.[18]

IV

The judgment of the Court of Appeals is reversed, and the case is remanded to the United States District Court for proceedings consistent with this opinion.

It is so ordered.

---

[18] We find it unnecessary to pass upon respondents' contention, raised in the courts below but not passed upon by the Court of Appeals, that interpleader should have been dismissed on the ground that the 11 Canadian claimants are "indispensable parties" who have not been properly served. The argument is that 28 U.S.C.A. § 2361 provides the exclusive mode of effecting service of process in statutory interpleader and that § 2361—which authorizes a district court to "issue its process for all claimants" but subsequently refers to service of "such process" by marshals "for the respective districts where the claimants reside or may be found"—does not permit service of process beyond the Nation's borders. Since our decision will require basic reconsideration of the litigation by the parties as well as the lower courts, there appears neither need nor necessity to determine this question at this time. We intimate no view as to the exclusivity of § 2361, whether it authorizes service of process in foreign lands, whether in light of the limitations we have imposed on the interpleader court's injunctive powers the Canadian claimants are in fact "indispensable parties" to the interpleader proceeding itself, or whether they render themselves amenable to service of process under § 2361 when they come into an American jurisdiction to establish their rights with respect either to the alleged tortfeasors or to the insurance fund. See 2 Moore, Fed.Prac. ¶ 4.20, at 1091–1105.

■ MR. JUSTICE DOUGLAS, dissenting.[*]

NOTE ON INTERPLEADER

1.   **What is interpleader?** *Tashire* is an example of what interpleader is not. What *is* interpleader? It is a special joinder device that allows a stakeholder to obtain a judicial determination that he owes an obligation to one of several competing claimants. A common example is a life insurance company where the policy holder has died, leaving two competing claimants to the policy proceeds. The company is willing to pay, but wants to pay only once. If the company must fight separate lawsuits with each of the two claimants, each suit could result in a judgment against the company. That result cannot be logically correct, for the company does not owe the money to both claimants. But the result is legally possible, given the res judicata rule that a person cannot be bound to the result, or to the facts found, in a suit in which she was not a party. Interpleader allows the insurance company to institute a suit in which it pays into the court the policy amount and asks the court to determine which of the competing claimants is entitled to the money. See, e.g., New York Life Insurance Co. v. Deshotel, 142 F.3d 873 (5th Cir. 1998) (interpleader proceeding to determine which of two beneficiaries entitled to policy proceeds); Metropolitan Life Insurance Co. v. Pearson, 6 F.Supp.2d 469 (D.Md. 1998) (same). See also Cohen v. Republic of the Philippines, 146 F.R.D. 90 (S.D.N.Y. 1993) (interpleader by art dealer to determine ownership of paintings once owned by the Marcoses); Indianapolis Colts v. Mayor and City Council of Baltimore, 733 F.2d 484 (7th Cir. 1984); 741 F.2d 954 (7th Cir. 1984); 775 F.2d 177 (7th Cir. 1985) (interpleader denied in dispute between Baltimore and Marion County, Indiana, over relocation of professional football team).

Traditional limitations on interpleader substantially restricted its availability. They were:

> 1.   The same thing, debt, or duty must be claimed by both or all the parties against whom the relief is demanded; 2. All their adverse titles or claims must be dependent, or be derived from a common source; 3. The person asking the relief—the plaintiff—must not have nor claim any interest in the subject-matter; 4. He must have incurred no independent liability to either of the claimants; that is, he must stand perfectly indifferent between them, in the position merely of stakeholder.

4 Pomeroy, Equity Jurisprudence § 1322 (3d ed. 1905). Modern interpleader rules and statutes have abandoned strict adherence to these requirements. This abandonment is sometimes explicitly signaled in the text of the rule or statute. For example 28 U.S.C. § 1335(a) allows not only interpleader, but also a proceeding "in the nature of interpleader."

Probably the most important modern departure from traditional interpleader is that the stakeholder is not required to disclaim all interest in the stake. For example, a life insurance company may interplead competing claimants (1) contending that no money is owed because the policy holder committed suicide, and (2) asking for a determination among competing claimants in the event the court finds the decedent did not commit suicide. Further, an interpleader proceeding is not confined narrowly to a decision

---

[*]   The dissenting opinion is omitted.

about ownership of the stake. Liability as among the claimants may be determined in the interpleader proceeding, as well as liability of the stakeholder to one or more of the claimants. Within broad limits, additional claims and parties may be added to the basic interpleader proceeding under relevant federal joinder rules. See 7 C. Wright, A. Miller, M. Kane, Federal Practice and Procedure § 1715 (2008).

Modern interpleader provisions now exist for both the state and federal courts. For representative state interpleader provisions, see Calif.C.Civ.P. §§ 386, 386.1, 386.5, 385.6; N.Y.C.P.L.R. §§ 1006, 2701, 2702. See Csohan v. United Benefit Life Ins. Co., 33 Ohio Op.2d 36, 200 N.E.2d 345 (1964), in which an Ohio state court stayed its hand to allow a California state court interpleader proceeding to go forward. For federal interpleader, see below.

2. History of the federal statutory interpleader. The federal interpleader statute was enacted in 1917 in response to New York Life Insurance Co. v. Dunlevy, 241 U.S. 518, 36 S.Ct. 613, 60 L.Ed. 1140 (1916). Joseph Gould, a Pennsylvania resident, purchased a "tontine" life insurance policy from New York Life. (A tontine policy pays off if the insured lives past a certain date, unlike a typical modern life insurance policy which pays off upon the death of the insured.) When Gould lived past the specified date, New York Life was required to pay the policy amount. But it was unclear whether the beneficiary was Gould or his daughter Effie Gould Dunlevy, who lived in California. A judgment creditor of Ms. Dunlevy garnished the life insurance policy in Pennsylvania. New York Life then sought interpleader in Pennsylvania state court to determine whether Gould or Dunlevy was the proper beneficiary under the policy (which would allow the court to determine whether garnishment by Dunlevy's judgment creditor was proper). Service was attempted against Dunlevy in California, but she did not appear in the Pennsylvania suit. The Pennsylvania court held that Gould was the proper beneficiary. (Given that a holding against Gould would have resulted in payment to Dunlevy's garnishing judgment creditor rather than to Dunlevy, was Dunlevy unhappy with this outcome? Should one suspect collusion between father and daughter?) After the Pennsylvania suit was concluded, Dunlevy filed suit in California against New York Life, claiming to be the true beneficiary. The United States Supreme Court affirmed a judgment for Dunlevy on the ground that she was not subject to personal jurisdiction in Pennsylvania and could not be bound by the result of the Pennsylvania suit.

The problem faced by New York Life in *Dunlevy*, and by any insurance company dealing with competing claimants in far-away states in 1916, was that limitations on a state court's personal jurisdiction meant that state-court interpleader sometimes could not authoritatively dispose of all claims. The solution was to take advantage of the scope of personal jurisdiction available to the federal sovereign. The 1917 federal interpleader statute provided for nationwide service of process, allowing a stakeholder to bring before a federal court all claimants found within the United States. (Notice footnote 18 of *Tashire*, in which the Court refuses to decide the extent of personal jurisdiction outside the United States.) The present-day successors to the 1917 statute are 28 U.S.C. §§ 1335, 1397, and 2361. Federal interpleader is the only statute asserting nationwide jurisdiction in cases where the substantive cause of action may be based only on state law. More typical assertions of nationwide jurisdiction are the federal antitrust and securities statutes.

3.   Federal statutory and rule interpleader. The federal interpleader statute was passed in 1917 and substantially revised in 1936. The Federal Rules of Civil Procedure, adopted in 1938, also provided for interpleader under the rules. Fed. R. Civ. P. 22. Statutory interpleader, however, continued (and continues) to exist, so that a litigant seeking interpleader in federal court today has a choice between statutory and rule interpleader. See Pan American Fire & Casualty Co. v. Revere, 188 F.Supp. 474 (E.D. La. 1960), for a useful analysis. There are small, but occasionally significant, differences between the two kinds of interpleader.

a.   Subject matter jurisdiction. (1) Statutory. Jurisdiction in statutory interpleader cases is based on diversity of citizenship as defined in 28 U.S.C. § 1335(a)(1). At least one of the competing claimants must be a citizen of a different state from another claimant. So long as that requirement is fulfilled, it does not matter that some claimants may be citizens of the same state, or that some claimants may be citizens of the same state as the stakeholder. This is so-called "minimal diversity," whose constitutionality had long been assumed but was explicitly confirmed in *Tashire*. The amount in controversy must be $500 or more. **(2) Rule.** Jurisdiction in rule interpleader cases is based on the general jurisdiction statutes. Most typically, jurisdiction is based on the general diversity statute, 28 U.S.C. § 1332. Under this statute, there must be "complete diversity"; that is, all claimants must be citizens of a different state from the stakeholder. It does not matter that some or all of the claimants may be citizens of the same state as each other. The amount in controversy must be more than $75,000. Jurisdiction may also be based on the existence of a federal question under 28 U.S.C. § 1331, but as a practical matter such suits are rare.

b.   Personal jurisdiction. (1) Statutory. Personal jurisdiction is available over any claimant found within the United States. 28 U.S.C. § 2361. The scope of personal jurisdiction over claimants outside the United States is uncertain. (See supra n. 2.) **(2) Rule.** Under Rule 4, personal jurisdiction is available to approximately the same extent as it would be in the state courts of the state in which the federal court is sitting.

c.   Venue. (1) Statutory. Venue is available in any judicial district in which one or more of the claimants resides. 28 U.S.C. § 1397. **(2) Rule.** Venue is available in (1) a judicial district where any defendant (claimant) resides, if all the defendants reside in the same state; (2) a judicial district in which a substantial part of the events or omissions giving rise to the claim occurred; or (3) a judicial district in which any defendant is subject to personal jurisdiction, if there is no district in which the suit may otherwise be brought. 28 U.S.C. § 1391(b). The availability of venue in the district where a substantial part of the event or omissions occurred, § 1391(b)(2), sometimes makes rule interpleader more attractive to the stakeholder than statutory interpleader.

d.   Injunctions against other proceedings. (1) Statutory. A federal court in a statutory interpleader case may enjoin claimants from instituting or prosecuting any suit in federal or state court that would affect the interpleader proceeding. 28 U.S.C. § 2361. **(2) Rule.** A federal court in a rule interpleader case may issue an injunction essentially comparable to that issued in a statutory interpleader case. There is a backhanded grant of authority for such an injunction in the federal Anti-injunction Act. 28 U.S.C.

§ 2283 (excluding interpleader suits from the Act's prohibition against injunctions).

   4. *Tashire.* Why did State Farm seek interpleader in federal district court in Oregon? Its maximum liability under its policy with Ellis Clark, the driver of the truck, was $20,000. Couldn't State Farm have given the $20,000 to Clark to settle claims as he wished, or to one of the claimants against Clark in full or partial settlement of the claim? The answer is "no." As the Supreme Court noted, State Farm had a contractual obligation to defend Clark in "actions covered by the policy," over and above its obligation to pay $20,000 in liability claims. The Court's opinion does not make clear how far that obligation went. For example, did State Farm's obligation to defend cease as soon as one of the cases settled or went to judgment for an amount equal to or greater than the policy amount? Insurance policies, as well as state laws, differ on the extent of an insurer's obligation to defend. See 1 A. Windt, Insurance Claims and Disputes § 4.32, Existence of Duty to Defend After Indemnity Duty Has Been Satisfied (3d ed. 1995). We can infer from State Farm's actions that its obligation to provide legal representation extended quite far and entailed considerable expense. State Farm sought to minimize that expense by interpleading all those claiming against its insured in a single forum. Defendant Greyhound quickly seized on State Farm's interpleader idea, joining State Farm's attempt to consolidate the litigation in the district court in Oregon. Unlike State Farm, whose monetary liability was limited to $20,000, Greyhound's liability was not limited, and Greyhound almost certainly had sufficient assets to satisfy all claims arising out of the accident.

   The Court in *Tashire* did not entirely forbid interpleader by liability insurers, but it was unwilling to allow interpleader by a $20,000 insurer when multiple suits were filed (and additional suits anticipated) in widely scattered courts, and when potential liability ran into the millions. If interpleader had been allowed in such a case, a very small tail would have wagged a very large dog. *Tashire* has been interpreted generally to bar interpleader in mass tort cases where the anticipated claims exceed the policy limits of the insured. See, e.g., Reliance National Insurance Co. v. Great Lakes Aviation, Ltd., 12 F.Supp.2d 854 (D.Ill.1998).

   The Court in *Tashire* did indicate that State Farm could use interpleader as a device to require that any judgments obtained against its insured be enforced in the district court in Oregon. From a standpoint of public policy and of fairness to the claimants from the limited fund of $20,000, this makes sense. But does State Farm have any interest in using interpleader for this limited purpose?

   5.   Compare multidistrict litigation under 28 U.S.C. § 1407. To put *Tashire* in perspective, compare what is allowed under 28 U.S.C. § 1407. Adopted a year after the Court's decision in *Tashire*, § 1407 allows transfer and consolidation in a single federal district court for pretrial proceedings in large-scale mass tort cases filed in multiple federal judicial districts, such as airplane crash or large-scale product liability cases, as well as antitrust or other statutory breach cases. Transfer and consolidation of cases filed in state court is not available under § 1407. Transfer and consolidation must be approved by a specially appointed Judicial Panel on Multidistrict Litigation. § 1407(b). Because of the relatively small scale of the *Tashire* "mass tort" and the relative simplicity of the factual issues typically involved in a traffic accident, it is unlikely that *Tashire* would have qualified for transfer and consolidation under § 1407. See 15 C. Wright, A. Miller, M. Kane, Federal Practice and Procedure § 3863 (2008). After pretrial proceedings (including summary judgment) are completed under § 1407, individual cases must be transferred back to their original judicial districts for trial. Lexecon Inc. v. Milberg Weiss Bershad Hynes & Lerach, 523 U.S. 26, 118 S.Ct. 956, 140 L.Ed.2d 62 (1998). Note, first, the limited application of § 1407 to large-scale mass torts (probably not including a bus accident like *Tashire*'s), and second, the limited scope of what may be accomplished under § 1407 compared to what State Farm and Greyhound tried to do in *Tashire*.

6. Additional reading. The classic academic treatment of interpleader is a series of articles by Chafee, Modernizing Interpleader, 30 Yale L.J. 814 (1921); Interpleader in the United States Courts, 41 Yale 1134 (1932), 42 Yale L.J. 41 (1932); The Federal Interpleader Act of 1936: I, 45 Yale L.J. 963 (1936); Federal Interpleader Since the Act of 1936, 49 Yale L.J. 377 (1940); Broadening the Second Stage of Interpleader, 56 Harv. L. Rev. 541 (1943); and Broadening the Second Stage of Federal Interpleader, 56 Harv. L. Rev. 929 (1943). An excellent treatment of early interpleader is Rogers, Historical Origins of Interpleader, 51 Yale L.J. 924 (1942). See also Clark on Code Pleading 427, 433 (2d ed. 1947); Hazard and Moskovitz, A Historical and Critical Analysis of Interpleader, 52 Calif. L. Rev. 706 (1964). For an analysis of modern federal interpleader, see 7 C. Wright, A. Miller, M. Kane, Federal Practice and Procedure §§ 1701–21 (2008).

C. CLASS ACTIONS

INTRODUCTION TO CLASS ACTIONS

The class action is a kind of "representative action," in which one or more "named parties" litigate on behalf of a group of similarly situated people who typically do not participate in the prosecution of the lawsuit. The named parties are parties to the suit in their personal capacities, but they also sue in a representative capacity—that is, as persons acting on behalf of the other "absent" members of the class. In appropriate circumstances, the named parties are permitted to proceed on behalf of the class members and to obtain a judgment binding on all class members. A class represented by individual named plaintiffs is known as a plaintiff class. The rules also permit a plaintiff to sue individual named defendants as representatives of a defendant class, though defendant class actions are far less common. In federal court, class actions are governed by Federal Rule of Civil Procedure 23, which we will examine in detail below.

Rule 23

The crucial defining characteristic of a class action is that a determination made at the request of a representative of a group can be binding on members of the group who are absent, unnamed, and sometimes unnotified. This is permitted even though the representative is usually both self-appointed and a stranger to the absentees. In other forms of representative actions, such as a suit by an executor on behalf of a decedent's estate or by a trustee on behalf of the trust, the connection between the representative and the represented non-party is relatively close. In the class action, however, the unnamed members of the class usually have no prior connection to the class representative and no advance opportunity to challenge the qualifications of those who undertake to speak on their behalf. See Restatement (Second) of Judgments §§ 41 and 42.

To say the least, the notion that a person is deemed to have had his day in court by virtue of the appearance of a stranger who purports to speak for him is, in Professor Chafee's phrase, "an incongruity." Z. Chafee, Some Problems of Equity 203 (1950). Yet the class action offers several significant potential benefits, both to litigants and the judicial system. A class action allows a large number of related claims to be "aggregated" together and resolved in a single case. Such aggregation may be beneficial to members of the plaintiff class who are relieved of the burdens of litigating individually, and to defendants who may prefer to resolve their liability on a large number of related claims in a single proceeding (or settlement) binding against all class members. Moreover, a class action makes possible the aggregation of many small-dollar claims against a defendant into a single large case. Such large cases are thought to be necessary to enforce the laws prohibiting a defendant's wrongful behavior, since without aggregation, such claims are too monetarily insignificant to warrant individual lawsuits. A class action also potentially offers substantial benefits to the court system due to its aggregation of huge numbers of claims into a single comprehensive proceeding.

Despite these potential benefits, such a proceeding involves serious threats to the rights and interests of absent members of the class. In particular, there is a risk that the class representative, or representatives, will not share the interests of absent class members or will not competently or loyally represent those interests. In some cases, the class representative or his lawyer may bring a suit or seek a remedy that is ultimately harmful to the class. In others, the representative may strike a lucrative settlement deal with the opposing party that benefits him but sacrifices the interests of the absentees. Because those risks are often very significant, the law treats class actions as justified only in limited circumstances, where the advantages of proceeding on a collective basis are substantial and sufficient steps have been taken to ensure adequacy of representation—that is, to reduce or eliminate the risk of incompetence or disloyalty on the part of the class representative or her lawyer.

In recent decades, the use of the class-action device has become both more frequent and controversial. Its increased use derives in part from the fact that modern society generates an increasing variety of legal controversies that directly affect the legal rights of many similarly situated persons, so that the perceived advantages of proceeding on a collective basis are often substantial. The increase in the frequency and importance of class actions also reflects the rise of creative and entrepreneurial plaintiffs' lawyers in the expanding fields of civil rights, consumer rights, federal regulatory law, and, increasingly, tort law. At the same time, the potential for disloyalty to class absentees, and hence the urgency of ensuring adequacy of representation, has also increased, because in a mass society the class representative is likely not only to be a stranger to other class members, but also to be selected by and in substantial measure under the control of the attorney for the class. Moreover, because liability to a large class might be enormous, even the threat of a meritless class action may induce a defendant to settle simply to avoid the risks and costs of litigation. In recent years, the Supreme Court has expressed increasing skepticism about, and some might even say hostility toward, class actions, as you will see in several of the cases in this chapter. As you consider these materials, ask yourself whether the Supreme Court is setting appropriate limits on the use of the class-action device.

HISTORICAL NOTE ON CLASS ACTIONS

Representative suits like the class action have existed in England since medieval times. The history of these actions is fascinating and is extensively explored in Yeazell, From Medieval Group Litigation to the Modern Class Action (1987). The modern version of the class action emerged initially from 18th and 19th century equity courts. Most of the law in this period centered on an issue that often arose at the outset of the action: an argument by one of the parties that the action should be dismissed because necessary parties had not been formally joined. At that point, the court had to decide whether the action could proceed on a representative basis in the absence of those parties. The core prerequisite for such an action was that the number of absent persons be so large as to render joinder impracticable. Once this prerequisite was met, courts permitted joinder in a loosely defined category of cases in which there was a strong similarity, often verging on identity, between the claims or defenses of the numerous parties, so that in the absence of class treatment, there was the potential for multiple lawsuits involving the party opposing the group and for inconsistent outcomes. See, e.g., City of London v. Perkins, 3 Bro.P.C. 157, 1 E.R. 1524 (1734) (suit by city against masters of vessels to establish validity of a duty imposed on cheese landed in port of London). In many leading cases, there was an additional element: a preexisting legal or customary relationship between the absentees and the representative party, as in the case of suits brought by some villagers on behalf of all other members of the village, or local officials on behalf of their community, Mayor of York v. Pilkington, 25 Eng. Rep. 946 (Ch. 1737) (suit by mayor on behalf of city residents in dispute over fishing rights) or by members of managers of an unincorporated association on behalf of others. See, e.g., Chancey v. May, Prec.Ch. 592, 24 E.R. 265 (Ch. 1722) (suit by managers of a brass works owned by unincorporated proprietors). The combination of close identity between the claims of the representatives and the absentees, as well as preexisting relationships between them, may have reassured the court that the representative would in fact take actions benefitting the absentees.

A second important category of cases in which courts allowed representatives to proceed without absentees involved claims by creditors against a debtor, or legatees against an estate. These cases featured a limited amount of money or property and a requirement that the funds be appropriately distributed among those with a claim to it. Accordingly, "no individual's claim could be resolved without a final accounting of all claims of all interested parties." Issacharoff, Governance and Legitimacy in the Law of Class Actions, 1999 Sup. Ct. Rev. 337, 358. A lively example of this kind of case involved the privateer bill for an accounting and distribution of the prize. Privateers were privately operated ships of war licensed by the English government to prey upon and seize ships and cargoes of enemy nations. Each crew member had a legal right to be paid a proportionate share of the prize. In a series of cases, the courts developed the doctrine that some members of the crew could seek a judgment on behalf of all crew members, where the number of crew members was great and some could not be joined because they were geographically dispersed, unidentifiable or dead.

From the mid-18th to the end of the 19th century, courts in class suits elaborated the standards for representative litigation when joinder was impracticable in terms of phrases such as "well defined community of interest" to describe what made up a class, and "common or general" to describe the legal problem class members shared. Compare Smith v. Swormstedt, 57 U.S. (16 How.) 288, 14 L.Ed. 942 (1853), with, for example, Weaver v. Pasadena Tournament of Roses Ass'n, 32 Cal.2d 833, 198 P.2d 514 (1948), and Brenner v. Title Guarantee & Trust Co., 276 N.Y. 230, 11 N.E.2d 890 (1937). Few if any of these cases gave explicit consideration to the question of why representative litigation was appropriate or of how to minimize its dangers.

From the outset, cases addressing the binding effect of a representative action upon dissatisfied absentees were much less frequent than those addressing whether cases could proceed on a representative basis. On the critical question of whether the judgment in a class suit was binding on persons who were within the class but who were not parties, the cases reached inconsistent results. Some early cases clearly held that a representative action could bind absentees, but others equivocated or found preclusion on other grounds. See Hazard, Gedid & Sowle, An Historical Analysis of the Binding Effect of Class Suits, 146 U. Pa. L. Rev. 1849 (1998). This anxiety and inconsistency continued in American law in the 19th century. Some authorities stated unequivocally that such actions were binding on absentees, Smith v. Swormstedt, 57 U.S. (16 How.) 288, 14 L. Ed. 942 (1853), but during the same period the federal equity rules explicitly provided that representative suits, though permissible, were "without prejudice to the claims and rights of the absent parties." In the early 20th century, the tide turned in favor of holding that class suits could bind members of the class who were neither joined as named parties nor aware of the litigation. See, e.g., Supreme Tribe of Ben-Hur v. Cauble, 255 U.S. 356, 41 S.Ct. 338, 65 L.Ed. 673 (1921). As you read the following materials, consider whether this trend is consistent with constitutional considerations of due process. For a provocative argument that the system has gone too far, see Redish, Wholesale Justice: Constitutional Democracy and the Problem of the Class Action Lawsuit (2009).

1. ADEQUACY OF REPRESENTATION AND RES JUDICATA IN CLASS ACTIONS

Hansberry v. Lee
Supreme Court of the United States, 1940.
311 U.S. 32, 61 S.Ct. 115, 85 L.Ed. 22.

■ MR. JUSTICE STONE delivered the opinion of the Court.

The question is whether the Supreme Court of Illinois, by its adjudication that petitioners in this case are bound by a judgment rendered in an earlier litigation to which they were not parties, has deprived them of the due process of law guaranteed by the Fourteenth Amendment.

Respondents brought this suit in the Circuit Court of Cook County, Illinois, to enjoin the breach by petitioners of an agreement restricting the use of land within a described area of the City of Chicago, which was alleged to have been entered into by some five hundred of the landowners. The agreement stipulated that for a specified period no part of the land should be "sold, leased to or permitted to be occupied by any person of the colored race," and provided that it should not be effective unless signed by the "owners of 95 per centum of the frontage," within the described area. The bill of complaint set up that the owners of 95 per cent of the frontage had signed; that respondents are owners of land within the restricted area who have either signed the agreement or acquired their land from others who did sign and that petitioners Hansberry, who are Negroes, have, with the alleged aid of the other petitioners and with knowledge of the agreement, acquired and are occupying land in the restricted area formerly belonging to an owner who had signed the agreement.

To the defense that the agreement had never become effective because owners of 95 per cent of the frontage had not signed it, respondents pleaded that that issue was res judicata by the decree in an earlier suit. Burke v. Kleiman, 277 Ill.App. 519. To this petitioners pleaded, by way of rejoinder, that they were not parties to that suit or bound by its decree, and that denial of their right to litigate, in the present suit, the issue of performance of the condition precedent to the validity of the agreement would be a denial of due process of law guaranteed by the Fourteenth Amendment. It does not appear, nor is it contended that any of petitioners is the successor in interest to or in privity with any of the parties in the earlier suit.

The circuit court, after a trial on the merits, found that owners of only about 54 per cent of the frontage had signed the agreement and that the only support of the judgment in the Burke case was a false and fraudulent stipulation of the parties that 95 per cent had signed. But it ruled that the issue of performance of the condition precedent to the validity of the agreement was res judicata as alleged and entered a decree for respondents. The Supreme Court of Illinois affirmed. 372 Ill. 369, 24 N.E.2d 37. We granted certiorari to resolve the constitutional question. 309 U.S. 652, 60 S.Ct. 889, 84 L.Ed. 1002.

The Supreme Court of Illinois, upon an examination of the record in Burke v. Kleiman, supra, found that that suit, in the Superior Court of Cook County, was brought by a landowner in the restricted area to enforce the agreement which had been signed by her predecessor in title, in behalf of herself and other property owners in like situation, against four named individuals who had acquired or asserted an interest in a plot of land formerly owned by another signer of the agreement; that upon stipulation of the parties in that suit that the agreement had been signed by owners of 95 per cent of all the frontage, the court had adjudged that the agreement was in force, that it was a covenant running with the land and binding all the land within the described area in the hands of the parties to the agreement and those claiming under them including defendants, and had entered its decree restraining the breach of the agreement by the defendants and those claiming under them, and that the appellate court had affirmed the decree. It found that the stipulation was untrue but held, contrary to the trial court, that it was not fraudulent or collusive. It also appears from the record in Burke v. Kleiman that the case was tried on an agreed statement of facts which raised only a single issue, whether by reason of changes in the restricted area, the agreement had ceased to be enforceable in equity.

From this the Supreme Court of Illinois concluded in the present case that Burke v. Kleiman was a "class" or "representative" suit and that in such a suit "where the remedy is pursued by a plaintiff who has the right to represent the class to which he belongs, other members of the class are bound by the results in the case unless it is reversed or set aside on direct proceedings"; [372 Ill. 369, 24 N.E.2d 37], that petitioners in the present suit were members of the class represented by the plaintiffs in the earlier suit and consequently were bound by its decree which had rendered the issue of performance of the condition precedent to the restrictive agreement res judicata, so far as petitioners are concerned. The court thought that the circumstance that the stipulation in the earlier suit that owners of 95 per cent of the frontage had signed the agreement was contrary to the fact as found in the present suit did not militate against this conclusion since the court in the earlier suit had jurisdiction to determine the fact as between the parties before it and that its determination, because of the representative character of the suit, even though erroneous, was binding on petitioners until set aside by a direct attack on the first judgment.

State courts are free to attach such descriptive labels to litigations before them as they may choose and to attribute to them such consequences as they think appropriate under state constitutions and laws, subject only to the requirements of the Constitution of the United States. But when the judgment of a state court, ascribing to the judgment of another court the binding force and effect of res judicata, is challenged for want of due process it becomes the duty of this Court to examine the course of procedure in both litigations to ascertain whether the litigant whose rights have thus been adjudicated has been afforded such notice and opportunity to be heard as are requisite to the due process which the Constitution prescribes. Western Life Indemnity Co. v. Rupp, 235 U.S. 261, 273, 35 S.Ct. 37, 40, 59 L.Ed. 220.

It is a principle of general application in Anglo-American jurisprudence that one is not bound by a judgment in personam in a litigation in which he is not designated as a party or to which he has not been made a party by service of process. Pennoyer v. Neff, 95 U.S. 714, 24 L.Ed. 565; 1 Freeman on Judgments, 5th Ed., § 407. A judgment rendered in such circumstances is not entitled to the full faith and credit which the Constitution and statute of the United States, R.S. § 905, 28 U.S.C. § 687, 28 U.S.C.A. § 687, prescribe, Pennoyer v. Neff, supra; Lafayette Ins. Co. v. French, 18 How. 404, 15 L.Ed. 451; Hall v. Lanning, 91 U.S. 160, 23 L.Ed. 271; Baker v. Baker, E. & Co., 242 U.S. 394, 37 S.Ct. 152, 61 L.Ed. 386, and judicial action enforcing it against the person or property of the absent party is not that due process which the Fifth and Fourteenth Amendments require. Postal Telegraph-Cable Co. v. Newport, 247 U.S. 464, 38 S.Ct. 566, 62 L.Ed. 1215; Old Wayne Mut. L. Ass'n v. McDonough, 204 U.S. 8, 27 S.Ct. 236, 51 L.Ed. 345.

To these general rules there is a recognized exception that, to an extent not precisely defined by judicial opinion, the judgment in a "class" or "representative" suit, to which some members of the class are parties, may bind members of the class or those represented who were not made parties to it. Smith v. Swormstedt, 16 How. 288, 14 L.Ed. 942; Royal Arcanum v. Green, 237 U.S. 531, 35 S.Ct. 724, 59 L.Ed. 1089, L.R.A. 1916A, 771; Hartford L. Ins. Co. v. Ibs, 237 U.S. 662, 35 S.Ct. 692, 59 L.Ed. 1165, L.R.A. 1916A, 765; Hartford Life Ins. Co. v. Barber, 245 U.S. 146, 38 S.Ct. 54, 62 L.Ed. 208; Supreme Tribe of Ben-Hur v. Cauble, 255

U.S. 356, 41 S.Ct. 338, 65 L.Ed. 673; cf. Christopher v. Brusselback, 302 U.S. 500, 58 S.Ct. 350, 82 L.Ed. 388.

The class suit was an invention of equity to enable it to proceed to a decree in suits where the number of those interested in the subject of the litigation is so great that their joinder as parties in conformity to the usual rules of procedure is impracticable. Courts are not infrequently called upon to proceed with causes in which the number of those interested in the litigation is so great as to make difficult or impossible the joinder of all because some are not within the jurisdiction or because their whereabouts is unknown or where if all were made parties to the suit its continued abatement by the death of some would prevent or unduly delay a decree. In such cases where the interests of those not joined are of the same class as the interests of those who are, and where it is considered that the latter fairly represent the former in the prosecution of the litigation of the issues in which all have a common interest, the court will proceed to a decree. Brown v. Vermuden, 1 Ch.Cas. 272; City of London v. Richmond, 2 Vern. 421; Cockburn v. Thompson, 16 Ves.Jr. 321; West v. Randall, Fed.Cas. No. 17,424, 2 Mason 181; Beatty v. Kurtz, 2 Pet. 566, 7 L.Ed. 521; Smith v. Swormstedt, supra; Supreme Tribe of Ben-Hur v. Cauble, supra; Story, Equity Pleading (2d Ed.) § 98.

It is evident that the considerations which may induce a court thus to proceed, despite a technical defect of parties, may differ from those which must be taken into account in determining whether the absent parties are bound by the decree or, if it is adjudged that they are, in ascertaining whether such an adjudication satisfies the requirement of due process and of full faith and credit. Nevertheless there is scope within the framework of the Constitution for holding in appropriate cases that a judgment rendered in a class suit is res judicata as to members of the class who are not formal parties to the suit. Here, as elsewhere, the Fourteenth Amendment does not compel state courts or legislatures to adopt any particular rule for establishing the conclusiveness of judgments in class suits [citations omitted], nor does it compel the adoption of the particular rules thought by this court to be appropriate for the federal courts. With a proper regard for divergent local institutions and interests, cf. Jackson County v. United States, 308 U.S. 343, 351, 60 S.Ct. 285, 288, 84 L.Ed. 313, this Court is justified in saying that there has been a failure of due process only in those cases where it cannot be said that the procedure adopted, fairly insures the protection of the interests of absent parties who are to be bound by it. Chicago, B. & Q.R. Co. v. Chicago, 166 U.S. 226, 235, 17 S.Ct. 581, 584, 41 L.Ed. 979.

It is familiar doctrine of the federal courts that members of a class not present as parties to the litigation may be bound by the judgment where they are in fact adequately represented by parties who are present, or where they actually participate in the conduct of the litigation in which members of the class are present as parties [citations omitted], or where the interest of the members of the class, some of whom are present as parties, is joint, or where for any other reason the relationship between the parties present and those who are absent is such as legally to entitle the former to stand in judgment for the latter. Smith v. Swormstedt, supra; cf. Christopher v. Brusselback, supra, 302 U.S. at pages 503, 504, 58 S.Ct. at page 352, 82 L.Ed. 388, and cases cited.

In all such cases, so far as it can be said that the members of the class who are present are, by generally recognized rules of law, entitled to stand in judgment for those who are not, we may assume for present purposes that such procedure affords a protection to the parties who are represented though absent, which would satisfy the requirements of due process and full faith and credit. See Bernheimer v. Converse, 206 U.S. 516, 27 S.Ct. 755, 51 L.Ed. 1163; Marin v. Augedahl, 247 U.S. 142, 38 S.Ct. 452, 62 L.Ed. 1038; Chandler v. Peketz, 297 U.S. 609, 56 S.Ct. 602, 80 L.Ed. 881. Nor do we find it necessary for the decision of this case to say that, when the only circumstance defining the class is that the determination of the rights of its members turns upon a single issue of fact or law, a state could not constitutionally adopt a procedure whereby some of the members of the class could stand in judgment for all, provided that the procedure were so devised and applied as to insure that those present are of the same class as those absent and that the litigation is so conducted as to insure the full and fair consideration of the common issue. Compare New England Divisions Case, 261 U.S. 184, 197, 43 S.Ct. 270, 275, 67 L.Ed. 605; Taggart v. Bremner, 7 Cir., 236 F. 544. We decide only that the procedure and the course of litigation sustained here by the plea of res judicata do not satisfy these requirements.

The restrictive agreement did not purport to create a joint obligation or liability. If valid and effective its promises were the several obligations of the signers and those claiming under them. The promises ran severally to every other signer. It is plain that in such circumstances all those alleged to be bound by the agreement would not constitute a single class in any litigation brought to enforce it. Those who sought to secure its benefits by enforcing it could not be said to be in the same class with or represent those whose interest was in resisting performance, for the agreement by its terms imposes obligations and confers rights on the owner of each plot of land who signs it. If those who thus seek to secure the benefits of the agreement were rightly regarded by the state Supreme Court as constituting a class, it is evident that those signers or their successors who are interested in challenging the validity of the agreement and resisting its performance are not of the same class in the sense that their interests are identical so that any group who had elected to enforce rights conferred by the agreement could be said to be acting in the interest of any others who were free to deny its obligation.

Because of the dual and potentially conflicting interests of those who are putative parties to the agreement in compelling or resisting its performance, it is impossible to say, solely because they are parties to it, that any two of them are of the same class. Nor without more, and with the due regard for the protection of the rights of absent parties which due process exacts, can some be permitted to stand in judgment for all.

It is one thing to say that some members of a class may represent other members in a litigation where the sole and common interest of the class in the litigation, is either to assert a common right or to challenge an asserted obligation. Smith v. Swormstedt, supra; Supreme Tribe of Ben-Hur v. Cauble, supra; Groves v. Farmers State Bank, 368 Ill. 35, 12 N.E.2d 618. It is quite another to hold that all those who are free alternatively either to assert rights or to challenge them are of a single class, so that any group merely because it is of the class so constituted, may be deemed adequately to represent any others of the class in litigating their interests in either alternative. Such a selection of representatives for purposes of litigation, whose substantial interests are not necessarily or even probably the same as those whom they are deemed to represent, does not afford that protection to absent parties which due process requires. The doctrine of representation of absent parties in a class suit has not hitherto been thought to go so far. See Terry v. Bank of Cape Fear, C.C., 20 F. 777, 781; Weidenfeld v. Northern Pac. Ry. Co., 8 Cir., 129 F. 305, 310; McQuillen v. National Cash Register Co., D.C., 22 F.Supp. 867, 873, affirmed, 4 Cir., 112 F.2d 877, 882; Brenner v. Title Guarantee & Trust Co., 276 N.Y. 230, 11 N.E.2d 890, 114 A.L.R. 1010; cf. Wabash R.R. Co. v. Adelbert College, 208 U.S. 38, 28 S.Ct. 182, 52 L.Ed. 379; Coe v. Armour Fertilizer Works, 237 U.S. 413, 35 S.Ct. 625, 59 L.Ed. 1027. Apart from the opportunities it would afford for the fraudulent and collusive sacrifice of the rights of absent parties, we think that the representation in this case no more satisfies the requirements of due process than a trial by a judicial officer who is in such situation that he may have an interest in the outcome of the litigation in conflict with that of the litigants. Tumey v. Ohio, 273 U.S. 510, 47 S.Ct. 437, 71 L.Ed. 749, 50 A.L.R. 1243.

The plaintiffs in the Burke case sought to compel performance of the agreement in behalf of themselves and all others similarly situated. They did not designate the defendants in the suit as a class or seek any injunction or other relief against others than the named defendants, and the decree which was entered did not purport to bind others. In seeking to enforce the agreement the plaintiffs in that suit were not representing the petitioners here whose substantial interest is in resisting performance. The defendants in the first suit were not treated by the pleadings or decree as representing others or as foreclosing by their defense the rights of others, and even though nominal defendants, it does not appear that their interest in defeating the contract outweighed their interest in establishing its validity. For a court in this situation to ascribe to either the plaintiffs or defendants the performance of such functions on behalf of petitioners here, is to attribute to them a power that it cannot be said that they had assumed to exercise, and a responsibility which, in view of their dual interests it does not appear that they could rightly discharge.

Reversed.

■ MR. JUSTICE MCREYNOLDS, MR. JUSTICE ROBERTS and MR. JUSTICE REED concurred in the result.

NOTE ON *HANSBERRY V. LEE*

1. **Background.** The defendant, Carl A. Hansberry, had been, at various times, a Deputy United States Marshal, an inventor, a businessman, and a Republican candidate for Congress from Illinois. In 1964 his daughter Lorraine wrote in a letter to the *New York Times:*

> My father was typical of a generation of Negroes who believed that the "American way" could successfully be made to work to democratize the United States. Thus, twenty-five years ago, he spent a small personal fortune, his considerable talents, and many years of his life fighting, in association with NAACP attorneys,

Chicago's "restrictive covenants" in one of this nation's ugliest ghettoes.

That fight also required that our family occupy the disputed property in a hellishly hostile "white neighborhood" in which, literally, howling mobs surrounded our house. One of their missiles almost took the life of the then eight-year-old signer of this letter. My memories of this "correct" way of fighting white supremacy in America include being spat at, cursed, and pummeled in the daily trek to and from school. And I also remember my desperate and courageous mother, patrolling our household all night with a loaded German luger, doggedly guarding her four children, while my father fought the respectable part of the battle in the Washington court.

The fact that my father and the NAACP "won" a Supreme Court decision, in a now famous case which bears his name in the law books, is—ironically—the sort of "progress" our satisfied friends allude to when they presume to deride the more radical means of struggle. The cost, in emotional turmoil, time and money, which contributed to my father's early death as a permanently embittered exile in a foreign country when he saw that after such sacrificial efforts the Negroes of Chicago were as ghetto-locked as ever, does not seem to figure in their calculations.

L. Hansberry, To Be Young, Gifted and Black 9 (1969). The *Times* declined to publish the letter because it was "too personal." Id. at 246. Lorraine Hansberry is most noted for her prize-winning play, A Raisin in the Sun, portraying a black family's experiences in Chicago. The plot revolves around the family's decision whether to move into a white neighborhood. Ms. Hansberry died of cancer in 1965, at age 34.

As Ms. Hansberry's reminiscence indicates, *Hansberry v. Lee* was part of the long struggle to desegregate housing in Chicago. The personal and social background of the case is usefully described in Kamp, The History Behind *Hansberry v. Lee,* 20 U.C. Davis L. Rev. 481, 488 (1987).

2. The facts of *Hansberry v. Lee*. *Hansberry v. Lee* is the generally accepted starting point for the study of class actions. The question in the case is easy enough to state: Should Hansberry be bound in the present case by the decision of the Illinois Supreme Court in the earlier case of *Burke v. Kleiman*? The Court's answer is also clear enough: Hansberry should not be bound. But the Court's analysis is clouded and ambiguous.

a. Racially restrictive covenants running with the land. The facts of *Hansberry* revolve around a device in real-property law called a "restrictive covenant," which creates a restriction on the use of property that "runs with the land," that is, from present to future owners of the property. Its purpose is to bind not only the original parties who created the covenant, but also all those who take the property from, and are therefore in "privity of estate" with, the original covenanting parties. Setting aside the racially restrictive provisions at issue in *Hansberry*, restrictive covenants have a long history and often serve useful purposes. They have been used, and are used today, to supplement and sometimes even replace zoning restrictions as a way of controlling land use. For example, they can be used to specify and enforce height and design restrictions in a much more effective way than zoning ordinances.

The great utility of restrictive covenants is based precisely on their binding effect on people who are not parties to the original covenant, who buy in the chain of title from the covenanting parties, and who may wish to depart from the restrictions. For example, the present owner of land bound by a restriction controlling the height of buildings on the land may not sell to someone else and thereby remove the restriction from the land, allowing the new owner to build a high-rise. Because the covenant "runs with the land," it continues to restrict the use of the land, irrespective of the sale to a new owner, and irrespective of whether the new owner's interests were represented in any earlier litigation concerning the validity of the covenant. In our example, the covenant protects the original covenanting parties from the new owner buying the property and flouting the height restriction on the land. This is presumably fair because the new owner bought the land with knowledge of the restrictive covenant.

In 1940, when *Hansberry* was decided, racially restrictive covenants were common in many cities in the United States and were regularly enforced. In his excellent history of the case, Professor Tidmarsh explains that because racially restrictive zoning ordinances were unconstitutional, "private landowners banded together and voluntarily agreed not to sell or lease properties to African-Americans—'negroes' or 'coloreds,' as the covenants usually described them." Tidmarsh, The Story of *Hansberry*: The Foundation for Modern Class Actions, in Civil Procedure Stories 217 (Clermont ed., 2004). The lawyers in *Hansberry v. Lee* thought their case might be the occasion for striking down such covenants under the equal protection clause, but probably regarded their due process arguments as the more likely basis for reversal of the lower court. Kamp, at 493. The Supreme Court eventually struck down racially restrictive covenants as unconstitutional eight years later in the landmark case, Shelley v. Kraemer, 334 U.S. 1, 68 S.Ct. 836, 92 L.Ed. 1161 (1948).

b. *Burke v. Kleiman.* The key question in *Hansberry* is whether the Hansberrys were bound by the finding in *Burke v. Kleiman* that the racially restrictive covenant was valid and enforceable. In *Burke v. Kleiman,* Olive Burke, a property owner, sued to enforce a racially restrictive covenant in the "South Park" neighborhood of Chicago, seeking the eviction of an African-American man to whom property-owner Isaac Kleiman had leased an apartment. In her complaint, Burke asserted that she was bringing suit "on behalf of herself and on behalf of all other property owners in the district covered by" the covenant in question. The parties stipulated that 95% of the property owners in the district had signed the restrictive covenant, and Kleiman conceded that his property was covered by the covenant. Kleiman did not argue that the covenant never came into effect, as would have been the case if the owners of only 54% of the frontage in the subdivision had signed; rather, he contended only that conditions had so changed since the covenant was entered into that it was no longer enforceable. (Changed conditions are a standard ground for avoiding restrictive covenants that have ceased to serve their original purpose.) The trial court held that conditions had not changed to such an extent, enforced the covenant, and evicted the African-American tenant. The court of appeals affirmed. Burke v. Kleiman, 277 Ill.App. 519 (1934).

c.   The case against Hansberry. Hansberry later bought a house in the South Park neighborhood covered by the same racially restrictive covenant. The house had been owned by a signer of the original covenant, and subsequently by a bank. The bank then sold the property to another white buyer who, in turn, sold it to the Hansberrys for a quick profit. Six white property owners in the neighborhood then sued "on behalf of themselves and all others similarly situated" to enforce the covenant and evict the Hansberrys. The defendants in the lawsuit included both the Hansberrys and those who arranged the sale of the property to them (including, incidentally, James Burke, whose wife, Olive, was the plaintiff in *Burke v. Kleiman*). The Supreme Court of Illinois held that the Hansberrys were bound by the holding in *Burke v. Kleiman* that the covenant was valid and enforceable because *Burke* had been brought as a "class or representative suit." It therefore bound all present and future property owners in the neighborhood, including the Hansberrys. Lee v. Hansberry, 372 Ill. 369, 24 N.E.2d 37 (1939). It was this decision that the plaintiffs successfully appealed to the Supreme Court.

3.   Lessons of *Hansberry v. Lee*. *Hansberry* is considered the foundation of the modern law of class actions. But what propositions does *Hansberry* stand for?

a.   Given that the case is one where impracticability of joinder would classically provide a rationale for a representative proceeding, why is the *Burke* class action, which was clearly designated as such, constitutionally insufficient to bind the Hansberrys to the outcome in the prior case? The critical language appears to be the following:

> It is one thing to say that some members of a class may represent other members in a litigation where the sole and common interest of the class in the litigation, is whether to assert a common right or to challenge and asserted obligation. It is quite another to hold that all those who are free alternatively either to assert rights or to challenge them are of a single class, so that any group, merely because it is of the class so constituted, may be deemed adequately to represent any others of the class in litigating their interests in either alternative. Such a selection of representatives for purposes of litigation, whose substantial interests are not necessarily or even probably the same as those whom they are deemed to represent, does not afford that protection to absent parties which due process requires.

Supra p. 645.

In the specific circumstances of this case, this language makes sense: in the earlier case, the Burkes could not have been adequate representatives of owners who wanted to sell or lease their property to African-Americans, because they obviously were interested in achieving exactly the opposite outcome. But does this mean that a representative class action can never bind an absentee who takes a different view from the named plaintiff of whether suit should be brought, or of the remedy to be sought, or of the fair terms of settlement? Or are there intermediate levels of disagreement or conflict of interest that might not preclude class treatment? In other words, how aligned to the interests of the representative and the class need to be in order for the representative to be deemed adequate?

During the second wave of school desegregation class actions brought in the 1970s, the named African-American plaintiffs often sought full integration of public school systems, while other African-American class members preferred remedies that led to less integration but that they believed would strengthen their own neighborhood schools. Bell, Serving Two Masters: Integration Ideals and Client Interests in School Desegregation Litigation, 85 Yale L.J. 470 (1976). When the Court in *Hansberry v. Lee* says that due process forbids representative litigation by class members "whose substantial interests are not necessarily or even probably the same as those they are deemed to represent" does it imply that those desegregation class actions were improper? For discussion, see Rhode, Class Conflicts in Class Actions, 34 Stan. L. Rev. 1183 (1982); Note, Conflicts in Class Actions and Protection of Absent Class Members, 91 Yale L.J. 590 (1982).

b.   If Burke could not represent those objecting to the enforcement of the covenant in the first action, could Kleiman have done so? The Court notes that the defendants in the case were not formally designated as a class. Had such a designation been made, would the judgment have been binding on the Hansberrys? What dangers are involved in allowing a plaintiff to designate defendants as class representatives? Does the Court's discussion of the issue suggest that those dangers were present in *Burke v. Kleiman*?

c.   What do you make of the Court's suggestion that the binding effect of a representative action may be limited to cases in which the absentees are "in fact adequately represented by parties who are present"? Did the defendants in the first case in fact provide adequate representation for the interest of absentees who were opposed to enforcement? If not, is it so clear that the Court has accepted the Illinois courts' finding that the stipulation in *Hansberry* was not collusive?

d.   Finally, imagine that the covenant in *Hansberry v. Lee* had been benign—controlling, for example, the height of a house that Hansberry could build. What would the Supreme Court's holding have been? Would the Court have allowed the Illinois Supreme Court to bind, as a matter of Illinois law, the seller (and therefore his purchaser) to the consequences of a non-fraudulent stipulation in earlier class action litigation involving a predecessor in title (or in Burke's case, his wife)? Does it violate federal constitutional due process to enforce a covenant against the buyer in such circumstances? Is it possible to think that if the covenant had served good rather than bad purposes the Supreme Court would have upheld the decision of the Illinois Supreme Court?

Another way of putting the foregoing point is that the issue of adequacy of representation arises in *Hansberry* only because the Court ignores without explanation an obvious alternative ground for treating the Hansberrys as bound by the prior judgment.

In any event, *Hansberry* remains relevant today. To begin with, the limitations on class actions found in federal Rule 23 are thought to ensure the constitutional due process requirement of adequate representation. Moreover, the *Hansberry* rule that a judgment is not binding on a person who was not so adequately represented is relevant in numerous modern contexts. See Taylor v. Sturgell, infra, p. 1091.

2. USES AND ADMINISTRATION OF CLASS SUITS

THE MODERN CLASS ACTION RULE: AN INTRODUCTION

The basis of modern class action practice in federal court is federal Rule 23. The original Rule 23, part of the 1938 federal rules package, attempted to make sense of the confusing class action jurisprudence of the late 19th and early 20th centuries by recognizing three settings in which representative proceedings were permitted, described in the rules as "true," "hybrid," and "spurious" class actions. The original Rule 23 also preserved 19th century ambivalence about whether the class action could bind absentees. Although the text of the Rule did not specify its preclusive effect, the drafters and the majority of courts that applied it took the view that both favorable and unfavorable judgments in "true" and "hybrid" class actions were binding on absent class members. Judgments in "spurious" class actions were not binding, though class members could, if they chose, take advantage of a judgment in favor of the class by intervening in the action, even after judgment. Hazard et al., 146 U. Pa. L. Rev. at 1938.

The classification of actions into "true," "hybrid," and "spurious" actions was confusing because the categories as defined did not relate in any obvious way to the reasons for allowing class action treatment. The distinction between the types of class actions regarded as binding and those that were nonbinding also wholly lacked a persuasive rationale. Hazard et al., 146 U. Pa. L. Rev. at 1941. The rule evoked acid criticism among the commentators. See Z. Chafee, supra, ch. 7; Note, Federal Class Actions: A Suggested Revision of Rule 23, 46 Colum. L. Rev. 818 (1946).

Rule 23 was revised in 1966 in an attempt to resolve the confusion. The revision had three goals: to define in a practical way the kinds of cases where the prospective benefits of class suit outweighed its disadvantages, to specify clearly that all class suits would be binding and delineate the scope of their preclusive effect, and to ensure that class actions were conducted to maximize their advantages and ensure fair representation of absent class members—the concern at the heart of *Hansberry v. Lee.* Advisory Committee Notes, 1966 Revision. See also Marcus, The History of the Modern Class Action, Part I: Sturm und Drang, 90 Wash. U. L. Rev. 587 (2014); Kaplan, Continuing Work of the Civil Committee: 1966 Amendments of the Federal Rules of Civil Procedure (I), 81 Harv. L. Rev. 356 (1967).

The basic structure of Rule 23 reflects the concerns of the drafters. Sections 23(a) and (b) seek to describe in practical terms the cases in which class action treatment will be permitted. Rule 23(a) prescribes the four basic elements—numerosity, commonality, typicality, and adequacy of representation—that all class actions must possess. Rule 23(b) defines three categories of cases in which, on certain specified additional conditions, actions having all four of the basic elements may be permitted to proceed on a class basis. In short, a putative class action must fulfill all four of the requirements of Rule 23(a) *and* the requirements of one of the 23(b) categories in order to be maintained.

Sections 23(c)–(h) describe the measures to be taken to determine the scope of the judgment rendered in the case and to ensure that the action is fairly conducted. These include a procedure, known as certification, in which the court is required to determine whether the requirements for class action treatment have been satisfied and to appoint class counsel. They also include a requirement of notice to absent class members in some cases. They also include a requirement for formal judicial review of any settlement or compromise of the class action in order to determine whether it is fair, reasonable and adequate. Finally, they provide for judicial review of any fee applications made by counsel in connections with the case. Practice under Rule 23 is sufficiently complicated to dominate an entire separate course in Complex Litigation, the leading casebook for which is Marcus, Sherman & Erichson, Complex Litigation (5th ed. 2010).

NOTE ON CLASS ACTIONS UNDER RULE 23

1.   **Rule 23(a): requirements applicable to all class actions.** Rule 23(a) provides that a class action may be brought either by a plaintiff class or against a defendant class ("[o]ne or more members of a class may sue or be sued as representative parties"). Plaintiff classes are much more common, but in appropriate circumstances defendant classes are very useful. Rule 23(a) then sets out the four requirements that all class actions must fulfill. The first and second requirements focus on the character of the class. The third and fourth focus on the nature of the party or parties seeking to represent the class. As Professor Tidmarsh writes, "A principal function of Rule 23(a) is to give effect to *Hansberry's* requirement of constitutionally adequate representation." Tidmarsh, supra, at 287. See if you can explain how each of the Rule 23(a) requirements serves this purpose.

a.   **Numerosity.** Rule 23(a)(1) requires that the class be so numerous that joinder of all members as individual named parties be "impracticable." If the class is not sufficiently "numerous," then there is no need to take the risks attendant to the class action—each plaintiff could simply join the lawsuit and prosecute her claim. There is no precise number below which class action treatment is unavailable, in part because the circumstances of individual cases may make joinder impracticable for reasons not entirely dependent on the number of would-be class members. A further reason for the imprecision of the numerosity requirement is variability of judicial attitudes and the discretion given to district judges. Classes as small as fourteen and sixteen have been certified. Jackson v. Danberg, 240 F.R.D. 145 (D. Del. 2007) (sixteen); Manning v. Princeton Consumer Discount Co., Inc., 390 F.Supp. 320, 324 (E.D. Pa. 1975) (fourteen). But would-be classes in the hundreds have been denied on numerosity grounds. See, e.g., Hum v. Dericks, 162 F.R.D. 628 (D. Haw. 1995); Minersville Coal Co. v. Anthracite Export Ass'n, 55 F.R.D. 426 (M.D. Pa. 1971).

b.   **Commonality.** Rule 23(a)(2) requires that there be questions of law or fact common to the class. This requirement had long been understood to not be particularly stringent, but this understanding may be obsolete after the Supreme Court's decision in Wal-Mart Stores, Inc. v. Dukes, 564 U.S. ___, 131 S.Ct. 2541, 180 L.Ed.2d 374 (2011), which will be discussed below. In *Wal-Mart*, the Court held: "Commonality requires the plaintiff to demonstrate that the class members have suffered the same injury." Id. at 2551 (internal quotation marks omitted).

c.   **Typicality.** Rule 23(a)(3) requires that the claims or defenses of the named ("representative") party or parties be typical of those of the class as a whole. To some degree, this requirement overlaps with that of subsection (a)(2), requiring that there be common questions of law or fact among members of the class, and (a)(4), requiring adequacy of representation.

However, typicality should be seen as an additional, free-standing requirement. The basic idea is that the named party or parties should have claims sufficiently similar to those of the class as a whole such that in representing their own interests they also represent the interests of the class members. "The typicality requirement is said to limit the class claims to those fairly encompassed by the named plaintiff's claims." General Telephone Co. v. EEOC, 446 U.S. 318, 330, 100 S.Ct. 1698, 64 L. Ed.2d 319 (1980). But courts have made clear that "interests and claims of Named Plaintiffs and class members need not be identical to satisfy typicality * * * Provided the claims of Named Plaintiffs and class members are based on the same legal or remedial theory, differing fact situations of the class members do not defeat typicality." D.G. ex rel. Stricklin v. Devaughn, 594 F.3d 1188 (10th Cir. 2011). If the class contains members with overlapping but distinct claims, it may be divided into subclasses, with different named parties representing each subclass. See Fed. R. Civ. P. 23(c)(4).

   d.   **Fair and adequate protection of the interests of the class.** Rule 23(a)(4) requires that the named party or parties provide fair and adequate protection of the interests of the class as a whole. Moreover, as *Hansberry* demonstrates, under the Due Process Clause, a judgment in a representative suit cannot be binding against a party that was not adequately represented. This requirement overlaps with the requirement that the claims or defenses of the named parties be typical of those of the class as a whole: "The commonality and typicality requirements of Rule 23(a) tend to merge. Both serve as guideposts for determining whether under the particular circumstances maintenance of a class action is economical and whether the named plaintiff's claim and the class claims are so interrelated that the interests of the class members will be fairly and adequately protected in their absence." General Telephone Co. v. Falcon, 457 U.S. 147, 157 n.13, 102 S.Ct. 2364, 72 L.Ed.2d 740 (1982).

   But the (a)(4) requirement goes beyond (a)(3). In part, as the Supreme Court said in *General Telephone Co. v. EEOC,* "[T]he adequate-representation requirement is typically construed to foreclose the class action where there is a conflict of interest between the named plaintiff and the members of the putative class." 446 U.S. at 331. The Supreme Court has also applied it to bar certification in cases where the class is defined to include representatives of groups of plaintiffs with sharply differing interests. Ortiz v. Fibreboard Corp., 527 U.S. 815, 119 S.Ct. 2295, 144 L.Ed.2d 715 (1999).

   2.   **Rule 23(b)(1)–(b)(2); non-opt out class actions.** Under the typology introduced by the 1966 revision, Rule 23(b) provides for three types of class actions. The first two are "mandatory" class actions, in that members of a properly certified class are not permitted to opt out of the action and under the rule are not entitled to notice of the filing of the action. The third type is not mandatory, in the sense that that class members must receive constitutionally adequate notice, and they have the right to opt out of the class (that is, choose not to be bound by the result). All class actions must meet the requirements of at least one of the three Rule 23(b) categories.

   a.   **Class actions under Rule 23(b)(1).** Class actions under Rule 23(b)(1) have the least clearly defined contours of the three kinds of class actions. Rule 23(b)(1)(A) takes the viewpoint of the party opposing the class, allowing class treatment when individually prosecuted suits would result in "incompatible standards of conduct for the party opposing the class." In general, a 23(b)(1)(A) class is appropriate when "practical necessity forces the opposing party to act in the same manner toward the individual class members and thereby makes inconsistent adjudications in separate actions unworkable or intolerable." 7A C. Wright, A. Miller, & M. Kane, Federal Practice and Procedure § 1773 (3d ed. 2005). See, e.g., Death Row Prisoners of Pennsylvania v. Ridge, 169 F.R.D. 618 (E.D. Pa. 1996) (class of death row inmates seeking determination of the applicability of the newly enacted federal habeas corpus statute, asserting a risk of inconsistent applications by state authorities); United States v. Truckee-Carson Irrigation Dist., 71 F.R.D. 10 (D. Nev. 1975) (class of holders of water "certificates" seeking determination of rights to water flowing from a common source).

The general practice in the Courts of Appeals is to certify a (b)(1)(A) class action only when injunctive or declaratory relief is sought. The rationale is given in In re Dennis Greenman Securities Litigation, 829 F.2d 1539, 1544 (11th Cir. 1987): "Many courts * * * have held that Rule 23(b)(1)(A) does not apply to actions seeking compensatory damages. * * * These courts reason that inconsistent standards for future conduct are not created because a defendant might be found liable to some plaintiffs and not to others. * * * Implicit in these decisions is the view that only actions seeking declaratory or injunctive relief can be certified under this section. * * * Underlying is the concern that if compensatory damage actions can be certified under Rule 23(b)(1)(A), then all actions could be certified under the section, thereby making the other sub-sections of Rule 23 meaningless, particularly Rule 23(b)(3)."

Rule 23(b)(1)(B) takes the viewpoint of the members of the class, allowing class treatment when individually prosecuted suits would "as a practical matter * * * be dispositive of the interests" of potential class members who have not brought individual suits, or would "impair or impede their ability to protect their interests." The most important kind of (b)(1)(B) class action is the so-called "limited fund" suit, in which class members claim an interest in a limited fund. The Supreme Court has recently suggested that presumptively, at least, limited fund class actions should be available only when (a) "the totals of the aggregated liquidated claims and the fund available for satisfying them, set definitely at their maximums, demonstrate the inadequacy of the fund to pay all the claims[;]" (b) "the whole of the inadequate fund [is] to be devoted to the overwhelming claims," with no funds being held back by the defendant; and (c) "the claimants identified by a common theory of recovery were treated equitably among themselves" and the "class will comprise everyone who might state a claim on a single or repeated set of facts, invoking a common theory of recovery, to be satisfied from the limited fund as the source of payment." Ortiz v. Fibreboard Corp., 527 U.S. 815, 838–39, 119 S.Ct. 2295, 144 L.Ed.2d 715 (1999).

b. Class actions under Rule 23(b)(2). Class actions under subsection Rule 23(b)(2) are available when the party opposing the class has "acted or refused to act on grounds that apply generally to the class," so that "final injunctive relief or corresponding declaratory relief" is "appropriate." Class actions under (b)(2) are sometimes called "injunction" class actions, but one should not overlook that (b)(2) class actions allow both injunctive and declaratory relief. Class actions under (b)(2) were expected by the rule drafters in 1966 to be primarily civil rights class actions, about which there had been some slight doubt prior to 1966. Many injunction class actions under (b)(2) have indeed been civil rights suits. But (b)(2) injunction class actions have been used in a wide range of non-civil rights suits as well. See Marcus, Flawed But Noble: Desegregation Litigation and its Implications for the Modern Class Action, 63 Fla. L. Rev. 657 (2011).

3. **Class actions under Rule 23(b)(3).** The requirements for certification under (b)(3) are different and more stringent than those under subsections (b)(1) and (b)(2). Questions of law or fact common to the class must "predominate" over questions affecting only individual class members, and the class action device must be "superior" to other available methods of adjudication. In addition, while notice is optional in (b)(1) and (b)(2) class actions, it is mandatory in (b)(3) class actions and class members must be afforded the right to opt out of the class. Damages class actions under (b)(3) are considered in greater detail in Note on the Requirements for Damages Class Actions Under Rule 23(b)(3), infra, p. 683.

A suit may be maintained under more than one subsection of Rule 23(b). If the class is simultaneously a (b)(1) and a (b)(2) class action, the hybrid nature of the class has little practical consequence. But if the class is simultaneously a (b)(3) class action and a (b)(1) or (b)(2) class action, there may be important practical consequences because of the notice and "opt-out" characteristics of a (b)(3) class. The special problems of hybrid class actions involving (b)(3) classes are considered, infra p. 689, in Note on Notice and Opt-Out Rights in Class Actions.

4. **Rule 23(c)—Determining by order whether to certify a class action; appointing class counsel; notice and membership in class; judgment; multiple classes and subclasses.** Rule 23(c) covers the critical decisions in managing the class action: whether to allow the suit to proceed as a class action, the requirement and form of notice; the definition of the class; and the potential for varying the class definition or the creation of subclasses.

a. **Certification under Rule 23(c)(1).** Rule 23(c)(1)(A) provides that a court shall determine by order whether to certify a class action "[a]t an early practicable time." The order may be altered or amended before final judgment. In deciding whether to certify a class, the court is not limited to the allegations of the pleadings. It can request evidence bearing on the propriety of class treatment, and in some cases it may be an abuse of discretion not to do so. General Telephone Co. of the Southwest v. Falcon, 457 U.S. 147, 102 S.Ct. 2364, 72 L.Ed.2d 740 (1982).

b. **Notice under Rule 23(c)(2).** Rule 23(c)(2) deals with notice. It expressly permits notice to class members under subsections (b)(1) and (b)(2) and requires it for class members of (b)(3) classes who can be identified through reasonable effort. The notice requirement will be considered in detail, infra p. 689, in Note on Notice and Opt-Out Rights in Class Actions.

c. **Scope of judgment under Rule 23(c)(3).** Rule 23(c)(3) requires that in a class action judgment the court must specify precisely who are members of the class. This requirement is designed to allow accurate determination of class membership for purposes of claim and issue preclusion.

d. **Restriction to certain issues, and subclasses under Rule 23(c)(4) and(c)(5).** Rule 23(c)(4) allows a court to certify a class as to certain issues only. For example, in a product liability case the court may certify for class treatment the question of the defectiveness of the product, leaving for individual treatment questions of individual damage. Subsection (c)(5) allows a court to certify subclasses when there is variation of claims or conflict among the members of the class. If subclasses are certified, named representatives of each subclass must meet the typicality and representativeness requirements of subsections 23(a)(3) and (4) for their subclasses and separate counsel must be appointed for each subclass. Ortiz v. Fibreboard Corporation, 527 U.S. 815, 856, 119 S.Ct. 2295, 144 L.Ed.2d 715 (1999).

5.   Rule 23(d)—orders in the conduct of a class action. Rule 23(d) gives considerable discretion to the district judge to manage the class action effectively. Of particular interest is subsection (d)(1)(B), explicitly authorizing the judge to require notice beyond that required under subsection (c)(2) "to protect class members and fairly conduct the action." The management of a complex class action is likely to involve the exercise of judgment and to require a number of discretionary procedural decisions. In the hands of an experienced and skilled judge, a class action can proceed fairly smoothly. In the hands of an impatient or unskilled judge, a class action can be a procedural disaster.

6.   Rule 23(e)—dismissal or compromise. Because the interests of the named class members or the interests of the lawyers representing the class may diverge from the interests of the unnamed class members, Rule 23(e) provides that class members must receive notice of any settlement and requires that the settlement be approved only after hearing and upon a finding that the settlement is fair reasonable and adequate. Settlement of class actions is considered in detail, infra p. 693.

7.   Rule 23(f)—interlocutory appeal of certification decisions. Rule 23(f) allows an interlocutory appeal of a district judge's certification decision if the court of appeals decides to permit the appeal. This amendment reflects the reality that the decision on whether to certify typically has enormous consequences for both plaintiff and defendant. Rule 23(f) was added to the Rule by amendment in 1998. Prior to the amendment, certification decisions were often difficult, and as a practical matter sometimes impossible, to appeal because class certification was not formally a final order in the case.

8.   Rule 23(g)–(h)—class counsel; attorney fees award. For many years, it has been clear that the competence and loyalty of class counsel, and the measures taken by the court to ensure them, are critical to the success of the class action device. The 2003 amendments to the class action rules make the importance of that issue explicit. Rule 23(g) requires the court to make a formal appointment of class counsel on the basis of a finding that the counsel will fairly and adequately represent the interests of the class. The rule permits the court to consider competing applications to serve as class counsel and to seek information about the competence and loyalty of class counsel, as well as their proposed terms for fees and costs. The order appointing class counsel may include express provisions with respect to fees and costs—in effect, the court may negotiate a fee agreement for the class members before class counsel is appointed. These provisions provide a framework that recognizes the recent practice of some courts in choosing class counsel in part based upon competitive bidding as to fees.

Rule 26(h) specifies the procedures for an award of fees to class counsel and costs. The source of those fees will often vary depending on the nature of the claim. In a civil rights class action, the source is likely to be a statutory award of attorneys' fees against the defendant. In an action for damages, the attorney may be entitled to statutory attorneys' fees if the class prevails or to an equitable share of the common fund created by the judgment or settlement awarded to the class. Traditionally, most such fees have been awarded on the basis of the so-called "lode star" rule, in which fees are calculated on the basis of the number of hours invested in the case by the lawyers for the class. In recent years, though, courts have increasingly awarded fees based upon a percentage of the recovery. And in some cases, courts have taken the initiative at the outset of the case, through an auction for class counsel, to obtain a formal fee contract specifying the fees payable by the class.

Wal-Mart Stores, Inc. v. Dukes

Supreme Court of the United States, 2011.
564 U.S. ___, 131 S.Ct. 2541, 180 L.Ed.2d 374.

■ JUSTICE SCALIA delivered the opinion of the Court

We are presented with one of the most expansive class actions ever. The District Court and the Court of Appeals approved the certification of a class comprising about one and a half million plaintiffs, current and former female employees of petitioner Wal-Mart who allege that the discretion exercised by their local supervisors over pay and promotion matters violates Title VII by discriminating against women. In addition to injunctive and declaratory relief, the plaintiffs seek an award of backpay. We consider whether the certification of the plaintiff class was consistent with Federal Rules of Civil Procedure 23(a) and (b)(2).

I

A

Petitioner Wal-Mart is the Nation's largest private employer. It operates four types of retail stores throughout the country: Discount Stores, Supercenters, Neighborhood Markets, and Sam's Clubs. Those stores are divided into seven nationwide divisions, which in turn comprise 41 regions of 80 to 85 stores apiece. Each store has between 40 and 53 separate departments and 80 to 500 staff positions. In all, Wal-Mart operates approximately 3,400 stores and employs more than one million people.

Pay and promotion decisions at Wal-Mart are generally committed to local managers' broad discretion, which is exercised "in a largely subjective manner." Local store managers may increase the wages of hourly employees (within limits) with only limited corporate oversight. As for salaried employees, such as store managers and their deputies, higher corporate authorities have discretion to set their pay within preestablished ranges.

Promotions work in a similar fashion. Wal-Mart permits store managers to apply their own subjective criteria when selecting candidates as "support managers," which is the first step on the path to management. Admission to Wal-Mart's management training program, however, does require that a candidate meet certain objective criteria, including an above-average performance rating, at least one year's tenure in the applicant's current position, and a willingness to relocate.

But except for those requirements, regional and district managers have discretion to use their own judgment when selecting candidates for management training. Promotion to higher office—*e.g.,* assistant manager, co-manager, or store manager—is similarly at the discretion of the employee's superiors after prescribed objective factors are satisfied.

B

The named plaintiffs in this lawsuit, representing the 1.5 million members of the certified class, are three current or former Wal-Mart employees who allege that the company discriminated against them on the basis of their sex by denying them equal pay or promotions, in violation of Title VII of the Civil Rights Act of 1964, 78 Stat. 253, as amended, 42 U.S.C. § 2000e–1 *et seq.*

Betty Dukes began working at a Pittsburgh, California, Wal-Mart in 1994. She started as a cashier, but later sought and received a promotion to customer service manager. After a series of disciplinary violations, however, Dukes was demoted back to cashier and then to greeter. Dukes concedes she violated company policy, but contends that the disciplinary actions were in fact retaliation for invoking internal complaint procedures and that male employees have not been disciplined for similar infractions. Dukes also claims two male greeters in the Pittsburgh store are paid more than she is.

Christine Kwapnoski has worked at Sam's Club stores in Missouri and California for most of her adult life. She has held a number of positions, including a supervisory position. She claims that a male manager yelled at her frequently and screamed at female employees, but not at men. The manager in question "told her to 'doll up,' to wear some makeup, and to dress a little better."

The final named plaintiff, Edith Arana, worked at a Wal-Mart store in Duarte, California, from 1995 to 2001. In 2000, she approached the store manager on more than one occasion about management training, but was brushed off. Arana concluded she was being denied opportunity for advancement because of her sex. She initiated internal complaint procedures, whereupon she was told to apply directly to the district manager if she thought her store manager was being unfair. Arana, however, decided against that and never applied for management training again. In 2001, she was fired for failure to comply with Wal-Mart's timekeeping policy.

These plaintiffs, respondents here, do not allege that Wal-Mart has any express corporate policy against the advancement of women. Rather, they claim that their local managers' discretion over pay and promotions is exercised disproportionately in favor of men, leading to an unlawful disparate impact on female employees, see 42 U.S.C. § 2000e–2(k). And, respondents say, because Wal-Mart is aware of this effect, its refusal to cabin its managers' authority amounts to disparate treatment, see § 2000e–2(a). Their complaint seeks injunctive and declaratory relief, punitive damages, and backpay. It does not ask for compensatory damages.

Importantly for our purposes, respondents claim that the discrimination to which they have been subjected is common to all Wal-Mart's female employees. The basic theory of their case is that a strong and uniform "corporate culture" permits bias against women to infect, perhaps subconsciously, the discretionary decisionmaking of each one of Wal-Mart's thousands of managers—thereby making every woman at the company the victim of one common discriminatory practice. Respondents therefore wish to litigate the Title VII claims of all female employees at Wal-Mart's stores in a nationwide class action.

C

Class certification is governed by Federal Rule of Civil Procedure 23. Under Rule 23(a), the party seeking certification must demonstrate, first, that:

"(1) the class is so numerous that joinder of all members is impracticable,

"(2) there are questions of law or fact common to the class,

"(3) the claims or defenses of the representative parties are typical of the claims or defenses of the class, and

"(4) the representative parties will fairly and adequately protect the interests of the class" (paragraph breaks added).

Second, the proposed class must satisfy at least one of the three requirements listed in Rule 23(b). Respondents rely on Rule 23(b)(2), which applies when "the party opposing the class has acted or refused to act on grounds that apply generally to the class, so that final injunctive relief or corresponding declaratory relief is appropriate respecting the class as a whole."[2] * * *

II

The class action is "an exception to the usual rule that litigation is conducted by and on behalf of the individual named parties only." In order to justify a departure from that rule, "a class representative must be part of the class and 'possess the same interest and suffer the same injury' as the class members." * * * Rule 23(a) ensures that the named plaintiffs are appropriate representatives of the class whose claims they wish to litigate. The Rule's four requirements—numerosity, commonality, typicality, and adequate representation—"effectively 'limit the class claims to those fairly encompassed by the named plaintiff's claims.' " General Telephone Co. of Southwest v. Falcon, 457 U.S. 147, 156 (1982).

A

The crux of this case is commonality—the rule requiring a plaintiff to show that "there are questions of law or fact common to the class." Rule 23(a)(2). That language is easy to misread, since "[a]ny competently crafted class complaint literally raises common 'questions.' " Nagareda, Class Certification in the Age of Aggregate Proof, 84 N.Y.U.L. Rev. 97, 131–132 (2009). For example: Do all of us plaintiffs indeed work for Wal-Mart? Do our managers have discretion over pay? Is that an unlawful employment practice? What remedies should we get? Reciting these questions is not sufficient to obtain class certification. Commonality

---

[2] * * * Rule 23(b)(3) states that a class may be maintained where "questions of law or fact common to class members predominate over any questions affecting only individual members," and a class action would be "superior to other available methods for fairly and efficiently adjudicating the controversy." The applicability of [this provision] to the plaintiff class is not before us.

requires the plaintiff to demonstrate that the class members "have suffered the same injury," *Falcon, supra,* at 157, 102 S.Ct. 2364. * * * Their claims must depend upon a common contention—for example, the assertion of discriminatory bias on the part of the same supervisor. That common contention, moreover, must be of such a nature that it is capable of classwide resolution—which means that determination of its truth or falsity will resolve an issue that is central to the validity of each one of the claims in one stroke.

* * *

Rule 23 does not set forth a mere pleading standard. A party seeking class certification must affirmatively demonstrate his compliance with the Rule—that is, he must be prepared to prove that there are *in fact* sufficiently numerous parties, common questions of law or fact, etc. We recognized in *Falcon* that "sometimes it may be necessary for the court to probe behind the pleadings before coming to rest on the certification question," 457 U.S., at 160, 102 S.Ct. 2364, and that certification is proper only if "the trial court is satisfied, after a rigorous analysis, that the prerequisites of Rule 23(a) have been satisfied," *id.,* at 161. Frequently that "rigorous analysis" will entail some overlap with the merits of the plaintiff's underlying claim. That cannot be helped. " '[T]he class determination generally involves considerations that are enmeshed in the factual and legal issues comprising the plaintiff's cause of action.' " *Falcon, supra,* at 160. Nor is there anything unusual about that consequence: The necessity of touching aspects of the merits in order to resolve preliminary matters, *e.g.,* jurisdiction and venue, is a familiar feature of litigation.

In this case, proof of commonality necessarily overlaps with respondents' merits contention that Wal-Mart engages in a *pattern or practice* of discrimination. That is so because, in resolving an individual's Title VII claim, the crux of the inquiry is "the reason for a particular employment decision." Here respondents wish to sue about literally millions of employment decisions at once. Without some glue holding the alleged *reasons* for all those decisions together, it will be impossible to say that examination of all the class members' claims for relief will produce a common answer to the crucial question *why was I disfavored.*

B

This Court's opinion in *Falcon* describes how the commonality issue must be approached. There [the Court explained]:

> "Conceptually, there is a wide gap between (a) an individual's claim that he has been denied a promotion [or higher pay] on discriminatory grounds, and his otherwise unsupported allegation that the company has a policy of discrimination, and (b) the existence of a class of persons who have suffered the same injury as that individual, such that the individual's claim and the class claim will share common questions of law or fact and that the individual's claim will be typical of the class claims."

Falcon suggested two ways in which that conceptual gap might be bridged. First, if the employer "used a biased testing procedure to evaluate both applicants for employment and incumbent employees, a class action on behalf of every applicant or employee who might have been prejudiced by the test clearly would satisfy the commonality and typicality requirements of Rule 23(a)." Second, "[s]ignificant proof that an employer operated under a general policy of discrimination conceivably could justify a class of both applicants and employees if the discrimination manifested itself in hiring and promotion practices in the same general fashion, such as through entirely subjective decisionmaking processes." We think that statement precisely describes respondents' burden in this case. The first manner of bridging the gap obviously has no application here; Wal-Mart has no testing procedure or other companywide evaluation method that can be charged with bias. The whole point of permitting discretionary decisionmaking is to avoid evaluating employees under a common standard.

The second manner of bridging the gap requires "significant proof" that Wal-Mart "operated under a general policy of discrimination." That is entirely absent here. Wal-Mart's announced policy forbids sex discrimination, and as the District Court recognized the company imposes penalties for denials of equal employment opportunity. The only evidence of a "general policy of discrimination" respondents produced was the testimony of Dr. William Bielby, their sociological expert. Relying on "social framework" analysis, Bielby testified that Wal-Mart has a "strong corporate culture" that makes it "vulnerable" to "gender bias." He could not, however, "determine with any specificity how regularly gender stereotypes play a meaningful role in employment decisions at Wal-Mart. . . . If Bielby admittedly has no answer to that question, we can safely disregard what he has to say. It is worlds away from "significant proof" that Wal-Mart "operated under a general policy of discrimination." * * * *

C

The only corporate policy that the plaintiffs' evidence convincingly establishes is Wal-Mart's "policy" of *allowing discretion* by local supervisors over employment matters. On its face, of course, that is just the opposite of a uniform employment practice that would provide the commonality needed for a class action; it is a policy *against having* uniform employment practices. It is also a very common and presumptively reasonable way of doing business—one that we have said "should itself raise no inference of discriminatory conduct," Watson v. Fort Worth Bank & Trust, 487 U.S. 977, 990, 108 S.Ct. 2777, 101 L.Ed.2d 827 (1988).

To be sure, we have recognized that, "in appropriate cases," giving discretion to lower-level supervisors can be the basis of Title VII liability under a disparate-impact theory—since "an employer's undisciplined system of subjective decisionmaking [can have] precisely the same effects as a system pervaded by impermissible intentional discrimination." *Id.,* at 990–991, 108 S.Ct. 2777. But the recognition that this type of Title VII claim "can" exist does not lead to the conclusion that every employee in a company using a system of discretion has such a claim in common. To the contrary, left to their own devices most managers in any corporation—and surely most managers in a corporation that forbids sex discrimination—would select sex-neutral, performance-based criteria for hiring and promotion that produce no actionable disparity at all. Others may choose to reward various attributes that produce disparate impact—such as scores on general aptitude tests or educational achievements. And still other managers may be guilty of intentional discrimination that produces a sex-based disparity. In such a company, demonstrating the invalidity of one manager's use of discretion will do nothing to demonstrate the invalidity of another's. A party seeking to certify a nationwide class will be unable to show that all the employees' Title VII claims will in fact depend on the answers to common questions. * * *

Because respondents provide no convincing proof of a companywide discriminatory pay and promotion policy, we have concluded that they have no established the existence of any common question.

III

We also conclude that respondents' claims for backpay were improperly certified under Federal Rule of Civil Procedure 23(b)(2). Our opinion in Ticor Title Ins. Co. v. Brown, 511 U.S. 117, 121, 114 S.Ct. 1359, 128 L.Ed.2d 33 (1994) (per curiam) expressed serious doubt about whether claims for monetary relief may be certified under that provision. We now hold that they may not, at least where (as here) the monetary relief is not incidental to the injunctive or declaratory relief.

A

Rule 23(b)(2) allows class treatment when "the party opposing the class has acted or refused to act on grounds that apply generally to the class, so that final injunctive relief or corresponding declaratory relief is appropriate respecting the class as a whole." One possible reading of this provision is that it applies *only* to requests for such injunctive or declaratory relief and does not authorize the class certification of monetary claims at all. We need not reach that broader question in this case, because we think that, at a minimum, claims for *individualized* relief (like the backpay at issue here) do not satisfy the Rule. The key to the (b)(2) class is "the indivisible nature of the injunctive or declaratory remedy warranted—the notion that the conduct is such that it can be enjoined or declared unlawful only as to all of the class members or as to none of them." In other words, Rule 23(b)(2) applies only when a single injunction or declaratory judgment would provide relief to each member of the class. It does not authorize class certification when each individual class member would be entitled to a *different* injunction or declaratory judgment against the defendant. Similarly, it does not authorize class certification when each class member would be entitled to an individualized award of monetary damages.

That interpretation accords with the history of the Rule. Because Rule 23 "stems from equity practice" that predated its codification, in determining its meaning we have previously looked to the historical models on which the Rule was based, As we observed in *Amchem [Products Inc. v. Windsor]*, "[c]ivil rights cases against parties charged with unlawful, class-based discrimination are prime examples" of what (b)(2) is meant to capture. 521 U.S. 591, 614 (1997). In particular, the Rule reflects a series of decisions involving challenges to racial segregation—conduct that was remedied by a single classwide order. In none of the cases cited by the Advisory Committee as examples of (b)(2)'s antecedents did the plaintiffs combine any claim for individualized relief with their classwide injunction.

Permitting the combination of individualized and classwide relief in a (b)(2) class is also inconsistent with the structure of Rule 23(b). Classes certified under (b)(1) and (b)(2) share the most traditional justifications for class treatment—that individual adjudications would be impossible or unworkable, as in a (b)(1) class, or that the relief sought must perforce affect the entire class at once, as in a (b)(2) class. For that reason these are also mandatory classes: The Rule provides no opportunity for (b)(1) or (b)(2) class members to opt out, and does not even oblige the District Court to afford them notice of the action. Rule 23(b)(3), by contrast, is an "adventuresome innovation" of the 1966 amendments, framed for situations "in which 'class-action treatment is not as clearly called for.'" It allows class certification in a much wider set of circumstances but with greater procedural protections. Its only prerequisites are that "the questions of law or fact common to class members predominate over any questions affecting only individual members, and that a class action is superior to other available methods for fairly and efficiently adjudicating the controversy." Rule 23(b)(3). And unlike (b)(1) and (b)(2) classes, the (b)(3) class is not mandatory; class members are entitled to receive "the best notice that is practicable under the circumstances" and to withdraw from the class at their option. See Rule 23(c)(2)(B).

Given that structure, we think it clear that individualized monetary claims belong in Rule 23(b)(3). The procedural protections attending the (b)(3) class—predominance, superiority, mandatory notice, and the right to opt out—are missing from (b)(2) not because the Rule considers them unnecessary, but because it considers them unnecessary *to a (b)(2) class*. When a class seeks an indivisible injunction benefitting all its members at once, there is no reason to undertake a case-specific inquiry into whether class issues predominate or whether class action is a superior method of adjudicating the dispute. Predominance and superiority are self-evident. But with respect to each class member's individualized claim for money, that is not so—which is precisely why (b)(3) requires the judge to make findings about predominance and superiority before allowing the class. Similarly, (b)(2) does not require that class members be given notice and optout rights, presumably because it is thought (rightly or wrongly) that notice has no purpose when the class is mandatory, and that depriving people of their right to sue in this manner complies with the Due Process Clause. In the context of a class action predominantly for money damages we have held that absence of notice and opt-out violates due process. See Phillips Petroleum Co. v. Shutts, 472 U.S. 797, 812 (1985). While we have never held that to be so where the monetary claims do not predominate, the serious possibility that it may be so provides an additional reason not to read Rule 23(b)(2) to include the monetary claims here.

B

Against that conclusion, respondents argue that their claims for backpay were appropriately certified as part of a class under Rule 23(b)(2) because those claims do not "predominate" over their requests for injunctive and declaratory relief. They rely upon the Advisory Committee's statement that Rule 23(b)(2) "does not extend to cases in which the appropriate final relief relates *exclusively or predominantly* to money damages." 39 F.R.D., at 102 (emphasis added). The negative implication, they argue, is that it *does* extend to cases in which the appropriate final relief relates only partially and nonpredominantly to money damages. Of course it is the Rule itself, not the Advisory Committee's description of it, that governs. And a mere negative inference does not in our view suffice to establish a disposition that has no basis in the Rule's text, and that does obvious violence to the Rule's structural features. The mere "predominance" of a proper (b)(2) injunctive claim does nothing to justify elimination of Rule 23(b)(3)'s procedural protections: It neither establishes the superiority of *class* adjudication over *individual* adjudication nor cures the notice and opt-out problems. We fail to see why the Rule should be read to nullify these protections whenever a plaintiff class, at its option, combines its monetary claims with a request—even a "predominating request"—for an injunction. * * * *

Finally, respondents argue that their backpay claims are appropriate for a (b)(2) class action because a backpay award is equitable in nature. The latter may be true, but it is irrelevant. The Rule does not speak of "equitable" remedies generally but of injunctions and declaratory judgments. As Title VII itself makes pellucidly clear, backpay is neither. See 42 U.S.C. § 2000e–5(g)(2)(B)(i) and (ii) (distinguishing between declaratory and injunctive relief and the payment of "backpay," see § 2000e–5(g)(2)(A)).

C

In *Allison v. Citgo Petroleum Corp.,* 151 F.3d 402, 415 (C.A.5 1998), the Fifth Circuit held that a (b)(2) class would permit the certification of monetary relief that is "incidental to requested injunctive or declaratory relief," which it defined as "damages that flow directly from liability to the class *as a whole* on the claims forming the basis of the injunctive or declaratory relief." In that court's view, such "incidental damage should not require additional hearings to resolve the disparate merits of each individual's case; it should neither introduce new substantial legal or factual issues, nor entail complex individualized determinations." *Ibid.* We need not decide in this case whether there are any forms of "incidental" monetary relief that are consistent with the interpretation of Rule 23(b)(2) we have announced and that comply with the Due Process Clause. Respondents do not argue that they can satisfy this standard, and in any event they cannot.

Contrary to the Ninth Circuit's view, Wal-Mart is entitled to individualized determinations of each employee's eligibility for backpay. Title VII includes a detailed remedial scheme. If a plaintiff prevails in showing that an employer has discriminated against him in violation of the statute, the court "may enjoin the respondent from engaging in such unlawful employment practice, and order such affirmative action as may be appropriate, [including] reinstatement or hiring of employees, with or without backpay . . . or any other equitable relief as the court deems appropriate." But if the employer can show that it took an adverse employment action against an employee for any reason other than discrimination, the court cannot order the "hiring, reinstatement, or promotion of an individual as an employee, or the payment to him of any backpay."

We have established a procedure for trying pattern-or-practice cases that gives effect to these statutory requirements. When the plaintiff seeks individual relief such as reinstatement or backpay after establishing a pattern or practice of discrimination, "a district court must usually conduct additional proceedings . . . to determine the scope of individual relief." At this phase, the burden of proof will shift to the company, but it will have the right to raise any individual affirmative defenses it may have, and to "demonstrate that the individual applicant was denied an employment opportunity for lawful reasons."

The Court of Appeals believed that it was possible to replace such proceedings with Trial by Formula. A sample set of the class members would be selected, as to whom liability for sex discrimination and the backpay owing as a result would be determined in depositions supervised by a master. The percentage of claims determined to be valid would then be applied to the entire remaining class, and the number of (presumptively) valid claims thus derived would be multiplied by the average backpay award in the sample set to arrive at the entire class recovery—without further individualized proceedings. We disapprove that novel project. Because the Rules Enabling Act forbids interpreting Rule 23 to "abridge, enlarge or modify any substantive right," 28 U.S.C. § 2072(b), a class cannot be certified on the premise that Wal-Mart will not be entitled to litigate its statutory defenses to individual claims. And because the necessity of that litigation will prevent backpay from being "incidental" to the classwide injunction, respondents' class could not be certified even assuming, *arguendo,* that "incidental" monetary relief can be awarded to a 23(b)(2) class. * * *

■ JUSTICE GINSBURG, with whom JUSTICE BREYER, JUSTICE SOTOMAYOR, and JUSTICE KAGAN join, concurring in part and dissenting in part.

The class in this case, I agree with the Court, should not have been certified under Federal Rule of Civil Procedure 23(b)(2). The plaintiffs, alleging discrimination in violation of Title VII, 42 U.S.C. § 2000e et seq., seek monetary relief that is not merely incidental to any injunctive or declaratory relief that might be available. A putative class of this type may be certifiable under Rule 23(b)(3), if the plaintiffs show that common class questions "predominate" over issues affecting individuals—e.g., qualification for, and the amount of, backpay or compensatory damages—and that a class action is "superior" to other modes of adjudication.

Whether the class the plaintiffs describe meets the specific requirements of Rule 23(b)(3) is not before the Court, and I would reserve that matter for consideration and decision on remand. The Court, however, disqualifies the class at the starting gate, holding that the plaintiffs cannot cross the "commonality" line set by Rule 23(a)(2). In so ruling, the Court imports into the Rule 23(a) determination concerns properly addressed in a Rule 23(b)(3) assessment.

I

A

Rule 23(a)(2) establishes a preliminary requirement for maintaining a class action: "[T]here are questions of law or fact common to the class." The Rule "does not require that all questions of law or fact raised in the litigation be common," 1 H. Newberg & A. Conte, Newberg on Class Actions § 3.10, pp. 3–48 to 3–49 (3d ed.1992); indeed, "[e]ven a single question of law or fact common to the members of the class will satisfy the commonality requirement," Nagareda, The Preexistence Principle and the Structure of the Class Action, 103 Colum. L.Rev. 149, 176, n. 110 (2003).

A "question" is ordinarily understood to be "[a] subject or point open to controversy." American Heritage Dictionary 1483 (3d ed.1992). See also Black's Law Dictionary 1366 (9th ed. 2009) (defining "question of fact" as "[a] disputed issue to be resolved . . . [at] trial" and "question of law" as "[a]n issue to be decided by the judge"). Thus, a "question" "common to the class" must be a dispute, either of fact or of law, the resolution of which will advance the determination of the class members' claims.

B

* * * The named plaintiffs, led by Betty Dukes, propose to litigate, on behalf of the class, allegations that Wal-Mart discriminates on the basis of gender in pay and promotions. They allege that the company "[r]eli[es] on gender stereotypes in making employment decisions such as . . . promotion[s][and] pay." Wal-Mart permits those prejudices to infect personnel decisions, the plaintiffs contend, by leaving pay and promotions in the hands of "a nearly all male managerial workforce" using "arbitrary and subjective criteria." Further alleged barriers to the advancement of female employees include the company's requirement, "as a condition of promotion to management jobs, that employees be willing to relocate." Absent instruction otherwise, there is a risk that managers will act on the familiar assumption that women, because of their services to husband and children, are less mobile than men. See Dept. of Labor, Federal Glass Ceiling Commission, Good for Business: Making Full Use of the Nation's Human Capital 151 (1995).

Women fill 70 percent of the hourly jobs in the retailer's stores but make up only "33 percent of management employees." 222 F.R.D., at 146. "[T]he higher one looks in the organization the lower the percentage of women." Id., at 155. The plaintiffs' "largely uncontested descriptive statistics" also show that women working in the company's stores "are paid less than men in every region" and "that the salary gap widens over time even for men and women hired into the same jobs at the same time." Ibid.; cf. Ledbetter v. Goodyear Tire & Rubber Co., 550 U.S. 618, 643, 127 S.Ct. 2162, 167 L.Ed.2d 982 (2007) (GINSBURG, J., dissenting). * * *

Wal-Mart's supervisors do not make their discretionary decisions in a vacuum. The District Court reviewed means Wal-Mart used to maintain a "carefully constructed . . . corporate culture," such as frequent meetings to reinforce the common way of thinking, regular transfers of managers between stores to ensure uniformity throughout the company, monitoring of stores "on a close and constant basis," and "Wal-Mart TV," "broadcas[t] . . . into all stores." Id., at 151–153 (internal quotation marks omitted).

The plaintiffs' evidence, including class members' tales of their own experiences, suggests that gender bias suffused Wal-Mart's company culture. * * * Finally, the plaintiffs presented an expert's appraisal to show that the pay and promotions disparities at Wal-Mart "can be explained only by gender discrimination and not by . . . neutral variables." * * *

C

The District Court's identification of a common question, whether Wal-Mart's pay and promotions policies gave rise to unlawful discrimination, was hardly infirm. The practice of delegating to supervisors large discretion to make personnel decisions, uncontrolled by formal standards, has long been known to have the potential to produce disparate effects. Managers, like all humankind, may be prey to biases of which they are unaware. The risk of discrimination is heightened when those managers are predominantly of one sex, and are steeped in a corporate culture that perpetuates gender stereotypes. * * *

We have held that "discretionary employment practices" can give rise to Title VII claims, not only when such practices are motivated by discriminatory intent but also when they produce discriminatory results. See Watson v. Fort Worth Bank & Trust, 487 U.S. 977, 988, 991, 108 S.Ct. 2777, 101 L.Ed.2d 827 (1988). * * *

The plaintiffs' allegations state claims of gender discrimination in the form of biased decisionmaking in both pay and promotions. The evidence reviewed by the District Court adequately demonstrated that resolving those claims would necessitate examination of particular policies and practices alleged to affect, adversely and globally, women employed at Wal-Mart's stores. Rule 23(a)(2), setting a necessary but not a sufficient criterion for class-action certification, demands nothing further.

II

A

The Court gives no credence to the key dispute common to the class: whether Wal-Mart's discretionary pay and promotion policies are discriminatory. "What matters," the Court asserts, "is not the raising of common 'questions,'" but whether there are "[d]issimilarities within the proposed class" that "have the potential to impede the generation of common answers." . . . The Court blends Rule 23(a)(2)'s threshold criterion with the more demanding criteria of Rule 23(b)(3), and thereby elevates the (a)(2) inquiry so that it is no longer "easily satisfied," 5 J. Moore et al., Moore's Federal Practice § 23.23[2], p. 23–72 (3d ed. 2011). Rule 23(b)(3) certification requires, in addition to the four 23(a) findings, determinations that "questions of law or fact common to class members predominate over any questions affecting only individual members" and that "a class action is superior to other available methods for . . . adjudicating the controversy."

The Court's emphasis on differences between class members mimics the Rule 23(b)(3) inquiry into whether common questions "predominate" over individual issues. And by asking whether the individual differences "impede" common adjudication, the Court duplicates 23(b)(3)'s question whether "a class action is superior" to other modes of adjudication. . . . "The Rule 23(b)(3) predominance inquiry" is meant to "tes[t] whether proposed classes are sufficiently cohesive to warrant adjudication by representation." Amchem Products, Inc. v. Windsor, 521 U.S. 591, 623, 117 S.Ct. 2231, 138 L.Ed.2d 689 (1997). If courts must conduct a "dissimilarities" analysis at the Rule 23(a)(2) stage, no mission remains for Rule 23(b)(3).

Because Rule 23(a) is also a prerequisite for Rule 23(b)(1) and Rule 23(b)(2) classes, the Court's "dissimilarities" position is far reaching. Individual differences should not bar a Rule 23(b)(1) or Rule 23(b)(2) class, so long as the Rule 23(a) threshold is met. * * *

B

The "dissimilarities" approach leads the Court to train its attention on what distinguishes individual class members, rather than on what unites them. Given the lack of standards for pay and promotions, the majority says, "demonstrating the invalidity of one manager's use of discretion will do nothing to demonstrate the invalidity of another's."

Wal-Mart's delegation of discretion over pay and promotions is a policy uniform throughout all stores. The very nature of discretion is that people will exercise it in various ways. A system of delegated discretion, Watson held, is a practice actionable under Title VII when it produces discriminatory outcomes. . . . That each individual employee's unique circumstances will ultimately determine whether she is entitled to backpay or damages, § 2000e–5(g)(2)(A) (barring backpay if a plaintiff "was refused . . . advancement . . . for any reason other than discrimination"), should not factor into the Rule 23(a)(2) determination.

* * *

The Court errs in importing a "dissimilarities" notion suited to Rule 23(b)(3) into the Rule 23(a) commonality inquiry. I therefore cannot join Part II of the Court's opinion.

NOTES AND QUESTIONS

1. **Overview.** The *Wal-Mart* decision addresses several important aspects of class action practice under Rule 23: the proper standard for a district court to apply in deciding whether to certify a class; what constitutes a "common question" sufficient to satisfy Rule 23(a)(2); and the question of whether and under what circumstances claims for monetary relief can be included in a class certified under Rule 23(b)(2).

2. **Standard to be applied by the district court at certification.** Over the years, there has been considerable uncertainty about the degree to which judges considering a class-certification motion should rely on the pleadings, or should instead inquire into the facts relevant to the elements of Rule 23 and make explicit findings concerning those elements. The *Wal-Mart* Court's statement that the plaintiff must "affirmatively demonstrate" that the elements of the Rule have been satisfied "in fact" aligns the Court with the weight of authority in the lower federal courts holding that factual determinations supporting Rule 23 findings must be based upon an appropriate evidentiary record (including discovery if necessary) and be made by a preponderance of the evidence. See, e.g., In re Hydrogen Peroxide Antitrust Litigation, 552 F.3d 305 (3d Cir. 2008). This trend is summarized in Marcus, Reviving Judicial Gatekeeping of Aggregation: Scrutinizing the Merits on Class Certification, 79 Geo. Wash. L. Rev. 324 (2011). Consider the effect of the Court's holding in this respect alongside its recent pleading decisions, discussed in Chapter 4.

Do a court's factual determinations at class certification infringe upon the parties' right to a jury trial? See Hazard, Fact Determinations in Rule 23 Class Actions, 82 Geo. Wash. L. Rev. 990 (2014). When a court makes such factual determinations, is it required to follow the Federal Rules of Evidence? See Mullenix, Putting Proponents to Their Proof: Evidentiary Rules at Class Certification, 82 Geo. Wash. L. Rev. 606 (2014).

3. The Rule 23(a)(2) commonality requirement. In *Wal-Mart* the Court says that the key to commonality under Rule 23(a)(2) is that the class claims must "depend on a common contention" whose determination "will resolve an issue that is central to the validity of each one of the class claims in one stroke." Because Rule 23(a)(2) requires only a single common question, often the common question requirement is easily satisfied. In an environmental case, for instance, the common question might be whether a company's discharge of pollutants exceeds the levels permitted by law. Alternatively, a common question may be shown when the claims in the case turn on the interpretation or truthfulness of a document, such as a consumer contract or a required written disclosure to shareholders of a publicly traded company. Or, in an antitrust case, a common question may be whether defendants conspired to create a monopoly. See generally 7A Wright, Miller & Kane, Federal Practice & Procedure § 1763. What was the "common question" asserted by the plaintiffs in *Wal-Mart*?

In the traditional model of a Rule 23(b)(2) civil rights class action, the common question was often the existence of an explicit policy of discrimination. Such a policy was at stake in perhaps the most famous class action of all: Brown v. Board of Education, 347 U.S. 453 (1954). According to the majority in *Wal-Mart*, would proof of an explicit company-wide policy of discrimination have sufficed to create a common question here? If so, why didn't the conceded existence of a company-wide policy of delegated subjective decision making at Wal-Mart establish the existence of a question common to all class members? Consider the Court's suggestion that a policy of delegated discretion, standing alone, was not unlawful—indeed that it was "a very common and presumptively reasonable way of doing business."

Prior to the Court's decision in *Wal-Mart*, the commonality requirement was thought to be a relatively low bar, almost an afterthought in many class actions. Do you think the Court has calibrated the commonality requirement correctly? For an argument that the Court has gone too far, see Spencer, Class Actions, Heightened Commonality, and Declining Access to Justice, 93 B.U. L. Rev. 441 (2013); Resnik, Fairness in Numbers: A Comment on AT&T v. Concepcion, Wal-Mart v. Dukes, and Turner v. Rogers, 125 Harv. L. Rev. 78 (2011). Do you agree with Justice Ginsburg's contention that the Court has conflated the commonality requirement of Rule 23(a)(2) with the predominance requirement of Rule 23(b)(3)? For a similar analysis, see Klonoff, The Decline of Class Actions, 90 Wash. U. L. Rev. 729 (2013).

4. The Court's rejection of plaintiffs' theory. In holding that the plaintiffs did not effectively establish commonality, the Court rejected the contention that Wal-Mart's discretionary employment policies produced discriminatory results because Wal-Mart's corporate culture embraced gender stereotypes. Compare Part II.B of the majority opinion with Part I.C of the dissent. Whose analysis do you find more persuasive? There is a wealth of material in the fields of sociology and psychology about the links between stereotyping and implicit biases and discrimination. For an introduction, see Heilman & Haynes, Subjectivity in the Appraisal Process, in Beyond Common Sense: Psychological Science in the Courtroom (Borgida & Fiske eds. 2008).

5. The Court's 23(b)(2) decision. All nine justices agree that the case was not properly brought under Rule 23(b)(2), despite the fact that the plaintiffs concededly sought substantial injunctive relief. Given the Court's unanimity on this question, should it have reached the question of whether the class met the commonality requirement?

In any event, according to the Court, the reason certification under Rule 23(b)(2) was improper in this case is that the claims for back pay are "individualized monetary claims." Why should claims for individualized monetary relief make a class action improper under Rule 23(b)(2)? Consider the different procedural requirements of class actions under Rule 23(b)(2) and 23(b)(3).

Why does the presence of individualized claims for damages call for more procedural protections than an action for a company-wide injunction? Part of the answer stems from the nature of the relief: an injunction is purely prospective and establishes a uniform standard of conduct for the defendant that will necessarily affect all present and future employees, whether there is a class action or not. Thus plaintiffs don't lose anything obvious by being included in a class and may gain by having their claims considered from a group-wide, rather than individual, perspective. The defendant may also benefit because class treatment eliminates the risk of separate actions leading to inconsistent injunctions. Part of the answer is efficiency: if a class action can be tried without individuated proof, the proceeding is vastly more efficient than a series of individual actions. In contrast, once individualized monetary relief is in play, there may be substantial variation in the actual harm suffered by individual plaintiffs, plaintiffs may have a stronger interest in controlling their own individual claims, defendants are much less likely to benefit from aggregation, and efficiency is much more elusive. Hence the Court argues, the more stringent tests for certification imposed by Rule 23(b)(3) are called for, as is the opportunity for the plaintiffs to opt out. Are these concerns sufficient to explain the Court's holding in *Wal-Mart*?

6. Can any monetary relief be awarded in a 23(b)(2) class action? Prior to the Court's decision, a number of lower courts had held that back pay remedies could be sought as part of a (b)(2) class action. See In re Monumental Life Ins. Co., 365 F.3d 408 (5th Cir. 2004); Robinson v. Metro-North R.R., 267 F.3d 147 (2d Cir. 2001). The Court's decision in *Wal-Mart* clearly establishes otherwise, at least where back pay determinations are necessarily individualized.

Does the Court's holding leave any room for plaintiffs ever to obtain significant monetary relief under Rule 23(b)(2)? Could there be cases where the determination of liability effectively determines the amount of individual damages? See Berger v. Xerox Corp. Retirement Income Guarantee Plan, 338 F.3d 755 (7th Cir. 2003) (23(b)(2) class action permitted when class-wide pension formula used by defendant was illegal; correct formula could be mechanically applied to compute each plaintiff's recovery). Would the due process clause still require the use of Rule 23(b)(3) in such cases, at least when the amount of monetary relief is more than trivial? Or does the fact that the fact and amount of monetary relief depend wholly on a common issue eliminate the need for such notice?

The Seventh Circuit has begun to answer these post-*Wal-Mart* questions. In Johnson v. Meriter Health Servs. Employee Ret. Plan, 702 F.3d 364 (7th Cir. 2012), a plaintiff class filed suit under ERISA, a federal statute establishing certain rules for employee retirement plans, alleging that they had not received all of the benefits to which they were entitled under their plan. The court rejected the argument that *Wal-Mart* precludes any monetary relief in a 23(b)(2) class action. It distinguished *Wal-Mart*, where a fair determination of pay could require an individualized hearing for each class member, noting the lack of notice or ability to opt out in a 23(b)(2) action. In this case, however, the court explained that it was possible that the "calculation of monetary relief will be mechanical, formulaic, a task not for a trier of fact but for a computer program," eliminating concerns about excessive individualized hearings on damages while still ensuring a fair award. Id. at 372. For further discussion of this question, see Klonoff, Class Actions for Monetary Relief Under Rule 23(b)(1)(A) and (b)(1)(B): Does Due Process Require Notice and Opt Out Rights?, 82 Geo. Wash. L. Rev. 798 (2014); Bradt, Much to Gain and Nothing to Lose: Implications of the History of the Declaratory Judgment for the (b)(2) Class Action, 58 Ark. L. Rev. 767 (2006).

7. Further reading. *Wal-Mart* has already spawned a large literature. In addition those cited above, other excellent articles include: Bone, The Misguided Search for Class Unity, 82 Geo. Wash. L. Rev. 651 (2014); Hines, The Unruly Class Action, 82 Geo. Wash. L. Rev. 718 (2014); Vairo, Is the Class Action Really Dead? Is That Good or Bad for Class Members?, 64 Emory L.J. 477 (2014); Rutherglen, The Way Forward After Wal-Mart, 88 Notre Dame L. Rev. 871 (2012).

Chandler v. Southwest Jeep-Eagle, Inc.

United States District Court, Northern District of Illinois, 1995.
162 F.R.D. 302.

■ CASTILLO, DISTRICT JUDGE

Plaintiff Raymond Chandler ("Chandler") sues defendants Southwest Jeep-Eagle, Inc. ("Southwest") and Calumet National Bank ("Calumet") seeking redress for alleged misrepresentations and unfair and deceptive practices in connection with Southwest's standard retail installment contract. Counts I and II of the complaint, the class claims, are alleged only against Southwest. Count I alleges that Southwest made certain misrepresentations in its retail installment contracts in violation of the Truth in Lending Act, 15 U.S.C. § 1601 et seq. ("TILA"). Count II alleges that the misrepresentations amounted to deceptive practices under the Illinois Consumer Fraud and Deceptive Business Practices Act, 815 ILCS 505/1 et seq. ("Consumer Fraud Act"). Counts III through VI are all claims brought by Chandler alone against Southwest and Calumet, the financial institution that financed the purchase. * * *

Pursuant to Federal Rule of Civil Procedure 23, Chandler moves for class certification with respect to counts I and II. Specifically, Chandler proposes that the class be defined as all persons who satisfy each of the following four criteria:

(i) they purchased a service contract or extended warranty from Southwest;

(ii) their transaction was financed by a retail installment contract;

(iii) their transaction was documented as a consumer transaction (i.e., TILA disclosures were made); and

(iv) the retail installment contract states that an amount was paid to a third party on account of an extended warranty or service contract that is other than the amount actually collected by the third party.

Plaintiff's Motion for Class Certification at 4.

With respect to count I, the TILA claim, the proposed class includes anyone whose retail installment contract is dated on or after October 12, 1993, one year prior to the date Chandler filed his original complaint. With respect to count II, the Consumer Fraud Act claim, the proposed class includes anyone whose retail installment contract was outstanding on or after October 12, 1991, three years prior to the date Chandler filed his original complaint. The different temporal parameters of the two classes is a product of the different statutes of limitation for TILA and the Consumer Fraud Act. A TILA action must be filed within one year of the contract date, 15 U.S.C. § 1640(e), while the Consumer Fraud Act has a three-year statute of limitations, 815 ILCS 505/10a(e).[1]

* * *

BACKGROUND

Southwest operates an automobile dealership. Calumet is a nationally chartered bank. On May 23, 1994, Chandler purchased from Southwest a used Chrysler automobile to be used for personal, family and household purposes. At the time he purchased the car, Chandler signed Southwest's standard motor vehicle retail installment sales contract, which was subsequently assigned to Calumet. Chandler also informed Southwest that he wished to purchase a full warranty from Chrysler that would be transferrable to another authorized Chrysler dealership for the purpose of repairs. Southwest informed Chandler that the price for a full warranty was $1,780.40 and provided Chandler with its standard service contract, on which the fee amount was listed under the subheading "Amounts Paid to Others for You," along with taxes, insurance premiums, and license, title, registration and filing fees, none of which were negotiable. Chandler signed the contract and paid the $1,780.40 fee to Southwest.

Chandler alleges, however, that Southwest only transferred a small portion of the $1,780.40 to Chrysler, retaining the balance, and that the fee amount was actually unilaterally determined by Southwest and therefore negotiable. Chandler charges that the method by which the cost was listed on the contract is misleading, unfair and deceptive. He alleges that Southwest intended him and other purchasers to rely on the misleading, unfair and deceptive representation and thus not attempt to negotiate the price of the service contract, allowing Southwest routinely to overcharge customers. He further alleges that had he known that the cost of the service contract was negotiable, neither he nor the average consumer would have paid as much.

Shortly after Chandler purchased his vehicle, it developed substantial mechanical problems. Chandler brought the car back to

---

[1] Although separate classes are at issue for each count because of these timing issues, the members' characteristics are materially identical. The difference in class size is solely the result of the different statutes of limitations for TILA and the Consumer Fraud Act. Because the operative facts and legal theory on which both claims are based are identical, for ease of exposition this opinion generally refers to both classes as a single unit.

Southwest numerous times for engine work and repairs to the radiator, tachometer, oil pressure and temperature gauges, air condenser, power steering, transmission, front wheel drive, alignment, internal computers and radio. Southwest, which kept the vehicle for lengthy periods of time, allegedly in order to complete the repairs, purportedly performed some repairs, but most of the problems remained uncorrected. Southwest refused Chandler's request to view the defective auto parts that Southwest allegedly had replaced.

After becoming frustrated with Southwest's inability to make the necessary repairs, Chandler took the vehicle to another authorized Chrysler dealer and requested service under the Chrysler service contract that he had purchased through Southwest. The dealer informed Chandler that the Chrysler warranty computer showed no record of Chandler's service contract, and refused to perform the necessary repairs. The dealer also informed Chandler that the vehicle model that Chandler had purchased from Southwest was the subject of several outstanding manufacturer's recalls with respect to which Southwest had not made repairs prior to selling the vehicle to Chandler. Chandler returned to Southwest for several more unsuccessful attempts to have the vehicle repaired. On September 13, 1994, Chandler revoked his acceptance of the vehicle on the basis of unmerchantability. Chandler claims that Southwest failed to make the necessary repairs to the defective vehicle as promised under the service contract and then fraudulently evaded responsibility for the car's condition.

ANALYSIS

Class Certification for Counts I and II

The party seeking class certification bears the burden of establishing that certification is proper. *Retired Chicago Police Ass'n v. City of Chicago*, 7 F.3d 584, 596 (7th Cir. 1993).

Rule 23 requires a two-step analysis to determine whether class certification is appropriate. First, the action must satisfy all four requirements of Rule 23(a). That is, "the plaintiff must meet the prerequisites of numerosity, commonality, typicality, and adequacy of representation." *Harriston v. Chicago Tribune Co.*, 992 F.2d 697, 703 (7th Cir. 1993) (internal quotation marks omitted). "All of these elements are prerequisites to certification; failure to meet any one of these precludes certification as a class." *Retired Chicago Police*, 7 F.3d at 596; *Harriston*, 992 F.2d at 703. Second, the action must satisfy one of the conditions of Rule 23(b). *Alliance to End Repression v. Rochford*, 565 F.2d 975, 977 (7th Cir. 1977). Chandler seeks certification under Rule 23(b)(3), which requires that questions of law or fact common to class members predominate over questions affecting only individual members, and that a class action be superior to other available methods for the fair and efficient adjudication of the controversy.

Chandler maintains that all of the requirements of Rule 23(a) and (b)(3) are met. Southwest contends that Chandler fails to meet any of Rule 23's requirements. Accordingly, we address each of the requirements for Rule 23(b)(3) certification in turn below.

A. Numerosity

Rule 23's first express requirement is that the class be "so numerous that joinder of all members is impracticable." Fed. R. Civ. P. 23(a)(1). The issue of whether the numerosity requirement is satisfied is extremely fact-specific. Courts have granted class certification to groups smaller than 30, see Riordan v. Smith Barney, 113 F.R.D. 60 (N.D. Ill. 1986) (finding 29 class members sufficient in securities fraud case where the class members were geographically diverse), and denied class certification in cases where the proposed class exceeded 100 members. Marcial v. Coronet Ins. Co., 880 F.2d 954 (7th Cir. 1989) (denying certification to proposed class of 400–600 members where class membership could only be determined by an inquiry into the individual circumstances of each member); In re Cardinal Indus., 139 Bankr. 703 (Bankr. S.D. Ohio 1991) (holding that 205 class members was not sufficient where joinder is practicable because the majority of class members were controlled by the same corporation); Liberty Lincoln-Mercury, Inc. v. Ford Marketing Corp., 149 F.R.D. 65 (D.N.J. 1993) (finding that 123 class members was not sufficient where the class members were large businesses capable of litigating their claims individually). As a general proposition, although the numerosity analysis does not rest on any magic number, permissive joinder is usually deemed impracticable where the class members number 40 or more. See H. Newberg, Class Actions § 305 (1992); Ikonen v. Hartz Mountain Corp., 122 F.R.D. 258, 262 (S.D. Cal. 1988). That standard is met in this case.

Southwest concedes that the proposed class would consist of approximately 50 members for purposes of the TILA claim [count I] and approximately 150 members for purposes of the Consumer Fraud Act claim [count II], but argues that these classes are insufficiently numerous to warrant certification. Southwest cites *Marcial, In re Cardinal Indus.,* and *Liberty Lincoln-Mercury* as support for its argument. However, in each of these cases, class certification was denied for reasons unrelated to numerosity. Moreover, the facts of this case are significantly different than those presented in the cases cited by Southwest. In the instant case, the dispute concerns a standard form document signed by all proposed class members, who are otherwise unrelated and would unlikely be motivated to bring individual actions given the relatively small size of the claim. These factors militate in favor of class certification even where the number of class members is relatively small. See, e.g., Swanson v. American Consumer Indus., 415 F.2d 1326, 1333 n.9 (7th Cir. 1969) (finding 40 class members sufficient for certification where individual class members are widely scattered and the amount at issue too small to warrant undertaking individual actions). In the instant case, the Court finds that the proposed classes are sufficiently numerous to make joinder impracticable. Accordingly, we find the numerosity requirement to be satisfied.

B. Commonality

Rule 23(a)(2) requires the presence of questions of law or fact common to the class. A "common nucleus of operative fact" is generally enough to satisfy the commonality requirement. Rosario v. Livaditis, 963 F.2d 1013, 1018 (7th Cir. 1992) (citing Franklin v. City of Chicago, 102 F.R.D. 944, 949–50 (N.D. Ill. 1984)). A common nucleus of operative fact is typically found where, as in the instant case, the defendants have engaged in standardized conduct toward members of the proposed class.

In the instant case, all proposed class members purchased a standard service contract from Southwest. Thus, their claims all involve the common question of whether the disclosure provisions of Southwest's standard retail installment contract violated TILA and/or the Consumer Fraud Act. Southwest contends that the commonality requirement is not met because each class member must prove reliance and actual damages. It is well-established, however, that the presence of some individualized *satisfied* issues does not overshadow the common nucleus of operative fact presented when the defendant has engaged in standardized conduct toward the class. Accordingly, we find that the commonality requirement is satisfied.

C. Typicality

Rule 23(a)(3) requires that the representative plaintiff's claims be typical of those of the class. This requirement focuses on whether the named representative's claim has the same essential characteristics of the claims of the class at large. A plaintiff's claim is typical "if it arises from the same event or practice or course of conduct that gives rise to the claims of other class members and his or her claims are based on the same legal theory." *De La Fuente,* 713 F.2d 225, 232 (7th Cir. 1983) (quoting H. Newberg, Class Actions § 115(b) at 185 (1977)). In this case, the legal theory underlying Chandler's class claims is that the standard retail installment contract provided to him and all other proposed class members violated TILA and/or the Consumer Fraud Act. Plainly, Chandler's TILA and Consumer Fraud Act claims arise out of the same course of conduct giving rise to the claims of the other class members. Southwest maintains, however, that Chandler is an atypical class representative because his own deposition testimony suggests that he did not rely on (or was not misled by) any alleged misrepresentation.[8]

It is clear that Chandler has fairly alleged that he relied upon and was deceived by Southwest's misrepresentation. Amended Complaint at ¶¶ 24, 28. Furthermore, Southwest reads Chandler's testimony selectively. In his deposition, Chandler clearly states that he believed that the amount charged would be transferred to the service contract provider. Plaintiff's Reply in Support of Motion for Class Certification at 9. Although Southwest may ultimately prove that Chandler did not rely on the alleged misrepresentation, the determination of whether *Satisfied* Chandler is a typical class member for purposes of class certification does not depend on the resolution of the merits of the case. The typicality requirement is satisfied.

---

[8] Southwest characterizes Chandler's deposition testimony as indicating that at the time of the transaction, he had no expectation one way or the other as to whether Southwest would be making a profit on the sale of the service contract. Defendant's Response in Opposition to Plaintiff's Motion for Class Certification at 6. Southwest argues that Chandler's statements indicate that because he did not consider at the time of the transaction whether Southwest was making a profit, he could not have been deceived by the contract terms. Accordingly, Southwest asserts that Chandler's claims could not be considered typical of class members who were allegedly misled by the contract. *See id.* at 7. It should be noted that Southwest's arguments really go to the merits of Chandler's claims rather than their typicality.

D.   Adequacy of Representation

Rule 23(a)(4)'s adequacy requirement has three elements: (1) the chosen class representative cannot have antagonistic or conflicting claims with other members of the class, *Rosario,* 963 F.2d 1013 (7th Cir. 1992); (2) the named representative must have a "sufficient interest in the outcome to ensure vigorous advocacy," *Riordan,* 113 F.R.D. 60, 64 (N.D. Ill. 1986); and, (3) counsel for the named plaintiff must be competent, experienced, qualified, and generally able to conduct the proposed litigation vigorously. *Id.* Southwest challenges Chandler's ability to satisfy the last of these three requirements.[9] Southwest notes that at least one judge has expressed doubt regarding Chandler's counsel's ability to represent a class. *See* Dartmouth Plan, Inc. v. Delgado, 87 CH 6676 (Cook Co. Cir. Court 1993). Notwithstanding the foregoing, this Court is satisfied that Chandler's attorneys have demonstrated that they possess the necessary qualifications to represent adequately a class of consumers under TILA and the Consumer Fraud Act. Chandler's attorneys have successfully prosecuted numerous consumer class actions—including actions before this Court. *See* Plaintiff's Memorandum in Support of Motion for Class Certification, App. G. In addition, a number of courts have commented favorably on their performance in class actions. See e.g., Bermudez v. First of Am. Bank, No. 93 C 3653 (N.D. Ill. Feb. 14, 1995); Brown v. Lasalle N.W. Nat'l Bank, 1993 U.S. Dist. LEXIS 11419, No. 92 C 8392, 1993 WL 313563 at *5 (N.D. Ill. Aug. 17, 1993); Johnson v. Steven Sims Subaru Leasing, 1993 U.S. Dist. LEXIS 8078, No. 92 C 6355, 1993 WL 761231 at *5 (N.D. Ill. June 9, 1993). Accordingly, we find that Chandler has met his burden of satisfying Rule 23(a)(4)'s adequacy of representation requirement.

E.   Predominance of Common Questions of Law or Fact

Class certification pursuant to Rule 23(b)(3) requires a determination that "questions of law or fact common to the members of the class predominate over any questions affecting only individual members, and that a class action is superior to other methods for the fair and efficient adjudication of the controversy." Fed. R. Civ. P. 23(b)(3).

1.   Common Questions of Law and Fact Predominate

Considerable overlap exists between Rule 23(a)(2)'s commonality prerequisite and 23(b)(3). Rule 23(a)(2) requires that common questions exist; Rule 23(b)(3) requires that they predominate. Many of the issues raised by Southwest relating to the relative importance of common issues have been addressed and disposed of above in the Court's discussion of Rule (a)(2)'s commonality requirement.

In considering whether common questions of law or fact predominate, the common issues need not be dispositive of the entire litigation. *Riordan,* 113 F.R.D. 60, 65 (N.D. Ill. 1986). "Instead, resolution of the predominance question tends to focus on the form trial on the issues would take, with consideration of whether the action would be manageable." Elliott v. ITT Corp., 150 F.R.D. 569, 577 (N.D. Ill. 1992)

---

[9]   Southwest somewhat half-heartedly asserts that Chandler is not personally motivated to pursue the claims on behalf of the class and that this action is driven by Chandler's counsel. However, Southwest has made no showing that Chandler is not an adequate representative of the class; and, the fact that Chandler's counsel has prosecuted numerous other class actions, standing alone, does not vitiate Chandler's role as a class representative.

(citing Simer v. Rios, 661 F.2d 655, 672–73 (7th Cir. 1981), cert. denied, 456 U.S. 917, 72 L.Ed.2d 177, 102 S.Ct. 1773 (1982)).

The predominance requirement is generally satisfied where a "common nucleus of operative fact" exists among all class members for which the law provides a remedy. Halverson v. Convenient Food Mart, 69 F.R.D. 331, 335 (N.D. Ill. 1974). Both TILA and the Consumer Fraud Act claims lend themselves readily to the finding that a common issue predominates over individual issues, as the principal question presented is whether the disclosure provisions of Southwest's standard retail installment contract provided to Chandler and all the proposed class members violated TILA and/or the Consumer Fraud Act.

Southwest suggests that the damages claimed by each class member can only be calculated by determining the extent of each individual's actual reliance on the alleged misrepresentation, and thus that common questions do not predominate. The Illinois Supreme Court has held, however, that reliance is not an element of a Consumer Fraud Act claim. Martin v. Heinold Commodities, 163 Ill. 2d 33, 643 N.E.2d 734, 754, 205 Ill. Dec. 443 (Ill. 1994). The question of reliance and individualized damages therefore does not arise at all in relation to the Consumer Fraud Act claim. With respect to the TILA claim, we note that predominance is not precluded even if individualized proof of damages is required. See, e.g., Rules Advisory Comm. Notes to 1966 Amends. to Rule 23, 39 F.R.D. 69, 103 (1966); Blackie v. Barrack, 524 F.2d 891, 905 (9th Cir. 1975), cert. denied, 429 U.S. 816, 50 L.Ed.2d 75, 97 S.Ct. 57 (1976) (noting that the amount of damages is invariably an individual question and does not defeat class action treatment); Heartland Communications, 161 F.R.D. 111, 1995 U.S. Dist. LEXIS 6207, 1995 WL 262631 at *4 (holding that the predominance requirement is satisfied even in the presence of individual questions where the critical issues are the defendant's standardized conduct towards class members and interpretation of the defendant's standard contract language). As long as the allocation of individualized damages does not create problems of unmanageability, which it does not in this case, a court may grant class certification. De La Fuente, 713 F.2d 225, 233 (holding that the administrative complications that may arise in calculating individual damages do not suffice to render district court's grant of class certification an abuse of discretion). For the foregoing reasons, this Court finds the predominance requirement to be satisfied.

2.   Class Action is Superior to Other Methods of Litigating This Matter

Rule 23(b)(3) provides a non-exhaustive list of factors for courts to consider in determining the superiority of class actions to individual litigation. These factors include the interest of individual members in individually controlling the litigation, the desirability of concentrating the litigation in the particular forum, and the manageability of the class action.

The Court finds that a class action is superior to other methods of litigating this matter for several reasons. First, as should be clear from the foregoing discussion, this case poses no unusual manageability concerns arising from either the size of the class or the adjudication of damages. Second, most of the proposed class members are individual consumers who are probably unaware of their rights under TILA and the Consumer Fraud Act. A class action would help to ensure that their rights are protected. Third, the size of each individual claim is relatively small. Class members, even if aware of their rights, likely would lack the initiative to bring suit individually. See Haynes v. Logan Furniture Mart, Inc., 503 F.2d 1161, 1164–65 (7th Cir. 1974) (finding "the improbability that large numbers of class members would possess the initiative to litigate individually" pertinent to superiority finding). Fourth, efficiency and consistency concerns favor trying the legality of a document challenged by all class members in one litigation, rather than forcing each proposed class member to litigate his or her claim individually. Scholes v. Stone, 143 F.R.D. 181 (N.D. Ill. 1992). In view of these considerations, the Court finds Rule 23(b)(3)'s superiority element to be satisfied.

Having determined that all of the prerequisites of Rule 23(a) are satisfied and that the action also meets the conditions of Rule 23(b)(3), the Court grants plaintiff's motion for class certification for counts I and II. This action may be maintained as a class action with the class defined, as in plaintiff's motion and memorandum in support of class certification, as follows:

(1)   Count I: All individuals who purchased a service contract from the defendant by means of a standard retail installment contract, dated on or after October 12, 1993, in which the TILA disclosures represented that the defendant paid an amount to a third party in exchange for a service contract that was different from the amount actually paid.

(2)   Count II: All individuals who purchased a service contract from the defendant by means of a standard retail installment contract, outstanding on or after October 12, 1991, in which the TILA disclosures represented that the defendant paid an amount to a third party in exchange for a service contract that was different from the amount actually paid.

* * *

Comcast Corp. v. Behrend

United States Supreme Court, 1995.
133 S.Ct. 1426, 185 L.Ed.2d 515.

■ JUSTICE SCALIA delivered the opinion of the Court.

The District Court and the Court of Appeals approved certification of a class of more than 2 million current and former Comcast subscribers who seek damages for alleged violations of the federal antitrust laws. We consider whether certification was appropriate under Federal Rule of Civil Procedure 23(b)(3).

I

Comcast Corporation and its subsidiaries, petitioners here, provide cable-television services to residential and commercial customers. From 1998 to 2007, petitioners engaged in a series of transactions that the parties have described as "clustering," a strategy of concentrating operations within a particular region. The region at issue here, which the parties have referred to as the Philadelphia "cluster" or the Philadelphia

"Designated Market Area" (DMA), includes 16 counties located in Pennsylvania, Delaware, and New Jersey. Petitioners pursued their clustering strategy by acquiring competitor cable providers in the region and swapping their own systems outside the region for competitor systems located in the region. For instance, in 2001, petitioners obtained Adelphia Communications' cable systems in the Philadelphia DMA, along with its 464,000 subscribers; in exchange, petitioners sold to Adelphia their systems in Palm Beach, Florida, and Los Angeles, California. As a result of nine clustering transactions, petitioners' share of subscribers in the region allegedly increased from 23.9 percent in 1998 to 69.5 percent in 2007.

The named plaintiffs, respondents here, are subscribers to Comcast's cable-television services. They filed a class-action antitrust suit against petitioners, claiming that petitioners entered into unlawful swap agreements, in violation of § 1 of the Sherman Act, and monopolized or attempted to monopolize services in the cluster, in violation of § 2. 15 U.S.C. §§ 1, 2. Petitioners' clustering scheme, respondents contended, harmed subscribers in the Philadelphia cluster by eliminating competition and holding prices for cable services above competitive levels.

Respondents sought to certify a class under Federal Rule of Civil Procedure 23(b)(3). That provision permits certification only if "the court finds that the questions of law or fact common to class members predominate over any questions affecting only individual members." The District Court held, and it is uncontested here, that to meet the predominance requirement respondents had to show (1) that the existence of individual injury resulting from the alleged antitrust violation (referred to as "antitrust impact") was "capable of proof at trial through evidence that [was] common to the class rather than individual to its members"; and (2) that the damages resulting from that injury were measurable "on a class-wide basis" through use of a "common methodology."

Respondents proposed four theories of antitrust impact: First, Comcast's clustering made it profitable for Comcast to withhold local sports programming from its competitors, resulting in decreased market penetration by direct broadcast satellite providers. Second, Comcast's activities reduced the level of competition from "overbuilders," companies that build competing cable networks in areas where an incumbent cable company already operates. Third, Comcast reduced the level of "benchmark" competition on which cable customers rely to compare prices. Fourth, clustering increased Comcast's bargaining power relative to content providers. Each of these forms of impact, respondents alleged, increased cable subscription rates throughout the Philadelphia DMA.

The District Court accepted the overbuilder theory of antitrust impact as capable of classwide proof and rejected the rest. Accordingly, in its certification order, the District Court limited respondents' "proof of antitrust impact" to "the theory that Comcast engaged in anticompetitive clustering conduct, the effect of which was to deter the entry of overbuilders in the Philadelphia DMA."

The District Court further found that the damages resulting from overbuilder-deterrence impact could be calculated on a classwide basis.

To establish such damages, respondents had relied solely on the testimony of Dr. James McClave. Dr. McClave designed a regression model comparing actual cable prices in the Philadelphia DMA with hypothetical prices that would have prevailed but for petitioners' allegedly anticompetitive activities. The model calculated damages of $875,576,662 for the entire class. As Dr. McClave acknowledged, however, the model did not isolate damages resulting from any one theory of antitrust impact. The District Court nevertheless certified the class.

A divided panel of the Court of Appeals affirmed. * * *

II

The class action is "an exception to the usual rule that litigation is conducted by and on behalf of the individual named parties only." Califano v. Yamasaki, 442 U.S. 682, 700–701, 99 S.Ct. 2545, 61 L.Ed.2d 176 (1979). To come within the exception, a party seeking to maintain a class action "must affirmatively demonstrate his compliance" with Rule 23. Wal-Mart Stores, Inc. v. Dukes, 564 U.S. ___, ___, 131 S.Ct. 2541, 2551–2552, 180 L.Ed.2d 374 (2011). The Rule "does not set forth a mere pleading standard." Ibid. Rather, a party must not only "be prepared to prove that there are in fact sufficiently numerous parties, common questions of law or fact," typicality of claims or defenses, and adequacy of representation, as required by Rule 23(a). Ibid. The party must also satisfy through evidentiary proof at least one of the provisions of Rule 23(b). The provision at issue here is Rule 23(b)(3), which requires a court to find that "the questions of law or fact common to class members predominate over any questions affecting only individual members."

Repeatedly, we have emphasized that it " 'may be necessary for the court to probe behind the pleadings before coming to rest on the certification question,' and that certification is proper only if 'the trial court is satisfied, after a rigorous analysis, that the prerequisites of Rule 23(a) have been satisfied.' " Ibid. (quoting General Telephone Co. of Southwest v. Falcon, 457 U.S. 147, 160–161, 102 S.Ct. 2364, 72 L.Ed.2d 740 (1982)). Such an analysis will frequently entail "overlap with the merits of the plaintiff's underlying claim." 564 U.S., at ___, 131 S.Ct., at 2551. That is so because the " 'class determination generally involves considerations that are enmeshed in the factual and legal issues comprising the plaintiff's cause of action.' " Ibid. (quoting Falcon, supra, at 160, 102 S.Ct. 2364).

The same analytical principles govern Rule 23(b). If anything, Rule 23(b)(3)'s predominance criterion is even more demanding than Rule 23(a). Amchem Products, Inc. v. Windsor, 521 U.S. 591, 623–624, 117 S.Ct. 2231, 138 L.Ed.2d 689 (1997). Rule 23(b)(3), as an " 'adventuresome innovation,' " is designed for situations " 'in which "class-action treatment is not as clearly called for." ' " Wal-Mart, supra, at ___, 131 S.Ct., at 2558 (quoting Amchem, 521 U.S., at 614–615, 117 S.Ct. 2231). That explains Congress's addition of procedural safeguards for (b)(3) class members beyond those provided for (b)(1) or (b)(2) class members (e.g., an opportunity to opt out), and the court's duty to take a " 'close look' " at whether common questions predominate over individual ones. Id. at 615, 117 S.Ct. 2231.

III

Respondents' class action was improperly certified under Rule 23(b)(3). By refusing to entertain arguments against respondents' damages model that bore on the propriety of class certification, simply because those arguments would also be pertinent to the merits determination, the Court of Appeals ran afoul of our precedents requiring precisely that inquiry. And it is clear that, under the proper standard for evaluating certification, respondents' model falls far short of establishing that damages are capable of measurement on a classwide basis. Without presenting another methodology, respondents cannot show Rule 23(b)(3) predominance: Questions of individual damage calculations will inevitably overwhelm questions common to the class. This case thus turns on the straightforward application of class-certification principles. * * *

A

We start with an unremarkable premise. If respondents prevail on their claims, they would be entitled only to damages resulting from reduced overbuilder competition, since that is the only theory of antitrust impact accepted for class-action treatment by the District Court. It follows that a model purporting to serve as evidence of damages in this class action must measure only those damages attributable to that theory. If the model does not even attempt to do that, it cannot possibly establish that damages are susceptible of measurement across the entire class for purposes of Rule 23(b)(3). Calculations need not be exact, see Story Parchment Co. v. Paterson Parchment Paper Co., 282 U.S. 555, 563, 51 S.Ct. 248, 75 L.Ed. 544 (1931), but at the class-certification stage (as at trial), any model supporting a "plaintiff's damages case must be consistent with its liability case, particularly with respect to the alleged anticompetitive effect of the violation." ABA Section of Antitrust Law, Proving Antitrust Damages: Legal and Economic Issues 57, 62 (2d ed. 2010); see, e.g., Image Tech. Servs. v. Eastman Kodak Co., 125 F.3d 1195, 1224 (C.A.9 1997). And for purposes of Rule 23, courts must conduct a " 'rigorous analysis' " to determine whether that is so. Wal-Mart, supra, at ___, 131 S.Ct., at 2551–2552.

The District Court and the Court of Appeals saw no need for respondents to "tie each theory of antitrust impact" to a calculation of damages. That, they said, would involve consideration of the "merits" having "no place in the class certification inquiry." That reasoning flatly contradicts our cases requiring a determination that Rule 23 is satisfied, even when that requires inquiry into the merits of the claim. Wal-Mart, supra, at ___, and n. 6, 131 S.Ct., at 2551–2552, and n. 6. The Court of Appeals simply concluded that respondents "provided a method to measure and quantify damages on a classwide basis," finding it unnecessary to decide "whether the methodology [was] a just and reasonable inference or speculative." 655 F.3d, at 206. Under that logic, at the class-certification stage any method of measurement is acceptable so long as it can be applied classwide, no matter how arbitrary the measurements may be. Such a proposition would reduce Rule 23(b)(3)'s predominance requirement to a nullity.

B

There is no question that the model failed to measure damages resulting from the particular antitrust injury on which petitioners' liability in this action is premised. The scheme devised by respondents' expert, Dr. McClave, sought to establish a "but for" baseline—a figure that would show what the competitive prices would have been if there had been no antitrust violations. Damages would then be determined by comparing to that baseline what the actual prices were during the charged period. The "but for" figure was calculated, however, by assuming a market that contained none of the four distortions that respondents attributed to petitioners' actions. In other words, the model assumed the validity of all four theories of antitrust impact initially advanced by respondents: decreased penetration by satellite providers, overbuilder deterrence, lack of benchmark competition, and increased bargaining power. At the evidentiary hearing, Dr. McClave expressly admitted that the model calculated damages resulting from "the alleged anticompetitive conduct as a whole" and did not attribute damages to any one particular theory of anticompetitive impact.

This methodology might have been sound, and might have produced commonality of damages, if all four of those alleged distortions remained in the case. * * *

For all we know, cable subscribers in Gloucester County may have been overcharged because of petitioners' alleged elimination of satellite competition (a theory of liability that is not capable of classwide proof); while subscribers in Camden County may have paid elevated prices because of petitioners' increased bargaining power vis-à-vis content providers (another theory that is not capable of classwide proof); while yet other subscribers in Montgomery County may have paid rates produced by the combined effects of multiple forms of alleged antitrust harm; and so on. The permutations involving four theories of liability and 2 million subscribers located in 16 counties are nearly endless.

In light of the model's inability to bridge the differences between supra-competitive prices in general and supra-competitive prices attributable to the deterrence of overbuilding, Rule 23(b)(3) cannot authorize treating subscribers within the Philadelphia cluster as members of a single class. Prices whose level above what an expert deems "competitive" has been caused by factors unrelated to an accepted theory of antitrust harm are not "anticompetitive" in any sense relevant here. "The first step in a damages study is the translation of the legal theory of the harmful event into an analysis of the economic impact of that event." Federal Judicial Center, Reference Manual on Scientific Evidence 432 (3d ed. 2011) (emphasis added). The District Court and the Court of Appeals ignored that first step entirely.

The judgment of the Court of Appeals for the Third Circuit is reversed. It is so ordered.

■ JUSTICE GINSBURG and JUSTICE BREYER, with whom JUSTICE SOTOMAYOR and JUSTICE KAGAN join, dissenting.

* * * To gain class-action certification under Rule 23(b)(3), the named plaintiff must demonstrate, and the District Court must find, "that the questions of law or fact common to class members predominate over any questions affecting only individual members." This predominance

requirement is meant to "tes[t] whether proposed classes are sufficiently cohesive to warrant adjudication by representation," Amchem Products, Inc. v. Windsor, 521 U.S. 591, 623, 117 S.Ct. 2231, 138 L.Ed.2d 689 (1997), but it scarcely demands commonality as to all questions. See 7AA C. Wright, A. Miller, & M. Kane, Federal Practice and Procedure § 1778, p. 121 (3d ed. 2005) (hereinafter Wright, Miller, & Kane). In particular, when adjudication of questions of liability common to the class will achieve economies of time and expense, the predominance standard is generally satisfied even if damages are not provable in the aggregate. See Advisory Committee's 1966 Notes on Fed. Rule Civ. Proc. 23, 28 U.S.C.App., p. 141 ("[A] fraud perpetrated on numerous persons by the use of similar misrepresentations may be an appealing situation for a class action, and it may remain so despite the need, if liability is found, for separate determination of the damages suffered by individuals within the class."); 7AA Wright, Miller, & Kane § 1781, at 235–237.

Recognition that individual damages calculations do not preclude class certification under Rule 23(b)(3) is well nigh universal. See 2 W. Rubenstein, Newberg on Class Actions § 4:54, p. 205 (5th ed. 2012) (ordinarily, "individual damage[s] calculations should not scuttle class certification under Rule 23(b)(3)"). Legions of appellate decisions across a range of substantive claims are illustrative. See, e.g., Tardiff v. Knox County, 365 F.3d 1, 6 (C.A.1 2004) (Fourth Amendment); Chiang v. Veneman, 385 F.3d 256, 273 (C.A.3 2004) (Equal Credit Opportunity Act); Bertulli v. Independent Assn. of Continental Pilots, 242 F.3d 290, 298 (C.A.5 2001) (Labor-Management Reporting and Disclosure Act and Railway Labor Act); Beattie v. CenturyTel, Inc., 511 F.3d 554, 564–566 (C.A.6 2007) (Federal Communications Act); Arreola v. Godinez, 546 F.3d 788, 801 (C.A.7 2008) (Eighth Amendment). Antitrust cases, which typically involve common allegations of antitrust violation, antitrust impact, and the fact of damages, are classic examples. . . . As this Court has rightly observed, "[p]redominance is a test readily met" in actions alleging "violations of the antitrust laws." Amchem, 521 U.S., at 625, 117 S.Ct. 2231.

* * * In the mine run of cases, it remains the "black letter rule" that a class may obtain certification under Rule 23(b)(3) when liability questions common to the class predominate over damages questions unique to class members. 2 Rubenstein, supra, § 4:54, at 208.

NOTE ON THE REQUIREMENTS FOR DAMAGES CLASS ACTIONS UNDER RULE 23(b)(3)

1.   **Federal Rule 23(b)(3) "damages" class actions.** Class actions under Rule 23(b)(3) were a significant innovation of the 1966 amendments. Subsection 23(b)(3) avoids using the word "damages," and indeed damages are clearly available in (b)(1) class actions and arguably to some slight extent even in (b)(2) class actions. Nonetheless, the primary function of subsection (b)(3) has been to provide an aggregation device for damage suits, and most class actions in which damages are sought are (b)(3) rather than (b)(1) or (b)(2) suits. There are two additional requirements for Rule 23(b)(3) class actions, over and above the general requirements of Rule 23(a): the court must find that (1) "questions of law or fact common to class members *predominate* over any questions affecting only individual members" of the

class (emphasis added), and (2) "that a class action is superior to other available methods for fairly and efficiently adjudicating the controversy." As described below in the Note on Notice and Opt Out Rights in Class Actions, infra, p. 689, Rule 23(c)(2) requires that in all (b)(3) class actions, "the court must direct to class members the best notice that is practicable under the circumstances, including individual notice to all members who can be identified through reasonable effort," and such notice must state that "that the court will exclude from the class any member who requests exclusion."

2.   Common questions must "predominate." Rule 23(a)(2) requires that there be "questions of law or fact common to the class" for any class action certified under Rule 23. The predominance requirement of Rule 23(b)(3) is significantly more stringent. "[T]he predominance criterion [of subsection (b)(3)] is far more demanding" than the commonality criterion of 23(a). Amchem Products, Inc. v. Windsor, 521 U.S. 591, 624, 117 S.Ct. 2231, 138 L.Ed.2d 689 (1997). Although the courts have not developed a precise formula for what predominance means in every case, it is clear that predominance should be found when "a class action would achieve economies of time, effort, and expense, and promote * * * uniformity of decision as to persons similarly situated, without sacrificing procedural fairness or bringing about other undesirable results." Id. at 615.

In damage class actions, the easier cases for predominance are those in which both the conduct of the defendant towards class members and the response of class members is uniform or highly standardized, and hence susceptible to common proof. An example might be a fraud claim based upon a public offering of securities pursuant to a written prospectus, in which all purchasers pay the same public offering price. In such cases, one can imagine common proof on almost every issue in the case, other than the number of shares purchased. Perhaps for that reason, the court in *Amchem* stated that "predominance is a test readily met in certain cases alleging consumer or securities fraud or violations of the antitrust laws." 521 U.S. at 625.

But, as *Comcast* shows, even in an antitrust case, the greater the potential for individual differences in the way that class members were treated by the defendant, or in the response of the class members to that treatment, the more difficult the predominance inquiry becomes. Is the court in *Chandler* correct in concluding that common questions predominate with respect to claims under the federal Truth in Lending Act? With respect to the representations made? With respect to reliance?

3.   Hurdles to predominance. In recent years, the two greatest hurdles to a finding of predominance have been (1) the existence of individual questions related to the liability and damages for individual members of the plaintiff class, and (2) the applicability of different states' laws to different members of the class.

a.   Individual issues. Since the mid-1990s, courts have grown increasingly wary of finding predominance when the circumstances of individual class members' claims affect the defendants' liability and the available damages. After all, courts have contended, if there would need to be a "mini-trial" to determine whether the defendant's conduct caused each plaintiff's injury, and, if so, what the specific plaintiff's damages would be, there would be little efficiency to be gained through use of the class-action device. Moreover, there would be heightened concerns that each individual's interests would not be effectively represented by the named plaintiff, whose circumstances might be unique in important ways. As a result, many courts consider the predominance hurdle to be quite high.

But as *Chandler* illustrates, in consumer-protection, securities, and antitrust cases, courts often have found predominance even when there are individual questions involving the amount of plaintiffs' damages. Predominance has historically been a bigger obstacle in so-called "mass tort" cases. Roughly speaking, there are two kinds of personal injury mass tort cases. One grows out of a single event affecting many people, as in an airplane crash case. The other grows out of multiple but linked events taking place over a fairly long period and affecting many people, as in a product liability or toxic pollution case. For some years after the amendment of Rule 23 in 1966, federal courts were unwilling, or at best very reluctant, to certify (b)(3) damages class actions in the latter type of mass tort cases.

Indeed, the drafters of the 1966 amendments to Rule 23 were skeptical of such class actions: "A 'mass accident' resulting in injuries to numerous persons is ordinarily not appropriate for a class action because of the likelihood that significant questions, not only of damages but of liability and defenses of liability, would be present, affecting the individuals in different ways. In these circumstances an action conducted nominally as a class action would degenerate in practice into multiple lawsuits separately tried." Fed. R. Civ. P. 23 Advisory Committee note. In addition, many mass tort cases claims are large enough to warrant pursuing as free-standing suits. As a result, during the late 1960's and 1970's, there was a strong reluctance in the federal judiciary to certify such actions.

In the 1980's, academic and judicial resistance to mass tort actions began to soften, in substantial part due to the tremendous problems created for the federal court system by the surge in asbestos cases. Cases in which class certification was granted include In re A.H. Robins Co., Inc., 880 F.2d 709 (4th Cir. 1989) (Dalkon Shield litigation); Jenkins v. Raymark Indus., Inc., 782 F.2d 468 (5th Cir. 1986) (asbestos litigation); In re Agent Orange Product Liability Litig., 100 F.R.D. 718 (E.D.N.Y.1983).

By the mid-1990's, however, the tide turned again. Courts began to show a resurgent skepticism about the certification of mass tort claims, particularly with respect to class claims involving nationwide classes and based on state law. See, e.g., Castano v. American Tobacco Co., 84 F.3d 734 (5th Cir. 1996) (rejecting class certification in case alleging fraud against tobacco manufacturers when "reliance must be proved in individual trials"); In re American Medical Sys., Inc., 75 F.3d 1069 (6th Cir. 1996) (reversing class certification in medical products liability case when "the products are different, each plaintiff has a unique complaint, and each receives different information and assurances from his treating physician").

At the forefront of the minds of judges in these cases was a newly prominent concern about the pressures on defendants to settle created by the class action. As Judge Posner explained:

> Suppose that 5,000 of the potential class members are not yet barred by the statute of limitations. And suppose the named plaintiffs * * * win the class portion of this case to the extent of establishing the defendants' liability under either of the two negligence theories. It is true that this would only be prima facie liability, that the defendants would have various defenses. But they could not be confident that the defenses would prevail. They might,

therefore, easily be facing $25 billion in potential liability (conceivably more), and with it bankruptcy. They may not wish to roll these dice. That is putting it mildly. They will be under intense pressure to settle. * * * If they settle, the class certification—the ruling that will have forced them to settle—will never be reviewed. * * * Judge Friendly, who was not given to hyperbole, called settlements induced by a small probability of an immense judgment in a class action "blackmail settlements." Henry J. Friendly, *Federal Jurisdiction: A General View* 120 (1973). Judicial concern about them is legitimate, not "sociological," as it was derisively termed in In re Sugar Antitrust Litigation, 559 F.2d 481, 483 n. 1 (9th Cir.1977).

In the Matter of Rhone Poulenc Rorer, Inc., 521 F.3d 1293 (7th Cir. 1995). Is it proper to refuse to certify an otherwise lawful class on the ground that certification will increase the pressure on the defendant to settle on terms favorable to the plaintiff class? Even if it is a proper ground, is a judge in a good position to assess the amount of pressure that will be produced by certification? See Silver, "We're Scared to Death": Class Certification and Blackmail, 78 N.Y. U. L. Rev. 1357 (2003) (answering no to both questions posed in text).

As *Comcast* shows, however, these concerns have application far beyond the mass tort area to areas once thought to be well within the predominance requirement, such as antitrust and consumer protection. As Professor Klonoff has summarized, "in recent years, the courts have made it far more difficult to certify class actions under (b)(3) by summarily finding, after identifying significant individualized issues, that predominance cannot be satisfied." Klonoff, The Decline of Class Actions, 90 Wash. U. L. Rev. 729 (2013).

The impact of *Comcast* in the lower courts remains to be seen. Courts remain divided in their interpretation of the opinion. See Note, Comcast Corp. v. Behrend and Chaos on the Ground, 81 U. Chi. L. Rev. 1213 (2014). Some courts have taken *Comcast* to mean that predominance cannot be satisfied in cases requiring any individualized determination of plaintiffs' damages. See In re Rail Freight Surcharge Litigation, 725 F.3d 244 (D.C. Cir. 2013); Martin v. Ford Motor Co., 292 F.R.D. 252 (E.D. Pa. 2013). Other courts, however, have not taken such a strict view, and have been willing to certify class actions based on common questions of liability and leaving individualized determinations of damages to later proceedings. See In re Whirlpool Corp. Front-Loading Washer Products Liab. Litig., 722 F.3d 838 (6th Cir. 2013); Leyva v. Medline Indus. Inc., 716 F.3d 510 (9th Cir. 2013). Based on these developments, is *Chandler* still good law after *Comcast*? And if the *Chandler* case came before you today as a district judge, how would you write the opinion?

b. Different states' laws applicable to class members' claims. The predominance question may depend importantly not just on common treatment of, and conduct by, class members, but on the sources of law underlying the plaintiffs' claims. A nationwide class action based on claims arising under federal law is much more likely to meet the predominance requirement than one in which the principal claims arise under state law, where the relevant state law differs from state to state. In brief, this is the problem: when class members are domiciled or injured in multiple states, choice-of-law rules often require application of different states' substantive laws to different class members. As a result, the claims of a class with members from all fifty states are potentially governed by all fifty states' laws. Courts have reached a near consensus that this renders the class uncertifiable under Rule 23(b)(3) for two reasons: first, the fact that different groups of plaintiffs' claims are governed by different laws means that the legal questions common to the class do not predominate over questions individual to each class member, and second, that the class is too difficult to manage through a trial, particularly when one considers the problem of instructing a jury. Federal courts now generally agree that, unless a class or subclass is governed by federal law or a single state's law, it cannot be certified under Rule 23. See York-Erwin, The Choice-of-Law Problem(s) in the Class Action Context, 84 N.Y.U. L. Rev. 1793 (2009); Silberman, The Role of Choice of Law in National Class Actions, 156 U. Pa. L. Rev. 2001 (2008).

4. **Class action must be "superior" to other methods of adjudication.** Rule 23(b)(3) requires that a class action must be "superior to other available methods for fairly and efficiently adjudicating the controversy." Subsections (b)(3)(A)–(D) provide a non-exhaustive list of factors to be considered in determining superiority. The first factor is the interest of class members in individually controlling the conduct of their own cases. As a practical matter, this factor is relevant only when the claims of absent parties have sufficient value to support an independent action. Even then, it arguably should be given little independent weight, for if notice to class members is fully effective to advise them of their rights, any potential member of a (b)(3) class who believes that an individual action is superior has the right to opt-out of the class under subsection (c)(2)(A).

The second factor is the extent and nature of any litigation already underway concerning the matter in controversy. Other pending litigation may demonstrate the potential for independent suits, and hence weigh against certification. The absence of other suits, on the other hand, can cut in favor of certification if it is viewed as demonstrating that single cases are uneconomic.

The third factor is the desirability of concentrating the litigation in the particular forum in which the suit is filed. In part, this is a consideration of the desirability of having a class action at all—that is, whether the litigation should be concentrated in a single forum. But in more important part, this is a consideration of the desirability of having a class action in *the particular forum chosen by plaintiffs*. For example, has the plaintiff engaged in forum shopping to such an extent that parties and witnesses will be seriously inconvenienced, or that the choice of law rules will result in the application of a particularly inappropriate substantive law to the controversy? To the extent that the problem is inconvenience of parties and witnesses, this may be alleviated through transfer of the suit under 28 U.S.C. § 1404(a). But to the extent that the problem is choice of law, this cannot be alleviated through transfer. See Van Dusen v. Barrack, 376 U.S. 612, 84 S.Ct. 805, 11 L.Ed.2d 945 (1964) (§ 1404(a) transfer results in a change of courtrooms, not a change of law), discussed supra p. 317, n. 5.

The fourth factor is the difficulties likely to be encountered in managing the class action, such as notice, discovery, trial, and remedy. In this sense, the superiority inquiry often overlaps with the predominance inquiry. When individual issues are found to predominate over the common ones, courts often note that such individual issues render the case impossible to "manage" both during the pretrial and trial phases of the litigation. See, e.g., Ahmad

v. Old Republic Nat. Title Ins. Co., 690 F.3d 698 (5th Cir. 2012); Rowden v. Pacific Parking Systems, Inc., 282 F.R.D. 581 (C.D. Cal. 2012). As the Fifth Circuit stated in the influential *Castano* case involving injuries caused by fraud by the tobacco industry, "After the class trial, the individual trials and appeals on comparative negligence and damages would have to take place. The net result could be that the class action device would lengthen, not shorten the time it takes for plaintiffs to reach final judgment." Castano v. American Tobacco Co., 84 F.3d 734, 751 (5th Cir. 1996).

Rule 23(b)(3) also directs courts to consider the alternatives to class action treatment that may provide more fair and efficient adjudication, and as to whether a class action might not be "superior." For example, using a pilot or "bellwether" suit with possible non-mutual offensive collateral estoppel effect may be more efficient than a class action. See, e.g., Yeager's Fuel, Inc. v. Pennsylvania Power & Light Co., 162 F.R.D. 482 (E.D.Pa.1995). Or consolidation of cases for pretrial proceedings under the multi-district litigation statute, 28 U.S.C. § 1407, may provide many of the economies of scale that a class action would provide. See discussion of § 1407, supra p. 320. Or, in situations where individual damage claims are large enough to support free-standing suits, traditional non-class suits may be superior. Note that in this context, courts often cite the risk of "blackmail settlements" described above. If the defendant is unfairly pressured to settle due to the existence of the class action, that may be reason to consider individual adjudication of plaintiffs' claims superior. See *Castano*, 84 F.3d at 751.

5.   Large scale, small claim class actions. From a plaintiff's perspective, one of the most important uses of Rule 23(b)(3) is to enable suits to be brought as part of a class action that, as a practical matter, could never have been brought as individual suits. "Class actions * * * may permit the plaintiffs to pool claims which would be uneconomical to litigate individually. For example, this lawsuit involves claims averaging about $100 per plaintiff; most of the plaintiffs would have no realistic day in court if a class action were not available." Phillips Petroleum Co. v. Shutts, 472 U.S. 797, 809, 105 S.Ct. 2965, 86 L.Ed.2d 628 (1985). The class action in *Chandler* made possible litigation that simply could not have been brought separately by the individual plaintiffs. How far should Rule 23 be allowed to give practical substance to what otherwise might have remained merely theoretical rights? Professors Burbank, Farhang, and Kritzer note that legislatures have considered the class action an essential tool for enforcement of regulatory policy through litigation, rather than through direct government regulation. Burbank, Farhang & Kritzer, Private Enforcement, 17 Lewis & Clark L. Rev. 637 (2014); see also Farhang, The Litigation State: Public Regulation and Private Lawsuits in the United States (2010).

But what if there is no statute creating the plaintiffs' cause of action? Professors Wright, Miller, and Kane write, "[I]t must be recognized that the effect of making Rule 23(b)(3) available is to enable recourse to the courts in situations in which it would otherwise be unavailable. This is not troublesome when the action is predicated on a statutory mandate that is designed to promote the private rectification of conduct thought undesirable or to effectuate some other expression of public policy. But the federal courts must consider the need to impose limits on litigation that does not fall within this category. Otherwise, Rule 23(b)(3) may become the source of trivial and burdensome lawsuits." 7A Wright, Miller, and Kane, Federal Practice and Procedure § 1779 (3d ed. 2005). Trivial from whose standpoint? Burdensome to whom? Where is a federal court to look to determine the purpose of a "statutory mandate" or to see "some other expression of public policy"? Should it look to Rule 23(b)(3) for such a purpose or expression? Does the Rules Enabling Act, which provides that the federal rules "shall not abridge, enlarge or modify any substantive right," prevent Rule 23(b)(3) from being used in this way? See 28 U.S.C. § 2072 and the discussion of *Shady Grove Orthopedic Assocs. v. Allstate Ins. Co.*, supra, at 392.

NOTE ON NOTICE AND OPT-OUT RIGHTS IN CLASS ACTIONS

1. The Rule 23(c)(2) requirement of notice in Rule 23(b)(3) class actions. Rule 23(c)(2) provides that in any (b)(3) class action "the court must direct to class members the best notice that is practicable under the circumstances, including individual notice to all members who can be identified through reasonable effort." The notice must advise the class member of her right to request exclusion from the class, of the fact that she will be included in the class judgment unless she requests exclusion, and of her right to enter a personal appearance in the action through separately retained counsel. The 2003 revisions to the rule contain an express requirement that the notice be in "plain, easily understood language."

What is the premise for requiring the notice specified in (c)(2) for class actions brought under Rule 23(b)(3), but not under Rules 23(b)(1) and (2)? Part of the answer must lie in the fact that an opt-out right cannot be effective without notice, and that the argument for allowing opt-out is often much stronger in a Rule 23(b)(3) class action.

From the perspective of a defendant facing the prospect of inconsistent injunctive remedies or sequential claims against a limited fund, allowing a representative action to bind the absentees is a critical means of preventing inconsistent outcomes or double liability. From the perspective of the represented class member, the non-opt-out class action recognizes that if any plaintiff is allowed to proceed individually, whether by seeking an injunction or by threatening to deplete the assets of a limited fund, the interests of absentees will necessarily be affected. In these circumstances, a class action arguably improves the situation of all absentees by directing explicit judicial attention to how their interests may differ from those of the class representative and to the measures that might be taken to protect their position. If there is no strong interest in opting out there is no strong argument for providing notice to that end.

A class action under Rule 23(b)(3) for money damages is importantly different. In the absence of a limited fund, an individual claim for damages by a class member does not inevitably affect the interests of absent class members or give rise to a substantial risk of unfairness to the defendant. The traditional argument for binding absent class members is therefore reduced in strength. In addition, if the claim for damages is sufficiently substantial, an absent class member may have strong reasons, stemming from the size or atypical attributes of his claim, to prefer to prosecute her own claim in a forum of her own choice, using her own lawyer, in a format that allows full consideration of the unique attributes of her claim.

2. *Eisen v. Carlisle & Jacquelin.* The leading case on the notice requirement under Rule 23(c)(2) is Eisen v. Carlisle & Jacquelin, 417 U.S. 156, 94 S.Ct. 2140, 40 L.Ed.2d 732 (1974). *Eisen* was an antitrust class-action brought on behalf of "odd-lot" (essentially small-time) traders against brokerage houses alleged to monopolize the market in odd-lot trading. As a result, class members paid defendants additional fees to trade, made possible by lack of competition in the industry. Class members' individual claims were, however, quite small; for example, the named plaintiff stood to recover only $70. This, therefore, was a classic example of the "small claim" class action—an action in which the individual claims were worth little, but when all of the class members' claims were aggregated, the damages became quite large. In *Eisen*, there were some six million class members, around two million of whom were readily identifiable by name and address. At the point the case reached the Supreme Court, the parties were arguing about two issues related to the notice required by Rule 23(c)(2): (1) must individual notice be mailed to all known class members, and (2) who must bear the cost?

The Supreme Court answered both questions straightforwardly: (1) Individual notice must be sent to all class members whose names and addresses can be ascertained through reasonable effort; and (2) the plaintiff must pay the cost of the notice. Both aspects of the *Eisen* holding are addressed below.

   3.   The required scope of notice under the Due Process Clause.
Eisen held explicitly that "individual notice must be sent to all class members whose names and addresses may be ascertained through reasonable effort." 417 U.S. at 176. In so holding, the Court stated that such notice was required by the plain language of Rule 23(c)(2). In coming to this conclusion, however, the Court drew upon its decision in Mullane v. Central Hanover Bank & Trust, 339 U.S. 306, 70 S.Ct. 652, 94 L.Ed. 865 (1950), supra p. 170. In *Mullane,* a bank administering pooled trust funds brought suit for an accounting. Potential adversaries in the suit were both income and principal beneficiaries of the trusts. The bank relied on a New York statute treating the suit as a quasi in rem proceeding and requiring only notice by publication. In a challenge by the representative of the income beneficiaries to the adequacy of notice, the Court stated that "[a]n elementary and fundamental requirement of due process in any proceeding which is to be accorded finality is notice reasonably calculated, under all the circumstances, to apprise interested parties of the pendency of the action and afford them an opportunity to present their objections." 339 U.S. at 314. Applying this principle, the Court held that publication notice did not satisfy constitutional due process, at least in the case of beneficiaries known to the trustee. This was the holding that the Court relied upon in *Eisen*. But at the same time, the Court in *Mullane* also held that due process did *not* require mailed notice to beneficiaries whose names and addresses were not known to the trustee:

> Whatever searches might be required in another situation under ordinary standards of diligence, in view of the character of the proceedings and the nature of the interests here involved we think them unnecessary. We recognize the practical difficulties and costs that would be attendant on frequent investigations into the status of great numbers of beneficiaries, many of whose interests in the common fund are so remote as to be ephemeral; and we have no doubt that such impracticable and extended searches are not required in the name of due process. The expense of keeping informed from day to day of substitutions among even current income beneficiaries and presumptive remaindermen, to say nothing of the far greater number of contingent beneficiaries, would

impose a severe burden on the plan, and would likely dissipate its advantages. These are practical matters in which we should be reluctant to disturb the judgment of the state authorities.

Supra pp. 175–176. This holding was not referred to in *Eisen*.

Is providing notice to the millions of holders of claims too small to warrant an individual action in *Eisen* more like providing notice to known beneficiaries in *Mullane* or more like providing notice to those beneficiaries "whose interests in the common fund are so remote as to be ephemeral * * * [and whose identification] would impose a severe burden on the plan and would likely dissipate its advantages?" Should it make a difference, as a constitutional matter, that the practical difficulties in *Mullane* concerned the costs of identifying interested parties, while in *Eisen* those difficulties concerned the costs of providing individualized mail notice to such parties?

If the claims are "wholly or predominately for money" damages, however, there is authority that notice is constitutionally required. In Phillips Petroleum Co. v. Shutts, 472 U.S. 797, 105 S.Ct. 2965, 86 L.Ed.2d 628 (1985), the Supreme Court held that a Kansas state court could exercise in personam jurisdiction over absent class members in an action brought under the Kansas equivalent of Rule 23(b)(3), even though the absent plaintiffs had no connection with Kansas other than the lawsuit itself, which had been filed in their name but without their prior knowledge. The key to the Court's holding was the nature of the proceeding in the Kansas court, in particular the plaintiffs' right to opt out of the class action. The Court held that due process required that the member "receive notice plus an opportunity to be heard and participate in the litigation," and that "at a minimum * * * an absent plaintiff [must] be provided with an opportunity to remove himself from the class." 472 U.S. at 812.

4.   What constitutes reasonable class notice? *Eisen* makes clear that Rule 23(c)(2) requires individual notice to all class members whose names and addresses can be identified through reasonable effort. But what about those who cannot be easily identified? Courts often read *Mullane* to "not require that notice be provided to every single class member if the circumstances would make such an expectation unreasonable and impracticable." Minter v. Wells Fargo Bank, N.A., 283 F.R.D. 268 (D. Md. 2012). As the Seventh Circuit recently held, "When reasonable effort would not suffice to identify the class members, notice by publication, imperfect though it is may be substituted." Hughes v. Kore of Indiana Enterprise, Inc., 731 F.3d 672 (7th Cir. 2013) (Posner, J.) (authorizing notice by publication of a class action against owners of ATMs via stickers on the ATMs and in a newspaper and on a website). Indeed, courts have often held that when all class members cannot be reasonably identified, notice by publication is sufficient to fill the gap. See Juris v. Inamed Corp., 685 F.3d 1294 (11th Cir. 2012) ("Where certain class members' names and addresses cannot be determined with reasonable efforts, notice by publication is generally considered adequate."); DeJulius v. New England Health Care Employees Pension Fund, 429 F.3d 935 (10th Cir. 2005) (authorizing notice by publication of settlement of a securities-fraud class action in the Investors Business Daily and the Kansas City Star).

The growth of the Internet has also had an effect on the definition of reasonable notice. More and more, courts are giving their blessing to notice schemes that make use primarily of the Internet. For instance, in Boundas

v. Abercrombie & Fitch Stores, Inc., 280 F.R.D. 408 (N.D. Ill. 2012), the defendant chain of stores gave out $25 gift cards to all customers who made purchases exceeding $100. Although the cards themselves stated that there was no expiration date, they were packaged in a sleeve that did state an expiration date. The company later voided all of the cards, and a plaintiff class of over 200,000 cardholders brought suit. In response to the defendant's claim that it had no records of most recipients of the gift cards, the court suggested that notice "might be provided, among other places, on Abercrombie's website or at Abercrombie store locations." For interesting discussions of how the Internet might impact Rule 23(c)(2)'s notice requirement, see Klonoff, Herrmann & Harrison, Making Class Actions Work: The Untapped Potential of the Internet, 13 J. Internet L. 1 (2009); Walters, "Best Notice Practicable" in the Twenty-First Century, 2003 U.C.L.A. J. L. Tech. 4.

5. **Who should bear the cost of notice?** In *Eisen*, the trial court recognized the problems created by the substantial cost of notice at the outset of the case:

> If the expense of notice is placed upon [petitioner], it would be the end of a possibly meritorious suit, frustrating both the policy behind private antitrust actions and the admonition that the new Rule 23 is to be given a liberal rather than a restrictive interpretation, *Eisen II* at 563. On the other hand, if costs were arbitrarily placed upon [respondents] at this point, the result might be the imposition of an unfair burden founded upon a groundless claim. In addition to the probability of encouraging frivolous class actions, such a step might also result in [respondents'] passing on to their customers, including many of the class members in this case, the expenses of defending these actions.

Eisen v. Carlisle & Jacquelin, 52 F.R.D. 253, 269 (S.D.N.Y. 1971). As a result, the trial court held a preliminary merits hearing to determine which party should bear the cost of notice. Because the plaintiffs had demonstrated a strong likelihood of success on the merits, the trial court decided that the defendants should bear 90% of the costs of the notice.

On appeal, the Supreme Court roundly rejected this approach. It both rejected the notion that anything in "the language or history of Rule 23 that gives a court any authority to conduct a preliminary inquiry into the merits of a suit in order to determine whether it may be maintained as a class action. * * * In the absence of any support under Rule 23, petitioner's effort to impose the cost of notice on respondents must fail. The usual rule is that a plaintiff must initially bear the cost of notice to the class. * * * Where, as here, the relationship between the parties is truly adversary, the plaintiff must pay for the cost of notice as part of the ordinary burden of financing his own suit." 417 U.S. at 178. In response to the argument that the cost of notice may render the litigation unviable, the Court stated, "There is nothing in Rule 23 to suggest that the notice requirements can be tailored to fit the pocketbooks of particular plaintiffs." Id. at 176.

The effect of the Court's holding is that representative parties in class actions must be prepared to bear significant costs at the outset of litigation. Moreover, if plaintiffs are successful, the costs of the notice will be deducted from the ultimate recovery. Was the Supreme Court right in *Eisen* that the plaintiffs should be required to bear the costs of notice? Would it be fair to require the defendants to bear some or all of the costs?

On a different note, is the basis for the Court's holding that Rule 23 does not authorize an inquiry into the merits of the litigation still good law after the Court's decisions in *Wal-Mart* and *Comcast*? Recall that in *Comcast*, the Court stated that "our cases requir[e] a determination that Rule 23 is satisfied, even when that requires inquiry into the merits of the claim." 133 S.Ct. at 1433. Indeed, as the Court recently stated, *Wal-Mart* and *Comcast* "have made clear that plaintiffs must actually prove—not simply plead—that their proposed class satisfies each requirement of Rule 23." Halliburton v. Erica P. John Fund, Inc., 563 U.S. ___, 134 S.Ct. 2398, 189 L.Ed.2d 339 (2014). Should the Court revisit its holding in *Eisen* in light of recent developments? See Marcus, Reviving Judicial Gatekeeping of Aggregation: Scrutinizing the Merits on Class Certification, 79 Geo. Wash. L. Rev. 324 (2011).

6. Notice in Rule 23(b)(1) and 23(b)(2) classes. There is nothing in Rule 23 that requires notice to members of (b)(1) and (b)(2) classes. That does not mean, however, that notice need never be provided in (b)(1) and (b)(2) class actions. The Due Process Clause may require notice even if the Rule does not. Under what circumstances might due process require notice in a class action? *Hansberry v. Lee* suggests one such class of cases: where there are special concerns about the adequacy of the class representative to speak for all class members, which might increase the need for monitoring by class members.

Second, Rule 23(d)(1) authorizes the district judge to require notice in some circumstances, providing that "the court may issue orders * * * to protect class members and fairly conduct the action * * * giving appropriate notice to some or all class members of: any step in the action; the proposed extent of the judgment; or the members' opportunity to signify whether they consider the representation fair and adequate, to intervene and present claims or defenses, or to otherwise come into the action." In addition, Rule 23(e) provides that "the court must direct notice" in the event of "settlement, voluntary dismissal or compromise" of a class action.

3.   SETTLEMENT OF CLASS SUITS

Pearson v. NBTY, Inc.

United States Court of Appeals for the Seventh Circuit, 2014.
772 F.3d 778.

■ POSNER, CIRCUIT JUDGE.

NBTY and its subsidiary Rexall Sundown manufacture vitamins and nutritional supplements, including glucosamine pills, which are dietary supplements designed to help people with joint disorders, such as osteoarthritis. Several class action suits have been filed in federal district courts across the country against NBTY, Rexall, and Target (a retail distributor of the pills, which are sold under brand names like "Osteo Bi-Flex" as well as in generic versions sold by pharmacies, such as CVS and Walgreen). The suits charge the defendants with violating several states' consumer protection laws by making false claims for glucosamine's efficacy, such as that it will "help rebuild cartilage," "support renewal of cartilage," help "maintain the structural integrity of joints," "lubricate joints," and "support [ ] mobility and flexibility."

Eight months after the plaintiffs filed suit in a federal district court in Illinois, class counsel in all six cases negotiated a nationwide settlement with NBTY and Rexall (for simplicity, we'll pretend there is a single defendant and call it "Rexall") and submitted it to that court for approval. For it is typical in class action cases of this sort—cases in which class counsel want to maximize the settlement and the defendants don't want to settle except for "global" peace—for the multiple class counsel to negotiate a single nationwide settlement and agree to submit it for approval to just one of the district courts in which the multiple actions had been filed.

The district judge approved the settlement, though with significant modifications. As approved, the settlement requires Rexall to cough up approximately $5.63 million—$1.93 million in fees to class counsel, plus an additional $179,676 in attorney expenses (attorneys' fees cover billable time and overhead expenses such as office space and secretaries, but clients typically are charged extra for such expenses as expert-consultant and expert-witness fees, PACER access, photocopies, and Westlaw research), $1.5 million in notice and administration costs, $1.13 million to the Orthopedic Research and Education Foundation, $865,284 to the 30,245 class members who submitted claims, and $30,000 to the six named plaintiffs ($5,000 apiece) as compensation for their role as the class representatives. The version of the settlement that had received preliminary approval had provided for even higher attorneys' fees—up to $4.5 million—with Rexall stipulating that it wouldn't challenge any attorney-fee requests by class counsel up to that amount. Such a stipulation is called a "clear-sailing" agreement.

* * *

The district judge valued the settlement at the maximum potential payment that class members could receive, which came to $20.2 million. That valuation, which played a critical role in the judge's decision as to how much to award class counsel in attorneys' fees, comprises $14.2 million for class members (based on the contrary-to-fact assumption that every one of the 4.72 million class members who had received postcard rather than publication notice of the class action would file a $3 claim), $1.5 million for the cost of notice to the class, and $4.5 million for fees to class counsel (the judge cut this amount but allowed the amount cut to revert to Rex-all pursuant to the kicker clause and adhered to the $20.2 million estimate of the overall value of the settlement). The judge excluded, however, both the cy pres award of $1.13 million in calculating the benefit to the class, for the obvious reason that the recipient of that award was not a member of the class, and the injunction, which he valued at zero, which was proper too, as we'll see.

The $20.2 million figure has barely any connection to the settlement's value to the class. Notice and fees, which together account for $6 million of the $20.2 million, are costs, not benefits. The attorneys' fees are of course not paid to the class members; and as we said in Redman v. RadioShack Corp., 768 F.3d 622, 630 (7th Cir.2014), "administrative costs should not have been included in calculating the division of the spoils between class counsel and class members. Those costs are part of the settlement but not part of the value received from the settlement by the members of the class. The costs therefore shed no light on the fairness of the division of the settlement pie between class counsel and class members." The $14.2 million "benefit" to the class members was a fiction too. Only 30,245 claims were filed, yielding total compensation for the class members of less than $1 million.

Because the amount of the attorneys' fees that the judge wanted to award class counsel—$1.93 million—was only 9.6 percent of $20.2 million, he thought the amount reasonable. But as we said in the Redman case, the "ratio that is relevant . . . is the ratio of (1) the fee to (2) the fee plus what the class members received." Id. Basing the award of attorneys' fees on this ratio, which shows how the aggregate value of the settlement is being split between class counsel and the class, gives class counsel an incentive to design the claims process in such a way as will maximize the settlement benefits actually received by the class, rather than to connive with the defendant in formulating claims-filing procedures that discourage filing and so reduce the benefit to the class. But $20.2 million is of course not the value of the settlement, defined as the sum of the awards to the class and to its lawyers. The class received a meager $865,284. This means the attorneys' fees represented not 9.6 percent of the aggregate value but an outlandish 69 percent. * * *

We can imagine a case in which a lawyer sets to work diligently to make a powerful case for his client, agrees to a fee that compensates him for the work necessary to litigate the case to a successful conclusion, and has a reasonable expectation of obtaining a judgment that will exceed the agreed-upon attorney's fee, but unforeseeable developments result in a judgment smaller than the agreed-upon fee, or even in a judgment for the defendant. In such a case the lawyer would have a right to his fee. But especially in consumer class actions, where the percentage of class members who file claims is often quite low (in this case it was 30,245 ÷ 12 million = .0025, or one quarter of one percent) . . . the presumption should we suggest be that attorneys' fees awarded to class counsel should not exceed a third or at most a half of the total amount of money going to class members and their counsel. In this case that range would be between $436,642 and $865,284—a far cry from the $1.93 million that the judge awarded, and absurdly far from the $4.5 million that class counsel requested, with the connivance of Rexall, which doubtless looked forward to recapturing, as it did, a big chunk of that amount. * * *

As experienced class action lawyers, class counsel in the present case must have known that the notice and claim forms, and the very modest monetary award that the average claimant would receive, were bound to discourage filings. The postcard sent to each of 4.72 million class members informs the recipient that to file a claim he must click on www.GlucosamineSettlement.com on his computer or cell-phone or call a toll-free phone number. (The website has changed since the deadline for filing claims; we base our discussion on printed copies in the record of the relevant screens of the website as it appeared during the claims period.) The opening screen of the website contains links to six documents. One is entitled "Full Class Notice," and if you clicked on it you would have seen a 10-page statement, largely repeating what was in the opening screen but adding more information about the case, and stating on the third page that "if you submit a claim postmarked or submitted online [by a specified date], you may be eligible to receive a check" of $3 for each bottle of the glucosamine pills you bought up to a total of 4 bottles, or $5 for up to 10 bottles if you provide proof of purchase.

Another of the links is captioned "Claim Form," and if you clicked on that you'd see a "Glucosamine Settlement Claim Form." The form required the claimant to list cash register receipts or other documentation indicating the date and place at which he or she had bought the product. The form advised the claimant that "The Claims Administrator and the Parties have the right to audit all claims for completeness, waste, fraud, and abuse. Filing a false claim may violate certain criminal or civil laws." Further, the claimant was—in boldface— required to "certify under penalty of perjury that the foregoing is true and correct to the best of my knowledge."

One would have thought, given the low ceiling on the amount of money that a member of the class could claim, that a sworn statement would be sufficient documentation, without requiring receipts or other business records likely to have been discarded. The requirement of needlessly elaborate documentation, the threats of criminal prosecution, and the fact that a claimant might feel obliged to wade through the five other documents accessible from the opening screen of the website, help to explain why so few recipients of the postcard notice bothered to submit a claim. It's hard to resist the inference that Rexall was trying to minimize the number of claims that class members would file, in order to minimize the cost of the settlement to it. . . . Class counsel could have done much better by the class had they been willing to accept lower fees in their negotiation with Rexall. But realism requires recognition that probably all that class counsel really care about is their fees—for $865,284 spread over 12 million class members is only 7 cents apiece.

The $1.13 million *cy pres* award to the orthopedic foundation did not benefit the class, except insofar as armed with this additional money the foundation may contribute to the discovery of new treatments for joint problems—a hopelessly speculative proposition. Cy pres (properly *cy près comme possible*, an Anglo-French term meaning "as near as possible") is the name of the doctrine that permits a benefit to be given other than to the intended beneficiary or for the intended purpose because changed circumstances make it impossible to carry out the benefactor's intent. A familiar example is that when polio was cured, the March of Dimes, a foundation that had been established in the 1930s at the behest of President Roosevelt to fight polio, was permitted to redirect its resources to improving the health of mothers and babies.

Since the joint problems that glucosamine is supposed to alleviate are the domain of orthopedic medicine, the choice of an orthopedic institute as a recipient of money left over after all approved class members' claims are paid is consistent with cy pres. But there is no validity to the $1.13 million cy pres award in this case. A cy pres award is supposed to be limited to money that can't feasibly be awarded to the intended beneficiaries, here consisting of the class members. Notice costing $1.5 million reached 4.72 million class members. Granted, doubling the expenditure would not have doubled the number of class members notified. The 4.72 million who received postcards were all those whom Rexall knew (through pharmacy loyalty programs and the like) to have bought its glucosamine pills, while notice by publication or via the

Internet tends to be ineffectual when the class consists of consumers. But the claims process could have been simplified. Or knowing that 4.72 million people had bought at least one bottle of its pills, Rexall could have mailed $3 checks to all 4.72 million postcard recipients. The Orthopedic Research and Education Foundation seems perfectly reputable, but it is entitled to receive money intended to compensate victims of consumer fraud only if it's infeasible to provide that compensation to the victims— which has not been demonstrated.

The 30-month "injunction," to which we now turn, is actually just a brief statement in the settlement agreement requiring Rexall to remove from its packaging claims listed in "Column 1" in an accompanying exhibit and replace them with claims listed in "Column 2." * * *

Given the emphasis that class counsel place on the fraudulent character of Rexall's claims, Rexall might have an incentive even without an injunction to change them. The injunction actually gives it protection by allowing it, with a judicial imprimatur (because it's part of a settlement approved by the district court), to preserve the substance of the claims by making—as we're about to see—purely cosmetic changes in wording, which Rexall in effect is seeking judicial approval of. For the injunction seems substantively empty. In place of "support[s] renewal of cartilage" Rexall is to substitute "contains a key building block of cartilage." We see no substantive change. For "works by providing the nourishment your body needs to build cartilage, lubricate, and strengthen your joints," is to be substituted "works by providing the nourishment your body needs to support cartilage, lubricate, and strengthen your joints." Finally, in place of "rebuilds cartilage," "repairs cartilage," or "renews cartilage" Rexall may instead advertise that its product "helps protect [or support] cartilage and helps with annoying flare-ups"; "helps to lubricate and cushion joints while supporting healthy connective tissue [or healthy cartilage]"; and that "just 'one' . . . caplet is all you need to help protect cartilage and help ease occasional joint stress." Again we can't see any substantive change.

* * * One would think that a purchaser who was convinced by the label that taking Rexall's glucosamine pills is all you need to "experience true joint comfort for yourself" would not be put off just because there is no claim that the pills achieve this miracle by rebuilding lost cartilage.

In light of the concerns we've expressed, we find it remarkable that at the oral argument of the appeal the lead class counsel told us, in justification of the injunction: "Well, from my perspective, the gain is that it's [that is, the deleted label claims are] no longer on the labeling and they're [that is, Rexall is] going to have to make a decision to put it back on. And so that in itself is an achievement because it has been on the labeling for over ten years." When one of the judges replied, "That's an achievement? I don't understand," the class lawyer replied: "I believe it's actually probably an unprecedented achievement but obviously you have your doubts." We're not the only doubters; the district judge deemed the value of the injunctive relief unascertainable (and so treated the value as zero). * * *

In closing we note with disapproval a quotation by class counsel from an opinion of ours that "because settlement of a class action, like settlement of any litigation, is basically a bargained exchange between the litigants, the judiciary's role is properly limited to the minimum necessary to protect the interests of the class and the public. Judges should not substitute their own judgment as to optimal settlement terms for the judgment of the litigants and their counsel." Armstrong v. Board of School Directors of City of Milwaukee, 616 F.2d 305, 315 (7th Cir. 1980). That quotation is from 34 years ago and in the decades since judges have accrued much more experience with class actions and have learned that class action settlements are often quite different from settlements of other types of cases, which indeed are bargained exchanges between the opposing litigants. Class counsel rarely have clients to whom they are responsive. The named plaintiffs in a class action, though supposed to be the representatives of the class, are typically chosen by class counsel; the other class members are not parties and have no control over class counsel. The result is an acute conflict of interest between class counsel, whose pecuniary interest is in their fees, and class members, whose pecuniary interest is in the award to the class. Defendants are interested only in the total costs of the settlement to them, and not in the division of the costs between attorneys' fees and payment to class members. We thus have "remarked the incentive of class counsel, in complicity with the defendant's counsel, to sell out the class by agreeing with the defendant to recommend that the judges approve a settlement involving a meager recovery for the class but generous compensation for the lawyers—the deal that promotes the self-interest of both class counsel and the defendant and is therefore optimal from the standpoint of their private interests." Eubank v. Pella Corp., 753 F.3d 718, 720 (7th Cir. 2014), quoting Creative Montessori Learning Centers v. Ashford Gear LLC, 662 F.3d 913, 918 (7th Cir. 2011), citing other opinions, in this and other circuits, recognizing the conflict of interest; see also Redman v. RadioShack Corp., supra, 768 F.3d at 629.

That is an accurate description of this case; and it is why objectors play an essential role in judicial review of proposed settlements of class actions and why judges must be both vigilant and realistic in that review. Theodore Frank and the other objectors flagged fatal weaknesses in the proposed settlement. The district judge made significant modifications in the settlement, but not enough. The settlement, a selfish deal between class counsel and the defendant, disserves the class. Class counsel shed crocodile tears over Rexall's misrepresentations, describing them as "demonstrably false," "consumer fraud," "false representations," and so on, and pointed out that most of the consumers of Rexall's glucosamine pills are elderly, bought the product in containers the labels of which recite the misrepresentations—and number some 12 million. Yet only one-fourth of one percent of these fraud victims will receive even modest compensation, and for a limited period the labels will be changed, in trivial respects unlikely to influence or inform consumers. And for conferring these meager benefits class counsel should receive almost $2 million?

The judgment is reversed and the case remanded for further proceedings consistent with this opinion.

NOTE ON CLASS ACTION SETTLEMENTS

1.   **Judicial review of class action settlements.** Rule 23(e) states that "claims, issues, or defenses of a certified class may be settled,

voluntarily dismissed, or compromised only with the court's approval." Class members must receive reasonable notice of the proposed settlement or compromise, even if the action is one under Rule 23(b)(1) or (b)(2) in which they have no right to opt out. The court must hold a hearing on the settlement and may not approve it unless the settlement is "fair, reasonable, and adequate." Under Rule 23(e)(5), any class member may object to the settlement proposal—hence the references to "objectors" in *Pearson*. In opt-out class actions certified under Rule 23(b)(3) the court may disapprove a settlement that does not give class members a renewed opportunity to opt out. The factors to be considered in reviewing the fairness of the settlement include:

> "(1) the complexity, expense and likely duration of the litigation * * *; (2) the reaction of the class to the settlement * * *; (3) the stage of the proceedings and the amount of discovery completed * * *; (4) the risks of establishing liability * * *; (5) the risks of establishing damages * * *; (6) the risks of maintaining the class action through trial * * *; (7) the ability of the defendants to withstand a greater judgment; (8) the range of reasonableness of the settlement fund in light of the best possible recovery * * *; (9) the range of reasonableness of the settlement fund to a possible recovery in light of all the attendant risks of litigation * * *."

In re Prudential Insurance Co. America Sales Practice Litigation Agent Actions, 148 F.3d 283, 317 (3d Cir. 1998).

2. The rationale for and limitations of judicial review. The provisions for review of class action settlements are consistent with the law governing other forms of representative action, which often require judicial approval of settlements.

As amply demonstrated by *Pearson*, the argument for judicial review of class action settlements is particularly strong because settlement presents special dangers that potential conflicts of interest built into the structure of the class action will become actual. Those conflicts may be between class representatives and absentees or between subgroups of absentees who have been combined in the same class. More commonly, they are between the interests of the lawyers for the class and all or part of the class. In an action for damages, there is a danger that the class representative and her lawyer may be bought off with a settlement that compensates them and leaves the absent class members with less than they deserve. In an action for a civil rights injunction, the named plaintiff or her lawyer may agree to relief that solves what they regard as the most serious problem faced by the class, while leaving other important class interests unaddressed. Class members are usually poorly positioned to monitor settlement because they lack information about both the evidence in the case and the bargaining leading to settlement, and sufficient financial stake in the outcome to acquire that information on their own. See Erichson & Zipursky, Consent Versus Closure, 96 Cornell L. Rev. 265 (2011).

Defendants often do not care whether a class action settlement is fair to particular class members or subclasses. Defendants' primary goal is simply to end the litigation. But defendants do have some incentive to settle on fair terms. The defendant's usual goal in settling is often to wrap up the entire dispute in a single transaction. Indeed, the defendant will sometimes pay a "peace premium" for a settlement that precludes virtually all claims in order to avoid overpaying to settle a collection of weak claims while the strongest opt out in order to continue litigation of their individual claims. Plus, the potentially disproportionate costs of facing a handful of claims may continue to attract negative publicity or act a drag on stock prices. Without the class action mechanism, claimants have a hard time credibly offering the defendant peace and capturing the associated premium because the rights to control the claims are widely dispersed among the individual claimants. But a class action settlement gives plaintiffs a low cost way to bundle their claims together for sale to the defendant as a single package, potentially leaving all parties better off. See Issacharoff & Rave, The BP Oil Spill Settlement and the Paradox of Public Litigation, 74 La. L. Rev. 397 (2014); Rave, Governing the Anticommons in Aggregate Litigation, 66 Vand. L. Rev. 1183 (2013).

Consider these arguments in light of the *Pearson* opinion. Is Judge Posner right to castigate the settlement? Would a better settlement have been possible? And is Judge Posner's concern for the compensation of the class members well founded, or should his concern be directed at whether the defendant has disgorged whatever unjust enrichment it derived from its misconduct?

3. Settlement classes. Rule 23 does not mention a "settlement class." But some federal courts in recent years have approved their use. They have been described as follows:

> The settlement class device * * * is a judicially crafted procedure. Usually, the request for a settlement class is presented to the court by both plaintiff(s) and defendant(s); having provisionally settled the case before seeking certification, the parties move for simultaneous class certification and settlement approval. Because this process is removed from the normal, adversarial, litigation mode, the class is certified for settlement purposes, not for litigation. Sometimes * * * the parties reach a settlement while the case is in litigation posture, only then moving the court, with the defendants' stipulation as to the class's compliance with the Rule 23 requisites, for class certification and settlement approval. In any event, the court disseminates notice of the proposed settlement and fairness hearing at the same time it notifies class members of the pendency of class action determination. Only when the settlement is about to be finally approved does the court formally certify the class, thus binding the interests of its members by the settlement.

In re GMC Pick-Up Truck Fuel Tank Products Liability Litig., 55 F.3d 768, 777–78 (3d Cir. 1995) (rejecting proposed settlement). For a useful analysis of five settlement class actions, see Tidmarsh, Mass Tort Settlement Class Actions: Five Case Studies (1998).

The settlement class device has great attraction in mass tort cases. A suitable settlement can so reduce litigation costs that defendants can save money even while the plaintiff class as a whole can obtain a larger recovery. But how can one determine that the settlement is fair in the sense that at least some of the savings achieved through settlement are going to the class members? And how can one determine that it is fair as among subclasses within the overall class?

In Amchem Products, Inc. v. Windsor, 521 U.S. 591, 117 S.Ct. 2231, 138 L.Ed.2d 689 (1997), the Supreme Court rejected a settlement class of plaintiffs asserting personal-injury claims against numerous asbestos manufacturers. In so holding, the Court explained that when certifying a settlement class, although "a district court need not inquire whether the case would present intractable management problems," the other requirements of Rule 23 "demand undiluted, even heightened attention. * * * Such attention is of vital importance, for a court asked to certify a settlement class will lack the opportunity, present when a case is litigated, to adjust the class, informed by the proceedings as they unfold." Id. at 620. Having held that the Rule 23 requirements apply to settlement classes with at least equal force as to class actions intended to be tried, the Court held that the plaintiff class failed the predominance requirement—due to differences among the plaintiffs regarding applicable law, causation, and damages—and the adequacy-of-representation requirement because those already sick with asbestos-related ailments seeking immediate payouts could not effective protect the interests of those whose injuries had not yet manifested.

In Ortiz v. Fibreboard Corp., 527 U.S. 815, 119 S.Ct. 2295, 144 L.Ed.2d 715 (1999), another asbestos personal-injury case, the trial court had certified a limited-fund class action under Rule 23(b)(1)(B), treating the defendant's insurance policy as establishing the universe of the limited fund. A single class was defined, consisting of present and future claimants, whether or not they were injured during the period when the defendant's principal insurance policy (the source of the limited fund) was in effect. The Court held that the failure to establish subclasses violated Rule 23:

> First, * * * a class divided between holders of present and future claims (some of the latter involving no physical injury and to claimants not yet born) requires division into homogeneous subclasses under Rule 23(c)(4)(B), with separate representation to eliminate conflicting interests of counsel. No such procedure was employed here, and the conflict was as contrary to the equitable obligation entailed by the limited fund rationale as it was to the requirements of structural protection applicable to all class actions under Rule 23(a)(4).
>
> Second, the class included those exposed to Fibreboard's asbestos products both before and after 1959. The date is significant, for that year saw the expiration of Fibreboard's insurance policy with Continental, the one that provided the bulk of the insurance funds for the settlement. Pre-1959 claimants accordingly had more valuable claims than post-1959 claimants, the consequence being a second instance of disparate interests within the certified class. While at some point there must be an end to reclassification with separate counsel, these two instances of conflict are well within the requirement of structural protection recognized in *Amchem*.

527 U.S. at 856–57.

Given the concerns the Supreme Court has had about the settlement class device, one can understand better its decision on the relevance of settlement to the certification decision. The Court has rejected any simple or uniform standard, saying that if management problems that would defeat class certification in a litigated case could be reduced by settlement, that difference could weigh in favor of certifying a settlement class. But, in the view of the Court, other criteria for certification—primarily those concerning the adequacy of representation—merit heightened scrutiny in certification of a settlement class. Considering the limits of the trial judge's ability to assess fairness in a settlement reached prior to the filing of any litigation, does it make sense to insist on a class definition that provides "structural assurance of fair and adequate representation of the diverse groups and individuals affected"? For an argument that settlement classes should be banned, see Erichson, The Problem of Settlement Class Actions, 82 Geo. Wash. L. Rev. 951 (2014). For the opposing view, see Campos, Mass Torts and Due Process, 65 Vand. L. Rev. 1069 (2012).

4. **"Coupon settlements."** As *Pearson* shows, many recent settlements have raised questions about the value of the remedy paid to the class. In settlements involving monetary awards, there may be uncertainty about how many class members will claim their award. In some cases, the settlement may provide that unclaimed funds revert to the defendant.

Some settlements in consumer class actions have not involved money but instead coupons entitling the plaintiff class members to purchase additional products from the defendant on a discounted basis. Defendants and lawyers for the settling plaintiff classes have typically argued that such settlements should be valued at the face amount of the coupons issued. Critics have argued that valuing coupon settlements on that basis overstates both their deterrent and compensatory effects. Such settlements do not necessarily deter because coupon-induced sales may still be profitable for defendants. They do not necessarily compensate because unless the there is a market in which the coupon can be sold, it is valueless to people who are not interested in purchasing the product. And because class counsel may be paid whether or not the coupons are redeemed, there is an additional concern that counsel could be selling out the class.

The Class Action Fairness Act of 2005, Pub. L. No. 109–2, 119 Stat. 4 (Feb. 18, 2005), contains several provisions regulating settlements. First, the Act specifies that if a proposed class action settlement includes coupons as part of the recovery awarded the class, "the portion of any attorney's fee award to class counsel that is attributable to the award of the coupons shall be based on the value to class members of the coupons that are redeemed." 28 U.S.C. § 1712(a). The Act also provides that if, following settlement, a portion of the coupons go unclaimed, the court may arrange for their distribution to "charitable or government organizations, as agreed to by the parties." 28 U.S.C. § 1712(e). Second, the Act provides that in cases where "any class member is obligated to pay sums to class counsel that would result in a net loss to the class member," the court may approve the settlement only if it finds that "nonmonetary benefits to the class member substantially outweigh the monetary loss." 28 U.S.C. § 1713. Third, the Act requires the parties to give detailed notice of proposed class action settlements to appropriate federal and state regulatory officials. 28 U.S.C. § 1715. Courts have so far been rigorous in applying this statute to ensure that coupon settlements provide substantial benefit to the class and that class counsel are not disproportionately rewarded. See, e.g., In re HP Inkjet Printer Litigation, 716 F.3d 1173 (9th Cir. 2013) (remanding settlement for reassessment of fee award in light of redemption value of the coupons); Radosti v. Envision EMI, LLC, 717 F. Supp. 2d 37 (D.D.C. 2010) (approving settlement when coupons "provide meaningful value to class members because of their high face value * * *, transferability, and their seven-year duration").

5. *Cy pres* settlements. One oft-included component of class settlements is the use of a *cy pres* remedy. The doctrine of *cy pres* derives from the law of trusts and estates, and it essentially provides that if the circumstances underlying a benefactor's gift have changed, such that achieving the exact purpose of that gift is impossible, courts may reform the terms of the gift to achieve a similar benefit. Hence the name, from the old French *cy pres comme possible*, or "as near as possible." Courts have applied this concept in the class action context to cases in which the class members are either unidentifiable or do not claim their awards. In such cases, the parties will agree, or the court will direct, that unclaimed funds, or some other portion of the settlement, will go to some charity or other organization whose activities are related to the purpose of the class action. In that sense, at least, the settlement will benefit the class, one step removed. Hence, in *Pearson*, the directive that money go to the Orthopedic Research and Education Foundation. Another example is Powell v. Georgia-Pacific Corp., 119 F.3d 703 (8th Cir. 1997), in which unclaimed funds in an employment discrimination class action were directed to a scholarship fund for African-American students. Sometimes, courts have approved giving unclaimed funds to unrelated charities and legal-aid societies. See In re Motorsports Merchandise Antitrust Litigation, 160 F. Supp. 2d 1392 (N.D. Ga. 2001) (nine charities including two legal-aid groups); Jones v. National Distillers, 56 F. Supp. 2d 355 (S.D.N.Y. 1999) (legal-aid society). Other cases are collected in Laycock, Modern American Remedies (4th ed. 2010).

Recently, *cy pres* settlements have been seriously criticized. Some argue that such settlements create opportunities to sell out the class and go beyond the power of the judge to compensate injured parties. See Redish, Julian & Zyontz, Cy Pres Relief and the Pathologies of the Modern Class Action: A Normative and Empirical Analysis, 62 Fla. L. Rev. 617 (2010). As *Pearson* illustrates, courts have begun to express increased skepticism toward *cy pres* remedies. See In re Baby Prods. Litig., 708 F.3d 163 (3d Cir. 2013); Klier v. Elf Autochem N.A., Inc., 658 F.3d 468 (5th Cir. 2011).

CHAPTER 6

DISCOVERY: REGULATING THE FLOW OF INFORMATION

A. THE SCOPE AND MECHANICS OF DISCOVERY

INTRODUCTORY NOTE ON DISCOVERY

1. **The functions of discovery.** Discovery is the legal process for compelling the disclosure of information relevant to disputed factual issues in litigation. The nominal purpose and principal justification for discovery is to enable more accurate outcomes in cases that are litigated on the merits or settled on the basis of expected trial outcomes. In an adversary system, the premise is that fuller disclosure will permit each party to present at trial the most favorable case that can be made on his behalf. The result should be more accurate trial outcomes. Discovery of the case that the other side plans to present—that is, of the information that it views as helping its cause—should reduce the risk of surprise. Discovery of information that the other side would never have presented voluntarily at trial will provide the trier of fact with a more complete view of the circumstances out of which the litigation arose.

An additional legitimate function of discovery is the promotion of settlement. The likelihood of settlement is increased as the parties' respective appraisals of the value of the case converge. The likelihood that the parties' pretrial estimates will converge is obviously affected by whether both parties have access to all information to be presented at trial, providing, of course, that the information is intelligently and realistically appraised by the attorneys. As the primary drafter of the 1938 federal Rules on discovery predicted, "one of the greatest uses of judicial procedure is to bring parties to a point where they will seriously discuss settlement. . . . Many a case would be settled, to the advantage of the parties and to the relief of the court, if the true situation could be disclosed before the trial begins." Sunderland, Scope and Method of Discovery Before Trial, 42 Yale L.J. 863 (1933).

Another important function of discovery is to make available prior to trial information revealing whether the case may be disposed of, in whole or in part, by summary judgment. In that setting, the use of discovery devices may allow a party to establish that a claim or defense has no evidentiary basis. But discovery can also help to ensure that the party opposing the motion has had a full opportunity to investigate the underlying factual issues before the court makes a ruling which deprives it of the right to a trial.

Discovery also has a number of uses not ordinarily thought of as legitimate. One is inflicting costs upon or harassing an opponent. The use of a discovery device is not made illegitimate simply because it is costly or unpleasant for the responding party. Conversely, discovery conducted solely in order to inflict costs is illegal for parties and unethical for lawyers. But between the poles of clearly acceptable and clearly abusive discovery, there is a range in which a litigant may maneuver, to the greater or lesser annoyance and expense of her opponent. The existence of that range of maneuver is a fact of life under modern procedure. Indeed, because typically the recipient of a discovery request must bear the costs of responding, even when discovery is legitimate it can be expensive and motivate settlement simply to avoid the costs of litigation. As noted in Chapter 4, supra, this concern was central to the Supreme Court's recent decision regarding pleading in Bell Atlantic Corp. v. Twombly, 550 U.S. 544, 127 S.Ct. 1955, 167 L.Ed.2d 929 (2007), in which the Court observed that "the threat of discovery expense will push cost-conscious defendants to settle even anemic cases." Id. at 559.

Another doubtful use of discovery may be to facilitate the "reconstruction" of evidence (that is, making up evidence) in anticipation of an opponent's proof at trial. Any such reconstruction by a litigant is, of course, improper. If done with the knowledge of counsel, it is a breach of ethics by the attorney. At the extreme, it is subornation of perjury by the attorney. But between the poles of refreshed memory and perjury is an area in which some litigants have made substantial travels, at times with the acquiescence of their attorneys.

2.   Federal and state discovery rules. Federal Rules 26–37 were a central component of the original 1938 Federal Rules of Civil Procedure. They worked a substantial change in the manner in which civil litigation was conducted, providing a much more effective mechanism than had previously existed for discovery of facts that the other side preferred not to become known. The discovery rules were substantially amended in 1970, in 1993 and again in 2000. (The discovery rules were also amended for non-substantive stylistic purposes in 2007. Significant amendments have been proposed for adoption in 2015, but they have not yet been passed on by the Supreme Court or Congress, as of the printing of this edition. See Note on the Proposed 2015 Discovery Rule Amendments, infra p. 732.) The states followed the lead of the 1938 federal discovery Rules in expanding the scope of discovery in their courts. With the exception of the mandatory disclosures required under the 1993 and 2000 amendments to the federal Rules (described below), discovery rules in state courts are substantially similar to their federal counterparts.

3.   Historical note. The discovery process inaugurated by the 1938 Federal Rules of Civil Procedure was revolutionary in American law. At common law, there was very little opportunity for pretrial discovery. Although there were some discovery devices available at equity and under the codes, these were relatively limited compared with the federal Rules regime. As Professor Langbein notes, a "common law litigant had no means of compelling the production of documents, and no opportunity before trial to examine to examine opposing parties or witnesses." Langbein, The Disappearance of Civil Trial, 122 Yale L.J. 522 (2012).

The principal architect of the federal discovery Rules was Professor Edson Sunderland. A progressive and legal realist, Sunderland believed that wide-ranging discovery, combined with simplified pleading, would lead to more effective administration of justice. See Burbank & Farhang, Litigation Reform: An Institutional Approach, 162 U. Pa. L. Rev. 1543 (2014). As Sunderland explained:

> It is probable that no procedural process offers greater opportunities for increasing the efficiency of the administration of justice than that of discovery before trial. Much of the delay in the preparation of a case, most of the lost effort in the course of the

trial, and a large part of the uncertainty in the outcome, result from the want of information on the part of litigants and their counsel as to the real nature of the respective claims and the facts upon which they rest.

False and fictitious causes and defenses thrive under a system of concealment and secrecy in the preliminary stages of litigation followed by surprise and confusion at the trial. Under such a system the merits of controversies are imperfectly understood by the parties, are inadequately presented to the courts, and too often fail to exert a controlling influence on the trial.

Sunderland, Foreword to Ragland, Discovery Before Trial (1932) (quoted in Subrin, Fishing Expeditions Allowed: The Historical Background of the 1938 Federal Discovery Rules, 39 B.C. L. Rev. 691 (1998)).

As Professor Hazard explains, the 1938 federal Rules regime, including the expansion of the scope of discovery and the availability of a variety of discovery tools, such as oral depositions and requests for the production of documents, redounds to the benefit of plaintiffs:

The powerful effects of the Federal Rules on discovery are augmented by their synergism with the pleading and joinder provisions. Pleading in general terms permits a claimant to prosecute another party without having to explain exactly why the party is being charged. The joinder of parties rules permit a civil prosecutor to proceed in quite the same way a criminal prosecutor goes after conspirators, giving all participants the ability to point fingers at each other. Correlatively, discovery facilitates adding parties whose participation in the transaction was not known at first. The open disclosure ethos of the Federal Rules makes them a boon to persons with legal grievances, that is, plaintiffs.

Hazard, Discovery Vices and Trans-Substantive Virtues in the Federal Rules of Civil Procedure, 137 U. Pa. L. Rev. 2237 (1989).

The plaintiff-friendliness of the federal Rules has never been lost on defendants, who have long fought to restrict the scope of discovery, which they contend is overly expensive, intrusive, and amenable to abuse by plaintiffs with meritless claims. Id. at 2243. In some cases, these concerns are well founded. As Professor Redish vividly explains,

Discovery is reminiscent of the invention of fire. Like fire, when used with proper restraint, discovery can be enormously valuable to achievement of the goals of the litigation matrix. But also like fire, when used carelessly or recklessly, discovery can also give rise to serious harm and destruction. * * * The problem, of course is finding ways to control such pathological discovery without either effectively destroying the beneficial effects of the discovery process or establishing control methods that are as economically inefficient as the abusive discover itself. This task has proven to be far more difficult than one might have hoped.

Redish, Pleading, Discovery, and the Federal Rules: Exploring the Foundations of Modern Procedure, 64 Fla. L. Rev. 845 (2012). The search for the optimal approach to discovery continues today. As you read the materials below, ask yourself whether the Rules properly balance the competing policy considerations.

Note on the Discovery Process and Discovery Tools

Discovery in civil suits is conducted using a variety of tools. Each tool has its own advantages and disadvantages, and an experienced litigator will have distinct preferences for one or another depending on the circumstances. Discovery is designed to operate, for the most part, without active involvement by the courts. When discovery works smoothly, as it often does, parties seek and provide information in a timely way without being ordered to do so by the court. Indeed, discovery is often heavily negotiated by the parties, with the rules providing only a baseline for such negotiations. When discovery works badly, as it sometimes does, parties and their lawyers may delay, harass, or obstruct one another, or refuse to provide requested information. If the discovery process breaks down, the court has the power to order recalcitrant parties to change their behavior and to award sanctions against them.

The grand tour of the discovery process below is necessarily abbreviated. Indeed, one could profitably devote an entire course to the study of discovery. Moreover, the nature of discovery is somewhat difficult to capture outside of the trenches of actual litigation—it is truly best learned through practice. But this description of the general course of discovery should leave you well equipped to enter practice with the baseline knowledge of the tools available to you and the system as a whole.

1. Informal investigation. Do not overlook the investigation that an attorney can, and should, undertake outside the compulsory structure of the formal discovery rules. Much of this discovery will take place before the suit is filed, as the attorney determines the strength of her case, explores the possibility of settlement, and decides whether a complaint should be filed. In a federal suit, some informal investigation will often have to take place before a complaint is filed in order to comply with Rule 11. Even after the complaint has been filed, some informal investigation will likely continue. The requirement of factual plausibility in pleading claims for relief imposed by the Supreme Court's recent decisions in *Twombly* and *Iqbal*, discussed supra p. 471–496, has made pre-filing investigation even more important.

Informal discovery includes interviews conducted by a lawyer, by an investigator employed in the lawyer's office, or by a licensed private investigator; review of documents held by various people; or visits to property that is the subject of the potential lawsuit. Sometimes the federal Freedom of Information Act, or state-law equivalents, can be usefully employed to obtain information in the hands of governmental bodies. Informal discovery has a number of advantages. It is usually far less expensive than formal discovery. For example, informal interviews are often easily arranged and quickly conducted; by contrast, formal depositions are often difficult to schedule and time-consuming to conduct. Further, informal discovery often gives an attorney considerable freedom to manage the information obtained. For example, if a potential witness in an informal interview says something unfavorable to the client, there is no rule requiring the lawyer to write it down and send it to the opposing counsel; by contrast, an unfavorable statement in a deposition is stated under oath, made in front of opposing counsel, and recorded for posterity.

The details of a formal discovery system differ from one jurisdiction to another, and a lawyer must follow carefully the applicable rules of the court in which he appears. The federal discovery rules are described in this note to give you an idea of a single, relatively coherent system. State discovery rules are similar in outline, though they vary from the federal pattern in some details.

   2.   **Meeting to draw up proposed discovery plan.** After the complaint is served, Rule 26(f) requires the parties to meet in order to develop a "proposed discovery plan." The plan should contain: any proposed changes to the mandatory disclosures required under Rule 26(a); any proposed changes in limitations on discovery; and a description of the parties' views on the subjects and timing of discovery. The initial discovery meeting is to be held "as soon as practicable": the outer limit for the meeting is 21 days prior to the final deadline for issuance of a scheduling order under Rule 16. This deadline in turn must be "within the earlier of 120 days after any defendant has been served with the complaint or 90 days after any defendant has appeared." Fed. R. Civ. P. 16(b)(2). The parties must submit a written report outlining the discovery plan to the court within 14 days of the meeting of the parties. Fed. R. Civ. P. 26(f)(2).

   3.   **Initial disclosures.** Except in certain limited classes of cases, the parties in federal court are required to make initial disclosures to each other of four classes of information: (i) names, addresses, and telephone numbers of individuals "likely to have discoverable information—along with the subjects of that information—that the disclosing party may use to support its claims or defenses, unless the use would be solely for impeachment;" (ii) copies, or descriptions by category and location, of documents, data compilations, and other tangible things "that the disclosing party may use to support its claims or defenses"; (iii) a computation of any category of damages claimed; and (iv) any insurance agreement out of which a judgment may be paid. Fed. R. Civ. P. 26(a)(1)(A)(i)–(iv). Unless otherwise agreed, the initial disclosures must be made within 14 days of the parties' meeting to prepare a discovery plan.

   Mandatory initial disclosure is a relatively new development in federal discovery practice. Until 1993, parties to federal litigation were under no obligation to produce information to their opponent in the absence of a formal request for such information. In 1993, the federal discovery rules were amended to require mandatory disclosure, but the disclosures of witnesses and documents under Rules 26(a)(1)(A)(i)–(ii) were limited to information relevant to disputed facts "alleged with particularity in the pleadings." The requirement of initial disclosure, without request from the other side, of information "relevant to disputed facts alleged with particularity in the pleadings" was extremely controversial because it required a party to make initial disclosure of information *unfavorable* to its case. In part for that reason, the 1993 version of Rule 26(a) allowed federal district courts to opt out of the mandatory disclosure regime. Many districts did so.

   Justice Scalia, joined by Justices Thomas and Souter, dissented from the transmittal to Congress of the 1993 rule requiring initial disclosures. He wrote,

> The proposed new regime does not fit comfortably within the American judicial system, which relies on adversarial litigation to develop the facts before a neutral decisionmaker. By placing upon lawyers the obligation to disclose information damaging to their clients—on their own initiative, and in a context where the lines between what must be disclosed and what need not be disclosed are

not clear but require the exercise of considerable judgment—the new Rule would place intolerable strain upon lawyers' ethical duty to represent their clients and not to assist the opposing side. Requiring a lawyer to make a judgment as to what information is 'relevant to disputed facts' plainly requires him to use his professional skills in the service of the adversary.

146 F.R.D. 507, 511 (1993). In 2000, Rule 26(a) was amended. Under the amended rule a party is only required to provide initial disclosure of information it "may use to support its claims or defenses"—that is, information *favorable* to its case. At the same time the requirement that a matter be pleaded with particularity in order to trigger mandatory disclosure was dropped.

4. **Scope of discovery.** The scope of American discovery is broader than in any other legal system in the world. Federal Rule 26(b)(1) is typical, providing that a party may obtain discovery concerning "any nonprivileged matter that is relevant to any party's claim or defense." Privileges are, for the most part, determined by rules and case law outside the discovery rules and will be considered later in this chapter, infra p. 738. Note also that the definition of the scope of discovery in Rule 26(b)(1) may soon be changing, see infra p. 732, Note on the Proposed 2015 Discovery Rule Amendments.

The scope of discovery goes well beyond learning what evidence the opposing side plans to introduce at trial or asking for production of specific identified documents. It also includes relatively open-ended investigation into categories of information that the opposing party may have no wish to reveal. To obtain discovery, the party seeking discovery need not demonstrate that the information sought would be admissible at trial. It is enough that the information sought "appears reasonably calculated to lead to the discovery of admissible evidence." Fed. R. Civ. P. 26(b)(1). Thus, for example, although hearsay evidence is often inadmissible at trial because of its unreliability, hearsay which seems reasonably likely to point the way toward admissible evidence is discoverable.

When using all of the discovery tools described below, the requesting party is also not required to identify particular items of information which it would like to see produced. Instead, it can proceed with a request that identifies the class or classes of information in which it has an interest.

5. **Depositions. a. In general.** A deposition is a formal questioning of a witness under oath. A deposition may be taken of any potential witness, whether or not a party. Typically it is conducted by a lawyer for a party. The lawyers for other parties to the case have the right to be present and to ask questions as well. The deposition is recorded for future reference. The traditional method of recording a deposition is for a stenographer to produce a typed transcript. A new and increasingly common method is to record the deposition on audio or videotape. A typed transcript of the deposition is typically used at trial, but in cases where the cost can be justified videotaped depositions are increasingly used at trial in presenting testimony of adverse parties.

The principal advantages of a deposition over other forms of discovery are that the deponent is answering directly rather than through her lawyer, that the deponent does not know in advance what the precise questions will be, and that the questioner can ask follow-up questions suggested by the answers given. Note, however, that a careful lawyer defending a deposition will prepare the deponent, covering beforehand the questions that are likely to be asked. Subtler advantages include the opportunity to assess potential witnesses (will they stand up under cross-examination; will they present a sympathetic and believable figure to the jury); the opportunity to assess a lawyer for the other side (is she well prepared and skillful); and the opportunity to show to the other side how well prepared and skillful you are. The greatest disadvantage of a deposition is its cost. At a minimum, it includes the cost of the lawyer preparing for, traveling to, and attending the deposition, and the reporter's fee for the transcript. The cost is even greater when one factors in the time of the lawyers for the other parties and the time of the witness. Videotaped depositions have the added costs associated with the taping. Subtler disadvantages include the danger of discovering and recording information unfavorable to one's client; and tipping one's hand on possible lines of analysis or attack.

Lawyers have certain rules of thumb about depositions. For example, a lawyer almost never deposes her own client, since she can learn everything she needs to know from an informal interview. And a lawyer deposes friendly witnesses relatively infrequently. The lawyer usually can learn enough from a friendly witness in an informal interview; in addition, the nuisance and formality of a deposition sometimes risk alienating the witness. There are exceptions, such as cases in which the client or witness is in failing health or may be out of the country at the time of trial. Unless court-imposed limitations on discovery or considerations of expense preclude a lawyer from doing so, a lawyer will ordinarily depose all important unfriendly witnesses. Sometimes, in corporate litigation, the most important deponent is a person far down in the defendant's corporate hierarchy who really knows what happened. Sometimes the most important deponent is the highest person in the hierarchy; once such a person is deposed, she may realize what an expense and embarrassment the lawsuit is going to be, and may agree to settle the case on favorable terms. Sometimes the order in which witnesses are deposed makes a difference in the effectiveness with which information is discovered.

An infrequently used device is a deposition on written questions. The lawyer prepares questions, which are sent to the deposition and asked by someone else. The witness answers under oath when the questions are read to him. The advantage of a deposition on written questions over a live deposition is that it is generally much cheaper. A severe, and usually overwhelming, disadvantage of a deposition on written questions is that the lawyer cannot ask follow up questions suggested by the answers.

   b.   Rule 30. Under Rule 30, a party may depose any person, whether or not a party, who possesses relevant information within the meaning of Rule 26. All parties to the suit must be given reasonable written notice of the time and place of the deposition. There is a presumptive upper limit of seven hours of deposition (a working day) for each witness, and a presumptive upper limit of ten depositions for each side, but these limits may be increased by agreement of the parties or by court order.

   c.   Conduct of the deposition. An attorney whose witness is being deposed may object to questions that are asked, but the range of permissible objections is narrower than that available at trial, since it is not a ground for objection that a question calls for inadmissible evidence. In some circumstances the lawyer may instruct the witness not to answer. Those circumstances are limited to (1) preservation of a privilege; (2) enforcement of a protective order limiting discovery; or (3) ending the deposition because of abusive behavior by the deposing party. Fed. R. Civ. P. 30(c)(2), (d)(3). An attorney whose witness is being deposed may cross-examine the deponent. Fed. R. Civ. P. 30(c). If a person impedes, delays, or frustrates fair examination of a deponent, the court may impose sanctions on that person. Sanctions can include attorney's fees incurred as a result of the improper behavior. Fed. R. Civ. P. 30(d)(2).

6. Interrogatories. a. In general. An interrogatory is a written question sent to a party that must be answered under oath and in writing. Interrogatories can only be sent to parties. (Non-parties can be deposed, however, and in some instances depositions on written questions can serve much the same function as interrogatories.) Interrogatories are inexpensive for the party asking the questions. Depending on the complexity of the answers required, they can be quite expensive for the party answering, who is obliged to respond with all relevant information reasonably available to her. Interrogatories, often accompanied by a request for production of documents, are usually the first formal discovery device used after the filing of a lawsuit.

Interrogatories are particularly useful in seeking what may be called "hard" information, such as names and addresses, document identification, and monetary calculations. Although interrogatories are addressed to a party, answers to interrogatories are in fact drafted by the party's lawyer. But even a creative lawyer will have difficulty avoiding questions such as, "What is the name and address of the doctor who treated you?" and "How much did that doctor charge you for her services?" Interrogatories can also be used, with more mixed success, to seek information about the other side's contentions. For example, plaintiff might ask, "Do you contend that plaintiff was outside the crosswalk when defendant's car struck him?" If the answer to that question is yes, the next interrogatory might ask for a listing of each item of evidence which the defendant believes supports that contention.

b. Rule 33. Answers to interrogatories are provided under oath, and must be signed by the party to which they are directed. There is a presumptive upper limit of 25 interrogatories (including "discrete subparts") submitted by one party to another. Interrogatories may ordinarily be submitted without special authorization, but leave of court is required to submit more than 25 interrogatories unless the parties are willing to stipulate to a larger number. Fed. R. Civ. P. 33(a). Objections to interrogatories must be stated with specificity by the lawyer for the party. Any grounds for objection not so stated are waived. To the extent that an interrogatory is not objectionable, it must be answered. Fed. R. Civ. P. 33(b)(1), (4).

7. Production of documents and things. a. In general. Depending on the type of case, document production can be either relatively unimportant or critical. An automobile accident case or a simple contract case will involve few documents. A major antitrust case, on the other hand, can involve thousands or hundreds of thousands of documents. In the latter case, document discovery is likely to be the single most important aspect of the litigation. Documents are usually sought from parties, but if necessary can be obtained by subpoena from non-parties.

In theory, discovery of documents is straightforward. A party asks—usually in interrogatories—what documents exist relevant to a particular issue and that they be produced. In practice, document discovery in large complex cases is difficult and expensive. Opposing parties are often reluctant to identify and hand over crucial documents, and are more than willing to identify and deliver large quantities of irrelevant documents that the requestor must wade through.

In some cases, physical objects are important pieces of evidence. For example, in a product liability case, a plaintiff may request that the product be made available for inspection and testing. In other cases, where the physical characteristics of land are at issue, a party may request access in order to inspect, measure, or photograph the land.

b.   Rule 34. A party may request another party to produce documents or tangible things for inspection, copying or testing; or to permit entry onto land or other physical property for inspection, measuring or photographing. Fed. R. Civ. P. 34(a). Leave of court is not required for such a request, and there is no presumptive upper limit on the number of documents or physical things that may be requested. Fed. R. Civ. P. 34(b). A non-party may be compelled by subpoena to produce documents and things, or to permit entry. Fed. R. Civ. P. 34(c); 45. Under Rule 45(d), a non-party may quash or modify a subpoena because of undue burden, privilege or other grounds.

8.   Physical and mental examinations. The most intrusive form of discovery is the compulsory physical examination. For that reason, such examinations are available only against parties and only when the physical or mental state of a party is in issue. In such cases, an opposing party may request an examination by a qualified expert. The court will ordinarily require a showing of "good cause" before allowing the examination. Fed. R. Civ. P. 35(a). The examination must be conducted by a "suitably licensed or certified examiner." For physical examinations, this is usually but not always a medical doctor; for mental examinations, a psychiatrist or psychologist. In most jurisdictions, the party seeking discovery chooses the examiner; in a few jurisdictions, the court chooses the examiner. The party obtaining the expert's report must, upon request, give a copy to the party who was examined. But the party who was examined must then turn over the results of any comparable examinations which she underwent from other experts. Fed. R. Civ. P. 35(b).

9.   Requests for admission. a. In general. A party may request that an opponent admit, for purposes of this case alone, that certain facts are true or that certain documents are genuine. Fed. R. Civ. P. 36. Requests for admission are usually made toward the end of the discovery phase of a suit, after other discovery tools have revealed the basic facts of the case. In theory, a request for admission might be, "Do you admit that your negligence caused plaintiff's injury?" If defendant is convinced that she will lose on the issue of liability, she could respond, "Yes," but such a response is very unlikely in a litigated case. Requests for admissions usually aim at secondary facts that are cumbersome to prove but unlikely to be seriously contested—for example, "Admit that X is the owner of a certain automobile." Admissions shorten and simplify a trial, and a litigant is often well advised to eliminate as many contestable issues as possible through requests for admission.

b.   Rule 36. A party may serve on another party a request for admission of the truth of any matter discoverable within the scope of the federal discovery rules. Ordinarily, if a party does not answer or object to a request for admission within 30 days, the matter is deemed admitted. Fed.

R. Civ. P. 36(a)(3). If the requested party objects or declines to admit, that party must state reasons for objecting or declining. Fed. R. Civ. P. 36(a)(4). Unless the court permits its withdrawal, an admission conclusively establishes the truth of the matter for purposes of the litigation. Fed. R. Civ. P. 36(b).

10. Motions for protective orders and motions to compel. Where a party believes that proposed discovery extends too broadly, threatens information that is exempt from discovery or confidential, or is too expensive or harassing, she may seek a protective order. A protective order may bar the discovery, limit it, specify conditions to protect against improper circulation or disclosure of confidential information or undue expense, or allocate costs as between the parties. Fed. R. Civ. P. 26(c). Alternatively, when a party makes an objection to requested discovery, the party seeking discovery may make a motion to compel compliance. Fed. R. Civ. P. 37(a)(1). Both motions for protective orders and motions to compel may be made only after the moving party has first "in good faith conferred or attempted to confer" with the opposing party or person in an effort to resolve the dispute without litigation. The court must award attorneys' fees against the party that loses a motion for a protective order or a motion to compel, unless the court finds that the losing party's position was "substantially justified." Fed. R. Civ. P. 37(a)(5).

As a general rule, courts do not relish repeatedly resolving discovery fights between parties who cannot work matters out for themselves. Sometimes, judges can get prickly. As one judge wrote in an order to the parties:

> When the undersigned accepted the appointment from the President of the United States of the position now held, he was ready to face the daily practice of law in federal courts with presumably competent lawyers. No one warned the undersigned that in many instances his responsibility would be the same as a person who supervised kindergarten. Frankly, the undersigned would guess the lawyers in this case did not attend kindergarten as they never learned how to get along well with others. Notwithstanding the history of filings and antagonistic motions full of personal insults and requiring multiple discovery hearings, earning the disgust of this Court, the lawyers continue ad infinitum. * * *

> The Court simply wants to scream to these lawyers, "Get a life," or "Do you have any other cases" or "When is the last time you registered for anger management classes?" * * * If the lawyers in this case do not change, immediately, their manner of practice and start conducting themselves as competent to practice in federal court, the Court will contemplate and may enter an order requiring the parties to obtain new counsel.

Klein-Becker, LLC v. Stanley, 2004 U.S. Dist. LEXIS 19107 (W.D. Tex. July 21, 2004).

11. Sanctions. When a party has disobeyed a court's order, or has abused the discovery process in an egregious way, the other party may wish to move for sanctions. The most common form of sanction is an award of costs, including attorneys' fees, caused by the discovery abuse. In extreme cases, a court may find a disputed fact against a party refusing to allow discovery, or even dismiss a cause of action (against a plaintiff) or enter judgment (against a defendant). For further discussion of these issues, see the Note on Discovery Ethics and Discovery Sanctions, infra p. 795.

Zubulake v. UBS Warburg LLC

United States District Court, Southern District of New York, 2003.
217 F.R.D. 309.

■ SCHEINDLIN, DISTRICT JUDGE:

The world was a far different place in 1849, when Henry David Thoreau opined (in an admittedly broader context) that "the process of discovery is very simple."[1] That hopeful maxim has given way to rapid technological advances, requiring new solutions to old problems. The issue presented here is one such problem, recast in light of current technology: To what extent is inaccessible electronic data discoverable, and who should pay for its production?

I.   INTRODUCTION

The Supreme Court recently reiterated that our "simplified notice pleading standard relies on liberal discovery rules and summary judgment motions to define disputed facts and issues and to dispose of unmeritorious claims."[2] Thus, it is now beyond dispute that "broad discovery is a cornerstone of the litigation process contemplated by the Federal Rules of Civil Procedure."[3] The Rules contemplate a minimal burden to bringing a claim; that claim is then fleshed out through vigorous and expansive discovery.[4]

In one context, however, the reliance on broad discovery has hit a roadblock. As individuals and corporations increasingly do business electronically—using computers to create and store documents, make deals, and exchange e-mails—the universe of discoverable material has expanded exponentially.[6] The more information there is to discover, the more expensive it is to discover all the relevant information until, in the end, "discovery is not just about uncovering the truth, but also about how much of the truth the parties can afford to disinter."[7]

This case provides a textbook example of the difficulty of balancing the competing needs of broad discovery and manageable costs. Laura Zubulake is suing UBS Warburg LLC, UBS Warburg, and UBS AG (collectively, "UBS" or the "Firm") under Federal, State and City law for gender discrimination and illegal retaliation. Zubulake's case is certainly

---

[1]   Henry David Thoreau, A Week on the Concord and Merrimack Rivers (1849).

[2]   Swierkiewicz v. Sorema, N.A., 534 U.S. 506, 512, 152 L.Ed.2d 1, 122 S.Ct. 992 (2002).

[3]   Jones v. Goord, 2002 U.S. Dist. LEXIS 8707, No. 95 Civ. 8026, 2002 WL 1007614, at *1 (S.D.N.Y. May 16, 2002).

[4]   See Hickman v. Taylor, 329 U.S. 495, 500–01, 91 L. Ed. 451, 67 S.Ct. 385 (1947).

[6]   Rowe Entm't, Inc. v. William Morris Agency, Inc., 205 F.R.D. 421, 429 (S.D.N.Y. 2002) (explaining that electronic data is so voluminous because, unlike paper documents, "the costs of storage are virtually nil. Information is retained not because it is expected to be used, but because there is no compelling reason to discard it"), aff'd, 2002 U.S. Dist. LEXIS 8308, 2002 WL 975713 (S.D.N.Y. May 9, 2002).

[7]   Rowe, 205 F.R.D. at 423.

not frivolous[8] and if she prevails, her damages may be substantial.[9] She contends that key evidence is located in various e-mails exchanged among UBS employees that now exist only on backup tapes and perhaps other archived media. According to UBS, restoring those e-mails would cost approximately $175,000.00, exclusive of attorney time in reviewing the e-mails. Zubulake now moves for an order compelling UBS to produce those e-mails at its expense.

II. BACKGROUND

A. Zubulake's Lawsuit

UBS hired Zubulake on August 23, 1999, as a director and senior salesperson on its U.S. Asian Equities Sales Desk (the "Desk"), where she reported to Dominic Vail, the Desk's manager. At the time she was hired, Zubulake was told that she would be considered for Vail's position if and when it became vacant.

In December 2000, Vail indeed left his position to move to the Firm's London office. But Zubulake was not considered for his position, and the Firm instead hired Matthew Chapin as director of the Desk. Zubulake alleges that from the outset Chapin treated her differently than the other members of the Desk, all of whom were male. In particular, Chapin "undermined Ms. Zubulake's ability to perform her job by, inter alia: (a) ridiculing and belittling her in front of co-workers; (b) excluding her from work-related outings with male co-workers and clients; (c) making sexist remarks in her presence; and (d) isolating her from the other senior salespersons on the Desk by seating her apart from them." No such actions were taken against any of Zubulake's male co-workers.

Zubulake ultimately responded by filing a Charge of (gender) Discrimination with the EEOC on August 16, 2001. On October 9, 2001, Zubulake was fired with two weeks' notice. On February 15, 2002, Zubulake filed the instant action, suing for sex discrimination and retaliation under Title VII, the New York State Human Rights Law, and the Administrative Code of the City of New York. UBS timely answered on March 12, 2002, denying the allegations. UBS's argument is, in essence, that Chapin's conduct was not unlawfully discriminatory because he treated everyone equally badly. * * *

B. The Discovery Dispute

Discovery in this action commenced on or about June 3, 2002, when Zubulake served UBS with her first document request. At issue here is request number twenty-eight, for "all documents concerning any communication by or between UBS employees concerning Plaintiff." The term document in Zubulake's request "includes, without limitation, electronic or computerized data compilations." On July 8, 2002, UBS responded by producing approximately 350 pages of documents,

---

[8]   Indeed, Zubulake has already produced a sort of "smoking gun": an e-mail suggesting that she be fired "ASAP" after her EEOC charge was filed, in part so that she would not be eligible for year-end bonuses. See 8/21/01 e-mail from Mike Davies to Rose Tong ("8/21/01 e-Mail").

[9]   At the time she was terminated, Zubulake's annual salary was approximately $500,000. Were she to receive full back pay and front pay, Zubulake estimates that she may be entitled to as much as $13,000,000 in damages, not including any punitive damages or attorney's fees.

including approximately 100 pages of e-mails. UBS also objected to a substantial portion of Zubulake's requests.

On September 12, 2002—after an exchange of angry letters and a conference before United States Magistrate Judge Gabriel W. Gorenstein—the parties reached an agreement (the "9/12/02 Agreement"). With respect to document request twenty-eight, the parties reached the following agreement, in relevant part:

> Defendants will ask UBS about how to retrieve e-mails that are saved in the firm's computer system and will produce responsive e-mails if retrieval is possible and Plaintiff names a few individuals.

Pursuant to the 9/12/02 Agreement, UBS agreed unconditionally to produce responsive e-mails from the accounts of five individuals named by Zubulake. * * * UBS was to produce such e-mails sent between August 1999 (when Zubulake was hired) and December 2001 (one month after her termination), to the extent possible.

UBS, however, produced no additional e-mails and insisted that its initial production (the 100 pages of e-mails) was complete. As UBS's opposition to the instant motion makes clear—although it remains unsaid—UBS never searched for responsive e-mails on any of its backup tapes. To the contrary, UBS informed Zubulake that the cost of producing e-mails on backup tapes would be prohibitive (estimated at the time at approximately $300,000.00).

Zubulake, believing that the 9/12/02 Agreement included production of e-mails from backup tapes, objected to UBS's nonproduction. In fact, Zubulake knew that there were additional responsive e-mails that UBS had failed to produce because she herself had produced approximately 450 pages of e-mail correspondence. Clearly, numerous responsive e-mails had been created and deleted[19] at UBS, and Zubulake wanted them.

On December 2, 2002, the parties again appeared before Judge Gorenstein, who ordered UBS to produce for deposition a person with knowledge of UBS's e-mail retention policies in an effort to determine whether the backup tapes contained the deleted e-mails and the burden of producing them. In response, UBS produced Christopher Behny, Manager of Global Messaging, who was deposed on January 14, 2003. Mr. Behny testified to UBS's e-mail backup protocol, and also to the cost of restoring the relevant data.

---

[19] The term "deleted" is sticky in the context of electronic data. " 'Deleting' a file does not actually erase that data from the computer's storage devices. Rather, it simply finds the data's entry in the disk directory and changes it to a 'not used' status—thus permitting the computer to write over the 'deleted' data. Until the computer writes over the 'deleted' data, however, it may be recovered by searching the disk itself rather than the disk's directory. Accordingly, many files are recoverable long after they have been deleted—even if neither the computer user nor the computer itself is aware of their existence. Such data is referred to as 'residual data.' " Shira A. Scheindlin & Jeffrey Rabkin, Electronic Discovery in Federal Civil Litigation: Is Rule 34 Up to the Task?, 41 B.C. L. Rev. 327, 337 (2000) (footnotes omitted). Deleted data may also exist because it was backed up before it was deleted. Thus, it may reside on backup tapes or similar media. Unless otherwise noted, I will use the term "deleted" data to mean residual data, and will refer to backed-up data as "backup tapes."

C. UBS's E-Mail Backup System

In the first instance, the parties agree that e-mail was an important means of communication at UBS during the relevant time period. Each salesperson, including the salespeople on the Desk, received approximately 200 e-mails each day. Given this volume, and because Securities and Exchange Commission regulations require it, UBS implemented extensive email backup and preservation protocols. In particular, e-mails were backed up in two distinct ways: on backup tapes and on optical disks.

1. Backup Tape Storage

UBS employees used a program called HP OpenMail, manufactured by Hewlett-Packard, for all work-related e-mail communications. With limited exceptions, all e-mails sent or received by any UBS employee are stored onto backup tapes. * * * *

Once e-mails have been stored onto backup tapes, the restoration process is lengthy. Each backup tape routinely takes approximately five days to restore, although resort to an outside vendor would speed up the process (at greatly enhanced costs, of course). * * *

Fortunately, NetBackup also created indexes of each backup tape. Thus, Behny was able to search through the tapes from the relevant time period and determine that the e-mail files responsive to Zubulake's requests are contained on a total of ninety-four backup tapes.

2. Optical Disk Storage

In addition to the e-mail backup tapes, UBS also stored certain e-mails on optical disks. * * * Internal e-mails, however, were not stored on this system.

UBS has retained each optical disk used since the system was put into place in mid-1998. Moreover, the optical disks are neither erasable nor rewritable. Thus, UBS has every e-mail sent or received by registered traders (except internal emails) during the period of Zubulake's employment, even if the e-mail was deleted instantaneously on that trader's system.

The optical disks are easily searchable using a program called Tumbleweed. * * *

III. LEGAL STANDARD

Federal Rules of Civil Procedure 26 through 37 govern discovery in all civil actions. As the Supreme Court long ago explained,

> The pre-trial deposition-discovery mechanism established by Rules 26 to 37 is one of the most significant innovations of the Federal Rules of Civil Procedure. Under the prior federal practice, the pre-trial functions of notice-giving issue-formulation and fact-revelation were performed primarily and inadequately by the pleadings. Inquiry into the issues and the facts before trial was narrowly confined and was often cumbersome in method. The new rules, however, restrict the pleadings to the task of general notice-giving and invest the deposition-discovery process with a vital role in the preparation for trial. The various instruments of discovery now serve (1) as a device, along with the pre-trial hearing under Rule 16, to

narrow and clarify the basic issues between the parties, and (2) as a device for ascertaining the facts, or information as to the existence or whereabouts of facts, relative to those issues. Thus civil trials in the federal courts no longer need to be carried on in the dark. The way is now clear, consistent with recognized privileges, for the parties to obtain the fullest possible knowledge of the issues and facts before trial.[29]

Consistent with this approach, Rule 26(b)(1) specifies that,

Parties may obtain discovery regarding any matter, not privileged, that is relevant to the claim or defense of any party, including the existence, description, nature, custody, condition, and location of any books, documents, or other tangible things and the identity and location of persons having knowledge of any discoverable matter. For good cause, the court may order discovery of any matter relevant to the subject matter involved in the action. Relevant information need not be admissible at the trial if the discovery appears reasonably calculated to lead to the discovery of admissible evidence. All discovery is subject to the limitations imposed by Rule 26(b)(2)(i), (ii), and (iii).

In turn, Rule 26(b)(2) imposes general limitations on the scope of discovery in the form of a "proportionality test":

The frequency or extent of use of the discovery methods otherwise permitted under these rules and by any local rule shall be limited by the court if it determines that: (i) the discovery sought is unreasonably cumulative or duplicative, or is obtainable from some other source that is more convenient, less burdensome, or less expensive; (ii) the party seeking discovery has had ample opportunity by discovery in the action to obtain the information sought; or (iii) the burden or expense of the proposed discovery outweighs its likely benefit, taking into account the needs of the case, the amount in controversy, the parties' resources, the importance of the issues at stake in the litigation, and the importance of the proposed discovery in resolving the issues.

Finally, "under [the discovery] rules, the presumption is that the responding party must bear the expense of complying with discovery requests, but [it] may invoke the district court's discretion under Rule 26(c) to grant orders protecting [it] from 'undue burden or expense' in doing so, including orders conditioning discovery on the requesting party's payment of the costs of discovery."

The application of these various discovery rules is particularly complicated where electronic data is sought because otherwise discoverable evidence is often only available from expensive-to-restore backup media. That being so, courts have devised creative solutions for balancing the broad scope of discovery prescribed in Rule 26(b)(1) with the cost-consciousness of Rule 26(b)(2). By and large, the solution has been to consider cost-shifting: forcing the requesting party, rather than the answering party, to bear the cost of discovery.

---

29   Hickman, 329 U.S. at 500–01.

By far, the most influential response to the problem of cost-shifting relating to the discovery of electronic data was given by United States Magistrate Judge James C. Francis IV of this district in *Rowe Entertainment.* Judge Francis utilized an eight-factor test to determine whether discovery costs should be shifted. Those eight factors are:

> (1) the specificity of the discovery requests; (2) the likelihood of discovering critical information; (3) the availability of such information from other sources; (4) the purposes for which the responding party maintains the requested data; (5) the relative benefits to the parties of obtaining the information; (6) the total cost associated with production; (7) the relative ability of each party to control costs and its incentive to do so; and (8) the resources available to each party.[30]

Both Zubulake and UBS agree that the eight-factor *Rowe* test should be used to determine whether cost-shifting is appropriate.

IV. DISCUSSION

A. Should Discovery of UBS's Electronic Data Be Permitted?

Under Rule 34, a party may request discovery of any document, "including writings, drawings, graphs, charts, photographs, phonorecords, and other data compilations. . . ." The "inclusive description" of the term document "accords with changing technology." "It makes clear that Rule 34 applies to electronics [sic] data compilations." Thus, "electronic documents are no less subject to disclosure than paper records." This is true not only of electronic documents that are currently in use, but also of documents that may have been deleted and now reside only on backup disks.

That being so, Zubulake is entitled to discovery of the requested e-mails so long as they are relevant to her claims, which they clearly are. As noted, e-mail constituted a substantial means of communication among UBS employees. To that end, UBS has already produced approximately 100 pages of e-mails, the contents of which are unquestionably relevant.

Nonetheless, UBS argues that Zubulake is not entitled to any further discovery because it already produced all responsive documents, to wit, the 100 pages of e-mails. This argument is unpersuasive for two reasons. First, because of the way that UBS backs up its e-mail files, it clearly could not have searched all of its e-mails without restoring the ninety-four backup tapes (which UBS admits that it has not done). UBS therefore cannot represent that it has produced all responsive emails. Second, Zubulake herself has produced over 450 pages of relevant e-mails, including e-mails that would have been responsive to her discovery requests but were never produced by UBS. These two facts strongly suggest that there are e-mails that Zubulake has not received that reside on UBS's backup media.

B. Should Cost-Shifting Be Considered?

Because it apparently recognizes that Zubulake is entitled to the requested discovery, UBS expends most of its efforts urging the court to shift the cost of production to "protect [it] . . . from undue burden or

---

[30]   205 F.R.D. at 429.

expense." Faced with similar applications, courts generally engage in some sort of cost-shifting analysis, whether the refined eight-factor *Rowe* test or a cruder application of Rule 34's proportionality test, or something in between.

The first question, however, is whether cost-shifting must be considered in every case involving the discovery of electronic data, which—in today's world—includes virtually all cases. In light of the accepted principle, stated above, that electronic evidence is no less discoverable than paper evidence, the answer is, "No." The Supreme Court has instructed that "the presumption is that the responding party must bear the expense of complying with discovery requests. . . ."[44] Any principled approach to electronic evidence must respect this presumption.

Courts must remember that cost-shifting may effectively end discovery, especially when private parties are engaged in litigation with large corporations. As large companies increasingly move to entirely paper-free environments, the frequent use of cost-shifting will have the effect of crippling discovery in discrimination and retaliation cases. This will both undermine the "strong public policy favoring resolving disputes on their merits,"[45] and may ultimately deter the filing of potentially meritorious claims.

Thus, cost-shifting should be considered only when electronic discovery imposes an "undue burden or expense" on the responding party.[46] The burden or expense of discovery is, in turn, "undue" when it "outweighs its likely benefit, taking into account the needs of the case, the amount in controversy, the parties' resources, the importance of the issues at stake in the litigation, and the importance of the proposed discovery in resolving the issues."[47]

Many courts have automatically assumed that an undue burden or expense may arise simply because electronic evidence is involved. This makes no sense. Electronic evidence is frequently cheaper and easier to produce than paper evidence because it can be searched automatically, key words can be run for privilege checks, and the production can be made in electronic form obviating the need for mass photocopying.

In fact, whether production of documents is unduly burdensome or expensive turns primarily on whether it is kept in an accessible or inaccessible format (a distinction that corresponds closely to the expense of production). In the world of paper documents, for example, a document is accessible if it is readily available in a usable format and reasonably indexed. Examples of inaccessible paper documents could include (a) documents in storage in a difficult to reach place; (b) documents converted to microfiche and not easily readable; or (c) documents kept haphazardly, with no indexing system, in quantities that make page-by-page searches impracticable. But in the world of electronic data, thanks

---

[44] Oppenheimer Fund, 437 U.S. at 358.

[45] Pecarsky v. Galaxiworld.com, Inc., 249 F.3d 167, 172 (2d Cir. 2001).

[46] Fed.R.Civ.P. 26(c).

[47] Fed.R.Civ.P. 26(b)(2)(iii). As noted, a court is also permitted to impose conditions on discovery when it might be duplicative, see Fed.R.Civ.P. 26(b)(2)(i), or when a reasonable discovery deadline has lapsed, see id. 26(b)(2)(ii). Neither of these concerns, however, is likely to arise solely because the discovery sought is of electronic data.

to search engines, any data that is retained in a machine readable format is typically accessible.

Whether electronic data is accessible or inaccessible turns largely on the media on which it is stored. Five categories of data, listed in order from most accessible to least accessible, are described in the literature on electronic data storage. [The five categories are (1) active, online data, such as hard disks; (2) near-line data, consisting of robotic storage devices containing removable media like optical disks; (3) offline storage, consisting of optical disks or magnetic tapes that have been removed from a machine and stored separately; (4) backup tapes; and (5) erased, fragmented or damaged data.]

Of these, the first three categories are typically identified as accessible, and the latter two as inaccessible. The difference between the two classes is easy to appreciate. Information deemed "accessible" is stored in a readily usable format. Although the time it takes to actually access the data ranges from milliseconds to days, the data does not need to be restored or otherwise manipulated to be usable. "Inaccessible" data, on the other hand, is not readily usable. Backup tapes must be restored using a process similar to that previously described, fragmented data must be de-fragmented, and erased data must be reconstructed, all before the data is usable. That makes such data inaccessible.

The case at bar is a perfect illustration of the range of accessibility of electronic data. As explained above, UBS maintains e-mail files in three forms: (1) active user e-mail files; (2) archived e-mails on optical disks; and (3) backup data stored on tapes. * * * For [active mail files and e-mails stored on optical disks] it would be wholly inappropriate to even consider cost-shifting. UBS maintains the data in an accessible and usable format, and can respond to Zubulake's request cheaply and quickly. Like most typical discovery requests, therefore, the producing party should bear the cost of production.

E-mails stored on backup tapes * * *, however, are an entirely different matter. Although UBS has already identified the ninety-four potentially responsive backup tapes, those tapes are not currently accessible. In order to search the tapes for responsive e-mails, UBS would have to engage in the costly and time-consuming process detailed above. It is therefore appropriate to consider cost shifting.

C. What Is the Proper Cost-Shifting Analysis?

In the year since *Rowe* was decided, its eight factor test has unquestionably become the gold standard for courts resolving electronic discovery disputes. But there is little doubt that the *Rowe* factors will generally favor cost-shifting. Indeed, of the handful of reported opinions that apply *Rowe* or some modification thereof, all of them have ordered the cost of discovery to be shifted to the requesting party.[63]

In order to maintain the presumption that the responding party pays, the cost-shifting analysis must be neutral; close calls should be resolved in favor of the presumption. The *Rowe* factors, as applied, undercut that presumption for three reasons. First, the *Rowe* test is incomplete. Second, courts have given equal weight to all of the factors,

---

[63]   See Murphy Oil, 2002 U.S. Dist. LEXIS 3196, 2002 WL 246439; Bristol-Myers Squibb, 205 F.R.D. 437; Byers, 2002 U.S. Dist. LEXIS 9861, 2002 WL 1264004.

when certain factors should predominate. Third, courts applying the *Rowe* test have not always developed a full factual record.

1. The Rowe Test Is Incomplete

a. A Modification of Rowe: Additional Factors

Certain factors specifically identified in the Rules are omitted from *Rowe's* eight factors. In particular, Rule 26 requires consideration of "the amount in controversy, the parties' resources, the importance of the issues at stake in the litigation, and the importance of the proposed discovery in resolving the issues."

Yet *Rowe* makes no mention of either the amount in controversy or the importance of the issues at stake in the litigation. These factors should be added. Doing so would balance the *Rowe* factor that typically weighs most heavily in favor of cost-shifting, "the total cost associated with production." The cost of production is almost always an objectively large number in cases where litigating cost-shifting is worthwhile. But the cost of production when compared to "the amount in controversy" may tell a different story. A response to a discovery request costing $100,000 sounds (and is) costly, but in a case potentially worth millions of dollars, the cost of responding may not be unduly burdensome.

Rowe also contemplates "the resources available to each party." But here too—although this consideration may be implicit in the *Rowe* test—the absolute wealth of the parties is not the relevant factor. More important than comparing the relative ability of a party to pay for discovery, the focus should be on the total cost of production as compared to the resources available to each party. Thus, discovery that would be too expensive for one defendant to bear would be a drop in the bucket for another.[66]

Last, "the importance of the issues at stake in the litigation" is a critical consideration, even if it is one that will rarely be invoked. For example, if a case has the potential for broad public impact, then public policy weighs heavily in favor of permitting extensive discovery. Cases of this ilk might include toxic tort class actions, environmental actions, so-called "impact" or social reform litigation, cases involving criminal conduct, or cases implicating important legal or constitutional questions.

b. A Modification of Rowe: Eliminating Two Factors

Two of the *Rowe* factors should be eliminated:

First, the *Rowe* test includes "the specificity of the discovery request." Specificity is surely the touchstone of any good discovery request, requiring a party to frame a request broadly enough to obtain relevant evidence, yet narrowly enough to control costs. But relevance and cost are already two of the *Rowe* factors (the second and sixth). Because the first and second factors are duplicative, they can be combined. Thus, the first factor should be: the extent to which the request is specifically tailored to discover relevant information.

Second, the fourth factor, "the purposes for which the responding party maintains the requested data" is typically unimportant. Whether

---

[66] UBS, for example, reported net profits after tax of 942 million Swiss Francs (approximately $716 million) for the third quarter of 2002 alone. See 11/12/02 UBS Press Release, available at http://www.ubswarburg.com/e/port_genint/index_genint.html.

the data is kept for a business purpose or for disaster recovery does not affect its accessibility, which is the practical basis for calculating the cost of production. * * *

c. A New Seven-Factor Test

Set forth below is a new seven-factor test based on the modifications to *Rowe* discussed in the preceding sections.

1. The extent to which the request is specifically tailored to discover relevant information;

2. The availability of such information from other sources;

3. The total cost of production, compared to the amount in controversy;

4. The total cost of production, compared to the resources available to each party;

5. The relative ability of each party to control costs and its incentive to do so;

6. The importance of the issues at stake in the litigation; and

7. The relative benefits to the parties of obtaining the information.

2. The Seven Factors Should Not Be Weighted Equally

Whenever a court applies a multi-factor test, there is a temptation to treat the factors as a check-list, resolving the issue in favor of whichever column has the most checks. But "we do not just add up the factors." When evaluating cost-shifting, the central question must be, does the request impose an "undue burden or expense" on the responding party? Put another way, "how important is the sought-after evidence in comparison to the cost of production?" The seven-factor test articulated above provide some guidance in answering this question, but the test cannot be mechanically applied at the risk of losing sight of its purpose.

Weighting the factors in descending order of importance may solve the problem and avoid a mechanistic application of the test. The first two factors—comprising the marginal utility test—are the most important. These factors include: (1) The extent to which the request is specifically tailored to discover relevant information and (2) the availability of such information from other sources. The substance of the marginal utility test was well described in *McPeek v. Ashcroft*:

> The more likely it is that the backup tape contains information that is relevant to a claim or defense, the fairer it is that the [responding party] search at its own expense. The less likely it is, the more unjust it would be to make the [responding party] search at its own expense. The difference is "at the margin."[74]

The second group of factors addresses cost issues: "How expensive will this production be?" and, "Who can handle that expense?" These factors include: (3) the total cost of production compared to the amount in controversy, (4) the total cost of production compared to the resources available to each party and (5) the relative ability of each party to control costs and its incentive to do so. The third "group"—(6) the importance of the litigation itself—stands alone, and as noted earlier will only rarely

---

[74] 202 F.R.D. at 34.

come into play. But where it does, this factor has the potential to predominate over the others. Collectively, the first three groups correspond to the three explicit considerations of Rule 26(b)(2)(iii). Finally, the last factor—(7) the relative benefits of production as between the requesting and producing parties—is the least important because it is fair to presume that the response to a discovery request generally benefits the requesting party. But in the unusual case where production will also provide a tangible or strategic benefit to the responding party, that fact may weigh against shifting costs.

D. A Factual Basis Is Required to Support the Analysis

Courts applying *Rowe* have uniformly favored cost-shifting largely because of assumptions made concerning the likelihood that relevant information will be found. * * *

But such proof will rarely exist in advance of obtaining the requested discovery. The suggestion that a plaintiff must not only demonstrate that probative evidence exists, but also prove that electronic discovery will yield a "gold mine," is contrary to the plain language of Rule 26(b)(1), which permits discovery of "any matter" that is "relevant to [a] claim or defense."

The best solution to this problem is found in *McPeek*:

> Given the complicated questions presented [and] the clash of policies . . . I have decided to take small steps and perform, as it were, a test run. Accordingly, I will order DOJ to perform a backup restoration of the e-mails attributable to Diegelman's computer during the period of July 1, 1998 to July 1, 1999. . . . The DOJ will have to carefully document the time and money spent in doing the search. It will then have to search in the restored e-mails for any document responsive to any of the plaintiff's requests for production of documents. Upon the completion of this search, the DOJ will then file a comprehensive, sworn certification of the time and money spent and the results of the search. Once it does, I will permit the parties an opportunity to argue why the results and the expense do or do not justify any further search.[76]

Requiring the responding party to restore and produce responsive documents from a small sample of backup tapes will inform the cost-shifting analysis laid out above.* * * [T]he entire cost-shifting analysis can be grounded in fact rather than guesswork.

> * * *

Accordingly, UBS is ordered to produce all responsive e-mails that exist on its optical disks or on its active servers (i.e., in HP OpenMail files) at its own expense. UBS is also ordered to produce, at its expense, responsive e-mails from any five backup tapes selected by Zubulake. UBS should then prepare an affidavit detailing the results of its search, as well as the time and money spent. After reviewing the contents of the backup tapes and UBS's certification, the Court will conduct the appropriate cost-shifting analysis.

---

[76] 202 F.R.D. at 34–35.

NOTE ON THE SCOPE AND COSTS OF DISCOVERY

1. **Costs and complexity of discovery.** The costs and complexity of discovery vary greatly depending on the amount and kinds of information thrown off by particular real-world interactions, the ease of identifying such information, and the stakes in the case.

Numerous studies have found that in both federal and state court, 40–50% or more of all cases filed have no discovery at all and that many other cases involve only a handful of discovery requests. Kakalik et al., Discovery Management: Further Analysis of the Civil Justice Reform Act Evaluation Data, 39 B.C. L. Rev. 613, 621–23, 635–37 (1998). Discovery in most small-stakes cases generally proceeds without incident and at a fairly low cost. Willging et al., An Empirical Study of Discovery and Disclosure Practice Under the 1993 Federal Rule Amendments, 39 B.C. L. Rev. 525, 531 (1998).

However, in cases where the stakes are higher, and the sources of information more various and difficult to locate, discovery can involve very high costs, in the hundreds of thousands or occasionally millions of dollars. These very high costs are typically confined to a small fraction, five percent or less, of the federal docket. This percentage is even lower in state courts. Reda, The Cost-and-Delay Narrative in Civil Justice Reform, 90 Or. L. Rev. 1085 (2012); Garth, Two Worlds of Civil Discovery: From Studies of Cost and Delay to the Markets in Legal Services and Legal Reform, 39 B.C. L. Rev. 597, 600–01 (1998).

2. **Judicial regulation of the discovery process.** Discovery is intended to be largely self-executing and self-regulating—and in most cases it is. Judicial involvement in the discovery process occurs only when there is a failure of voluntary compliance. The rules oblige the parties to attempt to negotiate a consensual resolution of their differences before burdening the court. Fed. R. Civ. P. 37(a)(1). In federal court, cases with modest amounts of discovery average roughly a contested discovery motion every other case. At the other extreme, in the small fraction (five to ten percent) of the federal caseload involving cases with the greatest amount of discovery, parties tend to resort to the court for help two or more times per case. Kakalik et al., 39 B.C. L. Rev. at 650. Within the federal system, rising numbers of cases with significant discovery disputes is one of the prime contributors to the growth in the use of federal magistrates. Magistrates are non-Article III judges who, as in *Zubulake*, decide many discovery disputes subject to review by federal district judges.

3. **Regulating the scope and costs of discovery.** As *Zubulake* indicates, the strong presumption in civil discovery is that if information is relevant and therefore discoverable, the responding party will bear the costs of producing information in a form suitable for examination. The costs for the producing party involve conducting an investigation to identify and screen responsive information and preparing witnesses for depositions. As a practical matter, in the overwhelming majority of cases the presumptive allocation of costs prevails.

In the sequel to the principal case, Zubulake v. UBS Warburg LLC, 216 F.R.D. 280 (S.D.N.Y. 2003), the sample of five backup tapes resulted in the production by defendant of some 600 e-mails (a total of 853 pages) responsive to Zubulake's document request. Zubulake argued that 68 of the 600 e-mails were "highly relevant to the issues in this case" and the court agreed, describing some of those e-mails as follows:

In particular, six e-mails singled out by Zubulake as particularly "striking" include:

- An e-mail from Hardisty, Chapin's supervisor, chastising Chapin for saying one thing and doing another with respect to Zubulake. Hardisty said, "As I see it, you do not appear to be upholding your end of the bargain to work with her." This e-mail stands in contrast to UBS's response to Zubulake's EEOC charges, which says that "Mr. Chapin was receptive to Mr. Hardisty's suggestions [for improving his relationship with Zubulake]."

- An e-mail from Chapin to one of his employees on the Desk, Joy Kim, suggesting to her how to phrase a complaint against Zubulake. A few hours later, Joy Kim did in fact send an e-mail to Chapin complaining about Zubulake, using precisely the same words that Chapin had suggested. But at his deposition (taken before these e-mails were restored), Chapin claimed that he did not solicit the complaint.

- An e-mail from Chapin to the human resources employee handling Zubulake's case listing the employees on the Desk and categorizing them as senior, mid-level, or junior salespeople. In its EEOC filing, however, UBS claimed in response to Zubulake's argument that she was the only senior salesperson on the desk, that it "does not categorize salespeople as 'junior' or 'senior.'" In addition, UBS claimed in its EEOC papers that there were four female salespeople on the Desk, but this e-mail shows only two.

- An e-mail from Chapin to Hardisty acknowledging that Zubulake's "ability to do a good job . . . is clear," and that she is "quite capable."

- An e-mail from Derek Hillan, presumably a UBS employee, to Chapin and Zubulake using vulgar language, although UBS claims that it does not tolerate such language.

- An e-mail from Michael Oertli, presumably a UBS employee, to Chapin explaining that UBS's poor performance in Singapore was attributable to the fact that it only "covered" eight or nine of twenty-two accounts, and not to Zubulake's poor performance, as UBS has argued.

216 F.R.D. at 285–86.

The defendant presented evidence that it had spent $11,524 in hiring a consultant to restore the emails from the five tapes. It also claimed to have spent a further $7,479 on reviewing the emails to screen for privilege prior to production, using a large law firm associate who charged $410 per hour and a paralegal who charged $170 per hour. It estimated costs to restore the remaining 89 backup tapes as $165,955 and the costs of having a lawyer or paralegal review them prior to production as $107,694. (These numbers are consistent with the findings of larger scale studies that, after controlling for all other variables, discovery costs tend to be consistently higher in cases involving larger law firms. Willging et al., 39 B.C. L. Rev. at 579–80.)

The court held that the plaintiff should pay 25% of the costs of restoring the backup tapes, but that the defendant should pay all its costs of having a lawyer or paralegal review the restored tapes prior to production, since those costs were incurred independently of the effort to make the evidence accessible. How would you, as a judge, have allocated the further costs of review and production as between plaintiff and defendant?

4. **Special rules governing electronic discovery.** The most important development of the last quarter-century in discovery has been the explosion of electronically stored information. *Zubulake* was at the forefront of this sea change, and it continues to be the leading case. Its author, Judge Scheindlin, is a leading authority on e-discovery and is a co-author of a casebook that serves as the primary resource on the subject. See Scheindlin, Capra & The Sedona Conference, Electronic Discovery and Digital Evidence (2d ed. 2012). In 2006, the federal Rules were amended to deal with issues of electronic discovery like those arising in *Zubulake*. The principal changes are as follows:

- Rule 16(b)(3)(B)(iii) states that a scheduling order may "provide for disclosure or discovery of electronically stored information."

- Rule 26(a)(1)(A)(ii) includes "electronically stored information" among the categories of information subject to mandatory initial disclosure.

- Rule 26(f)(3)(C) requires that discovery plans state the parties' views and proposals as to "any issues about disclosure or discovery of electronically stored information, including the form or forms in which it should be produced."

- Rule 26(b)(2)(B) is amended to deal specifically with problems of relevance, undue burden and cost sharing in the context of electronic discovery. Rule 26(b)(2)(B) now states that:

  A party need not provide discovery of electronically stored information from sources that the party identifies as not reasonably accessible because of undue burden or cost. On motion to compel discovery or for a protective order, the party from whom discovery is sought must show that the information is not reasonably accessible because of undue burden or cost. If that showing is made, the court may nonetheless order discovery from such sources if the requesting party shows good cause, considering the limitations of Rule 26(b)(2)(C). The court may specify conditions for discovery.

- Rule 34 is amended to permit the requesting party to specify the form in which "electronically stored information" should be produced. The responding party is then permitted to object to the chosen form. If the responding party objects, or if no form of production was specified, the responding party must state the form or forms of production it intends to use and must produce the information in a form or forms in which it is ordinarily maintained or in "a reasonably usable form or forms."

The Advisory Committee Note to amended Rule 26 states that under the Rule the party from whom discovery is sought may withhold from discovery information that it identifies as "not reasonably accessible." In the event that designation is contested, the party from whom discovery is sought has the burden of making an initial demonstration that the discovery sought will involve "undue burden or cost." After such a demonstration has been made, the burden is on the requesting party to show that that the burdens and costs of discovery are justified in the circumstances of the case. Among the considerations identified as relevant by the Committee are:

> (1) the specificity of the discovery request; (2) the quantity of information available from other and more easily accessed sources; (3) the failure to produce relevant information that seems likely to have existed but is no longer available on more easily accessed sources; (4) the likelihood of finding relevant, responsive information that cannot be obtained from other, more easily accessed sources; (5) predictions as to the importance and usefulness of the further information; (6) the importance of the issues at stake in the litigation; and (7) the parties' resources.

Fed. R. Civ. P. 26, 2006 Advisory Committee Note. The Note states that in some cases "the parties may need some focused discovery, which may include sampling of the sources" to determine the relevant costs and burdens and the potential contributions of the additional information to the litigation. And it allows the judge to condition discovery on, among other things, the "payment by the requesting party of part or all of the reasonable costs of obtaining information from sources that are not reasonably accessible." Id.

To what extent do these changes reflect the judge-made rule fashioned in *Zubulake*? To what extent do they depart from that rule? Does it seem likely that the application of the modified rule would have altered the decision-making process or outcome in that case? What effects do you think these rules have had on how corporations manage their information? See Ragan, Information Governance: It's a Duty and It's Smart Business, 19 Rich. J.L. & Tech. 12 (2013).

5. **The explosion of e-discovery and the use of "predictive coding."** The explosion of e-discovery continues to be a major story. Indeed, the enormous quantity of discoverable electronic material and the costs of reviewing and producing it are at the root of current proposals to amend the definition of the scope of discovery under Rule 26(b)(1). See infra p. 732, Note on the Proposed 2015 Discovery Rule Amendments. As Professor Marcus explains:

> Rule changes are not a sufficient measure of the prominence of e-discovery. A better measure is money. From next to nothing in 2000, an e-discovery industry has arisen that is expected to be worth $9.9 billion in 2017. That figure does not represent attorneys' fees, but rather the revenue of e-discovery providers. True, this development is part of a larger information-management evolution, but it is a very large part. It is large enough to get the attention of law firms; many of them now have e-discovery departments. It is also large enough to get the attention of law schools; at least sixty of those now (like Hastings) offer courses in e-discovery. In 2012,

the RAND Corporation published a study of the costs of e-discovery (and of attorney time involved in reviewing its fruits) and concluded that only predictive coding offered the promise of significantly curbing those costs. Since then, predictive coding has been the hottest topic on the e-discovery market; many vendors tout their product as "the best."

Marcus, "Looking Backward" to 1938, 162 U. Pa. L. Rev. 1691, 1724 (2014) (citing Pace & Zakaras, Where the Money Goes: Understanding Litigant Expenditures for Producing Electronic Discovery (2012)).

What is predictive coding? It can best be understood through comparison to traditional methods of document review. Typically, when responding to a request for production of documents under Rule 34, attorneys review their client's potentially relevant documents and divide them into two categories, those that are responsive to the request, and those that are non-responsive. Within the set of documents that are responsive to the request, the attorney then reviews the documents to see if they are shielded from disclosure by an applicable privilege, such as the attorney-client privilege or the work-product doctrine, discussed infra at p. 738. Predictive coding, in essence, attempts to replace the attorney with a computer in much of the document-review process. Magistrate Judge Peck explained the process in an influential recent decision:

> Unlike manual review, where the review is done by the most junior staff, computer-assisted coding involves a senior partner (or [small] team) who review and code a "seed set" of documents. The computer identifies properties of those documents that it uses to code other documents. As the senior reviewer continues to code more sample documents, the computer predicts the reviewer's coding. (Or, the computer codes some documents and asks the senior reviewer for feedback.)

> When the system's predictions and the reviewer's coding sufficiently coincide, the system has learned enough to make confident predictions for the remaining documents. Typically, the senior lawyer (or team) needs to review only a few thousand documents to train the computer.

> Some systems produce a simple yes/no as to relevance, while others give a relevance score (say, on a 0 to 100 basis) that counsel can use to prioritize review. For example, a score above 50 may produce 97% of the relevant documents, but constitutes only 20% of the entire document set.

> Counsel may decide, after sampling and quality control tests, that documents with a score of below 15 are so highly likely to be irrelevant that no further human review is necessary. Counsel can also decide the cost-benefit of manual review of the documents with scores of 15–50.

Moore v. Publicis Group, 287 F.R.D. 182 (S.D.N.Y. 2012). As the excerpt from Professor Marcus suggests, many believe that predictive coding may be the answer to the e-discovery puzzle. Do you believe the optimism is warranted? Judge Peck's opinion in *Moore* was the first to explicitly authorize predictive coding as a discovery method. How should courts supervise the process of "training" the computer, and quality control after the fact? Is the negotiation of predictive coding best left to the parties? More fundamentally, by placing such trust in the algorithm and by "deferring to the opinions of computer scientists and vendors," is "the bar ceding jurisdiction to self-interested parties" and "weakening the protections and legitimacy of our legal system"? See Remus, The Uncertain Promise of Predictive Coding, 99 Iowa L. Rev. 1691 (2014).

There is a burgeoning literature on predictive coding. For further reading, see McGinnis & Pearce, The Great Disruption: How Machine Intelligence Will Transform the Role of Lawyers in the Delivery of Legal Services, 82 Fordham L. Rev. 3041 (2014); Nasuti, Comment, Shaping the Technology of the Future: Predictive Coding in Discovery Case Law and Regulatory Disclosure Requirements, 93 N.C. L. Rev. 222 (2014); Yablon & Landsman-Roos, Predictive Coding: Emerging Questions & Concerns, 64 S.C. L. Rev. 633 (2014).

6. Appellate review of discovery orders. Can UBS do anything immediately to contest the trial court's decisions on the allocation of discovery costs? Probably not. Discovery orders ordinarily are not final judgments and hence ordinarily are not immediately appealable. Because so many cases subsequently settle or are disposed of on grounds unrelated to the discovery ruling, many discovery rulings do not survive to become appealable. One important consequence of non-appealability is that most of the law of discovery is made by trial courts and magistrates rather than appellate courts. See 15B Wright, Miller & Cooper Federal Practice and Procedure § 3914.23 (2008).

7. Comparison of American discovery practices with those of other countries. In the common law jurisdictions with which America shares litigation traditions, there is some pretrial discovery, principally of documents, but it is considerably narrower in scope than in American courts. In particular, the use of discovery for investigation is widely regarded as improper. In civil law jurisdictions (most of continental Europe, Latin America, and North Asia), American discovery is typically regarded with horror. In those systems, there is little or no compelled discovery of information unfavorable to a party's case and no discovery for investigative purposes.

Differences between common law and civil law discovery reflect contrasting arrangements for trial, conceptions of adjudication, and commitments to party control of litigation. First, in American litigation, the need to have a continuous and compact trial (largely for the convenience of lay jurors), means that all discovery must take place prior to and wholly separate from the trial. In such a system, there is every incentive to seek discovery broadly, since there will be no opportunity to remedy omissions once the trial begins. In a civil law proceeding, by contrast, the trial commences as soon as the pleadings are complete, and can be recessed to gather information as the judge thinks best. The judge manages both the discovery and the trial, seeking discovery only of the information he or she thinks needed for his or her purposes. Since all discovery must pass through the civil law judge, he or she has a powerful incentive to avoid irrelevant or duplicative discovery. Second, American discovery came of age when civil litigation was increasingly seen as a law enforcement device, in which private attorneys general played an important role. Conversely, civil law's "relative indifference to the completeness of the evidentiary material submitted to the court," sees adjudication more as resolving disputes on the parties' terms. M. Damaska, Evidence Law Adrift 114 (1997). For a comparison of American discovery practices with those of other industrialized countries, see Hazard, Discovery and the Role of the Judge in Civil Law Jurisdictions, 73 Notre Dame L.Rev.1017 (1998); Hazard, From Whom No Secrets Are Hid, 76 Tex. L. Rev. 1665 (1998).

8. **Discovery in international litigation.** Obtaining discovery from foreign parties subject to United States jurisdiction poses special problems, in part because of the vast difference between the scope of American discovery and that in other legal systems. Discovery of documents located in a foreign country is a particularly vexing problem. Many countries have enacted laws barring the production of documents in their jurisdiction for any proceeding in another country. Under these laws, the enforcement of a court order compelling discovery may open the producing party to criminal liability in the country where the documents are housed. In an effort to avoid these conflicts, the Hague Convention on the Taking of Evidence Abroad contains elaborate procedural provisions and specifications of the permitted scope of discovery. See Restatement (Third) of the Foreign Relations Law of the United States §§ 442, 473 (1987). Although the terms of the Hague Convention appear to preempt national law that is inconsistent, the United States Supreme Court has held that American discovery rules are not so preempted. But the Court refused to delineate standards for choosing between use of the federal Rules and use of the Hague Convention, leaving the line to be drawn by the trial court "based on its knowledge of the case and of the claims and interests of the parties and the governments whose statutes and policies they invoke." Société Nationale Industrielle Aerospatiale v. United States District Court, 482 U.S. 522, 107 S.Ct. 2542, 96 L.Ed.2d 461 (1987). For an example of the complexity and conflict engendered by differing American and civil law discovery regimes see Quaak v. Klynveld Peat Marwick Goerdeler Bedrijfsrevisoren, 361 F.3d 11 (1st Cir. 2004). The controversy resulting from conflicting national discovery regimes has spurred international efforts to develop transnational rules which might be used in international arbitrations and tribunals. Hazard & Taruffo, Transnational Rules of Civil Procedure: Rules and Commentary, 30 Cornell Int'l. L.J. 493 (1997), proposes an international discovery regime modeled on that in common law jurisdictions other than the United States, notably Great Britain, Canada and Australia, which would allow substantial document discovery, but would not allow for depositions or for the use of discovery for investigative purposes.

Parties in proceedings occurring overseas may sometimes be able to obtain discovery through courts in the United States. For example, a federal statute provides that a federal district court "may order" a person "resid[ing]" or "found" in the district to produce documents or provide testimony "for use in a proceeding in a foreign or international tribunal . . . upon application of any interested person." 28 U.S.C. § 1782(a). In Intel Corp. v. Advanced Micro Devices, Inc., 542 U.S. 241, 124 S.Ct. 2466, 159 L.Ed.2d 355 (2004), the Supreme Court held that this statute could be used to compel the production for use in a foreign proceeding of materials that would not be discoverable under the law of the foreign jurisdiction.

NOTE ON THE PROPOSED 2015 DISCOVERY RULE AMENDMENTS

1. **Proposed amendments to the federal discovery rules.** As of the printing of this edition, there are several significant amendments to the discovery rules working their way through the rulemaking process. As is

detailed below, the proposed amendments have generated enormous controversy. The proposed revisions are aimed at combating perceived increased costs of discovery, particularly in the era of dominant e-discovery. Supporters of the amendments argue that the proposed rule changes are a necessary counter-weight to the Rules' permissive approach to discovery; opponents contend that the proposed revisions will severely limit plaintiffs' ability to prevail on their claims by restricting access to information in the hands of defendants. A minority view is that the controversy is overblown.

The most important of these amendments is a proposed revision of Rule 26(b)(1), which defines the scope of discovery. There are three proposed changes to the current Rule.

First, Rule 26(b)(2)(C)(iii) currently provides that a court must "limit the extent or frequency of discovery" if it determines that "the burden or expense of the proposed discovery outweighs its likely benefit, considering the needs of the case, the amount in controversy, the parties' resources, the importance of the issues at stake in the action, and the importance of the discovery in resolving the issues." This is the so-called "proportionality" requirement. The proposed amendment would move this proportionality requirement into the definition of the scope of discovery, such that amended Rule 26(b)(1) would read:

> Parties may obtain discovery regarding any nonprivileged matter that is relevant to any party's claim or defense and proportional to the needs of the case, considering the importance of the issues at stake in the action, the amount in controversy, the parties' relative access to relevant information, the parties' resources, the importance of the discovery in resolving the issues, and whether the burden or expense of the proposed discovery outweighs its likely benefit.

The second major proposed amendment to Rule 26(b)(1) is to eliminate the current language allowing the court to order "discovery of any matter relevant to the subject matter involved in the action" upon a showing of good cause. In support of the proposed change, the Rules Committee reports that the "provision is virtually never used, and the proper focus of discovery is on the claims and defenses in the litigation." Memorandum on Proposed Amendments to the Federal Rules of Civil Procedure, June 14, 2014, available at http://www.uscourts.gov/uscourts/RulesAndPolicies/rules/Reports/ST09-2014.pdf.

The third proposed change to Rule 26(b)(1) is to replace the sentence that reads: "Relevant information need not be admissible at the trial if the discovery appears reasonably calculated to lead to the discovery of admissible evidence," with, "Information within the scope of discovery need not be admissible in evidence to be discoverable."

2.   The amendment process. The package of discovery-rule amendments grew out of a conference held at Duke University in May 2010, attended by prominent lawyers, judges, and academics, including many of those involved in the rulemaking process. Following the Duke Conference and additional public meetings, the Advisory Committee recommended a series of rule changes, including the changes to the definition of the scope of discovery under Rule 26(b)(1) and lowering the presumptive limits on depositions, interrogatories, and requests for admission. The Rules Committee then made the proposed amendments available for public comment and held several public hearings. The reaction was unprecedented. The Rules Committee received over 2,300 comments—prior to these amendments, no other proposed Rules changes had generated more than around 300 public comments in response.

Professor Richard Marcus, the Associate Reporter of the Civil Rules Advisory Committee, describes the public-comment period:

> Already the rules' current provisions that generally require responding parties to bear the costs of their responses to discovery have been assailed as "un-American," and the amendment package proposing some modest reduction of discovery have also been assailed as "un-American." Some comments come close to "May you burn in Hell."

Marcus, How to Steer an Ocean Liner, 18 Lewis & Clark L. Rev. 615 (2014).

After the public-comment period, the Rules Committee abandoned the proposed amendments reducing the presumptive limits on the discovery devices, but it left unchanged the above-noted changes to the scope of discovery under Rule 26(b)(1). As of this printing, the amendments have been sent for approval by the Judicial Conference. If the Judicial Conference and the Supreme Court approve the amendments, they will be sent to the Congress. The Report of the Committee on Rules of Practice and Procedure may be found at the federal courts' website, at http://www.uscourts.gov/us courts/RulesAndPolicies/rules/Reports/ST09-2014.pdf. If the Congress does not act, the amendments will go into effect on December 1, 2015.

3.   Reaction to the proposed amendments. As Professor Marcus notes, the response to the proposed changes has been intense, both in support and opposition. A good illustration of the positions different parties have taken is the testimony offered at a hearing conducted by the Senate Judiciary Committee on the amendments. All of the excerpts in this note may be found in United States Congress Senate Committee on the Judiciary, Changing the Rules: Will Limiting the Scope of Civil Discovery Diminish Accountability and Leave Americans Without Access to Justice?, 113th Cong., November 5, 2013. One witness at the hearing who spoke in favor of the proposed amendments was Andrew Pincus, a partner at the Mayer Brown law firm.

> The tremendous growth in the sheer quantity of electronically stored information combined with discovery rules formulated for the typewriter and paper era have produced a huge increase in discovery-related legal costs. A very recent study by the RAND Institute for Civil Justice, a widely recognized nonpartisan group, found a median cost of $1.8 million per case just for producing electronically stored information. The cost ranged from $17,000 in the smallest case to $27 million in the largest case.

> In addition, parties incur significant costs just to preserve electronically stored information, beginning when a claim is reasonably anticipated and during the entire course of the litigation. Otherwise, they face onerous sanctions in the event information later found to be subject to discovery is lost, even if that deletion is unintentional. * * *

> The principal proposed amendment relating to the scope of permissible discovery simply moves a standard already in the rule, requiring that discovery be proportional to the needs of the case in

order to give that standard added emphasis. It is hard to quarrel with the argument that discovery should be proportional, especially because the draft rule expressly includes factors other than the amount at stake in the litigation, such as the importance of the issues involved in the litigation, the need for discovery, and an overall cost-benefit determination. And judges will make the decision of what is proportional and what is not. We trust them to make many determinations, and there is no reason why they cannot make this one properly.

Again, this change * * * has an important benefit. It forces judges to engage in the discovery process when they decide these issues, and a big complaint from all lawyers on all sides is judges are not engaging enough early enough in the case. They do not manage, and the lawyers, left to their own devices, unfortunately, go off on a frolic. This will solve that problem.

Testifying in opposition to the amendments was Sherrilynn Ifill, Director-Counsel of the NAACP Legal Defense and Educational Fund. She contended:

For those of us who represent civil rights plaintiffs, discovery is the essential stage of any litigation, and that is, of course, because of the nature of our claims. The information that would support a claim of discrimination is often, as the Chairman pointed out, within the possession of the defendant. And the only way we can get that information is through the discovery process.

It is also true that one of the great successes of our work, the fact that we now find discrimination socially unacceptable, means that our ability to find that information, to gather that information, and to make a case for discrimination largely based on circumstantial evidence requires us to gather a range of information and data within the possession of the defendant. That information for us can only be obtained through discovery. * * *

At the outset, Chairman Coons talked about a worrisome set of cases and the potential for collateral consequences, and I think this is where the inquiry really is most appropriately targeted. Without question, there is a narrow band of cases, perhaps those discussed by Mr. Pincus, in which there are real problems with discovery and in which the costs are exorbitant. But those are not the majority of cases. As Professor Miller pointed out, no study has supported the idea that litigation has run amuck, either from costs or from overburdensome discovery. And the question is: What will we do with that small band of cases? And will we allow that small band of cases to essentially imbalance our civil litigation process against the vast majority of cases and in our instance, of course, civil rights cases?

For a trenchant discussion of these concerns, related to an earlier attempt to modify the discovery rules, see Thornburg, Giving the "Haves" A Little More: Considering the 1998 Discovery Proposals, 52 S.M.U. L. Rev. 229 (1999).

4. Perspectives from the bench. Numerous federal district judges have been among those who have responded to the proposed rule changes. One commenter who submitted a response to the proposed rule changes was Judge Scheindlin, the author of *Zubulake*. She offers an additional concern from the perspective of the trial judge—that placing the proportionality requirement in the definition of the scope of discovery will increase the volume of discovery motions, and that those motions will the difficult and time-consuming to resolve:

> The requesting party will say the case is worth one million dollars, and the producing party will say the case is worth ten thousand dollars. How will a court fairly decide the true amount in controversy at the very outset of the case? The producing party will say the burden or expense of the proposed discovery is very great— and it will cost us millions of dollars to retrieve the requested information—and the requesting party will say the producing party is exaggerating and the search and review can be done for far less if the requesting party uses less expensive and more efficient means to conduct the search. What a nightmare for the court! * * * How, exactly, can a court assess the benefit of materials that have not been identified—except in the most general way—at the very outset of the case? The proposal is not realistic.

Schiendin, D.J., Comments on Proposed Rules, Jan. 13, 2014.

Judge Rosenthal, a former chair of the Rules Committee, takes a contrary view. Writing with Professor Gensler, himself a former member of the Rules Committee, she responds:

> This "lack of information" critique is based on the premise that, at least at the beginning of the case, the judge does not have, and cannot get from the parties, the information needed to determine the point at which discovery becomes disproportionate. That is true in part, but irrelevant. It condemns the pursuit of proportionality for failing to achieve what it does not seek. The critique assumes that the judge's and lawyers' task is to define at the start what the outer boundaries of discovery will be throughout the case. That approach to proportionality—that approach to discovery management—defines the goal and the pursuit in exactly the wrong way. And it mistakenly transmogrifies an iterative process based on the judge's exercise of discretion informed by exchanges with, and information learned from, the parties into a ham-fisted variation on the set-it-and-forget-it mentality that impedes rather than facilitates effective case management.

> The key to achieving proportionality is not the early ability to find some clear line defining where discovery should end. Rather, proportionality requires making good judgments about *where and how discovery should begin*. In practically every case, at the Rule 16 initial pretrial conference, the parties and the judge can identify a core territory for discovery to begin. Who are the key people? What are the key documents or sources of information, and where are they to be found? Where is the "low-hanging fruit" that should be picked first and used to determine what other fruit is worth the added effort and cost to harvest? Targeted discovery is inherently proportional. When you start discovery by focusing on the best and most easily accessed sources of what appears to be the most important information, the benefit necessarily justifies the burden.

Gensler & Rosenthal, Four Years After Duke: Where Do We Stand on Calibrating the Pretrial Process, 18 Lewis & Clark L. Rev. 643 (2014). If you were a trial-court judge, would you be in favor of the proposed rule changes?

  5. Academic response. Academic response to the proposed changes has been split, as well. Professor Marcus believes "the rulemakers have sought (fairly successfully) to steer a middle course between the most aggressive supporters and critics." Marcus, "Looking Backward" to 1938, 162 U. Pa. L. Rev. 1691 (2014).

  But one concern expressed by several scholars is that the narrowing scope of discovery, in conjunction with the recent cases on pleading, class actions, summary judgment, and personal jurisdiction, represents a significant departure from the philosophy of the original federal Rules, which emphasized access to court and resolution of cases on the merits. Professor Miller opines:

>   [T]he proposed amendment to Rule 26(b)(1) represents a threat to the jugular of the discovery regime as we have known it. It would replace the longstanding principle that the scope of discovery embraces anything that is relevant to a claim or defense with dual requirements—note the use of the conjunctive "and" in the proposal—that the material sought be both relevant and proportionate according to five criteria that are both subjective and fact dependent. The Advisory Committee Note makes it clear that the proponent of discovery must show the request's relevance and proportionality. This is a dramatic reduction in the scope of discovery. It may well produce a tidal wave of defense motions to prevent discovery on the ground that one or more of the five proposed proportionality criteria is absent. The proposed amendments could produce increased motion practice costs, delays, consumption of judicial time better spent in other ways, fact-dependent hearings, inconsistent application, and potential restrictions on access to information needed to decide cases on their merits. These effects will fall most heavily on important areas of public policy—discrimination, consumer protection, and employment, for example. If promulgated these changes may well deter the institution of potentially meritorious claims for the violation of statutes enacted by Congress. The current proposals represent yet another procedural stop sign.

Prepared Statement of Arthur R. Miller, United States Cong. Senate Committee on the Judiciary, Changing the Rules: Will Limiting the Scope of Civil Discovery Diminish Accountability and Leave Americans Without Access to Justice?, November 5, 2013. See also Subrin & Main, The Fourth Era of American Civil Procedure, 162 U. Pa. L. Rev. 1839 (2014).

  Do you agree that the rule change will have such wide-ranging effects? Or, given that the proportionality limit is already in the current rules, is all of this much ado about very little?

B. PRIVILEGES AND TRIAL PREPARATION IMMUNITIES

1. THE ATTORNEY-CLIENT PRIVILEGE

Upjohn Co. v. United States

Supreme Court of the United States, 1981.
449 U.S. 383, 101 S.Ct. 677, 66 L.Ed.2d 584.

■ JUSTICE REHNQUIST delivered the opinion of the Court.

We granted certiorari in this case to address important questions concerning the scope of the attorney-client privilege in the corporate context and the applicability of the work-product doctrine in proceedings to enforce tax summonses. * * *

I

Petitioner Upjohn Co. manufactures and sells pharmaceuticals here and abroad. In January 1976 independent accountants conducting an audit of one of petitioner's foreign subsidiaries discovered that the subsidiary made payments to or for the benefit of foreign government officials in order to secure government business. The accountants so informed petitioner, Mr. Gerard Thomas, Upjohn's Vice-President, Secretary, and General Counsel. Thomas is a member of the Michigan and New York bars, and has been Upjohn's General Counsel for 20 years. He consulted with outside counsel and R.T. Parfet, Jr., Upjohn's Chairman of the Board. It was decided that the company would conduct an internal investigation of what were termed "questionable payments." As part of this investigation the attorneys prepared a letter containing a questionnaire which was sent to "All Foreign General and Area Managers" over the Chairman's signature. The letter began by noting recent disclosures that several American companies made "possibly illegal" payments to foreign government officials and emphasized that the management needed full information concerning any such payments made by Upjohn. The letter indicated that the Chairman had asked Thomas, identified as "the company's General Counsel," "to conduct an investigation for the purpose of determining the nature and magnitude of any payments made by the Upjohn Company or any of its subsidiaries to any employee or official of a foreign government." The questionnaire sought detailed information concerning such payments. Managers were instructed to treat the investigation as "highly confidential" and not to discuss it with anyone other than Upjohn employees who might be helpful in providing the requested information. Responses were to be sent directly to Thomas. Thomas and outside counsel also interviewed the recipients of the questionnaire and some 33 other Upjohn officers or employees as part of the investigation.

On March 26, 1976, the company voluntarily submitted a preliminary report to the Securities and Exchange Commission on Form 8–K disclosing certain questionable payments. A copy of the report was simultaneously submitted to the Internal Revenue Service, which immediately began an investigation to determine the tax consequences of the payments. Special agents conducting the investigation were given lists by Upjohn of all those interviewed and all who had responded to the questionnaire. On November 23, 1976, the Service issued a summons pursuant to 26 U.S.C. § 7602 demanding production of:

> "All files relative to the investigation conducted under the supervision of Gerard Thomas to identify payments to employees of foreign governments and any political contributions made by the Upjohn Company or any of its affiliates since January 1, 1971 and to determine whether any funds of the Upjohn Company had been improperly accounted for on the corporate books during the same period.

> "The records should include but not be limited to written questionnaires sent to managers of the Upjohn Company's foreign affiliates, and memoranda or notes of the interviews conducted in the United States and abroad with officers and employees of the Upjohn Company and its subsidiaries."

The company declined to produce the documents specified in the second paragraph on the grounds that they were protected from disclosure by the attorney-client privilege and constituted the work product of attorneys prepared in anticipation of litigation. On August 31, 1977, the United States filed a petition seeking enforcement of the summons under 26 U.S.C. §§ 7402(b) and 7604(a) in the United States District Court for the Western District of Michigan. * * *

II

Federal Rule of Evidence 501 provides that "the privilege of a witness . . . shall be governed by the principles of the common law as they may be interpreted by the courts of the United States in light of reason and experience." The attorney-client privilege is the oldest of the privileges for confidential communications known to the common law. 8 J. Wigmore, Evidence § 2290 (McNaughton rev. 1961). Its purpose is to encourage full and frank communication between attorneys and their clients and thereby promote broader public interests in the observance of law and administration of justice. The privilege recognizes that sound legal advice or advocacy serves public ends and that such advice or advocacy depends upon the lawyer being fully informed by the client. As we stated last Term in Trammel v. United States, 445 U.S. 40, 51, 100 S.Ct. 906, 913, 63 L.Ed.2d 186 (1980): "The lawyer-client privilege rests on the need for the advocate and counselor to know all that relates to the client's reasons for seeking representation if the professional mission is to be carried out." And in Fisher v. United States, 425 U.S. 391, 403, 96 S.Ct. 1569, 1577, 48 L.Ed.2d 39 (1976), we recognized the purpose of the privilege to be "to encourage clients to make full disclosures to their attorneys." This rationale for the privilege has long been recognized by the Court, see Hunt v. Blackburn, 128 U.S. 464, 470, 9 S.Ct. 125, 127, 32 L.Ed. 488 (1888) (privilege "is founded upon the necessity, in the interest and administration of justice, of the aid of persons having knowledge of the law and skilled in its practice, which assistance can only be safely and readily availed of when free from the consequences or the apprehension of disclosure"). Admittedly complications in the application of the privilege arise when the client is a corporation, which in theory is an artificial creature of the law, and not an individual; but this Court has assumed that the privilege applies when the client is a corporation, United States v. Louisville & Nashville R. Co., 236 U.S. 318, 336, 35 S.Ct.

363, 369, 59 L.Ed. 598 (1915), and the Government does not contest the general proposition.

The Court of Appeals, however, considered the application of the privilege in the corporate context to present a "different problem," since the client was an inanimate entity and "only the senior management, guiding and integrating the several operations, . . . can be said to possess an identity analogous to the corporation as a whole." 600 F.2d at 1226. The first case to articulate the so-called "control group test" adopted by the court below, Philadelphia v. Westinghouse Electric Corp., 210 F.Supp. 483, 485 (E.D.Pa.), petition for mandamus and prohibition denied sub nom. General Electric Co. v. Kirkpatrick, 312 F.2d 742 (C.A.3 1962), cert. denied, 372 U.S. 943, 83 S.Ct. 937, 9 L.Ed.2d 969 (1963), reflected a similar conceptual approach:

> "Keeping in mind that the question is, Is it the corporation which is seeking the lawyer's advice when the asserted privileged communication is made?, the most satisfactory solution, I think, is that if the employee making the communication, of whatever rank he may be, is in a position to control or even to take a substantial part in a decision about any action which the corporation may take upon the advice of the attorney, . . . then, in effect, *he is (or personifies) the corporation* when he makes his disclosure to the lawyer and the privilege would apply." (Emphasis supplied.)

Such a view, we think, overlooks the fact that the privilege exists to protect not only the giving of professional advice to those who can act on it but also the giving of information to the lawyer to enable him to give sound and informed advice. See *Trammel,* supra, at 51, 100 S.Ct., at 913; *Fisher,* supra, at 403, 96 S.Ct. at 1577. The first step in the resolution of any legal problem is ascertaining the factual background and sifting through the facts with an eye to the legally relevant. See ABA Code of Professional Responsibility, Ethical Consideration 4–1:

> "A lawyer should be fully informed of all the facts of the matter he is handling in order for his client to obtain the full advantage of our legal system. It is for the lawyer in the exercise of his independent professional judgment to separate the relevant and important from the irrelevant and unimportant. The observance of the ethical obligation of a lawyer to hold inviolate the confidences and secrets of his client not only facilitates the full development of facts essential to proper representation of the client but also encourages laymen to seek early legal assistance."

See also Hickman v. Taylor, 329 U.S. 495, 511, 67 S.Ct. 385, 393–394, 91 L.Ed. 451 (1947).

In the case of the individual client the provider of information and the person who acts on the lawyer's advice are one and the same. In the corporate context, however, it will frequently be employees beyond the control group as defined by the court below—"officers and agents . . . responsible for directing [the company's] actions in response to legal advice"—who will possess the information needed by the corporation's lawyers. Middle-level—and indeed lower-level—employees can, by actions within the scope of their employment, embroil the corporation in serious legal difficulties, and it is only natural that these employees would have the relevant information needed by corporate counsel if he is adequately to advise the client with respect to such actual or potential difficulties. This fact was noted in Diversified Industries, Inc. v. Meredith, 572 F.2d 596 (C.A.8 1977) (en banc):

> "In a corporation, it may be necessary to glean information relevant to a legal problem from middle management or non-management personnel as well as from top executives. The attorney dealing with a complex legal problem 'is thus faced with a "Hobson's choice." If he interviews employees not having "the very highest authority," their communications to him will not be privileged. If, on the other hand, he interviews *only* those employees with the "very highest authority," he may find it extremely difficult, if not impossible, to determine what happened.' " Id., at 608–609 (quoting Weinschel, Corporate Employee Interviews and the Attorney–Client Privilege, 12 B.C.Ind. & Comm.L.Rev. 873, 876 (1971)).

The control group test adopted by the court below thus frustrates the very purpose of the privilege by discouraging the communication of relevant information by employees of the client to attorneys seeking to render legal advice to the client corporation. The attorney's advice will also frequently be more significant to noncontrol group members than to those who officially sanction the advice, and the control group test makes it more difficult to convey full and frank legal advice to the employees who will put into effect the client corporation's policy. See, e.g., Duplan Corp. v. Deering Milliken, Inc., 397 F.Supp. 1146, 1164 (D.S.C.1974) ("After the lawyer forms his or her opinion, it is of no immediate benefit to the Chairman of the Board or the President. It must be given to the corporate personnel who will apply it").

The narrow scope given the attorney-client privilege by the court below not only makes it difficult for corporate attorneys to formulate sound advice when their client is faced with a specific legal problem but also threatens to limit the valuable efforts of corporate counsel to ensure their client's compliance with the law. In light of the vast and complicated array of regulatory legislation confronting the modern corporation, corporations, unlike most individuals, "constantly go to lawyers to find out how to obey the law," Burnham, The Attorney-Client Privilege in the Corporate Arena, 24 Bus.Law. 901, 913 (1969), particularly since compliance with the law in this area is hardly an instinctive matter, see, e.g., United States v. United States Gypsum Co., 438 U.S. 422, 440–441, 98 S.Ct. 2864, 2875–2876, 57 L.Ed.2d 854 (1978) ("the behavior proscribed by the [Sherman] Act is often difficult to distinguish from the gray zone of socially acceptable and economically justifiable business conduct").[2] The test adopted by the court below is difficult to apply in practice, though no abstractly formulated and unvarying "test" will

---

[2]   The Government argues that the risk of civil or criminal liability suffices to ensure that corporations will seek legal advice in the absence of the protection of the privilege. This response ignores the fact that the depth and quality of any investigations to ensure compliance with the law would suffer, even were they undertaken. The response also proves too much, since it applies to all communications covered by the privilege: an individual trying to comply with the law or faced with a legal problem also has strong incentive to disclose information to his lawyer, yet the common law has recognized the value of the privilege in further facilitating communications.

necessarily enable courts to decide questions such as this with mathematical precision. But if the purpose of the attorney-client privilege is to be served, the attorney and client must be able to predict with some degree of certainty whether particular discussions will be protected. An uncertain privilege, or one which purports to be certain but results in widely varying applications by the courts, is little better than no privilege at all. The very terms of the test adopted by the court below suggest the unpredictability of its application. The test restricts the availability of the privilege to those officers who play a "substantial role" in deciding and directing a corporation's legal response. Disparate decisions in cases applying this test illustrate its unpredictability. Compare, e.g., Hogan v. Zletz, 43 F.R.D. 308, 315–316 (N.D.Okl.1967), aff'd in part sub nom. Natta v. Hogan, 392 F.2d 686 (C.A.10 1968) (control group includes managers and assistant managers of patent division and research and development department) with Congoleum Industries, Inc. v. GAF Corp., 49 F.R.D. 82, 83–85 (E.D.Pa.1969), aff'd, 478 F.2d 1398 (C.A.3 1973) (control group includes only division and corporate vice-presidents, and not two directors of research and vice-president for production and research).

The communications at issue were made by Upjohn employees[3] to counsel for Upjohn acting as such, at the direction of corporate superiors in order to secure legal advice from counsel. As the Magistrate found, "Mr. Thomas consulted with the Chairman of the Board and outside counsel and thereafter conducted a factual investigation to determine the nature and extent of the questionable payments *and to be in a position to give legal advice to the company with respect to the payments.*" (Emphasis supplied.) Information, not available from upper-echelon management, was needed to supply a basis for legal advice concerning compliance with securities and tax laws, foreign laws, currency regulations, duties to shareholders, and potential litigation in each of these areas. The communications concerned matters within the scope of the employees' corporate duties, and the employees themselves were sufficiently aware that they were being questioned in order that the corporation could obtain legal advice. The questionnaire identified Thomas as "the company's General Counsel" and referred in its opening sentence to the possible illegality of payments such as the ones on which information was sought. A statement of policy accompanying the questionnaire clearly indicated the legal implications of the investigation. The policy statement was issued "in order that there be no uncertainty in the future as to the policy with respect to the practices which are the subject of this investigation." It began "Upjohn will comply with all laws and regulations," and stated that commissions or payments "will not be used as a subterfuge for bribes or illegal payments" and that all payments must be "proper and legal." Any future agreements with foreign distributors or agents were to be approved "by a company attorney" and any questions concerning the policy were to be referred "to the company's General Counsel." This statement was issued to Upjohn employees

---

[3] Seven of the eighty-six employees interviewed by counsel had terminated their employment with Upjohn at the time of the interview. App. 33a–38a. Petitioner argues that the privilege should nonetheless apply to communications by these former employees concerning activities during their period of employment. Neither the District Court nor the Court of Appeals had occasion to address this issue, and we decline to decide it without the benefit of treatment below.

worldwide, so that even those interviewees not receiving a questionnaire were aware of the legal implications of the interviews. Pursuant to explicit instructions from the Chairman of the Board, the communications were considered "highly confidential" when made, and have been kept confidential by the company. Consistent with the underlying purposes of the attorney-client privilege, these communications must be protected against compelled disclosure.

The Court of Appeals declined to extend the attorney-client privilege beyond the limits of the control group test for fear that doing so would entail severe burdens on discovery and create a broad "zone of silence" over corporate affairs. Application of the attorney-client privilege to communications such as those involved here, however, puts the adversary in no worse position than if the communications had never taken place. The privilege only protects disclosure of communications; it does not protect disclosure of the underlying facts by those who communicated with the attorney:

> "[T]he protection of the privilege extends only to *communications* and not to facts. A fact is one thing and a communication concerning that fact is an entirely different thing. The client cannot be compelled to answer the question, 'What did you say or write to the attorney?' but may not refuse to disclose any relevant fact within his knowledge merely because he incorporated a statement of such fact into his communication to his attorney." Philadelphia v. Westinghouse Electric Corp., 205 F.Supp. 830, 831 (E.D.Pa.1962).

See also *Diversified Industries,* 572 F.2d, at 611; State ex rel. Dudek v. Circuit Court, 34 Wis.2d 559, 580, 150 N.W.2d 387, 399 (1967) ("the courts have noted that a party cannot conceal a fact merely by revealing it to his lawyer"). Here the Government was free to question the employees who communicated with Thomas and outside counsel. Upjohn has provided the IRS with a list of such employees, and the IRS has already interviewed some 25 of them. While it would probably be more convenient for the Government to secure the results of petitioner's internal investigation by simply subpoenaing the questionnaires and notes taken by petitioner's attorneys, such considerations of convenience do not overcome the policies served by the attorney-client privilege. As Justice Jackson noted in his concurring opinion in Hickman v. Taylor, 329 U.S., at 516, 67 S.Ct., at 396: "Discovery was hardly intended to enable a learned profession to perform its functions . . . on wits borrowed from the adversary."

Needless to say, we decide only the case before us, and do not undertake to draft a set of rules which should govern challenges to investigatory subpoenas. Any such approach would violate the spirit of Federal Rule of Evidence 501. See S. Rep. No. 93–1277, p. 13 (1974) ("the recognition of a privilege based on a confidential relationship . . . should be determined on a case-by-case basis"); Trammel, 445 U.S., at 47; United States v. Gillock, 445 U.S. 360, 367 (1980). While such a "case-by-case" basis may to some slight extent undermine desirable certainty in the boundaries of the attorney-client privilege, it obeys the spirit of the Rules. At the same time we conclude that the narrow "control group test" sanctioned by the Court of Appeals in this case cannot, consistent with "the principles of the common law as . . . interpreted . . . in the light of reason and experience," Fed. Rule Evid. 501, govern the development of the law in this area.

[Part III of the Court's opinion appears in the section on Work Product Immunity at p. 756 infra.]

NOTE ON THE ATTORNEY-CLIENT PRIVILEGE

1.   **Basis for the privilege.** The standard view is that the attorney-client privilege represents an investment by the legal system in encouraging legal advice. The premises are that a lawyer will give better advice if she fully understands the facts relevant to the client's problem, that the client's awareness of the privilege will encourage fuller disclosure to the lawyer, and that the client will generally follow the advice given. The potential costs of the privilege arise from the failure of these premises. In cases where the existence of the privilege does not result in improved communication (because the client would share information with the lawyer anyway) the privilege is not improving the lawyer's advice and is preventing the tribunal from receiving relevant information. The social value of the privilege thus depends critically on the extent to which its existence encourages information flow to the lawyer. How does the Court assess that likelihood? See in particular note 2 of the Court's opinion. The premise that better informed legal advice leads to more lawful conduct can also fail. In cases where better-informed advice encourages unlawful, rather than lawful behavior, the privilege produces additional costs that must be offset against its benefits.

2.   **Scope of the privilege.** The scope of the privilege varies somewhat from jurisdiction to jurisdiction, but Wigmore's classic formulation describes the core privilege:

> Where legal advice of any kind is sought from a professional legal advisor in his capacity as such, the communications relating to that purpose, made in confidence by the client, are at his instance permanently protected from disclosure by himself or by the legal advisor, except the protection be waived.

8 J. Wigmore, Evidence in Trials at Common Law § 2292 at 554 (McNaughton ed. 1961).

The attorney-client privilege is available to an individual or to an organization, including a corporation, a partnership, or a governmental organization. An attorney-client relationship is created when the client reasonably believes that the attorney is providing, or is willing to consider providing, legal services. The privilege extends to communications during discussions about whether the attorney will represent the client, even if the attorney is not, in the end, employed. The privilege also extends to advice given without charge.

As Justice Rehnquist notes in *Upjohn,* the privilege protects communications rather than facts. Under *Upjohn,* a question to a witness in the form, "What did you say to your company's lawyer about the payment made to General X (an official of a foreign government)?" is subject to objection as calling for the content of a privileged communication. But what about questions asking the witness, "What was the economic justification for the payment that your company made to General X?" or "What was said during the March 13 meeting between you and General X?" Could the company's lawyer instruct the client not to answer on the ground that the witness had also discussed those subjects with company counsel?

3. **The absolute quality of the privilege.** Unlike some other privileges (and unlike the immunities created for trial preparation materials and experts), the attorney-client privilege cannot be overcome by a showing that the information embodied in the protected communication is unavailable from any other source. Restatement (Third) of the Law Governing Lawyers § 77 (2000). This principle was strongly reaffirmed in Swidler & Berlin v. United States, 524 U.S. 399, 118 S.Ct. 2081, 141 L.Ed.2d 379 (1998). In that case, the Watergate Special Prosecutor investigating the apparent suicide of Assistant White House Counsel Vincent Foster sought access to notes of a conversation between Foster and his lawyer that took place shortly before Foster's death. The prosecutor unsuccessfully argued that the information was critically important to resolving the reasons for Foster's death and unavailable from any other source, and that since the client was dead the social interest in preserving his confidences was reduced.

4. **Claiming and waiving the privilege.** If a party withholds otherwise discoverable information because of claimed privilege, the claim must be made "expressly," and must describe the nature of the documents, communications, or tangible things not produced or disclosed" "in a manner that * * * will enable other parties to assess the claim." Fed. R. Civ. P. 26(b)(5)(A). Typically, this is accomplished through the creation of a "privilege log" by the party responding to a document request. In the log, often a large spreadsheet, the lawyer will describe the withheld documents and the nature of the privilege. In the age of electronic discovery, this is an extraordinarily expensive and time-consuming exercise for clients with a large amount of data. See Hopson v. Mayor and City Council of Baltimore, 232 F.R.D. 228 (D. Md. 2005).

The privilege can be waived by the client, either by voluntarily disclosing the communication or by failing to claim the privilege. This makes "implied waiver" a continuous risk, particularly when parties are producing large volumes of information under intense time pressure. See Marcus, The Perils of Privilege: Waiver and the Litigator, 84 Mich. L. Rev. 1605 (1986). In federal court, the problem of inadvertent waiver is now addressed directly by Rule 26(b)(5)(B) and Federal Rule of Evidence 502(b). Under Rule 26(b)(5)(B), if a party discloses information that it believes is subject to a claim of privilege, it may notify the party that received the information of the claim and its basis. At that point, the party who received the information must "return, sequester, or destroy" the material, must seek to retrieve it if it has been disclosed to other persons, but may present the question of privilege to the court for resolution. Under Rule 502(b), the privilege is not waived by inadvertent disclosure where the privilege holder took reasonable steps to rectify the error, including following Rule 26(b)(5)(B). For a comprehensive discussion of these rules in the digital age, see Grimm, Bergstrom & Kraeuter, Federal Rule of Evidence 502: Has It Lived Up to Its Potential, 17 Rich. J.L. & Tech. 8 (2011).

5. **Exceptions to the attorney-client privilege.** There are a number of exceptions to the attorney-client privilege under which confidential attorney-client communications do not qualify for protection. For example, communications are not protected "if the services of the lawyer were sought or obtained to enable or aid anyone to commit or plan to commit what the client knew or reasonably should have known to be a crime or fraud." Unif. R. Evid. 502(d) (1999). Communications "relevant to an issue of breach of duty by a lawyer to the client or by a client to the lawyer" are also not privileged. Id. The most common scenarios involve suits by clients for malpractice and suits by lawyers for unpaid fees. In addition, in most states, the privilege does not apply when disclosure of the communication is reasonably necessary for a lawyer to rebut an accusation of wrongdoing arising out of the lawyer's work for the client. See Qualcomm, Inc. v. Broadcom Corp., 2008 WL 638108 (S.D. Cal. 2008) (applying "self-defense" exception to the privilege when lawyers needed otherwise privileged documents to defend themselves against discovery sanctions). For other exceptions to the privilege, see id. And see also proposed (but ultimately rejected) Fed. R. Evid. 503, 56 F.R.D. 183, 235–37 (1973); American Law Institute, Restatement (Third) of the Law Governing Lawyers §§ 79–86 (2000).

6. **The distinction between the privilege and the ethical duty of confidentiality.** The privilege is a legal shield against compelled disclosure in legal proceedings. It is narrowly limited to information communicated in confidence to the attorney by the client. The attorney also owes the client a legal and ethical duty not to disclose information harmful to the client in the absence of legal compulsion to do so. The duty of confidentiality is broader than the privilege because it extends to all information that the lawyer has about the representation, not just privileged communications, and because it applies in all settings, not just in situations where compelled disclosure is sought. But the duty of confidentiality is not in itself a shield against compelled disclosure. That is, it does not authorize the lawyer to withhold non-privileged information that there is a legal or ethical obligation to disclose. For example, most jurisdictions require an attorney to reveal to a court the fact that her client has committed perjury, even when the basis for the attorney's knowledge is a client communication. See American Law Institute, Restatement (Third) of the Law Governing Lawyers, §§ 59–67, 120 (2000).

7. **The attorney-client privilege in a corporate setting.** As is apparent from *Upjohn*, the operation and justification of the attorney-client privilege is substantially different for an individual client and an organizational client such as a corporation. Prior to the Court's decision in *Upjohn*, some jurisdictions restricted the attorney-client privilege in a corporation to communications between the attorney and the "control group" in the corporation. The consequence of the control-group test was to inhibit the corporation in conducting investigations of legal matters in which low-level employees possessed relevant information. Are you convinced by the Court's opinion in *Upjohn* that the control group test should have been abandoned? *Upjohn* is a critically important precedent for corporations because it protects a wide array of communications associated with litigation and regulatory compliance. See, e.g., In re Kellogg Brown & Root, 756 F.3d 754 (D.C. Cir. 2014) (holding that the *Upjohn* privilege applies to internal corporate investigations undertaken to ensure compliance with regulations or company policies).

A lurking problem with the attorney-client privilege in the corporate setting is that a corporate employee—particularly a low-level employee outside the "control group"—cannot protect the information he provides to the corporation's attorney because he is not personally the lawyer's client, but merely an employee of the lawyer's corporate client. The corporation—

not the employee—will ultimately decide whether to assert the attorney-client privilege with respect to the communications made by the employee, or whether instead to use the information against the employee in disciplinary or termination proceedings, or to turn the employee's communications over to a prosecutor. When the lawyer for the corporation is aware that the employee may not be able to count on confidentiality, she must tell the employee. American Bar Association Model Rules of Professional Conduct, Rule 1.13(f). If the employee, so warned, knows that he cannot control disclosure of his confidences by the corporation, is it the attorney-client privilege that is causing the employee to talk to the corporation's lawyer or instead the threat of being fired if she refuses to do so? In this kind of case, is the privilege serving a different purpose: encouraging a corporation to conduct internal investigations through its general counsel's office, confident that any information revealed to the lawyers will be protected by the privilege, if that is what the corporation ultimately decides is in *its* best interests? See Green & Pogdor, Unregulated Internal Investigations: Achieving Fairness for Corporate Constituents, 54 B.C. L. Rev. 73 (2013); Geisel, *Upjohn* Warnings, the Attorney-Client Privilege, and Principles of Lawyer Ethics: Achieving Harmony, 65 U. Miami L. Rev. 109 (2010).

8. Additional reading. See Hazard, An Historical Perspective on the Attorney-Client Privilege, 66 Calif. L. Rev. 1061 (1978). For an excellent account of *Upjohn*, see Sexton, A Post-*Upjohn* Consideration of the Corporate Attorney-Client Privilege, 57 N.Y.U.L. Rev. 443 (1982). For a theoretical account of the value of attorney-client confidentiality in litigation, see Bundy & Elhauge, Do Lawyers Improve the Adversary System: A General Theory of Litigation Advice and Its Regulation, 79 Calif. L. Rev. 313, 401–13 (1991) (stressing that the key issue is the extent to which confidentiality actually increases communications between lawyer and client).

FURTHER NOTE ON PRIVILEGED MATTER

1. Other privileges. There are many privileges in addition to the attorney-client privilege, though none whose invocation is so frequent or whose influence is so pervasive. The most important constitutional privilege is the Fifth Amendment privilege against self-incrimination. The major statutory and common law privileges, widely recognized in American jurisdictions, include those for communications between doctor or psychotherapist and patient, communications between spouses, and communications between priest and penitent. There are also a variety of governmental privileges, including a limited privilege for state secrets and a privilege for communications within the executive branch of government. See also the formidable list of privileges in Continuing Education of the Bar, California Trial Objections (10th ed. 2004), and in United States v. American Tel. & Tel. Co., 86 F.R.D. 603 (D.D.C. 1979).

2. Self-incrimination. An individual who is a party or witness in a civil case may invoke the Fifth Amendment privilege as a basis for refusing to answer questions whose answers might reasonably tend to incriminate him. The cases are divided, but some have held that a plaintiff's invocation of the Fifth Amendment is not a basis for dismissing her suit. See Comment, Plaintiff as Deponent: Invoking the Fifth Amendment, 48 U. Chi. L. Rev. 158 (1981); e.g., Campbell v. Gerrans, 592 F.2d 1054 (9th Cir. 1979). At a minimum, however, a civil plaintiff's refusal to testify permits an adverse inference as to the matter inquired into. See Baxter v. Palmigiano, 425 U.S. 308, 96 S.Ct. 1551, 47 L.Ed.2d 810 (1976). Moreover, courts are wary of belated attempts to assert the privilege by parties who have already testified at depositions or submitted affidavits. See Nutramax Laboratories v. Twin Laboratories, 32 F. Supp. 2d 331 (D. Md. 1999).

2. WORK PRODUCT IMMUNITY

INTRODUCTORY NOTE ON THE WORK-PRODUCT DOCTRINE

In the original 1938 version of the federal Rules, there was no provision governing the discoverability of material covered under what has come to be known as the "work-product" doctrine. Roughly speaking, the work product of an attorney is material prepared in anticipation of litigation, including but not limited to statements taken from witnesses, notes taken at meetings with witnesses or other people knowledgeable about the matter in dispute, and memoranda summarizing legal research. In the mid-1940s, the Advisory Committee on the Civil Rules proposed to the Supreme Court an amendment to Rule 30(b) that would have codified a work-product doctrine covering such material, protecting it from discovery by adverse parties. Rather than forward the proposed amendment to Congress, the Supreme Court decided *Hickman v. Taylor.*

Hickman v. Taylor

Supreme Court of the United States, 1947.
329 U.S. 495, 67 S.Ct. 385, 91 L.Ed. 451.

■ MR. JUSTICE MURPHY delivered the opinion of the Court.

This case presents an important problem under the Federal Rules of Civil Procedure * * * as to the extent to which a party may inquire into oral and written statements of witnesses, or other information, secured by an adverse party's counsel in the course of preparation for possible litigation after a claim has arisen. Examination into a person's files and records, including those resulting from the professional activities of an attorney, must be judged with care. It is not without reason that various safeguards have been established to preclude unwarranted excursions into the privacy of a man's work. At the same time, public policy supports reasonable and necessary inquiries. Properly to balance these competing interests is a delicate and difficult task.

On February 7, 1943, the tug "J.M. Taylor" sank while engaged in helping to tow a car float of the Baltimore & Ohio Railroad across the Delaware River at Philadelphia. The accident was apparently unusual in nature, the cause of it still being unknown. Five of the nine crew members were drowned. Three days later the tug owners and the underwriters employed a law firm, of which respondent Fortenbaugh is a member, to defend them against potential suits by representatives of the deceased crew members and to sue the railroad for damages to the tug.

A public hearing was held on March 4, 1943, before the United States Steamboat Inspectors, at which the four survivors were examined. This testimony was recorded and made available to all interested parties. Shortly thereafter, Fortenbaugh privately interviewed the survivors and took statements from them with an eye toward the anticipated litigation; the survivors signed these statements on March 29. Fortenbaugh also interviewed other persons believed to have some information relating to the accident and in some cases he made memoranda of what they told him. At the time when Fortenbaugh secured the statements of the survivors, representatives of two of the deceased crew members had been in communication with him. Ultimately claims were presented by representatives of all five of the deceased; four of the claims, however, were settled without litigation. The fifth claimant, petitioner herein, brought suit in a federal court under the Jones Act on November 26, 1943, naming as defendants the two tug owners, individually and as partners, and the railroad.

One year later, petitioner filed 39 interrogatories directed to the tug owners. The 38th interrogatory read: "State whether any statements of the members of the crews of the Tugs 'J.M. Taylor' and 'Philadelphia' or of any other vessel were taken in connection with the towing of the car float and the sinking of the Tug 'John M. Taylor.' Attach hereto exact copies of all such statements if in writing, and if oral, set forth in detail the exact provisions of any such oral statements or reports."

Supplemental interrogatories asked whether any oral or written statements, records, reports or other memoranda had been made concerning any matter relative to the towing operation, the sinking of the tug, the salvaging and repair of the tug, and the death of the deceased. If the answer was in the affirmative, the tug owners were then requested to set forth the nature of all such records, reports, statements or other memoranda.

The tug owners, through Fortenbaugh, answered all of the interrogatories except No. 38 and the supplemental ones just described. While admitting that statements of the survivors had been taken they declined to summarize or set forth the contents. They did so on the ground that such requests called "for privileged matter obtained in preparation for litigation" and constituted "an attempt to obtain indirectly counsel's private files." It was claimed that answering these requests "would involve practically turning over not only the complete files, but also the telephone records and, almost, the thoughts of counsel."

In connection with the hearing on these objections, Fortenbaugh made a written statement and gave an informal oral deposition explaining the circumstances under which he had taken the statements. But he was not expressly asked in the deposition to produce the statements. The District Court for the Eastern District of Pennsylvania, sitting en banc, held that the requested matters were not privileged. 4 F.R.D. 479. The court then decreed that the tug owners and Fortenbaugh, as counsel and agent for the tug owners, forthwith "Answer Plaintiff's 38th interrogatory and supplementary interrogatories; produce all written statements of witnesses obtained by Mr. Fortenbaugh, as counsel and agent for Defendants; state in substance any fact concerning this case which Defendants learned through oral statements made by witnesses to Mr. Fortenbaugh whether or not included in his private memoranda and produce Mr. Fortenbaugh's memoranda containing statements of fact by witnesses or to submit these memoranda to the Court for determination of those portions which should be revealed to

Plaintiff." Upon their refusal, the court adjudged them in contempt and ordered them imprisoned until they complied.

The Third Circuit Court of Appeals, also sitting en banc, reversed the judgment of the District Court. 153 F.2d 212. It held that the information here sought was part of the "work product of the lawyer" and hence privileged from discovery under the Federal Rules of Civil Procedure. The importance of the problem, which has engendered a great divergence of views among district courts, led us to grant certiorari. 328 U.S. 876, 66 S.Ct. 1337.

The pre-trial deposition-discovery mechanism established by Rules 26 to 37 is one of the most significant innovations of the Federal Rules of Civil Procedure. Under the prior federal practice, the pre-trial functions of notice-giving, issue-formulation and fact-revelation were performed primarily and inadequately by the pleadings.[2] Inquiry into the issues and the facts before trial was narrowly confined and was often cumbersome in method. The new rules, however, restrict the pleadings to the task of general notice-giving and invest the deposition-discovery process with a vital role in the preparation for trial. The various instruments of discovery now serve (1) as a device, along with the pre-trial hearing under Rule 16, to narrow and clarify the basic issues between the parties, and (2) as a device for ascertaining the facts, or information as to the existence or whereabouts of facts, relative to those issues. Thus civil trials in the federal courts no longer need be carried on in the dark. The way is now clear, consistent with recognized privileges, for the parties to obtain the fullest possible knowledge of the issues and facts before trial.

There is an initial question as to which of the deposition-discovery rules is involved in this case. Petitioner, in filing his interrogatories, thought that he was proceeding under Rule 33. That rule provides that a party may serve upon any adverse party written interrogatories to be answered by the party served. The District Court proceeded on the same assumption in its opinion, although its order to produce and its contempt order stated that both Rules 33 and 34 were involved. * * *

* * *

But under the circumstances we deem it unnecessary and unwise to rest our decision upon this procedural irregularity, an irregularity which is not strongly urged upon us and which was disregarded in the two courts below. It matters little at this late stage whether Fortenbaugh fails to answer interrogatories filed under Rule 26 or under Rule 33 or whether he refuses to produce the memoranda and statements pursuant to a subpoena under Rule 45 or a court order under Rule 34. The deposition-discovery rules created integrated procedural devices. And the basic question at stake is whether any of those devices may be used to inquire into materials collected by an adverse party's counsel in the course of preparation for possible litigation. The fact that the petitioner may have used the wrong method does not destroy the main thrust of his attempt. Nor does it relieve us of the responsibility of dealing with the problem raised by that attempt. It would be inconsistent with the liberal

---

[2] "The great weakness of pleading as a means for developing and presenting issues of fact for trial lay in its total lack of any means for testing the factual basis for the pleader's allegations and denials." Sunderland, "The Theory and Practice of Pre-Trial Procedure," 36 Mich. L. Rev. 215, 216. See also Ragland, Discovery Before Trial (1932), ch. I.

atmosphere surrounding these rules to insist that petitioner now go through the empty formality of pursuing the right procedural device only to reestablish precisely the same basic problem now confronting us. We do not mean to say, however, that there may not be situations in which the failure to proceed in accordance with a specific rule would be important or decisive. But in the present circumstances, for the purposes of this decision, the procedural irregularity is not material. Having noted the proper procedure, we may accordingly turn our attention to the substance of the underlying problem.

In urging that he has a right to inquire into the materials secured and prepared by Fortenbaugh, petitioner emphasizes that the deposition-discovery portions of the Federal Rules of Civil Procedure are designed to enable the parties to discover the true facts and to compel their disclosure wherever they may be found. It is said that inquiry may be made under these rules, epitomized by Rule 26, as to any relevant matter which is not privileged; and since the discovery provisions are to be applied as broadly and liberally as possible, the privilege limitation must be restricted to its narrowest bounds. On the premise that the attorney-client privilege is the one involved in this case, petitioner argues that it must be strictly confined to confidential communications made by a client to his attorney. And since the materials here in issue were secured by Fortenbaugh from third persons rather than from his clients, the tug owners, the conclusion is reached that these materials are proper subjects for discovery under Rule 26.

As additional support for this result, petitioner claims that to prohibit discovery under these circumstances would give a corporate defendant a tremendous advantage in a suit by an individual plaintiff. Thus in a suit by an injured employee against a railroad or in a suit by an insured person against an insurance company the corporate defendant could pull a dark veil of secrecy over all the pertinent facts it can collect after the claim arises merely on the assertion that such facts were gathered by its large staff of attorneys and claim agents. At the same time, the individual plaintiff, who often has direct knowledge of the matter in issue and has no counsel until some time after his claim arises could be compelled to disclose all the intimate details of his case. By endowing with immunity from disclosure all that a lawyer discovers in the course of his duties, it is said, the rights of individual litigants in such cases are drained of vitality and the lawsuit becomes more of a battle of deception than a search for truth.

But framing the problem in terms of assisting individual plaintiffs in their suits against corporate defendants is unsatisfactory. Discovery concededly may work to the disadvantage as well as to the advantage of individual plaintiffs. Discovery, in other words, is not a one-way proposition. It is available in all types of cases at the behest of any party, individual or corporate, plaintiff or defendant. The problem thus far transcends the situation confronting this petitioner. And we must view that problem in light of the limitless situations where the particular kind of discovery sought by petitioner might be used.

We agree, of course, that the deposition-discovery rules are to be accorded a broad and liberal treatment. No longer can the time-honored cry of "fishing expedition" serve to preclude a party from inquiring into the facts underlying his opponent's case. Mutual knowledge of all the relevant facts gathered by both parties is essential to proper litigation. To that end, either party may compel the other to disgorge whatever facts he has in his possession. The deposition-discovery procedure simply advances the stage at which the disclosure can be compelled from the time of trial to the period preceding it, thus reducing the possibility of surprise. But discovery, like all matters of procedure, has ultimate and necessary boundaries. As indicated by Rules 30(b) and (d) and 31(d), limitations inevitably arise when it can be shown that the examination is being conducted in bad faith or in such a manner as to annoy, embarrass or oppress the person subject to the inquiry. And as Rule 26(b) provides, further limitations come into existence when the inquiry touches upon the irrelevant or encroaches upon the recognized domains of privilege.

We also agree that the memoranda, statements and mental impressions in issue in this case fall outside the scope of the attorney-client privilege and hence are not protected from discovery on that basis. It is unnecessary here to delineate the content and scope of that privilege as recognized in the federal courts. For present purposes, it suffices to note that the protective cloak of this privilege does not extend to information which an attorney secures from a witness while acting for his client in anticipation of litigation. Nor does this privilege concern the memoranda, briefs, communications and other writings prepared by counsel for his own use in prosecuting his client's case; and it is equally unrelated to writings which reflect an attorney's mental impressions, conclusions, opinions or legal theories.

But the impropriety of invoking that privilege does not provide an answer to the problem before us. Petitioner has made more than an ordinary request for relevant, non-privileged facts in the possession of his adversaries or their counsel. He has sought discovery as of right of oral and written statements of witnesses whose identity is well known and whose availability to petitioner appears unimpaired. He has sought production of these matters after making the most searching inquiries of his opponents as to the circumstances surrounding the fatal accident, which inquiries were sworn to have been answered to the best of their information and belief. Interrogatories were directed toward all the events prior to, during and subsequent to the sinking of the tug. Full and honest answers to such broad inquiries would necessarily have included all pertinent information gleaned by Fortenbaugh through his interviews with the witnesses. Petitioner makes no suggestion, and we cannot assume, that the tug owners or Fortenbaugh were incomplete or dishonest in the framing of their answers. In addition, petitioner was free to examine the public testimony of the witnesses taken before the United States Steamboat Inspectors. We are thus dealing with an attempt to secure the production of written statements and mental impressions contained in the files and the mind of the attorney Fortenbaugh without any showing of necessity or any indication or claim that denial of such production would unduly prejudice the preparation of petitioner's case or cause him any hardship or injustice. For aught that appears, the essence of what petitioner seeks either has been revealed to him already through the interrogatories or is readily available to him direct from the witnesses for the asking.

The District Court, after hearing objections to petitioner's request, commanded Fortenbaugh to produce all written statements of witnesses and to state in substance any facts learned through oral statements of witnesses to him. Fortenbaugh was to submit any memoranda he had made of the oral statements so that the court might determine what portions should be revealed to petitioner. All of this was ordered without any showing by petitioner, or any requirement that he make a proper showing, of the necessity for the production of any of this material or any demonstration that denial of the production would cause hardship or injustice. The court simply ordered production on the theory that the facts sought were material and were not privileged as constituting attorney-client communications.

In our opinion, neither Rule 26 nor any other rule dealing with discovery contemplates production under such circumstances. That is not because the subject matter is privileged or irrelevant, as those concepts are used in these rules. Here is simply an attempt, without purported necessity or justification, to secure written statements, private memoranda and personal recollections prepared or formed by an adverse party's counsel in the course of his legal duties. As such, it falls outside the arena of discovery and contravenes the public policy underlying the orderly prosecution and defense of legal claims. Not even the most liberal of discovery theories can justify unwarranted inquiries into the files and the mental impressions of an attorney.

Historically, a lawyer is an officer of the court and is bound to work for the advancement of justice while faithfully protecting the rightful interests of his clients. In performing his various duties, however, it is essential that a lawyer work with a certain degree of privacy, free from unnecessary intrusion by opposing parties and their counsel. Proper preparation of a client's case demands that he assemble information, sift what he considers to be the relevant from the irrelevant facts, prepare his legal theories and plan his strategy without undue and needless interference. That is the historical and the necessary way in which lawyers act within the framework of our system of jurisprudence to promote justice and to protect their clients' interests. This work is reflected, of course, in interviews, statements, memoranda, correspondence, briefs, mental impressions, personal beliefs, and countless other tangible and intangible ways—aptly though roughly termed by the Circuit Court of Appeals in this case as the "work product of the lawyer." Were such materials open to opposing counsel on mere demand, much of what is now put down in writing would remain unwritten. An attorney's thoughts, heretofore inviolate, would not be his own. Inefficiency, unfairness and sharp practices would inevitably develop in the giving of legal advice and in the preparation of cases for trial. The effect on the legal profession would be demoralizing. And the interests of the clients and the cause of justice would be poorly served. *[noted in class]*

We do not mean to say that all written materials obtained or prepared by an adversary's counsel with an eye toward litigation are necessarily free from discovery in all cases. Where relevant and non-privileged facts remain hidden in an attorney's file and where production of those facts is essential to the preparation of one's case, discovery may properly be had. Such written statements and documents might, under certain circumstances, be admissible in evidence or give clues as to the existence or location of relevant facts. Or they might be useful for purposes of impeachment or corroboration. And production might be justified where the witnesses are no longer available or can be reached only with difficulty. Were production of written statements and documents to be precluded under such circumstances, the liberal ideals of the deposition-discovery portions of the Federal Rules of Civil Procedure would be stripped of much of their meaning. But the general policy against invading the privacy of an attorney's course of preparation is so well recognized and so essential to an orderly working of our system of legal procedure that a burden rests on the one who would invade that privacy to establish adequate reasons to justify production through a subpoena or court order. That burden, we believe, is necessarily implicit in the rules as now constituted.

* * * No attempt was made to establish any reason why Fortenbaugh should be forced to produce the written statements. There was only a naked, general demand for these materials as of right and a finding by the District Court that no recognizable privilege was involved. That was insufficient to justify discovery under these circumstances and the court should have sustained the refusal of the tug owners and Fortenbaugh to produce.

[A]s to oral statements made by witnesses to Fortenbaugh, whether presently in the form of his mental impressions or memoranda, we do not believe that any showing of necessity can be made under the circumstances of this case so as to justify productions. Under ordinary conditions, forcing an attorney to repeat or write out all that witnesses have told him and to deliver an account to his adversary gives rise to grave dangers of inaccuracy and untrustworthiness. No legitimate purpose is served by such production. The practice forces the attorney to testify as to what he remembers or what he saw fit to write down regarding the witnesses' remarks. Such testimony would not qualify as evidence; and to use it for impeachment or corroborative purposes would make the attorney much less an officer of the court and much more an ordinary witness. The standards of the profession would thereby suffer.

* * * Petitioner's counsel frankly admits that he wants the oral statements only to help prepare himself to examine witnesses and to make sure that he has overlooked nothing. That is insufficient under the circumstances to permit him an exception to the policy underlying the privacy of Fortenbaugh's professional activities. If there should be a rare situation justifying production of these matters, petitioner's case is not of that type.

* * *

Affirmed.

■ MR. JUSTICE JACKSON, concurring.

* * *

The primary effect of the practice advocated here would be on the legal profession itself. But it too often is overlooked that the lawyer and the law office are indispensable parts of our administration of justice. Law-abiding people can go nowhere else to learn the ever changing and constantly multiplying rules by which they must behave and to obtain redress for their wrongs. The welfare and tone of the legal profession is therefore of prime consequence to society, which would feel the consequences of such a practice as petitioner urges secondarily but certainly.

* * *

Counsel for the petitioner candidly said on argument that he wanted this information to help prepare himself to examine witnesses, to make sure he overlooked nothing. He bases his claim to it in his brief on the view that the Rules were to do away with the old situation where a law suit developed into 'a battle of wits between counsel.' But a common law trial is and always should be an adversary proceeding. Discovery was hardly intended to enable a learned profession to perform its functions either without wits or on wits borrowed from the adversary.

The real purpose and the probable effect of the practice ordered by the district court would be to put trials on a level even lower than a "battle of wits." I can conceive of no practice more demoralizing to the Bar than to require a lawyer to write out and deliver to his adversary an account of what witnesses have told him. Even if his recollection were perfect, the statement would be his language permeated with his inferences. Every one who has tried it knows that it is almost impossible so fairly to record the expressions and emphasis of a witness that when he testifies in the environment of the court and under the influence of the leading question there will not be departures in some respects. Whenever the testimony of the witness would differ from the "exact" statement the lawyer had delivered, the lawyer's statement would be whipped out to impeach the witness. Counsel producing his adversary's "inexact" statement could lose nothing by saying, "Here is a contradiction, gentlemen of the jury. I do not know whether it is my adversary or his witness who is not telling the truth, but one is not." Of course, if this practice were adopted, that scene would be repeated over and over again. The lawyer who delivers such statements often would find himself branded a deceiver afraid to take the stand to support his own version of the witness's conversation with him, or else he will have to go on the stand to defend his own credibility—perhaps against that of his chief witness, or possibly even his client.

Every lawyer dislikes to take the witness stand and will do so only for grave reasons. This is partly because it is not his role; he is almost invariably a poor witness. But he steps out of professional character to do it. He regrets it; the profession discourages it. But the practice advocated here is one which would force him to be a witness, not as to what he has seen or done but as to other witnesses' stories, and not because he wants to do so but in self-defense.

And what is the lawyer to do who has interviewed one whom he believes to be a biased, lying or hostile witness to get his unfavorable statements and know what to meet? He must record and deliver such statements even though he would not vouch for the credibility of the witness by calling him. Perhaps the other side would not want to call him either, but the attorney is open to the charge of suppressing evidence at the trial if he fails to call such a hostile witness even though he never regarded him as reliable or truthful.

Having been supplied the names of the witnesses, petitioner's lawyer gives no reason why he cannot interview them himself. If an employee-witness refuses to tell his story, he, too, may be examined under the Rules. He may be compelled on discovery as fully as on the trial to disclose his version of the facts. But that is his own disclosure—it can be used to impeach him if he contradicts it and such a deposition is not useful to promote an unseemly disagreement between the witness and the counsel in the case.

* * *

Upjohn Co. v. United States
Supreme Court of the United States, 1981.
449 U.S. 383, 101 S.Ct. 677, 66 L.Ed.2d 584.

[Parts I and II of the Court's opinion are reproduced above in Section B.1.]

III

Our decision that the communications by Upjohn employees to counsel are covered by the attorney-client privilege disposes of the case so far as the responses to the questionnaires and any notes reflecting responses to interview questions are concerned. The summons reaches further, however, and Thomas has testified that his notes and memoranda of interviews go beyond recording responses to his questions. To the extent that the material subject to the summons is not protected by the attorney-client privilege as disclosing communications between an employee and counsel, we must reach the ruling by the Court of Appeals that the work-product doctrine does not apply to summonses issued under 26 U.S.C. § 7602.

The Government concedes, wisely, that the Court of Appeals erred and that the work-product doctrine does apply to IRS summonses. * * *

As we stated last Term, the obligation imposed by a tax summons remains "subject to the traditional privileges and limitations." United States v. Euge, 444 U.S. 707, 714, 100 S.Ct. 874, 879–880, 63 L.Ed.2d 141 (1980). Nothing in the language of the IRS summons provisions or their legislative history suggests an intent on the part of Congress to preclude application of the work-product doctrine. Rule 26(b)(3) codifies the work-product doctrine, and the Federal Rules of Civil Procedure are made applicable to summons enforcement proceedings by Rule 81(a)(3). See Donaldson v. United States, 400 U.S. 517, 528, 91 S.Ct. 534, 541, 27 L.Ed.2d 580 (1971). While conceding the applicability of the work-product doctrine, the Government asserts that it has made a sufficient showing of necessity to overcome its protections. The Magistrate apparently so found. The Government relies on the following language in *Hickman*:

> "We do not mean to say that all written materials obtained or prepared by an adversary's counsel with an eye toward litigation are necessarily free from discovery in all cases. Where relevant and nonprivileged facts remain hidden in an attorney's file and where production of those facts is essential to the preparation of one's case, discovery may properly be had. . . . And production might be justified where the witnesses are no longer available or may be reached only with difficulty." 329 U.S., at 511, 67 S.Ct., at 394.

The Government stresses that interviewees are scattered across the globe and that Upjohn has forbidden its employees to answer questions it considers irrelevant. The above-quoted language from *Hickman,* however, did not apply to "oral statements made by witnesses . . . whether presently in the form of [the attorney's] mental impressions or memoranda." Id., at 512, 67 S.Ct., at 394. As to such material the Court did "not believe that any showing of necessity can be made under the circumstances of this case so as to justify production. . . . If there should be a rare situation justifying production of these matters petitioner's case is not of that type." Id., at 512–513, 67 S.Ct., at 394–395. See also *Nobles,* supra, 422 U.S., at 252–253, 95 S.Ct., at 2177 (White, J., concurring). Forcing an attorney to disclose notes and memoranda of witnesses' oral statements is particularly disfavored because it tends to reveal the attorney's mental processes, 329 U.S., at 513, 67 S.Ct., at 394–395 ("what he saw fit to write down regarding witnesses' remarks"); id., at 516–517, 67 S.Ct., at 396 ("the statement would be his [the attorney's] language, permeated with his inferences") (Jackson, J., concurring).[8]

Rule 26 accords special protection to work product revealing the attorney's mental processes. The Rule permits disclosure of documents and tangible things constituting attorney work product upon a showing of substantial need and inability to obtain the equivalent without undue hardship. This was the standard applied by the Magistrate. Rule 26 goes on, however, to state that "[i]n ordering discovery of such materials when the required showing has been made, the court shall protect against disclosure of the mental impressions, conclusions, opinions or legal theories of an attorney or other representative of a party concerning the litigation." Although this language does not specifically refer to memoranda based on oral statements of witnesses, the *Hickman* court stressed the danger that compelled disclosure of such memoranda would reveal the attorney's mental processes. It is clear that this is the sort of material the draftsmen of the Rule had in mind as deserving special protection. See Notes of Advisory Committee on 1970 Amendment to Rules, 28 U.S.C.App., p. 442 * * *.

Based on the foregoing, some courts have concluded that *no* showing of necessity can overcome protection of work product which is based on oral statements from witnesses. See, e.g., In re Grand Jury Proceedings, 473 F.2d 840, 848 (C.A.8 1973) (personal recollections, notes and memoranda pertaining to conversation with witnesses); In re Grand Jury Investigation, 412 F.Supp. 943, 949 (E.D.Pa.1976) (notes of conversation with witness "are so much a product of the lawyer's thinking and so little probative of the witness's actual words that they are absolutely protected from disclosure"). Those courts declining to adopt an absolute rule have nonetheless recognized that such material is entitled to special protection. See, e.g., In re Grand Jury Investigation, 599 F.2d 1224, 1231 (C.A.3 1979) ("special considerations . . . must shape any ruling on the discoverability of interview memoranda . . . ; such documents will be

---

[8]   Thomas described his notes of the interviews as containing "what I consider to be the important questions, the substance of the responses to them, my beliefs as to the importance of these, my beliefs as to how they related to the inquiry, my thoughts as to how they related to other questions. In some instances they might even suggest other questions that I would have to ask or things that I needed to find elsewhere." 78–1 USTC ¶ 9277, p. 83,599.

discoverable only in a 'rare situation' "); Cf. In re Grand Jury Subpoena, 599 F.2d, at 511–512.

We do not decide the issue at this time. It is clear that the Magistrate applied the wrong standard when he concluded that the Government had made a sufficient showing of necessity to overcome the protections of the work-product doctrine. The Magistrate applied the "substantial need" and "without undue hardship" standard articulated in the first part of Rule 26(b)(3). The notes and memoranda sought by the Government here, however, are work product based on oral statements. If they reveal communications, they are, in this case, protected by the attorney-client privilege. To the extent they do not reveal communications, they reveal the attorneys' mental processes in evaluating the communications. As Rule 26 and *Hickman* make clear, such work product cannot be disclosed simply on a showing of substantial need and inability to obtain the equivalent without undue hardship.

While we are not prepared at this juncture to say that such material is always protected by the work-product rule, we think a far stronger showing of necessity and unavailability by other means than was made by the Government or applied by the magistrate in this case would be necessary to compel disclosure. * * *

[The concurring opinion of Burger, C.J., is omitted.]

NOTE ON THE WORK-PRODUCT DOCTRINE

1.   **Rule 26(b)(3).** As indicated in the introductory note, when *Hickman* was decided, the federal discovery rules provided no explicit protection for work-product materials. As the Court saw it, the material sought fell "outside the arena of discovery." In 1970, the Federal Rules of Civil Procedure were amended specifically to include the work-product doctrine. Under current Rule 26(b)(3), a party may not obtain in discovery material "prepared in anticipation of litigation or for trial by or for another party or its representative (including the other party's attorney, consultant, surety, indemnitor, insurer, or agent)" unless the party seeking discovery "has substantial need for the materials to prepare its case and cannot, without undue hardship, obtain their substantial equivalent by other means." Like a claim of privilege, a work-product claim must be made expressly and in enough detail to permit an assessment of the claim. Fed. R. Civ. P. 26(b)(5). Thirty-four states have adopted verbatim the work-product formulation contained in the version of Rule 26(b)(3) that predated the 2007 stylistic amendments. 8 Wright, Miller, & Marcus, Federal Practice & Procedure § 2023 nn. 27–28 (2008).

2.   **Compare the work-product doctrine and the attorney-client privilege.** The work-product doctrine and the attorney-client privilege are different in scope. The work-product doctrine only protects materials prepared in anticipation of litigation, whereas the attorney-client privilege protects communications made in connection with legal advice of any kind, whether or not related to litigation. On the other hand, the work-product doctrine covers information from other sources than the client, notably witness statements and document compilations. The work-product doctrine can be overcome if the information either cannot be obtained from other sources or can only be obtained with great difficulty, but there is no exception

to the attorney-client privilege based on the unavailability of the information from other sources.

3. **Coverage of Rule 26(b)(3). a. "Documents and tangible things."** Rule 26(b)(3) explicitly confers work-product protection on "documents and tangible things." What about an attorney's unrecorded recollection of a witness statement? Assume that a witness has made a statement to a party's attorney, which the attorney remembers clearly even though she did not write it down. For example, suppose a bartender had told Fortenbaugh that the master of the J.M. Taylor had been drinking heavily on the night of the accident. The adverse party then submits an interrogatory that calls for information covered in that witness statement. Is the statement protected as work product even though it is neither a "document" nor a "tangible thing"? The Court in *Hickman* sends a mixed message on whether such an unrecorded recollection is protected as work product. On the one hand, it protects "oral statements made by witnesses to Fortenbaugh, whether presently in the form of his mental impressions or memoranda." On the other, it states that "full and honest answers" to plaintiff's "broad inquiries would necessarily have included all pertinent information gleaned by [Fortenbaugh's] interviews with the witnesses." Courts appear to be divided on the question. Compare In re Pfohl Bros. Landfill Litig., 175 F.R.D. 13 (W.D.N.Y. 1997) (intangible work product not protected) with Maynard v. Whirlpool Corp., 160 F.R.D. 85 (S.D. W. Va. 1995) (intangible work product sought by deposition is protected). Should the issue of protection for information gathered from witnesses depend on how the question is asked? Is a request for "any information concerning the physical condition of the master or crew on the night of the accident" less objectionable than one which reads, "tate whether any member of the crew had been drinking?" Is an inquiry by interrogatory less objectionable than one by deposition? See Shapiro, Some Problems of Discovery in an Adversary System, 63 Minn. L. Rev. 1055, 1066–1072 (1979). See also Cooper, Work Product of the Rulemakers, 53 Minn. L. Rev. 1269, 1301 (1969).

b. **"Prepared in anticipation of litigation."** The Advisory Committee notes to Rule 26(b)(3) state that the rule provides no protection for materials prepared "in the ordinary course of business, or pursuant to public requirements unrelated to litigation, or for other nonlitigation purposes." The distinction is often important in cases involving insurance companies, who routinely investigate every claim made by or against an insured, APL Corp. v. Aetna Cas. & Sur. Co., 91 F.R.D. 10, 21 (D. Md. 1980), or involving organizational investigations of claims of discrimination, conducted pursuant to an internal equal opportunity policy. Long v. Anderson University, 204 F.R.D. 129 (D. Ind. 2001) (no protection), Miller v. Federal Express Corp., 186 F.R.D. 376 (W.D. Tenn. 1999) (same), Onwuka v. Federal Express Corp., 178 F.R.D. 508 (D. Minn. 1997) (same). To obtain work-product protection in such cases, it is not enough to show that documents were prepared in response to a specific claim: the person claiming immunity must show that the document "can fairly be said to have been prepared or obtained because of the prospect of litigation." 8 C. Wright, A. Miller & R. Marcus, Federal Practice & Procedure § 2024 (2014). Not infrequently work product prepared in anticipation of one case is later requested in another case that was not anticipated at the time of the original litigation. Earlier cases held that immunity was not available. But the weight of authority now holds that the material should be protected. Id.

What if mental impressions or legal theories are included in a document prepared as part of a company's normal course of business? The D.C. Circuit has held that such content was protected attorney work product. United States v. Deloitte LLP, 610 F.3d 129 (D.C. Cir. 2010) (holding that protection applies to material prepared in anticipation of litigation contained in regular annual audit). But courts have been loath to apply the protection to documents created in the normal course of business that do not contain legal strategies or observations about potential litigation. See Jumpsport, Inc. v. Jumpking, Inc., 213 F.R.D. 329 (N.D. Cal. 2004).

c. **"By or for another party or by or for that other party's representative."** Under Rule 26(b)(3), work product need not be prepared by a lawyer. See United States v. Deloitte LLP, 610 F.3d 129 (D.C. Cir. 2010) (applying protection to materials prepared by independent auditor). The rule in some states is narrower. Cal.C.Civ.P. § 2018.010 et seq. (extending protection only to "the work product of an attorney"); see also Bank of the Orient v. Superior Court, 67 Cal.App.3d 588, 136 Cal.Rptr. 741 (1977) (work-product protection not applicable where document was not prepared by an attorney or the agent of an attorney).

4. **Overcoming the work-product protection.** The question reserved in *Upjohn* concerning the showing required to compel disclosure of opinion work product has not made its way back to the Supreme Court. What kind of showing should be required to compel production of opinion work product? Those courts that have compelled disclosure of such information have limited disclosure to cases in which the lawyer's own views and conduct are directly at issue. Ferrara & DiMercurio, Inc. v. St. Paul Mercury Ins. Co., 173 F.R.D. 7 (D. Mass. 1997) (plaintiff claimed that defendant insurer had acted in bad faith in failing to settle a claim; attorney's mental impressions were directly relevant to determining the defendant's state of mind); see 8 Wright, Miller & Marcus, Federal Practice & Procedure § 2026 (2008).

5. **Further reading.** On the work product doctrine generally, see 8 Wright, Miller & Marcus §§ 2021 et seq.; Epstein, The Attorney-Client Privilege and the Work-Product Doctrine (4th ed. 2001); Beardslee, Taking the Business out of Work Product, 79 Fordham L. Rev. 1869 (2011); Thornburg, Rethinking Work Product, 77 Va. L. Rev. 1515 (1991); Special Project, The Work Product Doctrine, 68 Cornell L.Rev. 760 (1983).

3. DISCOVERY FROM EXPERTS

INTRODUCTORY NOTE ON EXPERT TESTIMONY AT TRIAL

1. **The role of the expert witness.** In American civil litigation, expert witnesses do not testify to the underlying facts of the dispute. Instead they offer judgments or opinions about what those evidentiary facts tend to establish. Expert witnesses are heavily used in civil litigation. Their testimony is often crucial to liability, causation, and damage issues. In some important classes of litigation, such as professional malpractice cases, the plaintiff ordinarily cannot proceed to trial unless she can present a qualified expert who will testify that the defendant's conduct failed to meet the applicable standard of professional care. Indeed, as a respected federal magistrate judge has recently written, "The federal courtroom has been overrun by experts." Lynch, Doctoring the Testimony: Physicians, Rule 26 and the Challenges of Causation Testimony, 33 Rev. Litig. 249 (2014).

A study of routine civil jury trials in California found that experts testified in 86% of all trials, and that in trials where experts were used an average of 3.8 experts testified. In two thirds of the cases where an expert testified for one party (57% of all cases), there was an expert in the same general field who testified for the opposing party, so that the jury was required to resolve a conflict in the views of experts from the same field. Gross, Expert Evidence, 1991 Wis. L. Rev. 1113, 1119–20.

Many experts are professional or semi-professional witnesses:

> Nearly 60% of the appearances by expert witnesses in California Superior Court civil jury trials were by witnesses who testified in such cases at least two times over a six-year period. For a particular appearance before a jury, the average number of times the same expert testified over a six-year period was 9.4; the median was 2.2. It is important to note that these numbers greatly underrepresent the experts' total experience in litigation. They do not, for instance, include testimony in criminal trials or in civil trials in courts other than California State Superior Courts. More important, the numbers do not catch the many cases in which the same experts were consulted, wrote reports, or even testified in depositions, but failed to testify in court because the cases were settled or dismissed before trial.
>
> One way to put the trial experience of witnesses in perspective is to compare it to that of trial lawyers. Judging from 1985–86 cases, when an attorney examines an expert witness in a civil jury trial in California, the expert is twice as likely to have testified in another such case in the preceding six months as the attorney is to have tried one (42% to 21%).

Id. at 1120.

2. **The use and misuse of expert witnesses.** Claimed misuse of expert witnesses is both an old, and a very modern, problem. In the overwhelming majority of cases, testifying experts are retained, prepared to testify, and compensated by the party who presents their testimony, raising serious concerns about bias. In an article arguing for mandatory use of neutral court-appointed expert witnesses, Professor Gross begins with a passage from J. Taylor, Treatise on the Law of Evidence (1848): " '[P]erhaps the testimony which least deserves credit with a jury is that of *skilled witnesses*. . . . [I]t is often quite surprising to see with what facility, and to what extent, their views can be made to correspond with the wishes and interests of the parties who call them.' " Id. at 1114 (emphasis in original).

In recent decades, as a role of scientific expert testimony has become more prominent, concern with bias has combined with concern about the legitimacy of some claims of expert knowledge. Professor Gross recounts the use of expert testimony in a modern product liability case, Wells by Maihafer v. Ortho Pharmaceutical Corp., 615 F. Supp. 262 (N.D. Ga. 1985):

> The main plaintiff, Katie Laurel Wells, was born with severe birth defects; her mother had used Ortho-Gynol Contraceptive Jelly—a spermicide manufactured by the defendant—both before and after Katie Wells' unplanned conception. [The judge, sitting without a jury, entered judgment for plaintiff of $5.1 million

dollars, which was reduced on appeal to $4.7 million. The Supreme Court denied certiorari.]

The contested issues in the *Wells* case turned entirely on conflicting expert testimony. [District] Judge Shoob explained carefully how he evaluated this evidence:

> [T]he Court considered each expert's background, training, experience, and familiarity with the circumstances of this particular case; and the Court evaluated the rationality and internal consistency of each expert's testimony in light of all the evidence presented. The Court paid close attention to each expert's demeanor and tone. Perhaps most important, the Court did its best to ascertain the motives, biases, and interests that might have influenced each expert's opinion.

This careful and methodical analysis led directly to the judgment: "With few exceptions, the Court found the testimony of plaintiffs' experts generally to be competent, credible, and directed to the specific circumstances of this case. The testimony of defendant's experts, in contrast, often indicated bias or inconsistency."

* * *

In most respects, Judge Shoob's opinion in *Wells* is a first rate specimen of judicial craft. It is clear, detailed and carefully reasoned. In form and manner, it is a model of what common law judges are supposed to do when they decide cases. Its content, however, is another matter. Unfortunately, Judge Shoob's decision is absolutely wrong. There is no scientifically credible evidence that Ortho-Gynol Contraceptive Jelly ever causes birth defects.

Id. at 1121–22.

3. Controlling expert testimony through qualification standards. An expert must be qualified by the court in order to testify. A full examination of the admissibility of expert-witness testimony is best left to the course in Evidence, but a brief primer will help you understand the special discovery rules for experts. Federal Rule of Evidence 702 provides:

> If scientific, technical, or other specialized knowledge will assist the trier of fact to understand the evidence or to determine a fact in issue, a witness qualified as an expert by knowledge, skill, experience, training, or education, may testify thereto in the form of an opinion or otherwise.

Rule 702 addresses the concern that expert testimony will carry substantial weight with a jury. As Judge Gertner has explained, "a certain patina attaches to an expert's testimony unlike any other witness; this is 'science,' a professional's judgment, the jury may think and give more credence to the testimony than it may deserve." United States v. Hines, 55 F. Supp. 2d 62, 64 (D. Mass. 1999).

Ordinarily, an expert must demonstrate her qualifications through evidence concerning her formal training or experience in the field in question. She also must demonstrate that the opinion she seeks to offer is sufficiently reliable. Prior to 1993 the standard most often followed by courts for determining the admissibility came from Frye v. United States, 293 F. 1013 (D.C. Cir. 1923). In *Frye*, the court opined:

> Just when a scientific principle or discovery crosses the line between the experimental and demonstrable stages is difficult to define. Somewhere in this twilight zone the evidential force of the principle must be recognized, and while the courts will go a long way in admitting experimental testimony deduced from a well-recognized scientific principle or discovery, the thing from which the deduction is made must be sufficiently established to have gained *general acceptance in the particular field in which it belongs.*

noted in class

Id. at 1014 (emphasis added). This "general acceptance" principle is intended to keep, in essence, "junk science" from presentation to a jury, which might give it more credit than it deserves. Put yourself in the role of a trial-court judge. From that perspective, how easy is it to apply the *Frye* test? What about from the perspective of an attorney?

In 1993, the Supreme Court held that Rule 702 superseded the common-law *Frye* test in Daubert v. Merrell Dow Pharmaceuticals, 509 U.S. 579, 113 S.Ct. 2786, 125 L.Ed.2d 469 (1993). In *Daubert*, the plaintiffs sought to present expert testimony that a prescription drug, Bendectin, caused birth defects, despite the lack of any published scientific studies so concluding. The Court held that the lack of published studies supporting the plaintiff's position did not automatically prevent their experts from qualifying under Rule 702.

According to *Daubert*, a judge presented with scientific testimony must make a preliminary assessment of the scientific validity and applicability of the testimony. The Court offered a non-exclusive list of factors to be considered, including whether the theory or technique in question can be (and has been) tested, whether it has been subjected to peer review and publication, its known or potential error rate and the existence and maintenance of standards controlling its operation, and whether it has attracted widespread acceptance within a relevant scientific community. The Court emphasized that "[v]igorous cross-examination, presentation of contrary evidence, and careful instruction on burden of proof are the traditional and appropriate means of attacking shaky but admissible evidence." 509 U.S. at 597. The standard for appellate review of a decision to admit or exclude expert scientific testimony under *Daubert* is whether the district court has abused its discretion. General Electric Co. v. Joiner, 522 U.S. 136, 118 S.Ct. 512, 139 L.Ed.2d 508 (1997). Moreover, the Court has made clear that the *Daubert* test applies to all expert testimony, whether or not that expertise might be considered "scientific" or not. Kumho Tire Co. v. Carmichael, 526 U.S. 137, 119 S.Ct. 1167, 143 L.Ed.2d 238 (1999) (applying *Daubert* test to testimony of "tire failure analyst" in product liability case). Is the *Daubert* test more or less liberal in its attitude toward expert testimony than *Frye*?

noted in class

Due to the deferential standard of review of *Joiner*, Rule 702 places a significant burden on the trial judge to play an active "gatekeeping role" by assessing the expert evidence. The result is that litigation of parties' "*Daubert* motions," i.e., motions to exclude expert evidence, is extensive (and expensive). Some judges have chafed at the responsibility placed on them to assess the reliability of scientific evidence, and others have argued that judges are ill-equipped to play that role. Do you agree that *Daubert* is more difficult to apply than *Frye*? Is this role any more challenging, or are judges any more ill-suited to perform this function than many others we require them to perform? See Bernstein, The Misbegotten Judicial Resistance to the *Daubert* Revolution, 89 Notre Dame L. Rev. 27 (2013); Allen & Nafisi, *Daubert* and its Discontents, 76 Brook. L. Rev. 131 (2010).

Some states continue to follow the *Frye* test for admissibility of expert testimony, such as New York. See Cornell v. 360 W. 51st St. Realty, LLC, 22 N.Y.3d 762, 9 N.E.3d 884 (2014). But the trend is toward widespread adoption of the *Daubert* test. See, e.g., Stephan, Out of the *Frye*-ing Pan: Florida Adopts the *Daubert* Standard for Admission of Expert Testimony, 4 Trial Advocate Q. 22 (2013). California has long stuck with the *Frye* approach, but there are signs that it might be leaning in the direction of adopting *Daubert*. See Faigman & Imwinkelried, Wading into the *Daubert* Tide: *Sargon Enterprises, Inc. v. University of Southern California*, 64 Hastings L.J. 1665 (2012).

4. Discovery from testifying experts. Given concerns about professional witnesses, bias, and scientific unreliability, and the importance of effective cross examination in combating all three, it is not surprising that the federal Rules reflect a steady broadening of discovery from and about testifying experts. Under the current federal rules, the identity of an expert witness who will present evidence at trial must be disclosed without a specific request from the other side. Fed. R. Civ. P. 26(a)(2)(A). Expert witnesses who are "retained or specially employed to provide expert testimony in the case" or "whose duties as the party's employee regularly involve giving expert testimony" must prepare and sign a report containing "(i) a complete statement of all opinions the witness will express and the basis and reasons for them; (ii) the data or other information considered by the witness in forming them; (iii) any exhibits that will be used * * *; (iv) the witness's qualifications, * * *; (v) a list of all other cases in which, during the preceding four years, the witness has testified as an expert; and (vi) a statement of the compensation to be paid for the study and testimony in the case." Fed. R. Civ. P. 26(a)(2)(B). These disclosures will ordinarily be made in accordance with a court-ordered discovery schedule, but must in any event be made no later than 90 days before trial. Fed. R. Civ. P. 26(a)(2)(C). Experts not required to submit a report under Rule 26(a)(2)(B) (usually those not retained for the purpose of providing expert testimony, such as a treating physician) need only disclose the subject matter and a summary of the facts and opinions on which they are expected to testify, as opposed to a more extensive report. Fed. R. Civ. P. 26(a)(2)(C).

A party may depose any person who has been identified as an expert by an opposing party and whose opinions may be presented at trial. Any deposition of the expert takes place only after the expert's report has been made available to the deposing party. Fed. R. Civ. P. 26(b)(4)(A). The deposing party is required to pay the expert a reasonable fee for the time spent on the deposition. Fed. R. Civ. P. 26(b)(4)(E).

The 2010 Amendments to Rule 26 make clear that the work-product protections of Rule 23(b)(3) apply to drafts of any expert report or disclosure, and to the communications between an expert providing a report and counsel for the party, except for communications (a) concerning compensation of the expert, (b) that identify facts or data provided by the attorney that the expert considered in forming the opinions expressed in the report, or (c) that identify assumptions provided by the attorney in forming the opinions to be expressed. Fed. R. Civ. P. 26(b)(4)(C).

Why do you suppose the Rules provide for such extensive disclosure and discovery of expert-witness testimony? What incentives do these Rules, and their exceptions, create for parties in preparation of expert testimony?

The required disclosures of Rule 26(a)(2) explicitly apply only to expert witnesses "a party may use at trial," as do the requirements and protections of Rules 26(b)(4)(A)–(C). What discovery is available from expert witnesses a party has consulted who will not be used at trial? Read carefully Rule 26(b)(4)(D) and then the following primary case. (Note that prior to 2010, the content of Rule 26(b)(4)(D) was found at 26(b)(4)(B). Don't let the renumbering of the Rule trip you up; the relevant content of the Rule has not changed, and *Ager* remains the leading case.)

Ager v. Jane C. Stormont Hospital and Training School for Nurses

United States Court of Appeals, Tenth Circuit, 1980.
622 F.2d 496.

■ BARRETT, CIRCUIT JUDGE.

Lynn R. Johnson, counsel for plaintiff Emily Ager, appeals from an order of the District Court adjudging him guilty of civil contempt. Jurisdiction vests by reason of 28 U.S.C.A. § 1826(b).

Emily was born April 4, 1955, at Stormont-Vail Hospital in Topeka, Kansas. During the second stage of labor, Emily's mother suffered a massive rupture of the uterine wall. The ensuing loss of blood led to Mrs. Ager's death. Premature separation of the placenta from the uterine wall also occurred, resulting in fetal asphyxia. Following Emily's delivery, it was discovered that she evidenced signs of severe neurological dysfunction. Today, she is mentally impaired and a permanently disabled quadraplegic with essentially no control over her body functions.

In March, 1977, Emily's father filed, on her behalf, a complaint for the damages sustained at her birth. The complaint alleges, in essence, that "the hemorrhaging and resultant death of her mother and the brain damage and other injuries which she sustained * * * while still in her mother's womb and/or during her delivery, were directly and proximately caused by the negligence and carelessness of the defendants (Stormont-Vail Hospital and Dr. Dan L. Tappen, the attending physician) which joined and concurred in causing plaintiff's mother's death and plaintiff's bodily injuries and damages and resultant disability." After joining the issues, Dr. Tappen propounded a series of interrogatories to the plaintiff. The specific interrogatories at issue here are:

    1.   Have you contacted any person or persons, whether they are going to testify or not, in regard to the care and treatment rendered by Dr. Dan Tappen involved herein?

    2.   If the answer to the question immediately above is in the affirmative, please set forth the name of said person or persons and their present residential and/or business address.

3.   If the answer to question #1 is in the affirmative, do you have any statements or written reports from said person or persons?

In response, plaintiff filed written objections, accompanied by a lengthy brief. Dr. Tappen answered the plaintiff's objections. The answer brief was treated by the United States Magistrate as a motion for an order compelling discovery pursuant to Fed.Rules Civ.Proc., rule 37(a), 28 U.S.C.A. Following his review, the Magistrate ordered the plaintiff to answer the interrogatories.* * *

Plaintiff's counsel answered the interrogatories in part, but failed to provide any information concerning consultative experts not expected to testify at trial. Plaintiff apparently based the refusal to answer on her contention that an expert who advises a party that his opinion will not aid the party in the trial of the case falls within the definition of experts informally consulted but not retained or specially employed.

     * * *

Rather than complying with the Magistrate's order, Ager sought review by the District Court pursuant to 28 U.S.C.A. § 636(b)(1)(A). The District Court denied plaintiff's motion for review as untimely. On reconsideration, the Court affirmed the Magistrate's order:

> In the context of this malpractice case the question is whether plaintiff must identify each and every doctor, physician or medical expert plaintiff's counsel retained or specially employed during pretrial investigation and preparation. The courts have been divided on the issue. Compare Weiner v. Bache Halsey Stuart, Inc., 76 F.R.D. 624 (S.D.Fla.1977), Baki v. B. F. Diamond Const. Co., 71 F.R.D. 179 (D.Md.1976), Sea Colony, Inc. v. Continental Ins. Co., 63 F.R.D. 113 (D.Del.1974) and Nemetz v. Aye, 63 F.R.D. 66 (W.D.Penn.1974) with Guilloz v. Falmouth Hospital Ass'n, Inc., 21 F.R.Serv.2d 1367 (D.Mass.1976) and Perry v. W. S. Darley & Co., 54 F.R.D. 278 (E.D.Wis.1971). The Magistrate relied upon Baki and Nemetz, supra, and held the identities of persons retained or specially employed for an opinion(i.e. to whom some consideration had been paid) to be discoverable. We have again read the Magistrate's Order and the suggestions of counsel. We find plaintiff's argument based upon the Advisory Committee Notes to be unpersuasive. After reviewing the cases and the suggestions of counsel we cannot find the Magistrate's Order to be "contrary to law." (Parenthetical remark in original text).

Plaintiff's counsel filed a formal response to the Court's order and refused to comply. The Court thereafter entered a civil contempt order against Johnson. Johnson was committed to the custody of the United States Marshal until his compliance with the Court's order. Execution of the custody order was stayed pending appeal, after Johnson posted a recognizance bond. The Court specifically found that the appeal was not frivolous or taken for purposes of delay.

The issues on appeal are whether: (1) the District Court erred in adjudging Johnson guilty of civil contempt; and (2) a party may routinely discover the names of retained or specially employed consultative non-witness experts, pursuant to Fed.Rules Civ.Proc., rule 26(b)(4)(B), 28

U.S.C.A, absent a showing of exceptional circumstances justifying disclosure.

[The court's extensive discussion of the validity of the contempt order is omitted.]

Validity of the Underlying Order

Having held that the viability of the contempt citation depends upon the validity of the underlying order, we now turn to the issue of whether a party may routinely discover the identities of non-witness expert consultants absent a showing of exceptional circumstances justifying disclosure.

Fed.Rules Civ.Proc., rule 26, 28 U.S.C.A., governs the scope of discovery concerning experts or consultants. Subdivision (b)(4) separates these experts into four categories, applying different discovery limitations to each:

> (1) Experts a party expects to use at trial.* * *
>
> (2) Experts retained or specially employed in anticipation of litigation or preparation for trial but not expected to be used at trial. Except as provided in rule 35 for an examining physician, the facts and opinions of experts in this category can be discovered only on a showing of exceptional circumstances.
>
> (3) Experts informally consulted in preparation for trial but not retained. No discovery may be had of the names or views of experts in this category.
>
> (4) Experts whose information was not acquired in preparation for trial. This class, which includes both regular employees of a party not specially employed on the case and also experts who were actors or viewers of the occurrences that gave rise to suit, is not included within Rule 26(b)(4) at all and facts and opinions they have are freely discoverable as with any ordinary witness. (Footnotes omitted).

Wright & Miller, Federal Practice and Procedure: Civil § 2029, (hereinafter cited as Wright & Miller).

We are here concerned only with the second and third category of experts.

> A. *Discovery of Experts Informally Consulted,*
> *But Not Retained or Specially Employed*

No provision in Fed.Rules Civ.Proc., rule 26(b)(4), 28 U.S.C.A., expressly deals with non-witness experts who are informally consulted by a party in preparation for trial, but not retained or specially employed in anticipation of litigation. The advisory committee notes to the rule indicate, however, that subdivision (b)(4)(B) "precludes discovery against experts who (are) informally consulted in preparation for trial, but not retained or specially employed." We agree with the District Court that this preclusion not only encompasses information and opinions developed in anticipation of litigation, but also insulates discovery of the identity and other collateral information concerning experts consulted informally. * * * Wright & Miller, Civil § 2033; 4 Moore's Federal Practice para. 26.66(4); Graham, Discovery of Experts Under Rule 26(b)(4) of the

Federal Rules of Civil Procedure: Part One, an Analytical Study, 1976 U.Ill.L.F. 895, 938–939 (hereinafter cited as Graham, Part One).

Relying on Professor Graham's article, Ager urges that "an expert 'would be considered informally consulted if, for any reason, the consulting party did not consider the expert of any assistance', and that '(a) consulting party may consider the expert of no assistance because of his insufficient credentials, his unattractive demeanor, or his excessive fees.'" Brief of appellant at p. 37, quoting, Graham, Part One at pp. 939–940 n. 182. This view is, of course, at odds with the Trial Court's ruling that:

> The (commonly accepted meaning) of the term "informally consulted" necessarily implies a consultation without formality. If one makes an appointment with a medical expert to discuss a case or examine records and give advice or opinion for which a charge is made and the charge is paid or promised what is informal about such consultation? On the other hand, an attorney meets a doctor friend at a social occasion or on the golf course and a discussion occurs concerning the case no charge is made or contemplated no written report rendered such could clearly be an "informal consultation."

We decline to embrace either approach in its entirety. In our view, the status of each expert must be determined on an ad hoc basis. Several factors should be considered (1) the manner in which the consultation was initiated; (2) the nature, type and extent of information or material provided to, or determined by, the expert in connection with his review; (3) the duration and intensity of the consultative relationship; and, (4) the terms of the consultation, if any (e. g. payment, confidentiality of test data or opinions, etc.). Of course, additional factors bearing on this determination may be examined if relevant.

Thus, while we recognize that an expert witness' lack of qualifications, unattractive demeanor, excessive fees, or adverse opinions may result in a party's decision not to use the expert at trial, nonetheless, there are situations where a witness is retained or specifically employed in anticipation of litigation prior to the discovery of such undesirable information or characteristics. On the other hand, a telephonic inquiry to an expert's office in which only general information is provided may result in informal consultation, even if a fee is charged, provided there is no follow-up consultation.

The determination of the status of the expert rests, in the first instance, with the party resisting discovery. Should the expert be considered informally consulted, that categorization should be provided in response. The propounding party should then be provided the opportunity of requesting a determination of the expert's status based on an in camera review by the court. Inasmuch as the District Court failed to express its views on this question, we deem it appropriate to remand rather than attempt to deal with the merits of this issue on appeal. Dandridge v. Williams, 397 U.S. 471, 476 n. 6, 90 S.Ct. 1153, 1157 n. 6, 25 L.Ed.2d 491 (1970). If the expert is considered to have been only informally consulted in anticipation of litigation, discovery is barred.

B. *Discovery of the Identities of Experts Retained or Specially Employed*

Subdivision (b)(4)(B) of rule 26 specifically deals with non-witness experts who have been retained or specially employed by a party in anticipation of litigation. The text of that subdivision provides that "facts or opinions" of non-witness experts retained or specially employed may only be discovered upon a showing of "exceptional circumstances under which it is impracticable for the party seeking discovery to obtain facts or opinions on the same subject by other means." Inasmuch as discovery of the identities of these experts, absent a showing of exceptional circumstances, was not expressly precluded by the text of subdivision (b)(4)(B), the District Court found the general provisions of rule 26(b)(1) controlling. Subdivision (b)(1) provides:

(b) Scope of Discovery. Unless otherwise limited by order of the court in accordance with these rules, the scope of discovery is as follows:

(1) *In General.* Parties may obtain discovery regarding any matter, not privileged, which is relevant to the subject matter involved in the pending action, . . . including the . . . identity and location of persons having knowledge of any discoverable matter. . . .

The District Court's ruling on this issue follows Arco Pipeline Co. v. S/S Trade Star, supra; Weiner v. Bache Halsey Stuart, Inc., supra; Baki v. B. F. Diamond Const. Co., supra; and Sea Colony, Inc. v. Continental Ins. Co., supra. Several decisions, however, have held that rule 26(b)(4)(B) requires a showing of exceptional circumstances before names of retained or specially employed consultants may be discovered. The advisory committee notes indicate that the structure of rule 26 was largely developed around the doctrine of unfairness designed to prevent a party from building his own case by means of his opponent's financial resources, superior diligence and more aggressive preparation. Dr. Tappen contends that "(d)iscoverability of the identity of an expert retained or specially employed by the other party but who is not to be called to testify hardly gives the discovering party a material advantage or benefit at the expense of the opposing party's preparation. Once those identities are disclosed, the discovering party is left to his own diligence and resourcefulness in contacting such experts and seeking to enlist whatever assistance they may be both able and willing to offer." Brief of appellee at pp. 12–13. The drafters of rule 26 did not contemplate such a result:

Subdivision (b)(4)(B) is concerned only with experts retained or specially consulted in relation to trial preparation. Thus the subdivision precludes discovery against experts who were informally consulted in preparation for trial, but not retained or specially employed. As an ancillary procedure, a party may *on a proper showing* require the other party to name experts retained or specially employed, but not those informally consulted. [Emphasis supplied].

We hold that the "proper showing" required to compel discovery of a non-witness expert retained or specially employed in anticipation of litigation corresponds to a showing of "exceptional circumstances under which it is impracticable for the party seeking discovery to obtain facts or opinions on the same subject by other means." Fed.Rules Civ.Proc., rule 26(b)(4)(B).

There are several policy considerations supporting our view. Contrary to Dr. Tappen's view, once the identities of retained or specially employed experts are disclosed, the protective provisions of the rule concerning facts known or opinions held by such experts are subverted. The expert may be contacted or his records obtained and information normally non-discoverable, under rule 26(b)(4)(B), revealed. Similarly, although perhaps rarer, the opponent may attempt to compel an expert retained or specially employed by an adverse party in anticipation of trial, but whom the adverse party does not intend to call, to testify at trial. Kaufman v. Edelstein, 539 F.2d 811 (2d Cir. 1976).[6] The possibility also exists, although we do not suggest it would occur in this case, or that it would be proper, that a party may call his opponent to the stand and ask if certain experts were retained in anticipation of trial, but not called as a witness, thereby leaving with the jury an inference that the retaining party is attempting to suppress adverse facts or opinions. Finally, we agree with Ager's view that "(d)isclosure of the identities of (medical) consultative experts would inevitably lessen the number of candid opinions available as well as the number of consultants willing to even discuss a potential medical malpractice claim with counsel. . . . (I)n medical malpractice actions (perhaps) more than any other type of litigation, the limited availability of consultative experts and the widespread aversion of many health care providers to assist plaintiff's counsel require that, absent special circumstances, discovery of the identity of evaluative consultants be denied. If one assumes that access to informed opinions is desirable in both prosecuting valid claims and eliminating groundless ones, a discovery practice that would do harm to these objectives should not be condoned."

In sum, we hold that the identity, and other collateral information concerning an expert who is retained or specially employed in anticipation of litigation, but not expected to be called as a witness at trial, is not discoverable except as "provided in Rule 35(b)[7] or upon a showing of exceptional circumstances under which it is impracticable for the party seeking discovery to obtain facts or opinions on the same subject by other means."[8] Fed.Rules Civ.Proc., rule 26(b)(4)(B), 28

---

[6]   We do not here decide the propriety of this action.

[7]   Rule 35(b), Fed.Rules Civ.Proc., 28 U.S.C.A., deals with the exchange of information concerning physical or mental examinations of persons. These provisions are not at issue here.

[8]   Professor Albert Sacks, reporter to the advisory committee, listed two examples of exceptional circumstances at a Practising Law Institute Seminar on Discovery held in Atlanta, Georgia, September 25–26, 1970:

(a) Circumstances in which an expert employed by the party seeking discovery could not conduct important experiments and test(s) because an item of equipment, etc., needed for the test(s) has been destroyed or is otherwise no longer available. If the party from whom discovery is sought had been able to have its experts test the item before its destruction or nonavailability, then information obtained from those tests might be discoverable.

(b) Circumstances in which it might be impossible for a party to obtain its own expert. Such circumstances would occur when the number of experts in a field is small and their time is already fully retained by others.

See: ALI–ABA, Civil Trial Manual p. 189.

U.S.C.A. The party "seeking disclosure under Rule 26(b)(4)(B) carries a heavy burden" in demonstrating the existence of exceptional circumstances. Hoover v. United States Dept. of Interior, 611 F.2d 1132, 1142 n.13 (5th Cir. 1980).

Disposition

The order of the District Court adjudging Lynn R. Johnson guilty of civil contempt is vacated. The cause is remanded. On remand, the status of the non-witness experts against whom discovery is sought should be undertaken as a two-step process. First, was the expert informally consulted in anticipation of litigation but not retained or specially employed? If so, no discovery may be had as to the identity or opinions of the expert. Second, if the expert was not informally consulted, but rather retained or specially employed in anticipation of litigation, but not expected to testify at trial, do exceptional circumstances exist justifying disclosure of the expert's identity, opinions or other collateral information?

Vacated and remanded.

NOTE ON DISCOVERY OF NON-TESTIFYING EXPERTS

1. **Retained non-testifying experts.** Suppose that one of the defendant's non-testifying experts in *Ager,* prior to being retained, had overheard the defendant Dr. Tappen say at a cocktail party that "I screwed up the Ager case?" Would such information be protected by Rule 26(b)(4)(B)?

Conversely, what if the plaintiff's non-testifying expert had concluded, after being retained, that Dr. Tappen's conduct met the relevant standard of care? Would such information be protected by Rule 26(b)(4)(B)? What is the rationale for protecting the views of retained non-testifying experts, formed in anticipation of trial, from discovery? If the non-testifying expert's views differ from those of the testifying expert why shouldn't the finder of fact learn of that difference? Is there value in allowing lawyers and parties to hear unfavorable views from their retained experts without fear that their views will reach the tribunal? Do the same rationales that justify presumptive protection for the views of non-testifying experts also justify protecting their identities? The holding in *Ager* is the majority view, but not all courts agree. See Eisai Co., Ltd. V. Teva Pharmaceuticals USA, Inc., 247 F.R.D. 440 (D.N.J. 2007) (holding that disclosure of a non-testifying expert's name is required "upon a simple showing of relevance"). See also Wright, Miller, Kane & Marcus, Federal Practice & Procedure § 2032 (2014).

The court in *Ager* assumes that disclosure of the identities of non-testifying experts might make it possible for the opposing party to contact and obtain the opinions of a retained non-testifying expert outside of the discovery process, although it reserves judgment on the propriety of such contact. The authorities now make it clear that such efforts are an improper attempt to interfere with a confidential relationship and can result in disqualification if the lawyer making the contact obtains protected work product or trial strategy of the opponent. Cordy v. Sherwin-Williams Co., 156 F.R.D. 575 (D.N.J. 1994); Shadow Traffic Network v. Superior Ct., 24 Cal.App.4th 1067, 29 Cal.Rptr.2d 693 (1994). Given this law, which makes informal contact with an opposing party's retained expert into something of a minefield for counsel, are there still reasons to want to protect the identity of non-testifying retained experts? Might malpractice plaintiffs find it more difficult to obtain the opinions of a non-testifying doctor if it were widely known in the medical community that the doctor did consulting work for malpractice claimants?

What counts as an exceptional circumstance justifying the disclosure of the identity and opinions of a non-testifying expert? What if the expert had access in the course of her work to evidence that is no longer available? What if a showing were made that no other qualified expert could be found who was willing to offer expert testimony on the topic? See R.C. Olmstead, Inc. v. CU Interface, LLC, 657 F. Supp. 2d 899 (N.D. Ohio 2009).

Former Senator (and once Vice-Presidential nominee) John Edwards of North Carolina had an extended career as a trial lawyer representing plaintiffs. One of his specialties was medical malpractice. In one medical malpractice case, Edwards' associate contacted 41 obstetricians. "Of these thirty-six either flatly refused to testify, would not return [the associate's] calls, or waffled so badly they essentially disqualified themselves as witnesses. That left five who were willing to testify. Of these, two were from in state, and one rambled so badly that we knew we couldn't put him on the stand. So our arsenal of home-grown OBs numbered exactly one." J. Edwards, Four Trials 68 (2003). Are exceptional circumstances demonstrated when there is a showing that a party has consulted with multiple experts in an apparent effort to find a favorable opinion? Coates v. AC & S, Inc., 133 F.R.D. 109 (E.D. La. 1990), held that proof that defendant had asked multiple pathologists to examine slides containing tissue samples taken from the plaintiff's deceased husband to determine the cause of death constituted a form of "shopping" for expertise and demonstrated exceptional circumstances warranting disclosure of the identities and opinions of the non-testifying experts. Is this result consistent with *Ager*? Does it represent sound policy? For an excellent discussion of these issues, see Gelbach, Expert Mining and Required Disclosure, 81 U. Chi. L. Rev. 131 (2014).

Note also that employing multiple experts may lead to the creation of discoverable material. Recently, the Eleventh Circuit held that the work-product doctrine does not protect an expert's "personal notes and communications with other experts." See Republic of Ecuador v. Hinchee, 741 F.3d 1185 (11th Cir. 2013).

2. Informally consulted experts. What rationale justifies a total ban on any discovery of informal consultations with experts that do not result in retaining the expert? What benefits would flow from free discoverability of informal consultations with experts? What harms might result from making such conversations discoverable?

Langbein, The German Advantage in Civil Procedure
52 U. Chi. L. Rev. 823, 835–40 (1985).

IV. EXPERTS

The European jurist who visits the United States and becomes acquainted with our civil procedure typically expresses amazement at our witness practice. His amazement turns to something bordering on disbelief when he discovers that we extend the sphere of partisan control to the selection and preparation of experts. In the Continental tradition experts are selected and commissioned by the court, although with great attention to safeguarding party interests. In the German system, experts are not even called witnesses. They are thought of as "judges' aides."

Perverse incentives. At the American trial bar, those of us who serve as expert witnesses are known as "saxophones." This is a revealing term, as slang often is. The idea is that the lawyer plays the tune, manipulating the expert as though the expert were a musical instrument on which the lawyer sounds the desired notes. I sometimes serve as an expert in trust and pension cases, and I have experienced the subtle pressures to join the team—to shade one's views, to conceal doubt, to overstate nuance, to downplay weak aspects of the case that one has been hired to bolster. Nobody likes to disappoint a patron; and beyond this psychological pressure is the financial inducement. Money changes hands upon the rendering of expertise, but the expert can run his meter only so long as his patron litigator likes the tune. Opposing counsel undertakes a similar exercise, hiring and schooling another expert to parrot the contrary position. The result is our familiar battle of opposing experts. The more measured and impartial an expert is, the less likely he is to be used by either side.

At trial, the battle of experts tends to baffle the trier, especially in jury courts. If the experts do not cancel each other out, the advantage is likely to be with the expert whose forensic skills are the more enticing. The system invites abusive cross-examination. Since each expert is party-selected and party-paid, he is vulnerable to attack on credibility regardless of the merits of his testimony. A defense lawyer recently bragged about his technique of cross-examining plaintiffs' experts in tort cases. Notice that nothing in his strategy varies with the truthfulness of the expert testimony he tries to discredit:

> A mode of attack ripe with potential is to pursue a line of questions which, by their form and the jury's studied observation of the witness in response, will tend to cast the expert as a "professional witness." By proceeding in this way, the cross-examiner will reap the benefit of a community attitude, certain to be present among several of the jurors, that bias can be purchased, almost like a commodity.

Thus, the systematic incentive in our procedure to distort expertise leads to a systematic distrust and devaluation of expertise. Short of forbidding the use of experts altogether, we probably could not have designed a procedure better suited to minimize the influence of expertise.

The Continental tradition. European legal systems are, by contrast, expert-prone. Expertise is frequently sought. The literature emphasizes the value attached to having expert assistance available to the courts in an age in which litigation involves facts of ever-greater technical difficulty. The essential insight of Continental civil procedure is that credible expertise must be neutral expertise. Thus, the responsibility for selecting and informing experts is placed upon the courts, although with important protections for party interests.

Selecting the expert. German courts obtain expert help in lawsuits the way Americans obtain expert help in business or personal affairs. If you need an architect, a dermatologist, or a plumber, you do not commission a pair of them to take preordained and opposing positions on your problem, although you do sometimes take a second opinion. Rather, you take care to find an expert who is qualified to advise you in an objective manner; you probe his advice as best you can; and if you find his advice persuasive, you follow it.

When in the course of winnowing the issues in a lawsuit a German court determines that expertise might help resolve the case, the court selects and instructs the expert. The court may decide to seek expertise on its own motion, or at the request of one of the parties. The code of civil procedure allows the court to request nominations from the parties—indeed, the code requires the court to use any expert upon whom the parties agree—but neither practice is typical. In general, the court takes the initiative in nominating and selecting the expert.

The only respect in which the code of civil procedure purports to narrow the court's discretion to choose the expert is a provision whose significance is less than obvious: "If experts are officially designated for certain fields of expertise, other persons should be chosen only when special circumstances require." One looks outside the code of civil procedure, to the federal statutes regulating various professions and trades, for the particulars on official designation. For the professions, the statutes typically authorize the official licensing bodies to assemble lists of professionals deemed especially suited to serve as experts. In other fields, the state governments designate quasi-public bodies [such as the regional chamber of commerce and industry] to compile such lists. * * *

Current practice. In 1984 I spent a little time interviewing judges in Frankfurt about their practice in selecting experts. My sample of a handful of judges is not large enough to impress statisticians, but I think the picture that emerges from serious discussion with people who operate the system is worth reporting. Among the judges with whom I spoke, I found unanimity on the proposition that the most important factor predisposing a judge to select an expert is favorable experience with that expert in an earlier case. Experts thus build reputations with the bench. Someone who renders a careful, succinct, and well-substantiated report and who responds effectively to the subsequent questions of the court and the parties will be remembered when another case arises in his specialty. Again we notice that German civil procedure tracks the patterns of decision-making in ordinary business and personal affairs: If you get a plumber to fix your toilet and he does it well, you incline to hire him again.

When judges lack personal experience with appropriate experts, I am told, they turn to the authoritative lists described above. If expertise is needed in a field for which official lists are unavailing, the court is thrown upon its own devices. The German judge then gets on the phone, working from party suggestions and from the court's own research, much in the fashion of an American litigator hunting for expertise. In these cases there is a tendency to turn, first, to the bodies that prepare expert lists in cognate areas; or, if none, to the universities and technical institutes.

If enough potential experts are identified to allow for choice, the court will ordinarily consult party preferences. * * * [A] litigant can formally challenge an expert's appointment only on the narrow grounds for which a litigant could seek to recuse a judge.

Preparing the expert. The court that selects the expert instructs him, in the sense of propounding the facts that he is to assume or to investigate, and in framing the questions that the court wishes the expert to address. In formulating the expert's task, as in other important steps in the conduct of the case, the court welcomes adversary suggestions. If the expert should take a view of premises (for example, in an accident case or a building-construction dispute), counsel for both sides will accompany him.

Safeguards. The expert is ordinarily instructed to prepare a written opinion. When the court receives that report, it is circulated to the litigants. The litigants commonly file written comments, to which the expert is asked to reply. The court on its own motion may also request the expert to amplify his views. If the expert's report remains in contention, the court will schedule a hearing at which counsel for a dissatisfied litigant can confront and interrogate the expert.

The code of civil procedure reserves to the court the power to order a further report by another expert if the court should deem the first report unsatisfactory. A litigant dissatisfied with the expert may encourage the court to invoke its power to name a second expert. * * * When, therefore, a litigant can persuade the court that an expert's report has been sloppy or partial, that it rests upon a view of the field that is not generally shared, or that the question referred to the expert is exceptionally difficult, the court will commission further expertise.

A litigant may also engage his own expert, much as is done in the Anglo-American procedural world, in order to rebut the court-appointed expert. The court will discount the views of a party-selected expert on account of his want of neutrality, but cases occur in which he nevertheless proves to be effective. Ordinarily, I am told, the court will not in such circumstances base its judgment directly upon the views of the party-selected expert; rather, the court will treat the rebuttal as ground for engaging a further court-appointed expert (called an *Oberexperte,* literally an "upper" or "superior" expert), whose opinion will take account of the rebuttal.

To conclude: In the use of expertise German civil procedure strikes an adroit balance between nonadversarial and adversarial values. Expertise is kept impartial, but litigants are protected against error or caprice through a variety of opportunities for consultation, confrontation, and rebuttal.

NOTE ON COURT-APPOINTED EXPERTS

1. **The case for and against court-appointed experts.** The traditional argument for the use of partisan experts argues that "all witnesses, regardless of who engaged them, identify closely with their own opinions, and unintentionally introduce, as a result, a certain degree of bias and deviation from their oath to tell the truth, the whole truth and nothing but the truth." Diamond, The Fallacy of the Impartial Expert, 3 Archives of Crim. Psychodynamics 221 (1959). In addition, it is argued that court-appointed experts will tend to be biased toward establishment points of view or to be less well funded and hence less thorough than party chosen and financed experts. Id.

In recent years, there has been strong academic support for increased use of court-appointed experts on grounds similar to those advanced by Professor Langbein. Gross, Expert Evidence, 1991 Wis. L. Rev. 1113. Professor Bernstein suggests that court-appointed experts ought to be appointed to assist judges is deciding whether parties' expert witnesses meet the standard required by *Daubert* under Federal Rule of Evidence 702. Bernstein, Expert Witnesses, Adversarial Bias, and (Partial) Failure of the *Daubert* Revolution, 93 Iowa L. Rev. 451 (2008). Professor Robertson has suggested that the judge appoint a third-party intermediary who would select experts based on fact patterns provided by the parties, a sort of "double blind" selection of experts. Robertson, Blind Expertise, 85 N.Y.U. L. Rev. 174 (2010).

Despite the academic critiques and creative proposals, courts appoint such experts only rarely. Professor Gross offers an explanation:

> The essential flaw in the existing schemes for appointment of experts is the absence of incentives to use them. Appointed experts are never required; they are a luxury that can be added to the existing apparatus. Judges, even lawyers, may favor the practice in principle, but in the heat of a particular case appointed experts are always dispensable. Worse, both judges and lawyers have strong motives to avoid them. Judges do not want to take on the tasks of seeking out witnesses and shaping their evidence, either because they lack the time and resources (or think they do), or because they feel it would be inappropriate, or for both reasons. Lawyers are disturbed by witnesses they cannot control. A voluntary procedure for appointing witnesses may be an attractive vehicle for obtaining impartial expert evidence; however, between the passivity of judges and the hostility of trial lawyers, it has no motor.

Id. at 1220. Professor Gross suggests that requiring the exclusive use of court-appointed experts would be politically unacceptable because it is too strongly counter to American traditions of party control of litigation, and suggests alternative means of decoupling expertise from the control of the parties. Id. at 1220–31.

In an illuminating recent article discussing the use of economic experts in antitrust cases, Professor Haw countered the recent enthusiasm for court-appointed experts:

> [There is] an obvious and perhaps devastating criticism of court-appointed expert witnesses: judges, like parties, are biased when it comes to choosing economic experts. For the parties, bias comes most powerfully from wanting to win, but for the judge, the source of bias is ideological. Economics, because of its tendency to make contingent claims rather than prove scientific truths, and because of its redistributive consequences, is political. In a world where judges appoint expert economists, we would expect an antitrust minimalist to testify at every Republican appointee's trial and a pro-liability/pro-regulation witness to testify at every Democratic appointee's trial. This might give antitrust trials some predictability, but not the kind we are looking for.
>
> Even a nonbiased judge will have a difficult time determining whether an expert represents the majority view. What criteria should she use in determining the status of an expert's opinion?

Most experts who want to be hired will want to describe themselves as occupying the heartland of economic thought. So in looking for help, a judge would have to make the very judgments she needs help for, resulting in a kind of "experimenter's regress." Rule 706 also has serious practical limitations. One theory put forth for why judges so infrequently use Rule 706 is that they do not know how to go about finding a reliable expert. There is no "yellow pages" of neutral, reliable practitioners of economics. And Rule 706 requires both parties to share the cost of the appointed expert, which has given some judges pause when the means of the parties are unequal.

Haw, Adversarial Economics in Antitrust Litigation: Losing Academic Consensus in the Battle of the Experts, 106 Nw. U. L. Rev. 1261, 1294 (2012).

2.   Recent uses of court-appointed experts. Perhaps the most prominent use of court-appointed experts in recent years was in connection with the Federal Breast Implant Multi-District Litigation. After the cases were transferred to a single court for pretrial purposes, the district judge commissioned a National Science Panel consisting of three experts from relevant fields. The panel produced a lengthy report finding that current scientific knowledge provided no support for the claim that silicone breast implants caused systemic disease. For an account of these cases, see Hooper, Cecil & Willging, Assessing Causation in Breast Implant Litigation: The Role of Science Panels, 64 Law & Contemp. Probs. 139 (2001). See also Hall v. Baxter Healthcare Corp., 947 F. Supp. 1387 (D. Or. 1996) (judge appointed technical advisors to assist the court in assessing evidence on causation).

C. CONFIDENTIALITY, PRIVACY AND PREVENTION OF HARASSMENT

AN INTRODUCTORY NOTE ON CONFIDENTIALITY

1.   Commercial confidentiality and discovery. Litigation often involves information whose disclosure or misuse could cause substantial damage to the party producing it. If the information falls outside the protection of any privilege or trial-preparation immunity, the remedy for the producing party is normally to seek a formal protective order from the court barring discovery of the material or restricting its use and dissemination by the party to whom the information is produced.

As the Supreme Court has recognized, "orders forbidding any disclosure of trade secrets or confidential commercial information are rare." Federal Open Market Committee v. Merrill, 443 U.S. 340, 363 n.24, 99 S.Ct. 2800, 61 L.Ed.2d 587 (1979); In re Cooper Tire & Rubber Co., 568 F.3d 1180 (10th Cir. 2009). If the information sought is relevant to a disputed issue in the case, a court will normally order production of the material. A vivid example is Coca-Cola Bottling Co. v. Coca-Cola Co., 107 F.R.D. 288 (D. Del. 1985). In a contractual dispute between Coca-Cola bottlers and Coca-Cola concerning the pricing of syrup for New Coke and Diet Coke, the bottlers sought to prove similarities between those products and Classic Coke and to that end sought to discover the formula for "the ingredient that gives Coca-Cola its distinctive taste * * * a secret combination of flavoring oils and ingredients known as 'Merchandise 7X.'" The court described Coca-Cola's submission in support of its motion for a protective order barring discovery:

To satisfy its burden of proving that the Coca-Cola formulae qualify for trade secret protection, defendant has submitted the affidavit of Robert A. Keller, Senior Vice President and General Counsel of the Company. According to the Keller affidavit, the Company has taken every precaution to prevent disclosure of the formula for "Merchandise 7X," the secret ingredient in old Coke. The written version of the secret formula is kept in a security vault at the Trust Company Bank in Atlanta, and that vault can only be opened by a resolution from the Company's Board of Directors. It is the Company's policy that only two persons in the Company shall know the formula at any one time, and that only those persons may oversee the actual preparation of Merchandise 7X. The Company refuses to allow the identity of those persons to be disclosed or to allow those persons to fly on the same airplane at the same time. The same precautions are taken regarding the secret formulae of the Company's other cola drinks—diet Coke, caffeine free diet Coke, TAB, caffeine free TAB, and caffeine free Coca-Cola. The secret formula for each drink is only known to three or four persons in the Company. Similar precautions attend the experimental formulae sought by plaintiffs.

The Keller affidavit further states that these secret formulae are highly valued assets of the Company and have never been disclosed to persons outside the Company. As an indication of the value the Company places on its secret formulae, Keller avers that the Company elected to forego producing Coca-Cola in India, a potential market of 550 million persons, because the Indian government required the Company to disclose the secret formula for Coca-Cola as a condition of doing business there.

Id. at 294.

The Court held that Merchandise 7X was a trade secret, but also found that it was relevant to disputed issues in the litigation. Noting that "[e]xcept for a few privileged matters, nothing is sacred in civil litigation," the court ordered that the formula be produced subject to an appropriate protective order restricting its use and dissemination. Id. at 290. Coca-Cola then refused to produce the relevant formulas, and the court awarded sanctions in the form of an order precluding Coca-Cola from contending that the secret formulas for the old and new products were different. Coca-Cola Bottling Co. v. Coca-Cola Co., 107 F.R.D. 288 (D. Del. 1985).

2.   Personal privacy. Discovery can also involve invasion of personal privacy. The most intrusive such invasions are the physical or mental examinations. The following case deals with the issues raised by such examinations.

Vinson v. Superior Court

Supreme Court of California, 1987.
43 Cal.3d 833, 239 Cal.Rptr. 292, 740 P.2d 404.

■ MOSK, JUSTICE.

The plaintiff in a suit for sexual harassment and intentional infliction of severe emotional distress petitions for a writ of mandate and/or prohibition to direct respondent court to forbid her pending psychiatric examination, or in the alternative to protect her from any inquiry into her sexual history, habits, or practices. She also requests that her attorney be allowed to attend the examination if it is held. We conclude that the examination should be permitted but that a writ should issue to restrict its scope. We further conclude that her counsel should not be present.

Plaintiff is a 59-year-old widow who in 1979 applied for a job in Oakland with a federally funded program, administered at the time by defendant Peralta Community College District, under the direction of co-defendant Grant. Plaintiff alleges that Grant, during an interview with her in a private cubicle, commented on how attractive she appeared for a woman of her age. He assertedly made some salacious observations regarding her anatomy and expressed his desires with regard thereto. He allegedly concluded the interview by intimating that acquiring the position was subject to a condition precedent: her acquiescence to his sexual yearnings. Plaintiff claims she declined his advances as unconscionable and left greatly distraught.

Unknown to Grant, plaintiff was later hired by defendant college district as a certification technician. She asserts that once he discovered she was working for the program, he had her transferred to the payroll unit, a position for which he apparently knew she had no training. Soon thereafter he terminated her employment.

Plaintiff filed suit on several causes of action, among them sexual harassment, wrongful discharge, and intentional infliction of emotional distress. Defendants' actions are said to have caused her to suffer continuing emotional distress, loss of sleep, anxiety, mental anguish, humiliation, reduced self-esteem, and other consequences.

Defendants moved for an order compelling her to undergo a medical and a psychological examination.[1] The examinations were meant to test the true extent of her injuries and to measure her ability to function in the workplace. Plaintiff opposed the motion as a violation of her right to privacy. In the alternative, if the court were to permit the examination she requested a protective order shielding her from any probing into her sexual history or practices, and asked that her attorney be allowed to attend in order to assure compliance with the order. The court granted the motion without imposing any of these limitations. Plaintiff petitioned the Court of Appeal for a writ of prohibition and/or mandate to direct the trial court to forbid the examination or to issue appropriate protective orders. The Court of Appeal denied the petition.

We use prerogative writs in discovery matters only to review questions that are of general importance to the trial courts and the profession, and when broad principles can be enunciated to guide the courts in future cases. As we shall see, intervening legislative enactments have partially resolved some of the issues raised by this petition. Nonetheless, important questions remain regarding the right of a defendant in a case alleging sexual harassment and emotional distress to conduct discovery and a plaintiff's countervailing right to privacy.

---

[1] We use the terms "psychiatric," "psychological" and "mental" examination interchangeably for the purposes of this issue.

I. *The Appropriateness of a Mental Examination*

Plaintiff first contends the psychiatric examination should not be permitted because it infringes on her right to privacy. Before we can entertain this constitutional question, we must determine the statutory scope of the discovery laws.[2]

Code of Civil Procedure section 2032, subdivision (a)[3], permits the mental examination of a party in any action in which the mental condition of that party is in controversy. Plaintiff disputes that her mental condition is in controversy. She points to Cody v. Marriott Corp. (D.Mass.1984) 103 F.R.D. 421, 422, a case interpreting rule 35(a) of the Federal Rules of Civil Procedure. Like the California rule that was patterned on it, rule 35 requires that physical or mental condition be "in controversy" before an examination is appropriate.[4] *Cody* was an employment discrimination case in which the plaintiffs alleged mental and emotional distress. The court held that the claim of emotional distress did not ipso facto place the plaintiff's mental state in controversy.

The reasoning of *Cody* rested in large part on Schlagenhauf v. Holder (1964) 379 U.S. 104, 85 S.Ct. 234, 13 L.Ed.2d 152, in which the United States Supreme Court examined the "in controversy" requirement. In *Schlagenhauf* the plaintiffs were passengers injured when their bus collided with the rear of a truck. The defendant truck company, in answer to a cross-claim by the codefendant bus company, charged that the bus driver had been unfit to drive and moved to have him undergo a mental and physical examination. The Supreme Court recognized that at times the pleadings may be sufficient to put mental or physical condition in controversy, as when a plaintiff in a negligence action alleges mental or physical injury. (Id. at p. 119, 85 S.Ct. at p. 243.) But it determined that the driver had not asserted his mental condition in support of or in a defense of a claim, nor did the general charge of negligence put his mental state in controversy. (Id. at pp. 119–122, 85 S.Ct. at pp. 243–245.) *Schlagenhauf* thus stands for the proposition that one party's unsubstantiated allegation cannot put the mental state of another in controversy.

It is another matter entirely, however, when a party places his *own* mental state in controversy by alleging mental and emotional distress. Unlike the bus driver in *Schlagenhauf,* who had a controversy thrust upon him, a party who chooses to allege that he has mental and emotional difficulties can hardly deny his mental state is in controversy. To the extent the decision in *Cody,* supra, 103 F.R.D. 421, is inconsistent

---

[2] Part 4, title 3, chapter 3, article 3, of the Code of Civil Procedure (§§ 2016–2036.5), the applicable legislation on depositions and discovery at the time this action began, has been repealed. (Stats.1986, ch. 1334, § 1.) The repeal was operative July 1, 1987, on which date a new article 3 (entitled the Civil Discovery Act of 1986) came into effect. The act provides, however, that the use of a discovery method initiated before July 1, 1987, will be governed by the law regulating that method at the time it was initiated. (Stats.1987, ch. 86, § 20). We must therefore apply the superseded discovery procedures to this case. But as we shall show by appropriate references to the new act, many of its relevant provisions are substantially similar.

[3] Unless otherwise noted, all further statutory references are to the Code of Civil Procedure, and this and all further references to sections 2016 to 2036 refer to the version of those sections operative until July 1, 1987.

[4] Because section 2032 was based on federal rule 35, judicial construction of the federal rule may be useful in construing section 2032. (Reuter v. Superior Court (1979) 93 Cal.App.3d 332, 337, 155 Cal.Rptr. 525.)

with this conclusion, we decline to follow it. (See also Reuter v. Superior Court, supra, 93 Cal.App.3d at p. 340, 155 Cal.Rptr. 525.)

In the case at bar, plaintiff haled defendants into court and accused them of causing her various mental and emotional ailments. Defendants deny her charges. As a result, the existence and extent of her mental injuries is indubitably in dispute. In addition, by asserting a causal link between her mental distress and defendants' conduct, plaintiff implicitly claims it was not caused by a preexisting mental condition, thereby raising the question of alternative sources for the distress. We thus conclude that her mental state is in controversy.

We emphasize that our conclusion is based solely on the allegations of emotional and mental damages in this case. A simple sexual harassment claim asking compensation for having to endure an oppressive work environment or for wages lost following an unjust dismissal would not normally create a controversy regarding the plaintiff's mental state. To hold otherwise would mean that every person who brings such a suit implicitly asserts he or she is mentally unstable, obviously an untenable proposition.

Determining that the mental or physical condition of a party is in controversy is but the first step in our analysis. In contrast to more pedestrian discovery procedures, a mental or physical examination requires the discovering party to obtain a court order. The court may grant the motion only for good cause shown. (§ 2032, subd. (a).)[5]

Section 2036 defines a showing of "good cause" as requiring that the party produce specific facts justifying discovery and that the inquiry be relevant to the subject matter of the action or reasonably calculated to lead to the discovery of admissible evidence.[6] The requirement of a court order following a showing of good cause is doubtless designed to protect an examinee's privacy interest by preventing an examination from becoming an annoying fishing expedition. While a plaintiff may place his mental state in controversy by a general allegation of severe emotional distress, the opposing party may not require him to undergo psychiatric testing solely on the basis of speculation that something of interest may surface. (Schlagenhauf v. Holder, supra, 379 U.S. at pp. 116–122, 85 S.Ct. at pp. 241–245.)

Plaintiff in the case at bar asserts that she continues to suffer diminished self-esteem, reduced motivation, sleeplessness, loss of appetite, fear, lessened ability to help others, loss of social contacts, anxiety, mental anguish, loss of reputation, and severe emotional distress. In their motion defendants pointed to these allegations. Because the truth of these claims is relevant to plaintiff's cause of action and justifying facts have been shown with specificity, good cause as to these assertions has been demonstrated. Subject to limitations necessitated by plaintiff's right to privacy, defendants must be allowed to investigate the continued existence and severity of plaintiff's alleged damages.

---

[5]   After July 1, 1987, this requirement is contained in section 2032, subdivision (d).

[6]   This section has been repealed and has apparently not been replaced by equivalent language. There is no indication, however, that the Legislature intended repeal of former section 2036 to change the requirements for good cause in regard to mental examinations.

II. *Privacy Limitations on the Scope of a Mental Examination*

If we find, as we do, that an examination may be ordered, plaintiff urges us to circumscribe its scope to exclude any probing into her sexual history, habits, or practices. Such probing, she asserts, would intrude impermissibly into her protected sphere of privacy. Furthermore, it would tend to contravene the state's strong interest in eradicating sexual harassment by means of private suits for damages. An examination into a plaintiff's past and present sexual practices would inhibit the bringing of meritorious sexual harassment actions by compelling the plaintiff— whose privacy has already been invaded by the harassment—to suffer another intrusion into her private life.

A right to privacy was recognized in the seminal case of Griswold v. Connecticut (1965) 381 U.S. 479, 85 S.Ct. 1678, 14 L.Ed.2d 510. It protects both the marital relationship (ibid.) and the sexual lives of the unmarried (Eisenstadt v. Baird (1972) 405 U.S. 438, 92 S.Ct. 1029, 31 L.Ed.2d 349). More significantly, California accords privacy the constitutional status of an "inalienable right," on a par with defending life and possessing property. (Cal.Const., art. I, § 1; White v. Davis (1975) 13 Cal.3d 757, 120 Cal.Rptr. 94, 533 P.2d 222.) California's privacy protection similarly embraces sexual relations. (See Fults v. Superior Court (1979) 88 Cal.App.3d 899, 152 Cal.Rptr. 210; Morales v. Superior Court (1979) 99 Cal.App.3d 283, 160 Cal.Rptr. 194.)

Defendants acknowledge plaintiff's right to privacy *in abstracto* but maintain she has waived it for purposes of the present suit. In addition, they urge us to take heed of their right to a fair trial, which they claim depends on a "meaningful" examination of plaintiff. Defendants contend they would not have requested a mental examination if plaintiff had simply brought a sexual harassment suit; but because she claims emotional and mental damage, they should be entitled to present expert testimony on the extent of the injury. Preparing such testimony, they suggest, requires not simply a mental examination, but one without substantial restrictions on its scope.

We cannot agree that the mere initiation of a sexual harassment suit, even with the rather extreme mental and emotional damage plaintiff claims to have suffered, functions to waive all her privacy interests, exposing her persona to the unfettered mental probing of defendants' expert. Plaintiff is not compelled, as a condition to entering the courtroom, to discard entirely her mantle of privacy. At the same time, plaintiff cannot be allowed to make her very serious allegations without affording defendants an opportunity to put their truth to the test.

In Britt v. Superior Court (1978) 20 Cal.3d 844, 143 Cal.Rptr. 695, 574 P.2d 766, we faced a similar conflict between discovery procedures and the parties' constitutional rights. The plaintiffs were property owners near an airport operated by the local port district. They sued the district for diminution of property values, personal injuries, and emotional disturbance brought about by the airport's activities. The defendant sought to discover the plaintiffs' entire medical history, including all illnesses, injuries, and mental or emotional disturbances for which they had sought treatment at any time in their lives. Furthermore, it asked for information regarding their membership in various community organizations.

Responding to the assertion that the plaintiffs had waived their right to privacy by bringing suit, we stated that "while the filing of a lawsuit may implicitly bring about a partial waiver of one's constitutional right of associational privacy, the scope of such 'waiver' must be narrowly rather than expansively construed, so that plaintiffs will not be unduly deterred from instituting lawsuits by the fear of exposure of their private associational affiliations and activities." (Id. at p. 859, 143 Cal.Rptr. 695, 574 P.2d 766.) Therefore, we noted, an implicit waiver of a party's constitutional rights encompasses only discovery directly relevant to the plaintiff's claim and essential to the fair resolution of the lawsuit. (Id. at p. 859, 143 Cal.Rptr. 695, 574 P.2d 766; see also In re Lifschutz (1970) 2 Cal.3d 415, 431, 85 Cal.Rptr. 829, 467 P.2d 557.)

Plaintiff's present mental and emotional condition is directly relevant to her claim and essential to a fair resolution of her suit; she has waived her right to privacy in this respect by alleging continuing mental ailments. But she has not, merely by initiating this suit for sexual harassment and emotional distress, implicitly waived her right to privacy in respect to her sexual history and practices. Defendants fail to explain why probing into this area is directly relevant to her claim and essential to its fair resolution. Plaintiff does not contend the alleged acts were detrimental to her present sexuality. Her sexual history is even less relevant to her claim. We conclude that she has not waived her right to sexual privacy.

But even though plaintiff retains certain unwaived privacy rights, these rights are not necessarily absolute. On occasion her privacy interests may have to give way to her opponent's right to a fair trial. Thus courts must balance the right of civil litigants to discover relevant facts against the privacy interests of persons subject to discovery. (Valley Bank of Nevada v. Superior Court (1975) 15 Cal.3d 652, 657, 125 Cal.Rptr. 553, 542 P.2d 977.)

Before proceeding, we note the Legislature recently enacted a measure designed to protect the privacy of plaintiffs in cases such as these. Section 2036.1 (operative until July 1, 1987; presently, substantially the same provision is contained in § 2017, subdivision (d)), provides that in a civil suit alleging conduct that constitutes sexual harassment, sexual assault, or sexual battery, any party seeking discovery concerning the plaintiff's sexual conduct with individuals other than the alleged perpetrator must establish specific facts showing good cause for that discovery, and that the inquiry is relevant to the subject matter and reasonably calculated to lead to the discovery of admissible evidence.[7] (See also Priest v. Rotary (N.D.Cal.1983) 98 F.R.D. 755.) We must determine whether the general balancing of interests embodied in this new legislation has obviated the need for us to engage in an individualized balancing of privacy with discovery in the case at bar.

In enacting the measure, the Legislature took pains to declare that "The discovery of sexual aspects of complainant's [sic] lives, as well as

---

[7]   Although the motion to order an examination was made before this provision went into effect, we apply the section to the case at bar because procedural changes generally govern pending as well as future cases. (Woodland Hills Residents Assn., Inc. v. City Council (1979) 23 Cal.3d 917, 930–932, 154 Cal.Rptr. 503, 593 P.2d 200; Pacific Vegetable Oil Corp. v. C.S.T., Ltd. (1946) 29 Cal.2d 228, 232–233, 174 P.2d 441; Sour v. Superior Court (1934) 1 Cal.2d 542, 545, 36 P.2d 373.)

those of their past and current friends and acquaintances, has the clear potential to discourage complaints and to annoy and harass litigants. . . . without protection against it, individuals whose intimate lives are unjustifiably and offensively intruded upon might face the 'Catch-22' of invoking their remedy only at the risk of enduring further intrusions into the details of their personal lives in discovery. . . . [¶] . . . Absent extraordinary circumstances, inquiry into those areas should not be permitted, either in discovery or at trial." (Stats.1985, ch. 1328, § 1.)[8]

Nowhere do defendants establish specific facts justifying inquiry into plaintiff's zone of sexual privacy or show how such discovery would be relevant. Rather they make only the most sweeping assertions regarding the need for wide latitude in the examination. Because good cause has not been shown, discovery into this area of plaintiff's life must be denied. Section 2036.1, thus amply protects plaintiff's privacy interests. We anticipate that in the majority of sexual harassment suits, a separate weighing of privacy against discovery will not be necessary. It should normally suffice for the court, in ruling on whether good cause exists for probing into the intimate life of a victim of sexual harassment, sexual battery, or sexual assault, to evaluate the showing of good cause in light of the legislative purpose in enacting this section and the plaintiff's constitutional right to privacy.

III. *Presence of Counsel*

In the event a limited psychiatric examination is proper, plaintiff urges us to authorize the attendance of her attorney. She fears that the examiner will stray beyond the permitted area of inquiry. Counsel would monitor the interview and shield her from inappropriate interrogation. And depicting the examination as an "alien and frankly hostile environment," she asserts that she needs her lawyer to provide her with aid and comfort.

Defendants, joined by amici California Psychiatric Association and Northern California Psychiatric Association, counter that a meaningful mental examination cannot be conducted with an attorney interposing objections. And if plaintiff's counsel is present, defense counsel would also seek to attend. Defendants maintain these adversaries would likely convert the examination into a chaotic deposition.

We contemplated whether counsel must be allowed to attend the psychiatric examination of a client in Edwards v. Superior Court (1976) 16 Cal.3d 905, 130 Cal.Rptr. 14, 549 P.2d 846. The plaintiff in *Edwards* alleged that because of the defendant school district's failure to properly instruct and supervise users of school equipment, she sustained physical and emotional injuries. The trial court granted a motion compelling her to undergo a psychiatric examination alone. Holding that the plaintiff

---

[8]   Plaintiff suggests that section 2036.1 does not adequately protect her privacy interests because section 2032 already requires "good cause" for a mental examination, and nothing is added by again requiring good cause for inquiry into a plaintiff's sexual history and practices. But the above-quoted legislative declaration accompanying section 2036.1, i.e., that inquiry into sexuality should not be permitted absent "extraordinary circumstances," suggests that a stronger showing of good cause must be made to justify inquiry into this topic than is needed for a general examination. Furthermore, section 2032 merely requires good cause for the examination as a whole; in emotional distress cases that will often be present. By contrast, a defendant in a sexual harassment case desiring to ask sex-related questions must show specific facts justifying that particular inquiry.

could not insist on the presence of her counsel, a majority of this court denied her petition for a peremptory writ.

The plaintiff in *Edwards* raised many of the points urged upon us here. She asserted that her attorney should be present to protect her from improper inquiries. We were skeptical that a lawyer, unschooled in the ways of the mental health profession, would be able to discern the psychiatric relevance of the questions. And the examiner should have the freedom to probe deeply into the plaintiff's psyche without interference by a third party. (Id. at p. 911, 130 Cal.Rptr. 14, 549 P.2d 846.) The plaintiff further suggested counsel should be present to lend her comfort and support in an inimical setting. We responded that an examinee could view almost any examination of this sort, even by her own expert, as somewhat hostile. Whatever comfort her attorney's handholding might afford was substantially outweighed by the distraction and potential disruption caused by the presence of a third person. (Ibid.) Finally, we concluded counsel's presence was not necessary to ensure accurate reporting. Verbatim transcription might inhibit the examinee, preventing an effective examination. Furthermore, other procedural devices—pretrial discovery of the examiner's notes or cross-examination, for example—were available for the plaintiff's protection. (Id. at pp. 911–912, 130 Cal.Rptr. 14, 549 P.2d 846.)

A number of federal courts have since pondered this question. The court in Zabkowicz v. West Bend Co. (E.D.Wis.1984) 585 F.Supp. 635, agreed that the plaintiff in an action charging sexual harassment and extreme emotional distress was entitled to have her attorney or a recording device present to ensure that the defendant's expert did not overstep his bounds. But in another federal case, Lowe v. Philadelphia Newspapers (E.D.Pa.1983) 101 F.R.D. 296, the court ruled the plaintiff could not have counsel present at the psychiatric examination, although she could have a psychiatrist or other medical expert as an observer. In *Lowe* there were indications the defense had engaged in offensive tactics during discovery, which may explain the court's willingness to allow third parties into the examination. In contrast, in Brandenberg v. El Al Israel Airlines (S.D.N.Y.1978) 79 F.R.D. 543, there were no signs portending abuse, and the court denied the plaintiff's request for the presence of her counsel. These cases suggest that in the federal courts a mental examinee has no absolute right to the presence of an attorney; but when the circumstances warrant it, the courts may fashion some means of protecting an examinee from intrusive or offensive probing.

Despite the dissent in *Edwards,* 16 Cal.3d 905, 914, 130 Cal.Rptr. 14, 549 P.2d 846 (dis. opn. by Sullivan, J. and Mosk, J.), we conclude that a reconsideration of that decision—which is barely 10 years old—is not justified.[9] We emphasize, however, that *Edwards* should be viewed as standing for the proposition that the presence of an attorney is not

---

[9] Section 2032, subdivision (g) (operative July 1, 1987), now specifically provides for the attendance of an attorney at a *physical* examination. (See Sharff v. Superior Court (1955) 44 Cal.2d 508, 282 P.2d 896.) Subdivision (g)(2) states, however, that nothing in the discovery statutes shall be construed to alter, amend, or affect existing case law with respect to the presence of counsel or other persons during a mental examination by agreement or court order. Had the Legislature felt it desirable to have counsel present at psychiatric examinations, it would certainly have provided for this in its thorough revision of the section. Indeed, in the course of that revision the Legislature considered and rejected a provision that would have annulled our decision in *Edwards* by permitting counsel to attend a mental examination.

Rule

required during a mental examination. In light of their broad discretion in discovery matters (see generally Greyhound Corp. v. Superior Court (1961) 56 Cal.2d 355, 15 Cal.Rptr. 90, 364 P.2d 266), trial courts retain the power to permit the presence of counsel or to take other prophylactic measures when needed.

Plaintiff makes no showing that the court abused its discretion in excluding her counsel from the examination. Her fears are wholly unfounded at this point; not a shred of evidence has been produced to show that defendants' expert will not respect her legitimate rights to privacy or might disobey any court-imposed restrictions. Plaintiff's apprehension appears to derive less from the reality of the proposed analysis than from the popular image of mental examinations.

Plaintiff's interests can be adequately protected without having her attorney present. In the first place, section 2032 requires the court granting a physical or mental examination to specify its conditions and scope. We must assume, absent evidence to the contrary, that the examiner will proceed in an ethical manner, adhering to these constraints. And if plaintiff truly fears that the examiner will probe into impermissible areas, she may record the examination on audio tape. This is an unobtrusive measure that will permit evidence of abuse to be presented to the court in any motion for sanctions.[10]

Plaintiff refers us to the history of psychiatric examinations for victims of sexual assault. Such examinations were widely viewed as inhibiting prosecutions for rape by implicitly placing the victim on trial, leading to a legislative prohibition of examinations to assess credibility. (Pen.Code, § 1112; see also Note, Psychiatric Examinations of Sexual Assault Victims: A Reevaluation (1982) 15 U.C.Davis L.Rev. 973.) The victim of sexual harassment is analogous to the prosecutrix in a rape case, plaintiff asserts, and she points to legislative findings that discovery of sexual aspects of complainants' lives "has the clear potential to discourage complaints." (Stats.1985, ch. 1328, § 1.) If we conclude on the basis of general considerations that a mental examination is appropriate and that it should occur without the presence of counsel, plaintiff urges us to adopt a special rule exempting those who bring harassment charges from either or both of these requirements.

We believe that in these circumstances such a special rule is unwarranted. In the first place, we should be guided by the maxim that *entia non sunt multiplicanda praeter necessitatem:* we should carve out exceptions from general rules only when the facts require it. The state admittedly has a strong interest in eradicating the evil of sexual harassment, and the threat of a mental examination could conceivably dampen a plaintiff's resolve to bring suit. But we have seen that those who allege harassment have substantial protection under existing procedural rules. In general it is unlikely that a simple sexual harassment suit will justify a mental examination. Such examinations may ordinarily be considered only in cases in which the alleged mental or emotional distress is said to be ongoing. When an examination is permitted, investigation by a psychiatrist into the private life of a

---

[10] We note that the new discovery act explicitly provides both examiners and examinees the opportunity to perpetuate the interview on audio tape. (§ 2032, subd. (g)(2) (operative July 1, 1987).)

plaintiff is severely constrained, and sanctions are available to guarantee those restrictions are respected.

Finally, the mental examination in this case largely grows out of plaintiff's emotional distress claim. We do not believe the state has a greater interest in preventing emotional distress in sexual harassment victims than it has in preventing such distress in the victims of any other tort.

* * *

NOTE ON PROTECTIVE ORDERS AND THE PUBLIC INTEREST

1. Standard provisions in protective orders. As *Vinson* demonstrates, protective orders may sometimes prevent discovery of the information sought. More often, they allow discovery but restrict the use or dissemination of the information disclosed. Common provisions are those limiting the use of covered information to the preparation and trial of the lawsuit in which they are produced, restricting the persons to whom the information may be disclosed, for example, to parties, their lawyers, and expert witnesses in the case, or requiring that information be examined in a specific place or specific manner. Permitted uses or recipients may be narrowed still further for information that is particularly sensitive. Typically, those given access to information pursuant to a protective order, including nonparty witnesses, are required to sign a writing certifying that they have read the order, agree to abide by it, and submit to the jurisdiction of the court in the event of a violation.

2. Protective orders and the First Amendment. Because information generated through discovery often has public significance and because a protective order is a government regulation of whether and how that information can be disseminated, the First Amendment may be implicated. Protective orders are a form of prior restraint of speech, a kind of regulation that has traditionally been thought to require very strong justification. In Seattle Times Co. v. Rhinehart, 467 U.S. 20, 104 S.Ct. 2199, 81 L.Ed.2d 17 (1984), the trial court had ordered defendant newspaper not to publish or use for any non-litigation purpose confidential information obtained in discovery concerning the plaintiff. The Supreme Court held that the First Amendment did not prohibit "a protective order * * * entered upon a showing of good cause * * * limited to the context of pretrial civil discovery, [that] does not restrict the dissemination of information gained from other sources." Id. at 37. The Court reasoned that "judicial limitations on a party's ability to disseminate information discovered in advance of trial implicate the First Amendment rights of the restricted party to a far lesser extent than would restraints on dissemination of information in a different context." Id. at 34. The trial court's authority to issue protective orders upon a showing of good cause was necessary given the liberal scope of pretrial discovery and the need to protect legitimate privacy interests. Moreover, in the case of pretrial discovery documents, the First Amendment interest was weaker because "pretrial depositions and interrogatories are not public components of a civil trial." Id. at 33. See Post, The Management of Speech: Discretion and Rights, 1984 Sup. Ct. Rev. 169. Would the Court's rationale extend to allowing the court to keep under seal information relied upon in reaching a decision on the merits? To allowing a closed trial? See Westmoreland v. Columbia Broadcasting System, Inc., 752 F.2d 16 (2d Cir. 1984) (public has a First Amendment right to attend a civil trial); Publicker Indus. Inc. v. Cohen, 733 F.2d 1059 (3d Cir. 1984) (same).

3.   Protective orders and the public interest: the problem of settlement. Whether information discovered in a civil suit may be sealed by the court at the request of one or both of the parties is an important question in some cases. The issue is most acute in product liability, environmental and discrimination cases, where discovery can lead to production of information indicating that non-parties have been or are threatened by the practices or products of the defendant. Sometimes the plaintiff seeks to reveal information to parties or potential parties in other similar suits, or to the public at large. Sometimes, however, the plaintiff is willing to agree as part of a settlement that the information be kept confidential, and to join with the defendant in a motion to seal the court's records. The settlement offer by the defendant in such cases will likely be higher because of the plaintiff's agreement; in effect, the plaintiff is selling back to the defendant the right to conceal information revealed during discovery.

A judge has considerable leeway to issue protective orders that will seal court records, including materials obtained in discovery. See, e.g., Fed. R. Civ. P. 26(c). What policies should inform a judge's decision to seal a deposition, or to keep confidential other information discovered during litigation? Free public access to information obtained through the publicly funded adjudicatory process? Protection of the public from hazards that would otherwise remain unknown? Protection of the already problematic discovery system from further disruptive factors? Protection of the freedom of litigants on both sides to settle a case on terms that seem to them appropriate?

To some degree, federal courts have been willing to modify or disregard protective orders even without the assistance of special statutes. In Olympic Refining Co. v. Carter, 332 F.2d 260 (9th Cir. 1964), an earlier antitrust suit brought by the United States had resulted in the discovery of information covered by confidentiality orders. The court in the current case conceded that the defendants in the earlier case had "provided a fuller disclosure than might otherwise have been required of them, * * * in reliance upon the entry and continuing effectiveness of the protective orders," but it concluded that the orders were "subject to modification to meet the reasonable needs of other parties in other litigation." Id. at 264. *Olympic* was followed in Wilk v. American Medical Ass'n, 635 F.2d 1295, 1299 (7th Cir. 1980), which modified an earlier protective order, saying, "where an appropriate modification of a protective order can place private litigants in a position they would otherwise reach only after repetition of another's discovery, such modification can be denied only where it would tangibly prejudice substantial rights of the party opposing the modification." See also Foltz v. State Farm Mut. Auto. Ins. Co., 331 F.3d 1122 (9th Cir. 2003).

D. DISCOVERY ETHICS AND DISCOVERY SANCTIONS

Stevenson v. Union Pacific Railroad Co.

United States Court of Appeals, Eighth Circuit, 2004.
354 F.3d 739.

■ HANSEN, CIRCUIT JUDGE:

This case arises out of a car-train grade crossing accident in which Frank Stevenson was injured and his wife was killed. In this diversity lawsuit against the Union Pacific Railroad Company ("Union Pacific" or "the Railroad"), a jury awarded damages to Mr. Stevenson and Rebecca Harshberger as Administratrix of Mary Stevenson's estate on claims of negligence. * * * We affirm in part and reverse and remand for a new trial. * * *

I.

On November 6, 1998, a Union Pacific train struck the Stevensons' vehicle as it crossed the tracks on Highway 364 in Vanndale, Arkansas. Mrs. Stevenson died as a result of the collision, and Mr. Stevenson suffered severe injuries and has no memory of the accident. Mr. Stevenson and the administratrix of his wife's estate filed this action alleging that the accident was caused by Union Pacific's negligence. * * *

The plaintiffs filed a motion for sanctions on the ground that Union Pacific had destroyed evidence, namely, a voice tape of conversations between the train crew and dispatch at the time of the accident and track maintenance records from before the accident. Union Pacific argued that sanctions were not justified because it destroyed the documents in good faith pursuant to its routine document retention policies. The district court granted the motion following a three-day evidentiary hearing. The district court imposed sanctions of an adverse inference instruction regarding the destroyed evidence and an award of costs and attorneys' fees incurred as a result of the spoliation of evidence. Stevenson v. Union Pacific R.R., 204 F.R.D. 425 (E.D. Ark. 2001).

Prior to trial, the plaintiffs filed a motion in limine, seeking to prohibit Union Pacific from calling witnesses to explain that it destroyed the tape and track maintenance records pursuant to its routine document retention policies. The district court granted the motion and, at the outset of trial, orally instructed the jury that the voice tape and track inspection records "were destroyed by the railroad and . . . should have been preserved," and that the jurors "may, but are not required to, assume that the contents of the voice tapes and track inspection records would have been adverse, or detrimental, to the defendant." The district court thus permitted the plaintiffs to immediately reference the destroyed material and the fact that Union Pacific willfully destroyed it, but denied Union Pacific any opportunity to offer its routine document retention policy as an innocent explanation for its destruction of the evidence.

The parties stipulated that the only liability issues for trial were (1) whether the train sounded its horn appropriately, (2) whether the vegetation at the crossing obstructed Mr. Stevenson's view, and (3) whether the crossing surface was negligently maintained. At the close of trial, over Union Pacific's renewed objection, the district court repeated the spoliation instruction to the jury: "You may, but are not required to, assume that the contents of the voice tape and track inspection records would have been adverse, or detrimental, to the defendant." Union Pacific moved for judgment as a matter of law on the horn claim, asserting that there was insufficient evidence from which the jury could find that the alleged failure to sound the horn was a proximate cause of the accident. The district court denied the motion.

The jury returned a general verdict in favor of the plaintiffs, awarding Mr. Stevenson $2,000,000 in damages and awarding the estate $10,000 for funeral and ambulance expenses. The district court entered judgment on these amounts and also awarded the plaintiffs $164,410.25 in costs and attorneys' fees on the sanctions order. Union Pacific appeals, asserting that * * * the district court abused its discretion in giving the adverse inference instruction, and that the district court abused its discretion by ordering attorneys' fees as sanctions. * * *

II.

* * * Both prior to the filing of the lawsuit and during its pendency, Union Pacific destroyed two types of evidence—the tape of any recorded voice radio communications between the train crew and dispatchers on the date of the accident and all track maintenance records close in time to the accident. The district court imposed sanctions for this conduct under its inherent power by giving an adverse inference instruction, refusing to permit testimony to rebut the adverse inference, and imposing an award of attorneys' fees.

"We review a [district] court's imposition of sanctions under its inherent power for an abuse of discretion." Dillon v. Nissan Motor Co., 986 F.2d 263, 267 (8th Cir. 1993); see also Chambers v. NASCO, Inc., 501 U.S. 32, 111 S.Ct. 2123, 115 L.Ed.2d 27 (1991) (discussing the inherent powers of federal courts). A court's inherent power includes the discretionary "ability to fashion an appropriate sanction for conduct which abuses the judicial process." Chambers, 501 U.S. at 44–45, 111 S.Ct. 2123. Our interpretation of Supreme Court authority concerning a court's inherent power to sanction counsels that a finding of bad faith is not always necessary to the court's exercise of its inherent power to impose sanctions. Id. at 267; Harlan v. Lewis, 982 F.2d 1255, 1260 (8th Cir. 1993) (noting bad faith requirement does not extend "to every possible disciplinary exercise of the court's inherent power"). The Union Pacific argues that the sanctions were an abuse of discretion because it did not engage in bad faith conduct by destroying evidence pursuant to document retention policies. We will consider the extent to which a finding of bad faith is necessary separately below with regard to each type of sanction employed. Finally, "whether the extent of a sanction is appropriate is a question peculiarly committed to the district court." Dillon, 986 F.2d at 268.

1.   The Adverse Inference Instruction

At the close of trial, over Union Pacific's renewed objection and as a sanction for the destruction of records, the district court instructed the jury, "[y]ou may, but are not required to, assume that the contents of the voice tape and track inspection records would have been adverse, or detrimental, to the defendant." Union Pacific asserts that the sanction of giving an adverse inference instruction in this case amounted to an abuse of discretion, citing both federal and Arkansas law. We need not decide and do not reach any choice of law question in this case because the standard is the same under either state or federal law—there must be a finding of intentional destruction indicating a desire to suppress the truth. See Lewy v. Remington Arms Co., 836 F.2d 1104, 1111–12 (8th Cir. 1988). * * *

The district court imposed this sanction of an adverse inference instruction after concluding that Union Pacific destroyed the voice tape in bad faith, and that Union Pacific destroyed the track maintenance records in circumstances where it "knew or should have known that the documents would become material" and "should have preserved them". The district court reached these conclusions after discussing the factors set forth in Lewy, requiring the court to consider (1) whether the record retention policy is reasonable considering the facts and circumstances surrounding those documents, (2) whether lawsuits or complaints have been filed frequently concerning the type of records at issue, and (3) whether the document retention policy was instituted in bad faith. 836 F.2d at 1112.

* * * In support of this proposition, we quoted Gumbs v. Int'l Harvester, Inc., 718 F.2d 88, 96 (3d Cir. 1983), which states that the adverse inference from the destruction of evidence arises only where the destruction was intentional "and indicates a fraud and a desire to suppress the truth, and it does not arise where the destruction was a matter of routine with no fraudulent intent." * * * We have never approved of giving an adverse inference instruction on the basis of prelitigation destruction of evidence through a routine document retention policy on the basis of negligence alone. Where a routine document retention policy has been followed in this context, we now clarify that there must be some indication of an intent to destroy the evidence for the purpose of obstructing or suppressing the truth in order to impose the sanction of an adverse inference instruction. See Lewy, 836 F.2d at 1112.

The facts here are as follows. The accident occurred on November 6, 1998. The Stevensons filed this lawsuit on September 20, 1999, and mailed their requests for production of the voice tape on October 25, 1999. By that time, Union Pacific had long since destroyed the voice tape from the November 6, 1998, accident by recording over it in accordance with the company's routine procedure of keeping voice tapes for 90 days and then reusing the tapes. The district court found that although Union Pacific's voice tape retention policy was not unreasonable or instituted in bad faith, it was unreasonable and amounted to bad faith conduct for Union Pacific to adhere to the principle in the circumstances of this case.

[handwritten margin note: Reasoning of the district court]

In support of its bad faith determination, the district court found that Union Pacific had been involved in many grade crossing collisions and knew that the taped conversations would be relevant in any potential litigation regarding an accident that resulted in death and serious injury. There was evidence that Mike Reed, a claims representative for Union Pacific, had received notice of the accident shortly after it occurred, and he immediately began his investigation by calling the Railroad's Risk Management Communications Center to get details about the accident. He also called the Harriman Dispatching Center in Omaha to request copies of the train orders and warrants, the train consist, and a dispatcher's record of the train's movement. He did not, however, request a copy of the voice tape. The district court listened to available samples of this type of voice tape and found that they generally contain evidence that is discoverable and useful in developing a case. Additionally, the district court found that Union Pacific had preserved such tapes in cases where it was helpful to Union Pacific's position. The district court also found that the plaintiffs were prejudiced by the destruction of this tape because there are no other records of comments between the train crew and dispatch contemporaneous to the accident. The district court thus held that sanctions were justified and that an adverse inference instruction was an appropriate sanction for the destruction of the voice tape.

After considering the record and the particular circumstances of this case, we conclude that, while this case tests the limits of what we are able to uphold as a bad faith determination, the district court did not abuse its discretion by sanctioning Union Pacific's prelitigation conduct of destroying the voice tape. See Lewy, 836 F.2d at 1112 (stating that "even if the court finds the policy to be reasonable given the nature of the documents subject to the policy, the court may find that under the particular circumstances certain documents should have been retained notwithstanding the policy"). The district court's bad faith determination is supported by Union Pacific's act of destroying the voice tape pursuant to its routine policy in circumstances where Union Pacific had general knowledge that such tapes would be important to any litigation over an accident that resulted in serious injury or death, and its knowledge that litigation is frequent when there has been an accident involving death or serious injury. While these are quite general considerations, an important factor here is that a voice tape that is the only contemporaneous recording of conversations at the time of the accident will always be highly relevant to potential litigation over the accident. We conclude that this weighs heavier in this case than the lack of actual knowledge that litigation was imminent at the time of the destruction. Additionally, the record indicates that Union Pacific made an immediate effort to preserve other types of evidence but not the voice tape, and the district court noted that Union Pacific was careful to preserve a voice tape in other cases where the tape proved to be beneficial to Union Pacific. The prelitigation destruction of the voice tape in this combination of circumstances, though done pursuant to a routine retention policy, creates a sufficiently strong inference of an intent to destroy it for the purpose of suppressing evidence of the facts surrounding the operation of the train at the time of the accident.

There must be a finding of prejudice to the opposing party before imposing a sanction for destruction of evidence. Dillon, 986 F.2d at 267. The requisite element of prejudice is satisfied by the nature of the evidence destroyed in this case. While there is no indication that the voice tape destroyed contained evidence that could be classified as a smoking-gun, the very fact that it is the only recording of conversations between the engineer and dispatch contemporaneous with the accident renders its loss prejudicial to the plaintiffs. We find no abuse of discretion in the district court's decision to sanction the Railroad through an adverse inference instruction for its prelitigation destruction of the voice tape.

As to the track maintenance inspection records, the Union Pacific demonstrated that its policy is to destroy them after one year and replace them with the new inspection records. These records generally note defects that appear at a crossing on the day of its inspection and list the name of the person who inspected the track on that particular day, but they would not show the exact condition of the tracks on the day of the accident. The Stevensons requested the production of track maintenance records for two years prior to the accident. Union Pacific made no effort to preserve these documents from its routine document destruction policy.

The district court said it was not persuaded that the document retention policy was instituted in bad faith, but "[a]s with the voice tape, however, [Union Pacific] knew or should have known that the documents would become material and should have preserved them." (Appellant's Add. at 12.) The "knew or should have known" language indicates a negligence standard, and as noted earlier, we have never approved of giving an adverse inference instruction on the basis of negligence alone. Even if the district court intended its findings to be the equivalent of a bad faith determination, we conclude that the findings regarding the prelitigation destruction of track maintenance records do not amount to a showing of bad faith and that the district court abused its discretion in giving the adverse inference instruction in relation to the destruction of all track maintenance records up to two years prior to the accident.

There is no showing here that Union Pacific knew that litigation was imminent when, prior to any litigation, it destroyed track maintenance records from up to two years prior to the accident pursuant to its document retention policy. * * * It appears that Union Pacific was not on notice that the track maintenance records should be preserved until it received the October 1999 request for production of documents, and the condition of the track was not formally put into issue until the second amendment to the complaint in May 2000. Thus, any bad faith determination regarding the prelitigation destruction of the track maintenance records is not supported by the record, and any adverse inference instruction based on any prelitigation destruction of track maintenance records would have been given in error.

Union Pacific continued destroying track maintenance records after this lawsuit was initiated. We find no abuse of discretion in the district court's decision to impose sanctions for the destruction of track maintenance records after the commencement of litigation and the filing of the plaintiffs' request for production of documents on October 25, 1999. At the time the plaintiffs requested the production of the track maintenance records, the records from October and November 1998 (closest in time to the accident and thus most relevant) would have been available, but Union Pacific made no effort to preserve them. Although Union Pacific's counsel did not send the discovery request to the claims agent, Mr. Fuller, until November 17, 1999, even then the records from November 1998 would have been available and could have been preserved, but they were not.

At the sanctions hearing, Union Pacific claimed innocence under its routine document retention policy and a lack of knowledge because the proper agents did not know that the records were relevant or where they were kept. Mr. Fuller testified that he did not know where the track inspection records were kept because this was his first grade crossing collision case. Distracted by a derailment and his own vacation, Mr.

Fuller did not start looking for the requested records until December 1999. The November 1998 records had been routinely destroyed by then. The district court did not credit the Railroad's claimed lack of knowledge because of its specific knowledge of and participation in this litigation, the actual notice of the document request, and the relevance of track maintenance documents to the pending litigation because they could have revealed the Railroad's extent of knowledge about the track conditions at the time of the accident. After the specific document request for track maintenance records, Union Pacific cannot rely on its routine document retention policy as a shield. See Lewy, 836 F.2d at 1112 (noting that "a corporation cannot blindly destroy documents and expect to be shielded by a seemingly innocuous document retention policy").

Sanctioning the ongoing destruction of records during litigation and discovery by imposing an adverse inference instruction is supported by either the court's inherent power or Rule 37 of the Federal Rules of Civil Procedure, even absent an explicit bad faith finding, and we conclude that the giving of an adverse inference instruction in these circumstances is not an abuse of discretion.

2.   Refusal to Allow Rebuttal

Union Pacific argues that even if the district court did not abuse its discretion by giving the adverse inference instruction as a sanction for the destruction of evidence in this case, the district court abused its discretion by not permitting it to offer a reasonable rebuttal to the inference. We agree.

The permissive language of Instruction Number 26 allowed, but did not require, the jury to draw an adverse inference from the destruction of evidence. A permissive inference is subject to reasonable rebuttal. See Webb v. District of Columbia, 146 F.3d 964, 974 n. 20 (D.C.Cir. 1998) (noting that "[a]lthough an adverse inference presumption should not test the limits of reason," it is a common sanction in response to the destruction of documents and the opposing party "would be entitled to attempt to rebut it"); Lamarca v. United States, 31 F.Supp.2d 110, 128 (E.D.N.Y.1999) ("An adverse inference that the missing evidence is harmful can be rebutted by an adequate explanation of the reason for non-production.") (internal quotation marks omitted). While the district court need not permit a complete retrial of the sanctions hearing during trial, unfair prejudice should be avoided by permitting the defendant to put on some evidence of its document retention policy and how it affected the destruction of the requested records as an innocent explanation for its conduct. Absent this opportunity, the jury is deprived of sufficient information on which to base a rational decision of whether to apply the adverse inference, and an otherwise permissive inference easily becomes an irrebuttable presumption.

The district court's timing of the instruction in this case also contributes to our finding of unfair prejudice by the exclusion of reasonable rebuttal testimony. At the very outset of trial, the district court informed the jury that the Railroad had destroyed evidence that should have been preserved, and the plaintiffs referred to this destruction throughout the trial. We see no need to unduly emphasize the adverse inference at the outset of trial, especially where there is no finding that the evidence destroyed was crucial to the case. No doubt the evidence destroyed was relevant and its destruction prejudiced the plaintiffs' discovery efforts, but in previous cases where we have sustained a sanction of precluding evidence completely or settling a disputed matter of fact (thus permitting no rebuttal), the offending party had destroyed the one piece of crucial physical evidence in the case. See Sylla-Sawdon v. Uniroyal Goodrich Tire Co., 47 F.3d 277, 280 (8th Cir.) (noting that the tires destroyed were "critical to this litigation"), cert. denied, 516 U.S. 822, 116 S.Ct. 84, 133 L.Ed.2d 42 (1995); Dillon, 986 F.2d at 266 (noting that the "crucial evidence" destroyed was the car that caused the injuries that were the subject of the lawsuit). No such finding exists here.

    3.   Attorneys' Fees

    The district court also awarded attorneys' fees as a sanction. * * * "Federal courts sitting in diversity can use their inherent power to assess attorney fees as a sanction for bad faith conduct even if the applicable state law does not recognize the bad faith exception to the general rule against fee shifting." Id. at 1435. This inherent power reaches conduct both before and during litigation as long as that conduct abuses the judicial process in some manner. A bad faith finding is specifically required in order to assess attorneys' fees. Dillon 986 F.2d at 266 (citing Chambers, 501 U.S. at 45–46, 111 S.Ct. 2123, and Roadway Express, Inc. v. Piper, 447 U.S. 752, 767, 100 S.Ct. 2455, 65 L.Ed.2d 488 (1980)). This bad faith conduct must have practiced a fraud upon the court or defiled "the temple of justice," Chambers, 501 U.S. at 46, 111 S.Ct. 2123, and cannot be based solely on the prelitigation conduct that led to the substantive claim of the case, Lamb Eng'g, 103 F.3d at 1435.

    Union Pacific argues that the district court erred by imposing an award of attorneys' fees on the basis of its prelitigation destruction of evidence. We found no abuse of discretion in the district court's conclusion that the prelitigation destruction of the voice tape amounted to bad faith conduct, but any award of attorneys' fees based on prelitigation destruction of track maintenance records may be unwarranted because it is not supported by a bad faith finding. Because part of the existing award might be based upon prelitigation conduct that does not amount to bad faith, we vacate the award of attorneys' fees and remand for recalculation under the bad faith standard. * * *

III.

    Accordingly, we affirm in part and reverse and remand for a new trial consistent with this opinion and for reconsideration of the amount of attorneys' fees. We affirm the judgment of the district court on the issues raised in the cross-appeal, and we dismiss without prejudice Mr. Stevenson's motion for additional sanctions.

NOTE ON DISCOVERY ETHICS AND DISCOVERY SANCTIONS

    1.   A prelude: the duty to preserve evidence. Laws often oblige parties to preserve evidence for purposes of regulatory oversight, even if no litigation is pending or threatened. Destruction, alteration, or failure to preserve evidence relevant to a pending or foreseeable case is known as "spoliation." Destruction or alteration that is specifically intended to obstruct or impede the use or production of evidence in a pending or contemplated civil case is a criminal offense under federal law and the law of many states. See, for example, 18 U.S.C. § 1519.

Destruction of documents accomplished without corrupt intent, whether negligently or because of mindless adherence to a company policy concerning retention of documents, may result in sanctions. There is an affirmative duty to preserve information once a party is aware of the prospect of litigation and the relevance of the information to the litigation. Those conditions are clearly met when a discovery request has been made, but can also be satisfied by the filing and service of a complaint, or simply by notice that litigation is likely to be commenced. See Micron Technology, Inc. v. Rambus, 645 F.3d 1311 (Fed. Cir. 2011).

In federal civil litigation the duty to preserve evidence is said to derive both from the discovery provisions of the Federal Rules of Civil Procedure and from the court's inherent power. Lawyers for a party facing the prospect of civil litigation have a duty "to ensure that relevant information is preserved by giving clear instructions to the client to preserve such information." Zubulake v. UBS Warburg LLC, 229 F.R.D. 422, 424 (S.D.N.Y. 2004). The common term for this is a "litigation hold." An effective litigation hold must be prompt, and it must be thorough, both in the scope of information preserved and the holders of documents to whom it is directed. See O'Shea et al., Using Legal Holds for Electronic Discovery, 40 Wm. Mitchell L. Rev. 462 (2014).

As *Union Pacific* demonstrates, proof that relevant evidence has been destroyed can lead to a variety of sanctions, including an instruction to the fact finder that it may infer that the evidence, had it survived, would have been damaging to the case of the party who failed to produce it (a so-called "spoliation inference"). In cases where the party's conduct is especially egregious, or the prejudice resulting from the spoliation is especially strong, dismissal is an appropriate sanction. See Leon v. IDX Systems Corp., 464 F.3d 951 (9th Cir. 2006) (affirming dismissal and monetary penalties as sanction against plaintiff who deleted thousands of documents from his laptop during the pendency of the litigation); Silvestri v. General Motors Corp., 271 F.3d 583 (4th Cir. 2001) (affirming dismissal when plaintiff did not preserve the crucial piece of evidence in the case). Were the sanctions in *Union Pacific* appropriate, considering the defendant's conduct and the prejudice suffered by the plaintiff? If you were Union Pacific's lawyer, what advice would you give them in crafting their document-retention policies going forward?

The problem of evidence preservation is particularly acute in the case of electronic information because the information is often widely dispersed (an employee may have data not only at work, but on her mobile device, laptop or home computer) and is constantly changing on account of routine back-up and deletion programs, as well as the day-to-day manipulation of data in the course of the company's business. The duty to preserve evidence involves suspending, insofar as possible, this routine alteration of existing information. But in recognition of the difficulty of achieving perfect compliance, the federal Rules now provide that absent exceptional circumstances sanctions should not be imposed for the failure to provide electronically stored information lost as a result of the "routine, good-faith operation of an electronic information system." Fed. R. Civ. P. 37(e).

A proposed amendment to Rule 37(e), which would go into effect on December 1, 2015, attempts to clarify practice in this area. If electronically stored information is lost because a party failed to take reasonable steps to preserve it, and that loss of information is prejudicial, the court may "order measures no greater than necessary to cure the prejudice." If the court finds that a party "has acted with the intent to deprive another party of the information's use in the litigation," the court may presume that the lost information was unfavorable to the party that failed to produce it, give an adverse-inference instruction to the jury, or dismiss the action. For a comprehensive review of sanctions under current Rule 37(e), see Willoughby, Jones & Antine, Sanctions for E-discovery Violations: By the Numbers, 60 Duke L.J. 789 (2010).

One problem courts and parties now find themselves grappling with is the duty of electronic-data preservation when it comes to social media. Multiple courts have now sanctioned parties for deleting information from their social-media accounts when it was reasonably foreseeable that data from those accounts would be sought in discovery. See, e.g., Gatto v. United Airlines, Inc., 2013 WL 1285285 (D.N.J. 2013). An egregious example is Allied Concrete Co. v. Lester, 285 Va. 295, 736 S.E.2d 699 (Va. 2013), in which plaintiff sought damages for mental anguish associated with the wrongful death of his wife in an automobile accident caused by defendant company's employee. Defense counsel apparently was able to access the plaintiff's Facebook page, where the plaintiff had recently posted a photograph of himself "accompanied by other individuals, holding a beer can, while wearing a T-shirt emblazoned with 'I ♥ hot moms.' " The defendant then issued a discovery request to the plaintiff seeking printouts of his "Facebook page including, but not limited to, all pictures, his profile, his message board, status updates, and all messages sent or received." After receiving the request, the plaintiff's attorney instructed a paralegal to tell the plaintiff to "clean up" his Facebook page because "we don't want any blow-ups of this stuff at trial." The plaintiff then deleted his Facebook account and responded to the discovery request the next day, stating that as of the date of signing he did not have a Facebook account. To make matters worse, the plaintiff then testified at his deposition that he never deactivated his Facebook page. The court did not look kindly on this conduct. It issued an adverse-inference instruction to the jury regarding the deleted material, and it sanctioned the plaintiff in the amount of $180,000 and his attorney in the amount of $542,000 to "cover the defendant's attorney's fees and costs in addressing and defending against the misconduct." Id. at 302–03.

2. The conventional view of the legal obligation to provide discovery. In thinking about the problem of discovery misconduct, one must consider the legal and ethical background. The background norm is non-disclosure. In general, a litigant in federal court has an affirmative obligation to disclose information harmful to its case only when such information is responsive to a lawful request for that information from an opposing party or from the court.

When the client has no legal obligation to disclose information harmful to its case, her lawyer normally has no right to disclose such information, because the lawyer is prohibited from disclosing or using confidential client information "if there is a reasonable prospect that doing so will adversely affect a material interest of the client or if the client has instructed the lawyer not to use or disclose such information." American Law Institute,

Restatement (Third) of the Law Governing Lawyers § 60(1)(a) (2000). Indeed, the ethical rule in every American jurisdiction but one requires a lawyer in an adversary proceeding to keep silent about the existence of information harmful to his client's case, and to make proper objections to its production or introduction into evidence, even when the lawyer knows that the evidence is authentic and that the effect of his conduct will be to produce a decision opposite from that which would have resulted from full disclosure. Id. at § 120, comment *d*. This obligation flows from the lawyers' duties of competence, confidentiality and loyalty to the client.

At the other extreme, all authorities agree that the lawyer for a party who has been asked for information within the scope of discovery (1) may not withhold, or assist the client in withholding, that information without a non-frivolous basis in law for doing so, such as a non-frivolous argument that the information was not requested or a non-frivolous objection to its production, see, e.g., Fed. R. Civ. P. 26(g); (2) must comply with any formal requirements governing the assertion of an objection, see. e.g., Fed. R. Civ. P. 26(b)(5), 33(b)(4), 34(b); and (3) may not make knowingly false factual or legal claims concerning discovery. American Law Institute, Restatement (Third) of the Law Governing Lawyers § 120(1).

3.   **An alternative view of the obligation to provide discovery.** An alternative view holds that the lawyer has an obligation to produce relevant non-privileged information unfavorable to her client even in the absence of a lawful request for it, at least when such disclosure is necessary to prevent the tribunal from acting under a clear misunderstanding of the evidence. This view has thus far been expressly adopted in only one jurisdiction and only in the limited case where non-disclosure is likely to mislead the tribunal. See New Jersey Rules of Professional Conduct Rule 3.3(a)(5) (lawyer may not "fail to disclose to the tribunal a material fact with knowledge that the tribunal may tend to be misled by such failure."). This view has, however, received significant support from judges and academic lawyers. See, e.g., Frankel, The Search for Truth: An Umpireal View, 123 U. Pa. L. Rev. 1031 (1975).

Academics have also argued that parties should have an affirmative obligation to disclose unfavorable information even in the absence of a request from the opponent. See Brazil, The Adversary Character of Civil Discovery, 31 Vand. L. Rev. 1295 (1978). This principle underlay the federal rulemakers' first attempt at mandatory disclosure in the 1993 amendments to Rule 26(a), which required disclosure of unfavorable information, even in the absence of a request from the opponent, if the information was relevant to a disputed issue alleged "with particularity" in the opposing party's complaint or answer. For discussion of this requirement, and of the sharp professional and judicial criticism that led to its abolition, see Note on the Discovery Process and Discovery Tools, supra p. 708.

4.   **The sources and frequency of discovery misconduct.** The right of clients (and the obligation of their lawyers) to withhold unfavorable information that has not been requested and to object to the production of requested information gives parties taking discovery a strong incentive to make broad requests for information and to press vigorously for full responses. Requests designed to foil lawful evasion will necessarily call for the production of at least some information that is irrelevant and potentially costly to produce. Accordingly, there is always some potential for the interplay of legitimate avoidance, broad demands, and legitimate resistance

to spin out of control, resulting in costly friction and combat. A further complication is that both avoidance-resistance and broad demands result in increased discovery costs for the opponent, and are often pursued, at least in part, for precisely that reason. The costs can be psychic as well as financial, so that lawyers or parties who are willing and able to deal out and absorb emotional abuse may have a significant strategic advantage. See e.g., Paramount Comm., Inc. v. QVC Network, Inc., 637 A.2d 34 (Del. 1994) (describing exceptionally abusive conduct by a lawyer defending a deposition). In such situations, parties may each conclude, in complete good faith, that the other side has behaved abusively. And once parties believe that the other side has cheated, it becomes psychologically easier to justify one's own cheating as a defense against the opponent's misconduct.

Despite these dynamics, it appears that cheating and contentiousness are far from epidemic. Sanctions are, in fact, relatively rarely awarded. See Emery G. Lee III, Federal Judicial Center: Motions for Sanctions Based on Spoliation of Evidence in Civil Cases (2011). Indeed, abuses may be uncommon in many types of cases, particularly those where the stakes are low, the amount of information to be discovered is limited and localized, and the local litigation bar is small or specialized, so that lawyers deal with each other frequently and can benefit themselves and their clients by maintaining a reputation for trustworthiness. In these cases, the opportunities for abuse are limited, and the incentives to cheat are small. Conversely, studies suggest that cases involving high stakes, large quantities of widely dispersed information, and lawyers in large urban communities, are more likely to generate conflict and misconduct. Studies also suggest that lawyers perceive higher levels of discovery misconduct in fields like products liability and civil rights, where obtaining full discovery from the defendant is often critical to the plaintiff's case. Kakalik et al., Discovery Management: Further Analysis of the Civil Justice Reform Act Evaluation Data, 39 B.C. L. Rev. 613 (1998); Willging et al., An Empirical Study of Discovery and Disclosure Practice Under the 1993 Federal Rule Amendments, 39 B.C. L. Rev. 525, 531 (1998).

6. The law and policy of discovery sanctions. Discovery sanctions are governed by federal Rules 26, 30 and 37. Note that federal Rule 11 does not apply to discovery. Fed. R. Civ. P. 11(d).

a. Rule 26(g). If a party or an attorney for a party violates the certification requirement of Rule 26(g) "without substantial justification," the court "must impose an appropriate sanction on the signer, the party on whose behalf the signer was acting, or both," which may include costs and attorneys' fees incurred by the opposing party.

b. Rule 30(g). If a party either fails to attend and proceed with a deposition of an opposing party that she "noticed" (i.e., scheduled), or fails to subpoena a witness for a deposition with the result that the witness does not appear and the opposing party incurs expense as a result of the non-appearance, the court may order the party to pay the expenses incurred by the opposing party, including reasonable attorneys' fees. See, e.g., Jones v. J.C. Penney's Dep't Stores, Inc., 228 F.R.D. 190 (W.D.N.Y. 2005) (imposing financial sanctions under Rule 30(g) where plaintiff failed to proceed with scheduled depositions absent a sufficient justification). Furthermore, in cases where one party does not proceed with a scheduled expert witness deposition or cancels that deposition at the last minute, courts may also order the delaying party to cover the fees related to the expert witness's time and travel. See, e.g., Barrett v. Brian Bemis Auto World, 230 F.R.D. 535, 537

(N.D. Ill. 2005) (ordering that defendant pay reasonable expenses related to both attorney and expert witness fees).

c.   **Rule 37.** Rule 37 deals expressly with sanctions for a variety of different types of misconduct. One important subparagraph provides that if a court orders a party who has made a formal objection to discovery to disclose information or to provide discovery, it must award costs, including attorneys' fees, to the party who moved for the order, unless (1) the moving party did not confer or attempt to confer in order to resolve the matter extrajudicially, (2) the uncooperative party was "substantially justified" in its action, or (3) there is some other reason making the award of expenses unjust. Fed. R. Civ. P. 37(a)(5)(A).

A second critical section provides that if a party disobeys a judicial order to disclose or to provide discovery, a court may order that: (i) the questions in dispute be taken as established against the party disobeying the order; (ii) the disobeying party be foreclosed from making claims or defenses, or entering matters into evidence; (iii) the pleadings (or parts of the pleadings) of the disobeying party be stricken; (iv) staying proceedings until the order is obeyed; (v) the action of the disobeying party be dismissed; (vi) rendering default judgment against the disobeying party; or (vii) the disobeying party be held in contempt. Fed. R. Civ. P. 37(b)(2)(A)(i)–(vii). Rule 37 further provides that "instead of or in addition" to the preceding, "the court must order the disobedient party, the attorney advising that party, or both to pay the reasonable expenses, including attorney's fees * * * unless the failure was substantially justified or other circumstances make an award of expenses unjust." Fed. R. Civ. P. 37(b)(2)(C).

Rule 37(c)–(d) also authorizes a variety of other sanctions for offenses as various as failing to comply with initial mandatory disclosure requirements or to timely amend a response rendered inaccurate by subsequent events, failure to admit under Rule 36, and failure to attend a deposition or to respond to interrogatories or requests for inspection.

The Supreme Court has made clear its impatience with parties who abuse the discovery process, and has admonished the courts of appeals to leave undisturbed sanctions imposed in the district courts unless there has been an abuse of discretion. National Hockey League v. Metropolitan Hockey Club, Inc., 427 U.S. 639, 642–43, 96 S.Ct. 2778, 49 L.Ed.2d 747 (1976). Despite the Supreme Court's suggestion, courts are reluctant to use the sanction of dismissal, since it effectively short-circuits the accurate determination of the merits that the discovery rules are intended to foster. For that reason, dismissal is normally restricted to cases in which the conduct of the party resisting discovery was intentional, in bad faith, and resulted in substantial prejudice to the opposing party. Compare FDIC v. Conner, 20 F.3d 1376 (5th Cir. 1994) (dismissal of plaintiff's action reversed where plaintiff's failure to obey a discovery order took place early in discovery and did not seriously interfere with defendant's preparation of the case) and Pressey v. Patterson, 898 F.2d 1018 (5th Cir. 1990) (default judgment on the issue of liability against civil rights defendant reversed; defendant's lack of cooperation, violation of discovery orders, and destruction of audiotape interview with a key witness were not sufficiently willful to warrant such a severe sanction) with Guggenheim Capital, LLC v. Birnbaum, 722 F.3d 444 (2d Cir. 2013) (default order affirmed where defendant displayed "sustained recalcitrance" and "willfully disobeyed" discovery orders); Angiodynamics, Inc. v. Biolitec AG, 991 F. Supp. 2d 283

(D. Mass. 2014) (awarding default judgment of $74,920,422 when "Plaintiff has been thwarted at virtually every turn by Defendants' outrageous misconduct").

CHAPTER 7

DISPOSITION WITHOUT TRIAL

A. INTRODUCTION

Trials are increasingly rare in American federal and state courts. In federal court, total dispositions increased more than five-fold between 1962 and 2012 from 50,320 to 271,572 cases, but civil trials declined during that same period from 5,802 to 3,165. The percentage of cases disposed of by trial in 1962 was 11.5%; in 2012 it was 1.2%—fewer than one case in 50. Administrative Office of the U.S. Courts, Annual Report of the Director 2012, Table C-4. In state court, the data are more fragmentary but show a similar trend. According to two prominent commentators, "the absolute number of civil trials in [the nation's most populous counties] decreased 51.8 percent from 1992 to 2005." Galanter & Frozena, A Grin Without a Cat: The Continuing Decline and Displacement of Trials in American Courts, Daedalus, Summer 2014.

The reasons for the decline in trials are not well understood. But it is clear that the decline in trials has increased the importance of mechanisms for resolving cases without trial. This chapter briefly reviews alternative ways of resolving cases without trial. It focuses on two highly significant modes of disposition: summary judgment and settlement. The potential for a case to end on a motion for summary judgment or by agreement of the parties looms large in the strategic thinking of any litigator from the outset of any case.

NOTE ON DEVICES TO AVOID PLENARY TRIAL

1. Dismissal for failure to state a claim and judgment on the pleadings. A motion in federal practice for dismissal for failure to state a claim under federal Rule 12(b)(6) provides a mechanism under which the defendant is able to test the sufficiency of the plaintiff's allegations as a matter of law. The truth of the plaintiff's allegations is assumed for purposes of the motion, and the question asked is whether a cause of action is stated on those assumed facts. See discussion in Chapter 4.

A motion for judgment on the pleadings challenges the legal sufficiency of a party's factual allegations or legal contentions, in the same manner as a motion to dismiss for failure to state a claim and a demurrer. See Hazard, Leubsdorf, & Bassett, Civil Procedure § 5.11 (6th ed. 2011). In federal practice, either party may move for judgment on the pleadings under Rule 12(c) after the pleadings are complete. If the defendant makes the motion, it is the equivalent of (and indeed is sometimes called) a motion to dismiss for failure to state a claim under Rule 12(b)(6). But note that a Rule 12(b)(6) motion may also be made before the pleadings are complete, or at trial. See Rule 12(h)(2). The legal standards for granting or denying Rule 12(c) and 12(b)(6) motions are identical. Patel v. Contemporary Classics of Beverly Hills, 258 F.3d 123, 126 (2d Cir. 2001).

Motions to dismiss for failure to state a claim and motions for judgment on the pleadings are based on the pleadings themselves, and are not used to test the truth of factual allegations. If litigants supplement any of these motions by presenting exhibits, affidavits, or other materials, the motions will be treated as motions for summary judgment. See Fed. R. Civ. P. 12(d). In that event, all parties will be given the opportunity to obtain and present evidentiary materials relevant to the motion, including, if appropriate, the opportunity to take relevant discovery.

2. **Voluntary dismissal. a. By plaintiff or by stipulation.** Under federal Rule 41(a)(1)(A)(i), a plaintiff may voluntarily dismiss her suit as of right simply by filing a notice of dismissal, so long as she does so before defendant has answered or moved for summary judgment. A voluntary dismissal under this rule is "without prejudice." That is, the plaintiff may file the suit again without being met by a defense of res judicata. The period during which plaintiff may voluntarily dismiss merely "by notice" can be substantial. For example, it is common for defendants, with consent of plaintiffs, to delay answering the complaint; or proceedings may be stayed for months without an answer being required. See, e.g., Merit Ins. Co. v. Leatherby Ins. Co., 581 F.2d 137 (7th Cir. 1978) (proceedings stayed for nine months to allow arbitration; plaintiff allowed to dismiss without prejudice).

Plaintiff has only one bite at the apple, however. The first voluntary dismissal by notice is without prejudice, but the second is with prejudice. Fed. R. Civ. P. 41(a)(1)(B). This limitation prevents plaintiff from harassing defendant by repeated filings and dismissals, and it prevents (or at least severely limits) judge-shopping through filing, dismissal, and refiling. Plaintiff may also dismiss without prejudice by stipulation of the parties. Fed. R. Civ. P. 41(a)(1)(A)(ii). There is no limit on the number of dismissals without prejudice by stipulation of the parties because the defendant is in a position to protect herself against abuses by refusing to acquiesce.

b. **By order of the court.** Federal Rule 41(a)(2) allows a district court to dismiss a complaint without prejudice "on terms that the court considers proper." Such conditions are usually imposed when the dismissal threatens unfairness to defendant, typically because she has invested a lot in defending the case. The most common such condition is a requirement that plaintiff pay all or part of defendant's costs or attorneys' fees. A dismissal under Rule 41(a)(2) may be reversed only for abuse of discretion. Metropolitan Fed. Bank of Iowa v. W.R. Grace & Co., 999 F.2d 1257, 1262 (8th Cir. 1993). Further, if defendant has filed a counterclaim, the court may not dismiss the complaint under Rule 41(a)(2) unless (1) there is an independent basis for jurisdiction that will allow the counterclaim to continue after dismissal of plaintiff's claim, or (2) defendant is willing to consent to dismissal of her counterclaim.

3. **Involuntary dismissal for failure to prosecute.** A suit may be dismissed from federal court for failure to prosecute under Rule 41(b). A dismissal is proper when, in a persistent course of conduct, the plaintiff has been dilatory in pursuing her suit. For example, she may fail to conduct discovery, fail to respond to telephone calls or correspondence, fail to appear at depositions or scheduled conferences, or the like. One recent such instance may be found in In re Asbestos Products Liability Litigation, 718 F.3d 236 (3d Cir. 2013), in which the Third Circuit affirmed a district court's dismissal under Rule 41(b) where the district court ordered plaintiffs to provide a complete history of their exposure to asbestos, and they failed to comply with the order. Sometimes a suit is dismissed under this provision when it is apparent that plaintiff is using the suit to harass defendant and has no intention of actually bringing the case to trial. Unless the court specifies

otherwise in its order of dismissal, a dismissal for failure to prosecute operates as an adjudication on the merits with res judicata effect. See, e.g., Link v. Wabash R. Co., 370 U.S. 626, 82 S.Ct. 1386, 8 L.Ed.2d 734 (1962); Jones v. Horne, 634 F.3d 588 (D.C. Cir. 2011).

4. Default and default judgment. The federal Rules draw a distinction between entry of "default," Fed. R. Civ. P. 55(a), and entry of "default judgment," Fed. R. Civ. P. 55(b). Entry of "default" under Rule 55(a) against a defendant is a simple entry by the court clerk indicating that a defendant has "failed to plead or otherwise defend." The failure may occur at the outset of the action, when a defendant fails to answer the summons and complaint, or later, as when a defendant fails to respond to a motion for summary judgment. By itself, entry of default does not terminate the case. But, unless vacated, it does bar the defendant from offering any further defense on issues of liability, as distinct from remedy.

Entry of "default judgment" under Rule 55(b) is actual entry of a *judgment* granting relief against a defendant. Such a judgment is on the merits and has res judicata consequences. When the defendant has been defaulted for failure to make a timely appearance in the action, defendant is not a minor or incompetent, and the judgment sought is for a "sum certain," the clerk, upon proper proof of those facts, must enter default judgment. Fed. R. Civ. P. 55(b)(1). In all other circumstances, the plaintiff must apply to the judge for entry of judgment. Fed. R. Civ. P. 55(b)(2). If defendant "has appeared personally or by a representative" before defaulting, Rule 55(b)(2) requires notice of the application for judgment. The party seeking relief is required to present evidence, at what is sometimes called the "prove-up," concerning the amount of damages to be awarded, and the party who has been defaulted is also entitled to be heard on the issue. In contrast to ordinary judgments, the relief granted in a default judgment cannot exceed that demanded in the complaint. Fed. R. Civ. P. 54(c). No judgment by default may be entered against the United States unless the claimant establishes his right to relief by "evidence that satisfies the court." Fed. R. Civ. P. 55(d).

An *entry* of default may be set aside for "good cause"; a *judgment* of default may be set aside only in accordance with the provisions of Rule 60(b), which is the rule that provides relief from judgments generally. Courts are more lenient in setting aside entry of default than in setting aside a default judgment, particularly when the motion to set aside the default is made promptly, the party who obtained the default has suffered little or no prejudice, and the defendant can show a meritorious defense. Shepard Claims Serv., Inc. v. William Darrah & Associates, 796 F.2d 190 (6th Cir. 1986). That said, courts tend to approach motions seeking relief from a default judgment with relative liberality because the merits of the case have not been considered. See generally 11 C. Wright, A. Miller & M. Kane, Federal Practice and Procedure § 2857 (2012).

A recurring question in cases under Rule 60(b) concerns whether a client can be relieved of a default judgment entered because his lawyer failed to file responsive papers in a timely manner. Most such cases arise under Rule 60(b)(1), which governs motions to set aside the judgment brought within a year of the judgment based upon "mistake, inadvertence, surprise, or excusable neglect." One can find numerous statements that courts refuse to relieve a client of a default judgment entered "due to the mistake or omission of his attorney by reason of the latter's ignorance of the law or of the rules of the court, or his inability to efficiently manage his caseload." United States v. Cirami, 535 F.2d 736, 739 (2d. Cir. 1976); see also Easley v. Kirmsee, 382 F.3d 693, 698 (7th Cir. 2004) ("attorney inattentiveness to litigation is not excusable, no matter what the resulting consequences the attorney's somnolent behavior may have on a litigant"). But many decisions display a more lenient approach. See, for example, Info. Sys. & Networks Corp. v. United States, 994 F.2d 792, 795 (Fed. Cir. 1993). The Supreme Court has described the term "excusable neglect" as a "somewhat elastic concept" that, "at least for purposes of Rule 60(b) * * * is understood to encompass situations in which the failure to comply with a filing deadline is attributable to negligence." Pioneer Inv. Servs. Co. v. Brunswick Assoc. Ltd. P'ship, 507 U.S. 380, 394, 113 S.Ct. 1489, 123 L.Ed. 2d 74 (1993).

In addition, a number of courts have granted parties relief from default judgment under Rule 60(b)(6), which these courts have held allows relief in "extraordinary circumstances," upon a showing that the lawyer's negligence was not ordinary, but rather gross or egregious. The nominal theory behind such cases is that while clients bear the risk of routine negligence, it is unfair to charge them with responsibility for more grievous forms of lawyer misconduct. See Lal v. California, 610 F.3d 518 (9th Cir. 2010) (granting such relief and cataloguing cases). A more persuasive explanation may be that in such cases the presumptive prejudice to the defaulting party is greater, since the gravity of the lawyer's misconduct suggests that his practice may no longer be a going concern and that he will be unable to satisfy a subsequent malpractice claim.

A defendant seeking to set aside a default does not always have to present proof that she has a meritorious defense to plaintiff's claim. In Peralta v. Heights Medical Center, Inc., 485 U.S. 80, 108 S.Ct. 896, 99 L.Ed.2d 75 (1988), defendant in a Texas state court case was not properly served with notice of the complaint. He never appeared in the case, and a default judgment was entered against him. The Supreme Court held that it violated the due process clause of the Fourteenth Amendment for Texas to require that defendant demonstrate a "meritorious defense" as a condition of reopening the default judgment. The theory of the Texas rule was apparently that there would be no purpose served by reopening the judgment if defendant would simply lose on the merits in any event. The Supreme Court disagreed, noting among other things that the defendant's property had been sold without his knowledge at a sheriff's sale in execution of the judgment: "[H]ad he had notice of the suit, he might have * * * worked out a settlement, or paid the debt. He would also have preferred to sell his property himself in order to raise funds rather than to suffer it sold at a constable's auction." Id. at 85. How far does *Peralta* go? It clearly applies to default judgment defendants who have not received proper notice and have not appeared in the suit at all. But it seems doubtful that the reasoning of the case extends to defendants who received proper notice, but subsequently defaulted. Courts in such cases often require a showing of a meritorious defense.

Entry of default judgment following a failure to appear or defend should be distinguished from default judgment imposed as a penalty for litigation misconduct. For example, in extreme cases, default judgment may be entered as a sanction for failure to obey discovery orders. Fed. R. Civ. P. 37(b)(2)(A)(vi).

B. SUMMARY JUDGMENT

1. THE MOVING PARTY'S OBLIGATION TO SUPPORT A SUMMARY JUDGMENT MOTION

Adickes v. S.H. Kress & Co.

Supreme Court of the United States, 1970.
398 U.S. 144, 90 S.Ct. 1598, 26 L.Ed.2d 142.

■ MR. JUSTICE HARLAN delivered the opinion of the Court.

Petitioner, Sandra Adickes, a white school teacher from New York, brought this suit in the United States District Court for the Southern District of New York against respondent S.H. Kress & Co. ("Kress") to recover damages under 42 U.S.C.A. § 1983[1] for an alleged violation of her constitutional rights under the Equal Protection Clause of the Fourteenth Amendment. The suit arises out of Kress' refusal to serve lunch to Miss Adickes at its restaurant facilities in its Hattiesburg, Mississippi, store on August 14, 1964, and Miss Adickes' subsequent arrest upon her departure from the store by the Hattiesburg police on a charge of vagrancy. At the time of both the refusal to serve and the arrest, Miss Adickes was with six young people, all Negroes, who were her students in a Mississippi "Freedom School" where she was teaching that summer. Unlike Miss Adickes, the students were offered service, and were not arrested.

Petitioner's complaint had two counts, each bottomed on § 1983 and each alleging that Kress had deprived her of the right under the Equal Protection Clause of the Fourteenth Amendment not to be discriminated against on the basis of race. The first count charged that Miss Adickes had been refused service by Kress because she was a "Caucasian in the company of Negroes." * * * [The District Court directed a verdict for respondent on this count.]

The second count of her complaint, alleging that both the refusal of service and her subsequent arrest were the product of a conspiracy between Kress and the Hattiesburg police, was dismissed before trial on a motion for summary judgment. The District Court ruled that petitioner had "failed to allege any facts from which a conspiracy might be inferred." 252 F.Supp., at 144. This determination was unanimously affirmed by the Court of Appeals, 409 F.2d, at 126–127.

Miss Adickes, in seeking review here, claims that the District Court erred both in directing a verdict on the substantive count, and in granting summary judgment on the conspiracy count. Last Term we granted certiorari, 394 U.S. 1011, 89 S.Ct. 1635, 23 L.Ed.2d 38 (1969), and we now reverse and remand for further proceedings on each of the two counts.

---

[1]   Rev.Stat. § 1979, 42 U.S.C.A. § 1983 provides:

"Every person who, under color of any statute, ordinance, regulation, custom, or usage, of any State or Territory, subjects, or causes to be subjected, any citizen of the United States or other person within the jurisdiction thereof to the deprivation of any rights, privileges, or immunities secured by the Constitution and laws, shall be liable to the party injured in an action at law, suit in equity, or other proper proceeding for redress."

As explained in Part I, because the respondent failed to show the absence of any disputed material fact, we think the District Court erred in granting summary judgment. * * *

I

Briefly stated, the conspiracy count of petitioner's complaint made the following allegations: While serving as a volunteer teacher at a "Freedom School" for Negro children in Hattiesburg, Mississippi, petitioner went with six of her students to the Hattiesburg Public Library at about noon on August 14, 1964. The librarian refused to allow the Negro students to use the library, and asked them to leave. Because they did not leave, the librarian called the Hattiesburg chief of police who told petitioner and her students that the library was closed, and ordered them to leave. From the library, petitioner and the students proceeded to respondent's store where they wished to eat lunch. According to the complaint, after the group sat down to eat, a policeman came into the store "and observed [Miss Adickes] in the company of the Negro students." A waitress then came to the booth where petitioner was sitting, took the orders of the Negro students, but refused to serve petitioner because she was a white person "in the company of Negroes." The complaint goes on to allege that after this refusal of service, petitioner and her students left the Kress store. When the group reached the sidewalk outside the store, "the Officer of the Law who had previously entered [the] store" arrested petitioner on a groundless charge of vagrancy and took her into custody.

On the basis of these underlying facts petitioner alleged that Kress and the Hattiesburg police had conspired (1) "to deprive [her] of her right to enjoy equal treatment and service in a place of public accommodation"; and (2) to cause her arrest "on the false charge of vagrancy."

A.   Conspiracies Between Public Officials and Private Persons—Governing Principles

The terms of § 1983 make plain two elements that are necessary for recovery. First, the plaintiff must prove that the defendant has deprived him of a right secured by the "Constitution and laws" of the United States. Second, the plaintiff must show that the defendant deprived him of this constitutional right "under color of any statute, ordinance, regulation, custom, or usage, of any State or Territory." This second element requires that the plaintiff show that the defendant acted "under color of law."[4]

As noted earlier we read both counts of petitioner's complaint to allege discrimination based on race in violation of petitioner's equal protection rights. Few principles of law are more firmly stitched into our constitutional fabric than the proposition that a State must not discriminate against a person because of his race or the race of his companions, or in any way act to compel or encourage racial segregation.[6] Although this is a lawsuit against a private party, not the State or one of its officials, our cases make clear that petitioner will have made out a

---

   [4]   See, e.g., Monroe v. Pape, 365 U.S. 167, 184, 187, 81 S.Ct. 473, 482, 484, 5 L.Ed.2d 492 (1961); United States v. Price, 383 U.S. 787, 793, 794, 86 S.Ct. 1152, 1156, 1157, 16 L.Ed.2d 267 (1966).

   [6]   E.g., Brown v. Board of Education, 347 U.S. 483, 74 S.Ct. 686, 98 L.Ed. 873 (1954); cf. Barrows v. Jackson, 346 U.S. 249, 73 S.Ct. 1031, 97 L.Ed. 1586 (1953).

violation of her Fourteenth Amendment rights and will be entitled to relief under § 1983 if she can prove that a Kress employee, in the course of employment, and a Hattiesburg policeman somehow reached an understanding to deny Miss Adickes service in the Kress store, or to cause her subsequent arrest because she was a white person in the company of Negroes.

The involvement of a state official in such a conspiracy plainly provides the state action essential to show a direct violation of petitioner's Fourteenth Amendment equal protection rights, whether or not the actions of the police were officially authorized, or lawful; Monroe v. Pape, 365 U.S. 167, 81 S.Ct. 473, 5 L.Ed.2d 492 (1961); see United States v. Classic, 313 U.S. 299, 326, 61 S.Ct. 1031, 1043, 85 L.Ed. 1368 (1941); Screws v. United States, 325 U.S. 91, 107–111, 65 S.Ct. 1031, 1038–1040, 89 L.Ed. 1495 (1945); Williams v. United States, 341 U.S. 97, 99–100, 71 S.Ct. 576, 578–579, 95 L.Ed. 774 (1951). Moreover, a private party involved in such a conspiracy, even though not an official of the State, can be liable under § 1983. "Private persons, jointly engaged with state officials in the prohibited action, are acting 'under color' of law for purposes of the statute. To act 'under color' of law does not require that the accused be an officer of the State. It is enough that he is a willful participant in joint activity with the State or its agents," United States v. Price, 383 U.S. 787, 794, 86 S.Ct. 1152, 1157 (1966).

B.   Summary Judgment

We now proceed to consider whether the District Court erred in granting summary judgment on the conspiracy count. In granting respondent's motion, the District Court simply stated that there was "no evidence in the complaint or in the affidavits and other papers from which a 'reasonably-minded person' might draw an inference of conspiracy," 252 F.Supp., at 144, aff'd, 409 F.2d, at 126–127. Our own scrutiny of the factual allegations of petitioner's complaint, as well as the material found in the affidavits and depositions presented by Kress to the District Court, however, convinces us that summary judgment was improper here, for we think respondent failed to carry its burden of showing the absence of any genuine issue of fact. Before explaining why this is so, it is useful to state the factual arguments, made by the parties concerning summary judgment, and the reasoning of the courts below.

In moving for summary judgment, Kress argued that "uncontested facts" established that no conspiracy existed between any Kress employee and the police. To support this assertion, Kress pointed first to the statements in the deposition of the store manager (Mr. Powell) that (a) he had not communicated with the police,[8] and that (b) he had, by a prearranged tacit signal,[9] ordered the food counter supervisor to see that

---

[8] In his deposition, Powell admitted knowing Hugh Herring, chief of police of Hattiesburg, and said that he had seen and talked to him on two occasions in 1964 prior to the incident with Miss Adickes. (App. 123–126). When asked how often the arresting officer, Ralph Hillman, came into the store, Powell stated that he didn't know precisely but "Maybe every day." However, Powell said that on August 14 he didn't recall seeing any policemen either inside or outside the store (App. 136), and he denied (1) that he had called the police, (2) that he had agreed with any public official to deny Miss Adickes the use of the library, (3) that he had agreed with any public official to refuse Miss Adickes service in the Kress store on the day in question, or (4) that he had asked any public official to have Miss Adickes arrested. App. 154–155.

[9] The signal, according to Powell, was a nod of his head. Powell claimed that at a meeting about a month earlier with Miss Baggett, the food counter supervisor, he "told her not to serve

Miss Adickes was refused service only because he was fearful of a riot in the store by customers angered at seeing a "mixed group" of whites and blacks eating together.[10] Kress also relied on affidavits from the Hattiesburg chief of police,[11] and the two arresting officers,[12] to the effect that store manager Powell had not requested that petitioner be arrested. Finally, Kress pointed to the statements in petitioner's own deposition that she had no knowledge of any communication between any Kress employee and any member of the Hattiesburg police, and was relying on circumstantial evidence to support her contention that there was an arrangement between Kress and the police.

---

the white person in the group if I . . . shook my head no. But, if I didn't give her any sign, to go ahead and serve anybody." App. 135.

Powell stated that he had prearranged this tacit signal with Miss Baggett because "there was quite a lot of violence . . . in Hattiesburg" directed towards whites "with colored people, in what you call a mixed group." App. 131.

[10] Powell described the circumstances of his refusal as follows:

"On this particular day, just shortly after 12 o'clock, I estimate there was 75 to 100 people in the store and the lunch counter was pretty—was pretty well to capacity there, full and I was going up towards the front of the store in one of the aisles, and looking towards the front of the store, and there was a group of colored girls, and a white woman who came into the north door, which was next to the lunch counter.

"And the one thing that really stopped me and called my attention to this group, was the fact that they were dressed alike. They all had on, what looked like a light blue denim skirt. And the best I can remember is that they were—they were almost identical, all of them. And they came into the door, and people coming in stopped to look, and they went on to the booths. And there happened to be two empty there. And one group of them and the white woman sat down in one, and the rest of them sat in the second group.

"And, almost immediately there—I mean this, it didn't take just a few seconds from the time they came into the door to sit down, but, already the people began to mill around the store and started coming over towards the lunch counter. And, by that time I was up close to the candy counter, and I had a wide open view there. And the people had real sour looks on their faces, nobody was joking, or being corny, or carrying on. They looked like a frightened mob. They really did. I have seen mobs before. I was in Korea during the riots in 1954 and 1955. And I know what they are. And this actually got me.

"I looked out towards the front, and we have what they call see-through windows. There is no backs to them. You can look out of the store right into the street. And the north window, it looks right into the lunch counter. 25 or 30 people were standing there looking in, and across the street even, in a jewelry store, people were standing there, and it looked really bad to me. It looked like one person could have yelled 'let's get them,' which has happened before, and cause this group to turn into a mob. And, so, quickly I just made up my mind to avoid the riot, and protect the people that were in the store, and my employees, as far as the people in the mob who were going to get hurt themselves. I just knew that something was going to break loose there." App. 133–134.

[11] The affidavit of the chief of police, who it appears was not present at the arrest, states in relevant part:

"Mr. Powell had made no request of me to arrest Miss Sandra Adickes or any other person, in fact, I did not know Mr. Powell personally until the day of this statement. [But cf. Powell's statement at his deposition, n. 8, supra.] Mr. Powell and I had not discussed the arrest of this person until the day of this statement and we had never previously discussed her in any way." (App. 107.)

[12] The affidavits of Sergeant Boone and Officer Hillman each state, in identical language:

"I was contacted on this date by Mr. John H. Williams, Jr., a representative of Genesco, owners of S.H. Kress and Company, who requested that I make a statement concerning alleged conspiracy in connection with the aforesaid arrest.

"This arrest was made on the public streets of Hattiesburg, Mississippi, and was an officers discretion arrest. I had not consulted with Mr. G.T. Powell, Manager of S.H. Kress and Company in Hattiesburg, and did not know his name until this date. No one at the Kress store asked that the arrest be made and I did not consult with anyone prior to the arrest." (App. 110, 112.)

Petitioner, in opposing summary judgment, pointed out that respondent had failed in its moving papers to dispute the allegation in petitioner's complaint, a statement at her deposition,[13] and an unsworn statement by a Kress employee,[14] all to the effect that there was a policeman in the store at the time of the refusal to serve her, and that this was the policeman who subsequently arrested her. Petitioner argued that although she had no knowledge of an agreement between Kress and the police, the sequence of events created a substantial enough possibility of a conspiracy to allow her to proceed to trial, especially given the fact that the noncircumstantial evidence of the conspiracy could only come from adverse witnesses. Further, she submitted an affidavit specifically disputing the manager's assertion that the situation in the store at the time of the refusal was "explosive," thus creating an issue of fact as to what his motives might have been in ordering the refusal of service.

We think that on the basis of this record, it was error to grant summary judgment. As the moving party, respondent had the burden of showing the absence of a genuine issue as to any material fact, and for these purposes the material it lodged must be viewed in the light most favorable to the opposing party.[15] Respondent here did not carry its burden because of its failure to foreclose the possibility that there was a policeman in the Kress store while petitioner was awaiting service, and that this policeman reached an understanding with some Kress employee that petitioner not be served.

It is true that Mr. Powell, the store manager, claimed in his deposition that he had not seen or communicated with a policeman prior to his tacit signal to Miss Baggett, the supervisor of the food counter. But respondent did not submit any affidavits from Miss Baggett,[16] or from

---

[13] When asked whether she saw any policeman in the store up to the time of the refusal of service, Miss Adickes answered: "My back was to the door, but one of my students saw a policeman come in." (App. 75.) She went on to identify the student as "Carolyn." At the trial, Carolyn Moncure, one of the students who was with petitioner, testified that "about five minutes" after the group had sat down and while they were still waiting for service, she saw a policeman come in the store. She stated: "[H]e came in the store, my face was facing the front of the store, and he came in the store and he passed, and he stopped right at the end of our booth, and he stood up and he looked around and he smiled, and he went to the back of the store, he came right back and he left out." (App. 302.) This testimony was corroborated by that of Dianne Moncure, Carolyn's sister, who was also part of the group. She testified that while the group was waiting for service, a policeman entered the store, stood "for awhile" looking at the group, and then "walked to the back of the store." (App. 291.)

[14] During discovery, respondent gave to petitioner an unsworn statement by Miss Irene Sullivan, a check-out girl. In this statement Miss Sullivan said that she had seen Patrolman Hillman come into the store "[s]hortly after 12:00 noon," while petitioner's group was in the store. She said that he had traded a "hello greeting" with her, and then walked past her check-out counter toward the back of the store "out of [her] line of vision." She went on: "A few minutes later Patrolman Hillman left our store by the northerly front door just slightly ahead of a group composed of several Negroes accompanied by a white woman. As Hillman stepped onto the sidewalk outside our store the police car pulled across the street and into an alley that is alongside our store. The police car stopped and Patrolman Hillman escorted the white woman away from the Negroes and into the police car." (App. 178.)

[15] See, e.g., United States v. Diebold, 369 U.S. 654, 655, 82 S.Ct. 993, 994, 8 L.Ed.2d 176 (1962); 6 V. Moore, Federal Practice ¶ 56.15[3] (2d ed. 1966).

[16] In a supplemental brief filed in this Court respondent lodged a copy of an unsworn statement by Miss Baggett denying any contact with the police on the day in question. Apart from the fact that the statement is unsworn, see Fed.Rules Civ.Proc. 56(e), the statement itself is not in the record of the proceedings below and therefore could not have been considered by the trial court. Manifestly, it cannot be properly considered by us in the disposition of the case.

Miss Freeman,[17] the waitress who actually refused petitioner service, either of whom might well have seen and communicated with a policeman in the store. Further, we find it particularly noteworthy that the two officers involved in the arrest each failed in his affidavit to foreclose the possibility (1) that he was in the store while petitioner was there; and (2) that, upon seeing petitioner with Negroes, he communicated his disapproval to a Kress employee, thereby influencing the decision not to serve petitioner.

Given these unexplained gaps in the materials submitted by respondent, we conclude that respondent failed to fulfill its initial burden of demonstrating what is a critical element in this aspect of the case—that there was no policeman in the store. If a policeman were present, we think it would be open to a jury, in light of the sequence that followed, to infer from the circumstances that the policeman and a Kress employee had a "meeting of the minds" and thus reached an understanding that petitioner should be refused service. Because "[o]n summary judgment the inferences to be drawn from the underlying facts contained in [the moving party's] materials must be viewed in the light most favorable to the party opposing the motion," United States v. Diebold, Inc., 369 U.S. 654, 655, 82 S.Ct. 993, 994 (1962), we think respondent's failure to show there was no policeman in the store requires reversal.

Pointing to Rule 56(e), as amended in 1963,[18] respondent argues that it was incumbent on petitioner to come forward with an affidavit properly asserting the presence of the policeman in the store, if she were to rely on that fact to avoid summary judgment. Respondent notes in this regard that none of the materials upon which petitioner relied met the requirements of Rule 56(e).[19]

This argument does not withstand scrutiny, however, for both the commentary on and background of the 1963 amendment conclusively show that it was not intended to modify the burden of the moving party under Rule 56(c) to show initially the absence of a genuine issue concerning any material fact.[20] The Advisory Committee note on the

---

During discovery, petitioner attempted to depose Miss Baggett. However, Kress successfully resisted this by convincing the District Court that Miss Baggett was not a "managing agent," and "was without power to make managerial decisions."

[17] The record does contain an unsworn statement by Miss Freeman in which she states that she "did not contact the police or ask anyone else to contact the police *to make the arrest which subsequently occurred.*" (App. 177.) (Emphasis added.) This statement, being unsworn, does not meet the requirements of Fed.Rules Civ.Proc. 56(e), and was not relied on by respondent in moving for summary judgment. Moreover, it does not foreclose the possibility that Miss Freeman was influenced in her refusal to serve Miss Adickes by some contact with a policeman present in the store.

[18] The amendment added the following to Rule 56(e):

"When a motion for summary judgment is made and supported as provided in this rule, an adverse party may not rest upon the mere allegations or denials of his pleading, but his response, by affidavits or as otherwise provided in this rule, must set forth specific facts showing that there is a genuine issue for trial. If he does not so respond, summary judgment, if appropriate, shall be entered against him."

[19] Petitioner's statement at her deposition, see n. 13, supra, was, of course, hearsay; and the statement of Miss Sullivan, see n. 14, supra, was unsworn. And, the rule specifies that reliance on allegations in the complaint is not sufficient. See Fed.Rule Civ.Proc. 56(e).

[20] The purpose of the 1963 amendment was to overturn a line of cases, primarily in the Third Circuit, that had held that a party opposing summary judgment could successfully create a dispute as to a material fact asserted in an affidavit by the moving party simply by relying on

amendment states that the changes were not designed to "affect the ordinary standards applicable to the summary judgment." And, in a comment directed specifically to a contention like respondent's, the Committee stated that "[w]here the evidentiary matter in support of the motion does not establish the absence of a genuine issue, summary judgment must be denied *even if no opposing evidentiary matter is presented*."[21] Because respondent did not meet its initial burden of establishing the absence of a policeman in the store, petitioner here was not required to come forward with suitable opposing affidavits.[22]

If respondent had met its initial burden by, for example, submitting affidavits from the policemen denying their presence in the store at the time in question, Rule 56(e) would then have required petitioner to have done more than simply rely on the contrary allegation in her complaint. To have avoided conceding this fact for purposes of summary judgment, petitioner would have had to come forward with either (1) the affidavit of someone who saw the policeman in the store or (2) an affidavit under Rule 56(f) explaining why at that time it was impractical to do so. Even though not essential here to defeat respondent's motion, the submission of such an affidavit would have been the preferable course for petitioner's counsel to have followed. As one commentator has said:

> "It has always been perilous for the opposing party neither to proffer any countering evidentiary materials nor file a 56(f) affidavit. And the peril rightly continues [after the amendment to Rule 56(e)]. Yet the party moving for summary judgment has the burden to show that he is entitled to judgment under established principles; and if he does not discharge that burden then he is not entitled to judgment. No defense to an insufficient showing is required." 6 J. Moore, Federal Practice ¶ 56.22[2], pp. 2824–2825 (2d ed. 1966).

II

There remains to be discussed the substantive count of petitioner's complaint, and the showing necessary for petitioner to prove that respondent refused her service "under color of any . . . custom, or usage, of [the] State" in violation of her rights under the Equal Protection Clause of the Fourteenth Amendment.

* * *

---

a contrary allegation in a well-pleaded complaint. E.g., Frederick Hart & Co. v. Recordgraph Corp., 169 F.2d 580 (1948); United States ex rel. Kolton v. Halpern, 260 F.2d 590 (1958). See Advisory Committee Note on 1963 Amendment to subdivision (e) of Rule 56.

[21] Ibid. (emphasis added).

[22] In First National Bank of Ariz. v. Cities Service, 391 U.S. 253, 88 S.Ct. 1575, 20 L.Ed.2d 569 (1968), the petitioner claimed that the lower courts had misapplied Rule 56(e) to shift the burden imposed by Rule 56(c). In rejecting this contention we said: "Essentially all that the lower courts held in this case was that Rule 56(e) placed upon [petitioner] the burden of producing evidence of the conspiracy he alleged only *after respondent . . . conclusively showed that the facts upon which he relied to support his allegation were not susceptible of the interpretation which he sought to give them*." Id., at 289, 88 S.Ct., at 1593. (Emphasis added.) In this case, on the other hand, we hold that respondent failed to show conclusively that a fact alleged by petitioner was "not susceptible" of an interpretation that might give rise to an inference of conspiracy.

The judgment of the Court of Appeals is reversed, and the case remanded to that court for further proceedings consistent with this opinion.[†]

NOTE ON SUMMARY JUDGMENT

1.   **The aims of summary judgment.** A trial is an expensive proposition. Holding a trial requires the expenditure of significant time, energy, and resources of courts, parties, witnesses, and often jurors. In a civil case, neither party is entitled to insist upon a costly trial if there is no demonstrable need for one. Summary judgment provides a means, short of trial, for identifying and deciding, on the merits, those claims, defenses, or issues where the evidence is so one-sided that a trial before a judge or jury with live testimony would be a waste of time and money. In the formulation used by federal Rule 56(a), formerly Rule 56(c), these are the cases where the record on the motion establishes that "there is no genuine dispute as to any material fact and the movant is entitled to judgment as a matter of law."

Sometimes summary judgment is appropriate when the parties have themselves eliminated any "genuine" factual issue by stipulation, so that the only question is what the law requires, and the judge can decide the matter based exclusively on the briefing and argument by the parties. More commonly, as in *Adickes*, the material facts are sharply contested. In such cases, the court must decide whether the factual dispute is "genuine" on some basis other than the conviction of the parties or the words of their pleadings, and whether the factual disputes are "material" in that they matter to the outcome of the case. But to preserve the cost advantage, this disposition must be "summary," which in practice means on the basis of a paper record and perhaps an oral argument by counsel, without convening a jury or hearing live testimony from witnesses. The rules governing the motion must therefore strike a balance between avoiding wasteful trials, on the one hand, and curtailing valuable opportunities to decide controversies in a richer evidentiary context that respects the right to jury trial.

Summary judgment has become an increasingly frequent mode of disposition in the federal courts. Studies suggest that the percentage of cases in which summary judgment motions are made and granted has increased sharply between 1960 and 2000, from approximately 1.8% in 1960 to approximately 7.7% in 2000. Burbank, Vanishing Trials and Summary Judgment in Federal Civil Cases: Drifting Toward Bethlehem or Gomorrah?, 1 J. of Empirical Legal Stud. 591 (2004). As noted above, over roughly the same period the rate of trial in federal court has gone from 11.5% of filed cases to about 1.2% of filed cases. Galanter & Frozena, A Grin Without a Cat: The Continuing Decline and Displacement of Trials in American Courts, Daedalus, Summer 2014 (noting that summary judgment "now accounts for far more terminations than trials").

2.   **Historical background.** The motion for summary judgment was an English procedural innovation of the mid-19th century and was initially restricted to actions on commercial paper. This was a narrow class of cases in which the critical evidence was likely to be documentary. Under code pleading, the expansion of summary judgment to other types of actions was

---

[†]   The separate opinions of Black, J., concurring in the judgment, Douglas, J., dissenting in part, and Brennan, J., concurring in part and dissenting in part, are omitted. Marshall, J., did not participate.

halting and hedged by technical restrictions excited by fears of its abuse. C. Clark, Handbook on the Law of Code Pleading 557–59 (2d ed. 1947). Federal Rule 56 made a major break with past practice by making summary judgment available to both plaintiffs and defendants in every category of claim and allowing parties to move for partial summary judgment limited to a single claim or issue.

During the early history of summary judgment, the view of many courts was that the pleading of the party moved against, particularly a verified pleading, was sufficient to controvert the evidence, however strong, in support of the motion. See the discussion in note 20 of *Adickes*. The general rule today is that pleadings, even if verified, cannot be relied on as evidence in opposition to a properly supported motion for summary judgment because pleadings are merely allegations, not evidence of the truth thereof. The point is made explicit in federal Rule 56(c)(1)(A), the original version of which was added in 1963: "A party asserting that a fact cannot be or is genuinely disputed must support the assertion by citing to particular parts of materials in the record, including depositions, documents, electronically stored information, affidavits or declarations, stipulations (including those made for purposes of the motion only), admissions, interrogatory answers, or other materials . . . ." As the Advisory Committee noted in 1963, "The very mission of the summary judgment procedure is to pierce the pleadings and to assess the proof in order to see whether there is a genuine need for trial."

3. Moving for and responding to the motion for summary judgment. The procedures and standards for obtaining a summary judgment in federal court are set forth in Rule 56, which was last significantly revised in 2010. The standard for summary judgment is set out in Rule 56(a), which provides that a "court shall grant summary judgment if the movant shows that there is no genuine dispute as to any material fact and the movant is entitled to judgment as a matter of law." Under Rule 56(b), the movant may file the motion at any time "until 30 days after the close of all discovery."

Rule 56(c)(1) spells out the procedures for making and opposing the motion. Both the moving party and the non-moving parties are required to "support" their assertions that particular facts cannot be or are genuinely disputed. The Rule recognizes two ways of providing such support. First, a party may cite "to particular parts of materials in the record." The requirement of citation to particular parts is sometimes described as requiring a "pin point citation" to specific portions of the relevant materials. The Rule provides a list of permitted materials to which the parties may cite. Second, a party may support its position by "showing that the materials cited do not establish the absence or presence of a genuine dispute, or that an adverse party cannot produce admissible evidence to support the fact." Consequently, under Rule 56(c)(2), a party may object to the material cited by the opposing party on the ground that it "cannot be presented in a form that would be admissible in evidence" at trial.

Under Rule 56(d), a party may oppose a motion for summary judgment on the ground that "it cannot present facts essential to justify its opposition." When the opposing party makes such a showing the court may, among other things, defer considering the motion, deny it, or allow time for further affidavits or discovery. The rule ensures that motions for summary judgment are not decided prematurely, before the opposing party has the opportunity to marshal the facts necessary to defeat the motion.

4.   Deciding a motion for summary judgment. As noted above, under Rule 56(a), if a party succeeds in showing that there is no genuine dispute of material fact and that it is entitled to judgment as a matter of law on a claim or defense, or part of a claim or defense, the court "*shall* grant summary judgment." (Emphasis added.) But the rule does provide the court some discretion in adjudicating motions for summary judgment. In deciding the motion, the court need only consider the materials cited by the parties, but it *may* consider other materials in the record. Fed. R. Civ. P. 56(c)(3). A good lawyer, however, should not count on the court doing so. Under Rule 56(e), if a party fails to support an assertion of fact or properly address another party's assertion of fact, the court may grant the party a further opportunity to do so, treat the fact as undisputed for the purposes of the motion, or grant summary judgment where the motion and supporting materials "show that the movant is entitled to it." Moreover, under Rule 56(f), the court may grant summary judgment without a motion or on grounds not identified by the parties. After giving notice and a reasonable opportunity to respond, the court may grant summary judgment to a non-movant, grant the motion on grounds not raised by a party, or consider summary judgment *sua sponte* (that is, without a motion by any party) after identifying the facts that may not genuinely be in dispute.

5.   The relationship between the standard for granting summary judgment and the burdens of production and persuasion. Evaluating a summary judgment motion under the "no genuine dispute of material fact" standard requires an understanding of the two burdens of proof discussed in Chapter 4 at p. 458. The *burden of production,* which typically falls on the plaintiff, requires the plaintiff to produce evidence at trial that meets a minimum standard of "sufficiency." If the plaintiff does not introduce sufficient evidence on each essential element of its case, the judge need not permit the plaintiff's case to go to the jury. Instead, pursuant to federal Rule 50, the trial judge is authorized to grant judgment as a matter of law against the plaintiff. How Rule 50 is used to enforce the burden of production at trial will be discussed below in Chapter 8. For now it is enough to understand that when applying the sufficiency standard under Rule 50, the court evaluates the evidentiary record and decides whether, in the court's judgment, there is enough evidence supporting the plaintiff's claim that the jury could reasonably decide the case in plaintiff's favor.

This evaluation is linked to *the burden of persuasion* by which the plaintiff would ultimately have to convince the jury, which in a civil case is typically "by a preponderance of the evidence" or "more likely than not." The question that the court asks in deciding the burden-of-production question is whether there is sufficient evidence favoring the plaintiff such that a reasonable jury *could* find in the plaintiff's favor under the applicable standard of persuasion. If the answer is yes, then there is an issue that needs to be resolved by the jury and that justifies proceeding to a full trial. If the answer is no, then there is, in the terminology of Rule 50, no "legally sufficient evidentiary basis" for a finding in favor of the plaintiff, no reason to proceed to trial, and judgment will be entered for the defendant as a matter of law.

Summary judgment, then, serves as a device that can be used *before* trial to determine whether a party who bears the burden of *production* will be able to meet it. Indeed, most motions for summary judgment are made by defendants against plaintiffs who bear the burden of production on their claims for relief. (Summary judgment motions by parties who bear the burden of production and persuasion are discussed at p. 829 infra.) In *Adickes*, for example, the plaintiff would have borne the burden of production at trial on the issue of conspiracy between S.H. Kress and the Hattiesburg police. The defendant's motion for summary judgment, in effect, sought to test the sufficiency of the plaintiff's evidence to satisfy this burden. The ultimate question for the court under the "no genuine dispute as to any material fact" standard is the same as for the sufficiency standard discussed above: Do the evidentiary materials submitted by the parties show that there is sufficient evidence supporting each element of plaintiff's case to permit a reasonable jury to find for the plaintiff? If yes, there is a genuine dispute of material fact worthy of submission to the jury and hence reason to expend the resources necessary to conduct a full trial. If no, then there is no genuine dispute of material fact, no reason to proceed to trial, and summary judgment will be entered for the defendant.

6. **The moving party's obligation to support a motion for summary judgment**. Summary judgment procedure is designed so that a moving party can "pierce" the plaintiff's pleading and force a test of the plaintiff's ability to meet its burden of production at trial. In other words, the motion puts the question of whether the plaintiff will be able to sufficiently prove the allegations in the complaint at trial. It does not follow, however, that the moving party should be entitled to force such a test without affirmatively demonstrating that there is reason to believe that the plaintiff will fail it. If a bare summary judgment motion by the defendant, unsupported by any evidentiary materials, were sufficient to oblige the plaintiff to demonstrate that she had a triable case, then summary judgment would function as a discovery device, forcing the plaintiff to preview her case prior to trial and, incidentally, spend a substantial sum opposing the motion. To avoid this outcome, Rule 56 has been interpreted as imposing an initial burden on the party moving for summary judgment to "support" the motion. If the motion is not adequately supported, the plaintiff need not submit *any* evidentiary materials in opposition and the court need not determine whether the plaintiff has passed the test of Rule 56(a).

7. **Understanding *Adickes***. Sandra Adickes contended that defendants had conspired to deprive her of her civil rights in violation of 42 U.S.C. § 1983. The Court discusses the essential elements of her case in Section I.A. To support the essential element of state involvement in a conspiracy with defendant Kress, Adickes contended that a policeman in the store had reached an understanding with some Kress employee to refuse service to her, and/or that a Kress employee had requested that the police arrest her. In light of the Supreme Court's recent jurisprudence on pleading discussed in Chapter 4, do you think that Adickes' complaint would survive a motion to dismiss for failure to state a claim upon which relief can be granted under the standard promulgated in *Twombly* and *Iqbal*?

It appears from the *Adickes* opinion that no potential witness for Adickes had observed any communication between a Kress employee and the police, and that no potential witness for the defendant had admitted to any such communication. Since there was no "direct" evidence of such communication, Plaintiff's case was based on "circumstantial" evidence, that is, on inferences that could reasonably be drawn from what witnesses did perceive. Hence the critical questions:

a. On the basis of the preceding discussion of the plaintiff's burden of production, how much admissible circumstantial evidence of communication between Kress and the police would Adickes have had to introduce at a trial to be able to survive a Rule 50 motion and get her case to the jury? Is Justice Harlan suggesting that it would have been enough for the plaintiff to introduce the testimony of a single competent witness who claimed to have actually seen a policeman in the Kress store, even if every witness for the defendant denied that any policeman was present and that any communication had occurred?

b. What specific evidentiary materials did Adickes identify in support of her claim that a policeman was in the Kress store prior to the arrest? Did those materials comply with Rule 56(c)'s requirements of form and admissibility? Compare Rule 56(c) and note 19 in the Court's opinion.

c. If Adickes presented no evidentiary materials that complied with Rule 56(c) to show the presence of a policeman in the Kress store prior to the refusal of service and arrest, why was it error for the district court to "pierce" the plaintiff's complaint, which had alleged that there was an officer in the store, and require her to present some evidence that would satisfy her burden of production on that issue? Is the problem that the defendant failed to meet its initial burden of supporting its motion under Rule 56?

d. How is it exactly that defendant Kress failed to support its motion? The Court makes reference to "unexplained gaps in the materials submitted by" defendant. What "unexplained gaps" is the Court referring to? With regard to the refusal of service, read carefully the deposition of Mr. Powell, and the statements made by other Kress employees reproduced in footnotes 14, 16, and 17 of the Court's opinion. With regard to both the arrest and the refusal of service, read carefully the deposition of Mr. Powell and the affidavits of the two arresting officers, Sergeant Boone and Officer Hillman, reproduced in footnote 12 of the Court's opinion.

e. What kind of statements in affidavits or depositions from the defendant's witnesses would have been sufficient to meet the defendant's initial burden of supporting the summary judgment motion under Rule 56? Why do you think the defendant's witnesses didn't provide such statements?

8. **Post-*Adickes* developments.** In the aftermath of *Adickes*, some courts took the view that to meet its burden under Rule 56, the moving party without the burden of proof was required to bear "the burden of affirmatively demonstrating that, with respect to every essential issue of each count in the complaint, there is no genuine issue of material fact." Reynolds Indus., Inc. v. Mobil Oil Corp., 569 F. Supp. 716, 718 (D. Mass. 1983). Other courts and commentators argued that, at a minimum, a moving party without the burden of proof should be required to support its motion with evidence that would have permitted a jury verdict in the moving party's favor. See Louis, Federal Summary Judgment Doctrine: A Critical Analysis, 83 Yale L.J. 745, 752 (1974) (citing cases). Some scholars argued that these approaches made summary judgment far too difficult, and in some cases impossible, to obtain. See, e.g., Currie, Thoughts on Directed Verdicts and Summary Judgments, 45 U. Chi. L. Rev. 72, 78–79 (1977).

In any event, as Judge Diane P. Wood of the Seventh Circuit has put it, "before 1986, the federal courts overwhelmingly took the position that Rule 56 was to be used sparingly." Wood, Summary Judgment and the Law of Unintended Consequences, 36 Okla. City U. L. Rev. 231, 239 (2011). Indeed, many courts stated that motions for summary judgment should be denied whenever "there is the slightest doubt as to the facts." Arnstein v. Porter, 154 F.2d 464, 468 (2d Cir. 1946). In 1986, however, the Supreme Court decided three cases now known as the "Summary Judgment Trilogy," one of which was the following primary case. As you read it, consider to what extent, if any, the Supreme Court broke with the past.

Celotex Corp. v. Catrett

Supreme Court of the United States, 1986.
477 U.S. 317, 106 S.Ct. 2548, 91 L.Ed.2d 265.

■ JUSTICE REHNQUIST delivered the opinion of the Court.

The United States District Court for the District of Columbia granted the motion of petitioner Celotex Corporation for summary judgment against respondent Catrett because the latter was unable to produce evidence in support of her allegation in her wrongful death complaint that the decedent had been exposed to petitioner's asbestos products. A divided panel of the Court of Appeals for the District of Columbia Circuit reversed, however, holding that petitioner's failure to support its motion with evidence tending to *negate* such exposure precluded the entry of summary judgment in its favor. 244 U.S.App.D.C. 160, 756 F.2d 181 (1985). * * *

Respondent commenced this lawsuit in September 1980, alleging that the death in 1979 of her husband, Louis H. Catrett, resulted from his exposure to products containing asbestos manufactured or distributed by 15 named corporations. Respondent's complaint sounded in negligence, breach of warranty, and strict liability. Two of the defendants filed motions challenging the District Court's *in personam* jurisdiction, and the remaining 13, including petitioner, filed motions for summary judgment. Petitioner's motion, which was first filed in September 1981, argued that summary judgment was proper because respondent had "failed to produce evidence that any [Celotex] product . . . was the proximate cause of the injuries alleged within the jurisdictional limits of [the District] Court." In particular, petitioner noted that respondent had failed to identify, in answering interrogatories specifically requesting such information, any witnesses who could testify about the decedent's exposure to petitioner's asbestos products. In response to petitioner's summary judgment motion, respondent then produced three documents which she claimed "demonstrate that there is a genuine material factual dispute" as to whether the decedent had ever been exposed to petitioner's asbestos products. The three documents included a transcript of a deposition of the decedent, a letter from an official of one of the decedent's former employers whom petitioner planned to call as a trial witness, and a letter from an insurance company to respondent's attorney, all tending to establish that the decedent had been exposed to petitioner's asbestos products in Chicago during 1970–1971. Petitioner, in turn, argued that the three documents were inadmissible hearsay and thus could not be considered in opposition to the summary judgment motion.

In July 1982, almost two years after the commencement of the lawsuit, the District Court granted all of the motions filed by the various defendants. The court explained that it was granting petitioner's summary judgment motion because "there [was] no showing that the plaintiff was exposed to the defendant Celotex's product in the District of Columbia or elsewhere within the statutory period." Respondent appealed only the grant of summary judgment in favor of petitioner, and a divided panel of the District of Columbia Circuit reversed. The majority of the Court of Appeals held that petitioner's summary judgment motion was rendered "fatally defective" by the fact that petitioner "made no effort to adduce *any* evidence, in the form of affidavits or otherwise, to support its motion." 244 U.S.App.D.C., at 163, 756 F.2d, at 184 (emphasis in original). According to the majority, Rule 56(e) of the Federal Rules of Civil Procedure, and this Court's decision in Adickes v. S.H. Kress & Co., 398 U.S. 144, 159, 90 S.Ct. 1598, 1609, 26 L.Ed.2d 142 (1970), establish that "the party opposing the motion for summary judgment bears the burden of responding *only after* the moving party has met its burden of coming forward with proof of the absence of any genuine issues of material fact." 244 U.S.App.D.C., at 163, 756 F.2d, at 184 (emphasis in original; footnote omitted). The majority therefore declined to consider petitioner's argument that none of the evidence produced by respondent in opposition to the motion for summary judgment would have been admissible at trial. Ibid. The dissenting judge argued that "[t]he majority errs in supposing that a party seeking summary judgment must always make an affirmative evidentiary showing, even in cases where there is not a triable, factual dispute." Id., at 167, 756 F.2d, at 188 (Bork, J., dissenting). According to the dissenting judge, the majority's decision "undermines the traditional authority of trial judges to grant summary judgment in meritless cases." Id., at 166, 756 F.2d, at 187.

We think that the position taken by the majority of the Court of Appeals is inconsistent with the standard for summary judgment set forth in Rule 56(c) of the Federal Rules of Civil Procedure. Under Rule 56(c), summary judgment is proper "if the pleadings, depositions, answers to interrogatories, and admissions on file, together with the affidavits, if any, show that there is no genuine issue as to any material fact and that the moving party is entitled to a judgment as a matter of law." In our view, the plain language of Rule 56(c) mandates the entry of summary judgment, after adequate time for discovery and upon motion, against a party who fails to make a showing sufficient to establish the existence of an element essential to that party's case, and on which that party will bear the burden of proof at trial. In such a situation, there can be "no genuine issue as to any material fact," since a complete failure of proof concerning an essential element of the nonmoving party's case necessarily renders all other facts immaterial. The moving party is "entitled to judgment as a matter of law" because the nonmoving party has failed to make a sufficient showing on an essential element of her case with respect to which she has the burden of proof. "[T]h[e] standard [for granting summary judgment] mirrors the standard for a directed verdict under Federal Rule of Civil Procedure 50(a). . . ." Anderson v. Liberty Lobby, Inc., 477 U.S. 242, 250, 106 S.Ct. 2505, 2511, 91 L.Ed.2d 202 (1986).

Of course, a party seeking summary judgment always bears the initial responsibility of informing the district court of the basis for its motion, and identifying those portions of "the pleadings, depositions, answers to interrogatories, and admissions on file, together with the affidavits, if any," which it believes demonstrate the absence of a genuine issue of material fact. But unlike the Court of Appeals, we find no express or implied requirement in Rule 56 that the moving party support its motion with affidavits or other similar materials *negating* the opponent's claim. On the contrary, Rule 56(c), which refers to "the affidavits, *if any*" (emphasis added), suggests the absence of such a requirement. And if there were any doubt about the meaning of Rule 56(c) in this regard, such doubt is clearly removed by Rules 56(a) and (b), which provide that claimants and defendants, respectively, may move for summary judgment *"with or without supporting affidavits"* (emphasis added). The import of these subsections is that, regardless of whether the moving party accompanies its summary judgment motion with affidavits, the motion may, and should, be granted so long as whatever is before the district court demonstrates that the standard for the entry of summary judgment, as set forth in Rule 56(c), is satisfied. One of the principal purposes of the summary judgment rule is to isolate and dispose of factually unsupported claims or defenses, and we think it should be interpreted in a way that allows it to accomplish this purpose.

Respondent argues, however, that Rule 56(e), by its terms, places on the nonmoving party the burden of coming forward with rebuttal affidavits, or other specified kinds of materials, only in response to a motion for summary judgment "made and supported as provided in this rule." According to respondent's argument, since petitioner did not "support" its motion with affidavits, summary judgment was improper in this case. But as we have already explained, a motion for summary judgment may be made pursuant to Rule 56 "with or without supporting affidavits." In cases like the instant one, where the nonmoving party will bear the burden of proof at trial on a dispositive issue, a summary judgment motion may properly be made in reliance solely on the "pleadings, depositions, answers to interrogatories, and admissions on file." Such a motion, whether or not accompanied by affidavits, will be "made and supported as provided in this rule," and Rule 56(e) therefore requires the nonmoving party to go beyond the pleadings and by her own affidavits, or by the "depositions, answers to interrogatories, and admissions on file," designate "specific facts showing that there is a genuine issue for trial."

We do not mean that the nonmoving party must produce evidence in a form that would be admissible at trial in order to avoid summary judgment. Obviously, Rule 56 does not require the nonmoving party to depose her own witnesses. Rule 56(e) permits a proper summary judgment motion to be opposed by any of the kinds of evidentiary materials listed in Rule 56(c), except the mere pleadings themselves, and it is from this list that one would normally expect the nonmoving party to make the showing to which we have referred.

The Court of Appeals in this case felt itself constrained, however, by language in our decision in Adickes v. S.H. Kress & Co., 398 U.S. 144, 90 S.Ct. 1598, 26 L.Ed.2d 142 (1970). There we held that summary judgment had been improperly entered in favor of the defendant restaurant in an action brought under 42 U.S.C. § 1983. In the course of its opinion, the *Adickes* Court said that "both the commentary on and the background of the 1963 Amendment conclusively show that it was not intended to modify the burden of the moving party . . . to show initially the absence of a genuine issue concerning any material fact." Id., at 159,

90 S.Ct., at 1609. We think that this statement is accurate in a literal sense, since we fully agree with the *Adickes* Court that the 1963 Amendment to Rule 56(e) was not designed to modify the burden of making the showing generally required by Rule 56(c). It also appears to us that, on the basis of the showing before the Court in *Adickes,* the motion for summary judgment in that case should have been denied. But we do not think the *Adickes* language quoted above should be construed to mean that the burden is on the party moving for summary judgment to produce evidence showing the absence of a genuine issue of material fact, even with respect to an issue on which the nonmoving party bears the burden of proof. Instead, as we have explained, the burden on the moving party may be discharged by "showing"—that is, pointing out to the District Court—that there is an absence of evidence to support the nonmoving party's case.

The last two sentences of Rule 56(e) were added, as this Court indicated in *Adickes,* to disapprove a line of cases allowing a party opposing summary judgment to resist a properly made motion by reference only to its pleadings. While the *Adickes* Court was undoubtedly correct in concluding that these two sentences were not intended to *reduce* the burden of the moving party, it is also obvious that they were not adopted to *add to* that burden. Yet that is exactly the result which the reasoning of the Court of Appeals would produce; in effect, an amendment to Rule 56(e) designed to *facilitate* the granting of motions for summary judgment would be interpreted to make it *more difficult* to grant such motions. Nothing in the two sentences themselves requires this result, for the reasons we have previously indicated, and we now put to rest any inference that they do so.

Our conclusion is bolstered by the fact that district courts are widely acknowledged to possess the power to enter summary judgments *sua sponte,* so long as the losing party was on notice that she had to come forward with all of her evidence. See 244 U.S.App.D.C., at 167–168, 756 F.2d, at 189 (Bork, J., dissenting); 10A C. Wright, A. Miller & M. Kane, Federal Practice and Procedure § 2720, pp. 28–29 (1983). It would surely defy common sense to hold that the District Court could have entered summary judgment *sua sponte* in favor of petitioner in the instant case, but that petitioner's filing of a motion requesting such a disposition precluded the District Court from ordering it.

Respondent commenced this action in September 1980, and petitioner's motion was filed in September 1981. The parties had conducted discovery, and no serious claim can be made that respondent was in any sense "railroaded" by a premature motion for summary judgment. Any potential problem with such premature motions can be adequately dealt with under Rule 56(f), which allows a summary judgment motion to be denied, or the hearing on the motion to be continued, if the nonmoving party has not had an opportunity to make full discovery.

In this Court, respondent's brief and oral argument have been devoted as much to the proposition that an adequate showing of exposure to petitioner's asbestos products was made as to the proposition that no such showing should have been required. But the Court of Appeals declined to address either the adequacy of the showing made by respondent in opposition to petitioner's motion for summary judgment, or the question whether such a showing, if reduced to admissible evidence, would be sufficient to carry respondent's burden of proof at trial. We think the Court of Appeals with its superior knowledge of local law is better suited than we are to make these determinations in the first instance.

The Federal Rules of Civil Procedure have for more than 50 years authorized motions for summary judgment upon proper showings of the lack of a genuine, triable issue of material fact. Summary judgment procedure is properly regarded not as a disfavored procedural shortcut, but rather as an integral part of the Federal Rules as a whole, which are designed "to secure the just, speedy and inexpensive determination of every action." Fed.Rule Civ.Proc. 1; see Schwarzer, Summary Judgment Under the Federal Rules: Defining Genuine Issues of Material Fact, 99 F.R.D. 465, 467 (1984). Before the shift to "notice pleading" accomplished by the Federal Rules, motions to dismiss a complaint or to strike a defense were the principal tools by which factually insufficient claims or defenses could be isolated and prevented from going to trial with the attendant unwarranted consumption of public and private resources. But with the advent of "notice pleading," the motion to dismiss seldom fulfills this function any more, and its place has been taken by the motion for summary judgment. Rule 56 must be construed with due regard not only for the rights of persons asserting claims and defenses that are adequately based in fact to have those claims and defenses tried to a jury, but also for the rights of persons opposing such claims and defenses to demonstrate in the manner provided by the Rule, prior to trial, that the claims and defenses have no factual basis.

The judgment of the Court of Appeals is accordingly reversed, and the case is remanded for further proceedings consistent with this opinion.

It is so ordered.

■ JUSTICE WHITE, concurring in the Court's opinion and judgment.

I agree that the Court of Appeals was wrong in holding that the moving defendant must always support his motion with evidence or affidavits showing the absence of a genuine dispute about a material fact. I also agree that the movant may rely on depositions, answers to interrogatories, and the like, to demonstrate that the plaintiff has no evidence to prove his case and hence that there can be no factual dispute. But the movant must discharge the burden the Rules place upon him: It is not enough to move for summary judgment without supporting the motion in any way or with a conclusory assertion that the plaintiff has no evidence to prove his case. A plaintiff need not initiate any discovery or reveal his witnesses or evidence unless required to do so under the discovery Rules or by court order. Of course, he must respond if required to do so; but he need not also depose his witnesses or obtain their affidavits to defeat a summary judgment motion asserting only that he has failed to produce any support for his case. It is the defendant's task to negate, if he can, the claimed basis for the suit.

Petitioner Celotex does not dispute that if respondent has named a witness to support her claim, summary judgment should not be granted without Celotex somehow showing that the named witness' possible testimony raises no genuine issue of material fact. It asserts, however, that respondent has failed on request produce any basis for her case.

Respondent, on the other hand, does not contend that she was not obligated to reveal her witnesses and evidence but insists that she has revealed enough to defeat the motion for summary judgment. Because the Court of Appeals found it unnecessary to address this aspect of the case, I agree that the case should be remanded for further proceedings.

■ JUSTICE BRENNAN, with whom THE CHIEF JUSTICE and JUSTICE BLACKMUN join, dissenting.

* * * [C]ourts must routinely decide summary judgment motions, and the Court's opinion will very likely create confusion. For this reason, even if I agreed with the Court's result, I would have written separately to explain more clearly the law in this area. However, because I believe that Celotex did not meet its burden of production under Federal Rule of Civil Procedure 56, I respectfully dissent from the Court's judgment.

* * *

The burden of production imposed by Rule 56 requires the moving party to make a prima facie showing that it is entitled to summary judgment. 10A Wright, Miller & Kane § 2727. The manner in which this showing can be made depends upon which party will bear the burden of persuasion on the challenged claim at trial. If the *moving* party will bear the burden of persuasion at trial, that party must support its motion with credible evidence—using any of the materials specified in Rule 56(c)— that would entitle it to a directed verdict if not controverted at trial. Ibid. Such an affirmative showing shifts the burden of production to the party opposing the motion and requires that party either to produce evidentiary materials that demonstrate the existence of a "genuine issue" for trial or to submit an affidavit requesting additional time for discovery. Ibid.; Fed.Rule Civ.Proc. 56(e), (f).

If the burden of persuasion at trial would be on the *nonmoving* party, the party moving for summary judgment may satisfy Rule 56's burden of production in either of two ways. First, the moving party may submit affirmative evidence that negates an essential element of the nonmoving party's claim. Second, the moving party may demonstrate to the Court that the nonmoving party's evidence is insufficient to establish an essential element of the nonmoving party's claim. See 10A Wright, Miller & Kane § 2727, pp. 130–131; Louis, Federal Summary Judgment Doctrine: A Critical Analysis, 83 Yale L.J. 745, 750 (1974) (hereinafter Louis). If the nonmoving party cannot muster sufficient evidence to make out its claim, a trial would be useless and the moving party is entitled to summary judgment as a matter of law. Anderson v. Liberty Lobby, Inc., 477 U.S. 242, 249, 106 S.Ct. 2505, 2511, 91 L.Ed.2d 202 (1986).

Where the moving party adopts this second option and seeks summary judgment on the ground that the nonmoving party—who will bear the burden of persuasion at trial—has no evidence, the mechanics of discharging Rule 56's burden of production are somewhat trickier. Plainly, a conclusory assertion that the nonmoving party has no evidence is insufficient. * * * Such a "burden" of production is no burden at all and would simply permit summary judgment procedure to be converted into a tool for harassment. See Louis 750–751. Rather, as the Court confirms, a party who moves for summary judgment on the ground that the nonmoving party has no evidence must affirmatively show the absence of evidence in the record. * * * This may require the moving party to depose the nonmoving party's witnesses or to establish the inadequacy of documentary evidence. If there is literally no evidence in the record, the moving party may demonstrate this by reviewing for the court the admissions, interrogatories and other exchanges between the parties that are in the record. Either way, however, the moving party must affirmatively demonstrate that there is no evidence in the record to support a judgment for the nonmoving party.

If the moving party has not fully discharged this initial burden of production, its motion for summary judgment must be denied, and the Court need not consider whether the moving party has met its ultimate burden of persuasion. Accordingly, the nonmoving party may defeat a motion for summary judgment that asserts that the nonmoving party has no evidence by calling the Court's attention to supporting evidence already in the record that was overlooked or ignored by the moving party. In that event, the moving party must respond by making an attempt to demonstrate the inadequacy of this evidence, for it is only by attacking all the record evidence allegedly supporting the nonmoving party that a party seeking summary judgment satisfies Rule 56's burden of production. Thus, if the record disclosed that the moving party had overlooked a witness who would provide relevant testimony for the nonmoving party at trial, the Court could not find that the moving party had discharged its initial burden of production unless the moving party sought to demonstrate the inadequacy of this witness' testimony. Absent such a demonstration, summary judgment would have to be denied on the ground that the moving party had failed to meet its burden of production under Rule 56.

　　* * *

II

I do not read the Court's opinion to say anything inconsistent with or different than the preceding discussion. My disagreement with the Court concerns the application of these principles to the facts of this case.

Defendant Celotex sought summary judgment on the ground that plaintiff had "failed to produce" any evidence that her decedent had ever been exposed to Celotex asbestos. Celotex supported this motion with a 2-page "Statement of Material Facts as to Which There is No Genuine Issue" and a 3-page "Memorandum of Points and Authorities" which asserted that the plaintiff had failed to identify any evidence in responding to two sets of interrogatories propounded by Celotex and that therefore the record was "totally devoid" of evidence to support plaintiff's claim.

Approximately three months earlier, Celotex had filed an essentially identical motion. Plaintiff responded to this earlier motion by producing three pieces of evidence which she claimed "[a]t the very least . . . demonstrate that there is a genuine factual dispute for trial:" (1) a letter from an insurance representative of another defendant describing asbestos products to which plaintiff's decedent had been exposed, id., at 160; (2) a letter from T.R. Hoff, a former supervisor of decedent, describing asbestos products to which decedent had been exposed, id., at 162; and (3) a copy of decedent's deposition from earlier workmen's compensation proceedings, id., at 164. Plaintiff also apparently indicated at that time that she intended to call Mr. Hoff as a witness at trial. Tr. of Oral Arg. 6–7, 27–29.

Celotex subsequently withdrew its first motion for summary judgment.[5] However, as a result of this motion, when Celotex filed its second summary judgment motion, the record *did* contain evidence—including at least one witness—supporting plaintiff's claim. Indeed, counsel for Celotex admitted to this Court at oral argument that Celotex was aware of this evidence and of plaintiff's intention to call Mr. Hoff as a witness at trial when the second summary judgment motion was filed. Tr. of Oral Arg. 5–7. Moreover, plaintiff's response to Celotex' second motion pointed to this evidence—noting that it had already been provided to counsel for Celotex in connection with the first motion—and argued that Celotex had failed to "meet its burden of proving that there is no genuine factual dispute for trial."

On these facts, there is simply no question that Celotex failed to discharge its initial burden of production. Having chosen to base its motion on the argument that there was no evidence in the record to support plaintiff's claim, Celotex was not free to ignore supporting evidence that the record clearly contained. Rather, Celotex was required, as an initial matter, to attack the adequacy of this evidence. Celotex' failure to fulfill this simple requirement constituted a failure to discharge its initial burden of production under Rule 56, and thereby rendered summary judgment improper.[6]

* * *

■ JUSTICE STEVENS, dissenting*

FURTHER NOTE ON THE MOVING PARTY'S BURDEN TO SUPPORT A SUMMARY JUDGMENT MOTION

1. **Understanding *Celotex*.** As in *Adickes,* the plaintiff in *Celotex* would have had both the burdens of production and persuasion on the issue of exposure had her claim gone to trial. As we will explore more fully below, there were questions about the adequacy of her evidence to meet those burdens. Yet the Court of Appeals held, on the basis of *Adickes*, that the defendant's motion for summary judgment had to be denied *without* examining the plaintiff's evidence because the defendant had failed to meet *its* burden in moving for summary judgment. What kind of showing does *Adickes* suggest should have been required to force an examination of the adequacy of the plaintiff's proof?

The Supreme Court reversed. What is your understanding of the reasoning by which the Court concluded that the defendant's support for its motion was sufficient to compel an evidentiary response from the plaintiff?

---

    [5]   Celotex apparently withdrew this motion because, contrary to the assertion made in the first summary judgment motion, its second set of interrogatories had not been served on the plaintiff.

    [6]   If the plaintiff had answered Celotex' second set of interrogatories with the evidence in her response to the first summary judgment motion, and Celotex had ignored those interrogatories and based its second summary judgment motion on the first set of interrogatories only, Celotex obviously could not claim to have discharged its Rule 56 burden of production. This result should not be different simply because the evidence plaintiff relied upon to support her claim was acquired by Celotex other than in plaintiff's answers to interrogatories.

    *   The dissenting opinion of Justice Stevens has been omitted.

Do you think that the defendant's showing on this issue should have been treated as sufficient?

2.   Does *Celotex* overrule *Adickes*? The Court in *Celotex* states that a defendant is not necessarily required when moving for summary judgment to use affidavits specifically to disprove plaintiff's allegations. Is *Celotex* therefore inconsistent with *Adickes*? In Nissan Fire & Marine Ins. Co. v. Fritz Cos., 210 F.3d 1099, 1103–04 (9th Cir. 2000), the court saw the following distinction between *Adickes* and *Celotex*:

> We believe that the perceived tension between *Adickes* and *Celotex* may be explained by the fact that the two cases focused on different questions. The central question in *Adickes* was whether the moving party had carried its initial burden of production by producing affirmative evidence negating an essential element of the nonmoving party's claim. The central question in *Celotex* was whether the moving party had carried its initial burden of production by showing that the nonmoving party did not have enough evidence to carry its ultimate burden of persuasion at trial. In other words, *Adickes* and *Celotex* dealt with the two different methods by which a moving party can carry its initial burden of production.

See also Carmona v. Toledo, 215 F.3d 124 (1st Cir. 2000) (adopting same view). If the Ninth Circuit is right, is it nonetheless true that Justice Rehnquist's opinion "somehow managed to gut [*Adickes*] without overruling it?" Shapiro, The Story of Celotex, in Civil Procedure Stories 343, 359 (Clermont ed. 2004).

Amended Rule 56(c)(1), which took effect in 2010, adopts essentially the distinction suggested by the Ninth Circuit in the *Nissan Fire* case, allowing a party to support a motion for summary judgment by citing particular parts of materials in the record or by showing that an adverse party cannot produce affirmative evidence to support the existence of a critical fact.

3.   The summary judgment "trilogy." During the same term that the Court decided *Celotex*, it decided two other important cases concerning summary judgment, Anderson v. Liberty Lobby, Inc., 477 U.S. 242, 106 S.Ct. 2505, 91 L.Ed.2d 202 (1986), and Matsushita Elec. Indus. Co. v. Zenith Radio Corp., 475 U.S. 574, 106 S.Ct. 1348, 89 L.Ed.2d 538 (1986). While *Celotex* concerned the required level of support for a motion by a party who did not bear the burden of persuasion, *Anderson* and *Matsushita* both involved the question of what was required for a non-moving plaintiff with the burden of persuasion to counter a properly supported motion. But both cases, together with *Celotex*, were widely interpreted as making summary judgment motions easier to win. Knight v. U.S. Fire Ins. Co., 804 F.2d 9 (2d Cir. 1986); Wald, Summary Judgment at Sixty, 76 Tex. L. Rev. 1897, 1914–15 (1998).

Recent studies indicate that there has indeed been an increase in the frequency with which summary judgment is sought and granted over the past forty years, but that the role of the "trilogy" in producing that change is uncertain. A study of summary judgment practice in six federal district courts between 1975 and 2000 shows increases in several important areas: the percentage of cases in which summary judgment motions were filed (from 12% in 1975 to 20% in 2000), the percentage of cases in which one or more summary judgments was granted (from 6% in 1975 to 12% in 2000), and the percentage of cases terminated by summary judgment (from 3.7% in 1975 to

7.7% in 2000). But the vast bulk of these increases predated the trilogy. Cecil, Miletich & Cort, Trends in Summary Judgment Practice: A Preliminary Analysis 1–3 (Federal Judicial Center 2001). The authors were unable to "isolate any effect from the Supreme Court trilogy." Id. at 6. Indeed, as Professor Mullenix has recently written, "inexorably one is led to the conclusion that the summary judgment trilogy, at twenty five, has been much ado about very little." Mullenix, The 25th Anniversary of the Summary Judgment Trilogy: Much Ado About Very Little, 43 Loy. U. Chi. L.J. 561 (2012).

Nevertheless, the prevailing view is that the prominence of summary judgment has significantly increased since the trilogy. As Judge Wood writes, the motion for summary judgment is "the one moment in litigation when all of that information collected in discovery is sure to be used." Wood, Summary Judgment and the Law of Unintended Consequences, 36 Okla. City U. L. Rev. 231, 245 (2011). Indeed, according to a survey of lawyers conducted by the American Bar Association, 50% of plaintiffs' lawyers and 47% of defense lawyers state that "discovery is used more to develop evidence for summary judgment than it is to understand the other party's claims and defenses for trial." Am. Bar Ass'n, Section of Litig. Member Survey on Civil Practice, Full Report at 71 (Dec. 11, 2009).

As a result, Judge Hornby argues, "[t]he term summary judgment suggests a judicial process that is simple, abbreviated, and inexpensive. But the federal summary judgment process is none of those. Lawyers say it's complicated and that judges try to avoid it. Clients say it's expensive and protracted. Judges say it's tedious and time consuming. The very name for the procedure is a near oxymoron that creates confusion and frustrates expectations." Hornby, Summary Judgment Without Illusions, 13 Green Bag 2d 273 (2010). Others, such as Professor Brunet, argue that "[s]ummary judgment *is* efficient" because it clarifies factual and legal issues before trial and "the settlement value of a case increases when a motion for summary judgment is denied . . . A party will be reluctant to file a Rule 56 motion if the risk of loss is unacceptable." Brunet, The Efficiency of Summary Judgment, 43 Loy. Chi. L. Rev. 689 (2012).

4. Supporting a motion for summary judgment when the moving party bears the burden of proof. Motions for summary judgment by parties who bear the burden of production and persuasion (typically plaintiffs) are relatively infrequent. To begin with, outside of certain commercial settings (such as those involving written contracts for a sum certain), there are few cases where the plaintiff has evidence sufficiently compelling to avoid a trial on all issues.

Such motions are very difficult to win because the burden of supporting them is so demanding. Post-*Celotex*, the party without the burden of production can move for summary judgment on the basis of a showing that the opposing party has nothing with which to meet his burden. But the party *with* the burden must make an initial demonstration not only that he has evidence that would allow a jury to find in his favor, but also that his evidence is so compelling that a judge or jury would not be permitted to reject it at trial. Since judges and juries have broad power to reject testimony on the basis of credibility or demeanor and to refuse to draw permissible inferences even from uncontested evidence, there may be cases where the motion must be viewed as inadequately supported even if it presents only sworn testimony favoring the moving party. As a result, although they are not impossible, motions for summary judgment by parties who bear the burdens of production and persuasion are far less likely to be successful. See, e.g., 10A C. Wright, A. Miller & M. Kane, Federal Practice and Procedure § 2729 (3d ed. 2012).

2. RESPONDING TO A PROPERLY SUPPORTED SUMMARY JUDGMENT MOTION

Tolan v. Cotton

Supreme Court of the United States, 2014.
572 U.S. ___, 134 S.Ct. 1861, 188 L.Ed.2d. 895.

■ PER CURIAM:

During the early morning hours of New Year's Eve, 2008, police sergeant Jeffrey Cotton fired three bullets at Robert Tolan; one of those bullets hit its target and punctured Tolan's right lung. At the time of the shooting, Tolan was unarmed on his parents' front porch about 15 to 20 feet away from Cotton. Tolan sued, alleging that Cotton had exercised excessive force in violation of the Fourth Amendment. The District Court granted summary judgment to Cotton, and the Fifth Circuit affirmed, reasoning that regardless of whether Cotton used excessive force, he was entitled to qualified immunity because he did not violate any clearly established right. 713 F. 3d 299 (2013). In articulating the factual context of the case, the Fifth Circuit failed to adhere to the axiom that in ruling on a motion for summary judgment, "[t]he evidence of the nonmovant is to be believed, and all justifiable inferences are to be drawn in his favor." Anderson v. Liberty Lobby, Inc., 477 U.S. 242, 255 (1986). For that reason, we vacate its decision and remand the case for further proceedings consistent with this opinion.

I

A

The following facts, which we view in the light most favorable to Tolan, are taken from the record evidence and the opinions below. At around 2:00 on the morning of December 31, 2008, John Edwards, a police officer, was on patrol in Bellaire, Texas, when he noticed a black Nissan sport utility vehicle turning quickly onto a residential street. The officer watched the vehicle park on the side of the street in front of a house. Two men exited: Tolan and his cousin, Anthony Cooper.

Edwards attempted to enter the license plate number of the vehicle into a computer in his squad car. But he keyed an incorrect character; instead of entering plate number 696BGK, he entered 695BGK. That incorrect number matched a stolen vehicle of the same color and make. This match caused the squad car's computer to send an automatic message to other police units, informing them that Edwards had found a stolen vehicle.

Edwards exited his cruiser, drew his service pistol and ordered Tolan and Cooper to the ground. He accused Tolan and Cooper of having stolen the car. Cooper responded, "That's not true." And Tolan explained, "That's my car." Tolan then complied with the officer's demand to lie face-down on the home's front porch.

As it turned out, Tolan and Cooper were at the home where Tolan lived with his parents. Hearing the commotion, Tolan's parents exited the front door in their pajamas. In an attempt to keep the misunderstanding from escalating into something more, Tolan's father instructed Cooper to lie down, and instructed Tolan and Cooper to say nothing. Tolan and Cooper then remained facedown.

Edwards told Tolan's parents that he believed Tolan and Cooper had stolen the vehicle. In response, Tolan's father identified Tolan as his son, and Tolan's mother explained that the vehicle belonged to the family and that no crime had been committed. Tolan's father explained, with his hands in the air, "[T]his is my nephew. This is my son. We live here. This is my house." Tolan's mother similarly offered, "[S]ir this is a big mistake. This car is not stolen. . . . That's our car."

While Tolan and Cooper continued to lie on the ground in silence, Edwards radioed for assistance. Shortly thereafter, Sergeant Jeffrey Cotton arrived on the scene and drew his pistol. Edwards told Cotton that Cooper and Tolan had exited a stolen vehicle. Tolan's mother reiterated that she and her husband owned both the car Tolan had been driving and the home where these events were unfolding. Cotton then ordered her to stand against the family's garage door. In response to Cotton's order, Tolan's mother asked, "[A]re you kidding me? We've lived her[e] 15 years. We've never had anything like this happen before."

The parties disagree as to what happened next. Tolan's mother and Cooper testified during Cotton's criminal trial[1] that Cotton grabbed her arm and slammed her against the garage door with such force that she fell to the ground. Tolan similarly testified that Cotton pushed his mother against the garage door. In addition, Tolan offered testimony from his mother and photographic evidence to demonstrate that Cotton used enough force to leave bruises on her arms and back that lasted for days. By contrast, Cotton testified in his deposition that when he was escorting the mother to the garage, she flipped her arm up and told him to get his hands off her. He also testified that he did not know whether he left bruises but believed that he had not.

The parties also dispute the manner in which Tolan responded. Tolan testified in his deposition and during the criminal trial that upon seeing his mother being pushed he rose to his knees. Edwards and Cotton testified that Tolan rose to his feet.

Both parties agree that Tolan then exclaimed, from roughly 15 to 20 feet away, 713 F. 3d, at 303, "[G]et your fucking hands off my mom." The parties also agree that Cotton then drew his pistol and fired three shots at Tolan. Tolan and his mother testified that these shots came with no verbal warning. One of the bullets entered Tolan's chest, collapsing his right lung and piercing his liver. While Tolan survived, he suffered a life-altering injury that disrupted his budding professional baseball career and causes him to experience pain on a daily basis.

---

[1] The events described here led to Cotton's criminal indictment in Harris County, Texas, for aggravated assault by a public servant. 713 F. 3d 299, 303 (CA5 2013). He was acquitted. Ibid. The testimony of Tolan's mother during Cotton's trial is a part of the record in this civil action.

B

In May 2009, Cooper, Tolan, and Tolan's parents filed this suit in the Southern District of Texas, alleging claims under Rev. Stat. §1979, 42 U.S.C. § 1983. Tolan claimed, among other things, that Cotton had used excessive force against him in violation of the Fourth Amendment. After discovery, Cotton moved for summary judgment, arguing that the doctrine of qualified immunity barred the suit. That doctrine immunizes government officials from damages suits unless their conduct has violated a clearly established right.

The District Court granted summary judgment to Cotton. 854 F. Supp. 2d 444 (S.D. Tex. 2012). It reasoned that Cotton's use of force was not unreasonable and therefore did not violate the Fourth Amendment. Id., at 477–478. The Fifth Circuit affirmed, but on a different basis. 713 F.3d 299. It declined to decide whether Cotton's actions violated the Fourth Amendment. Instead, it held that even if Cotton's conduct did violate the Fourth Amendment, Cotton was entitled to qualified immunity because he did not violate a clearly established right.

[handwritten margin note: Reasoning of Dist court and Court of Appeal]

In reaching this conclusion, the Fifth Circuit began by noting that at the time Cotton shot Tolan, "it was . . . clearly established that an officer had the right to use deadly force if that officer harbored an objective and reasonable belief that a suspect presented an 'immediate threat to [his] safety.' " Id., at 306 (quoting Deville v. Marcantel, 567 F. 3d 156, 167 (CA5 2009)). The Court of Appeals reasoned that Tolan failed to overcome the qualified-immunity bar because "an objectively-reasonable officer in Sergeant Cotton's position could have . . . believed" that Tolan "presented an 'immediate threat to the safety of the officers.' " 713 F. 3d, at 307. In support of this conclusion, the court relied on the following facts: the front porch had been "dimly-lit"; Tolan's mother had "refus[ed] orders to remain quiet and calm"; and Tolan's words had amounted to a "verba[l] threa[t]." Ibid. Most critically, the court also relied on the purported fact that Tolan was "moving to intervene in" Cotton's handling of his mother, id., at 305, and that Cotton therefore could reasonably have feared for his life, id., at 307. Accordingly, the court held, Cotton did not violate clearly established law in shooting Tolan. * * *

II

A

In resolving questions of qualified immunity at summary judgment, courts engage in a two-pronged inquiry. The first asks whether the facts, "[t]aken in the light most favorable to the party asserting the injury, . . . show the officer's conduct violated a [federal] right[.]" Saucier v. Katz, 533 U.S. 194, 201 (2001). When a plaintiff alleges excessive force during an investigation or arrest, the federal right at issue is the Fourth Amendment right against unreasonable seizures. Graham v. Connor, 490 U.S. 386, 394 (1989). The inquiry into whether this right was violated requires a balancing of " 'the nature and quality of the intrusion on the individual's Fourth Amendment interests against the importance of the governmental interests alleged to justify the intrusion.' " Tennessee v. Garner, 471 U.S. 1, 8 (1985); see Graham, supra, at 396.

The second prong of the qualified-immunity analysis asks whether the right in question was "clearly established" at the time of the violation. Hope v. Pelzer, 536 U.S. 730, 739 (2002). Governmental actors are "shielded from liability for civil damages if their actions did not violate 'clearly established statutory or constitutional rights of which a reasonable person would have known.'" Ibid. "[T]he salient question . . . is whether the state of the law" at the time of an incident provided "fair warning" to the defendants "that their alleged [conduct] was unconstitutional." Id. at 741.

Courts have discretion to decide the order in which to engage these two prongs. Pearson v. Callahan, 555 U.S. 223, 236 (2009). But under either prong, courts may not resolve genuine disputes of fact in favor of the party seeking summary judgment. See Brosseau v. Haugen, 543 U.S. 194, 195, n. 2 (2004) (per curiam); Saucier, supra, at 201; Hope, supra, at 733, n. 1. This is not a rule specific to qualified immunity; it is simply an application of the more general rule that a "judge's function" at summary judgment is not "to weigh the evidence and determine the truth of the matter but to determine whether there is a genuine issue for trial." Anderson, 477 U.S., at 249. Summary judgment is appropriate only if "the movant shows that there is no genuine issue as to any material fact and the movant is entitled to judgment as a matter of law." Fed. Rule Civ. Proc. 56(a). In making that determination, a court must view the evidence "in the light most favorable to the opposing party." Adickes v. S. H. Kress & Co., 398 U.S. 144, 157 (1970); see also Anderson, supra, at 255.

Our qualified-immunity cases illustrate the importance of drawing inferences in favor of the nonmovant, even when, as here, a court decides only the clearly-established prong of the standard. In cases alleging unreasonable searches or seizures, we have instructed that courts should define the "clearly established" right at issue on the basis of the "specific context of the case." Saucier, supra, at 201; see also Anderson v. Creighton, 483 U.S. 635–641 (1987). Accordingly, courts must take care not to define a case's "context" in a manner that imports genuinely disputed factual propositions. See Brosseau, supra, at 195, 198 (inquiring as to whether conduct violated clearly established law "'in light of the specific context of the case'" and construing "facts . . . in a light most favorable to" the nonmovant).

B

In holding that Cotton's actions did not violate clearly established law, the Fifth Circuit failed to view the evidence at summary judgment in the light most favorable to Tolan with respect to the central facts of this case. By failing to credit evidence that contradicted some of its key factual conclusions, the court improperly "weigh[ed] the evidence" and resolved disputed issues in favor of the moving party, Anderson, 477 U.S., at 249.

First, the court relied on its view that at the time of the shooting, the Tolans' front porch was "dimly-lit." 713 F. 3d, at 307. The court appears to have drawn this assessment from Cotton's statements in a deposition that when he fired at Tolan, the porch was "'fairly dark,'" and lit by a gas lamp that was "'decorative.'" Id. at 302. In his own deposition, however, Tolan's father was asked whether the gas lamp was in fact "more decorative than illuminating." He said that it was not. Moreover, Tolan stated in his deposition that two floodlights shone on the driveway during the incident, and Cotton acknowledged that there were two motion-activated lights in front of the house. And Tolan confirmed that at the time of the shooting, he was "not in darkness."

Second, the Fifth Circuit stated that Tolan's mother "refus[ed] orders to remain quiet and calm," thereby "compound[ing]" Cotton's belief that Tolan "presented an immediate threat to the safety of the officers." 713 F. 3d, at 307 (internal quotation marks omitted). But here, too, the court did not credit directly contradictory evidence. Although the parties agree that Tolan's mother repeatedly informed officers that Tolan was her son, that she lived in the home in front of which he had parked, and that the vehicle he had been driving belonged to her and her husband, there is a dispute as to how calmly she provided this information. Cotton stated during his deposition that Tolan's mother was "very agitated" when she spoke to the officers. By contrast, Tolan's mother testified at Cotton's criminal trial that she was neither "aggravated" nor "agitated."

Third, the Court concluded that Tolan was "shouting," 713 F. 3d, at 306, 308, and "verbally threatening" the officer, id., at 307, in the moments before the shooting. The court noted, and the parties agree, that while Cotton was grabbing the arm of his mother, Tolan told Cotton, "[G]et your fucking hands off my mom." But Tolan testified that he "was not screaming." And a jury could reasonably infer that his words, in context, did not amount to a statement of intent to inflict harm. . . . A jury could well have concluded that a reasonable officer would have heard Tolan's words not as a threat, but as a son's plea not to continue any assault of his mother.

Fourth, the Fifth Circuit inferred that at the time of the shooting, Tolan was "moving to intervene in Sergeant Cotton's" interaction with his mother. 713 F. 3d, at 305; see also id., at 308 (characterizing Tolan's behavior as "abruptly attempting to approach Sergeant Cotton," thereby "inflam[ing] an already tense situation"). The court appears to have credited Edwards' account that at the time of the shooting, Tolan was on both feet "[i]n a crouch" or a "charging position" looking as if he was going to move forward. Tolan testified at trial, however, that he was on his knees when Cotton shot him, a fact corroborated by his mother. Tolan also testified in his deposition that he "wasn't going anywhere," and emphasized that he did not "jump up."

Considered together, these facts lead to the inescapable conclusion that the court below credited the evidence of the party seeking summary judgment and failed properly to acknowledge key evidence offered by the party opposing that motion. And while "this Court is not equipped to correct every perceived error coming from the lower federal courts," Boag v. MacDougall, 454 U.S. 364, 366 (1982) (O'Connor, J., concurring), we intervene here because the opinion below reflects a clear misapprehension of summary judgment standards in light of our precedents. * * *

The witnesses on both sides come to this case with their own perceptions, recollections, and even potential biases. It is in part for that reason that genuine disputes are generally resolved by juries in our adversarial system. By weighing the evidence and reaching factual inferences contrary to Tolan's competent evidence, the court below neglected to adhere to the fundamental principle that at the summary judgment stage, reasonable inferences should be drawn in favor of the nonmoving party.

Applying that principle here, the court should have acknowledged and credited Tolan's evidence with regard to the lighting, his mother's demeanor, whether he shouted words that were an overt threat, and his positioning during the shooting. This is not to say, of course, that these are the only facts that the Fifth Circuit should consider, or that no other facts might contribute to the reasonableness of the officer's actions as a matter of law. Nor do we express a view as to whether Cotton's actions violated clearly established law. We instead vacate the Fifth Circuit's judgment so that the court can determine whether, when Tolan's evidence is properly credited and factual inferences are reasonably drawn in his favor, Cotton's actions violated clearly established law.

The judgment of the United States Court of Appeals for the Fifth Circuit is vacated, and the case is remanded for further proceedings consistent with this opinion.

■ JUSTICE ALITO, concurring.*

NOTE ON RESPONDING TO A PROPERLY SUPPORTED SUMMARY JUDGMENT MOTION

1. **The timing of summary judgment and the right to request further discovery.** Rule 56(b) provides that a motion for summary judgment may be made at any time until thirty days after the close of all discovery in the litigation. In theory, then, summary judgment can be sought very early in the case. In actual practice, however, summary judgment motions are typically made after substantial discovery has taken place. Recall the Court's statement in *Celotex*: "Any potential problem with * * * premature motions can be adequately dealt with under Rule 56(f) [now 56(d)], which allows a summary judgment motion to be denied, or the hearing on the motion to be continued, if the nonmoving party has not had an opportunity to make full discovery."

2. **The formal sufficiency of the response to a properly supported motion.** A party who bears the burden of proof on an issue may also decline to respond to a motion for summary judgment on the ground that, because the motion has not been properly supported, no response is required. But as Justice Harlan points out in *Adickes*, this course is risky. It has become riskier still since *Celotex* has relaxed and in certain ways blurred the standard for determining when a motion is properly supported. Accordingly, a cautious lawyer will almost always want to provide evidence in response to a summary judgment motion.

In planning and evaluating the non-moving party's response one needs to bear in mind the formal requirements of Rule 56 and the separate question of whether the materials, assuming that they meet the formal requirements, suffice to give rise to a "genuine dispute" of fact. The express language of Rule 56(c) is quite clear on the formal question: a response to a properly supported motion consists of affidavits, depositions and the like "made on personal knowledge," setting forth "facts that would be admissible in evidence" (no hearsay), and showing affirmatively the competence of the witness to testify. Justice Harlan's dictum in *Adickes* rejecting the unsworn

---

*   The concurring opinion of Justice Alito has been omitted.

statement by Irene Sullivan (the inaptly described "check out girl") and Adickes' hearsay statement in her own deposition suggest that these requirements must be taken seriously. So must Justice Rehnquist's statement in *Celotex* that "ordinarily" the opposition to a properly supported motion would be drawn from the list of approved evidentiary materials (other than pleadings) listed in Rule 56(c).

Is there any question that defendant's motion in *Tolan v. Cotton* was sufficient to meet its initial burden of supporting its motion under Rule 56? Or that plaintiff's submissions in response to the motion met the formal requirements of Rule 56?

3. **The parties' obligation to identify evidence.** Local rules in many district courts supplement Rule 56(c) by requiring a party opposing a motion for summary judgment to file a brief containing a statement of material facts in dispute, with "appropriate citations" to depositions, affidavits, and other evidence supporting the opposing party's position. See, e.g., Southern District of New York, Local Civil Rule 56.1. Litigants cannot afford to ignore such rules. See Waldridge v. American Hoechst Corp., 24 F.3d 918 (7th Cir. 1994) (affirming grant of summary judgment for failure to comply with local rule). Sometimes courts achieve the same result without the benefit of a local rule. For example, in Carmen v. San Francisco Unified School Dist., 237 F.3d 1026 (9th Cir. 2001), the court affirmed a summary judgment against plaintiff despite the district court's failure to consider a declaration supporting plaintiff's claim of discrimination which would have been sufficient to give rise to a material issue of fact. The court noted that plaintiff had failed to do anything to alert the court to the existence or content of the declaration: "The record in this case consists of six heavily stuffed folders of papers, eight or nine inches thick when pressed together. The declaration * * * was filed two years before the summary judgment motion at issue," and the trial court could not be reasonably be expected to remember it or to search the file. "Though the [district] court has discretion in appropriate circumstances to consider other materials [than those cited by the party opposing summary judgment], it need not do so." Id. at 1029–31.

4. **The standard when the motion is properly made and supported.** Prior to the 1986 trilogy, federal courts often stated that summary judgment should be denied when "there is the slightest doubt as to the facts." Arnstein v. Porter, 154 F.2d 464 (2d Cir. 1946). That statement is no longer representative of the law or practice under the federal Rules. The present accepted view is that in evaluating the response to a summary judgment motion the question is whether there are "any genuine factual issues that properly can be resolved only by a finder of fact because they may reasonably be resolved in favor of either party * * * [T]his standard mirrors the standard for a directed verdict [now judgment as a matter of law] under Federal Rule of Procedure 50(a)." Anderson v. Liberty Lobby, 477 U.S. 242, 250, 106 S.Ct. 2505, 91 L.Ed.2d 202 (1986); *accord*, Reeves v. Sanderson Plumbing Products, Inc., 530 U.S. 133, 150, 120 S.Ct. 2097, 147 L.Ed.2d 105 (2000). In *Reeves*, a case where the Court again drew an explicit parallel between the standards for decision under Rule 50 and Rule 56, the Court suggested that in deciding the question whether a reasonable jury could find in favor of the nonmoving party the court should review "all of the evidence in the record," draw "all reasonable inferences in favor of the nonmoving party," and not make "credibility determinations or weigh the evidence." Id.

[handwritten margin note: noted in class / Mirrors 50(a) standard]

Thus, "although the court should review the record as a whole, it must disregard all evidence favorable to the moving party that the jury is not required to believe." Id. at 151. What explains the shift from the "slightest doubt" standard to the current standard mirroring that for directed verdict? Do you think that shift is desirable?

5.   **Understanding** *Tolan*. *Tolan* provides a representative example of current summary judgment practice, in which the parties marshal all available evidence in order to demonstrate that material facts are, or are not, in dispute. Reconsider the notes following *Celotex*. In your view, does the type of practice exemplified by the parties in *Tolan* enhance efficiency or promote waste of resources for the parties and the court?

According to the Supreme Court in *Tolan*, what was the Fifth Circuit's mistake in granting summary judgment? Based on the available evidence in the record, where precisely did the Court of Appeals go wrong? Moreover, based on the Supreme Court's discussion, what is the appropriate task for a jury if the case goes to trial? And for the judge?

6.   **The relationship between the burden of persuasion and the standard for summary judgment; factually implausible claims.** *Adickes*, *Celotex*, and *Tolan* are cases in which the plaintiff's burden at trial was to prove its case by a preponderance of the evidence. Anderson v. Liberty Lobby, Inc., 477 U.S. 242, 106 S.Ct. 2505, 91 L.Ed.2d 202 (1986), presented the question of whether more stringent or more lenient burdens of persuasion are to be taken into account in ruling upon a summary judgment motion. Plaintiffs brought a libel suit against investigative reporter Jack Anderson and others based on articles portraying them as "neo-Nazi, anti-Semitic, racist and Fascist." Plaintiffs were "public figures" under New York Times v. Sullivan, 376 U.S. 254, 84 S.Ct. 710, 11 L.Ed.2d 686 (1964), which meant that they had to prove not only that the defendants' statements were false, but also that the defendants had published them with "actual malice," defined as knowledge that the statements were false or published with reckless disregard of their truth or falsity. Under the standard of *New York Times*, plaintiffs were required to prove their contentions with "convincing clarity," rather than merely by a preponderance of the evidence. The Court held that in ruling on the summary judgment motion the judge was required to "view the evidence presented through the prism of the substantive evidentiary burden," asking itself whether a "reasonable factfinder could conclude * * * that the plaintiff had shown actual malice with convincing clarity." 477 U.S. at 252–54. Should the requirement in *Tolan* that the plaintiff demonstrate that the defendant violated a "clearly established" right affect the evidence necessary to defeat summary judgment?

<h1 style="text-align:center">Scott v. Harris</h1>

Supreme Court of the United States, 2007.
550 U.S. 372, 127 S.Ct. 1769, 167 L.Ed.2d 686.

■ JUSTICE SCALIA delivered the opinion of the Court.

We consider whether a law enforcement official can, consistent with the Fourth Amendment, attempt to stop a fleeing motorist from continuing his public-endangering flight by ramming the motorist's car from behind. Put another way: Can an officer take actions that place a fleeing motorist at risk of serious injury or death in order to stop the motorist's flight from endangering the lives of innocent bystanders?

I

In March 2001, a Georgia county deputy clocked respondent's vehicle traveling at 73 miles per hour on a road with a 55-mile-per-hour speed limit. The deputy activated his blue flashing lights indicating that respondent should pull over. Instead, respondent sped away, initiating a chase down what is in most portions a two-lane road, at speeds exceeding 85 miles per hour. The deputy radioed his dispatch to report that he was pursuing a fleeing vehicle, and broadcast its license plate number. Petitioner, Deputy Timothy Scott, heard the radio communication and joined the pursuit along with other officers. In the midst of the chase, respondent pulled into the parking lot of a shopping center and was nearly boxed in by the various police vehicles. Respondent evaded the trap by making a sharp turn, colliding with Scott's police car, exiting the parking lot, and speeding off once again down a two-lane highway.

Following respondent's shopping center maneuvering, which resulted in slight damage to Scott's police car, Scott took over as the lead pursuit vehicle. Six minutes and nearly 10 miles after the chase had begun, Scott decided to attempt to terminate the episode by employing a "Precision Intervention Technique ('PIT') maneuver, which causes the fleeing vehicle to spin to a stop." Having radioed his supervisor for permission, Scott was told to " '[g]o ahead and take him out.' " Instead, Scott applied his push bumper to the rear of respondent's vehicle. As a result, respondent lost control of his vehicle, which left the roadway, ran down an embankment, overturned, and crashed. Respondent was badly injured and was rendered a quadriplegic.

Respondent filed suit against Deputy Scott and others under Rev. Stat. § 1979, alleging, *inter alia,* a violation of his federal constitutional rights, viz. use of excessive force resulting in an unreasonable seizure under the Fourth Amendment. In response, Scott filed a motion for summary judgment based on an assertion of qualified immunity. The District Court denied the motion, finding that "there are material issues of fact on which the issue of qualified immunity turns which present sufficient disagreement to require submission to a jury." On interlocutory appeal, the United States Court of Appeals for the Eleventh Circuit affirmed the District Court's decision to allow respondent's Fourth Amendment claim against Scott to proceed to trial. Taking respondent's view of the facts as given, the Court of Appeals concluded that Scott's actions could constitute "deadly force" under Tennessee v. Garner, 471 U.S. 1, 105 S.Ct. 1694, 85 L.Ed.2d 1 (1985), and that the use of such force in this context "would violate [respondent's] constitutional right to be free from excessive force during a seizure. Accordingly, a reasonable jury could find that Scott violated [respondent's] Fourth Amendment rights." The Court of Appeals further concluded that "the law as it existed [at the time of the incident], was sufficiently clear to give reasonable law enforcement officers 'fair notice' that ramming a vehicle under these circumstances was unlawful." The Court of Appeals thus concluded that Scott was not entitled to qualified immunity. We granted certiorari and now reverse.

II

In resolving questions of qualified immunity, courts are required to resolve a "threshold question: Taken in the light most favorable to the party asserting the injury, do the facts alleged show the officer's conduct violated a constitutional right? This must be the initial inquiry." *Saucier v. Katz,* 533 U.S. 194, 201, 121 S.Ct. 2151, 150 L.Ed.2d 272 (2001). If, and only if, the court finds a violation of a constitutional right, "the next, sequential step is to ask whether the right was clearly established . . . in light of the specific context of the case." Although this ordering contradicts "[o]ur policy of avoiding unnecessary adjudication of constitutional issues," *Ashwander v. TVA,* 297 U.S. 288, 346–347, 56 S.Ct. 466, 80 L.Ed. 688 (1936) (Brandeis, J., concurring)), we have said that such a departure from practice is "necessary to set forth principles which will become the basis for a [future] holding that a right is clearly established." *Saucier, supra,* at 201, 121 S.Ct. 2151. We therefore turn to the threshold inquiry: whether Deputy Scott's actions violated the Fourth Amendment.

III

A

The first step in assessing the constitutionality of Scott's actions is to determine the relevant facts. As this case was decided on summary judgment, there have not yet been factual findings by a judge or jury, and respondent's version of events (unsurprisingly) differs substantially from Scott's version. When things are in such a posture, courts are required to view the facts and draw reasonable inferences "in the light most favorable to the party opposing the [summary judgment] motion." *United States v. Diebold, Inc.,* 369 U.S. 654, 655, 82 S.Ct. 993, 8 L.Ed.2d 176 (1962)*(per curiam); Saucier, supra,* at 201, 121 S.Ct. 2151. In qualified immunity cases, this usually means adopting (as the Court of Appeals did here) the plaintiff's version of the facts.

There is, however, an added wrinkle in this case: existence in the record of a videotape capturing the events in question. There are no allegations or indications that this videotape was doctored or altered in any way, nor any contention that what it depicts differs from what actually happened. The videotape quite clearly contradicts the version of the story told by respondent and adopted by the Court of Appeals.[5] For example, the Court of Appeals adopted respondent's assertions that, during the chase, "there was little, if any, actual threat to pedestrians or other motorists, as the roads were mostly empty and [respondent] remained in control of his vehicle." Indeed, reading the lower court's opinion, one gets the impression that respondent, rather than fleeing from police, was attempting to pass his driving test:

> "[T]aking the facts from the non-movant's viewpoint, [respondent] remained in control of his vehicle, slowed for turns and intersections, and typically used his indicators for turns. He did not run any motorists off the road. Nor was he a threat to

---

[5]   Justice Stevens suggests that our reaction to the videotape is somehow idiosyncratic, and seems to believe we are misrepresenting its contents. (dissenting opinion) ("In sum, the factual statements by the Court of Appeals quoted by the Court . . . were entirely accurate"). We are happy to allow the videotape to speak for itself. See Record 36, Exh. A, available at http://www.supremecourtus.gov/opinions/video/scott_v_harris.rmvb and in Clerk of Court's case file.

pedestrians in the shopping center parking lot, which was free from pedestrian and vehicular traffic as the center was closed. Significantly, by the time the parties were back on the highway and Scott rammed [respondent], the motorway had been cleared of motorists and pedestrians allegedly because of police blockades of the nearby intersections."

The videotape tells quite a different story. There we see respondent's vehicle racing down narrow, two-lane roads in the dead of night at speeds that are shockingly fast. We see it swerve around more than a dozen other cars, cross the double-yellow line, and force cars traveling in both directions to their respective shoulders to avoid being hit.[6] We see it run multiple red lights and travel for considerable periods of time in the occasional center left-turn-only lane, chased by numerous police cars forced to engage in the same hazardous maneuvers just to keep up. Far from being the cautious and controlled driver the lower court depicts, what we see on the video more closely resembles a Hollywood-style car chase of the most frightening sort, placing police officers and innocent bystanders alike at great risk of serious injury.

At the summary judgment stage, facts must be viewed in the light most favorable to the nonmoving party only if there is a "genuine" dispute as to those facts. Fed. Rule Civ. Proc. 56(c). As we have emphasized, "[w]hen the moving party has carried its burden under Rule 56(c), its opponent must do more than simply show that there is some metaphysical doubt as to the material facts. . . . Where the record taken as a whole could not lead a rational trier of fact to find for the nonmoving party, there is no 'genuine issue for trial.'" Matsushita Elec. Industrial Co. v. Zenith Radio Corp., 475 U.S. 574, 586–587, 106 S.Ct. 1348, 89 L.Ed.2d 538 (1986) (footnote omitted). "[T]he mere existence of *some* alleged factual dispute between the parties will not defeat an otherwise properly supported motion for summary judgment; the requirement is that there be no *genuine* issue of *material* fact." Anderson v. Liberty Lobby, Inc., 477 U.S. 242, 247–248, 106 S.Ct. 2505, 91 L.Ed.2d 202 (1986). When opposing parties tell two different stories, one of which is blatantly contradicted by the record, so that no reasonable jury could believe it, a court should not adopt that version of the facts for purposes of ruling on a motion for summary judgment.

That was the case here with regard to the factual issue whether respondent was driving in such fashion as to endanger human life. Respondent's version of events is so utterly discredited by the record that no reasonable jury could have believed him. The Court of Appeals should not have relied on such visible fiction; it should have viewed the facts in the light depicted by the videotape.

---

[6]   Justice Stevens hypothesizes that these cars "had already pulled to the side of the road or were driving along the shoulder because they heard the police sirens or saw the flashing lights," so that "[a] jury could certainly conclude that those motorists were exposed to no greater risk than persons who take the same action in response to a speeding ambulance." It is not our experience that ambulances and fire engines careen down two-lane roads at 85-plus miles per hour, with an unmarked scout car out in front of them. The risk they pose to the public is vastly less than what respondent created here. But even if that were not so, it would in no way lead to the conclusion that it was unreasonable to eliminate the threat to life that respondent posed. Society accepts the risk of speeding ambulances and fire engines in order to save life and property; it need not (and assuredly does not) accept a similar risk posed by a reckless motorist fleeing the police.

B

Judging the matter on that basis, we think it is quite clear that Deputy Scott did not violate the Fourth Amendment. Scott does not contest that his decision to terminate the car chase by ramming his bumper into respondent's vehicle constituted a "seizure." "[A] Fourth Amendment seizure [occurs] . . . when there is a governmental termination of freedom of movement through means intentionally applied." It is also conceded, by both sides, that a claim of "excessive force in the course of making [a] . . . 'seizure' of [the] person . . . [is] properly analyzed under the Fourth Amendment's 'objective reasonableness' standard." Graham v. Connor, 490 U.S. 386, 388, 109 S.Ct. 1865, 104 L.Ed.2d 443 (1989).[7]

1

Respondent urges us to analyze this case as we analyzed *Garner*, 471 U.S. 1, 105 S.Ct. 1694, 85 L.Ed.2d 1. We must first decide, he says, whether the actions Scott took constituted "deadly force." (He defines "deadly force" as "any use of force which creates a substantial likelihood of causing death or serious bodily injury," *id.*, at 19, 105 S.Ct. 1694.) If so, respondent claims that *Garner* prescribes certain preconditions that must be met before Scott's actions can survive Fourth Amendment scrutiny: (1) The suspect must have posed an immediate threat of serious physical harm to the officer or others; (2) deadly force must have been necessary to prevent escape; and (3) where feasible, the officer must have given the suspect some warning. Since these *Garner* preconditions for using deadly force were not met in this case, Scott's actions were *per se* unreasonable.

Respondent's argument falters at its first step; *Garner* did not establish a magical on/off switch that triggers rigid preconditions whenever an officer's actions constitute "deadly force." *Garner* was simply an application of the Fourth Amendment's "reasonableness" test to the use of a particular type of force in a particular situation. *Garner* held that it was unreasonable to kill a "young, slight, and unarmed" burglary suspect by shooting him "in the back of the head" while he was running away on foot, and when the officer "could not reasonably have believed that [the suspect] . . . posed any threat," and "never attempted to justify his actions on any basis other than the need to prevent an escape." Whatever *Garner* said about the factors that *might have* justified shooting the suspect in that case such "preconditions" have scant applicability to this case, which has vastly different facts. "*Garner* had nothing to do with one car striking another or even with car chases in general. . . . A police car's bumping a fleeing car is, in fact, not much like a policeman's shooting a gun so as to hit a person." Nor is the threat posed by the flight on foot of an unarmed suspect even remotely comparable to the extreme danger to human life posed by respondent in this case. Although respondent's attempt to craft an easy-to-apply legal test in the Fourth Amendment context is admirable, in the end we must still slosh

Distinction between Garner and the present case

---

[7] Justice Stevens incorrectly declares this to be "a question of fact best reserved for a jury," and complains we are "usurp[ing] the jury's factfinding function." At the summary judgment stage, however, once we have determined the relevant set of facts and drawn all inferences in favor of the nonmoving party *to the extent supportable by the record,* see Part III–A, *supra,* the reasonableness of Scott's actions-or, in Justice Stevens' parlance, "[w]hether [respondent's] actions have risen to a level warranting deadly force," is a pure question of law.

our way through the factbound morass of "reasonableness." Whether or not Scott's actions constituted application of "deadly force," all that matters is whether Scott's actions were reasonable.

2

In determining the reasonableness of the manner in which a seizure is effected, "[w]e must balance the nature and quality of the intrusion on the individual's Fourth Amendment interests against the importance of the governmental interests alleged to justify the intrusion." Scott defends his actions by pointing to the paramount governmental interest in ensuring public safety, and respondent nowhere suggests this was not the purpose motivating Scott's behavior. Thus, in judging whether Scott's actions were reasonable, we must consider the risk of bodily harm that Scott's actions posed to respondent in light of the threat to the public that Scott was trying to eliminate. Although there is no obvious way to quantify the risks on either side, it is clear from the videotape that respondent posed an actual and imminent threat to the lives of any pedestrians who might have been present, to other civilian motorists, and to the officers involved in the chase. See Part III–A, *supra*. It is equally clear that Scott's actions posed a high likelihood of serious injury or death to respondent—though not the near *certainty* of death posed by, say, shooting a fleeing felon in the back of the head, or pulling alongside a fleeing motorist's car and shooting the motorist. So how does a court go about weighing the perhaps lesser probability of injuring or killing numerous bystanders against the perhaps larger probability of injuring or killing a single person? We think it appropriate in this process to take into account not only the number of lives at risk, but also their relative culpability. It was respondent, after all, who intentionally placed himself and the public in danger by unlawfully engaging in the reckless, high-speed flight that ultimately produced the choice between two evils that Scott confronted. Multiple police cars, with blue lights flashing and sirens blaring, had been chasing respondent for nearly 10 miles, but he ignored their warning to stop. By contrast, those who might have been harmed had Scott not taken the action he did were entirely innocent. We have little difficulty in concluding it was reasonable for Scott to take the action that he did.

But wait, says respondent: Couldn't the innocent public equally have been protected, and the tragic accident entirely avoided, if the police had simply ceased their pursuit? We think the police need not have taken that chance and hoped for the best. Whereas Scott's action—ramming respondent off the road—was *certain* to eliminate the risk that respondent posed to the public, ceasing pursuit was not. First of all, there would have been no way to convey convincingly to respondent that the chase was off, and that he was free to go. Had respondent looked in his rear-view mirror and seen the police cars deactivate their flashing lights and turn around, he would have had no idea whether they were truly letting him get away, or simply devising a new strategy for capture. Perhaps the police knew a shortcut he didn't know, and would reappear down the road to intercept him; or perhaps they were setting up a roadblock in his path. Given such uncertainty, respondent might have been just as likely to respond by continuing to drive recklessly as by slowing down and wiping his brow.[8]

Second, we are loath to lay down a rule requiring the police to allow fleeing suspects to get away whenever they drive *so recklessly* that they put other people's lives in danger. It is obvious the perverse incentives such a rule would create: Every fleeing motorist would know that escape is within his grasp, if only he accelerates to 90 miles per hour, crosses the double-yellow line a few times, and runs a few red lights. The Constitution assuredly does not impose this invitation to impunity-earned-by-recklessness. Instead, we lay down a more sensible rule: A police officer's attempt to terminate a dangerous high-speed car chase that threatens the lives of innocent bystanders does not violate the Fourth Amendment, even when it places the fleeing motorist at risk of serious injury or death.

* * *

The car chase that respondent initiated in this case posed a substantial and immediate risk of serious physical injury to others; no reasonable jury could conclude otherwise. Scott's attempt to terminate the chase by forcing respondent off the road was reasonable, and Scott is entitled to summary judgment. The Court of Appeals' decision to the contrary is reversed.

It is so ordered.

■ JUSTICE GINSBURG, concurring.

I join the Court's opinion and would underscore two points. First, I do not read today's decision as articulating a mechanical, *per se* rule. The inquiry described by the Court is situation specific. Among relevant considerations: Were the lives and well-being of others (motorists, pedestrians, police officers) at risk? Was there a safer way, given the time, place, and circumstances, to stop the fleeing vehicle? "[A]dmirable" as "[an] attempt to craft an easy-to-apply legal test in the Fourth Amendment context [may be]," the Court explains, "in the end we must still slosh our way through the factbound morass of 'reasonableness.'"

* * *

■ JUSTICE BREYER, concurring.

I join the Court's opinion with one suggestion and two qualifications. Because watching the video footage of the car chase made a difference to my own view of the case, I suggest that the interested reader take advantage of the link in the Court's opinion and watch it. Having done so, I do not believe a reasonable jury could, in this instance, find that Officer Timothy Scott (who joined the chase late in the day and did not know the specific reason why the respondent was being pursued) acted in violation of the Constitution.

* * *

---

[8] Contrary to Justice Stevens' assertions, we do not "assum[e] that dangers caused by flight from a police pursuit will continue after the pursuit ends," nor do we make any "factual assumptions," with respect to what would have happened if the police had gone home. We simply point out the *uncertainties* regarding what would have happened, in response to *respondent's* factual assumption that the high-speed flight would have ended.

Third, I disagree with the Court insofar as it articulates a *per se* rule. The majority states: "A police officer's attempt to terminate a dangerous high-speed car chase that threatens the lives of innocent bystanders does not violate the Fourth Amendment, even when it places the fleeing motorist at risk of serious injury or death." This statement is too absolute. As Justice Ginsburg points out, whether a high-speed chase violates the Fourth Amendment may well depend upon more circumstances than the majority's rule reflects. With these qualifications, I join the Court's opinion.

■ JUSTICE STEVENS, dissenting

Today, the Court asks whether an officer may "take actions that place a fleeing motorist at risk of serious injury or death in order to stop the motorist's flight from endangering the lives of innocent bystanders." Depending on the circumstances, the answer may be an obvious "yes," an obvious "no," or sufficiently doubtful that the question of the reasonableness of the officer's actions should be decided by a jury, after a review of the degree of danger and the alternatives available to the officer. A high speed chase in a desert in Nevada is, after all, quite different from one that travels through the heart of Las Vegas.

Relying on a *de novo* review of a videotape of a portion of a nighttime chase on a lightly traveled road in Georgia where no pedestrians or other "bystanders" were present, buttressed by uninformed speculation about the possible consequences of discontinuing the chase, eight of the jurors on this Court reach a verdict that differs from the views of the judges on both the District Court and the Court of Appeals who are surely more familiar with the hazards of driving on Georgia roads than we are. The Court's justification for this unprecedented departure from our well-settled standard of review of factual determinations made by a district court and affirmed by a court of appeals is based on its mistaken view that the Court of Appeals' description of the facts was "blatantly contradicted by the record" and that respondent's version of the events was "so utterly discredited by the record that no reasonable jury could have believed him."

Rather than supporting the conclusion that what we see on the video "resembles a Hollywood-style car chase of the most frightening sort,"[1] the tape actually confirms, rather than contradicts, the lower courts' appraisal of the factual questions at issue. More important, it surely does not provide a principled basis for depriving the respondent of his right to have a jury evaluate the question whether the police officers' decision to use deadly force to bring the chase to an end was reasonable.

Omitted from the Court's description of the initial speeding violation is the fact that respondent was on a four-lane portion of Highway 34 when the officer clocked his speed at 73 miles per hour and initiated the chase. More significant-and contrary to the Court's assumption that respondent's vehicle "force[d] cars traveling in both directions to their

---

[1] I can only conclude that my colleagues were unduly frightened by two or three images on the tape that looked like bursts of lightning or explosions, but were in fact merely the headlights of vehicles zooming by in the opposite lane. Had they learned to drive when most high-speed driving took place on two-lane roads rather than on superhighways-when split-second judgments about the risk of passing a slow-poke in the face of oncoming traffic were routine—they might well have reacted to the videotape more dispassionately.

respective shoulders to avoid being hit"—a fact unmentioned in the text of the opinion explains why those cars pulled over prior to being passed by respondent. The sirens and flashing lights on the police cars following respondent gave the same warning that a speeding ambulance or fire engine would have provided. The 13 cars that respondent passed on his side of the road before entering the shopping center, and both of the cars that he passed on the right after leaving the center, no doubt had already pulled to the side of the road or were driving along the shoulder because they heard the police sirens or saw the flashing lights before respondent or the police cruisers approached.[4] A jury could certainly conclude that those motorists were exposed to no greater risk than persons who take the same action in response to a speeding ambulance, and that their reactions were fully consistent with the evidence that respondent, though speeding, retained full control of his vehicle.

The police sirens also minimized any risk that may have arisen from running "multiple red lights." In fact, respondent and his pursuers went through only two intersections with stop lights and in both cases all other vehicles in sight were stationary, presumably because they had been warned of the approaching speeders. Incidentally, the videos do show that the lights were red when the police cars passed through them but, because the cameras were farther away when respondent did so and it is difficult to discern the color of the signal at that point, it is not entirely clear that he ran either or both of the red lights. In any event, the risk of harm to the stationary vehicles was minimized by the sirens, and there is no reason to believe that respondent would have disobeyed the signals if he were not being pursued.

My colleagues on the jury saw respondent "swerve around more than a dozen other cars," and "force cars traveling in both directions to their respective shoulders," but they apparently discounted the possibility that those cars were already out of the pursuit's path as a result of hearing the sirens. Even if that were not so, passing a slower vehicle on a two-lane road always involves some degree of swerving and is not especially dangerous if there are no cars coming from the opposite direction. At no point during the chase did respondent pull into the opposite lane other than to pass a car in front of him; he did the latter no more than five times and, on most of those occasions, used his turn signal. On none of these occasions was there a car traveling in the opposite direction. In fact, at one point, when respondent found himself behind a car in his own lane and there were cars traveling in the other direction, he slowed and waited for the cars traveling in the other direction to pass before overtaking the car in front of him while using his turn signal to do so. This is hardly the stuff of Hollywood. To the contrary, the video does not reveal any incidents that could even be remotely characterized as "close calls."

In sum, the factual statements by the Court of Appeals quoted by the Court were entirely accurate. That court did not describe respondent as a "cautious" driver as my colleagues imply, but it did correctly conclude that there is no evidence that he ever lost control of his vehicle. That court also correctly pointed out that the incident in the shopping center parking lot did not create any risk to pedestrians or other vehicles

---

4   Although perhaps understandable, because their volume on the sound recording is low (possibly due to sound proofing in the officer's vehicle), the Court appears to minimize the significance of the sirens audible throughout the tape recording of the pursuit.

because the chase occurred just before 11 p.m. on a weekday night and the center was closed. It is apparent from the record (including the videotape) that local police had blocked off intersections to keep respondent from entering residential neighborhoods and possibly endangering other motorists. I would add that the videos also show that no pedestrians, parked cars, sidewalks, or residences were visible at any time during the chase. The only "innocent bystanders" who were placed "at great risk of serious injury," were the drivers who either pulled off the road in response to the sirens or passed respondent in the opposite direction when he was driving on his side of the road.

I recognize, of course, that even though respondent's original speeding violation on a four-lane highway was rather ordinary, his refusal to stop and subsequent flight was a serious offense that merited severe punishment. It was not, however, a capital offense, or even an offense that justified the use of deadly force rather than an abandonment of the chase. The Court's concern about the "imminent threat to the lives of any pedestrians who might have been present," while surely valid in an appropriate case, should be discounted in a case involving a nighttime chase in an area where no pedestrians were present.

What would have happened if the police had decided to abandon the chase? We now know that they could have apprehended respondent later because they had his license plate number. Even if that were not true, and even if he would have escaped any punishment at all, the use of deadly force in this case was no more appropriate than the use of a deadly weapon against a fleeing felon in Tennessee v. Garner, 471 U.S. 1, 105 S.Ct. 1694, 85 L.Ed.2d 1 (1985). In any event, any uncertainty about the result of abandoning the pursuit has not prevented the Court from basing its conclusions on its own factual assumptions.[5] The Court attempts to avoid the conclusion that deadly force was unnecessary by speculating that if the officers had let him go, respondent might have been "just as likely" to continue to drive recklessly as to slow down and wipe his brow. That speculation is unconvincing as a matter of common sense and improper as a matter of law. Our duty to view the evidence in the light most favorable to the nonmoving party would foreclose such speculation if the Court had not used its observation of the video as an excuse for replacing the rule of law with its ad hoc judgment. There is no evidentiary basis for an assumption that dangers caused by flight from a police pursuit will continue after the pursuit ends. * * *

* * *

Whether a person's actions have risen to a level warranting deadly force is a question of fact best reserved for a jury. Here, the Court has usurped the jury's factfinding function and, in doing so, implicitly labeled

[handwritten margin note: "Question of fact / question of law"]

---

[5] In noting that Scott's action "was *certain* to eliminate the risk that respondent posed to the public" while "ceasing pursuit was not," the Court prioritizes total elimination of the risk of harm to the public over the risk that respondent may be seriously injured or even killed. The Court is only able to make such a statement by assuming, based on its interpretation of events on the videotape, that the risk of harm posed in this case, and the type of harm involved, rose to a level warranting deadly force. These are the same types of questions that, when disputed, are typically resolved by a jury; this is why both the District Court and the Court of Appeals saw fit to have them be so decided. Although the Court claims only to have drawn factual inferences in respondent's favor "*to the extent supportable by the record*," its own view of the record has clearly precluded it from doing so to the same extent as the two courts through which this case has already traveled.

the four other judges to review the case unreasonable. It chastises the Court of Appeals for failing to "vie[w] the facts in the light depicted by the videotape" and implies that no reasonable person could view the videotape and come to the conclusion that deadly force was unjustified. However, the three judges on the Court of Appeals panel apparently did view the videotapes entered into evidence and described a very different version of events:

> "At the time of the ramming, apart from speeding and running two red lights, Harris was driving in a non-aggressive fashion (i.e., without trying to ram or run into the officers). Moreover, . . . Scott's path on the open highway was largely clear. The videos introduced into evidence show little to no vehicular (or pedestrian) traffic, allegedly because of the late hour and the police blockade of the nearby intersections. Finally, Scott issued absolutely no warning (e.g., over the loudspeaker or otherwise) prior to using deadly force." Harris v. Coweta County, 433 F.3d 807, 819, n. 14 (C.A.11 2005).

If two groups of judges can disagree so vehemently about the nature of the pursuit and the circumstances surrounding that pursuit, it seems eminently likely that a reasonable juror could disagree with this Court's characterization of events. Moreover, under the standard set forth in *Garner,* it is certainly possible that "a jury could conclude that Scott unreasonably used deadly force to seize Harris by ramming him off the road under the instant circumstances."

The Court today sets forth a *per se* rule that presumes its own version of the facts: "A police officer's attempt to terminate a dangerous high-speed car chase *that threatens the lives of innocent bystanders* does not violate the Fourth Amendment, even when it places the fleeing motorist at risk of serious injury or death." Not only does that rule fly in the face of the flexible and case-by-case "reasonableness" approach applied in *Garner* and Graham v. Connor, 490 U.S. 386, 109 S.Ct. 1865, 104 L.Ed.2d 443 (1989), but it is also arguably inapplicable to the case at hand, given that it is not clear that this chase threatened the life of any "innocent bystande[r]."[8] In my view, the risks inherent in justifying unwarranted police conduct on the basis of unfounded assumptions are unacceptable, particularly when less drastic measures—in this case, the use of stop sticks[9] or a simple warning issued from a loudspeaker—could have avoided such a tragic result. In my judgment, jurors in Georgia should be allowed to evaluate the reasonableness of the decision to ram respondent's speeding vehicle in a manner that created an obvious risk of death and has in fact made him a quadriplegic at the age of 19.

I respectfully dissent.

---

[8]   It is unclear whether, in referring to "innocent bystanders," the Court is referring to the motorists driving unfazed in the opposite direction or to the drivers who pulled over to the side of the road, safely out of respondent's and petitioner's path.

[9]   "Stop sticks" are a device which can be placed across the roadway and used to flatten a vehicle's tires slowly to safely terminate a pursuit.

NOTE ON *SCOTT V. HARRIS* AND THE STANDARD FOR SUMMARY JUDGMENT

1. **"We are happy to allow the videotape to speak for itself."** If you have not already done so, please take the majority up on the invitation in footnote 5 of its opinion. The video is readily available on the Internet.

2. **What did the Court decide?: The danger posed by Harris.** Did the Court hold that there was no issue of material fact with respect to the question of whether Harris's conduct posed "an actual and imminent threat to the lives" of pedestrians, civilian motorists, and the officers involved in the chase? If so, do you believe that the majority was correct in so holding? Did Justice Ginsburg or Justice Breyer decide that issue? If not, how did they avoid doing so?

3. **What did the Court decide?: The reasonableness of Scott's actions.** The majority opinion asserts that the reasonableness of Scott's "seizure" of Harris is a pure question of law. But to resolve that issue, the majority and the concurring opinions suggest, they must enter a "factbound morass." Justice Stevens in turn asserts that the issue of whether deadly force is warranted is "a question of fact best reserved for the jury." In personal injury actions brought under a negligence standard, the who, what, where, when, and how questions are typically viewed as questions of fact. The question of reasonableness, though apparently involving a question of "ought" rather than "is," is usually viewed as invoking the community standard of what the reasonably prudent person would do in the circumstances, and hence, except in the very clearest cases, as committed to the community's representatives on the jury. Hazard, Leubsdorf, & Bassett, Civil Procedure § 9.7 at 385 (6th ed. 2011). See also Simblest v. Maynard and Sioux City and Pacific R. Co. v. Stout in Chapter 8, *infra*. Is the majority taking the position that the reasonableness of the conduct of a law enforcement official under the Fourth Amendment is always a question of law for the Court? Or is it simply taking the position that on the facts no reasonable community could conclude that Scott's conduct was unreasonable? How do you understand the concurring Justices to have resolved that issue?

Are *Tolan* and *Scott* reconcilable? How would you distinguish them? In *Tolan*, which was decided seven years after *Scott*, the Court emphasized "the fundamental principle that at the summary judgment stage, reasonable inferences should be drawn in favor of the nonmoving party." Is *Scott* consistent with that principle?

4. **The role of race.** Can you tell from reading the Supreme Court's opinion what are the races of the respective participants in this episode? Would it affect your view of the case if you learned that the plaintiff was African American and that the defendant was white? Is this detail relevant to whether the case should have been decided at summary judgment or by a jury after trial?

5. **Alternative perspectives, alternative communities, and the role of the jury.** To see what prospective jurors might have made of *Scott*, three academics recently surveyed a diverse sample of 1,350 Americans (between 112 and 225 juries' worth, depending on the size of the jury). D. Kahan, D. Hoffman & D. Braman, Whose Eyes Are You Going to Believe? *Scott v. Harris* and the Perils of Cognitive Illiberalism, 122 Harv.L.Rev. 837 (2009). The participants were asked to read a factual synopsis of the case

drawn from the opinions and also were shown a condensed version of the videotape that contained all of the factual elements on which the majority and dissent disagreed. The videotape, like the one originally viewed by the Supreme Court, was in color rather than black and white, and hence potentially provided more detail than the black and white version on the Court's website. The authors asked the respondents to indicate the extent to which they agreed with a series of statements about: the degree of danger created by Harris's conduct, whether it was worth the danger to the public for the police to engage in a high-speed chase rather than arresting Harris later, the relative culpability of Harris and the police, and whether Scott's decision to use potentially deadly force was justified. They also collected demographic, cultural, and "worldview" data on the participants.

Based upon the survey responses and the demographic data, the authors identified differences between groups and, using advanced statistical techniques, also mapped the expected responses of four composite types, whom they described as follows.

Imagine four Americans. Ron, a white male who lives in Arizona, overcame his modest upbringing to become a self-made millionaire businessperson. He deeply resents government interference with markets but is otherwise highly respectful of authority, which he believes should be clearly delineated in all spheres of life. Politically, he identifies himself as a conservative Republican. Bernie, another white male, is a university professor who makes a modest salary and lives in Burlington, Vermont. He will go along with the left wing of the Democratic party, but thinks of himself as a 'social democrat.' He advocates highly egalitarian conditions in the home, in the workplace, and in society at large, and strongly supports government social welfare programs and regulations of every stripe. Linda is an African American woman employed as a social worker in Philadelphia, Pennsylvania. She is a staunch Democrat and unembarrassed to be characterized as a 'liberal.' Finally, there is Pat. Pat is the average American in every single respect: Pat earns the average income, has the average level of education, is average in ideology, is average in party identification, holds average cultural values, and is average even in race and gender. If placed on a jury, apprised of the basic issues and law and asked to watch the video in *Scott v. Harris*, what will these four individuals see on the tape, and how will the tape affect their views of how the case should come out prior to deliberating?

122 Harv. L. Rev. at 849–50. The group data showed a relatively large majority of respondents formed perceptions consistent with the Supreme Court majority. There were some marked differences by group, though. African Americans were markedly more likely to disagree with the Supreme Court. So were Democrats relative to Republicans, liberals relative to conservatives, Egalitarians relative to Hierarchs, and, on most measures, Communitarians relative to Individualists. Id. at 867.

When the data were analyzed in the framework of the four composite jurors, stark differences emerged. The discussion of two central issues is illustrative. The authors describe the:

deep *dissensus* that exists over whether the police should have engaged in a high-speed chase to apprehend Scott in the first place.

For Ron, this is a no-brainer: approximately three-quarters (76%,+/-2%) of the persons who share his defining characteristics disagree—about two-thirds (66%,+/-3%) either moderately or strongly—with the proposition that the "chase wasn't worth the danger to the public." Bernie and Linda, in contrast, generally *agree* with the same statement: 59% (+/-3%) of the persons who share Linda's characteristics either strongly or moderately agree the chase wasn't worth the risk, and another considerable slice (18%,+/-4%) "slightly agree"; 73% (+/-3) of the persons who share Bernie's characteristics agree (about half moderately or strongly) that the chase wasn't worth it. Pat leans toward Ron but is equivocal: 55% (+/-2%) of the members of the general population (according to the simulation) reject the claim that the chase wasn't worth the risk to the public, but the median citizen is only "slightly" inclined toward that position.

* * *

Bernie and Linda also don't agree with the *Scott* majority on the ultimate issue . . . Over three-fifths (65%, +/-2%) of the persons who share Linda's characteristics disagree—about one-half either strongly or moderately—with the statement that "[t]he danger that Harris's driving posed to the police and the public justified Officer Scott's decision to end the chase in a way that put Harris's own life in danger." Nearly three-fifths (58%, +/-2%) of the persons who hold Bernie's characteristics are also likely to believe that deadly force was unreasonable.

Pat does agree with the *Scott* majority, although not without a bit of equivocation. There is a 64% (+/-2%) chance that he/she will be only "slightly" inclined to agree, and over a 20% chance that he/she would conclude upon watching the tape that use of deadly force was unreasonable.

Ron again is emphatic. Over 80% of the individuals who share his characteristics would find the police acted reasonably.

Id. at 874, 878–79.

From this data, the authors argue that the *Scott* case lacked "the features that factual consensus must have before it can justify dispensing with jury deliberation." Id. at 886.

> "Precisely because juries can lend legitimacy to law by assuring *minorities* that their perspective is being respected, it surely isn't enough that 'the facts speak for themselves' for a large majority. If the minority's view of the facts reflects the minority's view of social reality, summary adjudication will deny the minority a basis to accept, or for the majority to demand that it accept, the law's view of the facts as its own."

Id.

"Under these circumstances," the authors argue, "ordering that the case be decided summarily based on the video was wrong precisely because doing so denied a dissenting group of citizens the respect they were owed, and hence denied the law the legitimacy it needs, when the law adopts a view of the facts that divides citizens on social, cultural and political lines." Id. at 887. If participation by outliers from groups with distinctive points of view is critical to the political function of the jury (and perhaps also to its accuracy), how can the participation of those groups be assured?

6. Applying the summary judgment standard. In recent years, it has been argued that "[t]he expanding federal caseload has contributed to a drift in many areas of federal litigation toward substituting summary judgment for trial." Wallace v. SMC Pneumatics, Inc., 103 F.3d 1394, 1397 (7th Cir. 1997) (Posner, J.). Is the Court's opinion in *Scott* an example of this drift? See, Miller, The Pretrial Rush to Judgment: Are the "Litigation Explosion," "Liability Crisis," and Efficiency Clichés Eroding Our Day in Court and Jury Trial Commitments?, 78 N.Y.U. L. Rev. 982 (2003).

7. Additional reading. For additional reading, see Coleman, Summary Judgment: What We Think We Know Versus What We Ought to Know, 43 Loy. Chi. L.J. 705 (2012); Gensler & Rosenthal, Managing Summary Judgment, 43 Loy. U. Chi. L. Rev. 1017 (2012); Wald, Summary Judgment at Sixty, 76 Tex. L. Rev. 1897 (1998); Issacharoff & Loewenstein, Second Thoughts about Summary Judgment, 100 Yale L.J. 73 (1990).

C. SETTLEMENT AND THE PRETRIAL CONFERENCE

INTRODUCTORY NOTE ON SETTLEMENT

1. The ubiquity of settlement. Settlement is the resolution of a dispute through a negotiated contract between the parties. Broadly speaking, settlement contracts involve two kinds of bargains. First, in the settlement of the typical claim for money damages the plaintiff exchanges all of her rights in her claim for a monetary payment from the defendant. Typically, the bargaining centers on the amount and timing of the payment. Second, in the settlement of a claim for injunctive relief, the claimant again surrenders her claim, but typically in exchange for a more complex set of promises about the defendant's future conduct. In such cases, the bargaining centers on the content and costs of those promises.

Settlement is by far the most common outcome in filed cases. Two-thirds or more of filed cases are resolved in that fashion. Galanter & Cahill, "Most Cases Settle": Judicial Promotion and Regulation of Settlements, 46 Stan. L. Rev. 1339 (1994).

The standard image of settlement is that it occurs "on the court house steps," immediately before trial. But in many fields of law, such as automobile personal injury cases, the vast majority of settlements occur before any litigation has been filed. The plaintiff may threaten litigation, and the defendant (or his insurer) may choose to avoid the filing of a complaint by preemptively settling. Moreover, once a complaint has been filed, settlement can happen at any time. A substantial number of cases settle immediately after the filing of the complaint without any further litigation activity; others settle before trial, others while the case is on appeal.

When a routine case is settled prior to filing, the plaintiff and defendant agree on a payment, the plaintiff signs and delivers a signed document "releasing" the defendant from her claim and/or promising not to bring suit, and the defendant gives the plaintiff a cashier's check. When a claim for damages is settled after filing, the defendant's settlement payment is typically conditioned upon the voluntary dismissal of the plaintiff's complaint with prejudice. Conversely, when a claim for injunctive relief is settled after filing, the agreement often becomes part of a court judgment entered on consent of the parties: a "consent decree."

Most dismissals pursuant to settlement do not require approval of the court. One exception is actions brought on behalf of minors, insane persons or incompetents. Another exception is class actions. See Fed. R. Civ. P. 23(e). Such settlements must be approved by the court. The obvious rationale for both exceptions is that the client (or client class) in such cases is often not able to protect itself against the misjudgment or self-interest of the lawyer.

2. How parties decide whether or not to settle. A party begins its settlement decision making by comparing the estimated value of continued litigation with the estimated value of settlement. Continued litigation may lead to a "fight to the finish" in which there is a judgment after a contested hearing or trial, an opinion on the merits, an appeal, and perhaps even post-judgment resistance to the court's decree. But the choice is not always so stark. Because settlement is always permitted, even during and after trial, often the choice is not between settlement and a contested trial or judgment, but between settlement now and settlement later. For simplicity in analysis, however, the following discussion will assume that the choice is between settlement and trial. To further simplify, we will focus on a claim for money damages—a products liability suit in which the plaintiff has suffered significant personal injury and in which the parties have completed discovery.

The law of agency and the law of professional ethics both assign the decision to settle to the client, unless the client has expressly or impliedly authorized the lawyer to make that decision for the client. American Law Institute, Restatement (Third) of the Law Governing Lawyers § 22. As a matter of lawyer-client relations, the lawyer is required to advise the client concerning the settlement decision and to abide by the client's decision whether to make or accept an offer at a specific amount. Opposing parties and courts are expected to understand that ordinarily it is the client rather than the lawyer who makes settlement decisions. Accordingly, opposing parties and courts are not entitled to rely upon a lawyer's representation that a case has been settled unless the client has, through its own actions or words, given them reason to believe that the lawyer has authority, not only to conduct the lawsuit or the negotiations, but also to conclude the deal.

a. Evaluating a claim. For both the plaintiff and defendant, settlement decision making has two elements: evaluation and bargaining. Each party has to form an idea of what the claim is worth, to its own side and to the opponent, before it can bargain sensibly over how much should be paid for it. Both sides need to estimate how likely it is that the plaintiff will win, what kind of recovery the plaintiff can expect, if she does win, and what it will cost to get there. Each of these estimates is uncertain. Parties must make necessarily imprecise prophecies about the evidence that will emerge, the skills of the lawyers on both sides, the reactions of the judge or jury, and the further costs of litigation, both out-of-pocket and emotional. Lawyers play the key role in this process of evaluation: they may profess optimism in public, but when they are helping their clients decide what the case is really worth, they must shift from forceful advocacy to dispassionate analysis.

Where the case involves money damages and the outcome is uncertain, lawyers necessarily have to estimate an *expected value* for the case. Often this estimate is done through tacit calculation, informally and by the seat of the pants. But some lawyers use more formal methods of analysis, and such methods are helpful to clarify what is going on. Plaintiff's lawyer multiplies the probability of success on the merits times the amount of the expected judgment. That gives her an expected payoff (before costs of litigation) for the case. If the plaintiff thinks that the odds of winning at trial are 60% and expects the jury to award a verdict of $300,000, then the expected value of the judgment is $180,000. From that amount, plaintiff must *subtract* the additional costs of going to trial—suppose they are $30,000. The expected value of the case to the plaintiff, after costs, is therefore $150,000.

The defendant's lawyer makes a similar evaluation of the expected outcome. If she agrees that the jury is likely to award $300,000 in damages, but thinks that there is only a 50% chance that plaintiff will prevail, then she will estimate the defendant's expected loss at $150,000. To that she has to *add* the defendant's expected costs of trial in the case—say they are $35,000. Thus, the defendant's expected loss from the case is $185,000.

With these estimates of expected value in hand, the lawyers will want to discuss with their clients (if they have not done so already) whether there are other factors, unique to the client, which would affect the valuation of the claim. Plaintiffs, for example, often need money now for basic needs. Also, many plaintiffs are risk averse: for them a 60% chance of winning $300,000 may well be worth considerably less than a certain payment of $180,000. If the plaintiff in this case needs money now or is risk averse, he may well place a personal value on continued prosecution that is lower than the lawyer's calculated value. Suppose that after conversation with his lawyer, plaintiff indicates to his lawyer that he would accept as little as $130,000 if a lump sum settlement can be accomplished promptly.

Assume that defendant is not worried about risk. But it does fear that the publicity accompanying a public trial and a negative verdict would harm the sales of its product and might attract unwanted attention from regulators. Suppose the defendant tells its lawyer that to avoid publicity it would pay an additional $25,000, that is, up to $210,000 to avoid a trial.

In this example, a necessary condition for settlement has been met: the least the plaintiff would accept in settlement is $130,000, considerably less than $210,000, which is the most the defendant would offer to settle the case. Thus, there is a "settlement gap"—a range of values where any bargain that is struck will make both parties better off by their own lights than continued litigation. The larger the settlement gap, the greater chance that the case will be settled.

Several factors bear on the likelihood and size of a settlement gap:

Expectations about the outcome. Parties can differ in their expectations about the probability of success or the damages to be awarded. For example, if the plaintiff thinks that his odds of winning are 80% and defendant thinks that plaintiff's odds of winning are only 20%, there is unlikely to be a settlement gap. Plaintiff will estimate the expected verdict, less costs, at $210,000. Defendant will estimate the expected verdict, plus costs, at $95,000. Even taking account of the plaintiff's need for money and risk aversion as well as the defendant's aversion to publicity, there is no basis for a settlement unless the parties' expectations change. Conversely, if the parties agree on the likelihood that plaintiff will prevail on liability and on the amount of damages, the settlement gap will grow.

Stakes. In general, the larger the financial, emotional, or ideological stakes, the harder the case will be to settle. This is so because when the stakes are high, even very small differences in the parties' expectations about how liability issues will be resolved can produce large differences between the parties' estimates of the value of the case. Moreover, litigation costs do not generally increase directly in proportion to stakes: a $500 million case does not cost 1,000 times more to try than a $500,000 case.

Costs. The greater the parties' costs of litigation, the greater the likelihood that there is a settlement gap. Even if the parties disagree substantially on the probable outcome, very high costs can make it in both parties' interest to settle rather than obtain a judicial resolution of their disagreement.

The parties' distinctive preferences and values. As the example illustrates, not every party values the experience of litigation the same way. One plaintiff may view having to testify as a terrifying cost of litigation; another may view it as a priceless benefit—an opportunity to tell her side of the story and obtain public vindication. There is more likely to be a settlement gap in litigation involving the first plaintiff than the second. Conversely, one defendant may view settlement of the plaintiff's claim as an intolerable stain on its reputation, while another dreads the exposure of a public trial. Litigation involving the first defendant is less likely to settle than litigation involving the second.

The role of the lawyer. Unless the client has delegated the decision to settle to the lawyer, the lawyer's job is to provide candid and accurate advice to the client on outcomes and costs. Inadequate preparation or analysis by the lawyer can increase or decrease the likelihood of settlement, depending on whether it leads to unwarranted optimism or unwarranted pessimism about the value of the case.

b. Bargaining to agreement. The existence of a settlement gap does not guarantee that settlement will occur. The parties must still reach agreement within that gap. They can do so by bargaining—that is, by discussing their positions and exchanging formal offers to settle the case. But bargaining is risky. A party may fear that by suggesting negotiations or making the first offer, it is signaling weakness to the opposing side. If defendant's offer to settle is too generous, or plaintiff's too stingy, it may cause the other side to reevaluate its opinion of the worth of the case and harden its position. Moreover, by making concessions, a party risks foregoing more of the joint gains from settlement than are necessary to reach agreement. For example, in our hypothetical bargaining situation, if plaintiff makes too low a demand, it will settle for much less than the $210,000 the defendant was willing to offer. If the defendant makes too high an offer, it will settle for much more than the $130,000 the plaintiff was prepared to accept. These risks may prevent either party from commencing bargaining or from making an offer within the settlement gap. To avoid leaving money on the table, the plaintiff might present a demand of $225,000, and the defendant might respond with an offer of $85,000. In that situation, there has been no offer within the settlement gap, even though the gap exists.

Even when a party receives an offer falling within the settlement gap, she may reject it if she thinks her opponent can be bluffed into sweetening the offer. In our example, plaintiff might offer to settle for $160,000, well within the settlement gap, but defendant may decide that plaintiff is bluffing and will ultimately agree to much less. If plaintiff does concede, the defendant will save even more. But if plaintiff makes no further concessions, the case may go to trial even though settlement for plaintiff's final demand would have made both parties better off and avoided the costs of trial. Complex factors determine the likelihood of a bargaining breakdown. Familiarity or a continuing relationship with an opponent may reduce a party's fear that the opponent will ruthlessly exploit concessions. In addition, disputants or lawyers who have dealt with each other previously are less likely to mistake each other's values, preferences, or likely courses of action, and hence are less likely to stumble into litigation in the mistaken belief that a better offer will surely be forthcoming.

The lawyer's role. More often than not, the same lawyers who act as advocates for the parties also conduct settlement bargaining. In this setting, their professional obligation to their client requires them to balance several potentially conflicting goals: on the one hand, the lawyer needs to induce enough interchange to determine whether a deal is possible at a price acceptable to the client and to signal to the opponent that such a deal may be possible. On the other hand, the lawyer wants to maintain a bargaining position that will capture as much as possible of the joint savings from settlement, and to bluff the other side into further concessions, if that is what the client wants to do. Moreover, the lawyer should put her self-interest to one side. It should be irrelevant to the bargaining process—and to the lawyer's advice to her client—that the lawyer might make more (or less) money if the case goes to trial. (Whether the lawyer will make more or less often depends on the nature of the lawyer's fee agreement with the client.)

      c.   **Changing understandings of the settlement process.** Poor preparation or poor judgment by a lawyer can lead to poor decisions to settle or litigate because lawyers fail to gather, properly evaluate, or properly communicate to the client the information needed for a sound decision. Apart from incompetence, there is a growing literature, much of it based on laboratory experiments, documenting psychological processes that may act as systematic barriers to settlement. Simply put, litigants and their lawyers both tend to think that their own position is both stronger on the facts and law—and more morally justified as well—than their opponents'. See Babcock et al., Biased Judgments of Fairness in Bargaining, 85 Am. Econ. Rev. 1337 (1995); Babcock et al., Creating Convergence: Debiasing Biased Litigants, 22 Law & Soc. Inquiry 913 (1997); Loewenstein et al., Self-Serving Assessments of Fairness and Pretrial Bargaining, 22 J. Legal Stud. 135 (1993); Mnookin, Why Negotiations Fail: An Exploration of Barriers to the Resolution of Conflict, 8 Ohio State J. on Disp. Resol. 235 (1993). There is also a theoretical literature suggesting that bargaining may have become more difficult to commence and bring to conclusion in a rapidly expanding litigation bar, where lawyers have many fewer repeat dealings. Gilson & Mnookin, Disputing Through Agents: Cooperation and Conflict Between Lawyers in Litigation, 94 Col. L. Rev. 509 (1994).

      3.   **The policy preference for settlement.** It has long been commonly stated that American law favors settlement and compromise. Williams v. First Nat'l Bank, 216 U.S. 582, 595, 30 S.Ct. 441, 54 L.Ed. 625 (1910). One can even find cases suggesting that "a bad settlement is almost always better than a good trial." In re Warner Communications Sec. Litig., 618 F. Supp. 735, 740 (S.D.N.Y. 1985), aff'd, 798 F.2d 35 (2d Cir. 1986). In federal court, the concrete expression of this policy preference is reflected in federal Rule 16, which establishes "facilitating settlement" as one of the explicit purposes of the pretrial conference. Fed. R. Civ. P. 16(a)(5). Indeed, under Rule 16(c), "the court may require that a party or its representative be present or reasonably available by other means to consider possible settlement" at a pretrial conference.

The drafters of Rule 16 favor settlement because it "eases crowded court dockets and results in savings to the litigants and the judicial system." Advisory Committee Note to Fed. R. Civ. P. 16. Others argue that settlement is a potentially superior form of justice, whether because it more accurately represents the parties' autonomous choices, better satisfies their underlying needs, or, in cases where the outcome of the trial is uncertain, finds a point between the parties' positions that reflects a more precise form of justice than any binary win-or-lose trial outcome. See, e.g., Menkel-Meadow, For and Against Settlement: Uses and Abuses of the Mandatory Settlement Conference, 33 UCLA L. Rev. 485 (1985) (arguing that settlement often better serves the parties' needs); Easterbrook, Justice and Contract in Consent Judgments, 1987 U. Chi. Legal F. 19, 24–25 (settlements generate more precise justice). Moreover, particularly in large cases such as mass torts, some argue that settlement is a necessary means of ensuring compensation to plaintiffs and deterrence of harms without overwhelming the legal system. See Isaacharoff & Klonoff, The Public Value of Settlement, 78 Fordham L. Rev. 1177 (2009). Professor Glover argues that the federal Rules should be reshaped to adapt to a world in which the vast majority of cases are—and ought to be—settled. Glover, The Federal Rules of Civil Settlement, 87 N.Y.U. L. Rev. 1713 (2012).

An alternative view argues that settlement represents a failure of our aspirations for justice. Critics wonder whether settlements that are driven primarily by the high costs and risks of litigation can be viewed as truly voluntary. They also fear that settlement has public costs. It prevents a public airing of evidence and arguments that may have wide significance for persons other than the disputants and reduces the occasions on which courts and juries are empowered to pronounce on issues of public importance. See Fiss, Against Settlement, 93 Yale L.J. 1073 (1984). For efforts to appraise these competing positions, see Galanter & Cahill, "Most Cases Settle": Judicial Promotion and Regulation of Settlements, 46 Stan. L. Rev. 1339 (1994); Bundy, The Policy in Favor of Settlement in an Adversary System, 44 Hastings L. J. 1 (1992).

For additional reading on settlement, see Symposium, Against Settlement—25 Years Later, 78 Fordham L. Rev. 1117 (2009); W. Brazil, Effective Approaches to Settlement: A Handbook for Judges and Lawyers (1988); D.M. Provine, Settlement Strategies for Federal District Judges (1986); Galanter, The Quality of Settlements, 1988 J. Disp. Resol. 55; Mnookin & Kornhauser, Bargaining in the Shadow of the Law: The Case of Divorce, 88 Yale L.J. 950 (1979).

Kothe v. Smith

United States Court of Appeals for the Second Circuit, 1985.
771 F.2d 667.

■ VAN GRAAFEILAND, CIRCUIT JUDGE

Dr. James Smith appeals from a judgment of the United States District Court for the Southern District of New York (Sweet, J.), which directed him to pay $1,000 to plaintiff-appellee's attorney, $1,000 to plaintiff-appellee's medical witness, and $480 to the Clerk of the Court. For the reasons hereinafter discussed, we direct that the judgment be vacated.

Patricia Kothe brought this suit for medical malpractice against four defendants, Dr. Smith, Dr. Andrew Kerr, Dr. Kerr's professional corporation, and Doctors Hospital, seeking $2 million in damages. She discontinued her action against the hospital four months prior to trial. She discontinued against Dr. Kerr and his corporation on the opening day of trial.

Three weeks prior thereto, Judge Sweet held a pretrial conference, during which he directed counsel for the parties to conduct settlement negotiations. Although it is not clear from the record, it appears that Judge Sweet recommended that the case be settled for between $20,000 and $30,000. He also warned the parties that, if they settled for a comparable figure after trial had begun, he would impose sanctions against the dilatory party. Smith, whose defense has been conducted throughout this litigation by his malpractice insurer, offered $5,000 on the day before trial, but it was rejected.

Although Kothe's attorney had indicated to Judge Sweet that his client would settle for $20,000, he had requested that the figure not be disclosed to Smith. Kothe's counsel conceded at oral argument that the lowest pretrial settlement demand communicated to Smith was $50,000. Nevertheless, when the case was settled for $20,000 after one day of trial, the district court proceeded to penalize Smith alone. In imposing the penalty, the court stated that it was "determined to get the attention of the carrier" and that "the carriers are going to have to wake up when a judge tells them that they want [sic] to settle a case and they don't want to settle it." Under the circumstances of this case, we believe that the district court's imposition of a penalty against Smith was an abuse of the sanction power given it by Fed. R. Civ. P. 16(f).

Although the law favors the voluntary settlement of civil suits, ABKCO Music, Inc. v. Harrisongs Music, Ltd., 722 F.2d 988, 997 (2d Cir. 1983), it does not sanction efforts by trial judges to effect settlements through coercion. Del Rio v. Northern Blower Co., 574 F.2d 23, 26 (1st Cir. 1978) (citing Wolff v. Laverne, Inc., 17 A.D.2d 213, 233 N.Y.S.2d 555 (1962), see MacLeod v. D.C. Transit System, Inc., 108 U.S. App. D.C. 399, 283 F.2d 194, 195 n.1 (D.C. Cir. 1960); 89 C.J.S., Trial, § 577 at 355. In the Wolff case, cited with approval in Del Rio, supra, the Court said:

> We view with disfavor all pressure tactics whether directly or obliquely, to coerce settlement by litigants and their counsel. Failure to concur in what the Justice presiding may consider an adequate settlement should not result in an imposition upon a

litigant or his counsel, who reject it, of any retributive sanctions not specifically authorized by law.

17 A.D.2d at 215. In short, pressure tactics to coerce settlement simply are not permissible. Schunk v. Schunk, 84 A.D.2d 904, 905, 446 N.Y.S.2d 672 (1981); Chomski v. Alston Cab Co., 32 A.D.2d 627, 299 N.Y.S.2d 896 (1969). "The judge must not compel agreement by arbitrary use of his power and the attorney must not merely submit to a judge's suggestion, though it be strongly urged." Brooks v. Great Atlantic & Pacific Tea Co., 92 F.2d 794, 796 (9th Cir. 1937).

Rule 16 of the Fed. R. Civ. P. was not designed as a means for clubbing the parties—or one of them—into an involuntary compromise. See Padovani v. Bruchhausen, 293 F.2d 546, 548 (2d Cir. 1961); Clark, To An Understanding Use of Pre-Trial, 1961, 29 F.R.D. 454, 456; Smith, Pretrial Conference—A Study of Methods, 1961, 29 F.R.D. 348, 353; Moskowitz, Glimpses of Federal Trials and Procedure, 1946, 4 F.R.D. 216, 218. Although subsection (c)(7) of Rule 16, added in the 1983 amendments of the Rule, was designed to encourage pretrial settlement discussions, it was not its purpose to "impose settlement negotiations on unwilling litigants." See Advisory Committee Note, 1983, 97 F.R.D. 205, 210.

We find the coercion in the instant case especially troublesome because the district court imposed sanctions on Smith alone. Offers to settle a claim are not made in a vacuum. They are part of a more complex process which includes "conferences, informal discussions, offers, counterdemands, more discussions, more haggling, and finally, in the great majority of cases, a compromise." J. & D. Sindell, Let's Talk Settlement 300 (1963). In other words, the process of settlement is a two-way street, and a defendant should not be expected to bid against himself. In the instant case, Smith never received a demand of less than $50,000. Having received no indication from Kothe that an offer somewhere in the vicinity of $20,000 would at least be given careful consideration, Smith should not have been required to make an offer in this amount simply because the court wanted him to.

Smith's attorney should not be condemned for changing his evaluation of the case after listening to Kothe's testimony during the first day of trial. As every experienced trial lawyer knows, the personalities of the parties and their witnesses play an important role in litigation. It is one thing to have a valid claim; it is quite another to convince a jury of this fact. It is not at all unusual, therefore, for a defendant to change his perception of a case based on the plaintiff's performance on the witness stand. We see nothing about that occurrence in the instant case that warranted the imposition of sanctions against the defendant alone.

Although we commend Judge Sweet for his efforts to encourage settlement negotiations, his excessive zeal leaves us no recourse but to remand the matter with instructions to vacate the judgment.

NOTE ON JUDICIAL MEDIATION AND SANCTIONS FOR REFUSAL TO SETTLE

1.   **Judicial mediation.** We have seen the Rule 16 pretrial conference before in connection with the court's management of civil discovery. The rule

also expressly authorizes a judicial role in the promotion of settlement. The court, at any pretrial conference, may "take appropriate action" with respect to "settling the case and using special procedures to assist in resolving the dispute when authorized by statute or local rule." Fed. R. Civ. P. 16(c)(2)(I).

It appears that Judge Sweet in *Kothe* acted as a "settlement judge." In part, he acted as a mediator. A mediator is a neutral third party who attempts to facilitate a negotiated resolution of a dispute. In classic mediation, the mediator lacks the power to decide the case. Essentially mediators perform two roles. First, they help the parties to think about their dispute more clearly and imaginatively. This may lead to the identification of a settlement gap that the parties had not themselves been able to identify. Second, mediators facilitate bargaining by creating conditions in which parties find it safer to exchange offers. Often both these roles require meeting separately with each of the parties or their lawyers—the commonly used term for this practice is "caucusing." Can you see the evidence that Judge Sweet sought to perform both the clarifying and facilitative roles in *Kothe*? That at least one of the parties caucused privately with him? Did Judge Sweet move beyond the role of mediator in threatening and then imposing sanctions for failure to settle?

   2.   The case for and against judicial mediation. Former Magistrate Judge Wayne Brazil, himself a well-known settlement judge, conducted a study of the attitudes of lawyers practicing in federal court towards judicial intervention in the settlement process. Most of those lawyers expressed the view that judicial mediation increases the likelihood of settlement and that settlement conferences should be mandatory in federal court. Magistrate Brazil's explanation for those results follows:

> Even though a large percentage of cases ultimately settle, the process through which the parties eventually reach agreement often is difficult to launch, then can be awkward, expensive, time-consuming and stressful. The route to resolution can be tortuously indirect and travel over it can be obstructed by emotion, posturing, and interpersonal friction. Counsel and clients can be distracted by irrelevancies and resources can be consumed by feints or maneuvers designed primarily to save face with opponents or to retain credibility with the people paying the bills. Parties and lawyers can be slow to feel confidence in the wisdom or fairness of proposals developed through such an awkward adversarial process, a process in which people assume that their opponents are not disclosing significant information and are offering only self-serving assessments of the implications of evidence and the relative strengths of competing positions.

> * * * [J]udicial involvement is likely to improve prospects for achieving settlement because judges are professional decision makers.

> Litigators, by contrast, are professional advocates. The skills that are central to the litigator's professional self-image and role revolve around marshaling evidence and arguments for one side, selecting and packaging information to make it as persuasive as possible. Lawyers are trained to uncover evidence, then to arrange its display to others; the others have ultimate responsibility to

decide what the evidence means. Thus, the litigator's job is to present persuasively, not to judge dispassionately.

Judges, on the other hand, are paid to make decisions, and to do so rationally and impartially. * * * To achieve their objective of making rational decisions * * * good judges become skillful at cutting through verbal and emotional camouflage to identify pivotal issues, at ferreting out the evidence, assessing credibility and analyzing strengths and weaknesses of arguments. The pursuit of fair solutions teaches judges to probe, to ask about matters not presented. The responsibility to make decisions puts a premium on efficiency. The responsibility to decide rationally sharpens the judge's analytical edge.

A judge who enters the settlement dynamic with these instincts and skills is in a position to make unique and valuable contributions. The presence of a judicial officer can create an expectation of decision making and can help overcome lawyers' and litigants' natural resistance to realistically assessing their positions. The judge can initiate settlement discussions earlier than counsel otherwise would and can relieve lawyers of the onus of being the first to suggest discussion of settlement. Some lawyers are reluctant to initiate settlement talks because they are afraid that raising the issue of settlement will be perceived by their opponents as a sign of weakness. That fear might help explain why so many of our respondents think settlement conferences should be mandatory in most actions and that judges should take steps to encourage settlement even when no one has asked them to.

Our data indicate, however, that lawyers believe that initiating dialogue about settlement is by no means the principal contribution judges can make to the process. What judges have to contribute to settlement that lawyers value most is skill in judging. Lawyers value penetrating, analytical exposition and thoughtful, objective, knowledgeable assessment. They want the judge's opinions. They want the judge's suggestions. They want the perspective of the experienced neutral. Data we discuss in a subsequent section shows that the judge's opinion that a settlement offer is reasonable is likely to have a great effect on a recalcitrant client, especially if that client is not often involved in litigation.

There are also many ways judges can contribute to the quality of the settlement dialogue itself: they can defuse emotions, set a constructive and analytical tone, help parties focus, and ask questions that expose underdeveloped areas. Judges can also help keep litigants talking when they otherwise might retreat into noncommunication. In these and other ways, a judicial officer can improve the civility, efficiency, and efficacy of the negotiation process.

W. Brazil, Settling Civil Disputes 44–46 (1985).

Professor Galanter and Ms. Cahill express a much more skeptical view of judicial involvement:

What do we know of the effects of judicial intervention on the number or quality of settlements? As to number, the available studies provide no basis for thinking judicial promotion leads to a number of settlements that is sufficiently higher than would otherwise occur to compensate for the opportunity costs of the judicial attention diverted from adjudication. * * * As to the effects of judicial promotion on the quality of settlements, we simply do not know. * * * Are settlements arranged by judges less variable, more principled, more reflective of the merits? No one knows.

Galanter & Cahill, "Most Cases Settle": Judicial Promotion and Regulation of Settlement, 46 Stan. L. Rev. 1339, 1388–89 (1994).

3.   Judicial mediation by the trial judge. Granting the force of Magistrate Judge Brazil's analysis, do you see any particular concerns with having Judge Sweet, who was also scheduled to preside at the trial of the case, act as a mediator in the dispute? With his helping the parties to evaluate their cases in private caucuses? With his participating in the exchange of settlement offers? With his formulating and communicating to the parties his best estimate of a fair settlement? Are those difficulties moderated by the fact that the case was to be tried by a jury? Would those concerns be eliminated if the parties had explicitly consented to have Judge Sweet mediate the case? See ADR Local Rule 7–2 (N.D. Cal.) (allowing the trial judge to conduct a settlement conference, in "his or her discretion," only upon written stipulation of the parties).

4.   Judicial mediation vs. private mediation. In most major cities, there are now a substantial number of professional mediators, usually lawyers or former judges, who are prepared, for a fee, to work with parties in helping to resolve their disputes. Where such mediators are available, what is the justification for using publicly paid judges to play a mediator's role rather than privately compensated mediators? Is there any justification for the judge doing any more than assuring that parties who wish to do so have in fact fully explored the question whether mediation would be useful to them—that is, if you will, for doing anything more than mediate the question of whether to engage a private mediator?

5.   Sanctions for refusal to make an offer. What was wrong with the sanction in *Kothe*? Was the problem with the sanction that the court lacked power to require the defendant to make any offer? Lacked power to require an offer at a specific amount? If Rule 16 does not specifically grant such a power, why shouldn't the court have the inherent power to order the defendant to make such an offer? Would you feel differently about requiring the defendant to respond if the plaintiff had actually offered to settle the case for $20,000? Or is there an inherent inconsistency between the reasons for favoring settlement and the idea of requiring a party to make or accept an offer at a specific amount?

In Dawson v. United States, 68 F.3d 886 (5th Cir. 1995), the district court sanctioned the United States for refusing to offer anything in settlement of a prisoner's Federal Tort Claims Act suit for damages, in supposed violation of a local court rule requiring "parties in every civil suit [to] make a good faith effort to settle." The court of appeals reversed, upholding the right of the United States to refuse to offer anything in settlement and instead insist on going to trial:

Early settlement of cases is an extremely laudable goal, which federal judges have considerable power to encourage and facilitate * * *. On the other hand, * * * parties may have valid and principled reasons for not wishing to settle particular cases. These reasons may not be based necessarily on the merits of a particular case, or the party's possible exposure in it, but because of the effect that a settlement might have on other pending or threatened litigation.

68 F.3d at 897.

Should it matter whether the reason for the defendant's failure to make an offer is in fact principled? In some types of cases, "repeat player" defendants pursue a strategy of "low ball" settlement offers. Such defendants know that many of the plaintiffs they oppose are so short of funds or worried about the stresses, risks, and delays of trial that they will accept an offer to settle that is worth much less than the "objective" value of their claim. The only way for defendants to identify such claimants, however, is to pursue a hardball negotiation strategy against all plaintiffs. Many plaintiffs will crack and accept the lower offer, saving the defendant substantial sums, but when the defendant's bluff is called, there will be a trial. See Gross & Syverud, Don't Try: Civil Jury Verdicts in a System Geared to Settlement, 44 UCLA L. Rev. 1, 53–56 (1996). Is the principle of paying as little as possible one that courts are bound to respect? Or is the problem that it is too hard to distinguish these cases from others where the defendant's reasons for refusing to settle may be more legitimate?

6. Sanctions for failure to participate or for failing to settle on time. Courts clearly have power under Rule 16 to compel the attendance of both lawyers and parties at pretrial settlement conferences. "If appropriate, the court may require that a party or its representative be present or reasonably available by other means to consider possible settlement." Fed. R. Civ. P. 16(c)(1). This language was added to Rule 16 in 1993 to confirm the result reached in G. Heileman Brewing Co. v. Joseph Oat Corp., 871 F.2d 648, 650 (7th Cir. 1989) (upholding, as an exercise of the court's inherent power, sanctions for failing to obey a court order to send a "corporate representative with power to settle" to a pretrial conference "to discuss disputed factual and legal issues and the possibility of settlement."). Why is it acceptable to require a party to attend a settlement conference, but not to require them to settle? In *Heileman*, Judge Richard Posner argued in dissent that, even if the court had authority to require a party's attendance, it lacked the power to require that a party send "an executive having 'full settlement authority' to the pretrial conference. This demand * * * would be defensible only if litigants had a duty to bargain in good faith over settlement before resorting to trial, and neither Rule 16 nor any other rule, statute, or doctrine imposes such a duty on federal litigants. There is no federal judicial power to compel settlement. Oat had made clear that it was not prepared to settle the case on any terms that required it to pay money. That was its prerogative, which once exercised made the magistrate's continued insistence on Oat's sending an executive to [the conference] arbitrary, unreasonable, willful, and indeed petulant." 871 F.2d at 658. Is there a good answer to Judge Posner's objection?

Can a party be sanctioned for failing to settle in accord with a court's pre-announced deadline for doing so? Newton v. A.C. & S., 918 F.2d 1121 (3d Cir. 1990) involved the following:

In an innovative effort to manage its trial docket, the district court instituted the practice of 'stacking' asbestos cases. Under this practice, the district court assigned the asbestos injury cases to a designated time slot. As a scheduled case is disposed of, either by

> trial or settlement, the district court moves the next case into the allotted slot. To give the parties of the next case in line sufficient notice of their trial date, the district court judge sets a deadline for settlement negotiations of two weeks prior to the trial date. If the litigants settle after the deadline, the district court imposes a fine regardless of fault and without a prior hearing.

Id. at 1125. The court of appeals upheld the court's power to set and enforce a deadline for settlement, but held that the automatic imposition of sanctions against both parties for failing to meet that deadline, without a prior hearing or determination of fault, violated the requirements of the Due Process Clause. Is the view of permissible coercion adopted in *Newton* consistent with that adopted in *Kothe*?

7.   Sanctions for failure to accept an offer: offer-of-settlement rules and offer-of-judgment rules. Both federal and state courts have offer-of-judgment or offer-of-settlement rules. Professors Anderson and Rowe have described such devices as follows:

> The essence of the offer of judgment or offer of settlement device * * * has been that a party * * * can formalize an offer to settle or to have judgment entered on certain terms, with the offeree exposed to adverse consequences if she does not accept the offer, and then fails to do well enough in the ultimate result as measured against the offer. To put the point another way, the rule makes "losers" suffer consequences, such as liability for post-offer costs or attorney fees, and the formal offer changes the benchmark of what counts as "losing" for purposes of determining cost or fee liability. A plaintiff, say, may win a verdict, but will incur liability for the defendant's reasonable post-offer costs or fees (or those incurred after expiration of the offer, to give the plaintiff time to consider it) if the verdict is not good enough in relation to a rejected defendant's offer.

Anderson & Rowe, Empirical Evidence on Settlement Devices: Does Rule 68 Encourage Settlement?, 71 Chi.-Kent L. Rev. 519, 520–21 (1995).

The federal offer-of-judgment rule, Rule 68, provides that at any time more than fourteen days before trial, "a party defending against a claim may serve on an opposing party an offer to allow judgment on specified terms[.] * * * If the judgment that the offeree finally obtains is not more favorable than the unaccepted offer, the offeree must pay the costs incurred after the offer was made." Rule 68 has some distinctive features.

First, the rule is not symmetrical. Only a defendant (or a plaintiff who is a defendant to a counterclaim) may make an offer of settlement under Rule 68. A plaintiff or counterclaimant may not make an offer under Rule 68.

Second, if the plaintiff is offered something in settlement by the defendant, and the plaintiff then recovers nothing at all at trial, the rule does not apply because the plaintiff did not obtain a "judgment." Thus, if the defendant offers $10,000 in settlement, the plaintiff refuses the offer, and the defendant prevails at trial, the rule does not award costs against the plaintiff. If, under the same circumstances, the plaintiff receives a judgment of $10, she owes costs. Delta Air Lines, Inc. v. August, 450 U.S. 346, 101 S.Ct. 1146, 67 L.Ed.2d 287 (1981).

Third, in most actions, the rule shifts only "costs" in the narrow technical sense, which do not include attorney's fees, the most important real cost of litigation. In a limited class of cases, however, the technical term "costs" may include attorney's fees. Marek v. Chesny, 473 U.S. 1, 105 S.Ct. 3012, 87 L.Ed.2d 1 (1985). In *Marek*, a civil rights case, the Supreme Court held that the term "costs" under Rule 68 includes attorney's fees under federal statutes which authorize the award of fees "as part of costs," including the Civil Rights Attorney's Fees Award of 1976, 42 U.S.C. § 1988. Under such a statute, a civil rights plaintiff who receives a Rule 68 offer faces two risks if she later recovers a judgment that doesn't better the offer: (a) payment of the other side's "costs" and (b) forfeiture of the attorney's fees she would otherwise obtain as a prevailing party. As construed in *Marek*, does Rule 68 violate the Rules Enabling Act, 28 U.S.C. § 2072(b) ("[s]uch rules shall not abridge, enlarge or modify any substantive right")?

Rule 68 has been heavily criticized. See, e.g., Burbank, Proposals to Amend Rule 68—Time to Abandon Ship, 19 U. Mich. J. L. Ref. 425 (1986); Miller, An Economic Analysis of Rule 68, 15 J. Legal Stud. 93 (1986). The Judicial Conference stated that the "rule has been rarely invoked and has been considered largely ineffective as a means of achieving its goals." But proposed modifications to make the rule available to both parties, to require that the offer be kept open for 30 days, and to make the sanction not merely costs but also the offering party's post-offer attorney's fees were never enacted. Among those opposing the modification were civil rights organizations, who objected that the stronger cost shifting provisions in the proposed new rule would work to the disadvantage of civil rights plaintiffs.

Recent articles on the operation of Rule 68 and analogous state rules include: Bone, To Encourage Settlement: Rule 68, Offers of Judgment, and the History of the Federal Rules of Civil Procedure, 102 Nw. U. L. Rev. 1561 (2008); Sherman, From "Loser Pays" to Modified Offer of Judgment Rules: Reconciling Incentives to Settle with Access to Justice, 76 Tex. L. Rev. 1863 (1998); Bonney, Tribeck, & Wrona, Rule 68: Awakening a Sleeping Giant, 65 Geo. Wash. L. Rev. 379 (1997).

In re Atlantic Pipe Corp.

United States Court of Appeals for the First Circuit, 2002.
304 F.3d 135.

■ SELYA, CIRCUIT JUDGE.

This mandamus proceeding requires us to resolve an issue of importance to judges and practitioners alike: Does a district court possess the authority to compel an unwilling party to participate in, and share the costs of, non-binding mediation conducted by a private mediator? We hold that a court may order mandatory mediation pursuant to an explicit statutory provision or local rule. We further hold that where, as here, no such authorizing medium exists, a court nonetheless may order mandatory mediation through the use of its inherent powers as long as the case is an appropriate one and the order contains adequate safeguards. Because the mediation order here at issue lacks such safeguards (although it does not fall far short), we vacate it and remand the matter for further proceedings.

I. BACKGROUND

In January 1996, Thames-Dick Superaqueduct Partners (Thames-Dick) entered into a master agreement with the Puerto Rico Aqueduct and Sewer Authority (PRASA) to construct, operate, and maintain the North Coast Superaqueduct Project (the Project). Thames-Dick granted subcontracts for various portions of the work, including a subcontract for construction management to Dick Corp. of Puerto Rico (Dick–PR), a subcontract for the operation and maintenance of the Project to Thames Water International, Ltd. (Thames Water), and a subcontract for the fabrication of pipe to Atlantic Pipe Corp. (APC). After the Project had been built, a segment of the pipeline burst. Thames-Dick incurred significant costs in repairing the damage. Not surprisingly, it sought to recover those costs from other parties. In response, one of PRASA's insurers filed a declaratory judgment action in a local court to determine whether Thames-Dick's claims were covered under its policy. The litigation ballooned, soon involving a number of parties and a myriad of issues above and beyond insurance coverage.

On April 25, 2001, the hostilities spilled over into federal court. Two entities beneficially interested in the master agreement—CPA Group International and Chiang, Patel & Yerby, Inc. (collectively CPA)—sued Thames-Dick, Dick–PR, Thames Water, and various insurers in the United States District Court for the District of Puerto Rico, seeking remuneration for consulting services rendered in connection with repairs to the Project. A googol of claims, counterclaims, cross-claims, and third-party complaints followed. Some of these were brought against APC (the petitioner here). To complicate matters, one of the defendants moved to dismiss on grounds that, inter alia, (1) CPA had failed to join an indispensable party whose presence would destroy diversity jurisdiction, and (2) the existence of the parallel proceeding in the local court counseled in favor of abstention.

While this motion was pending before the district court, Thames-Dick asked that the case be referred to mediation and suggested Professor Eric Green as a suitable mediator. The district court granted the motion over APC's objection and ordered non-binding mediation to proceed before Professor Green. The court pronounced mediation likely to conserve judicial resources; directed all parties to undertake mediation in good faith; stayed discovery pending completion of the mediation; and declared that participation in the mediation would not prejudice the parties' positions vis-a-vis the pending motion or the litigation as a whole. The court also stated that if mediation failed to produce a global settlement, the case would proceed to trial.

After moving unsuccessfully for reconsideration of the mediation order, APC sought relief by way of mandamus. Its petition alleged that the district court did not have the authority to require mediation (especially in light of unresolved questions as to the court's subject-matter jurisdiction) and, in all events, could not force APC to pay a share of the expenses of the mediation. We invited the other parties and the district judge to respond. See Fed. R. App. P. 21(b)(4)–(5). Several entities (including Thames-Dick, Dick–P.R., and Thames Water) opposed the petition. Two others (third-party defendants United States Fidelity & Guaranty Company and United Surety and Indemnity Company) filed a brief in support of APC. We assigned the case to the oral argument calendar and stayed the contemplated mediation pending our review.

Prior to argument in this court, two notable developments occurred. First, the district court considered and rejected the challenges to its exercise of jurisdiction. Second, APC rejected an offer by Thames-Dick to pay its share of the mediator's fees.

II. JURISDICTION

In an effort to shut off further debate, the respondents asseverate that mandamus is improper because APC will not suffer irreparable harm in the absence of such relief. They rest this asseveration on the notion that "mandamus is ordinarily appropriate [only] in those rare cases in which the issuance (or nonissuance) of an order presents a question anent the limits of judicial power, poses some special risk of irreparable harm to the appellant, and is palpably erroneous." United States v. Horn, 29 F.3d 754, 769 (1st Cir. 1994). The problem, however, is that these limitations typically apply only to supervisory mandamus. Id. at 769 & n.19. In the tiny class of cases in which advisory mandamus is appropriate, irreparable harm need not be shown. Id. at 769–70.

We believe that this case is fit for advisory mandamus because the extent of a trial court's power to order mandatory mediation presents a systemically important issue as to which this court has not yet spoken. See In re Prov. Journal Co., 293 F.3d 1, 9 (1st Cir. 2002) (discussing criteria for advisory mandamus). Moreover, that issue is capable of significant repetition prior to effective review. See Jennifer O'Hearne, Comment, Compelled Participation in Innovative Pretrial Proceedings, 84 Nw. U. L. Rev. 290, 317 (1989) (noting that, as a practical matter, lawyers often are unable to challenge pretrial innovations even when they may be invalid). That fact militates in favor of advisory mandamus. See Horn, 29 F.3d at 770. We conclude, therefore, that invoking advisory mandamus is prudent under the circumstances. Consequently, the existence vel non of irreparable harm is a non-issue. We turn, then, to the merits.

III. THE MERITS

There are four potential sources of judicial authority for ordering mandatory non-binding mediation of pending cases, namely, (a) the court's local rules, (b) an applicable statute, (c) the Federal Rules of Civil Procedure, and (d) the court's inherent powers. Because the district court did not identify the basis of its assumed authority, we consider each of these sources.

A. The Local Rules.

A district court's local rules may provide an appropriate source of authority for ordering parties to participate in mediation. See Rhea v. Massey-Ferguson, Inc., 767 F.2d 266, 268–69 (6th Cir. 1985) (per curiam). In Puerto Rico, however, the local rules contain only a single reference to any form of alternative dispute resolution (ADR). That reference is embodied in the district court's Amended Civil Justice Expense and Delay Reduction Plan (CJR Plan). See D.P.R. R. app. III.

The district court adopted the CJR Plan on June 14, 1993, in response to the directive contained in the Civil Justice Reform Act of 1990 (CJRA), 28 U.S.C. §§ 471–482. Rule V of the CJR Plan states:

> Pursuant to 28 U.S.C. § 473(b)(4), this Court shall adopt a method of Alternative Dispute Resolution ("ADR") through mediation by a judicial officer.
>
> Such a program would allow litigants to obtain from an impartial third party—the judicial officer as mediator—a flexible non-binding, dispute resolution process to facilitate negotiations among the parties to help them reach settlement.

D.P.R. R. app. III (R. V.). In addition to specifying who may act as a mediator, Rule V also limns the proper procedure for mediation sessions and assures confidentiality. See id.

The respondents concede that the mediation order in this case falls outside the boundaries of the mediation program envisioned by Rule V. It does so most noticeably because it involves mediation before a private mediator, not a judicial officer. Seizing upon this discrepancy, APC argues that the local rules limit the district court in this respect, and that the court exceeded its authority thereunder by issuing a non-conforming mediation order (i.e., one that contemplates the intervention of a private mediator). The respondents counter by arguing that the rule does not bind the district court because, notwithstanding the unambiguous promise of the CJR Plan (which declares that the district court "shall adopt a method of Alternative Dispute Resolution"), no such program has been adopted to date.

This is a powerful argument. APC does not contradict the respondents' assurance that the relevant portion of the CJR Plan has remained unimplemented, and we take judicial notice that there is no formal, ongoing ADR program in the Puerto Rico federal district court. Because that is so, we conclude that the District of Puerto Rico has no local rule in force that dictates the permissible characteristics of mediation orders. Consequently, APC's argument founders.[2]

B. The ADR Act.

There is only one potential source of statutory authority for ordering mandatory non-binding mediation here: the Alternative Dispute Resolution Act of 1998 (ADR Act), 28 U.S.C. §§ 651–658. Congress passed the ADR Act to promote the utilization of alternative dispute resolution methods in the federal courts and to set appropriate guidelines for their use. The Act lists mediation as an appropriate ADR process. Id. § 651(a). Moreover, it sanctions the participation of "professional neutrals from the private sector" as mediators. Id. § 653(b). Finally, the Act requires district courts to obtain litigants' consent only when they order arbitration, id. § 652(a), not when they order the use of other ADR mechanisms (such as non-binding mediation).

Despite the broad sweep of these provisions, the Act is quite clear that some form of the ADR procedures it endorses must be adopted in each judicial district by local rule. See id. § 651(b) (directing each district court to "devise and implement its own alternative dispute resolution

---

[2] This holding renders it unnecessary for us to discuss the respondents' alternate contention that the CJR Plan is a dead letter because the legislation that prompted its enactment—the CJRA—expired in 1997. See, e.g., Carl Tobias, Did the Civil Justice Reform Act of 1990 Actually Expire?, 31 U. Mich. J.L. Reform 887, 892 (1998) (exploring the uncertainty regarding whether the CJRA expired and whether local plans adopted pursuant to it are still effective).* * *

program, by local rule adopted under [28 U.S.C.] section 2071(a), to encourage and promote the use of alternative dispute resolution in its district"). In the absence of such local rules, the ADR Act itself does not authorize any specific court to use a particular ADR mechanism. Because the District of Puerto Rico has not yet complied with the Act's mandate, the mediation order here at issue cannot be justified under the ADR Act.

The respondents essay an end run around this lacuna: they contend (borrowing a phrase from the court below) that the "spirit" of the ADR Act authorizes the mediation order because the Act was intended to promote experimentation with ADR techniques. We reject this attempt to press the ADR Act into service by indirection.

Although the ADR Act was designed to promote the use of ADR techniques, Congress chose a very well-defined path: it granted each judicial district, rather than each individual judge, the authority to craft an appropriate ADR program. In other words, Congress permitted experimentation, but only within the disciplining format of district-wide local rules adopted with notice and a full opportunity for public comment. See 28 U.S.C. § 2071(b). To say that the Act authorized each district judge to disregard a district-wide ADR plan (or the absence of one) and fashion innovative procedures for use in specific cases is simply too much of a stretch.

We add, however, that although the respondents cannot use the ADR Act as a justification, neither can APC use it as a nullification. Noting that the Act requires the adoption of local rules establishing a formal ADR program, APC equates the absence of such rules with the absence of power to employ an ADR procedure (say, mediation) in a specific case. But that is wishful thinking: if one assumes that district judges possessed the power to require mediation prior to the passage of the ADR Act, there is nothing in the Act that strips them of that power. After all, even the adoption of a federal procedural rule does not implicitly abrogate a district court's inherent power to act merely because the rule touches upon the same subject matter. See Chambers v. Nasco, Inc., 501 U.S. 32, 42–43, 115 L.Ed.2d 27, 111 S.Ct. 2123 (1991) (rejecting the argument that the adoption of various provisions of the Civil Rules eliminated the district court's inherent power to impose other sanctions); Link v. Wabash R.R., 370 U.S. 626, 630, 8 L.Ed.2d 734, 82 S.Ct. 1386 (1963) (explaining that neither the permissive language of Fed. R. Civ. P. 41(b) nor the policy behind it justified a conclusion that it was meant to limit the district courts' inherent power to dismiss a case for want of prosecution).

The case before us is analogous to *Chambers* and *Link*. Even though Congress may cabin the district courts' inherent powers, its intention to do so must be clear and unmistakable. Not so here: we know of nothing in either the ADR Act or the policies that undergird it that can be said to restrict the district courts' authority to engage in the case-by-case deployment of ADR procedures. Hence, we conclude that where, as here, there are no implementing local rules, the ADR Act neither authorizes nor prohibits the entry of a mandatory mediation order.

C. The Civil Rules.

The respondents next argue that the district court possessed the authority to require mediation by virtue of the Federal Rules of Civil

Procedure. They concentrate their attention on Fed. R. Civ. P. 16, which states in pertinent part that "the court may take appropriate action[ ] with respect to . . . (9) settlement and the use of special procedures to assist in resolving the dispute when authorized by statute or local rule. . . ." Fed. R. Civ. P. 16(c)(9) [eds. note: now Rule 16(c)(2)(I)]. But the words "when authorized by statute or local rule" are a frank limitation on the district courts' authority to order mediation thereunder,[3] and we must adhere to that circumscription. See Schlagenhauf v. Holder, 379 U.S. 104, 121, 13 L.Ed.2d 152, 85 S.Ct. 234 (1964) (explaining that the Civil Rules "should not be expanded by disregarding plainly expressed limitations"). Because there is no statute or local rule authorizing mandatory private mediation in the District of Puerto Rico, see supra Parts III(A)–(B), Rule 16(c)(9) does not assist the respondents' cause.

D. Inherent Powers.

Even apart from positive law, district courts have substantial inherent power to manage and control their calendars. See *Link*, 370 U.S. at 630–31; see generally Brockton Sav. Bank v. Peat, Marwick, Mitchell & Co., 771 F.2d 5, 11 (1st Cir. 1985) (explaining that "the rules of civil procedure do not completely describe and limit the power of district courts"). This inherent power takes many forms. See Fed. R. Civ. P. 83(b) (providing that judges may regulate practice in any manner consistent with federal law and applicable rules). By way of illustration, a district court may use its inherent power to compel represented clients to attend pretrial settlement conferences, even though such a practice is not specifically authorized in the Civil Rules. See Heileman Brewing Co. v. Joseph Oat Corp., 871 F.2d 648, 650 (7th Cir. 1989) (en banc).

Of course, a district court's inherent powers are not infinite. There are at least four limiting principles. First, inherent powers must be used in a way reasonably suited to the enhancement of the court's processes, including the orderly and expeditious disposition of pending cases. Coyante v. P.R. Ports Auth., 105 F.3d 17, 23 (1st Cir. 1997). Second, inherent powers cannot be exercised in a manner that contradicts an applicable statute or rule. Chambers, 501 U.S. at 47. Third, the use of inherent powers must comport with procedural fairness. Id. at 50. And, finally, inherent powers "must be exercised with restraint and discretion." Id. at 44.

At one time, the inherent power of judges to compel unwilling parties to participate in ADR procedures was a hot-button issue for legal scholars. Compare, e.g., O'Hearne, supra at 320 (arguing that inherent power should not be used to compel participation in pretrial settlement proceedings), with Lucille M. Ponte, Putting Mandatory Summary Jury Trial Back on the Docket: Recommendations on the Exercise of Judicial Authority, 63 Fordham L. Rev. 1069, 1094 (1995) (urging the opposite conclusion). Although many federal district courts have forestalled further debate by adopting local rules that authorize specific ADR

---

[3]   We think it is pertinent here to quote the advisory committee's note:

The rule acknowledges the presence of statutes and local rules or plans that may authorize use of some [ADR] procedures even when not agreed to by the parties. The rule does not attempt to resolve questions as to the extent a court would be authorized to require such proceedings as an exercise of its inherent powers.

Fed. R. Civ. P. 16, advisory committee's note (1993 Amendment) (citations omitted).

procedures and outlaw others, e.g., D.N.H. R. 53.1 (permitting mandatory mediation); D. Me. R. 83.11 (permitting only voluntary mediation); D. Mass. R. 16.4 (permitting mandatory summary jury trials but only voluntary mediation), the District of Puerto Rico is not among them. Thus, we have no choice but to address the question head-on.

We begin our inquiry by examining the case law. In Strandell v. Jackson County, 838 F.2d 884 (7th Cir. 1987), the Seventh Circuit held that a district court does not possess inherent power to compel participation in a summary jury trial.[5] In the court's view, Fed. R. Civ. P. 16 occupied the field and prevented a district court from forcing "an unwilling litigant [to] be sidetracked from the normal course of litigation." Id. at 887. But the group that spearheaded the subsequent revision of Rule 16 explicitly rejected that interpretation. See Fed. R. Civ. P. 16, advisory committee's note (1993 Amendment) ("The [amended] rule does not attempt to resolve questions as to the extent a court would be authorized to require [ADR] proceedings as an exercise of its inherent powers."). Thus, we do not find Strandell persuasive on this point.

The *Strandell* court also expressed concern that summary jury trials would undermine traditional discovery and privilege rules by requiring certain disclosures prior to an actual trial. 838 F.2d at 888. We find this concern unwarranted. Because a summary jury trial (like a non-binding mediation) does not require any disclosures beyond what would be required in the ordinary course of discovery, its principal disadvantage to the litigants is that it may prevent them from saving surprises for the time of trial. Since trial by ambush is no longer in vogue, that interest does not deserve protection. See Fed. Reserve Bank v. Carey-Canada, Inc., 123 F.R.D. 603, 606 (D. Minn. 1988).

Relying on policy arguments, the Sixth Circuit also has found that district courts do not possess inherent power to compel participation in summary jury trials. See In re NLO, Inc., 5 F.3d 154, 157–58 (6th Cir. 1993). The court thought the value of a summary jury trial questionable when parties do not engage in the process voluntarily, and it worried that "too broad an interpretation of the federal courts' inherent power to regulate their procedure . . . encourages judicial high-handedness. . . ." Id. at 158 (citation and internal quotation marks omitted).

The concerns articulated by these two respected courts plainly apply to mandatory mediation orders. When mediation is forced upon unwilling litigants, it stands to reason that the likelihood of settlement is diminished. Requiring parties to invest substantial amounts of time and money in mediation under such circumstances may well be inefficient. Cf. Richard A. Posner, The Summary Jury Trial and Other Methods of Alternative Dispute Resolution: Some Cautionary Observations, 53 U. Chi. L. Rev. 366, 369–72 (1986) (offering a model to evaluate ADR techniques in terms of their capacity to encourage settlements).

The fact remains, however, that none of these considerations establishes that mandatory mediation is always inappropriate. There

---

[5]   A summary jury trial is an ADR technique in which the opposing attorneys present their case, in abbreviated form, to a mock jury, which proceeds to render a non-binding verdict. See In re NLO, Inc., 5 F.3d 154, 156 (6th Cir. 1993); see generally Thomas D. Lambros, The Summary Jury Trial Report to the Judicial Conference of the United States, 103 F.R.D. 461 (1984).

may well be specific cases in which such a protocol is likely to conserve judicial resources without significantly burdening the objectors' rights to a full, fair, and speedy trial. Much depends on the idiosyncracies of the particular case and the details of the mediation order.

In some cases, a court may be warranted in believing that compulsory mediation could yield significant benefits even if one or more parties object. After all, a party may resist mediation simply out of unfamiliarity with the process or out of fear that a willingness to submit would be perceived as a lack of confidence in her legal position. See Campbell C. Hutchinson, The Case for Mandatory Mediation, 42 Loy. L. Rev. 85, 89–90 (1996). In such an instance, the party's initial reservations are likely to evaporate as the mediation progresses, and negotiations could well produce a beneficial outcome, at reduced cost and greater speed, than would a trial. While the possibility that parties will fail to reach agreement remains ever present, the boon of settlement can be worth the risk.

This is particularly true in complex cases involving multiple claims and parties. The fair and expeditious resolution of such cases often is helped along by creative solutions—solutions that simply are not available in the binary framework of traditional adversarial litigation. Mediation with the assistance of a skilled facilitator gives parties an opportunity to explore a much wider range of options, including those that go beyond conventional zero-sum resolutions. Mindful of these potential advantages, we hold that it is within a district court's inherent power to order non-consensual mediation in those cases in which that step seems reasonably likely to serve the interests of justice. Cf. Reilly v. United States, 863 F.2d 149, 156–57 (1st Cir. 1988) (finding that district courts have inherent power to appoint technical advisors in especially complex cases).

E. The Mediation Order.

Our determination that the district courts have inherent power to refer cases to non-binding mediation is made with a recognition that any such order must be crafted in a manner that preserves procedural fairness and shields objecting parties from undue burdens. We thus turn to the specifics of the mediation order entered in this case. As with any exercise of a district court's inherent powers, we review the entry of that order for abuse of discretion. See Chambers, 501 U.S. at 50; Reilly, 863 F.2d at 156.

As an initial matter, we agree with the lower court that the complexity of this case militates in favor of ordering mediation. At last count, the suit involves twelve parties, asserting a welter of claims, counterclaims, cross-claims, and third-party claims predicated on a wide variety of theories. The pendency of nearly parallel litigation in the Puerto Rican courts, which features a slightly different cast of characters and claims that are related to but not completely congruent with those asserted here, further complicates the matter. Untangling the intricate web of relationships among the parties, along with the difficult and fact-intensive arguments made by each, will be time-consuming and will impose significant costs on the parties and the court. Against this backdrop, mediation holds out the dual prospect of advantaging the litigants and conserving scarce judicial resources.

In an effort to parry this thrust, APC raises a series of objections. Its threshold claim is that the district court erred in ordering mediation before resolving a pending motion to dismiss for lack of subject-matter jurisdiction (or, alternatively, to abstain). See, e.g., Bouchard Transp. Co. v. Fla. Dep't of Envtl. Prot., 91 F.3d 1445, 1448–49 (11th Cir. 1996) (vacating a mediation order and directing the lower court first to consider the objecting party's assertion of Eleventh Amendment immunity).

Given what has transpired, this argument is fruitless. While this proceeding was pending, the district court denied the motion in question and confirmed the existence of its subject-matter jurisdiction. See, CPA Group Int'l, Inc. v. Am. Int'l Ins. Co. No. 01–1483, slip op. at 16–25 (D.P.R. May 23, 2002). Thus, even if it were error to enter the mediation order before passing upon the motion to dismiss, the error was harmless; it would be an empty exercise to vacate the mediation order on this ground when the lower court has already rejected the challenges to its exercise of jurisdiction. See, e.g., Gibbs v. Buck, 307 U.S. 66, 78, 83 L. Ed. 1111, 59 S.Ct. 725 (1939); Aoude v. Mobil Oil Corp., 862 F.2d 890, 895 (1st Cir. 1988).

Next, APC posits that the appointment of a private mediator proposed by one of the parties is per se improper (and, thus, invalidates the order). We do not agree. The district court has inherent power to "appoint persons unconnected with the court to aid judges in the performance of specific judicial duties." Ex parte Peterson, 253 U.S. 300, 312, 64 L. Ed. 919, 40 S.Ct. 543 (1920). In the context of non-binding mediation, the mediator does not decide the merits of the case and has no authority to coerce settlement. Thus, in the absence of a contrary statute or rule, it is perfectly acceptable for the district court to appoint a qualified and neutral private party as a mediator. The mere fact that the mediator was proposed by one of the parties is insufficient to establish bias in favor of that party. Cf. TechSearch, L.L.C. v. Intel Corp., 286 F.3d 1360, 1379 n.3 (Fed. Cir. 2002) (noting that technical advisors typically would be selected from a list of candidates submitted by the parties).

We hasten to add that the litigants are free to challenge the qualifications or neutrality of any suggested mediator (whether or not nominated by a party to the case). APC, for example, had a full opportunity to present its views about the suggested mediator both in its opposition to the motion for mediation and in its motion for reconsideration of the mediation order. Despite these opportunities, APC offered no convincing reason to spark a belief that Professor Green, a nationally recognized mediator with significant experience in sprawling cases, is an unacceptable choice. When a court enters a mediation order, it necessarily makes an independent determination that the mediator it appoints is both qualified and neutral. Because the court made that implicit determination here in a manner that was procedurally fair (if not ideal), we find no abuse of discretion in its selection of Professor Green.[7]

---

[7] We say "not ideal" because, in an ideal world, it would be preferable for the district court, before naming a mediator, to solicit the names of potential nominees from all parties and to provide an opportunity for the parties to comment upon each others' proposed nominees.

APC also grouses that it should not be forced to share the costs of an unwanted mediation. We have held, however, that courts have the power under Fed. R. Civ. P. 26(f) to issue pretrial cost-sharing orders in complex litigation. See In re San Juan Dupont Plaza Hotel Fire Litig., 994 F.2d 956, 965 (1st Cir. 1993). Given the difficulties facing trial courts in cases involving multiple parties and multiple claims, we are hesitant to limit that power to the traditional discovery context. See id. This is especially true in complicated cases, where the potential value of mediation lies not only in promoting settlement but also in clarifying the issues remaining for trial.

The short of the matter is that, without default cost-sharing rules, the use of valuable ADR techniques (like mediation) becomes hostage to the parties' ability to agree on the concomitant financial arrangements. This means that the district court's inherent power to order private mediation in appropriate cases would be rendered nugatory absent the corollary power to order the sharing of reasonable mediation costs. To avoid this pitfall, we hold that the district court, in an appropriate case, is empowered to order the sharing of reasonable costs and expenses associated with mandatory non-binding mediation.

The remainder of APC's arguments are not so easily dispatched. Even when generically appropriate, a mediation order must contain procedural and substantive safeguards to ensure fairness to all parties involved. The mediation order in this case does not quite meet that test. In particular, the order does not set limits on the duration of the mediation or the expense associated therewith.

We need not wax longiloquent. As entered, the order simply requires the parties to mediate; it does not set forth either a timetable for the mediation or a cap on the fees that the mediator may charge. The figures that have been bandied about in the briefs—$900 per hour or $9,000 per mediation day—are quite large and should not be left to the mediator's whim. Relatedly, because the mediator is to be paid an hourly rate, the court should have set an outside limit on the number of hours to be devoted to mediation. Equally as important, it is trite but often true that justice delayed is justice denied. An unsuccessful mediation will postpone the ultimate resolution of the case—indeed, the district court has stayed all discovery pending the completion of the mediation—and, thus, prolong the litigation. For these reasons, the district court should have set a definite time frame for the mediation.

The respondents suggest that the district court did not need to articulate any limitations in its mediation order because the mediation process will remain under the district court's ultimate supervision; the court retains the ability to curtail any excessive expenditures of time or money; and a dissatisfied party can easily return to the court at any time. While this might be enough of a safeguard in many instances, the instant litigation is sufficiently complicated and the mediation efforts are likely to be sufficiently expensive that, here, reasonable time limits and fee constraints, set in advance, are appropriate.

A court intent on ordering non-consensual mediation should take other precautions as well. For example, the court should make it clear (as did the able district court in this case) that participation in mediation will not be taken as a waiver of any litigation position. The important point is that the protections we have mentioned are not intended to comprise an exhaustive list, but, rather, to illustrate that when a district court orders a party to participate in mediation, it should take care to assuage legitimate concerns about the possible negative consequences of such an order.

To recapitulate, we rule that a mandatory mediation order issued under the district court's inherent power is valid in an appropriate case. We also rule that this is an appropriate case. We hold, however, that the district court's failure to set reasonable limits on the duration of the mediation and on the mediator's fees dooms the decree.

IV. CONCLUSION

We admire the district court's pragmatic and innovative approach to this massive litigation. Our core holding—that ordering mandatory mediation is a proper exercise of a district court's inherent power, subject, however, to a variety of terms and conditions—validates that approach. We are mindful that this holding is in tension with the opinions of the Sixth and Seventh Circuits in *NLO* and *Strandell*, respectively, but we believe it is justified by the important goal of promoting flexibility and creative problem-solving in the handling of complex litigation.

That said, the need of the district judge in this case to construct his own mediation regime ad hoc underscores the greater need of the district court as an institution to adopt an ADR program and memorialize it in its local rules. In the ADR Act, Congress directed that "each United States district court shall authorize, by local rule under section 2071(a), the use of alternative dispute resolution processes in all civil actions." 28 U.S.C.§ 651(b). While Congress did not set a firm deadline for compliance with this directive, the statute was enacted four years ago. This omission having been noted, we are confident that the district court will move expediently to bring the District of Puerto Rico into compliance.

We need go no further. For the reasons set forth above, we vacate the district court's mediation order and remand for further proceedings consistent with this opinion. The district court is free to order mediation if it continues to believe that such a course is advisable or, in the alternative, to proceed with discovery and trial.

Vacated and remanded. Costs shall be taxed in favor of the petitioner.

NOTE ON COURT-ANNEXED ALTERNATIVE DISPUTE RESOLUTION

1. **The varieties of court-annexed alternative dispute resolution.** Over the past 25 years, there has been a considerable expansion in court-annexed programs aimed at facilitating settlement and reducing the costs and delays of litigation.

a. **Mediation.** Court-annexed mediation takes a number of forms. Judicial mediation has already been discussed. Other courts have full-time mediators on staff, have formed panels of private mediators to perform that role, or, as in *Atlantic Pipe,* appoint mediators based upon the nominations of the parties. Mediation proceedings are non-binding and confidential. Some states have identified classes of cases, such as child custody litigation, where the public interest in avoiding contested litigation is so strong that mediation s required as a condition of obtaining a trial. See, e.g., Cal. Fam. Code §§ 3161–3188 (mandatory child custody mediation).

b. Early neutral evaluation. Early neutral evaluation privatizes elements of pretrial management and judicial mediation. The parties meet for two hours, early in the litigation, with a neutral lawyer who specializes in the field that is the subject of their dispute. The parties make brief presentations of their cases, and receive a non-binding evaluation. The evaluator may also offer suggestions for case planning. Brazil, Early Neutral Evaluation (2012).

c. Court-annexed arbitration. Court-annexed arbitration programs typically establish a system of non-binding arbitration for claims for money damages. See, e.g., ADR Local Rule 5 (N.D.Cal.). The case is heard by an arbitrator or panel of three arbitrators. Most programs use lawyers from the community who have applied to serve, but some programs employ non-lawyer experts. Programs vary in the extent to which they contemplate discovery before the arbitration hearing. Arbitrators often have the power to relax the normal rules of evidence. At the hearing, the parties present the evidence and arguments supporting their claims and defenses. The arbitrator or panel then renders an award. In order to avoid any violation of the parties' jury trial rights, the award is non-binding. Either party may request a trial de novo, though some programs impose a sanction (such as the payment of the arbitrator's fees) upon a party who requests a de novo trial and fails to better the award. Hensler, What We Know and Don't Know About Court-Administered Arbitration, 69 Judicature 270 (1986).

d. Summary jury trial. Summary jury trial is a specialized, publicly subsidized form of the private alternative dispute resolution process known as a mini-trial. A mini-trial consists of counsel for the parties presenting severely abbreviated versions of their cases to an advisor or panel. In the classic private mini-trial, the advisor or panel consists of a neutral or neutrals, typically retired judges, lawyers, or people with expertise in the underlying subject matter of the dispute, who are retained by the parties and who render an advisory opinion. In cases involving disputes between organizations, the panel may include senior representatives of the organizations who meet after the mini-trial to attempt to negotiate a settlement.

In a summary jury trial, the mini-trial is conducted before a mock jury convened by the court from its jury pool. Typically, summary jury trial is used after discovery, when the parties have at least in theory had a full opportunity to investigate their claims, marshal their evidence, and identify the basis of their opponent's case. The lawyers begin with opening arguments, present an oral summary of the evidence supporting their position, and finish with closing arguments. The presentations are short, perhaps an hour per party. The judge instructs the jury, and the jury then deliberates and responds to a series of interrogatories about liability and damages. The advisory decision is intended to provide a basis for the parties to evaluate their claims and negotiate their way to a settlement. To preserve the settlement privilege, the entire process is confidential. For fuller description, see Brazil, Early Neutral Evaluation (2012); Lambros, The Summary Jury Trial and Other Alternative Methods of Dispute Resolution, 103 F.R.D. 461 (1984).

Much of the litigation concerning these devices concerns the source and scope of the court's authority to compel participation in these forms of alternative dispute resolution. Much of the most interesting scholarship, however, concerns their efficacy.

2. Authority to compel participation. In federal court, the issue of authority to compel participation is a matter of statute, rule, and case law. Most of the litigation has centered on judicial power to compel participation in summary jury trial, perhaps the most innovative and intrusive of the procedures. Strandell v. Jackson County, 838 F.2d 884 (7th Cir. 1987), held that neither Rule 16 nor the court's inherent power authorized compelling litigants to participate in summary jury trial; accord, In re NLO, 5 F.3d 154 (6th Cir. 1993). Other courts have taken a different view. Montgomery v. Louis Trauth Dairy, Inc., 164 F.R.D. 469 (S.D. Ohio 1996); Arabian American Oil Co. v. Scarfone, 119 F.R.D. 448 (M.D. Fla. 1988).

The Alternative Dispute Resolution Act of 1998, cited in *Atlantic Pipe*, requires all district courts "to authorize, by local rule adopted under section 2071(a), the use of alternative dispute resolution processes in all civil actions." 28 U.S.C. § 651(b). It also requires each district court to require by local rule that "litigants in all civil cases consider the use of an alternative dispute resolution process at an appropriate stage in the litigation." 28 U.S.C. § 652(a). The Act does not require that any alternative dispute resolution process be made mandatory, but it states that "any district court that elects to require the use of alternative dispute resolution in certain cases may do so only with respect to mediation, early neutral evaluation, and, if the parties consent, arbitration." Id. Doesn't the omission of summary jury trial from this list effectively answer the question whether parties to litigation in federal court can be compelled to participate in summary jury trial?

Was the *Atlantic Pipe* court correct to hold that the court's inherent power to compel mediation survived the qualifying language of former Rule 16(c)(9), now Rule 16(c)(2)(I) ("when authorized by state or local rule")? That it survived the enactment of the Alternative Dispute Resolution Act of 1998? What do you suppose was the congressional purpose underlying the legislative requirement that alternative dispute resolution programs be adopted by local rule? Do you think that the court was correct in finding authorization to shift the costs of mediation to unwilling parties in Rule 26(f), a provision dealing with discovery conferences?

3. The conditions justifying compelled participation. Assuming that the trial court had inherent power to order the parties to mediation and to make them pay for it, do you think that power was appropriately exercised in this case? Does the court identify any factor, other than the complexity of the case, which justifies the district court's decision? Does the fact that the district court ordered mediation before deciding that it had subject matter jurisdiction (i.e., power to hear the case) suggest over-eagerness to dispose of the case? How about the stay of discovery pending mediation? Does the court suggest any reason for believing that the parties are in a position to reach an informed resolution of the case at the pleading stage without access to relevant evidence?

4. The effectiveness of court-annexed alternative dispute resolution. The stated goals of court-annexed alternative dispute resolution programs are to reduce costs and delays and to improve the overall quality of justice for litigants. The evidence that they have done so is mixed. A comprehensive Rand Corporation study of four federal court mediation programs and two federal court neutral evaluation programs found that the programs had little effect on time and costs for the parties or the court. Kakalik et al., An Evaluation of Mediation and Early Neutral Evaluation Under the Civil Justice Reform Act (1996). Other studies suggest that strong, well-managed programs can reduce cost and delay for significant percentages of litigants. For discussion, see Brazil, Should Court-Sponsored ADR Survive?, 21 Ohio St. J. on Disp. Res. 241, 249–50 (2006). Studies almost universally show, however, that those who do pursue litigation far enough to reach an arbitration hearing express high satisfaction with having received an opportunity to tell their story to a neutral. Hensler, Does ADR Really Save Money? The Jury's Still Out, Nat'l L.J., Apr. 11, 1994, at C2; Hensler, Court-Annexed ADR in Donovan, Leisure, Newton & Irvine, ADR Practice Book (Wilkinson ed. 1990). Other scholars suggest that court-annexed arbitration programs may systematically disadvantage litigants of modest means. Bernstein, Understanding the Limits of Court-Connected ADR: A Critique of Federal Court-Annexed Arbitration Programs, 141 U. Pa. L. Rev. 2169 (1993).

The best explanation for these mixed results appears to run something like this. Alternative dispute resolution processes constitute an additional layer of procedure and costs between filing and trial. The theory behind such processes is that they will substitute for expensive trials, delivering settlements and party satisfaction at a lower cost to parties and the public. Undoubtedly, these devices have those cost-reducing and satisfaction-enhancing effects in one group of cases. But they also have other consequences. In a second group of cases, alternative dispute resolution does not bring about settlement and further litigation is required to resolve the case; in those cases alternative dispute resolution can increase costs and delays without offsetting benefits. Finally, in a third group of cases, alternative dispute resolution processes may prevent or delay settlement, in the following way. To the extent that alternative dispute resolution processes provide value for litigants, whether because they offer free legal advice and help with preparation (as in early neutral evaluation) or because they provide an inexpensive, but often highly valued, opportunity to be heard on the merits before a neutral (as in court-annexed arbitration), they will cause some litigants who would have settled earlier in the process to persist for longer in order to take advantage of the new procedure. E. Lind, et al. The Perception of Justice: Tort Litigants' Views of Trial, Court-Annexed Arbitration, and Judicial Settlement Conferences (1989). The mix of these effects depends critically on the quality of the program: how good are the neutrals, and how good is the program at screening to ensure that cases are forced to ADR only when they will benefit from it. In view of these findings, what is the strength of the case for compelling parties to resort to alternative dispute resolution procedures, as distinct from requiring them to "consider the use of an alternative dispute resolution process at an appropriate stage in the litigation"? 28 U.S.C. § 652(a).

INTRODUCTORY NOTE ON ARBITRATION

1. **Arbitration and private alternative dispute resolution.** Court adjudication and court-ordered mediation are, of course, not the only ways to settle disputes. Often parties will agree to an alternative form of

dispute resolution, such as private arbitration, to resolve their disagreements. Theoretically, such methods of "alternative dispute resolution," or ADR, are advantageous to the parties because they are faster, cheaper, and less formal than judicial proceedings. See, e.g., Menkel-Meadow, The Trouble with the Adversary System in a Post-Modern, Multicultural World, 1 J. Inst. Stud. Legal Ethics 49 (1996). On the other hand, some argue that ADR is less effective at protecting litigants' (particularly consumers') rights and may often be forced on parties without their knowing consent. See Resnik, Procedure as Contract, 80 Notre Dame L. Rev. 593 (2005). The literature debating the efficacy of ADR is vast, and the arguments generally resemble those explained above in the Introductory Note on Settlement, *infra*. For additional discussion, see, e.g., Symposium, Empirical Studies of Mandatory Arbitration, 41 U. Mich. J. L. Reform 777 (2008); Eisenberg & Miller, The Flight from Arbitration: An Empirical Study of Ex Ante Arbitration Clauses in the Contracts of Publicly Held Companies, 56 DePaul L. Rev. 335 (2007).

2. **Arbitration as a "creature of contract."** Parties must agree to arbitrate their disputes. Without such an agreement, the parties default to the standard litigation system—only by contract can a party be said to have waived his or her right to a "day in court." Parties, however, may agree to arbitration *ex ante*, meaning before a dispute arises, or *ex post*, meaning after the parties are already in conflict. The agreement to arbitrate often provides for a means of selecting an arbitrator (or panel of arbitrators) and for the procedures and law to be followed in the arbitration, including motion practice, discovery, and the fact-finding hearings. As a result, "[a]rbitration is thus not one procedure, but a family of procedures." Hazard, Leubsdorf & Bassett, Civil Procedure § 10.11 (6th ed. 2011). If one party to an agreement to arbitrate refuses to do so, or files an action in court, the other party's remedy is to file a motion to compel arbitration, essentially to enforce the arbitration agreement.

Agreements to arbitrate originally developed primarily as a means of resolving disputes in commercial relationships, typically between sophisticated parties. Indeed, numerous industries rely almost exclusively on arbitration to ensure speedy resolution of disputes by specialized tribunals. For example, arbitration of disputes is standard in the textile industry because the pace of the fashion industry demands quick and binding decisions. See, e.g., In re Cotton Yarn Antitrust Litig., 505 F.3d 274 (4th Cir. 2013); Chelsea Square Textiles, Inc. v. Bombay Dyeing & Mfg. Co., Ltd., 189 F.3d 289 (2d Cir. 1999).

Today, agreements to arbitrate have proliferated far beyond arm's-length contracts between commercial actors to many form contracts agreed to by employees and consumers. In fact, whether you are aware of it or not, you are almost certainly a party to many agreements to arbitrate disputes in standardized contracts to which you have agreed (just as you are likely a party to many forum-selection clauses, see Chapter 2, supra). See Resnik, Fairness in Numbers: A Comment on AT&T v. Concepcion, Walmart v. Dukes, and Turner v. Rogers, 125 Harv. L. Rev. 78 (2011).

AT&T Mobility LLC v. Concepcion

Supreme Court of the United States, 2011.
___ U.S. ___, 131 S.Ct. 1740, 179 L.Ed.2d 172.

■ JUSTICE SCALIA delivered the opinion of the Court.

Section 2 of the Federal Arbitration Act (FAA) makes agreements to arbitrate "valid, irrevocable, and enforceable, save upon such grounds as exist at law or in equity for the revocation of any contract." 9 U.S.C. § 2. We consider whether the FAA prohibits States from conditioning the enforceability of certain arbitration agreements on the availability of classwide arbitration procedures.

I

In February 2002, Vincent and Liza Concepcion entered into an agreement for the sale and servicing of cellular telephones with AT & T Mobility LCC (AT & T). The contract provided for arbitration of all disputes between the parties, but required that claims be brought in the parties' "individual capacity, and not as a plaintiff or class member in any purported class or representative proceeding." The agreement authorized AT & T to make unilateral amendments, which it did to the arbitration provision on several occasions.

The revised agreement provides that customers may initiate dispute proceedings by completing a one-page Notice of Dispute form available on AT & T's Web site. AT & T may then offer to settle the claim; if it does not, or if the dispute is not resolved within 30 days, the customer may invoke arbitration by filing a separate Demand for Arbitration, also available on AT & T's Web site. In the event the parties proceed to arbitration, the agreement specifies that AT & T must pay all costs for nonfrivolous claims; that arbitration must take place in the county in which the customer is billed; that, for claims of $10,000 or less, the customer may choose whether the arbitration proceeds in person, by telephone, or based only on submissions; that either party may bring a claim in small claims court in lieu of arbitration; and that the arbitrator may award any form of individual relief, including injunctions and presumably punitive damages. The agreement, moreover, denies AT & T any ability to seek reimbursement of its attorney's fees, and, in the event that a customer receives an arbitration award greater than AT & T's last written settlement offer, requires AT & T to pay a $7,500 minimum recovery and twice the amount of the claimant's attorney's fees.

The Concepcions purchased AT & T service, which was advertised as including the provision of free phones; they were not charged for the phones, but they were charged $30.22 in sales tax based on the phones' retail value. In March 2006, the Concepcions filed a complaint against AT & T in the United States District Court for the Southern District of California. The complaint was later consolidated with a putative class action alleging, among other things, that AT & T had engaged in false advertising and fraud by charging sales tax on phones it advertised as free.

In March 2008, AT & T moved to compel arbitration under the terms of its contract with the Concepcions. The Concepcions opposed the motion, contending that the arbitration agreement was unconscionable and unlawfully exculpatory under California law because it disallowed classwide procedures. The District Court denied AT & T's motion. It described AT & T's arbitration agreement favorably, noting, for example, that the informal dispute-resolution process was "quick, easy to use" and likely to "promp[t] full or . . . even excess payment to the customer without the need to arbitrate or litigate"; that the $7,500 premium functioned as "a substantial inducement for the consumer to pursue the claim in arbitration" if a dispute was not resolved informally; and that consumers who were members of a class would likely be worse off. Laster v. T-Mobile USA, Inc., 2008 WL 5216255, *11–*12 (S.D.Cal., Aug.11, 2008). Nevertheless, relying on the California Supreme Court's decision in Discover Bank v. Superior Court, 36 Cal.4th 148 (2005), the court found that the arbitration provision was unconscionable because AT & T had not shown that bilateral arbitration adequately substituted for the deterrent effects of class actions.

The Ninth Circuit affirmed, also finding the provision unconscionable under California law as announced in Discover Bank. * * *

II

The FAA was enacted in 1925 in response to widespread judicial hostility to arbitration agreements. See Hall Street Associates, L.L.C. v. Mattel, Inc., 552 U.S. 576, 581, 128 S.Ct. 1396, 170 L.Ed.2d 254 (2008). Section 2, the "primary substantive provision of the Act," Moses H. Cone Memorial Hospital v. Mercury Constr. Corp., 460 U.S. 1, 24, 103 S.Ct. 927, 74 L.Ed.2d 765 (1983), provides, in relevant part, as follows:

> "A written provision in any maritime transaction or a contract evidencing a transaction involving commerce to settle by arbitration a controversy thereafter arising out of such contract or transaction . . . shall be valid, irrevocable, and enforceable, save upon such grounds as exist at law or in equity for the revocation of any contract." 9 U.S.C. § 2.

We have described this provision as reflecting both a "liberal federal policy favoring arbitration," Moses H. Cone, supra, at 24, 103 S.Ct. 927, and the "fundamental principle that arbitration is a matter of contract," Rent-A-Center, West, Inc. v. Jackson, 561 U.S. 63, ___, 130 S.Ct. 2772, 2776, 177 L.Ed.2d 403 (2010). In line with these principles, courts must place arbitration agreements on an equal footing with other contracts, Buckeye Check Cashing, Inc. v. Cardegna, 546 U.S. 440, 443, 126 S.Ct. 1204, 163 L.Ed.2d 1038 (2006), and enforce them according to their terms, Volt Information Sciences, Inc. v. Board of Trustees of Leland Stanford Junior Univ., 489 U.S. 468, 478, 109 S.Ct. 1248, 103 L.Ed.2d 488 (1989).

The final phrase of § 2, however, permits arbitration agreements to be declared unenforceable "upon such grounds as exist at law or in equity for the revocation of any contract." This saving clause permits agreements to arbitrate to be invalidated by "generally applicable contract defenses, such as fraud, duress, or unconscionability," but not by defenses that apply only to arbitration or that derive their meaning from the fact that an agreement to arbitrate is at issue. . . . The question in this case is whether § 2 preempts California's rule classifying most collective-arbitration waivers in consumer contracts as unconscionable. We refer to this rule as the Discover Bank rule. * * *

In Discover Bank, the California Supreme Court . . . held as follows:

"[W]hen the waiver is found in a consumer contract of adhesion in a setting in which disputes between the contracting parties predictably involve small amounts of damages, and when it is alleged that the party with the superior bargaining power has carried out a scheme to deliberately cheat large numbers of consumers out of individually small sums of money, then . . . the waiver becomes in practice the exemption of the party 'from responsibility for [its] own fraud, or willful injury to the person or property of another.' Under these circumstances, such waivers are unconscionable under California law and should not be enforced." Id., at 162, 30 Cal.Rptr.3d 76, 113 P.3d, at 1110 (quoting Cal. Civ.Code Ann. § 1668).

California courts have frequently applied this rule to find arbitration agreements unconscionable. * * *

III

A

The Concepcions argue that the Discover Bank rule, given its origins in California's unconscionability doctrine and California's policy against exculpation, is a ground that "exist[s] at law or in equity for the revocation of any contract" under FAA § 2. * * *

When state law prohibits outright the arbitration of a particular type of claim, the analysis is straightforward: The conflicting rule is displaced by the FAA. Preston v. Ferrer, 552 U.S. 346, 353, 128 S.Ct. 978, 169 L.Ed.2d 917 (2008). But the inquiry becomes more complex when a doctrine normally thought to be generally applicable, such as duress or, as relevant here, unconscionability, is alleged to have been applied in a fashion that disfavors arbitration. * * *

Although § 2's saving clause preserves generally applicable contract defenses, nothing in it suggests an intent to preserve state-law rules that stand as an obstacle to the accomplishment of the FAA's objectives. Cf. Geier v. American Honda Motor Co., 529 U.S. 861, 872, 120 S.Ct. 1913, 146 L.Ed.2d 914 (2000); Crosby v. National Foreign Trade Council, 530 U.S. 363, 372–373, 120 S.Ct. 2288, 147 L.Ed.2d 352 (2000). As we have said, a federal statute's saving clause " 'cannot in reason be construed as [allowing] a common law right, the continued existence of which would be absolutely inconsistent with the provisions of the act. In other words, the act cannot be held to destroy itself.' " American Telephone & Telegraph Co. v. Central Office Telephone, Inc., 524 U.S. 214, 227–228, 118 S.Ct. 1956, 141 L.Ed.2d 222 (1998) (quoting Texas & Pacific R. Co. v. Abilene Cotton Oil Co., 204 U.S. 426, 446, 27 S.Ct. 350, 51 L.Ed. 553 (1907)).

* * * The overarching purpose of the FAA, evident in the text of §§ 2, 3, and 4, is to ensure the enforcement of arbitration agreements according to their terms so as to facilitate streamlined proceedings. Requiring the availability of classwide arbitration interferes with fundamental attributes of arbitration and thus creates a scheme inconsistent with the FAA.

B

The "principal purpose" of the FAA is to "ensur[e] that private arbitration agreements are enforced according to their terms." Volt, 489 U.S., at 478, 109 S.Ct. 1248; see also Stolt-Nielsen S.A. v. AnimalFeeds Int'l Corp., 559 U.S. 662, ___, 130 S.Ct. 1758, 1763, 176 L.Ed.2d 605 (2010). This purpose is readily apparent from the FAA's text. Section 2 makes arbitration agreements "valid, irrevocable, and enforceable" as written (subject, of course, to the saving clause); § 3 requires courts to stay litigation of arbitral claims pending arbitration of those claims "in accordance with the terms of the agreement"; and § 4 requires courts to compel arbitration "in accordance with the terms of the agreement" upon the motion of either party to the agreement (assuming that the "making of the arbitration agreement or the failure . . . to perform the same" is not at issue). In light of these provisions, we have held that parties may agree to limit the issues subject to arbitration, Mitsubishi Motors Corp. v. Soler Chrysler-Plymouth, Inc., 473 U.S. 614, 628, 105 S.Ct. 3346, 87 L.Ed.2d 444 (1985), to arbitrate according to specific rules, Volt, supra, at 479, 109 S.Ct. 1248, and to limit with whom a party will arbitrate its disputes, Stolt-Nielsen, supra, at ___, 130 S.Ct. at 1773.

The point of affording parties discretion in designing arbitration processes is to allow for efficient, streamlined procedures tailored to the type of dispute. It can be specified, for example, that the decisionmaker be a specialist in the relevant field, or that proceedings be kept confidential to protect trade secrets. And the informality of arbitral proceedings is itself desirable, reducing the cost and increasing the speed of dispute resolution.

* * *

Contrary to the dissent's view, our cases place it beyond dispute that the FAA was designed to promote arbitration. They have repeatedly described the Act as "embod[ying] [a] national policy favoring arbitration," Buckeye Check Cashing, 546 U.S., at 443, 126 S.Ct. 1204, and "a liberal federal policy favoring arbitration agreements, notwithstanding any state substantive or procedural policies to the contrary," Moses H. Cone, 460 U.S., at 24, 103 S.Ct. 927; see also Hall Street Assocs., 552 U.S., at 581, 128 S.Ct. 1396. Thus, in Preston v. Ferrer, holding preempted a state-law rule requiring exhaustion of administrative remedies before arbitration, we said: "A prime objective of an agreement to arbitrate is to achieve 'streamlined proceedings and expeditious results,'" which objective would be "frustrated" by requiring a dispute to be heard by an agency first. 552 U.S., at 357–358, 128 S.Ct. 978. That rule, we said, would "at the least, hinder speedy resolution of the controversy." Id., at 358, 128 S.Ct. 978.[5]

California's Discover Bank rule similarly interferes with arbitration. Although the rule does not require classwide arbitration, it allows any party to a consumer contract to demand it ex post. The rule is limited to adhesion contracts, Discover Bank, 36 Cal.4th at 162–163, but the times in which consumer contracts were anything other than adhesive are long past. Carbajal v. H & R Block Tax Servs., Inc., 372 F.3d 903, 906 (7th Cir. 2004); see also Hill v. Gateway 2000, Inc., 105 F.3d 1147, 1149 (C.A.7 1997). The rule also requires that damages be predictably small, and that the consumer allege a scheme to cheat consumers. Discover Bank, supra, at 162–163, 30 Cal.Rptr.3d 76, 113 P.3d, at 1110. The former requirement, however, is toothless and malleable (the Ninth Circuit has held that damages of $4,000 are sufficiently small, see Oestreicher v. Alienware Corp., 322 Fed.Appx. 489, 492 (2009) (unpublished)), and the latter has no limiting effect, as all that is required is an allegation. Consumers remain free to bring and resolve their disputes on a bilateral basis under Discover Bank, and some may well do so; but there is little incentive for lawyers to arbitrate on behalf of individuals when they may do so for a class and reap far higher fees in the process. And faced with inevitable class arbitration, companies would have less incentive to continue resolving potentially duplicative claims on an individual basis.

* * * [C]lass arbitration, to the extent it is manufactured by Discover Bank rather than consensual, is inconsistent with the FAA.

First, the switch from bilateral to class arbitration sacrifices the principal advantage of arbitration—its informality—and makes the process slower, more costly, and more likely to generate procedural morass than final judgment. "In bilateral arbitration, parties forgo the procedural rigor and appellate review of the courts in order to realize the benefits of private dispute resolution: lower costs, greater efficiency and speed, and the ability to choose expert adjudicators to resolve specialized disputes." 559 U.S., at ___, 130 S.Ct. at 1775. But before an arbitrator may decide the merits of a claim in classwide procedures, he must first decide, for example, whether the class itself may be certified, whether the named parties are sufficiently representative and typical, and how discovery for the class should be conducted. A cursory comparison of bilateral and class arbitration illustrates the difference. According to the American Arbitration Association (AAA), the average consumer arbitration between January and August 2007 resulted in a disposition on the merits in six months, four months if the arbitration was conducted by documents only. AAA, Analysis of the AAA's Consumer Arbitration Caseload, online at http://www.adr.org/si.asp?id=5027 (all Internet materials as visited Apr. 25, 2011, and available in Clerk of Court's case file). As of September 2009, the AAA had opened 283 class arbitrations. Of those, 121 remained active, and 162 had been settled, withdrawn, or dismissed. Not a single one, however, had resulted in a final award on the merits. * * *

Second, class arbitration requires procedural formality. The AAA's rules governing class arbitrations mimic the Federal Rules of Civil Procedure for class litigation. And while parties can alter those procedures by contract, an alternative is not obvious. If procedures are too informal, absent class members would not be bound by the arbitration. For a class-action money judgment to bind absentees in litigation, class representatives must at all times adequately represent absent class members, and absent members must be afforded notice, an opportunity to be heard, and a right to opt out of the class. Phillips Petroleum Co. v. Shutts, 472 U.S. 797, 811–812, 105 S.Ct. 2965, 86 L.Ed.2d 628 (1985). At least this amount of process would presumably be required for absent parties to be bound by the results of arbitration.

We find it unlikely that in passing the FAA Congress meant to leave the disposition of these procedural requirements to an arbitrator. Indeed, class arbitration was not even envisioned by Congress when it passed the FAA in 1925; as the California Supreme Court admitted in Discover

Bank, class arbitration is a "relatively recent development." 36 Cal.4th at 163. And it is at the very least odd to think that an arbitrator would be entrusted with ensuring that third parties' due process rights are satisfied.

Third, class arbitration greatly increases risks to defendants. Informal procedures do of course have a cost: The absence of multilayered review makes it more likely that errors will go uncorrected. Defendants are willing to accept the costs of these errors in arbitration, since their impact is limited to the size of individual disputes, and presumably outweighed by savings from avoiding the courts. But when damages allegedly owed to tens of thousands of potential claimants are aggregated and decided at once, the risk of an error will often become unacceptable. Faced with even a small chance of a devastating loss, defendants will be pressured into settling questionable claims. Other courts have noted the risk of "in terrorem" settlements that class actions entail, see, e.g., Kohen v. Pacific Inv. Management Co. LLC, 571 F.3d 672, 677–678 (C.A.7 2009), and class arbitration would be no different.

     * * *

The dissent claims that class proceedings are necessary to prosecute small-dollar claims that might otherwise slip through the legal system. But States cannot require a procedure that is inconsistent with the FAA, even if it is desirable for unrelated reasons. Moreover, the claim here was most unlikely to go unresolved. As noted earlier, the arbitration agreement provides that AT & T will pay claimants a minimum of $7,500 and twice their attorney's fees if they obtain an arbitration award greater than AT & T's last settlement offer. The District Court found this scheme sufficient to provide incentive for the individual prosecution of meritorious claims that are not immediately settled, and the Ninth Circuit admitted that aggrieved customers who filed claims would be "essentially guarantee[d]" to be made whole, 584 F.3d, at 856, n. 9. Indeed, the District Court concluded that the Concepcions were better off under their arbitration agreement with AT & T than they would have been as participants in a class action, which "could take months, if not years, and which may merely yield an opportunity to submit a claim for recovery of a small percentage of a few dollars." Laster, 2008 WL 5216255, at *12.

     * * *

Because it "stands as an obstacle to the accomplishment and execution of the full purposes and objectives of Congress," Hines v. Davidowitz, 312 U.S. 52, 67, 61 S.Ct. 399, 85 L.Ed. 581 (1941), California's Discover Bank rule is preempted by the FAA. The judgment of the Ninth Circuit is reversed, and the case is remanded for further proceedings consistent with this opinion.

It is so ordered.

■ JUSTICE BREYER, with whom JUSTICE GINSBURG, JUSTICE KAGAN, and JUSTICE SOTOMAYOR join, dissenting:*

The Federal Arbitration Act says that an arbitration agreement "shall be valid, irrevocable, and enforceable, save upon such grounds as exist at law or in equity for the revocation of any contract." 9 U.S.C. § 2

---

*   The concurring opinion by Justice Thomas is omitted.

(emphasis added). California law sets forth certain circumstances in which "class action waivers" in any contract are unenforceable. In my view, this rule of state law is consistent with the federal Act's language and primary objective. It does not "stan[d] as an obstacle" to the Act's "accomplishment and execution." Hines v. Davidowitz, 312 U.S. 52, 67, 61 S.Ct. 399, 85 L.Ed. 581 (1941). And the Court is wrong to hold that the federal Act pre-empts the rule of state law.

I

The California law in question consists of an authoritative state-court interpretation of two provisions of the California Civil Code. The first provision makes unlawful all contracts "which have for their object, directly or in-directly, to exempt anyone from responsibility for his own . . . violation of law." Cal. Civ.Code Ann. § 1668 (West 1985). The second provision authorizes courts to "limit the application of any unconscionable clause" in a contract so "as to avoid any unconscionable result." § 1670.5(a).

The specific rule of state law in question consists of the California Supreme Court's application of these principles to hold that "some" (but not "all") "class action waivers" in consumer contracts are exculpatory and unconscionable under California "law." Discover Bank v. Superior Ct., 36 Cal.4th 148, 160 (2005). In particular, in Discover Bank the California Supreme Court stated that, when a class-action waiver

> "is found in a consumer contract of adhesion in a setting in which disputes between the contracting parties predictably involve small amounts of damages, and when it is alleged that the party with the superior bargaining power has carried out a scheme to deliberately cheat large numbers of consumers out of individually small sums of money, then . . . the waiver becomes in practice the exemption of the party 'from responsibility for [its] own fraud, or willful injury to the person or property of another.'" Id. at 162–163.

In such a circumstance, the "waivers are unconscionable under California law and should not be enforced." Id. at 163.

The Discover Bank rule does not create a "blanket policy in California against class action waivers in the consumer context." * * * Instead, it represents the "application of a more general [unconscionability] principle." Gentry v. Superior Ct., 42 Cal.4th 443, 457 (2007). Courts applying California law have enforced class-action waivers where they satisfy general unconscionability standards. . . . And even when they fail, the parties remain free to devise other dispute mechanisms, including informal mechanisms that, in context, will not prove unconscionable. See Volt Information Sciences, Inc. v. Board of Trustees of Leland Stanford Junior Univ., 489 U.S. 468, 479, 109 S.Ct. 1248, 103 L.Ed.2d 488 (1989).

II

A

The Discover Bank rule is consistent with the federal Act's language. It "applies equally to class action litigation waivers in contracts without arbitration agreements as it does to class arbitration waivers in contracts with such agreements." Linguistically speaking, it falls directly within the scope of the Act's exception permitting courts to refuse to enforce arbitration agreements on grounds that exist "for the revocation of any contract." 9 U.S.C. § 2 (emphasis added). The majority agrees.

B

The Discover Bank rule is also consistent with the basic "purpose behind" the Act. Dean Witter Reynolds Inc. v. Byrd, 470 U.S. 213, 219, 105 S.Ct. 1238, 84 L.Ed.2d 158 (1985). We have described that purpose as one of "ensur[ing] judicial enforcement" of arbitration agreements. Ibid.; see also Marine Transit Corp. v. Dreyfus, 284 U.S. 263, 274, n. 2, 52 S.Ct. 166, 76 L.Ed. 282 (1932) (" 'The purpose of this bill is to make valid and enforceable agreements for arbitration' " (quoting H.R.Rep. No. 96, 68th Cong., 1st Sess., 1 (1924); emphasis added)); 65 Cong. Rec.1931 (1924) ("It creates no new legislation, grants no new rights, except a remedy to enforce an agreement in commercial contracts and in admiralty contracts"). As is well known, prior to the federal Act, many courts expressed hostility to arbitration, for example by refusing to order specific performance of agreements to arbitrate. See S.Rep. No. 536, 68th Cong., 1st Sess., 2 (1924). The Act sought to eliminate that hostility by placing agreements to arbitrate " 'upon the same footing as other contracts.' " Scherk v. Alberto-Culver Co., 417 U.S. 506, 511, 94 S.Ct. 2449, 41 L.Ed.2d 270 (1974) (quoting H.R.Rep. No. 96, at 2; emphasis added).

Congress was fully aware that arbitration could provide procedural and cost advantages. The House Report emphasized the "appropriate[ness]" of making arbitration agreements enforceable "at this time when there is so much agitation against the costliness and delays of litigation." Id. at 2. And this Court has acknowledged that parties may enter into arbitration agreements in order to expedite the resolution of disputes.

But we have also cautioned against thinking that Congress' primary objective was to guarantee these particular procedural advantages. Rather, that primary objective was to secure the "enforcement" of agreements to arbitrate. Dean Witter, 470 U.S., at 221, 105 S.Ct. 1238. See also id. at 219, 105 S.Ct. 1238 (we "reject the suggestion that the overriding goal of the Arbitration Act was to promote the expeditious resolution of claims"); id. at 219, 217–218, 105 S.Ct. 1238 ("[T]he intent of Congress" requires us to apply the terms of the Act without regard to whether the result would be "possibly inefficient"); cf. id., at 220, 105 S.Ct. 1238 (acknowledging that "expedited resolution of disputes" might lead parties to prefer arbitration). The relevant Senate Report points to the Act's basic purpose when it says that "[t]he purpose of the [Act] is clearly set forth in section 2," S.Rep. No. 536, at 2 (emphasis added), namely, the section that says that an arbitration agreement "shall be valid, irrevocable, and enforceable, save upon such grounds as exist at law or in equity for the revocation of any contract," 9 U.S.C. § 2.

Thus, insofar as we seek to implement Congress' intent, we should think more than twice before invalidating a state law that does just what § 2 requires, namely, puts agreements to arbitrate and agreements to litigate "upon the same footing."

III

The majority's contrary view (that Discover Bank stands as an "obstacle" to the accomplishment of the federal law's objective, ante, at 9–18) rests primarily upon its claims that the Discover Bank rule increases the complexity of arbitration procedures, thereby discouraging parties from entering into arbitration agreements, and to that extent discriminating in practice against arbitration. These claims are not well founded.

For one thing, a state rule of law that would sometimes set aside as unconscionable a contract term that forbids class arbitration is not (as the majority claims) like a rule that would require "ultimate disposition by a jury" or "judicially monitored discovery" or use of "the Federal Rules of Evidence." Unlike the majority's examples, class arbitration is consistent with the use of arbitration. It is a form of arbitration that is well known in California and followed elsewhere. . . . Indeed, the AAA has told us that it has found class arbitration to be "a fair, balanced, and efficient means of resolving class disputes." Brief for AAA as Amicus Curiae in Stolt-Nielsen S.A. v. AnimalFeeds Int'l Corp., O.T.2009, No. 08–1198, p. 25 (hereinafter AAA Amicus Brief). And unlike the majority's examples, the Discover Bank rule imposes equivalent limitations on litigation; hence it cannot fairly be characterized as a targeted attack on arbitration.

Where does the majority get its contrary idea—that individual, rather than class, arbitration is a "fundamental attribut[e]" of arbitration? The majority does not explain. And it is unlikely to be able to trace its present view to the history of the arbitration statute itself.

When Congress enacted the Act, arbitration procedures had not yet been fully developed. Insofar as Congress considered detailed forms of arbitration at all, it may well have thought that arbitration would be used primarily where merchants sought to resolve disputes of fact, not law, under the customs of their industries, where the parties possessed roughly equivalent bargaining power. * * * This last mentioned feature of the history—roughly equivalent bargaining power—suggests, if anything, that California's statute is consistent with, and indeed may help to further, the objectives that Congress had in mind.

Regardless, if neither the history nor present practice suggests that class arbitration is fundamentally incompatible with arbitration itself, then on what basis can the majority hold California's law pre-empted?

For another thing, the majority's argument that the Discover Bank rule will discourage arbitration rests critically upon the wrong comparison. The majority compares the complexity of class arbitration with that of bilateral arbitration. And it finds the former more complex. But, if incentives are at issue, the relevant comparison is not "arbitration with arbitration" but a comparison between class arbitration and judicial class actions. After all, in respect to the relevant set of contracts, the Discover Bank rule similarly and equally sets aside clauses that forbid class procedures—whether arbitration procedures or ordinary judicial procedures are at issue.

Why would a typical defendant (say, a business) prefer a judicial class action to class arbitration? AAA statistics "suggest that class arbitration proceedings take more time than the average commercial arbitration, but may take less time than the average class action in court." AAA Amicus Brief 24 (emphasis added). Data from California courts confirm that class arbitrations can take considerably less time than in-court proceedings in which class certification is sought. Compare ante, at 14 (providing statistics for class arbitration), with Judicial Council of California, Administrative Office of the Courts, Class Certification in California: Second Interim Report from the Study of California Class Action Litigation 18 (2010) (providing statistics for class-action litigation in California courts). And a single class proceeding is surely more efficient than thousands of separate proceedings for identical claims. Thus, if speedy resolution of disputes were all that mattered, then the Discover Bank rule would reinforce, not obstruct, that objective of the Act.

The majority's related claim that the Discover Bank rule will discourage the use of arbitration because "[a]rbitration is poorly suited to . . . higher stakes" lacks empirical support. Ante, at 16. Indeed, the majority provides no convincing reason to believe that parties are unwilling to submit high-stake disputes to arbitration. And there are numerous counterexamples. Loftus, Rivals Resolve Dispute Over Drug, Wall Street Journal, Apr. 16, 2011, p. B2 (discussing $500 million settlement in dispute submitted to arbitration); Ziobro, Kraft Seeks Arbitration In Fight With Starbucks Over Distribution, Wall Street Journal, Nov. 30, 2010, p. B10 (describing initiation of an arbitration in which the payout "could be higher" than $1.5 billion); Markoff, Software Arbitration Ruling Gives I.B.M. $833 Million From Fujitsu, N.Y. Times, Nov. 30, 1988, p. A1 (describing both companies as "pleased with the ruling" resolving a licensing dispute).

    ***

What rational lawyer would have signed on to represent the Concepcions in litigation for the possibility of fees stemming from a $30.22 claim? See, e.g., Carnegie v. Household Int'l, Inc., 376 F.3d 656, 661 (C.A.7 2004) ("The realistic alternative to a class action is not 17 million individual suits, but zero individual suits, as only a lunatic or a fanatic sues for $30"). In California's perfectly rational view, nonclass arbitration over such sums will also sometimes have the effect of depriving claimants of their claims (say, for example, where claiming the $30.22 were to involve filling out many forms that require technical legal knowledge or waiting at great length while a call is placed on hold). Discover Bank sets forth circumstances in which the California courts believe that the terms of consumer contracts can be manipulated to insulate an agreement's author from liability for its own frauds by "deliberately cheat[ing] large numbers of consumers out of individually small sums of money." Why is this kind of decision—weighing the pros and cons of all class proceedings alike—not California's to make?

Finally, the majority can find no meaningful support for its views in this Court's precedent. The federal Act has been in force for nearly a century. We have decided dozens of cases about its requirements. We have reached results that authorize complex arbitration procedures. E.g., Mitsubishi Motors, 473 U.S., at 629, 105 S.Ct. 3346 (antitrust claims arising in international transaction are arbitrable). We have upheld nondiscriminatory state laws that slow down arbitration proceedings. E.g., Volt Information Sciences, 489 U.S., at 477–479, 109 S.Ct. 1248

(California law staying arbitration proceedings until completion of related litigation is not pre-empted). But we have not, to my knowledge, applied the Act to strike down a state statute that treats arbitrations on par with judicial and administrative proceedings. Cf. Preston, 552 U.S., at 355–356, 128 S.Ct. 978 (Act pre-empts state law that vests primary jurisdiction in state administrative board).

* * *

These cases do not concern the merits and demerits of class actions; they concern equal treatment of arbitration contracts and other contracts. Since it is the latter question that is at issue here, I am not surprised that the majority can find no meaningful precedent supporting its decision.

IV

By using the words "save upon such grounds as exist at law or in equity for the revocation of any contract," Congress retained for the States an important role incident to agreements to arbitrate. 9 U.S.C. § 2. Through those words Congress reiterated a basic federal idea that has long informed the nature of this Nation's laws. We have often expressed this idea in opinions that set forth presumptions. See, e.g., Medtronic, Inc. v. Lohr, 518 U.S. 470, 485, 116 S.Ct. 2240, 135 L.Ed.2d 700 (1996) ("[B]ecause the States are independent sovereigns in our federal system, we have long presumed that Congress does not cavalierly pre-empt state-law causes of action"). But federalism is as much a question of deeds as words. It often takes the form of a concrete decision by this Court that respects the legitimacy of a State's action in an individual case. Here, recognition of that federalist ideal, embodied in specific language in this particular statute, should lead us to uphold California's law, not to strike it down. We do not honor federalist principles in their breach.

With respect, I dissent.

NOTE ON *CONCEPCION* AND THE FEDERAL ARBITRATION ACT

1. **The Federal Arbitration Act.** In 1924, Congress passed the Federal Arbitration Act, 9 U.S.C. §§ 1–16, with relatively little fanfare. Agitation for the passage of the federal act came primarily from the American Bar Association, which had succeeded in getting numerous similar state arbitration acts passed over the prior decade. This movement for arbitration statutes sought to overturn the common law rules then in force allowing for revocation of agreements to arbitrate and courts' refusals to stay litigation in favor of arbitration. Although proponents of these statutes also sought legislation in all fifty states, they deemed a federal statute necessary in order to ensure that arbitration agreements would be enforced in the federal courts. See generally MacNeil, American Arbitration Law (1992); Horton, Federal Arbitration Act Preemption, Purposivism, and State Public Policy, 101 Geo. L.J. 1217 (2013).

The FAA's crucial provisions are found in sections 2–4. Section 2 provides that:

> A written provision in any maritime transaction or a contract evidencing a transaction involving commerce to settle by arbitration a controversy thereafter arising out of such contract or transaction, or the refusal to perform the whole or any part thereof,

or an agreement in writing to submit to arbitration an existing
controversy arising out of such a contract, transaction, or refusal,
shall be valid, irrevocable, and enforceable, save upon such grounds
as exist at law or in equity for the revocation of any contract.

9 U.S.C. § 2. Section 3 provides for a stay of litigation while a dispute covered
by an arbitration agreement is pending, and Section 4 allows a party to an
arbitration agreement to bring an action in federal court to compel
arbitration. 9 U.S.C. §§ 3–4. Since the passage of the Act, arbitration
enormously has increased, and litigation over the meaning of the Act has
centered on questions about its scope: What arbitration agreements are
enforceable under the Act, and how far does the force of the Act extend in the
face of potentially conflicting state law?

   2. *Wilko v. Swan.* The Supreme Court first addressed the
applicability of the FAA to a federal statutory claim in 1953 in Wilko v. Swan,
346 U.S. 427, 74 S.Ct. 182, 98 L.Ed.2d 168 (1953). Wilko involved a
misrepresentation claim against a brokerage firm under the Securities Act
of 1933 and a mandatory arbitration clause in the original contract between
the plaintiff and the firm. The question in the case was whether section 14
of the Securities Act, which voids any "condition, stipulation, or provision
binding any person acquiring any security to waiver compliance with any
provision" of the Act, barred enforcement of the arbitration clause. The Court
held that it did. Justice Reed, writing for the majority, explicitly recognized
a conflict between the FAA and the Securities Act, writing that "[t]wo
policies, not easily reconcilable, are involved in this case." Reed noted that
the FAA "afforded participants in transactions subject to its legislative power
an opportunity to secure prompt, economical, and adequate solution of
controversies through arbitration if the parties are willing to accept less
certainty of legally correct adjustment," and that the Securities Act
"protect[s] the rights of investors and had forbidden a waiver of any of those
rights." Under the circumstances, the Court held that a contract agreeing to
arbitrate a claim under the Securities Act was invalid, on the ground that
such contracts were typically the result of the disparity of bargaining power
between the seller and the buyer that the Securities Act sought to protect.

   3. Post-*Wilko* developments. Although *Wilko* seemed to evince a
policy of rejecting agreements to arbitrate claims when doing so would
potentially harm parties with limited bargaining power, the Court has
moved away from that position in a series of cases that culminated in
Concepcion. For instance, despite historical evidence seemingly to the
contrary, the Supreme Court held in 1984 that the Act not only applies in
state court, but also preempts state law barring arbitration of certain
agreements. Southland Corp. v. Keating, 465 U.S. 1, 104 S.Ct. 852, 79
L.Ed.2d 1 (1984). In so doing, the Court stated that in passing the FAA,
"Congress declared a national policy favoring arbitration and withdrew the
power of the states to require a judicial forum for the resolution of claims the
parties agreed to resolve by arbitration." Id. at 10.

   The Court subsequently held that antitrust claims were arbitrable in
Mitsubishi Motors Corp. v. Soler Chrysler-Plymouth, 473 U.S. 614, 105 S.Ct.
3346, 87 L.Ed.2d 444 (1985). The case involved a motion to compel
arbitration by the Japanese automaker against one of its Puerto Rico-based
dealers. In its opinion, which reversed the First Circuit's refusal to enforce
the motion to compel, the Court stated that because "we are well past the
time when judicial suspicion of the desirability of arbitration and of the

competence of arbitral tribunals inhibited the development of arbitration as an alternative means of dispute resolution," there was no reason to depart from the strong national policy in favor of arbitration in the case of statutory claims. Id. at 626–27. Moreover, the Court both endorsed and enforced the parties' decision to "trade[ ] the procedures and opportunity for review of the courtroom for the simplicity, informality, and expedition of arbitration." Id. at 628.

Given the holding in *Mitsubishi*, it was perhaps inevitable that the Court would eventually overturn *Wilko*, which it did in Rodriguez v. Shearson/American Express, Inc., 490 U.S. 477, 109 S.Ct. 1917, 104 L.Ed.2d 526 (1989). In so doing, the Court made clear that "to the extent that *Wilko* rested on suspicion of arbitration as a method of weakening the protections afforded in the substantive law to would-be complainants, it has fallen far out of step with our current strong endorsement of the federal statutes favoring this method of resolving disputes." Id. at 481. For additional reading about the progression of this case law, see MacNeil, American Arbitration Law (1992).

4. Understanding *Concepcion*. *Concepcion* involved a standardized consumer contract, the kind often referred to as a "contract of adhesion." Like the cruise-line ticket in *Carnival Cruise Lines, Inc. v. Shute*, supra Chapter 2, the Concepcions cannot be said to have bargained for the terms in the agreement in any realistic sense. Do you agree with the Supreme Court that such arbitration agreements in standard-form contracts with individual consumers should be enforced? Are these consumers being deprived of a day in court, or are they in fact benefitting from a better and less expensive remedy?

Concepcion, of course, goes further than simply enforcing an arbitration clause in a form contract because it also enforces a requirement that any such claim be brought in the parties' "individual capacity, and not as a plaintiff or class member in any purported class or representative proceeding." Why did California's *Discover Bank* rule invalidate this contractual provision? And why, according to Justice Scalia, does the Federal Arbitration Act preempt the *Discover Bank* rule?

Numerous commentators and proponents of consumer class actions have decried the result in *Concepcion*, even suggesting that *Concepcion* may "signify death for the legal claims of many potential plaintiffs." Sternlight, Tsunami: AT&T Mobility v. Concepcion Impedes Access to Justice, 90 Or. L. Rev. 703, 704 (2012); Aragaki, AT&T Mobility v. Concepcion and the Antidiscrimination Theory of FAA Preemption, 4 Y.B. Arb. & Med. 39, 41 (2013). Some have argued that, post-*Concepcion*, many corporations will insert arbitration clauses with class-action waivers in their standard contracts and that "most class cases will not survive the impending tsunami of class action waivers." Gilles & Friedman, After Class: Aggregate Litigation in the Wake of *AT&T v. Concepcion*, 79 U. Chi. L. Rev. 623, 630 (2012).

Some commentators have taken the position that *Concepcion* does not obliterate all potential state efforts to invalidate class-action waivers. See Alexander, To Skin a Cat: Qui Tam Actions as a State Legislative Response to Concepcion, 46 U. Mich. J. L. Reform 1203 (2013); Wolff, Is There Life After Concepcion? State Courts, State Law, and the Mandate of Arbitration, 56 St. Louis U. L. J. 1269 (2012). If you were a state-court judge or legislator, what tools would you consider still available to strike down a class-action waiver in an arbitration agreement?

  5. ***Italian Colors.*** The Supreme Court returned to the issue of class-action waivers in arbitration agreements in 2013 in American Express Co. v. Italian Colors Restaurant, 570 U.S. ___ , 133 S.Ct. 2304, 486 L.Ed.2d 417 (2013). Italian Colors, an Italian restaurant in Oakland, California, sued American Express for violations of Section 1 of the Sherman Act. In essence, the plaintiff alleged that American Express improperly used its market power to require merchants to pay inflated fees in order to accept purchases on American Express credit cards and sought to represent a class of similarly situated merchants. The standard agreement between merchants and American Express contained an arbitration clause that prohibited class actions. The Second Circuit rejected the arbitration clause on the ground that "enforcement of the action would effectively preclude any action seeking to vindicate the statutory rights asserted by the plaintiffs." Italian Colors Rest. v. Am. Express Travel Related Servs. Co., 554 F.3d 300, 304 (2d Cir. 2009). The court of appeals reached this conclusion on the basis of expert testimony offered by the plaintiffs to the effect that antitrust claims were so expensive to litigate that the plaintiffs' "claims cannot reasonably be pursued at individual actions, whether in federal court or in arbitration." Id. at 313. The Supreme Court reversed the Second Circuit in a 5–3 decision.

  The majority, per Justice Scalia, held that the FAA required enforcement of the arbitration clause, including the class-action waiver. In response to the Second Circuit's contention that enforcement of the class-action waiver would make the plaintiffs' small individual claims impossible to vindicate, the Court held that "the fact that [a claim] is not worth the expense involved in *proving* a statutory remedy does not constitute the elimination of the *right to pursue* that remedy." 133 S.Ct. at 2311. The majority added that acceptance of the Second Circuit's case-by-case assessment of whether a class-action waiver prevents vindication of statutory rights would "undoubtedly destroy the prospect of speedy resolution that arbitration in general that bilateral arbitration in particular was meant to secure." Id. at 2312.

  Justice Kagan dissented, joined by Justices Ginsburg and Breyer. (Justice Sotomayor did not participate because she had been part of the Second Circuit panel that heard the case.) In her dissent, Justice Kagan described her view of the Court's holding: "The monopolist gets to use its monopoly power to insist on a contract effectively depriving its victims of all legal recourse. And here is the nutshell version of today's opinion, admirably flaunted rather than camouflaged: Too darn bad." Id. at 2313. The dissenters would have preferred adoption of the following rule: "When an arbitration agreement prevents the effective vindication of federal rights, a party may go to court." Id. at 2317.

  Do you think such an "effective vindication" exception would be appropriate? Would it conflict with the reasonable expectations of parties to a contract containing an arbitration clause? What criteria would courts use in applying such an exception?

  Do you think either Justice Scalia or Justice Kagan effectively resolved the tension between the policies underlying the antitrust laws and the Federal Arbitration Act? Would a compromise position have been possible?

See Bradt, Resolving Intrastate Conflicts of Laws: The Example of the
Federal Arbitration Act, 91 Wash. U. L. Rev. ___ (2015).

CHAPTER 8

TRIAL

A. THE SIGNIFICANCE AND STRUCTURE OF TRIAL

NOTE ON THE SIGNIFICANCE AND STRUCTURE OF TRIAL

1. **The significance of trial.** The public image of civil litigation centers on a contested trial before a jury. But in American civil litigation trials are increasingly infrequent. In federal court, trials have declined from 18.9% of all dispositions in 1938 (the year the Federal Rules of Civil Procedure were adopted), to 11.5% of dispositions in 1962, to around 1% of total dispositions in 2012. Figures for the courts of general jurisdiction in twenty-two states show a similar trend: jury trials declined by 34% between 1962 and 2002. Galanter & Frozena, A Grin Without a Cat: The Continuing Decline & Displacement of Trials in American Courts, Daedalus (Summer 2014). This decline appears to be part of a long-term trend. The limited available data suggest that in the nineteenth century trial rates were in the range of 25–35% or even higher. Id. As Professor Langbein recently summarized, "A striking trend in the administration of civil justice in the United States in recent decades has been the virtual abandonment of the centuries-old institution of trial." Langbein, The Disappearance of Civil Trial in the United States, 122 Yale L.J. 522 (2012).

But it would be a mistake to infer from the decline in the frequency of trials that trial is no longer an important mode of disposition. For in those cases that do survive the pretrial gauntlet, trials are more complex and the stakes are higher. In federal courts, the percentage of trials lasting four days or more nearly doubled between 1965 and 2008 from 15% to 27%. The evidence also suggests that the average stakes in those cases, whether in money or principle, are considerably higher than in those tried in the past. Moreover, although the statistics demonstrate that trials in courts have declined significantly, "trial-like" proceedings in arbitration and administrative tribunals have become more prominent. Kritzer, The Trials and Tribulations of Counting Trials, 62 DePaul L. Rev. 415 (2013).

More fundamentally, the institutions of trial potentially have an influence on every case, whether or not it is tried—the threat of trial looms over all party behavior, from the outset of a potential legal dispute. (That threat arguably looms even larger for lawyers with little experience trying cases.) For those cases that are resolved by settlement, the anticipated outcome of a trial, and the costs of achieving that outcome, provide the alternative to which the parties compare their settlement options and in whose "shadow" they try to bargain to agreement. Mnookin & Kornhauser, Bargaining in the Shadow of the Law: The Case of Divorce, 88 Yale L.J. 950 (1979); Galanter, The Civil Jury as Regulator of the Litigation Process, 1990 U. Chi. Legal F. 201. In theory, a trial process that produces unbiased and precise outcomes will cast a benign shadow over settlement. Conversely, a process that is biased, arbitrary, or excessively costly can be expected to strengthen the hand of the undeserving. Just as important, the ability to achieve a fair outcome in settlement depends upon the anticipated strength of one's case at trial, both in terms of underlying evidence and the skill of the advocate. Thus, the trial process can drive choices made not just at the time of settlement, but earlier in the case, when selecting counsel and the forum in which the case will be heard. As a matter of institutional design, the fact that many cases are eligible to be tried by jury means that trial ordinarily must be continuous and concentrated. This is in turn a major factor in American civil procedure's sharp separation between pre-trial, where the pleadings are evaluated and the evidence marshaled, and trial, where the evidence is presented to the fact-finder. See Von Mehren, The Significance for Procedural Practice and Theory of the Concentrated Trial: Comparative Remarks, in 2 Europaisches Rechtsdenken in Geschichte und Gegenwart: Festschrift für Helmut Coing (Horn ed. 1982).

2. **The structure of trial.** The best way to get a realistic grasp of an adversary proceeding—short of participating in one, preferably as an attorney—is to watch a well-conducted trial from beginning to end. But the following brief description of the structure of a trial may help. At the outset, it is important to note that a trial may proceed before a judge or a jury. A trial before a judge is referred to as a "bench trial." Trial to a jury is the more common mode of disposition in federal court: as of 2002 about two-thirds of all trials were to a jury. Galanter, 1 J. Empirical Legal Stud. at 464. In state court, though, the vast majority of trials (97%) are conducted before a judge. Id. at 506–08.

Jury trial is more formal than trial to a judge alone. Trial to a judge by definition lacks such devices as selecting and instructing the jury, and may also differ in the degree of adherence to evidence rules, formality or orderliness of proceeding, and psychological overtones. After all, in a bench trial, the judge need not worry about whether inadmissible evidence or argument is presented to a jury. But the two modes of trial are similar in their basic structure, and an explanation of the more formal jury-trial process roughly serves for both. For purposes of this text, we take as the norm the typical case of one plaintiff against one defendant concerning one principal transaction. Multi-party causes obviously may present additional complexities. See also Note on the Structure of a Lawsuit, supra p. 1.

After the pleadings, discovery proceedings, and pretrial motions have been completed or otherwise disposed of, prescribed machinery is available to move the case along. In some places the machinery is very simple: the clerk is required by local rule or custom to calendar the case for trial on his own initiative when the pleadings are closed, and then to notify the parties accordingly. More typically, however, it is incumbent on one of the parties to take some initiative to put the case on the trial calendar. The mechanics of different jurisdictions vary in detail but essentially the problem is one of requesting the clerk to calendar the case and of notifying the adversary.

When the time for trial arrives, the court assembles a group of prospective jurors selected through a system that is more or less elaborate, depending on the community involved. The prospective jurors are put on oath to answer truthfully the questions asked them on their voir dire examination, which is the inquiry conducted by the judge, counsel, or both, to find out whether they are suitable jurors. When the required number of jurors is selected (usually twelve or six), the jury is sworn to try the case according to the law and the evidence. The tribunal is now fully formed and ready to try the case.

The party with the burden of proof on the principal issues, almost always the plaintiff, then begins presenting his case by making an opening statement to the jury. The purpose of this statement is to outline the plaintiff's evidence so as to help the jury follow it intelligently. Usually, the defendant makes her opening statement immediately after the plaintiff completes his, although the defendant may wait until the plaintiff's evidence has been presented.

After completing his opening statement (and after defendant makes hers, unless she defers it) the plaintiff proceeds to present his evidence, oral, documentary, and "real," i.e., actual objects such as clothing, a damaged car, or whatever else may have evidentiary value in the case. This part of the proceeding is called the plaintiff's "case in chief." Usually, the plaintiff's lawyer exercises his own judgment as to the best order in which to call witnesses and present documents, and often the order is quite significant tactically. Sometimes by local rule a particular order may be partially prescribed, as where the plaintiff himself, in the absence of good reason to the contrary, is required to take the stand first if he is to testify in his case in chief.

As each witness for plaintiff takes the stand and is sworn, he is first directly examined by plaintiff's lawyer. To begin, the lawyer will ask preliminary questions designed to introduce the witness to the tribunal and to show his acquaintance with the facts involved: questions as to his name, address, family status, occupation, and his connection with the case on trial. The law of evidence has elaborate rules governing the method of getting information from witnesses. Some of these rules are essentially forensic in nature, i.e., primarily geared to assuring orderliness and discipline in procedure. These concern, for example, the format of testimony, whether in the witness's own narrative or question-and-answer style; the phraseology of questions, the general rule being against leading questions on direct examination; the extent of the judge's questioning; the manner of objecting to improper questions; the authentication of documents or other items of real evidence; the manner of attacking witnesses' credibility; and many similar matters. As to the forensic rules, the trial judge often has a large measure of discretion to permit departure from the norm. For example, she may permit leading questions to be asked of a child or other inarticulate person. Other rules governing evidence are more substantive in their nature and cannot be departed from except, sometimes, by waiver of the party entitled to their benefit, e.g., the hearsay rule. All of these rules, the forensic and substantive ones, constitute the subject matter of the course in Evidence.

After the plaintiff's lawyer has completed his direct examination of a witness, defendant's lawyer may cross-examine the witness. Cross examination, which has been described as the greatest engine for discovery of the truth ever devised, plays a more significant role in Anglo-American adjudication than in most other systems. Generally the purposes of cross examination are (i) to draw out whatever in the witness's knowledge potentially is favorable to the cross examiner, for in an adversary system the direct examiner will have focused on facts favorable to his side; (ii) to expose deficiencies of observation or narration (whether deliberate or unintentional) respecting the parts of the witness's direct testimony favorable to the party who called him; and (iii) to establish bias, self-interest, or any other characteristic of the witness which in normal human experience might indicate distortion of the facts by the witness (this is a form of "impeachment" of the witness). Various rules of evidence limit cross examination to the scope of the direct examination. After the cross examination is completed, plaintiff may conduct redirect examination of the witness. Normally redirect examination is limited to matters gone into on cross examination, but the judge may exercise discretion to relieve plaintiff's lawyer from this restriction during redirect examination and thus permit new matters to be presented. Then there may be re-cross examination, normally limited to the redirect, and the process may be continued back and forth until the witness's knowledge or the judge's patience is exhausted.

When the plaintiff has presented all of his witnesses and documentary and real evidence, he "rests." This means he turns the forum over to the defendant. Various devices are then customarily available to the defendant with which to attempt to take the case away from the jury, i.e., have a result favorable to defendant immediately proclaimed by the judge "as a matter of law." These devices include motions for nonsuits and directed verdicts, or, in federal court, motions for judgment as a matter of law. Assuming that defendant does not attempt to use any such device because she is confident none would be successful, or having made the attempt fails therein, she then proceeds to present her own "case in chief" to the jury. Each witness she calls is, in turn, subject to cross examination by plaintiff. After defendant rests plaintiff may move for a directed verdict in his favor, which would be granted only if the defense as a matter of law was inadequate to controvert plaintiff's established claim.

If plaintiff does not make a motion for a directed verdict or does not prevail on one, he may then present rebuttal evidence. Normally he is limited to rebutting defendant's case in chief, although the trial court may grant plaintiff an opportunity to correct inadvertent omissions in his case in chief. Then the defendant may present her "surrebuttal," normally limited to meeting plaintiff's rebuttal, and the process may go on, much as with the individual witness, until both sides have exhausted all they wish and are permitted to present. After both sides have rested, either or both may move for a directed verdict or judgment as a matter of law, a condition precedent in some jurisdictions to a motion after the trial for a judgment notwithstanding the verdict.

If the judge decides to let the case go to the jury, the next step usually is the closing arguments of counsel. Typically, plaintiff opens with his principal argument; then defendant argues; then plaintiff sometimes has a short time to conclude. Then come the judge's instructions to the jury on the controlling legal principles. (In a few jurisdictions, the instructions may be before argument. And in almost all jurisdictions the judge may give some instructions at appropriate times earlier in the trial. This is most likely to be done when the case is particularly complicated.) In a few jurisdictions, the judge may comment on the evidence, frankly giving her opinion as to which witnesses were, and which were not, likely telling the truth. Elsewhere, she may marshal the evidence, that is, summarize it, for the jury. But in most jurisdictions her instructions consist only of the applicable principles of law. Sometimes they are given orally only; sometimes they are reduced to writing and taken by the jury to the deliberation room. After the instructions, the case is submitted to the jury for deliberation and rendition of its verdict, which can be general, special, or general with answers to interrogatories. After the verdict is read, the jury is dismissed, with thanks. Various post-trial motions, including those for judgment notwithstanding the verdict or a new trial, are then available to the loser.

B. THE FINAL PRETRIAL CONFERENCE AND THE PRETRIAL ORDER

NOTE ON THE FINAL PRETRIAL CONFERENCE AND THE PRETRIAL ORDER

1. **The pretrial conference as a preparation for trial.** In common-law procedure, "the judge had little or no contact with the case before trial." Langbein, The Disappearance of Civil Trial in the United States, 122 Yale L. J. 522 (2012). The original federal Rules included a provision for a "pretrial conference" between the trial judge and the parties prior to the trial's commencement. The original vision of the pretrial conference was based on the idea of a single meeting shortly before the trial. In current practice, as we have seen, judges are encouraged to make use of pretrial conferences at all stages of the case, particularly in the scheduling and management of motion practice, discovery, and in the promotion of settlement. In cases of significant complexity, there may be many conferences devoted to such matters well before there is even any trial in prospect. Indeed, as Judge Rosenthal, the former Chair of Civil Rules Committee, and Professor Gensler recently put it, there is a strong consensus that "the remedy . . . for reducing unnecessary costs and delay was more and better judicial pretrial case management." Rosenthal & Gensler, Four Years After Duke: Where Do We Stand on Calibrating the Pretrial Process?, 18 Lewis & Clark L. Rev. 643 (2014).

In those cases where trial is a serious prospect (a class of cases which includes many that will settle on the eve of, or even during, trial or jury deliberations) the final pretrial conference also sets a plan for the trial that may follow. Typically, the parties are required to file separate or joint statements before the final pretrial conference. Contents may include: statements of the factual and legal issues that are undisputed, and those that remain in dispute; listings of expected witnesses and exhibits and anticipated issues concerning the admissibility of evidence; proposed further amendments to the pleadings; and an account of any pending settlement discussions. See, e.g., Civil L.R. 16–9 (N.D. Cal.). In federal court, the planning process is facilitated by Rule 26(a)(3), which requires each party to disclose at least 30 days in advance of trial a detailed description of the witnesses that it plans to present through live testimony, the witnesses whose testimony will be presented by deposition, and identification of documents and other evidence to be offered. Against this background, parties are then expected to present, again in advance of trial, most of their objections to the admissibility of depositions, documents, and other exhibits, on pain of being found to have waived those objections at trial. Fed. R. Civ. P. 26(a)(3). At the conference, the judge may seek further narrowing of the issues by concession or stipulation and resolve in advance issues concerning the scope and admissibility of the parties' evidence. See Fed. R. Civ. P. 16(c)(1)–(2)(d). Increasingly, courts will also use the final pretrial conference to establish limits on the presentation of evidence by limiting the numbers of witnesses who will testify or by setting time limits for the presentation of evidence, for example, a set number of hours for the plaintiff's case and cross-examination of the defendant's witnesses and an equal number for the defendant's case and cross-examination of the plaintiff's witnesses. See Fed. R. Civ. P. 16(c).

2.   The pretrial order. The final pretrial conference culminates in the issuance of a final pretrial order. The order has no set content—or rather, its content is determined in some measure by the parties, and where the parties cannot agree, by the judge conducting the conference. But it is common for the order to recite the undisputed facts and the contentions of the parties as they are expected to be presented at trial and to specify, to the extent feasible, the proofs expected to be offered. The statement of the contested issues in the final pretrial order is viewed as superseding the underlying pleadings. Moreover, at least in federal court, it may be modified "only to prevent manifest injustice." Fed. R. Civ. P. 16(e). Accordingly, a party who offers claims or evidence relevant to issues that were disputed in the parties' pleadings but were conceded or not identified as contested in the final pretrial order may find that the evidence is no longer admissible. Hunt v. County of Orange, 672 F.2d 606 (9th Cir. 2012); Smith v. Washington Sheraton Corp., 135 F.3d 779 (D.C. Cir. 1998). As the First Circuit recently held, "Because the resulting pretrial order issued under Rule 16 is intended to shape the contours of the ensuing trial by setting forth the legal theories upon which the parties intend to rely, claims or defenses omitted from the pretrial order are waived, whether or not properly raised in the pleadings." In re Net-Velazquez, 625 F.3d 34 (1st Cir. 2010) (citations omitted).

C. THE RIGHT TO JURY TRIAL

NOTE ON THE RIGHT TO JURY TRIAL

1.   The right to jury trial in federal trial courts. Assuming a party is able to surmount all of the obstacles of the pretrial process, the question remains: "When am I entitled to a trial by jury, and on what issues?" First, it is important to note that the right to a civil jury trial is waivable. A party who wants a jury trial typically must demand it far in advance of the trial's actually beginning. In the federal system, federal Rules 38 and 39 govern jury-trial demands, see Note on Demanding and Waiving Jury Trial, infra, p. 917. Second, a jury trial may be available with respect to some but not all of the issues in the case. Third, whether a party is entitled to a jury trial and what the characteristics of that trial will be depend on the rules of the court where the case is being litigated. In the federal courts, the right to a jury trial is governed by the Seventh Amendment to the U.S. Constitution.

The U.S. Constitution, Art. III, Sec. 2, Clause 3 provides: "The trial of all crimes, except in cases of impeachment, shall be by jury * * *." The body of the Constitution, however, says nothing about jury trial in civil cases. But the Seventh Amendment, proposed by the first Congress along with the other first ten amendments popularly known as "A Bill of Rights" and effective in 1791, provides:

> In suits at common law, where the value in controversy shall exceed twenty dollars, the right of trial by jury shall be preserved, and no fact tried by a jury, shall be otherwise re-examined in any court of the United States, than according to the rules of the common law.

The Seventh Amendment applies *only* to lawsuits brought in federal court. The first ten amendments were originally intended as checks only on the federal government, not on the states. The story of the extension, largely during the second half of the twentieth century, of many of the guarantees of the Bill of Rights to the states through their "selective incorporation" into the Due Process Clause of the Fourteenth Amendment is one of the most important chapters of American constitutional history, and you will study it in detail in Constitutional Law. In 1968, the Supreme Court, noting that trial by jury in *criminal* cases is fundamental to the American scheme of justice, held that the Fourteenth Amendment guarantees a right of jury trial in all state criminal cases which—were they to be tried in federal court—would come within the Sixth Amendment's guarantee. Duncan v. Louisiana, 391 U.S. 145, 88 S.Ct. 1444, 20 L.Ed.2d 491 (1968). But the federal constitutional guarantee of jury trial in *civil* cases has *not* been incorporated into the Fourteenth Amendment. So far as the federal Constitution is concerned, a state is free to modify or wholly abolish trial by jury in civil cases. See Walker v. Sauvinet, 92 U.S. 90, 23 L.Ed. 678 (1876). At least, such a generalization may still be taken as the starting point, although there may be exceptions, of uncertain dimension, in cases where a state court enforces a federal cause of action. See Dice v. Akron, Canton, & Youngstown R. R., supra Chapter 3, p. 410.

2. What does the Seventh Amendment "preserve?"

a. The meaning of "trial by jury." Note that the Seventh Amendment states that "the right to trial by jury shall be preserved." So, the Supreme Court has held, in order to ascertain the scope and meaning of the Seventh Amendment, "resort must be had to the appropriate rules of the common law established at the time of the adoption of that constitutional provision in 1791." Dimick v. Schiedt, 293 U.S. 474, 476, 55 S.Ct. 296, 79 L.Ed. 603 (1935). As a result, "[t]he right of trial by jury thus preserved is the right which existed under the English common law when the [Seventh] Amendment was adopted." Baltimore & Carolina Line v. Redman, 295 U.S. 654, 657, 55 S.Ct. 890, 79 L.Ed. 1636 (1935).

What was "trial by jury" at the English common law in 1791? Capital Traction Co. v. Hof, 174 U.S. 1, 13–14, 19 S.Ct. 580, 43 L.Ed. 873 (1899) says:

> "Trial by jury," in the primary and usual sense of the term at the common law and in the American constitutions, is not merely a trial by a jury of twelve men before an officer vested with authority to cause them to be summoned and impaneled, to administer oaths to them and to the constable in charge, and to enter judgment and issue execution on their verdict; but it is a trial by a jury of twelve men, in the presence and under the superintendence of a judge empowered to instruct them on the law and to advise them on the facts, and (except on acquittal of a criminal charge) to set aside their verdict if in his opinion it is against the law or the evidence. This proposition has been so generally admitted, and so seldom contested, that there has been little occasion for its distinct assertion. Yet there are unequivocal statements of it to be found in the books.

Compare Patton v. United States, 281 U.S. 276, 288, 50 S.Ct. 253, 74 L.Ed. 854 (1930), a felony prosecution, where the Court, after quoting Art. III, Sec. 2, Clause 3 and the Sixth Amendment of the Constitution, said:

> [W]e first inquire what is embraced by the phrase "trial by jury."
> That it means a trial by jury as understood and applied at common
> law, and includes all the essential elements as they were recognized
> in this country and England when the Constitution was adopted, is
> not open to question. Those elements were: (1) That the jury should
> consist of twelve men, neither more nor less; (2) that the trial
> should be in the presence and under the superintendence of a judge
> having power to instruct them as to the law and advise them in
> respect of the facts; and (3) that the verdict should be unanimous.

See generally Henderson, The Background of the Seventh Amendment, 80
Harv. L. Rev. 289 (1966); Wolfram, The Constitutional History of the
Seventh Amendment, 57 Minn. L. Rev. 639 (1973).

As we will see, modern civil juries, though they continue to decide cases
"in the presence and under the superintendence of a judge," are no longer all
male, often sit in groups as small as six, and, at least as a matter of
constitutional law, may also be permitted to render a non-unanimous
verdict. How these innovations have been squared with the "preservation" of
the eighteenth century jury trial is one of the topics we will explore below.
See Note on Jury Size and Unanimity, infra, p. 935.

**b.   The scope of the jury trial right: the meaning of "actions at
common law."** Again, take a look at the text of the Seventh Amendment. It
preserves the right to trial by jury "[i]n suits at common law, where the value
in controversy shall exceed twenty dollars." The primary constitutional
question is not what a jury trial *is*, but rather when a litigant is entitled to
one. The adopters of the Seventh Amendment simply referred to then-
contemporary practice. This might have seemed a sensible, even elegant,
solution to the problem of specifying when a jury was constitutionally
guaranteed. But for us it is less helpful. In fact, in modern times, it has
proved deeply problematic.

For an English or American lawyer in the late eighteenth century the
term "actions at common law" would have clearly been understood as
referring to the practice, then common in both England and most of the
thirteen colonies, of maintaining two primary sets of trial courts: courts of
law, in which jury trials were mostly available, and courts of equity, in which
they mostly were not. Almost all of the thirteen colonies, and their successors
the original thirteen states, had a jurisprudence preserving the division
between law and equity courts, but these bodies of law were both spotty and
inconsistent. Accordingly, the Supreme Court made the decision, early on,
that the term "actions at common law" would be defined by reference to the
practice of English courts in 1791, the date of the adoption of the Bill of
Rights, rather than by reference to colonial practice.

Even within the English court system, however, the division of
jurisdiction between the law courts and the equity courts was not always
clear, and some disputes could be litigated in either court system depending
on how the case was characterized and the nature of the relief sought.
Moreover, in at least some cases, the equity courts would refer a factual
question to the law courts for jury determination before proceeding to grant
relief in equity. See Chesnin & Hazard, Chancery Procedure and the Seventh
Amendment: Jury Trial of Issues in Equity Cases Before 1791, 83 Yale L.J.
999 (1974). Compare Langbein, Fact Finding in the English Court of
Chancery: A Rebuttal, 83 Yale L.J. 1620 (1974) (showing that the category

of cases in which equity deferred to jury fact-finding in the law courts was quite small). Though it is fascinating and important, a complete review of the history of the development of the courts of law and equity in England is far beyond the scope of this casebook. A concise introduction may be found at Langbein, Lerner & Smith, History of the Common Law (2009). Suffice it to say for our purposes that by 1791 the division of jurisdiction between the law and equity courts was quite muddled. Making matters worse, the courts of law and equity had developed quite distinct procedural practices, the most important distinction being the availability of a jury in courts of law and the lack thereof in courts of equity.

Despite the lack of clarity of the practice that existed at the time in even the best-developed system, the framers apparently felt that the common law/equity distinction provided a workable test for when a jury is required by the Constitution. Or, at the very least, the adoption of the existing practice without further clarification was an acceptable political resolution of an issue upon which the ratification of the Constitution was thought to depend.

Unfortunately, the framers' formulation has proved difficult to apply. The Seventh Amendment is not written in the broad and general language that characterizes most of the Constitution. Rather, it is tied to a specific (and in today's terms almost comical) dollar value, and to a system of courts and procedure existing at a specific time. Not only did inflation radically change the practical operation of the amendment, but the English court system was in transition even as the amendment was being adopted, and it was never precisely replicated in the United States in any event. For instance, when Congress established the federal court system under the Judiciary Act of 1789, it did not create separate equity and law courts. It retained different procedures approximately corresponding to the two sets of English courts, but created a single set of federal courts to hear cases on either the law "side" or the equity "side." In other words, the federal courts had a "split personality" from the beginning and used different procedures depending on whether the case being heard was deemed legal or equitable.

Beginning in the nineteenth century, procedural reformers began to recognize the unnecessary complication of states' maintaining two separate court systems whose jurisdictions overlapped and which had different procedural rules, and they began the movement to "merge" law and equity procedure into one unified system. New York, for instance, adopted such a single set of procedural rules in its courts in the 1848 Field Code. Subrin, David Dudley Field and the Field Code: A Historical Analysis of an Earlier Procedural Vision, 6 Law & Hist. Rev. 311 (1988). In 1938, the federal courts finally adopted a single set of procedural rules applicable to all civil cases except those brought in admiralty. As federal Rule 2 states: "There is one form of action—the civil action." So, post 1938, in the federal courts the split between "the law side and the equity side" was purportedly a thing of the past.

Adding to the complexity, in the years following 1791 a number of new causes of action were developed, both common law and statutory, many of which did not have equivalents or even close analogues in the old law or equity courts. The difficulty has become particularly acute since the middle of the twentieth century with the explosive growth of the regulatory state, which has brought with it both new causes of action and a new system of administrative courts.

The Seventh Amendment thus provides a specific and narrow historical test which has become more and more difficult to apply as the legal world resembles less and less the world for which it was originally designed. As you read the cases that follow, ask yourself how we can best resolve the dilemma presented by the amendment: What does it mean to "preserve" the "right to trial by jury" in a world that is so different from the world that existed when those words were written?

3.   State constitutional provisions guaranteeing jury trial. As noted above, states are not bound by the Seventh Amendment or by Supreme Court decisions construing it. But most states guarantee jury trials at least in those civil cases that, prior to the merger of law and equity, were "actions at law." Louisiana has no constitutional right to jury trial in civil cases, see Deutsch, Jury Trials Under the Federal Rules and the Louisiana Practice, 3 La. L. Rev. 422 (1941), and the constitutions of Colorado, Art. II, Sec. 23, and Wyoming, Art. 1, Sec. 9, have only indirect provisions respecting civil jury trial. In the other states the constitutional guarantees of jury trial in civil cases usually are phrased in strong but not very detailed language. The constitutional authors generally were content to provide that trial by jury "shall remain inviolate forever," "shall remain inviolate," "shall be secured," "shall remain as heretofore," etc. See W. Blume, American Civil Procedure 370 (1955). At least implicitly, the purport is that the right shall remain in substance as it was when the state constitutional provision was adopted. "It is the right to trial by jury as it existed at common law which is preserved; and what that right is, is a purely historical question, a fact which is to be ascertained like any other social, political or legal fact. The right is the historical right enjoyed at the time it was guaranteed by the Constitution. It is necessary, therefore, to ascertain what was the rule of the English common law upon this subject in 1850." People v. One 1941 Chevrolet Coupe, 37 Cal. 2d 283, 287, 231 P.2d 832 (1951).

4.   Further reading. There is an enormous literature on the civil jury. The classic book on American juries is H. Kalven & H. Zeisel, The American Jury (1966). Other useful books include V. Hans & N. Vidmar, American Juries (2007) and Verdict: Assessing the Civil Jury System (Litan ed. 1993), which contains an exceptional collection of useful essays. For a much harsher view of jury performance see S. Adler, The Jury: Trial and Error in the American Courtroom (1994). Useful recent articles include Symposium, The Jury at a Crossroad, 78 Chi.-Kent L. Rev. 907 (2003); Note, Developments in the Law: The Civil Jury, 110 Harv. L. Rev. 1408 (1997); and Symposium, Jury Research and Reform, 79 Judicature 214 (1996).

1.   THE RIGHT TO JURY TRIAL IN A MERGED SYSTEM OF LAW AND EQUITY

American Life Ins. Co. v. Stewart

Supreme Court of the United States, 1937.
300 U.S. 203, 57 S.Ct. 377, 81 L.Ed. 605.

■ MR. JUSTICE CARDOZO delivered the opinion of the Court.

In these cases suits have been brought for the cancellation of policies of life insurance on the ground of fraud in their procurement, the policies providing that they shall cease to be contestable unless contest shall be begun within a stated time. The question to be determined is the existence, in the circumstances, of a remedy in equity.

On February 23, 1932, petitioner, a Colorado corporation, issued to Reese Smith Stewart, a citizen of Kansas, two policies of life insurance, each for $5,000, one payable to his son, who is a respondent in No. 440, and the other payable to his wife, who is a respondent in No. 441. Each policy contains a provision that it 'shall be incontestable, except for nonpayment of the premium, after one year from its date of issue if the Insured be then living, otherwise after two years from its date of issue.' On May 31, 1932, three months and eight days after obtaining the insurance, the insured died, having made in his application fraudulent misstatements, or so the insurer charges, as to his health and other matters material to the risk. On September 3, 1932, the insurer brought suit to cancel the insurance, a separate suit for each policy, (the executrix of the insured being joined as a defendant with the respective beneficiaries.) The complaint in each suit refers in a paragraph numbered 8 to the provision that the policy shall be incontestable after the lapse of two years. In the same paragraph it states in substance that the beneficiary may delay the commencement of the action at law till the time for contest has gone by, or, beginning such an action within the period, may afterwards dismiss it and then begin anew. The insurer asks the court to act while yet the barrier is down.

On September 26, 1932, the defendants moved in each suit to dismiss the bill for want of equity. On October 11, 1932, the beneficiaries began actions at law in the same court to recover the insurance. On October 29, the insurer filed its supplemental bills setting forth the pendency of the actions at law, and praying an injunction against their continued prosecution. On July 28, 1933, the District Court denied the motions to dismiss, without passing, however, on motions made by the insurer to enjoin the actions at law. On August 29, a stipulation was signed and filed in each case that 'the suit in equity shall be tried' by the court 'before said law action is tried, Provided, however, that the issues in said law action shall in the meantime be made up in order that said law issues thus joined shall stand ready for trial, with the understanding that said law issues, if any remain for trial, shall be tried as soon after the trial of the suit in equity as the court shall determine,' and this stipulation was approved by the court and an order made accordingly. On October 10, 1933, the defendants in each of the equity suits filed their answers to the bills, denying the fraud, admitting the making of the 'incontestability clause' as stated in paragraph 8, and as to the other allegations of that paragraph denying any knowledge or information sufficient to form a belief. The answers did not state that the remedy at law was adequate.

Upon the trial of the suits in equity, the District Court found the fraudulent representations charged in the complaints, and decreed the cancellation and surrender of the policies. There was an appeal to the Circuit Court of Appeals for the Tenth Circuit, where the decree was reversed, one judge dissenting, the court holding that the insurer had an adequate remedy at law. 80 F. (2d) 600; 85 F.(2d) 791. We granted certiorari to settle an important question, and one likely to recur, as to the scope of equitable remedies.

No doubt it is the rule, and one recently applied in decisions of this court, that fraud in the procurement of insurance is provable as a defense in an action at law upon the policy, resort to equity being unnecessary to render that defense available. Enelow v. New York Life Ins. Co., 293 U.S. 379, 385, 55 S.Ct. 310, 312, 79 L.Ed. 440; Adamos v. New York Life Ins. Co., 293 U.S. 386, 55 S.Ct. 315, 79 L.Ed. 444; Phoenix Mut. L. Insurance Co. v. Bailey, 13 Wall. 616, 20 L.Ed. 501; Cable v. United States Life Ins. Co., 191 U.S. 288, 306, 24 S.Ct. 74, 48 L.Ed. 188. That being so, an insurer, though the victim of a fraud, may commonly stand aside and await the hour of attack. But this attitude of aloofness may at times be fraught with peril. If the policy is to become incontestable soon after the death of the insured, the insurer becomes helpless if he must wait for a move by some one else, who may prefer to remain motionless till the time for contest has gone by. A 'contest' within the purview of such a contract has generally been held to mean a present contest in a court, not a notice of repudiation or of a contest to be waged thereafter. See, e.g., Killian v. Metropolitan Life Ins. Co., 251 N.Y. 44, 48, 166 N.E. 798, 64 A.L.R. 956; New York Life Ins. Co. v. Hurt (C.C.A.) 35 F.(2d) 92, 95; Harnischfeger Sales Corp. v. National Life Ins. Co. (C.C.A.) 72 F.(2d) 921, 922. Accordingly an insurer, who might otherwise be condemned to loss through the mere inaction of an adversary, may assume the offensive by going into equity and there praying cancellation. This exception to the general rule has been allowed by the lower federal courts with impressive uniformity. It has had acceptance in the state courts. It was recognized only recently in an opinion of this court, though the facts were not such as to call for its allowance. Enelow v. New York Life Ins. Co., supra, 293 U.S. 379, at page 384, 55 S.Ct. 310, 312, 79 L.Ed. 440.

The argument is made, however, that the insurer, even if privileged to sue in equity, should not have gone there quite so quickly. Six months and ten days had gone by since the policies were issued. There would be nearly a year and a half more before the bar would become absolute. But how long was the insurer to wait before assuming the offensive, and how was it to know where the beneficiaries would be if it omitted to strike swiftly? Often a family breaks up and changes its abode after the going of its head. The like might happen to this family. To say that the insurer shall keep watch of the coming and going of the survivors is to charge it with a heavy burden. The task would be hard enough if beneficiaries were always honest. The possibility of bad faith, perhaps concealed and hardly provable, accentuates the difficulty. There are statements by judges of repute which suggest a possibility that the contest barrier may stand though the holder of the policy has gone to foreign lands. New York Life Ins. Co. v. Panagiotopoulos (C.C.A.) 80 F.(2d) 136, 139. There are statements that it will stand though an action at law, brought within the period, has been dismissed or discontinued later. See New York Life Ins. Co. v. Seymour (C.C.A.) 45 F. (2d) 47, 48, 73 A.L.R. 1523; Harnischfeger Sales Corp. v. National Life Ins. Co. (C.C.A.) 72 F.(2d) 921, 925; New York Life Ins. Co. v. Truesdale (C.C.A.) 79 F.(2d) 481, 485, with which contrast New York Life Ins. Co. v. Miller (C.C.A.) 73 F.(2d) 350, 355, 97 A.L.R. 562; Thomas v. Metropolitan Life Ins. Co., 135 Kan. 381, 387, 10 P.(2d) 864, 85 A.L.R. 229, and Powell v. Mutual Life Ins. Co., 313 Ill. 161, 170, 144 N.E. 825, 36 A.L.R. 1239. Whether such statements go too far we are not required to determine, for a slight variance in the facts, as, e.g., in the rule prevailing in the jurisdiction where the final suit is brought, may have a bearing on the conclusion. At least in such warnings there are possibilities of danger which a cautious insurer would not put aside as visionary. 'Where equity can give relief, plaintiff ought not to be compelled to speculate upon the change of his obtaining relief at law.' Davis v. Wakelee, 156 U.S. 680, 688, 15 S.Ct. 555, 558, 39 L.Ed. 578. To this must be added the danger that witnesses may disappear and evidence be lost. A remedy at law does not exclude one in equity unless it is equally prompt and certain and in other ways efficient. 'It must be a remedy which may be resorted to without impediment created otherwise than by the act of the party.' Cable v. United States Life Ins. Co., supra, 191 U.S. 288, at page 303, 24 S.Ct. 74, 76, 48 L.Ed. 188. Here the insurer had no remedy at law at all except at the pleasure of an adversary. There was neither equality in efficiency nor equality in certainty nor equality in promptness. 'The remedy at law cannot be adequate if its adequacy depends upon the will of the opposing party.' Bank of Kentucky v. Stone (C.C.) 88 F. 383, 391; cf. Lincoln National Life Ins. Co. v. Hammer (C.C.A.) 41 F.(2d) 12, 16. To make a contract incontestable after the lapse of a brief time is to confer upon its holder extraordinary privileges. We must be on our guard against turning them into weapons of oppression.

The argument is made that the suits in equity should have been dismissed when it appeared upon the trial that after the filing of the bills, and in October, 1932, the beneficiaries of the policies had sued on them at law. But the settled rule is that equitable jurisdiction existing at the filing of a bill is not destroyed because an adequate legal remedy may have become available thereafter. Dawson v. Kentucky Distilleries Co., 255 U.S. 288, 296, 41 S.Ct. 272, 275, 65 L.Ed. 638; Lincoln National Life Ins. Co. v. Hammer, supra; New York Life Ins. Co. v. Seymour, supra. There is indeed, a possibility that the bringing of actions of law might have been used by the respondents to their advantage if they had not chosen by a stipulation to throw the possibility away. A court has control over its own docket. Landis v. North American Co., December 7, 1936, 299 U.S. 248, 57 S.Ct. 163, 81 L.Ed. 153. In the exercise of a sound discretion it may hold one lawsuit in abeyance to abide the outcome of another, especially where the parties and the issues are the same. Id. If request had been made by the respondents to suspend the suits in equity till the other causes were disposed of, the District Court could have considered whether justice would not be done by pursuing such a course, the remedy in equity being exceptional and the outcome of necessity. Cf. Harnischfeger Sales Corp. v. National Life Ins. Co. (C.C.A.) 72 F.(2d) 921, 922, 923. There would be many circumstances to be weighed, as, for instance, the condition of the court calendar, whether the insurer had been precipitate or its adversaries dilatory, as well as other factors. In the end, benefit and hardship would have to be set off, the one against the other, and a balance ascertained. Landis v. North American Co., supra. But respondents, as already indicated, gave that possibility away. They stipulated that the issues in equity should be tried in advance of those at law, and that only such issues, if any, as were left should be disposed of later on. The cases were allowed to stand as if challenge to the suits had been made by a demurrer only. So challenged, they prevail.

The decree should be reversed, and the cause remanded to the Court of Appeals for a consideration of the merits and for other proceedings in accord with this opinion.

Reversed.

Beacon Theatres, Inc. v. Westover

Supreme Court of the United States, 1959.
359 U.S. 500, 79 S.Ct. 948, 3 L.Ed.2d 988.

■ MR. JUSTICE BLACK delivered the opinion of the Court.

Petitioner, Beacon Theatres, Inc., sought by mandamus to require a district judge in the Southern District of California to vacate certain orders alleged to deprive it of a jury trial of issues arising in a suit brought against it by Fox West Coast Theatres, Inc. The Court of Appeals for the Ninth Circuit refused the writ, holding that the trial judge had acted within his proper discretion in denying petitioner's request for a jury. 252 F.2d 864. We granted certiorari, 356 U.S. 956, 78 S.Ct. 996, 2 L.Ed.2d 1064, because "Maintenance of the jury as a fact-finding body is of such importance and occupies so firm a place in our history and jurisprudence that any seeming curtailment of the right to a jury trial should be scrutinized with the utmost care." Dimick v. Schiedt, 293 U.S. 474, 486, 55 S.Ct. 296, 301, 79 L.Ed. 603.

Fox had asked for declaratory relief against Beacon alleging a controversy arising under the Sherman Antitrust Act, 15 U.S.C. §§ 1, 2, and under the Clayton Act, 15 U.S.C. § 15, which authorizes suits for treble damages against Sherman Act violators. According to the complaint Fox operates a movie theatre in San Bernardino, California, and has long been exhibiting films under contracts with movie distributors. These contracts grant it the exclusive right to show "first run" pictures in the "San Bernardino competitive area" and provide for "clearance"—a period of time during which no other theatre can exhibit the same pictures. After building a drive-in theatre about 11 miles from San Bernardino, Beacon notified Fox that it considered contracts barring simultaneous exhibitions of first-run films in the two theatres to be overt acts in violation of the antitrust laws. Fox's complaint alleged that this notification, together with threats of treble damage suits against Fox and its distributors, gave rise to "duress and coercion" which deprived Fox of a valuable property right, the right to negotiate for exclusive first-run contracts. Unless Beacon was restrained, the complaint continued, irreparable harm would result. Accordingly, while its pleading was styled a "Complaint for Declaratory Relief," Fox prayed both for a declaration that a grant of clearance between the Fox and Beacon theatres is reasonable and not in violation of the antitrust laws, and for an injunction, pending final resolution of the litigation, to prevent Beacon from instituting any action under the antitrust laws against Fox and its distributors arising out of the controversy alleged in the complaint. Beacon filed an answer, a counterclaim against Fox, and a cross-claim against an exhibitor who had intervened. These denied the threats and asserted that there was no substantial competition between the two theatres, that the clearances granted were therefore unreasonable, and that a conspiracy existed between Fox and its distributors to manipulate contracts and clearances so as to restrain trade and monopolize first-run pictures in violation of the antitrust laws. Treble damages were asked.

Beacon demanded a jury trial of the factual issues in the case as provided by Federal Rule of Civil Procedure 38(b). The District Court, however, viewed the issues raised by the "Complaint for Declaratory Relief," including the question of competition between the two theatres, as essentially equitable. Acting under the purported authority of Rules 42(b) and 57, it directed that these issues be tried to the court before jury determination of the validity of the charges of antitrust violations made in the counterclaim and cross-claim.[3] A common issue of the "Complaint for Declaratory Relief," the counterclaim, and the cross-claim was the reasonableness of the clearances granted to Fox, which depended, in part, on the existence of competition between the two theatres. Thus the effect of the action of the District Court could be, as the Court of Appeals believed, "to limit the petitioner's opportunity fully to try to a jury every issue which has a bearing upon its treble damage suit," for determination of the issue of clearances by the judge might "operate either by way of res judicata or collateral estoppel so as to conclude both parties with respect thereto at the subsequent trial of the treble damage claim." 252 F.2d at page 874.

The District Court's finding that the Complaint for Declaratory Relief presented basically equitable issues draws no support from the Declaratory Judgment Act, 28 U.S.C. §§ 2201, 2202; Fed.Rules Civ.Proc. 57. That statute, while allowing prospective defendants to sue to establish their nonliability, specifically preserves the right to jury trial for both parties. It follows that if Beacon would have been entitled to a jury trial in a treble damage suit against Fox it cannot be deprived of that right merely because Fox took advantage of the availability of declaratory relief to sue Beacon first. Since the right to trial by jury applies to treble damage suits under the antitrust laws, and is, in fact, an essential part of the congressional plan for making competition rather than monopoly the rule of trade, see Fleitmann v. Welsbach Street Lighting Co., 240 U.S. 27, 29, 36 S.Ct. 233, 234, 60 L.Ed. 505, the Sherman and Clayton Act issues on which Fox sought a declaration were essentially jury questions.

Nevertheless the Court of Appeals refused to upset the order of the district judge. It held that the question of whether a right to jury trial existed was to be judged by Fox's complaint read as a whole. In addition to seeking a declaratory judgment, the court said, Fox's complaint can be read as making out a valid plea for injunctive relief, thus stating a claim traditionally cognizable in equity. A party who is entitled to maintain a suit in equity for an injunction, said the court, may have all the issues in his suit determined by the judge without a jury regardless of whether legal rights are involved. The court then rejected the argument that equitable relief, traditionally available only when legal remedies are inadequate, was rendered unnecessary in this case by the filing of the counterclaim and cross-claim which presented all the issues necessary to a determination of the right to injunctive relief. Relying on American Life Ins. Co. v. Stewart, 300 U.S. 203, 215, 57 S.Ct. 377, 380, 81 L.Ed. 605, decided before the enactment of the Federal Rules of Civil Procedure, it invoked the principle that a court sitting in equity could retain jurisdiction even though later a legal remedy became available. In such

---

[3]   Fed.Rules Civ.Proc., 42(b) reads: "The court in furtherance of convenience or to avoid prejudice may order a separate trial of any claim, cross-claim, counterclaim, or third-party claim, or of any separate issue or of any number of claims, cross-claims, counterclaims, third-party claims, or issues." Rule 57 reads in part: "The court may order a speedy hearing of an action for a declaratory judgment and may advance it on the calendar."

instances the equity court had discretion to enjoin the later lawsuit in order to allow the whole dispute to be determined in one case in one court. Reasoning by analogy, the Court of Appeals held it was not an abuse of discretion for the district judge, acting under Federal Rule of Civil Procedure 42(b), to try the equitable cause first even though this might, through collateral estoppel, prevent a full jury trial of the counterclaim and cross-claim which were as effectively stopped as by an equity injunction.

Beacon takes issue with the holding of the Court of Appeals that the complaint stated a claim upon which equitable relief could be granted. As initially filed, the complaint alleged that threats of lawsuits by petitioner against Fox and its distributors were causing irreparable harm to Fox's business relationships. The prayer for relief, however, made no mention of the threats but asked only that pending litigation of the claim for declaratory judgment, Beacon be enjoined from beginning any lawsuits under the antitrust laws against Fox and its distributors arising out of the controversy alleged in the complaint. Evidently of the opinion that this prayer did not state a good claim for equitable relief, the Court of Appeals construed it to include a request for an injunction against threats of lawsuits. This liberal construction of a pleading is in line with Rule 8 of the Federal Rules of Civil Procedure. See Conley v. Gibson, 355 U.S. 41, 47–48, 78 S.Ct. 99, 102–103, 2 L.Ed.2d 80. But this fact does not solve our problem. Assuming that the pleadings can be construed to support such a request and assuming additionally that the complaint can be read as alleging the kind of harassment by a multiplicity of lawsuits which would *traditionally* have justified equity to take jurisdiction and settle the case in one suit, we are nevertheless of the opinion that, under the Declaratory Judgment Act and the Federal Rules of Civil Procedure, neither claim can justify denying Beacon a trial by jury of all the issues in the antitrust controversy.

The basis of injunctive relief in the federal courts has always been irreparable harm and inadequacy of legal remedies. At least as much is required to justify a trial court in using its discretion under the Federal Rules to allow claims of equitable origins to be tried ahead of legal ones, since this has the same effect as an equitable injunction of the legal claims. And it is immaterial in judging if that discretion is properly employed, that before the Federal Rules and the Declaratory Judgment Act were passed, courts of equity, exercising a jurisdiction separate from courts of law, were, in some cases, allowed to enjoin subsequent legal actions between the same parties involving the same controversy. This was because the subsequent legal action, though providing an opportunity to try the case to a jury, might not protect the right of the equity plaintiff to a fair and orderly adjudication of the controversy. See, e.g., New York Life Ins. Co. v. Seymour, 6 Cir., 45 F.2d 47, 73 A.L.R. 1523. Under such circumstances the legal remedy could quite naturally be deemed inadequate. Inadequacy of remedy and irreparable harm are practical terms, however. As such their existence today must be determined, not by precedents decided under discarded procedures, but in the light of the remedies now made available by the Declaratory Judgment Act and the Federal Rules.

Viewed in this manner, the use of discretion by the trial court under Rule 42(b) to deprive Beacon of a full jury trial on its counterclaim and cross-claim, as well as on Fox's plea for declaratory relief, cannot be justified. Under the Federal Rules the same court may try both legal and equitable causes in the same action. Fed.Rules Civ.Proc. 1, 2, 18. Thus any defenses, equitable or legal, Fox may have to charges of antitrust violations can be raised either in its suit for declaratory relief or in answer to Beacon's counterclaim. On proper showing, harassment by threats of other suits, or other suits actually brought, involving the issues being tried in this case, could be temporarily enjoined pending the outcome of this litigation. Whatever permanent injunctive relief Fox might be entitled to on the basis of the decision in this case could, of course, be given by the court after the jury renders its verdict. In this way the issues between these parties could be settled in one suit giving Beacon a full jury trial of every antitrust issue. By contrast, the holding of the court below while granting Fox no additional protection unless the avoidance of jury trial be considered as such, would compel Beacon to split his antitrust case, trying part to a judge and part to a jury. Such a result, which involves the postponement and subordination of Fox's own legal claim for declaratory relief as well as of the counterclaim which Beacon was compelled by the Federal Rules to bring, is not permissible.

Our decision is consistent with the plan of the Federal Rules and the Declaratory Judgment Act to effect substantial procedural reform while retaining a distinction between jury and nonjury issues and leaving substantive rights unchanged.[12] Since in the federal courts equity has always acted only when legal remedies were inadequate, the expansion of adequate legal remedies provided by the Declaratory Judgment Act and the Federal Rules necessarily affects the scope of equity. Thus, the justification for equity's deciding legal issues once it obtains jurisdiction, and refusing to dismiss a case, merely because subsequently a legal remedy becomes available, must be re-evaluated in the light of the liberal joinder provisions of the Federal Rules which allow legal and equitable causes to be brought and resolved in one civil action. Similarly the need for, and therefore, the availability of such equitable remedies as Bills of Peace, *Quia Timet* and Injunction must be reconsidered in view of the existence of the Declaratory Judgment Act as well as the liberal joinder provision of the Rules. This is not only in accord with the spirit of the Rules and the Act but is required by the provision in the Rules that "[t]he right of trial by jury as declared by the Seventh Amendment to the Constitution or as given by a statute of the United States shall be preserved . . . inviolate."[16]

If there should be cases where the availability of declaratory judgment or joinder in one suit of legal and equitable causes would not in all respects protect the plaintiff seeking equitable relief from irreparable harm while affording a jury trial in the legal cause, the trial court will necessarily have to use its discretion in deciding whether the

---

[12] See 28 U.S.C. § 2072; Fed.Rules Civ.Proc., 39(a), 57. * * *

[16] Fed.Rules Civ.Proc., 38(a). In delegating to the Supreme Court responsibility for drawing up rules, Congress declared that: "Such rules shall not abridge, enlarge or modify any substantive right and shall preserve the right of trial by jury as at common law and as declared by the Seventh Amendment to the Constitution." 28 U.S.C. § 2072, 28 U.S.C.A. § 2072. The Seventh Amendment reads: "In Suits at common law, where the value in controversy shall exceed twenty dollars, the right of trial by jury shall be preserved, and no fact tried by a jury, shall be otherwise reexamined in any Court of the United States, than according to the rules of the common law."

legal or equitable cause should be tried first. Since the right to jury trial is a constitutional one, however, while no similar requirement protects trials by the court, that discretion is very narrowly limited and must, wherever possible, be exercised to preserve jury trial. As this Court said in Scott v. Neely, 140 U.S. 106, 109–110, 11 S.Ct. 712, 714, 35 L.Ed. 358: "In the Federal courts this [jury] right cannot be dispensed with, except by the assent of the parties entitled to it; nor can it be impaired by any blending with a claim, properly cognizable at law, of a demand for equitable relief in aid of the legal action, or during its pendency." This long-standing principle of equity dictates that only under the most imperative circumstances, circumstances which in view of the flexible procedures of the Federal Rules we cannot now anticipate, can the right to a jury trial of legal issues be lost through prior determination of equitable claims. As we have shown, this is far from being such a case.

Respondent claims mandamus is not available under the All Writs Act, 28 U.S.C. § 1651, 28 U.S.C.A. § 1651. Whatever differences of opinion there may be in other types of cases, we think the right to grant mandamus to require jury trial where it has been improperly denied is settled.

The judgment of the Court of Appeals is reversed.

Reversed.

■ MR. JUSTICE FRANKFURTER took no part in the consideration or decision of this case.

■ MR. JUSTICE STEWART, with whom MR. JUSTICE HARLAN and MR. JUSTICE WHITTAKER concur, dissenting.

* * *

The complaint filed by Fox stated a claim traditionally cognizable in equity. That claim, in brief, was that Beacon had wrongfully interfered with the right of Fox to compete freely with Beacon and other distributors for the licensing of films for first-run exhibition in the San Bernardino area. The complaint alleged that the plaintiff was without an adequate remedy at law and would be irreparably harmed unless the defendant were restrained from continuing to interfere—by coercion and threats of litigation—with the plaintiff's lawful business relationships.

The Court of Appeals found that the complaint, although inartistically drawn, contained allegations entitling the petitioner to equitable relief. That finding is accepted in the prevailing opinion today. If the complaint had been answered simply by a general denial, therefore, the issues would under traditional principles have been triable as a proceeding in equity. Instead of just putting in issue the allegations of the complaint, however, Beacon filed pleadings which affirmatively alleged the existence of a broad conspiracy among the plaintiff and other theatre owners to monopolize the first-run exhibition of films in the San Bernardino area to refrain from competing among themselves, and to discriminate against Beacon in granting film licenses. Based upon these allegations, Beacon asked damages in the amount of $300,000. Clearly these conspiracy allegations stated a cause of action triable as of right by a jury. What was demanded by Beacon, however, was a jury trial not only of this cause of action, but also of the issues presented by the original complaint.

Upon motion of Fox the trial judge ordered the original action for declaratory and equitable relief to be tried separately to the court and in advance of the trial of the defendant's counterclaim and cross-claim for damages. The court's order, which carefully preserved the right to trial by jury upon the conspiracy and damage issues raised by the counterclaim and cross-claim, was in conformity with the specific provisions of the Federal Rules of Civil Procedure.[3] Yet it is decided today that the Court of Appeals must compel the district judge to rescind it.

Assuming the existence of a factual issue common both to the plaintiff's original action and the defendant's counterclaim for damages, I cannot agree that the District Court must be compelled to try the counterclaim first. It is, of course, a matter of no great moment in what order the issues between the parties in the present litigation are tried. What is disturbing is the process by which the Court arrives at its decision—a process which appears to disregard the historic relationship between equity and law.

I.

The Court suggests that "the expression of adequate legal remedies provided by the Declaratory Judgment Act . . . necessarily affects the scope of equity." Does the Court mean to say that the mere availability of an action for a declaratory judgment operates to furnish "an adequate remedy at law" so as to deprive a court of equity of the power to act? That novel line of reasoning is at least implied in the Court's opinion. But the Declaratory Judgment Act did not "expand" the substantive law. That Act merely provided a new statutory remedy, neither legal nor equitable, but available in the areas of both equity and law. When declaratory relief is sought, the right to trial by jury depends upon the basic context in which the issues are presented. See Moore's Federal Practice (2d ed.) §§ 38.29, 57.30; Borchard, Declaratory Judgments (2d ed.), 399–404. If the basic issues in an action for declaratory relief are of a kind traditionally cognizable in equity, e.g., a suit for cancellation of a written instrument, the declaratory judgment is not a "remedy at law." If, on the other hand, the issues arise in a context traditionally cognizable at common law, the right to a jury trial of course remains unimpaired, even though the only relief demanded is a declaratory judgment.

Thus, if in this case the complaint had asked merely for a judgment declaring that the plaintiff's specified manner of business dealings with distributors and other exhibitors did not render it liable to Beacon under the antitrust laws, this would have been simply a "juxtaposition of parties" case in which Beacon could have demanded a jury trial. But the complaint in the present case, as the Court recognizes, presented issues of exclusively equitable cognizance, going well beyond a mere defense to any subsequent action at law. Fox sought from the court protection against Beacon's allegedly unlawful interference with its business relationships—protection which this Court seems to recognize might not have been afforded by a declaratory judgment, unsupplemented by equitable relief. The availability of a declaratory judgment did not,

---

[3]   Rule 42(b) provides: "(b) Separate Trials. The court in furtherance of convenience or to avoid prejudice may order a separate trial of any claim, cross-claim, counterclaim, or third-party claim, or of any separate issue or of any number of claims, cross-claims, counterclaims, third-party claims, or issues." * * *

therefore, operate to confer upon Beacon the right to trial by jury with respect to the issues raised by the complaint.

II.

The Court's opinion does not, of course, hold or even suggest that a court of equity may never determine "legal rights." For indeed it is precisely such rights which the Chancellor, when his jurisdiction has been properly invoked, has often been called upon to decide. Issues of fact are rarely either "legal" or "equitable." All depends upon the context in which they arise. The examples cited by Chief Judge Pope in his thorough opinion in the Court of Appeals in this case are illustrative: ". . . [I]n a suit by one in possession of real property to quiet title, or to remove a cloud on title, the court of equity may determine the legal title. In a suit for specific performance of a contract, the court may determine the making, validity and the terms of the contract involved. In a suit for an injunction against trespass to real property the court may determine the legal right of the plaintiff to the possession of that property. Cf. Pomeroy, Equity Jurisprudence, 5th ed., §§ 138–221, 221a, 221b, 221d, 250." 252 F.2d 864, 874.

Though apparently not disputing these principles, the Court holds, quite apart from its reliance upon the Declaratory Judgment Act, that Beacon by filing its counterclaim and cross-claim acquired a right to trial by jury of issues which otherwise would have been properly triable to the court. Support for this position is found in the principle that, "in the federal courts equity has always acted only when legal remedies were inadequate. . . ." Yet that principle is not employed in its traditional sense as a limitation upon the exercise of power by a court of equity. This is apparent in the Court's recognition that the allegations of the complaint entitled Fox to equitable relief—relief to which Fox would not have been entitled if it had had an adequate remedy at law. Instead, the principle is employed today to mean that because it is possible under the counterclaim to have a jury trial of the factual issue of substantial competition, that issue must be tried by a jury, even though the issue was primarily presented in the original claim for equitable relief. This is a marked departure from long-settled principles.

It has been an established rule "that equitable jurisdiction existing at the filing of a bill is not destroyed because an adequate legal remedy may have become available thereafter." American Life Ins. Co. v. Stewart, 300 U.S. 203, 215, 57 S.Ct. 377, 380, 81 L.Ed. 605. See Dawson v. Kentucky Distilleries & Warehouse Co., 255 U.S. 288, 296, 41 S.Ct. 272, 275, 65 L.Ed. 638. It has also been long settled that the District Court in its discretion may order the trial of a suit in equity in advance of an action at law between the same parties, even if there is a factual issue common to both. In the words of Mr. Justice Cardozo, writing for a unanimous Court in American Life Ins. Co. v. Stewart, supra:

> "A court has control over its own docket. . . . In the exercise of a sound discretion it may hold one lawsuit in abeyance to abide the outcome of another, especially where the parties and the issues are the same. . . . If request had been made by the respondents to suspend the suits in equity till the other causes were disposed of, the District Court could have considered whether justice would not be done by pursuing such a course,

the remedy in equity being exceptional and the outcome of
necessity. . . . There would be many circumstances to be
weighed, as, for instance, the condition of the court calendar,
whether the insurer had been precipitate or its adversaries
dilatory, as well as other factors. In the end, benefit and
hardship would have to be set off, the one against the other, and
a balance ascertained." 300 U.S. 203, 215–216, 57 S.Ct. 377,
380.

III.

The Court today sweeps away these basic principles as "precedents
decided under discarded procedures." It suggests that the Federal Rules
of Civil Procedure have somehow worked an "expansion of adequate legal
remedies" so as to oust the District Courts of equitable jurisdiction, as
well as to deprive them of their traditional power to control their own
dockets. But obviously the Federal Rules could not and did not "expand"
the substantive law one whit.[10]

Like the Declaratory Judgment Act, the Federal Rules preserve
inviolate the right to trial by jury in actions historically cognizable at
common law, as under the Constitution they must. They do not create a
right of trial by jury where that right "does not exist under the
Constitution or statutes of the United States." Rule 39(a). Since Beacon's
counterclaim was compulsory under the Rules, see Rule 13(a), it is
apparent that by filing it Beacon could not be held to have waived its jury
rights. Compare American Mills Co. v. American Surety Co., 260 U.S.
360, 43 S.Ct. 149, 67 L.Ed. 306. But neither can the counterclaim be held
to have transformed Fox's original complaint into an action at law. See
Bendix Aviation Corp. v. Glass, D.C., 81 F.Supp. 645.

The Rules make possible the trial of legal and equitable claims in
the same proceeding, but they expressly affirm the power of a trial judge
to determine the order in which claims shall be heard. Rule 42(b).
Certainly the Federal Rules were not intended to undermine the basic
structure of equity jurisprudence, developed over the centuries and
explicitly recognized in the United States Constitution.

For these reasons I think the petition for a writ of mandamus should
have been dismissed.

NOTES AND QUESTIONS

1. **The holding in *Beacon Theatres*.** The holding in *Beacon
Theatres* has two significant parts. First, the Court holds that a declaratory
judgment is a "legal" remedy for purposes of the Seventh Amendment if the
underlying issues in the action are legal in nature. A declaratory judgment
was at the time a relatively new remedy, and its status under the Seventh
Amendment was not clear. Although it was available in the state courts
somewhat earlier, it was not available in federal court until the passage of
the federal Declaratory Judgment Act in 1934. 28 U.S.C. §§ 2201–2202.
Hazard, Leubsdorf, & Bassett, Civil Procedure § 12.11, at 565 (6th ed. 2011),
states, "[I]f the declaratory remedy were analyzed by historical analogy to

---

[10] Congressional authorization of the Rules expressly provided that "Said rules shall
neither abridge, enlarge, nor modify the substantive rights of any litigant." 48 Stat. 1064. See
28 U.S.C. § 2072, 28 U.S.C.A. § 2072.

the legal-equitable dichotomy in remedies, it most clearly resembled equitable relief."

Second, the Court holds that in a suit where the determination of a factual issue is relevant to both legal and equitable claims presented in the same action, the determination must be made by a jury. Isn't the dissent correct that this holding reverses the result in *American Life Insurance Co. v. Stewart*? (Note that *American Life Insurance* was decided one year before the merger of law and equity accomplished by the adoption of the Federal Rules of the Civil Procedure in 1938, and its Rule 2.) Are you convinced that the merger under the Rules changed the constitutional analysis under the Seventh Amendment, requiring the result in *Beacon Theaters*? Which of the two cases reaches the more practical result?

2. **An abandonment of the historical test?** In praising *Beacon Theatres,* Professor John McCoid wrote, "If *Beacon* is to be read as holding that the grant of a jury trial is constitutionally compelled, as distinguished from merely permitted constitutionally, at its core must be the view that the command of the seventh amendment is one of adherence to a principle rather than to a particular set of results. * * * The abstract view that the right is a matter of principle fits well with the conception of the Constitution as a durable document providing continuingly useful standards for an evolving society." McCoid, Procedural Reform and the Right to Jury Trial: A Study of *Beacon Theatres, Inc. v. Westover,* 116 U. Pa. L. Rev. 1, 11–12 (1967). Note that Professor McCoid did not emphasize the historical faithfulness of the decision to English practice in 1791, but rather its supposedly principled basis. Is that a helpful way to think about the Seventh Amendment? What is the principle on which *Beacon Theatres* is based?

3. **The transforming effect of merger on other traditionally equitable claims.** In Dairy Queen, Inc. v. Wood, 369 U.S. 469, 82 S.Ct. 894, 8 L.Ed.2d 44 (1962), defendant had contracted with Dairy Queen to use its trademark in parts of Pennsylvania. Dairy Queen claimed that defendant breached the contract, and sought (1) an injunction against defendant's continuing use of the trademark; (2) an equitable "accounting" to determine the amount of money owed to Dairy Queen, and a judgment for that amount; and (3) an injunction to prevent defendant from collecting money from Dairy Queen stores in its territory. All three remedies sought were traditionally equitable. The Supreme Court, in an opinion by Justice Black, held that the Seventh Amendment required a jury trial on all factual issues related to Dairy Queen's claim for monetary relief.

The Court in *Dairy Queen* found that the claim for an accounting was a legal rather than an equitable issue for purposes of the Seventh Amendment. The Court recognized that an accounting was a traditional equitable proceeding, but said:

> The respondents' contention that this money claim is "purely equitable" is based primarily upon the fact that their complaint is cast in terms of an "accounting," rather than in terms of an action for "debt" or "damages." But the constitutional right to trial by jury cannot be made to depend upon the choice of words used in the pleadings. The necessary prerequisite to the right to maintain a suit for an equitable accounting, like all other equitable remedies, is, as we pointed out in Beacon Theatres, the absence of an adequate remedy at law. Consequently, in order to maintain such

a suit on a cause of action cognizable at law, as this one is, the plaintiff must be able to show that the "accounts between the parties" are of such a "complicated nature" that only a court of equity can satisfactorily unravel them. In view of the powers given to the District Courts by Federal Rule of Civil Procedure 53(b) to appoint masters to assist the jury in those exceptional cases where the legal issues are too complicated for the jury adequately to handle alone, the burden of such a showing is considerably increased and it will indeed be a rare case in which it can be met.

Id. at 477–78. How faithful to history is Justice Black's analysis? It is often said that equitable remedies are available only when legal remedies are inadequate. But does this proposition avoid the fact that in 1791 an accounting would have been available in equity on facts comparable to those in *Dairy Queen*?

The Court in *Dairy Queen* also emphatically reaffirmed the core holding of *Beacon Theatres* that a jury is required to decide all common factual issues:

> The holding in *Beacon Theatres* was that where both legal and equitable issues are presented in a single case, "only under the most imperative circumstances, circumstances which in view of the flexible procedures of the Federal Rules we cannot now anticipate, can the right to a jury trial of legal issues be lost through prior determination of equitable claims." That holding, of course, applies whether the trial judge chooses to characterize the legal issues presented as "incidental" to equitable issues or not. Consequently, in a case such as this where there cannot even be a contention of such "imperative circumstances," Beacon Theatres requires that any legal issues for which a trial by jury is timely and properly demanded be submitted to a jury.

Id. at 472–73.

In Ross v. Bernhard, 396 U.S. 531, 90 S.Ct. 733, 24 L.Ed.2d 729 (1970), the Court upheld a right to jury trial in a shareholders' derivative suit for damages. A shareholders' derivative suit is a device by which a shareholder of a corporation may bring suit on a corporation's behalf when the corporation itself refuses to do so. The Court noted that during the nineteenth century a shareholders' derivative suit was available only in equity and not at law. But it held that in the post-merger procedural world, a Seventh Amendment analysis should be based on the character of the substantive claims rather the procedural device by which they came into court. The Court therefore upheld the right to jury trial for all the damage claims because, if sued upon by the corporation directly, those claims would have carried a right to a jury. Is this analysis faithful to the historical approach to deciding such questions?

4. **Limiting the preclusive effect of judicial fact-finding.** At issue in *Beacon Theatres* and *Dairy Queen* is a form of issue preclusion, which we will study in detail in Chapter 9. In brief, the doctrine of issue preclusion provides that individual issues fully litigated and decided in one action may not be relitigated in a subsequent action. In other words, whatever was decided regarding the issue in the first action is controlling in the second; the issue may not be reargued. It was assumed in both *Beacon Theatres* and *Dairy Queen* that any factual determination, once made, would govern the rest of the proceedings in the case. The Court in *Beacon Theatres* held that

the jury should go first in order to avoid the preclusive effect of the judge's factual determinations—if the judge had decided the issue first, his decision would have been final, meaning the jury would not be able to address the issue. Should this principle of priority for jury determinations extend beyond the situation where the legal and equitable claims are asserted in the same action? In *Parklane Hosiery Co. v. Shore*, 439 U.S. 322, 99 S.Ct. 645, 58 L.Ed.2d 552 (1979), infra p. 1104, a federal district judge, in a previous equitable proceeding brought by the federal Securities and Exchange Commission, had found that defendant Parklane made material misstatements in documents distributed to investors. In a separate damage suit brought by the investors themselves, Parklane relied on *Beacon Theatres* to argue that it was entitled to a redetermination by a jury of the factual issues common to the two suits. The Court rejected the argument, characterizing *Beacon Theatres* as "enunciat[ing] no more than a general prudential rule." Id. at 334. Justice Rehnquist dissented, arguing that defendant was entitled under the Seventh Amendment to a redetermination by a jury. Note that *Parklane,* like *American Life Insurance Co. v. Stewart* and unlike *Beacon Theatres* and *Dairy Queen*, involved two separate suits.

5.   Justice Black's view of jury trial. Justice Hugo Black, the author of *Beacon Theatres* and *Dairy Queen*, consistently favored an expansive view of entitlement to jury trials. Justice Black was a U.S. Senator when he was nominated for the Supreme Court by President Roosevelt, but he had been an extremely successful plaintiff's attorney in Alabama before going into politics. In a reminiscence, Justice Black wrote about a case in which he had been a private prosecutor. The defendant, a woman with a taste for race tracks, had stolen some bonds from an unsympathetic wealthy woman.

> I had a number of real close friends on the jury that tried that case. My good friend, Reese Murray, a former FBI Agent, was representing the defendant. Reese started after the "Special Prosecutor for Money" at the very beginning and kept up his attacks to the very end. The lady whose bonds were alleged to have been stolen cannot truthfully be said to have strengthened her case. She was a richly dressed widow who came into the courtroom with black silks that swished as she walked. In her hands she carried a lorgnette, which now and then, especially when looking at the jury, she put to her eyes. When asked if she owned the bonds, her answer to me was: "Mr. Black, you will have to ask my broker for a description of the bonds. You know I do not keep up with things like that." Suffice it to say, her broker did give the jury an accurate description of the bonds, and the description was that which other evidence showed to be the same as bonds the defendant sold at the races in New Orleans.

> After the jury came in with its prompt verdict of acquittal, a friend on the jury who had borrowed three dollars from me at the Knights of Pythias Lodge came by my office to pay me for the loan. I asked him how the jury returned its verdict. His answer, which I think I shall never forget, was: "Hugo, do you think the jury would convict a woman for stealing from that damned old * * *?"

> This story may be thought by many to present an irrefutable argument against the jury system, but who can say such a result would not have been accepted by the Founders, who provided for

such trials by the friends, neighbors, and acquaintances of the defendants?

H. Black & E. Black, Mr. Justice and Mrs. Black: The Memoirs of Hugo L. Black and Elizabeth Black 61 (1986).

Professor McCoid concluded his article,

> [*Beacon Theatres*] requires a determination whether previous inadequacy of a legal remedy, which hitherto justified the exercise of equity jurisdiction, has been cured by changes to procedure. . . . [It asserts] that the seventh amendment's protection is based on a jurisdictional principle, rather than a conglomeration of jurisdictional results dictated by discarded procedures; jurisdiction is determined in light of existing, not past, procedure.

> * * *

> [*Beacon Theatres*] clearly enlarges enjoyment of jury trial as of right and reflects a basic pro-jury bias. That it should do so is quite clear, in view of the pro-jury bias of the Constitution.

116 U. Pa. L. Rev. at 23–24. Are Justice Black in his opinions, Professor McCoid in his article, and Justice Black in his reminiscence all saying the same thing in different language? For a similar argument for a "dynamic" view of the Seventh Amendment see Wolfram, The Constitutional History of the Seventh Amendment, 57 Minn. L. Rev. 639, 744–45 (1973).

6.   State constitutions and the doctrine of *Beacon Theatres*. The state courts have not escaped, any more than have the federal courts, the difficult questions of right to jury trial in the unified civil action after merger of law and equity. But they have often declined to adopt the solutions chosen by the U.S. Supreme Court. Contrary to *Beacon Theatres*, California has a preference for prior trial of equitable issues. Connell v. Bowes, 19 Cal.2d 870, 872, 123 P.2d 456, 457 (1942); Raedeke v. Gibraltar Sav. & Loan Ass'n, 10 Cal.3d 665, 670, 111 Cal.Rptr. 693, 517 P.2d 1157 (1974). New York has also rejected the rule in *Beacon Theatres*. Phoenix Mutual Life Ins. Co. v. Conway, 11 N.Y.2d 367, 183 N.E.2d 754, 229 N.Y.S.2d 740 (1962).

NOTE ON DEMANDING AND WAIVING JURY TRIAL

1.   Strategic considerations in choosing a jury trial. Of course, all of this confusion matters only if there is some reason a party prefers a trial before a jury rather than a judge. The choice between a judge or a jury is widely perceived as important. Experienced litigators claim to have a feel for how judges and juries react, and they have distinct preferences for juries in certain kinds of cases. There is a substantial literature showing differences in plaintiff win rates before judges and juries, and in some fields, such as products liability and medical malpractice, plaintiffs win much more often before judges. But it is not clear whether this is attributable to real differences in the ways that judges and juries decide cases or to how lawyers select the cases in which jury trial is demanded based upon their perceptions (or misperceptions) of how judges and juries differ. See Clermont & Eisenberg, Litigation Realities, 88 Cornell L. Rev. 119, 143–46 (2002). In addition to any generic differences between judges and juries, the decision to choose or waive a jury may depend on lawyers' perceptions of the relative competence and impartiality of the judges and juries in the particular community where the case will be tried, the strength of their claim or defense (conventional wisdom is that weaker plaintiff's cases have a better chance before a jury), and considerations of cost and convenience (jury trials cost more, take longer and are often more difficult to schedule).

2. Procedure in federal court. Under Rule 38, a party waives her right to jury trial if she does not timely demand it. See Fed. R. Civ. P. 38(b) ("On any issue triable of right by a jury, a party may demand a jury trial by (1) serving the other parties with a written demand—which may be included in a pleading—no later than 14 days after the last pleading directed to the issue is served; and (2) filing the demand [with the court] in accordance with Rule 5(d)."); Fed. R. Civ. P. 38(d) ("A party waives jury trial unless its demand is properly served and filed. A proper demand may be withdrawn only if the parties consent."). The requirements of Rule 38 differ from the pre-Rules practice under which, in the absence of an express waiver, jury trial followed as a matter of course in actions at law. Experienced practitioners who desire jury trial in federal court follow the wise custom authorized by Rule 38(b) of endorsing the demand for a jury on the complaint when they represent the plaintiff, and on the answer when they represent the defendant and plaintiff has not demanded a jury. Under Rule 39(b) the court in its discretion on motion may relieve a party from the consequences of his waiver by ordering a jury trial "on any issues for which a jury trial might have been demanded." But a practitioner seeking a jury trial should not rely on the court to save his or her bacon. Many courts refuse to order a jury trial when it has not been timely requested "unless some cause beyond mere inadvertence is shown." Richardson v. Stanley Works, Inc., 597 F.3d 1288, 1297 (Fed. Cir. 2010).

3. Procedure in removed cases. Suppose an action commenced in state court is duly removed to federal court under 28 U.S.C. § 1441. Must the party desiring a jury make a demand in federal court, and if so, when? See the somewhat complicated answer in Fed. R. Civ. P. 81(c).

2. THE MODERN HISTORICAL TEST

Chauffeurs v. Terry

Supreme Court of the United States, 1990.
494 U.S. 558, 110 S.Ct. 1339, 108 L.Ed.2d 519.

■ JUSTICE MARSHALL delivered the opinion of the Court except as to Part III–A.

This case presents the question whether an employee who seeks relief in the form of backpay for a union's alleged breach of its duty of fair representation has a right to trial by jury. We hold that the Seventh Amendment entitles such a plaintiff to a jury trial.

I

McLean Trucking Company and the Chauffeurs, Teamsters, and Helpers Local Union No. 391 were parties to a collective-bargaining agreement that governed the terms and conditions of employment at McLean's terminals. The 27 respondents were employed by McLean as truckdrivers in bargaining units covered by the agreement, and all were members of the Union. In 1982 McLean implemented a change in operations that resulted in the elimination of some of its terminals and the reorganization of others. [As a result of the change in operations, respondent union members filed grievances against McLean, and requested their union to represent them in prosecuting these grievances.]

* * *

[After a series of grievances,] respondents filed an action in District Court, alleging that McLean had breached the collective-bargaining agreement in violation of § 301 of the Labor Management Relations Act, 1947, 61 Stat. 156, 29 U.S.C. § 185 (1982 ed.),[1] and that the Union had violated its duty of fair representation. Respondents requested a permanent injunction requiring the defendants to cease their illegal acts and to reinstate them to their proper seniority status; in addition, they sought, *inter alia,* compensatory damages for lost wages and health benefits. In 1986 McLean filed for bankruptcy; subsequently, the action against it was voluntarily dismissed, along with all claims for injunctive relief.

Respondents had requested a jury trial in their pleadings. The Union moved to strike the jury demand on the ground that no right to a jury trial exists in a duty of fair representation suit. The District Court denied the motion to strike. After an interlocutory appeal, the Fourth Circuit affirmed the trial court, holding that the Seventh Amendment entitled respondents to a jury trial of their claim for monetary relief. 863 F.2d 334 (1988). We granted the petition for certiorari to resolve a circuit conflict on this issue, and now affirm the judgment of the Fourth Circuit.

II

The duty of fair representation is inferred from unions' exclusive authority under the National Labor Relations Act, 29 U.S.C. § 159(a), to represent all employees in a bargaining unit. The duty requires a union "to serve the interests of all members without hostility or discrimination toward any, to exercise its discretion with complete good faith and honesty, and to avoid arbitrary conduct." A union must discharge its duty both in bargaining with the employer and in its enforcement of the resulting collective bargaining agreement. Thus, the Union here was required to pursue respondents' grievances in a manner consistent with the principles of fair representation.

Because most collective-bargaining agreements accord finality to grievance or arbitration procedures established by the collective-bargaining agreement, an employee normally cannot bring a § 301 action against an employer unless he can show that the union breached its duty of fair representation in its handling of his grievance. DelCostello v. Teamsters, 462 U.S. 151, 163–164, 103 S.Ct. 2281, 2289–2290, 76 L.Ed.2d 476 (1983). Whether the employee sues both the labor union and the employer or only one of those entities, he must prove the same two facts to recover money damages: that the employer's action violated the terms of the collective-bargaining agreement and that the union

---

[1]   Section 301(a) of the Labor Management Relations Act, 1947, provides for suits by and against labor unions:

"Suits for violation of contracts between an employer and a labor organization representing employees in an industry affecting commerce as defined in this chapter, or between any such labor organizations, may be brought in any district court of the United States having jurisdiction of the parties, without respect to the amount in controversy or without regard to the citizenship of the parties." 29 U.S.C. § 185(a).

breached its duty of fair representation. Id., at 164–165, 103 S.Ct., at 2290–2291.

III

We turn now to the constitutional issue presented in this case—whether respondents are entitled to a jury trial. The Seventh Amendment provides that "[i]n Suits at common law, where the value in controversy shall exceed twenty dollars, the right of trial by jury shall be preserved." The right to a jury trial includes more than the common-law forms of action recognized in 1791; the phrase "Suits at common law" refers to "suits in which *legal* rights [are] to be ascertained and determined, in contradistinction to those where equitable rights alone [are] recognized, and equitable remedies [are] administered." Parsons v. Bedford, 3 Pet. 433, 447, 7 L.Ed. 732 (1830); see also ibid. ("[T]he amendment then may well be construed to embrace all suits which are not of equity and admiralty jurisdiction, whatever may be the peculiar form which they may assume to settle legal rights"). The right extends to causes of action created by Congress. Tull v. United States, 481 U.S. 412, 417, 107 S.Ct. 1831, 1835, 95 L.Ed.2d 365 (1987). Since the merger of the systems of law and equity, see Fed.Rule Civ.Proc. 2, this Court has carefully preserved the right to trial by jury where legal rights are at stake. As the Court noted in Beacon Theatres, Inc. v. Westover, " 'Maintenance of the jury as a fact-finding body is of such importance and occupies so firm a place in our history and jurisprudence that any seeming curtailment of the right to a jury trial should be scrutinized with the utmost care.' " 359 U.S. 500, 501, 79 S.Ct. 948, 952, 3 L.Ed.2d 988 (1959) (quoting Dimick v. Schiedt, 293 U.S. 474, 486, 55 S.Ct. 296, 301, 79 L.Ed. 603 (1935)).

To determine whether a particular action will resolve legal rights, we examine both the nature of the issues involved and the remedy sought. "First, we compare the statutory action to 18th-century actions brought in the courts of England prior to the merger of the courts of law and equity. Second, we examine the remedy sought and determine whether it is legal or equitable in nature." *Tull,* supra, 481 U.S., at 417–418, 107 S.Ct., at 1835–1836 (citations omitted). The second inquiry is the more important in our analysis. Granfinanciera, S.A. v. Nordberg, 492 U.S. 33, 42, 109 S.Ct. 2782, 2789, 106 L.Ed.2d 26 (1989).

A

An action for breach of a union's duty of fair representation was unknown in 18th-century England; in fact, collective-bargaining was unlawful. We must therefore look for an analogous cause of action that existed in the 18th century to determine whether the nature of this duty of fair representation suit is legal or equitable.

The Union contends that this duty of fair representation action resembles a suit brought to vacate an arbitration award because respondents seek to set aside the result of the grievance process. In the 18th Century, an action to set aside an arbitration award was considered equitable. 2 J. Story, Commentaries on Equity Jurisprudence § 1452, pp. 789–790 (13th ed. 1886) (equity courts had jurisdiction over claims that an award should be set aside on the ground of "mistake of the arbitrators"); see, e.g., Burchell v. Marsh, 17 How. 344, 15 L.Ed. 96 (1855) (reviewing bill in equity to vacate an arbitration award). In support of its characterization of the duty of fair representation claim, the Union cites United Parcel Serv., Inc. v. Mitchell, 451 U.S. 56, 101 S.Ct. 1559, 67 L.Ed.2d 732 (1981), in which we held that, for purposes of selecting from various state statutes an appropriate limitations period for a § 301 suit against an employer, such a suit was more analogous to a suit to vacate an arbitration award than to a breach of contract action. Id., at 62, 101 S.Ct., at 1563.

The arbitration analogy is inapposite, however, to the Seventh Amendment question posed in this case. No grievance committee has considered respondents' claim that the Union violated its duty of fair representation; the grievance process was concerned only with the employer's alleged breach of the collective-bargaining agreement. * * *

The Union next argues that respondents' duty of fair representation action is comparable to an action by a trust beneficiary against a trustee for breach of fiduciary duty. Such actions were within the exclusive jurisdiction of courts of equity. 2 Story, supra, § 960, p. 266; Restatement (Second) of Trusts § 199(c) (1959). This analogy is far more persuasive than the arbitration analogy. Just as a trustee must act in the best interests of the beneficiaries, 2A A. Scott, Law of Trusts § 170 (4th ed. 1987), a union, as the exclusive representative of the workers, must exercise its power to act on behalf of the employees in good faith, Vaca v. Sipes, 386 U.S., at 177, 87 S.Ct., at 909–910. Moreover, just as a beneficiary does not directly control the actions of a trustee, 3 Scott, supra, § 187, an individual employee lacks direct control over a union's actions taken on his behalf, see Cox, The Legal Nature of Collective Bargaining Agreements, 57 Mich.L. Rev. 1, 21 (1958).

The trust analogy extends to a union's handling of grievances. In most cases, a trustee has the exclusive authority to sue third parties who injure the beneficiaries' interest in the trust, 4 Scott, supra, § 282, pp. 25–29, including any legal claim the trustee holds in trust for the beneficiaries, Restatement (Second) of Trusts, supra, § 82, comment a. The trustee then has the sole responsibility for determining whether to settle, arbitrate, or otherwise dispose of the claim. Restatement (Second) of Trusts, supra, § 192. Similarly, the union typically has broad discretion in its decision whether and how to pursue an employee's grievance against an employer. Just as a trust beneficiary can sue to enforce a contract entered into on his behalf by the trustee only if the trustee "improperly refuses or neglects to bring an action against the third person," Restatement (Second) of Trusts, supra, § 282(2), so an employee can sue his employer for a breach of the collective-bargaining agreement only if he shows that the union breached its duty of fair representation in its handling of the grievance.

Respondents contend that their duty of fair representation suit is less like a trust action than an attorney malpractice action, which was historically an action at law, see, e.g., Russell v. Palmer, 2 Wils.K.B. 325, 95 Eng.Rep. 837 (1767). In determining the appropriate statute of limitations for a hybrid § 301/DFR action, this Court in DelCostello noted in dictum that an attorney malpractice action is "the closest state-law analogy for the claim against the union." 462 U.S., at 167, 103 S.Ct., at 2292. The Court in DelCostello did not consider the trust analogy, however. Presented with a more complete range of alternatives, we find that, in the context of the Seventh Amendment inquiry, the attorney malpractice analogy does not capture the relationship between the union and the represented employees as fully as the trust analogy does.

The attorney malpractice analogy is inadequate in several respects. Although an attorney malpractice suit is in some ways similar to a suit alleging a union's breach of its fiduciary duty, the two actions are fundamentally different. The nature of an action is in large part controlled by the nature of the underlying relationship between the parties. Unlike employees represented by a union, a client controls the significant decisions concerning his representation. Moreover, a client can fire his attorney if he is dissatisfied with his attorney's performance. This option is not available to an individual employee who is unhappy with a union's representation, unless a majority of the members of the bargaining unit share his dissatisfaction. See J.I. Case Co. v. NLRB, 321 U.S. 332, 338–339, 64 S.Ct. 576, 580–581, 88 L.Ed. 762 (1944). Thus, we find the malpractice analogy less convincing than the trust analogy.

Nevertheless, the trust analogy does not persuade us to characterize respondents' claim as wholly equitable. The Union's argument mischaracterizes the nature of our comparison of the action before us to 18th-century forms of action. As we observed in Ross v. Bernhard, 396 U.S. 531, 90 S.Ct. 733, 24 L.Ed.2d 729 (1970), "The Seventh Amendment question depends on the nature of the *issue* to be tried rather than the character of the overall action." Id., at 538, 90 S.Ct., at 738 (emphasis added) (finding a right to jury trial in a shareholder's derivative suit, a type of suit traditionally brought in courts of equity, because plaintiffs' case presented legal issues of breach of contract and negligence). As discussed above, * * * * to recover from the Union here, respondents must prove both that McLean violated § 301 by breaching the collective-bargaining agreement and that the Union breached its duty of fair representation. When viewed in isolation, the duty of fair representation issue is analogous to a claim against a trustee for breach of fiduciary duty. The § 301 issue, however, is comparable to a breach of contract claim—a legal issue.

Respondents' action against the Union thus encompasses both equitable and legal issues. The first part of our Seventh Amendment inquiry, then, leaves us in equipoise as to whether respondents are entitled to a jury trial.

B

Our determination under the first part of the Seventh Amendment analysis is only preliminary. Granfinanciera, S.A. v. Nordberg, 492 U.S., at 47, 109 S.Ct., at 2793. In this case, the only remedy sought is a request for compensatory damages representing backpay and benefits. Generally, an action for money damages was "the traditional form of relief offered in the courts of law." Curtis v. Loether, 415 U.S. 189, 196, 94 S.Ct. 1005, 1009, 39 L.Ed.2d 260 (1974). This Court has not, however, held that "any award of monetary relief must *necessarily* be 'legal' relief." Ibid. (emphasis added). See also *Granfinanciera,* supra, 492 U.S., at 86, n. 9, 109 S.Ct., at 2814, n. 9 (WHITE, J., dissenting). Nonetheless, because we conclude that the remedy respondents seek has none of the attributes that must be present before we will find an exception to the general rule and characterize damages as equitable, we find that the remedy sought by respondents is legal.

First, we have characterized damages as equitable where they are restitutionary, such as in "action[s] for disgorgement of improper profits," *Tull,* 481 U.S., at 424, 107 S.Ct., at 1839. The backpay sought by respondents is not money wrongfully held by the Union, but wages and benefits they would have received from McLean had the Union processed the employees' grievances properly. Such relief is not restitutionary.

Second, a monetary award "incidental to or intertwined with injunctive relief" may be equitable. *Tull,* supra, 481 U.S., at 424, 107 S.Ct., at 1839. Because respondents seek only money damages, this characteristic is clearly absent from the case.

The Union argues that the backpay relief sought here must nonetheless be considered equitable because this Court has labeled backpay awarded under Title VII [of the Civil Rights Act of 1964], 42 U.S.C. § 2000e et seq., as equitable. See Albemarle Paper Co. v. Moody, 422 U.S. 405, 415–418, 95 S.Ct. 2362, 2370–2372, 45 L.Ed.2d 280 (1975) (characterizing backpay awarded against employer under Title VII as equitable in context of assessing whether judge erred in refusing to award such relief). It contends that the Title VII analogy is compelling in the context of the duty of fair representation because its backpay provision was based on the NLRA provision governing backpay awards for unfair labor practices, 29 U.S.C. § 160(c) (1982 ed.) ("[W]here an order directs reinstatement of an employee, back pay may be required of the employer or labor organization"). See Albemarle Paper Co. v. Moody, supra, at 419, 95 S.Ct., at 2372. We are not convinced.

The Court has never held that a plaintiff seeking backpay under Title VII has a right to a jury trial. See Lorillard v. Pons, 434 U.S. 575, 581–582, 98 S.Ct. 866, 870–871, 55 L.Ed.2d 40 (1978). Assuming, without deciding, that such a Title VII plaintiff has no right to a jury trial, the Union's argument does not persuade us that respondents are not entitled to a jury trial here. Congress specifically characterized backpay under Title VII as a form of "equitable relief." 42 U.S.C. § 2000e–5(g) ("[T]he court may . . . order such affirmative action as may be appropriate, which may include, but is not limited to, reinstatement or hiring of employees, with or without back pay . . . , or any other equitable relief as the court deems appropriate"). See also Curtis v. Loether, supra, 415 U.S., at 196–197, 94 S.Ct., at 1009–1010 (distinguishing backpay under Title VII from damages under Title VIII, the fair housing provision of the Civil Rights Act, 42 U.S.C. §§ 3601–3619, which the Court characterized as "legal" for Seventh Amendment purposes). Congress made no similar pronouncement regarding the duty of fair representation. Furthermore, the Court has noted that backpay sought from an employer under Title VII would generally be restitutionary in nature, see Curtis v. Loether, supra, at 197, 94 S.Ct., at 1010, in contrast to the damages sought here from the Union. Thus, the remedy sought in this duty of fair representation case is clearly different from backpay sought for violations of Title VII.

* * *

We hold, then, that the remedy of backpay sought in this duty of fair representation action is legal in nature. Considering both parts of the Seventh Amendment inquiry, we find that respondents are entitled to a jury trial on all issues presented in their suit.

IV

On balance, our analysis of the nature of respondents' duty of fair representation action and the remedy they seek convinces us that this action is a legal one. Although the search for an adequate 18th-century analog revealed that the claim includes both legal and equitable issues, the money damages respondents seek are the type of relief traditionally awarded by courts of law. Thus, the Seventh Amendment entitles respondents to a jury trial, and we therefore affirm the judgment of the Court of Appeals.

It is so ordered.

■ JUSTICE BRENNAN, concurring in part and concurring in the judgment.

I agree with the Court that respondents seek a remedy that is legal in nature and that the Seventh Amendment entitles respondents to a jury trial on their duty of fair representation claims. I therefore join Parts I, II, III–B, and IV of the Court's opinion. I do not join that part of the opinion which reprises the particular historical analysis this Court has employed to determine whether a claim is a "Suit at common law" under the Seventh Amendment because I believe the historical test can and should be simplified.

The current test, first expounded in Curtis v. Loether, 415 U.S. 189, 194, 94 S.Ct. 1005, 1008, 39 L.Ed.2d 260 (1974), requires a court to compare the right at issue to 18th-century English forms of action to determine whether the historically analogous right was vindicated in an action at law or in equity, and to examine whether the remedy sought is legal or equitable in nature. However, this Court, in expounding the test, has repeatedly discounted the significance of the analogous form of action for deciding where the Seventh Amendment applies. I think it is time we dispense with it altogether. I would decide Seventh Amendment questions on the basis of the relief sought. If the relief is legal in nature, i.e., if it is the kind of relief that historically was available from courts of law, I would hold that the parties have a constitutional right to a trial by jury—unless Congress has permissibly delegated the particular dispute to a non-Article III decisionmaker and jury trials would frustrate Congress' purposes in enacting a particular statutory scheme.

I believe that our insistence that the jury trial right hinges in part on a comparison of the substantive right at issue to forms of action used in English courts 200 years ago needlessly convolutes our Seventh Amendment jurisprudence. For the past decade and a half, this Court has explained that the two parts of the historical test are not equal in weight, that the nature of the remedy is more important than the nature of the right. Since the existence of a right to jury trial therefore turns on the nature of the remedy, absent congressional delegation to a specialized decisionmaker, there remains little purpose to our rattling through dusty attics of ancient writs. The time has come to borrow William of Occam's razor and sever this portion of our analysis.

We have long acknowledged that, of the factors relevant to the jury trial right, comparison of the claim to ancient forms of action, "requiring extensive and possibly abstruse historical inquiry, is obviously the most difficult to apply." Ross v. Bernhard, 396 U.S. 531, 538, n. 10, 90 S.Ct. 733, 738, n. 10, 24 L.Ed.2d 729 (1970). Requiring judges, with neither the training nor time necessary for reputable historical scholarship, to root through the tangle of primary and secondary sources to determine which of a hundred or so writs is analogous to the right at issue has embroiled courts in recondite controversies better left to legal historians.* * *.

To be sure, it is neither unusual nor embarrassing for members of a court to disagree and disagree vehemently. But it better behooves judges to disagree within the province of judicial expertise. Furthermore, inquiries into the appropriate historical analogs for the rights at issue are not necessarily susceptible of sound resolution under the best of circumstances. As one scholar observes: "[T]he line between law and equity (and therefore between jury and non-jury trial) was not a fixed and static one. There was a continual process of borrowing by one jurisdiction from the other; there were less frequent instances of a sloughing off of older functions. . . . The borrowing by each jurisdiction from the other was not accompanied by an equivalent sloughing off of functions. This led to a very large overlap between law and equity." James, Right to a Jury Trial in Civil Actions, 72 Yale L.J. 655, 658–659 (1963).

In addition, modern statutory rights did not exist in the 18th-century and even the most exacting historical research may not elicit a clear historical analog. The right at issue here, for example, is a creature of modern labor law quite foreign to Georgian England. * * *

To rest the historical test required by the Seventh Amendment solely on the nature of the relief sought would not, of course, offer the federal courts a rule that is in all cases self-executing. Courts will still be required to ask which remedies were traditionally available at law and which only in equity. But this inquiry involves fewer variables and simpler choices, on the whole, and is far more manageable than the scholasticist debates in which we have been engaged. Moreover, the rule I propose would remain true to the Seventh Amendment, as it is undisputed that, historically, "[j]urisdictional lines [between law and equity] were primarily a matter of remedy." McCoid, Procedural Reform and the Right to Jury Trial: A Study of *Beacon Theatres, Inc. v. Westover,* 116 U.Pa.L. Rev. 1 (1967). See also Redish, Seventh Amendment Right to Jury Trial: A Study in the Irrationality of Rational Decision Making, 70 Nw.U.L. Rev. 486, 490 (1975) ("In the majority of cases at common law, the equitable or legal nature of a suit was determined not by the substantive nature of the cause of action but by the remedy sought").[7]

This is not to say that the resulting division between claims entitled to jury trials and claims not so entitled would exactly mirror the division between law and equity in England in 1791. But it is too late in the day for this Court to profess that the Seventh Amendment preserves the right

---

[7] There are, to be sure, some who advocate abolishing the historical test altogether. See, e.g., Wolfram, The Constitutional History of the Seventh Amendment, 57 Minn.L. Rev. 639, 742–747 (1973). Contrary to the intimations in JUSTICE KENNEDY'S dissent, see post, at 1359–1360, I am not among them. I believe that it is imperative to retain a historical test, for determining when parties have a right to jury trial, for precisely the same reasons JUSTICE KENNEDY does. It is mandated by the language of the Seventh Amendment and it is a bulwark against those who would restrict a right our forefathers held indispensable. Like JUSTICE KENNEDY, I have no doubt that courts can and do look to legal history for the answers to constitutional questions, see post, at 1359, and therefore the Seventh Amendment test I propose today obliges courts to do exactly that.

Where JUSTICE KENNEDY and I differ is in our evaluations of which historical test provides the more reliable results. * * *

to jury trial only in cases that would have been heard in the British law courts of the 18th century. * * *

Indeed, given this Court's repeated insistence that the nature of the remedy is always to be given more weight than the nature of the historically analogous right, it is unlikely that the simplified Seventh Amendment analysis I propose will result in different decisions than the analysis in current use. In the unusual circumstance that the nature of the remedy could be characterized equally as legal or equitable, I submit that the comparison of a contemporary statutory action unheard of in the 18th century to some ill-fitting ancient writ is too shaky a basis for the resolution of an issue as significant as the availability of a trial by jury. If, in the rare case, a tie-breaker is needed, let us break the tie in favor of jury trial.

What Blackstone described as "the glory of the English law" and "the most transcendent privilege which any subject can enjoy," 3 W. Blackstone, Commentaries *379, was crucial in the eyes of those who founded this country. The encroachment on civil jury trial by colonial administrators was a "deeply divisive issue in the years just preceding the outbreak of hostilities between the colonies and England," and all thirteen States reinstituted the right after hostilities ensued. Wolfram, The Constitutional History of the Seventh Amendment, 57 Minn.L. Rev. 639, 654–655 (1973). "In fact, '[t]he right to trial by jury was probably the only one universally secured by the first American constitutions.'" Id., at 655 (quoting L. Levy, Freedom of Speech and Press in Early American History—Legacy of Suppression 281 (1963 reprint)). Fear of a federal government that had not guaranteed jury trial in civil cases, voiced first at the Philadelphia Convention in 1787 and regularly during the ratification debates, was the concern that precipitated the maelstrom over the need for a bill of rights in the United States Constitution. Wolfram, supra, at 657–660.

This Court has long recognized the caliber of this right. In Parsons v. Bedford, 3 Pet. 433, 446, 7 L.Ed. 732 (1830), Justice Story stressed: "The trial by jury is justly dear to the American people. It has always been an object of deep interest and solicitude, and every encroachment upon it has been watched with great jealousy." Similarly, in Jacob v. New York City, 315 U.S. 752, 752–753, 62 S.Ct. 854, 854–855, 86 L.Ed. 1166 (1942), we said that "[t]he right of jury trial in civil cases at common law is a basic and fundamental feature of our system of federal jurisprudence . . . [a] right so fundamental and sacred to the citizen [that it] should be jealously guarded by the courts."

We can guard this right and save our courts from needless and intractable excursions into increasingly unfamiliar territory simply by retiring that prong of our Seventh Amendment test which we have already cast into a certain doubt. If we are not prepared to accord the nature of the historical analog sufficient weight for this factor to affect the outcome of our inquiry, except in the rarest of hypothetical cases, what reason do we have for insisting that federal judges proceed with this arduous inquiry? It is time we read the writing on the wall, especially as we ourselves put it there.

■ JUSTICE STEVENS, concurring in part and concurring in the judgment.

* * *

■ JUSTICE KENNEDY, with whom JUSTICE O'CONNOR and JUSTICE SCALIA join, dissenting.

* * *

I

Both the union and the respondents identify historical actions to which they find the duty of fair representation action most analogous. The union contends that the action resembles a traditional equitable suit by a beneficiary against a trustee for failing to pursue a claim that he holds in trust. See, e.g., Caffrey v. Darby, 6 Ves.Jun. 489, 495–496, 31 Eng.Rep. 1159, 1162 (Ch. 1801); Restatement (Second) of Trusts § 205(a), and Illustration 2, pp. 458, 459 (1957) (Restatement). In other words, the union compares itself to a trustee that, in its discretion, has decided not to press certain claims. The respondents argue that the duty of fair representation action resembles a traditional legal malpractice suit by a client against his lawyer for mishandling a claim. See, e.g., Pitt v. Yalden, 4 Burr. 2060, 98 Eng.Rep. 74 (K.B.1767); Russell v. Palmer, 2 Wils.K.B. 325, 95 Eng.Rep. 837 (1767). They contend that the union, when acting as their legal representative, had a duty to press their grievances.

* * *

II

The Court relies on two lines of precedents to overcome the conclusion that the trust action should serve as the controlling model. The first consists of cases in which the Court has considered simplifications in litigation resulting from modern procedural reforms in the federal courts. JUSTICE MARSHALL asserts that these cases show that the Court must look at the character of individual issues rather than claims as a whole. * * * The second line addresses the significance of the remedy in determining the equitable or legal nature of an action for the purpose of choosing the most appropriate analogy. Under these cases, the Court decides that the respondents have a right to a jury because they seek money damages. * * * These authorities do not support the Court's holding.

* * *

III

The Court must adhere to the historical test in determining the right to a jury because the language of the Constitution requires it. The Seventh Amendment "preserves" the right to jury trial in civil cases. We cannot preserve a right existing in 1791 unless we look to history to identify it. Our precedents are in full agreement with this reasoning and insist on adherence to the historical test. No alternatives short of rewriting the Constitution exist. If we abandon the plain language of the Constitution to expand the jury right, we may expect Courts with opposing views to curtail it in the future.

It is true that a historical inquiry into the distinction between law and equity may require us to enter into a domain becoming less familiar with time. Two centuries have passed since the Seventh Amendment's ratification and the incompleteness of our historical records makes it difficult to know the nature of certain actions in 1791. The historical test, nonetheless, has received more criticism than it deserves. Although our application of the analysis in some cases may seem biased in favor of jury trials, the test has not become a nullity. We do not require juries in all statutory actions. The historical test, in fact, resolves most cases without difficulty. See C. Wright, Law of Federal Courts § 92, p. 609 (4th ed. 1983) ("[T]he vast and controversial literature that has developed as to the scope of the jury right is, fortunately, not in proportion to the practical importance of the problem in the actual working of the courts").

I would hesitate to abandon or curtail the historical test out of concern for the competence of the Court to understand legal history. We do look to history for the answers to constitutional questions. See, e.g., Fay v. Noia, 372 U.S. 391, 399–415, 83 S.Ct. 822, 827–836, 9 L.Ed.2d 837 (1963) (opinion of BRENNAN, J.); Atascadero State Hospital v. Scanlon, 473 U.S. 234, 260–302, 105 S.Ct. 3142, 3156–3178, 87 L.Ed.2d 171 (1985) (BRENNAN, J., dissenting). Although opinions will differ on what this history shows, the approach has no less validity in the Seventh Amendment context than elsewhere.

If Congress has not provided for a jury trial, we are confined to the Seventh Amendment to determine whether one is required. Our own views respecting the wisdom of using a jury should be put aside. Like JUSTICE BRENNAN, I admire the jury process. Other judges have taken the opposite view. See, e.g., J. Frank, Law and the Modern Mind 170–185 (1931). But the judgment of our own times is not always preferable to the lessons of history. Our whole constitutional experience teaches that history must inform the judicial inquiry. Our obligation to the Constitution and its Bill of Rights, no less than the compact we have with the generation that wrote them for us, do not permit us to disregard provisions that some may think to be mere matters of historical form.

* * *

NOTES AND QUESTIONS

1. **A limit to the principle of *Beacon Theatres*?** The plaintiff's complaint in *Terry* contained a claim for back pay—that is, a claim for a monetary award that in premerger practice could have been brought only on the equity side of a federal court. Based upon the holdings and reasoning in *Beacon Theatres*, *Dairy Queen*, and *Ross v. Bernhard* shouldn't the Court have simply held that the merger of law and equity in effect transformed that equitable monetary claim into a legal claim for money damages triable as of right to a jury? Justice Brennan, in his concurring opinion, would have simplified the inquiry by focusing solely on the nature of the remedy: "If [the remedy] is the kind of relief that historically was available from courts of law, I would hold that the parties have a constitutional right to a trial by jury—unless Congress has permissibly delegated the particular dispute to a non-Article III decisionmaker and jury trials would frustrate Congress' purposes in enacting a particular statutory scheme." Isn't Justice Brennan's test the one that is most consistent with the *Beacon Theatres* line of cases? Why do you suppose that Justice Marshall's opinion does not follow, or even mention, that route? Is the principle underlying *Beacon Theatres* now dead as a source of new doctrine?

2. **The workability of the historical test.** Justice Marshall's opinion takes history seriously in the sense of analyzing carefully the cause of action and the nature of the remedy and comparing them to analogous

causes of action and remedies at law and in equity. How different is his approach from Justice Black's or Justice Brennan's? Is it more satisfactory?

Justice Kennedy is right in saying that the constitutional question of entitlement to a jury under the Seventh Amendment has a clear answer in most cases. This is surely so in ordinary tort or contract cases where damages are sought. It is usually so in statutory cases where damages are provided as a remedy. And even in cases like *Chauffeurs v. Terry,* the answer, once given by the Supreme Court, will be clear from that time forward. But that it is does not make borderline questions under new statutes any easier; and it does not necessarily make the answer ultimately given by the Supreme Court a particularly good one from the standpoint of fairness and efficiency in adjudication. What relevance, for example, does the question of whether unions are more analogous to eighteenth-century trustees or eighteenth-century lawyers have to do with whether jury or judge trial should be preferred as a matter of accuracy, fairness, legitimacy or cost?

Justice Brennan's test is probably easier to apply than the test applied in *Chauffeurs.* It may also make more sense as a practical matter. Justice Brennan's test would generally mean that a jury trial is available when monetary relief is sought, but not when injunctive or specific (i.e., specific performance) relief is sought. Moreover, the questions involved in granting injunctive or specific relief are often more subtle and multifaceted than those in granting monetary relief. Finally, relief usually presents a one-time, fairly straightforward question of how much A owes to B. Moreover, monetary relief is often backward-looking and its regulatory effects are indirect. Injunctive relief, in contrast, will directly regulate future real-world conduct. Not only are the regulatory stakes arguably higher, but injunctive or specific relief can present recurring questions because litigants sometimes seek modification or vacation of prior orders. A jury culled from the general population and sitting as a one-time event cannot provide effective ongoing supervision.

Why do you suppose there is no discussion of the desirability or practicality of jury trial in either the majority or dissenting opinions in the case? Do you suppose that the Justices have no views on those issues? Is it a virtue or vice of the historical test that it does not allow for discussion of those views?

3. **The right to jury trial under statutes prohibiting racial discrimination.** In Curtis v. Loether, 415 U.S. 189, 94 S.Ct. 1005, 39 L.Ed.2d 260 (1974), the Court upheld a right to jury trial in a damage action under Title VIII of the Civil Rights Act of 1968, 42 U.S.C. § 3612, which forbids racial discrimination in housing. The Court, in an opinion by Justice Marshall, held:

> A damages action under the statute sounds basically in tort—the statute merely defines a new legal duty, and authorizes the courts to compensate a plaintiff for the injury caused by the defendant's wrongful breach. As the Court of Appeals noted, this cause of action is analogous to a number of tort actions recognized at common law. More important, the relief sought here—actual and punitive damages—is the traditional form of relief offered in the courts of law.

Id. at 195–96. White defendant landlords, rather than the black would-be tenant, had sought the jury trial. The Court recognized "the possibility that jury prejudice may deprive a victim of discrimination of the verdict to which he or she is entitled," but found the decision controlled by "the clear command of the Seventh Amendment." Id. at 198.

Title VII of the Civil Rights Act of 1964 forbids racial discrimination in employment. 42 U.S.C. § 2000e et seq. The Supreme Court has repeatedly declined to say whether there is a right to jury trial in a suit for back pay under Title VII. See Landgraf v. USI Film Prods., 511 U.S. 244, 252 n.4, 114 S.Ct. 1483, 128 L.Ed.2d 229 (1994); Lytle v. Household Mfg., Inc., 494 U.S. 545, 549 n.1, 110 S.Ct. 1331, 108 L.Ed.2d 504 (1990); Lorillard v. Pons, 434 U.S. 575, 581–82, 98 S.Ct. 866, 55 L.Ed.2d 40 (1978); Curtis v. Loether, 415 U.S. 189, 196–97, 94 S.Ct. 1005, 1009–10, 39 L.Ed.2d 260 (1974). The lower federal courts have generally held that there is no right to jury trial in Title VII back pay suits. See, e.g., Keller v. Prince George's County, 827 F.2d 952 (4th Cir. 1987), Johnson v. Georgia Highway Express, 417 F.2d 1122 (5th Cir. 1969). In 1991, Congress provided by statute for jury trial in Title VII cases for compensatory and punitive damages. (Compensatory damages, as defined in the statute, do not include back pay.) 42 U.S.C. § 1981a(c). Do you suppose that Justice Marshall's reluctance to embrace Justice Brennan's approach has anything to do with concern about its effect on the right to jury trial in Title VII cases seeking back pay relief?

NOTE ON CONGRESSIONAL POWER TO REQUIRE NON-JURY TRIAL BEFORE AN ADMINISTRATIVE OR LEGISLATIVE TRIBUNAL

1.   **Administrative and legislative tribunals.** Article III of the Constitution, the so-called "judicial article," authorizes the creation of federal courts. Article III courts include the U.S. district courts, courts of appeal, and Supreme Court. Article III judges have constitutionally guaranteed life tenure "during good behavior," and constitutional protection against diminution in salary. However, for practical reasons and in particular circumstances, Congress has created "administrative" and "legislative" courts outside the strictures of Article III. Administrative courts are courts within federal administrative agencies. Such courts may adjudicate regulatory violations and award sanctions or, as in the case of the Social Security Administration, they may decide disputed claims for benefits. Legislative courts are nonadministrative courts with specialized geographical or subject matter jurisdictions. Specialized geographical courts exist in the District of Columbia and some federal territories. Specialized subject matter courts include the Tax Court and the U.S. Claims Court. The magistrate courts and the bankruptcy courts are subordinate to the federal district courts and have specialized jurisdictions. Judges appointed to non-Article III courts have statutorily, but not constitutionally, guaranteed terms in office and salaries.

2.   **No right to jury trial in government enforcement actions before an administrative tribunal.** The growth of the administrative state and proliferation of federal agencies with the power to inflict civil penalties present a complicated Seventh Amendment problem. On several occasions, the Court has had to address whether such regulatory schemes are inconsistent with the Seventh Amendment.

In NLRB v. Jones & Laughlin Steel Corp., 301 U.S. 1, 57 S.Ct. 615, 81 L.Ed. 893 (1937), the Court approved the administrative scheme set up to regulate unfair labor practices by the National Labor Relations Act. Under the Act, Congress created an administrative tribunal, the National Labor Relations Board, to determine whether a defendant had committed an unfair labor practice and to award the remedy of back pay if appropriate. Defendant Jones & Laughlin contended that this scheme deprived it of its Seventh Amendment right to a jury trial. The Court rejected this argument, stating that: "The instant case is not a suit at common law or in the nature of such a suit. The proceeding is one unknown to the common law. *It is a statutory proceeding.* Reinstatement of the employee and payment for time lost *are requirements [administratively] imposed for violation of the statute and are remedies appropriate to its enforcement.* The contention under the Seventh Amendment is without merit." Id. at 48–49.

In Atlas Roofing Co. v. Occupational Safety and Health Review Commission, 430 U.S. 442, 97 S.Ct. 1261, 51 L.Ed.2d 464 (1977), the Supreme Court reaffirmed this view. Atlas Roofing involved the Occupational Safety and Health Act of 1974 (OSHA). The Act allowed Department of Labor inspectors to determine whether employers were in violation of the Act and issue an abatement order and a civil monetary penalty. An alleged violator could appeal the inspector's determination to an administrative law judge, and then to the Occupational Health and Safety Review Commission, and then to the appropriate federal court of appeals. In reviewing the Commission's decision, the court of appeals is required to consider conclusive the Commission's findings of fact, so long as they are "supported by substantial evidence." Atlas Roofing contended that this scheme deprived it of its right to a jury trial. The Supreme Court disagreed unanimously. Writing for the Court, Justice White held:

> [W]hen Congress creates new statutory "public rights," it may assign their adjudication to an administrative agency with which a jury trial would be incompatible, without violating the Seventh Amendment's injunction that jury trial is to be "preserved" in "suits at common law." Congress is not required by the Seventh Amendment to choke the already crowded federal courts with new types of litigation or prevented from committing some new types of litigation to administrative agencies with special competence in the relevant field. This is the case even if the Seventh Amendment would have required a jury where the adjudication of those rights is assigned to a federal court of law instead of an administrative agency.

The Court founded its ruling on the historical argument that factfinding "was never the exclusive province of the jury under either the English or American legal systems at the time of the adoption of the Seventh Amendment; and the question whether a fact would be found by a jury turned to a considerable degree on the nature of the forum in which a litigant found himself." Because tribunals that did not use juries were ubiquitous when the Seventh Amendment was written, it could not be that the Congress is now powerless to create tribunals that do not use juries to find facts.

3. Defining public and private rights in administrative tribunals. If Congress can avoid a jury by the expedient of assigning a dispute to an administrative agency, is Congress free to evade the Seventh Amendment at will? The Court's answer in *Atlas Roofing* is that if a case involves a "public right," Congress is free to assign it to an administrative agency without trial by jury.

When the Supreme Court has focused specifically on whether Congress has the power to eliminate the right to trial by jury at the same time that it assigns cases to an administrative tribunal, the Court has offered two different conceptions of "public rights." The first, and narrower, conception is that public rights are limited to the definition offered in *Atlas Roofing*—cases in which the government is involved as a party in its sovereign capacity enforcing a federal statute. This definition of public rights would prohibit, for example, the establishment of an administrative tribunal in which private plaintiffs were required to try occupational injury claims against their employers.

At times, however, the Court has expressed a broader conception. In Granfinanciera, S.A. v. Nordberg, 492 U.S. 33, 109 S.Ct. 2782, 106 L.Ed.2d 26 (1989), the Court stated, in dictum, that Congress may dispense with trial by jury in all cases "involving statutory rights that are integral parts of a public regulatory scheme and whose adjudication Congress has assigned to an administrative agency or specialized court of equity [that is, a bankruptcy court]. Whatever terminological distinctions *Atlas Roofing* may have suggested, we now refer to those rights as 'public' rather than 'private.' " 492 U.S. at 55 n.10. This definition would seem to allow Congress to assign traditionally jury triable private claims to trial in an administrative agency provided that Congress had reenacted the claim as a federal statutory right and assigned it to a federal administrative tribunal as part of an effort to reform or systematize the operation of the law in the field.

Finally, in construing the arguably different question of the scope of congressional power to assign public rights cases to administrative courts in "a particularized area of law," the Court has held that such an assignment can also encompass related common law claims, like claims for damages for breach of contract, even though those claims are "private" and have historically been jury triable as of right. Commodity Futures Trading Comm'n v. Schor, 478 U.S. 833, 106 S.Ct. 3245, 92 L.Ed.2d 675 (1986). The *Schor* Court did not, however, give any express consideration to the Seventh Amendment implications of its holding or the tension between that holding and its prior formulations of the term "public rights."

4.   *Atlas Roofing* not applicable to "legislative" courts. The principle of *Atlas Roofing* applies to administrative courts, but not to non-Article III "legislative" courts. In Pernell v. Southall Realty, 416 U.S. 363, 94 S.Ct. 1723, 40 L.Ed.2d 198 (1974), the Court held that there was a Seventh Amendment right to jury trial in an action to recover real property in the courts of the District of Columbia. The troublesome question in the case had been whether an action to recover real property is an action at law, and therefore within the Seventh Amendment jury trial guarantee. The Supreme Court assumed without discussion that the Seventh Amendment applied to civil suits in the courts of the District of Columbia, even though they are non-Article III legislative courts.

5.   Additional reading. For criticism of *Atlas Roofing*, see Kirst, Administrative Penalties and the Civil Jury: The Supreme Court's Assault on the Seventh Amendment, 126 U. Pa. L. Rev. 1281 (1978). For a vigorous argument that the Supreme Court's distinction between private rights and public rights suits is without historical foundation, see Redish & LaFave, Seventh Amendment Right to Jury Trial in Non-Article III Proceedings: A Study in Dysfunctional Constitutional Theory, 4 Wm. & Mary Bill Rts. J. 407 (1995).

3. FUNCTIONAL CONSIDERATIONS IN DETERMINING THE SCOPE OF THE RIGHT TO JURY TRIAL: THE DISTINCTIVE COMPETENCIES OF JUDGE AND JURY

Robert MacCoun, Inside the Black Box: What Empirical Research Tells Us About Decisionmaking by Civil Juries[*]

Several legal scholars have pointed out that the appropriate standard by which to evaluate the quality of jury performance is not some absolute benchmark of perfection, but rather the performance of the most likely alternative factfinder, the trial judge. Or, to extend this argument, the arbitrator, or the expert tribunal. In this section, I will review the limited research that is available on this question.

One approach is to compare verdicts in bench trials and in jury trials. David Rottman's recent study of state courts found that across all tort cases, mean and median awards were larger for juries than for judges. Moreover, awards were considerably more variable in jury trials than in bench trials. Rottman did not attribute these results to judge-jury differences in decisionmaking, however; he argued that the differences are probably attributable to differences in case factors that determine litigants' choice of forum. In another study, Donald Wittman compared jury and arbitration awards and found that juries were more variable than arbitrators. Like Rottman, he noted that forum selection processes could make juries look more unpredictable, even if, ceteris paribus, they were equally inconsistent.

A fascinating new study by Kevin Clermont and Theodore Eisenberg contrasts plaintiff win rates in federal civil bench trials and in federal civil jury trials. The authors argue that their data refute both popular and academic views. The popular view is that juries are pro-plaintiff, suggesting that the ratio of plaintiff victories at bench trial and at jury trial ("the win ratio") should be [less] than 1.00. The academic view following [the logic that easy cases settle and only close (i.e., 50–50) cases are tried], is that the win ratio should equal 1.00 because [in both judge and jury-tried cases only the very close 50–50 cases should go to trial, resulting in equal numbers of plaintiffs' and defendants' wins.] In fact, Clermont and Eisenberg found that the win ratio was 1.15 for motor vehicle torts, 1.71 for products liability torts, and 1.72 for medical malpractice torts. In other words, plaintiffs won more cases before judges than before juries. Does this mean that juries actually have a pro-defendant bias in civil cases? Like Rottman and Wittman, Clermont and Eisenberg point out that such results could be caused by the case selection processes that determine whether a case is settled, taken to a judge, or taken to a jury. They raise three possibilities: same treatment but different cases; different treatment but same cases; or different treatment and different cases. Their analyses argue for the latter, but they acknowledge that these results are not yet fully understood.

One way of getting around the selection problem is to examine how juries and other factfinders decide the same cases. Kalven and Zeisel's seminal University of Chicago Jury Project compared the verdicts of

---

[*]   In Verdict: Assessing the Civil Jury System 137, 164–169 (R. Litan ed. 1993).

juries with the verdicts that trial judges reported they would have rendered had they tried the case. Kalven and Zeisel found that judges agreed with the jury's verdict about 80 percent of the time and that judges were as likely to agree with juries in complex cases as in simpler cones. In the cases where both agreed that the defendant was liable, 23 percent of the time the jury awarded more, 17 percent of the time the judge said he would have awarded more, and only 4 percent of the time were they in close agreement. On average, the jury awards were 20 percent higher than those the judges would have recommended. Juries found against corporations only 2 percent more often than did judges, but when corporations were liable, juries awarded 25 percent more. One drawback of this study is that judges did not render their verdict recommendations prior to learning the jury's verdict; it is possible that their responses partially reflect their attitudes toward the jury system in addition to their evaluation of the cases at hand.

* * *

Two recent studies have directly compared decisionmaking by college students and trial judges in the same fictitious cases. One study, discussed earlier, found no differences between these groups in evaluations of blameworthiness, although legal liability judgments were not assessed. In a recent set of experiments on the evaluation of statistical evidence, Gary Wells found a remarkable convergence of liability verdicts for college students and for trial judges. Students and judges not only responded almost identically to the same evidence; they also reacted almost identically to experimental *variations* in the evidence. Wells found that many judges demonstrated fallacious statistical reasoning of the sort that has been documented with students and other populations.

A limitation of many of these studies is that they rarely compare the processes by which juries, judges and arbitrators make decisions. This makes it difficult to draw any inferences about fact finding competence from their findings, for agreement rates tell us nothing about relative or absolute accuracy. Future research might overcome this limitation by assessing factfinding performance using direct measures of accuracy, such as the amount and accuracy of information recalled, comprehension of expert testimony, and so forth. Although we know that jurors can make mistakes, no solid evidence suggests that they are less competent than judges as fact finders, and juries might conceivably be more competent at some tasks.

Some readers will greet with some skepticism the notion that juries might out perform judges. After all, judges are drawn from a more restrictive population than jurors, they are specially trained in the law, and they quickly accumulate a great deal more trial experience than most jurors are ever likely to get. But unlike judges (in the typical bench trial), jurors perform in groups rather than individually. Social psychologists have been comparing individual and group performance for decades, and considerable evidence shows that groups outperform individuals on a variety of intellectual tasks, including recall of factual material, generation of solutions to problems, and correction of errors. Of course, these studies typically compared the average performance of individuals and groups sampled from the same population, which is analogous to comparing a single juror to a group of jurors or a single judge to a group of judges. Nonetheless, the heterogeneity of the jury might be a benefit in complex cases. Juries might actually be better suited than judges for coping with some dimensions of complex litigation.

      * * *

A reasoned evaluation of civil-jury performance should be premised on explicit performance criteria. Scholars have identified a variety of standards that legal experts and lay citizens have used to evaluate jury performance. I have summarized and integrated these criteria in Figure 5–1. [The standards summarized by Professor MacCoun are representativeness, impartiality, legal competence, accuracy of decision, consistency of decision, dispute resolution, legitimacy, and efficiency.]

These criteria aren't completely independent of each other; instead, they are loosely coupled. For example, high accuracy would seem to imply high consistency (but only if we know which cases to compare), whereas high consistency needn't imply high accuracy. Fact finding competence and impartiality are presumably prerequisites for accuracy, but we can rarely assess decision accuracy directly; indeed, if we knew the right verdict, we wouldn't need a jury. Thus we use other criteria as imperfect proxies for accuracy. When the correct answer isn't known, citizens tend to evaluate legal decisions in terms of the apparent fairness of the procedures that produced them.

Given what we know so far, what's my scorecard for figure 5–1? This is a judgment call involving some speculation beyond existing data, but based upon what we now know, I would give judges the edge on legal competence and efficiency, but juries the edge on representativeness, dispute resolution and legitimacy. Factfinding competence, decision consistency, and decision accuracy are uncertain, but I would expect groups to outperform individuals, the average judge to outperform the average juror, and the appropriate expert to outperform the average judge and the average juror. Thus juries should outperform jurors, judicial panels should outperform judges, and expert panels should outperform lone experts, but it is anybody's guess how juries stack up against lone experts or lone judges. *Impartiality* is a question mark. I've cited evidence that jurors are vulnerable to extralegal biases, but we know that judges are also vulnerable in this regard, even with the best of intentions.

NOTE ON THE STRENGTHS OF THE JURY AND THE JURISPRUDENCE OF JURY SIZE AND UNANIMITY

1. **Empirical evidence on the relative performance of judges and juries.** A significant number of scholars have expressed a view of the relative performance of judges and juries similar to, or in some cases, even more optimistic than that expressed by Professor MacCoun. See, e.g., Vidmar, The Performance of the American Civil Jury: An Empirical Perspective, 40 Ariz. L. Rev. 849 (1998). This is true even in relatively specialized fields, such as medical malpractice. Struve, Doctors, the Adversary System, and Procedural Reform of Medical Liability Litigation, 72 Fordham L. Rev. 943 (2004) (summarizing data showing agreement between assessments of juries and doctors on medical liability); Vidmar, 40 Ariz. L. Rev. at 884–85 (describing agreement between juror and lawyer assessment of pain and suffering awards). An emergent view questions

whether juries fully realize the claimed advantages of group decision making, arguing that group polarization of the deliberative process may sometimes cause the jury to reach extreme results, results more severe than the view of any single group member. See David Schkade et al., Deliberating About Dollars: The Severity Shift, 100 Colum. L. Rev. 1139 (2000) (showing that jury deliberations can result in punitive damage awards higher than the award originally preferred by the median jury member.) For discussion, see Cass Sunstein, Group Judgments: Deliberation, Statistical Means, and Information Markets, 80 N.Y.U. L. Rev. 962 (2005).

2. **Traditional twelve-person unanimous jury.** At common law, the traditional jury was composed of twelve people who were required to reach a unanimous verdict, in both criminal and civil cases. In the past several decades, both the size and unanimity traditions have been seriously eroded.

3. **Size.** One setting where the Seventh Amendment has encountered the social science of jury behavior is the question of jury size. Many states now use juries of fewer than twelve people. Since the constitutional guarantee of the Seventh Amendment does not apply to the states, there is no federal constitutional requirement that the states have civil juries, let alone juries of a certain size. In practice, many states have civil juries of fewer than twelve; six jurors is the most common number. In Williams v. Florida, 399 U.S. 78, 90 S.Ct. 1893, 26 L.Ed.2d 446 (1970), the Supreme Court upheld the constitutionality of a state's use of a six-person jury in a criminal case. But six is the lower limit. See Ballew v. Georgia, 435 U.S. 223, 98 S.Ct. 1029, 55 L.Ed.2d 234 (1978) (holding unconstitutional a state criminal jury of five persons).

In Colgrove v. Battin, 413 U.S. 149, 93 S.Ct. 2448, 37 L.Ed.2d 522 (1973), the Supreme Court, in a five-to-four decision, upheld the constitutionality of a six-person civil jury in federal court: "[B]y referring to the 'common law,' the Framers of the Seventh Amendment were concerned with preserving the *right* of trial by jury in civil cases where it existed at common law, rather than the various incidents of trial by jury." Id. at 155–56. On the question whether six was too few, the Court wrote, "We had no difficulty reaching the conclusion in *Williams* that a jury of six would guarantee an accused the trial by jury secured by Art. III and the Sixth Amendment. Significantly, our determination that there was 'no discernible difference between the results reached by the two different-sized juries' drew largely on the results of studies of the operations of juries of six in civil cases. Since then, much has been written about the six-member jury, but nothing that persuades us to depart from the conclusion reached in *Williams*." Id. at 158–59.

The Court's conclusion in *Colegrove v. Battin* that there is "no discernible difference" between six- and twelve-person juries has been discredited. The best available evidence suggests that larger juries are more likely than smaller juries to remember and understand evidence and instructions, less likely to render extreme verdicts at the high or low end, and much more likely to be representative of the communities from which they are drawn. Hans, The Power of Twelve: The Impact of Jury Size and Unanimity on Jury Decision Making, 4 Del. L. Rev. 1 (2001). In one study comparing eight- and twelve-member juries in California, 20% of eight-person juries included no African Americans, compared to 8.7% of the twelve-person juries, and 31% of the eight-person juries included no Hispanic jurors, compared to 19% of the twelve-person juries. Id. See also Rachlinski, The Story of *Colgrove*: Social Science on Trial, in Civil Procedure Stories 371, 379–80 (Clermont ed., 2004). For an eloquent argument, on historical and modern-day policy grounds, for the retention of the twelve-person civil jury, see Arnold, Trial by Jury: The Constitutional Right to a Jury of Twelve in Civil Trials, 22 Hofstra L. Rev. 1 (1993). Given Professor MacCoun's suggested criteria for evaluating the performance of the jury, isn't it quite clear that shifting from a twelve- to a six-person jury, while increasing efficiency, tends to erode many of the advantages that jury decision making may have over judicial decision making?

Federal Rule 48 provides that a jury shall be not fewer than six nor more than twelve. Under Rules 47 and 48, as amended in 1991, there are no alternate jurors. A juror may be excused for good cause at any time during trial or deliberations. Rule 47(c). Diminution in jury size is not grounds for mistrial unless the number of jurors falls below six. The Advisory Committee notes offer this advice: "[I]t will ordinarily be prudent and necessary, in order to provide for sickness or disability among jurors, to seat more than six jurors." All jurors who have heard the evidence and arguments will participate in the deliberations and verdict, even if that number turns out to be more than six. Unless the parties otherwise stipulate, no verdict may be taken from a jury that has been reduced to fewer than six. Fed. R. Civ. P. 48.

4. **Unanimity.** The Supreme Court has sustained the constitutionality of nonunanimous jury verdicts in state court criminal cases. See, e.g., Johnson v. Louisiana, 406 U.S. 356, 92 S.Ct. 1620, 32 L.Ed.2d 152 (1972) (9/12 majority of jurors constitutional); Apodaca v. Oregon, 406 U.S. 404, 92 S.Ct. 1628, 32 L.Ed.2d 184 (1972) (10/12 majority constitutional). But see Burch v. Louisiana, 441 U.S. 130, 99 S.Ct. 1623, 60 L.Ed.2d 96 (1979) (5/6 majority in a "nonpetty" offense unconstitutional). There is no federal constitutional requirement of any particular majority of jurors in state-court civil cases. Many states allow non-unanimous jury verdicts in civil cases. Zeisel, The Verdict of Five Out of Six Civil Jurors: Constitutional Problems, 1982 Am. B. Found. Res. J. 141, 155 (1982). See, e.g., Calif.C.Civ.P. §, 618 (three-fourths); N.Y.C.P.L.R. § 4113(a) (five-sixths). Studies suggest that relaxing the requirement of unanimity tends to weaken the position of those who hold minority positions on the jury, leads to less complete discussion of the evidence, and marginally decreases the number of hung juries. Hans, 4 Del. L. Rev. at 22–29.

Rule 48(a) requires unanimous verdicts in civil cases "[u]nless the parties stipulate otherwise." The requirement of unanimity in federal district courts applies even in diversity cases tried in states that permit nonunanimous verdicts. See, e.g., Masino v. Outboard Marine Corp., 652 F.2d 330 (3d Cir. 1981) (requiring unanimity of eight-person jury in diversity case when Pennsylvania permitted verdict by 5/6 majority).

Markman v. Westview Instruments, Inc.

Supreme Court of the United States, 1996.
517 U.S. 370, 116 S.Ct. 1384, 134 L.Ed.2d 577.

■ JUSTICE SOUTER delivered the opinion of the Court.

The question here is whether the interpretation of a so called patent claim, the portion of the patent document that defines the scope of the patentee's rights, is a matter of law reserved entirely for the court, or subject to a Seventh Amendment guarantee that a jury will determine the meaning of any disputed term of art about which expert testimony is offered. We hold that the construction of a patent, including terms of art within its claim, is exclusively within the province of the court.

I

The Constitution empowers Congress "to promote the Progress of Science and useful Arts, by securing for limited Times to Authors and Inventors the exclusive Right to their respective Writings and Discoveries." Art. I, § 8, cl. 8. Congress first exercised this authority in 1790, when it provided for the issuance of "letters patent," Act of Apr. 10, 1790, ch. 7, § 1, 1 Stat. 109, which, like their modern counterparts, granted inventors "the right to exclude others from making, using, offering for sale, selling, or importing the patented invention," in exchange for full disclosure of an invention. It has long been understood that a patent must describe the exact scope of an invention and its manufacture to "secure to [the patentee] all to which he is entitled, [and] to apprise the public of what is still open to them." Under the modern American system, these objectives are served by two distinct elements of a patent document. First, it contains a specification describing the invention "in such full, clear, concise, and exact terms as to enable any person skilled in the art . . . to make and use the same." Second, a patent includes one or more "claims," which "particularly poin[t] out and distinctly clai[m] the subject matter which the applicant regards as his invention." 35 U.S.C. § 112. "A claim covers and secures a process, a machine, a manufacture, a composition of matter, or a design, but never the function or result of either, nor the scientific explanation of their operation." The claim "define[s] the scope of a patent grant," and functions to forbid not only exact copies of an invention, but products that go to "the heart of an invention but avoids the literal language of the claim by making a noncritical change."[1] In this opinion, the word "claim" is used only in this sense peculiar to patent law.

Noted in class

Characteristically, patent lawsuits charge what is known as infringement, and rest on allegations that the defendant "without authority ma[de], used or [sold the] patented invention, within the United States during the term of the patent therefor. . . ." 35 U.S.C. § 271(a). Victory in an infringement suit requires a finding that the patent claim "covers the alleged infringer's product or process," which in turn necessitates a determination of "what the words in the claim mean."

product

Petitioner in this infringement suit, Markman, owns United States Reissue Patent No. 33,054 for his "Inventory Control and Reporting System for Drycleaning Stores." The patent describes a system that can monitor and report the status, location, and movement of clothing in a dry-cleaning establishment. The Markman system consists of a keyboard and data processor to generate written records for each transaction, including a bar code readable by optical detectors operated by employees,

---

[1] Thus, for example, a claim for a ceiling fan with three blades attached to a solid rod connected to a motor would not only cover fans that take precisely this form, but would also cover a similar fan that includes some additional feature, e. g., such a fan with a cord or switch for turning it on and off, and may cover a product deviating from the core design in some noncritical way, e. g., a three-bladed ceiling fan with blades attached to a hollow rod connected to a motor.

who log the progress of clothing through the dry-cleaning process. Respondent Westview's product also includes a keyboard and processor, and it lists charges for the dry-cleaning services on bar-coded tickets that can be read by portable optical detectors.

Markman brought an infringement suit against Westview and Althon Enterprises, an operator of dry-cleaning establishments using Westview's products (collectively, Westview). Westview responded that Markman's patent is not infringed by its system because the latter functions merely to record an inventory of receivables by tracking invoices and transaction totals, rather than to record and track an inventory of articles of clothing. Part of the dispute hinged upon the meaning of the word "inventory," a term found in Markman's independent claim 1, which states that Markman's product can "maintain an inventory total" and "detect and localize spurious additions to inventory." The case was tried before a jury, which heard, among others, a witness produced by Markman who testified about the meaning of the claim language.

After the jury compared the patent to Westview's device, it found an infringement of Markman's independent claim 1 and dependent claim 10.[2] The District Court nevertheless granted Westview's deferred motion for judgment as a matter of law, one of its reasons being that the term "inventory" in Markman's patent encompasses "both cash inventory and the actual physical inventory of articles of clothing." Under the trial court's construction of the patent, the production, sale, or use of a tracking system for dry cleaners would not infringe Markman's patent unless the product was capable of tracking articles of clothing throughout the cleaning process and generating reports about their status and location. Since Westview's system cannot do these things, the District Court directed a verdict on the ground that Westview's device does not have the "means to maintain an inventory total" and thus cannot "'detect and localize spurious additions to inventory as well as spurious deletions therefrom,'" as required by claim 1.

Markman appealed, arguing it was error for the District Court to substitute its construction of the disputed claim term "inventory" for the construction the jury had presumably given it. The United States Court of Appeals for the Federal Circuit affirmed, holding the interpretation of claim terms to be the exclusive province of the court and the Seventh Amendment to be consistent with that conclusion. Markman sought our review on each point, and we granted certiorari. We now affirm.

II

The Seventh Amendment provides that "in Suits at common law, where the value in controversy shall exceed twenty dollars, the right of trial by jury shall be preserved. . . ." U.S. Const., Amdt. 7. Since Justice Story's day, United States v. Wonson, 1 Gall. 5, 28 F. Cas. 745, 750 (No. 16,750) (CC Mass. 1812), we have understood that "the right of trial by jury thus preserved is the right which existed under the English common law when the Amendment was adopted." Baltimore & Carolina Line, Inc. v. Redman, 295 U.S. 654, 657, 79 L. Ed. 1636, 55 S.Ct. 890 (1935). In

---

[2] Dependent claim 10 specifies that, in the invention of claim 1, the input device is an alpha-numeric keyboard in which single keys may be used to enter the attributes of the items in question.

keeping with our longstanding adherence to this "historical test," Wolfram, The Constitutional History of the Seventh Amendment, 57 Minn. L. Rev. 639, 640–643 (1973), we ask, first, whether we are dealing with a cause of action that either was tried at law at the time of the founding or is at least analogous to one that was, see, e. g., Tull v. United States, 481 U.S. 412, 417, 95 L.Ed.2d 365, 107 S.Ct. 1831 (1987). If the action in question belongs in the law category, we then ask whether the particular trial decision must fall to the jury in order to preserve the substance of the common-law right as it existed in 1791.

A

As to the first issue, going to the character of the cause of action, "the form of our analysis is familiar. 'First we compare the statutory action to 18th-century actions brought in the courts of England prior to the merger of the courts of law and equity.'" Granfinanciera, S. A. v. Nordberg, 492 U.S. 33, 42, 106 L.Ed.2d 26, 109 S.Ct. 2782 (1989) (citation omitted). Equally familiar is the descent of today's patent infringement action from the infringement actions tried at law in the 18th century, and there is no dispute that infringement cases today must be tried to a jury, as their predecessors were more than two centuries ago. See, e. g., Bramah v. Hardcastle, 1 Carp. P. C. 168 (K. B. 1789).

B

This conclusion raises the second question, whether a particular issue occurring within a jury trial (here the construction of a patent claim) is itself necessarily a jury issue, the guarantee being essential to preserve the right to a jury's resolution of the ultimate dispute. In some instances the answer to this second question may be easy because of clear historical evidence that the very subsidiary question was so regarded under the English practice of leaving the issue for a jury. But when, as here, the old practice provides no clear answer, we are forced to make a judgment about the scope of the Seventh Amendment guarantee without the benefit of any foolproof test.

The Court has repeatedly said that the answer to the second question "must depend on whether the jury must shoulder this responsibility as necessary to preserve the 'substance of the common-law right of trial by jury.'" Tull v. United States, supra, at 426 (emphasis added) (quoting Colgrove v. Battin, 413 U.S. 149, 157, 37 L.Ed.2d 522, 93 S.Ct. 2448 (1973)); see also Baltimore & Carolina Line, supra, at 657. "'"Only those incidents which are regarded as fundamental, as inherent in and of the essence of the system of trial by jury, are placed beyond the reach of the legislature."'" Tull v. United States, supra, at 426 (citations omitted); see also Galloway v. United States, 319 U.S. 372, 392, 87 L. Ed. 1458, 63 S.Ct. 1077 (1943).

The "substance of the common-law right" is, however, a pretty blunt instrument for drawing distinctions. We have tried to sharpen it, to be sure, by reference to the distinction between substance and procedure. We have also spoken of the line as one between issues of fact and law.

But the sounder course, when available, is to classify a mongrel practice (like construing a term of art following receipt of evidence) by using the historical method, much as we do in characterizing the suits and actions within which they arise. Where there is no exact antecedent, the best hope lies in comparing the modern practice to earlier ones whose allocation to court or jury we do know, seeking the best analogy we can draw between an old and the new, see Tull v. United States, supra, at 420–421 (we must search the English common law for "appropriate analogies" rather than a "precisely analogous common-law cause of action").

C

"Prior to 1790 nothing in the nature of a claim had appeared either in British patent practice or in that of the American states," Lutz, Evolution of the Claims of U.S. Patents, 20 J. Pat. Off. Soc. 134 (1938), and we have accordingly found no direct antecedent of modern claim construction in the historical sources. Claim practice did not achieve statutory recognition until the passage of the Act of 1836, and inclusion of a claim did not become a statutory requirement until 1870; see 1 A. Deller, Patent Claims § 4, p. 9 (2d ed. 1971). Although, as one historian has observed, as early as 1850 "judges were . . . beginning to express more frequently the idea that in seeking to ascertain the invention 'claimed' in a patent the inquiry should be limited to interpreting the summary, or 'claim,' " Lutz, supra, at 145, "the idea that the claim is just as important if not more important than the description and drawings did not develop until the Act of 1870 or thereabouts." Deller, supra, § 4, at 9.

At the time relevant for Seventh Amendment analogies, in contrast, it was the specification, itself a relatively new development, H. Dutton, The Patent System and Inventive Activity During the Industrial Revolution, 1750–1852, pp. 75–76 (1984), that represented the key to the patent. Thus, patent litigation in that early period was typified by so-called novelty actions, testing whether "any essential part of [the patent had been] disclosed to the public before," and "enablement" cases, in which juries were asked to determine whether the specification described the invention well enough to allow members of the appropriate trade to reproduce it.

The closest 18th-century analogue of modern claim construction seems, then, to have been the construction of specifications, and as to that function the mere smattering of patent cases that we have from this period shows no established jury practice sufficient to support an argument by analogy that today's construction of a claim should be a guaranteed jury issue. Few of the case reports even touch upon the proper interpretation of disputed terms in the specifications at issue, and none demonstrates that the definition of such a term was determined by the jury. This absence of an established practice should not surprise us, given the primitive state of jury patent practice at the end of the 18th century, when juries were still new to the field. * * *

Markman seeks to supply what the early case reports lack in so many words by relying on decisions like Turner v. Winter, 1 T. R. 602, 99 Eng. Rep. 1274 (K. B. 1787), and Arkwright v. Nightingale, Dav. Pat. Cas. 37 (C. P. 1785), to argue that the 18th-century juries must have acted as definers of patent terms just to reach the verdicts we know they rendered in patent cases turning on enablement or novelty. But the conclusion simply does not follow. There is no more reason to infer that juries supplied plenary interpretation of written instruments in patent litigation than in other cases implicating the meaning of documentary terms, and we do know that in other kinds of cases during this period judges, not juries, ordinarily construed written documents.[7] The probability that the judges were doing the same thing in the patent litigation of the time is confirmed by the fact that as soon as the English reports did begin to describe the construction of patent documents, they show the judges construing the terms of the specifications. This evidence is in fact buttressed by cases from this Court; when they first reveal actual practice, the practice revealed is of the judge construing the patent. These indications of our patent practice are the more impressive for being all of a piece with what we know about the analogous contemporary practice of interpreting terms within a land patent, where it fell to the judge, not the jury, to construe the words.

D

Losing, then, on the contention that juries generally had interpretive responsibilities during the 18th century, Markman seeks a different anchor for analogy in the more modest contention that even if judges were charged with construing most terms in the patent, the art of defining terms of art employed in a specification fell within the province of the jury. Again, however, Markman has no authority from the period in question, but relies instead on the later case of Neilson v. Harford, Webs. Pat. Cas. 328 (Exch. 1841). There, an exchange between the judge and the lawyers indicated that although the construction of a patent was ordinarily for the court, id., at 349 (Alderson, B.), judges should "leav[e] the question of words of art to the jury," id., at 350 (Alderson, B.); see also id., at 370 (judgment of the court); Hill v. Evans, 4 De. G. F. & J. 288, 293–294, 45 Eng. Rep. 1195, 1197 (Ch. 1862). Without, however, in any way disparaging the weight to which Baron Alderson's view is entitled, the most we can say is that an English report more than 70 years after the time that concerns us indicates an exception to what probably had been occurring earlier.[9] In place of Markman's inference that this exceptional practice existed in 1791 there is at best only a possibility that it did, and for anything more than a possibility we have found no scholarly authority.

III

Since evidence of common-law practice at the time of the framing does not entail application of the Seventh Amendment's jury guarantee to the construction of the claim document, we must look elsewhere to

---

[7]   See, e. g., Devlin, Jury Trial of Complex Cases: English Practice at the Time of the Seventh Amendment, 80 Colum. L. Rev. 43, 75 (1980); Weiner, The Civil Jury Trial and the Law-Fact Distinction, 54 Calif. L. Rev. 1867, 1932 (1966). For example, one historian observed that it was generally the practice of judges in the late 18th century "to keep the construction of writings out of the jury's hands and reserve it for themselves," a "safeguard" designed to prevent a jury from "construing or refining it at pleasure." 9 J. Wigmore, Evidence § 2461, p. 194 (J. Chadbourn rev. ed. 1981) (emphasis in original; internal quotation marks omitted). The absence of any established practice supporting Markman's view is also shown by the disagreement between Justices Willis and Buller, reported in Macbeath v. Haldimand, 1 T. R. 173, 180–182, 99 Eng. Rep. 1036, 1040–1041 (K. B. 1786), as to whether juries could ever construe written documents when their meaning was disputed.

[9]   In explaining that judges generally construed all terms in a written document at the end of the 18th century, one historian observed that "interpretation by local usage for example (today the plainest case of legitimate deviation from the normal standard) was still but making its way." 9 Wigmore, Evidence § 2461, at 195; see also id., at 195, and n. 6 (providing examples of this practice). We need not in any event consider here whether our conclusion that the Seventh Amendment does not require terms of art in patent claims to be submitted to the jury supports a similar result in other types of cases.

characterize this determination of meaning in order to allocate it as between court or jury. We accordingly consult existing precedent[10] and consider both the relative interpretive skills of judges and juries and the statutory policies that ought to be furthered by the allocation.

A

The two elements of a simple patent case, construing the patent and determining whether infringement occurred, were characterized by the former patent practitioner, Justice Curtis. "The first is a question of law, to be determined by the court, construing the letters-patent, and the description of the invention and specification of claim annexed to them. The second is a question of fact, to be submitted to a jury." Winans v. Denmead, [56 U.S. 330, 338, 15 HOW 330, 338, 14 L. Ed. 717 (1854)]; see Winans v. New York & Erie R. Co., supra, at 100; Hogg v. Emerson, supra, at 484; cf. Parker v. Hulme, supra, at 1140.

In arguing for a different allocation of responsibility for the first question, Markman relies primarily on two cases, Bischoff v. Wethered, 76 U.S. 812, 9 Wall. 812, 19 L. Ed. 829 (1870), and Tucker v. Spalding, 80 U.S. 453, 13 Wall. 453, 20 L. Ed. 515 (1872). These are said to show that evidence of the meaning of patent terms was offered to 19th-century juries, and thus to imply that the meaning of a documentary term was a jury issue whenever it was subject to evidentiary proof. That is not what Markman's cases show, however.

* * * *

Bischoff does not then, as Markman contends, hold that the use of expert testimony about the meaning of terms of art requires the judge to submit the question of their construction to the jury. It is instead a case in which the Court drew a line between issues of document interpretation and product identification, and held that expert testimony was properly presented to the jury on the latter, ultimate issue, whether the physical objects produced by the patent were identical. The Court did not see the decision as bearing upon the appropriate treatment of disputed terms. As the opinion emphasized, the Court's "view of the case is not intended to, and does not, trench upon the doctrine that the construction of written instruments is the province of the court alone. It is not the construction of the instrument, but the character of the thing invented, which is sought in questions of identity and diversity of inventions." Id., at 816 (emphasis added). *Tucker*, the second case proffered by Markman, is to the same effect. Its reasoning rested expressly on *Bischoff*, and it just as clearly noted that in addressing the ultimate issue of mixed fact and law, it was for the court to "lay down to the jury the law which should govern them." *Tucker, supra*, at 455.

If the line drawn in these two opinions is a fine one, it is one that the Court has drawn repeatedly in explaining the respective roles of the jury and judge in patent cases, and one understood by commentators writing

---

[10]   Because we conclude that our precedent supports classifying the question as one for the court, we need not decide either the extent to which the Seventh Amendment can be said to have crystallized a law/fact distinction, cf. Ex parte Peterson, 253 U.S. 300, 310, 64 L. Ed. 919, 40 S.Ct. 543 (1920); Walker v. New Mexico & Southern Pacific R. Co., 165 U.S. 593, 597, 41 L. Ed. 837, 17 S.Ct. 421 (1897), or whether post-1791 precedent classifying an issue as one of fact would trigger the protections of the Seventh Amendment if (unlike this case) there were no more specific reason for decision.

in the aftermath of the cases Markman cites. Walker, for example, read *Bischoff* as holding that the question of novelty is not decided by a construction of the prior patent, "but depends rather upon the outward embodiment of the terms contained in the [prior patent]; and that such outward embodiment is to be properly sought, like the explanation of latent ambiguities arising from the description of external things, by evidence in pais." A. Walker, Patent Laws § 75, p. 68 (3d ed. 1895). He also emphasized in the same treatise that matters of claim construction, even those aided by expert testimony, are questions for the court:

> "Questions of construction are questions of law for the judge, not questions of fact for the jury. As it cannot be expected, however, that judges will always possess the requisite knowledge of the meaning of the terms of art or science used in letters patent, it often becomes necessary that they should avail themselves of the light furnished by experts relevant to the significance of such words and phrases. The judges are not, however, obliged to blindly follow such testimony." Id., § 189, at 173 (footnotes omitted).

* * * *

In sum, neither *Bischoff* nor *Tucker* indicates that juries resolved the meaning of terms of art in construing a patent, and neither case undercuts Justice Curtis's authority.

B

Where history and precedent provide no clear answers, functional considerations also play their part in the choice between judge and jury to define terms of art. We said in Miller v. Fenton, 474 U.S. 104, 114, 88 L.Ed.2d 405, 106 S.Ct. 445 (1985), that when an issue "falls somewhere between a pristine legal standard and a simple historical fact, the fact/law distinction at times has turned on a determination that, as a matter of the sound administration of justice, one judicial actor is better positioned than another to decide the issue in question." So it turns out here, for judges, not juries, are the better suited to find the acquired meaning of patent terms.

The construction of written instruments is one of those things that judges often do and are likely to do better than jurors unburdened by training in exegesis. Patent construction in particular "is a special occupation, requiring, like all others, special training and practice. The judge, from his training and discipline, is more likely to give a proper interpretation to such instruments than a jury; and he is, therefore, more likely to be right, in performing such a duty, than a jury can be expected to be." Parker v. Hulme, 18 F. Cas. at 1140. Such was the understanding nearly a century and a half ago, and there is no reason to weigh the respective strengths of judge and jury differently in relation to the modern claim; quite the contrary, for "the claims of patents have become highly technical in many respects as the result of special doctrines relating to the proper form and scope of claims that have been developed by the courts and the Patent Office." Woodward, Definiteness and Particularity in Patent Claims, 46 Mich. L. Rev. 755, 765 (1948).

Markman would trump these considerations with his argument that a jury should decide a question of meaning peculiar to a trade or profession simply because the question is a subject of testimony requiring credibility determinations, which are the jury's forte. It is, of course, true that credibility judgments have to be made about the experts who testify in patent cases, and in theory there could be a case in which a simple credibility judgment would suffice to choose between experts whose testimony was equally consistent with a patent's internal logic. But our own experience with document construction leaves us doubtful that trial courts will run into many cases like that. In the main, we expect, any credibility determinations will be subsumed within the necessarily sophisticated analysis of the whole document, required by the standard construction rule that a term can be defined only in a way that comports with the instrument as a whole. Thus, in these cases a jury's capabilities to evaluate demeanor, cf. Miller, supra, at 114, 117, to sense the "mainsprings of human conduct," Commissioner v. Duberstein, 363 U.S. 278, 289, 4 L.Ed.2d 1218, 80 S.Ct. 1190 (1960), or to reflect community standards, United States v. McConney, 728 F.2d 1195, 1204 (CA9 1984) (en banc), are much less significant than a trained ability to evaluate the testimony in relation to the overall structure of the patent. The decisionmaker vested with the task of construing the patent is in the better position to ascertain whether an expert's proposed definition fully comports with the specification and claims and so will preserve the patent's internal coherence. We accordingly think there is sufficient reason to treat construction of terms of art like many other responsibilities that we cede to a judge in the normal course of trial, notwithstanding its evidentiary underpinnings.

C

Finally, we see the importance of uniformity in the treatment of a given patent as an independent reason to allocate all issues of construction to the court. As we noted in General Elec. Co. v. Wabash Appliance Corp., 304 U.S. 364, 369, 82 L. Ed. 1402, 58 S.Ct. 899 (1938), "the limits of a patent must be known for the protection of the patentee, the encouragement of the inventive genius of others and the assurance that the subject of the patent will be dedicated ultimately to the public." Otherwise, a "zone of uncertainty which enterprise and experimentation may enter only at the risk of infringement claims would discourage invention only a little less than unequivocal foreclosure of the field," United Carbon Co. v. Binney & Smith Co., 317 U.S. 228, 236, 87 L. Ed. 232, 63 S.Ct. 165 (1942), and "the public [would] be deprived of rights supposed to belong to it, without being clearly told what it is that limits these rights." Merrill v. Yeomans, 94 U.S. 568, 573, 24 L. Ed. 235 (1877). It was just for the sake of such desirable uniformity that Congress created the Court of Appeals for the Federal Circuit as an exclusive appellate court for patent cases, H. R. Rep. No. 97–312, pp. 20–23 (1981), observing that increased uniformity would "strengthen the United States patent system in such a way as to foster technological growth and industrial innovation." Id., at 20.

Uniformity would, however, be ill served by submitting issues of document construction to juries. Making them jury issues would not, to be sure, necessarily leave evidentiary questions of meaning wide open in every new court in which a patent might be litigated, for principles of issue preclusion would ordinarily foster uniformity. Cf. Blonder-Tongue Laboratories, Inc. v. University of Ill. Foundation, 402 U.S. 313, 28 L.Ed.2d 788, 91 S.Ct. 1434 (1971). But whereas issue preclusion could not be asserted against new and independent infringement defendants even within a given jurisdiction, treating interpretive issues as purely legal will promote (though it will not guarantee) intrajurisdictional certainty through the application of stare decisis on those questions not yet subject to interjurisdictional uniformity under the authority of the single appeals court.

    * * *

Accordingly, we hold that the interpretation of the word "inventory" in this case is an issue for the judge, not the jury, and affirm the decision of the Court of Appeals for the Federal Circuit.

It is so ordered.

NOTE ON "THE PRACTICAL ABILITIES AND LIMITATIONS OF JURIES" AS A FACTOR DETERMINING THE SCOPE OF THE JURY TRIAL RIGHT

1. **The practical abilities and limitations of juries.** In Ross v. Bernhard, 396 U.S. 531, 538 n.10, 90 S.Ct. 733, 24 L.Ed.2d 729 (1970), the Supreme Court stated that whether an issue was "legal" and hence jury triable as of right was determined "by considering, first, the pre-merger custom with reference to such questions; second, the remedy sought; and, third, the practical abilities and limitations of juries." The last of these factors is not consistently mentioned, let alone taken into account, in subsequent Seventh Amendment decisions. But it has sometimes played a role in the Court's jurisprudence, most prominently in *Markman*. The practical effect of *Markman* upon an infringement claim for money damages is to create a bifurcated proceeding: the trial court holds an initial hearing to determine the scope of the patent claim and then there is a separate trial before the jury to determine whether the claim has been infringed and the amount of damages.

Is it so clear that the historical impasse outlined in *Markman* is real? After all, in *Chauffeurs v. Terry,* a majority of the Justices agreed that the most important (or in Justice Brennan's case, the decisive) factor in determining the scope of the jury trial right is the remedy sought. Does the Court in *Markman* give any weight at all to the fact that the plaintiff was seeking money damages? Should it have done so? Assuming that there was in fact no clear answer in the historical record, is it so clear that the judge is the superior decisionmaker? As the Court admits, claim construction typically involves competing testimony from expert witnesses. Moreover, it determines the scope of a lawful monopoly. Is there an argument for allowing the jury to make that decision? Is *Markman* further evidence that the populist preference for jury trial reflected in *Beacon Theaters* is no longer an active element of Seventh Amendment jurisprudence?

2. **Superior judicial competence and congressional power to require trial to the court.** In Tull v. United States, 81 U.S. 412, 107 S.Ct. 1831, 95 L.Ed.2d 365 (1987), the issue was whether the a defendant in an action seeking civil fines for violation of the federal Clean Water Act had a right to jury trial on the issues of liability and remedy. The Court found that the closest common-law analogy to an action for statutory penalties was an action for debt. It further held that "a civil penalty was a type of remedy at common law that could only be enforced in courts of law." Id. at 422. It held,

unanimously, that the issue of *liability* for a fine was jury triable as of right. But it then held that Congress had the power to require judicial determination of the *amount* of the penalty, notwithstanding the Seventh Amendment. The Court stated that the Seventh Amendment was "silent on the question whether a jury must determine the remedy in a trial in which it must determine liability." Id. at 425–26. It then held, citing *Colgrove v. Battin*, that the jury's determination of the amount of the penalty was not essential to preserve "the substance of the common law-right of trial by jury." Id. at 426. The Court reasoned that:

> Congress' assignment of the determination of the amount of civil penalties to trial judges * * * does not infringe on the constitutional right to a jury trial. Since Congress itself may fix the civil penalties, it may delegate that determination to trial judges. In this case, highly discretionary calculations that take into account multiple factors are necessary in order to set civil penalties under the Clean Water Act. These are the kinds of calculations traditionally performed by judges. We therefore hold that a determination of a civil penalty is not an essential function of a jury trial, and that the Seventh Amendment does not require a jury trial for that purpose in a civil action.

Id. at 426–27.

In Feltner v. Columbia Pictures Television, Inc., 523 U.S. 340, 118 S.Ct. 1279, 140 L.Ed.2d 438 (1998), plaintiff sought statutory damages under the federal Copyright Act. As in *Tull*, there was no dispute about the constitutional right to a jury determination of liability. The disputed point was whether the jury must also determine the amount. Although, as in *Tull*, the relevant legislation, Section 504(c)(1) of the Copyright Act, provided for determination of damages by "the court," the Supreme Court held that the Seventh Amendment required that the determination of the amount of statutory damages be made by a jury. The Court distinguished *Tull* on two grounds. First, in contrast to the silence of the historical record in *Tull*, the historical evidence showed clearly that eighteenth-century English juries had determined the amount of damages in copyright cases. Second, "the awarding of civil penalties to the Government could be viewed as analogous to sentencing in a criminal proceeding. * * * Here, of course, there is no similar analogy." Id. at 355. Can *Tull* and *Feltner* be reconciled so easily? The distinction drawn between the two cases based upon the alleged analogy between the judge's power to determine the amount of a civil penalty in *Tull* and the judge's power to determine a criminal sentence seems doubtful, particularly in the wake of Supreme Court decisions holding that all facts relied upon by the judge as a basis for increasing a criminal sentence must be found by a jury. Blakely v. Washington, 542 U.S. 296, 124 S.Ct. 2531, 159 L.Ed.2d 403 (2004). Is it a viable distinction that *Tull* involved fines whose level depended upon multiple factors and were administered as part of a complex regulatory regime? Or should *Tull* now be viewed as a case, like *Markman*, where the judge's presumed superior competence simply served as a tie breaker when the historical evidence was indeterminate?

3. **A possible complexity exception to the Seventh Amendment.** The Supreme Court has not decided whether there is a complexity exception to the Seventh Amendment. In *Dairy Queen v. Wood*, supra p. 914, n. 3, the Supreme Court held out the possibility that the accounting sought by Dairy Queen would be cognizable in equity if

" 'accounts between the parties' are of such a 'complicated nature' that only a court of equity can satisfactorily unravel them." 369 U.S. at 478. Though the issue whether complexity can create a constitutional requirement that the case be tried to a judge has never returned to the Supreme Court, it has been the subject of decisions in the lower federal courts.

In re Japanese Elec. Prods. Antitrust Litig., 631 F.2d 1069 (3d Cir. 1980), involved claims by two U.S. electronics manufacturers against the major Japanese electronics manufacturers and many of their subsidiaries. The claims centered on alleged worldwide, multi-year conspiracies involving defendants and many other coconspirators to sell televisions and other electronic goods at below cost with the aim of driving the plaintiffs out of business. The conduct was alleged to violate both antitrust and antidumping statutes and the remedies included treble damages, a legal claim that would normally have entitled the plaintiffs to trial by jury. Discovery in the case consumed nine years and resulted in the production of millions of documents and over 100,000 pages of deposition transcript. Trial was predicted to last for a year. The defendants moved to strike the plaintiffs' demand for jury trial, arguing that the proof of the claims would be too burdensome and complicated for the jury.

The court of appeals rejected the argument that the Seventh Amendment itself contained a complexity exception, finding no basis to "conclude that complexity alone ever was an established basis of equitable jurisdiction" in English practice in 1791. 631 F.2d at 1083. But the court recognized, in dictum, that the right to an accurate determination under the Due Process Clause of the Fifth Amendment could trump the Seventh Amendment right to jury trial:

> * * * the law presumes that a jury will decide rationally; it will resolve each disputed issue on the basis of a fair and reasonable assessment of the evidence and a fair and reasonable application of relevant legal rules.

> * * *

> Therefore, we find the most reasonable accommodation between the requirements of the fifth and seventh amendments to be a denial of jury trial when a jury will not be able to perform its task of rational decisionmaking with a reasonable understanding of the evidence and the relevant legal standards. In lawsuits of this complexity, the interests protected by this procedural rule of due process carry greater weight than the interests served by the constitutional guarantee of jury trial. Consequently, we shall not read the seventh amendment to guarantee the right to jury trial in these suits.

613 F.2d at 1084, 1086. The court rejected the argument that the jury was just as competent as a judge to decide a complex case. Because the jury has "both particular strengths and weaknesses in deciding complex cases * * * [a] litigant might prove that a particular suit is too complex for a jury. Because of the important due process rights implicated, a litigant should have the opportunity to make that showing." Id. at 1086. In contrast, "[a] general presumption that a judge is capable of deciding an extraordinarily complex case * * * is reasonable." Id. at 1086–87. The court remanded for a

determination whether the case was too complex to be tried to the jury, but the case was resolved before the district court ruled on that issue.

In a strong dissent, Judge Gibbons argued against the recognition of a Due Process override of the Seventh Amendment in complex cases. The complexity in the case, he argued, was the result of liberal permissive joinder of claims and parties under the federal Rules. Since the joinder rules were nonconstitutional, the proper solution in cases of disturbingly high complexity was to deny the nonconstitutional permissive right of joinder, not the constitutionally protected right to jury trial. And once the case was pared down in this way, he said: "I cannot conceive of a case in which what would be a separate claim for relief at common law, sufficiently comprehensible to a trial judge to satisfy due process, would be too complex for trial to a jury." Id. at 1092. In In re United States Financial Securities Litigation, 609 F.2d 411 (9th Cir. 1979), the trial judge denied a jury demand in a group of consolidated cases arising out of the collapse of a large financial and real estate firm, on the ground that the "legal and factual issues were of such complexity as to be beyond the practical abilities and limitations of a jury." Id. at 413. In another two-to-one decision, the Court of Appeals for the Ninth Circuit reversed, refusing to find either a complexity exception to the Seventh Amendment or a due process right to a nonjury determination in complex cases under the Fifth Amendment.

4. **The performance of juries in complex cases and the scholarship of the complexity exception.** There are several studies of the performance of civil juries in complex cases. For a balanced and relatively optimistic view, see Lempert, Civil Juries and Complex Cases: Taking Stock After Twelve Years, in Verdict: Assessing the Civil Jury System 181 (R. Litan ed., 1993). A much more negative, but unsystematic, account is S. Adler, The Jury: Trial and Error in the American Courtroom 218–42 (1994); see also Sanders, The Jury Deliberation in a Complex Case: Havner v. Merrell Dow Pharmaceuticals, 16 Just. Sys. J. 45, 57 (1993). There is a large literature on the law of the complexity exception, much of it financed by litigants. Commissioned studies in academic law journals are relatively rare. That there are so many on a single topic is extraordinary, reflecting the amount of money at stake in cases to which the complexity exception might apply. For one of the studies financed by plaintiffs in the *Japanese Electronic Products Litigation*, see Arnold, A Historical Inquiry into the Right to Trial by Jury in Complex Civil Litigation, 128 U. Pa. L. Rev. 829 (1980) (arguing against a complexity exception). For one of several financed by defendant International Business Machines in a series of antitrust cases, see Devlin, Jury Trial of Complex Cases: English Practice at the Time of the Seventh Amendment, 80 Colum. L. Rev. 43 (1980). For noncommissioned studies see Jorde, The Seventh Amendment Right to Jury Trial of Antitrust Issues, 69 Calif. L. Rev. 1 (1981); Kane, Civil Jury Trial: The Case for Reasoned Iconoclasm, 28 Hastings L.J. 1 (1976).

5. **Strategies for improving jury performance.** Many have argued that the difficulties that jurors may experience with complex cases can be ameliorated or eliminated with measures designed to facilitate decisionmaking by the jury, including oral and written preliminary instructions, permitting note taking and the use of notebooks, permitting juror questioning of witnesses, encouraging the use of summaries or excerpts, and permitting interim arguments during the presentation of evidence to explain the structure of the party's case. Schwarzer, Reforming

Jury Trial, 132 F.R.D. 575 (1991); Friedland, The Competency and Responsibility of Jurors in Deciding Cases, 85 Nw. L. Rev. 190 (1990). The mixed evidence on the effectiveness of such techniques is assessed in Heuer & Penrod, Trial Complexity, 18 Law & Hum. Behav. 29 (1994).

D. SELECTION OF THE TRIER OF FACT

1. THE JURY

INTRODUCTORY NOTE ON SELECTION OF THE JURY

Jury selection takes place in two stages. First, a group of potential jurors is assembled at the courthouse. These potential jurors are called the jury "panel," or "venire." ("Venir" is the French infinitive "to come.") Practices vary from jurisdiction to jurisdiction as to how the panel is chosen. Second, the actual jury is chosen from the members of the panel, through a process called "voir dire." ("Voir dire" is the combination of two French infinitives, "to see" and "to say.") Voir dire consists of questioning potential jurors to determine possible bias that would allow challenge for cause, or to reveal information that would induce a party to exercise a peremptory challenge. In the northern United States, voir dire is generally pronounced "vwoir deer"; in the southern United States, "vwoir dire," as in "dire consequences." Law dictionaries translate "voir dire" as "to tell the truth," but this is a loose approximation of the French, as well as a loose approximation of what sometimes happens.

a. THE JURY PANEL

Omotosho v. Giant Eagle, Inc.

Northern District of Ohio, 2014.
997 F. Supp. 2d 792.

■ PEARSON, J.

Plaintiff Ernest E. Omotosho presents the Court with a motion for a new trial. A trial of Plaintiff's claim that he was wrongfully discharged from employment because of his race, African American, resulted in an unanimous verdict in favor of Defendant Giant Eagle, Inc. No African Americans sat on the jury that rendered the verdict. No African Americans were on the panel from which the jury was selected. Plaintiff asserts that he was denied his right to a jury selected from a fair cross section of the community, and, therefore, the jury selection process used by the Northern District of Ohio failed to comply with the Jury Selection and Service Act of 1968 ("JSSA"), 28 U.S.C. § 1861 *et seq*.

The Court has considered the briefs submitted by the parties, studied the evidence, and reviewed the governing law. The evidence shows that African Americans are significantly underrepresented in the pool of qualified candidates available for jury service in Youngstown, Ohio. Although the Court believes that measures can and must be undertaken to improve this shortcoming of the jury selection process, Plaintiff's motion for a new trial is denied because he did not make a *prima facie* showing that the fair cross section requirement of the JSSA was violated.

I.   Factual and Procedural Background

This case had its genesis in the decision of Defendant, a regional supermarket chain, to fire Plaintiff as a stock clerk because he allegedly consumed an unpaid food item in violation of Defendant's workplace policy. Count One of the complaint alleged that white employees had committed similar or worse infractions but, unlike Plaintiff, were not terminated from employment, and that Plaintiff's discharge "violated [his] rights to be free from racial discrimination." * * *

The parties forewent the filing of summary judgment motions and commenced a jury trial. * * * The only matter to be tried was Count One: Plaintiff's claim of unlawful discharge on the basis of his race. After a three-day trial, an eight-member jury, all of whom were Caucasian, returned an unanimous verdict in favor of Defendant.

The issue of the jury's racial composition was first raised by Plaintiff at the start of *voir dire*. He remarked to the Court that none of the twenty-four individuals comprising the panel that appeared for jury service were African American. He then moved to "stop the *voir dire* proceedings and conduct a hearing on the process that led us to have a [panel] of all Caucasian[s] and no African-Americans." The Court— although observing that there appeared to be no African American panelists—denied Plaintiff's motion. Even so, the Court informed the parties that it would hold a hearing after the completion of *voir dire* and invite a representative from the Clerk's Office to answer questions regarding the jury selection procedures. At the conclusion of that hearing, which was held prior to opening statements, Plaintiff moved for a "mistrial." He contended that a fair jury had not been selected and that "the statistical likelihood of pooling a 24-member panel that includes no African-Americans in an evenhanded system would be virtually zero." The Court again denied Plaintiff's motion. Nevertheless, because the Clerk's Office representative conceded that she was not qualified to answer all of Plaintiff's questions, and because Plaintiff had not been given an adequate opportunity to examine the relevant data, the Court allowed Plaintiff to "take up the issue again" after he had a chance to investigate the jury selection procedures further.

Plaintiff did not offer additional evidence to support his jury challenge until after the trial. After the Court entered judgment in favor of Defendant, Plaintiff timely moved for a new trial pursuant to Rule 59. Plaintiff claims he was denied his right under the JSSA to a jury selected from a fair cross section of the community. * * *

III. Discussion

The motion before the Court raises questions concerning whether) @ issue
Plaintiff received his statutory entitlements under the JSSA. The act declares that "[i]t is the policy of the United States that all litigants in Federal courts entitled to trial by jury shall have the right to grand and petit juries selected at random from a fair cross section of the community in the district or division wherein the court convenes." 28 U.S.C. § 1861. The "fair cross section" language is drawn from the Supreme Court's jurisprudence defining criminal defendants' rights to a fair jury under the Sixth Amendment. *In re United States*, 426 F.3d 1, 8 (1st Cir.2005).

Although the Sixth Amendment does not govern civil cases; *Turner v. Rogers,* ___ U.S. ___, 131 S.Ct. 2507, 2516, 180 L.Ed.2d 452 (2011); the Sixth Circuit and its sister courts have adopted the test for evaluating constitutional fair cross section claims as the standard for analyzing fair cross section claims under the JSSA, which applies to civil cases. *United States v. Allen,* 160 F.3d 1096, 1102 (6th Cir.1998), *cert. denied,* 526 U.S. 1044, 119 S.Ct. 1345, 143 L.Ed.2d 508 (1999); *see United States v. Royal,* 174 F.3d 1, 6 (1st Cir.1999); *United States v. Shinault,* 147 F.3d 1266, 1270–71 (10th Cir.), *cert. denied,* 525 U.S. 988, 119 S.Ct. 459, 142 L.Ed.2d 411 (1998); *United States v. Clifford,* 640 F.2d 150, 155–56 (8th Cir.1981). To establish a *prima facie* violation of the fair cross section requirement, a litigant must demonstrate:

(1) that the group alleged to be excluded is a 'distinctive' group in the community;

(2) that the representation of this group in venires from which juries are selected is not fair and reasonable in relation to the number of such persons in the community;

and (3) that this underrepresentation is due to systematic exclusion of the group in the jury-selection process.

Duren v. Missouri, 439 U.S. 357, 364, 99 S.Ct. 664, 58 L.Ed.2d 579 (1979).

There is no dispute that African Americans are a "distinctive" group in the community. The salient questions raised by Plaintiff's motion are whether the remaining *Duren* requirements are met. Plaintiff asserts that the evidence he marshals conclusively shows that, here in Youngstown, the representation of African Americans in jury panels (interchangeably used with "venires") is not fair and reasonable in relation to the African American presence in the community, and African Americans are systematically excluded from the jury selection process. The Court examines the evidence in the sections below.

A.   JSSA's Statutory Requirements

[The court first held that the plaintiff's motion for a new trial was both timely and properly asserted under the statute.]

B.   Fair and Reasonable Representation

Plaintiff argues that the representation of African Americans on Youngstown jury panels is not fair and reasonable in relation to the representation of African Americans in the community. As evidence, Plaintiff points out that no African Americans appeared on the panel from which jurors were selected for his trial. Plaintiff also submits a report prepared by the Clerk of Court, known as an "AO 12," which analyzes the operation of the jury selection plan in Youngstown. One function of the AO 12 is to compare the demographic characteristics of a particular qualified jury wheel against the demographic characteristics of the corresponding community. The proffered report reveals that as of March 14, 2012, African Americans comprised only 3.46% of the 2,458 names in the qualified jury wheel for Youngstown, even though African Americans are 9.5% of the voting-age population in the Youngstown community.

The disparity must be understood in the context of the Northern District of Ohio's jury selection procedures. The district consists of four geographic divisions: Akron, Cleveland, Toledo, and Youngstown (the division where the instant Court sits). In the Northern District of Ohio, as in other federal judicial districts, the jury selection process is governed by a "written plan" adopted by the district court in accordance with the JSSA. 28 U.S.C. § 1863(a). The jury selection plan must comply with the JSSA's provisions and must also be approved by a reviewing panel consisting of the members of the Judicial Council of the Sixth Circuit. *Id.*

The district's current plan prescribes that the source of names from which potential jurors are selected shall be from the general election voter registration lists provided by the Ohio Secretary of State. Following each presidential election, names are randomly drawn from these lists and placed in a master jury wheel designated for a geographic division. The master jury wheel contains names of individuals residing within the division to whom juror qualification questionnaires are mailed. The Clerk determines, based on the information returned, whether an individual is unqualified, exempt, or excused from jury service. The names of those whom are deemed to be qualified for service are then placed in a qualified jury wheel. The qualified wheel holds the names of individuals whom, from time to time, are randomly selected by the Clerk to be issued summonses for jury service. In June 2013, the month of Plaintiff's trial, the Youngstown division was relying on the master wheel created after the 2008 presidential election.

The AO 12 for Youngstown discloses an underrepresentation of African Americans in the source of names from which qualified individuals are chosen for jury service. Although the AO 12 does not provide precise information regarding the demographic composition of venires, or jury panels, the report serves as a reliable proxy because veniremen are randomly selected from the qualified jury wheel. The disproportionate representation of groups within a qualified wheel, therefore, may provide a basis for a fair cross section claim. *See United States v. Jackman,* 46 F.3d 1240, 1244 (2d Cir.1995) ("fair cross-section requirement applies only to the larger pool serving as the source of names . . . . In other words, the Sixth Amendment guarantees the *opportunity* for a representative jury venire" [citation omitted; emphasis in original]). The mere underrepresentation of a distinctive group does not, alone, adversely implicate the fair cross section requirement. Plaintiff must, pursuant to *Duren,* show that the underrepresentation is "not fair and reasonable." In that regard, Plaintiff urges the Court to view the evidence through two lenses: absolute disparity and comparative disparity. These statistical concepts are ably summarized by the Tenth Circuit as follows:

> Absolute disparity measures the difference between the percentage of a group in the general population and its percentage in the qualified wheel. For instances, if Asians constitute 10% of the general population and 5% of the qualified wheel, the absolute disparity is 5%. Comparative disparity measures the *decreased likelihood* that members of an underrepresented group will be called for jury service, in contrast to what their presence in the community suggests it should be. This figure is determined by dividing the absolute disparity of the group by that group's percentage in the general population. In the example above, the comparative disparity is 50%: Asians are half as likely to be on venires as they would be if represented in proportion to their numbers in the community.

Shinault, 147 F.3d at 1272 (emphasis in original). According to the AO 12, the underrepresentation of African Americans in the Youngstown qualified jury wheel is 6.04%, as measured by the absolute disparity method, and 63.7%, as measured by the comparative disparity method. * * *

[T]he comparative disparity analysis can be misleading when members of a group compose only a small percentage of those eligible for jury service. *Berghuis v. Smith,* 559 U.S. 314, 329, 130 S.Ct. 1382, 176 L.Ed.2d 249 (2010). To illustrate: if the community contained only one member of a particular group, and that member was not included in the jury wheel, the comparative disparity would be 100% even though a jury without that member would "clearly" form a fair cross section of the community. * * *

"[T]he debate about use of absolute disparity versus comparative disparity has existed for at least 25 years." *Royal,* 174 F.3d at 6 n. 3. The Court need not, however, delve further into this subject in order to conclude that the numbers shown by Plaintiff are dismal. African Americans constitute a substantial segment of the Youngstown population—nearly 10%—yet they comprised only one-third of that figure in the qualified wheel, as reported by the AO 12. Plaintiff's expert in statistics, Guant-Hwa Andy Chang, opines that this difference causes African Americans to be underrepresented on jury panels 95.12% of the time. Excusing this shortfall through application of the 10% absolute disparity marker cannot be countenanced. "[T]o hold otherwise would prevent fair cross-section claims in areas where the minority population was less than 10%." *Ambrose v. Booker,* 684 F.3d 638, 643 (6th 2012), *cert. denied,* ___ U.S. ___, 133 S.Ct. 993, 184 L.Ed.2d 771 (2013).

The population of African Americans in Youngstown is not so slight as to disfavor the comparative disparity analysis, which shows that African Americans were 63.7% less likely to be called for jury service than they would have been if they were proportionally represented in the qualified wheel. This likelihood is significant, and its effects can be pernicious. No expert is needed for the Court to perceive that this degree of African American underrepresentation in the jury selection process can diminish the quality of jury deliberations, frustrate the ability of juries to reach decisions reflecting "the community's sense of justice," and threaten the public's confidence in the fairness and impartiality of our judicial system. *See Batson v. Kentucky,* 476 U.S. 79, 87, 106 S.Ct. 1712, 90 L.Ed.2d 69 (1986). * * *

The Clerk of Court has assured that, as of December 6, 2013, the qualified wheel for Youngstown has markedly improved since it was analyzed in the 2012 AO 12; the proportion of African Americans has increased to 5.41%. While this percentage is healthier, it does not excuse or redeem the wheel's deficiencies at the time of the report. It is also not a percentage that should be institutionally regarded as acceptable when it remains, in fact, highly unsatisfactory. Efforts must be made to understand why the qualified wheel so materially underrepresents African Americans in Youngstown. The evaluation and adoption of methods to improve—and maintain over time—the representative characteristic of the qualified wheel is imperative to the fair administration of justice, and must be made a top priority in this district.

Notwithstanding the above, the Court will refrain from ruling on whether Plaintiff's evidence satisfies the second prong of the *Duren* test. Such a ruling need not be made because, as will be explained below, Plaintiff fails to satisfy the third prong of the test, which requires that he demonstrate that African Americans are systematically excluded from the jury selection process.

C.   Systematic Exclusion

Plaintiff claims that two factors work in tandem to systematically exclude African Americans from the jury selection process. First, Plaintiff contends that "it is well known that African-Americans have a comparatively high rate of mobility." Second, Plaintiff argues that the Northern District of Ohio fails to update the addresses of the individuals whose names are in the master jury wheel. According to Plaintiff's theory, African Americans are therefore less likely to receive and return the juror qualification questionnaires mailed by the Clerk's Office, which, in turn, causes them to be underrepresented in the qualified jury wheel.

Before turning to the evidence, the Court first considers whether Plaintiff's theory describing systematic exclusion can prevail as a matter of law. Systematic exclusion means that "the cause of the underrepresentation . . . [was] inherent in the particular jury-selection process utilized." *Duren,* 439 U.S. at 366, 99 S.Ct. 664.

The classic examples of systematic exclusion are found in the cases of *Taylor* and *Duren. Taylor* involved a Louisiana law requiring that a woman could not be selected for jury service unless she had previously filed a written declaration of her desire to serve. *Taylor v. Louisiana,* 419 U.S. 522, 523, 95 S.Ct. 692, 42 L.Ed.2d 690 (1975). The Supreme Court held that the law, which did not apply to men, and which caused women to account for no more than 10% of the jury wheel, systematically excluded women from jury service. *Id.* at 524 and 538, 95 S.Ct. 692. In *Duren,* both the questionnaires and the summonses mailed to prospective jurors specially allowed women to claim automatic exemptions from jury service. 439 U.S. at 361, 99 S.Ct. 664. As a result of these exemptions, only 26.7% of those summoned for jury service were women, and only 14.5% of those who appeared in venires during the period in which the defendant's jury was chosen were female. *Id.* at 367, 99 S.Ct. 664. The Supreme Court held that the resulting disproportionate exclusion of women "was quite obviously due to the *system* by which juries are selected," which system was "the operation of Missouri's exemption criteria . . . as implemented in Jackson County." *Id.* (emphasis in original).

After *Duren* and *Taylor,* circuit courts, including the Sixth Circuit, have stated that a group is not systematically excluded if prospective jurors are "gathered without *active* discrimination." *Polk,* 1996 WL 47110 at *2 (emphasis added); *see Barber v. Ponte,* 772 F.2d 982, 997 (1st Cir.1985) ("courts have tended to allow a fair degree of leeway in designating jurors so long as the state or community does not *actively* prevent people from serving or actively discriminate" [emphasis in original]), *cert. denied,* 475 U.S. 1050, 106 S.Ct. 1272, 89 L.Ed.2d 580 (1986); *United States v. Cecil,* 836 F.2d 1431, 1446 (4th Cir.) (*quoting Ponte*), *cert. denied,* 487 U.S. 1205, 108 S.Ct. 2846, 101 L.Ed.2d 883

(1988). Active discrimination need not involve the intent to discriminate. * * *

The Court is not aware of any case that has found that a group was systematically excluded because insufficient effort was made to mitigate the effects of the group's relatively higher geographic mobility. Plaintiff states that, to his knowledge, "no court has previously considered the issue." In fact, some courts have declared that the influence of social and economic factors on juror participation cannot demonstrate the systematic exclusion of a distinctive group. *See, e.g., People v. Smith,* 463 Mich. 199, 206, 615 N.W.2d 1 (2000) ("Sixth Amendment does not require [the government] to counteract these factors"). These courts take the view that "under the systematic exclusion requirement the assessment of jury representativeness should take into account only 'affirmative government action' and not 'private sector influences.'" *United States v. Purdy,* 946 F.Supp. 1094, 1103 (D.Conn.1996) (*quoting Rioux,* 930 F.Supp. at 1572–73).

The Sixth Circuit has not foreclosed the consideration of social and economic factors in the systematic exclusion analysis. Rather, it has observed: "[T]he Sixth Amendment is concerned with social or economic factors when the particular *system* of selecting jurors makes such factors relevant to who is placed on the qualifying list and who is ultimately called to or excused from service on a venire panel." *Berghuis,* 543 F.3d at 341. The system at issue in *Berghuis* involved, among other things, a county's practice of allowing prospective jurors to "essentially 'opt out' of jury service" if jury duty would constitute a hardship based on child care concerns, transportation issues, or the inability to take time from work. *Id.* at 340. The panel concluded that African Americans were systematically excluded from jury selection because the evidence showed that the county's automatic granting of these excuses disproportionately impacted African American prospective jurors, and effectively removed the randomness from the jury selection process. *Id.* at 340.

The force causing the underrepresentation in *Berghuis* is, however, materially distinguishable from the influence claimed here. The exclusionary force in that case was the county's active elimination of African Americans from jury service, which, although unintentional, was claimed to have caused the underrepresentation at issue. In other words, the culprit was the system of "opt-out" procedures as implemented by the county. To the contrary, Plaintiff does not, in the present case, claim that African Americans in Youngstown are being actively eliminated from jury service. Rather, he complains about the system's *inaction,* or lack of effort, in offsetting the private sector influence of geographic mobility. This claim does not fall within the penumbra of conduct that has been understood by courts to constitute the systematic exclusion of a distinctive group. *See Bates v. United States,* 473 Fed.Appx. 446, 451 (6th Cir.2012). * * *

At its core, Plaintiff's theory describing the systematic exclusion of African Americans impugns the way voter registration lists are used in this district. Because, according to Plaintiff, African Americans are more likely to change residences, the addresses culled from the voter lists will more likely become inaccurate with respect to African Americans over time. Plaintiff thus maintains that "the use of only voter registration lists that did not produce a jury pool made up of a fair cross section of the community violated the JSSA."

Yet, "[v]oter registration lists are the presumptive statutory source for potential jurors." *United States v. Odeneal,* 517 F.3d 406, 412 (6th Cir.2008). The juror selection plan for this district, which prescribes the use of the voter registration lists, was approved by the Chief Judge and by a reviewing panel consisting of the members of the Judicial Council of the Sixth Circuit. "The use of voter registration lists has been consistently upheld against both statutory and constitutional challenge, unless the voter list in question had been compiled in a discriminatory manner." *Cecil,* 836 F.2d at 1446. * * * This fact is instructive, for it underscores the principle that individual decisions whether to vote, like individual decisions whether to move, are products of private choices the ramifications of which are tolerated within the sanctioned, objective system. Therefore, a system that relies exclusively on voter lists without resorting to measures that offset private-choice forces is not a system that actively or intentionally discriminates against any group. *Rule*

Finally, other circuits have considered and rejected the theory offered by Plaintiff. * * * Because the Sixth Circuit has yet to consider the issue, the Court follows the course charted by the Second and Tenth Circuits and holds that a group is not systematically excluded from the jury selection process when the system of selecting jurors does not proactively counteract the effects of the group's comparably higher rate of mobility. This is *not* to say that proactive measures should not be taken. Emphatically, they should (see Part IIIB). The impetus to do so, however, must arise from an institutional commitment to improve our system of justice for all who come before it, and not from the baseline obligations imposed by the fair cross section requirement. * * *

IV. Conclusion

Because Plaintiff has failed to show that African Americans in Youngstown, Ohio, are systematically excluded from the jury selection process, the Court denies Plaintiff's motion for a new trial. Although the motion is denied, the Court cannot ignore the startling evidence showing that African Americans have been, and are likely to continue to be, seriously underrepresented in the pool of qualified candidates available for jury service in Youngstown. This underrepresentation hobbles the judicial system by diminishing the quality of jury deliberations, obstructing the capacity of juries to reach decisions reflecting the community's sense of justice, and threatening public confidence in the fairness and impartiality of the courts. The Court will not pretend that a solution is readily or easily available. To preserve the promise of the fair and equal administration of justice, a greater commitment must be made to study, understand, and combat this insidious problem.

IT IS SO ORDERED.

NOTE ON THE JURY PANEL AND THE REQUIREMENTS OF REPRESENTATIVENESS

1. Basic legal requirements governing the selection of the panel. Federal practice in choosing both criminal and civil jury panels has been governed since 1968 by the Jury Selection and Service Act, 28 U.S.C.

§§ 1861–1878. The Act provides that "all litigants in Federal courts entitled to trial by jury" shall be entitled to a jury panel "selected at random from a fair cross section of the community," and requires that "[n]o citizen shall be excluded from [jury] service * * * on account of race, color, religion, sex, national origin, or economic status." §§ 1861, 1862. Each federal district court is required to "devise and place into operation a written plan for random selection of grand and petit jurors * * * designed to achieve the objectives" of the statute. 28 U.S.C. § 1863(a). In a civil case, a litigant may move to stay the proceedings on the ground of "substantial failure to comply" with the statute, provided that the challenge is made by the earlier of (a) "before the voir dire examination" or (b) "within seven days after the party discovered or could have discovered, by the exercise of diligence, the grounds therefor." 28 U.S.C. § 1867(c).

These statutory commands, binding only in federal court, parallel and implement two independent constitutional requirements that are binding in both state and federal court. The first is the prohibition on intentional discrimination against individual jurors imposed by the Fourteenth and Fifth Amendments in civil and criminal cases. The second is a requirement, derived from the Sixth Amendment, and applicable in criminal cases only, that the jury panel must be drawn "from a fair cross section of the community." In federal court, as noted, the statute extends the fair cross section requirement to civil cases explicitly and gives civil litigants standing to enforce it. In state courts the panel from which civil and criminal petit juries are chosen is almost always the same. Thus, in state courts a decision upholding (or striking down) the manner in which a panel is assembled in a criminal case will, as a practical matter, determine the way a panel is assembled in a civil case.

Intentional exclusion from jury panels on the basis of race (also now prohibited by 28 U.S.C. § 1862) has been forbidden by the Equal Protection Clause of the Fourteenth Amendment (and in federal courts, by the Due Process Clause of the Fifth Amendment) for over one hundred years. Strauder v. West Virginia, 100 U.S. 303, 25 L.Ed. 664 (1880).

Demonstrating a failure to comply with "fair cross section" requirement, in contrast, does not require proof of intentional discrimination. See, e.g., Alexander v. Louisiana, 405 U.S. 625, 92 S.Ct. 1221, 31 L.Ed.2d 536 (1972) (forbidding exclusion of minorities); Castaneda v. Partida, 430 U.S. 482, 97 S.Ct. 1272, 51 L.Ed.2d 498 (1977) (same); Taylor v. Louisiana, 419 U.S. 522, 95 S.Ct. 692, 42 L.Ed.2d 690 (1975) (exclusion of women). The defendant may challenge the composition of the jury panel even if he is not of the same race or gender as those excluded. Peters v. Kiff, 407 U.S. 493, 92 S.Ct. 2163, 33 L.Ed.2d 83 (1972).

The Court has reasoned that the values protected by the "fair cross section" requirement include prevention of bias in fact-finding:

> The purpose of a jury is to guard against the exercise of arbitrary power—to make available the commonsense judgment of the community as a hedge against the overzealous or mistaken prosecutor and in preference to the professional or perhaps overconditioned or biased response of a judge. * * * This prophylactic vehicle is not provided if the jury pool is made up of only special segments of the populace or if large, distinctive groups are excluded from the pool * * * "Trial by jury presupposes a jury

drawn from a pool broadly representative of the community as well as impartial in a specific case. . . . [The] broad representative character of the jury should be maintained, partly as assurance of a diffused impartiality and partly because sharing in the administration of justice is a phase of civic responsibility." Thiel v. Southern Pacific Co., 328 U.S. 217, 227 (1946) (Frankfurter, J., dissenting).

Taylor v. Louisiana, 419 U.S. at 530–31.

2. Administering the fair cross section requirement.

a. Cognizable groups. Cognizable groups under the "fair cross section" requirement are principally those protected from discrimination by the anti-bias norms of the Equal Protection Clause, including racial, ethnic, or religious minorities, and women. Courts have generally rejected the notion that groups defined by age or educational status have a sufficiently unique perspective or point of view to qualify as "cognizable" for purposes of the requirement. See, e.g., Johnson v. McCaughtry, 92 F.3d 585 (7th Cir. 1996) (persons 18–25 or over 70 not "cognizable groups"); State v. Porro, 152 N.J.Super. 259, 377 A.2d 950 (1977) (students not a cognizable group). Under the federal statute, and under many state constitutions, the fair cross section requirement has been extended to "economic status," a category not traditionally recognized under the Equal Protection Clause. See Thiel v. Southern Pacific Co., 328 U.S. 217, 66 S.Ct. 984, 90 L.Ed. 1181 (1946) (automatic exclusion of "daily wage workers" struck down under federal court's supervisory power).

b. Measuring underrepresentation. In Duren v. Missouri, 439 U.S. 357, 364, 99 S.Ct. 664, 58 L.Ed.2d 579 (1979), a twelve-person jury was composed entirely of men. The adult population in the county from which the panel was chosen was 54% women. During the month in which the jury was chosen, 15.5% of the panel members were women. The actual jury was chosen from a panel consisting of 5 women and 53 men. The disparity between men and women appears to have resulted primarily from a provision of Missouri law under which women could claim automatic exemption from jury service, simply on the ground that they were women. The disparity in *Duren* was very large in both absolute (38.5%) and relative (71%) terms. Where the excluded group is a minority, though, as in *Omotosho*, often the absolute disparity number is small, but the relative disparity is large. In general, courts faced with such cases have used absolute disparity as the measure and have required substantial absolute disparities, on the order of 10%, in order to find a prima facie violation. See United States v. McAnderson, 914 F.2d 934, 941 (7th Cir. 1990) (12% blacks on the jury venire vs. 20% in the community; actual disparity of 8% and comparative disparity of 40%, were not unfair or unreasonable); People v. Morales, 48 Cal.3d 527, 257 Cal.Rptr. 64, 770 P.2d 244 (1989) (suggesting that 9–11% actual, and 41–52% relative, disparity among Hispanic jurors was not unreasonable). Does use of the "absolute disparity" standard ensure adequate participation of minority jurors in the fair cross section?

c. Systematic exclusion. The classic forms of systematic exclusion involved more or less transparent efforts to exclude racial minorities from participation in grand and petit juries. In other cases, the purpose of the exclusion may at least on its face appear well intentioned. The automatic exemption for women in *Duren* is an example, as was the automatic exclusion of working-class jurors in *Thiel v. Southern Pacific*, which was justified on the ground that working-class jurors invariably claimed and obtained individual hardship excuses. But as the *Omotosho* case makes clear, when the challenged provisions of law are neutral on their face with respect to the underrepresented group, the challenge will normally fail. See also People v. Currie, 87 Cal. App. 4th 225, 104 Cal.Rptr.2d 430 (Cal. Ct. App. 2001).

   d.   Justifying systematic underrepresentation. Once a prima facie case has been established, the state can justify its selection process only by showing that a "significant state interest" is "manifestly and primarily advanced" by those aspects of the selection process that result in the exclusion. *Duren,* 439 U.S. at 367. The Court struck down the provision but noted that other exemptions with disproportionate impact but not articulated in terms of gender might survive. For example, the Court wrote, "We recognize that a State may have an important interest in assuring that those members of the family responsible for the care of children are available to do so. An exemption appropriately tailored to this interest would, we think, survive a fair-cross-section challenge." Id. at 370.

   3.   The process for selecting the jury panel. Selection of the jury begins with the source list. Federal district courts are authorized to use lists of registered or actual voters. They are also required to supplement those lists with "some other source of names * * * where necessary to foster the policy and protect the rights" secured by the Act. 28 U.S.C. § 1863(b)(2). As of 1997, about seventeen federal districts had done some form of supplementation, typically with lists of licensed drivers. Bueker, Jury Source Lists: Does Supplementation Really Work? 82 Cornell L. Rev. 390 (1997). State practice is more varied, but the normal practice is to use only lists of registered voters.

   Typically, a group of names is then randomly selected from the master source list using the "master jury wheel," which in most districts is a computer programmed to make a random selection from the (also computerized) source list. The names randomly selected from the source list are then sent a qualification questionnaire. Those questionnaires are designed to provide information about whether jurors are qualified to serve and whether they are exempt or excused from service.

      a.   Qualifications. The qualifications for jury service are as follows: the person must be a citizen of the United States, eighteen or over, a resident of the judicial district for one year, and able to fill out the jury form in, and to speak, the English language, physically and mentally capable of serving, and not charged or convicted of a state or federal felony. 28 U.S.C. § 1865. Most states have similar qualification requirements. Calif.C.Civ.P. § 203(a).

      b.   Exemptions. Those who are exempt from jury service include members of the Armed Forces of the United States, state and local police officers, and public officers in the executive, legislative, or judicial branches of federal, state, and local government. 28 U.S.C. § 1863(b)(6).

      c.   Excuses. Any prospective juror can be excused if service would involve "undue hardship or extreme inconvenience." 28 U.S.C. § 1866(c)(1). The court may also, if it chooses, identify classes of jurors who should be excused from jury service on the ground of hardship or extreme inconvenience if they so request. Districts have discretion in selecting such categories: they often include persons over 70, professionals in active practice (doctors, nurses, lawyers, clergy, teachers), persons with active care and custody obligations for younger children, and people who have recently served on another jury or grand jury. 28 U.S.C. § 1863(b)(5)(a).

In addition to information about qualifications and exemptions, the questionnaire also requests information on the juror's gender, race, and economic status, while explaining that the information need not be supplied, that it is being gathered solely to ensure that the jury meets the requirements of the statute, and that it is not relevant to whether the juror qualifies. If questionnaires are returned incomplete, or not returned at all, the court may send them again. In theory, the court may also sanction those who fail to respond, though in practice this almost never occurs. 28 U.S.C. § 1864(b).

Using the questionnaires, the court eliminates prospective jurors whose answers indicate that they are unqualified or exempt in order to create a qualified jury wheel, consisting of a list of jurors who are ready to be summoned. Jurors whose names are on the qualified jury wheel are then randomly selected and summoned to the court in sufficient numbers to meet the anticipated demand for jurors in cases going to trial. 28 U.S.C. § 1866. Failure to respond to a summons is punishable by a fine, but in practice those who fail to respond are rarely sanctioned for failing to do so. Jurors who appear at the courthouse may request an excuse for hardship. Many such requests are granted; those whose requests have been denied may renew them before the judge. From those jurors that remain, a randomly selected group is assembled and sent to the courtroom where they will undergo voir dire.

4. Tensions between the selection process and the ideal of a "representative panel." There is general agreement that current selection procedures in the federal courts and in most state courts, though facially neutral, result in juries that significantly underrepresent racial minorities, particular African Americans, Hispanics, Asian and Pacific Islanders, and Native Americans. This appears to be so for several reasons.

First, registered voter lists tend to have higher percentages of whites than the general population and lower percentages of blacks, Latinos, and Asian and Pacific Islanders. Consider some rough national comparisons between the population of registered voters and the voting age population as a whole: Whites are overrepresented in the pool of registered voters compared to the voting age population as a whole by about 1.5%. Voting-age African Americans are underrepresented in the pool of registered voters by about 3%. Americans of Hispanic origin are underrepresented by about 13%, and Asian and Pacific Islanders by 18%. When the source list is actual voters, underrepresentation of Hispanics and Asian and Pacific Islanders increases significantly. U.S. Census Bureau, Reported Voting and Registration, by Race, Hispanic Origin, Sex and Age, for the United States, November 2000; Kairys, Kadane, and Lehoczky, Jury Representativeness: A Mandate for Multiple Source Lists, 65 Calif. L. Rev. 776, 807–08 (1977).

Numerous constitutional challenges have been made to the use of voter lists. All but one have failed. The sole exception is People v. Harris, 36 Cal.3d

36, 201 Cal.Rptr. 782, 679 P.2d 433 (1984), in which the Supreme Court of California held that the use of registered voter lists resulted in unconstitutional underrepresentation of African Americans and Hispanics under both the federal and California Constitutions. California now provides by statute that the combined lists of registered voters and of licensed drivers (plus holders of Department of Motor Vehicles identification cards) "shall be considered inclusive of a representative cross section of the population." Calif.C.Civ.P. § 197(b). Other lists such as customer mailing lists, telephone directories, and utility company lists, may also be used. Calif.C.Civ.P. § 197(a). There is little evidence, however, that supplementing juror lists actually increases minority representation. See Bueker, Jury Source Lists: Does Supplementation Really Work?, 82 Cornell L. Rev. 390 (1997).

Failures to respond, exclusions, and excuses from jury service may also alter the composition of the jury panel. Not every person who is sent a summons to appear as a juror or asked to return a questionnaire in fact does so. Sometimes the mail from the court is undeliverable and sometimes the person receiving it simply fails to respond. Because minorities are significantly more likely to move than whites, their mail from the court is much more likely to go undelivered. Sanctions for failing to appear or respond are modest and rarely enforced. In addition, fees for jury service are much lower than market wages (in California, for example, the fee is $15 per day). Qualification standards also operate to exclude some minority groups. The general disqualification of persons charged or convicted of a felony has a disproportionate influence on minority representation. So does the requirement of English language competence. Finally, hardship excuses also exacerbate minority underrepresentation. Persons with less than a high school education and low incomes ($15,000 in late 1980s dollars) are significantly more likely to be excused for hardship. J. Munsterman et al., The Relationship of Juror Fees and Terms of Service to Jury System Performance 52–53 (1991). Low income and lower education levels are more prevalent in some minority communities. As the *Omotosho* case indicates, courts have generally rejected challenges to underrepresentation resulting from these factors on the ground that they result from practices that either do not systemically exclude minorities or have substantial independent justifications.

5. Race-conscious and race-neutral remedies for underrepresentation. In United States v. Ovalle, 136 F.3d 1092 (6th Cir. 1998), the Jury Selection Plan for the Eastern District of Michigan provided that to achieve a "qualified jury wheel" representing a fair cross section, "if the Court determines that a cognizable group of persons is substantially overrepresented in the qualified jury wheel, the Chief Judge shall order the Clerk to remove randomly a specific number of names so that the population of each cognizable group in the qualified wheel closely approximates the percentage of the population of each place of holding court." On the basis of a finding that black jurors were subject to 16% comparative underrepresentation in the qualified jury pool, the court ordered the removal from the master list of 877 (approximately 20%) of the white and other qualified jurors. Although the resulting plan ensured that African Americans were represented on the jury wheel in proportion to their percentage of the adult population, the court held that the plan unconstitutionally discriminated against excluded jurors in violation of the Due Process Clause of the Fifth Amendment. "Rather than affirmatively removing otherwise qualified jurors because of their racial status, alternative methods of broadening membership in the jury pool could have been utilized." Id. at 1106. Would such alternative measures be constitutional if targeted by race? For defenses of affirmative action in jury selection, see, Alschuler, Racial Quotas and the Jury, 44 Duke L.J. 704 (1995); King, Racial Jurymandering: Cancer or Cure? A Contemporary Review of Affirmative Action in Jury Selection, 68 N.Y.U. L. Rev. 707 (1993). Among the more or less race-neutral measures proposed to improve minority jury service are stronger steps to enforce jury summonses, higher juror fees, and sending proportionally more questionnaires or summonses to residents of political subdivisions with low response rates. See, e.g., Ellis & Diamond, Race, Diversity and Jury Composition: Battering and Bolstering Legitimacy, 78 Chi.-Kent L. Rev. 1033 (2003).

6.   Geographical variation. Different judicial districts and counties often have substantially different populations. The general practice is to draw from the geographical area of the jurisdiction in which the court sits. This can have profound consequences for a jury panel drawn from a "fair cross section of the community." Thus, both studies and anecdotal evidence indicate that juries in predominantly minority inner-city communities are much more likely than juries in surrounding suburban counties both to find liability and to award higher damages when they do find liability. Hayes, Bronx Cheer; Inner-City Jurors Tend to Rebuff Prosecutors and to Back Plaintiffs; They Identify With the Poor and Dislike the Powerful, Say Lawyers on Both Sides; No Negligence, but Pay Up, Wall St. J., Mar. 24, 1992, at 1. More broadly based studies show a strong positive correlation between the size of jury awards and the percentage of the vicinage that consists of racial minorities living in poverty. Helland & Tabarrok, Race, Poverty, and American Tort Awards: Evidence from Three Data Sets, 32 J. Legal. Stud. 27 (2003).

b.   VOIR DIRE

NOTE ON VOIR DIRE

1.   The process of voir dire. In voir dire, a group of jurors randomly drawn from those that show up at the courthouse are placed under oath and questioned by the judge who will preside at trial (common in federal court) or by the lawyers for the parties (common in state court). The answers to the questions posed provide the basis for the lawyers to challenge particular jurors, either for cause or peremptorily. Questions may be posed to the assembled jurors as a group, with jurors asked to respond with a show of hands. Or they may be posed to jurors individually, sometimes with detailed and pointed follow-up.

The amount of energy invested in voir dire varies considerably among different court systems. Voir dire is usually more perfunctory in federal court than in state court. Rule 47(a) gives broad discretion to the individual district judge. Most federal judges conduct their own questioning of prospective jurors, usually, but not always, asking questions submitted by the parties. Lawyers for the parties are seldom permitted to ask questions directly. In at least two reported cases, verdicts have been overturned for failure of the district judge to ask pertinent questions requested by one of the parties, but such cases are extremely rare. See Fietzer v. Ford Motor Co., 622 F.2d 281 (7th Cir. 1980) (in suit arising out of collision and fire involving Mercury Comet, failure to ask questions about prospective juror's involvement with rear-end collisions and burn injuries, and ownership of this brand of automobile); Kiernan v. Van Schaik, 347 F.2d 775 (3d Cir. 1965) (in personal injury suit, failure to ask questions about prospective jurors' relationships with insurance companies). The advantage of the federal practice is that a jury is seated relatively quickly. The disadvantage is that the parties in federal court voir dire will ordinarily not learn as much about the prospective jurors as they would in a state court voir dire. But it is not clear that a different quality of justice is administered by federal juries than by state juries, nor, if there is a difference in quality, that it is due to different practices on voir dire.

The common practice in state court is to allow extensive voir dire questioning by the attorneys for the parties. The California practice is prescribed by statute:

> To select a fair and impartial jury in civil jury trials, the trial judge shall examine the prospective jurors. Upon completion of the judge's initial examination, counsel for each party shall have the right to examine, by oral and direct questioning, any of the prospective jurors in order to enable counsel to intelligibly exercise both peremptory challenges and challenges for cause. During any examination conducted by counsel for the parties, the trial judge should permit liberal and probing examination calculated to discover bias or prejudice with regard to the circumstances of the particular case. The fact that a topic has been included in the judge's examination should not preclude additional nonrepetitive or nonduplicative questioning in the same area by counsel.

Calif.C.Civ.P. § 222.5. Social science research suggests that prospective jurors are more likely to respond truthfully and fully to questions asked by lawyers than to questions asked by judges. See, e.g., Jones, Judge- Versus Attorney-Conducted Voir Dire, 11 Law & Hum. Behav. 131 (1987). Attorney questioning during voir dire provides not only an opportunity to elicit information to assist in choosing the jury, but also an occasion to educate likely jurors about the case they will be asked to decide. A skillful lawyer during voir dire can sometimes establish a rapport with a jury, lay a foundation for evidence she will present, and plant seeds of doubt about her opponent's case.

Imperfections in voir dire often go undetected or uncorrected. In McDonough Power Equipment, Inc. v. Greenwood, 464 U.S. 548, 104 S.Ct. 845, 78 L.Ed.2d 663 (1984), a juror failed to respond to a question asking a group of jurors whether they or any members of their immediate family had sustained any severe injury resulting in any disability or prolonged pain and suffering, even though his son had suffered a broken leg on account of an exploding truck tire. The juror served on the trial jury. When the truth was brought out in post-trial proceedings, he explained that he did not think that a broken leg was a "serious" injury involving prolonged pain and suffering. The Court held that a new trial would be warranted only if the question was material, the answer was dishonest, and a correct response would have provided a valid ground for a challenge for cause. The fact that an answer curtailed the opportunity to ask further questions of the juror or to exercise a peremptory challenge was insufficient to set aside the verdict.

2.   Challenges for cause and peremptory challenges. Sometimes the information elicited on voir dire indicates sufficient bias or appearance of bias that the potential juror is excused for cause. In federal court, the standards for disqualification for cause are a matter of federal common law. Many states have statutes specifying the grounds for challenge for cause. For example, Cal.C.Civ.P. §§ 227–230. Cases in which bias or prejudice will be presumed commonly include a family or business relationship with a party, serving as an employee of a corporate party, or witnessing or personal knowledge of the disputed events.

Assuming that a juror does not obviously fall within one of the specified categories, the judge has substantial discretion in deciding whether actual prejudgment or bias has been demonstrated. Although the juror may express views favorable to one side or another, the court may still allow her on the jury if the judge finds credible her assurances that she can put any prior predispositions to one side and decide the case on the basis of the evidence.

When the information elicited does not warrant a challenge for cause, or where the court denies one, but one of the parties is nevertheless uncomfortable having that person on the jury, the party may exercise a peremptory challenge, and the potential juror will be excused. No reason need be given for a peremptory challenge.

A party has an unlimited number of challenges for cause, but a limited number of peremptory challenges. In civil cases in federal court, each party has three peremptory challenges. 28 U.S.C. § 1870. The number of state-court peremptory challenges varies from state to state. California and Texas each permit six peremptory challenges in civil cases. Calif.C.Civ.P. § 231(c); Tex.R.Civ.P. § 233. In civil cases, the same number of peremptory challenges is typically allowed, irrespective of the type of suit. In criminal cases, a higher or lower number of challenges is allowed, depending on the seriousness of the crime charged.

3.   **Legal protection of challenges for cause.** In Ross v. Oklahoma, 487 U.S. 81, 108 S.Ct. 2273, 101 L.Ed.2d 80 (1988), a state trial court wrongly refused to grant a challenge for cause, forcing a criminal defendant in a capital case to use a peremptory challenge to strike the potential juror. The defendant used all his peremptory challenges, but did not challenge for cause any of the jurors who comprised the jury that decided the case. The Supreme Court held that the wrongful denial of the challenge for cause did not deny the defendant due process under the Fourteenth Amendment to the Constitution.

Compare *Ross* to Kirk v. Raymark Industries, 61 F.3d 147 (3d Cir. 1995), in which the district court in a civil case wrongly refused to grant two challenges for cause, forcing the defendant to use two of its three peremptory challenges to strike those prospective jurors. (Recall that parties in civil cases in federal court are each entitled to three peremptory challenges. 28 U.S.C. § 1870.) The Court of Appeals held that "the remedy for impairment or denial or the statutory right to exercise peremptory challenges is per se reversal without any requirement of proving prejudice." Id. at 162. Note that defendant's unsuccessful argument in *Ross* was based on a constitutional right to due process; in *Kirk,* by contrast, defendant's successful argument was based on a statutory right under § 1870.

Edmonson v. Leesville Concrete, Inc.

Supreme Court of the United States, 1991.
500 U.S. 614, 111 S.Ct. 2077, 114 L.Ed.2d 660.

■ JUSTICE KENNEDY delivered the opinion of the Court.

We must decide in the case before us whether a private litigant in a civil case may use peremptory challenges to exclude jurors on account of their race. Recognizing the impropriety of racial bias in the courtroom, we hold the race-based exclusion violates the equal protection rights of the challenged jurors. This civil case originated in a United States District Court, and we apply the equal protection component of the Fifth Amendment's Due Process Clause. See Bolling v. Sharpe, 347 U.S. 497, 74 S.Ct. 693, 98 L.Ed. 884 (1954).

I

Thaddeus Donald Edmonson, a construction worker, was injured in a job-site accident at Fort Polk, Louisiana, a federal enclave. Edmonson sued Leesville Concrete Company for negligence in the United States District Court for the Western District of Louisiana, claiming that a Leesville employee permitted one of the company's trucks to roll backward and pin him against some construction equipment. Edmonson invoked his Seventh Amendment right to a trial by jury.

During *voir dire,* Leesville used two of its three peremptory challenges authorized by statute to remove black persons from the prospective jury. Citing our decision in Batson v. Kentucky, 476 U.S. 79, 106 S.Ct. 1712, 90 L.Ed.2d 69 (1986), Edmonson, who is himself black, requested that the District Court require Leesville to articulate a race-neutral explanation for striking the two jurors. The District Court denied the request on the ground that *Batson* does not apply in civil proceedings. As impaneled, the jury included 11 white persons and 1 black person. The jury rendered a verdict for Edmonson, assessing his total damages at $90,000. It also attributed 80% of the fault to Edmonson's contributory negligence, however, and awarded him the sum of $18,000.

Edmonson appealed, and a divided panel of the Court of Appeals for the Fifth Circuit reversed, holding that our opinion in *Batson* applies to a private attorney representing a private litigant and that peremptory challenges may not be used in a civil trial for the purpose of excluding jurors on the basis of race. 860 F.2d 1308 (1988). * * *

The full court then ordered rehearing en banc. A divided en banc panel affirmed the judgment of the District Court, holding that a private litigant in a civil case can exercise peremptory challenges without accountability for alleged racial classifications. 895 F.2d 218 (C.A.5 1990). * * * We granted certiorari, and now reverse the Court of Appeals.

II

A

In Powers v. Ohio, 499 U.S. 400, 111 S.Ct. 1364, 113 L.Ed.2d 411 (1991), we held that a criminal defendant, regardless of his or her race, may object to a prosecutor's race-based exclusion of persons from the petit jury. Our conclusion rested on a two-part analysis. First, following our opinions in *Batson* and in Carter v. Jury Commission of Greene County, 396 U.S. 320, 90 S.Ct. 518, 24 L.Ed.2d 549 (1970), we made clear that a prosecutor's race-based peremptory challenge violates the equal protection rights of those excluded from jury service. 499 U.S., at 407–409. Second, we relied on well-established rules of third-party standing to hold that a defendant may raise the excluded jurors' equal protection rights. Id., at 410–15.

* * *

That an act violates the Constitution when committed by a government official, however, does not answer the question whether the same act offends constitutional guarantees if committed by a private litigant or his attorney. The Constitution's protections of individual liberty and equal protection apply in general only to action by the government. National Collegiate Athletic Assn. v. Tarkanian, 488 U.S. 179, 191, 109 S.Ct. 454, 461, 102 L.Ed.2d 469 (1988). Racial discrimination, though invidious in all contexts, violates the Constitution only when it may be attributed to state action. Moose Lodge No. 107 v. Irvis, 407 U.S. 163, 172, 92 S.Ct. 1965, 1971, 32 L.Ed.2d 627 (1972). Thus, the legality of the exclusion at issue here turns on the extent to which a litigant in a civil case may be subject to the Constitution's restrictions.

The Constitution structures the National Government, confines its actions, and, in regard to certain individual liberties and other specified matters, confines the actions of the States. With a few exceptions, such as the provisions of the Thirteenth Amendment, constitutional guarantees of individual liberty and equal protection do not apply to the actions of private entities. *Tarkanian,* supra, 488 U.S., at 191, 109 S.Ct., at 461; Flagg Bros., Inc. v. Brooks, 436 U.S. 149, 156, 98 S.Ct. 1729, 1733, 56 L.Ed.2d 185 (1978). This fundamental limitation on the scope of constitutional guarantees "preserves an area of individual freedom by limiting the reach of federal law" and "avoids imposing on the State, its agencies or officials, responsibility for conduct for which they cannot fairly be blamed." Lugar v. Edmondson Oil Co., 457 U.S. 922, 936–937, 102 S.Ct. 2744, 2753, 73 L.Ed.2d 482 (1982). One great object of the Constitution is to permit citizens to structure their private relations as they choose subject only to the constraints of statutory or decisional law.

To implement these principles, courts must consider from time to time where the governmental sphere ends and the private sphere begins. Although the conduct of private parties lies beyond the Constitution's scope in most instances, governmental authority may dominate an activity to such an extent that its participants must be deemed to act with the authority of the government and, as a result, be subject to constitutional constraints. This is the jurisprudence of state action, which explores the "essential dichotomy" between the private sphere and the public sphere, with all its attendant constitutional obligations. *Moose Lodge,* supra, 407 U.S., at 172, 92 S.Ct., at 1971.

* * *

* * * It cannot be disputed that, without the overt, significant participation of the government, the peremptory challenge system, as well as the jury trial system of which it is a part, simply could not exist. [P]eremptory challenges have no utility outside the jury system, a system which the government alone administers. In the federal system, Congress has established the qualifications for jury service, see 28 U.S.C. § 1865, and has outlined the procedures by which jurors are selected. To this end, each district court in the federal system must adopt a plan for locating and summoning to the court eligible prospective jurors. 28 U.S.C. § 1863; see, e.g., Jury Plan for the United States District Court for the Western District of Louisiana (on file with Administrative Office of United States Courts). This plan, as with all other trial court procedures, must implement statutory policies of random juror selection from a fair cross section of the community, 28 U.S.C. § 1861, and non-exclusion on account of race, color, religion, sex, national origin, or economic status, 18 U.S.C. § 243; 28 U.S.C. § 1862. Statutes prescribe many of the details of the jury plan, 28 U.S.C. § 1863, defining the jury wheel, § 1863(b)(4), voter lists, §§ 1863(b)(2), 1869(c), and jury commissions, § 1863(b)(1). A statute also authorizes the establishment of procedures for assignment to grand and petit juries, § 1863(b)(8), and for lawful excuse from jury service, §§ 1863(b)(5), (6).

At the outset of the selection process, prospective jurors must complete jury qualification forms as prescribed by the Administrative Office of the United States Courts. See 28 U.S.C. § 1864. Failure to do so may result in fines and imprisonment, as might a willful misrepresentation of a material fact in answering a question on the form. Ibid. In a typical case, counsel receive these forms and rely on them when exercising their peremptory strikes. See G. Bermant, Jury Selection Procedures in United States District Courts 7–8, (Federal Judicial Center 1982). The Clerk of the United States District Court, a federal official, summons potential jurors from their employment or other pursuits. They are required to travel to a United States courthouse, where they must report to juror lounges, assembly rooms, and courtrooms at the direction of the court and its officers. Whether or not they are selected for a jury panel, summoned jurors receive a per diem fixed by statute for their service. 28 U.S.C. § 1871.

The trial judge exercises substantial control over *voir dire* in the federal system. See Fed.Rule Civ.Proc. 47. The judge determines the range of information that may be discovered about a prospective juror, and so affects the exercise of both challenges for cause and peremptory challenges. In some cases, judges may even conduct the entire *voir dire* by themselves, a common practice in the District Court where the instant case was tried. See Louisiana Rules of Court, Local Rule W.D.La. 13.02 (1990). The judge oversees the exclusion of jurors for cause, in this way determining which jurors remain eligible for the exercise of peremptory strikes. In cases involving multiple parties, the trial judge decides how peremptory challenges shall be allocated among them. 28 U.S.C. § 1870. When a lawyer exercises a peremptory challenge, the judge advises the juror he or she has been excused.

As we have outlined here, a private party could not exercise its peremptory challenges absent the overt, significant assistance of the court. The government summons jurors, constrains their freedom of movement, and subjects them to public scrutiny and examination. The party who exercises a challenge invokes the formal authority of the court, which must discharge the prospective juror, thus effecting the "final and practical denial" of the excluded individual's opportunity to serve on the petit jury. Virginia v. Rives, 100 U.S. 313, 322, 25 L.Ed. 667 (1880). Without the direct and indispensable participation of the judge, who beyond all question is a state actor, the peremptory challenge system would serve no purpose. By enforcing a discriminatory peremptory challenge, the court "has not only made itself a party to the [biased act], but has elected to place its power, property and prestige behind the [alleged] discrimination." Burton v. Wilmington Parking Authority, 365 U.S., at 725, 81 S.Ct., at 862. In so doing, the government has "create[d] the legal framework governing the [challenged] conduct," *National Collegiate Athletic Assn.*, 488 U.S., at 192, 109 S.Ct., at 462, and in a significant way has involved itself with invidious discrimination.

* * *

Race discrimination within the courtroom raises serious questions as to the fairness of the proceedings conducted there. Racial bias mars the integrity of the judicial system and prevents the idea of democratic government from becoming a reality. Rose v. Mitchell, 443 U.S. 545, 556, 99 S.Ct. 2993, 3000, 61 L.Ed.2d 739 (1979); Smith v. Texas, 311 U.S. 128, 130, 61 S.Ct. 164, 165, 85 L.Ed. 84 (1940). In the many times we have addressed the problem of racial bias in our system of justice, we have not "questioned the premise that racial discrimination in the qualification or selection of jurors offends the dignity of persons and the integrity of the courts." *Powers*, 499 U.S., at 402, 111 S.Ct., at 1366. To permit racial exclusion in this official forum compounds the racial insult inherent in judging a citizen by the color of his or her skin.

* * *

III

It remains to consider whether a prima facie case of racial discrimination has been established in the case before us, requiring Leesville to offer race-neutral explanations for its peremptory challenges. In *Batson,* we held that determining whether a prima facie case has been established requires consideration of all relevant circumstances, including whether there has been a pattern of strikes against members of a particular race. 476 U.S., at 96–97, 106 S.Ct., at 1722–23. The same approach applies in the civil context, and we leave it to the trial courts in the first instance to develop evidentiary rules for implementing our decision.

The judgment is reversed, and the case is remanded for further proceedings consistent with our opinion.

It is so ordered.

■ JUSTICE O'CONNOR, with whom THE CHIEF JUSTICE and JUSTICE SCALIA join, dissenting.

The Court concludes that the action of a private attorney exercising a peremptory challenge is attributable to the government and therefore may compose a constitutional violation. This conclusion is based on little more than that the challenge occurs in the course of a trial. Not everything that happens in a courtroom is state action. A trial, particularly a civil trial, is by design largely a stage on which private parties may act; it is a forum through which they can resolve their disputes in a peaceful and ordered manner. The government erects the platform; it does not thereby become responsible for all that occurs upon it. As much as we would like to eliminate completely from the courtroom the specter of racial discrimination, the Constitution does not sweep that broadly. Because I believe that a peremptory strike by a private litigant is fundamentally a matter of private choice and not state action, I dissent.

* * *

Racism is a terrible thing. It is irrational, destructive, and mean. Arbitrary discrimination based on race is particularly abhorrent when manifest in a courtroom, a forum established by the government for the resolution of disputes through "quiet rationality." See ante, at 2088. But not every opprobrious and inequitable act is a constitutional violation. The Fifth Amendment's Due Process Clause prohibits only actions for which the Government can be held responsible. The Government is not responsible for everything that occurs in a courtroom. The Government is not responsible for a peremptory challenge by a private litigant. I respectfully dissent.

■ JUSTICE SCALIA, dissenting.

* * *

The concrete benefits of the Court's newly discovered constitutional rule are problematic. It will not necessarily be a net help rather than hindrance to minority litigants in obtaining racially diverse juries. In criminal cases, Batson v. Kentucky, 476 U.S. 79, 106 S.Ct. 1712, 90 L.Ed.2d 69 (1986), already prevents the *prosecution* from using race-based strikes. The effect of today's decision (which logically must apply to criminal prosecutions) will be to prevent the *defendant* from doing so— so that the minority defendant can no longer seek to prevent an all-white jury, or to seat as many jurors of his own race as possible. To be sure, it is ordinarily more difficult to *prove* race-based strikes of white jurors, but defense counsel can generally be relied upon to do what we say the Constitution requires. So in criminal cases, today's decision represents a net loss to the minority litigant. In civil cases that is probably not true— but it does not represent an unqualified gain either. *Both* sides have peremptory challenges, and they are sometimes used to *assure* rather than to *prevent* a racially diverse jury.

The concrete costs of today's decision, on the other hand, are not at all doubtful; and they are enormous. We have now added to the duties of already-submerged state and federal trial courts the obligation to assure that race is not included among the other factors (sex, age, religion, political views, economic status) used by private parties in exercising their peremptory challenges. That responsibility would be burden enough if it were not to be discharged through the adversary process; but of course it is. When combined with our decision this Term in Powers v. Ohio, 499 U.S. 400, 111 S.Ct. 1364, 113 L.Ed.2d 411 (1991), which held that the party objecting to an allegedly race-based peremptory challenge need not be of the same race as the challenged juror, today's decision means that *both* sides, in *all* civil jury cases, no matter what their race (and indeed, even if they are artificial entities such as corporations), may lodge racial-challenge objections and, after those objections have been considered and denied, appeal the denials—with the consequence, if they are successful, of having the judgments against them overturned. Thus, yet another complexity is added to an increasingly Byzantine system of justice that devotes more and more of its energy to sideshows and less and less to the merits of the case. Judging by the number of *Batson* claims that have made their way even as far as this Court under the *pre-Powers* regime, it is a certainty that the amount of judges' and lawyers' time devoted to implementing today's newly discovered Law of the Land will be enormous. That time will be diverted from other matters, and the overall system of justice will certainly suffer. Alternatively, of course, the States and Congress may simply abolish peremptory challenges, which would cause justice to suffer in a different fashion.

Although today's decision neither follows the law nor produces desirable concrete results, it certainly has great symbolic value. To overhaul the doctrine of state action in this fashion—what a magnificent demonstration of this institution's uncompromising hostility to race-based judgments, even by private actors! The price of the demonstration is, alas, high, and much of it will be paid by the minority litigants who use our courts. I dissent.

FURTHER NOTE ON VOIR DIRE

1. **The *Batson* test for unlawful discrimination in the use of peremptory challenges.** In Batson v. Kentucky, 476 U.S. 79, 106 S.Ct. 1712, 90 L.Ed.2d 69 (1986), the Court held that race-based peremptory challenges violate the Equal Protection Clause of the Fourteenth Amendment. The test articulated in *Batson* is as follows:

> * * * To establish [a prima facie case of race-based peremptory challenge], a defendant first must show that he is a member of a cognizable racial group, * * * and that the prosecutor has exercised peremptory challenges to remove from the venire members of the defendant's race. Second, the defendant is entitled to rely on the fact, as to which there can be no dispute, that peremptory challenges constitute a jury selection practice that permits "those to discriminate who are of a mind to discriminate." * * * Finally, the defendant must show that these facts and any other relevant circumstances raise an inference that the prosecutor used that practice to exclude the veniremen from the petit jury on account of their race. This combination of factors in the empaneling of the petit jury, as in the selection of the venire, raised the necessary inference of purposeful discrimination.
>
> In deciding whether the defendant has made the requisite showing, the trial court should consider all relevant circumstances. For example, a "pattern" of strikes against black jurors included in the particular venire might give rise to an inference of discrimination. Similarly, the prosecutor's questions and statements during *voir dire* examination and in exercising his challenges may support or refute an inference of discriminatory purpose. These examples are merely illustrative. * * *
>
> Once the defendant makes a prima facie showing, the burden shifts to the State to come forward with a neutral explanation for challenging black jurors. Though this requirement imposes a limitation in some cases on the full peremptory character of the historic challenge, we emphasize that the prosecutor's explanation need not rise to the level justifying exercise of challenge for cause. * * * But the prosecutor may not rebut the defendant's prima facie case of discrimination by stating merely that he challenged jurors of the defendant's race on the assumption—or his intuitive

judgment—that they would be partial to the defendant because of their shared race. * * * Just as the Equal Protection Clause forbids the States to exclude black persons from the venire on the assumption that blacks as a group are unqualified to serve as jurors, * * * so it forbids the States to strike black veniremen on the assumption that they will be biased in a particular case simply because the defendant is black. * * * Nor may the prosecutor rebut the defendant's case merely by denying that he had a discriminatory motive or "affirm[ing] [his] good faith in making individual selections." * * * The prosecutor therefore must articulate a neutral explanation related to the particular case to be tried.

Id. at 96–98.

Justice Marshall concurred in the judgment, but argued that the difficulty of building a prima facie case and the ease of making up a plausible neutral explanation meant that the *Batson* rule was likely to be ineffective in detecting and preventing race-based challenges. Instead, he argued, peremptories should be banned from the criminal justice system altogether. Id. at 107.

Five years after *Batson*, the Court modified the first requirement for a prima facie case, holding that a criminal defendant may object to race-based peremptory challenges even if the challenged jurors are of a different race from the defendant. Powers v. Ohio, 499 U.S. 400, 111 S.Ct. 1364, 113 L.Ed.2d 411 (1991)(petit jurors).

2.   What counts as a "race-neutral" justification? In Hernandez v. New York, 500 U.S. 352, 111 S.Ct. 1859, 114 L.Ed.2d 395 (1991), the prosecutor explained peremptory strikes of two Latino prospective jurors in a trial of a Spanish-speaking Latino defendant. The Supreme Court upheld the trial court's decision accepting as both "race-neutral" and truthful the prosecutor's explanation that the two jurors, who spoke Spanish, might not accept fully the translation into English by the court interpreter.

In Purkett v. Elem, 514 U.S. 765, 115 S.Ct. 1769, 131 L.Ed.2d 834 (1995) (per curiam), the Supreme Court further softened *Batson*'s requirement of a race-neutral explanation for a peremptory strike. Defendant in a state court robbery case objected under *Batson* to the prosecutor's use of two of his six peremptories to exclude black men. The prosecutor explained one of his strikes: " 'I struck [him] because of his long hair. He had long curly hair. He had the longest hair of anybody on the panel so far. He appeared to me to not be a good juror for that fact, the fact that he had long hair hanging down shoulder length, curly, unkempt hair. Also he had a mustache and a goatee type beard.' " Id. at 766. In a federal habeas corpus challenge to defendant's conviction, the court of appeals held that the exclusion of that juror violated *Batson*: "[T]he prosecution must at least articulate some plausible race-neutral reason for believing those factors will somehow affect the person's ability to perform his or her duties as a juror. In the present case, the prosecutor's comments * * * do not constitute such legitimate race-neutral reasons[.]" Elem v. Purkett, 25 F.3d 679, 683 (8th Cir. 1994).

The Supreme Court disagreed:

[O]nce the opponent of a peremptory challenge has made out a prima facie case of racial discrimination (step one), the burden of production shifts to the proponent of the strike to come forward with a race-neutral explanation (step two). If a race-neutral explanation is tendered, the trial court must then decide (step three) whether the opponent of the strike has proved purposeful racial discrimination. * * * The second step of this process does not demand an explanation that is persuasive, or even plausible. * * *

* * * It is not until the *third* step that the persuasiveness of the justification becomes relevant—the step in which the trial court determines whether the opponent of the strike has carried his burden of proving purposeful discrimination. * * *. At that stage, implausible or fantastic justifications may (and probably will) be found to be pretexts for purposeful discrimination. But to say that a trial judge *may choose to disbelieve* a silly or superstitious reason at step three is quite different from saying that a trial judge *must terminate* the inquiry at step two when the race-neutral reason is silly or superstitious.

514 U.S. at 767–68 (emphasis in original). The Court's analysis in *Purkett* has two consequences. First, a prosecutor can satisfy his burden at step two by advancing any reason at all so long as it is race-neutral. Second, a reviewing court—on direct appeal or on habeas corpus—will have to give some kind of deference to the fact-finding of the trial judge at step three. On federal habeas corpus, the state trial judge's finding of fact must be "presumed to be correct" by the reviewing court. Id. at 769.

The limit of the Supreme Court's tolerance for questionable *Batson* trial court findings was tested in Miller-El v. Dretke, 361 F.3d 849 (5th Cir. 2004), a case in which the prosecutor used ten of fourteen peremptory strikes against African Americans. Of the African-American jurors who survived challenge for cause, the prosecutor removed ten of eleven (91%) from the panel, while removing only four of thirty-one (13%) of the white jurors. There was evidence of differential questioning of African Americans, of manipulation of the selection process to increase the likelihood of African Americans being dropped from the jury, and of a long standing policy of systematic racial discrimination by the relevant prosecutor's office. Moreover, several justifications given for striking African-American jurors appeared to apply equally well to white jurors who were not struck. In a habeas corpus proceeding, the Fifth Circuit held that the prisoner had failed to show by clear and convincing evidence that the state court's finding of no discrimination was incorrect. The Supreme Court reversed, finding that the defendant had presented clear and convincing evidence of discrimination. Miller-El v. Dretke, 545 U.S. 231, 125 S.Ct. 2317, 162 L.Ed.2d 196 (2005).

3. How has *Batson* worked in practice? Justice Marshall's concern about the effectiveness of *Batson* appears to have been borne out in practice. After an extensive study of *Batson* challenges reported in appellate opinions, Professor Kenneth Melilli concluded that "*Batson* has [not] effectively circumscribed race- and gender-based peremptory challenges; toward that end, *Batson* is almost surely a failure." Melilli, *Batson* in Practice: What We Have Learned About *Batson* and Peremptory Challenges, 71 Notre Dame L. Rev. 447, 503 (1996); see also Marder, *Batson* Revisited, 97 Iowa L. Rev. 1612 (2012).

4. Should peremptory challenges be abolished? What is at stake in preserving peremptory challenges? In favor of such challenges, it can be argued that voir dire practices are often perfunctory and imperfect, particularly in federal court, that lawyers need to be free to question jurors vigorously (and then to excuse peremptorily any they may have offended by doing so), and that judges may sometimes err in failing to grant challenges for cause.

At the same time, there is a substantial and largely skeptical literature on the effectiveness of attorney voir dire and peremptory challenges in eliminating biased jurors. Writing over two decades ago, Professor MacCoun stated that "a large body of systematic empirical research has called into question the efficacy of both traditional and scientific jury selection strategies. In general, the demographic characteristics, personality traits, and general attitudes of jurors have weak and unreliable effects on verdicts." MacCoun, Inside the Black Box: What Empirical Research Tells Us About Decisionmaking by Civil Juries, in Verdict: Assessing the Civil Jury System 137, 151 (R. Litan ed., 1993). Another summary of the literature estimated that attorneys operating on the basis of their own hunches showed "low accuracy" (sometimes worse than random guessing) in distinguishing favorable and unfavorable jurors, and concluded that at best "attorney selection strategies * * * exercise a small influence on the outcomes of a few cases." Hastie, Is Attorney-Conducted Voir Dire an Effective Procedure for the Selection of Impartial Juries?, 40 Am. U. L. Rev. 703, 714, 717 (1991). "Scientific jury selection" does somewhat better. This technique relies less on attorneys' gut instincts than on "survey analyses and the clinical judgments of psychologists and psychiatrists. This technique factors in the results of statistical analyses of surveys conducted in the venue to identify juror background characteristics associated with a bias toward either side of the case." Id. at 719. Lawyers using these techniques appear to do about 5–10% better than random guessing in predicting juror attitudes. Id. See also Strier & Shestowsky, Profiling the Profilers: A Study of the Trial Consulting Profession, Its Impact on Trial Justice, and What, If Anything, to Do About It, 1999 Wis. L. Rev. 441.

It appears that the most successful uses of peremptories, at least from the point of view of the party making them, are likely to be based on "juror background characteristics associated with a bias"—that is, on group-based generalizations whose application to individuals may often violate the Equal Protection Clause. In this connection, recall the study of composite jurors discussed in connection with *Scott v. Harris, supra* Chapter 7, which showed stark and predictable differences in the way that particular juror types viewed the questions of excessive force raised in that case, based in part on their membership in particular cognizable social groups. In contrast, ad hoc "seat of the pants" justifications like those offered in cases like *Hernandez* and *Purkett*, even if sincerely proffered, are very unlikely to be correct or to have much influence on the accuracy or fairness of the jury's determinations. Professor Nancy Marder, following in Justice Marshall's footsteps, has argued for the abolition of peremptory challenges altogether. Marder, Beyond Gender: Peremptory Challenges and the Roles of the Jury, 73 Tex. L. Rev. 1041 (1995). For a thoughtful discussion, see Leong, Civilizing *Batson*, 97 Iowa L. Rev. 1561 (2012); Underwood, Ending Race Discrimination in Jury Selection: Whose Right Is It Anyway?, 92 Colum. L. Rev. 725 (1992).

5.   Expanding the protected categories. In J.E.B. v. Alabama ex rel. T.B., 511 U.S. 127, 114 S.Ct. 1419, 128 L.Ed.2d 89 (1994), a civil paternity and child support suit brought by the state of Alabama on behalf of the mother against the alleged father, the state had ten peremptory strikes and defendant J.E.B. had eleven. The venire panel consisted of 24 women and 12 men. One woman and two men were excused for cause, leaving 23 women and 10 men. The state struck one woman and nine men. J.E.B. struck 10 women and then used his final strike to eliminate the last man, resulting in a jury of 12 women. The jury returned a verdict finding that J.E.B. was the father, and the court entered an order directing him to pay child support. The Alabama Court of Appeals refused to extend *Batson* to gender-based strikes, and affirmed.

The Supreme Court reversed, holding that gender-based peremptory challenges violate the Equal Protection Clause of the Fourteenth Amendment. "Discrimination in jury selection, whether based on race or on gender, causes harm to the litigants, the community, and the individual jurors who are wrongfully excluded from participation in the judicial process. * * * Equal opportunity to participate in the fair administration of justice is fundamental to our democratic system. It not only furthers the goals of the jury system. It reaffirms the promise of equality under the law—that all citizens, regardless of race, ethnicity, or gender, have the chance to take part directly in our democracy." Id. at 140, 145–46.

The Ninth Circuit recently held, in SmithKline Beecham v. Abbott Laboratories, 740 F.3d 471 (9th Cir. 2014), that the Equal Protection Clause prohibits peremptory strikes based on sexual orientation. The underlying dispute in the case involved antitrust, contract, and unfair-trade-practices claims regarding the pricing of HIV medications. At jury selection, defendant Abbott Labs used a peremptory challenge against the only self-identified gay member of the venire, apparently based "on a discriminatory assumption that [the juror] could not impartially evaluate the case based on his sexual orientation." Id. at 477. The court held that the *Batson* doctrine applies to peremptory challenges based on sexual orientation:

> As illustrated by this case, permitting a strike based on sexual orientation would send the false message that gays and lesbians could not be trusted to reason fairly on issues of great import to the community or the nation. Strikes based on preconceived notions of the identities, preferences, and biases or gays and lesbians reinforce and perpetuate these stereotypes. The Constitution cannot countenance "state-sponsored group stereotypes rooted in, and reflective of, historical prejudice." J.E.B., 511 U.S. at 128.

> The history of exclusion of gays and lesbians from democratic institutions and the pervasiveness of stereotypes about the group lead us to conclude that *Batson* applies to peremptory strikes based on sexual orientation.

Id. at 486.

6.   Additional reading. There is a large literature on voir dire, and the *Batson* doctrine. A sampling includes Symposium Twenty-Five Years of *Batson*, 97 Iowa L. Rev. 1393 (2012); Page, *Batson*'s Blind Spot, 85 B.U. L. Rev. 155 (2005); Alschuler, The Supreme Court and the Jury: Voir Dire, Peremptory Challenges, and the Review of Jury Verdicts, 56 U. Chi. L. Rev. 153 (1989); Babcock, Voir Dire: Preserving "Its Wonderful Power," 27 Stan. L. Rev. 545 (1975); Zeisel and Diamond, The Effect of Peremptory Challenges on Jury and Verdict: An Experiment in a Federal District Court, 30 Stan. L. Rev. 491 (1978).

2. THE JUDGE

Caperton v. A.T. Massey Coal Co., Inc.

Supreme Court of the United States, 2009.
556 U.S. 868, 129 S.Ct. 2252, 173 L.Ed.2d 1208.

■ JUSTICE KENNEDY delivered the opinion of the Court.

In this case the Supreme Court of Appeals of West Virginia reversed a trial court judgment, which had entered a jury verdict of $50 million. Five justices heard the case, and the vote to reverse was 3 to 2. The question presented is whether the Due Process Clause of the Fourteenth Amendment was violated when one of the justices in the majority denied a recusal motion. The basis for the motion was that the justice had received campaign contributions in an extraordinary amount from, and through the efforts of, the board chairman and principal officer of the corporation found liable for the damages.

Under our precedents there are objective standards that require recusal when "the probability of actual bias on the part of the judge or decisionmaker is too high to be constitutionally tolerable." *Withrow v. Larkin*, 421 U.S. 35, 47, 95 S.Ct. 1456, 43 L.Ed.2d 712 (1975). Applying those precedents, we find that, in all the circumstances of this case, due process requires recusal.

I

In August 2002 a West Virginia jury returned a verdict that found respondents A.T. Massey Coal Co. and its affiliates (hereinafter Massey) liable for fraudulent misrepresentation, concealment, and tortious interference with existing contractual relations. The jury awarded petitioners Hugh Caperton, Harman Development Corp., Harman Mining Corp., and Sovereign Coal Sales (hereinafter Caperton) the sum of $50 million in compensatory and punitive damages.

In June 2004 the state trial court denied Massey's post-trial motions challenging the verdict and the damages award, finding that Massey "intentionally acted in utter disregard of [Caperton's] rights and ultimately destroyed [Caperton's] businesses because, after conducting cost-benefit analyses, [Massey] concluded it was in its financial interest to do so." * * *

Don Blankenship is Massey's chairman, chief executive officer, and president. After the verdict but before the appeal, West Virginia held its 2004 judicial elections. Knowing the Supreme Court of Appeals of West Virginia would consider the appeal in the case, Blankenship decided to support an attorney who sought to replace Justice McGraw. Justice McGraw was a candidate for reelection to that court. The attorney who sought to replace him was Brent Benjamin.

In addition to contributing the $1,000 statutory maximum to Benjamin's campaign committee, Blankenship donated almost $2.5 million to "And For The Sake Of The Kids," a political organization formed under 26 U.S.C. § 527. The § 527 organization opposed McGraw and supported Benjamin. Blankenship's donations accounted for more than two-thirds of the total funds it raised. This was not all. Blankenship spent, in addition, just over $500,000 on independent expenditures—for direct mailings and letters soliciting donations as well as television and newspaper advertisements—" 'to support . . . Brent Benjamin.' "

To provide some perspective, Blankenship's $3 million in contributions were more than the total amount spent by all other Benjamin supporters and three times the amount spent by Benjamin's own committee. Caperton contends that Blankenship spent $1 million more than the total amount spent by the campaign committees of both candidates combined.

Benjamin won. He received 382,036 votes (53.3%), and McGraw received 334,301 votes (46.7%).

In October 2005, before Massey filed its petition for appeal in West Virginia's highest court, Caperton moved to disqualify now-Justice Benjamin under the Due Process Clause and the West Virginia Code of Judicial Conduct, based on the conflict caused by Blankenship's campaign involvement. Justice Benjamin denied the motion in April 2006. He indicated that he "carefully considered the bases and accompanying exhibits proffered by the movants." But he found "no objective information . . . to show that this Justice has a bias for or against any litigant, that this Justice has prejudged the matters which comprise this litigation, or that this Justice will be anything but fair and impartial." In December 2006 Massey filed its petition for appeal to challenge the adverse jury verdict. The West Virginia Supreme Court of Appeals granted review.

In November 2007 that court reversed the $50 million verdict against Massey. The majority opinion, authored by then-Chief Justice Davis and joined by Justices Benjamin and Maynard, found that "Massey's conduct warranted the type of judgment rendered in this case." It reversed, nevertheless, based on two independent grounds—first, that a forum-selection clause contained in a contract to which Massey was not a party barred the suit in West Virginia, and, second, that res judicata barred the suit due to an out-of-state judgment to which Massey was not a party. Justice Starcher dissented, stating that the "majority's opinion is morally and legally wrong." * * *

The court granted rehearing. . . . Justice Benjamin again refused to withdraw[.] * * * In April 2008 a divided court again reversed the jury verdict, and again it was a 3-to-2 decision [with Justice Benjamin again in the majority].

We granted certiorari.

II

It is axiomatic that "[a] fair trial in a fair tribunal is a basic requirement of due process." *Murchison, supra,* at 136, 75 S.Ct. 623. As the Court has recognized, however, "most matters relating to judicial disqualification [do] not rise to a constitutional level." *FTC v. Cement Institute,* 333 U.S. 683, 702, 68 S.Ct. 793, 92 L.Ed. 1010 (1948). The early and leading case on the subject is *Tumey v. Ohio,* 273 U.S. 510, 47 S.Ct. 437, 71 L.Ed. 749 (1927). There, the Court stated that "matters of kinship, personal bias, state policy, remoteness of interest, would seem generally to be matters merely of legislative discretion." *Id.,* at 523, 47 S.Ct. 437.

The *Tumey* Court concluded that the Due Process Clause incorporated the common-law rule that a judge must recuse himself when he has "a direct, personal, substantial, pecuniary interest" in a case. *Ibid.* This rule reflects the maxim that "[n]o man is allowed to be a judge in his own cause; because his interest would certainly bias his judgment, and, not improbably, corrupt his integrity." The Federalist No. 10, p. 59 (J. Cooke ed.1961) (J. Madison); see Frank, Disqualification of Judges, 56 Yale L.J. 605, 611–612 (1947) (same). Under this rule, "disqualification for bias or prejudice was not permitted"; those matters were left to statutes and judicial codes. *Lavoie, supra,* at 820, 106 S.Ct. 1580. Personal bias or prejudice "alone would not be sufficient basis for imposing a constitutional requirement under the Due Process Clause." *Lavoie, supra,* at 820, 106 S.Ct. 1580.

As new problems have emerged that were not discussed at common law, however, the Court has identified additional instances which, as an objective matter, require recusal. These are circumstances "in which experience teaches that the probability of actual bias on the part of the judge or decisionmaker is too high to be constitutionally tolerable." *Withrow,* 421 U.S., at 47, 95 S.Ct. 1456. To place the present case in proper context, two instances where the Court has required recusal merit further discussion.

A

The first involved the emergence of local tribunals where a judge had a financial interest in the outcome of a case, although the interest was less than what would have been considered personal or direct at common law.

This was the problem addressed in *Tumey*. There, the mayor of a village had the authority to sit as a judge (with no jury) to try those accused of violating a state law prohibiting the possession of alcoholic beverages. Inherent in this structure were two potential conflicts. First, the mayor received a salary supplement for performing judicial duties, and the funds for that compensation derived from the fines assessed in a case. No fines were assessed upon acquittal. The mayor-judge thus received a salary supplement only if he convicted the defendant. 273 U.S., at 520, 47 S.Ct. 437. Second, sums from the criminal fines were deposited to the village's general treasury fund for village improvements and repairs. *Id.,* at 522, 47 S.Ct. 437.

The Court held that the Due Process Clause required disqualification " both because of [the mayor-judge's] direct pecuniary interest in the outcome, and because of his official motive to convict and to graduate the fine to help the financial needs of the village." *Id.,* at 535, 47 S.Ct. 437. It so held despite observing that "[t]here are doubtless mayors who would not allow such a consideration as $12 costs in each case to affect their judgment in it." *Id.,* at 532, 47 S.Ct. 437. The Court articulated the controlling principle:

> "Every procedure which would offer a possible temptation to the average man as a judge to forget the burden of proof required to convict the defendant, or which might lead him not to hold the balance nice, clear and true between the State and the accused, denies the latter due process of law." *Ibid.*

The Court was thus concerned with more than the traditional common-law prohibition on direct pecuniary interest. It was also concerned with a more general concept of interests that tempt adjudicators to disregard neutrality. * * *

B

The second instance requiring recusal that was not discussed at common law emerged in the criminal contempt context, where a judge had no pecuniary interest in the case but was challenged because of a conflict arising from his participation in an earlier proceeding. This Court characterized that first proceeding (perhaps pejoratively) as a " 'one-man grand jury.' " *Murchison,* 349 U.S., at 133, 75 S.Ct. 623.

In that first proceeding, and as provided by state law, a judge examined witnesses to determine whether criminal charges should be brought. The judge called the two petitioners before him. One petitioner answered questions, but the judge found him untruthful and charged him with perjury. The second declined to answer on the ground that he did not have counsel with him, as state law seemed to permit. The judge charged him with contempt. The judge proceeded to try and convict both petitioners. *Id.,* at 134–135, 75 S.Ct. 623.

This Court set aside the convictions on grounds that the judge had a conflict of interest at the trial stage because of his earlier participation followed by his decision to charge them. The Due Process Clause required disqualification. The Court recited the general rule that "no man can be a judge in his own case," adding that "no man is permitted to try cases where he has an interest in the outcome." *Id.,* at 136, 75 S.Ct. 623. It noted that the disqualifying criteria "cannot be defined with precision. Circumstances and relationships must be considered." *Ibid.* These circumstances and the prior relationship required recusal: "Having been a part of [the one-man grand jury] process a judge cannot be, in the very nature of things, wholly disinterested in the conviction or acquittal of those accused." *Id.,* at 137, 75 S.Ct. 623. That is because "[a]s a practical matter it is difficult if not impossible for a judge to free himself from the influence of what took place in his 'grand-jury' secret session." *Id.,* at 138, 75 S.Ct. 623. * * *

III

Based on the principles described in these cases we turn to the issue before us. This problem arises in the context of judicial elections, a framework not presented in the precedents we have reviewed and discussed.

Caperton contends that Blankenship's pivotal role in getting Justice Benjamin elected created a constitutionally intolerable probability of actual bias. Though not a bribe or criminal influence, Justice Benjamin would nevertheless feel a debt of gratitude to Blankenship for his extraordinary efforts to get him elected. That temptation, Caperton claims, is as strong and inherent in human nature as was the conflict the Court confronted in *Tumey* [ ] when a mayor-judge (or the city) benefited financially from a defendant's conviction, as well as the conflict identified in *Murchison* [ ]when a judge was the object of a defendant's contempt.

Justice Benjamin was careful to address the recusal motions and explain his reasons why, on his view of the controlling standard, disqualification was not in order. In four separate opinions issued during the course of the appeal, he explained why no actual bias had been established. He found no basis for recusal because Caperton failed to provide "objective evidence" or "objective information," but merely "subjective belief" of bias. Nor could anyone "point to any actual conduct or activity on [his] part which could be termed 'improper.' " In other words, based on the facts presented by Caperton, Justice Benjamin conducted a probing search into his actual motives and inclinations; and he found none to be improper. We do not question his subjective findings of impartiality and propriety. Nor do we determine whether there was actual bias.

Following accepted principles of our legal tradition respecting the proper performance of judicial functions, judges often inquire into their subjective motives and purposes in the ordinary course of deciding a case. This does not mean the inquiry is a simple one. "The work of deciding cases goes on every day in hundreds of courts throughout the land. Any judge, one might suppose, would find it easy to describe the process which he had followed a thousand times and more. Nothing could be farther from the truth." B. Cardozo, The Nature of the Judicial Process 9 (1921). * * *

The difficulties of inquiring into actual bias, and the fact that the inquiry is often a private one, simply underscore the need for objective rules. Otherwise there may be no adequate protection against a judge who simply misreads or misapprehends the real motives at work in deciding the case. The judge's own inquiry into actual bias, then, is not one that the law can easily superintend or review, though actual bias, if disclosed, no doubt would be grounds for appropriate relief. In lieu of exclusive reliance on that personal inquiry, or on appellate review of the judge's determination respecting actual bias, the Due Process Clause has been implemented by objective standards that do not require proof of actual bias. * * *

We turn to the influence at issue in this case. Not every campaign contribution by a litigant or attorney creates a probability of bias that requires a judge's recusal, but this is an exceptional case. . . . We conclude that there is a serious risk of actual bias—based on objective and reasonable perceptions—when a person with a personal stake in a particular case had a significant and disproportionate influence in placing the judge on the case by raising funds or directing the judge's election campaign when the case was pending or imminent. The inquiry centers on the contribution's relative size in comparison to the total amount of money contributed to the campaign, the total amount spent in the election, and the apparent effect such contribution had on the outcome of the election.

Applying this principle, we conclude that Blankenship's campaign efforts had a significant and disproportionate influence in placing Justice Benjamin on the case. Blankenship contributed some $3 million to unseat the incumbent and replace him with Benjamin. His contributions eclipsed the total amount spent by all other Benjamin supporters and exceeded by 300% the amount spent by Benjamin's campaign committee. Caperton claims Blankenship spent $1 million more than the total amount spent by the campaign committees of both candidates combined.

Massey responds that Blankenship's support, while significant, did not cause Benjamin's victory. In the end the people of West Virginia elected him, and they did so based on many reasons other than Blankenship's efforts. Massey points out that every major state newspaper, but one, endorsed Benjamin. * * *

Whether Blankenship's campaign contributions were a necessary and sufficient cause of Benjamin's victory is not the proper inquiry. Much like determining whether a judge is actually biased, proving what ultimately drives the electorate to choose a particular candidate is a difficult endeavor, not likely to lend itself to a certain conclusion. This is particularly true where, as here, there is no procedure for judicial factfinding and the sole trier of fact is the one accused of bias. Due process requires an objective inquiry into whether the contributor's influence on the election under all the circumstances "would offer a possible temptation to the average . . . judge to . . . lead him not to hold the balance nice, clear and true." *Tumey, supra,* at 532, 47 S.Ct. 437. In an election decided by fewer than 50,000 votes (382,036 to 334,301), see Blankenship's campaign contributions—in comparison to the total amount contributed to the campaign, as well as the total amount spent in the election—had a significant and disproportionate influence on the electoral outcome. And the risk that Blankenship's influence engendered actual bias is sufficiently substantial that it "must be forbidden if the guarantee of due process is to be adequately implemented." *Withrow, supra,* at 47, 95 S.Ct. 1456.

The temporal relationship between the campaign contributions, the justice's election, and the pendency of the case is also critical. It was reasonably foreseeable, when the campaign contributions were made, that the pending case would be before the newly elected justice. The $50 million adverse jury verdict had been entered before the election, and the Supreme Court of Appeals was the next step once the state trial court dealt with post-trial motions. So it became at once apparent that, absent recusal, Justice Benjamin would review a judgment that cost his biggest donor's company $50 million. Although there is no allegation of a *quid pro quo* agreement, the fact remains that Blankenship's extraordinary contributions were made at a time when he had a vested stake in the outcome. Just as no man is allowed to be a judge in his own cause, similar fears of bias can arise when—without the consent of the other parties— a man chooses the judge in his own cause. And applying this principle to the judicial election process, there was here a serious, objective risk of actual bias that required Justice Benjamin's recusal.

Justice Benjamin did undertake an extensive search for actual bias. But, as we have indicated, that is just one step in the judicial p objective standards may also require recusal whether or not actu exists or can be proved. . . . We find that Blankenship's significe disproportionate influence—coupled with the temporal relat between the election and the pending case—" ' "offer a temptation to the average . . . judge to . . . lead him not to hold the nice, clear and true." ' " *Lavoie,* 475 U.S., at 825, 106 S.Ct. 1580. these extreme facts the probability of actual bias rises unconstitutional level.

IV

Our decision today addresses an extraordinary situation where the Constitution requires recusal. Massey and its *amici* predict that various adverse consequences will follow from recognizing a constitutional violation here—ranging from a flood of recusal motions to unnecessary interference with judicial elections. We disagree. The facts now before us are extreme by any measure. The parties point to no other instance involving judicial campaign contributions that presents a potential for bias comparable to the circumstances in this case.

It is true that extreme cases often test the bounds of established legal principles, and sometimes no administrable standard may be available to address the perceived wrong. But it is also true that extreme cases are more likely to cross constitutional limits, requiring this Court's intervention and formulation of objective standards. This is particularly true when due process is violated. * * *

This Court's recusal cases are illustrative. In each case the Court dealt with extreme facts that created an unconstitutional probability of bias that " 'cannot be defined with precision.' " *Lavoie,* 475 U.S., at 822, 106 S.Ct. 1580 (quoting *Murchison,* 349 U.S., at 136, 75 S.Ct. 623). Yet the Court articulated an objective standard to protect the parties' basic right to a fair trial in a fair tribunal. The Court was careful to distinguish the extreme facts of the cases before it from those interests that would not rise to a constitutional level. . . . In this case we do nothing more than what the Court has done before.

As such, it is worth noting the effects, or lack thereof, of the Court's prior decisions. Even though the standards announced in those cases raised questions similar to those that might be asked after our decision today, the Court was not flooded with *Monroeville* or *Murchison* motions. That is perhaps due in part to the extreme facts those standards sought to address. Courts proved quite capable of applying the standards to less extreme situations. * * *

"The Due Process Clause demarks only the outer boundaries of judicial disqualifications. Congress and the states, of course, remain free to impose more rigorous standards for judicial disqualification than those we find mandated here today." *Lavoie, supra,* at 828, 106 S.Ct. 1580. Because the codes of judicial conduct provide more protection than due process requires, most disputes over disqualification will be resolved without resort to the Constitution. Application of the constitutional standard implicated in this case will thus be confined to rare instances.

The judgment of the Supreme Court of Appeals of West Virginia is reversed, and the case is remanded for further proceedings not inconsistent with this opinion.

■ CHIEF JUSTICE ROBERTS, with whom JUSTICE SCALIA, JUSTICE THOMAS, and JUSTICE ALITO join, dissenting.

I, of course, share the majority's sincere concerns about the need to maintain a fair, independent, and impartial judiciary—and one that appears to be such. But I fear that the Court's decision will undermine rather than promote these values.

Until today, we have recognized exactly two situations in which the Federal Due Process Clause requires disqualification of a judge: when the judge has a financial interest in the outcome of the case, and when the judge is trying a defendant for certain criminal contempts. Vaguer notions of bias or the appearance of bias were never a basis for disqualification, either at common law or under our constitutional precedents. Those issues were instead addressed by legislation or court rules.

Today, however, the Court enlists the Due Process Clause to overturn a judge's failure to recuse because of a "probability of bias." Unlike the established grounds for disqualification, a "probability of bias" cannot be defined in any limited way. The Court's new "rule" provides no guidance to judges and litigants about when recusal will be constitutionally required. This will inevitably lead to an increase in allegations that judges are biased, however groundless those charges may be. The end result will do far more to erode public confidence in judicial impartiality than an isolated failure to recuse in a particular case.

I

There is a "presumption of honesty and integrity in those serving as adjudicators." *Withrow v. Larkin,* 421 U.S. 35, 47, 95 S.Ct. 1456, 43 L.Ed.2d 712 (1975). All judges take an oath to uphold the Constitution and apply the law impartially, and we trust that they will live up to this promise. See *Republican Party of Minn. v. White,* 536 U.S. 765, 796, 122 S.Ct. 2528, 153 L.Ed.2d 694 (2002). * * *

In any given case, there are a number of factors that could give rise to a "probability" or "appearance" of bias: friendship with a party or lawyer, prior employment experience, membership in clubs or associations, prior speeches and writings, religious affiliation, and countless other considerations. We have never held that the Due Process Clause requires recusal for any of these reasons, even though they could be viewed as presenting a "probability of bias." Many state *statutes* require recusal based on a probability or appearance of bias, but "that alone would not be sufficient basis for imposing a *constitutional* requirement under the Due Process Clause." *Lavoie, supra,* at 820, 106 S.Ct. 1580 (emphasis added). States are, of course, free to adopt broader recusal rules than the Constitution requires—and every State has—but these developments are not continuously incorporated into the Due Process Clause.

II

In departing from this clear line between when recusal is constitutionally required and when it is not, the majority repeatedly emphasizes the need for an "objective" standard. The majority's analysis is "objective" in that it does not inquire into Justice Benjamin's motives or decisionmaking process. But the standard the majority articulates— "probability of bias"—fails to provide clear, workable guidance for future cases. At the most basic level, it is unclear whether the new probability of bias standard is somehow limited to financial support in judicial elections, or applies to judicial recusal questions more generally.

But there are other fundamental questions as well. With little help from the majority, courts will now have to determine:

1.   How much money is too much money? What level of contribution or expenditure gives rise to a "probability of bias"?

2.   How do we determine whether a given expenditure is "disproportionate"? Disproportionate *to what* ?

3.   Are independent, non-coordinated expenditures treated the same as direct contributions to a candidate's campaign? What about contributions to independent outside groups supporting a candidate?

4.   Does it matter whether the litigant has contributed to other candidates or made large expenditures in connection with other elections?

5.   Does the amount at issue in the case matter? What if this case were an employment dispute with only $10,000 at stake? What if the plaintiffs only sought non-monetary relief such as an injunction or declaratory judgment?

6.   Does the analysis change depending on whether the judge whose disqualification is sought sits on a trial court, appeals court, or state supreme court?

7.   How long does the probability of bias last? Does the probability of bias diminish over time as the election recedes? Does it matter whether the judge plans to run for reelection?

8.   What if the "disproportionately" large expenditure is made by an industry association, trade union, physicians' group, or the plaintiffs' bar? Must the judge recuse in all cases that affect the association's interests? Must the judge recuse in all cases in which a party or lawyer is a member of that group? Does it matter how much the litigant contributed to the association?

9.   What if the case involves a social or ideological issue rather than a financial one? Must a judge recuse from cases involving, say, abortion rights if he has received "disproportionate" support from individuals who feel strongly about either side of that issue? If the supporter wants to help elect judges who are "tough on crime," must the judge recuse in all criminal cases?

10.   What if the candidate draws "disproportionate" support from a particular racial, religious, ethnic, or other group, and the case involves an issue of particular importance to that group?

[Justice Roberts continued in this vein, offering thirty more questions about the applicability of the majority's holding.]

These are only a few uncertainties that quickly come to mind. Judges and litigants will surely encounter others when they are forced to, or wish to, apply the majority's decision in different circumstances. Today's opinion requires state and federal judges simultaneously to act as political scientists (why did candidate X win the election?), economists (was the financial support disproportionate?), and psychologists (is there likely to be a debt of gratitude?).

The Court's inability to formulate a "judicially discernible and manageable standard" strongly counsels against the recognition of a novel constitutional right. * * *

III

A

To its credit, the Court seems to recognize that the inherently boundless nature of its new rule poses a problem. But the majority's only answer is that the present case is an "extreme" one, so there is no need to worry about other cases. * * *

But this is just so much whistling past the graveyard. Claims that have little chance of success are nonetheless frequently filed. The success rate for certiorari petitions before this Court is approximately 1.1%, and yet the previous Term some 8,241 were filed. Every one of the "*Caperton* motions" or appeals or § 1983 actions will claim that the judge is biased, or probably biased, bringing the judge and the judicial system into disrepute. And all future litigants will assert that their case is *really* the most extreme thus far.

Extreme cases often test the bounds of established legal principles. There is a cost to yielding to the desire to correct the extreme case, rather than adhering to the legal principle. That cost has been demonstrated so often that it is captured in a legal aphorism: "Hard cases make bad law." * * *

B

And why is the Court so convinced that this is an extreme case? It is true that Don Blankenship spent a large amount of money in connection with this election. But this point cannot be emphasized strongly enough: Other than a $1,000 direct contribution from Blankenship, *Justice Benjamin and his campaign had no control over how this money was spent.* Campaigns go to great lengths to develop precise messages and strategies. An insensitive or ham-handed ad campaign by an independent third party might distort the campaign's message or cause a backlash against the candidate, even though the candidate was not responsible for the ads. See *Buckley v. Valeo,* 424 U.S. 1, 47, 96 S.Ct. 612, 46 L.Ed.2d 659 (1976) (*per curiam*) ("Unlike contributions, such independent expenditures may well provide little assistance to the candidate's campaign and indeed may prove counterproductive"); see also Brief for Conference of Chief Justices as Amicus Curiae 27, n. 50 (citing examples of judicial elections in which independent expenditures backfired and hurt the candidate's campaign). The majority repeatedly characterizes Blankenship's spending as "contributions" or "campaign contributions," but it is more accurate to refer to them as "independent expenditures." Blankenship only "contributed" $1,000 to the Benjamin campaign.

Moreover, Blankenship's independent expenditures do not appear "grossly disproportionate" compared to other such expenditures in this very election. "And for the Sake of the Kids"—an independent group that received approximately two-thirds of its funding from Blankenship— spent $3,623,500 in connection with the election. But large independent expenditures were also made in support of Justice Benjamin's opponent. "Consumers for Justice"—an independent group that received large contributions from the plaintiffs' bar—spent approximately $2 million in this race. And Blankenship has made large expenditures in connection with several previous West Virginia elections, which undercuts any notion that his involvement in this election was "intended to influence the outcome" of particular pending litigation.

It is also far from clear that Blankenship's expenditures affected the outcome of this election. Justice Benjamin won by a comfortable 7-point margin (53.3% to 46.7%). Many observers believed that Justice Benjamin's opponent doomed his candidacy by giving a well-publicized speech that made several curious allegations; this speech was described in the local media as " deeply disturbing" and worse. Justice Benjamin's opponent also refused to give interviews or participate in debates. All but one of the major West Virginia newspapers endorsed Justice Benjamin. Justice Benjamin just might have won because the voters of West Virginia thought he would be a better judge than his opponent. Unlike the majority, I cannot say with any degree of certainty that Blankenship "cho[se] the judge in his own cause." I would give the voters of West Virginia more credit than that.

* * *

It is an old cliché, but sometimes the cure is worse than the disease. I am sure there are cases where a "probability of bias" should lead the prudent judge to step aside, but the judge fails to do so. Maybe this is one of them. But I believe that opening the door to recusal claims under the Due Process Clause, for an amorphous "probability of bias," will itself bring our judicial system into undeserved disrepute, and diminish the confidence of the American people in the fairness and integrity of their courts. I hope I am wrong.

I respectfully dissent.

■ JUSTICE SCALIA, dissenting.

The principal purpose of this Court's exercise of its certiorari jurisdiction is to clarify the law. As THE CHIEF JUSTICE's dissent makes painfully clear, the principal consequence of today's decision is to create vast uncertainty with respect to a point of law that can be raised in all litigated cases in (at least) those 39 States that elect their judges. This course was urged upon us on grounds that it would preserve the public's confidence in the judicial system.

The decision will have the opposite effect. What above all else is eroding public confidence in the Nation's judicial system is the perception that litigation is just a game, that the party with the most resourceful lawyer can play it to win, that our seemingly interminable legal proceedings are wonderfully self-perpetuating but incapable of delivering real-world justice. The Court's opinion will reinforce that perception, adding to the vast arsenal of lawyerly gambits what will come to be known as the *Caperton* claim. The facts relevant to adjudicating it will have to be litigated—and likewise the law governing it, which will be indeterminate for years to come, if not forever. Many billable hours will be spent in poring through volumes of campaign finance reports, and many more in contesting nonrecusal decisions through every available means.

A Talmudic maxim instructs with respect to the Scripture: "Turn it over, and turn it over, for all is therein." 8 e Babylonian Talmud: Seder Nezikin, Tractate Aboth, Ch. V, Mishnah 22, pp. 76–77 (I. Epstein ed.1935). (footnote omitted). Divinely inspired text may contain the answers to all earthly questions, but the Due Process Clause most assuredly does not. The Court today continues its quixotic quest to right all wrongs and repair all imperfections through the Constitution. Alas, the quest cannot succeed—which is why some wrongs and imperfections have been called nonjusticiable. In the best of all possible worlds, should judges sometimes recuse even where the clear commands of our prior due process law do not require it? Undoubtedly. The relevant question, however, is whether we do more good than harm by seeking to correct this imperfection through expansion of our constitutional mandate in a manner ungoverned by any discernable rule. The answer is obvious.

NOTE ON THE RECUSAL OR DISQUALIFICATION OF THE JUDGE

1. **Foundations: due process and judicial neutrality.** Neutrality implies isolation: from the political process, from the parties, and from the outcome of the dispute. It is clear that certain kinds of structural forms of bias violate the Due Process Clause. Consider Mayor Pugh, of the Village of North College Hill, Ohio, who presided over a town court established to hear violations of the state's Prohibition Act. The enabling legislation provided that the Mayor's additional compensation for taking on the responsibility of presiding over liquor cases was to be paid solely as a fraction of any fines that he awarded against defendants (a fee contingent on conviction) and that an additional substantial portion of the fines that he levied against defendants was to be paid in support of the Village's budget. In Tumey v. Ohio, 273 U.S. 510, 47 S.Ct. 437, 71 L.Ed. 749 (1927), both the personal and the institutional conflicts of interest created by this "eat what you kill" system of adjudication were held sufficient to give rise to a violation of due process.

In Aetna Life Ins. Co. v. LaVoie, 475 U.S. 813, 106 S.Ct. 1580, 89 L.Ed.2d 823 (1986), Justice Embry of the Alabama Supreme Court was one of the majority in an unsigned per curiam five-to-four decision affirming a judgment awarding $3.5 million in compensatory and punitive damages for an insurer's bad faith failure to pay a claim. Among the contested issues on appeal were the quantum of evidence sufficient to create a triable issue of fact on the issue of bad faith and the amount of punitive damages. It later emerged that Justice Embry had written the opinion, and that at the time of the decision, he had personally filed two actions against other insurers in an Alabama trial court, one a class action in which he was lead plaintiff on behalf of all state employees; both actions alleged bad faith failure to pay claims and sought punitive damages. Subsequently the class action settled and Justice Embry received $30,000 as part of the settlement. The Supreme Court held that Justice Embry's participation in a decision whose outcome bore directly on the strength of both the liability and damage elements of his pending claims was so direct, personal, substantial, and pecuniary as to violate Aetna's due process rights. Conversely, the interest that the other justices might have had as members of the class of all state employees was not sufficiently direct and personal to require disqualification, given that they did not know of the class action at the time of the original decision, that no class had been certified, and that no relief had been awarded.

2. *Caperton* **and judicial elections.** In *Caperton*, the Supreme Court decided five to four that Mr. Blankenship's expenditures in the judicial election constituted an "extreme case" requiring Justice Benjamin's recusal—as a matter of constitutional due process. But as Justice Roberts

suggests in dissent, is this really such an extreme case, and was Justice Benjamin unconstitutionally partial?

Moreover, does the *Caperton* opinion imply that the practice in thirty states of electing judges is unconstitutional? Professor Redish and Ms. Aronoff suggest so, arguing that an elected judge can never be sufficiently neutral. They contend that "life tenure, or, at the very least, some form of formal term limit is required by the Due Process Clause to assure constitutionally required judicial independence. As radical as this recommendation may be, we argue that there is no other way to assure the appearance or reality of fairness, both of which lie at the core of the due process guarantee." Redish & Aronoff, The Real Constitutional Problem with State Judicial Selection: Due Process, Judicial Retention, and the Dangers of Popular Constitutionalism, 56 Wm. & Mary L. Rev. 1 (2014). Are they right? Are there other reforms that could enhance judicial neutrality short of requiring life tenure? See Bassett & Perschbacher, The Elusive Goal of Impartiality, 97 Iowa L. Rev. 181 (2011).

Such concerns about partiality regularly arise in states with elected judiciaries where judges depend heavily on political contributions from lawyers who regularly appear before them. For example, in Aguilar v. Anderson, 855 S.W.2d 799 (Tex. Ct. App. 1993), the trial judge personally solicited a contribution from a party's lawyer while the lawyer had a case pending before him and then granted summary judgment in favor of the lawyer's client. The Texas Court of Appeal affirmed the judge's denial of a motion to recuse. The court noted that Texas courts had "repeatedly rejected the notion that a judge's acceptance of campaign contributions from lawyers creates bias necessitating recusal, or even an appearance of impropriety." Id. at 802. Moreover, "the contribution was small, the trial judge maintained a voluntary policy of accepting only very limited contributions from any single source and the contributing lawyer was not even lead attorney for defendants." Id. Noting that the standard for disqualification was whether the judge's impartiality might reasonably be questioned, a concurring judge argued that "a 'reasonable person' must be aware of the 'facts of life' which surround the judiciary. In states which elect judges, the 'reasonable person' must know that judges have to stand for election on a regular basis, that elections cost money and that in metropolitan areas and state-wide races those races are very expensive for an effective campaign." Id. at 805. But in Pierce v. Pierce, 39 P.3d 791 (Okla. 2001), the Oklahoma Supreme Court held that it was a violation of the Due Process Clause for a judge to preside over a divorce in which a party's lawyer and that lawyer's son had each given the legal maximum of $5,000 to the judge's campaign and had raised additional funds for him while the case was pending before the judge. Would these cases come out the same way after *Caperton*?

3.   Is the *Caperton* cure worse than the disease? In *Caperton*, the dissenting justices express concerns that the majority's somewhat vague constitutional standard will open the floodgates to judicial-recusal motions and sow deep uncertainty about elected judges' fitness to hear cases. At least in the first few years following the Court's decision that worry appears to have been unfounded. Cases applying the constitutional rule from *Caperton* have been rare, see, e.g., State v. Sawyer, 305 P.3d 608 (Kan. 2013), and one commentator has opined that "[w]e have now had enough experience since *Caperton* was decided in 2009 to know that *Caperton*-like disqualification motions will not become *de rigeur*." Smith & Peck, A Jurist and a Lawyer

Consider Judicial Recusal After *Caperton*, Judges' J. (Summer 2013); see also Stempel, Playing Forty Questions: Responding to Justice Roberts's Concerns in *Caperton* and Some Tentative Answers About Operationalizing Judicial Recusal and Due Process, 39 Sw. L. Rev. 1 (2009). Even if the courts have not been swamped with recusal motions based on *Caperton*, has the Supreme Court created a workable standard, or is jurisprudence on this issue destined to simply be *ad hoc*?

4. **Judicial-recusal statutes.** Although *Caperton* and the cases on which it is based establish a due process right to recusal in extreme cases, the states and the federal government are free to, and have, passed statutes stricter than the constitutional standard. Under 28 U.S.C. § 455(a), a federal judge "shall disqualify himself in any proceeding in which his impartiality might reasonably be questioned." The statute goes on to provide a list of specific circumstances under which a judge must recuse himself, including when the judge "in private practice . . . served as lawyer in the matter in controversy," the judge is related to the parties or lawyers, or, most commonly, when the judge "knows that he . . . has a financial interest in the subject matter in controversy or in a party to the proceeding, or any other interest that could be substantially affected by the outcome of the proceeding." 28 U.S.C. § 455(b).

Although the general duty to recuse under § 455(a) is open-ended, the requirement to recuse based on a financial interest in the litigation is strict. Not only does the statute require the judge to recuse himself when he is aware of a financial interest, it requires him to "inform himself about his personal and fiduciary financial interests, and make a reasonable effort to inform himself about the personal financial interests of his spouse and minor children residing in his household." 28 U.S.C. § 455(c). Nevertheless, the statute also provides that if a judge has "devoted substantial judicial time" to a case and later finds out that he has a financial interest, the judge may avoid disqualification by divesting himself of the "interest that provides grounds for the disqualification." 28 U.S.C. § 455(f).

5. **Personal commitments and attitudes.** While the rules with respect to financial disqualification are detailed and strict, those with respect to political leanings or attitudes are inexplicit, and judges are rarely disqualified on those grounds. In Pennsylvania v. International Union of Operating Engineers, 388 F. Supp. 155 (E.D. Pa. 1974), a race discrimination suit against a union, the union moved to disqualify Judge Leon Higginbotham, an African American, on the grounds, inter alia, that during the pendency of the case he had given a speech to the Association for the Study of Afro-American Life and History criticizing recent Supreme Court opinions dealing with race discrimination. Judge Higginbotham said that he did "not see the [Supreme] Court of the 1970's or envision the Court of the 1980's as the major instrument for significant change and improvement in the quality of race relations in America," and concluding that "we must make major efforts in other forums without exclusive reliance on the federal legal process." Id. at 157. The speech was given prominent coverage in The Philadelphia Inquirer. The affidavit in support of recusal went on to state that the judge "identified * * * with causes of blacks, including the cause of correction of social injustices which [he believed had] been caused to blacks," and that he had made himself "a participant in those causes, including the cause of correction of social injustices which [he believed had] been caused to blacks." Id. at 158. Taking these facts as true, the judge held that they did

not constitute grounds for recusal, noting that nothing he had said made any reference to the parties or the disputed issues in the case before him. Judge Higginbotham later published a scholarly book on the history of race during the colonial period. Higginbotham, In the Matter of Color (Oxford Univ. Press 1998). Is this result in this case consistent with 28 U.S.C § 455(a)'s requirement that the judge should recuse when his or her impartiality might reasonably be questioned? For an eloquent defense of Supreme Court justices sitting to decide cases involving issues on which they expressed public views before coming to the Court, see Justice Rehnquist's opinion in Laird v. Tatum, 409 U.S. 824, 93 S.Ct. 7, 34 L.Ed.2d 50 (1972).

6.   **Actions and attitudes arising from the conduct of the case.** Under the so called "extrajudicial source" doctrine, actions taken and statements made by the judge on the basis of events occurring in the case—as distinct from attitudes or communications that predate or occur independently of the proceedings—are typically not a basis for recusal. The reason behind the rule is that judges will naturally, and indeed are required to, form views of the case based upon the record and the proceedings before them. Thus, judicial rulings made in the course of the case and "opinions formed by the judge on the basis of facts introduced or events occurring in the course of the current proceedings, or of prior proceedings," are not a basis for recusal unless they can be shown to derive from sources outside the record or "they display a deep-seated favoritism or antagonism that would make fair judgment impossible." Liteky v. United States, 510 U.S. 540, 555, 114 S.Ct. 1147, 127 L.Ed.2d 474 (1994). "Thus, judicial remarks during the course of a trial that are critical or disapproving of, or even hostile to, counsel, the parties, or their cases, ordinarily do not support a bias or partiality challenge." Id. Nor do "expressions of impatience, dissatisfaction, annoyance, and even anger, that are within the bounds of what imperfect men and women, even after having been confirmed as federal judges, sometimes display. A judge's ordinary efforts at courtroom administration—even a stern and short-tempered judge's ordinary efforts at courtroom administration—remain immune." Id. at 55–56.

7.   **Extrajudicial commentary on a pending case.** In United States v. Microsoft Corp., 253 F.3d 34 (D.C. Cir. 2001), the court of appeals reviewed the district judge's finding that Microsoft Corporation violated the federal antitrust laws. After the close of the taking of evidence in the district court, the judge had given a number of interviews to reporters on condition that the interviews be "embargoed" until after he announced his decision. Some interviews lasted many hours. Among other things, Judge Jackson was reported as saying that Bill Gates' "testimony is without credibility." "[I]f I were able to propose a remedy of my devising, I'd require Mr. Gates to write a book report" on Napoleon "because I think [Gates] has a Napoleonic concept of himself and his company, an arrogance that derives from power and unalloyed success, with no leavening hard experience, no reverses." A reporter wrote that the judge had said that he could not "get out of his mind the group picture he had seen of Bill Gates and Paul Allen and their shaggy-haired first employees at Microsoft." He saw in the picture "a smart-mouthed young kid who had extraordinary ability and needs a little discipline. I've often said to colleagues that Gates would be better off if he had finished Harvard." Id. at 110.

In an extraordinary rebuke, the court of appeals wrote:

> Canon 3A(6) of the Code of Conduct for United States Judges requires federal judges to "avoid public comment on the merits of [ ] pending or impending" cases. Canon 2 tells judges to "avoid impropriety and the appearance of impropriety in all activities," on the bench and off. Canon 3A(4) forbids judges to initiate or consider ex parte communications on the merits of pending or impending proceedings. Section 455(a) of the Judicial Code requires judges to recuse themselves when their "impartiality might reasonably be questioned." 28 U.S.C. § 455(a).
>
> All indications are that the District Judge violated each of these ethical precepts by talking about the case with reporters. The violations were deliberate, repeated, egregious, and flagrant. The only serious question is what consequence should follow.

Id. at 107. On the merits, the court affirmed in part and reversed in part, and remanded for further proceedings. It disqualified the judge from sitting on the case on remand.

Recently, the Second Circuit disqualified the well-respected district judge adjudicating the litigation challenging the "stop and frisk" practices of the New York City Police Department. Judge Scheindlin had given several interviews regarding the case, including to the Associated Press, The New Yorker, and the New York Law Journal. Although the court took pains to note that it made no findings that Judge Scheindlin had engaged in any judicial misconduct, the court decided that her "appearance of impartiality may reasonably be questioned." The court stated:

> While nothing prohibits a judge from giving an interview to the media, and while one who gives an interview cannot predict with certainty what the writer will say, judges who affiliate themselves with news stories by participating in interviews run the risk that the resulting stories may contribute to the appearance of partiality. It is perhaps illustrative of how such situations can get out of the control of the judge that, later in The New Yorker piece, the article quotes a former law clerk of Judge Scheindlin: "As one of her former law clerks put it, 'What you have to remember about the judge is that she thinks cops lie.'"
>
> Further, in those two articles, as well as the New York Law Journal article, Judge Scheindlin describes herself as a jurist who is skeptical of law enforcement, in contrast to certain of her colleagues, whom she characterizes as inclined to favor the government. Given the heightened and sensitive public scrutiny of these cases, interviews in which the presiding judge draws such distinctions between herself and her colleagues might lead a reasonable observer to question the judge's impartiality.

Ligon v. City of New York, 736 F.3d 118 (2014) (per curiam). Was the Second Circuit's decision too cautious? And will the Second Circuit's disqualification order "have a sad effect on the public role that judges play?" Bazelon, Shut Up, Judge!, Slate (Nov. 1, 2013).

    8. Insubstantial claims of bias. The other side of the coin is that a judge has an obligation not to recuse herself unless the charge of actual or apparent bias really holds water:

> [D]isqualification is appropriate only if the facts provide what an objective, knowledgeable member of the public would find to be a *reasonable basis* for doubting the judge's impartiality. Were less required, a judge could abdicate in difficult cases at the mere sound of controversy, or *a litigant could avoid adverse decisions by alleging the slightest of factual bases for bias.*

El Fenix de Puerto Rico v. M/Y JOHANNY, 36 F.3d 136, 141 (1st Cir. 1994) (emphases in original). Sometimes a judge with an interest in a case must preside because there is effectively no wholly disinterested judge available. In In re Virginia Elec. & Power Co., 539 F.2d 357 (4th Cir. 1976), the District Judge, as a customer of Virginia Electric and Power (VEPCO), stood to receive a refund of $70–$100 if VEPCO prevailed in the suit. The judge notified the parties of his possible refund as soon as he became aware of it. Neither party objected until after almost four months and ten pretrial orders, when Sun Shipbuilding moved for recusal. (It does not appear from the opinion whether the orders were unfavorable to Sun Shipbuilding.) The district judge recused himself, but the court of appeals reversed, pointing out that every judge in Virginia was a VEPCO customer.

9.   **The procedure for recusal.** There are two federal recusal statutes, 28 U.S.C. §§ 144 and 455. Section 144 applies only to district judges. It provides, "Whenever a party to any proceeding in a district court makes and files a timely and sufficient affidavit that the judge before whom the matter is pending has a personal bias or prejudice against him in favor of any adverse party, such judge shall proceed no further therein, but another judge shall be assigned to hear such proceeding." "Personal bias or prejudice" are not defined in § 144. A judge challenged under § 144 may herself decide whether, assuming the truth of the matters stated, the affidavit is "timely" and "sufficient." Berger v. United States, 255 U.S. 22, 41 S.Ct. 230, 65 L.Ed. 481 (1922). If a timely affidavit accompanying a § 144 recusal motion is held to be "sufficient," a different judge must conduct a hearing into the truth of the matters asserted in the affidavit. See United States v. Azhocar, 581 F.3d 735 (9th Cir. 1978) ("Only after the legal sufficiency of the affidavit is determined does it become the duty of the judge to 'proceed no further' in the case."). Section 455 applies to all federal Justices, judges, and magistrate judges. It contains a long and very specific list of criteria requiring recusal. It does not contain an explicit timeliness requirement. A judge challenged under § 455 may, in her discretion, refer a recusal motion to another judge for decision, or she may decide it herself. If she decides it herself, she may decide disputed factual matters. See 13D Wright, Miller, Cooper & Freer, Federal Practice & Procedure §§ 3550–51 (2014).

A procedure allowing a challenged judge to decide a recusal motion herself is arguably justified on the ground that it prevents the disruption of referring the recusal question to another judge, but it is also a deterrent against moving for recusal. A motion for recusal may be, and often is, taken personally by the challenged judge. See, e.g., Duplan Corp. v. Deering Milliken, Inc., 400 F. Supp. 497 (D.S.C. 1975).

E. THE PROVINCE OF THE JURY

1. TAKING THE CASE FROM THE JURY

INTRODUCTORY NOTE ON TAKING THE CASE FROM THE JURY

The strongest control of jury functioning by the judge is taking the case away from the jury and entering a judgment that the judge thinks correct. This can be done at trial by what has been traditionally been called a directed verdict, or after trial by judgment notwithstanding the verdict (judgment n.o.v.). The terminology under the federal Rules, since a 1991 amendment, is judgment as a matter of law, which is the equivalent of both a directed verdict and a judgment notwithstanding the verdict. See Fed. R. Civ. P. 50. A less extreme method of jury control by the judge is taking the case away from the jury but ordering a new trial before a different jury. See Fed. R. Civ. P. 59. These devices will be examined below.

Simblest v. Maynard

United States Court of Appeals for the Second Circuit, 1970.
427 F.2d 1.

■ TIMBERS, DISTRICT JUDGE.

We have before us another instance of Vermont justice—this time at the hands of a federal trial judge who, correctly applying the law, set aside a $17,125 plaintiff's verdict and entered judgment n.o.v. for defendant, Rule 50(b), Fed. R. Civ. P., in a diversity negligence action arising out of an intersection collision between a passenger vehicle driven by plaintiff and a fire engine driven by defendant in Burlington, Vermont, during the electric power blackout which left most of New England in darkness on the night of November 9, 1965. We affirm.

I

Plaintiff, a citizen and resident of New Hampshire, was 66 years of age at the time of the accident. He was a distributor of reference books and had been in Burlington on business for three days prior to the accident. He was an experienced driver, having driven an average of some 54,000 miles per year since 1922. He was thoroughly familiar with the intersection in question. His eyesight was excellent and his hearing was very good.

Defendant, a citizen of Vermont, had resided in Burlington for 44 years. He had been a full time fireman with the Burlington Fire Department for 17 years. He was assigned to and regularly drove the 500 gallon pumper which he was driving at the time of the accident. He was thoroughly familiar with the intersection in question.

The accident occurred at the intersection of Main Street (U.S. Route 2), which runs generally east and west, and South Willard Street (U.S. Routes 2 and 7), which runs generally north and south. The neighborhood is partly business, partly residential. At approximately the center of the intersection there was an overhead electrical traffic control signal designed to exhibit the usual red and green lights.

At the time of the accident, approximately 5:27 P.M., it was dark, traffic was light and the weather was clear. Plaintiff was driving his 1964 Chrysler station wagon in a westerly direction on Main Street, approaching the intersection. Defendant was driving the fire engine, in response to a fire alarm, in a southerly direction on South Willard Street, also approaching the intersection.

Plaintiff testified that the traffic light was green in his favor as he approached and entered the intersection; but that when he had driven part way through the intersection the power failure extinguished all lights within his range of view, including the traffic light. All other witnesses, for both plaintiff and defendant, testified that the power failure occurred at least 10 to 15 minutes prior to the accident; and there was no evidence, except plaintiff's testimony, that the traffic light was operating at the time of the accident.

Plaintiff also testified that his speed was 12 to 15 miles per hour as he approached the intersection. He did not look to his right *before* he entered the intersection;[1] after looking to his left, to the front and to the rear (presumably through a rear view mirror), he looked to his right for the first time *when he was one-half to three-quarters of the way through the intersection* and then for the first time saw the fire engine within 12 feet of him. He testified that he did not hear the fire engine's siren or see the flashing lights or any other lights on the fire engine.

Plaintiff further testified that his view to the north (his right) as he entered the intersection was obstructed by various objects, including traffic signs, trees on Main Street and a Chamber of Commerce information booth on Main Street east of the intersection. All of the evidence, including the photographs of the intersection, demonstrates that, despite some obstruction of plaintiff's view to the north, he could have seen the approaching fire engine if he had looked between the obstructions and if he had looked to the north after he passed the information booth. One of plaintiff's own witnesses, Kathleen Burgess,

---

[1]   Plaintiff has stated in his brief in this Court that "as he approached the intersection, he *did* look to his right" (Appellant's Brief, 5); and he emphasizes "the only direct evidence on this point . . . from the plaintiff who testified as follows:

"Q. You did look to the right? A. Oh yes, sir. I sure did." (Appellant's Brief, 12–13.)

We find this testimony, lifted out of context, unfortunately to have created a mistaken impression on a critical issue in the case.

Plaintiff's complete direct testimony as to when he looked to his right, and in the sequence given, is as follows:

"*Direct Examination* (By Mr. Grussing) . . .

Q. Now, tell us, Mr. Simblest, in your own words, just what occurred when you entered that intersection. A. Well, I will repeat. I had the 'green' light with me, proceeded through, was talf (sic) to 3/4 through the street, looked to my right, and within 12 feet of me, here is a big, massive fire truck. . . . (Tr. 17)

. . .

Q. Did you, as you approached this intersection, did you look to your right at all to see what was coming out of the intersection? A. Coming into an intersection with people ready to go across, with fairly decent eyesight I could see from the left to the right to the front, and I had already watched in the rear before they got to that angle.

Q. You did look to the right? A. Oh, yes, sir. I sure did.

Q. Were you able, or did you see this truck approaching? A. Within '12' feet. It was too late.

Q. The first time you saw it, it was within 12 feet of you? A. That is right." (Tr. 19)

testified that "maybe five to ten seconds previous to when he was struck he might have seen the fire truck," referring to the interval of time after plaintiff passed the information booth until the collision.

Defendant testified that, accompanied by Captain Fortin in the front seat, he drove the fire engine from the Mansfield Avenue Fire Station, seven and one-half blocks away from the scene of the accident, in the direction of the fire on Maple Street. While driving in a southerly direction on South Willard Street and approaching the intersection with Main Street, the following warning devices were in operation on the fire engine: the penetrator making a wailing sound; the usual fire siren; a flashing red light attached to the dome of the fire engine; two red lights on either side of the cab; and the usual headlights. Defendant saw plaintiff's car east of the information booth and next saw it as it entered the intersection. Defendant testified that he was traveling 20 to 25 miles per hour as he approached the intersection;[2] he slowed down, applied his brakes and turned the fire engine to his right, in a westerly direction, in an attempt to avoid the collision. He estimated that he was traveling 15 to 20 miles per hour at the time of impact. A police investigation found a 15 foot skid mark made by the fire engine but no skid marks made by plaintiff's car.

The fire engine struck plaintiff's car on the right side, in the area of the fender and front door. Plaintiff's head struck the post on the left side of his car, causing him to lose consciousness for about a minute. He claims that this injury aggravated a chronic pre-existing degenerative arthritic condition of the spine.

Other witnesses who virtually bracketed the intersection from different vantage points were called. Frank Valz, called by plaintiff, was looking out a window in a building on the northeast corner of the intersection; he saw the fire engine when it was a block north of the intersection; he heard its siren and saw its flashing red lights. Kathleen Burgess, another of plaintiff's witnesses (referred to above), was driving in a northerly direction on South Willard Street, just south of the intersection; seeing the fire engine when it was a block north of the intersection, she pulled over to the curb and stopped; she saw its flashing lights, but did not hear its siren. Holland Smith and Irene Longe, both called by defendant, were in the building at the southwest corner of the intersection; as the fire engine approached the intersection, they each heard its warning signals and saw its flashing lights in operation.

Defendant's motions for a directed verdict at the close of plaintiff's case and at the close of all the evidence having been denied and the jury having returned a plaintiff's verdict, defendant moved to set aside the verdict and the judgment entered thereon and for entry of judgment n.o.v. in accordance with his motion for a directed verdict. Chief Judge Leddy filed a written opinion granting defendant's motion.

On appeal plaintiff urges that the district court erred in granting defendant's motion for judgment n.o.v. or, in the alternative, in declining to charge the jury on the doctrine of last clear chance. We affirm both rulings of the district court.

---

[2] The maximum speed attributed to the fire engine as it approached the intersection was 30 to 35 miles per hour (testimony of Captain Fortin).

II

In determining whether the motion for judgment n.o.v. should have been granted, a threshold question is presented as to the correct standard to be applied. This standard has been expressed in various ways. Simply stated, it is whether the evidence is such that, without weighing the credibility of the witnesses or otherwise considering the weight of the evidence, there can be but one conclusion as to the verdict that reasonable men could have reached. See, e.g., Brady v. Southern Railway Company, 320 U.S. 476, 479–80 (1943); O'Connor v. Pennsylvania Railroad Company, 308 F.2d 911, 914–15 (2 Cir. 1962). See also 5 Moore's Federal Practice ¶ 50.02[1], at 2320–23 (2d ed. 1968); Wright, Law of Federal Courts § 95, at 425 (2d ed. 1970). On a motion for judgment n.o.v., the evidence must be viewed in the light most favorable to the party against whom the motion is made and he must be given the benefit of all reasonable inferences which may be drawn in his favor from that evidence. O'Connor v. Pennsylvania Railroad Company, supra, at 914–15; 5 Moore, supra, at 2325; Wright, supra, at 425.

We acknowledge that it has not been settled in a diversity action whether, in considering the evidence in the light most favorable to the party against whom the motion is made, the court may consider all the evidence or only the evidence favorable to such party and the uncontradicted, unimpeached evidence unfavorable to him. Under Vermont law, all the evidence may be considered. Kremer v. Fortin, 119 Vt. 1, 117 A.2d 245 (1955) (intersection collision between fire engine and passenger car). Plaintiff here urges that under the federal standard only evidence favorable to him should have been considered, citing Wilkerson v. McCarthy, 336 U.S. 53, 57 (1949). As plaintiff reads that case, the court below should not have considered anything else, not even the uncontradicted, unimpeached evidence unfavorable to him. However, we are committed to a contrary view in a diversity case. O'Connor v. Pennsylvania Railroad Company, supra.

The Supreme Court at least twice has declined to decide whether the state or federal standard as to the sufficiency of the evidence is controlling on such motions in diversity cases. Mercer v. Theriot, 377 U.S. 152, 156 (1964) (per curiam); Dick v. New York Life Insurance Company, 359 U.S. 437, 444–45 (1959). Our Court likewise has declined to decide this issue in recent cases. Mull v. Ford Motor Company, 368 F.2d 713, 716 n. 4 (2 Cir. 1966); Hooks v. New York Central Railroad Company, 327 F.2d 259, 261 n. 2 (2 Cir. 1964); Jacobs v. Great Atlantic & Pacific Tea Company, 324 F.2d 50, 51 n. 1 (2 Cir. 1963); Evans v. S.J. Groves & Sons Company, 315 F.2d 335, 342 n. 2 (2 Cir. 1963). See 5 Moore, supra, at 2347–50.[3]

See especially the comprehensive opinion of the Fifth Circuit in Boeing Company v. Shipman, 411 F.2d 365 (5 Cir. 1969) (en banc), holding (1) that in diversity cases a federal rather than state standard should be applied in testing the sufficiency of the evidence in connection

---

[3]   Assuming that the federal standard were controlling, plaintiff's contention that under that standard evidence introduced by the moving party may not be considered is open to question. Plaintiff relies on Wilkerson v. McCarthy, 336 U.S. 53, 57 (1949). But most Courts of Appeals have held that evidence introduced by the moving party may be considered, distinguishing *Wilkerson* on the ground that FELA cases are *sui generis*. 5 Moore, supra, at 2329.

with motions for a directed verdict and for judgment n.o.v.; (2) that the FELA standard for testing the sufficiency of the evidence on such motions is not applicable in diversity cases; and (3) that the federal standard to be applied in diversity cases requires the court to consider "all of the evidence—not just that evidence which supports the nonmover's case— but in the light and with all reasonable inferences most favorable to the party opposed to the motion." 411 F.2d at 374.

Our careful review of the record in the instant case leaves us with the firm conviction that, under either the Vermont standard or the more restrictive federal standard, plaintiff was contributorily negligent as a matter of law; and that Chief Judge Leddy correctly set aside the verdict and entered judgment for defendant n.o.v. O'Connor v. Pennsylvania Railroad Company, supra, at 914; Presser Royalty Company v. Chase Manhattan Bank, 272 F.2d 838, 840 (2 Cir. 1959).

Under the Vermont standard which permits all the evidence to be considered, Kremer v. Fortin, supra, plaintiff was so clearly guilty of contributory negligence that no further dilation is required.

Under the more restrictive federal standard—i.e., considering only the evidence favorable to plaintiff and the uncontradicted, unimpeached evidence unfavorable to him—while a closer question is presented than under the Vermont standard, we nevertheless hold that plaintiff was guilty of contributory negligence as a matter of law.[4]

In our view, applying the federal standard, the critical issue in the case is whether the fire engine was sounding a siren or displaying a red light as it approached the intersection immediately before the collision. Upon this critical issue, Chief Judge Leddy accurately and succinctly summarized the evidence as follows:

> "All witnesses to the accident, except the plaintiff, testified that the fire truck was sounding a siren or displaying a flashing red light. All of the witnesses except Miss Burgess and the plaintiff testified that the fire truck was sounding its siren and displaying a flashing red light."

The reason such evidence is critical is that under Vermont law, 23 V.S.A. § 1033, upon the approach of a fire department vehicle which is sounding a siren or displaying a red light, or both, all other vehicles are required to pull over to the right lane of traffic and come to a complete stop until the emergency vehicle has passed.[5] Since the emergency provision of this statute supersedes the general right of way statute regarding intersections controlled by traffic lights, 23 V.S.A. § 1054, the lone testimony of plaintiff that the traffic light was green in his favor as

---

[4] We emphasize that, solely for the purpose of testing the validity of plaintiff's claim under the federal standard, we assume without deciding that the federal standard is as stated. But compare, e.g., Boeing Company v. Shipman, supra note 3, at 373–75.

[5] 23 V.S.A. § 1033, in relevant part, provides:

"Except as hereinafter provided, all vehicles shall give the right of way to other vehicles approaching at intersecting highways from the right; and shall have the right of way over those approaching from the left; provided that upon the approach of an ambulance, police or fire department vehicle which is sounding a siren or displaying a red light or both, all other vehicles shall pull to the right of the lane of traffic and come to a complete stop until such emergency vehicle has passed. . . ."

Violation of this statute under Vermont law constitutes prima facie evidence of negligence. Dashnow v. Myers, 121 Vt. 273, 155 A.2d 859 (1959).

he approached and entered the intersection is of no moment. And since the emergency provision of 23 V.S.A. § 1033 becomes operative if *either* the siren is sounding *or* a red light is displayed on an approaching fire engine, we focus upon plaintiff's own testimony that he did not see the fire engine's flashing light, all other witnesses having testified that the red light was flashing.

As stated above, plaintiff testified that he first saw the fire engine when he was one-half to three-quarters of the way through the intersection and when the fire engine was within 12 feet of his car. At the speed at which the fire engine was traveling, plaintiff had approximately one-third of a second[6] in which to observe the fire engine prior to the collision. Accepting plaintiff's testimony that his eyesight was excellent, and assuming that the fire engine's flashing red light was revolving as rapidly as 60 revolutions per minute, plaintiff's one-third of a second observation does not support an inference that the light was not operating, much less does it constitute competent direct evidence to that effect. Opportunity to observe is a necessary ingredient of the competency of eyewitness evidence. Plaintiff's opportunity to observe, accepting his own testimony, simply was too short for his testimony on the operation of the light to be of any probative value whatsoever.

Plaintiff's testimony that he did not see the fire engine's flashing red light, in the teeth of the proven physical facts, we hold is tantamount to no proof at all on that issue. O'Connor v. Pennsylvania Railroad Company, supra, at 915. As one commentator has put it, ". . . the question of the total absence of proof quickly merges into the question whether the proof adduced is so insignificant as to be treated as the equivalent of the absence of proof." 5 Moore, supra, at 2320. If plaintiff had testified that he had not looked to his right at all, he of course would have been guilty of contributory negligence as a matter of law. We hold that his testimony in fact was the equivalent of his saying that he did not look at all.

Chief Judge Leddy concluded that plaintiff was guilty of contributory negligence as a matter of law; accordingly, he set aside the verdict and entered judgment n.o.v. for defendant. We agree.

III

Plaintiff urges in the alternative the claim that the district court erred in declining to charge the jury on the doctrine of last clear chance; of course this doctrine is relevant only if plaintiff was guilty of contributory negligence. Since we hold, as did Chief Judge Leddy, that plaintiff was contributorily negligent, his last clear chance claim is properly before us.

Moreover, we reject defendant's contentions that plaintiff failed properly to plead the doctrine of last clear chance (the complaint was amended to reflect such claim); and that plaintiff's requests to charge on the doctrine consisted of mere abstract propositions of law (the trial judge

---

[6]   This is the arithmetical mean (.322 seconds) between the maximum and minimum time intervals, according to the evidence, within which plaintiff could have observed the fire engine travel 12 feet. The minimum interval (.230 seconds) is based on Captain Fortin's testimony that the fire engine was traveling 35 miles per hour as it approached the intersection (supra note 2); the maximum interval (.414 seconds) is based on defendant's testimony that he was traveling 20 miles per hour (supra pages 3 and 4).

denied plaintiff's request to charge on last clear chance on the ground that "I do not think there is any evidence to support it").

We turn directly to whether there was evidence sufficient to warrant charging the jury on the issue of last clear chance. In addition to the usual essential elements of last clear chance, Vermont law requires the existence of a period of time during which *plaintiff,* in the exercise of due care, *could not* have avoided the accident *and* during which *defendant,* in the exercise of due care, *could* have avoided the accident. Spencer v. Fondry, 122 Vt. 149, 152, 167 A.2d 372 (1960).

Plaintiff's claim regarding last clear chance is pegged entirely on the theory that, there being no traffic behind his car, defendant should have seen such absence of traffic and should have had sufficient time to turn the fire engine to his left, rather than to his right, and thus to maneuver it into the space to the rear of plaintiff's car.

We agree with Chief Judge Leddy's ruling, directed precisely to plaintiff's claim in this respect, in refusing to charge on the doctrine of last clear chance:

> "The evidence is that, as I recall it, that while there was sufficient space behind the rear of the plaintiff's car and the easterly line of Willard Street, all of the testimony is that at the rate of speed the truck was going and because of the closeness of the two vehicles, it was impossible for the truck to make a maneuvering to go through that space, and that was testified to by the driver and also Miss Burgess who was parked on the opposite side of the intersection."

We hold, assuming *arguendo* there was an interval of time during which plaintiff in the exercise of due care could not have avoided the accident, that—based on the proven physical facts regarding the speed of the fire engine and the proximity of the two vehicles referred to above— the overwhelming, uncontroverted evidence demonstrates that defendant in the exercise of due care simply could not have avoided the accident. Spencer v. Fondry, supra, at 152.

Affirmed.

NOTE ON DEVICES FOR TAKING A CASE FROM THE JURY

1. **History and terminology.** At common law there was a device for taking a case from the jury, in addition to nonsuit and directed verdict, known as the demurrer to the evidence. Gibson v. Hunter, 2 H. Blackst. 187, 126 E.R. 499 (House of Lords, 1793). See also Galloway v. United States, 319 U.S. 372, 391 n.23, 63 S.Ct. 1077, 87 L.Ed. 1458 (1943). At one time, the judge after granting a motion for directed verdict literally directed the jury to return a verdict for one party or the other. If the jury failed to return the verdict as directed, the judge had the power to enter the proper verdict himself. Umsted v. Scofield Eng'g Constr. Co., 203 Cal. 224, 226, 263 P. 799, 799 (1928). The common practice now is for the judge simply to enter the verdict. See Calif.C.Civ.P. § 630(e), "The order of the court granting the motion for directed verdict is effective without any assent of the jury." The federal courts abandoned the formalistic and annoying ritual of actually directing the jury to return a particular verdict by amendment to Fed. R. Civ. P. 50 in 1963.

The federal Rules have now abandoned the vocabulary of motion for directed verdict and motion for judgment notwithstanding the verdict. Both are now called motions for judgment as a matter of law. Fed. R. Civ. P. 50(a), (b). Indeed, the amended Rule 50 considers preverdict and post-verdict motions to be the same thing; the post-verdict motion is simply a "renewed motion." Fed. R. Civ. P. 50(b). A motion for judgment as a matter of law may be made "at any time before the case is submitted to the jury." Fed. R. Civ. P. 50(a). A motion for judgment as a matter of law made after return of the verdict by the jury (i.e., a "renewed motion") will not be entertained unless the moving party first made the motion before the case was submitted to the jury. Fed. R. Civ. P. 50(b).

2.   The relationship between the standard for granting directed verdict and the burdens of production and persuasion. Like a motion for summary judgment, a motion for judgment as a matter of law (or directed verdict) tests the sufficiency of the nonmoving party's evidence to meet its *burden of production*. This evaluation is linked to the *burden of persuasion* by which the party would ultimately have to convince the jury, which in a civil case is typically "by a preponderance" or "more likely than not."

The present federal standard for granting a judgment as a matter of law is substantially the same as the federal standard articulated by the *Simblest* court. In deciding the question whether a reasonable jury could find in favor of the nonmoving party, the court should review "all of the evidence in the record," "draw all reasonable inferences in favor of the non moving party," and "not make credibility determinations or weigh the evidence." Reeves v. Sanderson Plumbing Prods., Inc., 530 U.S. 133, 150, 120 S.Ct. 2097, 147 L.Ed.2d 105 (2000). Thus, "although the court should review the record as a whole, it must disregard all evidence favorable to the moving party that the jury is not required to believe." Id. at 151. Was this standard properly applied in *Simblest*? Did the court resolve all issues of credibility in favor of nonmoving party? Did it draw all reasonable inferences from the evidence, so credited, in favor of the moving party?

One way of understanding the function of the motion for judgment as matter of law and related devices is as a means of preserving the integrity of the substantive law. Or put another way, to give the jury unlimited power to find the facts also gives them the power to alter the law in their discretion. Was the jury in *Simblest* seeking to alter the applicable substantive law? If so, was the court right to stop it from doing so? For discussion, see Noah, Civil Jury Nullification, 86 Iowa L. Rev. 1601 (2001).

3.   Practical considerations in taking the case from the jury. Trial judges usually do not grant motions for directed verdicts or (in the new federal terminology) preverdict motions for judgment as a matter of law. If the judge grants the preverdict motion, ending the case, and the court of appeals decides she was wrong to do so, the trial will have to be held all over again. If the judge grants a post-verdict motion and the court of appeals decides she was wrong to do so, the verdict can be reinstated. And there is always the chance that the jury will agree that nonmoving party's case lacks merit, obviating the need to decide the motion. In describing federal practice, Professors Wright and Miller advise, "Even at the close of all the evidence it may be desirable to refrain from granting a motion for judgment as a matter of law despite the fact that it would be possible for the district court to do so." 9B C. Wright & A. Miller, Federal Practice and Procedure § 2533 (3d ed.

2008). See generally Cooper, Directions for Directed Verdicts: A Compass for Federal Courts, 55 Minn. L. Rev. 903 (1971).

4.   Directing a verdict for the party with the burden of proof. Directing a verdict for the party having the burden of proof may involve different considerations from directing a verdict against such a party. An outstanding discussion in the case law is Ferdinand v. Agricultural Ins. Co., 22 N.J. 482, 126 A.2d 323 (1956). See 9B C. Wright & A. Miller, Federal Practice and Procedure § 2535 (3d ed. 2008); Carmichael, Directing a Verdict in Favor of the Party with the Burden of Proof, 16 Wake Forest L. Rev. 607 (1980).

Sioux City & Pacific Railroad Co. v. Stout

Supreme Court of the United States, 1873.
84 U.S. (17 Wall.) 657, 21 L.Ed. 745.

Henry Stout, a child six years of age and living with his parents, sued, by his next friend, the Sioux City and Pacific Railroad Company, in the court below, to recover damages for an injury sustained upon a turntable belonging to the said company. The turntable was in an open space, about eighty rods from the company's depot, in a hamlet or settlement of one hundred to one hundred and fifty persons. Near the turntable was a travelled road passing through the depot grounds, and another travelled road near by. On the railroad ground, which was not inclosed or visibly separated from the adjoining property, was situated the company's station-house, and about a quarter of a mile distant from this was the turntable on which the plaintiff was injured. There were but few houses in the neighborhood of the turntable, and the child's parents lived in another part of the town, and about three-fourths of a mile distant. The child, without the knowledge of his parents, set off with two other boys, the one nine and the other ten years of age, to go to the depot, with no definite purpose in view. When the boys arrived there, it was proposed by some of them to go to the turntable to play. The turntable was not attended or guarded by any servant of the company, was not fastened or locked, and revolved easily on its axis. Two of the boys began to turn it, and in attempting to get upon it, the foot of the child (he being at the time upon the railroad track) was caught between the end of the rail on the turntable as it was revolving, and the end of the iron rail on the main track of the road, and was crushed.

One witness, then a servant of the company, testified that he had previously seen boys playing at the turntable, and had forbidden them from playing there. But the witness had no charge of the table, and did not communicate the fact of having seen boys playing there, to any of the officers or servants of the company having the table in charge.

One of the boys, who was with the child when injured, had previously played upon the turntable when the railroad men were working on the track, in sight, and not far distant.

It appeared from the testimony that the child had not, before the day on which he was now injured, played at the turntable, or had, indeed, ever been there.

The table was constructed on the railroad company's own land, and, the testimony tended to show, in the ordinary way. It was a skeleton turntable, that is to say, it was not planked between the rails, though it had one or two loose boards upon the ties. There was an iron latch fastened to it which turned on a hinge, and, when in order, dropped into an iron socket on the track, and held the table in position while using. The catch of this latch was broken at the time of the accident. The latch, which weighed eight or ten pounds, could be easily lifted out of the catch and thrown back on the table, and the table was allowed to be moved about. This latch was not locked, or in any way fastened down before it was broken, and all the testimony on that subject tended to show that it was not usual for railroad companies to lock or guard turntables, but that it was usual to have a latch with a catch, or draw-bolt, to keep them in position when used.

The record stated that "the counsel for the defendant disclaimed resting their defence on the ground that the plaintiff's parents were negligent, or that the plaintiff (considering his tender age) was negligent, but rested their defence on the ground that the company was not negligent, and asserted that the injury to the plaintiff was accidental or brought upon himself."

On the question whether there was negligence on the part of the railway company in the management or condition of its turntable, the judge charged the jury—"that to maintain the action it must appear by the evidence that the turntable, in the condition, situation, and place where it then was, was a dangerous machine, one which, if unguarded or unlocked, would be likely to cause injury to children; that if in its construction and the manner in which it was left it was not dangerous in its nature, the defendants were not liable for negligence; that they were further to consider whether, situated as it was as the defendants' property in a small town, somewhat remote from habitations, there was negligence in not anticipating that injury might occur if it was left unlocked or unguarded; that if they did not have reason to anticipate that children would be likely to resort to it, or that they would be likely to be injured if they did resort to it, then there was no negligence."

The jury found a verdict of $7500 for the plaintiff, from the judgment upon which this writ of error was brought.

■ MR. JUSTICE HUNT delivered the opinion of the court.

* * *

2d. Was there negligence on the part of the railway company in the management or condition of its turntable?

The charge on this point * * * was an impartial and intelligent one. Unless the defendant was entitled to an order that the plaintiff be nonsuited, or, as it is expressed in the practice of the United States courts, to an order directing a verdict in its favor, the submission was right. If, upon any construction which the jury was authorized to put upon the evidence, or by any inferences they were authorized to draw from it, the conclusion of negligence can be justified, the defendant was not entitled to this order, and the judgment cannot be disturbed. To express it affirmatively, if from the evidence given it might justly be inferred by the jury that the defendant, in the construction, location, management, or condition of its machine had omitted that care and attention to prevent the occurrence of accidents which prudent and careful men ordinarily bestow, the jury was at liberty to find for the plaintiff.

That the turntable was a dangerous machine, which would be likely to cause injury to children who resorted to it, might fairly be inferred from the injury which actually occurred to the plaintiff. There was the same liability to injury to him, and no greater, that existed with reference to all children. When the jury learned from the evidence that he had suffered a serious injury, by his foot being caught between the fixed rail of the road-bed and the turning rail of the table they were justified in believing that there was a probability of the occurrence of such accidents.

So, in looking at the remoteness of the machine from inhabited dwellings, when it was proved to the jury that several boys from the hamlet were at play there on this occasion, and that they had been at play upon the turntable on other occasions, and within the observation and to the knowledge of the employees of the defendant, the jury were justified in believing that children would probably resort to it, and that the defendant should have anticipated that such would be the case.

As it was in fact, on this occasion, so it was to be expected that the amusement of the boys would have been found in turning this table while they were on it or about it. This could certainly have been prevented by locking the turntable when not in use by the company. It was not shown that this would cause any considerable expense or inconvenience to the defendant. It could probably have been prevented by the repair of the broken latch. This was a heavy catch which, by dropping into a socket, prevented the revolution of the table. There had been one on this table weighing some eight or ten pounds, but it had been broken off and had not been replaced. It was proved to have been usual with railroad companies to have upon their turntables a latch or bolt, or some similar instrument. The jury may well have believed that if the defendant had incurred the trifling expense of replacing this latch, and had taken the slight trouble of putting it in its place, these very small boys would not have taken the pains to lift it out, and thus the whole difficulty have been avoided. Thus reasoning, the jury would have reached the conclusion that the defendant had omitted the care and attention it ought to have given, that it was negligent, and that its negligence caused the injury to the plaintiff. The evidence is not strong and the negligence is slight, but we are not able to say that there is not evidence sufficient to justify the verdict. We are not called upon to weigh, to measure, to balance the evidence, or to ascertain how we should have decided if acting as jurors. The charge was in all respects sound and judicious, and there being sufficient evidence to justify the finding, we are not authorized to disturb it.

3d. It is true, in many cases, that where the facts are undisputed the effect of them is for the judgment of the court, and not for the decision of the jury. This is true in that class of cases where the existence of such facts come in question rather than where deductions or inferences are to be made from the facts. If a deed be given in evidence, a contract proven, or its breach testified to, the existence of such deed, contract or breach, there being nothing in derogation of the evidence, is no doubt to be ruled as a question of law. In some cases, too, the necessary inference from the proof is so certain that it may be ruled as a question of law. If a sane man voluntarily throws himself in contact with a passing engine, there being nothing to counteract the effect of this action, it may be ruled as a matter of law that the injury to him resulted from his own fault, and that no action can be sustained by him or his representatives. So if a coach-driver intentionally drives within a few inches of a precipice, and an accident happens, negligence may be ruled as a question of law. On the other hand, if he had placed a suitable distance between his coach and the precipice, but by the breaking of a rein or an axle, which could not have been anticipated, an injury occurred, it might be ruled as a question of law that there was no negligence and no liability. But these are extreme cases. The range between them is almost infinite in variety and extent. It is in relation to these intermediate cases that the opposite rule prevails. Upon the facts proven in such cases, it is a matter of judgment and discretion, of sound inference, what is the deduction to be drawn from the undisputed facts. Certain facts we may suppose to be clearly established from which one sensible, impartial man would infer that proper care had not been used, and that negligence existed; another man equally sensible and equally impartial would infer that proper care had been used, and that there was no negligence. It is this class of cases and those akin to it that the law commits to the decision of a jury. Twelve men of the average of the community, comprising men of education and men of little education, men of learning and men whose learning consists only in what they have themselves seen and heard, the merchant, the mechanic, the farmer, the laborer; these sit together, consult, apply their separate experience of the affairs of life to the facts proven, and draw a unanimous conclusion. This average judgment thus given it is the great effort of the law to obtain. It is assumed that twelve men know more of the common affairs of life than does one man, that they can draw wiser and safer conclusions from admitted facts thus occurring than can a single judge.

In no class of cases can this practical experience be more wisely applied than in that we are considering. We find, accordingly, although not uniform or harmonious, that the authorities justify us in holding in the case before us, that although the facts are undisputed it is for the jury and not for the judge to determine whether proper care was given, or whether they establish negligence.

* * *

It has been already shown that the facts proved justified the jury in finding that the defendant was guilty of negligence, and we are of the opinion that it was properly left to the jury to determine that point.

Upon the whole case, the judgment must be affirmed.

NOTE ON THE JURY'S ROLE IN NEGLIGENCE CASES

1. **Distinguishing *Simblest* and *Stout*.** In *Simblest v. Maynard*, the court held, in substance, that it was undisputed that the fire engine's lights had been flashing, and directed a verdict against the plaintiff. In *Stout*, the court finds the facts undisputed, but allows the case to go to the jury. What explains the difference between the two cases? Why is the jury's power illegitimate in one but not in the other? On the general problem of functions of court and jury in negligence cases, see Prosser and Keeton, Torts 235 et seq. (5th ed. 1984); James, Functions of Judge and Jury in Negligence Cases,

58 Yale L.J. 667 (1949); cf. 9 Wigmore on Evidence § 2494 (Chadbourn ed., 1981).

2.   Jury lawmaking outside of the law of negligence. Reconsider the facts of *Scott v. Harris*, supra p. 836. Recall that in that case, the Supreme Court held that Scott's conduct in ramming Harris's car constituted a reasonable seizure under the Fourth Amendment as a matter of law. Assuming arguendo that the videotape in that case conclusively established the facts of the matter, should the question whether the police officers acted reasonably in their own defense still have been submitted to the jury under the rationale of the *Stout* decision? If not, why not?

2.   PUTTING THE CASE TO THE JURY: INSTRUCTIONS AND THE FORM OF THE VERDICT

Once the decision is made to allow the jury to evaluate the evidence, that evaluation is framed and in some measure controlled by the instructions given by the court, and the form of the verdict. Each is discussed in turn below.

NOTE ON INSTRUCTIONS TO THE JURY

1.   The content of instructions to the jury. Instructions to the jury state the rules of substantive law that the jury must apply. They also advise the jury concerning their task as finder of fact, explaining the applicable burden of persuasion and the jury's role as the arbiter of credibility and the drawer of reasonable inferences. Where the issue is one for the court, the judge may give a so-called "binding instruction" which tells the jurors how they must decide the issue.

The judge may also sum up the evidence and comment on issues of credibility, weight, and inference, so long as her comments make it clear to the jury that the power to decide those questions remains with them. The power to comment on the evidence is used more frequently and more extensively in federal court than in most state courts, but is today rarely employed even in federal court. Compare Evans v. Wright, 505 F.2d 287 (4th Cir. 1974) ("a United States district judge is not a bump on a log"), with People v. Rincon-Pineda, 14 Cal.3d 864, 886, 123 Cal.Rptr. 119, 538 P.2d 247 (1975) (stating that the power to comment on the evidence and testimony and credibility of witnesses "is to be exercised with great care, lest the province of the jury as trier of fact be invaded"). And a few states purport to prohibit the practice altogether. See, e.g., Ariz. Const. Art. 6, § 27 ("Judges shall not charge juries with respect to matters of fact, nor comment thereon, but shall declare the law.").

2.   The process of framing instructions to the jury. Even if the parties request no instructions, the judge has an obligation to instruct with respect to the basic rules of substantive law as they apply to the principal elements of the case. Moreover, the judge may give instructions going beyond the practical minimum even if the parties do not request them. In practice, however, there is a significant adversarial element in the framing of the instructions, in two senses.

First, the content of instructions is often contested. In both state and federal court, the parties file written requests for instructions. Ordinarily the parties will present different views both of what the substantive law requires and of what instructions are warranted given the evidence on particular issues. The judge must resolve those issues, and will often hear argument before doing so.

Second, although failure to give an instruction that is obviously necessary (or the giving of an instruction that is obviously wrong) may sometimes constitute plain error warranting a reversal even in the absence of a request or objection below, a party who fails to request a proper instruction, or who fails to object to an improper one, is ordinarily out of luck. Federal Rule 51 provides: "A court may consider a plain error in the instructions that has not been preserved as required by Rule 51(d)(1) if the error affects substantial rights."

3. **The timing of instructions.** Rule 51 allows the judge to give instructions before or after arguments of counsel. In most states, judges instruct after the arguments of counsel, but increasingly courts have used their discretion to instruct whenever they deem it most helpful to the jury. In complex cases, the judge may give preliminary instructions before the jury hears any evidence in order to allow them to make sense of the evidence in the case. For studies of the effectiveness of early instruction, showing mixed results, see Ellsworth & Reifman, Juror Comprehension and Public Policy: Perceived Problems and Proposed Solutions, 6 Psychol., Pub. Pol'y & Law 788, 803 (2000).

4. **Appellate review.** If an objection to an instruction has been properly preserved, the reviewing court will reverse if the following four conditions are met: (a) the requested (but not given) instruction was not covered by another instruction; (b) the requested instruction was a correct statement of the law; (c) the issue on which the instruction was requested was properly before the jury; and (d) that the failure to give the requested instruction was prejudicial, not harmless error. Hazard, Leubsdorf & Bassett, Civil Procedure § 11.22, at 497 (6th ed. 2011).

5. **Form instructions and juror comprehension.** It has been observed that "juries have the disadvantage * * * of being treated like children while the testimony is going on, but then being doused with a kettleful of law during the charge that would make a third-year law-student blanch." C. Bok, I, Too, Nicodemus 261–62 (1946). There is a tension in instructing juries between ensuring technical legal accuracy and consistency, on the one hand, and ensuring jury comprehension on the other. Most states have sought to ensure the first two goals through the adoption of form instructions. For many years, the California practice was much affected by the statewide availability of the Book of Approved Jury Instructions, popularly known as BAJI, originated in Los Angeles Superior Court. BAJI was supplemented by CALJIC, a counterpart for criminal cases. These manuals contained hundreds of model jury instructions covering the issues recurring in jury cases. Similar pattern instructions are in use in many jurisdictions. See Devitt, Blackmar & Wolff, Federal Jury Practice and Instructions (4th ed. 1987). For example, the Ninth Circuit has a list of model jury instructions for civil cases available on the court's website.

Pattern instructions ensure convenience and doctrinal purity, but jurors often don't understand them. See, e.g., Tiersma, The Rocky Road to Legal Reform: Improving the Language of Jury Instructions, 66 Brook. L. Rev. 1081 (2001); Ellsworth & Reifman, Juror Comprehension and Public Policy: Perceived Problems and Proposed Solutions, 6 Psychol., Pub. Pol'y & Law

788 (2000). Professors Ellsworth and Reifman summarize the evidence: " 'Study after study has shown that jurors do not understand the law they are given, often performing at no better than chance level on objective tests of comprehension.' " Id. at 796. Appellate courts have proven unsympathetic to juries who express their confusion. In some jurisdictions case law holds that it is a sufficient answer to the jury's questions simply to reread the instruction; in others it may be reversible error if the trial court attempts to answer jury requests for clarification in "every day" language. People v. Ruge, 35 Cal.Rptr.2d 830 (Cal. Ct. App. 1994); People v. Garcia, 54 Cal.App.3d 61, 126 Cal.Rptr. 275 (1975). For a sharp critique of this body of law, see Saks, Judicial Nullification, 68 Ind. L.J. 1281, 1283 (1993) ("judges routinely nullify the law by rendering it meaningless, thereby compelling jurors to invent the law themselves.")

A number of studies suggest that intensive redrafting, in consultation with experts in psycholinguistics, may raise comprehension rates substantially (perhaps into the 80% range), but few jurisdictions have undertaken such efforts as yet. Ellsworth & Reifman, 6 Psych. Pub. Pol'y & Law at 802. A notable exception is California, which has adopted "plain language" civil jury instructions. Judicial Council of California Civil Jury Instructions (2005), informally known at CACI (pronounced "Casey") (http://www.courtinfo.ca.gov/reference/documents/civiljuryinst.pdf). A pair of examples gives some flavor of the change:

BAJI 2.21 (old instruction):

Failure of recollection is common. Innocent misrecollection is not uncommon.

CACI 107 (new instruction):

People often forget things or make mistakes in what they remember.

BAJI 2.60 (old instruction):

"Preponderance of the evidence" means evidence that has more convincing force than that opposed to it. If the evidence is so evenly balanced that you are unable to say that the evidence on either side of an issue preponderates, your finding on that issue must be against the party who had the burden of proving it.

CACI 200 (new instruction):

A party must persuade you, by the evidence presented in court, that what he or she is required to prove is more likely to be true than not true. This is referred to as "the burden of proof."

NOTE ON GENERAL AND SPECIAL VERDICTS

1.   The general verdict. The verdict usually employed in a jury trial is a "general" verdict. The jury is given two forms (unless the case involves multiple parties). One form, for plaintiff, is essentially, "We find for plaintiff in the amount of $_____." The other is "We find for defendant." The general verdict obviously conceals the reasoning process by which the jury reached its conclusion, and this is one of its great practical and perhaps theoretical virtues. It would be impractical to require the jury to agree on a narrative statement of the basis of its verdict in all cases. Still, if the jury were required to indicate its basic findings, this would perhaps (a) improve the jury's deliberative process and understanding of the law by identifying the issues to be decided and providing a decision tree for resolving them, and (b) reduce the need for retrials or outright reversal by making it possible to identify with greater precision whether errors by the court or jury actually contaminated the decision reached or were in fact harmless. The special verdict, in which the jury is required to render "a special written finding on each issue of fact" is one means for attempting to achieve this goal. Fed. R. Civ. P. 49(a).

2. **The special verdict and its antecedents.** At common law, there was a device known as the special verdict requiring the jury to find specifically on all the issues essential to the plaintiff's case. The use of this device was very tricky, owing partly to ambiguities in the term "issue" and to inevitable errors in drafting statements of issues. See Hazard, Leubsdorf & Bassett, Civil Procedure § 11.23 (6th ed. 2011). A few states, notably Texas, used special verdicts for many years notwithstanding that their virtue was fully offset by their complexity and vulnerability to error. The federal Rules and most state procedures have permissible variations. In addition to the special verdict, in which the jury must decide each element in the case, Rule 49(b) permits the court to submit a general verdict form to the jury accompanied by written interrogatories as to one or more issues of fact whose decision is necessary to a verdict.

A number of commentators and a few judges have strongly urged wider use of the special verdict or the general verdict accompanied by answers to interrogatories, especially in complex cases. The classic, tendentious statement of this view is by Judge Jerome Frank in Skidmore v. Baltimore & Ohio R.R., 167 F.2d 54 (2d Cir. 1948): "The general verdict is as inscrutable and essentially mysterious as the judgment which issued from the ancient oracle of Delphi." Those who oppose the use of the special verdict typically stress its greater complexity and its tendency to reduce the power of the jury to bring popular norms into the decision-making process. Its use is normally discretionary with the trial court, see 9A C. Wright & A. Miller, Federal Practice and Procedure §§ 2505, 2511 (2008).

3. **The problem of inconsistency.** When a court uses a general verdict accompanied by interrogatories the possibility arises that the jury's answers to an interrogatory may be inconsistent with the general verdict. For example, the general verdict may be in favor of the plaintiff, but the jury's answer to an interrogatory may appear to negate the element of causation. In general, courts have an obligation to try to reconcile apparent inconsistencies. Gallick v. Baltimore & Ohio R. R., 372 U.S. 108, 83 S.Ct. 659, 9 L.Ed.2d 618 (1963): Hasson v. Ford Motor Co., 19 Cal.3d 530, 540, 138 Cal.Rptr. 705, 564 P.2d 857 (1977) ("The general and special verdicts must be beyond possibility of reconciliation under any possible application of the evidence and instructions.") But if the finding cannot be reconciled with the verdict, the verdict cannot stand. See, e.g., Guidry v. Kem Mfg. Co., 598 F.2d 402 (5th Cir. 1979). The trial judge confronted with such a verdict has discretion to enter judgment on the specific findings, to resubmit the issues to the jury for clarification or to order a new trial. More troublesome is the case where answers to interrogatories are inconsistent with each other, and also inconsistent with the general verdict. In such cases, the judge must either resubmit to the jury or grant a new trial. Fed. R. Civ. P. 49(b). See also Olander, Resolving Inconsistencies in Federal Special Verdicts, 53 Fordham L. Rev. 1089 (1985); For a sustained analysis supporting a preference for the

general verdict, see Thornburg, The Power and the Process: Instructions and the Civil Jury, 66 Fordham L. Rev. 1837 (1998).

3. MOTIONS AFTER VERDICT

INTRODUCTORY NOTE ON POST-TRIAL MOTIONS

1.   **Entry of judgment.** After the verdict in a case tried to a jury, or after the decision by the judge in a nonjury case, judgment should be entered forthwith. See Fed. R. Civ. P. 58. Entry of judgment has significance for a variety of purposes, the most important of which is computation of time during which an appeal must be taken. The date of entry of judgment also determines the time within which most post-trial motions may be made.

2.   **The variety of post-trial motions.** There are essentially two things that can be done through a motion after a jury trial, other than allowing the verdict and judgment to stand. One is to enter judgment against the verdict-winner, i.e., judgment as a matter of law (in federal court) or judgment notwithstanding the verdict (in many state courts); the other is to order a new trial. Judgment as a matter of law, like summary judgment and directed verdict, raises the issue of the sufficiency of the evidence to support the verdict and should be granted only when the evidence is insufficient to permit a reasonable jury to find for the verdict winner under the applicable burden of persuasion. In essence, by granting such a motion, the court is holding that the jury's verdict is indefensible.

A new trial can be appropriate either because the evidence is weak (although not necessarily weak enough to justify judgment as a matter of law) or because procedural errors contaminated the proceeding, e.g., there was improperly admitted evidence, improper conduct or argument during trial, or error in instructions. The forms of contamination that might justify a new trial are practically infinite. Perhaps in recognition of the difficulty of enumeration, Rule 59(a) provides that a new trial may be awarded "for any reason for which a new trial has heretofore been granted in an action at law in federal court." In addition, a new trial may be granted on the ground of "newly discovered" evidence. To obtain relief on this ground, the applicant must show that she used due diligence before and during trial to ferret out the evidence belatedly discovered. This requirement is rather rigidly applied in most federal courts, see 11 C. Wright, A. Miller & M. Kane, Federal Practice and Procedure § 2808 (2014); Owens v. International Paper Co., 528 F.2d 606 (5th Cir. 1976).

NOTE ON SETTING ASIDE A VERDICT BASED ON JURY MISCONDUCT

1.   **Impeaching the verdict based on jury misconduct.** In jury trials, there are many mishaps that can occur in the jury room. The traditional common-law rule was that a juror could not be heard to impeach his verdict. In other words, testimony of a juror would not be received to show that some mishap had occurred in the jury's performance of its functions. The result is that the content of jury deliberations is nearly sacrosanct. This rule had the intended effect of making it difficult to show that jury misconduct had occurred and hence to have a verdict set aside on the ground of such misconduct. See Hazard, Leubsdorf & Bassett, Civil Procedure

§ 11.27 (6th ed. 2011); Comment, Impeachment of Jury Verdicts by Jurors: A Proposal, 1969 U. Ill. L. F. 388. In recent years, however, this rule has been somewhat relaxed as some state and federal courts began to recognize limited exceptions to the traditional rule. The most accepted such exception permitted juror testimony that some "extraneous matter" had influenced the jury's verdict. See Mueller & Kirkpatrick, Federal Evidence § 6:16. For instance, Federal Rule of Evidence 606(b) provides:

> Upon an inquiry into the validity of a verdict or indictment, a juror may not testify as to any matter or statement occurring during the course of the jury's deliberations or to the effect of anything upon that or any other juror's mind or emotions as influencing the juror to assent to or dissent from the verdict or indictment or concerning the juror's mental processes in connection therewith. But a juror may testify about (1) whether extraneous prejudicial information was improperly brought to the jury's attention, (2) whether any outside influence was improperly brought to bear upon any juror, or (3) whether there was a mistake in entering the verdict on to the verdict form. A juror's affidavit or evidence of any statement by the juror may not be received on a matter about which the juror would be precluded from testifying.

The rule allows admission of testimony that "[b]ribery, private communication with a party, improper remarks by a court officer or other outside, consulting documents not in evidence, and the like" tainted the jury's verdict. Hazard, Leubsdorf & Bassett, Civil Procedure § 11.27 (6th ed. 2011).

2. **The limited reach of Federal Rule of Evidence 606(b).** Although Federal Rule of Evidence 606(b) provides an exception to the traditional common-law approach, the Supreme Court has repeatedly made it clear that such an exception is quite limited in scope. Strikingly, in Tanner v. United States, 483 U.S. 107, 107 S.Ct. 2739, 97 L.Ed.2d 90 (1987), the Court held that Rule 606(b) barred testimony by jurors that their colleagues were under the influence of alcohol, marijuana, and cocaine during the trial. In so holding, the Court stated that jury deliberations must be shielded from public scrutiny. Otherwise, "full and frank discussion in the jury room, jurors' willingness to return an unpopular verdict, and the community's trust in a system that relies on the decisions of laypeople would all be undermined by a barrage of post-verdict scrutiny of juror conduct." The Court rejected the argument that substance abuse constituted an "outside influence" under Rule 606(b), holding that "drugs or alcohol voluntarily ingested by a juror seems no more an 'outside influence' than a virus, poorly prepared food, or lack of sleep." Recently, the Court reaffirmed the reasoning in *Tanner*, unanimously holding that "Rule 606(b) precludes a party seeking a new trial from using one juror's affidavit of what another juror said in deliberations to demonstrate the other juror's dishonesty during voir dire." Warger v. Shauers, 574 U.S. ___ , 135 S.Ct. 531, 190 L.Ed.2d 422 (2014).

3. **The jury as black box.** Professor Albert Alschuler bitterly criticizes *Tanner*: "A legal system that would knowingly permit a drunken, dozing tribunal of the sort described in *Tanner* to send people to prison has little claim to respect." Alschuler, The Supreme Court and the Jury: Voir Dire, Peremptory Challenges, and the Review of Jury Verdicts, 56 U. Chi. L. Rev. 153, 228 (1989). Comparing the carefully articulated procedural protections in place at voir dire, including *Batson*'s protection against

racially biased peremptory challenges, with the lack of protections later in the process, Alschuler writes:

> [W]e have captured the worst of two worlds, creating burdensome, unnecessary and ineffective jury controls at the front end of the criminal trial while failing to implement badly needed controls at the back end. Although we have devoted substantial resources to implementing our front-end procedures, we generally have refused to expend significant resources to determine whether they have worked. Indeed, we often have turned aside clear evidence of their failure.

Id. at 154–55. For additional criticism of *Tanner* and Federal Rule of Evidence 606(b), see Cammack, The Jurisprudence of Jury Trials: The No Impeachment Rule and the Conditions for Legitimate Legal Decisionmaking, 64 U. Colo. L. Rev. 57 (1993).

With *Tanner* compare Krouse v. Graham, 19 Cal. 3d 59, 137 Cal. Rptr. 863, 562 P.2d 1022 (1977), applying a similar California rule but reaching a contrary result. See also Attridge v. Cencorp Div., 836 F.2d 113 (2d Cir. 1987) (Rule 606(b) did not preclude inquiry after jurors were discharged to determine whether verdict they designated as "Total Verdict Amount" incorporated 20% reduction for plaintiff's negligence); United States v. Bailey, 834 F.2d 218 (1st Cir. 1987) (permitting interrogation of former jurors in defense to criminal charge of bribing jury).

NOTE ON SETTING ASIDE THE VERDICT BASED ON THE SUFFICIENCY OR WEIGHT OF THE EVIDENCE

1.   Post-trial motions based upon the sufficiency or weight of the evidence. Post-trial motions may seek to control the jury without reviewing the manner of its deliberations, by demonstrating that the evidence submitted does not warrant the verdict rendered. The available motions are those for a new trial on the ground of insufficiency of the evidence, which results in the case being tried again before another jury, and for renewed judgment as a matter of law (in federal court) or judgment notwithstanding the verdict (in many state courts), which results in the immediate entry of judgment against the verdict-winner. When judgment as a matter of law is granted the verdict-winner has no chance to supplement the proofs offered in the first trial. On the other hand, if judgment as a matter of law is granted, the verdict-winner has an immediate appeal which may result in reinstatement of the verdict. By contrast, when a new trial is granted the verdict-winner in the first trial generally cannot appeal until after the new trial has gone to judgment; if the verdict-winner in the first trial has lost in the second, she has the heavy burden on appeal of showing that the original verdict should displace the second verdict. See Evers v. Equifax, Inc., 650 F.2d 793 (5th Cir. 1981).

2.   The requirement of a motion for judgment as a matter of law before submission to the jury. The requirement in federal Rule 50(b) that there have been a prior motion for a judgment as a matter of law was originally understood to be required to conform to practice in trials at "common law" and hence by the Seventh Amendment. See Slocum v. New York Life Ins. Co., 228 U.S. 364, 33 S.Ct. 523, 57 L.Ed. 879 (1913). Today, it is independently justified as a device for giving the party moved against fair notice of evidentiary problems in its case while there is still time to correct them. The former requirement that the original motion for judgment as a matter of law be made at the close of all the evidence has now been relaxed: the motion may now be made at any time before the case is submitted to the jury. But a lawyer who fails to make such a motion (if there are good grounds for it) does her client a major disservice. Although a court does have the power to award a judgment as a matter of law even if a party does not move for it properly, this power is both discretionary and invoked extraordinarily rarely and only to prevent manifest injustice. See Procter & Gamble Co. v. Amway Corp., 242 F.3d 539, 559 (5th Cir. 2001); Zeigler v. Fisher-Price, Inc., 302 F. Supp. 2d 999, 1007 (N.D. Iowa 2004).

Spurlin v. General Motors Corp.

United States Court of Appeals for the Fifth Circuit, 1976.
528 F.2d 612.

■ TUTTLE, CIRCUIT JUDGE:

This diversity suit arises out of a school bus crash which occurred in Morgan County, Alabama, on April 23, 1968, when the bus's brakes failed. Two wrongful death suits and twenty-two personal injury actions were filed, on behalf of the children who were in the bus at the time, against the manufacturer of the school bus chassis, General Motors Corporation. Following consolidation of the cases for trial by the district court,[1] a six-person jury heard evidence for approximately two weeks. The court then submitted the cases on the theory of alleged negligent design of the braking system, and the jury returned a verdict for the plaintiffs, awarding damages in the amount of $70,000 each in the wrongful death cases. The district court, however, granted defendant's post-trial motions for judgment notwithstanding the verdict and, in the alternative, a new trial, on the ground that the verdict was not supported by the evidence. This appeal followed. We consider the district court's two post-trial rulings in turn, beginning with its grant of General Motors' motion for judgment notwithstanding the verdict.

I.   CORRECTNESS OF THE DISTRICT COURT'S GRANT
     OF JUDGMENT NOTWITHSTANDING THE VERDICT

A.   *The Standard of Review.*

The applicable standard of review for judging the correctness of a district court's grant or denial of a motion for judgment notwithstanding the verdict was carefully delineated by this court in Boeing Co. v. Shipman, 411 F.2d 365 (5th Cir. 1969) (en banc):

> "On motions for directed verdict and for judgment notwithstanding the verdict the Court should consider all of the evidence—not just that evidence which supports the nonmover's case—but in the light and with all reasonable inferences most favorable to the party opposed to the motion. . . . [I]f there is substantial evidence opposed to the motions, that is, evidence of such quality and weight that reasonable and fair-minded men in the exercise of impartial judgment might reach different

---

[1]   Over defendant's objection, the district court consolidated all of the cases for trial on the issue of liability, and additionally consolidated the two wrongful death actions for trial on the issue of damages. The latter were brought under the Alabama Homicide Act, Title 7, § 119, under which a successful plaintiff is awarded punitive rather than compensatory damages.

conclusions, the motions shall be denied, and the case submitted to the jury. . . . There must be a conflict on substantial evidence to create a jury question. However, it is the function of the jury as the traditional finder of the facts, and not the Court, to weigh conflicting evidence and inferences, and determine the credibility of witnesses." 411 F.2d at 374–375 (footnotes omitted).

* * * It is important to note * * * that defendant General Motors has not assigned, as separate grounds for cross-appeal, the commission of any errors by the district court in admitting into evidence any particular items or testimony given by any of the witnesses. This Court, therefore, is not required to consider the issue of the scope of the evidence which was properly before the jury in reaching its verdict, but is free to examine and rely upon all the evidence which the district court charged the jury it could consider in deciding the case.

B.   *Plaintiffs' Theory of Recovery.*

Briefly stated, the theory upon which the cases were submitted to the jury was one of alleged negligent design of the bus's braking system by General Motors, coupled with a failure to warn of the unique problems and need for frequent servicing and maintenance associated with operating school buses. Specifically, the plaintiffs contended that the braking system with which the 1965 66-passenger school bus at issue was equipped was not reasonably safe for the use for which it was intended in that: (1) the single hydraulic braking system on the bus was a dangerous system because of the inevitability of total failure of braking power in the event of a loss of brake fluid through undetected leakage; (2) there was no effective emergency brake on the bus, only a parking brake which was not intended to stop a loaded, moving vehicle such as this one; and (3) there was no warning device of any sort, such as a gauge or warning light, to indicate when the brake fluid in the reservoir was running low. Furthermore, the plaintiffs alleged, the owner's manual which came with the bus suggested brake fluid level checks only every 6,000 miles, which on a school bus would be only once a year, whereas safe maintenance practices would actually require checking the brake fluid in such a vehicle every two weeks to a month.

* * * C.   *Sufficiency of the Evidence Under the Boeing Co. Test.*

* * * While it is unnecessary to catalogue in detail the evidence presented on these issues at trial, a brief summary of the mechanics involved in the braking system in use on this particular bus, and the testimony offered by witnesses on both sides regarding its safety will serve to support our holding that there was sufficient "substantial evidence" as required by Boeing Co. v. Shipman, supra, for the jury to have found that the braking system on the bus was not reasonably safe and consequently that GM had breached its duty as a manufacturer.

The bus which crashed was a 1965 66-passenger school bus, the chassis portion of which was designed and built by General Motors. It was equipped with a single hydraulic braking system, containing a single reservoir in the master cylinder supplying all of the brake fluid which transmits pressure to the brake cylinders on each wheel. In such a system, a leak which exhausts the brake fluid in the reservoir causes a sudden and total failure of braking ability, as happened in this case. A dual hydraulic braking system, on the other hand, is equipped with two brake fluid reservoirs, each of which services the brake cylinders on two separate wheels, so that in the event of loss of fluid from one of the reservoirs, whether from leakage or some other cause, the vehicle continues to have braking power on the wheels serviced by the other reservoir. The only other braking mechanism with which the bus in this case was equipped was a parking brake, which by the admission of all those who testified at the trial was never intended to function as an emergency brake.

We find that the evidence offered at trial on the safety of the braking system as described above was more than sufficient to withstand a motion for judgment n.o.v. under the test set out in *Boeing*. Although a GM Senior Design Engineer, Paul Fisher, testified that he considered a dual hydraulic braking system to be less reliable than a single system (because of the existence of more parts and consequently a greater possibility that one of them could malfunction), the plaintiffs put on expert testimony that the single hydraulic braking system in use on the bus at issue was not reasonably safe for the purpose for which it was intended. Both of plaintiffs' expert witnesses, Professor Milton Koenig, a professor of mechanical engineering at Wayne State University in Detroit, and Dr. Leslie W. Ball, Director of Safety at Marshall Space Flight Center in Huntsville, Alabama, were found by the district court to be qualified to give expert opinions on the braking design issues on which they testified. Both Professor Koenig and Dr. Ball stated several times during their testimony that they considered a single hydraulic braking system such as was used on the bus in this case to be "inherently unsafe" or "not reasonably safe." Certainly the jury could have found, from this expert testimony admitted by the district court, that the braking system on the bus was not a sufficiently safe one.

* * *

Plaintiffs introduced into evidence copies of the 1965 GM owner's and shop maintenance manuals, both of which stated the fluid in the brake fluid reservoir should be checked every 6,000 miles. In addition, the owner's manual stated that "[t]he Chevrolet braking system requires very little care. The braking system should be checked occasionally for indications of fluid leaks. If leaks are found necessary repairs should be made at once. Keep the brakes properly adjusted, check all vacuum hose connections for leaks." The 1965 truck shop manual contained only the following additional warning: "Sustained heavy duty and high speed operation, or operation under adverse conditions may require more frequent servicing."

Plaintiffs alleged, and sought to prove, that these statements in the manuals were inadequate and grossly misleading in that checking the brake fluid level on a school bus every 6,000 miles would mean inspecting it only once a year, whereas GM engineers who testified at trial admitted that it would be necessary to check the fluid level on a school bus several times a month in order to conform with good maintenance practices. Plaintiffs' experts, Professor Koenig and Dr. Ball, testified that in their opinions the manuals were misleading and inaccurate with respect to the frequency of servicing which should have been stated as required for school bus operations. GM's Field Maintenance Supervisor also testified that the fluid level on a school bus should be checked once a week, but insisted that at yearly seminars held by him and attended by school bus maintenance personnel, (including some from Morgan County) verbal instructions were given that school bus braking systems required at least weekly checks of the level of the brake fluid. Such supplemental verbal instructions, it was urged, were certainly sufficient to cure any deficiency in the written ones in the manuals.

Given the existence of all this conflicting evidence bearing on the issue of the adequacy of the warnings in the two GM manuals that came with the bus chassis purchased by Morgan County in 1964, this Court is of the opinion that sufficient evidence was adduced at trial to create a jury issue on the negligence *vel non* of the Morgan County officials and whether such negligence, if it occurred, was foreseeable by GM. With respect to the possibility of intervening negligence in the form of the bus driver's failure to notice operational signs indicating possible loss of brake fluid, we note that the driver denied noticing either any signs of leakage or the gradual development of any significant "give" in his brake pedal prior to the accident, thus creating a jury question on this issue also.

From the above analysis, then, it appears that there was ample evidence introduced at trial under the Boeing Co. v. Shipman test to warrant submitting the issue of proximate cause to the jury. Since we have already determined that there was sufficient evidence to go to the jury on the breach of duty issue, it follows that the plaintiffs put on the kind and quantity of evidence which this Court had held is required to withstand a defense motion for judgment n.o.v., and the district court's grant of that motion by GM must therefore be reversed.

II.   THE ALTERNATIVE ORDER GRANTING THE MOTION FOR NEW TRIAL

We now turn to a consideration of the propriety of the district court's alternative grant of a new trial on the ground that the evidence was insufficient to support the jury verdict. We think it critical that the case law on this point be read against the background of the Seventh Amendment, which provides that

"[i]n Suits at common law, where the value in controversy shall exceed twenty dollars, the right of trial by jury shall be preserved, and no fact tried by a jury, shall be otherwise reexamined in any Court of the United States, than according to the rules of the common law." U.S. Const.Amend. VII.

While this constitutional provision obviously cannot be applied so as to foreclose any scrutiny of a jury's fact-findings, it expresses in clear terms the principle that facts once found by a jury in the context of a civil trial are not to be reweighed and a new trial granted lightly.

The general rule, as uniformly stated by the commentators and applied by the courts, is that a district court's grant of a new trial is within the discretion of the court, and is ordinarily nonreviewable save for an abuse of that discretion. Montgomery Ward & Co. v. Duncan, 311 U.S. 243, 61 S.Ct. 189, 85 L.Ed. 147 (1940); see generally 6A Moore's Federal Practice, ¶ 59.08[5]. Several jurisdictions, however, have carefully distinguished the situation where the trial court has granted a new trial on the grounds of insufficiency of the evidence, since by so doing the court is in a sense intruding upon the jury's function and affecting a litigant's Seventh Amendment rights. Appellate courts in these jurisdictions are more exacting in reviewing such a new trial grant. See, e.g., Lind v. Schenley Industries, Inc., 278 F.2d 79 (3d Cir.), cert. denied, 364 U.S. 835, 81 S.Ct. 58, 5 L.Ed.2d 60 (1960); Cities Service Oil Co. v. Launey, 403 F.2d 537 (5th Cir. 1968); Duncan v. Duncan, 377 F.2d 49, 52–55 (6th Cir.), cert. denied, 389 U.S. 913, 88 S.Ct. 239, 19 L.Ed.2d 260 (1967); Fireman's Fund Ins. Co. v. Aalco Wrecking Co., Inc., 466 F.2d 179 (8th Cir. 1972), cert. denied, 410 U.S. 930, 93 S.Ct. 1371, 35 L.Ed.2d 592 (1973).

The standard adopted by this Court is that the district court should not grant a new trial motion unless the jury verdict is "at least . . . against the *great* weight of the evidence." Cities Service Oil Co. v. Launey, supra, at 540 (emphasis in the original). A rule which would permit a court to grant a new trial when the verdict was merely against the "greater weight" of the evidence, this Court said, "would destroy the role of the jury as the principal trier of the facts, and would enable the trial judge to disregard the jury's verdict at will." Id.

Applying the test enunciated in *Cities Service,* we conclude after careful examination of the record, that the district court erred in granting a new trial in the alternative. Without reiterating in detail any of the evidence previously discussed, it should be clear from the preceding section of this opinion that the evidence was at most conflicting on the issues of negligent design and proximate cause. In such a situation, as the Supreme Court has stated,

> "[c]ourts are not free to reweigh the evidence and set aside the jury verdict merely because the jury could have drawn different inferences or conclusions or because judges feel that other results are more reasonable." Tennant v. Peoria & Pekin Union Ry., 321 U.S. 29, 35, 64 S.Ct. 409, 412, 88 L.Ed. 520 (1944).

Factors this Court has previously considered in reviewing a district court's alternative grant of a new trial include, among others, the simplicity or complexity of the issues, the degree to which the evidence presented was in dispute, and whether any "undesirable or pernicious element" occurred or was introduced into the trial. O'Neil v. W.R. Grace & Co., 410 F.2d 908, 913, 915 (5th Cir. 1969). Examining this case in light of those factors, we find that both the issue as to the reasonable safety of the single hydraulic braking system without an emergency brake backup, and the issue as to the "state of the art" in the automotive industry in 1964 were sufficiently simple so as not to form a basis for granting a new trial. Juries are constantly being called upon to pass upon negligent design issues in the products liability area, and the sometimes confusing amount and type of technical testimony that was elicited on the design issue at the trial of this case should not as a matter of law have precluded the jury that heard the case from being able fully to comprehend and assess the basic safety and technological feasibility issues involved.

Furthermore, there have been no allegations that the case was improperly tried, or that counsel on either side made prejudicial statements; this appeal has been argued, by counsel for both parties, solely on the issue of the sufficiency of the evidence to support the jury verdict. Finally, the fact that the evidence, as we have observed, was conflicting on certain elements of appellants' case, is not enough in itself to justify the district court's decision to grant a new trial. Tennant v. Peoria & Pekin Union Ry. Co., supra.

NOTE ON APPELLATE REVIEW OF POST-TRIAL MOTIONS

1. **Judgment as a matter of law and new trial in the alternative.** A party will often move in the alternative either for judgment as a matter of law (judgment n.o.v.) or for a new trial. Rule 50(c) requires that the district court rule on both motions at the same time, even if ruling on one motion seems to make ruling on the other unnecessary. There are several possible scenarios. First, if the judge denies both the motion for judgment as a matter of law and the motion for a new trial, the original judgment becomes final and appealable and the denial of both motions can be considered on appeal. Second, if, as in *Spurlin*, the judge grants the motion for judgment as a matter of law, there will also be an appealable final judgment because the grant of that motion ends the case. When that occurs, the ruling granting or denying the new trial motion will be treated as conditional. The court of appeals will reach the new trial motion only if it decides that judgment as a matter of law was improperly granted. Finally, if the judge denies the motion for judgment as a matter of law, but grants the motion for a new trial, then the matter will proceed to the second trial without an appeal, because the grant of a new trial means there is no appealable, final order.

2. **Appellate review of grants or denials of new trial based on the weight of the evidence.** The terms "weight" or "great weight" of the evidence imply a different inquiry than the question of sufficiency of the evidence to permit a verdict for the winner. In judging sufficiency, courts are not permitted to resolve issues of credibility or conflicting inferences. In deciding issues of "weight," however, courts must, in some measure, assess both credibility and inference. Though this may seem a grave intrusion into the jury's province, it is also one that was clearly sanctioned in common law courts in 1791.

Traditionally decisions granting or denying a new trial on the ground of the weight of the evidence are treated with great deference by reviewing courts. Since the question to be decided necessarily involves some attention to issues of credibility and inference as well as some knowledge of the actual performance of the trial jury (as contrasted with the hypothetical trial jury that would decide a second trial), the trial judge may have a great deal more relevant information than the court of appeals. Deference will be greatest when the judge denies the motion, since the policy of preserving trial by jury and the policy of deference to the trial judge are mutually reinforcing. After some years of serious doubt, the Supreme Court has settled that decisions refusing to grant a new trial can be reviewed on appeal consistent with the Seventh Amendment. Gasperini v. Center for Humanities, Inc., 518 U.S. 415, 116 S.Ct. 2211, 135 L.Ed.2d 659 (1996). But outright reversals in such cases are rare, although they do happen. See Dadurian v. Underwriters at Lloyd's, 787 F.2d 756 (1st Cir. 1986). Conversely, when the judge decides against the jury, the concern arises that the judge may have substituted her judgment for the jury's—acting in effect as a "thirteenth juror"—rather than correcting a probable error. In those cases, as *Spurlin* indicates, deference to the trial judge's ruling is likely to be greater when the judge is able to point to specific features of the trial to which she had superior access and that demonstrate the risk of error. In state courts, the standard for the grant of a new trial is sometimes more lenient ("against the weight of the evidence") and trial judges determinations may receive greater deference. See, e.g., Mann v. Hunt, 283 A.D. 140, 126 N.Y.S.2d 823 (1953).

3. **Granting judgment as a matter of law against the verdict winner.** While the verdict loser in the trial court ordinarily has every incentive to seek both judgment as a matter of law and a new trial, the verdict winner may well not, even if it may have good solid claims of legal error (for example, that its case would have been stronger still if the court had not improperly excluded certain evidence). What happens, then, to the verdict winner's potential claims for a new trial if it should lose the motion for judgment as a matter of law? If the decision is made in the trial court, the party has 28 days from entry of the judgment to file any motion it may have for a new trial. But what if judgment as a matter of law is entered on appeal? In Weisgram v. Marley, 528 U.S. 440, 120 S.Ct. 1011, 145 L.Ed.2d 958 (2000), plaintiff prevailed at trial and defendant's motions for judgment as a matter of law and a new trial were denied. On appeal, the court of appeals held that plaintiff's expert evidence was inadmissible and that in the absence of such evidence plaintiff's case failed to meet the Rule 50 standard of legal sufficiency. It then granted judgment as a matter of law for the defendant, ending the case. The Supreme Court held that while the appellate court was not required to enter judgment for the defendant, and was required to remain alert to the possibility that the verdict-winning plaintiff had a claim for a new trial worthy of presentation to the district court, it had not abused its discretion in granting judgment for defendant because the insufficiency of the evidence was clear and because the verdict winner, despite ample opportunity to do so, had not indicated any grounds on which it might have sought a new trial. See also Neely v. Martin K. Eby Constr. Co., 386 U.S. 317, 87 S.Ct. 1072, 18 L.Ed.2d 75 (1967).

4. **Evidence of appellate attitudes toward verdict-winners.** The attitude toward jury verdicts reflected in *Spurlin* may no longer be typical of federal appellate judges. A recent study of civil jury trials on appeal found that defendants succeeded more than plaintiffs on appeal from civil trials, and especially from jury trials. Defendants that appealed their losses after trial obtained reversals at a 28% rate, while losing plaintiffs succeeded in only 15% of their appeals, with the spread increasing to 31% and 13% for appeals from jury trials. Because the authors of the study could find no reason for thinking that the appealed cases were a biased sample of the underlying disputes, they concluded that in the federal system:

> appellate courts are indeed more favorable to defendants than are trial judges and juries. * * * The appellate judges seem to act on their perceptions of the trial courts' being pro-plaintiff. That tendency would be appropriate if the trial courts were in fact biased in favor of the plaintiff. As empirical evidence has accumulated refuting a trial court bias, however, the appellate judges' perceptions increasingly appear to be misperceptions. If misperceptions are in play, then this appellate leaning in favor of the defendant is a cause for concern.

Clermont & Eisenberg, Plaintiphobia in the Appellate Courts: Civil Rights Really Do Differ from Negotiable Instruments, 2002 U. Ill. L. Rev. 947, 949.

O'Gee v. Dobbs Houses, Inc.

United States Court of Appeals for the Second Circuit, 1978.
570 F.2d 1084.

■ LUMBARD, CIRCUIT JUDGE:

This appeal and cross-appeal arise out of an incident that took place during a United Airlines flight on April 23, 1972, as a result of which Kathleen O'Gee (now Mrs. Kathleen Collins), a United flight attendant, claimed to have suffered injuries to her back. The incident occurred when O'Gee attempted to reposition a large piece of kitchen equipment loaded on board the plane by Dobbs Houses, Inc. [Dobbs], a caterer. Defendant Dobbs appeals from a jury verdict against it in the amount of $170,000, and third-party defendant United cross-appeals from the dismissal of its counterclaim against Dobbs for indemnification of costs.

We affirm the judgment against Dobbs on the issues of liability, but remand to the district court with instructions to grant Dobbs a new trial on the issue of damages unless, within a reasonable time, plaintiff signifies willingness to accept a reduction of damages to $85,000. We reverse the dismissal of United's counterclaim.

I.   FACTS

[Plaintiff injured her back while handling an eight hundred pound airline cold-buffet which had been filled with food prepared by the defendant. She charged that the defendant had failed to fulfil its duty to lock the unit down after delivering to the plane, and that she had injured her back when the unit shifted in flight and she was required to push on it and latch it back in place.]

* * *

During the remainder of April 23, O'Gee had a "very bad backache," of which she complained to another stewardess and the flight engineer. She returned to work on April 24 and 25, but suffered pain and stiffness throughout both days. On April 26, she reported to a United medical officer, who gave her medication and requested that she return before her next flight. Over the next fourteen months, O'Gee saw several physicians, both in New York City and in Rochester, where her parents lived. Her problem was variously diagnosed as back sprain, a slipped disk, and a herniated disk. Much of this period was spent either in bed or in therapy; attempts to resume work in July and again in October of 1972 were unsuccessful. Finally, in May of 1973, O'Gee underwent a laminectomy for the removal of a herniated disk from her back. After a period of recuperation, she returned to work at United (on smaller planes than formerly) in September of 1973. Thereafter, O'Gee lost no further time from work as a result of the April, 1972, incident, and even received commendations for perfect records in 1975 and 1976.

O'Gee brought suit against Dobbs, alleging that her injury was the result of the defendant's negligence in placing and securing the buffet unit on the plane. Dobbs impleaded United, claiming that any injury sustained resulted from defects in United's equipment. United counterclaimed against Dobbs for costs and counsel fees, citing the indemnity clause of its contract with Dobbs.

At trial, O'Gee did not call to testify any of the doctors she had consulted in the two years immediately following the incident.[5] Rather, she relied for her medical testimony exclusively on Dr. Leo J. Koven, who first saw her in December of 1976, but who was given access to the findings of the Rochester doctors who had recommended and performed the laminectomy, as well as to her hospital records. Dr. Koven was permitted to testify, over strenuous objection, to the opinions of other doctors O'Gee had seen, as he had learned of them through their reports, and through the history he had taken from O'Gee herself.

Following a seven-day jury trial, a special verdict was returned finding Dobbs negligent, its negligence 100% responsible for plaintiff's damages, and O'Gee entitled to $170,000. A motion to set aside the verdict as excessive was denied; so was United's attempt to press its claim under the indemnification agreement. On appeal, Dobbs alleges:

1.   That the evidence was insufficient to permit a jury verdict on the issues of Dobbs' negligence and causation;

2.   That the trial court erred in making reference to the so-called 'emergency doctrine' in its charge to the jury;

3.   That the trial court erred in permitting Dr. Koven to testify about other doctors' opinions; and

4.   That the trial court erred in refusing to set aside the verdict as excessive.

On its cross-appeal, United alleges that the terms of its indemnification agreement with Dobbs require that Dobbs be found liable to United for any expenses incurred in defending against the third-party complaint.

II.   SUFFICIENCY OF EVIDENCE

[The court held that the evidence was sufficient to sustain a jury verdict on the issues of liability and that the plaintiff's expert had properly been permitted to testify concerning other doctors' opinions.]

* * *

V.   DAMAGES

Dobbs argues that the $170,000 verdict for O'Gee is excessive. We laid down the standard for review of the size of a verdict sixteen years ago:

We hold we have the power to review the order of a trial judge refusing to set aside a verdict as excessive. If we reverse, it must be because of an abuse of discretion. If the question of excessiveness is close or in balance, we must affirm. The very nature of the problem counsels restraint. Just as the trial judge is not called upon to say whether the amount is higher than he personally would have awarded, so are we appellate judges not to decide whether we would have set aside the verdict if we were presiding at the trial, but whether the amount is so high that it would be a denial of justice to permit it to stand. We must give the benefit of every doubt to the judgment of the trial judge; but

---

[5]   One of the doctors O'Gee consulted in 1972, Dr. Jack Kapland, was called by Dobbs, and gave testimony hostile to O'Gee.

surely there must be an upper limit, and whether that has been surpassed is not a question of fact with respect to which reasonable men may differ, but a question of law.

Dagnello v. Long Island Railroad Co., 289 F.2d 797, 806 (2d Cir. 1961) (footnote omitted). Whatever the opinion of the trial court,[7] we must make our own assessment of the evidence to determine whether there has been a denial of justice.

We believe that the denial of the motion to set aside the verdict as excessive was, in this case, an abuse of discretion. O'Gee alleged $10,000 in actual lost wages, for the fourteen months in 1972 and 1973 when she did not work. There was no evidence supporting any finding of future wage loss, since no time at all was lost as a result of the incident after September of 1973—in fact, no claim is made for such future wage loss. Moreover, any physical problems resulting from the incident have not prevented O'Gee from performing her duties as a United stewardess (albeit on smaller planes) in an apparently satisfactory fashion, and from winning commendations for reliability and perfect records in 1975 and 1976.

Indeed, when O'Gee returned to work temporarily in October of 1972, she was found to be—and certified by her signature that she agreed she was—in good health. Further evidence of this is provided by O'Gee's 1971 and 1972 tax returns that were presented to the jury. In 1971, when she was presumably working full time, O'Gee earned approximately $6982. In 1972, during which she missed five months, she earned approximately $6411. Apparently her condition did not prevent her from working substantial amounts of overtime.

On appeal, it was argued that O'Gee suffered humiliation and a loss of prestige as a result of being forced to work on smaller planes than she had formerly. Suffice it to say that we do not find this, even in conjunction with the other items of damage alleged, to justify an award of $170,000. Consequently, we conclude that Dobbs is entitled to a new trial on the issue of damages, unless O'Gee is willing to accept a reduction of the judgment to $85,000, one half of the present figure.

[The court's discussion of United's cross-appeal is omitted.]

* * *

Affirmed in part, reversed in part, remanded in part with instructions.

■ FEINBERG, CIRCUIT JUDGE (concurring in part and dissenting in part):

I concur in so much of the majority opinion as affirms Dobbs' liability to plaintiff Kathleen O'Gee and reverses the dismissal of United's counterclaim. I emphatically dissent from the reduction of plaintiff's damages from $170,000 to $85,000, on pain of a new trial.

Plaintiff at the time of the incident complained of was 23 years old. The jury could have found—and presumably did, in view of the size of the verdict—the following: Before the injury to plaintiff's back, she was in "very good health" and had never had any back problems. Plaintiff had been "very active" and regularly skied, played tennis, used a small

---

7   Judge Weinstein remarked to counsel that any verdict up to $200,000 would be permitted to stand as justified by the evidence.

sailboat and enjoyed gardening. As a result of the accident, she was completely bedridden in early 1973 for a while and in severe pain. Despite the use of a back brace at this time, plaintiff was unable to straighten her back and continued to have "a lot of pain."

In May 1973, plaintiff suffered the distress, both physical and mental, and the risk of a myelogram immediately followed by a laminectomy to remove a herniated disc. After this operation, she had to "learn to walk all over again" and has been in pain every day. She cannot play tennis and has given up attempts to ski again. She took her sailboat out once but found it "too much for [her] back." She has married since the accident, but has trouble with household chores and does no more gardening.

Despite these medical procedures and a regimen of pain-producing daily exercises, plaintiff still has some numbness, mechanical disability, and recurrent pain for which she takes medication. The onset of her menstrual period increases her discomfort since her back swells and she experiences numbness running down her right leg as far as the calf. Moreover, pregnancy would assuredly aggravate her back condition. She has a 3 1/2 inch permanent scar on her lower back. Dr. Koven testified that there was evidence of an "ongoing disability or derangement in the lower portion of the back, which was also producing pressure on the nerve root." He concluded that this condition was permanent, but that it might be relieved by a fusion operation, although such an operation is not always successful. Without a fusion, according to the doctor, plaintiff will continue to have pain. Plaintiff was 28 at the time of trial with a life expectancy of almost 50 years. As a result of this injury, she was out of work a total of 14 months and lost $10,000 in wages.

The jury found that defendant Dobbs was negligent and that its negligence caused plaintiff's injury. As a result of that negligence, plaintiff has suffered severely in the past and will do so in the future. Her life has been radically and permanently changed. She is no longer a young woman in exuberant good health able to do what she wants. Now, her activities are limited and she has pain every day, and the years ahead are not promising.

In view of the substantial past and future pain and suffering, the loss of wages, the permanent disabilities, and the loss of enjoyment of life[2] reflected in this record, I find it hard to understand how the majority can say that the $170,000 jury verdict "is irrational or so high as to shock the judicial conscience," Batchkowsky v. Penn Central Co., 525 F.2d 1121, 1124 (2d Cir. 1975). In *Batchkowsky*, we reiterated this test for the invocation of appellate remittitur after the trial judge has denied a similar motion. The reluctance to interfere with both the Seventh Amendment guarantee and the experience of the trial bench, which that test reflects, is especially relevant here where Judge Weinstein, after viewing all the evidence, stated that he would have sustained a verdict

---

[2] The federal courts, including this circuit, have long recognized that loss of enjoyment of life, such as inability to play tennis, ski, sail, or fully enjoy homelife activities, is a compensable element of damages. See Lebrecht v. Bethlehem Steel Corp., 402 F.2d 585, 591–92 (2d Cir. 1968); Downie v. United States Lines Co., 359 F.2d 344, 347 n.7 (3d Cir. 1966) (en banc); Hanson v. Reiss Steamship Co., 184 F. Supp. 545, 552 (D. Del. 1960).

of up to $200,000.[4] The jury verdict is still within the boundaries of prior cases, see, e.g., Chiarello v. Domenico Bus Service, Inc., 542 F.2d 883 (2d Cir. 1976).[5] Moreover, we must be aware that whether plaintiff's recovery is $85,000 or $170,000, either sum will be subject to the ravages of inflation, about which the jury was not instructed. Under all the circumstances, judicial "shock" at the larger figure but not for the former draws a line whose basis eludes me. In sum, I would affirm the amount of the jury verdict.

NOTE ON EXCESSIVE OR INADEQUATE VERDICTS

1. **The standard for excessiveness or inadequacy of compensatory damages.** Among the jury determinations that must have sufficient support in the evidence is the amount of damages. In cases where the measure of damages is relatively definite, there is little difficulty determining whether an award by the jury is supported by sufficient evidence. It is rare in such cases that a jury makes a wildly inappropriate award, although sometimes the jury may compromise the question of liability and return a verdict for half of the plaintiff's clearly proven damages. In personal injury and other cases where the measure of damages for pain and suffering is imprecise, however, the question whether the damages are excessive or inadequate yields correspondingly indeterminate answers. Nevertheless, the law is that the trial judge must set aside a verdict when its amount is not supported by the evidence. But as *O'Gee* demonstrates, what amount of damages is within the limits of reasonableness for a given set of injuries can be the subject of profound disagreement among judges. The formulations used by reviewing courts provide limited guidance. Compare Joan W. v. City of Chicago, 771 F.2d 1020 (7th Cir. 1985) ("monstrously excessive") with Dedman v. McKinley, 238 Iowa 886, 892, 29 N.W.2d 337, 340 (1947) (so excessive as to "shock the conscience").

2. **Remittitur.** If the trial judge thinks the damage award of the verdict is excessive or inadequate, it makes sense that she be able to adjust the verdict to bring it within the limits of reasonableness without having to require a new trial. But this involves directly substituting her appraisal of damages for that of the jury, thus "invading the province" of the jury and to that extent denying the parties the right of jury trial on the damages issue. Many years ago a way around this difficulty was devised: At the hearing on the defendant's motion for a new trial, the judge would indicate what he thought was the upper limit of a reasonable verdict; he then conditionally granted the motion for a new trial with the order being ineffective if the plaintiff consented to accept a judgment in the reduced amount. The justifying theory was that the defendant was not being denied jury trial, because he already had appeared before a jury on the question of damages, and that plaintiff was not being denied jury trial because she was consenting to the reduced verdict rather than insisting on her right to put the question

---

[4]   Judge Weinstein further observed that "the woman has suffered very serious injuries and suffered great pain, and I think the verdict was just."

[5]   In *Chiarello*, in an opinion by Judge Lumbard, we sustained a recovery for $669,910, of which $275,548 represented pain and suffering after being discounted for future value, 542 F.2d at 886 n.4. The plaintiff in that case, like plaintiff O'Gee, primarily suffered from a herniated disc. Moreover, the plaintiff in *Chiarello* only had a 32-year life expectancy whereas the plaintiff here had a 49.9-year life expectancy.

of damages to another jury. This procedure is called "remittitur." See Dimick v. Schiedt, 293 U.S. 474, 55 S.Ct. 296, 79 L.Ed. 603 (1935).

Remittitur is allowed in federal courts only on condition that the plaintiff has the choice between either accepting the lower damage amount or being allowed another jury trial. See Hetzel v. Prince William County, 523 U.S. 208, 118 S.Ct. 1210, 140 L.Ed.2d 336 (1998), in which the Supreme Court held that a reduction in damages without offering plaintiff the choice of another jury trial violated the jury trial guarantee of the Seventh Amendment. Under federal law, a party who accepts the reduced verdict cannot then appeal to seek reinstatement of the original verdict, the theory being that she has consented to the reduced award. Donovan v. Penn Shipping Co., 429 U.S. 648, 97 S.Ct. 835, 51 L.Ed.2d 112 (1977); Note, Remittitur Practice in the Federal Courts, 76 Colum. L. Rev. 299 (1976). In fact, of course, the consent is not freely given: the plaintiff is choosing between (1) a reduction in the amount won before the jury and (2) the costs, delays and uncertainties of retrying the case before a new jury, who in many instances will have to redetermine issues of liability as well as issues of damages. Moreover, the costs, delays, and uncertainties cannot normally be avoided by direct appeal, since the grant of a new trial will normally not be immediately appealable. Remittitur is not universally accepted. For example, Missouri abolished remittitur on the ground that it is an unnecessary practice leading to inconsistent results, but its state legislature restored the practice by statute. See Badahman v. Catering St. Louis, 395 S.W.2d 29 (Mo. 2013).

3. **Additur.** A corresponding device, called "additur," can be used to deal with an inadequate verdict: The trial judge denies plaintiff's motion for a new trial, on the condition that defendant agree to increase the award to an amount specified by the judge. This procedure has not been adopted in the federal courts; it was thought to invade the jury's province because the amount fixed by the judge was outside the range of the amount pronounced by the jury. Dimick v. Schiedt, supra. The logic of the Supreme Court's position that additur invades the province of the jury, but remittitur does not, has been heavily and justly criticized. Many state courts permit additur. See Jehl v. Southern Pacific Co., 66 Cal.2d 821, 59 Cal.Rptr. 276, 427 P.2d 988 (1967), codified at Calif.C.Civ.P. § 662.5, which provides that the trial court may increase or decrease a verdict to that amount which "the court in its independent judgment determines from the evidence to be fair and reasonable." See Note, California Restores Additur, 8 Santa Clara Law. 123 (1967). See generally Hazard, Leubsdorf & Bassett, Civil Procedure § 11.29 (6th ed. 2011).

4. **Judicial supervision and the "runaway jury."** Judicial power to reduce damage awards is of considerable practical importance in many kinds of civil litigation. Popular coverage of civil litigation focuses on the dramatic and the unusual—and hence, it turns out, on the big verdicts. A study that sampled mass-media accounts of civil litigation found that the mean of the verdicts reported in the mass media was between four and fourteen times higher than the actual mean verdict in the full sample of cases (depending on the source of the estimate for the mean) and between five and thirty-four times the median award. Bailis and MacCoun, Estimating Liability Risks with the Media as Your Guide: A Content Analysis of Media Coverage of Civil Litigation, 20 Law & Hum. Behav. 419, 426 (1996). The reality is that very high awards are infrequent, and when they occur, they

are frequently reduced by trial judges or appellate courts. U.S. Gen. Accounting Office, Pub. No. GAO/HRD–89–99, Product Liability: Verdicts and Case Resolution in Five States 45 tbl. 3.5 (1989) (in a five state study of product liability cases from 1983 to 1985 awards were reduced in 50% of the cases; on average 76% of the verdict amount was paid); Broder, Characteristics of Million Dollar Awards: Jury Verdicts and Final Disbursements, 11 Just. Sys. J. 349, 353 (1986) (74% of verdicts of $1 million and above returned in 1984 and 1985 were reduced; 43% of the money originally awarded paid to plaintiffs); additional studies are cited in Vidmar, The Performance of the American Civil Jury: An Empirical Perspective, 40 Ariz. L. Rev. 849, 893–95 (1998).

5. Punitive damages. Judges also retain the power to reduce punitive damages awards, using the same discretionary standards as in cases involving compensatory damages, and that power is frequently exercised to reduce or eliminate such damages altogether. Rustad, Unraveling Punitive Damages: Current Data and Further Inquiry, 1998 Wis. L. Rev. 15, 40–44 (citing studies).

State and federal law also impose substantive limitations on the amount of punitive damages. State statutes can take the form of a concrete dollar limit, a limitation of punitive damages to a multiple of the amount of compensatory damages, or a limitation of punitive damages to a specified fraction of the defendant's net worth. See Note on Remedies, supra Chapter 1. The federal constitutional standard, derived from the Due Process Clause, is that an award of punitive damages may not be "grossly excessive" in proportion to the wrong committed. To assess proportionality, the Supreme Court looks at three "guideposts": the reprehensibility of the defendant's conduct, the ratio between the punitive damage award, and the severity of the harm inflicted or threatened (often, but not always, measured by the compensatory damage award), and the ratio between the punitive damage award and monetary sanctions set by the legislature for similar misconduct. The Court has twice applied its new standard to invalidate state court punitive damage awards as excessive. State Farm Mutual Automobile Ins. Co. v. Campbell, 538 U.S. 408, 123 S.Ct. 1513, 155 L.Ed.2d 585 (2003) (insurance bad faith; compensatory award of $1 million; punitive award of $146 million); BMW of North America, Inc. v. Gore, 517 U.S. 559, 116 S.Ct. 1589, 134 L.Ed.2d 809 (1996) (consumer deception; compensatory award $4,000; punitive award $2 million).

The substantive requirement of proportionality under the Due Process Clause is accompanied by unusual procedural requirements. Both state and federal courts are required to conduct appellate review of punitive damage awards. Honda Motor Co. v. Oberg, 512 U.S. 415, 432, 114 S.Ct. 2331, 129 L.Ed.2d 336 (1994). Moreover, in applying the constitutional standard of proportionality, the reviewing court may not defer to the trial judge's informed discretion. Instead, the reviewing court must apply a standard of de novo review. Cooper Indus., Inc. v. Leatherman Tool Group, Inc., 532 U.S. 424, 121 S.Ct. 1678, 149 L.Ed.2d 674 (2001). Finally, when an award fails the test of proportionality, the remedy is not remittitur. Instead, the court should simply reduce the award to the constitutionally acceptable maximum.

In the *State Farm* case, the court outlined a series of guidelines for proportionality, stating that where the compensatory damages award is substantial in practice "few awards exceeding a single-digit ratio between punitive and compensatory damages, to a significant degree, will satisfy Due

Process." 538 U.S. at 425. It remains to be seen how this presumptive limit of 10–1 will play out in practice. One thing the Court has made clear is that the harm against which the multiple is measured cannot include an award for harm to persons other than the plaintiff. Thus, the Court has held that in an action brought by an individual, the actual or potential harm to persons other than the plaintiff may be considered in evaluating the reprehensibility of the defendant's conduct, but not in determining the measure of actual harm against which the ratio of punitive damages to harm is calculated. Philip Morris USA v. Williams, 549 U.S. 346, 127 S.Ct. 1057, 166 L.Ed.2d 940 (2007). In any event, the 10–1 limitation, the Court said, is not a "bright-line" rule. It might not apply, for example, when " 'a particularly egregious act resulted in relatively low economic damages' " or where the conduct was hard to detect and the monetary value of the harm difficult to determine. For a lively application of the former exception, see Mathias v. Accor Econ. Lodging, Inc., 347 F.3d 672 (7th Cir. 2003) (upholding a 36–1 ratio in a case involving bed bug bites resulting from an infestation "of farcical proportions" in a Red Roof Inn.)

F. DECISIONS IN JUDGE-TRIED CASES

NOTE ON THE STRUCTURE OF A NON-JURY TRIAL

The trial of a case to the court sitting without a jury proceeds substantially in the same way as a trial to a jury. See Note on the Structure of a Lawsuit, supra p. 1. The only formal differences in federal practice concern the reception of offers of proof under Federal Rule of Evidence 103(c) and the requirement of findings of fact and conclusions of law under Rule 52 and the related provision therein as to the scope of appellate review of the trial judge's findings of fact. However, the style of presentation of a case to a judge may be considerably different from a jury case. For example:

> Many judges indicate they do not want an opening statement (because they have read the pleadings, pretrial order, or trial briefs and believe they know what the case is about); if such a statement is made, its content is usually somewhat different from an opening to a jury.

> The rules of evidence, particularly the hearsay rule, are applied in more relaxed fashion and the reception of inadmissible evidence is very unlikely to be regarded as reversible error.

> The judge may intervene in examination of witnesses more readily, uninhibited by concern for prejudicing the jury.

> Examination of witnesses and admission of real evidence (documents, etc.) usually is more expedited.

> The judge may ask that final argument take the form of written submissions rather than an oral presentation.

> The judge is not obliged to render a decision before adjourning, and may take the case under submission for a prolonged period.

For an interesting comparison between trial procedure in civil law systems, where trials are ordinarily to the court without a jury, see Damaska, Presentation of Evidence and Factfinding Precision, 123 U. Pa. L. Rev. 1083 (1975). Perhaps most important, a case tried to a judge is different from a jury trial because there is one finder of fact, whose predispositions may be crucial. The question of the circumstances under which a party may disqualify a judge who might be adversely predisposed is sometimes critical. See Note on the Recusal of the Judge, supra.

Anderson v. City of Bessemer City

Supreme Court of the United States, 1985.
470 U.S. 564, 105 S.Ct. 1504, 84 L.Ed.2d 518.

■ JUSTICE WHITE delivered the opinion of the Court.

In Pullman-Standard v. Swint, 456 U.S. 273 (1982), we held that a District Court's finding of discriminatory intent in an action brought under Title VII of the Civil Rights Act of 1964, 42 U.S.C. § 2000e *et seq.*, is a factual finding that may be overturned on appeal only if it is clearly erroneous. In this case, the Court of Appeals for the Fourth Circuit concluded that there was clear error in a District Court's finding of discrimination and reversed. Because our reading of the record convinces us that the Court of Appeals misapprehended and misapplied the clearly-erroneous standard, we reverse.

I

Early in 1975, officials of respondent Bessemer City, North Carolina, set about to hire a new Recreation Director for the city. Although the duties that went with the position were not precisely delineated, the new Recreation Director was to be responsible for managing all of the city's recreational facilities and for developing recreational programs—athletic and otherwise—to serve the needs of the city's residents. A five-member committee selected by the Mayor was responsible for choosing the Recreation Director. Of the five members, four were men; the one woman on the committee, Mrs. Auddie Boone, served as the chairperson.

Eight persons applied for the position of Recreation Director. Petitioner, at the time a 39-year-old schoolteacher with college degrees in social studies and education, was the only woman among the eight. The selection committee reviewed the resumes submitted by the applicants and briefly interviewed each of the jobseekers. Following the interviews, the committee offered the position to Mr. Donald Kincaid, a 24-year-old who had recently graduated from college with a degree in physical education. All four men on the committee voted to offer the job to Mr. Kincaid; Mrs. Boone voted for petitioner.

Believing that the committee had passed over her in favor of a less qualified candidate solely because she was a woman, petitioner filed discrimination charges with the Charlotte District Office of the Equal Employment Opportunity Commission. In July 1980 (five years after petitioner filed the charges), the EEOC's District Director found that there was reasonable cause to believe that petitioner's charges were true and invited the parties to attempt a resolution of petitioner's grievance through conciliation proceedings. The EEOC's efforts proved unsuccessful, and in due course, petitioner received a right-to-sue letter.

Petitioner then filed this Title VII action in the United States District Court for the Western District of North Carolina. After a 2-day trial during which the court heard testimony from petitioner, Mr. Kincaid, and the five members of the selection committee, the court issued a brief memorandum of decision setting forth its finding that petitioner was entitled to judgment because she had been denied the position of Recreation Director on account of her sex. In addition to laying out the rationale for this finding, the memorandum requested that petitioner's counsel submit proposed findings of fact and conclusions of law expanding upon those set forth in the memorandum. Petitioner's counsel complied with this request by submitting a lengthy set of proposed findings; the court then requested and received a response setting forth in detail respondent's objections to the proposed findings—objections that were, in turn, answered by petitioner's counsel in a somewhat less lengthy reply. After receiving these submissions, the court issued its own findings of fact and conclusions of law. 557 F.Supp. 412, 413–419 (1983).

As set forth in the formal findings of fact and conclusions of law, the court's finding that petitioner had been denied employment by respondent because of her sex rested on a number of subsidiary findings. First, the court found that at the time the selection committee made its choice, petitioner had been better qualified than Mr. Kincaid to perform the range of duties demanded by the position. The court based this finding on petitioner's experience as a classroom teacher responsible for supervising schoolchildren in recreational and athletic activities, her employment as a hospital recreation director in the late 1950's, her extensive involvement in a variety of civic organizations, her knowledge of sports acquired both as a high school athlete and as a mother of children involved in organized athletics, her skills as a public speaker, her experience in handling money (gained in the course of her community activities and in her work as a bookkeeper for a group of physicians), and her knowledge of music, dance, and crafts. The court found that Mr. Kincaid's principal qualifications were his experience as a student teacher and as a coach in a local youth basketball league, his extensive knowledge of team and individual sports, acquired as a result of his lifelong involvement in athletics, and his formal training as a physical education major in college. Noting that the position of Recreation Director involved more than the management of athletic programs, the court concluded that petitioner's greater breadth of experience made her better qualified for the position.

Second, the court found that the male committee members had in fact been biased against petitioner because she was a woman. The court based this finding in part on the testimony of one of the committee members that he believed it would have been "real hard" for a woman to handle the job and that he would not want his wife to have to perform the duties of the Recreation Director. The finding of bias found additional support in evidence that another male committee member had told Mr. Kincaid, the successful applicant, of the vacancy and had also solicited applications from three other men, but had not attempted to recruit any women for the job.

Also critical to the court's inference of bias was its finding that petitioner, alone among the applicants for the job, had been asked whether she realized the job would involve night work and travel and whether her husband approved of her applying for the job. The court's finding that the committee had pursued this line of inquiry only with petitioner was based on the testimony of petitioner that these questions had been asked of her and the testimony of Mrs. Boone that similar questions had not been asked of the other applicants. Although Mrs. Boone also testified that during Mr. Kincaid's interview, she had made a "comment" to him regarding the reaction of his new bride to his taking the position of Recreation Director, the court concluded that this comment was not a serious inquiry, but merely a "facetious" remark prompted by Mrs. Boone's annoyance that only petitioner had been questioned about her spouse's reaction. The court also declined to credit the testimony of one of the male committee members that Mr. Kincaid had been asked about his wife's feelings "in a way" and the testimony of another committeeman that all applicants had been questioned regarding their willingness to work at night and their families' reaction to night work. The court concluded that the finding that only petitioner had been seriously questioned about her family's reaction suggested that the male committee members believed women had special family responsibilities that made certain forms of employment inappropriate.

Finally, the court found that the reasons offered by the male committee members for their choice of Mr. Kincaid were pretextual. The court rejected the proposition that Mr. Kincaid's degree in physical education justified his choice, as the evidence suggested that where male candidates were concerned, the committee valued experience more highly than formal training in physical education.[1] The court also rejected the claim of one of the committeemen that Mr. Kincaid had been hired because of the superiority of the recreational programs he planned to implement if selected for the job. The court credited the testimony of one of the other committeemen who had voted for Mr. Kincaid that the programs outlined by petitioner and Mr. Kincaid were substantially identical.

On the basis of its findings that petitioner was the most qualified candidate, that the committee had been biased against hiring a woman, and that the committee's explanations for its choice of Mr. Kincaid were pretextual, the court concluded that petitioner had met her burden of establishing that she had been denied the position of Recreation Director because of her sex. Petitioner having conceded that ordering the city to hire her would be an inappropriate remedy under the circumstances, the court awarded petitioner backpay in the amount of $30,397 and attorney's fees of $16,971.59.

The Fourth Circuit reversed the District Court's finding of discrimination. 717 F.2d 149 (1983). In the view of the Court of Appeals, three of the District Court's crucial findings were clearly erroneous: the finding that petitioner was the most qualified candidate, the finding that petitioner had been asked questions that other applicants were spared, and the finding that the male committee members were biased against hiring a woman. Having rejected these findings, the Court of Appeals concluded that the District Court had erred in finding that petitioner had been discriminated against on account of her sex.

---

[1] The evidence established that the committee members had initially favored a third candidate, Bert Broadway, and had decided not to hire him only because he stated that he was unwilling to move to Bessemer City. Mr. Broadway had two years of experience as a community recreation director; but like petitioner, he lacked a college degree in physical education.

II

We must deal at the outset with the Fourth Circuit's suggestion that "close scrutiny of the record in this case [was] justified by the manner in which the opinion was prepared," *id.*, at 156—that is, by the District Court's adoption of petitioner's proposed findings of fact and conclusions of law. The court recalled that the Fourth Circuit had on many occasions condemned the practice of announcing a decision and leaving it to the prevailing party to write the findings of fact and conclusions of law. See, *e. g.*, Cuthbertson v. Biggers Bros., Inc., 702 F.2d 454 (1983); EEOC v. Federal Reserve Bank of Richmond, 698 F.2d 633 (1983); Chicopee Mfg. Corp. v. Kendall Co., 288 F.2d 719 (1961). The court rejected petitioner's contention that the procedure followed by the trial judge in this case was proper because the judge had given respondent an opportunity to object to the proposed findings and had not adopted petitioner's findings verbatim. According to the court, the vice of the procedure lay in the trial court's solicitation of findings after it had already announced its decision and in the court's adoption of the "substance" of petitioner's proposed findings.

We, too, have criticized courts for their verbatim adoption of findings of fact prepared by prevailing parties, particularly when those findings have taken the form of conclusory statements unsupported by citation to the record. We are also aware of the potential for overreaching and exaggeration on the part of attorneys preparing findings of fact when they have already been informed that the judge has decided in their favor. Nonetheless, our previous discussions of the subject suggest that even when the trial judge adopts proposed findings verbatim, the findings are those of the court and may be reversed only if clearly erroneous.

In any event, the District Court in this case does not appear to have uncritically accepted findings prepared without judicial guidance by the prevailing party. The court itself provided the framework for the proposed findings when it issued its preliminary memorandum, which set forth its essential findings and directed petitioner's counsel to submit a more detailed set of findings consistent with them. Further, respondent was provided and availed itself of the opportunity to respond at length to the proposed findings. Nor did the District Court simply adopt petitioner's proposed findings: the findings it ultimately issued—and particularly the crucial findings regarding petitioner's qualifications, the questioning to which petitioner was subjected, and bias on the part of the committeemen—vary considerably in organization and content from those submitted by petitioner's counsel. Under these circumstances, we see no reason to doubt that the findings issued by the District Court represent the judge's own considered conclusions. There is no reason to subject those findings to a more stringent appellate review than is called for by the applicable rules.

III

Because a finding of intentional discrimination is a finding of fact, the standard governing appellate review of a district court's finding of discrimination is that set forth in Federal Rule of Civil Procedure 52(a): "Findings of fact shall not be set aside unless clearly erroneous, and due regard shall be given to the opportunity of the trial court to judge of the credibility of the witnesses." The question before us, then, is whether the Court of Appeals erred in holding the District Court's finding of discrimination to be clearly erroneous.

) @ issue

Although the meaning of the phrase "clearly erroneous" is not immediately apparent, certain general principles governing the exercise of the appellate court's power to overturn findings of a district court may be derived from our cases. The foremost of these principles, as the Fourth Circuit itself recognized, is that "[a] finding is 'clearly erroneous' when although there is evidence to support it, the reviewing court on the entire evidence is left with the definite and firm conviction that a mistake has been committed." United States v. United States Gypsum Co., 333 U.S. 364, 395 (1948). This standard plainly does not entitle a reviewing court to reverse the finding of the trier of fact simply because it is convinced that it would have decided the case differently. The reviewing court oversteps the bounds of its duty under Rule 52(a) if it undertakes to duplicate the role of the lower court. "In applying the clearly erroneous standard to the findings of a district court sitting without a jury, appellate courts must constantly have in mind that their function is not to decide factual issues *de novo.*" Zenith Radio Corp. v. Hazeltine Research, Inc., 395 U.S. 100, 123 (1969). If the district court's account of the evidence is plausible in light of the record viewed in its entirety, the court of appeals may not reverse it even though convinced that had it been sitting as the trier of fact, it would have weighed the evidence differently. Where there are two permissible views of the evidence, the factfinder's choice between them cannot be clearly erroneous.

Rule

Rule

This is so even when the district court's findings do not rest on credibility determinations, but are based instead on physical or documentary evidence or inferences from other facts. To be sure, various Court of Appeals have on occasion asserted the theory that an appellate court may exercise *de novo* review over findings not based on credibility determinations.* * * [B]ut it is impossible to trace the theory's lineage back to the text of Rule 52(a), which states straightforwardly that "findings of fact shall not be set aside unless clearly erroneous." That the Rule goes on to emphasize the special deference to be paid credibility determinations does not alter its clear command: Rule 52(a) "does not make exceptions or purport to exclude certain categories of factual findings from the obligation of a court of appeals to accept a district court's findings unless clearly erroneous." *Pullman-Standard* v. *Swint,* 456 U.S., at 287.

The rationale for deference to the original finder of fact is not limited to the superiority of the trial judge's position to make determinations of credibility. The trial judge's major role is the determination of fact, and with experience in fulfilling that role comes expertise. Duplication of the trial judge's efforts in the court of appeals would very likely contribute only negligibly to the accuracy of fact determination at a huge cost in diversion of judicial resources. In addition, the parties to a case on appeal have already been forced to concentrate their energies and resources on persuading the trial judge that their account of the facts is the correct one; requiring them to persuade three more judges at the appellate level is requiring too much. As the Court has stated in a different context, the trial on the merits should be "the 'main event' . . . rather than a "tryout on the road.'" Wainwright v. Sykes, 433 U.S. 72, 90 (1977). For these

parties have already persuaded the trial court of their position reasons, review of factual findings under the clearly-erroneous standard—with its deference to the trier of fact—is the rule, not the exception.

When findings are based on determinations regarding the credibility of witnesses, Rule 52(a) demands even greater deference to the trial court's findings; for only the trial judge can be aware of the variations in demeanor and tone of voice that bear so heavily on the listener's understanding of and belief in what is said. See Wainwright v. Witt, 469 U.S. 412 (1985). This is not to suggest that the trial judge may insulate his findings from review by denominating them credibility determinations, for factors other than demeanor and inflection go into the decision whether or not to believe a witness. Documents or objective evidence may contradict the witness' story; or the story itself may be so internally inconsistent or implausible on its face that a reasonable factfinder would not credit it. Where such factors are present, the court of appeals may well find clear error even in a finding purportedly based on a credibility determination. But when a trial judge's finding is based on his decision to credit the testimony of one of two or more witnesses, each of whom has told a coherent and facially plausible story that is not contradicted by extrinsic evidence, that finding, if not internally inconsistent, can virtually never be clear error.

IV

Application of the foregoing principles to the facts of the case lays bare the errors committed by the Fourth Circuit in its employment of the clearly-erroneous standard. In detecting clear error in the District Court's finding that petitioner was better qualified than Mr. Kincaid, the Fourth Circuit improperly conducted what amounted to a *de novo* weighing of the evidence in the record. The District Court's finding was based on essentially undisputed evidence regarding the respective backgrounds of petitioner and Mr. Kincaid and the duties that went with the position of Recreation Director. The District Court, after considering the evidence, concluded that the position of Recreation Director in Bessemer City carried with it broad responsibilities for creating and managing a recreation program involving not only athletics, but also other activities for citizens of all ages and interests. The court determined that petitioner's more varied educational and employment background and her extensive involvement in a variety of civic activities left her better qualified to implement such a rounded program than Mr. Kincaid, whose background was more narrowly focused on athletics.

The Fourth Circuit, reading the same record, concluded that the basic duty of the Recreation Director was to implement an athletic program, and that the essential qualification for a successful applicant would be either education or experience specifically related to athletics.[2] Accordingly, it seemed evident to the Court of Appeals that Mr. Kincaid was in fact better qualified than petitioner.

---

[2] The Fourth Circuit thus saw no inconsistency between the statement of the male committee members that they preferred Bert Broadway because of his experience and their claim that they had selected Mr. Kincaid over petitioner because of his formal training. See n. 1, *supra*. In the view of the Court of Appeals, this demonstrated only that Mr. Broadway had relevant experience and Mr. Kincaid had relevant education, while petitioner had neither.

Based on our own reading of the record, we cannot say that either interpretation of the facts is illogical or implausible. Each has support in inferences that may be drawn from the facts in the record; and if either interpretation had been drawn by a district court on the record before us, we would not be inclined to find it clearly erroneous. The question we must answer, however, is not whether the Fourth Circuit's interpretation of the facts was clearly erroneous, but whether the District Court's finding was clearly erroneous. The District Court determined that petitioner was better qualified, and, as we have stated above, such a finding is entitled to deference notwithstanding that it is not based on credibility determinations. When the record is examined in light of the appropriately deferential standard, it is apparent that it contains nothing that mandates a finding that the District Court's conclusion was clearly erroneous.

Somewhat different concerns are raised by the Fourth Circuit's treatment of the District Court's finding that petitioner, alone among the applicants for the position of Recreation Director, was asked questions regarding her spouse's feelings about her application for the position. Here the error of the Court of Appeals was its failure to give due regard to the ability of the District Court to interpret and discern the credibility of oral testimony. The Court of Appeals rested its rejection of the District Court's finding of differential treatment on its own interpretation of testimony by Mrs. Boone—the very witness whose testimony, in the view of the District Court, supported the finding. In the eyes of the Fourth Circuit, Mrs. Boone's testimony that she had made a "comment" to Mr. Kincaid about the feelings of his wife (a comment judged "facetious" by the District Court) conclusively established that Mr. Kincaid, and perhaps other male applicants as well, had been questioned about the feelings of his spouse.

Mrs. Boone's testimony on this point, which is set forth in the margin,[3] is certainly not free from ambiguity. But Mrs. Boone several

---

3

"Q: Did the committee members ask that same kind of question of the other applicants?

"A: Not that I recall.

"Q: Do you deny that the other applicants, aside from the plaintiff, were asked about the prospect of working at night in that position?

"A: Not to my knowledge.

"Q: Are you saying they were not asked that?

"A: They were not asked, not in the context that they were asked of Phyllis. I don't know whether they were worried because Jim wasn't going to get his supper or what. You know, that goes both ways.

"Q: Did you tell Phyllis Anderson that Donnie Kincaid was not asked about night work?

"A: He wasn't asked about night work.

"Q: That answers one question. Now, let's answer the other one. Did you tell Phyllis Anderson that, that Donnie Kincaid was not asked about night work?

"A: Yes, after the interviews—I think the next day or sometime, and I know—may I answer something?

"Q: If it's a question that has been asked; otherwise, no. It's up to the Judge to say.

"A: You asked if there was any question asked about—I think Donnie was just married, and I think I made the comment to him personally—and your new bride won't mind.

"Q: So, you asked him yourself about his own wife's reaction?

"A: No, no.

"Q: That is what you just said.

times stated that other candidates had not been questioned about the reaction of their wives—at least, "not in the same context" as had petitioner. And even after recalling and calling to the attention of the court that she had made a comment on the subject to Mr. Kincaid, Mrs. Boone denied that she had "asked" Mr. Kincaid about his wife's reaction. Mrs. Boone's testimony on these matters is not inconsistent with the theory that her remark was not a serious inquiry into whether Mr. Kincaid's wife approved of his applying for the position. Whether the judge's interpretation is actually correct is impossible to tell from the paper record, but it is easy to imagine that the tone of voice in which the witness related her comment, coupled with her immediate denial that she had questioned Mr. Kincaid on the subject, might have conclusively established that the remark was a facetious one. We therefore cannot agree that the judge's conclusion that the remark was facetious was clearly erroneous.

* * *

Once the trial court's characterization of Mrs. Boone's remark is accepted, it is apparent that the finding that the male candidates were not seriously questioned about the feelings of their wives cannot be deemed clearly erroneous. The trial judge was faced with the testimony of three witnesses, one of whom (Mrs. Boone) stated that none of the other candidates had been so questioned, one of whom (a male committee member) testified that Mr. Kincaid had been asked such a question "in a way," and one of whom (another committeeman) testified that all the candidates had been subjected to similar questioning. None of these accounts is implausible on its face, and none is contradicted by any reliable extrinsic evidence. Under these circumstances, the trial court's decision to credit Mrs. Boone was not clearly erroneous.

The Fourth Circuit's refusal to accept the District Court's finding that the committee members were biased against hiring a woman was based to a large extent on its rejection of the finding that petitioner had been subjected to questioning that the other applicants were spared. Given that that finding was not clearly erroneous, the finding of bias cannot be termed erroneous: it finds support not only in the treatment of petitioner in her interview, but also in the testimony of one committee member that he believed it would have been difficult for a woman to perform the job and in the evidence that another member solicited applications for the position only from men.[4]

Our determination that the findings of the District Court regarding petitioner's qualifications, the conduct of her interview, and the bias of the male committee members were not clearly erroneous leads us to conclude that the court's finding that petitioner was discriminated against on account of her sex was also not clearly erroneous. The District

---

"Mr. Gibson: Objection, Your Honor.

"[The] Court: Sustained. You don't have to rephrase the answer."

[4] The Fourth Circuit's suggestion that any inference of bias was dispelled by the fact that each of the male committee members was married to a woman who had worked at some point in the marriage is insufficient to establish that the finding of bias was clearly erroneous. Although we decline to hold that a man's attitude toward his wife's employment is irrelevant to the question whether he may be found to have a bias against working women, any relevance the factor may have in a particular case is a matter for the district court to weigh in its consideration of bias, not the court of appeals.

Court's findings regarding petitioner's superior qualifications and the bias of the selection committee are sufficient to support the inference that petitioner was denied the position of Recreation Director on account of her sex. Accordingly, we hold that the Fourth Circuit erred in denying petitioner relief under Title VII.

In so holding, we do not assert that our knowledge of what happened 10 years ago in Bessemer City is superior to that of the Court of Appeals; nor do we claim to have greater insight than the Court of Appeals into the state of mind of the men on the selection committee who rejected petitioner for the position of Recreation Director. Even the trial judge, who has heard the witnesses directly and who is more closely in touch than the appeals court with the milieu out of which the controversy before him arises, cannot always be confident that he "knows" what happened. Often, he can only determine whether the plaintiff has succeeded in presenting an account of the facts that is more likely to be true than not. Our task—and the task of appellate tribunals generally— is more limited still: we must determine whether the trial judge's conclusions are clearly erroneous. On the record before us, we cannot say that they are. Accordingly, the judgment of the Court of Appeals is

Reversed.

[The opinions of JUSTICE POWELL, concurring, and JUSTICE BLACKMUN, concurring in the judgment, are omitted.]

NOTE ON FINDINGS OF FACT AND CONCLUSIONS OF LAW

1.   The rationale of *Anderson*. Does the scope of review of district court findings of fact differ in any significant way from the scope of review for findings by a jury? If so, is that difference justified? If not, should there be a difference? Recall that there is no Seventh Amendment restriction on the standard of review to be applied in judge-tried cases.

Shortly after the Court's decision in *Anderson*, Rule 52(a) was amended to make it clear that it applies to review of findings based on documentary evidence. What is the rationale for deferring to trial court fact-finding in cases where the evidence presents no issues of credibility or demeanor? Is the issue of discrimination, like negligence, one that varies with local conditions and norms? If so, can judges be trusted to recognize and apply those norms? Or is the issue simply not important enough to warrant reexamination by the court of appeals? When the issue is deemed more important, the scope of appellate review of judicial findings often becomes less deferential. Bose Corp. v. Consumers Union, 466 U.S. 485, 104 S.Ct. 1949, 80 L.Ed.2d 502 (1984) (de novo review for issues of fact bearing on the exercise of First Amendment rights).

The Supreme Court recently directed its attention toward Rule 52(a) in Teva Pharmaceuticals USA, Inc. v. Sandoz, Inc., 574 U.S. ___, 135 S.Ct. 831, ___ L.Ed.2d ___ (2015). The case involved the appropriate standard of review of a district court's factfinding when performing claim construction in a patent case. The Court had previously held, in Markman v. Westview Instruments, Inc, supra p. 937, that claim construction is a job for the judge and not the jury. In *Teva*, the Court, applying the "clear command" of *Anderson*, held that when a judge finds facts that serve as the "evidentiary underpinnings" for a claim construction, those findings are reviewed for clear error, and not de novo. The dispute in *Teva* centered on the district court's finding regarding the definition of the term "molecular weight." For our purposes, it is not necessary to delve into the scientific arguments. We need only note that the district court resolved the dispute by deciding a battle of competing expert witnesses. This factual determination based on the evidence, according to the Court, was entitled to deference under Rule 52(a). As the Court explained,

> While we held in *Markman* that the ultimate issue of the proper construction of a claim should be treated as a question of law, we also recognized that in patent construction subsidiary factfinding is sometimes necessary. * * * [Rule 52(a)] requires appellate courts to review all such subsidiary factual findings under the "clearly erroneous standard." * * *

> * * * A district court judge who has presided over, and listened to, the entirely of a proceeding has a comparatively greater opportunity to gain that familiarity than an appeals court judge who must read a written transcript or perhaps just those portions to which the parties have referred.

Is this the correct result? Does the conclusion in *Anderson* that a district court's findings of fact are entitled to deference apply equally to a district court's interpretation of the meaning of a term when the evidence relied on is presented by expert and not lay witnesses?

2. **Findings of fact and conclusions of law.** Federal Rule 52(a) applies to judgments in favor of either plaintiff or defendant. Note that findings of fact are required not only after trials without a jury or with an advisory jury, but also when the judge grants or refuses an interlocutory injunction under Rule 65. See Rules 52(a), 65(d). Is the trial court justified in asking the prevailing counsel to prepare the findings? The practice is more common in state than in federal court, in substantial part because of the greater case load and relatively smaller professional staffs on the state courts. Federal courts sometime ask counsel to prepare findings, and it is not improper to do so. See Citizens for Balanced Env't & Transp., Inc. v. Volpe, 650 F.2d 455 (2d Cir. 1981). In some cases, the practice is abused, causing appellate courts to swallow hard and losing litigants to choke. See, e.g., Monroe County Conservation Council, Inc. v. Adams, 566 F.2d 419, 425 n.7 (2d Cir. 1977) ("[T]he district judge adopted the [prevailing party's] proposed findings of fact and conclusions of law in their entirety, omitting the formality of retyping, on the day following oral argument, during the course of which he indicated that he had not yet read the voluminous documents upon which his decision hinged.").

3. **Findings of fact and post-trial motions.** There is greater flexibility in dealing with post-trial motions in judge-tried as contrasted with jury-tried cases. Thus, a motion for amended findings under Rule 52(b) may be blended with a motion for a new trial under Rule 59. Rule 59(a) provides, "After a nonjury trial, the court may, on motion for a new trial, open the judgment if one has been entered, take additional testimony, amend findings of fact and conclusions of law or make new ones, and direct the entry of a new judgment." In effect a motion for a new trial in a court-tried case may result under this rule essentially in a *continuation* of the original trial, rather than in a *new* trial in whole or part. See 12 Moore's Federal Practice ¶ 59.07. See also Fed. R. Civ. P. 58 on entry of judgment.

G. THE JUDGMENT

NOTE ON ENTERING AND ENFORCING THE JUDGMENT

1.   The variety of issues raised by judgments. A judgment or decree is the ultimate outcome of the litigation process. Many principles of widely differing scope, significance, and function are subsumed under the term "judgments." Those focused on in this note include the constituents of a judgment, the difference between its *rendition* and *entry,* and its effective date for such important purposes as terminating the power of the trial court over the case, commencement of the time to appeal, and issuance of a writ of execution. They also include some introductory material on enforcing judgments. Aspects of the judgment are considered at many other places in these materials: (1) the jurisdictional prerequisites for a valid judgment, considered in Chapter 2; (2) relief from judgments, considered in the Note on Default Judgment in Chapter 7; (3) the preclusive effect of judgments and the recognition of judgments in other states, considered in Chapter 9. A careful reading of Rules 54, 58, and 79 is a good start in dealing with judgments. The course in Conflict of Laws deals with problems related to the recognition and enforcement of judgments in detail.

2.   The entry of the judgment. A judgment is simply a legal document which describes the final decree of the court. Although at common law, a judgment could sometimes become effective before being entered, the federal Rules provide that judgment is effective only upon entry. Fed. R. Civ. P. 58. Entry consists of the clerk making a notation in a book (now typically an "electronic book") known as the "civil docket" indicating that the judgment has been rendered. The book is kept on a case-by-case basis, with each event in the litigation recorded as it occurs. The entry will typically be brief, stating that judgment is now entered and, at least in a simpler case, reciting the relief decreed. Fed. R. Civ. P. 79. In actions where the judgment is relatively simple (where a jury has rendered a general verdict or the judge has decided a case in which relief is limited to a sum certain and costs or no relief is granted), the clerk is authorized to prepare, sign, and enter the judgment into the civil docket without intervention by the parties or the court. Where the judgment is to be based upon a special verdict, a general verdict accompanied by special interrogatories, or a more elaborate judicial decision, the court is required to approve the form of the judgment, after which the clerk shall enter it.

3.   The legal significance of entry. Entry of the judgment triggers the time periods for post-trial motions under Rules 50 and 59. It also triggers the time to file an appeal: 30 days in a civil case in which neither the United States nor an officer or agency is a party; 60 days otherwise. Fed. R. App. P. 4.

Entry of the judgment is also a necessary condition for the validity of actions taken on the basis of the judgment, such as an execution on and sale of property owned by the defendant to satisfy the judgment. Jackson v. Sears, Roebuck & Co., 83 Ariz. 20, 315 P.2d 871 (1957) (applying the Arizona versions of federal Rules 58 and 79). Indeed, actions taken on the basis of a judgment which has not been entered are legally void. Id.

4.   The form of the judgment. The judgment is required to embodied in a separate document, distinct from, for example, the jury verdict or judicial findings and conclusions on which it is based. A suggested form for

Judgment on a Jury Verdict (Fed. R. Civ. P. Appendix of Forms, Form 70) follows:

United States District Court for the Southern

District of New York

A.B., Plaintiff   JUDGMENT

v.

C.D., Defendant

This action was tried by a jury with Judge Jane Marshall presiding, and the jury has rendered a verdict.

It is ordered that:

[the plaintiff A.B. recover from the defendant C.D. the amount of _____, with interest thereon at the rate of _____%, along with costs.]

[the plaintiff recover nothing, the action be dismissed on the merits, and the defendant C.D. recover costs from the plaintiff A.B.]

Date:

_____

Clerk of Court

This form is designed for simple cases in which Rule 58(a) approves the signature and entry of judgment by the clerk acting alone. But it also shows the basic issues that must be addressed in any judgment involving a claim for relief: the amount awarded, if any; the amount of any prejudgment interest; and the allocation of costs. A judgment must be sufficiently definite and certain so that a party can comply with its provisions. In cases involving monetary awards, that means that the amount awarded must usually be clearly specified in the judgment. Kittle v. Lang, 107 Cal.App.2d 604, 237 P.2d 673 (1951). In more complex cases, the form of judgment must be reviewed by the court to determine whether it actually reflects what has been decided. The court is empowered to request attorneys to submit proposed forms of judgment for approval where it deems that doing so would save time or lead to a more accurate record. Fed. R. Civ. P. 58.

5. Judgment as to fewer than all claims. Rule 54(b) permits the court to direct the entry of a final judgment "as to one or more, but fewer than all, claims or parties." Being final, such partial judgments are appealable. See Kallay, A Study in Rule-Making by Decision: California

Courts Adopt Federal Rule of Civil Procedure 54(b), 13 Sw. U. L. Rev. 87 (1982).

6. Enforcement of money judgments. a. Procedure for enforcement. Often the losing party satisfies the judgment by simply paying the required sum. But sometimes affirmative steps to enforce the judgment are needed. Judgments for the payment of money are enforced by a writ of execution, issued by the court and addressed to the sheriff, directing the seizure of the judgment debtor's nonexempt property and the public sale of that property. From the sale proceeds are deducted the costs of the sale, prior encumbrances, and the judgment debt, with the balance, if any, returned to the judgment debtor. See Laycock, Modern American Remedies 830–31 (4th ed. 2010). In federal court, money judgments are enforced in accordance with the practice and procedure of the state in which the federal court sits, unless there is a preempting federal statute. Fed. R. Civ. P. 69(a). When a judgment has been paid, the judgment creditor is generally required to sign and file a form entitled "Satisfaction of Judgment."

b. Enforcement of judgments from or in foreign jurisdictions. Judgments rendered in other jurisdictions cannot be enforced in the same manner as domestic money judgments. Traditionally, execution was possible only after the foreign judgment had been "domesticated" by a suit on the foreign judgment and the rendition of a domestic judgment for the amount of the foreign judgment. Because of the delay and red tape involved in this procedure, many jurisdictions have adopted a "registration" procedure instead. American money judgments, even if rendered by courts with in personam and subject matter jurisdiction, are not always enforceable in foreign countries. The subject is complex and cannot be fully explored in a brief note. A useful article is Brand, Enforcement of Foreign Money-Judgments in the United States: In Search of Uniformity and International Acceptance, 67 Notre Dame L. Rev. 253 (1991). See also the thoughtful discussion in Degnan and Kane, The Exercise of Jurisdiction Over and Enforcement of Judgments Against Alien Defendants, 39 Hastings L.J. 799 (1988).

7. Enforcement of judgments ordering specific acts. When a judgment orders a party to perform a specific act, such as the execution or delivery of a deed or other document, and the party fails to perform within the time ordered, the court generally will direct that the act be done by some other person authorized by the court to act for the recalcitrant party, and at his expense. In a proper case the court may hold the disobedient party in contempt and issue a writ of attachment, garnishment, or execution. If the property is within its jurisdiction, the court, rather than ordering conveyance of the property, may simply enter a judgment divesting the party of title to the property and vesting title in others. See Fed. R. Civ. P. 70. The Supreme Court has held, however, that a state need not enforce an injunction issued by a sister state that impermissibly interferes with the functioning of that state's judicial system, such as an antisuit injunction. See Baker v. General Motors Corp., 522 U.S. 222 (1998).

Lemoge v. United States of America

United States Court of Appeals, Ninth Circuit, 2009.
587 F.3d 1188.

■ GOULD, CIRCUIT JUDGE:

Mark and Roxina Lemoge appeal the district court's denial of their motion to set aside the dismissal of their action for personal injuries under the Federal Torts Claims Act (FTCA) against the United States and to extend time to serve the summons and complaint. The issue is whether the district court abused its discretion under Federal Rule of Civil Procedure 60(b) by denying the Lemoges relief from the dismissal. * * * We reverse and remand.

I

In April 2004, Mark Lemoge suffered a serious leg injury at a military facility when a concrete park bench collapsed and fell on him. In April 2006, the Lemoges filed an administrative tort claim pursuant to the FTCA with the Department of the Navy concerning that injury.

The Lemoges' administrative tort claim was denied, after which, on April 5, 2007, the Lemoges filed a personal injury action against the United States in the United States District Court for the Southern District of California. In June 2007, Mark Caruana, counsel for the Lemoges, sent a copy of the summons and complaint to the Navy's administrative-claims attorney. On September 5, 2007, a Navy attorney forwarded correspondence to Caruana stating that the United States Attorney's office needed to be served. On September 18, 2007, the district court issued an order to show cause why the action should not be dismissed for failure to serve the government with the summons and complaint pursuant to Federal Rule of Civil Procedure 4(m), which requires the defendant to be served within 120 days after the complaint is filed. On October 9, 2007, hearing nothing from the Lemoges, the district court sua sponte dismissed the Lemoges' action without prejudice.

During the time in which the Lemoges were to have served the summons and complaint, Caruana suffered medical complications, including a staph infection, from an injury to his leg. Over several months, Caruana underwent three surgeries, skin grafts, extensive therapy, and a full regimen of medications. Caruana states he was not able to "connect the dots" and therefore did not timely serve the summons and complaint and was not aware of the order to show cause or the dismissal.

Caruana subsequently discovered that the case had been dismissed. The Lemoges concede that because more than six months have passed since the denial of their FTCA claim, they are time-barred from re-filing their action under 28 U.S.C. § 2401(b). Thus, on May 8, 2008, Caruana, on behalf of the Lemoges, filed a motion to set aside the dismissal and extend time to serve the summons and complaint (the "Motion"). * * *

The district court denied the Lemoges' Motion orally at the end of a July 7, 2008, hearing, and confirmed the denial through an order filed one week later. The district court construed the Lemoges' Motion as a motion for relief under Federal Rule of Civil Procedure 60(b)(1) for excusable neglect. Despite accepting that Caruana had suffered medical injuries requiring extensive treatment, the district court concluded that none of Caruana's explanations justified the significant passage of time before the Motion was filed. The district court also concluded that the government would be unfairly prejudiced if the Lemoges' action was reopened because the government relied on its dismissal in settling the Granite State Action.

The Lemoges appeal the district court's denial of their Motion.

II

A district court's denial of relief from a final judgment, order, or proceeding under Federal Rule of Procedure 60(b) is reviewed for abuse of discretion. De Saracho v. Custom Food Mach., Inc., 206 F.3d 874, 880 (9th Cir.2000). A district court abuses its discretion by denying relief under Rule 60(b) when it makes an error of law or relies on a clearly erroneous factual determination. Bateman v. U.S. Postal Serv., 231 F.3d 1220, 1223 (9th Cir.2000).

Federal Rule of Civil Procedure 60(b)(1) provides as follows: "On motion and just terms, the court may relieve a party or its legal representative from a final judgment, order, or proceeding for the following reasons: [ ] mistake, inadvertence, surprise, or excusable neglect."

Excusable neglect "encompass[es] situations in which the failure to comply with a filing deadline is attributable to negligence," Pioneer Inv. Servs. Co. v. Brunswick Assocs. Ltd., 507 U.S. 380, 394, 113 S.Ct. 1489, 123 L.Ed.2d 74 (1993), and includes "omissions caused by carelessness," id. at 388, 113 S.Ct. 1489. The determination of whether neglect is excusable "is at bottom an equitable one, taking account of all relevant circumstances surrounding the party's omission." Id. at 395, 113 S.Ct. 1489. To determine when neglect is excusable, we conduct the equitable analysis specified in Pioneer by examining "at least four factors: (1) the danger of prejudice to the opposing party; (2) the length of the delay and its potential impact on the proceedings; (3) the reason for the delay; and (4) whether the movant acted in good faith." Bateman, 231 F.3d at 1223–24 (citing Pioneer, 507 U.S. at 395, 113 S.Ct. 1489). Although Pioneer involved excusable neglect under Federal Rule of Bankruptcy Procedure 9006(b), in Briones v. Riviera Hotel & Casino, 116 F.3d 379 (9th Cir.1997), we concluded that the Pioneer standard governs analysis of excusable neglect under Rule 60(b)(1). See id. at 381, 113 S.Ct. 1489.

A

We conclude that the district court did not identify the Pioneer-Briones standard or correctly conduct the Pioneer-Briones analysis and that this was an abuse of discretion. While the district court conducted analysis related to the first three factors, the district court did not consider the fourth factor, good faith, or, as required under the circumstances of this case, the prejudice the Lemoges would suffer if their Motion was denied.

The district court did not cite to Pioneer or Briones or list the Pioneer-Briones factors. In Bateman, we held that district courts should explicitly use the Pioneer-Briones framework for analysis of excusable neglect under Rule 60(b)(1)[.] * * *

As in Bateman, here "[t]he court did not . . . mention the equitable test established by Pioneer " or "spell[ ] out the equitable test." Id. at 1224. It is not, moreover, merely a matter of the district court not citing and stating the test required by Pioneer and by Briones. More importantly, we are concerned that the substance of the district court's analysis wholly omitted discussion of one of the four factors said to be relevant by the Supreme Court in Pioneer. Therefore, following the test stated by us recently in United States v. Hinkson, we conclude that the district court abused its discretion by not "identif[ying] the correct legal rule" and omitting analysis of an important part of that rule. 585 F.3d 1247, 1261 (9th Cir.2009) (en banc). * * *

Rule

The district court conducted some analysis relevant to the Pioneer-Briones factors: the district court stated that the government would be unfairly prejudiced if the case were reopened, that the Lemoges' Motion came seven months after the case was dismissed, and that Caruana's explanations did not justify the significant passage of time before relief was requested. This discussion loosely fits within the framework of the first three Pioneer-Briones factors. But the district court did not conduct any analysis relevant to the fourth factor, good faith. * * *

Not discussing good faith here does not seem to us to be an irrelevancy. It is difficult to even assess whether this case is close without knowing whether Caruana acted in good faith in connection with his delays and with his explanations that attributed the delays to his own injury. * * *

Moreover, in the circumstances of this case, we think that the district court also erred in its analysis of prejudice by not considering the prejudice the Lemoges would suffer if they were denied relief. In Pioneer, the Supreme Court stated that "all relevant circumstances" must be considered. 507 U.S. at 395, 113 S.Ct. 1489. We stated in Briones that "[t]hese four enumerated factors" are "not an exclusive list." 116 F.3d at 381. Although prejudice to the movant is not an explicit Pioneer-Briones factor, and is not a factor that we think should be assessed in each and every case evaluating a Rule 60(b) motion, prejudice to the movant, in a case such as that before us, is one of the "relevant circumstances" that should be considered when evaluating excusable neglect.

* * * Here, the district court acknowledged the Lemoges' argument that they would be prejudiced by the denial of relief because they would be barred by the statute of limitations from re-filing their action. But the district court neither considered prejudice to the Lemoges in its analysis of prejudice, nor gave it any apparent weight.

B

Turning to its application of the specific Pioneer-Briones factors, the district court in our view erred by concluding that the Lemoges did not establish excusable neglect sufficient for relief under Rule 60(b)(1). First, the government would not be prejudiced if the Lemoges were granted relief; instead, the Lemoges would suffer the "ultimate" prejudice absent relief because the statute of limitations on their claim has run. Second, the length of the delay was not unreasonable given the circumstances. Third, Caruana offered credible reasons for the delay. Fourth, there is no indication that Caruana or the Lemoges acted in bad faith. * * *

Prejudice to the Lemoges if relief is denied is an important consideration under these circumstances. The Lemoges' Rule 60(b)(1) motion seeks to set aside a dismissal for non-compliance with Rule 4(m)'s service requirements. The Lemoges cannot re-file their action because the statute of limitations has run. And the government will not be prejudiced if the Lemoges are granted relief. In contrast to the lack of prejudice to the government if the Lemoges are granted relief, the Lemoges will suffer substantial prejudice absent relief because they cannot re-file their action. Indeed, the Lemoges would endure the ultimate prejudice of being forever barred from pursuing their claims.

As to the second factor, the length of the delay, Federal Rule of Civil Procedure 60(c) requires that a Rule 60(b) motion be made "within a reasonable time" and "no more than a year after the entry of the judgment or order or the date of the proceeding." "What constitutes 'reasonable time' depends upon the facts of each case, taking into consideration the interest in finality, the reason for delay, the practical ability of the litigant to learn earlier of the grounds relied upon, and prejudice to the other parties." Ashford v. Steuart, 657 F.2d 1053, 1055 (9th Cir.1981) (per curiam).

The Lemoges' Motion was brought within a year of the dismissal and within a reasonable amount of time. The Lemoges sought relief about seven months after the case was dismissed. According to the district court, in spite of Caruana's third surgery in November, he should have been able to tend to his law practice by, at the latest, March 2008, but did not bring the Motion until May. Under the district court's view, Caruana waited at least two months after he should have been able to return to his law practice before filing the Motion. But this delay is insubstantial when viewed in light of Caruana's traumatic medical issues that still afflicted him as of the time of the hearing. Caruana testified at the hearing that while his most recent surgery was in November 2007, the surgeries were ongoing and he was still experiencing swelling. It is understandable that, as a sole practitioner, it would take Caruana months to get back on his feet and to catch up on the status of his cases while recovering from surgery. Under the totality of the circumstances, the Lemoges brought the Motion within a reasonable time.

As to the third factor, the reason for the delay, the district court erred in its conclusion that Caruana did not provide adequate reasons for the delay. Caruana's inability to identify the correct agency to serve may have been negligent, and seriously so, but it was nonetheless, in the circumstances here, excusable negligence if merely a good-faith mistake. Caruana's June 2007 letter to the Navy, sent before his medical problems arose, demonstrates that he was trying to ascertain how to successfully prosecute the Lemoges' FTCA claim. The district court noted that Caruana "was expressly informed by letter dated September 5, 2007 . . . [that] the proper agency for service of any civil complaint was the United States Attorney's Office" and was later notified through the district court's order to show cause that service had not been completed. But Caruana's medical problems, which the district court accepted, explain why Caruana did not review the Navy attorney's September 5, 2007, letter, why he did not respond to the district court's order to show cause, and why he did not file the Motion until seven months after the case had been dismissed. There is no question that Caruana could have handled his practice better, but under the circumstances, Caruana provided adequate reasons for the delay.

As to the fourth factor, good faith, the district court did not discuss this factor. We conclude that "there is no evidence that [Caruana] acted with anything less than good faith. His errors resulted from negligence and carelessness, not from deviousness or willfulness." Laurino, 279 F.3d at 753 (quoting Bateman, 231 F.3d at 1225). The government argues that even though the district court did not discuss good faith, we should infer that the district court believed that Caruana failed his clients by not diligently pursuing his cases. The government's argument is misplaced. The district court merely concluded that Caruana did not provide an adequate reason for not diligently prosecuting the Lemoges' action. See id. We do not infer from this that the district court found that Caruana acted in bad faith. To the contrary, the district court appeared to be sympathetic to the injured status and situation of Caruana. The district judge stated at the hearing, "I hate to sound like I am hard hearted about [granting relief], but . . . I just [don't] think [the legal standard] can be met in this case." If any inference at all can be drawn, it would be that the district court did not think that Caruana acted in bad faith, but felt compelled, erroneously, to deny relief on other grounds.

In sum, we conclude that under the total circumstances, the Lemoges have demonstrated excusable neglect. We therefore reverse the district court's denial of the Rule 60(b)(1) Motion and consequent continued dismissal of the case because the complete test from Pioneer-Briones was not recognized by the district court and because each of the Pioneer-Briones factors, as we consider this appeal, weighs in favor of granting relief to the Lemoges. * * *

* * * On remand, the district court is instructed to grant the Lemoges' Motion and enter an order providing the Lemoges a reasonable amount of time to serve the government with the summons and complaint.

REVERSED and REMANDED.

NOTE ON EXTRAORDINARY RELIEF FROM JUDGMENTS

1. **Historical antecedents.** Historically, there were three methods of obtaining relief from a judgment: (1) making a motion in the action in which the judgment was rendered; (2) bringing a separate suit in equity to set aside the judgment; and (3) in the case of a "void" judgment (typically one rendered without jurisdiction), awaiting the time when the judgment was relied on (for example, when an attempt was made to enforce it through execution) and defensively asserting that the judgment was void. This note discusses modern variations of all three methods.

2. **Motion in the action in which the judgment was rendered.** The procedure of relief by motion in the court where the judgment was rendered has been enlarged by statute to include all the grounds formerly available through the other mechanisms for seeking relief. See Fed. R. Civ. P. 60(b). This motion is generally the preferred, and most effective, procedure. See, e.g., Restatement (Second) of Judgments § 78. On the history of federal Rule 60(b), see Moore and Rogers, Federal Relief from Civil Judgments, 55 Yale L.J. 623 (1946). See also Note, Relief from Final

Judgment Under Rule 60(b)(1) Due to Judicial Errors of Law, 83 Mich.L. Rev. 1571 (1985).

Federal Rule 60(b) provides for six categories of relief. The first three are subject to a one-year limitation period and the last three are not. The three grounds subject to the one year limit are:

(1) mistake, inadvertence, surprise, or excusable neglect; (2) newly discovered evidence that, with reasonable diligence, could not have been discovered in time to move for a new trial under Rule 59(b); (3) fraud (whether previously called intrinsic or extrinsic), misrepresentation, or misconduct by an opposing party.

The other three grounds are subject to a requirement that they be brought within a reasonable time. They are:

(4) the judgment is void; (5) the judgment has been satisfied, released or discharged; it is based on an earlier judgment that has been reversed or vacated; or applying it prospectively is no longer equitable; or (6) any other reason that justifies relief.

3. General conditions. The text and structure of Rule 60(b) is misleading in several respects. The first is that it fails to identify certain prerequisites for the motion that apply to most of the categories. As Professors Hazard, Leubsdorf, and Bassett point out:

Except when the judgment is 'void,' * * * the decisional law * * * requires that the following conditions be satisfied:

1. The moving party must have acted with reasonable promptness and diligence after having discovered the grounds on which the motion is based. Diligence after discovery is required even within the one-year period imposed on the first three categories of 60(b) relief.

2. The moving party must have a claim or defense of substantial merit that can be asserted if the judgment is set aside.

3. Granting the motion must not unfairly jeopardize interests of reliance that have taken shape on the basis of the judgment.

4. The grounds advanced must not have been previously adjudicated in the original action or in some previous effort to obtain relief from the judgment and must not be grounds the applicant could have asserted by appeal from the judgment.

Hazard, Leubsdorf & Bassett, Civil Procedure § 15.15, at 714 (6th ed. 2011).

4. The divide between default judgments and judgments on the merits. Although Rule 60(b) says nothing about it, in fact motions to set aside default judgments are treated with greater leniency than motions to set aside judgments entered after both sides have been heard and the court has invested effort in rendering a decision. And, as *Lemoge* demonstrates, when a party finds itself unable to seek relief due to its attorney's failure to prosecute the case, courts are occasionally willing to use Rule 60(b) to save the party's claim even if the statute of limitations has run. Assuming that the basic conditions for the motion identified above have been satisfied, courts will often vacate default judgments within the one-year period on the basis of "excusable neglect." Some circuits will also allow vacation of default judgments under Rule 60(b)(6) even after the one-year period, if there is a showing that the default resulted from gross or egregious negligence by the party's prior attorney. For further discussion and citations see Note on Devices to Avoid Plenary Trial, p. 803 supra.

5.   Overlapping categories. As the case of default judgments illustrates, the specific grounds for relief under Rule 60(b)(1)–(5) appear to overlap with the catchall provision 60(b)(6). In particular, it seems impossible to distinguish "mistake * * * or excusable neglect" referred to in Rule 60(b)(1) from "any other reason that justifies relief," referred to in Rule 60(b)(6). Courts that are stingy about granting relief give a narrow reading to Rule 60(b)(6), see Ackermann v. United States, 340 U.S. 193, 71 S.Ct. 209, 95 L.Ed. 207 (1950); see also DeWeerth v. Baldinger, 38 F.3d 1266 (2d Cir. 1994), supra p. 415, in which the court of appeals refused to reopen a judgment even after it had become clear that it had made a mistake in applying New York law. But other decisions give Rule 60(b) a more generous interpretation. See United States v. Karahalias, 205 F.2d 331 (2d Cir. 1953); Liljeberg v. Health Services Acquisition Corp., 486 U.S. 847, 108 S.Ct. 2194, 100 L.Ed.2d 855 (1988). The result is some degree of confusion. See generally Kane, Relief From Federal Judgments: A Morass Unrelieved by Rule, 30 Hastings L.J. 41 (1978).

6.   Recurring problems: newly discovered evidence and fraud. In order to succeed on a motion based on newly discovered evidence the party must demonstrate not only that it has satisfied the general conditions for relief identified above, but also that the evidence (a) was in existence at the time of the judgment, (b) would likely have led to a different result in the case, and (c) could not have been uncovered through ordinary discovery procedures. Given the scope of modern discovery, such a showing will ordinarily be very difficult to make. Courts are especially reluctant to award relief under Rule 60(b)(2) when it appears that the plaintiff could have discovered the relevant evidence before filing his case. See, e.g., Fisher v. Kadant, Inc., 589 F.3d 505 (1st Cir. 2009) (refusing to grant Rule 60(b)(2) relief and noting that "[t]he customary practice is to investigate first and sue later, not vice-versa").

Historically the law distinguished between extrinsic fraud, which justified relief from judgment, and intrinsic fraud, which did not. Extrinsic fraud was said to consist of actions that prevented a party from obtaining a fair hearing on its case, such as bribery of the judge or jury or fraudulently inducing a party not to appear in court. Intrinsic fraud included the use of perjured testimony or forged documents. It was argued that discovery and cross-examination were an adequate remedy for intrinsic fraud. The courts were probably also influenced by the consideration that recognizing intrinsic fraud as a ground for relief would lead to a sharp increase in motions to vacate. Another line of cases grants relief for a separate category of "fraud on the court," in which perjured or forged evidence is no longer treated as intrinsic because it is not only the court, but also the opposing party, that has been misled. Hazel-Atlas Glass Co. v. Hartford-Empire Co., 322 U.S. 238, 64 S.Ct. 997, 88 L.Ed. 1250 (1944). Rule 60(b)(3) purports to abolish the distinction between intrinsic and extrinsic fraud, but the distinction still survives in many state courts. Kulchar v. Kulchar, 1 Cal.3d 467, 471, 82 Cal.Rptr. 489, 462 P.2d 17 (1969).

Many 60(b)(3) motions in federal court now center on failure to comply with discovery obligations, typically by withholding damaging documents. In order to succeed on the motion to vacate a party must show her opponent's fraud, misrepresentation or misconduct by "clear and convincing evidence," and must further demonstrate that the failure to comply prevented the party from fully and fairly presenting her case, because, for example, it "precluded inquiry into a plausible theory of the case, denied access to evidence that would have been probative of an important issue, or closed off a potentially fruitful avenue of direct or cross examination." Anderson v. Cryovac, Inc., 862 F.2d 910, 924 (1st Cir. 1988). (*Anderson* is the denouement of the toxic tort litigation described in Jonathan Harr's A Civil Action and the film of the same name). For contrasting applications of this approach, compare Rozier v. Ford Motor Co., 573 F.2d 1332 (5th Cir. 1978) (reversing the trial court and granting relief) with Anderson v. Beatrice Foods Co., 900 F.2d 388 (1st Cir. 1990) (affirming the trial court's denial of relief).

7.   **Separate suit to set aside the judgment.** A separate suit may also be employed to set aside the judgment. Specific provision is made for such a suit in Rule 60(d), in addition to the six grounds for relief from judgment enumerated at the beginning of the rule: "[The] rule does not limit a court's power to: (1) entertain an independent action to relieve a party from a judgment, order, or proceeding; * * * or set aside a judgment for fraud on the court."

In United States v. Beggerly, 524 U.S. 38, 118 S.Ct. 1862, 1868, 141 L.Ed.2d 32 (1998), the Supreme Court held that an "independent action" under Rule 60 is available only to "prevent a grave miscarriage of justice." The United States had brought an earlier quiet-title action (the *Adams* litigation), concerning land on Horn Island in Mississippi, in 1979. At various times, Horn Island had been controlled by France, Britain, and Spain, and it eventually came under the control of the United States in 1803 as part of the Louisiana Purchase. During the *Adams* litigation, United States government officials searched public title records and could find no indication that any part of Horn Island had ever been granted to a private landowner. The *Adams* litigation was settled in 1982 after the United States agreed to pay a sum of money to those who claimed title to land on the island, and judgment was entered on the settlement. Some time later, a specialist employed by respondents found documents in the National Archives that, according to her, indicated that the island had passed into private hands by a grant from the Spanish government in 1781. If that were true, title to Horn Island would not have passed to the United States in 1803, but rather would have remained in respondents' predecessors in title. In 1994, respondents filed a new quiet title action seeking to reopen the judgment entered in the *Adams* litigation twelve years earlier, relying on the provision of Rule 60 allowing for an "independent action." The Court held that these facts did not amount to a "grave miscarriage of justice" that would bring the case within the "independent action" provision.

8.   **Defending against enforcement of a void judgment.** A litigant may choose to defend against enforcement of a prior judgment on the ground that the judgment was void. The most common situation is one in which defendant is sued in a forum that he believes has no *in personam* jurisdiction over him. He may make a special appearance in that forum to argue the question of jurisdiction; if he does, he must abide by the jurisdictional decision of that forum. See Baldwin v. Iowa State Traveling Men's Ass'n, 283 U.S. 522, 51 S.Ct. 517, 75 L.Ed. 1244 (1931). Alternatively, he may decline to appear in the original forum, suffer a default judgment, and then collaterally attack that judgment in any forum in which the plaintiff seeks

to enforce it. See discussion, supra p. 213, Note on *Insurance Corp. of Ireland* and Special Appearance.

9.   **Recalling the mandate of an appellate court.** The counterpart in the appellate court to relief from judgment in the trial court is "recall of the mandate." Recalls of mandates by appellate courts are generally based on common law principles rather than rules or statutes. A federal appellate court will recall its mandate "to protect the integrity of its own processes," and only for "good cause" and in "exceptional circumstances." See, e.g., Zipfel v. Halliburton Co., 861 F.2d 565, 566–67 (9th Cir. 1988). In Calderon v. Thompson, 523 U.S. 538, 118 S.Ct. 1489, 140 L.Ed.2d 728 (1998) (reversing recall of mandate), the Supreme Court held that a court of appeals can recall its mandate in a habeas corpus case brought by a state prisoner under sentence of death only to "avoid a miscarriage of justice as defined by our habeas corpus jurisprudence." See generally Comment, Recall of Appellate Mandates in Federal Civil Litigation, 64 Cornell L. Rev. 704 (1979); Ulrich, Thompson & Kessler, Sidley & Austin, Federal Appellate Practice Guide, Ninth Circuit § 9.18 (1994).

CHAPTER 9

PRECLUSIVE EFFECT OF PRIOR ADJUDICATION

A. RES JUDICATA AND COLLATERAL ESTOPPEL

INTRODUCTORY NOTE ON RES JUDICATA (CLAIM PRECLUSION) AND COLLATERAL ESTOPPEL (ISSUE PRECLUSION)

A final judgment is a final judicial pronouncement on the matters adjudicated by the court. What are the purposes of giving finality to a judgment? Some are fairly obvious. Finality allows the parties repose. For the winner, such repose is clearly welcome; for the loser, it is greeted with, at best, mixed emotions. Finality also allows the parties and others affected by the result to plan for the future once judgment is rendered. And finality conserves judicial time, allowing a court to move on to other judicial business. Other purposes may be more subtle. For example, finality may save the court system the embarrassment that would result if the same matter were litigated more than once and the courts were to give different answers to the same question.

Most of the drawbacks of finality are also fairly obvious. What if the parties did not know (and could not have discovered) relevant information prior to the judgment, but discover such information afterwards? What if a person affected by the judgment was not alerted to the litigation until after judgment is rendered? What if the court simply made a mistake?

Res judicata (meaning "thing adjudicated") is frequently used as an umbrella term referring to finality of judgments. Res judicata in this broad sense is conventionally divided into two categories—res judicata (used in a narrow sense) and collateral estoppel. The terms res judicata (in the narrow sense) and collateral estoppel are used more or less interchangeably with the more modern terms, claim preclusion and issue preclusion.

Stated briefly, res judicata (claim preclusion) refers to the finality attached to a final judgment granting or denying plaintiff's claim or claims. If plaintiff wins her claim against defendant, that claim and related claims are *merged* in the judgment, and plaintiff may not bring those claims in future litigation against the same defendant. If plaintiff loses her claim against defendant, that claim and related claims are *barred* in future litigation brought by plaintiff against the same defendant. The definition of "same" and "related" claim varies somewhat from one jurisdiction to another.

Stated briefly, collateral estoppel (issue preclusion) refers to the finality attached to a final decision on a particular issue of fact or law. If two adverse parties actually litigate an issue of fact or law, if there was a fair opportunity to litigate that issue, if the issue was actually decided by a court, and if the issue was necessary to the court's judgment, the party who lost on that issue may not relitigate it in subsequent litigation against the same party. Under some circumstances, the party who lost on that issue may not relitigate against a new party.

The Restatement (Second) of Judgments § 17 largely encapsulates the foregoing:

> A valid and final personal judgment is conclusive between the parties, except on appeal or other direct review, to the following extent:
>
> (1) If the judgment is in favor of the plaintiff, the claim is extinguished and merged in the judgment and a new claim may arise on the judgment (see § 18);
>
> (2) If the judgment is in favor of the defendant, the claim is extinguished and the judgment bars a subsequent action on that claim (see § 19);
>
> (3) A judgment in favor of either the plaintiff or the defendant is conclusive, in a subsequent action between them on the same or a different claim, with respect to any issue actually litigated and determined if its determination was essential to that judgment (see § 27).

Although res judicata (in the broad sense) comes into play only after final judgment is rendered, the doctrine has important consequences before litigation is begun. A lawyer contemplating filing suit must be aware of the consequences of the judgment she seeks. For example, depending on what she wishes to accomplish and on the applicable res judicata (claim preclusion) rules in the jurisdiction, the lawyer may choose to file a complaint containing either some or all of plaintiff's claims against defendant. (In the great majority of cases, it will be in plaintiff's interest to file a complaint containing all related claims.) Similarly, depending on what she wishes to accomplish and on the applicable collateral estoppel (issue preclusion) rules, the lawyer may choose to name one party, some parties, or all possible parties, as defendant or defendants in the first suit. Depending on the collateral estoppel consequences, a non-party may choose to intervene in ongoing litigation.

B. PRECLUSION BETWEEN THE SAME PARTIES

1. INTRODUCTION

Federated Department Stores, Inc. v. Moitie

Supreme Court of the United States, 1981.
452 U.S. 394, 101 S.Ct. 2424, 69 L.Ed.2d 103.

■ JUSTICE REHNQUIST delivered the opinion of the Court.

The only question presented in this case is whether the Court of Appeals for the Ninth Circuit validly created an exception to the doctrine of res judicata. * * *

I

In 1976 the United States brought an antitrust action against petitioners, owners of various department stores, alleging that they had violated § 1 of the Sherman Act, 15 U.S.C. § 1, by agreeing to fix the retail price of women's clothing sold in northern California. Seven parallel civil actions were subsequently filed by private plaintiffs seeking treble damages on behalf of proposed classes of retail purchasers, including that of respondent Moitie in state court (*Moitie I*) and respondent Brown (*Brown I*) in the United States District Court for the Northern District of California. Each of these complaints tracked almost verbatim the allegations of the Government's complaint, though the *Moitie I* complaint referred solely to state law. All of the actions originally filed in the District Court were assigned to a single federal judge, and the *Moitie I* case was removed there on the basis of diversity of citizenship and federal question jurisdiction. The District Court dismissed all of the actions "in their entirety" on the ground that plaintiffs had not alleged an "injury" to their "business or property" within the meaning of § 4 of the Clayton Act, 15 U.S.C. § 15. Weinberg v. Federated Department Stores, 426 F.Supp. 880 (1977).

[handwritten margin note: Moitie = state court]

Plaintiffs in five of the [seven] suits appealed that judgment to the Court of Appeals for the Ninth Circuit. The single counsel representing Moitie and Brown, however, chose not to appeal and instead refiled the two actions in state court, *Moitie II* and *Brown II*. Although the complaints purported to raise only state-law claims, they made allegations similar to those made in the prior complaints, including that of the Government. Petitioners removed these new actions to the District Court for the Northern District of California and moved to have them dismissed on the ground of res judicata. In a decision rendered July 8, 1977, the District Court first denied respondents' motion to remand. It held that the complaints, though artfully couched in terms of state law, were "in many respects identical" with the prior complaints, and were thus properly removed to federal court because they raised "essentially federal law" claims. The court then concluded that because *Moitie II* and *Brown II* involved the "same parties, the same alleged offenses, and the same time periods" as *Moitie I* and *Brown I,* the doctrine of res judicata required that they be dismissed this time. Moitie and Brown appealed.

Pending that appeal, this Court on June 11, 1979 decided Reiter v. Sonotone Corp., 442 U.S. 330, 99 S.Ct. 2326, 60 L.Ed.2d 931, holding that retail purchasers can suffer an "injury" to their "business or property" as those terms are used in § 4 of the Clayton Act. On June 25, 1979, the Court of Appeals for the Ninth Circuit reversed and remanded the five cases which had been decided with *Moitie I* and *Brown I,* the cases that had been appealed, for further proceedings in light of *Reiter.*

When *Moitie II* and *Brown II* finally came before the Court of Appeals for the Ninth Circuit, the court reversed the decision of the District Court dismissing the cases. 611 F.2d 1267.[2] Though the court recognized that a "strict application of the doctrine of *res judicata* would

---

[2] The Court of Appeals also affirmed the District Court's conclusion that *Brown II* was properly removed to federal court, reasoning that the claims presented were "federal in nature." We agree that at least some of the claims had a sufficient federal character to support removal. As one treatise puts it, courts "will not permit plaintiff to use artful pleading to close off defendant's right to a federal forum . . . [and] occasionally the removal court will seek to determine whether the real nature of the claim is federal, regardless of plaintiff's characterization." 14 Wright, Miller & Cooper, Federal Practice and Procedure § 3722, pp. 565–566 (1976) (citing cases). The District Court applied that settled principle to the facts of this case. After "an extensive review and analysis of the origins and substance of" the two *Brown* complaints, it found, and the Court of Appeals expressly agreed, that respondents had attempted to avoid removal jurisdiction by "artful[ly]" casting their "essentially federal law claims" as state-law claims. We will not question here that factual finding. * * *

preclude our review of the instant decision," id., at 1269, it refused to apply the doctrine to the facts of this case. It observed that the other five litigants in the *Weinberg* cases had successfully appealed the decision against them. It then asserted that "non-appealing parties may benefit from a reversal when their position is closely interwoven with that of appealing parties," and concluded that "because the instant dismissal rested on a case that has been effectively overruled," the doctrine of res judicata must give way to "public policy" and "simple justice." Id., at 1269–1270. * * *

II

There is little to be added to the doctrine of res judicata as developed in the case law of this Court. A final judgment on the merits of an action precludes the parties or their privies from relitigating issues that were or could have been raised in that action. Commissioner v. Sunnen, 333 U.S. 591, 597, 68 S.Ct. 715, 719, 92 L.Ed. 898 (1948); Cromwell v. County of Sac, 94 U.S. 351, 352–353, 24 L.Ed. 195 (1877). Nor are the res judicata consequences of a final, unappealed judgment on the merits altered by the fact that the judgment may have been wrong or rested on a legal principle subsequently overruled in another case. * * * As this Court explained in Baltimore S.S. Co. v. Phillips, 274 U.S. 316, 325, 47 S.Ct. 600, 604, 71 L.Ed. 1069 (1927), an "erroneous conclusion" reached by the court in the first suit does not deprive the defendants in the second action "of their right to rely upon the plea of *res judicata*. . . . A judgment merely voidable because based upon an erroneous view of the law is not open to collateral attack, but can be corrected only by a direct review and not by bringing another action upon the same cause [of action]." We have observed that "the indulgence of a contrary view would result in creating elements of uncertainty and confusion and in undermining the conclusive character of judgments, consequences which it was the very purpose of the doctrine of *res judicata* to avert." Reed v. Allen, 286 U.S. 191, 201, 52 S.Ct. 532, 534, 76 L.Ed. 1054 (1932).

In this case, the Court of Appeals conceded that the "strict application of the doctrine of *res judicata*" required that *Brown II* be dismissed. By that, the court presumably meant that the "technical elements" of res judicata had been satisfied, namely, that the decision in *Brown I* was a final judgment on the merits and involved the same claims and the same parties as *Brown II*.[3] The court, however, declined to dismiss *Brown II* because, in its view, it would be unfair to bar respondents from relitigating a claim so "closely interwoven" with that of the successfully appealing parties. We believe that such an unprecedented departure from accepted principles of res judicata is unwarranted. Indeed, the decision below is all but foreclosed by our prior case law.

* * *

* * * [T]his Court recognizes no general equitable doctrine, such as that suggested by the Court of Appeals, which countenances an exception to the finality of a party's failure to appeal merely because his rights are "closely interwoven" with those of another party. * * *

---

[3]   The dismissal for failure to state a claim under Fed.Rule Civ.Proc. 12(b)(6) is a "judgment on the merits." See Angel v. Bullington, 330 U.S. 183, 190, 67 S.Ct. 657, 661, 91 L.Ed. 832 (1947); Bell v. Hood, 327 U.S. 678, 66 S.Ct. 773, 90 L.Ed. 939 (1946).

The Court of Appeals also rested its opinion in part on what it viewed as "simple justice." But we do not see the grave injustice which would be done by the application of accepted principles of res judicata. "Simple justice" is achieved when a complex body of law developed over a period of years is evenhandedly applied. The doctrine of res judicata serves vital public interests beyond any individual judge's ad hoc determination of the equities in a particular case. There is simply "no principle of law or equity which sanctions the rejection by a federal court of the salutary principle of *res judicata*." Heiser v. Woodruff, 327 U.S. 726, 733, 66 S.Ct. 853, 856, 90 L.Ed. 970 (1946). The Court of Appeals' reliance on "public policy" is similarly misplaced. This Court has long recognized that "[p]ublic policy dictates that there be an end of litigation; that those who have contested an issue shall be bound by the result of the contest, and that matters once tried shall be considered forever settled as between the parties." Baldwin v. Traveling Men's Assn., 283 U.S. 522, 525, 51 S.Ct. 517, 518, 75 L.Ed. 1244 (1931). We have stressed that "[the] doctrine of *res judicata* is not a mere matter of practice or procedure inherited from a more technical time than ours. It is a rule of fundamental and substantial justice, 'of public policy and of private peace,' which should be cordially regarded and enforced by the courts. . . ." Hart Steel Co. v. Railroad Supply Co., 244 U.S. 294, 299, 37 S.Ct. 506, 507, 61 L.Ed. 1148 (1917). * * *

Respondents * * * argue that "the district court's dismissal on grounds of *res judicata* should be reversed, and the district court directed to grant respondent's motion to remand to the California state court." * * * In their view, *Brown I* cannot be considered res judicata as to their state law claims, since *Brown I* raised only federal-law claims and *Brown II* raised additional state-law claims not decided in *Brown I*, such as unfair competition, fraud and restitution.

It is unnecessary for this Court to reach that issue. It is enough for our decision here that *Brown I* is res judicata as to respondents' federal law claims. Accordingly, the judgment of the Court of Appeals is reversed, and the cause remanded for proceedings consistent with this opinion.

It is so ordered.

■ JUSTICE BLACKMUN, with whom JUSTICE MARSHALL joins, concurring in the judgment.

While I agree with the result reached in this case, I write separately to state my views on two points.

First, I, for one, would not close the door upon the possibility that there are cases in which the doctrine of res judicata must give way to what the Court of Appeals referred to as "overriding concerns of public policy and simple justice." 611 F.2d 1267, 1269 (C.A.9 1980). Professor Moore has noted: "Just as res judicata is occasionally qualified by an overriding, competing principle of public policy, so occasionally it needs an equitable tempering." 1B Moore's Federal Practice ¶ 0.405[12], p. 791 (1980) (footnote omitted). See also Reed v. Allen, 286 U.S. 191, 209, 52 S.Ct. 532, 537, 76 L.Ed. 1054 (1932) (Cardozo, J., joined by Brandeis and Stone, JJ., dissenting) ("A system of procedure is perverted from its proper function when it multiplies impediments to justice without the warrant of clear necessity"). But this case is clearly not one in which equity requires that the doctrine give way. Unlike the nonappealing party in *Reed,* respondents were not "caught in a mesh of procedural complexities." Ibid. Instead, they made a deliberate tactical decision not to appeal. Nor would public policy be served by making an exception to the doctrine in this case; to the contrary, there is a special need for strict application of res judicata in complex multiple party actions of this sort so as to discourage "break-away" litigation. Cf. Reiter v. Sonotone Corp., 442 U.S. 330, 345, 99 S.Ct. 2326, 2334, 60 L.Ed.2d 931 (1979). Finally, this is not a case "where the rights of appealing and nonappealing parties are so interwoven or dependent upon each other as to require a reversal of the whole judgment when a part thereof is reversed." See Ford Motor Credit Co. v. Uresti, 581 S.W.2d 298, 300 (Tex.Civ.App.1979).

Second, and in contrast, I would flatly hold that *Brown I* is res judicata as to respondents' state law claims. Like the District Court, the Court of Appeals found that those state law claims were simply disguised federal claims; since respondents have not cross-petitioned from that judgment, their argument that this case should be remanded to state court should be itself barred by res judicata. More important, even if the state and federal claims are distinct, respondents' failure to allege the state claims in *Brown I* manifestly bars their allegation in *Brown II.* The dismissal of *Brown I* is res judicata not only as to all claims respondents actually raised, but also as to all claims that could have been raised. See Commissioner v. Sunnen, 333 U.S. 591, 597, 68 S.Ct. 715, 719, 92 L.Ed. 898 (1948); Restatement (Second) of Judgments § 61.1 (Tent. Draft No. 5, Mar. 10, 1978). Since there is no reason to believe that it was clear at the outset of this litigation that the District Court would have declined to exercise pendent jurisdiction over state claims, respondents were obligated to plead those claims if they wished to preserve them. See id., § 61.1, Comment (e). Because they did not do so, I would hold the claims barred.

■ JUSTICE BRENNAN, dissenting.

In its eagerness to correct the decision of the Court of Appeals for the Ninth Circuit, the Court today disregards statutory restrictions on federal-court jurisdiction, and, in the process, confuses rather than clarifies long-established principles of res judicata. I therefore respectfully dissent.

[Justice Brennan first argues that removal of *Brown II,* a non-diversity suit based solely on state law, was improper.]

III

Even assuming that this Court and the lower federal courts have jurisdiction to decide this case, however, I dissent from the Court's disposition of the res judicata issue. * * *

Like Justice Blackmun, I would hold that the dismissal of *Brown I* is res judicata not only as to every matter that was actually litigated, but also as to every ground or theory of recovery that might also have been presented. * * * B.J. Moore & T. Currier, Moore's Federal Practice ¶ 0.410 [2]. p. 1163 (1980). An unqualified dismissal on the merits of a substantial federal antitrust claim precludes relitigation of the same claim on a state-law theory. *Woods Exploration & Producing Co. v. Aluminum Co. of America,* 438 F.2d 1286, 1312–1315 (C.A.5 1971), cert. denied, 404 U.S. 1047 (1972); *Ford Motor Co. v. Superior Court,* 35 Cal. App. 3d 676, 680, 110 Cal. Rptr. 59, 61–62 (1973); See Restatement

(Second) of Judgments § 61.1, Reporter's Note to Illustration 10, 1978). The Court's failure to acknowledge this basic principle can only create doubts and confusion where none were before, and may encourage litigants to split their causes of action, state from federal, in the hope that they might win a second day in court.

* * *

INTRODUCTORY NOTE

1. The consequence of allowing a case to go to final judgment. Moitie and Brown paid a high price for not appealing the adverse judgment of the district court in their first suit. Once they allowed that judgment to become final, it was res judicata as to their federal anti-trust claims (and probably their state anti-trust claims, too). Sometimes it is obvious that an appeal is so unlikely to succeed that it is not worth the time and money to pursue it. But, as seen in *Moitie*, it is sometimes very much worth keeping a case alive by pursuing an appeal.

2. Cautionary tales. In Lim v. Central DuPage Hospital, 972 F.2d 758 (7th Cir. 1992), plaintiff Lim, a physician, was denied staff privileges at the Central DuPage Hospital. He filed suit based on race discrimination and violation of federal antitrust law. He voluntarily dismissed his antitrust claim when the Seventh Circuit, in a separate suit, Ezpeleta v. Sisters of Mercy Health Corp., 800 F.2d 119, 122 (7th Cir. 1986), warned that it considered antitrust claims for denial of hospital staff privileges legally frivolous and subject to sanctions under federal Rule 11. (Rule 11 was then in its strict form, prior to its amendment in 1993.) Two years later, the Supreme Court overruled *Ezpeleta* in Patrick v. Burget, 486 U.S. 94, 108 S.Ct. 1658, 100 L.Ed.2d 83 (1988). By then, Lim's first suit was on appeal to the Seventh Circuit. Lim unsuccessfully sought to revive his antitrust claim in the court of appeals. He then filed a new, second suit in district court based on his antitrust claim. On appeal from the district court in that case, the court of appeals held that he was barred by claim preclusion because he should have kept the antitrust claim in the first suit despite the explicit threat of Rule 11 sanctions. In *Ezpeleta*, the court of appeals had been so confident of its judgment that it wrote, "[A]ny future antitrust challenges to decisions regarding staff privileges under the Indiana medical peer review process may be deemed frivolous because of the clear bar of the state action doctrine. * * * In this very expensive area of litigation, we must require that attorneys think before they file. Cf. Stewart v. RCA Corp., 790 F.2d 624, 631 (7th Cir. 1986) (Rule 11 *requires* lawyers to think first and file later, on pain of personal liability)." Do you blame Dr. Lim for withdrawing his antitrust claim in the face of this warning? Is something wrong with the law of claim preclusion if it produces this result? Or was there something wrong with the Seventh Circuit's view of Rule 11? With the Seventh Circuit's view of its own infallibility?

In McKnight v. General Motors Corp., 511 U.S. 659, 114 S.Ct. 1826, 128 L.Ed.2d 655 (1994) (per curiam), the Supreme Court rapped the knuckles of the Seventh Circuit for behavior similar to its behavior in *Ezpeleta* and *Lim*. Plaintiff appealed a district court dismissal of his suit under § 101 of the Civil Rights Act of 1991, arguing that § 101 did not have retroactive application. The then-rule in the Seventh Circuit was that § 101 did apply retroactively. The Seventh Circuit sanctioned the attorney $500 for bringing a frivolous appeal. The Supreme Court reversed the sanction, noting that there were conflicting decisions in several district courts and that the Supreme Court had not yet ruled on the question: "Filing an appeal was the only way petitioner could preserve the issue pending a possible favorable decision by this Court." In separate cases, the Supreme Court decided the merits of the § 101 issue adversely to the position advocated by plaintiff in *McKnight*. Landgraf v. USI Film Products, 511 U.S. 244, 114 S.Ct. 1483, 128 L.Ed.2d 229 (1994); Rivers v. Roadway Express, Inc., 511 U.S. 298, 114 S.Ct. 1510, 128 L.Ed.2d 274 (1994). Indeed, by the time the Supreme Court issued its opinion in *McKnight* it had already issued opinions in *Landgraf* and *Rivers*. But the fact that plaintiff's position on § 101 did not prevail does not mean that his appeal was frivolous.

2. RES JUDICATA (CLAIM PRECLUSION)

Davis v. Dallas Area Rapid Transit

United States Court of Appeals for the Fifth Circuit, 2004.
383 F.3d 309.

■ PRADO, CIRCUIT JUDGE.

Cedric Davis and Rufus Johnson appeal from the district court's entry of summary judgment in favor of defendants, Dallas Area Rapid Transit and Dallas Area Rapid Transit Chief of Police Juan Rodriguez, in a suit alleging race discrimination, retaliation, and hostile work environment under Title VII of 42 U.S.C. § 2000e et seq. ("Title VII"), 42 U.S.C. § 1981(a), 42 U.S.C. § 1983, and 42 U.S.C. § 1988. The district court held that Appellants failed to raise a fact question on their claims regarding their nonselection for promotions to lieutenant, and that their remaining claims were barred by res judicata. For the reasons stated below, we AFFIRM the judgment of the district court.

BACKGROUND

Cedric Davis and Rufus Johnson ("Appellants"), African-American males, first collectively filed suit against their employer, Dallas Area Rapid Transit ("DART"), and DART Chief of Police Juan Rodriguez ("Chief Rodriguez"), on November 16, 2001 ("Davis I"). In Davis I, Appellants alleged race discrimination and retaliation under Title VII and violations of the First and Fourteenth Amendments under 42 U.S.C. § 1983. The claims in Davis I were based on alleged conduct by DART and Chief Rodriguez occurring between November 1998 and February 2001, during Appellants' employment at DART as police officers.[2] In February 2002, the district court dismissed the claims in Davis I with prejudice.

On June 26, 2002, Appellants filed the current lawsuit against DART ("Davis II"), alleging race discrimination, retaliation, and hostile work environment in violation of Title VII and 42 U.S.C. § 1981(a). Appellants amended their complaint in Davis II on January 28, 2003 to include parallel claims against Chief Rodriguez under 42 U.S.C. § 1983

---

[2] Johnson is still employed with DART as a corporal. Davis voluntarily resigned from DART in January 2003.

and 42 U.S.C. § 1988[4] for violations of the First and Fourteenth Amendments. The claims in Davis II were predicated on various alleged incidents of discrimination and retaliation occurring between March 2001 and April 2002, including complaints that Appellants had been wrongly excluded from the lieutenant promotion process between December 2001 and April 2002.

On June 24, 2003, the district court entered summary judgment in favor of DART and Chief Rodriguez in Davis II. The court held that Appellants failed to present a genuine issue of material fact about whether their nonselection for lieutenant promotions was based on either race discrimination or retaliation. The court concluded that Appellants' remaining claims, predating and unrelated to the lieutenant promotion process at DART, were precluded as res judicata by the judgment in Davis I. Appellants timely appealed the district court's judgment in Davis II.

ANALYSIS

Res Judicata

The doctrine of res judicata, or claim preclusion, forecloses relitigation of claims that were or could have been raised in a prior action. Allen v. McCurry, 449 U.S. 90, 94, 101 S.Ct. 411, 66 L.Ed.2d 308 (1980). Four elements must be met for a claim to be barred by res judicata:

(1) the parties in both the prior suit and current suit must be identical;

(2) a court of competent jurisdiction must have rendered the prior judgment;

(3) the prior judgment must have been final and on the merits; and

(4) the plaintiff must raise the same cause of action in both suits.

Howe v. Vaughan, 913 F.2d 1138, 1143–44 (5th Cir.1990).

In the district court, the first three factors of the res judicata analysis were not disputed. Only the fourth factor—whether the causes of action were the same in both suits—was at issue. The district court concluded that the claims in Davis II, which were based on alleged conduct predating the DART lieutenant promotion process, were part of the same cause of action as the claims in Davis I and could have been litigated in Davis I. Therefore, the district court held that res judicata precluded relitigation of those claims ("barred claims").

In our review of the district court's res judicata ruling, we must determine (1) whether the barred claims were part of the same cause of action as the claims in Davis I, and (2) whether the barred claims could have been advanced in Davis I. The res judicata effect of a prior judgment is a question of law that we review de novo. See Procter & Gamble Co. v. Amway Corp., 242 F.3d 539, 546 (5th Cir.2001).

To determine whether the prior and current suits involve the same cause of action, we apply the "transactional" test. Nilsen v. City of Moss Point, 701 F.2d 556, 560 (5th Cir.1983). Under the transactional test, a

---

[4]   42 U.S.C. § 1988 is an attorney's fee provision.

prior judgment's preclusive effect extends to all rights of the plaintiff "with respect to all or any part of the transaction, or series of connected transactions, out of which the [original] action arose." Petro-Hunt, L.L.C. v. United States, 365 F.3d 385, 395–96 (5th Cir.2004) (quoting the Restatement (Second) of Judgments § 24(1) (1982)). What grouping of facts constitutes a "transaction" or a "series of transactions" must "be determined pragmatically, giving weight to such considerations as whether the facts are related in time, space, origin, or motivation, whether they form a convenient trial unit, and whether their treatment as a unit conforms to the parties' expectations or business understanding or usage." Id. (quoting the Restatement (Second) of Judgments § 24(2) (1982)). The critical issue under the transactional test is whether the two actions are based on the "same nucleus of operative facts." Id. at 396 (quoting In re Southmark Corp., 163 F.3d 925, 934 (5th Cir.1999)). Thus, we must review the facts contained in each complaint to determine whether they are part of the same transaction or series of transactions, which arise from the same nucleus of operative facts.

Appellants filed Davis I on November 16, 2001. The complaint accused DART and Chief Rodriguez of discrimination and retaliation based on alleged conduct that occurred between November 1998 and February 2001. Davis I alleged, among other things, that Johnson was wrongly refused medical leave and that Appellants were denied promotions to the position of sergeant in February 2001. The complaint alleged that the wrongful conduct toward the Appellants was motivated by racial discrimination and was retaliation for previous Equal Employment Opportunity Commission ("EEOC") charges the Appellants had filed. Appellants complained that they were subjected to retaliation and discrimination at DART because they "continue to publicly speak out against race discrimination." Davis I was dismissed with prejudice in February 2002.

On June 26, 2002, Appellants filed Davis II. The complaint in Davis II also alleges discrimination and retaliation by DART and Chief Rodriguez. The barred claims allege conduct occurring between March and November 2001, including: an unwarranted Internal Affairs investigation in July 2001; and a baseless order by Chief Rodriguez to take a polygraph test in August 2001, which DART Executive Vice President Victor Burke later rescinded as retaliatory. The Davis II complaint maintains that the alleged wrongful conduct was motivated by race discrimination, by the Appellants' public criticism of DART and Chief Rodriguez at a DART board meeting, and by prior complaints to the EEOC.

Appellants assert that the barred claims in Davis II cannot be considered part of the same series of transactions as those in Davis I, because the conduct alleged in Davis II (spanning March 2001 to April 2002) was different from that alleged in Davis I (spanning November 1998 to February 2001). We have held that "subsequent wrongs" by a defendant constitute new causes of action, see Blair v. City of Greenville, 649 F.2d 365, 368 (5th Cir.1981), and that "[a] Title VII plaintiff is free to bring successive actions, claiming in each that his employer has taken retaliatory actions against him more recent than the prior lawsuit," Dawkins v. Nabisco, Inc., 549 F.2d 396, 397 (5th Cir.1977). However, Appellants are not aided by these principles—the "subsequent wrongs" we previously considered occurred either after the plaintiffs had filed their prior lawsuit or after the district court had entered judgment in the prior lawsuit. Here, the conduct they alleged in Davis II occurred before Davis I was filed.

time line issue in the present case

Under the transactional test's pragmatic considerations, the barred claims in Davis II and the wrongs alleged in Davis I constitute a series of connected transactions and are the same claim. While factual allegations articulated in the two complaints differ, all of the claims in question originate from the same continuing course of allegedly discriminatory conduct by DART and Chief Rodriguez. Additionally, both lawsuits cite the same motivation for the alleged discrimination—that Appellants "continue to publicly speak out against race discrimination [at DART]." This statement, from the Davis I complaint in November 2001, presumably refers, in part, to Appellants' public complaints of discrimination at the May 2001 DART board meeting and their prior EEOC charges. In Davis II, Appellants also claim, explicitly and implicitly, that these charges against DART and Chief Rodriguez motivated the alleged retaliatory conduct.

In addition, the claims precluded in Davis II were so connected in time and space with the claims in Davis I, that they could have, and should have, been brought in the first action to create a single, convenient trial unit. Res judicata "bars all claims that were or could have been advanced in support of the cause of action on the occasion of its former adjudication [.]" Nilsen, 701 F.2d at 560 (emphasis in original). The barred claims were predicated on conduct that allegedly occurred before Appellants filed Davis I in November 2001. Hence, Appellants could have included these claims in the earlier suit.

Appellants argue, however, that they properly excluded these claims from Davis I because they did not receive EEOC right-to-sue letters on the underlying allegations until April 1, 2002. A right-to-sue letter is a condition precedent to filing a Title VII claim. See 42 U.S.C. § 2000e–5(f)(1); Pinkard v. Pullman-Standard, 678 F.2d 1211, 1215 (5th Cir.1982). In July 2001, before filing Davis I, Appellants filed charges against DART and Chief Rodriguez with the EEOC.[5] The charges alleged that the July 2001 Internal Affairs investigation constituted harassment and retaliation for Appellants' prior criticism of DART and Chief Rodriguez. By the time Appellants received the right-to-sue letters on April 1, 2002, judgment had been entered in Davis I for over a month. Hence, Appellants maintain that even if some of the allegations in Davis I and Davis II were part of the same cause of action and overlapped temporally, the Davis II claims should not be barred because Appellants were not able to bring them in Davis I. The district court disagreed, noting that:

> [w]hile Title VII requires exhaustion of administrative remedies before a federal claim may be brought, there were options available to Plaintiffs other than simply choosing between their claims. Plaintiffs could have filed the suit and requested a stay pending the conclusion of the administrative proceedings on the two EEOC complaints at issue in this discussion, or Plaintiffs

---

[5] Appellants also filed a complaint with DART's internal Equal Employment Office regarding the same matters described in the July 2001 EEOC Charges. In August 2001, they received a finding that Chief Rodriguez had retaliated against them.

could have delayed filing the first suit until the administrative proceedings were completed.

This circuit has never directly addressed whether a Title VII claim may be barred by res judicata if, at the time of the earlier suit, the plaintiffs have not yet received a right-to-sue letter. However, several of our sister circuits have answered this question in the affirmative.

The district court in this case relied on Woods v. Dunlop Tire Corp., 972 F.2d 36 (2d Cir.1992), in which the Second Circuit held that a plaintiff's Title VII claims were barred by res judicata even though she had not received a right-to-sue letter at the time she filed her lawsuit. In Woods, the plaintiff's Title VII claims arose out of the same transaction as a previously filed Labor Management Relations Act ("LMRA") claim. Id. at 38. Although the plaintiff did not have a right-to-sue letter from the EEOC when she initiated the LMRA action, the court reasoned that to avoid the sting of res judicata, the plaintiff could have filed her LMRA claim, sought a stay in the district court pending the outcome of her EEOC proceedings, and then joined her Title VII claims once she received her right-to-sue letter. Id. at 41. In reaching this conclusion, the Second Circuit noted that "the language and policy of Title VII do not undercut the application of res judicata, and we see no reason militating against application of well-settled claim preclusion principles." Id. at 39.

Several other circuits have similarly held that Title VII claims were barred where plaintiffs failed to take measures to avoid preclusion under res judicata while they pursued the requisite Title VII remedies. * * *

We agree with the Second Circuit's reasoning in Woods that a plaintiff who brings a Title VII action and files administrative claims with the EEOC must still comply "with general rules governing federal litigation respecting other potentially viable claims." 972 F.2d at 39–40. Because the barred claims arose from the same nucleus of operative fact as the claims in Davis I and they predate that action, Appellants were on notice to include those claims in Davis I. To prevent their claims from being precluded, Appellants could have requested a stay in Davis I until they received their letters. Accordingly, we affirm the district court's determination that Appellants' claims predating and unrelated to the lieutenant promotion process were barred by res judicata.

Claims Related to Lieutenant Promotion Process

Appellants' remaining claims allege that their exclusion from the lieutenant promotion process at DART, which occurred between December 2001 and April 2002, was motivated by race discrimination and was retaliatory. [The district court had not dismissed the appellants's claims relating to the lieutenant promotion process based on res judicata. Rather, it had reached the merits of the claims and had granted summary judgment against the appellants. Without discussing res judicata, the court of appeals affirmed this grant of summary judgment.]

AFFIRMED.

NOTE ON RES JUDICATA (CLAIM PRECLUSION)

1. **Historical background.** The early common law had no doctrine of res judicata in the modern sense. Unless the statute of limitations

prevented him from so doing, a plaintiff often could sue under one writ and, if unsuccessful, thereafter sue on another. To the extent that the writs were mutually exclusive, this privilege theoretically worked out fairly: if plaintiff failed in the first action because the wrong writ was chosen, in justice he should be able to try again with the correct writ. But by the middle of the 18th century, the courts had so expanded the scope of many writs that there were large areas of overlap. Hence, a plaintiff often could bring successive actions on different writs, asserting substantially the same claim. To meet this evasion of the limits of the writ structure, the common law courts fashioned the doctrine of "election of remedies": A plaintiff who chose a writ was deemed to have "elected" his remedy and was precluded from subsequently using another writ. The rule thus accomplished many of the same objectives as the present rules of merger and bar under modern res judicata law. See Hitchin v. Campbell, 2 W. Blackstone 827, 96 E.R. 487 (K.B. 1771).

2. **Res judicata (claim preclusion) under § 24 of the Restatement (Second) of Judgments.** In all modern res judicata schemes, there is a general rule against "splitting claims." "Claim" has a special meaning under § 24 of the Restatement (Second) of Judgments for purposes of res judicata (claim preclusion). In this context, "claim" has an unusually broad definition. A "claim" includes all causes of action that are transactionally related:

> (1) When a valid and final judgment rendered in an action extinguishes the plaintiff's claim pursuant to the rules of merger or bar (see §§ 18, 19), the claim extinguished includes all rights of the plaintiff to remedies against the defendant *with respect to all or any part of the transaction, or series of connected transactions, out of which the actions arose.*

> (2) What factual grouping constitutes a "transaction", and what groupings constitute a "series", are to be determined pragmatically, giving weight to such considerations as whether the facts are related in time, space, origin, or motivation, whether they form a convenient trial unit, and whether their treatment as a unit conforms to the parties' expectations or business understanding or usage.

(Emphasis added.)

3. **Section 24 of the Second Restatement in federal court.** Despite the Supreme Court's reluctance in *Moitie* to apply § 24 of the Second Restatement to Brown's state-law claim in *Brown II*, federal courts routinely apply § 24, as indicated by Justices Blackmun and Brennan. If the Supreme Court had applied § 24 in *Moitie*, the state antitrust action would almost certainly have been dismissed as arising out of the same transaction or series of connection transactions as the federal antitrust action.

4. **Use it or lose it.** The prohibition against "claim splitting" means that a second suit is precluded not only as to all causes of action that *were* brought in the first suit, but also as to all causes of action that *could have been brought* in that suit, so long as the later causes of action were part of the same "claim" as in the first suit. That is, once a plaintiff brings suit, he must assert all causes of action arising out of the same "claim." If he fails to assert such a cause of action, and the first suit goes to final judgment, he may not thereafter assert that cause of action in a later suit.

5.   The *Davis* case. The *Davis* case is a good example of a federal court relying on § 24 for the definition of a "claim" for purposes of res judicata (claim preclusion).

a.   Time of bringing suit. Note that if plaintiffs Davis and Johnson's second suit, *Davis II*, had been based entirely on events occurring after filing the complaint in their first suit, *Davis I*, the second suit would have been allowed, even if the events were part of a continuous series of transactions. The problem was that the events at issue in *Davis II* took place early enough that they could have been litigated in *Davis I*.

b.   The "right-to-sue" letter. The court's opinion does not say it explicitly, but we may infer that Davis and Johnson had received EEOC right-to-sue letters specifically addressing the claims they litigated in *Davis I*. But at the time they filed *Davis I*, they had not yet received additional right-to-sue letters addressing the retaliation and other claims they sought to bring in *Davis II*. Davis and Johnson seem to have thought (or, more accurately, their lawyers seem to have thought) that the normal rules of res judicata were suspended while they waited for "right-to-sue" letters from the EEOC authorizing suit based on the later events that were the subject of *Davis II*. As the court makes plain, however, there were ways to litigate in the first suit claims based on those later events. Other federal courts follow the same rule with respect to right-to-sue letters issued by the EEOC. See, e.g., Havercombe v. Department of Education, 250 F.3d 1 (1st Cir. 2001); Owens v. Kaiser Foundation Health Plan, Inc., 244 F.3d 708 (9th Cir. 2001).

c.   The exclusion from the lieutenant promotion process. The court of appeals does not perform a res judicata analysis of Davis and Johnson's causes of action alleging exclusion from the lieutenant promotion process. This appears to be a result of the manner in which the district court dealt with this cause of action. The district court addressed the lieutenant promotion process on the merits without addressing res judicata. The court of appeals then affirmed that part of the decision on the merits, also not addressing res judicata. If the court of appeals had addressed the res judicata question, it is possible that the lieutenant promotion process causes of action were sufficiently related that they too would have been held barred by res judicata.

6.   Narrower definition of "claim" in some state courts. Some state courts define "claim" more narrowly than § 24. For example, California defines claim as a "primary right." If two suits are based on different "primary rights," the second suit is permitted even if it arises out of the same transaction or occurrence as the first suit. The definition of "primary right" under California law is often a matter of some difficulty, even for California lawyers and judges. In Dunkin v. Boskey, 82 C.A.4th 171, 98 Cal.Rptr.2d 44 (2000), plaintiff was sterile because of testicular cancer. His long-time partner (to whom he was not married) had a child through artificial insemination from an anonymous donor. After the birth of the child, plaintiff was listed on her birth certificate as her father. He cared for the girl as if she were his own child, but he never adopted her. The mother later broke off the relationship with the plaintiff and took the girl away. Plaintiff first brought an unsuccessful suit against the mother to establish his parental rights. He then brought a second suit against the mother for breach of a contract under which she had allegedly agreed to allow him to help raise the child. The California court of appeal held that the second suit was not barred by res judicata because the theories of the two suits were not based on the same "primary right." See also Le Parc Community Ass'n v. Workers' Compensation Appeals Board, 110 C.A.4th 1161, 2 Cal.Rptr.3d 408 (2003) (negligence suit by employee against an uninsured employer not based on the same "primary right" as a workers' compensation claim against that employer). The California Supreme Court has hinted—but only hinted—that it might eventually adopt the Second Restatement approach. See Mycogen Corp. v. Monsanto Co., 28 Cal.4th 888, 909 n.13, 123 Cal.Rptr.2d 432, 51 P.3d 297 (2002).

Some other states also have narrow definitions of "claim." See, e.g., the Arizona rule articulated in E.C. Garcia & Co. v. Arizona State Dept. of Revenue, 178 Ariz. 510, 520, 875 P.2d 169, 179 (Ct.App.1993) ("Two causes of action which arise out of the same transaction or occurrence are not the same for purposes of res judicata if proof of different or additional facts will be required to establish them."); Torcasso v. Standard Outdoor Sales, Inc., 157 Ill.2d 484, 193 Ill.Dec. 192, 626 N.E.2d 225 (1993); Butler v. Reeder, 628 So.2d 99 (Ct.App.La. 1993).

7. Compare "transaction" in the Federal Rules of Civil Procedure. Section 24(1) of the Second Restatement uses the familiar phraseology "transaction, or series of connected transactions, out of which the actions arose." Compare similar language in Rule 13(a) (compulsory counterclaim) ("arises out of the transaction or occurrence that is the subject matter of the opposing party's claim"); Rule 13(g) (cross-claim) ("arises out of the transaction or occurrence that is the subject matter of the original action or of a counterclaim, or if the claim relates to any property that is the subject matter of the original action"); Rule 14(a)(2)(D) and (a)(3) (impleader) (third-party defendant may assert against the plaintiff "any claim arising out of the transaction or occurrence that is the subject matter of the plaintiff's claim against the third-party plaintiff"; the plaintiff may assert any claim against the third-party defendant "arising out of the transaction or occurrence that is the subject matter of the plaintiff's claim against the third-party plaintiff"); Rule 20(a) (permissive joinder of parties) (parties may join together as plaintiffs if they assert a right to relief "arising out of the same transaction, occurrence, or series of transactions or occurrences" and if "any question of law or fact common to all plaintiffs will arise in the action").

8. No bright-line definition of claim in § 24. Section 24 does not provide a bright-line definition of "claim." The definitions of the terms "transaction" and "series," as used in Section 24(1), are not self-evident, and they are not necessarily synonymous with those terms as they are used in the federal Rules. Indeed, the definitions may not even be consistent from one application of § 24 to another. Section 24(2) is worth quoting again: "What factual grouping constitutes a 'transaction,' and what groupings constitute a 'series,' are to be determined pragmatically, giving weight to such considerations as whether the facts are related in time, space, origin, or motivation, whether they form a convenient trial unit, and whether their treatment as a unit conforms to the parties' expectations or business understanding or usage."

Consider the following two examples. First, imagine that a state prisoner brings a civil rights suit under 42 U.S.C. § 1983 contending that the prison unconstitutionally limited his access to court by imposing unreasonable restrictions on access to the prison law library and to word processing. After the prisoner wins (or loses) that suit, he files another § 1983 access-to-court suit, this time complaining that the prison unreasonably restricts access to photocopiers. The second suit is almost certainly barred by res judicata (claim preclusion) as arising out of the same "transaction, or series of connected transactions."

Second, imagine that a class action was brought under § 1983 on behalf of all of the prisoners in that prison, alleging unconstitutional actions by the prison officials, including limitations on court access. The plaintiff class wins (or loses) the suit, including its claim of unconstitutional denial of court access. Several years later, an individual prisoner in that prison brings a § 1983 access-to-court suit, contending that during the time period covered by the class action he was unreasonably denied access to photocopiers. This prisoner was an unnamed member of the class in the earlier suit. Is his individual suit barred by res judicata (claim preclusion)? Applying § 24, the court of appeals said no:

> We do not believe that all facts related to court access . . . create one transaction and a single claim.* * * Especially taking into account that the first action was a class action for which [the individual plaintiff in the second suit] was an unnamed, absent class member, his claim should not be precluded. * * * Arguably, everything related to prison life could conceivably be deemed part of "a series of transactions" when a broad-based class action is brought, but if this is how claim preclusion is defined in the class action context, it would essentially make class actions obsolete. After one prisoner class action had been filed, no "related" claims could ever be filed. No responsible attorney would ever file a class action challenging a prison condition, because by doing so, all future claims by prisoners challenging an unconstitutional condition could be barred—even if the specific issue was never raised in the previous litigation.

Hiser v. Franklin, 94 F.3d 1287, 1292–93 (9th Cir. 1996).

9. Res judicata and compulsory counterclaims. Section 22 of the Second Restatement provides:

> (1) Where the defendant may interpose a claim as a counterclaim but he fails to do so, he is not thereby precluded from subsequently maintaining an action on that claim, except as stated in Subsection (2).

> (2) A defendant who may interpose a claim as a counterclaim in an action but fails to do so is precluded, after the rendition of the judgment in that action, from maintaining an action on the claim if:

>> (a) The counterclaim is required to be interposed by a compulsory counterclaim statute or rule of court[.]

When a compulsory counterclaim rule is written in terms of the same "transaction or occurrence" as the claim brought by plaintiff, the effect of § 22 on defendants will be roughly the same as the effect of § 24 on plaintiffs. See, e.g., Fed. R. Civ. P. 13(a); Calif.C.Civ.P. § 426.30(a) ("[I]f a party against whom a complaint has been filed and served fails to allege in a cross-complaint any related cause of action which (at the time of serving his answer to the complaint) he has against the plaintiff, such party may not thereafter in any other action assert against the plaintiff the related cause of action not pleaded."). The sanction for failure to assert a compulsory counterclaim is not provided in federal Rule 13(a), but the general view is that the consequence is the same as that explicitly provided in Calif.C.Civ.P. § 426.30(a) and indicated in § 22 of the Second Restatement. See, e.g., Currie Medical Specialties, Inc. v. Bowen, 136 Cal.App.3d 774, 776, 186 Cal.Rptr. 543 (1982) (under Calif.C.Civ.P. § 426.30 a failure to assert a compulsory counterclaim in federal court bars that claim in a later suit in California state court).

10. Res judicata and intervenors. If a party intervenes in a suit, that party must pursue its claims in that suit or be barred by claim preclusion later. In Local 322, Allied Industrial Workers of America v. Johnson Controls, Inc., 969 F.2d 290 (7th Cir. 1992), Local 322 filed suit against Johnson Controls in federal district court under Title VII of the Civil Rights Act of 1964. Without dismissing its action in the district court, Local 322 intervened in a similar federal court action brought by the United Auto Workers (UAW) against Johnson Controls while that case was on appeal to the Seventh Circuit. After the Seventh Circuit decided in favor of Johnson Controls, the UAW petitioned for a writ of certiorari to the Supreme Court. Local 322 declined to join the petition, thus letting the Seventh Circuit's decision become final as to its claim. (Recall that this is essentially what happened in *Moitie* when Moitie and Brown chose not to appeal.) Local 322 then sought to revive its earlier action in the district court, but the district court held that it was barred by res judicata (claim preclusion). When Local 322 appealed the district court's res judicata ruling, the Seventh Circuit not only ruled against it, but also issued an order to show cause why it should not be sanctioned for bringing a frivolous appeal. To add insult to injury, the Supreme Court granted the UAW's petition for certiorari and held for the UAW on the merits. See International Union, United Automobile, Aerospace and Agricultural Implement Workers of America, UAW v. Johnson Controls, Inc., 499 U.S. 187, 111 S.Ct. 1196, 113 L.Ed.2d 158 (1991).

11. Modification of res judicata by statute. A statute may qualify or abrogate the application of the rules of claim preclusion in order to serve the particular purposes of the statute. See, e.g., Barrentine v. Arkansas-Best Freight System, Inc., 450 U.S. 728, 101 S.Ct. 1437, 67 L.Ed.2d 641 (1981) (unfavorable determination of wage claim in collective bargaining arbitration does not preclude employee's assertion of Fair Labor Standards Act claim based on the same conduct); Vestal and Hill, Preclusion in Labor Controversies, 35 Okla.L.Rev. 281 (1982); Restatement (Second) of Judgments § 26(d). See the analysis in Jackson, Matheson and Piskorski, The Proper Role of Res Judicata and Collateral Estoppel in Title VII Suits, 79 Mich.L.Rev. 1485 (1981); cf. Note, Res Judicata in Title VII Actions, 27 B.C.L.Rev. 173 (1985).

12. Court may raise res judicata defense on its own motion. Ordinarily, a defense of res judicata (claim preclusion) should be raised by the party advantaged by the defense. But a court may raise the question of claim preclusion on its own motion for the sake of judicial economy. See Alyeska Pipeline Serv. Co. v. United States, 231 Ct.Cl. 540, 688 F.2d 765 (1982).

Staats v. County of Sawyer

United States Court of Appeals for the Seventh Circuit, 2000.
220 F.3d 511.

■ D. WOOD, CIRCUIT JUDGE.

In September 1994, Edward Staats learned that he suffers from bipolar disorder. He received treatment for it, but when he attempted to return to his job as personnel director for Sawyer and Bayfield Counties, Wisconsin (the Counties), he was told that the job had been eliminated. Believing that this was a poor disguise for disability discrimination, he pursued his state administrative remedies. Ultimately, the Labor and Industry Review Commission (LIRC) rejected his claims, and the Circuit Court for LaCrosse County affirmed that decision. Meanwhile, Staats had also filed charges with the federal Equal Employment Opportunity Commission (EEOC), which in due course issued him a right-to-sue letter. This case followed in federal court. The district court dismissed Staats's claims under Titles I and II of the Americans with Disabilities Act (ADA) and the Rehabilitation Act of 1973 on the ground of claim preclusion. Because we find that Wisconsin would permit claim splitting under the circumstances presented here, we reverse and remand for further proceedings.

I

There is little more to the underlying facts than we have already recounted. Staats began working as the full-time personnel director for the Counties in May 1993 under an arrangement whereby he split his time between them. Either county was entitled to terminate the agreement by filing written notice before September 1 of the year preceding termination. Everything proceeded smoothly until September 1994, when Staats began acting strangely. He was hospitalized the same month for his bi-polar disorder; in October, he was hospitalized again and remained in the hospital until mid-November. In late November 1994, he attempted to return to work. At that point, the Counties told him that he needed a release from his doctor. He complied, but the work release his doctor gave him restricted him to "working no more than 40 hours per week, taking no work home to complete after hours, attending regular therapy sessions with psychiatrists, in complian[ce] with his medication, monthly laboratory testing of medication blood level and abstinence from alcohol for the next 90 days." In mid-December 1994, one of Staats's treating physicians completed a medical form indicating that Staats was able to perform work as a personnel director as of November 20, 1994.

A return to work, however, was not in Staats's future. Instead, on December 19, the Counties' attorney informed Staats that he could continue to work until the end of the calendar year, at which time his job position itself would be eliminated. On March 3, 1995, Staats filed a claim of employment discrimination with the State of Wisconsin Equal Rights Division, alleging violations of the Wisconsin Fair Employment Act (WFEA), Wis. Stat. § 111.31 et seq. The Equal Rights Division found probable cause to believe that the Counties had discriminated against Staats and certified the matter to a hearing before an administrative law judge. After a full hearing on the merits, the ALJ issued a decision concluding that the Counties had violated the WFEA and had failed to determine what sort of accommodation Staats might need.

The Counties appealed the decision to the LIRC. Conducting the appeal on the record, the LIRC reversed the ALJ's decision. It found that although the Counties had eliminated Staats's position because of his disability, the Counties had not violated the WFEA. Staats sought review of the LIRC decision in state court under the Wisconsin state administrative review procedures. See Wis. Stat. § 111.395. The state court conducted a review limited to the administrative record, as it was required to do by statute. See Wis. Stat. § 227.57. It upheld the LIRC's decision. See id. Staats did not appeal.

Two weeks after Staats filed his complaint with the Equal Rights Division, he cross-filed with the EEOC. Sometime in May 1998, he received his right-to-sue letter from the EEOC and shortly thereafter filed the present action in federal district court. His complaint alleged that the Counties had discriminated against him because of his disability (bi-polar disorder) by failing to provide reasonable accommodations for him and eliminating his position, in violation of Titles I and II of the Americans with Disabilities Act, 42 U.S.C. § 12101, et seq., and the Rehabilitation Act of 1973, as amended, 29 U.S.C. § 794, et seq. The Counties filed a motion for summary judgment on the basis that the state court decision affirming the decision of the LIRC barred the federal court action under the doctrine of claim preclusion. See 28 U.S.C. § 1738; Northern States Power Co. v. Bugher, 189 Wis.2d 541, 525 N.W.2d 723, 728–29 (1995). The district court agreed and entered judgment for the Counties; Staats now appeals.

II

* * *

Staats suggests three reasons why the state court judgment does not bar his claims under the federal anti-discrimination laws: (1) Wisconsin law would not give the state court judgment preclusive effect; (2) the state court had limited jurisdiction in conducting its review of the administrative decision and therefore Staats could not have brought his federal claims in the earlier proceeding; and (3) the standards and remedies provided by Wisconsin discrimination law are narrower than those of federal law, and so an exception to claim preclusion should apply.

As we recently observed in Froebel v. Meyer, 217 F.3d 928 (7th Cir.2000), the federal court was required to give the Wisconsin court's judgment the same full faith and credit that it would have received in a Wisconsin court. Id. at 936; 28 U.S.C. § 1738. * * *

* * * In Froebel, we reviewed the principles that govern in Wisconsin:

The Wisconsin Supreme Court recently summarized its approach to deciding when a subsequent action is barred in Sopha v. Owens-Corning Fiberglas Corp., 230 Wis.2d 212, 601 N.W.2d 627 (1999). There the court indicated that three factors had to be present in order to preclude the later action: (1) identity between the parties or their privies in the prior and present suits; (2) prior litigation resulted in a final judgment on the merits by a court with jurisdiction; and (3) identity of the causes of action in the two suits. 601 N.W. at 637.

Froebel, 217 F.3d at 936. See also Northern States Power, 525 N.W.2d at 728; Patzer v. Board of Regents of the University of Wisconsin System, 763 F.2d 851, 855 (7th Cir.1985).

The first requirement—identity of the parties—is plainly met here, as Staats and the Counties were the opposing parties in both cases. We assume for the sake of argument that the third requirement—identity of claim—is also satisfied, under the transactional approach that prevails in Wisconsin. See Northern States Power, 525 N.W.2d at 728–29; Parks v. City of Madison, 171 Wis.2d 730, 492 N.W.2d 365, 370 (App.1992), citing Juneau Square Corp. v. First Wisconsin National Bank, 122 Wis.2d 673, 364 N.W.2d 164, 170 (App.1985). Staats's WFEA, ADA, and Rehabilitation Act claims arose out of the same basic factual situation and the same basic conduct of the Counties: the elimination of his position of employment. Under the transactional approach, Wisconsin would probably find that these claims are the same. See Brye v. Brakebush, 32 F.3d 1179, 1184 (7th Cir.1994); DePratt v. West Bend Mutual Ins. Co., 113 Wis.2d 306, 334 N.W.2d 883, 886 (1983) ("[The] claim is coterminous with the transaction, regardless of the number of substantive theories or variant forms of relief flowing from these theories; the transaction is the basis of the litigative unit or entity which may not be split."), quoting Restatement (Second) of Judgments § 24 cmt. a.

As in Froebel, the problem arises with the second factor—whether this is the kind of final judgment to which Wisconsin gives preclusive effect. As we explained in Froebel, there are really two elements to this inquiry: finality and jurisdiction. Here, it is undisputed that the state court's review of the LIRC decision concluded with a final judgment. Its finality is unaffected by the fact that the procedures governing this type of proceeding are somewhat truncated and the standard of review is quite deferential. Standing behind the court's judgment were adversarial administrative proceedings with sufficient procedural safeguards for the state court findings to satisfy due process. See Kremer, 456 U.S. at 483–85, 102 S.Ct. 1883.

As in Froebel, however, we must also consider the jurisdiction of the state agency and state court, because the second factor used by the Wisconsin Supreme Court requires consideration of the jurisdiction of the first forum. * * * Under Wisconsin's law of judgments, "[t]he earlier judgment is conclusive 'as to all matters which were litigated or which might have been litigated' in that proceeding." Jantzen v. Baker, 131 Wis.2d 507, 388 N.W.2d 660, 662 (App.1986), quoting DePratt, 334 N.W.2d at 885, quoted in Parks, 492 N.W.2d at 368 (emphasis from Jantzen). This proposition is reflected in the Second Restatement:

> A given claim may find support in theories or grounds arising from both state and federal law. When the plaintiff brings an action on the claim in a court, either state or federal, in which there is no jurisdictional obstacle to his advancing both theories or grounds, but he presents only one of them, and judgment is entered with respect to it, he may not maintain a second action in which he tenders the other theory or ground. If however, the court in the first action would clearly not have had jurisdiction to entertain the omitted theory or ground (or, having jurisdiction, would clearly have declined to exercise it as a

matter of discretion), then a second action in a competent court presenting the omitted theory or ground should be held not precluded.

Restatement (Second) of Judgments, § 25 cmt. e; see also id. § 26(1)(c).

Under this reasoning, if there was a forum in which all claims arising out of the single transaction could have been brought, and the plaintiff chooses a forum of limited jurisdiction instead, then the plaintiff's other claims are barred by the doctrine of claim preclusion, because the other claims could have been brought in the forum of general jurisdiction. If, on the other hand, no such forum exists, and the plaintiff is forced to split her claims, a suit in one forum does not bar the plaintiff from also bringing suit in another. See Marrese v. American Academy of Orthopaedic Surgeons, 470 U.S. 373, 382–83 & n. 3, 105 S.Ct. 1327, 84 L.Ed.2d 274 (1985).

We explained Waid v. Merrill Area Public Schools, 91 F.3d 857 (7th Cir.1996), why claim preclusion does not require litigants to choose between claims:

> For example, if state law creates a right and gives a state agency exclusive original jurisdiction over claims relating to that right, pursuit of a claim with the agency does not preclude the subsequent pursuit of related claims based on federal or state rights that could not have been asserted before the agency. Because the principles of claim preclusion do not require plaintiffs to make this kind of choice, she may therefore proceed in the forum of limited and exclusive jurisdiction without losing the opportunity to later litigate the claims not within that forum's jurisdictional competency.

Id. at 865, citing Restatement (Second) of Judgments § 26. Waid, which involved the same administrative scheme before us now, held that because the jurisdiction of the Equal Rights Division is limited, its decision did not preclude a plaintiff from bringing a separate action in federal court to assert federal claims arising from the same factual situation. Id. at 865–66. See also Jones v. City of Alton, 757 F.2d 878, 886–87 (7th Cir.1985) (holding federal claims and defenses were not precluded where plaintiff tried to raise them in state proceedings but they were improperly excluded).

We find Waid indistinguishable from the present case. The Equal Rights Division's jurisdiction is limited; it can hear claims brought under WFEA but not the federal anti-discrimination statutes. Even though in a free-standing case the Wisconsin state courts could have heard Staats's federal law claims, see Yellow Freight System, Inc. v. Donnelly, 494 U.S. 820, 821, 110 S.Ct. 1566, 108 L.Ed.2d 834 (1990), the Equal Rights Division could not: it lacked jurisdiction to do so. See Waid, 91 F.3d at 865. Thus, it was impossible for Staats to raise his federal claims in addition to his WFEA claims in his action brought before the Equal Rights Division. Conversely, the Equal Rights Division was the exclusive forum in which Staats could bring his WFEA claims: the WFEA does not create a private right of action, see Bourque v. Wausau Hosp. Ctr., 145 Wis.2d 589, 427 N.W.2d 433, 437 (App.1988); Bachand v. Connecticut Gen. Life Ins. Co., 101 Wis.2d 617, 305 N.W.2d 149, 152 (App.1981), and

Staats therefore could not assert his WFEA claims in state or federal court.

The net result was that Staats had no way to consolidate his WFEA, ADA, and Rehabilitation Act claims in any single forum. He was forced to split his claims and litigate them in separate fora. See Parks, 492 N.W.2d at 369–70 (holding prior federal court action did not preclude plaintiff's later state action where federal court declined to retain jurisdiction over pendent state claims after granting summary judgment for defendant on federal claims). Cf. Balcerzak v. City of Milwaukee, 163 F.3d 993, 997 (7th Cir.1998) (holding plaintiff's § 1983 claims were precluded where, due to his litigation strategy, he chose not to raise government defendant's race discrimination as a defense to his termination in state proceedings); Humphrey v. Tharaldson Enters., Inc., 95 F.3d 624, 627 (7th Cir.1996) (holding plaintiff's federal claims precluded when he chose to file state law claims in administrative forum of limited jurisdiction where state law provided a private right of action).

* * *

* * * In short, because the WFEA claims had to be adjudicated in a forum of limited jurisdiction, Staats is not precluded from bringing his federal claims in another forum.

* * *

The judgment of the district court is REVERSED and the case is REMANDED for further proceedings consistent with this opinion.

FURTHER NOTE ON RES JUDICATA (CLAIM PRECLUSION)

1. **Exceptions to the general rule against claim splitting.** Section 26 of the Second Restatement provides:

(1) When any of the following circumstances exists, the general rule of § 24 does not apply to extinguish the claim, and part or all of the claim subsists as a possible basis for a second action by the plaintiff against the defendant:

(a) The parties have agreed in terms or in effect that the plaintiff may split his claim, or the defendant has acquiesced therein;

(b) The court in the first action has expressly reserved the plaintiff's right to maintain the second action; or

(c) *The plaintiff was unable to rely on a certain theory of the case or to seek a certain remedy or form of relief in the first action because of the limitations on the subject matter jurisdiction of the courts or restrictions on their authority to entertain multiple theories or demands for multiple remedies or forms of relief in a single action, and the plaintiff desires in the second action to rely on that theory or to seek that remedy or form of relief;* or

(d) The judgment in the first action was plainly inconsistent with the fair and equitable implementation of a statutory or constitutional scheme, or it is the sense of the scheme that the plaintiff should be permitted to split his claim; or

(e)   For reasons of substantive policy in a case involving a continuing or recurrent wrong, the plaintiff is given an option to sue once for the total harm, both past and prospective, or to sue from time to time for the damages incurred to the date of suit, and chooses the later course; or

(f)   It is clearly and convincingly shown that the policies favoring preclusion of a second action are overcome for an extraordinary reason, such as the apparent invalidity of a continuing restraint or condition having a vital relation to personal liberty or the failure of the prior litigation to yield a coherent disposition of the controversy.

(Emphasis added.) The court relied on the exception contained in § 26(c) (italicized above) to allow Staats to bring his federal discrimination claim under Title VII despite the fact that his earlier litigation of his state discrimination claim arose out of the same "transaction." Section 26(c) is commonly applied by other courts. See, e.g., Parker v. Blauvelt Volunteer Fire Company, 93 N.Y.2d 343, 690 N.Y.S.2d 478, 712 N.E.2d 647 (1999).

2.   Limitation on the exception contained in § 26(c). The exception to the "use it or lose it" principle of § 24 seen in *Staats* is limited. Comment g to § 24 notes that if a plaintiff has a choice between two forums— one with restricted jurisdiction such that it cannot entertain all of plaintiff's claim, and the other with unrestricted jurisdiction—the plaintiff chooses the restricted forum at his peril. Comment g provides:

The rule stated in this Section as to splitting a claim is applicable although the first action is brought in a court which has no jurisdiction to give a judgment for more than a designated amount. When the plaintiff brings an action in such a court and recovers judgment for the maximum amount which the court can award, he is precluded from thereafter maintaining an action for balance of his claim. . . . It is assumed here that a court was available to the plaintiff *in the same system of courts*—say a court of general jurisdiction in the same state—where he could have sued for the entire amount. . . . The plaintiff, having voluntarily brought his action in a court which can grant him only limited relief, cannot insist upon maintaining another action on the claim.

(Emphasis added.)

The United States Supreme Court has strongly hinted that it believes Comment g may apply not only to courts within the "system" of courts of a single state, but to federal and state courts within the federal "system." See Marrese v. American Academy of Orthopaedic Surgeons, 470 U.S. 373, 382 n.3, 105 S.Ct. 1327, 84 L.Ed.2d 274 (1985). That is, if a plaintiff has a choice between a state court that can hear only plaintiff's state claim, and a federal court that can hear both plaintiff's federal and state claim, a plaintiff could be barred from bringing her federal claim in federal court if she brings her state claim first in state court. The court of appeals in *Staats* clearly reads Comment g that way. However, when the first court is a state court, the res judicata consequence of a first state court suit depends not on federal law but on the res judicata law of that state. The legislature or the highest court of the state will have the final say on what that state law is. See further discussion of interjurisdictional preclusion, infra, p. 1116.

3. **Traps for the unwary.** Litigants should be aware of two traps.

a. **"Claim" does not differentiate between state and federal causes of action.** "Claim" is not defined, for purposes of res judicata, in terms of state or federal substantive law. So long as the forum in which the first suit is filed is jurisdictionally competent to hear state and federal causes of action within the scope of the claim, the plaintiff must assert all of his causes of action—both state and federal—in that first suit. A plaintiff should not make the mistake of thinking that he may file his state causes of action in state court and save his federal causes of action for a later federal court suit, or vice versa. See discussion of the scope of federal court subject matter jurisdiction over claims based on state law under the supplemental jurisdiction statute, 28 U.S.C. § 1367, supra p. 260.

b. **Choose the more jurisdictionally competent forum.** If plaintiff has two causes of action and has a choice between two courts—one that can hear both of plaintiff's claims, and one that can hear only one of them—§ 26(c) and Comment g to § 24 instruct her to choose the more jurisdictionally competent forum. Choosing the jurisdictionally restricted forum runs the risk that she will not be able to bring her other cause of action in the other forum in a second suit.

3. Collateral Estoppel (Issue Preclusion)

Introductory Note on Collateral Estoppel (Issue Preclusion)

1. **Collateral estoppel (issue preclusion) under the Restatement (Second) of Judgments.** Section 27 of the Second Restatement provides:

> When an issue of fact or law is actually litigated and determined by a valid and final judgment, and the determination is essential to the judgment, the determination is conclusive in a subsequent action between the parties, whether on the same or a different claim.

A more elaborate statement is:

> [A] judgment in a prior proceeding bars a party and its privies from relitigating an issue if, but "only if:" (1) the issues in both proceedings are identical, (2) the issue in the prior proceeding was actually litigated and actually decided, (3) there was full and fair opportunity to litigate in the prior proceeding, and (4) the issue previously litigated was necessary to support a valid and final judgment on the merits.

NLRB v. Thalbo Corp., 171 F.3d 102, 109 (2d Cir. 1999).

2. **Issue of fact or law.** Traditionally, the rule of issue preclusion applied only to issues of fact; stare decisis applied to issues of law. But the modern view applies preclusion to both. See Restatement Second of Judgments § 28, Comment b; see also Hazard, Preclusion as to Issues of Law: The Legal System's Interest, 70 Iowa L.Rev. 81 (1984); Buckley, Issue Preclusion and Issues of Law: A Doctrinal Framework Based on Rules of Recognition, Jurisdiction and Legal History, 24 Hous.L.Rev. 875 (1987). The

extension of issue preclusion to issues of law may be traceable in part to the weakening of stare decisis.

3. "Ultimate" and "mediate" facts. Judge Learned Hand drew a distinction between "ultimate" and "mediate" facts in The Evergreens v. Nunan, 141 F.2d 927 (2d Cir. 1944). Most analysts were not able to see the difference, or that it was relevant. It is now generally accepted that the question is not whether the fact was ultimate or mediate, but whether it was treated as important and necessary to the decision in the first action. See Restatement (Second) of Judgments § 27, Comment j; Synanon Church v. United States, 820 F.2d 421 (D.C. Cir. 1987). The more important questions are whether it was foreseeable that the factual issue might come up in later litigation, and whether the party had an adequate incentive to litigate the issue the first time. Compare Yates v. United States, 354 U.S. 298, 77 S.Ct. 1064, 1 L.Ed.2d 1356 (1957), with Dobbins v. Title Guar. & Trust Co., 22 Cal.2d 64, 136 P.2d 572 (1943).

a.   IDENTICAL ISSUE ACTUALLY LITIGATED AND DETERMINED

B & B Hardware, Inc. v. Hargis Industries, Inc.

Supreme Court of the United States, 2015.
575 U.S. ___, 135 S.Ct. 1293, ___ L.Ed.2d ___.

■ JUSTICE ALITO delivered the opinion of the Court.

Sometimes two different tribunals are asked to decide the same issue. When that happens, the decision of the first tribunal usually must be followed by the second, at least if the issue is really the same. Allowing the same issue to be decided more than once wastes litigants' resources and adjudicators' time, and it encourages parties who lose before one tribunal to shop around for another. The doctrine of collateral estoppel or issue preclusion is designed to prevent this from occurring.

This case concerns the application of issue preclusion in the context of trademark law. Petitioner, B & B Hardware, Inc. (B & B), and respondent Hargis Industries, Inc. (Hargis), both use similar trademarks; B & B owns SEALTIGHT while Hargis owns SEALTITE. Under the Lanham Act, 15 U.S.C. § 1051 *et seq.*, an applicant can seek to register a trademark through an administrative process within the United States Patent and Trademark Office (PTO). But if another party believes that the PTO should not register a mark because it is too similar to its own, that party can oppose registration before the Trademark Trial and Appeal Board (TTAB). Here, Hargis tried to register the mark SEALTITE, but B & B opposed SEALTITE's registration. After a lengthy proceeding, the TTAB agreed with B & B that SEALTITE should not be registered.

In addition to permitting a party to object to the registration of a mark, the Lanham Act allows a mark owner to sue for trademark infringement. Both a registration proceeding and a suit for trademark infringement, moreover, can occur at the same time. In this case, while the TTAB was deciding whether SEALTITE should be registered, B & B and Hargis were also litigating the SEALTIGHT versus SEALTITE dispute in federal court. In both registration proceedings and infringement litigation, the tribunal asks whether a likelihood of confusion exists between the mark sought to be protected (here, SEALTIGHT) and the other mark (SEALTITE).

The question before this Court is whether the District Court in this case should have applied issue preclusion to the TTAB's decision that SEALTITE is confusingly similar to SEALTIGHT. Here, the Eighth Circuit rejected issue preclusion for reasons that would make it difficult for the doctrine ever to apply in trademark disputes. We disagree with that narrow understanding of issue preclusion. Instead, consistent with principles of law that apply in innumerable contexts, we hold that a court should give preclusive effect to TTAB decisions if the ordinary elements of issue preclusion are met. We therefore reverse the judgment of the Eighth Circuit and remand for further proceedings.

I

A

Trademark law has a long history, going back at least to Roman times. See Restatement (Third) of Unfair Competition § 9, Comment *b* (1993). The principle underlying trademark protection is that distinctive marks—words, names, symbols, and the like—can help distinguish a particular artisan's goods from those of others. *Ibid.* One who first uses a distinct mark in commerce thus acquires rights to that mark. See 2 J. McCarthy, Trademarks and Unfair Competition § 16:1 (4th ed.2014) (hereinafter McCarthy). Those rights include preventing others from using the mark. See 1 A. LaLonde, Gilson on Trademarks § 3.02[8] (2014) (hereinafter Gilson).

Though federal law does not create trademarks, see, *e.g., Trade-Mark Cases,* 100 U.S. 82, 92, 25 L.Ed. 550 (1879), Congress has long played a role in protecting them. In 1946, Congress enacted the Lanham Act, the current federal trademark scheme. As relevant here, the Lanham Act creates at least two adjudicative mechanisms to help protect marks. First, a trademark owner can register its mark with the PTO. Second, a mark owner can bring a suit for infringement in federal court.

Registration is significant. The Lanham Act confers "important legal rights and benefits" on trademark owners who register their marks. 3 McCarthy § 19:3, at 19–21; see also *id.,* § 19:9, at 19–34 (listing seven of the "procedural and substantive legal advantages" of registration). Registration, for instance, serves as "constructive notice of the registrant's claim of ownership" of the mark. 15 U.S.C. § 1072. It also is "prima facie evidence of the validity of the registered mark and of the registration of the mark, of the owner's ownership of the mark, and of the owner's exclusive right to use the registered mark in commerce on or in connection with the goods or services specified in the certificate." § 1057(b). And once a mark has been registered for five years, it can become "incontestable." §§ 1065, 1115(b).

To obtain the benefits of registration, a mark owner files an application with the PTO. § 1051. The application must include, among other things, "the date of the applicant's first use of the mark, the date of the applicant's first use of the mark in commerce, the goods in connection with which the mark is used, and a drawing of the mark." § 1051(a)(2). The usages listed in the application—*i.e.,* those goods on which the mark appears along with, if applicable, their channels of distribution—are critical. * * * The PTO generally cannot register a mark which "so resembles" another mark "as to be likely, when used on or in connection with the goods of the applicant, to cause confusion, or to cause mistake, or to deceive." 15 U.S.C. § 1052(d).

If a trademark examiner believes that registration is warranted, the mark is published in the Official Gazette of the PTO. § 1062. At that point, "[a]ny person who believes that he would be damaged by the registration" may "file an opposition." § 1063(a). Opposition proceedings occur before the TTAB (or panels thereof). § 1067(a). The TTAB consists of administrative trademark judges and high-ranking PTO officials, including the Director of the PTO and the Commissioner of Trademarks. § 1067(b).

Opposition proceedings before the TTAB are in many ways "similar to a civil action in a federal district court." * * * These proceedings, for instance, are largely governed by the Federal Rules of Civil Procedure and Evidence. See 37 CFR §§ 2.116(a), 2.122(a) (2014). The TTAB also allows discovery and depositions. See §§ 2.120, 2.123(a). The party opposing registration bears the burden of proof, see § 2.116(b), and if that burden cannot be met, the opposed mark must be registered, see 15 U.S.C. § 1063(b).

The primary way in which TTAB proceedings differ from ordinary civil litigation is that "proceedings before the Board are conducted in writing, and the Board's actions in a particular case are based upon the written record therein." * * * Even so, the TTAB allows parties to submit transcribed testimony, taken under oath and subject to cross-examination, and to request oral argument. See 37 CFR §§ 2.123, 2.129.

When a party opposes registration because it believes the mark proposed to be registered is too similar to its own, the TTAB evaluates likelihood of confusion by applying some or all of the 13 factors set out in *In re E.I. DuPont DeNemours & Co.*, 476 F.2d 1357 (CCPA 1973). After the TTAB decides whether to register the mark, a party can seek review in the U.S. Court of Appeals for the Federal Circuit, or it can file a new action in district court. See 15 U.S.C. § 1071. In district court, the parties can conduct additional discovery and the judge resolves registration *de novo.* § 1071(b)[.] * * *

The Lanham Act, of course, also creates a federal cause of action for trademark infringement. The owner of a mark, whether registered or not, can bring suit in federal court if another is using a mark that too closely resembles the plaintiff's. The court must decide whether the defendant's use of a mark in commerce "is likely to cause confusion, or to cause mistake, or to deceive" with regards to the plaintiff's mark. See 15 U.S.C. § 1114(1)(a) (registered marks); § 1125(a)(1)(A) (unregistered marks). In infringement litigation, the district court considers the full range of a mark's usages, not just those in the application.

B

Petitioner B & B and respondent Hargis both manufacture metal fasteners. B & B manufactures fasteners for the aerospace industry, while Hargis manufactures fasteners for use in the construction trade. Although there are obvious differences between space shuttles and A-frame buildings, both aerospace and construction engineers prefer fasteners that seal things tightly. Accordingly, both B & B and Hargis want their wares associated with tight seals. A feud of nearly two decades has sprung from this seemingly commonplace set of facts.

In 1993 B & B registered SEALTIGHT for "threaded or unthreaded metal fasteners and other related hardwar[e]; namely, self-sealing nuts, bolts, screws, rivets and washers, all having a captive o-ring, for use in the aerospace industry." * * * In 1996, Hargis sought to register SEALTITE for "self-piercing and self-drilling metal screws for use in the manufacture of metal and post-frame buildings." * * * B & B opposed Hargis' registration because, although the two companies sell different products, it believes that SEALTITE is confusingly similar to SEALTIGHT.

The twists and turns in the SEALTIGHT versus SEALTITE controversy are labyrinthine. The question whether either of these marks should be registered, and if so, which one, has bounced around within the PTO for about two decades; related infringement litigation has been before the Eighth Circuit three times; and two separate juries have been empaneled and returned verdicts. The full story could fill a long, unhappy book.

 For purposes here, we pick up the story in 2002, when the PTO published SEALTITE [as a registered mark of Hargis] in the Official Gazette. This prompted opposition proceedings before the TTAB, complete with discovery, including depositions. B & B argued that SEALTITE could not be registered because it is confusingly similar to SEALTIGHT. B & B explained, for instance, that both companies have an online presence, the largest distributor of fasteners sells both companies' products, and consumers sometimes call the wrong company to place orders. Hargis rejoined that the companies sell different products, for different uses, to different types of consumers, through different channels of trade.

Invoking a number of the *DuPont* factors, the TTAB sided with B & B. The Board considered, for instance, whether SEALTIGHT is famous (it's not, said the Board), how the two products are used (differently), how much the marks resemble each other (very much), and whether customers are actually confused (perhaps sometimes). * * * Concluding that "the most critical factors in [its] likelihood of confusion analysis are the similarities of the marks and the similarity of the goods," * * * the TTAB determined that SEALTITE—when "used in connection with 'self-piercing and self-drilling metal screws for use in the manufacture of metal and post-frame buildings' "—could not be registered because it "so resembles" SEALTIGHT when "used in connection with fasteners that provide leakproof protection from liquids and gases, fasteners that have a captive o-ring, and 'threaded or unthreaded metal fastners and other related hardware . . . for use in the aerospace industry' as to be likely to cause confusion[.]" * * * Despite a right to do so, Hargis did not seek judicial review in either the Federal Circuit or District Court.

All the while, B & B had sued Hargis for infringement. Before the District Court ruled on likelihood of confusion, however, the TTAB announced its decision. After a series of proceedings not relevant here, B & B argued to the District Court that Hargis could not contest likelihood of confusion because of the preclusive effect of the TTAB decision. The District Court disagreed, reasoning that the TTAB is not an Article III court. The jury returned a verdict for Hargis, finding no likelihood of confusion.

B & B appealed to the Eighth Circuit. Though accepting for the sake of argument that agency decisions can ground issue preclusion, the panel majority affirmed for three reasons: first, because the TTAB uses different factors than the Eighth Circuit to evaluate likelihood of confusion; second, because the TTAB placed too much emphasis on the appearance and sound of the two marks; and third, because Hargis bore the burden of persuasion before the TTAB, while B & B bore it before the District Court. 716 F.3d 1020 (2013). Judge Colloton dissented, concluding that issue preclusion should apply. After calling for the views of the Solicitor General, we granted certiorari. 573 U.S. ___ (2014).

II

The first question that we must address is whether an agency decision can ever ground issue preclusion. The District Court rejected issue preclusion because agencies are not Article III courts. The Eighth Circuit did not adopt that view, and, given this Court's cases, it was right to take that course.

This Court has long recognized that "the determination of a question directly involved in one action is conclusive as to that question in a second suit." *Cromwell v. County of Sac*, 94 U.S. 351, 354, 24 L.Ed. 195 (1877). The idea is straightforward: Once a court has decided an issue, it is "forever settled as between the parties," *Baldwin v. Iowa State Traveling Men's Assn.*, 283 U.S. 522, 525, 51 S.Ct. 517, 75 L.Ed. 1244 (1931), thereby "protect[ing]" against "the expense and vexation attending multiple lawsuits, conserv[ing] judicial resources, and foster[ing] reliance on judicial action by minimizing the possibility of inconsistent verdicts," *Montana v. United States*, 440 U.S. 147, 153–154, 99 S.Ct. 970, 59 L.Ed.2d 210 (1979). In short, "a losing litigant deserves no rematch after a defeat fairly suffered." *Astoria Fed. Sav. & Loan Assn. v. Solimino*, 501 U.S. 104, 107, 111 S.Ct. 2166, 115 L.Ed.2d 96 (1991).

Although the idea of issue preclusion is straightforward, it can be challenging to implement. The Court, therefore, regularly turns to the Restatement (Second) of Judgments for a statement of the ordinary elements of issue preclusion. * * *

Both this Court's cases and the Restatement make clear that issue preclusion is not limited to those situations in which the same issue is before two *courts*. Rather, where a single issue is before a court and an administrative agency, preclusion also often applies. Indeed, this Court has explained that because the principle of issue preclusion was so "well established" at common law, in those situations in which Congress has authorized agencies to resolve disputes, "courts may take it as given that Congress has legislated with the expectation that the principle [of issue preclusion] will apply except when a statutory purpose to the contrary is evident." *Astoria, supra*, at 108. This reflects the Court's longstanding view that " '[w]hen an administrative agency is acting in a judicial capacity and resolves disputed issues of fact properly before it which the parties have had an adequate opportunity to litigate, the courts have not hesitated to apply res judicata to enforce repose.' " *University of Tenn. v. Elliott*, 478 U.S. 788, 797–798, 106 S.Ct. 3220, 92 L.Ed.2d 635 (1986) (quoting *United States v. Utah Constr. & Mining Co.*, 384 U.S. 394, 422, 86 S.Ct. 1545, 16 L.Ed.2d 642 (1966))[.] * * *

Although apparently accepting *Astoria* and *Utah Construction*, Hargis argues that we should not read the Lanham Act (or, presumably, many other federal statutes) as authorizing issue preclusion. Otherwise, Hargis warns, the Court would have to confront " 'grave and doubtful questions' as to the Lanham Act's consistency with the Seventh Amendment and Article III of the Constitution." * * * We are not persuaded.

At the outset, we note that Hargis does not argue that giving issue preclusive effect to the TTAB's decision would be unconstitutional. Instead, Hargis contends only that we should read the Lanham Act narrowly because a broad reading *might* be unconstitutional. * * *

We reject Hargis' statutory argument that we should jettison administrative preclusion in whole or in part to avoid potential constitutional concerns. As to the Seventh Amendment, for instance, the Court has already held that the right to a jury trial does not negate the issue-preclusive effect of a judgment, even if that judgment was entered by a juryless tribunal. See *Parklane Hosiery Co. v. Shore*, 439 U.S. 322, 337, 99 S.Ct. 645, 58 L.Ed.2d 552 (1979). It would seem to follow naturally that although the Seventh Amendment creates a jury trial right in suits for trademark damages, see *Dairy Queen, Inc. v. Wood*, 369 U.S. 469, 477, 479–480, 82 S.Ct. 894, 8 L.Ed.2d 44 (1962), TTAB decisions still can have preclusive effect in such suits. * * *

The claim that we should read the Lanham Act narrowly to avoid Article III concerns is equally unavailing[.] * * * [I]n *Elliott*, the Court, relying on *Utah Construction*, explained that absent a contrary indication, Congress presumptively intends that an agency's determination (there, a state agency) has preclusive effect. 478 U.S., at 796–799; see also *Astoria*, 501 U.S., at 110 (recognizing the "presumption"). To be sure, the Court has never addressed whether such preclusion offends Article III. But because this Court's cases are so clear, there is no ambiguity for this Court to sidestep through constitutional avoidance.

III

The next question is whether there is an "evident" reason why Congress would not want TTAB decisions to receive preclusive effect, even in those cases in which the ordinary elements of issue preclusion are met. *Astoria*, *supra*, at 108. We conclude that nothing in the Lanham Act bars the application of issue preclusion in such cases.

The Lanham Act's text certainly does not forbid issue preclusion. Nor does the Act's structure. Granted, one can seek judicial review of a TTAB registration decision in a *de novo* district court action, and some courts have concluded from this that Congress does not want unreviewed TTAB decisions to ground issue preclusion. See, *e.g.*, *American Heritage Life Ins. Co. v. Heritage Life Ins. Co.*, 494 F.2d 3, 9–10 (C.A.5 1974). But that conclusion does not follow. Ordinary preclusion law teaches that if a party to a court proceeding does not challenge an adverse decision, that decision can have preclusive effect in other cases, even if it would have been reviewed *de novo*. See Restatement (Second) of Judgments § 28, Comment *a* and Illustration 1 (explaining that the failure to pursue an appeal does not undermine issue preclusion and including an example of an apparently unappealed district court's dismissal for failure to state a claim); cf. *Federated Department Stores, Inc. v. Moitie*, 452 U.S. 394, 398, 101 S.Ct. 2424, 69 L.Ed.2d 103 (1981) (noting "the res judicata consequences of a final, unappealed judgment on the merits").

    * * *

What matters here is that registration is not a prerequisite to an infringement action. Rather, it is a separate proceeding to decide separate rights. Neither is issue preclusion a one-way street. When a district court, as part of its judgment, decides an issue that overlaps with part of the TTAB's analysis, the TTAB gives preclusive effect to the court's judgment. * * *

Hargis also argues that allowing TTAB decisions to have issue-preclusive effect will adversely affect the registration process. Because of the TTAB's " 'limited jurisdiction' " and " 'the narrowness of the issues' " before it, Hargis contends, the Court should infer that TTAB proceedings are supposed to be more streamlined than infringement litigation. * * * But, the argument goes, if TTAB decisions can have issue-preclusive effect in infringement litigation, parties may spend more time and energy before the TTAB, thus bogging down the registration process. This concern does not change our conclusion. Issue preclusion is available unless it is "evident," *Astoria, supra*, at 108, that Congress does not want it. Here, if a streamlined process in all registration matters was particularly dear to Congress, it would not have authorized *de novo* challenges for those "dissatisfied" with TTAB decisions. 15 U.S.C. § 1071(b). Plenary review serves many functions, but ensuring a streamlined process is not one of them. Moreover, as explained below, for a great many registration decisions issue preclusion obviously will not apply because the ordinary elements will not be met. For those registrations, nothing we say today is relevant.

IV

At last we turn to whether there is a categorical reason why registration decisions can never meet the ordinary elements of issue preclusion, *e.g.*, those elements set out in § 27 of the Restatement (Second) of Judgments. Although many registrations will not satisfy those ordinary elements, that does not mean that none will. We agree with Professor McCarthy that issue preclusion applies where "the issues in the two cases are indeed identical and the other rules of collateral estoppel are carefully observed." 6 McCarthy § 32:99, at 32–244; see also 3 Gilson § 11.08[4][i][iii][B], p. 11–319 ("Ultimately, Board decisions on likelihood of confusion . . . should be given preclusive effect on a case-by-case basis").

A

The Eighth Circuit's primary objection to issue preclusion was that the TTAB considers different factors than it does. Whereas the TTAB employs some or all of the *DuPont* factors to assess likelihood of confusion, the Eighth Circuit looks to similar, but not identical, factors identified in *SquirtCo v. Seven-Up Co.*, 628 F.2d 1086, 1091 (C.A.8 1980). The court's instinct was sound: "[I]ssues are not identical if the second action involves application of a different legal standard, even though the factual setting of both suits may be the same." 18 C. Wright, A. Miller, &

E. Cooper, Federal Practice & Procedure § 4417, p. 449 (2d ed.2002) (hereinafter Wright & Miller). Here, however, the same likelihood-of-confusion standard applies to both registration and infringement.

To begin with, it does not matter that registration and infringement are governed by different statutory provisions. Often a single standard is placed in different statutes; that does not foreclose issue preclusion. See, *e.g., Smith v. Bayer Corp.*, 564 U.S. ___, 131 S.Ct. 2368, 180 L.Ed.2d 341 (2011). Neither does it matter that the TTAB and the Eighth Circuit use different factors to assess likelihood of confusion. For one thing, the factors are not fundamentally different, and "[m]inor variations in the application of what is in essence the same legal standard do not defeat preclusion." *Id.*, at 2378 n.9. More important, if federal law provides a single standard, parties cannot escape preclusion simply by litigating anew in tribunals that apply that one standard differently. A contrary rule would encourage the very evils that issue preclusion helps to prevent.

The real question, therefore, is whether likelihood of confusion for purposes of registration is the same standard as likelihood of confusion for purposes of infringement. We conclude it is, for at least three reasons. First, the operative language is essentially the same; the fact that the registration provision separates "likely" from "to cause confusion, or to cause mistake, or to deceive" does not change that reality. See 2 Gilson § 5.01[2][a], at 5–17 (explaining that "the same statutory test" applies). Second, the likelihood-of-confusion language that Congress used in these Lanham Act provisions has been central to trademark registration since at least 1881. See Act of Mar. 3, 1881, ch. 138, § 3, 21 Stat. 503 (using a "likely to cause confusion" standard for registration). That could hardly have been by accident. And third, district courts can cancel registrations during infringement litigation, just as they can adjudicate infringement in suits seeking judicial review of registration decisions. See 15 U.S.C. § 1119; 3 McCarthy § 21:20. There is no reason to think that the same district judge in the same case should apply two separate standards of likelihood of confusion.

Hargis responds that the text is not actually the same because the registration provision asks whether the marks "resemble" each other, 15 U.S.C. § 1052(d), while the infringement provision is directed towards the "use in commerce" of the marks, § 1114(1). Indeed, according to Hargis, the distinction between "resembl[ance]" and "use" has been key to trademark law for over a century. There is some force to this argument. It is true that "a party opposing an application to register a mark before the Board often relies only on its federal registration, not on any common-law rights in usages not encompassed by its registration," and "the Board typically analyzes the marks, goods, and channels of trade only as set forth in the application and in the opposer's registration, regardless of whether the actual usage of the marks by either party differs." Brief for United States as *Amicus Curiae* 23[.] * * * This means that unlike in infringement litigation, "[t]he Board's determination that a likelihood of confusion does or does not exist will not resolve the confusion issue with respect to non-disclosed usages." Brief for United States as *Amicus Curiae* 23.

Hargis' argument falls short, however, because it mistakes a reason not to apply issue preclusion in some or even many cases as a reason never to apply issue preclusion. Just because the TTAB does not always consider the same usages as a district court does, it does not follow that the Board applies a different standard to the usages it does consider. If a mark owner uses its mark in ways that are materially the same as the usages included in its registration application, then the TTAB is deciding the same likelihood-of-confusion issue as a district court in infringement litigation. By contrast, if a mark owner uses its mark in ways that are materially unlike the usages in its application, then the TTAB is not deciding the same issue. Thus, if the TTAB does not consider the marketplace usage of the parties' marks, the TTAB's decision should "have no later preclusive effect in a suit where actual usage in the marketplace is the paramount issue." 6 McCarthy § 32:101, at 32–246.

Materiality, of course, is essential—trivial variations between the usages set out in an application and the use of a mark in the marketplace do not create different "issues," just as trivial variations do not create different "marks." * * *

    * * *

[T]he Eighth Circuit erred in holding that issue preclusion could not apply here because the TTAB relied too heavily on "appearance and sound." App. to Pet. for Cert. 10a. Undoubtedly there are cases in which the TTAB places more weight on certain factors than it should. When that happens, an aggrieved party should seek judicial review. The fact that the TTAB may have erred, however, does not prevent preclusion. As Judge Colloton observed in dissent, " 'issue preclusion prevent[s] relitigation of wrong decisions just as much as right ones.' " 716 F.3d, at 1029 (quoting *Clark v. Clark*, 984 F.2d 272, 273 (C.A.8 1993)); see also Restatement (Second) of Judgments § 28, Comment *j*, at 284 (explaining that "refusal to give the first judgment preclusive effect should not . . . be based simply on a conclusion that [it] was patently erroneous").

B

Hargis also argues that registration is categorically incompatible with issue preclusion because the TTAB uses procedures that differ from those used by district courts. Granted, "[r]edetermination of issues is warranted if there is reason to doubt the quality, extensiveness, or fairness of procedures followed in prior litigation." *Montana*, 440 U.S., at 164, n. 11; see also *Parklane Hosiery*, 439 U.S., at 331, and n. 15 (similar). But again, this only suggests that sometimes issue preclusion might be inappropriate, not that it always is.

No one disputes that the TTAB and district courts use different procedures. Most notably, district courts feature live witnesses. Procedural differences, by themselves, however, do not defeat issue preclusion. Equity courts used different procedures than did law courts, but that did not bar issue preclusion. See *id.*, at 333. Nor is there reason to think that the state agency in *Elliott* used procedures identical to those in federal court; nonetheless, the Court held that preclusion could apply. See 478 U.S., at 796–799. Rather than focusing on whether procedural differences exist—they often will—the correct inquiry is whether the procedures used in the first proceeding were fundamentally poor, cursory, or unfair. See *Montana*, 440 U.S., at 164, n. 11.

Here, there is no categorical "reason to doubt the quality, extensiveness, or fairness," *ibid.*, of the agency's procedures. In large part they are exactly the same as in federal court. * * *

The Eighth Circuit likewise erred by concluding that Hargis bore the burden of persuasion before the TTAB. B & B, the party opposing registration, bore the burden, see 37 CFR § 2.116(b); TTAB Manual § 702.04(a), just as it did in the infringement action. * * *

C

Hargis also contends that the stakes for registration are so much lower than for infringement that issue preclusion should never apply to TTAB decisions. Issue preclusion may be inapt if "the amount in controversy in the first action [was] so small in relation to the amount in controversy in the second that preclusion would be plainly unfair." Restatement (Second) of Judgments § 28, Comment j, at 283–284. After all, "[f]ew . . . litigants would spend $50,000 to defend a $5,000 claim." Wright & Miller § 4423, at 612. Hargis is wrong, however, that this exception to issue preclusion applies to every registration. To the contrary: When registration is opposed, there is good reason to think that both sides will take the matter seriously.

The benefits of registration are substantial. Registration is "prima facie evidence of the validity of the registered mark," 15 U.S.C. § 1057(b), and is a precondition for a mark to become "incontestable," § 1065. Incontestability is a powerful protection. See, e.g., *Park 'N Fly, Inc. v. Dollar Park & Fly, Inc.*, 469 U.S. 189, 194, 105 S.Ct. 658, 83 L.Ed.2d 582 (1985) (holding that an incontestable mark cannot be challenged as merely descriptive); see also *id.*, at 193 (explaining that "Congress determined that . . . 'trademarks should receive nationally the greatest protection that can be given them' " and that "[a]mong the new protections created by the Lanham Act were the statutory provisions that allow a federally registered mark to become incontestable" (quoting S.Rep. No. 1333, 79th Cong., 2d Sess., 6 (1946))).

The importance of registration is undoubtedly why Congress provided for *de novo* review of TTAB decisions in district court. It is incredible to think that a district court's adjudication of particular usages would not have preclusive effect in another district court. Why would unchallenged TTAB decisions be different? Congress' creation of this elaborate registration scheme, with so many important rights attached and backed up by plenary review, confirms that registration decisions can be weighty enough to ground issue preclusion.

V

For these reasons, the Eighth Circuit erred in this case. On remand, the court should apply the following rule: So long as the other ordinary elements of issue preclusion are met, when the usages adjudicated by the TTAB are materially the same as those before the district court, issue preclusion should apply.

The judgment of the United States Court of Appeals for the Eighth Circuit is reversed, and the case is remanded for further proceedings consistent with this opinion.

It is so ordered.

■ JUSTICE GINSBURG, concurring.

The Court rightly recognizes that "for a great many registration decisions issue preclusion obviously will not apply." * * * That is so because contested registrations are often decided upon "a comparison of the marks in the abstract and apart from their marketplace usage." 6 J. McCarthy, Trademarks and Unfair Competition § 32:101, p. 32–247 (4th ed.2014). When the registration proceeding is of that character, "there will be no [preclusion] of the likel[ihood] of confusion issue . . . in a later infringement suit." *Ibid.* On that understanding, I join the Court's opinion.

■ JUSTICE THOMAS, with whom JUSTICE SCALIA joins, dissenting.

The Court today applies a presumption that when Congress enacts statutes authorizing administrative agencies to resolve disputes in an adjudicatory setting, it intends those agency decisions to have preclusive effect in Article III courts. That presumption was first announced in poorly supported dictum in a 1991 decision of this Court, and we have not applied it since. Whatever the validity of that presumption with respect to statutes enacted after its creation, there is no justification for applying it to the Lanham Act, passed in 1946. Seeing no other reason to conclude that Congress implicitly authorized the decisions of the Trademark Trial and Appeal Board (TTAB) to have preclusive effect in a subsequent trademark infringement suit, I would affirm the decision of the Court of Appeals.

* * *

NOTE ON IDENTICAL ISSUE ACTUALLY LITIGATED AND DECIDED

1.   Purposes of collateral estoppel (issue preclusion). What are the purposes of the doctrine of collateral estoppel? An obvious purpose is judicial efficiency. If a court, or court-like body, has already determined an issue, a later court does not have to spend time redetermining the same issue. A less obvious purpose is maintaining judicial consistency (and the facade of correctness). Many judicial decisions are little more than guesses—educated and careful guesses, but guesses nonetheless. Some procedural rules openly acknowledge this fact. For example, the normal burden of proof in a civil case is "preponderance of the evidence." To satisfy the preponderance burden, a plaintiff need only persuade a court that it is 51% likely that the truth is as she has portrayed it. If truth seeking were the overriding consideration, we might not have a doctrine of collateral estoppel. If a question or law or fact is litigated a second time, the parties might in many instances do a better job of getting the relevant law or evidence before the court, with the consequence that the answer of the second court would be more likely to be correct than the answer of the first court.

2.   Preclusion based on adjudication by an administrative agency. The dissenters in *B & B Hardware* object to giving issue preclusive effect to an adjudicative decision by an administrative agency, in this case the Trademark Trial and Appeal Board ("TTAB"). However, preclusive effect has been given to administrative adjudications for several decades. To be the basis for issue preclusion, the administrative process must resemble fairly closely a conventional judicial process—with a neutral adjudicator, with sufficient opportunity for discovery, and with adequate means to assess the strength and reliability of the evidence. The Court in *B & B Hardware* notes that the TTAB does not take live testimony. Should that have been a ground for refusing to give issue preclusive effect to the TTAB's registration decision? Is there something about a trademark registration decision that makes live testimony unnecessary?

3. **Same (or identical) issue.** The Court in *B & B Hardware* concludes that the "same" issue is presented to the TTAB in a registration proceeding as to a federal district court in an infringement suit. The issue in both instances is whether there is a "likelihood of confusion." It does not matter, writes the Court, that the factors that guide the TTAB and the district court in deciding likelihood of confusion are not precisely the same. Why doesn't it matter? Does it follow from the mere fact that the issue is formally described in the same way (likelihood of confusion) that the TTAB and the district court actually decide the same issue? Even when the TTAB and the district court use different criteria to determine whether there is a likelihood of confusion? Did you notice that the Court frames the question as whether the TTAB and the district court decide the "same," rather than the "identical," issue? Is the Court's avoidance of the commonly used term in issue preclusion ("identical") a signal that the Court realizes that the use of different criteria of decision inescapably present the possibility that the TTAB and the district court might decide slightly different issues?

4. **Different issue.** The Court writes that the range of uses described in a registration proceeding might be narrower than the range of actual uses of the product or service. A registration proceeding cannot be the basis for issue preclusion in an infringement suit when the range of uses at issue in the suit is broader than in the registration proceeding. Thus, while the Court holds that issue preclusion in a trademark infringement suit will sometimes be available based on a registration decision by the TTAB, this will not always be so. Indeed, the Court writes, "[F]or a great many registration decisions issue preclusion obviously will not apply because the ordinary elements [of issue preclusion] will not be met." Justice Ginsburg is careful to quote this language in her concurrence, explaining that when the range of uses is different, the issue of "likelihood of confusion" is different.

5. **Erroneous first decision.** The Court openly confesses that the TTAB might make an erroneous registration decision. But the Court says this does not matter: "The fact that the TTAB may have erred * * * does not prevent preclusion." Should it matter?

6. **Actually litigated.** For determination of an issue to be preclusive in later litigation, it must have been "actually litigated" in the earlier litigation. "Actually litigated," in this context, means that the parties are genuinely adverse on this issue, and that evidence on the issue was presented to the court. If a party concedes an issue, that issue has not been litigated. It does not matter that some evidence was presented or even that the court may have made a factual finding. For example, in Troutt v. Colorado Western Insurance Co., 246 F.3d 1150 (9th Cir. 2001), the state court had made a finding that alcohol use had contributed to an accident. When the issue of alcohol use was raised in a later case, the court refused to apply collateral estoppel: "The alcohol issue was not raised by the parties in their pleadings [in the earlier state case], nor was it developed at trial or through motions practice. Rather, the state court's findings seem to be based primarily on Troutt's admission of liability." Id. at 1158. Similarly, an issue is not actually litigated if the parties stipulate to its resolution.

The rule used to be that an issue between parties on the same side of a litigation, for example between co-defendants, was never actually litigated. The modern rule is that the issue can be actually litigated if the parties were antagonistic to each other on the issue. See, e.g., Nevada v. United States, 463 U.S. 110, 103 S.Ct. 2906, 77 L.Ed.2d 509 (1983); McLellan v. Columbus I–70 West Auto-Truckstop, Inc., 525 F.Supp. 1233 (N.D.Ill.1981); Restatement (Second) of Judgments § 38. A difficult problem is presented by a default judgment entered after defendant has made some kind of appearance. An issue may have been litigated in some sense, but it has not been resolved by the court on the basis of conflicting submissions. There is some authority also giving it issue preclusive effect, but the dominant view is to the contrary. See Restatement Second of Judgments § 27, Reporter's Note. Compare Kaspar Wire Works, Inc. v. Leco Engineering & Mach., Inc., 575 F.2d 530 (5th Cir. 1978), with Barber v. International Brotherhood of Boilermakers, 778 F.2d 750 (11th Cir. 1985). See also Kaufman v. Eli Lilly & Co., 65 N.Y.2d 449, 492 N.Y.S.2d 584, 482 N.E.2d 63 (1985) (issue preclusion denied as to issue of law which defendant did not contest in the prior litigation).

7. Actually determined. Some courts have refused to apply issue preclusion where there is evidence that the issue was decided by a jury compromise. See Restatement Second of Judgments § 29(5) (no use of issue preclusion when "based on a compromise verdict or finding"); Taylor v. Hawkinson, 47 Cal.2d 893, 306 P.2d 797 (1957) (compromise verdict cannot be used); Katz v. Eli Lilly & Co., 84 F.R.D. 378 (E.D.N.Y.1979) (interrogation of jurors in the first case permitted to determine whether they had compromised). See also Milks v. Eli Lilly & Co., 94 F.R.D. 674 (S.D.N.Y.1982); Note, Use of Juror Depositions to Bar Collateral Estoppel, 34 Vand.L.Rev. 143 (1981). Absent evidence of jury compromise, however, the stated (but not always observed) rule is that preclusion is applied no matter how irregular or erroneous the prior judgment was. See, e.g., Shaid v. Consolidated Edison Co., 95 A.D.2d 610, 467 N.Y.S.2d 843 (1983); Eichman v. Fotomat Corp., 759 F.2d 1434 (9th Cir. 1985).

b. FULL AND FAIR OPPORTUNITY TO LITIGATE, AND NECESSARY TO THE JUDGMENT

Jacobs v. CBS Broadcasting

United States Court of Appeals for the Ninth Circuit, 2002.
291 F.3d 1173.

■ GRABER, J.

Plaintiffs Mike Jacobs, Jr., William Webb, and Westwind Releasing Corporation filed this action against Defendant CBS Broadcasting, Inc., alleging that CBS had breached a contract to give Plaintiffs production credit when it produced a television series called *Early Edition*. The district court granted summary judgment to CBS on the ground that an earlier nonjudicial proceeding precluded Plaintiffs from bringing their claim to court. We reverse because that nonjudicial proceeding was too informal to have preclusive effect.

* * *

Michael Givens is a script writer and a member of the Writers' Guild of America (WGA). Givens wrote a script titled *The Fourth Estate a/k/a/ Final Edition* (*Final Edition*). Westwind optioned Final Edition for the purpose of securing a television broadcast commitment from a network. Under the agreement between Givens and Westwind, any writing credit to be accorded Givens was to be determined pursuant to the WGA's Minimum Basic Agreement (MBA) credit-determination procedures. Givens was entitled to additional compensation under the contract only if the WGA awarded him a "written by" or "screenplay by" credit.

CBS later agreed with Westwind to acquire the broadcast rights to *Final Edition* (First Agreement). In a second contract, CBS bought all rights to *Final Edition* from Westwind and Givens (Second Agreement). The Second Agreement provided that, *"[i]f a project is produced based upon the literary property*, CBS agrees . . . to provide credit to William Webb and Mike Jacobs, Jr. as Co Executive Producers (or Executive Producers at CBS' election) on a shared card." (Emphasis added.) The Second Agreement also incorporated the provision in the original contract between Givens and Westwind stating that any writing credit for Givens would be governed by the WGA's credit-determination procedures.

CBS eventually participated in the production of a series called *Early Edition*, which shared a common premise with Givens' *Final Edition* script.[1] However, when the Notice of Tentative Writing Credits for Early Edition was issued, Givens was not listed as a "participating writer" who was entitled to receive credit. Givens complained to the WGA, citing those provisions of the MBA setting forth the circumstances under which WGA members such as Givens are entitled to writing credit. The WGA responded by suspending the credits process and informing Columbia Tristar, one of the producers of *Early Edition*, that if *Early Edition* aired with credits different from those that the WGA ultimately found to be proper, the WGA would pursue damages on behalf of the WGA-credited writers.

The WGA undertook an investigation and concluded that Givens was not a "participating writer" of *Early Edition*. Givens sought review of the participating-writer decision but, after engaging in additional investigation, the WGA reaffirmed its conclusion that Givens was not entitled to writing credit. After this second determination, Givens asked the WGA to reconsider its decision. The WGA again decided that Givens was not entitled to credit. In a letter to Givens, the WGA noted that its determination that Givens was not a participating writer precluded it from representing him in any subsequent writing-credit arbitration against CBS.

While Givens was pursuing his WGA appeals, Givens, Jacobs, Webb, and Westwind filed this action [against CBS] in Los Angeles County Superior Court. They argued that the Early Edition project was "based upon" the literary property *Final Edition* and that, accordingly, CBS had breached its contract by not providing them with writing and production credit. CBS removed the action to federal court. * * * [Givens entered into

---

[1] In Early Edition and Final Edition, a man is able to predict the future when he comes into possession of the next day's newspaper, and he attempts to alter events that are yet to occur.

a separate arbitration with CBS, which he lost. At that point, Givens dropped out of the federal court suit.]

CBS then filed a motion for summary judgment against the remaining Plaintiffs, who seek production credit regardless of who actually wrote the *Early Edition* scripts. [CBS argued] that Plaintiffs' claims for production credit were entirely derivative of Givens' claim for writing credit[.] The district court * * * granted summary judgment [to CBS on the] ground that the * * * WGA participating-writer determination involving Givens had a nonmutual collateral estoppel effect[2] on Plaintiffs' action. Plaintiffs filed a timely notice of appeal.

* * *

CBS argues that the WGA's determination that Givens was not a participating writer precludes Plaintiffs from litigating whether *Early Edition* is "based upon" *Final Edition*. To prevail, CBS must establish that the WGA participating-writer proceeding satisfies the requirements for application of collateral estoppel. Lucido v. Superior Court, 51 Cal.3d 335, 272 Cal.Rptr. 767, 795 P.2d 1223, 1225 (1990) ("The party asserting collateral estoppel bears the burden of establishing these requirements" under California law.); Hydranautics v. FilmTec Corp., 204 F.3d 880, 885 (9th Cir.2000) (same under federal law).

* * *

Under California law, CBS must demonstrate that the WGA participating-writer determination was adjudicatory in nature before that determination can have collateral estoppel effect. See Vandenberg v. Superior Court, 21 Cal.4th 815, 88 Cal.Rptr.2d 366, 982 P.2d 229, 237 (1999) (stating criterion). * * * Plaintiffs argue * * * that the district court erred in giving the WGA participating-writer determination preclusive effect because that determination lacked the procedural safeguards that California courts require. We agree.

Rule

In order to have an issue-preclusive effect in a later judicial action in California, an arbitration must have been conducted with certain procedural safeguards. As the California Supreme Court recently explained:

> Whether collateral estoppel is fair and consistent with public policy in a particular case depends in part upon the character of the forum that first decided the issue later sought to be foreclosed. In this regard, courts consider the judicial nature of the prior forum, i.e., its legal formality, the scope of its jurisdiction, and its procedural safeguards, particularly including the opportunity for judicial review of adverse rulings.

Vandenberg, 88 Cal.Rptr.2d 366, 982 P.2d at 237. The California Courts of Appeal have similarly noted that it is "appropriate to give collateral estoppel effect to findings made during an arbitration, *so long as the arbitration had the elements of an adjudicatory procedure.*" Kelly v. Vons

---

2. Under the doctrine of nonmutual collateral estoppel, it is not necessary that the earlier and later proceedings involve the same parties or their privies. To the contrary, a nonparty to the earlier proceeding may invoke the doctrine against a party who is bound by the proceeding. Vandenberg v. Superior Court, 21 Cal.4th 815, 88 Cal.Rptr.2d 366, 982 P.2d 229, 237 (1999). The district court in this case applied the doctrine of nonmutual collateral estoppel, holding that, because Plaintiffs were in privity with Givens, CBS could invoke the WGA participating-writer determination against them even though CBS had not been a party to that proceeding.

Cos., 67 Cal.App.4th 1329, 79 Cal.Rptr.2d 763, 767 (1998) (emphasis added)[.] * * * The need for procedural safeguards and legal formality is especially acute in the circumstances of this case because "collateral estoppel is invoked by a nonparty to the prior litigation. Such cases require close examination to determine whether nonmutual use of the doctrine is fair and appropriate." Vandenberg, 88 Cal.Rptr.2d 366, 982 P.2d at 237 (citations omitted); see also Benasra v. Mitchell Silberberg & Knupp, 96 Cal.App.4th 96, 116 Cal.Rptr.2d 644, 652 (2002) (same).

When deciding whether an arbitration was sufficiently adjudicatory in nature, courts apply the same standards used to determine whether an administrative proceeding should have collateral estoppel effect. See Restatement (Second) of Judgments, §§ 83(2), 84(3)(b) (1980); Kelly, 79 Cal.Rptr.2d at 767; see also Vandenberg, 88 Cal.Rptr.2d 366, 982 P.2d at 237 (relying on cases discussing the collateral estoppel effect of administrative proceedings). Accordingly, courts must examine such factors as whether

> (1) the [arbitration] was conducted in a judicial-like adversary proceeding; (2) the proceedings required witnesses to testify under oath; (3) the [arbitral] determination involved the adjudicatory application of rules to a single set of facts; (4) the proceedings were conducted before an impartial hearing officer; (5) the parties had the right to subpoena witnesses and present documentary evidence; and (6) the [arbitrator] maintained a verbatim record of the proceedings. Additional factors include whether the hearing officer's decision was adjudicatory and in writing with a statement of reasons. Finally, [whether] that reasoned decision [was] adopted by the director of the agency with the potential for later judicial review.

Imen v. Glassford, 201 Cal.App.3d 898, 247 Cal.Rptr. 514, 518 (1988) (citing People v. Sims, 32 Cal.3d 468, 186 Cal.Rptr. 77, 651 P.2d 321, 328–29 (1982)); see also Kelly, 79 Cal.Rptr.2d at 767 (explaining that an arbitration should provide parties "the opportunity for a hearing before an impartial and qualified officer, at which they may give formal recorded testimony under oath, cross-examine and compel the testimony of witnesses, and obtain a written statement of decision"); cf. Plaine v. McCabe, 797 F.2d 713, 720 (9th Cir.1986) (giving an administrative proceeding collateral estoppel effect because "[t]he fairness hearing was conducted similarly to a court proceeding. It was an adversary proceeding in which opposing parties were present and represented by counsel and were allowed to call, examine, cross-examine, and subpoena witnesses. . . . [T]estimony was to be submitted under oath or affirmation and a verbatim transcript was required.").

The WGA participating-writer determination did not provide the requisite procedural safeguards to give it issue-preclusive effect in California. The determination was made after an informal "investigation" into Givens' claims. The WGA did not take formal testimony from interested parties but, instead, engaged in "discussions" with Givens, his agent, CBS, and Columbia Tristar. Givens had no opportunity to cross-examine witnesses. Neither did Jacobs or Webb. Further, none of them had a right to examine the evidence presented by CBS and others. Givens and CBS simply provided the WGA with relevant information about the development of each project, and the WGA arrived at its conclusions through an examination of those materials. Finally, the WGA's participating-writer determination was subject to only very limited judicial review.

Thus, although undoubtedly conducted with care and in good faith, the WGA participating-writer proceeding was insufficiently formal and provided too few procedural safeguards to constitute an adjudicatory proceeding. Because the remaining Plaintiffs did not agree to litigate their entitlement to production credit in an informal arbitral forum, under California law the WGA's decision on writing credit does not preclude the litigation of Plaintiffs' claims in a judicial proceeding.

REVERSED and REMANDED for further proceedings consistent with this opinion.

NOTE ON FULL AND FAIR OPPORTUNITY TO LITIGATE, AND NECESSARY TO THE JUDGMENT

1. **Full and fair opportunity to litigate.** The "full and fair opportunity to litigate" requirement may be satisfied by a non-judicial proceeding, but, as the *Jacobs* case makes clear, that proceeding must be sufficiently formal and must offer sufficient procedural safeguards that the proceeding approximates a judicial proceeding. See Carlisle, Getting a Full Bite of the Apple: When Should the Doctrine of Issue Preclusion Make an Administrative or Arbitral Determination Binding in a Court of Law?, 55 Fordham L.Rev. 63 (1986), and Shell, Res Judicata and Collateral Estoppel Effects of Commercial Arbitration, 35 U.C.L.A.L.Rev. 623 (1988).

2. **Administrative agency determinations.** Administrative agencies have jurisdiction to adjudicate many types of claims. These adjudications usually are subject to some kind of judicial review on the record compiled in the administrative proceeding. The old rule was that because administrative adjudications were not judicial adjudications, they had no preclusive effect beyond the immediate proceeding. But administrative adjudication has gradually been formalized so that it is often hardly distinguishable from judicial adjudication: Pleadings, discovery, adversarial evidentiary presentations, and legal argument before an administrative law judge are all typical features today. Administrative proceedings that approximate court litigation in affording the parties a "full and fair" opportunity to litigate are generally treated as equivalent to court litigation for purposes of collateral estoppel. See, e.g., United States v. Utah Constr. & Mining Co., 384 U.S. 394, 86 S.Ct. 1545, 16 L.Ed.2d 642 (1966). However, some administrative proceedings are quite informal, and are not entitled to collateral estoppel effect. See, e.g., Littlejohn v. United States, 321 F.3d 915 (9th Cir. 2003) (refusing to give collateral estoppel effect to administrative decision of Veterans Administration (VA) granting benefits because of the "claimant-friendly," "non-adversarial" proceedings before the VA).

The general rule is that findings in state administrative proceedings will have preclusive effect in a later federal court suit between the same parties. Kremer v. Chemical Constr. Corp., 456 U.S. 461, 102 S.Ct. 1883, 72 L.Ed.2d 262 (1982). The Supreme Court has made clear, however, that the general rule is only a starting presumption and that the intent of Congress under a particular statute will control. For example, a plaintiff who has been unsuccessful in a state administrative proceeding alleging age discrimination may thereafter bring suit in federal court under the federal

Age Discrimination and Employment Act of 1967. Astoria Federal Sav. & Loan Ass'n v. Solimino, 501 U.S. 104, 111 S.Ct. 2166, 115 L.Ed.2d 96 (1991). See also University of Tennessee v. Elliott, 478 U.S. 788, 106 S.Ct. 3220, 92 L.Ed.2d 635 (1986) (findings in unreviewed state administrative proceeding not given preclusive effect on employee's Title VII discrimination claims, but given preclusive effect on claims under 42 U.S.C.A. § 1983). See Restatement (Second) of Judgments § 83; Carlisle, supra; Note, Res Judicata Effects of State Agency Decisions in Title VII Actions, 70 Cornell L.Rev. 695 (1985).

3.   **Affirmance on appeal.** In some circumstances, the unavailability of an appeal prevents a judicial determination from having collateral estoppel effect. In Johnson v. Watkins, 101 F.3d 792 (2d Cir. 1996), Johnson was prosecuted in New York state court for illegal possession of a weapon. Johnson sought to suppress the evidence of the weapon on the ground that he had been searched incident to an illegal arrest. He contended that the arrest was illegal because it had been effected without probable cause. The judge in the criminal case held that there had been probable cause for the arrest, and he refused to suppress the weapon. At trial, Johnson was acquitted. He then brought a civil suit in federal court for false arrest. The arresting police officers sought to preclude Johnson from trying the issue of whether there had been probable cause to arrest him, based on the collateral estoppel effect of the judge's ruling at the criminal trial. Johnson was unable to appeal the state court's adverse determination of probable cause because he was acquitted. Because there had been no appeal, the federal court held that the probable cause determination could not be given collateral estoppel effect in his later civil trial. It wrote that under New York law "[i]f a party has not had an opportunity to appeal an adverse finding, then it has not had a full and fair opportunity to litigate that issue." Id. at 795.

4.   **Burden of proof.** Should the determination of an issue under a preponderance of the evidence standard be preclusive in a later proceeding where the burden of proof is higher, or where the burden is on the other party? The Second Restatement says it should not. See § 28(4). Courts generally follow the practice recommended by the Restatement. See, e.g., Freeman United Coal Mining Co. v. Office of Workers' Compensation Program, 20 F.3d 289, 294 (7th Cir. 1994) ("Collateral estoppel should not apply where the party against whom preclusion is sought faced a heavier burden of persuasion in the first action compared with the second."). What about the reverse? If a criminal defendant is convicted based on a jury's conclusion that he committed the act in question "beyond a reasonable doubt," should the criminal conviction be given collateral effect in a later civil proceeding brought against that defendant?

5.   **Essential to the judgment.** What if a court grants a judgment for the plaintiff based on two, or perhaps three, alternative findings of fact or law? In a later proceeding should any, or all, of these findings be given collateral estoppel effect? The competing ideas are that (1) an alternative determination is no less such for being alternative, especially given the multi-issue, alternative theory modes of litigation that are common in modern procedure, and (2) an alternative determination is dictum in the sense that the court would have reached the same result with or without the determination. The Second Restatement takes the position that an alternative determination is not conclusive unless both alternatives are reviewed and decided on appeal, which may be a strange compromise. Restatement (Second) of Judgments § 27, Comments i, j, and o. The case law

is not entirely consistent, but most decisions exhibit a strong suspicion of alternative determinations. See, e.g., Connors v. Tanoma Mining Co., 953 F.2d 682 (D.C. Cir. 1992).

6. Law of the case and direct estoppel. Related to but distinct from collateral estoppel is the "law of the case" doctrine, under which a determination of an issue of law at one stage of a case becomes the law of that case and, absent a change in circumstances, will not be reexamined in a subsequent stage of the case. A common application of the doctrine is where the issue has once been considered in an appeal and then, following remand and further proceedings in the lower court, comes up again in a subsequent appeal in the same case. See, e.g., Bray v. Cox, 38 N.Y.2d 350, 379 N.Y.S.2d 803, 342 N.E.2d 575 (1976); Jordan v. Jordan, 132 Ariz. 38, 643 P.2d 1008 (1982); Fine v. Bellefonte Underwriters Ins. Co., 758 F.2d 50 (2d Cir. 1985); Bigbee v. Pacific Tel. & Tel. Co., 34 Cal.3d 49, 192 Cal.Rptr. 857, 665 P.2d 947 (1983); Steinman, Law of the Case: A Judicial Puzzle in Consolidated and Transferred Cases and in Multidistrict Litigation, 135 U.Pa.L.Rev. 595 (1987); Vestal, Law of the Case: Single-Suit Preclusion, 1967 Utah L.Rev. 1. See also Hayman Cash Register Co. v. Sarokin, 669 F.2d 162 (3d Cir. 1982). Compare United States v. Burns, 662 F.2d 1378 (11th Cir. 1981) (refusing to apply law of the case where manifest injustice would result). Similar to the *law* of the case doctrine is the rule that a finding of *fact* at one stage of a case ordinarily precludes relitigation of that factual issue in another stage of the case, a consequence sometimes called "direct estoppel."

7. Judicial estoppel. A related doctrine is "judicial estoppel," under which a party is precluded from asserting inconsistent positions in successive litigations. Although the doctrine is not uniformly applied, it generally precludes a litigant who was successful in the first litigation from asserting an inconsistent position in later litigation; however, if the litigant was *un*successful in the earlier litigation, judicial estoppel will not prevent him from taking a later inconsistent position. For an argument that judicial estoppel is incompatible with the basic philosophy of modern pleading that permits a litigant to take inconsistent positions, see Note, Judicial Estoppel—Beating Shields into Swords and Back Again, 139 U.Pa.L.Rev. 1711, 1755 (1991).

4. IDENTITY OF PARTIES

Taylor v. Sturgell

Supreme Court of the United States, 2008.
553 U.S. 880, 128 S.Ct. 2161, 171 L.Ed.2d 155.

■ JUSTICE GINSBURG delivered the opinion of the Court.

"It is a principle of general application in Anglo-American jurisprudence that one is not bound by a judgment *in personam* in a litigation in which he is not designated as a party or to which he has not been made a party by service of process." Hansberry v. Lee, 311 U.S. 32, 40, 61 S.Ct. 115, 85 L.Ed. 22 (1940). Several exceptions, recognized in this Court's decisions, temper this basic rule. In a class action, for example, a person not named as a party may be bound by a judgment on the merits of the action, if she was adequately represented by a party who actively participated in the litigation. See id., at 41, 61 S.Ct. 115. In this case, we consider for the first time whether there is a "virtual representation" exception to the general rule against precluding nonparties. Adopted by a number of courts, including the courts below in the case now before us, the exception so styled is broader than any we have so far approved.

The virtual representation question we examine in this opinion arises in the following context. Petitioner Brent Taylor filed a lawsuit under the Freedom of Information Act seeking certain documents from the Federal Aviation Administration. Greg Herrick, Taylor's friend, had previously brought an unsuccessful suit seeking the same records. The two men have no legal relationship, and there is no evidence that Taylor controlled, financed, participated in, or even had notice of Herrick's earlier suit. Nevertheless, the D.C. Circuit held Taylor's suit precluded by the judgment against Herrick because, in that court's assessment, Herrick qualified as Taylor's "virtual representative."

We disapprove the doctrine of preclusion by "virtual representation," and hold, based on the record as it now stands, that the judgment against Herrick does not bar Taylor from maintaining this suit.

I

The Freedom of Information Act (FOIA) accords "any person" a right to request any records held by a federal agency. No reason need be given for a FOIA request, and unless the requested materials fall within one of the Act's enumerated exemptions, the agency must "make the records promptly available" to the requester. If an agency refuses to furnish the requested records, the requester may file suit in federal court and obtain an injunction "order[ing] the production of any agency records improperly withheld."

The courts below held the instant FOIA suit barred by the judgment in earlier litigation seeking the same records. Because the lower courts' decisions turned on the connection between the two lawsuits, we begin with a full account of each action.

A

The first suit was filed by Greg Herrick, an antique aircraft enthusiast and the owner of an F-45 airplane, a vintage model manufactured by the Fairchild Engine and Airplane Corporation (FEAC) in the 1930's. In 1997, seeking information that would help him restore his plane to its original condition, Herrick filed a FOIA request asking the Federal Aviation Administration (FAA) for copies of any technical documents about the F-45 contained in the agency's records.

To gain a certificate authorizing the manufacture and sale of the F-45, FEAC had submitted to the FAA's predecessor, the Civil Aeronautics Authority, detailed specifications and other technical data about the plane. Hundreds of pages of documents produced by FEAC in the certification process remain in the FAA's records. The FAA denied Herrick's request, however, upon finding that the documents he sought are subject to FOIA's exemption for "trade secrets and commercial or financial information obtained from a person and privileged or confidential." In an administrative appeal, Herrick urged that FEAC and its successors had waived any trade-secret protection. The FAA thereupon contacted FEAC's corporate successor, respondent Fairchild

Corporation (Fairchild). Because Fairchild objected to release of the documents, the agency adhered to its original decision.

Herrick then filed suit in the U.S. District Court for the District of Wyoming. Challenging the FAA's invocation of the trade-secret exemption, Herrick placed heavy weight on a 1955 letter from FEAC to the Civil Aeronautics Authority. The letter authorized the agency to lend any documents in its files to the public "for use in making repairs or replacement parts for aircraft produced by Fairchild." Herrick v. Garvey, 298 F.3d 1184, 1193 (C.A.10 2002) (internal quotation marks omitted). This broad authorization, Herrick maintained, showed that the F-45 certification records held by the FAA could not be regarded as "secre[t]" or "confidential" within the meaning of § 552(b)(4).

Rejecting Herrick's argument, the District Court granted summary judgment to the FAA.* * *

On appeal, the Tenth Circuit agreed with Herrick that the 1955 letter had stripped the requested documents of trade-secret protection. But the Court of Appeals upheld the District Court's alternative determination-i.e., that Fairchild had restored trade-secret status by objecting to Herrick's FOIA request. On that ground, the appeals court affirmed the entry of summary judgment for the FAA.

In so ruling, the Tenth Circuit noted that Herrick had failed to challenge two suppositions underlying the District Court's decision. First, the District Court assumed trade-secret status could be "restored" to documents that had lost protection. Second, the District Court also assumed that Fairchild had regained trade-secret status for the documents even though the company claimed that status only "after Herrick had initiated his request" for the F-45 records. The Court of Appeals expressed no opinion on the validity of these suppositions.

B

The Tenth Circuit's decision issued on July 24, 2002. Less than a month later, on August 22, petitioner Brent Taylor—a friend of Herrick's and an antique aircraft enthusiast in his own right—submitted a FOIA request seeking the same documents Herrick had unsuccessfully sued to obtain. When the FAA failed to respond, Taylor filed a complaint in the U.S. District Court for the District of Columbia. Like Herrick, Taylor argued that FEAC's 1955 letter had stripped the records of their trade-secret status. But Taylor also sought to litigate the two issues concerning recapture of protected status that Herrick had failed to raise in his appeal to the Tenth Circuit.

After Fairchild intervened as a defendant, the District Court in D.C. concluded that Taylor's suit was barred by claim preclusion; accordingly, it granted summary judgment to Fairchild and the FAA. The court acknowledged that Taylor was not a party to Herrick's suit. Relying on the Eighth Circuit's decision in Tyus v. Schoemehl, 93 F.3d 449 (1996), however, it held that a nonparty may be bound by a judgment if she was "virtually represented" by a party.

* * * *

The record before the District Court in Taylor's suit revealed the following facts about the relationship between Taylor and Herrick: Taylor is the president of the Antique Aircraft Association, an organization to which Herrick belongs; the two men are "close associate[s];" Herrick asked Taylor to help restore Herrick's F-45, though they had no contract or agreement for Taylor's participation in the restoration; Taylor was represented by the lawyer who represented Herrick in the earlier litigation; and Herrick apparently gave Taylor documents that Herrick had obtained from the FAA during discovery in his suit.

Fairchild and the FAA conceded that Taylor had not participated in Herrick's suit. The D.C. District Court determined, however, that Herrick ranked as Taylor's virtual representative because the facts fit each of the other six indicators on the Eighth Circuit's list. Accordingly, the District Court held Taylor's suit, seeking the same documents Herrick had requested, barred by the judgment against Herrick.

The D.C. Circuit affirmed. * * *

[T]he D.C. Circuit announced its own five-factor test. * * * * * *

We granted certiorari to resolve the disagreement among the Circuits over the permissibility and scope of preclusion based on "virtual representation."

II

The preclusive effect of a federal-court judgment is determined by federal common law. See Semtek Int'l Inc. v. Lockheed Martin Corp., 531 U.S. 497, 507–508, 121 S.Ct. 1021, 149 L.Ed.2d 32 (2001). For judgments in federal-question cases-for example, Herrick's FOIA suit-federal courts participate in developing "uniform federal rule[s]" of res judicata, which this Court has ultimate authority to determine and declare. Id., at 508, 121 S.Ct. 1021. The federal common law of preclusion is, of course, subject to due process limitations. See Richards v. Jefferson County, 517 U.S. 793, 797, 116 S.Ct. 1761, 135 L.Ed.2d 76 (1996).

Taylor's case presents an issue of first impression in this sense: Until now, we have never addressed the doctrine of "virtual representation" adopted (in varying forms) by several Circuits and relied upon by the courts below. Our inquiry, however, is guided by well-established precedent regarding the propriety of nonparty preclusion. We review that precedent before taking up directly the issue of virtual representation.

A

The preclusive effect of a judgment is defined by claim preclusion and issue preclusion, which are collectively referred to as "res judicata." Under the doctrine of claim preclusion, a final judgment forecloses "successive litigation of the very same claim, whether or not relitigation of the claim raises the same issues as the earlier suit." Issue preclusion, in contrast, bars "successive litigation of an issue of fact or law actually litigated and resolved in a valid court determination essential to the prior judgment," even if the issue recurs in the context of a different claim. By "preclud[ing] parties from contesting matters that they have had a full and fair opportunity to litigate," these two doctrines protect against "the expense and vexation attending multiple lawsuits, conserv[e] judicial resources, and foste[r] reliance on judicial action by minimizing the possibility of inconsistent decisions." Montana v. United States, 440 U.S. 147, 153–154, 99 S.Ct. 970, 59 L.Ed.2d 210 (1979).

A person who was not a party to a suit generally has not had a "full and fair opportunity to litigate" the claims and issues settled in that suit. The application of claim and issue preclusion to nonparties thus runs up against the "deep-rooted historic tradition that everyone should have his own day in court." Richards, 517 U.S., at 798, 116 S.Ct. 1761 (internal quotation marks omitted). Indicating the strength of that tradition, we have often repeated the general rule that "one is not bound by a judgment in personam in a litigation in which he is not designated as a party or to which he has not been made a party by service of process." Hansberry, 311 U.S., at 40, 61 S.Ct. 115. See also, e.g., Richards, 517 U.S., at 798, 116 S.Ct. 1761; Martin v. Wilks, 490 U.S. 755, 761, 109 S.Ct. 2180, 104 L.Ed.2d 835 (1989); Zenith Radio Corp. v. Hazeltine Research, Inc., 395 U.S. 100, 110, 89 S.Ct. 1562, 23 L.Ed.2d 129 (1969).

B

Though hardly in doubt, the rule against nonparty preclusion is subject to exceptions. For present purposes, the recognized exceptions can be grouped into six categories.

First, "[a] person who agrees to be bound by the determination of issues in an action between others is bound in accordance with the terms of his agreement." 1 Restatement (Second) of Judgments § 40, p. 390 (1980) (hereinafter Restatement). * * * We have never had occasion to consider this ground for nonparty preclusion, and we express no view on it here.

Second, nonparty preclusion may be justified based on a variety of pre-existing "substantive legal relationship[s]" between the person to be bound and a party to the judgment. Shapiro 78. See also Richards, 517 U.S., at 798, 116 S.Ct. 1761. Qualifying relationships include, but are not limited to, preceding and succeeding owners of property, bailee and bailor, and assignee and assignor. See 2 Restatement §§ 43–44, 52, 55. These exceptions originated "as much from the needs of property law as from the values of preclusion by judgment." 18A C. Wright, A. Miller, & E. Cooper, Federal Practice and Procedure § 4448, p. 329 (2d ed.2002) (hereinafter Wright & Miller). The substantive legal relationships justifying preclusion are sometimes collectively referred to as "privity." * * * The term "privity," however, has also come to be used more broadly, as a way to express the conclusion that nonparty preclusion is appropriate on any ground. See 18A Wright & Miller § 4449, pp. 351–353, and n. 33 (collecting cases). To ward off confusion, we avoid using the term "privity" in this opinion.

Third, we have confirmed that, "in certain limited circumstances," a nonparty may be bound by a judgment because she was "adequately represented by someone with the same interests who [wa]s a party" to the suit. Richards, 517 U.S., at 798, 116 S.Ct. 1761 (internal quotation marks omitted). Representative suits with preclusive effect on nonparties include properly conducted class actions * * * and suits brought by trustees, guardians, and other fiduciaries[.] * * *

Fourth, a nonparty is bound by a judgment if she "assume[d] control" over the litigation in which that judgment was rendered. Montana, 440 U.S., at 154, 99 S.Ct. 970. See also Schnell v. Peter Eckrich & Sons, Inc., 365 U.S. 260, 262, n. 4, 81 S.Ct. 557, 5 L.Ed.2d 546 (1961); 1 Restatement § 39. * * *

Fifth, a party bound by a judgment may not avoid its preclusive force by relitigating through a proxy. Preclusion is thus in order when a person who did not participate in a litigation later brings suit as the designated representative of a person who was a party to the prior adjudication. See Chicago, R.I. & P.R. Co. v. Schendel, 270 U.S. 611, 620, 623, 46 S.Ct. 420, 70 L.Ed. 757 (1926); 18A Wright & Miller § 4454, pp. 433–434. * * *

Sixth, in certain circumstances a special statutory scheme may "expressly foreclos[e] successive litigation by nonlitigants . . . if the scheme is otherwise consistent with due process." Martin, 490 U.S., at 762, n. 2, 109 S.Ct. 2180. Examples of such schemes include bankruptcy and probate proceedings, see ibid., and quo warranto actions or other suits that, "under [the governing] law, [may] be brought only on behalf of the public at large," Richards, 517 U.S., at 804, 116 S.Ct. 1761.

III

Reaching beyond these six established categories, some lower courts have recognized a "virtual representation" exception to the rule against nonparty preclusion. * * *

The D.C. Circuit, the FAA, and Fairchild have presented three arguments in support of an expansive doctrine of virtual representation. We find none of them persuasive.

A

The D.C. Circuit purported to ground its virtual representation doctrine in this Court's decisions stating that, in some circumstances, a person may be bound by a judgment if she was adequately represented by a party to the proceeding yielding that judgment. But the D.C. Circuit's definition of "adequate representation" strayed from the meaning our decisions have attributed to that term.

In Richards, we reviewed a decision by the Alabama Supreme Court holding that a challenge to a tax was barred by a judgment upholding the same tax in a suit filed by different taxpayers. 517 U.S., at 795–797, 116 S.Ct. 1761. The plaintiffs in the first suit "did not sue on behalf of a class," their complaint "did not purport to assert any claim against or on behalf of any nonparties," and the judgment "did not purport to bind" nonparties. Id., at 801, 116 S.Ct. 1761. There was no indication, we emphasized, that the court in the first suit "took care to protect the interests" of absent parties, or that the parties to that litigation "understood their suit to be on behalf of absent [parties]." Id., at 802, 116 S.Ct. 1761. In these circumstances, we held, the application of claim preclusion was inconsistent with "the due process of law guaranteed by the Fourteenth Amendment." Id., at 797, 116 S.Ct. 1761.

* * *

We restated Richards' core holding in South Central Bell Telephone Co. v. Alabama, 526 U.S. 160, 119 S.Ct. 1180, 143 L.Ed.2d 258 (1999). In that case, as in Richards, the Alabama courts had held that a judgment rejecting a challenge to a tax by one group of taxpayers barred a subsequent suit by a different taxpayer. See 526 U.S., at 164–165, 119 S.Ct. 1180. In South Central Bell, however, the nonparty had notice of the original suit and engaged one of the lawyers earlier employed by the original plaintiffs. See id., at 167–168, 119 S.Ct. 1180. Under the D.C. Circuit's decision in Taylor's case, these factors apparently would have sufficed to establish adequate representation. Yet South Central Bell held that the application of res judicata in that case violated due process. Our inquiry came to an end when we determined that the original plaintiffs had not understood themselves to be acting in a representative capacity and that there had been no special procedures to safeguard the interests of absentees.

Our decisions recognizing that a nonparty may be bound by a judgment if she was adequately represented by a party to the earlier suit thus provide no support for the D.C. Circuit's broad theory of virtual representation.

B

Fairchild and the FAA do not argue that the D.C. Circuit's virtual representation doctrine fits within any of the recognized grounds for nonparty preclusion. Rather, they ask us to abandon the attempt to delineate discrete grounds and clear rules altogether. Preclusion is in order, they contend, whenever "the relationship between a party and a non-party is 'close enough' to bring the second litigant within the judgment." Courts should make the "close enough" determination, they urge, through a "heavily fact-driven" and "equitable" inquiry. Only this sort of diffuse balancing, Fairchild and the FAA argue, can account for all of the situations in which nonparty preclusion is appropriate.

We reject this argument for three reasons. First, our decisions emphasize the fundamental nature of the general rule that a litigant is not bound by a judgment to which she was not a party. See, e.g., Richards, 517 U.S., at 798–799, 116 S.Ct. 1761; Martin, 490 U.S., at 761–762, 109 S.Ct. 2180. Accordingly, we have endeavored to delineate discrete exceptions that apply in "limited circumstances." Id., at 762, n. 2, 109 S.Ct. 2180. Respondents' amorphous balancing test is at odds with the constrained approach to nonparty preclusion our decisions advance.

* * * *

Our second reason for rejecting a broad doctrine of virtual representation rests on the limitations attending nonparty preclusion based on adequate representation. A party's representation of a nonparty is "adequate" for preclusion purposes only if, at a minimum: (1) the interests of the nonparty and her representative are aligned, see Hansberry, 311 U.S., at 43, 61 S.Ct. 115; and (2) either the party understood herself to be acting in a representative capacity or the original court took care to protect the interests of the nonparty, see Richards, 517 U.S., at 801–802, 116 S.Ct. 1761; supra, at 2173–2174. In addition, adequate representation sometimes requires (3) notice of the original suit to the persons alleged to have been represented, see Richards, 517 U.S., at 801, 116 S.Ct. 1761. Richards suggested that notice is required in some representative suits, e.g., class actions seeking monetary relief. See 517 U.S., at 801, 116 S.Ct. 1761 (citing Hansberry v. Lee, 311 U.S. 32, 40, 61 S.Ct. 115, 85 L.Ed. 22 (1940), Eisen v. Carlisle & Jacquelin, 417 U.S. 156, 177, 94 S.Ct. 2140, 40 L.Ed.2d 732 (1974), and Mullane v. Central Hanover Bank & Trust Co., 339 U.S. 306, 319, 70 S.Ct. 652, 94 L.Ed. 865 (1950)). But we assumed without deciding that a lack of notice might be overcome in some circumstances. See Richards, 517 U.S., at 801, 116 S.Ct. 1761. In the class-action context, these limitations are implemented by the procedural safeguards contained in Federal Rule of Civil Procedure 23.

An expansive doctrine of virtual representation, however, would "recogniz[e], in effect, a common-law kind of class action." Tice, 162 F.3d, at 972 (internal quotation marks omitted). That is, virtual representation would authorize preclusion based on identity of interests and some kind of relationship between parties and nonparties, shorn of the procedural protections prescribed in Hansberry, Richards, and Rule 23. These protections, grounded in due process, could be circumvented were we to approve a virtual representation doctrine that allowed courts to "create de facto class actions at will." Tice, 162 F.3d, at 973.

Third, a diffuse balancing approach to nonparty preclusion would likely create more headaches than it relieves. Most obviously, it could significantly complicate the task of district courts faced in the first instance with preclusion questions. * * * Preclusion doctrine, it should be recalled, is intended to reduce the burden of litigation on courts and parties. Cf. Montana, 440 U.S., at 153–154, 99 S.Ct. 970. "In this area of the law," we agree, " 'crisp rules with sharp corners' are preferable to a round-about doctrine of opaque standards."

C

Finally, * * * the FAA maintains that nonparty preclusion should apply more broadly in "public-law" litigation than in "private-law" controversies. To support this position, the FAA offers two arguments. First, the FAA urges, our decision in Richards acknowledges that, in certain cases, the plaintiff has a reduced interest in controlling the litigation "because of the public nature of the right at issue." * * *

Taylor's FOIA action falls within the category described in Richards, the FAA contends, because "the duty to disclose under FOIA is owed to the public generally." The opening sentence of FOIA, it is true, states that agencies "shall make [information] available to the public." Equally true, we have several times said that FOIA vindicates a "public" interest. The Act, however, instructs agencies receiving FOIA requests to make the information available not to the public at large, but rather to the "person" making the request. Thus, in contrast to the public-law litigation contemplated in Richards, a successful FOIA action results in a grant of relief to the individual plaintiff, not a decree benefiting the public at large.

* * *

The FAA next argues that "the threat of vexatious litigation is heightened" in public-law cases because "the number of plaintiffs with standing is potentially limitless." FOIA does allow "any person" whose request is denied to resort to federal court for review of the agency's determination. Thus it is theoretically possible that several persons could coordinate to mount a series of repetitive lawsuits.

But we are not convinced that this risk justifies departure from the usual rules governing nonparty preclusion. First, stare decisis will allow courts swiftly to dispose of repetitive suits brought in the same circuit. Second, even when stare decisis is not dispositive, "the human tendency not to waste money will deter the bringing of suits based on claims or issues that have already been adversely determined against others."

Shapiro 97. This intuition seems to be borne out by experience: The FAA has not called our attention to any instances of abusive FOIA suits in the Circuits that reject the virtual-representation theory respondents advocate here.

IV

For the foregoing reasons, we disapprove the theory of virtual representation on which the decision below rested. The preclusive effects of a judgment in a federal-question case decided by a federal court should instead be determined according to the established grounds for nonparty preclusion described in this opinion. See Part II–B, supra.

* * *

* * * We now turn back to Taylor's action to determine whether * * * the result reached by the courts below can be justified on one of the recognized grounds for nonparty preclusion.

A

It is uncontested that four of the six grounds for nonparty preclusion have no application here: There is no indication that Taylor agreed to be bound by Herrick's litigation, that Taylor and Herrick have any legal relationship, that Taylor exercised any control over Herrick's suit, or that this suit implicates any special statutory scheme limiting relitigation. Neither the FAA nor Fairchild contends otherwise.

It is equally clear that preclusion cannot be justified on the theory that Taylor was adequately represented in Herrick's suit. Nothing in the record indicates that Herrick understood himself to be suing on Taylor's behalf, that Taylor even knew of Herrick's suit, or that the Wyoming District Court took special care to protect Taylor's interests. Under our pathmarking precedent, therefore, Herrick's representation was not "adequate." See Richards, 517 U.S., at 801–802, 116 S.Ct. 1761.

That leaves only the fifth category: preclusion because a nonparty to an earlier litigation has brought suit as a representative or agent of a party who is bound by the prior adjudication. Taylor is not Herrick's legal representative and he has not purported to sue in a representative capacity. He concedes, however, that preclusion would be appropriate if respondents could demonstrate that he is acting as Herrick's "undisclosed agen[t]."

* * * We therefore remand to give the courts below an opportunity to determine whether Taylor, in pursuing the instant FOIA suit, is acting as Herrick's agent. Taylor concedes that such a remand is appropriate.

We have never defined the showing required to establish that a nonparty to a prior adjudication has become a litigating agent for a party to the earlier case. Because the issue has not been briefed in any detail, we do not discuss the matter elaborately here. We note, however, that courts should be cautious about finding preclusion on this basis. A mere whiff of "tactical maneuvering" will not suffice; instead, principles of agency law are suggestive. They indicate that preclusion is appropriate only if the putative agent's conduct of the suit is subject to the control of the party who is bound by the prior adjudication. See 1 Restatement (Second) of Agency § 14, p. 60 (1957) ("A principal has the right to control the conduct of the agent with respect to matters entrusted to him.").

On remand, Fairchild suggests, Taylor should bear the burden of proving he is not acting as Herrick's agent. * * * Fairchild justifies this proposed burden-shift on the ground that "it is unlikely an opposing party will have access to direct evidence of collusion."

We reject Fairchild's suggestion. Claim preclusion, like issue preclusion, is an affirmative defense. See Fed. Rule Civ. Proc. 8(c); Blonder-Tongue, 402 U.S., at 350, 91 S.Ct. 1434. Ordinarily, it is incumbent on the defendant to plead and prove such a defense, see Jones v. Bock, 549 U.S. 199, 204, 127 S.Ct. 910, 166 L.Ed.2d 798 (2007), and we have never recognized claim preclusion as an exception to that general rule, see 18 Wright & Miller § 4405, p. 83 ("[A] party asserting preclusion must carry the burden of establishing all necessary elements."). We acknowledge that direct evidence justifying nonparty preclusion is often in the hands of plaintiffs rather than defendants. See, e.g., Montana, 440 U.S., at 155, 99 S.Ct. 970 (listing evidence of control over a prior suit). But "[v]ery often one must plead and prove matters as to which his adversary has superior access to the proof." 2 K. Broun, McCormick on Evidence § 337, p. 475 (6th ed.2006). In these situations, targeted interrogatories or deposition questions can reduce the information disparity. We see no greater cause here than in other matters of affirmative defense to disturb the traditional allocation of the proof burden.

* * *

For the reasons stated, the judgment of the United States Court of Appeals for the District of Columbia Circuit is vacated, and the case is remanded for further proceedings consistent with this opinion.

NOTE ON PRECLUSION OF NON-PARTIES

1.   The general principle. Everyone is entitled to his or her "day in court." The Supreme Court put it this way: "[There is a] general consensus in Anglo-American jurisprudence that one is not bound by a judgment *in personam* in a litigation in which he is not designated as a party or to which he has not been made a party by service of process. * * * This rule is part of *our deep-rooted historic tradition that everyone should have his own day in court.*" Richards v. Jefferson County, 517 U.S. 793, 798, 116 S.Ct. 1761, 135 L.Ed.2d 76 (1996) (citations and quotation marks omitted) (emphasis added). But as may be seen from the Court's discussion in *Taylor v. Sturgell* there are some exceptions. Under some circumstances, someone else's day in court may turn out be yours, too.

2.   Tidying up the vocabulary. The Court in *Taylor v. Sturgell* is careful to distance itself from two terms that have been used to describe situations in which someone will be bound by an adverse result in litigation conducted by someone else—"privity" and "virtual representation."

The term "privity" has been used in preclusion law and elsewhere to describe someone who has a sufficiently close relationship with another person that she can be bound to the same legal obligations as that other person. For example, in property law an owner of property who is in "privity of estate" with a prior owner may be bound to an obligation that "runs with the land." In preclusion law, a person in privity with a party is precluded by prior litigation to the same extent as that party. The Court noted in 1996 in the *Richards* case that the boundaries of privity, as used in preclusion law, had expanded in recent years: "[A]lthough there are clearly constitutional limits on the 'privity' exception, the term 'privity' is now used to describe various relationships between litigants that would not have come with the traditional definitions of that term." In the preclusion context, the Court now seems ready to abandon the use of the term altogether.

The term "virtual representation" was, for a time, commonly used to describe a relationship resulting in a non-party being bound to the result obtained in a litigation in which her interest was represented by someone else. But the meaning of "virtual representation" was always somewhat imprecise. In Tice v. American Airlines, Inc., 162 F.3d 966, 971 (7th Cir. 1998), the court wrote that "the term 'virtual representation' has cast more shadows than light."

3.   Categories of cases in which one need not have been a party to the prior litigation. The Court in *Taylor v. Sturgell* carefully outlines six categories of cases in which one need not have been a party to the prior litigation in order to be bound by an adverse ruling or result. The most important, in the sense of the most commonly recurring, of the categories are the following:

a.   Consent. A non-party may consent to be bound by the result of litigation. Sometimes the agreement is entered into as part of the litigation process. For example, a third-party defendant impleaded by the defendant under Rule 14 may agree to be bound by the court's determination of liability of the defendant to the plaintiff, leaving for subsequent litigation only the question whether the third-party defendant must indemnify the defendant. Restatement (Second) of Judgments, § 40, comm. a, illustr. 1. Sometimes the agreement precedes the litigation. For example, in Tennessee Ass'n of Health Maintenance Organizations, Inc. v. Grier, 262 F.3d 559 (6th Cir. 2001), a health care provider contracted with the State of Tennessee to follow guidelines or rules developed by the State. When the State was sued by federal Medicaid recipients, the State agreed to a judgment under which a number of its reimbursement procedures were changed. The health care provider was not a party to the suit, but it was precluded by its contract with the State from challenging the procedures specified in the judgment. Consent will not be inferred lightly. For example, in South Central Bell Telephone Co. v. Alabama, 526 U.S. 160, 168, 119 S.Ct. 1180, 143 L.Ed.2d 258 (1999), a party asked that its suit be "held in abeyance" until another suit, involving different parties but raising the same issue, was resolved. The Supreme Court held that this request was not an agreement to be bound by the result in the other suit, but was, rather, merely a "routine request for a continuance."

b.   Pre-existing formal relationships. Certain formal relationships result in preclusion of non-parties. For example, a beneficiary of an estate will be bound by the result of litigation undertaken by the trustee of the estate. Similarly, someone for whom an executor, administrator, guardian, or conservator has been appointed for purposes of litigation will be bound by the result of that litigation. Restatement (Second) of Judgments, § 41. The relationships that qualify for preclusion under this heading may be found in the second and third categories listed by the Court in *Taylor v. Sturgell*.

c.   Control. If a non-party substantially controls the litigation behavior of a party, the non-party may be bound by that litigation. In the formulation of the Second Restatement:

> A person who is not a party to an action but who controls or substantially participates in the control of the presentation on behalf of a party is bound by the determination of issues decided as though he were a party.

Restatement (Second) of Judgements, § 39.

In Montana v. United States, 440 U.S. 147, 99 S.Ct. 970, 59 L.Ed.2d 210 (1979), a contractor on a federal dam project brought a state court suit against the State of Montana, contending that a Montana gross receipts tax unconstitutionally discriminated against the United States and its contractors. The United States was not a party to the contractor's suit. After the contractor lost its suit, the United States filed its own suit against the State based on the same contention, this time in federal district court. The Supreme Court held that the United States had so controlled the contractor's state court suit that it was bound by the holding in that suit. The United States had (1) required the contractor to file its suit; (2) reviewed and approved the complaint in the contractor's suit; (3) paid the contractor's costs and attorneys' fees; (4) directed that an appeal be taken from the adverse judgment of the trial court; (5) appeared and submitted an amicus brief in the Montana Supreme Court; (6) caused the contractor to file a notice of appeal to the United States Supreme Court; and (7) caused the abandonment of the appeal to the Supreme Court. Id. at 155. Compare Metro Industries, Inc. v. Sammi Corp., 82 F.3d 839, 848 n.6 (9th Cir. 1996), in which the parties in the first and second suits had the same attorney, had aligned interests on the question at issue, and argued similar theories of liability. The court nevertheless refused to find that there was sufficient control of the first suit by the party to the second suit.

In Headwaters, Inc. v. U.S. Forest Service, 399 F.3d 1047 (9th Cir. 2005), plaintiffs in the first suit brought suit against the United States Forest Service, challenging timber sales on Forest Service land. That suit was dismissed with prejudice shortly after filing. One of the plaintiffs in that suit then filed a second suit against the Forest Service challenging the same sales. That suit was dismissed based on claim preclusion. A third suit was then filed against the Forest Service challenging the same sale, this time by a plaintiff who had not participated in either of the first two suits. The plaintiff in the third suit was represented by the same lawyer as the plaintiff in the second suit. The court held that there was insufficient evidence of control over the plaintiffs' conduct in the first suit by the plaintiff in the third suit, and that preclusion was therefore not proper. Is there something different about a public interest case against the government, brought by the same lawyer, where many potential plaintiffs are available to bring essentially the same suit? The Supreme Court's discussion in *Taylor v. Sturgell* suggests that there may be. Does the holding in *Headwaters* give too much freedom to a public interest firm to relitigate when the first plaintiff loses her suit, simply by filing a new suit on behalf of new plaintiff? How difficult would it be to show—if it is in fact true—that the public interest law firm rather than the plaintiffs controlled the litigation in both the first and second suit? Should control by the firm, as distinct from control by the plaintiffs, result in preclusion in the second suit?

d. Class actions. Unnamed parties in class actions are bound to the result in a properly certified class action. Federal Rule 23 provides carefully structured protections of unnamed class members, including requirements that there be questions of law or fact common to the class; that the claims or defenses of the named representatives be typical of the claims or defenses of the unnamed class members; that the named representatives fairly and adequately protect the interests of the unnamed class members; that there be adequate notice to the unnamed class members; and that the court approve any proposed settlement of the action.

4. Relitigation through a proxy. One of the Court's categories in *Taylor v. Sturgell* is relitigation through a proxy. The litigation in *Taylor v. Sturgell* may or may not fall into this category. The Court remands to the district court for further proceedings to determine whether it does. That is, the Court remands for a determination whether Taylor, the plaintiff in the second FOIA suit, is acting as a proxy for Herrick, the losing plaintiff in the first FOIA suit. The evidence is clear that Taylor did not control Herrick in the first suit. But the evidence is unclear as to whether Herrick is now controlling Taylor. Note how careful the Court is to warn the district court not to conclude too easily that Herrick is controlling Taylor

C. PRECLUSION AGAINST OTHER PARTIES

INTRODUCTORY NOTE ON COLLATERAL ESTOPPEL (ISSUE PRECLUSION) AGAINST OTHER PARTIES

A judgment may have collateral estoppel (issue preclusion) effect not only between the parties to the original proceeding, but also between such a party and one who was not a party to the first action.

1. The mutuality rule. Suppose that A claims to be injured as the result of acts of B and C. A sues B, but loses on the ground that no injury was proven. Suppose A now sues C for the same injury. Should A be bound by the earlier finding that he suffered no injury?

As the law of res judicata stood until about 1940, the answer was that A would not be bound. This was by virtue of the "mutuality" rule, which went like this: Collateral estoppel should apply only when it can apply "mutually." One party should not be bound by a judgment unless, if the judgment had gone the other way, the opposing party would also have been bound; conversely, a party could not invoke a judgment as binding in his favor unless it would have been binding on the other party had it gone the other way. Thus, in the hypothetical above, A would not be bound because C, having not been a party to the first action, would not have been bound if A won. See Millar, The Historical Relation of Estoppel by Record to Res Judicata, 35 Ill.L.Rev. 41 (1940).

The old mutuality rule was always subject to exceptions. Most of the exceptions were subsumed under the category of "privity." If a person was in privity with a winner, he could take advantage of that winner's victory on the issue in question, despite the mutuality rule. See, e.g., Portland Gold Mining Co. v. Stratton's Independence, Ltd., 158 Fed. 63 (8th Cir. 1907). Similarly, if a person was in "privity" with a loser on the issue, he was bound even though he never had his day in court.

2. Preclusion in favor of third parties. The modern rule on non-mutual collateral estoppel (issue preclusion) derives from Bernhard v. Bank of America, 19 Cal.2d 807, 122 P.2d 892 (1942). In the first proceeding, the heirs of an elderly woman sued a man who had acted as her financial advisor, contending that he had stolen her money by transferring it into his own bank account. The heirs lost, on a finding that the money had been given to the defendant as a gift. In the second proceeding, the heirs sued the bank that had made the transfer, contending that the transfer was improper and that the bank should have taken care to prevent it. The bank asserted that the prior judgment was conclusive against the heirs on the factual issue of the legitimacy of the transfer. The court applied preclusion, rejecting the mutuality rule and allowing non-mutual collateral estoppel by the defendant in the second suit against an unsuccessful plaintiff in the first suit. According to the *Bernhard* court, the critical questions were: "Was the issue decided in the prior adjudication identical with the one presented in the action in question? Was there a final judgment on the merits? Was the party against whom the plea is asserted a party or in privity with a party to the prior adjudication?" 122 P.2d at 895. *Bernhard v. Bank of America* had a slow start in gaining adherents, but is now the accepted rule. See, e.g., Restatement (Second) of Judgments § 29; Schwartz v. Public Adm'r, 24 N.Y.2d 65, 298 N.Y.S.2d 955, 246 N.E.2d 725 (1969); and *Parklane Hosiery Co. v. Shore*, which follows.

Parklane Hosiery Co. v. Shore

Supreme Court of the United States, 1979.
439 U.S. 322, 99 S.Ct. 645, 58 L.Ed.2d 552.

■ MR. JUSTICE STEWART delivered the opinion of the Court.

This case presents the question whether a party who has had issues of fact adjudicated adversely to it in an equitable action may be collaterally estopped from relitigating the same issues before a jury in a subsequent legal action brought against it by a new party.

The respondent brought this stockholder's class action against the petitioners in a Federal District Court. The complaint alleged that the petitioners, Parklane Hosiery Company, Inc. (Parklane), and 13 of its officers, directors, and stockholders, had issued a materially false and misleading proxy statement in connection with a merger. The proxy statement, according to the complaint, had violated §§ 14(a), 10(b), and 20(a) of the Securities Exchange Act of 1934, 48 Stat. 895, 891, 899, as amended, 15 U.S.C. §§ 78n(a), 78j(b), and 78t(a), as well as various rules and regulations promulgated by the Securities and Exchange Commission (SEC). The complaint sought damages, rescission of the merger, and recovery of costs.

Before this action came to trial, the SEC filed suit against the same defendants in the Federal District Court, alleging that the proxy statement that had been issued by Parklane was materially false and misleading in essentially the same respects as those that had been alleged in the respondent's complaint. Injunctive relief was requested. After a 4-day trial, the District Court found that the proxy statement was materially false and misleading in the respects alleged, and entered a declaratory judgment to that effect. SEC v. Parklane Hosiery Co., 422 F.Supp. 477. The Court of Appeals for the Second Circuit affirmed this judgment. 558 F.2d 1083.

The respondent in the present case then moved for partial summary judgment against the petitioners, asserting that the petitioners were collaterally estopped from relitigating the issues that had been resolved against them in the action brought by the SEC.[2] The District Court denied the motion on the ground that such an application of collateral estoppel would deny the petitioners their Seventh Amendment right to a jury trial. The Court of Appeals for the Second Circuit reversed, holding that a party who has had issues of fact determined against him after a full and fair opportunity to litigate in a nonjury trial is collaterally estopped from obtaining a subsequent jury trial of these same issues of fact. 565 F.2d 815. The appellate court concluded that "the Seventh Amendment preserves the right to jury trial only with respect to issues of fact, [and] once those issues have been fully and fairly adjudicated in a prior proceeding, nothing remains for trial, either with or without a jury." Id., at 819. Because of an intercircuit conflict, we granted certiorari. 435 U.S. 1006, 98 S.Ct. 1875, 56 L.Ed.2d 387.

I

The threshold question to be considered is whether, quite apart from the right to a jury trial under the Seventh Amendment, the petitioners can be precluded from relitigating facts resolved adversely to them in a prior equitable proceeding with another party under the general law of collateral estoppel. Specifically, we must determine whether a litigant who was not a party to a prior judgment may nevertheless use that judgment "offensively" to prevent a defendant from relitigating issues resolved in the earlier proceeding.[4]

A

Collateral estoppel, like the related doctrine of res judicata,[5] FN5 has the dual purpose of protecting litigants from the burden of relitigating an identical issue with the same party or his privy and of promoting judicial economy by preventing needless litigation. Blonder-Tongue Laboratories, Inc. v. University of Illinois Foundation, 402 U.S. 313, 328–329, 91 S.Ct. 1434, 1442–1443, 28 L.Ed.2d 788. Until relatively recently, however, the scope of collateral estoppel was limited by the doctrine of mutuality of parties. Under this mutuality doctrine, neither party could use a prior judgment as an estoppel against the other unless

---

[2] A private plaintiff in an action under the proxy rules is not entitled to relief simply by demonstrating that the proxy solicitation was materially false and misleading. The plaintiff must also show that he was injured and prove damages. Mills v. Electric Auto-Lite, 396 U.S. 375, 386–390, 90 S.Ct. 616, 622–624, 24 L.Ed.2d 593. Since the SEC action was limited to a determination of whether the proxy statements contained materially false and misleading statements, the respondent conceded that he would still have to prove these other elements of his prima facie case in the private action. The petitioner's right to a jury trial on those remaining issues is not contested.

[4] In this context, offensive use of collateral estoppel occurs when the plaintiff seeks to foreclose the defendant from litigating an issue the defendant has previously litigated unsuccessfully in an action with another party. Defensive use occurs when a defendant seeks to prevent a plaintiff from asserting a claim the plaintiff has previously litigated and lost against another defendant.

[5] Under the doctrine of res judicata, a judgment on the merits in a prior suit bars a second suit involving the same parties or their privies based on the same cause of action. Under the doctrine of collateral estoppel, on the other hand, the second action is upon a different cause of action and the judgment in the prior suit precludes relitigation of issues actually litigated and necessary to the outcome of the first action. 1B J. Moore, Federal Practice ¶ 0.405[1], pp. 622–624 (2d ed. 1974); e.g., Lawlor v. National Screen Serv. Corp., 349 U.S. 322, 326, 75 S.Ct. 865, 867, 99 L.Ed. 1122 (1955); Commissioner of Internal Revenue v. Sunnen, 333 U.S. 591, 597, 68 S.Ct. 715, 719, 92 L.Ed. 898 (1948); Cromwell v. County of Sac, 94 U.S. 351, 352–353, 24 L.Ed. 195 (1876).

both parties were bound by the judgment. Based on the premise that it is somehow unfair to allow a party to use a prior judgment when he himself would not be so bound,[7] the mutuality requirement provided a party who had litigated and lost in a previous action an opportunity to relitigate identical issues with new parties.

By failing to recognize the obvious difference in position between a party who has never litigated an issue and one who has fully litigated and lost, the mutuality requirement was criticized almost from its inception. Recognizing the validity of this criticism, the Court in Blonder-Tongue Laboratories, Inc. v. University of Illinois Foundation, supra, abandoned the mutuality requirement, at least in cases where a patentee seeks to relitigate the validity of a patent after a federal court in a previous lawsuit has already declared it invalid. The "broader question" before the Court, however, was "whether it is any longer tenable to afford a litigant more than one full and fair opportunity for judicial resolution of the same issue." 402 U.S., at 328, 91 S.Ct., at 1442. The Court strongly suggested a negative answer to that question[.] * * * :

B

The *Blonder-Tongue* case involved defensive use of collateral estoppel—a plaintiff was estopped from asserting a claim that the plaintiff had previously litigated and lost against another defendant. The present case, by contrast, involves offensive use of collateral estoppel—a plaintiff is seeking to estop a defendant from relitigating the issues which the defendant previously litigated and lost against another plaintiff. In both the offensive and defensive use situations, the party against whom estoppel is asserted has litigated and lost in an earlier action. Nevertheless, several reasons have been advanced why the two situations should be treated differently.

First, offensive use of collateral estoppel does not promote judicial economy in the same manner as defensive use does. Defensive use of collateral estoppel precludes a plaintiff from relitigating identical issues by merely "switching adversaries." Bernhard v. Bank of America Nat. Trust & Savings Assn., 19 Cal.2d, at 813, 122 P.2d, at 895. Thus defensive collateral estoppel gives a plaintiff a strong incentive to join all potential defendants in the first action if possible. Offensive use of collateral estoppel, on the other hand, creates precisely the opposite incentive. Since a plaintiff will be able to rely on a previous judgment against a defendant but will not be bound by that judgment if the defendant wins, the plaintiff has every incentive to adopt a "wait and see" attitude, in the hope that the first action by another plaintiff will result in a favorable judgment. Thus offensive use of collateral estoppel will likely increase rather than decrease the total amount of litigation, since potential plaintiffs will have everything to gain and nothing to lose by not intervening in the first action.

A second argument against offensive use of collateral estoppel is that it may be unfair to a defendant. If a defendant in the first action is sued for small or nominal damages, he may have little incentive to defend

---

[7]   It is a violation of due process for a judgment to be binding on a litigant who was not a party nor a privy and therefore has never had an opportunity to be heard. Blonder-Tongue Laboratories, Inc. v. University of Illinois Foundation, 402 U.S. 313, 329, 91 S.Ct. 1434, 1443, 28 L.Ed.2d 788; Hansberry v. Lee, 311 U.S. 32, 40, 61 S.Ct. 115, 117, 85 L.Ed. 22.

vigorously, particularly if future suits are not foreseeable. The Evergreens v. Nunan, 141 F.2d 927, 929 (C.A.2); cf. Berner v. British Commonwealth Pac. Airlines, 346 F.2d 532 (C.A.2) (application of offensive collateral estoppel denied where defendant did not appeal an adverse judgment awarding damages of $35,000 and defendant was later sued for over $7 million). Allowing offensive collateral estoppel may also be unfair to a defendant if the judgment relied upon as a basis for the estoppel is itself inconsistent with one or more previous judgments in favor of the defendant.[14] Still another situation where it might be unfair to apply offensive estoppel is where the second action affords the defendant procedural opportunities unavailable in the first action that could readily cause a different result.[15]

C

We have concluded that the preferable approach for dealing with these problems in the federal courts is not to preclude the use of offensive collateral estoppel, but to grant trial courts broad discretion to determine when it should be applied. The general rule should be that in cases where a plaintiff could easily have joined in the earlier action or where, either for the reasons discussed above or for other reasons, the application of offensive estoppel would be unfair to a defendant, a trial judge should not allow the use of offensive collateral estoppel.

In the present case, however, none of the circumstances that might justify reluctance to allow the offensive use of collateral estoppel is present. The application of offensive collateral estoppel will not here reward a private plaintiff who could have joined in the previous action, since the respondent probably could not have joined in the injunctive action brought by the SEC even had he so desired.[17] Similarly, there is no unfairness to the petitioners in applying offensive collateral estoppel in this case. First, in light of the serious allegations made in the SEC's complaint against the petitioners, as well as the foreseeability of subsequent private suits that typically follow a successful government judgment, the petitioners had every incentive to litigate the SEC lawsuit fully and vigorously. Second, the judgment in the Commission action was not inconsistent with any previous decision. Finally, there will in the respondent's action be no procedural opportunities available to the

---

[14] In Professor Currie's familiar example, a railroad collision injures 50 passengers all of whom bring separate actions against the railroad. After the railroad wins the first 25 suits, a plaintiff wins in suit 26. Professor Currie argues that offensive use of collateral estoppel should not be applied so as to allow plaintiffs 27 through 50 automatically to recover. Currie, Mutuality of Estoppel: Limits of the *Bernhard* Doctrine, 9 Stan.L.Rev. 281, 304 (1957). See Restatement (Second) of Judgments (Tentative Draft No. 2, 1975) § 88(4).

[15] If, for example, the defendant in the first action was forced to defend in an inconvenient forum and therefore was unable to engage in full scale discovery or call witnesses, application of offensive collateral estoppel may be unwarranted. Indeed, differences in available procedures may sometimes justify not allowing a prior judgment to have estoppel effect in a subsequent action even between the same parties, or where defensive estoppel is asserted against a plaintiff who has litigated and lost. The problem of unfairness is particularly acute in cases of offensive estoppel, however, because the defendant against whom estoppel is asserted typically will not have chosen the forum in the first action. See id., § 88(2) and Comment d.

[17] SEC v. Everest Management Corp., 2nd Cir., 475 F.2d 1236, 1240 ("the complicating effect of the additional issues and the additional parties outweighs any advantage of a single disposition of the common issues"). Moreover, consolidation of a private action with one brought by the SEC without its consent is prohibited by statute. 15 U.S.C. § 78u(g).

petitioner that were unavailable in the first action of a kind that might be likely to cause a different result.[19]

We conclude, therefore, that none of the considerations that would justify a refusal to allow the use of offensive collateral estoppel is present in this case. Since the petitioners received a "full and fair" opportunity to litigate their claims in the SEC action, the contemporary law of collateral estoppel leads inescapably to the conclusion that the petitioners are collaterally estopped from relitigating the question of whether the proxy statements were materially false and misleading.

II

The question that remains is whether, notwithstanding the law of collateral estoppel, the use of offensive collateral estoppel in this case would violate the petitioners' Seventh Amendment right to a jury trial.

A

"[T]he thrust of the [Seventh] Amendment was to preserve the right to jury trial as it existed in 1791." Curtis v. Loether, 415 U.S. 189, 193, 94 S.Ct. 1005, 1007, 39 L.Ed.2d 260. At common law, a litigant was not entitled to have a jury determine issues that had been previously adjudicated by a chancellor in equity. Hopkins v. Lee, 6 Wheat. 109; Smith v. Kernochen, 7 How. 198, 217–218, 12 L.Ed. 666; Brady v. Daly, 175 U.S. 148, 158–159, 20 S.Ct. 62, 66, 44 L.Ed. 109; Shapiro & Coquillette, The Fetish of Jury Trials in Civil Cases: A Comment on Rachal v. Hill, 85 Harv.L.Rev. 442, 448–458 (1971).

Recognition that an equitable determination could have collateral estoppel effect in a subsequent legal action was the major premise of this Court's decision in Beacon Theatres v. Westover, 359 U.S. 500, 79 S.Ct. 948, 3 L.Ed.2d 988. In that case the plaintiff sought a declaratory judgment that certain arrangements between it and the defendant were not in violation of the antitrust laws, and asked for an injunction to prevent the defendant from instituting an antitrust action to challenge the arrangements. The defendant denied the allegations and counterclaimed for treble damages under the antitrust laws, requesting a trial by jury of the issues common to both the legal and equitable claims. The Court of Appeals upheld denial of the request, but this Court reversed, stating that:

> "[T]he effect of the action of the District Court could be, as the Court of Appeals believed, 'to limit the petitioner's opportunity fully to try to a jury every issue which has a bearing upon its treble damage suit,' for determination of the issue of clearances by the judge might 'operate either by way of res judicata or collateral estoppel so as to conclude both parties with respect thereto at the subsequent trial of the treble damage claim.'" Id., at 504, 79 S.Ct., at 953.

It is thus clear that the Court in the *Beacon Theatres* case thought that if an issue common to both legal and equitable claims was first

---

[19] It is true, of course, that the petitioners in the present action would be entitled to a jury trial of the issues bearing on whether the proxy statement was materially false and misleading had the SEC action never been brought—a matter to be discussed in Part II of this opinion. But the presence or absence of a jury as fact-finder is basically neutral, quite unlike, for example, the necessity of defending the first lawsuit in an inconvenient forum.

determined by a judge, relitigation of the issue before a jury might be foreclosed by res judicata or collateral estoppel. To avoid this result, the Court held that when legal and equitable claims are joined in the same action, the trial judge has only limited discretion in determining the sequence of trial and "that discretion . . . must, wherever possible, be exercised to preserve jury trial." Id., at 510, 79 S.Ct., at 956.

Both the premise of *Beacon Theatres,* and the fact that it enunciated no more than a general prudential rule were confirmed by this Court's decision in Katchen v. Landy, 382 U.S. 323, 86 S.Ct. 467, 15 L.Ed.2d 391. In that case the Court held that a bankruptcy court, sitting as a statutory court of equity, is empowered to adjudicate equitable claims prior to legal claims, even though the factual issues decided in the equity action would have been triable by a jury under the Seventh Amendment if the legal claims had been adjudicated first. * * *

B

Despite the strong support to be found both in history and in the recent decisional law of this Court for the proposition that an equitable determination can have collateral estoppel effect in a subsequent legal action, the petitioners argue that application of collateral estoppel in this case would nevertheless violate their Seventh Amendment right to a jury trial. The petitioners contend that since the scope of the Amendment must be determined by reference to the common law as it existed in 1791, and since the common law permitted collateral estoppel only where there was mutuality of parties, collateral estoppel cannot constitutionally be applied when such mutuality is absent.

The petitioners have advanced no persuasive reason, however, why the meaning of the Seventh Amendment should depend on whether or not mutuality of parties is present. A litigant who has lost because of adverse factual findings in an equity action is equally deprived of a jury trial whether he is estopped from relitigating the factual issues against the same party or a new party. In either case, the party against whom estoppel is asserted has litigated questions of fact, and has had the facts determined against him in an earlier proceeding. In either case there is no further factfinding function for the jury to perform, since the common factual issues have been resolved in the previous action. Cf. Ex parte Peterson, 253 U.S. 300, 310, 40 S.Ct. 543, 547, 64 L.Ed. 919 ("No one is entitled in a civil case to trial by jury, unless and except so far as there are issues of fact to be determined").

The Seventh Amendment has never been interpreted in the rigid manner advocated by the petitioners. On the contrary, many procedural devices developed since 1791 that have diminished the civil jury's historic domain have been found not to be inconsistent with the Seventh Amendment. * * *

* * *

The law of collateral estoppel, like the law in other procedural areas defining the scope of the jury's function, has evolved since 1791. * * * [T]hese developments are not repugnant to the Seventh Amendment simply for the reason that they did not exist in 1791. Thus if, as we have held, the law of collateral estoppel forecloses the petitioners from relitigating the factual issues determined against them in the SEC action, nothing in the Seventh Amendment dictates a different result, even though because of lack of mutuality there would have been no collateral estoppel in 1791.

The judgment of the Court of Appeals is

Affirmed.

■ MR. JUSTICE REHNQUIST, dissenting.

* * *

I

The Seventh Amendment provides:

> "In Suits at common law, where the value in controversy shall exceed twenty dollars, the right of trial by jury shall be preserved, and no fact tried by a jury, shall be otherwise reexamined in any Court of the United States, than according to the rules of common law."

The history of the Seventh Amendment has been amply documented by this Court and by legal scholars, and it would serve no useful purpose to attempt here to repeat all that has been written on the subject. Nonetheless, the decision of this case turns on the scope and effect of the Seventh Amendment, which, perhaps more than with any other provision of the Constitution, are determined by reference to the historical setting in which the Amendment was adopted. See Colgrove v. Battin, 413 U.S. 149, 152, 93 S.Ct. 2448, 2450, 37 L.Ed.2d 522 (1973). It therefore is appropriate to pause to review, albeit briefly, the circumstances preceding and attending the adoption of the Seventh Amendment as a guide in ascertaining its application to the case at hand.

A

It is perhaps easy to forget, now more than 200 years removed from the events, that the right of trial by jury was held in such esteem by the colonists that its deprivation at the hands of the English was one of the important grievances leading to the break with England. See Sources and Documents Illustrating the American Revolution 1764–1788 and the Formation of the Federal Constitution 94 (S. Morison 2d ed. 1929); R. Pound, The Development of Constitutional Guarantees of Liberty 69–72 (1957); C. Ubbelohde, The Vice-Admiralty Courts and the American Revolution 208–211 (1960). The extensive use of vice-admiralty courts by colonial administrators to eliminate the colonists' right of jury trial was listed among the specific offensive English acts denounced in the Declaration of Independence. And after war had broken out, all of the 13 newly formed States restored the institution of civil jury trial to its prior prominence; 10 expressly guaranteed the right in their state constitutions and the 3 others recognized it by statute or by common practice. Indeed, "[t]he right to trial by jury was probably the only one universally secured by the first American state constitutions. . . ." L. Levy, Legacy of Suppression: Freedom of Speech and Press in Early American History 281 (1960).[5]

* * *

---

[5]   When Congress in 1787 adopted the Northwest Ordinance for governance of the territories west of the Appalachians, it included a guarantee of trial by jury in civil cases. 2 Thorpe 960–961.

B

The Seventh Amendment requires that the right of trial by jury be "preserved." Because the Seventh Amendment demands preservation of the jury trial right, our cases have uniformly held that the content of the right must be judged by historical standards. Thus, in Baltimore & Carolina Line, Inc. v. Redman, 295 U.S. 654, 657, 55 S.Ct. 890, 891, 79 L.Ed. 1636 (1935), the Court stated that "[t]he right of trial by jury thus preserved is the right which existed under the English common law when the amendment was adopted." And in Dimick v. Schiedt, 293 U.S. 474, 476, 55 S.Ct. 296, 297, 79 L.Ed. 603 (1935), the Court held: "In order to ascertain the scope and meaning of the Seventh Amendment, resort must be had to the appropriate rules of the common law established at the time of the adoption of that constitutional provision in 1791." If a jury would have been impaneled in a particular kind of case in 1791, then the Seventh Amendment requires a jury trial today, if either party so desires.

To be sure, it is the substance of the right of jury trial that is preserved, not the incidental or collateral effects of common-law practice in 1791. "The aim of the amendment, as this Court has held, is to preserve the substance of the common-law right of trial by jury, as distinguished from mere matters of form or procedure, and particularly to retain the common-law distinction between the province of the court and that of the jury. . . ." Baltimore & Carolina Line, Inc. v. Redman, 295 U.S., at 657, 55 S.Ct., at 891. "The Amendment did not bind the federal courts to the exact procedural incidents or details of jury trial according to the common law of 1791, any more than it tied them to the common-law system of pleading or the specific rules of evidence then prevailing." Galloway v. United States, 319 U.S. 372, 390, 63 S.Ct. 1077, 1087, 87 L.Ed. 1458 (1943).

To say that the Seventh Amendment does not tie federal courts to the exact procedure of the common law in 1791 does not imply, however, that any nominally "procedural" change can be implemented, regardless of its impact on the functions of the jury. For to sanction creation of procedural devices which limit the province of the jury to a greater degree than permitted at common law in 1791 is in direct contravention of the Seventh Amendment. And since we deal here not with the common law *qua* common law but with the Constitution, no amount of argument that the device provides for more efficiency or more accuracy or is fairer will save it if the degree of invasion of the jury's province is greater than allowed in 1791. To rule otherwise would effectively permit judicial repeal of the Seventh Amendment because nearly any change in the province of the jury, no matter how drastic the diminution of its functions, can always be denominated "procedural reform."

* * *

C

Judged by the foregoing principles, I think it is clear that petitioners were denied their Seventh Amendment right to a jury trial in this case. Neither respondent nor the Court doubt that at common law as it existed in 1791, petitioners would have been entitled in the private action to have a jury determine whether the proxy statement was false and misleading in the respects alleged. The reason is that at common law in 1791, collateral estoppel was permitted only where the parties in the first action were identical to, or in privity with, the parties to the subsequent action. It was not until 1971 that the doctrine of mutuality was abrogated by this Court in certain limited circumstances. Blonder-Tongue Laboratories, Inc. v. University of Illinois Foundation, 402 U.S. 313, 91 S.Ct. 1434, 28 L.Ed.2d 788. But developments in the judge-made doctrine of collateral estoppel, however salutary, cannot, consistent with the Seventh Amendment, contract in any material fashion the right to a jury trial that a defendant would have enjoyed in 1791. In the instant case, resort to the doctrine of collateral estoppel does more than merely contract the right to a jury trial: It eliminates the right entirely and therefore contravenes the Seventh Amendment.

　　　* * *

II

Even accepting, *arguendo,* the majority's position that there is no violation of the Seventh Amendment here, I nonetheless would not sanction the use of collateral estoppel in this case. The Court today holds:

> "The general rule should be that in cases where a plaintiff could easily have joined in the earlier action or where, either for the reasons discussed above or for other reasons, the application of offensive collateral estoppel would be unfair to a defendant, a trial judge should not allow the use of offensive collateral estoppel." * * *

In my view, it is "unfair" to apply offensive collateral estoppel where the party who is sought to be estopped has not had an opportunity to have the facts of his case determined by a jury. Since in this case petitioners were not entitled to a jury trial in the Securities and Exchange Commission (SEC) lawsuit, I would not estop them from relitigating the issues determined in the SEC suit before a jury in the private action. I believe that several factors militate in favor of this result.

First, the use of offensive collateral estoppel in this case runs counter to the strong federal policy favoring jury trials, even if it does not, as the majority holds, violate the Seventh Amendment. The Court's decision in Beacon Theatres, Inc. v. Westover, 359 U.S. 500, 79 S.Ct. 948, 3 L.Ed.2d 988 (1959), exemplifies that policy. In *Beacon Theatres* the Court held that where both equitable and legal claims or defenses are presented in a single case, "only under the most imperative circumstances, circumstances which in view of the flexible procedures of the Federal Rules we cannot now anticipate, can the right to a jury trial of legal issues be lost through prior determination of equitable claims." Id., at 510–511, 79 S.Ct., at 957. * * *

Second, I believe that the opportunity for a jury trial in the second action could easily lead to a different result from that obtained in the first action before the court and therefore that it is unfair to estop petitioners from relitigating the issues before a jury. This is the position adopted in the Restatement (Second) of Judgments, which disapproves of the application of offensive collateral estoppel where the defendant has an opportunity for a jury trial in the second lawsuit that was not available in the first action. The Court accepts the proposition that it is unfair to apply offensive collateral estoppel "where the second action affords the defendant procedural opportunities unavailable in the first action that could readily cause a different result." * * * Differences in discovery opportunities between the two actions are cited as examples of situations where it would be unfair to permit offensive collateral estoppel. [Ante], n. 15. But in the Court's view, the fact that petitioners would have been entitled to a jury trial in the present action is not such a "procedural opportunit[y]" because "the presence or absence of a jury as factfinder is basically *neutral,* quite unlike, for example, the necessity of defending the first lawsuit in an inconvenient forum." * * * (emphasis added).

As is evident from the prior brief discussion of the development of the civil jury trial guarantee in this country, those who drafted the Declaration of Independence and debated so passionately the proposed Constitution during the ratification period, would indeed be astounded to learn that the presence or absence of a jury is merely "neutral," whereas the availability of discovery, a device unmentioned in the Constitution, may be controlling. It is precisely because the Framers believed that they might receive a different result at the hands of a jury of their peers than at the mercy of the sovereign's judges, that the Seventh Amendment was adopted. And I suspect that anyone who litigates cases before juries in the 1970's would be equally amazed to hear of the supposed lack of distinction between trial by court and trial by jury. The Court can cite no authority in support of this curious proposition. The merits of civil juries have been long debated, but I suspect that juries have never been accused of being merely "neutral" factors.

* * *

NOTE ON NONMUTUAL COLLATERAL ESTOPPEL

1.   Defensive and offensive collateral estoppel. The decision in *Bernhard v. Bank of America,* discussed supra p. 1103, n. 2, allowing defensive use of collateral estoppel by a non-party to the prior litigation, has now met with general approval. See Blonder-Tongue Laboratories, Inc. v. University of Illinois Foundation, 402 U.S. 313, 91 S.Ct. 1434, 28 L.Ed.2d 788 (1971), discussed in *Parklane*; Restatement (Second) of Judgments § 29. Offensive use of collateral estoppel by a non-party raises more difficult problems, as indicated by *Parklane*. In addition to the fairness concerns expressed by the Court in *Parklane,* critics have doubted the efficiency rationale of the doctrine. See Flanagan, Offensive Collateral Estoppel: Inefficiency and Foolish Consistency, 1982 Ariz.St.L.J. 45; Callen, Efficiency After All: A Reply to Professor Flanagan's Theory of Offensive Collateral Estoppel, 1983 Ariz.St.L.J. 799. See also Green, The Inability of Offensive Collateral Estoppel to Fulfill Its Promise: An Examination of Estoppel in Asbestos Litigation, 70 Iowa L.Rev. 141 (1984). Nevertheless, courts appear ready to apply collateral estoppel offensively, at least against private parties, where it would not be inequitable to do so. See Restatement (Second) of Judgments § 29. Different rules apply where the government is a party, as discussed below.

2.   Settlement to avoid preclusion. Litigants sometimes settle a case to avoid the preclusion that would result from an unfavorable judgment. This might happen, for example, in a product liability case where additional cases involving the same product are waiting in the wings. In a jurisdiction that allows offensive non-mutual collateral estoppel, the plaintiff in the first case may have a bargaining advantage because of the asymmetry of non-mutual estoppel. The plaintiff has no greater interest in the litigation than the amount at stake in the case itself. That is not so for the defendant, for if it loses the first case the application of collateral estoppel could result in an automatic finding of liability in all cases waiting to be tried. The potential adverse consequence of an adverse judgment is thus much greater than simply the amount of liability in the first case. The first plaintiff may be able to take advantage of that potential liability by extracting a larger pretrial settlement from the defendant than would be available if only liability in the first suit were at issue. See Note, Exposing the Extortion Gap: An Economic Analysis of the Rules of Collateral Estoppel, 105 Harv.L.Rev. 1940 (1992). By the same token, if the plaintiff goes to trial and wins, the successive plaintiffs are "free riders" on the first plaintiff's victory, since issue preclusion from the first case increases the value of the later cases.

What about a settlement after a trial court judgment that goes against the defendant? A losing defendant may wish to settle a suit after judgment while the case is still pending on appeal, in return for the winner's agreement to vacate the judgment as part of the settlement. A vacatur of the judgment has the effect of wiping off the books the trial court's determination. If a plaintiff's judgment that has issue preclusion consequences can be vacated pursuant to a settlement, the potential liability of the defendant to subsequent plaintiffs increases the bargaining power (and thus the settlement price) of the successful plaintiff. To what extent does such a settlement undercut the public interest? See Note, Avoiding Issue Preclusion by Settlement Conditioned Upon the Vacatur of Entered Judgments, 96 Yale L.J. 860 (1987); Note, Collateral Estoppel Effects of Judgments Vacated Pursuant to Settlement, 1987 U.Ill.L.Rev. 731; Comment, The Impact of Collateral Estoppel on Postjudgment Settlements, 15 Sw.U.L.Rev. 343 (1985).

In U.S. Bancorp Mortgage Co. v. Bonner Mall Partnership, 513 U.S. 18, 26–7, 115 S.Ct. 386, 130 L.Ed.2d 233 (1994), the Supreme Court held that vacatur of a lower court decision pursuant to settlement should be allowed only in "exceptional circumstances":

> "Judicial settlements are presumptively correct and valuable to the community as a whole. They are not merely the property of private litigants. * * * " [citation omitted] Congress has prescribed a primary route, by appeal as of right and certiorari, through which parties may seek relief from the legal consequences of judicial judgments. To allow a party who steps off the statutory path to employ the secondary remedy of vacatur as a refined form of collateral attack on the judgment would—quite apart from any considerations of fairness to the parties—disturb the orderly operation of the federal judicial system.

For discussion see Fisch, Rewriting History: The Propriety of Eradicating Prior Decisional Law Through Settlement and Vacatur, 76 Cornell L.Rev. 589 (1990); Resnik, Whose Judgment? Vacating Judgments, Preferences for Settlement, and the Role of Adjudication at the Close of the Twentieth Century, 41 U.C.L.A.L.Rev. 1471 (1994).

3.   Preclusive effects of a criminal conviction. A criminal conviction can be relied on for preclusive effect in a subsequent civil action in which the criminal defendant is a party. Convictions for major offenses are generally thought to be reliable and a proper subject for collateral estoppel, but there are some doubts about the reliability of convictions for minor offenses. For example, many states provide that a conviction for a motor vehicle violation may not be used to establish civil liability. There are similar reliability concerns about convictions based on guilty pleas, due to the harsh realities of the plea bargaining process. See Bower v. O'Hara, 759 F.2d 1117 (3d Cir. 1985) (guilty plea not preclusive in later civil action). Among other things, a defendant's guilt is not "actually litigated" in reaching the agreement to plead guilty. For a general discussion, see Thau, Collateral Estoppel and the Reliability of Criminal Determinations: Theoretical, Practical, and Strategic Implications for Criminal and Civil Litigation, 70 Geo.L.J. 1079 (1982); Shapiro, Should a Guilty Plea Have Preclusive Effect?, 70 Iowa L.Rev. 27 (1984).

In situations where collateral estoppel does not apply, a criminal conviction is at least admissible as proof that the defendant was convicted of the crime. See Fed.R.Evid. 803(22) (felony conviction).

4. Preclusion against the United States. The United States and other governments are generally subject to claim preclusion. See United States v. Mendoza, 464 U.S. 154, 104 S.Ct. 568, 78 L.Ed.2d 379 (1984); Montana v. United States, 440 U.S. 147, 99 S.Ct. 970, 59 L.Ed.2d 210 (1979). The United States is also generally subject to issue preclusion where the party seeking to invoke collateral estoppel was a party to the prior litigation. Montana v. United States, supra. See also Levin and Leeson, Issue Preclusion Against the United States Government, 70 Iowa L.Rev. 113 (1984).

But the Supreme Court has held that offensive nonmutual collateral estoppel should not be available against the United States. *United States v. Mendoza*, supra. The Court distinguished private from governmental parties, reasoning that the efficiency interests underlying the doctrine are outweighed by the doctrine's particular adverse effect on the government: (1) the government is more likely than any private party to litigate with different parties over the same legal issue, both because of the breadth of its litigation relationships and because of the nature of the issues the government litigates, particularly constitutional issues; (2) the government would be forced to revise its strategic and tactical policies as to whether to appeal a case, and might have to appeal in every case to avoid foreclosing further review of the issue if it were treated like a private party for purposes of preclusion; and (3) the Supreme Court would be deprived of the benefit of multiple determinations by courts of appeals on difficult legal questions because the development of such diverse judicial views would be frozen by the first final judgment. For a critical analysis of the Supreme Court's "blunt approach" in *Mendoza* and a suggestion that nonmutual issue preclusion should occasionally be available against states, see Comment, Nonmutual Issue Preclusion against States, 109 Harv.L.Rev. 792 (1996).

Although there is no nonmutual issue preclusion against the United States, holdings in earlier cases do make some difference. In Allbritton v. Commissioner of Internal Revenue, 37 F.3d 183, 184–5 (5th Cir. 1994), the Internal Revenue Service asserted a position that had already been rejected by two courts of appeals and several district courts. The Fifth Circuit took a dim view of the government's position:

> The government's assessment of deficiencies in the Taxpayers' income taxes, and its appeal based on the same statutory interpretation previously rejected by the Fourth Circuit, the

Federal Circuit, and several district courts constitutes 'circuit shopping' at the Taxpayers' expense in the hopes of creating a circuit conflict. * * * [W]hile the Commissioner is free by law to relitigate prior lost issues in other circuits, he does so at the risk of incurring the obligation to reimburse the taxpayer. [I]n continuing to litigate this issue despite constant jurisprudence to the contrary, the Commissioner is not substantially justified and should bear all reasonable costs of Taxpayers' litigation [including attorneys' fees].

D. RECOGNITION OF JUDGMENTS FROM OTHER JURISDICTIONS

1. INTERSTATE RECOGNITION OF JUDGMENTS

Fauntleroy v. Lum

Supreme Court of the United States, 1908.
210 U.S. 230, 28 S.Ct. 641, 52 L.Ed. 1039.

■ MR. JUSTICE HOLMES delivered the opinion of the Court:

This is an action upon a Missouri judgment, brought in a court of Mississippi. The declaration set forth the record of the judgment. The defendant pleaded that the original cause of action arose in Mississippi out of a gambling transaction in cotton futures; that he declined to pay the loss; that the controversy was submitted to arbitration, the question as to the illegality of the transaction, however, not being included in the submission; that an award was rendered against the defendant; that thereafter, finding the defendant temporarily in Missouri, the plaintiff brought suit there upon the award; that the trial court refused to allow the defendant to show the nature of the transaction, and that, by the laws of Mississippi, the same was illegal and void, but directed a verdict if the jury should find that the submission and award were made, and remained unpaid; and that a verdict was rendered and the judgment in suit entered upon the same. (The plaintiff in error is an assignee of the judgment, but nothing turns upon that.) The plea was demurred to on constitutional grounds, and the demurrer was overruled, subject to exception. Thereupon replications were filed, again setting up the Constitution of the United States (art. 4, § 1), and were demurred to. The supreme court of Mississippi held the plea good and the replications bad, and judgment was entered for the defendant. Thereupon the case was brought here.

The main argument urged by the defendant to sustain the judgment below is addressed to the jurisdiction of the Mississippi courts.

The laws of Mississippi make dealing in futures a misdemeanor, and provide that contracts of that sort, made without intent to deliver the commodity or to pay the price, "shall not be enforced by any court." Annotated Code of 1892, §§ 1120, 1121, 2117. The defendant contends that this language deprives the Mississippi courts of jurisdiction, and that the case is like Anglo-American Provision Co. v. Davis Provision Co., 191 U.S. 373, 48 L.Ed. 225, 24 Sup.Ct.Rep. 92. There the New York statutes refused to provide a court into which a foreign corporation could come, except upon causes of action arising within the state, etc.; and it was held that the state of New York was under no constitutional obligation to give jurisdiction to its supreme court against its will. One question is whether that decision is in point.

No doubt it sometimes may be difficult to decide whether certain words in a statute are directed to jurisdiction or to merits; but the distinction between the two is plain. One goes to the power, the other only to the duty, of the court. Under the common law it is the duty of a court of general jurisdiction not to enter a judgment upon a parol promise made without consideration; but it has power to do it, and, if it does, the judgment is unimpeachable, unless reversed. Yet a statute could be framed that would make the power, that is, the jurisdiction, of the court, dependent upon whether there was a consideration or not. Whether a given statute is intended simply to establish a rule of substantive law, and thus to define the duty of the court, or is meant to limit its power, is a question of construction and common sense. When it affects a court of general jurisdiction, and deals with a matter upon which that court must pass, we naturally are slow to read ambiguous words as meaning to leave the judgment open to dispute, or as intended to do more than to fix the rule by which the court should decide.

The case quoted concerned a statute plainly dealing with the authority and jurisdiction of the New York court. The statute now before us seems to us only to lay down a rule of decision. The Mississippi court in which this action was brought is a court of general jurisdiction and would have to decide upon the validity of the bar, if the suit upon the award or upon the original cause of action had been brought there. The words "shall not be enforced by any court" are simply another, possibly less emphatic, way of saying that an action shall not be brought to enforce such contracts. As suggested by the counsel for the plaintiff in error, no one would say that the words of the Mississippi statute of frauds, "An action shall not be brought whereby to charge a defendant," Code 1892, § 4225, go to the jurisdiction of the court. Of course it could be argued that logically they had that scope, but common sense would revolt. See 191 U.S. 375, 48 L.Ed. 227, 24 Sup.Ct.Rep. 92. * * *

The doctrine laid down by Chief Justice Marshall was "that the judgment of a state court should have the same credit, validity, and effect in every other court in the United States which it had in the state where it was pronounced, and that whatever pleas would be good to a suit thereon in such state, and none others, could be pleaded in any other court in the United States." Hampton v. M'Connel, 3 Wheat. 234, 4 L.Ed. 378. There is no doubt that this quotation was supposed to be an accurate statement of the law as late as Christmas v. Russell, 5 Wall. 290, 18 L.Ed. 475, where an attempt of Mississippi, by statute, to go behind judgments recovered in other states, was declared void, and it was held that such judgments could not be impeached even for fraud.

     * * *

We assume that the statement of Chief Justice Marshall is correct. It is confirmed by the act of May 26, 1790, chap. 11, 1 Stat. at L. 122 (Rev.Stat. § 905, U.S.Comp.Stat.1901, p. 677), providing that the said records and judicial proceedings "shall have such faith and credit given to them in every court within the United States as they have by law or usage in the courts of the state from whence the said records are or shall be taken." See further Tilt v. Kelsey, 207 U.S. 43, 57, ante, 1, 28 Sup.Ct.Rep. 1. Whether the award would or would not have been conclusive, and whether the ruling of the Missouri court upon that matter was right or wrong, there can be no question that the judgment was conclusive in Missouri on the validity of the cause of action. Pitts v. Fugate, 41 Mo. 405; State ex rel. Hudson v. Trammel, 106 Mo. 510, 17 S.W. 502; Re Copenhaver, 118 Mo. 377, 40 Am.St.Rep. 382, 24 S.W. 161. A judgment is conclusive as to all the *media concludendi* (United States v. California & O. Land Co., 192 U.S. 355, 48 L.Ed. 476, 24 Sup.Ct.Rep. 266); and it needs no authority to show that it cannot be impeached either in or out of the state by showing that it was based upon a mistake of law. Of course, a want of jurisdiction over either the person or the subject-matter might be shown. Andrews v. Andrews, 188 U.S. 14, 47 L.Ed. 366, 23 Sup.Ct.Rep. 237; Clarke v. Clarke, 178 U.S. 186, 44 L.Ed. 1028, 20 Sup.Ct.Rep. 873. But, as the jurisdiction of the Missouri court is not open to dispute, the judgment cannot be impeached in Mississippi even if it went upon a misapprehension of the Mississippi law. See Godard v. Gray, L.R. 6 Q.B. 139; MacDonald v. Grand Trunk R. Co., 71 N.H. 448, 59 L.R.A. 448, 93 Am.St.Rep. 550, 52 Atl. 982; Peet v. Hatcher, 112 Ala. 514, 57 Am.St.Rep. 45, 21 So. 711.

We feel no apprehensions that painful or humiliating consequences will follow upon our decision. No court would give judgment for a plaintiff unless it believed that the facts were a cause of action by the law determining their effect. Mistakes will be rare. In this case the Missouri court no doubt supposed that the award was binding by the law of Mississippi. If it was mistaken, it made a natural mistake. The validity of its judgment, even in Mississippi, is, as we believe, the result of the Constitution as it always has been understood, and is not a matter to arouse the susceptibilities of the states, all of which are equally concerned in the question and equally on both sides.

Judgment reversed.

■ MR. JUSTICE WHITE, with whom concurs MR. JUSTICE HARLAN, MR. JUSTICE MCKENNA, and MR. JUSTICE DAY, dissenting:

* * *

When the Constitution was adopted the principles of comity by which the decrees of the courts of one state were entitled to be enforced in another were generally known; but the enforcement of those principles by the several states had no absolute sanction, since they rested but in comity. Now, it cannot be denied that, under the rules of comity recognized at the time of the adoption of the Constitution, and which, at this time, universally prevail, no sovereignty was or is under the slightest moral obligation to give effect to a judgment of another sovereignty, when to do so would compel the state in which the judgment was sought to be executed to enforce an illegal and prohibited contract, when both the contract and all the acts done in connection with its performance had taken place in the latter state. This seems to me conclusive of this case, since, both in treatises of authoritative writers (Story, Confl.L. § 609), and by repeated adjudications of this court, it has been settled that the purpose of the due faith and credit clause was not to confer any new power, but simply to make obligatory that duty which, when the Constitution was adopted, rested, as has been said, in comity alone.

Without citing the numerous decisions which so hold, reference is made to a few of the leading cases in which the prior rulings of this court were reviewed, the foregoing principle was stated, and the scope of the due faith and credit clause was fully expounded: Thompson v. Whitman, 18 Wall. 457, 21 L.Ed. 897; Wisconsin v. Pelican Ins. Co., 127 U.S. 265, 32 L.Ed. 239, 8 Sup.Ct.Rep. 1370; Cole v. Cunningham, 133 U.S. 107, 33 L.Ed. 538, 10 Sup.Ct.Rep. 269; Andrews v. Andrews, 188 U.S. 14, 47 L.Ed. 366, 23 Sup.Ct.Rep. 237. A more particular review of those cases will demonstrate why my conviction is that the decision in this case overrules the cases cited.

* * *

NOTE ON FULL FAITH AND CREDIT

1. Recognition of judgments. Before the adoption of the Constitution, each state was considered a separate sovereign entity, and recognition of judgments of sister states was governed by the doctrine of comity. To help forge one nation out of many, the framers of the Constitution included the Full Faith and Credit Clause, Article IV, section 1, which provides:

> Full Faith and Credit shall be given in each State to the public Acts, Records, and judicial Proceedings of every other State; And the Congress may by general Laws prescribe the Manner in which such Acts, Records and Proceedings shall be proved, and the Effect thereof.

The Clause covers "public acts" and "records" as well as judgments, but the history of its legal development and implementation has mainly concerned judgments.

A judgment of one state must be recognized by other states under the Full Faith and Credit Clause. See Restatement (Second) of Conflict of Laws § 93 et seq.; Reynolds, The Iron Law of Full Faith and Credit, 53 Md.L.Rev. 412 (1994). The issue preclusive effects of such judgments, stemming from the Full Faith and Credit Clause, are somewhat uncertain. See Scoles, Interstate Preclusion by Prior Litigation, 74 Nw.U.L.Rev. 742 (1979); Casad, Intersystem Preclusion and the Restatement (Second) of Judgments, 66 Cornell L.Rev. 510 (1981). See generally, Erichson, Interjurisdictional Preclusion, 96 Mich.L.Rev. 945 (1998).

Full faith and credit mandates that a state must give at least as much effect to the judgment of the rendering state as would the rendering state itself. But a state sometimes gives effect to other states' judgments even when not compelled to do so by full faith and credit. For example, if the rendering state adheres to the old mutuality rule, the enforcing state may disregard that rule and give a non-party the benefit of preclusion when a court of the rendering state would not. See Hart v. American Airlines, Inc., 61 Misc.2d 41, 304 N.Y.S.2d 810 (Sup.Ct.1969). Is that fair? What if the now-precluded party did not foresee the possibility of later litigation in a forum not adhering to the mutuality rule? See generally von Mehren and Trautman, Recognition of Foreign Adjudications: A Survey and a Suggested Approach, 81 Harv.L.Rev. 1601 (1968).

Not all judgments are entitled to full faith and credit. Judgments that are not final in the rendering state are not entitled to full faith and credit in other states. Judgments not "on the merits," i.e., judgments based on procedural faults rather than on substantive law, need not be given preclusive effect. Judgments based on faulty jurisdiction, venue, parties, pleading, or the statute of limitations thus generally are not subject to the Full Faith and Credit Clause. Moreover, where the rendering court has entered a substantive judgment, that judgment may be attacked in another state if the rendering state did not have jurisdiction over the subject matter or over the parties. However, if the rendering court itself considered its own jurisdiction, a finding in favor of territorial jurisdiction is entitled to res judicata effect on that issue, and the only avenue of relief is an appeal from the judgment of the rendering court. See *Parsons Steel, Inc. v. First Alabama Bank*, infra p. 1128. As seen in *Fauntleroy v. Lum*, erroneous judgments on the merits, by a court with jurisdiction over the person and the subject matter, are entitled to full faith and credit.

Where there are inconsistent judgments, the later judgment is entitled to full faith and credit, not the earlier one. Valley National Bank of Arizona v. A.E. Rouse & Co., 121 F.3d 1332 (9th Cir. 1997). The failure of the second judgment to give full faith and credit to the first judgment is res judicata on that issue and may be corrected only on appeal from the second judgment. See Treinies v. Sunshine Mining Co., 308 U.S. 66, 60 S.Ct. 44, 84 L.Ed. 85 (1939); *Parsons Steel*, infra p. 1128. See also, Ruth Bader Ginsburg, Judgments in Search of Full Faith and Credit: The Last-in-Time Rule for Conflicting Judgments, 82 Harv. L.Rev. 798 (1969).

2.   Enforcement of judgments. A domestic judgment is enforced by a writ of execution issued by the courts of the state in which the judgment was rendered. A judgment of another state, however, traditionally could not be enforced directly by a domestic writ of execution; rather, the judgment creditor had to bring an independent action based on the foreign judgment in order to obtain a domestic judgment, which then could be enforced by a writ of execution. To eliminate the delays and technicalities of this procedure, many states have adopted the Uniform Enforcement of Foreign Judgments Act, 13 U.L.A. 152 (Master ed. 1986), or a similar act. The pertinent sections of the Uniform Act provide:

§ 1. Definition.

In this Act "foreign judgment" means any judgment, decree, or order of a court of the United States or of any other court which is entitled to full faith and credit in this state.

§ 2. Filing and Status of Foreign Judgments.

A copy of any foreign judgment authenticated in accordance with the act of Congress or the statutes of this state may be filed in the office of the Clerk of any [District Court of any city or county] of this state. The Clerk shall treat the foreign judgment in the same manner as a judgment of the [District Court of any city or county] of this state. A judgment so filed has the same effect and is subject to the same procedures, defenses and proceedings for reopening, vacating, or staying as a judgment of a [District Court of any city or county] of this state and may be enforced or satisfied in like manner.

§ 3. Notice of Filing.

(a) At the time of the filing of the foreign judgment, the judgment creditor or his lawyer shall make and file with the Clerk of Court an affidavit setting forth the name and last known post office address of the judgment debtor, and the judgment creditor.

(b) Promptly upon the filing of the foreign judgment and the affidavit, the Clerk shall mail notice of the filing of the foreign judgment to the judgment debtor at the address given and shall make a note of the mailing in the docket. The notice shall include the name and post office address of the judgment creditor and the judgment creditor's lawyer, if any, in this state. In addition, the judgment creditor may mail a notice of the filing of the judgment to the judgment debtor and may file proof of mailing with the Clerk. Lack of mailing notice of filing by the Clerk shall not affect the enforcement proceedings if proof of mailing by the judgment creditor has been filed.

* * *

§ 4. Stay.

(a) If the judgment debtor shows the [District Court of any city or county] that an appeal from the foreign judgment is pending or will be taken, or that a stay of execution has been granted, the court shall stay enforcement of the foreign judgment until the appeal is concluded, the time for appeal expires, or the stay of execution expires or is vacated, upon proof that the judgment debtor has furnished the security for the satisfaction of the judgment required by the state in which it was rendered.

* * *

§ 6. Optional Procedure.

The right of a judgment creditor to bring an action to enforce his judgment instead of proceeding under this Act remains unimpaired.

On the general problems of enforcing a foreign judgment, see P. Hay, P. Borchers, and S. Symeonides, Conflict of Laws § 24.12 (5th ed. 2010).

2. STATE-FEDERAL AND FEDERAL-STATE RECOGNITION OF JUDGMENTS

Marrese v. American Academy of Orthopaedic Surgeons

Supreme Court of the United States, 1985.
470 U.S. 373, 105 S.Ct. 1327, 84 L.Ed.2d 274.

■ JUSTICE O'CONNOR delivered the opinion of the Court.

This case concerns the preclusive effect of a state court judgment in a subsequent lawsuit involving federal antitrust claims within the exclusive jurisdiction of the federal courts. The Court of Appeals for the Seventh Circuit, sitting en banc, held as a matter of federal law that the earlier state court judgments barred the federal antitrust suit. 726 F.2d 1150 (1984). * * *

I

Petitioners are board-certified orthopaedic surgeons who applied for membership in respondent American Academy of Orthopaedic Surgeons (Academy). Respondent denied the membership applications without providing a hearing or a statement of reasons. In November 1976, petitioner Dr. Treister filed suit in the Circuit Court of Cook County, State of Illinois, alleging that the denial of membership in the Academy violated associational rights protected by Illinois common law. Petitioner Dr. Marrese separately filed a similar action in state court. Neither petitioner alleged a violation of state antitrust law in his state court action; nor did either petitioner contemporaneously file a federal antitrust suit. The Illinois Appellate Court ultimately held that Dr. Treister's complaint failed to state a cause of action, Treister v. American Academy of Orthopaedic Surgeons, 78 Ill.App.3d 746, 33 Ill.Dec. 501, 396 N.E.2d 1225 (1979), and the Illinois Supreme Court denied leave to appeal. 79 Ill.2d 630 (1980). After the Appellate Court ruled against Dr. Treister, the Circuit Court dismissed Dr. Marrese's complaint.

In March 1980, petitioners filed a federal antitrust suit in the United States District Court for the Northern District of Illinois based on the same events underlying their unsuccessful state court actions. As amended, the complaint alleged that respondent Academy possesses monopoly power, that petitioners were denied membership in order to discourage competition, and that their exclusion constituted a boycott in violation of § 1 of the Sherman Act, 15 U.S.C. § 1. Respondent filed a motion to dismiss arguing that claim preclusion barred the federal antitrust claim because the earlier state court actions concerned the same facts and were dismissed with prejudice.[1] In denying this motion, the District Court reasoned that state courts lack jurisdiction over federal antitrust claims, and therefore a state court judgment cannot have claim preclusive effect in a subsequent federal antitrust suit. * * * In a divided vote, the Court of Appeals held that claim preclusion barred the federal antitrust suit * * *. 726 F.2d 1150 (C.A.7 1984).

* * *

III

The issue presented by this case is whether a state court judgment may have preclusive effect on a federal antitrust claim that could not have been raised in the state proceeding. Although federal antitrust claims are within the exclusive jurisdiction of the federal courts, see, e.g., General Investment Co. v. Lake Shore & M.S.R. Co., 260 U.S. 261, 286–288, 43 S.Ct. 106, 116–117, 67 L.Ed. 244 (1922), the Court of Appeals ruled that the dismissal of petitioners' complaints in state court barred them from bringing a claim based on the same facts under the Sherman Act. The Court of Appeals erred by suggesting that in these

---

[1] In this opinion we use the term "claim preclusion" to refer to "res judicata" in a narrow sense, i.e., the preclusive effect of a judgment in foreclosing litigation of matters that should have been raised in an earlier suit. In contrast, we use the term "issue preclusion" to refer to the effect of a judgment in foreclosing relitigation of a matter that has been litigated and decided. See Migra v. Warren City School Dist. Bd. of Ed., 465 U.S. 75, 77, n. 1, 104 S.Ct. 892, 894, n. 1, 79 L.Ed.2d 56 (1984).

circumstances a federal court should determine the preclusive effect of a state court judgment without regard to the law of the State in which judgment was rendered.

The preclusive effect of a state court judgment in a subsequent federal lawsuit generally is determined by the full faith and credit statute, which provides that state judicial proceedings "shall have the same full faith and credit in every court within the United States . . . as they have by law or usage in the courts of such State . . . from which they are taken." 28 U.S.C. § 1738. This statute directs a federal court to refer to the preclusion law of the State in which judgment was rendered. "It has long been established that § 1738 does not allow federal courts to employ their own rules of res judicata in determining the effect of state judgments. Rather, it goes beyond the common law and commands a federal court to accept the rules chosen by the State from which the judgment is taken." Kremer v. Chemical Construction Corp., 456 U.S. 461, 481–482, 102 S.Ct. 1883, 1897, 72 L.Ed.2d 262 (1982); see also Allen v. McCurry, 449 U.S. 90, 96, 101 S.Ct. 411, 415, 66 L.Ed.2d 308 (1980). Section 1738 embodies concerns of comity and federalism that allow the States to determine, subject to the requirements of the statute and the Due Process Clause, the preclusive effect of judgments in their own courts. See Kremer, supra, 456 U.S., at 478, 481–483, 102 S.Ct., at 1897–1898. Cf. Riley v. New York Trust Co., 315 U.S. 343, 349, 62 S.Ct. 608, 612, 86 L.Ed. 885 (1942) (discussing preclusive effect of state judgment in proceedings in another State).

The fact that petitioners' antitrust claim is within the exclusive jurisdiction of the federal courts does not necessarily make § 1738 inapplicable to this case. Our decisions indicate that a state court judgment may in some circumstances have preclusive effect in a subsequent action within the exclusive jurisdiction of the federal courts. Without discussing § 1738, this Court has held that the issue preclusive effect of a state court judgment barred a subsequent patent suit that could not have been brought in state court. Becher v. Contoure Laboratories, Inc., 279 U.S. 388, 49 S.Ct. 356, 73 L.Ed. 752 (1929). Moreover, Kremer held that § 1738 applies to a claim of employment discrimination under Title VII of the Civil Rights Act of 1964, 78 Stat. 253, as amended, 42 U.S.C. § 2000e et seq., although the Court expressly declined to decide whether Title VII claims can be brought only in federal courts. 456 U.S., at 479, n. 20, 102 S.Ct., at 1896, n. 20. Kremer implies that absent an exception to § 1738, state law determines at least the issue preclusive effect of a prior state judgment in a subsequent action involving a claim within the exclusive jurisdiction of the federal courts.

More generally, Kremer indicates that § 1738 requires a federal court to look first to state preclusion law in determining the preclusive effects of a state court judgment. Cf. Haring v. Prosise, 462 U.S. 306, 314, and n. 8, 103 S.Ct. 2368, 2373, and n. 8, 76 L.Ed.2d 595 (1983); Smith, Full Faith and Credit and Section 1983: A Reappraisal, 63 N.C.L.Rev. 59, 110–111 (1984). The Court's analysis in Kremer began with the finding that state law would in fact bar relitigation of the discrimination issue decided in the earlier state proceedings. That finding implied that the plaintiff could not relitigate the same issue in federal court unless some exception to § 1738 applied. Kremer observed that "an exception to § 1738 will not be recognized unless a later statute contains an express or implied repeal." Title VII does not expressly repeal § 1738, and the Court concluded that the statutory provisions and legislative history do not support a finding of implied repeal. We conclude that the basic approach adopted in *Kremer* applies in a lawsuit involving a claim within the exclusive jurisdiction of the federal courts.

To be sure, a state court will not have occasion to address the specific question whether a state judgment has issue or claim preclusive effect in a later action that can be brought only in federal court. Nevertheless, a federal court may rely in the first instance on state preclusion principles to determine the extent to which an earlier state judgment bars subsequent litigation. Cf. FDIC v. Eckhardt, 691 F.2d 245, 247–248 (C.A.6 1982) (applying state law to determine preclusive effect on claim within concurrent jurisdiction of state and federal courts). *Kremer* illustrates that a federal court can apply state rules of issue preclusion to determine if a matter actually litigated in state court may be relitigated in a subsequent federal proceeding.

With respect to matters that were not decided in the state proceedings, we note that claim preclusion generally does not apply where "[t]he plaintiff was unable to reply on a certain theory of the case or to seek a certain remedy because of the limitations on the subject matter jurisdiction of the courts. . . ." Restatement (Second) of Judgments § 26(1)(c) (1982). If state preclusion law includes this requirement of prior jurisdictional competency, which is generally true, a state judgment will *not* have claim preclusive effect on a cause of action within the exclusive jurisdiction of the federal courts. Even in the event that a party asserting the affirmative defense of claim preclusion can show that state preclusion rules in some circumstances bar a claim outside the jurisdiction of the court that rendered the initial judgment, the federal court should first consider whether application of the state rules would bar the particular federal claim.

Reference to state preclusion law may make it unnecessary to determine if the federal court, as an exception to § 1738, should refuse to give preclusive effect to a state court judgment. The issue whether there is an exception to § 1738 arises only if state law indicates that litigation of a particular claim or issue should be barred in the subsequent federal proceeding. To the extent that state preclusion law indicates that a judgment normally does not have claim preclusive effect as to matters that the court lacked jurisdiction to entertain, lower courts and commentators have correctly concluded that a state court judgment does not bar a subsequent federal antitrust claim. See 726 F.2d, at 1174 (Cudahy, J., dissenting) (citing cases); 692 F.2d, at 1099 (Stewart, J., dissenting); Restatement, supra, § 25(1), Comment e; id. § 26(1)(c), Illustration 2; 18 C. Wright, A. Miller, & E. Cooper, Federal Practice and Procedure § 4470, pp. 687–688 (1981). Unless application of Illinois preclusion law suggests, contrary to the usual view, that petitioners' federal antitrust claim is somehow barred, there will be no need to decide in this case if there is an exception to § 1738.[3]

---

[3] The Chief Justice notes that preclusion rules bar the splitting of a cause of action between a court of limited jurisdiction and one of general jurisdiction, and suggests that state requirements of jurisdictional competency may leave unclear whether a state court action precludes a subsequent federal antitrust claim. * * * The rule that the judgment of a court of limited jurisdiction concludes the entire claim assumes that the plaintiff might have commenced

The Court of Appeals did not apply the approach to § 1738 that we have outlined. Both the plurality opinion, see 726 F.2d, at 1154, and the concurring opinion, see id., at 1163–1164 (Flaum, J.), express the view that § 1738 allows a federal court to give a state court judgment greater preclusive effect than the state courts themselves would give to it. This proposition, however, was rejected by Migra v. Warren City School Dist. Bd. of Ed., 465 U.S. 75, 104 S.Ct. 892, 79 L.Ed.2d 56 (1984), a case decided shortly after the Court of Appeals announced its decision in the instant case. In *Migra,* a discharged schoolteacher filed suit under 42 U.S.C. § 1983 in federal court after she prevailed in state court on a contract claim involving the same underlying events. The Federal District Court dismissed the § 1983 action as barred by claim preclusion. The opinion of this Court emphasized that under § 1738, state law determined the preclusive effect of the state judgment. Because it was unclear from the record whether the District Court's ruling was based on state preclusion law, we remanded for clarification on this point. Such a remand obviously would have been unnecessary were a federal court free to give greater preclusive effect to a state court judgment than would the judgment-rendering State. See id., at 88, 104 S.Ct., at 900 (WHITE, J., concurring).

We are unwilling to create a special exception to § 1738 for federal antitrust claims that would give state court judgments greater preclusive effect than would the courts of the State rendering the judgment. Cf. Haring v. Prosise, 462 U.S., at 317–318, 103 S.Ct., at 2375 (refusing to create special preclusion rule for § 1983 claim subsequent to plaintiff's guilty plea). The plurality opinion for the Court of Appeals relied on Federated Department Stores, Inc. v. Moitie, 452 U.S. 394, 101 S.Ct. 2424, 69 L.Ed.2d 103 (1981), to observe that the doctrine of claim preclusion protects defendants from repetitive lawsuits based on the same conduct, 726 F.2d, at 1152, and that there is a practical need to require plaintiffs "to litigate their claims in an economical and parsimonious fashion." We agree that these are valid and important concerns, and we note that under § 1738 state issue preclusion law may promote the goals of repose and conservation of judicial resources by preventing the relitigation of certain issues in a subsequent federal proceeding. See *Kremer,* 456 U.S., at 485, 102 S.Ct., at 1899 (state judgment barred subsequent Title VII action in federal court).

If we had a single system of courts and our only concerns were efficiency and finality, it might be desirable to fashion claim preclusion rules that would require a plaintiff to bring suit initially in the forum of most general jurisdiction, thereby resolving as many issues as possible in one proceeding. See Restatement (Second) of Judgments § 24 Comment *g* (1982); C. Wright, A. Miller, & E. Cooper, supra, § 4407, p.

---

his action in a court *in the same system of courts* that was competent to give full relief. See Restatement (Second) of Judgments § 24, Comment *g* (1982). Moreover, the jurisdictional competency requirement generally is understood to imply that state court litigation based on a state statute analogous to a federal statute, e.g., a state antitrust law, does not bar subsequent attempts to secure relief in federal court if the state court lacked jurisdiction over the federal statutory claim. Id. § 26(1)(c), Illustration 2. Although a particular State's preclusion principles conceivably could support a rule similar to that proposed by The Chief Justice, * * * where state preclusion rules do not indicate that a claim is barred, we do not believe that federal courts should fashion a federal rule to preclude a claim that could not have been raised in the state proceedings.

51; id. § 4412, p. 93. The decision of the Court of Appeals approximates such a rule inasmuch as it encourages plaintiffs to file suit initially in federal district court and to attempt to bring any state law claims pendent to their federal antitrust claims. Whether this result would reduce the overall burden of litigation is debatable, see 726 F.2d, at 1181–1182 (Cudahy, J., dissenting); C. Wright, A. Miller, & E. Cooper, supra, § 4407, pp. 51–52, and we decline to base our interpretation of § 1738 on our opinion on this question.

More importantly, we have parallel systems of state and federal courts, and the concerns of comity reflected in § 1738 generally allow States to determine the preclusive scope of their own courts' judgments. See *Kremer,* 456 U.S., at 481–482, 102 S.Ct., at 1897; Allen v. McCurry, 449 U.S., at 96, 101 S.Ct., at 415; cf. Currie, Res Judicata: The Neglected Defense, 45 U.Chi.L.Rev. 317, 327 (1978) (state policies may seek to limit preclusive effect of state court judgment). These concerns certainly are not made less compelling because state courts lack jurisdiction over federal antitrust claims. We therefore reject a judicially created exception to § 1738 that effectively holds as a matter of federal law that a plaintiff can bring state law claims initially in state court only at the cost of forgoing subsequent federal antitrust claims. Federated Department Stores, Inc. v. Moitie does not suggest a contrary conclusion. That case did not involve § 1738; rather it held that "accepted principles of res judicata" determine the preclusive effect of a federal court judgment.

In this case the Court of Appeals should have first referred to Illinois law to determine the preclusive effect of the state judgment. Only if state law indicates that a particular claim or issue would be barred, is it necessary to determine if an exception to § 1738 should apply. Although for purposes of this case, we need not decide if such an exception exists for federal antitrust claims, we observe that the more general question is whether the concerns underlying a particular grant of exclusive jurisdiction justify a finding of an implied partial repeal of § 1738. Resolution of this question will depend on the particular federal statute as well as the nature of the claim or issue involved in the subsequent federal action. Our previous decisions indicate that the primary consideration must be the intent of Congress. See *Kremer,* 456 U.S., at 470–476, 102 S.Ct., at 1891–1894 (finding no congressional intent to depart from § 1738 for purposes of Title VII); cf. Brown v. Felsen, 442 U.S. 127, 138, 99 S.Ct. 2205, 2212, 60 L.Ed.2d 767 (1979) (finding congressional intent that state judgments would not have claim preclusive effect on dischargeability issue in bankruptcy).

* * * Before this Court, the parties have continued to disagree about the content of Illinois preclusion law. We believe that this dispute is best resolved in the first instance by the District Court.

* * *

The judgment of the Court of Appeals is reversed, and the case is remanded for further proceedings consistent with this opinion.

It is so ordered.

■ JUSTICE BLACKMUN and JUSTICE STEVENS took no part in the consideration or decision of this case.

■ CHIEF JUSTICE BURGER, concurring in the judgment.

I agree with the Court's implicit conclusion that the Court of Appeals approached 28 U.S.C. § 1738 too narrowly and technically by holding it irrelevant on the ground that Illinois law does not address the preclusive effect of a state court judgment on a federal antitrust suit. * * *

* * * The principles of Illinois res judicata doctrine appear to be indeterminate as to whether petitioners' ability to raise state antitrust claims in their prior state court suits should preclude their assertion of essentially the same claims in the present federal action. This indeterminancy arises from the fact that the Illinois courts have not addressed whether the notion of "questions which could have been raised" should be applied narrowly or broadly. No Illinois court has considered how the jurisdictional competency requirement should apply in the type of situation presented by this case, where the same theory of recovery may be asserted under different statutes. Nor has any Illinois court considered whether res judicata precludes splitting a cause of action between a court of limited jurisdiction and one of general jurisdiction.[3]

Hence it is likely that the principles of Illinois claim preclusion law do not speak to the preclusive effect that petitioners' state court judgments should have on the present action. In this situation, it may be consistent with § 1738 for a federal court to formulate a federal rule to resolve the matter. If state law is simply indeterminate, the concerns of comity and federalism underlying § 1738 do not come into play. At the same time, the federal courts have direct interests in ensuring that their resources are used efficiently and not as a means of harassing defendants with repetitive lawsuits, as well as in ensuring that parties asserting federal rights have an adequate opportunity to litigate those rights. Given the insubstantiality of the state interests and the weight of the federal interests, a strong argument could be made that a federal rule would be more appropriate than a creative interpretation of ambiguous state law.[4] When state law is indeterminate or ambiguous, a clear federal

---

[3]   Compare Restatement (Second) of Judgments § 24, comment g, illus. 14:

"In an automobile collision, A is injured and his car damaged as a result of the negligence of B. Instead of suing in a court of general jurisdiction of the state, A brings his action for the damage to his car in a justice's court, which has jurisdiction in actions for damage to property but has no jurisdiction in actions for injury to the person. Judgment is rendered for A for the damage to the car. A cannot thereafter maintain an action against B to recover for the injury to his person arising out of the same collision."

See also 18 C. Wright, A. Miller, & E. Cooper, Federal Practice and Procedure § 4412, p. 95 (1981), stating that the "general rule" in state courts is that "[a] second action will not be permitted on parts of a single claim that could have been asserted in a court of broader jurisdiction simply because the plaintiff went first to a court of limited jurisdiction in the same state that could not hear them." The holding in Lucas v. Le Compte, 42 Ill. 303 (1866), is similar to this "general rule," but that holding was based on a construction of an Illinois statute, Ill.Rev.Stat., ch. 59, § 35 (1845), which (a) has been repealed, see Act of Apr. 15, 1965, 1965 Ill.Laws 331, and (b) had a broader preclusive effect than general Illinois res judicata doctrine has. Clancey v. McBride, 338 Ill. 35, 169 N.E. 729 (1929), involved the same circumstances as the above-quoted illustration from the Restatement. The court resolved the case, however, without reference to the limited jurisdiction of the justice's court, by concluding that injury to the person and injury to property are distinct legal wrongs that can be the subject of separate lawsuits.

[4]   By contrast, when a federal court construes substantive rights and obligations under state law in the context of a diversity action, the federal interest is insignificant and the state's

rule would promote substantive interests as well: "Uncertainty intrinsically works to defeat the opportunities for repose and reliance sought by the rules of preclusion, and confounds the desire for efficiency by inviting repetitious litigation to test the preclusive effects of the first effort." 18 C. Wright, A. Miller, & E. Cooper, supra, n. 3, § 4407, at 49.

A federal rule might be fashioned from the test, which this Court has applied in other contexts, that a party is precluded from asserting a claim that he had a "full and fair opportunity" to litigate in a prior action. See, e.g., Kremer v. Chemical Construction Corp., 456 U.S. 461, 485, 102 S.Ct. 1883, 1899, 72 L.Ed.2d 262 (1982); Allen v. McCurry, 449 U.S. 90, 95, 101 S.Ct. 411, 415, 66 L.Ed.2d 308 (1980); Montana v. United States, 440 U.S. 147, 153, 99 S.Ct. 970, 973, 59 L.Ed.2d 210 (1979); Blonder-Tongue Laboratories, Inc. v. University of Illinois Foundation, 402 U.S. 313, 328, 91 S.Ct. 1434, 1442, 28 L.Ed.2d 788 (1971). Thus, if a state statute is identical in all material respects with a federal statute within exclusive federal jurisdiction, a party's ability to assert a claim under the state statute in a prior state court action might be said to have provided, in effect, a "full and fair opportunity" to litigate his rights under the federal statute. Cf. Derish v. San Mateo-Burlingame Board of Realtors, 724 F.2d 1347 (C.A.9 1983); Nash County Board of Education v. Biltmore Co., 640 F.2d 484 (CA4), cert. denied, 454 U.S. 878, 102 S.Ct. 359, 70 L.Ed.2d 188 (1981).

The Court will eventually have to face these questions; I would resolve them now.

Parsons Steel, Inc. v. First Alabama Bank

Supreme Court of the United States, 1986.
474 U.S. 518, 106 S.Ct. 768, 88 L.Ed.2d 877.

■ JUSTICE REHNQUIST delivered the opinion of the Court.

* * *

Petitioners Parsons Steel, Inc., and Jim and Melba Parsons sued respondents First Alabama Bank of Montgomery and Edward Herbert, a bank officer, in Alabama state court in February 1979, essentially alleging that the bank had fraudulently induced the Parsons to permit a third person to take control of a subsidiary of Parsons Steel and eventually to obtain complete ownership of the subsidiary. The subsidiary was adjudicated an involuntary bankrupt in April 1979, and the trustee in bankruptcy was added as a party plaintiff in the state action. In May 1979 Parsons Steel and the Parsons sued the bank in the United States District Court for the District of Alabama, alleging that the same conduct on the part of the bank that was the subject of the state-court suit also violated the Bank Holding Company Act (BHCA) amendments, 12 U.S.C. §§ 1971–1978. The trustee in bankruptcy chose not to participate in the federal action.

The parties conducted joint discovery in the federal and state actions. The federal action proceeded to trial on the issue of liability before the state action went to trial. A jury returned a verdict in favor of

---

interest is much more direct than it is in the present situation, even if the relevant state law is ambiguous.

petitioners, but the District Court granted judgment n.o.v. to the bank. That judgment was affirmed on appeal. Parsons Steel, Inc. v. First Alabama Bank of Montgomery, 679 F.2d 242 (C.A.11 1982). After the federal judgment was entered, respondents pleaded in the state action the defenses of res judicata and collateral estoppel based on that judgment. The Alabama court, however, ruled that res judicata did not bar the state action. Almost a year after the federal judgment was entered, the state complaint was amended to include a Uniform Commercial Code (UCC) claim that the bank's foreclosure sale of the subsidiary's assets was commercially unreasonable. A jury returned a general verdict in favor of petitioners, awarding a total of four million and one dollars in damages.

Having lost in state court, respondents returned to the District Court that had previously entered judgment in the bank's favor and filed the present injunctive action against petitioners, the plaintiffs in the state action. The District Court found that the federal BHCA suit and the state action were based on the same factual allegations and claimed substantially the same damages. The court held that the state claims should have been raised in the federal action as pendent to the BHCA claim and accordingly that the BHCA judgment barred the state claims under res judicata. Determining that the Alabama judgment in effect nullified the earlier federal-court judgment in favor of the bank, the District Court enjoined petitioners from further prosecuting the state action.

A divided panel of the Court of Appeals affirmed in relevant part, holding that the issuance of the injunction was not "an abuse of discretion" by the District Court. 747 F.2d 1367, 1381 (1984). The majority first agreed with the District Court that the fraud and UCC claims presented issues of fact and law that could have been and should have been raised in the same action as the BHCA claim. Thus the parties to the BHCA action and their privies, including the trustee in bankruptcy, were barred by res judicata from raising these claims in state court after the entry of the federal judgment.

The majority then held that the injunction was proper under the so-called "relitigation exception" to the Anti-Injunction Act, 28 U.S.C. § 2283, which provides:

> "A court of the United States may not grant an injunction to stay proceedings in a State court except as expressly authorized by Act of Congress, or where necessary in aid of its jurisdiction, or *to protect or effectuate its judgments*"(emphasis added).

In reaching this holding, the majority explicitly declined to consider the possible preclusive effect, pursuant to the Full Faith and Credit Act, 28 U.S.C. § 1738,[2] of the state court's determination after full litigation by the parties that the earlier federal-court judgment did not bar the state action. According to the majority, "while a federal court is generally bound by other state court determinations, the relitigation exception empowers a federal court to be the final adjudicator as to the *res judicata*

---

[2]   The Full Faith and Credit Act provides, in pertinent part, that state judicial proceedings "shall have the same full faith and credit in every court within the United States . . . as they have by law or usage in the courts of such State . . . from which they are taken."

effects of its prior judgments on a subsequent state action." 747 F.2d, at 1376 (footnote omitted).

Finally, the majority ruled that respondents had not waived their right to an injunction by waiting until after the trial in the state action was completed. The majority concluded that the state-court pleadings were so vague that it was not clear until after trial that essentially the same cause of action was involved as the BHCA claim and that the earlier federal judgment was in danger of being nullified. According to the majority, the Anti-Injunction Act does not limit the power of a federal court to protect its judgment "to specific points in time in state court trials or appellate procedure." Id., at 1377.

* * *

In our view, the majority of the Court of Appeals gave unwarrantedly short shrift to the important values of federalism and comity embodied in the Full Faith and Credit Act. As recently as last March, in Marrese v. American Academy of Orthopaedic Surgeons, 470 U.S. 373, 105 S.Ct. 1327, 84 L.Ed.2d 274 (1985), we reaffirmed our holding in Migra v. Warren City School Dist. Bd. of Education, 465 U.S. 75, 104 S.Ct. 892, 79 L.Ed.2d 56 (1984), that under the Full Faith and Credit Act a federal court must give the same preclusive effect to a state-court judgment as another court of that State would give. "It has long been established that § 1738 does not allow federal courts to employ their own rules of res judicata in determining the effect of state judgments. Rather, it goes beyond the common law and commands a federal court to accept the rules chosen by the State from which the judgment is taken." Kremer v. Chemical Construction Corp., 456 U.S. 461, 481–482, 102 S.Ct. 1883, 1898, 72 L.Ed.2d 262 (1982). The Full Faith and Credit Act thus "allow[s] the States to determine, subject to the requirements of the statute and the Due Process Clause, the preclusive effect of judgments in their own courts." Marrese, supra, at 380, 105 S.Ct. at 1332.

In the instant case, however, the Court of Appeals did not consider the possible preclusive effect under Alabama law of the state-court judgment, and particularly of the state court's resolution of the res judicata issue, concluding instead that the relitigation exception to the Anti-Injunction Act limits the Full Faith and Credit Act. We do not agree. "[A]n exception to § 1738 will not be recognized unless a later statute contains an express or implied partial repeal." Kremer, supra, at 468, 102 S.Ct., at 1890; Allen v. McCurry, 449 U.S. 90, 99, 101 S.Ct. 411, 417, 66 L.Ed.2d 308 (1980). Here, as in Kremer, there is no claim of an express repeal; rather, the Court of Appeals found an implied repeal. " 'It is, of course, a cardinal principle of statutory construction that repeals by implication are not favored,' Radzanower v. Touche Ross & Co., 426 U.S. 148, 154 [96 S.Ct. 1989, 1993, 48 L.Ed.2d 540] (1976); United States v. United Continental Tuna Corp., 425 U.S. 164, 168 [96 S.Ct. 1319, 1323, 47 L.Ed.2d 653] (1976), and whenever possible, statutes should be read consistently." 456 U.S., at 468, 102 S.Ct., at 1890. We believe that the Anti-Injunction Act and the Full Faith and Credit Act can be construed consistently, simply by limiting the relitigation exception of the Anti-Injunction Act to those situations in which the state court has not yet ruled on the merits of the res judicata issue. Once the state court has finally rejected a claim of res judicata, then the Full Faith and Credit Act becomes applicable and federal courts must turn to state law to determine the preclusive effect of the state court's decision.

The contrary holding of the Court of Appeals apparently was based on the fact that Congress in 1948 amended the Anti-Injunction Act to overrule this Court's decision in Toucey v. New York Life Insurance Co., 314 U.S. 118, 62 S.Ct. 139, 86 L.Ed. 100 (1941), in favor of the understanding of prior law expressed in Justice Reed's dissenting opinion. See Revisor's Note to 1948 Revision of Anti-Injunction Act, 28 U.S.C., p. 377. But the instant case is a far cry from *Toucey,* and one may fully accept the logic of Justice Reed's dissent without concluding that it sanctions the result reached by the Court of Appeals here. In each of the several cases involved in *Toucey,* the prevailing party in the federal action sought an injunction against relitigation in state court as soon as the opposing party commenced the state action, and before there was any resolution of the res judicata issue by the state court. In the instant case, on the other hand, respondents chose to fight out the res judicata issue in state court first, and only after losing there did they return to federal court for another try.

The Court of Appeals also felt that the District Court's injunction would discourage inefficient simultaneous litigation in state and federal courts on the same issue—that is, the res judicata effect of the prior federal judgment. But this is one of the costs of our dual court system:

> "In short, the state and federal courts had concurrent jurisdiction in this case, and neither court was free to prevent either party from simultaneously pursuing claims in both courts." Atlantic Coast Line R. Co. v. Locomotive Engineers, 398 U.S. 281, 295, 90 S.Ct. 1739, 1747, 26 L.Ed.2d 234 (1970).

* * *

We hold, therefore, that the Court of Appeals erred by refusing to consider the possible preclusive effect, under Alabama law, of the state-court judgment. Even if the state court mistakenly rejected respondents' claim of res judicata, this does not justify the highly intrusive remedy of a federal-court injunction against the enforcement of the state-court judgment. Rather, the Full Faith and Credit Act requires that federal courts give the state court judgment, and particularly the state court's resolution of the res judicata issue, the same preclusive effect it would have had in another court of the same State. Challenges to the correctness of a state court's determination as to the conclusive effect of a federal judgment must be pursued by way of appeal through the state-court system and certiorari from this Court. See Angel v. Bullington, 330 U.S. 183, 67 S.Ct. 657, 91 L.Ed. 832 (1947).

We think the District Court is best situated to determine and apply Alabama preclusion law in the first instance. Should the District Court conclude that the state-court judgment is not entitled to preclusive effect under Alabama law and the Full Faith and Credit Act, it would then be in the best position to decide the propriety of a federal-court injunction under the general principles of equity, comity, and federalism discussed in Mitchum v. Foster, 407 U.S. 225, 243, 92 S.Ct. 2151, 2162, 32 L.Ed.2d 705 (1972).

The judgment of the Court of Appeals is reversed, and the case is remanded for further proceedings consistent with this opinion.

NOTE ON INTERJURISDICTIONAL PRECLUSION

1.   State-federal and federal-state preclusion. When the first suit is in the court of one state and the second suit in the court of another state, the Full Faith and Credit Clause of the Constitution dictates the preclusive effect of the judgment rendered by the court of the first state. See *Fauntleroy v. Lum* and Note on Full Faith and Credit, supra p. 1116. We can call these instances of state-state recognition. What about situations where the first suit is in state court and the second in federal court (state-federal preclusion)? What about situations where the first suit is in federal court and the second in state court (federal-state preclusion)?

a.   State-federal preclusion. As seen in *Marrese* and *Parsons Steel*, state-federal preclusion is governed by the federal Full Faith and Credit Act, 28 U.S.C. § 1738. Those cases show the strictness with which the federal courts adhere to the statutory language, holding that there are no implied exceptions (*Marrese*), not even for an erroneous failure to honor a prior federal judgment (*Parsons Steel*). Section 1738 has been construed to require that the federal court in the second case give precisely the same preclusive effect the rendering state court would have given had the second case been brought in a court of that state, no more and no less. See, e.g., Migra v. Warren City School District Bd. of Education, 465 U.S. 75, 81, 104 S.Ct. 892, 79 L.Ed.2d 56 (1984) ("It is now settled that a federal court must give to a state court judgment the same preclusive effect as would be given that judgment under the law of the State in which the judgment was rendered."); Kremer v. Chemical Construction Corp., 456 U.S. 461, 466, 102 S.Ct. 1883, 72 L.Ed.2d 262 (1982) ("Section 1738 requires federal courts to give the same preclusive effect to state court judgments that those judgments would be given in the courts of the State from which the judgments emerged.").

The Supreme Court has expanded *Marrese* beyond litigated judgments to include court-approved settlements. In Matsushita Electric Industrial Co. v. Epstein, 516 U.S. 367, 373, 116 S.Ct. 873, 878, 134 L.Ed.2d 6 (1996), a disputed tender offer and corporate acquisition resulted in two shareholder class actions, one in state court and one in federal court. The state court action, filed in Delaware, was based on state law, and the federal court action was based on federal securities laws. Suits based on federal securities laws are within the exclusive jurisdiction of the federal courts. The state court suit was terminated first, in a judgment incorporating a court-approved settlement. The settlement purported to resolve all state and federal claims against the defendants even though the state court did not have (and indeed could not have had) the federal claims before it. The Supreme Court held that the state court settlement was entitled to whatever preclusive effect the Delaware courts would have given it. "[W]e conclude that § 1738 is generally applicable in cases in which the state court judgment at issue incorporates a class action settlement releasing claims solely within the jurisdiction of the federal courts." The Court then analyzed Delaware law and concluded that if otherwise valid the settlement was preclusive as to both the state and federal claims. For discussion, see Kahan and Silberman, *Matsushita* and Beyond: The Role of State Courts in Class Actions Involving Exclusive Federal Claims, 1996 Sup.Ct.Rev. 219.

In Baker v. General Motors Corp., 522 U.S. 222, 118 S.Ct. 657, 139 L.Ed.2d 580 (1998), the Supreme Court held that 28 U.S.C. § 1738 does not require a federal court to obey a state court decree enjoining a party from testifying in later suits. In the first suit, plaintiff Elwell sued his employer, General Motors Corporation, in Michigan state court for wrongful discharge. During fifteen of his thirty years at GM, Elwell had studied fires in GM vehicles. Elwell and GM settled the state court suit. Pursuant to the settlement, the court entered a judgment enjoining Elwell from "testifying, without the prior written consent of General Motors Corporation, either upon deposition or at trial, as an expert witness, or as a witness of any kind, and from consulting with attorneys or their agents in any litigation * * * involving General Motors Corporation[.]"

In a separate suit brought in federal district court in Missouri, plaintiffs' mother was burned to death in a General Motors vehicle. Over GM's objection, plaintiffs called Elwell as a witness. The Supreme Court held that the Michigan state court decree could not prevent Elwell from testifying:

> Michigan's judgment * * * cannot reach beyond the Elwell-GM controversy to control proceedings against GM brought in other States, by other parties, asserting claims the merits of which Michigan has not considered. Michigan has no power over those parties, and no basis for commanding them to become intervenors in the Elwell-GM dispute. * * * Most essentially, Michigan lacks authority to control courts elsewhere by precluding them, in actions brought by strangers to the Michigan litigation, from determining for themselves what witnesses are competent to testify and what evidence is relevant and admissible in their search for the truth. * * * Michigan's decree could operate against Elwell to preclude him from *volunteering* his testimony. * * * But a Michigan court cannot, by entering the injunction to which Elwell and GM stipulated, dictate to a court in another jurisdiction that evidence relevant in [this] case—a controversy to which Michigan is foreign—shall be inadmissible.

Id. at 238 (emphasis in original).

b.   Federal-state preclusion. In cases in which the first suit is brought in federal court and the second suit in state court, there is no applicable constitutional or statutory provision. In early cases, the Supreme Court appeared to believe that federal-state preclusion was governed by the federal full faith and credit statute, 28 U.S.C. § 1738. See, e.g., Embry v. Palmer, 107 U.S. 3, 2 S.Ct. 25, 27 L.Ed. 346 (1882). The Court no longer holds that view. In Semtek International, Inc. v. Lockheed Martin Corp., 531 U.S. 497, 508, 121 S.Ct. 1021, 149 L.Ed.2d 32 (2001), the Court specifically stated what had been assumed to be true: federal-state preclusion is governed by federal common law. The Court wrote in *Semtek*, "[N]o federal textual provision addresses the claim-preclusion effect of a federal-court judgment in a federal-question case, yet we have long held that States cannot give those judgments merely whatever effect they would give their own judgments, but must accord them the effect that this Court prescribes." Id. at 507.

Applying federal common law in *Semtek*, the Court distinguished between federal question and diversity cases. In federal question cases, a uniform federal common law of preclusion applies to determine the preclusive effect of the federal court's judgment. That has been the interpretation of *Semtek* in the state courts. See, e.g., Wong v. Cayetano, 111 Hawai'i 462, 143 P.3d 1, 16 (2006); Better Boating Ass'n v. BMG Chart

Products, Inc., 61 Mass.App.Ct. 542, 813 N.E.2d 851, 858 (2004). In diversity cases, federal common law dictates that it is the preclusion law of the state in which the federal court sits that applies to determine the preclusive effect of that court's judgment. The Court wrote, as to diversity cases, "Since state, rather than federal, substantive law is at issue there is no need for a uniform federal rule." 531 U.S. at 508. The Court cautioned, however, that "in situations in which the state law is incompatible with federal interests" a uniform federal rule might govern. Id. at 509.

For thoughtful academic analyses of *Semtek*, see Burbank, *Semtek*, Forum Shopping, and Federal Common Law, 77 Notre Dame L.Rev. 1027, 1042 (2002); Woolley, The Sources of Federal Preclusion Law after *Semtek*, 72 U.Cin.L.Rev. 527 (2003); Dudley and Rutherglen, Deforming the Federal Rules: An Essay on What's Wrong with the Recent *Erie* Decisions, 92 Va.L.Rev. 707 (2006).

2. Federal injunctions to "protect or effectuate" federal judgments in later state court proceedings. A federal court has the power under the federal All Writs Act, 28 U.S.C. § 1651, and the relitigation exception of the federal Anti-Injunction Act, 28 U.S.C. § 2283, to issue injunctions to "protect or effectuate its judgments."

a. Availability of federal injunction. The Supreme Court has had little hesitation in affirming or encouraging timely sought injunctions under the relitigation exception to the Anti-Injunction Act. In Chick Kam Choo v. Exxon Corp., 486 U.S. 140, 108 S.Ct. 1684, 100 L.Ed.2d 127 (1988), a federal district court dismissed several federal-law claims on the merits, held that Texas choice-of-law rules required that Singapore rather than Texas substantive law applied to another claim, and dismissed the Singapore-law claim under *forum non conveniens*. Plaintiff then refiled in Texas state court. The federal district court enjoined state court relitigation of both the *forum non conveniens* question and the choice-of-law question. The Supreme Court held that the federal district court had no authority to enjoin relitigation of the *forum non conveniens* ruling in state court because the district court had decided that question under federal law applicable only as to the federal forum, and the state court was free to decide it under Texas law as to the Texas forum. However, the Court held that the federal district court had the authority to enjoin relitigation of the choice-of-law ruling because the district court had already decided that question under Texas choice-of-law rules, just as the Texas court was now being asked to do. In Rivet v. Regions Bank of Louisiana, 522 U.S. 470, 118 S.Ct. 921, 926 n. 3, 139 L.Ed.2d 912 (1998), the Court reaffirmed the availability of a federal district court injunction under the relitigation exception.

Lower courts grant injunctions under the relitigation exception with some frequency. See, e.g., In re Dublin Securities, 133 F.3d 377 (6th Cir. 1997); In re SDDS, Inc., 97 F.3d 1030 (8th Cir. 1996); Deus v. Allstate Insurance Co., 15 F.3d 506 (5th Cir. 1994); Santopadre v. Pelican Homestead & Savings Association, 937 F.2d 268 (5th Cir. 1991); Golden v. Pacific Maritime Association, 786 F.2d 1425 (9th Cir. 1986); Bank of Heflin v. Miles, 621 F.2d 108 (5th Cir. 1980); Seaboard Coast Line R. Co. v. Union Camp Corp., 613 F.2d 604 (5th Cir. 1980). But the availability of an injunction is subject to normal equitable considerations, and its issuance is within the discretion of the district judge. As it remanded in *Chick Kam Choo*, the Supreme Court cautioned, "[T]he fact that an injunction may issue under the Anti-Injunction Act does not mean that it must issue. On remand the District

Court should decide whether it is appropriate to enter an injunction." 486 U.S. at 151.

b.   Timeliness in seeking the federal injunction. In *Parsons Steel*, the Supreme Court held that an injunction against relitigation must be timely sought in federal court. It wrote, "We believe that the Anti-Injunction Act and the Full Faith and Credit Act can be construed consistently, simply by limiting the relitigation exception of the Anti-Injunction Act to those situations in which the state court has not yet ruled on the merits of the res judicata issue. Once the state court has finally rejected a claim of res judicata, then the Full Faith and Credit Act becomes applicable[.]" What, exactly, does the Court mean? The state court might "rule" on the res judicata issue long before any judgment is rendered. The Full Faith and Credit Act, 28 U.S.C. § 1738, is ordinarily triggered by the rendering of a judgment of the state court, even though the actual wording of the Act is "proceedings" rather than "judgment." Indeed, the Supreme Court wrote later in *Parsons Steel*, "[T]he Full Faith and Credit Act requires that federal courts give the state court *judgment* * * * the same preclusive effect it would have had in another court of the same state." (Emphasis added.)

On remand in *Parsons Steel,* the district court continued its injunction against further state court proceedings on the ground the injunction had issued while post-trial motions were still pending in the state court and before any final judgment had been entered. The court of appeals affirmed. First Alabama Bank v. Parsons Steel, Inc., 825 F.2d 1475 (11th Cir. 1987), cert. denied sub nom. McGregor v. First Alabama Bank, 484 U.S. 1060, 108 S.Ct. 1015, 98 L.Ed.2d 980 (1988). Most circuits follow the approach of the Eleventh Circuit, allowing a federal court to enjoin a state court proceeding under the relitigation exception to the Anti-Injunction Act, even after the state court has ruled that it will not honor the federal court judgment, so long as the state court has not rendered a final judgment that would trigger the operation of the Full Faith and Credit Act. For example, in Bryan v. BellSouth Communications, Inc., 492 F.3d 231, 240 (4th Cir. 2007), the Fourth Circuit wrote, "[U]nder North Carolina law, the state-court order in this case denying BellSouth's motion to dismiss is not a final order and is not entitled to *res judicata* effect. * * * Accordingly, the issuance of an injunction in this case is not barred by *Parsons Steel*." See also, e.g., Duffy & McGovern Accommodation Services v. QCI Marine Offshore, Inc., 448 F.3d 825 (5th Cir. 2006); Amalgamated Sugar Co. v. NL Industries, 825 F.2d 634 (2d Cir. 1987).

However, the Seventh Circuit has adopted a different approach. In Ramsden v. AgriBank, 214 F.3d 865 (7th Cir. 2000), the court recognized that the Full Faith and Credit Act did not apply because the state court had not entered a final judgment, even though it had ruled that the federal court judgment was not entitled to preclusive effect. Therefore, the relitigation exception to the Anti-Injunction Act allowed the district court to enjoin the state court litigation. But the court nonetheless held that the federal court injunction should not issue, based on comity concerns. It wrote, "Once a state court considers a res judicata defense and rules that a prior federal judgment does not actually bar a claim, the affront of federal court intervention stripping the state court of power to continue is greatly magnified." Id. at 870. See also Brother Records, Inc. v. Jardine, 432 F.3d 939, 944 (9th Cir. 2005); Kaempfer v. Brown, 684 F.Supp. 319 (D.D.C. 1988).

A cautious litigant wanting preclusion in state court based on a federal court judgment will be well advised to seek an injunction from the federal court as an initial matter, rather than presenting the preclusion question to the state court and seeking the injunction only if the state court rules against him.

3.   International recognition. Judgments of foreign countries are not covered by either the Full Faith and Credit Clause of the Constitution or the statutory provisions of the Full Faith and Credit Act. Absent a treaty, each state in the international community may decide for itself the extent to which it will recognize a judgment of a foreign nation. This voluntary process of giving recognition is known as "comity." In general, judgments of foreign countries will be recognized if the foreign judgment was obtained in accordance with American concepts of minimal due process, namely proper jurisdiction, adequate notice, and a fair hearing. See Restatement (Third) of the Foreign Relations Law of the United States § 481 et seq. In Hilton v. Guyot, 159 U.S. 113, 16 S.Ct. 139, 40 L.Ed. 95 (1895), the Supreme Court added a reciprocity requirement, namely, that a judgment of a United States court would be recognized by the country whose judgment was presented for recognition. The reciprocity doctrine is in some disrepute today. See P. Hay, P. Borchers, and S. Simeonides, Conflict of Laws § 24.33 (5th ed. 2010).

The Uniform Money-Judgments Recognition Act, 13 U.L.A. 261 (Master ed. 1986), provides for the recognition and enforcement of money judgments of foreign nations, but lists the following grounds for non-recognition:

§ 4.   [Grounds for Non-recognition]

(a)   A foreign judgment is not conclusive if

(1)   the judgment was rendered under a system which does not provide impartial tribunals or procedures compatible with the requirements of due process of law;

(2)   the foreign court did not have personal jurisdiction over the defendant; or

(3)   the foreign court did not have jurisdiction over the subject matter.

(b)   A foreign judgment need not be recognized if

(1)   the defendant in the proceedings in the foreign court did not receive notice of the proceedings in sufficient time to enable him to defend;

(2)   the judgment was obtained by fraud;

(3)   the [cause of action] [claim for relief] on which the judgment is based is repugnant to the public policy of this state;

(4)   the judgment conflicts with another final and conclusive judgment;

(5)   the proceeding in the foreign court was contrary to an agreement between the parties under which the dispute in question was to be settled otherwise than by proceedings in that court; or

(6)   in the case of jurisdiction based only on personal service, the foreign court was a seriously inconvenient forum for the trial of the action.

The Restatement (Third) of the Foreign Relations Law of the United States, §§ 481, 482, provides for the recognition and enforcement of a money judgment of a foreign country under substantially the same criteria, with the difference that the Restatement lists lack of subject matter jurisdiction of the foreign court as a ground for the discretionary denial of recognition, while the Uniform Law lists it as a mandatory ground for denial.

4. Additional reading. An excellent analysis of state-federal preclusion problems is Erichson, Interjurisdictional Preclusion, 96 Mich.L.Rev. 945 (1998). See also Lenich, The Collateral Estoppel Effect of State Court Judgments in Federal Antitrust Actions: Unmaking the Judge-Made Law, 38 Rutgers L.Rev. 241 (1986); Corr, Supreme Court Doctrine in the Trenches: The Case of Collateral Estoppel, 27 Wm. & Mary L.Rev. 35 (1986); Symposium (on res judicata), 70 Iowa L.Rev. 13 (1984); Note, Erie and the Preclusive Effect of Federal Diversity Judgments, 85 Colum.L.Rev. 1505 (1985); Symposium, Preclusion in a Federal System, 70 Cornell L.Rev. 599 (1985).

CHAPTER 10

REVIEW OF THE DISPOSITION

INTRODUCTORY NOTE ON APPELLATE REVIEW

It has long been recognized in Anglo-American law that a person or entity against whom a final judgment has been rendered in an action involving substantial stakes should have the right to appeal to a higher court. In the American system, there are variations among the state courts and between the state and federal courts, but the general structure of appellate court systems is more or less the same for all of these courts.

The essentials of the federal court system are as follows. There are three statutorily prescribed levels of federal courts created under Article III of the Constitution—the district courts, the courts of appeals, and the Supreme Court. Article III judges are appointed for life, only subject to removal by Congress by impeachment.

The district courts are trial courts, located in all major and some mid-sized American cities. The district courts are divided into ninety-four districts. Populous states have several districts; some sparsely populated states have only one. See, e.g., the Southern District of New York (Manhattan), the Northern District of Illinois (the Chicago area), the Central District of California (the Los Angeles area), the District of New Hampshire (all of New Hampshire), and the District of Alaska (all of Alaska). With rare exceptions, district judges act alone in deciding cases. Magistrate judges, appointed for a term years by the district courts, assist the district courts in various ways. The manner in which they act depends in part on the policies of the particular district in which they sit. In some districts, with the consent of the parties, magistrate judges hear civil cases in the same manner as district judges. Bankruptcy judges, appointed for a term of years by the circuit courts, decide bankruptcy cases. District courts hear appeals from decisions of the bankruptcy judges. Neither magistrate judges nor bankruptcy judges are Article III judges.

Circuit courts of appeal hear appeals from decisions of the district courts. There are twelve geographically based circuits. Eleven of them are numbered; the twelfth is the Court of Appeals for the District of Columbia. The Ninth Circuit is largest circuit, with twenty-nine active judges and comprising Alaska, Arizona, California, Idaho, Hawai'i, Montana, Nevada, Oregon, Washington, Guam, and the Northern Mariana Islands. The First Circuit is the smallest, with six active judges and comprising Massachusetts, Rhode Island, New Hampshire, Maine, and Puerto Rico. There have been intermittent calls to divide the Ninth Circuit, on the ostensible ground that it is too big to function efficiently. In the view of one of the authors of this casebook, the Ninth Circuit functions very efficiently, precisely because of its large size. In his view, the boutique circuits on the East Coast—the First, Second and Third—should be combined into a single circuit. (This is only partly a joke.) There is one named circuit, the Court of Appeals for the Federal Circuit, whose jurisdiction is based on subject matter rather than geography. It has exclusive jurisdiction over appeals from the district courts in patent cases. Because of the small number of cases heard by the U.S.

Supreme Court, a decision by the court of appeals is almost always, in practical effect, the final decision.

Courts of appeals typically sit in panels of three judges. In a few important cases in which a three-judge panel may have reached a decision at odds with the view of the majority of the active judges on the circuit, a court of appeals may rehear the appeal *en banc*. In every circuit except the Ninth, all of the active judges on the circuit sit on the *en banc* panel. The Ninth Circuit practice is not to rehear the appeal with all twenty-nine circuit judges, although it has the legal authority to do so. Instead, it rehears cases *en banc* with panels of eleven judges—the chief judge and ten circuit judges drawn at random.

The Supreme Court reviews decisions of the federal courts of appeals, and, in rare cases, decisions of specially constituted three-judge district courts. It also reviews decisions of state supreme courts on issues of federal law. For more than a century, the Supreme Court has had nine Justices. That number is set by statute rather than by the Constitution. During its first hundred years, there were as few as five and as many as ten Justices. For most of the twentieth century, the Supreme Court's appellate docket was divided between cases heard on appeal as a matter of right, and cases heard by writ of certiorari as a matter of discretion. In the 1980s, about 10% of the Supreme Court's docket was made up of mandatory appeals, although the Court had by that time developed a practice under which these appeals were largely treated as if they were petitions for writs of certiorari. In 1988, Congress amended the Court's appellate jurisdictional statute to eliminate virtually all of the Court's mandatory appellate jurisdiction, leaving only its certiorari jurisdiction. At present, the Supreme Court receives about 10,000 petitions for a writ of certiorari per year. The Court decides about seventy-five to eighty cases per year, including cases coming up from both the federal and state courts. As these numbers make clear, the Court's central function is not to correct errors committed by the lower courts (although in any given year it typically reverses the lower court in somewhere between 75% and 80% of the cases it hears). Rather, the Supreme Court is essentially a policy-level court, deciding unanswered questions of law, deciding questions of law on which the lower courts have divided, and re-deciding questions of law that had previously been regarded as settled.

Although there is variation from state to state, court systems in the states are organized similarly. Populous states have three levels of courts, as in the federal system, with the state supreme court often hearing civil cases and noncapital criminal cases only as a matter of discretionary review. Several sparsely populated states have only two levels of courts, with a mandatory jurisdiction in the state supreme court over appeals from the trial courts. Most state supreme courts have seven justices. Unlike federal judges, state court judges are subject to removal from office by popular vote.

A. MECHANICS OF TAKING AN APPEAL

Professors Wright and Kane have summarized admirably the procedure for taking an appeal from a decision of a federal district court. They write:

> Under the rules the timely filing of a simple notice of appeal [under Federal Rule of Appellate Procedure 4] is the only step required to take an appeal. * * *

[A]n appellant who has filed a notice of appeal cannot then sit back and do nothing until the case is called for argument. The appellant must pay the required fees, give security for costs, if the court so requires in a civil case, file the record on appeal, and file its brief and appendix, but none of these steps is jurisdictional. The appeal may be dismissed for failure to take these further steps at the proper time, but the matter is within the discretion of the court of appeals. It need not dismiss the appeal and ordinarily will not do so in the absence of prejudice to the appellee.

[The only exceptions to this general pattern are interlocutory appeals under 28 U.S.C. § 1292(b), appeals from partial summary judgments under Rule 54(b), appeals from grants or denials of class action certification under Rule 23(f), and appeals from grants or denials of motions to remand to state court under the Class Action Fairness Act, 28 U.S.C. § 1443(c). The party seeking to bring the appeal in these cases must obtain the approval of the court of appeals.]

The notice of appeal, as described in Appellate Rule 3(c), is an extremely simple document. Some notice of appeal, regarded as sufficient by the appellate court, must be filed, because the notice of appeal is the one jurisdictional prerequisite to an appeal. The courts are very liberal, however, in entertaining an appeal even when the notice fails to comply with the rule. The notice should not be used as a technical trap for the unwary drafter, and a defective notice of appeal should not warrant dismissal for want of jurisdiction if the intention to appeal from a specific judgment may be reasonably inferred from the text of the notice and the defect has not materially misled the appellee. This has been fully understood by the courts. * * *

         * * *

In civil cases the notice of appeal must be filed within 30 days after entry of judgment except when the United States is a party to the suit, in which case 60 days is allowed. * * * [T]he time for noticing the appeal now may be extended an additional 30 days if a party shows "excusable neglect" or "good cause." * * *

It is important to observe that it is the "filing" of the notice within the designated time that is required. Service on the opposing party will not do. Neither will deposit in the mail if the notice is not actually received in the clerk's office within the designated time, though an exception has been made in extreme cases. If the clerk actually receives the notice, however, the clerk cannot refuse to file it on the ground that his fee has not been paid.

Certain posttrial motions suspend the finality of the judgment and the time for giving notice of appeal runs from the entry of the order granting or denying the motions. * * * In civil cases the time is extended by: a motion for judgment under Civil Rule 50(b); a motion to amend the findings under Rule 52(b); a motion for a new trial or to alter or amend the judgment under Rule 59; or a motion for relief under Rule 60. A motion for attorney's fees under Rule 54 also has this effect, but only if the district court has extended the time for appeal [under] Rule 58. A posttrial motion must itself be timely if it is to extend the time for appeal.

* * * [Appellate Rule 4(a)(4)] provides that a notice of appeal filed before the disposition of one of the specified posttrial motions becomes effective upon disposition of the motion. Thus, a notice filed before the filing of one of the specified motions, or after the filing of a motion but before its disposition, is in effect suspended until the motion is disposed of, whereupon the previously filed notice effectively places jurisdiction in the court of appeals. That earlier notice brings the underlying case, as well as any orders specified in that notice, to the court of appeals. If a party wishes to appeal from the disposition of the motion, or from any alteration of the judgment made as a result of the motion, the party must amend the earlier notice of appeal—or file a notice of appeal if the party has not appealed earlier—to indicate this.

An appellee may defend a judgment on any ground consistent with the record, even if rejected in the lower court. But it cannot attack the decree with a view either to enlarging its own rights thereunder or to lessening the rights of its adversary unless it files a cross-appeal, whether what it seeks is to correct an error or to supplement the decree with respect to a matter not dealt with below. * * * [I]f one party files a timely notice of appeal, any other party may file a notice of appeal within 14 days of the filing of the first notice or within the time in which the party might otherwise have given notice of appeal, whichever period last expires.

* * *

Appellate Rules 10 and 11 prescribe how the record on appeal is to be prepared and transmitted to the appellate court. The record on appeal is defined [in Appellate Rule 10(a)] as being "(1) the original papers and exhibits filed in the district court; (2) the transcript of proceedings, if any; and (3) a certified copy of the docket entries prepared by the clerk." * * *

In addition to the record, of which only a single copy is required, some provision must be made for putting into the hands of each of the judges who will hear the appeal those portions of the record that are of particular significance. [This may be done, depending on the practice in the particular circuit, by preparing either an "appendix" or "excerpts of record." The appendix and excerpts of record, usually far shorter than the actual district court record, are distributed to each of the judges hearing the appeal.]

C. Wright and M. Kane, Law of Federal Courts § 104 (7th ed. 2011) (footnotes omitted) (reprinted with permission). See also Levy, The Mechanics of Federal Appeals: Uniformity and Case Management in the Circuit Courts, 61 Duke L.J. 315 (2011).

B. WHEN CAN AN APPEAL BE TAKEN?

1. THE FINAL JUDGMENT RULE

Cox Broadcasting Corp. v. Cohn

Supreme Court of the United States, 1975.
420 U.S. 469, 95 S.Ct. 1029, 43 L.Ed.2d 328.

■ MR. JUSTICE WHITE delivered the opinion of the Court.

The issue before us in this case is whether, consistently with the First and Fourteenth Amendments, a State may extend a cause of action for damages for invasion of privacy caused by the publication of the name of a deceased rape victim which was publicly revealed in connection with the prosecution of the crime.

I

In August 1971, appellee's 17-year-old daughter was the victim of a rape and did not survive the incident. * * *

In May 1972, appellee brought an action for money damages against appellants, * * * claiming that his right to privacy had been invaded by the television broadcasts giving the name of his deceased daughter. Appellants admitted the broadcasts but claimed that they were privileged under both state law and the First and Fourteenth Amendments. The trial court, rejecting appellants' constitutional claims and holding that the Georgia statute gave a civil remedy to those injured by its violation, granted summary judgment to appellee as to liability, with the determination of damages to await trial by jury.

On appeal, the Georgia Supreme Court, in its initial opinion, held that * * * the complaint stated a cause of action "for the invasion of the appellee's right of privacy, or for the tort of public disclosure"—a "common law tort exist[ing] in this jurisdiction without the help of the statute that the trial judge in this case relied on." Id., at 62, 200 S.E.2d, at 130. Although the privacy invaded was not that of the deceased victim, the father was held to have stated a claim for invasion of his own privacy by reason of the publication of his daughter's name. The court explained, however, that liability did not follow as a matter of law and that summary judgment was improper; whether the public disclosure of the name actually invaded appellee's "zone of privacy," and if so, to what extent, were issues to be determined by the trier of fact. Also, "in formulating such an issue for determination by the fact-finder, it is reasonable to require the appellee to prove that the appellants invaded his privacy with wilful or negligent disregard for the fact that reasonable men would find the invasion highly offensive." Id., at 64, 200 S.E.2d, at 131. The Georgia Supreme Court did agree with the trial court, however, that the First and Fourteenth Amendments did not, as a matter of law, require judgment for appellants. * * *

* * *

II

Appellants invoke the appellate jurisdiction of this Court under 28 U.S.C.A. § 1257(2) and, if that jurisdictional basis is found to be absent, through a petition for certiorari under 28 U.S.C.A. § 2103. * * *

* * *

Since 1789, Congress has granted this Court appellate jurisdiction with respect to state litigation only after the highest state court in which judgment could be had has rendered a "[f]inal judgment or decree." Title 28 U.S.C.A. § 1257 retains this limitation on our power to review cases coming from state courts. The Court has noted that "[c]onsiderations of English usage as well as those of judicial policy" would justify an interpretation of the final-judgment rule to preclude review "where anything further remains to be determined by a State court, no matter how dissociated from the only federal issue that has finally been adjudicated by the highest court of the State." Radio Station WOW, Inc. v. Johnson, 326 U.S. 120, 124, 65 S.Ct. 1475, 1478, 89 L.Ed. 569 (1945). But the Court there observed that the rule had not been administered in such a mechanical fashion and that there were circumstances in which there has been "a departure from this requirement of finality for federal appellate jurisdiction." Ibid.

These circumstances were said to be "very few," ibid.; but as the cases have unfolded, the Court has recurringly encountered situations in which the highest court of a State has finally determined the federal issue present in a particular case, but in which there are further proceedings in the lower state courts to come. There are now at least four categories of such cases in which the Court has treated the decision on the federal issue as a final judgment for the purposes of 28 U.S.C.A. § 1257 and has taken jurisdiction without awaiting the completion of the additional proceedings anticipated in the lower state courts. In most, if not all, of the cases in these categories, these additional proceedings would not require the decision of other federal questions that might also require review by the Court at a later date, and immediate rather than delayed review would be the best way to avoid "the mischief of economic waste and of delayed justice," Radio Station WOW, Inc. v. Johnson, supra, at 124, 65 S.Ct., at 1478, as well as precipitate interference with state litigation. In the cases in the first two categories considered below, the federal issue would not be mooted or otherwise affected by the proceedings yet to be had because those proceedings have little substance, their outcome is certain, or they are wholly unrelated to the federal question. In the other two categories, however, the federal issue would be mooted if the petitioner or appellant seeking to bring the action here prevailed on the merits in the later state-court proceedings, but there is nevertheless sufficient justification for immediate review of the federal question finally determined in the state courts.

In the first category are those cases in which there are further proceedings—even entire trials—yet to occur in the state courts but where for one reason or another the federal issue is conclusive or the outcome of further proceedings preordained. In these circumstances, because the case is for all practical purposes concluded, the judgment of the state court on the federal issue is deemed final. In Mills v. Alabama, 384 U.S. 214, 86 S.Ct. 1434, 16 L.Ed.2d 484 (1966), for example, a demurrer to a criminal complaint was sustained on federal constitutional grounds by a state trial court. The State Supreme Court reversed, remanding for jury trial. This Court took jurisdiction on the reasoning that the appellant had no defense other than his federal claim and could not prevail at trial on the facts or any nonfederal ground. To dismiss the appeal "would not only be an inexcusable delay of the benefits Congress intended to grant by providing for appeal to this Court, but it would also result in a completely unnecessary waste of time and energy in judicial systems already troubled by delays due to congested dockets." Id., at 217–218, 86 S.Ct., at 1436 (footnote omitted).

Second, there are cases such as *Radio Station WOW,* supra, and Brady v. Maryland, 373 U.S. 83, 83 S.Ct. 1194, 10 L.Ed.2d 215 (1963), in which the federal issue, finally decided by the highest court in the State, will survive and require decision regardless of the outcome of future state-court proceedings. In *Radio Station WOW,* the Nebraska Supreme Court directed the transfer of the properties of a federally licensed radio station and ordered an accounting, rejecting the claim that the transfer order would interfere with the federal license. The federal issue was held reviewable here despite the pending accounting on the "presupposition . . . that the federal questions that could come here have been adjudicated by the State court, and that the accounting which remains to be taken could not remotely give rise to a federal question . . . that may later come here. . . ." 326 U.S., at 127, 65 S.Ct., at 1480. The judgment rejecting the federal claim and directing the transfer was deemed "dissociated from a provision for an accounting even though that is decreed in the same order." Id., at 126, 65 S.Ct., at 1479. Nothing that could happen in the course of the accounting, short of settlement of the case, would foreclose or make unnecessary decision on the federal question. Older cases in the Court had reached the same result on similar facts. Carondelet Canal & Nav. Co. v. Louisiana, 233 U.S. 362, 34 S.Ct. 627, 58 L.Ed. 1001 (1914); Forgay v. Conrad, 6 How. 201, 12 L.Ed. 404 (1848). In the latter case, the Court, in an opinion by Mr. Chief Justice Taney, stated that the Court had not understood the final-judgment rule "in this strict and technical sense, but has given [it] a more liberal, and, as we think, a more reasonable construction, and one more consonant to the intention of the legislature." Id., at 203.

In the third category are those situations where the federal claim has been finally decided, with further proceedings on the merits in the state courts to come, but in which later review of the federal issue cannot be had, whatever the ultimate outcome of the case. Thus, in these cases, if the party seeking interim review ultimately prevails on the merits, the federal issue will be mooted; if he were to lose on the merits, however, the governing state law would not permit him again to present his federal claims for review. The Court has taken jurisdiction in these circumstances prior to completion of the case in the state courts. California v. Stewart, 384 U.S. 436, 86 S.Ct. 1602, 16 L.Ed.2d 694 (1966) (decided with Miranda v. Arizona), epitomizes this category. There the state court reversed a conviction on federal constitutional grounds and remanded for a new trial. Although the State might have prevailed at trial, we granted its petition for certiorari and affirmed, explaining that the state judgment was "final" since an acquittal of the defendant at trial would preclude, under state law, an appeal by the State. Id., at 498 n. 71, 86 S.Ct., at 1640.

A recent decision in this category is North Dakota State Board of Pharmacy v. Snyder's Drug Stores, Inc., 414 U.S. 156, 94 S.Ct. 407, 38 L.Ed.2d 379 (1973), in which the Pharmacy Board rejected an application for a pharmacy operating permit relying on a state statute specifying ownership requirements which the applicant did not meet. The State Supreme Court held the statute unconstitutional and remanded the matter to the Board for further consideration of the application, freed from the constraints of the ownership statute. The Board brought the case here, claiming that the statute was constitutionally acceptable under modern cases. After reviewing the various circumstances under which the finality requirement has been deemed satisfied despite the fact that litigation had not terminated in the state courts, we entertained the case over claims that we had no jurisdiction. The federal issue would not survive the remand, whatever the result of the state administrative proceedings. The Board might deny the license on state-law grounds, thus foreclosing the federal issue, and the Court also ascertained that under state law the Board could not bring the federal issue here in the event the applicant satisfied the requirements of state law except for the invalidated ownership statute. Under these circumstances, the issue was ripe for review.[10]

Lastly, there are those situations where the federal issue has been finally decided in the state courts with further proceedings pending in which the party seeking review here might prevail on the merits on nonfederal grounds, thus rendering unnecessary review of the federal issue by this Court, and where reversal of the state court on the federal issue would be preclusive of any further litigation on the relevant cause of action rather than merely controlling the nature and character of, or determining the admissibility of evidence in, the state proceedings still to come. In these circumstances, if a refusal immediately to review the state court decision might seriously erode federal policy, the Court has entertained and decided the federal issue, which itself has been finally determined by the state courts for purposes of the state litigation.

In Construction Laborers v. Curry, 371 U.S. 542, 83 S.Ct. 531, 9 L.Ed.2d 514 (1963), the state courts temporarily enjoined labor union picketing over claims that the National Labor Relations Board had exclusive jurisdiction of the controversy. The Court took jurisdiction for two independent reasons. First, the power of the state court to proceed in the face of the preemption claim was deemed an issue separable from the merits and ripe for review in this Court, particularly "when postponing review would seriously erode the national labor policy requiring the subject matter of respondents' cause to be heard by the . . . Board, not by the state courts." Id., at 550, 83 S.Ct., at 536. Second, the Court was convinced that in any event the union had no defense to the entry of a permanent injunction other than the preemption claim that had already

---

[10]   Cohen v. Beneficial Industrial Loan Corp., 337 U.S. 541, 69 S.Ct. 1221, 93 L.Ed. 1528 (1949), was a diversity action in the federal courts in the course of which there arose the question of the validity of a state statute requiring plaintiffs in stockholder suits to post security for costs as a prerequisite to bringing the action. The District Court held the state law inapplicable, the Court of Appeals reversed, and this Court, after granting certiorari, held that the issue of security for costs was separable from and independent of the merits and that if review were to be postponed until the termination of the litigation, "it will be too late effectively to review the present order and the rights conferred by the statute, if it is applicable, will have been lost, probably irreparably." Id., at 546, 69 S.Ct., at 1225.

been ruled on in the state courts. Hence the case was for all practical purposes concluded in the state tribunals.

In Mercantile National Bank v. Langdeau, 371 U.S. 555, 83 S.Ct. 520, 9 L.Ed.2d 523 (1963), two national banks were sued, along with others, in the courts of Travis County, Tex. The claim asserted was conspiracy to defraud an insurance company. The banks as a preliminary matter asserted that a special federal venue statute immunized them from suit in Travis County and that they could properly be sued only in another county. Although trial was still to be had and the banks might well prevail on the merits, the Court, relying on *Curry,* entertained the issue as a "separate and independent matter, anterior to the merits and not enmeshed in the factual and legal issues comprising the plaintiff's cause of action." Id., at 558, 83 S.Ct., at 522. Moreover, it would serve the policy of the federal statute "to determine now in which state court appellants may be tried rather than to subject them . . . to long and complex litigation which may all be for naught if consideration of the preliminary question of venue is postponed until the conclusion of the proceedings." Ibid.

Miami Herald Publishing Co. v. Tornillo, 418 U.S. 241, 94 S.Ct. 2831, 41 L.Ed.2d 730 (1974), is the latest case in this category. There a candidate for public office sued a newspaper for refusing, allegedly contrary to a state statute, to carry his reply to the paper's editorial critical of his qualifications. The trial court held the act unconstitutional, denying both injunctive relief and damages. The State Supreme Court reversed, sustaining the statute against the challenge based upon the First and Fourteenth Amendments and remanding the case for a trial and appropriate relief, including damages. The newspaper brought the case here. We sustained our jurisdiction, relying on the principles elaborated in the *North Dakota* case and observing:

> "Whichever way we were to decide on the merits, it would be intolerable to leave unanswered, under these circumstances, an important question of freedom of the press under the First Amendment; an uneasy and unsettled constitutional posture of § 104.38 could only further harm the operation of a free press. Mills v. Alabama, 384 U.S. 214, 221–222, 86 S.Ct. 1434, 1438, 16 L.Ed.2d 484 (1966) (Douglas, J., concurring). See also Organization for a Better Austin v. Keefe, 402 U.S. 415, 418 n., 91 S.Ct. 1575, 1577, 29 L.Ed.2d 1 (1971)." 418 U.S., at 247 n. 6, 94 S.Ct., at 2834.

In light of the prior cases, we conclude that we have jurisdiction to review the judgment of the Georgia Supreme Court rejecting the challenge under the First and Fourteenth Amendments to the state law authorizing damage suits against the press for publishing the name of a rape victim whose identity is revealed in the course of a public prosecution. The Georgia Supreme Court's judgment is plainly final on the federal issue and is not subject to further review in the state courts. Appellants will be liable for damages if the elements of the state cause of action are proved. They may prevail at trial on nonfederal grounds, it is true, but if the Georgia court erroneously upheld the statute, there should be no trial at all. Moreover, even if appellants prevailed at trial and made unnecessary further consideration of the constitutional question, there would remain in effect the unreviewed decision of the

State Supreme Court that a civil action for publishing the name of a rape victim disclosed in a public judicial proceeding may go forward despite the First and Fourteenth Amendments. Delaying final decision of the First Amendment claim until after trial will "leave unanswered . . . an important question of freedom of the press under the First Amendment," "an uneasy and unsettled constitutional posture [that] could only further harm the operation of a free press." *Tornillo,* supra, 418 U.S., at 247 n. 6, 94 S.Ct., at 2834. On the other hand, if we now hold that the First and Fourteenth Amendments bar civil liability for broadcasting the victim's name, this litigation ends. Given these factors—that the litigation could be terminated by our decision on the merits and that a failure to decide the question now will leave the press in Georgia operating in the shadow of the civil and criminal sanctions of a rule of law and a statute the constitutionality of which is in serious doubt—we find that reaching the merits is consistent with the pragmatic approach that we have followed in the past in determining finality. See Gillespie v. United States Steel Corp., 379 U.S. 148, 85 S.Ct. 308, 13 L.Ed.2d 199 (1964); Radio Station WOW, Inc. v. Johnson, 326 U.S., at 124, 65 S.Ct., at 1478; Mills v. Alabama, 384 U.S., at 221–222, 86 S.Ct., at 1438–1439 (Douglas, J., concurring).

> * * *

■ The concurring opinions of JUSTICE POWELL and JUSTICE DOUGLAS and the dissenting opinion of JUSTICE REHNQUIST are omitted.

■ MR. JUSTICE STEVENS took no part in the consideration or decision of this case.

NOTE ON THE FINAL JUDGMENT RULE AS APPLIED TO SUPREME COURT REVIEW OF STATE COURT DECISIONS

1.   **The final judgment rule.** The general rule, followed in both federal and state courts, is that an appeal may be taken only from a final judgment of the trial court. The final judgment rule is embodied in two federal statutes, one dealing with cases coming up from state court, the other with cases coming up from federal court. As a general proposition, it makes sense to wait until the trial is over and judgment is rendered before allowing appeals of trial court rulings. If parties could appeal every adverse trial court ruling as soon as that ruling is made, there would be frequent appeals and almost interminable trials. If the parties are obliged to wait until entry of final judgment, some rulings will not be appealed. The winner at trial is not likely to appeal at all, except sometimes (and quite rarely) as a cross-appeal. Mid-trial rulings that go against the eventual winner of the suit thus almost always become irrelevant. The loser at trial may (and most likely will) choose to appeal only the most important rulings by the judge. By the time of the judgment, it will be clear that some adverse rulings did not make any actual difference to the outcome of the case, so some mid-trial rulings that went against the eventual loser will not be appealed. Finally, many judgments are simply never appealed. Even though an appeal might have been attractive on one or more issues in the middle of trial if an appeal had then been available, by the time the trial has finished and the judgment has been entered the losing party may conclude that an appeal is a waste of time and money.

2. Review of state court decisions by the U.S. Supreme Court. The statute at issue in *Cox Broadcasting*, 28 U.S.C. § 1257(a) in its current form, deals with review of decisions of state courts by the U.S. Supreme Court. Section 1257(a) provides that "final judgments or decrees rendered by the highest court of a State in which a decision could be had, may be reviewed by the Supreme Court * * *." The final judgment rule performs a different function in cases coming to the Supreme Court from the state courts than in cases coming to the federal courts of appeals from the federal district courts. There are two important differences. First, the Supreme Court does not have jurisdiction to review all of the questions decided by the state court. It can review only decisions on issues of federal law. If it is clear that the Supreme Court's decision on the issue of federal law will under no circumstances make any difference to the outcome of the case, and would hence be merely "advisory," the Court will not decide the issue. Michigan v. Long, 463 U.S. 1032, 103 S.Ct. 3469, 77 L.Ed.2d 1201 (1983). Second, as indicated in the note at the beginning of this chapter, the Supreme Court is a policy-level court. It is not a court of error correction. With rare exceptions, by the time a case gets to the Supreme Court an appellate court has already had an opportunity to correct trial court errors. This is doubly true in cases coming up from the state courts, where Supreme Court review typically follows review by two state appellate courts.

In the materials that follow, you will see various federal statutory and rule-based mechanisms that allow interlocutory review by federal courts of appeals of decisions by federal district courts. There are no such statutory or rule-based mechanisms authorizing interlocutory review by the Supreme Court of state court decisions. Can you see why this is so?

3. Four categories of state court decisions reviewable under *Cox Broadcasting* despite the absence of a "final judgment or decree." The Court in *Cox Broadcasting* describes four categories of cases in which the final judgment rule of § 1257(a) is satisfied despite the fact that the state court judgment is not, in fact, final. Note that the text of § 1257(a) does not provide for exceptions to its final judgment rule. The four categories of reviewable decisions are all judge-made exceptions to the final judgment rule of § 1257(a). First, there may be further proceedings in the state courts after the decision of the Supreme Court, but "for one reason or another the federal issue is conclusive or the outcome of further proceedings preordained." Second, there may be further proceedings in the state courts, but the federal issue that has already been finally decided by the state court "will survive and require decision regardless of the outcome of future state-court proceedings." Third, there may be further proceedings in the state courts, but Supreme Court review of the federal issue that has already been finally decided "cannot be had, whatever the ultimate outcome of the case." Fourth, there may be further proceedings in the state courts in which state-law issues may determine the outcome of the case in the absence of Supreme Court review of the federal issue, but "reversal of the state court on the federal issue would be preclusive of any further litigation on the relevant cause of action."

Is there a common theme to these four judge-made exceptions to the ostensibly categorical final judgment rule in § 1257(a)? Are all four exceptions designed to facilitate the Supreme Court's role as policy-level court? Do the four exceptions belie the description of the role of the Supreme

Court by Chief Justice Roberts in his confirmation hearings as merely "calling balls and strikes"?

4.   No direct appeal from state courts to lower federal courts. There is no federal statute—indeed, there is no constitutional authority for such a statute—authorizing direct appellate review of decisions of state courts by federal district courts or courts of appeals. Rooker v. Fidelity Trust Co., 263 U.S. 413 (1923); District of Columbia Court of Appeals v. Feldman, 460 U.S. 462 (1983). Federal district courts have statutory authority to review state court criminal judgments on habeas corpus, but habeas review is a collateral attack rather than direct review. See 28 U.S.C. § 2254.

Mohawk Industries, Inc. v. Norman Carpenter

Supreme Court of the United States, 2009.
558 U.S. 100, 130 S.Ct. 599, 175 L.Ed.2d 458.

■ JUSTICE SOTOMAYOR delivered the opinion of the Court.

Section 1291 of the Judicial Code confers on federal courts of appeals jurisdiction to review "final decisions of the district courts." 28 U.S.C. § 1291. Although "final decisions" typically are ones that trigger the entry of judgment, they also include a small set of prejudgment orders that are "collateral to" the merits of an action and "too important" to be denied immediate review. Cohen v. Beneficial Industrial Loan Corp., 337 U.S. 541, 546 (1949). In this case, petitioner Mohawk Industries, Inc., attempted to bring a collateral order appeal after the District Court ordered it to disclose certain confidential materials on the ground that Mohawk had waived the attorney-client privilege. The Court of Appeals dismissed the appeal for want of jurisdiction.

The question before us is whether disclosure orders adverse to the attorney-client privilege qualify for immediate appeal under the collateral order doctrine. Agreeing with the Court of Appeals, we hold that they do not. Postjudgment appeals, together with other review mechanisms, suffice to protect the rights of litigants and preserve the vitality of the attorney-client privilege.

I

In 2007, respondent Norman Carpenter, a former shift supervisor at a Mohawk manufacturing facility, filed suit in the United States District Court for the Northern District of Georgia, alleging that Mohawk had terminated him in violation of 42 U.S.C. § 1985(2) and various Georgia laws. According to Carpenter's complaint, his termination came after he informed a member of Mohawk's human resources department in an e-mail that the company was employing undocumented immigrants. At the time, unbeknownst to Carpenter, Mohawk stood accused in a pending class-action lawsuit of conspiring to drive down the wages of its legal employees by knowingly hiring undocumented workers in violation of federal and state racketeering laws. See Williams v. Mohawk Indus., Inc., No. 4:04-cv-00003-HLM (ND Ga., Jan. 6, 2004). Company officials directed Carpenter to meet with the company's retained counsel in the Williams case, and counsel allegedly pressured Carpenter to recant his statements. When he refused, Carpenter alleges, Mohawk fired him under false pretenses.

After learning of Carpenter's complaint, the plaintiffs in the *Williams* case sought an evidentiary hearing to explore Carpenter's allegations. In its response to their motion, Mohawk described Carpenter's accusations as "pure fantasy" and recounted the "true facts" of Carpenter's dismissal. According to Mohawk, Carpenter himself had "engaged in blatant and illegal misconduct" by attempting to have Mohawk hire an undocumented worker. The company "commenced an immediate investigation," during which retained counsel interviewed Carpenter. Because Carpenter's "efforts to cause Mohawk to circumvent federal immigration law" "blatantly violated Mohawk policy," the company terminated him.

As these events were unfolding in the *Williams* case, discovery was underway in Carpenter's case. Carpenter filed a motion to compel Mohawk to produce information concerning his meeting with retained counsel and the company's termination decision. Mohawk maintained that the requested information was protected by the attorney-client privilege.

The District Court agreed that the privilege applied to the requested information, but it granted Carpenter's motion to compel disclosure after concluding that Mohawk had implicitly waived the privilege through its representations in the *Williams* case. * * * The court declined to certify its order for interlocutory appeal under 28 U.S.C. § 1292(b). But, recognizing "the seriousness of its [waiver] finding," it stayed its ruling to allow Mohawk to explore other potential "avenues to appeal . . . , such as a petition for mandamus or appealing this Order under the collateral order doctrine." * * *

Mohawk filed a notice of appeal and a petition for a writ of mandamus to the Eleventh Circuit. The Court of Appeals dismissed the appeal for lack of jurisdiction under 28 U.S.C. § 1291, holding that the District Court's ruling did not qualify as an immediately appealable collateral order within the meaning of *Cohen,* 337 U.S. 541. "Under *Cohen,*" the Court of Appeals explained, "an order is appealable if it (1) conclusively determines the disputed question; (2) resolves an important issue completely separate from the merits of the action; and (3) is effectively unreviewable on appeal from a final judgment." 541 F. 3d 1048, 1052 (2008) (*per curiam*). According to the court, the District Court's waiver ruling satisfied the first two of these requirements but not the third, because "a discovery order that implicates the attorney-client privilege" can be adequately reviewed "on appeal from a final judgment." *Ibid.* The Court of Appeals also rejected Mohawk's mandamus petition, finding no "clear usurpation of power or abuse of discretion" by the District Court. *Id.,* at 1055. We granted certiorari to resolve a conflict among the Circuits concerning the availability of collateral appeals in the attorney-client privilege context.[1]

---

[1] Three Circuits have permitted collateral order appeals of attorney-client privilege rulings. See *In re Napster, Inc. Copyright Litigation,* 479 F. 3d 1078, 1087–1088 (CA9 2007); *United States* v. *Philip Morris Inc.,* 314 F. 3d 612, 617–621 (CADC 2003); *In re Ford Motor Co.,* 110 F. 3d 954, 957–964 (CA3 1997). The remaining Circuits to consider the question have found such orders nonappealable. See, *e.g., Boughton* v. *Cotter Corp.,* 10 F. 3d 746, 749–750 (CA10 1993); *Texaco Inc.* v. *Louisiana Land & Exploration Co.,* 995 F. 2d 43, 44 (CA5 1993); *Reise* v. *Board of Regents,* 957 F. 2d 293, 295 (CA7 1992); *Chase Manhattan Bank, N. A.* v. *Turner &*

II

A

By statute, Courts of Appeals "have jurisdiction of appeals from all final decisions of the district courts of the United States,... except where a direct review may be had in the Supreme Court." 28 U.S.C. § 1291. A "final decisio[n]" is typically one "by which a district court disassociates itself from a case." *Swint* v. *Chambers County Comm'n,* 514 U.S. 35, 42 (1995). This Court, however, "has long given" § 1291 a "practical rather than a technical construction." *Cohen,* 337 U.S., at 546. As we held in *Cohen,* the statute encompasses not only judgments that "terminate an action," but also a "small class" of collateral rulings that, although they do not end the litigation, are appropriately deemed "final." *Id.,* at 545–546. "That small category includes only decisions that are conclusive, that resolve important questions separate from the merits, and that are effectively unreviewable on appeal from the final judgment in the underlying action." *Swint,* 514 U.S., at 42.

In applying *Cohen*'s collateral order doctrine, we have stressed that it must "never be allowed to swallow the general rule that a party is entitled to a single appeal, to be deferred until final judgment has been entered." *Digital Equipment Corp.* v. *Desktop Direct, Inc.,* 511 U.S. 863, 868 (1994) (citation omitted); see also *Will* v. *Hallock,* 546 U.S. 345, 350 (2006) ("emphasizing [the doctrine's] modest scope"). Our admonition reflects a healthy respect for the virtues of the final-judgment rule. Permitting piecemeal, prejudgment appeals, we have recognized, undermines "efficient judicial administration" and encroaches upon the prerogatives of district court judges, who play a "special role" in managing ongoing litigation. *Firestone Tire & Rubber Co.* v. *Risjord,* 449 U.S. 368, 374 (1981); see also *Richardson-Merrell Inc.* v. *Koller,* 472 U.S. 424, 436 (1985) ("[T]he district judge can better exercise [his or her] responsibility [to police the prejudgment tactics of litigants] if the appellate courts do not repeatedly intervene to second-guess prejudgment rulings").

The justification for immediate appeal must therefore be sufficiently strong to overcome the usual benefits of deferring appeal until litigation concludes. This requirement finds expression in two of the three traditional *Cohen* conditions. The second condition insists upon "*important* questions separate from the merits." *Swint,* 514 U.S., at 42 (emphasis added). More significantly, "the third *Cohen* question, whether a right is `adequately vindicable' or 'effectively reviewable,' simply cannot be answered without a judgment about the value of the interests that would be lost through rigorous application of a final judgment requirement." *Digital Equipment,* 511 U.S., at 878–879. That a ruling "may burden litigants in ways that are only imperfectly reparable by appellate reversal of a final district court judgment . . . has never sufficed." *Id.,* at 872. Instead, the decisive consideration is whether delaying review until the entry of final judgment "would imperil a substantial public interest" or "some particular value of a high order." *Will,* 546 U.S., at 352–353.

Newall, PLC, 964 F. 2d 159, 162–163 (CA2 1992); *Quantum Corp.* v. *Tandon Corp.,* 940 F. 2d 642, 643–644 (CA Fed. 1991).

In making this determination, we do not engage in an "individualized jurisdictional inquiry." *Coopers & Lybrand* v. *Livesay,* 437 U.S. 463, 473 (1978). Rather, our focus is on "the entire category to which a claim belongs." *Digital Equipment,* 511 U.S., at 868. As long as the class of claims, taken as a whole, can be adequately vindicated by other means, "the chance that the litigation at hand might be speeded, or a 'particular injustic[e]' averted," does not provide a basis for jurisdiction under § 1291. *Ibid.* (quoting *Van Cauwenberghe* v. *Biard,* 486 U.S. 517, 529 (1988) (alteration in original)).

B

In the present case, the Court of Appeals concluded that the District Court's privilege-waiver order satisfied the first two conditions of the collateral order doctrine—conclusiveness and separateness—but not the third—effective unreviewability. Because we agree with the Court of Appeals that collateral order appeals are not necessary to ensure effective review of orders adverse to the attorney-client privilege, we do not decide whether the other *Cohen* requirements are met.

Mohawk does not dispute that "we have generally denied review of pretrial discovery orders." *Firestone,* 449 U.S., at 377; see also 15B C. Wright, A. Miller, & E. Cooper, Federal Practice and Procedure § 3914.23, p. 123 (2d ed. 1992) (hereinafter Wright & Miller) ("[T]he rule remains settled that most discovery rulings are not final"). Mohawk contends, however, that rulings implicating the attorney-client privilege differ in kind from run-of-the-mill discovery orders because of the important institutional interests at stake. According to Mohawk, the right to maintain attorney-client confidences—the *sine qua non* of a meaningful attorney-client relationship—is "irreparably destroyed absent immediate appeal" of adverse privilege rulings. * * *

We readily acknowledge the importance of the attorney-client privilege, which "is one of the oldest recognized privileges for confidential communications." *Swidler & Berlin* v. *United States,* 524 U.S. 399, 403 (1998). By assuring confidentiality, the privilege encourages clients to make "full and frank" disclosures to their attorneys, who are then better able to provide candid advice and effective representation. *Upjohn Co.* v. *United States,* 449 U.S. 383, 389 (1981). This, in turn, serves "broader public interests in the observance of law and administration of justice." *Ibid.*

The crucial question, however, is not whether an interest is important in the abstract; it is whether deferring review until final judgment so imperils the interest as to justify the cost of allowing immediate appeal of the entire class of relevant orders. We routinely require litigants to wait until after final judgment to vindicate valuable rights, including rights central to our adversarial system. See, *e.g., Richardson-Merrell,* 472 U.S., at 426 (holding an order disqualifying counsel in a civil case did not qualify for immediate appeal under the collateral order doctrine); *Flanagan* v. *United States,* 465 U.S. 259, 260 (1984) (reaching the same result in a criminal case, notwithstanding the Sixth Amendment rights at stake). In *Digital Equipment,* we rejected an assertion that collateral order review was necessary to promote "the public policy favoring voluntary resolution of disputes." 511 U.S., at 881. "It defies common sense," we explained, "to maintain that parties' readiness to settle will be significantly dampened (or the corresponding public interest impaired) by a rule that a district court's decision to let allegedly barred litigation go forward may be challenged as a matter of right only on appeal from a judgment for the plaintiff's favor." *Ibid.*

We reach a similar conclusion here. In our estimation, postjudgment appeals generally suffice to protect the rights of litigants and assure the vitality of the attorney-client privilege. Appellate courts can remedy the improper disclosure of privileged material in the same way they remedy a host of other erroneous evidentiary rulings: by vacating an adverse judgment and remanding for a new trial in which the protected material and its fruits are excluded from evidence.

Dismissing such relief as inadequate, Mohawk emphasizes that the attorney-client privilege does not merely "prohibi[t] use of protected information at trial"; it provides a "right not to disclose the privileged information in the first place." * * * Mohawk is undoubtedly correct that an order to disclose privileged information intrudes on the confidentiality of attorney-client communications. But deferring review until final judgment does not meaningfully reduce the *ex ante* incentives for full and frank consultations between clients and counsel.

One reason for the lack of a discernible chill is that, in deciding how freely to speak, clients and counsel are unlikely to focus on the remote prospect of an erroneous disclosure order, let alone on the timing of a possible appeal. Whether or not immediate collateral order appeals are available, clients and counsel must account for the possibility that they will later be required by law to disclose their communications for a variety of reasons—for example, because they misjudged the scope of the privilege, because they waived the privilege, or because their communications fell within the privilege's crime-fraud exception. Most district court rulings on these matters involve the routine application of settled legal principles. They are unlikely to be reversed on appeal, particularly when they rest on factual determinations for which appellate deference is the norm. See, *e.g., Richardson-Merrell,* 472 U.S., at 434 ("Most pretrial orders of district judges are ultimately affirmed by appellate courts."); *Reise* v. *Board of Regents,* 957 F. 2d 293, 295 (CA7 1992) (noting that "almost all interlocutory appeals from discovery orders would end in affirmance" because "the district court possesses discretion, and review is deferential"). The breadth of the privilege and the narrowness of its exceptions will thus tend to exert a much greater influence on the conduct of clients and counsel than the small risk that the law will be misapplied.

Moreover, were attorneys and clients to reflect upon their appellate options, they would find that litigants confronted with a particularly injurious or novel privilege ruling have several potential avenues of review apart from collateral order appeal. First, a party may ask the district court to certify, and the court of appeals to accept, an interlocutory appeal pursuant to 28 U.S.C. § 1292(b). The preconditions for § 1292(b) review—"a controlling question of law," the prompt resolution of which "may materially advance the ultimate termination of the litigation"—are most likely to be satisfied when a privilege ruling involves a new legal question or is of special consequence, and district courts should not hesitate to certify an interlocutory appeal in such cases. Second, in extraordinary circumstances—*i.e.,* when a disclosure order "amount[s] to a judicial usurpation of power or a clear abuse of discretion," or otherwise works a manifest injustice—a party may petition the court of appeals for a writ of mandamus. *Cheney* v. *United States Dist. Court for D. C.,* 542 U.S. 367, 390 (2004) (citation and internal quotation marks omitted); see also *Firestone,* 449 U.S., at 378–379, n. 13.[2] While these discretionary review mechanisms do not provide relief in every case, they serve as useful "safety valve[s]" for promptly correcting serious errors. *Digital Equipment,* 511 U.S., at 883.

Another long-recognized option is for a party to defy a disclosure order and incur court-imposed sanctions. District courts have a range of sanctions from which to choose, including "directing that the matters embraced in the order or other designated facts be taken as established for purposes of the action," "prohibiting the disobedient party from supporting or opposing designated claims or defenses," or "striking pleadings in whole or in part." Fed. Rule Civ. Proc. 37(b)(2)(i)–(iii). Such sanctions allow a party to obtain postjudgment review without having to reveal its privileged information. Alternatively, when the circumstances warrant it, a district court may hold a noncomplying party in contempt. The party can then appeal directly from that ruling, at least when the contempt citation can be characterized as a criminal punishment. See, *e.g., Church of Scientology of Cal.* v. *United States,* 506 U.S. 9, 18, n. 11 (1992); *Firestone,* 449 U.S., at 377; *Cobbledick* v. *United States,* 309 U.S. 323, 328 (1940); see also Wright & Miller § 3914.23, at 140–155.

These established mechanisms for appellate review not only provide assurances to clients and counsel about the security of their confidential communications; they also go a long way toward addressing Mohawk's concern that, absent collateral order appeals of adverse attorney-client privilege rulings, some litigants may experience severe hardship. Mohawk is no doubt right that an order to disclose privileged material may, in some situations, have implications beyond the case at hand. But the same can be said about many categories of pretrial discovery orders for which collateral order appeals are unavailable. As with these other orders, rulings adverse to the privilege vary in their significance; some may be momentous, but others are more mundane. Section 1292(b) appeals, mandamus, and appeals from contempt citations facilitate immediate review of some of the more consequential attorney-client privilege rulings. Moreover, protective orders are available to limit the spillover effects of disclosing sensitive information. That a fraction of orders adverse to the attorney-client privilege may nevertheless harm individual litigants in ways that are "only imperfectly reparable" does not justify making all such orders immediately appealable as of right under § 1291. *Digital Equipment,* 511 U.S., at 872.

In short, the limited benefits of applying "the blunt, categorical instrument of § 1291 collateral order appeal" to privilege-related disclosure orders simply cannot justify the likely institutional costs. *Id.,* at 883. Permitting parties to undertake successive, piecemeal appeals of all adverse attorney-client rulings would unduly delay the resolution of district court litigation and needlessly burden the Courts of Appeals. See Wright & Miller § 3914.23, at 123 ("Routine appeal from disputed

---

[2] Mohawk itself petitioned the Eleventh Circuit for a writ of mandamus. * * * It has not asked us to review the Court of Appeals' denial of that relief.

discovery orders would disrupt the orderly progress of the litigation, swamp the courts of appeals, and substantially reduce the district court's ability to control the discovery process."); cf. *Cunningham* v. *Hamilton County,* 527 U.S. 198, 209 (1999) (expressing concern that allowing immediate appeal as of right from orders fining attorneys for discovery violations would result in "the very sorts of piecemeal appeals and concomitant delays that the final judgment rule was designed to prevent"). Attempting to downplay such concerns, Mohawk asserts that the three Circuits in which the collateral order doctrine currently applies to adverse privilege rulings have seen only a trickle of appeals. But this may be due to the fact that the practice in all three Circuits is relatively new and not yet widely known. Were this Court to approve collateral order appeals in the attorney-client privilege context, many more litigants would likely choose that route. They would also likely seek to extend such a ruling to disclosure orders implicating many other categories of sensitive information, raising an array of line-drawing difficulties.[3]

C

In concluding that sufficiently effective review of adverse attorney-client privilege rulings can be had without resort to the *Cohen* doctrine, we reiterate that the class of collaterally appealable orders must remain "narrow and selective in its membership." *Will,* 546 U.S., at 350. This admonition has acquired special force in recent years with the enactment of legislation designating rulemaking, "not expansion by court decision," as the preferred means for determining whether and when prejudgment orders should be immediately appealable. *Swint,* 514 U.S., at 48. Specifically, Congress in 1990 amended the Rules Enabling Act, 28 U.S.C. § 2071 *et seq.,* to authorize this Court to adopt rules "defin[ing] when a ruling of a district court is final for the purposes of appeal under section 1291." § 2072(c). Shortly thereafter, and along similar lines, Congress empowered this Court to "prescribe rules, in accordance with [§ 2072], to provide for an appeal of an interlocutory decision to the courts of appeals that is not otherwise provided for under [§ 1292]." § 1292(e). These provisions, we have recognized, "warran[t] the Judiciary's full respect." *Swint,* 514 U.S., at 48; see also *Cunningham,* 527 U.S., at 210.

Indeed, the rulemaking process has important virtues. It draws on the collective experience of bench and bar, see 28 U.S.C. § 2073, and it facilitates the adoption of measured, practical solutions. We expect that the combination of standard postjudgment appeals, § 1292(b) appeals, mandamus, and contempt appeals will continue to provide adequate protection to litigants ordered to disclose materials purportedly subject to the attorney-client privilege. Any further avenue for immediate appeal of such rulings should be furnished, if at all, through rulemaking, with the opportunity for full airing it provides.

---

[3] Participating as *amicus curiae* in support of respondent Carpenter, the United States contends that collateral order appeals should be available for rulings involving certain governmental privileges "in light of their structural constitutional grounding under the separation of powers, relatively rare invocation, and unique importance to governmental functions." Brief for United States as *Amicus Curiae* 28. We express no view on that issue.

* * *

In sum, we conclude that the collateral order doctrine does not extend to disclosure orders adverse to the attorney-client privilege. Effective appellate review can be had by other means. Accordingly, we affirm the judgment of the Court of Appeals for the Eleventh Circuit.

It is so ordered.

■ The concurring opinion of JUSTICE THOMAS is omitted.

NOTE ON THE FINAL JUDGMENT RULE AS APPLIED TO REVIEW OF FEDERAL DISTRICT COURT DECISIONS

1.   The final judgment rule as applied to federal district court decisions. The final judgment rule for review of federal district court decisions is embodied in 28 U.S.C. § 1291. It provides, "The courts of appeals * * * shall have jurisdiction of appeals from all final decisions of the district courts of the United States * * * ." "Federal appellate jurisdiction generally depends on the existence of a decision by the District Court that 'ends the litigation on the merits and leaves nothing for the court to do but execute the judgment.'" Cooper & Lybrand v. Livesay, 437 U.S. 463, 467, 98 S.Ct. 2454, 57 L.Ed.2d 351 (1978). To be final within the meaning of § 1291, the judgment must resolve all claims against all parties. As indicated in *Mohawk*, however, there are a number of exceptions to the final judgment rule of § 1291.

2.   The collateral order doctrine. The modern foundational case for the collateral order doctrine is Cohen v. Beneficial Loan Corp., 337 U.S. 541, 69 S.Ct. 1221, 93 L.Ed.2d 1528 (1949). The Court admitted frankly that the text of § 1291 did not provide for any exception, but provided a judge-made exception to allow review of a nonfinal order. It wrote:

> [Interlocutory review is available] in that small class [of cases] which finally determine claims of right separate from, and collateral to, rights asserted in the action, too important to be denied review and too independent of the cause itself to require that appellate consideration be deferred until the whole case is adjudicated. The Court has long given this provision of the statute this practical rather than a technical construction.

Id. at 546. The Court later "distilled" the collateral order doctrine down to three conditions that must be fulfilled before a nonfinal order can be appealed: "that an order [1] conclusively determine the disputed question, [2] resolve an important issue completely separate from the merits of the action, and [3] be effectively unreviewable on appeal from a final judgment." Will v. Hallock, 546 U.S. 345, 349, 126 S.Ct. 952, 163 L.Ed.2d 836 (2006) (internal quotation marks omitted).

3.   *Mohawk* decision. The Court in *Mohawk* considers the second and third *Cohen* conditions together, looking both at the importance of the right at issue and the ability effectively to vindicate that right without interlocutory review. The Court does not dispute the importance of the right, but holds that it can be adequately protected by various means short of interlocutory review under the collateral order doctrine. Among the means suggested by the Court are interlocutory review under 28 U.S.C. §1292(b), mandamus, defiance of a discovery order and being held in criminal contempt, and a protective order. How convinced are you of the adequacy of these means of protecting the right?

In the Court's view, the primary function of the attorney-client privilege is the encouragement it offers to clients to share information with their attorneys. The Court tells us that the possibility that a privileged communication might later be subject to discovery by an adversary is not likely to deter the sharing of information. If encouragement of sharing information is the central purpose of the attorney-client privilege, and the only harm that might come from a mistaken order by the district court is a marginally greater reluctance of a client to share information, the Court may be correct that the right can be adequately protected by the means it suggests. But what other possible harms? What if the client shared information that is useful to an adverse party in planning its litigationg strategy, and the case tis then tried based on that strategy? What if the client shared intensely personal and embarrassing information with her attorney, and that information must now be revealed, not to a friend but to an adversary?

4.   Application of *Mohawk* to other privileges. After *Mohawk*, it seems almost certain that district court orders mandating discovery of information arguably protected by other privileges, such as priest-penitent and doctor-patient, are not reviewable under the collateral order doctrine. Should the Court's analysis of the attorney-client privilege in *Mohawk* apply equally to the priest-penitent and doctor-patient privileges?

5.   Examples. An order rejecting the defense of qualified immunity— either on a Rule 12(b)(6) motion or on summary judgment—to a police officer is immediately appealable under the collateral order doctrine. Behrens v. Pelletier, 516 U.S. 299, 116 S.Ct. 834, 133 L.Ed.2d 773 (1996); Mitchell v. Forsyth, 472 U.S. 511, 105 S.Ct. 2806, 86 L.Ed.2d 411 (1985). An order denying the defense of sovereign immunity under the Eleventh Amendment is also immediately appealable. Puerto Rico Aqueduct & Sewer Authority v. Metcalf & Eddy, Inc., 506 U.S. 139, 113 S.Ct. 684, 121 L.Ed.2d 605 (1993). An order refusing to enforce a forum-selection clause is not immediately appealable. Lauro Lines S.R.L. v. Chasser, 490 U.S. 495, 109 S.Ct. 1976, 104 L.Ed.2d 548 (1989). An order rejecting a claim to immunity based on a settlement agreement is not immediately appealable. Digital Equipment Corp. v. Desktop Direct, Inc., 511 U.S. 863, 114 S.Ct. 1992, 128 L.Ed.2d 842 (1994).

6.   Appeals under 28 U.S.C. § 1292. a. § 1292(a). A grant, denial, modification, or continuation of an injunction is immediately appealable. Carson v. American Brands, Inc., 450 U.S. 79, 101 S.Ct. 993, 67 L.Ed.2d (1981). The most frequent application of § 1292(a) is appeals from grants or denials of preliminary injunctions. See, e.g., Coalition for Economic Equity v. Wilson, 122 F.3d 692 (9th Cir. 1997) (sustaining constitutionality of Proposition 209, California's anti-affirmative action initiative). **b. § 1292(b).** If a district judge believes that an otherwise nonappealable order "involves a controlling question of law as to which there is substantial ground for difference of opinion and that an appeal from the order may materially advance the ultimate termination of the litigation," she "shall so state in writing" in the order. 28 U.S.C. § 1292(b). If an appeal from such an order is taken within ten days, the court of appeals in its discretion may decide to hear the appeal.

7.   Appeals under federal Rule 54(b). A district judge "may direct the entry of a final judgment as to one or more but fewer than all of the claims or parties," but "only upon an express determination that there is no just reason for delay." A final judgment under Rule 54(b) may be appealed, even though the rest of the case continues to be litigated in the district court. The court of appeals will hear the appeal if it determines that entry of judgment under Rule 54(b) was proper. See Curtiss-Wright Corp. v. General Electric Co., 446 U.S. 1, 100 S.Ct. 1460, 64 L.Ed.2d 1 (1980). The general standard is that a Rule 54(b) final judgment must aid in the "expeditious determination" of the entire case. Texaco, Inc. v. Ponsoldt, 939 F.2d 794, 798 (9th Cir. 1991).

8.   Appeals under federal Rule 23(f). An order of the district court granting or denying class certification under Rule 23 may be appealed, provided that the appeal is brought within ten days of the order, and that the court of appeals accepts the appeal. Rule 23(f) was added to Rule 23 in 1996. Courts of appeal are reluctant to hear appeals under Rule 23(f). See Chamberlain v. Ford Motor Co., 402 F.3d 952 (9th Cir. 2005) ("We begin with the premise that Rule 23(f) review should be a rare occurrence."); Prado-Steiman v. Bush, 221 F.3d 1266 (11th Cir. 2000); Blair v. Equifax Check Services, 181 F.3d 832 (7th Cir. 1999).

9.   Appeals under 28 U.S.C. § 1453(c). Under the Class Action Fairness Act (CAFA), a court of appeals has discretion to hear an appeal from a district court order granting or denying a motion to remand a class action to the state court in which the action was originally filed. If an appeal is accepted, the deadlines are extraordinarily short. Absent an extension, the court of appeals must render judgment not later than sixty days after the appeal is *filed* (not sixty days after completion of briefing or after oral argument). One extension not to exceed ten days may be granted if the parties agree or if there is "good cause shown." See McAtee v. Capital One, 479 F.3d 1143 (9th Cir. 2007); Progressive West v. Preciado, 479 F.3d 1014 (9th Cir. 2007).

10.   Additional reading. For useful academic writing on the problems posed by the final judgment rule and its various exceptions, see Shah, Increase Access to the Appellate Courts: A Critical Look at Modernizing the Final Judgment Rule, 11 Seton Hall Rev. 40 (2014); Lammon, Rules, Standards, and Experimentation in Appellate Jurisdiction, 74 Ohio St. L.J. 423 (2013); Feldman, An Appeal for Immediate Appealability: Applying the Collateral Order Doctrine to Orders Denying Appointed Counsel in Civil Rights Cases, Geo. L.J. 1717 (2011); Steinman, Reinventing Appellate Jurisdiction, 48 Boston Coll. L.Rev. 1237 (2007); André, The Final Judgment Rule and Party Appeals of Civil Contempt Orders, 55 N.Y.U.L.Rev. 1041 (1980); Redish, The Pragmatic Approach to Appealability in the Federal Courts, 75 Colum.L.Rev. 89 (1975).

2. MANDAMUS

Kerr v. United States District Court

Supreme Court of the United States, 1976.
426 U.S. 394, 96 S.Ct. 2119, 48 L.Ed.2d 725.

■ MR. JUSTICE MARSHALL delivered the opinion of the Court.

Petitioners, defendants in a class action, sought issuance of writs of mandamus from the United States Court of Appeals for the Ninth Circuit to compel the District Court to vacate two discovery orders. The Court of Appeals refused to issue the writs. We hold that in the circumstances of this case—and particularly in light of the availability of an alternative, less extreme, path to modification of the challenged discovery orders—issuance of the writ is inappropriate. We therefore affirm.

I

Seven prisoners in the custody of the Department of Corrections of the State of California filed a class action in the United States District Court for the Northern District of California on behalf of themselves and "on behalf of all adult male felons who now are, as well as all adult male felons who in the future will be, in the custody of the California Department of Corrections, whether confined in an institution operated by the Department or on parole." Among the defendants in the action are petitioners in this case: the individual members of the California Adult Authority, the Administrative Officer of the California Adult Authority, and the Director of Corrections of the State of California. Plaintiffs' complaint alleges substantial constitutional violations in the manner in which the California Adult Authority carries out its function of determining the length and conditions of punishment for convicted criminal offenders.

In the course of discovery, plaintiffs submitted requests for the production of a number of documents pursuant to Fed.Rule Civ.Proc. 34. Petitioners' subsequent two petitions for writs of mandamus were concerned with two classes of documents that were part of these requests. The first class, part of a series of requests first made in June 1973, and which will be referred to here as the "Adult Authority files," is generally comprised of the personnel files of all members and employees of the Adult Authority, all Adult Authority documents relating to its past, present or future operation, and all memoranda written by the Chairman of the Adult Authority within the preceding five years. The second class of documents with which we are concerned was first requested by plaintiffs in November 1973, and will be referred to here as the "prisoners' files." Plaintiffs requested the opportunity to examine the files of every twentieth inmate at each California Department of Corrections institution; the class of documents, therefore, is comprised of the correctional files of a sample of the prisoners in the custody of the California Department of Corrections.

When presented with the request for the Adult Authority files, petitioners objected, claiming that the files were irrelevant, confidential, and privileged, and suggesting that they should not be required to turn over the files to plaintiffs without prior *in camera* review by the District Court to evaluate the claims of privilege. Plaintiffs moved, pursuant to

Fed.Rule Civ.Proc. 37, for an order compelling discovery. The District Court referred the matter to a Magistrate for findings and recommendations, and the Magistrate recommended that the District Court order production of the Adult Authority files without undertaking an *in camera* inspection of the files. The District Court accepted the Magistrate's recommendations and ordered the production of the documents. Seeking to limit distribution of the personnel files of the Adult Authority members and their employees, however, the District Court issued a protective order limiting the number of people associated with the plaintiffs who could examine those documents:

> "[N]o personnel file of any member of the Adult Authority, hearing representative or executive officer, nor any copy of any of its contents, shall be shown to any person except counsel of record for the plaintiffs and no more than a total of two investigators designated by such counsel, and then only to the extent necessary to the conduct of this action."

Dissatisfied with the District Court's ruling, petitioners filed a petition for a writ of mandamus under 28 U.S.C.A. § 1651(a),[3] requesting the Court of Appeals for the Ninth Circuit to vacate the District Court's order granting plaintiffs' motion to compel discovery. The Court of Appeals denied the petition in an opinion filed on January 17, 1975. 511 F.2d 192. * * *

A similar course was followed with regard to the requests for the prisoners' files. When petitioners, asserting grounds of privilege, objected to the requests, plaintiffs filed a motion to compel production which the District Court referred for findings and recommendations to a Magistrate. The Magistrate recommended that petitioners be required to produce up to 200 prisoner files subject to a protective order "that would restrict examination and inspection of inmate files to attorneys for plaintiffs and for their use only in connection with this lawsuit." * * * The District Court accepted the Magistrate's recommendation, but added to the recommended protective order a requirement that no prisoner's file be turned over for examination without the inmate's consent. Petitioners then filed a petition for mandamus which the Court of Appeals denied by order and without opinion on December 18, 1974.

Petitioners sought review in this Court of the denial of both petitions. We granted certiorari. 421 U.S. 987, 95 S.Ct. 1988, 44 L.Ed.2d 476 (1975).

II

The remedy of mandamus is a drastic one, to be invoked only in extraordinary situations. Will v. United States, 389 U.S. 90, 95, 88 S.Ct. 269, 273, 19 L.Ed.2d 305 (1967); Bankers Life & Cas. Co. v. Holland, 346 U.S. 379, 382–385, 74 S.Ct. 145, 147–149, 98 L.Ed. 106 (1953); Ex parte Fahey, 332 U.S. 258, 259, 67 S.Ct. 1558, 1559, 91 L.Ed. 2041 (1947). As we have observed, the writ "has traditionally been used in the federal courts only 'to confine an inferior court to a lawful exercise of its prescribed jurisdiction or to compel it to exercise its authority when it is its duty to do so.'" Will v. United States, 389 U.S., at 95, 88 S.Ct., at 273,

---

[3] Title 28 U.S.C.A. § 1651(a) provides: "The Supreme Court and all courts established by Act of Congress may issue all writs necessary or appropriate in aid of their respective jurisdictions and agreeable to the usages and principles of law."

quoting Roche v. Evaporated Milk Assn., 319 U.S. 21, 26, 63 S.Ct. 938, 941, 87 L.Ed. 1185 (1943). And, while we have not limited the use of mandamus by an unduly narrow and technical understanding of what constitutes a matter of "jurisdiction," Will v. United States, 389 U.S., at 95, 88 S.Ct., at 273, the fact still remains that "only exceptional circumstances amounting to a judicial 'usurpation of power' will justify the invocation of this extraordinary remedy." Ibid.

Our treatment of mandamus within the federal court system as an extraordinary remedy is not without good reason. As we have recognized before, mandamus actions such as the one involved in the instant case "have the unfortunate consequence of making the [district court] judge a litigant, obliged to obtain personal counsel or to leave his defense to one of the litigants [appearing] before him" in the underlying case. Bankers Life & Cas. Co. v. Holland, 346 U.S., at 384–385, 74 S.Ct., at 149, quoting Ex parte Fahey, 332 U.S., at 260, 67 S.Ct., at 1559. More importantly, particularly in an era of excessively crowded lower court dockets, it is in the interest of the fair and prompt administration of justice to discourage piecemeal litigation. It has been Congress' determination since the Judiciary Act of 1789 that as a general rule "appellate review should be postponed . . . until after final judgment has been rendered by the trial court." Will v. United States, 389 U.S., at 96, 88 S.Ct., at 274; Parr v. United States, 351 U.S. 513, 520–521, 76 S.Ct. 912, 917–918, 100 L.Ed. 1377 (1956). A judicial readiness to issue the writ of mandamus in anything less than an extraordinary situation would run the real risk of defeating the very policies sought to be furthered by that judgment of Congress.

As a means of implementing the rule that the writ will issue only in extraordinary circumstances, we have set forth various conditions to its issuance. Among these are that the party seeking issuance of the writ have no other adequate means to attain the relief he desires, Roche v. Evaporated Milk Assn., 319 U.S., at 26, 63 S.Ct., at 941, and that he satisfy "the burden of showing that [his] right to issuance of the writ is 'clear and indisputable.' " Bankers Life & Cas. Co. v. Holland, 346 U.S., at 384, 74 S.Ct., at 148, quoting United States ex rel. Bernardin v. Duell, 172 U.S. 576, 582, 19 S.Ct. 286, 287, 43 L.Ed. 559 (1899); Will v. United States, 389 U.S., at 96, 88 S.Ct., at 274. Moreover, it is important to remember that issuance of the writ is in large part a matter of discretion with the court to which the petition is addressed. Schlagenhauf v. Holder, 379 U.S. 104, 112 n. 8, 85 S.Ct. 234, 239, 13 L.Ed.2d 152 (1964); Parr v. United States, 351 U.S., at 520, 76 S.Ct., at 917. See also Technitrol Inc. v. McManus, 405 F.2d 84 (CA8), cert. denied, 394 U.S. 997, 89 S.Ct. 1591, 22 L.Ed.2d 775 (1969); Pacific Car and Foundry Co. v. Pence, 403 F.2d 949 (C.A.9 1968).

When looked at in the framework of these factors, it would appear that the actions of the Court of Appeals in this case should be affirmed. What petitioners are seeking here is not a declaration that the documents in question are absolutely privileged and that plaintiffs can never have access to any of them. On the contrary, petitioners request only that "production of the confidential documents not be compelled without a prior informed determination by the district court that plaintiffs' need for them in the action below outweighs their confidentiality." Brief for Petitioners 77–78. Petitioners ask in essence only that the District Court review the challenged documents *in camera* before passing on whether each one individually should or should not be disclosed. But the Court of Appeals' opinion dealing with the Adult Authority files did not foreclose the possible necessity of such *in camera* review. Its denial of the writ was based largely on the grounds that the governmental privilege had not been asserted personally by anyone eligible to assert it, and that it had not been asserted with the requisite specificity. The court apparently left open the opportunity for petitioners to return to the District Court, assert the privilege more specifically and through responsible officials, and then have their request for an *in camera* review of the materials by the District Court reconsidered in a different light:

> "Since there may be information in the requested documents which should be protected, the petitioners may assert a privilege to a particular document or class of documents, and perhaps seek *in camera* inspection, at the time the documents are discovered in the district court." 511 F.2d, at 198–199.

Petitioners contend that by denying the petition for mandamus the Court of Appeals has afforded them no remedy at all. To the contrary, we read the above quoted language of the opinion as providing petitioners an avenue far short of mandamus to achieve precisely the relief they seek.

To the extent that the opinion below might be regarded as ambiguous, we are fortified in our reading of it by a recognition of the serious consequences which could flow from an unwarranted failure to grant petitioners the opportunity to have the documents reviewed by the trial judge *in camera* before being compelled to turn them over. Petitioners' claims of privilege rest in large part on the notion that turning over the requested documents would result in substantial injury to the State's prison-parole system by unnecessarily chilling the free and uninhibited exchange of ideas between staff members within the system, by causing the unwarranted disclosure and consequent drying up of confidential sources, and in general by unjustifiably compromising the confidentiality of the system's records and personnel files. In light of the potential seriousness of these considerations and in light of the fact that the weight to be accorded them will inevitably vary with the nature of the specific documents in question, it would seem that an *in camera* review of the documents is a relatively costless and eminently worthwhile method to insure that the balance between petitioners' claims of irrelevance and privilege and plaintiffs' asserted need for the documents is correctly struck. Indeed, this Court has long held the view that *in camera* review is a highly appropriate and useful means of dealing with claims of governmental privilege. E.g., United States v. Nixon, 418 U.S. 683, 706, 94 S.Ct. 3090, 3106, 41 L.Ed.2d 1039 (1974); United States v. Reynolds, 345 U.S. 1, 73 S.Ct. 528, 97 L.Ed. 727 (1953).

Insofar as discovery of the prisoners' files is concerned, it is true that the Court of Appeals' order denying the petition for a writ of mandamus with regard to those files was issued without any statement of reasons for the denial. However, there is no reason to think that by its order the Court of Appeals meant to foreclose petitioners from following precisely the same avenue with regard to the prisoners' files as it gave them the opportunity to follow with regard to the Adult Authority files.

We are thus confident that the Court of Appeals did in fact intend to afford the petitioners the opportunity to apply for and, upon proper application, receive *in camera* review. Accordingly the orders of the Court of Appeals are affirmed.

So ordered.

NOTE ON MANDAMUS

1. **An extraordinary remedy.** A writ of mandamus is an extraordinary remedy, available under the All Writs Act, 28 U.S.C. § 1651(a). As the Court says in *Kerr*, "The remedy of mandamus is a drastic one, to be invoked only in extraordinary situations." Note that the effect of the writ can sometimes be achieved even when it is denied, as in the court of appeals' opinion in *Kerr*. The Supreme Court opinion appears to be artfully written so that it ostensibly limits use of mandamus for interlocutory review while carefully "saving" the Court's earlier decisions that had enlarged its use, for example, Schlagenhauf v. Holder, 379 U.S. 104, 85 S.Ct. 234, 13 L.Ed.2d 152 (1964), where mandamus was granted to review an order dealing with the scope of discovery. The decision in *Kerr* nevertheless seems to have presaged a restrictive view of interlocutory review by mandamus in the federal system. See Allied Chem. Corp. v. Daiflon, Inc., 449 U.S. 33, 101 S.Ct. 188, 66 L.Ed.2d 193 (1980), reversing a circuit court's issuance of mandamus to prevent a new trial in a district court.

2. **Criteria for granting mandamus.** The articulated criteria for granting a writ of mandamus vary slightly from circuit to circuit, but there is general agreement that mandamus should be rarely granted, and that the right to the writ should be "clear and indisputable." Calderon v. United States District Court, 103 F.3d 72, 74 (9th Cir. 1996). The criteria in the Ninth Circuit, not all of which are likely to be present in any single case are the so-called *Bauman* factors: (1) there is no other adequate means, such as direct appeal, of obtaining the relief sought; (2) the petitioner will be damaged or prejudiced in a way not correctable on appeal; (3) the district court's order is clearly erroneous as a matter of law; (4) the district court's order is an often-repeated error, or manifests a persistent disregard of the federal rules; and (5) the district court's order raises new and important problems, or issues of law of first impression. See Bauman v. United States District Court, 557 F.2d 650, 654–55 (9th Cir. 1977). Not surprisingly, district judges hate to be "mandamused" by the court of appeals. In their view, being reversed on appeal is already bad enough; being mandamused is even worse.

3. **A substitute for appellate review?** The Supreme Court allowed mandamus as a substitute for appellate review of a final judgment in Thermtron Products, Inc. v. Hermansdorfer, 423 U.S. 336, 96 S.Ct. 584, 46 L.Ed.2d 542 (1976). After a diversity case had been removed from state to federal court under 28 U.S.C. § 1441, Judge Hermansdorfer remanded it to state court on the ground that his docket was too crowded. Despite the language of 28 U.S.C. § 1447(d) providing that a remand order of a removed case is "not reviewable on appeal or otherwise," the Court held that mandamus was an appropriate mechanism to correct Judge Hermansdorfer's obviously incorrect, indeed willfully incorrect, remand. See Hermann, Thermtron Revisited: When and How Federal Trial Court Remand Orders are Reviewable, 19 Ariz. St. L.J. 395 (1987).

4.   Examples of use of mandamus. For various situations in which mandamus has been granted by the court of appeals, see Bonner and Appler, Interlocutory Appeals and Mandamus, 4 Litigation 25, 25–26 (1978). Writs have been issued when the district judge refused to dismiss a case although jurisdiction is lacking or a meritorious preliminary defense exists; stayed trial proceedings pending arbitration, exhaustion of some administrative remedy or resolution of a related case in another forum; quashed writs of attachment or garnishment filed before the trial to ensure any judgment can be satisfied; denied permission to file a cross-claim or other pleading amendment, or refuses to permit intervention; refused to permit depositions of certain individuals, or grants permission to take inappropriate depositions or improperly limits or conditions depositions; entered orders limiting or denying discovery, or requires the production of privileged material; refused to recuse himself. The authors add that seeking mandamus "has frequently been useful even where the writ does not issue. Often the court will review the merits of the request, state how it believes the trial judge should have decided the issue, but decline to issue the writ for technical reasons * * *. It is rare that the district court does not 'get the message' and grant the relief voluntarily." Id. at 29. See also Berger, The Mandamus Power of the United States Courts of Appeal, 31 Buff.L.Rev. 37 (1982).

5.   Mandamus in privilege cases. The Court in *Mohawk* suggested that mandamus would be a useful remedy in cases in which the district court improperly granted a motion to compel production of information protected by the attorney-client privilege. Based on what you now know about mandamus, how likely is it that someone seeking review of an order to reveal information arguably protected under the attorney-client privilege will be able to obtain a writ of mandamus?

3.   REVIEWABILITY OF CONTENTIONS

Bankers Life & Casualty Co. v. Crenshaw

Supreme Court of the United States, 1988.
486 U.S. 71, 108 S.Ct. 1645, 100 L.Ed.2d 62.

■ JUSTICE MARSHALL delivered the opinion of the Court.

* * *

I

This action grows out of allegations that appellant Bankers Life and Casualty Company refused in bad faith to pay appellee Lloyd Crenshaw's insurance claim for loss of a limb. According to testimony at trial, appellee was injured on January 6, 1979, when a car alternator he was repairing rolled off his workbench and landed on his foot. Three days later, after the injury had not responded to home treatment, appellee went to the emergency room of the local Air Force Base hospital. Hospital doctors prescribed a splint, crutches, and pain medication, and told appellee to return in a week. Appellee revisited the hospital three times over the next five days, each time complaining of continuing pain in his foot. By the last visit, appellee's foot had swollen and begun to turn blue, and the examining doctor recommended a surgery consultation. Appellee was admitted to the hospital, where, on January 17, an Air Force general surgeon determined that a surgical amputation was necessary. The following day, appellee's leg was amputated below the knee.

At the time of the amputation, appellee was insured under a group policy issued by appellant. The policy provided a $20,000 benefit for loss of limb due to accidental bodily injury. In April of 1979, appellee submitted a claim under the policy. Appellant denied the claim. The apparent basis for the denial was an opinion of appellant's Medical Director, Dr. Nathaniel McParland, that the cause of the amputation was not appellee's accident but a pre-existing condition of arteriosclerosis, a degenerative vascular disease. Appellee responded to the company's denial by furnishing a statement signed by three doctors who treated him at the hospital. They stated that appellee's arteriosclerosis was "an underlying condition and not the immediate cause of the gangrenous necrosis. The precipating [sic] event must be considered to be the trauma which initially brought him to the Emergency Room on 9 January." 483 So.2d 254, 261 (Miss.1985). Dr. McParland and a company analyst concluded that this statement was inconsequential, and appellant adhered to its position that the arteriosclerosis was responsible for the loss of limb.

Appellee persisted in his efforts to recover under the policy, eventually hiring an attorney, and appellant persisted in its intransigence. In its correspondence with appellee and his attorney, appellant repeatedly asserted that appellee had not suffered an injury as defined in the policy, that is, a " 'bodily injury, causing the loss while this policy is in force, directly and independently of all other causes and effected solely through an accidental bodily injury to the insured person.' " Id., at 262, quoting letter of Apr. 8, 1980, from Wm. Herzau to appellee. In contemporaneous internal memoranda, however, appellant noted that notwithstanding the policy language, appellee was entitled to recovery under Mississippi law if his injury had "aggravate[d], render[ed] active, or set in motion a latent or dormant pre-existing physical condition or disease." Id., at 262, 263. The memoranda also demonstrated that appellant knew its files were incomplete yet never attempted to obtain appellee's medical records, most notably his emergency room report, even though Mississippi law and internal company procedures required such efforts.

After appellant again denied the claim on the ground that there was no evidence that appellee's " 'injury caused this loss "directly and independently of all other causes," ' " see id., at 263, appellee brought this suit in Mississippi state court. His complaint requested $20,000 in actual damages, and, as amended, $1,635,000 in punitive damages for the tort of bad-faith refusal to pay an insurance claim. The jury awarded appellee the $20,000 provided by the policy and punitive damages of $1.6 million.

The Mississippi Supreme Court affirmed the jury verdict without modification. It concluded that the punitive damages award was not excessive in light of appellant's financial worth and the degree of its wrongdoing. See id., at 279. * * * In its appeal to the Mississippi Supreme Court, appellant did not raise a federal constitutional challenge to the size of the punitive damages award.[1] Following the affirmance of the jury

---

[1] Appellant did offer on appeal a federal due process challenge based on the alleged "chilling effect" of unrestricted punitive damages awards on the exercise of a litigant's right of

verdict, appellant filed a petition for rehearing. Appellant argued in the petition that "[t]he punitive damage verdict was clearly excessive, not reasonably related to any legitimate purpose, constitutes excessive fine, and violates constitutional principles." App. to Juris. Statement 139a. An accompanying brief asserted that the punitive damage award violated "due process, equal protection, and other constitutional standards." Id., at 151a. * * *

II

Appellant focuses most of its efforts in this appeal to challenging the punitive damages award of $1.6 million. It contends foremost that the award violates the Eighth Amendment's guarantee that "excessive fines [shall not be] imposed." U.S. Const., Amdt. 8. Appellant argues first, that the Excessive Fines Clause applies to punitive damages awards rendered in civil cases, and second, that the particular award in this case was constitutionally excessive. In addition to its excessive fines claim, appellant challenges the punitive damage award in this case on the grounds that it violates the Due Process Clause and the Contract Clause. Although we noted probable jurisdiction as to all of the questions presented in appellant's jurisdictional statement, appellant's challenges to the size of the punitive damages award do not fall within our appellate jurisdiction. See 28 U.S.C. § 1257(2). We therefore treat them as if contained in a petition for a writ of certiorari, and our unrestricted notation of probable jurisdiction of the appeal is to be understood as a grant of the writ as to these claims. See Mishkin v. New York, 383 U.S. 502, 512, 86 S.Ct. 958, 965, 16 L.Ed.2d 56 (1966). We conclude, however, that these claims were not raised and passed upon in state court, and we decline to reach them here. See ibid. ("The issue thus remains within our certiorari jurisdiction, and we may, for good reason, even at this stage, decline to decide the merits of the issue, much as we would dismiss a writ of certiorari as improvidently granted").

Appellant maintains that it raised its various challenges to the size of the punitive damage award in its petition for rehearing before the Mississippi Supreme Court. In urging us to entertain the claims, appellant relies on our decision in Hathorn v. Lovorn, 457 U.S. 255, 262–265, 102 S.Ct. 2421, 2426–2428, 72 L.Ed.2d 824 (1982), in which we accepted certiorari jurisdiction of claims that were raised, but not passed upon, in the Mississippi Supreme Court on petition for rehearing. *Hathorn* would be apposite were we to conclude that appellant had adequately raised its claims on rehearing. But appellant's petition for rehearing alleged only that the punitive damage award "was clearly excessive, not reasonably related to any legitimate purpose, constitutes excessive fine, and violates constitutional principles." App. to Juris. Statement 139a. The vague appeal to constitutional principles does not preserve appellant's Contract Clause or due process claim. A party may not preserve a constitutional challenge by generally invoking the Constitution in state court and awaiting review in this Court to specify the constitutional provision it is relying upon. Cf. Taylor v. Illinois, 484 U.S. 400, 407 n. 9, 108 S.Ct. 646, 651 n. 9, 98 L.Ed.2d 798 (1988) ("A generic reference to the Fourteenth Amendment is not sufficient to

---

access to the courts. See App. to Juris. Statement 135a. We read this attack on the alleged open-endedness of Mississippi's punitive damages awards to be distinct from the attack on the size of the particular award that appellant has waged before this Court.

preserve a constitutional claim based on an unidentified provision of the Bill of Rights . . .").

Appellant's reference to the excessiveness of the punitive damage award more colorably raises a cognizable constitutional challenge to the size of the award, one based on the Excessive Fines Clause of the Eighth Amendment. But this language as well is too oblique to allow us to conclude that appellant raised before the Mississippi Supreme Court the federal claim it now urges us to resolve. As this Court stated in Webb v. Webb, 451 U.S. 493, 501, 101 S.Ct. 1889, 1894, 68 L.Ed.2d 392 (1981), "[a]t the minimum . . . there should be no doubt from the record that a claim under a *federal* statute or the *Federal* Constitution was presented in the state courts and that those courts were apprised of the nature or substance of the federal claim at the time and in the manner required by the state law." Although the petition for rehearing alleges that the fine is excessive, it does not indicate that the fine is excessive as a constitutional matter, be it state or federal. It certainly does not identify the Excessive Fines Clause of the Eighth Amendment to the Federal Constitution as the source of appellant's claim. Indeed, the crucial language from appellant's petition contains no reference whatsoever to the Eighth Amendment, the Federal Constitution, or federal law. This failure to invoke the Federal Constitution is especially problematic in this case because the Mississippi Constitution contains its own Excessive Fines Clause. Miss.Const. Art. 3, § 28. Thus, even if the Mississippi Supreme Court understood appellant to be offering a constitutional challenge, it may very well have taken that challenge to be anchored in the state constitution. Cf. *Webb,* supra, at 496–498, 101 S.Ct., at 1891–1892 (finding that party's reference to "full faith and credit" in state court proceedings had failed to raise a federal constitutional claim even though the state constitution contained no full faith and credit clause); id., at 502–503, 101 S.Ct., at 1894–1895 (MARSHALL, J., dissenting). We therefore conclude that appellant's Eighth Amendment challenge, like its other challenges to the size of the punitive damage award, was not properly raised below.[2]

Whether appellant's failure to raise these claims in the Mississippi courts deprives us of all power to review them under our certiorari jurisdiction is an unsettled question. As Chief Justice Rehnquist wrote for the Court in Illinois v. Gates, 462 U.S. 213, 103 S.Ct. 2317, 76 L.Ed.2d 527 (1983), the cases have been somewhat inconsistent in their characterization of the "not pressed or passed upon below" rule. Early opinions seemed to treat the requirement as jurisdictional, whereas more recent cases clearly view the rule as merely a prudential restriction that does not pose an insuperable bar to our review. See id., at 218–219, 103 S.Ct., at 2321–2322 (discussing cases). We are not called on today to conclusively characterize the "not pressed or passed upon below" rule,

---

[2] Similarly, appellant's challenges in this Court to the size of the punitive damage award in no way qualify as "mere enlargements" of claims made before the Mississippi Supreme Court. Under the mere enlargement doctrine, "[p]arties are not confined here to the same arguments which were advanced in the courts below upon a Federal question there discussed." Dewey v. Des Moines, 173 U.S. 193, 198, 19 S.Ct. 379, 380, 43 L.Ed. 665 (1899). See also Stanley v. Illinois, 405 U.S. 645, 658, n. 10, 92 S.Ct. 1208, 1216, n. 10, 31 L.Ed.2d 551 (1972). *Dewey* makes clear, however, that the federal question must be brought to the attention of the court below in some manner. "A claim or right which has never been made or asserted cannot be said to have been denied by a judgment which does not refer to it." 173 U.S., at 200, 19 S.Ct., at 381.

however, because assuming that the rule is merely prudential, we believe that the more prudent course in this case is to decline to review appellant's claims.

In determining whether to exercise jurisdiction over questions not properly raised below, the Court has focused on the policies that animate the "not pressed or passed upon below" rule. These policies are first, comity to the States, and second, a constellation of practical considerations, chief among which is our own need for a properly developed record on appeal. See Webb v. Webb, supra, 451 U.S., at 500–501, 101 S.Ct., at 1893–1894. Because the chief issue appellant would have us resolve—whether the Eighth Amendment's Excessive Fines Clause serves to limit punitive damages in state civil cases—is a question of some moment and difficulty, these policies apply with special force. See Illinois v. Gates, supra, 462 U.S., at 224, 103 S.Ct., at 2325 ("Where difficult issues of great public importance are involved, there are strong reasons to adhere scrupulously to the customary limitations on our discretion"); Mishkin v. New York, 383 U.S., at 512–513, 86 S.Ct., at 965 ("The far-reaching and important questions tendered by this claim are not presented by the record with sufficient clarity to require or justify their decision"). Our review of appellant's claim now would short-circuit a number of less intrusive, and possibly more appropriate, resolutions: the Mississippi State Legislature might choose to enact legislation addressing punitive damage awards for bad-faith refusal to pay insurance claims;[3] failing that, the Mississippi state courts may choose to resolve the issue by relying on the state constitution or on some other adequate and independent nonfederal ground; and failing that, the Mississippi Supreme Court will have its opportunity to decide the question of federal law in the first instance, while any ultimate review of the question that we might undertake will gain the benefit of a well-developed record and a reasoned opinion on the merits. We think it unwise to foreclose these possibilities, and therefore decline to address appellant's challenges to the size of the punitive damage award.

* * *

■ JUSTICE STEVENS and JUSTICE KENNEDY took no part in the consideration or decision of this case.

■ JUSTICE WHITE, with whom JUSTICE SCALIA joins, concurring.

I join Parts I and III of the Court's opinion but not Part II. I continue to believe that "the statute which gives us jurisdiction in this cause, 28 U.S.C. § 1257(3), prevents us from deciding federal constitutional claims raised here for the first time on review of state-court decisions. Cardinale v. Louisiana, 394 U.S. 437, 438–439 [89 S.Ct. 1161, 1162–1163, 22 L.Ed.2d 398]." Illinois v. Gates, 462 U.S. 213, 247, 103 S.Ct. 2317, 2337, 76 L.Ed.2d 527 (1983) (WHITE, J., concurring in the judgment). Thus, I disagree with the Court's analysis—under "prudential" standards—of appellant's preservation of its challenge to the punitive damage award here. * * * Ultimately, because the majority properly declines to address

---

[3] Several States have enacted limits on punitive damages in specified types of causes of action. See, e.g., Fla.Stat.Ann. § 713.31(2)(c) (1988) (fraudulent filing of mechanics' lien); Wash.Rev.Code § 9A.36.080 (1987) (malicious harassment); Cal.Civ.Code Ann. § 1787.3 (West 1985) (consumer credit denial).

claims which I believe are not within this Court's jurisdiction, I concur in Part II's result, but not its reasoning.

■ JUSTICE O'CONNOR, with whom JUSTICE SCALIA joins, concurring in part and concurring in the judgment.

I do not agree with the Court's analysis of our jurisdiction over appellant's federal due process claim. I therefore do not join Part II or footnote 1 of the Court's opinion. I join the remainder of the opinion, and I agree with the analysis of Part II insofar as claims under the Excessive Fines Clause and Contract Clause are concerned. Moreover, for the reasons given below, I ultimately concur in the Court's judgment with respect to the due process claim as well.

In its brief on appeal to the Mississippi Supreme Court, appellant expressly invoked the Due Process Clause of the Fourteenth Amendment and argued that Mississippi law chilled its fundamental right of access to the courts by authorizing unlimited punitive damages. App. to Juris. Statement 135a. The Court does not acknowledge this argument in its discussion of why the due process claim was not raised and passed upon below, but only notes that appellant did not present a due process argument clearly in its petition for rehearing. * * * The Court suggests that it need not consider the due process argument raised in appellant's brief to the Mississippi Supreme Court because it is "distinct from the attack on the size of the particular award that appellant has waged before this Court." * * * Standing alone, this observation is insufficient to deprive this Court of jurisdiction over appellant's due process claim. "Parties are not confined here to the same arguments which were advanced in the courts below upon a Federal question there discussed." Dewey v. Des Moines, 173 U.S. 193, 197–198, 19 S.Ct. 379, 380–381, 43 L.Ed. 665 (1899). See Illinois v. Gates, 462 U.S. 213, 248, 103 S.Ct. 2317, 2337, 76 L.Ed.2d 527 (1983) (WHITE, J., concurring in judgment).

Accordingly, the Court should examine the federal due process argument that appellant makes in this Court to determine whether it is "only an enlargement" of the due process argument it raised below. See Dewey, supra, 173 U.S., at 197, 19 S.Ct., at 380. In its principal brief in this Court, appellant contends that the Mississippi Supreme Court changed its standard for judging when an insurer may be liable for punitive damages and applied the new standard retroactively to this case. Appellant explains that it therefore had no advance notice of what conduct could render it liable for punitive damages. Citing cases in which this Court has struck down criminal statutes as void for vagueness, e.g., Roberts v. United States Jaycees, 468 U.S. 609, 104 S.Ct. 3244, 82 L.Ed.2d 462 (1984); Giaccio v. Pennsylvania, 382 U.S. 399, 86 S.Ct. 518, 15 L.Ed.2d 447 (1966), appellant maintains that this violated the Due Process Clause. Brief for Appellant 40–43. Then, in a supplemental brief filed after argument with the Court's leave, appellant expands the due process argument pressed below and mounts a more general attack on permitting juries to impose unlimited punitive damages on an ad hoc basis. Post-argument Brief for Appellant 4–10.

Appellant has touched on a due process issue that I think is worthy of the Court's attention in an appropriate case. Mississippi law gives juries discretion to award any amount of punitive damages in any tort case in which a defendant acts with a certain mental state. In my view, because of the punitive character of such awards, there is reason to think that this may violate the Due Process Clause.

Punitive damages are awarded not to compensate for injury but, rather, "to punish reprehensible conduct and to deter its future occurrence." Gertz v. Welch, Inc., 418 U.S. 323, 350, 94 S.Ct. 2997, 3012, 41 L.Ed.2d 789 (1974). Punitive damages are not measured against actual injury, so there is no objective standard that limits their amount. Hence, "the impact of these windfall recoveries is unpredictable and potentially substantial." Electrical Workers v. Foust, 442 U.S. 42, 50, 99 S.Ct. 2121, 2127, 60 L.Ed.2d 698 (1979). For these reasons, the Court has forbidden the award of punitive damages in defamation suits brought by private plaintiffs, *Gertz,* supra, 418 U.S., at 349–359, 94 S.Ct., at 3011–3012, and in unfair representation suits brought against unions under the Railway Labor Act, *Electrical Workers,* supra, 442 U.S., at 52, 99 S.Ct., at 2128. For similar reasons, the Court should scrutinize carefully the procedures under which punitive damages are awarded in civil lawsuits.

Under Mississippi law, the jury may award punitive damages for any common law tort committed with a certain mental state, that is, "for a willful and intentional wrong, or for such gross negligence and reckless negligence as is equivalent to such a wrong." 483 So.2d 254, 269 (Miss.1985) (opinion below). Although this standard may describe the required mental state with sufficient precision, the amount of the penalty that may ensue is left completely indeterminate. As the Mississippi Supreme Court said, "the determination of the amount of punitive damages is a matter committed solely to the authority and discretion of the jury." Id., at 278. This grant of wholly standardless discretion to determine the severity of punishment appears inconsistent with due process. The Court has recognized that "vague sentencing provisions may pose constitutional questions if they do not state with sufficient clarity the consequences of violating a given criminal statute." United States v. Batchelder, 442 U.S. 114, 123, 99 S.Ct. 2198, 2204, 60 L.Ed.2d 755 (1979). Nothing in Mississippi law warned appellant that by committing a tort that caused $20,000 of actual damages, it could expect to incur a $1.6 million punitive damage award.

This due process question, serious as it is, should not be decided today. The argument was not appellant's principal submission to this Court. The analysis in the briefs and the discussion at oral argument were correspondingly abbreviated. Although the Court could assert jurisdiction over the due process question on the theory that the argument made here was a "mere enlargement" of the due process argument raised below, it would not be prudent to do so. Accordingly, I concur in the Court's judgment on this question and would leave for another day the consideration of these issues.

■ JUSTICE SCALIA, concurring in part and concurring in the judgment.

I join Part I (except for footnote 1) and Part III of the opinion of the Court, and concur in its judgment. As to Part II, I agree with Justice White that the question of our entertaining the issues there discussed should be resolved as a matter of law, and not of discretion, and I therefore join his opinion. The Court having chosen not to follow that course, I agree with Justice O'Connor regarding the basis on which our discretion should be exercised concerning the due process claim, and therefore join her opinion.

■ JUSTICE BLACKMUN's opinion, concurring in part and dissenting in part, is omitted.

NOTES AND QUESTIONS

1. **Federal claims in the Supreme Court that were not pressed or passed upon in the state court.** In *Bankers Life*, the defendant contended in the Supreme Court that the amount of punitive damages was excessive, in violation of various provisions of the federal Constitution. The Court writes that the question whether it has the authority to entertain a challenge not pressed or passed upon in the state court below is unsettled. The Court does not answer that unsettled question, but on the assumption that it does have the authority, it declines as a matter of comity and prudence to entertain the challenge. Seventeen years later, in Howell v. Mississippi, 543 U.S. 440, 125 S.Ct. 856, 160 L.Ed.2d 873 (2005), the Court again refused to answer the question whether it had the authority to address a challenge not pressed or passed upon in the state court below. Howell was a state prisoner under sentence of death who sought to bring a direct appeal of his conviction. He contended that the state court had violated his Eighth and Fourteenth Amendment rights in refusing to give a requested jury instructed. The Court initially granted a writ of certiorari, but then dismissed the writ as improvidently granted because Howell had not raised his federal claim in the Mississippi state courts.

It is easy to see why the Supreme Court would hesitate to rule on a claim or defense not pressed or passed upon in the state court. But it is also easy to see why, from time to time, in its function as a policy-level court, the Court would be tempted to decide to rule on a claim or defense not raised below. Recall what the Court did in *Erie v. Tompkins*, supra, Chapter 3. Justice Brandeis began his opinion for the Court: "The question for decision is whether the oft-challenged doctrine of Swift v. Tyson shall now be disapproved." "The question for decision" had not been raised by the parties or passed upon by the courts below. To distinguish *Bankers Life* and *Howell* from *Erie*, is it a sufficient answer that the Court in *Erie* was reviewing a decision by a federal court of appeals rather than by a state court?

2. **More common issues concerning the scope and manner of appellate review.** While interesting, the unsettled issue in *Bankers Life* and *Howell* arises rarely and only in a very specific context. Other issues concerning appellate review are recurring and workaday. A few examples follow.

a. **Argument not made in the district court.** The general rule is that a court of appeal will not address an argument not made below, but there are two well-established exceptions to the general rule. The first is that a court of appeals can affirm the district court on any ground, even if the argument was not raised or addressed in the district court. The second is that a court of appeals can affirm or reverse based on an argument not made below when "the issue presented is purely one of law and either does not depend on the factual record developed below, or the pertinent record has been fully developed." Bolker v. Commissioner of Internal Revenue, 760 F.2d 1039, 1042 (9th Cir. 1985). Also, as you will recall from Chapter 2, supra, either a party or the court of appeals may raise the issue of lack of subject matter jurisdiction for the first time on appeal. See Louisville & Nashville R.R. Co. v. Mottley, 211 U.S. 149, 29 S.Ct. 42, 53 L.Ed.2d 126 (1908).

b.   Objections not made in the district court. Ordinarily, objections to rulings by the district court, such as the admission or exclusion of evidence, are waived if not made at the time of the ruling. Under Rule 51(d)(2), however, a failure to make a timely objection to a jury instruction does not waive the objection. Appellate review of a jury instruction in the absence of an objection in the district court is for "plain error." "Plain error" must not only be "plain" in the sense of obvious; it must also "affect substantial rights" and "seriously affect the fairness, integrity or public reputation of judicial proceedings." Henderson v. United States, 568 U.S. ___, 133 S.Ct. 1121, 1126, 185 L.Ed.2d 85 (2013).

c.   De novo, clear error, and abuse of discretion. When objections are properly made and preserved, the court of appeals reviews questions of law, including judgments "as a matter of law" under Rules 50 and 56, de novo. It reviews findings of fact by the district court for "clear error." And it reviews matters committed to the discretion of the district court for "abuse of discretion." The Supreme Court briskly summarized: "Traditionally, decisions on 'questions of law' are 'reviewable de novo,' decisions on 'questions of fact' are 'reviewable for clear error,' and decisions on 'matters of discretion' are 'reviewable for 'abuse of discretion.' " Highmark, Inc. v. Allcare Health Management System, Inc., 572 U.S.___, 234 S.Ct. 1744, 1748, 188 L.Ed.2d 829 (2014).

INDEX

References are to Pages